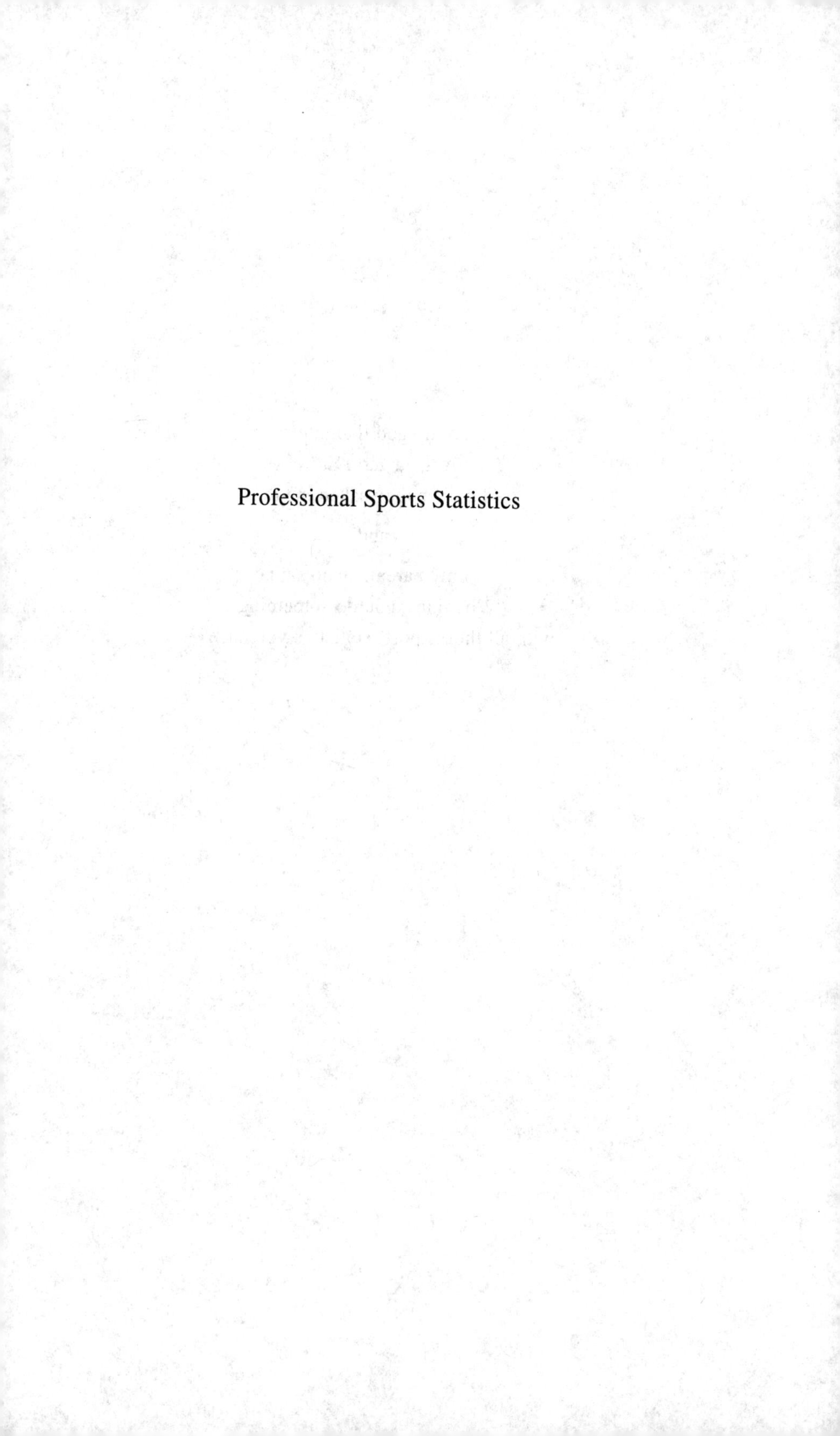

Professional Sports Statistics

To my god-daughters,
Angela and Laurie,
"because they asked me to,"

and

to my parents, who said,
"Why don't you do something
with all those sports statistics you have?"

Professional Sports Statistics

A North American Team-by-Team, and Major Non-Team Events, Year-by-Year Reference, 1876 through 1996

K. MICHAEL GASCHNITZ

McFarland & Company, Inc., Publishers
Jefferson, North Carolina, and London

British Library Cataloguing-in-Publication data are available

Library of Congress Cataloguing-in-Publication Data

Gaschnitz, K. Michael.
Professional sports statistics : a North American team-by-team, and major non-team events, year-by-year reference, 1876 through 1996 / by K. Michael Gaschnitz.
p. cm.
Includes bibliographical references.
ISBN 0-7864-0299-7 (library binding : 40# alkaline paper) ∞
1. Professional sports—North America—History—Statistics.
I. Title.
GV581.G37 1997
796.04'4'097021—dc21 97-13593
CIP

Manufactured in the United States of America

McFarland & Company, Inc., Publishers
Box 611, Jefferson, North Carolina 28640

Contents

Introduction

The idea for this book first took root when I was a boy in Western Canada in the late 1960's. In rural Canada there was not much opportunity for a kid on a farm to travel to many other parts of the world and most of my experiences of the outside world would come from the television and from books. As with most Canadian boys, I would spend my Saturday nights watching *Hockey Night in Canada,* usually from the cities of Toronto and Montreal but once in a while from a far off American city. During the summers and fall we would also watch CFL football from such exotic cities as Regina, Calgary and Winnipeg. This television experience first stirred my interests in sports.

Soon I became interested in how statistics were used to measure sports performance. It seemed to me that sports, unlike other activities, was the one human pursuit that could be measured and preserved for history's sake. Then around 1970 my father bought me my first sports book, full of statistics and stories, and with that I was hooked. My father provided the incentive for my compiling statistics.

The five years of work which went into this book included two summers of almost daily trips to local libraries poring over old microfilm and back issues of various magazines. Exciting as this may have been, the research didn't end there. It also involved contacting the public relations departments of many of the teams included in this book, and most of them were very helpful in supplying information. Many other sources were also consulted, including Charles L. Coleman's excellent *The Trail of the Stanley Cup* which gives a wonderful account of the early years of pro hockey. Michael Benson's *Ballparks of North America* is an invaluable source for those interested in the history of major and minor league baseball stadiums and makes the reader almost feel as if they are at the ballpark. Special thanks goes to David Biesel the author of *Can You Name That Team?*, an excellent book detailing the origins of the nicknames for most major league professional teams and many minor league teams.

A complete list of sources is included in the Bibliography beginning on page 1337.

Many older sports enthusiasts, followers of the Olympics and college sports and raised on the legends of Jim Thorpe and the Four Horsemen, Notre Dame's legendary backfield, may think that professional sports are a relatively new phenomenon, but professional sports have existed nearly as long as man has taken part in organized athletics.

This book will not begin with statistics from ancient civilizations, as needless to say reports from that era are sketchy, nor for partly the same reason will it deal with North America's first organized professional sports league, baseball's National Association, organized in 1871. Because of its erratic scheduling and poor organization, most sports historians do not consider the National Association to be a "major" league.

Many of the leagues included in the book are all but forgotten but were at the time serious rivals to the more familiar leagues.

This book covers only the teams in those leagues that are considered major league. Minor league professional teams are beyond the scope of this book.

The coverage begins with the formation of the National League of baseball on February 2, 1876, the oldest North American professional sports league in existence. The National League has had many rivals throughout the years, including the Federal League, the Players League, the American Association and others, and they are all covered here. As is the case with most leagues that try to compete with an established league they were ultimately unsuccessful. The established leagues would usually have the best facilities, be based in cities with larger populations and would have a well established core of fans, thus usually making any rival league a losing proposition.

The Pacific Coast Hockey Association and the Western Canada Hockey League were both equals to the more established National Hockey League and for a time carried on a heated bidding war for players. The National Hockey League, organized in Montreal, November 22, 1917, was not the first organized professional hockey league. This distinction instead belongs to the International Professional League, organized in Houghton, Michigan, in 1903; because of its regional nature and its brief history no statistics are included here. Those of many of the NHL's antecedent leagues as well as its early rivals in the PCHA and the WCHL and the more recent World Hockey Association are, however.

Statistics from many of the early basketball leagues are included. One may trace the history of many of today's multimillion-dollar, multinational franchises back to their beginnings as small time regional clubs run on a shoestring budget. You will also find the records from the NBA's only serious rival, the American Basketball Association.

Although the predecessor to the NFL was first organized in 1920 as the American Football Association, the scheduling was very erratic and organization was poor and the Association does not warrant inclusion in this book. Coverage has instead begun with the renaming of the league in 1922 as the National Football League. Statistics from the NFL's numerous competitors, such as the World Football League, the United States Football League and the Canadian Football League, are included as well.

The CFL, a highly entertaining league, can trace its history back to the early years of the century. The Grey Cup game, symbolic of Canadian Football supremacy, predates the formation of the NFL by 11 years. The records of the CFL are given only from the year 1950 to the present. It was in 1950 that, for the first time, the Toronto Argonauts paid all of their players, thus making the team a fully professional team.

Included also are yearly standing from the North American Soccer League and the two leagues which merged to form the NASL.

The book is divided into two sections. The first section includes the year-by-year standings of the different leagues and the various teams which made up the leagues. After the league standings are listed the coaching changes from the previous year, the top five individual leaders in various statistical categories, award winners, all-star teams, all-star game results, and Hall of Fame inductees. Following these regular season results are found the results of every playoff game in which the various teams have participated. Also included are some of the important rule changes and any items of importance or interest which may have occurred during the year.

In the first section one is able to find out that in 1961 Roger Maris hit 61 home runs, the West Division defeated the East division 153-131 in the NBA All-Star Game, the Washington Redskins won only one game all season in the NFL, the Winnipeg Blue Bombers won the CFL's Grey Cup, Bernie "Boom-Boom" Geoffrion scored 50 goals during the NHL campaign and Gene Littler won the U.S. Open Golf Championship. In the first section comparisons can be made between the performances of various leagues, teams, and individuals during each season.

Although most of the focus of this book is on team sports, included also are some of the major individual sports such as the Indianapolis 500, the Kentucky Derby and others.

The second section of the book deals with the individual teams. Included in this section are the yearly standings of the various teams, as well as yearly playoff results and the team's coaching history. I have also included a listing of the home cities of the various teams as well as a rudimentary family tree showing the movements of a team from one city to another. Also included is a short description of how the team acquired its nickname.

The baseball, football and soccer seasons all take place during one calendar year, while basketball and hockey seasons take place in two calendar years. The 1944-45 hockey season, for example will be found in the year of 1945 not 1944.

The method of listing the dates of a team's coaching history depends upon the league in which a team played. If the person coached a soccer, baseball or football team the date listed indicates the actual years of the coach's employment. In the case of a basketball or hockey team the matter changes somewhat. If the date indicated shows a coach was fired in 1983, it may mean either he was fired in the latter half of the 1982-83 season or the early part of the 1983-84 season. The first section of the book reveals the exact seasons in which a team hired or fired its coach.

No matter whether a team has changed cities in which they were based or whether they have just changed their name, each franchise has been treated as a separate entity. So for example, one will not find the statistics for the Alberta Oilers listed with those of the Edmonton Oilers. Also those teams, such as the Oakland Raiders, which relocated to another city and then returned at a later time are given separate entries.

Also in the second section is found information on the various teams' home venues. Only the stadiums in which a team has played the majority of its home games are listed. Not included are NHL or NBA neutral site games, or stadiums in which a team has been forced to play temporarily because of external circumstances. Seating capacities listed for the various venues change from year to year or sport to sport. Listed are the building's most recent seating capacity for stadiums still in use and the seating capacity at the time of use for those facilities or teams no longer operating. The dates listed after the seating capacity indicates the year from which the seating capacity figures are taken. If no date is indicated, the capacity figure reflects the stadium's capacity at some time during the team's use of that building.

Many of the formative teams of various leagues (especially baseball) were known by many different names and early newspaper accounts would often refer to a specific team using a variety of different names. The nicknames of the teams used in this book are the most common ones.

Year-by-Year Sports Statistics

AWARDS

American Basketball Association

Coach of the Year--Awarded to the coach of the year in the ABA.

Most Valuable Player--Awarded to the ABA's most valuable player.

Rookie of the Year--Awarded to the ABA's top rookie.

Canadian Football League

Annis Stukus Trophy--Awarded to the coach of the year as selected by the Football Reporters of Canada.

CFL Awards--see Schenley Awards.

Dave Dryburgh Trophy--Awarded to the player who leads the Western Division in scoring at the end of the regular season.

DeMarco-Becket Memorial Trophy--Originally presented to the most outstanding lineman in the Western Division. From 1974 the award has been presented to the most outstanding offensive lineman in the Western Division.

Dr. Beattie Martin Trophy--Awarded to the outstanding Canadian player in the Western Division since 1971. Prior to this the trophy was presented to the top Canadian rookie in the Western Division. This trophy was replaced by the Jackie Parker Trophy in 1974.

Eddie James Memorial Trophy--Awarded to the leading rusher in the Western Division.

Frank M. Gibson Trophy--Presented to the outstanding rookie in the Eastern Division.

GMC Awards--see Schenley Awards.

Grey Cup Most Outstanding Defensive Star--Awarded to the most outstanding defensive player in the Grey Cup Game. Awarded from 1974 to 1990.

Grey Cup Most Outstanding Offensive Star--Awarded to the most outstanding offensive player in the Grey Cup Game. Awarded from 1974 to 1990.

Grey Cup Most Valuable Canadian--Awarded to the most outstanding Canadian player of the Grey Cup Game. First awarded in 1971.

Grey Cup Most Valuable Player--Awarded to the most valuable player in the Grey Cup Game.

Gruen Trophy--Awarded to the outstanding Canadian rookie in the Eastern Division. Awarded from 1950 to 1972.

Jackie Parker Trophy--Awarded to the Western Division's top rookie.

James P. McCaffrey Trophy--Presented to the outstanding defensive player in the Eastern Division.

James S. Dixon Trophy--Awarded to the champion of the Eastern Division.

Jeff Nicklin Memorial Trophy--Awarded to the most outstanding player in the Western Division since 1973. Prior to this the trophy was presented to the player considered the most valuable to his team in the Western Division.

Jeff Russel Memorial Trophy--From 1950 to 1972 the trophy was presented to the Eastern Division player thought to possess the highest qualities of courage, fair play and sportsmanship. From 1973 to 1995 the trophy has been presented to most outstanding player in the Eastern Division.

Leo Dandurand Trophy--Awarded to the outstanding offensive lineman in the Eastern Division.

Lew Hayman Trophy--Awarded to the outstanding Canadian player in the Eastern Division.

N.J. Taylor Trophy--Presented annually to the Western Division championship team.

Norm Fieldgate Trophy--Awarded to the outstanding defensive player in the Western Division from 1978 to the present. Prior to this the trophy was awarded to the champion of the Western Division.

Schenley Award Most Outstanding Canadian--Awarded to the outstanding Canadian player in the CFL, replaced by the CFL Awards in 1988.

Schenley Award Most Outstanding Defensive Player--Awarded to the most outstanding defensive player. Prior to 1974 only one award was presented to both offensive and defensive linemen.

Schenley Award Most Outstanding Lineman--Awarded to the most outstanding offensive or defensive lineman from 1955 to 1973.

Schenley Award Most Outstanding Offensive Lineman--Awarded to the most outstanding offensive lineman. Prior to 1974 only one award was presented to both offensive and defensive lineman.

Schenley Award Most Outstanding Player--Awarded to the most outstanding player in the CFL.

Schenley Award Most Outstanding Rookie--Awarded to the top rookie in the CFL.

Terry Evanshen Award--Replaced the Jeff Russell Memorial Trophy beginning in 1995.

Major League Baseball

ALCS Most Valuable Player--Awarded to the player contributing the most to his team's success in the American League Championship Series.

Arch Ward Memorial Trophy--Presented to the All-Star Game most valuable player. Known as the Commissioner's Trophy from 1970 to 1984.

Baseball Writers Award--Presented to the most valuable player in each league as chosen by the Baseball Writers Association of America. First presented in 1930.

Chalmers Award--Presented by the Chalmers automobile company to the most valuable player in each league. The award was presented from 1911 to 1914.

Chronicle-Telegraph Cup--Championship trophy awarded to the winner of the National League playoffs winner in 1900.

Cy Young Award--Presented to the best pitcher in each league as voted on by the Baseball Writers Association of America. The Award was introduced in 1955 with only one award being presented each year from then until 1966.

League Award--Presented by the member clubs to the most valuable player in each league. Awarded from 1922 to 1929.

NLCS Most Valuable Player--Awarded to the player contributing the most to his team's success in the National League Championship Series.

Rookie of the Year--Awarded to the top rookie in each league as voted on by the Baseball Writers Association of America. Only one award was awarded in 1947 and 1948 and separate awards were presented for each league beginning in 1949.

Sporting News Executive of the Year--Awarded to the top executive in Major League Baseball as chosen by "The Sporting News."

Sporting News Manager of the Year--Awarded to the top manager in Major League Baseball as chosen by "The Sporting News". A combined award was given from 1936 to 1985. Separate awards were given for each league beginning in 1986.

Sporting News Most Valuable Player--Awarded to the most valuable player in each league as chosen by "The Sporting News." Awarded from 1929 to 1945.

Sporting News Pitcher of the Year--Awarded to the top pitcher of the year in each league as chosen by "The Sporting News."

Sporting News Player of the Year--Awarded to the most valuable player of the year as chosen by "The Sporting News." First awarded in 1948.

Sporting News Rookie of the Year--Awarded to the top rookie in each league as chosen by "The Sporting News". One award was given out from 1946 to 1948 and in 1950. Two awards were given out in 1949 and from 1951 to 1962. Four awards were given out beginning in 1963 for best rookie and best rookie pitcher in each league.

Temple Cup--Awarded to the winner of the playoff between the 1st place team and the 2nd place team in the National League from 1894 to 1897.

World Series Most Valuable Player--Presented to the player having contributed most to his team's success during the World Series.

National Basketball Association

Court Vision Award--First awarded in 1995 to the player who leads the league in the statistics of (steals and assists divided by turnovers).

Defensive Player of the Year--Awarded to the NBA's defensive player of the year as selected by the NBA writers and broadcasters.

Eddie Gottlieb Trophy--Awarded to the NBA's top rookie as selected by the NBA's writers and broadcasters.

Executive of the Year--Awarded to the executive of the year as selected by the "Sporting News."

Good Hands Award --This trophy is awarded for ball handling.

J. Walter Kennedy Citizenship Award--Awarded to the player displaying outstanding qualities of citizenship.

Larry O'Brien Trophy--Awarded to the NBA championship team. The trophy replaced the Walter A. Brown Trophy.

Maurice Podoloff Trophy--Awarded to the NBA's most valuable player. The trophy was awarded by the NBA players until 1979-1980 and by the NBA writers and broadcasters since 1980-1981.

Most Improved Player--Awarded to the most improved player as selected by the NBA writers and broadcasters.

NBA Finals Most Valuable Player--Awarded to the NBA player adjudged to have been the most valuable player to his team in the post season as selected by "Sport Magazine."

Red Auerbach Trophy--Awarded to the NBA Coach of the Year.

Schick Award--Awarded to the player contributing most to his team's success. The award winner is determined by a computer formula.

Sixth Man Award--This award is presented in recognition of players who are non-starters.

Walter A. Brown Trophy--Awarded to the NBA championship team. The award was renamed the Larry O'Brien Trophy after NBA President Larry O'Brien who retired in 1984.

National Football League

Associated Press Most Valuable Player--First awarded in 1957 and is presented to the most valuable player in the NFL as selected by the Associated Press.

Bert Bell Memorial Trophy--Presented annually to the NFL rookie of the year as chosen by a panel on behalf of "The World Almanac". First presented in 1964.

Bert Bell Trophy--Presented to the NFL's most valuable player. The trophy is presented by the Maxwell Club of Philadelphia and was first awarded in 1959.

Dan McGuire Award--see Pro Bowl MVP.

George Halas Trophy--Awarded annually to the best defensive player in the NFL.

Jim Thorpe Trophy--Awarded to the NFL most valuable player as selected by the NFL Players Association and presented by The World Almanac.

Joe. F. Carr Trophy--Presented to the NFL's most valuable player. First presented in 1938, the trophy was retired in 1947.

Pete Rozelle Award--see Super Bowl MVP.

Pro Bowl MVP--Awarded annually to the player thought to have contributed the most to his team during the NFL Pro Bowl Game. The award's name was changed to the Dan McGuire Award in 1985.

Professional Football Writers Association Most Valuable Player--Awarded since 1976 to the NFL's most valuable player.

Rookie of the Year--Awarded annually to the rookie of the year in each conference as selected by news service sports editors.

Super Bowl MVP--Awarded to the most valuable player in the Super Bowl, and was presented by "Sport Magazine". The award was renamed the Pete Rozelle Award in 1990 and presented by the NFL.

UPI AFC-AFL Player of the Year--Presented to the player of the year in the American Football League from 1960 to 1969 and the American Football Conference since 1970.

UPI AFC-AFL Coach of the Year--Presented to the coach of the year in the American Football League from 1960 to 1969 and the American Football Conference since 1970.

UPI AFC-AFL Rookie of the Year--Presented to the top rookie in the American Football League from 1960 to 1969 and the American Football Conference since 1970.

UPI NFL-NFC Coach of the Year--Presented to the top coach in the NFL since 1955 and the National Football Conference since 1970.

UPI NFL-NFC Rookie of the Year--Presented to the rookie of the year in the NFL from 1955 to 1969 and the National Football Conference since 1970.

UPI NFL-NFC Player of the Year--Presented to the player of the year in the National Football Conference since 1970.

UPI Most Valuable Player--Awarded to the most valuable player in the NFL from 1953 to 1969.

National Hockey League

Alka-Seltzer Plus Award--Presented to the player, having played a minimum of 60 games, who leads the league in plus-minus statistics at the end of the regular season. The award was first presented in 1989-1990 by Miles Inc. (see Emery Edge Award).

Art Ross Trophy--Presented to the player who leads the league in scoring during the regular season. The trophy was first presented in 1947.

Bill Masterton Memorial Trophy--Awarded to the player who best exemplifies the qualities of perseverance, sportsmanship and dedication to hockey. First presented in 1968 to honor Bill Masterton who died January 15, 1968 after a collision during a game.

Bud Light/NHL Man of the Year--Awarded to the player recognized in the community as a positive role model through his conduct on and off the ice. First awarded in 1988.

Calder Trophy--Awarded to the player judged to be the most proficient in his first year of competition in the NHL. First awarded in 1936-1937 and was replaced by the Calder Memorial Trophy in 1943 after the death of NHL President Frank Calder.

Calder Memorial Trophy--see Calder Trophy.

Clarence S. Campbell Bowl--The Bowl was first awarded in 1967 to the champions of the West Division. Since the 1981-82 season the Bowl has been awarded to the team which advances to the Stanley Cup finals as winners of the Campbell Conference.

Conn Smythe Trophy--Awarded to the player adjudged to have been the most valuable to his team in the playoffs. First awarded in 1964.

Dodge Performance of the Year--Awarded to either the outstanding team or individual player performance of the year. The award was presented only in 1988 and 1989.

Dodge Performer of the Year--Awarded to the NHL's most outstanding performer in the regular season. The award was only presented from 1985 to 1990.

Dodge Ram Tough Award--Awarded to the player who wins the overall Ram Tough statistical category (combined total of power play, shorthanded, game winning and game tying goals). Awarded from 1988 to 1991.

Emery Edge Award--Presented from 1982-83 to 1987-1988 (see Alka Seltzer Plus Award).

Frank J. Selke Trophy--Awarded to the forward who best excels in the defensive aspects of the game. First awarded in 1977 by the NHL's Board of Governors.

Hart Memorial Trophy--see Hart Trophy.

Hart Trophy--Awarded to the player adjudged to be the most valuable to his team. The trophy was donated in 1923 and retired to the Hockey Hall of Fame in 1960. The trophy was replaced by the Hart Memorial Trophy.

James Norris Memorial Trophy--Awarded to the defenseman who demonstrates throughout the season the greatest all around ability in that position. First awarded in 1953 by the children of James Norris.

King Clancy Memorial Trophy--Awarded to the player who best exemplifies leadership qualities on and off the ice and has made a noteworthy humanitarian contribution in his community. First presented by the NHL Board of Governors in 1988.

Lady Byng Memorial Trophy--see Lady Byng Trophy.

Lady Byng Trophy--Awarded to the player adjudged to have exhibited the best type of sportsmanship and gentlemanly conduct combined with a high standard of play. The trophy was first presented in 1925 and given to Frank Boucher to keep after he won it seven times in eight years. Lady Byng presented another trophy in 1936, and after her death in 1949 the league presented the Lady Byng Memorial Trophy in her honor.

Lester B. Pearson Award--Awarded to the NHL's outstanding player as selected by the members of the National Hockey League Player Association. First presented in 1970.

Lester Patrick Trophy--Awarded for outstanding service to hockey in the United States. First presented in 1966 by the New York Rangers.

O'Brien Cup--Awarded to the team finishing first in the league during the regular season. First presented in the 1917-1918 season the award was originally emblematic of the championship of the National Hockey Association and presented by J. Ambrose O'Brien founder of the NHA. The Cup was replaced by the Prince of Wales Trophy in 1924-25 (see Prince of Wales Trophy and President's Trophy).

President's Trophy--Awarded to the team finishing first overall during the regular season. First presented in 1985-1986.

Prince of Wales Trophy--First awarded in 1924-25 the trophy was presented to the team finishing first overall during the regular season. From 1927-28 through 1937-38 the trophy went to the team finishing first in the American Division. From 1938-39 through 1966-67 it again went to the team finishing first overall. From 1967-68 through 1973-74 the trophy was presented to the winner of the East Division. From 1974-75 through 1980-81 it went to the team finishing first overall in the Prince of Wales Conference. Beginning in 1981-82 it went to the playoff champion of the Prince of Wales Conference.

Pro Set/NHL Player of the Year Award--Awarded to the NHL's most valuable player in the regular season. First awarded in 1991.

Stanley Cup--From 1893 to 1910 the Cup was awarded to the amateur hockey champions of Canada. Since then it has been awarded to the professional hockey champions and has been in sole possession of the NHL since 1946.

Trico Goaltender Award--Awarded to the goaltender with the best save percentage during the regular season. Awarded from 1989 to 1991.

Vezina Trophy--Awarded to the goaltender judged to have been the best at his position during the regular season as voted by the general managers of the league. From 1927 through 1980-81 the trophy was presented to the goaltender(s) of the club allowing the fewest goals against it (see Jennings Trophy).

William M. Jennings Trophy--Awarded to the goaltender(s) having played a minimum of 25 games to the team with the fewest goals against it. First presented in 1981-1982 by the NHL's Board of Governors (see Vezina Trophy).

North American Soccer League

Coach of the Year--Awarded to the NASL coach of the year.

Lead Goalkeeper --Awarded to the goalkeeper with the most saves.

MVP Award--Awarded to the player adjudged to be the most valuable player to his team during the regular season.

Rookie of the Year--Awarded to the NASL player judged to have been the best player in his first year of competition.

World Hockey Association

Avco World Trophy--Emblematic of the championship of the WHA.

Ben Hatskin Trophy--Presented to the best goaltender during the regular season in the WHA.

Bill Hunter Trophy--Awarded to the regular season scoring champion.

Dennis Murphy Trophy--Awarded to the best defenseman during the regular season.

Gordie Howe Trophy--Awarded to the most valuable player during the regular season.

Lou Kaplan Trophy--Presented to the rookie of the year.

Most Valuable Player in the Playoffs--Awarded to the player judged to be the most valuable player to his team during the playoffs. First presented in 1974-75.

Paul Deneau Trophy--Presented to the most gentlemanly player during the regular season in the WHA.

Robert Schmertz Trophy--Awarded to the coach of the year.

List of Abbreviations

Leagues

AA	American Association (1882-1891)
AAFC	All-American Football Conference (1946-1949)
ABA	American Basketball Association (1968-1976)
ABL	American Basketball League (1926-1931)
AFL	American Football League (1960-1969)
AL	American League (1901 to present)
BAA	Basketball Association of America (1947-1949)
CFC	Canadian Football Council (1956-1957)
CFL	Canadian Football League (1958 to present)
CRU	Canadian Rugby Union (1950-1955)
ECHA	Eastern Canada Hockey Association (1909)
FL	Federal League (1914-1915)
NASL	North American Soccer League (1968-1984)
NBA	National Basketball Association (1950 to present)
NBL	National Basketball League (1938-1949)
NFL	National Football League (1922 to present)
NHA	National Hockey Association (1910-1917)
NHL	National Hockey League (1918 to present)
NL	National League (1876 to present)
NPSL	National Professional Soccer League (1967)
PCHA	Pacific Coast Hockey Association (1912-1924)
PL	Player's League (1890)
UA	Union Association (1884)
USA	United Soccer Association (1967)
USFL	United States Football League (1983-1985)
WCHA	Western Canada Hockey Association (1922-1924)
WCHL	Western Canada Hockey League (1925)
WFL	World Football League (1974-1975) (1992)
WHA	World Hockey Association (1973-1979)
WHL	Western Hockey League (1926)
WLAF	World League of American Football (1991)

ALCS-American League Championship Series, Ave-Average, BP-Bonus Points, Conf.-Conference, Div.-Division, ERA-Earned Run Average, GA-Goals Against, GAA-Goals Against Average, GB-Games Behind, GF-Goals For, GP-Games Played, L-Losses, MVP-Most Valuable Player, NLCS-National League Championship Series, OR-Opponents Runs, PA-Points Against, PCT-Percentage, PF-Points For, PPGA-Points per Game Against, PPGF-Points per Game For, PTS-Points, R-Runs, RBI-Runs Batted In, T-Ties, UPI-United Press International, W-Wins

Figure in brackets indicates extra innings or overtime.

1876

BASEBALL
National League

Team Name	W	L	Pct	GB	R	OR
Chicago White Stockings	52	14	.788	-	624	257
St. Louis Reds	45	19	.703	6	386	229
Hartford Blues	47	21	.691	6	429	261
Boston Red Caps	39	31	.557	15	471	450
Louisville Colonels	30	36	.455	22	280	344
New York Mutuals	21	35	.375	26	260	412
Philadelphia Athletics	14	45	.237	34.5	378	534
Cincinnati Reds	9	56	.138	42.5	238	579

Coaches

Chicago--Al Spalding 52-14; St. Louis--Harmon Dehlman 45-19; Hartford--Bob Ferguson 47-21; Boston--Harry Wright 9-31; Louisville--Chick Fulmer 30-36; New York--Bill Cammeyer 21-35; Philadelphia--Al Wright 14-45; Cincinnati--Charlie Gould 9-56

League Leaders

Batting Average

Ross Barnes	.429
George Hall	.366
Cap Anson	.356
John Peters	.351
Cal McVey	.347

Home Runs

George Hall	5
Charley Jones	4
Lew Brown	2
Jimmy Hallinan	2
Jack Manning	2

RBI

Deacon White	60
Cap Anson	59
Paul Hines	59
Ross Barnes	59
Cal McVey	53

ERA

George Bradley	1.23
Jim Devlin	1.56
Bill Cummings	1.67
Tommy Bond	1.68
Al Spalding	1.75

Wins

Al Spalding	46
George Bradley	45
Tommy Bond	31
Jim Devlin	30
Bob Mathews	21

Saves

Jack Manning	5
George Zettlein	2
Cal McVey	2
Joe Borden	1
George Bradley	1

Strikeouts

Jim Devlin	122
George Bradley	103
Tommy Bond	88
Al Spalding	39
Bob Mathews	37

Notes

The National League was founded on February 2, 1876 in New York City by William A. Hulbert and other club delegates, with Morgan G. Bulkeley as the first President.

Other Sports

Horseracing--Kentucky Derby won by Vagrant (time 2:38.25, purse $2,950).
previous years race won by Aristides (time 2:37.75, purse $2,850).

1877

BASEBALL
National

Team Name	W	L	Pct	GB	R	OR
Boston Red Caps	42	18	.700	-	419	263
Louisville Colonels	35	25	.583	7	339	288
Hartford Blues	31	27	.534	10	341	311
St. Louis Reds	28	32	.467	14	284	318
Chicago White Stockings	26	33	.441	15.5	366	375
Cincinnati Reds	15	42	.263	25.5	291	485

Coaching Changes

Louisville--Jack Chapman 35-25; Cincinnati--Lip Pike 3-11, Bob Addy 12-31; St. Louis--John Lucas 14-12, George McManus 14-20.

League Leaders

Batting Average

Deacon White	.387
Jack Cassidy	.378
Cal McVey	.368
Jim O'Rourke	.362
Cap Anson	.337

Home Runs

Lip Pike	4
George Shaffer	3
Charley Jones	2
Deacon White	2
Charles Snyder	2

RBI

Deacon White	49
John Peters	41
Ezra Sutton	39
Charley Jones	38
Tom York	37

ERA

Tommy Bond	2.11
Terry Larkin	2.14
Jim Devlin	2.25
Fred Nichols	2.60
Joe Blong	2.74

Wins

Tommy Bond	40
Jim Devlin	35
Terry Larkin	29
George Bradley	18
Fred Nichols	18

Saves

Cal McVey	2
Al Spalding	1
Jack Manning	1

Strikeouts

Tommy Bond	170
Jim Devlin	141
Terry Larkin	96
Fred Nichols	80
George Bradley	59

Rules

Time at bat not charged to a batter for a base on balls.

Notes

William Hulbert became the second President of the National League.

Other Sports

Horseracing--Kentucky Derby won by Baden Baden (time 2:38, purse $3,300).

1878

BASEBALL
National League

Team Name	W	L	Pct	GB	R	OR
Boston Red Caps	41	19	.683	-	298	241
Cincinnati Reds	37	23	.617	4	333	281
Providence Grays	33	27	.550	8	353	337
Chicago White Stockings	30	30	.500	11	371	331
Indianapolis Hoosiers	24	36	.400	17	293	328
Milwaukee Brewers	15	45	.250	26	256	386

Coaching Changes

Cincinnati--Cal McVey 37-23; Providence--George Ware 33-27; Chicago--Bob Ferguson 30-30; Indianapolis--John Clapp 24-36; Milwaukee--Jack Chapman 15-45.

League Leaders

Batting Average		Home Runs		RBI	
Paul Hines	.358	Paul Hines	4	Paul Hines	50
Abner Dalrymple	.354	Charley Jones	3	Lew Brown	43
Bob Ferguson	.351	Russ McKelvey	2	Cap Anson	40
Joe Start	.351	Cal McVey	2	Bob Ferguson	39
Cap Anson	.341	Monte Ward	1	Charley Jones	39

ERA		Wins		Saves	
Monte Ward	1.51	Tommy Bond	40	Tom Healey	1
Jim McCormick	1.69	Will White	30		
Will White	1.79	Terry Larkin	29		
Sam Weaver	1.95	Monte Ward	22		
Tommy Bond	2.06	Ed Nolan	13		

Strikeouts	
Tommy Bond	182
Will White	169
Terry Larkin	163
Ed Nolan	125
Monte Ward	116

Other Sports

Horseracing--Kentucky Derby won by Day Star (time 2:37.25, purse $4,050).

1879

BASEBALL
National League

Team Name	W	L	Pct	GB	R	OR
Providence Grays	59	25	.702	-	612	355
Boston Red Caps	54	30	.643	5	562	348
Buffalo Bisons	46	32	.590	10	394	365
Chicago White Stockings	46	33	.582	10.5	437	411
Cincinnati Reds	43	37	.538	14	485	464
Cleveland Blues	27	55	.329	31	322	461
Syracuse Stars	22	48	.314	30	276	462
Troy Trojans	19	56	.253	35.5	321	543

Coaching Changes

Providence--George Wright 59-25; Buffalo--John Clapp 46-32; Chicago--Cap Anson 46-33; Cincinnati--Deacon White 8-8, Cal McVey 35-29; Cleveland--Jim McCormick 27-55; Syracuse--Mike Dorgan 22-48; Troy--Horace Phillips 12-46, Bob Ferguson 7-10.

League Leaders

Batting Average

Paul Hines	.357
Jim O'Rourke	.348
Mike Kelly	.348
John O'Rourke	.341
Deacon White	.330

Home Runs

Charley Jones	9
John O'Rourke	6
Dan Brouthers	4
Charlie Eden	3
Lew Brown	2

RBI

John O'Rourke	62
Charley Jones	62
Lou Dickerson	57
Cal McVey	55
Deacon White	52

ERA

Tommy Bond	1.96
Will White	1.99
Monte Ward	2.15
James Galvin	2.28
Bob Mathews	2.29

Wins

Monte Ward	47
Will White	43
Tommy Bond	43
James Galvin	37
Terry Larkin	31

Saves

Charles Foley	1
Monte Ward	1
Bob Mathews	1

Strikeouts

Monte Ward	239
Will White	232
Jim McCormick	197
Tommy Bond	155
Terry Larkin	142

Other Sports

Horseracing--Kentucky Derby won by Lord Murphy (time 2:37, purse $3,550).

1880

BASEBALL
National League

Team Name	W	L	Pct	GB	R	OR
Chicago White Stockings	67	17	.798	-	538	317
Providence Grays	52	32	.619	15	419	299
Cleveland Blues	47	37	.560	20	387	337
Troy Trojans	41	42	.494	25.5	392	438
Worcester Brown Stockings	40	43	.482	26.5	412	370
Boston Red Caps	40	44	.476	27	416	456
Buffalo Bisons	24	58	.293	42	331	502
Cincinnati Reds	21	59	.263	44	296	472

Coaching Changes
Providence--Jim Bullock 52-32; Troy--Bob Ferguson 41-42; Worcester--Frank Bancroft 40-43; Buffalo--Bill McGunnigle 4-13, Sam Crane 20-45; Cincinnati--John Clapp 21-59.

League Leaders

Batting Average		Home Runs		ERA	
George Gore	.360	Harry Stovey	6	Tim Keefe	0.86
Cap Anson	.337	Jim O'Rourke	6	George Bradley	1.38
Roger Connor	.330	Charley Jones	5	Monte Ward	1.74
Abner Dalrymple	.330	Fred Dunlap	4	Fred Goldsmith	1.75
Tom Burns	.309	John O'Rourke	3	Jim McCormick	1.85

Wins		Saves		Strikeouts	
Jim McCormick	45	Lee Richmond	3	Larry Corcoran	268
Larry Corcoran	43	Larry Corcoran	2	Jim McCormick	260
Monte Ward	38	Fred Corey	2	Lee Richmond	243
Mickey Welch	34	George Bradley	1	Monte Ward	230
Lee Richmond	32	Tom Poorman	1	Will White	161

Notes
Base on balls on eight balls instead of nine.
John Richmond of Worchester pitched the first perfect game.

Other Sports
Horseracing--Kentucky Derby won by Fonso (time 2:37.5, purse $3,800).

1881

BASEBALL
National League

Team Name	W	L	Pct	GB	R	OR
Chicago White Stockings	56	28	.667	-	550	379
Providence Grays	47	37	.560	9	447	426
Buffalo Bisons	45	38	.542	10.5	440	447
Detroit Wolverines	41	43	.488	15	439	429
Troy Trojans	39	45	.464	17	399	429
Boston Red Caps	38	45	.458	17.5	349	410
Cleveland Blues	36	48	.429	20	392	414
Worcester Brown Stockings	32	50	.390	23	410	492

Coaching Changes

Providence--Jim Bullock 17-17, Bob Morrow 30-20; Buffalo--Jim O'Rourke 45-38; Detroit--Frank Bancroft 41-43; Cleveland--Mike McGeary 36-48; Worcester--Freeman Brown 32-50.

League Leaders

Batting Average

Cap Anson	.399
Martin Powell	.338
Jack Rowe	.333
Joe Start	.328
Fred Dunlap	.325

Home Runs

Dan Brouthers	8
Charlie Bennett	7
Jack Farrell	5
Tom Burns	4
Fred Dunlap	3

RBI

Cap Anson	82
Charlie Bennett	64
Michael Kelly	55
Monte Ward	53
Hardy Richardson	53

ERA

Stump Weidman	1.80
Monte Ward	2.13
George Derby	2.20
Larry Corcoran	2.31
James Galvin	2.37

Wins

Jim Whitney	31
Larry Corcoran	31
George Derby	29
James Galvin	28
Jim McCormick	26

Saves

Bob Mathews	2
John Morrill	1

Strikeouts

George Derby	212
Jim McCormick	178
Jim Whitney	162
Lee Richmond	156
Larry Corcoran	150

Other Sports

Horseracing--Kentucky Derby won by Hindoo (time 2:40, purse $4,410).

1882

BASEBALL
National League

Team Name	W	L	Pct	GB	R	OR
Chicago White Stockings	55	29	.655	-	604	353
Providence Grays	52	32	.619	3	463	356
Boston Red Caps	45	39	.536	10	472	414
Buffalo Bisons	45	39	.536	10	500	461
Cleveland Blues	42	40	.512	12	402	411
Detroit Wolverines	42	41	.506	12.5	407	488
Troy Trojans	35	48	.422	19.5	430	522
Worcester Brown Stockings	18	66	.214	37	379	652

Coaching Changes

Providence--Harry Wright 52-32; Boston--John Morrill 45-39; Cleveland--Ford Evans 42-40; Worcester--Freeman Brown 4-19, Tommy Bond 5-22, Jack Chapman 9-25.

League Leaders

Batting Average

Dan Brouthers	.368
Cap Anson	.362
Roger Connor	.330
Joe Start	.329
Jim Whitney	.323

Home Runs

George Wood	7
Dan Brouthers	6
Mike Muldoon	6
Jim Whitney	5
Charlie Bennett	5

ERA

Larry Corcoran	1.95
Charles Radbourne	2.09
Jim McCormick	2.37
Fred Goldsmith	2.42
Tim Keefe	2.50

Wins

Jim McCormick	36
Charles Radbourn	33
James Galvin	28
Fred Goldsmith	28
Larry Corcoran	27

Saves

Monte Ward	1

Strikeouts

Charles Radbourn	201
Jim McCormick	200
George Derby	182
Jim Whitney	180
Larry Corcoran	170

American Association

Team Name	W	L	Pct	GB	R	OR
Cincinnati Red Stockings	55	25	.688	-	489	268
Philadelphia Athletics	41	34	.547	11.5	406	389
Louisville Eclipse	42	38	.525	13	443	352
Pittsburgh Alleghenys	39	39	.500	15	428	418
St. Louis Browns	37	43	.463	18	399	496
Baltimore Orioles	19	54	.260	32.5	273	515

Coaching

Cincinnati--Pop Snyder 55-25; Philadelphia--Lew Simmons 20-19, Charlie Mason 21-15; Louisville--John Dyler 6-7, Bill Reccius 24-18, Leech Maskrey 12-13; Pittsburgh--Al Pratt 39-39; St. Louis--Ned Cuthbert 37-43, Ed Brown 10-11; Baltimore--Henry Myers 19-54

League Leaders

Batting Average		Home Runs		ERA	
Pete Browning	.378	Oscar Walker	7	John Driscoll	1.21
Warren Carpenter	.342	Pete Browning	5	Guy Hecker	1.30
Ed Swartwood	.329	Ed Swartwood	5	Harry McCormick	1.52
Jack O'Brien	.303	Bill Taylor	4	Will White	1.54
William Wolf	.299	Jack O'Brien	3	Tony Mullane	1.88

Wins		Saves		Strikeouts	
Will White	40	Ed Fusselbach	1	Tony Mullane	170
Tony Mullane	30			Harry Salisbury	135
Sam Weaver	26			George McGinnis	134
George McGinnis	25			Will White	122
Harry Salisbury	20			Sam Weaver	104

Notes

Justus Thorner of Cincinnati and H.D. Knight of Pittsburgh formed the American Association. Paul Hines of the Providence Grays becomes the first fielder to wear sunglasses in the field. The American Association charges 25 cents admission to its games while the National League is charging 50 cents to most of its games.

Other Sports

Horseracing--Kentucky Derby won by Apollo (time 2:40.25, purse $4,560).

1883

BASEBALL
National League

Team Name	W	L	Pct	GB	R	OR
Boston Beaneaters	63	35	.643	-	669	456
Chicago White Stockings	59	39	.602	4	679	540
Providence Grays	58	40	.592	5	636	436
Cleveland Blues	55	42	.567	7.5	476	443
Buffalo Bisons	52	45	.536	10.5	614	576
New York Gothams	46	50	.479	16	530	577
Detroit Wolverines	40	58	.408	23	524	650
Philadelphia Phillies	17	81	.173	46	437	887

Coaching Changes

Boston--Jack Burdock 31-26, John Morrill 32-9; Cleveland--Frank Bancroft 55-42; New York--John Clapp 46-50; Detroit--Jack Chapman 40-58; Philadelphia--Bob Ferguson 4-13, Blondie Purcell 13-68.

League Leaders

Batting Average		Home Runs		ERA	
Dan Brouthers	.374	William Ewing	10	Jim McCormick	1.84
Roger Connor	.357	Joe Hornung	8	Charles Radbourne	2.05
George Gore	.334	Jerry Denny	8	Jim Whitney	2.24
Jack Burdock	.330	Monte Ward	7	Will Sawyer	2.36
Jim O'Rourke	.328	John Morrill	6	Hugh Daily	2.42

Wins		Saves		Strikeouts	
Charles Radbourn	48	Jim Whitney	2	Jim Whitney	345
James Galvin	46	Stump Weidman	2	Charles Radbourn	315
Jim Whitney	37	George Derby	1	James Galvin	279
Larry Corcoran	34	Charlie Buffinton	1	Larry Corcoran	216
Jim McCormick	28	Jim McCormick	1	Charlie Buffinton	188

Notes

A.G. Mills succeeded William Hulbert to become the third President of the National League. Hugh Dailey of the Cleveland Spiders threw a no-hitter against the Philadelphia Phillies to lead his team to a 1-0 victory. Dailey only had one arm.

American Association

Team Name	W	L	Pct	GB	R	OR
Philadelphia Athletics	66	32	.673	-	720	547
St. Louis Browns	65	33	.663	1	549	409
Cincinnati Red Stockings	61	37	.622	5	662	413
New York Metropolitans	54	42	.563	11	498	405
Louisville Eclipse	52	45	.536	13.5	564	562
Columbus Discoverers	32	65	.330	33.5	476	659
Pittsburgh Alleghenys	31	67	.316	35	525	728
Baltimore Orioles	28	68	.292	37	471	742

Coaching Changes

St. Louis--Ted Sullivan 53-27, Charlie Comiskey 12-6; New York--Jim Mutrie 54-42; Louisville--Bill Reccius 12-10, Leech Maskrey 24-16, Joe Gerhardt 16-19; Columbus--Horace Phillips 32-65; Pittsburgh--Al Pratt 12-20, Ormond Butler 17-36, Joe Battin 2-11; Baltimore--Bill Barnie 28-68; Philadelphia--Lew Simmons 66-32.

League Leaders

Batting Average		**Home Runs**		**ERA**	
Ed Swartwood	.356	Harry Stovey	14	Will White	2.09
Pete Browning	.338	Charley Jones	11	Tony Mullane	2.19
Jim Clinton	.313	John Reilly	9	Ren Deagle	2.31
Dave Rowe	.313	Tom Brown	5	George McGinnis	2.33
John Reilly	.311	Charles Fulmer	5	Tim Keefe	2.41

Wins		**Saves**		**Strikeouts**	
Will White	43	Tony Mullane	1	Tim Keefe	361
Tim Keefe	41	Bob Barr	1	Bob Mathews	203
Tony Mullane	35			Tony Mullane	191
Bob Mathews	30			Frank Mountain	159
George McGinnis	28			Guy Hecker	153

Franchise Changes

NL-Boston Red Caps changed name to Boston Beaneaters.
Troy Trojans became New York Gothams.
Worchester became Philadelphia Phillies.

Other Sports

Horseracing--Kentucky Derby won by Leonatus (time 2:43, purse $3,760).

1884

BASEBALL
National League

Team Name	W	L	Pct	GB	R	OR
Providence Grays	84	28	.750	-	665	388
Boston Beaneaters	73	38	.658	10.5	684	468
Buffalo Bisons	64	47	.577	19.5	700	626
Chicago White Stockings	62	50	.554	22	834	647
New York Gothams	62	50	.554	22	693	623
Philadelphia Phillies	39	73	.348	45	549	824
Cleveland Blues	35	77	.313	49	458	716
Detroit Wolverines	28	84	.250	56	445	736

Coaching Changes

Providence--Frank Bancroft 84-28; Boston--John Morrill 73-38; New York--James Price 56-42, Monte Ward 6-8; Philadelphia--Harry Wright 39-73; Cleveland--Charlie Hackett 35-77.

League Leaders

Batting Average		Home Runs		ERA	
Michael Kelly	.354	Ned Williamson	27	Charles Radbourne	1.38
Jim O'Rourke	.347	Fred Pfeffer	25	Charlie Sweemey	1.55
Ezra Sutton	.346	Abner Dalrymple	22	Charles Getzein	1.95
Cap Anson	.335	Cap Anson	21	James Galvin	1.99
Dan Brouthers	.327	Dan Brouthers	14	Jim Whitney	2.09

Wins		Saves		Strikeouts	
Charles Radbourn	60	John Morrill	2	Charles Radbourn	441
Charles Buffinton	48	Jim O'Rourke	1	Charles Buffinton	417
James Galvin	46	Charles Radbourn	1	James Galvin	369
Mickey Welch	39	Charlie Ferguson	1	Mickey Welch	345
Larry Corcoran	35	Charlie Sweeney	1	Larry Corcoran	272

American Association

Team Name	W	L	Pct	GB	R	OR
New York Metropolitans	75	32	.701	-	734	423
Columbus Discoverers	69	39	.639	6.5	585	459
Louisville Eclipse	68	40	.630	7.5	573	425
St. Louis Browns	67	40	.626	8	658	539
Cincinnati Red Stockings	68	41	.624	8	754	512
Baltimore Orioles	63	43	.594	11.5	636	515
Philadelphia Athletics	61	46	.570	14	700	546
Toledo Blue Stockings	46	58	.442	27.5	463	571
Brooklyn Bridegrooms	40	64	.385	33.5	476	644
Richmond Virginias	12	30	.286	30.5	194	294
Pittsburgh Alleghenys	30	78	.278	45.5	406	725
Indianapolis Hoosiers	29	78	.271	46	462	755
Washington Nationals	12	51	.190	41	248	481

Coaching Changes

Columbus--Gus Schmelz 69-39; Louisville--Joe Gerhardt 39-18, Mike Walsh 29-22; St. Louis--Jimmy Williams 67 40; Cincinnati--Will White 43-25, Pop Snyder 25-16; Philadelphia--Charlie Mason 28-23, Bill Sharsig 33-23; Toledo--Charlie Morton 46-58; Brooklyn--George Taylor 40-64; Richmond--Felix Moses 12-30; Pittsburgh--Joe Battin 1-3, George Creamer 2-7, Denny McKnight 12-17, Bob Ferguson 5-21, Horace Phillips 10-30; Indianapolis--Jim Gifford 25-59, Bill Watkins 4-19; Washington--Holly Hollingshead 12-51.

League Leaders

Batting Average		Home Runs		ERA	
Dave Orr	.354	John Reilly	11	Guy Hecker	1.80
John Reilly	.339	Harry Stovey	10	Dave Foutz	2.18
Pete Browning	.336	Dave Orr	9	Ed Morris	2.18
Harry Stovey	.326	Charley Jones	7	Tim Keefe	2.29
Fred Lewis	.323	Fred Mann	7	Frank Mountain	2.45

Wins		Saves		Strikeouts	
Guy Hecker	52	Thomas Burns	1	Guy Hecker	385
Tim Keefe	37	Hank O'Day	1	James Henderson	346
Jack Lynch	37	Frank Mountain	1	Tony Mullane	329
Tony Mullane	37			Tim Keefe	323
Ed Morris	34			Larry McKeon	308

World Series

October 23	Providence Grays	6	at	New York Metropolitans	0
October 24	Providence Grays	3	at	New York Metropolitans	1
October 25	Providence Grays	12	at	New York Metropolitans	2

Notes

Moses Fleetwood "Fleet" Walker of the Toledo Blue Stockings became the first black player in major league baseball. His brother Welday Walker also played with Toledo this year.

Union Association

Team Name	W	L	Pct	GB	R	OR
St. Louis Maroons	94	19	.832	-	887	429
Milwaukee Unions	8	4	.667	35.5	53	34
Cincinnati Outlaw Reds	69	36	.657	21	703	466
Baltimore Unions	58	47	.552	32	662	627
Boston Unions	58	51	.532	34	636	558
Chicago-Pittsburgh	41	50	.451	42	438	482
Washington Nationals	47	65	.420	46.5	572	679
Philadelphia Keystones	21	46	.313	50	414	545
St. Paul Saints	2	6	.250	39.5	24	57
Altoona Pride	6	19	.240	44	90	216
Kansas City Unions	16	63	.203	61	311	618
Wilmington Quicksteps	2	16	.111	44.5	35	114

Coaching

St. Louis--Henry Lucas 94-19; Milwaukee--Tom Loftus 8-4; Cincinnati--Dan O'Leary 33-29, Sam Crane 36-7; Baltimore--Charlie Levis 53-35, Bill Henderson 5-12; Boston--Tim Murnane 8-17, Tom Furniss 4-6, Jake Morse 46-28; Chicago/Pittsburgh--Ed Hengle 34-39, Joe Battin 1-5, Joe Ellick 6-6; Washington--Mike Scanlon 47-65; Philadelphia--Fergy Malone 11-30, Tom Pratt 10-16; St. Paul--A.M. Thompson 2-6; Altoona--Ed Curtis 6-19; Kansas City--Ted Sullivan 16-63; Wilmington--Joe Simmons 2-16

League Leaders

Batting Average		Home Runs		ERA	
Fred Dunlap	.412	Fred Dunlap	13	Jim McCormick	1.54
George Shaffer	.360	Edward Crane	12	Bill Taylor	1.68
Harry Moore	.336	Charlie Levis	6	Henry Boyle	1.74
Jack Gleason	.324	Joe Flynn	4	Fred Shaw	1.77
Emmett Seery	.313	Henry Boyle	4	Charlie Sweeney	1.83

Wins		Saves		Strikeouts	
Bill Sweeney	40	Bill Taylor	4	Hugh Daily	483
Hugh Daily	28	Lou Sylvester	1	Bill Sweeney	374
George Bradley	25	Henry Boyle	1	Fred Shaw	309
Bill Taylor	25	Fred Dunlap	1	Bill Wise	268
Charlie Sweeney	24	Lew Brown	1	Walter Burke	255

Notes

St. Louis millionaire Henry Lucas formed the Union Association in 1884 but it only lasted one year.

Other Sports

Horseracing--Kentucky Derby won by Buchanan (time 2:40.25, purse $3,990).

1885

BASEBALL
National League

Team Name	W	L	Pct	GB	R	OR
Chicago White Stockings	87	25	.777	-	834	470
New York Gothams	85	27	.759	2	691	370
Philadelphia Phillies	56	54	.509	30	513	511
Providence Grays	53	57	.482	33	442	531
Boston Beaneaters	46	66	.411	41	528	589
Detroit Wolverines	41	67	.380	44	514	582
Buffalo Bisons	38	74	.339	49	495	761
St. Louis Maroons	36	72	.333	49	390	593

Coaching Changes

New York--Jim Mutrie 85-27; Detroit--Charlie Morton 18-39, Bill Watkins 23-28; Buffalo--Jack Chapman 12-19, George Hughson 18-33, Pud Galvin 8-22; St.Louis--Henry Lucas 36-72.

League Leaders

Batting Average		Home Runs		ERA	
Roger Connor	.371	Abner Dalrymple	11	Tim Keefe	1.58
Dan Brouthers	.359	Michael Kelly	9	Mickey Welch	1.66
Mike Dorgan	.326	Sam Thompson	7	John Clarkson	1.85
Hardy Richardson	.319	Dan Brouthers	7	Charles Baldwin	1.86
George Gore	.313	Tom Burns	7	Charles Radbourne	2.20

Wins		Saves		Strikeouts	
John Clarkson	53	Ned Williamson	2	John Clarkson	308
Mickey Welch	44	Fred Pfeffer	2	Mickey Welch	258
Tim Keefe	32	Mickey Welch	1	Charlie Buffinton	242
Charles Radbourne	28	Charles Baldwin	1	Tim Keefe	230
Charlie Ferguson	26	Pud Galvin	1	Jim Whitney	200

Notes

Nicholas Young succeeded A.G. Mills as President of the National League.

American Association

Team Name	W	L	Pct	GB	R	OR
St. Louis Browns	79	33	.705	-	677	461
Cincinnati Red Stockings	63	49	.563	16	642	575
Pittsburgh Alleghenys	56	55	.505	22.5	547	539
Philadelphia Athletics	55	57	.491	24	764	691
Brooklyn Bridegrooms	53	59	.473	26	624	650
Louisville Eclipse	53	59	.473	26	564	598
New York Metropolitans	44	64	.407	33	526	688
Baltimore Orioles	41	68	.376	36.5	541	683

Coaching Changes

Cincinnati--O.P. Caylor 63-49; Pittsburgh--Horace Phillips 56-55; Philadelphia--Lon Knight 16-19, Charlie Mason 17-21, Bill Sharsig 9-2-17; Brooklyn--Joe Doyle 13-20, Charlie Hackett 15-25, Charlie Byrne 25-14; Louisville--Jim Hart 53-59; New York--Jim Gifford 44-64; St. Louis--Charlie Comiskey 79-33.

League Leaders

Batting Average		**Home Runs**		**ERA**	
Pete Browning	.362	Harry Stovey	13	Bob Caruthers	2.07
Dave Orr	.342	Frank Fennelly	10	Guy Hecker	2.18
Henry Larkin	.329	Pete Browning	9	Ed Morris	2.35
Charley Jones	.322	Henry Larkin	8	Bob Mathews	2.43
Harry Stovey	.315	Dave Orr	6	Dave Foutz	2.63

Wins		**Saves**		**Strikeouts**	
Bob Caruthers	40	Thomas Burns	3	Ed Morris	298
Ed Morris	39	Phil Reccius	1	Bob Mathews	286
Dave Foutz	33	Joe Sommer	1	James Henderson	263
Henry Porter	33	John Corkhill	1	Guy Hecker	209
Bob Mathews	30	Bill Terry	1	Henry Porter	197

World Series

October 14	St. Louis Browns	5	at	Chicago White Stockings	5
October 15	Chicago White Stockings	5	at	St. Louis Browns	4
October 16	Chicago White Stockings	4	at	St. Louis Browns	7
October 17	Chicago White Stockings	2	at	St. Louis Browns	3
October 22	Chicago White Stockings	9		St. Louis Browns	2*
October 23	Chicago White Stockings	9		St. Louis Browns	2#
October 24	St. Louis Browns	13		Chicago White Stockings	4#

*Game played in Pittsburgh
#Game played in Cincinnati

Other Sports

Horseracing--Kentucky Derby won by Joe Cotton (time 2:37.2, purse $4,630).

1886

BASEBALL

National League

Team Name	W	L	Pct	GB	R	OR
Chicago White Stockings	90	34	.726	-	900	555
Detroit Wolverines	87	36	.707	2.5	829	538
New York Giants	75	44	.630	12.5	692	558
Philadelphia Phillies	71	43	.623	14	621	498
Boston Beaneaters	56	61	.479	30.5	657	661
St. Louis Maroons	43	79	.352	46	547	712
Kansas City Cowboys	30	91	.248	58.5	494	872
Washington Senators	28	92	.233	60	445	791

Coaching Changes

Detroit--Bill Watkins 87-36; St. Louis--Gus Schmelz 43-79; Kansas City--Dave Rowe 30-91; Washington--Mike Scanlon 13-66, John Gaffney 15-26.

League Leaders

Batting Average

Michael Kelly	.388
Cap Anson	.371
Dan Brouthers	.370
Roger Connor	.355
Hardy Richardson	.351

Home Runs

Hardy Richardson	11
Dan Brouthers	11
Cap Anson	10
Paul Hines	9
Jerry Denny	9

RBI

Cap Anson	147
Fred Pfeffer	95
Sam Thompson	89
Jack Rowe	87
Monte Ward	81

ERA

Charlie Ferguson	1.98
Charles Baldwin	2.24
John H. Boyle	2.24
John Flynn	2.24
John Clarkson	2.41

Wins

Charles Baldwin	42
Tim Keefe	41
John Clarkson	36
Mickey Welch	33
Charles Getzein	30

Saves

Charlie Ferguson	2
John Flynn	1
James Ryan	1
James Devlin	1
Ned Williamson	1

Strikeouts

Charles Baldwin	323
John Clarkson	313
Tim Keefe	291
Mickey Welch	272
Bill Stemmyer	239

American Association

Team Name	W	L	Pct	GB	R	OR
St. Louis Browns	93	46	.669	-	944	592
Pittsburgh Alleghenys	80	57	.584	12	810	647
Brooklyn Bridegrooms	76	61	.555	16	832	832
Louisville Eclipse	66	70	.485	25.5	833	805
Cincinnati Red Stockings	65	73	.471	27.5	883	865
Philadelphia Athletics	63	72	.467	28	772	942
New York Metropolitans	53	82	.393	38	628	766
Baltimore Orioles	48	83	.366	41	625	878

Coaching Changes

Brooklyn--Charlie Byrne 76-61; Philadelphia--Lew Simmons 41-55, Bill Sharsig 22-17; New York--Jim Gifford 6-12, Bob Ferguson 47-70.

League Leaders

Battling Average		Home Runs		ERA	
Guy Hecker	.341	Harry Stovey	7	Dan Foutz	2.11
Pete Browning	.340	Dave Orr	7	Bob Caruthers	2.32
Dave Orr	.338	John McPhee	7	Thomas Ramsey	2.45
Bob Caruthers	.334	Frank Fennelly	6	Ed Morris	2.45
James O'Neill	.328	John Milligan	5	James Galvin	2.67

Wins		Saves		Strikeouts	
Ed Morris	41	Fred Ely	1	Matt Kilroy	513
Dan Foutz	41	Ed Morris	1	Thomas Ramsey	499
Thomas Ramsey	38	Joe Strauss	1	Ed Morris	326
Tony Mullane	33	Dan Foutz	1	Dan Foutz	283
Bob Caruthers	30	Nat Hudson	1	Tony Mullane	250

World Series

October 18	St. Louis Browns	0	at	Chicago White Stockings	6
October 19	St. Louis Browns	12	at	Chicago White Stockings	0
October 20	St. Louis Browns	4	at	Chicago White Stockings	11
October 21	Chicago White Stockings	5	at	St. Louis Browns	8
October 22	Chicago White Stockings	3	at	St. Louis Browns	10
October 23	Chicago White Stockings	3	at	St. Louis Browns	4

Rules

Pitchers box changed to 4x7 feet instead of 6x6 feet.
Base on balls on 7 balls.

Franchise Changes

NL--New York Gothams changed name to New York Giants.

Other Sports

Horseracing--Kentucky Derby won by Ben Ali (time 2:36.5, purse $4,890).

1887

BASEBALL
National League

Team Name	W	L	Pct	GB	R	OR
Detroit Wolverines	79	45	.637	-	969	714
Philadelphia Phillies	75	48	.610	3.5	901	702
Chicago White Stockings	71	50	.587	6.5	813	716
New York Giants	68	55	.553	10.5	816	723
Boston Beaneaters	61	60	.504	16.5	831	792
Pittsburgh Alleghenys	55	69	.444	24	621	750
Washington Senators	46	76	.377	32	601	818
Indianapolis Hoosiers	37	89	.294	43	628	965

Coaching Changes

Pittsburgh--Horace Phillips 55-69; Washington--John Gaffney 46-76; Indianapolis--Walter Burnham 6-22, Fred Thomas 11-18, Horace Fogel 20-49.

League Leaders

Batting Average	
Sam Thompson	.372
Cap Anson	.347
Dan Brouthers	.338
Monte Ward	.338
Sam Wise	.334

Home Runs	
Bill O'Brien	19
Roger Connor	17
Fred Pfeffer	16
George Wood	14
Dan Brouthers	12

RBI	
Sam Thompson	166
Roger Connor	104
Cap Anson	102
Dan Brouthers	101
Jerry Denny	97

Stolen Bases	
Monte Ward	111
Jim Fogarty	102
Michael Kelly	84
Ned Hanlon	69
Jack Glassock	62

ERA	
Dan Casey	2.86
Pete Conway	2.90
Charlie Ferguson	3.00
John Clarkson	3.08
Tim Keefe	3.10

Wins	
John Clarkson	38
Tim Keefe	35
Charlie Getzein	29
James Galvin	28
Dan Casey	28

Strikeouts	
John Clarkson	237
Tim Keefe	186
Mark Baldwin	164
Charlie Buffinton	160
Jim Whitney	146

Notes

The Chicago White Stockings become the first team to engage in spring training. They were preparing for a preseason series against the St. Louis Browns in Hot Springs, Arkansas.

American Association

Team Name	W	L	PCT	GB	R	OR
St. Louis Browns	95	40	.704	-	1131	761
Cincinnati Red Stockings	81	54	.600	14	892	745
Baltimore Orioles	77	58	.570	18	975	861
Louisville Eclipse	76	60	.559	19.5	956	854
Philadelphia Athletics	64	69	.481	30	893	890
Brooklyn Bridegrooms	60	74	.448	34.5	904	918
New York Metropolitans	44	89	.331	50	754	1093
Cleveland Spiders	39	92	.298	54	729	1112

Coaching Changes

Cincinnati--Gus Schmelz 81-54; Louisville--John Kelly 76-60; Philadelphia--Frank Bancroft 22-25, Bill Sharsig 42-44; New York--Bob Ferguson 6-24, Dave Orr 28-36, O.P. Caylor 10-29; Cleveland--Jimmy Williams 39-92.

League Leaders

Batting Average		Home Runs		Stolen Bases	
James O'Neill	.435	James O'Neill	14	Arlie Latham	129
Pete Browning	.402	John Reilly	10	Charlie Comiskey	117
Dave Orr	.368	Thomas Burns	9	Pete Browning	103
Dennis Lyons	.367	Bob Caruthers	8	John McPhee	95
Bob Caruthers	.357	James Davis	8	Mike Griffin	94

ERA		Wins		Saves	
Elmer Smith	2.94	Matt Kilroy	46	William Terry	3
Matt Kilroy	3.07	Tom Ramsey	37	Charles King	1
Bob Gilks	3.08	Elmer Smith	34	Bill Serad	1
Tony Mullane	3.24	Charles King	32	Guy Hecker	1
Bob Caruthers	3.30	Tony Mullane	31		

Strikeouts	
Tom Ramsey	355
Matt Kilroy	217
John Smith	206
Gus Weyhing	193
Elmer Smith	176

World Series

October 10	Detroit Wolverines	1	at	St. Louis Browns	6
October 11	Detroit Wolverines	5	at	St. Louis Browns	3
October 12	St. Louis Browns	1	at	Detroit Wolverines	2
October 13	Detroit Wolverines	8		St. Louis Browns	0*
October 14	St. Louis Browns	5		Detroit Wolverines	2**
October 15	Detroit Wolverines	9		St. Louis Browns	0***
October 17	Detroit Wolverines	3		St. Louis Browns	1#
October 18	Detroit Wolverines	9		St. Louis Browns	2##
October 19	Detroit Wolverines	4		St. Louis Browns	2#

October 21	St. Louis Browns	11		Detroit Wolverines	4###
October 21	Detroit Wolverines	13		St. Louis Browns	3@
October 22	St. Louis Browns	5		Detroit Wolverines	1**
October 24	St. Louis Browns	3	at	Detroit Wolverines	6
October 25	Detroit Wolverines	4		St. Louis Browns	3@@
October 26	Detroit Wolverines	2	at	St. Louis Browns	9

*Game played in Pittsburgh
**Game played in Brooklyn
***Game played in New York
#Game played in Philadelphia
##Game played in Boston
###Game played in Washington
@Game played in Baltimore
@@Game played in Chicago

Rules

Batter no longer allowed to call for a high or low pitch.
Base on balls on 5 balls.

Other Sports

Horseracing--Kentucky Derby won by Montrose (time 2:39.25, purse $4,200).

1888

BASEBALL
National League

Team Name	W	L	Pct	GB	R	OR
New York Giants	84	47	.641	-	659	479
Chicago White Stockings	77	58	.570	9	734	659
Philadelphia Phillies	69	61	.531	14.5	535	509
Boston Beaneaters	70	64	.522	15.5	669	619
Detroit Wolverines	68	63	.519	16	721	629
Pittsburgh Alleghenys	66	68	.493	19.5	534	580
Indianapolis Hoosiers	50	85	.370	36	603	731
Washington Senators	48	86	.358	37.5	482	731

Coaching Changes

Detroit--Bill Watkins 49-45, Bob Leadley 19-18; Indianapolis--Harry Spence 50-85; Washington--Walter Hewitt 12-29, Ted Sullivan 36-57.

League Leaders

Batting Average

Cap Anson	.344
Jimmy Ryan	.332
Michael Kelly	.318
Dan Brouthers	.307
William Ewing	.306

Home Runs

Jimmy Ryan	16
Roger Connor	14
Jerry Denny	12
Cap Anson	12
Dick Johnston	12

RBI

Cap Anson	84
Bill Nash	75
Jack Rowe	74
Ned Williamson	73
Michael Kelly	71

Stolen Bases

William Hoy	82
Emmett Seery	80
Billy Sunday	71
Fred Pfeffer	64
Jimmy Ryan	60

ERA

Tim Keefe	1.74
Ben Sanders	1.90
Charlie Buffinton	1.91
Mickey Welch	1.93
Bill Sowders	2.07

Wins

Tim Keefe	33
John Clarkson	33
Pete Conway	30
Ed Morris	29
Charlie Buffinton	29

Saves

George Wood	2
Edward Crane	1
George Van Haltren	1

Strikeouts

Tim Keefe	333
John Clarkson	223
Charlie Getzein	202
Charlie Buffinton	199
Hank O'Day	186

Rules

Strike out on 3 strikes.

American Association

Team Name	W	L	Pct	GB	R	OR
St. Louis Browns	92	43	.681	-	789	501
Brooklyn Bridegrooms	88	52	.629	6.5	758	584
Philadelphia Athletics	81	52	.609	10	827	594
Cincinnati Red Stockings	80	54	.597	11.5	745	628
Baltimore Orioles	57	80	.416	36	653	779
Cleveland Spiders	50	82	.379	40.5	651	839
Louisville Eclipse	48	87	.356	44	689	870
Kansas City Blues	43	89	.326	47.5	579	896

Coaching Changes

Brooklyn--Bill McGunnigle 88-52; Philadelphia--Bill Sharsig 81-52; Cleveland--Jimmy Williams 19-41, Tom Lofthus 31-41; Louisville--John Kerins 11-32, Mordecai Davidson 37-55; Kansas City--Dave Rowe 14-35, Sam Barkley 26-43, Bill Watkins 3-11.

League Leaders

Batting Average		Home Runs		RBI	
James O'Neill	.335	John Reilly	13	John Reilly	103
John Reilly	.321	Harry Stovey	9	Henry Larkin	101
Pete Browning	.313	Henry Larkin	7	Dave Foutz	99
Hubert Collins	.307	Denny Lyons	6	James O'Neill	98
Dave Orr	.305	Tommy Tucker	6	John Corkhill	93

Stolen Bases		ERA		Wins	
Arlie Latham	109	Charlie King	1.64	Charlie King	45
Hugh Nicol	103	Ed Seward	2.01	Ed Seward	35
Curt Welch	95	William Terry	2.03	Bob Caruthers	29
Tom McCarthy	93	Mickey Hughes	2.13	Gus Weyhing	28
Harry Stovey	87	Elton Chamberlain	2.19	Lee Viau	27

Saves		Strikeouts	
Tony Mullane	1	Ed Seward	272
John Corkhill	1	Charlie King	258
Bob Gilks	1	Tom Ramsey	228
		Edward Bakely	212
		Gus Weyhing	204

World Series

October 16	St. Louis Browns	1	at	New York Giants	2
October 17	St. Louis Browns	3	at	New York Giants	0
October 18	St. Louis Browns	2	at	New York Giants	4
October 19	New York Giants	6		St. Louis Browns	3*
October 20	St. Louis Browns	4	at	New York Giants	6
October 22	New York Giants	12		St. Louis Browns	5**

*Game played in Brooklyn
**Game played in Philadelphia

October 24	New York Giants	5	at	St. Louis Browns	7
October 25	New York Giants	11	at	St. Louis Browns	3
October 26	New York Giants	11	at	St. Louis Browns	14
October 27	New York Giants	7	at	St. Louis Browns	18

Franchise Changes

AA--New York Metropolitans became the Kansas City Blues.

Other Sports

Horseracing--Kentucky Derby won by Macbeth (time 2:38.25, purse $4,740).

1889

BASEBALL
National League

Team Name	W	L	Pct	GB	R	OR
New York Giants	83	43	.659	-	935	708
Boston Beaneaters	83	45	.648	1	826	626
Chicago White Stockings	67	65	.508	19	867	814
Philadelphia Phillies	63	64	.496	20.5	742	748
Pittsburgh Alleghenys	61	71	.462	25	726	801
Cleveland Spiders	61	72	.459	25.5	656	720
Indianapolis Hoosiers	59	75	.440	28	819	894
Washington Senators	41	83	.331	41	632	892

Coaching Changes

Boston--Jim Hart 83-45; Pittsburgh--Horace Phillips 28-43, Fred Dunlap 7-9, Ned Hanlon 26-19; Cleveland--Tom Lofthus 61-72; Indianapolis--Frank Bancroft 25-42, Jack Glasscock 34-33; Washington--John Morrill 13-39, Arthur Irwin 28.

League Leaders

Batting Average		Home Runs		RBI	
Dan Brouthers	.373	Sam Thompson	20	Roger Connor	130
Jack Glassock	.352	Jerry Denny	18	Dan Brouthers	118
Mike Tiernan	.335	Jimmy Ryan	17	Cap Anson	117
Fred Carroll	.330	Roger Connor	13	Jerry Denny	112
Bill Ewing	.327	Hugh Duffy	12	Sam Thompson	111

Stolen Bases		ERA		Wins	
Jim Fogarty	99	John Clarkson	2.73	John Clarkson	49
Michael Kelly	68	Edward Bakely	2.96	Charlie Buffinton	28
Tom Brown	63	Mickey Welch	3.02	Tim Keefe	28
Monte Ward	62	Charlie Buffinton	3.24	Mickey Welch	27
Jack Glassock	57	Tim Keefe	3.31	James Galvin	23

Saves		Strikeouts	
Bill Bishop	2	John Clarkson	284
Bill Sowders	2	Tim Keefe	209
Mickey Welch	2	Harry Staley	159
Mike Madden	1	Charlie Buffinton	153
William Gleason	1	Charlie Getzein	139

American Association

Team Name	W	L	Pct	GB	R	OR
Brooklyn Bridegrooms	93	44	.679	-	995	706
St. Louis Browns	90	45	.667	2	957	680
Philadelphia Athletics	75	58	.564	16	880	787
Cincinnati Red Stockings	76	63	.547	18	897	769
Baltimore Orioles	70	65	.519	22	791	795
Columbus Discoverers	60	78	.435	33.5	779	924
Kansas City Blues	55	82	.401	38	852	1031
Louisville Eclipse	27	111	.196	66.5	632	1091

Coaching Changes

Columbus--Al Buckenberger 60-78; Kansas City--Bill Watkins 55-82; Louisville--Thomas "Dude" Esterbrook 2-8, William Wolf 15-51, Dan Shannon 9-43, Jack Chapman 1-9.

League Leaders

Battling Average

Tommy Tucker	.372
James O'Neill	.335
Denny Lyons	.329
Dave Orr	.327
Jim Holliday	.321

Home Runs

Harry Stovey	19
Jim Holliday	19
Charlie Duffee	15
John Milligan	12
Denny Lyons	9

RBI

Harry Stovey	119
Dave Foutz	113
James O'Neill	110
Lou Bierbauer	105
Jim Holliday	104

Stolen Bases

Billy Hamilton	111
William O'Brien	91
Herman Long	89
Hugh Nicol	80
Arlie Latham	69

ERA

Jack Stivetts	2.25
Jesse Duryea	2.56
Matt Kilroy	2.85
Gus Weyhing	2.95
Elton Chamberlain	2.97

Wins

Bob Caruthers	40
Charles King	34
Elton Chamberlain	32
Jesse Duryea	32
Gus Weyhing	30

Saves

Tony Mullane	5
Scott Stratton	1
John Sowders	1
Jack Stivens	1

Strikeouts

Mark Baldwin	368
Matt Kilroy	217
Gus Weyhing	213
Elton Chamberlain	202
Charles King	188

World Series

October 18	Brooklyn Bridegrooms	12	at	New York Giants	10
October 19	New York Giants	6	at	Brooklyn Bridegrooms	2
October 22	Brooklyn Bridegrooms	8	at	New York Giants	7
October 23	New York Giants	7	at	Brooklyn Bridegrooms	10
October 24	New York Giants	11	at	Brooklyn Bridegrooms	3
October 25	Brooklyn Bridegrooms	1	at	New York Giants	2
October 26	Brooklyn Bridegrooms	7	at	New York Giants	11
October 28	New York Giants	16	at	Brooklyn Bridegrooms	7
October 29	Brooklyn Bridegrooms	2	at	New York Giants	3

Other Sports

Horseracing--Kentucky Derby won by Spokane (time 2:34.5, purse $4,970).
Boxing--John L. Sullivan beat Jake Kilrain in 75 rounds to retain the title.

Notes

The fight between Sullivan and Kilrain was the last championship bare-knuckles bout.

1890

BASEBALL
National League

Team Name	W	L	Pct	GB	R	OR
Brooklyn Bridegrooms	86	43	.667	-	884	620
Chicago White Stockings	84	53	.613	6	847	692
Philadelphia Phillies	78	54	.591	9.5	823	707
Cincinnati Reds	77	55	.583	10.5	753	633
Boston Beaneaters	76	57	.571	12	763	593
New York Giants	63	68	.481	24	713	698
Cleveland Spiders	44	88	.333	43.5	630	832
Pittsburgh Innocents	23	113	.169	66.5	597	1235

Coaching Changes

Brooklyn--Bill McGunnigle 86-43; Cincinnati--Tom Loftus 77--55; Boston-Frank Selee 76-57; Cleveland--Gus Schmelz 21-55, Bob Leadley 23-33; Pittsburgh--Guy Hecker 23-113.

League Leaders

Batting Average		Home Runs		RBI	
Jack Glassock	.336	Walt Wilmot	14	Tom Burns	128
Bill Hamilton	.325	Mike Tiernan	13	Cap Anson	107
Jack Clements	.315	Tom Burns	13	Sam Thompson	102
Bill O'Brien	.314	Herman Long	8	Walt Wilmot	99
Sam Thompson	.313	Jack Clements	7	Dave Foutz	98

Stolen Bases		ERA		Wins	
Bill Hamilton	102	Billy Rhines	1.95	Bill Hutchison	42
Hubert Collins	85	Kid Nichols	2.21	Bill Gleason	38
Billy Sunday	84	Amos Rusie	2.56	Tom Lovett	30
Walt Wilmot	76	Bill Gleason	2.63	Amos Rusie	29
Mike Tiernan	56	Bill Hutchison	2.70	Billy Rhines	28

Saves		Strikeouts	
Bill Hutchison	2	Amos Rusie	341
Dave Foutz	2	Bill Hutchison	289
Bill Gleason	2	Kid Nichols	222
Tony Mullane	1	Bill Gleason	222
Pat Luby	1	William Terry	185

American Association

Team Name	W	L	Pct	GB	R	OR
Louisville Eclipse	88	44	.667	-	819	588
Columbus Discoverers	79	55	.590	10	831	617
St. Louis Browns	78	58	.574	12	870	736
Toledo Maumees	68	64	.515	20	739	689
Rochester Beau Brummels	63	63	.500	22	709	711
Brooklyn-Baltimore	41	92	.308	47.5	674	925
Syracuse Stars	55	72	.433	30.5	698	831
Philadelphia Athletics	54	78	.409	34	702	945

Coaching Changes

Louisville--Jack Chapman 88-44; Columbus--Al Buckenberger 42-42, Gus Schmelz 37-13; St. Louis--Tom McCarthy 13-13, James Roseman 32-19, Charles Campau 33-26; Toledo--Charlie Morton 68-64; Rochester--Pat Powers 63-63; Brooklyn/Baltimore--Jim Kennedy 26-73, Bill Barnie 15-19; Syracuse--George Frazer 55-72.

League Leaders

Batting Average

William Wolf	.363
Denny Lyons	.354
Tom McCarthy	.350
John Johnson	.346
Clarence Childs	.345

Home Runs

Charles Campau	10
Ed Cartwright	8
Jack Stivetts	7
Denny Lyons	7
Perry Werdey	6

Stolen Bases

Tom McCarthy	83
Ted Scheffler	77
Bill Van Dyke	73
Curt Welch	72
Ed Dailey	62

ERA

Scott Stratton	2.36
Phil Ehret	2.53
Frank Knauss	2.81
Elton Chamberlain	2.83
John Healy	2.89

Wins

John McMahon	36
Scott Stratton	34
Hank Gastright	30
Bob Barr	28
Jack Stivetts	27

Saves

Herb Goodall	4
Philip Ehret	2
Frank Knauss	1
Bob Miller	1
Bill Whitrock	1

Strikeouts

John McMahon	291
Jack Stivetts	289
Tom Ramsey	257
John Healy	225
Bob Barr	209

World Series

October 17	Brooklyn Bridegrooms	9	at	Louisville Eclipse	0
October 18	Brooklyn Bridegrooms	5	at	Louisville Eclipse	3
October 20	Brooklyn Bridegrooms	7	at	Louisville Eclipse	7
October 21	Brooklyn Bridegrooms	4	at	Louisville Eclipse	5
October 25	Louisville Eclipse	2	at	Brooklyn Bridegrooms	7
October 27	Louisville Eclipse	9	at	Brooklyn Bridegrooms	8
October 28	Louisville Eclipse	6	at	Brooklyn Bridegrooms	2

Players League

Team Name	W	L	Pct	GB	R	OR
Boston Reds	81	48	.628	-	992	767
Brooklyn Wonders	76	56	.576	6.5	964	893
New York Giants	74	57	.565	8	1018	875
Chicago Pirates	75	62	.547	10	886	770
Philadelphia Quakers	68	63	.519	14	941	855
Pittsburgh Burghers	60	68	.469	20.5	835	892
Cleveland Infants	55	75	.423	26.5	849	1027
Buffalo Bisons	36	96	.273	46.5	793	1199

Coaching

Boston-- Michael "King" Kelly 81-48; Brooklyn--Monte Ward 76-56; New York--William Ewing 74-57; Chicago--Charlie Comiskey 75-62; Philadelphia--Ben Hilt 17-19, Jim Fogarty 30-19, Charlie Buffinton 21-25; Pittsburgh--Ned Hanlon 60-68; Cleveland--Jay Faatz 10-25, Henry Larkin 27-33, Patsy Tebeau 18-17; Buffalo--Jack Rowe 36-96

League Leaders

Batting Average		Home Runs		RBI	
Pete Browning	.373	Roger Connor	13	Hardy Richardson	143
Dave Orr	.373	Hardy Richardson	11	Dave Orr	124
Jim O'Rourke	.360	Harry Stovey	11	Jake Beckley	120
Roger Connor	.349	George Gore	10	Jim O'Rourke	115
Jim Ryan	.340	Jake Beckley	10	Henry Larkin	112

Stolen Bases		ERA		Wins	
Harry Stovey	97	Charles King	2.69	Mark Baldwin	34
Tom Brown	79	Harry Staley	3.23	Gus Weyhing	30
Hugh Duffy	78	Mark Baldwin	3.31	Charles King	30
Ned Hanlon	65	Charles Radbourn	3.31	Charles Radbourn	27
Monte Ward	63	Tim Keefe	3.38	Hank O'Day	23

Saves		Strikeouts	
Hank O'Day	3	Mark Baldwin	211
George Hemming	3	Charles King	185
Con Murphy	2	Gus Weyhing	177
George Van Haltren	2	John Ewing	145
Bill Daley	2	Harry Staley	145

Notes

A small organization, The Brotherhood of Professional Ball Players, founded the Players League which could not compete with the two established leagues and disbanded after one season.

Franchise Changes

NL--Pittsburgh changed name from Alleghenys to Innocents.
AA--Brooklyn team moved to Baltimore in mid-season.

Other Sports

Horseracing--Kentucky Derby won by Riley (time 2:45, purse $5,460).

1891

BASEBALL
National League

Team Name	W	L	Pct	GB	R	OR
Boston Beaneaters	87	51	.630	-	847	658
Chicago White Stockings	82	53	.607	3.5	832	730
New York Giants	71	61	.538	13	754	711
Philadelphia Phillies	68	69	.496	18.5	756	773
Cleveland Spiders	65	74	.468	22.5	835	888
Brooklyn Bridegrooms	61	76	.445	25.5	765	820
Cincinnati Reds	56	81	.409	30.5	646	790
Pittsburgh Pirates	55	80	.407	30.5	679	744

Coaching Changes

Cleveland--Bob Leadley 31-34, Patsy Tebeau 34-40; Brooklyn--Monte Ward 61-76; Pittsburgh--Ned Hanlon 31-47, Bill McGunnigle 24-33.

League Leaders

Batting Average

Bill Hamilton	.340
James Holliday	.319
Pete Browning	.317
Jack Clements	.310
Mike Tiernan	.306

Home Runs

Mike Tiernan	17
Harry Stovey	16
Walt Wilmot	11
James Holliday	9
Bill Dahlen	9

RBI

Cap Anson	120
Billy Nash	95
Harry Stovey	95
Jim O'Rourke	95
Roger Connor	94

Stolen Bases

Bill Hamilton	111
Arlie Latham	87
Mike Griffin	65
Herman Long	60
Monte Ward	57

ERA

John Ewing	2.27
Kid Nichols	2.39
Amos Rusie	2.55
Harry Staley	2.58
Mark Baldwin	2.76

Wins

Bill Hutchison	43
Amos Rusie	33
John Clarkson	33
Kid Nichols	30
Cy Young	27

Saves

Kid Nichols	3
John Clarkson	3
John Thornton	2
Cy Young	2
John Sharrot	1

Strikeouts

Amos Rusie	337
Bill Hutchison	261
Kid Nichols	240
Mark Baldwin	197
Charles King	160

World Series

October 17	Boston Beaneaters	0	at	Cleveland Spiders	0
October 18	Boston Beaneaters	4	at	Cleveland Spiders	3
October 19	Boston Beaneaters	3	at	Cleveland Spiders	2
October 21	Cleveland Spiders	0	at	Boston Beaneaters	4
October 22	Cleveland Spiders	7	at	Boston Beaneaters	12
October 24	Cleveland Spiders	3	at	Boston Beaneaters	8

Franchise Changes

Louisville, Washington and Baltimore moved to the National League from the American Association.

Other Sports

Horseracing--Kentucky Derby won by Azra (time 2:41.5, purse $4,230).
Heavyweight Boxing--James Corbett defeated John L. Sullivan in 21 rounds.

Notes

The fight between Corbett and Sullivan was the first fight where big gloves were used.

1893

BASEBALL
National League

Team Name	W	L	Pct	GB	R	OR
Boston Beaneaters	86	43	.667	-	1008	795
Pittsburgh Pirates	81	48	.628	5	970	766
Cleveland Spiders	73	55	.570	12.5	976	839
Philadelphia Phillies	72	57	.558	14	1011	841
New York Giants	68	64	.515	19.5	941	845
Brooklyn Bridegrooms	65	63	.508	20.5	775	845
Cincinnati Reds	65	63	.508	20.5	759	814
Baltimore Orioles	60	70	.462	26.5	820	893
Chicago White Stockings	56	71	.441	29	829	874
St. Louis Browns	57	75	.432	30.5	745	829
Louisville Colonels	50	75	.400	34	759	942
Washington Senators	40	89	.310	46	722	1032

Coaching Changes

Pittsburgh--Al Buckenberger 81-48; New York--Monte Ward 68-64; Brooklyn--Dave Foutz 65-63; Baltimore--Ned Hanlon 60-70; St. Louis--Bill Watkins 57-7-5; Louisville--Bill Barnie 50-75; Washington--Jim O'Rourke 40-89.

League Leaders

Batting Average

Bill Hamilton	.380
Sam Thompson	.370
Ed Delahanty	.368
Hugh Duffy	.363
George Davis	.355

Home Runs

Ed Delahanty	19
Jack Clements	17
Mike Tiernan	15
Bobby Lowe	13
Roger Connor	11

RBI

Ed Delahanty	146
Ed McKean	133
Sam Thompson	126
Billy Nash	123
William Ewing	122

Stolen Bases

Tom Brown	66
Tommy Dowd	59
Arlie Latham	57
Eddie Burke	54
Steve Brodie	49

ERA

Ted Breitenstein	3.18
Amos Rusie	3.23
Cy Young	3.26
Philip Ehret	3.44
Art Clarkson	3.48

Wins

Frank Killen	35
Cy Young	34
Kid Nichols	34
Amos Rusie	33
Bill Kennedy	26

Saves

Mark Baldwin	2
Tony Mullane	2
Frank Donnelly	2
Frank Dwyer	2
Charles Hastings	1

Strikeouts

Amos Rusie	208
Bill Kennedy	107
Ted Breitenstein	102
Cy Young	102
Gus Weyhing	101

Rules

Pitching distance lengthened to 60 ft. 6in.

Other Sports

Horseracing--Kentucky Derby won by Lookout (time 2:39.2.5, purse $4,090).

1894

BASEBALL
National League

Team Name	W	L	Pct	GB	R	OR
Baltimore Orioles	89	39	.695	-	1171	820
New York Giants	88	44	.667	3	940	789
Boston Beaneaters	83	49	.629	8	1222	1002
Philadelphia Phillies	71	57	.555	18	1143	966
Brooklyn Bridegrooms	70	61	.534	20.5	1021	1007
Cleveland Spiders	68	61	.527	21.5	932	896
Pittsburgh Pirates	65	65	.500	25	955	972
Chicago Colts	57	75	.432	34	1041	1066
St. Louis Browns	56	76	.424	35	771	954
Cincinnati Reds	55	75	.423	35	910	1085
Washington Senators	45	87	.341	46	882	1122
Louisville Colonels	36	94	.277	54	692	1001

Coaching Changes

Philadelphia--Arthur Irwin 71-57; Pittsburgh--Al Buckenberger 53-55, Connie Mack 12-10; St. Louis--George Miller 56-76; Washington--Gus Schmelz 45-87.

League Leaders

Batting Average

Hugh Duffy	.440
George Turner	.416
Sam Thompson	.407
Ed Delahanty	.407
Bill Hamilton	.404

Home Runs

Hugh Duffy	18
Bobby Lowe	17
Bill Joyce	17
Bill Dahlen	15
Sam Thompson	13

RBI

Hugh Duffy	145
Sam Thompson	141
Ed Delahanty	131
Walt Wilmot	130
Dan Brouthers	128

Stolen Bases

Bill Hamilton	98
John McGraw	78
Walt Wilmot	74
Tom Brown	66
Bill Lange	65

ERA

Amos Rusie	2.78
Jouett Meekin	3.70
George Mercer	3.76
Cy Young	3.94
Jack Taylor	4.08

Wins

Amos Rusie	36
Jouett Meekin	33
Kid Nichols	32
Ted Breitenstein	27
Ed Stein	27

Saves

Tony Mullane	4
Bill Hawke	3
George Mercer	3
Hank Gastright	2
Bill Kennedy	1

Strikeouts

Amos Rusie	195
Ted Breitenstein	140
Jouett Meekin	133
Pink Hawley	120
Kid Nichols	113

Temple Cup

October 4	New York Giants	4	at	Baltimore Orioles	1
October 5	New York Giants	9	at	Baltimore Orioles	6
October 6	Baltimore Orioles	1	at	New York Giants	4
October 8	Baltimore Orioles	3	at	New York Giants	16

Rules

Batter charged with a strike for hitting a foul bunt.

Franchise Changes

NL--Chicago White Stockings changed name to Chicago Colts.

Other Sports

Horseracing--Kentucky Derby won by Chant (time 2:41, purse $4,020).
Heavyweight Boxing--James Corbett knocked-out Charley Mitchell in 3 rounds.

1895

BASEBALL
National League

Team Name	W	L	Pct	GB	R	OR
Baltimore Orioles	87	43	.669	-	1009	646
Cleveland Spiders	84	46	.646	3	917	720
Philadelphia Phillies	78	53	.595	9.5	1068	957
Chicago Colts	72	58	.554	15	866	854
Brooklyn Bridegrooms	71	60	.542	16.5	867	834
Boston Beaneaters	71	60	.542	16.5	907	826
Pittsburgh Pirates	71	61	.538	17	811	787
Cincinnati Reds	66	64	.508	21	903	854
New York Giants	66	65	.504	21.5	852	834
Washington Senators	43	85	.336	43	837	1048
St. Louis Browns	39	92	.298	48.5	1090	1032
Louisville Colonels	35	96	.267	52.5	698	1090

Coaching Changes

Pittsburgh--Connie Mack 71-61; Cincinnati--William Ewing 66-64; New York--George Davis 17-17, Jack Doyle 31-31, Harvey Watkins 18-17; St. Louis--Al Buckenberger 16-23, Joe Quinn 13-27, Lew Phelan 8-21, Chris Von Der Ahe 2-12; Louisville--John McCloskey 35-96.

League Leaders

Batting Average

Jesse Burkett	.409
Ed Delahanty	.404
Jack Clements	.394
Sam Thompson	.392
Bill Lange	.389

Home Runs

Sam Thompson	18
Bill Joyce	17
Jack Clements	13
Ed Delahanty	11
Bill Lange	10

RBI

Sam Thompson	165
Joe Kelley	134
Steve Brodie	134
Hugh Jennings	125
Ed McKean	119

Stolen Bases

Bill Hamilton	97
Bill Lange	67
John McGraw	61
Joe Kelley	54
Jake Stenzel	53

ERA

Al Maul	2.45
John McMahon	2.94
Pink Hawley	3.18
Bill Hoffer	3.21
John Foreman	3.22

Wins

Cy Young	35
Pink Hawley	31
Bill Hoffer	31
Kid Nichols	30
John B. Taylor	26

Saves

Ernie Beam	3
Tom Parrott	3
Kid Nichols	3
Bill Phillips	2
John Malarkey	2

Strikeouts

Amos Rusie	201
Pink Hawley	142
Kid Nichols	140
Ted Breitenstein	127
Cy Young	121

Temple Cup

October 2	Baltimore Orioles	4	at	Cleveland Spiders	5
October 3	Baltimore Orioles	2	at	Cleveland Spiders	7
October 5	Baltimore Orioles	1	at	Cleveland Spiders	7
October 7	Cleveland Spiders	0	at	Baltimore Orioles	5
October 8	Cleveland Spiders	5	at	Baltimore Orioles	2

Other Sports

Horseracing--Kentucky Derby won by Halma (time 2:37.5, purse $2,970).
Golf--U.S. Open won by Horace Rawlings with a score of 173.

1896

BASEBALL
National League

Team Name	W	L	Pct	GB	R	OR
Baltimore Orioles	90	39	.698	-	995	662
Cleveland Spiders	80	48	.625	9.5	840	650
Cincinnati Reds	77	50	.606	12	783	620
Boston Beaneaters	74	57	.565	17	860	761
Chicago Colts	71	57	.555	18.5	815	799
Pittsburgh Pirates	66	63	.512	24	787	741
New York Giants	64	67	.489	27	829	821
Philadelphia Phillies	62	68	.477	28.5	890	891
Brooklyn Bridegrooms	58	73	.443	33	692	764
Washington Senators	58	73	.443	33	818	920
St. Louis Browns	40	90	.308	50.5	593	929
Louisville Colonels	38	93	.290	53	653	997

Coaching Changes

New York--Arthur Irwin 38-53, Bill Joyce 26-14; Philadelphia--Billy Nash 62-68; St. Louis--Harry Diddlebock 7-11, Arlie Latham 0-2, Chris Von Der Ahe 0-2, Roger Connor 9-37, Tommy Dowd 24-38; Louisville--John McCloskey 9-34, Bill McGunnigle 29-59.

League Leaders

Batting Average		Home Runs		RBI	
Jesse Burkett	.410	Bill Joyce	14	Ed Delahanty	126
Hugh Jennings	.401	Ed Delahanty	13	Hugh Jennings	121
Ed Delahanty	.397	Sam Thompson	12	Hugh Duffy	112
Willie Keeler	.386	Roger Connor	11	Ed McKean	112
Mike Tiernan	.369	Bill Dahlen	9	Henry Reitz	106

Stolen Bases		ERA		Wins	
Joe Kelley	87	Billy Rhines	2.45	Kid Nichols	30
Bill Lange	84	Kid Nichols	2.83	Frank Killen	30
Bill Hamilton	83	George Cuppy	3.12	Cy Young	28
Charles Miller	76	Frank Dwyer	3.15	Jouett Meekin	26
Jack Doyle	73	Cy Young	3.24	Bill Hoffer	25

Saves		Strikeouts	
Cy Young	3	Cy Young	140
William Hill	2	Pink Hawley	137
Chauncey Fisher	2	Frank Killen	134
Charlie Hastings	1	Ted Breitenstein	114
Bill Kissinger	1	Jouett Meekin	110

Temple Cup

October 2	Baltimore Orioles	7	at	Cleveland Spiders	1
October 3	Cleveland Spiders	2	at	Baltimore Orioles	7
October 5	Cleveland Spiders	2	at	Baltimore Orioles	6
October 8	Baltimore Orioles	5	at	Cleveland Spiders	0

Other Sports

Horseracing--Kentucky Derby won by Ben Brush (time 2:07.75, purse $4,850).
Golf--U.S. Open won by James Foulis with a score of 152.

Notes

The Kentucky Derby was changed from 11.5 miles to 11.25 miles.

1897

BASEBALL
National League

Team Name	W	L	Pct	GB	R	OR
Boston Beaneaters	93	39	.705	-	1025	665
Baltimore Orioles	90	40	.692	2	964	674
New York Giants	83	48	.634	9.5	895	695
Cincinnati Reds	76	56	.576	17	763	705
Cleveland Spiders	69	62	.527	23.5	773	680
Brooklyn Bridegrooms	61	71	.462	32	802	845
Washington Senators	61	71	.462	32	781	793
Pittsburgh Pirates	60	71	.458	32.5	676	835
Chicago Colts	59	73	.447	34	832	894
Philadelphia Phillies	55	77	.417	38	752	792
Louisville Colonels	52	78	.400	40	669	859
St. Louis Browns	29	102	.221	63.5	588	1083

Coaching Changes

New York--Bill Joyce 83-48; Brooklyn--Bill Barnie 61-71; Washington--Gus Schmelz 9-25, Tom Brown 52-46; Pittsburgh--Patrick Donovan 60-71; Philadelphia--George Stallings 55-77; Louisville--Jim Rogers 17-26, Fred Clarke 35-52; St. Louis--Tommy Dowd 6-25, Hugh Nicol 9-29, Bill Hallman 13-4, Chris Von Der Ahe 1-2.

League Leaders

Batting Average

Willie Keeler	.424
Fred Clarke	.390
Jesse Burkett	.383
Ed Delahanty	.377
Joe Kelley	.362

Home Runs

Hugh Duffy	11
George Davis	10
Napoleon Lajoie	9
Jake Beckley	8
Mike Grady	7

RBI

George Davis	134
Jimmy Collins	132
Hugh Duffy	129
Napoleon Lajoie	127
Joe Kelley	118

Stolen Bases

Bill Lange	73
Jake Stenzel	69
Bill Hamilton	66
George Davis	65
Willie Keeler	64

ERA

Amos Rusie	2.54
Kid Nichols	2.64
Jerry Nops	2.81
Joe Corbett	3.11
Jack Powell	3.16

Wins

Kid Nichols	31
Amos Rusie	28
Fred Klobedanz	26
Joe Corbett	24
Ted Breitenstein	23

Saves

Kid Nichols	3
Jim Sullivan	2
Mike Sullivan	2
Philip Ehret	2
Jack Taylor	2

Strikeouts

Jim McJames	156
James Seymour	149
Joe Corbett	149
Amos Rusie	135
Kid Nichols	127

Temple Cup

October 4	Baltimore Orioles	12	at	Boston Beaneaters	13
October 5	Baltimore Orioles	13	at	Boston Beaneaters	11
October 6	Baltimore Orioles	8	at	Boston Beaneaters	3
October 9	Boston Beaneaters	11	at	Baltimore Orioles	12
October 11	Boston Beaneaters	3	at	Baltimore Orioles	9

Other Sports

Horseracing--Kentucky Derby won by Typhoon II (time 2:12.5, purse $4,850).
Heavyweight Boxing--Bob Fitzsimmons defeated James J. Corbett in 14 rounds.
Golf--U.S. Open won by Joe Lloyd with a score of 162.

1898

BASEBALL
National League

Team Name	W	L	Pct	GB	R	OR
Boston Beaneaters	102	47	.685	-	872	614
Baltimore Orioles	96	53	.644	6	933	623
Cincinnati Reds	92	60	.605	11.5	831	740
Chicago Orphans	85	65	.567	17.5	828	679
Cleveland Spiders	81	68	.544	21	730	683
Philadelphia Phillies	78	71	.523	24	823	784
New York Giants	77	73	.513	25.5	837	800
Pittsburgh Pirates	72	76	.486	29.5	634	694
Louisville Colonels	70	81	.464	33	728	833
Brooklyn Bridegrooms	54	91	.372	46	638	811
Washington Senators	51	101	.336	52.5	704	939
St. Louis Cardinals	39	111	.260	63.5	571	929

Coaching Changes

Chicago--Tom Burns 85-65; Philadelphia--George Stallings 19-27, Bill Shettsline 59-44; New York--Bill Joyce 23-21, Cap Anson 9-13, Bill Joyce 45-39; Pittsburgh--Bill Watkins 72-76; Louisville--Fred Clarke 70-81; Brooklyn--Bill Barnie 15-20, Mike Griffin 1-3, Charlie Ebbets 38-68; Washington--Tom Brown 3-13, Jack Doyle 20-24, James "Deacon" McGuire 19-49, Arthur Irwin 9-15; St. Louis--Tim Hurst 39-111.

League Leaders

Batting Average		Home Runs		RBI	
Willie Keeler	.385	Jimmy Collins	15	Napoleon Lajoie	127
Bill Hamilton	.369	Honus Wagner	10	Jimmy Collins	111
John McGraw	.342	Bill Joyce	10	Joe Kelley	110
Elmer Smith	.342	John Anderson	9	Hugh Duffy	108
Jesse Burkett	.341	Ed McKean	9	Dan McGann	106

Stolen Bases		ERA		Wins	
Ed Delahanty	58	Clark Griffith	1.88	Kid Nichols	32
Bill Hamilton	54	Al Maul	2.10	Bert Cunningham	28
Gene DeMontreville	49	Kid Nichols	2.13	Pink Hawley	27
Charlie Dexter	44	Jim McJames	2.36	Jim McJames	27
John McGraw	43	James Callahan	2.46	Ted Lewis	26

Saves		Strikeouts	
Kid Nichols	3	Cy Seymour	239
Jesse Tannehill	2	Jim McJames	178
Bill Damman	2	Victor Willis	160
Charles Hickman	2	Kid Nichols	138
Ted Lewis	2	Wiley Piatt	121

Franchise Changes

NL--Chicago Colts changed name to Chicago Orphans.
St. Louis Browns became known as St. Louis Cardinals.

Other Sports

Horseracing--Kentucky Derby won by Plaudit (time 2:09, purse $4,850).
Golf--U.S. Open won by Fred Herd with a score of 328.

1899

BASEBALL
National League

Team Name	W	L	Pct	GB	R	OR
Brooklyn Superbas	101	47	.682	-	892	658
Boston Beaneaters	95	57	.625	8	858	645
Philadelphia Phillies	94	58	.618	9	916	743
Baltimore Orioles	86	62	.581	15	827	691
St. Louis Cardinals	84	67	.556	18.5	819	739
Cincinnati Reds	83	67	.553	19	856	770
Pittsburgh Pirates	76	73	.510	25.5	834	765
Chicago Cubs	75	73	.507	26	812	763
Louisville Colonels	75	77	.493	28	827	775
New York Giants	60	90	.400	42	734	863
Washington Senators	54	98	.355	49	743	983
Cleveland Spiders	20	134	.130	84	529	1252

Coaching Changes

Brooklyn--Ned Hanlon 101-47; Philadelphia--Bill Shettsline 94-58; Baltimore--John McGraw 86-62; St. Louis--Patsy Tebeau 84-67; Pittsburgh--Bill Watkins 8-16, Patrick Donovan 68-57; New York--John Day 30-40, Fred Hoey 30-50; Washington--Arthur Irwin 54-98; Cleveland--Lave Cross 8-30, Joe Quinn 12-104.

League Leaders

Batting Average		Home Runs		RBI	
Ed Delahanty	.410	John Freeman	25	Ed Delahanty	137
Jesse Burkett	.396	Bobby Wallace	12	John Freeman	122
John McGraw	.391	Jim Williams	9	Jim Williams	116
Willie Keeler	.379	Ed Delahanty	9	Honus Wagner	113
Jim Williams	.355	Sam Mertes	9	Bobby Wallace	108

Stolen Bases		ERA		Wins	
Jim Sheckard	77	Al Orth	2.49	James J. Hughes	28
John McGraw	73	Victor Willis	2.50	Joe McGinnity	28
John Heidrick	55	Cy Young	2.58	Victor Willis	27
James Holmes	50	Bill Bernhard	2.65	Cy Young	26
Fred Clarke	49	Joe McGinnity	2.68	Jesse Tannehill	24

Saves		Strikeouts	
Sam Leever	3	Frank Hahn	145
Victor Willis	2	Cy Seymour	142
Jack Dunn	2	Sam Leever	121
John B. Taylor	2	Victor Willis	120
Bill Kennedy	2	Ed Doheny	115

Franchise Changes

NL--Brooklyn Bridegrooms became known as Brooklyn Superbas.
Chicago Orphans became known as Chicago Cubs.

Other Sports

Horseracing--Kentucky Derby won by Manuel (time 2:12, purse $4,850).
Heavyweight Boxing--James Jeffries beat Bob Fitzsimmons in 11 rounds.
James Jeffries beat Tom Sharkey in 25 rounds.
Golf--U.S. Open won by Willie Smith with a score of 315.

1900

BASEBALL
National League

Team Name	W	L	Pct	GB	R	OR
Brooklyn Superbas	82	54	.603	-	816	722
Pittsburgh Pirates	79	60	.568	4.5	733	612
Philadelphia Phillies	75	63	.543	8	810	792
Boston Beaneaters	66	72	.478	17	778	739
Chicago Cubs	65	75	.464	19	635	751
St. Louis Cardinals	65	75	.464	19	744	748
Cincinnati Reds	62	77	.446	21.5	703	745
New York Giants	60	78	.435	23	713	823

Coaching Changes

Pittsburgh--Fred Clarke 79-60; Chicago--Tom Loftus 65-75; St. Louis--Patsy Tebeau 48-55, Louie Heilbroner 17-20; Cincinnati--Bob Allen 62-77; New York--William Ewing 21-41, George Davis 39-37.

League Leaders

Batting Average		Home Runs		RBI	
Honus Wagner	.381	Herman Long	12	Elmer Flick	110
Elmer Flick	.367	Elmer Flick	11	Ed Delahanty	109
Jesse Burkett	.363	Mike Donlin	10	Honus Wagner	100
Willie Keeler	.362	Charles Hickman	9	Jimmy Collins	95
John McGraw	.344	Bill Sullivan	8	Jake Beckley	94

Stolen Bases		ERA		Wins	
George Van Haltren	45	Rube Waddell	2.37	Joe McGinnity	28
Patsy Donovan	45	Ned Garvin	2.41	Jesse Tannehill	20
Jimmy Barrett	44	John W. Taylor	2.55	Bill Dinneen	20
Willie Keeler	41	Sam Leever	2.71	Bill Kennedy	20
Sam Mertes	38	Willie Sudhoff	2.76	Charles Phillippe	20

Saves		Strikeouts	
Frank Kitson	4	Rube Waddell	130
Bill Bernhard	2	Frank Hahn	127
George Cuppy	1	Cy Young	115
Jack Chesbro	1	Ned Garvin	107
Jack Taylor	1	Bill Dinneen	107

Chronicle Telegraph Cup

October 15	Brooklyn Superbas	5	at	Pittsburgh Pirates	2
October 16	Brooklyn Superbas	4	at	Pittsburgh Pirates	2
October 17	Brooklyn Superbas	0	at	Pittsburgh Pirates	10
October 18	Brooklyn Superbas	6	at	Pittsburgh Pirates	1

Franchise Changes

NL--Louisville Colonels merged with the Pittsburgh Pirates.

Other Sports

Horseracing--Kentucky Derby won by Lieut. Gibson (time 2:06.25, purse $4,850).
Heavyweight Boxing--James Jeffries knocked out James Corbett in 23 rounds.
Golf-- U.S. Open won by Harry Vardon with a score of 313.

1901

BASEBALL
National League

Team Name	W	L	Pct	GB	R	OR
Pittsburgh Pirates	90	49	.647	-	776	534
Philadelphia Phillies	83	57	.593	7.5	668	543
Brooklyn Superbas	79	57	.581	9.5	744	600
St. Louis Cardinals	76	64	.543	14.5	792	689
Boston Beaneaters	69	69	.500	20.5	530	556
Chicago Cubs	53	86	.381	37	578	698
New York Giants	52	85	.380	37	544	755
Cincinnati Reds	52	87	.374	38	561	818

Coaching Changes

St. Louis--Patrick Donovan 76-64; New York--George Davis 52-85; Cincinnati--John McPhee 52-87.

League Leaders

Batting Average

Jesse Burkett	.376
Ed Delahanty	.354
Jim Sheckard	.354
Honus Wagner	.353
Willie Keeler	.339

Home Runs

Sam Crawford	16
Jim Sheckard	11
Jesse Burkett	10
Ed Delahanty	8
Elmer Flick	8

RBI

Honus Wagner	126
Ed Delahanty	108
Sam Crawford	104
Jim Sheckard	104
Bobby Wallace	91

Stolen Bases

Honus Wagner	49
Tully Hartsel	41
Sammy Strang	40
Dick Harley	37
Clarence Beaumont	36

ERA

Jesse Tannehill	2.18
Charles Phillippe	2.22
Al Orth	2.27
Victor Willis	2.36
Jack Chesbro	2.38

Wins

Bill Donovan	27
Jack Harper	23
Frank Hahn	22
Red Donahue	22
Jack Chesbro	21

Saves

Jack Powell	3
Willie Sudhoff	2
Frank Kitson	2
Charles Phillippe	2
Bill Phyle	1

Strikeouts

Frank Hahn	239
Bill Donovan	226
Tom Hughes	225
Christy Mathewson	221
Rube Waddell	172

Rules

Any foul ball not caught on the fly is a strike unless the batter has two strikes on him.

American League

Team Name	W	L	Pct	GB	R	OR
Chicago White Sox	83	53	.610	-	819	632
Boston Somersets	79	57	.581	4	759	608
Detroit Tigers	74	61	.548	8.5	742	696
Philadelphia Athletics	74	62	.544	9	805	760
Baltimore Orioles	68	65	.511	13.5	761	750
Washington Senators	61	73	.455	21	683	771
Cleveland Bronchos	55	82	.401	28.5	666	831
Milwaukee Brewers	48	89	.350	35.5	641	828

Coaching

Chicago--Clark Griffith 83-53; Boston--Jimmy Collins 79-57; Detroit--George Stallings 74-61; Philadelphia--Connie Mack 74-62; Baltimore--John McGraw 68-65; Washington--Jim Manning 61-73; Cleveland--Jim McAleer 55-82; Milwaukee--Hugh Duffy 48-89

League Leaders

Batting Average		Home Runs		RBI	
Napoleon Lajoie	.426	Napoleon Lajoie	14	Napoleon Lajoie	125
Mike Donlin	.340	John Freeman	12	John Freeman	114
John Freeman	.339	Mike Grady	9	John Anderson	99
Ralph Seybold	.334	Harry Davis	8	Sam Mertes	98
Jimmy Collins	.332	Ralph Seybold	8	James Williams	96

Stolen Bases		ERA		Wins	
Frank Isbell	52	Cy Young	1.62	Cy Young	33
Sam Mertes	46	James Callahan	2.42	Joe McGinnity	24
Fielder Jones	38	Joe Yeager	2.61	Clark Griffith	24
Cy Seymour	38	Clark Griffith	2.67	Roscoe Miller	23
Oliver Pickering	36	George Winter	2.80	Charles Fraser	22

Saves		Strikeouts	
Bill Hoffer	3	Cy Young	158
Joe McGinnity	3	Roy Patterson	127
Ned Garvin	2	Pete Dowling	124
Erwin Harvey	1	Ned Garvin	122
Wiley Piatt	1	Charles Fraser	110

Notes

Through the efforts of Ban Johnson and Charlie Comiskey the American League was formed from the Western Association, a minor league circuit which Johnson had taken over in 1894. The Western Association changed its name to the American League in 1900 and placed clubs in several Eastern cities and began raiding National League talent and reached major league status in 1901. Johnson was named as first President of the league.

Other Sports

Horseracing--Kentucky Derby won by His Eminence (time 2:67-75, purse $4,850).
Heavyweight Boxing--James Jeffries knocked out Gus Ruhlin in 5 rounds.
Golf--U.S. Open was won by Willie Anderson in a playoff with Alex Smith with scores of 331-331; 85-86

1902

BASEBALL
National League

Team Name	W	L	Pct	GB	R	OR
Pittsburgh Pirates	103	36	.741	-	775	440
Brooklyn Superbas	75	63	.543	27.5	564	519
Boston Beaneaters	73	64	.533	29	571	515
Cincinnati Reds	70	70	.500	33.5	632	566
Chicago Cubs	68	69	.496	34	530	501
St. Louis Cardinals	56	78	.418	44.5	517	695
Philadelphia Phillies	56	81	.409	46	484	649
New York Giants	48	88	.353	53.5	401	589

Coaching Changes

Boston--Al Buckenberger 73-64; Cincinnati--John McPhee 27-37, Frank Bancroft 10-7, Joe Kelley 33-26; Chicago--Frank Selee 68-69; New York--Horace Fogel 18-23, George Smith 5-27, John McGraw 25-38.

League Leaders

Batting Average		Home Runs		RBI	
Clarence Beaumont	.357	Tommy Leach	6	Honus Wagner	91
Sam Crawford	.333	Jake Beckley	5	Tommy Leach	85
Willie Keeler	.333	Tom McCreery	4	Sam Crawford	78
Honus Wagner	.330	Jim Sheckard	4	Bill Dahlen	74
Jake Beckley	.330	Steve Brodie	3	Bill Bransfield	69

Stolen Bases		ERA		Wins	
Honus Wagner	42	John W. Taylor	1.33	Jack Chesbro	28
Jimmy Slagle	40	Frank Hahn	1.76	Victor Willis	27
Patrick Donovan	34	Jesse Tannehill	1.95	Togie Pittinger	27
Clarence Beaumont	33	Carl Lundgren	1.97	John W. Taylor	22
George Smith	32	Charles Phillippe	2.05	Frank Hahn	22

Saves		Strikeouts	
Victor Willis	3	Victor Willis	225
Sam Leever	2	Guy White	185
Tully Sparks	1	Togie Pittinger	174
Bob Rhodes	1	Bill Donovan	170
Ed Murphy	1	Christy Mathewson	159

American League

Team Name	W	L	Pct	GB	R	OR
Philadelphia Athletics	83	53	.610	-	775	636
St. Louis Browns	78	58	.574	5	619	607
Boston Somersets	77	60	.562	6.5	664	600
Chicago White Sox	74	60	.552	8	675	602
Cleveland Blues	69	67	.507	14	686	667
Washington Senators	61	75	.449	22	709	790
Detroit Tigers	52	83	.385	30.5	566	657
Baltimore Orioles	50	88	.362	34	715	850

Coaching Changes

St. Louis--Jimmy McAleer 78-58; Cleveland--Bill Armour 69-67; Washington--Tom Loftus 61-75; Detroit--Frank Dwyer 52-83; Baltimore--John McGraw 28-34, Wilbert Robinson 22-54.

League Leaders

Batting Average		Home Runs		RBI	
Napoleon Lajoie	.378	Ralph Seybold	16	John Freeman	121
Ed Delahanty	.376	Charles Hickman	11	Charles Hickman	110
Charles Hickman	.361	John Freeman	11	Lave Cross	108
Pat Dougherty	.342	Bill Bradley	11	Ralph Seybold	97
Lave Cross	.342	Ed Delahanty	10	Ed Delahanty	93

Stolen Bases		ERA		Wins	
Tully Hartsel	47	Ed Siever	1.91	Cy Young	32
Sam Mertes	46	Rube Waddell	2.05	Rube Waddell	25
Dave Fultz	44	Bill Bernhard	2.15	Red Donahue	22
Billy Gilbert	38	Cy Young	2.15	Jack Powell	21
Frank Isbell	38	Ned Garvin	2.21	Bill Dinneen	21

Saves		Strikeouts	
Jack Powell	3	Rube Waddell	210
Fred Mitchell	1	Cy Young	160
Lewis Wiltse	1	Jack Powell	137
Clarence Wright	1	Bill Dinneen	136
Roscoe Miller	1	Eddie Plank	107

Franchise Changes

AL--Milwaukee Brewers became the St. Louis Browns.
Cleveland changed name from Bronchos to Blues.

Other Sports

Horseracing--Kentucky Derby won by Alan-A-Dale (time 2:08.75, purse $4,850).
Heavyweight Boxing--James Jeffries knocked out Bob Fitzsimmons in 8 rounds.
Golf--U.S. Open won by L. Auchterlonie with a score of 307.

1903

BASEBALL
National League

Team Name	W	L	Pct	GB	R	OR
Pittsburgh Pirates	91	49	.650	-	792	613
New York Giants	84	55	.604	6.5	729	548
Chicago Cubs	82	56	.594	8	695	594
Cincinnati Reds	74	65	.532	16.5	764	749
Brooklyn Superbas	70	66	.515	19	666	674
Boston Beaneaters	58	80	.420	32	575	661
Philadelphia Phillies	49	86	.363	39.5	618	743
St. Louis Cardinals	43	94	.314	46.5	505	762

Coaching Changes

New York--John McGraw 84-55; Cincinnati--Joe Kelley 74-65; Philadelphia--Charles Zimmer 49-86.

League Leaders

Batting Average		Home Runs		RBI	
Honus Wagner	.355	Jim Sheckard	9	Sam Mertes	104
Fred Clarke	.351	Tommy Leach	7	Honus Wagner	101
Mike Donlin	.351	Sam Mertes	7	Jack Doyle	91
Roger Bresnahan	.350	Mike Donlin	7	Tommy Leach	87
Cy Seymour	.342	Patrick Moran	7	Harry Steinfeldt	83

Stolen Bases		ERA		Wins	
Jim Sheckard	67	Sam Leever	2.06	Joe McGinnity	32
Frank Chance	67	Christy Mathewson	2.26	Christy Mathewson	29
Sam Strang	46	Jake Weimer	2.30	Sam Leever	25
Honus Wagner	46	Charles Phillippe	2.43	Charles Phillippe	24
Sam Mertes	45	Joe McGinnity	2.43	Frank Hahn	22

Saves		Strikeouts	
Roscoe Miller	3	Christy Mathewson	267
Carl Lundgren	3	Joe McGinnity	171
Ed Doheny	2	Ned Garvin	154
Charles Phillippe	2	Togie Pittinger	140
Ned Garvin	2	Jake Weimer	128

Notes

Henry Pullman succeeded Nicholas Young as the President of the National League.

American League

Team Name	W	L	Pct	GB	R	OR
Boston Somersets	91	47	.659	-	707	505
Philadelphia Athletics	75	60	.556	14.5	597	519
Cleveland Blues	77	63	.550	15	639	578
New York Highlanders	72	62	.537	17	579	573
Detroit Tigers	65	71	.478	25	567	539
St. Louis Browns	65	74	.468	26.5	500	525
Chicago White Sox	60	77	.438	30.5	516	613
Washington Senators	43	94	.314	47.5	438	691

Coaching Changes

New York--Clark Griffith 72-62; Detroit--Ed Barrow 65-71; Chicago--James Callahan 60-77.

League Leaders

Batting Average

Napoleon Lajoie	.344
Sam Crawford	.335
Pat Dougherty	.331
Jim Barrett	.315
Bill Bradley	.313

Home Runs

John F. Freeman	13
Charles Hickman	12
Albert Ferris	9
Ralph Seybold	8
Jim Ryan	7

RBI

John Freeman	104
Charles Hickman	97
Napoleon Lajoie	93
Lave Cross	90
Sam Crawford	89

Stolen Bases

Harry Bay	45
Oliver Pickering	40
James Holmes	35
Pat Dougherty	35
William Conroy	33

ERA

Earl Moore	1.77
Cy Young	2.08
Bill Bernhard	2.12
Guy White	2.13
Adrian Joss	2.15

Wins

Cy Young	28
Eddie Plank	23
Jack Chesbro	21
Bill Dinneen	21
Rube Waddell	21

Saves

George Mullin	3
Jack Powell	2
Cy Young	2
Frank Owen	1
Earl Moore	1

Strikeouts

Rube Waddell	302
Bill Donovan	187
Eddie Plank	176
Cy Young	176
George Mullin	170

World Series

October 1	Pittsburgh Pirates	7	at	Boston Somersets	3
October 2	Pittsburgh Pirates	0	at	Boston Somersets	3
October 3	Pittsburgh Pirates	4	at	Boston Somersets	2
October 6	Boston Somersets	4	at	Pittsburgh Pirates	5
October 7	Boston Somersets	11	at	Pittsburgh Pirates	2
October 8	Boston Somersets	6	at	Pittsburgh Pirates	3
October 10	Boston Somersets	7	at	Pittsburgh Pirates	3
October 13	Pittsburgh Pirates	0	at	Boston Somersets	3

Franchise Changes

AL--Baltimore Orioles became the New York Highlanders.

Other Sports

Horseracing--Kentucky Derby won by Judge Himes (time 2:09, purse $4,850).
Heavyweight Boxing--James Jeffries knocked out James Corbett in 10 rounds.
Golf--U.S. Open won by Willie Anderson with a score of 307.

1904

BASEBALL
National League

Team Name	W	L	Pct	GB	R	OR
New York Giants	106	47	.693	-	744	476
Chicago Cubs	93	60	.608	13	597	517
Cincinnati Reds	88	65	.575	18	692	547
Pittsburgh Pirates	87	66	.569	19	675	586
St. Louis Cardinals	75	79	.487	31.5	602	595
Brooklyn Superbas	56	97	.366	50	497	614
Boston Beaneaters	55	98	.359	51	491	752
Philadelphia Phillies	52	100	.342	53.5	571	782

Coaching Changes

St. Louis--Kid Nichols 75-79; Philadelphia--Hugh Duffy 52-100.

League Leaders

Batting Average		Home Runs		RBI	
Honus Wagner	.349	Harry Lumley	9	Bill Dahlen	80
Mike Donlin	.329	Dave Brain	7	Sam Mertes	78
Jake Beckley	.325	Charles Dooin	6	Harry Lumley	78
Mike Grady	.313	Frank Chance	6	Honus Wagner	75
Cy Seymour	.313	Patrick Dolan	6	Tom Corcoran	74

Stolen Bases		ERA		Wins	
Honus Wagner	53	Joe McGinnity	1.61	Christy Mathewson	34
Sam Mertes	47	Ned Garvin	1.68	Joe McGinnity	33
Bill Dahlen	47	Mordecai Brown	1.86	Jack Harper	23
Dan McGann	42	Jake Weimer	1.91	Luther Taylor	22
Frank Chance	42	Kid Nichols	2.02	Kid Nichols	21

Saves		Strikeouts	
Joe McGinnity	5	Christy Mathewson	212
George Wiltse	3	Victor Willis	196
Leon Ames	3	Jake Weimer	177
Bill Milligan	2	Togie Pittinger	146
Herb Briggs	2	Joe McGinnity	144

American League

Team Name	W	L	Pct	GB	R	OR
Boston Somersets	95	59	.617	-	608	466
New York Highlanders	92	59	.609	1.5	598	526
Chicago White Sox	89	65	.578	6	600	482
Cleveland Blues	86	65	.570	7.5	647	482
Philadelphia Athletics	81	70	.536	12.5	557	503
St. Louis Browns	65	87	.428	29	481	604
Detroit Tigers	62	90	.408	32	505	627
Washington Senators	38	113	.252	55.5	437	743

Coaching Changes

Chicago--James Callahan 22-18, Fielder Jones 67-47; Detroit--Ed Barrow 32-46, Bobby Lowe 30-44; Washington--Malachi Kittredge 1-16, Patrick Donovan 37-97.

League Leaders

Batting Average		Home Runs		RBI	
Napoleon Lajoie	.376	Harry Davis	10	Napoleon Lajoie	102
Willie Keeler	.343	John Freeman	7	John Freeman	84
Harry Davis	.309	Daniel Murphy	7	Bill Bradley	83
Elmer Flick	.306	John Ganzel	6	John Anderson	82
Bill Bradley	.300	Fred Parent	6	Daniel Murphy	77

Stolen Bases		ERA		Wins	
Elmer Flick	38	Adrian Joss	1.59	Jack Chesbro	41
Harry Bay	38	Rube Waddell	1.62	Cy Young	27
John Heidrick	35	Otto Hess	1.67	Eddie Plank	26
George Davis	32	Guy White	1.78	Rube Waddell	25
William Conroy	30	Jack Chesbro	1.82	Bill Bernhard	23

Saves		Strikeouts	
Casey Patten	2	Rube Waddell	349
Clark Griffith	1	Jack Chesbro	239
Ed Walsh	1	Jack Powell	202
Thomas Hughes	1	Eddie Plank	201
Frank Kitson	1	Cy Young	200

Notes

There was no World Series this year.
The International Pro League, the first professional hockey league was founded in Houghton Michigan. It was a professional league but not a "major" league and no statistics are available. There would not be another professional hockey league for 5 more years.

Other Sports

Horseracing--Kentucky Derby won by Elwood (time 2:08.5, purse $4,850).
Heavyweight Boxing--James Jeffries knocked out Jack Munroe in 2 rounds.
Golf--U.S. Open won by Willie Anderson with a score of 303.

1905

BASEBALL
National League

Team Name	W	L	Pct	GB	R	OR
New York Giants	105	48	.686	-	780	504
Pittsburgh Pirates	96	57	.627	9	692	569
Chicago Cubs	92	61	.601	13	667	442
Philadelphia Phillies	83	69	.546	21.5	708	603
Cincinnati Reds	79	74	.516	26	736	691
St. Louis Cardinals	58	96	.377	47.5	534	741
Boston Beaneaters	51	103	.331	54.5	467	733
Brooklyn Superbas	48	104	.316	56.5	506	807

Coaching Changes

Chicago--Frank Selee 52-38, Frank Chance 40-23; St. Louis--Kid Nichols 19-29, Jimmy Burke 17-32, Stanley Robison 22-35; Boston--Fred Tenney 51-103.

League Leaders

Batting Average		Home Runs		RBI	
Cy Seymour	.377	Fred Odwell	9	Cy Seymour	121
Honus Wagner	.363	Cy Seymour	8	Sam Mertes	108
Mike Donlin	.356	Bill Dahlen	7	Honus Wagner	101
Clarence Beaumont	.328	Mike Donlin	7	Sherry Magee	98
Roy Thomas	.317	Harry Lumley	7	John Titus	89

Stolen Bases		ERA		Wins	
Bill Maloney	59	Christy Mathewson	1.27	Christy Mathewson	32
Art Devlin	59	Ed Reulbach	1.42	Togie Pittinger	23
Honus Wagner	57	Bob Wicker	2.02	Leon Ames	22
Sam Mertes	52	Herbert Briggs	2.14	Joe McGinnity	21
Sherry Magee	48	Mordecai Brown	2.17	Sam Leever	20

Saves		Strikeouts	
Claude Elliot	6	Christy Mathewson	206
Joe McGinnity	3	Leon Ames	198
George Wiltse	3	Orval Overall	173
Mike Lynch	2	Bob Ewing	164
Togie Pittinger	2	Irv Young	156

American League

Team Name	W	L	Pct	GB	R	OR
Philadelphia Athletics	92	56	.622	-	617	486
Chicago White Sox	92	60	.605	2	613	443
Detroit Tigers	79	74	.516	15.5	511	608
Boston Puritans	78	74	.513	16	583	557
Cleveland Naps	76	78	.494	19	559	582
New York Highlanders	71	78	.477	21.5	587	644
Washington Senators	64	87	.424	29.5	560	613
St. Louis Browns	54	99	.353	40.5	509	606

Coaching Changes

Cleveland--Napoleon Lajoie 76-78; Chicago--Fielder Jones 92-60; Washington--Jake Stahl 64-87; Detroit--Bill Armour 79-74.

League Leaders

Batting Average

Elmer Flick	.306
Willie Keeler	.302
Harry Bay	.298
Sam Crawford	.297
Frank Isbell	.296

Home Runs

Harry Davis	8
George Stone	7
Ralph Seybold	6
Danny Murphy	6
Albert Ferris	6

RBI

Harry Davis	83
Lave Cross	77
John Donahue	76
Sam Crawford	75
Terry Turner	72

Stolen Bases

Dan Hoffman	46
Dave Fultz	44
Jake Stahl	41
Harry Bay	36
Tully Hartsel	36

ERA

Rube Waddell	1.48
Guy White	1.76
Cy Young	1.82
Andy Coakley	1.84
Nick Altrock	1.88

Wins

Eddie Plank	26
Rube Waddell	24
Nick Altrock	22
George Mullin	22
Ed Killian	22

Saves

Rube Waddell	4
Clark Griffith	3
Chief Bender	3
Bill Wolfe	2
Jim Buchanan	2

Strikeouts

Rube Waddell	287
Cy Young	210
Eddie Plank	210
Harry Howell	198
Frank Smith	171

World Series

October 9	New York Giants	3	at	Philadelphia Athletics	0
October 10	Philadelphia Athletics	3	at	New York Giants	0
October 12	New York Giants	9	at	Philadelphia Athletics	0
October 13	Philadelphia Athletics	0	at	New York Giants	1
October 14	Philadelphia Athletics	0	at	New York Giants	2

Franchise Changes

AL--Boston Somersets changed name to Boston Puritans.
Cleveland Blues changed name to Cleveland Naps.

Other Sports

Horseracing--Kentucky Derby won by Agile (time 2:10.75, purse $4,850).
Heavyweight Boxing--James Jeffries retires. Marvin Hart knocked out Jack Root in 12 rounds to claim the title. Jack O'Brien also claimed the title.
Golf--U.S. Open won by Willie Anderson with a score of 314.

1906

BASEBALL
National League

Team Name	W	L	Pct	GB	R	OR
Chicago Cubs	116	36	.763	-	704	381
New York Giants	96	56	.632	20	625	508
Pittsburgh Pirates	93	60	.608	23.5	622	464
Philadelphia Phillies	71	82	.464	45.5	530	568
Brooklyn Superbas	66	86	.434	50	495	620
Cincinnati Reds	64	87	.424	51.5	530	582
St. Louis Cardinals	52	98	.347	63	475	620
Boston Beaneaters	49	102	.325	66.5	408	646

Coaching Changes

Chicago--Frank Chance 116-36; Brooklyn--Patrick Donovan 66-86; Cincinnati--Ned Hanlon 64-87; St. Louis--John McCloskey 52-98.

League Leaders

Batting Average		Home Runs		RBI	
Honus Wagner	.339	Tim Jordan	12	Harry Steinfeldt	83
Harry Steinfeldt	.327	Harry Lumley	9	Jim Nealon	83
Harry Lumley	.324	Cy Seymour	8	Cy Seymour	80
Sammy Strang	.319	Frank Schulte	7	Tim Jordan	78
Frank Chance	.319	John Bates	6	Frank Chance	71

Stolen Bases		ERA		Wins	
Frank Chance	57	Mordecai Brown	1.04	Joe McGinnity	26
Sherry Magee	55	Jack Priester	1.56	Mordecai Brown	25
Art Devlin	54	Ed Reulbach	1.65	Sam Leever	22
Honus Wagner	53	Victor Willis	1.73	Victor Willis	22
Johnny Evers	49	Albert Leifield	1.87	Christy Mathewson	21

Saves		Strikeouts	
George Ferguson	6	Fred Beebe	171
Elmer Stricklett	5	Francis Pfeffer	158
George Wiltse	5	Leon Ames	156
Harry McIntire	3	Jack Priester	153
Mordecai Brown	3	John Lush	151

American League

Team Name	W	L	Pct	GB	R	OR
Chicago White Sox	93	58	.616	-	570	460
New York Highlanders	90	61	.596	3	643	544
Cleveland Naps	89	64	.582	5	663	482
Philadelphia Athletics	78	67	.538	12	561	536
St. Louis Browns	76	73	.510	16	565	501
Detroit Tigers	71	78	.477	21	518	596
Washington Senators	55	95	.367	37.5	518	670
Boston Puritans	49	105	.318	45.5	462	711

Coaching Changes

Boston--Jimmy Collins 44-92, Charles Stahl 5-13.

League Leaders

Batting Average		Home Runs		RBI	
George Stone	.358	Harry Davis	12	Harry Davis	96
Napoleon Lajoie	.355	Charles Hickman	9	Napoleon Lajoie	91
Hal Chase	.323	George Stone	6	George Davis	80
Bill Congalton	.320	Ralph Seybold	5	Jimmy Williams	77
Ralph Seybold	.316	William Conroy	4	Hal Chase	76

Stolen Bases		ERA		Wins	
Elmer Flick	39	Guy White	1.52	Al Orth	25
John Anderson	39	Barney Pelty	1.59	Jack Chesbro	22
Frank Isbell	37	Adrian Joss	1.72	Adrian Joss	21
Dave Altizer	37	Jack Powell	1.77	Nick Altrock	21
John Donahue	36	Bob Rhoads	1.80	Bob Rhoads	21

Saves		Strikeouts	
Chief Bender	3	Rube Waddell	196
Otto Hess	3	Cy Falkenberg	178
Frank Smith	2	Ed Walsh	171
John Eubank	2	Otto Hess	167
Barney Pelty	2	Chief Bender	159

World Series

October 9	Chicago White Sox	2	at	Chicago Cubs	1
October 10	Chicago Cubs	7	at	Chicago White Sox	1
October 11	Chicago White Sox	3	at	Chicago Cubs	0
October 12	Chicago Cubs	1	at	Chicago White Sox	0
October 13	Chicago White Sox	8	at	Chicago Cubs	6
October 14	Chicago Cubs	3	at	Chicago White Sox	8

Other Sports

Horseracing--Kentucky Derby won by Sir Huon (time 2:08.80, purse $4,850).
Heavyweight Boxing--Tommy Burns defeated Marvin Hart in 20 rounds.
Jack O'Brien and Tommy Burns fought to a draw in 20 rounds.
Golf--U.S. Open won by Alex Smith with a score of 295.

1907

BASEBALL
National League

Team Name	W	L	Pct	GB	R	OR
Chicago Cubs	107	45	.704	-	570	390
Pittsburgh Pirates	91	63	.591	17	634	507
Philadelphia Phillies	83	64	.565	21.5	514	481
New York Giants	82	71	.536	25.5	573	511
Brooklyn Superbas	65	83	.439	40	446	522
Cincinnati Reds	66	87	.431	41.5	524	514
Boston Doves	58	90	.392	47	503	651
St. Louis Cardinals	52	101	.340	55.5	419	607

Coaching Changes

Philadelphia--Bill Murray 83-64.

League Leaders

Batting Average

Honus Wagner	.350
Sherry Magee	.328
Clarence Beaumont	.322
Tommy Leach	.303
Cy Seymour	.294

Home Runs

Dave Brain	10
Harry Lumley	9
John Murray	7
Honus Wagner	6
George Browne	5

RBI

Sherry Magee	85
Ed Abbaticchio	82
Honus Wagner	82
Cy Seymour	75
Harry Steinfeldt	70

Stolen Bases

Honus Wagner	61
Johnny Evers	46
Sherry Magee	46
Tommy Leach	43
Art Devlin	38

ERA

Jack Priester	1.15
Carl Lundgren	1.17
Mordecai Brown	1.39
Sam Leever	1.66
Ed Reulbach	1.69

Wins

Christy Mathewson	23
Orval Overall	23
Tully Sparks	21
Victor Willis	21
Albert Leifield	21

Saves

Joe McGinnity	4
Mordecai Brown	3
Orval Overall	3
Charles Phillippe	2
Christy Mathewson	2

Strikeouts

Christy Mathewson	178
Bob Ewing	147
Leon Ames	146
Fred Beebe	141
Orval Overall	139

American League

Team Name	W	L	Pct	GB	R	OR
Detroit Tigers	92	58	.613	-	696	519
Philadelphia Athletics	88	57	.607	1.5	582	509
Chicago White Sox	87	64	.576	5.5	584	475
Cleveland Naps	85	67	.559	8	528	523
New York Highlanders	70	78	.473	21	604	671
St. Louis Browns	69	83	.454	24	538	560
Boston Red Sox	59	90	.396	32.5	466	556
Washington Senators	49	102	.325	43.5	505	690

Coaching Changes

Detroit--Hugh Jennings 92-58; Boston--Cy Young 3-4, George Huff 3-5, Bob Unglaub 8-20, James "Deacon" McGuire 45-61; Washington--Joe Cantillon 49-102.

League Leaders

Batting Average

Ty Cobb	.350
Sam Crawford	.323
George Stone	.320
Elmer Flick	.302
Simon Nicholls	.302

Home Runs

Harry Davis	8
Ty Cobb	5
Ralph Seybold	5
Dan Hoffman	4
Albert Ferris	4

RBI

Ty Cobb	119
Ralph Seybold	92
Harry Davis	87
Sam Crawford	81
Bobby Wallace	70

Stolen Bases

Ty Cobb	49
Elmer Flick	41
William Conroy	41
Bob Ganley	40
Dave Altizer	38

ERA

Ed Walsh	1.60
Ed Killian	1.78
Adrian Joss	1.83
Walter Johnson	1.87
Harry Howell	1.93

Wins

Adrian Joss	27
Bill Donovan	26
Ed Walsh	25
Guy White	25
Ed Killian	24

Saves

Bill Dinneen	4
Chief Bender	3
Cy Young	3
Harry Howell	3
Jack Coombs	2

Strikeouts

Rube Waddell	232
Ed Walsh	206
Eddie Plank	183
Jimmy Dygert	151
Cy Young	147

World Series

October 8	Detroit Tigers	3	at	Chicago Cubs	3 [12]
October 9	Detroit Tigers	1	at	Chicago Cubs	3
October 10	Detroit Tigers	1	at	Chicago Cubs	5
October 11	Chicago Cubs	6	at	Detroit Tigers	1
October 12	Chicago Cubs	2	at	Detroit Tigers	0

Rules

All appearances by a player in an official League game count as a game played (AL).

Other Sports

Horseracing--Kentucky Derby won by Pink Star (time 2:12.6, purse $4,850).
Heavyweight Boxing--Tommy Burns defeated Jack O'Brien in 20 rounds.
Tommy Burns knocked-out Bill Squires in 1 round.
Tommy Burns knocked out Gunner Moir in 10 rounds.
Golf--U.S. Open won by Alex Rose with a score of 302.

Franchise Changes

NL--Boston Beaneaters changed name to Boston Doves.
AL--Boston Puritans changed name to Boston Red Sox.

Notes

The Interprovincial Rugby Football Union, a forerunner of the Canadian Football League was formed this year but it was not professional. The CFL would not become fully professional until 1950.

1908

BASEBALL
National League

Team Name	W	L	Pct	GB	R	OR
Chicago Cubs	99	55	.643	-	625	457
New York Giants	98	56	.636	1	652	458
Pittsburgh Pirates	98	56	.636	1	585	474
Philadelphia Phillies	83	71	.539	16	503	446
Cincinnati Reds	73	81	.474	26	488	542
Boston Doves	63	91	.409	36	537	621
Brooklyn Superbas	53	101	.344	46	375	515
St. Louis Cardinals	49	105	.318	50	372	624

Coaching Changes

Cincinnati--John Ganzel 73-81; Boston--Joe Kelley 63-91.

League Leaders

Batting Average		Home Runs		RBI	
Honus Wagner	.354	Tim Jordan	12	Honus Wagner	109
Mike Donlin	.334	Honus Wagner	10	Mike Donlin	106
Larry Doyle	.308	John Murray	7	Cy Seymour	92
Bill Bransfield	.304	Joe Tinker	6	Bill Bransfield	71
Johnny Evers	.300	Mike Donlin	6	Joe Tinker	68

Stolen Bases		ERA		Wins	
Honus Wagner	53	Christy Mathewson	1.43	Christy Mathewson	35
John Murray	48	Mordecai Brown	1.47	Mordecai Brown	27
Hans Lobert	47	George McQuillan	1.53	Victor Willis	24
Sherry Magee	40	Howie Camnitz	1.56	Ed Reulbach	24
Johnny Evers	36	Andy Coakley	1.78	Nick Maddox	23

Saves		Strikeouts	
Mordecai Brown	5	Christy Mathewson	259
Christy Mathewson	5	George Rucker	199
Joe McGinnity	4	Orval Overall	167
Bob Ewing	3	Arthur Raymond	145
Luther Taylor	2	Ed Reulbach	133

American League

Team Name	W	L	Pct	GB	R	OR
Detroit Tigers	90	63	.588	-	645	552
Cleveland Naps	90	64	.584	.5	570	471
Chicago White Sox	88	64	.579	1.5	535	480
St. Louis Browns	83	69	.546	6.5	543	478
Boston Red Sox	75	79	.487	15.5	563	515
Philadelphia Athletics	68	85	.444	22	487	554
Washington Senators	67	85	.441	22.5	479	530
New York Highlanders	51	103	.331	39.5	458	700

Coaching Changes

Boston--James "Deacon" McGuire 53-62, Fred Lake 22-17; New York--Clark Griffith 24-32, Norman Elberfeld 27-71.

League Leaders

Batting Average		Home Runs		RBI	
Ty Cobb	.324	Sam Crawford	7	Ty Cobb	108
Sam Crawford	.311	Bill Hinchman	6	Sam Crawford	80
Harry Gessler	.308	Harry Davis	5	Albert Ferris	74
Charles Hemphill	.297	Harry Niles	5	Napoleon Lajoie	74
Matty McIntyre	.295	George Stone	5	Claude Rossman	71

Stolen Bases		ERA		Wins	
Patsy Dougherty	47	Adrian Joss	1.16	Ed Walsh	39
Charlie Hemphill	42	Cy Young	1.26	Adrian Joss	24
Herman Schaefer	40	Ed Walsh	1.42	Ed Summers	24
Ty Cobb	39	Walter Johnson	1.64	Cy Young	21
Josh Clarke	37	Ed Summers	1.64	Rube Waddell	19

Saves		Strikeouts	
Ed Walsh	7	Ed Walsh	269
Tom Hughes	4	Rube Waddell	232
Rube Waddell	3	Tom Hughes	165
Jack Chesbro	3	Jimmy Dygert	164
Nick Altrock	2	Walter Johnson	160

World Series

October 9	Chicago Cubs	10	at	Detroit Tigers	6
October 11	Detroit Tigers	1	at	Chicago Cubs	6
October 12	Detroit Tigers	8	at	Chicago Cubs	3
October 13	Chicago Cubs	3	at	Detroit Tigers	0
October 14	Chicago Cubs	2	at	Detroit Tigers	0

Other Sports

Horseracing--Kentucky Derby won by Stone Street (time 2:15.2, purse $4,850).
Heavyweight Boxing--Tommy Burns knocked-out Jack Palmer in 4 rounds.
Tommy Burns knocked-out Jem Roche in 1 round.
Tommy Burns knocked-out Jewey Smith in 5 rounds.
Tommy Burns knocked-out Bill Squires in 8 rounds.
Tommy Burns knocked-out Bill Squires in 13 rounds.
Tommy Burns knocked-out Bill Lang in 2 rounds.
Jack Johnson stopped Tommy Burns in 14 rounds.
Golf--U.S. Open won by Fred McLeod with a score of 322.

Notes

The first professional hockey league in Canada, the Ontario Professional Hockey League, was formed this year but it was not considered a major league.
The fight between Johnson and Burns was stopped by the police.

1909

BASEBALL
National League

Team Name	W	L	Pct	GB	R	OR
Pittsburgh Pirates	110	42	.724	-	701	448
Chicago Cubs	104	49	.680	6.5	632	376
New York Giants	92	61	.601	18.5	621	546
Cincinnati Reds	77	76	.503	33.5	603	599
Philadelphia Phillies	74	79	.484	36.5	514	518
Brooklyn Superbas	55	98	.359	55.5	442	627
St. Louis Cardinals	54	98	.355	56	583	728
Boston Pilgrims	45	108	.294	65.5	427	681

Coaching Changes

Cincinnati--Clark Griffith 77-76; Brooklyn--Harry Lumley 55-98; St. Louis--Roger Bresnahan 54-98; Boston--Frank Bowerman 23-55, Harry Smith 22-53.

League Leaders

Batting Average

Honus Wagner	.339
Mike Mitchell	.310
Dick Hoblitzell	.308
Larry Doyle	.301
Al Bridwell	.295

Home Runs

John Murray	7
Tommy Leach	6
Larry Doyle	6
Beals Becker	6
Honus Wagner	5

RBI

Honus Wagner	100
John Murray	91
John Miller	87
Mike Mitchell	86
Ed Konetchy	80

Stolen Bases

Bob Bescher	54
John Murray	48
Dick Egan	39
Sherwood Magee	38
Al Burch	38

ERA

Christy Mathewson	1.14
Mordecai Brown	1.31
Orval Overall	1.42
Howie Camnitz	1.62
Floyd Kroh	1.65

Wins

Mordecai Brown	26
Howie Camnitz	24
Christy Mathewson	24
Victor Willis	23
Orval Overall	21

Saves

Mordecai Brown	7
James Crandall	4
Howie Camnitz	3
George Wiltse	3
Al Mattern	3

Strikeouts

Orval Overall	205
George Rucker	201
Earl Moore	173
Mordecai Brown	172
Leon Ames	156

American League

Team Name	W	L	Pct	GB	R	OR
Detroit Tigers	98	54	.645	-	666	493
Philadelphia Athletics	95	58	.621	3.5	600	414
Boston Red Sox	88	63	.583	9.5	590	561
Chicago White Sox	78	74	.513	20	494	465
New York Highlanders	74	77	.490	23.5	591	580
Cleveland Naps	71	82	.464	27.5	519	543
St. Louis Browns	61	89	.407	36	443	574
Washington Senators	42	110	.276	56	382	655

Coaching Changes

Boston--Fred Lake 88-63; Chicago--Billy Sullivan 78-74; New York--George Stallings 74-77; Cleveland--Napoleon Lajoie 57-57, James "Deacon" McGuire 14-25.

League Leaders

Batting Average

Ty Cobb	.377
Eddie Collins	.346
Napoleon Lajoie	.324
Sam Crawford	.314
Harry Lord	.311

Home Runs

Ty Cobb	9
Tris Speaker	7
Sam Crawford	6
Jake Stahl	6
Danny Murphy	5

RBI

Ty Cobb	107
Sam Crawford	97
Frank Baker	85
Tris Speaker	77
Harry Davis	75

Stolen Bases

Ty Cobb	76
Eddie Collins	67
Owen Bush	53
Harry Lord	36
Patsy Dougherty	36

ERA

Harry Krause	1.39
Ed Walsh	1.41
Chief Bender	1.66
Eddie Plank	1.70
Adrian Joss	1.71

Wins

George Mullin	29
Frank Smith	24
Ed Willett	21
Eddie Plank	19
Ed Summers	19

Saves

Frank Arellanes	7
Jack Warhop	4
Jack Powell	3
Tom Hughes	3
Jack Quinn	2

Strikeouts

Frank Smith	177
Walter Johnson	164
Charles Berger	162
Chief Bender	161
Rube Waddell	141

World Series

October 8	Detroit Tigers	1	at	Pittsburgh Pirates	4
October 9	Detroit Tigers	7	at	Pittsburgh Pirates	2
October 11	Pittsburgh Pirates	8	at	Detroit Tigers	6
October 12	Pittsburgh Pirates	0	at	Detroit Tigers	5
October 13	Detroit Tigers	4	at	Pittsburgh Pirates	8
October 14	Pittsburgh Pirates	4	at	Detroit Tigers	5
October 16	Pittsburgh Pirates	8	at	Detroit Tigers	0

HOCKEY
Eastern Canada Hockey Association

Team Name	GP	W	L	T	GF	GA	Pts	Pct
Ottawa Senators	12	10	2	0	117	63	20	.833
Montreal Wanderers	12	9	3	0	82	61	18	.750
Quebec Bulldogs	12	3	0	0	78	106	6	.250
Montreal Shamrocks	12	2	10	0	56	103	4	.167

Coaching

Not Available

League Leaders

Goals		Points		GAA		Wins	
Marty Walsh	38	Marty Walsh	38	Riley Hern	5.03	Percy Lesueur	10
Herb Jordan	29	Herb Jordan	29	Percy Lesueur	5.25	Riley Hern	9
Bruce Stuart	22	Bruce Stuart	22	W. Baker	8.53	Paddy Moran	3
Chubby Power	22	Chubby Power	22	Paddy Moran	8.83	W. Baker	2
Albert Kerr	20	Albert Kerr	20				

Stanley Cup Playoffs*

December 28	Edmonton Thistles	3	at	Montreal Wanderers	7
December 30	Edmonton Thistles	7	at	Montreal Wanderers	6

Notes

The Eastern Canada Hockey Association was formed November 4th, 1908, when Montreal and the Victorias resigned from the Eastern Canada Amateur Hockey Association and left all the remaining teams as professional. The league decided to drop the word amateur from its title. Joe Power is named as first President of the Eastern Canada Hockey Association.

*--As Stanley Cup champion for the 1907-1908 season, the Montreal Wanderers accepted a challenge from Edmonton, the Alberta champions and played a two game series at the start of the 1908-1909 season. Ottawa as champions for the 1908-1909 season were awarded the Stanley Cup and were not involved in any playoffs.

Franchise Changes

NL--Boston Doves changed name to Boston Pilgrims.

Other Sports

Horseracing--Kentucky Derby won by Wintergreen (time 2:08.2, purse $4,850).
Heavyweight Boxing--Jack Johnson and Jack O'Brien fought to a 6 round draw.
Jack Johnson and Tony Ross fought to a 6 round draw.
Jack Johnson and Al Kaufman, 10 rounds, no decision.
Jack Johnson knocked-out Stanley Ketchell in 12 rounds.
Golf--U.S. Open won by George Sargent with a score of 290.

1910

BASEBALL
National League

Team Name	W	L	Pct	GB	R	OR
Chicago Cubs	104	50	.675	-	711	497
New York Giants	91	63	.591	13	715	545
Pittsburgh Pirates	86	67	.562	17.5	655	576
Philadelphia Phillies	78	75	.510	25.5	674	682
Cincinnati Reds	75	79	.487	29	620	665
Brooklyn Superbas	64	90	.416	40	497	622
St. Louis Cardinals	63	90	.412	40.5	637	717
Boston Pilgrims	53	100	.346	50.5	495	700

Coaching Changes

Philadelphia--Charles Dooin 78-75; Brooklyn--Bill Dahlen 64-90; Boston--Fred Lake 53-100.

League Leaders

Batting Average

Sherry Magee	.331
Vin Campbell	.326
Arthur Hofman	.325
Fred Snodgrass	.321
Honus Wagner	.320

Home Runs

Fred Beck	10
Fred Schulte	10
Larry Doyle	8
Jake Daubert	8
John Flynn	6

RBI

Sherry Magee	123
Mike Mitchell	88
John Murray	87
Arthur Hofman	86
Honus Wagner	81

Stolen Bases

Bob Bescher	70
John Murray	57
George Paskert	51
Sherry Magee	49
Josh Devore	43

ERA

George McQuillan	1.60
Leonard Cole	1.80
Mordecai Brown	1.86
Christy Mathewson	1.89
Leon Ames	2.22

Wins

Christy Mathewson	27
Mordecai Brown	21
Earl Moore	21
Leonard Cole	20
Charles Adams	18

Saves

Mordecai Brown	7
Harry Gaspar	5
James Crandall	4
Charles Phillippe	4
Lewis Richie	3

Strikeouts

Earl Moore	185
Christy Mathewson	184
Sam Frock	171
Louis Drucke	151
Napoleon Rucker	147

American League

Team Name	W	L	Pct	GB	R	OR
Philadelphia Athletics	102	48	.680	-	672	439
New York Highlanders	88	63	.583	14.5	629	502
Detroit Tigers	86	68	.558	18	679	580
Boston Red Sox	81	72	.529	22.5	637	564
Cleveland Naps	71	81	.467	32	539	654
Chicago White Sox	68	85	.444	35.5	456	495
Washington Senators	66	85	.437	36.5	498	552
St. Louis Browns	47	107	.305	57	454	778

Coaching Changes

New York--George Stallings 79-61, Hal Chase 9-2; Boston--Patrick Donovan 81-72; Cleveland--James "Deacon" McGuire 71-81; Chicago--Hugh Duffy 68-85; Washington--Jim McAleer 66-85; St. Louis--Jack O'Connor 47-107.

League Leaders

Batting Average		Home Runs		RBI	
Ty Cobb	.385	Jake Stahl	10	Sam Crawford	120
Napoleon Lajoie	.384	Ty Cobb	8	Ty Cobb	91
Tris Speaker	.340	George Lewis	8	Eddie Collins	81
Eddie Collins	.322	Tris Speaker	7	Jake Stahl	77
John Knight	.312	Sam Crawford	5	Napoleon Lajoie	76

Stolen Bases		ERA		Wins	
Eddie Collins	81	Ed Walsh	1.27	Jack Coombs	30
Ty Cobb	65	Jack Coombs	1.30	Russ Ford	26
Owen Bush	49	Walter Johnson	1.35	Walter Johnson	24
Rollie Zeider	49	Harry Morgan	1.55	Chief Bender	22
Clyde Milan	44	Chief Bender	1.58	George Mullin	21

Saves		Strikeouts	
Ed Walsh	6	Walter Johnson	313
Charley Hall	5	Ed Walsh	258
Fred Falkenberg	4	Jack Coombs	224
Fred Harkness	3	Russ Ford	209
Elmer Koestner	2	Chief Bender	155

World Series

October 17	Chicago Cubs	1	at	Philadelphia Athletics	4
October 18	Chicago Cubs	3	at	Philadelphia Athletics	9
October 20	Philadelphia Athletics	12	at	Chicago Cubs	5
October 22	Philadelphia Athletics	3	at	Chicago Cubs	4 [10]
October 23	Philadelphia Athletics	7	at	Chicago Cubs	2

Notes

Thomas Lynch succeeded Henry Pullman as President of the National League when Henry Pullman died. William Howard Taft became the first U.S. President to throw out a baseball to open the major league baseball season.

HOCKEY
National Hockey Association

Team Name	GP	W	L	T	GF	GA	Pts	Pct
Montreal Wanderers	12	11	1	0	91	41	22	.917
Ottawa Senators	12	9	3	0	89	66	18	.750
Renfrew Creamery Kings	12	8	3	1	96	54	17	.708
Cobalt Silver Kings	12	4	8	0	79	104	8	.333
Haileybury Comets	12	4	8	0	77	83	8	.333
Montreal Shamrocks	12	3	8	1	52	95	7	.292
Montreal Canadiens	12	2	10	0	59	100	4	.167

Coaching Changes

Not available.

League Leaders

Goals

Harry Smith	29
Marty Walsh	23
Lester Patrick	22
Herb Clarke	22
Horace Gaul	22

Points

Harry Smith	29
Marty Walsh	23
Lester Patrick	22
Herb Clarke	22
Horace Gaul	22

GAA

Riley Hern	3.42
Bert Lindsay	4.50
Jack Winchester	5.20
Percy Lesueur	5.50
Paddy Moran	7.27

Wins

Riley Hern	12
Percy Lesueur	9
Bert Lindsay	8
Chief Jones	4

Shutouts

Riley Hern	1

Stanley Cup Playoffs*

January 5	Galt	3	at	Ottawa Senators	12
January 7	Galt	1	at	Ottawa Senators	3
January 18	Edmonton Thistles	4	at	Ottawa Senators	8
January 20	Edmonton Thistles	7	at	Ottawa Senators	13
March 12	Berlin Dutchmen	3	at	Montreal Wanderers	7**

*As Stanley Cup champion for the 1908-1909 season the Ottawa Senators accepted a challenge from Galt, champions of the Ontario Professional Hockey League and Edmonton champions of Alberta at the start of the 1909-1910 season and won 4 straight games.
**Wanderers as champions of the National Hockey Association took possession of the Stanley Cup and accepted a challenge from Berlin, champions of the OPHL for the 1909-1910 season and defeated them in a single game series.

Notes

The ECHA was disbanded and the teams decided to form the Canadian Hockey Association which also disbanded after a few games. Four teams from the CHA then joined the National Hockey Association which was formed December 2 1909, in Montreal. M. Doheny is named first President of the NHA.
Frank and Lester Patrick sign with Renfrew of the National Hockey Association. They are paid $3,000 each for playing approximately 12 games each.
Fred Taylor of the Renfrew Creamery Kings earned approximately $5,200 for playing12 games to become one of the highest paid athletes in pro sports. Unlike modern players Taylor usually played the whole game as did most of the players at the time.

Other Sports

Horseracing--Kentucky Derby won by Donau (time 2:06.4, purse $4,850).
Heavyweight Boxing--Jack Johnson knocked-out Jim Jeffries in 15 rounds.
Golf--U.S. Open won by Alex Smith with a score of 298.

1911

BASEBALL
National league

Team Name	W	L	Pct	GB	R	OR
New York Giants	99	54	.647	-	756	542
Chicago Cubs	92	62	.597	7.5	757	607
Pittsburgh Pirates	85	69	.552	14.5	744	560
Philadelphia Phillies	79	73	.520	19.5	658	673
St. Louis Cardinals	75	74	.503	22	671	745
Cincinnati Reds	70	83	.458	29	682	700
Brooklyn Dodgers	64	86	.427	33.5	539	659
Boston Pilgrims	44	107	.291	54	699	1020

Coaching Changes

Boston--Fred Tenney 44-107.

League Leaders

Batting Average

Honus Wagner	.334
Roy Miller	.333
John Meyers	.332
Fred Clarke	.324
Art Fletcher	.319

Home Runs

Frank Schulte	21
Fred Luderus	16
Sherry Magee	15
Larry Doyle	13
Owen Wilson	12

RBI

Owen Wilson	107
Frank Schulte	107
Fred Luderus	99
Sherry Magee	94
Roy Miller	91

Stolen Bases

Bob Bescher	80
Josh Devore	61
Fred Snodgrass	51
Fred Merkle	49
John Murray	48

ERA

Christy Mathewson	1.99
Lew Richie	2.31
Charles Adams	2.33
Rube Marquard	2.50
Grover Alexander	2.57

Wins

Grover Alexander	28
Rube Marquard	25
Christy Mathewson	24
Bob Harmon	23
Charles Adams	22

Saves

Mordecai Brown	13
James Crandall	5
Napoleon Rucker	4
George Chalmers	4
Bill Schardt	4

Strikeouts

Rube Marquard	237
Grover Alexander	227
Napoleon Rucker	190
Earl Moore	174
Bob Harmon	144

American League

Team Name	W	L	Pct	GB	R	OR
Philadelphia Athletics	101	50	.669	-	861	601
Detroit Tigers	89	65	.578	13.5	831	777
Cleveland Naps	80	73	.523	22	691	709
Chicago White Sox	77	74	.510	24	717	627
Boston Red Sox	78	75	.510	24	680	647
New York Highlanders	76	76	.500	25.5	686	726
Washington Senators	64	90	.416	38.5	624	760
St. Louis Browns	45	107	.296	56.5	567	810

Coaching Changes

Cleveland--James "Deacon" McGuire 6-11, George Stovall 74-62; New York--Hal Chase 76-76; St. Louis--Bobby Wallace 45-107.

League Leaders

Batting Average

Ty Cobb	.420
Joe Jackson	.408
Sam Crawford	.378
Eddie Collins	.365
William Cree	.348

Home Runs

Frank Baker	9
Ty Cobb	8
Tris Speaker	8
George Lewis	7
Joe Jackson	7

RBI

Ty Cobb	127
Fred Baker	115
Sam Crawford	115
Frank Bodie	97
Jim Delahanty	94

Stolen Bases

Ty Cobb	83
Clyde Milan	58
William Cree	48
James Callahan	45
Harry Lord	43

ERA

Vean Gregg	1.81
Walter Johnson	1.89
Joe Wood	2.02
Eddie Plank	2.10
Chief Bender	2.16

Wins

Jack Coombs	29
Ed Walsh	26
Walter Johnson	25
Vean Gregg	23
Eddie Plank	22

Saves

Ed Walsh	7
Joe Wood	5
Eddie Plank	5
Charley Hall	5
Chief Bender	4

Strikeouts

Ed Walsh	255
Joe Wood	231
Walter Johnson	207
Jack Coombs	185
Russ Ford	158

World Series

October 14	Philadelphia Athletics	1	at	New York Giants	2
October 16	New York Giants	1	at	Philadelphia Athletics	3
October 17	Philadelphia Athletics	3	at	New York Giants	2 [11]
October 24	New York Giants	2	at	Philadelphia Athletics	4
October 25	New York Giants	4	at	Philadelphia Athletics	3 [10]
October 26	New York Giants	2	at	Philadelphia Athletics	13

Individual Awards

Chalmers Award--Frank Schulte (Chicago Cubs NL)
Ty Cobb (Detroit Tigers AL)

HOCKEY

National Hockey Association

Team Name	GP	W	L	T	GF	GA	Pts	Pct
Ottawa Senators	16	13	3	0	122	69	26	.813
Montreal Canadiens	16	8	8	0	66	62	16	.500
Renfrew Creamery Kings	16	8	8	0	91	101	16	.500
Montreal Wanderers	16	7	9	0	73	88	14	.438
Quebec Bulldogs	16	4	12	0	65	97	8	.250

Coaching*

Canadiens--George Kennedy 8-8; Wanderers--Dick Boon 7-9

League Leaders

Goals		Points		GAA	
Marty Walsh	37	Marty Walsh	37	Georges Vezina	3.88
Albert Kerr	32	Albert Kerr	32	Percy Lesueur	4.31
Don Smith	28	Don Smith	28	Riley Hern	5.50
Bruce Ridpath	22	Bruce Ridpath	22	Paddy Moran	6.06
Odie Cleghorn	20	Odie Cleghorn	20	Bert Lindsay	6.31

Wins		Shutouts	
Percy Lesueur	13	Percy Lesueur	1
Georges Vezina	8		
Bert Lindsay	8		
Riley Hern	7		
Paddy Moran	4		

Stanley Cup Playoffs

March 13	Galt	4	at	Ottawa Senators	7
March 16	Port Arthur	4	at	Ottawa Senators	13

Rules

The game was to consist of 3 twenty minute periods instead of 2 thirty minute periods as had been the situation before.

Notes

Emmett Quinn is named President of the National Hockey Association.
Ottawa Senators as champions of the NHA took possession of the Stanley Cup. They were challenged for the Cup by Galt of the OPHL, who they defeated 7 to 4. Ottawa was then challenged by Port Arthur of the New Ontario League and they defeated them 13 to 4.
Brothers Odie and Sprague Cleghorn signed with Renfrew of the NHA for $1,000 each, Odie playing 16 games and Sprague playing 12 games.

Franchise Changes

NL--Brooklyn Superbas changed name to Brooklyn Dodgers.

Other Sports

Horseracing--Kentucky Derby won by Meridian (time 2:05, purse $4,850).
Golf--U.S. Open won by John McDermott with a score of 307.
Auto Racing--Indianapolis 500 won by Ray Harroun (6hr., 41min., 8sec., ave. speed 74.7 MPH).

*Not complete

1912

BASEBALL
National League

Team Name	W	L	Pct	GB	R	OR
New York Giants	103	48	.682	-	823	571
Pittsburgh Pirates	93	58	.616	10	751	565
Chicago Cubs	91	59	.607	11.5	756	666
Cincinnati Reds	75	78	.490	29	656	722
Philadelphia Phillies	73	79	.480	30.5	670	689
St. Louis Cardinals	63	90	.412	41	659	825
Brooklyn Dodgers	58	95	.379	46	651	748
Boston Braves	52	101	.340	52	693	873

Coaching Changes

Cincinnati--Hank O'Day 75-78; Boston--Johnny Kling 52-101.

League Leaders

Batting Average

Heinie Zimmerman	.372
John Meyers	.358
Bill Sweeney	.344
John Evers	.341
Larry Doyle	.330

Home Runs

Heinie Zimmerman	14
Frank Schulte	12
Cliff Cravath	11
Owen Wilson	11
Fred Merkle	11

RBI

Heinie Zimmerman	103
Honus Wagner	102
Bill Sweeney	100
Owen Wilson	95
John Murray	92

Stolen Bases

Bob Bescher	67
Max Carey	45
Fred Snodgrass	43
John Murray	38
Fred Merkle	37

ERA

Jeff Tesreau	1.96
Christy Mathewson	2.12
Napoleon Rucker	2.21
Hank Robinson	2.26
Eppa Rixey	2.50

Wins

Rube Marquard	27
Larry Cheney	26
Claude Hendrix	23
Christy Mathewson	23
Howie Camnitz	22

Saves

Harry Sallee	6
Napoleon Rucker	4
Christy Mathewson	4
Ed Reulbach	3
Hubbard Purdue	3

Strikeouts

Grover Alexander	195
Claude Hendrix	176
Rube Marquard	175
John Benton	162
Napoleon Rucker	151

American League

Team Name	W	L	Pct	GB	R	OR
Boston Red Sox	105	47	.691	-	800	544
Washington Senators	91	61	.599	14	698	581
Philadelphia Athletics	90	62	.592	15	780	656
Chicago White Sox	78	76	.506	28	640	647
Cleveland Molly McGuires	75	78	.490	30.5	680	681
Detroit Tigers	69	84	.451	36.5	720	768
St. Louis Browns	53	101	.344	53	556	790
New York Highlanders	50	102	.329	55	632	839

Coaching Changes

Boston--Jake Stahl 105-47; Washington--Clark Griffith 91-61; Chicago--James Callahan 78-76; Cleveland--Harry Davis 54-71, Joe Birmingham 21-7; St. Louis--Bob Wallace 12-27, George Stovall 41-74; New York--Harry Wolverton 50-102.

League Leaders

Batting Average		**Home Runs**		**RBI**	
Ty Cobb	.410	Frank Baker	10	Frank Baker	130
Joe Jackson	.395	Tris Speaker	9	Sam Crawford	109
Tris Speaker	.383	Ty Cobb	7	George Lewis	109
Napoleon Lajoie	.368	Danny Moeller	6	John McInnis	101
Eddie Collins	.348	Guy Zinn	6	Napoleon Lajoie	90

Stolen Bases		**ERA**		**Wins**	
Clyde Milan	88	Walter Johnson	1.39	Joe Wood	34
Eddie Collins	63	Joe Wood	1.91	Walter Johnson	32
Ty Cobb	61	Ed Walsh	2.15	Ed Walsh	27
Tris Speaker	52	Eddie Plank	2.22	Eddie Plank	25
Rollie Zeider	47	Ray Collins	2.53	Bob Groom	24

Saves		**Strikeouts**	
Ed Walsh	10	Walter Johnson	296
Hugh Bedient	3	Joe Wood	258
Walter Johnson	3	Ed Walsh	254
Frank Lange	3	Vean Gregg	184
Jean Dubuc	3	Bob Groom	179

World Series

October 8	Boston Red Sox	4	at	New York Giants	3
October 9	New York Giants	6	at	Boston Red Sox	6 [11]
October 10	New York Giants	2	at	Boston Red Sox	1
October 11	Boston Red Sox	3	at	New York Giants	1
October 12	New York Giants	1	at	Boston Red Sox	2
October 14	Boston Red Sox	2	at	New York Giants	5
October 15	New York Giants	11	at	Boston Red Sox	4
October 16	New York Giants	2	at	Boston Red Sox	3 [10]

Individual Awards

Chalmers Award--Larry Doyle (New York Giants NL)
Tris Speaker (Boston Red Sox AL)

HOCKEY
National Hockey Association

Team Name	GP	W	L	T	GF	GA	Pts	Pct
Quebec Bulldogs	18	10	8	0	81	79	20	.556
Ottawa Senators	18	9	9	0	99	93	18	.500
Montreal Wanderers	18	9	9	0	95	96	18	.500
Montreal Canadiens	18	8	10	0	59	66	16	.444

Coaching Changes

Not Available.

League Leaders

Goals		Points		GAA	
Skene Ronan	35	Skene Ronan	35	Georges Vezina	3.67
Didier Pitre	28	Didier Pitre	28	Paddy Moran	4.39
Ernie Russell	27	Ernie Russell	27	Broughton	4.50
Albert Kerr	25	Albert Kerr	25	Percy Lesueur	5.17
Odie Cleghorn	23	Odie Cleghorn	23	Art Boyce	5.75

Wins		Shutouts	
Paddy Moran	10	Broughton	1
Percy Lesueur	9		
Georges Vezina	8		

Stanley Cup Playoffs

March 11	Moncton	3	at	Quebec Bulldogs	9
March 13	Moncton	0	at	Quebec Bulldogs	8

Rules

Six man hockey was introduced this year.
Players on National Hockey Association teams were required to wear identifying numbers on the left arm of their uniform, although mid-way through the season the rule was modified so that the number had to be worn on the front of the uniform.
Quebec as champions of the National Hockey Association were awarded the Stanley Cup and accepted a challenge from Moncton of the Maritime Professional Hockey League and defeated them in two straight games.

Pacific Coast Hockey Association

Team Name	GP	W	L	T	GF	GA	Pts	Pct
New Westminster Royals	15	9	6	0	78	77	18	.600
Vancouver Millionaires	15	7	8	0	102	94	14	.467
Victoria Senators	16	7	9	0	81	90	14	.438

Coaching

New Westminster--Jim Gardner 9-6-0; Vancouver--Frank Patrick 7-8-0; Victoria--Lester Patrick 7-9-0

League Leaders

Goals		Points		GAA	
Newsy Lalonde	27	Newsy Lalonde	27	Hugh Lehman	5.13
Harry Hyland	26	Harry Hyland	26	Bert Lindsay	5.63
Tom Dunderdale	24	Tom Dunderdale	24	Allan Parr	6.27
Frank Patrick	23	Frank Patrick	23		
Don Smith	19	Don Smith	19		

Wins	
Hugh Lehman	9
Bert Lindsay	7
Allan Parr	7

Notes

The Pacific Coast Hockey Association was organized this year in Vancouver on December 7, 1911 by Frank and Lester Patrick. W.P. Irving is named first President of the league.
The Denman Arena was the first arena in Canada with artificial ice.

Franchise Changes

NL--Boston Pilgrims became Boston Braves.
AL--Cleveland Naps became known as the Cleveland Molly McGuires.

Other Sports

Horseracing--Kentucky Derby won by Worth (time 2:09.4, purse $4,850).
Heavyweight Boxing--Jack Johnson won by points over Jim Flynn in 9 rounds.
Golf--U.S. Open won by John McDermott with a score of 294.
Auto Racing--Indianapolis 500 won by Joe Dawson (ave. speed 78.70 MPH).

Notes

The fight between Johnson and Flynn was stopped by the police.

1913

BASEBALL
National League

Team Name	W	L	Pct	GB	R	OR
New York Giants	101	51	.664	-	684	502
Philadelphia Phillies	88	63	.583	12.5	693	636
Chicago Cubs	88	65	.575	13.5	720	640
Pittsburgh Pirates	78	71	.523	21.5	673	585
Boston Braves	69	82	.457	31.5	641	690
Brooklyn Dodgers	65	84	.436	34.5	595	613
Cincinnati Reds	64	89	.418	37.5	607	714
St. Louis Cardinals	51	99	.340	49	523	756

Coaching Changes

Chicago--Johnny Evers 88-65; Boston--George Stallings 69-82; Cincinnati--Joe Tinker 64-89; St. Louis--Miller Huggins 51-99.

League Leaders

Batting Average

Jake Daubert	.350
Gavvy Cravath	.341
Jim Viox	.317
Joe Tinker	.317
Beals Becker	.316

Home Runs

Clifford Cravath	19
Fred Luderus	18
Vic Saier	14
Sherry Magee	11
Owen Wilson	10

RBI

Clifford Cravath	128
Heinie Zimmerman	95
Vic Saier	92
John Miller	90
Fred Luderus	86

Stolen Bases

Max Carey	61
Ralph Myers	57
John Lobert	41
George Burns	40
George Cutshaw	39

ERA

Christy Mathewson	2.06
Charles Adams	2.15
Jeff Tesreau	2.17
Al Demaree	2.21
George Pearce	2.31

Wins

Tom Seaton	27
Christy Mathewson	25
Rube Marquard	24
Jeff Tesreau	22
Grover Alexander	22

Saves

Larry Cheney	11
Mordecai Brown	6
James Crandall	6
Harry Sallee	5
Claude Hendrix	3

Strikeouts

Tom Seaton	168
Jeff Tesreau	167
Grover Alexander	159
Rube Marquard	151
Charles Adams	144

League Leaders

Goals		Points		GAA	
Tom Dunderdale	24	Tom Dunderdale	24	Bert Lindsay	3.73
Carl Kendall	16	Carl Kendall	16	Hugh Lehman	4.57
Frank Patrick	15	Frank Patrick	15	Allan Parr	5.56
Ran McDonald	15	Ran McDonald	15	Foxy Smith	10.00
Lester Patrick	14	Lester Patrick	14		

Wins		Shutouts	
Bert Lindsay	10	Bert Lindsay	1
Allan Parr	7		
Hugh Lehman	6		
Foxy Smith	0		

Notes

C.E. Doherty succeeded W.P. Irving as President of the Pacific Coast Hockey Association.

Franchise Changes

NL--New York Highlanders changed name to New York Yankees.
PCHA--Victoria Senators changed name to Victoria Aristocrats.

Other Sports

Horseracing--Kentucky Derby won by Donerail (time 2:04.8, purse $5,475).
Heavyweight Boxing--Jack Johnson knocked-out Andre Spaul in 2 rounds.
Jack Johnson and Jim Johnson fought to a 10 round draw.
Golf--U.S. Open won by Francis Ouimet with a score of 304.
Auto Racing--Indianapolis 500 won by Jules Goux (ave. speed 76.92 MPH).

1914

BASEBALL
National League

Team Name	W	L	Pct	GB	R	OR
Boston Braves	94	59	.614	-	657	548
New York Giants	84	70	.545	10.5	672	576
St. Louis Cardinals	81	72	.529	13	558	540
Chicago Cubs	78	76	.506	16.5	605	638
Brooklyn Dodgers	75	79	.487	19.5	622	612
Philadelphia Phillies	74	80	.481	20.5	651	673
Pittsburgh Pirates	69	85	.448	25.5	503	540
Cincinnati Reds	60	94	.390	34.5	530	671

Coaching Changes

Chicago--Hank O'Day 78-76; Brooklyn--Wilbert Robinson 75-79; Cincinnati--Charles Herzog 60-94.

League Leaders

Batting Average		Home Runs		RBI	
Jake Daubert	.329	Gavvy Cravath	19	Sherry Magee	103
Beals Becker	.325	Vic Saier	18	Gavvy Cravath	100
Jack Dalton	.319	Sherry Magee	15	Zack Wheat	89
Zack Wheat	.319	Fred Luderus	12	John Miller	88
Casey Stengel	.316	Joe A. Connolly	9	Heinie Zimmerman	87

Stolen Bases		ERA		Wins	
George Burns	62	Bill Doak	1.72	Grover Alexander	27
Charles Herzog	46	Bill James	1.90	Dick Rudolph	27
Alvin Dolan	42	Jeff Pfeffer	1.97	Jeff Tesreau	26
Max Carey	38	James Vaughn	2.05	Bill James	26
Bob Bescher	36	Harry Sallee	2.10	Christy Mathewson	24

Saves		Strikeouts	
Leon Ames	6	Grover Alexander	214
Harry Sallee	6	Jeff Tesreau	189
Larry Cheney	5	James Vaughn	165
George McQuillan	4	Larry Cheney	157
Jeff Pfeffer	4	Bill James	156

Notes

John Tener succeeded Thomas Lynch as President of the National League.

American League

Team Name	W	L	Pct	GB	R	OR
Philadelphia Athletics	99	53	.651	-	749	520
Boston Red Sox	91	62	.595	8.5	588	511
Washington Senators	81	73	.526	19	572	519
Detroit Tigers	80	73	.523	19.5	615	618
St. Louis Browns	71	82	.464	28.5	523	614
Chicago White Sox	70	84	.455	30	487	568
New York Yankees	70	84	.455	30	536	550
Cleveland Molly McGuires	51	102	.333	48.5	538	708

Coaching Changes

Boston--Bill Carrigan 91-62; St. Louis--Branch Rickey 71-82; New York--Frank Chance 61-76, Roger Peckinpaugh 9-8.

League Leaders

Batting Average		Home Runs		RBI	
Ty Cobb	.368	Frank Baker	8	Sam Crawford	104
Eddie Collins	.344	Sam Crawford	8	John McInnis	95
Tris Speaker	.338	Jack Fournier	6	Tris Speaker	90
Joe Jackson	.338	Tilly Walker	6	Frank Baker	89
Frank Baker	.319	George H. Burns	5	Eddie Collins	85

Stolen Bases		ERA		Wins	
Fred Maisel	74	Dutch Leonard	1.01	Walter Johnson	28
Eddie Collins	58	George Foster	1.65	Harry Coveleski	21
Tris Speaker	42	Walter Johnson	1.72	Ray Collins	20
Burt Shotton	40	Ernie Shore	1.89	George Dauss	19
Clyde Milan	38	Ray Caldwell	1.94	Ray Caldwell	18

Saves		Strikeouts	
Jack Bentley	4	Walter Johnson	225
Roy Mitchell	4	Willie Mitchell	179
Urban Faber	4	Dutch Leonard	174
Dutch Leonard	4	Jim Shaw	164
Alex Main	3	George Dauss	150

World Series

October 9	Boston Braves	7	at	Philadelphia Athletics	1
October 10	Boston Braves	1	at	Philadelphia Athletics	0
October 12	Philadelphia Athletics	4	at	Boston braves	5 [12]
October 13	Philadelphia Athletics	1	at	Boston Braves	3

Individual Awards

Chalmers Award--Johnny Evers (Boston Braves NL)
Eddie Collins (Philadelphia Athletics AL)

Federal League

Team Name	W	L	Pct	GB	R	OR
Indianapolis Federal Hoosiers	88	65	.575	-	762	622
Chicago Whales	87	67	.565	1.5	621	517
Baltimore Terrapins	84	70	.545	4.5	645	628
Buffalo Blues	80	71	.530	7	620	602
Brooklyn Tip-Tops	77	77	.500	11.5	662	677
Kansas City Packers	67	84	.444	20	644	683
Pittsburgh Rebels	64	86	.427	22.5	605	698
St. Louis Terriers	62	89	.411	25	565	697

Coaching

Indianapolis--Bill Phillips 88-65; Chicago--Joe Tinker 87-67; Baltimore--Otto Knabe 84-70; Buffalo--Larry Schlafly 80-71; Brooklyn--Bill Bradley 77-77; Kansas City--George Stovall 67-84; Pittsburgh--Harry Gessler 6-12, Ennis Oakes 58-74; St. Louis--Mordecai "Three Finger" Brown 50-63, Fielder Jones 12-26

League Leaders

Batting Average		Home Runs		RBI	
Benny Kauff	.370	Edward Zwilling	15	Frank LaPorte	107
Steve Evans	.348	Bill Kenworthy	15	Steve Evans	96
Ted Easterly	.335	Charlie Hanford	13	Edward Zwilling	95
Albert Shaw	.324	Steve Evans	12	Benny Kauff	95
Vin Campbell	.318	Ed Lennox	11	Bill Kenworthy	91

Stolen Bases		ERA		Wins	
Benny Kauff	75	Adam Johnson	1.58	Claude Hendrix	29
Bill McKechnie	47	Claude Hendrix	1.69	Cy Falkenberg	25
Ralph Myers	43	Russ Ford	1.82	Tom Seaton	25
Chet Chadbourne	42	Charles Watson	2.01	George Suggs	25
Max Flack	37	Cy Falkenberg	2.22	Jack Quinn	25

Saves		Strikeouts	
Russ Ford	6	Cy Falkenberg	236
Claude Hendrix	5	Earl Moseley	205
Irvin Wilhelm	4	Claude Hendrix	189
Gene Packard	4	Tom Seaton	172
Dave Davenport	4	Bob Groom	167

Notes

James A. Gilmore, president of the minor Federal League brought the league into direct competition with the two established leagues.

HOCKEY

National Hockey Association

Team Name	GP	W	L	T	GF	GA	Pts	Pct
Montreal Canadiens	20	13	7	0	85	65	26	.650
Toronto Blueshirts	20	13	7	0	93	65	26	.650
Quebec Bulldogs	20	12	8	0	111	73	24	.600
Ottawa Senators	20	11	9	0	65	71	22	.550
Montreal Wanderers	20	7	13	0	102	125	14	.350
Toronto Ontarios	20	4	16	0	61	118	8	.200

Coaching Changes*

Toronto Ontarios--Jim Murphy 4-16; Toronto Blueshirts--Jack Marshall 13-7; Montreal--George Kennedy 13-7.

League Leaders

Goals		Points		GAA	
Tommy Smith	39	Tommy Smith	39	Georges Vezina	3.25
Harry Hyland	31	Harry Hyland	31	Harry Holmes	3.25
Gordon Roberts	30	Gordon Roberts	30	Clint Benedict	3.29
Jack McDonald	26	Jack McDonald	26	Paddy Moran	3.65
Joe Malone	24	Joe Malone	24	Percy Leseur	3.69

Wins		Shutouts	
Harry Holmes	13	Percy Lesueur	1
Georges Vezina	13	Harry Holmes	1
Paddy Moran	12	Georges Vezina	1
Percy Leseur	7	Paddy Moran	1
Clint Benedict	5		

Rules

The referee was to drop the puck on face-offs instead of placing it on the ice and calling "Play."

Pacific Coast Hockey Association

Team Name	GP	W	L	T	GF	GA	Pts	Pct
Victoria Aristocrats	15	10	5	0	80	67	20	.667
New Westminster Royals	16	7	9	0	75	81	14	.438
Vancouver Millionaires	15	6	9	0	76	83	12	.400

Coaching Changes

Not available.

*Not complete

League Leaders

Goals		Points		GAA		Wins	
Tom Dunderdale	23	Tom Dunderdale	23	Bert Lindsay	4.47	Bert Lindsay	10
Eddie Oatman	22	Eddie Oatman	22	Hugh Lehman	5.06	Hugh Lehman	7
Albert Kerr	20	Albert Kerr	20	Allan Parr	5.53	Allan Parr	6
Ken Mallen	20	Ken Mallen	20				
Fred Taylor	18	Fred Taylor	18				

All Star Team

Goal	Hugh Lehman (New Westminster Royals)
Defense	Ernie Johnson (New Westminster Royals)
Defense	Frank Patrick (Vancouver Millionaires)
Rover Center	Fred Taylor (Vancouver Millionaires)
Center	Tom Dunderdale (Victoria Aristocrats)
Right Wing	Eddie Oatman (New Westminster Royals)
Left Wing	Albert Kerr (Victoria Aristocrats)

Stanley Cup Playoffs

March 7	Toronto Blueshirts	0	at	Montreal Canadiens	2
March 11	Montreal Canadiens	0	at	Toronto Blueshirts	6
March 14	Victoria Aristocrats	2	at	Toronto Blueshirts	5
March 17	Victoria Aristocrats	5	at	Toronto Blueshirts	6
March 19	Victoria Aristocrats	1	at	Toronto Blueshirts	2

Rules

PCHA--Bluelines were introduced to divide the ice surface into 3 zones.

Notes

Frank Patrick is named President of the PCHA.
Toronto Blueshirts defeated Montreal Canadiens for the championship of the NHA, 6 goals to 2. Toronto was then challenged for the Stanley Cup by Victoria of the PCHA and defeated them 3 games to 0.

Franchise Changes

NHA--Toronto Tecumsehs changed their name to Toronto Ontarios.

Other Sports

Horseracing--Kentucky Derby won by Old Rosebud (time 2:03.4, purse $9,125).
Heavyweight Boxing--Jack Johnson defeated Frank Moran in 20 rounds.
Golf--U.S. Open was won by Walter Hagen with a score of 290.
Auto Racing--Indianapolis 500 was won by Rene Thomas (time 6hr, 3min, 45sec, ave speed 82.47 MPH).

1915

BASEBALL
National League

Team Name	W	L	Pct	GB	R	OR
Philadelphia Phillies	90	62	.592	-	589	463
Boston Braves	83	69	.546	7	582	545
Brooklyn Dodgers	80	72	.526	10	536	560
Chicago Cubs	73	80	.477	17.5	570	620
Pittsburgh Pirates	73	81	.474	18	557	520
St. Louis Cardinals	72	81	.471	18.5	590	601
Cincinnati Reds	71	83	.461	20	516	585
New York Giants	69	83	.454	21	582	628

Coaching Changes

Philadelphia--Pat Moran 90-62; Chicago--Roger Bresnahan 73-80.

League Leaders

Batting Average		Home Runs		RBI	
Larry Doyle	.320	Gavvy Cravath	24	Gavvy Cravath	115
Fred Luderus	.315	Cy Williams	13	Sherry Magee	87
Tom Griffith	.307	Frank Schulte	12	Tom Griffith	85
Bill Hinchman	.307	Vic Saier	11	Honus Wagner	78
Jake Daubert	.301	Beals Becker	11	Bill Hinchman	77

Stolen Bases		ERA		Wins	
Max Carey	36	Grover Alexander	1.22	Grover Alexander	31
Charles Herzog	35	Fred Toney	1.58	Dick Rudolph	21
Doug Baird	29	Al Mamaux	2.04	Erskine Mayer	21
Vic Saier	29	Jeff Pfeffer	2.10	Al Mamaux	21
George Cutshaw	28	Tom Hughes	2.12	Tom Hughes	20

Saves		Strikeouts	
John Benton	5	Grover Alexander	241
Tom Hughes	5	Jeff Tesreau	176
Wilbur Cooper	4	Tom Hughes	171
Dan Griner	3	Al Mamaux	152
Jim Lavender	3	James Vaughn	148

Rules

The National League introduces a rule making it mandatory for all teams to have canvases ready to cover the field in case of rain.

American League

Team Name	W	L	Pct	GB	R	OR
Boston Red Sox	101	50	.669	-	668	499
Detroit Tigers	100	54	.649	2.5	778	573
Chicago White Sox	93	61	.604	9.5	717	509
Washington Senators	85	68	.556	17	571	492
New York Yankees	69	83	.454	32.5	583	596
St. Louis Browns	63	91	.409	39.5	521	693
Cleveland Indians	57	95	.375	44.5	539	670
Philadelphia Athletics	43	109	.283	58.5	545	890

Coaching Changes

Chicago--Clarence Rowland 93-61; New York--Bill Donovan 69-83; Cleveland--Joe Birmingham 12-16, Lee Fohl 45-79.

League Leaders

Batting Average		Home Runs		RBI	
Ty Cobb	.369	Robert Roth	7	Sam Crawford	112
Eddie Collins	.332	Reuben Oldring	6	Bobby Veach	112
Jack Fournier	.322	George Burns	5	Ty Cobb	99
Tris Speaker	.322	Jack Fournier	5	John F. Collins	85
John McInnis	.314	Luke Boone	5	Joe Jackson	81

Stolen Bases		ERA		Wins	
Ty Cobb	96	Joe Wood	1.49	Walter Johnson	28
Fred Maisel	51	Walter Johnson	1.55	Urban Faber	24
Eddie Collins	46	Ernie Shore	1.64	Jim Scott	24
Burt Shotton	43	Jim Scott	2.03	George Dauss	23
Clyde Milan	40	Ray Fisher	2.11	Harry Coveleski	23

Saves		Strikeouts	
Carl Mays	7	Walter Johnson	203
Harry Coveleski	4	Urban Faber	182
Carl Weilman	4	John Wyckoff	157
Samuel Jones	4	Harry Coveleski	150
Bill Steen	4	Willie Mitchell	149

World Series

October 8	Boston Red Sox	1	at	Philadelphia Phillies	3
October 9	Boston Red Sox	2	at	Philadelphia Phillies	1
October 11	Philadelphia Phillies	1	at	Boston Red Sox	2
October 12	Philadelphia Phillies	1	at	Boston Red Sox	2
October 13	Boston Red Sox	5	at	Philadelphia Phillies	4

Federal League

Team Name	W	L	Pct	GB	R	OR
Chicago Whales	86	66	.566	-	641	538
St. Louis Terriers	87	67	.565	-	634	528
Pittsburgh Rebels	86	67	.562	.5	592	524
Kansas City Packers	81	72	.529	5.5	547	551
Newark Peppers	80	72	.526	6	585	562
Buffalo Blues	74	78	.487	12	574	634
Brooklyn Tip-Tops	70	82	.461	16	647	673
Baltimore Terrapins	47	107	.305	40	550	760

Coaching Changes

St. Louis--Fielder Jones 87-67; Pittsburgh--Ennis Oakes 86-67; Newark--Bill Phillips 26-27, Bill McKechnie 54 45; Buffalo--Larry Schlafly 14-29, Walter Blair 1-1, Harry Lord 59-48; Brooklyn--Lee Magee 53-64, John Ganzel 17-18.

League Leaders

Batting Average		Home Runs		RBI	
Benny Kauff	.342	Hal Chase	17	Edward Zwilling	94
Bill Fischer	.329	Edward Zwilling	13	Ed Konetchy	93
Lee Magee	.323	Benny Kauff	12	Hal Chase	89
Ed Konetchy	.314	Ed Konetchy	10	Benny Kauff	83
Max Flack	.314	Michael Walsh	9	William Borton	83

Stolen Bases		ERA		Wins	
Benny Kauff	55	Earl Moseley	1.91	George McConnell	24
Mike Mowrey	40	Eddie Plank	2.08	Frank Allen	23
James Kelly	38	Mordecai Brown	2.09	Dave Davenport	22
Max Flack	37	George McConnell	2.20	James Crandall	22
Lee Magee	34	Dave Davenport	2.20	Nick Cullop	22

Saves		Strikeouts	
Hugh Bedient	10	Dave Davenport	229
George Wiltse	5	Al Schulz	160
Eros Barger	5	George McConnell	151
Bill Upham	4	Eddie Plank	147
Tom Seaton	4	Fred Anderson	142

HOCKEY
National Hockey Association

Team Name	GP	W	L	T	GF	GA	Pts	Pct
Ottawa Senators	20	14	6	0	74	65	28	.700
Montreal Wanderers	20	14	6	0	127	82	28	.700
Quebec Bulldogs	20	11	9	0	85	85	22	.550
Toronto Blueshirts	20	8	12	0	66	84	16	.400
Toronto Ontarios/Shamrock	20	7	13	0	76	96	14	.350
Montreal Canadiens	20	6	14	0	65	81	12	.300

Coaching Changes*

Ontarios/Shamrocks--Jimmy Murphy 7-13; Ottawa--Frank Shaughnessy (record unknown); Canadiens--George Kennedy 6-14.

League Leaders

Goals		Points		GAA	
Tommy Smith	39	Tommy Smith	39	Clint Benedict	3.25
Didier Pitre	30	Didier Pitre	30	Georges Vezina	4.05
Gordon Roberts	29	Gordon Roberts	29	Charlie McCarthy	4.10
Harry Broadbent	24	Harry Broadbent	24	Harry Holmes	4.20
Harry Hyland	23	Harry Hyland	23	Paddy Moran	4.25

Wins	
Clint Benedict	14
Charlie McCarthy	14
Paddy Moran	11
Harry Holmes	8
Percy Lesueur	7

Pacific Coast Hockey Association

Team Name	GP	W	L	T	GF	GA	Pts	Pct
Vancouver Millionaires	17	13	4	0	115	71	26	.765
Portland Rosebuds	18	9	9	0	91	83	18	.500
Victoria Aristocrats	17	4	13	0	64	116	8	.235

Coaching Changes

Portland--Pete Muldoon 9-9.

League Leaders

Goals		Assists		GAA	
Mickey Mackay	34	Mickey Mackay	34	Hugh Lehman	4.18
Fred Taylor	23	Fred Taylor	23	Mike Mitchell	4.61
Frank Nighbor	22	Frank Nighbor	22	Bert Lindsay	6.82
Eddie Oatman	22	Eddie Oatman	22		
Ran McDonald	22	Ran McDonald	22		

Wins		Shutouts	
Hugh Lehman	13	Hugh Lehman	1
Mike Mitchell	9		
Bert Lindsay	4		

*Not complete

All Star Team

Goal	Hugh Lehman (Vancouver Millionaires)
Defense	Ernie Johnson (Portland Rosebuds)
Defense	Lester Patrick (Victoria Aristocrats)
Rover	Fred Taylor (Vancouver Millionaires)
Center	Mickey Mackay (Vancouver Millionaires)
Right Wing	Eddie Oatman (Portland Rosebuds)
Left Wing	Frank Nighbor (Vancouver Millionaires)

Stanley Cup Playoffs

March 10	Montreal Wanderers	0	at	Ottawa Senators	4
March 13	Ottawa Senators	0	at	Montreal Wanderers	1
March 22	Ottawa Senators	2	at	Vancouver Millionaires	6
March 24	Ottawa Senators	3	at	Vancouver Millionaires	8
March 26	Ottawa Senators	3	at	Vancouver Millionaires	12

Notes

Ottawa as champions of the NHA were challenged for the Stanley Cup by Vancouver, champions of the PCHA and were defeated by Vancouver 3 games to 0.
In the Stanley Cup finals 2 games were played under western rules and 1 game played under eastern rules.

Franchise Changes

AL--Cleveland Molly McGuires changed name to Cleveland Indians.
NHA--Toronto Ontarios changed name to Toronto Shamrocks midway through the year.
PCHA--New Westminster Royals became the Portland Rosebuds.

Other Sports

Horseracing--Kentucky Derby won by Regret (time 2:05.4, purse $11,450).
Heavyweight Boxing--Jess Willard knocked-out Jack Johnson in 26 rounds.
Golf--U.S. Open won by J.D. Travers with a score of 297.
Auto Racing--Indianapolis 500 won by Ralph de Palma (ave. speed 89.84 MPH).

1916

BASEBALL
National League

Team Name	W	L	Pct	GB	R	OR
Brooklyn Dodgers	94	60	.610	-	585	467
Philadelphia Phillies	91	62	.595	2.5	581	489
Boston Braves	89	63	.586	4	542	453
New York Giants	86	66	.566	7	597	503
Chicago Cubs	67	86	.438	26.5	520	541
Pittsburgh Pirates	65	89	.422	29	484	586
Cincinnati Reds	60	93	.392	33.5	505	622
St. Louis Cardinals	60	93	.392	33.5	476	629

Coaching Changes

Chicago--Joe Tinker 67-86; Pittsburgh--James Callahan 65-89; Cincinnati--Charles Herzog 34-49, Ivy Wingo 1-1, Christy Mathewson 25-43.

League Leaders

Batting Average		Home Runs		RBI	
Hal Chase	.339	Cy Williams	12	Heinie Zimmerman	83
Jake Daubert	.316	Dave Robertson	12	Hal Chase	82
Bill Hinchman	.315	Gavvy Cravath	11	Bill Hinchman	76
Rogers Hornsby	.313	Benny Kauff	9	Benny Kauff	74
Zack Wheat	.312	Zack Wheat	9	Zack Wheat	73

Stolen Bases		ERA		Wins	
Max Carey	63	Grover Alexander	1.55	Grover Alexander	33
Benny Kauff	40	Rube Marquard	1.58	Jeff Pfeffer	25
Bob Bescher	39	Eppa Rixey	1.85	Eppa Rixey	22
George Burns	37	Wilbur Cooper	1.87	Al Mamaux	21
Charles Herzog	34	Jeff Pfeffer	1.92	Al Demaree	19

Saves		Strikeouts	
Leon Ames	7	Grover Alexander	167
Gene Packard	5	Larry Cheney	166
Tom L. Hughes	5	Al Mamaux	163
Rube Marquard	4	Fred Toney	146
Chief Bender	3	James Vaughn	144

American League

Team Name	W	L	Pct	GB	R	OR
Boston Red Sox	91	63	.591	-	548	480
Chicago White Sox	89	65	.578	2	601	500
Detroit Tigers	87	67	.565	4	673	573
New York Yankees	80	74	.519	11	575	561
St. Louis Browns	79	75	.513	12	591	545
Cleveland Indians	77	77	.500	14	630	621
Washington Senators	76	77	.497	14.5	534	543
Philadelphia Athletics	36	117	.235	54.5	447	776

Coaching Changes

St. Louis--Fielder Jones 79-75; Cleveland--Lee Fohl 77-77.

League Leaders

Batting Average		Home Runs		RBI	
Tris Speaker	.386	Wally Pipp	12	Del Pratt	103
Ty Cobb	.371	Frank Baker	10	Wally Pipp	93
Joe Jackson	.341	Wally Schang	7	Bobby Veach	91
Amos Strunk	.316	Oscar Felsch	7	Tris Speaker	79
Larry Gardner	.308	Ty Cobb	5	Joe Jackson	78

Stolen Bases		ERA		Wins	
Ty Cobb	68	Babe Ruth	1.75	Walter Johnson	25
Armando Marsans	46	Eddie Cicotte	1.78	Bob Shawkey	23
Burt Shotton	41	Walter Johnson	1.89	Babe Ruth	23
Eddie Collins	40	Harry Coveleski	1.97	Harry Coveleski	22
Tris Speaker	35	Urban Faber	2.02	George Dauss	19

Saves		Strikeouts	
Bob Shawkey	9	Walter Johnson	228
Jim Bagby	5	Elmer Myers	182
Dutch Leonard	5	Babe Ruth	170
Eddie Cicotte	4	Joe Bush	157
Allan Russell	4	Harry Harper	149

World Series

October 7	Brooklyn Dodgers	5	at	Boston Red Sox	6
October 9	Brooklyn Dodgers	1	at	Boston Red Sox	2 [14]
October 10	Boston Red Sox	3	at	Brooklyn Dodgers	4
October 11	Boston Red Sox	6	at	Brooklyn Dodgers	2
October 12	Brooklyn Dodgers	1	at	Boston Red Sox	4

Notes

On June 26 in a game against Chicago the Cleveland Indians of the American League became the first baseball team to wear numbers on their uniform sleeves to help fans identify the players.

HOCKEY

National Hockey Association

Team Name	GP	W	L	T	GF	GA	Pts	Pct
Montreal Canadiens	24	16	7	1	104	76	33	.688
Ottawa Senators	24	13	11	0	78	72	26	.542
Quebec Bulldogs	24	10	12	2	91	98	22	.458
Montreal Wanderers	24	10	14	0	90	116	20	.417
Toronto Blueshirts	24	9	14	1	97	98	19	.396

Coaching Changes*

Ottawa--Alf Smith 13-11; Toronto Blueshirts--Jack Marshall 9-14-1.

League Leaders

Goals		Points		GAA	
Newsy Lalonde	31	Newsy Lalonde	31	Clint Benedict	3.00
Joe Malone	26	Joe Malone	26	Georges Vezina	3.17
Cy Denneny	26	Cy Denneny	26	Paddy Moran	3.73
Didier Pitre	23	Didier Pitre	23	Percy Lesueur	4.00
Gordon Keats	22	Gordon Keats	22	Bert Lindsay	4.78

Wins		Shutouts	
Georges Vezina	16	Clint Benedict	1
Clint Benedict	13	Percy Lesueur	1
Bert Lindsay	10	Bert Lindsay	1
Paddy Moran	9		
Percy Leseur	9		

Pacific Coast Hockey Association

Team Name	GP	W	L	T	GF	GA	Pts	Pct
Portland Rosebuds	18	13	5	0	71	50	26	.722
Vancouver Millionaires	18	9	9	0	75	69	18	.500
Seattle Metropolitans	18	9	9	0	68	67	18	.500
Victoria Aristocrats	18	5	13	0	74	102	10	.278

Coaching Changes*

Vancouver--Frank Patrick 9-9; Victoria--Lester Patrick 5-13; Seattle--Pete Muldoon 13-5-0.

League Leaders

Goals		Points		GAA	
Bernie Morris	23	Fred Taylor	36	Tom Murray	2.78
Fred Taylor	22	Bernie Morris	32	Harry Holmes	3.72
Charles Tobin	21	Albert Kerr	30	Hugh Lehman	3.83
Lloyd Cook	18	Charles Tobin	29	Fred McCulloch	5.67
Albert Kerr	16	Lester Patrick	24		

*Not complete

Wins		**Shutouts**	
Tom Murray	13	Tom Murray	2
Harry Holmes	9		
Hugh Lehman	9		
Fred McCulloch	5		

Stanley Cup Playoffs

March 20	Portland Rosebuds	2	at	Montreal Canadiens	0
March 22	Portland Rosebuds	1	at	Montreal Canadiens	2
March 25	Portland Rosebuds	3	at	Montreal Canadiens	6
March 28	Portland Rosebuds	6	at	Montreal Canadiens	5
March 30	Portland Rosebuds	1	at	Montreal Canadiens	2

Franchise Changes

None

Other Sports

Horseracing--Kentucky Derby won by George Smith (time 2:04, purse $9,750).
Heavyweight Boxing--Jess Willard and Frank Moran fought to a 10 round no decision.
Golf--U.S. Open won by Chick Evans with a score of 286.
Auto Racing--Indianapolis 500 won by Daxio Resta (average speed 83.26 MPH).

1917

BASEBALL
National League

Team Name	W	L	Pct	GB	R	OR
New York Giants	98	56	.636	-	635	457
Philadelphia Phillies	87	65	.572	10	578	501
St. Louis Cardinals	82	70	.539	15	531	568
Cincinnati Reds	78	76	.506	20	601	611
Chicago Cubs	74	80	.481	24	552	553
Boston Braves	72	81	.471	25.5	536	558
Brooklyn Dodgers	70	81	.464	26.5	511	566
Pittsburgh Pirates	51	103	.331	47	464	594

Coaching Changes

Cincinnati--Christy Mathewson 78-76; Chicago--Fred Mitchell 74-80; Pittsburgh--James Callahan 20-40, Honus Wagner 1-4, Hugo Bezdek 30-59.

League Leaders

Batting Average

Edd Roush	.341
Rogers Hornsby	.327
Zack Wheat	.312
Benny Kauff	.308
Henry Groh	.304

Home Runs

Dave Robertson	12
Gavvy Cravath	12
Rogers Hornsby	8
Dave Hickman	6
Larry Doyle	6

RBI

Heinie Zimmerman	102
Hal Chase	86
Gavvy Cravath	83
Casey Stengel	73
Fred Luderus	72

Stolen Bases

Max Carey	46
George Burns	40
Benny Kauff	30
Walter Maranville	27
Doug Baird	26

ERA

Grover Alexander	1.86
William Perritt	1.88
Ferdie Schupp	1.95
Pete Schneider	1.98
James Vaughn	2.01

Wins

Grover Alexander	30
Fred Toney	24
James Vaughn	23
Ferdie Schupp	21
Pete Schneider	20

Saves

Harry Sallee	4
Leon Ames	3
Sherrod Smith	3
John Benton	3
Fred Anderson	3

Strikeouts

Grover Alexander	201
James Vaughn	195
Phil Douglas	151
Ferdie Schupp	147
Pete Schneider	142

American League

Team Name	W	L	Pct	GB	R	OR
Chicago White Sox	100	54	.649	-	657	464
Boston Red Sox	90	62	.592	9	556	453
Cleveland Indians	88	66	.571	12	584	543
Detroit Tigers	78	75	.510	21.5	639	577
Washington Senators	74	79	.484	25.5	543	566
New York Yankees	71	82	.464	28.5	524	560
St. Louis Browns	57	97	.370	43	511	687
Philadelphia Athletics	55	98	.359	44.5	527	691

Coaching Changes

Boston--Jack Barry 90-62.

League Leaders

Batting Average		Home Runs		RBI	
Ty Cobb	.383	Wally Pipp	9	Bobby Veach	103
George Sisler	.353	Bobby Veach	8	Oscar Felsch	102
Tris Speaker	.352	Ty Cobb	7	Ty Cobb	102
Bobby Veach	.319	Frank Bodie	7	Harry Heilmann	86
Oscar Felsch	.308	Frank Baker	6	Joe Jackson	75

Stolen Bases		ERA		Wins	
Ty Cobb	55	Eddie Cicotte	1.53	Eddie Cicotte	28
Eddie Collins	53	Carl Mays	1.74	Babe Ruth	24
Ray Chapman	52	Stan Coveleski	1.81	Walter Johnson	23
Robert Roth	51	Urban Faber	1.92	Jim Bagby	23
George Sisler	37	Ewell Russell	1.95	Carl Mays	22

Saves		Strikeouts	
Dave Danforth	7	Walter Johnson	188
Jim Bagby	6	Eddie Cicotte	150
Bernie Boland	6	Dutch Leonard	144
Ewell Russell	4	Stan Coveleski	133
Fred Coumbe	4	Babe Ruth	128

World Series

October 6	New York Giants	1	at	Chicago White Sox	2
October 7	New York Giants	2	at	Chicago White Sox	7
October 10	Chicago White Sox	0	at	New York Giants	2
October 11	Chicago White Sox	0	at	New York Giants	5
October 13	New York Giants	5	at	Chicago White Sox	8
October 15	Chicago White Sox	4	at	New York Giants	2

HOCKEY
National Hockey Association

First Half

Team Name	GP	W	L	T	GF	GA	Pts	Pct
Montreal Canadiens	10	7	3	0	58	38	14	.700
Ottawa Senators	10	7	3	0	56	41	14	.700
228th Battalion	10	6	4	0	70	57	12	.600
Toronto Blueshirts	10	5	5	0	50	45	10	.500
Montreal Wanderers	10	3	7	0	56	72	6	.300
Quebec Bulldogs	10	2	8	0	43	80	4	.200

Second Half

Team Name	GP	W	L	T	GF	GA	Pts	Pct
Ottawa Senators	10	8	2	0	63	22	16	.800
Quebec Bulldogs	10	8	2	0	54	46	16	.800
Montreal Canadiens	10	3	7	0	31	42	6	.200
Toronto Blueshirts	4	2	2	0	14	16	4	.500
Montreal Wanderers	10	2	8	0	38	65	4	.200
228th Battalion	4	0	4	0	3	12	0	.000

Coaching Changes*

228th Battalion--L.W. Reade 6-8; Ottawa--Eddie Gerard 15-5.

League Leaders

Goals		Points		GAA		Shutouts	
Joe Malone	41	Joe Malone	41	Clint Benedict	2.78	Clint Benedict	1
Frank Nighbor	41	Frank Nighbor	41	Georges Vezina	4.00	Howie Lockhart	1
Odie Cleghorn	28	Odie Cleghorn	28	Bill Nicholson	4.00		
Newsy Lalonde	27	Newsy Lalonde	27	Sam Hebert	5.60		
Jack Darragh	26	Jack Darragh	26	Howie Lockhart	5.75		

Notes

Frank Robinson succeeded Emmett Quinn as President of the National Hockey Association.
The National Hockey Association decided to play a split schedule with the winner of the first half to play the winner of the second half for the league championship.
The Toronto Blueshirts and the 228th Battalion, an army team based in Toronto, dropped out midway through the second half of the schedule.

Pacific Coast Hockey Association

Team Name	GP	W	L	T	GF	GA	Pts	Pct
Seattle Metropolitans	24	16	8	0	125	80	32	.667
Vancouver Millionaires	23	14	9	0	131	124	28	.607
Portland Rosebuds	24	9	15	0	114	112	18	.375
Spokane Canaries	23	8	15	0	89	143	16	.348

Coaching Changes

Portland--Tom Scott 9-15-0.

*Not complete

League Leaders

Goals		Assists		Points	
Gordie Roberts	43	Barney Stanley	18	Bernie Morris	54
Bernie Morris	37	Bernie Morris	17	Gordie Roberts	53
Frank Foyston	36	Fred Taylor	15	Frank Foyston	48
Dick Irvin	35	Jack Walker	15	Dick Irvin	46
Barney Stanley	28	Fred Harris	13	Barney Stanley	46

GAA		Wins		Shutouts	
Harry Holmes	3.33	Harry Holmes	16	Harry Holmes	2
Tom Murray	4.67	Hugh Lehman	14		
Hugh Lehman	5.39	Tom Murray	9		
Norm Fowler	6.22	Norm Fowler	8		

Stanley Cup Playoffs

March 7	Ottawa Senators	2	at	Montreal Canadiens	5
March 10	Montreal Canadiens	2	at	Ottawa Senators	4
March 17	Montreal Canadiens	8	at	Seattle Metropolitans	4
March 20	Montreal Canadiens	1	at	Seattle Metropolitans	6
March 23	Montreal Canadiens	1	at	Seattle Metropolitans	4
March 25	Montreal Canadiens	1	at	Seattle Metropolitans	9

Franchise Changes

PCHA--Victoria Aristocrats became the Spokane Canaries.

Other Sports

Horseracing--Kentucky Derby won by Omar Khayyam (time 2:04.6, purse $16,600).

Notes

There was no U.S. Open golf championship or Indianapolis 500 this year because of the war.

1918

BASEBALL
National League

Team Name	W	L	Pct	GB	R	OR
Chicago Cubs	84	45	.651	-	538	391
New York Giants	71	53	.573	10.5	480	423
Cincinnati Reds	68	60	.531	15.5	538	496
Pittsburgh Pirates	65	60	.520	17	466	411
Brooklyn Dodgers	57	69	.452	25.5	360	459
Philadelphia Phillies	55	68	.447	26	430	507
Boston Braves	53	71	.427	28.5	424	469
St. Louis Cardinals	51	78	.395	33	454	534

Coaching Changes

Cincinnati--Christy Mathewson 61-57, Heinie Groh 7-3; Pittsburgh--Hugo Bezdek 65-60; St. Louis--Jack Hendricks 51-78.

League Leaders

Batting Average

Zack Wheat	.335
Edd Roush	.333
Henry Groh	.320
Charlie Hollocher	.316
Jake Daubert	.308

Home Runs

Gavvy Cravath	8
Walton Cruise	6
Cy Williams	6
Rogers Hornsby	5
Edd Roush	5

RBI

Sherry Magee	76
George Cutshaw	68
Fred Luderus	67
James Smith	65
Fred Merkle	65

Stolen Bases

Max Carey	58
George Burns	40
Charlie Hollocher	26
Doug Baird	25
George Cutshaw	25

ERA

James Vaughn	1.74
George Tyler	2.00
Wilbur Cooper	2.11
Phil Douglas	2.13
Burleigh Grimes	2.14

Wins

James Vaughn	22
Claude Hendrix	19
Wilbur Cooper	19
Burleigh Grimes	19
George Tyler	19

Saves

Fred Anderson	3
Joe Oeschger	3
Fred Toney	3
Wilbur Cooper	3
Harry Sallee	2

Strikeouts

James Vaughn	148
Wilbur Cooper	117
Burleigh Grimes	113
George Tyler	102
Art Nehf	96

Notes

John Heydler became the eighth President of the National League, succeeding John Tener.

American League

Team Name	W	L	Pct	GB	R	OR
Boston Red Sox	75	51	.595	-	473	381
Cleveland Indians	73	56	.566	3.5	510	447
Washington Senators	72	56	.563	4	461	392
New York Yankees	60	63	.488	13.5	491	474
St. Louis Browns	60	64	.484	14	426	448
Chicago White Sox	57	67	.460	17	457	443
Detroit Tigers	55	71	.437	20	473	555
Philadelphia Athletics	52	76	.406	24	412	563

Coaching Changes

Boston--Ed Barrow 75-51; New York--Miller Huggins 60-63; St. Louis--Fielder Jones 23-24, Jimmy Austin 6-8, Jimmy Burke 29-32.

League Leaders

Batting Average		Home Runs		RBI	
Ty Cobb	.382	Clarence Walker	11	Bobby Veach	78
George H. Burns	.352	Babe Ruth	11	George H. Burns	70
George Sisler	.341	Frank Baker	6	Joe Wood	66
Tris Speaker	.318	George H. Burns	6	Babe Ruth	66
Frank Baker	.306	Harry Heilmann	5	Ty Cobb	64

Stolen Bases		ERA		Wins	
George Sisler	45	Walter Johnson	1.27	Walter Johnson	23
Robert Roth	35	Stan Coveleski	1.82	Stan Coveleski	22
Ty Cobb	34	Allen Sotheron	1.94	Carl Mays	21
Ray Chapman	30	Scott Perry	1.98	Scott Perry	21
Tris Speaker	27	Joe Bush	2.11	George Mogridge	17

Saves		Strikeouts	
Jim Bagby	6	Walter Johnson	162
George Mogridge	5	Jim Shaw	129
Bob Geary	3	Joe Bush	125
Allan Russell	3	Guy Morton	123
Fred Coumbe	3	Carl Mays	114

World Series

September 5	Boston Red Sox	1	at	Chicago Cubs	0
September 6	Boston Red Sox	1	at	Chicago Cubs	3
September 7	Boston Red Sox	2	at	Chicago Cubs	1
September 9	Chicago Cubs	2	at	Boston Red Sox	3
September 10	Chicago Cubs	3	at	Boston Red Sox	0
September 11	Chicago Cubs	1	at	Boston Red Sox	2

HOCKEY
National Hockey League
First Half

Team Name	GP	W	L	T	GF	GA	Pts	Pct
Montreal Canadiens	14	10	4	0	81	47	20	.714
Toronto Arenas	14	8	6	0	71	75	16	.571
Ottawa Senators	14	5	9	0	67	79	10	.357
Montreal Wanderers	6	1	5	0	17	35	2	.167

Second Half

Team Name	GP	W	L	T	GF	GA	Pts	Pct
Toronto Arenas	8	5	3	0	37	34	10	.625
Ottawa Senators	8	4	4	0	35	35	8	.500
Montreal Canadians	8	3	5	0	34	37	6	.375

Coaching Changes

Canadiens--George Kennedy 13-9; Toronto--Dick Carroll 13-9; Ottawa--Eddie Gerard 9-13; Wanderers--Art Ross 1-5.

League Leaders

Goals		Points		Penalty Minutes	
Joe Malone	44	Joe Malone	44	Joe Hall	60
Cy Denneny	36	Cy Denneny	36	Ken Randall	55
Reg Noble	28	Reg Noble	28	Harry Hyland	34
Newsy Lalonde	23	Newsy Lalonde	23	Cy Denneny	34
Corb Denneny	20	Corb Denneny	20	Russell Crawford	33

GAA		Wins		Shutouts	
Georges Vezina	4.00	Georges Vezina	13	Georges Vezina	1
Harry Holmes	4.75	Harry Holmes	10	Clint Benedict	1
Clint Benedict	5.18	Clint Benedict	9		
Bert Lindsay	5.83	Arthur Brooks	2		
Arthur Brooks	6.00	Sam Hebert	1		

Rules

A goaltender was now allowed to drop to his knees to make a save, before this a goaltender was not allowed to leave his feet.

Notes

The National Hockey League was organized November 26th, 1917, in Montreal after the NHA disbanded following a season of strife and disorganization. Frank Calder became the first President of the League.
The Montreal Wanderers dropped out of the league after their arena burned down.

NHL Playoffs

March 11	Montreal Canadiens	3	at	Toronto Arenas	7
March 13	Toronto Arenas	3	at	Montreal Canadiens	4

Pacific Coast Hockey Association

Team Name	GP	W	L	T	GF	GA	Pts	Pct
Seattle Metropolitans	18	11	7	0	67	65	22	.611
Vancouver Millionaires	18	9	9	0	70	60	18	.500
Portland Rosebuds	18	7	11	0	63	75	14	.389

Coaching Changes

Portland--Pete Muldoon 7-11-0.

League Leaders

Goals

Fred Taylor	32
Gordon Roberts	20
Bernie Morris	20
Tom Dunderdale	14
Charles Tobin	13

Points

Fred Taylor	32
Gordon Roberts	20
Bernie Morris	20
Tom Dunderdale	14
Charles Tobin	13

GAA

Hugh Lehman	3.33
Norm Fowler	3.61
Tom Murray	4.17

Wins

Norm Fowler	11
Hugh Lehman	9
Tom Murray	7

Shutouts

Hugh Lehman	1
Norm Fowler	1

All Star Teams

First Team		Second Team
Hugh Lehman	Goal	Norm Fowler
Ernie Johnson	Point	Lester Patrick
Bobbie Rowe	Cover Point	Lloyd Cook
Fred Taylor	Rover	Alf Barbour
Bernie Morris	Center	Mickey Mackay
Charlie Tobin	Right Wing	Eddie Oatman
Frank Foyston	Left Wing	Barney Stanley

PCHA Playoffs

March 11	Seattle Metropolitans	2	at	Vancouver Millionaires	2
March 13	Vancouver Millionaires	1	at	Seattle Metropolitans	0

Stanley Cup Playoffs

March 20	Vancouver Millionaires	3	at	Toronto Arenas	5
March 23	Vancouver Millionaires	6	at	Toronto Arenas	4
March 26	Vancouver Millionaires	3	at	Toronto Arenas	6
March 28	Vancouver Millionaires	8	at	Toronto Arenas	1
March 30	Vancouver Millionaires	1	at	Toronto Arenas	2

Franchise Changes

NHL--Toronto Blueshirts became Toronto Arenas.

Other Sports

Horseracing--Kentucky Derby won by Exterminator (time 2:10.8, purse $14,700).

1919

BASEBALL
National League

Team Name	W	L	Pct	GB	R	OR
Cincinnati Reds	96	44	.686	-	578	402
New York Giants	87	53	.621	9	605	470
Chicago Cubs	75	65	.536	21	454	407
Pittsburgh Pirates	71	68	.511	24.5	472	466
Brooklyn Dodgers	69	71	.493	27	525	513
Boston Braves	57	82	.410	38.5	465	563
St. Louis Cardinals	54	83	.394	40.5	463	552
Philadelphia Phillies	47	90	.343	47.5	510	699

Coaching Changes

St. Louis--Branch Rickey 54-83; Philadelphia--Jack Coombs l8-44, Gavvy Cravath 29-46; Cincinnati--Pat Moran 96-44.

League Leaders

Batting Average

Edd Roush	.321
Rogers Hornsby	.318
Ross Youngs	.311
Henry Groh	.310
Milt Stock	.307

Home Runs

Gavvy Cravath	12
Benny Kauff	10
Cy Williams	9
Rogers Hornsby	8
Larry Doyle	7

RBI

Henry Myers	73
Rogers Hornsby	71
Edd Roush	71
Benny Kauff	67
Henry Groh	63

Stolen Bases

George Burns	40
George Cutshaw	36
Carson Bigbee	31
Jack Smith	30
Charles Herzog	28

ERA

Grover Alexander	1.72
James Vaughn	1.79
Walt Ruether	1.82
Fred Toney	1.84
Charles Adams	1.98

Wins

Jesse Barnes	25
James Vaughn	21
Harry Sallee	21
Horace Eller	20
Walt Ruether	19

Saves

Oscar Tuero	4
Jean Dubuc	3
Adolfo Luque	3
Jimmy Ring	3
Al Demaree	2

Strikeouts

James Vaughn	141
Horace Eller	137
Grover Alexander	121
Lee Meadows	116
Wilbur Cooper	106

American League

Team Name	W	L	Pct	GB	R	OR
Chicago White Sox	88	52	.629	-	668	534
Cleveland Indians	84	55	.604	3.5	634	535
New York Yankees	80	59	.576	7.5	582	514
Detroit Tigers	80	60	.571	8	620	582
St. Louis Browns	67	72	.482	20.5	535	567
Boston Red Sox	66	71	.482	20.5	565	552
Washington Senators	56	84	.400	32	533	570
Philadelphia Athletics	36	104	.257	52	459	742

Coaching Changes

Chicago--Bill Gleason 88-52; Cleveland--Lee Fohl 45-34, Tris Speaker 39-21; St. Louis--Jimmy Burke 67-72.

League Leaders

Batting Average		Home Runs		RBI	
Ty Cobb	.384	Babe Ruth	29	Babe Ruth	114
Bobby Veach	.355	Tilly Walker	10	Bobby Veach	101
George Sisler	.352	Frank Baker	10	Joe Jackson	96
Joe Jackson	.351	George Sisler	10	Harry Heilmann	93
Ira Flagstead	.331	Elmer J. Smith	9	George Lewis	89

Stolen Bases		ERA		Wins	
Eddie Collins	33	Walter Johnson	1.49	Eddie Cicotte	29
George Sisler	28	Eddie Cicotte	1.82	Stan Coveleski	24
Ty Cobb	28	Carl Weilman	2.07	Claud Williams	23
Sam Rice	26	Carl Mays	2.11	George Dauss	21
Harry Hooper	23	Al Sothoron	2.20	Jim Bagby	17

Saves		Strikeouts	
Allan Russell	5	Walter Johnson	147
Bob Shawkey	4	Jim Shaw	128
Jim Shaw	4	Claud Williams	125
Al Sothoron	3	Bob Shawkey	122
Stan Coveleski	3	Stan Coveleski	118

World Series

October 1	Chicago White Sox	1	at	Cincinnati Reds	9
October 2	Chicago White Sox	2	at	Cincinnati Reds	4
October 3	Cincinnati Reds	0	at	Chicago White Sox	3
October 4	Cincinnati Reds	2	at	Chicago White Sox	0
October 6	Cincinnati Reds	5	at	Chicago White Sox	0
October 7	Chicago White Sox	5	at	Cincinnati Reds	4 [10]
October 8	Chicago White Sox	4	at	Cincinnati Reds	1
October 9	Cincinnati Reds	10	at	Chicago White Sox	5

HOCKEY
National Hockey League

First Half

Team Name	GP	W	L	T	GF	GA	Pts	Pct
Montreal Canadiens	10	7	3	0	57	50	14	.700
Ottawa Senators	10	5	5	0	39	39	10	.500
Toronto Arenas	10	3	7	0	42	49	6	.300

Second Half

Team Name	GP	W	L	T	GF	GA	Pts	Pct
Ottawa Senators	8	7	1	0	32	14	14	.875
Montreal Canadiens	8	3	5	0	31	28	6	.375
Toronto Arenas	8	2	6	0	22	43	4	.250

Coaching Changes

Ottawa--Alf Smith 12-6.

League Leaders

Goals

Newsy Lalonde	23
Odie Cleghorn	23
Frank Nighbor	18
Cy Denneny	18
Didier Pitre	14

Assists

Newsy Lalonde	9
Odie Cleghorn	6
Ken Randall	6
Sprague Cleghorn	6
Eddie Gerard	6

Points

Newsy Lalonde	32
Odie Cleghorn	29
Frank Nighbor	22
Cy Denneny	22
Didier Pitre	18

Penalty Minutes

Joe Hall	85
Russell Crawford	51
Bert Corbeau	51
Cy Denneny	43
Newsy Lalonde	40

GAA

Clint Benedict	2.94
Georges Vezina	4.33
Harry Holmes	4.50
Bert Lindsay	5.19

Wins

Clint Benedict	12
Georges Vezina	10
Bert Lindsay	5
Harry Holmes	0

Shutouts

Clint Benedict	2
Georges Vezina	1

NHL Playoffs

February 22	Ottawa Senators	4	at	Montreal Canadiens	8
February 27	Montreal Canadiens	5	at	Ottawa Senators	3
March 1	Ottawa Senators	3	at	Montreal Canadiens	6
March 3	Montreal Canadiens	3	at	Ottawa Senators	6
March 6	Ottawa Senators	2	at	Montreal Canadiens	4

Rules

Kicking the puck was made legal.

The introduction of bluelines and forward passing within the center ice zone were adopted in the NHL this season.

Notes

The Stanley Cup playoffs were not completed this year because of the influenza epidemic that was sweeping the world at the time. Many players became ill and Joe Hall of the Canadiens died because of the virus.

Pacific Coast Hockey Association

Team Name	GP	W	L	T	GF	GA	Pts	Pct
Vancouver Millionaires	20	12	8	0	72	55	24	.600
Seattle Metropolitans	20	11	9	0	66	46	22	.550
Victoria Aristocrats	20	7	13	0	44	81	14	.350

Coaching Changes

Seattle--Pete Muldoon 11-9-0.

League Leaders

Goals		Points		GAA	
Fred Taylor	23	Fred Taylor	36	Harry Holmes	2.30
Bernie Morris	22	Bernie Morris	29	Hugh Lehman	2.75
Fred Harris	19	Fred Harris	25	Tom Murray	4.05
Frank Foyston	15	Frank Foyston	19		
Cully Wilson	11	Russell Stanley	18		

Wins		Shutouts	
Hugh Lehman	12	Tom Murray	2
Harry Holmes	11	Hugh Lehman	1
Tom Murray	7		

PCHA Playoffs

March 12	Vancouver Millionaires	1	at	Seattle Metropolitans	6
March 14	Seattle Metropolitans	1	at	Vancouver Millionaires	4

Rules

A delayed penalty system was adopted to assure that neither team would be more than one player short at any time.

Stanley Cup Playoffs

March 19	Montreal Canadiens	0	at	Seattle Metropolitans	7
March 22	Montreal Canadiens	4	at	Seattle Metropolitans	2
March 24	Montreal Canadiens	2	at	Seattle Metropolitans	7
March 26	Montreal Canadiens	0	at	Seattle Metropolitans	0 [20:00]
March 30	Montreal Canadiens	4	at	Seattle Metropolitans	3 [15:51]

Franchise Changes

PCHA--Portland Rosebuds became Victoria Aristocrats.

Other Sports

Horseracing--Kentucky Derby won by Sir Barton (time 2:09.8, purse $20,825).
Heavyweight Boxing--Jack Dempsey knocked out Jess Willard in 3 rounds.
Golf--U.S.-Open won by Walter Hagen with a score of 301.
Auto Racing--Indianapolis 500 won by "Howdy" Wilcox (ave. speed 88.06 MPH).

1920

BASEBALL

National League

Team Name	W	L	Pct	GB	R	OR
Brooklyn Dodgers	93	61	.604	-	660	528
New York Giants	86	68	.558	7	682	543
Cincinnati Reds	82	71	.536	10.5	639	569
Pittsburgh Pirates	79	75	.513	14	530	552
Chicago Cubs	75	79	.487	18	619	635
St. Louis Cardinals	75	79	.487	18	675	682
Boston Braves	62	90	.408	30	523	670
Philadelphia Phillies	62	91	.405	30.5	565	714

Coaching Changes

Pittsburgh--George Gibson 79-75; Philadelphia--Gavvy Cravath 62-91.

League Leaders

Batting Average

Rogers Hornsby	.370
Ross Youngs	.351
Edd Roush	.339
Zack Wheat	.328
Cy Williams	.325

Home Runs

Cy Williams	15
Emil Meusel	14
George Kelly	11
Dave Robertson	10
Austin McHenry	10

RBI

Rogers Hornsby	94
George Kelly	94
Edd Roush	90
Pat Duncan	83
Henry Myers	80

Stolen Bases

Max Carey	52
Edd Roush	36
Frank Frisch	34
Carson Bigbee	31
Alfred Neale	29

ERA

Grover Alexander	1.91
Charles Adams	2.16
Burleigh Grimes	2.22
Wilbur Cooper	2.39
Walt Ruether	2.47

Wins

Grover Alexander	27
Wilbur Cooper	24
Burleigh Grimes	23
Art Nehf	21
Fred Toney	21

Saves

Bill Sherdel	6
Grover Alexander	5
Hugh McQuillan	5
Bill Hubbell	4
Al Mamaux	4

Strikeouts

Grover Alexander	173
James Vaughn	131
Burleigh Grimes	131
Jesse Haines	120
Ferdie Schupp	119

American League

Team Name	W	L	Pct	GB	R	OR
Cleveland Indians	98	56	.636	-	857	642
Chicago White Sox	96	58	.623	2	794	666
New York Yankees	95	59	.617	3	839	629
St. Louis Browns	76	77	.497	21.5	797	766
Boston Red Sox	72	81	.471	25.5	651	699
Washington Senators	68	84	.447	29	723	802
Detroit Tigers	61	93	.396	37	651	832
Philadelphia Athletics	48	106	.312	50	555	831

Coaching Changes

Cleveland--Tris Speaker 98-56.

League Leaders

Batting Average		Home Runs		RBI	
George Sisler	.407	Babe Ruth	54	Babe Ruth	137
Tris Speaker	.388	George Sisler	19	Bill Jacobson	122
Joe Jackson	.382	Tilly Walker	17	George Sisler	122
Babe Ruth	.376	Oscar Felsch	14	Joe Jackson	121
Eddie Collins	.369	Elmer J. Smith	12	Larry Gardner	118

Stolen Bases		ERA		Wins	
Sam Rice	63	Bob Shawkey	2.45	Jim Bagby	31
George Sisler	42	Stan Coveleski	2.49	Carl Mays	26
Robert Roth	24	Urban Shocker	2.71	Stan Coveleski	24
Mike Menosky	23	Jim Bagby	2.89	Urban Faber	23
Jack Tobin	21	Urban Faber	2.99	Claud Williams	22

Saves		Strikeouts	
Urban Shocker	5	Stan Coveleski	133
Richard Kerr	5	Claud Williams	128
Bill Burwell	4	Bob Shawkey	126
Walter Johnson	3	Urban Faber	108
Jack Quinn	3	Urban Shocker	107

World Series

October 5	Cleveland Indians	3	at	Brooklyn Dodgers	1
October 6	Cleveland Indians	0	at	Brooklyn Dodgers	3
October 7	Cleveland Indians	1	at	Brooklyn Dodgers	2
October 9	Brooklyn Dodgers	1	at	Cleveland Indians	5
October 10	Brooklyn Dodgers	1	at	Cleveland Indians	8
October 11	Brooklyn Dodgers	0	at	Cleveland Indians	1
October 12	Brooklyn Dodgers	0	at	Cleveland Indians	3

Rules

Spitballs and other unorthodox pitches were abolished. Each team could name 2 spitball pitchers for the 1920 season and none during the following seasons (NL, AL).

Stolen bases are not credited to a player if no effort is made to put him out (NL, AL).

Notes

Kenesaw Mountain Landis is appointed as the first Commissioner of baseball

Ray Chapman, Cleveland Indians shortstop died after being hit in the head by a pitch by Carl Mays of the New York Yankees. Mays was later exonerated of any blame.

Eight Chicago White Sox players were indicted and charged with complicity to fix the 1919 World Series. The players were Eddie Cicotte, "Shoeless Joe" Jackson, Oscar Felsch, Charles Risberg, George Weaver, Arnold Gandil, Claude Williams and Fred McMullin.

HOCKEY
National Hockey League
First Half

Team Name	GP	W	L	T	GF	GA	Pts	Pct
Ottawa Senators	12	9	3	0	59	23	18	.750
Montreal Canadiens	12	8	4	0	62	51	16	.667
Toronto St. Patricks	12	5	7	0	52	62	10	.417
Quebec Bulldogs	12	2	10	0	44	81	4	.167

Second Half

Team Name	GP	W	L	T	GF	GA	Pts	Pct
Ottawa Senators	12	10	2	0	62	41	20	.833
Toronto St. Patricks	12	7	5	0	67	44	14	.583
Montreal Canadiens	12	5	7	0	67	62	10	.417
Quebec Bulldogs	12	2	10	0	47	96	4	.167

Coaching History

Ottawa--Pete Green 19-5; Toronto--Frank Heffernan 5-7, Harry Sproule 7-5; Quebec--Mike Quinn 4-20.

League Leaders

Goals

Joe Malone	39
Newsy Lalonde	36
Frank Nighbor	26
Reg Noble	24
Corb Denneny	23

Assists

Corb Denneny	12
Ken Randall	7
Frank Nighbor	7
Reg Noble	7
Didier Pitre	7

Points

Joe Malone	45
Newsy Lalonde	42
Corb Denneny	35
Frank Nighbor	33
Reg Noble	31

Penalty Minutes

Carl Wilson	79
Sprague Cleghorn	62
Bert Corbeau	59
Reg Noble	51
Ken Randall	43

GAA

Clint Benedict	2.67
Ivan Mitchell	4.47
Georges Vezina	4.67
Frank Brophy	7.12

Wins

Clint Benedict	19
Georges Vezina	13
Ivan Mitchell	7
Howie Lockhart	4
Frank Brophy	3

Shutouts

Clint Benedict	5

Pacific Coast Hockey Association

Team Name	GP	W	L	T	GF	GA	Pts	Pct
Seattle Metropolitans	22	12	10	0	59	55	24	.545
Vancouver Millionaires	22	11	11	0	75	65	22	.500
Victoria Aristocrats	22	10	12	0	57	71	20	.455

Coaching Changes

None.

League Leaders

Goals		Points		GAA	
Frank Foyston	26	Tom Dunderdale	33	Harry Holmes	2.50
Tom Dunderdale	25	Frank Foyston	29	Hugh Lehman	2.95
Alf Skinner	16	Fred Harris	24	Norm Fowler	3.23
Gordon Roberts	15	Eddie Oatman	24		
Fred Harris	14	Gordon Roberts	19		

Wins		Shutouts	
Harry Holmes	12	Harry Holmes	4
Hugh Lehman	11	Hugh Lehman	1
Norm Fowler	10	Norm Fowler	1

PCHA Playoffs

March 12	Vancouver Millionaires	3	at	Seattle Metropolitans	1
March 15	Seattle Metropolitans	6	at	Vancouver Millionaires	0

Stanley Cup Playoffs

March 22	Seattle Metropolitans	2	at	Ottawa Senators	3
March 24	Seattle Metropolitans	0	at	Ottawa Senators	3
March 27	Seattle Metropolitans	3	at	Ottawa Senators	1
March 30	Seattle Metropolitans	5	at	Ottawa Senators	2
April 1	Seattle Metropolitans	1	at	Ottawa Senators	6

Franchise Changes

NHL--Toronto Arenas changed name to Toronto St. Patricks.

Other Sports

Horseracing--Kentucky Derby won by Paul Jones (time 2:09, purse $30,375).
Heavyweight Boxing--Jack Dempsey knocked-out Billy Miske in 3 rounds.
Jack Dempsey knocked-out Bill Brennan in 12 rounds.
Golf--U.S. Open won by Edward Ray with a score of 295.
Auto Racing--Indianapolis 500 won by Gaston Chevrolet (ave speed 88.50 MPH).
Tennis--U.S. Open won by Bill Tilden in the men's singles
U.S. Open won by William Johnston and Clarence Griffin in the men's doubles.

1921

BASEBALL
National League

Team Name	W	L	Pct	GB	R	OR
New York Giants	94	59	.614	-	840	637
Pittsburgh Pirates	90	63	.588	4	692	595
St. Louis Cardinals	87	66	.569	7	809	681
Boston Braves	79	74	.516	15	721	697
Brooklyn Dodgers	77	75	.507	16.5	667	681
Cincinnati Reds	70	83	.458	24	618	649
Chicago Cubs	64	89	.418	30	668	773
Philadelphia Phillies	51	103	.331	43.5	617	919

Coaching Changes

Boston--Fred Mitchell 79-74; Chicago--Johnny Evers 42-56, Bill Killefer 22-33; Philadelphia--Bill Donovan 31-71, Irvin Wilhelm 20-32.

League Leaders

Batting Average

Rogers Hornsby	.397
Edd Roush	.352
Austin McHenry	.350
Walton Cruise	.346
Jack Fournier	.343

Home Runs

George Kelly	23
Rogers Hornsby	21
Cy Williams	18
Austin McHenry	17
Jack Fournier	16

RBI

Rogers Hornsby	126
George Kelly	122
Ross Youngs	102
Austin McHenry	102
Frank Frisch	100

Stolen Bases

Frank Frisch	49
Max Carey	37
Jim Johnston	28
Sam Bohne	26
Walter Maranville	25

ERA

Bill Doak	2.59
Charles Adams	2.64
Charles Glazner	2.77
Eppa Rixey	2.78
Burleigh Grimes	2.83

Wins

Wilbur Cooper	22
Burleigh Grimes	22
Art Nehf	20
Joe Oeschger	20
Eppa Rixey	19

Saves

Lou North	7
Jesse Barnes	6
Hugh McQuillan	5
Walter Betts	4
Hal Carlson	4

Strikeouts

Burleigh Grimes	136
Wilbur Cooper	134
Adolfo Luque	102
Hugh McQuillan	94
Charles Glazner	88

Notes

Fans attending National League baseball games were allowed to keep any balls knocked into the stands. Prior to this police would order fans to throw the balls back onto the field.

The first baseball game broadcast on radio took place August 5, 1921. Station KDKA broadcast from Pittsburgh's Forbes Field as the Pirates defeated Philadelphia 8-5.

American League

Team Name	W	L	Pct	GB	R	OR
New York Yankees	98	55	.641	-	948	708
Cleveland Indians	94	60	.610	4.5	925	712
St. Louis Browns	81	73	.526	17.5	835	845
Washington Senators	80	73	.523	18	704	738
Boston Red Sox	75	79	.487	23.5	668	696
Detroit Tigers	71	82	.464	27	883	852
Chicago White Sox	62	92	.403	36.5	683	858
Philadelphia Athletics	53	100	.346	45	657	894

Coaching Changes

St. Louis--Lee Fohl 81-73; Washington--George McBride 80-73; Boston--Hugh Duffy 75-79; Detroit--Ty Cobb 71-82.

League Leaders

Batting Average		Home Runs		RBI	
Harry Heilmann	.394	Babe Ruth	59	Babe Ruth	170
Ty Cobb	.389	Bob Meusel	24	Harry Heilmann	139
Babe Ruth	.378	Ken Williams	24	Bob Meusel	135
George Sisler	.371	Tilly Walker	23	Bobby Veach	128
Tris Speaker	.362	Harry Heilmann	19	Ken Williams	117

Stolen Bases		ERA		Wins	
George Sisler	35	Urban Faber	2.48	Carl Mays	27
Stanley Harris	29	George Mogridge	3.00	Urban Shocker	27
Sam Rice	25	Carl Mays	3.05	Urban Faber	25
Ty Cobb	22	Waite Hoyt	3.09	Stan Coveleski	23
Ernie Johnson	22	Sam Jones	3.22	Sam Jones	23

Saves		Strikeouts	
Jim Middleton	7	Walter Johnson	143
Carl Mays	7	Urban Shocker	132
Carl Holling	4	Bob Shawkey	126
Jim Bagby	4	Urban Faber	124
Ray Caldwell	4	Dutch Leonard	120

World Series

(all games were played at the Polo Grounds)

October 5	New York Yankees	3	at	New York Giants	0
October 6	New York Giants	0	at	New York Yankees	3
October 7	New York Yankees	5	at	New York Giants	13
October 9	New York Giants	4	at	New York Yankees	2
October 10	New York Yankees	3	at	New York Giants	1
October 11	New York Giants	8	at	New York Yankees	5
October 12	New York Yankees	1	at	New York Giants	2
October 13	New York Giants	1	at	New York Yankees	0

HOCKEY
National Hockey League

First Half

Team Name	GP	W	L	T	GF	GA	Pts	Pct
Ottawa Senators	10	8	2	0	49	23	16	.800
Toronto St. Patricks	10	5	5	0	39	47	10	.500
Montreal Canadiens	10	4	6	0	37	51	8	.400
Hamilton Tigers	10	3	7	0	34	38	6	.300

Second Half

Team Name	GP	W	L	T	GF	GA	Pts	Pct
Toronto St. Patricks	14	10	4	0	66	53	20	.714
Montreal Canadiens	14	9	5	0	75	48	18	.643
Ottawa Senators	14	6	8	0	48	52	12	.429
Hamilton Tigers	14	3	11	0	58	94	6	.214

Coaching Changes

Toronto--Dick Carroll 15-9; Montreal--Leo Dandurand 13-11; Hamilton--Percy Thompson 7-17.

League Leaders

Goals		Assists		Points	
Cecil Dye	35	Hugh Cameron	9	Newsy Lalonde	40
Cy Denneny	34	Louis Berlinquette	9	Cy Denneny	39
Newsy Lalonde	32	Joe Matte	9	Cecil Dye	37
Joe Malone	28	Newsy Lalonde	8	Joe Malone	32
Corb Denneny	19	George Prodgers	8	Hugh Cameron	27

Penalty Minutes		GAA		Wins	
Bert Corbeau	86	Clint Benedict	3.13	Clint Benedict	14
Bill Couture	74	Vernon Forbes	3.90	Vernon Forbes	13
Harry Mummery	68	Georges Vezina	4.13	Georges Vezina	13
Ken Randall	58	Howie Lockhart	5.50	Howie Lockhart	7
Reg Noble	54	Ivan Mitchell	5.50	Ivan Mitchell	2

Shutouts	
Clint Benedict	2
Georges Vezina	1
Howie Lockhart	1

NHL Playoffs

March 10	Toronto St. Patricks	0	at	Ottawa Senators	5
March 14	Ottawa Senators	2	at	Toronto St. Patricks	0

Pacific Coast Hockey Association

Team Name	GP	W	L	T	GF	GA	Pts	Pct
Vancouver Millionaires	24	13	11	0	86	78	26	.542
Seattle Metropolitans	24	12	11	1	77	68	25	.521
Victoria Cougars	24	10	13	1	71	88	21	.438

Coaching Changes

None.

League Leaders

Goals		Points		GAA	
Frank Foyston	24	Frank Fredrickson	32	Harry Holmes	2.83
Jim Riley	23	Fred Harris	32	Hugh Lehman	3.25
Alf Skinner	20	Frank Foyston	31	Norm Fowler	3.67
Frank Fredrickson	19	Jack Adams	30		
Jack Adams	17	Jim Riley	28		

Wins		Shutouts	
Hugh Lehman	13	Hugh Lehman	3
Harry Holmes	12	Norm Fowler	3
Norm Fowler	10		

PCHA Playoffs

March 14	Seattle Metropolitans	0	at	Vancouver Millionaires	7
March 16	Vancouver Millionaires	6	at	Seattle Metropolitans	2

Stanley Cup Playoffs

March 21	Ottawa Senators	1	at	Vancouver Millionaires	3
March 24	Ottawa Senators	4	at	Vancouver Millionaires	3
March 28	Ottawa Senators	3	at	Vancouver Millionaires	2
March 31	Ottawa Senators	2	at	Vancouver Millionaires	3
April 4	Ottawa Senators	2	at	Vancouver Millionaires	1

Franchise Changes

NHL--Quebec Bulldogs became the Hamilton Tigers.
PCHA--Victoria Aristocrats changed name to Victoria Cougars.

Other Sports

Horseracing--Kentucky Derby won by Behave Yourself (time 2:04.2, purse $38,450).
Heavyweight Boxing--Jack Dempsey knocked-out George Carpentier in 4 rounds.
Golf--U.S. Open won by James Barnes with a score of 289.
Auto Racing--Indianapolis 500 won by Thomas Milton (ave. speed 89.62 MPH).
Tennis--U.S. Open won by Bill Tilden in the men's singles.
U.S. Open won by Bill Tilden and Vincent Richards in the men's doubles.

Notes

The heavyweight boxing match between Dempsey and Carpentier on July 2 was the first title fight broadcast on radio.

1922

BASEBALL
National League

Team Name	W	L	Pct	GB	R	OR
New York Giants	93	61	.604	-	852	658
Cincinnati Reds	86	68	.558	7	766	677
Pittsburgh Pirates	85	69	.552	8	865	736
St. Louis Cardinals	85	69	.552	8	863	819
Chicago Cubs	80	74	.519	13	771	808
Brooklyn Dodgers	76	78	.494	17	743	754
Philadelphia Phillies	57	96	.373	35.5	738	920
Boston Braves	53	100	.346	39.5	596	822

Coaching Changes

Pittsburgh--George Gibson 32-33, Bill McKechnie 53-36; Chicago--Bill Killefer 80-74; Philadelphia--Irvin Wilhelm 57-96.

League Leaders

Batting Average

Rogers Hornsby	.401
Ray Grimes	.354
Lawrence Miller	.352
Carson Bigbee	.350
James Tierney	.345

Home Runs

Rogers Hornsby	42
Cy Williams	26
George Kelly	17
Cliff Lee	17
Zack Wheat	16

RBI

Rogers Hornsby	152
Emil Meusel	132
Zack Wheat	112
George Kelly	107
Ray Grimes	99

Stolen Bases

Max Carey	51
Frank Frisch	31
George Burns	30
Walter Maranville	24
Carson Bigbee	24

ERA

Wilfred Ryan	3.01
Pete Donahue	3.12
Wilbur Cooper	3.18
Art Nehf	3.29
Adolfo Luque	3.31

Wins

Eppa Rixey	25
Wilbur Cooper	23
Walt Ruether	21
Art Nehf	19
Jeff Pfeffer	19

Saves

Claude Jonnard	5
Lou North	4
Ernest Osborne	3
Tony Kaufmann	3
Al Mamaux	3

Strikeouts

Dazzy Vance	134
Wilbur Cooper	129
Jimmy Ring	116
John Morrison	104
Burleigh Grimes	99

American League

Team Name	W	L	Pct	GB	R	OR
New York Yankees	94	60	.610	-	758	618
St. Louis Browns	93	61	.604	1	867	643
Detroit Tigers	79	75	.513	15	828	791
Cleveland Indians	78	76	.506	16	768	817
Chicago White Sox	77	77	.500	17	691	691
Washington Senators	69	85	.448	25	650	706
Philadelphia Athletics	65	89	.422	29	705	830
Boston Red Sox	61	93	.396	33	598	769

Coaching Changes

Washington--Clyde Milan 69-85.

League Leaders

Batting Average

George Sisler	.420
Ty Cobb	.401
Tris Speaker	.378
Harry Heilmann	.356
Bing Miller	.336

Home Runs

Ken Williams	39
Tilly Walker	37
Babe Ruth	35
Bing Miller	21
Harry Heilmann	21

RBI

Ken Williams	155
Bobby Veach	126
Marty McManus	109
George Sisler	105
Bill Jacobson	102

Stolen Bases

George Sisler	51
Ken Williams	37
Stanley Harris	25
Ernie Johnson	21
Eddie Collins	20

ERA

Urban Faber	2.80
Herman Pillette	2.85
Bob Shawkey	2.91
Urban Shocker	2.97
Walter Johnson	2.99

Wins

Eddie Rommel	27
Joe Bush	26
Urban Shocker	24
George Uhle	22
Urban Faber	21

Saves

Sam Jones	8
Hubert Pruett	7
Wayne Wright	5
Elam Vangilder	4
George Dauss	4

Strikeouts

Urban Shocker	149
Urban Faber	148
Bob Shawkey	130
Howard Ehmke	108
Walter Johnson	105

World Series

(all games played at the Polo Grounds)

October 4	New York Yankees	2	at	New York Giants	3
October 5	New York Giants	3	at	New York Yankees	3 [10]
October 6	New York Yankees	0	at	New York Giants	3
October 7	New York Giants	4	at	New York Yankees	3
October 8	New York Yankees	3	at	New York Giants	5

Individual Awards

League Award--George Sisler (St. Louis Browns AL)

FOOTBALL
National Football League

Team Name	GP	W	L	T	PF	PA	Pct
Canton Bulldogs	12	10	0	2	184	15	.917
Chicago Bears	12	9	3	0	123	44	.750
Chicago Cardinals	11	8	3	0	96	50	.727
Toledo Maroons	9	5	2	2	94	59	.667
Rock Island Independents	7	4	2	1	154	27	.643
Racine Legions	11	6	4	1	122	56	.591
Dayton Triangles	8	4	3	1	80	52	.563
Green Bay Packers	11	4	3	3	70	54	.550
Buffalo All Americans	10	5	4	1	87	41	.550
Akron Pros	10	3	5	2	146	95	.400
Milwaukee Badgers	9	2	4	3	51	71	.389
Oorang Indians	8	2	6	0	51	184	.250
Minneapolis Marines	4	1	3	0	19	40	.250
Louisville Brecks	4	1	3	0	13	140	.250
Rochester Jeffersons	5	0	4	1	13	76	.100
Hammond Pros	6	0	5	1	0	69	.083
Evansville Crimson Giants	3	0	3	0	6	88	.000
Columbus Panhandles	7	0	7	0	18	156	.000

Coaching

Canton--Guy Chamberlin 10-0-2; Chicago Bears--George Halas 9-3-0; Chicago Cardinals--Paddy Driscoll 8-3-0; Toledo--Gil Falcon 5-2-2; Rock Island--Jimmy Conzelman 4-2-1; Racine--Babe Ruetz 6-4-1; Dayton--Carl Storck 4-3-1; Green Bay--Earl Lambeau 4-3-3; Buffalo--Tom Hughitt 5-4-1; Akron--Brooke Brewer & Paul Sheeks 3-5-2; Milwaukee--Fritz Pollard 2-4-3; Oorang--Jim Thorpe 2-6-0; Louisville--Hubert Wiggs 1-3-0; Rochester--Leo Lyons 0-4-1; Evansville--Frank Fausch 0-3-0; Columbus--Frank Nesser 0-7-0; Hammond--(unknown); Minneapolis--(unknown)

League Leaders

Points		Field Goals	
Hank Gillo	52	Paddy Driscoll	8
Jimmy Conzelman	48	Hank Gillo	6
Dutch Sternaman	41	Dutch Sternaman	6
Paddy Driscoll	40	Arnie Horween	3
Ed Shaw	38	Frank Morrissey	3

Notes

The National Football League was formed this year from the American Professional Football Association which had been formed two years earlier. George Halas of the Chicago Bears suggested the name. From 1922 to 1933 the League teams played erratic schedules and rules were not standardized.

Tackle Duke Slater of the Milwaukee Badgers became the first black player in major league professional football.

HOCKEY

National Hockey League

Team Name	GP	W	L	T	GF	GA	Pts	Pct
Ottawa Senators	24	14	8	2	106	84	30	.625
Toronto St. Patricks	24	13	10	1	98	97	27	.563
Montreal Canadiens	24	12	11	1	88	94	25	.521
Hamilton Tigers	24	7	17	0	88	105	14	.292

Coaching Changes

Toronto--Eddie Powers 13-10-1.

League Leaders

Goals		Assists		Points	
Harry Broadbent	30	Harry Broadbent	14	Harry Broadbent	44
Cecil Dye	30	Leo Reise	14	Cy Denneny	40
Cy Denneny	28	Cy Denneny	12	Cecil Dye	37
Joe Malone	23	Eddie Gerard	9	Joe Malone	30
Odie Cleghorn	21	Reg Noble	8	Hugh Cameron	27

Penalty Minutes		GAA		Wins	
Sprague Cleghorn	63	Clint Benedict	3.50	Clint Benedict	14
Corb Denneny	28	Georges Vezina	3.92	Georges Vezina	12
Odie Cleghorn	26	John Roach	4.14	John Roach	11
Bert Corbeau	26	Howie Lockhart	4.38	Howie Lockhart	6
Harry Broadbent	24			Ivan Mitchell	2

Shutouts	
Clint Benedict	2

NHL Playoffs

March 11	Ottawa Senators	4	at	Toronto St. Patricks	5
March 13	Toronto St. Patricks	0	at	Ottawa Senators	0

Pacific Coast Hockey Association

Team Name	GP	W	L	T	GF	GA	Pts	Pct
Seattle Metropolitans	24	12	11	1	65	64	25	.521
Vancouver Millionaires	24	12	12	0	77	68	24	.500
Victoria Cougars	24	11	12	1	61	71	23	.479

Coaching Changes

None.

League Leaders

Goals		Points		GAA	
Jack Adams	25	Jack Adams	29	Harry Holmes	2.67
Frank Foyston	16	Mickey Mackay	26	Hugh Lehman	2.82
Jim Riley	16	Frank Fredrickson	25	Norm Fowler	2.92
Mickey Mackay	15	Bernie Morris	24	Tom Murray	3.00
Frank Fredrickson	15	Frank Foyston	23		

Wins		Shutouts	
Harry Holmes	12	Harry Holmes	4
Hugh Lehman	12	Hugh Lehman	4
Norm Fowler	11		
Tom Murray	0		

PCHA Playoffs

March 3	Vancouver Millionaires	1	at	Seattle Metropolitans	0
March 6	Seattle Metropolitans	0	at	Vancouver Millionaires	1

Rules

The Pacific Coast Hockey Association introduced the penalty shot this year.

Western Canada Hockey Association

Team Name	GP	W	L	T	GF	GA	Pts	Pct
Edmonton Eskimos	24	15	9	0	117	76	30	.625
Regina Capitals	24	14	10	0	94	78	28	.583
Calgary Tigers	24	14	10	0	75	62	28	.583
(Saskatoon Sheiks)	14	4	10	0	43	77	8	.286
(Moose Jaw Orphans)	10	1	9	0	24	60	2	.100

Coaches

Edmonton--Ken Mckenzie 15-9-0; Regina Wes Champ 14-10-0; Calgary--Barney Stanley 14-10-0; Saskatoon/Moose Jaw--Bob Pinder 5-19-0

League Leaders

Goals		Assists		Points	
Gordon Keats	29	Gordon Keats	25	Gordon Keats	54
Barney Stanley	26	Joe Simpson	13	George Hay	33
Ty Arbour	25	George Hay	11	Ty Arbour	31
George Hay	22	Elmer Nagle	7	Barney Stanley	30
Dick Irvin	19	Dick Irvin	7	Joe Simpson	28

GAA		Wins		Shutouts	
Hal Winkler	2.36	Bill Laird	14	Charles Reid	2
Charles Reid	2.58	Charles Reid	14	Hal Winkler	1
Bill Laird	3.12	Hal Winkler	10		
Wilf Talbot	4.13	Sam Hebert	5		
Sam Hebert	5.70	Wilf Talbot	4		

WCHA Playoffs

March 2	Regina Capitals	1	at	Calgary Tigers	0
March 3	Calgary Tigers	1	at	Regina Capitals	1
March 4	Edmonton Eskimos	1	at	Regina Capitals	1
March 6	Regina Capitals	2	at	Edmonton Eskimos	1

Western Playoffs

March 8	Regina Capitals	2	at	Vancouver Millionaires	1
March 11	Vancouver Millionaires	4	at	Regina Capitals	0

Stanley Cup Playoffs

March 17	Vancouver Millionaires	4	at	Toronto St. Patricks	3
March 20	Vancouver Millionaires	1	at	Toronto St. Patricks	2 [4:50]
March 23	Vancouver Millionaires	3	at	Toronto St. Patricks	0
March 25	Vancouver Millionaires	0	at	Toronto St. Patricks	6
March 28	Vancouver Millionaires	1	at	Toronto St. Patricks	5

Notes

The Western Canada Hockey League was organized this year with E.L. Richardson as president.

Franchise Changes

WCHL--Saskatoon Sheiks moved to Moose Jaw midway through the season.

Other Sports

Horseracing--Kentucky Derby won by Morvich (time 2:04.6, purse $53,775).
Golf--U.S. Open won by Gene Sarazen with a score of 288.
Auto Racing--Indianapolis 500 won by James Murphy (ave. speed 94.48 MPH).
Tennis--U.S. Open won by Bill Tilden in the men's singles.
U.S. Open won by Bill Tilden and Vincent Richards in the men's doubles

1923

BASEBALL
National League

Team Name	W	L	Pct	GB	R	OR
New York Giants	95	58	.621	-	854	679
Cincinnati Reds	91	63	.591	4.5	708	629
Pittsburgh Pirates	87	67	.565	8.5	786	696
Chicago Cubs	83	71	.539	12.5	756	704
St. Louis Cardinals	79	74	.516	16	746	732
Brooklyn Dodgers	76	78	.494	19.5	753	741
Boston Braves	54	100	.351	41.5	636	798
Philadelphia Phillies	50	104	.325	45.5	748	1008

Coaching Changes

Pittsburgh--Bill McKechnie 87-67; Philadelphia--Art Fletcher 50-104.

League Leaders

Batting Average

Rogers Hornsby	.384
Jim Bottomley	.371
Jack Fournier	.351
Edd Roush	.351
Frank Frisch	.348

Home Runs

Cy Williams	41
Jack Fournier	22
Lawrence Miller	20
Emil Meusel	19
Rogers Hornsby	17

RBI

Emil Meusel	125
Cy Williams	114
Frank Frisch	111
George Kelly	103
Jack Fournier	102

Stolen Bases

Max Carey	51
George Grantham	43
Cliff Heathcote	32
Jack Smith	32
Frank Frisch	29

ERA

Adolfo Luque	1.93
Eppa Rixey	2.80
Vic Keen	3.00
Tony Kaufmann	3.10
Jesse Haines	3.11

Wins

Adolfo Luque	27
John Morrison	25
Grover Alexander	22
Burleigh Grimes	21
Pete Donahue	21

Saves

Claude Jonnard	5
Wilfred Ryan	4
Art Decatur	3
John Stuart	3
Jack Bentley	3

Strikeouts

Dazzy Vance	197
Adolfo Luque	151
Burleigh Grimes	119
John Morrison	114
Jimmy Ring	112

American League

Team Name	W	L	Pct	GB	R	OR
New York Yankees	98	54	.645	-	823	622
Detroit Tigers	83	71	.539	16	831	741
Cleveland Indians	82	71	.536	16.5	888	746
Washington Senators	75	78	.490	23.5	720	747
St. Louis Browns	74	78	.487	24	688	720
Philadelphia Athletics	69	83	.454	29	661	761
Chicago White Sox	69	85	.448	30	692	741
Boston Red Sox	61	91	.401	37	584	809

Coaching Changes

Washington--Owen Bush 75-78; St. Louis--Lee Fohl 51-49, Jimmy Austin 23-29; Boston--Frank Chance 61-91.

League Leaders

Batting Average		Home Runs		RBI	
Harry Heilmann	.403	Babe Ruth	41	Babe Ruth	130
Babe Ruth	.393	Ken Williams	29	Tris Speaker	130
Tris Speaker	.380	Harry Heilmann	18	Harry Heilmann	115
Eddie Collins	.360	Tris Speaker	17	Joe Sewell	109
Ken Williams	.357	Frank Brower	16	Wally Pipp	108

Stolen Bases		ERA		Wins	
Eddie Collins	47	Stan Coveleski	2.76	George Uhle	26
John Mostil	41	Waite Hoyt	3.02	George Dauss	21
Stanley Harris	23	Elam Vangilder	3.06	Sam Jones	21
Sam Rice	20	George Mogridge	3.11	Urban Shocker	20
Charlie Jamieson	19	Eddie Rommel	3.27	Howard Ehmke	20

Saves		Strikeouts	
Allan Russell	9	Walter Johnson	130
Jack Quinn	7	Joe Bush	125
Bill Harriss	6	Bob Shawkey	125
Bert Cole	5	Howard Ehmke	121
Urban Shocker	5	Urban Shocker	109

World Series

October 10	New York Giants	5	at	New York Yankees	4
October 11	New York Yankees	4	at	New York Giants	2
October 12	New York Giants	1	at	New York Yankees	0
October 13	New York Yankees	8	at	New York Giants	4
October 14	New York Giants	1	at	New York Yankees	8
October 15	New York Yankees	6	at	New York Giants	4

Individual Awards

League Award--Babe Ruth (New York Yankees AL)

FOOTBALL
National Football League

Team Name	GP	W	L	T	PF	PA	Pct
Canton Bulldogs	12	11	0	1	246	19	.958
Chicago Bears	12	9	2	1	123	35	.792
Green Bay Packers	10	7	2	1	85	34	.750
Milwaukee Badgers	12	7	2	3	100	49	.708
Chicago Cardinals	12	8	4	0	161	56	.667
Cleveland Indians	7	3	1	3	52	49	.643
Duluth Eskimos	7	4	3	0	35	33	.571
Columbus Tigers	10	5	4	1	119	35	.550
Buffalo All Americans	11	4	4	3	81	43	.500
Racine Legions	10	4	4	2	86	86	.500
Rock Island Independents	8	2	3	3	84	62	.438
Toledo Maroons	7	2	3	2	23	60	.429
Minneapolis Marines	9	2	5	2	48	87	.333
St. Louis Browns	7	1	4	2	14	39	.286
Hammond Pros	7	1	5	1	14	59	.214
Dayton Triangles	8	1	6	1	16	95	.188
Akron Pros	7	1	6	0	25	74	.143
Oorang Indians	11	1	10	0	49	247	.045
Rochester Jeffersons	2	0	2	0	0	116	.000
Louisville Brecks	3	0	3	0	0	83	.000

Coaching Changes

Milwaukee--Jimmy Conzelman 7-2-3; Chicago Cardinals--Arnold Horween 8-4-0; Cleveland--Gene Edwards 3-1-3; Duluth--Joe Sternaman 4-3-0; Columbus--Pete Stinchcomb 1-2-1, Gus Tebell 4-2-0; Rock Island--Dale Sies 2-3-3; Toledo--Clarence Horning 2-3-2; Minneapolis--Harry Mehre 2-5-2; St. Louis--Ollie Kraehe 1-4-2; Hammond--Fritz Pollard 1-5-1; Akron--Carl Cramer 1-6-0; Louisville--Jim Kendrick 0-3-0; Racine--(unknown).

League Leaders

Points		Field Goals	
Paddy Driscoll	78	Paddy Driscoll	10
Pete Henry	58	Pete Henry	9
Dutch Sternaman	51	Hank Gillo	8
Ben Winkelman	45	Cub Buck	6
Hank Gillo	44	Frank Morrissey	6

HOCKEY
National Hockey League

Team Name	GP	W	L	T	GF	GA	Pts	Pct
Ottawa Senators	24	14	9	1	77	54	29	.604
Montreal Canadiens	24	13	9	2	73	61	28	.583
Toronto St. Patricks	24	13	10	1	82	88	27	.563
Hamilton Tigers	24	6	18	0	81	110	12	.250

Coaching Changes

Toronto--Charlie Querrie 3-3-0, Jack Adams 10-7-1; Hamilton--Art Ross 6-18-0.

League Leaders

Goals		Assists		Points	
Cecil Dye	26	Edmond Bouchard	12	Cecil Dye	37
Bill Boucher	25	Cecil Dye	11	Cy Denneny	33
Cy Denneny	23	Cy Denneny	10	Bill Boucher	29
Odie Cleghorn	18	Reg Noble	10	Jack Adams	27
Jack Adams	18	George Boucher	9	Odie Cleghorn	25

Penalty Minutes		GAA		Wins	
Bill Boucher	52	Clint Benedict	2.25	Clint Benedict	14
Ken Randall	51	Georges Vezina	2.54	Georges Vezina	13
Carl Wilson	46	John Roach	3.67	John Roach	13
George Boucher	44	Vernon Forbes	4.58	Vernon Forbes	6
Jack Adams	42				

Shutouts	
Clint Benedict	4
Georges Vezina	2
John Roach	1

NHL Playoffs

March 7	Ottawa Senators	2	at	Montreal Canadiens	0
March 9	Montreal Canadiens 2		at	Ottawa Senators	1

Pacific Coast Hockey Association

Team Name	GP	W	L	T	GF	GA	Pts	Pct
Vancouver Maroons	30	17	12	1	116	88	35	.583
Victoria Cougars	30	16	14	0	94	85	32	.533
Seattle Metropolitans	30	15	15	0	100	106	30	.500

Coaching Changes

None.

League Leaders

Goals		Points		GAA	
Frank Fredrickson	41	Frank Fredrickson	56	Hugh Lehman	2.44
Mickey Mackay	27	Mickey Mackay	37	Norm Fowler	2.83
Jim Riley	22	Lloyd Cook	29	Harry Holmes	3.53
Bernie Morris	21	Frank Foyston	28	Charlie Reid	5.40
Frank Foyston	20				

Wins		Shutouts	
Hugh Lehman	16	Hugh Lehman	4
Norm Fowler	16	Norm Fowler	4
Harry Holmes	15	Harry Holmes	3
		Charles Reid	1

PCHA Playoffs

March 7	Vancouver Maroons	3	at	Victoria Cougars	0
March 12	Victoria Cougars	3	at	Vancouver Maroons	2

Western Canada Hockey Association

Team Name	GP	W	L	T	GF	GA	Pts	Pct
Edmonton Eskimos	30	19	10	1	112	90	39	.650
Regina Capitals	30	16	14	0	93	97	32	.533
Calgary Tigers	30	12	18	0	91	106	24	.400
Saskatoon Sheiks	30	8	20	2	91	125	18	.300

Coaching Changes

Regina--Barney Stanley 16-14-0; Calgary--Herb Gardiner 12-18-0; Saskatoon--Newsy Lalonde 8-20-2.

League Leaders

Goals		Assists		Points	
Newsy Lalonde	30	Art Gagne	21	Art Gagne	43
George Hay	28	Gordon Keats	15	Gordon Keats	39
Gordon Keats	24	Bill Cook	15	George Hay	37
Harry Oliver	23	Joe Simpson	14	Newsy Lalonde	34
Art Gagne	22	Harry Oliver	9	Harry Oliver	32

GAA		Wins		Shutouts	
Bill Laird	3.04	Hal Winkler	17	Bill Laird	3
Hal Winkler	3.11	Bill Laird	16	Hal Winkler	1
Bill Binney	3.35	Bill Binney	7	Bill Binney	1
Charles Reid	3.75	Charles Reid	5	Tom Murray	1
Sam Hebert	4.17	Tom Murray	4		

WCHA Playoffs

March 14	Edmonton Eskimos	1	at	Regina Capitals	0
March 16	Regina Capitals	3	at	Edmonton Eskimos	3

Stanley Cup Playoffs

March 16	Ottawa Senators	1	at	Vancouver Maroons	0
March 19	Ottawa Senators	1	at	Vancouver Maroons	4
March 23	Ottawa Senators	3	at	Vancouver Maroons	2
March 26	Ottawa Senators	5	at	Vancouver Maroons	1
March 29	Ottawa Senators	2	at	Edmonton Eskimos	1 [2:08]**
March 31	Ottawa Senators	1	at	Edmonton Eskimos	0**

Notes

The WCHA and the PCHA played an interlocking schedule.

**Games played in Vancouver

Franchise Changes

WCHA--Vancouver Millionaires changed name to Vancouver Maroons.
WCHL--Moose Jaw Orphans became the Saskatoon Sheiks.
NFL--Columbus Panhandles became the Columbus Tigers.

Other Sports

Horseracing--Kentucky Derby won by Zev (time 2:05.4; purse $53,600).
Heavyweight Boxing--Jack Dempsey won on points from Tom Gibbons in 15 rounds.
Jack Dempsey knocked-out Luis Firpo in 2 rounds.
Golf--U.S. Open won by Bobby Jones with a score of 296.
Auto Racing--Indianapolis 500 won by Thomas Milton (ave. speed 90.95 MPH).
Tennis--U.S. Open won by Bill Tilden in the men's singles.
U.S. Open won by Bill Tilden and Brian Norton in the men's doubles.

1924

BASEBALL

National League

Team Name	W	L	Pct	GB	R	OR
New York Giants	93	60	.608	-	857	641
Brooklyn Dodgers	92	62	.597	1.5	717	675
Pittsburgh Pirates	90	63	.588	3	724	588
Cincinnati Reds	83	70	.542	10	649	579
Chicago Cubs	81	72	.529	12	698	699
St. Louis Cardinals	65	89	.422	28.5	740	750
Philadelphia Phillies	55	96	.364	37	676	849
Boston Braves	53	100	.346	40	520	800

Coaching Changes

Cincinnati--Jack Hendricks 83-70; Boston--Dave Bancroft 53-100.

League Leaders

Batting Average		Home Runs		RBI	
Rogers Hornsby	.424	Jack Fournier	27	George Kelly	136
Zack Wheat	.375	Rogers Hornsby	25	Jack Fournier	116
Ross Youngs	.356	Cy Williams	24	Glenn Wright	111
Kiki Cuyler	.354	George Kelly	21	Jim Bottomley	111
Edd Roush	.348	Gabby Hartnett	16	Emil Meusel	102

Stolen Bases		ERA		Wins	
Max Carey	49	Dazzy Vance	2.16	Dazzy Vance	28
Kiki Cuyler	32	Hugh McQuillan	2.69	Burleigh Grimes	22
Cliff Heathcote	26	Eppa Rixey	2.76	Carl Mays	20
Jack Smith	24	Emil Yde	2.83	Wilbur Cooper	20
Pie Traynor	24	Grover Alexander	3.03	Ray Kremer	18

Saves		Strikeouts	
Frank May	6	Dazzy Vance	262
Wilfred Ryan	5	Burleigh Grimes	135
Claude Jonnard	5	Adolfo Luque	86
John Couch	3	John Morrison	85
Walt Ruether	3	Tony Kaufmann	79

American League

Team Name	W	L	Pct	GB	R	OR
Washington Senators	92	62	.597	-	755	613
New York Yankees	89	63	.586	2	798	667
Detroit Tigers	86	68	.558	6	849	796
St. Louis Browns	74	78	.487	17	764	797
Philadelphia Athletics	71	81	.467	20	685	778
Cleveland Indians	67	86	.438	24.5	755	814
Boston Red Sox	67	87	.435	25	725	801
Chicago White Sox	66	87	.431	25.5	793	858

Coaching Changes

Washington--Stanley Harris 92-62; St. Louis--George Sisler 74-78; Boston--Lee Fohl 67-87; Chicago--Johnny Evers 66-87.

League Leaders

Batting Average		Home Runs		RBI	
Babe Ruth	.378	Babe Ruth	46	Leon Goslin	129
Charlie Jamieson	.359	Joe Hauser	27	Babe Ruth	121
Bibb Falk	.352	Bill Jacobson	19	Bob Meusel	120
Eddie Collins	.349	Ken Williams	18	Joe Hauser	115
John Bassler	.346	Ike Boone	13	Harry Heilmann	113

Stolen Bases		ERA		Wins	
Eddie Collins	42	Walter Johnson	2.72	Walter Johnson	23
Bob Meusel	26	Tom Zachary	2.75	Herb Pennock	21
Sam Rice	24	Herb Pennock	2.83	Hollis Thurston	20
Ty Cobb	23	Stan Baumgartner	2.88	Joe Shaute	20
Charlie Jamieson	21	Sherrod Smith	3.02	Howard Ehmke	19

Saves		Strikeouts	
Fred Marberry	15	Walter Johnson	158
Allan Russell	8	Howard Ehmke	119
Jack Quinn	7	Bob Shawkey	114
George Dauss	6	Herb Pennock	101
George Connally	6	Urban Shocker	84

World Series

October 4	New York Giants	4	at	Washington Senators	3 [12]
October 5	New York Giants	3	at	Washington Senators	4
October 6	Washington Senators	4	at	New York Giants	6
October 7	Washington Senators	7	at	New York Giants	4
October 8	Washington Senators	2	at	New York Giants	6
October 9	New York Giants	1	at	Washington Senators	2
October 10	New York Giants	3	at	Washington Senators	4

Individual Awards

League Award--Dazzy Vance (Brooklyn Dodgers NL)
Walter Johnson (Washington Senators AL)

FOOTBALL
National Football League

Team Name	GP	W	L	T	PF	PA	Pct
Cleveland Bulldogs	9	7	1	1	229	60	.833
Duluth Kelleys	6	5	1	0	56	16	.833
Frankford Yellow Jackets	14	11	2	1	326	109	.821
Chicago Bears	11	6	1	4	136	55	.727
Rock Island Independents	10	6	2	2	98	44	.700
Green Bay Packers	11	7	4	0	108	38	.636
Racine Legions	10	4	3	3	69	47	.550
Chicago Cardinals	10	5	4	1	90	67	.550
Buffalo Bisons	11	6	5	0	120	140	.545
Columbus Tigers	8	4	4	0	91	68	.500
Hammond Pros	5	2	2	1	18	45	.500
Milwaukee Badgers	13	5	8	0	142	188	.385
Akron Pros	8	2	6	0	59	132	.250
Dayton Triangles	8	2	6	0	45	148	.250
Kansas City Cowboys	9	2	7	0	46	124	.222
Kenosha Maroons	6	0	5	1	18	127	.083
Minneapolis Marines	6	0	6	0	14	108	.000
Rochester Jeffersons	7	0	7	0	7	156	.000

Coaching Changes

Cleveland--Guy Chamberlin 7-1-1; Duluth--Dewey Scanlon 5-1-0; Frankford--Robert Berryman 11-2-1; Rock Island--John Armstrong 6-2-2; Columbus--Jim Weaver 4-4-0; Akron--Jim Flower 2-6-0; Kansas City--LeRoy Andrews 2-7-0; Kenosha--Earl Potteiger 0-5-1; Minneapolis--Joe Brandy 0-6-0; Rochester--Jerry Noonan 0-7-0; Racine--(unknown).

League Leaders

Points		Field Goals	
Tex Hamer	75	Hank Gillo	8
Joey Sternaman	73	Joey Sternaman	8
Ben Boynton	59	Paddy Driscoll	7
Hank Gillo	48	Red Dunn	7
John Storer	48	Jim Welsh	6

Notes

Scheduling continued to be erratic in the NFL and many teams would schedule games against weaker teams in order to better their records.

HOCKEY
National Hockey League

Team Name	GP	W	L	T	GF	GA	Pts	Pct
Ottawa Senators	24	16	8	0	74	54	32	.667
Montreal Canadiens	24	13	11	0	59	48	26	.542
Toronto St. Patricks	24	10	14	0	59	85	20	.417
Hamilton Tigers	24	9	15	0	63	68	18	.375

American League

Team Name	W	L	Pct	GB	R	OR
Washington Senators	96	55	.636	-	829	669
Philadelphia Athletics	88	64	.579	8.5	830	714
St. Louis Browns	82	71	.536	15	897	909
Detroit Tigers	81	73	.526	16.5	903	829
Chicago White Sox	79	75	.513	18.5	811	771
Cleveland Indians	70	84	.455	27.5	782	810
New York Yankees	69	85	.448	28.5	706	774
Boston Red Sox	47	105	.309	49.5	639	921

Coaching Changes

Chicago--Eddie Collins 79-75.

League Leaders

Batting Average		Home Runs		RBI	
Harry Heilmann	.393	Bob Meusel	33	Bob Meusel	138
Tris Speaker	.389	Ken Williams	25	Harry Heilmann	133
Al Simmons	.384	Babe Ruth	25	Al Simmons	129
Ty Cobb	.378	Al Simmons	24	Leon Goslin	113
Ivy Wingo	.370	Lou Gehrig	20	Earl Sheely	111

Stolen Bases		ERA		Wins	
John Mostil	43	Stan Coveleski	2.84	Eddie Rommel	21
Leon Goslin	26	Herb Pennock	2.96	Ted Lyons	21
Sam Rice	26	Walter Johnson	3.07	Stan Coveleski	20
Eddie Collins	19	George Datiss	3.16	Walter Johnson	20
Ike Davis	19	Ted Blankenship	3.16	Bill Harriss	19

Saves		Strikeouts	
Fred Marberry	15	Robert Grove	116
George Connally	8	Walter Johnson	108
Jesse Doyle	8	Howard Ehmke	95
George Walberg	7	Bill Harriss	95
Elam Vangilder	6	Sam Jones	92

World Series

October 7	Washington Senators	4	at	Pittsburgh Pirates	1
October 8	Washington Senators	2	at	Pittsburgh Pirates	3
October 10	Pittsburgh Pirates	3	at	Washington Senators	4
October 11	Pittsburgh Pirates	3	at	Washington Senators	4
October 12	Pittsburgh Pirates	6	at	Washington Senators	3
October 13	Washington Senators	2	at	Pittsburgh Pirates	3
October 15	Washington Senators	7	at	Pittsburgh Pirates	9

Individual Awards

League Award--Rogers Hornsby (St. Louis Cardinals NL)
Roger Peckinpaugh (Washington Senators AL)

FOOTBALL
National Football League

Team Name	GP	W	L	T	PF	PA	Pct
Pottsville Maroons	12	10	2	0	270	45	.833
Chicago Cardinals	14	11	2	1	230	65	.821
Detroit Panthers	12	8	2	2	129	39	.750
New York Giants	12	8	4	0	122	67	.667
Frankford Yellow Jackets	20	13	7	0	190	169	.650
Akron Pros	8	4	2	2	65	51	.625
Chicago Bears	17	9	5	3	158	96	.618
Green Bay Packers	13	8	5	0	151	110	.615
Rock Island Independents	11	5	3	3	99	58	.591
Providence Steam Roller	12	6	5	1	111	101	.542
Canton Bulldogs	8	4	4	0	50	73	.500
Cleveland Bulldogs	14	5	8	1	75	135	.393
Kansas City Cowboys	8	2	5	1	65	97	.313
Buffalo Bisons	9	1	6	2	33	113	.222
Hammond Pros	5	1	4	0	23	87	.200
Rochester Jeffersons	7	0	6	1	26	111	.071
Dayton Triangles	8	0	7	1	3	84	.063
Duluth Kelleys	3	0	3	0	6	25	.000
Milwaukee Badgers	6	0	6	0	7	191	.000
Columbus Tigers	9	0	9	0	28	124	.000

Coaching Changes

Pottsville--Dick Rauch 10-2-0; Chicago Cardinals--Norman Barry 11-2-1; Detroit--Jimmy Conzelman 8-2-2; New York Giants--Bob Folwell 8-4-0; Frankford--Guy Chamberlin 13-7-0; Akron--George Berry 4-0-2, Fritz Pollard 0-2-0; Rock Island--Rube Ursella 5-3-3; Providence--Archie Golembeski 6-5-1; Canton--Harry Robb 4-4-0; Buffalo--Walt Koppisch 1-6-2; Hammond--Doc Young 0-1-0, Fritz Pollard 1-3-0; Rochester--Cecil Griggs 0-6 1; Milwaukee--John Bryan 0-6-0.

League Leaders

Points		Field Goals	
Charlie Berry	74	Paddy Driscoll	11
Paddy Driscoll	67	Bull Behman	5
Joey Sternaman	62	Charlie Berry	3
Hal Erickson	48	Doc Elliot	3
Tony Latone	48	Dutch Hendrian	3

Notes

Harold "Red" Grange earned $30,000 for playing just one game with the Chicago Bears.

HOCKEY
National Hockey League

Team Name	GP	W	L	T	GF	GA	Pts	Pct
Hamilton Tigers	30	19	10	1	90	60	39	.650
Toronto St. Patricks	30	19	11	0	90	84	38	.633
Montreal Canadiens	30	17	11	2	93	56	36	.600
Ottawa Senators	30	17	12	1	83	66	35	.583
Montreal Maroons	30	9	19	2	45	65	20	.333
Boston Bruins	30	6	24	0	49	119	12	.200

Coaching Changes

Hamilton--Jim Gardner 19-10-1; Maroons--Eddie Gerard 9-19-2; Boston--Art Ross 6-24-0.

League Leaders

Goals		Assists		Points	
Cecil Dye	38	Cy Denneny	15	Cecil Dye	44
Howie Morenz	30	Bill Boucher	13	Cy Denneny	43
Aurel Joliat	29	Clarence Day	12	Aurel Joliat	40
Cy Denneny	28	Aurel Joliat	11	Howie Morenz	37
Jack Adams	21	Jack Adams	8	Bill Boucher	31

Penalty Minutes		GAA		Wins	
Bill Boucher	92	Georges Vezina	1.87	Vernon Forbes	19
Aurel Joliat	85	Vernon Forbes	2.00	John Roach	19
Sprague Cleghorn	82	Clint Benedict	2.17	Georges Vezina	17
Reginald Smith	81	Alex Connell	2.20	Alex Connell	17
George Boucher	80	John Roach	2.80	Clint Benedict	9

Shutouts	
Alex Connell	7
Vernon Forbes	6
Georges Vezina	5
Clint Benedict	2
Charles Stewart	2

NHL Playoffs

March 11	Toronto St. Patricks	2	at	Montreal Canadiens	3
March 13	Montreal Canadiens	2	at	Toronto St. Patricks	0

Individual Awards

Hart Trophy--Billy Burch (Hamilton Tigers)
Lady Byng Trophy--Frank Nighbor (Ottawa Senators)

Rules

Kicking the puck in the neutral zone is legalized.

Western Canada Hockey League

Team Name	GP	W	L	T	GF	GA	Pts	Pct
Calgary Tigers	28	17	11	0	96	80	34	.607
Saskatoon Crescents	28	16	11	1	102	75	33	.589
Victoria Cougars	28	16	12	0	84	63	32	.571
Edmonton Eskimos	28	14	13	1	97	109	29	.518
Vancouver Maroons	28	12	16	0	91	102	24	.429
Regina Capitals	28	8	20	0	82	123	16	.286

Coaching Changes

None.

League Leaders

Goals		Assists		Points	
Mickey Mackay	29	Frank Boucher	15	Mickey Mackay	35
Frank Fredrickson	22	Bob Trapp	13	Frank Boucher	32
Gordon Keats	21	Harry Oliver	12	Gordon Keats	30
Bill Cook	18	Bill Cook	12	Harry Oliver	30
Harry Oliver	18	Joe Simpson	10	Bill Cook	30

GAA		Wins		Shutouts	
Harry Holmes	2.25	Hal Winkler	17	Harry Holmes	3
George Hainsworth	2.68	Harry Holmes	16	George Hainsworth	2
Hugh Lehman	2.73	George Hainsworth	16	Hal Winkler	2
Hal Winkler	2.86	Hugh Lehman	7	Norm Fowler	1
Herb Stuart	4.00	Herb Stuart	7	Herb Stuart	1

WCHL Playoffs

March 6	Saskatoon Crescents	1	at	Victoria Cougars	3
March 10	Victoria Cougars	3	at	Saskatoon Crescents	3
March 14	Victoria Cougars	1	at	Calgary Tigers	1
March 18	Calgary Tigers	0	at	Victoria Cougars	2

Stanley Cup Playoffs

March 21	Montreal Canadiens	2	at	Victoria Cougars	5
March 23	Victoria Cougars	3	at	Montreal Canadiens	1**
March 27	Montreal Canadiens	4	at	Victoria Cougars	2
March 30	Montreal Canadiens	1	at	Victoria Cougars	6

Notes

After the PCHA disbanded, Victoria and Vancouver were allowed to join the WCHL.
In the Stanley Cup playoffs of this year Victoria made full use of line changes, the first time this tactic had been tried.

Other Sports

Horseracing--Kentucky Derby won by Flying Ebony (time 2:07.6, purse $52,950).
Golf--U.S. Open won by William McFarlane in a playoff with Bobby Jones with a score of 291. (tie breaking rounds of 75-75, 73-72)
Auto Racing--Indianapolis 500 won by Peter de Paolo (ave. speed 101.13 MPH).
Tennis--U.S. Open won by Bill Tilden in the men's singles.
U.S. Open won by Norris Williams and Vincent Richards in the men's doubles.

Notes

Station WGN in Chicago broadcast the first Kentucky Derby on May 2.

**Game played in Vancouver

1926

BASEBALL
National League

Team Name	W	L	Pct	GB	R	OR
St. Louis Cardinals	89	65	.578	-	817	678
Cincinnati Reds	87	67	.565	2	747	651
Pittsburgh Pirates	84	69	.549	4.5	769	689
Chicago Cubs	82	72	.532	7	682	602
New York Giants	74	77	.490	13.5	663	668
Brooklyn Dodgers	71	82	.464	17.5	623	705
Boston Braves	66	86	.434	22	624	719
Philadelphia Phillies	58	93	.384	29.5	687	900

Coaching Changes

St. Louis--Rogers Hornsby 89-65; Chicago--Joe McCarthy 82-72.

League Leaders

Batting Average		Home Runs		RBI	
Eugene Hargrave	.353	Lewis Wilson	21	Jim Bottomley	120
Walter Christensen	.350	Jim Bottomley	19	Lewis Wilson	109
Earl Smith	.346	Cy Williams	18	Les Bell	100
Cy Williams	.345	Les Bell	17	Bill Southworth	99
Paul Waner	.336	Bill Southworth	16	Wally Pipp	99

Stolen Bases		ERA		Wins	
Kiki Cuyler	35	Ray Kremer	2.61	Lee Meadows	20
Earl Adams	27	Charlie Root	2.82	Ray Kremer	20
Taylor Douthit	23	Jesse Petty	2.84	Pete Donahue	20
Frank Frisch	23	Fred Fitzsimmons	2.88	Flint Rhem	20
Ross Youngs	21	Tony Kaufmann	3.02	Carl Mays	19

Saves		Strikeouts	
Lloyd Davies	6	Dazzy Vance	140
Jack Scott	5	Charlie Root	127
Ray Kremer	5	Frank May	103
Rube Ehrhardt	4	Larry Benton	103
Joe Bush	3	Jesse Petty	101

American League

Team Name	W	L	Pct	GB	R	OR
New York Yankees	91	63	.591	-	847	713
Cleveland Indians	88	66	.571	3	738	612
Philadelphia Athletics	83	67	.553	6	677	570
Washington Senators	81	69	.540	8	802	761
Chicago White Sox	81	72	.529	9.5	730	665
Detroit Tigers	79	75	.513	12	793	830
St. Louis Browns	62	92	.403	29	682	845
Boston Red Sox	46	107	.301	44.5	562	835

Coaching Changes

None.

League Leaders

Batting Average

Henry Manush	.378
Babe Ruth	.372
Bob Fothergill	.367
Harry Heilmann	.367
George Burns	.358

Home Runs

Babe Ruth	47
Al Simmons	19
Tony Lazzeri	18
Ken Williams	17
Leon Goslin	17

RBI

Babe Ruth	155
George Burns	114
Tony Lazzeri	114
Al Simmons	109
Bibb Falk	108

Stolen Bases

John Mostil	35
Sam Rice	25
Bill Hunnefield	24
Earl McNeely	18
Joe Sewell	17

ERA

Robert Grove	2.51
George Uhle	2.83
Ted Lyons	3.01
Eddie Rommel	3.08
Stan Coveleski	3.12

Wins

George Uhle	27
Herb Pennock	23
Urban Shocker	19
Ted Lyons	18
Waite Hoyt	16

Saves

Fred Marberry	22
George Dauss	9
Robert Grove	6
Joe Pate	6
Sam Jones	5

Strikeouts

Robert Grove	194
George Uhle	159
Tom Thomas	127
Walter Johnson	125
Earl Whitehill	109

World Series

October 2	St. Louis Cardinals	1	at	New York Yankees	2
October 3	St. Louis Cardinals	6	at	New York Yankees	2
October 5	New York Yankees	0	at	St. Louis Cardinals	4
October 6	New York Yankees	10	at	St. Louis Cardinals	5
October 7	New York Yankees	3	at	St. Louis Cardinals	2 [10]
October 9	St. Louis Cardinals	10	at	New York Yankees	2
October 10	St. Louis Cardinals	3	at	New York Yankees	2

Individual Awards

League Award--Bob O'Farrell (St. Louis Cardinals NL)
George Burns (Cleveland Indians AL)

BASKETBALL
American Basketball League
First Half

Team Name	GP	W	L	Pct	GB
Brooklyn Arcadians	16	12	4	.750	-
Washington Palace Five	16	11	5	.688	1
Cleveland Rosenblums	16	10	6	.625	2
Rochester Centrals	16	9	7	.563	3
Ft. Wayne Caseys	16	7	9	.438	5
Boston Whirlwinds	16	6	10	.375	6
Chicago Bruins	16	6	10	.375	6
Detroit Paluski Post Five	16	6	10	.375	6
Buffalo Germans	16	5	11	.313	7

Second Half

Cleveland Rosenblums	14	13	1	.929	-
Washington Palace Five	14	11	3	.786	2
Rochester Centrals	14	9	5	.643	4
Brooklyn Arcadians	14	7	7	.500	6
Ft. Wayne Caseys	14	6	8	.429	7
Buffalo Germans	14	5	9	.357	8
Chicago Bruins	14	3	11	.214	10
Detroit Paluski Post Five	14	2	12	.143	11

Coaching *

Cleveland--Marty Friedman 23-7; Washington--Ray Kennedy 22-8; Brooklyn--Gary Schmeelk 19-11; Chicago--George Halas 9-21; Buffalo--Allie Heerdt 10-20

League Leaders

Field Goals		Free Throws		Points	
Rusty Saunders	74	Rusty Saunders	93	Rusty Saunders	241
Honey Russell	69	Ray Kennedy	86	Honey Russell	221
Ray Kennedy	67	Elmer Ripley	84	Ray Kennedy	220
Nat Hickey	66	Honey Russell	83	Elmer Ripley	200
Red Conaty	64	Marty Barry	77	Nat Hickey	196

ABL Playoffs

Cleveland beat Brooklyn 3 games to 2.

Notes

The American Basketball League was formed this year with Joe Carr as its head. Boston dropped out of the ABL after the first half.

*Not complete

FOOTBALL

National Football League

Team Name	GP	W	L	T	PF	PA	Pct
Frankford Yellow Jackets	16	14	1	1	236	49	.906
Chicago Bears	16	12	1	3	216	63	.844
Pottsville Maroons	13	10	2	1	155	29	.808
Kansas City Cowboys	11	8	3	0	76	53	.727
Green Bay Packers	13	7	3	3	151	61	.654
New York Giants	13	8	4	1	147	45	.654
Los Angeles Buccaneers	10	6	3	1	77	57	.650
Duluth Eskimos	14	6	5	3	113	81	.536
Buffalo Bisons	10	4	4	2	53	62	.500
Chicago Cardinals	12	5	6	1	74	98	.458
Providence Steam Roller	13	5	7	1	83	103	.423
Detroit Panthers	12	4	6	2	107	70	.417
Akron Indians	8	1	4	3	23	89	.313
Hartford Blues	10	3	7	0	57	99	.300
Brooklyn Lions	11	3	8	0	60	150	.273
Dayton Triangles	6	1	4	1	15	82	.250
Milwaukee Badgers	9	2	7	0	41	66	.222
Racine Tornadoes	5	1	4	0	8	92	.200
Canton Bulldogs	13	1	9	3	46	161	.192
Columbus Tigers	7	1	6	0	26	93	.143
Hammond Pros	4	0	4	0	3	56	.000
Louisville Colonels	4	0	4	0	0	108	.000

Coaching Changes

Los Angeles--Brick Muller & Tut Imlay 6-3-1; New York--Joe Alexander 8-4-1; Buffalo-- Jim Kendrick 4-4-2; Providence--Jim Laird 5-7-1; Hartford--Jack Keough 3-7-0; Brooklyn--Robert Berryman 3-8-0; Akron--Fritz Pollard & Rube Ursella 1-4-3; Racine--Hank Gillo & Wallace Barr 1-4-0; Columbus--John Heldt 1-6-0; Canton--Harry Robb & Pete Henry 1-9-3; Hammond--Doc Young 0-4-0; Louisville--Len Sachs 0-4-0.

League Leaders

Points		Field Goals	
Paddy Driscoll	86	Paddy Driscoll	12
Ernie Nevers	62	Al Bloodgood	8
Curly Oden	60	Johnny Budd	6
McBride	48	Ernie Nevers	4
Ben Jones	48	Red Dunn 4	

HOCKEY
National Hockey League

Team Name	GP	W	L	T	GF	GA	Pts	Pct
Ottawa Senators	36	24	8	4	77	42	52	.722
Montreal Maroons	36	20	11	5	91	73	45	.625
Pittsburgh Pirates	36	19	16	1	82	70	39	.542
Boston Bruins	36	17	15	4	92	85	38	.528
New York Americans	36	12	20	4	68	89	28	.389
Toronto St. Patricks	36	12	21	3	92	114	27	.375
Montreal Canadiens	36	11	24	1	79	108	23	.319

Coaching Changes

Pittsburgh--Odie Cleghorn 19-16-1; New York--Tommy Gorman 12-20-4; Canadiens--Cecil Hart 11-24-1.

League Leaders

Goals		Assists		Points	
Nels Stewart	34	Frank Nighbor	13	Nels Stewart	42
Carson Cooper	28	Cy Denneny	12	Cy Denneny	36
Jimmy Herberts	26	Aurel Joliat	9	Jimmy Herberts	31
Cy Denneny	24	Reginald Smith	9	Carson Cooper	31
Howie Morenz	23	Reg Noble	9	Howie Morenz	26

Penalty Minutes		GAA		Wins	
Bert Corbeau	121	Alex Connell	1.17	Alex Connell	24
Nels Stewart	119	Roy Worters	1.94	Clint Benedict	20
Harry Broadbent	112	Clint Benedict	2.03	Roy Worters	18
Bill Boucher	112	Charles Stewart	2.29	Charles Stewart	17
Albert Siebert	108	Vernon Forbes	2.47	Vernon Forbes	12

Shutouts	
Alex Connell	15
Roy Worters	7
Clint Benedict	6
Charles Stewart	6
Vernon Forbes	2

NHL Playoffs

March 20	Montreal Maroons	3	at	Pittsburgh Pirates	1
March 23	Pittsburgh Pirates	3	at	Montreal Maroons	3
March 25	Ottawa Senators	1	at	Montreal Maroons	1
March 27	Montreal Maroons	1	at	Ottawa Senators	0

Individual Awards

Hart Trophy--Nels Stewart (Montreal Maroons)
Lady Byng Trophy--Frank Nighbor (Ottawa Senators)

Rules

The delayed penalty rule was adopted in the NHL.

Western Hockey League

Team Name	GP	W	L	T	GF	GA	Pts	Pct
Edmonton Eskimos	30	19	11	0	94	77	38	.633
Saskatoon Crescents	30	18	11	1	93	64	37	.617
Victoria Cougars	30	15	11	4	68	53	34	.567
Portland Rosebuds	30	12	16	2	84	110	26	.433
Calgary Tigers	30	10	17	3	71	80	23	.383
Vancouver Maroons	30	10	18	2	64	90	22	.367

Coaching Changes

Portland--Pete Muldoon 12-16-2.

League Leaders

Goals		Assists		Points	
Bill Cook	31	Corb Denneny	15	Bill Cook	41
Dick Irvin	31	George Hay	12	Dick Irvin	36
Art Gagne	22	Harry Oliver	12	Art Gagne	33
Gordon Keats	19	Art Gagne	11	Corb Denneny	33
Corb Denneny	18	Gordon Keats	10	George Hay	31

GAA		Wins		Shutouts	
Harry Holmes	1.77	Herb Stuart	19	Hal Winkler	6
George Hainsworth	2.13	George Hainsworth	18	Harry Holmes	4
Herb Stuart	2.57	Harry Holmes	15	George Hainsworth	4
Hal Winkler	2.67	Red McCusker	12	Hugh Lehman	3
Hugh Lehman	3.00	Hal Winkler	10	Herb Stuart	2

WHL Playoffs

March 12	Victoria Cougars	3	at	Saskatoon Crescents	3
March 16	Saskatoon Crescents	0	at	Victoria Cougars	1
March 20	Edmonton Eskimos	1	at	Victoria Cougars	3
March 22	Victoria Cougars	2		Edmonton Eskimos	2**

Stanley Cup Playoffs

March 30	Victoria Cougars	0	at	Montreal Maroons	3
April 1	Victoria Cougars	0	at	Montreal Maroons	3
April 3	Victoria Cougars	3	at	Montreal Maroons	2
April 6	Victoria Cougars	0	at	Montreal Maroons	2

Notes

The Western Canada Hockey League dropped the word Canada from its name but this was its last season.

Franchise Changes

NHL--Hamilton Tigers became New York Americans.
WHL--Regina Capitals became Portland Rosebuds.
NFL--Duluth Kelleys changed name to Duluth Eskimos.
Akron Pros changed name to Akron Indians.

**Game played in Vancouver

Other Sports

Horseracing--Kentucky Derby won by Bubbling Over (time 2:03.8, purse $50,075).
Heavyweight Boxing--Gene Tunney beat Jack Dempsey in 10 rounds.
Golf--U.S. Open won by Bobby Jones with a score of 293.
Auto Racing--Indianapolis 500 won by Frank Lockhart (ave. speed 95.88 MPH).
Tennis--U.S. Open won by Rene Lacoste in the men's singles.
U.S. Open won by Norris Williams and Vincent Richards in the men's doubles.

1927

BASEBALL

National League

Team Name	W	L	Pct	GB	R	OR
Pittsburgh Pirates	94	60	.610	-	817	659
St. Louis Cardinals	92	61	.601	1.5	754	665
New York Giants	92	62	.597	2	817	720
Chicago Cubs	85	68	.556	8.5	750	661
Cincinnati Reds	75	78	.490	18.5	643	653
Brooklyn Dodgers	65	88	.425	28.5	541	619
Boston Braves	60	94	.390	34	651	771
Philadelphia Phillies	51	103	.331	43	678	903

Coaching Changes

Pittsburgh--Owen Bush 94-60; St. Louis--Bob O'Farrell 92-61; Philadelphia--John McInnis 51-103.

League Leaders

Batting Average		Home Runs		RBI	
Paul Waner	.380	Lewis Wilson	30	Paul Waner	131
Rogers Hornsby	.361	Cy Williams	30	Lewis Wilson	129
Lloyd Waner	.355	Rogers Hornsby	26	Rogers Hornsby	125
Riggs Stephenson	.344	Bill Terry	20	Jim Bottomley	124
Pie Traynor	.342	Jim Bottomley	19	Bill Terry	121

Stolen Bases		ERA		Wins	
Frank Frisch	48	Ray Kremer	2.47	Charlie Root	26
Max Carey	32	Grover Alexander	2.52	Jesse Haines	24
Harvey Hendrick	29	Dazzy Vance	2.70	Carmen Hill	22
Earl Adams	26	Jesse Haines	2.72	Grover Alexander	21
Lance Richbourg	24	Jesse Petty	2.98	Ray Kremer	19

Saves		Strikeouts	
Bill Sherdel	6	Dazzy Vance	184
George Mogridge	5	Charlie Root	145
Art Nehf	5	Frank May	121
Frank Henry	4	Burleigh Grimes	102
James Elliot	3	Jesse Petty	101

American League

Team Name	W	L	Pct	GB	R	OR
New York Yankees	110	44	.714	-	975	599
Philadelphia Athletics	91	63	.591	19	841	726
Washington Senators	85	69	.552	25	782	730
Detroit Tigers	82	71	.536	27.5	845	805
Chicago White Sox	70	83	.458	39.5	662	708
Cleveland Indians	66	87	.431	43.5	668	766
St. Louis Browns	59	94	.386	50.5	724	904
Boston Red. Sox	51	103	.331	59	597	856

Coaching Changes

Detroit--George Moriarty 82-71; Chicago--Ray Schalk 70-83; Cleveland--Jack McCallister 66-87; St. Louis--Dan Howley 59-94; Boston--Bill Carrigan 51-103.

League Leaders

Batting Average		Home Runs		RBI	
Harry Heilmann	.398	Babe Ruth	60	Lou Gehrig	175
Al Simmons	.392	Lou Gehrig	47	Babe Ruth	164
Lou Gehrig	.373	Tony Lazzeri	18	Leon Goslin	120
Bob Fothergill	.359	Ken Williams	17	Harry Heilmann	120
Ty Cobb	.357	Al Simmons	15	Bob Fothergill	114

Stolen Bases		ERA		Wins	
George Sisler	27	Waite Hoyt	2.63	Ted Lyons	22
Bob Meusel	24	Urban Shocker	2.84	Waite Hoyt	22
Johnny Neun	22	Ted Lyons	2.84	Robert Grove	20
Tony Lazzeri	22	Irving Hadley	2.85	Herb Pennock	19
Ty Cobb	22	Tom Thomas	2.98	Wilcy Moore	19

Saves		Strikeouts	
Garland Braxton	13	Robert Grove	174
Wilcy Moore	13	Rube Walberg	136
Robert Grove	9	Tom Thomas	107
Fred Marberry	9	Horace Lisenbee	105
Joe Pate	6	Garland Braxton	95

World Series

October 5	New York Yankees	5	at	Pittsburgh Pirates	4
October 6	New York Yankees	6	at	Pittsburgh Pirates	2
October 7	Pittsburgh Pirates	1	at	New York Yankees	8
October 8	Pittsburgh Pirates	3	at	New York Yankees	4

Individual Awards

League Award--Paul Waner (Pittsburgh Pirates NL)
Lou Gehrig (New York Yankees AL)

Notes

Ernest Barnard replaced Ban Johnson as President of the American League.

BASKETBALL
American Basketball League

First Half

Team Name	GP	W	L	Pct	GB
Cleveland Rosenblums	21	17	4	.810	-
Washington Palace Five	21	16	5	.762	1
Philadelphia Warriors	21	14	7	.667	3
Brooklyn Arcadians	21	13	8	.619	4
Ft. Wayne Hoosiers	21	8	13	.381	9
Rochester Centrals	21	8	13	.381	9
Chicago Bruins	21	7	14	.333	10
Baltimore Orioles	21	1	20	.048	16

Second Half

Brooklyn Arcadians	21	19	2	.905	-
Ft. Wayne Hoosiers	21	15	6	.714	4
Washington Palace Five	21	14	7	.667	5
Philadelphia Warriors	21	10	11	.476	9
Cleveland Rosenblums	21	9	12	.429	10
Chicago Bruins	21	6	15	.286	13
Rochester Centrals	21	6	15	.286	13
Baltimore Orioles	21	5	16	.238	14

Coaching Changes*

Philadelphia--Eddie Gottlieb 24-18; Baltimore--Johnny Beckman 6-36.

League Leaders

Field Goals		Free Throws		Points	
Rusty Saunders	119	Benny Borgmann	206	Rusty Saunders	399
Nat Hickey	103	Chick Passon	181	Benny Borgmann	380
Chick Passon	93	Ray Kennedy	172	Chick Passon	367
Johnny Beckman	91	Carl Husta	162	Nat Hickey	343
Benny Borgmann	87	Rusty Saunders	161	Carl Husta	330

ABL Playoffs

Brooklyn beat Cleveland 3 games to 0.

Notes

The Brooklyn and Detroit teams dropped out of the league after the start of the season. The games of the Detroit team were stricken from the standings and the record of the Brooklyn team was taken over by the New York Celtics which at the time was a non-league barnstorming team.

FOOTBALL

National Football League

Team Name	GP	W	L	T	PF	PA	Pct
New York Giants	13	11	1	1	197	20	.885
Green Bay Packers	10	7	2	1	113	43	.750
Chicago Bears	14	9	3	2	149	98	.714
Cleveland Bulldogs	13	8	4	1	209	107	.654
Providence Steam Roller	14	8	5	1	105	88	.607
New York Yankees	16	7	8	1	143	174	.469
Frankford Yellow Jackets	18	6	9	3	155	166	.417
Pottsville Maroons	13	5	8	0	80	163	.385
Chicago Cardinals	11	3	7	1	69	134	.318
Dayton Triangles	8	1	6	1	15	58	.188
Duluth Eskimos	9	1	8	0	68	134	.111
Buffalo Bisons	5	0	5	0	8	123	.000

Coaching Changes

Giants--Earl Potteiger 11-1-1; Cleveland--LeRoy Andrews 8-4-1; Providence--Jimmy Conzelman 8-5-1; Yankees--Ralph Scott 7-8-1; Frankford--Adolph Youngstrom 4-5-2, Charley Moran 2-4-1; Cardinals--Guy Chamberlin 3-7-1; Dayton--Lou Mahrt 1-6-1; Duluth--Ernie Nevers 1-8-0; Buffalo--Dim Batterson 0-5-0.

*Not complete

League Leaders

Points		Field Goals	
Jack McBride	57	Ken Mercer	5
Eddie Tryon	48	Gus Sonnenberg	3
Al Bloodgood	45	Charley Moran	3
Paddy Driscoll	45	Jack McBride	2
Ken Mercer	40	Paddy Driscoll	2

HOCKEY
National Hockey League

Canadian Division

Team Name	GP	W	L	T	GF	GA	Pts	Pct
Ottawa Senators	44	30	10	4	86	69	64	.727
Montreal Canadiens	44	28	14	2	99	67	58	.659
Montreal Maroons	44	20	20	4	71	68	44	.500
New York Americans	44	17	25	2	82	91	36	.409
Toronto Maple Leafs	44	15	24	5	79	94	35	.398

American Division

Team Name	GP	W	L	T	GF	GA	Pts	Pct
New York Rangers	44	25	13	6	95	72	56	.636
Boston Bruins	44	21	20	3	97	89	45	.511
Chicago Black Hawks	44	19	22	3	115	116	41	.466
Pittsburgh Pirates	44	15	26	3	79	108	33	.375
Detroit Cougars	44	12	28	4	76	105	28	.318

Coaching Changes

Ottawa--Dave Gill 30-10-4; Americans--Newsy Lalonde 17-25-2; Toronto--Conn Smythe 15-24-5; Rangers--Lester Patrick 25-13-6; Chicago--Pete Muldoon 19-22-3; Detroit--Art Duncan 12-18-4.

League Leaders

Goals		Assists		Points	
Bill Cook	33	Dick Irvin	18	Bill Cook	37
Howie Morenz	25	Frank Boucher	15	Dick Irvin	36
Cecil Dye	25	Frank Fredrickson	13	Howie Morenz	32
Billy Burch	19	Irvine Bailey	13	Frank Fredrickson	31
Frank Fredrickson	18	King Clancy	10	Cecil Dye	30

Penalty Minutes		GAA		Wins	
Nels Stewart	133	George Hainsworth	1.52	Alex Connell	30
Eddie Shore	130	Clint Benedict	1.52	George Hainsworth	28
Reginald Smith	125	Lorne Chabot	1.56	Lorne Chabot	22
Albert Siebert	116	Alex Connell	1.57	Clint Benedict	20
George Boucher	115	Hal Winkler	1.81	Hugh Lehman	19

Shutouts

George Hainsworth	14
Clint Benedict	13
Alex Connell	13
Lorne Chabot	10
Vernon Forbes	8

Stanley Cup Playoffs

March 29	Montreal Canadiens	1	at	Montreal Maroons	1
March 29	Boston Bruins	6		Chicago Black Hawks	1**
March 31	Montreal Maroons	0	at	Montreal Canadiens	1 [12:05]
March 31	Chicago Black Hawks	4	at	Boston Bruins	4
April 2	Ottawa Senators	4	at	Montreal Canadiens	0
April 2	New York Rangers	0	at	Boston Bruins	0
April 4	Montreal Canadiens	1	at	Ottawa Senators	1
April 4	Boston Bruins	3	at	New York Rangers	1
April 7	Ottawa Senators	0	at	Boston Bruins	0 [20:00]
April 9	Ottawa Senators	3	at	Boston Bruins	1
April 11	Boston Bruins	1	at	Ottawa Senators	1 [20:00]
April 13	Boston Bruins	1	at	Ottawa Senators	3

Individual Awards

Hart Trophy--Herb Gardiner (Montreal Canadiens)
Lady Byng Trophy--Billy Burch (New York Americans)
Vezina Trophy--George Hainsworth (Montreal Canadiens)

Notes

After the WHL disbanded many players joined the NHL. The Chicago Black Hawks were formed from the nucleus of the Portland Rosebuds.

Franchise Changes

NHL--Toronto St. Patricks changed name to Toronto Maple Leafs.
ABL--Ft. Wayne Caseys changed name to Ft. Wayne Hoosiers.

Other Sports

Horseracing--Kentucky Derby won by Whiskery (time 2:06, purse $51,000).
Heavyweight Boxing--Gene Tunney Defeated Jack Dempsey in a 10 round decision.
Golf--U.S. Open won by Tommy Armour in a playoff with Harry Cooper with a score of 301-301, 76-79.
Auto Racing--Indianapolis 500 won by George Souders (ave. speed 97.54 MPH).
Tennis--U.S. Open won by Rene Lacoste in the men's singles.
U.S. Open won by Bill Tilden and Francis Hunter in the men's doubles.

**Game played in New York

1928

BASEBALL
National League

Team Name	W	L	Pct	GB	R	OR
St. Louis Cardinals	95	59	.617	-	807	636
New York Giants	93	61	.604	2	807	653
Chicago Cubs	91	63	.591	4	714	615
Pittsburgh Pirates	85	67	.559	9	837	704
Cincinnati Reds	78	74	.513	16	648	686
Brooklyn Dodgers	77	76	.503	17.5	665	640
Boston Braves	50	103	.327	44.5	631	878
Philadelphia Phillies	43	109	.283	51	660	957

Coaching Changes

St. Louis--Bill McKechnie 95-59; Boston--Jack Slattery 11-20, Rogers Hornsby 39-83; Philadelphia--Burt Shotton 43-109.

League Leaders

Batting Average

Rogers Hornsby	.387
Paul Waner	.370
Fred Lindstrom	.358
George Sisler	.340
Floyd Herman	.340

Home Runs

Jim Bottomley	31
Lewis Wilson	31
Charles Hafey	27
Del Bissonette	25
Rogers Hornsby	21

RBI

Jim Bottomley	136
Pie Traynor	124
Lewis Wilson	120
Charles Hafey	111
Fred Lindstrom	107

Stolen Bases

Kiki Cuyler	37
Frank Frisch	29
Curt Walker	19
Fresco Thompson	19
Max Carey	18

ERA

Dazzy Vance	2.09
John Blake	2.47
Art Nehf	2.65
Bill Clark	2.68
Larry Benton	2.73

Wins

Larry Benton	25
Burleigh Grimes	25
Dazzy Vance	22
Bill Sherdel	21
Jesse Haines	20

Saves

Hal Haid	5
Bill Sherdel	5
Larry Benton	4
Hal Carlson	4
Bill Doak	3

Strikeouts

Dazzy Vance	200
Pat Malone	155
Charlie Root	122
Burleigh Grimes	97
Larry Benton	90

American League

Team Name	W	L	Pct	GB	R	OR
New York Yankees	101	53	.656	-	894	685
Philadelphia Athletics	98	55	.641	2.5	829	615
St. Louis Browns	82	72	.532	19	772	742
Washington Senators	75	79	.487	26	718	705
Chicago White Sox	72	82	.468	29	656	725
Detroit Tigers	68	86	.442	33	744	804
Cleveland Indians	62	92	.403	39	674	830
Boston Red Sox	57	96	.373	43.5	589	770

Coaching Changes

Chicago--Ray Schalk 32-42, Lena Blackburne 40-40; Cleveland--Roger Peckinpaugh 62-92.

League Leaders

Batting Average

Leon Goslin	.379
Henry Manush	.378
Lou Gehrig	.374
Al Simmons	.351
Tony Lazzeri	.332

Home Runs

Babe Ruth	54
Lou Gehrig	27
Leon Goslin	17
Joe Hauser	16
Al Simmons	15

RBI

Lou Gehrig	142
Babe Ruth	142
Bob Meusel	113
Henry Manush	108
Al Simmons	107

Stolen Bases

Charles Myer	30
Johnny Mostil	23
Harry Rice	20
Oswald Bluege	18
Bill Cissell	18

ERA

Garland Braxton	2.51
Herb Pennock	2.56
Robert Grove	2.58
Sam Jones	2.84
Jack Quinn	2.90

Wins

George Pipgras	24
Robert Grove	24
Waite Hoyt	23
Alvin Crowder	21
Sam Gray	20

Saves

Waite Hoyt	8
Willis Hudlin	7
Garland Braxton	6
Ted Lyons	6
Elam Vangilder	5

Strikeouts

Robert Grove	183
George Pipgras	139
Tom Thomas	129
Charles Ruffing	118
George Earnshaw	117

World Series

October 4	St. Louis Cardinals	1	at	New York Yankees	4
October 5	St. Louis Cardinals	3	at	New York Yankees	9
October 7	New York Yankees	7	at	St. Louis Cardinals	3
October 9	New York Yankees	7	at	St. Louis Cardinals	3

Individual Awards

League Award--Jim Bottomley (St. Louis Cardinals NL)
Mickey Cochrane (Philadelphia Athletics AL)

BASKETBALL
American Basketball League

Eastern Division

Team Name	GP	W	L	Pct	GB
New York Celtics	49	40	9	.899	-
Philadelphia Warriors	51	30	21	.588	11
(Washington Palace Five)	20	6	14	.300	19.5
(Brooklyn Visitations)	31	19	12	.613	7
Rochester Centrals	52	24	28	.462	17.5

Western Division

Team Name	GP	W	L	Pct	GB
Ft. Wayne Hoosiers	51	27	24	.529	-
Cleveland Rosenblums	51	22	29	.431	5
Detroit Cardinals	18	5	13	.278	11
Chicago Bruins	49	13	36	.265	13

Coaching Changes*

Cleveland--Dave Kerr 22-29; Ft. Wayne--Frank Morgenweck 27-24; New York--John Whitty 40-9; Chicago--George Halas 13-36.

League Leaders

Points

Davey Banks	406
Harry Topel	402
Benny Borgmann	391
Nat Hickey	356
Honey Russell	339

ABL Playoffs

Ft. Wayne beat Cleveland 2 games to 0. New York beat Philadelphia 2 games to 0.
New York beat Ft. Wayne 3 games to 1.

FOOTBALL
National Football League

Team Name	GP	W	L	T	PF	PA	Pct
Providence Steam Roller	11	8	1	2	128	42	.818
Frankford Yellow Jackets	16	11	3	2	175	84	.750
Detroit Wolverines	10	7	2	1	189	76	.750
Green Bay Packers	13	6	4	3	120	92	.577
Chicago Bears	13	7	5	1	182	85	.577
New York Giants	13	4	7	2	79	136	.385
New York Yankees	13	4	8	1	103	179	.346
Pottsville Maroons	10	2	8	0	74	134	.200
Chicago Cardinals	6	1	5	0	7	107	.167
Dayton Triangles	7	0	7	0	9	131	.000

*Not complete

Coaching Changes

Frankford--Ed Weir 11-3-2; Detroit--LeRoy Andrews 7-2-1; Yankees--Dick Rauch 4-8-1; Pottsville--Pete Henry 2-8-0; Cardinals--Fred Gillies 1-5-0; Dayton--Fay Abbott 0-7-0.

League Leaders

Points		Field Goals	
Verne Lewellen	54	Harry O'Boyle	2
Gibby Welch	48	Gus Sonnenberg	1
Ben Friedman	43	Fay Abbott	1
Tiny Feather	42	Bruce Caldwell	1
Ken Mercer	38	Red Dunn	1

HOCKEY
National Hockey League

Canadian Division

Team Name	GP	W	L	T	GF	GA	Pts	Pct
Montreal Canadiens	44	26	11	7	116	48	59	.670
Montreal Maroons	44	24	14	6	96	77	54	.614
Ottawa Senators	44	20	14	10	78	57	50	.568
Toronto Maple Leafs	44	18	18	8	89	88	44	.500
New York Americans	44	11	27	6	63	128	29	.330

American Division

Team Name	GP	W	L	T	GF	GA	Pts	Pct
Boston Bruins	44	20	13	11	77	70	51	.580
New York Rangers	44	19	16	9	94	79	47	.534
Pittsburgh Pirates	44	19	17	8	67	76	46	.523
Detroit Cougars	44	19	19	6	88	79	44	.500
Chicago Black Hawks	44	7	34	3	68	134	17	.139

Coaching Changes

Americans--Wilfred Green 11-27-6; Detroit--Jack Adams 19-19-6; Chicago--Barney Stanley 4-17-2, Hugh Lehman 3-17-1.

League Leaders

Goals		Assists		Points	
Howie Morenz	33	Howie Morenz	18	Howie Morenz	51
Aurel Joliat	28	Bill Cook	14	Aurel Joliat	39
Nels Stewart	27	George Hay	13	Frank Boucher	35
Frank Boucher	23	Frank Boucher	12	George Hay	35
George Hay	22	Sylvio Mantha	11	Nels Stewart	34

Penalty Minutes		GAA		Wins	
Eddie Shore	165	George Hainsworth	1.09	George Hainsworth	26
Ivan Johnson	146	Alex Connell	1.30	Clint Benedict	24
Albert Siebert	109	Hal Winkler	1.59	Alex Connell	20
Clarence Bowcher	106	Roy Worters	1.73	Hal Winkler	20
Aurel Joliat	105	Clint Benedict	1.73	Lorne Chabot	19

Shutouts

Hal Winkler	15
Alex Connell	15
George Hainsworth	13
Roy Worters	11
Lorne Chabot	11

Stanley Cup Playoffs

March 27	Montreal Maroons	1	at	Ottawa Senators	0
March 27	Pittsburgh Pirates	0	at	New York Rangers	4
March 29	Ottawa Senators	1	at	Montreal Maroons	2
March 29	Pittsburgh Pirates	4	at	New York Rangers	2
March 31	Montreal Canadiens	2	at	Montreal Maroons	2
April 1	Boston Bruins	1	at	New York Rangers	1
April 3	Montreal Maroons	1	at	Montreal Canadiens	0 [8:20]
April 3	New York Rangers	4	at	Boston Bruins	1
April 5	New York Rangers	0	at	Montreal Maroons	2
April 7	New York Rangers	2	at	Montreal Maroons	1 [7:05]
April 10	New York Rangers	0	at	Montreal Maroons	2
April 12	New York Rangers	1	at	Montreal Maroons	0
April 14	New York Rangers	2	at	Montreal Maroons	1

Individual Awards

Hart Trophy--Howie Morenz (Montreal Canadiens)
Lady Byng Trophy--Frank Boucher (New York Rangers)
Vezina Trophy--George Hainsworth (Montreal Canadiens)

Rules

Teams were to change ends after each period.

Franchise Changes

ABL--Brooklyn Arcadians changed name officially to New York Celtics.
Washington Palace Five became Brooklyn Visitation mid-way through the season.

Other Sports

Horseracing--Kentucky Derby won by Reigh Count (time 2:10.4, purse $55,375).
Heavyweight Boxing--Gene Tunney knocked-out Tom Heeney in 11 rounds.
Golf--U.S. Open won by John Farrell in a playoff with Bobby Jones (playoff rounds of 294-294, 143-144).
Auto Racing--Indianapolis 500 won by Louis Meyer (ave. speed of 99.48 MPH).
Tennis--U.S. Open won by Henri Cochet in the men's singles.
U.S. Open won by George Lott and John Hennessey in the men's doubles.

Notes

Gene Tunney retired this year after his fight with Heeney.

1929

BASEBALL
National League

Team Name	W	L	Pct	GB	R	OR
Chicago Cubs	98	54	.645	-	982	758
Pittsburgh Pirates	88	65	.575	10.5	904	780
New York Giants	84	67	.556	13.5	897	709
St. Louis Cardinals	78	74	.513	20	831	806
Philadelphia Phillies	71	82	.464	27.5	897	1032
Brooklyn Dodgers	70	83	.458	28.5	755	888
Cincinnati Reds	66	88	.429	33	686	760
Boston Braves	56	88	.364	43	657	876

Coaching Changes

Pittsburgh--Owen Bush 67-51, Jewel Ens 21-14; St. Louis--Bill Southworth 43-45, Charles Street 2-0, Bill McKechnie 33-29; Boston--Emil Fuchs 56-98.

League Leaders

Batting Average

Francis O'Doul	.398
Floyd Herman	.381
Rogers Hornsby	.380
Bill Terry	.372
Riggs Stephenson	.362

Home Runs

Charles Klein	43
Mel Ott	42
Rogers Hornsby	40
Lewis Wilson	39
Francis O'Doul	32

RBI

Lewis Wilson	159
Mel Ott	151
Rogers Hornsby	149
Charles Klein	145
Jim Bottomley	137

Stolen Bases

Kiki Cuyler	43
Evar Swanson	33
Frank Frisch	24
Floyd Herman	21
Ethan Allen	21

ERA

Bill Walker	3.09
Burleigh Grimes	3.13
Charlie Root	3.47
Pat Malone	3.57
Charles Lucas	3.60

Wins

Pat Malone	22
Charles Lucas	19
Charlie Root	19
Ray Kremer	18
Carl Hubbell	18

Saves

Guy Bush	8
John Morrison	8
Lou Koupal	6
Phil Collins	5
Steve Swetonic	5

Strikeouts

Pat Malone	166
Bill Clark	140
Dazzy Vance	126
Charlie Root	124
Carl Hubbell	106

American League

Team Name	W	L	Pct	GB	R	OR
Philadelphia Athletics	104	46	.693	-	901	615
New York Yankees	88	66	.571	18	899	775
Cleveland Indians	81	71	.533	24	717	736
St. Louis Browns	79	73	.520	26	733	713
Washington Senators	71	81	.467	34	730	776
Detroit Tigers	70	84	.455	36	926	928
Chicago White Sox	59	93	.388	46	627	792
Boston Red Sox	58	96	.377	48	605	803

Coaching Changes

New York--Miller Huggins 82-61, Art Fletcher 6-5; Washington--Walter Johnson 71-81; Detroit--Stanley "Bucky" Harris 70-84; Chicago--Lena Blackburne 50-93.

League Leaders

Batting Average		Home Runs		RBI	
Lew Fonseca	.369	Babe Ruth	46	Al Simmons	157
Al Simmons	.365	Lou Gehrig	35	Babe Ruth	154
Henry Manush	.355	Al Simmons	34	Dale Alexander	137
Tony Lazzeri	.354	Jimmie Foxx	33	Lou Gehrig	126
Jimmie Foxx	.354	Dale Alexander	25	Harry Heilmann	120

Stolen Bases		ERA		Wins	
Charlie Gehringer	28	Robert Grove	2.81	George Earnshaw	24
Bill Cissell	26	Fred Marberry	3.06	Wes Ferrell	21
Bing Miller	24	Tom Thomas	3.19	Robert Grove	20
Jack Rothrock	23	George Earnshaw	3.29	Fred Marberry	19
Roy Johnson	20	Willis Hudlin	3.34	George Pipgras	18

Saves		Strikeouts	
Fred Marberry	11	Robert Grove	170
Wilcy Moore	8	George Earnshaw	149
Bill Shores	7	George Pipgras	125
Wes Ferrell	5	Fred Marberry	121
Lil Stoner	4	Charles Ruffing	109

World Series

October 8	Philadelphia Athletics	3	at	Chicago Cubs	1
October 9	Philadelphia Athletics	9	at	Chicago Cubs	3
October 11	Chicago Cubs	3	at	Philadelphia Athletics	1
October 12	Chicago Cubs	8	at	Philadelphia Athletics	10
October 14	Chicago Cubs	2	at	Philadelphia Athletics	3

Individual Awards

League Award--Rogers Hornsby (Chicago Cubs NL)
Sporting News MVP--AL Simmons (Philadelphia Athletics AL)

Notes

On May 13, the New York Yankees and Cleveland Indians become the first teams to wear numbers on the backs of their uniforms on what will become a full time basis.

BASKETBALL
American Basketball League

First Half

Team Name	GP	W	L	Pct	GB
Cleveland Rosenblums	28	19	9	.679	-
Ft. Wayne Hoosiers	28	18	10	.643	1
Brooklyn Visitations	27	15	12	.556	3.5
Chicago Bruins	27	15	12	.556	3.5
New York Hakoahs	29	13	16	.448	6.5
Trenton Bengals	28	12	16	.429	7
Rochester Centrals	26	11	15	.423	7
Paterson Whirlwinds	25	6	19	.240	11.5

Second Half

Team Name	GP	W	L	Pct	GB
Ft. Wayne Hoosiers	14	11	3	.786	-
Brooklyn Visitations	14	10	4	.714	1
Cleveland Rosenblums	14	10	4	.714	1
Rochester Centrals	14	7	7	.500	4
New York Hakoahs	14	5	9	.357	6
Trenton Bengals	12	4	8	.333	6
Chicago Bruins	14	4	10	.286	7
Paterson Whirlwinds	12	3	9	.250	7

Coaching Changes*

Chicago--George Halas 19-22; Paterson--Frank Morgenweck 9-28.

League Leaders

Field Goals		Free Throws		Points	
Nat Hickey	124	Benny Borgmann	125	Benny Borgmann	325
Tom Barlow	120	Carl Husta	83	Nat Hickey	322
Lou Rabin	110	Al Kellett	79	Carl Husta	285
Red Conaty	107	Nat Hickey	74	Lou Rabin	274
Rusty Saunders	104	Johnny Beckman	67	Tom Barlow	274

ABL Playoffs

Cleveland beat Ft. Wayne 4 games to 0.

Notes

The American Basketball League named John J. O'Brien as league President.

*Not complete

FOOTBALL
National Football League

Team Name	GP	W	L	T	PF	PA	Pct
Green Bay Packers	13	12	0	1	198	22	.962
New York Giants	14	12	1	1	298	77	.893
Frankford Yellow Jackets	18	9	4	5	129	128	.639
Chicago Cardinals	13	6	6	1	154	83	.500
Boston Bulldogs	8	4	4	0	98	73	.500
Orange Tornadoes	11	3	4	4	35	80	.455
Staten Island Stapletons	10	3	4	3	89	65	.450
Providence Steam Roller	12	4	6	2	107	117	.417
Chicago Bears	14	4	8	2	110	207	.357
Buffalo Bisons	9	1	7	1	48	142	.167
Minneapolis Redjackets	10	1	9	0	42	185	.100
Dayton Triangles	6	0	6	0	7	136	.000

Coaching Changes

New York--LeRoy Andrews 12-1-1; Frankford--Russell Behman 9-4-5; Cardinals--Dewey Scanlon 6-6-1; Boston--Dick Rauch 4-4-0; Orange--John Depler 3-4-4; Staten Island--Doug Wycoff 3-4-3; Buffalo--Al Jolley 1-7-1; Minneapolis--Herb Joesting 1-9-0.

League Leaders

Points		Field Goals	
Ernie Nevers	85	Red Dunn	2
Tom Plansky	62	Ken Mercer	2
Len Sedbrook	60	Tony Plansky	2
Tony Latone	54	Chuck Weimer	2
Ray Flaherty	49	Herb Bizer	1

HOCKEY
National Hockey league

Canadian Division

Team Name	GP	W	L	T	GF	GA	Pts	Pct
Montreal Canadiens	44	22	7	15	71	43	59	.670
New York Americans	44	19	13	12	53	53	50	.568
Toronto Maple Leafs	44	21	18	5	85	69	47	.534
Ottawa Senators	44	14	17	13	54	67	41	.466
Montreal Maroons	44	15	20	9	67	65	39	.443

American Division

Team Name	GP	W	L	T	GF	GA	Pts	Pct
Boston Bruins	44	26	13	5	89	52	57	.648
New York Rangers	44	21	13	10	72	65	52	.591
Detroit Cougars	44	19	16	9	72	63	47	.534
Pittsburgh Pirates	44	9	27	8	46	80	26	.295
Chicago Black. Hawks	44	7	29	8	33	85	22	.250

Coaching Changes

Americans--Tommy Gorman 19-13-12; Boston--Cy Denneny 26-13-5; Chicago--Herb Gardiner 7-29-8.

League Leaders

Goals		Assists		Points	
Irvine Bailey	22	Frank Boucher	16	Irvine Bailey	32
Nels Stewart	21	Andy Blair	15	Nels Stewart	29
Carson Cooper	18	Gerry Lowrey	12	Carson Cooper	27
Howie Morenz	17	Irvine Bailey	10	Howie Morenz	27
Harry Oliver	17	Howie Morenz	10	Andy Blair	27

Penalty Minutes		GAA		Wins	
Mervyn Dutton	139	George Hainsworth	0.98	Cecil Thompson	26
Lionel Conacher	132	Cecil Thompson	1.18	George Hainsworth	22
Reginald Smith	120	Roy Worters	1.21	John Roach	21
Eddie Shore	96	Clarence Dolson	1.43	Lorne Chabot	20
Art Smith	91	John Roach	1.48	Clarence Dolson	19

Shutouts	
George Hainsworth	22
Roy Worters	13
John Roach	13
Cecil Thompson	12
Lorne Chabot	12

Stanley Cup Playoffs

March 19	New York Americans	0	at	New York Rangers	0
March 19	Toronto Maple Leafs	3	at	Detroit Cougars	1
March 19	Montreal Canadiens	0	at	Boston Bruins	1
March 21	New York Rangers	1	at	New York Americans	0 [29:50]
March 21	Detroit Cougars	1	at	Toronto Maple Leafs	4
March 21	Montreal Canadiens	0	at	Boston Bruins	1
March 23	Boston Bruins	3	at	Montreal Canadiens	2
March 24	Toronto Maple Leafs	0	at	New York Rangers	1
March 26	New York Rangers	2	at	Toronto Maple Leafs	1 [2:03]
March 28	New York Rangers	0	at	Boston Bruins	2
March 29	Boston Bruins	2	at	New York Rangers	1

Individual Awards

Hart Trophy--Roy Worters (New York Americans)
Lady Byng Trophy--Frank Boucher (New York Rangers)
Vezina Trophy--George Hainsworth (Montreal Canadiens)

Rules

The NHL introduced overtime this year. This was to be of 10 minutes duration and if the score was still tied at the end of this period the game was to be called a draw.

Franchise Changes

None

Other Sports

Horseracing--Kentucky Derby won by Clyde Van Dusen (time 2:10.8, purse $53,950).
Golf--U.S. Open won by Bobby Jones in a playoff with Al Espinosa (294-294, 141-164).
Auto Racing--Indianapolis 500 won Ray Keech (ave speed 97.58 MPH).
Tennis--U.S. Open won by Bill Tilden in the men's singles.
U.S. Open won by George Lott and John Doeg in the men's doubles.

1930

BASEBALL
National League

Team Name	W	L	Pct	GB	R	OR
St. Louis Cardinals	92	62	.597	-	1004	784
Chicago Cubs	90	64	.584	2	998	870
New York Giants	87	67	.565	5	959	814
Brooklyn Dodgers	86	68	.558	6	871	738
Pittsburgh Pirates	80	74	.519	12	891	928
Boston Braves	70	84	.455	22	693	835
Cincinnati Reds	59	95	.383	33	665	857
Philadelphia Phillies	52	102	.338	40	944	1199

Coaching Changes

St. Louis--Charles Street 92-62; Chicago--Joe McCarthy 86-64, Rogers Hornsby 4-0; Pittsburgh--Jewel Ens 80-74; Boston--Bill McKechnie 70-84; Cincinnati--Dan Howley 59-95.

League Leaders

Batting Average

Bill Terry	.401
Floyd Herman	.393
Charles Klein	.386
Francis O'Doul	.383
Fred Lindstrom	.379

Home Runs

Lewis Wilson	56
Charles Klein	40
Wally Berger	38
Gabby Hartnett	37
Floyd Herman	35

RBI

Lewis Wilson	190
Charles Klein	170
Kiki Cuyler	134
Floyd Herman	130
Bill Terry	129

Stolen Bases

Kiki Cuyler	37
Floyd Herman	18
Paul Waner	18
Joe Stripp	15
Frank Frisch	15

ERA

Dazzy Vance	2.61
Carl Hubbell	3.76
Bill Walker	3.93
Pat Malone	3.94
Burleigh Grimes	4.07

Wins

Pat Malone	20
Ray Kremer	20
Freddie Fitzsimmons	19
Carl Hubbell	17
Erv Brame	17

Saves

Herman Bell	8
Joe Heving	6
Bill Clark	6
Jim Lindsey	5
Steve Swetonic	5

Strikeouts

Bill Hallahan	177
Dazzy Vance	173
Pat Malone	142
Charlie Root	124
Carl Hubbell	117

American League

Team Name	W	L	Pct	GB	R	OR
Philadelphia Athletics	102	52	.662	-	951	751
Washington Senators	94	60	.610	8	892	689
New York Yankees	86	68	.558	16	1062	898
Cleveland Indians	81	73	.526	21	890	915
Detroit Tigers	75	79	.487	27	783	833
St. Louis Browns	64	90	.416	38	751	886
Chicago White Sox	62	92	.403	40	729	884
Boston Red Sox	52	102	.338	50	612	814

Coaching Changes

New York--Bob Shawkey 86-68; St. Louis--Bill Killefer 64-90; Chicago--Owen-Bush 62-92; Boston--Charles Wagner 52-102.

League Leaders

Batting Average		Home Runs		RBI	
Al Simmons	.381	Babe Ruth	49	Lou Gehrig	174
Lou Gehrig	.379	Lou Gehrig	41	Al Simmons	165
Babe Ruth	.359	Leon Goslin	37	Jimmie Foxx	156
Carl Reynolds	.359	Jimmie Foxx	37	Babe Ruth	153
Mickey Cochrane	.357	Al Simmons	36	Leon Goslin	138

Stolen Bases		ERA		Wins	
Marty McManus	23	Robert Grove	2.54	Robert Grove	28
Charlie Gehringer	19	Wes Ferrell	3.31	Wes Farrell	25
Roy Johnson	17	Walter Stewart	3.45	Ted Lyons	22
Leon Goslin	17	George Uhle	3.65	George Earnshaw	22
Joe Cronin	17	Irving Hadley	3.73	Walter Stewart	20

Saves		Strikeouts	
Robert Grove	9	Robert Grove	209
Jack Quinn	6	George Earnshaw	193
Garland Braxton	6	Irving Hadley	162
Charlie Sullivan	5	Wes Ferrell	143
Hal McKain	5	Charles Ruffing	131

World Series

October 1	St. Louis Cardinals	2	at	Philadelphia Athletics	5
October 2	St. Louis Cardinals	1	at	Philadelphia Athletics	6
October 4	Philadelphia Athletics	0	at	St. Louis Cardinals	5
October 5	Philadelphia Athletics	1	at	St. Louis Cardinals	3
October 6	Philadelphia Athletics	2	at	St. Louis Cardinals	0
October 8	St. Louis Cardinals	1	at	Philadelphia Athletics	7

Individual Awards

Baseball Writers Award--Hack Wilson (Chicago Cubs NL)
Joe Cronin (Washington Senators AL)
Sporting News MVP--Bill Terry (New York Giants NL)
Joe Cronin (Washington Senators AL)

BASKETBALL
American Basketball League

First Half

Team Name	GP	W	L	Pct	GB
Cleveland Rosenblums	24	17	7	.738	-
Brooklyn Visitations	24	15	9	.625	2
Rochester Centrals	24	14	10	.583	3
Ft. Wayne Hoosiers	24	12	12	.500	5
Chicago Bruins	24	12	12	.500	5
Paterson Whirlwinds	24	10	14	.417	7
Syracuse All-Americans	24	4	20	.167	13

Second Half

Team Name	GP	W	L	Pct	GB
Rochester Centrals	30	19	11	.633	-
Cleveland Rosenblums	30	18	12	.600	1
Chicago Bruins	30	17	13	.567	2
Brooklyn Visitations	30	15	15	.500	4
Ft. Wayne Hoosiers	30	13	17	.433	6
Paterson Whirlwinds	30	8	22	.267	11

Coaching Changes*

Rochester--Frank Morgenweck 36-18; Cleveland--Dave Kerr 35-19.

League Leaders

Field Goals		Free Throws		Points	
Benny Borgmann	149	Benny Borgmann	118	Benny Borgmann	416
Carl Husta	135	Gordon Chizmadia	117	Gordon Chizmadia	343
Nat Hickey	133	Davey Banks	63	Carl Husta	331
Davey Banks	122	Carl Husta	61	Nat Hickey	317
Gordon Chizmadia	113	Joe Brennan	61	Davey Banks	307

ABL Playoffs

Rochester	20	Cleveland	16
Cleveland	18	Rochester	17
Cleveland	23	Rochester	16
Cleveland	18	Rochester	13
Cleveland	21	Rochester	15

Notes

The Syracuse All-Americans and the New York Celtics joined the ABL this season but due to financial problems New York played only 10 games and then dropped out of the league. All of New York's games were stricken from the standings. Syracuse only played 20 games and then dropped out of the league, their remaining 4 games in the first half were forfeited to their scheduled opponents.

*Not complete

FOOTBALL
National Football League

Team Name	GP	W	L	T	PF	PA	Pct
New York Giants	17	13	4	0	308	98	.765
Green Bay Packers	14	10	3	1	234	111	.750
Chicago Bears	14	9	4	1	169	71	.679
Brooklyn Dodgers	12	7	4	1	154	59	.625
Providence Steam Roller	11	6	4	1	90	125	.591
Staten Island Stapletons	12	5	5	2	95	112	.500
Portsmouth Spartans	14	5	6	3	176	161	.464
Chicago Cardinals	13	5	6	2	128	132	.462
Frankford Yellow Jackets	18	4	13	1	113	321	.250
Minneapolis Redjackets	9	1	7	1	27	165	.167
Newark Tornadoes	12	1	10	1	51	190	.125

Coaching Changes

Bears--Ralph Jones 9-4-1; Brooklyn--Al Jolley 7-4-1; Cardinals--Ernie Nevers 5-6-2; Portsmouth--Hal Griffen 5-6-3; Minneapolis--George Gibson 1-7-1; Newark--John Depler 1-10-1.

League Leaders

Points		Field Goals	
Jack McBride	57	Frosty Peters	2
Ben Friedman	55	Ben Friedman	1
Vern Lewellen	54	Ernie Nevers	1
Ken Strong	53	Ken Strong	1
Ernie Nevers	48	Butch Meeker	1

HOCKEY
National Hockey League

Canadian Division

Team Name	GP	W	L	T	GF	GA	Pts	Pct
Montreal Maroons	44	23	16	5	141	114	51	.580
Montreal Canadiens	44	21	14	9	142	114	51	.580
Ottawa Senators	44	21	15	8	138	118	50	.568
Toronto Maple Leafs	44	17	21	6	116	124	40	.455
New York Americans	44	14	25	5	113	161	33	.375

American Division

Team Name	GP	W	L	T	GF	GA	Pts	Pct
Boston Bruins	44	38	5	1	179	98	77	.875
Chicago Black Hawks	44	21	18	5	117	111	47	.534
New York Rangers	44	17	17	10	136	143	44	.500
Detroit Cougars	44	14	24	6	117	133	34	.386
Pittsburgh Pirates	44	5	36	3	102	185	13	.148

Coaching Changes

Maroons--Duncan Munro 23-16-5; Ottawa--Edward "Newsy" Lalonde 21-15-8; Americans--Lionel Conacher 14 25-5; Boston--Art Ross 38-5-1; Chicago--Tom Shaughnessy 10-8-3, Bill Tobin 11-10-2; Pittsburgh--Frank Fredrickson 5-36-3.

League Leaders

Goals		**Assists**		**Points**	
Ralph Weiland	43	Frank Boucher	36	Ralph Weiland	73
Dit Clapper	41	Norman Gainor	31	Frank Boucher	62
Howie Morenz	40	Ralph Weiland	30	Dit Clapper	61
Nels Stewart	39	Bill Cook	30	Bill Cook	59
Hector Kilrea	36	King Clancy	23	Hector Kilrea	58

Penalty Minutes		**GAA**		**Wins**	
Joe Lamb	119	Cecil Thompson	2.23	Cecil Thompson	38
Sylvio Mantha	108	James Walsh	2.47	Alex Connell	21
Eddie Shore	105	Chuck Gardiner	2.52	Chuck Gardiner	21
Red Dutton	98	George Hainsworth	2.57	George Hainsworth	20
Harvey Rockburn	97	Lorne Chabot	2.69	John Roach	17

Shutouts	
Lorne Chabot	6
George Hainsworth	4
Cecil Thompson	3
Chuck Gardiner	3
James Walsh	2

Stanley Cup Playoffs

March 20	New York Rangers	1	at	Ottawa Senators	1
March 20	Boston Bruins	2	at	Montreal Maroons	1 [45:35]
March 22	Boston Bruins	4	at	Montreal Maroons	2
March 23	Montreal Canadiens	1	at	Chicago Black Hawks	0
March 23	Ottawa Senators	2	at	New York Rangers	5
March 25	Montreal Maroons	1	at	Boston Bruins	0 [26:37]
March 26	Chicago Black Hawks	2	at	Montreal Maroons	2 [51:43]
March 27	Montreal Maroons	1	at	Boston Bruins	5
March 28	New York Rangers	1	at	Montreal Canadiens	2 [68:52]
March 30	Montreal Canadiens	2	at	New York Rangers	0
April 1	Montreal Canadiens	3	at	Boston Bruins	0
April 3	Boston Bruins	3	at	Montreal Canadiens	4

Individual Awards

Hart Trophy--Nels Stewart (Montreal Maroons)
Lady Byng Trophy--Frank Boucher (New York Rangers)
Vezina Trophy--Cecil Thompson (Boston Bruins)

Rules

Kicking the puck was made legal in all areas of the ice.
Forward passing was now allowed within all three zones but not across the bluelines.
Offsides were abolished altogether which permitted players to stand anywhere on the ice regardless of where the puck was. This rule itself was done away with one-third of the way through the year.

Franchise Changes

NFL--Orange Tornadoes became the Newark Tornadoes.

Other Sports

Horseracing--Kentucky Derby won by Gallant Fox (time 2:07.6 purse $50,725).
Heavyweight Boxing--Max Schmeling defeated Jack Sharkey in 4 rounds when Sharkey fouled Schmeling.
Golf--U.S. Open won by Bobby Jones with a score of 287.
Auto Racing--Indianapolis 500 won by William Arnold (ave. speed 100.488 MPH).
Tennis--U.S. Open won by John Doeg in the men's singles.
U.S. Open won by George Lott and John Doeg in the men's doubles.

1931

BASEBALL
National League

Team Name	W	L	Pct	GB	R	OR
St. Louis Cardinals	101	53	.656	-	815	614
New York Giants	87	65	.572	13	768	599
Chicago Cubs	84	70	.545	17	828	710
Brooklyn Dodgers	79	73	.520	21	681	673
Pittsburgh Pirates	75	79	.487	26	636	691
Philadelphia Phillies	66	88	.429	35	684	828
Boston Braves	64	90	.416	37	533	680
Cincinnati Red	58	96	.377	43	592	742

Coaching Changes

Chicago--Rogers Hornsby 84-70.

League Leaders

Batting Average

Charles Hafey	.349
Bill Terry	.349
Jim Bottomley	.348
Charles Klein	.337
Francis O'Doul	.336

Home Runs

Charles Klein	31
Mel Ott	29
Wally Berger	19
Floyd Herman	18
Russell Arlett	18

RBI

Charles Klein	121
Mel Ott	115
Bill Terry	112
Pie Traynor	103
Floyd Herman	97

Stolen Bases

Frank Frisch	28
Floyd Herman	17
John Martin	16
Earl Adams	16
George Watkins	15

ERA

Bill Walker	2.26
Carl Hubbell	2.66
Ed Brandt	2.92
Henry Meine	2.98
Syl Johnson	3.00

Wins

Bill Hallahan	19
James Elliot	19
Henry Meine	19
Paul Derringer	18
Ed Brandt	18

Saves

Jack Quinn	15
Jim Lindsey	7
James Elliot	5
Bill Hallahan	4
Phil Collins	4

Strikeouts

Bill Hallahan	159
Carl Hubbell	156
Dazzy Vance	150
Paul Derringer	134
Charlie Root	131

American League

Team Name	W	L	Pct	GB	R	OR
Philadelphia Athletics	107	45	.704	-	858	626
New York Yankees	94	59	.614	13.5	1067	760
Washington Senators	92	62	.597	16	843	691
Cleveland Indians	78	76	.506	30	885	833
St. Louis Browns	63	91	.409	45	722	870
Boston Red. Sox	62	90	.408	45	625	800
Detroit Tigers	61	93	.396	47	651	836
Chicago White Sox	56	97	.366	51.5	704	939

Coaching Changes

New York--Joe McCarthy 94-59; Boston--John Collins 62-90.

League Leaders

Batting Average		Home Runs		RBI	
Al Simmons	.390	Babe Ruth	46	Lou Gehrig	184
Babe Ruth	.373	Lou Gehrig	46	Babe Ruth	163
Eddie Morgan	.351	Earl Averill Sr.	32	Earl Averill Sr.	143
Mickey Cochrane	.349	Jimmie Foxx	30	Al Simmons	128
Lou Gehrig	.341	Leon Goslin	24	Joe Cronin	126

Stolen Bases		ERA		Wins	
Ben Chapman	61	Robert Grove	2.06	Robert Grove	31
Roy Johnson	33	Lefty Gomez	2.63	Wes Ferrell	22
Jack Burns	19	Lloyd Brown	3.20	Lefty Gomez	21
Tony Lazzeri	18	Fred Marberry	3.45	George Earnshaw	21
Bill Cissell	18	George Uhle	3.50	Rube Walberg	20

Saves		Strikeouts	
Wilcy Moore	10	Robert Grove	175
Irving Hadley	8	George Earnshaw	152
Chad Kimsey	7	Lefty Gomez	150
Fred Marberry	7	Charles Ruffing	132
George Earnshaw	6	Irving Hadley	124

World Series

October 1	Philadelphia Athletics	6	at	St. Louis Cardinals	2
October 2	Philadelphia Athletics	0	at	St. Louis Cardinals	2
October 5	St. Louis Cardinals	5	at	Philadelphia Athletics	2
October 6	St. Louis Cardinals	0	at	Philadelphia Athletics	3
October 7	St. Louis Cardinals	5	at	Philadelphia Athletics	1
October 9	Philadelphia Athletics	8	at	St. Louis Cardinals	1
October 10	Philadelphia Athletics	2	at	St. Louis Cardinals	4

Individual Awards

Baseball Writers Award--Frank Frisch (St. Louis Cardinals NL)
Robert Grove (Philadelphia Athletics AL)
Sporting News MVP--Charles Klein (Philadelphia Phillies NL)
Lou Gehrig (New York Yankees AL)

Rules

A fair ball which bounces over or through a fence or into the stands is considered a ground rule double instead of a home run (NL and AL).

Notes

William Harridge replaced Ernest Barnard as President of the American League.

BASKETBALL
American Basketball League

First Half

Team Name	GP	W	L	Pct	GB
Brooklyn Visitations	21	14	7	.667	-
Ft. Wayne Hoosiers	22	13	9	.591	1.5
Rochester Centrals	19	10	9	.526	3
Paterson Crescents	18	9	9	.500	3.5
Cleveland Rosenblums	12	6	6	.500	3.5
Toledo Red Man Tobaccos	21	8	13	.381	6
Chicago Bruins	21	7	14	.333	7

Second Half

Team Name	GP	W	L	Pct	GB
Ft. Wayne Hoosiers	16	11	5	.688	-
Chicago Bruins	16	11	5	.688	-
Brooklyn Visitations	16	8	8	.500	3
Rochester Centrals	15	5	10	.333	5
Toledo Red Man Tobaccos	15	4	11	.274	6.5

Coaching Changes

Not Available.

League Leaders

Field Goals		Free Throws		Points	
Benny Borgmann	111	Benny Borgmann	68	Benny Borgmann	290
Davey Banks	94	Davey Banks	66	Davey Banks	254
Willie Scrill	87	Al Kellett	55	Manny Hirsch	211
Manny Hirsch	81	Manny Hirsch	49	Willie Scrill	203
Frank Shimek	78	Frank Shimek	47	Frank Shimek	203

ABL Playoffs

Ft. Wayne 20 Chicago 16
Brooklyn beat Ft. Wayne 4 games to 2.

Rules

A rule was instituted in the ABL which prohibited a player from holding the ball in the foul lane for more than 3 seconds.

Notes

This was the last season for the ABL as a major league.
Cleveland and Paterson dropped out of the ABL mid-way through the season. Ft. Wayne defeated Chicago 1 game to 0 to decide the winner of the second half of the ABL season.

FOOTBALL
National Football League

Team Name	GP	W	L	T	PF	PA	Pct
Green Bay Packers	14	12	2	0	291	87	.857
Portsmouth Spartans	14	11	3	0	175	77	.786
Chicago Bears	13	8	5	0	145	92	.615
Chicago Cardinals	9	5	4	0	120	128	.556
New York Giants	14	7	6	1	154	100	.536
Providence Steam Roller	11	4	4	3	78	127	.500
Staten Island Stapletons	11	4	6	1	79	118	.409
Cleveland Indians	10	2	8	0	45	137	.200
Frankford Yellow Jackets	8	1	6	1	13	99	.188
Brooklyn Dodgers	14	2	12	0	64	199	.143

Coaching Changes

Portsmouth--George "Potsy" Clark 11-3-0; Chicago Cardinals--LeRoy Andrews 1-2-0, Ernie Nevers 4-2-0; Providence--Ed Robinson 4-4-3; Staten Island--Hinky Haines 4-6-1; Cleveland--Harry Workman 2-8-0; Brooklyn--John Depler 2-12-0.

League Leaders

Points		Field Goals	
Johnny Blood	72	Ken Strong	2
Ernie Nevers	66	Ernie Nevers	1
Dutch Clark	60	Hap Moran	1
Ken Strong	53	Glenn Presnell	1
Red Grange	42	Luke Johnses	1

HOCKEY
National Hockey League

Canadian Division

Team Name	GP	W	L	T	GF	GA	Pts	Pct
Montreal Canadiens	44	26	10	8	129	89	60	.682
Toronto Maple Leafs	44	22	13	9	118	99	53	.602
Montreal Maroons	44	20	18	6	105	106	46	.523
New York Americans	44	18	16	10	76	74	46	.523
Ottawa Senators	44	10	30	4	91	142	24	.273

American Division

Team Name	GP	W	L	T	GF	GA	Pts	Pct
Boston Bruins	44	28	10	6	143	90	62	.705
New York Rangers	44	23	17	8	134	112	54	.614
Chicago Black Hawks	44	24	17	3	108	78	51	.580
Detroit Falcons	44	16	21	7	102	105	39	.443
Philadelphia Quakers	44	4	36	4	76	184	12	.136

Coaching Changes

Toronto--Conn Smythe 1-0-1, Art Duncan 21-13-8; Maroons--Duncan Munro 14-13-5, George Boucher 6-5-1; Americans--Eddie Gerard 18-16-10; Chicago--Dick Irvin 24-17-3; Philadelphia--Cooper Smeaton 4-36-4.

League Leaders

Goals

Charlie Conacher	31
Bill Cook	30
Howie Morenz	28
Nels Stewart	25
Ebbie Goodfellow	25

Assists

Joe Primeau	32
Frank Boucher	27
Ebbie Goodfellow	23
Howie Morenz	23
Aurel Joliat	22

Points

Howie Morenz	51
Ebbie Goodfellow	48
Charlie Conacher	43
Irvin Bailey	42
Bill Cook	42

Penalty Minutes

Harvey Rockburn	118
Eddie Shore	105
D'Arcy Coulson	103
Art Shields	98
Joe Lamb	91

GAA

Roy Worters	1.68
Chuck Gardiner	1.77
John Roach	1.98
George Hainsworth	2.02
Cecil Thompson	2.05

Wins

Cecil Thompson	28
George Hainsworth	26
Chuck Gardiner	24
Lorne Chabot	21
John Roach	19

Shutouts

Chuck Gardiner	12
George Hainsworth	8
Roy Worters	8
John Roach	7
Lorne Chabot	6

Stanley Cup Playoffs

March 24	Chicago Black Hawks	2	at	Toronto Maple Leafs	2
March 24	Montreal Maroons	1	at	New York Rangers	5
March 24	Montreal Canadiens	4	at	Boston Bruins	5 [18:56]
March 26	Toronto Maple Leafs	1	at	Chicago Black Hawks	2 [19:20]
March 26	New York Rangers	3	at	Montreal Maroons	0
March 26	Montreal Canadiens	1	at	Boston Bruins	0
March 28	Boston Bruins	2	at	Montreal Canadiens	4 [5:10]
March 29	New York Rangers	0	at	Chicago Black Hawks	2
March 30	Boston Bruins	3	at	Montreal Canadiens	1
March 31	Chicago Black Hawks	1	at	New York Rangers	0
April 1	Boston Bruins	2	at	Montreal Canadiens	3 [19:00]
April 3	Montreal Canadiens	2	at	Chicago Black Hawks	1
April 5	Montreal Canadiens	1	at	Chicago Black Hawks	2 [24:50]
April 9	Chicago Black Hawks	3	at	Montreal Canadiens	2 [53:50]
April 11	Chicago Black Hawks	2	at	Montreal Canadiens	4
April 14	Chicago Black Hawks	0	at	Montreal Canadiens	2

All Star Teams

First Team		Second Team
Charlie Gardiner	Goal	Cecil Thompson
Eddie Shore	Defense	Sylvio Mantha
King Clancy	Defense	Ivan Johnson
Howie Morenz	Center	Frank Boucher
Bill Cook	Right Wing	Aubrey Clapper
Aurel Joliat	Left Wing	Frederick Cook
Lester Patrick	Coach	Dick Irvin

Individual Awards

Hart Trophy--Howie Morenz (Montreal Canadiens)
Lady Byng Trophy--Frank Boucher (New York Rangers)
Vezina Trophy--Roy Worters (New York Americans)

Notes

In a playoff game between the Canadiens and Bruins, Bruins coach Art Ross pulled his goaltender in favor of an extra attacker. It was the first time this tactic had ever been tried in hockey.

Rules

Forward passing was allowed from the neutral zone across the attacking blueline as long as no attacking player preceded the puck into the zone.

Franchise Changes

NHL--Detroit Cougars changed name to Detroit Falcons.
Pittsburgh Pirates became the Philadelphia Quakers.
ABL--Paterson Whirlwinds changed name to Paterson Crescents.

Other Sports

Horseracing--Kentucky Derby won by Twenty Grand (time 2:01.8, purse $48,725).
Heavyweight Boxing--Max Schmeling knocked-out Young Stribling in 15 rounds.
Golf--U.S. Open won by Billy Burke in a playoff with George Von Elm (scores of 292-292, 149-149, 148-149).
Auto Racing--Indianapolis 500 won by Louis Schneider (ave. speed 96.629 MPH).
Tennis--U.S. Open won by H. Ellsworth Vines in the men's singles.
U.S. Open won by Wilmer Allison and John Van Ryn in the men's doubles.

1932

BASEBALL

National League

Team Name	W	L	Pct	GB	R	OR
Chicago Cubs	90	64	.584	-	720	633
Pittsburgh Pirates	86	68	.558	4	701	711
Brooklyn Dodgers	81	73	.526	9	752	747
Philadelphia Phillies	78	76	.506	12	844	796
Boston Braves	77	77	.500	13	649	655
New York Giants	72	82	.468	18	755	706
St. Louis Cardinals	72	82	.468	18	684	717
Cincinnati Reds	60	94	.390	30	575	715

Coaching Changes

Chicago--Rogers Hornsby 53-44, Charlie Grimm 37-20; Pittsburgh--George Gibson 86-68; Brooklyn--Max Carey 81-73; New York--John McGraw 17-23, Bill Terry 55-59.

League Leaders

Batting Average		Home Runs		RBI	
Francis O'Doul	.368	Charles Klein	38	Don Hurst	143
Bill Terry	.350	Mel Ott	38	Charles Klein	137
Charles Klein	.348	Bill Terry	28	Art Whitney	124
Paul Waner	.341	Don Hurst	24	Lewis Wilson	123
Don Hurst	.339	Lewis Wilson	23	Mel Ott	123

Stolen Bases		ERA		Wins	
Charles Klein	20	Lon Warneke	2.37	Lon Warneke	22
Tony Piet	19	Carl Hubbell	2.50	Bill Clark	20
Frank Frisch	18	Walter Betts	2.80	Guy Bush	19
George Watkins	18	Steve Swetonic	2.82	Carl Hubbell	18
George Davis	16	Charles Lucas	2.94	Larry French	18

Saves		Strikeouts	
Jack Quinn	8	Jay Dean	191
Ray Benge	6	Carl Hubbell	137
Ben Cantwell	5	Pat Malone	120
Dolf Luque	5	James Carleton	113
Joe Shaute	4	Bob Brown	110

American League

Team Name	W	L	Pct	GB	R	OR
New York Yankees	107	47	.695	-	1002	724
Philadelphia Athletics	94	60	.610	13	981	752
Washington Senators	93	61	.604	14	840	716
Cleveland Indians	87	65	.572	19	845	747
Detroit Tigers	76	75	.503	29.5	799	787
St. Louis Browns	63	91	.409	44	736	898
Chicago White Sox	49	102	.325	56.5	667	897
Boston Red Sox	43	111	.279	64	566	915

Coaching Changes

Chicago--Lew Fonseca 49-102; Boston--John Collins 11-46, Marty McManus 32-65.

League Leaders

Batting Average		Home Runs		RBI	
Dale Alexander	.367	Jimmie Foxx	58	Jimmie Foxx	169
Jimmie Foxx	.364	Babe Ruth	41	Lou Gehrig	151
Lou Gehrig	.349	Al Simmons	35	Al Simmons	151
Henry Manush	.342	Lou Gehrig	34	Babe Ruth	137
Babe Ruth	.341	Earl Averill	32	Earl Averill	124

Stolen Bases		ERA		Wins	
Ben Chapman	38	Robert Grove	2.84	Alvin Crowder	26
Gerald Walker	30	Charles Ruffing	3.09	Robert Grove	25
Roy Johnson	20	Ted Lyons	3.28	Lefty Gomez	24
Bill Cissell	18	Alvin Crowder	3.33	Wes Ferrell	23
Lu Blue	17	Tom Bridges	3.36	Monte Weaver	22

Saves		Strikeouts	
Fred Marberry	13	Charles Ruffing	190
Wilcy Moore	8	Robert Grove	188
Chester Hogsett	7	Lefty Gomez	176
Robert Grove	7	Irving Hadley	145
Urban Faber	6	George Pipgras	111

World Series

September 28	Chicago Cubs	6	at	New York Yankees	12
September 29	Chicago Cubs	2	at	New York Yankees	5
October 1	New York Yankees	7	at	Chicago Cubs	5
October 2	New York Yankees	13	at	Chicago Cubs	6

Individual Awards

Baseball Writers Award--Charles Klein (Philadelphia Phillies NL)
Jimmie Foxx (Philadelphia Athletics AL)
Sporting News MVP--Charles Klein (Philadelphia Phillies NL)
Jimmie Foxx (Philadelphia Athletics AL)

FOOTBALL
National Football League

Team Name	GP	W	L	T	PF	PA	Pct
Green Bay Packers	14	10	3	1	152	63	.750
Chicago Bears	14	7	1	6	160	44	.714
Portsmouth Spartans	12	6	2	4	116	71	.667
Boston Braves	10	4	4	2	55	79	.500
New York Giants	12	4	6	2	93	113	.417
Brooklyn Dodgers	12	3	9	0	63	131	.250
Chicago Cardinals	10	2	6	2	72	114	.300
Staten Island Stapletons	12	2	7	3	77	173	.292

Coaching Changes
Boston--Lud Wray 4-4-2; Brooklyn--Ben Friedman 3-9-0; Cardinals--Jack Chevigny 2-6-2; Staten Island--Hal Hanson 2-7-3.

League Leaders

Points		Field Goals	
Dutch Clark	55	Dutch Clark	3
Red Grange	42	Tiny Engebretsen	1
Ray Flaherty	30	Ben Friedman	1
Jack Grossman	30	Stu Wilson	1
Luke Johnses	26		

Rules
Passing was legalized anywhere behind the line of scrimmage.

HOCKEY
National Hockey League

Canadian Division

Team Name	GP	W	L	T	GF	GA	Pts	Pct
Montreal Canadiens	48	25	16	7	128	111	57	.594
Toronto Maple Leafs	48	23	18	7	133	127	53	.552
Montreal Maroons	48	19	22	7	142	139	45	.469
New York Americans	48	16	24	8	95	142	40	.417

American Division

Team Name	GP	W	L	T	GF	GA	Pts	Pct
New York Rangers	48	23	17	8	134	112	54	.563
Chicago Black Hawks	48	18	19	11	86	101	47	.490
Detroit Falcons	48	18	20	10	95	108	46	.479
Boston Bruins	48	15	21	12	122	117	42	.438

Coaching Changes
Toronto--Art Duncan 0-3-2, Dick Irvin 23-15-5; Maroons--Sprague Cleghorn 19-22-7; Chicago--Emil Iverson 18-19-11.

League Leaders

Goals

Charlie Conacher	34
Bill Cook	34
Harvey Jackson	28
Howie Morenz	24
Cecil Dillon	23

Assists

Joe Primeau	37
Reginald Smith	33
Harvey Jackson	25
Howie Morenz	25
Aurel Joliat	24

Points

Harvey Jackson	53
Joe Primeau	50
Howie Morenz	49
Charlie Conacher	48
Bill Cook	48

Penalty Minutes

Red Dutton	107
Ivan Johnson	106
Red Horner	97
Dave Trottier	94
Earl Seibert	88

GAA

Chuck Gardiner	1.92
Alex Connell	2.25
George Hainsworth	2.29
John Roach	2.33
Lorne Chabot	2.41

Wins

George Hainsworth	25
John Roach	23
Lorne Chabot	22
Alex Connell	18
Chuck Gardiner	18

Shutouts

John Roach	9
Cecil Thompson	9
George Hainsworth	6
Alex Connell	6
Roy Worters	5

Stanley Cup Playoffs

March 24	New York Rangers	3	at	Montreal Canadiens	4
March 26	New York Rangers	4	at	Montreal Canadiens	3 [59:32]
March 27	Montreal Canadiens	0	at	New York Rangers	1
March 27	Toronto Maple Leafs	0	at	Chicago Black Hawks	2
March 27	Montreal Maroons	1	at	Detroit Falcons	1
March 29	Chicago Black Hawks	0	at	Toronto Maple Leafs	6
March 29	Montreal Canadiens	2	at	New York Rangers	5
March 31	Toronto Maple Leafs	1	at	Montreal Maroons	1
April 2	Montreal Maroons	2	at	Toronto Maple Leafs	3 [17:59]
April 5	Toronto Maple Leafs	6	at	New York Rangers	4
April 7	Toronto Maple Leafs	6		New York Rangers	2*
April 9	New York Rangers	4	at	Toronto Maple Leafs	6

All Star Teams

First Team		Second Team
Charlie Gardiner	Goal	Roy Worters
Eddie Shore	Defense	Sylvio Mantha
Ivan Johnson	Defense	King Clancy
Howie Morenz	Center	Reginald Smith
Bill Cook	Right Wing	Charlie Conacher
Harvey Jackson	Left Wing	Aurel Joliat
Lester Patrick	Coach	Dick Irvin

*Game played in Boston

Individual Awards

Hart Trophy--Howie Morenz (Montreal Canadiens)
Lady Byng Trophy--Joe Primeau (Toronto Maple Leafs)
Vezina Trophy--Chuck Gardiner (Chicago Black Hawks)

Franchise Changes

None

Other Sports

Horseracing--Kentucky Derby won by Burgoo King (time 2:05.2, purse $52,350).
Heavyweight Boxing--Jack Sharkey defeated Max Schmeling in a 15 round decision.
Golf--U.S. Open won by Gene Sarazen with a score of 286.
Auto Racing--Indianapolis 500 won by Fred Frame (ave. speed 104.144 MPH).
Tennis--U.S. Open won by H. Ellsworth Vines in the men's singles.
U.S. Open won by H. Ellsworth Vines and Keith Gledhill in the men's doubles.

1933

BASEBALL
National League

Team Name	W	L	Pct	GB	R	OR
New York Giants	91	61	.599	-	636	515
Pittsburgh Pirates	87	67	.565	5	667	619
Chicago Cubs	86	68	.558	6	646	536
Boston Braves	83	71	.539	9	552	531
St. Louis Cardinals	82	71	.536	9.5	687	609
Brooklyn Dodgers	65	88	.425	26.5	617	695
Philadelphia Phillies	60	92	.395	31	607	760
Cincinnati Reds	58	94	.382	33	496	643

Coaching Changes

New York--Bill Terry 91-61; Chicago--Charlie Grimm 86-68; St. Louis--Charles Street 46-45, Frank Frisch 36-26; Cincinnati--Owen Bush 58-94.

League Leaders

Batting Average		Home Runs		RBI	
Charles Klein	.368	Charles Klein	28	Charles Klein	120
Virgil Davis	.349	Wally Berger	27	Wally Berger	106
Tony Piet	.323	Mel Ott	23	Mel Ott	103
Bill Terry	.322	Joe Medwick	18	Joe Medwick	98
Wes Schulmerich	.318	Johnny Vergez	16	Joe Vaughan	97

Stolen Bases		ERA		Wins	
John Martin	26	Carl Hubbell	1.66	Carl Hubbell	23
Frank Frisch	18	Lon Warneke	2.00	Ben Cantwell	20
Charles Fullis	18	Hal Schumacher	2.16	Guy Bush	20
Charles Klein	15	Ed Brandt	2.60	Jay Dean	20
Ernie Orsatti	14	Charlie Root	2.60	Hal Schumacher	19

Saves		Strikeouts	
Phil Collins	6	Jay Dean	199
Herman Bell	5	Carl Hubbell	156
Bill M. Harris	5	Jim Carleton	147
Carl Hubbell	5	Lon Warneke	133
Dolf Luque	4	Roy Parmelee	132

American League

Team Name	W	L	Pct	GB	R	OR
Washington Senators	99	53	.651	-	850	665
New York Yankees	91	59	.607	7	927	768
Philadelphia Athletics	79	72	.523	19.5	875	853
Cleveland Indians	75	76	.497	23.5	654	669
Detroit Tigers	75	79	.487	25	722	733
Chicago White Sox	67	83	.447	31	683	814
Boston Red Sox	63	86	.423	34.5	700	758
St. Louis Browns	55	96	.364	43.5	669	820

Coaching Changes

Washington--Joe Cronin 99-53; Cleveland--Roger Peckinpaugh 26-25, Walter Johnson 49-51; Boston--Marty McManus 63-86; St. Louis--Bill Killefer 34-59, Al Sothoron 1-3, Rogers Hornsby 20-34; Detroit--Stanley "Bucky" Harris 73-79, Del Baker 2-0.

League Leaders

Batting Average		Home Runs		RBI	
Jimmie Foxx	.356	Jimmie Foxx	48	Jimmie Foxx	163
Henry Manush	.336	Babe Ruth	34	Lou Gehrig	139
Lou Gehrig	.334	Lou Gehrig	32	Al Simmons	119
Al Simmons	.331	Bob Johnson	21	Joe Cronin	118
Charlie Gehringer	.325	Tony Lazzeri	18	Joe Kuhel	107

Stolen Bases		ERA		Wins	
Ben Chapman	27	Monte Pearson	2.33	Alvin Crowder	24
Gerald Walker	26	Mel Harder	2.95	Robert Grove	24
Evar Swanson	19	Tom Bridges	3.09	Earl Whitehill	22
Joe Kuhel	17	Lefty Gomez	3.18	Oral Hildebrand	16
Bill Werber	15	Robert Grove	3.20	Lefty Gomez	16

Save		Strikeouts	
Jack Russell	13	Lefty Gomez	163
Chester Hogsett	9	Irving Hadley	149
Wilcy Moore	8	Charles Huffing	122
Robert Grove	6	Tom Bridges	120
Joe Heving	6	Johnny Allen	119

All-Star Game

(Comiskey Park, Chicago)

July 6	American League	4	National League	2

World Series

October 3	Washington Senators	2	at	New York Giants	4
October 4	Washington Senators	1	at	New York Giants	6
October 5	New York Giants	0	at	Washington Senators	4
October 6	New York Giants	2	at	Washington Senators	1 [11]
October 7	New York Giants	4	at	Washington Senators	3

Individual Awards

Baseball Writers Award--Carl Hubbell (New York Giants NL)
Jimmie Foxx (Philadelphia Athletics AL)
Sporting News MVP--Carl Hubbell (New York Giants NL)
Jimmie Foxx (Philadelphia Athletics AL)

FOOTBALL
National Football League

East Division

Team Name	GP	W	L	T	PF	PA	Pct
New York Giants	14	11	3	0	244	101	.786
Brooklyn Dodgers	10	5	4	1	93	54	.550
Boston Redskins	12	5	5	2	103	97	.500
Philadelphia Eagles	9	3	5	1	77	158	.389
Pittsburgh Pirates	11	3	6	2	67	208	.364

West Division

Team Name	GP	W	L	T	PF	PA	Pct
Chicago Bears	13	10	2	1	133	82	.808
Portsmouth Spartans	11	6	5	0	128	87	.545
Green Bay Packers	13	5	7	1	170	107	.423
Cincinnati Reds	10	3	6	1	38	110	.350
Chicago Cardinals	11	1	9	1	52	101	.136

Coaching Changes

Brooklyn--Cap McEwen 5-4-1; Boston--"Lone Star" Dietz 5-5-2; Philadelphia--Lud Wray 3-5-1: Pittsburgh--Tap Dauds 3-6-2; Chicago Bears--George Halas 10-2-1; Cincinnati--Al Jolley 0-3-0, Mike Palm 3-3-1; Chicago Cardinals--Paul Schissler 1-9-1.

League Leaders

Yards Rushing		Yards Passing		Passing %	
Jim Musick	809	Harry Newman	973	Ben Friedman	53
Cliff Battles	737	Glenn Presnell	774	Bob Monnet	50
Bronko Nagurski	533	Arnie Herber	656	Chris Cagle	42
Glenn Presnell	522	Ben Friedman	597	Arnie Herber	40
Swede Hanson	494	Keith Molesworth	421	Harry Newman	39

Receiving Yards		Receptions		Field Goals	
Paul Moss	383	"Shipwreck" Kelly	22	Ken Strong	5
Ray Tesser	274	Bill Hewitt	16	Jack Manders	5
Bill Hewitt	274	Roger Grove	15	Glenn Presnell	5
"Shipwreck" Kelly	246	Lavie Dilweg	14	Algy Clark	4
Lavie Dilweg	225	Ray Tesser	14	Mose Kelsch	3

NFL Championship

December 17	New York Giants	21	at	Chicago Bears	23

Rules

The ball was to be brought in ten yards from the sidelines on any play ending within 5 yards of the sidelines.

HOCKEY
National Hockey League

Canadian Division

Team Name	GP	W	L	T	GF	GA	Pts	Pct
Toronto Maple Leafs	48	24	18	6	119	111	54	.563
Montreal Maroons	48	22	20	6	135	119	50	.521
Montreal Canadiens	48	18	25	5	92	115	41	.427
New York Americans	48	15	22	11	91	118	41	.427
Ottawa Senators	48	11	27	10	88	131	32	.333

American Division

Team Name	GP	W	L	T	GF	GA	Pts	Pct
Boston Bruins	48	25	15	8	124	88	58	.604
Detroit Falcons	48	25	15	8	111	93	58	.604
New York Rangers	48	23	17	8	135	107	54	.563
Chicago Black Hawks	48	16	20	12	88	101	44	.458

Coaching Changes

Toronto--Dick Irvin 24-18-6; Maroons--Eddie Gerard 22-20-6; Canadiens--Edward "Newsy" Lalonde 18-25-5; Americans--Joe Simpson 15-22-11; Ottawa--Cy Denneny 11-27-10; Chicago--Emil Iverson 8-9-6, Tommy Gorman 8-11-6.

League Leaders

Goals		Assists		Points	
Bill Cook	28	Frank Boucher	28	Bill Cook	50
Harvey Jackson	27	Eddie Shore	27	Harvey Jackson	44
Marty Barry	24	Paul Haynes	25	Larry Northcott	43
Fred Cook	22	Norman Himes	25	Reg Smith	41
Larry Northcott	22	Johnny Gagnon	23	Paul Haynes	41

Penalty Minutes		GAA		Wins	
Red Horner	144	Cecil Thompson	1.83	Cecil Thompson	25
Ivan Johnson	127	John Roach	1.94	John Roach	25
Art Shields	119	Chuck Gardiner	2.10	Lorne Chabot	24
Eddie Shore	102	Andy Aitkenhead	2.23	Andy Aitkenhead	23
Vern Ayres	97	David Kerr	2.32	George Hainsworth	18

Shutouts	
Cecil Thompson	11
John Roach	9
George Hainsworth	7
Lorne Chabot	5
Chuck Gardiner	5

Stanley Cup Playoffs

March 25	Detroit Falcons	2	at	Montreal Maroons	0
March 25	Toronto Maple Leafs	1	at	Boston Bruins	2 [14:14]
March 26	Montreal Canadiens	2	at	New York Rangers	5
March 28	Montreal Maroons	2	at	Detroit Falcons	3
March 28	New York Rangers	3	at	Montreal Canadiens	3
March 28	Toronto Maple Leafs	1	at	Boston Bruins	0 [15:03]
March 30	Boston Bruins	2	at	Toronto Maple Leafs	1 [4:23]
March 30	Detroit Falcons	0	at	New York Rangers	2
April 1	Boston Bruins	3	at	Toronto Maple Leafs	5
April 2	New York Rangers	4	at	Detroit Falcons	3
April 3	Boston Bruins	0	at	Toronto Maple Leafs	1 [104:46]
April 4	Toronto Maple Leafs	1	at	New York Rangers	5
April 8	New York Rangers	3	at	Toronto Maple Leafs	1
April 11	New York Rangers	2	at	Toronto Maple Leafs	3
April 13	New York Rangers	1	at	Toronto Maple Leafs	0 [7:33]

All Star Teams

First Team		Second Team
John Roach	Goal	Charlie Gardiner
Eddie Shore	Defense	King Clancy
Ivan Johnson	Defense	Lionel Conacher
Frank Boucher	Center	Howie Morenz
Bill Cook	Right Wing	Charlie Conacher
Lawrence Northcott	Left Wing	Harvey Jackson
Lester Patrick	Coach	Dick Irvin

Individual Awards

Calder Trophy--Carl Voss (New York Rangers/Detroit Falcons)
Hart Trophy--Eddie Shore (Boston Bruins)
Lady Byng Trophy--Frank Boucher (New York Rangers)
Vezina Trophy--Cecil Thompson (Boston Bruins)

Rules

Playing with a broken stick was made illegal.

Notes

The National Hockey League abolished the two referee officiating system in favor of a referee and a judge of play who would be responsible for calling off-sides.

Franchise Changes

NFL--Boston Braves changed name to Boston Redskins.

Other Sports

Horseracing--Kentucky Derby won by Broker's Tip (time 2:06.8, purse $48,925).
Heavyweight Boxing--Primo Carnera knocked-out Jack Sharkey in 6 rounds.
Primo Carnera defeated Paulino Uzcudun in 15 rounds.
Golf--U.S. Open won by Johnny Goodman with a score of 287.
Auto Racing--Indianapolis 500 won by Louis Meyer (ave. speed 104.089 MPH).
Tennis--U.S. Open won by Fred Perry in the men's singles.
U.S. Open won by George Lott and Lester Stoefen in the men's doubles.

1934

BASEBALL
National League

Team Name	W	L	Pct	GB	R	OR
St. Louis Cardinals	95	58	.621	-	799	656
New York Giants	93	60	.608	2	760	583
Chicago Cubs	86	65	.570	8	705	639
Boston Braves	78	73	.517	16	683	714
Pittsburgh Pirates	74	76	.493	19.5	735	713
Brooklyn Dodgers	71	81	.467	23.5	748	795
Philadelphia Phillies	56	93	.376	37	675	794
Cincinnati Reds	52	99	.344	42	590	801

Coaching Changes

St. Louis--Frank Frisch 95-58; Pittsburgh--George Gibson 27-24, Harold Traynor--47-52; Brooklyn--Casey Stengel 71-81; Philadelphia--Jim Wilson 56-93; Cincinnati--Bob O'Farrell 26-58, Burt Shotton 1-0, Chuck Dressen 25-41.

League Leaders

Batting Average		Home Runs		RBI	
Paul Waner	.362	Mel Ott	35	Mel Ott	135
Bill Terry	.354	Jim Collins	35	Jim Collins	128
Kiki Cuyler	.338	Wally Berger	34	Wally Berger	121
Jim Collins	.333	Gabby Hartnett	22	Joe Medwick	106
Joe Vaughan	.333	Chuck Klein	20	Gus Suhr	103

Stolen Bases		ERA		Wins	
John Martin	23	Carl Hubbell	2.30	Jay Dean	30
Kiki Cuyler	15	Jay Dean	2.66	Hal Schumacher	23
Dick Bartell	13	Curt Davis	2.95	Lon Warneke	22
Danny Taylor	12	Fred Fitzsimmons	3.04	Carl Hubbell	21
Stan Hack	11	Bill Walker	3.12	Paul Dean	19

Saves		Strikeouts	
Carl Hubbell	8	Jay Dean	195
Dolf Luque	7	Van Mungo	184
Jay Dean	7	Paul Dean	150
Herman Bell	6	Lon Warneke	143
Al Smith	5	Paul Derringer	122

Notes

The Cincinnati Reds became the first team to fly by airplane to another city for a road game.

American League

Team Name	W	L	Pct	GB	R	OR
Detroit Tigers	101	53	.656	-	958	708
New York Yankees	94	60	.610	7	842	669
Cleveland Indians	85	69	.552	16	814	763
Boston Red Sox	76	76	.500	24	820	775
Philadelphia Athletics	68	82	.453	31	764	838
St. Louis Browns	67	85	.441	33	674	800
Washington Senators	66	86	.434	34	729	806
Chicago White Sox	53	99	.349	47	704	946

Coaching Changes

Detroit--Mickey Cochrane 101-53; Cleveland--Walter Johnson 85-69; Boston--Stanley Harris 76-76; St.Louis--Rogers Hornsby 67-85; Chicago--Lew Fonseca 4-13, Jimmy Dykes 49-86.

League Leaders

Batting Average		Home Runs		RBI	
Lou Gehrig	.363	Lou Gehrig	49	Lou Gehrig	165
Charlie Gehringer	.356	Jimmie Foxx	44	Hal Trosky	142
Henry Manush	.349	Hal Trosky	35	Hank Greenberg	139
Al Simmons	.344	Bob Johnson	34	Jimmie Foxx	130
Joe Vosmik	.341	Earl Averill	31	Charlie Gehringer	127

Stolen Bases		ERA		Wins	
Bill Werber	40	Lefty Gomez	2.33	Lefty Gomez	26
Joyner White	28	Mel Harder	2.61	Tom Rowe	24
Ben Chapman	26	John Murphy	3.12	Tom Bridges	22
Pete Fox	25	Eldon Auker	3.42	Mel Harder	20
Gerald Walker	20	Tom Rowe	3.45	Charles Ruffing	19

Saves		Strikeouts	
Jack Russell	7	Lefty Gomez	158
Lloyd Brown	6	Tom Bridges	151
Bobo Newsom	5	Tom Rowe	149
Joe Heving	4	Charles Ruffing	149
Jack Knott	4	Monte Pearson	140

All-Star Game

(Polo Grounds, New York)

July 10	American League	9	National League	7

World Series

October 3	St. Louis Cardinals	8	at	Detroit Tigers	3
October 4	St. Louis Cardinals	2	at	Detroit Tigers	3 [12]
October 5	Detroit Tigers	1	at	St. Louis Cardinals	4
October 6	Detroit Tigers	10	at	St. Louis Cardinals	4
October 7	Detroit Tigers	3	at	St. Louis Cardinals	1
October 8	St. Louis Cardinals	4	at	Detroit Tigers	3
October 9	St. Louis Cardinals	11	at	Detroit Tigers	0

Individual Awards

Baseball Writers Award--Jay Dean (St. Louis Cardinals NL)
Mickey Cochrane (Detroit Tigers AL)
Sporting News MVP--Jay Dean (St. Louis Cardinals NL)
Lou Gehrig (New York Yankees AL)

FOOTBALL
National Football League
East Division

Team Name	GP	W	L	T	PF	PA	Pct
New York Giants	13	8	5	0	147	107	.615
Boston Redskins	12	6	6	0	107	94	.500
Brooklyn Dodgers	11	4	7	0	61	153	.364
Philadelphia Eagles	11	4	7	0	127	85	.364
Pittsburgh Pirates	12	2	10	0	51	206	.167

West Division

Team Name	GP	W	L	T	PF	PA	Pct
Chicago Bears	13	13	0	0	286	86	1.000
Detroit Lions	13	10	3	0	238	59	.769
Green Bay Packers	13	7	6	0	156	112	.538
Chicago Cardinals	11	5	6	0	80	84	.455
(Cincinnati Reds)	8	0	8	0	10	243	.000
(St. Louis Gunners)	3	1	2	0	27	61	.333

Coaching Changes

Pittsburgh--Luby DiMelio 2-10-0; Detroit--Potsy Clark 10-3-0; Cincinnati--Algy Clark 0-8-0; St. Louis--Mike Palm 1-2-0.

League Leaders

Yards Rushing		Yards Passing		Passing % (40 attempts)	
Beattie Feathers	1004	Arnie Herber	799	Dutch Clark	47
Swede Hanson	805	Warren Heller	511	Harry Newman	38
Dutch Clark	763	Dutch Clark	383	Arnie Herber	37
Bronko Nagurski	586	Harry Newman	366	Bob Monnet	34
Warren Heller	528	Harp Vaughan	272	Ed Matesic	33

Receiving Yards		Receptions		Field Goals	
Harry Eliding	257	Joe Carter	16	Jack Manders	10
Joe Carter	238	Red Badgro	16	Ken Strong	4
Joe Skladany	222	Ben Smith	12	Ralph Kercheval	4
Red Badgro	206	Charley Malone	11	Dutch Clark	4
Ben Smith	190	Joe Skladany	10	Glenn Presnell	4

NFL Championship

December 9	Chicago Bears	13	at	New York Giants	30

Notes

The Cincinnati Reds of the NFL folded with 3 games remaining in the season and a new team was formed. This team was called the St. Louis Gunners, an independent team which had been operating in the area.

HOCKEY
National Hockey League

Canadian Division

Team Name	GP	W	L	T	GF	GA	Pts	Pct
Toronto Maple Leafs	48	26	13	9	174	119	61	.635
Montreal Canadiens	48	22	20	6	99	101	50	.521
Montreal Maroons	48	19	18	11	117	122	49	.510
New York Americans	48	15	23	10	104	132	40	.417
Ottawa Senators	48	13	29	6	115	143	32	.333

American Division

Team Name	GP	W	L	T	GF	GA	Pts	Pct
Detroit Red Wings	48	24	14	10	113	98	58	.604
Chicago Black Hawks	48	20	17	11	88	83	51	.531
New York Rangers	48	21	19	8	120	113	50	.521
Boston Bruins	48	18	25	5	111	130	41	.427

Coaching Changes

Ottawa--George Boucher 13-29-6; Chicago--Tom Gorman 20-17-11.

League Leaders

Goals		Assists		Points	
Charlie Conacher	32	Joe Primeau	32	Charlie Conacher	52
Marty Barry	27	Frank Boucher	30	Joe Primeau	46
Aurel Joliat	22	Cecil Dillon	26	Frank Boucher	44
John Sorrell	21	Elwin Romnes	21	Marty Barry	39
Nels Stewart	21	Charlie Conacher	20	Cecil Dillon	39

Penalty Minutes		GAA		Wins	
Red Horner	146	Wilfred Cude	1.57	George Hainsworth	26
Lionel Conacher	87	Chuck Gardiner	1.73	Lorne Chabot	21
Ivan Johnson	86	Roy Worters	2.08	Andy Aitkenhead	21
Nels Stewart	68	Lorne Chabot	2.15	Chuck Gardiner	20
Earl Seibert	66	Andy Aitkenhead	2.35	Dave Kerr	19

Shutouts	
Chuck Gardiner	10
Lorne Chabot	8
Andy Aitkenhead	7
Dave Kerr	6
Wilfred Cude	5

Stanley Cup Playoffs

March 20	New York Rangers	0	at	Montreal Maroons	0
March 22	Chicago Black Hawks	3	at	Montreal Canadiens	2
March 22	Detroit Red Wings	2	at	Toronto Maple Leafs	1 [1:33]
March 24	Detroit Red Wings	6	at	Toronto Maple Leafs	3
March 25	Montreal Canadiens	1	at	Chicago Black Hawks	1 [11:05]
March 25	Montreal Maroons	2	at	New York Rangers	1
March 26	Toronto Maple Leafs	3	at	Detroit Red Wings	1
March 28	Toronto Maple Leafs	5	at	Detroit Red Wings	1
March 28	Chicago Black Hawks	3	at	Montreal Maroons	0
March 30	Toronto Maple Leafs	0	at	Detroit Red Wings	1
April 1	Montreal Maroons	2	at	Chicago Black Hawks	3
April 3	Chicago Black Hawks	2	at	Detroit Red Wings	1
April 5	Chicago Black Hawks	4	at	Detroit Red Wings	1
April 8	Detroit Red Wings	5	at	Chicago Black Hawks	2
April 10	Detroit Red Wings	0	at	Chicago Black Hawks	1 [30:05]

All Star Teams

First Team		Second Team
Charlie Gardiner	Goal	Roy Worters
King Clancy	Defense	Eddie Shore
Lionel Conacher	Defense	Ivan Johnson
Frank Boucher	Center	Joe Primeau
Charlie Conacher	Right Wing	Bill Cook
Harvey Jackson	Left Wing	Aurel Joliat
Lester Patrick	Coach	Dick Irvin

Individual Awards

Calder Trophy--Russ Blinco (Montreal Maroons)
Hart Trophy--Aurel Joliat (Montreal Canadiens)
Lady Byng Trophy--Frank Boucher (New York Rangers)
Vezina Trophy--Chuck Gardiner (Chicago Black Hawks)

Franchise Changes

NHL--Detroit Falcons changed name to Detroit Red Wings.
NFL--Portsmouth Spartans became the Detroit Lions.

Other Sports

Horseracing--Kentucky Derby won by Cavalcade (time 2:04, purse $28,175).
Heavyweight Boxing--Primo Carnera defeated Tommy Loughran in 15 rounds.
Max Baer knocked-out Primo Carnera in 11 rounds.
Golf--U.S. Open won by Olin Dutra with a score of 293.
Auto Racing--Indianapolis 500 won by William Cummings (ave. speed 104.863 MPH)
Tennis--U.S. Open won by Fred Perry in the men's singles.
U.S. Open won by George Lott and Lester Stoefen in the men's doubles.

1935

BASEBALL

National League

Team Name	W	L	Pct	GB	R	OR
Chicago Cubs	100	54	.649	-	847	597
St. Louis Cardinals	96	58	.623	4	829	625
New York Giants	91	62	.595	8.5	770	675
Pittsburgh Pirates	86	67	.562	13.5	743	647
Brooklyn Dodgers	70	83	.458	29.5	711	767
Cincinnati Reds	68	85	.444	31.5	646	772
Philadelphia Phillies	64	89	.418	35.5	685	871
Boston Braves	38	115	.248	61.5	575	852

Coaching Changes

Pittsburgh--Harold Traynor 86-67; Cincinnati--Chuck Dressen 68-85.

League Leaders

Batting Average		Home Runs		RBI	
Joe Vaughan	.385	Wally Berger	34	Wally Berger	130
Joe Medwick	.353	Mel Ott	31	Joe Medwick	126
Gabby Hartnett	.344	Dolf Camilli	25	Jim Collins	122
Ernie Lombardi	.343	Jim Collins	23	Mel Ott	114
Billy Herman	.341	Joe Medwick	23	Hank Leiber	107

Stolen Bases		ERA		Wins	
August Galan	22	Cy Blanton	2.58	Jay Dean	28
John Martin	20	Bill Swift	2.70	Carl Hubbell	23
Frenchy Bordagaray	18	Hal Schumacher	2.89	Paul Derringer	22
Ival Goodman	14	Larry French	2.96	Bill Lee	20
Stan Hack	14	Bill Lee	2.96	Lon Warneke	20

Saves		Strikeouts	
Emil Leonard	8	Jay Dean	182
Syl Johnson	6	Carl Hubbell	150
Waite Hoyt	6	Van Mungo	143
Don Brennan	5	Paul Dean	143
Allyn Stout	5	Cy Blanton	142

Notes

Ford Frick succeeded John Heydler as President of the National League.
The first night game between major league baseball teams was played on May 24th, when the Cincinnati Reds defeated the Phillies 2 to 1 in Cincinnati.

American League

Team Name	W	L	Pct	GB	R	OR
Detroit Tigers	93	58	.616	-	919	665
New York Yankees	89	60	.597	3	818	632
Cleveland Indians	82	71	.536	12	776	739
Boston Red Sox	78	75	.510	16	718	732
Chicago White Sox	74	78	.487	19.5	738	750
Washington Senators	67	86	.438	27	823	903
St. Louis Browns	65	87	.428	28.5	718	930
Philadelphia Athletics	58	91	.389	34	710	869

Coaching Changes

Cleveland--Walter Johnson 46-48, Steve O'Neill 36-23; Boston--Joe Cronin 78-75; Chicago--Jim Dykes 74-78; Washington--Stanley Harris 67-86.

League Leaders

Batting Average		Home Runs		RBI	
Charles Myer	.349	Jimmie Foxx	36	Hank Greenberg	170
Joe Vosmik	.348	Hank Greenberg	36	Lou Gehrig	119
Jimmie Foxx	.346	Lou Gehrig	30	Jimmie Foxx	115
Roger Cramer	.332	Bob Johnson	28	Hal Trosky	113
Charlie Gehringer	.330	Hal Trosky	26	Julius Solters	112

Stolen Bases		ERA		Wins	
Bill Werber	29	Robert Grove	2.70	Wes Ferrell	25
Lyn Lary	28	Ted Lyons	3.02	Mel Harder	22
Mel Almada	20	Charles Ruffing	3.12	Tom Bridges	21
Joyner White	19	Lefty Gomez	3.18	Robert Grove	20
Ben Chapman	17	Mel Harder	3.29	Tom Rowe	19

Saves		Strikeouts	
Jack Knott	7	Tom Bridges	163
Whit Wyatt	5	Tom Rowe	140
Chester Hogsett	5	Lefty Gomez	138
John Murphy	5	Robert Grove	121
Oral Hildebrand	5	John Allen	113

All-Star Game

(Municipal Stadium, Cleveland)

July 8	American League	4	National League	1

World Series

October 2	Chicago Cubs	3	at	Detroit Tigers	0
October 3	Chicago Cubs	3	at	Detroit Tigers	8
October 4	Detroit Tigers	6	at	Chicago Cubs	5 [11]
October 5	Detroit Tigers	2	at	Chicago Cubs	1
October 6	Detroit Tigers	1	at	Chicago Cubs	3
October 7	Chicago Cubs	3	at	Detroit Tigers	4

Individual Awards

Baseball Writers Award--Gabby Hartnett (Chicago Cubs NL)
Hank Greenberg (Detroit Tigers AL)
Sporting News MVP--Joe Vaughan (Pittsburgh Pirates NL)
Hank Greenberg (Detroit Tigers AL)

FOOTBALL
National Football League

East Division

Team Name	GP	W	L	T	PF	PA	Pct
New York Giants	12	9	3	0	180	96	.750
Brooklyn Dodgers	12	5	6	1	90	141	.458
Pittsburgh Pirates	12	4	8	0	100	209	.333
Boston Redskins	11	2	8	1	65	123	.227
Philadelphia Eagles	11	2	9	0	60	179	.182

West Division

Team Name	GP	W	L	T	PF	PA	Pct
Detroit Lions	12	7	3	2	191	111	.667
Green Bay Packers	12	8	4	0	181	96	.667
Chicago Bears	12	6	4	2	192	106	.583
Chicago Cardinals	12	6	4	2	99	97	.583

Coaching Changes

Brooklyn--Paul Schissler 5-6-1; Pittsburgh--Joe Bach 4-8-0; Boston--Eddie Casey 2-8-1; Cardinals--Milan Creighton 6-4-2.

League Leaders

Yards Rushing		Yards Passing		Passing % (40 attempts)	
Doug Russell	499	Ed Danowski	795	Ed Danowski	50
Ernie Caddel	450	Arnie Herber	729	Bob Monnet	47
Kink Richards	449	John Gildea	529	Phil Sarboe	46
Bill Shepherd	425	Bernie Masterson	456	Bill Shepherd	44
Dutch Clark	412	Bob Monnett	454	Bernie Masterson	41

Receiving Yards		Receptions		Field Goals	
Charley Malone	433	Tod Goodwin	26	Armand Nicolai	7
Tod Goodwin	432	Johnny Blood	25	Bill Smith	6
Don Hutson	420	Bill Smith	24	Ralph Kercheval	5
Johnny Blood	404	Charley Malone	22	Glenn Presnell	4
Bill Smith	318	Luke Johnses	19	Riley Smith	4

NFL Championship

December 15	New York Giants	7	at	Detroit Lions	26

HOCKEY
National Hockey League

Canadian Division

Team Name	GP	W	L	T	GF	GA	Pts	Pct
Toronto Maple Leafs	48	30	14	4	157	111	64	.667
Montreal Maroons	48	24	19	5	123	92	53	.552
Montreal Canadiens	48	19	23	6	110	145	44	.458
New York Americans	48	12	27	9	100	142	33	.344
St. Louis Eagles	48	11	31	6	86	144	28	.292

American Division

Team Name	GP	W	L	T	GF	GA	Pts	Pct
Boston Bruins	48	26	16	6	129	112	58	.604
Chicago Black Hawks	48	26	17	5	118	88	57	.594
New York Rangers	48	22	20	6	137	139	50	.521
Detroit Red Wings	48	19	22	7	127	114	45	.469

Coaching Changes

Maroons--Tommy Gorman 24-19-5; Canadiens--Edward "Newsy" Lalonde 5-8-3, Leo Dandurand 14-15-3; St. Louis--Eddie Gerard 2-11-0, George Boucher 9-20-6; Boston--Frank Patrick 26-16-6; Chicago--Clem Laughlin 26-17-5.

League Leaders

Goals		Assists		Points	
Charlie Conacher	36	Art Chapman	34	Charlie Conacher	57
Cecil Dillon	25	Frank Boucher	32	Syd Howe	47
Syd Howe	22	Larry Aurie	29	Larry Aurie	46
Harvey Jackson	22	Herb Lewis	27	Frank Boucher	45
Nels Stewart	21	Syd Howe	25	Harvey Jackson	44

Penalty Minutes		GAA		Wins	
Red Horner	125	Lorne Chabot	1.83	George Hainsworth	30
Irvine Frew	89	Alex Connell	1.92	Cecil Thompson	26
Earl Seibert	86	Norman Smith	2.08	Lorne Chabot	26
Albert Siebert	80	George Hainsworth	2.31	Alex Connell	24
Ralph Bowman	72	Cecil Thompson	2.33	Dave Kerr	19

Shutouts	
Alex Connell	9
Lorne Chabot	8
George Hainsworth	8
Cecil Thompson	8
Dave Kerr	8

Stanley Cup Playoffs

Date	Visitor	Score		Home	Score
March 23	Toronto Maple Leafs	0	at	Boston Bruins	1 [33:26]
March 23	Chicago Black Hawks	0	at	Montreal Maroons	0
March 24	Montreal Canadiens	1	at	New York Rangers	2
March 26	Montreal Maroons	1	at	Chicago Black Hawks	0 [4:02]
March 26	Toronto Maple Leafs	2	at	Boston Bruins	0
March 26	New York Rangers	4	at	Montreal Canadiens	4
March 28	Boston Bruins	0	at	Toronto Maple Leafs	3
March 28	Montreal Maroons	2	at	New York Rangers	1
March 30	Boston Bruins	1	at	Toronto Maple Leafs	2
March 30	New York Rangers	3	at	Montreal Maroons	3
April 4	Montreal Maroons	3	at	Toronto Maple Leafs	2 [5:28]
April 6	Montreal Maroons	3	at	Toronto Maple Leafs	1
April 9	Toronto Maple Leafs	1	at	Montreal Maroons	4

All Star Teams

First Team		Second Team
Lorne Chabot	Goal	Cecil Thompson
Eddie Shore	Defense	Cy Wentworth
Earl Seibert	Defense	Art Coulter
Frank Boucher	Center	Ralph Weiland
Charlie Conacher	Right Wing	Aubrey Clapper
Harvey Jackson	Left Wing	Aurel Joliat
Lester Patrick	Coach	Dick Irvin

Individual Awards

Calder Trophy--David Schriner (New York Americans)
Hart Trophy--Eddie Shore (Boston Bruins)
Lady Byng Trophy--Frank Boucher (New York Rangers)
Vezina Trophy--Lorne Chabot (Chicago Black Hawks)

Rules

The penalty shot rule was introduced.

Franchise Changes

NHL--Ottawa Senators became the St. Louis Eagles.

Other Sports

Horseracing--Kentucky Derby won by Omaha (time 2:05, purse $39,525).
Heavyweight Boxing--James J. Braddock defeated Max Baer in 15 rounds.
Golf--U.S. Open won by Sam Parks Jr. with a score of 299.
Auto Racing--Indianapolis 500 won by Kelly Petillo (ave speed 106.240 MPH).
Tennis--U.S. Open won by Wilmer Allison in the men's singles.
U.S. Open won by Wilmer Allison and John Van Ryn in the men's doubles.
U.S. Open won by Helen Jacobs in the women's singles.
U.S. Open won by Helen Jacobs and Sarah P. Fabyan in the women's doubles.
U.S. Open won by Sarah P. Fabyan and Enrique Maier in the mixed doubles.

1936

BASEBALL
National League

Team Name	W	L	Pct	GB	R	OR
New York Giants	92	62	.597	-	742	621
Chicago Cubs	87	67	.565	5	755	603
St. Louis Cardinals	87	67	.565	5	795	794
Pittsburgh Pirates	84	70	.545	8	804	718
Cincinnati Reds	74	80	.481	18	722	760
Boston Bees	71	83	.461	21	631	715
Brooklyn Dodgers	67	87	.435	25	662	752
Philadelphia Phillies	54	100	.351	38	726	874

Coaching Changes

None.

League Leaders

Batting Average		Home Runs		RBI	
Paul Waner	.373	Mel Ott	33	Joe Medwick	138
Ernest Phelps	.367	Dolf Camilli	28	Mel Ott	135
Joe Medwick	.351	Wally Berger	25	Gus Suhr	118
Frank Demaree	.350	Chuck Klein	25	Chuck Klein	104
Joe Vaughan	.335	John Mize	19	Dolf Camilli	102

Stolen Bases		ERA		Wins	
John Martin	23	Carl Hubbell	2.31	Carl Hubbell	26
Stan Hack	17	Dan MacFayden	2.87	Jay Dean	24
Stu Martin	17	Jay Dean	3.17	Paul Derringer	19
Lou Chiozza	17	Charles Lucas	3.18	Larry French	18
Kiki Cuyler	16	Bill Lee	3.31	Bill Lee	18

Saves		Strikeouts	
Jay Dean	11	Van Mungo	238
Don Brennan	9	Jay Dean	195
Bob Smith	8	Cy Blanton	127
Dick Coffman	7	Carl Hubbell	123
Syl Johnson	7	Paul Derringer	121

American League

Team Name	W	L	Pct	GB	R	OR
New York Yankees	102	51	.667	-	1065	731
Detroit Tigers	83	71	.539	19.5	921	871
Chicago White Sox	81	70	.536	20	920	873
Washington Senators	82	71	.536	20	889	799
Cleveland Indians	80	74	.519	22.5	921	862
Boston Red Sox	74	80	.481	28.5	775	764
St. Louis Browns	57	95	.375	44.5	804	1064
Philadelphia Athletics	53	100	.346	49	714	1045

Coaching Changes

Cleveland--Steve O'Neill 80-74.

League Leaders

Batting Average		**Home Runs**		**RBI**	
Luke Appling	.388	Lou Gehrig	49	Hal Trosky	162
Earl Averill	.378	Hal Trosky	42	Lou Gehrig	152
Bill Dickey	.362	Jimmie Foxx	41	Jimmie Foxx	143
Charlie Gehringer	.354	Joe DiMaggio	29	Henry Bonura	138
Lou Gehrig	.354	Earl Averill	28	Julius Solters	134

Stolen Bases		**ERA**		**Wins**	
Lyn Lary	37	Robert Grove	2.81	Tom Bridges	23
Jake Powell	26	John Allen	3.44	Vern Kennedy	21
Bill Werber	23	Pete Appleton	3.53	Wes Ferrell	20
Roy Hughes	20	Tom Bridges	3.60	Charles Ruffing	20
Ben Chapman	20	Monte Pearson	3.71	John Allen	20

Saves		**Strikeouts**	
Pat Malone	9	Tom Bridges	175
Jack Knott	6	John Allen	165
Clint Brown	5	Bobo Newsom	156
John Murphy	5	Robert Grove	130
Oral Hildebrand	4	Monte Pearson	118

All-Star Game

(Braves Field, Boston)

July 7	National League	4	American League	3

World Series

September 30	New York Yankees	1	at	New York Giants	6
October 2	New York Yankees	18	at	New York Giants	4
October 3	New York Giants	1	at	New York Yankees	2
October 4	New York Giants	2	at	New York Yankees	5
October 5	New York Giants	5	at	New York Yankees	4 [10]
October 6	New York Yankees	13	at	New York Giants	5

Individual Awards

Baseball Writers Award--Carl Hubbell (New York Giants NL)
Lou Gehrig (New York Yankees AL)
Sporting News Executive of the Year--Branch Rickey (St. Louis Cardinals NL)
Sporting News Manager of the Year--Joe McCarthy (New York Yankees AL)
Sporting News MVP--Carl Hubbell (New York Giants NL)
Lou Gehrig (New York Yankees AL)

Hall of Fame Inductees

Ty Cobb, Walter Johnson, Christy Mathewson, Babe Ruth, Honus Wagner

FOOTBALL
National Football League

East Division

Team Name	GP	W	L	T	PF	PA	Pct
Boston Redskins	12	7	5	0	149	110	.583
Pittsburgh Pirates	12	6	6	0	98	187	.500
New York Giants	12	5	6	1	115	163	.458
Brooklyn Dodgers	12	3	8	1	92	161	.292
Philadelphia Eagles	12	1	11	0	51	206	.083

West Division

Team Name	GP	W	L	T	PF	PA	Pct
Green Bay Packers	12	10	1	1	248	118	.875
Chicago Bears	12	9	3	0	222	94	.750
Detroit Lions	12	8	4	0	235	102	.667
Chicago Cardinals	12	3	8	1	74	143	.292

Coaching Changes

Boston--Ray Flaherty 7-5-0; Philadelphia--Bert Bell 1-11-0.

League Leaders

Yards Rushing		Yards Passing		Passing % (40 attempts)	
Tuffy Leemans	830	Arnie Herber	1239	Dutch Clark	54
Ace Gutowsky	827	Ed Matesic	850	Ed Matesic	46
Dutch Clark	628	Phil Sarboe	680	Ed Danowski	45
Cliff Battles	614	Pug Vaughan	546	Arnie Herber	45
George Grosvenor	612	Ed Danowski	515	Phil Sarboe	41

Receiving Yards		Receptions		Field Goals	
Don Hutson	526	Don Hutson	34	Armand Nicolai	7
Bill Smith	414	Bill Smith	20	Jack Manders	7
Bill Hewitt	358	Ernie Caddel	19	Riley Smith	4
Eggs Manske	325	Wayne Millner	18	Ernie Smith	4
Jeff Barrett	268	Eggs Manske	17	Dutch Clark	4

NFL Championship

(Polo Grounds, New York)

December 13	Green Bay Packers	21	Boston Redskins	6

HOCKEY
National Hockey League

Canadian Division

Team Name	GP	W	L	T	GF	GA	Pts	Pct
Montreal Maroons	48	22	16	10	114	106	54	.563
Toronto Maple Leafs	48	23	19	6	126	106	52	.542
New York Americans	48	16	25	7	109	122	39	.406
Montreal Canadiens	48	11	26	11	82	123	33	.344

American Division

Team Name	GP	W	L	T	GF	GA	Pts	Pct
Detroit Red Wings	48	24	16	8	124	103	56	.583
Boston Bruins	48	22	20	6	92	83	50	.521
Chicago Black Hawks	48	21	19	8	93	92	50	.521
New York Rangers	48	19	17	12	91	96	50	.521

Coaching Changes

Americans--Red Dutton 16-25-7; Canadiens--Sylvio Mantha 11-26-11.

League Leaders

Goals

Charlie Conacher	23
Bill Thoms	23
Marty Barry	21
David Schriner	19
Reg Smith	19

Assists

Art Chapman	28
David Schriner	26
Elwin Romnes	25
Herb Lewis	23
Paul Thompson	23

Points

David Schriner	45
Marty Barry	40
Paul Thompson	40
Charlie Conacher	38
Reg Smith	38

Penalty Minutes

Red Horner	167
Art Shields	81
Reg Smith	75
Charlie Conacher	74
Red Dutton	69

GAA

Cecil Thompson	1.71
Mike Karakas	1.92
Dave Kerr	2.02
Norman Smith	2.15
George Hainsworth	2.21

Wins

Norman Smith	24
George Hainsworth	23
Cecil Thompson	22
Mike Karakas	21
Dave Kerr	18

Shutouts

Cecil Thompson	10
Mike Karakas	9
Dave Kerr	8
George Hainsworth	8
Wilfred Cude	6

Stanley Cup Playoffs

March 24	Toronto Maple Leafs	0	at	Boston Bruins	3
March 24	Chicago Black Hawks	0	at	New York Americans	3
March 24	Detroit Red Wings	1	at	Montreal Maroons	0 [116:30]
March 26	Boston Bruins	3	at	Toronto Maple Leafs	8
March 26	New York Americans	4	at	Chicago Black Hawks	5
March 26	Detroit Red Wings	3	at	Montreal Maroons	0
March 28	New York Americans	1	at	Toronto Maple Leafs	3
March 29	Montreal Maroons	1	at	Detroit Red Wings	2
March 31	Toronto Maple Leafs	0	at	New York Americans	1
April 2	New York Americans	1	at	Toronto Maple Leafs	3
April 5	Toronto Maple Leafs	1	at	Detroit Red Wings	3
April 7	Toronto Maple Leafs	4	at	Detroit Red Wings	9
April 9	Detroit Red Wings	3	at	Toronto Maple Leafs	4 [31:00]
April 11	Detroit Red Wings	3	at	Toronto Maple Leafs	2

All Star Teams

First Team		Second Team
Cecil Thompson	Goal	Wilf Cude
Eddie Shore	Defense	Earl Seibert
Albert Siebert	Defense	Ebbie Goodfellow
Reginald Smith	Center	Bill Thoms
Charlie Conacher	Right Wing	Cecil Dillon
Dave Schriner	Left Wing	Paul Thompson
Lester Patrick	Coach	Tommy Gorman

Individual Awards

Calder Trophy--Mike Karakas (Chicago Black Hawks)
Hart Trophy--Eddie Shore (Boston Bruins)
Lady Byng Trophy--Elwin Romnes (Chicago Black Hawks)
Vezina Trophy--Cecil Thompson (Boston Bruins)

Franchise Changes

NL--Boston Braves changed name to Boston Bees.

Other Sports

Horseracing--Kentucky Derby won by Bold Venture (time 2:03.6, purse $37,725).
Golf--U.S. Open won by Tony Manero with a score of 282.
Auto Racing--Indianapolis 500 won by Louis Meyer (ave. speed 109.069 MPH).
Tennis--U.S. Open won by Fred Perry in the men's singles.
U.S. Open won by Don Budge and C. Gene Mako in the men's doubles.
U.S. Open won by Alice Marble in the women's singles.
U.S. Open won by M.G. Van Ryn and Carolin Babcock in the women's doubles.
U.S. Open won by Alice Marble and C. Gene Mako in the mixed doubles.

1937

BASEBALL
National League

Team Name	W	L	Pct	GB	R	OR
New York Giants	95	57	.625	-	732	602
Chicago Cubs	93	61	.604	3	811	682
Pittsburgh Pirates	86	68	.558	10	704	646
St. Louis Cardinals	81	73	.526	15	789	733
Boston Bees	79	73	.520	16	579	556
Brooklyn Dodgers	62	91	.405	33.5	616	772
Philadelphia Phillies	61	92	.399	34.5	724	869
Cincinnati Reds	56	98	.364	40	612	707

Coaching Changes

Brooklyn--Burleigh Grimes 62-91; Cincinnati--Chuck Dressen 51-78, Bobby Wallace 5-20.

League Leaders

Batting Average

Joe Medwick	.374
Johnny Mize	.364
Gabby Hartnett	.354
Paul Waner	.354
Art Whitney	.341

Home Runs

Mel Ott	31
Joe Medwick	31
Dolf Camilli	27
Johnny Mize	25
August Galan	18

RBI

Joe Medwick	154
Frank Demaree	115
Johnny Mize	113
Bob Swift	97
Mel Ott	95

Stolen Bases

August Galan	23
Stan Hack	16
George Scharein	13
Harry Lavagetto	13
Terry Moore	13

ERA

Jim Turner	2.38
Cliff Melton	2.61
Jay Dean	2.69
Russ Bauers	2.88
Lou Fette	2.88

Wins

Carl Hubbell	22
Jim Turner	20
Cliff Melton	20
Lou Fette	20
Lon Warneke	18

Saves

Mace Brown	7
Cliff Melton	7
Lee Grissom	6
Al Hollingsworth	5
Charlie Root	5

Strikeouts

Carl Hubbell	159
Lee Grissom	149
Cy Blanton	143
Cliff Melton	142
Wayne LaMaster	135

American League

Team Name	W	L	Pct	GB	R	OR
New York Yankees	102	52	.662	-	979	671
Detroit Tigers	89	65	.578	13	935	841
Chicago White Sox	86	68	.558	16	780	730
Cleveland Indians	83	71	.539	19	817	768
Boston Red Sox	80	72	.526	21	821	775
Washington Senators	73	80	.477	28.5	757	841
Philadelphia Athletics	54	97	.358	46.5	699	854
St. Louis Browns	46	108	.299	56	715	1023

Coaching Changes

St. Louis--Rogers Hornsby 25-50, Jim Bottomley 21-58.

League Leaders

Batting Average		Home Runs		RBI	
Charlie Gehringer	.371	Joe DiMaggio	46	Hank Greenberg	183
Lou Gehrig	.351	Hank Greenberg	40	Joe DiMaggio	167
Joe DiMaggio	.346	Lou Gehrig	37	Lou Gehrig	159
Zeke Bonura	.345	Jimmie Foxx	36	Bill Dickey	133
Cecil Travis	.344	Rudy York	35	Hal Trosky	128

Stolen Bases		ERA		Wins	
Ben Chapman	35	Lefty Gomez	2.33	Lefty Gomez	21
Bill Werber	35	Monty Stratton	2.40	Charles Ruffing	20
Gerald Walker	23	Johnny Allen	2.55	Roxie Lawson	18
Jesse Hill	18	Charles Ruffing	2.98	Eldon Auker	17
Luke Appling	18	Robert Grove	3.02	Robert Grove	17

Saves		Strikeouts	
Clint Brown	18	Lefty Gomez	194
John Murphy	10	Bobo Newsom	166
Jack Wilson	7	Robert Grove	153
Pat Malone	6	Bob Feller	150
Joe Heving	5	Tom Bridges	138

All-Star Game

(Griffith Stadium, Washington)

July 7	American League	8	National League	3

World Series

October 6	New York Giants	1	at	New York Yankees	8
October 7	New York Giants	1	at	New York Yankees	8
October 8	New York Yankees	5	at	New York Giants	1
October 9	New York Yankees	3	at	New York Giants	7
October 10	New York Yankees	4	at	New York Giants	2

Individual Awards

Baseball Writers Award--Joe Medwick (St. Louis Cardinals NL)
Charlie Gehringer (Detroit Tigers AL)
Sporting News Executive of the Year--Ed Barrow (New York Yankees AL)
Sporting News Manager of the Year--Bill McKechnie (Boston Bees NL)
Sporting News MVP--Joe Medwick (St. Louis Cardinals NL)
Charlie Gehringer (Detroit Tigers AL)

Hall of Fame Inductees

Morgan Bulkeley, Ban Johnson, Napoleon Lajoie, Connie Mack, John McGraw, Tris Speaker, George Wright, Cy Young

FOOTBALL
National Football League

East Division

Team Name	GP	W	L	T	PF	PA	Pct
Washington Redskins	11	8	3	0	195	120	.727
New York Giants	11	6	3	2	128	109	.636
Pittsburgh Pirates	11	4	7	0	122	145	.364
Brooklyn Dodgers	11	3	7	1	82	174	.318
Philadelphia Eagles	11	2	8	1	86	177	.227

West Division

Team Name	GP	W	L	T	PF	PA	Pct
Chicago Bears	11	9	1	1	201	100	.864
Green Bay Packers	11	7	4	0	220	122	.636
Detroit Lions	11	7	4	0	180	105	.636
Chicago Cardinals	11	5	5	1	135	165	.500
Cleveland Rams	11	1	10	0	175	207	.091

Coaching Changes

Washington--Ray Flaherty 8-3-0; Pittsburgh--Johnny Blood 4-7-0; Brooklyn--Potsy Clark 3-7-1; Detroit--Dutch Clark 7-4-0; Cleveland--Hugo Bezdek 1-10-0.

League Leaders

Yards Rushing		Yards Passing		Passing % (40 attempts)	
Cliff Battles	874	Sam Baugh	1127	Bob Monnett	51
Clark Hinkle	552	Ed Danowski	814	Ed Danowski	49
Bull Karcis	511	Pat Coffee	804	Sam Baugh	47
Dutch Clark	468	Arnie Herber	676	Ace Parker	46
George Grosvenor	461	Bernie Masterson	615	Arnie Herber	45

Receiving Yards		Receptions		Field Goals	
Gaynell Tinsley	675	Don Hutson	41	Jack Manders	8
Don Hutson	552	Gaynell Tinsley	36	Riley Smith	5
Jeff Barrett	461	Charley Malone	28	Tilly Manton	5
Charley Malone	419	Jeff Barrett	20	Regis Monahan	5
Joe Carter	282	Bill Hewitt	16	Armand Niccolai	4

NFL Championship

December 12	Washington Redskins	28	at	Chicago Bears	21

HOCKEY
National Hockey League

Canadian Division

Team Name	GP	W	L	T	GF	GA	Pts	Pct
Montreal Canadiens	48	24	18	6	115	111	54	.563
Montreal Maroons	48	22	17	9	126	110	53	.552
Toronto Maple Leafs	48	22	21	5	119	115	49	.510
New York Americans	48	15	29	4	122	161	34	.354

American Division

Team Name	GP	W	L	T	GF	GA	Pts	Pct
Detroit Red Wings	48	25	14	9	128	102	59	.615
Boston Bruins	48	23	18	7	120	110	53	.552
New York Rangers	48	19	20	9	117	106	47	.490
Chicago Black Hawks	48	14	27	7	99	131	35	.365

Coaching Changes

Canadiens--Cecil Hart 24-18-6; Boston--Art Ross 23-18-7.

League Leaders

Goals		Assists		Points	
Larry Aurie	23	Syl Apps	29	David Schriner	46
Nels Stewart	23	Marty Barry	27	Syl Apps	45
Butch Keeling	22	Bob Gracie	25	Marty Barry	44
Harvey Jackson	21	David Schriner	25	Larry Aurie	43
David Schriner	21	Bill Cowley	22	Harvey Jackson	40

Penalty Minutes		GAA		Wins	
Red Horner	124	Norman Smith	2.13	Norman Smith	25
Art Shields	94	Dave Kerr	2.19	Cecil Thompson	23
Lionel Conacher	64	Bill Beveridge	2.24	Wilfred Cude	22
Jack Portland	58	Wilfred Cude	2.25	Walter Broda	22
Joe Jerwa	57	Cecil Thompson	2.29	Dave Kerr	19

Shutouts	
Norman Smith	6
Cecil Thompson	6
Wilfred Cude	5
Mike Karakas	5
Dave Kerr	4

Stanley Cup Playoffs

March 23	Boston Bruins	1	at	Montreal Maroons	4
March 23	New York Rangers	3	at	Toronto Maple Leafs	0
March 23	Montreal Canadiens	0	at	Detroit Red Wings	4
March 25	Montreal Maroons	0	at	Boston Bruins	4
March 25	Toronto Maple Leafs	1	at	New York Rangers	2 [13:05]
March 25	Montreal Canadiens	1	at	Detroit Red Wings	5
March 27	Detroit Red Wings	1	at	Montreal Canadiens	3
March 28	Montreal Maroons	4	at	Boston Bruins	1
March 30	Detroit Red Wings	1	at	Montreal Canadiens	3
April 1	Detroit Red Wings	2	at	Montreal Canadiens	1 [51:49]
April 1	Montreal Maroons	0	at	New York Rangers	1
April 3	New York Rangers	4	at	Montreal Maroons	0
April 6	Detroit Red Wings	1	at	New York Rangers	5
April 8	New York Rangers	2	at	Detroit Red Wings	4
April 11	New York Rangers	1	at	Detroit Red Wings	0
April 13	New York Rangers	0	at	Detroit Red Wings	1
April 15	New York Rangers	0	at	Detroit Red Wings	3

All Star Teams

First Team		Second Team
Norm Smith	Goal	Wilf Cude
Albert Siebert	Defense	Earl Seibert
Ebbie Goodfellow	Defense	Lionel Conacher
Marty Barry	Center	Art Chapman
Larry Aurie	Right Wing	Cecil Dillon
Harvey Jackson	Left Wing	Dave Schriner
Jack Adams	Coach	Cecil Hart

Individual Awards

Calder Trophy--Syl Apps (Toronto Maple Leafs)
Hart Trophy--Albert Siebert (Montreal Canadiens)
Lady Byng Trophy--Marty Barry (Detroit Red Wings)
Vezina Trophy--Norm Smith (Detroit Red Wings)

Notes

The National Hockey League took full control of the New York Americans from Bill Dwyer.

Franchise Changes

NFL--Boston Redskins became Washington Redskins.

Other Sports

Horseracing--Kentucky Derby won by War Admiral (time 2:03.2, purse $52,050).
Heavyweight Boxing--Joe Louis knocked-out James J. Braddock in 8 rounds.
Joe Louis defeated Tommy Farr in 15 rounds.
Golf--U.S. Open won by Ralph Guldahl with a score of 281.
Auto Racing--Indianapolis 500 won by Wilbur Shaw (ave. speed 113.580 MPH).
Tennis--U.S. Open won by Don Budge in the men's singles.
U.S. Open won by Baron G. von Cramm and Henner Henkel in the men's doubles.
U.S. Open won by Anita Lizana in the women's singles.
U.S. Open won by Sarah P. Fabyan and Alice Marble in the women's doubles.
U.S. Open won by Sarah P. Fabyan and Don Budge in the mixed doubles.

1938

BASEBALL
National League

Team Name	W	L	Pct	GB	R	OR
Chicago Cubs	89	63	.586	-	713	598
Pittsburgh Pirates	86	64	.573	2	707	630
New York Giants	83	67	.553	5	705	637
Cincinnati Reds	82	68	.547	6	723	634
Boston Bees	77	75	.507	12	561	618
Brooklyn Dodgers	69	80	.463	18.5	704	710
St. Louis Cardinals	71	80	.470	17.5	725	721
Philadelphia Phillies	45	105	.300	43	550	840

Coaching Changes

Chicago--Charlie Grimm 45-36, Gabby Hartnett 44-27; Cincinnati--Bill McKechnie 82-68; Boston--Casey Stengel 77-75; St. Louis--Frank Frisch 62-72, Mike Gonzalez 9-8; Philadelphia--Jimmie Wilson 45-103, Hans Lobert 0-2.

League Leaders

Batting Average		Home Runs		RBI	
Ernie Lombardi	.342	Mel Ott	36	Joe Medwick	122
Johnny Mize	.337	Ival Goodman	30	Mel Ott	116
Frank McCormick	.327	Johnny Mize	27	Johnny Rizzo	111
Joe Medwick	.322	Dolf Camilli	24	Frank McCormick	106
Joe Vaughan	.322	Johnny Rizzo	23	Johnny Mize	102

Stolen Bases		ERA		Wins	
Stan Hack	16	Bill Lee	2.66	Bill Lee	22
Harry Lavagetto	15	Paul Derringer	2.93	Paul Derringer	21
Ernie Koy	15	Dan MacFayden	2.95	Clay Bryant	19
Don Gutteridge	14	Bob Klinger	2.99	Bob Weiland	16
Joe Vaughan	14	Fred Fitzsimmons	3.02	Mace Brown	15

Saves		Strikeouts	
Dick Coffman	12	Clay Bryant	135
Charlie Root	8	Paul Derringer	132
Luke Hamlin	6	John Vander Meer	125
Dick Errickson	6	Bill Lee	121
Walter Brown	5	Bob Weiland	117

American League

Team Name	W	L	Pct	GB	R	OR
New York Yankees	99	53	.651	-	966	710
Boston Red Sox	88	61	.591	9.5	902	751
Cleveland Indians	86	66	.566	13	847	782
Detroit Tigers	84	70	.545	16	862	795
Washington Senators	75	76	.497	23.5	814	873
Chicago White Sox	65	83	.439	32	709	752
St. Louis Browns	55	97	.362	44	755	962
Philadelphia Athletics	53	99	.349	46	726	956

Coaching Changes

Cleveland--Ossie Vitt 86-66; Detroit--Mickey Cochrane 47-50, Del Baker 37-20; St. Louis--Charles Street 55-97.

League Leaders

Batting Average		Home Runs		RBI	
Jimmie Foxx	.349	Hank Greenberg	58	Jimmie Foxx	175
Jeff Heath	.343	Jimmie Foxx	50	Hank Greenberg	146
Ben Chapman	.340	Harlond Clift	34	Joe DiMaggio	140
Charles Myer	.336	Rudy York	33	Rudy York	127
Cecil Travis	.335	Joe DiMaggio	32	Harlond Clift	118

Stolen Bases		ERA		Wins	
Frank Crosetti	27	Robert Grove	3.08	Charles Ruffing	21
Lynford Lary	23	Charles Ruffing	3.31	Bobo Newsom	20
Bill Werber	19	Lefty Gomez	3.35	Lefty Gomez	18
John Lewis	17	Emil Leonard	3.43	Bob Feller	17
Pete Fox	16	Thornton Lee	3.49	Mel Harder	17

Saves		Strikeouts	
John Murphy	11	Bob Feller	240
John Humphries	6	Bobo Newsom	226
Archie McKain	6	Howard Mills	134
Nelson Potter	5	Lefty Gomez	129
Pete Appleton	5	Charles Ruffing	127

All-Star Game
(Crosley Field, Cincinnati)

July 6	National League	4	American League	1

World Series

October 5	New York Yankees	3	at	Chicago Cubs	1
October 6	New York Yankees	6	at	Chicago Cubs	3
October 8	Chicago Cubs	2	at	New York Yankees	5
October 9	Chicago Cubs	3	at	New York Yankees	8

Individual Awards

Baseball Writers Award--Ernie Lombardi (Cincinnati Reds NL)
Jimmie Foxx (Boston Red Sox AL)
Sporting News Executive of the Year--Warren Giles (Cincinnati Reds NL)
Sporting News Manager of the Year--Joe McCarthy (New York Yankees AL)
Sporting News MVP--Ernie Lombardi (Cincinnati Reds NL)
Jimmie Foxx (Boston Red Sox AL)

Hall of Fame Inductees

Grover Alexander, Alexander Cartwright, Henry Chadwick

BASKETBALL

National Basketball League

East Division

Team Name	GP	W	L	PPGF	PPGA	Pct	GB
Akron Firestone Non-Skids	18	14	4	40.1	34.0	.778	-
Akron Goodyear Wing-Foots	18	13	5	35.8	27.7	.722	1
Pittsburgh Pirates	13	8	5	37.3	33.4	.615	3.5
Buffalo Bisons	9	3	6	29.1	30.6	.333	6.5
Warren Penn Oilers	12	3	9	26.5	38.6	.250	8
Columbus Athletic Supply	13	1	12	25.6	38.7	.077	10.5

West Division

Team Name	GP	W	L	PPGF	PPGA	Pct	GB
Oshkosh All-Stars	14	12	2	49.1	35.2	.857	-
Whiting Ciesar All-Americans	15	12	3	41.3	37.3	.800	.5
Fort Wayne Zollner Pistons	20	13	7	40.4	31.6	.650	2
Indianapolis Kautskys	13	4	9	36.3	37.7	.308	7.5
Richmond King Clothiers	3	1	2	29.1	37.6	.333	5.5
Cincinnati Comellos	7	2	5	29.1	37.6	.286	6.5
Kankakee Gallagher Trojans	14	3	11	33.3	53.3	.214	9
Dayton Metros	13	2	11	31.5	37.6	.154	9.5

Coaching

Non-Skids--Paul Sheeks 14-4; Akron--Lefty Byers 13-5; Pittsburgh--Dudey Moore 8-5; Buffalo--Allie Heerdt 3-6; Warren Penn--Gerry Archibald 3-9; Columbus--Cookie Cunningham 1-12; Oshkosh--Lon Darling 12-2; Whiting--Whitey Wickhorst 12-3; Fort Wayne--Byron Evard 13-7; Indianapolis--Frank Kautsky 4-9; Richmond/Cincinnati--Bob McConachie 1-4, John Wiethe 2-3; Kankakee--Don Betourne 3-11; Dayton--Bill Hosket 2-11

League Leaders

Field Goals		Free Throws		Points	
Leroy Edwards	83	Soup Cable	45	Leroy Edwards	210
Bart Quinn	71	Leroy Edwards	44	Bart Quinn	170
Jack Ozburn	59	Johnny Wooden	39	Scotty Armstrong	147
Chuck Bloedorn	58	Scotty Armstrong	35	Jack Ozburn	144
Vince McGowan	57	Bob Kessler	31	Vince McGowan	144

NBL Championship

Akron Firestone Non-Skids	21	at	Akron Goodyear Wingfoots	26
Akron Goodyear Wingfoots	37	at	Akron Firestone Non-Skids	31
Oshkosh All Stars	40	at	Whiting Ciesar All-Americans	33
Whiting Ciesar All Americans	38	at	Oshkosh All Stars	41
Akron Goodyear Wingfoots	29	at	Oshkosh All Stars	28
Oshkosh All Stars	39	at	Akron Goodyear Wingfoots	31
Akron Goodyear Wingfoots	35	at	Oshkosh All Stars	27

Rules

The NBL could not agree on a uniform policy concerning the center jump and as a compromise the decision to use the center jump was left to the home team.

Notes

The National Basketball League was formed this year, when three large corporations decided to enter the sport of pro basketball. Firestone, Goodyear and General Electric who had each fielded amateur teams in the previous years decided to run their teams against professionals. They joined with ten independent teams and formed the NBL with Hubert Johnson as the commissioner.
The Richmond team folded after the season began and moved to Cincinnati.

FOOTBALL
National Football League

East Division

Team Name	GP	W	L	T	PF	PA	Pct
New York Giants	11	8	2	1	194	79	.773
Washington Redskins	11	6	3	2	148	154	.636
Brooklyn Dodgers	11	4	4	3	131	161	.500
Philadelphia Eagles	11	5	6	0	154	164	.455
Pittsburgh Pirates	11	2	9	0	79	169	.182

West Division

Team Name	GP	W	L	T	PF	PA	Pct
Green Bay Packers	11	8	3	0	223	118	.727
Detroit Lions	11	7	4	0	119	108	.636
Chicago Bears	11	6	5	0	194	148	.545
Cleveland Rams	11	4	7	0	131	215	.364
Chicago Cardinals	11	2	9	0	111	168	.182

Coaching Changes

Cleveland--Hugo Bezdek 0-3-0, Art Lewis 4-4-0.

League Leaders

Yards Rushing		Yards Passing		Passing % (40 attempts)	
Whizzer White	567	Ace Parker	865	Ed Danowski	54
Tuffy Leemans	463	Sam Baugh	853	Bob Monnett	54
Bill Shepherd	455	Ed Danowski	848	John Robbins	54
Cecil Isbell	445	Bernie Masterson	848	Sam Baugh	49
Ace Gutowsky	444	Cecil Isbel	659	Bill Hartman	49

Receiving Yards		Receptions		Field Goals	
Don Hutson	548	Gaynell Tinsley	41	Ward Cuff	5
Gaynell Tinsley	516	Don Hutson	32	Ralph Kercheval	5
Jim Benton	418	Joe Carter	27	Regis Monahan	4
Joe Carter	386	Charley Malone	24	Jack Manders	3
Bill Smith	338	Jim Benton	21	Clarke Hinkle	3

Pro Bowl Game
(Wrigley Field, Los Angeles)

January 15 1939 New York Giants 13 All-Stars 10

NFL Championship

December 11 Green Bay Packers 17 at New York Giants 23

Individual Awards

Joe F. Carr Trophy--Mel Hein (New York Giants)

HOCKEY
National Hockey League

Canadian Division

Team Name	GP	W	L	T	GF	GA	Pts	Pct
Toronto Maple Leafs	48	24	15	9	151	127	57	.594
New York Americans	48	19	18	11	110	111	49	.510
Montreal Canadians	48	18	17	13	123	128	49	.510
Montreal Maroons	48	12	30	6	101	149	30	.313

American Division

Team Name	GP	W	L	T	GF	GA	Pts	Pct
Boston Bruins	48	30	11	7	142	89	67	.698
New York Rangers	48	27	15	6	149	96	60	.625
Chicago Black Hawks	48	14	25	9	97	139	37	.385
Detroit Red Wings	48	12	25	11	99	133	35	.365

Coaching Changes

Maroons--"King" Clancy 6-11-1, Tommy Gorman 6-19-5; Chicago--Bill Stewart 14-25-9.

League Leaders

Goals		Assists		Points	
Gord Drillon	26	Syl Apps	29	Gord Drillon	52
George Mantha	23	Gord Drillon	26	Syl Apps	50
Paul Thompson	22	Phil Watson	25	Paul Thompson	44
Syl Apps	21	Bill Thoms	24	George Mantha	42
Cecil Dillon	21	Clint Smith	23	Cecil Dillon	39

Penalty Minutes		GAA		Wins	
Red Horner	92	Cecil Thompson	1.85	Cecil Thompson	30
Art Coulter	90	Dave Kerr	2.00	Dave Kerr	27
Ott Heller	68	Earl Robertson	2.31	Walter Broda	24
Joe Cooper	57	Walter Broda	2.65	Earl Robertson	19
Walter Pratt	56	Wilfred Cude	2.68	Wilfred Cude	18

Shutouts

Dave Kerr	8
Cecil Thompson	7
Earl Robertson	6
Walter Broda	6
Wilfred Cude	3

Stanley Cup Playoffs

March 22	New York Americans	2	at	New York Rangers	1 [21:25]
March 22	Chicago Black Hawks	4	at	Montreal Canadiens	6
March 24	New York Rangers	4	at	New York Americans	3
March 24	Montreal Canadiens	0	at	Chicago Black Hawks	4
March 24	Boston Bruins	0	at	Toronto Maple Leafs	1 [21:31]
March 26	Chicago Black Hawks	3	at	Montreal Canadiens	2 [11:49]
March 26	Boston Bruins	1	at	Toronto Maple Leafs	2
March 27	New York Americans	3	at	New York Rangers	2 [60:40]
March 29	Toronto Maple Leafs	3	at	Boston Bruins	2 [10:04]
March 29	Chicago Black Hawks	1	at	New York Americans	3
March 31	New York Americans	0	at	Chicago Black Hawks	1
April 3	Chicago Black Hawks	3	at	New York Americans	2
April 5	Chicago BlackHawks	3	at	Toronto Maple Leafs	1
April 7	Chicago Black Hawks	1	at	Toronto Maple Leafs	5
April 10	Chicago Black Hawks	1	at	Chicago Black Hawks	2
April 12	Toronto Maple Leafs	1	at	Chicago Black Hawks	4

All Star Teams

First Team		Second Team
Cecil Thompson	Goal	Dave Kerr
Eddie Shore	Defense	Art Coulter
Albert Siebert	Defense	Earl Seibert
Bill Cowley	Center	Syl Apps
Cecil Dillon	Right Wing	Cecil Dillon
Gord Drillon	(tied)	Gord Drillon
Paul Thompson	Left Wing	Hector Blake
Lester Patrick	Coach	Art Ross

Individual Awards

Calder Trophy--Carl Dahlstrom (Chicago Black Hawks)
Hart Trophy--Eddie Shore (Boston Bruins)
Lady Byng Trophy--Gordie Drillon (Toronto Maple Leafs)
Vezina Trophy--Cecil Thompson (Boston Bruins)

Rules

Icing the puck became illegal. Should the defending team shoot the puck over the opposing team's goal line from their side of the red line the puck would be brought back to the defender's own end for a face-off.

Other Sports

Horseracing--Kentucky Derby won by Lawrin (time 2:04.8, purse $47,050).
Heavyweight Boxing--Joe Louis knocked-out Nathan Mann in 3 rounds.
Joe Louis knocked-out Harry Thomas in 5 rounds.
Joe Louis knocked-out Max Schmeling in 1 round.
Golf--U.S. Open won by Ralph Guldahl with a score of 284.
Auto Racing--Indianapolis 500 won by Floyd Roberts (ave. speed 117.200 MPH)
Tennis--U.S. Open won by Don Budge in the men's singles.
U.S. Open won by Don Budge and Gene Mako in the men's doubles.
U.S. Open won by Alice Marble in the women's singles.
U.S. Open won by Alice Marble and Sarah P. Fabyan in the women's doubles.
U.S. Open won by Alice Marble and Don Budge in the mixed doubles.

1939

BASEBALL
National League

Team Name	W	L	Pct	GB	R	OR
Cincinnati Reds	97	57	.630	-	767	595
St. Louis Cardinals	92	61	.601	4.5	779	633
Brooklyn Dodgers	84	69	.549	12.5	708	645
Chicago Cubs	84	70	.545	13	724	678
New York Giants	77	74	.510	18.5	703	685
Pittsburgh Pirates	68	85	.444	28.5	666	721
Boston Bees	63	88	.417	32.5	572	659
Philadelphia Phillies	45	106	.298	50.5	553	856

Coaching Changes

St. Louis--Ray Blades 92-61; Brooklyn--Leo Durocher 84-69; Chicago--Gabby Hartnett 84-70; Philadelphia--James Prothro 45-106.

League Leaders

Batting Average		Home Runs		RBI	
Johnny Mize	.349	Johnny Mize	28	Frank McCormick	128
Frank McCormick	.332	Mel Ott	27	Joe Medwick	117
Joe Medwick	.332	Dolf Camilli	26	Johnny Mize	108
Paul Waner	.328	Hank Leiber	24	Dolf Camilli	104
Morris Arnovich	.324	Enie Lombardi	20	Hank Leiber	88

Stolen Bases		ERA		Wins	
Stan Hack	17	Bill Walters	2.29	Bill Walters	27
Lee Handley	17	Carl Hubbell	2.75	Paul Derringer	25
Bill Werber	15	Hugh Casey	2.93	Curt Davis	22
Harry Lavagetto	14	Paul Derringer	2.93	Luke Hamlin	20
John Hassett	13	Lou Fette	2.96	Bill Lee	19

Saves		Strikeouts	
Bob Bowman	9	Claude Passeau	137
Clyde Shoun	9	Bill Walters	137
Walter Brown	7	Mort Cooper	130
Mace Brown	7	Paul Derringer	128
Curt Davis	7	Bill Lee	105

American League

Team Name	W	L	Pct	GB	R	OR
New York Yankees	106	45	.702	-	967	556
Boston Red Sox	89	62	.589	17	890	795
Cleveland Indians	87	67	.565	20.5	797	700
Chicago White Sox	85	69	.552	22.5	755	737
Detroit Tigers	81	73	.526	26.5	849	762
Washington Senators	65	87	.428	41.5	702	797
Philadelphia Athletics	55	97	.362	51.5	711	1022
St. Louis Browns	43	111	.279	64.5	733	1035

Coaching Changes

Detroit--Del Baker 81-73; St. Louis--Fred Haney 43-111.

League Leaders

Batting Average		Home Runs		RBI	
Joe DiMaggio	.381	Jimmie Foxx	35	Ted Williams	145
Jimmie Foxx	.360	Hank Greenberg	33	Joe DiMaggio	126
Bob Johnson	.338	Ted Williams	31	Bob Johnson	114
Hal Trosky	.335	Joe DiMaggio	30	Hank Greenberg	112
Charlie Keller	.334	Joe Gordon	28	Joe Gordon	111

Stolen Bases		ERA		Wins	
George Case	51	Robert Grove	2.54	Bob Feller	24
Pete Fox	23	Ted Lyons	2.76	Charles Ruffing	21
Mike Kreevich	23	Bob Feller	2.85	Bobo Newsom	20
Barney McCosky	20	Charles Ruffing	2.93	Emil Leonard	20
Ben Chapman	18	Lefty Gomez	3.41	Tom Bridges	17

Saves		Strikeouts	
John Murphy	19	Bob Feller	246
Clint Brown	18	Bobo Newsom	192
Alfred Dean	7	Tom Bridges	129
Joe Heving	7	Johnny Rigney	119
Pete Appleton	6	Ken Chase	118

All-Star Game

(Yankee Stadium, New York)

July 11	American League	3		National League	1

World Series

October 4	Cincinnati Reds	1	at	New York Yankees	2
October 5	Cincinnati Reds	0	at	New York Yankees	4
October 7	New York Yankees	7	at	Cincinnati Reds	3
October 8	New York Yankees	7	at	Cincinnati Reds	4 [10]

Individual Awards

Baseball Writers Award--Bill Walters (Cincinnati Reds NL)
Joe DiMaggio (New York Yankees AL)
Sporting News Executive of the Year--Larry MacPhail (Brooklyn Dodgers NL)
Sporting News Manager of the Year--Leo Durocher (Brooklyn Dodgers NL)
Sporting News MVP--Bill Walters (Cincinnati Reds NL)
Joe DiMaggio (New York Yankees AL)

Hall of Fame Inductees

Cap Anson, Eddie Collins, Charlie Comiskey, Candy Cummings, William Ewing, Lou Gehrig, Willie Keeler, Charles Radbourne, George Sisler, Albert Spalding

Notes

The first major league baseball game to be televised was a doubleheader between the Brooklyn Dodgers and the Cincinnati Reds on August 26th, 1939. The game was telecast by station W2XBS, New York City and used two cameras.

BASKETBALL
National Basketball League

East Division

Team Name	GP	W	L	PPGF	PPGA	Pct	GB
Akron Firestone Non-Skids	27	24	3	44.6	35.9	.889	-
Akron Goodyear Wingfoots	28	14	14	34.1	35.5	.509	10.5
(Warren Penn Oilers)	19	9	10	38.1	39.6	.471	11
(Cleveland White Horses)	9	5	4	38.1	39.6	.556	10
Pittsburgh Pirates	27	13	14	36.9	39.3	.481	11

West Division

Team Name	GP	W	L	PPGF	PPGA	Pct	GB
Oshkosh All-Stars	28	17	11	41.2	36.1	.607	-
Indianapolis Kautskys	26	13	13	43.3	43.6	.500	3
Sheboygan Redskins	28	11	17	35 6	37.5	.393	6
Hammond Ciesar All-Americans	28	4	24	36 0	42.1	.143	13

Coaching Changes

Warren Penn/Cleveland--Gerry Archibald 14-14; Indianapolis--Bob Nipper 13-13; Sheboygan--"Doc" Schutte 11-17; Hammond--Whitey Wickhorst 4-24.

League Leaders

Field Goals		Free Throws		Points	
Leroy Edwards	124	Leroy Edwards	86	Leroy Edwards	334
Soup Cable	99	Jewell Young	72	Jewell Young	264
Walt Stankey	97	Buddy Jeannette	65	Soup Cable	262
Jewell Young	96	Soup Cable	64	Bill Laughlin	232
Bill Laughlin	92	Paul Birch	51	Paul Sokody	223

NBL Championship

Oshkosh All-Stars	38	at	Akron Firestone Non-Skids	50
Oshkosh All-Stars	38	at	Akron Firestone Non-Skids	36
Akron Firestone Non-Skids	40	at	Oshkosh All-Stars	29
Akron Firestone Non-Skids	37	at	Oshkosh All-Stars	49
Akron Firestone Non-Skids	37	at	Oshkosh All-Stars	30

Notes

The Warren Penn Oilers folded after the start of the season and became the Cleveland White Horses.

FOOTBALL
National Football League

East Division

Team Name	GP	W	L	T	PF	PA	Pct
New York Giants	11	9	1	1	168	85	.864
Washington Redskins	11	8	2	1	242	94	.773
Brooklyn Dodgers	11	4	6	1	108	219	.409
Philadelphia Eagles	11	1	9	1	105	200	.136
Pittsburgh Steelers	11	1	9	1	114	216	.136

West Division

Team Name	GP	W	L	T	PF	PA	Pct
Green Bay Packers	11	9	2	0	233	153	.818
Chicago Bears	11	8	3	0	298	157	.727
Detroit Lions	11	6	5	0	145	150	.545
Cleveland Rams	11	5	5	1	195	164	.500
Chicago Cardinals	11	1	10	0	84	254	.091

Coaching Changes

Pittsburgh--Johnny Blood 0-3-0, Walt Kiesling 1-6-1; Detroit--Gus Henderson 6-5-0; Cleveland--Dutch Clark 5-5-l; Cardinals--Ernie Nevers 1-10-0.

League Leaders

Yards Rushing		Yards Passing		Passing % (40 attempts)	
Bill Osmanski	699	Davey O'Brien	1324	Frankie Filchock	62
Andy Farkas	547	Parker Hall	1227	Johnny Pingel	56
Joe Maniaci	544	Arnie Herber	1107	Sam Baugh	55
Pug Manders	482	Frankie Filchock	1094	Parker Hall	51
Parker Hall	458	Ace Parker	977	Davey O'Brien	49

Receiving Yards		Receptions		Field Goals	
Don Hutson	846	Don Hutson	34	Ward Cuff	7
Perry Schwartz	550	Perry Schwartz	33	Ralph Kercheval	6
Andy Farkas	437	Vic Spadaccini	32	Ken Strong	4
Sam Boyd	423	Red Ramsey	31	Tiny Engebretsen	4
Dick Plasman	403	Jim Benton	27	Chuck Hanneman	4

Pro Bowl Game
(Gilmore Stadium, Los Angeles)

January 14 1940	Green Bay Packers	16	All-Stars	7

NFL Championship

December 10	New York Giants	0	at	Green Bay Packers	27

Individual Awards

Joe F. Carr Trophy--Parker Hall (Cleveland Rams)

Notes

Carl Storck replaced Joe Carr as President of the National Football League.
The first professional football game was also telecast this year. The game was telecast by station W2XBS, New York City and showed the Brooklyn Dodgers defeating the Philadelphia Eagles, 23 to 14 on October 22, 1939.

HOCKEY
National Hockey League

Team Name	GP	W	L	T	GF	GA	Pts	Pct
Boston Bruins	48	36	10	2	156	76	74	.771
New York Rangers	48	26	16	6	149	105	58	.604
Toronto Maple Leafs	48	19	20	9	114	107	47	.490
New York Americans	48	17	21	10	119	157	44	.458
Detroit Red Wings	48	18	24	6	197	128	42	.438
Montreal Canadiens	48	15	24	9	115	146	39	.406
Chicago Black Hawks	48	12	28	8	91	132	32	.333

Coaching Changes

Montreal--Cecil Hart 6-18-6, Jules Dugal 9-6-3; Chicago--Bill Stewart 8-10-3, Paul Thompson 4-18-5.

League Leaders

Goals		Assists		Points	
Roy Conacher	26	Bill Cowley	34	Hector Blake	47
Hector Blake	24	Paul Haynes	33	David Schriner	44
Alex Shibicky	24	David Schriner	31	Bill Cowley	42
Clint Smith	21	Marty Barry	28	Clint Smith	41
Bryan Hextall	20	Tom Anderson	27	Marty Barry	41

Penalty Minutes		GAA		Wins	
Red Horner	85	Frank Brimsek	1.58	Frank Brimsek	33
Muzz Patrick	72	Dave Kerr	2.19	Dave Kerr	26
Art Coulter	58	Walter Broda	2.23	Walter Broda	19
Stewart Evans	58	Cecil Thompson	2.49	Earl Robertson	17
Earl Seibert	57	Mike Karakas	2.75	Cecil Thompson	16

Shutouts	
Frank Brimsek	10
Walter Broda	8
Dave Kerr	6
Mike Karakas	5
Cecil Thompson	4

Stanley Cup Playoffs

March 21	New York Americans	0	at	Toronto Maple Leafs	4
March 21	Detroit Red Wings	0	at	Montreal Canadiens	2
March 21	Boston Bruins	2	at	New York Rangers	1 [59:25]

March 23	Toronto Maple Leafs	2	at	New York Americans	0
March 23	Montreal Canadiens	3	at	Detroit Red Wings	7
March 23	New York Rangers	2	at	Boston Bruins	3 [8:24]
March 26	Montreal Canadiens	0	at	Detroit Red Wings	1 [7:47]
March 26	New York Rangers	1	at	Boston Bruins	4
March 28	Boston Bruins	1	at	New York Rangers	2
March 28	Detroit Red Wings	1	at	Toronto Maple Leafs	4
March 30	New York Rangers	2	at	Boston Bruins	1 [17:19]
March 30	Toronto Maple Leafs	1	at	Detroit Red Wings	3
April 1	Boston Bruins	1	at	New York Rangers	3
April 1	Detroit Red Wings	4	at	Toronto Maple Leafs	5 [5:42]
April 2	New York Rangers	1	at	Boston Bruins	2 [48:00]
April 6	Toronto Maple Leafs	1	at	Boston Bruins	2
April 9	Toronto Maple Leafs	3	at	Boston Bruins	2 [10:38]
April 11	Boston Bruins	3	at	Toronto Maple Leafs	1
April 13	Boston Bruins	2	at	Toronto Maple Leafs	0
April 16	Toronto Maple Leafs	1	at	Boston Bruins	3

All Star Teams

First Team		Second Team
Frank Brimsek	Goal	Earl Robertson
Eddie Shore	Defense	Earl Seibert
Aubrey Clapper	Defense	Art Coulter
Syl Apps	Center	Neil Colville
Gord Drillon	Right Wing	Bobby Bauer
Hector Blake	Left Wing	John Gottselig
Art Ross	Coach	Mervyn Dutton

Individual Awards

Calder Trophy--Frank Brimsek (Boston Bruins)
Hart Trophy--Hector Blake (Montreal Canadiens)
Lady Byng Trophy--Clint Smith (New York Rangers)
Vezina Trophy--Frank Brimsek (Boston Bruins)

Notes

The NHL did away with the Canadian and American Divisions after the Montreal Maroons dropped out of the league.

Rules

The penalty shot line was abolished. Now the player taking a penalty shot was allowed to skate towards the goal.

Franchise Changes

NFL--Pittsburgh Pirates changed name to Pittsburgh Steelers.
NBL--Warren Penn became the Cleveland White Horses.
Whiting Ciesar All-Americans became the Hammond Ciesar All-Americans.

Other Sports

Horseracing--Kentucky Derby won by Johnstown (time 2:03.4, purse $46,350).
Heavyweight Boxing--Joe Louis knocked-out John H. Lewis in 1 round.

Joe Louis knocked-out Jack Roper in 1 round.
Joe Louis knocked-out Tony Galento in 4 rounds.
Joe Louis knocked-out Bob Pastor in 11 rounds.

Golf--U.S. Open won by Byron Nelson in a playoff with Craig Wood and Denny Shute (Tie-breaking rounds of 284-284-284; 68- 68-76; 70-73).

Auto Racing--Indianapolis 500 won by Wilbur Shaw (ave. speed 115.035 MPH).

Tennis--U.S. Open won by Bobby Riggs in the men's singles.
U.S. Open won by Adrian Quist and John Bromwich in the men's doubles.
U.S. Open won by Alice Marble in the women's singles.
U.S. Open won by Alice Marble and Sarah P. Fabyan in the women's doubles.
U.S. Open won by Alice Marble and Harry Hopman in the mixed doubles.

Notes

The first tennis tournament was telecast this year. Station W2XBS of New York City telecast the Eastern Grass Court Championship on August 9 from New York. They used a telescopic lens and an iconoscope to obtain closeups of important points.

1940

BASEBALL
National League

Team Name	W	L	Pct	GB	R	OR
Cincinnati Reds	100	53	.654	-	707	528
Brooklyn Dodgers	88	65	.575	12	697	621
St. Louis Cardinals	84	69	.549	16	747	699
Pittsburgh Pirates	78	76	.506	22.5	809	783
Chicago Cubs	75	79	.487	25.5	681	636
New York Giants	72	80	.474	27.5	663	659
Boston Bees	65	87	.428	34.5	623	745
Philadelphia Phillies	50	103	.327	50	494	750

Coaching Changes

St. Louis--Ray Blades 15-24, Mike Gonzalez 0-5, Bill Southworth 69-40; Pittsburgh--Frank Frisch 78-76.

League Leaders

Batting Average

Debs Garms	.355
Ernie Lombardi	.319
John Cooney	.318
Stan Hack	.317
Johnny Mize	.314

Home Runs

Johnny Mize	43
Bill Nicholson	25
John Rizzo	24
Dolf Camilli	23
Vince DiMaggio	19

RBI

Johnny Mize	137
Frank McCormick	127
Maurice Van Robays	116
Elburt Fletcher	104
Babe Young	101

Stolen Bases

Linus Frey	22
Stan Hack	21
Terry Moore	18
Bill Werber	16
Harold Reese	15

ERA

Bill Walters	2.48
Claude Passeau	2.50
Truett Sewell	2.80
Fred Fitzsimmons	2.81
Jim Turner	2.89

Wins

Bill Walters	22
Paul Derringer	20
Claude Passeau	20
Fred Fitzsimmons	16
Truett Sewell	16

Saves

Mace Brown	7
Walter Brown	7
Joe Beggs	7
Claude Passeau	5
Clyde Shoun	5

Strikeouts

Kirby Higbe	137
Whit Wyatt	124
Claude Passeau	124
Hal Schumacher	123
Paul Derringer	115

American League

Team Name	W	L	Pct	GB	R	OR
Detroit Tigers	90	64	.584	-	888	717
Cleveland Indians	89	65	.578	1	710	637
New York Yankees	88	66	.571	2	817	671
Boston Red Sox	82	72	.532	8	872	825
Chicago White Sox	82	72	.532	8	735	672
St. Louis Browns	67	87	.435	23	757	882
Washington Senators	64	90	.416	26	665	811
Philadelphia Athletics	54	100	.351	36	703	932

Coaching Changes

None.

League Leaders

Batting Average		Home Runs		RBI	
Joe DiMaggio	.352	Hank Greenberg	41	Hank Greenberg	150
Luke Appling	.348	Jimmie Foxx	36	Rudy York	134
Ted Williams	.344	Rudy York	33	Joe DiMaggio	133
Ray Radcliff	.342	Bob Johnson	31	Jimmie Foxx	119
Hank Greenberg	.340	Joe DiMaggio	31	Ted Williams	113

Stolen Bases		ERA		Wins	
George Case	35	Ernie Bonham	1.90	Bob Feller	27
Gerald Walker	21	Bob Feller	2.61	Bobo Newsom	21
Joe Gordon	18	Bobo Newsom	2.83	Al Milnar	18
John Lewis	15	John Rigney	3.11	Sid Hudson	17
Mike Kreevich	15	Eddie Smith	3.21	Tom Rowe	16

Saves		Strikeouts	
Al Benton	17	Bob Feller	261
Clint Brown	10	Bobo Newsom	164
John Murphy	9	John Rigney	141
Ed Heusser	5	Tom Bridges	133
John Allen	5	Ken Chase	129

All-Star Game

(Sportsman's Park, St. Louis)

July 10	National League	4	American League	0

World Series

October 2	Detroit Tigers	7	at	Cincinnati Reds	2
October 3	Detroit Tigers	3	at	Cincinnati Reds	5
October 4	Cincinnati Reds	4	at	Detroit Tigers	7
October 5	Cincinnati Reds	5	at	Detroit Tigers	2
October 6	Cincinnati Reds	0	at	Detroit Tigers	8
October 7	Detroit Tigers	0	at	Cincinnati Reds	4
October 8	Detroit Tigers	1	at	Cincinnati Reds	2

Individual Awards

Baseball Writers Award--Frank McCormick (Cincinnati Reds NL)
Hank Greenberg (Detroit Tigers AL)
Sporting News Executive of the Year--W.O. Briggs Sr. (Detroit Tigers AL)
Sporting News Manager of the Year--Bill McKechnie (Cincinnati Reds NL)
Sporting News MVP--Frank McCormick (Cincinnati Reds NL)
Hank Greenberg (Detroit Tigers AL)

BASKETBALL

National Basketball League

East Division

Team Name	GP	W	L	PPGF	PPGA	Pct	GB
Akron Firestone Non-Skids	27	18	9	44.2	40.8	.667	-
Detroit Eagles	27	17	10	39.8	36.6	.630	1
Akron Goodyear Wingfoots	28	14	14	37.4	37.0	.500	4.5
Indianapolis Kautskys	28	9	19	41.5	45.6	.321	9.5
West Division							
Oshkosh All-Stars	28	15	13	42.7	40.2	.536	-
Sheboygan Redskins	28	15	13	36.7	38.3	.536	-
Chicago Bruins	28	14	14	36.8	36.4	.500	1
Hammond Ciesar All-Americans	28	9	19	36.9	40.8	.321	6

Coaching Changes

Detroit--Gerry Archibald 17-10; Wingfoots--Ray Detrick 14-14; Sheboygan--Frank Zummach 15-13; Chicago--Sam Lifschulz 14-14; Hammond--Lou Boudreau 1-4, Eddie Ciesar 0-2, Leo Bereolos 8-13.

League Leaders

Field Goals		Free Throws		Points	
Ernie Andres	130	Leroy Edwards	139	Leroy Edwards	361
Mike Novak	114	Ben Stephens	113	Ben Stephens	295
Leroy Edwards	111	Bobby Neu	71	Mike Novak	293
Wibs Kautz	105	Jewell Young	70	Ernie Andres	292
Jack Ozburn	102	Mike Novak	65	Wibs Kautz	273

NBL Championship

Detroit Eagles	35	at	Akron Firestone Non-Skids	48
Akron Firestone Non-Skids	37	at	Detroit Eagles	49
Detroit Eagles	35	at	Akron Firestone Non-skids	46
Sheboygan Redskins	24	at	Oshkosh All-Stars	41
Oshkosh All-Stars	42	at	Sheboygan Redskins	43
Oshkosh All-Stars	31	at	Sheboygan Redskins	29
Akron Firestone Non-Skids	37	at	Oshkosh All-Stars	47
Akron Firestone Non-Skids	46	at	Oshkosh All-Stars	60
Oshkosh All-Stars	32	at	Akron Firestone Non-Skids	35
Oshkosh All-Stars	40	at	Akron Firestone Non-Skids	41
Oshkosh All-Stars	50	at	Akron Firestone Non-Skids	61

Notes

Station W2XBS televised the first basketball game this year. The telecast took place on February 28th, featuring a game between two university teams.

FOOTBALL
National Football League

East Division

Team Name	GP	W	L	T	PF	PA	Pct
Washington Redskins	11	9	2	0	245	142	.818
Brooklyn Dodgers	11	8	3	0	186	120	.727
New York Giants	11	6	4	1	131	133	.591
Pittsburgh Steelers	11	2	7	2	60	178	.273
Philadelphia Eagles	11	1	10	0	111	211	.091

West Division

Team Name	GP	W	L	T	PF	PA	Pct
Chicago Bears	11	8	3	0	238	152	.727
Green Bay Packers	11	6	4	1	238	155	.591
Detroit Lions	11	5	5	1	138	153	.500
Cleveland Rams	11	4	6	1	171	191	.409
Chicago Cardinals	11	2	7	2	139	222	.273

Coaching Changes

Brooklyn--Jock Sutherland 8-3-0; Pittsburgh--Walt Kiesling 2-7-2; Detroit--Potsy Clark5-5-1; Cardinals--Jim Conzelman 2-7-2.

League Leaders

Yards Rushing		Yards Passing		Passing % (40 attempts)	
Whizzer White	514	Sam Baugh	1367	Sam Baugh	63
Johnny Drake	480	Davey O'Brien	1290	Frank Filchock	52
Tuffy Leemans	474	Parker Hall	1108	Cotton Price	50
Banks McFadden	411	Cecil Isbell	1037	Eddie Miller	48
Dick Todd	408	Sid Luckman	941	Sid Luckman	46

Receiving Yards		Receptions		Field Goals	
Don Looney	707	Don Looney	58	Clarke Hinkle	9
Don Hutson	664	Don Hutson	45	Armand Niccolai	6
Dick Todd	402	Jim Johnston	29	Ward Cuff	5
Perry Schwartz	370	Vic Spadaccini	22	Ralph Kercheval	4
Jim Benton	351	Jim Benton	22	Jack Manders	2

Pro Bowl Game
(Gilmore Stadium, Los Angeles)

December 29	Chicago Bears	28		All-Stars	14

NFL Championship

December 8	Chicago Bears	73	at	Washington Redskins	0

Individual Awards

Joe F. Carr Trophy--Ace Parker (Brooklyn Dodgers)

HOCKEY

National Hockey League

Team Name	GP	W	L	T	GF	GA	Pts	Pct
Boston Bruins	48	31	12	5	170	98	67	.698
New York Rangers	48	27	11	10	136	77	64	.667
Toronto Maple Leafs	48	25	17	6	134	110	56	.583
Chicago Black Hawks	48	23	19	6	112	120	52	.542
Detroit Red Wings	48	16	26	6	90	126	38	.396
New York Americans	48	15	29	4	106	140	34	.354
Montreal Canadiens	48	10	33	5	90	167	25	.260

Coaching Changes

Boston--Ralph Weiland 31-12-5; Rangers--Frank Boucher 27-11-10; Chicago--Paul Thompson 23-19-6; Montreal--Alfred Lepine 10-33-5.

League Leaders

Goals		Assists		Points	
Bryan Hextall	24	Milt Schmidt	30	Milt Schmidt	52
Woody Dumart	22	Bill Cowley	27	Bob Bauer	43
Milt Schmidt	22	Bob Bauer	26	Woody Dumart	43
Herb Cain	21	Syd Howe	23	Bill Cowley	40
Gord Drillon	21	Woody Dumart	21	Gord Drillon	40

Penalty Minutes		GAA		Wins	
Red Horner	87	Dave Kerr	1.60	Frank Brimsek	31
Art Coulter	68	Paul Goodman	2.00	Dave Kerr	27
Elton Chamberlain	63	Frank Brimsek	2.04	Walter Broda	25
Jack Church	62	Walter Broda	2.30	Paul Goodman	16
Walter Pratt	61	Cecil Thompson	2.61	Cecil Thompson	16

Shutouts	
Dave Kerr	8
Frank Brimsek	6
Earl Robertson	6
Paul Goodman	4
Walter Broda	4

Stanley Cup Playoffs

March 19	Chicago Black Hawks	2	at	Toronto Maple Leafs	3 [6:35]
March 19	New York Americans	1	at	Detroit Red Wings	2 [00:25]
March 19	Boston Bruins	0	at	New York Rangers	4
March 21	Toronto Maple Leafs	2	at	Chicago Black Hawks	1
March 21	New York Rangers	2	at	Boston Bruins	4
March 22	Detroit Red Wings	4	at	New York Americans	5
March 24	New York Rangers	3	at	Boston Bruins	4
March 24	New York Americans	1	at	Detroit Red Wings	3

March 26	Boston Bruins	0	at	New York Rangers	1
March 26	Detroit Red Wings	1	at	Toronto Maple Leafs	2
March 28	New York Rangers	1	at	Boston Bruins	0
March 30	Boston Bruins	1	at	New York Rangers	4
April 2	Toronto Maple Leafs	1	at	New York Rangers	2 [15:30]
April 3	Toronto Maple Leafs	2	at	New York Rangers	6
April 6	New York Rangers	1	at	Toronto Maple Leafs	1
April 9	New York Rangers	0	at	Toronto Maple Leafs	3
April 11	New York Rangers	2	at	Toronto Maple Leafs	1 [31:43]
April 13	New York Rangers	3	at	Toronto Maple Leafs	2 [2:07]

All Star Teams

First Team		Second Team
Dave Kerr	Goal	Frank Brimsek
Aubrey Clapper	Defense	Art Coulter
Ebbie Goodfellow	Defense	Earl Seibert
Milt Schmidt	Center	Neil Colville
Bryan Hextall	Right Wing	Bobby Bauer
Hector Blake	Left Wing	Woody Dumart
Paul Thompson	Coach	Frank Boucher

Individual Awards

Calder Trophy--Kilby MacDonald (New York Rangers)
Hart Trophy--Ebenezer Goodfellow (Detroit Red Wings)
Lady Byng Trophy--Bobby Bauer (Boston Bruins)
Vezina Trophy--Dave Kerr (New York Rangers)

Notes

Station W2XBS, New York, televised the first professional hockey game on February 25th. In the game between the New York Rangers and the Canadiens, the Rangers won 6-2.

Franchise Changes

NFL--Cleveland White Horses became the Detroit Eagles.

Other Sports

Horseracing--Kentucky Derby won by Gallahadion (time 2:05, purse $60,150).
Heavyweight Boxing-- Joe Louis defeated Arturo Godoy in 15 rounds.
Joe Louis knocked-out Johnny Paychek in 2 rounds.
Joe Louis knocked-out Arturo Godoy in 8 rounds.
Joe Louis knocked-out Al McCoy in 6 rounds.
Golf--U.S. Open won by Lawson Little in a playoff with Gene Sarazen (rounds of 287-287, 70-73).
Auto Racing--Indianapolis 500 won by Wilbur Shaw (ave. speed 114.277 MPH).
Tennis--U.S. Open won by Don McNeill in the men's singles.
U.S. Open won by Jack Kramer and Frederick Schroeder Jr. in the men's doubles.
U. S. Open won by Alice Marble in the women's singles.
U.S. Open won by Alice Marble and Sarah P. Fabyan in the women's doubles.
U.S. Open won by Alice Marble and Bobby Riggs in the mixed doubles.

1941

BASEBALL

National League

Team Name	W	L	Pct	GB	R	OR
Brooklyn Dodgers	100	54	.649	-	800	581
St. Louis Cardinals	97	56	.634	2.5	734	589
Cincinnati Reds	88	66	.571	12	616	564
Pittsburgh Pirates	81	73	.526	19	690	643
New York Giants	74	79	.484	25.5	667	706
Chicago Cubs	70	84	.455	30	666	670
Boston Braves	62	92	.403	38	592	720
Philadelphia Phillies	43	111	.279	57	501	793

Coaching Changes

St. Louis--Bill Southworth 97-56; Chicago--Jim Wilson 70-84.

League Leaders

Batting Average

Pete Reiser	.343
John Cooney	.319
Joe Medwick	.318
Stan Hack	.317
Johnny Mize	.317

Home Runs

Dolf Camilli	34
Mel Ott	27
Bill Nicholson	26
Babe Young	25
Babe Dahlgren	23

RBI

Dolf Camilli	120
Babe Young	104
Vince DiMaggio	100
Johnny Mize	100
Bill Nicholson	98

Stolen Bases

Dan Murtaugh	18
Stan Benjamin	17
Linus Frey	16
Lee Handley	16
John Hopp	15

ERA

Elmer Riddle	2.24
Whit Wyatt	2.34
Ernie White	2.40
John Vander Meer	2.82
Bill Walters	2.83

Wins

Kirby Higbe	22
Whit Wyatt	22
Elmer Riddle	19
Bill Walters	19
Ernie White	17

Saves

Walter Brown	8
Hugh Casey	7
Bill Crouch	7
Ike Pearson	6
Ira Hutchinson	5

Strikeouts

John Vander Meer	202
Whit Wyatt	176
Bill Walters	129
Kirby Higbe	121
Mort Cooper	118

American League

Team Name	W	L	Pct	GB	R	OR
New York Yankees	101	53	.656	-	830	631
Boston Red Sox	84	70	.545	17	865	750
Chicago White Sox	77	77	.500	24	638	649
Cleveland Indians	75	79	.487	26	677	668
Detroit Tigers	75	79	.487	26	686	743
St. Louis Browns	70	84	.455	31	765	823
Washington Senators	70	84	.455	31	728	798
Philadelphia Athletics	64	90	.416	37	713	840

Coaching Changes

Cleveland--Roger Peckinpaugh 75-79; St. Louis--Fred Haney 15-29, Luke Sewell 55-55.

League Leaders

Batting Average		Home Runs		RBI	
Ted Williams	.406	Ted Williams	37	Joe DiMaggio	125
Cecil Travis	.359	Charlie Keller	33	Jeff Heath	123
Joe DiMaggio	.357	Tom Henrich	31	Charlie Keller	122
Jeff Heath	.340	Joe DiMaggio	30	Ted Williams	120
Dick Siebert	.334	Rudy York	27	Rudy York	111

Stolen Bases		ERA		Wins	
George Case	33	Thornton Lee	2.37	Bob Feller	25
Joe Kuhel	20	Charlie Wagner	3.07	Thornton Lee	22
Jeff Heath	18	Marius Russo	3.09	Dick Newsome	19
Mike Kreevich	17	Bob Feller	3.15	Emil Leonard	18
Jim Tabor	17	Eddie Smith	3.18	Lefty Gomez	15

Saves		Strikeouts	
John Murphy	15	Bob Feller	260
Al Benton	7	Bobo Newsom	175
Tom Ferrick	7	Thornton Lee	130
Mike Ryba	6	John Rigney	119
Joe Heving	5	Mickey Harris	111

All-Star Game

(Briggs Stadium, Detroit)

July 8	American League	7	National League	5

World Series

October 1	Brooklyn Dodgers	2	at	New York Yankees	3
October 2	Brooklyn Dodgers	3	at	New York Yankees	2
October 4	New York Yankees	2	at	Brooklyn Dodgers	1
October 5	New York Yankees	7	at	Brooklyn Dodgers	4
October 6	New York Yankees	3	at	Brooklyn Dodgers	1

Individual Awards

Baseball Writers Award--Dolf Camilli (Brooklyn Dodgers NL)
Joe DiMaggio (New York Yankees AL)
Sporting News Executive of the Year--Ed Barrow (New York Yankees AL)
Sporting News Manager of the Year--Billy Southworth (St. Louis Cardinals NL)
Sporting News MVP--Dolf Camilli (Brooklyn Dodgers NL)
Joe DiMaggio (New York Yankees AL)

BASKETBALL
National Basketball League

Team Name	GP	W	L	PPGF	PPGA	Pct	GB
Oshkosh All-Stars	24	18	6	42.2	37.1	.750	-
Sheboygan Redskins	24	13	11	36.1	34.7	.542	5
Akron Firestone Non-Skids	24	13	11	42.3	40.4	.542	5
Detroit Eagles	24	12	12	40.5	43.7	.500	6
Chicago Bruins	24	11	13	38.0	37.2	.458	7
Akron Goodyear Wing-Foots	24	11	13	38.6	38.8	.458	7
Hammond Ciesar All-Americans	24	6	18	38.6	44.4	.250	12

Coaching Changes

Detroit--Dutch Dehnert 12-12; Chicago--Frank Linskey 11-13; Hammond--Carl Anderson 6-18.

League Leaders

Field Goals		Free Throws		Points	
Ben Stephens	98	Leroy Edwards	76	Ben Stephens	265
Ed Sadowski	95	Jake Pelkington	70	Ed Sadowski	256
Wibs Kautz	94	Ben Stephens	69	Bill Hapac	227
Jack Ozburn	88	Bill Hapac	67	Wibs Kautz	227
Buddy Jeannette	75	Ed Sadowski	66	Jack Ozburn	211

NBL Championship

Oshkosh All-Stars	30	at	Akron Firestone Non-Skids	28
Akron Firestone Non-Skids	41	at	Oshkosh All-Stars	47
Sheboygan Redskins	32	at	Detroit Eagles	43
Detroit Eagles	19	at	Sheboygan Redskins	22
Detroit Eagles	40	at	Sheboygan Redskins	54
Oshkosh All-Stars	53	at	Sheboygan Redskins	38
Sheboygan Redskins	38	at	Oshkosh All-Stars	44
Sheboygan Redskins	36	at	Oshkosh All-Stars	54

FOOTBALL
National Football League

East Division

Team Name	GP	W	L	T	PF	PA	Pct
New York Giants	11	8	3	0	238	114	.727
Brooklyn Dodgers	11	7	4	0	158	127	.636
Washington Redskins	11	6	5	0	176	174	.545
Philadelphia Eagles	11	2	8	1	119	218	.227
Pittsburgh Steelers	11	1	9	1	103	276	.136

West Division

Team Name	GP	W	L	T	PF	PA	Pct
Chicago Bears	11	10	1	0	396	147	.909
Green Bay Packers	11	10	1	0	258	120	.909
Detroit Lions	11	4	6	1	121	195	.409
Chicago Cardinals	11	3	7	1	127	197	.318
Cleveland Rams	11	2	9	0	116	244	.182

Coaching Changes

Philadelphia--Greasy Neale 2-8-1; Pittsburgh--Bert Bell 0-2-0, Buff Donelli 0-4-0, Walt Kiesling 1-3-1; Detroit--Bill Edwards 4-6-1.

League Leaders

Yards Rushing		Yards Passing		Passing % (40 attempts)	
Pug Manders	486	Cecil Isbell	1479	Sid Luckman	57
George McAfee	474	Sammy Baugh	1236	Cecil Isbell	57
Marshall Goldberg	427	Sid Luckman	1181	Sam Baugh	55
Norm Standlee	414	Tommy Thompson	974	Tommy Thompson	53
Clarke Hinkle	393	Parker Hall	883	Ace Parker	50

Receiving Yards		Receptions		Field Goals	
Don Hutson	738	Don Hutson	58	Clarke Hinkle	6
Bill Dewell	352	Dick Humbert	29	Ward Cuff	5
Perry Schwartz	343	Bill Dewell	28	Andy Marefos	4
Dick Humbert	332	Perry Schwartz	24	Bill Daddio	4
Ward Cuff	317	Lou Brock	22	Bob Masterson	3

Punt Return Yards	
Whizzer White	262
Lee Gentry	238
Art Jones	232
George Franck	194
Tuffy Leemans	170

Pro Bowl Game
(Polo Grounds, New York)

January 4 1942	Chicago Bears	35		All-Stars	24

NFL Championship

December 14	Green Bay Packers	14	at	Chicago Bears	33
December 21	New York Giants	9	at	Chicago Bears	37

Individual Awards

Joe F. Carr Trophy--Don Hutson (Green Bay Packers)

Notes

Elmer Layden became the first Commissioner of the National Football League when the league replaced the office of President with a commissioner.

HOCKEY
National Hockey League

Team Name	GP	W	L	T	GF	GA	Pts	Pct
Boston Bruins	48	27	8	13	168	102	67	.698
Toronto Maple Leafs	48	28	14	6	145	99	62	.646
Detroit Red Wings	48	21	16	11	112	102	53	.552
New York Rangers	48	21	19	8	143	125	50	.521
Chicago Black Hawks	48	16	25	7	112	139	39	.406
Montreal Canadiens	48	16	26	6	121	147	38	.396
New York Americans	48	8	29	11	99	186	27	.186

Coaching Changes

Toronto--Clarence "Hap" Day 28-14-6; Montreal--Dick Irvin 16-26-6.

League Leaders

Goals		Assists		Points	
Bryan Hextall	26	Bill Cowley	45	Bill Cowley	62
Roy Conacher	24	Neil Colville	28	Syl Apps	44
David Schriner	24	Bill Taylor	26	Gord Drillon	44
Gord Drillon	23	Milt Schmidt	25	Bryan Hextall	44
Syl Apps	20	Phil Watson	25	Lynn Patrick	44

Penalty Minutes		GAA		Wins	
Jim Orlando	99	Walter Broda	2.06	Walter Broda	28
Cliff Goupille	81	Frank Brimsek	2.13	Frank Brimsek	27
Elton Chamberlain	75	John Mowers	2.13	John Mowers	21
Joe Cooper	66	Dave Kerr	2.60	Dave Kerr	21
Des Smith	61	Paul Goodman	2.62	Bert Gardiner	13

Shutouts	
Frank Brimsek	6
Walter Broda	4
John Mowers	4
Dave Kerr	2
Paul Goodman	2

Stanley Cup Playoffs

March 20	Montreal Canadiens	1	at	Chicago Black Hawks	2
March 20	New York Rangers	1	at	Detroit Red Wings	2 [12:01]
March 20	Toronto Maple Leafs	0	at	Boston Bruins	3
March 22	Chicago Black Hawks	3	at	Montreal Canadiens	4 [34:04]
March 22	Toronto Maple Leafs	5	at	Boston Bruins	3
March 23	Detroit Red Wings	1	at	New York Rangers	3
March 25	Montreal Canadiens	2	at	Chicago Black Hawks	3
March 25	New York Rangers	2	at	Detroit Red Wings	3
March 25	Boston Bruins	2	at	Toronto Maple Leafs	7
March 27	Chicago Black Hawks	1	at	Detroit Red Wings	3
March 27	Boston Bruins	2	at	Toronto Maple Leafs	1
March 29	Toronto Maple Leafs	2	at	Boston Bruins	1 [17:31]
March 30	Detroit Red Wings	2	at	Chicago Black Hawks	1 [9:15]
April 1	Boston Bruins	2	at	Toronto Maple Leafs	1
April 3	Toronto Maple Leafs	1	at	Boston Bruins	2
April 6	Detroit Red Wings	2	at	Boston Bruins	3
April 8	Detroit Red Wings	1	at	Boston Bruins	2
April 10	Boston Bruins	4	at	Detroit Red Wings	2
April 12	Boston Bruins	3	at	Detroit Red Wings	1

All Star Teams

First Team		Second Team
Walter Broda	Goal	Frank Brimsek
Aubrey Clapper	Defense	Earl Seibert
Wally Stanowski	Defense	Ott Heller
Bill Cowley	Center	Syl Apps
Bryan Hextall	Right Wing	Bobby Bauer
Dave Schriner	Left Wing	Woody Dumart
Ralph Weiland	Coach	Dick Irvin

Individual Awards

Calder Trophy--John Quilty (Montreal Canadiens)
Hart Trophy--Bill Cowley (Boston Bruins)
Lady Byng Trophy--Bobby Bauer (Boston Bruins)
Vezina Trophy--Walter Broda (Toronto Maple Leafs)

Notes

Flooding the ice between periods of a hockey game became mandatory.

Franchise Changes

NL--Boston Bees changed their name back to Boston Braves.

Other Sports

Horseracing--Kentucky Derby won by Whirlaway (time 2:01.4, purse $61,275).
Heavyweight Boxing--Joe Louis knocked-out Red Berman in 5 rounds.
Joe Louis knocked-out Gus Dorazio in 2 rounds.
Joe Louis knocked-out Abe Simon in 13 rounds.
Joe Louis knocked-out Tony Musto in 9 rounds.
Joe Louis beat Buddy Baer in 7 rounds on a disqualification.
Joe Louis knocked-out Billy Conn in 13 rounds.
Joe Louis knocked-out Lou Nova in 6 rounds.
Joe Louis knocked-out Buddy Baer in 1 round.
Golf--U.S. Open won by Craig Wood with a score of 284.
Auto Racing--Indianapolis 500 won by Floyd Davis and Mauri Rose (ave. speed 115.117 MPH).
Tennis--U.S. Open won by Bobby Riggs in the men's singles.
U.S. Open won by Jack Kramer and Frederick Schroeder Jr. in the men's doubles.
U.S. Open won by Sarah P. Cooke in the women's singles.
U.S. Open won by Sarah P. Cooke and Margaret Osborne in the women's doubles
U.S. Open won by Sarah P. Cooke and Jack Kramer in the mixed doubles.

1942

BASEBALL

National League

Team Name	W	L	Pct	GB	R	OR
St. Louis Cardinals	106	48	.688	-	755	482
Brooklyn Dodgers	104	50	.675	2	742	510
New York Giants	85	67	.559	20	675	600
Cincinnati Reds	76	76	.500	29	527	545
Pittsburgh Pirates	66	81	.449	36.5	585	631
Chicago Cubs	68	86	.442	38	591	665
Boston Braves	59	89	.399	44	515	645
Philadelphia Phillies	42	109	.278	62.5	394	706

Coaching Changes

New York--Mel Ott 85-67; Philadelphia--Hans Lobert 42-109.

League Leaders

Batting Average

Ernie Lombardi	.330
Enos Slaughter	.318
Stan Musial	.315
Pete Reiser	.310
Johnny Mize	.305

Home Runs

Mel Ott	30
Johnny Mize	26
Dolf Camilli	26
Bill Nicholson	21
Max West	16

RBI

Johnny Mize	110
Dolf Camilli	109
Enos Slaughter	98
Joe Medwick	96
Mel Ott	93

Stolen Bases

Pete Reiser	20
Harold Reese	15
Froilan Fernandez	15
Lennie Merullo	14
John Hopp	14

ERA

Mort Cooper	1.78
John Beazley	2.13
Curtis Davis	2.36
John Vander Meer	2.43
Bill Lohrman	2.48

Wins

Mort Cooper	22
John Beazley	21
Whit Wyatt	19
Claude Passeau	19
John Vander Meer	18

Saves

Hugh Casey	13
Ace Adams	11
Joe Beggs	8
John Sain	6
Harry Gumbert	5

Strikeout

John Vander Meer	186
Mort Cooper	152
Kirby Higbe	115
Bill Walters	109
Reuben Melton	107

American League

Team Name	W	L	Pct	GB	R	OR
New York Yankees	103	51	.669	-	801	507
Boston Red Sox	93	59	.612	9	761	594
St. Louis Browns	82	69	.543	19.5	730	637
Cleveland Indians	75	79	.487	28	590	659
Detroit Tigers	73	81	.474	30	589	587
Chicago White Sox	66	82	.446	34	538	609
Washington Senators	62	89	.411	39.5	653	817
Philadelphia Athletics	55	99	.357	48	549	801

Coaching Changes

St. Louis--Luke Sewell 82-69; Cleveland--Lou Boudreau 75-79.

League Leaders

Batting Average		Home Runs		RBI	
Ted Williams	.356	Ted Williams	36	Ted Williams	137
John Pesky	.331	Chester Laabs	27	Joe DiMaggio	114
Stan Spence	.323	Charlie Keller	26	Charlie Keller	108
Joe Gordon	.322	Joe DiMaggio	21	Joe Gordon	103
George Case	.320	Rudy York	21	Bob Doerr	102

Stolen Bases		ERA		Wins	
George Case	44	Ted Lyons	2.10	Cecil Hughson	22
James Vernon	25	Ernie Bonham	2.27	Ernie Bonham	21
Joe Kuhel	22	Spud Chandler	2.38	Jim Bagby	17
Phil Rizzuto	22	Hal Newhouser	2.45	Phil Marchildon	17
Myril Hoag	17	Henry Borowy	2.52	Spud Chandler	16

Saves		Strikeouts	
John Murphy	11	Cecil Hughson	113
Mace Brown	6	Bobo Newsom	113
Joe Haynes	6	Al Benton	110
George Caster	5	Phil Marchildon	110
Hal Newhouser	5	John Niggeling	107

All-Star Game

(Polo Grounds, New York)

July 6	American League	3	National League	1

World Series

September 30	New York Yankees	7	at	St. Louis Cardinals	4
October 1	New York Yankees	3	at	St. Louis Cardinals	4
October 3	St. Louis Cardinals	2	at	New York Yankees	0
October 4	St. Louis Cardinals	9	at	New York Yankees	6
October 5	St. Louis Cardinals	4	at	New York Yankees	2

Individual Awards

Baseball Writers Award--Mort Cooper (St. Louis Cardinals NL)
Joe Gordon (New York Yankees AL)
Sporting News Executive of the Year--Branch Rickey (St. Louis Cardinals NL)
Sporting News Manager of the Year--Billy Southworth (St. Louis Cardinals NL)
Sporting News MVP--Mort Cooper (St. Louis Cardinals NL)
Joe Gordon (New York Yankees AL)

Hall of Fame Inductee

Rogers Hornsby

BASKETBALL
National Basketball League

Team Name	GP	W	L	PPGF	PPGA	Pct	GB
Oshkosh All-Stars	24	20	4	49.3	40.7	.833	-
Fort Wayne Zollner Pistons	24	15	9	47.0	44.4	.625	5
Akron Goodyear Wingfoots	24	15	9	45.4	40.8	.625	5
Indianapolis Kautskys	23	12	11	41.5	41.2	.522	7.5
Sheboygan Redskins	24	10	14	39.3	42.4	.417	10
Chicago Bruins	23	8	15	41.8	44.6	.348	11.5
Toledo Jim White Chevrolets	24	3	21	39.7	51.2	.125	17

Coaching Changes

Fort Wayne--Carl Bennett 15-9; Chicago--Jack Tierney 8-15; Toledo--Tommy Edwards 3-21; Indianapolis--(unknown).

League Leaders

Field Goals		Free Throws		Points	
Chuck Chuckovits	143	Chuck Chuckovits	120	Chuck Chuckovits	406
Bobby McDermott	115	Leroy Edwards	92	Bobby McDermott	277
Ed Dancker	98	George Glamack	82	Jewell Young	263
Jewell Young	93	Jewell Young	77	Leroy Edwards	262
George Glamack	87	John Townsend	63	George Glamack	256

NBL Championship

Oshkosh All Stars	40	at	Indianapolis Kautskys	33
Indianapolis Kautskys	48	at	Oshkosh All-Stars	64
Fort Wayne Zollner Pistons	30	at	Akron Goodyear Wingfoots	46
Akron Goodyear Wingfoots	48	at	Fort Wayne Zollner Pistons	51
Akron Goodyear Wingfoots	43	at	Fort Wayne Zollner Pistons	49
Oshkosh All-Stars	43	at	Fort Wayne Zollner Pistons	61
Fort Wayne Zollner Pistons	60	at	Oshkosh All-Stars	68
Fort Wayne Zollner Pistons	46	at	Oshkosh All-Stars	52

FOOTBALL
National Football League

East Division

Team Name	GP	W	L	T	PF	PA	Pct
Washington Redskins	11	10	1	0	227	102	.909
Pittsburgh Steelers	11	7	4	0	167	119	.636
New York Giants	11	5	5	1	155	139	.500
Brooklyn Dodgers	11	3	8	0	100	168	.273
Philadelphia Eagles	11	2	9	0	134	239	.182

West Division

Team Name	GP	W	L	T	PF	PA	Pct
Chicago Bears	11	11	0	0	376	84	1.000
Green Bay Packers	11	8	2	1	300	215	.773
Cleveland Rams	11	5	6	0	150	207	.455
Chicago Cardinals	11	3	8	0	98	209	.273
Detroit Lions	11	0	11	0	38	263	.000

Coaching Changes

Pittsburgh--Walt Kiesling 7-4-0; Brooklyn--Mike Getto 3-8-0; Bears--George Halas 6-0-0, Luke Johnses--Hunk Anderson--Paddy Driscoll 5-0-0; Detroit--Bill Edwards 0-3-0, Bull Karcis 0-8-0.

League Leaders

Yards Rushing		**Yards Passing**		**Passing %** (40 attempts)	
Bill Dudley	696	Cecil Isbell	2021	Sam Baugh	59
Meril Condit	647	Sam Baugh	1524	Sid Luckman	54
Gary Famiglietti	503	Tommy Thompson	1410	Cecil Isbell	54
Andy Farkas	468	Bud Schwenk	1360	Tuffy Leemans	51
Dick Riffle	467	Sid Luckman	1023	Tommy Thompson	47

Receiving Yards		**Receptions**		**Field Goals**	
Don Hutson	1211	Don Hutson	74	Bill Daddio	5
Ray McLean	571	Pop Ivy	27	Frank Maznicki	4
Andy Uram	420	Dante Magnani	24	Ted Fritsch	4
Jim Benton	345	Jim Benton	23	Ward Cuff	3
Dick Todd	328	Dick Todd	23	Meril Condit	3

Punt Return Yards		**Kickoff Return Yards**	
Bill Dudley	271	Marshall Goldberg	393
Ernie Steele	264	Bill Dudley	298
Andy Farkas	219	Dante Magnani	250
Meril Condit	210	Merle Hapes	215
Andy Tomasic	199	Pug Manders	210

Pro Bowl Game

(Shibe Park, Philadelphia)

December 27	All-Stars	17		Washington Redskins	14

NFL Championship

December 13	Chicago Bears	6	at	Washington Redskins	14

Individual Awards

Joe F. Carr Trophy--Don Hutson (Green Bay Packers)

Notes

After George Halas joined the navy he handed the coaching reins to Johnses, Anderson, and Driscoll who were co-coaches.

HOCKEY

National Hockey League

Team Name	GP	W	L	T	GF	GA	Pts	Pct
New York Rangers	48	29	17	2	177	143	60	.625
Toronto Maple Leafs	48	27	18	3	158	136	57	.594
Boston Bruins	48	25	17	6	160	118	56	.583
Chicago Black Hawks	48	22	23	3	145	155	47	.490
Detroit Red Wings	48	19	25	4	140	147	42	.438
Montreal Canadiens	48	18	27	3	134	173	39	.406
Brooklyn Americans	48	16	29	3	133	175	35	.365

Coaching Changes

Boston--Art Ross 2.5-17-6.

League Leaders

Goals		Assists		Points	
Lynn Patrick	32	Phil Watson	37	Bryan Hextall	56
Roy Conacher	24	Bryan Hextall	32	Lynn Patrick	54
Bob Hamill	24	Sid Abel	31	Don Grosso	53
Bryan Hextall	24	Don Grosso	30	Phil Watson	52
Don Grosso	23	Eddie Wares	29	Sid Abel	49

Penalty Minutes		GAA		Wins	
Pat Egan	124	Frank Brimsek	2.45	Jim Henry	29
Jim Orlando	111	Walter Broda	2.83	Walter Broda	27
Jack Stewart	93	Jim Henry	2.98	Frank Brimsek	24
Des Smith	70	John Mowers	3.06	Sam LoPresti	21
Bingo Kampman	67	Sam LoPresti	3.23	John Mowers	19

Shutouts	
Walter Broda	6
John Mowers	5
Frank Brimsek	3
Sam LoPresti	3
Jim Henry	2

Stanley Cup Playoffs

March 21	New York Rangers	1	at	Toronto Maple Leafs	3
March 22	Toronto Maple Leafs	4	at	New York Rangers	2
March 22	Boston Bruins	2	at	Chicago Black Hawks	1 [5:51]
March 22	Montreal Canadiens	1	at	Detroit Red Wings	2
March 24	Chicago Black Hawks	4	at	Boston Bruins	0
March 24	Detroit Red Wings	0	at	Montreal Canadiens	5
March 24	Toronto Maple Leafs	0	at	New York Rangers	3
March 26	Chicago Black Hawks	2	at	Boston Bruins	3
March 26	Montreal Canadiens	2	at	Detroit Red Wings	6
March 28	New York Rangers	1	at	Toronto Maple Leafs	2
March 29	Toronto Maple Leafs	1	at	New York Rangers	3
March 29	Detroit Red Wings	6	at	Boston Bruins	4
March 31	New York Rangers	2	at	Toronto Maple Leafs	3
March 31	Boston Bruins	1	at	Detroit Red Wings	3
April 4	Detroit Red Wings	3	at	Toronto Maple Leafs	2
April 7	Detroit Red Wings	4	at	Toronto Maple Leafs	2
April 9	Toronto Maple Leafs	2	at	Detroit Red Wings	5
April 12	Toronto Maple Leafs	4	at	Detroit Red Wings	3
April 14	Detroit Red Wings	3	at	Toronto Maple Leafs	9
April 16	Toronto Maple Leafs	3	at	Detroit Red Wings	0
April 18	Detroit Red Wings	1	at	Toronto Maple Leafs	3

All Star Teams

First Team		Second Team
Frank Brimsek	Goal	Walter Broda
Earl Seibert	Defense	Pat Egan
Tommy Anderson	Defense	Wilfrid McDonald
Syl Apps	Center	Phil Watson
Bryan Hextall	Right Wing	Gord Drillon
Lynn Patrick	Left Wing	Sid Abel
Frank Boucher	Coach	Paul Thompson

Individual Awards

Calder Trophy--Grant Warwick (New York Rangers)
Hart Trophy--Tommy Anderson (New York Americans)
Lady Byng Trophy--Syl Apps (Toronto Maple Leafs)
Vezina Trophy--Frank Brimsek (Boston Bruins)

Franchise Changes

New York Americans changed name to Brooklyn Americans.

Other Sports

Horseracing--Kentucky Derby won by Shut Out (time 2:04.4, purse $64,225).
Heavyweight Boxing--Joe Louis knocked-out Abe Simon in 6 rounds.
Tennis--U.S. Open won by Frederick Schroeder Jr. in the men's singles.
U.S. Open won by Gardner Mulloy and William Talbert in the men's doubles.
U.S. Open won by Pauline Betz in the women's singles.
U.S. Open won by A. Louise Brough and Margaret Osborne in the women's doubles.
U.S. Open won by A. Louise Brough and Frederick Schroeder Jr. in the mixed doubles.

Notes

There was no Indianapolis 500 or U.S. Open golf tournament this year due to the war.

1943

BASEBALL
National league

Team Name	W	L	Pct	GB	R	OR
St. Louis Cardinals	105	49	.682	-	679	475
Cincinnati Reds	87	67	.565	18	608	543
Brooklyn Dodgers	81	72	.529	23.5	716	674
Pittsburgh Pirates	80	74	.519	25	669	605
Chicago Cubs	74	79	.484	30.5	632	600
Boston Braves	68	85	.444	36.5	465	612
Philadelphia Blue Jays	64	90	.416	41	571	676
New York Giants	55	98	.359	49.5	558	713

Coaching Changes

Philadelphia--Stanley Harris 40-53, Fred Fitzsimmons 24-37.

League Leaders

Batting Average		Home Runs		RBI	
Stan Musial	.357	Bill Nicholson	29	Bill Nicholson	128
Billy Herman	.330	Mel Ott	18	Bob Elliot	101
Walker Cooper	.318	Ron Northey	16	Billy Herman	100
Bob Elliot	.315	Coaker Triplett	15	Vince DiMaggio	88
Nicholas Witek	.314	Vince DiMaggio	15	Walker Cooper	81

Stolen Bases		ERA		Wins	
Joe Vaughan	20	Howard Pollet	1.75	Elmer Riddle	21
Harry Lowrey	13	Max Lanier	1.90	Mort Cooper	21
Frank Gustine	12	Mort Cooper	2.30	Truett Sewell	21
Jim Russell	12	Whit Wyatt	2.49	Hiram Bithorn	18
Charles Workman	12	Truett Sewell	2.54	Al Javery	17

Saves		Strikeouts	
Les Webber	10	John Vander Meer	174
Ace Adams	9	Mort Cooper	141
Clyde Shoun	7	Al Javery	134
Joe Beggs	6	Max Lanier	123
Edward Head	6	Kirby Higbe	108

American League

Team Name	W	L	Pct	GB	R	OR
New York Yankees	98	56	.636	-	669	542
Washington Senators	84	69	.549	13.5	666	595
Cleveland Indians	82	71	.536	15.5	600	577
Chicago White Sox	82	72	.532	16	573	594
Detroit Tigers	78	76	.506	20	632	560
St. Louis Browns	72	80	.474	25	596	604
Boston Red Sox	68	84	.447	29	563	607
Philadelphia Athletics	49	105	.318	49	497	717

Coaching Changes

Washington--Ossie Bluege 84-69; Detroit--Steve O'Neill 78-76.

League Leaders

Batting Average		**Home Runs**		**RBI**	
Luke Appling	.328	Rudy York	34	Rudy York	118
Dick Wakefield	.316	Charlie Keller	31	Nick Etten	107
Ralph Hodgin	.314	Vern Stephens	22	Billy Johnson	94
Roger Cramer	.300	Jeff Heath	18	Vern Stephens	91
George Case	.294	Joe Gordon	17	Stan Spence	88

Stolen Bases		**ERA**		**Wins**	
George Case	61	Spud Chandler	1.64	Paul Trout	20
Wally Moses	56	Ernie Bonham	2.27	Spud Chandler	20
Thurman Tucker	29	Tommy Bridoes	2.39	Early Wynn	18
Luke Appling	27	Paul Trout	2.48	Al Smith	17
Mickey Vernon	24	Butch Wensloff	2.54	Jim Bagby	17

Saves		**Strikeouts**	
Gordon Maltzberger	14	Allie Reynolds	151
Mace Brown	9	Hal Newhouser	144
Joe Heving	9	Spud Chandler	134
George Caster	8	Tom Bridges	124
John Murphy	8	Virgil Trucks	118

All-Star Game

(Shibe Park, Philadelphia)

July 13	American League	5	National League	3

World Series

October 5	St. Louis Cardinals	2	at	New York Yankees	4
October 6	St. Louis Cardinals	4	at	New York Yankees	3
October 7	St. Louis Cardinals	2	at	New York Yankees	6
October 10	New York Yankees	2	at	St. Louis Cardinals	1
October 11	New York Yankees	2	at	St. Louis Cardinals	0

Individual Awards

Baseball Writers Award--Stan Musial (St. Louis Cardinals NL)
Spud Chandler (New York Yankees AL)
Sporting News Executive of the Year--Clark Griffiths (Washington Senators AL)
Sporting News Manager of the Year--Joe McCarthy (New York Yankees AL)
Sporting News MVP--Stan Musial (St. Louis Cardinals NL)
Spud Chandler (New York Yankees AL)

BASKETBALL
National Basketball League

Team Name	GP	W	L	PPGF	PPGA	Pct	GB
Fort Wayne Zollner Pistons	23	17	6	51.1	46.4	.739	-
Sheboygan Redskins	23	12	11	43.2	43.7	.522	5
Oshkosh All-Stars	23	11	12	44.4	44.2	.478	6
Chicago Studebakers	23	8	15	48.2	50.8	.348	9
Toledo Jim White Chevrolets	4	0	4	38.8	48.0	.000	7.5

Coaching Changes

Sheboygan--Carl Roth 12-11; Chicago--John Jordan 8-15; Toledo--Sid Goldberg 0-4.

League Leaders

Field Goals		Free Throws		Points	
Bobby McDermott	132	Bernie Price	77	Bobby McDermott	316
Ed Dancker	96	Leroy Edwards	72	Ed Dancker	240
Rube Lautenschlager	88	Jake Pelkington	70	Jake Pelkington	236
Sonny Boswell	88	Sonny Boswell	53	Sonny Boswell	229
Ralph Vaughn	86	Bobby McDermott	52	Ralph Vaughn	222

NBL Championship

Chicago Studebakers	37	at	Fort Wayne Zollner Pistons	49
Fort Wayne Zollner Pistons	32	at	Chicago Studebakers	45
Chicago Studebakers	32	at	Fort Wayne Zollner Pistons	44
Oshkosh All-Stars	38	at	Sheboygan Redskins	50
Sheboygan Redskins	56	at	Oshkosh All-Stars	47
Sheboygan Redskins	55	at	Fort Wayne Zollner Pistons	50
Fort Wayne Zollner Pistons	50	at	Sheboygan Redskins	45 [OT]
Sheboygan Redskins	30	at	Fort Wayne Zollner Pistons	29

FOOTBALL
National Football League

East Division

Team Name	GP	W	L	T	PF	PA	Pct
Washington Redskins	10	6	3	1	229	137	.650
New York Giants	10	6	3	1	197	170	.650
Philadelphia Eagles-Pittsburgh Steelers	10	5	4	1	225	200	.550
Brooklyn Dodgers	10	2	8	0	65	234	.200

West Division

Team Name	GP	W	L	T	PF	PA	Pct
Chicago Bears	10	8	1	1	303	157	.850
Green Bay Packers	10	7	2	1	264	172	.750
Detroit Lions	10	3	6	1	178	218	.350
Chicago Cardinals	10	0	10	0	95	238	.000

Coaching Changes

Washington--Dutch Bergman 6-3-1; Philadelphia/Pittsburgh--Greasy Neale & Walt Kiesling 5-4-1; Brooklyn--Pete Cairthorn 2-8-0; Chicago Bears--Luke Johnses & Hunk Anderson & Paddy Driscoll 8-1-1; Detroit--Gus Dorais 3-6-1; Cardinals--Phil Handler 0-10-0.

League Leaders

Yards Rushing		Yards Passing		Passing % (40 attempts)	
Bill Paschal	572	Sid Luckman	2194	Sam Baugh	56
Jack Hinkle	571	Sam Baugh	1754	Sid Luckman	54
Harry Clark	556	Tony Canadeo	875	Irv Comp	50
Ward Cuff	523	Roy Zimmerman	846	Dean McAdams	49
Tony Canadeo	489	Frank Sinkwich	699	George Cafego	49

Receiving Yards		Receptions		Field Goals	
Don Hutson	776	Don Hutson	47	Ward Cuff	3
Wilbur Moore	537	Joe Aguirre	37	Don Hutson	3
Harry Clark	535	Wilbur Moore	30	Bob Snyder	2
Harry Jacunski	528	Eddie Rucinski	26	Augie Lio	2
Ray McLean	435	Harry Jacunski	24	Bob Masterson	1

Punt Return Yards		Kickoff Return Yards	
Frank Sinkwich	228	Ken Heineman	442
Bob Seymour	173	Harry Clark	326
Andy Farkas	168	Andy Farkas	279
Harry Clark	158	Ned Mathews	246
Ernie Steele	152	Tony Canadeo	242

NFL Championship

December 19	Washington Redskins	28	at	New York Giants	0
December 26	Washington Redskins	21	at	Chicago Bears	41

Individual Awards

Joe F. Carr Trophy--Sid Luckman (Chicago Bears)

HOCKEY
National Hockey league

Team Name	GP	W	L	T	GF	GA	Pts	Pct
Detroit Red Wings	50	25	14	11	169	124	61	.610
Boston Bruins	50	24	17	9	195	176	57	.570
Toronto Maple Leafs	50	22	19	9	198	159	53	.530
Montreal Canadiens	50	19	19	12	181	191	50	.500
Chicago Black Hawks	50	17	18	15	179	180	49	.490
New York Rangers	50	11	31	8	161	253	30	.300

Coaching Changes

None.

League Leaders

Goals		Assists		Points	
Doug Bentley	33	Bill Cowley	45	Doug Bentley	73
Joseph Benoit	30	Max Bentley	44	Bill Cowley	72
Gord Drillon	28	Herb O'Connor	43	Max Bentley	70
Robert Hamill	28	Billy Taylor	42	Lynn Patrick	61
Bill Cowley	27	Elmer Lach	40	Lorne Carr	60

Penalty Minutes		GAA		Wins	
Jim Orlando	99	John Mowers	2.47	John Mowers	25
Reg Hamilton	68	Walter Broda	3.18	Frank Brimsek	24
Jack Stewart	68	Frank Brimsek	3.52	Walter Broda	22
Elton Chamberlain	67	Bert Gardiner	3.58	Paul Bibeault	19
Vic Myles	57	Paul Bibeault	3.81	Bert Gardiner	17

Shutouts	
John Mowers	6
Walter Broda	1
Frank Brimsek	1
Bert Gardiner	1
Paul Bibeault	1

Stanley Cup Playoffs

March 21	Toronto Maple Leafs	2	at	Detroit Red Wings	4
March 21	Montreal Canadiens	4	at	Boston Bruins	5 [12:30]
March 23	Toronto Maple Leafs	3	at	Detroit Red Wings	2 [70:18]
March 23	Montreal Canadiens	3	at	Boston Bruins	5
March 25	Detroit Red Wings	4	at	Toronto Maple Leafs	2
March 25	Boston Bruins	3	at	Montreal Canadiens	2 [3:20]
March 27	Detroit Red Wings	3	at	Toronto Maple Leafs	6
March 27	Boston Bruins	0	at	Montreal Canadiens	4
March 28	Toronto Maple Leafs	2	at	Detroit Red Wings	4
March 30	Detroit Red Wings	3	at	Toronto Maple Leafs	2 [9:21]
March 30	Montreal Canadiens	4	at	Boston Bruins	5 [3:41]
April 1	Boston Bruins	2	at	Detroit Red Wings	6
April 4	Boston Bruins	3	at	Detroit Red Wings	4
April 7	Detroit Red Wings	4	at	Boston Bruins	0
April 8	Detroit Red Wings	2	at	Boston Bruins	0

All Star Teams

First Team		Second Team
John Mowers	Goal	Frank Brimsek
Earl Seibert	Defense	Jack Crawford
Jack Stewart	Defense	Bill Hollett
Bill Cowley	Center	Syl Apps
Lorne Carr	Right Wing	Bryan Hextall
Doug Bentley	Left Wing	Lynn Patrick
Jack Adams	Coach	Art Ross

Individual Awards

Calder Trophy--Gaye Stewart (Toronto Maple Leafs)
Hart Trophy--Bill Cowley (Boston Bruins)
Lady Byng Trophy--Max Bentley (Chicago Black Hawks)
Vezina Trophy--Johnny Mowers (Detroit Red Wings)

Notes

When Frank Calder died on February 4,1943 Red Dutton succeeded him as President of the National Hockey League.

Franchise Changes

NL--Philadelphia Phillies changed name to Philadelphia Blue Jays.
NFL--Pittsburgh Steelers and Philadelphia Eagles merged and played home games in both cities.

Other Sports

Horseracing--Kentucky Derby won by Count Fleet (time 2:04, purse $60,725).
Tennis--U.S. Open won by Joseph Hunt in the men's singles.
U.S. Open won by Jack Kramer and Frank Parker in the men's doubles.
U.S. Open won by Pauline Betz in the women's singles.
U.S. Open won by A. Louise Brough and Margaret Osborne in the women's doubles.
U.S. Open won by Margaret Osborne and William Talbert in the mixed doubles.

Notes

There was no Indianapolis 500 or U.S. Open Golf Championship held this year due to the war.

1944

BASEBALL
National League

Team Name	W	L	Pct	GB	R	OR
St. Louis Cardinals	105	49	.682	-	772	490
Pittsburgh Pirates	90	63	.588	14.5	744	662
Cincinnati Red Legs	89	65	.578	16	573	537
Chicago Cubs	75	79	.487	30	702	669
New York Giants	67	87	.435	38	682	773
Boston Braves	65	89	.422	40	593	674
Brooklyn Dodgers	63	91	.409	42	690	832
Philadelphia Blue Jays	61	92	.399	43.5	539	658

Coaching Changes

Chicago--Jim Wilson 1-9, Roy Johnson 0-1, Charlie Grimm 74-69; Boston--Bob Coleran 65-89; Philadelphia--Fred Fitzsimmons 61-92.

League Leaders

Batting Average		Home Runs		RBI	
Fred Walker	.357	Bill Nicholson	33	Bill Nicholson	122
Stan Musial	.347	Mel Ott	26	Bob Elliot	108
Joe Medwick	.337	Ron Northey	22	Ron Northey	104
John Hopp	.336	Frank McCormick	20	Ray Sanders	102
Phil Cavarretta	.321	George Kurowski	20	Frank McCormick	102

Stolen Bases		ERA		Wins	
John Barrett	28	Ed Heusser	2.38	Bill Walters	23
Tony Lupien	18	Bill Walters	2.40	Mort Cooper	22
Roy Hughes	16	Mort Cooper	2.46	Bill Voiselle	21
John Hopp	15	Max Lanier	2.65	Truett Sewell	21
John Kerr	14	Ted Wilks	2.65	Jim Tobin	18

Saves		Strikeouts	
Ace Adams	13	Bill Voiselle	161
Xavier Rescigno	5	Max Lanier	141
Fred Schmidt	5	Al Javery	137
Arthur Cuccurullo	4	Ken Raffensberger	136
Curt Davis	4	Fritz Ostermueller	97

American League

Team Name	W	L	Pct	GB	R	OR
St. Louis Browns	89	65	.578	-	684	587
Detroit Tigers	88	66	.571	1	658	581
New York Yankees	83	71	.539	6	674	617
Boston Red Sox	77	77	.500	12	739	676
Cleveland Indians	72	82	.468	17	643	677
Philadelphia Athletics	72	82	.468	17	525	594
Chicago White Sox	71	83	.461	18	543	662
Washington Senators	64	90	.416	25	592	664

Coaching Changes

None.

League Leaders

Batting Average		Home Runs		RBI	
Lou Boudreau	.327	Nick Etten	22	Vern Stephens	109
Bobby Doerr	.325	Vern Stephens	20	Bob Johnson	106
Bob Johnson	.324	John Lindell	18	John Lindell	103
George Stirnweiss	.319	Stan Spence	18	Stan Spence	100
Stan Spence	.316	Rudy York	18	Rudy York	98

Stolen Bases		ERA		Wins	
George Stirnweiss	55	Paul Trout	2.12	Hal Newhouser	29
George Case	49	Hal Newhouser	2.22	Paul Trout	27
Glenn Myatt	26	Cecil Hughson	2.26	Nelson Potter	19
Wally Moses	21	John Niggeling	2.32	Cecil Hughson	18
Don Gutteridge	20	Jack Kramer	2.49	Henry Borowy	17

Saves		Strikeouts	
Joe Berry	12	Hal Newhouser	187
Gordon Maltzberger	12	Paul Trout	144
George Caster	12	Bobo Newsom	142
Joe Hevin'	10	Jack Kramer	124
Frank Barrett	8	John Niggeling	121

All-Star Game

(Forbes Field, Pittsburgh)

July 11	National League	7	American League	1

World Series

October 4	St. Louis Browns	2	at	St. Louis Cardinals	1
October 5	St. Louis Browns	2	at	St. Louis Cardinals	3 [11]
October 6	St. Louis Cardinals	2	at	St. Louis Browns	6
October 7	St. Louis Cardinals	5	at	St. Louis Browns	1
October 8	St. Louis Cardinals	2	at	St. Louis Browns	0
October 9	St. Louis Browns	1	at	St. Louis Cardinals	3

Individual Awards

Baseball Writers Award--Marty Marion (St. Louis Cardinals NL)
Hal Newhouser (Detroit Tigers AL)
Sporting News Executive of the Year--William DeWitt (St. Louis Browns AL)
Sporting News Manager of the Year--Luke Sewell (St. Louis Browns AL)
Sporting News MVP--Marty Marion (St. Louis Cardinals NL)
Bobby Doerr (Boston Red Sox AL)

Hall of Fame Inductees

Kenesaw Mountain Landis

Notes

Happy Chandler replaced Kenesaw Mountain Landis as Commissioner of baseball.

BASKETBALL
National Basketball League

Team Name	GP	W	L	PPGF	PPGA	Pct	GB
Fort Wayne Zollner Pistons	22	18	4	47.2	41.2	.818	-
Sheboygan Redskins	22	14	8	41.5	40.9	.636	4
Oshkosh All-Stars	22	7	15	42.1	43.5	.318	11
Cleveland Chase Brass	18	3	15	42.1	48.4	.167	13

Coaching Changes

Cleveland--Vito Kubilus 3-15.

League Leaders

Field Goals		Free Throws		Points	
Bob McDermott	123	Mel Riebe	97	Mel Riebe	323
Mel Riebe	113	Clint Wager	72	Bob McDermott	306
Clint Wager	79	Bob McDermott	60	Clint Wager	230
Ed Dancker	70	Ed Dancker	52	Ed Dancker	192
Rube Lautenschlager	68	Leroy Edwards	52	Buddy Jeannette	184

NBL Championship

Cleveland Chase Brass	37	at	Fort Wayne Zollner Pistons	64
Fort Wayne Zollner Pistons	42	at	Cleveland Chase Brass	31
Oshkosh All-Stars	31	at	Sheboygan Redskins	32
Sheboygan Redskins	32	at	Oshkosh All-Stars	34
Oshkosh All-Stars	27	at	Sheboygan Redskins	40
Fort Wayne Zollner Pistons	55	at	Sheboygan Redskins	53
Fort Wayne Zollner Pistons	36	at	Sheboygan Redskins	26
Sheboygan Redskins	38	at	Fort Wayne Zollner Pistons	48

FOOTBALL
National Football league
East Division

Team Name	GP	W	L	T	PF	PA	Pct
New York Giants	10	8	1	1	206	75	.850
Philadelphia Eagles	10	7	1	2	267	131	.800
Washington Redskins	10	6	3	1	169	180	.650
Boston Yanks	10	2	8	0	82	233	.200
Brooklyn Tigers	10	0	10	0	69	166	.000

West Division

Team Name	GP	W	L	T	PF	PA	Pct
Green Bay Packers	10	8	2	0	238	141	.800
Chicago Bears	10	6	3	1	258	172	.650
Detroit Lions	10	6	3	1	216	151	.650
Cleveland Rams	10	4	6	0	188	224	.400
Chicago Cardinals-Pittsburgh Steelers	10	0	10	0	108	328	.000

Coaching Changes

Philadelphia--Greasy Neale 7-1-2; Washington--Dud DeGroot 6-3-1; Boston--Herb Kopf 2-8-0; Brooklyn--Pete Cawthorn & Ed Kuhale & Frank Bridges 0-10-0; Cleveland--Buff Donelli 4-6-0; Cardinals/Pittsburgh--Phil Handler & Walt Kiesling 0-10-0.

League Leaders

Yards Rushing		Yards Passing		Passing % (40 attempts)	
Bill Paschal	737	Irv Comp	1159	Frank Filchock	57
John Grigas	610	Frank Filchock	1139	Sam Baugh	56
Frank Sinkwich	563	Frank Sinkwich	1060	Sid Luckman	50
Hank Margarita	463	Sid Luckman	1018	Bob Westfall	49
Steve Van Buren	444	Sam Baugh	849	George Cafego	48

Receiving Yards		Receptions		Field Goals	
Don Hutson	866	Don Hutson	58	Ken Strong	6
Jim Benton	505	Jim Benton	39	Roy Zimmerman	4
Dave Diehl	426	Joe Aguirre	34	Joe Aguirre	4
Wilbur Moore	424	Wilbur Moore	33	Lou Zontini	3
Ray McLean	414	Les Dye	24	Augie Lio	2

Punt Return Yards		Kickoff Return Yards	
Bob Davis	271	John Grigas	471
Steve Van Buren	230	Bob Thurbon	291
Ernie Steele	181	Ted Fritsch	288
Frank Sinkwich	148	Albie Reisz	285
Frank Seno	129	Hank Margarita	279

NFL Championship

December 17	Green Bay Packers	14	at	New York Giants	7

Individual Awards

Joe F. Carr Trophy--Frank Sinkwich (Detroit Lions)

HOCKEY
National Hockey League

Team Name	GP	W	L	T	GF	GA	Pts	Pct
Montreal Canadiens	50	38	5	7	234	109	83	.830
Detroit Red Wings	50	26	18	6	214	177	58	.580
Toronto Maple Leafs	50	23	23	4	214	174	50	.500
Chicago Black Hawks	50	22	23	5	178	187	49	.490
Boston Bruins	50	19	26	5	223	268	43	.430
New York Rangers	50	6	39	5	162	310	17	.170

Coaching Changes

None.

League Leaders

Goals		Assists		Points	
Doug Bentley	38	Clint Smith	49	Herb Cain	82
Herb Cain	36	Elmer Lach	48	Doug Bentley	77
Lorne Carr	36	Herb Cain	46	Lorne Carr	74
Carl Liscombe	36	Herb O'Connor	42	Carl Liscombe	73
Mud Bruneteau	35	Bill Cowley	41	Elmer Lach	72

Penalty Minutes		GAA		Wins	
Mike McMahon	98	Bill Durnan	2.18	Bill Durnan	38
Pat Egan	95	Paul Bibeault	3.00	Conrad Dion	17
Elton Chamberlain	85	Mike Karakas	3.04	Bert Gardiner	17
Bob Dill	66	Conrad Dion	3.08	Paul Bibeault	13
Phil Watson	61	Jim Franks	4.06	Mike Karakas	12

Shutouts	
Paul Bibeault	5
Mike Karakas	3
Bill Durnan	2
Jim Franks	1
Conrad Dion	1

Stanley Cup Playoffs

March 21	Toronto Maple Leafs	3	at	Montreal Canadiens	1
March 21	Chicago Black Hawks	2	at	Detroit Red Wings	1
March 23	Toronto Maple Leafs	1	at	Montreal Canadiens	5
March 23	Chicago Black Hawks	1	at	Detroit Red Wings	4
March 25	Montreal Canadiens	2	at	Toronto Maple Leafs	1
March 26	Detroit Red Wings	0	at	Chicago Black Hawks	2

March 28	Montreal Canadiens	4	at	Toronto Maple Leafs	1
March 28	Detroit Red Wings	1	at	Chicago Black Hawks	7
March 30	Toronto Maple Leafs	0	at	Montreal Canadiens	11
March 30	Chicago Black Hawks	5	at	Detroit Red Wings	2
April 4	Chicago Black Hawks	1	at	Montreal Canadiens	5
April 6	Montreal Canadiens	3	at	Chicago Black Hawks	1
April 9	Montreal Canadiens	3	at	Chicago Black Hawks	2
April 13	Chicago Black Hawks	4	at	Montreal Canadiens	5 [9:12]

All Star Teams

First Team		Second Team
Bill Durnan	Goal	Paul Bibeault
Earl Seibert	Defense	Emile Bouchard
Walter Pratt	Defense	Aubrey Clapper
Bill Cowley	Center	Elmer Lach
Lorne Carr	Right Wing	Maurice Richard
Doug Bentley	Left Wing	Herb Cain
Dick Irvin	Coach	Clarence Day

Individual Awards

Calder Memorial Trophy--Gus Bodnar (Toronto Maple Leafs)
Hart Trophy--Walter Pratt (Toronto Maple Leafs)
Lady Byng Trophy--Clint Smith (Chicago Black Hawks)
Vezina Trophy--Bill Durnan (Montreal Canadiens)

Rules

The center ice red line was introduced to the NHL, and it was now legal to pass from the defensive zone to the center ice zone. With the third line on the ice surface it was now possible to make two line passes and the league adopted a rule forbidding this.

Franchise Changes

NL--Cincinnati- Reds changed name to Cincinnati Red Legs.
NFL--Pittsburgh Steelers and Philadelphia Eagles merger broke up this year and the Steelers then merged with the Chicago Cardinals.
NFL--Brooklyn. Dodgers changed name to Brooklyn Tigers.

Other Sports

Horseracing--Kentucky Derby won by Pensive (time 2,:04.2, purse $64,675).
Tennis--U.S. Open won by Frank Parker in the men's singles.
U.S. Open won by Don McNeill and Robert Falkenburg in the men's doubles.
U.S. Open won by Pauline Betz in the women's singles.
U.S. Open won by Louise Brough and Margaret Osborne in the women's doubles.
U.S. Open won by Margaret Osborne and William Talbert in the mixed doubles.

Notes

There was no Indianapolis 500 or U.S. Open Golf Championship held this year due to the war.

1945

BASEBALL
National League

Team Name	W	L	Pct	GB	R	OR
Chicago Cubs	98	56	.636	-	735	532
St. Louis Cardinals	95	59	.617	3	756	583
Brooklyn Dodgers	87	67	.565	11	795	724
Pittsburgh Pirates	82	72	.532	16	750	686
New York Giants	78	74	.513	19	668	700
Boston Braves	67	85	.441	30	721	728
Cincinnati Red Legs	61	93	.396	37	536	694
Philadelphia Phillies	46	108	.299	52	548	865

Coaching Changes

Chicago--Charlie Grimm 98-56; Boston--Bob Coleran 42-49, Del Bissonette 25-36; Philadelphia--Fred Fitzsimmons17-50, Ben Chapman 29-58.

League Leaders

Batting Average

Phil Cavarretta	.355
Tom Holmes	.352
Goodwin Rosen	.325
Stan Hack	.323
George Kurowski	.323

Home Runs

Tom Holmes	28
Chuck Workman	25
Elvin Adams	22
Mel Ott	21
George Kurowski	21

RBI

Fred Walker	124
Tom Holmes	117
Luis Olmo	110
Andy Pafko	110
Elvin Adams	109

Stolen Bases

Albert Schoendienst	26
John Barrett	25
Dain Clay	19
Jim Russell	15
Luis Olmo	15

ERA

Hank Borowy	2.13
Claude Passeau	2.46
Harry Brecheen	2.52
Bill Walters	2.68
Hank Wyse	2.68

Wins

Charles Barrett	23
Hank Wyse	22
Ken Burkhart	19
Hal Gregg	18
Claude Passeau	17

Saves

Andy Karl	15
Ace Adams	15
Xavier Rescigno	9
Don Hendrickson	5
Cyril Buker	5

Strikeouts

Charles Roe	148
Hal Gregg	139
Ken Burkhart	115
Van Lingle Mungo	101
John Hutchings	99

American League

Team Name	W	L	Pct	GB	R	OR
Detroit Tigers	88	65	.575	-	633	565
Washington Senators	87	67	.565	1.5	622	562
St. Louis Browns	81	70	.536	6	597	548
New York Yankees	81	71	.533	6.5	676	606
Cleveland Indians	73	72	.503	11	557	548
Chicago White Sox	71	78	.477	15	596	633
Boston Red Sox	71	83	.461	17.5	599	674
Philadelphia Athletics	52	98	.347	34.5	494	638

Coaching Changes

None.

League Leaders

Batting Average

George Stirnweiss	.309
Tony Cuccinello	.308
John Dickshot	.302
Bob Estalella	.299
George Myatt	.296

Home Runs

Vern Stephens	24
Roy Cullenbine	18
Nick Etten	18
Rudy York	18
Jeff Heath	15

RBI

Nick Etten	111
Roy Cullenbine	93
Vern Stephens	89
Rudy York	87
George Binks	81

Stolen Bases

George Stirnweiss	33
George Myatt	30
George Case	30
George Metkovich	19
John Dickshot	18

ERA

Hal Newhouser	1.81
Al Benton	2.02
Roger Wolff	2.12
Emil Leonard	2.13
Thornton Lee	2.44

Wins

Hal Newhouser	25
David Ferriss	21
Roger Wolff	20
Steve Gromek	19
Paul Trout	18

Saves

Jim Turner	10
Joe Berry	5
Frank Overmire	4
Eddie Klieman	4
Earl Caldwell	4

Strikeouts

Hal Newhouser	212
Nelson Potter	129
Bobo Newsom	127
Allie Reynolds	112
Thornton Lee	108

World Series

October 3	Chicago Cubs	9	at	Detroit Tigers	0
October 4	Chicago Cubs	1	at	Detroit Tigers	4
October 5	Chicago Cubs	3	at	Detroit Tigers	0
October 6	Detroit Tigers	4	at	Chicago Cubs	1
October 7	Detroit Tigers	8	at	Chicago Cubs	4
October 8	Detroit Tigers	7	at	Chicago Cubs	8 [12]
October 10	Detroit Tigers	9	at	Chicago Cubs	3

Individual Awards

Baseball Writers Award--Phil Cavarretta (Chicago Cubs NL)
Hal Newhouser (Detroit Tigers AL)
Sporting News Executive of the Year--Philip Wrigley (Chicago Cubs NL)
Sporting News Manager of the Year--Ossie Bluege (Washington Senators AL)
Sporting News MVP--Tom Holmes (Boston Braves NL)
Eddie Mayo (Detroit Tigers AL)

Hall of Fame Inductees

Roger Bresnahan, Dan Brouthers, Fred Clarke, Jimmie Collins, Ed Delahanty, Hugh Duffy, Hugh Jennings, Mike Kelly, Jim O'Rourke, Wilbert Robinson

BASKETBALL
National Basketball League
East Division

Team Name	GP	W	L	PPGF	PPGA	Pct	GB
Fort Wayne Zollner Pistons	30	25	5	56.9	50.2	.833	-
Cleveland Allmen Transfers	30	13	17	51.0	51.0	.433	12
Pittsburgh Raiders	30	7	23	48.7	55.5	.233	18

West Division

Team Name	GP	W	L	PPGF	PPGA	Pct	GB
Sheboygan Redskins	30	19	11	49.8	46.0	.633	-
Chicago American Gears	30	14	16	51.6	53.9	.467	5
Oshkosh All-Stars	30	12	18	46.9	48.2	.400	7

Coaching Changes

Cleveland--Jeff Carlin 13-17; Pittsburgh--Joe Urso 7-23; Sheboygan--Dutch Dehnert 19-11; Chicago--Jack Tierney 14-16.

League Leaders

Field Goals		Free Throws		Points	
Bobby McDermott	258	Mel Riebe	161	Mel Riebe	607
Mel Riebe	223	Leroy Edwards	157	Bobby McDermott	603
Stan Patrick	187	Bobby McDermott	87	Stan Patrick	458
Huck Hartman	127	Stan Patrick	84	Leroy Edwards	407
Leroy Edwards	125	Buddy Jeannette	82	Huck Hartman	327

NBL Championship

Cleveland Allmen Transfers	50	at	Fort Wayne Zollner Pistons	78
Cleveland Allmen Transfers	51	at	Fort Wayne Zollner Pistons	58
Chicago American Gears	50	at	Sheboygan Redskins	49
Sheboygan Redskins	49	at	Chicago American Gears	36
Chicago American Gears	27	at	Sheboygan Redskins	57
Fort Wayne Zollner Pistons	53	at	Sheboygan Redskins	65
Fort Wayne Zollner Pistons	47	at	Sheboygan Redskins	50
Sheboygan Redskins	47	at	Fort Wayne Zollner Pistons	58
Sheboygan Redskins	41	at	Fort Wayne Zollner Pistons	58
Sheboygan Redskins	49	at	Fort Wayne Zollner Pistons	59

FOOTBALL
National Football League
East Division

Team Name	GP	W	L	T	PF	PA	Pct
Washington Redskins	10	8	2	0	209	121	.800
Philadelphia Eagles	10	7	3	0	272	133	.700
New York Giants	10	3	6	1	179	198	.350
Boston Yanks	10	3	6	1	123	211	.350
Pittsburgh Steelers	10	2	8	0	79	220	.200

West Division

Team Name	GP	W	L	T	PF	PA	Pct
Cleveland Rams	10	9	1	0	244	136	.900
Detroit Lions	10	7	3	0	195	194	.700
Green Bay Packers	10	6	4	0	258	173	.600
Chicago Bears	10	3	7	0	192	235	.300
Chicago Cardinals	10	1	9	0	98	228	.100

Coaching Changes

Pittsburgh--Jim Leonard 2-8-0; Cleveland--Adam Walsh 9-1-0; Chicago Bears--Luke Johnses & Hunk Anderson & Paddy Driscoll 1-7-0, George Halas 2-0-0; Cardinals--Phil Handler 1-9-0.

League Leaders

Yards Rushing		Yards Passing		Passing % (40 attempts)	
Steve Van Buren	832	Sid Luckman	1725	Sam Baugh	70
Frank Akins	797	Sam Baugh	1669	Sid Luckman	54
Hank Margarita	497	Bob Waterfield	1609	Bob Waterfield	52
Fred Gehrke	467	Paul Christman	1147	Roy Zimmerman	51
Jim Gillette	390	Roy Zimmerman	991	John Hovious	48

Receiving Yards		Receptions		Field Goals	
Jim Benton	1067	Don Hutson	47	Joe Aguirre	7
Don Hutson	834	Jim Benton	45	Ken Strong	6
Frank Liebel	593	Ken Kavanaugh	35	Roy Zimmerman	4
Ken Kavanaugh	539	Steve Bagarus	35	Augie Lio	4
Steve Bagarus	517	George Wilson	28	Ben Agajanian	4

Punt Return Yards		Kickoff Return Yards	
Steve Bagarus	251	Frank Seno	408
Dave Ryan	220	Steve Van Buren	373
Busit Warren	168	Steve Bagarus	325
Steve Van Buren	154	John Martin	302
Ward Cuff	124	Ted Fritsch	279

NFL Championship

December 16	Washington Redskins	14	at	Cleveland Rams	15

Individual Awards

Joe F. Carr Trophy--Bob Waterfield (Cleveland Rams)

HOCKEY
National Hockey League

Team Name	GP	W	L	T	GF	GA	Pts	Pct
Montreal Canadiens	50	38	8	4	228	121	80	.800
Detroit Red Wings	50	31	14	5	218	161	67	.670
Toronto Maple Leafs	50	24	22	4	183	161	52	.520
Boston Bruins	50	16	30	4	179	219	36	.360
Chicago Black Hawks	50	13	30	7	171	174	33	.330
New York Rangers	50	11	29	10	154	147	32	.320

Coaching Changes

Chicago--Paul Thompson 0-1-0, John Gottselig 13-29-7.

League Leaders

Goals

Rocket Richard	50
Hector Blake	29
Ted Kennedy	29
Bill Mosienko	28
David Schriner	27

Assists

Elmer Lach	54
Bill Cowley	40
Hector Blake	38
Gus Bodnar	36
Syd Howe	36

Points

Elmer Lach	80
Rocket Richard	73
Hector Blake	67
Bill Cowley	65
Ted Kennedy	54

Penalty Minutes

Pat Egan	86
Bob Dill	69
Leo Lamoureux	58
Joe Cooper	50
Bob Davidson	49

GAA

Bill Durnan	2.42
Frank McCool	3.22
Harry Lumley	3.22
Conrad Dion	3.25
Mike Karakas	3.90

Wins

Bill Durnan	38
Harry Lumley	24
Frank McCool	24
Mike Karakas	12
Ken McAuley	11

Shutouts

Mike Karakas	4
Frank McCool	4
Harry Lumley	1
Ken McAuley	1
Bill Durnan	1

Stanley Cup Playoffs

March 20	Toronto Maple Leafs	1	at	Montreal Canadiens	0
March 20	Boston Bruins	4	at	Detroit Red Wings	3
March 22	Toronto Maple Leafs	3	at	Montreal Canadiens	2
March 22	Boston Bruins	4	at	Detroit Red Wings	2
March 24	Montreal Canadiens	4	at	Toronto Maple Leafs	1
March 25	Detroit Red Wings	3	at	Boston Bruins	2
March 27	Montreal Canadiens	3	at	Toronto Maple Leafs	4 [12:36]
March 27	Detroit Red Wings	3	at	Boston Bruins	2
March 29	Toronto Maple Leafs	3	at	Montreal Canadiens	10
March 29	Boston Bruins	2	at	Detroit Red Wings	3 [17:21]
March 31	Montreal Canadiens	2	at	Toronto Maple Leafs	3
April 1	Detroit Red Wings	3	at	Boston Bruins	5

April 3	Boston Bruins	3	at	Detroit Red Wings	5
April 6	Toronto Maple Leafs	1	at	Detroit Red Wings	0
April 8	Toronto Maple Leafs	2	at	Detroit Red Wings	0
April 12	Detroit Red Wings	0	at	Toronto Maple Leafs	1
April 14	Detroit Red Wings	5	at	Toronto Maple Leafs	3
April 19	Toronto Maple Leafs	0	at	Detroit Red Wings	2
April 21	Detroit Red Wings	1	at	Toronto Maple Leafs	0 [14:16]
April 22	Toronto Maple Leafs	2	at	Detroit Red Wings	1

All Star Teams

First Team		Second Team
Bill Durnan	Goal	Mike Karakas
Emile Bouchard	Defense	Glen Harmon
Bill Hollett	Defense	Walter Pratt
Elmer Lach	Center	Bill Cowley
Maurice Richard	Right Wing	Bill Mosienko
Hector Blake	Left Wing	Syd Howe
Dick Irvin	Coach	Jack Adams

Individual Awards

Calder Memorial Trophy--Frank McCool (Toronto Maple Leafs)
Hart Trophy--Elmer Lach (Montreal Canadiens)
Lady Byng Trophy--Bill Mosienko (Chicago Black Hawks)
Vezina Trophy--Bill Durnan (Montreal Canadiens)

Hall of Fame Inductees

Sir Montagu Allan, Dan Bain, Hobey Baker, Russel Bowie, Charlie Gardiner, Eddie Gerard, Frank McGee, Howie Morenz, Tommy Phillips, Harvey Pulford, Art Ross, Lord Stanley of Preston, Hod Stuart, Georges Vezina

Franchise Changes

NL--Philadelphia Blue Jays changed name back to Philadelphia Phillies.
NFL--Pittsburgh Steelers and Chicago Cardinals went their separate ways this season.

Other Sports

Horseracing--Kentucky Derby won by Hoop Jr. (time 2:07, purse $64,850).
Tennis--U.S. Open won by Frank Parker in the men's singles.
U.S. Open won by Gardnar Mulloy and William Talbert in the men's doubles.
U.S. Open won by Sarah Cooke in the women's singles.
U.S. Open won by A. Louise Brough and Margaret Osborne in the women's doubles.
U.S. Open won by Margaret Osborne and William Talbert in the mixed doubles.

Notes

There was no Indianapolis 500 or U.S. Open Golf Championship held this year due to the year.

1946

BASEBALL
National League

Team Name	W	L	Pct	GB	R	OR
St. Louis Cardinals	98	58	.628	-	712	545
Brooklyn Dodgers	96	60	.615	2	701	570
Chicago Cubs	82	71	.536	14.5	626	581
Boston Braves	81	72	.529	15.5	630	592
Philadelphia Phillies	69	85	.448	28	560	705
Cincinnati Reds	67	87	.435	30	523	570
Pittsburgh Pirates	63	91	.409	34	552	668
New York Giants	61	93	.396	36	612	685

Coaching Changes

St. Louis--Eddie Dyer 98-58; Boston--Bill Southworth 81-72; Philadelphia--Ben Chapman 69-85; Pittsburgh--FrankFrisch 62-89, Virgil Davis 1-2.

League Leaders

Batting Average		Home Runs		RBI	
Stan Musial	.365	Ralph Kiner	23	Enos Slaughter	130
John Hopp	.333	John Mize	22	Fred Walker	116
Fred Walker	.319	Enos Slaughter	18	Stan Musial	103
Del Ennis	.313	Del Ennis	17	George Kurowski	89
Tom Holmes	.310	Ron Northey	16	Ralph Kiner	81

Stolen Bases		ERA		Wins	
Pete Reiser	34	Howard Pollet	2.10	Howard Pollet	21
Bert Haas	22	John Sain	2.21	John Sain	20
John Hopp	21	Joe Beggs	2.32	Kirby Higbe	17
Bob Adams	16	Ewell Blackwell	2.45	Murry Dickson	15
Fred Walker	14	Harry Brecheen	2.49	Harry Brecheen	15

Saves		Strikeouts	
Ken Raffensberger	6	John Schmitz	135
Andy Karl	5	Kirby Higbe	134
Hugh Casey	5	John Sain	129
Art Herring	5	Dave Koslo	121
Howard Pollet	5	Harry Brecheen	117

Notes

St. Louis Cardinals defeated Brooklyn 2 games to 1 in a playoff for the championship of the NL.

American league

Team Name	W	L	Pct	GB	R	OR
Boston Red Sox	104	50	.675	-	792	594
Detroit Tigers	92	62	.597	12	704	567
New York Yankees	87	67	.565	17	684	547
Washington Senators	76	78	.494	28	608	706
Chicago White Sox	74	80	.481	30	562	595
Cleveland Indians	68	86	.442	36	537	637
St. Louis Browns	66	88	.429	38	621	711
Philadelphia Athletics	49	105	.318	55	529	680

Coaching Changes

New York--Joe McCarthy 22-13, Bill Dickey 57-48, John Neun 8-6; Chicago--Jim Dykes 10-20,Ted Lyons 64-60; St. Louis--Luke Sewell 53-71, Zack Taylor 13-17.

League Leaders

Batting Average		Home Runs		RBI	
Mickey Vernon	.353	Hank Greenberg	44	Hank Greenberg	127
Ted Williams	.342	Ted Williams	38	Ted Williams	123
John Pesky	.335	Charlie Keller	30	Rudy York	119
George Kell	.322	Pat Seerey	26	Bobby Doerr	116
Dom DiMaggio	.316	Joe DiMaggio	25	Charlie Keller	101

Stolen Bases		ERA		Wins	
George Case	28	Hal Newhouser	1.94	Bob Feller	26
George Stirnweiss	18	Spud Chandler	2.10	Hal Newhouser	26
Eddie Lake	15	Bob Feller	2.18	David Ferriss	25
Phil Rizzuto	14	Bill Bevens	2.23	Spud Chandler	20
Don Kolloway	14	Paul Trout	2.34	Cecil Hughson	20

Saves		Strikeouts	
Bob Klinger	9	Bob Feller	348
Earl Caldwell	8	Hal Newhouser	275
John Murphy	7	Cecil Hughson	172
Tom Ferrick	6	Virgil Trucks	161
Steve Gromek	4	Paul Trout	151

All-Star Game

(Fenway Park, Boston)

July 9	American League	12	National League	0

World Series

October 6	Boston Red Sox	3	at	St. Louis Cardinals	2 [10]
October 7	Boston Red Sox	0	at	St. Louis Cardinals	3
October 9	St. Louis Cardinals	0	at	Boston Red Sox	4
October 10	St. Louis Cardinals	12	at	Boston Red Sox	3
October 11	St. Louis Cardinals	3	at	Boston Red Sox	6
October 13	Boston Red Sox	1	at	St. Louis Cardinals	4
October 15	Boston Red Sox	3	at	St. Louis Cardinals	4

Individual Awards

Baseball Writers Award--Stan Musial (St. Louis Cardinals NL)
Ted Williams (Boston Red Sox AL)
Sporting News Executive of the Year--Thomas Yawkey (Boston Red Sox AL)
Sporting News Manager of the Year--Eddie Dyer (St. Louis Cardinals NL)
Sporting News Rookie of the Year--Del Ennis (Philadelphia Phillies NL)

Hall of Fame Inductees

Jesse Burkett, Frank Chance, Jack Chesbro, John Evers, Clark Griffith, Tom McCarthy, Joe, McGinnity, Eddie Plank, Joe Tinker, George Waddell, Ed Walsh

BASKETBALL
National Basketball League

East Division

Team Name	GP	W	L	PPGF	PPGA	Pct	GB
Fort Wayne Zollner Pistons	34	26	8	58.7	51.0	.765	-
Rochester Royals	34	24	10	56.8	50.8	.706	2
Youngstown Bears	33	13	20	46.6	50.5	.394	12.5
Cleveland Allmen Transfers	33	4	29	46.1	56.4	.121	21.5

West Division

Team Name	GP	W	L	PPGF	PPGA	Pct	GB
Sheboygan Redskins	34	21	13	51.0	48.2	.618	-
Oshkosh All-Stars	34	19	15	53.4	49.2	.559	2
Chicago American Gears	34	17	17	48.4	51.6	.500	4
Indianapolis Kautskys	32	10	22	46.4	49.8	.313	10

Coaching Changes

Rochester--Les Harrison 24-10; Youngstown--Paul Birch 13-20; Chicago--Swede Roos 17-17; Indianapolis Nat Hickey 10-22.

League Leaders

Field Goals		Free Throws		Points	
Bob Carpenter	186	Leroy Edwards	119	Bob Carpenter	473
Bobby McDermott	184	George Glamack	115	Bobby McDermott	458
Ed Dancker	162	Buddy Jeannette	105	George Glamack	417
George Glamack	151	Bob Carpenter	101	Ed Dancker	393
Red Holzman	143	Bobby McDermott	90	Red Holzman	363

NBL Championship

Rochester Royals	44	at	Fort Wayne Zollner Pistons	54
Rochester Royals	58	at	Fort Wayne Zollner Pistons	52
Fort Wayne Zollner Pistons	52	at	Rochester Royals	58
Fort Wayne Zollner Pistons	54	at	Rochester Royals	70
Oshkosh All-Stars	45	at	Sheboygan Redskins	46
Oshkosh All-Stars	53	at	Sheboygan Redskins	41
Sheboygan Redskins	58	at	Oshkosh All-Stars	52
Sheboygan Redskins	42	at	Oshkosh All-Stars	68
Oshkosh All-Stars	46	at	Sheboygan Redskins	65
Sheboygan Redskins	50	at	Rochester Royals	60
Sheboygan Redskins	54	at	Rochester Royals	61
Rochester Royals	66	at	Sheboygan Redskins	48

Notes

Ward Lambert is named Commissioner of the National Basketball League.
George Mikan signed one of basketball's first big contracts when he signed with the Chicago American Gears for $60,000 over five years.

FOOTBALL
National Football League

East Division

Team Name	GP	W	L	T	PF	PA	Pct
New York Giants	11	7	3	1	236	162	.682
Philadelphia Eagles	11	6	5	0	231	220	.545
Washington Redskins	11	5	5	1	171	191	.500
Pittsburgh Steelers	11	5	5	1	136	117	.500
Boston Yanks	11	2	8	1	189	273	.227

West Division

Team Name	GP	W	L	T	PF	PA	Pct
Chicago Bears	11	8	2	1	289	193	.773
Los Angeles Rams	11	6	4	1	277	257	.591
Green Bay Packers	11	6	5	0	148	158	.545
Chicago Cardinals	11	6	5	0	260	198	.545
Detroit Lions	11	1	10	0	142	310	.091

Coaching Changes

Washington--Turk Edwards 5-5-1; Pittsburgh--Jock Sutherland 5-5-1; Bears--George Halas 8-2-1; Los Angeles--Adam Walsh 6-4-1; Cardinals--Jim Conzelman 6-5-0.

League Leaders

Yards Rushing		Yards Passing		Passing% (40 attempts)	
Bill Dudley	604	Sid Luckman	1826	Tommy Thompson	55
Pat Harder	545	Bob Waterfield	1747	Sam Baugh	54
Steve Van Buren	529	Paul Christman	1656	Frank Filchock	51
Hugh Gallarneau	476	Paul Governali	1293	Bob Waterfield	51
Tony Canadeo	476	Frank Filchock	1262	Roy Zimmerman	50

Receiving Yards		Receptions		Field Goals	
Jim Benton	981	Jim Benton	63	Ted Fritsch	9
Bill Dewell	643	Hal Crisler	32	Bob Waterfield	6
Mal Kutner	634	Steve Bagarus	31	Augie Lio	6
Jack Ferrante	451	Jack Ferrante	28	Dick Poillon	6
Steve Bagarus	438	Bill Dewell	27	Ward Cuff	5

Punt Return Yards		Kickoff Return Yards	
Bill Dudley	385	Sonny Karnofsky	599
Steve Bagarus	192	Frank Seno	408
Frank Seno	176	Steve Bagarus	332
Bosh Pritchard	166	Steve Van Buren	319
Jim Youel	150	Dave Ryan	308

NFL Championship

December 15	Chicago Bears	24	at	New York Giants	14

Individual Awards

Joe F. Carr Trophy--Bill Dudley (Pittsburgh Steelers)

Notes

Bert Bell replaced Elmer Layden becoming the second Commissioner of the National Football League.
With air travel becoming more commonplace the major leagues of football spread out to the west coast. The NFL had a west coast team based in Los Angeles in 1926 but it played road games only.

All-American Football Conference

East Division

Team Name	GP	W	L	T	PF	PA	Pct
New York Yankees	14	10	3	1	270	192	.750
Brooklyn Dodgers	14	3	10	1	226	339	.250
Buffalo Bisons	14	3	10	1	249	370	.250
Miami Seahawks	14	3	11	0	167	378	.214

West Division

Team Name	GP	W	L	T	PF	PA	Pct
Cleveland Browns	14	12	2	0	423	137	.857
San Francisco 49ers	14	9	5	0	307	189	.643
Los Angeles Dons	14	7	5	2	305	290	.571
Chicago Rockets	14	5	6	3	263	315	.464

Coaching Changes

New York--Ray Flaherty 10-3-1; Brooklyn--Mal Stevens 2-4-1, Cliff Battles 1-6-0; Buffalo--Red Dawson 3-10-1; Miami--Jack Meagher 1-5-0, Hamp Pool 2-6-0; Cleveland--Paul Brown 12-2-0; San Francisco--Buck Shaw 9-5-0; Los Angeles--Dud Degroot 7-5-2; Chicago--Dick Hanley 1-1-1, Bob Dove & Ned Mathews & Willie Wilkin 2-2-1, Pat Boland 2-3-1.

League Leaders

Yards Rushing		Yards Passing		Passing % (40 attempts)	
Spec Sanders	709	Glenn Dobbs	1886	Charlie O'Rourke	58
Norm Standlee	651	Otto Graham	1834	Otto Graham	55
Vic Kulbitski	605	Frank Albert	1404	Ace Parker	54
Marion Motley	601	Bob Hoernschemeyer	1266	Frank Albert	53
"Special Delivery" Jones	539	Charlie O'Rourke	1250	Angelo Bertelli	53

Receiving Yards		Receptions		Field Goals	
Dante Lavelli	843	Dante Lavelli	40	Lou Groza	13
Alyn Beals	586	Alyn Beals	40	Steve Nemeth	9
Mac Speedie	564	Saxon Judd	34	Harvey Johnson	6
Fay King	466	Fay King	30	Phil Martinovich	5
Saxon Judd	443	"Crazy Legs" Hirsch	27	Joe Vetrano	4

Punt Return Yards		Kickoff Return Yards	
Chuck Fenenbock	299	Chuck Fenenbock	479
Spec Sanders	257	Steve Juzwik	452
Ken Casanega	248	Spec Sanders	395
"Crazy Legs" Hirsch	235	"Crazy Legs" Hirsch	384
Bob Seymour	211	Monk Gafford	345

AAFC Championship

December 22	New York Yankees	9	at	Cleveland Browns	14

Notes

The All-American Football Conference was organized this year by Arch Ward who was sports editor of the Chicago Tribune.

HOCKEY
National Hockey League

Team Name	GP	W	L	T	GF	GA	Pts	Pct
Montreal Canadiens	50	28	17	5	172	134	61	.610
Boston Bruins	50	24	18	8	167	156	56	.560
Chicago Black Hawks	50	23	20	7	200	178	53	.530
Detroit Red Wings	50	20	20	10	146	159	50	.500
Toronto Maple Leafs	50	19	24	7	174	185	45	.450
New York Rangers	50	13	28	9	144	191	35	.350

Coaching Changes

Boston--Dit Clapper 24-18-8; Chicago--John Gottselig 23-20-7.

League Leaders

Goals		Assists		Points	
Gaye Stewart	37	Elmer Lach	34	Max Bentley	61
Max Bentley	30	Max Bentley	31	Gaye Stewart	52
Hector Blake	29	Bill Mosienko	30	Hector Blake	50
Rocket Richard	27	Ab DeMarco	27	Clint Smith	50
Clint Smith	26	Alex Kaleta	27	Rocket Richard	48

Penalty Minutes		GAA		Wins	
Jack Stewart	73	Bill Durnan	2.60	Bill Durnan	24
Bep Guidolin	62	Paul Bibeault	2.88	Mike Karakas	22
John Mariucci	58	Harry Lumley	3.18	Harry Lumley	20
Emil Bouchard	52	Frank Brimsek	3.26	Frank Brimsek	16
Rocket Richard	50	Mike Karakas	3.46	Charlie Rayner	12

Shutouts	
Bill Durnan	4
Harry Lumley	2
Paul Bibeault	2
Frank Brimsek	2
Mike Karakas	1

Stanley Cup Playoffs

March 19	Chicago Black Hawks	2	at	Montreal Canadiens	6
March 19	Detroit Red Wings	1	at	Boston Bruins	3
March 21	Chicago Black Hawks	1	at	Montreal Canadiens	5
March 21	Detroit Red Wings	3	at	Boston Bruins	0
March 24	Montreal Canadiens	8	at	Chicago Black Hawks	2
March 24	Boston Bruins	5	at	Detroit Red Wings	2
March 26	Montreal Canadiens	7	at	Chicago Black Hawks	2
March 26	Boston Bruins	4	at	Detroit Red Wings	1
March 28	Detroit Red Wings	3	at	Boston Bruins	4 [9:05]
March 30	Boston Bruins	3	at	Montreal Canadiens	4 [9:08]
April 2	Boston Bruins	2	at	Montreal Canadiens	3 [16:55]
April 4	Montreal Canadiens	4	at	Boston Bruins	2
April 7	Montreal Canadiens	2	at	Boston Bruins	3 [15:13]
April 9	Boston Bruins	3	at	Montreal Canadiens	6

All Star Teams

First Team		Second Team
Bill Durnan	Goal	Frank Brimsek
Jack Crawford	Defense	Ken Reardon
Emile Bouchard	Defense	Jack Stewart
Max Bentley	Center	Elmer Lach
Maurice Richard	Right Wing	Bill Mosienko
Gaye Stewart	Left Wing	Hector Blake
Dick Irvin	Coach	John Gottselig

Individual Awards

Calder Memorial Trophy--Edgar Laprade (New York Rangers)
Hart Trophy--Max Bentley (Chicago Black Hawks)
Lady Byng Trophy--Hector Blake (Montreal Canadiens)
Vezina Trophy--Bill Durnan (Montreal Canadiens)

Notes

The NHL added a second linesman this year.
Clarence Campbell succeeded Red Dutton as President of the National Hockey League and began his reign as the longest serving head of a major league sports organization. Campbell was eventually to serve 32 years as President of the NHL.

Franchise Changes

NL--Cincinnati Red Legs changed their name back to Cincinnati Reds.
NFL--Cleveland Rams became Los Angeles Rams.
Pittsburgh Raiders became the Youngstown Bears.

Other Sports

Horseracing--Kentucky Derby won by Assault (2:06.6, purse $96,400).
Heavyweight Boxing--Joe Louis knocked-out Billy Conn in 8 rounds.
Joe Louis knocked--out Tami Mauriello in 1 round.
Golf--U.S. Open won by Lloyd Mangrum in a 3 way playoff with Byron Nelson and Vic Ghezzi with scores of 284 284-284,72-72-72, 72-73-73.
Auto Racing--Indianapolis 500 won by George Robson (ave speed 114.820 MPH)
Tennis--U.S. Open won by Jack Kramer in the men's singles.
U.S. Open won by Gardnar Mulloy and William Talbert in the men's doubles.
U.S. Open won by Pauline Betz in the women's singles.
U.S. Open won by Louise Brough and Margaret Osborne in the women's doubles.
U.S. Open won by Margaret Osborne and William Talbert in the mixed doubles.

Notes

The heavyweight fight between Louis and Conn was the first heavyweight fight to be telecast. It was telecast from New York by station WNBT-TV on June 19.

1947

BASEBALL
National League

Team Name	W	L	Pct	GB	R	OR
Brooklyn Dodgers	94	60	.610	-	774	668
St. Louis Cardinals	89	65	.578	5	780	634
Boston Braves	86	68	.558	8	701	622
New York Giants	81	73	.526	13	830	761
Cincinnati Reds	73	81	.474	21	681	755
Chicago Cubs	69	85	.448	25	567	722
Philadelphia Phillies	62	92	.403	32	589	687
Pittsburgh Pirates	62	92	.403	32	744	817

Coaching Changes

Brooklyn--Clyde Sukeforth 1-0, Burt Shotton 93-60; Cincinnati--John Neun 73-81; Pittsburgh--Bill Herman 61-92, Bill Burwell 1-0.

League Leaders

Batting Average		Home Runs		RBI	
Harry Walker	.363	Johnny Mize	51	Johnny Mize	138
Bob Elliot	.317	Ralph Kiner	51	Ralph Kiner	127
Phil Cavarretta	.314	Willard Marshall	36	Walker Cooper	122
Ralph Kiner	.313	Walker Cooper	35	Bob Elliot	113
Stan Musial	.312	Bobby Thomson	29	Willard Marshall	107

Stolen Bases		ERA		Wins	
Jackie Robinson	29	Warren Spahn	2.33	Ewell Blackwell	22
Pete Reiser	14	Ewell Blackwell	2.47	Johnny Sain	21
Harry Walker	13	Ralph Branca	2.67	Ralph Branca	21
Johnny Hopp	13	Emil Leonard	2.68	Warren Spahn	21
Earl Torgeson	11	Murry Dickson	3.07	Larry Jansen	21

Saves		Strikeouts	
Hugh Casey	18	Ewell Blackwell	193
Ken Trinkle	10	Ralph Branca	148
Harry Gumbert	10	Johnny Sain	132
Hank Behrman	8	Warren Spahn	123
Emil Kush	5	George Munger	123

Notes

Jackie Robinson became the first black to play in either the NL or the AL when he played in an exhibition game on April 11.

American League

Team Name	W	L	Pct	GB	R	OR
New York Yankees	97	57	.630	-	794	568
Detroit Tigers	85	69	.552	12	714	642
Boston Red Sox	83	71	.539	14	720	669
Cleveland Indians	80	74	.519	17	687	588
Philadelphia Athletics	78	76	.506	19	633	614
Chicago White Sox	70	84	.455	27	553	661
Washington Senators	64	90	.416	33	496	675
St. Louis Browns	59	95	.383	38	564	744

Coaching Changes

New York--Stanley Harris 97-57; Chicago--Ted Lyons 70-84; St. Louis--Herold Rue 59-95.

League Leaders

Batting Average		Home Runs		RBI	
Ted Williams	.343	Ted Williams	32	Ted Williams	114
Barney McCosky	.328	Joe Gordon	29	Tom Henrich	98
Johnny Pesky	.324	Jeff Heath	27	Joe DiMaggio	97
Taft Wright	.324	Roy Cullenbine	24	Jake Jones	96
George Kell	.320	Rudy York	21	Billy Johnson	95

Stolen Bases		ERA		Wins	
Bob Dillinger	34	Spud Chandler	2.46	Bob Feller	20
Dave Philley	21	Bob Feller	2.68	Allie Reynolds	19
Johnny Pesky	12	Dick Fowler	2.81	Phil Marchildon	19
Mickey Vernon	12	Ed Lopat	2.81	Joe Dobson	18
Elmer Valo	11	Hal Newhouser	2.87	Fred Hutchinson	18

Saves		Strikeouts	
Joe Page	17	Bob Feller	196
Eddie Klieman	17	Hal Newhouser	176
Russ Christopher	12	W. Masterson	135
Tom Ferrick	9	Allie Reynolds	129
Earl Caldwell	8	Phil Marchildon	128

All-Star Game

(Wrigley Field, Chicago)

July 8	American League	2		National League	1

World Series

September 30	Brooklyn Dodgers	3	at	New York Yankees	5
October 1	Brooklyn Dodgers	3	at	New York Yankees	10
October 2	New York Yankees	8	at	Brooklyn Dodgers	9
October 3	New York Yankees	2	at	Brooklyn Dodgers	3
October 4	New York Yankees	2	at	Brooklyn Dodgers	1
October 5	Brooklyn Dodgers	8	at	New York Yankees	6
October 6	Brooklyn Dodgers	2	at	New York Yankees	5

Individual Awards

Baseball Writers Award--Bob Elliott (Boston Braves NL)
Joe DiMaggio (New York Yankees AL)
Rookie of the Year--Jackie Robinson (Brooklyn Dodgers NL)
Sporting News Executive of the Year--Branch Rickey (Brooklyn Dodgers NL)
Sporting News Manager of the Year--Stanley Harris (New York Yankees AL)
Sporting News Rookie of the Year--Jackie Robinson (Brooklyn Dodgers NL)

Hall of Fame Inductees

Mickey Cochrane, Frank Frisch, Robert Grove, Carl Hubbell

BASKETBALL
National Basketball League
East Division

Team Name	GP	W	L	PPGF	PPGA	Pct	GB
Rochester Royals	44	31	13	62.9	56.5	.705	-
Fort Wayne Zollner Pistons	44	25	19	58.3	55.6	.568	6
Toledo Jeeps	44	21	23	57.3	56.0	.477	10
Syracuse Nationals	44	21	23	55.8	55.5	.477	10
(Buffalo Bisons)	12	4	8	49.1	51.8	.333	16
(Tri-Cities Blackhawks)	32	15	17	49.1	51.8	.469	10
Youngstown Bears	44	12	32	53.5	60.1	.273	19

West Division

Team Name	GP	W	L	PPGF	PPGA	Pct	GB
Oshkosh All-Stars	44	28	16	58.0	55.3	.636	-
Indianapolis Kautskys	44	27	17	56.9	53.1	.614	1
Chicago American Gears	44	26	18	58.4	54.3	.591	2
Sheboygan Redskins	44	26	18	54.5	53.0	.591	2
Anderson Duffy Packers	44	24	20	59.7	58.5	.545	4
Detroit Gems	44	4	40	47.6	63.0	.091	24

Coaching Changes

Rochester--Ed Malanowicz & Les Harrison 31-13; Fort Wayne--Bob McDermott 7-7, Carl Bennett 18-12; Toledo--Julie Rivlin 21-23; Syracuse--Ben Borgmann 21-23; Tri-Cities--Nat Hickey 19-25; Youngstown--Frank Shannon 12-32; Indianapolis--Ernie Andres 21-13, Bob Dietz & Herm Schaefer 6-4; Chicago--Davey Banks 4-4, Harry Foote 4-4, Bob McDermott 18-10; Sheboygan--Doxie Moore 26-18; Anderson--Murray Mendenhall 24-20; Detroit--Joel Mason 3-13, Fred Campbell 1-27.

League Leaders

Field Goals		Free Throws		Free Throw Att		Points	
Hal Tidrick	232	George Sobek	179	Arnie Risen	276	Al Cervi	632
Fred Lewis	230	Al Cervi	176	Don Otten	261	Fred Lewis	585
Al Cervi	228	Arnie Risen	174	George Sobek	248	Arnie Risen	582
Red Holzman	227	Don Otten	169	Jerry Rizzo	238	Hal Tidrick	579
Arnie Risen	204	Jerry Rizzo	169	Al Cervi	236	Don Otten	569

NBL Championship

Syracuse Nationals	64	at	Rochester Royals	66
Rochester Royals	61	at	Syracuse Nationals	64
Syracuse Nationals	48	at	Rochester Royals	54
Rochester Royals	62	at	Syracuse Nationals	57
Toledo Jeeps	38	at	Fort Wayne Zollner Pistons	65
Toledo Jeeps	31	at	Fort Wayne Zollner Pistons	54
Fort Wayne Zollner Pistons	46	at	Toledo Jeeps	56
Fort Wayne Zollner Pistons	53	at	Toledo Jeeps	58
Toledo Jeeps	46	at	Fort Wayne Zollner Pistons	64
Fort Wayne Zollner Pistons	49	at	Rochester Royals	58
Rochester Royals	49	at	Fort Wayne Zollner Pistons	56
Fort Wayne Zollner Pistons	47	at	Rochester Royals	76
Chicago American Gears	74	at	Indianapolis Kautskys	72
Chicago American Gears	69	at	Indianapolis Kautskys	61
Indianapolis Kautskys	68	at	Chicago American Gears	67
Indianapolis Kautskys	55	at	Chicago American Gears	54
Indianapolis Kautskys	62	at	Chicago American Gears	76
Oshkosh All-Stars	48	at	Sheboygan Redskins	54
Oshkosh All-Stars	35	at	Sheboygan Redskins	40
Sheboygan Redskins	44	at	Oshkosh All-Stars	53
Sheboygan Redskins	47	at	Oshkosh All-Stars	49
Oshkosh All-Stars	54	at	Chicago American Gears	60
Chicago American Gears	61	at	Oshkosh All-Stars	60
Chicago American Gears	65	at	Rochester Royals	71
Chicago American Gears	67	at	Rochester Royals	63
Rochester Royals	70	at	Chicago American Gears	78
Rochester Royals	68	at	Chicago American Gears	79

Notes

The Buffalo Bisons folded after 12 games and became the Tri-Cities Blackhawks.

Basketball Association of America
East Division

Team Name	GP	W	L	PPGF	PPGA	Pct	GB
Washington Capitols	60	49	11	73.8	63.9	.817	-
Philadelphia Warriors	60	35	25	68.6	65.2	.583	14
New York Knickerbockers	60	33	27	64.7	64.0	.550	16
Providence Steamrollers	60	28	32	72.5	74.2	.467	21
Toronto Huskies	60	22	38	66.6	71.0	.367	27
Boston Celtics	60	22	38	60.1	65.0	.367	27

West Division

Team Name	GP	W	L	PPGF	PPGA	Pct	GB
Chicago Stags	61	39	22	77.0	73.3	.639	-
St. Louis Bombers	61	38	23	66.6	64.1	.623	1
Cleveland Rebels	60	30	30	70.9	71.8	.500	8.5
Detroit Falcons	60	20	40	63.3	65.3	.333	18.5
Pittsburgh Ironmen	60	15	45	61.2	67.6	.250	23.5

Coaching

Washington--Red Auerbach 49-11; Philadelphia--Ed Gottlieb 35-25; New York--Neil Cohalan33-27; Providence--Bob Morris 28-32; Toronto--Ed Sadowski 3-9, Lew Hayman 0-1, Dick Fitzgerald 2-1, Red Rolfe 17-27; Boston--Honey Russell 22-38; Chicago--Ole Olsen 39-22; St. Louis--Ken Loeffler 38-23; Cleveland--Dutch Dehnert 17-20, Roy Clifford 13-10; Detroit--Glenn Curtis 12-22, Cincy Sachs 8-18; Pittsburgh--Paul Birch l5-45

League Leaders

Field Goals		**Free Throws**		**Free Throw Att.**	
Joe Fulks	475	Joe Fulks	439	Joe Fulks	601
Bob Feerick	364	Leo Mogus	235	Stan Miasek	385
Max Zaslofsky	336	Stan Miasek	233	Chick Halbert	356
Stan Miasek	331	Coulby Gunther	226	Coulby Gunther	351
Ed Sadowski	329	Ed Sadowski	219	Earl Shannon	348

Points		**Assists**		**Fouls**	
Joe Fulks	1389	Ernie Calverly	202	Stan Miasek	208
Bob Feerick	926	Kenny Sailors	134	Joe Fulks	199
Stan Miasek	895	Ossie Schectman	109	Hank Beenders	196
Ed Sadowski	877	Howie Dallmar	104	Ed Sadowski	194
Max Zaslofsky	877	Mickey Rottner	93	Ernie Calverly	191

BAA Championship

April 2	St. Louis Bombers	68	at	Philadelphia Warriors	73
April 2	N.Y. Knickerbockers	51	at	Cleveland Rebels	77
April 2	Chicago Stags	81	at	Washington Capitols	65
April 3	Chicago Stags	69	at	Washington Capitols	53
April 5	Philadelphia Warriors	51	at	St. Louis Bombers	73
April 5	Cleveland Rebels	74	at	N.Y. Knickerbockers	86
April 6	Philadelphia Warriors	75	at	St. Louis Bombers	59
April 8	Washington Capitols	55	at	Chicago Stags	67
April 9	Cleveland Rebels	71	at	N.Y. Knickerbockers	93
April 10	Chicago Stags	69	at	Washington Capitols	76
April 12	Washington Capitols	67	at	Chicago Stags	55
April 12	N.Y. Knickerbockers	70	at	Philadelphia Warriors	82
April 13	Washington Capitols	61	at	Chicago Stags	66
April 14	Philadelphia Warriors	72	at	N.Y. Knickerbockers	53
April 16	Chicago Stags	71	at	Philadelphia Warriors	84
April 17	Chicago Stags	75	at	Philadelphia Warriors	85
April 19	Philadelphia Warriors	75	at	Chicago Stags	72
April 20	Philadelphia Warriors	73	at	Chicago Stags	74
April 22	Chicago Stags	80	at	Philadelphia Warriors	83

All Star Teams

First Team

Joe Fulks (Philadelphia Warriors)
Bob Feerick (Washington Capitols)
Stan Miasek (Detroit Falcons)
"Bones" McKinney (Washington Capitols)
Max Zaslofsky (Chicago Stags)

Second Team

Ernie Calverly (Providence Steamrollers)
Frank Baumholtz (Cleveland Rebels)
John Logan (St. Louis Bombers)
Chuck Halbert (Chicago Stags)
Fred Scolari (Washington Capitols)

Notes

The operators of the major sports arenas looking for ways to fill their arenas on dates not taken by hockey or college basketball formed the Basketball Association of America. This group was headed by Walter Brown of Boston. Maurice Podoloff was named as first Commissioner of the league.

FOOTBALL
National Football League

East Division

Team Name	GP	W	L	T	PF	PA	Pct
Philadelphia Eagles	12	8	4	0	308	242	.667
Pittsburgh Steelers	12	8	4	0	240	259	.667
Boston Yanks	12	4	7	1	168	256	.375
Washington Redskins	12	4	8	0	295	367	.333
New York Giants	12	2	8	2	190	309	.250

West Division

Team Name	GP	W	L	T	PF	PA	Pct
Chicago Cardinals	12	9	3	0	306	231	.750
Chicago Bears	12	8	4	0	363	241	.667
Green Bay Packers	12	6	5	1	274	210	.542
Los Angeles Rams	12	6	6	0	259	214	.500
Detroit Lions	12	3	9	0	231	305	.250

Coaching Changes

Boston--Clipper Smith 4-7-1; Los Angeles--Bob Snyder 6-6-0.

League Leaders

Yards Rushing		Yards Passing		Passing % (40 attempts)	
Steve Van Buren	1008	Sam Baugh	2938	Sam Baugh	59
Johnny Clement	670	Sid Luckman	2712	Sid Luckman	54
Tony Canadeo	464	Paul Christman	2191	Clyde LeForce	54
Ken Washington	444	Paul Governali	1775	Tom Thompson	53
Walt Schlinkman	439	Tom Thompson	1680	Paul Christman	46

Receiving Yards		Receptions		Field Goals	
Mal Kutner	944	Jim Keane	64	Pat Harder	7
Jim Keane	910	Bob Nussbaumer	47	Ward Cuff	7
Ken Kavanaugh	818	Mal Kutner	43	Bob Waterfield	7
Don Currivan	782	Bill Dewell	42	Joe Glamp	6
Nolan Luhn	696	Nolan Luhn	42	Ted Fritsch	6

Punt Return Yards		Kickoff Return Yards	
Walt Slater	435	Eddie Saenz	797
Tommy Harmon	392	Frank Seno	636
Eddie Saenz	308	Walt Slater	480
Bosh Pritchard	271	Bill Dudley	359
George McAfee	261	Charlie Trippi	321

NFL Championship

December 21	Philadelphia Eagles	21	at	Pittsburgh Steelers	0
December 28	Philadelphia Eagles	21	at	Chicago Cardinals	28

Notes

Frank Filchock and Merle Hapes of the New York Giants were suspended for "actions detrimental to the National Football League and professional football" for becoming involved in a plot by gamblers to fix the 1946 NFL championship game between the Bears and Giants.

All-American Football Conference
East Division

Team Name	GP	W	L	T	PF	PA	Pct
New York Yankees	14	11	2	1	378	239	.821
Buffalo Bills	14	8	4	2	320	288	.643
Brooklyn Dodgers	14	3	10	1	181	340	.250
Baltimore Colts	14	2	11	1	167	377	.179
West Division							
Cleveland Browns	14	12	1	1	410	185	.893
San Francisco 49ers	14	8	4	2	327	264	.643
Los Angeles Dons	14	7	7	0	328	256	.500
Chicago Rockets	14	1	13	0	263	425	.071

Coaching Changes

Brooklyn--Cliff Battles 3-10-1: Baltimore--Cecil Isbell 2-11-1; Los Angeles--Dud Degroot 5-5-0, Mel Hein & Ted Shipkey 2-2-0: Chicago--Jim Crowley 0-10-0, Hamp Pool 1-3-0.

League Leaders

Yards Rushing		Yards Passing		Passing % (40 attempts)	
Spec Sanders	1432	Otto Graham	2753	Otto Graham	61
John Strzykalski	906	Bud Schwenk	2236	Al Dekdebrun	60
Marion Motley	889	George Ratterman	1840	Spec Sanders	54
Chet Mutryn	868	Frank Albert	1692	Frank Albert	53
Buddy Young	712	Sam Vacanti	1571	Bud Schwenk	51

Receiving Yards		Receptions		Field Goals	
Mac Speedie	1146	Mac Speedie	67	Ben Agajanian	15
Dante Lavelli	799	Dante Lavelli	49	Lou Groza	7
Ray Ramsey	768	Alyn Beals	47	Harvey Johnson	7
Bill Hillenbrand	702	Lamar Davis	46	Joe Vetrano	4
Alyn Beals	655	Bill Hillenbrand	39	John Rokisky	4

Punt Return Yards		Kickoff Return Yards	
Charlie O'Rourke	215	Chet Mutryn	691
Chuck Fenenbock	210	Spec Sanders	593
Bill Hillenbrand	201	Monk Gafford	565
Chet Mutryn	187	Bill Hillenbrand	466
Monk Gafford	186	Chuck Fenenbock	452

AAFC Championship

December 14	Cleveland Browns	14	at	New York Yankees	3

HOCKEY
National Hockey League

Team Name	GP	W	L	T	GF	GA	Pts	Pct
Montreal Canadiens	60	34	16	10	189	138	78	.650
Toronto Maple Leafs	60	31	19	10	209	172	72	.600
Boston Bruins	60	26	23	11	190	175	63	.525
Detroit Red Wings	60	22	27	11	190	193	55	.458
New York Rangers	60	22	32	6	167	186	50	.417
Chicago Black Hawks	60	19	37	4	193	274	42	.350

Coaching Changes

None.

League Leaders

Goals		Assists		Points	
Rocket Richard	45	Billy Taylor	46	Max Bentley	72
Bob Bauer	30	Max Bentley	43	Rocket Richard	71
Roy Conacher	30	Milt Schmidt	35	Billy Taylor	63
Max Bentley	29	Doug Bentley	34	Milt Schmidt	62
Ted Kennedy	28	Ted Kennedy	32	Ted Kennedy	60

Penalty Minutes		GAA		Wins	
Gus Mortson	133	Bill Durnan	2.30	Bill Durnan	34
John Mariucci	110	Walter Broda	2.87	Walter Broda	31
Elton Chamberlain	97	Frank Brimsek	2.92	Frank Brimsek	26
Jim Thomson	97	Chuck Rayner	3.05	Chuck Rayner	22
Bill Ezinicki	93	Harry Lumley	3.06	Harry Lumley	22

Shutouts	
Chuck Rayner	5
Walter Broda	4
Bill Durnan	4
Harry Lumley	3
Frank Brimsek	3

Stanley Cup Playoffs

March 25	Boston Bruins	1	at	Montreal Canadiens	3
March 26	Detroit Red Wings	2	at	Toronto Maple Leafs	3 [3:05]
March 27	Boston Bruins	1	at	Montreal Canadiens	2 [5:38]
March 29	Montreal Canadiens	2	at	Boston Bruins	4
March 29	Detroit Red Wings	9	at	Toronto Maple Leafs	1
April 1	Montreal Canadiens	5	at	Boston Bruins	1
April 1	Toronto Maple Leafs	4	at	Detroit Red Wings	1
April 3	Boston Bruins	3	at	Montreal Canadiens	4 [36:40]
April 3	Toronto Maple Leafs	4	at	Detroit Red Wings	1
April 5	Detroit Red Wings	1	at	Toronto Maple Leafs	6
April 8	Toronto Maple Leafs	0	at	Montreal Canadiens	6
April 10	Toronto Maple Leafs	4	at	Montreal Canadiens	0

April 12	Montreal Canadiens	2	at	Toronto Maple Leafs	4
April 15	Montreal Canadiens	1	at	Toronto Maple Leafs	2 [16:36]
April 17	Toronto Maple Leafs	1	at	Montreal Canadiens	3
April 19	Montreal Canadiens	1	at	Toronto Maple Leafs	2

All Star Teams

First Team		Second Team
Bill Durnan	Goal	Frank Brimsek
Ken Reardon	Defense	Jack Stewart
Emile Bouchard	Defense	Bill Quackenbush
Milt Schmidt	Center	Max Bentley
Maurice Richard	Right Wing	Bobby Bauer
Doug Bentley	Left Wing	Woody Dumart

Individual Awards

Art Ross Trophy--Max Bentley (Chicago Black Hawks)
Calder Memorial Trophy--Howie Meeker (Toronto Maple Leafs)
Hart Trophy--Rocket Richard (Montreal Canadiens)
Lady Byng Trophy--Bobby Bauer (Boston Bruins)
Vezina Trophy--Bill Durnan (Montreal Canadiens NHL)

Hall of Fame Inductees

Frank Calder, Dit Clapper, Bill Hewitt, Aurel Joliat, Francis Nelson, Frank Nighbor, William Northey, Lester Patrick, John Ross Robertson, Claude Robinson, Eddie Shore, James T. Sutherland, Cyclone Taylor,

Notes

Stanley Cup trustee P.D. Ross turned over full possession of the Stanley Cup to the NHL. The Cup had in theory been a challenge trophy, although the NHL had been the sole league competing for the trophy since 1927.

Franchise Changes

AAFC--Buffalo Bisons changed name to Buffalo Bills.

Other Sports

Horseracing--Kentucky Derby won by Jet Pilot (time 2:06.6, purse $92,160).
Heavyweight Boxing--Joe Louis defeated Joe Walcott in a 15 round split decision.
Golf--U.S. Open won by Lew Worsham in a playoff with Sam Snead (score of 282-282, 69-70).
Auto Racing--Indianapolis 500 won by Mauri Rose (ave. speed 116.338 MPH).
Tennis--U.S. Open won by Jack Kramer in the men's singles.
U.S. Open won by Jack Kramer and Frederick Schroeder Jr. in the men's doubles.
U.S. Open won by Louise Brough in the women's singles.
U.S. Open won by Louise Brough and Margaret Osborne in the women's doubles.
U.S. Open won by Louise Brough and John Bromwich in the mixed doubles.

1948

BASEBALL

National League

Team Name	W	L	Pct	GB	R	OR
Boston Braves	91	62	.595	-	739	584
St. Louis Cardinals	85	69	.552	6.5	742	646
Brooklyn Dodgers	84	70	.545	7.5	744	667
Pittsburgh Pirates	83	71	.539	8.5	706	699
New York Giants	78	76	.506	13.5	780	704
Philadelphia Phillies	66	88	.429	25.5	591	729
Cincinnati Reds	64	89	.418	27	588	752
Chicago Cubs	64	90	.416	27.5	597	706

Coaching Changes

Brooklyn--Leo Durocher 36-37, Burt Shotton 48-33; Pittsburgh--Bill Meyer 83-71; New York--Mel Ott 27-38, Leo Durocher 51-38; Philadelphia--Ben Chapman 37-42, Allen Cooke 6-5, Eddie Sawyer 23-41; Cincinnati--John Neun 44-56, Bill Walters 20-33.

League Leaders

Batting Average		Home Runs		RBI	
Stan Musial	.376	Ralph Kiner	40	Stan Musial	131
Richie Ashburn	.333	Johnny Mize	40	Johnny Mize	125
Tom Holmes	.325	Stan Musial	39	Ralph Kiner	123
Alvin Dark	.322	Hank Sauer	35	Sid Gordon	107
Enos Slaughter	.321	Sid Gordon	30	Andy Pafko	101

Stolen Bases		ERA		Wins	
Richie Ashburn	32	Harry Brecheen	2.24	Johnny Sain	24
Harold Reese	25	Emil Leonard	2.51	Harry Brecheen	20
Stan Rojek	24	Johnny Sain	2.60	John Schmitz	18
Jackie Robinson	22	John Schmitz	2.64	Larry Jansen	18
Earl Torgeson	19	Rex Barney	3.10	John Vandermeer	17

Saves		Strikeouts	
Harry Gumbert	17	Harry Brecheen	149
Ted Wilks	13	Rex Barney	138
Kirby Higbe	10	Johnny Sain	137
Hank Behrman	7	Larry Jansen	126
Ken Trinkle	7	Ralph Branca	122

American League

Team Name	W	L	Pct	GB	R	OR
Cleveland Indians	97	58	.626	-	840	568
Boston Red Sox	96	59	.619	1	907	720
New York Yankees	94	60	.610	2.5	857	633
Philadelphia Athletics	84	70	.545	12.5	729	735
Detroit Tigers	78	76	.506	18.5	700	726
St. Louis Browns	59	94	.386	37	671	849
Washington Senators	56	97	.366	40	578	796
Chicago White Sox	51	101	.336	44.5	559	814

Coaching Changes

Boston--Joe McCarthy 96-59; St. Louis--Zack Taylor 59-94; Washington--Joe Kuhel 56-97.

League Leaders

Batting Average		Home Runs		RBI	
Ted Williams	.369	Joe DiMaggio	39	Joe DiMaggio	155
Lou Boudreau	.355	Joe Gordon	32	Vern Stephens	137
Dale Mitchell	.336	Ken Keltner	31	Ted Williams	127
Al Zarilla	.329	Vern Stephens	29	Joe Gordon	124
Barney McCosky	.326	Bobby Doerr	27	Hank Majeski	120

Stolen Bases		ERA		Wins	
Bob Dillinger	28	Gene Bearden	2.43	Hal Newhouser	21
Gil Coan	23	Bob Lemon	2.82	Bob Lemon	20
Mickey Vernon	15	Hal Newhouser	3.01	Gene Bearden	20
Dale Mitchell	13	Mel Parnell	3.14	Vic Raschi	19
Thurman Tucker	11	Paul Trout	3.43	Bob Feller	19

Saves		Strikeouts	
Russ Christopher	17	Bob Feller	164
Joe Page	16	Bob Lemon	147
Tom Ferrick	10	Hal Newhouser	143
Art Houtteman	10	Lou Brissie	127
Howie Judson	8	Vic Raschi	124

All-Star Game

(Sportsman's Park, St. Louis)

July 13	American League	5		National League	2

World Series

October 6	Cleveland Indians	0	at	Boston Braves	1
October 7	Cleveland Indians	4	at	Boston Braves	1
October 8	Boston Braves	0	at	Cleveland Indians	2
October 9	Boston Braves	1	at	Cleveland Indians	2
October 10	Boston Braves	11	at	Cleveland Indians	5
October 11	Cleveland Indians	4	at	Boston Braves	3

Individual Awards

Baseball Writers Award--Stan Musial (St. Louis Cardinals NL)
Lou Boudreau (Cleveland Indians AL)
Rookie of the Year--Alvin Dark (Boston Braves NL)
Sporting News Executive of the Year--Bill Veeck (Cleveland Indians AL)
Sporting News Manager of the Year--Bill Meyer (Pittsburgh Pirates NL)
Sporting News Pitcher of the Year Johnny Sain (Boston Braves NL)
Bob Lemon (Cleveland Indians AL)
Sporting News Player of the Year--Stan Musial (St. Louis Cardinals NL)
Lou Boudreau (Cleveland Indians AL)
Sporting News Rookie of the Year--Richie Ashburn (Philadelphia Phillies NL)

Hall of Fame Inductees

Herb Pennock, Harold Traynor

BASKETBALL
National Basketball League

East Division

Team Name	GP	W	L	PPGF	PPGA	Pct	GB
Rochester Royals	60	44	16	64.6	58.2	.733	-
Anderson Duffy Packers	60	42	18	65.0	59.4	.700	2
Fort Wayne Zollner Pistons	60	40	20	59.9	56.9	.667	4
Syracuse Nationals	60	24	36	59.3	62.5	.400	20
Toledo Jeeps	59	22	37	55.8	57.1	.373	21.5
Flint Dow A.C.'s	60	8	52	58.4	69.4	.133	36

West Division

Team Name	GP	W	L	PPGF	PPGA	Pct	GB
Minneapolis Lakers	60	43	17	64.1	56.6	.717	-
Tri-Cities Blackhawks	60	30	30	60.9	61.1	.500	13
Oshkosh All-Stars	60	29	31	59.7	59.6	.483	14
Indianapolis Kautskys	59	24	35	60.2	63.2	.407	18.5
Sheboygan Redskins	60	23	37	56.8	60.9	.383	20

Coaching Changes

Rochester--Eddie Malanowicz 44-16; Fort Wayne--Carl Bennett 40-20; Flint--Jim Walsh 0-21, Matt Zunic 8-50; Minneapolis--John Kundla 43-17; Tri-Cities--Nat Hickey 8-12, Bobby McDermott 22-18; Indianapolis--Glenn Curtis 2-2, Leo Klier 1-1, Bruce Hale 21-32.

League Leaders

Field Goals		Free Throws		Free Throw Att.	
George Mikan	406	George Mikan	383	George Mikan	509
Jim Pollard	310	Bob Calihan	260	Don Otten	392
Don Otten	282	Don Otten	260	Bob Calihan	371
Mike Todorovich	277	Gene Englund	242	Mike Todorovich	343
Stanley Von Nieda	276	Mike Todorovich	223	Gene Englund	333

George Mikan	1195
Don Otten	824
Bob Calihan	806
Mike Todorovich	777
Jim Pollard	760

NBL Championship

Rochester Royals	65	at	Fort Wayne Zollner Pistons	56
Rochester Royals	64	at	Fort Wayne Zollner Pistons	68
Fort Wayne Zollner Pistons	47	at	Rochester Royals	64
Fort Wayne Zollner Pistons	62	at	Rochester Royals	71
Syracuse Nationals	56	at	Anderson Duffy Packers	73
Syracuse Nationals	54	at	Anderson Duffy Packers	72
Anderson Duffy Packers	79	at	Syracuse Nationals	68
Rochester Royals	71	at	Anderson Duffy Packers	66
Anderson Duffy Packers	76	at	Rochester Royals	69
Anderson Duffy Packers	48	at	Rochester Royals	74
Oshkosh All Stars	68	at	Minneapolis Lakers	80
Oshkosh All Stars	65	at	Minneapolis Lakers	88
Minneapolis Lakers	51	at	Oshkosh All-Stars	69
Minneapolis Lakers	61	at	Oshkosh All-Stars	55
Tri-Cities Blackhawks	77	at	Indianapolis Kautskys	67
Tri-Cities Blackhawks	70	at	Indianapolis Kautskys	89
Indianapolis Kautskys	59	at	Tri-Cities Blackhawks	70
Indianapolis Kautskys	61	at	Tri-Cities Blackhawks	74
Minneapolis Lakers	98	at	Tri-Cities Blackhawks	79
Tri-Cities Blackhawks	59	at	Minneapolis Lakers	83
Rochester Royals	72	at	Minneapolis Lakers	80
Rochester Royals	67	at	Minneapolis Lakers	82
Minneapolis Lakers	60	at	Rochester Royals	74
Minneapolis Lakers	75	at	Rochester Royals	65

Notes

Doxie Moore replaced Ward Lambert as Commissioner of the National Basketball League for the upcoming 1948-1949 season when Lambert resigned due to poor health.

Basketball Association of America
East Division

Team Name	GP	W	L	PPGF	PPGA	Pct	GB
Philadelphia Warriors	48	27	21	73.4	72.1	.563	-
New York Knickerbockers	48	26	22	74.5	71.4	.542	1
Boston Celtics	48	20	28	68.8	72.7	.417	7
Providence Steamrollers	48	6	42	69.1	80.7	.125	21

West Division

Team Name	GP	W	L	PPGF	PPGA	Pct	GB
St. Louis Bombers	48	29	19	71.5	69.5	.604	-
Baltimore Bullets	48	28	20	74.4	70.5	.583	1
Chicago Stags	48	28	20	75.8	73.2	.583	1
Washington Capitols	48	28	20	73.7	71.1	.583	1

Coaching Changes

New York--Joe Lapchick 26-22-; Providence--Hank Soar 2-17, Nat Hickey 4-25; Baltimore--Buddy Jeannette 28-20.

League Leaders

Field Goals		Free Throws		Free Throw Att	
Max Zaslofsky	373	Joe Fulks	297	Ed Sadowski	422
Joe Fulks	326	Ed Sadowski	294	Joe Fulks	390
Ed Sadowski	308	Max Zaslofsky	261	Max Zaslofsky	333
Bob Feerick	293	Johnny Logan	202	Stan Miasek	310
Carl Braun	276	Buddy Jeannette	191	Johnny Logan	272

Points		Assists		Fouls	
Max Zaslofsky	1007	Howie Dallmar	120	Chuck Gilmur	231
Joe Fulks	949	Ernie Calverly	119	Red Rocha	209
Ed Sadowski	910	Jim Seminoff	89	Gene Vance	193
Bob Feerick	775	Chuck Gilmur	77	Stan Miasek	192
Stan Miasek	716	Andy Phillip	74	Ed Sadowski	182

BAA Championship

Date	Team	Score		Team	Score
March 23	Washington Capitols	70	at	Chicago Stags	74
March 23	Philadelphia Warriors	58	at	St. Louis Bombers	60
March 25	Baltimore Bullets	75	at	Chicago Stags	72
March 25	Philadelphia Warriors	65	at	St. Louis Bombers	64
March 27	N.Y. Knickerbockers	81	at	Baltimore Bullets	85
March 27	St. Louis Bombers	56	at	Philadelphia Warriors	84
March 28	Baltimore Bullets	69	at	N.Y. Knickerbockers	79
March 28	Chicago Stags	79	at	Boston Celtics	72
March 30	St. Louis Bombers	56	at	Philadelphia Warriors	51
March 31	Chicago Stags	77	at	Boston Celtics	81
April 1	N.Y. Knickerbockers	77	at	Baltimore Bullets	84
April 1	Philadelphia Warriors	62	at	St. Louis Bombers	69
April 2	Chicago Stags	81	at	Boston Celtics	74
April 3	St. Louis Bombers	61	at	Philadelphia Warriors	84
April 6	Philadelphia Warriors	85	at	St. Louis Bombers	46
April 7	Baltimore Bullets	73	at	Chicago Stags	67
April 8	Chicago Stags	72	at	Baltimore Bullets	89
April 10	Baltimore Bullets	60	at	Philadelphia Warriors	71
April 13	Baltimore Bullets	66	at	Philadelphia Warriors	63
April 15	Philadelphia Warriors	70	at	Baltimore Bullets	72
April 17	Philadelphia Warriors	75	at	Baltimore Bullets	78
April 20	Baltimore Bullets	82	at	Philadelphia Warriors	91
April 21	Philadelphia Warriors	73	at	Baltimore Bullets	88

All Star Teams

First Team

Joe Fulks (Philadelphia Warriors)
Max Zaslofsky (Chicago Stags)
Ed Sadowski (Boston Celtics)
Howie Dallmar (Philadelphia Warriors)
Bob Feerick (Washington Capitols)

Second Team

John Logan (St. Louis Bombers)
Carl Braun (N.Y. Knickerbockers)
Stan Miasek (Chicago Stags)
Fred Scolari (Washington Capitols)
Buddy Jeannette (Baltimore Bullets)

Notes

Three teams tied for the last playoff spots behind St. Louis and a playoff was necessary to determine the other two playoff teams. Baltimore defeated Chicago 75-72 for second place and Chicago defeated Washington 75-72 for third place.

FOOTBALL
National Football League
East Division

Team Name	GP	W	L	T	PF	PA	Pct
Philadelphia Eagles	12	9	2	1	376	156	.792
Washington Redskins	12	7	5	0	291	287	.583
N.Y. Giants	12	4	8	0	297	388	.333
Pittsburgh Steelers	12	4	8	0	200	243	.333
Boston Yanks	12	3	9	0	174	372	.250

West Division

Team Name	GP	W	L	T	PF	PA	Pct
Chicago Cardinals	12	11	1	0	395	226	.917
Chicago Bears	12	10	2	0	375	151	.833
Los Angeles Rams	12	6	5	1	327	269	.542
Green Bay Packers	12	3	9	0	154	290	.250
Detroit Lions	12	2	10	0	200	407	.167

Coaching Changes

Pittsburgh--John Michelosen 4-8-0; Los Angeles--Clark Shaughnessy 6-5-1; Detroit--Bo McMillin 2-10-0.

League Leaders

Yards Rushing		Yards Passing		Passing % (40 attempts)	
Steve Van Buren	945	Sam Baugh	2599	Sam Baugh	59
Charlie Trippi	690	Charlie Conerly	2175	Tom Thompson	57
Elmer Angsman	638	Tom Thompson	1965	Sid Luckman	55
Camp Wilson	612	Jim Hardy	1390	John Lujack	55
Tony Canadeo	598	Bob Waterfield	1354	Charlie Conerly	54

Receiving Yards		Receptions		Field Goals	
Mal Kutner	943	Tom Fears	51	Cliff Patton	8
Pete Phios	766	Pete Pihos	46	Pat Harder	7
Tom Fears	698	Mal Kutner	41	Bob Waterfield	6
Val Jansante	623	Bill Swiacki	39	Ted Fritsch	6
Hal Crisler	599	Val Jansante	39	Dick Poillon	5

Punt Return Yards		Kickoff Return Yards	
George McAfee	417	Dan Sandifer	594
Jerry Davis	334	Joe Scott	569
Bosh Pritchard	282	Bill Paschal	498
Dan Sandifer	236	Fred Gehrke	464
Pat McHugh	220	Jerry Davis	437

NFL Championship

December 19	Chicago Cardinals	0	at	Philadelphia Eagles	7

All-American Football Conference
East Division

Team Name	GP	W	L	T	PF	PA	Pct
Buffalo Bills	14	7	7	0	360	358	.500
Baltimore Colts	14	7	7	0	333	327	.500
New York Yankees	14	6	8	0	265	301	.429
Brooklyn Dodgers	14	2	12	0	253	387	.143

West Division

Team Name	GP	W	L	T	PF	PA	Pct
Cleveland Browns	14	14	0	0	389	190	1.000
San Francisco 49ers	14	12	2	0	495	248	.857
Los Angeles Dons	14	7	7	0	258	305	.500
Chicago Rockets	14	1	13	0	202	439	.071

Coaching Changes

New York--Ray Flaherty 2-6-0, Red Steader 4-2-0; Brooklyn Carl Voyles 2-12-0; Los Angeles--Jim Phelan 7-7-0; Chicago--Ed McKeever 1-13-0.

League Leaders

Yards Rushing		Yards Passing		Passing % (40 attempts)	
Marion Motley	964	Otto Graham	2713	Frank Albert	58
John Strzykalski	915	George Ratterman	2577	Y.A. Tittle	56
Chet Mutryn	823	Y.A. Tittle	2522	Otto Graham	52
Spec Sanders	759	Glenn Dobbs	2403	Glenn Dobbs	50
Lou Tomasetti	716	Frank Albert	1990	George Ratterman	50

Receiving Yards		Receptions		Field Goals	
Bill Hillenbrand	970	Mac Speedie	58	Rex Grossman	10
Al Baldwin	916	Al Baldwin	54	Lou Groza	8
Mac Speedie	816	Billy Hillenbrand	50	Joe Vetrano	5
Chet Mutryn	794	Fay King	50	Ben Agajanian	5
Lamar Davis	765	Alyn Beals	46	Jim McCarthy	2

Punt Return Yards		Kickoff Return Yards	
Herm Wedemeyer	368	Monk Gafford	559
Rex Bumgardner	336	Chet Mutryn	500
Jim Cason	309	Forrest Hall	369
Bill Reinhard	276	Bob Pfohl	366
Cliff Lewis	258	Billy Hillenbrand	356

AAFC Championship

December 12	Buffalo Bills	28	at	Baltimore Colts	17
December 19	Buffalo Bills	7	at	Cleveland Browns	49

HOCKEY
National Hockey League

Team Name	GP	W	L	T	GF	GA	Pts	Pct
Toronto Maple Leafs	60	32	15	13	182	143	77	.642
Detroit Red Wings	60	30	18	12	187	148	72	.600
Boston Bruins	60	23	24	13	167	168	59	.492
New York Rangers	60	21	26	13	176	201	55	.458
Montreal Canadiens	60	20	29	11	147	169	51	.425
Chicago Black Hawks	60	20	34	6	195	225	46	.383

Coaching Changes

Detroit--Tommy Ivan 30-18-12; Chicago--John Gottselig 7-20-2, Charlie Conacher 13-14-4.

League Leaders

Goals		Assists		Points	
Ted Lindsay	33	Doug Bentley	37	Elmer Lach	61
Elmer Lach	30	Herb O'Connor	36	Herb O'Connor	60
Rocket Richard	28	Edgar Laprade	34	Doug Bentley	57
Gaye Stewart	27	Elmer Lach	31	Gaye Stewart	56
Max Bentley	26	Sid Abel	30	Max Bentley	54

Penalty Minutes		GAA		Wins	
Bill Barilko	147	Walter Broda	2.38	Walter Broda	32
Ken Reardon	129	Harry Lumley	2.46	Harry Lumley	30
Gus Mortson	118	Bill Durnan	2.77	Frank Brimsek	23
Bill Ezinicki	97	Frank Brimsek	2.80	Bill Durnan	20
Ted Lindsay	95	Jim Henry	3.19	Emile Francis	18

Shutouts	
Harry Lumley	7
Bill Durnan	5
Walter Broda	5
Frank Brimsek	3
Jim Henry	2

All-Star Game
(Maple Leaf Gardens, Toronto)

October 13 1947	All-Stars	4	Toronto Maple Leafs	3

Stanley Cup Playoffs

March 24	Boston Bruins	4	at	Toronto Maple Leafs	5 [17:30]
March 24	New York Rangers	1	at	Detroit Red Wings	2
March 26	New York Rangers	2	at	Detroit Red Wings	5
March 27	Boston Bruins	3	at	Toronto Maple Leafs	5
March 28	Detroit Red Wings	2	at	New York Rangers	3
March 30	Toronto Maple Leafs	5	at	Boston Bruins	1
March 30	Detroit Red Wings	1	at	New York Rangers	3
April 1	Toronto Maple Leafs	2	at	Boston Bruins	3

April 1	New York Rangers	1	at	Detroit Red Wings	3
April 3	Boston Bruins	2	at	Toronto Maple Leafs	3
April 4	Detroit Red Wings	4	at	New York Rangers	2
April 7	Detroit Red Wings	3	at	Toronto Maple Leafs	5
April 10	Detroit Red Wings	2	at	Toronto Maple Leafs	4
April 11	Toronto Maple Leafs	2	at	Detroit Red Wings	0
April 14	Toronto Maple Leafs	7	at	Detroit Red Wings	2

All Star Teams

First Team		Second Team
Walter Broda	Goal	Frank Brimsek
Bill Quackenbush	Defense	Ken Reardon
Jack Stewart	Defense	Neil Colville
Elmer Lach	Center	Herb O'Connor
Maurice Richard	Right Wing	Norman Poile
Ted Lindsay	Left Wing	Gaye Stewart

Individual Awards

Art Ross Trophy--Elmer Lach (Montreal Canadiens)
Calder Memorial Trophy--Jim McFadden (Detroit Red Wings)
Hart Trophy--Herbert O'Connor (New York Rangers)
Lady Byng Trophy--Herbert O'Connor (New York Rangers)
Vezina Trophy--Walter Broda (Toronto Maple Leafs)

Other Sports

Horseracing--Kentucky Derby won by Citation (time 2:05.4, purse $83,400).
Heavyweight Boxing--Joe Louis knocked-out Joe Walcott in 11 rounds.
Golf--U.S. Open won by Ben Hogan with a score of 276.
Auto Racing--Indianapolis 500 won by Mauri Rose (ave. speed 119.813 MPH).
Tennis--U.S Open won by Pancho Gonzales in the men's singles.
U.S. Open won by Gardner Mulloy and William Talbert in the men's doubles.
U.S. Open won by Margaret 0. du Pont in the women's singles.
U.S. Open won by Margaret 0. du Pont and Louise Brough in the women's doubles.
U.S. Open won by Louise Brough and Thomas Brown Jr. in the mixed doubles.

1949

BASEBALL
National League

Team Name	W	L	Pct	GB	R	OR
Brooklyn Dodgers	97	57	.630	-	879	651
St. Louis Cardinals	96	58	.623	1	766	616
Philadelphia Phillies	81	73	.526	16	662	668
Boston Braves	75	79	.487	22	706	719
New York Giants	73	81	.474	24	736	693
Pittsburgh Pirates	71	83	.461	26	681	760
Cincinnati Reds	62	92	.403	35	627	770
Chicago Cubs	61	93	.396	36	593	773

Coaching Changes

Brooklyn--Burt Shotton 97-57; Philadelphia--Eddie Sawyer 81-73; New York--Leo Durocher73-81; Cincinnati--Bill Walters 61-90, Luke Sewell 1-2; Chicago--Charlie Grimm 19-31, Frank Frisch 42-62.

League Leaders

Batting Average		Home Runs		RBI	
Jackie Robinson	.342	Ralph Kiner	54	Ralph Kiner	127
Stan Musial	.338	Stan Musial	36	Jackie Robinson	124
Enos Slaughter	.336	Hank Sauer	31	Stan Musial	123
Carl Furillo	.322	Bobby Thomson	27	Gil Hodges	115
Ralph Kiner	.310	Sid Gordon	26	Del Ennis	110

Stolen Bases		ERA		Wins	
Jackie Robinson	37	Dave Koslo	2.50	Warren Spahn	21
Harold Reese	26	Howard Pollet	2.77	Howard Pollet	20
Hal Jeffcoat	12	Charles Roe	2.79	Ken Raffensberger	18
Gene Hermanski	12	Ken Heintzelman	3.02	Don Newcombe	17
Duke Snider	12	Warren Spahn	3.07	Russ Meyer	17

Saves		Strikeouts	
Ted Wilks	9	Warren Spahn	151
Nelson Potter	7	Don Newcombe	149
Jim Konstanty	7	Larry Jansen	113
Gerry Staley	6	Ralph Branca	109
Ervin Palica	6	Charles Roe	109

American League

Team Name	W	L	Pct	GB	R	OR
New York Yankees	97	57	.630	-	829	637
Boston Red Sox	96	58	.623	1	896	667
Cleveland Indians	89	65	.578	8	675	574
Detroit Tigers	87	67	.565	10	751	655
Philadelphia Athletics	81	73	.526	16	726	725
Chicago White Sox	63	91	.409	34	648	737
St. Louis Browns	53	101	.344	44	667	913
Washington Senators	50	104	.325	47	584	868

Coaching Changes

New York--Casey Stengel 97-57; Detroit--Robert Rolfe 87-67; Chicago--Jack Onslow 63-91.

League Leaders

Batting Average

George Kell	.343
Ted Williams	.343
Bob Dillinger	.324
Dale Mitchell	.317
Bobby Doerr	.309

Home Runs

Ted Williams	43
Vern Stephens	39
Tom Henrich	24
Larry Doby	24
Jack Graham	24

RBI

Ted Williams	159
Vern Stephens	159
Vic Wertz	133
Bobby Doerr	109
Sam Chapman	108

Stolen Bases

Bob Dillinger	20
Phil Rizzuto	18
Elmer Valo	14
Dave Philley	13
Sherry Robertson	10

ERA

Mel Parnell	2.77
Virgil Trucks	2.81
Bob Lemon	2.99
Ed Lopat	3.26
Bill Wight	3.31

Wins

Mel Parnell	25
Ellis Kinder	23
Bob Lemon	22
Vic Raschi	21
Alex Kellner	20

Saves

Joe Page	27
Al Benton	10
Tom Ferrick	6
Satchel Paige	5
Walt Masterson	4

Strikeouts

Virgil Trucks	153
Hal Newhouser	144
Bob Lemon	138
Ellis Kinder	138
Tommy Byrne	129

All-Star Game

(Ebbets Field, Brooklyn)

July 12	American League	11	National League	7

World Series

October 5	Brooklyn Dodgers	0	at	New York Yankees	1
October 6	Brooklyn Dodgers	1	at	New York Yankees	0
October 7	New York Yankees	4	at	Brooklyn Dodgers	3
October 8	New York Yankees	6	at	Brooklyn Dodgers	4
October 9	New York Yankees	10	at	Brooklyn Dodgers	6

Individual Awards

Baseball Writers Award--Jackie Robinson (Brooklyn Dodgers NL)
Ted Williams (Boston Red Sox AL)
Rookie of the Year Don Newcombe (Brooklyn Dodgers NL)
Roy Sievers (St. Louis Browns AL)
Sporting News Executive of the Year--Robert Carpenter (Philadelphia Phillies NL)
Sporting News Manager of the Year--Casey Stengel (New York Yankees AL)
Sporting News Pitcher of the Year--Howie Pollet (St. Louis Cardinals NL)
Ellis Kinder (Boston Red Sox AL)
Sporting News Player of the Year--Enos Slaughter (St. Louis Cardinals NL)
Ted Williams (Boston Red Sox AL)
Sporting News Rookie of the Year--Roy Sievers (St. Louis Browns AL)
Don Newcombe (Brooklyn Dodgers NL)

Hall of Fame Inductees

Mordecai Brown, Charlie Gehringer, Kid Nichols

BASKETBALL
National Basketball League
East Division

Team Name	GP	W	L	PPGF	PPGA	Ave	GB
Anderson Duffy Packers	64	49	15	72.1	63.1	.766	-
Syracuse Nationals	63	40	23	66.5	63.8	.635	8.5
Hammond Calumet Buccaneers	62	21	41	61.0	64.9	.339	17
(Detroit Vagabond Kings)	19	2	17	61.1	75.2	.105	
(Dayton Rens)	40	14	26	56.7	61.7	.350	30.5

West Division

Team Name	GP	W	L	PPGF	PPGA	Ave	GB
Oshkosh All-Stars	64	37	27	60.9	59.0	.578	-
Tri-Cities Blackhawks	64	36	28	65.1	62.4	.563	1
Sheboygan Redskins	64	35	29	62.0	61.7	.547	2
Waterloo Hawks	62	30	32	58.9	59.2	.484	6
Denver Nuggets	62	18	44	58.2	64.1	.290	18

Coaching Changes

Syracuse--Al Cervi 40-23; Hammond--Bob Carpenter 11-16, George Sobek 10-25; Detroit--Del Loranger 2-17; Dayton--Pop Gates 14-26; Oshkosh--Lon Darling 8-4, Gene Englund 29-23; Tri-Cities--Bob McDermott 25-20, Roger Potter 11-8; Sheboygan--Ken Suesens 35-29; Waterloo--Charley Shipp 30-32; Denver--Ralph Bishop 18-44.

League Leaders

Field Goals		Free Throws		Free Throw Att	
Dick Mehen	315	Don Otten	297	Don Otten	424
Don Otten	301	Al Cervi	287	Gene Englund	393
Harry Boykoff	293	Gene Englund	282	Al Cervi	382
Gene Englund	284	Dolph Schayes	267	Dolph Schayes	370
Dolph Schayes	271	George Sobek	232	George Sobek	322

Points

Don Otten	899
Gene Englund	850
Dick Mehen	841
Dolph Schayes	809
Harry Boykoff	777

NBL Championship

Anderson Duffy Packers	89	at	Syracuse Nationals	74
Anderson Duffy Packers	62	at	Syracuse Nationals	80
Syracuse Nationals	59	at	Anderson Duffy Packers	76
Syracuse Nationals	84	at	Anderson Duffy Packers	90
Syracuse Nationals	80	at	Hammond Calumet Buccaneers	69
Hammond Calumet Buccaneers	66	at	Syracuse Nationals	72
Tri-Cities Blackhawks	66	at	Oshkosh All-Stars	68
Tri-Cities Blackhawks	59	at	Oshkosh All-Stars	73
Oshkosh All-Stars	64	at	Tri-Cities Blackhawks	70
Oshkosh All-Stars	70	at	Tri-Cities Blackhawks	69
Sheboygan Redskins	60	at	Tri-Cities Blackhawks	75
Tri-Cities Blackhawks	59	at	Sheboygan Redskins	51
Anderson Duffy Packers	74	at	Oshkosh All-Stars	70
Anderson Duffy Packers	72	at	Oshkosh All-Stars	70
Oshkosh All-Stars	64	at	Anderson Duffy Packers	88

Notes

The Detroit Vagabond Kings folded and their record was assumed by the New York Rens a formerly powerful all black touring team. The team for this season was based in Dayton but played a majority of their games on the road.
This was the last season for three different leagues. The BAA and the NBL merged to become the NBA and the AAFC merged with the NFL

Basketball Association of America
East Division

Team Name	GP	W	L	PPGF	PPGA	Pct	GB
Washington Capitols	60	38	22	81.8	79.4	.633	-
New York Knickerbockers	60	32	28	79.2	77.7	.533	6
Baltimore Bullets	60	29	31	83.6	82.2	.483	9
Philadelphia Warriors	60	28	32	83.7	83.4	.467	10
Boston Celtics	60	25	35	76.6	79.5	.417	13
Providence Steamrollers	60	12	48	78.5	87.6	.200	26

West Division

Team Name	GP	W	L	PPGF	PPGA	Pct	GB
Rochester Royals	60	45	15	84.0	77.4	.750	-
Minneapolis Lakers	60	44	16	84.0	76.7	.733	1
Chicago Stags	60	38	22	84.0	80.0	.633	7
St. Louis Bombers	60	29	31	75.8	79.4	.483	16
Fort Wayne Zollner Pistons	60	22	38	74.3	77.5	.367	21
Indianapolis Jets	60	18	42	74.7	79.4	.300	27

Coaching Changes

Boston--Doggie Julian 25-35; Providence--Ken Loeffler 12-48; Rochester--Les Harrison 45-15; Minneapolis--John Kundla 44-16; Chicago--Ole Olsen 28-21, Phil Brownstein 10-1; St. Louis--Grady Lewis 29-31; Fort Wayne--Carl Bennett 0-6, Curly Armstrong 22-32; Indianapolis--Bruce Hale 4-13, Burl Friddle 14-29.

League Leaders

Field Goals		Free Throws		Free Throw Att	
George Mikan	583	George Mikan	532	George Mikan	689
Joe Fulks	529	Joe Fulks	502	Joe Fulks	638
Max Zaslofsky	425	Max Zaslofsky	347	Arnie Risen	462
Belus Smawley	352	Arnie Risen	305	Max Zaslofsky	413
Arnie Risen	345	Ken Sailors	281	Ken Sailors	367

Points		Assists		Fouls	
George Mikan	1698	Bob Davies	321	Ed Sadowski	273
Joe Fulks	1560	Andy Phillip	319	Joe Fulks	262
Max Zaslofsky	1197	John Logan	276	George Mikan	260
Arnie Risen	995	Ernie Calverly	251	Lee Knorek	258
Ed Sadowski	920	George Senesky	233	Kleggie Hermsen	257

BAA Championship

March 22	St. Louis Bombers	64	at	Rochester Royals	93
March 23	Washington Capitols	92	at	Philadelphia Warriors	70
March 23	N.Y. Knickerbockers	81	at	Baltimore Bullets	82
March 23	Rochester Royals	66	at	St. Louis Bombers	64
March 23	Chicago Stags	77	at	Minneapolis Lakers	84
March 24	Philadelphia Warriors	78	at	Washington Capitols	80
March 24	Baltimore Bullets	82	at	N.Y. Knickerbockers	84
March 24	Minneapolis Lakers	101	at	Chicago Stags	85
March 26	Baltimore Bullets	99	at	N.Y. Knickerbockers	103 [OT]
March 27	Minneapolis Lakers	80	at	Rochester Royals	79
March 29	N.Y. Knickerbockers	71	at	Washington Capitols	77
March 29	Minneapolis Lakers	67	at	Rochester Royals	55*
March 31	Washington Capitols	84	at	N.Y. Knickerbockers	86 [OT]
April 2	N.Y. Knickerbockers	76	at	Washington Capitols	84
April 4	Washington Capitols	84	at	Minneapolis Lakers	88
April 6	Washington Capitols	62	at	Minneapolis Lakers	76
April 8	Minneapolis Lakers	94	at	Washington Capitols	74
April 9	Minneapolis Lakers	71	at	Washington Capitols	83
April 11	Minneapolis Lakers	66	at	Washington Capitols	74
April 13	Minneapolis Lakers	77	at	Washington Capitols	56*

All Star Teams

First Team	Second Team
George Mikan (Minneapolis Lakers)	Arnie Risen (Rochester Royals)
Joe Fulks (Philadelphia Warriors)	Bob Feerick (Washington Capitols)
Bob Davies (Rochester Royals)	"Bones" McKinney (Washington Capitols)
Max Zaslofsky (Chicago Stags)	Ken Sailors (Providence Steamrollers)
Jim Pollard (Minneapolis Lakers)	John Logan (St. Louis Bombers)

*Game was played in St. Paul

FOOTBALL
National Football League
East Division

Team Name	GP	W	L	T	PF	PA	Pct
Philadelphia Eagles	12	11	1	0	364	134	.917
Pittsburgh Steelers	12	6	5	1	224	214	.542
New York Giants	12	6	6	0	287	298	.500
Washington Redskins	12	4	7	1	268	339	.375
New York Bulldogs	12	1	10	1	153	368	.125

West Division

Team Name	GP	W	L	T	PF	PA	Pct
Los Angeles Rams	12	8	2	2	360	239	.750
Chicago Bears	12	9	3	0	332	218	.750
Chicago Cardinals	12	6	5	1	360	301	.542
Detroit Lions	12	4	8	0	237	259	.333
Green Bay Packers	12	2	10	0	114	329	.167

Coaching Changes

Washington--John Whelchel 2-4-1, Herman Ball 2-3-0; Cardinals--Buddy Parker & Phil Handler 2-4-0, Buddy Parker 4-1-1; Bulldogs--Charley Ewart 1-10-1.

League Leaders

Yards Rushing		Yards Passing		Passing % (40 attempts)	
Steve Van Buren	1146	John Lujack	2658	Sam Baugh	57
Tony Canadeo	1052	Bob Waterfield	2168	Norm Van Brocklin	55
Elmer Angsman	674	Chuck Conerly	2138	Tom Thompson	54
"Choo-Choo" Roberts	634	Sam Baugh	1903	John Lujack	52
Jerry Nuzum	611	Bobby Layne	1796	Bob Waterfield	52

Receiving Yards		Receptions		Field Goals	
Bob Mann	1014	Tom Fears	77	Cliff Patton	9
Tom Fears	1013	Bob Mann	66	Bob Waterfield	9
Hugh Taylor	781	Bill Chipley	57	Ben Agajanian	8
"Choo-Choo" Roberts	711	Bill Swiacki	47	George Blanda	7
Jim Keane	696	Jim Keane	47	Vinnie Yablonskie	5

Punt Return Yards		Kickoff Return Yards	
"Vitamin" Smith	427	Don Doll	536
Em Tunnell	315	Don Sandifer	518
Red Cochran	314	Jack Salschneider	474
Wally Triplett	281	Ed Saenz	465
George McAfee	279	Charlie Trippi	427

NFL Championship

December 18	Philadelphia Eagles	14	at	Los Angeles Rams	0

All-American Football Conference

Team Name	GP	W	L	T	PF	PA	Pct
Cleveland Browns	12	9	1	2	339	171	.833
San Francisco 49ers	12	9	3	0	416	227	.750
New York Yankees	12	8	4	0	196	206	.667
Buffalo Bills	12	5	5	2	236	256	.500
Chicago Hornets	12	4	8	0	179	268	.333
Los Angeles Dons	12	4	8	0	253	322	.333
Baltimore Colts	12	1	11	0	172	341	.083

Coaching Changes

New York--Red Steader 8-4-0; Buffalo--Red Dawson 1-3-1, Clem Crowe 4-2-1; Chicago--Ray Flaherty 4-8-0; Baltimore--Cecil Isbell 0-4-0, Walt Driskill 1-7-0.

League Leaders

Yards Rushing		Yards Passing		Passing % (40 attempts)	
Joe Perry	783	Otto Graham	2785	George Ratterman	58
Chet Mutryn	696	Y.A. Tittle	2209	Otto Graham	56
Marion Motley	570	Frankie Albert	1862	Y.A. Tittle	51
Ollie Cline	518	Bob Hoernschemeyer	1063	John Clement	51
Buddy Young	495	John Clement	906	Frank Albert	50

Receiving Yards		Receptions		Field Goals	
Mac Speedie	1028	Mac Speedie	62	Harvey Johnson	7
Al Baldwin	719	Al Baldwin	53	Rex Grassman	6
Alyn Beals	678	Alyn Beals	44	Jim McCarthy	6
Billy Stone	621	Dan Edwards	42	Chet Adams	4
Dick Wilkins	589	Lamar Davis	38	Bob Nelson	3

Punt Return Yards		Kickoff Return Yards	
Jim Cason	351	Herm Wedemeyer	602
Sam Cathcart	306	Billy Grimes	411
Bob Livingstone	292	Ray Ramsey	407
Pete Layden	287	Bob Hoernschemeyer	373
Herm Wedemeyer	221	Joe Perry	337

AAFC Championship

December 11	San Francisco 49ers	7	at	Cleveland Browns	21

HOCKEY

National Hockey League

Team Name	GP	W	L	T	GF	GA	Pts	Pct
Detroit Red Wings	60	34	19	7	195	145	75	.625
Boston Bruins	60	29	23	8	178	163	66	.550
Montreal Canadiens	60	28	23	9	152	126	65	.542
Toronto Maple Leafs	60	22	25	13	147	161	57	.475
Chicago Black Hawks	60	21	31	8	173	211	50	.417
New York Rangers	60	18	31	11	133	172	47	.392

Coaching Changes

Chicago--Charlie Conacher 21-31-8; New York--Frank Boucher 6-11-6, Lynn Patrick 12-20-5.

League Leaders

Goals		Assists		Points	
Sid Abel	28	Doug Bentley	43	Roy Conacher	68
Roy Conacher	26	Roy Conacher	42	Doug Bentley	66
Jim Conacher	26	Ted Lindsay	30	Sid Abel	54
Harry Watson	26	Paul Ronty	29	Ted Lindsay	54
Ted Lindsay	24	Sid Abel	26	Paul Ronty	49

Penalty Minutes		GAA		Wins	
Bill Ezinicki	145	Bill Durnan	2.10	Harry Lumley	34
Bep Guidolin	116	Harry Lumley	2.42	Bill Durnan	28
Elton Chamberlain	111	Walter Broda	2.68	Frank Brimsek	26
Rocket Richard	110	Frank Brimsek	2.72	Walter Broda	22
Ken Reardon	103	Chuck Rayner	2.90	Jim Henry	21

Shutouts	
Bill Durnan	10
Chuck Rayner	7
Harry Lumley	6
Walter Broda	5
Gordon Henry	1

All-Star Game

(Chicago Stadium, Chicago)

November 3 1948	All-Stars	3	Toronto Maple Leafs	1

Stanley Cup Playoffs

Date	Visitor			Home	
March 22	Montreal Canadiens	1	at	Detroit Red Wings	2 [44:52]
March 22	Toronto Maple Leafs	3	at	Boston Bruins	0
March 24	Montreal Canadiens	4	at	Detroit Red Wings	3 [2:59]
March 24	Toronto Maple Leafs	3	at	Boston Bruins	2
March 26	Detroit Red Wings	2	at	Montreal Canadiens	3
March 26	Boston Bruins	5	at	Toronto Maple Leafs	4 [16:41]
March 29	Detroit Red Wings	3	at	Montreal Canadiens	1
March 29	Boston Bruins	1	at	Toronto Maple Leafs	3
March 30	Toronto Maple Leafs	3	at	Boston Bruins	2
March 31	Montreal Canadiens	1	at	Detroit Red Wings	3
April 2	Detroit Red Wings	1	at	Montreal Canadiens	3
April 5	Montreal Canadiens	1	at	Detroit Red Wings	3
April 8	Toronto Maple Leafs	3	at	Detroit Red Wings	2 [17:31]
April 10	Toronto Maple Leafs	3	at	Detroit Red Wings	1
April 13	Detroit Red Wings	1	at	Toronto Maple Leafs	3
April 16	Detroit Red Wings	1	at	Toronto Maple Leafs	3

All Star Teams

First Team		Second Team
Bill Durnan	Goal	Chuck Rayner
Bill Quackenbush	Defense	Glen Harmon
Jack Stewart	Defense	Ken Reardon
Sid Abel	Center	Doug Bentley
Maurice Richard	Right Wing	Gordie Howe
Roy Conacher	Left Wing	Ted Lindsay

Individual Awards

Art Ross Trophy--Roy Conacher (Chicago Black Hawks)
Calder Memorial Trophy--Pentti Lund (New York Rangers)
Hart Trophy--Sid Abel (Detroit Red Wings)
Lady Byng Trophy--Bill Quackenbush (Detroit Red Wings)
Vezina Trophy--Bill Durnan (Montreal Canadiens)

Franchise Changes

NFL--Boston Yankees became the New York Bulldogs.,
AAFC--Chicago Rockets changed name to Chicago Hornets.
NBL--Detroit Vagabond Kings became the Dayton Rens part way through the season.

Other Sports

Horseracing--Kentucky Derby won by Ponder (time 2:04.2, purse $91,600).
Heavyweight Boxing--Ezzard Charles defeated Joe Walcott in 15 rounds.
Ezzard Charles knocked-out Pat Valentino in 8 rounds, and clinched the title.
Golf--U.S. Open won by Cary Middlecoff with a score of 286.
Auto Racing--Indianapolis 500 won by William Holland (ave. speed 121.327 MPH).
Tennis--U.S. Open won by Pancho Gonzales in the men's singles.
U.S. Open won by John Bromwich and William Sidwell in the men's singles.
U.S. Open won by Margaret 0. du Pont in the women's singles.
U.S. Open won by Louise Brough and Margaret 0. du Pont in the women's doubles.
U.S. Open won by Louise Brough and Eric Sturgess in the mixed doubles.

1950

BASEBALL
National League

Team Name	W	L	Pct	GB	R	OR
Philadelphia Phillies	91	63	.591	-	722	624
Brooklyn Dodgers	89	65	.578	2	847	724
New York Giants	86	68	.558	5	735	643
Boston Braves	83	71	.539	8	785	736
St. Louis Cardinals	78	75	.510	12.5	693	670
Cincinnati Reds	66	87	.431	24.5	654	734
Chicago Cubs	64	89	.418	26.5	643	772
Pittsburgh Pirates	57	96	.373	33.5	681	857

Coaching Changes

Cincinnati--Luke Sewell 66-87; Chicago--Frank Frisch 64-89.

League Leaders

Batting Average		Home Runs		RBI	
Stan Musial	.346	Ralph Kiner	47	Del Ennis	126
Jackie Robinson	.328	Andy Pafko	36	Ralph Kiner	118
Duke Snider	.321	Hank Sauer	32	Gil Hodges	113
Del Ennis	.311	Gil Hodges	32	Ted Kluszewski	111
Ted Kluszewski	.307	Roy Campanella	31	Stan Musial	109

Stolen Bases		ERA		Wins	
Sam Jethroe	35	Jim Hearn	1.94	Warren Spahn	21
Harold Reese	17	Jim Konstanty	2.66	Robin Roberts	20
Duke Snider	16	Sal Maglie	2.71	Johnny Sain	20
Earl Torgeson	15	Nicholas Church	2.73	Elwin Roe	19
Richie Ashburn	14	Ewell Blackwell	2.97	Don Newcombe	19

Saves		Strikeouts	
Jim Konstanty	22	Warren Spahn	191
Bill Werle	8	Ewell Blackwell	188
Ralph Branca	7	Larry Jansen	161
Bob Hogue	7	Robin Roberts	146
Emil Leonard	6	Curt Simmons	146

American League

Team Name	W	L	Pct	GB	R	OR
New York Yankees	98	56	.636	-	914	691
Detroit Tigers	95	59	.617	3	837	713
Boston Red Sox	94	60	.610	4	1027	804
Cleveland Indians	92	62	.597	6	806	654
Washington Senators	67	87	.435	31	690	813
Chicago White Sox	60	94	.390	38	625	749
St. Louis Browns	58	96	.377	40	684	916
Philadelphia Athletics	52	102	.338	46	670	913

Coaching Changes

Boston--Joe McCarthy 32-30, Steve O'Neill 62-30; Washington--Stanley Harris 67-87; Chicago--Jack Onslow 8-22, John Corriden 52-72.

League Leaders

Batting Average		Home Runs		RBI	
Bill Goodman	.354	Al Rosen	37	Walt Dropo	144
George Kell	.340	Walt Dropo	34	Vern Stephens	144
Dom DiMaggio	.328	Joe DiMaggio	32	Yogi Berra	124
Larry Doby	.326	Vern Stephens	30	Vic Wertz	123
Al Zarilla	.325	Gus Zernial	29	Joe DiMaggio	122

Stolen Bases		ERA		Wins	
Dom DiMaggio	15	Early Wynn	3.20	Bob Lemon	23
Phil Rizzuto	12	Ned Garver	3.39	Vic Raschi	21
Elmer Valo	12	Bob Feller	3.43	Art Houtteman	19
Gil Coan	10	Ed Lopat	3.47	Early Wynn	18
Johnny Lipon	9	Art Houtteman	3.54	Ed Lopat	18

Saves		Strikeouts	
Mickey Harris	15	Bob Lemon	170
Joe Page	13	Allie Reynolds	160
Tom Ferrick	11	Vic Raschi	155
Ellis Kinder	9	Early Wynn	143
Lou Brissie	8	Bob Feller	119

All-Star Game

(Comiskey Park, Chicago)

July 11	National League	4	American League	3

World Series

October 4	New York Yankees	1	at	Philadelphia Phillies	0
October 5	New York Yankees	2	at	Philadelphia Phillies	1 [10]
October 6	Philadelphia Phillies	2	at	New York Yankees	3
October 7	Philadelphia Phillies	2	at	New York Yankees	5

Individual Awards

Baseball Writers Award--Jim Konstanty (Philadelphia Phillies NL)
Phil Rizzuto (New York Yankees AL)
Rookie of the Year--Sam Jethroe (Boston Braves NL)
Walt Dropo (Boston Red Sox AL)
Sporting News Executive of the Year--George Weiss (New York Yankees AL)
Sporting News Manager of the Year--Robert Rolfe (Detroit Tigers AL)
Sporting News Pitcher of the Year--Jim Konstanty (Philadelphia Phillies NL)
Bob Lemon (Cleveland Indians AL)
Sporting News Player of the Year--Ralph Kiner (Pittsburgh Pirates NL)
Phil Rizzuto (New York Yankees AL)
Sporting News Rookie of the Year--Whitey Ford (New York Yankees AL)

Rules

The strike zone was to include only the area from the batter's armpits to the top of his knees (NL and AL).

BASKETBALL
National Basketball Association

Eastern Division

Team Name	GP	W	L	PPGF	PPGA	Pct	GB
Syracuse Nationals	64	51	13	84.8	76.7	.797	-
New York Knickerbockers	68	40	28	80.7	78.6	.588	13
Washington Capitols	68	32	36	76.5	77.4	.471	21
Philadelphia Warriors	68	26	42	73.3	76.4	.382	27
Baltimore Bullets	68	25	43	73.1	78.7	.368	28
Boston Celtics	68	22	46	79.7	82.2	.324	31

Central Division

Team Name	GP	W	L	PPGF	PPGA	Pct	GB
Minneapolis Lakers	68	51	17	84.1	75.7	.750	-
Rochester Royals	68	51	17	82.4	74.6	.750	-
Fort Wayne Zollner Pistons	68	40	28	79.3	77.9	.588	11
Chicago Stags	68	40	28	78.7	77.1	.588	11
St. Louis Bombers	68	26	42	73.7	76.5	.382	25

Western Division

Team Name	GP	W	L	PPGF	PPGA	Pct	GB
Indianapolis Olympians	64	39	25	85.8	82.1	.609	-
Anderson Duffey Packers	64	37	27	87.3	83.6	.578	2
Tri-Cities Blackhawks	64	29	35	83.0	83.6	.453	10
Sheboygan Redskins	62	22	40	82.4	87.8	.355	16
Waterloo Hawks	62	19	43	79.4	84.9	.306	19
Denver Nuggets	62	11	51	77.7	89.1	.177	27

Coaching

Denver--Jim Darden 11-51; Minneapolis--John Kundla 51-17; Rochester--Les Harrison 51-17; Fort Wayne--Murray Mendenhall 40-28; Chicago--Phil Brownstein 40-28; St. Louis--Grady Lewis 26-42; Syracuse--Al Cervi 51-13; New York--Joe Lapchick 40-28; Washington--Bob Feerick 32-36; Philadelphia--Eddie Gottlieb 26-42; Baltimore--Buddy Jeannette 25-43; Boston--Doggie Julian 22-46; Indianapolis--Cliff Barker 39-25; Anderson--Howie Schultz 21-14, Ike Duffey 1-2, Doxie Moore 15-11; Tri-Cities--Roger Potter 1-6, Red Auerbach 28-29; Sheboygan--Ken Suesens 22-40; Waterloo--Charley Shipp 8-27, Jack Smiley 11-16

League Leaders

Field Goals

George Mikan	649
Alex Groza	521
Max Zaslofsky	397
Jim Pollard	394
Carl Braun	373

Free Throws

George Mikan	567
Alex Groza	454
Frank Brian	402
Ed Macauley	379
Dolph Schayes	376

Assists

Dick McGuire	386
Andy Phillip	377
Bob Davies	294
George Senesky	264
Al Cervi	264

Points

George Mikan	1865
Alex Groza	1496
Frank Brian	1138
Max Zaslofsky	1115
Ed Macauley	1081

Fouls

George Mikan	297
Bob Brannum	279
Chuck Gilmur	275
Charlie Black	273
Bob Brown	269

NBA Championship

March 20	Chicago Stags	69	at	Ft. Wayne Zollner Pistons	86
March 21	Minneapolis Lakers	78	at	Rochester Royals	76
March 21	N.Y. Knickerbockers	90	at	Washington Capitols	87
March 21	Sheboygan Redskins	85	at	Indianapolis Olympians	86
March 21	Tri-Cities Blackhawks	77	at	Anderson Duffy Packers	89
March 22	Philadelphia Warriors	76	at	Syracuse Nationals	93
March 22	Washington Capitols	83	at	N.Y. Knickerbockers	103
March 22	Chicago Stags	75	at	Minneapolis Lakers	85
March 23	Syracuse Nationals	59	at	Philadelphia Warriors	53
March 23	Ft. Wayne Zollner Pistons	90	at	Rochester Royals	84
March 23	Indianapolis Olympians	85	at	Sheboygan Redskins	95
March 23	Anderson Duffy Packers	75	at	Tri-Cities Blackhawks	76
March 24	Tri-Cities Blackhawks	71	at	Anderson Duffy Packers	94
March 25	Minneapolis Lakers	75	at	Chicago Stags	67
March 25	Rochester Royals	78	at	Ft. Wayne Zollner Pistons	79 [OT]
March 25	Sheboygan Redskins	84	at	Indianapolis Olympians	91
March 26	N.Y. Knickerbockers	83	at	Syracuse Nationals	91 [OT]
March 27	Ft. Wayne Zollner Pistons	79	at	Minneapolis Lakers	93
March 28	Minneapolis Lakers	89	at	Ft. Wayne Zollner Pistons	82
March 28	Anderson Duffy Packers	74	at	Indianapolis Olympians	77
March 30	Syracuse Nationals	76	at	N.Y. Knickerbockers	80
March 30	Indianapolis Olympians	67	at	Anderson Duffy Packers	84
April 1	Anderson Duffy Packers	67	at	Indianapolis Olympians	65
April 2	N.Y. Knickerbockers	80	at	Syracuse Nationals	91
April 5	Anderson Duffy Packers	50	at	Minneapolis Lakers	75
April 6	Minneapolis Lakers	90	at	Anderson Duffy Packers	71
April 8	Minneapolis Lakers	68	at	Syracuse Nationals	66
April 9	Minneapolis Lakers	85	at	Syracuse Nationals	91
April 14	Minneapolis Lakers	91		Syracuse Nationals	77 **
April 16	Minneapolis Lakers	77		Syracuse Nationals	69 **
April 20	Minneapolis Lakers	76	at	Syracuse Nationals	83
April 23	Syracuse Nationals	95	at	Minneapolis Lakers	110

All Star Teams

First Team	Second Team
George Mikan (Minneapolis Lakers)	Frank Brian (Anderson Duffy Packers)
Jim Pollard (Minneapolis Lakers)	Fred Schaus (Ft Wayne Zollner Pistons)
Alex Groza (Indianapolis Olympians)	Dolph Schayes (Syracuse Nationals)
Bob Davies (Rochester Royals)	Al Cervi (Syracuse Nationals)
Max Zaslofsky (Chicago Stags)	Ralph Beard (Indianapolis Olympians)

Notes

The NBA was formed this year from a merger of the NBL and the BAA and the league faced huge scheduling problems because of the merger, as flying was not yet common in the pro sports leagues. The Eastern and Central Divisions played 68 games except for Syracuse which played 64 games, the same amount as the Western Division teams.
Charles Henry Cooper became the first black player to play in the NBA when he played for Fort Wayne on November 1, 1950. There had been other blacks to play major league basketball earlier and in fact had been whole teams comprised of black players in previous leagues.
Maurice Podoloff was named as the first Commissioner of the NBA.

**Games played in St. Paul

FOOTBALL
National Football league

American Conference

Team Name	GP	W	L	T	PF	PA	Pct
Cleveland Browns	12	10	2	0	310	144	.833
New York Giants	12	10	2	0	268	150	.833
Philadelphia Eagles	12	6	6	0	254	141	.500
Pittsburgh Steelers	12	6	6	0	180	195	.500
Chicago Cardinals	12	5	7	0	233	287	.417
Washington Redskins	12	3	9	0	232	326	.250

National Conference

Team Name	GP	W	L	T	PF	PA	Pct
Los Angeles Rams	12	9	3	0	466	309	.750
Chicago Bears	12	9	3	0	279	207	.750
New York Yanks	12	7	5	0	366	367	.583
Detroit Lions	12	6	6	0	321	285	.500
Green Bay Packers	12	3	9	0	244	406	.250
San Francisco 49ers	12	3	9	0	213	300	.250
Baltimore Colts	12	1	11	0	213	462	.083

Coaching Changes

Cleveland--Paul Brown 10-2-0; Cardinals--Curly Lambeau 5-7-0; Washington--Herman Ball 3-9-0; Los Angeles--Joe Stydahar 9-3-0; Yanks--Red Steader 7-5-0; Green Bay--Gene Ronzani 3-9-0; San Francisco--Buck Shaw 3-9-0; Baltimore--Clem Crowe 1-11-0.

League Leaders

Yards Rushing		Yards Passing		Passing % (40 attempts)	
Marion Motley	810	Bobby Layne	2323	Bob Waterfield	57
Frank Ziegler	733	George Ratterman	2251	John Rauch	57
Joe Geri	705	Norm Van Brocklin	2061	Norm Van Brocklin	55
Eddie Price	703	Otto Graham	1943	Sam Baugh	54
Joe Perry	647	Y.A. Tittle	1884	Otto Graham	54

Receiving Yards		Receptions		Field Goals	
Tom Fears	1116	Tom Fears	84	Lou Groza	13
Cloyce Box	1009	Dan Edwards	52	Cliff Patton	8
Bob Shaw	971	Cloyce Box	50	Joe Geri	8
Hugh Taylor	833	Paul Salata	50	Doak Walker	8
Dan Edwards	775	Bob Shaw	48	Bob Waterfield	7

Punt Return Yards		Kickoff Return Yards	
Billy Grimes	555	"Vitamin" Smith	742
Em Tunnell	305	Don Paul	693
George McAfee	284	Billy Grimes	600
Herb Rich	276	Buddy Young	536
"Vitamin" Smith	218	George Taliaferro	473

Pro Bowl Game

(Memorial Coliseum, Los Angeles)

January 14 1951	American Conference	28		National Conference	27

NFL Championship

December 17	Chicago Bears	14	at	Los Angeles Rams	24
December 17	New York Giants	3	at	Cleveland Browns	8
December 24	Los Angeles Rams	28	at	Cleveland Browns	30

Individual Awards

Pro Bowl M.V.P.--Otto Graham (Cleveland Browns)

Rules

The free substitution rule was permanently adopted which meant that most players would no longer have to play both ways and would allow for the development of offensive and defensive specialists.

Notes

After the death of the AAFC, Cleveland, San Francisco, and Baltimore moved into the NFL and the remaining players were spread around the league.

Dan Sherby is named president of the American Conference and Emil Fisher is named president of the National Conference of the National Football League.

Frank Filchock was reinstated this year by the NFL Commissioner Bert Bell, Filchock had been suspended in 1947 for being involved with gamblers.

Canadian Rugby Union

Interprovincial Rugby Football Union

Team Name	GP	W	L	T	PF	PA	Pts	Pct
Hamilton Tiger--Cats	12	7	5	0	231	217	14	.583
Toronto Argonauts	12	6	5	1	291	187	13	.542
Montreal Alouettes	12	6	6	0	192	261	12	.500
Ottawa Rough Riders	12	4	7	1	182	231	9	.375

Western Interprovincial Football Union

Team Name	GP	W	L	T	PF	PA	Pts	Pct
Winnipeg Blue Bombers	14	10	4	0	221	156	20	.714
Saskatchewan Roughriders	14	7	7	0	207	177	14	.500
Edmonton Eskimos	14	7	7	0	201	197	14	.500
Calgary Stampeders	14	4	10	0	152	251	8	.286

Coaching

Winnipeg--Frank Larson 10 4 0; Hamilton--Carl Voyles 7-5-0; Toronto--Frank Clair 12-6-5; Calgary--Les Lear 4-10-0; Edmonton--Annis Stukus 7-7-0; Montreal--Lew Hayman 6-6-0; Ottawa--Wally Masters 4-7-1; Saskatchewan--Fred Grant 7-7-0

League Leaders

Yards Rushing		Yards Passing		Passing %		Receiving Yards	
Tom Casey	637	Lindy Berry	2201	Keith Spaith	49	Morris Bailey	1060
				Lindy Berry	49		

Receptions		Punting Average		Points	
Morris Bailey	67	Keith Spaith	41.5	Edgar Jones	108

Grey Cup Championship

October 28	Edmonton Eskimos	24	at	Saskatchewan Roughriders	1
November 4	Winnipeg Blue Bombers	16	at	Edmonton Eskimos	17
November 11	Edmonton Eskimos	12	at	Winnipeg Blue Bombers	22
November 11	Toronto Argonauts	11	at	Hamilton Tiger-Cats	13
November 13	Edmonton Eskimos	6	at	Winnipeg Blue Bombers	29
November 15	Hamilton Tiger-Cats	6	at	Toronto Argonauts	24
November 18	Toronto Balmy Beach	13	at	Toronto Argonauts	43
November 25	Winnipeg Blue Bombers	0	at	Toronto Argonauts	13

Individual Awards

Dave Dryburgh Memorial Trophy--Joe Aguirre (Winnipeg Blue Bombers)
Dr. Beattie Martin Trophy--Gordon Brown (Calgary Stampeders)
Eddie James Memorial Trophy--Tom Casey (Winnipeg Blue Bombers)
Gruen Trophy--Bob McDonald (Hamilton Tiger-Cats)
Jeff Nicklin Memorial Trophy--Lindy Berry (Edmonton Eskimos)
Jeff Russel Memorial Trophy--Don Loney (Ottawa Rough Riders)

Notes

A forerunner of the Canadian Football League, the Canadian Rugby Union became fully professional this year when the Toronto Argonauts became professional. The IRFU and WIFU were separate members of the CRU which was formed in 1891. They did not play interlocking schedules.

HOCKEY
National Hockey League

Team Name	GP	W	L	T	GF	GA	Pts	Pct
Detroit Red Wings	70	37	19	14	229	164	88	.629
Montreal Canadiens	70	29	22	19	164	150	77	.550
Toronto Maple Leafs	70	31	27	12	176	173	74	.529
New York Rangers	70	28	31	11	170	189	67	.479
Boston Bruins	70	22	32	16	198	228	60	.429
Chicago Black Hawks	70	22	38	10	203	244	54	.386

Coaching Changes

New York--Lynn Patrick 28-31-11; Boston--George Boucher 22-32-16.

League Leaders

Goals		Assists		Points	
Rocket Richard	43	Ted Lindsay	55	Ted Lindsay	78
Gordie Howe	35	Paul Ronty	36	Sid Abel	69
Sid Abel	34	Sid Abel	35	Gordie Howe	68
Metro Prystai	29	Bep Guidolin	34	Rocket Richard	65
John Peirson	27	Doug Bentley	33	Paul Ronty	59

Penalty Minutes		GAA		Wins	
Bill Ezinicki	144	Bill Durnan	2.20	Harry Lumley	33
Gus Kyle	143	Harry Lumley	2.35	Walter Broda	30
Ted Lindsay	141	Walter Broda	2.48	Chuck Rayner	28
Bill Gadsby	138	Chuck Rayner	2.62	Bill Durnan	26
Gus Mortson	125	Jack Gelineau	3.28	Frank Brimsek	22

Shutouts

Walter Broda	9
Bill Durnan	8
Harry Lumley	7
Chuck Rayner	6
Gerry McNeil	1

All-Star Game

(Maple Leaf Gardens, Toronto)

October 10 1949	All-Stars	3	Toronto Maple Leafs	1

Stanley Cup Playoffs

March 28	Toronto Maple Leafs	5	at	Detroit Red Wings	0
March 29	Montreal Canadiens	1	at	New York Rangers	3
March 30	Toronto Maple Leafs	1	at	Detroit Red Wings	3
April 1	New York Rangers	3	at	Montreal Canadiens	2
April 1	Detroit Red Wings	0	at	Toronto Maple Leafs	2
April 2	Montreal Canadiens	1	at	New York Rangers	4
April 4	Detroit Red Wings	2	at	Toronto Maple Leafs	1 [20:38]
April 4	New York Rangers	2	at	Montreal Canadiens	3 [15:19]
April 6	Toronto Maple Leafs	2	at	Detroit Red Wings	0
April 6	New York Rangers	3	at	Montreal Canadiens	0
April 8	Detroit Red Wings	4	at	Toronto Maple Leafs	0
April 9	Toronto Maple Leafs	0	at	Detroit Red Wings	1 [8:39]
April 11	New York Rangers	1	at	Detroit Red Wings	4
April 13	New York Rangers	3		Detroit Red Wings	1 *
April 15	Detroit Red Wings	4		New York Rangers	0 *
April 17	New York Rangers	4	at	Detroit Red Wings	3 [8:54]
April 20	New York Rangers	2	at	Detroit Red Wings	1 [1:38]
April 22	New York Rangers	4	at	Detroit Red Wings	5
April 23	New York Rangers	3	at	Detroit Red Wings	4 [28:31]

All Star Teams

First Team		Second Team
Bill Durnan	Goal	Chuck Rayner
Gus Mortson	Defense	Leo Reise
Ken Reardon	Defense	Leonard Kelly
Sid Abel	Center	Ted Kennedy
Maurice Richard	Right Wing	Gordie Howe
Ted Lindsay	Left Wing	Tony Leswick

*Game played in Toronto

Individual Awards

Art Ross Trophy--Ted Lindsay (Detroit Red Wings)
Calder Memorial Trophy--Jack Gelineau (Boston Bruins)
Hart Trophy--Chuck Rayner (New York Rangers)
Lady Byng Trophy--Edgar Laprade (New York Rangers)
Vezina Trophy--Bill Durnan (Montreal Canadiens)

Hall of Fame Inductees

Scotty Davidson, Graham Drinkwater, Mike Grant, Si Griffis, Newsy Lalonde, Joe Malone, George Richardson, Harry Trihey,

Notes

The white ice surface was made mandatory

Franchise Changes

NFL--New York Bulldogs changed name to New York Yanks.

Other Sports

Horseracing--Kentucky Derby won by Middleground (time 2:01.6, purse $92,650).
Heavyweight Boxing--Ezzard Charles knocked-out Freddy Beshore in 14 rounds.
Ezzard Charles defeated Joe Louis in 15 rounds and gained universal recognition as world champion.
Ezzard Charles knocked-out Nick Barone in 11 rounds.
Golf--U.S. Open won by Ben Hogan in a playoff with Lloyd Mangrum and George Fazio (scoresof287-287-287, 69-73-75)
Auto Racing--Indianapolis 500 won by John Parsons (ave. speed 124.002 MPH).
Tennis--U.S. Open won by Arthur Larsen in the men's singles.
U.S. Open won by John Bromwich and Frank Sedgman in the men's doubles.
U.S. Open won by Margaret O. du Pont in the women's singles.
U.S. Open won by Louise Brough and Margaret O. du Pont in the women's doubles.
U.S. Open won by Margaret O. du Pont and Kenneth MacGregor in the mixed doubles.

1951

BASEBALL
National League

Team Name	W	L	Pct	GB	R	OR
New York Giants	98	59	.624	-	781	641
Brooklyn Dodgers	97	60	.618	1	855	672
St. Louis Cardinals	81	73	.526	15.5	683	671
Boston Braves	76	78	.494	20.5	723	662
Philadelphia Phillies	73	81	.474	23.5	648	644
Cincinnati Reds	68	86	.442	28.5	559	667
Pittsburgh Pirates	64	90	.416	32.5	689	845
Chicago Cubs	62	92	.403	34.5	614	750

Coaching Changes

Brooklyn--Chuck Dressen 97-60; St. Louis--Marty Marion 81-73; Boston--Bill Southworth 28-31, Tom Holmes 48-47; Chicago--Frank Frisch 35-45, Phil Cavaretta 27-47.

League Leaders

Batting Average		Home Runs		RBI	
Stan Musial	.355	Ralph Kiner	42	Monte Irvin	121
Richie Ashburn	.344	Gil Hodges	40	Ralph Kiner	109
Jackie Robinson	.338	Roy Campanella	33	Sid Gordon	109
Roy Campanella	.325	Stan Musial	32	Roy Campanella	108
Monte Irvin	.312	Bobby Thomson	32	Stan Musial	108

Stolen Bases		ERA		Wins	
Sam Jethroe	35	Chet Nichols	2.88	Larry Jansen	23
Richie Ashburn	29	Sal Maglie	2.93	Sal Maglie	23
Jackie Robinson	25	Warren Spahn	2.98	Elwin Roe	22
Harold Reese	20	Robin Roberts	3.03	Warren Spahn	22
Earl Torgeson	20	Elwin Roe	3.04	Robin Roberts	21

Saves		Strikeouts	
Ted Wilks	13	Don Newcombe	164
Frank Smith	11	Warren Spahn	164
Jim Konstanty	9	Sal Maglie	146
Al Brazle	7	Larry Jansen	145
Clyde Kina	6	Bob Rush	129

Notes

New York defeated Brooklyn 2 games to 1 in a playoff game to determine the championship of the NL.
Ford Frick replaced Happy Chandler as the commissioner of baseball and Warren Giles replaced Frick as President of the National League.

American League

Team Name	W	L	Pct	GB	R	OR
New York Yankees	98	56	.636	-	798	621
Cleveland Indians	93	61	.604	5	696	594
Boston Red Sox	87	67	.565	11	804	725
Chicago White Sox	81	73	.526	17	714	644
Detroit Tigers	73	81	.474	25	685	741
Philadelphia Athletics	70	84	.455	28	736	745
Washington Senators	62	92	.403	36	672	764
St. Louis Browns	52	102	.338	46	611	882

Coaching Changes

Chicago--Paul Richards 81-73; Philadelphia--Jim Dykes 70-84.Cleveland--Al Lopez 93-61; Boston--Steve O'Neill 87-67.

League Leaders

Batting Average		Home Runs		RBI	
Ferris Fain	.344	Gus Zernial	33	Gus Zernial	129
Minnie Minoso	.326	Ted Williams	30	Ted Williams	126
George Kell	.319	Ed Robinson	29	Ed Robinson	117
Ted Williams	.318	Luke Easter	27	Luke Easter	103
Nelson Fox	.313	Vic Wertz	27	Al Rosen	102

Stolen Bases		ERA		Wins	
Minnie Minoso	31	Saul Rogovin	2.78	Bob Feller	22
Jim Bushy	26	Ed Lopat	2.91	Ed Lopat	21
Phil Rizzuto	18	Early Wynn	3.02	Vic Raschi	21
Chico Carrasquel	14	Billy Pierce	3.03	Mike Garcia	20
Gil McDougald	14	Allie Reynolds	3.05	Ned Garver	20

Saves		Strikeouts	
Ellis Kinder	14	Vic Raschi	164
Carl Scheib	10	Early Wynn	133
Lou Brissie	9	Bob Lemon	132
Allie Reynolds	7	Ted Gray	131
Mike Garcia	6	Mickey McDermott	127

All-Star Game

(Briggs Stadium, Detroit)

July 10	National League	8	American League	3

World Series

October 4	New York Giants	5	at	New York Yankees	1
October 5	New York Giants	1	at	New York Yankees	3
October 6	New York Yankees	2	at	New York Giants	6
October 8	New York Yankees	6	at	New York Giants	2
October 9	New York Yankees	13	at	New York Giants	1
October 10	New York Giants	3	at	New York Yankees	4

Individual Awards

Baseball Writers Award--Roy Campanella (Brooklyn Dodgers NL)
Yogi Berra (New York Yankees AL)
Rookie of the Year--Willie Mays (New York Giants NL)
Gil McDougald (New York Yankees AL)
Sporting News Executive of the Year--George Weiss (New York Yankees AL)
Sporting News Manager of the Year--Leo Durocher (New York Giants NL)
Sporting News Pitcher of the Year--Elwin Roe (Brooklyn Dodgers NL)
Bob Feller (Cleveland Indians AL)
Sporting News Player of the Year--Stan Musial (St. Louis Cardinals NL)
Ferris Fain (Philadelphia Athletics AL)
Sporting News Rookie of the Year--Willie Mays (New York Giants NL)
Minnie Minoso (Chicago White Sox AL)

Hall of Fame Inductees

Jimmie Foxx, Mel Ott

BASKETBALL
National Basketball Association

Eastern Division

Team Name	GP	W	L	PPGF	PPGA	Pct	GB
Philadelphia Warriors	66	40	26	85.4	81.6	.606	-
Boston Celtics	69	39	30	85.2	85.5	.565	2.5
New York Knickerbockers	66	36	30	85.8	85.4	.545	4
Syracuse Nationals	66	32	34	86.1	85.5	.485	8
Baltimore Bullets	66	24	42	82.0	84.3	.364	16
Washington Capitols	35	10	25	81.3	86.0	.286	14.5

Western Division

Team Name	GP	W	L	PPGF	PPGA	Pct	GB
Minneapolis Lakers	68	44	24	82.8	77.4	.647	-
Rochester Royals	68	41	27	84.6	81.7	.603	3
Fort Wayne Zollner Pistons	68	32	36	84.1	86.0	.471	12
Indianapolis Olympians	68	31	37	81.7	84.1	.456	13
Tri-Cities Blackhawks	68	25	43	84.3	88.1	.368	19

Coaching Changes

Boston--Red Auerbach 39-30; Baltimore--Buddy Jeannette 14-23, Walt Budko 10-19; Tri-Cities--Dave McMillan 9-14, John Logan 2-1, Mike Todorovich 14-28; Washington--Bones McKinney 10-25.

League Leaders

Field Goals		Free Throws		Assists	
George Mikan	678	George Mikan	576	Andy Phillip	414
Alex Groza	492	Ed Macauley	466	Dick McGuire	400
Ed Macauley	459	Dolph Schayes	457	George Senesky	342
Joe Fulks	429	Alex Groza	445	Bob Cousy	341
Ralph Beard	409	Frank Brian	418	Ralph Beard	318

Points		Fouls	
George Mikan	1932	George Mikan	308
Alex Groza	1429	Arnie Johnson	290
Ed Macauley	1384	Paul Arizin	284
Joe Fulks	1236	Arnie Risen	278
Frank Brian	1144	Alex Hannum	271

All-Star Game

(Boston Gardens, Boston)

March 2	East Division	111	West Division	94

NBA Championship

March 20	N.Y. Knickerbockers	83	at	Boston Celtics	69
March 20	Syracuse Nationals	91	at	Philadelphia Warriors	89 [OT]
March 20	Ft. Wayne Zollner Pistons	81	at	Rochester Royals	110
March 21	Indianapolis Olympians	81	at	Minneapolis Lakers	95
March 22	Boston Celtics	78	at	N.Y. Knickerbockers	92
March 22	Philadelphia Warriors	78	at	Syracuse Nationals	90
March 22	Rochester Royals	78	at	Ft. Wayne Zollner Pistons	83
March 23	Minneapolis Lakers	88	at	Indianapolis Olympians	108
March 24	Ft. Wayne Zollner Pistons	78	at	Rochester Royals	97
March 25	Indianapolis Olympians	80	at	Minneapolis Lakers	85
March 28	Syracuse Nationals	92	at	N.Y. Knickerbockers	103
March 29	Rochester Royals	73	at	Minneapolis Lakers	76
March 29	N.Y. Knickerbockers	80	at	Syracuse Nationals	102
March 31	Rochester Royals	70	at	Minneapolis Lakers	66
March 31	Syracuse Nationals	75	at	N.Y. Knickerbockers	97
April 1	Minneapolis Lakers	70	at	Rochester Royals	83
April 1	N.Y. Knickerbockers	83	at	Syracuse Nationals	90
April 3	Minneapolis Lakers	75	at	Rochester Royals	80
April 4	Syracuse Nationals	81	at	N.Y. Knickerbockers	83
April 7	N.Y. Knickerbockers	65	at	Rochester Royals	92
April 8	N.Y. Knickerbockers	84	at	Rochester Royals	99
April 11	Rochester Royals	78	at	N.Y. Knickerbockers	71
April 13	Rochester Royals	73	at	N.Y. Knickerbockers	79
April 15	N.Y. Knickerbockers	92	at	Rochester Royals	89
April 18	Rochester Royals	73	at	N.Y. Knickerbockers	80
April 21	N.Y. Knickerbockers	75	at	Rochester Royals	79

All Star Teams

First Team	Second Team
George Mikan (Minneapolis Lakers)	Dolph Schayes (Syracuse Nationals)
Alex Groza (Indianapolis Olympians)	Frank Brian (Tri-Cities Blackhawks)
Ed Macauley (Boston Celtics)	Vern Mikkelsen (Minneapolis Lakers)
Bob Davies (Rochester Royals)	Joe Fulks (Philadelphia Warriors)
Ralph Beard (Indianapolis Olympians)	Dick McGuire (N.Y. Knickerbockers)

Individual Awards

NBA All Star Game MVP--Ed Macauley (Boston Celtics)

FOOTBALL
National Football League

American Conference

Team Name	GP	W	L	T	PF	PA	Pct
Cleveland Browns	12	11	1	0	331	152	.917
New York Giants	12	9	2	1	254	161	.792
Washington Redskins	12	5	7	0	183	296	.417
Pittsburgh Steelers	12	4	7	1	183	235	.375
Philadelphia Eagles	12	4	8	0	234	264	.333
Chicago Cardinals	12	3	9	0	210	287	.250

National Conference

Team Name	GP	W	L	T	PF	PA	Pct
Los Angeles Rams	12	8	4	0	392	261	.667
Detroit Lions	12	7	4	1	336	259	.625
San Francisco 49ers	12	7	4	1	255	205	.625
Chicago Bears	12	7	5	0	286	282	.583
Green Bay Packers	12	3	9	0	254	375	.250
New York Yanks	12	1	9	2	241	382	.167

Coaching Changes

Washington--Herman Ball 0-3-0, Dick Todd 5-4-0; Philadelphia--Bo McMillin 2-0-0, Wayne Millner 2-8-0; Cardinals--Curly Lambeau 2-8-0, Phil Handler & Cecil Isbell 1-1-0; Detroit--Buddy Parker 7-4-1.

League Leaders

Yards Rushing

Eddie Price	971
Rob Goode	951
Dan Towler	854
Bob Hoernschemeyer	678
Joe Perry	677

Yards Passing

Bobby Layne	2403
Otto Graham	2205
Bob Celeri	1797
Norm Van Brocklin	1725
Bob Waterfield	1566

Passing %
(40 attempts)

Bob Thomason	57
Y.A. Tittle	55
Otto Graham	55
Frank Albert	54
Norm Van Brocklin	52

Receiving Yards

Elroy Hirsch	1495
Gordon Soltau	826
Fran Polsfoot	796
Bob Mann	696
Dorne Dibble	613

Receptions

Elroy Hirsch	66
Gordon Soltau	59
Fran Polsfoot	57
Bob Mann	50
Dante Lavelli	43

Field Goals

Bob Waterfield	13
Ray Poole	12
Lou Groza	10
Bill Dudley	10
Joe Geri	7

Punt Return Yards

Em Tunnell	489
Jack Christiansen	343
Joe Arenas	272
Ray Mathews	231
Buddy Young	231

Kickoff Return Yards

George Taliaferro	622
Billy Grimes	582
Dom Moselle	547
Joe Arenas	542
Al Pollard	464

Pro Bowl Game
(Memorial Coliseum, Los Angeles)

January 12 1952	National Conference	30		American Conference	13

NFL Championship

December 23	Cleveland Browns	17	at	Los Angeles Rams	24

Individual Awards

Pro Bowl MVP--Dan Towler (Los Angeles Rams)

Canadian Rugby Union
Interprovincial Rugby Football Union

Team Name	GP	W	L	T	PF	PA	Pts	Pct
Ottawa Rough Riders	12	7	5	0	218	197	14	.583
Hamilton Tiger Cats	12	7	5	0	229	131	14	.583
Toronto Argonauts	12	7	5	0	226	205	14	.583
Montreal Alouettes	12	3	9	0	146	286	6	.250

Western Interprovincial Football Union

Team Name	GP	W	L	T	PF	PA	Pts	Pct
Saskatchewan Roughriders	14	8	6	0	277	219	16	.571
Edmonton Eskimos	14	8	6	0	306	262	16	.571
Winnipeg Blue Bombers	14	8	6	0	303	311	16	.571
Calgary Stampeders	14	4	10	0	205	299	8	.286

Coaching Changes

Ottawa--Clem Crowe 7-5-0; Saskatchewan--H. Smith 8-6-0; Winnipeg--George Trafton 8-6-0.

League Leaders

Yards Rushing		Yards Passing		Passing %		Receiving Yards	
Normie Kwong	933	Jack Jacobs	3248	Jack Jacobs	57	Neill Armstrong	1024
Receptions		**Punting Average**		**Points**			
Bob Shaw	61	Glenn Dobbs	44.2	Bob Shaw	61		

Grey Cup Championship

October 27	Winnipeg Blue Bombers	1	at	Edmonton Eskimos	4
November 3	Saskatchewan Roughriders	11	at	Edmonton Eskimos	15
November 7	Hamilton Tiger-Cats	24	at	Toronto Argonauts	7
November 10	Edmonton Eskimos	5	at	Saskatchewan Roughriders	12
November 12	Edmonton Eskimos	18	at	Saskatchewan Roughriders	19
November 12	Toronto Argonauts	21	at	Hamilton Tiger-Cats	7
November 14	Ottawa Rough Riders	17	at	Hamilton Tiger-Cats	7
November 17	Hamilton Tiger-Cats	9	at	Ottawa Rough Riders	11
November 21	Sarnia Imperials	17	at	Ottawa Rough Riders	43
November 24	Ottawa Rough Riders	21		Saskatchewan Rough Riders	14*

*Game played in Toronto

Individual Awards

Dave Dryburgh Memorial Trophy--Bob Shaw (Calgary Stampeders)
Dr. Beattie Martin Trophy--Jim Chambers (Edmonton Eskimos)
Eddie James Memorial Trophy--Normie Kwong (Edmonton Eskimos)
Gruen Trophy--Bruno Bitkowski (Ottawa Rough Riders)
Jeff Nicklin Memorial Trophy--Glen Dobbs (Saskatchewan Roughriders)
Jeff Russel Memorial Trophy--Bruce Cummings (Ottawa Rough Riders)

Notes

E. Kent Phillips was appointed Commissioner of the Western Interprovincial Football Union.

HOCKEY

National Hockey League

Team Name	GP	W	L	T	GF	GA	Pts	Pct
Detroit Red Wings	70	44	13	13	236	139	101	.721
Toronto Maple Leafs	70	41	16	13	212	138	95	.679
Montreal Canadiens	70	25	30	15	173	184	65	.464
Boston Bruins	70	22	30	18	178	197	62	.443
New York Rangers	70	20	29	21	169	201	61	.436
Chicago Black Hawks	70	13	47	10	171	280	36	.257

Coaching Changes

Toronto--Joe Primeau 41-16-13; Boston--Lynn Patrick 22-30-18; New York--Neil Colville 20-29-21; Chicago--Ebbie Goodfellow 13-47-10.

League Leaders

Goals		Assists		Points	
Gordie Howe	43	Gordie Howe	43	Gordie Howe	86
Rocket Richard	42	Ted Kennedy	43	Rocket Richard	66
Tod Sloan	31	Max Bentley	41	Max Bentley	62
Sid Smith	30	Milt Schmidt	39	Sid Abel	61
Roy Conacher	26	Sid Abel	38	Milt Schmidt	61

Penalty Minutes		GAA		Wins	
Gus Mortson	142	Al Rollins	1.77	Terry Sawchuk	44
Tom Johnson	128	Terry Sawchuk	1.99	Al Rollins	27
Bill Ezinicki	119	Gerry McNeil	2.63	Gerry McNeil	25
Tony Leswick	112	Jack Gelineau	2.81	Jack Gelineau	22
Ted Lindsay	110	Chuck Rayner	2.85	Chuck Rayner	19

Shutouts	
Terry Sawchuk	11
Gerry McNeil	6
Walter Broda	6
Al Rollins	5
Jack Gelineau	4

All-Star Game

(Olympia Stadium, Detroit)

October 8 1950	Detroit Red Wings	7		All-Stars	1

Stanley Cup Playoffs

March 27	Montreal Canadiens	3	at	Detroit Red Wings	2 [61:09]
March 28	Boston Bruins	2	at	Toronto Maple Leafs	0
March 29	Montreal Canadiens	1	at	Detroit Red Wings	0 [42:20]
March 31	Detroit Red Wings	2	at	Montreal Canadiens	0
March 31	Boston Bruins	1	at	Toronto Maple Leafs	1 [20:00]
April 1	Toronto Maple Leafs	3	at	Boston Bruins	0
April 3	Detroit Red Wings	4	at	Montreal Canadiens	1
April 3	Toronto Maple Leafs	3	at	Boston Bruins	1
April 5	Montreal Canadiens	5	at	Detroit Red Wings	2
April 7	Boston Bruins	1	at	Toronto Maple Leafs	4
April 7	Detroit Red Wing	2	at	Montreal Canadiens	3
April 8	Toronto Maple Leafs	6	at	Boston Bruins	0
April 11	Montreal Canadiens	2	at	Toronto Maple Leafs	3 [5:51]
April 14	Montreal Canadiens	3	at	Toronto Maple Leafs	2 [2:55]
April 17	Toronto Maple Leafs	2	at	Montreal Canadiens	1 [4:47]
April 19	Toronto Maple Leafs	3	at	Montreal Canadiens	2 [5:15]
April 21	Montreal Canadiens	2	at	Toronto Maple Leafs	3 [2:53]

All Star Teams

First Team		Second Team
Terry Sawchuk	Goal	Chuck Rayner
Leonard Kelly	Defense	Jim Thomson
Bill Quackenbush	Defense	Leo Reise
Milt Schmidt	Center	Sid Abel
	(tied)	Ted Kennedy
Gordie Howe	Right Wing	Maurice Richard
Ted Lindsay	Left Wing	Sid Smith

Individual Awards

Art Ross Trophy--Gordie Howe (Detroit Red Wings)
Calder Memorial Trophy--Terry Sawchuk (Detroit Red Wings)
Hart Trophy--Milt Schmidt (Boston Bruins)
Lady Byng Trophy--Leonard Kelly (Detroit Red Wings)
Vezina Trophy--Al Rollins (Toronto Maple Leafs)

Franchise Changes

NONE

Other Sports

Horseracing--Kentucky Derby won by Count Turf (time 2:02.6, purse $98,050).
Heavyweight Boxing--Ezzard Charles knocked-out Lee Oma in 10 rounds. Ezzard Charles defeated Joe Walcott in 15 rounds. Ezzard Charles defeated Joey Maxim in 15 rounds. Joe Walcott knocked-out Ezzard Charles in 7 rounds.
Golf--U.S. Open won by Ben Hogan with a score of 287.
Auto Racing--Indianapolis 500 won by Lee Wallard (ave. speed of 126.244 MPH).
Tennis--U.S. Open won by Frank Sedgman in the men's singles.
U.S. Open won by Frank Sedgman and Kenneth McGregor in the men's doubles.
U.S. Open won by Maureen Connolly in the women's singles.
U.S. Open won by Doris Hart and Shirley Fry in the women's doubles.
U.S. Open won by Doris Hart and Frank Sedgman in the mixed doubles.

1952

BASEBALL
National League

Team Name	W	L	Pct	GB	R	OR
Brooklyn Dodgers	96	57	.627	-	775	603
New York Giants	92	62	.597	4.5	722	639
St. Louis Cardinals	88	66	.571	8.5	677	630
Philadelphia Phillies	87	67	.565	9.5	657	552
Chicago Cubs	77	77	.500	19.5	628	631
Cincinnati Reds	69	85	.448	27.5	615	659
Boston Braves	64	89	.418	32	569	651
Pittsburgh Pirates	42	112	.273	54.5	515	793

Coaching Changes

St. Louis--Eddie Stanky 88-66; Philadelphia--Eddie Sawyer 28-35, Steve O'Neill--59-32; Chicago--Phil Cavarretta 77-77; Cincinnati--Luke Sewell 39-59, Earle Brocker 3-2, Rogers Hornsby 27-24; Boston--Tom Holmes 13-22, Charlie Grimm 51-67.

League Leaders

Batting Average

Stan Musial	.336
Frank Baumholtz	.325
Ted Kluszewski	.320
Jackie Robinson	.308
Duke Snider	.303

Home Runs

Hank Sauer	37
Ralph Kiner	37
Gil Hodges	32
Sid Gordon	25
Eddie Mathews	25

RBI

Hank Sauer	121
Bobby Thomson	108
Del Ennis	107
Gil Hodges	102
Enos Slaughter	101

Stolen Bases

Harold Reese	30
Sam Jethroe	28
Jackie Robinson	24
Richie Ashburn	16
Dee Fondy	13

ERA

Hoyt Wilhelm	2.43
Warren Hacker	2.58
Robin Roberts	2.59
Billy Loes	2.69
Bob Rush	2.70

Wins

Robin Roberts	28
Sal Maglie	18
Bob Rush	17
Gerry Staley	17
Ken Raffensberger	17

Saves

Al Brazle	16
Joe Black	15
Hoyt Wilhelm	11
Emil Leonard	11
Frank Smith	7

Strikeouts

Warren Spahn	183
Bob Rush	157
Robin Roberts	148
Wilmer Mizell	146
Curt Simmons	141

American League

Team Name	W	L	Pct	GB	R	OR
New York Yankees	95	59	.617	-	727	557
Cleveland Indians	93	61	.604	2	763	606
Chicago White Sox	81	73	.526	14	610	568
Philadelphia Athletics	79	75	.513	16	664	723
Washington Senators	78	76	.506	17	598	608
Boston Red Sox	76	78	.494	19	668	658
St. Louis Browns	64	90	.416	31	604	733
Detroit Tigers	50	104	.325	45	557	738

Coaching Changes

Boston--Lou Boudreau 76-78; St. Louis--Rogers Hornsby 22-28, Marty Marion 42-62; Detroit--Robert Rolfe 23-49, Fred Hutchinson 27-55.

League Leaders

Batting Average		Home Runs		RBI	
Ferris Fain	.327	Larry Doby	32	Al Rosen	105
Dale Mitchell	.323	Luke Easter	31	Ed Robinson	104
Mickey Mantle	.311	Yogi Berra	30	Larry Doby	104
George Kell	.311	Walt Dropo	29	Gus Zernial	100
Gene Woodling	.309	Gus Zernial	29	Yogi Berra	98

Stolen Bases		ERA		Wins	
Minnie Minoso	22	Allie Reynolds	2.06	Bobbie Shantz	24
Jim Rivera	21	Mike Garcia	2.37	Early Wynn	23
Jackie Jensen	18	Bobbie Shantz	2.48	Mike Garcia	22
Phil Rizzuto	17	Bob Lemon	2.50	Bob Lemon	22
F. Throneberry	16	Joe Dobson	2.51	Allie Reynolds	20

Saves		Strikeouts	
Harry Dorish	11	Allie Reynolds	160
Satchel Paige	10	Early Wynn	153
John Sain	7	Bobbie Shantz	152
Al Benton	6	Billy Pierce	144
Luis Aloma	6	Mike Garcia	143

All-Star Game
(Shibe Park, Philadelphia)

July 8	National League	3	American League	2

World Series

October 1	New York Yankees	2	at	Brooklyn Dodgers	4
October 2	New York Yankees	7	at	Brooklyn Dodgers	1
October 3	Brooklyn Dodgers	5	at	New York Yankees	3
October 4	Brooklyn Dodgers	0	at	New York Yankees	2
October 5	Brooklyn Dodgers	6	at	New York Yankees	5 [11]
October 6	New York Yankees	3	at	Brooklyn Dodgers	2
October 7	New York Yankees	4	at	Brooklyn Dodgers	2

Individual Awards

Baseball Writers Award--Hank Sauer (Chicago Cubs NL)
Bobby Shantz (Philadelphia Athletics AL)
Rookie of the Year--Joe Black (Brooklyn Dodgers NL)
Harry Byrd (Philadelphia Athletics AL)
Sporting News Executive of the Year--George Weiss (New York Yankees AL)
Sporting News Manager of the Year--Eddie Stanky (St. Louis Cardinals NL)
Sporting News Pitcher of the Year--Robin Roberts (Philadelphia Phillies NL)
Bobby Shantz (Philadelphia Athletics AL)
Sporting News Player of the Year--Hank Sauer (Chicago Cubs NL)
Luke Easter (Cleveland Indians AL)
Sporting News Rookie of the Year--Joe Black (Brooklyn Dodgers NL)
Clint Courtney (St. Louis Browns AL)

Hall of Fame Inductees

Harry Heilmann, Paul Waner

BASKETBALL
National Basketball Association

Eastern Division

Team Name	GP	W	L	PPGF	PPGA	Pct	GB
Syracuse Nationals	66	40	26	86.7	82.2	.606	-
Boston Celtics	66	39	27	91.3	87.3	.591	1
New York Knickerbockers	66	37	29	85.0	84.2	.561	3
Philadelphia Warriors	66	33	33	86.5	87.8	.500	7
Baltimore Bullets	66	20	46	81.5	89.0	.303	20

Western Division

Team Name	GP	W	L	PPGF	PPGA	Pct	GB
Rochester Royals	66	41	25	86.2	82.9	.621	-
Minneapolis Lakers	66	40	26	85.6	79.5	.606	1
Indianapolis Olympians	66	34	32	82.9	82.8	.515	7
Fort Wayne Zollner Pistons	66	29	37	78.0	80.1	.439	12
Milwaukee Hawks	66	17	49	73.2	81.2	.258	24

Coaching Changes

Baltimore--Fred Scolari 12-27, Chick Reiser 8-19; Indianapolis--Herm Schaeffer 34-32; Fort Wayne--Paul Birch 29-37; Milwaukee--Doxie Moore 17-49.

League Leaders

Field Goals		Free Throws		Assists	
Paul Arizin	548	Paul Arizin	578	Andy Phillip	539
George Mikan	545	Ed Macauley	496	Bob Cousy	441
Bob Cousy	512	George Mikan	433	Bob Davies	390
Jim Pollard	411	Bob Cousy	409	Dick McGuire	388
Larry Foust	390	Bobby Wanzer	377	Fred Scolari	303

Points		Fouls	
Paul Arizin	1674	George Mikan	286
George Mikan	1523	Vern Mikkelsen	282
Bob Cousy	1433	Don Boven	271
Ed Macauley	1264	Bob Davies	269
Bob Davies	1052	Jack Kerris	265

All-Star Game
(Boston Gardens, Boston)

February 11	East Division	108		West Division	91

NBA Championship

March 18	Ft. Wayne Zollner Pistons	78	at	Rochester Royals	95
March 19	N.Y. Knickerbockers	94	at	Boston Celtics	105
March 20	Philadelphia Warriors	83	at	Syracuse Nationals	102
March 20	Rochester Royals	92	at	Ft. Wayne Zollner Pistons	86
March 22	Syracuse Nationals	95	at	Philadelphia Warriors	100
March 23	Philadelphia Warriors	73	at	Syracuse Nationals	84
March 23	Boston Celtics	97	at	N.Y. Knickerbockers	101
March 23	Indianapolis Olympians	70	at	Minneapolis Lakers	78
March 25	Minneapolis Lakers	94	at	Indianapolis Olympians	87
March 26	N.Y. Knickerbockers	88	at	Boston Celtics	87 [OT]
March 29	Minneapolis Lakers	78	at	Rochester Royals	88
March 30	Minneapolis Lakers	83	at	Rochester Royals	78
April 2	N.Y. Knickerbockers	87	at	Syracuse Nationals	85
April 3	N.Y. Knickerbockers	92	at	Syracuse Nationals	102
April 4	Syracuse Nationals	92	at	N.Y. Knickerbockers	99
April 5	Rochester Royals	67	at	Minneapolis Lakers	77
April 6	Rochester Royals	80	at	Minneapolis Lakers	82
April 8	Syracuse Nationals	93	at	N.Y. Knickerbockers	100
April 12	Minneapolis Lakers	83	at	N.Y. Knickerbockers	79 *[OT]
April 13	N.Y. Knickerbockers	80	at	Minneapolis Lakers	72 *
April 16	Minneapolis Lakers	82	at	N.Y. Knickerbockers	77
April 18	Minneapolis Lakers	89	at	N.Y. Knickerbockers	90 [OT]
April 20	Minneapolis Lakers	102	at	N.Y. Knickerbockers	89 *
April 23	Minneapolis Lakers	68	at	N.Y. Knickerbockers	76
April 25	N.Y. Knickerbockers	65	at	Minneapolis Lakers	82

All Star Teams

First Team	Second Team
George Mikan (Minneapolis Lakers)	Larry Foust (Ft. Wayne Zollner Pistons)
Ed Macauley (Boston Celtics)	Vern Mikkelsen (Minneapolis Lakers)
Paul Arizin (Philadelphia Warriors)	Jim Pollard (Minneapolis Lakers)
Bob Cousy (Boston Celtics)	Bob Wanzer (Rochester Royals)
Bob Davies (Rochester Royals)	Andy Phillip (Philadelphia Warriors)
Dolph Schayes (Syracuse Nationals)	

Individual Awards

NBA All Star Game MVP--Paul Arizin (Philadelphia Warriors)

Rules

The foul lane was widened to 12 ft. from 6 ft.

*Games played in St. Paul

FOOTBALL
National Football League

American Conference

Team Name	GP	W	L	T	PF	PA	Pct
Cleveland Browns	12	8	4	0	310	213	.667
New York Giants	12	7	5	0	234	231	.583
Philadelphia Eagles	12	7	5	0	252	271	.583
Pittsburgh Steelers	12	5	7	0	300	273	.417
Chicago Cardinals	12	4	8	0	172	221	.333
Washington Redskins	12	4	8	0	240	287	.333

National Conference

Team Name	GP	W	L	T	PF	PA	Pct
Detroit Lions	12	9	3	0	344	192	.750
Los Angeles Rams	12	9	3	0	349	234	.750
San Francisco 49ers	12	7	5	0	285	221	.583
Green Bay Packers	12	6	6	0	295	312	.500
Chicago Bears	12	5	7	0	245	326	.417
Dallas Texans	12	1	11	0	182	427	.083

Coaching Changes

Philadelphia--Jim Trimble 7-5-0; Pittsburgh--Joe Bach 5-7-0; Cardinals--Joe Kuharich 4-8-0; Washington--Curly Lambeau 4-8-0; Los Angeles--Joe Stydahar 0-1-0, Hamp Pool 9-2-0; Dallas--Jim Phelan 1-11-0.

League Leaders

Yards Rushing		Yards Passing		Passing % (40 attempts)	
Dan Towler	894	Otto Graham	2816	Norm Van Brocklin	55
Eddie Price	748	Jim Finks	2307	Frank Albert	55
Joe Perry	725	Bobby Layne	1999	Harry Gilmer	53
Hugh McElhenny	684	Norm Van Brocklin	1736	Tobin Rote	52
Bob Hoernschemeyer	457	Eddie LeBaron	1420	Bob Williams	52

Receiving Yards		Receptions		Field Goals	
Billy Howton	1231	Mac Speedie	62	Lou Groza	19
Bud Grant	997	Bud Grant	56	Bob Walston	11
Hugh Taylor	961	Elbie Nickel	55	Pat Harder	11
Cloyce Box	924	Gordie Soltau	55	Bob Waterfield	11
Mac Speedie	911	Don Stonesifer	54	Ray Poole	10

Punt Return Yards		Kickoff Return Yards	
Em Tunnell	411	Buddy Young	643
Ray Mathews	397	Ollie Matson	624
John Williams	366	Lynn Chandnois	599
Woodley Lewis	351	Bill Baggett	567
Jack Christiansen	322	Al Pollard	528

Pro Bowl Game

(Memorial Coliseum, Los Angeles)

January 10 1953	National Conference	27		American Conference	7

NFL Championship

December 21	Los Angeles Rams	21	at	Detroit Lions	31
December 28	Detroit Lions	17	at	Cleveland Browns	7

Individual Awards

Pro-Bowl MVP--Don Doll (Detroit Lions)

Canadian Rugby Union
Interprovincial Rugby Football Union

Team Name	GP	W	L	T	PF	PA	Pts	Pct
Hamilton Tiger-Cats	12	9	2	1	268	162	19	.792
Toronto Argonauts	12	7	4	1	265	191	15	.625
Ottawa Rough Riders	12	5	7	0	200	238	10	.417
Montreal Alouettes	12	2	10	0	136	278	4	.167

Western Interprovincial Football Union

Team Name	GP	W	L	T	PF	PA	Pts	Pct
Winnipeg Blue Bombers	16	12	3	1	394	211	25	.781
Edmonton Eskimos	16	9	6	1	291	280	19	.594
Calgary Stampeders	16	7	9	0	293	340	14	.438
Saskatchewan Roughriders	16	3	13	0	216	363	6	.188

Coaching Changes

Edmonton--Frank Filchock 9-6-1; Montreal--Doug "Peahead" Walker 2-10-0; Saskatchewan--Glenn Dobbs 3-13-0.

League Leaders

Yards Rushing		Yards Passing		Passing %		Receiving Yards	
Johnnie Bright	815	Jack Jacobs	2586	Jack Jacobs	51	Bob Shaw	1094
						Paul Salata	1088

Receptions		Punting Average		Points	
Paul Salata	65	Butch Avinger	44.7	Bob Shaw	110

Grey Cup

October 22	Edmonton Eskimos	12	at	Calgary Stampeders	31
October 25	Calgary Stampeders	7	at	Edmonton Eskimos	30
October 30	Winnipeg Blue Bombers	28	at	Edmonton Eskimos	12
November 8	Edmonton Eskimos	18	at	Winnipeg Blue Bombers	12
November 11	Edmonton Eskimos	22	at	Winnipeg Blue Bombers	11
November 15	Toronto Argonauts	22	at	Hamilton tiger-cats	6
November 19	Hamilton Tiger-Cats	27	at	Toronto Argonauts	11
November 22	Hamilton Tiger-Cats	7	at	Toronto Argonauts	12
November 26	Sarnia Imperials	15	at	Toronto Argonauts	34
November 29	Edmonton Eskimos	11	at	Toronto Argonauts	21

Individual Awards

Dave Dryburgh Memorial Trophy--Bob Shaw (Calgary Stampeders)
Dr. Beattie Martin Trophy--Lorne Benson (Winnipeg Blue Bombers)
Eddie James Memorial Trophy--Johnny Bright (Calgary Stampeders)
Gruen Trophy--Johnny Fedosoff (Toronto Argonauts)
Jeff Nicklin Memorial Trophy--Jack Jacobs (Winnipeg Blue Bombers)
Jeff Russel Memorial Trophy--Vince Mazza (Hamilton Tiger-Cats)

HOCKEY
National Hockey League

Team Name	GP	W	L	T	GF	GA	Pts	Pct
Detroit Red Wings	70	44	14	12	215	133	100	.714
Montreal Canadiens	70	34	26	10	195	164	78	.557
Toronto Maple Leafs	70	29	25	16	168	157	74	.529
Boston Bruins	70	25	29	16	162	176	66	.471
New York Rangers	70	23	34	13	192	219	59	.421
Chicago Black hawks	70	17	44	9	158	241	43	.307

Coaching Changes

New York--Neil Colville 6-12-5, Bill Cook 17-22-8.

League Leaders

Goals		Assists		Points	
Gordie Howe	47	Elmer Lach	50	Gordie Howe	86
Bill Mosienko	31	Don Raleigh	42	Ted Lindsay	69
Ted Lindsay	30	Gordie Howe	39	Elmer Lach	65
Bernie Geoffrion	30	Ted Lindsay	39	Don Raleigh	61
Maurice Richard	27	Sid Abel	36	Sid Smith	57

Penalty Minutes		GAA		Wins	
Gus Kyle	127	Terry Sawchuk	1.90	Terry Sawchuk	44
Ted Lindsay	123	Al Rollins	2.22	Gerry McNeil	34
Fern Flaman	110	Gerry McNeil	2.34	Al Rollins	29
Gus Mortson	106	Jim Henry	2.51	Jim Henry	25
Al Dewsbury	99	Chuck Rayner	3.00	Chuck Rayner	18

Shutouts	
Terry Sawchuk	12
Jim Henry	7
Al Rollins	5
Gerry McNeil	5
Chuck Rayner	2

All-Star Game
(Maple Leaf Gardens, Toronto)

October 9 1951	1st Team	2	2nd Team	2

Stanley Cup Playoffs

March 25	Toronto Maple Leafs	0	at	Detroit Red Wings	3
March 25	Boston Bruins	1	at	Montreal Canadiens	5
March 27	Toronto Maple Leafs	0	at	Detroit Red Wings	1
March 27	Boston Bruins	0	at	Montreal Canadiens	4
March 29	Detroit Red Wings	6	at	Toronto Maple Leafs	2
March 30	Montreal Canadiens	1	at	Boston Bruins	4
April 1	Detroit Red Wings	3	at	Toronto Maple Leafs	1
April 1	Montreal Canadiens	2	at	Boston Bruins	3
April 3	Boston Bruins	1	at	Montreal Canadiens	0
April 6	Montreal Canadiens	3	at	Boston Bruins	2 [27:49]
April 8	Boston Bruins	1	at	Montreal Canadiens	3
April 10	Detroit Red Wings	3	at	Montreal Canadiens	1
April 12	Detroit Red Wings	2	at	Montreal Canadiens	1
April 13	Montreal Canadiens	0	at	Detroit Red Wings	3
April 15	Montreal Canadiens	0	at	Detroit Red Wings	3

All Star Teams

First Team		Second Team
Terry Sawchuk	Goal	Jim Henry
Leonard Kelly	Defense	Hy Buller
Doug Harvey	Defense	Jim Thomson
Elmer Lach	Center	Milt Schmidt
Gordie Howe	Right Wing	Maurice Richard
Ted Lindsay	Left Wing	Sid Smith

Individual Awards

Art Ross Trophy--Gordie Howe (Detroit Red Wings)
Calder Memorial Trophy--Bernie Geoffrion (Montreal Canadiens)
Hart Trophy--Gordie Howe (Detroit Red Wings)
Lady Byng Trophy--Sid Smith (Toronto Maple Leafs)
Vezina Trophy--Terry Sawchuk (Detroit Red Wings)

Hall of Fame Inductees

Dickie Boon, Bill Cook, Frank Goheen, Ernest Johnson, Mickey MacKay

Rules

The goal crease was enlarged to 4ft. x 8ft. from 3ft- x 7ft., and the face-off circles were enlarged to a 15 ft. radius from a 10 ft. radius.

Franchise Changes

NFL--New York Yanks became the Dallas Texans.
NBA--Tri-Cities Blackhawks became the Milwaukee Hawks.

Other Sports

Horseracing--Kentucky Derby won by Hill Gail (time 2:01.6, purse $96,300).
Heavyweight Boxing--Joe Walcott defeated Ezzard Charles in 15 rounds.
Rocky Marciano knocked out Joe Walcott in 13 rounds.
Golf--U.S. Open won by Julius Boros with a score of 281.
Auto Racing--Indianapolis 500 won by Troy Ruttman (ave. speed 128.922 MPH).
Tennis--U.S. Open won by Frank Sedgman in the men's singles.
U.S. Open won by Mervyn Rose and E. Victor Seixas Jr. in the men's doubles.
U.S. Open won by Maureen Connolly in the women's singles.
U.S. Open won by Doris Hart and Shirley Fry in the women's doubles.
U.S. Open won by Doris Hart and Frank Sedgman in the mixed doubles.

1953

BASEBALL
National League

Team Name	W	L	Pct	GB	R	OR
Brooklyn Dodgers	105	49	.682	-	955	689
Milwaukee Braves	92	62	.597	13	738	589
Philadelphia Phillies	83	71	.539	22	716	666
St. Louis Cardinals	83	71	.539	22	768	713
New York Giants	70	84	.455	35	768	747
Cincinnati Reds	68	86	.442	37	714	788
Chicago Cubs	65	89	.422	40	633	835
Pittsburgh Pirates	50	104	.325	55	622	887

Coaching Changes

Milwaukee--Charlie Grimm 92-62; Philadelphia--Steve O'Neill 83-71; Cincinnati--Rogers Hornsby 64-82, Buster Mills 4-4; Pittsburgh--Fred Haney 50-104.

League Leaders

Batting Average		Home Runs		RBI	
Carl Furillo	.344	Eddie Mathews	47	Roy Campanella	142
Red Schoendienst	.342	Duke Snider	42	Eddie Mathews	135
Stan Musial	.337	Roy Campanella	41	Duke Snider	126
Duke Snider	.336	Ted Kluszewski	40	Del Ennis	125
Don Mueller	.333	Ralph Kiner	35	Gil Hodges	122

Stolen Bases		ERA		Wins	
Bill Bruton	26	Warren Spahn	2.10	Warren Spahn	23
Harold Reese	22	Robin Roberts	2.75	Robin Roberts	23
Jim Gilliam	21	Bob Buhl	2.97	Carl Erskine	20
Jackie Robinson	17	Harvey Haddix	3.06	Harvey Haddix	20
Duke Snider	16	John Antonelli	3.18	Gerry Staley	18

Saves		Strikeouts	
Al Brazle	18	Robin Roberts	198
Hoyt Wilhelm	15	Carl Erskine	187
Jim Hughes	9	Wilmer Mizell	173
Lew Burdette	8	Harvey Haddix	163
Emil Leonard	8	Warren Spahn	148

American League

Team Name	W	L	Pct	GB	R	OR
New York Yankees	99	52	.656	-	801	547
Cleveland Indians	92	62	.597	8.5	770	627
Chicago White Sox	89	65	.578	11.5	716	592
Boston Red Sox	84	69	.549	16	656	632
Washington Senators	76	76	.500	23.5	687	614
Detroit Tigers	60	94	.390	40.5	695	923
Philadelphia Athletics	59	95	.383	41.5	632	799
St. Louis Browns	54	100	.351	46.5	555	778

Coaching Changes

Detroit--Fred Hutchinson 60-94; St. Louis--Marty Marion 54-100.

League Leaders

Batting Average		Home Runs		RBI	
Mickey Vernon	.337	Al Rosen	43	Al Rosen	145
Al Rosen	.336	Gus Zernial	42	Mickey Vernon	115
Billy Goodman	.313	Larry Doby	29	Ray Boone	114
Minnie Minoso	.313	Yogi Berra	27	Gus Zernial	108
Jim Bushy	.312	Ray Boone	26	Yogi Berra	108

Stolen Bases		ERA		Wins	
Minnie Minoso	25	Ed Lopat	2.42	Bob Porterfield	22
Jim Rivera	22	Billy Pierce	2.72	Mel Parnell	21
Jackie Jensen	18	Virgil Trucks	2.93	Bob Lemon	21
Dave Philley	13	John Sain	3.00	Virgil Trucks	20
Jim Bushy	13	Edward Ford	3.00	Mickey McDermott	18

Saves		Strikeouts	
Ellis Kinder	27	Billy Pierce	186
Harry Dorish	18	Virgil Trucks	149
Allie Reynolds	13	Early Wynn	138
Satchel Paige	11	Mel Parnell	136
John Sain	9	Mike Garcia	134

All-Star Game

(Crosley Field, Cincinnati)

July 14	National League	5	American League	1

World Series

September 30	Brooklyn Dodgers	5	at	New York Yankees	9
October 1	Brooklyn Dodgers	2	at	New York Yankees	4
October 2	New York Yankees	2	at	Brooklyn Dodgers	3
October 3	New York Yankees	3	at	Brooklyn Dodgers	7
October 4	New York Yankees	11	at	Brooklyn Dodgers	7
October 5	Brooklyn Dodgers	3	at	New York Yankees	4

Individual Awards

Baseball Writers Award--Roy Campanella (Brooklyn Dodgers NL)
Al Rosen (Cleveland Indians AL)
Rookie of the Year--Jim Gilliam (Brooklyn Dodgers NL)
Harvey Kuenn (Detroit Tigers AL)
Sporting News Executive of the Year--Louis Perini (Milwaukee Braves NL)
Sporting News Manager of the Year--Casey Stengel (New York Yankees AL)
Sporting News Pitcher of the Year--Warren Spahn (Milwaukee Braves NL)
Bob Porterfield (Washington Senators AL)
Sporting News Player of the Year--Roy Campanella (Brooklyn Dodgers NL)
Al Rosen (Cleveland Indians AL)
Sporting News Rookie of the Year--Jim Gilliam (Brooklyn Dodgers NL)
Harvey Kuenn (Detroit Tigers AL)

Hall of Fame Inductees

Ed Barrow, Charles Bender, Tom Connolly, Jay Dean, Bill Klem, Al Simmons, Bobby Wallace, Harry Wright

BASKETBALL

National Basketball Association

Eastern Division

Team Name	GP	W	L	PPGF	PPGA	Pct	GB
New York Knickerbockers	70	47	23	85.5	80.3	.671	-
Syracuse Nationals	71	47	24	85.6	81.3	.662	.5
Boston Celtics	71	46	25	88.1	85.8	.648	1.5
Baltimore Bullets	70	16	54	84.4	90.9	.229	31
Philadelphia Warriors	69	12	57	80.2	88.9	.174	34.5

Western Division

Team Name	GP	W	L	PPGF	PPGA	Pct	GB
Minneapolis Lakers	70	48	22	85.3	79.2	.686	-
Rochester Royals	70	44	26	86.3	83.5	.629	4
Fort Wayne Zollner Pistons	69	36	33	81.0	81.1	.522	11.5
Indianapolis Olympians	71	28	43	74.6	77.4	.394	20.5
Milwaukee Hawks	71	27	44	75.9	78.8	.380	21.5

Coaching Changes

Baltimore--Chick Reiser 0-3, Clair Bee 16-51; Milwaukee--Fuzzy Levane 27-44.

League Leaders

Field Goals		Free Throws		Assists	
Neil Johnston	504	Neil Johnston	556	Bob Cousy	547
George Mikan	500	Dolph Schayes	512	Andy Phillip	397
Bob Cousy	464	Ed Macauley	500	George King	364
Ed Macauley	451	Bob Cousy	479	Dick McGuire	296
Jack Nichols	425	George Mikan	442	Paul Seymour	294

Points		Fouls	
Neil Johnston	1564	Don Meineke	334
George Mikan	1442	Joe Fulks	319
Bob Cousy	1407	Joe Graboski	303
Ed Macauley	1402	George Mikan	290
Dolph Schayes	1262	Vern Mikkelson	289

All-Star Game

(at Memorial Coliseum, Ft. Wayne)

January 13	West Division	79		East Division	75

NBA Championship

March 17	Baltimore Bullets	62	at	N.Y. Knickerbockers	80
March 19	Boston Celtics	87	at	Syracuse Nationals	81
March 20	N.Y. Knickerbockers	90	at	Baltimore Bullets	81
March 20	Ft. Wayne Zollner Pistons	84	at	Rochester Royals	77
March 21	Syracuse Nationals	105	at	Boston Celtics	111 [OT]
March 22	Rochester Royals	83	at	Ft. Wayne Zollner Pistons	71
March 22	Indianapolis Olympians	69	at	Minneapolis Lakers	85
March 23	Minneapolis Lakers	81	at	Indianapolis Olympians	79
March 24	Ft. Wayne Zollner Pistons	67	at	Rochester Royals	65
March 25	Boston Celtics	91	at	N.Y. Knickerbockers	95
March 26	Ft. Wayne Zollner Pistons	73	at	Minneapolis Lakers	83
March 26	N.Y. Knickerbockers	70	at	Boston Celtics	86
March 28	Ft. Wayne Zollner Pistons	75	at	Minneapolis Lakers	82
March 28	Boston Celtics	82	at	N.Y. Knickerbockers	101
March 29	N.Y. Knickerbockers	82	at	Boston Celtics	75
March 30	Minneapolis Lakers	95	at	Ft. Wayne Zollner Pistons	98
April 1	Minneapolis Lakers	82	at	Ft. Wayne Zollner Pistons	85
April 2	Ft. Wayne Zollner Pistons	58	at	Minneapolis Lakers	74
April 4	N.Y. Knickerbockers	96	at	Minneapolis Lakers	88
April 5	N.Y. Knickerbockers	71	at	Minneapolis Lakers	73
April 7	Minneapolis Lakers	90	at	N.Y. Knickerbockers	75
April 8	Minneapolis Lakers	71	at	N.Y. Knickerbockers	69
April 10	Minneapolis Lakers	91	at	N.Y. Knickerbockers	84

All Star Teams

First Team	Second Team
George Mikan (Minneapolis Lakers)	Bill Sharman (Boston Celtics)
Bob Cousy (Boston Celtics)	Vern Mikkelsen (Minneapolis Lakers)
Neil Johnston (Philadelphia Warriors)	Bob Wanzer (Rochester Royals)
Ed Macauley (Boston Celtics)	Bob Davies (Rochester Royals)
Dolph Schayes (Syracuse Nationals)	Andy Phillip (Philadelphia Warriors)

Individual Awards

Eddie Gottlieb Trophy--Don Meineke (Fort Wayne Zollner Pistons)
NBA All Star Game MVP--George Mikan (Minneapolis Lakers)

FOOTBALL
National Football League

Eastern Conference

Team Name	GP	W	L	T	PF	PA	Pct
Cleveland Browns	12	11	1	0	348	162	.917
Philadelphia Eagles	12	7	4	1	352	215	.625
Washington Redskins	12	6	5	1	208	215	.542
Pittsburgh Steelers	12	6	6	0	211	263	.500
New York Giants	12	3	9	0	179	277	.250
Chicago Cardinals	12	1	10	1	190	337	.125

Western Conference

Team Name	GP	W	L	T	PF	PA	Pct
Detroit Lions	12	10	2	0	271	205	.833
San Francisco 49ers	12	9	3	0	372	237	.750
Los Angeles Rams	12	8	3	1	366	236	.708
Chicago Bears	12	3	8	1	218	262	.292
Baltimore Colts	12	3	9	0	182	350	.250
Green Bay Packers	12	2	9	1	200	338	.208

Coaching Changes

Cardinals--Joe Stydahar 1-10-1; Baltimore--Keith Molesworth 3-9-0; Green Bay--Gene Ronzani 2-7-1, Hugh Devore & Ray McLean 0-2-0.

League Leaders

Yards Rushing		Yards Passing		Passing % (40 attempts)	
Joe Perry	1018	Otto Graham	2722	Otto Graham	65
Dan Towler	879	Bob Thomason	2462	Y.A. Tittle	58
Skeets Quinlan	705	Norm Van Brocklin	2393	George Ratterman	56
"Choo-Choo" Justice	616	George Blanda	2164	Norm Van Brocklin	55
Fran Rogel	527	Y.A. Tittle	2121	Bob Thomason	53

Receiving Yards		Receptions		Field Goals	
Pete Pihos	1049	Pete Pihos	63	Lou Groza	23
Elroy Hirsch	941	Elbie Nickel	62	Doak Walker	12
Jim Dooley	841	Elroy Hirsch	61	Bill Dudley	11
Bill Wilson	840	Don Stonesifer	56	Gord Soltau	10
Dante Lavelli	783	Jim Dooley	53	Ben Agajanian	10

Punt Return Yards		Kickoff Return Yards	
Woodley Lewis	267	Woodley Lewis	830
Charlie Trippi	239	Al Carmichael	641
Em Tunnell	223	Lynn Chandnois	610
Al Carmichael	199	Joe Arenas	551
John Williams	172	Em Tunnell	479

Pro-Bowl Game

(Memorial Coliseum, Los Angeles)

January 17 1954	Eastern Conference	20		Western Conference	9

NFL Championship

December 27	Cleveland Browns	16	at	Detroit Lions	17

Individual Awards

Pro-Bowl MVP--Chuck Bednarik (Philadelphia Eagles)
U.P.I. Most Valuable Player--Otto Graham (Cleveland Browns)

Canadian Rugby Union
Interprovincial Rugby Football Union

Team Name	GP	W	L	T	PF	PA	Pts	Pct
Montreal Alouettes	14	8	6	0	292	229	16	.571
Hamilton Tiger-Cats	14	8	6	0	229	247	16	.571
Ottawa Rough Riders	14	7	7	0	266	238	14	.500
Toronto Argonauts	14	5	9	0	172	249	10	.357

Western Interprovincial Football Union

Team Name	GP	W	L	T	PF	PA	Pts	Pct
Edmonton Eskimos	16	12	4	0	276	157	24	.750
Saskatchewan Roughriders	16	8	7	1	243	239	17	.531
Winnipeg Blue Bombers	16	8	8	0	226	226	16	.500
Calgary Stampeders	16	3	12	1	190	313	7	.219

Coaching Changes

Edmonton--Darrell Royal 12-4-0; Saskatchewan--Frank Filchock 8-7-1; Calgary--Bob Snyder 3-12-1.

League Leaders

Yards Rushing		Yards Passing		Passing %		Receptions	
Billy Vessels	926	Jack Jacobs	1924	Jack Jacobs	58	Bud Grant	68

Punting Average		Points	
Rod Pantages	44.4	Gene Roberts	88

Grey Cup

October 28	Saskatchewan Roughriders	5	at	Winnipeg Blue Bombers	43
October 31	Winnipeg Blue Bombers	17	at	Saskatchewan Roughriders	18
November 7	Winnipeg Blue Bombers	7	at	Edmonton Eskimos	25
November 11	Edmonton Eskimos	17	at	Winnipeg Blue Bombers	21
November 14	Winnipeg Blue Bombers	30	at	Edmonton Eskimos	24
November 18	Montreal Alouettes	12	at	Hamilton Tiger-Cats	37
November 22	Hamilton Tiger-Cats	22	at	Montreal Alouettes	11
November 22	Toronto Balmy Beach	4	at	Winnipeg Blue Bombers	24
November 28	Hamilton Tiger-Cats	12		Winnipeg Blue Bombers	6*

*Game played in Toronto

Individual Awards

Dave Dryburgh Memorial Trophy--Bud Korchak (Winnipeg Blue Bombers)
Dr. Beattie Martin Trophy--Gordon Sturtridge (Saskatchewan Roughriders)
Eddie James Memorial Trophy--Billy Vessels (Edmonton Eskimos)
Gruen Trophy--Bob Dawson (Hamilton Tiger-Cats)
Jeff Nicklin Memorial Trophy--John Henry Johnson (Calgary Stampeders)
Jeff Russel Memorial Trophy--Bob Cunningham (Ottawa Rough Riders)
Schenley Award Most Outstanding Player--Billy Vessels (Edmonton Eskimos)

Notes

Sydney Halter replaced Kent Phillips as Commissioner of the Western Interprovincial Football Union.

HOCKEY

National Hockey League

Team Name	GP	W	L	T	GF	GA	Pts	Pct
Detroit Red Wings	70	36	16	18	222	133	90	.643
Montreal Canadiens	70	28	23	19	155	148	75	.536
Boston Bruins	70	28	29	13	152	172	69	.493
Chicago Black Hawks	70	27	28	15	169	175	69	.493
Toronto Maple Leafs	70	27	30	13	156	167	67	.479
New York Rangers	70	17	37	16	152	211	50	.357

Coaching Changes

Chicago--Sid Abel 27-28-15; New York--Bill Cook 17-37-16.

League Leaders

Goals		Assists		Points	
Gordie Howe	49	Gordie Howe	46	Gordie Howe	95
Ted Lindsay	32	Alex Delvecchio	43	Ted Lindsay	71
Wally Hergesheimer	30	Ted Lindsay	39	Rocket Richard	61
Rocket Richard	28	Paul Ronty	38	Wally Hergesheimer	59
Fleming MacKell	27	Metro Prystai	34	Alex Delvecchio	59

Penalty Minutes		GAA		Wins	
Rocket Richard	112	Terry Sawchuk	1.90	Terry Sawchuk	32
Ted Lindsay	111	Gerry McNeil	2.12	Jim Henry	28
Fern Flaman	110	Harry Lumley	2.39	Al Rollins	27
George Gee	99	Jim Henry	2.46	Harry Lumley	27
Al Dewsbury	97	Al Rollins	2.50	Gerry McNeil	25

Shutouts	
Harry Lumley	10
Gerry McNeil	10
Terry Sawchuk	9
Jim Henry	7
Al Rollins	6

All-Star Game

(Olympia Stadium, Detroit)

October 5 1952	1st Team	1		2nd Team	1

Stanley Cup Playoffs

March 24	Boston Bruins	0	at	Detroit Red Wings	7
March 24	Chicago Black Hawks	1	at	Montreal Canadiens	3
March 26	Boston Bruins	5	at	Detroit Red Wings	3
March 26	Chicago Black Hawks	3	at	Montreal Canadiens	4
March 29	Detroit Red Wings	1	at	Boston Bruins	2 [12:29]
March 29	Montreal Canadiens	1	at	Chicago Black Hawks	2 [5:18]
March 31	Detroit Red Wings	2	at	Boston Bruins	6
March 31	Montreal Canadiens	1	at	Chicago Black Hawks	3
April 2	Boston Bruins	4	at	Detroit Red Wings	6
April 2	Chicago Black Hawks	4	at	Montreal Canadiens	2
April 4	Montreal Canadiens	3	at	Chicago Black Hawks	0
April 5	Detroit Red Wings	2	at	Boston Bruins	4
April 7	Chicago Black Hawks	1	at	Montreal Canadiens	4
April 9	Boston Bruins	2	at	Montreal Canadiens	4
April 11	Boston Bruins	4	at	Montreal Canadiens	1
April 12	Montreal Canadiens	3	at	Boston Bruins	0
April 14	Montreal Canadiens	7	at	Boston Bruins	3
April 16	Boston Bruins	0	at	Montreal Canadiens	1 [1:22]

All Star Teams

First Team		Second Team
Terry Sawchuk	Goal	Gerry McNeil
Leonard Kelly	Defense	Bill Quackenbush
Doug Harvey	Defense	Bill Gadsby
Fleming Mackell	Center	Alex Delvecchio
Gordie Howe	Right Wing	Maurice Richard
Ted Lindsay	Left Wing	Bert Olmstead

Individual Awards

Art Ross Trophy--Gordie Howe (Detroit Red Wings)
Calder Memorial Trophy--Lorne Worsley (New York Rangers)
Hart Trophy--Gordie Howe (Detroit Red Wings)
Lady Byng Trophy--Leonard Kelly (Detroit Red Wings)
Vezina Trophy--Terry Sawchuk (Detroit Red Wings)

Franchise Changes

NL--Boston Braves became the Milwaukee Braves.
NFL--Dallas Texans became the Baltimore Colts.

Other Sports

Horseracing--Kentucky Derby won by Dark Star (time 2:02, purse $90,050).
Heavyweight Boxing--Rocky Marciano knocked-out Joe Walcott in 1 round.
Rocky Marciano knocked-out Roland LaStarza in 11 rounds.
Golf--U.S. Open won by Ben Hogan with a score of 283.
Auto Racing--Indianapolis 500 won by Bill Vukovich (ave. speed 128.740 MPH).
Tennis--U.S. Open won by Tony Trabert in the men's singles.
U.S. Open won by Rex Hartwig and Mervyn Rose in the men's doubles.
U.S. Open won by Maureen Connolly in the women's singles.
U.S. Open won by Doris Hart and Shirley Fry in the women's doubles.
U.S. Open won by Doris Hart and E. Victor Seixas Jr. in the mixed doubles.

1954

BASEBALL
National League

Team Name	W	L	Pct	GB	R	OR
New York Giants	97	57	.630	-	732	550
Brooklyn Dodgers	92	62	.597	5	778	740
Milwaukee Braves	89	65	.578	8	670	556
Philadelphia Phillies	75	79	.487	22	659	614
Cincinnati Reds	74	80	.481	23	729	763
St. Louis Cardinals	72	82	.468	25	799	790
Chicago Cubs	64	90	.416	33	700	766
Pittsburgh Pirates	53	101	.344	44	557	845

Coaching Changes

Cincinnati--George Tebbetts 74-80; Brooklyn--Walter Alston 92-62; Philadelphia--Steve O'Neill 40-37,Terry Moore 35-42; Chicago--Stan Hack 64-90.

League Leaders

Batting Average		Home Runs		RBI	
Willie Mays	.345	Ted Kluszewski	49	Ted Kluszewski	141
Don Mueller	.342	Gil Hodges	42	Gil Hodges	130
Duke Snider	.341	Willie Mays	41	Duke Snider	130
Stan Musial	.330	Hank Sauer	41	Stan Musial	126
Ted Kluszewski	.326	Eddie Mathews	40	Del Ennis	119

Stolen Bases		ERA		Wins	
Bill Bruton	34	John Antonelli	2.30	Robin Roberts	23
John Temple	21	Lew Burdette	2.76	Warren Spahn	21
Dee Fondy	20	Curt Simmons	2.81	John Antonelli	21
Wally Moon	18	Ruben Gomez	2.88	Harvey Haddix	18
Richie Ashburn	11	Gene Conley	2.96	Carl Erskine	18

Saves		Strikeouts	
Jim Hughes	24	Robin Roberts	185
Frank Smith	20	Harvey Haddix	184
Marv Grissom	19	Carl Erskine	166
Dave Jolly	10	John Antonelli	152
John Hetki	9	Warren Spahn	136

American League

Team Name	W	L	Pct	GB	R	OR
Cleveland Indians	111	43	.721	-	746	504
New York Yankees	103	51	.669	8	805	563
Chicago White Sox	94	60	.610	17	711	521
Boston Red Sox	69	85	.448	42	700	728
Detroit Tigers	68	86	.442	43	584	664
Washington Senators	66	88	.429	45	632	680
Baltimore Orioles	54	100	.351	57	483	668
Philadelphia Athletics	51	103	.331	60	542	875

Coaching Changes

Philadelphia--Eddie Joost 51-103; Chicago--Paul Richards 91-54, Marty Marion 3-6; Baltimore--Jimmy Dykes 54-100.

League Leaders

Batting Average		Home Runs		RBI	
Bob Avila	.341	Larry Doby	32	Larry Doby	126
Minnie Minoso	.320	Ted Williams	29	Yogi Berra	125
Irv Noren	.319	Mickey Mantle	27	Jackie Jensen	117
Nelson Fox	.319	Jackie Jensen	25	Minnie Minoso	116
Yogi Berra	.307	Al Rosen	24	Al Rosen	102

Stolen Bases		ERA		Wins	
Jackie Jensen	22	Mike Garcia	2.64	Bob Lemon	23
Minnie Minoso	18	Sandy Consuegra	2.69	Early Wynn	23
Jim Rivera	18	Bob Lemon	2.72	Bob Grim	20
Jim Bushy	17	Early Wynn	2.73	Mike Garcia	19
Forrest Jacobs	17	Steve Gromek	2.74	Virgil Trucks	19

Saves		Strikeouts	
John Sain	22	Bob Turley	185
Ellis Kinder	15	Early Wynn	155
Ray Narleski	13	Virgil Trucks	152
Hal Newhouser	7	Billy Pierce	148
Don Mossi	7	Jack Harshman	134

All-Star Game

(Municipal Stadium, Cleveland)

July 13	American League	11	National League	9

World Series

September 29	Cleveland Indians	2	at	New York Giants	5 [10]
September 30	Cleveland Indians	1	at	New York Giants	3
October 1	New York Giants	6	at	Cleveland Indians	2
October 2	New York Giants	7	at	Cleveland Indians	4

Individual Awards

Baseball Writers Award--Willie Mays (New York Giants NL)
Yogi Berra (New York Yankees AL)
Rookie of the Year--Wally Moon (St. Louis Cardinals NL)
Bob Grim (New York Yankees AL)
Sporting News Executive of the Year--Horace Stoneman (New York Giants NL)
Sporting News Manager of the Year--Leo Durocher (New York Giants NL)
Sporting News Pitcher of the Year--John Antonelli (New York Giants NL)
Bob Lemon (Cleveland Indians AL)
Sporting News Player of the Year--Willie Mays (New York Giants NL)
Bobby Avila (Cleveland Indians AL)
Sporting News Rookie of the Year--Wally Moon (St. Louis Cardinals NL)
Bob Grim (New York Yankees AL)

Hall of Fame Inductees

Bill Dickey, Walter Maranville, Bill Terry

Rules

Batter credited with a sacrifice fly and not charged with a time at bat if he hits a fly ball, but the runner scored on the catch (NL and AL).

Notes

The Major League Baseball Players Association was formed July 12th of this year.

BASKETBALL
National Basketball Association

Eastern Division

Team Name	GP	W	L	PPGF	PPGA	Pct	GB
New York Knickerbockers	72	44	28	79.0	79.1	.611	-
Boston Celtics	72	42	30	87.7	85.4	583	2
Syracuse Nationals	72	42	30	83.5	78.6	.583	2
Philadelphia Warriors	72	29	43	78.2	80.4	.403	15
Baltimore Bullets	72	16	56	78.3	85.1	.222	28

Western Division

Team Name	GP	W	L	PPGF	PPGA	Pct	GB
Minneapolis Lakers	72	46	26	81.7	78.3	.639	-
Rochester Royals	72	44	28	79.8	77.3	.611	2
Fort Wayne Zollner Pistons	72	40	32	77.0	76.1	.556	6
Milwaukee Hawks	72	21	51	70.0	75.3	.292	31

Coaching Changes

Baltimore--Clair Bee 16-56; Milwaukee--Fuzzy Levane 11-35, Red Holzman 10-16.

League Leaders

Field Goals		Free Throws		Assists	
Neil Johnston	591	Neil Johnston	577	Bob Cousy	518
Bob Cousy	486	Dolph Schayes	488	Andy Phillip	449
Ed Macauley	462	Ray Felix	449	Paul Seymour	364
George Mikan	441	Harry Gallatin	433	Dick McGuire	354
Bill Sharman	412	George Mikan	424	Bob Davies	323

Points		Fouls	
Neil Johnston	1759	Earl Lloyd	303
Bob Cousy	1383	Arnie Risen	284
Ed Macauley	1344	Bob Brannum	280
George Mikan	1306	Alex Hannum	279
Ray Felix	1269	Paul Hoffman	271

All-Star Game

(at Madison Square Garden, New York)

January 21	East Division	98		West Division	93 [OT]

NBA Championship

March 16	Boston Celtics	93	at	N.Y. Knickerbockers	71
March 16	Ft. Wayne Zollner Pistons	75	at	Rochester Royals	82
March 17	Syracuse Nationals	96	at	Boston Celtics	95 [OT]
March 17	Rochester Royals	88	at	Minneapolis Lakers	109
March 18	N.Y. Knickerbockers	68	at	Syracuse Nationals	75
March 18	Minneapolis Lakers	90	at	Ft. Wayne Zollner Pistons	85
March 20	N.Y. Knickerbockers	78	at	Boston Celtics	79
March 20	Ft. Wayne Zollner Pistons	73	at	Minneapolis Lakers	78
March 21	Syracuse Nationals	103	at	N.Y. Knickerbockers	99
March 21	Rochester Royals	89	at	Ft. Wayne Zollner Pistons	71
March 22	Boston Celtics	85	at	Syracuse Nationals	98
March 23	Minneapolis Lakers		at	Rochester Royals	(canceled)
March 24	Rochester Royals	76	at	Minneapolis Lakers	89
March 25	Boston Celtics	94	at	Syracuse Nationals	109
March 27	Minneapolis Lakers	73	at	Rochester Royals	74
March 27	Syracuse Nationals	83	at	Boston Celtics	76
March 28	Rochester Royals	72	at	Minneapolis Lakers	82
March 31	Syracuse Nationals	68	at	Minneapolis Lakers	79
April 3	Syracuse Nationals	62	at	Minneapolis Lakers	60
April 4	Minneapolis Lakers	81	at	Syracuse Nationals	67
April 8	Minneapolis Lakers	69	at	Syracuse Nationals	80
April 10	Minneapolis Lakers	84	at	Syracuse Nationals	73
April 11	Syracuse Nationals	65	at	Minneapolis Lakers	63
April 12	Syracuse Nationals	80	at	Minneapolis Lakers	87

All Star Teams

First Team	Second Team
Bob Cousy (Boston Celtics)	Ed Macauley (Boston Celtics)
Neil Johnston (Philadelphia Warriors)	Jim Pollard (Minneapolis Lakers)
George Mikan (Minneapolis Lakers)	Carl Braun (N.Y. Knickerbockers)
Dolph Schayes (Syracuse Nationals)	Bob Wanzer (Rochester Royals)
Harry Gallatin (N.Y. Knickerbockers)	Paul Seymour (Syracuse Nationals)

Individual Awards

Eddie Gottlieb Trophy--Ray Felix (Baltimore Bullets)
NBA All Star Game MVP--Bob Cousy (Boston Celtics)

Notes

Jack Molinas of the Ft. Wayne Zollner Pistons was banned from the NBA for betting on his own team's games.

FOOTBALL

National Football League

Eastern Conference

Team Name	GP	W	L	T	PF	PA	Pct
Cleveland Browns	12	9	3	0	336	162	.750
Philadelphia Eagles	12	7	4	1	284	230	.625
New York Giants	12	7	5	0	293	184	.583
Pittsburgh Steelers	12	5	7	0	219	263	.417
Washington Redskins	12	3	9	0	207	432	.250
Chicago Cardinals	12	2	10	0	183	347	.167

Western Conference

Team Name	GP	W	L	T	PF	PA	Pct
Detroit Lions	12	9	2	1	337	189	.792
Chicago Bears	12	8	4	0	301	279	.667
San Francisco 49ers	12	7	4	1	313	251	.625
Los Angeles Rams	12	6	5	1	314	285	.542
Green Bay Packers	12	4	8	0	234	251	.333
Baltimore Colts	12	3	9	0	131	279	.250

Coaching Changes

New York--Jim Lee Howell 7-5-0; Pittsburgh--Walt Kiesling 5-7-0; Washington--Joe Kuharich 3-9-0; Green Bay--Lisle Blackbourne 4-8-0; Baltimore--Weeb Ewbank 3-9-0.

League Leaders

Yards Rushing		Yards Passing		Passing % (40 attempts)	
Joe Perry	1049	Norm Van Brocklin	2637	George Ratterman	60
John Johnson	681	Tobin Rote	2311	Otto Graham	59
Tank Younger	610	Y.A. Tittle	2205	Y.A. Tittle	58
Dan Towler	599	Otto Graham	2092	Tom Dublinski	56
Mo Bassett	588	Jim Finks	2003	Bobby Layne	55

Receiving Yards		Receptions		Field Goals	
Bob Boyd	1212	Pete Pihos	60	Lou Groza	16
Harlon Hill	1124	Bill Wilson	60	Ben Agajanian	13
Pete Pihos	872	Bob Boyd	53	Doak Walker	11
Bill Wilson	830	Bill Howton	52	Gord Soltau	11
Dante Lavelli	802	Dante Lavelli	47	Fred Cone	9

Punt Return Yards		Kickoff Return Yards	
Veryl Switzer	306	Woodley Lewis	836
Jack Christiansen	225	Les Goble	749
Herb Johnson	164	Dale Atkeson	623
Jerry Williams	153	Al Carmichael	531
Bill Reynolds	138	Verl Switzer	500

Pro Bowl Game

(Memorial Coliseum, Los Angeles)

January 16, 1955	Western Conference	26		Eastern Conference	19

NFL Championship

December 26	Detroit Lions	10	at	Cleveland Browns	56

Individual Awards

Pro-Bowl MVP--Billy Wilson (San Francisco 49ers)
U.P.I. MVP--Joe Perry (San Francisco 49ers)

Canadian Rugby Union
Interprovincial Rugby Football Union

Team Name	GP	W	L	T	PF	PA	Pts	Pct
Montreal Alouettes	14	11	3	0	341	148	22	.786
Hamilton Tiger-Cats	14	9	5	0	275	207	18	.643
Toronto Argonauts	14	6	8	0	212	265	12	.429
Ottawa Rough Riders	14	2	12	0	129	337	4	.143

Western Interprovincial Football Union

Team Name	GP	W	L	T	PF	PA	Pts	Pct
Edmonton Eskimos	16	11	5	0	255	163	22	.688
Saskatchewan Roughriders	16	10	4	2	239	204	22	.688
Winnipeg Blue Bombers	16	8	6	2	202	190	18	.563
Calgary Stampeders	16	8	8	0	271	165	16	.500
British Columbia Lions	16	1	15	0	100	345	2	.063

Coaching Changes

Edmonton--Frank Ivy 11-5-0; Winnipeg--Allie Sherman 8-6-2; Calgary--Larry Siemering 8-8-0; British Columbia--Annis Stukus 1-15-0.

League Leaders

Yards Rushing

Howard Waugh 1043

Yards Passing

Sam Etcheverry 3610

Passing %

Frank Tripucka 59

Receiving Yards

Al Pfeifer 1142
Red O'Quinn 1024

Receptions

Al Pfeifer 68

Punting Average

Larry Isbell 46.3

Points

Joe Aguirre 85

Grey Cup

October 30	Saskatchewan Roughriders	14	at	Winnipeg Blue Bombers	14
November 1	Winnipeg Blue Bombers	13	at	Saskatchewan Roughriders	11
November 6	Winnipeg Blue Bombers	3	at	Edmonton Eskimos	9
November 11	Edmonton Eskimos	6	at	Winnipeg Blue Bombers	12
November 13	Winnipeg Blue Bombers	5	at	Edmonton Eskimos	10
November 17	Montreal Alouettes	14	at	Hamilton Tiger-Cats	9
November 20	Hamilton Tiger-Cats	19	at	Montreal Alouettes	24
November 20	K-W Dutchmen	6	at	Edmonton Eskimos	28
November 27	Edmonton Eskimos	26		Montreal Alouettes	25*

Individual Awards

Dave Dryburgh Memorial Trophy--Joe Aguirre (Saskatchewan Roughriders)
Dr. Beattie Martin Trophy--Lynn Bottoms (Calgary Stampeders)
Eddie James Memorial Trophy--Howard Waugh (Calgary Stampeders)
Gruen Trophy--Ron Howell (Hamilton Tiger-Cats)
Jeff Nicklin Memorial Trophy--Jackie Parker (Edmonton Eskimos)
Jeff Russel Memorial Trophy--Sam Etcheverry (Montreal Alouettes)
Schenley Award Most Outstanding Canadian--Gerry James (Winnipeg Blue Bombers)
Schenley Award Most Outstanding Player--Sam Etcheverry (Montreal Alouettes CRU)

HOCKEY
National Hockey League

Team Name	GP	W	L	T	GF	GA	Pts	Pct
Detroit Red Wings	70	37	19	14	191	132	88	.629
Montreal Canadiens	70	35	24	11	195	141	81	.579
Toronto Maple Leafs	70	32	24	14	152	131	78	.557
Boston Bruins	70	32	28	10	177	181	74	.529
New York Rangers	70	29	31	10	161	182	68	.486
Chicago Black Hawks	70	12	51	7	133	242	31	.221

Coaching Changes

Toronto--Francis "King" Clancy 32-24-14; New York--Frank Boucher 12-20-6, Murray Patrick 17-11-4.

League Leaders

Goals		Assists		Points	
Rocket Richard	37	Gordie Howe	48	Gordie Howe	81
Gordie Howe	33	Bert Olmstead	37	Rocket Richard	67
Bernie Geoffrion	29	Ted Lindsay	36	Ted Lindsay	62
Wally Hergesheimer	27	Larry Wilson	33	Bernie Geoffrion	54
Ted Lindsay	26	Earl Reibel	33	Bert Olmstead	52

Penalty Minutes		GAA		Wins	
Gus Mortson	132	Harry Lumley	1.86	Terry Sawchuk	35
Rocket Richard	112	Terry Sawchuk	1.94	Harry Lumley	32
Ted Lindsay	110	Gerry McNeil	2.15	Jim Henry	32
Doug Harvey	110	Jim Henry	2.59	Johnny Bower	29
Ivan Irwin	109	Johnny Bower	2.60	Gerry McNeil	28

*Game played in Toronto

Shutouts

Harry Lumley	13
Terry Sawchuk	12
Jim Henry	8
Gerry McNeil	6
Jacques Plante	5

All-Star Game
(The Forum, Montreal)

October 3 1953	All-Stars	3	Montreal Canadiens	1

Stanley Cup Playoffs

March 23	Toronto Maple Leafs	0	at	Detroit Red Wings	5
March 23	Boston Bruins	0	at	Montreal Canadiens	2
March 25	Toronto Maple Leafs	3	at	Detroit Red Wings	1
March 25	Boston Bruins	1	at	Montreal Canadiens	8
March 27	Detroit Red Wings	3	at	Toronto Maple Leafs	1
March 28	Montreal Canadiens	4	at	Boston Bruins	3
March 30	Detroit Red Wings	2	at	Toronto Maple Leafs	1
March 30	Montreal Canadiens	2	at	Boston Bruins	0
April 1	Toronto Maple Leafs	3	at	Detroit Red Wings	4 [21:01]
April 4	Montreal Canadiens	1	at	Detroit Red Wings	3
April 6	Montreal Canadiens	3	at	Detroit Red Wings	1
April 8	Detroit Red Wings	5	at	Montreal Canadiens	2
April 10	Detroit Red Wings	2	at	Montreal Canadiens	0
April 11	Montreal Canadiens	1	at	Detroit Red Wings	0 [5:45]
April 13	Detroit Red Wings	1	at	Montreal Canadiens	4
April 16	Montreal Canadiens	1	at	Detroit Red Wings	2 [4:29]

All Star Team

First Team		Second Team
Harry Lumley	Goal	Terry Sawchuk
Leonard Kelly	Defense	Bill Gadsby
Doug Harvey	Defense	Tim Horton
Ken Mosdell	Center	Ted Kennedy
Gordie Howe	Right Wing	Maurice Richard
Ted Lindsay	Left Wing	Ed Sanford

Individual Awards

Art Ross Trophy--Gordie Howe (Detroit Red Wings)
Calder Memorial Trophy--Camille Henry (New York Rangers)
Hart Trophy--Al Rollins (Chicago Black Hawks)
James Norris Trophy--Leonard Kelly (Detroit Red Wings)
Lady Byng Trophy--Leonard Kelly (Detroit Red Wings)
Vezina Trophy--Harry Lumley (Toronto Maple Leafs)

Franchise Changes

AL--St. Louis Browns became the Baltimore Orioles.

Other Sports

Horseracing--Kentucky Derby won by Determine (time 2:03, purse $102,050).
Heavyweight Boxing--Rocky Marciano defeated Ezzard Charles in 15 rounds.
Rocky Marciano knocked-out Ezzard Charles in 8 rounds.
Golf-U.S. Open won by Ed Furgol with a score of 284.
Auto Racing--Indianapolis 500 won by Bill Vukovich (ave. speed 130.840 MPH)
Tennis--U.S. Open won by E. Victor Seixas Jr. in the men's singles.
U.S. Open won by E. Victor Seixas Jr. and Tony Trabert in the men's doubles.
U.S. Open won by Doris Hart in the women's singles.
U.S. Open won by Doris Hart and Shirley Fry in the women's doubles.
U.S. Open won by Doris Hart and E. Victor Seixas Jr. in the mixed doubles.

1955

BASEBALL
National League

Team Name	W	L	Pct	GB	R	OR
Brooklyn Dodgers	98	55	.641	-	857	650
Milwaukee Braves	85	69	.552	13.5	743	668
New York Giants	80	74	.519	18.5	702	673
Philadelphia Phillies	77	77	.500	21.5	675	666
Cincinnati Reds	75	79	.487	23.5	761	684
Chicago Cubs	72	81	.471	26	626	713
St. Louis Cardinals	68	86	.442	30.5	654	757
Pittsburgh Pirates	60	94	.390	38.5	560	767

Coaching Changes

Philadelphia--Mayo Smith 77-77; St. Louis--Eddie Stanky 17-19, Harry Walker 51-67.

League Leaders

Batting Average

Richie Ashburn	.338
Willie Mays	.319
Stan Musial	.319
Roy Campanella	.318
Hank Aaron	.314

Home Runs

Willie Mays	51
Ted Kluszewski	47
Ernie Banks	44
Duke Snider	42
Eddie Mathews	41

RBI

Duke Snider	136
Willie Mays	127
Del Ennis	120
Ernie Banks	117
Ted Kluszewski	113

Stolen Bases

Bill Bruton	25
Willie Mays	24
Ken Boyer	22
John Temple	19
Jim Gilliam	15

ERA

Bob Friend	2.83
Don Newcombe	3.20
Bob Buhl	3.21
Warren Spahn	3.26
Robin Roberts	3.28

Wins

Robin Roberts	23
Don Newcombe	20
Joe Nuxhall	17
Warren Spahn	17
Bob Friend	14

Saves

Jack Meyer	16
Ed Roebuck	12
Hershell Freeman	11
Clement Labine	11
Marv Grissom	8

Strikeouts

Sam Jones	198
Robin Roberts	160
Harvey Haddix	150
Don Newcombe	143
John Antonelli	143

American League

Team Name	W	L	Pct	GB	R	OR
New York Yankees	96	58	.623	-	762	569
Cleveland Indians	93	61	.604	3	698	601
Chicago White Sox	91	63	.591	5	725	557
Boston Red Sox	84	70	.545	12	755	652
Detroit Tigers	79	75	.513	17	775	658
Kansas City Athletics	63	91	.409	33	638	911
Baltimore Orioles	57	97	.370	39	540	754
Washington Senators	53	101	.344	43	598	789

Coaching Changes

Chicago--Marty Marion 91-63; Boston--Michael Higgins 84-70; Detroit--Stanley Harris 79-75; K. C. --Lou Boudreau 63-91; Baltimore--Paul Richards 57-97; Washington--Chuck Dressen 53-101.

League Leaders

Batting Average		Home Runs		RBI	
Al Kaline	.340	Mickey Mantle	37	Jack Jensen	116
Victor Power	.319	Gus Zernial	30	Ray Boone	116
George Kell	.312	Ted Williams	28	Yogi Berra	108
Nelson Fox	.311	Yogi Berra	27	Roy Sievers	106
Harvey Kuenn	.306	Norm Zauchin	27	Al Kaline	102

Stolen Bases		ERA		Wins	
Jim Rivera	25	Bill Pierce	1.97	Bob Lemon	18
Minnie Minoso	19	Edward Ford	2.63	Edward Ford	18
Jack Jensen	16	Early Wynn	2.82	Frank Sullivan	18
Jim Bushy	12	Herb Score	2.85	Bob Turley	17
Al Smith	11	Frank Sullivan	2.91	Early Wynn	17

Saves		Strikeouts	
Ray Narieski	19	Herb Score	245
Tom Gorman	18	Bob Turley	210
Ellis Kinder	18	Bill Pierce	157
Jim Konstanty	11	Edward Ford	137
Tom Morgan	10	Bill Hoeft	133

All-Star Game

(County Stadium, Milwaukee)

July 12	National League	6		American League	5

World Series

September 28	Brooklyn Dodgers	5	at	New York Yankees	6
September 29	Brooklyn Dodgers	2	at	New York Yankees	4
September 30	New York Yankees	3	at	Brooklyn Dodgers	8
October 1	New York Yankees	5	at	Brooklyn Dodgers	8
October 2	New York Yankees	3	at	Brooklyn Dodgers	5
October 3	Brooklyn Dodgers	1	at	New York Yankees	5
October 4	Brooklyn Dodgers	2		New York Yankees	0

Individual Awards

Baseball Writers Award--Roy Campanella (Brooklyn Dodgers NL)
Yogi Berra (New York Yankees AL)
Rookie of the Year--Bill Virdon (St. Louis Cardinals NL)
Herb Score (Cleveland Indians AL)
Sporting News Executive of the Year--Walter O'Malley (Brooklyn Dodgers NL)
Sporting News Manager of the Year--Walter Alston (Brooklyn Dodgers NL)
Sporting News Pitcher of the Year--Robin Roberts (Philadelphia Phillies NL)
Whitey Ford (New York Yankees AL)
Sporting News Player of the Year--Duke Snider (Brooklyn Dodgers NL)
Al Kaline (Detroit Tigers AL)
Sporting News Rookie of the Year--Bill Virdon (St. Louis Cardinals NL)
Herb Score (Cleveland Indians AL)
World Series MVP--Johnny Podres (Brooklyn Dodgers NL)

Hall of Fame Inductees

Frank Baker, Joe DiMaggio, Gabby Hartnett, Ted Lyons, Ray Schalk, Clarence Vance

BASKETBALL
National Basketball Association

Eastern Division

Team Name	GP	W	L	PPGF	PPGA	Pct	GB
Syracuse Nationals	72	43	29	91.1	89.7	.597	-
New York Knickerbockers	72	38	34	92.7	92.6	.528	5
Boston Celtics	72	36	36	101.4	101.5	.500	7
Philadelphia Warriors	72	33	39	93.2	93.5	.458	10

Western Division

Team Name	GP	W	L	PPGF	PPGA	Pct	GB
Fort Wayne Zollner Pistons	72	43	29	92.4	90.0	.597	-
Minneapolis Lakers	72	40	32	95.6	94.5	.556	3
Rochester Royals	72	29	43	90.8	92.4	.403	14
Milwaukee Hawks	72	26	46	87.4	90.4	.361	17

Coaching Changes

Fort Wayne--Charlie Eckman 43-29; Milwaukee--Red Holzman 26-46.

League Leaders

Field Goals		Free Throws		Assists	
Paul Arizin	529	Neil Johnston	589	Bob Cousy	557
Bob Cousy	522	Dolph Schayes	489	Dick McGuire	542
Neil Johnston	521	Bob Cousy	460	Andy Phillip	491
Bob Pettit	520	Paul Arizin	454	Paul Seymour	483
Clyde Lovellette	519	Vern Mikkelsen	447	Slater Martin	427

Points		Fouls	
Neil Johnston	1631	Vern Mikkelsen	319
Paul Arizin	1512	Bob Harrison	291
Bob Cousy	1504	Ray Felix	286
Bob Pettit	1466	Earl Lloyd	283
Frank Selvy	1348	Chuck Share	273

All-Star Game

(at Madison Square Garden, New York)

January 18	East Division	100		West Division	91

NBA Playoffs

March 15	N.Y. Knickerbockers	101	at	Boston Celtics	122
March 16	Minneapolis Lakers	82		Rochester Royals	78*
March 16	Boston Celtics	95	at	N.Y. Knickerbockers	102
March 18	Minneapolis Lakers	92	at	Rochester Royals	94
March 19	Minneapolis Lakers	119		Rochester Royals	110*

*Games played in St. Paul

March 19	Boston Celtics	116	at	N.Y. Knickerbockers	109
March 20	Ft. Wayne Zollner Pistons	96		Minneapolis Lakers	79**
March 22	Boston Celtics	100	at	Syracuse Nationals	110
March 22	Ft. Wayne Zollner Pistons	98		Minneapolis Lakers	97#[OT]
March 23	Ft. Wayne Zollner Pistons	91	at	Minneapolis Lakers	99 [OT]
March 24	Boston Celtics	110	at	Syracuse Nationals	116
March 26	Syracuse Nationals	97	at	Boston Celtics	100 [OT]
March 27	Syracuse Nationals	110	at	Boston Celtics	94
March 27	Ft. Wayne Zollner Pistons	105	at	Minneapolis Lakers	96
March 31	Ft. Wayne Zollner Pistons	82	at	Syracuse Nationals	86
April 2	Ft. Wayne Zollner Pistons	84	at	Syracuse Nationals	87
April 3	Ft. Wayne Zollner Pistons	96		Syracuse Nationals	89#
April 5	Ft. Wayne Zollner Pistons	109		Syracuse Nationals	102#
April 7	Ft. Wayne Zollner Pistons	74		Syracuse Nationals	71#
April 9	Ft. Wayne Zollner Pistons	104	at	Syracuse Nationals	109
April 10	Ft. Wayne Zollner Pistons	91		Syracuse Nationals	92

All Star Teams

First Team

Neil Johnston (Philadelphia Warriors)
Bob Cousy (Boston Celtics)
Dolph Schayes (Syracuse Nationals)
Bob Pettit (Milwaukee Hawks)
Larry Foust (Ft. Wayne Zollner Pistons)

Second Team

Vern Mikkelsen (Minneapolis Lakers)
Harry Gallatin (N.Y. Knickerbockers)
Paul Seymour (Syracuse Nationals)
Slater Martin (Minneapolis Lakers)
Bill Sharman (Boston Celtics)

Individual Awards

Eddie Gottlieb Trophy--Bob Pettit (Milwaukee Hawks)
NBA All Star Game MVP--Bill Sharman (Boston Celtics)

Rules

The 24 second clock was introduced this year which forced teams to shoot within 24 seconds of gaining possession of the ball.
Teams were limited to 5 fouls per period; when a team received its 6th foul of the period, the opponent would receive a penalty shot on all free throw situations.

FOOTBALL
National Football League

Eastern Conference

Team Name	GP	W	L	T	PF	PA	Pct
Cleveland Browns	12	9	2	1	349	218	.792
Washington Redskins	12	8	4	0	246	222	.667
New York Giants	12	6	5	1	267	223	.542
Chicago Cardinals	12	4	7	1	224	252	.375
Philadelphia Eagles	12	4	7	1	248	231	.375
Pittsburgh Steelers	12	4	8	0	195	285	.333

**Game played in Elkhart, Indiana
#Game played in Indianapolis

Western Conference

Los Angeles Rams	12	8	3	1	260	231	.708
Chicago Bears	12	8	4	0	294	251	.667
Green Bay Packers	12	6	6	0	258	276	.500
Baltimore Colts	12	5	6	1	214	239	.458
San Francisco 49ers	12	4	8	0	216	298	.333
Detroit Lions	12	3	9	0	230	275	.250

Coaching Changes

Cardinals--Ray Richards 4-7-1; Los Angeles--Sid Gillman 8-3-1; San Francisco--Red Steader 4-8-0.

League Leaders

Yards Rushing		**Yards Passing**		**Passing %** (40 attempts)	
Alan Ameche	961	Jim Finks	2270	George Ratterman	68
Howie Ferguson	859	Y.A. Tittle	2185	Ted Marchibroda	56
Curley Morrison	824	Tobin Rote	1977	Otto Graham	53
Ron Waller	716	Norm Van Brocklin	1890	Norm Van Brocklin	53
Joe Perry	701	Bobby Layne	1830	Bobby Layne	53

Receiving Yards		**Receptions**		**Field Goals**	
Pete Pihos	864	Pete Pihos	62	Fred Cone	16
Bill Wilson	831	Bill Wilson	53	Les Richter	13
Harlon Hill	789	Tom Fears	44	Lou Groza	11
Ray Mathews	762	Bill Howton	44	George Blanda	11
Bill Howton	697	Dave Middleton	44	Ben Agajanian	10

Punt Return Yards		**Kickoff Return Yards**	
Ollie Matson	245	Sid Watson	716
Scooter Scudero	241	Scooter Scudero	699
Frank Bernardi	163	Joe Arenas	594
Veryl Switzer	158	Ron Drzewiecki	591
Don Paul	148	Ron Waller	461

Pro Bowl Game

(Memorial Coliseum, Los Angeles)

January 15 1956	Eastern Conference	31		Western Conference	30

NFL Championship

December 26	Cleveland Browns	38	at	Los Angeles Rams	14

Individual Awards

Jim Thorpe Trophy--Harlon Hill (Chicago Bears)
Pro-Bowl MVP--Ollie Matson (Chicago Cardinals)
U.P.I. NFL-NFC Coach of the Year--Joe Kuharich (Washington Redskins)
U.P.I. NFL-NFC Rookie of the Year--Alan Ameche (Baltimore Colts)
U.P.I. MVP--Otto Graham (Cleveland Browns)

Canadian Rugby Union
Interprovincial Rugby Football Union

Team Name	GP	W	L	T	PF	PA	Pts	Pct
Montreal Alouettes	12	9	3	0	388	214	18	.750
Hamilton Tiger-Cats	12	8	4	0	271	193	16	.667
Toronto Argonauts	12	4	8	0	239	328	8	.333
Ottawa Rough Riders	12	3	9	0	174	337	6	.250

Western Interprovincial Football Union

Team Name	GP	W	L	T	PF	PA	Pts	Pct
Edmonton Eskimos	16	14	2	0	286	117	28	.875
Saskatchewan Roughriders	16	10	6	0	270	245	20	.625
Winnipeg Blue Bombers	16	7	9	0	210	195	14	.438
British Columbia Lions	16	5	11	0	211	330	10	.313
Calgary Stampeders	16	4	12	0	209	299	8	.250

Coaching Changes

Toronto--Bill Swiacki 4-8-0; Ottawa--Chan Caldwell 3-9-0; Calgary--Jack Hennemier 4-12-0.

League Leaders

Yards Rushing

Normie Kwong	1250
Pat Abbruzzi	1248
Gerry James	1205

Yards Passing

Sam Etcheverry	3610

Passing %

Sam Etcheverry	57
Don Klosterman	57
Frank Tripucka	57

Receiving Yards

Al Pfeifer	1342
Red O'Quinn	1097
Willie Roberts	1091

Receptions

Red O'Quinn	78

Punting Average

Cam Fraser	47.4

Points

Al Pfeifer	98

All-Star Game
(at Varsity Stadium, Toronto)

December 3	East	6	West	6

Grey Cup

November 5	Winnipeg Blue Bombers	16	at	Saskatchewan Roughriders	7
November 7	Saskatchewan Roughriders	9	at	Winnipeg Blue Bombers	8
November 10	Edmonton Eskimos	29	at	Winnipeg Blue bombers	6
November 12	Toronto Argonauts	32	at	Hamilton Tiger-Cats	28
November 16	Winnipeg Blue Bombers	6	at	Edmonton Eskimos	26
November 19	Toronto Argonauts	36	at	Montreal Alouettes	38
November 26	Edmonton Eskimos	34		Montreal Alouettes	19*

*Game played in Vancouver

Individual Awards

Dave Dryburgh Memorial Trophy--Ken Carpenter (Saskatchewan Roughriders)
Dr. Beattie Martin Trophy--Jarry Lunn (Saskatchewan Roughriders)
Eddie James Memorial Trophy--Normie Kwong (Edmonton Eskimos)
Gruen Trophy--Ed Mularchyk (Ottawa Rough Riders)
Jeff Nicklin Memorial Trophy--Ken Carpenter (Saskatchewan Roughriders)
Jeff Russel Memorial Trophy--Avatus Stone (Ottawa Rough Riders)
Schenley Award Most Outstanding Canadian--Normie Kwong (Edmonton Eskimos)
Schenley Award Most Outstanding Lineman--Tex Coulter (Montreal Alouettes)
Schenley Award Most Outstanding Player--Pat Abbruzzi (Montreal Alouettes)

HOCKEY
National Hockey League

Team Name	GP	W	L	T	GF	GA	Pts	Pct
Detroit Red Wings	70	42	17	11	204	134	95	.679
Montreal Canadiens	70	41	18	11	228	157	93	.664
Toronto Maple Leafs	70	24	24	22	147	135	70	.500
Boston Bruins	70	23	26	21	169	188	67	.479
New York Rangers	70	17	35	18	150	210	52	.371
Chicago Black Hawks	70	13	40	17	161	235	43	.307

Coaching Changes

Detroit--Jimmy Skinner 42-17-11; Boston--Lynn Patrick 10-14-6, Milt Schmidt 13-12-15; New York--Murray Patrick 17-35-18; Chicago--Frank Eddolls 13-40-17.

League Leaders

Goals		Assists		Points	
Rocket Richard	38	Bert Olmstead	48	Bernie Geoffrion	75
Bernie Geoffrion	38	Doug Harvey	43	Rocket Richard	74
Jean Beliveau	37	Ted Kennedy	42	Jean Beliveau	73
Sid Smith	33	George Sullivan	42	Earl Reibel	66
Gordie Howe	29	Earl Reibel	41	Gordie Howe	62

Penalty Minutes		GAA		Wins	
Fern Flaman	150	Harry Lumley	1.94	Terry Sawchuk	40
Tony Leswick	137	Terry Sawchuk	1.96	Jacques Plante	31
Gord Hollingworth	135	Jacques Plante	2.14	Harry Lumley	24
Gus Mortson	133	John Henderson	2.49	Lorne Worsley	15
Rocket Richard	125	Lorne Worsley	3.03	John Henderson	15

Shutouts	
Terry Sawchuk	12
Harry Lumley	8
John Henderson	5
Jacques Plante	5
Lorne Worsley	4

All-Stars Game

(Olympia Stadium, Detroit)

October 2 1954	All-Stars	2		Detroit Red Wings	2

Stanley Cup Playoffs

March 22	Toronto Maple Leafs	4	at	Detroit Red Wings	7
March 22	Boston Bruins	0	at	Montreal Canadiens	2
March 24	Toronto Maple Leafs	1	at	Detroit Red Wings	2
March 24	Boston Bruins	1	at	Montreal Canadiens	3
March 26	Detroit Red Wings	2	at	Toronto Maple Leafs	1
March 27	Montreal Canadiens	2	at	Boston Bruins	4
March 29	Detroit Red Wings	3	at	Toronto Maple Leafs	0
March 29	Montreal Canadiens	4	at	Boston Bruins	3 [3:05]
March 31	Boston Bruins	1	at	Montreal Canadiens	5
April 3	Montreal Canadiens	2	at	Detroit Red Wings	4
April 5	Montreal Canadiens	1	at	Detroit Red Wings	7
April 7	Detroit Red Wings	2	at	Montreal Canadiens	4
April 9	Detroit Red Wings	3	at	Montreal Canadiens	5
April 10	Montreal Canadiens	1	at	Detroit Red Wings	5
April 12	Detroit Red Wings	3	at	Montreal Canadiens	6
April 14	Montreal Canadiens	1	at	Detroit Red Wings	3

All Star Teams

First Team		Second Team
Harry Lumley	Goal	Terry Sawchuk
Doug Harvey	Defense	Bob Goldham
Leonard Kelly	Defense	Fern Flaman
Jean Beliveau	Center	Ken Mosdell
Maurice Richard	Right Wing	Bernie Geoffrion
Sid Smith	Left Wing	Danny Lewicki

Individual Awards

Art Ross Trophy--Bernie Geoffrion (Montreal Canadiens)
Calder Memorial Trophy--Ed Litzenberger (Montreal Canadiens/Chicago Black Hawks)
Hart Trophy--Ted Kennedy (Toronto Maple Leafs)
James Norris Trophy--Doug Harvey (Montreal Canadiens)
Lady Byng Memorial Trophy--Sid Smith (Toronto Maple Leafs)
Vezina Trophy--Terry Sawchuk (Detroit Red Wings)

Notes

Fans in Montreal rioted following the suspension of superstar Rocket Richard after he punched linesman Cliff Thompson in the face. The game of March 17 was forfeited after the first period, and the riot resulting from the suspension of Richard and the forfeiting of the game ended in 60 arrests and thousands of dollars in damage.

Franchise Changes

AL--Philadelphia Athletics became the Kansas City Athletics.

Other Sports

Horseracing--Kentucky Derby won by Swaps (time 2:01.8, purse $108,400).
Heavyweight Boxing--Rocky Marciano knocked-out Don Cockell in 9 rounds.
Rocky Marciano knocked-out Archie Moore in 9 rounds.
Golf--U.S. Open won by Jack Fleck in a playoff with Ben Hogan (scores of 287-287, 69-72).
Auto Racing--Indianapolis 500 won by Bob Sweikert (ave. speed 128.209 MPH).
Tennis--U.S. Open won by Tony Trabert in the men's singles.
U.S. Open won by Kosei Kamo and Atsushi Miyagi in the men's doubles.
U.S. Open won by Doris Hart in the women's singles.
U.S. Open won by Louise Brough and Margaret O. du Pont in the women's doubles.
U.S. Open won by Doris Hart and Victor Seixas Jr. in the mixed doubles.

1956

BASEBALL

National League

Team Name	W	L	Pct	GB	R	OR
Brooklyn Dodgers	93	61	.604	-	720	601
Milwaukee Braves	92	62	.597	1	709	569
Cincinnati Reds	91	63	.591	2	775	658
St. Louis Cardinals	76	78	.494	17	678	698
Philadelphia Phillies	71	83	.461	22	668	738
New York Giants	67	87	.435	26	540	650
Pittsburgh Pirates	66	88	.429	27	588	653
Chicago Cubs	60	94	.390	33	597	708

Coaching Changes

Milwaukee--Charlie Grimm 24-22, Fred Haney 68-40; St. Louis--Fred Hutchinson 76-78; New York--Bill Rigney 67-87; Pittsburgh--Bob Bragan 66-88.

League Leaders

Batting Average		Home Runs		RBI	
Hank Aaron	.328	Duke Snider	43	Stan Musial	109
Bill Virdon	.319	Joe Adcock	38	Joe Adcock	103
Roberto Clemente	.311	Frank Robinson	38	Ted Kluszewski	102
Stan Musial	.310	Eddie Mathews	37	Duke Snider	101
Ken Boyer	.306	Wally Post	36	Ken Boyer	98

Stolen Bases		ERA		Wins	
Willie Mays	40	Lew Burdette	2.70	Don Newcombe	27
Jim Gilliam	21	Warren Spahn	2.78	Warren Spahn	20
Bill White	15	John Antonelli	2.86	John Antonelli	20
John Temple	14	Sal Maglie	2.87	Lew Burdette	19
Harold Reese	13	Don Newcombe	3.06	Brooks Lawrence	19

Saves		Strikeouts	
Clement Labine	19	Sam Jones	176
Hershell Freeman	18	Harvey Haddix	170
Joseph Lown	13	Bob Friend	166
Don Bessent	9	Robin Roberts	157
Larry Jackson	9	Wilmer Mizell	153

American League

Team Name	W	L	Pct	GB	R	OR
New York Yankees	97	57	.630	-	857	631
Cleveland Indians	88	66	.571	9	712	581
Chicago White Sox	85	69	.552	12	776	634
Boston Red Sox	84	70	.545	13	780	751
Detroit Tigers	82	72	.532	15	789	699
Baltimore Orioles	69	85	.448	28	571	705
Washington Senators	59	95	.383	38	652	924
Kansas City Athletics	52	102	.338	45	619	831

Coaching Changes

None.

League Leaders

Batting Average		Home Runs		RBI	
Mickey Mantle	.353	Mickey Mantle	52	Mickey Mantle	130
Ted Williams	.345	Vic Wertz	32	Al Kaline	128
Harvey Kuenn	.332	Yogi Berra	30	Vic Wertz	106
Charlie Maxwell	.326	Roy Sievers	29	Harry Simpson	105
Bob Nieman	.320	Charlie Maxwell	28	Yogi Berra	105

Stolen Bases		ERA		Wins	
Luis Aparicio	21	Edward Ford	2.47	Frank Lary	21
Jim Rivera	20	Herb Score	2.53	Bob Lemon	20
Bob Avila	17	Early Wynn	2.72	Herb Score	20
Minnie Minoso	12	Bob Lemon	3.03	Bill Pierce	20
John Francona	11	Jack Harshman	3.10	Bill Hoeft	20

Saves		Strikeouts	
George Zuverink	16	Herb Score	263
Don Mossi	11	Bill Pierce	192
Tom Morgan	11	Paul Foytack	184
Ivan Delock	9	Bill Hoeft	172
Bob Shantz	9	Frank Lary	165

All-Star Game

(Griffith Stadium, Washington)

July 10	National League	7	American League	3

World Series

October 3	New York Yankees	3	at	Brooklyn Dodgers	6
October 5	New York Yankees	8	at	Brooklyn Dodgers	13
October 6	Brooklyn Dodgers	3	at	New York Yankees	5
October 7	Brooklyn Dodgers	2	at	New York Yankees	6
October 8	Brooklyn Dodgers	0	at	New York Yankees	2
October 9	New York Yankees	0	at	Brooklyn Dodgers	1 [11]
October 10	New York Yankees	9	at	Brooklyn Dodgers	0

Individual Awards

Baseball Writers Award--Don Newcombe (Brooklyn Dodgers NL)
Mickey Mantle (New York Yankees AL)
Cy Young Award--Don Newcombe (Brooklyn Dodgers NL)
Rookie of the Year--Frank Robinson (Cincinnati Reds NL)
Luis Aparicio (Chicago White Sox AL)
Sporting News Executive of the Year--Gabe Paul (Cincinnati Reds NL)
Sporting News Manager of the Year--George Tebbetts (Cincinnati Reds NL)
Sporting News Pitcher of the Year--Don Newcombe (Brooklyn Dodgers NL)
Bill Pierce (Chicago White Sox AL)
Sporting News Player of the Year--Hank Aaron (Milwaukee Braves NL)
Mickey Mantle (New York Yankees AL)
Sporting News Rookie of the Year--Frank Robinson (Cincinnati Reds NL)
Luis Aparicio (Chicago White Sox AL)
World Series MVP--Don Larsen (New York Yankees AL)

Hall of Fame Inductees

Joe Cronin, Hank Greenberg

BASKETBALL
National Basketball Association

Eastern Division

Team Name	GP	W	L	PPGF	PPGA	Pct	GB
Philadelphia Warriors	72	45	27	103.1	98.8	.625	-
Boston Celtics	72	39	33	106.0	105.3	.542	6
Syracuse Nationals	72	35	37	96.9	96.9	.486	10
New York Knickerbockers	72	35	37	100.2	100.6	.486	10

Western Division

Team Name	GP	W	L	PPGF	PPGA	Pct	GB
Fort Wayne Zollner Pistons	72	37	35	94.4	93.7	.514	-
Minneapolis Lakers	72	33	39	99.3	100.2	.458	4
St. Louis Hawks	72	33	39	96.6	98.0	.458	4
Rochester Royals	72	31	41	95.8	98.7	.431	6

Coaching Changes

Philadelphia--George Senesky 45-27; New York--Joe Lapchick 26-25, Vince Boryla 9-12; St. Louis--Red Holzman 33-39; Rochester--Bobby Wanzer 31-41.

League Leaders

Field Goals		Free Throws		Assists	
Bob Pettit	646	Bob Pettit	557	Bob Cousy	642
Paul Arizin	617	Neil Johnston	549	Jack George	457
Clyde Lovellette	594	Dolph Schayes	542	Slater Martin	445
Bill Sharman	538	Frank Selvy	537	George King	410
Neil Johnston	499	Paul Arizin	507	Andy Phillip	410

Points		Fouls	
Bob Pettit	1849	Vern Mikkelsen	319
Paul Arizin	1741	Chuck Share	318
Neil Johnston	1547	Arnie Risen	300
Clyde Lovellette	1526	Ray Felix	293
Dolph Schayes	1472	Dick Ricketts	287

All-Star Game

(at Rochester War Memorial Coliseum, Rochester)

January 24	West Division	108	East Division	94

NBA Playoffs

March 15	New York Knickerbockers	77	at	Syracuse Nationals	82
March 16	Minneapolis Lakers	103	at	St. Louis Hawks	97
March 17	Syracuse Nationals	93	at	Boston Celtics	110
March 17	Minneapolis Lakers	115	at	St. Louis Hawks	116
March 19	Boston Celtics	98	at	Syracuse Nationals	101
March 19	St. Louis Hawks	75	at	Minneapolis Lakers	133
March 21	Syracuse Nationals	102	at	Boston Celtics	97
March 21	St. Louis Hawks	116	at	Minneapolis Lakers	115
March 22	St. Louis Hawks	86	at	Fort Wayne Zollner Pistons	85
March 23	Syracuse Nationals	87	at	Philadelphia Warriors	109
March 24	Ft. Wayne Zollner Pistons	74	at	St. Louis Hawks	84
March 25	Philadelphia Warriors	118	at	Syracuse Nationals	122
March 25	St. Louis Hawks	84	at	Fort Wayne Zollner Pistons	107
March 27	Syracuse Nationals	96	at	Philadelphia Warriors	119
March 27	Ft. Wayne Zollner Pistons	93	at	St. Louis Hawks	84
March 28	Philadelphia Warriors	104	at	Syracuse Nationals	108
March 29	Syracuse Nationals	104	at	Philadelphia Warriors	109
March 29	St. Louis Hawks	97	at	Fort Wayne Zollner Pistons	102
March 31	Ft. Wayne Zollner Pistons	94	at	Philadelphia Warriors	98
April 1	Philadelphia Warriors	83	at	Fort Wayne Zollner Pistons	84
April 3	Ft. Wayne Zollner Pistons	96	at	Philadelphia Warriors	100
April 5	Philadelphia Warriors	107	at	Fort Wayne Zollner Pistons	105
April 7	Ft. Wayne Zollner Pistons	88	at	Philadelphia Warriors	99

All Star Teams

First Team	Second Team
Bob Pettit (St. Louis Hawks)	Dolph Schayes (Syracuse Nationals)
Paul Arizin (Philadelphia Warriors)	Maurice Stokes (Rochester Royals)
Neil Johnston (Philadelphia Warriors)	Clyde Lovellette (Minneapolis Lakers)
Bob Cousy (Boston Celtics)	Slater Martin (Minneapolis Lakers)
Bill Sharman (Boston Celtics)	Jack George (Philadelphia Warriors)

Individual Awards

Eddie Gottlieb Trophy--Maurice Stokes (Rochester Royals)
Maurice Podoloff Trophy--Bob Pettit (St. Louis Hawks)
NBA All Star Game MVP--Bob Pettit (St. Louis Hawks)

FOOTBALL
National Football League

Eastern Conference

Team Name	GP	W	L	T	PF	PA	Pct
New York Giants	12	8	3	1	264	197	.708
Chicago Cardinals	12	7	5	0	240	182	.583
Washington Redskins	12	6	6	0	183	225	.500
Cleveland Browns	12	5	7	0	167	177	.417
Pittsburgh Steelers	12	5	7	0	217	250	.417
Philadelphia Eagles	12	3	8	1	143	215	.292

Western Conference

Team Name	GP	W	L	T	PF	PA	Pct
Chicago Bears	12	9	2	1	363	246	.792
Detroit Lions	12	9	3	0	300	188	.750
San Francisco49ers	12	5	6	1	233	284	.458
Baltimore Colts	12	5	7	0	270	322	.417
Green Bay Packers	12	4	8	0	264	342	.333
Los Angeles Rams	12	4	8	0	291	307	.333

Coaching Changes

Philadelphia--Hugh Devore 3-8-1; Bears--Paddy Driscoll 9-2-1; San Francisco--Frankie Albert 5-6-1.

League Leaders

Yards Rushing		**Yards Passing**		**Passing %** (40 attempts)	
Rick Casares	1126	Tobin Rote	2203	George Ratterman	68
Ollie Matson	924	Bobby Layne	1909	George Shaw	60
Hugh McElhenny	916	Ed Brown	1667	Harry Gilmer	59
Alan Ameche	858	Y.A. Tittle	1641	Ed Brown	57
Frank Gifford	819	Ted Marchibroda	1585	Y.A. Tittle	57

Receiving Yards		**Receptions**		**Field Goals**	
Bill Howton	1188	Bill Wilson	60	Sam Baker	17
Harlon Hill	1128	Bill Howton	55	Gord Soltau	13
Bill Wilson	889	Frank Gifford	51	George Blanda	12
Jim Mutscheller	715	Harlon Hill	47	Bobby Layne	12
Leon Clarke	650	Jim Mutscheller	44	Lou Groza	11

Punt Return Yards		**Kickoff Return Yards**	
Carl Taseff	233	Al Carmichael	927
Frank Bernardi	217	Joe Arenas	801
Ken Konz	187	Tom Wilson	477
Al Carmichael	165	Don Bingham	444
Ken Keller	146	Jack Losch	390

Pro Bowl Game

(Memorial Coliseum, Los Angeles)

January 13 1957	Western Conference	19	Eastern Conference	10

NFL Championship

December 30	Chicago Bears	7	at	New York Giants	47

Individual Awards

Jim Thorpe Trophy--Frank Gifford (New York Giants)
Pro-Bowl MVP--Bert Rechichar (Baltimore Colts)
Ernie Stautner (Pittsburgh Steelers)
U.P.I. NFL-NFC Coach of the Year--Buddy Parker (Detroit Lions)
U.P.I. NFL-NFC Rookie of the Year--Lenny Moore (Baltimore Colts)
U.P.I. MVP--Frank Gifford (New York Giants)

Rules

NFL commissioner Bert Bell banned all electronic communication between coaches and on field players. Before this many teams had radio receivers installed in the quarterbacks helmets.

Notes

The NFL signed a contract with CBS television network for coverage of all league games, although home games were blacked out within a 50 mile radius.

Canadian Football Council
Interprovincial Rugby Football Union

Team Name	GP	W	L	T	PF	PA	Pts	Pct
Montreal Alouettes	14	10	4	0	478	361	20	.714
Hamilton Tiger-Cats	14	7	7	0	383	385	14	.500
Ottawa Rough Riders	14	7	7	0	326	359	14	.500
Toronto Argonauts	14	4	10	0	331	413	8	.286

Western Interprovincial Football Union

Team Name	GP	W	L	T	PF	PA	Pts	Pct
Edmonton Eskimos	16	11	5	0	358	235	22	.688
Saskatchewan Roughriders	16	10	6	0	353	272	20	.625
Winnipeg Blue Bombers	16	9	7	0	315	228	18	.563
British Columbia Lions	16	6	10	0	251	361	12	.375
Calgary Stampeders	16	4	12	0	229	410	8	.250

Coaching Changes

Hamilton--Jim Trimble 7-7-0; Ottawa--Frank Clair 7-7-0; British Columbia--Clem Crowe 6-10-0; Calgary--Jack Hennemier 2-2-0, Otis Douglas 2-10-0.

League Leaders

Yards Rushing

Normie Kwong	1437
Earl Lunsford	1283
Bob McNamara	1101
Pat Abbruzzi	1062

Yards Passing

Sam Etcheverry	4723

Passing %

Sam Etcheverry	62

Receiving Yards

Hal Patterson	1914
Bob Simpson	1030

Receptions

Hal Patterson	88

Punting Average

Cam Fraser	46.0

Points

Buddy Leake	103

All-Star Game
(at Empire Stadium, Vancouver)

December 8	West	15		East	0

Grey Cup

November 3	Winnipeg Blue Bombers	7	at	Saskatchewan Roughriders	42
November 5	Saskatchewan	8	at	Winnipeg Blue Bombers	19
November 7	Ottawa Rough Riders	21	at	Hamilton Tiger-Cats	46
November 10	Edmonton Eskimos	22	at	Saskatchewan Roughriders	23
November 10	Montreal Alouettes	30	at	Hamilton Tiger-Cats	21
November 12	Saskatchewan	12	at	Edmonton Eskimos	20
November 17	Saskatchewan	7	at	Edmonton Eskimos	51
November 17	Hamilton Tiger-Cats	41	at	Montreal Alouettes	48
November 24	Edmonton Eskimos	50		Montreal Alouettes	27 *

Individual Awards
Dave Dryburgh Memorial Trophy--Buddy Leake (Winnipeg Blue Bombers)
Dr. Beattie Martin Trophy--Norm Rauhaus (Winnipeg Blue Bombers)
Eddie James Memorial Trophy--Normie Kwong (Edmonton Eskimos)
Gruen Trophy--Tommy Grant (Hamilton Tiger-Cats)
Jeff Nicklin Memorial Trophy--Jackie Parker (Edmonton Eskimos)
Jeff Russel Memorial Trophy--Hal Patterson (Montreal Alouettes)
Schenley Award Most Outstanding Canadian--Normie Kwong (Edmonton Eskimos)
Schenley Award Most Outstanding Lineman--Kaye Vaughan (Ottawa Rough Riders)
Schenley Award Most Outstanding Player--Hal Patterson (Montreal Alouettes)

Notes
The Canadian Rugby Union changed its name to the Canadian Football Council on January 22, 1956. Sydney Halter was named as first Commissioner.

HOCKEY
National Hockey League

Team Name	GP	W	L	T	GF	GA	Pts	Pct
Montreal Canadiens	70	45	15	10	222	131	100	.714
Detroit Red Wings	70	30	24	16	183	148	76	.543
New York Rangers	70	32	28	10	204	203	74	.529
Toronto Maple Leafs	70	24	33	13	153	181	61	.436
Boston Bruins	70	23	34	13	147	185	59	.421
Chicago Black Hawks	70	19	39	12	155	216	50	.357

Coaching Changes
Montreal--Hector Blake 45-15-10; New York--Phil Watson 32-28-10; Boston--Milt Schmidt 23-34-13; Chicago--Dick Irvin 19-39-12.

League Leaders

Goals		Assists		Points	
Jean Beliveau	47	Bert Olmstead	56	Jean Beliveau	88
Gordie Howe	38	Andy Bathgate	47	Gordie Howe	79
Rocket Richard	38	Bill Gadsby	42	Rocket Richard	71
Tod Sloan	37	Jean Beliveau	41	Bert Olmstead	70
Bernie Geoffrion	29	Gordie Howe	41	Tod Sloan	66

*Game played in Toronto

Penalty Minutes		GAA		Wins	
Lou Fontinato	202	Jacques Plante	1.86	Jacques Plante	42
Ted Lindsay	161	Glenn Hall	2.11	Lorne Worsley	32
Jean Beliveau	148	Terry Sawchuk	2.66	Glenn Hall	30
Bob Armstrong	122	Harry Lumley	2.71	Terry Sawchuk	22
Vic Stasiuk	118	Lorne Worsley	2.90	Harry Lumley	21

Shutouts

Glenn Hall	12
Terry Sawchuk	9
Jacques Plante	7
Lorne Worsley	4
Harry Lumley	3

All-Star Game
(Olympia Stadium, Detroit)

October 2 1955	Detroit Red Wings	3		All-Stars	1

Stanley Cup Playoffs

March 20	New York Rangers	1	at	Montreal Canadiens	7
March 20	Toronto Maple Leafs	2	at	Detroit Red Wings	3
March 22	New York Rangers	4	at	Montreal Canadiens	2
March 22	Toronto Maple Leafs	1	at	Detroit Red Wings	3
March 24	Montreal Canadiens	3	at	New York Rangers	1
March 24	Detroit Red Wings	5	at	Toronto Maple Leafs	4 [4:22]
March 25	Montreal Canadiens	5	at	New York Rangers	3
March 27	Detroit Red Wings	0	at	Toronto Maple Leafs	2
March 27	New York Rangers	0	at	Montreal Canadiens	7
March 29	Toronto Maple Leafs	1	at	Detroit Red Wings	3
March 31	Detroit Red Wings	4	at	Montreal Canadiens	6
April 3	Detroit Red Wings	1	at	Montreal Canadiens	5
April 5	Montreal Canadiens	1	at	Detroit Red Wings	3
April 8	Montreal Canadiens	3	at	Detroit Red Wings	0
April 10	Detroit Red Wings	1	at	Montreal Canadiens	3

All Star Teams

First Team		Second Team
Jacques Plante	Goal	Glenn Hall
Doug Harvey	Defense	Leonard Kelly
Bill Gadsby	Defense	Tom Johnson
Jean Beliveau	Center	Tod Sloan
Maurice Richard	Right Wing	Gordie Howe
Ted Lindsay	Left Wing	Bert Olmstead

Individual Awards

Art Ross Trophy--Jean Beliveau (Montreal Canadiens)
Calder Memorial Trophy--Glenn Hall (Detroit Red Wings)
Hart Trophy--Jean Beliveau (Montreal Canadiens)
James Norris Trophy--Doug Harvey (Montreal Canadiens)
Lady Byng Memorial Trophy--Earl Reibel (Detroit Red Wings)
Vezina Trophy--Jacques Plante (Montreal Canadiens)

Franchise Changes

NBA--Milwaukee Hawks became the St. Louis Hawks.

Other Sports

Horseracing--Kentucky Derby won by Needles (time 2:03.2, purse $123,450).

Heavyweight Boxing--Floyd Patterson knocked-out Archie Moore in -5 rounds, to claim the title.

Golf--U.S. Open won by Cary Middlecoff with a score of 281.

Auto Racing--Indianapolis 500 won by Pat Flaherty (ave. speed 128.490 MPH).

Tennis--U.S. Open won by Ken Rosewall in the men's singles.
U.S. Open won by Ken Rosewall and Lewis Hoad in the men's doubles.
U.S. Open won by Shirley J. Fry in the women's singles.
U.S. Open won by A. Louise Brough and Margaret 0. du Pont in the women's doubles.
U.S. Open won by Margaret 0. du Pont and Ken Rosewall in the mixed doubles.

1957

BASEBALL
National League

Team Name	W	L	Pct	GB	R	OR
Milwaukee Braves	95	39	.617	-	772	613
St. Louis Cardinals	87	67	.565	8	737	666
Brooklyn Dodgers	84	70	.545	11	690	591
Cincinnati Reds	80	74	.519	15	747	781
Philadelphia Phillies	77	77	.500	18	623	656
New York Giants	69	85	.448	26	643	701
Chicago Cubs	62	92	.403	33	628	722
Pittsburgh Pirates	62	92	.403	33	586	696

Coaching Changes

Milwaukee--Fred Haney 95-59; Chicago--Bob Scheffing 62-92; Pittsburgh--Bobby Bragan 36-67, Danny Murtaugh 26-25.

League Leaders

Batting Average

Stan Musial	.351
Willie Mays	.333
Frank Robinson	.322
Hank Aaron	.322
Dick Groat	.315

Home Runs

Hank Aaron	44
Ernie Banks	43
Duke Snider	40
Willie Mays	35
Eddie Mathews	32

RBI

Hank Aaron	132
Del Ennis	105
Ernie Banks	102
Stan Musial	102
Gil Hodges	98

Stolen Bases

Willie Mays	38
Jim Gilliam	26
Don Blasingame	21
John Temple	19
Chico Fernandez	18

ERA

John Podres	2.66
Don Drysdale	2.69
Warren Spahn	2.69
Bob Buhl	2.74
Vern Law	2.87

Wins

Warren Spahn	21
Jack Sanford	19
Bob Buhl	18
Don Drysdale	17
Lew Burdette	17

Saves

Clement Labine	17
Marv Grissom	14
Joseph Lown	12
Hoyt Wilhelm	11
Dick Farrell	10

Strikeouts

Jack Sanford	188
Dick Drott	170
Moe Drabowsky	170
Sam Jones	154
Don Drysdale	148

American League

Team Name	W	L	Pct	GB	R	OR
New York Yankees	98	56	.636	-	723	534
Chicago White Sox	90	64	.584	8	707	566
Boston Red Sox	82	72	.532	16	721	668
Detroit Tigers	78	76	.506	20	614	614
Baltimore Orioles	76	76	.500	21	597	588
Cleveland Indians	76	77	.497	21.5	682	722
Kansas City Athletics	59	94	.386	38.5	563	710
Washington Senators	55	99	.357	43	603	808

Coaching Changes

Chicago--Al Lopez 90-64; Detroit--Jack Tighe 78-76; Cleveland--Kerby Farrell 76-77; Kansas City--Lou Boudreau 36-67, Harry Craft 23-21; Washington--Charles Dressen 5-16, Harry "Cookie" Lavagetto 50-83.

League Leaders

Batting Average		Home Runs		RBI	
Ted Williams	.388	Roy Sievers	42	Roy Sievers	114
Mickey Mantle	.365	Ted Williams	38	Vic Wertz	105
Gene Woodling	.321	Mickey Mantle	34	Frank Malzone	103
Bob Boyd	.318	Vic Wertz	28	Minnie Minoso	103
Nelson Fox	.317	Gus Zernial	27	Jack Jensen	103

Stolen Bases		ERA		Wins	
Luis Aparicio	28	Bob Shantz	2.45	Jim Bunning	20
Jim Rivera	18	Tom Sturdivant	2.54	Bill Pierce	20
Minnie Minoso	18	Jim Bunning	2.69	Dick Donovan	16
Mickey Mantle	16	Bob Turley	2.71	Tom Sturdivant	16
Jim Landis	14	Frank Sullivan	2.73	Tom Brewer	16

Saves		Strikeouts	
Bob Grim	19	Early Wynn	184
Ray Narleski	16	Jim Bunning	182
Ike Delock	11	Cliff Johnson	177
George Zuverink	9	Bill Pierce	171
Gene Clevenger	8	Bob Turley	152

All-Star Game

(Busch Stadium, St. Louis)

July 9	American League	6	National League	5

World Series

October 2	Milwaukee Braves	1	at	New York Yankees	3
October 3	Milwaukee Braves	4	at	New York Yankees	2
October 5	New York Yankees	12	at	Milwaukee Braves	3
October 6	New York Yankees	5	at	Milwaukee Braves	7 [10]
October 7	New York Yankees	0	at	Milwaukee Braves	1
October 9	Milwaukee Braves	2	at	New York Yankees	3
October 10	Milwaukee Braves	5	at	New York Yankees	0

Individual Awards

Baseball Writers Award--Hank Aaron (Milwaukee Braves NL)
Mickey Mantle (New York Yankees AL)
Cy Young Award--Warren Spahn (Milwaukee Braves NL)
Rookie of the Year--Jack Sanford (Philadelphia Phillies NL)
Tony Kubek (New York Yankees AL)
Sporting News Executive of the Year--France Lane (St. Louis Cardinals NL)
Sporting News Manager of the Year--Fred Hutchinson (St. Louis Cardinals NL)
Sporting News Pitcher of the Year--Warren Spahn (Milwaukee Braves NL)
Bill Pierce (Chicago White Sox AL)
Sporting News Player of the Year--Stan Musial (St. Louis Cardinals NL)
Ted Williams (Boston Red Sox AL)
Sporting News Rookie of the Year--Ed Bouchee (Philadelphia Phillies NL)
Jack Sanford (Philadelphia Phillies NL)
Tony Kubek (New York Yankees AL)
World Series MVP--Lew Burdette (Milwaukee Braves NL)

Hall of Fame Inductees

Sam Crawford, Joe McCarthy

BASKETBALL
National Basketball Association

Eastern Division

Team Name	GP	W	L	PPGF	PPGA	Pct	GB
Boston Celtics	72	44	28	105.5	100.2	.611	-
Syracuse Nationals	72	38	34	99.7	101.1	.528	6
Philadelphia Warriors	72	37	35	100.4	98.8	.514	7
New York Knickerbockers	72	36	36	100.8	100.9	.500	8

Western Division

Team Name	GP	W	L	PPGF	PPGA	Pct	GB
St. Louis Hawks	72	34	38	98.5	98.6	.472	-
Minneapolis Lakers	72	34	38	102.3	103.1	.472	-
Fort Wayne Pistons	72	34	38	96.4	98.7	.472	-
Rochester Royals	72	31	41	93.4	95.6	.431	3

Coaching Changes

Syracuse--Al Cervi 4-8, Paul Seymour 34-26; New York--Vince Boryla 36-36; St. Louis--Red Holzman 14-19, Slater Martin 5-3, Alex Hannum 15-16.

League Leaders

Field Goals		Free Throws		Assists	
Paul Arizin	613	Dolph Schayes	625	Bob Cousy	478
Bob Pettit	613	Paul Arizin	591	Jack McMahon	367
Clyde Lovellette	574	Neil Johnston	535	Maurice Stokes	331
George Yardley	522	Bob Pettit	529	Jack George	307
Neil Johnston	520	George Yardley	503	Slater Martin	269

Points		Fouls	
Paul Arizin	1817	Vern Mikkelsen	312
Bob Pettit	1755	Dick Ricketts	307
Dolph Schayes	1617	Tom Heinsohn	304
Neil Johnston	1575	Maurice Stokes	287
George Yardley	1547	Ray Felix	284

All-Star Game

(at Boston Gardens, Boston)

January 15	East Division	109	West Division	97

NBA Playoffs

March 14	Fort Wayne Pistons	103	at	St. Louis Hawks	115
March 16	Syracuse Nationals	103	at	Philadelphia Warriors	96
March 16	Minneapolis Lakers	111	at	St. Louis Hawks	114
March 17	Fort Wayne Pistons	127	at	Minneapolis Lakers	131
March 18	Philadelphia Warriors	80	at	Syracuse Nationals	91
March 19	Minneapolis Lakers	110	at	Fort Wayne Pistons	108
March 21	Syracuse Nationals	90	at	Boston Celtics	108
March 21	Minneapolis Lakers	109	at	St. Louis Hawks	118
March 23	Boston Celtics	120	at	Syracuse Nationals	105
March 24	Minneapolis Lakers	104	at	St. Louis Hawks	106
March 24	Syracuse Nationals	80	at	Boston Celtics	83
March 25	St. Louis Hawks	143	at	Minneapolis Lakers	135 [OT]
March 30	St. Louis Hawks	125	at	Boston Celtics	123 [OT]
March 31	St. Louis Hawks	99	at	Boston Celtics	119
April 6	Boston Celtics	98	at	St. Louis Hawks	100
April 7	Boston Celtics	123	at	St. Louis Hawks	118
April 9	St. Louis Hawks	109	at	Boston Celtics	124
April 11	Boston Celtics	94	at	St. Louis Hawks	96
April 13	St. Louis Hawks	123	at	Boston Celtics	125 [OT]

All Star Teams

First Team	Second Team
Paul Arizin (Philadelphia Warriors)	George Yardley (Fort Wayne Pistons)
Dolph Schayes (Syracuse Nationals)	Maurice Stokes (Rochester Royals)
Bob Pettit (St. Louis Hawks)	Neil Johnston (Philadelphia Warriors)
Bob Cousy (Boston Celtics)	Dick Garmaker (Minneapolis Lakers)
Bill Sharman (Boston Celtics)	Slater Martin (St. Louis Hawks)

Individual Awards

Eddie Gottlieb Trophy--Tommy Heinsohn (Boston Celtics)
Maurice Podoloff Trophy--Bob Cousy (Boston Celtics)
NBA All Star Game MVP--Bob Cousy (Boston Celtics)

FOOTBALL
National Football League

Eastern Conference

Team Name	GP	W	L	T	PF	PA	Pct
Cleveland Browns	12	9	2	1	269	172	.792
New York Giants	12	7	5	0	254	211	.583
Pittsburgh Steelers	12	6	6	0	161	178	.500
Washington Redskins	12	5	6	1	251	230	.458
Philadelphia Eagles	12	4	8	0	173	230	.333
Chicago Cardinals	12	3	9	0	200	299	.250

Western Conference

Team Name	GP	W	L	T	PF	PA	Pct
Detroit Lions	12	8	4	0	251	231	.667
San Francisco 49ers	12	8	4	0	260	264	.667
Baltimore Colts	12	7	5	0	303	235	.583
Los Angeles Rams	12	6	6	0	307	278	.500
Chicago Bears	12	5	7	0	203	211	.417
Green Bay Packers	12	3	9	0	218	311	.250

Coaching Changes

Pittsburgh--Buddy Parker 6-6-0; Detroit--George Wilson 8-4-0.

League Leaders

Yards Rushing		Yards Passing		Passing % (40 attempts)	
Jim Brown	942	John Unitas	2550	Y.A. Tittle	63
Rick Casares	700	Y.A. Tittle	2157	Ed LeBaron	59
Don Besseler	673	Norm Van Brocklin	2105	Tom O'Connell	57
John Johnson	621	Earl Morrall	1900	John Unitas	57
Tom Wilson	616	Chuck Conerly	1712	Chuck Conerly	55

Receiving Yards		Receptions		Field Goals	
Ray Berry	800	Bill Wilson	52	Lou Groza	15
Billy Wilson	757	Ray Berry	47	Sam Baker	14
Bill Howton	727	Jack McClairen	46	George Blanda	14
Lenny Moore	687	Frank Gifford	41	Fred Cone	12
Jack McClairen	630	Lenny Moore	40	Paige Cothren	11

Punt Return Yards		Kickoff Return Yards	
Bert Zagers	217	Al Carmichael	690
Al Carmichael	190	Woodley Lewis	682
Woodley Lewis	175	Joe Arenas	657
Billy Wells	143	Gene Filipski	613
Yale Lary	139	Jon Arnett	504

Pro-Bowl Game
(Memorial Coliseum, Los Angeles)

January 12 1958	Western Conference	26	Eastern Conference	7

NFL Championship

December 22	Detroit Lions	31	at	San Francisco 49ers	27
December 29	Cleveland Browns	14	at	Detroit Lions	59

Individual Awards

AP MVP--Jim Brown (Cleveland Browns)
Jim Thorpe Trophy--John Unitas (Baltimore Colts)
Pro-Bowl MVP--Hugh McElhenny (San Francisco 49ers)
Gene Brito (Washington Redskins)
U.P.I. NFL-NFC Coach of the Year--Paul Brown (Cleveland Browns)
U.P.I. NFL-NFC Rookie of the Year--Jim Brown (Cleveland Browns)
U.P.I. MVP--Y.A. Tittle (San Francisco 49ers)

Canadian Football Council
Interprovincial Rugby Football Union

Team Name	GP	W	L	T	PF	PA	Pts	Pct
Hamilton Tiger-Cats	14	10	4	0	250	189	20	.714
Ottawa Rough Riders	14	8	6	0	326	237	16	.571
Montreal Alouettes	14	6	8	0	287	301	12	.429
Toronto Argonauts	14	4	10	0	274	410	8	.286

Western Interprovincial Football Union

Team Name	GP	W	L	T	PF	PA	Pts	Pct
Edmonton Eskimos	16	14	2	0	475	142	28	.875
Winnipeg Blue Bombers	16	12	4	0	406	300	24	.750
Calgary Stampeders	16	6	10	0	221	413	12	.375
British Columbia Lions	16	4	11	1	284	369	9	.281
Saskatchewan Roughriders	16	3	12	1	276	438	7	.219

Coaching Changes

Toronto--Hamp Pool 4-10-0; Winnipeg--Bud Grant 12-4-0; Calgary--Otis Douglas 6-10-0.

League Leaders

Yards Rushing

Johnny Bright	1679
Gerry James	1192
Gerry McDougall	1053
Normie Kwong	1050

Yards Passing

Sam Etcheverry 3341

Passing %

Sam Etcheverry 53

Receiving Yards

Red O'Quinn 1006

Receptions

Red O'Quinn 61

Punting Average

Cam Fraser 46.0

Points

Gerry James 131

All-Star Game
(at McGill Stadium, Montreal)

December 7	East	20	West	2

Grey Cup

November 9	Calgary Stampeders	13	at	Winnipeg Blue Bombers	13
November 11	Winnipeg Blue Bombers	15	at	Calgary Stampeders	3
November 13	Montreal Alouettes	24	at	Ottawa Rough Riders	15
November 16	Edmonton Eskimos	7	at	Winnipeg Blue Bombers	19
November 16	Hamilton Tiger-Cats	17	at	Montreal Alouettes	10
November 20	Winnipeg Blue Bombers	4	at	Edmonton Eskimos	5
November 23	Winnipeg Blue Bombers	17	at	Edmonton Eskimos	2 [OT]
November 23	Montreal Alouettes	1	at	Hamilton Tiger-Cats	23
November 30	Hamilton Tiger-Cats	32		Winnipeg Blue Bombers	7 *

Individual Awards

Dave Dryburgh Memorial Trophy--Gerry James (Winnipeg Blue Bombers)
DeMarco-Becket Memorial Trophy--Art Walker (Edmonton Eskimos)
Dr. Beattie Martin Trophy--Mike Lashuk (Edmonton Eskimos)
Eddie James Memorial Trophy--Johnny Bright (Edmonton Eskimos)
Gruen Trophy--Gary Williams (Toronto Argonauts)
Jeff Nicklin Memorial Trophy--Jackie Parker (Edmonton Eskimos)
Jeff Russel Memorial Trophy--Dick Shatto (Toronto Argonauts)
Schenley Award Most Outstanding Canadian--Gerry James (Winnipeg Blue Bombers)
Schenley Award Most Outstanding Lineman--Kaye Vaughan (Ottawa Rough Riders)
Schenley Award Most Outstanding Player--Jackie Parker (Edmonton Eskimos)

Rules

Interference by eligible blockers legal up to the 5 yard line.

Notes

The first Grey Cup game telecast coast to coast in Canada took place on November 30th. TV rights brought $125,000.

HOCKEY

National Hockey League

Team Name	GP	W	L	T	GF	GA	Pts	Pct
Detroit Red Wings	70	38	20	12	198	157	88	.629
Montreal Canadiens	70	35	23	12	210	155	82	.586
Boston Bruins	70	34	24	12	195	174	80	.571
New York Rangers	70	26	30	14	184	227	66	.471
Toronto Maple Leafs	70	21	34	15	174	192	57	.407
Chicago Black Hawks	70	16	39	15	169	225	47	.336

Coaching Changes

Toronto--Howie Meeker 21-34-15; Chicago--Tommy Ivan 16-39-15.

League Leaders

Goals		Assists		Points	
Gordie Howe	44	Ted Lindsay	55	Gordie Howe	89
Jean Beliveau	33	Jean Beliveau	51	Ted Lindsay	85
Rocket Richard	33	Andy Bathgate	50	Jean Beliveau	84
Ed Litzenberger	32	Gordie Howe	45	Andy Bathgate	77
Real Chevrefils	31	Doug Harvey	44	Ed Litzenberger	64

*Game played in Toronto

Penalty Minutes		**GAA**		**Wins**	
Gus Mortson	147	Jacques Plante	2.02	Glenn Hall	38
Lou Fontinato	139	Glenn Hall	2.24	Jacques Plante	31
Leo Labine	128	Terry Sawchuk	2.38	Lorne Worsley	26
Pierre Pilote	117	Don Simmons	2.42	Ed Chadwick	21
Jack Evans	110	Ed Chadwick	2.74	Al Rollins	16

Strikeouts

Jacques Plante	9
Ed Chadwick	5
Glenn Hall	4
Don Simmons	4
Al Rollins	3

All Star Game

(The Forum, Montreal)

October 9 1956	All-Stars	1		Montreal Canadiens	1

Stanley Cup Playoffs

March 26	Boston Bruins	3	at	Detroit Red Wings	1
March 26	Montreal Canadiens	4	at	New York Rangers	1
March 28	Boston Bruins	2	at	Detroit Red Wings	7
March 28	Montreal Canadiens	3	at	New York Rangers	4 [13:38]
March 30	New York Rangers	3	at	Montreal Canadiens	8
March 31	Detroit Red Wings	3	at	Boston Bruins	4
April 2	Detroit Red Wings	0	at	Boston Bruins	2
April 2	New York Rangers	1	at	Montreal Canadiens	3
April 4	New York Rangers	3	at	Montreal Canadiens	4 [2:11]
April 4	Boston Bruins	4	at	Detroit Red Wings	3
April 6	Boston Bruins	1	at	Montreal Canadiens	5
April 9	Boston Bruins	0	at	Montreal Canadiens	1
April 11	Montreal Canadiens	4	at	Boston Bruins	2
April 14	Montreal Canadiens	0	at	Boston Bruins	2
April 16	Boston Bruins	1	at	Montreal Canadiens	5

All Star Teams

First Team		Second Team
Glenn Hall	Goal	Jacques Plante
Doug Harvey	Defense	Fern Flaman
Leonard Kelly	Defense	Bill Gadsby
Jean Beliveau	Center	Ed Litzenberger
Gordie Howe	Right Wing	Maurice Richard
Ted Lindsay	Left Wing	Real Chevrefils

Individual Awards

Art Ross Trophy--Gordie Howe (Detroit Red Wings)
Calder Memorial Trophy--Larry Regan (Boston Bruins)
Hart Trophy--Gordie Howe (Detroit Red Wings)
James Norris Trophy--Doug Harvey (Montreal Canadiens)
Lady Byng Memorial Trophy--Andy Hebenton (New York Rangers)
Vezina Trophy--Jacques Plante (Montreal Canadiens)

Rules

A player serving a minor penalty was allowed to return to the ice if a power play goal was scored. This rule resulted from the fact that the Montreal team had a very devastating power play and would score many goals on just one penalty.

Notes

The National Hockey League Player's Association was formed this year.

Franchise Changes

NBA--Fort Wayne Zollner Pistons became Fort Wayne Pistons.

Other Sports

Horseracing--Kentucky Derby won by Iron Liege (time 2:02.2, purse $107,950).
Heavyweight Boxing--Floyd Patterson knocked-out Hurricane Jackson in 10 rounds.
Floyd Patterson knocked-out Pete Rademacher in 6 rounds.
Golf--U.S. Open won by Dick Mayer in a playoff with Cary Middlecoff (scores of 282-282, 72-79).
Auto Racing--Indianapolis 500 won by Sam Hanks (ave. speed 135.601 MPH).
Tennis--U.S. Open won by Malcolm Anderson in the men's singles.
U.S. Open won by Ashley Cooper and Neale Fraser in the men's doubles.
U.S. Open won by Althea Gibson in the women's singles.
U.S. Open won by Louise Brough and Margaret O. du Pont in the women's doubles.
U.S. Open won by Althea Gibson and Kurt Nielsen in the mixed doubles.

1958

BASEBALL
National League

Team Name	W	L	Pct	GB	R	OR
Milwaukee Braves	92	62	.597	-	675	541
Pittsburgh Pirates	84	70	.545	8	662	607
San Francisco Giants	80	74	.519	12	727	698
Cincinnati Reds	76	78	.494	16	695	621
Chicago Cubs	72	82	.468	20	709	725
St. Louis Cardinals	72	82	.468	20	619	704
Los Angeles Dodgers	71	83	.461	21	668	761
Philadelphia Phillies	69	85	.448	23	664	762

Coaching Changes

Pittsburgh--Danny Murtaugh 84-70; San Francisco--Bill Rigney 80-74; Cincinnati--George "Birdie" Tebbetts 52-61, Jimmy Dykes-24-17; St. Louis--Fred Hutchinson 69-75, Stan Hack 3-7; Los Angeles--Walter Alston 71-83; Philadelphia--Mayo Smith 399-44, Eddie Sawyer 30-41.

League Leaders

Batting Average		Home Runs		RBI	
Richie Ashburn	.350	Ernie Banks	47	Ernie Banks	129
Willie Mays	.347	Frank Thomas	35	Frank Thomas	109
Stan Musial	.337	Eddie Mathews	31	Harry Anderson	97
Hank Aaron	.326	Frank Robinson	31	Willie Mays	96
Bob Skinner	.321	Hank Aaron	30	Orlando Cepeda	96

Stolen Bases		ERA		Wins	
Willie Mays	31	Stuart Miller	2.47	Warren Spahn	22
Richie Ashburn	30	Sam Jones	2.88	Bob Friend	22
Tony Taylor	21	Lew Burdette	2.91	Lew Burdette	20
Don Blasingame	20	Warren Spahn	3.07	Bob Purkey	17
Jim Gilliam	18	Robin Roberts	3.24	Robin Roberts	17

Saves		Strikeouts	
Roy Face	20	Sam Jones	225
Clement Labine	14	Warren Spahn	150
Dick Farrell	11	John Podres	143
John Klippstein	10	John Antonelli	143
Marv Grissom	10	Bob Friend	135

Notes

The National League finally moved to the West coast with the transfer of the New York Giants to San Francisco and the Brooklyn Dodgers to Los Angeles.

American League

Team Name	W	L	Pct	GB	R	OR
New York Yankees	92	62	.597	-	759	577
Chicago White Sox	82	72	.532	10	634	615
Boston Red Sox	79	75	.513	13	697	691
Cleveland Indians	77	76	.503	14.5	694	635
Detroit Tigers	77	77	.500	15	659	606
Baltimore Orioles	74	79	.484	17.5	521	575
Kansas City Athletics	73	81	.474	19	642	713
Washington Senators	61	93	.396	31	553	747

Coaching Changes

Cleveland--Bob Bragan 31-36, Joe Gordon 46-40; Detroit--Jack Tighe 21-28, Bill Norman 56-49; Kansas City--Harry Craft 73-81; Washington--Harry "Cookie" Lavagetto 61-93.

League Leaders

Batting Average		Home Runs		RBI	
Ted Williams	.328	Mickey Mantle	42	Jack Jensen	122
Pete Runnels	.322	Rocky Colavito	41	Rocky Colavito	113
Harvey Kuenn	.319	Roy Sievers	39	Roy Sievers	108
Al Kaline	.313	Bob Cerv	38	Bob Cerv	104
Vic Power	.312	Jack Jensen	35	Mickey Mantle	97

Stolen Bases		ERA		Wins	
Luis Aparicio	29	Edward Ford	2.01	Bob Turley	21
Jim Rivera	21	Bill Pierce	2.68	Bill Pierce	17
Jim Landis	19	Jack Harshman	2.89	Cal McLish	16
Mickey Mantle	18	Frank Lary	2.90	Frank Lary	16
Minnie Minoso	14	Bill O'Dell	2.97	Arnie Portocarrero	15

Saves		Strikeouts	
Ryne Duren	20	Early Wynn	179
Dick Hyde	18	Jim Bunning	177
Leo Kiely	12	Bob Turley	168
Murray Wall	10	Jack Harshman	161
Joseph Lown	8	Camilo Pascual	146

All-Star Game

(Memorial Stadium, Baltimore)

July 8	American League	4	National League	3

World Series

October 1	New York Yankees	3	at	Milwaukee Braves	4 [10]
October 2	New York Yankees	5	at	Milwaukee Braves	13
October 4	Milwaukee Braves	0	at	New York Yankees	4
October 5	Milwaukee Braves	3	at	New York Yankees	0
October 6	Milwaukee Braves	0	at	New York Yankees	7
October 8	New York Yankees	4	at	Milwaukee Braves	3 [10]
October 9	New York Yankees	6	at	Milwaukee Braves	2

Individual Awards

Baseball Writers Award--Ernie Banks (Chicago Cubs NL)
Jackie Jensen (Boston Red Sox AL)
Cy Young Award--Bob Turley (New York Yankees ,AL)
Rookie of the Year--Orlando Cepeda (San Francisco Giants NL)
Albert Pearson (Washington Senators AL)
Sporting News Executive of the Year--Joe Brown (Pittsburgh Pirates NL)
Sporting News Manager of the Year--Casey Stengel (New York Yankees AL)
Sporting News Pitcher of the Year--Warren Spahn (Milwaukee Braves NL)
Bob Turley (New York Yankees AL)
Sporting News Player of the Year--Ernie Banks (Chicago Cubs NL)
Jackie Jensen (Boston Red Sox AL)
Sporting News Rookie of the Year--Orlando Cepeda (San Francisco Giants NL)
Carlton Willey (Milwaukee Braves NL)
Albert Pearson (Washington Senators AL)
Ryne Duren (New York Yankees AL)
World Series MVP--Bob Turley (New York Yankees AL)

BASKETBALL
National Basketball Association

Eastern Division

Team Name	GP	W	L	PPGF	PPGA	Pct	GB
Boston Celtics	72	49	23	109.9	104.4	.681	-
Syracuse Nationals	72	41	31	107.2	105.1	.569	8
Philadelphia Warriors	72	37	35	104.3	104.4	.514	12
New York Knickerbockers	72	35	37	112.1	110.8	.486	14

Eastern Division

Team Name	GP	W	L	PPGF	PPGA	Pct	GB
St. Louis Hawks	72	41	31	107.5	106.2	.569	-
Detroit Pistons	72	33	39	105.3	107.7	.458	8
Cincinnati Royals	72	33	39	101.7	103.1	.458	8
Minneapolis Lakers	72	19	53	105.1	111.5	.264	22

Coaching Changes

Syracuse--Paul Seymour 41-31; St. Louis--Alex Hannum 41-31; Detroit--Charlie Eckman 9-16, Red Rocha 24-23; Cincinnati--Bobby Wanzer 33-39; Minneapolis--George Mikan 9-30, Johnny Kundla 10-23.

League Leaders

Field Goals		Free Throws		Assists	
Clyde Lovellette	679	George Yardley	655	Bob Cousy	463
George Yardley	673	Dolph Schayes	629	Dick McGuire	454
Dolph Schayes	581	Bob Pettit	557	Maurice Stokes	403
Bob Pettit	581	Kenny Sears	452	Carl Braun	393
Bill Sharman	550	Neil Johnston	442	George King	337

Points		**Fouls**	
George Yardley	2001	Walter Dukes	311
Dolph Schayes	1791	Larry Foust	299
Bob Pettit	1719	Vern Mikkelsen	299
Clyde Lovellette	1659	Ray Felix	283
Paul Arizin	1406	Chuck Share	279

All-Star Game

(at St. Louis Arena, St. Louis)

January 21	East Division	130	West Division	118

NBA Playoffs

March 15	Philadelphia Warriors	82	at	Syracuse Nationals	86
March 15	Cincinnati Royals	93	at	Detroit Pistons	100
March 16	Syracuse Nationals	93	at	Philadelphia Warriors	95
March 16	Detroit Pistons	124	at	Cincinnati Royals	104
March 18	Philadelphia Warriors	101	at	Syracuse Nationals	88
March 19	Philadelphia Warriors	98	at	Boston Celtics	107
March 19	Detroit Pistons	111	at	St. Louis Hawks	114
March 22	Boston Celtics	109	at	Philadelphia Warriors	87
March 22	St. Louis Hawks	99	at	Detroit Pistons	96
March 23	Philadelphia Warriors	92	at	Boston Celtics	106
March 23	Detroit Pistons	109	at	St. Louis Hawks	89
March 25	St. Louis Hawks	145	at	Detroit Pistons	101
March 26	Boston Celtics	97	at	Philadelphia Warriors	111
March 27	Detroit Pistons	96	at	St. Louis Hawks	120
March 27	Philadelphia Warriors	88	at	Boston Celtics	93
March 29	St. Louis Hawks	104	at	Boston Celtics	102
March 30	St. Louis Hawks	112	at	Boston Celtics	136
April 2	Boston Celtics	108	at	St. Louis Hawks	111
April 5	Boston Celtics	109	at	St. Louis Hawks	98
April 9	St. Louis Hawks	102	at	Boston Celtics	100
April 12	Boston Celtics	109	at	St. Louis Hawks	110

All Star Teams

First Team	Second Team
Dolph Schayes (Syracuse Nationals)	Cliff Hagan (St. Louis Hawks)
George Yardley (Detroit Pistons)	Maurice Stokes (Cincinnati Royals)
Bob Pettit (St. Louis Hawks)	Bill Russell (Boston Celtics)
Bob Cousy (Boston Celtics)	Tom Gola (Philadelphia Warriors)
Bill Sharman (Boston Celtics)	Slater Martin (St. Louis Hawks)

Individual Awards

Eddie Gottlieb Trophy--Woody Sauldsberry (Philadelphia Warriors)
Maurice Podoloff Trophy--Bill Russell (Boston Celtics)
NBA All Star Game MVP--Bob Pettit (St. Louis Hawks)

Notes

Dolph Schayes of the Syracuse Nationals of the NBA became the highest scoring professional basketball player of all time when he surpassed George Mikan's previous total of 11,764 points. Schayes scored 23 points on January 12 to lead his team to a 135-109 win over the Detroit Pistons.

FOOTBALL
National Football League

Eastern Conference

Team Name	GP	W	L	T	PF	PA	Pct
New York Giants	12	9	3	0	246	183	.750
Cleveland Browns	12	9	3	0	302	217	.750
Pittsburgh Steelers	12	7	4	1	261	230	.625
Washington Redskins	12	4	7	1	214	268	.375
Chicago Cardinals	12	2	9	1	261	356	.208
Philadelphia Eagles	12	2	9	1	235	306	.208

Western Conference

Team Name	GP	W	L	T	PF	PA	Pct
Baltimore Colts	12	9	3	0	381	203	.750
Chicago Bears	12	8	4	0	298	230	.667
Los Angeles Rams	12	8	4	0	344	278	.667
San Francisco 49ers	12	6	6	0	257	324	.500
Detroit Lions	12	4	7	1	261	276	.375
Green Bay Packers	12	1	10	1	193	382	.125

Coaching Changes

Cardinals--Frank Ivy 2-9-1; Philadelphia--Buck Shaw 2-9-1; Bears--George Halas 8-4-0; Green Bay--Ray McLean 1-10-1.

League Leaders

Yards Rushing		Yards Passing		Passing % (40 attempts)	
Jim Brown	1527	Bill Wade	2875	John Brodie	60
Alan Ameche	791	Bobby Layne	2510	Y.A. Tittle	58
Joe Perry	758	Norm Van Brocklin	2409	Milt Plum	54
Tom Tracy	714	John Unitas	2007	Ed LeBaron	54
Jon Arnett	683	Tobin Rote	1678	M.C. Reynolds	54

Receiving Yards		Receptions		Field Goals	
Del Shofner	1097	Pete Retzlaff	56	Tom Miner	14
Lenny Moore	938	Ray Berry	56	Paige Cothren	14
Jim Orr	910	Del Shofner	51	Sam Baker	13
Ray Berry	794	Lenny Moore	50	Pat Summerall	12
Pete Retzlaff	766	Clyde Conner	49	Paul Hornung	11

Punt Return Yards		Kickoff Return Yards	
Jon Arnett	223	Jim Sears	756
Carl Taseff	196	Al Carmichael	700
Yale Lary	196	Ollie Matson	497
Bob Mitchell	165	Bob Mitchell	454
Bill Wells	158	Sid Watson	443

Pro Bowl Game
(Memorial Coliseum, Los Angeles)

January 11 1959	Eastern Conference	28	Western Conference	21

NFL Championship

December 21	Cleveland Browns	0	at	New York Giants	10
December 28	Baltimore Colts	23	at	New York Giants	17 [OT]

Individual Awards

AP MVP--Gino Marchetti (Baltimore Colts)
Jim Thorpe Trophy--Jim Brown (Cleveland Browns)
Pro Bowl MVP--Frank Gifford (New York Giants)
Doug Atkins (Chicago Bears)
Rookie of the Year--Bobby Mitchell (Cleveland Browns)
U.P.I. NFL-NFC Coach of the Year--Weeb Ewbank (Baltimore Colts)
U.P.I. NFL-NFC Rookie of the Year--Jim Orr (Pittsburgh Steelers)
U.P.I. MVP--Jim Brown (Cleveland Browns)

Notes

The NFL championship game went into overtime, the first time the game had gone into overtime since the rule had been adopted in 1955.

Canadian Football League
Interprovincial Rugby Football Union

Team Name	GP	W	L	T	PF	PA	Pts	Pct
Hamilton Tiger-Cats	14	10	3	1	291	235	21	.750
Montreal Alouettes	14	7	6	1	265	269	15	.536
Ottawa Rough Riders	14	6	8	0	233	243	12	.429
Toronto Argonauts	14	4	10	0	266	308	8	.286

Western Interprovincial Football Union

Team Name	GP	W	L	T	PF	PA	Pts	Pct
Winnipeg Blue Bombers	16	13	3	0	361	182	26	.813
Edmonton Eskimos	16	9	6	1	312	292	19	.594
Saskatchewan Roughriders	16	7	7	2	320	324	16	.500
Calgary Stampeders	16	6	9	1	314	312	13	.406
British Columbia Lions	16	3	13	0	202	399	6	.188

Coaching Changes

Toronto--Hamp Pool 4-10-0; Edmonton--Sam Lyle 9-6-1; Saskatchewan--George Terlep7-7-2; British Columbia--Clem Crowe 0-6-0, Dan Edwards 3-7-0.

League Leaders

Yards Rushing

Johnny Bright	1722
Cookie Gilchrist	1254
Leo Lewis	1160
Gerry McDougall	1109
Normie Kwong	1033

Yards Passing

Sam Etcheverry	3548

Passing %

Sam Etcheverry	58

Receiving Yards

Jack Hill	1065

Receptions

Red O'Quinn	65

Punting Average

Cam Fraser	45.6

Points

Jack Hill	145

All-Star Game
(Civic Stadium, Hamilton)

December 6	West	9	East	3

Grey Cup Playoffs

November 8	Edmonton Eskimos	27	at	Saskatchewan Roughriders	11
November 11	Saskatchewan Roughriders	1	at	Edmonton Eskimos	31
November 12	Ottawa Rough Riders	26	at	Montreal Alouettes	12
November 15	Winnipeg Blue Bombers	30	at	Edmonton Eskimos	7
November 15	Hamilton Tiger-Cats	35	at	Ottawa Rough Riders	7
November 19	Edmonton Eskimos	30	at	Winnipeg blue Bombers	7
November 22	Ottawa Rough Riders	7	at	Hamilton Tiger-Cats	19
November 22	Edmonton Eskimos	7	at	Winnipeg Blue Bombers	23
November 29	Winnipeg Blue Bombers	35	at	Hamilton Tiger-Cats	28 *

Individual Awards

Dave Dryburgh Memorial Trophy--Jack Hill (Saskatchewan Roughriders)
DeMarco-Becket Memorial Trophy--Don Luzzi (Calgary Stampeders)
Dr. Beattie Martin Trophy--Walt Radzick (Calgary Stampeders)
Eddie James Memorial Trophy--Johnny Bright (Edmonton Eskimos)
Gruen Trophy--Ron Brewer (Toronto Argonauts)
Jeff Nicklin Memorial Trophy--Jackie Parker (Edmonton Eskimos)
Jeff Russel Memorial Trophy--Sam Etcheverry (Montreal Alouettes)
Schenley Award Most Outstanding Canadian--Ron Howell (Hamilton Tiger-Cats)
Schenley Award Most Outstanding Lineman--Don Luzzi (Calgary Stampeders)
Schenley Award Most Outstanding Player--Jackie Parker (Edmonton Eskimos)

Notes

The Canadian Football Council withdrew from the Canadian Rugby Union and renamed itself the Canadian Football League.

HOCKEY
National Hockey League

Team Name	GP	W	L	T	GF	GA	Pts	Pct
Montreal Canadiens	70	43	17	10	250	158	96	.686
New York Rangers	70	32	25	13	195	188	77	.550
Detroit Red Wings	70	29	29	12	176	207	70	.500
Boston Bruins	70	27	28	15	199	194	69	.493
Chicago Black Hawks	70	24	39	7	163	202	55	.393
Toronto Maple Leafs	70	21	38	11	192	226	53	.379

Coaching Changes

Detroit--Jim Skinner 13-17-7, Sid Abel 16-12-5; Chicago--Rudy Pilous 24-39-7; Toronto--Bill Reay 21-38-11.

*Game played in Vancouver

League Leaders

Goals		Assists		Points	
Dickie Moore	36	Henri Richard	52	Dickie Moore	84
Gordie Howe	33	Dickie Moore	48	Henri Richard	80
Ed Litzenberger	32	Andy Bathgate	48	Andy Bathgate	78
Camille Henry	32	Gordie Howe	44	Gordie Howe	77
Andy Bathgate	30	Fleming Mackell	40	Bronco Horvath	66

Penalty Minutes		GAA		Wins	
Lou Fontinato	152	Jacques Plante	2.11	Jacques Plante	34
Forbes Kennedy	135	Lorne Worsley	2.32	Terry Sawchuk	29
Doug Harvey	131	Don Simmons	2.50	Glenn Hall	24
Ted Lindsay	110	Harry Lumley	2.84	Lorne Worsley	21
Jack Evans	108	Glenn Hall	2.89	Ed Chadwick	21

Shutouts	
Jacques Plante	9
Glenn Hall	7
Don Simmons	5
Ed Chadwick	4
Lorne Worsley	4

All-Star Game

(The Forum, Montreal)

October 5 1957	All-Stars	5	Montreal Canadiens	3

Stanley Cup Playoffs

March 25	Detroit Red Wings	1	at	Montreal Canadiens	8
March 25	Boston Bruins	3	at	New York Rangers	5
March 27	Detroit Red Wings	1	at	Montreal Canadiens	5
March 27	Boston Bruins	4	at	New York Rangers	3 [4:46]
March 29	New York Rangers	0	at	Boston Bruins	5
March 30	Montreal Canadiens	2	at	Detroit Red Wings	1 [11:52]
April 1	New York Rangers	5	at	Boston Bruins	2
April 1	Montreal Canadiens	4	at	Detroit Red Wings	3
April 3	New York Rangers	1	at	Boston Bruins	6
April 5	New York Rangers	2	at	Boston Bruins	8
April 8	Boston Bruins	1	at	Montreal Canadiens	2
April 10	Boston Bruins	5	at	Montreal Canadiens	2
April 13	Montreal Canadiens	3	at	Boston Bruins	0
April 15	Montreal Canadiens	1	at	Boston Bruins	3
April 17	Boston Bruins	2	at	Montreal Canadiens	3 [5:451
April 20	Montreal Canadiens	5	at	Boston Bruins	3

All Star Teams

First Team		Second Team
Glenn Hall	Goal	Jacques Plante
Doug Harvey	Defense	Fern Flaman
Bill Gadsby	Defense	Marcel Pronovost
Henri Richard	Center	Jean Beliveau
Gordie Howe	Right Wing	Andy Bathgate
Dickie Moore	Left Wing	Camille Henry

Individual Awards

Art Ross Trophy--Dickie Moore (Montreal Canadiens)
Calder Memorial Trophy--Frank Mahovlich (Toronto Maple Leafs)
Hart Trophy--Gordie Howe (Detroit Red Wings)
James Norris Trophy--Doug Harvey (Montreal Canadiens)
Lady Byng Memorial Trophy--Camille Henry (New York Rangers)
Vezina Trophy--Jacques Plante (Montreal Canadiens)

Hall of Fame Inductees

Frank Boucher, King Clancy, Sprague Cleghorn, Alex Connell, George Dudley, Mervyn Dutton, Frank Foyston, Frank Frederickson, Herb Gardiner, George Hay, Dick Irvin Sr., Ching Johnson, Gordon Keats, Hugh Lehman, George McNamara, Paddy Moran, James Norris Sr., Frank Patrick, Allan Pickard, Senator Donat Raymond, Conn Smythe, Lloyd Turner

Notes

Willie O'Ree became the first black to play in the NHL when he appeared in a game on January 18th helping his Boston team to defeat Montreal 3 to 0.

Franchise Changes

NL--New York Giants became the San Francisco Giants.
NL--Brooklyn Dodgers became the Los Angeles Dodgers.
NBA--Fort Wayne Pistons became the Detroit Pistons.
NBA--Rochester Royals became the Cincinnati Royals.

Other Sports

Horseracing--Kentucky Derby won by Tim Tam (time 2:05, purse $116,400).
Heavyweight Boxing--Floyd Patterson knocked-out Roy Harris in 12 rounds.
Golf--U.S. Open won by Tommy Bolt with a score of 283.
Auto Racing--Indianapolis 500 won by Jimmy Bryan (ave. speed 133.791 MPH)
Tennis--U.S. Open won by Ashley Cooper in the men's singles.
U.S. Open won by Hamilton Richardson and Alejandro Olmedo in the men's doubles.
U.S. Open won by Althea Gibson in the women's singles.
U.S. Open won by Darlene Hard and Jeanne Arth in the women's doubles.
U.S. Open won by Margaret O. du Pont and Neale Fraser in the mixed doubles.

1959

BASEBALL
National League

Team Name	W	L	Pct	GB	R	OR
Los Angeles Dodgers	88	68	.564	-	705	670
Milwaukee Braves	86	70	.551	2	724	623
San Francisco Giants	83	71	.539	4	705	613
Pittsburgh Pirates	78	76	.506	9	651	680
Chicago Cubs	74	80	.481	13	673	688
Cincinnati Reds	74	80	.481	13	764	738
St. Louis Cardinals	71	83	.461	16	641	725
Philadelphia Phillies	64	90	.416	23	599	725

Coaching Changes

Cincinnati--Mayo Smith 35-45, Fred Hutchinson 39-35; St. Louis--Solomon Hemus 71-83; Philadelphia--Eddie Sawyer 64-90.

League Leaders

Batting Average		Home Runs		RBI	
Hank Aaron	.355	Eddie Mathews	46	Ernie Banks	143
Joe Cunningham	.345	Ernie Banks	45	Frank Robinson	125
Orlando Cepeda	.317	Hank Aaron	39	Hank Aaron	123
Vada Pinson	.316	Frank Robinson	36	Gus Bell	115
Willie Mays	.313	Willie Mays	34	Eddie Mathews	114

Stolen Bases		ERA		Wins	
Willie Mays	27	Sam Jones	2.83	Warren Spahn	21
Orlando Cepeda	23	Stu Miller	2.84	Sam Jones	21
Tony Taylor	23	Bob Buhl	2.86	Lew Burdette	21
Jim Gilliam	23	Warren Spahn	2.96	John Antonelli	19
Vada Pinson	21	Vernon Law	2.98	Roy Face	18

Saves		Strikeouts	
Lindy McDaniel	15	Don Drysdale	242
Don McMahon	15	Sam Jones	209
Don Elston	13	Sandy Koufax	173
Bill Henry	12	John Antonelli	165
Roy Face	10	Mike McCormick	151

Notes

Los Angeles defeated Milwaukee 2 games to 0 in a playoff for the National League pennant.

American League

Team Name	W	L	Pct	GB	R	OR
Chicago White Sox	94	60	.610	-	669	588
Cleveland Indians	89	65	.578	5	745	646
New York Yankees	79	75	.513	15	687	647
Detroit Tigers	76	78	.494	18	713	732
Boston Red Sox	75	79	.487	19	726	696
Baltimore Orioles	74	80	.481	20	551	621
Kansas City Athletics	66	88	.429	28	681	760
Washington Senators	63	91	.409	31	619	701

Coaching Changes

Cleveland--Joe Gordon 89-65; Detroit--Bill Norman 2-15, Jimmy Dykes 74-63; Boston--Michael Higgins 31-42, Rudy York 0-1, Bill Jurges 44-36.

League Leaders

Batting Average

Harvey Kuenn	.353
Al Kaline	.327
Pete Runnels	.314
Nelson Fox	.306
Minnie Minoso	.302

Home Runs

Rocky Colavito	42
Harmon Killebrew	42
Jim Lemon	33
Charlie Maxwell	31
Mickey Mantle	31

RBI

Jack Jensen	112
Rocky Colavito	111
Harmon Killebrew	105
Jim Lemon	100
Charlie Maxwell	95

Stolen Bases

Lou Aparicio	56
Mickey Mantle	21
Jack Jensen	20
Jim Landis	20
Bob Allison	13

ERA

Hoyt Wilhelm	2.19
Camilo Pascual	2.64
Bob Shaw	2.69
Art Ditmar	2.90
Jerry Walker	2.92

Wins

Early Wynn	22
Cal McLish	19
Bob Shaw	18
Don Mossi	17
Frank Lary	17

Saves

Joseph Lown	15
Ryne Duren	14
Bill Loes	14
Gerry Staley	14
Mike Fornieles	11

Strikeouts

Jim Bunning	201
Camilo Pascual	185
Early Wynn	179
Herb Score	147
Hoyt Wilhelm	139

All-Star Games

(Forbes Field, Pittsburgh)

July 7	National League	5	American League	4

(Memorial Coliseum, Los Angeles)

August 3	American League	5	National League	3

World Series

October 1	Los Angeles Dodgers	0	at	Chicago White Sox	11
October 2	Los Angeles Dodgers	4	at	Chicago White Sox	3
October 4	Chicago White Sox	1	at	Los Angeles Dodgers	3
October 5	Chicago White Sox	4	at	Los Angeles Dodgers	5
October 6	Chicago White Sox	1	at	Los Angeles Dodgers	0
October 8	Los Angeles Dodgers	9	at	Chicago White Sox	3

Individual Awards

Baseball Writers Award--Ernie Banks (Chicago Cubs NL)
Nelson Fox (Chicago White Sox AL)
Cy Young Award--Early Wynn (Chicago White Sox AL)
Rookie of the Year--Willie McCovey (San Francisco Giants NL)
Bob Allison (Washington Senators AL)
Sporting News Executive of the Year--Buzzie Bavasi (Los Angeles Dodgers NL)
Sporting News Manager of the Year--Walter Alston (Los Angeles Dodgers NL)
Sporting News Pitcher of the Year--Sam Jones (San Francisco Giants NL)
Early Wynn (Chicago White Sox AL)
Sporting News Player of the Year--Ernie Banks (Chicago Cubs NL)
Nelson Fox (Chicago White Sox AL)
Sporting News Rookie of the Year--Willie McCovey (San Francisco Giants NL)
Bob Allison (Washington Senators AL)
World Series MVP--Larry Sherry (Los Angeles Dodgers NL)

Hall of Fame Inductees

Zack Wheat

Notes

Joe Cronin replaced William Harridge as President of the American League.
Professional baseball fields constructed after June 1, 1958 must have a minimum distance of 325 feet on both the first and third base foul lines to the outfield fence, and a minimum of 400 feet to the center field fence.

BASKETBALL
National Basketball Association

Eastern Division

Team Name	GP	W	L	PPGF	PPGA	Pct	GB
Boston Celtics	72	52	20	116.4	109.9	.722	-
New York Knickerbockers	72	40	32	110.3	110.1	.556	12
Syracuse Nationals	72	35	37	113.1	109.1	.486	17
Philadelphia Warriors	72	32	40	103.3	106.3	.444	20

Western Division

Team Name	GP	W	L	PPGF	PPGA	Pct	GB
St. Louis Hawks	72	49	23	108.8	105.1	.681	-
Minneapolis Lakers	72	33	39	106.0	107.3	.458	16
Detroit Pistons	72	28	44	105.1	106.6	.389	21
Cincinnati Royals	72	19	53	103.1	112.0	.264	30

Coaching Changes

New York--Fuzzy Levane 40-32; Philadelphia--Al Cervi 32 -40; St. Louis--Andy Phillip 6-4, Ed MacAuley 43-19; Minneapolis--Johnny Kundla 33-39; Detroit--Red Rocha 28-44; Cincinnati--Bobby Wanzer 3-35, Tom Marshall 16-38.

League Leaders

Field Goals		Free Throws		Assists	
Bob Pettit	719	Bob Pettit	667	Bob Cousy	557
Jack Twyman	710	Paul Arizin	587	Dick McGuire	443
Cliff Hagan	646	Elgin Baylor	532	Larry Costello	379
Paul Arizin	632	Dolph Schayes	526	Richie Guerin	364
Elgin Baylor	605	Kenny Sears	506	Carl Braun	349

Points		Fouls	
Bob Pettit	2105	Walter Dukes	332
Jack Twyman	1857	Earl Lloyd	291
Paul Arizin	1851	Jim Loscutoff	285
Elgin Baylor	1742	Dolph Schayes	280
Cliff Hagan	1707	Jack Twyman	277

All-Star Game

(at Olympia Stadium, Detroit)

January 23	West Division	124	East Division	108

NBA Playoffs

March 13	Syracuse Nationals	129	at	N.Y. Knickerbockers	123
March 14	Detroit Pistons	89	at	Minneapolis Lakers	92
March 15	N.Y. Knickerbockers	115	at	Syracuse Nationals	131
March 15	Minneapolis Lakers	103	at	Detroit Pistons	117
March 18	Syracuse Nationals	109	at	Boston Celtics	131
March 18	Detroit Pistons	102	at	Minneapolis Lakers	129
March 21	Boston Celtics	118	at	Syracuse Nationals	120
March 21	Minneapolis Lakers	90	at	St. Louis Hawks	124
March 22	Syracuse Nationals	111	at	Boston Celtics	133
March 22	St. Louis Hawks	98	at	Minneapolis Lakers	106
March 24	Minneapolis Lakers	97	at	St. Louis Hawks	127
March 25	Boston Celtics	107	at	Syracuse Nationals	119
March 26	St. Louis Hawks	98	at	Minneapolis Lakers	108
March 28	Syracuse Nationals	108	at	Boston Celtics	129
March 28	Minneapolis Lakers	98	at	St. Louis Hawks	97 [OT]
March 29	Boston Celtics	121	at	Syracuse Nationals	133
March 29	St. Louis Hawks	104	at	Minneapolis Lakers	106
April 1	Syracuse Nationals	125	at	Boston Celtics	130
April 4	Minneapolis Lakers	115	at	Boston Celtics	118
April 5	Minneapolis Lakers	108	at	Boston Celtics	128
April 7	Boston Celtics	123	at	Minneapolis Lakers	120*
April 9	Boston Celtics	118	at	Minneapolis Lakers	113

All Star Teams

First Team	Second Team
Bob Pettit (St. Louis Hawks)	Paul Arizin (Philadelphia Warriors)
Elgin Baylor (Minneapolis Lakers)	Cliff Hagan (St. Louis Hawks)
Bill Russell (Boston Celtics)	Dolph Schayes (Syracuse Nationals)
Bob Cousy (Boston Celtics)	Slater Martin (St. Louis Hawks)
Bill Sharman (Boston Celtics)	Richie Guerin (N.Y. Knickerbockers)

*Game was played in St. Paul

Individual Awards

Eddie Gottlieb Trophy--Elgin Baylor (Minneapolis Lakers)
Maurice Podoloff Trophy--Bob Pettit (St. Louis Hawks)
NBA All Star Game MVP--Bob Pettit (St. Louis Hawks)
Elgin Baylor (Minneapolis Lakers)

Hall of Fame Inductees

Phog Allen, Dr. Clifford Carlson, First Team, Dr. Luther Gulick, Edward Hickox, Charles Hyatt, Matthew Kennedy, Hank Luisetti, Dr. Walter Meanwell, George Mikan, Ralph Morgan, Dr. James Naismith, Harold Olsen, Original Celtics, John Schommer, Amos Alonzo Stagg, Oswald Tower

FOOTBALL
National Football League

Eastern Conference

Team Name	GP	W	L	T	PF	PA	Pct
New York Giants	12	10	2	0	284	170	.833
Cleveland Browns	12	7	5	0	270	214	.583
Philadelphia Eagles	12	7	5	0	268	278	.583
Pittsburgh Steelers	12	6	5	1	257	216	.542
Washington Redskins	12	3	9	0	185	350	.250
Chicago Cardinals	12	2	10	0	234	324	.167

Western Conference

Team Name	GP	W	L	T	PF	PA	Pct
Baltimore Colts	12	9	3	0	374	251	.750
Chicago Bears	12	8	4	0	252	196	.667
Green Bay Packers	12	7	5	0	248	246	.583
San Francisco 49ers	12	7	5	0	255	237	.583
Detroit Lions	12	3	8	1	203	275	.292
Los Angeles Rams	12	2	10	0	242	315	.167

Coaching Changes

Washington--Mike Nixon 3-9-0; Green Bay--Vince Lombardi 7-5-0; San Francisco--Red Hickey 7-5-0.

League Leaders

Yards Rushing		Yards Passing		Passing % (40 attempts)	
Jim Brown	1329	Johnny Unitas	2899	Milt Plum	59
J. D. Smith	1036	Norm Van Brocklin	2617	Billy Wade	59
Ollie Matson	863	Billy Wade	2001	Chuck Conerly	58
Tom Tracy	794	Milt Plum	1992	Norm Van Brocklin	56
Bobby Mitchell	743	Bobby Layne	1986	Johnny Unitas	53

Receiving Yards		Receptions		Field Goals	
Ray Berry	959	Ray Berry	66	Pat Summerall	20
Del Shofner	936	Tom McDonald	47	Tom Davis	12
Lenny Moore	846	Lenny Moore	47	Bobby Layne	11
Tom McDonald	846	Del Shofner	47	Sam Baker	10
Frank Gifford	768	Jim Mutscheller	44	John Aveni	10

Punt Return Yards		Kickoff Return Yards	
Bill Stacy	281	Lenny Lyles	565
Jon Arnett	184	Dick James	503
Bob Mitchell	177	Bill Butler	472
John Morris	171	John Sample	457
Bill Butler	163	Tom McDonald	444

Pro Bowl Game
(Memorial Coliseum, Los Angeles)

January 17 1960	Western Conference	38		Eastern Conference	21

NFL Championship

December 27	New York Giants	16	at	Baltimore Colts	31

Individual Awards

AP MVP--Charley Conerly (New York Giants)
Bert Bell Trophy--Johnny Unitas (Baltimore Colts)
Jim Thorpe Trophy--Charley Conerly (New York Giants)
Pro Bowl MVP--Johnny Unitas (Baltimore Colts)
Gene Lipscomb (Baltimore Colts)
Rookie of the Year--Nick Pietrosante (Detroit Lions)
U.P.I. NFL-NFC Coach of the Year--Vince Lombardi (Green Bay Packers)
U.P.I. NFL-NFC Rookie of the Year--Boyd Dowler (Green Bay Packers)
U.P.I. MVP--Johnny Unitas (Baltimore Colts)

Notes

Long time NFL commissioner, Bert Bell, died of a heart attack on October 11, Austin Gunsel the league treasurer, temporarily replaced him.

Canadian Football League
Interprovincial Rugby Football Union

Team Name	GP	W	L	T	PF	PA	Pts	Pct
Hamilton Tiger-Cats	14	10	4	0	298	162	20	.714
Ottawa Rough Riders	14	8	6	0	275	217	16	.571
Montreal Alouettes	14	6	8	0	193	305	12	.429
Toronto Argonauts	14	4	10	0	192	274	8	.286

Western Interprovincial Football Union

Team Name	GP	W	L	T	PF	PA	Pts	Pct
Winnipeg Blue Bombers	16	12	4	0	418	272	24	.750
Edmonton Eskimos	16	10	6	0	370	221	20	.625
British Columbia Lions	16	9	7	0	306	301	18	.563
Calgary Stampeders	16	8	8	0	356	301	16	.500
Saskatchewan Roughriders	16	1	15	0	212	567	2	.063

Coaching Changes

Toronto--Hamp Pool 3-7-0, Steve Owen l-3-0; Edmonton--Eagle Keys 10-6-0; British Columbia--Wayne Robinson 9-7-0; Saskatchewan--George Terlep 0-9-0 Frank Tripucka 1-6-0.

League Leaders

Yards Rushing		Yards Passing		Passing%	
Johnny Bright	1340	Sam Etcheverry	3133	Joe Kapp	60
Dave Thelen	1339	Joe Bob Smith	1108		
Charlie Shepard	1076				
Earl Lunsford	1027				
Gerry McDougall	1010				

Receiving Yards		Receptions		Points	
Ernie Pitts	1126	Ernie Pitts	68	Jackie Parker	109

Grey Cup Playoffs

October 31	Edmonton Eskimos	20	at	British Columbia Lions	8
November 4	British Columbia Lions	7	at	Edmonton Eskimos	41
November 7	Montreal Alouettes	0	at	Ottawa Rough Riders	43
November 11	Winnipeg Blue Bombers	19	at	Edmonton Eskimos	11
November 14	Hamilton Tiger-Cats	5	at	Ottawa Rough Riders	17
November 14	Edmonton Eskimos	8	at	Winnipeg Blue Bombers	16
November 21	Ottawa Rough Riders	7	at	Hamilton Tiger-Cats	21
November 28	Winnipeg Blue Bombers	21		Hamilton Tiger-Cats	7 *

Individual Awards

Dave Dryburgh Memorial Trophy--Jackie Parker (Edmonton Eskimos)
DeMarco-Becket Memorial Trophy--Art Walker (Edmonton Eskimos)
Dr. Beattie Martin Trophy--Henry Janzen (Winnipeg Blue Bombers)
Eddie James Memorial Trophy--Johnny Bright (Edmonton Eskimos)
Grey Cup MVP--Charlie Shepard (Winnipeg Blue Bombers)
Gruen Trophy--Joe Poirier (Ottawa Rough Riders)
Jeff Nicklin Memorial Trophy--Jackie Parker (Edmonton Eskimos)
Jeff Russel Memorial Trophy--Russ Jackson (Ottawa Rough Riders)
Schenley Award Most Outstanding Canadian--Russ Jackson (Ottawa Rough Riders)
Schenley Award Most Outstanding Lineman--Roger Nelson (Edmonton Eskimos)
Schenley Award Most Outstanding Player--Johnny Bright (Edmonton Eskimos)

HOCKEY
National Hockey League

Team Name	GP	W	L	T	GF	GA	Pts	Pct
Montreal Canadiens	70	39	18	13	258	158	91	.650
Boston Bruins	70	32	29	9	205	215	73	.521
Chicago Black-Hawks	70	28	29	13	197	208	69	.493
Toronto Maple Leafs	70	27	32	11	189	201	65	.464
New York Rangers	70	26	32	12	201	217	64	.457
Detroit Red Wings	70	25	37	8	167	218	58	.414

Coaching Changes

Toronto--Billy Reay 5-12-3, George Imlach 22-20-8; Detroit--Sid Abel 25-37-8.

*Game played in Toronto

League Leaders

Goals		Assists		Points	
Jean Beliveau	45	Dickie Moore	55	Dickie Moore	96
Dickie Moore	41	Andy Bathgate	48	Jean Beliveau	91
Andy Bathgate	40	Jean Beliveau	46	Andy Bathgate	88
Ed Litzenberger	33	Gordie Howe	46	Gordie Howe	78
Andy Hebenton	33	Bill Gadsby	46	Ed Litzenberger	77

Penalty Minutes		GAA		Wins	
Ted Lindsay	184	Jacques Plante	2.16	Jacques Plante	38
Lou Fontinato	149	Johnny Bower	2.74	Glenn Hall	28
Carl Brewer	125	Glenn Hall	2.97	Lorne Worsley	26
Jim Bartlett	118	Lorne Worsley	3.07	Don Simmons	24
Eddie Shack	109	Ed Chadwick	3.10	Terry Sawchuk	23

Shutouts	
Jacques Plante	9
Terry Sawchuk	5
Ed Chadwick	3
Don Simmons	3
Johnny Bower	3

All-Star Game

(The Forum, Montreal)

October 4 1958	Montreal Canadiens	6	All-Stars	3

Stanley Cup Playoffs

March 24	Chicago Black Hawks	2	at	Montreal Canadiens	4
March 24	Toronto Maple Leafs	1	at	Boston Bruins	5
March 26	Chicago Black Hawks	1	at	Montreal Canadiens	5
March 26	Toronto Maple Leafs	2	at	Boston Bruins	4
March 28	Montreal Canadiens	2	at	Chicago Black Hawks	4
March 28	Boston Bruins	2	at	Toronto Maple Leafs	3 [5:021
March 31	Montreal Canadiens	1	at	Chicago Black Hawks	3
March 31	Boston Bruins	2	at	Toronto Maple Leafs	3 [11:21]
April 2	Chicago Black Hawks	2	at	Montreal Canadiens	4
April 2	Toronto Maple Leafs	4	at	Boston Bruins	1
April 4	Montreal Canadiens	5	at	Chicago Black Hawks	4
April 4	Boston Bruins	5	at	Toronto Maple Leafs	4
April 7	Toronto Maple Leafs	3	at	Boston Bruins	2
April 9	Toronto Maple Leafs	3	at	Montreal Canadiens	5
April 11	Toronto Maple Leafs	1	at	Montreal Canadiens	3
April 14	Montreal Canadiens	2	at	Toronto Maple Leafs	3 [10:06]
April 16	Montreal Canadiens	3	at	Toronto Maple Leafs	2
April 18	Toronto Maple Leafs	3	at	Montreal Canadiens	5

All Star Teams

First Team		Second Team
Jacques Plante	Goal	Terry Sawchuk
Tom Johnson	Defense	Marcel Pronovost
Bill Gadsby	Defense	Doug Harvey
Jean Beliveau	Center	Henri Richard
Andy Bathgate	Right Wing	Gordie Howe
Dickie Moore	Left Wing	Alex Delvecchio

Individual Awards

Art Ross Trophy--Dickie Moore (Montreal Canadiens)
Calder Memorial Trophy--Ralph Backstrom (Montreal Canadiens)
Hart Trophy--Andy Bathgate (New York Rangers)
James Norris Trophy--Tom Johnson (Montreal Canadiens)
Lady Byng Memorial Trophy--Alex Delvecchio (Detroit Red Wings)
Vezina Trophy--Jacques Plante (Montreal Canadiens)

Hall of Fame Inductees

Jack Adams, Cy Denneny, Cecil Thompson

Franchise Changes

None

Other Sports

Horseracing--Kentucky Derby won by Tomy Lee (time 2:02.2, purse $119,650).
Heavyweight Boxing--Floyd Patterson knocked-out Brian London in 11 rounds.
Ingemar Johansson knocked-out Floyd Patterson in 3 rounds.
Golf--U.S. Open won by Billy Casper with a score of 282.
Auto Racing--Indianapolis 500 won by Rodger Ward (ave. speed 135.857 MPH)
Tennis--U.S. Open won by Neale Fraser in the men's singles.
U.S. Open won by Neale Fraser and Roy Emerson in the men's doubles.
U.S. Open won by Maria Bueno in the women's doubles.
U.S. Open won by Darlene Hard and Jeanne Arth in the women's doubles.
U.S. Open won by Margaret 0. du Pont and Neale Fraser in the mixed doubles.

1960

BASEBALL
National League

Team Name	W	L	Pct	GB	R	OR
Pittsburgh Pirates	95	59	.617	-	734	593
Milwaukee Braves	88	66	.571	7	724	658
St. Louis Cardinals	86	68	.558	9	639	616
Los Angeles Dodgers	82	72	.532	13	662	593
San Francisco Giants	79	75	.513	16	671	631
Cincinnati Reds	67	87	.435	28	640	692
Chicago Cubs	60	94	.390	35	634	776
Philadelphia Phillies	59	95	.383	36	546	691

Coaching Changes

Milwaukee--Charles Dressen 88-66; San Francisco--Bill Rigney 33-2-5, Tom Sheehan 46-50; Cincinnati--Fred Hutchinson 67-87; Chicago--Charlie Grimm 6-11, Lou Boudreau 54-83; Philadelphia--Eddie Sawyer 0-1, Andy Cohen 1-0, Gene Mauch 58-94.

League Leaders

Batting Average		Home Runs		RBI	
Dick Groat	.325	Ernie Banks	41	Hank Aaron	126
Willie Mays	.319	Hank Aaron	40	Eddie Mathews	124
Roberto Clemente	.314	Eddie Mathews	39	Ernie Banks	117
Ken Boyer	.304	Ken Boyer	32	Willie Mays	103
Wally Moon	.299	Frank Robinson	31	Ken Boyer	97

Stolen Bases		ERA		Wins	
Maury Wills	50	Mike McCormick	2.70	Ernie Broglio	21
Vada Pinson	32	Ernie Broglio	2.74	Warren Spahn	21
Tony Taylor	26	Don Drysdale	2.84	Vernon Law	20
Willie Mays	25	Stan Williams	3.00	Lew Burdette	19
Bill Bruton	22	Bob Friend	3.00	Sam Jones	18

Saves		Strikeouts	
Lindy McDaniel	26	Don Drysdale	246
Roy Face	24	Sandy Koufax	197
Bill Henry	17	Sam Jones	190
Jim Brosnan	12	Ernie Broglio	188
Dick Farrell	11	Bob Friend	183

American League

Team Name	W	L	Pct	GB	R	OR
New York Yankees	97	57	.630	-	746	627
Baltimore Orioles	89	65	.578	8	682	606
Chicago White Sox	87	67	.565	10	741	617
Cleveland Indians	76	78	.494	21	667	693
Washington Senators	73	81	.474	24	672	696
Detroit Tigers	71	83	.461	26	633	644
Boston Red Sox	65	89	.422	32	658	775
Kansas City Athletics	58	96	.377	39	615	756

Coaching Changes

Cleveland--Joe Gordon 49-46, Joyner White 1-0, Jim Dykes 26-32; Detroit--Jim Dykes 44-52, Bill Hitchcock 1-0, Joe Gordon 26-31; Boston--Bill Jurges 34-47, Michael Higgins 31-42; Kansas City--Bob Elliot 58-96.

League Leaders

Batting Average		Home Runs		RBI	
Pete Runnels	.320	Mickey Mantle	40	Roger Maris	112
Al Smith	.315	Roger Maris	39	Minnie Minoso	105
Minnie Minoso	.311	Jim Lemon	38	Vic Wertz	103
Bill Skowron	.309	Rocky Colavito	35	Jim Lemon	100
Harvey Kuenn	.308	Harmon Killebrew	31	Jim Gentile	98

Stolen Bases		ERA		Wins	
Lou Aparicio	51	Frank Baumann	2.67	Jim Perry	18
Jim Landis	23	Jim Bunning	2.79	Chuck Estrada	18
Lenny Green	21	Hal Brown	3.06	Leo Daley	16
Al Kaline	19	Art Ditmar	3.06	Art Ditmar	15
Jim Piersall	18	Edward Ford	3.08	Milt Pappas	15

Saves		Strikeouts	
Mike Fornieles	14	Jim Bunning	201
John Klippstein	14	Pedro Ramos	160
Ray Moore	13	Early Wynn	158
Bob Shantz	11	Frank Lary	149
Hank Aguirre	10	Chuck Estrada	144

All-Star Games

(Municipal Stadium, Kansas City)

July 11	National League	5	American League	3

(Yankee Stadium, New York)

July 13	National League	6	American League	0

World Series

October 5	New York Yankees	4	at	Pittsburgh Pirates	6
October 6	New York Yankees	16	at	Pittsburgh Pirates	3
October 8	Pittsburgh Pirates	0	at	New York Yankees	10
October 9	Pittsburgh Pirates	3	at	New York Yankees	2
October 10	Pittsburgh Pirates	5	at	New York Yankees	2
October 12	New York Yankees	12	at	Pittsburgh Pirates	0
October 13	New York Yankees	9	at	Pittsburgh Pirates	10

Individual Awards

Baseball Writers Award--Dick Groat (Pittsburgh Pirates NL)
Roger Maris(New York Yankees AL)
Cy Young Award--Vernon Law (Pittsburgh Pirates NL)
Rookie of the Year--Frank Howard (Los Angeles Dodgers NL)
Ron Hansen (Baltimore Orioles AL)
Sporting News Executive of the Year--George Weiss (New York Yankees AL)
Sporting News Manager of the Year--Danny Murtaugh (Pittsburgh Pirates NL)
Sporting News Pitcher of the Year--Vernon Law (Pittsburgh Pirates NL)
Chuck Estrada (Baltimore Orioles AL)
Sporting News Player of the Year--Dick Groat (Pittsburgh Pirates NL)
Roger Maris(New York Yankees AL)
Sporting News Rookie of the Year--Frank Howard (Los Angeles Dodgers NL)
Ron Hansen (Baltimore Orioles AL)
World Series MVP--Bobby Richardson (New York Yankees AL)

BASKETBALL
National Basketball Association
Eastern Division

Team Name	GP	W	L	PPGF	PPGA	Pct	GB
Boston Celtics	75	59	16	124.5	116.2	.787	-
Philadelphia Warriors	75	49	26	118.6	116.4	.653	10
Syracuse Nationals	75	45	30	118.9	116.4	.600	14
New York Knickerbockers	75	27	48	117.3	119.6	.360	32

Western Division

Team Name	GP	W	L	PPGF	PPGA	Pct	GB
St. Louis Hawks	75	46	29	113.4	110.7	.613	-
Detroit Pistons	75	30	45	111.6	115.0	.400	16
Minneapolis Lakers	75	25	50	107.3	111.4	.333	21
Cincinnati Royals	75	19	56	111.1	117.4	.253	27

Coaching Changes

Philadelphia--Neil Johnston 49-26; New York--Fuzzy Levane 8-19, Carl Braun 19-29; St. Louis--Ed Macauley 46-29; Cincinnati--Tom Marshall 19-56 Detroit--Red Rocha 13-21, Dick McGuire 17-24; Minneapolis--John Castellani 11-25, Jim Pollard 14-25.

League Leaders

Field Goals		Free Throws		Assists	
Wilt Chamberlain	1065	Jack Twyman	598	Bob Cousy	715
Jack Twyman	870	Wilt Chamberlain	577	Guy Rodgers	482
Elgin Baylor	755	Elgin Baylor	564	Richie Guerin	468
Cliff Hagan	719	Bob Pettit	544	Larry Costello	449
Tom Heinsohn	673	Dolph Schayes	533	Tom Gola	409

Points		Fouls	
Wilt Chamberlain	2707	Tom Gola	311
Jack Twyman	2338	Walter Dukes	310
Elgin Baylor	2074	Bailey Howell	282
Bob Pettit	1882	Tom Heinsohn	275
Cliff Hagan	1859	Jack Twyman	275

All-Star Game
(Convention Hall, Philadelphia)

January 22	East Division	125		West Division	115

NBA Playoffs

March 11	Syracuse Nationals	92	at	Philadelphia Warriors	115
March 12	Minneapolis Lakers	113	at	Detroit Pistons	112
March 13	Philadelphia Warriors	119	at	Syracuse Nationals	125
March 13	Detroit Pistons	99	at	Minneapolis Lakers	114
March 14	Syracuse Nationals	112	at	Philadelphia Warriors	132
March 16	Philadelphia Warriors	105	at	Boston Celtics	111
March 16	Minneapolis Lakers	99	at	St. Louis Hawks	112
March 17	Minneapolis Lakers	120	at	St. Louis Hawks	113
March 18	Boston Celtics	110	at	Philadelphia Warriors	115
March 19	St. Louis Hawks	93	at	Minneapolis Lakers	89
March 19	Philadelphia Warriors	90	at	Boston Celtics	120
March 20	St. Louis Hawks	101	at	Minneapolis Lakers	103
March 20	Boston Celtics	112	at	Philadelphia Warriors	104
March 22	Minneapolis Lakers	117	at	St. Louis Hawks	110 [OT]
March 22	Philadelphia Warriors	128	at	Boston Celtics	107
March 24	St. Louis Hawks	117	at	Minneapolis Lakers	96
March 24	Boston Celtics	119	at	Philadelphia Warriors	117
March 26	Minneapolis Lakers	86	at	St. Louis Hawks	97
March 27	St. Louis Hawks	122	at	Boston Celtics	140
March 29	St. Louis Hawks	113	at	Boston Celtics	103
April 2	Boston Celtics	102	at	St. Louis Hawks	86
April 3	Boston Celtics	96	at	St. Louis Hawks	106
April 5	St. Louis Hawks	102	at	Boston Celtics	127
April 7	Boston Celtics	102	at	St. Louis Hawks	105
April 9	St. Louis Hawks	103	at	Boston Celtics	122

All Star Teams

First Team	Second Team
Bob Pettit (St. Louis Hawks)	Jack Twyman (Cincinnati Royals)
Elgin Baylor (Minneapolis Lakers)	Dolph Schayes (Syracuse Nationals)
Wilt Chamberlain (Philadelphia Warriors)	Bill Russell (Boston Celtics)
Bob Cousy (Boston Celtics)	Richie Guerin (N.Y. Knickerbockers)
Gene Shue (Detroit Pistons)	Bill Sharman (Boston Celtics)

Individual Awards

Eddie Gottlieb Trophy--Wilt Chamberlain (Philadelphia Warriors)
Maurice Podoloff Trophy--Wilt Chamberlain (Philadelphia Warriors)
NBA All Star Game MVP--Wilt Chamberlain (Philadelphia Warriors)

Hall of Fame Inductees

Ernest Blood, Victor Hanson, George Hepbron, Frank Keaney, Ward Lambert, Edward Macauley, Branch McCracken, Charles Murphy, H. V. Porter, John Wooden

FOOTBALL
National Football League

Eastern Conference

Team Name	GP	W	L	T	PF	PA	Pct
Philadelphia Eagles	12	10	2	0	321	246	.833
Cleveland Browns	12	8	3	1	362	217	.708
New York Giants	12	6	4	2	271	261	.583
St. Louis Cardinals	12	6	5	1	288	230	.542
Pittsburgh Steelers	12	5	6	1	240	275	.458
Washington Redskins	12	1	9	2	178	309	.167

Western Conference

Team Name	GP	W	L	T	PF	PA	Pct
Green Bay Packers	12	8	4	0	332	209	.667
Detroit Lions	12	7	5	0	239	212	.583
San Francisco 49ers	12	7	5	0	208	205	.583
Baltimore Colts	12	6	6	0	288	234	.500
Chicago Bears	12	5	6	1	194	299	.458
Los Angeles Rams	12	4	7	1	265	297	.375
Dallas Cowboys	12	0	11	1	177	369	.042

Coaching Changes

St. Louis--Frank Ivy 6-5-1; Los Angeles--Bob Waterfield 4-7-1; Dallas--Tom Landry 0-11-1.

League Leaders

Yards Rushing		Yards Passing		Passing % (40 attempts)	
Jim Brown	1257	John Unitas	3099	Earl Morrall	65
Jim Taylor	1101	Norm Van Brocklin	2471	Milt Plum	60
John Crow	1071	Milt Plum	2297	Billy Wade	58
Nick Pietrosante	872	Bobby Layne	1814	Bart Starr	57
J.D. Smith	780	Eddie LeBaron	1736	Ralph Guglielmi	56

Receiving Yards		Receptions		Field Goals	
Ray Berry	1298	Ray Berry	74	Tommy Davis	19
Buddy Dial	972	Sonny Randle	62	Bob Khayat	15
Lenny Moore	936	Jim Phillips	52	Paul Hornung	15
Sonny Randle	893	Jim Gibbons	51	Bob Walston	14
Jim Phillips	883	Pete Retzlaff	46	Jerry Perry	13

Punt Return Yards		Kickoff Return Yards	
Abe Woodson	174	Ted Dean	533
Bill Stits	166	Lenny Lyles	526
Bill Butler	131	Tom Franckhauser	526
Preston Carpenter	120	John Sample	519
Willie Wood	106	Sam Horner	511

Pro Bowl Game
(Memorial Coliseum, Los Angeles)

January 15 1961	Western Conference	35	Eastern Conference	31

NFL Championship

December 26	Green Bay Packers	13	at	Philadelphia Eagles	17

Individual Awards

AP MVP--Norm Van Brocklin (Philadelphia Eagles)
Joe Schmidt (Detroit Lions)
Bert Bell--Norm Van Brocklin (Philadelphia Eagles)
Jim Thorpe Trophy--Norm Van Brocklin (Philadelphia Eagles)
Pro Bowl MVP--John Unitas (Baltimore Colts)
Sam Huff (New York Giants)
Rookie of the Year--Gail Cogdill (Detroit Lions)
Abner Haynes (Dallas Texans)
U.P.I. MVP-Norm Van Brocklin (Philadelphia Eagles)
U.P.I. NFL-NFC Coach of the Year--Buck Shaw (Philadelphia Eagles)
U.P.I. NFL-NFC Rookie of the Year --Gail Cogdill (Detroit Lions)

Notes

Pete Rozelle was named as the new Commissioner of the NFL.

American Football League
Eastern Division

Team Name	GP	W	L	T	PF	PA	Pct
Houston Oilers	14	10	4	0	379	285	.714
New York Titans	14	7	7	0	382	399	.500
Buffalo Bills	14	5	8	1	296	303	.393
Boston Patriots	14	5	9	0	286	349	.357

Western Division

Team Name	GP	W	L	T	PF	PA	Pct
Los Angeles Chargers	14	10	4	0	373	336	.714
Dallas Texans	14	8	6	0	362	253	.571
Oakland Raiders	14	6	8	0	319	388	.429
Denver Broncos	14	4	9	1	309	393	.321

Coaching

Houston--Lou Rymkus 10-4-0; New York--Sammy Baugh 7-7-0; Buffalo--Buster Ramsey 5-8-1; Boston--Lou Saban 5-9-0; Los Angeles--Sid Gillman 10-4-0; Dallas--Hank Stram 8-6-0; Oakland--Eddie Erdalatz 6-8-0; Denver--Frank Filchock 4-9-1

League Leaders

Yards Rushing		Yards Passing		Passing % (40 attempts)	
Abner Haynes	875	Frank Tripucka	3038	Hunter Enis	56
Paul Lowe	855	Jack Kemp	3018	Tom Flores	54
Bill Cannon	644	Al Dorow	2748	Jack Lee	53
Dave Smith	643	Butch Songin	2476	Jack Kemp	52
Tony Teresa	608	Cotton Davidson	2474	Frank Tripucka	52

Receiving Yards		Receptions		Field Goals	
Bill Groman	1473	Lionel Taylor	92	Gene Mingo	18
Don Maynard	1265	Bill Groman	72	George Blanda	15
Lionel Taylor	1235	Don Maynard	72	Ben Agajanian	13
Art Powell	1167	Art Powell	69	Jack Spikes	13
Chris Burford	789	Abner Haynes	55	Bill Shockley	9

Punt Return Yards		Kickoff Return Yards	
Abner Haynes	215	Leon Burton	897
John Robinson	207	Jack Larscheid	852
Jack Larscheid	106	Dick Christy	617
Dick Harris	105	Paul Lowe	611
Jim Sears	101	Ken Hall	594

AFL Championship

January 1 (1961) Los Angeles Chargers 16 at Houston Oilers 24

Individual Awards

U.P.I. AFL-AFC Coach of the Year--Lou Rymkus (Houston Oilers)
U.P.I. AFL-AFC Player of the Year--Abner Haynes (Dallas Texans)
U.P.I. AFL-AFC Rookie of the Year--Abner Haynes (Dallas Texans)

Notes

The American Football League was formed this year with Joe Foss as the commissioner.
The league signed a national television contract with ABC which provided each team with 150,000 dollars.

Canadian Football League
Eastern Conference

Team Name	GP	W	L	T	PF	PA	Pts	Pct
Toronto Argonauts	14	10	4	0	370	265	20	.714
Ottawa Rough Riders	14	9	5	0	400	283	18	.643
Montreal Alouettes	14	5	9	0	340	458	10	.357
Hamilton Tiger-Cats	14	4	10	0	273	377	8	.286

Western Interprovincial Football Union

Team Name	GP	W	L	T	PF	PA	Pts	Pct
Winnipeg Blue Bombers	16	14	2	0	453	239	28	.875
Edmonton Eskimos	16	10	6	0	318	225	20	.625
Calgary Stampeders	16	6	8	2	374	404	14	.438
British Columbia Lions	16	5	9	2	296	356	12	.375
Saskatchewan Roughriders	16	2	12	2	205	422	6	.188

Coaching Changes

Toronto--Lou Agase 10-4-0; Montreal--Perry Moss 5-9-0; Calgary--Otis Douglas 1-3-0, Steve Owen 5-5-2; Saskatchewan--Ken Carpenter 2-12-2.

League Leaders

Yards Rushing		Yards Passing		Passing %	
Dave Thelen	1407	Tobin Rote	4247	Tobin Rote	57
Earl Lunsford	1343				
Johnny Bright	1268				
Willie Fleming	1051				
Ron Stewart	1020				

Receiving Yards		Receptions		Points	
Dave Mann	1382	Dave Mann	61	Cookie Gilchrist	115
Hal Patterson	1121	Hal Patterson	61	Gerry James	114

Grey Cup Playoffs

November 2	Calgary Stampeders	7	at	Edmonton Eskimos	30
November 5	Montreal Alouettes	14	at	Ottawa Rough Riders	30
November 5	Edmonton Eskimos	40	at	Calgary Stampeders	21
November 12	Winnipeg Blue Bombers	22	at	Edmonton Eskimos	16
November 12	Toronto Argonauts	21	at	Ottawa Rough Riders	33
November 14	Edmonton Eskimos	10	at	Winnipeg Blue Bombers	5
November 19	Edmonton Eskimos	4	at	Winnipeg Blue Bombers	2
November 20	Ottawa Rough Riders	21	at	Toronto Argonauts	20
November 26	Ottawa Rough Riders	16		Edmonton Eskimos	6 *

Individual Awards

Dave Dryburgh Memorial Trophy--Gerry James (Winnipeg Blue Bombers)
DeMarco-Becket Memorial Trophy--Frank Rigney (Winnipeg Blue Bombers)
Dr. Beattie Martin Trophy--Neal Beaumont (British Columbia Lions)
Eddie James Memorial Trophy--Earl Lunsford (Calgary Stampeders)
Grey Cup MVP--Ron Stewart (Ottawa Rough Riders)
Gruen Trophy--Bill Mitchell (Toronto Argonauts)
Jeff Nicklin Memorial Trophy--Jackie Parker (Edmonton Eskimos)
Jeff Russel Memorial Trophy--Ron Stewart (Ottawa Rough Riders)
Schenley Award Most Outstanding Canadian--Ron Stewart (Ottawa Rough Riders)
Schenley Award Most Outstanding Lineman--Herb Gray (Winnipeg Blue Bombers)
Schenley Award Most Outstanding Player--Jackie Parker (Edmonton Eskimos)

Notes

The Interprovincial Rugby Football Union changed its name to the Eastern Football Conference.

HOCKEY

National Hockey League

Team Name	GP	W	L	T	GF	GA	Pts	Pct
Montreal Canadiens	70	40	18	12	255	178	92	.657
Toronto Maple Leafs	70	35	26	9	199	195	79	.564
Chicago Black Hawks	70	28	29	13	191	180	69	.493
Detroit Red Wings	70	26	29	15	186	197	67	.479
Boston Bruins	70	28	34	8	220	241	64	.457
New York Rangers	70	17	38	15	187	247	49	.350

*Game played in Vancouver

Coaching Changes

Toronto--George Imlach 35-26-9; New York--Phil Watson 3-9-3, Alf Pike 14-29-12.

League Leaders

Goals		Assists		Points	
Bobby Hull	39	Don McKenney	49	Bobby Hull	81
Bronco Horvath	39	Andy Bathgate	48	Bronco Horvath	80
Jean Beliveau	34	Gordie Howe	45	Jean Beliveau	74
Dean Prentice	32	Henri Richard	43	Andy Bathgate	74
Bernie Geoffrion	30	Dickie Moore	42	Henri Richard	73

Penalty Minutes		GAA		Wins	
Carl Brewer	150	Jacques Plante	2.54	Jacques Plante	40
Lou Fontinato	137	Glenn Hall	2.57	Johnny Bower	34
Vic Stasiuk	121	Terry Sawchuk	2.69	Glenn Hall	28
Stan Mikita	119	Johnny Bower	2.73	Terry Sawchuk	24
Fern Flaman	112	Don Simmons	3.36	Harry Lumley	18

Shutouts	
Glenn Hall	6
Terry Sawchuk	5
Johnny Bower	5
Jacques Plante	3
Don Simmons	2

All-Star Game

(The Forum, Montreal)

October 3 1959	Montreal Canadiens	6	All-Stars	1

Stanley Cup Playoffs

March 23	Detroit Red Wings	2	at	Toronto Maple Leafs	1
March 24	Chicago Black Hawks	3	at	Montreal Canadiens	4
March 26	Detroit Red Wings	2	at	Toronto Maple Leafs	4
March 26	Chicago Black Hawks	3	at	Montreal Canadiens	4 [8:38]
March 27	Toronto Maple Leafs	5	at	Detroit Red Wings	4 [43:00]
March 29	Montreal Canadiens	4	at	Chicago Black Hawks	0
March 29	Toronto Maple Leafs	1	at	Detroit Red Wings	2 [1:54]
March 31	Montreal Canadiens	2	at	Chicago Black Hawks	0
April 2	Detroit Red Wings	4	at	Toronto Maple Leafs	5
April 3	Toronto Maple Leafs	4	at	Detroit Red Wings	2
April 7	Toronto Maple Leafs	2	at	Montreal Canadiens	4
April 9	Toronto Maple Leafs	1	at	Montreal Canadiens	2
April 12	Montreal Canadiens	5	at	Toronto Maple Leafs	2
April 14	Montreal Canadiens	4	at	Toronto Maple Leafs	0

All Star Teams

First Team		Second Team
Glenn Hall	Goal	Jacques Plante
Doug Harvey	Defense	Allan Stanley
Marcel Pronovost	Defense	Pierre Pilote
Jean Beliveau	Center	Bronco Horvath
Gordie Howe	Right Wing	Bernie Geoffrion
Bobby Hull	Left Wing	Dean Prentice

Individual Awards

Art Ross Trophy--Bobby Hull (Chicago Black Hawks)
Calder Memorial Trophy--Bill Hay (Chicago Black Hawks)
Hart Memorial Trophy--Gordie Howe (Detroit Red Wings)
James Norris Trophy--Doug Harvey (Montreal Canadiens)
Lady Byng Memorial Trophy--Don McKenney (Boston Bruins)
Vezina Trophy--Jacques Plante (Montreal Canadiens)

Hall of Fame Inductees

George Boucher, John Kilpatrick, Sylvio Mantha, Frank Selke, Jack Walker

Franchise Changes

NFL--Chicago Cardinals became the St. Louis Cardinals.

Other Sports

Horseracing--Kentucky Derby won by Venetian Way (time 2:02.4, purse $114,850).
Heavyweight Boxing--Floyd Patterson knocked-out Ingemar Johansson in 5 rounds.
Golf--U.S. Open won by Arnold Palmer with a score of 280.
Auto Racing--Indianapolis 500 won by Jim Rathmann (ave. speed 138-757 MPH).
Tennis--U.S. Open won by Neale Fraser in the men's singles.
U.S. Open won by Neale Fraser and Roy Emerson in the men's doubles.
U.S. Open won by Darlene Hard in the women's singles.
U.S. Open won by Darlene Hard and Maria Bueno in the women's doubles.
U.S. Open won by Margaret du Pont and Neale Fraser in the mixed doubles.

Notes

Floyd Patterson became the first heavyweight to regain the title.

1961

BASEBALL
National League

Team Name	W	L	Pct	GB	R	OR
Cincinnati Reds	93	61	.604	-	710	653
Los Angeles Dodgers	89	65	.578	4	735	697
San Francisco Giants	85	69	.552	8	773	655
Milwaukee Braves	83	71	.539	10	712	656
St. Louis Cardinals	80	74	.519	13	703	668
Pittsburgh Pirates	75	79	.487	18	694	675
Chicago Cubs	64	90	.416	29	689	800
Philadelphia Phillies	47	107	.305	46	584	796

Coaching Changes

San Francisco--Alvin Dark85-69; Milwaukee--Chuck Dressen 71-58, George "Birdie" Tebbetts 12-13; St. Louis--Solomon Hemus 33-41, Johnny Keane 47-33; Chicago--Avitus Himsl 10-21, Harry Kraft--7-9, Elvin Tappe 42-53, Lou Klein 5-7; Philadelphia--Gene Mauch 47-107.

League Leaders

Batting Average		Home Runs		RBI	
Roberto Clemente	.351	Orlando Cepeda	46	Orlando Cepeda	142
Vada Pinson	.343	Willie Mays	40	Frank Robinson	124
Ken Boyer	.329	Frank Robinson	37	Willie Mays	123
Wally Moon	.328	Dick Stuart	35	Hank Aaron	120
Hank Aaron	.327	Joe Adcock	35	Dick Stuart	117

Stolen Bases		ERA		Wins	
Maury Wills	35	Warren Spahn	3.02	Warren Spahn	21
Vada Pinson	23	Jim O'Toole	3.10	Joe Jay	21
Frank Robinson	22	Curt Simmons	3.13	Jim O'Toole	19
Hank Aaron	21	Mike McCormick	3.20	John Podres	18
Willie Mays	18	Bob Gibson	3.24	Sandy Koufax	18

Saves		Strikeouts	
Stuart Miller	17	Sandy Koufax	269
Roy Face	17	Stan Williams	205
Jim Brosnan	16	Don Drysdale	182
Bill Henry	16	Jim O'Toole	178
Larry Sherry	15	Bob Gibson	166

American League

Team Name	W	L	Pct	GB	R	OR
New York Yankees	109	53	.673	-	827	612
Detroit Tigers	101	61	.623	8	841	671
Baltimore Orioles	95	67	.586	14	691	588
Chicago White Sox	86	76	.531	23	765	726
Cleveland Indians	78	83	.484	30.5	737	752
Boston Red Sox	76	86	.469	33	729	792
Minnesota Twins	70	90	.438	38	707	778
Los Angeles Angels	70	91	.435	38.5	744	784
Kansas City Athletics	61	100	.379	47.5	683	863
Washington Senators	61	100	.379	47.5	618	776

Coaching Changes

New York--Ralph Houk 109-53; Detroit--Bob Scheffing 101-61; Baltimore--Paul Richards 84-47, Lum Harris 11-20; Cleveland Jim Dykes 78-82, Mel Harder 0-1; Boston--Michael Higgins 76-86; Minnesota--Harry Lavagetto 29-45, Sam Mele 41-45; Los Angeles--Bill Rigney 70-91; Kansas City--Joe Gordon 26-43, Hank Bauer 35-57; Washington--James Vernon 61-l00.

League Leaders

Batting Average

Norm Cash	.361
Al Kaline	.324
Jimmy Piersall	.322
Mickey Mantle	.317
Jim Gentile	.302

Home Runs

Roger Maris	61
Mickey Mantle	54
Harmon Killebrew	46
Jim Gentile	46
Rocky Colavito	45

RBI

Roger Maris	142
Jim Gentile	141
Rocky Colavito	140
Norm Cash	132
Mickey Mantle	128

Stolen Bases

Lou Aparicio	53
Dick Howser	37
Jake Wood	30
Charles Hinton	22
Bill Bruton	22

ERA

Dick Donovan	2.40
Bill Stafford	2.68
Don Mossi	2.96
Milt Pappas	3.04
Juan Pizarro	3.05

Wins

Edward Ford	25
Frank Lary	23
Steve Barber	18
Jim Bunning	17
Ralph Terry	16

Saves

Luis Arroyo	29
Hoyt Wilhelm	18
Mike Fornieles	15
Ray Moore	14
Terry Fox	12

Strikeouts

Camilo Pascual	221
Edward Ford	209
Jim Bunning	194
Juan Pizarro	188
Ken McBride	180

All-Star Game

(Candlestick Park, San Francisco)

July 11	National League	5	American League	4

(Fenway Park, Boston)

July 31	National League	1	American League	1

World Series

October 4	Cincinnati Reds	0	at	New York Yankees	2
October 5	Cincinnati Reds	6	at	New York Yankees	2
October 7	New York Yankees	3	at	Cincinnati Reds	2
October 8	New York Yankees	7	at	Cincinnati Reds	0
October 9	New York Yankees	13	at	Cincinnati Reds	5

Individual Awards

Baseball Writers Award--Frank Robinson (Cincinnati Reds NL)
Roger Maris (New York Yankees AL)
Cy Young Award--Whitey Ford (New York Yankees AL)
Rookie of the Year--Billy Williams (Chicago Cubs NL)
Don Schwall (Boston Red Sox AL)
Sporting News Executive of the Year--Dan Topping (New York Yankees AL)
Sporting News Manager of the Year--Ralph Houk (New York Yankees AL)
Sporting News Pitcher of the Year--Warren Spahn (Milwaukee Braves NL)
Whitey Ford (New York Yankees AL)
Sporting News Player of the Year--Frank Robinson (Cincinnati Reds NL)
Roger Maris (New York Yankees AL)
Sporting News Rookie of the Year--Billy Williams (Chicago Cubs NL)
Ken Hunt (Cincinnati Reds NL)
Dick Howser (Kansas City Royals AL)
Don Schwall (Boston Red Sox AL)
World Series MVP--Whitey Ford (New York Yankees AL)

Hall of Fame Inductees

Max Carey, Billy Hamilton

Notes

The Washington Senators became the Minnesota Twins and a new team was formed in Washington.

BASKETBALL
National Basketball Association

Eastern Division

Team Name	GP	W	L	PPGF	PPGA	Pct	GB
Boston Celtics	79	57	22	119.7	114.1	.722	-
Philadelphia Warriors	79	46	33	121.0	120.1	.582	11
Syracuse Nationals	79	38	41	121.3	119.2	.481	19
New York Knickerbockers	79	21	58	113.7	120.1	.266	36

Western Division

Team Name	GP	W	L	PPGF	PPGA	Pct	GB
St. Louis Hawks	79	51	28	118.8	116.5	.646	-
Los Angeles Lakers	79	36	43	114.0	114.1	.456	15
Detroit Pistons	79	34	45	118.6	121.0	.430	17
Cincinnati Royals	79	33	46	117.9	121.3	.418	18

Coaching Changes

Syracuse--Alex Hannum 38-41; New York--Carl Braun 21-58; St. Louis--Paul Seymour 51-28; Los Angeles--Fred Schaus 36-43; Detroit--Dick McGuire 34-45; Cincinnati--Charlie Wolf 33-46.

League Leaders

Field Goals		Free Throws		Assists	
Wilt Chamberlain	1251	Dolph Schayes	680	Oscar Robertson	690
Elgin Baylor	931	Elgin Baylor	676	Guy Rodgers	677
Jack Twyman	796	Oscar Robertson	653	Bob Cousy	587
Bob Pettit	769	Bailey Howell	601	Gene Shue	530
Oscar Robertson	756	Bob Pettit	582	Richie Guerin	503

Points		Fouls	
Wilt Chamberlain	3033	Paul Arizin	335
Elgin Baylor	2538	Tom Gola	321
Oscar Robertson	2165	Walter Dukes	313
Bob Pettit	2120	Richie Guerin	310
Jack Twyman	1997	Ray Felix	302

All-Star Game

(Onodaga County War Memorial Coliseum, Syracuse)

January 17	West Division	153	East Division	131

NBA Playoffs

March 14	Syracuse Nationals	115	at	Philadelphia Warriors	107
March 14	Detroit Pistons	102	at	Los Angeles Lakers	120
March 15	Detroit Pistons	118	at	Los Angeles Lakers	120
March 16	Philadelphia Warriors	114	at	Syracuse Nationals	115
March 17	Los Angeles Lakers	113	at	Detroit Pistons	124
March 18	Los Angeles Lakers	114	at	Detroit Pistons	123
March 18	Syracuse Nationals	106	at	Philadelphia Warriors	103
March 19	Detroit Pistons	120	at	Los Angeles Lakers	137
March 19	Syracuse Nationals	115	at	Boston Celtics	128
March 21	Boston Celtics	98	at	Syracuse Nationals	115
March 21	Los Angeles Lakers	122	at	St. Louis Hawks	118
March 22	Los Angeles Lakers	106	at	St. Louis Hawks	121
March 23	Syracuse Nationals	110	at	Boston Celtics	133
March 24	St. Louis Hawks	112	at	Los Angeles Lakers	118
March 25	Boston Celtics	120	at	Syracuse Nationals	107
March 25	St. Louis Hawks	118	at	Los Angeles Lakers	117
March 26	Syracuse Nationals	101	at	Boston Celtics	123
March 27	Los Angeles Lakers	121	at	St. Louis Hawks	112
March 29	St. Louis Hawks	114	at	Los Angeles Lakers	113 [OT]
April 1	Los Angeles Lakers	103	at	St. Louis Hawks	105
April 2	St. Louis Hawks	95	at	Boston Celtics	129
April 5	St. Louis Hawks	108	at	Boston Celtics	116
April 8	Boston Celtics	120	at	St. Louis Hawks	124
April 9	Boston Celtics	119	at	St. Louis Hawks	104
April 11	St. Louis Hawks	112	at	Boston Celtics	121

All Star Teams

First Team	Second Team
Elgin Baylor (Los Angeles Lakers)	Dolph Schayes (Syracuse Nationals)
Bob Pettit (St. Louis Hawks)	Tom Heinsohn (Boston Celtics)
Wilt Chamberlain (Philadelphia Warriors)	Bill Russell (Boston Celtics)
Bob Cousy (Boston Celtics)	Larry Costello (Syracuse Nationals)
Oscar Robertson (Cincinnati Royals)	Gene Shue (Detroit Pistons)

Individual Awards

Eddie Gottlieb Trophy--Oscar Robertson (Cincinnati Royals)
Maurice Podoloff Trophy--Bill. Russell (Boston Celtics)
NBA All Star Game MVP--Oscar Robertson (Cincinnati Royals)

Hall of Fame Inductees

Bennie Borgmann, Buffalo Germans, Forrest DeBernardi, George Hoyt, George Keogan, Bob Kurland, John J. O'Brien, Andy Phillip, Ernest Quigley, John Roosma, Leonard Sachs, Arthur Schabinger, Christian Steinmetz, David Tobey, Arthur Trester, Edward Wachter, David Walsh

FOOTBALL

National Football League

Eastern Conference

Team Name	GP	W	L	T	PF	PA	Pct
New York Giants	14	10	3	1	368	220	.750
Philadelphia Eagles	14	10	4	0	361	297	.714
Cleveland Browns	14	8	5	1	319	270	.607
St. Louis Cardinals	14	7	7	0	279	267	.500
Pittsburgh Steelers	14	6	8	0	295	287	.429
Dallas Cowboys	14	4	9	1	236	380	.321
Washington Redskins	14	1	12	1	174	392	.107

Western Conference

Team Name	GP	W	L	T	PF	PA	Pct
Green Bay Packers	14	11	3	0	391	223	.786
Detroit Lions	14	8	5	1	270	258	.607
Baltimore Colts	14	8	6	0	302	307	.571
Chicago Bears	14	8	6	0	326	302	.571
San Francisco 49ers	14	7	6	1	346	272	.538
Los Angeles Rams	14	4	10	0	263	333	.286
Minnesota Vikings	14	3	11	0	285	407	.214

Coaching Changes

New York--Allie Sherman 10-3-1; Philadelphia--Nick Skorich 10-4-0; St. Louis--Frank, Ivy 5-7-0, Chuck Drulis & Ray Prochaska & Ray Willsey 2-0; Washington--Bill McPeak 1-12-1; Minnesota --Norm Van Brocklin 3-11-0.

League Leaders

Yards Rushing		Yards Passing		Passing % (40 attempts)	
Jim Brown	1408	Sonny Jurgensen	3723	Milt Plum	59
Jim Taylor	1307	John Unitas	2990	Bart Starr	58
Alex Webster	928	John Brodie	2588	Y.A. Tittle	57
Nick Piettrosante	841	Bart Starr	2418	Rudy Bukich	57
J.D. Smith	823	Milt Plum	2416	Sonny Jurgensen	56

Receiving Yards		Receptions		Field Goals	
Tom McDonald	1144	Jim Phillips	78	Steve Myhra	21
Del Shofner	1125	Ray Berry	75	Lou Groza	16
Jim Phillips	1092	Del Shofner	68	Lou Michaels	15
Mike Ditka	1076	Tom McDonald	64	Paul Hornung	15
Buddy Dial	1047	Mike Ditka	56	Jim Martin	15

Punt Return Yards		Kickoff Return Yards	
John Sample	283	Tim Brown	811
Willie Wood	225	Abe Woodson	782
Bob Boyd	173	Dick Bass	698
Abe Woodson	172	Jim Steffen	691
Bob Mitchell	164	Lenny Lyles	672

Pro Bowl Game

(Memorial Coliseum, Los Angeles)

January 14 1962	Western Conference	31		Eastern Conference	30

NFL Championship

December 31	New York Giants	0	at	Green Bay Packers	37

Individual Awards

AP MVP--Paul Hornung (Green Bay Packers)
Bert Bell Trophy--Paul Hornung (Green Bay Packers)
Jim Thorpe Trophy--Y.A. Tittle (New York Giants)
Pro-Bowl MVP--Jim Brown (Cleveland Browns)
Henry Jordan (Green Bay Packers)
Rookie of the Year--Mike Ditka (Chicago Bears)
U.P.I. MVP-Paul Hornung (Green Bay Packers)
U.P.I. NFL-NFC Coach of the Year--Allie Sherman (New York Giants)
U.P.I. NFL-NFC Rookie of the Year--Mike Ditka (Chicago Bears)

Notes

NFL commissioner Pete Rozelle successfully persuaded Congress to pass a bill officially exempting the league's package deal with CBS from anti-trust legislation.

American Football league
Eastern Division

Team Name	GP	W	L	T	PF	PA	Pct
Houston Oilers	14	10	3	1	513	242	.750
Boston Patriots	14	9	4	1	413	313	.679
New York Titans	14	7	7	0	301	390	.500
Buffalo Bills	14	6	8	0	294	342	.429

Western Division

Team Name	GP	W	L	T	PF	PA	Pct
San Diego Chargers	14	12	2	0	396	219	.857
Dallas Texans	14	6	8	0	334	343	.429
Denver Broncos	14	3	11	0	251	432	.214
Oakland Raiders	14	2	12	0	237	458	.143

Coaching Changes

Houston--Lou Rymkus 1-3-1, Wally Lemm 9-0-0; Boston--Lou Saban 2-3-0, Mike Holovak 7-1-1; San Diego--Sid Gillman 12-2-0; Oakland--Marty Feldman 2-12-0.

League Leaders

Yards Rushing		**Yards Passing**		**Passing %** (40 attempts)	
Bill Cannon	948	George Blanda	3330	Babe Parilli	53
Bill Mathis	846	Jack Kemp	2686	George Blanda	52
Abner Haynes	841	Al Dorow	2651	Jack Lee	52
Paul Lowe	767	Cotton Davidson	2445	Tom Flores	52
Charley Tolar	577	Tom Flores	2176	Frank Tripucka	49

Receiving Yards		**Receptions**		**Field Goals**	
Charley Hennigan	1746	Lionel Taylor	100	Gino Cappelletti	17
Lionel Taylor	1176	Charley Hennigan	82	George Blanda	16
Bill Groman	1175	Art Powell	71	George Blair	13
Dave Kocourek	1055	Dave Kocourek	55	George Fleming	11
Art Powell	881	Chris Burford	51	Joe Hergert	6

Punt Return Yards		**Kickoff Return Yards**	
Dick Christy	383	Frank Jackson	645
Al Frazier	231	George Fleming	588
Claude Gibson	209	Al Frazier	504
Abner Haynes	196	Dave Grayson	453
Keith Lincoln	150	Bill Cannon	439

All Star Game
(Balboa Stadium, San Diego)

January 7 1962	West Division	47		East Division	27

AFL Championship

December 24	Houston Oilers	10	at	San Diego Chargers	3

Individual Awards

AFL All Star Game MVP--Cotton Davidson (Oakland Raiders)
Rookie of the Year--Earl Faison (San Diego Chargers)
U.P.I. AFL-AFC Coach of the Year--Wally Lemm (Houston Oilers)
U.P.I. AFL-AFC Player of the Year--George Blanda (Houston Oilers)
U.P.I. AFL-AFC Rookie of the Year--Earl Faison (San Diego Chargers)

Canadian Football League
Eastern Conference

Team Name	GP	W	L	T	PF	PA	Pts	Pct
Hamilton Tiger-Cats	14	10	4	0	340	393	20	.714
Ottawa Rough Riders	14	8	6	0	359	285	16	.571
Toronto Argonauts	14	7	6	1	255	258	15	.536
Montreal Alouettes	14	4	9	1	213	225	9	.321

Western Conference

Team Name	GP	W	L	T	PF	PA	Pts	Pct
Winnipeg Blue Bombers	16	13	3	0	360	251	26	.813
Edmonton Eskimos	16	10	5	1	334	257	21	.656
Calgary Stampeders	16	7	9	0	300	311	14	.438
Saskatchewan Roughriders	16	5	10	1	211	314	11	.344
British Columbia Lions	16	1	13	2	215	393	4	.125

Coaching Changes

Saskatchewan--Steve Owen 5-10-1; British Columbia--Wayne Robinson 0-7-1, Dave Skrien 1-6-1; Calgary--Bobby Dobbs 7-9-0.

League Leaders

Yards Rushing		Yards Passing		Passing %	
Earl Lunsford	1794	Tobin Rote	3093	Tobin Rote	57
Johnny Bright	1350				
Don Clark	1143				
Leo Lewis	1035				
Dave Thelen	1032				

Receptions		Points	
Dave Mann	53	Jackie Parker	104

Grey Cup Playoffs

November 11	Edmonton Eskimos	8	at	Calgary Stampeders	10
November 11	Toronto Argonauts	43	at	Ottawa Rough Riders	19
November 13	Calgary Stampeders	17	at	Edmonton Eskimos	18
November 18	Winnipeg Blue Bombers	14	at	Calgary Stampeders	1
November 19	Hamilton Tiger-Cats	7	at	Toronto Argonauts	25
November 22	Calgary Stampeders	14	at	Winnipeg Blue Bombers	43
November 25	Toronto Argonauts	2	at	Hamilton Tiger Cats	48 [OT]
December 2	Winnipeg Blue Bombers	21		Hamilton Tiger-Cats	14 [OT]*

*Game played in Toronto

Individual Awards

Annis Stukus Trophy--Jim Trimble (Hamilton Tiger-Cats)
Dave Dryburgh Memorial Trophy--Jackie Parker (Edmonton Eskimos)
DeMarco-Becket Memorial Trophy--Frank Rigney (Winnipeg Blue Bombers)
Dr. Beattie Martin Trophy--Larry Robinson (Calgary Stampeders)
Eddie James Memorial Trophy--Earl Lunsford (Calgary Stampeders)
Grey Cup MVP--Ken Ploen (Winnipeg Blue Bombers)
Gruen Trophy--Gino Beretta (Montreal Alouettes)
Jeff Nicklin Memorial Trophy--Jackie Parker (Edmonton Eskimos)
Jeff Russel Memorial Trophy--Bob-Jack Oliver (Montreal Alouettes)
Schenley Award Most Outstanding Canadian--Tony Pajaczkowski (Calgary Stampeders)
Schenley Award Most Outstanding Lineman--Frank Rigney (Winnipeg Blue Bombers)
Schenley Award Most Outstanding Player--Bernie Faloney (Hamilton Tiger-Cats)

Rules

Four backs were permitted unlimited blocking on rushing plays if they lined up outside the ends.

Notes

This years Grey Cup game was the first game to go into overtime.
Western Interprovincial Football Union changed its name to the Western Football Conference. Partial interlocking play was introduced between the Eastern and Western Conferences.

HOCKEY
National Hockey League

Team Name	GP	W	L	T	GF	GA	Pts	Pct
Montreal Canadiens	70	41	19	10	254	188	92	.657
Toronto Maple Leafs	70	39	19	12	234	176	90	.643
Chicago Black Hawks	70	29	24	17	198	180	75	.536
Detroit Red Wings	70	25	29	16	195	215	66	.471
New York Rangers	70	22	38	10	204	248	54	.386
Boston Bruins	70	15	42	13	176	154	43	.307

Coaching Changes

New York--Alf Pike 22-38-10.

League Leaders

Goals		Assists		Points	
Bernie Geoffrion	50	Jean Beliveau	58	Bernie Geoffrion	95
Frank Mahovlich	48	Leonard Kelly	50	Jean Beliveau	90
Dickie Moore	35	Gordie Howe	49	Frank Mahovlich	84
Jean Beliveau	32	Andy Bathgate	48	Andy Bathgate	77
Bobby Hull	31	Bill Hay	48	Gordie Howe	72

Penalty Minutes		GAA		Wins	
Pierre Pilote	165	Johnny Bower	2.50	Johnny Bower	33
Reg Fleming	145	Charlie Hodge	2.53	Glenn Hall	29
Jean-Guy Talbot	143	Glenn Hall	2.57	Jacques Plante	22
Frank Mahcvlich	131	Jacques Plante	2.80	Charlie Hodge	19
Eric Nesterenko	125	Hank Bassen	2.89	Lorne Worsley	19

Shutouts

Glenn Hall	6
Charlie Hodge	4
Jacques Plante	2
Terry Sawchuk	2
Johnny Bower	2

All Star Game

(The Forum, Montreal)

October 1 1960	All Stars	2	Montreal Canadiens	1

Stanley Cup Playoffs

March 21	Chicago Black Hawks	2	at	Montreal Canadiens	6
March 22	Detroit Red Wings	2	at	Toronto Maple Leafs	3 [24:51]
March 23	Chicago Black Hawks	4	at	Montreal Canadiens	3
March 25	Detroit Red Wings	4	at	Toronto Maple Leafs	2
March 26	Montreal Canadiens	1	at	Chicago Black Hawks	2 [52:12]
March 26	Toronto Maple Leafs	0	at	Detroit Red Wings	2
March 28	Montreal Canadiens	5	at	Chicago Black Hawks	2
March 28	Toronto Maple Leafs	1	at	Detroit Red Wings	4
April 1	Chicago Black Hawks	3	at	Montreal Canadiens	0
April 1	Detroit Red Wings	3	at	Toronto Maple Leafs	2
April 4	Montreal Canadiens	0	at	Chicago Black Hawks	3
April 6	Detroit Red Wings	2	at	Chicago Black Hawks	3
April 8	Chicago Black Hawks	1	at	Detroit Red Wings	3
April 10	Detroit Red Wings	1	at	Chicago Black Hawks	3
April 12	Chicago Black Hawks	1	at	Detroit Red Wings	2
April 14	Detroit Red Wings	3	at	Chicago Black Hawks	6
April 16	Chicago Black Hawks	5	at	Detroit Red Wings	1

All Star Teams

First Team		Second Team
Johnny Bower	Goal	Glenn Hall
Doug Harvey	Defense	Allan Stanley
Marcel Pronovost	Defense	Pierre Pilote
Jean Beliveau	Center	Henri Richard
Bernie Geoffrion	Right Wing	Gordie Howe
Frank Mahovlich	Left Wing	Dickie Moore

Individual Awards

Art Ross Trophy--Bernie Geoffrion (Montreal Canadiens)
Calder Memorial Trophy--Dave Keon (Toronto Maple Leafs)
Hart Memorial Trophy--Bernie Geoffrion (Montreal Canadiens)
James Norris Trophy--Doug Harvey (Montreal Canadiens)
Lady Byng Memorial Trophy--Leonard Kelly (Toronto Maple Leafs)
Vezina Trophy--Johnny Bower (Toronto Maple Leafs)

Hall of Fame Inductees

Syl Apps Sr., George Brown, Charlie Conacher, Hap Day, Chaucer Elliot, George Hainsworth, Joe Hall, Mickey Ion, Percy LeSueur, Paul Loicq, Frank Rankin, Maurice Richard, Milt Schmidt, Oliver Seibert, Cooper Smeaton, Bruce Stuart, Fred Waghorn

Rules

Clubs were allowed to dress 16 skaters instead of 17 as had been the case previously.

Franchise Changes

AL--Washington Senators became the Minnesota Twins.
AFL--Los Angeles Chargers became the San Diego Chargers.
NBA--Minneapolis Lakers became the Los Angeles Lakers.

Other Sports

Horseracing--Kentucky Derby won by Carry Back (time 2:04, purse $120,500).
Heavyweight Boxing--Floyd Patterson knocked-out Ingemar Johansson in 6 rounds.
Floyd Patterson knocked-out Tom McNeeley in 4 rounds.
Golf--U.S. Open won by Gene Littler with a score of 281.
Auto Racing--Indianapolis 500 won by A.J. Foyt (ave. speed 139.131 MPH).
Tennis--U.S. Open won by Roy Emerson in the men's singles.
U.S. Open won by Dennis Ralston and Chuck McKinley in the men's doubles.
U.S. Open won by Darlene Hard in the women's singles.
U.S. Open won by Darlene Hard and Lesley Turner in the women's doubles.
U.S. Open won by Margaret Smith and Robert Mark in the mixed doubles.

1962

BASEBALL
National League

Team Name	W	L	Pct	GB	R	OR
San Francisco Giants	103	62	.624	-	878	690
Los Angeles Dodgers	102	63	.618	1	842	697
Cincinnati Reds	98	64	.605	3.5	802	685
Pittsburgh Pirates	93	68	.578	8	706	626
Milwaukee Braves	86	76	.531	15.5	730	665
St. Louis Cardinals	84	78	.519	17.5	774	664
Philadelphia Phillies	81	80	.503	20	705	759
Houston Colt 45s	64	96	.400	36.5	592	717
Chicago Cubs	59	103	.364	42.5	632	827
New York Mets	40	120	.250	60.5	617	948

Coaching Changes

Milwaukee--George Tebbetts 86-76; St. Louis--John Keane 84-78; Houston--Harry Craft 64-96; Chicago--Elvin Tappe 4-16, Lou Klein 12-18, Charlie Metro 43-69; New York--Casey Stengel 40-120.

League Leaders

Batting Average		Home Runs		RBI	
Tom Davis	.346	Willie Mays	49	Tom Davis	153
Frank Robinson	.342	Hank Aaron	45	Willie Mays	141
Bill White	.324	Frank Robinson	39	Frank Robinson	136
Hank Aaron	.323	Ernie Banks	37	Hank Aaron	128
George Altman	.318	Orlando Cepeda	35	Frank Howard	119

Stolen Bases		ERA		Wins	
Maury Wills	104	Sandy Koufax	2.54	Don Drysdale	25
Willie Davis	32	Bob Shaw	2.80	Jack Sanford	24
Vada Pinson	26	Bob Purkey	2.81	Bob Purkey	23
Julian Javier	26	Don Drysdale	2.83	Joe Jay	21
Tony Taylor	20	Bob Gibson	2.85	Art Mahaffey	19

Saves		Strikeouts	
Elroy Face	28	Don Drysdale	232
Ron Perranoski	20	Sandy Koufax	216
Stu Miller	19	Bob Gibson	208
Lindy McDaniel	14	Dick Farrell	203
Jim Brosnan	13	Bill O'Dell	195

Notes

San Francisco defeated Los Angeles in a playoff for the championship of the NL 2 games to 1.
The National League expanded to 10 teams this year with the addition of the Houston Colt 45's and the New York Mets.

American League

Team Name	W	L	Pct	GB	R	OR
New York Yankees	96	66	.593	-	817	680
Minnesota Twins	91	71	.562	5	798	713
Los Angeles Angels	86	76	.531	10	718	706
Detroit Tigers	85	76	.528	10.5	758	692
Chicago White Sox	85	77	.525	11	707	658
Cleveland Indians	80	82	.494	16	682	745
Baltimore Orioles	77	85	.475	19	652	680
Boston Red Sox	76	84	.475	19	707	756
Kansas City Athletics	72	90	.444	24	745	837
Washington Senators	60	101	.373	35.5	599	716

Coaching Changes

Minnesota--Sam Mele 91-71; Cleveland--Mel McGaha 80-82; Baltimore--Billy Hitchcock 77-85; Kansas City--Hank Bauer 72-90.

League Leaders

Batting Average		Home Runs		RBI	
Pete Runnels	.326	Harmon Killebrew	48	Harmon Killebrew	126
Floyd Robinson	.312	Norm Cash	39	Norm Siebern	117
Charles Hinton	.310	Rocky Colavito	37	Rocky Colavito	112
Norm Siebern	.308	Leon Wagner	37	Floyd Robinson	109
Brooks Robinson	.303	Jim Gentile	33	Leon Wagner	107

Stolen Bases		ERA		Wins	
Lou Aparicio	31	Hank Aguirre	2.21	Ralph Terry	23
Charles Hinton	28	Robin Roberts	2.78	Camilo Pascual	20
Jake Wood	24	Edward Ford	2.90	Dick Donovan	20
Ed Charles	20	Dean Chance	2.96	Ray Herbert	20
Dick Howser	19	Eddie Fisher	3.10	Jim Bunning	19

Saves		Strikeouts	
Dick Radatz	24	Camilo Pascual	206
Marshall Bridges	18	Jim Bunning	184
Terry Fox	16	Ralph Terry	176
Hoyt Wilhelm	15	Jim Kaat	173
Gary Bell	12	Juan Pizarro	173

All Star Game

(RFK Stadium, Washington)

July 10	National League	3	American league	1

(Comiskey Park I, Chicago)

July 30	American league	9	National League	4

World Series

October 4	New York Yankees	6	at	San Francisco Giants	2
October 5	New York Yankees	0	at	San Francisco Giants	2
October 7	San Francisco Giants	2	at	New York Yankees	3
October 8	San Francisco Giants	7	at	New York Yankees	3
October 10	San Francisco Giants	3	at	New York Yankees	5
October 15	New York Yankees	2	at	San Francisco Giants	5
October 16	New York Yankees	1	at	San Francisco Giants	0

Individual Awards

Arch Ward Memorial Trophy--Maury Wills (Los Angeles Dodgers NL)
Baseball Writers Award--Maury Wills (Los Angeles Dodgers NL)
Mickey Mantle (New York Yankees AL)
Cy Young Award--Don Drysdale (Los Angeles Dodgers NL)
Rookie of the Year--Ken Hubbs (Chicago Cubs NL)
Tom Tresh (New York Yankees AL)
Sporting News Executive of the Year--Fred Haney (Los Angeles Dodgers NL)
Sporting News Manager of the Year--Bill Rigney (Los Angeles Dodgers NL)
Sporting News Pitcher of the Year--Don Drysdale (Los Angeles Dodgers NL)
Dick Donovan (Cleveland Indians AL)
Sporting News Player of the Year--Maury Wills (Los Angeles Dodgers NL)
Mickey Mantle (New York Yankees AL)
Sporting News Rookie of the Year--Ken Hubbs (Chicago Cubs NL)
Tom Tresh (New York Yankees AL)
World Series MVP--Ralph Terry (New York Yankees AL)

Hall of Fame Inductees

Bob Feller, Bill McKechnie, Jackie Robinson, Edd Roush

BASKETBALL
National Basketball Association

Eastern Division

Team Name	GP	W	L	PPGF	PPGA	Pct	GB
Boston Celtics	80	60	20	121.1	111.9	.750	-
Philadelphia Warriors	80	49	31	125.4	122.7	.613	11
Syracuse Nationals	80	41	39	120.7	118.4	.513	19
New York Knickerbockers	80	29	51	114.8	119.7	.363	31

Western Division

Team Name	GP	W	L	PPGF	PPGA	Pct	GB
Los Angeles Lakers	80	54	26	118.5	116.3	.675	-
Cincinnati Royals	80	43	37	123.1	121.3	.538	11
Detroit Pistons	80	37	43	115.4	117.1	.463	17
St. Louis Hawks	80	29	51	118.9	122.1	.363	25
Chicago Packers	80	18	62	110.9	119.4	.225	36

Coaching Changes

Philadelphia--Frank McGuire 49-31; New York--Eddie Donovan 29-51; St. Louis--Paul Seymour 5-9, Fuzzy Levane 20-40, Bob Pettit 4-2; Chicago--Jim Pollard 18-62.

League Leaders

Field Goals		Free Throws		Assists	
Wilt Chamberlain	1597	Wilt Chamberlain	835	Oscar Robertson	899
Walt Bellamy	973	Jerry West	712	Guy Rodgers	663
Bob Pettit	867	Oscar Robertson	700	Bob Cousy	584
Oscar Robertson	866	Bob Pettit	695	Richie Guerin	539
Richie Guerin	839	Richie Guerin	625	Gene Shue	465

Points		Fouls	
Wilt Chamberlain	4029	Tom Meschery	330
Walt Bellamy	2495	Walter Dukes	327
Oscar Robertson	2432	Jack Twyman	323
Bob Pettit	2429	Bailey Howell	317
Jerry West	2310	Guy Rodgers	312

All Star Game

(Kiel Auditorium, St. Louis)

January 16	West Division	150		East Division	130

NBA Playoffs

Date	Visitor	Score		Home	Score
March 16	Syracuse Nationals	103	at	Philadelphia Warriors	110
March 16	Cincinnati Royals	122	at	Detroit Pistons	123
March 17	Detroit Pistons	107	at	Cincinnati Royals	129
March 18	Philadelphia Warriors	97	at	Syracuse Nationals	82
March 18	Cincinnati Royals	107	at	Detroit Pistons	118
March 19	Syracuse Nationals	101	at	Philadelphia Warriors	100
March 20	Detroit Pistons	112	at	Cincinnati Royals	111
March 20	Philadelphia Warriors	99	at	Syracuse Nationals	106
March 22	Syracuse Nationals	104	at	Philadelphia Warriors	121
March 24	Philadelphia Warriors	89	at	Boston Celtics	117
March 24	Detroit Pistons	108	at	Los Angeles Lakers	132
March 25	Detroit Pistons	112	at	Los Angeles Lakers	127
March 27	Boston Celtics	106	at	Philadelphia Warriors	113
March 27	Los Angeles Lakers	111	at	Detroit Pistons	106
March 28	Philadelphia Warriors	114	at	Boston Celtics	129
March 29	Los Angeles Lakers	117	at	Detroit Pistons	118
March 31	Boston Celtics	106	at	Philadelphia Warriors	110
March 31	Detroit Pistons	132	at	Los Angeles Lakers	125
April 1	Philadelphia Warriors	104	at	Boston Celtics	119
April 3	Los Angeles Lakers	123	at	Detroit Pistons	117
April 3	Boston Celtics	99	at	Philadelphia Warriors	109
April 5	Philadelphia Warriors	107	at	Boston Celtics	109
April 7	Los Angeles Lakers	108	at	Boston Celtics	122
April 8	Los Angeles Lakers	129	at	Boston Celtics	122
April 10	Boston Celtics	115	at	Los Angeles Lakers	117
April 11	Boston Celtics	115	at	Los Angeles Lakers	103
April 14	Los Angeles Lakers	126	at	Boston Celtics	121
April 16	Boston Celtics	119	at	Los Angeles Lakers	105
April 18	Los Angeles Lakers	107	at	Boston Celtics	110 [OT]

All Star Teams

First Team	Second Team
Bob Pettit (St. Louis Hawks)	Tom Heinsohn (Boston Celtics)
Elgin Baylor (Los Angeles Lakers)	Jack Twyman (Cincinnati Royals)
Wilt Chamberlain (Philadelphia Warriors)	Bill Russell (Boston Celtics)
Jerry West (Los Angeles Lakers)	Richie Guerin (N.Y. Knickerbockers)
Oscar Robertson (Cincinnati Royals)	Bob Cousy (Boston Celtics)

Individual Awards

Eddie Gottlieb Trophy--Walt Bellamy (Chicago Packers)
Maurice Podoloff Trophy--Bill Russell (Boston Celtics)
NBA All Star Game MVP--Bob Pettit (St. Louis Hawks)

Hall of Fame Inductees

Jack McCracken, Frank Morgenweck, Pat Page, Lynn St. John, Barney Sedran, John Thompson

Notes

The Chicago Packers joined the NBA this year and was the first new franchise in the league.
On March 2, 1962 Wilt Chamberlain of the Philadelphia Warriors scored 100 points against the New York Knickerbockers to lead the Warriors to a 169-147 victory.

FOOTBALL
National Football League

Eastern Conference

Team Name	GP	W	L	T	PF	PA	Pct
New York Giants	14	12	2	0	398	283	.857
Pittsburgh Steelers	14	9	5	0	312	363	.643
Cleveland Browns	14	7	6	1	291	257	.536
Washington Redskins	14	5	7	2	305	376	.429
Dallas Cowboys	14	5	8	1	398	402	.393
St. Louis Cardinals	14	4	9	1	287	361	.321
Philadelphia Eagles	14	3	10	1	282	356	.250

Western Conference

Team Name	GP	W	L	T	PF	PA	Pct
Green Bay Packers	14	13	1	0	415	148	.929
Detroit Lions	14	11	3	0	315	177	.786
Chicago Bears	14	9	5	0	321	287	.643
Baltimore Colts	14	7	7	0	293	288	.500
San Francisco 49ers	14	6	8	0	282	331	.429
Minnesota Vikings	14	2	11	1	254	410	.179
Los Angeles Rams	14	1	12	1	220	334	.107

Coaching Changes

St. Louis--Wally Lemm 4-9-1; Los Angeles--Bob Waterfield 1-7-0, Harland Svare 0-5-1.

League Leaders

Yards Rushing		Yards Passing		Passing % (40 attempts)	
Jim Taylor	1474	Sonny Jurgensen	3261	Bart Starr	62
John Johnson	1141	Y.A. Tittle	3224	Earl Morrall	62
Dick Bass	1033	Billy Wade	3172	Frank Ryan	58
Jim Brown	996	Johnny Unitas	2967	John Brodie	58
Don Perkins	945	Norm Snead	2926	Johnny Unitas	57

Receiving Yards		Receptions		Field Goals	
Bobby Mitchell	1384	Bob Mitchell	72	Lou Michaels	26
Sonny Randle	1158	Sonny Randle	63	Don Chandler	19
Tom McDonald	1146	Bobby Conrad	62	Lou Groza	14
Del Shofner	1133	Jim Phillips	60	Sam Baker	14
Frank Clarke	1043	Tom McDonald	58	Roger LeClerc	13

Punt Return Yards		Kickoff Return Yards	
Pat Studstill	457	Abe Woodson	1157
Willie Wood	273	Dick James	889
John Morris	208	Tim Brown	831
Abe Woodson	179	John Counts	784
Bill Butler	169	Amos Marsh	725

Pro Bowl Game

(Memorial Coliseum, Los Angeles)

January 13 1963	Eastern Conference	30		Western Conference	20

NFL Championship

December 30	Green Bay Packers	16	at	New York Giants	7

Individual Awards

AP MVP--Jim Taylor (Green Bay Packers)
Bert Bell Trophy--Andy Robustelli (New York Giants)
Jim Thorpe Trophy--Jim Taylor (Green Bay Packers)
Pro Bowl MVP--Jim Brown (Cleveland Browns)
Gene Lipscomb (Pittsburgh Steelers)
Rookie of the Year--Ronnie Bull (Chicago Bears)
Jim Thorpe Trophy--Jim Taylor (Green Bay Packers)
U.P.I. MVP--Y.A. Tittle (New York Giants)
U.P.I. NFL-NFC Coach of the Year--Allie Sherman (New York Giants)
U.P.I. NFL-NFC Rookie of the Year--Ronnie Bull (Chicago Bears)

Rules

Grabbing another player's face mask was made illegal.

American Football League
Eastern Division

Team Name	GP	W	L	T	PF	PA	Pct
Houston Oilers	14	11	3	0	387	270	.786
Boston Patriots	14	9	4	1	346	295	.679
Buffalo Bills	14	7	6	1	309	272	.536
New York Titans	14	5	9	0	278	423	.357

Western Division

Team Name	GP	W	L	T	PF	PA	Pct
Dallas Texans	14	11	3	0	389	233	.786
Denver Broncos	14	7	7	0	353	334	.500
San Diego Chargers	14	4	10	0	314	392	.286'
Oakland Raiders	14	1	13	0	213	370	.071

Coaching Changes

Houston--Frank Ivy 11-3-0; Boston--Mike Holovak 9-4-1; Buffalo--Lou Saban 7-6-1; New York--Bulldog Turner 5-9-0; Denver--Jack Faulkner 7-7-0; Oakland--Marty Feldman 0-5-0; Red Conkright 1-8-0.

League Leaders

Yards Rushing		Yards Passing		Passing % (40attempts)	
Cookie Gilchrist	1096	Frank Tripucka	2917	Len Dawson	61
Abner Haynes	1049	George Blanda	2810	Frank Tripucka	55
Charley Tolar	1012	Len Dawson	2759	Babe Parilli	55
Clem Daniels	766	Babe Parilli	1988	Hunter Enis	53
Curtis McClinton	604	Cotton Davidson	1977	Jack Lee	52

Receiving Yards		Receptions		Field Goals	
Art Powell	1130	Lionel Taylor	77	Gene Mingo	27
Don Maynard	1041	Art Powell	64	Gino Cappelletti	20
Lionel Taylor	908	Dick Christy	62	George Blair	17
Jim Colclough	868	Bo Dickinson	60	Bill Shockley	13
Charley Hennigan	867	Don Maynard	56	Tom Brooker	12

Punt Return Yards		Kickoff Return Yards	
Dick Christy	250	Dick Christy	824
Bob Jancik	164	Jerry Robinson	748
Bob Garner	162	Bo Roberson	748
Ron Burton	122	Bob Jancik	726
Abner Haynes	119	Larry Garron	686

All-Star Game
(Balboa Stadium, San Diego)

January 13 1963	West Division	21		East Division	14

AFL Championship

December 23	Dallas Texans	20	at	Houston Oilers	17

Individual Awards

AFL All Star Game MVP--Curtis McClinton (Dallas Texans)
Earl Faison (San Diego Chargers)
Rookie of the Year--Curtis McClinton (Dallas Texans)
U.P.I. AFL-AFC Coach of the Year--Jack Faulkner (Denver Broncos)
U.P.I. AFL-AFC Player of the Year--Cookie Gilchrist (Buffalo Bills)
U.P.I. AFL-AFC Rookie of the Year--Curtis McClinton (Dallas Texans)

Notes

The AFL championship game went into a second overtime quarter before the outcome was decided.

Canadian Football League
Eastern Conference

Team Name	GP	W	L	T	PF	PA	Pts	Pct
Hamilton Tiger-Cats	14	9	4	1	358	286	19	.679
Ottawa Rough Riders	14	6	7	1	339	302	13	.464
Montreal Alouettes	14	4	7	3	308	309	11	.393
Toronto Argonauts	14	4	10	0	250	378	8	.286

Western Conference

Team Name	GP	W	L	T	PF	PA	Pts	Pct
Winnipeg Blue Bombers	16	11	5	0	385	291	22	.688
Calgary Stampeders	16	9	6	1	352	335	19	.594
Saskatchewan Roughriders	16	8	7	1	268	336	17	.531
British Columbia Lions	16	7	9	0	346	342	14	.438
Edmonton Eskimos	16	6	9	1	310	346	13	.406

Coaching Changes

Toronto--Lou Agase 0-3-0, Nobby Wirkowski 4-7-0; British Columbia--Dave Skrien 7-9-0.

League Leaders

Yards Rushing		Yards Passing		Passing %	
George Dixon	1520	Joe Kapp	3279	Joe Kapp	55
Nub Beamer	1161			Tobin Rote	54
Earl Lunsford	1016				

Receptions		Points	
Tommy Joe Coffey	65	Tommy Joe Coffey	129

Grey Cup Playoffs

November 10	Saskatchewan	0	at	Calgary Stampeders	25
November 10	Montreal Alouettes	18	at	Ottawa Rough Riders	17
November 12	Calgary Stampeders	18	at	Saskatchewan Roughriders	7
November 17	Winnipeg Blue Bombers	14	at	Calgary Stampeders	20
November 17	Hamilton Tiger-Cats	28	at	Montreal Alouettes	17
November 21	Calgary Stampeders	11	at	Winnipeg Blue Bombers	19
November 24	Montreal Alouettes	21	at	Hamilton Tiger-Cats	30
November 24	Calgary Stampeders	7	at	Winnipeg Blue Bombers	12
December 1	Winnipeg Blue Bombers	28		Hamilton Tiger-Cats	27 *

*Game played in Toronto

Individual Awards

Annis Stukus Trophy--Steve Owen (Saskatchewan Roughriders)
Dave Dryburgh Memorial Trophy--Tommy Joe Coffey (Edmonton Eskimos)
DeMarco-Becket Memorial Trophy--Tom Brown (British Columbia Lions)
Dr. Beattie Martin Trophy--Ted Frechette (Edmonton Eskimos)
Eddie James Memorial Trophy--Nub Beamer (British Columbia Lions)
Grey Cup MVP--Leo Lewis (Winnipeg Blue Bombers)
Gruen Trophy--Whit Tucker (Ottawa Rough Riders)
Jeff Nicklin Memorial Trophy--Eagle Day (Calgary Stampeders)
Jeff Russel Memorial Trophy--George Dixon (Montreal Alouettes)
Schenley Award Most Outstanding Canadian--Harvey Wylie (Calgary Stampeders)
Schenley Award Most Outstanding Lineman--John Barrow (Hamilton Tiger-Cats)
Schenley Award Most Outstanding Player--George Dixon (Montreal Alouettes)

Notes

Two football Halls of Fame were established this year with the founding of the Canadian Football Hall of Fame in Hamilton and the Football Hall of Fame in Canton Ohio.
This year's Grey Cup game was stopped by fog with 9 minutes and 29 seconds left to play, the remainder of the game was played the following day.

HOCKEY
National Hockey League

Team Name	GP	W	L	T	GF	GA	Pts	Pct
Montreal Canadiens	70	42	14	14	259	166	98	.700
Toronto Maple Leafs	70	37	22	11	232	180	85	.607
Chicago Black Hawks	70	31	26	13	217	186	75	.536
New York Rangers	70	26	32	12	195	207	64	.457
Detroit Red Wings	70	23	33	14	184	219	60	.429
Boston Bruins	70	15	47	8	177	306	38	.271

Coaching Changes

New York--Doug Harvey 26-32-12; Boston--Phil Watson 15-47-8.

League Leaders

Goals		Assists		Points	
Bobby Hull	50	Andy Bathgate	56	Bobby Hull	84
Gordie Howe	33	Stan Mikita	52	Andy Bathgate	84
Frank Mahovlich	33	Bill Hay	52	Gordie Howe	77
Claude Provost	33	Gordie Howe	44	Stan Mikita	77
Gilles Tremblay	32	Alex Delvecchio	43	Frank Mahovlich	71

Penalty Minutes		GAA		Wins	
Lou Fontinato	167	Jacques Plante	2.37	Jacques Plante	42
Ted Green	116	Johnny Bower	2.58	Johnny Bower	32
Bob Pulford	98	Glenn Hall	2.66	Glenn Hall	31
Pierre Pilote	97	Hank Bassen	2.81	Lorne Worsley	22
Bob Baun	94	Lorne Worsley	2.97	Terry Sawchuk	14

Shutouts

Glenn Hall	9
Terry Sawchuk	5
Jacques Plante	4
Hank Bassen	3
John Bower	2

All Star Game

(Chicago Stadium, Chicago)

October 7 1961	All Stars	3	Chicago Black Hawks	1

Stanley Cup Playoffs

March 27	Chicago Black Hawks	1	at	Montreal Canadiens	2
March 27	New York Rangers	2	at	Toronto Maple Leafs	4
March 29	Chicago Black Hawks	3	at	Montreal Canadiens	4
March 29	New York Rangers	1	at	Toronto Maple Leafs	2
April 1	Montreal Canadiens	1	at	Chicago Black Hawks	4
April 1	Toronto Maple Leafs	4	at	New York Rangers	5
April 3	Montreal Canadiens	3	at	Chicago Black Hawks	5
April 3	Toronto Maple Leafs	2	at	New York Rangers	4
April 5	Chicago Black Hawks	4	at	Montreal Canadiens	3
April 5	New York Rangers	2	at	Toronto Maple Leafs	3 [24:23]
April 7	New York Rangers	1	at	Toronto Maple Leafs	7
April 8	Montreal Canadiens	0	at	Chicago Black Hawks	2
April 10	Chicago Black Hawks	1	at	Toronto Maple Leafs	4
April 12	Chicago Black Hawks	2	at	Toronto Maple Leafs	3
April 15	Toronto Maple Leafs	0	at	Chicago Black Hawks	3
April 17	Toronto Maple Leafs	1	at	Chicago Black Hawks	4
April 19	Chicago Black Hawks	4	at	Toronto Maple Leafs	8
April 22	Toronto Maple Leafs	2	at	Chicago Black Hawks	1

All Star Teams

First Team		Second Team
Jacques Plante	Goal	Glenn Hall
Doug Harvey	Defense	Carl Brewer
Jean-Guy Talbot	Defense	Pierre Pilote
Stan Mikita	Center	Dave Keon
Andy Bathgate	Right Wing	Gordie Howe
Bobby Hull	Left Wing	Frank Mahovlich

Individual Awards

Art Ross Trophy--Bobby Hull (Chicago Black Hawks)
Calder Memorial Trophy--Bobby Rousseau (Montreal Canadiens)
Hart Memorial Trophy--Jacques Plante (Montreal Canadiens)
James Norris Trophy--Doug Harvey (New York Rangers)
Lady Byng Memorial Trophy--Dave Keon (Toronto Maple Leafs)
NHL All Star Game MVP--Eddie Shack (Toronto Maple Leafs)
Vezina Trophy--Jacques Plante (Montreal Canadiens)

Hall of Fame Inductees

Frank Ahearn, Harry Broadbent, Walter Brown, Harold Cameron, Russell Crawford, Jack Darragh, Jimmy Gardner, Billy Gilmour, Wilfred Green, Riley Hern, Tom Hooper, Fred Hume, Bouse Hutton, Harry Hyland, Jack Laviolette, Fred Maxwell, Billy McGimsie, Reg Noble, James Norris Jr., John O'Brien, Didier Pitre, Mike Rodden, Jack Ruttan, David Schriner, Harold Simpson, Alfred Smith, Frank Smith, Barney Stanley, Nels Stewart, Marty Walsh, Harry Watson, Harry Westwick, Fred Whitcroft, Gordon Wilson

Other Sports

Horseracing--Kentucky Derby won by Decidedly (time 2:00.4, purse $119,650).
Heavyweight Boxing--Sonny Liston knocked-out Floyd Patterson in 1 round.
Golf--U.S. Open won by Jack Nicklaus in a playoff with Arnold Palmer (scores of 283-283, 71-74).
Auto Racing--Indianapolis 500 won by Rodger Ward (ave. speed 140.292 MPH).
Tennis--U.S. Open won by Rod Laver in the men's singles.
U.S. Open won by Rafael Osuna and Antonio Palafox in the men's doubles.
U.S. Open won by Margaret Smith in the women's singles.
U.S. Open won by Maria Bueno and Darlene Hard in the women's doubles.
U.S. Open won by Margaret Smith and Fred Stolle in the mixed doubles.

1963

BASEBALL
National League

Team Name	W	L	Pct	GB	R	OR
Los Angeles Dodgers	99	63	.611	-	640	550
St. Louis Cardinals	93	69	.574	6	747	628
San Francisco Giants	88	74	.543	11	725	641
Philadelphia Phillies	87	75	.537	12	642	578
Cincinnati Reds	86	76	.531	13	648	594
Milwaukee Braves	84	78	.519	15	677	603
Chicago Cubs	82	80	.506	17	570	578
Pittsburgh Pirates	74	88	.457	25	567	595
Houston Colt 45s	66	96	.407	33	464	640
New York Mets	51	111	.315	48	501	774

Coaching Changes

Milwaukee--Bob Bragan 84-78; Chicago--Bob Kennedy 82-80.

League Leaders

Batting Average

Tom Davis	.326
Roberto Clemente	.320
Dick Groat	.319
Hank Aaron	.319
Orlando Cepeda	.316

Home Runs

Hank Aaron	44
Willie McCovey	44
Willie Mays	38
Orlando Cepeda	34
Frank Howard	28

RBI

Hank Aaron	130
Ken Boyer	111
Bill White	109
Vada Pinson	106
Willie Mays	103

Stolen Bases

Maury Wills	40
Hank Aaron	31
Vada Pinson	27
Frank Robinson	26
Willie Davis	25

ERA

Sandy Koufax	1.88
Dick Ellsworth	2.11
Bob Friend	2.34
Juan Marichal	2.41
Curt Simmons	2.48

Wins

Juan Marichal	25
Sandy Koufax	25
Warren Spahn	23
Jim Maloney	23
Dick Ellsworth	22

Saves

Lindy McDaniel	22
Ron Perranoski	21
Elroy Face	16
Jack Baldschun	16
Bill Henry	14

Strikeouts

Sandy Koufax	306
Jim Maloney	265
Don Drysdale	251
Juan Marichal	248
Bob Gibson	204

American League

Team Name	W	L	Pct	GB	R	OR
New York Yankees	104	57	.646	-	714	547
Chicago White Sox	94	68	.580	10.5	683	544
Minnesota Twins	91	70	.565	13	767	602
Baltimore Orioles	86	76	.531	18.5	644	621
Cleveland Indians	79	83	.488	25.5	635	702
Detroit Tigers	79	83	.488	25.5	700	703
Boston Red Sox	76	85	.472	28	666	704
Kansas City Athletics	73	89	.451	31.5	615	704
Los Angeles Angels	70	91	.435	34	597	660
Washington Senators	56	106	.346	48.5	578	812

Coaching Changes

Cleveland--George Tebbetts 79-83; Detroit--Bob Scheffing 24-36, Charles Dressen 55-47; Boston--John Pesky 76-85; Kansas City--Ed Lopat 73-89; Washington--James Vernon 14-26, Gil Hodges 42-80.

League Leaders

Batting Average		Home Runs		RBI	
Carl Yastrzemski	.321	Harmon Killebrew	45	Dick Stuart	118
Al Kaline	.312	Dick Stuart	42	Al Kaline	101
Richard Rollins	.307	Bob Allison	35	Harmon Killebrew	96
Albert Pearson	.304	Jimmie Hall	33	Rocky Colavito	91
Pete Ward	.295	Elston Howard	28	Bob Allison	91

Stolen Bases		ERA		Wins	
Lou Aparicio	40	Gary Peters	2.33	Edward Ford	24
Charles Hinton	25	Juan Pizarro	2.39	Jim Bouton	21
Russ Snyder	18	Camilo Pascual	2.46	Camilo Pascual	21
Jake Wood	18	Jim Bouton	2.53	Bill Monbouquette	20
Albert Pearson	17	Al Downing	2.56	Steve Barber	20

Saves		Strikeouts	
Stu Miller	27	Camilo Pascual	202
Dick Radatz	25	Jim Bunning	196
Bill Dailey	21	Dick Stigman	193
Hoyt Wilhelm	21	Gary Peters	189
John Wyatt	21	Edward Ford	189

All Star Game

(Cleveland Stadium, Cleveland)

July 9	National League	5		American League	3

World Series

October 2	Los Angeles Dodgers	5	at	New York Yankees	2
October 3	Los Angeles Dodgers	4	at	New York Yankees	1
October 5	New York Yankees	0	at	Los Angeles Dodgers	1
October 6	New York Yankees	1	at	Los Angeles Dodgers	2

Individual Awards

Arch Ward Memorial Trophy--Willie Mays (San Francisco Giants NL)
Baseball Writers Award--Sandy Koufax (Los Angeles Dodgers NL)
Elston Howard (New York Yankees AL)
Cy Young Award--Sandy Koufax (Los Angeles Dodgers NL)
Rookie of the Year--Pete Rose (Cincinnati Reds NL)
Gary Peters (Chicago White Sox AL)
Sporting News Executive of the Year--Bing Devine (St. Louis Cardinals NL)
Sporting News Manager of the Year--Walter Alston (Los Angeles Dodgers NL)
Sporting News Pitcher of the Year--Sandy Koufax (Los Angeles Dodgers NL)
Whitey Ford (New York Yankees AL)
Sporting News Player of the Year--Hank Aaron (Milwaukee Braves NL)
Al Kaline (Detroit Tigers AL)
Sporting News Rookie of the Year--Pete Rose (Cincinnati Reds NL)
Ray Culp (Philadelphia Phillies NL)
Pete Ward (Chicago White Sox AL)
Gary Peters (Chicago White Sox AL)
World Series MVP--Sandy Koufax (Los Angeles Dodgers NL)

Hall of Fame Inductees

John Clarkson, Elmer Flick, Sam Rice, Eppa Rixey

Rules

Strike zone to include area from the top of the shoulder to the bottom of the knee (NL, AL).

BASKETBALL
National Basketball Association
Eastern Division

Team Name	GP	W	L	PPGF	PPGA	Pct	GB
Boston Celtics	80	58	22	118.8	111.6	.725	-
Syracuse Nationals	80	48	32	121.6	117.8	.600	10
Cincinnati Royals	80	42	38	119.0	117.8	.525	16
New York Knickerbockers	80	21	59	110.5	117.7	.356	37

Western Division

Team Name	GP	W	L	PPGF	PPGA	Pct	GB
Los Angeles Lakers	80	53	27	115.5	112.4	.663	-
St. Louis Hawks	80	48	32	109.6	107.8	.600	5
Detroit Pistons	80	34	46	113.9	117.6	.425	19
San Francisco Warriors	80	31	49	118.5	120.6	.388	22
Chicago Zephyrs	80	25	55	109.9	113.9	.313	28

Coaching Changes

St. Louis--Harry Gallatin 48-32; San Francisco--Bob Feerick 31-49; Chicago--Jack McMahon 12-26, Bob Leonard 13-29.

League Leaders

Field Goals		Free Throws		Assists	
Wilt Chamberlain	1463	Bob Pettit	685	Guy Rodgers	825
Elgin Baylor	1029	Elgin Baylor	661	Oscar Robertson	758
Walt Bellamy	840	Wilt Chamberlain	660	Bob Cousy	515
Oscar Robertson	825	Oscar Robertson	614	Sihugo Green	422
Bob Pettit	778	Walt Bellamy	553	Elgin Baylor	386

Points		Fouls	
Wilt Chamberlain	3586	Zelmo Beaty	312
Elgin Baylor	2719	Bailey Howell	300
Oscar Robertson	2264	Bob Boozer	299
Bob Pettit	2241	Guy Rodgers	296
Walt Bellamy	2233	Tom Gola	295

All Star Game

(Los Angeles Sports Arena, Los Angeles)

January 16	East Division	115	West Division	108

Notes

J. Walter Kennedy replaced Maurice Podoloff to become the second commissioner of the NBA.

NBA Playoffs

March 19	Cincinnati Royals	120	at	Syracuse Nationals	123
March 20	Detroit Pistons	99	at	St. Louis Hawks	118
March 21	Syracuse Nationals	115	at	Cincinnati Royals	133
March 22	Detroit Pistons	108	at	St. Louis Hawks	122
March 23	Cincinnati Royals	117	at	Syracuse Nationals	121
March 24	St. Louis Hawks	103	at	Detroit Pistons	107
March 24	Syracuse Nationals	118	at	Cincinnati Royals	125
March 26	St. Louis Hawks	104	at	Detroit Pistons	100
March 26	Cincinnati Royals	131	at	Syracuse Nationals	127 [OT]
March 28	Cincinnati Royals	135	at	Boston Celtics	132
March 29	Boston Celtics	125	at	Cincinnati Royals	102
March 31	Cincinnati Royals	121	at	Boston Celtics	116
March 31	St. Louis Hawks	104	at	Los Angeles Lakers	112
April 2	St. Louis Hawks	99	at	Los Angeles Lakers	101
April 3	Boston Celtics	128	at	Cincinnati Royals	110
April 4	Los Angeles Lakers	112	at	St. Louis Hawks	125
April 6	Cincinnati Royals	120	at	Boston Celtics	125
April 6	Los Angeles Lakers	114	at	St. Louis Hawks	124
April 7	Boston Celtics	99	at	Cincinnati Royals	109
April 7	St. Louis Hawks	100	at	Los Angeles Lakers	123
April 9	Los Angeles Lakers	113	at	St. Louis Hawks	121
April 10	Cincinnati Royals	131	at	Boston Celtics	142
April 11	St. Louis Hawks	100	at	Los Angeles Lakers	115
April 14	Los Angeles Lakers	114	at	Boston Celtics	117
April 16	Los Angeles Lakers	106	at	Boston Celtics	113
April 17	Boston Celtics	99	at	Los Angeles Lakers	119
April 19	Boston Celtics	108	at	Los Angeles Lakers	105
April 21	Los Angeles Lakers	126	at	Boston Celtics	119
April 24	Boston Celtics	112	at	Los Angeles Lakers	109

All Star Teams

First Team	Second Team
Elgin Baylor (Los Angeles Lakers)	Tom Heinsohn (Boston Celtics)
Bob Pettit (St. Louis Hawks)	Bailey Howell (Detroit Pistons)
Bill Russell (Boston Celtics)	Wilt Chamberlain (San Francisco Warriors)
Oscar Robertson (Cincinnati Royals)	Bob Cousy (Boston Celtics)
Jerry West (Los Angeles Lakers)	Hal Greer (Syracuse Nationals)

Individual Awards

Eddie Gottlieb Trophy--Terry Dischinger (Chicago Zephyrs)
Maurice Podoloff Trophy--Bill Russell (Boston Celtics)
NBA All Star Game MVP--Bill Russell (Boston Celtics)
Red Auerbach Trophy--Harry Gallatin (St. Louis Hawks)

Hall of Fame Inductees

Robert Gruenig, New York Renaissance, William Reid

FOOTBALL
National Football League

Eastern Conference

Team Name	GP	W	L	T	PF	PA	Pct
New York Giants	14	11	3	0	448	280	.786
Cleveland Browns	14	10	4	0	343	262	.714
St. Louis Cardinals	14	9	5	0	341	283	.643
Pittsburgh Steelers	14	7	4	3	321	295	.607
Dallas Cowboys	14	4	10	0	305	378	.286
Washington Redskins	14	3	11	0	279	398	.214
Philadelphia Eagles	14	2	10	2	242	381	.214

Western Conference

Team Name	GP	W	L	T	PF	PA	Pct
Chicago Bears	14	11	1	2	301	144	.857
Green Bay Packers	14	11	2	1	369	206	.821
Baltimore Colts	14	8	6	0	316	285	.571
Detroit Lions	14	5	8	1	326	265	.393
Minnesota Vikings	14	5	8	1	309	390	.393
Los Angeles Rams	14	5	9	0	210	350	.357
San Francisco 49ers	14	2	12	0	198	391	.357

Coaching Changes

Cleveland--Blanton Collier 10-4-0; Baltimore--Don Shula 8-6-0; Los Angeles--Harland Svare 5-9-0; San Francisco--Red Hickey 0-3-0; Jack Christiansen 2-9-0.

League Leaders

Yards Rushing		**Yards Passing**		**Passing %** (40 attempts)	
Jim Brown	1863	John Unitas	3481	Rudy Bukich	67
Jim Taylor	1018	Charley Johnson	3280	Y.A. Tittle	60
Tim Brown	841	Y.A. Tittle	3145	John Unitas	58
John Johnson	773	Norm Snead	3043	Fran Tarkenton	57
Tom Mason	763	Ed Brown	2982	Billy Wade	54

Receiving Yards		**Receptions**		**Field Goals**	
Bob Mitchell	1436	Bobby Conrad	73	Jim Martin	24
Buddy Dial	1295	Bobby Mitchell	69	Lou Michaels	21
Del Shofner	1181	Terry Barr	66	Don Chandler	18
Terry Barr	1086	Del Shofner	64	Jerry Kramer	16
Sonny Randle	1014	Buddy Dial	60	Lou Groza	15

Punt Return Yards		Kickoff Return Yards	
Tom Watkins	399	Tim Brown	945
Jerry Logan	279	Abe Woodson	935
Bill Butler	220	Dick James	830
Dick James	214	Carver Shannon	823
Brady Keys	198	Bill Butler	713

Pro Bowl Game
(Memorial Coliseum, Los Angeles)

January 12 1964	Western Conference	31		Eastern Conference	17

NFL Championship

December 29	New York Giants	10	at	Chicago Bears	14

Individual Awards

AP MVP--Y.A. Tittle (New York Giants)
Bert Bell Trophy--Jim Brown (Cleveland Browns)
Jim Thorpe Trophy--Jim Brown (Cleveland Browns)
Y.A. Tittle (New York Giants)
Pro Bowl MVP--Johnny Unitas (Baltimore Colts)
Gino Marchetti (Baltimore Colts)
Rookie of the Year--Paul Flatley (Minnesota Vikings)
U.P.I. MVP--Jim Brown (Cleveland Browns)
U.P.I. NFL-NFC Coach of the Year--George Halas (Chicago Bears)
U.P.I. NFL-NFC Rookie of the Year--Paul Flatley (Minnesota Vikings)

Hall of Fame Inductees

Sammy Baugh, Bert Bell, Joe Carr, Dutch Clark, Red Grange, George Halas, Mel Hein, Pete Henry, Cal Hubbard, Don Hutson, Curly Lambeau, Tim Mara, George Marshall, Johnny (Blood) McNally, Bronko Nagurski, Ernie Nevers

Notes

Alex Karras and Paul Hornung of Green Bay were suspended indefinitely for betting on games. Five members of the Detroit team were fined $2,000 each for betting on the championship games.

American Football League
Eastern Division

Team Name	GP	W	L	T	PF	PA	Pct
Boston Patriots	14	7	6	1	327	257	.536
Buffalo Bills	14	7	6	1	304	291	.536
Houston Oilers	14	6	8	0	302	372	.429
New York Jets	14	5	8	1	249	399	.393

Western Division

Team Name	GP	W	L	T	PF	PA	Pct
San Diego Chargers	14	11	3	0	399	256	.786
Oakland Raiders	14	10	4	0	363	288	.714
Kansas City Chiefs	14	5	7	2	347	263	.429
Denver Broncos	14	2	11	1	301	473	.179

Coaching Changes

New York--Weeb Ewbank 5-8-1; Oakland--Al Davis 10-4-0; Kansas City--Hank Stram 5-7-2.

League Leaders

Yards Rushing		Yards Passing		Passing % (40 attempts)	
Clem Daniels	1099	George Blanda	3003	Tobin Rote	59
Paul Lowe	1010	Jack Kemp	2914	Len Dawson	54
Cookie Gilchrist	979	Tobin Rote	2510	George Blanda	53
Keith Lincoln	826	Len Dawson	2389	Jack Kemp	51
Larry Garron	750	Babe Parilli	2335	Don Breaux	51

Receiving Yards		Receptions		Field Goals	
Art Powell	1304	Lionel Taylor	78	Gino Cappelletti	22
Lance Alworth	1206	Art Powell	73	George Blair	17
Lionel Taylor	1101	Bake Turner	71	Gene Mingo	16
Charley Hennigan	1051	Bill Miller	69	Mack Yoho	10
Bake Turner	1007	Chris Burford	68	George Blanda	9

Punt Return Yards		Kickoff Return Yards	
Claude Gibson	307	Bob Jancik	1317
Bob Suci	233	Charley Mitchell	954
Fred Glick	171	Bo Roberson	809
Ray Abruzzese	152	Larry Garron	693
Bob Jancik	145	Dick Christy	585

All Star Game

(Balboa Stadium, San Diego)

January 19 1964	Western Division	27		Eastern Division	24

AFL Championship

December 28	Boston Patriots	26	at	Buffalo Bills	8
January 5 1964	Boston Patriots	10	at	San Diego Chargers	51

Individual Awards

AFL All Star Game MVP--Keith Lincoln (San Diego Chargers)
Archie Matsos (Oakland Raiders)
Rookie of the Year--Billy Joe (Denver Broncos)
U.P.I. AFL-AFC Coach of the Year--Al Davis (Oakland Raiders)
U.P.I. AFL-AFC Player of the Year--Lance Alworth (San Diego Chargers)
U.P.I. AFL-AFC Rookie of the Year--Billy Joe (Denver Broncos)

Canadian Football league
Eastern Conference

Team Name	GP	W	L	T	PF	PA	Pts	Pct
Hamilton Tiger-Cats	14	10	4	0	312	214	20	.714
Ottawa Rough Riders	14	9	5	0	326	284	18	.643
Montreal Alouettes	14	6	8	0	277	297	12	.429
Toronto Argonauts	14	3	11	0	202	310	6	.214

Western Conference

British Columbia Lions	16	12	4	0	387	232	24	.750
Calgary Stampeders	16	10	4	2	427	323	22	.688
Saskatchewan Roughriders	16	7	7	2	223	266	16	.500
Winnipeg Blue Bombers	16	7	9	0	302	325	14	.438
Edmonton Eskimos	16	2	14	0	220	425	4	.125

Coaching Changes

Hamilton--Ralph Sazio 10-4-0; Montreal--Jim Trimble 6-8-0; Toronto--Nobby Wirkowski 3-11-0; Saskatchewan--Bob Shaw 7-7-2.

League Leaders

Yards Rushing		**Yards Passing**		**Passing %**	
Lovell Coleman	1343	Joe Kapp	3126	Joe Kapp	61
George Dixon	1270				
Willie Fleming	1234				

Receiving Yards		**Receptions**		**Points**	
Tommy Joe Coffey	1104	Bobby Taylor	74	George Fleming	135
Bobby Taylor	1057				

Grey Cup Playoffs

November 9	Saskatchewan Roughriders	9	at	Calgary Stampeders	35
November 9	Montreal Alouettes	5	at	Ottawa Rough Riders	17
November 11	Calgary Stampeders	12	at	Saskatchewan Roughriders	39
November 17	British Columbia Lions	19	at	Saskatchewan Roughriders	7
November 17	Hamilton Tiger-Cats	45	at	Ottawa Rough Riders	0
November 20	Saskatchewan Roughriders	13	at	British Columbia Lions	8
November 23	Saskatchewan Roughriders	1	at	British Columbia Lions	36
November 24	Ottawa Rough Riders	35	at	Hamilton Tiger-Cats	18
November 30	Hamilton Tiger-Cats	21	at	British Columbia Lions	10

Individual Awards

Annis Stukus Trophy--Dave Skrien (British Columbia Lions)
Dave Dryburgh Memorial Trophy--George Fleming (Winnipeg Blue Bombers)
DeMarco-Becket Memorial Trophy--Tom Brown (British Columbia Lions)
Dr. Beattie Martin Trophy--Peter Kempf (British Columbia Lions)
Eddie James Memorial Trophy--Lovell Coleman (Calgary Stampeders)
Gruen Trophy--Rick Black (Ottawa Rough Riders)
Jeff Nicklin Memorial Trophy--Joe Kapp (British Columbia Lions)
Jeff Russel Memorial Trophy--Garney Henley (Hamilton Tiger-Cats)
Schenley Award Most Outstanding Canadian--Russ Jackson (Ottawa Rough Riders)
Schenley Award Most Outstanding Lineman--Tom Brown (British Columbia Lions)
Schenley Award Most Outstanding Player--Russ Jackson (Ottawa Rough Riders)

Hall of Fame Inductees

Harry Batstone, Ormond Beach, Joe Breen, Wes Brown, Lionel Conacher, Ernest Cox, John DeGruchy, Seppi DuMoulin, Eddie Emerson, William Foulds, Hugh Gall, Lord Earl Grey, Harry Griffith, Frank Hannibal, Fritz Hanson, Jack Jacobs, Eddie James, Joe Krol, Smirle Lawson, Frank Leadlay, Percy Molson, Norman Perry, Russ Rebholz, Ted Reeve, Alvin Ritchie, Jeff Russel, Frank Shaughnessy, Benjamin Simpson, David Sprague, Piffles Taylor, Brian Timmis

HOCKEY
National Hockey League

Team Name	GP	W	L	T	GF	GA	Pts	Pct
Toronto Maple Leafs	70	35	23	12	221	180	82	.586
Chicago Black Hawks	70	32	21	17	194	178	81	.579
Montreal Canadiens	70	28	19	23	225	183	79	.564
Detroit Red Wings	70	32	25	13	200	194	77	.550
New York Rangers	70	22	36	12	211	233	56	.400
Boston Bruins	70	14	39	17	198	281	45	.321

Coaching Changes

New York--Murray Patrick 11-19-4, George Sullivan 11-17-8; Boston--Phil Watson 1-8-5, Milt Schmidt 13-31-12.

League Leaders

Goals		Assists		Points	
Gordie Howe	38	Henri Richard	50	Gordie Howe	86
Camille Henry	37	Jean Beliveau	49	Andy Bathgate	81
Frank Mahovlich	36	Gordie Howe	48	Stan Mikita	76
Andy Bathgate	35	Andy Bathgate	46	Frank Mahovlich	73
Parker MacDonald	33	Stan Mikita	45	Henri Richard	73

Penalty Minutes		GAA		Wins	
Howie Young	273	Terry Sawchuk	2.48	Glenn Hall	30
Carl Brewer	168	Jacques Plante	2.49	Terry Sawchuk	23
Lou Fontinato	141	Don Simmons	2.50	Jacques Plante	22
Ted Green	117	Glenn Hall	2.55	Lorne Worsley	22
Bill Gadsby	116	John Bower	2.62	John Bower	20

Shutouts	
Glenn Hall	5
Jacques Plante	5
Terry Sawchuk	3
John Bower	1
Don Simmons	1

All Star Game
(Maple Leaf Gardens, Toronto)

October 6 1962	Toronto Maple Leafs	4	All Stars	1

Stanley Cup Playoffs

Date	Visitor	Score		Home	Score
March 26	Montreal Canadiens	1	at	Toronto Maple Leafs	3
March 26	Detroit Red Wings	4	at	Chicago Black Hawks	5
March 28	Montreal Canadiens	2	at	Toronto Maple Leafs	3
March 28	Detroit Red Wings	2	at	Chicago Black Hawks	5
March 30	Toronto Maple Leafs	2	at	Montreal Canadiens	0
March 31	Chicago Black Hawks	2	at	Detroit Red Wings	4
April 2	Toronto Maple Leafs	1	at	Montreal Canadiens	3

April 2	Chicago Black Hawks	1	at	Detroit Red Wings	4
April 4	Montreal Canadiens	0	at	Toronto Maple Leafs	5
April 4	Detroit Red Wings	4	at	Chicago Black Hawks	2
April 7	Chicago Black Hawks	4	at	Detroit Red Wings	7
April 9	Detroit Red Wings	2	at	Toronto Maple Leafs	4
April 11	Detroit Red Wings	2	at	Toronto Maple Leafs	4
April 14	Toronto Maple Leafs	2	at	Detroit Red Wings	3
April 16	Toronto Maple Leafs	4	at	Detroit Red Wings	2
April 18	Detroit Red Wings	1	at	Toronto Maple Leafs	3

All Star Teams

First Team		Second Team
Glenn Hall	Goal	Terry Sawchuk
Pierre Pilote	Defense	Tim Horton
Carl Brewer	Defense	Elmer Vasko
Stan Mikita	Center	Henri Richard
Gordie Howe	Right Wing	Andy Bathgate
Frank Mahovlich	Left Wing	Bobby Hull

Individual Awards

Art Ross Trophy--Gordie Howe (Detroit Red Wings)
Calder Memorial Trophy--Kent Douglas (Toronto Maple Leafs)
Hart Memorial Trophy--Gordie Howe (Detroit Red Wings)
James Norris Trophy--Pierre Pilote (Chicago Black Hawks)
Lady Byng Memorial Trophy--Dave Keon (Toronto Maple Leafs)
NHL All Star Game MVP--Frank Mahovlich (Toronto Maple Leafs)
Vezina Trophy--Glenn Hall (Chicago Black Hawks)

Hall of Fame Inductees

Leo Dandurand, Ebbie Goodfellow, Tommy Gorman, Bob Hewitson, Frederick McLaughlin, Joe Primeau, Earl Seibert

Notes

The National Hockey League introduces their first amateur draft. Garry Monohan is chosen first overall by the Montreal Canadiens.

Franchise Changes

AFL--New York Titans became the New York Jets.
Dallas Texans became the Kansas City Chiefs.
NBA--Philadelphia Warriors became the San Francisco Warriors.
Chicago Packers became the Chicago Zephyrs.

Other Sports

Horseracing--Kentucky Derby won by Chateaugay (time 2:01.8, purse $108,900).
Heavyweight Boxing--Sonny Liston knocked-out Floyd Patterson in 1 round.
Golf--U.S. Open won by Julius Boros in a playoff with Jacky Cupit and Arnold Palmer (scores of 293-293-293, 70-73-76).
Auto Racing--Indianapolis 500 won by Parnelli Jones (ave. speed 143.137 MPH).
Tennis--U.S. Open won by Rafael Osuna in the men's singles.
U.S. Open won by Dennis Ralston and Chuck McKinley in the men's doubles.
U.S. Open won by Maria Bueno in the women's singles.
U.S. Open won by Margaret Smith and Robyn Ebbern in the women's doubles.
U.S. Open won by Margaret Smith and Kenneth Fletcher in the mixed doubles.

1964

BASEBALL

National League

Team Name	W	L	Pct	GB	R	OR
St. Louis Cardinals	93	69	.574	-	715	652
Cincinnati Reds	92	70	.568	1	660	566
Philadelphia Phillies	92	70	.568	1	693	632
San Francisco Giants	90	72	.556	3	656	587
Milwaukee Braves	88	74	.543	5	803	744
Los Angeles Dodgers	80	82	.494	13	614	572
Pittsburgh Pirates	80	82	.494	13	663	636
Chicago Cubs	76	86	.469	17	649	724
Houston Colt 45s	66	96	.407	27	495	628
New York Mets	53	109	.327	40	569	776

Coaching Changes

Cincinnati--Fred Hutchinson 60-49, Dick Sisler 32-21; Houston--Harry Craft 61-88, Luman Harris 5-8.

League Leaders

Batting Average		Home Runs		RBI	
Roberto Clemente	.339	Willie Mays	47	Ken Boyer	119
Hank Aaron	.328	Billy Williams	33	Ron Santo	114
Joe Torre	.321	Orlando Cepeda	31	Willie Mays	111
Richie Allen	.318	Jim Hart	31	Joe Torre	109
Lou Brock	.315	John Callison	31	John Callison	104

Stolen Bases		ERA		Wins	
Maury Wills	53	Sandy Koufax	1.74	Larry Jackson	24
Lou Brock	43	Don Drysdale	2.18	Juan Marichal	21
Willie Davis	42	Chris Short	2.20	Ray Sadecki	20
Tom Harper	24	Juan Marichal	2.48	Tony Cloninger	19
Frank Robinson	23	Jim Bunning	2.63	Sandy Koufax	19

Saves		Strikeouts	
Hal Woodeshick	23	Bob Veale	250
Al McBean	22	Bob Gibson	245
Jack Baldschun	21	Don Drysdale	237
Lindy McDaniel	15	Sandy Koufax	223
Barney Schultz	14	Jim Bunning	219

American League

Team Name	W	L	Pct	GB	R	OR
New York Yankees	99	63	.611	-	730	577
Chicago White Sox	98	64	.605	1	642	501
Baltimore Orioles	97	65	.599	2	679	567
Detroit Tigers	85	77	.525	14	699	678
Los Angeles Angels	82	80	.506	17	544	551
Cleveland Indians	79	83	.488	20	689	693
Minnesota Twins	79	83	.488	20	737	678
Boston Red Sox	72	90	.444	27	688	793
Washington Senators	62	100	.383	37	578	733
Kansas City Athletics	57	105	.352	42	621	836

Coaching Changes

New York--Yogi Berra 99-63; Baltimore--Hank Bauer 97-65; Detroit--Charles Dressen 85-77; Boston--John Pesky 70-90, Bill Herman 2-0; Washington--Gil Hodges 62-100; Kansas City--Ed Lopat 17-35, Mel McGaha 40-70.

League Leaders

Batting Average		Home Runs		RBI	
Tony Oliva	.323	Harmon Killebrew	49	Brooks Robinson	118
Brooks Robinson	.317	John Powell	39	Dick Stuart	114
Elston Howard	.313	Mickey Mantle	35	Mickey Mantle	111
Mickey Mantle	.303	Rocky Colavito	34	Harmon Killebrew	111
Floyd Robinson	.301	Dick Stuart	33	Rocky Colavito	102

Stolen Bases		ERA		Wins	
Lou Aparicio	57	Dean Chance	1.65	Gary Peters	20
Al Weis	22	Joe Horlen	1.88	Dean Chance	20
Vic Davalillo	21	Edward Ford	2.13	Wally Bunker	19
Dick Howser	20	Gary Peters	2.50	Dave Wickersham	19
Chuck Hinton	17	Juan Pizarro	2.56	Juan Pizarro	19

Saves		Strikeouts	
Dick Radatz	29	Al Downing	217
Hoyt Wilhelm	27	Camilo Pascual	213
Stuart Miller	23	Dean Chance	207
John Wyatt	20	Gary Peters	205
Bob Lee	19	Mickey Lolich	192

All Star Game

(Shea Stadium, New York)

July 7	National League	7	American League	4

World Series

October 7	New York Yankees	5	at	St. Louis Cardinals	9
October 8	New York Yankees	8	at	St. Louis Cardinals	3
October 10	St. Louis Cardinals	1	at	New York Yankees	2
October 11	St. Louis Cardinals	4	at	New York Yankees	3
October 12	St. Louis Cardinals	5	at	New York Yankees	2 [10]
October 14	New York Yankees	8	at	St. Louis Cardinals	3
October 15	New York Yankees	5	at	St. Louis Cardinals	7

Individual Awards

Arch Ward Memorial Trophy--John Callison (Philadelphia Phillies NL)
Baseball Writers Award--Ken Boyer (St. Louis Cardinals NL)
Brooks Robinson (Baltimore Orioles AL)
Cy Young Award--Dean Chance (Los Angeles Angels AL)
Rookie of the Year--Richie Allen (Philadelphia Phillies NL)
Tony Oliva (Minnesota Twins AL)
Sporting News Executive of the Year--Bing Devine (St. Louis Cardinals NL)
Sporting News Manager of the Year--Johnny Keane (St. Louis Cardinals NL)
Sporting News Pitcher of the Year--Sandy Koufax (Los Angeles Dodgers NL)
Dean Chance (Los Angeles Angels AL)
Sporting News Player of the Year--Ken Boyer (St. Louis Cardinals NL)
Brooks Robinson (Baltimore Orioles AL)
Sporting News Rookie of the Year--Richie Allen (Philadelphia Phillies NL)
Bill McCool (Cincinnati Reds NL)
Tony Oliva (Minnesota Twins AL)
Wally Bunker (Baltimore Orioles AL)
World Series MVP--Bob Gibson (St. Louis Cardinals NL)

Hall of Fame Inductees

Luke Appling, Red Faber, Burleigh Grimes, Miller Huggins, Tim Keefe, Henry Manush, John Ward

BASKETBALL
National Basketball Association

Eastern Division

Team Name	GP	W	L	PPGF	PPGA	Pct	GB
Boston Celtics	80	59	21	113.0	105.1	.738	-
Cincinnati Royals	80	55	25	114.7	109.7	.688	4
Philadelphia 76ers	80	34	46	112.2	116.5	.425	25
New York Knickerbockers	80	22	58	112.2	119.6	.275	37

Western Division

Team Name	GP	W	L	PPGF	PPGA	Pct	GB
San Francisco Warriors	80	48	32	107.7	102.6	.600	-
St. Louis Hawks	80	46	34	110.0	108.4	.575	2
Los Angeles Lakers	80	42	38	109.7	108.7	.525	6
Baltimore Bullets	80	31	49	111.9	113.6	.388	17
Detroit Pistons	80	23	57	107.8	115.5	.288	25

Coaching Changes

Cincinnati--Jack McMahon 55-25; Philadelphia--Dolph Schayes 34-46; San Francisco--Alex Hannum 48-32; Baltimore--Bob Leonard 31-49; Detroit--Charlie Wolf 23-57.

League Leaders

Field Goals		Free Throws		Assists	
Wilt Chamberlain	1204	Oscar Robertson	800	Oscar Robertson	868
Oscar Robertson	840	Bob Pettit	608	Guy Rodgers	556
Walt Bellamy	811	Jerry West	584	K.C. Jones	407
Bob Pettit	791	Wilt Chamberlain	540	Jerry West	403
Elgin Baylor	756	Walt Bellamy	537	Wilt Chamberlain	403

Points		Fouls	
Wilt Chamberlain	2948	Wayne Embry	325
Oscar Robertson	2480	Terry Dischinger	321
Bob Pettit	2190	Gus Johnson	321
Walt Bellamy	2159	Jerry Lucas	300
Jerry West	2064	Bob Pettit	300

All Star Game

(Boston Gardens, Boston)

January 14	East Division	111	West Division	107

NBA Playoffs

March 21	Los Angeles Lakers	104	at	St. Louis Hawks	115
March 22	Philadelphia 76ers	102	at	Cincinnati Royals	127
March 22	Los Angeles Lakers	90	at	St. Louis Hawks	106
March 24	Cincinnati Royals	114	at	Philadelphia 76ers	122
March 25	St. Louis Hawks	105	at	Los Angeles Lakers	107
March 25	Philadelphia 76ers	89	at	Cincinnati Royals	101
March 28	St. Louis Hawks	88	at	Los Angeles Lakers	97
March 28	Cincinnati Royals	120	at	Philadelphia 76ers	129
March 29	Philadelphia 76ers	124	at	Cincinnati Royals	130
March 30	Los Angeles Lakers	108	at	St. Louis Hawks	121
March 31	Cincinnati Royals	87	at	Boston Celtics	103
April 1	St. Louis Hawks	116	at	San Francisco Warriors	111
April 2	Cincinnati Royals	90	at	Boston Celtics	101
April 3	St. Louis Hawks	85	at	San Francisco Warriors	120
April 5	Boston Celtics	102	at	Cincinnati Royals	92
April 5	San Francisco Warriors	109	at	St. Louis Hawks	113
April 7	Boston Celtics	93	at	Cincinnati Royals	102
April 8	San Francisco Warriors	111	at	St. Louis Hawks	109
April 9	Cincinnati Royals	95	at	Boston Celtics	109
April 10	St. Louis Hawks	97	at	San Francisco Warriors	121
April 12	San Francisco Warriors	95	at	St. Louis Hawks	123
April 16	St. Louis Hawks	95	at	San Francisco Warriors	105
April 18	Boston Celtics	108	at	San Francisco Warriors	96
April 20	San Francisco Warriors	101	at	Boston Celtics	124
April 22	Boston Celtics	91	at	San Francisco Warriors	115
April 24	Boston Celtics	98	at	San Francisco Warriors	95
April 26	San Francisco Warriors	99	at	Boston Celtics	105

All Star Teams

First Team	Second Team
Bob Pettit (St. Louis Hawks)	Tom Heinsohn (Boston Celtics)
Elgin Baylor (Los Angeles Lakers)	Jerry Lucas (Cincinnati Royals)
Wilt Chamberlain (San Francisco Warriors)	Bill Russell (Boston Celtics)
Oscar Robertson (Cincinnati Royals)	John Havlicek (Boston Celtics)
Jerry West (Los Angeles Lakers)	Hal Greer (Philadelphia 76ers)

Individual Awards

Eddie Gottlieb Trophy--Jerry Lucas (Cincinnati Royals)
Maurice Podoloff Trophy--Oscar Robertson (Cincinnati Royals)
NBA All Star Game MVP--Oscar Robertson (Cincinnati Royals)
Red Auerbach Trophy--Alex Hannum (San Francisco Warriors)

Hall of Fame Inductees

John Bunn, Harold Foster, Nat Holman, Ned Irish, William Jones, Kenneth Loeffler, Honey Russell

FOOTBALL
National Football League

Eastern Conference

Team Name	GP	W	L	T	PF	PA	Pct
Cleveland Browns	14	10	3	1	415	293	.750
St. Louis Cardinals	14	9	3	2	357	331	.714
Washington Redskins	14	6	8	0	307	305	.429
Philadelphia Eagles	14	6	8	0	312	313	.429
Dallas Cowboys	14	5	8	1	250	289	.393
Pittsburgh Steelers	14	5	9	0	253	315	.357
New York Giants	14	2	10	2	241	399	.214

Western Conference

Team Name	GP	W	L	T	PF	PA	Pct
Baltimore Colts	14	12	2	0	428	225	.857
Green Bay Packers	14	8	5	1	342	245	.607
Minnesota Vikings	14	8	5	1	355	296	.607
Detroit Lions	14	7	5	2	280	260	.571
Los Angeles Rams	14	5	7	2	283	339	.429
Chicago Bears	14	5	9	0	260	379	.357
San Francisco 49ers	14	4	10	0	236	330	.286

Coaching Changes

Philadelphia--Joe Kuharich 6-8-0; San Francisco--Jack Christiansen 4-10-0.

League Leaders

Yards Rushing		**Yards Passing**		**Passing %** (40 attempts)	
Jim Brown	1446	Charley Johnson	3045	Rudy Bukich	62
Jim Taylor	1169	Sonny Jurgensen	2934	Bart Starr	60
John Johnson	1048	John Unitas	2824	King Hill	56
Bill Brown	866	Fran Tarkenton	2506	Fran Tarkenton	56
Don Perkins	768	John Brodie	2498	Billy Wade	56

Receiving Yards		Receptions		Field Goals	
John Morris	1200	John Morris	93	Jim Bakken	25
Terry Barr	1030	Mike Ditka	75	Lou Groza	22
Frank Clarke	973	Frank Clarke	65	Fred Cox	21
Gary Ballman	935	Bobby Conrad	61	Bruce Gossett	18
Paul Warfield	920	Bob Mitchell	60	Lou Michaels	17

Punt Return Yards		Kickoff Return Yards	
Mel Renfro	418	Mel Renfro	1017
Willie Wood	252	Clarence Childs	987
Tom Watkins	238	Abe Woodson	880
Wendell Harris	214	Pat Studstill	708
Elijah Pitts	191	Tim Brown	692

Pro Bowl Game
(Memorial Coliseum, Los Angeles)

January 10, 1965 Western Conference 34 Eastern Conference 14

NFL Championship

December 27 Baltimore Colts 0 at Cleveland Browns 27

Individual Awards

AP MVP--Johnny Unitas (Baltimore Colts)
Bert Bell Trophy--Charlie Taylor (Washington Redskins) [World Almanac]
Bert Bell Trophy--Johnny Unitas (Baltimore Colts)
Jim Thorpe Trophy--Lenny Moore (Baltimore Colts)
Pro Bowl MVP--Fran Tarkenton (Minnesota Vikings)
Terry Barr (Detroit Lions)
Rookie of the Year--Charlie Taylor (Washington Redskins)
U.P.I. MVP--Johnny Unitas (Baltimore Colts)
U.P.I. NFL-NFC Coach of the Year--Don Shula (Baltimore Colts)
U.P.I. NFL-NFC Rookie of the Year--Charley Taylor (Washington Redskins)

Hall of Fame Inductees

Jimmy Conzelman, Ed Healey, Clarke Hinkle, Link Lyman, Mike Michalske, Art Rooney, George Trafton

American Football League
Eastern Division

Team Name	GP	W	L	T	PF	PA	Pct
Buffalo Bills	14	12	2	0	400	242	.857
Boston Patriots	14	10	3	1	365	297	.750
New York Jets	14	5	8	1	278	315	.393
Houston Oilers	14	4	10	0	310	355	.286

Western Division

Team Name	GP	W	L	T	PF	PA	Pct
San Diego Chargers	14	8	5	1	341	300	.607
Kansas City Chiefs	14	7	7	0	366	306	.500
Oakland Raiders	14	5	7	2	303	350	.429
Denver Broncos	14	2	11	1	240	438	.179

Coaching Changes

Houston--Sammy Baugh 4-10-0; Denver--Jack Faulkner 0-4-0, Mac Speedie 2-7-1.

League Leaders

Yards Rushing		Yards Passing		Passing% (40 attempts)	
Cookie Gilchrist	981	Babe Parilli	3465	Len Dawson	56
Matt Snell	948	George Blanda	3287	John Hadl	54
Clem Daniels	824	Len Dawson	2879	Eddie Wilson	53
Sid Blanks	756	Cotton Davidson	2497	George Blanda	52
Abner Haynes	697	Dick Wood	2298	Mickey Slaughter	51

Receiving Yards		Receptions		Field Goals	
Charley Hennigan	1546	Charley Hennigan	101	Gino Cappelletti	25
Art Powell	1361	Art Powell	76	Pete Gogolak	19
Lance Alworth	1235	Lionel Taylor	76	Mike Mercer	15
Elbert Dubenion	1139	Frank Jackson	62	Jim Turner	13
Bake Turner	974	Lance Alworth	61	George Blanda	13

Punt Return Yards		Kickoff Return Yards	
Claude Gibson	419	Odell Barry	1245
Hagood Clarke	317	Bo Roberson	975
Bob Jancik	220	J.D. Garrett	749
Lance Alworth	189	Dave Grayson	679
Bill Baird	170	Bill Cannon	518

All Star Game

(Jeppesen Stadium, Houston)

January 16 1965	West Division	38		East Division	14

AFL Championship

December 26	San Diego Chargers	7	at	Buffalo Bills	20

Individual Awards

AFL All Star Game MVP--Keith Lincoln (San Diego Chargers)
Willie Brown (Denver Broncos)
Rookie of the Year--Matt Snell (New York Jets)
U.P.I. AFL-AFC Coach of the Year--Lou Saban (Buffalo Bills)
U.P.I. AFL-AFC Player of the Year--Gino Cappelletti (Boston Patriots)
U.P.I. AFL-AFC Rookie of the Year--Matt Snell (New York Jets)

Canadian Football League
Eastern Conference

Team Name	GP	W	L	T	PF	PA	Pts	Pct
Hamilton Tiger-Cats	14	10	3	1	329	201	21	.750
Ottawa Rough Riders	14	8	5	1	313	228	17	.607
Montreal Alouettes	14	6	8	0	192	264	12	.429
Toronto Argonauts	14	4	10	0	243	332	8	.286

Western Conference

British Columbia Lions	16	11	2	3	328	168	25	.781
Calgary Stampeders	16	12	4	0	352	249	24	.750
Saskatchewan Roughriders	16	9	7	0	330	282	18	.563
Edmonton Eskimos	16	4	12	0	223	458	8	.250
Winnipeg Blue Bombers	16	1	14	1	270	397	3	.094

Coaching Changes

Edmonton--Neil Armstrong 4-12-0.

League Leaders

Yards Rushing

Lovell Coleman	1629
Ed Buchanan	1390
Bob Swift	1054
George Reed	1012

Yards Passing

Joe Kapp	2816

Passing %

Joe Kapp	59
Jackie Parker	59

Receiving Yards

Tommy Joe Coffey	1142
Tom Grant	1029
Hugh Campbell	1000

Receptions

Tommy Joe Coffey	81

Points

Larry Robinson	106

Grey Cup Playoffs

November 7	Calgary Stampeders	25	at	Saskatchewan Roughriders	34
November 7	Montreal Alouettes	0	at	Ottawa Rough Riders	27
November 9	Saskatchewan Roughriders	6	at	Calgary Stampeders	51
November 14	British Columbia Lions	24	at	Calgary Stampeders	10
November 14	Hamilton Tiger-Cats	13	at	Ottawa Rough Riders	30
November 18	Calgary Stampeders	14	at	British Columbia Lions	10
November 21	Ottawa Rough Riders	8	at	Hamilton Tiger-Cats	26
November 22	Calgary Stampeders	14	at	British Columbia Lions	33
November 28	British Columbia Lions	34		Hamilton Tiger-Cats	24 *

Individual Awards

Annis Stukus Trophy--Ralph Sazio (Hamilton Tiger-Cats)
Dave Dryburgh Memorial Trophy--Larry Robinson (Calgary Stampeders)
DeMarco-Becket Memorial Trophy--Tom Brown (British Columbia Lions)
Dr. Beattie Martin Trophy--Billy Cooper (Winnipeg Blue Bombers)
Eddie James Memorial Trophy--Lovell Coleman (Calgary Stampeders)
Gruen Trophy--Al Irwin (Montreal Alouettes)
Jeff Nicklin Memorial Trophy--Tom Brown (British Columbia Lions)
Jeff Russel Memorial Trophy--Dick Shatto (Toronto Argonauts)
Schenley Award Most Outstanding Canadian--Tommy Grant (Hamilton Tiger-Cats)
Schenley Award Most Outstanding Lineman--Tom Brown (British Columbia Lions)
Schenley Award Most Outstanding Player--Lovell Coleman (Calgary Stampeders)

Hall of Fame Inductees

Tom Casey, Ross Craig, Tony Golab, Ted Morris, Jack Newton, Mike Rodden, Paul Rowe, Bert Warwick, Huck Welch

*Game played in Toronto

HOCKEY
National Hockey League

Team Name	GP	W	L	T	GF	GA	Pts	Pct
Montreal Canadiens	70	36	21	13	209	167	85	.607
Chicago Black Hawks	70	36	22	12	218	169	84	.600
Toronto Maple Leafs	70	33	25	12	192	172	78	.557
Detroit Red Wings	70	30	29	11	191	204	71	.507
New York Rangers	70	22	38	10	186	242	54	.386
Boston Bruins	70	18	40	12	170	212	48	.343

Coaching Changes

Chicago--Billy Reay 36-22-12; New York--George Sullivan 22-38-10; Boston--Milt Schmidt 18-40-12.

League Leaders

Goals		Assists		Points	
Bobby Hull	43	Andy Bathgate	58	Stan Mikita	89
Stan Mikita	39	Stan Mikita	50	Bobby Hull	87
Ken Wharram	39	Jean Beliveau	50	Jean Beliveau	78
Camille Henry	29	Gordie Howe	47	Andy Bathgate	77
Jean Beliveau	28	Pierre Pilote	46	Gordie Howe	73

Penalty Minutes		GAA		Wins	
Vic Hadfield	151	Johnny Bower	2.11	Glenn Hall	34
Terry Harper	149	Charlie Hodge	2.26	Charlie Hodge	33
Stan Mikita	149	Glenn Hall	2.31	Johnny Bower	24
Ted Green	145	Terry Sawchuk	2.60	Terry Sawchuk	24
Reg Fleming	140	Eddie Johnston	3.01	Jacques Plante	22

Shutouts	
Charlie Hodge	8
Glenn Hall	7
Eddie Johnston	6
Terry Sawchuk	5
Johnny Bower	5

All Star Game
(Maple Leaf Gardens, Toronto)

October 5 1963	Toronto Maple Leafs	3	All Stars	3

Stanley Cup Playoffs

March 26	Toronto Maple Leafs	0	at	Montreal Canadiens	2
March 26	Detroit Red Wings	1	at	Chicago Black Hawks	4
March 28	Toronto Maple Leafs	2	at	Montreal Canadiens	1
March 29	Detroit Red Wings	5	at	Chicago Black Hawks	4
March 31	Montreal Canadiens	3	at	Toronto Maple Leafs	2
March 31	Chicago Black Hawks	0	at	Detroit Red Wings	3
April 2	Montreal Canadiens	3	at	Toronto Maple Leafs	5

April 2	Chicago Black Hawks	3	at	Detroit Red Wings	2 [8:21]
April 4	Toronto Maple Leafs	2	at	Montreal Canadiens	4
April 5	Detroit Red Wings	2	at	Chicago Black Hawks	3
April 7	Montreal Canadiens	0	at	Toronto Maple Leafs	3
April 7	Chicago Black Hawks	2	at	Detroit Red Wings	7
April 9	Toronto Maple Leafs	3	at	Montreal Canadiens	1
April 9	Detroit Red Wings	4	at	Chicago Black Hawks	2
April 11	Detroit Red Wings	2	at	Toronto Maple Leafs	3
April 14	Detroit Red Wings	4	at	Toronto Maple Leafs	3 [7:52]
April 16	Toronto Maple Leafs	3	at	Detroit Red Wings	4
April 18	Toronto Maple Leafs	4	at	Detroit Red Wings	2
April 21	Detroit Red Wings	2	at	Toronto Maple Leafs	1
April 23	Toronto Maple Leafs	4	at	Detroit Red Wings	3 [1:42]
April 25	Detroit Red Wings	0	at	Toronto Maple Leafs	4

All Star Teams

First Team		Second Team
Glenn Hall	Goal	Charlie Hodge
Pierre Pilote	Defense	Elmer Vasko
Tim Horton	Defense	Jacques Laperriere
Stan Mikita	Center	Jean Beliveau
Ken Wharram	Right Wing	Gordie Howe
Bobby Hull	Left Wing	Frank Mahovlich

Individual Awards

Art Ross Trophy--Stan Mikita (Chicago Black Hawks)
Calder Memorial Trophy--Jacques Laperriere (Montreal Canadiens)
Hart Memorial Trophy--Jean Beliveau (Montreal Canadiens)
James Norris Trophy--Pierre Pilote (Chicago Black Hawks)
Lady Byng Memorial Trophy--Ken Wharram (Chicago Black Hawks)
NHL ALL Star Game MVP--Jean Beliveau (Montreal Canadiens)
Vezina Trophy--Charlie Hodge (Montreal Canadiens)

Hall of Fame Inductees

Doug Bentley, Angus Campbell, Bill Chadwick, Francis Dilio, Bill Durnan, Albert Siebert, "Black Jack" Stewart

Franchise Changes

NBA--Syracuse Nationals became the Philadelphia 76ers.
Chicago Zephyrs became the Baltimore Bullets.

Other Sports

Horseracing--Kentucky Derby won by Northern Dancer (time 2:00, purse $114,300).
Heavyweight Boxing--Cassius Clay knocked-out Sonny Liston in 7 rounds.
Golf--U.S. Open won by Ken Venturi with a score of 278.
Auto Racing--Indianapolis 500 won by A.J. Foyt (ave. speed 147.350 MPH).
Tennis--U.S. Open won by Roy Emerson in the men's singles.
U.S. Open won by Dennis Ralston and Chuck McKinley in the men's doubles.
U.S. Open won by Maria Bueno in the women's singles.
U.S. Open won by Billie Jean Moffitt and Karen Susman in the women's doubles.
U.S. Open won by Margaret Smith and John Newcombe in the mixed doubles.

1965

BASEBALL

National League

Team Name	W	L	Pct	GB	R	OR
Los Angeles Dodgers	97	65	.599	-	608	521
San Francisco Giants	95	67	.586	2	682	593
Pittsburgh Pirates	90	72	.556	7	675	580
Cincinnati Reds	89	73	.549	8	825	704
Milwaukee Braves	86	76	.531	11	708	633
Philadelphia Phillies	85	76	.528	11.5	654	667
St. Louis Cardinals	80	81	.497	16.5	707	674
Chicago Cubs	72	90	.444	25	635	723
Houston Astros	65	97	.401	32	569	711
New York Mets	50	112	.309	47	495	752

Coaching Changes

San Francisco--Herman Franks 95-67; Pittsburgh--Harry Walker 90-72; Cincinnati--Dick Sisler 89-73; St. Louis--Albert Schoendienst 80-81; Chicago--Bob Kennedy 24-32, Lou Klein 48-58; Houston--Luman Harris 65-97; New York--Casey Stengel 31-64, Wes Westrum 19-48.

League Leaders

Batting Average

Roberto Clemente	.329
Hank Aaron	.318
Willie Mays	.317
Billy Williams	.315
Pete Rose	.312

Home Runs

Willie Mays	52
Willie McCovey	39
Billy Williams	34
Frank Robinson	33
Ron Santo	33

RBI

Deron Johnson	130
Frank Robinson	113
Willie Mays	112
Billy Williams	108
Willie Stargell	107

Stolen Bases

Maury Wills	94
Lou Brock	63
Jim Wynn	43
Tom Harper	35
Willie Davis	25

ERA

Sandy Koufax	2.04
Juan Marichal	2.13
Vernon Law	2.15
Jim Maloney	2.54
Jim Bunning	2.60

Wins

Sandy Koufax	26
Tony Cloninger	24
Don Drysdale	23
Juan Marichal	22
Sam Ellis	22

Saves

Ted Abernathy	31
Bill McCool	21
Frank Linzy	21
Hal Woodeschick	18
Bill O'Dell	18

Strikeouts

Sandy Koufax	382
Bob Veale	276
Bob Gibson	270
Jim Bunning	268
Jim Maloney	244

Notes

The first enclosed major league baseball stadium opened in the spring when the Houston Astrodome became the home of the Houston Astros.

American League

Team Name	W	L	Pct	GB	R	OR
Minnesota Twins	102	60	.630	-	774	600
Chicago White Sox	95	67	.586	7	647	555
Baltimore Orioles	94	68	.580	8	641	578
Detroit Tigers	89	73	.549	13	680	602
Cleveland Indians	87	75	.537	15	663	613
New York Yankees	77	85	.475	25	611	604
California Angels	75	87	.463	27	527	569
Washington Senators	70	92	.432	32	591	721
Boston Red Sox	62	100	.383	40	669	791
Kansas City Athletics	59	103	.364	43	585	755

Coaching Changes

New York--Johnny Keane 77-85; California--Bill Rigney 75-87; Boston--Bi11 Herman 62-100; Kansas City--Mel McGaha 5-21, Haywood Sullivan 54-82.

League Leaders

Batting Average		Home Runs		RBI	
Tony Oliva	.321	Tony Conigliaro	32	Rocky Colavito	108
Carl Yastrzemski	.312	Norm Cash	30	Willie Horton	104
Vic Davalillo	.301	Willie Horton	29	Tony Oliva	98
Brooks Robinson	.297	Leon Wagner	28	Felix Mantilla	92
Leon Wagner	.294	Fred Whitfield	26	Fred Whitfield	90

Stolen Bases		ERA		Wins	
Bert Campaneris	51	Sam McDowell	2.18	James Grant	21
Jose Cardenal	37	Eddie Fisher	2.40	Mel Stottlemyre	20
Zoilo Versalles	27	Wilfred Siebert	2.43	Jim Kaat	18
Lou Aparicio	26	George Brunet	2.56	Sam McDowell	17
Vic Davalillo	26	Pete Richert	2.60	Wilfred Siebert	16

Saves		Strikeouts	
Ron Kline	29	Sam McDowell	325
Eddie Fisher	24	Mickey Lolich	226
Stuart Miller	24	Denny McLain	192
Bob Lee	23	Wilfred Siebert	191
Dick Radatz	22	Al Downing	179

Notes

William Eckert became the fourth commissioner of baseball replacing Ford Frick and Emmett Ashford becomes the first black umpire to be hired by major league baseball.
Satchel Paige of the Kansas City Athletics became the oldest person to play major league professional sports when at the age of 59 he pitched 3 innings allowing 1 hit.
Major league baseball introduced their amateur draft.

All Star Game

(Metropolitan Stadium, Bloomington)

July 13	National League	6	American League	5

World Series

October 6	Los Angeles Dodgers	2	at	Minnesota Twins	8
October 7	Los Angeles Dodgers	1	at	Minnesota Twins	5
October 9	Minnesota Twins	0	at	Los Angeles Dodgers	4
October 10	Minnesota Twins	2	at	Los Angeles Dodgers	7
October 11	Minnesota Twins	0	at	Los Angeles Dodgers	7
October 13	Los Angeles Dodgers	1	at	Minnesota Twins	5
October 14	Los Angeles Dodgers	2	at	Minnesota Twins	0

Individual Awards

Arch Ward Memorial Trophy--Juan Marichal (San Francisco Giants NL)
Baseball Writers Award--Willie Mays (San Francisco Giants NL)
Zoilo Versalles (Minnesota Twins AL)
Cy Young Award--Sandy Koufax (Los Angeles Dodgers NL)
Rookie of the Year--Jim Lefebvre (Los Angeles Dodgers NL)
Curt Blefary (Baltimore Orioles AL)
Sporting News Executive of the Year--Calvin Griffith (Minnesota Twins AL)
Sporting News Manager of the Year--Sam Mele (Minnesota Twins AL)
Sporting News Pitcher of the Year--Sandy Koufax (Los Angeles Dodgers NL)
James Grant (Minnesota Twins AL)
Sporting News Player of the Year--Willie Mays (San Francisco Giants NL)
Tony Oliva (Minnesota Twins AL)
Sporting News Rookie of the Year--Joe Morgan (Houston Astros NL)
Frank Linzy (San Francisco Giants NL)
Curt Blefary (Baltimore Orioles AL)
Marcelino Lopez (California Angels AL)
World Series MVP--Sandy Koufax (Los Angeles Dodgers NL)

Hall of Fame Inductees

James Galvin

BASKETBALL
National Basketball Association

Eastern Division

Team Name	GP	W	L	PPGF	PPGA	Pct	GB
Boston Celtics	80	62	18	112.8	104.5	.775	-
Cincinnati Royals	80	48	32	114.2	111.9	.600	14
Philadelphia 76ers	80	40	40	112.5	112.7	.500	22
New York Knickerbockers	80	31	49	107.4	111.1	.388	31

Western Division

Team Name	GP	W	L	PPGF	PPGA	Pct	GB
Los Angeles Lakers	80	49	31	111.9	109.9	.613	-
St. Louis Hawks	80	45	35	108.8	105.8	.563	4
Baltimore Bullets	80	37	43	113.6	115.8	.463	12
Detroit Pistons	80	31	49	108.5	111.9	.388	18
San Francisco Warriors	80	17	63	105.8	112.0	.213	32

Coaching Changes

New York--Eddie Donovan 12-26, Harry Gallatin 19-23; St. Louis--Harry Gallatin 17-16, Richie Guerin 28-19; Baltimore--Buddy Jeannette 37-43; Detroit--Charlie Wolf 2-9, Dave DeBusschere 29-40.

League Leaders

Field Goals		Free Throws		Assists	
Wilt Chamberlain	1063	Oscar Robertson	665	Oscar Robertson	861
Jerry West	822	Jerry West	648	Guy Rodgers	565
Sam Jones	821	Walt Bellamy	515	K.C. Jones	437
Oscar Robertson	807	Bailey Howell	504	Len Wilkens	431
Elgin Baylor	763	Elgin Baylor	483	Bill Russell	410

Points		Fouls	
Wilt Chamberlain	2534	Bailey Howell	345
Jerry West	2292	Willis Reed	339
Oscar Robertson	2279	Zelmo Beaty	328
Sam Jones	2070	Kevin Loughery	320
Elgin Baylor	2009	Satch Sanders	318

All Star Game

(Kiel Auditorium, St. Louis)

January 13	East Division	124	West Division	123

NBA Playoffs

March 24	Philadelphia 76ers	119	at	Cincinnati Royals	117
March 24	Baltimore Bullets	108	at	St. Louis Hawks	105
March 26	Cincinnati Royals	121	at	Philadelphia 76ers	120
March 26	Baltimore Bullets	105	at	St. Louis Hawks	129
March 27	St. Louis Hawks	99	at	Baltimore Bullets	131
March 28	Philadelphia 76ers	108	at	Cincinnati Royals	94 [OT]
March 30	St. Louis Hawks	103	at	Baltimore Bullets	109
March 31	Cincinnati Royals	112	at	Philadelphia 76ers	119
April 3	Baltimore Bullets	115	at	Los Angeles Lakers	121
April 4	Philadelphia 76ers	98	at	Boston Celtics	108
April 5	Baltimore Bullets	115	at	Los Angeles Lakers	118
April 6	Boston Celtics	103	at	Philadelphia 76ers	109
April 7	Los Angeles Lakers	115	at	Baltimore Bullets	122
April 8	Philadelphia 76ers	94	at	Boston Celtics	112
April 9	Los Angeles Lakers	112	at	Baltimore Bullets	114
April 9	Boston Celtics	131	at	Philadelphia 76ers	134 [OT]
April 11	Baltimore Bullets	112	at	Los Angeles Lakers	120
April 11	Philadelphia 76ers	108	at	Boston Celtics	114
April 13	Los Angeles Lakers	117	at	Baltimore Bullets	115
April 15	Philadelphia 76ers	109	at	Boston Celtics	110
April 18	Los Angeles Lakers	110	at	Boston Celtics	142
April 19	Los Angeles Lakers	123	at	Boston Celtics	129
April 21	Boston Celtics	105	at	Los Angeles Lakers	126
April 23	Boston Celtics	112	at	Los Angeles Lakers	99
April 25	Los Angeles Lakers	96	at	Boston Celtics	129

All Star Teams

First Team	Second Team
Elgin Baylor (Los Angeles Lakers)	Bob Pettit (St. Louis Hawks)
Jerry Lucas (Cincinnati Royals)	Gus Johnson (Baltimore Bullets)
Bill Russell (Boston Celtics)	Wilt Chamberlain (San Francisco-Philadelphia)
Oscar Robertson (Cincinnati Royals)	Sam Jones (Boston Celtics)
Jerry West (Los Angeles Lakers)	Hal Greer (Philadelphia 76ers)

Individual Awards

Eddie Gottlieb Trophy--Willis Reed (New York Knickerbockers)
Maurice Podoloff Trophy--Bill Russell (Boston Celtics)
NBA All Star Game MVP--Jerry Lucas (Cincinnati Royals)
Red Auerbach Trophy--Red Auerbach (Boston Celtics)

Hall of Fame Inductees

Walter Brown, Paul Hinkle, Howard Hobson, Bill Mokray

FOOTBALL

National Football League

Eastern Conference

Team Name	GP	W	L	T	PF	PA	Pct
Cleveland Browns	14	11	3	0	363	325	.786
Dallas Cowboys	14	7	7	0	325	280	.500
New York Giants	14	7	7	0	270	338	.500
Washington Redskins	14	6	8	0	257	301	.429
Philadelphia Eagles	14	5	9	0	363	359	.357
St. Louis Cardinals	14	5	9	0	296	309	.357
Pittsburgh Steelers	14	2	12	0	202	397	.143

Western Conference

Team Name	GP	W	L	T	PF	PA	Pct
Green Bay Packers	14	10	3	1	316	224	.750
Baltimore Colts	14	10	3	1	389	284	.750
Chicago Bears	14	9	5	0	409	275	.643
San Francisco 49ers	14	7	6	1	421	402	.536
Minnesota Vikings	14	7	7	0	383	403	.500
Detroit Lions	14	6	7	1	257	295	.464
Los Angeles Rams	14	4	10	0	269	328	.286

Coaching Changes

Pittsburgh--Mike Nixon 2-12-0; Detroit--Harry Gilmer 6-7-1.

League Leaders

Yards Rushing		Yards Passing		Passing % (40 attempts)	
Jim Brown	1544	John Brodie	3112	John Brodie	62
Gale Sayers	867	Rudy Bukich	2641	John Unitas	58
Tim Brown	861	Fran Tarkenton	2609	Rudy Bukich	56
Ken Willard	778	John Unitas	2530	Bart Starr	56
Jim Taylor	734	Earl Morrall	2446	Buddy Humphrey	55

Receiving Yards		Receptions		Field Goals	
Dave Parks	1344	Dave Parks	80	Fred Cox	23
Pete Retzlaff	1190	Tom McDonald	67	Jim Bakken	21
Tom McDonald	1036	Pete Retzlaff	66	Lou Michaels	17
Bob Hayes	1003	Bob Mitchell	60	Don Chandler	17
Bob Conrad	909	Bernie Casey	59	Tom Davis	17

Punt Return Yards		Kickoff Return Yards	
Alvin Haymond	403	Kermit Alexander	741
Rickie Harris	377	Clarence Childs	718
Leroy Kelly	265	Al Nelson	683
Kermit Alexander	262	Abe Woodson	665
Gale Sayers	238	Irv Cross	662

Pro Bowl Game
(Memorial Coliseum, Los Angeles)

January 15 1966	Eastern Conference	36		Western Conference	7

NFL Championship

December 26	Baltimore Colts	10	at	Green Bay Packers	13 [OT]
January 2 1966	Cleveland Browns	12	at	Green Bay Packers	23

Individual Awards

AP MVP--Jim Brown (Cleveland Browns)
Bert Bell Trophy--Gale Sayers (Chicago Bears) [World Almanac]
Bert Bell Trophy--Pete Retzlaff (Philadelphia Eagles)
Jim Thorpe Trophy--Jim Brown (Cleveland Browns)
Pro Bowl MVP--Jim Brown (Cleveland Browns)
Dale Meinert (St. Louis Cardinals)
Rookie of the Year--Gale Sayers (Chicago Bears)
U.P.I. MVP--Jim Brown (Cleveland Browns)
U.P.I. NFL-NFC Coach of the Year--George Halas (Chicago Bears)
U.P.I. NFL-NFC Rookie of the Year--Gale Sayers (Chicago Bears)

Hall of Fame Inductees

Guy Chamberlin, Paddy Driscoll, Otto Graham, Sid Luckman, Steve Van Buren, Bob Waterfield

American Football League
Eastern Division

Team Name	GP	W	L	T	PF	PA	Pct
Buffalo Bills	14	10	3	1	313	226	.750
New York Jets	14	5	8	1	285	303	.393
Boston Patriots	14	4	8	2	244	302	.357
Houston Oilers	14	4	10	0	298	429	.286

Western Division

Team Name	GP	W	L	T	PF	PA	Pct
San Diego Chargers	14	9	2	3	340	227	.750
Oakland Raiders	14	8	5	1	298	239	.607
Kansas City Chiefs	14	7	5	2	322	285	.571
Denver Broncos	14	4	10	0	303	392	.286

Coaching Changes

Houston--Hugh Taylor 4-10-0; Denver--Mac Speedie 4-10-0.

League Leaders

Yards Rushing		Yards Passing		Passing % (40 attempts)	
Paul Lowe	1121	John Hadl	2798	Len Dawson	53
Cookie Gilchrist	954	Babe Parilli	2597	Mickey Slaughter	51
Clem Daniels	884	George Blanda	2542	Don Breaux	51
Matt Snell	763	Jack Kemp	2368	John Hadl	50
Curtis McClinton	661	Len Dawson	2262	Joe Namath	48

Receiving Yards		Receptions		Field Goals	
Lance Alworth	1602	Lionel Taylor	85	Pete Gogolak	28
Don Maynard	1218	Lance Alworth	69	Jim Turner	20
Lionel Taylor	1131	Don Maynard	68	Herb Travenio	18
Art Powell	800	Ode Burrell	55	Gino Cappelletti	17
Charley Frazier	717	Art Powell	52	Gary Kroner	13

Punt Return Yards		Kickoff Return Yards	
Speedy Duncan	464	Abner Haynes	901
Claude Gibson	357	Charley Warner	825
Willie Mitchell	242	Speedy Duncan	612
Butch Byrd	220	Odell Barry	611
Odell Barry	210	Bert Coan	479

All Star Game

(Rice Stadium, Houston)

January 15 1966	All Stars	30		Buffalo Bills	19

AFL Championship

December 26	Buffalo Bills	23	at	San Diego Chargers	0

Individual Awards

AFL All Star Game MVP--Joe Namath (New York Jets)
Frank Buncom (San Diego Chargers)
Rookie of the Year--Joe Namath (New York Jets)
U.P.I. AFL-AFC Coach of the Year--Lou Saban (Buffalo Bills)
U.P.I. AFL-AFC Player of the Year--Paul Lowe (San Diego Chargers)
U.P.I. AFL-AFC Rookie of the Year--Joe Namath (New York Jets)

Notes

Both the NFL and the AFL voted to expand to the American south for the following season.

Canadian Football League
Eastern Conference

Team Name	GP	W	L	T	PF	PA	Pts	Pct
Hamilton Tiger-Cats	14	10	4	0	281	153	20	.714
Ottawa Rough Riders	14	7	7	0	300	234	14	.500
Montreal Alouettes	14	5	9	0	183	215	10	.357
Toronto Argonauts	14	3	11	0	193	360	6	.214

Western Conference

Team Name	GP	W	L	T	PF	PA	Pts	Pct
Calgary Stampeders	16	12	4	0	340	243	24	.750
Winnipeg Blue Bombers	16	11	5	0	301	262	22	.688
Saskatchewan Roughriders	16	8	7	1	276	277	17	.531
British Columbia Lions	16	6	9	1	286	273	13	.406
Edmonton Eskimos	16	5	11	0	257	400	10	.313

Coaching Changes

Toronto--Bob Shaw 3-11-0; Calgary--Jerry Williams 12-4-0; Saskatchewan--Eagle Keys 8-7-1.

League Leaders

Yards Rushing		Yards Passing		Passing %	
George Reed	1768	Joe Kapp	2961	Bernie Faloney	54
Lovell Coleman	1509				
Dave Raimey	1052				

Receiving Yards		Receptions		Points	
Hugh Campbell	1329	Tommy Joe Coffey	81	Larry Robinson	95
Tommy Joe Coffey	1286				

Grey Cup Playoffs

November 6	Montreal Alouettes	7	at	Ottawa Rough Riders	36
November 7	Saskatchewan Roughriders	9	at	Winnipeg Blue Bombers	15
November 13	Winnipeg Blue Bombers	9	at	Calgary Stampeders	27
November 14	Hamilton Tiger-Cats	18	at	Ottawa Rough Riders	13
November 17	Calgary Stampeders	11	at	Winnipeg Blue bombers	15
November 20	Winnipeg Blue Bombers	19	at	Calgary Stampeders	12
November 20	Ottawa Rough Riders	7	at	Hamilton Tiger-Cats	7
November 27	Hamilton Tiger-Cats	22		Winnipeg Blue Bombers	16*

*Game played in Toronto

Individual Awards

Annis Stukus Trophy--Bud Grant (Winnipeg Blue Bombers)
Dave Dryburgh Memorial Trophy--Larry Robinson (Calgary Stampeders)
DeMarco-Becket Memorial Trophy--Dick Fouts (British Columbia Lions)
Dr. Beattie Martin Trophy--Ron Forwick (Edmonton Eskimos)
Eddie James Memorial Trophy--George Reed (Saskatchewan Roughriders)
Gruen Trophy--Terry Evanshen (Montreal Alouettes)
Jeff Nicklin Memorial Trophy George Reed (Saskatchewan Roughriders)
Jeff Russel Memorial Trophy--Bernie Faloney (Montreal Alouettes)
Schenley Award Most Outstanding Canadian--Zeno Karcz (Hamilton Tiger-Cats)
Schenley Award Most Outstanding Lineman--Wayne Harris (Calgary Stampeders)
Schenley Award Most Outstanding Player--George Reed (Saskatchewan Roughriders)

Hall of Fame Inductees

Harold Bailey, Ab Box, Dean Griffing, Bob Isbister Sr., Frank McGill, Clair Warner

HOCKEY
National Hockey League

Team Name	GP	W	L	T	GF	GA	Pts	Pct
Detroit Red Wings	70	40	23	7	224	175	87	.621
Montreal Canadiens	70	36	23	11	211	185	83	.593
Chicago Black Hawks	70	34	28	8	224	176	76	.543
Toronto Maple Leafs	70	30	26	14	204	173	74	.529
New York Rangers	70	20	38	12	179	246	52	.371
Boston Bruins	70	21	43	6	166	253	48	.343

Coaching Changes

None.

League Leaders

Goals		Assists		Points	
Norm Ullman	42	Stan Mikita	59	Stan Mikita	87
Bobby Hull	39	Gordie Howe	47	Norm Ullman	83
Gordie Howe	29	Pierre Pilote	45	Gordie Howe	76
Stan Mikita	28	Alex Delvecchio	42	Bobby Hull	71
Claude Provost	27	Norm Ullman	41	Alex Delvecchio	67

Penalty Minutes		GAA		Wins	
Carl Brewer	177	John Bower	2.38	Roger Crozier	40
Ted Lindsay	173	Roger Crozier	2.42	Charlie Hodge	26
Pierre Pilote	162	Glenn Hall	2.43	Glenn Hall	18
Bob Baun	160	Denis DeJordy	2.52	Terry Sawchuk	17
John Ferguson	156	Terry Sawchuk	2.56	Denis DeJordy	16

Shutouts	
Roger Crozier	6
Glenn Hall	4
John Bower	3
Denis DeJordy	3
Eddie Johnston	3

All Star Game

(Maple Leaf Gardens, Toronto)

October 10 1964	All Stars	3		Toronto Maple Leafs	2

Stanley Cup Playoffs

April 1	Chicago Black Hawks	3	at	Detroit Red Wings	4
April 1	Toronto Maple Leafs	2	at	Montreal Canadiens	3
April 3	Toronto Maple Leafs	1	at	Montreal Canadiens	3
April 4	Chicago Black Hawks	3	at	Detroit Red Wings	6
April 6	Detroit Red Wings	2	at	Chicago Black Hawks	5
April 6	Montreal Canadiens	2	at	Toronto Maple Leafs	3 [4:17]
April 8	Detroit Red Wings	1	at	Chicago Black Hawks	2
April 8	Montreal Canadiens	2	at	Toronto Maple Leafs	4
April 10	Toronto Maple Leafs	1	at	Montreal Canadiens	3
April 11	Chicago Black Hawks	2	at	Detroit Red Wings	4
April 13	Detroit Red Wings	0	at	Chicago Black Hawks	4
April 13	Montreal Canadiens	4	at	Toronto Maple Leafs	3 [16:33]
April 15	Chicago Black Hawks	4	at	Detroit Red Wings	2
April 17	Chicago Black Hawks	2	at	Montreal Canadiens	3
April 20	Chicago Black Hawks	0	at	Montreal Canadiens	2
April 22	Montreal Canadiens	1	at	Chicago Black Hawks	3
April 25	Montreal Canadiens	1	at	Chicago Black Hawks	5
April 27	Chicago Black Hawks	0	at	Montreal Canadiens	6
April 29	Montreal Canadiens	1	at	Chicago Black Hawks	2
May 1	Chicago Black Hawks	0	at	Montreal Canadiens	4

All Star Teams

First Team		Second Team
Roger Crozier	Goal	Charlie Hodge
Pierre Pilote	Defense	Bill Gadsby
Jacques Laperriere	Defense	Carl Brewer
Norm Ullman	Center	Stan Mikita
Claude Provost	Right Wing	Gordie Howe
Bobby Hull	Left Wing	Frank Mahovlich

Individual Awards

Art Ross Trophy--Stan Mikita (Chicago Black Hawks)
Calder Memorial Trophy--Roger Crozier (Detroit Red Wings)
Conn Smythe Trophy--Jean Beliveau (Montreal Canadiens)
Hart Memorial Trophy--Bobby Hull (Chicago Black Hawks)
James Norris Trophy--Pierre Pilote (Chicago Black Hawks)
Lady Byng Memorial Trophy--Bobby Hull (Chicago Black Hawks)
NHL All Star Game MVP--Gordie Howe (Detroit Red Wings)
Vezina Trophy--Johnny Bower and Terry Sawchuk (Toronto Maple Leafs)

Hall of Fame Inductees

Marty Barry, Clint Benedict, Art Farrell, Foster Hewitt, Red Horner, Syd Howe, Thomas Lockhart, Jack Marshall, Bill Mosienko, Blair Russel, Ernest Russell, Fred Scanlan

Franchise Changes

NL--Houston Colt 45s became the Houston Astros.
AL--Los Angeles Angels became the California Angels.

Other Sports

Horseracing--Kentucky Derby won by Lucky Debonair (time 2:01.2, purse $112,000).
Heavyweight Boxing--Cassius Clay knocked-out Sonny Liston in 1 round.
Cassius Clay knocked-out Floyd Patterson in 12 rounds.
Golf--U.S. Open won by Gary Player in a playoff with Kel Nagle (scores of 282-282, 71-74).
Auto Racing--Indianapolis 500 won by Jim Clark (ave. speed 150.686 MPH).
Tennis--U.S.. Open won by Manuel Santans in the men's singles.
U.S. Open won by Roy Emerson and Fred Stolle in the men's doubles.
U.S. Open won by Margaret Smith in the women's singles.
U.S. Open won by Carole C. Graebner and Nancy Richey in the women's doubles.
U.S. Open won by Margaret Smith and Fred Stolle in the mixed doubles.

1966

BASEBALL
National League

Team Name	W	L	Pct	GB	R	OR
Los Angeles Dodgers	95	67	.586	-	606	490
San Francisco Giants	93	68	.578	1.5	675	626
Pittsburgh Pirates	92	70	.568	3	759	641
Philadelphia Phillies	87	75	.537	8	696	640
Atlanta Braves	85	77	.525	10	782	683
St. Louis Cardinals	83	79	.512	12	571	577
Cincinnati Reds	76	84	.475	18	692	702
Houston Astros	72	90	.444	23	612	695
New York Mets	66	95	.410	28.5	587	761
Chicago Cubs	59	103	.364	36	644	809

Coaching Changes

Atlanta--Bob Bragan 52-59, Bill Hitchcock 33-18; Cincinnati--Don Heffner 37-46, Dave Bristol 39-38; Houston--Grady Hatton 72-90; New York--Wes Westrum 66-95; Chicago--Leo Durocher 59-103.

League Leaders

Batting Average		Home Runs		RBI	
Matty Alou	.342	Hank Aaron	44	Hank Aaron	127
Felipe Alou	.327	Richie Allen	40	Roberto Clemente	119
Rico Carty	.326	Willie Mays	37	Richie Allen	110
Richie Allen	.317	Willie McCovey	36	Willie Mays	103
Roberto Clemente	.317	Joe Torre	36	Bill White	103

Stolen Bases		ERA		Wins	
Lou Brock	74	Sandy Koufax	1.73	Sandy Koufax	27
Roland Jackson	49	Mike Cuellar	2.22	Juan Marichal	25
Maury Wills	38	Juan Marichal	2.23	Bob Gibson	21
Adolfo Phillips	32	Jim Bunning	2.41	Gaylord Perry	21
Tom Harper	29	Bob Gibson	2.44	Chris Short	20

Saves		Strikeouts	
Phil Regan	21	Sandy Koufax	317
Elroy Face	18	Jim Bunning	252
Bill McCool	18	Bob Veale	229
Frank Linzy	16	Bob Gibson	225
Claude Raymond	16	Juan Marichal	222

American League

Team Name	W	L	Pct	GB	R	OR
Baltimore Orioles	97	63	.606	-	755	601
Minnesota Twins	89	73	.549	9	663	581
Detroit Tigers	88	74	.543	10	719	698
Chicago White Sox	83	79	.512	15	574	517
Cleveland Indians	81	81	.500	17	574	586
California Angels	80	82	.494	18	604	643
Kansas City Athletics	74	86	.463	23	564	648
Washington Senators	71	88	.447	25.5	557	659
Boston Red Sox	72	90	.444	26	655	731
New York Yankees	70	89	.440	26.5	611	612

Coaching Changes

Detroit--Chuck Dressen 16-10, Bob Swift 32-25, Frank Skaff 40-39; Chicago--Eddie Stanky 83-79; Cleveland--George Tebbetts 66-57, George Strickland 15-24; Kansas City--Alvin Dark 74-86; Boston--Bill Herman 64-82, Pete Runnels 8-8; New York--Johnny Keane 4-16, Ralph Houk 66-73.

League Leaders

Batting Average

Frank Robinson	.316
Tony Oliva	.307
Al Kaline	.288
John Powell	.287
Harmon Killebrew	.281

Home Runs

Frank Robinson	49
Harmon Killebrew	39
John Powell	34
Norm Cash	32
Joe Pepitone	31

RBI

Frank Robinson	122
Harmon Killebrew	110
John Powell	109
Willie Horton	100
Brooks Robinson	100

Stolen Bases

Bert Campaneris	52
Don Buford	51
Tommie Agee	44
Lou Aparicio	25
Jose Cardenal	24

ERA

Gary Peters	1.98
Joe Horlen	2.43
Steve Hargan	2.48
Jim Perry	2.54
Tommy John	2.62

Wins

Jim Kaat	25
Denny McLain	20
Earl Wilson	18
Wilfred Siebert	16
Jim Palmer	15

Saves

Jack Aker	32
Ron Kline	23
Larry Sherry	20
Eddie Fisher	19
Stuart Miller	18

Strikeouts

Sam McDowell	225
Jim Kaat	205
Earl Wilson	200
Pete Richert	195
Gary Bell	194

All Star Game

(Busch Stadium, St. Louis)

July 12	National League	2		American League	1

World Series

October 5	Baltimore Orioles	5	at	Los Angeles Dodgers	2
October 6	Baltimore Orioles	6	at	Los Angeles Dodgers	0
October 8	Los Angeles Dodgers	0	at	Baltimore Orioles	1
October 9	Los Angeles Dodgers	0	at	Baltimore Orioles	1

Individual Awards

Arch Ward Memorial Trophy--Brooks Robinson (Baltimore Orioles AL)
Baseball Writers Award--Roberto Clemente (Pittsburgh Pirates NL)
Frank Robinson (Baltimore Orioles AL)
Cy Young Award--Sandy Koufax (Los Angeles Dodgers NL)
Rookie of the Year--Tommy Helms (Cincinnati Reds NL)
Tommie Agee (Chicago White Sox AL)
Sporting News Executive of the Year--Lee MacPhail (Commissioner's Office)
Sporting News Manager of the Year--Hank Bauer (Baltimore Orioles AL)
Sporting News Pitcher of the Year--Sandy Koufax (Los Angeles Dodgers NL)
Jim Kaat (Minnesota Twins AL)
Sporting News Player of the Year--Roberto Clemente (Pittsburgh Pirates NL)
Frank Robinson (Baltimore Orioles AL)
Sporting News Rookie of the Year--Tommy Helms (Cincinnati Reds NL)
Don Sutton (Los Angeles Dodgers NL)
Tommie Agee (Chicago White Sox AL)
Jim Nash (Kansas City Athletics AL)
World Series MVP--Frank Robinson (Baltimore Orioles AL)

Hall of Fame Inductees

Casey Stengel, Ted Williams

BASKETBALL
National Basketball Association
Eastern Division

Team Name	GP	W	L	PPGF	PPGA	Pct	GB
Philadelphia 76ers	80	55	25	117.3	112.7	.688	-
Boston Celtics	80	54	26	112.7	107.8	.675	1
Cincinnati Royals	80	45	35	117.8	116.6	.563	10
New York Knickerbockers	80	30	50	116.7	119.3	.375	25

Western Division

Team Name	GP	W	L	PPGF	PPGA	Pct	GB
Los Angeles Lakers	80	45	35	119.5	116.4	.563	-
Baltimore Bullets	80	38	42	118.3	119.5	.475	7
St. Louis Hawks	80	36	44	111.4	112.0	.450	9
San Francisco Warriors	80	35	45	115.5	118.2	.438	10
Detroit Pistons	80	22	58	110.3	117.2	.275	23

Coaching Changes

New York--Harry Gallatin 6-15, Dick McGuire 24-35; Baltimore--Paul Seymour 38-42; St. Louis--Richie Guerin 36-44; Detroit--Dave DeBusschere 22-58.

League Leaders

Field Goals		Free Throws		Assists	
Wilt Chamberlain	1074	Jerry West	840	Oscar Robertson	847
Oscar Robertson	818	Oscar Robertson	742	Guy Rodgers	846
Jerry West	818	Rick Barry	569	K.C. Jones	503
Rick Barry	745	Wilt Chamberlain	501	Jerry West	480
Hal Greer	703	Dick Barnett	467	Lenny Wilkens	429

Points		**Fouls**	
Wilt Chamberlain	2649	Zelmo Beaty	344
Jerry West	2476	Bill Bridges	333
Oscar Robertson	2378	Tom Gola	326
Rick Barry	2059	Willis Reed	323
Walt Bellamy	1820	Satch Sanders	317

All Star Game

(Cincinnati Gardens, Cincinnati)

January 11	East Division	137		West Division	94

NBA Playoffs

March 23	Cincinnati Royals	107	at	Boston Celtics	103
March 24	St. Louis Hawks	113	at	Baltimore Bullets	111
March 26	Boston Celtics	132	at	Cincinnati Royals	125
March 27	St. Louis Hawks	105	at	Baltimore Bullets	100
March 27	Cincinnati Royals	113	at	Boston Celtics	107
March 30	Baltimore Bullets	112	at	St. Louis Hawks	121
March 30	Boston Celtics	120	at	Cincinnati Royals	103
April 1	Cincinnati Royals	103	at	Boston Celtics	112
April 1	St. Louis Hawks	106	at	Los Angeles Lakers	129
April 3	Boston Celtics	115	at	Philadelphia 76ers	96
April 3	St. Louis Hawks	116	at	Los Angeles Lakers	125
April 6	Philadelphia 76ers	93	at	Boston Celtics	114
April 6	Los Angeles Lakers	113	at	St. Louis Hawks	120
April 7	Boston Celtics	105	at	Philadelphia 76ers	111
April 9	Los Angeles Lakers	107	at	St. Louis Hawks	95
April 10	Philadelphia 76ers	108	at	Boston Celtics	114 [OT]
April 10	St. Louis Hawks	112	at	Los Angeles Lakers	100
April 12	Boston Celtics	120	at	Philadelphia 76ers	112
April 13	Los Angeles Lakers	127	at	St. Louis Hawks	131
April 15	St. Louis Hawks	121	at	Los Angeles Lakers	130
April 17	Los Angeles Lakers	133	at	Boston Celtics	129 [OT]
April 19	Los Angeles Lakers	109	at	Boston Celtics	129
April 20	Boston Celtics	120	at	Los Angeles Lakers	106
April 22	Boston Celtics	122	at	Los Angeles Lakers	117
April 24	Los Angeles Lakers	121	at	Boston Celtics	117
April 26	Boston Celtics	115	at	Los Angeles Lakers	123
April 28	Los Angeles Lakers	93	at	Boston Celtics	95

All Star Teams

First Team

Rick Barry (San Francisco Warriors)
Jerry Lucas (Cincinnati Royals)
Wilt Chamberlain (Philadelphia 76ers)
Oscar Robertson (Cincinnati Royals)
Jerry West (Los Angeles Lakers)

Second Team

John Havlicek (Boston Celtics)
Gus Johnson (Baltimore Bullets)
Bill Russell (Boston Celtics)
Sam Jones (Boston Celtics)
Hal Greer (Philadelphia 76ers)

Individual Awards

Eddie Gottlieb Trophy--Rick Barry (San Francisco Warriors)
Maurice Podoloff Trophy--Wilt Chamberlain (Philadelphia 76ers)
NBA All Star Game MVP--Adrian Smith (Cincinnati Royals)
Red Auerbach Trophy--Dolph Schayes (Philadelphia 76ers)

Hall of Fame Inductees

Everett Dean, Joe Lapchick

FOOTBALL
National Football League

Eastern Conference

Team Name	GP	W	L	T	PF	PA	Pct
Dallas Cowboys	14	10	3	1	445	239	.750
Cleveland Browns	14	9	5	0	403	259	.643
Philadelphia Eagles	14	9	5	0	326	340	.643
St. Louis Cardinals	14	8	5	1	264	265	.607
Washington Redskins	14	7	7	0	351	355	.500
Pittsburgh Steelers	14	5	8	1	316	347	.393
Atlanta Falcons	14	3	11	0	204	437	.214
New York Giants	14	1	12	1	263	501	.107

Western Conference

Team Name	GP	W	L	T	PF	PA	Pct
Green Bay Packers	14	12	2	0	335	163	.857
Baltimore Colts	14	9	5	0	314	226	.643
Los Angeles Rams	14	8	6	0	289	212	.571
San Francisco 49ers	14	6	6	2	320	325	.500
Chicago Bears	14	5	7	2	234	272	.429
Detroit Lions	14	4	9	1	206	317	.321
Minnesota Vikings	14	4	9	1	292	304	.321

Coaching Changes

St. Louis--Charley Winner 8-5-1; Washington--Otto Graham 7-7-0; Pittsburgh--Bill Austin 5-8-1; Atlanta--Norb Hecker 3-11-0; Los Angeles--George Allen 8-6-0.

League Leaders

Yards Rushing		**Yards Passing**		**Passing %** (40 attempts)	
Gale Sayers	1231	Sonny Jurgensen	3209	Bart Starr	62
Leroy Kelly	1141	Frank Ryan	2974	Bill Munson	60
Dick Bass	1090	John Brodie	2810	Sonny Jurgensen	58
Bill Brown	829	Don Meredith	2805	Dennis Claridge	57
Ken Willard	763	John Unitas	2748	John Unitas	56

Receiving Yards		**Receptions**		**Field Goals**	
Pat Studstill	1266	Charley Taylor	72	Bruce Gossett	28
Bob Hayes	1232	Pat Studstill	67	Jim Bakken	23
Charley Taylor	1119	Dave Parks	66	Charlie Gogolak	22
Homer Jones	1044	Bob Hayes	64	Mike Clark	21
Dave Parks	974	Tom Moore	60	Lou Michaels	21

Punt Return Yards		Kickoff Return Yards	
Alvin Haymond	347	Ron Smith	1013
Jim Stiger	259	Kermit Alexander	984
John Roland	221	Clarence Childs	855
Kermit Alexander	198	Roy Shivers	762
John Robinson	185	Gale Sayers	718

Pro Bowl Game

(Memorial Coliseum, Los Angeles)

January 22 1967	Eastern Conference	20		Western Conference	10

NFL Championship

January 1 1967	Green Bay Packers	34	at	Dallas Cowboys	27

Individual Awards

AP MVP--Bart Starr (Green Bay Packers)
Bert Bell Trophy--Tommy Nobis (Atlanta Falcons) [World Almanac]
Bert Bell Trophy--Don Meredith (Dallas Cowboys)
George Halas Trophy--Larry Wilson (St. Louis Cardinals)
Jim Thorpe Trophy--Bart Starr (Green Bay Packers)
Pro Bowl MVP--Gale Sayers (Chicago Bears)
Floyd Peters (Philadelphia Eagles)
Rookie of the Year--John Roland (St. Louis Cardinals)
Super Bowl MVP--Bart Starr (Green Bay Packers)
U.P.I. MVP--Bart Starr (Green Bay Packers)
U.P.I. NFL-NFC Coach of the Year--Tom Landry (Dallas Cowboys)
U.P.I. NFL-NFC Rookie of the Year--John Roland (St. Louis Cardinals)

Hall of Fame Inductees

Bill Dudley, Joe Guyon, Arnie Herber, Walt Kiesling, George McAfee, Steve Owen, Hugh Ray, Bulldog Turner

American Football League
Eastern Division

Team Name	GP	W	L	T	PF	PA	Pct
Buffalo Bills	14	9	4	1	358	225	.679
Boston Patriots	14	8	4	2	315	283	.643
New York Jets	14	6	6	2	322	312	.500
Houston Oilers	14	3	11	0	335	396	.214
Miami Dolphins	14	3	11	0	213	362	.214

Western Division

Team Name	GP	W	L	T	PF	PA	Pct
Kansas City Chiefs	14	11	2	1	448	276	.821
Oakland Raiders	14	8	5	1	315	288	.607
San Diego Chargers	14	7	6	1	335	284	.536
Denver Broncos	14	4	10	0	196	381	.286

Coaching Changes

Buffalo--Joe Collier 9-4-1; Houston--Wally Lemm 3-11-0; Miami--George Wilson 3-11-0; Oakland--John Rauch 8-5-1; Denver--Mac Speedie 0-2-0, Ray Malavasi 4-8-0.

League Leaders

Yards Rushing		Yards Passing		Passing % (40 attempts)	
Jim Nance	1458	Joe Namath	3379	Len Dawson	56
Mike Garrett	801	John Hadl	2846	John Hadl	53
Clem Daniels	801	Babe Parilli	2721	John Stofa	51
Bob Burnett	766	Tom Flores	2638	Max Choboian	50
Wray Carlton	696	Len Dawson	2527	Joe Namath	49

Receiving Yards		Receptions		Field Goals	
Lance Alworth	1383	Lance Alworth	73	Mike Mercer	21
Otis Taylor	1297	George Sauer	63	Booth Lusteg	19
Charley Frazier	1129	Otis Taylor	58	Jim Turner	18
George Sauer	1079	Chris Burford	58	George Blanda	16
Art Powell	1026	Charley Frazier	57	Dick Van Raaphorst	16

Punt Return Yards		Kickoff Return Yards	
Rodger Bird	323	Bob Jancik	875
"Speedy" Duncan	238	Charley Warner	846
Ed Rutkowski	209	Joe Auer	698
Butch Byrd	186	Emmitt Thomas	673
Mike Garrett	139	Emerson Boozer	659

All Star Game

(Oakland--Alameda County Coliseum, Oakland)

January 21 1967	East Division	30		West Division	23

AFL Championship

January 1 1967	Kansas City Chiefs	31	at	Buffalo Bills	7

Super Bowl I

(Memorial Coliseum, Los Angeles)

January 15 1967	Green Bay Packers	35		Kansas City Chiefs	10

Individual Awards

AFL All Star Game MVP--Babe Parilli (Boston Patriots)
Verlon Biggs (New York Jets)
Rookie of the Year--Bobby Burnett (Buffalo Bills)
U.P.I. AFL-AFC Coach--Mike Holovak (Boston Patriots)
U.P.I. AFL-AFC Player of the Year--Jim Nance (Boston Patriots)
U.P.I. AFL-AFC Rookie of the Year--Bobby Burnett (Buffalo Bills)

Notes

Al Davis took over from Joe Foss as Commissioner of the American Football League.
Milt Woodard succeeded Al Davis as Commissioner of the American Football League.
It was announced in June of 1966 that both the NFL and the AFL would merge in the near future. The clubs would conduct a common draft and finish the season with the Super Bowl. Pete Rozelle would act as commissioner.

Canadian Football League
Eastern Conference

Team Name	GP	W	L	T	PF	PA	Pts	Pct
Ottawa Rough Riders	14	11	3	0	278	177	22	.786
Hamilton Tiger-Cats	14	9	5	0	264	160	18	.643
Montreal Alouettes	14	7	7	0	156	215	14	.500
Toronto Argonauts	14	5	9	0	182	271	10	.357

Western Conference

Team Name	GP	W	L	T	PF	PA	Pts	Pct
Saskatchewan Roughriders	16	9	6	1	351	318	19	.594
Winnipeg Blue Bombers	16	8	7	1	264	230	17	.531
Edmonton Eskimos	16	6	9	1	251	328	13	.406
Calgary Stampeders	16	6	9	1	227	259	13	.406
British Columbia Lions	16	5	11	0	254	269	10	.313

Coaching Changes

None.

League Leaders

Yards Rushing		Yards Passing		Passing %	
George Reed	1409	Ron Lancaster	2976	Joe Kapp	58
Dave Raimey	1223				
Don Lisbon	1007				

Receiving Yards		Receptions		Points	
Terry Evanshen	1200	Terry Evanshen	67	Hugh Campbell	102
Hugh Campbell	1109				

Grey Cup Playoffs

November	6	Edmonton Eskimos	8	at	Winnipeg Blue Bombers	16
November	6	Montreal Alouettes	14	at	Hamilton Tiger-Cats	24
November	13	Winnipeg Blue Bombers	7	at	Saskatchewan Roughriders	14
November	13	Ottawa Rough Riders	30	at	Hamilton Tiger-Cats	1
November	16	Saskatchewan Roughriders	21	at	Winnipeg Blue Bombers	19
November	19	Ottawa Rough Riders	42	at	Hamilton Tiger-Cats	16 *
November	26	Saskatchewan Roughriders	29	at	Ottawa Rough Riders	14 **

*Game played in Montreal
**Game played in Vancouver

Individual Awards

Annis Stukus Trophy--Frank Clair (Ottawa Rough Riders)
Dave Dryburgh Memorial Trophy--Hugh Campbell (Saskatchewan Roughriders)
DeMarco-Becket Memorial Trophy--Wayne Harris (Calgary Stampeders)
Dr. Beattie Martin Trophy--Garry Lefebvre (Edmonton Eskimos)
Eddie James Memorial Trophy--George Reed (Saskatchewan Roughriders)
Gruen Trophy--Mike Wadsworth (Toronto Argonauts)
Jeff Nicklin Memorial Trophy--Ron Lancaster (Saskatchewan Roughriders)
Jeff Russel Memorial Trophy--Gene Gaines (Ottawa Rough Riders)
Schenley Award Most Outstanding Canadian--Russ Jackson (Ottawa Rough Riders)
Schenley Award Most Outstanding Lineman--Wayne Harris (Calgary Stampeders)
Schenley Award Most Outstanding Player--Russ Jackson (Ottawa Rough Riders)

Hall of Fame Inductees

John Ferraro, Sydney Halter, Greg Kabat, Dave McCann, Silver Quilty, Hugh Stirling

Rules

Unlimited blocking on rushing plays is legalized

HOCKEY
National Hockey League

Team Name	GP	W	L	T	GF	GA	Pts	Pct
Montreal Canadiens	70	41	21	8	239	173	90	.643
Chicago Black Hawks	70	37	25	8	240	187	82	.586
Toronto Maple Leafs	70	34	25	11	208	187	79	.564
Detroit Red Wings	70	31	27	12	221	194	74	.529
Boston Bruins	70	21	43	6	174	275	48	.343
New York Rangers	70	18	41	11	195	261	47	.336

Coaching Changes

New York--George Sullivan 5-10-5, Emile Francis 13-31-6.

League Leaders

Goals		Assists		Points	
Bobby Hull	54	Stan Mikita	48	Bobby Hull	97
Frank Mahovlich	32	Bobby Rousseau	48	Stan Mikita	78
Norm Ullman	31	Jean Beliveau	48	Bobby Rousseau	78
Alex Delvecchio	31	Gordie Howe	46	Jean Beliveau	77
Stan Mikita	30	Bobby Hull	43	Gordie Howe	75

Penalty Minutes		GAA		Wins	
Reg Fleming	166	John Bower	2.25	Glenn Hall	34
John Ferguson	153	Lorne Worsley	2.36	Lorne Worsley	29
Bryan Watson	133	Charlie Hodge	2.58	Roger Crozier	28
Ted Green	113	Glenn Hall	2.63	John Bower	18
Vic Hadfield	112	Roger Crozier	2.78	Charlie Hodge	12

Shutouts

Roger Crozier	7
Glenn Hall	4
John Bower	3
Bruce Gamble	2
Cesare Maniago	2

All Star Game
(The Forum, Montreal)

October 20 1965	All Stars	5	Montreal Canadiens	2

Stanley Cup Playoffs

April 7	Toronto Maple Leafs	3	at	Montreal Canadiens	4
April 7	Detroit Red Wings	1	at	Chicago Black Hawks	2
April 9	Toronto Maple Leafs	0	at	Montreal Canadiens	2
April 10	Detroit Red Wings	7	at	Chicago Black Hawks	0
April 12	Montreal Canadiens	5	at	Toronto Maple Leafs	2
April 12	Chicago Black Hawks	2	at	Detroit Red Wings	1
April 14	Montreal Canadiens	4	at	Toronto Maple Leafs	1
April 14	Chicago Black Hawks	1	at	Detroit Red Wings	5
April 17	Detroit Red Wings	5	at	Chicago Black Hawks	3
April 19	Chicago Black Hawks	2	at	Detroit Red Wings	3
April 24	Detroit Red Wings	3	at	Montreal Canadiens	2
April 26	Detroit Red Wings	5	at	Montreal Canadiens	2
April 28	Montreal Canadiens	4	at	Detroit Red Wings	2
May 1	Montreal Canadiens	2	at	Detroit Red Wings	1
May 3	Detroit Red Wings	1	at	Montreal Canadiens	5
May 5	Montreal Canadiens	3	at	Detroit Red Wings	2 [2:20]

All Star Teams

First Team		Second Team
Glenn Hall	Goal	Lorne Worsley
Jacques Laperriere	Defense	Allan Stanley
Pierre Pilote	Defense	Pat Stapleton
Stan Mikita	Center	Jean Beliveau
Gordie Howe	Right Wing	Bobby Rousseau
Bobby Hull	Left Wing	Frank Mahovlich

Individual Awards

Art Ross Trophy--Bobby Hull (Chicago Black Hawks)
Calder Memorial Trophy--Brit Selby (Toronto Maple Leafs)
Conn Smythe Trophy--Roger Crozier (Detroit Red Wings)
Hart Memorial Trophy--Bobby Hull (Chicago Black Hawks)
James Norris Trophy--Jacques Laperriere (Montreal Canadiens)
Lady Byng Memorial Trophy--Alex Delvecchio (Detroit Red Wings)
Lester Patrick Trophy--Jack Adams
Vezina Trophy--Lorne Worsley and Charlie Hodge (Montreal Canadiens)

Hall of Fame Inductees

Max Bentley, Hector Blake, Butch Bouchard, Frank Brimsek, Clarence Campbell, Ted Kennedy, Elmer Lach, Ted Lindsay, Babe Pratt, Ken Reardon

Franchise Changes

NL--Milwaukee Braves became the Atlanta Braves.

Other Sports

Horseracing--Kentucky Derby won by Kauai King (time 2:02, purse $120,500).
Heavyweight Boxing--Cassius Clay defeated George Chuvalo in 15 rounds.
Cassius Clay knocked-out Henry Cooper in 6 rounds.
Cassius Clay knocked-out Brian London in 3 rounds.
Cassius Clay knocked-out Karl Mildenberger in 12 rounds,
Cassius Clay knocked-out Cleveland Williams in 3 rounds.
Golf--U.S. Open won by Billy Casper in a playoff with Arnold Palmer (scores of 278-278, 69-73).
Auto Racing--Indianapolis 500 won by Graham Hill (ave. speed 144.317 MPH).
Tennis--U.S. Open won by Fred Stolle in the men's singles.
U.S. Open won by Fred Stolle and Roy Emerson in the men's doubles.
U.S. Open won by Maria Bueno in the women's singles.
U.S. Open won by Maria Bueno and Nancy Richey in the women's doubles.
U.S. Open won by Donna Floyd Fales and Owen Davidson in the mixed doubles.

1967

BASEBALL
National League

Team Name	W	L	Pct	GB	R	OR
St. Louis Cardinals	101	60	.627	-	695	557
San Francisco Giants	91	71	.562	10.5	652	551
Chicago Cubs	87	74	.540	14	702	624
Cincinnati Reds	87	75	.537	14.5	604	563
Philadelphia Phillies	82	80	.506	19.5	612	581
Pittsburgh Pirates	81	81	.500	20.5	679	693
Atlanta Braves	77	85	.475	24.5	631	640
Los Angeles Dodgers	73	89	.451	28.5	519	595
Houston Astros	69	93	.426	32.5	626	742
New York Mets	61	101	.377	40.5	498	672

Coaching Changes

Cincinnati--Dave Bristol 87-75; Pittsburgh--Harry Walker 42-42, Danny Murtaugh 39-39; Atlanta--Billy Hitchcock 77-82, Ken Silvestri 0-3; New York--Wes Westrum 57-94, Francis Parker 4-7.

League Leaders

Batting Average		Home Runs		RBI	
Roberto Clemente	.357	Hank Aaron	39	Orlando Cepeda	111
Tony Gonzalez	.339	Jim Wynn	37	Roberto Clemente	110
Matty Alou	.338	Willie McCovey	31	Hank Aaron	109
Curt Flood	.335	Ron Santo	31	Jim Wynn	107
Rusty Staub	.333	Jim Hart	29	Tony Perez	102

Stolen Bases		ERA		Wins	
Lou Brock	52	Phil Niekro	1.87	Mike McCormick	22
Maury Wills	29	Jim Bunning	2.29	Ferguson Jenkins	20
Joe Morgan	29	Chris Short	2.39	Claude Osteen	17
Vada Pinson	26	Gary Nolan	2.58	Jim Bunning	17
Adolfo Phillips	24	Gaylord Perry	2.61	Bob Veale	16

Saves		Strikeouts	
Ted Abernathy	28	Jim Bunning	253
Frank Linzy	17	Ferguson Jenkins	236
Elroy Face	17	Gaylord Perry	230
Ron Perranoski	16	Gary Nolan	206
Joe Hoerner	15	Mike Cuellar	203

American League

Team Name	W	L	Pct	GB	R	OR
Boston Red Sox	92	70	.568	-	722	614
Detroit Tigers	91	71	.562	1	683	587
Minnesota Twins	91	71	.562	1	671	590
Chicago White Sox	89	73	.549	3	531	491
California Angels	84	77	.522	7.5	567	587
Baltimore Orioles	76	85	.472	15.5	654	592
Washington Senators	76	85	.472	15.5	550	637
Cleveland Indians	75	87	.463	17	559	613
New York Yankees	72	90	.444	20	522	621
Kansas City Athletics	62	99	.385	29.5	533	660

Coaching Changes

Boston--Dick Williams 92-70; Detroit--Mayo Smith 91-71; Minnesota--Sam Mele 25-2.5, Cal Ermer 66-46; Cleveland--Joe Adcock 75-87; New York--Ralph Houk 72-90; Kansas City--Alvin Dark 52-69, Luke Appling 10-30.

League Leaders

Batting Average		**Home Runs**		**RBI**	
Carl Yastrzemski	.326	Carl Yastrzemski	44	Carl Yastrzemski	121
Frank Robinson	.311	Harmon Killebrew	44	Harmon Killebrew	113
Al Kaline	.308	Frank Howard	36	Frank Robinson	94
George Scott	.303	Frank Robinson	30	Frank Howard	89
Paul Blair	.293	Al Kaline	25	Tony Oliva	83

Stolen Bases		**ERA**		**Wins**	
Bert Campaneris	55	Joe Horlen	2.06	Earl Wilson	22
Don Buford	34	Gary Peters	2.28	Jim Lonborg	22
Tommie Agee	28	Wilfred Siebert	2.38	Dean Chance	20
Tom McCraw	24	Tommy John	2.47	Joe Horlen	19
Horace Clarke	21	Jim Merritt	2.53	Denny McLain	17

Saves		**Strikeouts**	
Minnie Rojas	27	Jim Lonborg	246
Bob Locker	20	Sam McDowell	236
John Wyatt	20	Dean Chance	220
Horace Womack	18	Luis Tiant	219
Al Worthington	16	Gary Peters	215

All Star Game

(Anaheim Stadium, Anaheim)

July 11	National League	2	American League	1

World Series

October 4	St. Louis Cardinals	2	at	Boston Red Sox	1
October 5	St. Louis Cardinals	0	at	Boston Red Sox	5
October 7	Boston Red Sox	2	at	St. Louis Cardinals	5
October 8	Boston Red Sox	0	at	St. Louis Cardinals	6
October 9	Boston Red Sox	3	at	St. Louis Cardinals	1
October 11	St. Louis Cardinals	4	at	Boston Red Sox	8
October 12	St. Louis Cardinals	7	at	Boston Red Sox	2

Individual Awards

Arch Ward Memorial Trophy--Tony Perez (Cincinnati Reds NL)
Baseball Writers Award--Orlando Cepeda (St. Louis Cardinals NL)
Carl Yastrzemski (Boston Red Sox AL)
Cy Young Award--Mike McCormick (San Francisco Giants NL)
Jim Lonborg (Boston Red Sox AL)
Rookie of the Year--Tom Seaver (New York Mets NL)
Rod Carew (Minnesota Twins AL)
Sporting News Executive of the Year--Dick O'Connell (Boston Red Sox AL)
Sporting News Manager of the Year--Dick Williams (Boston Red Sox AL)
Sporting News Pitcher of the Year--Mike McCormick (San Francisco Giants NL)
Jim Lonborg (Boston Red Sox AL)
Sporting News Player of the Year--Orlando Cepeda (St. Louis Cardinals NL)
Carl Yastrzemski (Boston Red Sox AL)
Sporting News Rookie of the Year--Lee May (Cincinnati Reds NL)
Dick Hughes (St. Louis Cardinals NL)
Rod Carew (Minnesota Twins AL)
Tom Phoebus (Baltimore Orioles AL)
World Series MVP--Bob Gibson (St. Louis Cardinals NL)

Hall of Fame Inductees

Branch Rickey, Charles Ruffing, Lloyd Waner

BASKETBALL

National Basketball Association

Eastern Division

Team Name	GP	W	L	PPGF	PPGA	Pct	GB
Philadelphia 76ers	81	68	13	125.2	115.8	.840	-
Boston Celtics	81	60	21	119.3	111.3	.741	8
Cincinnati Royals	81	39	42	117.1	117.4	.481	29
New York Knickerbockers	81	36	45	116.4	119.4	.444	32
Baltimore Bullets	81	20	61	115.5	122.0	.247	48

Western Division

Team Name	GP	W	L	PPGF	PPGA	Pct	GB
San Francisco Warriors	81	44	37	122.4	119.5	.543	-
St. Louis Hawks	81	39	42	113.6	115.2	.481	5
Los Angeles Lakers	81	36	45	120.5	120.2	.444	8
Chicago Bulls	81	33	48	113.2	116.9	.407	11
Detroit Pistons	81	30	51	111.3	116.8	.370	14

Coaching Changes

Philadelphia--Alex Hannum 68-13; Boston--Bill Russell 60-21; New York--Dick McGuire 36-45; Baltimore--Mike Farmer 1-8, Buddy Jeannette 3-13, Gene Shue 16-40; San Francisco--Bill Sharman 44-37; Chicago--John Kerr 33-48; Detroit--Dave DeBusschere 28-45, Don Butcher 2-6.

League Leaders

Field Goals		Free Throws		Assists	
Rick Barry	1011	Rick Barry	753	Guy Rodgers	908
Oscar Robertson	838	Oscar Robertson	736	Oscar Robertson	845
Wilt Chamberlain	785	Jerry West	602	Wilt Chamberlain	630
Elgin Baylor	711	Lenny Wilkens	459	Bill Russell	472
Hal Greer	699	Chet Walker	445	Jerry West	447

Points		Fouls	
Rick Barry	2775	Joe Strawder	344
Oscar Robertson	2412	Bill Bridges	325
Wilt Chamberlain	1956	Hal Greer	302
Jerry West	1892	Dave DeBusschere	297
Elgin Baylor	1862	Bailey Howell	296

All Star Game

(Cow Palace, San Francisco)

January 10	West Division	135	East Division	120

Notes

Bill Russell of the Boston Celtics became the first black head coach in major league sports history.

NBA Playoffs

March 21	N.Y. Knickerbockers	110	at	Boston Celtics	140
March 21	Cincinnati Royals	120	at	Philadelphia 76ers	116
March 21	Chicago Bulls	100	at	St. Louis Hawks	114
March 21	Los Angeles Lakers	108	at	San Francisco Warriors	124
March 22	Philadelphia 76ers	123	at	Cincinnati Royals	102
March 23	St. Louis Hawks	113	at	Chicago Bulls	107
March 23	San Francisco Warriors	113	at	Los Angeles Lakers	102
March 24	Cincinnati Royals	106	at	Philadelphia 76ers	121
March 25	Boston Celtics	115	at	N.Y. Knickerbockers	108
March 25	Chicago Bulls	106	at	St. Louis Hawks	119
March 25	Philadelphia 76ers	112	at	Cincinnati Royals	94
March 26	N.Y. Knickerbockers	123	at	Boston Celtics	112
March 26	Los Angeles Lakers	115	at	San Francisco Warriors	122
March 28	Boston Celtics	118	at	N.Y. Knickerbockers	109
March 30	St. Louis Hawks	115	at	San Francisco Warriors	117
March 31	Boston Celtics	113	at	Philadelphia 76ers	127
April 1	St. Louis Hawks	136	at	San Francisco Warriors	143
April 2	Philadelphia 76ers	107	at	Boston Celtics	102
April 5	San Francisco Warriors	109	at	St. Louis Hawks	115
April 5	Boston Celtics	104	at	Philadelphia 76ers	115
April 8	San Francisco Warriors	104	at	St. Louis Hawks	109
April 9	Philadelphia 76ers	117	at	Boston Celtics	121
April 10	St. Louis Hawks	102	at	San Francisco Warriors	123

April 11	Boston Celtics	116	at	Philadelphia 76ers	140
April 12	San Francisco Warriors	112	at	St. Louis Hawks	107
April 14	San Francisco Warriors	135	at	Philadelphia 76ers	141 [OT]
April 16	San Francisco Warriors	95	at	Philadelphia 76ers	126
April 18	Philadelphia76ers	124	at	San Francisco Warriors	130
April 20	Philadelphia 76ers	122	at	San Francisco Warriors	108
April 23	San Francisco Warriors	117	at	Philadelphia 76ers	109
April 24	Philadelphia 76ers	125	at	San Francisco Warriors	122

All Star Teams

First Team

Rick Barry (San Francisco Warriors)
Elgin Baylor (Los Angeles Lakers)
Wilt Chamberlain (Philadelphia 76ers)
Jerry West (Los Angeles Lakers)
Oscar Robertson (Cincinnati Royals)

Second Team)

Willis Reed (N.Y. Knickerbockers)
Jerry Lucas (Cincinnati Royals)
Bill Russell (Boston Celtics)
Hal Greer (Philadelphia 76ers)
Sam Jones (Boston Celtics)

Individual Awards

Eddie Gottlieb Trophy--Dave Bing (Detroit Pistons)
Maurice Podoloff Trophy--Wilt Chamberlain (Philadelphia 76ers)
NBA All Star Game MVP--Rick Barry (San Francisco Warriors)
Red Auerbach Trophy--John Kerr (Chicago Bulls)

Hall of Fame Inductees

Clair Bee, Howard Cann, Amory Gill, Alvin Julian

FOOTBALL
National Football League

Eastern Conference
Capitol Division

Team Name	GP	W	L	T	PF	PA	Pct
Dallas Cowboys	14	9	5	0	342	268	.643
Philadelphia Eagles	14	6	7	1	351	409	.464
Washington Redskins	14	5	6	3	347	353	.464
New Orleans Saints	14	3	11	0	233	379	.214
Century Division							
Cleveland Browns	14	9	5	0	334	297	.643
New York Giants	14	7	7	0	369	379	.500
St. Louis Cardinals	14	6	7	1	333	356	.464
Pittsburgh Steelers	14	4	9	1	281	320	.321
Western Conference							
Central Division							
Green Bay Packers	14	9	4	1	332	209	.679
Chicago Bears	14	7	6	1	239	218	.536
Detroit Lions	14	5	7	2	260	259	.429
Minnesota Vikings	14	3	8	3	233	294	.321

Coastal Division

Los Angeles Rams	14	11	1	2	398	196	.857
Baltimore Colts	14	11	1	2	394	198	.857
San Francisco 49ers	14	7	7	0	273	337	.500
Atlanta Falcons	14	1	12	1	175	422	.107

Coaching Changes

New Orleans--Tom Fears 3-11-0; Detroit--Joe Schmidt 5-7-2; Minnesota--Bud Grant 3-8-3.

League Leaders

Yards Rushing		Yards Passing		Passing % (40 attempts)	
Leroy Kelly	1205	Sonny Jurgensen	3747	John Unitas	58
Dave Osborn	972	John Unitas	3428	Sonny Jurgensen	57
Gale Sayers	880	Norm Snead	3399	Zeke Bratkowski	56
John Roland	876	Fran Tarkenton	3088	Norm Snead	55
Mel Farr	860	Jim Hart	3008	Bart Starr	55

Receiving Yards		Receptions		Field Goals	
Ben Hawkins	1265	Charley Taylor	70	Jim Bakken	27
Homer Jones	1209	Jerry Smith	67	Bruce Gossett	20
Jack Smith	1205	Willie Richardson	63	Lou Michaels	20
Bob Hayes	998	Bob Mitchell	60	Don Chandler	19
Lance Rentzel	996	Ben Hawkins	59	Fred Cox	17

Punt Return Yards		Kickoff Return Yards	
Bob Hayes	276	Ron Smith	976
Doug Cunningham	249	Doug Cunningham	826
Ben Davis	229	Travis Williams	739
Rick Harris	208	Walter Roberts	737
Alvin Haymond	155	Ben Davis	708

Pro Bowl Game

(Memorial Coliseum, Los Angeles)

January 21 1968	Western Conference	38	Eastern Conference	20

NFL Playoffs

December 23	Green Bay Packers	28	at	Los Angeles Rams	7*
December 24	Cleveland Browns	14	at	Dallas Cowboys	52
December 31	Dallas Cowboys	17	at	Green Bay Packers	21

Individual Awards

AP MVP--Johnny Unitas (Baltimore Colts)
Bert Bell Trophy--Mel Farr (Detroit Lions) [World Almanac]
Bert Bell Trophy--Johnny Unitas (Baltimore Colts)
George Halas Trophy--Deacon Jones (Los Angeles Rams)
Jim Thorpe Trophy--Johnny Unitas (Baltimore Colts)

*Game played in Milwaukee

Pro Bowl MVP--Gale Sayers (Chicago Bears)
Dave Robinson (Green Bay Packers)
Rookie of the Year--Mel Farr (Detroit Lions)
Super Bowl MVP--Bart Starr (Green Bay Packers)
U.P.I. MVP--Johnny Unitas (Baltimore Colts)
U.P.I. NFL-NFC Coach of the Year--George Allen (Los Angeles Rams)
U.P.I. NFL-NFC Rookie of the Year--Mel Farr (Detroit Lions)

Hall of Fame Inductees

Chuck Bednarik, Charles Bidwell, Paul Brown, Bobby Layne, Dan Reeves, Ken Strong, Joe Stydahar, Emlen Tunnell

Notes

With a new team in New Orleans bringing the NFL membership to 16, the league divided into four four-team divisions.

American Football League
Eastern Division

Team Name	GP	W	L	T	PF	PA	Pct
Houston Oilers	14	9	4	1	258	199	.679
New York Jets	14	8	5	1	371	329	.607
Buffalo Bills	14	4	10	0	237	285	.286
Miami Dolphins	14	4	10	0	219	407	.286
Boston Patriots	14	3	10	1	280	389	.250

Western Division

Team Name	GP	W	L	T	PF	PA	Pct
Oakland Raiders	14	13	1	0	468	233	.929
Kansas City Chiefs	14	9	5	0	408	254	.643
San Diego Chargers	14	8	5	1	360	352	.607
Denver Broncos	14	3	11	0	256	409	.214

Coaching Changes

Denver--Lou Saban 3-11-0.

League Leaders

Yards Rushing		Yards Passing		Passing % (40 attempts)	
Jim Nance	1216	Joe Namath	4007	Len Dawson	58
Hoyle Granger	1194	John Hadl	3365	Joe Namath	53
Mike Garrett	1087	Daryle Lamonica	3228	Daryle Lamonica	52
Dick Post	663	Len Dawson	2651	John Hadl	51
Brad Hubbert	643	Jack Kemp	2503	Bob Griese	50

Receiving Yards		Receptions		Field Goals	
Don Maynard	1434	George Sauer	75	Jan Stenerud	21
George Sauer	1189	Don Maynard	71	George Blanda	20
Lance Alworth	1010	Jack Clancy	67	Jim Turner	17
Otis Taylor	958	Hewritt Dixon	59	Mike Mercer	16
Willie Frazier	922	Otis Taylor	59	Gino Cappelletti	16

Punt Return Yards		Kickoff Return Yards	
Rodger Bird	612	Noland Smith	1148
"Speedy" Duncan	434	Floyd Little	942
Floyd Little	270	Jay Cunningham	627
Bill Baird	219	Abner Haynes	569
Noland Smith	212	Earl Christy	521

All Star Game
(Gator Bowl, Jacksonville)

January 21 1968	East Division	25		West Division	24

AFL Playoffs

December 31	Houston Oilers	7	at	Oakland Raiders	40

Super Bowl II
(Orange Bowl, Miami)

January 14 1968	Green Bay Packers	33	at	Oakland Raiders	14

Individual Awards

AFL All Star Game MVP--"Speedy" Duncan (San Diego Chargers)
Joe Namath (New York Jets)
Don Maynard (New York Jets)
Rookie of the Year--George Webster (Houston Oilers)
U.P.I. AFL-AFC Coach of the Year--John Rauch (Oakland Raiders)
U.P.I. AFL-AFC Player of the Year--Daryle Lamonica (Oakland Raiders)
U.P.I. AFL-AFC Rookie of the Year--George Webster (Houston Oilers)

Canadian Football League
Eastern Conference

Team Name	GP	W	L	T	PF	PA	Pts	Pct
Hamilton Tiger-Cats	14	10	4	0	250	195	20	.714
Ottawa Rough Riders	14	9	4	1	337	207	19	.679
Toronto Argonauts	14	5	8	1	252	266	11	.393
Montreal Alouettes	14	2	12	0	166	302	4	.143

Western Conference

Team Name	GP	W	L	T	PF	PA	Pts	Pct
Calgary Stampeders	16	12	4	0	382	219	24	.750
Saskatchewan Roughriders	16	12	4	0	346	282	24	.750
Edmonton Eskimos	16	9	6	1	266	246	19	.594
Winnipeg Blue Bombers	16	4	12	0	212	414	8	.250
British Columbia Lions	16	3	12	1	239	319	7	.219

Coaching Changes

Toronto--Leo Cahill 5-8-1; Montreal--Darrell Mudra 2-12-0; Winnipeg--Joe Zaleski 4-12-0; British Columbia--Dave Skrien 0-4-0, Jim Champion 3-8-1.

League Leaders

Yards Rushing		Yards Passing		Passing %	
George Reed	1471	Peter Liske	4479	Peter Liske	60
Jim Thomas	1006				

Receiving Yards		Receptions		Points	
Terry Evanshen	1662	Terry Evanshen	96	Tommy Joe Coffey	107
Whit Tucker	1171				
Ken Nielsen	1121				

Grey Cup Playoffs

November 11	Edmonton Eskimos	5	at	Saskatchewan Roughriders	21
November 12	Toronto Argonauts	22	at	Ottawa Rough Riders	38
November 18	Saskatchewan Roughriders	11	at	Calgary Stampeders	15
November 18	Hamilton Tiger-Cats	11	at	Ottawa Rough Riders	3
November 22	Calgary Stampeders	9	at	Saskatchewan Roughriders	11
November 25	Ottawa Rough Riders	0	at	Hamilton Tiger-Cats	26
November 26	Saskatchewan Roughriders	17	at	Calgary Stampeders	13
December 2	Hamilton Tiger-Cats	24	at	Saskatchewan Roughriders	1*

Individual Awards

Annis Stukus Trophy--Jerry Williams (Calgary Stampeders)
Dave Dryburgh Memorial Trophy--Terry Evanshen (Calgary Stampeders)
DeMarco-Becket Trophy--John LaGrone (Edmonton Eskimos)
Dr. Beattie Martin Trophy--Ted Gerela (British Columbia Lions)
Eddie James Memorial Trophy--George Reed (Saskatchewan Roughriders)
Grey Cup MVP--Joe Zuger (Hamilton Tiger-Cats)
Gruen Trophy--Wayne Giardino (Ottawa Rough Riders)
Jeff Nicklin Memorial Trophy--Peter Liske (Calgary Stampeders)
Jeff Russel Memorial Trophy--Ron Stewart (Ottawa Rough Riders)
Schenley Award Most Outstanding Canadian--Terry Evanshen (Calgary Stampeders)
Schenley Award Most Outstanding Lineman--Ed McQuarters (Saskatchewan Roughriders)
Schenley Award Most Outstanding Player--Peter Liske (Calgary Stampeders)

Hall of Fame Inductees

Carl Cronin, Cap Fear, Jimmy McCaffrey

Notes

The CFL set up its offices in Toronto with Keith Davey as Commissioner Davey is succeeded on February 23rd by Ted Workman and then Allan McEachern.

*Game played in Ottawa

HOCKEY
National Hockey League

Team Name	GP	W	L	T	GF	GA	Pts	Pct
Chicago Black Hawks	70	41	17	12	264	170	94	.671
Montreal Canadiens	70	32	25	13	202	188	77	.550
Toronto Maple Leafs	70	32	27	11	204	211	75	.536
New York Rangers	70	30	28	12	188	189	72	.514
Detroit Red Wings	70	27	39	4	212	241	58	.414
Boston Bruins	70	17	43	10	182	253	44	.314

Coaching Changes

Toronto--George Imlach 25-26-9, Francis "King" Clancy 7-1-2; New York--Emile Francis 30-28-12; Boston--Harry Sinden 17-43-10.

League Leaders

Goals		Assists		Points	
Bobby Hull	52	Stan Mikita	62	Stan Mikita	97
Stan Mikita	35	Phil Goyette	49	Bobby Hull	80
Ken Wharram	31	Pierre Pilote	46	Norm Ullman	70
Bruce MacGregor	28	Norm Ullman	44	Ken Wharram	65
Rod Gilbert	28	Bobby Rousseau	44	Gordie Howe	65

Penalty Minutes		GAA		Wins	
John Ferguson	177	Glenn Hall	2.38	Ed Giacomin	30
Reg Fleming	146	Denis DeJordy	2.46	Denis DeJordy	22
Gary Bergman	129	Charlie Hodge	2.57	Roger Crozier	22
Ed Van Impe	111	Ed Giacomin	2.61	Glenn Hall	19
Bobby Orr	102	John Bower	2.64	Terry Sawchuk	15

Shutouts	
Ed Giacomin	9
Roger Crozier	4
Denis DeJordy	4
Charlie Hodge	3
Glenn Hall	2

All Star Game
(The Forum, Montreal)

January 18	Montreal Canadiens	3	All Stars	0

Stanley Cup Playoffs

April 6	Toronto Maple Leafs	2	at	Chicago Black Hawks	5
April 6	New York Rangers	4	at	Montreal Canadiens	6
April 8	New York Rangers	1	at	Montreal Canadiens	3
April 9	Toronto Maple Leafs	3	at	Chicago Black hawks	1
April 11	Montreal Canadiens	3	at	New York Rangers	2
April 11	Chicago Black Hawks	1	at	Toronto Maple Leafs	3
April 13	Montreal Canadiens	2	at	New York Rangers	1 [6:281]

April 13	Chicago Black Hawks	4	at	Toronto Maple Leafs	3
April 15	Toronto Maple Leafs	4	at	Chicago Black Hawks	2
April 18	Chicago Black Hawks	1	at	Toronto Maple Leafs	3
April 20	Toronto Maple Leafs	2	at	Montreal Canadiens	6
April 22	Toronto Maple Leafs	3	at	Montreal Canadiens	0
April 25	Montreal Canadiens	2	at	Toronto Maple Leafs	3 [28:26]
April 27	Montreal Canadiens	6	at	Toronto Maple Leafs	2
April 29	Toronto Maple Leafs	4	at	Montreal Canadiens	1
May 2	Montreal Canadiens	1	at	Toronto Maple Leafs	3

All Star Teams

First Team		Second Team
Ed Giacomin	Goal	Glenn Hall
Pierre Pilote	Defense	Tim Horton
Harry Howell	Defense	Bobby Orr
Stan Mikita	Center	Norm Ullman
Ken Wharram	Right Wing	Gordie Howe
Bobby Hull	Left Wing	Don Marshall

Individual Awards

Art Ross Trophy--Stan Mikita (Chicago Black Hawks)
Calder Memorial Trophy--Bobby Orr (Boston Bruins)
Conn Smythe Trophy--Dave Keon (Toronto Maple Leafs)
Hart Memorial Trophy--Stan Mikita (Chicago Black Hawks)
James Norris Trophy--Harry Howell (New York Rangers)
Lady Byng Memorial Trophy--Stan Mikita (Chicago Black Hawks)
Lester Patrick Trophy--Gordie Howe, Charles Adams, James Norris Sr.
NHL All Star Game MVP--Henri Richard (Montreal Canadiens)
Vezina Trophy--Glenn Hall and Denis Dejordy (Chicago Black Hawks)

Hall of Fame Inductees

Turk Broda, Neil Colville, Harry Oliver, Red Storey

Rules

Substitutions are allowed on coincidental major penalties.

Notes

The NHL was now prepared to expand the following season, with 6 franchises being awarded to American cities. This would mean the league would double in size.

SOCCER

United Soccer Association
Eastern Division

Team Name	GP	W	L	T	GF	GA	Pts	Pct
Washington Whips	12	5	2	5	19	11	15	.625
Cleveland Stokers	12	5	3	4	19	13	14	.583
Toronto City	12	4	3	5	23	17	13	.542
Detroit Cougars	12	3	3	6	11	18	12	.500
New York Skyliners	12	2	4	6	15	17	10	.417
Boston Rovers	12	2	7	3	12	26	7	.292

Western Division

Los Angeles Wolves	12	5	2	5	21	14	15	.625
San Francisco Golden Gate Gales	12	5	4	3	25	19	13	.542
Chicago Mustangs	12	3	2	7	20	14	13	.542
Houston Stars	12	4	4	4	19	18	12	.500
Vancouver Royals	12	3	4	5	20	28	11	.458
Dallas Tornado	12	3	6	3	14	23	9	.375

Coaching

Washington--Ed Turnbull 5-2-5; Cleveland--Tony Waddington 5-3-4; Toronto--Bob Shankly 4-3-5; Detroit--John Colrain 3-3-6; New York--Ondino Vierra 2-4-6; Boston--Liam Tuohy 2-7-3; Los Angeles--Ronnie Allen 5-2-5; San Francisco--Ernst Happel 5-4-3; Chicago--Manlio Scopigno 3-2-7; Houston--Matim Francisco 4-4-4; Vancouver--Ian McCall 3-4-5; Dallas--Jerry Kerr 3-6-3

League Leaders

Goals

Roberto Boninsegna	10
Henk Houwaart	9
Peter Dobing	7
Paulo Borges	6
Rene Pas	6

Points

Roberto Boninsegna	21
Henk Houwaart	20
Paulo Borges	15
Peter Dobing	14
Rene Pas	14

Shutouts

Robert Clark	5
John Kennedy	4
John Farmer	2

GAA
(540minutes)

Robert Clark	0.917
Phil Parkes	1.000
Pietro Pianta	1.004
John Kennedy	1.240
Osmar Migueluccil	1.390

USA Championship

July 15	Washington Whips	5	at	Los Angeles Wolves	6

All Star Teams

First Team		Second Team
Robert Clark	Goal	Gordon Banks
Mario Tito	Defender	Eric Skeels
Jose Fidelis	Defender	Jan Villerius
Pat Stanton	Defender	Joe Davis
Jim Baxter	Midfield	John Moore
Tom McMillan	Midfield	Miguel Longo
Ary Clemente	Midfield	Doug Smith
Paulo Borges	Forward	Henk Houwaart
Peter Dobing	Forward	Roberto Boninsegna
George Eastham	Forward	Benedicto Ribeiro
Roy Vernon	Forward	Peter Cormack

Notes

The North American Soccer League was formed this year by Jack Kent Cooke and others, but changed its name at the last minute to the United Soccer Association with Dick Walsh named as its first commissioner

The USA was the only one of the two professional soccer leagues league sanctioned by FIFA the governing body of international soccer.

National Professional Soccer League
Eastern Division

Team Name	GP	W	L	T	GF	GA	Pts	Pct
Baltimore Bays	32	14	9	9	53	47	162	.563
Philadelphia Spartans	32	14	9	9	53	43	157	.545
New York Generals	32	11	13	8	60	58	143	.496
Atlanta Chiefs	31	10	12	9	51	46	135	.484
Pittsburgh Phantoms	31	10	14	7	59	74	132	.473

Western Division

Team Name	GP	W	L	T	GF	GA	Pts	Pct
Oakland Clippers	32	19	8	5	64	34	185	.642
St. Louis Stars	32	14	11	7	54	57	156	.542
Chicago Spurs	32	10	11	11	50	55	142	.493
Toronto Falcons	32	10	17	5	59	70	127	.441
Los Angeles Toros	32	7	15	10	42	61	114	.396

Coaching

Baltimore--Doug Millward 14-9-9; Philadelphia--John Szep 14-9-9; New York--Freddie Goodwin 11-13-8; Atlanta--Phil Woosnam 10-12-9; Pittsburgh-- Janos Bedl, Co Prins, Pepino Gruber; Oakland--Ivan Toplak 19-8-5; St. Louis--Rudi Gutendorf 14-11-7; Chicago--Alan Rogers 10-11-11;Toronto--Hector Mariano 10-17-5; Los Angeles--Max Wozniak 7-15-10

League Leaders

Goals		Points		Shutouts	
Yanko Daucik	20	Yanko Daucik	48	Mirko Stojanovic	10
Willie Roy	17	Willie Roy	39	Terry Adlington	7
Eli Durate	15	Eli Durate	35	Gernot Fraydl	7
Manfred Rummel	14	Rudi Kolbl	34	Ernesto Lopera	4
George Kirby	14	Manfred Rummel	32	Sven Lindberg	3

GAA	
Mirko Stojanovic	1.00
Klaus Griletz	1.00
Ernesto Lopera	1.07
Terry Adlington	1.27
Sven Lindberg	1.37

NPSL Championship

September 3	Oakland Clippers	0	at	Baltimore Bays	1
September 9	Baltimore Bays	1	at	Oakland Clippers	4

All Star Team

Goal	Mirko Stojanovic (Oakland Clippers)
Defense	Mel Scott (Oakland Clippers)
Defense	Badu Da Cruz (Baltimore Bays)
Midfield	Juan Santisteban (Baltimore Bays)
Midfield	Ilija Mitic (Oakland Clippers)

Midfield	Ruben Navarro (Baltimore Bays)
Forward	Willie Roy (Chicago Spurs)
Forward	Co Prins (Pittsburgh Phantoms)
Forward	Mario Baesso (Oakland Clippers)
Forward	Art Welch (Baltimore Bays)
Forward	Emment Kapengwe (Atlanta Chiefs)

Individual Awards

Lead Goalkeeper Award--Mirko Stojanovic (Oakland Clippers)
Most Valuable Player--Ruben Navarro (Philadelphia Spartans)
Rookie of the Year--Willie Roy (Chicago Spurs)

Rules

Teams were awarded 6 points for a win and a bonus point for each goal scored up to a maximum of three per team per game.

Notes

Bill Cox and Richard Millen headed two groups which merged and formed the NPSL., and in a move unique to professional sports in North America imported 12 complete teams from overseas to represent the 12 cities in the league until they could acquire their own players for the following season with Ken Macker named as its first commissioner.
A minor scandal took place in the NPSL when it was announced that the CBS television network had its producers notify the referees via hidden walkie-talkies when they should whistle down an imaginary infringement so that commercials could be inserted into the play without any action being missed by the viewers.

Other Sports

Horseracing--Kentucky Derby won by Proud Clarion (time 2:00.6, purse $119,700).
Heavyweight Boxing--Cassius Clay defeated Ernie Terrell in 15 rounds.
Cassius Clay knocked-out Zora Folley in 7 rounds.
Golf--U.S. Open won by Jack Nicklaus with a score of 275.
Auto Racing--Indianapolis 500 won by A.J. Foyt (ave. speed 151.207 MPH).
Tennis--U.S. Open won by John Newcombe in the men's singles.
U.S. Open won by John Newcombe and Tony Roche in the men's doubles.
U.S. Open won by Billie Jean King in the women's singles.
U.S. Open won by Billie Jean King and Rosemary Casals in the women's doubles.
U.S. Open won by Billie Jean King and Owen Davidson in the mixed doubles.

Notes

Cassius Clay was stripped of his title for refusing to enter military service.

1968

BASEBALL
National League

Team Name	W	L	Pct	GB	R	OR
St. Louis Cardinals	97	65	.599	-	583	472
San Francisco Giants	88	74	.543	9	599	529
Chicago Cubs	84	78	.519	13	612	611
Cincinnati Reds	83	79	.512	14	690	673
Atlanta Braves	81	81	.500	16	514	549
Pittsburgh Pirates	80	82	.494	17	583	532
Los Angeles Dodgers	76	86	.469	21	470	509
Philadelphia Phillies	76	86	.469	21	543	615
New York Mets	73	89	.451	24	473	499
Houston Astros	72	90	.444	25	510	588

Coaching Changes

Atlanta--Luman Harris 81-81; Pittsburgh--Larry Shepard 80-82; Philadelphia--Gene Mauch 26-27, George Myatt 2-0, Bob Skinner 48 59; New York--Gil Hodges 73-89; Houston--Grady Hatton 23-38, Harry Walker 49-52.

League Leaders

Batting Average		Home Runs		RBI	
Pete Rose	.335	Willie McCovey	36	Willie McCovey	105
Matty Alou	.332	Richie Allen	33	Ron Santo	98
Felipe Alou	.317	Ernie Banks	32	Bill Williams	98
Alex Johnson	.312	Bill Williams	30	Tony Perez	92
Curt Flood	.301	Hank Aaron	29	Richie Allen	90

Stolen Bases		ERA		Wins	
Lou Brock	62	Bob Gibson	1.12	Juan Marichal	26
Maury Wills	52	Bob Bolin	1.99	Bob Gibson	22
Willie Davis	36	Bob Veale	2.05	Ferguson Jenkins	20
Hank Aaron	28	Jerry Koosman	2.08	Jerry Koosman	19
Cleon Jones	23	Steve Blass	2.12	Nelson Briles	19

Saves		Strikeouts	
Phil Regan	25	Bob Gibson	268
Joe Hoerner	17	Ferguson Jenkins	260
Clay Carroll	17	Bill Singer	227
Jim Brewer	14	Juan Marichal	218
Elroy Face	13	Ray Sadecki	206

American League

Team Name	W	L	Pct	GB	R	OR
Detroit Tigers	103	59	.636	-	671	492
Baltimore Orioles	91	71	.562	12	579	497
Cleveland Indians	86	75	.534	16.5	516	504
Boston Red Sox	86	76	.531	17	614	611
New York Yankees	83	79	.512	20	536	531
Oakland Athletics	82	80	.506	21	569	544
Minnesota Twins	79	83	.488	24	562	546
California Angels	67	95	.414	36	498	615
Chicago White Sox	67	95	.414	36	463	527
Washington Senators	65	96	.404	37.5	524	665

Coaching Changes

Baltimore--Hank Bauer 43-37, Earl Weaver 48-34; Cleveland--Alvin Dark 86-75; Oakland--Bob Kennedy 82-80; Minnesota--Cal Ermer 79-83; Chicago--Eddie Stanky 34-45, Les Moss 0-2, Al Lopez 33-48; Washington--Jim Lemon 65-96.

League Leaders

Batting Average		Home Runs		RBI	
Carl Yastrzemski	.301	Frank Howard	44	Ken Harrelson	109
Danny Cater	.290	Willie Horton	36	Frank Howard	106
Tony Oliva	.289	Ken Harrelson	35	Jim Northrup	90
Willie Horton	.285	Reggie Jackson	29	John Powell	85
Ted Uhlaender	.283	Norm Cash	25	Willie Horton	85

Stolen Bases		ERA		Wins	
Bert Campaneris	62	Luis Tiant	1.60	Denny McLain	31
Jose Cardenal	40	Sam McDowell	1.81	Dave McNally	22
Cesar Tovar	35	Dave McNally	1.95	Mel Stottlemyre	21
Don Buford	27	Denny McLain	1.96	Luis Tiant	21
Joe Foy	26	Tommy John	1.98	Jim Hardin	18

Saves		Strikeouts	
Al Worthington	18	Sam McDowell	283
Wilbur Wood	16	Denny McLain	280
Dennis Higgins	13	Luis Tiant	264
Vicente Romo	12	Dean Chance	234
Hoyt Wilhelm	12	Dave McNally	202

All Star Game

(The Astrodome, Houston)

July 9	National League	1	American League	0

Notes

Bowie Kuhn became the fifth Commissioner of major league baseball replacing William Eckert.

World Series

October 2	Detroit Tigers	0	at	St. Louis Cardinals	4
October 3	Detroit Tigers	8	at	St. Louis Cardinals	1
October 5	St. Louis Cardinals	7	at	Detroit Tigers	3
October 6	St. Louis Cardinals	10	at	Detroit Tigers	1
October 7	St. Louis Cardinals	3	at	Detroit Tigers	5
October 9	Detroit Tigers	13	at	St. Louis Cardinals	1
October 10	Detroit Tigers	4	at	St. Louis Cardinals	1

Individual Awards

Arch Ward Memorial Trophy--Willie Mays (San Francisco Giants NL)
Baseball Writers Award--Bob Gibson (St. Louis Cardinals NL)
Denny McLain (Detroit Tigers AL)
Cy Young Award--Bob Gibson (St. Louis Cardinals NL)
Denny McLain (Detroit Tigers AL)
Rookie of the Year--Johnny Bench (Cincinnati Reds NL)
Stan Bahnsen (New York Yankees AL)
Sporting News Executive of the Year--James Campbell (Detroit Tigers AL)
Sporting News Manager of the Year--Mayo Smith (Detroit Tigers AL)
Sporting News Pitcher of the Year--Bob Gibson (St. Louis Cardinals NL)
Denny McLain (Detroit Tigers AL)
Sporting News Player of the Year--Pete Rose (Cincinnati Reds NL)
Ken Harrelson (Boston Red Sox AL)
Sporting News Rookie of the Year--Johnny Bench (Cincinnati Reds NL)
Jerry Koosman (New York Mets NL)
Del Unser (Washington Senators AL)
Stan Bahnsen (New York Yankees AL)
World Series MVP--Mickey Lolich (Detroit Tigers AL)

Hall of Fame Inductees

Kiki Cuyler, Leon Goslin, Joe Medwick

BASKETBALL
National Basketball Association

Eastern Division

Team Name	GP	W	L	PPGF	PPGA	Pct	GB
Philadelphia 76ers	82	62	20	122.6	114.0	.756	-
Boston Celtics	82	54	28	116.1	112.0	.659	8
New York Knickerbockers	82	43	39	116.1	114.3	.524	19
Detroit Pistons	82	40	42	118.6	120.6	.488	22
Cincinnati Royals	82	39	43	116.6	217.4	.476	23
Baltimore Bullets	82	36	46	117.4	117.8	.439	26

Western Division

Team Name	GP	W	L	PPGF	PPGA	Pct	GB
St. Louis Hawks	82	56	26	113.0	110.3	.683	-
Los Angeles Lakers	82	52	30	121.2	115.6	.634	4
San Francisco Warriors	82	43	39	117.0	117.6	.524	13
Chicago Bulls	82	29	53	109.5	113.5	.354	27
Seattle SuperSonics	82	23	59	118.7	125.1	.280	33
San Diego Rockets	82	15	67	112.4	121.0	.183	41

Coaching Changes

New York--Dick McGuire 15-22, Red Holzman 28-17; Detroit--Don Butcher 40-42; Cincinnati--Ed Jucker 39-43; Baltimore--Gene Shue 36-46; Los Angeles--Butch Van Breda Kolff 52-30; Seattle--Al Bianchi 23-59; San Diego--Jack McMahon 15-67.

League Leaders

Field Goals		Free Throws		Assists	
Dave Bing	835	Oscar Robertson	576	Wilt Chamberlain	702
Wilt Chamberlain	819	Lenny Wilkens	546	Lenny Wilkens	679
Hal Greer	777	Rudy LaRusso	522	Oscar Robertson	633
Elgin Baylor	757	Earl Monroe	507	Dave Bing	509
Earl Monroe	742	Elgin Baylor	488	Walt Hazzard	493

Points		Fouls	
Dave Bing	2142	Bill Bridges	366
Elgin Baylor	2002	Willis Reed	343
Wilt Chamberlain	1992	Rudy LaRusso	337
Earl Monroe	1991	Clyde Lee	331
Hal Greer	1976	Tom Meschery	323

All Star Game

(Madison Square Garden, New York)

January 23	East Division	144		West Division	124

NBA Playoffs

March 22	N.Y. Knickerbockers	110	at	Philadelphia 76ers	118
March 22	San Francisco Warriors	111	at	St. Louis Hawks	106
March 23	Philadelphia 76ers	117	at	N.Y. Knickerbockers	128
March 23	San Francisco Warriors	103	at	St. Louis Hawks	111
March 24	Detroit Pistons	116	at	Boston Celtics	123
March 24	Chicago Bulls	101	at	Los Angeles Lakers	109
March 25	Boston Celtics	116	at	Detroit Pistons	126
March 25	Chicago Bulls	106	at	Los Angeles Lakers	111
March 26	St. Louis Hawks	109	at	San Francisco Warriors	124
March 27	Detroit Pistons	109	at	Boston Celtics	98
March 27	N.Y. Knickerbockers	132	at	Philadelphia 76ers	138 [OT]
March 27	Los Angeles Lakers	98	at	Chicago Bulls	104
March 28	Boston Celtics	135	at	Detroit Pistons	110
March 29	St. Louis Hawks	107	at	San Francisco Warriors	108
March 29	Los Angeles Lakers	93	at	Chicago Bulls	87
March 30	Philadelphia 76ers	98	at	N.Y. Knickerbockers	107
March 31	N.Y. Knickerbockers	107	at	Philadelphia 76ers	123
March 31	San Francisco Warriors	103	at	St. Louis Hawks	129
March 31	Detroit Pistons	96	at	Boston Celtics	110
March 31	Chicago Bulls	99	at	Los Angeles Lakers	122
April 1	Philadelphia 76ers	113	at	N.Y. Knickerbockers	97
April 1	Boston Celtics	111	at	Detroit Pistons	103
April 2	St. Louis Hawks	106	at	San Francisco Warriors	111
April 5	Boston Celtics	127	at	Philadelphia 76ers	118
April 5	San Francisco Warriors	105	at	Los Angeles Lakers	133
April 10	Philadelphia 76ers	115	at	Boston Celtics	106

April 10	San Francisco Warriors	112	at	Los Angeles Lakers	115
April 11	Boston Celtics	114	at	Philadelphia 76ers	122
April 11	Los Angeles Lakers	128	at	San Francisco Warriors	124
April 13	Los Angeles Lakers	106	at	San Francisco Warriors	100
April 14	Philadelphia 76ers	110	at	Boston Celtics	105
April 15	Boston Celtics	122	at	Philadelphia 76ers	104
April 17	Philadelphia 76ers	106	at	Boston Celtics	114
April 19	Boston Celtics	100	at	Philadelphia 76ers	96
April 21	Los Angeles Lakers	101	at	Boston Celtics	107
April 24	Los Angeles Lakers	123	at	Boston Celtics	113
April 26	Boston Celtics	127	at	Los Angeles Lakers	119
April 28	Boston Celtics	105	at	Los Angeles Lakers	119
April 30	Los Angeles Lakers	117	at	Boston Celtics	120 [OT]
May 2	Boston Celtics	124	at	Los Angeles Lakers	109

All Star Teams

First Team

Elgin Baylor (Los Angeles Lakers)
Jerry Lucas (Cincinnati Royals)
Wilt Chamberlain (Philadelphia 76ers)
Dave Bing (Detroit Pistons)
Oscar Robertson (Cincinnati Royals)

Second Team

Willis Reed (N.Y. Knickerbockers)
John Havlicek (Boston Celtics)
Bill Russell (Boston Celtics)
Hal Greer (Philadelphia 76ers)
Jerry West (Los Angeles Lakers)

Individual Awards

Eddie Gottlieb Trophy--Earl Monroe (Baltimore Bullets)
Maurice Podoloff Trophy--Wilt Chamberlain (Philadelphia 76ers)
NBA All Star Game MVP--Hal Greer (Philadelphia 76ers)
Red Auerbach Trophy--Richie Guerin (St. Louis Hawks)

Hall of Fame Inductees

Red Auerbach, Dutch Dehnert, Henry Iba, Adolph Rupp, Charles Taylor

American Basketball Association
Eastern Division

Team Name	GP	W	L	PPGF	PPGA	Pct	GB
Pittsburgh Pipers	78	54	24	111.9	108.7	.692	-
Minnesota Muskies	78	50	28	108.6	104.7	.641	4
Indiana Pacers	78	38	40	109.6	109.4	.487	16
Kentucky Colonels	78	36	42	104.5	105.2	.462	18
New Jersey Americans	78	36	42	110.8	112.4	.462	18

Western Division

Team Name	GP	W	L	PPGF	PPGA	Pct	GB
New Orleans Buccaneers	78	48	30	111.7	106.9	.615	-
Dallas Chaparrals	78	46	32	109.9	108.6	.590	2
Denver Rockets	78	45	33	105.7	101.5	.577	3
Houston Mavericks	78	29	49	103.5	107.8	.372	19
Anaheim Amigos	78	25	53	111.6	116.1	.321	23
Oakland Oaks	78	22	56	110.8	117.4	.282	26

Coaching

Pittsburgh--Vince Cazetta 54-24; Minnesota--Jim Pollard 50-28;Indiana--Larry Staverman 38-40; Kentucky--John Givens 5-12, Gene Rhodes 31-30; New Jersey--Max Zaslofsky 36-42; New Orleans--Babe McCarthy 48-30; Dallas--Cliff Hagan 46-32; Denver--Bob Bass 45-33; Houston--Slater Martin 29-49; Anaheim--Al Brightman 12-24, Harry Dinnel 13-29; Oakland--Bruce Hale 22-56

League Leaders

Field Goals		**Free Throws**		**Assists**	
Mel Daniels	669	Connie Hawkins	603	Larry Brown	506
Doug Moe	665	Doug Moe	551	Steve Chubin	364
Darrel Carrier	643	Larry Jones	530	Roger Brown	327
Charlie Williams	642	Steve Chubin	518	Connie Hawkins	320
Connie Hawkins	635	Fred Lewis	465	Charlie Beasley	290

Points		**Fouls**	
Doug Moe	1884	Dan Anderson	329
Connie Hawkins	1875	Art Becker	321
Darrel Carrier	1765	Goose Ligon	307
Larry Jones	1742	Les Hunter	297
Mel Daniels	1729	Roger Brown	296

All Star Game

(State Fairgrounds Arena, Indianapolis)

January 9	East Division	126	West Division	120

ABA Playoffs

March 23	Houston Mavericks	110	at	Dallas Chaparrals	111
March 24	Kentucky Colonels	102	at	Minnesota Muskies	115
March 25	Indiana Pacers	127	at	Pittsburgh Pipers	146
March 25	Houston Mavericks	97	at	Dallas Chaparrals	115
March 26	Indiana Pacers	108	at	Pittsburgh Pipers	121
March 26	Kentucky Colonels	100	at	Minnesota Muskies	95
March 26	Denver Rockets	104	at	New Orleans Buccaneers	130
March 26	Dallas Chaparrals	116	at	Houston Mavericks	103
March 27	Pittsburgh Pipers	133	at	Indiana Pacers	114
March 27	Minnesota Muskies	116	at	Kentucky Colonels	107
March 27	Denver Rockets	93	at	New Orleans Buccaneers	105
March 29	Minnesota Muskies	86	at	Kentucky Colonels	94
March 30	New Orleans Buccaneers	98	at	Denver Rockets	105
March 30	Kentucky Colonels	108	at	Minnesota Muskies	114
March 31	New Orleans Buccaneers	100	at	Denver Rockets	108
April 3	Denver Rockets	97	at	New Orleans Buccaneers	102
April 4	Minnesota Muskies	117	at	Pittsburgh Pipers	125
April 5	Dallas Chaparrals	99	at	New Orleans Buccaneers	104
April 6	Minnesota Muskies	137	at	Pittsburgh Pipers	123
April 9	Dallas Chaparrals	112	at	New Orleans Buccaneers	109
April 10	Pittsburgh Pipers	107	at	Minnesota Muskies	99
April 10	New Orleans Buccaneers	110	at	Dallas Chaparrals	107
April 11	New Orleans Buccaneers	119	at	Dallas Chaparrals	103
April 13	Pittsburgh Pipers	117	at	Minnesota Muskies	108

April 13	Dallas Chaparrals	107	at	New Orleans Buccaneers	108
April 14	Minnesota Muskies	105	at	Pittsburgh Pipers	114
April 18	New Orleans Buccaneers	112	at	Pittsburgh Pipers	120
April 20	New Orleans Buccaneers	109	at	Pittsburgh Pipers	100
April 24	Pittsburgh Pipers	101	at	New Orleans Buccaneers	109
April 25	Pittsburgh Pipers	106	at	New Orleans Buccaneers	105 [OT]
April 27	New Orleans Buccaneers	111	at	Pittsburgh Pipers	108
May 1	Pittsburgh Pipers	118	at	New Orleans Buccaneers	112
May 4	New Orleans Buccaneers	113	at	Pittsburgh Pipers	122

All Star Teams

First Team

Connie Hawkins (Pittsburgh Pipers)
Doug Moe (New Orleans Buccaneers)
Mel Daniels (Minnesota Muskies)
Larry Jones (Denver Rockets)
Charlie Williams (Pittsburgh Pipers)

Second Team

Roger Brown (Indiana Pacers)
Cincy Powell (Dallas Chaparrals)
John Beasley (Dallas Chaparrals)
Larry Brown (New Orleans Buccaneers)
Louie Dampier (Kentucky Colonels)

Individual Awards

ABA All Star Game MVP--Larry Brown (New Orleans Buccaneers)
Coach of the Year--Vince Cazetta (Pittsburgh Pipers)
Most Valuable Player--Connie Hawkins (Pittsburgh Pipers)
Rookie of the Year--Mel Daniels (Minnesota Muskies)

Rules

Field goals from beyond 25 feet counted as three points
The American Basketball Association adopted a 30 second clock which forced teams to shoot the ball within 30 seconds or give up the ball.

Notes

The ABA was formed this year by a group of California investors led by Gary Davidson. This was the first of three pro sports leagues founded by Gary Davidson.
NBA legend George Mikan became the first Commissioner of the American Basketball Association.
The ABA adopted the use of a red, white, and blue basketball instead of the traditional brown one.
Kentucky and New Jersey tied for fourth place in the ABA and were scheduled to play a tie breaker but a suitable arena could not be found and Kentucky was awarded fourth place by forfeit.

FOOTBALL
National Football League

Eastern Conference

Capitol Division

Team Name	GP	W	L	T	PF	PA	Pct
Dallas Cowboys	14	12	2	0	431	186	.857
New York Giants	14	7	7	0	294	325	.500
Washington Redskins	14	5	9	0	249	358	.357
Philadelphia Eagles	14	2	12	0	202	351	.143

Century Division

Cleveland Browns	14	10	4	0	394	273	.714
St. Louis Cardinals	14	9	4	1	325	289	.679
New Orleans Saints	14	4	9	1	246	327	.321
Pittsburgh Steelers	14	2	11	1	244	397	.179

Western Conference
Central Division

Minnesota Vikings	14	8	6	0	282	242	.571
Chicago Bears	14	7	7	0	250	333	.500
Green Bay Packers	14	6	7	1	281	227	.464
Detroit Lions	14	4	8	2	207	241	.357

Coastal Division

Baltimore Colts	14	13	1	0	402	144	.929
Los Angeles Rams	14	10	3	1	312	200	.750
San Francisco 49ers	14	7	6	1	303	310	.536
Atlanta Falcons	14	2	12	0	170	389	.143

Coaching Changes

Chicago--Jim Dooley 7-7-0; Green Bay--Phil Bengston 6-7-1; San Francisco--Dick Nolan 7-6-1; Atlanta--Norb Hecker 0-3-0, Norm Van Brocklin 2-9-0.

League Leaders

Yards Rushing		**Yards Passing**		**Passing %** (40 attempts)	
Leroy Kelly	1239	John Brodie	3020	Bart Starr	64
Ken Willard	967	Earl Morrall	2909	John Brodie	58
Tom Woodeshick	947	Fran Tarkenton	2555	Earl Morrall	57
Dick Hoak	858	Don Meredith	2500	Sonny Jurgensen	57
Gale Sayers	856	Bill Nelsen	2366	Bill Munson	55

Receiving Yards		**Receptions**		**Field Goals**	
Roy Jefferson	1074	Clifton McNeil	71	Mac Percival	25
Paul Warfield	1067	Roy Jefferson	58	Sam Baker	19
Homer Jones	1057	Dan Abramowicz	54	Charlie Durkee	19
Lance Rentzel	1009	Lance Rentzel	54	Fred Cox	19
Clifton McNeil	994	Bob Hayes	53	Don Cockroft	18

Punt Return Yards		**Kickoff Return Yards**	
Chuck Latourette	345	Chuck Latourette	1237
Bob Hayes	312	Cannonball Butler	799
Roy Jefferson	274	Ronnie Blye	734
Alvin Haymond	201	Ron Smith	718
Charlie West	201	Don Shy	682

Pro Bowl Game
(Memorial Coliseum, Los Angeles)

January 19 1969	Western Conference	10	Eastern Conference	7

Notes

A furor arose this year when NBC who were broadcasting the game between New York and Oakland, decided to preempt the last two minutes of the game to show the movie "Heidi". The network received so many protests that they promised never to do such a thing again.

NFL Playoffs

December 21	Dallas Cowboys	20	at	Cleveland Browns	31
December 22	Minnesota Vikings	14	at	Baltimore Colts	24
December 29	Baltimore Colts	34	at	Cleveland Browns	0

Individual Awards

AP MVP--Earl Morrall (Baltimore Colts)
Bert Bell Trophy--Earl McCullough (Detroit Lions) [World Almanac]
Bert Bell Trophy--Leroy Kelly (Cleveland Browns)
George Halas Trophy--Deacon Jones (Los Angeles Rams)
Jim Thorpe Trophy--Earl Morrall (Baltimore Colts)
Pro Bowl MVP--Roman Gabriel (Los Angeles Rams)
Merlin Olsen (Los Angeles Rams)
Rookie of the Year--Earl McCullouch (Detroit Lions)
U.P.I. MVP--Earl Morrall (Baltimore Colts)
U.P.I. NFL-NFC Coach of the Year--Don Shula (Baltimore Colts)
U.P.I. NFL-NFC Rookie of the Year--Earl McCullough (Detroit Lions)

Hall of Fame Inductees

Cliff Battles, Art Donovan, Elroy Hirsch, Wayne Millner, Marion Motley, Charley Trippi, Alex Wojciechowicz

American Football League
Eastern Division

Team Name	GP	W	L	T	PF	PA	Pct
New York Jets	14	11	3	0	419	280	.786
Houston Oilers	14	7	7	0	303	248	.500
Miami Dolphins	14	5	8	1	276	355	.393
Boston Patriots	14	4	10	0	229	406	.286
Buffalo Bills	14	1	12	1	199	367	.107

Western Division

Team Name	GP	W	L	T	PF	PA	Pct
Oakland Raiders	14	12	2	0	453	233	.857
Kansas City Chiefs	14	12	2	0	371	170	.857
San Diego Chargers	14	9	5	0	382	310	.643
Denver Broncos	14	5	9	0	255	404	.357
Cincinnati Bengals	14	3	11	0	215	329	.214

Coaching Changes

Cincinnati--Paul Brown 3-11-0; Buffalo--Joe Collier 0-2-0, Harvey Johnson 1-10-1.

League Leaders

Yards Rushing		Yards Passing		Passing% (40 attempts)	
Paul Robinson	1023	John Hadl	3473	Sam Wyche	64
Robert Holmes	866	Daryle Lamonica	3245	George Blanda	61
Hewritt Dixon	865	Joe Namath	3147	Len Dawson	59
Hoyle Granger	848	Bob Griese	2473	Dewey Warren	59
Dick Post	758	Len Dawson	2109	Jack Lee	56

Receiving Yards		Receptions		Field Goals	
Lance Alworth	1312	Lance Alworth	68	Jim Turner	34
Don Maynard	1297	George Sauer	66	Jan Stenerud	30
George Sauer	1141	Fred Biletnikoff	61	Dennis Partee	22
Warren Wells	1137	Karl Noonan	58	George Blanda	21
Gary Garrison	1103	Don Maynard	57	Gino Cappelletti	15

Punt Return Yards		Kickoff Return Yards	
Butch Atkinson	490	Max Anderson	971
Noland Smith	270	Willie Porter	812
Floyd Little	261	Butch Atkinson	802
Hagood Clarke	241	Zeke Moore	787
Larry Carwell	227	Floyd Little	649

All Star Game

(Gator Bowl, Jacksonville)

January 19 1969	West Division	38	East Division	25

AFL Playoffs

December 22	Kansas City Chiefs	6	at	Oakland Raiders	41
December 29	Oakland Raiders	23	at	New York Jets	27

Super Bowl III

(Orange Bowl, Miami)

January 12 1969	New York Jets	16	Baltimore Colts	7

Individual Awards

AFL All Star Game MVP--Len Dawson (Kansas City Chiefs)
George Webster (Houston Oilers)
Rookie of the Year--Paul Robinson (Cincinnati Bengals)
Super Bowl MVP--Joe Namath (New York Jets)
U.P.I. AFL-AFC Coach of the Year--Hank Stram (Kansas City Chiefs)
U.P.I. AFL-AFC Player of the Year--Joe Namath (New York Jets)
U.P.I. AFL-AFC Rookie of the Year--Paul Robinson (Cincinnati Bengals)

Notes

This was the year when Joe Namath of the New York Jets guaranteed that his team would win the Super Bowl when no AFL team had ever come close to winning it.

Canadian Football League
Eastern Conference

Team Name	GP	W	L	T	PF	PA	Pts	Pct
Ottawa Rough Riders	14	9	3	2	416	271	20	.714
Toronto Argonauts	14	9	5	0	284	266	18	.643
Hamilton Tiger-Cats	14	6	7	1	262	292	13	.464
Montreal Alouettes	14	3	9	2	234	327	8	.286

Western Conference

Team Name	GP	W	L	T	PF	PA	Pts	Pct
Saskatchewan Roughriders	16	12	3	1	345	223	25	.781
Calgary Stampeders	16	10	6	0	412	249	20	.625
Edmonton Eskimos	16	8	7	1	228	288	17	.531
British Columbia Lions	16	4	11	1	217	318	9	.281
Winnipeg Blue Bombers	16	3	13	0	210	374	6	.188

Coaching Changes

Hamilton--Joe Restic 6-7-1; Montreal--O. Kay Dalton 3-9-2; British Columbia--Jim Champion 4-11-1.

League Leaders

Yards Rushing		Yards Passing		Passing %	
George Reed	1222	Peter Liske	4333	Peter Liske	62
Jim Evenson	1220				
Bill Symons	1107				

Receiving Yards		Receptions		Points	
Herman Harrison	1306	Ken Nielsen	68	Ted Gerela	115
Ken Nielsen	1031				
Terry Evanshen	1002				

Grey Cup Playoffs

November 9	Hamilton Tiger-Cats	21	at	Toronto Argonauts	33
November 10	Edmonton Eskimos	13	at	Calgary Stampeders	29
November 16	Calgary Stampeders	32	at	Saskatchewan Roughriders	0
November 17	Ottawa Rough Riders	11	at	Toronto Argonauts	13
November 20	Saskatchewan Roughriders	12	at	Calgary Stampeders	25[OT]
November 23	Toronto Argonauts	14	at	Ottawa Rough Riders	36
November 30	Ottawa Rough Riders	24	at	Calgary Stampeders	21 *

*Game played in Toronto

Individual Awards

Annis Stukus Trophy--Eagle Keys (Saskatchewan Roughriders)
Dave Dryburgh Memorial Trophy--Ted Gerela (British Columbia Lions)
DeMarco-Becket Memorial Trophy--Ed McQuarters (Saskatchewan Roughriders)
Dr.. Beattie Martin Trophy--Dave Crammer (Calgary Stampeders)
Eddie James Memorial Trophy--George Reed (Saskatchewan Roughriders)
Grey Cup MVP--Vic Washington (Ottawa Rough Riders)
Gruen Trophy--Dave Knechtel (Toronto Argonauts)
Jeff Nicklin Memorial Trophy--Ron Lancaster (Saskatchewan Roughriders)
Jeff Russel Memorial Trophy--Larry Fairholm (Montreal Alouettes)
Schenley Award Most Outstanding Canadian--Ken Nielsen (Winnipeg Blue Bombers)
Schenley Award Most Outstanding Lineman Ken Lehmann (Ottawa Rough Riders)
Schenley Award Most Outstanding Player--Bill Symons (Toronto Argonauts)

Hall of Fame Inductees

Wes Cutler, Joseph Ryan, Joe Tubman

Notes

Jake Gaudaur was named as CFL commissioner.

HOCKEY
National Hockey League

Eastern Division

Team Name	GP	W	L	T	GF	GA	Pts	Pct
Montreal Canadiens	74	42	22	10	236	167	94	.635
New York Rangers	74	39	23	12	226	183	90	.608
Boston Bruins	74	37	27	10	259	216	84	.568
Chicago Black Hawks	74	32	26	16	212	222	80	.541
Toronto Maple Leafs	74	33	31	10	209	176	76	.514
Detroit Red Wings	74	27	35	12	245	257	66	.446

Western Division

Team Name	GP	W	L	T	GF	GA	Pts	Pct
Philadelphia Flyers	74	31	32	11	173	179	73	.493
Los Angeles Kings	74	31	33	10	200	224	72	.486
St. Louis Blues	74	27	31	16	177	191	70	.473
Minnesota North Stars	74	27	32	15	191	226	69	.466
Pittsburgh Penguins	74	27	34	13	195	216	67	.453
Oakland Seals	74	15	42	17	153	219	47	.318

Coaching Changes

Toronto--George Imlach 33-31-10; Philadelphia--Keith Allen 31-32-11; Los Angeles--Leonard "Red" Kelly 31-33-10; St. Louis--Lynn Patrick 4-10-2, Scotty Bowman 23-21-14; Minnesota--Wren Blair 27-32-15; Pittsburgh--George Sullivan 27-34-13; Oakland--Bert Olmstead 11-37-16, Gordon Fashoway 4-5-1.

League Leaders

Goals

Bobby Hull	44
Stan Mikita	40
Gordie Howe	39
Phil Esposito	35
Wayne Connelly	35

Assists

Phil Esposito	49
Rod Gilbert	48
Alex Delvecchio	48
Stan Mikita	47
Jean Ratelle	46

Points

Stan Mikita	87
Phil Esposito	84
Gordie Howe	82
Jean Ratelle	78
Rod Gilbert	77

Penalty Minutes

Barclay Plager	153
Don Awrey	150
Noel Picard	142
Ed Van Impe	141
Gary Dornhoefer	134

GAA

Lorne Worsley	1.98
John Bower	2.25
Doug Favell	2.27
Bruce Gamble	2.32
Ed Giacomin	2.44

Wins

Ed Giacomin	36
Rogie Vachon	23
Gerry Cheevers	23
Denis DeJordy	23
Cesare Maniago	21

Shutouts

Ed Giacomin	8
Cesare Maniago	6
Les Binkley	6
Glenn Hall	5
Bruce Gamble	5

All Star Game

(Maple Leaf Gardens, Toronto)

January 16	Toronto Maple Leafs	4	All Stars	3

Notes

The National Hockey League expanded this year with the 6 new teams forming the Western Division. These new teams drafted their players from the established teams.
The Oakland Seals began the season as the California Seals but changed their name on November 6th 1967.

Stanley Cup Playoffs

April 4	Boston Bruins	1	at	Montreal Canadiens	2
April 4	Chicago Black Hawks	1	at	New York Rangers	3
April 4	St. Louis Blues	1	at	Philadelphia Flyers	0
April 4	Minnesota North Stars	1	at	Los Angeles Kings	2
April 6	Boston Bruins	3	at	Montreal Canadiens	5
April 6	St. Louis Blues	3	at	Philadelphia Flyers	4
April 6	Minnesota North Stars	0	at	Los Angeles Kings	2
April 9	Montreal Canadiens	5	at	Boston Bruins	2
April 9	Chicago Black Hawks	1	at	New York Rangers	2
April 9	Los Angeles Kings	5	at	Minnesota North Stars	7
April 10	Philadelphia Flyers	2	at	St. Louis Blues	3 [24:10]
April 11	Montreal Canadiens	3	at	Boston Bruins	2
April 11	New York Rangers	4	at	Chicago Black Hawks	7
April 11	Philadelphia Flyers	2	at	St. Louis Blues	5
April 11	Los Angeles Kings	2	at	Minnesota North Stars	3
April 13	New York Rangers	1	at	Chicago Black Hawks	3
April 13	St. Louis Blues	1	at	Philadelphia Flyers	6

April 13	Minnesota North Stars	2	at	Los Angeles Kings	3
April 14	Chicago Black Hawks	2	at	New York Rangers	1
April 16	New York Rangers	1	at	Chicago Black Hawks	4
April 16	Philadelphia Flyers	2	at	St. Louis Blues	1 [31:38]
April 16	Los Angeles Kings	3	at	Minnesota North Stars	4 [9:11]
April 18	St. Louis Blues	3	at	Philadelphia Flyers	1
April 18	Minnesota North Stars	9	at	Los Angeles Kings	4
April 18	Chicago Black Hawks	2	at	Montreal Canadiens	9
April 20	Chicago Black Hawks	1	at	Montreal Canadiens	4
April 21	Minnesota North Stars	3	at	St. Louis Blues	5
April 22	St. Louis Blues	2	at	Minnesota North Stars	3 [3:41]
April 23	Montreal Canadiens	4	at	Chicago Black Hawks	2
April 25	Minnesota North Stars	5	at	St. Louis Blues	1
April 25	Montreal Canadiens	1	at	Chicago Black Hawks	2
April 27	Minnesota North Stars	3	at	St. Louis Blues	4 [1:32]
April 28	Chicago Black Hawks	3	at	Montreal Canadiens	4 [2:14]
April 29	Minnesota North Stars	2	at	St. Louis Blues	3 [17:27]
May 1	St. Louis Blues	1	at	Minnesota North Stars	5
May 3	Minnesota North Stars	1	at	St. Louis Blues	2 [22:50]
May 5	Montreal Canadiens	3	at	St. Louis Blues	2 [1:41]
May 7	Montreal Canadiens	1	at	St. Louis Blues	0
May 9	St. Louis Blues	3	at	Montreal Canadiens	4 [1:13]
May 11	St. Louis Blues	2	at	Montreal Canadiens	3

All Star Teams

First Team		Second Team
Lorne Worsley	Goal	Ed Giacomin
Bobby Orr	Defense	J.C. Tremblay
Tim Horton	Defense	Jim Neilson
Stan Mikita	Center	Phil Esposito
Gordie Howe	Right Wing	Rod Gilbert
Bobby Hull	Left Wing	John Bucyk

Individual Awards

Art Ross Trophy--Stan Mikita (Chicago Black Hawks)
Bill Masterton Trophy--Claude Provost (Montreal Canadiens)
Calder Memorial Trophy--Derek Sanderson (Boston Bruins)
Conn Smythe Trophy--Glenn Hall (St. Louis Blues)
Hart Memorial Trophy--Stan Mikita (Chicago Black Hawks)
James Norris Trophy--Bobby Orr (Boston Bruins)
Lady Byng Memorial Trophy--Stan Mikita (Chicago Black Hawks)
Lester Patrick Trophy--Thomas Lockhart and Walter Brown and John R. Kilpatrick
NHL All Star Game MVP--Bruce Gamble (Toronto Maple Leafs)
Vezina Trophy--Lorne Worsley and Rogie Vachon (Montreal Canadiens)

Hall of Fame Inductees

Bill Cowley, James Dunn, James Hendy

SOCCER
North American Soccer League

Eastern Conference
Atlantic Division

Team Name	GP	W	L	T	GF	GA	BP	Pts	Pct
Atlanta Chiefs	31	18	7	6	50	32	48	174	.624
Washington Whips	32	15	10	7	63	53	56	167	.580
New York Generals	32	12	8	12	62	54	36	164	.569
Baltimore Bays	32	13	16	3	42	43	41	128	.444
Boston Beacons	32	9	17	6	51	69	49	121	.420

Lakes Division

Team Name	GP	W	L	T	GF	GA	BP	Pts	Pct
Cleveland Stokers	32	14	7	11	62	44	58	175	.608
Chicago Mustangs	32	13	10	9	68	68	59	164	.569
Toronto Falcons	32	13	13	6	55	69	48	144	.500
Detroit Cougars	31	6	21	4	48	65	40	88	.315

Western Conference

Gulf Division

Team Name	GP	W	L	T	GF	GA	BP	Pts	Pct
Kansas City Spurs	32	16	11	5	61	43	47	158	.549
Houston Stars	32	14	12	6	58	41	48	150	.521
St. Louis Stars	32	12	14	6	47	59	40	130	.451
Dallas Tornado	32	22	6	4	28	109	28	52	.181

Pacific Division

Team Name	GP	W	L	T	GF	GA	BP	Pts	Pct
San Diego Toros	32	18	8	6	65	38	60	186	.646
Oakland Clippers	32	18	8	6	71	38	59	185	.642
Los Angeles Wolves	32	11	13	0	55	52	49	139	.483
Vancouver Royals	32	12	15	5	51	60	49	136	.472

Coaching Changes

Washington--Andre Nagy, Hicabi Emerkli ; Baltimore--Gordon Jago 13-16-3; Boston--Jack Mansell 9-17-6; Cleveland--Norman Low 14-7-11; Chicago--George Meyer 13-10-9; Toronto--Laddie Kubala 13-13-6; Detroit--Len Julians, Andre Nagy; Kansas City--Janos Bedl 16-11-5; Houston--Geza Henni 14-12-6; Dallas--Bob Kap, Keith Spurgeon ; San Diego--George Curtis, Angel Papadopolus ; Los Angeles--Ray Wood 11-13-8; Vancouver--Ferenc Puskas 12-15-5.

League Leaders

Goals		Points		GAA	
John Kowalik	30	John Kowalik	69	Ataulfo Sanchez	0.93
Cirilo Fernandez	30	Cirilio Fernandez	67	Vic Rouse	0.96
Iris DeBrito	21	Ilija Mitic	48	Mirko Stojanovic	1.12
Henry Klein	20	Henry Klein	44	Lief Neilsen	1.24
Ilija Mitic	18	Iris DeBrito	44	Bert Hoogerman	1.28

NASL Playoffs

September 11	Atlanta Chiefs	1	at	Cleveland Stokers	1
September 11	San Diego Toros	1	at	Kansas City Spurs	1
September 14	Cleveland Stokers	1	at	Atlanta Chiefs	2 [OT]
September 16	Kansas City Spurs	0	at	San Diego Toros	1 [OT]
September 21	Atlanta Chiefs	0	at	San Diego Toros	0
September 28	San Diego Toros	0	at	Atlanta Chiefs	3

All Star Teams

First Team		Second Team
Mirko Stojanovic	Goal	Vic Rouse
Mel Scott	Defender	John Worbye
Momcilio Gavric	Defender	John Cocking
David Davidovic	Midfield	Dennis Viollet
Ron Crisp	Midfield	Milan Cop
Ruben Navarro	Midfield	Tony Knapp
John Kowalik	Forward	Victorio Casa
Cirilo Fernandez	Forward	Mario Baesso
Jorgen Kristensen	Forward	Eric Barber
Casey Frankiewicz	Forward	Edvaldo Neto
llija Mitic	Forward	Enrique Mateos

Individual Awards

Coach of the Year--Phil Woosnam (Atlanta Chiefs)
Lead Goalkeeper Award--Ataulfo Sanchez (San Diego Toros)
Most Valuable Player--John Kowalik (Chicago Mustangs)
Rookie of the Year--Kaizer Motaung (Atlanta Chiefs)

Notes

Dick Walsh and Ken Macker were named co-Commissioners of the North American Soccer League.

Franchise Changes

AL--Kansas City Athletics moved to Oakland.
NASL--Chicago Spurs became the Kansas City Spurs.
Los Angeles Toros became the San Diego Toros.

Other Sports

Horseracing--Kentucky Derby won by Dancer's Image (time 2:02.2, purse $122,600).
Golf--U.S. Open won by Lee Trevino with a score of 275.
Auto Racing--Indianapolis 500 won by Bobby Unser (ave. speed 152.882 MPH).
Tennis--U.S. Open won by Arthur Ashe in the men's singles.
U.S. 0pen won by Robert Lutz and Stan Smith in the men's doubles.
U.S. Open won by Virginia Wade in the women's singles.
U.S. Open won by Maria Bueno and Margaret Court in the women's doubles.
U.S. Open won by Mary Ann Eisel and Peter Curtis in the mixed doubles.

Notes

Dancer's Image was disqualified from purse money in the Kentucky Derby because tests disclosed the presence of the pain killing drug phenylbutazone in his system. All wagers were paid on Dancer's Image but first place prize money was paid to Forward Pass which finished second.

1969

BASEBALL
National League
East

Team Name	W	L	Pct	GB	R	OR
New York Mets	100	62	.617	-	632	541
Chicago Cubs	92	70	.568	8	720	611
Pittsburgh Pirates	88	74	.543	12	725	652
St. Louis Cardinals	87	75	.537	13	595	540
Philadelphia Phillies	63	99	.389	37	645	745
Montreal Expos	52	110	.321	48	582	791

West

Team Name	W	L	Pct	GB	R	OR
Atlanta Braves	93	69	.574	-	691	631
San Francisco Giants	90	72	.556	3	713	636
Cincinnati Reds	89	73	.549	4	798	768
Los Angeles Dodgers	85	77	.525	8	645	561
Houston Astros	81	81	.500	12	676	668
San Diego Padres	52	110	.321	41	468	746

Coaching Changes

Pittsburgh--Larry Shepard 84-73, Alex Grammas 4-1; Philadelphia--Bob Skinner 44-64, George Myatt 19-35; Montreal--Gene Mauch 52-110; San Francisco--Clyde King 90-72; Houston--Harry Walker 81-81; San Diego--Preston Gomez 52-110.

League Leaders

Batting Average

Pete Rose	.348
Roberto Clemente	.345
Cleon Jones	.340
Matty Alou	.331
Willie McCovey	.320

Home Runs

Willie McCovey	45
Hank Aaron	44
Lee May	38
Tony Perez	37
Jim Wynn	33

RBI

Willie McCovey	126
Ron Santo	123
Tony Perez	122
Lee May	110
Ernie Banks	106

Stolen Bases

Lou Brock	53
Joe Morgan	49
Bobby Bonds	45
Maury Wills	40
Bob Tolan	26

ERA

Juan Marichal	2.10
Steve Carlton	2.17
Bob Gibson	2.18
Tom Seaver	2.21
Jerry Koosman	2.28

Wins

Tom Seaver	25
Phil Niekro	23
Juan Marichal	21
Ferguson Jenkins	21
Bill Hands	20

Saves

Fred Gladding	29
Wayne Granger	27
Cecil Upshaw	27
Jim Brewer	20
Phil Regan	17

Strikeouts

Ferguson Jenkins	273
Bob Gibson	269
Bill Singer	247
Don Wilson	235
Gaylord Perry	233

NLCS

October 4	New York Mets	9	at	Atlanta Braves	5
October 5	New York Mets	11	at	Atlanta Braves	6
October 6	Atlanta Braves	4	at	New York Mets	7

American League

East

Team Name	W	L	Pct	GB	R	OR
Baltimore Orioles	109	53	.673	-	779	517
Detroit Tigers	90	72	.556	19	701	601
Boston Red Sox	87	75	.537	22	743	736
Washington Senators	86	76	.531	23	694	644
New York Yankees	80	81	.497	28.5	562	587
Cleveland Indians	62	99	.385	46.5	573	717

West

Team Name	W	L	Pct	GB	R	OR
Minnesota Twins	97	65	.599	-	790	618
Oakland Athletics	88	74	.543	9	740	678
California Angels	71	91	.438	26	528	652
Kansas City Royals	69	93	.426	28	586	688
Chicago White Sox	68	94	.420	29	625	723
Seattle Pilots	64	98	.395	33	639	799

Coaching Changes

Baltimore--Earl Weaver 109-53; Boston--Dick Williams 82-71, Eddie Popowski 5-4;Washington--Ted Williams 86-76; Minnesota--Billy Martin 97-65; Oakland--Hank Bauer 80-69, John McNamara 8-5; California--Bill Rigney 11-28, Harold Phillips 6o-63; Kansas City--Joe Gordon 69-93; Chicago--Al Lopez 8-9, Don Gutteridge 60-85; Seattle--Joseph Schultz 64-98.

League Leaders

Batting Average		Home Runs		RBI	
Rod Carew	.332	Harmon Killebrew	49	Harmon Killebrew	140
Reg Smith	.309	Frank Howard	48	John Powell	121
Tony Oliva	.309	Reggie Jackson	47	Reggie Jackson	118
Frank Robinson	.308	Carl Yastrzemski	40	Sal Bando	113
John Powell	.304	Rico Petrocelli	40	Frank Howard	111

Stolen Bases		ERA		Wins	
Tom Harper	73	Dick Bosman	2.19	Denny McLain	24
Bert Campaneris	62	Jim Palmer	2.34	Mike Cuellar	23
Cesar Tovar	45	Mike Cuellar	2.38	Jim Perry	20
Pat Kelly	40	Andy Messersmith	2.52	Dave McNally	20
Joe Foy	37	Fred Peterson	2.55	Dave Boswell	20

Saves		Strikeouts	
Ron Perranoski	31	Sam McDowell	279
Ken Tatum	22	Mickey Lolich	271
Albert Lyle	17	Andy Messersmith	211
Dennis Higgins	16	Dave Boswell	190
Eddie Watt	16	Joe Coleman	182

All Star Game

(RFK Stadium, Washington)

July 23	National League	9		American League	3

ALCS

October 4	Minnesota Twins	3	at	Baltimore Orioles	4 [12]
October 5	Minnesota Twins	0	at	Baltimore Orioles	1 [11]
October 6	Baltimore Orioles	11	at	Minnesota Twins	2

World Series

October 11	New York Mets	1	at	Baltimore Orioles	4
October 12	New York Mets	2	at	Baltimore Orioles	1
October 14	Baltimore Orioles	0	at	New York Mets	5
October 15	Baltimore Orioles	1	at	New York Mets	2 [10]
October 16	Baltimore Orioles	3	at	New York Mets	5

Individual Awards

Arch Ward Memorial Trophy--Willie McCovey (San Francisco Giants NL)
Baseball Writers Award--Willie McCovey (San Francisco Giants NL)
Harmon Killebrew (Minnesota Twins AL)
Cy Young Award--Tom Seaver (New York Mets NL)
Denny McLain (Detroit Tigers AL)
Mike Cuellar (Baltimore Orioles AL)
Rookie of the Year--Ted Sizemore (Los Angeles Dodgers NL)
Lou Piniella (Kansas City Royals AL)
Sporting News Executive of the Year--John Murphy (New York Mets NL)
Sporting News Manager of the Year--Gil Hodges (New York Mets NL)
Sporting News Pitcher of the Year--Tom Seaver (New York Mets NL)
Denny McLain (Detroit Tigers AL)
Sporting News Player of the Year--Willie McCovey (San Francisco Giants NL)
Harmon Killebrew (Minnesota Twins AL)
Sporting News Rookie of the Year--Jose "Coco" Laboy (Montreal Expos NL)
Tom Griffin (Houston Astros NL)
Sporting News Rookie of the Year--Carlos May (Chicago White Sox AL)
Mike Nagy (Boston Red Sox AL)
World Series MVP--Don Clendendon (New York Mets NL)

Hall of Fame Inductees

Roy Campanella, Stan Coveleski, Waite Hoyt, Stan Musial

Rules

Strike zone to include area only from the armpit to the top of the knee (NL, AL).
Pitcher's mound lowered to 10 inches above the base lines and home plate (NL, AL).

BASKETBALL
National Basketball Association

Eastern Division

Team Name	GP	W	L	PPGF	PPGA	Pct	GB
Baltimore Bullets	82	57	25	116.4	112.1	.695	-
Philadelphia 76ers	82	55	27	118.9	113.8	.671	2
New York Knickerbockers	82	54	28	110.8	105.2	.659	3
Boston Celtics	82	48	34	111.0	105.4	.585	9
Cincinnati Royals	82	41	41	114.5	115.6	.500	16
Detroit Pistons	82	32	50	114.1	117.3	.390	25
Milwaukee Bucks	82	27	55	110.2	115.4	.329	30

Western Division

Team Name	GP	W	L	PPGF	PPGA	Pct	GB
Los Angeles Lakers	82	55	27	112.2	108.1	.671	-
Atlanta Hawks	82	48	34	111.3	109.4	.585	7
San Francisco Warriors	82	41	41	109.1	110.7	.500	14
San Diego Rockets	82	37	45	115.3	115.5	.451	18
Chicago Bulls	82	33	49	104.7	106.9	.402	22
Seattle SuperSonics	82	30	52	112.1	116.6	.366	25
Phoenix Suns	82	16	66	111.7	120.5	.195	39

Coaching Changes

Philadelphia--Jack Ramsay 55-27; New York--Red Holzman 54-28; Detroit--Don Butcher 10-12, Paul Seymour 22-38; Milwaukee--Larry Costello 27-55; Atlanta--Richie Guerin 48-34; San Francisco--George Lee 41-41; Chicago--Dick Motta 33-49; Phoenix--John Kerr 16-66.

League Leaders

Field Goals

Elvin Hayes	930
Earl Monroe	809
Bob Rule	776
Bill Cunningham	739
Hal Greer	732

Free Throws

Oscar Robertson	643
Bill Cunningham	556
Lenny Wilkens	547
Gail Goodrich	495
Jerry West	490

Assists

Oscar Robertson	772
Lenny Wilkins	674
Walt Frazier	635
Guy Rodgers	561
Dave Bing	546

Points

Elvin Hayes	2327
Earl Monroe	2065
Bill Cunningham	2034
Bob Rule	1965
Oscar Robertson	1955

Fouls

Bill Cunningham	329
Art Harris	326
Bob Rule	322
Walt Bellamy	320
Tom Boerwinkle	317

All Star Game
(Baltimore Civic Center, Baltimore)

January 14	East Division	123	West Division	112

NBA Playoffs

March 26	San Francisco Warriors	99	at	Los Angeles Lakers	94
March 26	Boston Celtics	114	at	Philadelphia 76ers	100
March 27	N.Y. Knickerbockers	113	at	Baltimore Bullets	101
March 27	San Diego Rockets	98	at	Atlanta Hawks	107
March 28	San Francisco Warriors	107	at	Los Angeles Lakers	101
March 28	Philadelphia 76ers	103	at	Boston Celtics	134
March 29	Baltimore Bullets	91	at	N.Y. Knickerbockers	107
March 29	San Diego Rockets	114	at	Atlanta Hawks	116
March 30	N.Y. Knickerbockers	119	at	Baltimore Bullets	116
March 30	Boston Celtics	125	at	Philadelphia 76ers	118
March 31	Los Angeles Lakers	115	at	San Francisco Warriors	98
April 1	Philadelphia 76ers	119	at	Boston Celtics	116
April 1	Atlanta Hawks	97	at	San Diego Rockets	104
April 2	Baltimore Bullets	108	at	N.Y. Knickerbockers	115
April 2	Los Angeles Lakers	103	at	San Francisco Warriors	88
April 4	San Francisco Warriors	98	at	Los Angeles Lakers	103
April 4	Boston Celtics	93	at	Philadelphia 76ers	90
April 4	Atlanta Hawks	112	at	San Diego Rockets	114
April 5	Los Angeles Lakers	118	at	San Francisco Warriors	78
April 6	San Diego Rockets	101	at	Atlanta Hawks	112
April 6	Boston Celtics	108	at	N.Y. Knickerbockers	100
April 7	Atlanta Hawks	108	at	San Diego Rockets	106
April 9	N.Y. Knickerbockers	97	at	Boston Celtics	112
April 10	Boston Celtics	91	at	N.Y. Knickerbockers	101
April 11	Atlanta Hawks	93	at	Los Angeles Lakers	95
April 13	Atlanta Hawks	102	at	Los Angeles Lakers	104
April 13	N.Y. Knickerbockers	96	at	Boston Celtics	97
April 14	Boston Celtics	104	at	N.Y. Knickerbockers	112
April 15	Los Angeles Lakers	80	at	Atlanta Hawks	99
April 17	Los Angeles Lakers	100	at	Atlanta Hawks	85
April 18	N.Y. Knickerbockers	105	at	Boston Celtics	106
April 20	Atlanta Hawks	96	at	Los Angeles Lakers	104
April 23	Boston Celtics	118	at	Los Angeles Lakers	120
April 25	Boston Celtics	112	at	Los Angeles Lakers	118
April 27	Los Angeles Lakers	105	at	Boston Celtics	111
April 29	Los Angeles Lakers	88	at	Boston Celtics	89
May 1	Boston Celtics	104	at	Los Angeles Lakers	117
May 3	Los Angeles Lakers	90	at	Boston Celtics	99
May 5	Boston Celtics	108	at	Los Angeles Lakers	106

All Star Teams

First Team

Bill Cunningham (Philadelphia 76ers)
Elgin Baylor (Los Angeles Lakers)
Wes Unseld (Baltimore Bullets)
Earl Monroe (Baltimore Bullets)
Oscar Robertson (Cincinnati Royals)

Second Team

John Havlicek (Boston Celtics)
Dave DeBusschere (Detroit-New York)
Willis Reed (N.Y. Knickerbockers)
Hal Greer (Philadelphia 76ers)
Jerry West (Los Angeles Lakers)

Individual Awards

Eddie Gottlieb Trophy--Wes Unseld (Baltimore Bullets)
Maurice Podoloff Trophy--Wes Unseld (Baltimore Bullets)
NBA All Star Game MVP--Oscar Robertson (Cincinnati Royals)

NBA Finals MVP--Jerry West (Los Angeles Lakers)
Red Auerbach Trophy--Gene Shue (Baltimore Bullets)

Hall of Fame Inductees

Ben Carnevale, Bob Davies

American Basketball Association
Eastern Division

Team Name	GP	W	L	PPGF	PPGA	Pct	GB
Indiana Pacers	78	44	34	119.6	115.5	.564	-
Miami Floridians	78	43	35	115.5	115.1	.551	1
Kentucky Colonels	78	42	36	111.2	111.0	.538	2
Minnesota Pipers	78	36	42	114.3	114.2	.462	8
New York Nets	78	17	61	108.5	117.2	.218	27

Western Division

Team Name	GP	W	L	PPGF	PPGA	Pct	GB
Oakland Oaks	78	60	18	126.5	118.1	.769	-
New Orleans Buccaneers	78	46	32	116.1	112.7	.590	14
Denver Rockets	78	44	34	114.9	113.4	.564	16
Dallas Chaparrals	78	41	37	111.0	111.7	.526	19
Los Angeles Stars	78	33	45	114.4	117.5	.423	27
Houston Mavericks	78	23	55	111.3	117.0	.295	37

Coaching Changes

Indiana--Larry Staverman 2-7, Bob Leonard 42-27; Miami--Jim Pollard 43-35; Kentucky--Gene Rhodes 42-36; Minnesota--Jim Harding 20-12, Vern Mikkelsen 6-7, Gus Young--10-23; New York--Max Zaslofsky 17-61; Oakland--Alex Hannum 60-18; Los Angeles--Bill Sharman 33-45; Houston--Slater Martin 3-9, Jim Weaver 20-46.

League Leaders

Field Goals		Free Throws		Assists	
Jim Jones	764	Larry Jones	591	Larry Brown	544
Larry Jones	759	Jim Jones	521	Don Freeman	501
Louie Dampier	713	Darrel Carrier	447	Louie Dampier	456
Mel Daniels	712	Roger Brown	442	Jim Jones	437
Don Freeman	651	Ron Boone	436	Roger Brown	345

Points		Fouls	
Larry Jones	2133	John Smith	328
Jim Jones	2050	Skip Thoren	324
Louie Dampier	1933	Kendall Rhine	321
Mel Daniels	1824	Goose Ligon	312
Will Somerset	1758	Gene Moore	311

All Star Game
(Freedom Hall, Louisville)

January 28	East Division	127	West Division	133

ABA Playoffs

April 5	Oakland Oaks	129	at	Denver Rockets	99
April 5	Dallas Chaparrals	106	at	New Orleans Buccaneers	129
April 6	Denver Rockets	122	at	Oakland Oaks	119
April 7	Minnesota Pipers	110	at	Miami Floridians	119
April 7	Dallas Chaparrals	108	at	New Orleans Buccaneers	122
April 8	Kentucky Colonels	128	at	Indiana Pacers	118
April 8	Denver Rockets	99	at	Oakland Oaks	121
April 9	Kentucky Colonels	115	at	Indiana Pacers	120
April 9	Minnesota Pipers	106	at	Miami Floridians	99
April 10	Oakland Oaks	108	at	Denver Rockets	109
April 10	New Orleans Buccaneers	106	at	Dallas Chaparrals	130
April 10	Indiana Pacers	111	at	Kentucky Colonels	130
April 10	Miami Floridians	93	at	Minnesota Pipers	109
April 12	Denver Rockets	118	at	Oakland Oaks	128
April 12	New Orleans Buccaneers	114	at	Dallas Chaparrals	107
April 12	Miami Floridians	116	at	Minnesota Pipers	109
April 13	Indiana Pacers	104	at	Kentucky Colonels	105 [OT]
April 13	Minnesota Pipers	107	at	Miami Floridians	122
April 13	Oakland Oaks	115	at	Denver Rockets	126
April 14	Kentucky Colonels	97	at	Indiana Pacers	116
April 14	Dallas Chaparrals	123	at	New Orleans Buccaneers	112
April 15	Indiana Pacers	107	at	Kentucky Colonels	89
April 15	Miami Floridians	100	at	Minnesota Pipers	105
April 15	New Orleans Buccaneers	118	at	Dallas Chaparrals	136
April 16	Denver Rockets	102	at	Oakland Oaks	115
April 17	Dallas Chaparrals	95	at	New Orleans Buccaneers	101
April 17	Kentucky Colonels	111	at	Indiana Pacers	120
April 19	Miami Floridians	137	at	Minnesota Pipers	128
April 19	New Orleans Buccaneers	118	at	Oakland Oaks	128
April 20	Miami Floridians	110	at	Indiana Pacers	126
April 21	New Orleans Buccaneers	124	at	Oakland Oaks	135
April 22	Miami Floridians	116	at	Indiana Pacers	131
April 23	Oakland Oaks	113	at	New Orleans Buccaneers	107
April 23	Indiana Pacers	119	at	Miami Floridians	105
April 25	Oakland Oaks	128	at	New Orleans Buccaneers	114
April 25	Indiana Pacers	110	at	Miami Floridians	114
April 26	Miami Floridians	105	at	Indiana Pacers	127
April 30	Indiana Pacers	114	at	Oakland Oaks	123
May 2	Indiana Pacers	150	at	Oakland Oaks	122
May 3	Oakland Oaks	134	at	Indiana Pacers	126 [OT]
May 5	Oakland Oaks	144	at	Indiana Pacers	117
May 7	Indiana Pacers	131	at	Oakland Oaks	135 [OT]

All Star Teams

First Team

Connie Hawkins (Minnesota Pipers)
Rick Barry (Oakland Oaks)
Mel Daniels (Indiana Pacers)
James Jones (New Orleans Buccaneers)
Larry Jones (Denver Rockets)

Second Team

John Beasley (Dallas Chaparrals)
Doug Moe (Oakland Oaks)
"Red" Robbins (New Orleans Buccaneers)
Don Freeman (Miami Floridians)
Louie Dampier (Kentucky Colonels)

Individual Awards

ABA All Star Game MVP--John Beasley (Dallas Chaparrals)
Coach of the Year--Alex Hannum (Oakland Oaks)
Most Valuable Player--Mel Daniels (Indiana Pacers)
Rookie of the Year--Warren Armstrong (Oakland Oaks)

Notes

Jim Gardner replaced George Mikan as Commissioner of the American Basketball Association on July 14 and was in turn replaced by Jack Dolph in October.
The Kentucky Colonels signed female jockey Penny Ann Early to a players contract. She threw the ball into play on an out-of-bounds play, the Colonels then immediately called time out and took her out of the line-up, and she was destined never to play professionally again.

FOOTBALL
National Football League

Eastern Conference
Capitol Division

Team Name	GP	W	L	T	PF	PA	Pct
Dallas Cowboys	14	11	2	1	369	223	.821
Washington Redskins	14	7	5	2	307	319	.571
New Orleans Saints	14	5	9	0	311	393	.357
Philadelphia Eagles	14	4	9	1	279	377	.321

Century Division

Team Name	GP	W	L	T	PF	PA	Pct
Cleveland Browns	14	10	3	1	351	300	.750
New York Giants	14	6	8	0	264	298	.429
St. Louis Cardinals	14	4	9	1	314	389	.321
Pittsburgh Steelers	14	1	13	0	218	404	.071

Western Conference

Central Division

Team Name	GP	W	L	T	PF	PA	Pct
Minnesota Vikings	14	12	2	0	379	133	.857
Detroit Lions	14	9	4	1	259	188	.679
Green Bay Packers	14	8	6	0	269	221	.571
Chicago Bears	14	1	13	0	210	339	.071

Coastal Division

Team Name	GP	W	L	T	PF	PA	Pct
Los Angeles Rams	14	11	3	0	320	243	.786
Baltimore Colts	14	8	5	1	279	268	.607
Atlanta Falcons	14	6	8	0	276	268	.429
San Francisco 49ers	14	4	8	2	277	319	.357

Coaching Changes

Washington--Vince Lombardi 7-5-2; Philadelphia--Jerry Williams 4-9-1; Pittsburgh--Chuck Noll 1-13-0; Atlanta--Norm Van Brocklin 6-8-0.

League Leaders

Yards Rushing		Yards Passing		Passing % (40 attempts)	
Gale Sayers	1032	Sonny Jurgensen	3102	Sonny Jurgensen	62
Calvin Hill	942	Fran Tarkenton	2918	Bart Starr	62
Tom Matte	909	Norm Snead	2768	Edd Hargett	60
Larry Brown	888	Bill Nelson	2743	Bob Berry	57
Tom Woodeshick	831	Craig Morton	2619	John Brodie	56

Receiving Yards		Receptions		Field Goals	
Harold Jackson	1116	Dan Abramowicz	73	Fred Cox	26
Roy Jefferson	1079	Charley Taylor	71	Errol Mann	25
Dan Abramowicz	1015	Roy Jefferson	67	Bruce Gossett	22
John Gilliam	997	Harold Jackson	65	Tom Dempsey	22
Lance Rentzel	960	Dave Williams	56	Mike Clark	20

Punt Return Yards		Kickoff Return Yards	
Alvin Haymond	435	Bo Scott	722
Charlie West	245	Preston Pearson	706
Lem Barney	191	Ron Smith	585
Travis Williams	189	Dave Hampton	582
Bill Bradley	181	Bob Williams	563

Pro Bowl Game

(Memorial Coliseum, Los Angeles)

January 18 1970	Western Conference	16	Eastern Conference	13

NFL Playoffs

December 27	Los Angeles Rams	20	at	Minnesota Vikings	23
December 28	Cleveland Browns	38	at	Dallas Cowboys	14
January 4 1970	Cleveland Browns	7	at	Minnesota Vikings	27

Individual Awards

AP MVP--Roman Gabriel (Los Angeles Rams)
Bert Bell Trophy--Calvin Hill (Dallas Cowboys) [World Almanac]
Bert Bell Trophy--Roman Gabriel (Los Angeles Rams)
George Halas Trophy--Dick Butkus (Chicago Bears)
Jim Thorpe Trophy--Roman Gabriel (Los Angeles Rams)
Pro Bowl MVP--Gale Sayers (Chicago Bears)
George Andrie (Dallas Cowboys)
Rookie of the Year--Calvin Hill (Dallas Cowboys)
U.P.I. MVP--Roman Gabriel (Los Angeles Rams)
U.P.I. NFL-NFC Coach of the Year--Bud Grant (Minnesota Vikings)
U.P.I. NFL-NFC Rookie of the Year--Calvin Hill (Dallas Cowboys)

Hall of Fame Inductees

Turk Edwards, Earl Neale, Leo Nomellini, Joe Perry, Ernie Stautner

American Football League
Eastern Division

Team Name	GP	W	L	T	PF	PA	Pct
New York Jets	14	10	4	0	353	269	.714
Houston Oilers	14	6	6	2	278	279	.500
Boston Patriots	14	4	10	0	266	316	.286
Buffalo Bills	14	4	10	0	230	359	.286
Miami Dolphins	14	3	10	1	233	332	.250

Western Division

Team Name	GP	W	L	T	PF	PA	Pct
Oakland Raiders	14	12	1	1	377	242	.893
Kansas City Chiefs	14	11	3	0	359	177	.786
San Diego Chargers	14	8	6	0	288	276	.571
Denver Broncos	14	5	8	1	297	344	.393
Cincinnati Bengals	14	4	9	1	280	367	.321

Coaching Changes

Boston--Clive Rush 4-10-0; Buffalo--John Rauch 4-10-0; Oakland--John Madden 12-1-1; San Diego--Sid Gillman 4-5-0, Charlie Waller 4-1-0.

League Leaders

Yards Rushing		Yards Passing		Passing % (40 attempts)	
Dick Post	873	Daryle Lamonica	3302	Bob Davis	60
Jim Nance	750	Joe Namath	2734	Len Dawson	59
Hoyle Granger	740	Pete Beathard	2455	Greg Cook	54
Mike Garrett	732	John Hadl	2253	Peter Liske	53
Floyd Little	729	Mike Taliaferro	2160	Daryle Lamonica	52

Receiving Yards		Receptions		Field Goals	
Warren Wells	1260	Lance Alworth	64	Jim Turner	32
Lance Alworth	1003	Fred Biletnikoff	54	Jan Stenerud	27
Don Maynard	938	Al Denson	53	George Blanda	20
Eric Crabtree	855	Alvin Reed	51	Roy Gerela	19
Fred Biletnikoff	837	Warren Wells	47	Bruce Alford	17

Punt Return Yards		Kickoff Return Yards	
Jerry LeVias	292	Mercury Morris	1136
Bill Thompson	288	Jerry LeVias	940
"Speedy" Duncan	280	Carl Garrett	792
Mike Battle	235	Mike Battle	750
Mercury Morris	172	Bubba Thornton	749

All Star Game
(Astrodome, Houston)

January 17 1970	West Division	26	East Division	3

AFL Playoffs

December 20	Kansas City Chiefs	13	at	New York Jets	6
December 21	Houston Oilers	7	at	Oakland Raiders	56
January 4 1970	Kansas City Chiefs	17	at	Oakland Raiders	7

Super Bowl IV
(Tulane Stadium, New Orleans)

January 11 1970	Kansas City Chiefs	23	Minnesota Vikings	7

Individual Awards
AFL All Star Game MVP--John Hadl (San Diego Chargers)
Rookie of the Year--Carl Garrett (Boston Patriots)
Super Bowl MVP--Len Dawson (Kansas City Chiefs)
U.P.I. AFL-AFC Coach of the Year--Paul Brown (Cincinnati Bengals)
U.P.I. AFL-AFC Player of the Year--Daryle Lamonica (Oakland Raiders)
U.P.I. AFL-AFC Rookie of the Year--Greg Cook (Cincinnati Bengals)

Canadian Football League
Eastern Conference

Team Name	GP	W	L	T	PF	PA	Pts	Pct
Ottawa Rough Riders	14	11	3	0	399	298	22	.786
Toronto Argonauts	14	10	4	0	406	280	20	.714
Hamilton Tiger-Cats	14	8	5	1	307	315	17	.607
Montreal Alouettes	14	2	10	2	304	395	6	.214

Western Conference

Team Name	GP	W	L	T	PF	PA	Pts	Pct
Saskatchewan Roughriders	16	13	3	0	392	261	26	.813
Calgary Stampeders	16	9	7	0	327	314	18	.563
British Columbia Lions	16	5	11	0	235	335	10	.313
Edmonton Eskimos	16	5	11	0	241	246	10	.313
Winnipeg Blue Bombers	16	3	12	1	192	359	7	.219

Coaching Changes
Calgary--Jim Duncan 9-7-0; British Columbia--Jim Champion 1-9-0, Jackie Parker 4-2-0.

League Leaders

Yards Rushing		Yards Passing		Passing %	
George Reed	1353	Russ Jackson	3641	Jerry Keeling	56
Jim Evenson	1287				
Dennis Duncan	1037				

Receiving Yards		Receptions		Points	
Margene Adkins	1402	Tommy Joe Coffey	71	Tommy Joe Coffey	148
Bobby Taylor	1183				
Tommy Joe Coffey	1110				
Herman Harrison	1043				

Grey Cup Playoffs

November 8	British Columbia Lions	21	at	Calgary Stampeders	35
November 9	Hamilton Tiger-Cats	9	at	Toronto Argonauts	15
November 15	Calgary Stampeders	11	at	Saskatchewan Roughriders	17
November 16	Ottawa Rough Riders	14	at	Toronto Argonauts	22
November 19	Saskatchewan Roughriders	36	at	Calgary Stampeders	13
November 22	Toronto Argonauts	3	at	Ottawa Rough Riders	32
November 30	Ottawa Rough Riders	29	at	Saskatchewan Roughriders	11*

Individual Awards

Annis Stukus Trophy--Frank Clair (Ottawa Rough Riders)
Dave Dryburgh Memorial Trophy--Jack Abendschan (Saskatchewan Roughriders)
DeMarco-Becket Memorial Trophy--Ed McQuarters (Saskatchewan Roughriders)
Dr. Beattie Martin Trophy--Dave Easley (British Columbia Lions)
Eddie James Memorial Trophy--George Reed (Saskatchewan Roughriders)
Grey Cup MVP--Russ Jackson (Ottawa Rough Riders)
Gruen Trophy--Al Phaneuf (Montreal Alouettes)
Jeff Nicklin Memorial Trophy--Ron Lancaster (Saskatchewan Roughriders)
Jeff Russel Memorial Trophy--Russ Jackson (Ottawa Rough Riders)
Schenley Award Most Outstanding Canadian--Russ Jackson (Ottawa Rough Riders)
Schenley Award Most Outstanding Lineman--John Lagrone (Edmonton Eskimos)
Schenley Award Most Outstanding Player--Russ Jackson (Ottawa Rough Riders)

Hall of Fame Inductees

Arthur Chipman, Andrew Davies, Abe Eliowitz, Sam Etcheverry, Normie Kwong, Art Stevenson,

Notes

This years Grey Cup game was the first to start and finish on a Sunday.

HOCKEY
National Hockey League

Eastern Division

Team Name	GP	W	L	T	GF	GA	Pts	Pct
Montreal Canadiens	76	46	19	11	271	202	103	.678
Boston Bruins	76	42	18	16	303	221	100	.658
New York Rangers	76	41	26	9	231	196	91	.599
Toronto Maple Leafs	76	35	26	15	234	217	85	.559
Detroit Red Wings	76	33	31	12	239	221	78	.513
Chicago Black Hawks	76	34	33	9	280	246	77	.507

Western Division

Team Name	GP	W	L	T	GF	GA	Pts	Pct
St. Louis Blues	76	37	25	14	204	157	88	.579
Oakland Seals	76	29	36	11	219	251	69	.454
Philadelphia Flyers	76	20	35	21	174	225	61	.401
Los Angeles Kings	76	24	42	10	185	260	58	.382
Pittsburgh Penguins	76	20	45	11	189	252	51	.336
Minnesota North Stars	76	18	43	15	189	270	51	.336

*Game played in Montreal

Coaching Changes

Montreal--Claude Ruel 46-19-11; New York--Bernie Geoffrion 22-18-3, Emile Francis 19-8-6; Detroit--Bill Gadsby 33-31-12; St. Louis--Scotty Bowman 37-25-14; Oakland--Fred Glover 29-36-11; Minnesota--Wren Blair l2-21-8, John Muckler 6-22-7.

League Leaders

Goals		Assists		Points	
Bobby Hull	58	Phil Esposito	77	Phil Esposito	126
Phil Esposito	49	Stan Mikita	67	Bobby Hull	107
Frank Mahovlich	49	Gordie Howe	59	Gordie Howe	103
Ken Hodge	45	Alex Delvecchio	58	Stan Mikita	97
Gordie Howe	44	Pat Stapleton	50	Ken Hodge	90

Penalty Minutes		GAA		Wins	
Forbes Kennedy	219	Jacques Plante	1.96	Ed Giacomin	37
Jim Dorey	200	Glenn Hall	2.17	Gerry Cheevers	28
John Ferguson	185	Lorne Worsley	2.25	Bruce Gamble	28
Carol Vadnais	151	Roy Edwards	2.54	Rogie Vachon	22
Don Awrey	149	Ed Giacomin	2.55	Denis DeJordy	22

Shutouts	
Glenn Hall	8
Ed Giacomin	7
Jacques Plante	5
Roy Edwards	4
Gary Smith	4

All Star Game

(The Forum, Montreal)

January 21	East Division	3	West Division	3

Stanley Cup Playoffs

April 2	New York Rangers	1	at	Montreal Canadiens	3
April 2	Toronto Maple Leafs	0	at	Boston Bruins	10
April 2	Philadelphia Flyers	2	at	St. Louis Blues	5
April 2	Los Angeles Kings	5	at	Oakland Seals	4 [0:19]
April 3	New York Rangers	2	at	Montreal Canadiens	5
April 3	Toronto Maple Leafs	0	at	Boston Bruins	7
April 3	Philadelphia Flyers	0	at	St. Louis Blues	5
April 3	Los Angeles Kings	2	at	Oakland Seals	4
April 5	Montreal Canadiens	4	at	New York Rangers	1
April 5	Boston Bruins	4	at	Toronto Maple Leafs	3
April 5	St. Louis Blues	3	at	Philadelphia flyers	0
April 5	Oakland Seals	5	at	Los Angeles Kings	2
April 6	Montreal Canadiens	4	at	New York Rangers	3
April 6	Boston Bruins	3	at	Toronto Maple Leafs	2
April 6	St. Louis Blues	4	at	Philadelphia Flyers	1
April 6	Oakland Seals	2	at	Los Angeles Kings	4
April 9	Los Angeles Kings	1	at	Oakland Seals	4
April 10	Oakland Seals	3	at	Los Angeles Kings	4

April 10	Boston Bruins	2	at	Montreal Canadiens	3 [0:42]
April 13	Los Angeles Kings	5	at	Oakland Seals	3
April 13	Boston Bruins	3	at	Montreal Canadiens	4 [4:55]
April 15	Los Angeles Kings	0	at	St. Louis Blues	3
April 17	Montreal Canadiens	0	at	Boston Bruins	5
April 17	Los Angeles Kings	2	at	St. Louis Blues	3
April 19	St. Louis Blues	5	at	Los Angeles Kings	2
April 20	Montreal Canadiens	2	at	Boston Bruins	3
April 20	St. Louis Blues	4	at	Los Angeles Kings	1
April 22	Boston Bruins	2	at	Montreal Canadiens	4
April 24	Montreal Canadiens	2	at	Boston Bruins	1 [11:28]
April 27	St. Louis Blues	1	at	Montreal Canadiens	3
April 29	St. Louis Blues	1	at	Montreal Canadiens	3
May 1	Montreal Canadiens	4	at	St. Louis Blues	0
May 4	Montreal Canadiens	2	at	St. Louis Blues	1

All Star Teams

First Team		Second Team
Glenn Hall	Goal	Ed Giacomin
Bobby Orr	Defense	Ted Green
Tim Horton	Defense	Ted Harris
Phil Esposito	Center	Jean Beliveau
Gordie Howe	Right Wing	Yvan Cournoyer
Bobby Hull	Left Wing	Frank Mahovlich

Individual Awards

Art Ross Trophy--Phil Esposito (Boston Bruins)
Bill Masterton Trophy--Ted Hampson (Oakland Seals)
Calder Memorial Trophy--Danny Grant (Minnesota North Stars)
Conn Smythe Trophy--Serge Savard (Montreal Canadiens)
Hart Memorial Trophy--Phil Esposito (Boston Bruins)
James Norris Trophy--Bobby Orr (Boston Bruins)
Lady Byng Memorial Trophy--Alex Delvecchio (Detroit Red Wings)
Lester Patrick Trophy--Bobby Hull and Edward Jeremiah
NHL All Star Game MVP--Frank Mahovlich (Detroit Red Wings)
Vezina Trophy--Jacques Plante and Glenn Hall (St. Louis Blues)

Hall of Fame Inductees

Sid Abel, Bryan Hextall, Red Kelly, George Leader, Bruce Norris, Roy Worters

SOCCER

North American Soccer League

Team Name	GP	W	L	T	GF	GA	BP	Pts	Pct
Kansas City Spurs	16	10	2	4	53	28	38	110	.764
Atlanta Chiefs	16	11	2	3	46	20	34	109	.757
Dallas Tornado	16	8	6	2	32	31	28	82	.569
St. Louis Stars	16	3	11	2	24	47	23	47	.326
Baltimore Bays	16	2	13	1	27	56	27	42	.292

Coaching Changes

Atlanta--Vic Crowe 11-2-3; Dallas--Ron Newman 8-6-2; St. Louis--Robert Kehoe 3-11-2.

League Leaders

Goals		Points		GAA	
Kaizer Motaung	16	Kaizer Motaung	36	Manfred Kammerer	1.07
George Benitez	15	George Benitez	35	Humberto Arrieta	1.57
Ilija Mitic	11	Ilija Mitic	26	Leonel Conde	1.75
Ademar Saccone	9	Fons Stoffels	23	Dave Jokerst	2.78
Fons Stoffels	8	Manfred Seissler	22	Orrie Banach	3.23

All Star Team

Goal	Leonel Conde (Kansas City Spurs)
Defender	John Borodiak (Baltimore Bays)
Defender	Kirk Apostolidis (Dallas Tornado)
Midfield	William Quiros (Kansas City Spurs)
Midfield	John Best (Dallas Tornado)
Midfield	Joe Puis (St. Louis Stars)
Forward	Pepe Fernandez (Kansas City Spurs)
Forward	Kaizer Motaung (Atlanta Chiefs)
Forward	Manfred Seissler (Kansas City Spurs)
Forward	llija Mitic (Dallas Tornado)
Forward	Emment Kapengwe (Atlanta Chiefs)
Forward	Art Welch (Baltimore Bays)

Individual Awards

Lead Goalkeeper Award--Manfred Kammerer (Atlanta Chiefs)
Most Valuable Player--Cirilio Fernandez (Kansas City Spurs)
Rookie of the Year--Siegfried Stritzi (Baltimore Bays)

Notes

Phil Woosnam was named as Commissioner of the North American Soccer League.
The NASL lost 12 teams this year and the league was in danger of collapsing.
The NASL did not hold any playoffs this year.

Franchise Changes

ABA--Anaheim Amigos moved to Los Angeles.
Minnesota Muskies moved to Miami.
Pittsburgh Pipers became the Minneapolis Pipers.
New Jersey Americans moved to New York.
NBA--St. Louis Hawks became the Atlanta Hawks.

Other Sports

Horseracing--Kentucky Derby won by Majestic Prince (time 2:01.8, purse $113,200).
Golf--U.S. Open won by Orville Moody with a score of 281.
Auto Racing--Indianapolis -500 won by Mario Andretti (ave. speed 156.867 MPH).
Tennis--U.S. Open won by Rod Laver in the men's singles.
U.S. Open won by Fred Stolle and Ken Rosewall in the men's doubles.
U.S. Open won by Margaret Smith Court in the women's singles.
U.S. Open won by Francoise Durr and Darlene Hard in the women's doubles.
U.S. Open won by Margaret Smith Court and Marty Riessen in the mixed doubles.

1970

BASEBALL
National League

East

Team Name	W	L	Pct	GB	R	OR
Pittsburgh Pirates	89	73	.549	-	729	664
Chicago Cubs	84	78	.519	5	806	679
New York Mets	83	79	.512	6	695	630
St. Louis Cardinals	76	86	.469	13	744	747
Philadelphia Phillies	73	88	.453	15.5	594	730
Montreal Expos	73	89	.451	16	687	807

West

Team Name	W	L	Pct	GB	R	OR
Cincinnati Reds	102	60	.630	-	775	681
Los Angeles Dodgers	87	74	.540	14.5	749	684
San Francisco Giants	86	76	.531	16	831	826
Atlanta Braves	76	86	.469	26	736	772
Houston Astros	79	83	.488	23	744	763
San Diego Padres	63	99	.389	39	681	788

Coaching Changes

Pittsburgh--Danny Murtaugh 89-73; Philadelphia--Frank Lucchesi 73-88; Cincinnati--George "Sparky" Anderson 102-60; San Francisco--Clyde King 19-25, Charlie Fox 67-51.

League Leaders

Batting Average

Rico Carty	.366
Joe Torre	.325
M. Sanguillen	.325
Bill Williams	.322
Wes Parker	.319

Home Runs

Johnny Bench	45
Bill Williams	42
Tony Perez	40
Willie McCovey	39
Hank Aaron	38

RBI

Johnny Bench	148
Tony Perez	129
Bill Williams	129
Willie McCovey	126
Hank Aaron	118

Stolen Bases

Bob Tolan	57
Lou Brock	51
Bob Bonds	48
Joe Morgan	42
Willie Davis	38

ERA

Tom Seaver	2.81
Wayne Simpson	3.02
Luke Walker	3.04
Bob Gibson	3.12
Jerry Koosman	3.14

Wins

Bob Perry	23
Gaylord Perry	23
Ferguson Jenkins	22
Jim Merritt	20
Gary Nolan	18

Saves

Wayne Granger	35
Dave Giustu	26
Jim Brewer	24
Claude Raymond	23
Dick Selma	22

Strikeouts

Tom Seaver	283
Bob Gibson	274
Ferguson Jenkins	274
Gaylord Perry	214
Ken Holtzman	202

NLCS

October 3	Cincinnati Reds	3	at	Pittsburgh Pirates	0 [10]
October 4	Cincinnati Reds	3	at	Pittsburgh Pirates	1
October 5	Pittsburgh Pirates	2	at	Cincinnati Reds	3

Notes

Charles Feeney succeeded Warren Giles as President of the National League.

American League

East

Team Name	W	L	Pct	GB	R	OR
Baltimore Orioles	108	54	.667	-	792	574
New York Yankees	93	69	.574	15	680	612
Boston Red Sox	87	75	.537	21	786	722
Detroit Tigers	79	83	.488	29	666	731
Cleveland Indians	76	86	.469	32	649	675
Washington Senators	70	92	.432	38	626	689

West

Team Name	W	L	Pct	GB	R	OR
Minnesota Twins	98	64	.605	-	744	605
Oakland Athletics	89	73	.549	9	678	593
California Angels	86	76	.531	12	631	630
Kansas City Royals	65	97	.401	33	611	705
Milwaukee Brewers	65	97	.401	33	613	751
Chicago White Sox	56	106	.346	42	633	822

Coaching Changes

Boston--Eddie Kasko 87-75; Minnesota--Bill Rigney 98-64; California--Harold Phillips 86-76; Oakland--John McNamara 89-73; Kansas City--Charlie Metro 19-35, Bob Lemon 46-62; Milwaukee--Dave Bristol 65-97; Chicago--Don Gutteridge 49-87, Bill Adair 4-6, Charles Tanner 3-13.

League Leaders

Batting Average		Home Runs		RBI	
Alex Johnson	.329	Frank Howard	44	Frank Howard	126
Carl Yastrzemski	.329	Harmon Killebrew	41	Tony Conigliaro	116
Tony Oliva	.325	Carl Yastrzemski	40	John Powell	114
Lou Aparicio	.313	Tony Conigliaro	36	Harmon Killebrew	113
Frank Robinson	.306	John Powell	35	Tony Oliva	107

Stolen Bases		ERA		Wins	
Bert Campaneris	42	Diego Segui	2.56	Mike Cuellar	24
Tom Harper	38	Jim Palmer	2.71	Dave McNally	24
Sandy Alomar	35	Clyde Wright	2.83	Jim Perry	24
Pat Kelly	34	Fred Peterson	2.91	Clyde Wright	22
Amos Otis	33	Sam McDowell	2.92	Fred Peterson	20

Saves		Strikeouts	
Ron Perranoski	34	Sam McDowell	304
Lindy McDaniel	29	Mickey Lolich	230
Darold Knowles	27	Bob Johnson	206
Tom Timmerman	27	Jim Palmer	199
James Grant	24	Ray Culp	197

All Star Game
(Riverfront Stadium, Cincinnati)

July 14	National League	5		American League	4

ALCS

October 3	Baltimore Orioles	10	at	Minnesota Twins	6
October 4	Baltimore Orioles	11	at	Minnesota Twins	3
October 5	Minnesota Twins	1	at	Baltimore Orioles	6

World Series

October 10	Baltimore Orioles	4	at	Cincinnati Reds	3
October 11	Baltimore Orioles	6	at	Cincinnati Reds	5
October 13	Cincinnati Reds	3	at	Baltimore Orioles	9
October 14	Cincinnati Reds	6	at	Baltimore Orioles	5
October 15	Cincinnati Reds	3	at	Baltimore Orioles	9

Individual Awards

Arch Ward Memorial Trophy--Carl Yastrzemski (Boston Red Sox AL)
Baseball Writers Award--Johnny Bench (Cincinnati Reds NL)
John Powell (Baltimore Orioles AL)
Cy Young Award--Bob Gibson (St. Louis Cardinals NL)
Jim Perry (Minnesota Twins AL)
Rookie of the Year--Carl Morton (Montreal Expos NL)
Thurman Munson (New York Yankees AL)
Sporting News Executive of the Year--Harry Dalton (Baltimore Orioles AL)
Sporting News Manager of the Year--Danny Murtaugh (Pittsburgh Pirates NL)
Sporting News Pitcher of the Year--Bob Gibson (St. Louis Cardinals NL)
Sam McDowell (Cleveland Indians AL)
Sporting News Player of the Year--Johnny Bench (Cincinnati Reds NL)
Harmon Killebrew (Minnesota Twins AL)
Sporting News Rookie of the Year--Bernie Carbo (Cincinnati Reds NL)
Carl Morton (Montreal Expos NL)
Roy Foster (Cleveland Indians AL)
Bert Blyleven (Minnesota Twins AL)
World Series MVP--Brooks Robinson (Baltimore Orioles AL)

Hall of Fame Inductees

Lou Boudreau, Earl Combs, Ford Frick, Jesse Haines

BASKETBALL
National Basketball Association
Eastern Division

Team Name	GP	W	L	PPGF	PPGA	Pct	GB
New York Knickerbockers	82	60	22	115.0	105.9	.732	-
Milwaukee Bucks	82	56	26	118.8	114.2	.683	4
Baltimore Bullets	82	50	32	120.7	118.6	.610	10
Philadelphia 76ers	82	42	40	121.9	118.5	.512	18
Cincinnati Royals	82	36	46	117.3	120.2	.439	24
Boston Celtics	82	34	48	114.9	116.8	.415	26
Detroit Pistons	82	31	51	112.8	116.1	.378	29

Western Division

Team Name	GP	W	L	PPGF	PPGA	Pct	GB
Atlanta Hawks	82	48	34	117.6	117.2	.585	-
Los Angeles Lakers	82	46	36	113.7	111.8	.561	2
Chicago Bulls	82	39	43	114.9	116.7	.476	9
Phoenix Suns	82	39	43	119.3	121.1	.476	9
Seattle SuperSonics	82	36	46	116.9	119.5	.439	12
San Francisco Warriors	82	30	52	111.1	115.6	.366	18
San Diego Rockets	82	27	55	118.7	121.8	.329	21

Coaching Changes

Cincinnati--Bob Cousy 36-46; Boston--Tom Heinsohn 34-48; Detroit--Butch Van Breda Kolff 31-51; Los Angeles--Joe Mullaney 46-36; Phoenix--John Kerr 15-23, Jerry Colangelo 24-20; Seattle--Lenny Wilkens 36-46; San Francisco--George Lee 22-30, Al Attles 8-22; San Diego--Jack McMahon 9-17, Alex Hannum 18-38.

League Leaders

Field Goals		Free Throws		Assists	
Lew Alcindor	938	Jerry West	647	Lenny Wilkens	683
Elvin Hayes	914	Connie Hawkins	577	Walt Frazier	629
Jerry West	831	Earl Monroe	532	Clem Haskins	624
Lou Hudson	830	Bill Cunningham	510	Gail Goodrich	605
Bill Cunningham	802	John Havlicek	488	Walt Hazzard	561

Points		Fouls	
Lew Alcindor	2361	Jim Davis	335
Jerry West	2309	Bill Cunningham	331
Elvin Hayes	2256	Norm Van Lier	329
Bill Cunningham	2114	Tom Meschery	317
Lou Hudson	2031	Mel Counts	304

All Star Game

(The Spectrum, Philadelphia)

January 20	East Division	142	West Division	135

NBA Playoffs

Date	Visitor	Score		Home	Score
March 25	Philadelphia 76ers	118	at	Milwaukee Bucks	125
March 25	Chicago Bulls	111	at	Atlanta Hawks	129
March 25	Phoenix Suns	112	at	Los Angeles Lakers	128
March 26	Baltimore Bullets	117	at	N.Y. Knickerbockers	120 [OT]
March 27	Philadelphia 76ers	112	at	Milwaukee Bucks	105
March 27	N.Y. Knickerbockers	106	at	Baltimore Bullets	99
March 28	Chicago Bulls	104	at	Atlanta Hawks	124
March 29	Phoenix Suns	114	at	Los Angeles Lakers	101
March 29	Baltimore Bullets	127	at	N.Y. Knickerbockers	113
March 30	Milwaukee Bucks	156	at	Philadelphia 76ers	120
March 31	Atlanta Hawks	106	at	Chicago Bulls	101
March 31	N.Y. Knickerbockers	92	at	Baltimore Bullets	102
April 1	Milwaukee Bucks	118	at	Philadelphia 76ers	111
April 2	Baltimore Bullets	80	at	N.Y. Knickerbockers	101
April 2	Los Angeles Lakers	98	at	Phoenix Suns	112
April 3	Philadelphia 76ers	106	at	Milwaukee Bucks	115
April 3	Atlanta Hawks	120	at	Chicago Bulls	131
April 4	Los Angeles Lakers	102	at	Phoenix Suns	112
April 5	Chicago Bulls	107	at	Atlanta Hawks	113
April 5	N.Y. Knickerbockers	87	at	Baltimore Bullets	96
April 5	Phoenix Suns	121	at	Los Angeles Lakers	138
April 6	Baltimore Bullets	114	at	N.Y. Knickerbockers	127
April 7	Los Angeles Lakers	104	at	Phoenix Suns	93
April 9	Phoenix Suns	94	at	Los Angeles Lakers	129
April 11	Milwaukee Bucks	102	at	N.Y. Knickerbockers	110
April 12	Los Angeles Lakers	119	at	Atlanta hawks	115
April 13	Milwaukee Bucks	111	at	N.Y. Knickerbockers	112
April 14	Los Angeles Lakers	105	at	Atlanta Hawks	94
April 16	Atlanta Hawks	114	at	Los Angeles Lakers	115 [OT]
April 17	N.Y. Knickerbockers	96	at	Milwaukee Bucks	101
April 19	N.Y. Knickerbockers	117	at	Milwaukee Bucks	105
April 19	Atlanta Hawks	114	at	Los Angeles Lakers	133
April 20	Milwaukee Bucks	96	at	N.Y. Knickerbockers	132
April 24	Los Angeles Lakers	112	at	N.Y. Knickerbockers	124
April 27	Los Angeles Lakers	105	at	N.Y. Knickerbockers	103
April 29	N.Y. Knickerbockers	111	at	Los Angeles Lakers	108 [OT]
May 1	N.Y. Knickerbockers	115	at	Los Angeles Lakers	121 [OT]
May 4	Los Angeles Lakers	100	at	N.Y. Knickerbockers	107
May 6	N.Y. Knickerbockers	113	at	Los Angeles Lakers	135
May 8	Los Angeles Lakers	99	at	N.Y. Knickerbockers	113

All Star Teams

First Team	Second Team
Bill Cunningham (Philadelphia 76ers)	John Havlicek (Boston Celtics)
Connie Hawkins (Phoenix Suns)	Gus Johnson (Baltimore Bullets)
Willis Reed (N.Y. Knickerbockers)	Lew Alcindor (Milwaukee Bucks)
Jerry West (Los Angeles Lakers)	Lou Hudson (Atlanta Hawks)
Walt Frazier (N.Y. Knickerbockers)	Oscar Robertson (Cincinnati Royals)

Individual Awards

Eddie Gottlieb Trophy--Lew Alcindor (Milwaukee Bucks)
Maurice Podoloff Trophy--Willis Reed (New York Knickerbockers)
NBA All Star Game MVP--Willis Reed (New York Knickerbockers)

NBA Finals MVP--Willis Reed (New York Knickerbockers)
Red Auerbach Trophy--Red Holzman (New York Knickerbockers)

Hall of Fame Inductees

Bob Cousy, Bob Pettit, Abe Saperstein

American Basketball Association
Eastern Division

Team Name	GP	W	L	PPGF	PPGA	Pct	GB
Indiana Pacers	84	59	25	113.2	109.8	.702	-
Kentucky Colonels	84	45	39	113.5	112.5	.536	14
Carolina Cougars	84	42	42	106.8	107.0	.500	17
New York Nets	84	39	45	108.9	109.8	.464	20
Pittsburgh Pipers	84	29	55	112.4	117.0	.345	30
Miami Floridians	84	23	61	113.2	118.3	.274	36

Western Division

Team Name	GP	W	L	PPGF	PPGA	Pct	GB
Denver Rockets	84	51	33	115.4	111.1	.607	-
Dallas Chaparrals	84	45	39	120.0	118.1	.536	6
Washington Capitols	84	44	40	118.2	118.8	.524	7
Los Angeles Stars	84	43	41	113.7	113.9	.512	8
New Orleans Buccaneers	84	42	42	107.9	107.1	.500	9

Coaching Changes

Indiana--Bob Leonard 59-25; Carolina--"Bones" McKinney 42-42; New York--York Larese 39-45; Pittsburgh--John Clark 14-25, Buddy Jeannette 15-30; Miami--Jim Pollard 5-15, Hal Blitman 18-46; Denver--John McLendon 9-19, Joe Belmont 42-14; Dallas--Cliff Hagan 22-21, Max Williams 23-18; Washington--Al Bianchi 44-40.

League Leaders

Field Goals		Free Throws		Assists	
Spencer Haywood	986	Don Freeman	626	Larry Brown	580
Bob Verga	867	Larry Jones	579	Mack Calvin	478
Don Freeman	766	Spencer Haywood	547	Bill Melchionni	457
Levern Tart	756	Mack Calvin	529	Louie Dampier	447
Louie Dampier	743	Don Sidle	469	Jeff Congdon	446

Points		Fouls	
Spencer Haywood	2519	Gene Moore	382
Bob Verga	2258	Goose Ligon	360
Don Freeman	2163	Les Hunter	335
Louie Dampier	2125	Ira Harge	328
Levern Tart	1935	Mel Daniels	309

All Star Game
(State Fairgrounds Arena, Indianapolis)

January 24	East Division	98	West Division	128

ABA Playoffs

April 17	Washington Capitols	111	at	Denver Rockets	130
April 17	New York Nets	122	at	Kentucky Colonels	118 [OT]
April 17	Los Angeles Stars	115	at	Dallas Chaparrals	103
April 18	Carolina Cougars	105	at	Indiana Pacers	123
April 18	New York Nets	111	at	Kentucky Colonels	113
April 18	Washington Capitols	135	at	Denver Rockets	143
April 18	Los Angeles Stars	121	at	Dallas Chaparrals	129
April 19	Carolina Cougars	98	at	Indiana Pacers	103
April 19	Kentucky Colonels	99	at	New York Nets	107
April 19	Denver Rockets	120	at	Washington Capitols	125
April 20	Dallas Chaparrals	116	at	Los Angeles Stars	104
April 22	Indiana Pacers	115	at	Carolina Cougars	106
April 22	Kentucky Colonels	128	at	New York Nets	101
April 22	Denver Rockets	114	at	Washington Capitols	131
April 22	Dallas Chaparrals	138	at	Los Angeles Stars	144
April 23	Washington Capitols	110	at	Denver Rockets	132
April 24	Indiana Pacers	110	at	Carolina Cougars	106
April 24	Los Angeles Stars	146	at	Dallas Chaparrals	139
April 25	Denver Rockets	111	at	Washington Capitols	116
April 26	New York Nets	127	at	Kentucky Colonels	112
April 26	Dallas Chaparrals	123	at	Los Angeles Stars	124
April 28	Washington Capitols	119	at	Denver Rockets	143
April 28	Kentucky Colonels	116	at	New York Nets	113
April 29	New York Nets	101	at	Kentucky Colonels	112
April 30	Los Angeles Stars	113	at	Denver Rockets	123 [OT]
May 1	Kentucky Colonels	114	at	Indiana Pacers	110
May 1	Los Angeles Stars	114	at	Denver Rockets	105
May 2	Kentucky Colonels	110	at	Indiana Pacers	121
May 3	Indiana Pacers	114	at	Kentucky Colonels	110
May 4	Denver Rockets	113	at	Los Angeles Stars	119
May 5	Indiana Pacers	111	at	Kentucky Colonels	103
May 5	Denver Rockets	110	at	Los Angeles Stars	114
May 6	Kentucky Colonels	103	at	Indiana Pacers	117
May 9	Los Angeles Stars	109	at	Denver Rockets	107
May 15	Los Angeles Stars	93	at	Indiana Pacers	109
May 17	Los Angeles Stars	111	at	Indiana Pacers	114
May 18	Indiana Pacers	106	at	Los Angeles Stars	109
May 21	Indiana Pacers	142	at	Los Angeles Stars	120
May 23	Los Angeles Stars	117	at	Indiana Pacers	113
May 25	Indiana Pacers	111	at	Los Angeles Stars	107

All Star Teams

First Team

Rick Barry (Washington Capitols)
Spencer Haywood (Denver Rockets)
Mel Daniels (Indiana Pacers)
Bob Verga (Carolina Cougars)
Larry Jones (Denver Rockets)

Second Team

Roger Brown (Indiana Pacers)
Bob Netolicky (Indiana Pacers)
"Red" Robbins (New Orleans Buccaneers)
Louie Dampier (Kentucky Colonels)
Don Freeman (Miami Floridians)

Individual Awards

ABA All Star Game MVP--Spencer Haywood (Denver Rockets)
Coach of the Year--Joe Belmont (Denver Rockets)
Bill Sharman (Los Angeles Stars)

Most Valuable Player--Spencer Haywood (Denver Rockets)
Rookie of the Year--Spencer Haywood (Denver Rockets)

FOOTBALL
National Football League

National Football Conference
Eastern Division

Team Name	GP	W	L	T	PF	PA	Pct
Dallas Cowboys	14	10	4	0	299	221	.714
New York Giants	14	9	5	0	301	270	.643
St. Louis Cardinals	14	8	5	1	325	228	.607
Washington Redskins	14	6	8	0	297	314	.429
Philadelphia Eagles	14	3	10	1	241	332	.250

Central Division

Team Name	GP	W	L	T	PF	PA	Pct
Minnesota Vikings	14	12	2	0	335	143	.857
Detroit Lions	14	10	4	0	347	202	.714
Chicago Bears	14	6	8	0	256	261	.429
Green Bay Packers	14	6	8	0	196	293	.429

Western Division

Team Name	GP	W	L	T	PF	PA	Pct
San Francisco 49ers	14	10	3	1	352	267	.750
Los Angeles Rams	14	9	4	1	325	202	.679
Atlanta Falcons	14	4	8	2	206	261	.357
New Orleans Saints	14	2	11	1	172	347	.179

American Football Conference

Eastern Division

Team Name	GP	W	L	T	PF	PA	Pct
Baltimore Colts	14	11	2	1	321	234	.821
Miami Dolphins	14	10	4	0	297	228	.714
New York Jets	14	4	10	0	255	286	.286
Buffalo Bills	14	3	10	1	204	337	.250
Boston Patriots	14	2	12	0	149	361	.143

Central Division

Team Name	GP	W	L	T	PF	PA	Pct
Cincinnati Bengals	14	8	6	0	312	255	.571
Cleveland Browns	14	7	7	0	286	265	.500
Pittsburgh Steelers	14	5	9	0	210	272	.357
Houston Oilers	14	3	10	1	217	352	.250

Western Division

Team Name	GP	W	L	T	PF	PA	Pct
Oakland Raiders	14	8	4	2	300	293	.643
Kansas City Chiefs	14	7	5	2	272	244	.571
San Diego Chargers	14	5	6	3	282	278	.464
Denver Broncos	14	5	8	1	253	264	.393

Coaching Changes

New York Giants--Alex Webster 9-5-0; Washington--Bill Austin 6-8-0; New Orleans--Tom Fears 1-5-1, J.D. Roberts 1-6-0; Baltimore--Don McCafferty 11-2-1; Miami--Don Shula 10-4-0; New York Jets--Weeb Ewbank 4-10-0; Buffalo--John Rauch 3-10-1; Boston--Clive Rush 1-6-0, John Mazur 1-6-0; Cincinnati--Paul Brown 8-6-0; Cleveland--Blanton Collier 7-7-0; Pittsburgh--Chuck Noll 5-9-0; Houston--Wally Lemm 3-10-1; Oakland--John Madden 8-4-2; Kansas City--Hank Stram 7-5-2; San Diego--Charlie Waller 5-6-3; Denver--Lou Saban 5-8-1.

League Leaders

Yards Rushing		**Yards Passing**		**Passing %** (40 attempts)	
Larry Brown	1125	John Brodie	2941	Greg Landry	61
Ron Johnson	1027	Fran Tarkenton	2777	Sonny Jurgensen	60
MacArthur Lane	977	Jim Hart	2575	John Brodie	59
Floyd Little	901	Roman Gabriel	2552	Bob Berry	58
Larry Csonka	874	Daryle Lamonica	2516	Bob Griese	58

Receiving Yards		**Receptions**		**Field Goals**	
Gene Washington	1100	Dick Gordon	71	Fred Cox	30
Marlin Briscoe	1036	Marlin Briscoe	57	Jan Stenerud	30
Dick Gordon	1026	Dan Abramowicz	55	David Ray	29
Gary Garrison	1006	Gene Washington	53	Pete Gogolak	25
John Gilliam	952	Jack Snow	51	Horst Muhlmann	25

Punt Return Yards		**Kickoff Return Yards**	
Bruce Taylor	516	Alvin Haymond	1022
Alvin Haymond	376	Mike Battle	891
Ron Gardin	330	"Mercury" Morris	812
Ed Podolak	311	Bill Walik	805
Jake Scott	290	Cecil Turner	752

Pro Bowl Game

(Memorial Coliseum, Los Angeles)

January 24 1971	National Conference	27	American Conference	6

NFL Playoffs

December 26	Cincinnati Bengals	0	at	Baltimore Colts	17
December 26	Detroit Lions	0	at	Dallas Cowboys	5
December 27	Miami Dolphins	14	at	Oakland Raiders	21
December 27	San Francisco 49ers	17	at	Minnesota Vikings	14
January 3 1971	Dallas Cowboys	17	at	San Francisco 49ers	10
January 3 1971	Oakland Raiders	17	at	Baltimore Colts	27

Super Bowl V

(Orange Bowl, Miami)

January 17 1971	Baltimore Colts	16	Dallas Cowboys	13

Individual Awards

AP MVP--John Brodie (San Francisco 49ers)
Bert Bell Trophy--Raymond Chester (Oakland Raiders) [World Almanac]
Bert Bell Trophy--George Blanda (Oakland Raiders)
George Halas Trophy--Dick Butkus (Chicago Bears)
Jim Thorpe Trophy--John Brodie (San Francisco 49ers)
Pro Bowl MVP--Mel Renfro (Dallas Cowboys)
Fred Carr (Green Bay Packers)
George Andrie (Dallas Cowboys)
Rookie of the Year--Bruce Taylor (San Francisco 49ers)
Dennis Shaw (Buffalo Bills)
Ray Chester (Oakland Raiders)
Super Bowl MVP--Chuck Howley (Dallas Cowboys)
U.P.I. AFC Coach of the Year--Don Shula (Miami Dolphins)
U.P.I. AFC Player of the Year--George Blanda (Oakland Raiders)
U.P.I. Rookie of the Year--Dennis Shaw (Buffalo Bills)
U.P.I. NFC Coach of the Year--Alex Webster (New York Giants)
U.P.I. NFC Player of the Year--John Brodie (San Francisco 49ers)
U.P.I. NFC Rookie of the Year--Bruce Taylor (San Francisco 49ers)

Hall of Fame Inductees

Jack Christiansen, Tom Fears, Hugh McElhenny, Pete Pihos

Notes

This was the first season for A.B.C.'s Monday Night Football.
This was the year when the NFL and the AFL merged under the NFL banner.

Canadian Football League
Eastern Conference

Team Name	GP	W	L	T	PF	PA	Pts	Pct
Hamilton Tiger-Cats	14	8	5	1	292	279	17	.607
Toronto Argonauts	14	8	6	0	329	290	16	.571
Montreal Alouettes	14	7	6	1	246	279	15	.536
Ottawa Rough Riders	14	4	10	0	255	279	8	.286

Western Conference

Team Name	GP	W	L	T	PF	PA	Pts	Pct
Saskatchewan Roughriders	16	14	2	0	369	206	28	.875
Edmonton Eskimos	16	9	7	0	282	287	18	.563
Calgary Stampeders	16	9	7	0	293	209	18	.563
British Columbia Lions	16	6	10	0	295	384	12	.375
Winnipeg Blue Bombers	16	2	14	0	184	332	4	.125

Coaching Changes

Montreal--Sam Etcheverry 7-6-1; Ottawa--Jack Gotta 4-10-0; Edmonton--Ray Jauch 9-7-0; British Columbia--Jackie Parker 6-10-0; Winnipeg--Jim Spavital 2-14-0.

League Leaders

Yards Rushing		Yards Passing		Passing % (200 attempts)	
Hugh McKinnis	1135	Ron Lancaster	2779	Ron Lancaster	53.0
Jim Evenson	1003	Gary Wood	2755	Don Jonas	53.0
Bill Symons	908	Paul Brothers	2604	Sonny Wade	52.8
Dave Raimey	839	Don Trull	2455	Paul Brothers	52.5
Dennis Duncan	823	Sonny Wade	2421	Wally Gabler	52.1

Receiving Yards		Receptions		Points	
Hugh Oldham	1043	Herman Harrison	70	Jack Abendschan	116
Jim Young	1041	Terry Swarn	61	Tommy Joe Coffey	113
Herman Harrison	1024	Dave Fleming	56	Ted Gerela	107
Terry Swarn	739	Jim Young	54	Dave Cutler	106
Mike Eben	733	D. Smith	54	Don Jonas	100

All Star Game

(Lansdowne Park, Ottawa)

July 2	All Stars	35		Ottawa Rough Riders	14

Grey Cup Playoffs

November 7	Montreal Alouettes	16	at	Toronto Argonauts	7
November 8	Calgary Stampeders	16	at	Edmonton Eskimos	9
November 14	Calgary Stampeders	28	at	Saskatchewan Roughriders	11
November 15	Hamilton Tiger-Cats	22	at	Montreal Alouettes	32
November 18	Saskatchewan Roughriders	11	at	Calgary Stampeders	3
November 21	Montreal Alouettes	11	at	Hamilton Tiger-Cats	4
November 22	Calgary Stampeders	15	at	Saskatchewan Roughriders	14
November 28	Montreal Alouettes	23		Calgary Stampeders	10*

Individual Awards

Annis Stukus Trophy--Ray Jauch (Edmonton Eskimos)
CFL All Star Game MVP--Ron Lancaster (Saskatchewan Roughriders)
Dave Dryburgh Memorial Trophy--Jack Abendschan (Saskatchewan Roughriders)
DeMarco-Becket Memorial Trophy--Greg Pipes (Edmonton Eskimos)
Dr. Beattie Martin Trophy--John Senst (Winnipeg Blue Bombers)
Eddie James Memorial Trophy--Hugh McKinnis (Calgary Stampeders)
Grey Cup MVP--Sonny Wade (Montreal Alouettes)
Gruen Trophy--Jim Corrigall (Toronto Argonauts)
Jeff Nicklin Memorial Trophy--Ron Lancaster (Saskatchewan Roughriders)
Jeff Russel Memorial Trophy--Bill Symons (Toronto Argonauts)
Schenley Award Most Outstanding Canadian--Jim Young (British Columbia Lions)
Schenley Award Most Outstanding Lineman--Wayne Harris (Calgary Stampeders)
Schenley Award Most Outstanding Player--Ron Lancaster (Saskatchewan Roughriders)

Hall of Fame Inductees

Johnny Bright, Kenneth Montgomery, Gordon Perry

*Game played in Toronto

Notes

Vancouver's Empire Stadium received Canada's first artificial turf.
The first CFL All-Star Game since 1958 was played on July 2nd.

HOCKEY

National Hockey League
Eastern Division

Team Name	GP	W	L	T	GF	GA	Pts	Pct
Chicago Black Hawks	76	45	22	9	250	170	99	.635
Boston Bruins	76	40	17	19	277	216	99	.635
Detroit Red Wings	76	40	21	15	246	199	95	.609
New York Rangers	76	38	22	16	246	189	92	.590
Montreal Canadiens	76	38	22	16	244	201	92	.590
Toronto Maple Leafs	76	29	34	13	222	242	71	.455

Western Division

Team Name	GP	W	L	T	GF	GA	Pts	Pct
St. Louis Blues	76	37	27	12	224	179	86	.551
Pittsburgh Penguins	76	26	38	12	182	238	64	.410
Minnesota North Stars	76	19	35	22	224	257	60	.385
Oakland Seals	76	22	40	14	169	243	58	.372
Philadelphia Flyers	76	17	35	24	197	225	58	.372
Los Angeles Kings	76	14	52	10	168	290	38	.244

Coaching Changes

Detroit--Bill Gadsby 2-1-0, Sid Abel 38-20-15; New York--Emile Francis 38-22-16; Toronto--John McLellan 29-34-13; Pittsburgh--Leonard "Red" Kelly 26-38-12; Minnesota--Wren Blair 9-13-10, Charlie Burns 10-22-12; Philadelphia--Vic Stasiuk 17-35-24; Los Angeles--Hal Laycoe 5-18-1, John Wilson 9-34-9.

League Leaders

Goals

Phil Esposito	43
Garry Unger	42
Stan Mikita	39
Frank Mahovlich	38
Bobby Hull	38

Assists

Bobby Orr	87
Phil Esposito	56
Tom Williams	52
Walt Tkaczuk	50
Phil Goyette	49

Points

Bobby Orr	120
Phil Esposito	99
Stan Mikita	86
Phil Goyette	78
Walt Tkaczuk	77

Penalty Minutes

Keith Magnuson	213
John Ferguson	139
Bobby Orr	125
Gary Bergman	122
Don Awrey	120

GAA

Ernie Wakely	2.11
Tony Esposito	2.17
Jacques Plante	2.19
Ed Giacomin	2.36
Roy Edwards	2.59

Wins

Tony Esposito	38
Ed Giacomin	35
Rogie Vachon	31
Roy Edwards	24
Gerry Cheevers	24

Shutouts

Tony Esposito	15
Ed Giacomin	6
Jacques Plante	5
Ernie Wakely	4
Rogie Vachon	4

All Star Game

(St. Louis Arena, St. Louis)

January 20	East Division	4		West Division	1

Stanley Cup Playoffs

April 8	Minnesota North Stars	2	at	St. Louis Blues	6
April 8	Detroit Red Wings	2	at	Chicago Black Hawks	4
April 8	New York Rangers	2	at	Boston Bruins	8
April 8	Oakland Seals	1	at	Pittsburgh Penguins	2
April 9	Detroit Red Wings	2	at	Chicago Black Hawks	4
April 9	New York Rangers	3	at	Boston Bruins	5
April 9	Oakland Seals	1	at	Pittsburgh Penguins	2
April 9	Minnesota North Stars	1	at	St. Louis Blues	2
April 11	Chicago Black Hawks	4	at	Detroit Red Wings	2
April 11	Boston Bruins	3	at	New York Rangers	4
April 11	Pittsburgh Penguins	5	at	Oakland Seals	2
April 11	St. Louis Blues	2	at	Minnesota North Stars	4
April 12	Chicago Black Hawks	4	at	Detroit Red Wings	2
April 12	Boston Bruins	2	at	New York Rangers	4
April 12	Pittsburgh Penguins	3	at	Oakland Seals	2 [8:28]
April 12	St. Louis Blues	0	at	Minnesota North Stars	4
April 14	New York Rangers	2	at	Boston Bruins	3
April 14	Minnesota North Stars	3	at	St. Louis Blues	6
April 16	Boston Bruins	4	at	New York Rangers	1
April 16	St. Louis Blues	4	at	Minnesota North Stars	2
April 19	Boston Bruins	6	at	Chicago Black Hawks	3
April 19	Pittsburgh Penguins	1	at	St. Louis Blues	3
April 21	Boston Bruins	4	at	Chicago Black Hawks	1
April 21	Pittsburgh Penguins	1	at	St. Louis Blues	4
April 23	Chicago Black Hawks	2	at	Boston Bruins	5
April 23	St. Louis Blues	2	at	Pittsburgh Penguins	3
April 26	Chicago Black Hawks	4	at	Boston Bruins	5
April 26	St. Louis Blues	1	at	Pittsburgh Penguins	2
April 28	Pittsburgh Penguins	0	at	St. Louis Blues	5
April 30	St. Louis Blues	4	at	Pittsburgh Penguins	3
May 3	Boston Bruins	6	at	St. Louis Blues	1
May 5	Boston Bruins	6	at	St. Louis Blues	2
May 7	St. Louis Blues	1	at	Boston Bruins	4
May 10	St. Louis Blues	3	at	Boston Bruins	4 [0:40]

All Star Teams

First Team		Second Team
Tony Esposito	Goal	Ed Giacomin
Bobby Orr	Defense	Carl Brewer
Brad Park	Defense	Jacques Laperriere
Phil Esposito	Center	Stan Mikita
Gordie Howe	Right Wing	John McKenzie
Bobby Hull	Left Wing	Frank Mahovlich

Individual Awards

Art Ross Trophy--Bobby Orr (Boston Bruins)
Bill Masterton Trophy--Pit Martin (Chicago Black Hawks)
Calder Memorial Trophy--Tony Esposito (Chicago Black Hawks)

Conn Smythe Trophy--Bobby Orr (Boston Bruins)
Hart Memorial Trophy--Bobby Orr (Boston Bruins)
James Norris Trophy--Bobby Orr (Boston Bruins)
Lady Byng Memorial Trophy--Phil Goyette (St. Louis Blues)
Lester Patrick Trophy--Eddie Shore and James Hendy
NHL All Star Game MVP--Bobby Hull (Chicago Black Hawks)
Vezina Trophy--Tony Esposito (Chicago Black Hawks)

Hall of Fame Inductees

Cecil Dye, Bill Gadsby, Tom Johnson, Bob LeBel

SOCCER
North American Soccer League

Northern Division

Team Name	GP	W	L	T	GF	GA	BP	Pts	Pct
Rochester Lancers	24	9	9	6	41	45	39	111	.514
Kansas City Spurs	24	8	10	6	42	44	34	100	.463
St. Louis Stars	24	5	17	2	26	71	24	60	.278

Southern Division

Team Name	GP	W	L	T	GF	GA	BP	Pts	Pct
Washington Darts	24	14	6	4	52	29	41	137	.634
Atlanta Chiefs	24	11	8	5	53	33	42	123	.569
Dallas Tornado	24	8	12	4	39	39	32	92	.426

Coaching Changes

Rochester--Alex Perolli, Charles Schiano, Sal DeRosa; Kansas City--Alan Rogers 8-10-6; St. Louis--Robert Kehoe, Don Range; Washington--Lincoln Phillips 14-6-4; Atlanta--Vic Rouse 11-8-5.

League Leaders

Goals		Points		Shutouts	
Kirk Apostolidis	16	Kirk Apostolidis	35	Lincoln Phillips	12
Leroy DeLeon	16	Carlos Metidieri	35	Leonel Conde	7
Carlos Metidieri	14	Leroy DeLeon	33	Ken Cooper	6
Art Welch	12	Art Welch	32	Vic Rouse	4
Nick Papadakis	11	Manfred Seissler	29	Manfred Kammerer	4

GAA	
Lincoln Phillips	0.95
Vic Rouse	1.07
Ken Cooper	1.45
Manfred Kammerer	1.58
Leonel Conde	1.65

NASL Championship

September 6	Washington Darts	0	at	Rochester Lancers	3
September 13	Rochester Lancers	1	at	Washington Darts	3

All Star Teams

First Team		Second Team
Lincoln Phillips	Goal	Leonel Conde
Charlie Mitchell	Defender	John Cocking
Uriel da Viega	Defender	Delroy Scott
Willie Evans	Midfield	Ray Bloomfield
John Best	Midfield	Roy Turner
Willie Fraser	Midfield	Bob DeLuca
Carlos Metidieri	Forward	Warren Archibald
Dave Metchik	Forward	Clarival Oliviera
Art Welch	Forward	Kirk Apostolidis
Leroy DeLeon	Forward	Mike Renshaw
Manfred Seissler	Forward	Pat McBride

Individual Awards

Lead Goalkeeper Award--Lincoln Phillips (Washington Darts)
Most Valuable Player--Carlos Metidieri (Rochester Lancers)
Rookie of the Year--Jim Leeker (St. Louis Stars)

Franchise Changes

AL--Seattle Pilots became the Milwaukee Brewers.
ABA--The Minnesota Pipers moved back to Pittsburgh.
ABA--The Houston Mavericks became the Carolina Cougars.
ABA--The Oakland Oaks became the Washington Capitols.

Other Sports

Horseracing--Kentucky Derby won by Dust Commander (time 2:03.4 purse $127,800).
Heavyweight Boxing--Joe Frazier knocked-out Jimmy Ellis in 5 rounds.
Joe Frazier knocked-out Bob Foster in 2 rounds.
Golf--U.S. Open won by Tony Jacklin with a score of 288.
Auto Racing--Indianapolis 500 won by Al Unser (ave. speed 155.749 MPH).
Tennis--U.S. Open won by Ken Rosewall in the men's singles.
U.S. Open won by Pierre Barthes and Nicki Pilic in the men's doubles.
U.S. Open won by Margaret Smith Court in the women's singles.
U.S. Open won by Margaret Smith Court and Judy Tegart Dalton in the women's doubles.
U.S. Open won by Margaret Smith Court and Marty Riessen in the mixed doubles.

1971

BASEBALL
National League

East

Team Name	W	L	Pct	GB	R	OR
Pittsburgh Pirates	97	65	.599	-	788	599
St. Louis Cardinals	90	72	.556	7	739	699
Chicago Cubs	83	79	.512	14	637	648
New York Mets	83	79	.512	14	588	550
Montreal Expos	71	90	.441	25.5	622	729
Philadelphia Phillies	67	95	.414	30	558	688

West

Team Name	W	L	Pct	GB	R	OR
San Francisco Giants	100	72	.556	-	706	644
Los Angeles Dodgers	89	73	.549	1	663	587
Atlanta Braves	82	80	.506	8	643	699
Cincinnati Reds	79	83	.488	11	586	581
Houston Astros	79	83	.488	11	585	567
San Diego Padres	61	100	.379	28.5	486	610

Coaching Changes

San Francisco--Charlie Fox 90-72.

League Leaders

Batting Average

Joe Torre	.363
Ralph Garr	.343
Glenn Beckert	.342
Roberto Clemente	.341
Hank Aaron	.327

Home Runs

Willie Stargell	48
Hank Aaron	47
Lee May	39
Deron Johnson	34
Earl Williams	33

RBI

Joe Torre	137
Willie Stargell	125
Hank Aaron	118
Bobby Bonds	102
Willie Montanez	99

Stolen Bases

Lou Brock	64
Joe Morgan	40
Ralph Garr	30
Bud Harrelson	28
Tommie Agee	28

ERA

Tom Seaver	1.76
Dave Roberts	2.10
Don Wilson	2.45
Ken Forsch	2.54
Don Sutton	2.55

Wins

Ferguson Jenkins	24
Al Downing	20
Steve Carlton	20
Tom Seaver	20
Dock Ellis	19

Saves

Dave Giusti	30
Mike Marshall	23
Jim Brewer	22
Jerry Johnson	18
Cecil Upshaw	17

Strikeouts

Tom Seaver	289
Ferguson Jenkins	263
Bill Stoneman	251
Clayton Kirby	231
Don Sutton	194

NLCS

October 2	Pittsburgh Pirates	4	at	San Francisco Giants	5
October 3	Pittsburgh Pirates	9	at	San Francisco Giants	4
October 5	San Francisco Giants	1	at	Pittsburgh Pirates	2
October 6	San Francisco Giants	5	at	Pittsburgh Pirates	9

American League
East

Team Name	W	L	Pct	GB	R	OR
Baltimore Orioles	101	57	.639	-	742	530
Detroit Tigers	91	71	.562	12	701	645
Boston Red Sox	85	77	.525	18	691	667
New York Yankees	82	80	.506	21	648	641
Washington Senators	63	96	.396	38.5	537	660
Cleveland Indians	60	102	.370	43	543	747

West

Team Name	W	L	Pct	GB	R	OR
Oakland Athletics	101	60	.627	-	691	564
Kansas City Royals	85	76	.528	16	603	566
Chicago White Sox	79	83	.488	22.5	617	597
California Angels	76	86	.469	25.5	511	576
Minnesota Twins	74	86	.463	26.5	654	670
Milwaukee Brewers	69	92	.429	32	534	609

Coaching Changes

Detroit--Billy Martin 91-71; Cleveland--Alvin Dark 42-61, John Lipon 18-41; Oakland--Dick Williams 101-60; Kansas City--Bob Lemon 85-76; Chicago--Charles Tanner 79-83.

League Leaders

Batting Average

Tony Oliva	.337
Bob Murcer	.331
Merv Rettenmund	.318
Cesar Tovar	.311
Rod Carew	.307

Home Runs

Bill Melton	33
Norm Cash	32
Reggie Jackson	32
Reg Smith	30
Frank Robinson	28

RBI

Harmon Killebrew	119
Frank Robinson	99
Reg Smith	96
Bob Murcer	94
Sal Bando	94

Stolen Bases

Amos Otis	52
Fred Patek	49
Sandy Alomar	39
Bert Campaneris	34
Vada Pinson	25

ERA

Vida Blue	1.82
Wilbur Wood	1.91
Jim Palmer	2.68
Mike Hedlund	2.71
Bert Blyleven	2.82

Wins

Mickey Lolich	25
Vida Blue	24
Wilbur Wood	22
Dave McNally	21
James Hunter	21

Saves

Ken Sanders	31
Ted Abernathy	23
Fred Scherman	20
Tom Burgmeier	17
Roland Fingers	17

Strikeouts

Mickey Lolich	308
Vida Blue	301
Joe Coleman	236
Bert Blyleven	224
Wilbur Wood	210

All Star Game
(Tiger Stadium, Detroit)

July 13	American League	6		National League	4

ALCS

October 3	Oakland Athletics	3	at	Baltimore Orioles	5
October 4	Oakland Athletics	1	at	Baltimore Orioles	5
October 5	Baltimore Orioles	5	at	Oakland Athletics	3

World Series

October 9	Pittsburgh Pirates	3	at	Baltimore Orioles	5
October 11	Pittsburgh Pirates	3	at	Baltimore Orioles	11
October 12	Baltimore Orioles	1	at	Pittsburgh Pirates	5
October 13	Baltimore Orioles	3	at	Pittsburgh Pirates	4
October 14	Baltimore Orioles	0	at	Pittsburgh Pirates	4
October 16	Pittsburgh Pirates	2	at	Baltimore Orioles	3 [10]
October 17	Pittsburgh Pirates	2	at	Baltimore Orioles	1

Individual Awards

Arch Ward Memorial Trophy--Frank Robinson (Baltimore Orioles AL)
Baseball Writers Award--Joe Torre (St. Louis Cardinals NL)
Vida Blue (Oakland Athletics AL)
Cy Young Award--Ferguson Jenkins (Chicago Cubs NL)
Vida Blue (Oakland Athletics AL)
Rookie of the Year--Earl Williams (Atlanta Braves NL)
Chris Chambliss (Cleveland Indians AL)
Sporting News Executive of the Year--Cedric Tallis (Kansas City Royals AL)
Sporting News Manager of the Year--Charlie Fox (San Francisco Giants NL)
Sporting News Pitcher of the Year--Ferguson Jenkins (Chicago Cubs NL)
Vida Blue (Oakland Athletics AL)
Sporting News Player of the Year--Joe Torre (St. Louis Cardinals NL)
Tony Oliva (Minnesota Twins AL)
Sporting News Rookie of the Year--Earl Williams (Atlanta Braves NL)
Reggie Cleveland (St. Louis Cardinals NL)
Chris Chambliss (New York Yankees AL)
Bill Parsons (Milwaukee Brewers AL)
World Series MVP--Roberto Clemente (Pittsburgh Pirates NL)

Hall of Fame Inductees

Dave Bancroft, Jake Beckley, Charles Hafey, Harry Hooper, Joe Kelley, Rube Marquard, Satchel Paige, George Weiss

BASKETBALL
National Basketball Association

Atlantic Division

Team Name	GP	W	L	PPGF	PPGA	Pct	GB
New York Knickerbockers	82	52	30	110.1	105.0	.634	-
Philadelphia 76ers	82	47	35	114.8	113.3	.573	5
Boston Celtics	82	44	38	117.2	115.1	.537	8
Buffalo Braves	82	22	60	105.5	112.1	.268	30

Central Division

Baltimore Bullets	82	42	40	112.9	112.3	.512	-
Atlanta Hawks	82	36	46	114.0	115.8	.439	6
Cincinnati Royals	82	33	49	116.0	119.2	.402	9
Cleveland Cavaliers	82	15	67	102.1	113.3	.183	27

Midwest Division

Milwaukee Bucks	82	66	16	118.4	106.2	.805	-
Chicago Bulls	82	51	31	110.6	105.4	.622	15
Phoenix Suns	82	48	34	113.8	111.9	.585	18
Detroit Pistons	82	45	37	110.1	110.9	.549	21

Pacific Division

Los Angeles Lakers	82	48	34	114.8	111.7	.585	-
San Francisco Warriors	82	41	41	107.1	108.5	.500	7
San Diego Rockets	82	40	42	113.2	113.4	.488	8
Seattle SuperSonics	82	38	44	115.0	117.0	.463	10
Portland Trail Blazers	82	29	53	115.5	120.0	.354	19

Coaching Changes

Buffalo--Dolph Schayes 22-60; Cleveland--Bill Fitch 15-67; Phoenix--Cotton Fitzsimmons 48-34; San Francisco--Al Attles 41-41; San Diego--Alex Hannum 40-42; Portland--Rolland Todd 29-53.

League Leaders

Field Goals		Free Throws		Assists	
Lew Alcindor	1063	Dave Bing	615	Norm Van Lier	832
Elvin Hayes	948	John Havlicek	554	Oscar Robertson	668
John Havlicek	892	Dick Van Arsdale	553	Lenny Wilkens	654
Lou Hudson	829	Jerry West	525	John Havlicek	607
Dave Bing	799	Stu Lantz	519	Walt Frazier	536

Points		Fouls	
Lew Alcindor	2596	Dave Cowens	350
Elvin Hayes	2350	Don Adams	344
John Havlicek	2338	Norm Van Lier	343
Dave Bing	2213	John Trapp	337
Bob Love	2043	Bill Cunningham	328

All Star Game

(San Diego Sports Arena, San Diego)

January 12	West Division	108	East Division	107

NBA Playoffs

March 24	Chicago Bulls	99	at	Los Angeles Lakers	100
March 24	Philadelphia 76ers	126	at	Baltimore Bullets	112
March 25	Atlanta Hawks	101	at	N.Y. Knickerbockers	112
March 26	Chicago Bulls	95	at	Los Angeles Lakers	105
March 26	Baltimore Bullets	119	at	Philadelphia 76ers	107

March 27	Milwaukee Bucks	107	at	San Francisco Warriors	96
March 27	Atlanta Hawks	113	at	N.Y. Knickerbockers	104
March 28	N.Y. Knickerbockers	110	at	Atlanta Hawks	95
March 28	Philadelphia 76ers	103	at	Baltimore Bullets	111
March 28	Los Angeles Lakers	98	at	Chicago Bulls	106
March 29	Milwaukee Bucks	104	at	San Francisco Warriors	90*
March 30	N.Y. Knickerbockers	113	at	Atlanta Hawks	107
March 30	Milwaukee Bucks	114	at	San Francisco Warriors	102*
March 30	Baltimore Bullets	120	at	Philadelphia 76ers	105
March 30	Los Angeles Lakers	102	at	Chicago Bulls	112
April 1	Atlanta Hawks	107	at	N.Y. Knickerbockers	111
April 1	Milwaukee Bucks	104	at	San Francisco Warriors	106
April 1	Philadelphia 76ers	104	at	Baltimore Bullets	103
April 1	Chicago Bulls	86	at	Los Angeles Lakers	115
April 3	Baltimore Bullets	94	at	Philadelphia 76ers	98
April 4	Milwaukee Bucks	136	at	San Francisco Warriors	86*
April 4	Philadelphia 76ers	120	at	Baltimore Bullets	128
April 4	Los Angeles Lakers	99	at	Chicago Bulls	113
April 6	Chicago Bulls	98	at	Los Angeles Lakers	109
April 6	Baltimore Bullets	111	at	N.Y. Knickerbockers	112
April 9	Baltimore Bullets	88	at	N.Y. Knickerbockers	107
April 9	Los Angeles Lakers	85	at	Milwaukee Bucks	106
April 11	N.Y. Knickerbockers	88	at	Baltimore Bullets	114
April 11	Los Angeles Lakers	73	at	Milwaukee Bucks	91
April 14	N.Y. Knickerbockers	80	at	Baltimore Bullets	101
April 14	Milwaukee Bucks	107	at	Los Angeles Lakers	118
April 16	Baltimore Bullets	84	at	N.Y. Knickerbockers	89
April 16	Milwaukee Bucks	117	at	Los Angeles Lakers	94
April 18	N.Y. Knickerbockers	96	at	Baltimore Bullets	113
April 18	Los Angeles Lakers	98	at	Milwaukee Bucks	116
April 19	Baltimore Bullets	93	at	N.Y. Knickerbockers	91
April 21	Baltimore Bullets	88	at	Milwaukee Bucks	98
April 25	Milwaukee Bucks	102	at	Baltimore Bullets	83
April 28	Baltimore Bullets	99	at	Milwaukee Bucks	107
April 30	Milwaukee Bucks	118	at	Baltimore Bullets	106

All Star Teams

First Team	Second Team
John Havlicek (Boston Celtics)	Gus Johnson (Baltimore Bullets)
Bill Cunningham (Philadelphia 76ers)	Bob Love (Chicago Bulls)
Lew Alcindor (Milwaukee Bucks)	Willis Reed (N.Y. Knickerbockers)
Jerry West (Los Angeles Lakers)	Walt Frazier (N.Y. Knickerbockers)
Dave Bing (Detroit Pistons)	Oscar Robertson (Milwaukee Bucks)

Individual Awards

Eddie Gottlieb Trophy--Dave Cowens (Boston Celtics)
Geoff Petrie (Portland Trail Blazers)
Maurice Podoloff Trophy--Lew Alcindor (Milwaukee Bucks)
NBA All Star Game MVP--Lenny Wilkens (Seattle SuperSonics)
NBA Finals MVP--Lew Alcindor (Milwaukee Bucks)
Red Auerbach Trophy--Dick Motta (Chicago Bulls)

*Games played in Madison, Wisconsin

Hall of Fame Inductees

Edgar Diddle, Bob Douglas, Paul Endacott, Max Friedman, Eddie Gottlieb, Clifford Wells

American Basketball Association
Eastern Division

Team Name	GP	W	L	PPGF	PPGA	Pct	GB
Virginia Squires	84	55	29	123.3	119.7	.655	-
Kentucky Colonels	84	44	40	122.3	122.1	.524	11
New York Nets	84	40	44	111.0	111.6	.476	15
Floridians	84	37	47	114.0	115.6	.440	18
Pittsburgh Condors	84	36	48	119.1	121.8	.429	19
Carolina Cougars	84	34	50	115.3	119.4	.405	21

Western Division

Team Name	GP	W	L	PPGF	PPGA	Pct	GB
Indiana Pacers	84	58	26	119.1	113.1	.690	-
Utah Stars	84	57	27	119.0	111.9	.679	1
Memphis Pros	84	41	43	109.2	109.9	.488	17
Texas Chaparrals	84	30	54	121.5	124.5	.357	28
Denver Rockets	84	30	54	118.6	122.7	.357	28

Coaching Changes

Virginia--Al Bianchi 55-29; Kentucky--Gene Rhodes 10-5, Alex Groza 2-0, Frank Ramsey 32-35; New York--Lou Carnesecca 40-44; Floridians--Hal Blitman 18-30, Bob Bass 19-17; Pittsburgh--Jack McMahon 36-48; Carolina--Bones McKinney 17-25; Jerry Steele 17-25; Utah--Bill Sharman 57-27; Memphis--Babe McCarthy 41-43; Texas--Max Williams 5-14, Bill Blakeley 25-40; Denver--Joe Belmont 3-10, Stan Albeck 27-44.

League Leaders

Field Goals		Free Throws		Assists	
Dan Issel	938	Mack Calvin	696	Bill Melchianni	672
Charlie Scott	902	Larry Cannon	606	Mack Calvin	619
John Brisker	898	Dan Issel	604	Charlie Scott	472
Larry Jones	764	Charlie Scott	456	Jim Jones	468
Larry Cannon	751	Rick Barry	451	George Lehmann	464

Points		Fouls	
Dan Issel	2480	Wendell Ladner	334
John Brisker	2315	Mike Lewis	332
Charlie Scott	2276	"Goose" Ligon	331
Mack Calvin	2201	Cincy Powell	323
Larry Cannon	2126	Dan Issel	323

All Star Game
(Greensboro Coliseum, Greensboro)

January 23	East Division	126	West Division	122

ABA Playoffs

April 2	Floridians	112	at	Kentucky Colonels	116
April 2	New York Nets	105	at	Virginia Squires	113
April 2	Memphis Pros	98	at	Indiana Pacers	114
April 2	Texas Chaparrals	115	at	Utah Stars	125
April 3	Texas Chaparrals	107	at	Utah Stars	137
April 3	Memphis Pros	104	at	Indiana Pacers	106
April 4	Floridians	110	at	Kentucky Colonels	120
April 4	New York Nets	108	at	Virginia Squires	114
April 4	Utah Stars	113	at	Texas Chaparrals	101
April 5	Indiana Pacers	91	at	Memphis Pros	90
April 6	Kentucky Colonels	102	at	Floridians	120
April 6	Virginia Squires	131	at	New York Nets	135
April 6	Utah Stars	128	at	Texas Chaparrals	107
April 7	Virginia Squires	127	at	New York Nets	130
April 7	Indiana Pacers	102	at	Memphis Pros	101
April 8	Kentucky Colonels	117	at	Floridians	129
April 9	New York Nets	124	at	Virginia Squires	127
April 10	Floridians	101	at	Kentucky Colonels	118
April 10	Virginia Squires	118	at	New York Nets	114
April 12	Kentucky Colonels	112	at	Floridians	103
April 12	Utah Stars	120	at	Indiana Pacers	118
April 14	Utah Stars	107	at	Indiana Pacers	120
April 15	Kentucky Colonels	136	at	Virginia Squires	132
April 17	Kentucky Colonels	122	at	Virginia Squires	142
April 17	Indiana Pacers	108	at	Utah Stars	121
April 19	Virginia Squires	150	at	Kentucky Colonels	137
April 20	Indiana Pacers	99	at	Utah Stars	126
April 21	Virginia Squires	110	at	Kentucky Colonels	128
April 22	Utah Stars	109	at	Indiana Pacers	127
April 23	Kentucky Colonels	115	at	Virginia Squires	107
April 24	Indiana Pacers	105	at	Utah Stars	102
April 24	Virginia Squires	117	at	Kentucky Colonels	129
April 28	Utah Stars	108	at	Indiana Pacers	101
May 3	Kentucky Colonels	117	at	Utah Stars	136
May 5	Kentucky Colonels	125	at	Utah Stars	138
May 7	Utah Stars	110	at	Kentucky Colonels	116
May 8	Utah Stars	125	at	Kentucky Colonels	129 [OT]
May 12	Kentucky Colonels	127	at	Utah Stars	137
May 15	Utah Stars	101	at	Kentucky Colonels	105
May 18	Kentucky Colonels	121	at	Utah Stars	131

All Star Teams

First Team	Second Team
Roger Brown (Indiana Pacers)	John Brisker (Pittsburgh Condors)
Rick Barry (New York Nets)	Joe Caldwell (Carolina Cougars)
Mel Daniels (Indiana Pacers)	Zelmo Beaty (Utah Stars)
Mack Calvins (Floridians)	Dan Issel (Kentucky Colonels)
Charlie Scott (Virginia Squires)	Don Freeman (Texas Chaparrals)
	Larry Cannon (Denver Rockets)

Individual Awards

ABA All Star Game MVP--Mel Daniels (Indiana Pacers)
Coach of the Year--Al Bianchi (Virginia Squires)
Most Valuable Player--Mel Daniels (Indiana Pacers)
Rookie of the Year--Dan Issel (Kentucky Colonels)
Charlie Scott (Virginia Squires)

FOOTBALL
National Football League
National Football Conference
Eastern Division

Team Name	GP	W	L	T	PF	PA	Pct
Dallas Cowboys	14	11	3	0	406	222	.786
Washington Redskins	14	9	4	1	276	190	.679
Philadelphia Eagles	14	6	7	1	221	302	.464
St. Louis Cardinals	14	4	9	1	231	279	.321
New York Giants	14	4	10	0	228	362	.286

Central Division

Team Name	GP	W	L	T	PF	PA	Pct
Minnesota Vikings	14	11	3	0	245	139	.786
Detroit Lions	14	7	6	1	341	286	.536
Chicago Bears	14	6	8	0	185	276	.429
Green Bay Packers	14	4	8	2	274	298	.357

Western Division

Team Name	GP	W	L	T	PF	PA	Pct
San Francisco 49ers	14	9	5	0	300	216	.643
Los Angeles Rams	14	8	5	1	313	260	.607
Atlanta Falcons	14	7	6	1	274	277	.536
New Orleans Saints	14	4	8	2	266	347	.357

American Football Conference
Eastern Division

Team Name	GP	W	L	T	PF	PA	Pct
Miami Dolphins	14	10	3	1	315	174	.750
Baltimore Colts	14	10	4	0	313	140	.714
New England Patriots	14	6	8	0	238	325	.429
New York Jets	14	6	8	0	212	299	.429
Buffalo Bills	14	1	13	0	184	394	.071

Central Division

Team Name	GP	W	L	T	PF	PA	Pct
Cleveland Browns	14	9	5	0	285	273	.643
Pittsburgh Steelers	14	6	8	0	246	292	.429
Houston Oilers	14	4	9	1	251	330	.321
Cincinnati Bengals	14	4	10	0	284	265	.286

Western Division

Team Name	GP	W	L	T	PF	PA	Pct
Kansas City Chiefs	14	10	3	1	302	208	.750
Oakland Raiders	14	8	4	2	344	278	.643
San Diego Chargers	14	6	8	0	311	341	.429
Denver Broncos	14	4	9	1	203	275	.321

Coaching Changes

Washington--George Allen 9-4-1; Philadelphia--Jerry Williams 0-3-0, Ed Khayat 6-4-1; St. Louis--Bob Hollway 4-9-1; Green Bay--Dan Devine 4-8-2; Los Angeles--Tom Prothro 8-5-1; New Orleans--J.D. Roberts 4-8-2; New England--John Mazur 6-8-0; Buffalo--Harvey Johnson 1-13-0; Cleveland--Nick Skorich 9-5-0; Houston--Ed Hughes 4-9-1; San Diego--Sid Gillman 4-6-0, Harland Svare 2-2-0; Denver--Lou Saban 2-6-1, Jerry Smith 2-3-0.

League Leaders

Yards Rushing		**Yards Passing**		**Passing %** (40 attempts)	
Floyd Little	1133	John Hadl	3075	Virgil Carter	62
John Brockington	1105	John Brodie	2642	Roger Staubach	60
Larry Csonka	1051	Fran Tarkenton	2567	Bob Berry	60
Steve Owens	1035	Len Dawson	2504	Fran Tarkenton	59
Willie Ellison	1000	Bill Nelson	2319	Len Dawson	55

Receiving Yards		**Receptions**		**Field Goals**	
Otis Taylor	1110	Fred Biletnikoff	61	Curt Knight	29
Paul Warfield	996	Bob Tucker	59	Garo Yepremian	28
Fred Biletnikoff	929	Otis Taylor	57	Jan Stenerud	26
Gary Garrison	889	Ted Kwalick	52	Jim Turner	25
Gene Washington	884	Randy Vataha	51	Bruce Gossett	23

Punt Return Yards		**Kickoff Return Yards**	
Jake Scott	318	Dave Hampton	1314
Leroy Kelly	292	Rocky Thompson	947
Bill Thompson	274	Vic Washington	858
Jon Staggers	262	Linzy Cole	834
Bruce Taylor	235	Cliff Harris	823

Pro Bowl Game

(Memorial Coliseum, Los Angeles)

January 23 1972	American Conference	26		National Conference	13

NFL Playoffs

December 25	Dallas Cowboys	20	at	Minnesota Vikings	12
December 25	Miami Dolphins	27	at	Kansas City Chiefs	24 [OT]
December 26	Washington Redskins	20	at	San Francisco 49ers	24
December 26	Baltimore Colts	20	at	Cleveland Browns	3
January 2 1972	Baltimore Colts	0	at	Miami Dolphins	21
January 2 1972	San Francisco 49ers	3	at	Dallas Cowboys	14

Super Bowl VI

(Tulane Stadium, New Orleans)

January 16 1972	Dallas Cowboys	24	Miami Dolphins	3

Individual Awards

AP MVP--Alan Page (Minnesota Vikings)
Bert Bell Trophy--Jim Plunkett (New England Patriots) [World Almanac]
John Brockington (Green Bay Packers)
Bert Bell Trophy--Roger Staubach (Dallas Cowboys)

George Halas Trophy--Alan Page (Minnesota Vikings)
Carl Eller (Minnesota Vikings)
Jim Thorpe Trophy--Bob Griese (Miami Dolphins)
Pro Bowl MVP--Jan Stenerud (Kansas City Chiefs)
Willie Lanier (Kansas City Chiefs)
Rookie of the Year--John Brockington (Green Bay Packers)
Jim Plunkett (New England Patriots)
Isiah Robertson (Los Angeles Rams)
Super Bowl MVP--Roger Staubach (Dallas Cowboys)
U.P.I. AFC Coach of the Year--Don Shula (Miami Dolphins)
U.P.I. AFC Player of the Year--Otis Taylor (Kansas City Chiefs)
U.P.I. AFC Rookie of the Year--Jim Plunkett (New England Patriots)
U.P.I. NFC Coach of the Year--George Allen (Washington Redskins)
U.P.I. NFC Player of the Year--Alan Page (Minnesota Vikings)
U.P.I. NFC Rookie of the Year--John Brockington (Green Bay Packers)

Hall of Fame Inductees

Jim Brown, Bill Hewitt, Bruiser Kinard, Vince Lombardi, Andy Robustelli, Y.A. Tittle, Norm Van Brocklin

Canadian Football League
Eastern Conference

Team Name	GP	W	L	T	PF	PA	Pts	Pct
Toronto Argonauts	14	10	4	0	289	248	20	.714
Hamilton Tiger-Cats	14	7	7	0	242	246	14	.500
Ottawa Rough Riders	14	6	8	0	291	277	12	.429
Montreal Alouettes	14	6	8	0	226	248	12	.429

Western Conference

Team Name	GP	W	L	T	PF	PA	Pts	Pct
Calgary Stampeders	16	9	6	1	290	218	19	.594
Saskatchewan Roughriders	16	9	6	1	347	316	19	.594
Winnipeg Blue Bombers	16	7	8	1	366	349	15	.469
British Columbia Lions	16	6	9	1	282	363	13	.406
Edmonton Eskimos	16	6	10	0	237	305	12	.375

Coaching Changes

Hamilton--Al Darrow 7-7-0; Saskatchewan--Dave Skrien 9-6-1; British Columbia--Eagle Keys 6-9-1.

League Leaders

Yards Rushing		Yards Passing		Passing% (100 attempts)	
Jim Evenson	1237	Don Jonas	4036	Jerry Keeling	58.4
George Reed	1146	Ron Lancaster	2759	Gary Wood	56.0
Leon McQuay	977	Joe Theisman	2440	Don Moorhead	53.8
Hugh McKinnis	910	Sonny Wade	2090	Joe Theisman	53.2
Mack Herron	900	Jerry Keeling	2038	Don Jonas	52.1

Receiving Yards		Receptions		Points	
Jim Thorpe	1436	Jim Thorpe	70	Don Jonas	121
Bob LaRose	1080	Herman Harrison	70	Jack Abendschan	94
Herm Harrison	980	Bob Larose	58	Gerry Organ	92
Terry Evenshen	852	Jim Young	55	Dave Cutler	85
George McGowan	827	Terry Evenshen	50	Larry Robinson	81

All Star Game
(Autostade, Montreal)

June 29	All Stars	30		Montreal Alouettes	13

Grey Cup Playoffs

November 6	Winnipeg Blue Bombers	23	at	Saskatchewan Roughriders	34
November 7	Ottawa Rough Riders	4	at	Hamilton Tiger-Cats	23
November 13	Saskatchewan Roughriders	21	at	Calgary Stampeders	30
November 14	Toronto Argonauts	23	at	Hamilton Tiger-Cats	8
November 17	Calgary Stampeders	23	at	Saskatchewan Roughriders	21
November 20	Hamilton Tiger-Cats	17	at	Toronto Argonauts	17
November 28	Calgary Stampeders	14		Toronto Argonauts	11*

Individual Awards

Annis Stukus Trophy--Leo Cahill (Toronto Argonauts)
CFL All Star Game MVP--Bill Symons (Toronto Argonauts)
Dave Dryburgh Memorial Trophy--Don Jonas (Winnipeg Blue Bombers)
DeMarco Becket Memorial Trophy--Wayne Harris (Calgary Stampeders)
Dr. Beattie Martin Trophy--Bob Kraemer (Winnipeg Blue Bombers)
Eddie James Memorial Trophy--Jim Evenson (British Columbia Lions)
Grey Cup Most Valuable Canadian--Dick Suderman (Calgary Stampeders)
Grey Cup MVP--Wayne Harris (Calgary Stampeders)
Gruen Trophy--Jim Foley (Montreal Alouettes)
Jeff Nicklin Memorial Trophy--Don Jonas (Winnipeg Blue Bombers)
Jeff Russel Memorial Trophy--Mel Profit (Toronto Argonauts)
Schenley Award Most Outstanding Canadian--Terry Evanshen (Montreal Alouettes)
Schenley Award Most Outstanding Lineman--Wayne Harris (Calgary Stampeders)
Schenley Award Most Outstanding Player--Don Jonas (Winnipeg Blue Bombers)

Hall of Fame Inductees

Leonard Back, Jackie Parker, Hal Patterson

*Game played in Vancouver

HOCKEY
National Hockey League
Eastern Division

Team Name	GP	W	L	T	GF	GA	Pts	Pct
Boston Bruins	78	57	14	7	399	207	121	.776
New York Rangers	78	49	18	11	259	177	109	.699
Montreal Canadiens	78	42	23	13	291	216	97	.622
Toronto Maple Leafs	78	37	33	8	248	211	82	.526
Buffalo Sabres	78	24	39	15	217	291	63	.404
Vancouver Canucks	78	24	46	8	229	296	56	.359
Detroit Red Wings	78	22	45	11	209	308	55	.353

Western Division

Team Name	GP	W	L	T	GF	GA	Pts	Pct
Chicago Black Hawks	78	40	20	9	277	184	107	.686
St. Louis Blues	78	34	25	19	223	208	87	.558
Philadelphia Flyers	78	28	33	17	207	225	73	.468
Minnesota North Stars	78	28	34	16	191	223	72	.462
Los Angeles Kings	78	25	40	13	239	303	63	.404
Pittsburgh Penguins	78	21	37	20	221	240	62	.397
California Golden Seals	78	20	53	5	199	320	45	.288

Coaching Changes

Boston--Tom Johnson 57-14-7; Montreal--Claude Ruel 11-8-4, Al MacNeil 31-15-9; Buffalo--George Imlach 24-39-15; Vancouver--Hal Laycoe 24-46-8; Detroit--Ned Harkness 9-7-3, Doug Barkley 13-38-8; St. Louis--Al Arbour 21-15-14, Scotty Bowman 13-10-5; Minnesota--Jack Gordon 28-34-16; Los Angeles--Larry Regan 25-40-13; California--Fred Glover 20-53-5.

League Leaders

Goals

Phil Esposito	76
John Bucyk	51
Bobby Hull	44
Ken Hodge	43
Dennis Hull	40

Assists

Bobby Orr	102
Phil Esposito	76
John Bucyk	65
Ken Hodge	62
Wayne Cashman	58

Points

Phil Esposito	152
Bobby Orr	139
John Bucyk	116
Ken Hodge	105
Bobby Hull	96

Penalty Minutes

Keith Magnuson	291
Dennis Hextall	217
Jim Dorey	198
Pete Mahovlich	181
Tracy Pratt	179

GAA

Jacques Plante	1.88
Ed Giacomin	2.16
Tony Esposito	2.27
Gilles Villemure	2.30
Glenn Hall	2.42

Wins

Tony Esposito	35
Ed Johnston	30
Gerry Cheevers	27
Ed Giacomin	27
Jacques Plante	24

Shutouts

Ed Giacomin	8
Tony Esposito	6
Cesare Maniago	5
Jacques Plante	4
Ed Johnston	4

All Star Game
(Boston Gardens, Boston)

January 19	West Division	2		East Division	1

Stanley Cup Playoffs

April 7	Montreal Canadiens	1	at	Boston Bruins	3
April 7	Toronto Maple Leafs	4	at	New York Rangers	5
April 7	Philadelphia Flyers	2	at	Chicago Black Hawks	5
April 7	Minnesota North Stars	3	at	St. Louis Blues	2
April 8	Montreal Canadiens	7	at	Boston Bruins	5
April 8	Toronto Maple Leafs	4	at	New York Rangers	1
April 8	Philadelphia Flyers	2	at	Chicago Black Hawks	6
April 8	Minnesota North Stars	2	at	St. Louis Blues	4
April 10	Boston Bruins	1	at	Montreal Canadiens	3
April 10	New York Rangers	1	at	Toronto Maple Leafs	3
April 10	Chicago Black Hawks	3	at	Philadelphia Flyers	2
April 10	St. Louis Blues	3	at	Minnesota North Stars	0
April 11	Boston Bruins	5	at	Montreal Canadiens	2
April 11	New York Rangers	4	at	Toronto Maple Leafs	2
April 11	Chicago Black Hawks	6	at	Philadelphia Flyers	2
April 11	St. Louis Blues	1	at	Minnesota North Stars	2
April 13	Montreal Canadiens	3	at	Boston Bruins	7
April 13	Toronto Maple Leafs	1	at	New York Rangers	3
April 13	Minnesota North Stars	4	at	St. Louis Blues	3
April 15	Boston Bruins	3	at	Montreal Canadiens	8
April 15	New York Rangers	2	at	Toronto Maple Leafs	1 [9:07]
April 15	St. Louis Blues	2	at	Minnesota North Stars	5
April 18	Montreal Canadiens	4	at	Boston Bruins	2
April 18	New York Rangers	2	at	Chicago Black Hawks	1 [1:37]
April 20	Minnesota North Stars	2	at	Montreal Canadiens	7
April 20	New York Rangers	0	at	Chicago Black Hawks	3
April 22	Minnesota North Stars	6	at	Montreal Canadiens	3
April 22	Chicago Black Hawks	1	at	New York Rangers	4
April 24	Montreal Canadiens	6	at	Minnesota North Stars	3
April 25	Chicago Black Hawks	7	at	New York Rangers	1
April 25	Montreal Canadiens	2	at	Minnesota North Stars	5
April 27	New York Rangers	2	at	Chicago Black Hawks	3 [6:35]
April 27	Minnesota North Stars	1	at	Montreal Canadiens	6
April 29	Montreal Canadiens	3	at	Minnesota North Stars	2
April 29	Chicago Black Hawks	2	at	New York Rangers	3 [41:29]
May 2	New York Rangers	2	at	Chicago Black Hawks	4
May 4	Montreal Canadiens	1	at	Chicago Black Hawks	2 [21:11]
May 6	Montreal Canadiens	3	at	Chicago Black Hawks	5
May 9	Chicago Black Hawks	2	at	Montreal Canadiens	4
May 11	Chicago Black Hawks	2	at	Montreal Canadiens	5
May 13	Montreal Canadiens	0	at	Chicago Black Hawks	2
May 16	Chicago Black Hawks	3	at	Montreal Canadiens	4
May 18	Montreal Canadiens	3	at	Chicago Black Hawks	2

All Star Teams

First Team		Second Team
Ed Giacomin	Goal	Jacques Plante
Bobby Orr	Defense	Brad Park
J.C. Tremblay	Defense	Pat Stapleton
Phil Esposito	Center	Dave Keon
Ken Hodge	Right Wing	Yvan Cournoyer
John Bucyk	Left Wing	Bobby Hull

Individual Awards

Art Ross Trophy--Phil Esposito (Boston Bruins)
Bill Masterton Trophy--Jean Ratelle (New York Rangers)
Calder Memorial Trophy--Gil Perreault (Buffalo Sabres)
Conn Smythe Trophy--Ken Dryden (Montreal Canadiens)
Hart Memorial Trophy--Bobby Orr (Boston Bruins)
James Norris Trophy--Bobby Orr (Boston Bruins)
Lady Byng Memorial Trophy--John Bucyk (Boston Bruins)
Lester Patrick Trophy--William M. Jennings, John Sollenberger and Terry Sawchuk.
Lester B. Pearson Award--Phil Esposito (Boston Bruins)
NHL All Star Game MVP--Bobby Hull (Chicago Black Hawks)
Vezina Trophy--Ed Giacomin and Gilles Villemure (New York Rangers)

Hall of Fame Inductees

Busher Jackson, Gordon Roberts, Terry Sawchuk, Ralph Weiland, Arthur Wirtz,

Rules

Curvature for stick blades which had been set at one inch was now limited to one-half inch.

SOCCER

North American Soccer League

Northern Division

Team Name	GF	W	L	T	GF	GA	BP	Pts	Pct
Rochester Lancers	24	13	5	6	48	31	45	141	.653
New York Cosmos	24	9	10	5	51	55	48	117	.542
Toronto Metros	24	5	10	9	32	47	32	89	.412
Montreal Olympiques	24	4	15	5	29	58	26	65	.301

Southern Division

Team Name	GF	W	L	T	GF	GA	BP	Pts	Pct
Atlanta Chiefs	24	12	7	5	35	29	33	120	.556
Dallas Tornado	24	10	6	8	38	24	35	119	.551
Washington Darts	24	8	6	10	36	34	33	111	.514
St. Louis Stars	24	6	13	5	37	47	35	86	.398

Coaching Changes

Rochester--Sal DeRosa 13-5-6; New York--Gordon Bradley 9-10-5; Toronto--Graham Leggat 5-10-9; Montreal--Renato Tofani 4-15-5; Washington--Alan Rogers 8-6-10; St. Louis--George Meyer; Casey Frankiewicz.

League Leaders

Goals		Points		Shutouts	
Carlos Metidieri	19	Carlos Metidieri	46	Mirko Stojanovic	8
Randy Horton	16	Randy Horton	37	Manfred Kammerer	8
Casey Frankiewicz	14	Casey Frankiewicz	33	Leonel Conde	4
Manfred Seissler	10	Jorge Siega	27	Claude Campos	3
Jorge Siega	9	Manfred Seissler	27	Orest Banach	2

GAA	
Mirko Stojanovic	0.79
Claude Campos	1.11
Manfred Kammerer	1.14
Orest Banach	1.31
Leonel Conde	1.38

NASL Playoffs

September 1	Dallas Tornado	1	at	Rochester Lancers	2 [OT]
September 2	New York Cosmos	0	at	Atlanta Chiefs	1 [OT]
September 4	Rochester Lancers	1	at	Dallas Tornado	3
September 5	Atlanta Chiefs	2	at	New York Cosmos	0
September 8	Dallas Tornado	2	at	Rochester Lancers	1 [OT]
September 12	Dallas Tornado	1	at	Atlanta Chiefs	2 [OT]
September 15	Atlanta Chiefs	1	at	Dallas Tornado	4
September 19	Dallas Tornado	2	at	Atlanta Chiefs	0

All Star Teams

First Team		Second Team
Mirko Stojanovic	Goal	Leonel Conde
Dick Hall	Defender	Clive Charles
Willie Evans	Defender	Uriel da Viega
Peter Short	Defender	John Cocking
John Best	Defender	Charlie Mitchell
Dragan Popovic	Midfield	Francisco Escos
Siggy Stritzi	Midfield	Felix Correia
Carlos Metidieri	Forward	Warren Archibald
Randy Horton	Forward	Casey Frankiewicz
Kaizer Motaung	Forward	Franco Gallina
Manfred Seissler	Forward	Jorge Siega

Individual Awards

Lead Goalkeeper Award--Mirko Stojanovic (Dallas Tornado)
Most Valuable Player--Carlos Metidieri (Rochester Lancers)
Rookie of the Year--Randy Horton (New York Cosmos)

Franchise Changes

NHL--Oakland Seals became the California Golden Seals after two games.
NFL--Boston Patriots became the New England Patriots.
ABA--Washington Capitols became the Virginia Squires based in Norfolk and surrounding cities
Los Angeles Stars became the Utah Stars.
New Orleans Buccaneers became the Memphis Pros.

Dallas Chaparrals became the Texas Chaparrals.
Miami Floridians became the Floridians.
Pittsburgh Pipers became the Pittsburgh Condors.

Other Sports

Horseracing--Kentucky Derby won by Canonero II (time 2:03.2, purse $145,500).
Heavyweight Boxing--Joe Frazier defeated Muhammad Ali in 15 rounds.
Golf--U.S. Open won by Lee Trevino in a playoff with Jack Nicklaus (scores of 280-280, 68-71).
Auto Racing--Indianapolis 500 won by Al Unser (ave. speed 157.735 MPH).
Tennis--U.S. Open won by Stan Smith in the men's singles.
U.S. Open won by John Newcombe and Roger Taylor in the men's doubles.
U.S. Open won by Billie Jean King in the women's singles.
U.S. Open won by Rosemary Casals and Judy Tegart Dalton in the women's doubles.
U.S. Open won by Billie Jean King and Owen Davidson in the mixed doubles.

1972

BASEBALL
National League

East

Team Name	W	L	Pct	GB	R	OR
Pittsburgh Pirates	96	59	.619	-	691	512
Chicago Cubs	85	70	.548	11	685	567
New York Mets	83	73	.532	13.5	528	578
St. Louis Cardinals	75	81	.481	21.5	568	600
Montreal Expos	70	86	.449	26.5	513	609
Philadelphia Phillies	59	97	.378	37.5	503	635

West

Team Name	W	L	Pct	GB	R	OR
Cincinnati Reds	95	59	.617	-	707	557
Houston Astros	84	69	.549	10.5	708	636
Los Angeles Dodgers	85	70	.548	10.5	584	527
Atlanta Braves	70	84	.445	25	628	730
San Francisco Giants	69	86	.445	26.5	662	649
San Diego Padres	58	95	.379	36.5	488	665

Coaching Changes

Pittsburgh--Bill Virdon 96-59; Chicago--Leo Durocher 46-44, Walter Lockman 39-26; New York--Yogi Berra 83-73; Philadelphia--Frank Lucchesi 26-50, Paul Owens 33-47; Houston--Harry Walker 67-54, Francis Parker 1-0, Leo Durocher 16-15; Atlanta--Luman Harris 47-57, Eddie Mathews 23-27; San Diego--Preston Gomez 4-7, Don Zimmer 54-88.

League Leaders

Batting Average		Home Runs		RBI	
Billy Williams	.333	Johnny Bench	40	Johnny Bench	125
Ralph Garr	.325	Nate Colbert	38	Billy Williams	122
Cesar Cedeno	.320	Billy Williams	37	Willie Stargell	112
Bob Watson	.312	Hank Aaron	34	Nate Colbert	111
Al Oliver	.312	Willie Stargell	33	Lee May	98

Stolen Bases		ERA		Wins	
Lou Brock	63	Steve Carlton	1.97	Steve Carlton	27
Joe Morgan	58	Gary Nolan	1.99	Tom Seaver	21
Cesar Cedeno	55	Don Sutton	2.08	Claude Osteen	20
Bobby Bonds	44	Jon Matlack	2.32	Ferguson Jenkins	20
Bob Tolan	42	Bob Gibson	2.46	Steve Blass	19

Saves		Strikeouts	
Clay Carroll	37	Steve Carlton	310
Frank McGraw	27	Tom Seaver	249
Dave Giusti	22	Bob Gibson	208
Mike Marshall	18	Don Sutton	207
Jack Aker	17	Ferguson Jenkins	184

NLCS

October 7	Cincinnati Reds	1	at	Pittsburgh Pirates	5
October 8	Cincinnati Reds	5	at	Pittsburgh Pirates	3
October 9	Pittsburgh Pirates	3	at	Cincinnati Reds	2
October 10	Pittsburgh Pirates	1	at	Cincinnati Reds	7
October 11	Pittsburgh Pirates	3	at	Cincinnati Reds	4

American League

East

Team Name	W	L	Pct	GB	R	OR
Detroit Tigers	86	70	.551	-	558	514
Boston Red Sox	85	70	.548	.5	640	620
Baltimore Orioles	80	74	.519	5	519	430
New York Yankees	79	76	.510	6.5	557	527
Cleveland Indians	72	84	.462	14	472	519
Milwaukee Brewers	65	91	.417	21	493	595

West

Team Name	W	L	Pct	GB	R	OR
Oakland Athletics	93	62	.600	-	604	457
Chicago White Sox	87	67	.565	5.5	566	535
Minnesota Twins	77	77	.500	15.5	537	535
Kansas City Royals	76	78	.494	16.5	580	545
California Angels	75	80	.484	18	454	533
Texas Rangers	54	100	.351	38.5	461	628

Coaching Changes

Cleveland--Ken Aspromonte 72-84; Milwaukee--Dave Bristol 10-20, Roy McMillan 1-1, Del Crandall 54-70; Minnesota--Bill Rigney 36-34, Frank Quilici 41-43; California--Del Rice 75-80; Texas--Ted Williams 54-100.

League Leaders

Batting Average		Home Runs		RBI	
Rod Carew	.318	Richie Allen	37	Richie Allen	113
Lou Piniella	.312	Bobby Murcer	33	John Mayberry	100
Richie Allen	.308	Harmon Killebrew	26	Bobby Murcer	96
Carlos May	.308	Mike Epstein	26	George Scott	88
Joe Rudi	.305	Reggie Jackson	25	John Powell	81

Stolen Bases		ERA		Wins	
Bert Campaneris	52	Luis Tiant	1.91	Wilbur Wood	24
Dave Nelson	51	Gaylord Perry	1.92	Gaylord Perry	24
Fred Patek	33	James Hunter	2.04	Mickey Lolich	22
Pat Kelly	32	Jim Palmer	2.07	Jim Palmer	21
Amos Otis	28	Roger Nelson	2.08	Stan Bahnsen	21

Saves		Strikeouts	
Albert Lyle	35	Nolan Ryan	329
Terry Forster	29	Mickey Lolich	250
Roland Fingers	21	Gaylord Perry	234
Wayne Granger	19	Bert Blyleven	228
Ken Sanders	17	Joe Coleman	222

All Star Game

(Atlanta Fulton County Stadium, Atlanta)

July 25	National League	4	American League	3

ALCS

October 7	Detroit Tigers	2	at	Oakland Athletics	3 [11]
October 8	Detroit Tigers	0	at	Oakland Athletics	5
October 10	Oakland Athletics	0	at	Detroit Tigers	3
October 11	Oakland Athletics	3	at	Detroit Tigers	4 [10]
October 12	Oakland Athletics	2	at	Detroit Tigers	1

World Series

October 14	Oakland Athletics	3	at	Cincinnati Reds	2
October 15	Oakland Athletics	2	at	Cincinnati Reds	1
October 18	Cincinnati Reds	10	at	Oakland Athletics	0
October 19	Cincinnati Reds	2	at	Oakland Athletics	3
October 20	Cincinnati Reds	5	at	Oakland Athletics	4
October 21	Oakland Athletics	1	at	Cincinnati Reds	8
October 22	Oakland Athletics	3	at	Cincinnati Reds	2

Individual Awards

Arch Ward Memorial Trophy--Joe Morgan (Cincinnati Reds NL)
Baseball Writers Award--Johnny Bench (Cincinnati Reds NL)
Dick Allen (Chicago White Sox AL)
Cy Young Award--Steve Carlton (Philadelphia Phillies NL)
Gaylord Perry (Cleveland Indians AL)
Rookie of the Year--Jon Matlack (New York Mets NL)
Carlton Fisk (Boston Red Sox AL)
Sporting News Executive of the Year--Roland Hemond (Chicago White Sox AL)
Sporting News Manager of the Year--Charles Tanner (Chicago White Sox AL)
Sporting News Pitcher of the Year--Steve Carlton (Philadelphia Phillies NL)
Wilbur Wood (Chicago White Sox AL)
Sporting News Player of the Year--Billy Williams (Chicago Cubs NL)
Dick Allen (Chicago White Sox AL)
Sporting News Rookie of the Year--Dave Rader (San Francisco Giants NL)
Jon Matlack (New York Mets NL)
Carlton Fisk (Boston Red Sox AL)
Dick Tidrow (Cleveland Indians AL)
World Series MVP--Gene Tenace (Oakland Athletics AL)

Hall of Fame Inductees

Yogi Berra, Josh Gibson, Vernon Gomez, Will Harridge, Sandy Koufax, Buck Leonard, Early Wynn, Ross Youngs

BASKETBALL
National Basketball Association

Atlantic Division

Team Name	GP	W	L	PPGF	PPGA	Pct	GB
Boston Celtics	82	56	26	115.6	110.8	.683	-
New York Knickerbockers	82	48	34	107.1	104.7	.585	8
Philadelphia 76ers	82	30	52	112.2	115.9	.366	26
Buffalo Braves	82	22	60	102.0	111.3	.268	34

Central Division

Team Name	GP	W	L	PPGF	PPGA	Pct	GB
Baltimore Bullets	82	38	44	107.1	108.3	.463	-
Atlanta Hawks	82	36	46	109.5	111.3	.439	2
Cincinnati Royals	82	30	52	107.8	111.8	.366	8
Cleveland Cavaliers	82	23	59	105.8	113.4	.280	15

Midwest Division

Team Name	GP	W	L	PPGF	PPGA	Pct	GB
Milwaukee Bucks	82	63	19	114.6	103.5	.768	-
Chicago Bulls	82	57	25	111.2	102.9	.695	6
Phoenix Suns	82	49	33	116.3	110.8	.598	14
Detroit Pistons	82	26	56	109.1	115.9	.317	37

Pacific Division

Team Name	GP	W	L	PPGF	PPGA	Pct	GB
Los Angeles Lakers	82	69	13	121.0	108.7	.841	-
Golden State Warriors	82	51	31	108.2	107.4	.622	18
Seattle SuperSonics	82	47	35	109.2	108.8	.573	22
Houston Rockets	82	34	48	109.7	111.2	.415	35
Portland Trail Blazers	82	18	64	106.8	116.5	.220	51

Coaching Changes

Buffalo--Dolph Schayes 0-1, John McCarthy 22-59; Detroit--Butch van Breda Kolff 6-6, Earl Lloyd 20-50; Los Angeles--Bill Sharman 69-13; Golden State--Al Attles 51-31; Houston--Tex Winter 34-48; Portland--Rolland Todd 12-44, Stu Inman 6-20.

League Leaders

Field Goals		Free Throws		Assists	
Kareem Abdul-Jabbar	1159	Nate Archibald	677	Lenny Wilkens	766
John Havlicek	897	Dick Van Arsdale	529	Jerry West	747
Bob Lanier	834	Jerry West	515	Nate Archibald	701
Elvin Hayes	832	Archie Clark	507	John Havlicek	614
Gail Goodrich	826	Kareem Abdul-Jabbar	504	Archie Clark	613

Points		Fouls	
Kareem Abdul-Jabbar	2822	Dave Cowens	314
John Havlicek	2252	Jerry Sloan	309
Nate Archibald	2145	Elmore Smith	306
Gail Goodrich	2127	Nate Williams	300
Elvin Hayes	2063	Calvin Murphy	298

All Star Game

(The Forum, Los Angeles)

January 18	West Division	112		East Division	110

NBA Playoffs

March 28	Golden State Warriors	117	at	Milwaukee Bucks	106
March 28	Chicago Bulls	80	at	Los Angeles Lakers	95
March 29	Atlanta Hawks	108	at	Boston Celtics	126
March 30	Golden State Warriors	93	at	Milwaukee Bucks	118
March 30	Chicago Bulls	124	at	Los Angeles Lakers	131
March 31	Boston Celtics	104	at	Atlanta Hawks	113
March 31	N.Y. Knickerbockers	116	at	Baltimore Bullets	108 [OT]
April 1	Milwaukee Bucks	122	at	Golden State Warriors	94
April 2	Los Angeles Lakers	108	at	Chicago Bulls	101
April 2	Atlanta Hawks	113	at	Boston Celtics	136
April 2	Baltimore Bullets	88	at	N.Y. Knickerbockers	110
April 4	Milwaukee Bucks	106	at	Golden State Warriors	99
April 4	Los Angeles Lakers	108	at	Chicago Bulls	97
April 4	Boston Celtics	110	at	Atlanta Hawks	112
April 4	N.Y. Knickerbockers	103	at	Baltimore Bullets	104
April 6	Golden State Warriors	100	at	Milwaukee Bucks	108
April 6	Baltimore Bullets	98	at	N.Y. Knickerbockers	104
April 7	Atlanta Hawks	114	at	Boston Celtics	124
April 9	N.Y. Knickerbockers	106	at	Baltimore Bullets	82
April 9	Boston Celtics	127	at	Atlanta Hawks	118
April 9	Milwaukee Bucks	93	at	Los Angeles Lakers	72
April 11	Baltimore Bullets	101	at	N.Y. Knickerbockers	107
April 12	Milwaukee Bucks	134	at	Los Angeles Lakers	135
April 13	N.Y. Knickerbockers	116	at	Boston Celtics	94
April 14	Los Angeles Lakers	108	at	Milwaukee Bucks	105
April 16	Boston Celtics	105	at	N.Y. Knickerbockers	106
April 16	Los Angeles Lakers	88	at	Milwaukee Bucks	114
April 18	Milwaukee Bucks	90	at	Los Angeles Lakers	115
April 19	N.Y. Knickerbockers	109	at	Boston Celtics	115
April 21	Boston Celtics	98	at	N.Y. Knickerbockers	116
April 22	Los Angeles Lakers	104	at	Milwaukee Bucks	100
April 23	N.Y. Knickerbockers	111	at	Boston Celtics	103
April 26	N.Y. Knickerbockers	114	at	Los Angeles Lakers	92
April 30	N.Y. Knickerbockers	92	at	Los Angeles Lakers	106
May 3	Los Angeles Lakers	107	at	N.Y. Knickerbockers	96
May 5	Los Angeles Lakers	116	at	N.Y. Knickerbockers	111 [OT]
May 7	N.Y. Knickerbockers	100	at	Los Angeles Lakers	114

All Star Teams

First Team	Second Team
John Havlicek (Boston Celtics)	Bob Love (Chicago Bulls)
Spencer Haywood (Seattle SuperSonics)	Bill Cunningham (Philadelphia 76ers)
Kareem Abdul-Jabbar (Milwaukee Bucks)	Wilt Chamberlain (Los Angeles Lakers)
Jerry West (Los Angeles Lakers)	Nate Archibald (Cincinnati Royals)
Walt Frazier (N.Y. Knickerbockers)	Archie Clark (Philadelphia-Baltimore)

Individual Awards

Eddie Gottlieb Trophy--Sidney Wicks (Portland Trail Blazers)
Maurice Podoloff Trophy--Kareem Abdul-Jabbar (Milwaukee Bucks)
NBA All Star Game MVP--Jerry West (Los Angeles Lakers)
NBA Finals MVP--Wilt Chamberlain (Los Angeles Lakers)
Red Auerbach Trophy--Bill Sharman (Los Angeles Lakers)

Hall of Fame Inductees

Johnny Beckman, Bruce Drake, Dutch Lonborg, Elmer Ripley, Adolph Schayes, John Wooden

American Basketball Association

Eastern Division

Team Name	GP	W	L	PPGF	PPGA	Pct	GB
Kentucky Colonels	84	68	16	116.0	107.0	.810	-
Virginia Squires	84	45	39	118.9	118.0	.536	23
New York Nets	84	44	40	112.8	112.4	.524	24
Floridians	84	36	48	112.8	114.3	.429	32
Carolina Cougars	84	35	49	114.8	118.1	.417	33
Pittsburgh Condors	84	25	59	119.2	126.4	.298	43

Western Division

Team Name	GP	W	L	PPGF	PPGA	Pct	GB
Utah Stars	84	60	24	117.8	112.1	.714	-
Indiana Pacers	84	47	37	112.9	110.3	.560	13
Dallas Chaparrals	84	42	42	104.4	104.3	.500	18
Denver Rockets	84	34	50	111.9	113.1	.405	26
Memphis Pros	84	26	58	107.5	113.0	.310	34

Coaching Changes

Kentucky--Joe Mullaney 68-16; Floridians--Bob Bass 36-48; Carolina--Tom Meschery 35-49; Pittsburgh--Jack McMahon 4-6, Mark Binstein 21-43; Utah--LaDell Andersen 60-24; Dallas--Tom Nissalke 42-42; Denver--Alex Hannum 34-50.

League Leaders

Field Goals		Free Throws		Assists	
Charlie Scott	985	Rick Barry	641	Bill Melchionni	669
Dan Issel	972	Mack Calvin	611	Larry Brown	549
Ralph Simpson	920	Dan Issel	591	Louis Dampier	515
Julius Erving	910	Charlie Scott	525	Warren Jabali	495
Rick Barry	902	Zelmo Beaty	522	Jim Jones	485

Points		Fouls	
Dan Issel	2538	Wendell Ladner	347
Charlie Scott	2524	Julius Keye	346
Rick Barry	2518	Wilbert Jones	322
Ralph Simpson	2300	Mike Lewis	315
Julius Erving	2290	Zelmo Beaty	315

All Star Game
(Freedom Hall, Louisville)

January 29	East Division	142		West Division	115

ABA Playoffs

March 31	Denver Rockets	96	at	Indiana Pacers	102
March 31	Floridians	107	at	Virginia Squires	114 [OT]
April 1	New York Nets	122	at	Kentucky Colonels	108
April 1	Floridians	100	at	Virginia Squires	125
April 1	Dallas Chaparrals	96	at	Utah Stars	106
April 1	Denver Rockets	106	at	Indiana Pacers	105
April 3	Dallas Chaparrals	107	at	Utah Stars	113
April 4	New York Nets	105	at	Kentucky Colonels	90
April 4	Virginia Squires	118	at	Floridians	113
April 4	Indiana Pacers	122	at	Denver Rockets	120 [OT]
April 5	Utah Stars	96	at	Dallas Chaparrals	89
April 5	Kentucky Colonels	105	at	New York Nets	99
April 6	Virginia Squires	115	at	Floridians	106
April 6	Indiana Pacers	96	at	Denver Rockets	112
April 7	Kentucky Colonels	92	at	New York Nets	100
April 7	Utah Stars	103	at	Dallas Chaparrals	99
April 8	New York Nets	93	at	Kentucky Colonels	109
April 8	Denver Rockets	79	at	Indiana Pacers	91
April 9	Indiana Pacers	99	at	Denver Rockets	106
April 10	Kentucky Colonels	96	at	New York Nets	101
April 13	Denver Rockets	89	at	Indiana Pacers	91
April 13	New York Nets	91	at	Virginia Squires	138
April 15	Indiana Pacers	100	at	Utah Stars	108
April 15	New York Nets	106	at	Virginia Squires	115
April 17	Indiana Pacers	109	at	Utah Stars	117
April 19	Utah Stars	111	at	Indiana Pacers	116
April 22	Utah Stars	108	at	Indiana Pacers	118
April 24	Virginia Squires	117	at	New York Nets	119
April 24	Indiana Pacers	130	at	Utah Stars	139
April 26	Virginia Squires	107	at	New York Nets	118
April 26	Utah Stars	99	at	Indiana Pacers	105
April 29	New York Nets	107	at	Virginia Squires	116
May 1	Virginia Squires	136	at	New York Nets	146
May 1	Indiana Pacers	117	at	Utah Stars	113
May 4	New York Nets	94	at	Virginia Squires	88
May 6	New York Nets	103	at	Indiana Pacers	124
May 9	New York Nets	117	at	Indiana Pacers	115
May 12	Indiana Pacers	114	at	New York Nets	108
May 15	Indiana Pacers	105	at	New York Nets	110
May 18	New York Nets	99	at	Indiana Pacers	100
May 20	Indiana Pacers	108	at	New York Nets	105

All Star Teams

First Team	Second Teams
Rick Barry (New York Nets)	Willie Wise (Utah Stars)
Dan Issel (Kentucky Colonels)	Julius Erving (Virginia Squires)
Artis Gilmore (Kentucky Colonels)	Zelmo Beaty (Utah Stars)
Don Freeman (Dallas Chaparrals)	Ralph Simpson (Denver Rockets)
Bill Melchionni (New York Nets)	Charlie Scott (Virginia Squires)

Individual Awards

ABA All Star Game MVP--Dan Issel (Kentucky Colonels)
Coach of the Year--Tom Nissalke (Dallas Chaparrals)
Most Valuable Player--Artis Gilmore (Kentucky Colonels)
Rookie of the Year--Artis Gilmore (Kentucky Colonels)

Notes

Bob Carlson replaced Jack Dolph as Commissioner of the American Basketball Association.

FOOTBALL

National Football League
National Football Conference
Eastern Division

Team Name	GP	W	L	T	PF	PA	Pct
Washington Redskins	14	11	3	0	336	218	.786
Dallas Cowboys	14	10	4	0	319	240	.714
New York Giants	14	8	6	0	331	247	.571
St. Louis Cardinals	14	4	9	1	193	303	.321
Philadelphia Eagles	14	2	11	1	145	352	.179

Central Division

Team Name	GP	W	L	T	PF	PA	Pct
Green Bay Packers	14	10	4	0	304	226	.714
Detroit Lions	14	8	5	1	339	290	.607
Minnesota Vikings	14	7	7	0	301	252	.500
Chicago Bears	14	4	9	1	225	275	.321

Western Division

Team Name	GP	W	L	T	PF	PA	Pct
San Francisco 49ers	14	8	5	1	353	249	.607
Atlanta Falcons	14	7	7	0	269	274	.500
Los Angeles Rams	14	6	7	1	291	286	.464
New Orleans Saints	14	2	11	1	215	361	.179

American Football Conference
Eastern Division

Team Name	GP	W	L	T	PF	PA	Pct
Miami Dolphins	14	14	0	0	385	171	1.000
New York Jets	14	7	7	0	367	324	.500
Baltimore Colts	14	5	9	0	235	252	.357
Buffalo Bills	14	4	9	1	257	377	.321
New England Patriots	14	3	11	0	192	446	.214

Central Division

Team Name	GP	W	L	T	PF	PA	Pct
Pittsburgh Steelers	14	11	3	0	343	175	.786
Cleveland Browns	14	10	4	0	268	249	.714
Cincinnati Bengals	14	8	6	0	299	229	.571
Houston Oilers	14	1	13	0	164	380	.071

Western Division

Oakland Raiders	14	10	3	1	365	248	.750
Kansas City Chiefs	14	8	6	0	287	254	.571
Denver Broncos	14	5	9	0	325	350	.357
San Diego Chargers	14	4	9	1	264	344	.321

Coaching Changes

Philadelphia--Ed Khayat 2-11-1; Chicago--Abe Gibron 4-9-1; Baltimore--Don McCafferty 1-4-0, John Sandusky 4-5-0; Buffalo--Lou Saban 4-9-1; New England--John Mazur 2-7-0, Phil Bengston 1-4-0; Houston--Bill Peterson 1-13-0; Denver--John Ralston 5-9-0; San Diego--Harland Svare 4-9-1.

League Leaders

Yards Rushing		**Yards Passing**		**Passing %** (40 attempts)	
O.J. Simpson	1251	Joe Namath	2816	Sonny Jurgensen	66
Larry Brown	1216	Archie Manning	2781	John Brodie	64
Ron Johnson	1182	Fran Tarkenton	2651	Norm Snead	60
Larry Csonka	1117	John Hadl	2449	Ken Stabler	60
Marv Hubbard	1100	Craig Morton	2396	Fran Tarkenton	57

Receiving Yards		**Receptions**		**Field Goals**	
Harold Jackson	1048	Harold Jackson	62	Chester Marcol	33
John Gilliam	1035	Fred Biletnikoff	58	Roy Gerela	28
Gene Washington	918	Chip Myers	57	Horst Muhlmann	27
Rich Caster	833	Otis Taylor	57	Bob Howfield	27
Otis Taylor	821	Bob Tucker	55	Garo Yepremian	24

Punt Return Yards		**Kickoff Return Yards**	
Bruce Laird	303	Margene Adkins	1020
Tom Casanova	289	Ron Smith	924
Jim Bertelson	232	Bruce Laird	843
Ralph McGill	219	Rocky Thompson	821
Ken Ellis	215	Vic Washington	771

Pro Bowl Game

(Texas Stadium, Irving Texas)

January 21 1973	American Conference	33	National Conference	28

NFL Playoffs

December 23	Dallas Cowboys	30	at	San Francisco 49ers	28
December 23	Oakland Raiders	7	at	Pittsburgh Steelers	13
December 24	Green Bay Packers	3	at	Washington Redskins	16
December 24	Cleveland Browns	14	at	Miami Dolphins	20
December 31	Dallas Cowboys	3	at	Washington Redskins	26
December 31	Miami Dolphins	21	at	Pittsburgh Steelers	17

Super Bowl VII

(Memorial Coliseum, Los Angeles)

January 14 1973	Miami Dolphins	14	Washington Redskins	7

Individual Awards

AP MVP--Larry Brown (Washington Redskins)
Bert Bell Trophy--Franco Harris (Pittsburgh Steelers) [World Almanac]
Willie Buchanan (Green Bay Packers)
Bert Bell Trophy--Larry Brown (Washington Redskins)
George Halas Trophy--Joe Greene (Pittsburgh Steelers)
Jim Thorpe Trophy--Larry Brown (Washington Redskins)
Pro Bowl MVP--O.J. Simpson (Buffalo Bills)
Rookie of the Year--Franco Harris (Pittsburgh Steelers)
Willie Buchanan (Green Bay Packers)
Chester Marcol (Green Bay Packers)
Super Bowl MVP--Jake Scott (Miami Dolphins)
U.P.I. AFC Coach of the Year--Chuck Noll (Pittsburgh Steelers)
U.P.I. AFC Player of the Year--O.J. Simpson (Buffalo Bills)
U.P.I. AFC Rookie of the Year--Franco Harris (Pittsburgh Steelers)
U.P.I. NFC Coach of the year--Dan Devine (Green Bay Packers)
U.P.I. NFC Player of the Year--Larry Brown (Washington Redskins)
U.P.I. NFC Rookie of the Year--Chester Marcol (Green Bay Packers)

Hall of Fame Inductees

Lamar Hunt, Gino Marchetti, Ollie Matson, Clarence Parker

Canadian Football League
Eastern Conference

Team Name	GP	W	L	T	PF	PA	Pts	Pct
Hamilton Tiger-Cats	14	11	3	0	372	262	22	.786
Ottawa Rough Riders	14	11	3	0	298	228	22	.786
Montreal Alouettes	14	4	10	0	246	353	8	.286
Toronto Argonauts	14	3	11	0	254	298	6	.214

Western Conference

Team Name	GP	W	L	T	PF	PA	Pts	Pct
Winnipeg Blue Bombers	16	10	6	0	401	300	20	.625
Edmonton Eskimos	16	10	6	0	380	368	20	.625
Saskatchewan Roughriders	16	8	8	0	330	283	16	.500
Calgary Stampeders	16	6	10	0	331	394	12	.375
British Columbia Lions	16	5	11	0	254	380	10	.313

Coaching Changes

Hamilton--Jerry Williams 11-3-0.

League Leaders

Yards Rushing		Yards Passing		Passing %	
Mack Herron	1527	Don Jonas	3583	Don Jonas	56
Dave Buchanan	1163				
George Reed	1069				
George McGowan	1015				
Gerry Shaw	1002				

Receiving Yards		Receptions		Points	
Jim Young	1362	Jim Thorpe	70	Gerry Organ	131
Jim Thorpe	1260				
Eric Allen	1067				

All Star Game
(McMahon Stadium, Calgary)

June 28	Calgary Stampeders	23		All Stars	22

Grey Cup Playoffs

November 11	Montreal Alouettes	11	at	Ottawa Rough Riders	14
November 12	Saskatchewan Roughriders	8	at	Edmonton Eskimos	6
November 18	Hamilton Tiger-Cats	7	at	Ottawa Rough Riders	19
November 19	Saskatchewan Roughriders	27	at	Winnipeg Blue Bombers	24
November 26	Ottawa Rough Riders	8	at	Hamilton Tiger-Cats	23
December 3	Saskatchewan Roughriders	10	at	Hamilton Tiger-Cats	13

Individual Awards

Annis Stukus Trophy--Jack Gotta (Ottawa Rough Riders)
Dave Dryburgh Memorial Trophy--Dave Cutler (Edmonton Eskimos)
DeMarco-Becket Memorial Trophy--John Helton (Calgary Stampeders)
Dr. Beattie Martin Trophy--Walt McKee (Winnipeg Blue Bombers)
Eddie James Memorial Trophy--Mack Herron (Winnipeg Blue Bombers)
Grey Cup Most Valuable Canadian--Ian Sunter (Hamilton Tiger-Cats)
Grey Cup MVP--Chuck Ealey (Hamilton Tiger-Cats)
Gruen Trophy--Bob Richardson (Hamilton Tiger-Cats)
Jeff Nicklin Memorial Trophy--Mack Herron (Winnipeg Blue Bombers)
Jeff Russel Memorial Trophy-Garney Henley (Hamilton Tiger--Cats)
Schenley Award Most Outstanding Canadian--Jim Young (British Columbia Lions)
Schenley Award Most Outstanding Lineman--John Helton (Calgary Stampeders)
Schenley Award Most Outstanding Player--Garney Henley (Hamilton Tiger-Cats)
Schenley Award Most Outstanding Rookie--Chuck Ealey (Hamilton Tiger-Cats)

HOCKEY

National Hockey League
Eastern Division

Team Name	GP	W	L	T	GF	GA	Pts	Pct
Boston Bruins	78	54	13	11	330	204	119	.763
New York Rangers	78	48	17	13	317	192	109	.699
Montreal Canadiens	78	46	16	16	307	205	108	.692
Toronto Maple Leafs	78	33	11	14	209	208	80	.513
Detroit Red Wings	78	33	35	10	261	262	76	.487
Buffalo Sabres	78	16	43	19	203	289	51	.327
Vancouver Canucks	78	20	50	8	203	287	48	.308

Western Division

Chicago Black Hawks	78	46	17	15	256	166	107	.686
Minnesota North Stars	78	37	29	12	212	191	86	.551
St. Louis Blues	78	28	39	11	208	247	67	.429
Pittsburgh Penguins	78	26	38	14	220	258	66	.423
Philadelphia Flyers	78	26	38	14	200	236	66	.423
California Golden Seals	78	21	39	18	216	288	60	.385
Los Angeles Kings	78	20	49	9	206	305	49	.314

Coaching Changes

Montreal--Scotty Bowman 46-16-16; Toronto--John McLellan 24-28-11, "King" Clancy 9-3-3; Detroit--Doug Barkley 3-8-0, John Wilson 30-27-10; Buffalo--George Imlach 8-23-10, Floyd Smith 0-1-0, Joe Crozier 8-19-9; St. Louis--Sid Abel 3-6-1, Bill McCreary 6-14-4, Al Arbour 19-19-6; Philadelphia--Fred Shero 26-38-14; California--Fred Glover 0-1-2, Vic Stasiuk 21-38-16; Los Angeles--Larry Regan 2-7-1, Fred Glover 18-42-8.

League Leaders

Goals		Assists		Points	
Phil Esposito	66	Bobby Orr	80	Phil Esposito	133
Vic Hadfield	50	Phil Esposito	67	Bobby Orr	117
Yvan Cournoyer	47	Jean Ratelle	63	Jean Ratelle	109
Jean Ratelle	46	Vic Hadfield	56	Vic Hadfield	106
Rick Martin	44	Fred Stanfield	56	Rod Gilbert	97

Penalty Minutes		GAA		Wins	
Bryan Watson	212	Tony Esposito	1.77	Ken Dryden	39
Keith Magnuson	201	Gilles Villemure	2.09	Tony Esposito	31
Gary Dornhoefer	183	Lorne Worsley	2.12	Gerry Cheevers	27
Barclay Plager	176	Ken Dryden	2.24	Ed Johnston	27
Rick Foley	168	Gary Smith	2.42	Gilles Villemure	24

Shutouts	
Tony Esposito	9
Ken Dryden	8
Doug Favell	5
Gilles Meloche	4
Al Smith	4

All Star Game

(Metropolitan Sports Center, Minneapolis)

January 25	East Division	3		West Division	2

Stanley Cup Playoffs

April 5	St. Louis Blues	0	at	Minnesota North Stars	3
April 5	Toronto Maple Leafs	0	at	Boston Bruins	5
April 5	Montreal Canadiens	2	at	New York Rangers	3
April 5	Pittsburgh Penguins	1	at	Chicago Black Hawks	3
April 6	Toronto Maple Leafs	4	at	Boston Bruins	3 [2:58]

April 6	Montreal Canadiens	2	at	New York Rangers	5
April 6	Pittsburgh Penguins	2	at	Chicago Black Hawks	3
April 6	St. Louis Blues	5	at	Minnesota North Stars	6 [1:36]
April 8	Boston Bruins	2	at	Toronto Maple Leafs	0
April 8	New York Rangers	1	at	Montreal Canadiens	2
April 8	Chicago Black Hawks	2	at	Pittsburgh Penguins	0
April 8	Minnesota North Stars	1	at	St. Louis Blues	2
April 9	Boston Bruins	5	at	Toronto Maple Leafs	4
April 9	New York Rangers	6	at	Montreal Canadiens	4
April 9	Chicago Black Hawks	6	at	Pittsburgh Penguins	5 [0:12]
April 9	Minnesota North Stars	2	at	St. Louis Blues	3
April 11	Toronto Maple Leafs	2	at	Boston Bruins	3
April 11	Montreal Canadiens	2	at	New York Rangers	1
April 11	St. Louis Blues	3	at	Minnesota North Stars	4
April 13	New York Rangers	3	at	Montreal Canadiens	2
April 13	Minnesota North Stars	2	at	St. Louis Blues	4
April 16	St. Louis Blues	2	at	Minnesota North Stars	1 [10:07]
April 16	New York Rangers	3	at	Chicago Black Hawks	2
April 18	St. Louis Blues	1	at	Boston Bruins	6
April 18	New York Rangers	5	at	Chicago Black Hawks	3
April 20	St. Louis Blues	2	at	Boston Bruins	10
April 20	Chicago Black Hawks	2	at	New York Rangers	3
April 23	Boston Bruins	7	at	St. Louis Blues	2
April 23	Chicago Black Hawks	2	at	New York Rangers	6
April 25	Boston Bruins	5	at	St. Louis Blues	3
April 30	New York Rangers	5	at	Boston Bruins	6
May 2	New York Rangers	1	at	Boston Bruins	2
May 4	Boston Bruins	2	at	New York Rangers	5
May 7	Boston Bruins	3	at	New York Rangers	2
May 9	New York Rangers	3	at	Boston Bruins	2
May 11	Boston Bruins	3	at	New York Rangers	0

All Star Teams

First Team		Second Team
Tony Esposito	Goal	Ken Dryden
Bobby Orr	Defense	Bill White
Brad Park	Defense	Pat Stapleton
Phil Esposito	Center	Jean Ratelle
Rod Gilbert	Right Wing	Yvan Cournoyer
Bobby Hull	Left Wing	Vic Hadfield

Individual Awards

Art Ross Trophy--Phil Esposito (Boston Bruins)
Bill Masterton Trophy--Bobby Clarke (Philadelphia Flyers)
Calder Memorial Trophy--Ken Dryden (Montreal Canadiens)
Conn Smythe Trophy--Bobby Orr (Boston Bruins)
Hart Memorial Trophy--Bobby Orr (Boston Bruins)
James Norris Trophy--Bobby Orr (Boston Bruins)
Lady Byng Memorial Trophy--Jean Ratelle (New York Rangers)
Lester Patrick Trophy--Clarence Campbell, John Kelly, Ralph Weiland, James Norris.
Lester B. Pearson Award--Jean Ratelle (New York Rangers)
NHL All Star Game MVP--Bobby Orr (Boston Bruins)
Vezina Trophy--Tony Esposito and Gary Smith (Chicago Black Hawks)

Hall of Fame Inductees

Weston Adams, Jean Beliveau, Bernie Geoffrion, Harry Holmes, Gordie Howe, Hooley Smith

Rules

The third man to enter a fight was to be given a game misconduct.

SOCCER

North American Soccer League
Northern Division

Team Name	GP	W	L	T	GF	GA	BP	Pts	Pct
New York Cosmos	14	7	3	4	28	16	23	77	.611
Rochester Lancers	14	6	5	3	20	22	19	64	.508
Montreal Olympiques	14	4	5	5	19	20	18	57	.452
Toronto Metros	14	4	6	4	18	22	17	53	.421

Southern Division

Team Name	GP	W	L	T	GF	GA	BP	Pts	Pct
St. Louis Stars	14	7	4	3	20	14	18	69	.548
Dallas Tornado	14	6	5	3	15	12	15	60	.476
Atlanta Chiefs	14	5	6	3	19	18	17	56	.444
Miami Gatos	14	3	8	3	17	32	17	44	.349

Coaching Changes

Rochester--Adolfo Gori 6-5-3; Montreal--Graham Adams 4-5-5; St. Louis--Casey Frankiewicz 7-4-3; Miami--Sal DeRosa, Norm Sutherland.

League Leaders

Goals		Points		Shutouts	
Randy Horton	9	Randy Horton	22	Ken Cooper	6
Michael Dillon	8	Michael Dillon	18	Manfred Kammerer	4
Paul Child	8	Paul Child	17	Claude Campos	4
Willie Roy	7	Warren Archibald	17	Sam Nusum	4
Warren Archibald	6	Willie Roy	16	Paulo Dias	3

GAA	
Ken Cooper	0.86
Mike Winter	1.00
Manfred Kammerer	1.14
Richard Blackmore	1.14
Dick Howard	1.31

NASL Playoffs

August 15	Rochester Lancers	0	at	St. Louis Stars	2
August 19	Dallas Tornado	0	at	New York Cosmos	1
August 26	St. Louis Stars	1	at	New York Cosmos	2

All Star Teams

First Team		Second Team
Ken Cooper	Goal	Dick Howard
John Best	Defender	Dick Hall
John Sewell	Defender	Clive Charles
Peter Short	Defender	Wilf Tranter
Willie Evans	Defender	Brian Rowan
John Kerr	Midfield	Francisco Escos
Graeme Souness	Midfield	Dave Metchik
Pat McBride	Midfield	Siggy Stritzi
Randy Horton	Forward	Carlos Metidieri
Paul Child	Forward	Art Welch
Michael Dillon	Forward	Jorge Siega

Individual Awards

Lead Goalkeeper Award--Ken Cooper (Dallas Tornado)
Coach of the Year--Casey Frankiewicz (St. Louis Stars)
Most Valuable Player--Randy Horton (New York Cosmos)
Rookie of the Year--Mike Winter (St. Louis Stars)

Franchise Changes

AL--Washington Senators became the Texas Rangers.
NBA--San Diego Rockets became the Houston Rockets.
NBA--San Francisco Warriors changed their name to Golden State Warriors.
ABA--Texas Chaparrals became the Dallas Chaparrals.
NASL--Washington Darts became the Miami Gatos.

Other Sports

Horseracing--Kentucky Derby won by Riva Ridge (time 2:01.8, purse $140,300).
Heavyweight Boxing--Joe Frazier knocked-out Terry Daniels in 4 rounds.
Joe Frazier knocked-out Ron Stander in 5 rounds.
Golf--U.S. Open won by Jack Nicklaus with a score of 290.
Auto Racing--Indianapolis 500 won by Mark Donahue (ave. speed 163.465 MPH).
Tennis--U.S. Open won by Ilie Nastase in the men's singles.
U.S. Open won by Cliff Drysdale and Roger Taylor in the men's doubles.
U.S. Open won by Billie Jean King in the women's singles.
U.S. Open won by Francoise Durr and Betty Stove in the women's doubles.
U.S. Open won by Margaret Smith Court and Marty Riessen in the mixed doubles.

1973

BASEBALL
National League

East

Team Name	W	L	Pct	GB	R	OR
New York Mets	82	79	.509	-	608	588
St. Louis Cardinals	81	81	.500	1.5	643	603
Pittsburgh Pirates	80	82	.494	2.5	704	693
Montreal Expos	79	83	.488	3.5	668	702
Chicago Cubs	77	84	.478	5	614	655
Philadelphia Phillies	71	91	.438	11.5	642	717

West

Team Name	W	L	Pct	GB	R	OR
Cincinnati Reds	99	63	.611	-	741	557
Los Angeles Dodgers	95	66	.590	3.5	675	565
San -Francisco Giants	88	74	.543	11	739	702
Houston Astros	82	80	.506	17	681	672
Atlanta Braves	76	85	.472	22.5	799	774
San Diego Padres	60	102	.370	39	548	770

Coaching Changes

Pittsburgh--Bill Virdon 67-69, Danny Murtaugh 13-13; Chicago--Walter Lockman 77-84; Philadelphia--Danny Ozark 71-91; Houston--Leo Durocher 82-80; Atlanta--Eddie Mathews 76-85; San Diego--Don Zimmer 60-102.

League Leaders

Batting Average

Pete Rose	.338
Cesar Cedeno	.320
Garry Maddox	.319
Tony Perez	.314
Bob Watson	.312

Home Runs

Willie Stargell	44
Dave Johnson	43
Darrell Evans	41
Hank Aaron	40
Bobby Bonds	39

RBI

Willie Stargell	119
Lee May	105
Johnny Bench	104
Darrell Evans	104
Ken Singleton	103

Stolen Bases

Lou Brock	70
Joe Morgan	67
Cesar Cedeno	56
Bobby Bonds	43
Dave Lopes	36

ERA

Tom Seaver	2.08
Don Sutton	2.42
Wayne Twitchell	2.50
Mike Marshall	2.66
Andy Messersmith	2.70

Wins

Ron Bryant	24
Jack Billingham	19
Tom Seaver	19
Don Sutton	18
Don Gullett	18

Saves

Mike Marshall	31
Tug McGraw	25
Dave Giusti	20
Jim Brewer	20
Bob Locker	18

Strikeouts

Tom Seaver	251
Steve Carlton	223
Jon Matlack	205
Don Sutton	200
Andy Messersmith	177

NLCS

October 6	New York Mets	1	at	Cincinnati Reds	2
October 7	New York Mets	5	at	Cincinnati Reds	0
October 8	Cincinnati Reds	2	at	New York Mets	9
October 9	Cincinnati Reds	2	at	New York Mets	1 [12]
October 10	Cincinnati Reds	2	at	New York Mets	7

American League

East

Team Name	W	L	Pct	GB	R	OR
Baltimore Orioles	97	65	.599	-	754	561
Boston Red Sox	89	73	.549	8	738	647
Detroit Tigers	85	77	.525	12	642	674
New York Yankees	80	82	.494	17	641	610
Milwaukee Brewers	74	88	.457	23	708	731
Cleveland Indians	71	91	.438	26	679	826

West

Team Name	W	L	Pct	GB	R	OR
Oakland Athletics	94	68	.580	-	758	615
Kansas City Royals	88	74	.543	6	754	752
Minnesota Twins	81	81	.500	13	738	692
California Angels	79	83	.488	15	629	657
Chicago White Sox	77	85	.475	17	652	705
Texas Rangers	57	105	.352	37	619	844

Coaching Changes

Detroit--Billy-Martin 76-67, Joseph Schultz 9-10; Milwaukee--Del Crandall 74-88; Kansas City--Jack McKeon 88-74; Minnesota--Frank Quilici 8i-81; California--Bob Winkles 79-83; Texas--"Whitey" Herzog 47-91, Billy Martin 9-14, Del Wilber 1-0.

League Leaders

Batting Average		Home Runs		RBI	
Rod Carew	.350	Reggie Jackson	32	Reggie Jackson	117
George Scott	.306	Frank Robinson	30	George Scott	107
Tom Davis	.306	Jeff Burroughs	30	John Mayberry	100
Bob Murcer	.304	Sal Bando	29	Sal Bando	98
Dave May	.303	Carlton Fisk	26	Frank Robinson	97

Stolen Bases		ERA		Wins	
Tom Harper	54	Jim Palmer	2.40	Wilbur Wood	24
Bill North	53	Bert Blyleven	2.52	Joe Coleman	23
Dave Nelson	43	Bill Lee	2.74	Jim Palmer	22
Rod Carew	41	Nolan Ryan	2.87	James Hunter	21
Fred Patek	36	George Medich	2.91	Ken Holtzman	21

Saves		Strikeouts	
John Hiller	38	Nolan Ryan	383
Albert Lyle	27	Bert Blyleven	258
Rollie Fingers	22	Bill Singer	241
Doug Bird	20	Gaylord Perry	238
Cecilio Acosta	18	Mickey Lolich	214

All Star Game

(Royals Stadium, Kansas City)

July 24	National League	7		American League	1

ALCS

October 6	Oakland Athletics	0	at	Baltimore Orioles	6
October 7	Oakland Athletics	6	at	Baltimore Orioles	3
October 9	Baltimore Orioles	1	at	Oakland Athletics	2 [11]
October 10	Baltimore Orioles	5	at	Oakland Athletics	4
October 11	Baltimore Orioles	0	at	Oakland Athletics	3

World Series

October 13	New York Mets	1	at	Oakland Athletics	2
October 14	New York Mets	10	at	Oakland Athletics	7 [12]
October 16	Oakland Athletics	3	at	New York Mets	2
October 17	Oakland Athletics	1	at	New York Mets	6
October 18	Oakland Athletics	0	at	New York Mets	2
October 20	New York Mets	1	at	Oakland Athletics	3
October 21	New York Mets	2	at	Oakland Athletics	5

Individual Awards

Arch Ward Memorial Trophy--Bobby Bonds (San Francisco Giants NL)
Baseball Writers Award--Pete Rose (Cincinnati Reds NL)
Reggie Jackson (Oakland Athletics AL)
Cy Young Award--Tom Seaver (New York Mets NL)
Jim Palmer (Baltimore Orioles AL)
Rookie of the Year--Gary Matthews (San Francisco Giants NL)
Al Bumbry (Baltimore Orioles AL)
Sporting News Executive of the Year--Bob Howsam (Cincinnati Reds NL)
Sporting News Manager of the Year--Gene Mauch (Montreal Expos NL)
Sporting News Pitcher of the Year--Ron Bryant (San Francisco Giants NL)
Jim Palmer (Baltimore Orioles AL)
Sporting News Player of the Year--Bobby Bonds (San Francisco Giants NL)
Reggie Jackson (Oakland Athletics AL)
Sporting News Rookie of the Year--Gary Matthews (San Francisco Giants NL)
Steve Rogers(Montreal Expos NL)
Al Bumbry(Baltimore Orioles AL)
Steve Bushy (Kansas City Royals AL)
World Series MVP--Reggie Jackson (Oakland Athletics AL)

Hall of Fame Inductees

Roberto Clemente, Bill Evans, Monte Irvin, George Kelly, Warren Spahn, Mickey Welch

Rules

The American League voted unanimously to adopt the designated hitter rule on a three year experimental basis.

BASKETBALL
National Basketball Association

Atlantic Division

Team Name	GP	W	L	PPGF	PPGA	Pct	GB
Boston Celtics	82	68	14	112.7	104.5	.829	-
New York Knickerbockers	82	57	25	105.0	98.2	.695	11
Buffalo Braves	82	21	61	103.3	112.5	.256	47
Philadelphia 76ers	82	9	73	104.1	116.2	.110	59

Central Division

Team Name	GP	W	L	PPGF	PPGA	Pct	GB
Baltimore Bullets	82	52	30	105.0	101.6	.634	-
Atlanta Hawks	82	46	36	112.4	112.3	.561	6
Houston Rockets	82	33	49	112.8	114.5	.402	19
Cleveland Cavaliers	82	32	50	102.7	105.3	.390	20

Midwest Division

Team Name	GP	W	L	PPGF	PPGA	Pct	GB
Milwaukee Bucks	82	60	22	107.2	99.0	.732	-
Chicago Bulls	82	51	31	104.1	100.6	.622	9
Detroit Pistons	82	40	42	110.3	110.0	.488	20
Kansas City-Omaha Kings	82	36	46	107.6	110.5	.439	24

Pacific Division

Team Name	GP	W	L	PPGF	PPGA	Pct	GB
Los Angeles Lakers	82	60	22	111.7	103.2	.732	-
Golden State Warriors	82	47	35	108.8	105.7	.573	13
Phoenix Suns	82	38	44	111.6	112.9	.463	22
Seattle SuperSonics	82	26	56	103.7	109.6	.317	34
Portland Trail Blazers	82	21	61	106.2	112.4	.256	39

Coaching Changes

Buffalo--Jack Ramsay 21-61; Philadelphia--Roy Rubin 4-47, Kevin Loughery 5-26; Houston--Tex Winter 17-30, Johnny Egan 16-19; Detroit--Earl Lloyd 2-5, Ray Scott 38-37; Kansas City-Omaha--Bob Cousy 36-46; Phoenix--Butch Van Breda Kolff 3-5, Jerry Colangelo 35-39; Seattle--Tom Nissalke 13-32, Bucky Buckwalter 13-24; Portland--Jack McCloskey 21-61.

League Leaders

Field Goals		Free Throws		Assists	
Nate Archibald	1028	Nate Archibald	663	Nate Archibald	910
Kareem Abdul-Jabbar	982	Pete Maravich	485	Dave Bing	637
Spencer Haywood	889	Spencer Haywood	473	Lenny Wilkens	628
Geoff Petrie	836	Dave Bing	456	Norm Van Lier	567
Lou Hudson	816	Charlie Scott	436	Oscar Robertson	551

Points		Fouls	
Nate Archibald	2719	Neal Walk	323
Kareem Abdul-Jabbar	2292	Dave Cowens	311
Spencer Haywood	2251	Charlie Scott	306
Pete Maravich	2063	Lloyd Neal	305
Charlie Scott	2048	Mike Newlin	301

All Star Game

(Chicago Stadium, Chicago)

January 23	East Division	104		West Division	84

NBA Playoffs

March 30	Golden State Warriors	90	at	Milwaukee Bucks	110
March 30	Baltimore Bullets	83	at	N.Y. Knickerbockers	95
March 30	Chicago Bulls	104	at	Los Angeles Lakers	107 [OT]
April 1	Baltimore Bullets	103	at	N.Y. Knickerbockers	123
April 1	Atlanta Hawks	109	at	Boston Celtics	134
April 1	Golden State Warriors	95	at	Milwaukee Bucks	92
April 1	Chicago Bulls	93	at	Los Angeles Lakers	108
April 4	Boston Celtics	126	at	Atlanta Hawks	113
April 4	N.Y. Knickerbockers	103	at	Baltimore Bullets	96
April 5	Milwaukee Bucks	113	at	Golden State Warriors	93
April 6	Atlanta Hawks	118	at	Boston Celtics	105
April 6	N.Y. Knickerbockers	89	at	Baltimore Bullets	97
April 6	Los Angeles Lakers	86	at	Chicago Bulls	96
April 7	Milwaukee Bucks	97	at	Golden State Warriors	102
April 8	Boston Celtics	94	at	Atlanta Hawks	97
April 8	Baltimore Bullets	99	at	N.Y. Knickerbockers	109
April 8	Los Angeles Lakers	94	at	Chicago Bulls	98
April 10	Golden State Warriors	100	at	Milwaukee Bucks	97
April 10	Chicago Bulls	102	at	Los Angeles Lakers	123
April 11	Atlanta Hawks	101	at	Boston Celtics	108
April 13	Boston Celtics	121	at	Atlanta Hawks	103
April 13	Milwaukee Bucks	86	at	Golden State Warriors	100
April 13	Los Angeles Lakers	93	at	Chicago Bulls	101
April 15	Chicago Bulls	92	at	Los Angeles Lakers	95
April 15	N.Y. Knickerbockers	108	at	Boston Celtics	134
April 17	Golden State Warriors	99	at	Los Angeles Lakers	101
April 18	Boston Celtics	96	at	N.Y. Knickerbockers	129
April 19	Golden State Warriors	93	at	Los Angeles Lakers	104
April 20	N.Y. Knickerbockers	98	at	Boston Celtics	91
April 21	Los Angeles Lakers	126	at	Golden State Warriors	70
April 21	Boston Celtics	110	at	N.Y. Knickerbockers	117 [OT]
April 23	Los Angeles Lakers	109	at	Golden State Warriors	117
April 25	Golden State Warriors	118	at	Los Angeles Lakers	128
April 25	N.Y. Knickerbockers	97	at	Boston Celtics	98
April 27	Boston Celtics	110	at	N.Y. Knickerbockers	100
April 29	N.Y. Knickerbockers	94	at	Boston Celtics	78
May 1	N.Y. Knickerbockers	112	at	Los Angeles Lakers	115
May 3	N.Y. Knickerbockers	99	at	Los Angeles Lakers	95
May 6	Los Angeles Lakers	83	at	N.Y. Knickerbockers	87
May 8	Los Angeles Lakers	98	at	N.Y. Knickerbockers	103
May 10	N.Y. Knickerbockers	102	at	Los Angeles Lakers	93

All Star Teams

First Team

John Havlicek (Boston Celtics)
Spencer Haywood (Seattle SuperSonics)
Kareem Abdul-Jabbar (Milwaukee Bucks)
Nate Archibald (Kansas City-Omaha)
Jerry West (Los Angeles Lakers)

Second Team

Elvin Hayes (Baltimore Bullets)
Rick Barry (Golden State Warriors)
Dave Cowens (Boston Celtics)
Walt Frazier (N.Y. Knickerbockers)
Pete Maravich (Atlanta Hawks)

Individual Awards

Eddie Gottlieb Trophy--Bob McAdoo (Buffalo Braves)
Maurice Podoloff Trophy--Dave Cowens (Boston Celtics)
NBA All Star Game MVP--Dave Cowens (Boston Celtics)
NBA Executive of the Year--Joe Axelson (Kansas City-Omaha)
NBA Finals MVP--Willis Reed (New York Knickerbockers)
Red Auerbach Trophy--Tommy Heinsohn (Boston Celtics)

Hall of Fame Inductees

Harry Fisher, Maurice Podoloff, Ernest Schmidt

American Basketball Association

Eastern Division

Team Name	GP	W	L	PPGF	PPGA	Pct	GB
Carolina Cougars	84	57	27	115.6	110.7	.679	-
Kentucky Colonels	84	56	28	111.9	105.5	.667	1
Virginia Squires	84	42	42	115.4	115.8	.500	15
New York Nets	84	30	54	103.6	110.1	.357	27
Memphis Tams	84	24	60	111.5	118.1	.286	33

Western Division

Team Name	GP	W	L	PPGF	PPGA	Pct	GB
Utah Stars	84	55	29	115.6	110.0	.655	-
Indiana Pacers	84	51	33	114.7	112.5	.607	4
Denver Rockets	84	47	37	110.8	107.6	.560	8
San Diego Conquistadors	84	30	54	109.0	113.3	.357	25
Dallas Chaparrals	84	28	56	110.7	115.1	.333	27

Coaching Changes

Carolina--Larry Brown 57-27; Memphis--Bob Bass 24-60; San Diego--K.C. Jones 30-54; Dallas--Babe McCarthy 24-48, Dave Brown 4-8.

League Leaders

Field Goals		Free Throws		Assists	
Dan Issel	902	George Thompson	549	Chuck Williams	582
Julius Erving	894	George McGinnis	517	Warren Jabali	539
George McGinnis	868	Mack Calvin	500	Bill Cunningham	530
Bill Cunningham	771	Chuck Williams	493	Louie Dampier	521
Stew Johnson	769	Dan Issel	485	Al Smith	477

Points		Fouls	
Dan Issel	2292	Gene Moore	369
Julius Erving	2268	George McGinnis	348
George McGinnis	2261	Tom Owens	318
Bill Cunningham	2028	Mel Daniels	315
Ralph Simpson	1890	Bill Cunningham	309

All Star Game

(The Salt Palace, Salt Lake City)

February 6	East Division	111	West Division	123

ABA Playoffs

Date	Visitor	Score		Home	Score
March 30	New York Nets	96	at	Carolina Cougars	104
March 30	Virginia Squires	101	at	Kentucky Colonels	129
March 31	Denver Rockets	91	at	Indiana Pacers	114
March 31	New York Nets	114	at	Carolina Cougars	111
April 1	Virginia Squires	109	at	Kentucky Colonels	94
April 1	Denver Rockets	93	at	Indiana Pacers	106
April 2	San Diego Conquistadors	93	at	Utah Stars	107
April 3	Carolina Cougars	101	at	New York Nets	91
April 3	Kentucky Colonels	115	at	Virginia Squires	113
April 3	Indiana Pacers	94	at	Denver Rockets	105
April 4	San Diego Conquistadors	92	at	Utah Stars	103
April 5	Carolina Cougars	112	at	New York Nets	108
April 5	Indiana Pacers	97	at	Denver Rockets	95
April 6	New York Nets	113	at	Carolina Cougars	136
April 6	Kentucky Colonels	108	at	Virginia Squires	90
April 7	Virginia Squires	103	at	Kentucky Colonels	114
April 7	Utah Stars	97	at	San Diego Conquistadors	96
April 7	Denver Rockets	107	at	Indiana Pacers	121
April 8	Utah Stars	120	at	San Diego Conquistadors	98
April 11	Kentucky Colonels	113	at	Carolina Cougars	103
April 12	Indiana Pacers	107	at	Utah Stars	124
April 14	Indiana Pacers	116	at	Utah Stars	110
April 14	Kentucky Colonels	105	at	Carolina Cougars	125
April 16	Utah Stars	108	at	Indiana Pacers	118
April 16	Carolina Cougars	94	at	Kentucky Colonels	108
April 18	Utah Stars	104	at	Indiana Pacers	103
April 18	Carolina Cougars	102	at	Kentucky Colonels	91
April 19	Indiana Pacers	104	at	Utah Stars	102
April 20	Kentucky Colonels	107	at	Carolina Cougars	112
April 21	Carolina Cougars	100	at	Kentucky Colonels	119
April 21	Utah Stars	98	at	Indiana Pacers	107
April 24	Kentucky Colonels	107	at	Carolina Cougars	96
April 28	Indiana Pacers	111	at	Kentucky Colonels	107
April 30	Indiana Pacers	102	at	Kentucky Colonels	114
May 3	Kentucky Colonels	92	at	Indiana Pacers	88
May 5	Kentucky Colonels	86	at	Indiana Pacers	90
May 8	Indiana Pacers	89	at	Kentucky Colonels	86
May 10	Kentucky Colonels	109	at	Indiana Pacers	93
May 12	Indiana Pacers	88	at	Kentucky Colonels	81

All Star Teams

First Team

Bill Cunningham (Carolina Cougars)
Julius Erving (Virginia Squires)
Artis Gilmore (Kentucky Colonels)
James Jones (Utah Stars)
Warren Jabali (Denver Rockets)

Second Team

George McGinnis (Indiana Pacers)
Dan Issel (Kentucky Colonels)
Mel Daniels (Indiana Pacers)
Ralph Simpson (Denver Rockets)
Mack Calvin (Carolina Cougars)

Individual Awards

ABA All Star Game MVP--Warren Jabali (Denver Rockets)
Coach of the Year--Larry Brown (Carolina Cougars)
Most Valuable Player--Billy Cunningham (Carolina Cougars)
Rookie of the Year--Brian Taylor (New York Nets)

Notes

Mike Storen became the ABA's new Commissioner, replacing Bob Carlson.

FOOTBALL
National Football League

National Football Conference
Eastern Division

Team Name	GP	W	L	T	PF	PA	Pct
Dallas Cowboys	14	10	4	0	382	203	.714
Washington Redskins	14	10	4	0	325	198	.714
Philadelphia Eagles	14	5	8	1	310	393	.393
St. Louis Cardinals	14	4	9	1	286	365	.321
New York Giants	14	2	11	1	226	362	.179

Central Division

Team Name	GP	W	L	T	PF	PA	Pct
Minnesota Vikings	14	12	2	0	296	168	.857
Detroit Lions	14	6	7	1	271	247	.464
Green Bay Packers	14	5	7	2	202	259	.429
Chicago Bears	14	3	11	0	195	334	.214

Western Division

Team Name	GP	W	L	T	PF	PA	Pct
Los Angeles Rams	14	12	2	0	388	178	.857
Atlanta Falcons	14	9	5	0	318	224	.643
San Francisco 49ers	14	5	9	0	262	319	.357
New Orleans Saints	14	5	9	0	163	312	.357

American Football Conference

Eastern Division

Team Name	GP	W	L	T	PF	PA	Pct
Miami Dolphins	14	12	2	0	343	150	.857
Buffalo Bills	14	9	5	0	259	230	.643
New England Patriots	14	5	9	0	258	300	.357
New York Jets	14	4	10	0	240	306	.286
Baltimore Colts	14	4	10	0	226	341	.286

Central Division

Team Name	GP	W	L	T	PF	PA	Pct
Cincinnati Bengals	14	10	4	0	286	231	.714
Pittsburgh Steelers	14	10	4	0	347	210	.714
Cleveland Browns	14	7	5	2	234	255	.571
Houston Oilers	14	1	13	0	199	467	.071

Western Division

Team Name	GP	W	L	T	PF	PA	Pct
Oakland Raiders	14	9	4	1	292	175	.679
Denver Broncos	14	7	5	2	354	296	.571
Kansas City Chiefs	14	7	5	2	231	192	.571
San Diego Chargers	14	2	11	1	188	386	.179

Coaching Changes

Philadelphia--Mike McCormack 5-8-l; St. Louis--Don Coryell 4-9-1; Detroit--Don McCafferty 6-7-1; Los Angeles--Chuck Knox 12-2-0; New Orleans--John North 5-9-0; New England--Chuck Fairbanks 5-9-0; Baltimore--Howard Schnellenberger 4-10-0; Houston--Bill Peterson 0-5-0, Sid Gillman 1-8-0; San Diego--Harland Svare 1-6-1, Ron Waller 1-5-0.

League Leaders

Yards Rushing		**Yards Passing**		**Passing %** (40 attempts)	
O.J. Simpson	2003	Roman Gabriel	3219	Len Dawson	65
John Brocklington	1144	Jim Plunkett	2550	Ken Stabler	63
Calvin Hill	1142	Charley Johnson	2465	Roger Staubach	63
Lawrence McCutcheon	1097	Roger Staubach	2428	Fran Tarkenton	62
Larry Csonka	1003	Ken Anderson	2428	Sonny Jurgensen	60

Receiving Yards		**Receptions**		**Field Goals**	
Harold Carmichael	1116	Harold Carmichael	67	David Ray	30
John Gilliam	907	Charlie Taylor	59	Roy Gerela	29
Harold Jackson	874	Fred Willis	57	Nick Mike-Mayer	26
Charlie Young	854	Charlie Young	57	Bruce Gossett	26
Isaac Curtis	843	Ed Pololak	55	Garo Yepremian	25

Punt Return Yards		**Kickoff Return Yards**	
Bill Thompson	366	Mack Herron	1092
Ray Brown	360	Herb Mul-Key	1011
Ron Smith	352	Ron Smith	947
Butch Atkinson	336	Bob Gresham	723
Glen Edwards	336	Alvin Haymond	703

Pro Bowl Game
(Arrowhead Stadium, Kansas City)

January 20 1974	American Conference	15	National Conference	13

NFL Playoffs

December 22	Washington Redskins	20	at	Minnesota Vikings	27
December 22	Pittsburgh Steelers	14	at	Oakland Raiders	33
December 23	Los Angeles Rams	16	at	Dallas Cowboys	27
December 23	Cincinnati Bengals	16	at	Miami Dolphins	34
December 30	Minnesota Vikings	27	at	Dallas Cowboys	10
December 30	Oakland Raiders	10	at	Miami Dolphins	27

Super Bowl VIII
(Rice Stadium, Houston)

January 13 1974	Miami Dolphins	24	Minnesota Vikings	7

Individual Awards

AP MVP--O.J. Simpson (Buffalo Bills)
Bert Bell Trophy--Booby Clark (Cincinnati Bengals) [World Almanac]
Chuck Foreman (Minnesota Vikings)
Bert Bell Trophy--O.J. Simpson (Buffalo Bills)
George Halas Trophy--Dick Anderson (Miami Dolphins)
Alan Page (Minnesota Vikings)
Jim Thorpe Trophy--O.J. Simpson (Buffalo Bills)
Pro Bowl MVP--Garo Yepremian (Miami Dolphins)

Rookie of the Year--Chuck Foreman (Minnesota Vikings)
Booby Clark (Cincinnati Bengals)
Wally Chambers (Chicago Bears)
Charles Young (Philadelphia Eagles)
Super Bowl MVP--Larry Csonka (Miami Dolphins)
U.P.I. AFC Coach of the Year--John Ralston (Denver Broncos)
U.P.I. AFC Player of the Year--O.J. Simpson (Buffalo Bills)
U.P.I. AFC Rookie of the Year--Booby Clark (Cincinnati Bengals)
U.P.I. NFC Coach of the Year--Chuck Knox(Los Angeles Rams)
U.P.I. NFC Player of the Year--John Hadl (Los Angeles Rams)
U.P.I. NFC Rookie of the Year--Charles Young (Philadelphia Eagles)

Hall of Fame Inductees

Raymond Berry, Jim Parker, Joe Schmidt

Notes

When the U.S. Congress passed a bill forbidding television blackouts of NFL games sold out 48 hours ahead of time, the league televised home games for the first time in years, albeit reluctantly. O.J. Simpson of the Buffalo Bills became the first man to rush for over 2,000 yards, when he rushed for 2,003 yards.

Canadian Football League
Eastern Conference

Team Name	GP	W	L	T	PF	PA	Pts	Pct
Ottawa Rough Riders	14	9	5	0	275	234	18	.643
Toronto Argonauts	14	7	5	2	265	231	16	.571
Montreal Alouettes	14	7	6	1	273	238	15	.536
Hamilton Tiger-Cats	14	7	7	0	304	263	14	.500

Western Conference

Team Name	GP	W	L	T	PF	PA	Pts	Pct
Edmonton Eskimos	16	9	5	2	329	284	20	.625
Saskatchewan Roughriders	16	10	6	0	360	287	20	.625
British Columbia Lions	16	5	9	2	261	328	12	.375
Calgary Stampeders	16	6	10	0	214	368	12	.375
Winnipeg Blue Bombers	16	4	11	1	267	315	9	.281

Coaching Changes

Toronto--John Rauch 7-5-2; Montreal--Marv Levy 7-6-1; Saskatchewan--John Payne 10-6-0; Calgary--Jim Duncan 5-8-0, Jim Wood 1-2-0.

League Leaders

Yards Rushing		Yards Passing		Passing %	
Roy Bell	1455	Ron Lancaster	3767	Jim Jones	61.5
Andy Hopkins	1223	Don Jonas	3363	Bruce Lemmerman	59.5
George Reed	1193	Peter Liske	2861	Tom Wilkinson	59.5
John Musso	1029	Joe Theisman	2496	Chuck Ealey	58.6
John Harvey	1024	Chuck Ealey	2312	Don Moorhead	57.6

Receiving Yards		Receptions		Points	
George McGowan	1123	George McGowan	81	Dave Cutler	133
Tom Campana	910	Tom Forzani	62	Gerry Organ	123
Bob LaRose	855	Rudy Linterman	60	Jack Abendschan	110
Johnny Rodgers	841	Tom Campana	57	Ian Sunter	102
Eric Allen	797	Bob Kraemer	47	Zenon Andrusyshyn	100

All Star Game
(Ivor Wynne Stadium, Hamilton)

June 27	All Stars	22	Hamilton Tiger-Cats	11

Grey Cup Playoffs

November 11	British Columbia Lions	13	at	Saskatchewan Roughriders	33
November 11	Montreal Alouettes	32	at	Toronto Argonauts	10 [OT]
November 18	Montreal Alouettes	13	at	Ottawa Rough Riders	23
November 18	Saskatchewan Roughriders	23	at	Edmonton Eskimos	25
November 25	Ottawa Rough Riders	22	at	Edmonton Eskimos	18 *

Individual Awards

Annis Stukus Trophy--Jack Gotta (Ottawa Rough Riders)
CFL All Star Game MVP--Peter Dalla Riva (Montreal Alouettes)
Dave Dryburgh Memorial Trophy--Dave Cutler (Edmonton Eskimos)
DeMarco-Becket Memorial Trophy--Ray Nettles (British Columbia Lions)
Dr. Beattie Martin Trophy--Lorne Richardson (Saskatchewan Roughriders)
Eddie James Memorial Trophy--Roy Bell (Edmonton Eskimos)
Grey Cup Most Valuable Canadian--Garry Lefebvre (Edmonton Eskimos)
Grey Cup MVP--Charlie Brandon (Ottawa Rough Riders)
Gruen Trophy--Bob Richardson(Hamilton Tiger-Cats)
Jeff Nicklin Memorial Trophy--George McGowan (Edmonton Eskimos)
Jeff Russel Memorial Trophy--John Harvey (Montreal Alouettes)
Schenley Award Most Outstanding Canadian--Gerry Organ (Ottawa Rough Riders)
Schenley Award Most Outstanding Lineman--Ray Nettles (British Columbia Lions)
Schenley Award Most Outstanding Player--George McGowan (Edmonton Eskimos)
Schenley Award Most Outstanding Rookie--Johnny Rodgers (Montreal Alouettes)

Hall of Fame Inductees

Russ Jackson, Leo Lewis, Moe Lieberman

HOCKEY
National Hockey League

Eastern Division

Team Name	GP	W	L	T	GF	GA	Pts	Pct
Montreal Canadiens	78	52	10	16	329	184	120	.769
Boston Bruins	78	51	22	5	330	235	107	.686
New York Rangers	78	47	23	8	297	208	102	.654
Buffalo Sabres	78	37	27	14	257	219	88	.564
Detroit Red Wings	78	37	29	12	265	243	86	.551
Toronto Maple Leafs	78	27	41	10	247	279	64	.410
Vancouver Canucks	78	22	47	9	233	339	53	.340
New York Islanders	78	12	60	6	170	347	30	.192

*Game played in Toronto

Western Division

Chicago Black Hawks	78	42	27	9	284	225	93	.596
Philadelphia Flyers	78	37	30	11	296	256	85	.545
Minnesota North Stars	78	37	30	11	254	230	85	.545
St. Louis Blues	78	32	34	12	233	251	76	.487
Pittsburgh Penguins	78	32	37	9	257	265	73	.468
Los Angeles Kings	78	31	36	11	232	245	73	.468
Atlanta Flames	78	25	38	15	191	239	65	.417
California Golden Seals	78	16	46	16	213	323	48	.308

Coaching Changes

Boston--Tom Johnson 31-16-5, Armand Guidolin 20-6-0; Buffalo--Joe Crozier 37-27-14; Detroit--John Wilson 37-29-12; Toronto--John McLellan 27-41-10; Vancouver--Vic Stasiuk 22-47-9; Islanders--Phil Goyette 6-4o-4, Earl Ingarfield 6-20-2; St. Louis--Al Arbour 2-6-5, Jean-Guy Talbot 30-28-7; Pittsburgh--Leonard Kelly 17-19-6, Ken Schinkel 15-18-3; Los Angeles--Bob Pulford 31-36-11; Atlanta--Bernie Geoffrion 25-38-15; California--Gary Young 2-7-3, Fred Glover 14-39-13.

League Leaders

Goals		Assists		Points	
Phil Esposito	55	Phil Esposito	75	Phil Esposito	130
Mickey Redmond	52	Bobby Orr	72	Bobby Clarke	104
Rick MacLeish	50	Bobby Clarke	67	Bobby Orr	101
Jacques Lemaire	44	Pit Martin	61	Rick MacLeish	100
Jim Pappin	41	Gil Perreault	60	Jacques Lemaire	95

Penalty Minutes		GAA		Wins	
Dave Schultz	259	Ken Dryden	2.26	Ken Dryden	33
Bob Kelly	238	Gilles Villemure	2.29	Tony Esposito	32
Steve Durbano	231	Tony Esposito	2.51	Roy Edwards	27
Andre Dupont	215	Roy Edwards	2.63	Ed Giacomin	26
Don Saleski	205	Dave Dryden	2.65	Ed Johnston	24

Shutouts	
Ken Dryden	6
Roy Edwards	6
Cesare Maniago	5
Ed Johnston	5
Tony Esposito	4

All Star Game

(Madison Square Garden, New York)

January 30	East Division	5	West Division	4

Stanley Cup Playoffs

April 4	Buffalo Sabres	1	at	Montreal Canadiens	2
April 4	New York Rangers	6	at	Boston Bruins	2
April 4	St. Louis Blues	1	at	Chicago Black Hawks	7
April 4	Minnesota North Stars	3	at	Philadelphia Flyers	0
April 5	Buffalo Sabres	3	at	Montreal Canadiens	7

April 5	New York Rangers	4	at	Boston Bruins	2
April 5	St. Louis Blues	0	at	Chicago Black Hawks	1
April 5	Minnesota North Stars	1	at	Philadelphia Flyers	4
April 7	Montreal Canadiens	5	at	Buffalo Sabres	2
April 7	Boston Bruins	4	at	New York Rangers	2
April 7	Chicago Black Hawks	5	at	St. Louis Blues	2
April 7	Philadelphia Flyers	0	at	Minnesota North Stars	5
April 8	Montreal Canadiens	1	at	Buffalo Sabres	5
April 8	Boston Bruins	0	at	New York Rangers	4
April 8	Chicago Black Hawks	3	at	St. Louis Blues	5
April 8	Philadelphia Flyers	3	at	Minnesota North Stars	0
April 10	Buffalo Sabres	3	at	Montreal Canadiens	2 [9:18]
April 10	New York Rangers	6	at	Boston Bruins	3
April 10	St. Louis Blues	1	at	Chicago Black Hawks	6
April 10	Minnesota North Stars	2	at	Philadelphia Flyers	3 [8:35]
April 12	Montreal Canadiens	4	at	Buffalo Sabres	2
April 12	Philadelphia Flyers	4	at	Minnesota North Stars	1
April 12	New York Rangers	4	at	Chicago Black Hawks	1
April 14	Philadelphia Flyers	5	at	Montreal Canadiens	4 [2:56]
April 15	New York Rangers	4	at	Chicago Black Hawks	5
April 17	Philadelphia Flyers	3	at	Montreal Canadiens	4 [6:45]
April 17	Chicago Black Hawks	2	at	New York Rangers	1
April 19	Montreal Canadiens	2	at	Philadelphia Flyers	1
April 19	Chicago Black Hawks	3	at	New York Rangers	1
April 22	Montreal Canadiens	4	at	Philadelphia Flyers	1
April 24	New York Rangers	1	at	Chicago Black Hawks	4
April 24	Philadelphia Flyers	3	at	Montreal Canadiens	5
April 29	Chicago Black Hawks	3	at	Montreal Canadiens	8
May 1	Chicago Black Hawks	1	at	Montreal Canadiens	4
May 3	Montreal Canadiens	4	at	Chicago Black Hawks	7
May 6	Montreal Canadiens	4	at	Chicago Black Hawks	0
May 8	Chicago Black Hawks	8	at	Montreal Canadiens	7
May 10	Montreal Canadiens	6	at	Chicago Black Hawks	4

All Star Teams

First Team		Second Team
Ken Dryden	Goal	Tony Esposito
Bobby Orr	Defense	Brad Park
Guy Lapointe	Defense	Bill White
Phil Esposito	Center	Bobby Clarke
Mickey Redmond	Right Wing	Yvan Cournoyer
Frank Mahovlich	Left Wing	Dennis Hull

Individual Awards

Art Ross Trophy--Phil Esposito (Boston Bruins)
Bill Masterton Trophy--Lowell MacDonald (Pittsburgh Penguins)
Calder Memorial Trophy--Steve Vickers (New York Rangers)
Conn Smythe Trophy--Yvan Cournoyer (Montreal Canadiens)
Hart Memorial Trophy--Bobby Clark (Philadelphia Flyers)
James Norris Trophy--Bobby Orr (Boston Bruins)
Lady Byng Memorial Trophy--Gil Perreault (Buffalo Sabres)
Lester Patrick Trophy--Walter Bush Jr.
Lester B. Pearson Award--Bobby Clarke (Philadelphia Flyers)

NHL All Star Game MVP--Greg Polis (Pittsburgh Penguins)
Vezina Trophy--Ken Dryden (Montreal Canadiens)

Hall of Fame Inductees

Doug Harvey, Hartland Molson, Chuck Rayner, Tom Smith, Frank Udvari

World Hockey Association
Eastern Division

Team Name	GP	W	L	T	GF	GA	Pts	Pct
New England Whalers	78	46	30	2	318	263	94	.603
Cleveland Crusaders	78	43	32	3	287	239	89	.571
Philadelphia Blazers	78	38	40	0	288	305	76	.487
Ottawa Nationals	78	35	39	4	279	301	74	.474
Quebec Nordiques	78	33	40	5	276	313	71	.455
New York Raiders	78	33	43	2	303	334	68	.436

Western Division

Team Name	GP	W	L	T	GF	GA	Pts	Pct
Winnipeg Jets	78	43	31	4	285	249	90	.577
Houston Aeros	78	39	35	4	284	269	82	.526
Los Angeles Sharks	78	37	35	6	259	250	80	.513
Alberta Oilers	78	38	37	3	269	256	79	.506
Minnesota Fighting Saints	78	38	37	3	250	269	79	.506
Chicago Cougars	78	26	50	2	245	295	54	.346

Coaching

New England--Jack Kelley 46-30-2; Cleveland--Bill Needham 43-32-3; Philadelphia--John McKenzie 1-6-0, Phil Watson 37-34-0; Ottawa--Bill Harris 35-39-4; Quebec--Maurice Richard 1-1-0, Maurice Filion 32-39-5; New York--Camille Henry 33-43-2; Winnipeg--Bob Hull 43-31-4; Houston--Bill Dineen 39-35-4; Los Angeles--Terry Slater 37-35-6; Alberta--Ray Kinasewich 38-37-3; Minnesota--Glen Sonmor 39-37-3; Chicago--Marcel Pronovost 26-50-2

League Leaders

Goals

Danny Lawson	61
Tom Webster	53
Bobby Hull	51
Ron Ward	51
Andre Lacroix	50

Assists

J.C. Tremblay	75
Andre Lacroix	74
Ron Ward	67
Norm Beaudin	65
Bob Sicinski	63

Points

Andre Lacroix	124
Ron Ward	118
Danny Lawson	106
Tom Webster	103
Bobby Hull	103

Penalty Minutes

John Schella	239
Tom Gilmore	191
Don Paradise	189
John Arbour	188
Jim Cardiff	185

GAA
(1,560 minutes)

Gerry Cheevers	2.84
Joe Daley	2.90
Russ Gillow	2.91
Wayne Rutledge	3.00
Jack Norris	3.06

Wins

Bernie Parent	33
Gerry Cheevers	32
Al Smith	31
Jack Norris	28
Ernie Wakely	26

Shutouts		**Save %**	
Gerry Cheevers	5	Gerry Cheevers	.912
Mike Curran	4	Mike Curran	.908
Al Smith	3	Wayne Rutledge	.907
Joe Daley	2	Jim McLeod	.904
Russ Gillow	2	Jack Norris	.902

All Star Game

(Colisee de Quebec, Quebec City)

January 6	East Division	6	West Division	2

WHA Playoffs

April 4	Philadelphia Blazers	2	at	Cleveland Crusaders	3 [5:47]
April 5	Los Angeles Sharks	2	at	Houston Aeros	7
April 6	Minnesota Fighting Saints	1	at	Winnipeg Jets	3
April 7	Ottawa Nationals	2	at	New England Whalers	6
April 7	Philadelphia Blazers	1	at	Cleveland Crusaders	7
April 7	Los Angeles Sharks	4	at	Houston Aeros	2
April 8	Ottawa Nationals	3	at	New England Whalers	4 [3:37]
April 8	Minnesota Fighting Saints	2	at	Winnipeg Jets	5
April 8	Cleveland Crusaders	3	at	Philadelphia Blazers	1
April 10	Winnipeg Jets	4	at	Minnesota Fighting Saints	6
April 10	Ottawa Nationals	4	at	New England Whalers	2 *
April 11	Winnipeg Jets	3	at	Minnesota Fighting Saints	2 [9:49]
April 11	Cleveland Crusaders	6	at	Philadelphia Blazers	2
April 11	Houston Aeros	2	at	Los Angeles Sharks	3
April 12	New England Whalers	7	at	Ottawa Nationals	3 *
April 13	Houston Aeros	3	at	Los Angeles Sharks	2 [3:12]
April 14	Ottawa Nationals	4	at	New England Whalers	5 [3:47]
April 15	Minnesota Fighting Saints	5	at	Winnipeg Jets	8
April 15	Los Angeles Sharks	3	at	Houston Aeros	6
April 17	Houston Aeros	3	at	Los Angeles Sharks	2
April 18	Cleveland Crusaders	2	at	New England Whalers	3
April 19	Cleveland Crusaders	2	at	New England Whalers	3
April 20	Houston Aeros	1	at	Winnipeg Jets	5
April 21	New England Whalers	5	at	Cleveland Crusaders	4
April 22	Houston Aeros	0	at	Winnipeg Jets	2
April 22	New England Whalers	2	at	Cleveland Crusaders	5
April 24	Winnipeg Jets	4	at	Houston Aeros	2
April 26	Cleveland Crusaders	1	at	New England Whalers	3
April 26	Winnipeg Jets	3	at	Houston Aeros	0
April 29	Winnipeg Jets	2	at	New England Whalers	7
May 2	New England Whalers	7	at	Winnipeg Jets	4
May 3	New England Whalers	3	at	Winnipeg Jets	4
May 5	Winnipeg Jets	2	at	New England Whalers	4
May 6	Winnipeg Jets	6	at	New England Whalers	9

*Games played in Toronto

All Star Teams

Position	First Team	Second Team	Third Team
Goal	Gerry Cheevers	Bernie Parent	Al Smith
Defense	J.C. Tremblay	Jim Dorey	Rick Ley
Defense	Paul Shmyr	Larry Hornung	Ted Green
Left Wing	Bobby Hull	Gary Jarrett	Wayne Carleton
Center	Andre Lacroix	Ron Ward	Chris Bordeleau
Right Wing	Danny Lawson	Tom Webster	Norm Beaudin

Individual Awards

Ben Hatskin Trophy--Gerry Cheevers (Cleveland Crusaders)
Bill Hunter Trophy--Andre Lacroix (Philadelphia Blazers)
Dennis Murphy Trophy--J.C. Tremblay(Quebec Nordiques)
Gordie Howe Trophy--Bobby Hull (Winnipeg Jets)
Lou Kaplan Trophy--Terry Caffrey (New England Whalers)
Paul Deneau Trophy--Ted Hampson (Minnesota Fighting Saints)
Robert Schmertz Trophy--Jack Kelley (New England Whalers)
WHA All Star Game MVP--Wayne Carleton (Ottawa Nationals)

Rules

The WHA adopted a 10 minute overtime period if the game ended in a tie after regulation time.

Notes

The World Hockey Association was formed this year when Gary Davidson and Dennis Murphy, decided to form a new league to take on the NHL
A controversy arose over the final playoff spot in the Western Division of the WHA. Although the guidelines for playoff qualification had been prearranged at the beginning of the season, it was decided that Alberta and Minnesota should play a special playoff game to decide who was to receive the final playoff spot. Minnesota won the game.

SOCCER

North American Soccer League

Eastern Division

Team Name	GP	W	L	T	GF	GA	BP	Pts	Pct
Philadelphia Atoms	19	9	2	8	29	14	26	104	.608
New York Cosmos	19	7	5	7	31	23	28	91	.532
Miami Toros	19	8	5	6	26	21	22	88	.515

Northern Division

Team Name	GP	W	L	T	GF	GA	BP	Pts	Pct
Toronto Metros	19	6	4	9	32	18	26	89	.520
Montreal Olympiques	19	5	10	4	25	32	22	64	.374
Rochester Lancers	19	4	9	6	17	27	17	59	.345

Southern Division

Team Name	GP	W	L	T	GF	GA	BP	Pts	Pct
Dallas Tornado	19	11	4	4	36	25	33	111	.649
St. Louis Stars	19	7	7	5	27	27	25	82	.480
Atlanta Apollos	19	3	9	7	23	40	23	62	.363

Coaching Changes

Philadelphia--Al Miller 9-2-8; Miami--John Young 8-5-6; Toronto--Arthur Rodrigues 6-4-9; Rochester--Sal DeRosa 4-9-6; Atlanta--Ken-Bracewell 3-9-7.

League Leaders

Goals		Points		Shutouts	
Warren Archibald	12	Kyle Rote	30	Ruben Montoya	7
Ilijah Mitic	12	Warren Archibald	29	Bob Rigby	6
Andy Provan	11	Andy Provan	28	Dick Howard	6
Joe Fink	11	Gene Geimer	25	Ken Cooper	5
Kyle Rote	10	Ilija Mitic	25	Jerry Sularz	5

GAA

Bob Rigby	0.62
Dick Howard	1.00
Ruben Montoya	1.11
Ken Cooper	1.17
Jerry Sularz	1.22

NASL Playoffs

August 15	New York Cosmos	0	at	Dallas Tornado	1
August 18	Toronto Metros	0	at	Philadelphia Atoms	3
August 25	Philadelphia Atoms	2	at	Dallas Tornado	0

All Star Teams

First Team		Second Team
Ken Cooper	Goal	Bob Rigby
John Best	Defense	Bob Smith
Chris Dunleavy	Defense	Derek Trevis
David Sadler	Defense	Dick Hall
Brian Rowan	Defense	Roy Evans
Ilija Mitic	Midfield	Pat McBride
Fernando Pinto	Midfield	Francisco Escos
Ian McPhee	Midfield	Roberto Aguirre
Andy Provan	Forward	Joe Fink
Jim Fryatt	Forward	Rick Reynolds
Warren Archibald	Forward	Randy Horton

Individual Awards

Lead Goalkeeper Award--Bob Rigby (Philadelphia Atoms)
Coach of the Year--Al Miller (Philadelphia Atoms)
Most Valuable Player--Warren Archibald (Miami Toros)
Rookie of the Year--Kyle Rote Jr. (Dallas Tornado).

Rules

A new off-side rule in the NASL stated that an attacking player could not be ruled off-side until within 35 yards of his opponents goal. An extra line running across the width of the field was drawn at each end to mark the off-side zone.

Notes

The Philadelphia Atoms became one of the few first year teams to win a championship of a major professional sports league.

Franchise Changes

NBA--Cincinnati Royals became the Kansas City-Omaha Kings.
ABA--Memphis Pros became the Memphis Tams.

Other Sports

Horseracing--Kentucky Derby won by Secretariat (time 1:59.4, purse $155,050).
Heavyweight Boxing--George Foreman knocked-out Joe Frazier in 2 rounds.
George Foreman knocked-out Joe Roman in 1 round.
Golf--U.S. Open won by Johnny Miller with a score of 279.
Auto Racing--Indianapolis 500 won Gordon Johncock (ave. speed 159.014 MPH).
Tennis--U.S. Open won by John Newcombe in the men's singles.
U.S. Open won by John Newcombe and Owen Davidson in the men's doubles.
U.S. Open won by Margaret Smith Court in the women's singles.'
U.S. Open won by Margaret Smith Court and Virginia Wade in the women's doubles.
U.S. Open won by Billie Jean King and Owen Davidson in the mixed doubles.

1974

BASEBALL
National League

East

Team Name	W	L	Pct	GB	R	OR
Pittsburgh Pirates	88	74	.543	-	751	657
St. Louis Cardinals	86	75	.534	1.5	677	643
Philadelphia Phillies	80	82	.494	8	676	701
Montreal Expos	79	82	.491	8.5	662	657
New York Mets	71	91	.438	17	572	646
Chicago Cubs	66	96	.407	22	669	326

West

Team Name	W	L	Pct	GB	R	OR
Los Angeles Dodgers	102	60	.630	-	798	561
Cincinnati Reds	98	64	.605	4	776	631
Atlanta Braves	88	74	.543	14	661	563
Houston Astros	81	81	.500	21	653	632
San Francisco Giants	72	90	.444	30	634	723
San Diego Padres	60	102	.370	42	541	830

Coaching Changes

Pittsburgh--Danny Murtaugh 88-74; Chicago--Walter Lockman 41-52, Jim Marshall 25-44; Atlanta--Eddie Mathews 50-49, Clyde King 38-25; Houston--Preston Gomez 81-81; San Francisco--Charlie Fox 34-42, Wes Westrum 38-48; San Diego--John McNamara 60-102.

League Leaders

Batting Average		Home Runs		RBI	
Ralph Garr	.353	Mike Schmidt	36	Johnny Bench	129
Al Oliver	.321	Johnny Bench	33	Mike Schmidt	116
Greg Gross	.314	Jim Wynn	32	Steve Garvey	111
Bill Buckner	.314	Tony Perez	28	Jim Wynn	108
Richard Zisk	.313	Cesar Cedeno	26	Ted Simmons	103

Stolen Bases		ERA		Wins	
Lou Brock	118	Lee Capra	2.28	Phil Niekro	20
Dave Lopes	59	Phil Niekro	2.38	Andy Messersmith	20
Joe Morgan	58	Jon Matlack	2.41	Jack Billingham	19
Cesar Cedeno	57	Mike Marshall	2.42	Don Sutton	19
Larry Lintz	50	Andy Messersmith	2.59	Don Gullett	17

Saves		Strikeouts	
Mike Marshall	21	Steve Carlton	240
Randy Moffitt	15	Andy Messersmith	221
Pedro Borbon	14	Tom Seaver	201
Dave Giusti	12	Jon Matlack	195
Tom House	11	Phil Niekro	195

NLCS

October 5	Los Angeles Dodgers	3	at	Pittsburgh Pirates	0
October 6	Los Angeles Dodgers	5	at	Pittsburgh Pirates	2
October 8	Pittsburgh Pirates	7	at	Los Angeles Dodgers	0
October 9	Pittsburgh Pirates	1	at	Los Angeles Dodgers	12

American League
East

Team Name	W	L	Pct	GB	R	OR
Baltimore Orioles	91	71	.562	-	659	612
New York Yankees	89	73	.549	2	671	623
Boston Red Sox	84	78	.519	7	696	661
Cleveland Indians	77	85	.475	14	662	694
Milwaukee Brewers	76	86	.469	15	647	660
Detroit Tigers	72	90	.444	19	620	768

West

Team Name	W	L	Pct	GB	R	OR
Oakland Athletics	90	72	.556	-	689	551
Texas Rangers	84	76	.525	5	690	698
Minnesota Twins	82	80	.506	8	673	669
Chicago White Sox	80	80	.500	9	684	721
Kansas City Royals	77	85	.475	13	667	662
California Angels	68	94	.420	22	618	657

Coaching Changes

New York--Bill Virdon 89-73; Boston--Darrell Johnson 84-78; Detroit--Ralph Houk 72-90; Oakland--Alvin Dark 90-72; Texas--Billy Martin 84-76; California--Bobby Winkles 32-46, Dick Williams 36-48.

League Leaders

Batting Average		Home Runs		RBI	
Rod Carew	.364	Richie Allen	32	Jeff Burroughs	118
Jorge Orto	.316	Reggie Jackson	29	Sal Bando	103
Hal McRae	.310	Gene Tenace	26	Joe Rudi	99
Lou Piniella	.305	Jeff Burroughs	25	Ken Henderson	95
Elliot Maddox	.303	Bob Darwin	25	Bob Darwin	94

Stolen Bases		ERA		Wins	
Bill North	54	James Hunter	2.49	Ferguson Jenkins	25
Rod Carew	38	Gaylord Perry	2.52	James Hunter	25
John Lowenstein	36	Andy Hassler	2.61	Mike Cuellar	22
Bert Campaneris	34	Bert Blyleven	2.66	Steve Bushy	22
Fred Patek	33	Alan Fitzmorris	2.79	Luis Tiant	22

Saves		Strikeouts	
Terry Forster	24	Nolan Ryan	367
Tom Murphy	20	Bert Blyleven	249
Bill Campbell	19	Ferguson Jenkins	225
Rollie Fingers	18	Gaylord Perry	216
Tom Buskey	18	Mickey Lolich	202

All Star Game

(Three Rivers Stadium, Pittsburgh)

July 23	National League	7		American League	2

ALCS

October 5	Baltimore Orioles	6	at	Oakland Athletics	3
October 6	Baltimore Orioles	0	at	Oakland Athletics	5
October 8	Oakland Athletics	1	at	Baltimore Orioles	0
October 9	Oakland Athletics	2	at	Baltimore Orioles	1

World Series

October 12	Oakland Athletics	3	at	Los Angeles Dodgers	2
October 13	Oakland Athletics	2	at	Los Angeles Dodgers	3
October 15	Los Angeles Dodgers	2	at	Oakland Athletics	3
October 16	Los Angeles Dodgers	2	at	Oakland Athletics	5
October 17	Los Angeles Dodgers	2	at	Oakland Athletics	3

Individual Awards

Arch Ward Memorial Trophy--Steve Garvey (Los Angeles Dodgers NL)
Baseball Writers Award--Steve Garvey (Los Angeles Dodgers NL)
Jeff Burroughs (Texas Rangers AL)
Cy Young Award--Mike Marshall (Los Angeles Dodgers NL)
Jim Hunter (Oakland Athletics AL)
Rookie of the Year--Bake McBride (St. Louis Cardinals NL)
Mike Hargrove (Texas Rangers AL)
Sporting News Executive of the Year--Gabe Paul (New York Yankees AL)
Sporting News Manager of the Year--Bill Virdon (New York Yankees AL)
Sporting News Pitcher of the Year--Mike Marshall (Los Angeles Dodgers NL)
Jim Hunter (Oakland Athletics AL)
Sporting News Player of the Year--Lou Brock (St. Louis Cardinals NL)
Jeff Burroughs (Texas Rangers AL)
Sporting News Rookie of the Year--Greg Gross (Houston Astros NL)
John D'Acquisto (San Francisco Giants NL)
Mike Hargrove (Texas Rangers AL)
Frank Tanana (California Angels AL)
World Series MVP--Rollie Fingers (Oakland Athletics AL)

Hall of Fame Inductees

"Cool Papa" Bell, Jim Bottomley, John Conlan, Edward "Whitey" Ford, Mickey Mantle, Sam Thompson

Notes

Lee McPhail replaced Joe Cronin as President of the American League.

BASKETBALL
National Basketball Association

Atlantic Division

Team Name	GP	W	L	PPGF	PPGA	Pct	GB
Boston Celtics	82	56	26	109.0	105.1	.683	-
New York Knickerbockers	82	49	33	101.3	98.5	.598	7
Buffalo Braves	82	42	40	111.6	111.8	.512	14
Philadelphia 76ers	82	25	57	101.2	107.5	.305	31

Central Division

Capital Bullets	82	47	35	101.9	100.4	.573	-
Atlanta Hawks	82	35	47	108.6	110.0	.427	12
Houston Rockets	82	32	50	107.4	107.6	.390	15
Cleveland Cavaliers	82	29	53	100.3	104.6	.354	18

Midwest Division

Milwaukee Bucks	82	59	23	107.1	99.0	.720	-
Chicago Bulls	82	54	28	102.0	98.7	.659	5
Detroit Pistons	82	52	30	104.4	100.3	.634	7
Kansas City-Omaha Kings	82	33	49	102.0	105.8	.402	26

Pacific Division

Los Angeles Lakers	82	47	35	109.2	108.3	.573	-
Golden State Warriors	82	44	38	109.9	107.3	.537	3
Seattle SuperSonics	82	36	46	107.0	109.5	.439	11
Phoenix Suns	82	30	52	107.9	111.5	.366	17
Portland Trail Blazers	82	27	55	106.8	111.6	.329	20

Coaching Changes

Philadelphia--Gene Shue 25-57; Capital-K.C. Jones 47-35; Atlanta--Cotton Fitzsimmons 35-47; Houston--John Egan 32-50; Detroit--Ray Scott 52-30; K.C./Omaha--Bob Cousy 6-14, Draff Young 0-4, Phil Johnson 27-31; Seattle--Bill Russell 36-46; Phoenix--John MacLeod 30-52.

League Leaders

Field Goals

Kareem Abdul-Jabbar	948
Bob McAdoo	901
Pete Maravich	819
Rick Barry	796
Rudy Tomjanovich	788

Free Throws

Gail Goodrich	508
Pete Maravich	469
Bob McAdoo	459
Chet Walker	439
Rick Barry	417

Assists

Ernie DiGregorio	663
Calvin Murphy	603
Dave Bing	555
Walt Frazier	551
Norm Van Lier	548

Points

Bob McAdoo	2261
Kareem Abdul-Jabbar	2191
Pete Maravich	2107
Gail Goodrich	2076
Rick Barry	2009

Fouls

Kevin Porter	3602
Kareem Abdul-Jabbar	3548
Dave Cowens	3352
Walt Frazier	3338
Jim McMillan	3322

All Star Game

(The Kingdome, Seattle)

January 15	West Division	134	East Division	123

NBA Playoffs

March 29	Capitals Bullets	91	at	N.Y. Knickerbockers	102
March 29	Los Angeles Lakers	95	at	Milwaukee Bucks	99
March 30	Buffalo Braves	97	at	Boston Celtics	107
March 30	Detroit Pistons	97	at	Chicago Bulls	88

March 31	Los Angeles Lakers	90	at	Milwaukee Bucks	109
March 31	N.Y. Knickerbockers	87	at	Capital Bullets	99
April 1	Chicago Bulls	108	at	Detroit Pistons	103
April 2	Boston Celtics	105	at	Buffalo Braves	115
April 2	Milwaukee Bucks	96	at	Los Angeles Lakers	98
April 2	Capital Bullets	88	at	N.Y. Knickerbockers	79
April 3	Buffalo Braves	107	at	Boston Celtics	120
April 4	Milwaukee Bucks	112	at	Los Angeles Lakers	90
April 5	N.Y. Knickerbockers	101	at	Capital Bullets	93[OT]
April 5	Detroit Pistons	83	at	Chicago Bulls	84
April 6	Boston Celtics	102	at	Buffalo Braves	104
April 7	Los Angeles Lakers	92	at	Milwaukee Bucks	114
April 7	Capital Bullets	105	at	N.Y. Knickerbockers	106
April 7	Chicago Bulls	87	at	Detroit Pistons	102
April 9	Buffalo Braves	97	at	Boston Celtics	100
April 9	Detroit Pistons	94	at	Chicago Bulls	98
April 10	N.Y. Knickerbockers	92	at	Capital Bullets	109
April 11	Chicago Bulls	88	at	Detroit Pistons	92
April 12	Boston Celtics	106	at	Buffalo Braves	104
April 12	Capital Bullets	81	at	N.Y. Knickerbockers	91
April 13	Detroit Pistons	94	at	Chicago Bulls	96
April 14	N.Y. Knickerbockers	88	at	Boston Celtics	113
April 16	Boston Celtics	111	at	N.Y. Knickerbockers	99
April 16	Chicago Bulls	85	at	Milwaukee Bucks	101
April 18	Milwaukee Bucks	113	at	Chicago Bulls	111
April 19	N.Y. Knickerbockers	103	at	Boston Celtics	100
April 20	Chicago Bulls	90	at	Milwaukee Bucks	113
April 21	Boston Celtics	98	at	N.Y. Knickerbockers	91
April 22	Milwaukee Bucks	115	at	Chicago Bulls	99
April 24	N.Y. Knickerbockers	94	at	Boston Celtics	105
April 28	Boston Celtics	98	at	Milwaukee Bucks	83
April 30	Boston Celtics	96	at	Milwaukee Bucks	105 [OT]
May 3	Milwaukee Bucks	83	at	Boston Celtics	95
May 5	Milwaukee Bucks	97	at	Boston Celtics	89
May 7	Boston Celtics	96	at	Milwaukee Bucks	87
May 10	Milwaukee Bucks	102	at	Boston Celtics	101 [OT]
May 12	Boston Celtics	102	at	Milwaukee Bucks	87

All Star Teams

First Team	Second Team
John Havlicek (Boston Celtics)	Elvin Hayes (Capital Bullets)
Rick Barry (Golden State Warriors)	Spencer Haywood (Seattle SuperSonics)
Kareem Abdul-Jabbar (Milwaukee Bucks)	Bob McAdoo (Buffalo Braves)
Walt Frazier (N.Y. Knickerbockers)	Dave Bing (Detroit Pistons)
Gail Goodrich (Los Angeles Lakers)	Norm Van Lier (Chicago Bulls)

Individual Awards

Eddie Gottlieb Trophy--Ernie DiGregorio (Buffalo Braves)
Maurice Podoloff Trophy--Kareem Abdul-Jabbar (Los Angeles Lakers)
NBA All Star Game MVP--Bob Lanier (Detroit Pistons)
NBA Executive of the Year--Eddie Donovan (Buffalo Braves)
NBA Finals MVP--John Havlicek (Boston Celtics)
Red Auerbach Trophy--Ray Scott (Detroit Pistons)

Hall of Fame Inductees

Joseph Brennan, Emil Liston, Bill Russell, Robert Vandivier

American Basketball Association
Eastern Division

Team Name	GP	W	L	PPGF	PPGA	Pct	GB
New York Nets	84	55	29	109.4	104.0	.655	-
Kentucky Colonels	84	53	31	107.4	103.3	.631	2
Carolina Cougars	84	47	37	110.5	107.0	.560	8
Virginia Squires	84	28	56	106.4	111.3	.333	27
Memphis Tams	84	21	63	101.2	108.2	.250	34

Western Division

Team Name	GP	W	L	PPGF	PPGA	Pct	GB
Utah Stars	84	51	33	105.1	104.7	.607	-
Indiana Pacers	84	46	38	105.8	105.0	.548	5
San Antonio Spurs	84	45	39	97.6	96.7	.536	6
Denver Rockets	84	37	47	113.2	115.7	.440	14
San Diego Conquistadors	84	37	47	107.0	107.5	.440	14

Coaching Changes

New York--Kevin Loughery 55-29; Kentucky--Babe McCarthy 53-31; Memphis--Butch Van Breda Kolff 21-63; Utah--Joe Mullaney 51-33; San Antonio--Tom Nissalke 45-39; San Diego--Wilt Chamberlain 37-47.

League Leaders

Field Goals		Free Throws		Assists	
Julius Erving	914	Mack Calvin	490	Al Smith	619
Dan Issel	829	George McGinnis	488	Chuck Williams	557
George McGinnis	789	Dan Issel	457	Louie Dampier	473
Stew Johnson	716	Julius Erving	454	Julius Erving	434
Willie Wise	714	George Thompson	410	Jim Jones	429

Points		Fouls	
Julius Erving	2299	Jim Chones	347
Dan Issel	2118	Ted McClain	326
George McGinnis	2071	George McGinnis	325
Willie Wise	1826	Rick Jones	319
George Gervin	1730	George Carter	308

All Star Game

(Norfolk Scope, Norfolk)

January 30	East Division	128	West Division	112

ABA Playoffs

March 29	Virginia Squires	96	at	New York Nets	108
March 30	San Diego Conquistadors	99	at	Utah Stars	114
March 30	San Antonio Spurs	113	at	Indiana Pacers	109
April 1	Virginia Squires	110	at	New York Nets	129

April 1	Carolina Cougars	102	at	Kentucky Colonels	118
April 1	San Diego Conquistadors	105	at	Utah Stars	119
April 1	San Antonio Spurs	101	at	Indiana Pacers	128
April 3	Indiana Pacers	96	at	San Antonio Spurs	115
April 3	Utah Stars	96	at	San Diego Conquistadors	97
April 4	Utah Stars	98	at	San Diego Conquistadors	100
April 4	New York Nets	115	at	Virginia Squires	116
April 4	Indiana Pacers	91	at	San Antonio Spurs	89
April 5	Kentucky Colonels	99	at	Carolina Cougars	96
April 6	Kentucky Colonels	120	at	Carolina Cougars	110
April 6	San Diego Conquistadors	93	at	Utah Stars	100
April 6	San Antonio Spurs	100	at	Indiana Pacers	105
April 7	New York Nets	116	at	Virginia Squires	88
April 8	Virginia Squires	96	at	New York Nets	108
April 8	Carolina Cougars	119	at	Kentucky Colonels	128
April 8	Utah Stars	110	at	San Diego Conquistadors	99
April 10	Indiana Pacers	86	at	San Antonio Spurs	102
April 12	San Antonio Spurs	86	at	Indiana Pacers	97
April 13	Kentucky Colonels	106	at	New York Nets	119
April 13	Indiana Pacers	96	at	Utah Stars	105
April 15	Kentucky Colonels	80	at	New York Nets	99
April 15	Indiana Pacers	102	at	Utah Stars	106
April 17	New York Nets	89	at	Kentucky Colonels	87
April 17	Utah Stars	99	at	Indiana Pacers	90
April 18	Utah Stars	107	at	Indiana Pacers	118
April 20	New York Nets	103	at	Kentucky Colonels	90
April 22	Indiana Pacers	110	at	Utah Stars	101
April 25	Utah Stars	89	at	Indiana Pacers	91
April 27	Indiana Pacers	87	at	Utah Stars	109
April 30	Utah Stars	85	at	New York Nets	89
May 4	Utah Stars	94	at	New York Nets	118
May 6	New York Nets	103	at	Utah Stars	100 [OT]
May 8	New York Nets	89	at	Utah Stars	97
May 10	Utah Stars	100	at	New York Nets	111

All Star Teams

First Team

Julius Erving (New York Nets)
George McGinnis (Indiana Pacers)
Artis Gilmore (Kentucky Colonels)
James Jones (Utah Stars)
Mack Calvin (Carolina Cougars)

Second Team

Dan Issel (Kentucky Colonels)
Willie Wise (Utah Stars)
Swen Nater (San Antonio Spurs)
Ron Boone (Utah Stars)
Louie Dampier (Kentucky Colonels)

Individual Awards

ABA All Star Game MVP--Artis Gilmore (Kentucky Colonels)
Coach of the Year--Babe McCarthy (Kentucky Colonels)
Joe Mullaney (Utah Stars)
Most Valuable Player--Julius Erving (New York Nets)
Rookie of the Year--Swen Nater (Virginia Squires)

Notes

The ABA continued its head office merry-go-round with Tedd Munchak replacing Mike Storen as Commissioner.

FOOTBALL
National Football League

National Football Conference
Eastern Division

Team Name	GP	W	L	T	PF	PA	Pct
St. Louis Cardinals	14	10	4	0	285	218	.714
Washington Redskins	14	10	4	0	320	196	.714
Dallas Cowboys	14	8	6	0	297	235	.571
Philadelphia Eagles	14	7	7	0	242	217	.500
New York Giants	14	2	12	0	195	299	.143

Central Division

Team Name	GP	W	L	T	PF	PA	Pct
Minnesota Vikings	14	10	4	0	310	195	.714
Detroit Lions	14	7	7	0	256	270	.500
Green Bay Packers	14	6	8	0	210	206	.429
Chicago Bears	14	4	10	0	152	279	.286

Western Division

Team Name	GP	W	L	T	PF	PA	Pct
Los Angeles Rams	14	10	4	0	263	181	.714
San Francisco 49ers	14	6	8	0	226	236	.429
New Orleans Saints	14	5	9	0	166	263	.357
Atlanta Falcons	14	3	11	0	111	271	.214

American Football Conference

Eastern Division

Team Name	GP	W	L	T	PF	PA	Pct
Miami Dolphins	14	11	3	0	327	216	.786
Buffalo Bills	14	9	5	0	264	244	.643
New England Patriots	14	7	7	0	348	289	.500
New York Jets	14	7	7	0	279	300	.500
Baltimore Colts	14	2	12	0	190	329	.143

Central Division

Team Name	GP	W	L	T	PF	PA	Pct
Pittsburgh Steelers	14	10	3	1	305	189	.750
Cincinnati Bengals	14	7	7	0	283	259	.500
Houston Oilers	14	7	7	0	236	282	.500
Cleveland Browns	14	4	10	0	251	344	.286

Western Division

Team Name	GP	W	L	T	PF	PA	Pct
Oakland Raiders	14	12	2	0	355	228	.857
Denver Broncos	14	7	6	1	302	294	.536
Kansas City Chiefs	14	5	9	0	233	293	.357
San Diego Chargers	14	5	9	0	212	285	.357

Coaching Changes

New York Giants--Bill Arnsparger 2-12-0; Detroit--Rick Forzano 7-7-0; Atlanta--Norm Van Brocklin 2-6-0, Marion Campbell 1-5-0; New York Jets--Charley Winner 7-7-0; Baltimore--Howard Schnellenberger 0-3-0, Joe Thomas 2-9-0; Houston--Sid Gillman 7-7-0; San Diego--Tom Prothro 5-9-0.

League Leaders

Yards Rushing		Yards Passing		Passing % (40 attempts)	
Otis Armstrong	1407	Ken Anderson	2667	Bob Berry	71
Don Woods	1162	Joe Namath	2616	Ken Anderson	65
O.J. Simpson	1125	Fran Tarkenton	2598	Sonny Jurgensen	64
Larry McCutcheon	1109	Roger Staubach	2552	Norm Snead	61
Franco Harris	1006	Ken Stabler	2469	Bob Griese	60

Receiving Yards		Receptions		Field Goals	
Cliff Branch	1092	Lydell Mitchell	72	Chester Marcol	25
Drew Pearson	1087	Charlie Young	63	Errol Mann	23
Gary Garrison	785	Drew Pearson	62	Roy Gerela	20
Mel Gray	770	Cliff Branch	60	John Leypoldt	19
Ron Jessie	761	Harold Carmichael	56	Mark Moseley	18

Punt Return Yards		Kickoff Return Yards	
Lynn Swann	577	Lou Piccone	961
Mack Herron	517	Wallace Francis	947
Ron Smith	486	Jimmie Jones	927
Bill Johnson	409	Dennis Morgan	823
Don Walker	384	Bill Johnson	785

Pro Bowl Game

(Orange Bowl, Miami)

January 20 1975	National Conference	17	American Conference	10

NFL Playoffs

December 21	St. Louis Cardinals	14	at	Minnesota Vikings	30
December 21	Miami Dolphins	26	at	Oakland Raiders	28
December 22	Washington Redskins	10	at	Los Angeles Rams	19
December 22	Buffalo Bills	14	at	Pittsburgh Steelers	32
December 29	Los Angels Rams	10	at	Minnesota Vikings	14
December 29	Pittsburgh Steelers	24	at	Oakland Raiders	13

Super Bowl IX

(Tulane Stadium, New Orleans)

January 12 1975	Pittsburgh Steelers	16	Minnesota Vikings	6

Individual Awards

A.P. MVP--Ken Stabler (Oakland Raiders)
Bert Bell Trophy--Don Woods (San Diego Chargers) [World Almanac]
Bert Bell Trophy--Merlin Olsen (Los Angeles Rams)
George Halas Trophy--Joe Greene (Pittsburgh Steelers)
Jim Thorpe Trophy--Ken Stabler (Oakland Raiders)
Pro Bowl MVP--James Harris (Los Angeles Rams)
Rookie of the Year--Don Woods (San Diego Chargers)
Jack Lambert (Pittsburgh Steelers)
Super Bowl MVP--Franco Harris (Pittsburgh Steelers)
U.P.I. AFC Coach of the Year--Sid Gillman (Houston Oilers)
U.P.I. AFC Player of the Year--Ken Stabler (Oakland Raiders)

U.P.I. AFC Rookie of the Year--Don Woods (San Diego Chargers)
U.P.I. NFC Coach of the Year--Don Coryell (St. Louis Cardinals)
U.P.I. NFC Player of the Year--Jim Hart (St. Louis Cardinals)
U.P.I. NFC Rookie of the Year--John Hicks (New York Giants)

Hall of Fame Inductees

Tony Canadeo, Bill George, Lou Groza, Dick Lane

Rules

Missed field goals that travel into the end zone would be brought back to the line of scrimmage

Notes

The NFL moved the goal posts to the rear of the end zone where they had been until 1933, and an extra sudden death period was added for all tie games during the season.

Canadian Football League

Eastern Conference

Team Name	GP	W	L	T	PF	PA	Pts	Pct
Montreal Alouettes	16	9	5	2	339	271	20	.625
Ottawa Rough Riders	16	7	9	0	261	271	14	.438
Hamilton Tiger-Cats	16	7	9	0	279	313	14	.438
Toronto Argonauts	16	6	9	1	281	314	13	.406

Western Conference

Team Name	GP	W	L	T	PF	PA	Pts	Pct
Edmonton Eskimos	16	10	5	1	345	247	21	.656
Saskatchewan Roughriders	16	9	7	0	305	289	18	.563
British Columbia Lions	16	8	8	0	306	299	16	.500
Winnipeg Blue Bombers	16	8	8	0	258	350	16	.500
Calgary Stampeders	16	6	10	0	285	305	12	.375

Coaching Changes

Ottawa--George Brancato 7-9-0; Toronto--John Rauch 3-4-0, Joe Moss 3-5-1; Winnipeg--Bud Riley 8-8-0; Calgary--Jim Wood 6-10-0.

League Leaders

Yards Rushing		Yards Passing		Passing % (200 attempts)	
George Reed	1447	Peter Liske	3259	Tom Wilkinson	66.0
Roy Bell	1341	Ron Lancaster	2873	Bill Etter	59.6
Lou Harris	1239	Mike Rae	2501	Peter Liske	58.2
Monroe Eley	1176	Don Moorhead	2478	Ron Lancaster	56.2
Steve Ferrughelli	1134	Jim Jones	2297	Don Moorhead	53.3

Receiving Yards		Receptions		Points	
Johnny Rodgers	1024	Rudy Linterman	64	Dave Cutler	144
Rudy Linterman	951	Tom Forzani	61	Ian Sunter	141
Rhome Nixon	850	Tony Gabriel	61	Zenon Andrusyshyn	134
Tom Forzani	841	Johnny Rodgers	60	Gerry Organ	134
Tony Gabriel	795	Bobby Thompson	56	Don Sweet	109

All Star Game
(Lansdowne Park, Ottawa)

June 26	Ottawa Rough Riders	25		All Stars	22

Grey Cup Playoffs

November 10	British Columbia Lions	14	at	Saskatchewan Roughriders	24
November 10	Hamilton Tiger-Cats	19	at	Ottawa Rough Riders	21
November 17	Saskatchewan Roughriders	27	at	Edmonton Eskimos	31
November 17	Ottawa Rough Riders	4	at	Montreal Alouettes	14
November 24	Montreal Alouettes	20	at	Edmonton Eskimos	7*

Individual Awards

Annis Stukus Trophy--Marv Levy (Montreal Alouettes)
CFL All Star Game MVP--Rhome Nixon (Ottawa Rough Riders)
Dave Dryburgh Memorial Trophy--Dave Cutler (Edmonton Eskimos)
DeMarco-Becket Memorial Trophy--Curtis Wester (British Columbia Lions)
Dr. Beattie Martin Trophy--Rudy Linterman (Calgary Stampeders)
Eddie James Memorial Trophy--George Reed (Saskatchewan Roughriders)
Grey Cup Most Outstanding Defensive Star--Junior Ah You (Montreal Alouettes)
Grey Cup Most Outstanding Offensive Star--Sonny Wade (Montreal Alouettes)
Grey Cup Most Valuable Canadian--Don Sweet (Montreal Alouettes)
Jackie Parker Trophy--Tom Scott (Winnipeg Blue Bombers)
Jeff Nicklin Memorial Trophy--Tom Wilkinson (Edmonton Eskimos)
Jeff Russel Memorial Trophy--Johnny Rodgers (Montreal Alouettes)
Norm Fieldgate Trophy--John Helton (Calgary Stampeders)
Schenley Award Most Outstanding Canadian--Tony Gabriel (Hamilton Tiger-Cats)
Schenley Award Most Outstanding Defensive Player--John Helton (Calgary Stampeders)
Schenley Award Most Outstanding Offensive Lineman--Ed George (Montreal Alouettes)
Schenley Award Most Outstanding Player--Tom Wilkinson (Edmonton Eskimos)
Schenley Award Most Outstanding Rookie--Sam Cvijanovich (Toronto Argonauts)

Hall of Fame Inductees

Andrew Currie, George Dixon, Bernie Faloney, Billy Hughes, Les Lear, Martin Ruby, Annis Stukus

World Football League
Eastern Division

Team Name	GP	W	L	T	PF	PA	Pct
Florida Blazers	20	14	6	0	419	280	.700
Charlotte Stars	20	10	10	0	467	350	.500
Philadelphia Bell	19	8	11	0	491	413	.421
Jacksonville Sharks	14	4	10	0	258	358	.286

Central Division

Team Name	GP	W	L	T	PF	PA	Pct
Memphis Southmen	20	17	3	0	629	365	.850
Birmingham Americans	20	15	5	0	500	394	.750
Chicago Fire	19	7	12	0	446	600	.368
Detroit Wheels	14	1	13	0	209	358	.071

*Game played in Vancouver

Western Division

Southern California Sun	20	13	7	0	486	341	.650
The Hawaiins	20	9	11	0	413	422	.450
Portland Storm	20	7	12	1	264	426	.375
{Houston Texans }	12	3	8	1	113	269	.292
{Shreveport Steamers}	8	4	4	0	127	146	.500

Coaching

Florida--Jack Pardee 14-6-0; Charlotte--Babe Parilli 10-10-0; Philadelphia--Ron Waller 8-11-0; Jacksonville--Bud Asher 2-4-0, Charlie Tate 2-6-0 ; Memphis--John McVay 17-3-0; Birmingham--Jack Gotta 15-5-0; Chicago--Jim Spavital 7-12-0; Detroit--Dan Boisture 1-13-0; Southern California--Tom Fears 13-7-0; Hawaiins--Mike Giddings 9-11-0; Portland--Dick Coury 7-12-1; Houston/Shreveport--Jim Garret 7-12-1

League Leaders

Rushing Yards		Passing Yards		Receptions	
Tom Reamon	1576	Tony Adams	3905	Tim Delaney	89 for 1232 yds.
J.J. Jennings	1524	King Corcoran	3631	Rick Eber	66 for 771 yds.
Jim Nance	1240	Bob Davis	2977	James McAlister	65 for 772 yds.
John Land	1136	Virgil Carter	2629	Dennis Homan	61 for 930 yds.
Rufus Ferguson	1086	John Huarte	2416	Alfred Jenkins	60 for 1326 yds.

WFL Playoffs

November 21	Philadelphia Bell	3	at	Florida Blazers	18
November 21	Hawaiins	34	at	Southern California Sun	14
November 29	Florida Blazers	18	at	Memphis Southmen	15
November 30	Hawaiins	19	at	Birmingham Americans	22
December 5	Florida Blazers	21	at	Birmingham Americans	22

Individual Awards

Most Valuable Players--Tommy Reamon (Florida Blazers), J.J. Jennings (Memphis Southmen) Tony Adams (Southern California Sun)

Notes

Gary Davidson was named as Commissioner of the World Football League.

HOCKEY

National Hockey League
Eastern Division

Team Name	GP	W	L	T	GF	GA	Pts	Pct
Boston Bruins	78	52	17	9	349	221	113	.724
Montreal Canadiens	78	45	24	9	293	240	99	.635
New York Rangers	78	40	24	14	300	251	94	.603
Toronto Maple Leafs	78	35	27	16	274	230	86	.551
Buffalo Sabres	78	32	34	12	242	250	76	.487
Detroit Red Wings	78	29	39	10	255	319	68	.436
Vancouver Canucks	78	24	43	11	224	296	59	.378
New York Islanders	78	19	41	18	182	247	56	.359

Western Division

Philadelphia Flyers	78	50	16	12	273	164	112	.718
Chicago Black Hawks	78	41	14	23	272	164	105	.673
Los Angeles Kings	78	33	33	12	233	231	78	.500
Atlanta Flames	78	30	34	14	214	238	74	.474
Pittsburgh Penguins	78	28	41	9	242	273	65	.417
St. Louis Blues	78	26	40	12	206	248	64	.410
Minnesota North Stars	78	23	38	17	235	195	63	.404
California Golden Seals	78	13	55	10	195	342	36	.231

Coaching Changes

Boston--Armand Guidolin 52-17-9; Rangers--Larry Popein 18-14-9, Emile Francis 22-10-5; Toronto--Leonard Kelly 35-27-16; Detroit--Ted Garvin 2-9-1, Alex Delvecchio 27-30-9; Vancouver--Bill McCreary 9-25-7, Phil Maloney 15-18-4; Islanders--Al Arbour 19-41-18; Pittsburgh--Ken Schinkel 14-31-5, Marc Boileau 14-10-4; St. Louis--Jean-Guy Talbot 22-25-8, Lou Angotti 4-15-4; Minnesota--Jack Gordon 3-8-6, Parker MacDonald 20-30-11; California--Fred Glover 11-38-8, Marshall Johnston 2-17-2.

League Leaders

Goals		**Assists**		**Points**	
Phil Esposito	68	Bobby Orr	90	Phil Esposito	145
Rick Martin	52	Phil Esposito	77	Bobby Orr	122
Mickey Redmond	51	Dennis Hextall	62	Ken Hodge	105
Ken Hodge	50	Syl Apps Jr.	61	Wayne Cashman	89
Bill Goldsworthy	48	Andre Boudrias	59	Bobby Clarke	87
Penalty Minutes		**Plus/Minus**		**GAA**	
Dave Schultz	348	Bobby Orr	84	Bernie Parent	1.89
Andre Dupont	216	Al Sims	64	Tony Esposito	2.04
Garry Howatt	204	Phil Esposito	51	Doug Favell	2.71
Phil Russell	184	Bill White	51	Wayne Thomas	2.76
Denis Potvin	175	Wayne Cashman	49	Dan Bouchard	2.77
Wins		**Shutouts**			
Bernie Parent	47	Bernie Parent	12		
Tony Esposito	34	Tony Esposito	10		
Gilles Gilbert	34	Gilles Gilbert	6		
Ed Giacomin	30	Dan Bouchard	5		
Rogie Vachon	28	Rogie Vachon	5		

All Star Game

(The Stadium, Chicago)

January 29	West Division	6		East Division	4

Stanley Cup Playoffs

April 9	Atlanta Flames	1	at	Philadelphia Flyers	4
April 10	Toronto Maple Leafs	0	at	Boston Bruins	1
April 10	Los Angeles Kings	1	at	Chicago Black Hawks	3
April 10	New York Rangers	4	at	Montreal Canadiens	1

April 11	Toronto Maple Leafs	3	at	Boston Bruins	6
April 11	New York Rangers	1	at	Montreal Canadiens	4
April 11	Los Angeles Kings	1	at	Chicago Black Hawks	4
April 11	Atlanta Flames	1	at	Philadelphia Flyers	5
April 12	Philadelphia Flyers	4	at	Atlanta Flames	1
April 13	Montreal Canadiens	4	at	New York Rangers	2
April 13	Chicago Black Hawks	1	at	Los Angeles Kings	0
April 13	Boston Bruins	6	at	Toronto Maple Leafs	3
April 14	Boston Bruins	4	at	Toronto Maple Leafs	3 [1:27]
April 14	Montreal Canadiens	4	at	New York Rangers	6
April 14	Chicago Black Hawks	1	at	Los Angeles Kings	5
April 14	Philadelphia Flyers	4	at	Atlanta Flames	3 [5:40]
April 16	New York Rangers	3	at	Montreal Canadiens	2 [4:07]
April 16	Los Angeles Kings	0	at	Chicago Black Hawks	1
April 18	Montreal Canadiens	2	at	New York Rangers	5
April 18	Chicago Black Hawks	4	at	Boston Bruins	2
April 20	New York Rangers	0	at	Philadelphia Flyers	4
April 21	Chicago Black Hawks	6	at	Boston Bruins	8
April 23	New York Rangers	2	at	Philadelphia Flyers	5
April 23	Boston Bruins	3	at	Chicago Black Hawks	4 [3:48]
April 25	Philadelphia Flyers	3	at	New York Rangers	5
April 25	Boston Bruins	5	at	Chicago Black Hawks	2
April 28	Philadelphia Flyers	1	at	New York Rangers	2 [4:20]
April 28	Chicago Black Hawks	2	at	Boston Bruins	6
April 30	New York Rangers	1	at	Philadelphia Flyers	4
April 30	Boston Bruins	4	at	Chicago Black Hawks	2
May 2	Philadelphia Flyers	1	at	New York Rangers	4
May 5	New York Rangers	3	at	Philadelphia Flyers	4
May 7	Philadelphia Flyers	2	at	Boston Bruins	3
May 9	Philadelphia Flyers	3	at	Boston Bruins	2 [12:01]
May 12	Boston Bruins	1	at	Philadelphia Flyers	4
May 14	Boston Bruins	2	at	Philadelphia Flyers	4
May 16	Philadelphia Flyers	1	at	Boston Bruins	5
May 19	Boston Bruins	0	at	Philadelphia Flyers	1

All Star Teams

First Team		Second Team
Bernie Parent	Goal	Tony Esposito
Bobby Orr	Defense	Bill White
Brad Park	Defense	Barry Ashbee
Phil Esposito	Center	Bobby Clarke
Ken Hodge	Right Wing	Mickey Redmond
Richard Martin	Left Wing	Wayne Cashman

Individual Awards

Art Ross Trophy--Phil Esposito (Boston Bruins)
Bill Masterton Trophy--Henri Richard (Montreal Canadiens)
Calder Memorial Trophy--Denis Potvin (New York Islanders)
Conn Smythe Trophy--Bernie Parent (Philadelphia Flyers)
Hart Memorial Trophy--Phil Esposito (Boston Bruins)
Jack Adams Award--Fred Shero (Philadelphia Flyers)
James Norris Trophy--Bobby Orr (Boston Bruins)

Lady Byng Memorial Trophy--John Bucyk (Boston Bruins)
Lester Patrick Trophy--Alex Delvecchio, Murray Murdoch, Weston Adams Sr., Charles Crovat
Lester B. Pearson Award--Phil Esposito (Boston Bruins)
NHL All Star Game MVP--Garry Unger (St. Louis Blues)
Vezina Trophy--Bernie Parent (Philadelphia Flyers)
Tony Esposito (Chicago Black Hawks)

Hall of Fame Inductees

Billy Burch, Art Coulter, Tom Dunderdale, Charles Hay, Tommy Ivan, Dickie Moore, Anatoli Tarasov, Carl Voss

World Hockey Association
Eastern Division

Team Name	GP	W	L	T	GF	GA	Pts	Pct
New England Whalers	78	43	31	4	291	260	90	.577
Toronto Toros	78	41	33	4	304	272	86	.551
Cleveland Crusaders	78	37	32	9	266	264	83	.532
Chicago Cougars	78	38	35	5	271	273	81	.519
Quebec Nordiques	78	38	36	4	306	280	80	.513
(New York Golden Blades)	20	6	12	2	47	80	14	.350
(New Jersey Knights)	58	26	30	2	221	233	54	.466

Western Division

Team Name	GP	W	L	T	GF	GA	Pts	Pct
Houston Aeros	78	48	25	5	318	219	101	.647
Minnesota Fighting Saints	78	44	32	2	332	275	90	.577
Edmonton Oilers	78	38	37	3	268	269	79	.506
Winnipeg Jets	78	34	39	5	264	296	73	.468
Vancouver Blazers	78	27	50	1	278	345	55	.353
Los Angeles Sharks	78	25	53	0	239	339	50	.321

Coaching Changes

New England--Ron Ryan 43-31-4; Toronto--Billy Harris 41-33-4; Chicago--Pat Stapleton 38-35-5; Quebec--Jacques Plante 38-36-4; New York--Camille Henry 6-12-2; New Jersey--Harry Howell 26-30-2; Minnesota--Harry Neale 44-32-2; Edmonton--Brian Shaw 38-37-3; Vancouver--John McKenzie 3-4-0, Phil Watson 3-9-0, Andy Bathgate 21-37-1; Los Angeles--Ted Slater 5-14-0, Ted McCaskill 20-39-0.

League Leaders

Goals		Assists		Points	
Mike Walton	57	Andre Lacroix	80	Mike Walton	117
Bobby Hull	53	Gordie Howe	69	Andre Lacroix	111
Danny Lawson	50	Bryan Campbell	62	Gordie Howe	100
Tom Webster	43	Mike Walton	60	Bobby Hull	95
Frank Hughes	42	Andre Hinse	56	Wayne Connelly	95

Penalty Minutes		GAA (1,560 minutes)		Wins	
Gord Gallant	223	Don McLeod	2.56	Don McLeod	33
Doug Barrie	214	Gerry Cheevers	3.03	Al Smith	30
John Arbour	192	Al Smith	3.08	Gerry Cheevers	30
Colin Campbell	191	Cam Newton	3.14	Gilles Gratton	26
Jim Cardiff	188	Jack Norris	3.21	Cam Newton	25

Shutouts		**Save %**	
Gerry Cheevers	4	Don McLeod	.911
Don McLeod	3	Mike Curran	.910
Ernie Wakely	3	Gerry Cheevers	.906
Pete Donnelly	3	John Garrett	.903
Mike Curran	2	Richard Brodeur	.901

All Star Game

(St. Paul Civic Center, St. Paul)

January 3	East Division	8		West Division	4

WHA Playoffs

April 6	Edmonton Oilers	1	at	Minnesota Fighting Saints	2
April 6	Chicago Cougars	4	at	New England Whalers	6
April 7	Cleveland Crusaders	0	at	Toronto Toros	4
April 7	Edmonton Oilers	5	at	Minnesota Fighting Saints	8
April 7	Chicago Cougars	3	at	New England Whalers	4 [2:05]
April 8	Houston Aeros	5	at	Winnipeg Jets	2
April 9	New England Whalers	6	at	Chicago Cougars	8
April 9	Cleveland Crusaders	3	at	Toronto Toros	4
April 10	Houston Aeros	3	at	Winnipeg Jets	2
April 10	Minnesota Fighting Saints	6	at	Edmonton Oilers	2
April 10	New England Whalers	1	at	Chicago Cougars	2 [17:45]
April 12	Minnesota Fighting Saints	1	at	Edmonton Oilers	2
April 12	Chicago Cougars	4	at	New England Whalers	2
April 12	Toronto Toros	4	at	Cleveland Crusaders	2
April 13	Winnipeg Jets	1	at	Houston Aeros	10
April 13	Toronto Toros	2	at	Cleveland Crusaders	3
April 14	Edmonton Oilers	4	at	Minnesota Fighting Saints	5
April 14	Winnipeg Jets	4	at	Houston Aeros	5
April 14	New England Whalers	2	at	Chicago Cougars	0
April 15	Cleveland Crusaders	1	at	Toronto Toros	4
April 16	Chicago Cougars	3	at	New England Whalers	2
April 18	Minnesota Fighting Saints	5	at	Houston Aeros	4
April 19	Chicago Cougars	4	at	Toronto Toros	6
April 20	Minnesota Fighting Saints	2	at	Houston Aeros	5
April 21	Houston Aeros	1	at	Minnesota Fighting Saints	4
April 22	Chicago Cougars	4	at	Toronto Toros	3
April 28	Houston Aeros	4	at	Minnesota Fighting Saints	1
April 28	Toronto Toros	2	at	Chicago Cougars	3*
April 29	Minnesota Fighting Saints	4	at	Houston Aeros	9
April 29	Toronto Toros	7	at	Chicago Cougars	6*
May 1	Houston Aeros	3	at	Minnesota Fighting Saints	1
May 1	Chicago Cougars	3	at	Toronto Toros	5
May 4	Toronto Toros	2	at	Chicago Cougars	9*
May 6	Chicago Cougars	5	at	Toronto Toros	2
May 12	Houston Aeros	3	at	Chicago Cougars	2*
May 15	Houston Aeros	6	at	Chicago Cougars	1*
May 17	Chicago Cougars	4	at	Houston Aeros	7
May 19	Chicago Cougars	2	at	Houston Aeros	6

*Games played in Mt. Prospect, Illinois

All Star Teams

First Team		Second Team
Don MacLeod	Goal	Gerry Cheevers
Pat Stapleton	Defense	J.C. Tremblay
Paul Shmyr	Defense	Al Hamilton
Andre Lacroix	Center	Wayne Carleton
Gordie Howe	Right Wing	Mike Walton
Bobby Hull	Left Wing	Mark Howe

Individual Awards

Ben Hatskin Trophy--Don McLeod (Houston Aeros)
Bill Hunter Trophy--Mike Walton (Minnesota Fighting Saints)
Dennis Murphy Trophy--Pat Stapleton (Chicago Cougars)
Gordie Howe Trophy--Gordie Howe (Houston Aeros)
Lou Kaplan Trophy--Mark Howe (Houston Aeros)
Paul Deneau Trophy--Ralph Backstrom (Chicago Cougars)
Robert Schmertz Trophy--Billy Harris (Toronto Toros)
WHA All Star Game MVP--Mike Walton (Minnesota Fighting Saints)

Notes

Dennis Murphy replaced Gary Davidson as president of the World Hockey Association.
The New England franchise moved from Boston to Hartford but retained the original name.

SOCCER

North American Soccer League
Northern Division

Team Name	GP	W	L	T	GF	GA	BP	Pts	Pct
Boston Minutemen	20	10	9	1	36	23	31	94	.522
Toronto Metros	20	9	10	1	30	31	30	87	.483
Rochester Lancers	20	8	10	2	23	30	23	77	.428
New York Cosmos	20	4	14	2	28	40	28	58	.322

Eastern Division

Team Name	GP	W	L	T	GF	GA	BP	Pts	Pct
Miami Toros	20	9	5	6	38	24	35	107	.594
Baltimore Comets	20	10	8	2	42	46	39	105	.583
Philadelphia Atoms	20	8	11	1	25	25	23	74	.411
Washington Diplomats	20	7	12	1	29	36	25	70	.389

Central Division

Team Name	GP	W	L	T	GF	GA	BP	Pts	Pct
Dallas Tornado	20	9	8	3	39	27	37	100	.556
St.. Louis Stars	20	4	15	1	27	42	27	54	.300
Denver Dynamos	20	5	15	0	21	42	19	49	.272

Western Division

Team Name	GP	W	L	T	GF	GA	BP	Pts	Pct
Los Angeles Aztecs	20	11	7	2	41	36	38	110	.611
San Jose Earthquakes	20	9	8	3	43	38	40	103	.572
Seattle Sounders	20	10	7	3	37	17	32	101	.561
Vancouver Whitecaps	20	5	11	4	29	30	28	70	.389

Coaching Changes

Boston--Hubert Vogelsinger 10-9-1; Rochester--Bill Hughes , John Petrossi, Ted Dumitru; Baltimore--Doug Millward 10-8-2; Washington--Dennis Viollet 7-12-1; St. Louis--John Sewell 4-15-1; Denver--Ken Bracewell 5-15-0; Los Angeles--Alex Perolli 11-7-2; San Jose-Gabbo Gavric 7-7-0, Ivan Toplak 2-1-3; Seattle--John Best 10-7-3; Vancouver--Jim Easton 5-11-4.

League Leaders

Goals		Points		Shutouts	
Paul Child	15	Paul Child	36	Ken Cooper	9
Peter Silvester	14	Peter Silvester	31	Barry Watling	8
Steven David	13	Doug McMillan	30	Claude Campos	8
David Butler	10	John Rowlands	28	Ian McKechnie	5
Doug McMillan	10	Steven David	26	Bob Rigby	5

GAA	
Barry Watling	0.80
Ian McKechnie	0.94
Bob Rigby	1.10
Ken Cooper	1.10
Claude Campos	1.14

NASL Playoffs

August 14	San Jose Earthquakes	0	at	Dallas Tornado	3
August 15	Baltimore Comets	0	at	Boston Minutemen	1
August 17	Boston Minutemen	0	at	Los Angeles Aztecs	2
August 17	Dallas Tornado	1	at	Miami Toros	3
August 25	Los Angeles Aztecs	4	at	Miami Toros	3 [OT]

All Star Teams

First Team		Second Team
Barry Watling	Goal	Bob Rigby
Dick Hall	Defender	Ralph Wright
Albert Jackson	Defender	Derek Trevis
Chris Dunleavy	Defender	Jim Gabriel
Geoff Butler	Defender	Brian Rowan
Ronnie Sharp	Midfield	Hank Liotart
llija Mitic	Midfield	Luis Marotte
Roberto Aguirre	Midfield	Fernando Pinto
Paul Child	Forward	Ade Coker
John Rowlands	Forward	Doug McMillan
Peter Silvester	Forward	Warren Archibald

Individual Awards

Coach of the Year--John Young (Miami Toros)
Lead Goalkeeper Award--Barry Watling (Seattle Sounders)
Most Valuable Player--Peter Silvester (Baltimore Comets)
Rookie of the Year--Douglas McMillan (Los Angeles Aztecs)

Rules

The NASL introduced the tie breaker rule this year in an attempt to lessen the number of tie games. Whenever the game was tied after the regulation 90 minutes the game would be decided by penalty kicks, the teams alternately taking five turns each, the winner would be the team scoring the most goals, or if the tie remained after five attempts, the team scoring more than the other after equal numbers of additional attempts.

Franchise Changes

WHA--Ottawa Nationals became the Toronto Toros.
New York Raiders changed their name to New York Golden Blades and then became the New Jersey Knights after 20 games.
Alberta Oilers became the Edmonton Oilers.
Philadelphia Blazers became the Vancouver Blazers
NBA--Baltimore Bullets became the Capital Bullets based in Washington D.C.
ABA--Dallas Chaparrals became the San Antonio Spurs.

Other Sports

Horseracing--Kentucky Derby won by Cannonade (time 2:04, purse $274,000).
Heavyweight Boxing--George Foreman knocked-out Ken Norton in 2 rounds.
Muhammad Ali knocked-out George Foreman in 8 rounds.
Golf--U.S. Open won by Hale Irwin with a score of 287.
Auto Racing--Indianapolis 500 won by Johnny Rutherford (ave. speed 158.589 MPH).
Tennis--U.S. Open won by Jimmy Connors in the men's singles.
U.S. Open won by Bob Lutz and Stan Smith in the men's doubles.
U.S. Open won by Billie Jean King in the women's singles.
U.S. Open won by Billie Jean King and Rosemary Casals in the women's doubles.
U.S. Open won by Pam Teeguarden and Geoff Masters in the mixed doubles.

1975

BASEBALL
National League

East

Team Name	W	L	Pct	GB	R	OR
Pittsburgh Pirates	92	69	.571	-	712	565
Philadelphia Phillies	86	76	.531	6.5	735	694
New York Mets	82	80	.506	10.5	646	625
St. Louis Cardinals	82	80	.506	10.5	662	689
Chicago Cubs	75	87	.463	17.5	712	827
Montreal Expos	75	87	.463	17.5	601	690

West

Team Name	W	L	Pct	GB	R	OR
Cincinnati Reds	108	54	.667	-	840	586
Los Angeles Dodgers	88	74	.543	20	648	534
San Francisco Giants	80	81	.497	27.5	659	671
San Diego Padres	71	91	.438	37	552	683
Atlanta Braves	67	94	.416	40.5	584	739
Houston Astros	64	97	.398	43.5	664	711

Coaching Changes

New York--Yogi Berra 56-53, Roy McMillan 26-27; Chicago--Jim Marshall 75-87; San Francisco Wes Westrum 80-81; Atlanta--Clyde King 59-76, Connie Ryan 8-18; Houston--Preston Gomez 47-80, Bill Virdon 17-17.

League Leaders

Batting Average		Home Runs		RBI	
Bill Madlock	.354	Mike Schmidt	38	Greg Luzinski	120
Ted Simmons	.332	Don Kingman	36	Johnny Bench	110
Manny Sanguillen	.328	Greg Luzinski	34	Tony Perez	109
Joe Morgan	.327	Johnny Bench	28	Daniel Staub	105
Bob Watson	.324	Dave Parker	25	Dave Parker	101

Stolen Bases		ERA		Wins	
Dave Lopes	77	Randy Jones	2.24	Tom Seaver	22
Joe Morgan	67	Andy Messersmith	2.29	Randy Jones	20
Lou Brock	56	Tom Seaver	2.38	Andy Messersmith	19
Cesar Cedeno	50	Jerry Reuss	2.54	Jerry Reuss	18
Jose Cardenal	34	Bob Forsch	2.86	Burt Hooten	18

Saves		Strikeouts	
Al Hrabosky	22	Tom Seaver	243
Rawly Eastwick	22	John Montefusco	215
Dave Giusti	17	Andy Messersmith	213
Darold Knowles	15	Steve Carlton	192
Will McEnaney	15	J.R. Richard	176

NLCS

October 4	Pittsburgh Pirates	3	at	Cincinnati Reds	8
October 5	Pittsburgh Pirates	1	at	Cincinnati Reds	6
October 7	Cincinnati Reds	5	at	Pittsburgh Pirates	3 [10]

American League

East

Team Name	W	L	Pct	GB	R	OR
Boston Red Sox	95	65	.594	-	796	709
Baltimore Orioles	90	69	.566	4.5	682	553
New York Yankees	83	77	.519	12	681	588
Cleveland Indians	79	80	.497	15.5	688	703
Milwaukee Brewers	68	94	.420	28	675	792
Detroit Tigers	57	102	.358	37.5	570	786

West

Team Name	W	L	Pct	GB	R	OR
Oakland Athletics	98	64	.605	-	758	606
Kansas City Royals	91	71	.562	7	710	649
Texas Rangers	79	83	.488	19	714	733
Minnesota Twins	76	83	.478	20.5	724	736
Chicago White Sox	75	86	.466	22.5	655	703
California Angels	72	89	.447	25.5	628	723

Coaching Changes

New York--Bill Virdon 53-51, Billy Martin 30-26; Cleveland--Frank Robinson 79-80; Kansas City--Jack McKeon 50-46, Dorrel "Whitey" Herzog 41-25; Texas--Billy Martin 44-51, Frank Lucchesi 35-32; California--Dick Williams 72-89.

League Leaders

Batting Average		Home Runs		RBI	
Rod Carew	.359	George Scott	36	George Scott	109
Fred Lynn	.331	Reggie Jackson	36	John Mayberry	106
Thurman Munson	.318	John Mayberry	34	Fred Lynn	105
Jim Rice	.309	Bobby Bonds	32	Reggie Jackson	104
Claudell Washington	.308	Gene Tenace	29	Jim Rice	102

Stolen Bases		ERA		Wins	
Mickey Rivers	70	Jim Palmer	2.09	James Hunter	23
Claudell Washington	40	James Hunter	2.58	Jim Palmer	23
Amos Otis	39	Dennis Eckersley	2.60	Vida Blue	22
Rod Carew	35	Frank Tanana	2.62	Jim Kaat	20
Jerry Remy	34	Ed Figueroa	2.91	Mike Torrez	20

Saves		Strikeouts	
Rich Gossage	26	Frank Tanana	269
Rollie Fingers	24	Bert Blyleven	233
Tom Murphy	20	Gaylord Perry	233
Dave LaRoache	17	Jim Palmer	193
Dick Drago	15	Vida Blue	189

All Star Game
(County Stadium, Milwaukee)

July 15	National League	6		American League	3

ALCS

October 4	Oakland Athletics	1	at	Boston Red Sox	7
October 5	Oakland Athletics	2	at	Boston Red Sox	6
October 7	Boston Red Sox	5	at	Oakland Athletics	3

World Series

October 11	Cincinnati Reds	0	at	Boston Red Sox	6
October 12	Cincinnati Reds	3	at	Boston Red Sox	2
October 14	Boston Red Sox	5	at	Cincinnati Reds	6 [10]
October 15	Boston Red Sox	5	at	Cincinnati Reds	4
October 16	Boston Red Sox	2	at	Cincinnati Reds	6
October 21	Cincinnati Reds	6	at	Boston Red Sox	7 [12]
October 22	Cincinnati Reds	4	at	Boston Red Sox	3

Individual Awards

Arch Ward Memorial Trophy--Bill Madlock (Chicago Cubs NL)
John Matlock (New York Mets NL)
Baseball Writers Award--Joe Morgan (Cincinnati Reds NL)
Fred Lynn (Boston Red Sox AL)
Cy Young Award--Tom Seaver (New York Mets NL)
Jim Palmer (Baltimore Orioles AL)
Rookie of the Year--John Montefusco (San Francisco Giants NL)
Fred Lynn (Boston Red Sox AL)
Sporting News Executive of the Year--Dick O'Connell (Boston Red Sox AL)
Sporting News Manager of the Year--Darrell Johnson (Boston Red Sox AL)
Sporting News Pitcher of the Year--Tom Seaver (New York Mets NL)
Jim Palmer (Baltimore Orioles AL)
Sporting News Player of the Year--Joe Morgan (Cincinnati Reds NL)
Fred Lynn (Boston Red Sox AL)
Sporting News Rookie of the Year--Gary Carter (Montreal Expos NL)
John Montefusco (San Francisco Giants NL)
Fred Lynn (Boston Red Sox AL)
Dennis Eckersley (Cleveland Indians AL)
World Series MVP--Pete Rose (Cincinnati Reds NL)

Hall of Fame Inductees

Earl Averill, Stanley "Bucky" Harris, Billy Herman, Judy Johnson, Ralph Kiner

Rules

The American League decided to adopt the designated hitter rule on a permanent basis.

Notes

Jim "Catfish" Hunter became the first free agent in baseball history.
Frank Robinson became the first black manager in baseball history when he was named manager of the Cleveland Indians.

BASKETBALL
National Basketball Association

Atlantic Division

Team Name	GP	W	L	PPGF	PPGA	Pct	GB
Boston Celtics	82	60	22	106.5	100.8	.732	-
Buffalo Braves	82	49	33	107.8	105.6	.598	11
New York Knickerbockers	82	40	42	100.4	101.7	.488	20
Philadelphia 76ers	82	34	48	99.8	102.8	.415	26

Central Division

Team Name	GP	W	L	PPGF	PPGA	Pct	GB
Washington Bullets	82	60	22	104.7	97.5	.732	-
Houston Rockets	82	41	41	103.9	102.9	.500	19
Cleveland Cavaliers	82	40	42	99.0	99.4	.488	20
Atlanta Hawks	82	31	51	105.1	106.5	.378	29
New Orleans Jazz	82	23	59	101.5	109.3	.280	37

Midwest Division

Team Name	GP	W	L	PPGF	PPGA	Pct	GB
Chicago Bulls	82	47	35	98.1	95.0	.573	-
Kansas City-Omaha Kings	82	44	38	101.4	101.6	.537	3
Detroit Pistons	82	40	42	98.9	100.3	.488	7
Milwaukee Bucks	82	38	44	100.7	100.5	.463	9

Pacific Division

Team Name	GP	W	L	PPGF	PPGA	Pct	GB
Golden State Warriors	82	48	34	108.5	105.2	.585	-
Seattle SuperSonics	82	43	39	103.1	103.1	.524	5
Portland Trail Blazers	82	38	44	105.8	103.3	.463	10
Phoenix Suns	82	32	50	101.2	103.6	.390	16
Los Angeles Lakers	82	30	52	103.2	107.2	.366	18

Coaching Changes

Washington--K.C. Jones 60-22; New Orleans--Scotty Robertson 1-14, Elgin Baylor 0-1, Butch Van Breda Kolff 22-44; Kansas City/Omaha--Phil Johnson 44-38; Portland--Lenny Wilkens 38-44.

League Leaders

Field Goals

Bob McAdoo	1095
Rick Barry	1028
Kareem Abdul-Jabbar	812
Nate Archibald	759
Elvin Hayes	739

Free Throws

Nate Archibald	652
Bob McAdoo	641
Chet Walker	413
Elvin Hayes	409
Rick Barry	394

Assists

Kevin Porter	650
Dave Bing	610
Nate Archibald	557
Randy Smith	534
Slick Watts	499

Points

Bob McAdoo	2831
Rick Barry	2450
Nate Archibald	2170
Kareem Abdul-Jabbar	1949
Elvin Hayes	1887

Fouls

Phil Jackson	330
Bob Dandridge	330
Kevin Porter	320
Cliff Ray	305
Ron Behagen	301

All Star Game

(Arizona Veterans' Memorial Coliseum, Phoenix)

January 14	East Division	108		West Division	102

NBA Playoffs

April 8	N.Y. Knickerbockers	84	at	Houston Rockets	99
April 8	Detroit Pistons	77	at	Seattle SuperSonics	90
April 9	K.C.-Omaha Kings	89	at	Chicago Bulls	95
April 10	Houston Rockets	96	at	N.Y. Knickerbockers	106
April 10	Seattle SuperSonics	106	at	Detroit Pistons	122
April 10	Buffalo Braves	113	at	Washington Bullets	102
April 12	N.Y. Knickerbockers	86	at	Houston Rockets	118
April 12	Detroit Pistons	93	at	Seattle SuperSonics	100
April 12	Washington Bullets	120	at	Buffalo Braves	106
April 13	Chicago Bulls	95	at	K.C.-Omaha Kings	102
April 14	Houston Rockets	106	at	Boston Celtics	123
April 14	Seattle SuperSonics	96	at	Golden State Warriors	123
April 16	Houston Rockets	100	at	Boston Celtics	123
April 16	Seattle SuperSonics	100	at	Golden State Warriors	99
April 16	Buffalo Braves	96	at	Washington Bullets	111
April 16	K.C.-Omaha Kings	90	at	Chicago Bulls	93
April 17	Golden State Warriors	105	at	Seattle SuperSonics	96
April 18	Washington Bullets	102	at	Buffalo Braves	108
April 18	Chicago Bulls	100	at	K.C.-Omaha Kings	104 [OT]
April 19	Boston Celtics	102	at	Houston Rockets	117
April 19	Golden State Warriors	94	at	Seattle SuperSonics	111
April 20	Buffalo Braves	93	at	Washington Bullets	97
April 20	K.C.-Omaha Kings	77	at	Chicago Bulls	104
April 22	Boston Celtics	122	at	Houston Rockets	117
April 22	Seattle SuperSonics	100	at	Golden State Warriors	124
April 23	Washington Bullets	96	at	Buffalo Braves	102
April 23	Chicago Bulls	101	at	K.C.-Omaha Kings	89
April 24	Golden State Warriors	105	at	Seattle SuperSonics	96
April 24	Houston Rockets	115	at	Boston Celtics	128
April 25	Buffalo Braves	96	at	Washington Bullets	115
April 27	Washington Bullets	100	at	Boston Celtics	95
April 27	Chicago Bulls	89	at	Golden State Warriors	107
April 30	Boston Celtics	92	at	Washington Bullets	117
April 30	Golden State Warriors	89	at	Chicago Bulls	90
May 3	Washington Bullets	90	at	Boston Celtics	101
May 4	Golden State Warriors	101	at	Chicago Bulls	108
May 6	Chicago Bulls	106	at	Golden State Warriors	111
May 7	Boston Celtics	108	at	Washington Bullets	119
May 8	Chicago Bulls	89	at	Golden State Warriors	79
May 9	Washington Bullets	99	at	Boston Celtics	103
May 11	Golden State Warriors	86	at	Chicago Bulls	72
May 11	Boston Celtics	92	at	Washington Bullets	98
May 14	Chicago Bulls	79	at	Golden State Warriors	83
May 18	Golden State Warriors	101	at	Washington Bullets	95
May 20	Washington Bullets	91	at	Golden State Warriors	92
May 23	Washington Bullets	101	at	Golden State Warriors	109
May 25	Golden State Warriors	96	at	Washington Bullets	95

All Star Teams

First Team	Second Team
Rick Barry (Golden State Warriors)	John Havlicek (Boston Celtics)
Elvin Hayes (Washington Bullets)	Spencer Haywood (Seattle SuperSonics)
Bob McAdoo (Buffalo Braves)	Dave Cowens (Boston Celtics)
Nate Archibald (Kansas City-Omaha)	Phil Chenier (Washington Bullets)
Walt Frazier (N.Y. Knickerbockers)	Jo Jo White (Boston Celtics)

Individual Awards

Eddie Gottlieb Trophy--Keith Wilkes (Golden State Warriors)
J. Walter Kennedy Award--Wes Unseld (Washington Bullets)
Maurice Podoloff Trophy--Bob McAdoo (Buffalo Braves)
NBA All Star Game MVP--Walt Frazier (New York Knickerbockers)
NBA Executive of the Year--Dick Vertlieb (Golden State Warriors)
NBA Finals MVP--Rick Barry (Golden State Warriors)
Maurice Podoloff Trophy--Bob McAdoo (Buffalo Braves)
Red Auerbach Trophy--Phil Johnson (Kansas City-Omaha)

Hall of Fame Inductees

Tom Gola, Edward Krause, Harry Litwack, Bill Sharman

Notes

Larry O'Brien succeeded J. Walter Kennedy as Commissioner of the National Basketball Association.

American Basketball Association
Eastern Division

Team Name	GP	W	L	PPGF	PPGA	Pct	GB
Kentucky Colonels	84	58	26	108.9	101.7	.690	-
New York Nets	84	58	26	111.1	103.4	.690	-
Spirits of St. Louis	84	32	52	109.0	113.4	.381	26
Memphis Sounds	84	27	57	103.6	108.9	.321	31
Virginia Squires	84	15	69	99.0	109.5	.179	43

Western Division

Team Name	GP	W	L	PPGF	PPGA	Pct	GB
Denver Nuggets	84	65	19	118.7	111.4	.774	-
San Antonio Spurs	84	51	33	113.4	109.2	.607	14
Indiana Pacers	84	45	39	112.8	111.7	.536	20
Utah Stars	84	38	46	101.3	102.9	.452	27
San Diego Conquistadors	84	31	53	109.9	115.5	.369	34

Coaching Changes

Kentucky--Hubie Brown 58-26; St. Louis--Bob MacKinnon 32-52; Memphis--Joe Mullaney 27-57; Denver--Larry Brown 65-19; San Antonio--Tom Nissalke 18-10, Bob Bass 33-23; Utah--Bucky Buckwalter 24-32, Tom Nissalke 14-14; San Diego--Alex Groza 15-23, Beryl Shipley 16-30.

League Leaders

Field Goals		Free Throws		Assists	
Julius Erving	914	George McGinnis	545	Chuck Williams	576
George McGinnis	873	Julius Erving	486	Mack Calvin	570
Ron Boone	872	Mack Calvin	475	George McGinnis	495
Artis Gilmore	784	James Silas	430	Julius Erving	462
George Gervin	784	Artis Gilmore	412	Louie Dampier	449

Points		Fouls	
George McGinnis	2353	Wilbert Jones	353
Julius Erving	2343	Darnell Hillman	330
Ron Boone	2117	Marvin Barnes	328
Artis Gilmore	1981	Artis Gilmore	318
George Gervin	1965	Mike Jackson	308

All Star Game

(HemisFair Arena, San Antonio)

January 28	East Division	151		West Division	124

ABA Playoffs

April 5	Indiana Pacers	122	at	San Antonio Spurs	119 [OT]
April 6	Memphis Sounds	91	at	Kentucky Colonels	98
April 6	Spirits of St. Louis	105	at	New York Nets	111
April 6	Utah Stars	107	at	Denver Nuggets	122
April 7	Indiana Pacers	98	at	San Antonio Spurs	93
April 7	Utah Stars	120	at	Denver Nuggets	126
April 8	Memphis Sounds	105	at	Kentucky Colonels	119
April 9	Spirits of St. Louis	115	at	New York Nets	97
April 9	Denver Nuggets	108	at	Utah Stars	122
April 10	Kentucky Colonels	101	at	Memphis Sounds	80
April 10	San Antonio Spurs	103	at	Indiana Pacers	113
April 11	New York Nets	108	at	Spirits of St. Louis	113
April 11	Kentucky Colonels	93	at	Memphis Sounds	107
April 11	Denver Nuggets	110	at	Utah Stars	132
April 12	San Antonio Spurs	110	at	Indiana Pacers	109
April 12	Utah Stars	119	at	Denver Nuggets	130
April 13	Memphis Sounds	99	at	Kentucky Colonels	111
April 13	New York Nets	89	at	Spirits of St. Louis	100
April 14	Indiana Pacers	117	at	San Antonio Spurs	123
April 14	Denver Nuggets	115	at	Utah Stars	113
April 15	Spirits of St. Louis	108	at	New York Nets	107
April 16	San Antonio Spurs	100	at	Indiana Pacers	115
April 20	Indiana Pacers	128	at	Denver Nuggets	131
April 21	Spirits of St. Louis	109	at	Kentucky Colonels	112
April 22	Indiana Pacers	131	at	Denver Nuggets	124
April 23	Spirits of St. Louis	103	at	Kentucky Colonels	108
April 24	Denver Nuggets	112	at	Indiana Pacers	118
April 25	Kentucky Colonels	97	at	Spirits of St. Louis	103
April 25	Denver Nuggets	126	at	Indiana Pacers	109
April 27	Kentucky Colonels	117	at	Spirits of St. Louis	98
April 27	Indiana Pacers	109	at	Denver Nuggets	90

April 28	Spirits of St. Louis	103	at	Kentucky Colonels	123
April 30	Denver Nuggets	104	at	Indiana Pacers	99
May 3	Indiana Pacers	104	at	Denver Nuggets	96
May 13	Indiana Pacers	94	at	Kentucky Colonels	120
May 15	Indiana Pacers	93	at	Kentucky Colonels	95
May 17	Kentucky Colonels	109	at	Indiana Pacers	101
May 19	Kentucky Colonels	86	at	Indiana Pacers	94
May 22	Indiana Pacers	105	at	Kentucky Colonels	110

All Star Teams

First Team

Julius Erving (New York Nets)
George McGinnis (Indiana Pacers)
Artis Gilmore (Kentucky Colonels)
Mack Calvin (Denver Nuggets)
Ron Boone (Utah Stars)

Second Team

Marvin Barnes (Spirits of St. Louis)
George Gervin (San Antonio Spurs)
Swen Nater (San Antonio Spurs)
Brian Taylor (New York Nets)
James Silas (San Antonio Spurs)

Individual Awards

ABA All Star Game MVP--Freddie Lewis (Spirits of St. Louis)
Coach of the Year--Larry Brown (Denver Nuggets)
Most Valuable Player--George McGinnis (Indiana Pacers)
Julius Erving (New York Nets)
Rookie of the Year--Marvin Barnes (Spirits of St. Louis)

FOOTBALL
National Football League

National Football Conference
Eastern Division

Team Name	GP	W	L	T	PF	PA	Pct
St. Louis Cardinals	14	11	3	0	356	276	.786
Dallas Cowboys	14	10	4	0	350	268	.714
Washington Redskins	14	8	6	0	325	276	.571
New York Giants	14	5	9	0	216	306	.357
Philadelphia Eagles	14	4	10	0	226	302	.286

Central Division

Team Name	GP	W	L	T	PF	PA	Pct
Minnesota Vikings	14	12	2	0	377	180	.857
Detroit Lions	14	7	7	0	245	262	.500
Chicago Bears	14	4	10	0	191	379	.286
Green Bay Packers	14	4	10	0	226	285	.286

Western Division

Team Name	GP	W	L	T	PF	PA	Pct
Los Angeles Rams	14	12	2	0	312	135	.857
San Francisco 49ers	14	5	9	0	255	286	.357
Atlanta Falcons	14	4	10	0	240	289	.286
New Orleans Saints	14	2	12	0	165	360	.143

American Football Conference

Eastern Division

Baltimore Colts	14	10	4	0	395	269	.714
Miami Dolphins	14	10	4	0	357	222	.714
Buffalo Bills	14	8	6	0	420	355	.571
New York Jets	14	3	11	0	258	438	.214
New England Patriots	14	3	11	0	258	358	.214

Central Division

Pittsburgh Steelers	14	12	2	0	373	162	.857
Cincinnati -Bengals	14	11	3	0	340	246	.786
Houston Oilers	14	10	4	0	293	226	.714
Cleveland Browns	14	3	11	0	218	372	.214

Western Division

Oakland Raiders	14	11	3	0	375	255	.786
Denver Broncos	14	6	8	0	254	307	.429
Kansas City Chiefs	14	5	9	0	282	341	.357
San Diego Chargers	14	2	12	0	189	345	.143

Coaching Changes

Chicago--Jack Pardee 4-10-0; Green Bay--Bart Starr 4-10-0; Atlanta--Marion Campbell 4-10-0; New Orleans--John North 1-5-0; Ernie Hefferle 1-7-0; Baltimore--Ted Marchibroda 10-4-0; New York Jets--Charley Winner 2-7-0, Ken Shipp 1-4-0; Houston--Bum Phillips 10-4-0; Cleveland--Forrest Gregg 3-11-0; Kansas City--Paul Wiggin 5-9-0.

League Leaders

Yards Rushing		**Yards Passing**		**Passing %** (140 attempts)	
O.J. Simpson	1817	Ken Anderson	3169	Len Dawson	66.4
Franco Harris	1246	Fran Tarkenton	2994	Fran Tarkenton	64.2
Lydell Mitchell	1193	Roger Staubach	2666	Bob Griese	61.8
Jim Otis	1076	Jim Hart	2507	Ken Anderson	60.5
Chuck Foreman	1070	Bert Jones	2483	Bert Jones	59.0

Receiving Yards		**Receptions**		**Field Goals**	
Ken Burrough	1063	Chuck Foreman	73	Toni Fritsch	22
Isaac Curtis	934	Lydell Mitchell	60	Jan Stenerud	22
Mel Gray	926	Reg Rucker	60	Jim Turner	21
Cliff Branch	893	Ken Payne	58	Tom Dempsey	21
Drew Pearson	822	Bob Chandler	55	Horst Muhlmann	20

Punt Return Yards		**Kickoff Return Yards**	
Neal Colzie	655	Rick Upchurch	1084
Billy Johnson	610	Steve Odom	1034
Virgil Livers	456	Terry Metcalfe	960
Mike Fuller	410	Vic Washington	923
Howard Stevens	396	Kent Carter	879

Pro Bowl Game

(Louisiana Superdome, New Orleans)

January 26 1976	National Conference	23		American Conference	20

NFL Playoffs

December 27	St. Louis Cardinals	23	at	Los Angeles Rams	35
December 27	Baltimore Colts	10	at	Pittsburgh Steelers	28
December 28	Dallas Cowboys	17	at	Minnesota Vikings	14
December 28	Cincinnati Bengals	28	at	Oakland Raiders	31
January 4 1976	Dallas Cowboys	37	at	Los Angeles Rams	7
January 4 1976	Oakland Raiders	10	at	Pittsburgh Steelers	16

Super Bowl X

(Orange Bowl, Miami)

January 18 1976	Pittsburgh Steelers	21		Dallas Cowboys	17

Individual Awards

A.P. MVP--Fran Tarkenton (Minnesota Vikings)
Bert Bell Trophy--Robert Brazile (Houston Oilers) [World Almanac]
Steve Bartkowski (Atlanta Falcons)
Bert Bell Trophy--Fran Tarkenton (Minnesota Vikings)
George Halas Trophy--Mel Blount (Dallas Cowboys)
Curley Culp (Kansas City Chiefs)
Jack Youngblood (Los Angeles Rams)
Jim Thorpe Trophy--Fran Tarkenton (Minnesota Vikings)
Pro Bowl MVP--Billy Johnson (Houston Oilers)
Rookie of the Year--Mike Thomas (Washington Redskins)
Robert Brazile (Houston Oilers)
Super Bowl MVP--Lynn Swann (Pittsburgh Steelers)
U.P.I. AFC Coach of the Year--Ted Marchibroda (Baltimore Colts)
U.P.I. AFC Player of the Year--O.J. Simpson (Buffalo Bills)
U.P.I. AFC Rookie of the Year--Robert Brazile (Houston Oilers)
U.P.I. NFC Coach of the Year--Tom Landry (Dallas Cowboys)
U.P.I. NFC Player of the Year--Fran Tarkenton (Minnesota Vikings)
U.P.I. NFC Rookie of the Year--Mike Thomas (Washington Redskins)

Hall of Fame Inductees

Roosevelt Brown, George Connor, Dante Lavelli, Lenny Moore

Notes

NFL referees were equipped with wireless microphones for all games.
The divisional winners with the highest won-lost percentage were made the home team for the divisional playoffs, and the surviving winners with the highest percentage made home team for the championship game.

Canadian Football League
Eastern Conference

Team Name	GP	W	L	T	PF	PA	Pts	Pct
Ottawa Rough Riders	16	10	5	1	394	280	21	.656
Montreal Alouettes	16	9	7	0	353	345	18	.563
Hamilton Tiger-Cats	16	5	10	1	284	395	11	.344
Toronto Argonauts	16	5	10	1	261	324	11	.344

Western Conference

Edmonton Eskimos	16	12	4	0	432	370	24	.750
Saskatchewan Roughriders	16	10	5	1	373	390	21	.656
Winnipeg Blue Bombers	16	6	8	2	340	383	14	.438
Calgary Stampeders	16	6	10	0	387	363	12	.375
British Columbia Lions	16	6	10	0	276	331	12	.375

Coaching Changes

Hamilton--Jerry Williams 5-9-0, Bob Krouse 0-1-1; Toronto--Russ Jackson 5-10-1; Calgary--Jim Wood 4-6-0, Bob Baker 2-4-0; British Columbia--Eagle Keys 1-5-0, Cal Murphy 5-5-0.

League Leaders

Yards Rushing		Yards Passing		% (100 Attempts)	
Willie Burden	1896	Ron Lancaster	3545	Tom Wilkinson	63.6
George Reed	1454	Tom Wilkinson	2859	Tom Clements	57.1
Art Green	1188	Peter Liske	2310	Bruce Lemmerman	57.1
Doyle Orange	1055	Joe Pisarcik	2252	Joe Pisarcik	56.6
Roy Bell	1006	Tom Clements	2013	Jerry Keeling	54.4

Receiving Yards		Receptions		Points	
George McGowan	1472	George McGowan	98	Dave Cutler	169
Rhett Dawson	1191	Rhett Dawson	69	Gerry Organ	124
Tony Gabriel	1115	Tony Gabriel	65	Zenon Andrusyshyn	121
Tom Forzani	971	Mike Eben	63	Cyril McFall	111
Terry Evenshen	970	Peter Dalla Riva	56	Ian Sunter	109

Grey Cup Playoffs

November 8	Winnipeg Blue Bombers	24	at	Saskatchewan Roughriders	42
November 9	Hamilton Tiger-Cats	12	at	Montreal Alouettes	35
November 15	Montreal Alouettes	20	at	Ottawa Rough Riders	10
November 16	Saskatchewan Roughriders	18	at	Edmonton Eskimos	30
November 23	Edmonton Eskimos	9	at	Montreal Alouettes	8*

Individual Awards

Annis Stukus Trophy--George Brancato (Ottawa Rough Riders)
Dave Dryburgh Memorial Trophy--Dave Cutler (Edmonton Eskimos)
DeMarco-Becket Memorial Trophy--Charlie Turner (Edmonton Eskimos)
Dr. Beattie Martin Trophy--Tom Forzani (Calgary Stampeders)
Eddie James Memorial Trophy--Willie Burden (Calgary Stampeders)
Frank M. Gibson Trophy--Tom Clements (Ottawa Rough Riders)
Grey Cup Most Outstanding Defensive Star--Lewis Cook (Montreal Alouettes)
Grey Cup Most Outstanding Offensive Star--Steve Ferrughelli (Montreal Alouettes)
Grey Cup Most Valuable Canadian--Dave Cutler (Edmonton Eskimos)
Jackie Parker Trophy--Larry Cameron (British Columbia Lions)

*Game played in Calgary

James P. McCaffrey Trophy--Jim Corrigall (Toronto Argonauts)
Jeff Nicklin Memorial Trophy--Willie Burden (Calgary Stampeders)
Jeff Russel Memorial Trophy--Johnny Rodgers (Montreal Alouettes)
Leo Dandurand Trophy--Dave Braggins (Montreal Alouettes)
Lou Hayman Trophy--Jim Foley (Ottawa Rough Riders)
Norm Fieldgate Trophy--Bill Baker (British Columbia Lions)
Schenley Award Most Outstanding Canadian--Jim Foley (Ottawa Rough Riders)
Schenley Award Most Outstanding Defensive Player--Jim Corrigall (Toronto Argonauts)
Schenley Award Most Outstanding Offensive Lineman--Charlie Turner (Edmonton Eskimos CFL)
Schenley Award Most Outstanding Player--Willie Burden (Calgary Stampeders)
Schenley Award Most Outstanding Rookie--Tom Clements (Ottawa Rough Riders)

Hall of Fame Inductees

Byron Bailey, Tom Brook, Lew Hayman, Ken Ploen, Dick Shatto, Herb Trawick

Notes

The CFL introduced the two point convert.

World Football League
Eastern Division

Team Name	GP	W	L	T	PF	PA	Pct
Birmingham Vulcans	12	9	3	0	257	186	.750
Memphis Southmen	11	7	4	0	254	206	.636
Jacksonville Express	11	6	5	0	227	247	.545
Charlotte Hornets	11	6	5	0	225	199	.545
Philadelphia Bell	11	4	7	0	195	237	.364

Western Division

Team Name	GP	W	L	T	PF	PA	Pct
Southern California Sun	12	7	5	0	354	341	.583
San Antonio Wings	13	7	6	0	364	268	.538
Shreveport Steamer	12	5	7	0	276	313	.417
The Hawaiins	11	4	7	0	210	281	.364
Portland Thunder	11	4	7	0	213	239	.364
Chicago Wind	5	1	4	0	67	124	.200

Coaching Changes

Birmingham--Marvin Bass 9-3-0; Jacksonville--Charlie Tate 6-5-0; Charlotte--Bob Gibson 6-5-0; Philadelphia--Willie Wood 4-7-0; San Antonio--Steve Moss 7-6-0; Shreveport--Marshall Taylor 5-7-0; Portland--Greg Barton 4-7-0; Chicago--Abe Gibron 1-4-0.

League Leaders

Rushing Yards		Passing Yards		Receptions	
Anthony Davis	1200	John Walton	2405	Ed Richardson	46 for 682 yds.
Art Cantrelle	814	Edd Hargett	2100	Tim Delaney	44 for 594 yds.
Rufus Ferguson	768	George Mira	1675	Terry Lindsey	43 for 669 yds.
Jim Nance	767	Danny White	1445	Dennis Hughes	36 for 552 yds.
Al Haywood	687	Pat Haden	1404	Ed Marshall	31 for 582 yds.

WFL Championship

The World Football League did not hold any playoffs this season as the league disbanded before the season ended.

Notes

Chris Hemmeter succeeded Gary Davidson as head of the World Football League but the league folded part way through its second season.

HOCKEY
National Hockey League
Campbell Conference
Patrick Division

Team Name	GP	W	L	T	GF	GA	Pts	Pct
Philadelphia Flyers	80	51	18	11	293	181	113	.706
New York Rangers	80	37	29	14	319	276	88	.550
New York Islanders	80	33	25	22	264	221	88	.550
Atlanta Flames	80	34	31	15	243	233	83	.519

Smythe Division

Team Name	GP	W	L	T	GF	GA	Pts	Pct
Vancouver Canucks	80	38	32	10	271	254	86	.538
St. Louis Blues	80	35	31	14	269	267	84	.525
Chicago Black Hawks	80	37	35	8	268	241	89	.513
Minnesota North Stars	80	23	50	7	221	341	53	.331
Kansas City Scouts	80	15	54	11	184	328	41	.256

Prince of Wales Conference

Norris Division

Team Name	GP	W	L	T	GF	GA	Pts	Pct
Montreal Canadiens	80	47	14	19	374	225	113	.706
Los Angeles Kings	80	42	17	21	269	185	105	.656
Pittsburgh Penguins	80	37	28	15	326	289	89	.556
Detroit Red Wings	80	23	45	12	259	335	58	.363
Washington Capitals	80	8	67	5	181	446	21	.131

Adams Division

Team Name	GP	W	L	T	GF	GA	Pts	Pct
Buffalo Sabres	80	49	16	15	354	240	113	.706
Boston Bruins	80	40	26	14	345	245	94	.588
Toronto Maple Leafs	80	31	33	16	280	309	78	.488
California Golden Seals	80	19	48	13	212	316	51	.319

Coaching Changes

Rangers--Emile Francis 37-29-14; Atlanta--Bernie Geoffrion 22-20-10, Fred Creighton 12-11-5; Vancouver--Phil Maloney 38-32-10; St. Louis--Lou Angotti 2-5-2, Lynn Patrick 1-0-1, Gary Young 32-26-11; Minnesota--Jack Gordon 11-23-5, Charlie Burns 12-27-2; Kansas City--Armand Guidolin 15-54-11; Pittsburgh--Marc Boileau 37-28-15; Detroit--Alex Delvecchio 23-45-12; Washington--Jim Anderson 4-45-5, George Sullivan 2-17-0, Milt Schmidt 2-5-0; Boston--Don Cherry 40-26-14; Buffalo--Floyd Smith 49-16-15.

League Leaders

Goals		Assists		Points	
Phil Esposito	61	Bobby Orr	89	Bobby Orr	135
Guy Lafleur	53	Bobby Clarke	89	Phil Esposito	127
Rick Martin	52	Pete Mahovlich	82	Marcel Dionne	121
Danny Grant	50	Marcel Dionne	74	Guy Lafleur	119
Marcel Dionne	47	Phil Esposito	66	Pete Mahovlich	117

Penalty Minutes		**Plus/Minus**		**GAA**	
Dave Schultz	472	Bobby Orr	80	Bernie Parent	2.03
Andre Dupont	276	Bobby Clarke	79	Rogie Vachon	2.24
Phil Russell	260	Serge Savard	71	Ken Dryden	2.69
Bryan Watson	238	Don Luce	61	Tony Esposito	2.74
Bob Gassoff	222	Larry Robinson	61	Billy Smith	2.78

Wins		**Shutouts**	
Bernie Parent	44	Bernie Parent	12
Tony Esposito	34	Rogie Vachon	6
Gary Smith	32	Tony Esposito	6
Ken Dryden	30	Phil Myre	5
Rogie Vachon	27	Ken Dryden	4

All Star Game
(The Forum, Montreal)

January 21	Wales Conference	7		Campbell Conference	1

Stanley Cup Playoffs

April 8	Toronto Maple Leafs	2	at	Los Angeles Kings	3 [8:53]
April 8	Chicago Black Hawks	2	at	Boston Bruins	8
April 8	St. Louis Blues	3	at	Pittsburgh Penguins	4
April 8	New York Islanders	3	at	New York Rangers	2
April 10	Los Angeles Kings	2	at	Toronto Maple Leafs	3 [10:19]
April 10	Boston Bruins	3	at	Chicago Black Hawks	4 [7:33]
April 10	Pittsburgh Penguins	5	at	St. Louis Blues	3
April 10	New York Rangers	8	at	New York Islanders	3
April 11	Toronto Maple Leafs	2	at	Los Angeles Kings	1
April 11	Chicago Black Hawks	6	at	Boston Bruins	4
April 11	New York Islanders	4	at	New York Rangers	3 [0:11]
April 13	Toronto Maple Leafs	3	at	Philadelphia Flyers	6
April 13	Chicago Black Hawks	1	at	Buffalo Sabres	4
April 13	New York Islanders	4	at	Pittsburgh Penguins	5
April 13	Vancouver Canucks	2	at	Montreal Canadiens	6
April 15	Toronto Maple Leafs	0	at	Philadelphia Flyers	3
April 15	Chicago Black Hawks	1	at	Buffalo Sabres	3
April 15	Vancouver Canucks	2	at	Montreal Canadiens	1
April 15	New York Islanders	1	at	Pittsburgh Penguins	3
April 17	Philadelphia Flyers	2	at	Toronto Maple Leafs	0
April 17	Buffalo Sabres	4	at	Chicago Black Hawks	5 [2:31]
April 17	Montreal Canadiens	4	at	Vancouver Canucks	1
April 17	Pittsburgh Penguins	6	at	New York Islanders	4
April 19	Philadelphia Flyers	4	at	Toronto Maple Leafs	3 [1:45]
April 19	Montreal Canadiens	4	at	Vancouver Canucks	0
April 20	Buffalo Sabres	6	at	Chicago Black Hawks	2
April 20	Pittsburgh Penguins	1	at	New York Islanders	3
April 22	Chicago Black Hawks	1	at	Buffalo Sabres	3
April 22	Vancouver Canucks	4	at	Montreal Canadiens	5 [17:46]
April 22	New York Islanders	4	at	Pittsburgh Penguins	2
April 24	Pittsburgh Penguins	1	at	New York Islanders	4
April 26	New York Islanders	1	at	Pittsburgh Penguins	0
April 27	Montreal Canadiens	5	at	Buffalo Sabres	6 [4:42]

April 29	New York Islanders	0	at	Philadelphia Flyers	4
April 29	Montreal Canadiens	2	at	Buffalo Sabres	4
May 1	New York Islanders	4	at	Philadelphia Flyers	5 [2:56]
May 1	Buffalo Sabres	0	at	Montreal Canadiens	7
May 3	Buffalo Sabres	2	at	Montreal Canadiens	8
May 4	Philadelphia Flyers	1	at	New York Islanders	0
May 6	Montreal Canadiens	4	at	Buffalo Sabres	5 [5:56]
May 7	Philadelphia Flyers	3	at	New York Islanders	4 [1:53]
May 8	Buffalo Sabres	4	at	Montreal Canadiens	3
May 8	New York Islanders	5	at	Philadelphia Flyers	1
May 11	Philadelphia Flyers	1	at	New York Islanders	2
May 13	New York Islanders	1	at	Philadelphia Flyers	4
May 15	Buffalo Sabres	1	at	Philadelphia Flyers	4
May 18	Buffalo Sabres	1	at	Philadelphia Flyers	2
May 20	Philadelphia Flyers	4	at	Buffalo Sabres	5 [18:29]
May 22	Philadelphia Flyers	2	at	Buffalo Sabres	4
May 25	Buffalo Sabres	1	at	Philadelphia Flyers	5
May 27	Philadelphia Flyers	2	at	Buffalo Sabres	0

All Star Teams

First Team		Second Team
Bernie Parent	Goal	Rogatien Vachon
Bobby Orr	Defense	Guy Lapointe
Denis Potvin	Defense	Borje Salming
Bobby Clarke	Center	Phil Esposito
Guy Lafleur	Right Wing	Rene Robert
Richard Martin	Left Wing	Steve Vickers

Individual Awards

Art Ross Trophy--Bobby Orr (Boston Bruins)
Bill Masterton Trophy--Don Luce (Buffalo Sabres)
Calder Memorial Trophy--Eric Vail (Atlanta Flames)
Conn Smythe Trophy--Bernie Parent (Philadelphia Flyers)
Hart Memorial Trophy--Bobby Clarke (Philadelphia Flyers)
Jack Adams Award--Bob Pulford (Los Angeles Kings)
James Norris Trophy--Bobby Orr (Boston Bruins)
Lady Byng Memorial Trophy--Marcel Dionne (Detroit Red Wings)
Lester B. Pearson Award--Bobby Orr (Boston Bruins)
Lester Patrick Trophy--Donald Clark, Bill Chadwick, Tommy Ivan.
NHL All Star Game MVP--Syl Apps Jr. (Pittsburgh Penguins)
Vezina Trophy--Bernie Parent (Philadelphia Flyers)

Hall of Fame Inductees

George Armstrong, Irwin Bailey, Frank Buckland, Gord Drillon, Glenn Hall, William Jennings, Pierre Pilote

Notes

NHL clubs played an 80 game schedule an increase of 2 games from the previous season.

World Hockey Association
Canadian Division

Team Name	GP	W	L	T	GF	GA	Pts	Pct
Quebec Nordiques	78	46	32	0	331	299	92	.590
Toronto Toros	78	43	33	2	349	304	88	.564
Winnipeg Jets	78	38	35	5	322	293	81	.519
Vancouver Blazers	78	37	39	2	256	270	76	.487
Edmonton Oilers	78	36	38	4	279	279	76	.487

Western Division

Team Name	GP	W	L	T	GF	GA	Pts	Pct
Houston Aeros	78	53	25	0	369	247	106	.679
San Diego Mariners	78	43	31	4	326	268	90	.577
Minnesota Fighting Saints	78	42	33	3	308	279	87	.558
Phoenix Roadrunners	78	39	31	8	300	265	86	.551
(Michigan Stags)	43	14	26	3	107	179	31	.360
(Baltimore Blades)	35	7	27	1	98	162	15	.214

Eastern Division

Team Name	GP	W	L	T	GF	GA	Pts	Pct
New England Whalers	78	43	30	5	274	279	91	.583
Cleveland Crusaders	78	35	40	3	236	258	73	.468
Chicago Cougars	78	30	47	1	261	312	61	.391
Indianapolis Racers	78	18	57	3	216	338	39	.250

Coaching Changes

Quebec--Jean Guy Gendron 46-32-0; Toronto--Billy Harris- 22-17-1, Bob LeDuc 21-16-1; Winnipeg--Rudy Pilous 34-26-5, Bobby Hull 4-9-0; Vancouver--Joe Crozier 37-39-2; Edmonton--Brian Shaw 30-26-3, Bill Hunter 6-12-1; New England--Ron Ryan 40-28-5, Jack Kelley 3-2-0; Cleveland--John Hanna 14-18-1, Jack Vivian 21-22-2; Indianapolis--Gerry Moore 18-57-3; San Diego--Harry Howell 43-31-4; Phoenix--Sandy Hucul 39-31-8; Michigan/Baltimore--John Wilson 21-53-4.

League Leaders

Goals		Assists		Points	
Bobby Hull	77	Andre Lacroix	106	Andre Lacroix	147
Serge Bernier	54	Ulf Nilsson	94	Bobby Hull	142
Wayne Rivers	54	Larry Lund	75	Serge Bernier	122
Anders Hedberg	53	Serge Bernier	68	Ulf Nilsson	120
Tom Simpson	52	Wayne Dillon	66	Larry Lund	108

Penalty Minutes		GAA (1,560 minutes)		Wins	
Gord Gallant	203	Ron Grahame	3.03	Don McLeod	33
John Hughes	201	Bob Whidden	3.23	Al Smith	33
Ron Busniuk	176	W. Rutledge	3.23	Ron Grahame	33
John Schella	176	Ernie Wakely	3.25	Gilles Gratton	30
Cam Connor	168	Gerry Cheevers	3.26	John Garrett	30

Shutouts		**Save %**	
Ron Grahame	4	Gerry Cheevers	.905
Gerry Cheevers	4	John Garrett	.905
Ernie Wakely	3	Bob Whidden	.903
Wayne Rutledge	2	Ron Grahame	.900
Ken Brown	2	Ernie Wakely	.900

All Star Game
(Northlands Coliseum, Edmonton)

January 21	West Division	6	East Division	4

WHA Playoffs

April 8	Phoenix Roadrunners	2	at	Quebec Nordiques	5
April 9	Minnesota Fighting Saints	6	at	New England Whalers	5
April 9	Toronto Toros	3	at	San Diego Mariners	5
April 10	Cleveland Crusaders	5	at	Houston Aeros	8
April 10	Phoenix Roadrunners	2	at	Quebec Nordiques	6
April 11	Minnesota Fighting Saints	2	at	New England Whalers	3 [6:46]
April 12	Cleveland Crusaders	3	at	Houston Aeros	5
April 12	Quebec Nordiques	3	at	Phoenix Roadrunners	0
April 12	Toronto Toros	6	at	San Diego Mariners	7
April 13	Houston Aeros	1	at	Cleveland Crusaders	3
April 13	New England Whalers	3	at	Minnesota Fighting Saints	8
April 14	San Diego Mariners	2	at	Toronto Toros	5
April 15	Quebec Nordiques	5	at	Phoenix Roadrunners	6 [3:27]
April 15	New England Whalers	5	at	Minnesota Fighting Saints	2
April 15	Houston Aeros	7	at	Cleveland Crusaders	2
April 16	San Diego Mariners	5	at	Toronto Toros	6
April 17	Cleveland Crusaders	1	at	Houston Aeros	3
April 17	Phoenix Roadrunners	2	at	Quebec Nordiques	4
April 18	Minnesota Fighting Saints	4	at	New England Whalers	0
April 18	Toronto Toros	3	at	San Diego Mariners	4
April 19	New England Whalers	1	at	Minnesota Fighting Saints	6
April 21	San Diego Mariners	6	at	Toronto Toros	4
April 22	Minnesota Fighting Saints	1	at	Quebec Nordiques	4
April 24	Minnesota Fighting Saints	5	at	Quebec Nordiques	3
April 25	Houston Aeros	4	at	San Diego Mariners	0
April 26	Quebec Nordiques	6	at	Minnesota Fighting Saints	1
April 27	Houston Aeros	2	at	San Diego Mariners	1
April 27	Quebec Nordiques	2	at	Minnesota Fighting Saints	4
April 29	San Diego Mariners	0	at	Houston Aeros	6
April 29	Minnesota Fighting Saints	3	at	Quebec Nordiques	6
May 1	San Diego Mariners	4	at	Houston Aeros	5 [00:27]
May 1	Quebec Nordiques	4	at	Minnesota Fighting Saints	2
May 3	Quebec Nordiques	2	at	Houston Aeros	6
May 6	Quebec Nordiques	3	at	Houston Aeros	5
May 10	Houston Aeros	2	at	Quebec Nordiques	0
May 12	Houston Aeros	7	at	Quebec Nordiques	2

All Star Teams

First Team		Second Team
Ron Grahame	Goal	Gerry Cheevers
J.C. Tremblay	Defense	Poul Popiel
Kevin Morrison	Defense	Barry Long
Andre Lacroix	Center	Serge Bernier
Gordie Howe	Right Wing	Anders Hedberg
Bobby Hull	Left Wing	Marc Tardif

Individual Awards

Ben Hatskin Trophy--Ron Grahame (Houston Aeros)
Bill Hunter Trophy--Andre Lacroix (San Diego Mariners)
Dennis Murphy Trophy--J.C. Tremblay (Quebec Nordiques)
Gordie Howe Trophy--Bobby Hull (Winnipeg Jets)
Lou Kaplan Trophy--Anders Hedberg (Winnipeg Jets)
Paul Deneau Trophy--Mike Rodgers (Edmonton Oilers)
Robert Schmertz Trophy--Sandy Hucul (Phoenix Roadrunners)
WHA All Star Game MVP--Rejean Houle (Quebec Nordiques)
WHA MVP in Playoffs--Ron Grahame (Houston Aeros)

Notes

Dennis Murphy resigned as president of the WHA and was replaced by Ben Hatskin.
The WHA moved its head office from Santa Ana, California to Toronto and realigned into three divisions; East West and Canadian.

SOCCER
North American Soccer League

Northern Division

Team Name	GP	W	L	GF	GA	BP	Pts	Pct
Boston Minutemen	22	13	9	41	29	38	116	.586
Toronto Metro-Croatia	22	13	9	39	28	36	114	.576
New York Cosmos	22	10	12	39	38	31	91	.460
Rochester Lancers	22	6	16	29	49	28	64	.323
Hartford Bicentennials	22	6	16	27	51	25	61	.308

Eastern Division

Team Name	GP	W	L	GF	GA	BP	Pts	Pct
Tampa Bay Rowdies	22	16	6	46	27	39	135	.682
Miami Toros	22	14	8	47	30	39	123	.621
Washington Diplomats	22	12	10	42	47	40	112	.566
Philadelphia Atoms	22	10	12	33	42	30	90	.455
Baltimore Comets	22	9	13	34	52	33	87	.439

Central Division

Team Name	GP	W	L	GF	GA	BP	Pts	Pct
St. Louis Stars	22	13	9	38	34	37	115	.581
Chicago Sting	22	12	10	39	33	34	106	.535
Denver Dynamos	22	9	13	37	42	31	85	.429
Dallas Tornado	22	9	13	33	38	29	83	.419
San Antonio Thunder	22	6	16	24	46	23	59	.298

Western Division

Portland Timbers	22	16	6	43	27	42	138	.697
Seattle Sounders	22	15	7	42	28	39	129	.652
Los Angeles Aztecs	22	12	10	42	33	35	107	.540
Vancouver Whitecaps	22	11	11	38	28	33	99	.500
San Jose Earthquakes	22	8	14	37	48	35	83	.419

Coaching Changes

Toronto--Ivan Markovic 13-0-0; Rochester--Ted Dumitru 6-16-0; Tampa Bay--Eddie Firmani 16-6-0; Hartford--Manfred Schellscheidt 6-16-0; Miami--Greg Meyers 14-8-0; Chicago--Bill Foulkes 12-10-0; Denver--John Young 9-13-0; San Antonio--Alex Perolli 1-8-0, Don Batie 5-8-0; Portland--Vic Crowe 16-6-0; Los Angeles--Terry Fisher l2-10-0; San Jose-Gabbo Gavric 3-1-0, Ivan Toplak 5-13-0.

League Leaders

Goals		Points		Shutouts	
Steven David	23	Steven David	52	Zeljko Bilecki	8
Derek Smethurst	18	Gordon Hill	39	Shep Messing	6
Gordon Hill	16	Derek Smethurst	39	Barry Watling	6
Peter Withe	16	Peter Withe	38	Graham Brown	5
Tommy Ord	16	Uri Banhoffer	37	Greg Weber	5

GAA	
Shep Messing	0.93
Barry Watling	1.15
Graham Brown	1.20
Zeljko Bilecki	1.25
Greg Weber	1.34

NASL Playoffs

August 12	Seattle Sounders	1	at	Portland Timbers	2 [OT]
August 13	Los Angeles Aztecs	1	at	St. Louis Stars	2
August 13	Miami Toros	2	at	Boston Minutemen	1 [OT]
August 13	Toronto Metro-Croatia	0	at	Tampa Bay Rowdies	1
August 16	Miami Toros	0	at	Tampa Bay Rowdies	3
August 17	St. Louis Stars	0	at	Portland Timbers	1
August 24	Tampa Bay Rowdies	2	at	Portland Timbers	0 *

All Star Teams

First Team		Second Team
Peter Bonetti	Goal	Ken Cooper
Bob Smith	Defender	Tony Want
Mike England	Defender	Stewart Jump
Werner Roth	Defender	Ralph Wright
Farrukh Quraishi	Defender	Charlie Mitchell
Arfon Griffiths	Midfield	Barry Powell
Ronnie Sharp	Midfield	John Boyle
Antonio Simoes	Midfield	Bob Hope
Steven David	Forward	Peter Withe
Pele	Forward	Tommy Ord
Gordon Hill	Forward	Stewart Scullion

*Game played in San Jose

Individual Awards

Coach of the Year--John Sewell (St. Louis Stars)
Lead Goalkeeper Award--Shep Messing (Boston Minutemen)
Most Valuable Player--Steven David (Miami Toros)
Rookie of the Year--Chris Bahr (Philadelphia Atoms)

Franchise Changes

WHA--New Jersey Knights became the San Diego Mariners.
Los Angeles Sharks became the Michigan Stags and then the Baltimore Blades.
WFL--Birmingham Americans became the Birmingham Vulcans.
Jacksonville Sharks became the Jacksonville Express.
Charlotte Stars became the Charlotte Hornets.
Portland Storm became the Portland Thunder.
Chicago Fire became the Chicago Winds.
NBA--Capital Bullets became the Washington Bullets.
ABA--Carolina Cougars became the Spirits of St. Louis
Memphis Tams became the Memphis Sounds.
Denver Rockets became the Denver Nuggets
NASL Toronto Metros became the Toronto Metro-Croatia

Other Sports

Horseracing--Kentucky Derby won by Foolish Pleasure (time 2:02, purse $209,611).
Heavyweight Boxing--Muhammad Ali knocked-out Chuck Wepner in 15 rounds.
Muhammad Ali knocked-out Ron Lyle in 11 rounds.
Muhammad Ali defeated Joe Bugner in 15 rounds.
Muhammad Ali knocked-out Joe Frazier in 14 rounds.
Golf--U.S. Open won by Lou Graham with a score of 287.
Auto Racing--Indianapolis 500 won by Bobby Unser (ave. speed 149.213 MPH).
Tennis--U.S. Open won by Manuel Orantes in the men's singles.
U.S. Open won by Jimmy Connors and Ilie Nastase in the men's doubles.
U.S. Open won by Chris Evert in the women's singles.
U.S. Open won by Margaret Court and Virginia Wade in the women's doubles.
U.S. Open won by Rosemary Casals and Dick Stockton in the mixed doubles.

1976

BASEBALL
National League

East

Team Name	W	L	Pct	GB	R	OR
Philadelphia Phillies	101	61	.623	-	770	557
Pittsburgh Pirates	92	70	.568	9	708	630
New York Mets	86	76	.531	15	615	538
Chicago Cubs	75	87	.463	26	611	728
St. Louis Cardinals	72	90	.444	29	629	671
Montreal Expos	55	107	.340	46	531	734

West

Team Name	W	L	Pct	GB	R	OR
Cincinnati Reds	102	60	.630	-	857	633
Los Angeles Dodgers	92	70	.568	10	608	543
Houston Astros	80	82	.494	22	625	657
San Francisco Giants	74	88	.457	28	595	686
San Diego Padres	73	89	.451	29	570	662
Atlanta Braves	70	92	.432	32	620	700

Coaching Changes

New York--Joe Frazier 86-76; Montreal--Karl Kuehl 43-85, Charlie Fox 12-22; Houston--Bill Virdon 80-82; San Francisco--Bill Rigney 74-88; Atlanta--Dave Bristol 70-92.

League Leaders

Batting Average
(450 at bats)

Bill Madlock	.339
Ken Griffey	.336
Garry Maddox	.330
Pete Rose	.323
Joe Morgan	.320

Home Runs

Mike Schmidt	38
Dave Kingman	37
Rick Monday	32
George Foster	29
Joe Morgan	27

RBI

George Foster	121
Joe Morgan	111
Mike Schmidt	107
Bob Watson	102
Greg Luzinski	95

Stolen Bases

Davey Lopes	63
Joe Morgan	60
Frank Taveras	58
Cesar Cedeno	58
Lou Brock	56

ERA
(162 innings)

John Denny	2.52
Doug Rau	2.57
Tom Seaver	2.59
Jerry Koosman	2.70
Randy Jones	2.74

Wins

Randy Jones	22
Jerry Koosman	21
Don Sutton	21
J.R. Richard	20
Steve Carlton	20

Saves

Rawly Eastwick	26
Skip Lockwood	19
Ken Forsch	19
Charlie Hough	18
Butch Metzger	16

Strikeouts

Tom Seaver	235
J.R. Richard	214
Jerry Koosman	200
Steve Carlton	195
Phil Niekro	173

NLCS

October 9	Cincinnati Reds	6	at	Philadelphia Phillies	3
October 10	Cincinnati Reds	6	at	Philadelphia Phillies	2
October 12	Philadelphia Phillies	6	at	Cincinnati Reds	7

American League
East

Team Name	W	L	Pct	GB	R	OR
New York Yankees	97	62	.610	-	730	575
Baltimore Orioles	88	74	.543	10.5	619	598
Boston Red Sox	83	79	.512	15.5	716	660
Cleveland Indians	81	78	.509	16	615	615
Detroit Tigers	74	87	.460	24	609	709
Milwaukee Brewers	66	95	.410	32	570	655

West

Team Name	W	L	Pct	GB	R	OR
Kansas City Royals	90	72	.556	-	713	611
Oakland Athletics	87	74	.540	2.5	686	598
Minnesota Twins	85	77	.525	5	743	704
California Angels	76	86	.469	14	550	631
Texas Rangers	76	86	.469	14	616	652
Chicago White Sox	64	97	.398	25.5	586	745

Coaching Changes

New York--Billy Martin 97-62; Boston--Darrell Johnson 41-45, Don Zimmer 42-34; Milwaukee Alex Grammas 66-95; Kansas City--Dorrel "Whitey" Herzog 90-72; Oakland Charles Tanner 87-74; Minnesota--Gene Mauch 85-77; California--Dick Williams 39-57, Norm Sherry 37-29; Texas--Frank Lucchesi 76-86; Chicago--Paul Richards 64-97.

League Leaders

Batting Average (450 at bats)		Home Runs		RBI	
George Brett	.333	Graig Nettles	32	Lee May	109
Hal McRae	.332	Reggie Jackson	27	Thurman Munson	105
Rod Carew	.331	Sal Bando	27	Carl Yastrzemski	102
Lyman Bostock	.323	George Hendrick	25	Larry Hisle	96
Ron LeFlore	.316	Lee May	25	Rusty Staub	96

Stolen Bases		ERA (162 innings)		Wins	
Bill North	75	Mark Fidrych	2.34	Jim Palmer	22
Ron LeFlore	58	Vida Blue	2.36	Luis Tiant	21
Bert Campaneris	54	Frank Tanana	2.44	Wayne Garland	20
Don Baylor	52	Mike Torrez	2.50	Mark Fidrych	19
Fred Patek	51	Jim Palmer	2.51	Ed Figueroa	19

Saves		Strikeouts	
Albert Lyle	23	Nolan Ryan	327
Dave LaRoche	21	Frank Tanana	261
Rollie Fingers	20	Bert Blyleven	219
Bill Campbell	20	Dennis Eckersley	200
Mark Littell	16	James Hunter	173

All Star Game

(Veterans Stadium, Philadelphia)

July 13	National League	7		American League	1

ALCS

October 9	New York Yankees	4	at	Kansas City Royals	1
October 10	New York Yankees	3	at	Kansas City Royals	7
October 12	Kansas City Royals	3	at	New York Yankees	5
October 13	Kansas City Royals	7	at	New York Yankees	4
October 14	Kansas City Royals	6	at	New York Yankees	7

World Series

October 16	New York Yankees	1	at	Cincinnati Reds	5
October 17	New York Yankees	3	at	Cincinnati Reds	4
October 19	Cincinnati Reds	6	at	New York Yankees	2
October 21	Cincinnati Reds	7	at	New York Yankees	2

Individual Awards

Arch Ward Memorial Trophy--George Foster (Cincinnati Reds NL)
Baseball Writers Award--Joe Morgan (Cincinnati Reds NL)
Thurman Munson (New York Yankees AL)
Cy Young Award--Randy Jones (San Diego Padres NL)
Jim Palmer (Baltimore Orioles AL)
Rookie of the Year--Butch Metzger (San Diego Padres NL)
Pat Zachry (Cincinnati Reds NL)
Mark Fidrych (Detroit Tigers AL)
Sporting News Executive of the Year--Joe Burke (Kansas City Royals AL)
Sporting News Manager of the Year--Danny Ozark (Philadelphia Phillies NL)
Sporting News Pitcher of the Year--Randy Jones (San Diego Padres NL)
Jim Palmer (Baltimore Orioles AL)
Sporting News Player of the Year--George Foster (Cincinnati Reds NL)
Thurman Munson (New York Yankees AL)
Sporting News Rookie of the Year--Larry Herndon (San Francisco Giants NL)
Butch Metzger (San Diego Padres NL)
Butch Wynegar (Minnesota Twins AL)
Mark Fidrych (Detroit Tigers AL)
World Series MVP--Johnny Bench (Cincinnati Reds NL)

Hall of Fame Inductees

Oscar Charleston, Roger Connor, Cal Hubbard, Bob Lemon, Fred Lindstrom, Robin Roberts

Notes

Major league baseball began its 100th season with a player lockout but the dispute was resolved before the season began.

BASKETBALL
National Basketball Association

Eastern Conference
Atlantic Division

Team Name	GP	W	L	PPGF	PPGA	Pct	GB
Boston Celtics	82	54	28	106.2	103.9	.659	-
Philadelphia 76ers	82	46	36	106.5	106.3	.561	8
Buffalo Braves	82	46	36	107.3	106.4	.561	8
New York Knickerbockers	82	38	44	102.7	103.9	.463	16

Central Division

Team Name	GP	W	L	PPGF	PPGA	Pct	GB
Cleveland Cavaliers	82	49	33	101.7	99.2	.598	-
Washington Bullets	82	48	34	102.8	100.4	.585	1
Houston Rockets	82	40	42	106.2	107.0	.488	9
New Orleans Jazz	82	38	44	104.1	105.0	.463	11
Atlanta Hawks	82	29	53	102.6	105.5	.354	20

Western Conference

Midwest Division

Team Name	GP	W	L	PPGF	PPGA	Pct	GB
Milwaukee Bucks	82	38	44	101.8	103.3	.463	-
Detroit Pistons	82	36	46	104.9	106.0	.439	2
Kansas City Kings	82	31	51	103.3	106.2	.378	7
Chicago Bulls	82	24	58	95.9	98.8	.293	14

Pacific Division

Team Name	GP	W	L	PPGF	PPGA	Pct	GB
Golden State Warriors	82	59	23	109.8	103.1	.720	-
Seattle SuperSonics	82	43	39	106.4	106.7	.524	16
Phoenix Suns	82	42	40	105.1	104.5	.512	17
Los Angeles Lakers	82	40	42	106.9	106.8	.488	19
Portland Trail Blazers	82	37	45	104.1	105.3	.451	22

Coaching Changes

New-Orleans--Butch van Breda Kolff 38-44; Atlanta--Lowell "Cotton" Fitzsimmons 28-46, Gene Tormohlen 1-7; Detroit--Ray Scott 17-25, Herb Brown 19-21.

League Leaders

Field Goals		Free Throws		Assists	
Bob McAdoo	934	Bob McAdoo	559	Slick Watts	661
Kareem Abdul-Jabbar	914	Nate Archibald	501	Nate Archibald	615
Fred Brown	742	John Drew	488	Cal Murphy	596
Nate Archibald	717	George McGinnis	475	Norm Van Lier	500
Rick Barry	707	Kareem Abdul-Jabbar	447	Rick Barry	496

Points		**Rebounds per Game**	
Bob McAdoo	2427	Kareem Abdul-Jabbar	16.9
Kareem Abdul-Jabbar	2275	Dave Cowens	16.0
Nate Archibald	1935	Wes Unseld	13.3
Randy Smith	1787	Paul Silas	12.7
George McGinnis	1769	Sam Lacey	12.6

All Star Game

(The Spectrum, Philadelphia)

February 3	East Division	123		West Division	109

NBA Playoffs

April 13	Detroit Pistons	110	at	Milwaukee Bucks	107
April 13	Washington Bullets	100	at	Cleveland Cavaliers	95
April 13	Phoenix Suns	99	at	Seattle SuperSonics	102
April 15	Buffalo Braves	95	at	Philadelphia 76ers	89
April 15	Milwaukee bucks	123	at	Detroit Pistons	126
April 15	Cleveland Cavaliers	80	at	Washington Bullets	79
April 15	Phoenix Suns	116	at	Seattle SuperSonics	111
April 16	Philadelphia 76ers	131	at	Buffalo Braves	106
April 17	Washington Bullets	76	at	Cleveland Cavaliers	88
April 18	Buffalo Braves	124	at	Philadelphia 76ers	123 [OT]
April 18	Detroit Pistons	107	at	Milwaukee Bucks	104
April 18	Seattle SuperSonics	91	at	Phoenix Suns	103
April 20	Detroit Pistons	103	at	Golden State Warriors	127
April 20	Seattle SuperSonics	114	at	Phoenix Suns	130
April 21	Buffalo Braves	98	at	Boston Celtics	107
April 21	Cleveland Cavaliers	98	at	Washington Bullets	109
April 22	Detroit Pistons	123	at	Golden State Warriors	111
April 22	Washington Bullets	91	at	Cleveland Cavaliers	92
April 23	Buffalo Braves	96	at	Boston Celtics	101
April 24	Golden State Warriors	113	at	Detroit Pistons	96
April 25	Boston Celtics	93	at	Buffalo Braves	98
April 25	Phoenix Suns	108	at	Seattle SuperSonics	114
April 26	Golden State Warriors	102	at	Detroit Pistons	106
April 26	Cleveland Cavaliers	98	at	Washington Bullets	102 [OT]
April 27	Seattle SuperSonics	112	at	Phoenix Suns	123
April 28	Boston Celtics	122	at	Buffalo Braves	124
April 28	Detroit Pistons	109	at	Golden State Warriors	128
April 29	Washington Bullets	85	at	Cleveland Cavaliers	87
April 30	Buffalo Braves	88	at	Boston Celtics	99
April 30	Golden State Warriors	118	at	Detroit Pistons	116 [OT]
May 2	Boston Celtics	104	at	Buffalo Braves	100
May 2	Phoenix Suns	103	at	Golden State Warriors	128
May 5	Phoenix Suns	108	at	Golden State Warriors	101
May 6	Cleveland Cavaliers	99	at	Boston Celtics	111
May 7	Golden State Warriors	99	at	Phoenix Suns	91
May 9	Cleveland Cavaliers	89	at	Boston Celtics	94
May 9	Golden State Warriors	129	at	Phoenix Suns	133 [OT]
May 11	Boston Celtics	78	at	Cleveland Cavaliers	83
May 12	Phoenix Suns	95	at	Golden State Warriors	111
May 14	Boston Celtics	87	at	Cleveland Cavaliers	106
May 14	Golden State Warriors	104	at	Phoenix Suns	105

May 16	Cleveland Cavaliers	94	at	Boston Celtics	99
May 16	Phoenix Suns	94	at	Golden State Warriors	86
May 18	Boston Celtics	94	at	Cleveland Cavaliers	87
May 23	Phoenix Suns	87	at	Boston Celtics	98
May 27	Phoenix Suns	90	at	Boston Celtics	105
May 30	Boston Celtics	98	at	Phoenix Suns	105
June 2	Boston Celtics	107	at	Phoenix Suns	109
June 4	Phoenix Suns	126	at	Boston Celtics	128 [OT]
June 6	Boston Celtics	87	at	Phoenix Suns	80

All Star Teams

First Team	Second Team
Rick Barry (Golden State Warriors)	Elvin Hayes (Washington Capitals)
George McGinnis (Philadelphia 76ers)	John Havlicek (Boston Celtics)
Kareem Abdul-Jabbar (Los Angeles Lakers)	Dave Cowens (Boston Celtics)
Nate Archibald (Kansas City Kings)	Randy Smith (Buffalo Braves)
Pete Maravich (New Orleans Jazz)	Phil Smith (Golden State Warriors)

Individual Awards

Eddie Gottlieb Trophy--Alvan Adams (Phoenix Suns)
Executive of the Year--Jerry Colangelo (Phoenix Suns)
J. Walter Kennedy Citizenship Award--Slick Watts (Seattle SuperSonics)
Maurice Podoloff Trophy--Kareem Abdul-Jabbar (Los Angeles Lakers)
NBA All Star Game MVP--Dave Bing (Washington Bullets)
NBA Finals MVP--JoJo White (Boston Celtics)
Red Auerbach Trophy--Bill Fitch (Cleveland Cavaliers)

Hall of Fame Inductees

Elgin Baylor, Charles Cooper, Lauren Gale, William Johnson, Frank McGuire

American Basketball Association

Team Name	**GP**	**W**	**L**	**PPGF**	**PPGA**	**Pct**	**GB**
Denver Nuggets	84	60	24	121.9	115.9	.714	-
New York Nets	84	55	29	111.8	108.8	.655	5
San Antonio Spurs	84	50	34	115.6	111.6	.595	10
Kentucky Colonels	84	46	38	111.0	110.2	.548	14
Indiana Pacers	84	39	45	112.9	112.6	.464	21
St. Louis Spirits	84	35	49	108.9	112.1	.417	25
Virginia Squires	83	15	68	106.9	116.6	.181	44.5
San Diego Sails	11	3	8	98.8	103.5	.273	36.5
Utah Stars	16	4	12	114.9	116.6	.125	34

Coaching Changes

San Antonio--Bob Bass 50-34; St. Louis--Rod Thorn 20-279 Joe Mullaney 15-22; Virginia--Al Bianchi 1-6, Mack Calvin 0-6, Bill Musselman 4-22, Jack Ankerson 1-1, Zelmo Beaty 9-33; San Diego--Bill Musselman 3-8; Utah--Tom Nissalke 4-12.

League Leaders

Free Throws % (150 complete)		Field Goals		Assists	
Bill Keller	.896	Julius Erving	915	Don Buse	689
Jim Eakins	.888	David Thompson	804	Ralph Simpson	597
Mack Calvin	.888	Artis Gilmore	773	Louie Dampier	467
James Silas	.872	Bill Knight	768	James Silas	452
Ron Boone	.871	Dan Issel	751	Julius Erving	423

Points		Rebounds per Game	
Julius Erving	2462	Artis Gilmore	15.51
David Thompson	2158	Maurice Lucas	11.28
Artis Gilmore	2067	Caldwell Jones	11.22
James Silas	2000	Larry Kenon	11.07
Bill Knight	1969	Julius Erving	11.01

All Star Game

(McNichols Sports Arena, Denver)

January 27	Denver Nuggets	144	All Stars	138

ABA Playoffs

April 8	Indiana Pacers	109	at	Kentucky Colonels	120
April 9	San Antonio Spurs	101	at	New York Nets	116
April 10	Kentucky Colonels	95	at	Indiana Pacers	109
April 11	San Antonio Spurs	105	at	New York Nets	79
April 12	Indiana Pacers	99	at	Kentucky Colonels	100
April 14	New York Nets	103	at	San Antonio Spurs	111
April 15	Kentucky Colonels	107	at	Denver Nuggets	110
April 17	Kentucky Colonels	138	at	Denver Nuggets	119
April 18	New York Nets	110	at	San Antonio Spurs	108
April 19	San Antonio Spurs	108	at	New York Nets	110
April 19	Denver Nuggets	114	at	Kentucky Colonels	126
April 21	New York Nets	105	at	San Antonio Spurs	106
April 21	Denver Nuggets	108	at	Kentucky Colonels	106
April 22	Kentucky Colonels	117	at	Denver Nuggets	127
April 24	San Antonio Spurs	114	at	New York Nets	121
April 25	Denver Nuggets	115	at	Kentucky Colonels	119
April 28	Kentucky Colonels	110	at	Denver Nuggets	133
May 1	New York Nets	120	at	Denver Nuggets	118
May 4	New York Nets	121	at	Denver Nuggets	127
May 6	Denver Nuggets	111	at	New York Nets	117
May 8	Denver Nuggets	112	at	New York Nets	121
May 11	New York Nets	110	at	Denver Nuggets	118
May 13	Denver Nuggets	106	at	New York Nets	112

All Star Teams

First Team	Second Team
Julius Erving (New York Nets)	David Thompson (Denver Nuggets)
Bill Knight (Indiana Pacers)	Bobby Jones (Denver Nuggets)
Artis Gilmore (Kentucky Colonels)	Dan Issel (Denver Nuggets)
James Silas (San Antonio Spurs)	Don Buse (Indiana Pacers)
Ralph Simpson (Denver Nuggets)	George Gervin (San Antonio Spurs)

Individual Awards

ABA All star Game MVP--David Thompson (Denver Nuggets)
Coach of the Year--Larry Brown (Denver Nuggets)
Most Valuable Player--Julius Erving (New York Nets)
Rookie of the Year--David Thompson (Denver Nuggets)

FOOTBALL
National Football League
National Football Conference
Eastern Division

Team Name	GP	W	L	T	PF	PA	Pct
Dallas Cowboys	14	11	3	0	296	194	.786
Washington Redskins	14	10	4	0	291	217	.714
St. Louis Cardinals	14	10	4	0	309	267	.714
Philadelphia Eagles	14	4	10	0	165	286	.286
New York Giants	14	3	11	0	170	250	.214

Central Division

Team Name	GP	W	L	T	PF	PA	Pct
Minnesota Vikings	14	11	2	1	305	176	.821
Chicago Bears	14	7	7	0	253	216	.500
Detroit Lions	14	6	8	0	262	220	.429
Green Bay Packers	14	5	9	0	218	299	.357

Western Division

Team Name	GP	W	L	T	PF	PA	Pct
Los Angeles Rams	14	10	3	1	351	190	.750
San Francisco 49ers	14	8	6	0	270	190	.571
Atlanta Falcons	14	4	10	0	172	312	.286
New Orleans Saints	14	4	10	0	253	346	.286
Seattle Seahawks	14	2	12	0	229	429	.143

American Football Conference

Eastern Division

Team Name	GP	W	L	T	PF	PA	Pct
Baltimore Colts	14	11	3	0	417	246	.786
New England Patriots	14	11	3	0	376	236	.786
Miami Dolphins	14	6	8	0	263	264	.429
New York Jets	14	3	11	0	169	383	.214
Buffalo Bills	14	2	12	0	245	363	.143

Central Division

Team Name	GP	W	L	T	PF	PA	Pct
Pittsburgh Steelers	14	10	4	0	342	138	.714
Cincinnati Bengals	14	10	4	0	335	210	.714
Cleveland Browns	14	9	5	0	267	287	.643
Houston Oilers	14	5	9	0	222	273	.357

Western Division

Team Name	GP	W	L	T	PF	PA	Pct
Oakland Raiders	14	13	1	0	350	237	.929
Denver Broncos	14	9	5	0	315	206	.643
San Diego Chargers	14	6	8	0	248	285	.429
Kansas City Chiefs	14	5	9	0	290	376	.357
Tampa Bay Buccaneers	14	0	14	0	125	412	.000

Coaching Changes

Philadelphia--Dick Vermeil 4-10-0; N.Y. Giants--Bill Arnsparger 0-7-0, John McVay 3-4-0; Detroit--Rick Forzano 1-3-0, Tom Hudspeth 5-5-0; San Francisco--Monte Clark 8-6-0; Atlanta--Marion Campbell 1-4-0, Pat Peppler 3-6-0; New Orleans--Hank Stram 4-10-0; Seattle--Jack Patera 2-12-0; N.Y. Jets--Lou Holtz 3-10-0, Mike Holovak 0-1-0; Buffalo--Lou Saban 2-3-0, Jim Ringo 0-9-0; Cincinnati--Bill Johnson 10-4-0; Tampa Bay--John McKay 0-14-0.

League Leaders

Yards Rushing		**Yards Passing**		**Passing %** (200 attempts)	
O.J. Simpson	1503	Bert Jones	3104	Ken Stabler	66.7
Walter Payton	1390	Fran Tarkenton	2961	Fran Tarkenton	61.9
Delvin Williams	1203	Jim Hart	2946	Bert Jones	60.3
Lydell Mitchell	1200	Ken Stabler	2737	Bob Griese	59.6
Lawrence McCutcheon	1168	Roger Staubach	2715	Dan Fouts	57.9

Receiving Yards		**Receptions**		**Field Goals**	
Charlie Joiner	1056	MacArthur Lane	66	Mark Moseley	22
Ken Burrough	932	Bob Chandler	61	Jan Stenerud	21
Sam White	906	Lydell Mitchell	60	Jim Bakken	20
Bob Chandler	824	Drew Pearson	58	Toni Linhart	20
Frank Grant	818	Chuck Foreman	55	Fred Cox	19

Punt Return Yards		**Kickoff Return Yards**	
Ed Brown	646	Willie Shelby	761
Mike Haynes	608	Brian Baschnagel	754
Rick Upchurch	536	Ed Brown	738
Butch Johnson	489	Howard Stevens	710
Neal Colzie	448	Butch Johnson	693

Pro Bowl Game
(Kingdome, Seattle)

January 17 1977	American Conference	24	National Conference	14

NFL Playoffs

December 18	Washington Redskins	20	Minnesota Vikings	35
December 18	New England Patriots	21	Oakland Raiders	24
December 19	Los Angeles Rams	14	Dallas Cowboys	12
December 19	Pittsburgh Steelers	40	Baltimore Colts	14
December 26	Los Angeles Rams	13	Minnesota Vikings	24
December 26	Pittsburgh Steelers	7	Oakland Raiders	24

Super Bowl XI
(Rose Bowl, Pasadena)

January 9 1977	Oakland Raiders	32	Minnesota Vikings	14

Individual Awards

A.P. MVP--Bert Jones (Baltimore Colts)
Bert Bell Trophy--Mike Haynes (New England Patriots) [World Almanac]
Bert Bell Trophy--Ken Stabler (Oakland Raiders)
P.F.W.A. MVP--Bert Jones (Baltimore Colts)
George Halas Trophy--Wally Chambers (Chicago Bears)
Jack Lambert (Pittsburgh Steelers)
Jerry Sherk (Cleveland Browns)

Jim Thorpe Trophy--Bert Jones (Baltimore Colts)
Pro Bowl MVP--Mel Blount (Pittsburgh Steelers)
Rookie of the Year--Mike Haynes (New England Patriots)
Sammy White (Minnesota Vikings)
Super Bowl MVP--Fred Biletnikoff (Oakland Raiders)
U.P.I. AFC Coach of the Year--Chuck Fairbanks (New England Patriots)
U.P.I. AFC Player of the Year--Bert Jones (Baltimore Colts)
U.P.I. AFC Rookie of the Year--Mike Haynes (New England Patriots)
U.P.I. NFL Coach of the Year--Jack Pardee (Chicago Bears)
U.P.I. NFC Player of the Year--Chuck Foreman (Minnesota Vikings)
U.P.I. NFC Rookie of the Year--Sammy White (Minnesota Vikings)

Hall of Fame Inductees

Ray Flaherty, Len Ford, Jim Taylor

Notes

The NFL introduced the 30 second clock which was to be visible to all players and fans.
The Dallas Cowboys became the first wild card team to play in the Super Bowl.
Linebacker Larry Ball played on this season's 0-14 Tampa Bay Buccaneers. In 1972 Ball played on Miami's 14-0 Super Bowl winning team.

Canadian Football League

Eastern Conference

Team Name	GP	W	L	T	PF	PA	Pts	Pct
Ottawa Rough Riders	16	9	6	1	411	346	19	.594
Hamilton Tiger-Cats	16	8	8	0	269	348	16	.500
Montreal Alouettes	16	7	8	1	305	273	15	.469
Toronto Argonauts	16	7	8	1	289	354	15	.469

Western Conference

Team Name	GP	W	L	T	PF	PA	Pts	Pct
Saskatchewan Roughriders	16	11	5	0	427	238	22	.688
Winnipeg Blue Bombers	16	10	6	0	384	316	20	.625
Edmonton Eskimos	16	9	6	1	311	367	19	.594
British Columbia Lions	16	5	9	2	308	336	12	.375
Calgary Stampeders	16	2	12	2	316	442	6	.188

Coaching Changes

Hamilton--George Dickson 0-2-0, Bob Shaw 8-6-0; British Columbia--Cal Murphy 5-9-2; Calgary--Bob Baker 0-9-1, Joe Tiller 2-3-1.

League Leaders

Yards Rushing		Yards Passing		Passing % (200 attempts)	
Jim Washington	1277	Ron Lancaster	3869	Ron Lancaster	60.1
Art Green	1257	Dieter Brock	3101	Tom Clements	59.9
Mike Strickland	1119	Tom Clements	2856	Dieter Brock	55.5
Andy Hopkins	1075	Sonny Wade	2504	Chuck Ealey	53.9
Jim Edwards	1046	Bruce Lemmerman	2271	Sonny Wade	53.7

Receiving Yards		Receptions		Points	
Tony Gabriel	1320	Tony Gabriel	72	Bernie Ruoff	152
Rhett Dawson	996	Rhett Dawson	65	Don Sweet	141
Tom Scott	968	George McGowan	60	Bob Macoritti	133
Jim Foley	847	Tom Forzani	57	Lui Passaglia	128
George McGowan	833	Jim Edwards	57	Dave Cutler	126

All Star Game

(Clarke Stadium, Edmonton)

May 29	Western Conference	27	Eastern Conference	16

Grey Cup Playoffs

November 13	Montreal Alouettes	0	at	Hamilton Tiger-Cats	23
November 14	Edmonton Eskimos	14	at	Winnipeg Blue bombers	12
November 20	Edmonton Eskimos	13	at	Saskatchewan Roughriders	23
November 21	Hamilton Tiger-Cats	15	at	Ottawa Rough Riders	17
November 28	Ottawa Rough Riders	23	at	Saskatchewan Roughriders	20*

Individual Awards

Annis Stukus Trophy--Bob Shaw (Hamilton Tiger-Cats)
Dave Dryburgh Memorial Trophy--Bernie Ruoff (Winnipeg Blue Bombers)
DeMarco-Becket Memorial Trophy--Al Wilson (British Columbia Lions)
Dr. Beattie Martin Trophy--Bill Baker (British Columbia Lions)
Eddie James Memorial Trophy--Jim Washington (Winnipeg Blue Bombers)
Frank M. Gibson Trophy--Neil Lumsden (Toronto Argonauts)
Grey Cup Most Outstanding Defensive Star--Cleveland Vann (Saskatchewan Roughriders)
Grey Cup Most Outstanding Offensive Star--Tom Clements (Ottawa Rough Riders)
Grey Cup Most Valuable Canadian--Tony Gabriel (Ottawa Rough Riders)
Jackie Parker Trophy--John Sciarra (British Columbia Lions)
James P. McCaffrey Trophy--Granville Liggins (Toronto Argonauts)
Jeff Nicklin Memorial Trophy--Ron Lancaster (Saskatchewan Roughriders)
Jeff Russel Memorial Trophy--Jimmy Edwards (Hamilton Tiger-Cats)
Leo Dandurand Trophy--Dan Yochum (Montreal Alouettes)
Lew Hayman Trophy--Tony Gabriel (Ottawa Rough Riders)
Norm Fieldgate Trophy--Bill Baker (British Columbia Lions)
Schenley Award Most Outstanding Canadian--Tony Gabriel (Ottawa Rough Riders)
Schenley Award Most Outstanding Defensive Player--Bill Baker (British Columbia Lions)
Schenley Award Most Outstanding Offensive Lineman--Dan Yochum (Montreal Alouettes)
Schenley Award Most Outstanding Player--Ron Lancaster (Saskatchewan Roughriders)
Schenley Award Most Outstanding Rookie--John Sciarra (British Columbia Lions)

Hall of Fame Inductees

John Barrow, Wayne Harris, Chester McCance, Bob Simpson, Harry Spring

*Game played in Toronto

HOCKEY

National Hockey League
Campbell Conference

Patrick Division

Team Name	GP	W	L	T	GF	GA	Pts	Pct
Philadelphia Flyers	80	51	13	16	348	209	118	.738
New York Islanders	80	42	21	17	297	190	101	.631
Atlanta Flames	80	35	33	12	262	237	82	.513
New York Rangers	80	29	42	9	262	333	67	.419

Smythe Division

Team Name	GP	W	L	T	GF	GA	Pts	Pct
Chicago Black Hawks	80	32	30	18	254	261	82	.513
Vancouver Canucks	80	33	32	15	271	272	81	.506
St. Louis Blues	80	29	37	14	249	290	72	.450
Minnesota North Stars	80	20	53	7	195	303	47	.294
Kansas City Scouts	80	12	56	12	190	351	36	.225

Prince of Wales Conference

Norris Division

Team Name	GP	W	L	T	GF	GA	Pts	Pct
Montreal Canadiens	80	58	11	11	337	174	127	.794
Los Angeles Kings	80	38	33	9	263	265	85	.531
Pittsburgh Penguins	80	35	33	12	339	303	82	.513
Detroit Red Wings	80	26	44	10	226	300	62	.388
Washington Capitals	80	11	59	10	224	394	32	.200

Adams Division

Team Name	GP	W	L	T	GF	GA	Pts	Pct
Boston Bruins	80	48	15	17	313	237	113	.706
Buffalo Sabres	80	46	21	13	339	240	105	.656
Toronto Maple Leafs	80	34	31	15	294	276	83	.519
California Golden Seals	80	27	42	11	250	278	65	.406

Coaching Changes

Atlanta--Fred Creighton 35-33-12; Rangers--Ron Stewart 15-20-4, John Ferguson 14-22-5; St. Louis--Garry Young 9-15-5, Lynn Patrick 3-5-0, Leo Boivin 17-17-9; Minnesota--Ted Harris 20-53-7; Kansas City--Armand Guidolin 11-30-4, Sid Abel 0-3-0, Ed Bush 1-23-8; Pittsburgh--Marc Boileau 15-23 5, Ken Schinkel 20-10-7; Detroit--Doug Barkley 7-15-4, Alex Delvecchio 19-29-6; Washington Milt Schmidt 3-28-5, Tom McVie 8-31-5; California--Jack Evans 27-42-11.

League Leaders

Goals		Assists		Points	
Reg Leach	61	Bobby Clarke	89	Guy Lafleur	125
Guy Lafleur	56	Pete Mahovlich	71	Bobby Clarke	119
Pierre Larouche	53	Guy Lafleur	69	Gil Perreault	113
Jean Pronovost	52	Gil Perreault	69	Bill Barber	112
Dan Gare	50	Denis Potvin	67	Pierre Larouche	111

Penalty Minutes		**Plus/Minus**		**GAA** (1,600 minutes)	
Bryan Watson	322	Bobby Clarke	83	Ken Dryden	2.03
Dave Schultz	307	Bill Barber	74	Glenn Resch	2.07
Bob Gassoff	306	Reg Leach	73	Dan Bouchard	2.54
Dennis Polonich	302	Steve Shutt	73	Wayne Stephenson	2.58
Dave Williams	299	Pete Mahovlich	71	Billy Smith	2.61

Wins		**Shutouts**	
Ken Dryden	42	Ken Dryden	8
Wayne Stephenson	40	Glenn Resch	7
Gilles Gilbert	33	Rogie Vachon	5
Tony Esposito	30	Tony Esposito	4
Gerry Desjardins	29	Jim Rutherford	4

All Star Game
(The Spectrum, Philadelphia)

January 20	Wales Conference	7		Campbell Conference	5

Stanley Cup Playoffs

April 6	Buffalo Sabres	2	at	St. Louis Blues	5
April 6	Pittsburgh Penguins	1	at	Toronto Maple Leafs	4
April 6	Vancouver Canucks	3	at	New York Islanders	5
April 6	Atlanta Flames	1	at	Los Angeles Kings	2
April 7	Los Angeles Kings	1	at	Atlanta Flames	0
April 8	St. Louis Blues	2	at	Buffalo Sabres	3 [11:43]
April 8	Toronto Maple Leafs	0	at	Pittsburgh Penguins	2
April 8	New York Islanders	3	at	Vancouver Canucks	1
April 9	St. Louis Blues	1	at	Buffalo Sabres	2 [14:27]
April 9	Pittsburgh Penguins	0	at	Toronto Maple Leafs	4
April 11	Los Angeles Kings	0	at	Boston Bruins	4
April 11	Chicago Black Hawks	0	at	Montreal Canadiens	4
April 11	New York Islanders	3	at	Buffalo Sabres	5
April 12	Toronto Maple Leafs	1	at	Philadelphia Flyers	4
April 13	Toronto Maple Leafs	1	at	Philadelphia Flyers	3
April 13	Los Angeles Kings	3	at	Boston Bruins	2 [0:27]
April 13	Chicago Black Hawks	1	at	Montreal Canadiens	3
April 13	New York Islanders	2	at	Buffalo Sabres	3 [14:04]
April 15	Philadelphia Flyers	4	at	Toronto Maple Leafs	5
April 15	Boston Bruins	4	at	Los Angeles Kings	6
April 15	Montreal Canadiens	2	at	Chicago Black Hawks	1
April 15	Buffalo Sabres	3	at	New York Islanders	5
April 17	Philadelphia Flyers	3	at	Toronto Maple Leafs	4
April 17	Boston Bruins	3	at	Los Angeles Kings	0
April 17	Buffalo Sabres	2	at	New York Islanders	4
April 18	Montreal Canadiens	4	at	Chicago Black Hawks	1
April 20	Toronto Maple Leafs	1	at	Philadelphia Flyers	7
April 20	Los Angeles Kings	1	at	Boston Bruins	7
April 20	New York Islanders	4	at	Buffalo Sabres	3
April 22	Philadelphia Flyers	5	at	Toronto Maple Leafs	8
April 22	Boston Bruins	3	at	Los Angeles Kings	4 [18:28]
April 22	Buffalo Sabres	2	at	New York Islanders	3
April 25	Toronto Maple Leafs	3	at	Philadelphia Flyers	7

April 25	Los Angeles Kings	0	at	Boston Bruins	3
April 27	New York Islanders	2	at	Montreal Canadiens	3
April 27	Boston Bruins	4	at	Philadelphia Flyers	2
April 29	New York Islanders	3	at	Montreal Canadiens	4
April 29	Boston Bruins	1	at	Philadelphia Flyers	2 [13:38]
May 1	Montreal Canadiens	3	at	New York Islanders	2
May 2	Philadelphia Flyers	5	at	Boston Bruins	2
May 4	Montreal Canadiens	2	at	New York Islanders	5
May 4	Philadelphia Flyers	4	at	Boston Bruins	2
May 6	New York Islanders	2	at	Montreal Canadiens	5
May 6	Boston Bruins	3	at	Philadelphia Flyers	6
May 9	Philadelphia Flyers	3	at	Montreal Canadiens	4
May 11	Philadelphia Flyers	1	at	Montreal Canadiens	2
May 13	Montreal Canadiens	3	at	Philadelphia Flyers	2
May 16	Montreal Canadiens	5	at	Philadelphia Flyers	3

All Star Teams

First Team		Second Team
Ken Dryden	Goal	Glenn Resch
Denis Potvin	Defense	Borje Salming
Brad Park	Defense	Guy Lapointe
Bobby Clarke	Center	Gilbert Perreault
Guy Lafleur	Right Wing	Reggie Leach
Bill Barber	Left Wing	Richard Martin

Individual Awards

Art Ross Trophy--Guy Lafleur (Montreal Canadiens)
Bill Masterton Trophy--Rod Gilbert (New Yolk Rangers)
Calder Memorial Trophy--Bryan Trottier (New York Islanders)
Conn Smythe Trophy--Reggie Leach (Philadelphia Flyers)
Hart Memorial Trophy--Bobby Clarke (Philadelphia Flyers)
Jack Adams Award--Don Cherry (Boston Bruins)
James Norris Trophy--Denis Potvin (New York Islanders)
Lady Byng Memorial Trophy--Jean Ratelle (New York Rangers/Boston Bruins)
Lester B. Pearson Award--Guy Lafleur (Montreal Canadiens)
Lester Patrick Trophy--Stan Mikita, George Leader, Bruce Norris.
NHL All Star Game MVP--Pete Mahovlich (Montreal Canadiens)
Vezina Trophy--Ken Dryden (Montreal Canadiens)

Hall of Fame Inductees

Johnny Bower, Dr. Jack Gibson, Philip Ross, Bill Quackenbush, Bill Wirtz

World Hockey Association

Canadian Division

Team Name	GP	W	L	T	GF	GA	Pts	Pct
Winnipeg Jets	81	52	27	2	345	254	106	.654
Quebec Nordiques	81	50	27	4	371	316	104	.642
Calgary Cowboys	80	41	35	4	307	282	86	.538
Edmonton Oilers	81	27	49	5	268	345	59	.364
Toronto Toros	81	24	52	5	335	398	53	.327

Western Division

Houston Aeros	80	53	27	0	341	263	106	.663
Phoenix Roadrunners	80	39	35	6	302	287	84	.525
San Diego Mariners	80	36	38	6	303	290	78	.488
Minnesota Fighting Saints	59	30	25	4	211	212	64	.542
(Denver Spurs)	34	14	19	1	114	142	29	.426
(Ottawa Civics)	7	0	7	0	20	30	0	.000

Eastern Division

Indianapolis Racers	80	35	39	6	245	247	76	.475
Cleveland Crusaders	80	35	40	5	273	279	75	.469
New England Whalers	80	33	40	7	255	290	73	.456
Cincinnati Stingers	80	35	44	1	285	340	71	.444

Coaching Changes

Winnipeg--Bobby Kromm 52-27-2; Calgary--Joe Crozier 41-35-4; Edmonton--Clare Drake 18-28-2, Bill Hunter 9-21-3; Toronto Bob Baun 15-35-5, Gilles Leger 9-17-0; Indianapolis--Jacques Demers 35-39-6; Cleveland--John Wilson 35-40-5; New England--Jack Kelley14-16-3, Don Blackburn l4-18-3, Harry Neale 5-6-1; Cincinnati--Terry Slater 35-44-l; San Diego Ron Ingram 36-38-6; Denver/Ottawa--Jean-Guy Talbot 14-26-1.

League Leaders

Goals		**Assists**		**Points**	
Marc Tardif	71	Marc Tardif	77	Marc Tardif	148
Real Cloutier	60	J.C. Tremblay	77	Bobby Hull	123
Vaclav Nedomansky	56	Ulf Nilsson	76	Real Cloutier	114
Bobby Hull	53	Robbie Ftorek	72	Ulf Nilsson	114
Rejean Houle	51	Chris Bordeleau	72	Robbie Ftorek	113

Penalty Minutes		**GAA** (1,560 minutes)		**Wins**	
Curtis Brackenbury	365	Michel Dion	2.74	Richard Brodeur	44
Kim Clackson	351	Joe Daley	2.84	Joe Daley	41
Gord Gallant	297	Jack Norris	3.18	Ron Grahame	39
Cam Connor	295	Ernie Wakely	3.26	Ernie Wakely	35
Pierre Roy	258	Ron Grahame	3.27	Don McLeod	30

Shutouts		**Save %** (1,560 minutes)	
Joe Daley	5	Michel Dion	.910
Ron Grahame	3	Joe Daley	.903
Ernie Wakely	3	Ron Grahame	.896
John Garrett	3	John Garrett	.896
Christer Abrahamsson	2	Ernie Wakely	.895

All Star Game

(The Coliseum, Richfield, Ohio)

January 13	Canada	6	USA	1

WHA Playoffs

April 9	Cleveland Crusaders	3	at	New England Whalers	5
April 9	San Diego Mariners	1	at	Phoenix Roadrunners	3
April 9	Edmonton Oilers	3	at	Winnipeg Jets	7
April 10	Calgary Cowboys	3	at	Quebec Nordiques	1
April 10	New England Whalers	6	at	Cleveland Crusaders	1
April 10	Phoenix Roadrunners	2	at	San Diego Mariners	4
April 11	Edmonton Oilers	4	at	Winnipeg Jets	5 [0:54]
April 11	Calgary Cowboys	8	at	Quebec Nordiques	4
April 11	New England Whalers	3	at	Cleveland Crusaders	2
April 13	San Diego Mariners	4	at	Phoenix Roadrunners	6
April 14	Winnipeg Jets	3	at	Edmonton Oilers	2
April 14	Quebec Nordiques	2	at	Calgary Cowboys	3
April 15	Phoenix Roadrunners	1	at	San Diego Mariners	5
April 16	Winnipeg Jets	7	at	Edmonton Oilers	2
April 16	Quebec Nordiques	4	at	Calgary Cowboys	3
April 16	New England Whalers	4	at	Indianapolis Racers	1
April 17	San Diego Mariners	2	at	Phoenix Roadrunners	1
April 17	New England Whalers	0	at	Indianapolis Racers	4
April 18	Calgary Cowboys	6	at	Quebec Nordiques	4
April 21	Indianapolis Racers	0	at	New England Whalers	3
April 21	San Diego Mariners	4	at	Houston Aeros	8
April 23	Indianapolis Racers	1	at	New England Whalers	2
April 23	San Diego Mariners	1	at	Houston Aeros	3
April 23	Calgary Cowboys	1	at	Winnipeg Jets	6
April 24	New England Whalers	0	at	Indianapolis Racers	4
April 25	Houston Aeros	8	at	San Diego Mariners	4
April 25	Calgary Cowboys	2	at	Winnipeg Jets	3
April 27	Indianapolis Racers	5	at	New England Whalers	3
April 27	Houston Aeros	2	at	San Diego Mariners	3
April 28	Winnipeg Jets	6	at	Calgary Cowboys	3
April 28	San Diego Mariners	3	at	Houston Aeros	2
April 29	New England Whalers	6	at	Indianapolis Racers	0
April 30	Houston Aeros	3	at	San Diego Mariners	2
April 30	Winnipeg Jets	3	at	Calgary Cowboys	7
May 2	Calgary Cowboys	0	at	Winnipeg Jets	2
May 5	New England Whalers	4	at	Houston Aeros	2
May 7	New England Whalers	2	at	Houston Aeros	5
May 9	Houston Aeros	1	at	New England Whalers	4
May 11	Houston Aeros	4	at	New England Whalers	3
May 13	New England Whalers	3	at	Houston Aeros	4
May 15	Houston Aeros	1	at	New England Whalers	6
May 16	New England Whalers	0	at	Houston Aeros	2
May 20	Winnipeg Jets	4	at	Houston Aeros	3
May 23	Winnipeg Jets	5	at	Houston Aeros	4
May 25	Houston Aeros	3	at	Winnipeg Jets	6
May 27	Houston Aeros	1	at	Winnipeg Jets	9

All Star Teams

First Team		Second Team
Joe Daley	Goal	Ron Grahame
Paul Shmyr	Defense	Kevin Morrison
J.C. Tremblay	Defense	Pat Stapleton
Ulf Nilsson	Center	Robbie Ftorek
Anders Hedberg	Right Wing	Real Cloutier
Marc Tardif	Left Wing	Bobby Hull

Individual Awards

Ben Hatskin Trophy--Michel Dion (Indianapolis Racers)
Bill Hunter Trophy--Marc Tardif (Quebec Nordiques)
Dennis Murphy Trophy--Paul Shmyr (Cleveland Crusaders)
Howe Trophy--Marc Tardif (Quebec Nordiques)
Lou Kaplan Trophy--Mark Napier (Toronto Toros)
Paul Deneau Trophy--Vaclav Nedomansky (Toronto Toros)
Robert Schmertz Trophy--Bobby Kromm (Winnipeg Jets)
WHA All Star Game MVP--Real Cloutier (Quebec Nordiques)
Paul Shmyr (Cleveland Crusaders)
WHA MVP in Playoffs--Ulf Nilsson (Winnipeg Jets)

Notes

Bill MacFarland became President and Chief Operating Officer of the WHA.

SOCCER

North American Soccer League

Northern Division

Team Name	GP	W	L	GF	GA	BP	Pts	Pct
Chicago Sting	24	15	9	52	32	42	132	.611
Toronto Metro-Croatia	24	15	9	38	30	33	123	.569
Rochester Lancers	24	13	11	36	32	36	114	.528
Hartford Bicentennials	24	12	12	37	56	35	107	.495
Boston Minutemen	24	7	17	35	64	32	74	.343

Eastern Division

Team Name	GP	W	L	GF	GA	BP	Pts	Pct
Tampa Bay Rowdies	24	18	6	58	30	46	154	.713
New York Cosmos	24	16	8	65	34	52	148	.685
Washington Diplomats	24	14	10	46	38	42	126	.583
Philadelphia Atoms	24	8	16	32	49	32	80	.370
Miami Toros	24	6	18	29	58	28	63	.292

Southern Division

Team Name	GP	W	L	GF	GA	BP	Pts	Pct
San Jose Earthquakes	24	14	10	47	30	39	123	.569
Dallas Tornado	24	13	11	44	45	39	117	.542
Los Angeles Aztecs	24	12	12	43	44	36	108	.500
San Antonio Thunder	24	12	12	38	32	35	107	.495
San Diego Jaws	24	9	15	29	47	28	82	.380

Western Division

Minnesota Kicks	24	15	9	54	33	48	138	.639
Seattle Sounders	24	14	10	40	31	39	123	.569
Vancouver Whitecaps	24	14	10	38	30	36	120	.556
Portland Timbers	24	8	16	23	40	23	71	.329
St. Louis Stars	24	5	19	28	57	28	58	.269

Coaching Changes

Toronto--Ivan Markovic 10-6, Domagoj Kapetanovic 5-3; Rochester--Don Popovic 13-11; Boston--Hubert Vogelsinger 5-4, John Bertos 6-11; New York--Gordon Bradley 8-2, Ken Furphy 8-6; Philadelphia--Jesus Ponce 8-16; San Jose--Gabbo Gavric 14-10; Dallas--Al Miller 13-11; San Antonio--Don Batie 12-12; San Diego--Derek Trevis 9-15; Minnesota--Freddie Goodwin 15-19; Vancouver--Richard Krautzun 14-10.

League Leaders

Goals		**Points**		**Shutouts**	
Derek Smethurst	20	Giorgio Chinaglia	49	Tony Chursky	9
Giorgio Chinaglia	19	Derek Smethurst	45	Paolo Cimpiel	9
Mike Stojanovic	17	Pele	44	Arnold Mausser	6
Alan Willey	16	Mike Stojanovic	41	Mervyn Cawston	6
Eusebio (Ferreira)	16	Alan Willey	39	Phil Parkes	6

GAA
(1365 minutes)

Tony Chursky	0.91
Mike Hewitt	0.92
Paolo Cimpiel	0.96
Arnold Mausser	1.17
Mervyn Cawston	1.20

NASL Playoffs

August 17	Washington Diplomats	0	at	New York Cosmos	2
August 18	Rochester Lancers	1	at	Toronto Metro-Croatia	2
August 18	Los Angeles Aztecs	0	at	Dallas Tornado	2
August 18	Vancouver Whitecaps	0	at	Seattle Sounders	1
August 20	Dallas Tornado	0	at	San Jose Earthquakes	2
August 20	Toronto Metro-Croatia	3	at	Chicago Sting	2
August 20	New York Cosmos	1	at	Tampa Bay Rowdies	3
August 21	Seattle Sounders	0	at	Minnesota Kicks	3
August 24	Toronto Metro-Croatia	2	at	Tampa Bay Rowdies	0
August 25	San Jose Earthquakes	1	at	Minnesota Kicks	3
August 28	Toronto Metro-Croatia	3		Minnesota Kicks	0*

*Game played in Seattle

All Star Teams

First Team		Second Team
Arnold Mausser	Goal	Eric Martin
Bobby Moore	Defender	Stewart Jump
Mike England	Defender	George Ley
Tommy Smith	Defender	Ron Webster
Keith Eddy	Defender	Bobby Smith
Ramon Mifflin	Midfield	Alan West
Antonio Simoes	Midfield	Bob Hope
Rodney Marsh	Midfield	Al Trost
George Best	Forward	Derek Smethurst
Pele	Forward	Stewart Scullion
Giorgio Chinaglia	Forward	Jeff Bourne

Individual Awards

Coach of the Year--Eddie Firmani (Tampa Bay Rowdies)
Lead Goalkeeper Award--Tony Chursky (Seattle Sounders)
Most Valuable Player--Pele (New York Cosmos)
Rookie of the Year--Steve Pecher (Dallas Tornado)

Franchise Changes

WHA--Vancouver Blazers became the Calgary Cowboys.
Denver Spurs became the Ottawa Civics after 34 games and then folded completely.
NBA--Kansas City-Omaha Kings became the Kansas City Kings.
ABA--San Diego Conquistadors became the San Diego Sails.
Baltimore Comets became the San Diego Jaws.
Denver Dynamos became the Minnesota Kicks.

Other Sports

Horseracing--Kentucky Derby won by Bold Forbes (time 2:01.6, purse $165,200).
Heavyweight Boxing--Muhammad Ali knocked-out Jean-Pierre Coopman in 5 rounds.
Muhammad Ali defeated Jimmy Young in 15 rounds.
Muhammad Ali knocked-out Richard Dunn in 5 rounds.
Muhammad Ali defeated Ken Norton in 15 rounds.
Golf--U.S. Open won by Andy North with a score of 285.
Auto Racing--Indianapolis 500 won by Johnny Rutherford (ave. speed 148.725 MPH).
Tennis--U.S. Open won by Jimmy Connors in the men's singles.
U.S. Open won by Marty Riessen and Tom Okker in the men's doubles.
U.S. Open won by Chris Evert in the women's singles.
U.S. Open won by Linky Boshoff and Ilana Kloss in the women's doubles.
U.S. Open won by Billie Jean King and Phil Dent in the mixed doubles.

1977

BASEBALL
National League
East

Team Name	W	L	Pct	GB	R	OR
Philadelphia Phillies	101	61	.623	-	847	668
Pittsburgh Pirates	96	66	.593	5	734	665
St. Louis Cardinals	83	79	.512	18	737	688
Chicago Cubs	81	81	.500	20	692	739
Montreal Expos	75	87	.463	26	665	736
New York Mets	64	98	.395	37	587	663

West

Team Name	W	L	Pct	GB	R	OR
Los Angeles Dodgers	98	64	.605	-	769	582
Cincinnati Reds	88	74	.543	10	802	725
Houston Astros	81	81	.500	17	680	650
San Francisco Giants	75	87	.463	23	673	711
San Diego Padres	69	93	.426	29	692	834
Atlanta Braves	61	101	.377	37	678	895

Coaching Changes

Pittsburgh--Charles Tanner 96-66; St. Louis--Vern Rapp 83-79; Chicago--Herman Franks 81-81; Montreal--Dick Williams 75-87; New York--Joe Frazier 15-29, Joe Torre 49-69; Los Angeles--Tom Lasorda 98-64; San Francisco--Joe Altobelli 75-87; San Diego--John McNamara 20-28, Al Dark 49-55; Atlanta--Dave Bristol 8-21, Ted Turner 0-1, Vern Benson 1-0, Dave Bristol 52-79.

League Leaders

Batting Average
(450 at bats)

Dave Parker	.338
Renaldo Stennett	.336
Garry Templeton	.322
George Foster	.320
Ken Griffey	.318

Home Runs

George Foster	52
Jeff Burroughs	41
Greg Luzinski	39
Mike Schmidt	38
Steve Garvey	33

RBI

George Foster	149
Greg Luzinski	130
Steve Garvey	115
Jeff Burroughs	114
Bob Watson	110

Stolen Bases

Frank Taveras	70
Cesar Cedeno	61
Gene Richards	56
Omar Moreno	53
Joe Morgan	49

ERA
(162 innings)

John Candelaria	2.34
Tom Seaver	2.59
Burt Hooton	2.62
Steve Carlton	2.64
Tommy John	2.78

Wins

Steve Carlton	23
Tom Seaver	21
Rick Reuschel	20
John Candelaria	20
Bob Forsch	20

Saves

Rollie Fingers	35
Bruce Sutter	31
Rich Gossage	26
Charlie Hough	22
Skip Lockwood	20

Strikeouts

Phil Niekro	262
J.R. Richard	214
Steve Rogers	206
Steve Carlton	198
Tom Seaver	196

NLCS

October 4	Philadelphia Phillies	7	at	Los Angeles Dodgers	5
October 5	Philadelphia Phillies	1	at	Los Angeles Dodgers	7
October 7	Los Angeles Dodgers	6	at	Philadelphia Phillies	5
October 8	Los Angeles Dodgers	4	at	Philadelphia Phillies	1

Notes

Lou Brock broke Ty Cobb's all time base stealing record when he stole his 893rd base.

American League
East

Team Name	W	L	Pct	GB	R	OR
New York Yankees	100	62	.617	-	831	651
Boston Red Sox	97	64	.602	2.5	859	712
Baltimore Orioles	97	64	.602	2.5	719	653
Detroit Tigers	74	88	.457	26	714	751
Cleveland Indians	71	90	.441	28.5	676	739
Milwaukee Brewers	67	95	.414	33	639	765
Toronto Blue Jays	54	107	.335	45.5	605	822

West

Team Name	W	L	Pct	GB	R	OR
Kansas City Royals	102	60	.600	-	822	651
Texas Rangers	94	68	.580	8	767	657
Chicago White Sox	90	72	.556	12	844	771
Minnesota Twins	84	77	.522	17.5	867	776
California Angels	74	88	.457	28	675	695
Seattle Mariners	64	98	.395	38	624	855
Oakland Athletics	63	98	.391	38.5	605	749

Coaching Changes

Boston--Don Zimmer 97-64; Cleveland--Frank Robinson 26-31, Jeff Torborg 45-59; Toronto--Roy Hartsfield 54-107; Texas--Frank Lucchesi 31-31, Eddie Stanky 1-0, Connie Ryan 2-4, Bill Hunter 60-33; Chicago--Bob Lemon 90-72; California--Norm Sherry 39-42, Dave Garcia 35-46; Seattle--Darrell Johnson 64-98; Oakland--Jack McKeon 26-27, Bobby Winkles 37-71.

League Leaders

Batting Average (450 at bats)		**Home Runs**		**RBI**	
Rod Carew	.388	Jim Rice	39	Larry Hisle	119
Lyman Bostock	.336	Bobby Bonds	37	Bobby Bonds	115
Ken Singleton	.328	Graig Nettles	37	Jim Rice	114
Mickey Rivers	.326	George Scott	33	Butch Hobson	112
Ron Leflore	.325	Reggie Jackson	32	Al Cowens	112

Stolen Bases		**ERA** (162 innings)		**Wins**	
Fred Patek	53	Frank Tanana	2.54	Jim Palmer	20
Mitchell Page	42	Bert Blyleven	2.72	Dennis Leonard	20
Jerry Remy	41	Nolan Ryan	2.77	Dave Goltz	20
Bobby Bonds	41	Ron Guidry	2.82	Nolan Ryan	19
Ron LeFlore	39	Jim Palmer	2.91	Jim Colborn	18

Saves		Strikeouts	
Bill Campbell	31	Nolan Ryan	341
George Lyle	26	Dennis Leonard	244
Lerrin LaGrow	25	Frank Tanana	205
Jim Kern	18	Jim Palmer	193
Enrique Romo	16	Dennis Eckersley	191

All Star Game

(Yankee Stadium, New York)

July 19	National League	7		American League	5

ALCS

October 5	Kansas City Royals	7	at	New York Yankees	2
October 6	Kansas City Royals	2	at	New York Yankees	6
October 7	New York Yankees	2	at	Kansas City Royals	6
October 8	New York Yankees	6	at	Kansas City Royals	4
October 9	New York Yankees	5	at	Kansas City Royals	3

World Series

October 11	Los Angeles Dodgers	3	at	New York Yankees	4 [12]
October 12	Los Angeles Dodgers	6	at	New York Yankees	1
October 14	New York Yankees	5	at	Los Angeles Dodgers	3
October 15	New York Yankees	4	at	Los Angeles Dodgers	2
October 16	New York Yankees	4	at	Los Angeles Dodgers	10
October 18	Los Angeles Dodgers	4	at	New York Yankees	8

Individual Awards

Arch Ward Memorial Trophy--Don Sutton (Los Angeles Dodgers NL)
Baseball Writers Award--George Foster (Cincinnati Reds NL)
Rod Carew (Minnesota Twins AL)
Cy Young Award--Steve Carlton (Philadelphia Phillies NL)
Sparky Lyle (New York Yankees AL)
NLCS MVP--Dusty Baker (Los Angeles Dodgers NL)
Rookie of the Year--Andre Dawson (Montreal Expos NL)
Eddie Murray (Baltimore Orioles AL)
Sporting News Executive of the Year--Bill Veeck (Chicago White Sox AL)
Sporting News Manager of the Year--Earl Weaver (Baltimore Orioles AL)
Sporting News Pitcher of the Year--Steve Carlton (Philadelphia Phillies NL),
Nolan Ryan (California Angels AL)
Sporting News Player of the Year--George Foster (Cincinnati Reds NL)
Rod Carew (Minnesota Twins AL)
Sporting News Rookie of the Year--Andre Dawson (Montreal Expos NL)
Bob Owchinko (San Diego Padres NL)
Mitchell Page (Oakland Athletics AL)
Dave Rozema (Detroit Tigers AL)
World Series MVP--Reggie Jackson (New York Yankees AL)

Hall of Fame Inductees

Ernie Banks, Martin Dihigo, John Henry Lloyd, Al Lopez, Amos Rusie, Joe Sewell

BASKETBALL

National Basketball Association

Eastern Conference
Atlantic Division

Team Name	GP	W	L	PPGF	PPGA	Pct	GB
Philadelphia 76ers	82	50	32	110.2	106.2	.610	-
Boston Celtics	82	44	38	104.5	106.5	.537	6
New York Knickerbockers	82	40	42	108.6	108.6	.488	10
Buffalo Braves	82	30	52	105.0	109.5	.366	20
New York Nets	82	22	60	95.9	102.7	.268	28

Central Division

Team Name	GP	W	L	PPGF	PPGA	Pct	GB
Houston Rockets	82	40	33	106.4	104.8	.598	-
Washington Bullets	82	48	34	105.5	104.5	.585	1
San Antonio Spurs	82	44	38	115.0	114.4	.537	5
Cleveland Cavaliers	82	43	39	102.1	101.0	.524	6
New Orleans Jazz	82	35	47	104.6	107.4	.427	14
Atlanta Hawks	82	31	51	102.4	106.4	.378	18

Western Conference

Midwest Division

Team Name	GP	W	L	PPGF	PPGA	Pct	GB
Denver Nuggets	82	50	32	112.6	107.4	.610	-
Detroit Pistons	82	44	38	109.4	110.4	.537	6
Chicago Bulls	82	44	38	98.9	98.0	.537	6
Kansas City Kings	82	40	42	107.7	106.8	.488	10
Indiana Pacers	82	36	46	106.8	108.6	.439	14
Milwaukee Bucks	82	30	52	108.4	111.5	.366	20

Pacific Division

Team Name	GP	W	L	PPGF	PPGA	Pct	GB
Los Angeles Lakers	82	50	29	106.9	104.1	.646	-
Portland Trail Blazers	82	49	33	111.7	106.2	.598	4
Golden State Warriors	82	46	36	110.9	107.7	.561	7
Seattle SuperSonics	82	40	42	104.0	105.5	.488	13
Phoenix Suns	82	34	48	104.9	104.2	.415	19

Coaching Changes

Buffalo--Tates Locke 16-30, Bob MacKinnon 3-4, Joe Mullaney 11-18; Houston--Tom Nissalke 49-33; Washington--Dick Motta 48-34; San Antonio--Doug Moe 44-38; New Orleans--Butch van Breda Kolff 14-12, Elgin Baylor 21-35; Atlanta--Hubert Brown 31-51; New York Nets--Kevin Loughery 22-60; Denver--Larry Brown 50-32; Detroit--Herb Brown 44-38; Chicago--Ed Badger 44 38; Indiana--Bob Leonard 36-46; Milwaukee--Larry Costello 3-15, Don Nelson 27-37; Los Angeles--Jerry West 53-29; Portland--Jack Ramsay 49-33.

League Leaders

Field Goals		Free Throws		Assists	
Kareem Abdul-Jabbar	888	Pete Maravich	501	Don Buse	685
Pete Maravich	886	David Thompson	477	Norm Van Lier	636
Bill Knight	831	Adrian Dantley	476	Slick Watts	630
David Thompson	824	Dan Issel	445	Tom Henderson	598
Elvin Hayes	760	George Gervin	443	Kevin Porter	592

Points		Rebounds per Game	
Pete Maravich	2273	Bill Walton	14.4
Kareem Abdul-Jabbar	2152	Kareem Abdul-Jabbar	13.3
David Thompson	2125	Moses Malone	13.1
Bill Knight	2075	Artis Gilmore	13.0
Elvin Hayes	1942	Bob McAdoo	12.9

All Star Game

(The Mecca, Milwaukee)

February 13	West Division	125	East Division	124

NBA Playoffs

April 12	San Antonio Spurs	94	at	Boston Celtics	104
April 12	Detroit Pistons	95	at	Golden State Warriors	90
April 12	Chicago Bulls	83	at	Portland Trail Blazers	96
April 13	Cleveland Cavaliers	100	at	Washington Bullets	109
April 14	Golden State Warriors	138	at	Detroit Pistons	108
April 15	Boston Celtics	113	at	San Antonio Spurs	109
April 15	Washington Bullets	83	at	Cleveland Cavaliers	91
April 15	Portland Trail Blazers	104	at	Chicago Bulls	107
April 17	Detroit Pistons	101	at	Golden State Warriors	109
April 17	Cleveland Cavaliers	98	at	Washington Bullets	104
April 17	Chicago Bulls	98	at	Portland Trail Blazers	106
April 17	Boston Celtics	113	at	Philadelphia 76ers	111
April 19	Washington Bullets	111	at	Houston Rockets	101
April 20	Boston Celtics	101	at	Philadelphia 76ers	113
April 20	Golden State Warriors	106	at	Los Angeles Lakers	115
April 20	Portland Trail Blazers	101	at	Denver Nuggets	100
April 21	Washington Bullets	118	at	Houston Rockets	124 [OT]
April 22	Philadelphia 76ers	109	at	Boston Celtics	100
April 22	Golden State Warriors	86	at	Los Angeles Lakers	95
April 22	Portland Trail Blazers	110	at	Denver Nuggets	121
April 24	Philadelphia 76ers	119	at	Boston Celtics	124
April 24	Los Angeles Lakers	105	at	Golden State Warriors	109
April 24	Houston Rockets	90	at	Washington Bullets	93
April 24	Denver Nuggets	106	at	Portland Trail Blazers	110
April 26	Los Angeles Lakers	103	at	Golden State Warriors	114
April 26	Houston Rockets	107	at	Washington Bullets	103
April 26	Denver Nuggets	96	at	Portland Trail Blazers	105
April 27	Boston Celtics	91	at	Philadelphia 76ers	110
April 29	Philadelphia 76ers	108	at	Boston Celtics	113
April 29	Golden State Warriors	105	at	Los Angeles Lakers	112
April 29	Washington Bullets	115	at	Houston Rockets	123

May 1	Boston Celtics	77	at	Philadelphia 76ers	83
May 1	Los Angeles Lakers	106	at	Golden State Warriors	115
May 1	Houston Rockets	108	at	Washington Bullets	103
May 1	Portland Trail Blazers	105	at	Denver Nuggets	114 [OT]
May 2	Denver Nuggets	92	at	Portland Trail Blazers	108
May 4	Golden State Warriors	84	at	Los Angeles Lakers	97
May 5	Houston Rockets	117	at	Philadelphia 76ers	128
May 6	Portland Trail Blazers	121	at	Los Angeles Lakers	109
May 8	Houston Rockets	97	at	Philadelphia 76ers	106
May 8	Portland Trail Blazers	99	at	Los Angeles Lakers	97
May 10	Los Angeles Lakers	97	at	Portland Trail Blazers	102
May 11	Philadelphia 76ers	94	at	Houston Rockets	118
May 13	Los Angeles Lakers	101	at	Portland Trail Blazers	105
May 13	Philadelphia 76ers	107	at	Houston Rockets	95
May 15	Houston Rockets	118	at	Philadelphia 76ers	115
May 17	Philadelphia 76ers	112	at	Houston Rockets	109
May 22	Portland Trail Blazers	101	at	Philadelphia 76ers	107
May 26	Portland Trail Blazers	89	at	Philadelphia 76ers	107
May 29	Philadelphia 76ers	107	at	Portland Trail Blazers	129
May 31	Philadelphia 76ers	98	at	Portland Trail Blazers	130
June 3	Portland Trail Blazers	110	at	Philadelphia 76ers	104
June 5	Philadelphia 76ers	107	at	Portland Trail Blazers	109

All Star Teams

First Team	Second Team
Elvin Hayes (Washington Capitals)	Julius Erving (Philadelphia 76ers)
David Thompson (Denver Nuggets)	George McGinnis (Philadelphia 76ers)
Kareem Abdul-Jabbar (Los Angeles Lakers)	Bill Walton (Portland Trail Blazers)
Pete Maravich (New Orleans Jazz)	George Gervin (San Antonio Spurs)
Paul Westphal (Phoenix Suns)	Jo Jo White (Boston Celtics)

Individual Awards

Eddie Gottlieb Trophy--Adrian Dantley (Buffalo Braves)
Executive of the Year--Ray Patterson (Houston Rockets)
J. Walter Kennedy Citizenship Award--Dave Bing (Washington Bullets)
Maurice Podoloff Trophy--Kareem Abdul-Jabbar (Los Angeles Lakers)
NBA All Star Game MVP--Julius Erving (Philadelphia 76ers)
NBA Finals MVP--Bill Walton (Portland Trail Blazers)
Red Auerbach Trophy--Tom Nissalke (Houston Rockets)

Hall of Fame Inductees

Paul Arizin, Joe Fulks, Clifford Hagan, John Nucatola, Jim Pollard

Notes

The American Basketball Association did not operate this year on a major league level.

FOOTBALL

National Football League

National Football Conference
Eastern Division

Team Name	GP	W	L	T	PF	PA	Pct
Dallas Cowboys	14	12	2	0	345	212	.857
Washington Redskins	14	9	5	0	196	189	.643
St. Louis Cardinals	14	7	7	0	272	287	.500
New York Giants	14	5	9	0	181	265	.357
Philadelphia Eagles	14	5	9	0	220	207	.357

Central Division

Team Name	GP	W	L	T	PF	PA	Pct
Minnesota Vikings	14	9	5	0	231	227	.643
Chicago Bears	14	9	5	0	255	253	.643
Detroit Lions	14	6	8	0	183	252	.429
Green Bay Packers	14	4	10	0	134	219	.286
Tampa Bay Buccaneers	14	2	12	0	103	223	.143

Western Division

Team Name	GP	W	L	T	PF	PA	Pct
Los Angeles Rams	14	10	4	0	302	146	.714
Atlanta Falcons	14	7	7	0	179	120	.500
San Francisco 49ers	14	5	9	0	220	260	.357
New Orleans Saints	14	3	11	0	232	336	.214

American Football Conference

Eastern Division

Team Name	GP	W	L	T	PF	PA	Pct
Baltimore Colts	14	10	4	0	295	221	.714
Miami Dolphins	14	10	4	0	313	197	.714
New England Patriots	14	9	5	0	278	217	.643
New York Jets	14	3	11	0	191	300	.214
Buffalo Bills	14	3	11	0	160	313	.214

Central Division

Team Name	GP	W	L	T	PF	PA	Pct
Pittsburgh Steelers	14	9	5	0	283	243	.643
Cincinnati Bengals	14	8	6	0	238	235	.571
Houston Oilers	14	8	6	0	299	230	.571
Cleveland Browns	14	6	8	0	269	267	.429

Western Division

Team Name	GP	W	L	T	PF	PA	Pct
Denver Broncos	14	12	2	0	274	148	.857
Oakland Raiders	14	11	3	0	351	230	.786
San Diego Chargers	14	7	7	0	222	205	.500
Seattle Seahawks	14	5	9	0	282	373	.357
Kansas City Chiefs	14	2	12	0	225	349	.143

Coaching Changes

Giants--John McVay 5-9-0; Detroit--Tom Hudspeth 6-8-0; Atlanta--Leeman Bennett 7-7-0; San Francisco--Ken Meyer 5-9-0; Jets--Walt Michaels 3-11-0; Buffalo--Jim Ringo 3-11-0; Cleveland Forrest Gregg 6-7-0, Dick Modzelewski 0-1-0; Denver--Red Miller 12-2-0; Kansas City--Paul Wiggin 1-6-0, Tom Bettio 1-6-0.

League Leaders

Yards Rushing		**Yards Passing**		**Passing %** (195 attempts)	
Walter Payton	1852	Joe Ferguson	2803	Fran Tarkenton	60.1
Mark van Eeghen	1273	Bert Jones	2686	Bob Griese	58.6
Lawrence McCutcheon	1238	Roger Staubach	2620	Roger Staubach	58.2
Franco Harris	1162	Jim Hart	2542	Ken Stabler	57.5
Lydell Mitchell	1159	Terry Bradshaw	2523	Brian Sipe	57.4

Receiving Yards		**Receptions**		**Field Goals**	
Drew Pearson	870	Lydell Mitchell	71	Mark Moseley	21
James Scott	809	Bob Chandler	60	Errol Mann	20
Lynn Swann	789	Clark Gaines	55	Chris Bahr	19
John Stallworth	784	Nat Moore	52	Rafael Septien	18
Nat Moore	765	Ahmad Rashad	51	Efren Herrera	18

Punt Return Yards		**Kickoff Return Yards**	
Rick Upchurch	653	Bruce Harper	1035
Billy Johnson	539	Paul Hofer	871
Larry Marshall	489	Ray Clayborn	869
Eddie Brown	452	Eddie Brown	852
Bruce Harper	425	Al Hunter	820

Pro Bowl Game

(Tampa Stadium, Tampa)

January 23 1978	National Conference	14		American Conference	13

NFL Playoffs

December 24	Oakland Raiders	37	at	Baltimore Colts	31
December 24	Pittsburgh Steelers	21	at	Denver Broncos	34
December 26	Chicago Bears	7	at	Dallas Cowboys	37
December 26	Minnesota Vikings	14	at	Los Angeles Rams	7
January 1 1978	Minnesota Vikings	6	at	Dallas Cowboys	23
January 1 1978	Oakland Raiders	17	at	Denver Broncos	20

Super Bowl XII

(Louisiana Superdome, New Orleans)

January 15 1978	Dallas Cowboys	27	Denver Broncos	10

Individual Awards

A.P. MVP--Walter Payton (Chicago Bears)
Bert Bell Trophy--Tony Dorsett (Dallas Cowboys) [World Almanac)
Bert Bell Trophy--Bob Griese (Miami Dolphins)
George Halas Trophy--Harvey Martin (Dallas Cowboys)
P.F.W.A. MVP--Walter Payton (Chicago Bears)

Pro Bowl MVP--Walter Payton (Chicago Bears)
Rookie of the Year--Tony Dorsett (Dallas Cowboys)
Super Bowl MVP--Harvey Martin (Dallas Cowboys)
Randy White (Dallas Cowboys)
Jim Thorpe Trophy--Walter Payton (Chicago Bears)
U.P.I. AFC Coach of the Year--Red Miller (Denver Broncos)
U.P.I. AFC Player of the Year--Craig Morton (Denver Broncos)
U.P.I. AFC Rookie of the Year--A.J. Duhe (Miami Dolphins)
U.P.I. NFC Coach of the Year--Leeman Bennett (Atlanta Falcons)
U.P.I. NFC Player of the Year--Walter Payton (Chicago Bears)
U.P.I. NFC Rookie of the Year--Tony Dorsett (Dallas Cowboys)

Hall of Fame Inductees

Frank Gifford, Forrest Gregg, Gale Sayers, Bart Starr, Bill Willis

Rules

Defenders were permitted to make contact with eligible receivers only once.

Notes

Chicago Bears Walter Payton set a single game rushing record with 275 yards on November 20. The NFL Players Association and the NFL Management Council ratified a collective bargaining agreement extending until 1982. The total cost of the agreement was estimated to be 107 million dollars.

Canadian Football League
Eastern Conference

Team Name	GP	W	L	T	PF	PA	Pts	Pct
Montreal Alouettes	16	11	5	0	311	245	22	.688
Ottawa Rough Riders	16	8	8	0	368	344	16	.500
Toronto Argonauts	16	6	10	0	251	266	12	.375
Hamilton Tiger-Cats	16	5	11	0	283	394	10	.313

Western Conference

Team Name	GP	W	L	T	PF	PA	Pts	Pct
Edmonton Eskimos	16	10	6	0	412	320	20	.625
British Columbia Lions	16	10	6	0	369	326	20	.625
Winnipeg Blue Bombers	16	10	6	0	382	336	20	.625
Saskatchewan Roughriders	16	8	8	0	330	389	16	.500
Calgary Stampeders	16	4	12	0	241	327	8	.250

Coaching Changes

Toronto--Leo Cahill 6-10-0; Hamilton--Bob Shaw 5-11-0; Edmonton--Hugh Campbell 10-6-0; British Columbia--Vic Rapp 10-6-0; Saskatchewan--Jim Eddy 8-8-0; Calgary--Jack Gotta 4-12-0.

League Leaders

Yards Rushing		**Yards Passing**		**Passing %** (200 attempts)	
Jimmy Edwards	1581	Ron Lancaster	3072	Tom Clements	61.0
Jim Washington	1262	Dieter Brock	3063	Tom Wilkinson	59.8
Willie Burden	1032	Tom Clements	2804	Dieter Brock	57.8
Richard Holmes	1016	Jerry Tagge	2787	Jim Jones	57.6
Jim Germany	1004	John Hufnagel	2276	Ron Lancaster	56.7

Receiving Yards		Receptions		Points	
Tony Gabriel	1362	Molly McGee	68	Dave Cutler	195
Tom Scott	1079	Gord Paterson	67	Lui Passaglia	157
Steve Mazurak	978	Tom Scott	66	Don Sweet	136
Tom Forzani	894	Tony Gabriel	65	Bernie Ruoff	134
Gord Paterson	882	Willie Burden	63	Jerry Organ	130

All Star Game

(Exhibition Stadium, Toronto)

June 4	Eastern Conference	20		Western Conference	19

Grey Cup Playoffs

November 12	Winnipeg Blue Bombers	32	at	British Columbia Lions	33
November 13	Toronto Argonauts	16	at	Ottawa Rough Riders	21
November 19	Ottawa Rough Riders	18	at	Montreal Alouettes	21
November 20	British Columbia Lions	1	at	Edmonton Eskimos	38
November 27	Montreal Alouettes	41		Edmonton Eskimos	6*

Individual Awards

Annis Stukus Trophy--Vic Rapp (British Columbia Lions)
CFL All Star Game MVP--Jimmy Jones (Hamilton Tiger-Cats)
Chuck Zapiec (Montreal Alouettes)
Dave Dryburgh Memorial Trophy--Dave Cutler (Edmonton Eskimos)
DeMarco-Becket Memorial Trophy--Al Wilson (British Columbia Lions)
Dr. Beattie Martin Trophy--Gord Paterson (Winnipeg Blue Bombers)
Eddie James Memorial Trophy--Jim Washington (Winnipeg Blue Bombers)
Frank M. Gibson Trophy--Mike Murphy (Ottawa Rough Riders)
Grey Cup Most Outstanding Defensive Star--Glen Weir (Montreal Alouettes)
Grey Cup Most Outstanding Offensive Star--Sonny Wade (Montreal Alouettes)
Grey Cup Most Valuable Canadian--Don Sweet (Montreal Alouettes)
Jackie Parker Trophy--Leon Bright (British Columbia Lions)
James P. McCaffrey Trophy--Glen Weir (Montreal Alouettes)
Jeff Nicklin Memorial Trophy--Jerry Tagge (British Columbia Lions)
Jeff Russel Memorial Trophy--Jimmy Edwards (Hamilton Tiger-Cats)
Leo Dandurand Trophy--Mike Wilson (Toronto Argonauts)
Lew Hayman Trophy--Tony Gabriel (Ottawa Rough Riders)
Norm Fieldgate Trophy--Dan Kepley (Edmonton Eskimos)
Schenley Award Most Outstanding Canadian--Tony Gabriel (Ottawa Rough Riders)
Schenley Award Most Outstanding Defensive Player--Dan Kepley (Edmonton Eskimos)
Schenley Award Most outstanding Offensive Lineman--Al Wilson (British Columbia Lions)
Schenley Award Most Outstanding Player--Jimmy Edwards (Hamilton Tiger-Cats)
Schenley Award Most Outstanding Rookie--Leon Bright (British Columbia Lions)

Hall of Fame Inductees

Tommy Joe Coffey, Hap Shouldice, Ron Stewart

Notes

The Grey Cup game was played before a record crowd of 68,318 in Montreal's Olympic Stadium.

*Game played in Montreal

HOCKEY
National Hockey League

Clarence Campbell Conference
Patrick Division

Team Name	GP	W	L	T	GF	GA	Pts	Pct
Philadelphia Flyers	80	48	16	16	323	213	112	.700
New York Islanders	80	47	21	12	288	196	106	.663
Atlanta Flames	80	34	34	12	264	265	80	.500
New York Rangers	80	29	37	14	272	310	72	.450

Smythe Division

Team Name	GP	W	L	T	GF	GA	Pts	Pct
St. Louis Blues	80	32	39	9	239	276	73	.456
Minnesota North Stars	80	23	39	18	240	310	64	.400
Chicago Black Hawks	80	26	43	11	240	298	63	.394
Vancouver Canucks	80	25	42	13	235	294	63	.394
Colorado Rockies	80	20	46	14	226	307	54	.338

Prince of Wales Conference

Norris Division

Team Name	GP	W	L	T	GF	GA	Pts	Pct
Montreal Canadiens	80	60	8	12	387	171	132	.825
Los Angeles Kings	80	34	31	15	271	241	83	.519
Pittsburgh Penguins	80	34	33	13	240	252	81	.506
Washington Capitals	80	24	42	14	221	307	62	.388
Detroit Red Wings	80	16	55	9	183	309	41	.256

Adams Division

Team Name	GP	W	L	T	GF	GA	Pts	Pct
Boston Bruins	80	49	23	8	312	240	106	.663
Buffalo Sabres	80	48	24	8	301	220	104	.650
Toronto Maple Leafs	80	33	32	15	301	285	81	.506
Cleveland Barons	80	25	42	13	240	383	63	.394

Coaching Changes

Rangers--John Ferguson 29-37-14; St.Louis--Emile Francis 32-39-9; Chicago--Billy Reay 10-19-5, Bill White 16-24-6; Vancouver--Phil Maloney 9-23-3, Orland Kurtenbach 16-19-10; Colorado--John Wilson 20-46-14; Pittsburgh--Ken Schinkel 34-33-13; Washington--Tom McVie 24-42-14; Detroit--Alex Delvecchio 13-26-5, Larry Wilson 3 29-4; Cleveland--Jack Evans 25-42-13.

League Leaders

Goals		Assists		Points	
Steve Shutt	60	Guy Lafleur	80	Guy Lafleur	136
Guy Lafleur	56	Marcel Dionne	69	Marcel Dionne	122
Marcel Dionne	53	Tim Young	66	Steve Shutt	105
Rick MacLeish	49	Larry Robinson	66	Rick MacLeish	97
Lanny McDonald	46	Borje Salming	66	Gil Perreault	95

Penalty Minutes		Plus/Minus		GAA	
				(1,600 minutes)	
Dave Williams	338	Larry Robinson	120	Ken Dryden	2.14
Dennis Polonich	274	Guy Lafleur	89	Glenn Resch	2.28
Bob Gassoff	254	Steve Shutt	88	Billy Smith	2.50
Phil Russell	233	Serge Savard	79	Gerry Desjardins	2.63
Dave Schultz	232	Jacques Lemaire	70	Bernie Parent	2.71

Wins		Shutouts	
Ken Dryden	41	Ken Dryden	10
Bernie Parent	35	Rogie Vachon	8
Rogie Vachon	33	Bernie Parent	5
Gerry Desjardins	31	Glenn Resch	4
Gerry Cheevers	30	Mike Palmateer	4

All Star Game

(Pacific Coliseum, Vancouver)

January 25	Wales Conference	4	Campbell Conference	3

Stanley Cup Playoffs

April 5	Chicago Black Hawks	2	at	New York Islanders	5
April 5	Minnesota North Stars	2	at	Buffalo Sabres	4
April 5	Toronto Maple Leafs	4	at	Pittsburgh Penguins	2
April 5	Atlanta Flames	2	at	Los Angeles Kings	5
April 7	Chicago Black Hawks	1	at	New York Islanders	2
April 7	Buffalo Sabres	7	at	Minnesota North Stars	1
April 7	Pittsburgh Penguins	6	at	Toronto Maple Leafs	4
April 7	Los Angeles Kings	2	at	Atlanta Flames	3
April 9	Toronto Maple Leafs	5	at	Pittsburgh Penguins	2
April 9	Atlanta Flames	2	at	Los Angeles Kings	4
April 11	Toronto Maple Leafs	3	at	Philadelphia Flyers	2
April 11	Los Angeles Kings	3	at	Boston Bruins	8
April 11	St. Louis Blues	2	at	Montreal Canadiens	7
April 11	Buffalo Sabres	2	at	New York Islanders	4
April 13	Toronto Maple Leafs	4	at	Philadelphia Flyers	1
April 13	Los Angeles Kings	2	at	Boston Bruins	6
April 13	St. Louis Blues	0	at	Montreal Canadiens	3
April 13	Buffalo Sabres	2	at	New York Islanders	4
April 15	Philadelphia Flyers	4	at	Toronto Maple Leafs	3 [2:55]
April 15	Boston Bruins	7	at	Los Angeles Kings	6
April 15	New York Islanders	4	at	Buffalo Sabres	3
April 16	Montreal Canadiens	5	at	St. Louis Blues	1
April 17	Philadelphia Flyers	6	at	Toronto Maple Leafs	5 [19:10]
April 17	Boston Bruins	4	at	Los Angeles Kings	7
April 17	Montreal Canadiens	4	at	St. Louis blues	1
April 17	New York Islanders	4	at	Buffalo Sabres	3
April 19	Toronto Maple Leafs	0	at	Philadelphia Flyers	2
April 19	Los Angeles Kings	3	at	Boston Bruins	1
April 21	Philadelphia Flyers	4	at	Toronto Maple Leafs	3
April 21	Boston Bruins	4	at	Los Angeles Kings	3
April 23	New York Islanders	3	at	Montreal Canadiens	4
April 24	Boston Bruins	4	at	Philadelphia Flyers	3 [2:57]
April 26	New York Islanders	0	at	Montreal Canadiens	3

April 26	Boston Bruins	5	at	Philadelphia Flyers	4 [10:07]
April 28	Montreal Canadiens	3	at	New York Islanders	5
April 28	Philadelphia Flyers	1	at	Boston Bruins	2
April 30	Montreal Canadiens	4	at	New York Islanders	0
May 1	Philadelphia Flyers	0	at	Boston Bruins	3
May 3	New York Islanders	4	at	Montreal Canadiens	3 [3:58]
May 5	Montreal Canadiens	2	at	New York Islanders	1
May 7	Boston Bruins	3	at	Montreal Canadiens	7
May 10	Boston Bruins	0	at	Montreal Canadiens	3
May 12	Montreal Canadiens	4	at	Boston Bruins	2
May 14	Montreal Canadiens	2	at	Boston Bruins	1 [4:32]

All Star Teams

First Team		Second Team
Ken Dryden	Goal	Rogatien Vachon
Larry Robinson	Defense	Denis Potvin
Borje Salming	Defense	Guy Lapointe
Marcel Dionne	Center	Gilbert Perreault
Guy Lafleur	Right Wing	Lanny McDonald
Steve Shutt	Left Wing	Richard Martin

Individual Awards

Art Ross Trophy--Guy Lafleur (Montreal Canadiens)
Bill Masterton Trophy--Ed Westfall (New York Islanders)
Calder Memorial Trophy--Willi Plett (Atlanta Flames)
Conn Smythe Trophy--Guy Lafleur (Montreal Canadiens)
Hart Memorial Trophy--Guy Lafleur (Montreal Canadiens)
Jack Adams Award--Scotty Bowman (Montreal Canadiens)
James Norris Trophy--Larry Robinson (Montreal Canadiens)
Lady Byng Memorial Trophy--Marcel Dionne (Los Angeles Kings)
Lester B. Pearson Award--Guy Lafleur (Montreal Canadiens)
Lester Patrick Trophy--Johnny Bucyk, Murray Armstrong, John Mariucci.
NHL All Star Game MVP--Rick Martin (Buffalo Sabres)
Vezina Trophy--Ken Dryden (Montreal Canadiens)
Michel Larocque (Montreal Canadiens)

Hall of Fame Inductees

"Bunny" Ahearne, Harold Ballard, Joseph Cattarinich, Alex Delvecchio, Tim Horton

Rules

The fighting rule is amended to provide a major and a game misconduct penalty to a player judged to be the instigator in a fight.

Notes

Clarence Campbell retired as President of the NHL and was succeeded by John Ziegler.

World Hockey Association
Eastern Division

Team Name	GP	W	L	T	GF	GA	Pts	Pct
Quebec Nordiques	81	47	31	3	353	295	97	.599
Cincinnati Stingers	81	39	37	5	354	303	83	.512
Indianapolis Racers	81	36	37	8	276	305	80	.494
New England Whalers	81	35	40	6	275	290	76	.469
Birmingham Bulls	81	31	46	4	289	309	66	.407
Minnesota Fighting Saints	42	19	18	5	136	129	43	.512

Western Division

Team Name	GP	W	L	T	GF	GA	Pts	Pct
Houston Aeros	80	50	24	6	320	241	106	.663
Winnipeg Jets	80	46	32	2	366	291	94	.588
San Diego Mariners	81	40	37	4	284	283	84	.519
Edmonton Oilers	81	34	43	4	243	304	72	.444
Calgary Cowboys	81	31	43	7	252	296	69	.426
Phoenix Roadrunners	80	28	48	4	281	383	60	.375

Coaching Changes

Quebec Marc Boileau 47-31-3; New England--Harry Neale 35-40-6; Birmingham--Gilles Leger 7-16-1; Pat Kelly 24-30-3; Minnesota--Glen Sonmor 19-18-5; Edmonton--Armand Guidolin 25-36-2, Glen Sather 9-7-2; Phoenix--Al Rollins 28-48-4.

League Leaders

Goals

Anders Hedberg	70
Real Cloutier	66
Mark Napier	60
Richard LeDuc	52
Blaine Stoughton	52

Assists

Ulf Nilsson	85
Andre Lacroix	82
Real Cloutier	75
Chris Bordeleau	75
Robbie Ftorek	71

Points

Real Cloutier	141
Anders Hedberg	131
Ulf Nilsson	124
Robbie Ftorek	117
Andre Lacroix	114

Penalty Minutes

Frank Beaton	274
Paul Baxter	244
Ron Busniuk	224
Cam Connor	224
Bill Butters	215

GAA
(1,560 minutes)

Ron Grahame	2.74
Ernie Wakely	3.09
Wayne Rutledge	3.15
Joe Daley	3.24
Michel Dion	3.36

Wins

Joe Daley	39
Richard Brodeur	29
Ron Grahame	27
Don McLeod	25
John Garrett	24

Shutouts

John Garrett	4
Ken Broderick	4
Ron Grahame	4
Jacques Caron	3
Wayne Rutledge	3

All Star Game
(Hartford Civic Center)

January 18	East Division	4	West Division	2

WHA Playoffs

April 9	New England Whalers	2	at	Quebec Nordiques	5
April 9	Indianapolis Racers	4	at	Cincinnati Stingers	3 [48:40]
April 10	San Diego Mariners	1	at	Winnipeg Jets	5
April 12	New England Whalers	3	at	Quebec Nordiques	7
April 12	Indianapolis Racers	7	at	Cincinnati Stingers	2
April 12	San Diego Mariners	1	at	Winnipeg Jets	4
April 13	Edmonton Oilers	3	at	Houston Aeros	4 [13:11]
April 14	Quebec Nordiques	4	at	New England Whalers	3 [1:50]
April 14	Cincinnati Stingers	3	at	Indianapolis Racers	5
April 15	Edmonton Oilers	2	at	Houston Aeros	6
April 16	Quebec Nordiques	4	at	New England Whalers	6
April 16	Cincinnati Stingers	1	at	Indianapolis Racers	3
April 16	Winnipeg Jets	4	at	San Diego Mariners	5
April 17	Houston Aeros	2	at	Edmonton Oilers	7
April 17	Winnipeg Jets	4	at	San Diego Mariners	6
April 19	New England Whalers	0	at	Quebec Nordiques	3
April 20	Houston Aeros	4	at	Edmonton Oilers	1
April 20	San Diego Mariners	0	at	Winnipeg Jets	3
April 22	Edmonton Oilers	3	at	Houston Aeros	4
April 22	Winnipeg Jets	1	at	San Diego Mariners	3
April 23	Indianapolis Racers	1	at	Quebec Nordiques	3
April 24	San Diego Mariners	3	at	Winnipeg Jets	7
April 25	Indianapolis Racers	3	at	Quebec Nordiques	8
April 26	Winnipeg Jets	4	at	Houston Aeros	3 [8:05]
April 28	Quebec Nordiques	6	at	Indianapolis Racers	5 [5:29]
April 28	Winnipeg Jets	2	at	Houston Aeros	7
April 30	Quebec Nordiques	0	at	Indianapolis Racers	2
April 30	Houston Aeros	3	at	Winnipeg Jets	4
May 1	Houston Aeros	4	at	Winnipeg Jets	6
May 2	Indianapolis Racers	3	at	Quebec Nordiques	8
May 3	Winnipeg Jets	2	at	Houston Aeros	3
May 5	Houston Aeros	3	at	Winnipeg Jets	6
May 11	Winnipeg Jets	2	at	Quebec Nordiques	1
May 15	Winnipeg Jets	1	at	Quebec Nordiques	6
May 18	Quebec Nordiques	1	at	Winnipeg Jets	6
May 20	Quebec Nordiques	4	at	Winnipeg Jets	2
May 22	Winnipeg Jets	3	at	Quebec Nordiques	8
May 24	Quebec Nordiques	3	at	Winnipeg Jets	12
May 26	Winnipeg Jets	2	at	Quebec Nordiques	8

All Star Teams

First Team		Second Team
John Garrett	Goal	Joe Daley
Darryl Maggs	Defense	Poul Popiel
Ron Plumb	Defense	Mark Howe
Robbie Ftorek	Center	Ulf Nilsson
Anders Hedberg	Right Wing	Real Cloutier
Marc Tardif	Left Wing	Rick Dudley

Individual Awards

Ben Hatskin Trophy--Ron Grahame (Houston Aeros)
Bill Hunter Trophy--Real Cloutier (Quebec Nordiques)

Dennis Murphy Trophy--Ron Plumb (Cincinnati Stingers)
Gordie Howe Trophy--Robbie Ftorek (Phoenix Roadrunners)
Lou Kaplan Trophy--George Lyle (New England Whalers)
Paul Deneau Trophy--Dave Keon (Minnesota Fighting Saints/New England Whalers)
Robert Schmertz Trophy--Bill Dineen (Houston Aeros)
WHA All Star Game MVP--Louis Levasseur (Minnesota Fighting Saints)
Willy Lindstrom (Winnipeg Jets)
WHA MVP in Playoffs--Serge Bernier (Quebec Nordiques)

Notes

The WHA again realigned its divisions, this time it divided into East and West Division. Howard Baldwin became President of the World Hockey Association with Ben Hatskin as Chairman of the Board. The league offices moved to Hartford from Toronto.

SOCCER

North American Soccer League

Northern Division

Team Name	GP	W	L	GF	GA	BP	Pts	Pct
Toronto Metro-Croatia	26	13	13	42	38	37	115	.491
St. Louis Stars	26	12	14	33	35	32	104	.444
Rochester Lancers	26	11	15	34	41	33	99	.423
Chicago Sting	26	10	16	31	43	28	88	.376
Connecticut Bicentennials	26	7	19	34	65	30	72	.308

Eastern Division

Team Name	GP	W	L	GF	GA	BP	Pts	Pct
Fort Lauderdale Strikers	26	19	7	49	29	47	161	.688
Cosmos	26	15	11	60	39	50	140	.598
Tampa Bay Rowdies	26	14	12	55	45	47	131	.560
Washington Diplomats	26	10	16	32	49	32	92	.393

Southern Division

Team Name	GP	W	L	GF	GA	BP	Pts	Pct
Dallas Tornado	26	18	8	56	37	53	161	.688
Los Angeles Aztecs	26	15	11	65	54	57	147	.628
San Jose Earthquakes	26	14	12	37	44	35	119	.509
Team Hawaii	26	11	15	45	59	41	106	.453
Las Vegas Quicksilvers	26	11	15	38	44	37	103	.440

Western Division

Team Name	GP	W	L	GF	GA	BP	Pts	Pct
Minnesota Kicks	26	16	10	44	36	41	136	.581
Vancouver Whitecaps	26	14	12	43	46	40	124	.530
Seattle Sounders	26	14	12	43	34	39	123	.526
Portland Timbers	26	10	16	39	42	38	98	.419

Coaching Changes

Toronto--Ivan Sangullian 13-13; Chicago--Bill Foulkes 4-10, Willy Roy 6-6; Connecticut--Bobby Thomson 1-12, Malcolm Musgrove 6-7; Fort Lauderdale--Ron Newman 19-7; Cosmos--Gordon Bradley 12-8, Eddie Firmani 3-3;Tampa Bay--Eddie Firmani 7-3, John Boyle 7-9; Washington--Dennis Viollet 6-9, Alan Spavin 4-7; Team Hawaii--Hubert Vogelsinger 8-9, Charlie Mitchell 3-6; Las Vegas--Derek Trevis 10-10, Jim Fryatt 1-5; Vancouver--Eckhard Krautzun 3-3, Holger Osieck 0-3, Tony Waiters 11-6; Seattle--Jim Gabriel 14-12; Portland--Brian Tiler 10-16.

League Leaders

Goals		**Points**		**Shutouts**	
Steve David	26	Steve David	58	Zeljko Bilecki	10
Derek Smethurst	19	Derek Smethurst	42	Gordon Banks	9
Giorgio Chinaglia	15	George Best	40	Ken Cooper	8
Mike Stojanovic	14	Giorgio Chinaglia	38	Geoff Barnett	8
Alan Willey	14	Mike Stojanovic	33	Mike Hewitt	8

GAA
(1,170 minutes)

Ken Cooper	0.90
Gordon Banks	1.12
John Jackson	1.18
Zeljko Bilecki	1.21
Geoff Barnett	1.25

NASL Playoffs

August 10	San Jose Earthquakes	1	at	Los Angeles Aztecs	2
August 10	Seattle Sounders	2	at	Vancouver Whitecaps	0
August 10	Tampa Bay Rowdies	0	at	Cosmos	3
August 10	Rochester Lancers	1	at	St. Louis Stars	0 [SO]
August 13	Toronto Metro-Croatia	0	at	Rochester Lancers	1 [SO]
August 14	Seattle Sounders	2	at	Minnesota Kicks	1 [SO]
August 14	Dallas Tornado	1	at	Los Angeles Aztecs	3
August 14	Ft. Lauderdale Strikers	3	at	Cosmos	8
August 16	Rochester Lancers	1	at	Toronto Metro-Croatia	0
August 17	Los Angeles Aztecs	5	at	Dallas Tornado	1
August 17	Cosmos	3	at	Fort Lauderdale Strikers	2 [SO]
August 17	Minnesota Kicks	0	at	Seattle Sounders	1
August 21	Seattle Sounders	3	at	Los Angeles Aztecs	1
August 21	Cosmos	2	at	Rochester Lancers	1
August 24	Rochester Lancers	1	at	Cosmos	4
August 25	Los Angeles Aztecs	0	at	Seattle Sounders	1
August 28	Cosmos	2	at	Seattle Sounders	1 *

All Star Teams

First Team		Second Team
Gordon Banks	Goal	Alan Mayer
Franz Beckenbauer	Defender	Ray Evans
Mike England	Defender	Steve Pecher
Bruce Wilson	Defender	Humberto
Mel Machin	Defender	George Ley
		Arsene Auguste
George Best	Midfield	Charlie Cooke
Wolfgang Suhnholz	Midfield	Vito Dimitrijevic
Alan West	Midfield	Rodney Marsh
Steve David	Forward	Mike Stojanovic
Pele	Forward	Steve Wegerle
Derek Smethurst	Forward	Buzz Parsons

*Game played in Portland

Individual Awards

Coach of the Year--Ron Newman (Fort Lauderdale Strikers)
Lead Goalkeeper Award--Ken Cooper (Dallas Tornado)
Most Valuable Player--Franz Beckenbauer (New York Cosmos)
Rookie of the Year--Jim McAlister (Seattle Sounders)

Notes

The shootout was introduced this year to replace the penalty kick tie-breaker.

Franchise Changes

NHL--Kansas City Scouts became Colorado Rockies
California Golden Seals became the Cleveland Barons.
WHA--Toronto Toros became the Birmingham Bulls
Cleveland Crusaders became the Minnesota Fighting Saints.
NASL--Hartford Bicentennials became the Connecticut Bicentennials.
Miami Toros became the Fort Lauderdale Strikers.
New York Cosmos became known simply as the Cosmos.
San Antonio Thunder became Team Hawaii.
San Diego Jaws became the Las Vegas Quicksilvers.

Other Sports

Horseracing--Kentucky Derby won by Seattle Slew (time 2:02.2, purse $214,700).
Heavyweight Boxing--Muhammad Ali defeated Alfredo Evangelista in 15 rounds.
Muhammad Ali defeated Ernie Shavers in 15 rounds.
Golf--U.S. Open won by Hubert Green with a, score of 278.
Auto Racing--Indianapolis 500 won by A.J. Foyt (ave. speed 161.331 MPH).
Tennis--U.S. Open won by Guillermo Vilas in the men's singles.
U.S. Open won by Bob Hewitt and Frew McMillan in the men's doubles.
U.S. Open won by Chris Evert in the women's singles.
U.S. Open won by Betty Stove and Martina Navratilova in the women's doubles.
U.S. Open won by Betty Stove and Frew McMillan in the mixed doubles.

Notes

Seattle Slew won horse racing's Triple Crown.
A.J. Foyt won his fourth Indianapolis 500 auto race.

1978

BASEBALL
National League

East

Team Name	W	L	Pct	GB	R	OR
Philadelphia Phillies	90	72	.556	-	708	586
Pittsburgh Pirates	88	73	.547	1.5	684	637
Chicago Cubs	79	83	.488	11	664	724
Montreal Expos	76	86	.469	14	633	611
St. Louis Cardinals	69	93	.426	21	600	657
New York Mets	66	96	.407	24	607	690

West

Team Name	W	L	Pct	GB	R	OR
Los Angeles Dodgers	95	67	.586	-	727	573
Cincinnati Reds	92	69	.571	2.5	710	688
San Francisco Giants	89	73	.549	6	613	594
San Diego Padres	84	78	.519	11	591	598
Houston Astros	74	88	.457	21	605	634
Atlanta Braves	69	93	.426	26	600	750

Coaching Changes

St. Louis--Vern Rapp 6-10, Jack Krol 1-1, Ken Boyer 62-82; New York--Joe Torre 66-96; San Diego--Roger Craig 84-78; Atlanta--Bobby Cox 69-93.

League Leaders

Batting Average (440 at bats)		Home Runs		RBI	
Dave Parker	.334	George Foster	40	George Foster	120
Bill Buckner	.323	Greg Luzinski	35	Dave Parker	117
Steve Garvey	.316	Dave Parker	30	Steve Garvey	113
Jose Cruz	.315	Reggie Smith	29	Greg Luzinski	101
Bill Madlock	.309	Dave Kingman	28	Jack Clark	98

Stolen Bases		ERA (162 innings)		Wins	
Omar Moreno	71	Craig Swan	2.43	Gaylord Perry	21
Frank Taveras	46	Steve Rogers	2.47	Ross Grimsley	20
Dave Lopes	45	Pete Vukovich	2.55	Phil Niekro	19
Ivan DeJesus	41	Bob Knepper	2.63	Burt Hooton	19
Ozzie Smith	40	Burt Hooton	2.71	Vida Blue	18

Saves		Strikeouts	
Rollie Fingers	37	J.R. Richard	303
Kent Tekulve	31	Phil Niekro	248
Doug Bair	28	Tom Seaver	226
Bruce Sutter	27	Bert Blyleven	182
Terry Forster	22	John Montefusco	177

NLCS

October 4	Los Angeles Dodgers	9	at	Philadelphia Phillies	5
October 5	Los Angeles Dodgers	4	at	Philadelphia Phillies	0
October 6	Philadelphia Phillies	9	at	Los Angeles Dodgers	4
October 7	Philadelphia Phillies	3	at	Los Angeles Dodgers	4 [10]

American League

East

Team Name	W	L	Pct	GB	R	OR
New York Yankees	100	63	.613	-	735	582
Boston Red Sox	99	64	.607	1	796	657
Milwaukee Brewers	93	69	.574	6.5	804	650
Baltimore Orioles	90	71	.559	9	659	633
Detroit Tigers	86	76	.531	13.5	714	653
Cleveland Indians	69	90	.434	29	639	694
Toronto Blue Jays	59	102	.366	40	590	775

West

Team Name	W	L	Pct	GB	R	OR
Kansas City Royals	90	70	.568	-	743	634
California Angels	87	75	.537	5	691	666
Texas Rangers	87	75	.537	5	692	632
Minnesota Twins	73	89	.451	19	666	678
Chicago White Sox	71	90	.441	20.5	634	731
Oakland Athletics	69	93	.426	23	532	690
Seattle Mariners	56	104	.350	35	614	834

Coaching Changes

New York--Billy Martin 52-42, Dick Howser 0-1, Bob Lemon 48-20; Milwaukee--George Bamberger 93-69; Cleveland--Jeff Torborg 69-90; California--Dave Garcia 25-21, Jim Fregosi 62-54; Texas--Bill Hunter 86-75, Pat Corrales 1-0; Chicago--Bob Lemon 34-40, Larry Doby 37-50; Oakland--Bobby Winkles 24-15, Jack McKeon 45-78.

League Leaders

Batting Average
(440 at bats)

Rod Carew	.333
Al Oliver	.324
Jim Rice	.315
Lou Piniella	.314
Ben Oglivie	.303

Home Runs

Jim Rice	46
Don Baylor	34
Larry Hisle	34
Andre Thornton	33
Gorman Thomas	32

RBI

Jim Rice	139
Rusty Staub	121
Larry Hisle	115
Andre Thornton	105
Rico Carty	99

Stolen Bases

Ron LeFlore	68
Julio Cruz	59
Elliot Wills	52
Miguel Dilone	50
Willie Wilson	46

ERA
(162innings)

Ron Guidry	1.74
Jon Matlack	2.30
Mike Caldwell	2.37
Jim Palmer	2.46
Dave Goltz	2.50

Wins

Ron Guidry	25
Mike Caldwell	22
Jim Palmer	21
Dennis Leonard	21
Ed Figueroa	20

Saves		Strikeouts	
Rich Gossage	27	Nolan Ryan	260
Dave LaRoche	25	Ron Guidry	248
Don Stanhouse	24	Dennis Leonard	183
Mike Marshall	21	Mike Flanagan	167
Al Hrabosky	20	Dennis Eckersley	162

All Star Game
(San Diego Stadium, San Diego)

July 11	National League	7		American League	3

ALCS

October 3	New York Yankees	7	at	Kansas City Royals	1
October 4	New York Yankees	4	at	Kansas City Royals	10
October 6	Kansas City Royals	5	at	New York Yankees	6
October 7	Kansas City Royals	1	at	New York Yankees	2

World Series

October 10	New York Yankees	5	at	Los Angeles Dodgers	11
October 11	New York Yankees	3	at	Los Angeles Dodgers	4
October 13	Los Angeles Dodgers	1	at	New York Yankees	5
October 14	Los Angeles Dodgers	3	at	New York Yankees	4 [10]
October 15	Los Angeles Dodgers	2	at	New York Yankees	12
October 17	New York Yankees	7	at	Los Angeles Dodgers	2

Individual Awards

Arch Ward Memorial Trophy--Steve Garvey (Los Angeles Dodgers NL)
Baseball Writers Award--Dave Parker (Pittsburgh Pirates NL)
Jim Rice (Boston Red Sox AL)
Cy Young Award--Gaylord Perry (San Diego Padres NL)
Ron Guidry (New York Yankees AL)
NLCS MVP--Steve Garvey (Los Angeles Dodgers NL)
Rookie of the Year--Bob Horner (Atlanta Braves NL)
Lou Whitaker (Detroit Tigers AL)
Sporting News Executive of the Year--Spec Richardson (San Francisco Giants NL)
Sporting News Manager of the Year--George Bamberger (Milwaukee Brewers AL)
Sporting News Pitcher of the Year--Vida Blue (San Francisco Giants NL)
Ron Guidry (New York Yankees AL)
Sporting News Player of the Year--Dave Parker (Pittsburgh Pirates NL)
Jim Rice (Boston Red Sox AL)
Sporting News Rookie of the Year--Bob Horner (Atlanta Braves NL)
Don Robinson (Pittsburgh Pirates NL)
Paul Molitor (Milwaukee Brewers AL)
Rich Gale (Kansas City Royals AL)
World Series MVP--Bucky Dent (New York Yankees AL)

Hall of Fame Inductees

Addie Joss, Larry MacPhail, Eddie Mathews

BASKETBALL

National Basketball Association

Eastern Conference
Atlantic Division

Team Name	GP	W	L	PPGF	PPGA	Pct	GB
Philadelphia 76ers	82	55	27	114.7	109.6	.671	-
New York Knickerbockers	82	43	39	113.4	114.0	.524	12
Boston Celtics	82	32	50	105.7	107.7	.390	23
Buffalo Braves	82	27	55	105.3	109.0	.329	28
New Jersey Nets	82	24	58	106.7	112.5	.293	31

Central Division

Team Name	GP	W	L	PPGF	PPGA	Pct	GB
San Antonio Spurs	82	52	30	114.5	111.1	.634	-
Washington Bullets	82	44	38	110.3	109.4	.537	8
Cleveland Cavaliers	82	43	39	104.4	103.9	.524	9
Atlanta Hawks	82	41	41	103.7	103.9	.500	11
New Orleans Jazz	82	39	43	107.6	109.5	.476	13
Houston Rockets	82	28	54	103.8	107.8	.341	24

Western Conference

Midwest Division

Team Name	GP	W	L	PPGF	PPGA	Pct	GB
Denver Nuggets	82	48	34	111.8	110.9	.585	-
Milwaukee Bucks	82	44	38	112.4	113.0	.537	4
Chicago Bulls	82	40	42	103.9	104.8	.488	8
Detroit Pistons	82	38	44	109.0	110.2	.463	10
Kansas City Kings	82	31	51	109.5	111.4	.378	17
Indiana Pacers	82	31	51	108.6	111.1	.378	17

Pacific Division

Team Name	GP	W	L	PPGF	PPGA	Pct	GB
Portland Trail Blazers	82	58	24	107.7	101.5	.707	-
Phoenix Suns	82	49	33	112.3	108.6	.598	9
Seattle SuperSonics	82	47	35	104.5	102.9	.573	11
Los Angeles Lakers	82	45	37	110.3	107.6	.549	13
Golden State Warriors	82	43	39	106.1	105.7	.524	15

Coaching Changes

Philadelphia--Gene Shue 2-4, Bill Cunningham 53-23; New York--Willis Reed 43-39; Boston--Tom Heinsohn 11-23, Tom Sanders 21-27; Buffalo--Lowell "Cotton" Fitzsimmons 27-55; New Jersey--Kevin Loughery 24-58; New Orleans--Elgin Baylor 39-43; Milwaukee--Don Nelson 44-38; Detroit--Herb Brown 9-15, Bob Kauffman 29-29; Kansas City--Phil Johnson 13-24, Larry Staverman 18-27; Seattle--Bob Hopkins 5-17, Lenny Wilkens 42-18.

League Leaders

Field Goals		Free Throws		Assists	
George Gervin	864	Adrian Dantley	541	Kevin Porter	837
Calvin Murphy	852	David Thompson	520	John Lucas	768
David Thompson	826	George Gervin	504	Rick Sobers	584
Bob McAdoo	814	Artis Gilmore	471	Norm Nixon	553
Paul Westphal	809	Bob McAdoo	469	Norm Van Lier	531

Points		Rebounds per Game	
George Gervin	2232	Truck Robinson	15.7
David Thompson	2172	Moses Malone	15.0
Bob McAdoo	2097	Dave Cowens	14.0
Randy Smith	2021	Elvin Hayes	13.3
Paul Westphal	2014	Swen Nater	13.2

All Star Game

(The Omni, Atlanta)

February 5	East Division	133	West Division	125

NBA Championship

April 11	Milwaukee Bucks	111	at	Phoenix Suns	103
April 12	N.Y. Knickerbockers	132	at	Cleveland Cavaliers	114
April 12	Atlanta Hawks	94	at	Washington Bullets	103
April 12	Los Angeles Lakers	90	at	Seattle SuperSonics	102
April 14	Cleveland Cavaliers	107	at	N.Y. Knickerbockers	109
April 14	Phoenix Suns	90	at	Milwaukee Bucks	94
April 14	Washington Bullets	107	at	Atlanta Hawks	103 [OT]
April 14	Seattle SuperSonics	99	at	Los Angeles Lakers	105
April 16	Los Angeles Lakers	102	at	Seattle SuperSonics	111
April 16	N.Y. Knickerbockers	90	at	Philadelphia 76ers	130
April 16	Washington Bullets	103	at	San Antonio Spurs	114
April 18	N.Y. Knickerbockers	100	at	Philadelphia 76ers	119
April 18	Seattle SuperSonics	104	at	Portland Trail Blazers	95
April 18	Washington Bullets	121	at	San Antonio Spurs	117
April 18	Milwaukee Bucks	103	at	Denver Nuggets	119
April 20	Philadelphia 76ers	137	at	N.Y. Knickerbockers	126
April 21	Seattle SuperSonics	93	at	Portland Trail Blazers	96
April 21	San Antonio Spurs	105	at	Washington Bullets	118
April 21	Milwaukee Bucks	111	at	Denver Nuggets	127
April 23	Philadelphia 76ers	112	at	N.Y. Knickerbockers	107
April 23	Portland Trail Blazers	84	at	Seattle SuperSonics	99
April 23	San Antonio Spurs	95	at	Washington Bullets	98
April 23	Denver Nuggets	112	at	Milwaukee Bucks	143
April 25	Washington Bullets	105	at	San Antonio Spurs	116
April 25	Denver Nuggets	118	at	Milwaukee Bucks	104
April 26	Portland Trail Blazers	98	at	Seattle SuperSonics	100
April 28	San Antonio Spurs	100	at	Washington Bullets	103
April 28	Milwaukee Bucks	117	at	Denver Nuggets	112
April 30	Seattle SuperSonics	89	at	Portland Trail Blazers	113

April 30	Denver Nuggets	91	at	Milwaukee Bucks	119
April 30	Washington Bullets	122	at	Philadelphia 76ers	117
May 1	Portland Trail Blazers	94	at	Seattle SuperSonics	105
May 3	Milwaukee Bucks	110	at	Denver Nuggets	116
May 3	Washington Bullets	104	at	Philadelphia 76ers	110
May 5	Seattle SuperSonics	107	at	Denver Nuggets	116
May 5	Philadelphia 76ers	108	at	Washington Bullets	123
May 7	Seattle SuperSonics	121	at	Denver Nuggets	111
May 7	Philadelphia 76ers	105	at	Washington Bullets	121
May 10	Denver Nuggets	91	at	Seattle SuperSonics	105
May 10	Washington Bullets	94	at	Philadelphia 76ers	107
May 12	Denver Nuggets	94	at	Seattle SuperSonics	100
May 12	Philadelphia 76ers	99	at	Washington Bullets	101
May 14	Seattle SuperSonics	114	at	Denver Nuggets	123
May 17	Denver Nuggets	108	at	Seattle SuperSonics	123
May 21	Washington Bullets	102	at	Seattle SuperSonics	106
May 25	Seattle SuperSonics	98	at	Washington Bullets	106
May 28	Seattle SuperSonics	93	at	Washington Bullets	92
May 30	Washington Bullets	120	at	Seattle SuperSonics	116 [OT]
June 2	Washington Bullets	94	at	Seattle SuperSonics	98
June 4	Seattle SuperSonics	82	at	Washington Bullets	117
June 7	Washington Bullets	105	at	Seattle SuperSonics	99

All Star Teams

First Team	Second Team
Leonard Robinson (New Orleans Jazz)	Walter Davis (Phoenix Suns)
Julius Erving (Philadelphia 76ers)	Maurice Lucas (Portland Trail Blazers)
Bill Walton (Portland Trail Blazers)	Kareem Abdul-Jabbar (Los Angeles Lakers)
George Gervin (San Antonio Spurs)	Paul Westphal (Phoenix Suns)
David Thompson (Denver Nuggets)	Pete Maravich (New Orleans Jazz)

Individual Awards

Eddie Gottlieb Trophy--Walter Davis (Phoenix Suns)
Executive of the Year--Bob Ferry (Washington Bullets)
J. Walter Kennedy Award--Bob Lanier (Detroit Pistons)
Maurice Podoloff Trophy--Bill Walton (Portland Trail Blazers)
NBA All Star Game MVP--Randy Smith (Buffalo Braves)
NBA Finals MVP--Wes Unseld (Washington Bullets)
Red Auerbach Trophy--Hubie Brown (Atlanta Hawks)

Hall of Fame Inductees

Sam Barry, Wilt Chamberlain, James Enright, Edgar Hickey, Raymond Meyer, John McLendon, Peter Newell

FOOTBALL

National Football League
National Football Conference
Eastern Division

Team Name	GP	W	L	T	PF	PA	Pct
Dallas Cowboys	16	12	4	0	384	208	.750
Philadelphia Eagles	16	9	7	0	270	250	.563
Washington Redskins	16	8	8	0	273	283	.500
St. Louis Cardinals	16	6	10	0	248	296	.375
New York Giants	16	6	10	0	264	298	.375

Central Division

Team Name	GP	W	L	T	PF	PA	Pct
Minnesota Vikings	16	8	7	1	294	306	.531
Green Bay Packers	16	8	7	1	249	269	.531
Detroit Lions	16	7	9	0	290	300	.438
Chicago Bears	16	7	9	0	253	274	.438
Tampa Bay Buccaneers	16	5	11	0	241	259	.313

Western Division

Team Name	GP	W	L	T	PF	PA	Pct
Los Angeles Rams	16	12	4	0	316	245	.750
Atlanta Falcons	16	9	7	0	240	290	.563
New Orleans Saints	16	7	9	0	281	298	.438
San Francisco 49ers	16	2	14	0	219	350	.125

American Football Conference

Eastern Division

Team Name	GP	W	L	T	PF	PA	Pct
New England Patriots	16	11	5	0	358	286	.688
Miami Dolphins	16	11	5	0	372	254	.688
New York Jets	16	8	8	0	359	364	.500
Buffalo Bills	16	5	11	0	302	354	.313
Baltimore Colts	16	5	11	0	239	421	.313

Central Division

Team Name	GP	W	L	T	PF	PA	Pct
Pittsburgh Steelers	16	14	2	0	356	195	.875
Houston Oilers	16	10	6	0	283	298	.625
Cleveland Browns	16	8	8	0	334	356	.500
Cincinnati Bengals	16	4	12	0	252	284	.250

Western Division

Team Name	GP	W	L	T	PF	PA	Pct
Denver Broncos	16	10	6	0	282	198	.625
Oakland Raiders	16	9	7	0	311	283	.563
San Diego Chargers	16	9	7	0	355	309	.563
Seattle Seahawks	16	9	7	0	345	358	.563
Kansas City Chiefs	16	4	12	0	243	327	.250

Coaching Changes

Washington--Jack Pardee 8-8-0; St. Louis--Bud Wilkinson 6-10-0; Detroit--Monte Clark 7-0-0; Chicago--Neill Armstrong 7-9-0; Los Angeles--Ray Malavasi 12-4-0; New Orleans--Dick Nolan 7-9-0; San Francisco--Pete McCulley 1-8-0, Fred O'Connor 1-6-0; New England--Chuck Fairbanks 11-4-0, Ron Erhardt and Hank Bullough 0-1-0; Buffalo--Chuck Knox 5-11-0; Cleveland--Sam Rutigliano 8-8-0; Cincinnati--Bill Johnson 0-5-0, Homer Rice 4-7-0; San Diego--Tom Prothro 1-3-0, Don Coryell 8-4-0; Kansas City--Marv Levy 4-12-0.

League Leaders

Yards Rushing		**Yards Passing**		**Passing %** (300 attempts)	
Earl Campbell	1450	Fran Tarkenton	3468	Bob Griese	63.0
Walter Payton	1395	Archie Manning	3416	Archie Manning	61.8
Tony Dorsett	1325	Jim Zorn	3283	Fran Tarkenton	60.3
Delvin Williams	1258	Roger Staubach	3190	Dan Fouts	58.8
Wilbert Montgomery	1220	Jim Hart	3121	Ken Stabler	58.4

Receiving Yards		**Receptions**		**Field Goals**	
Wes Walker	1169	Rickey Young	88	Frank Corral	29
Steve Largent	1168	Tony Galbreath	74	Pat Leahy	22
Harold Carmichael	1072	Steve Largent	71	Joe Danelo	21
John Jefferson	1001	Ahmad Rashad	66	Benny Ricardo	20
Pat Tilley	900	Pat Tilley	62	Jan Stenerud	20

Punt Return Yards		**Kickoff Return Yards**	
Jack Wallace	618	Larry Anderson	930
Rick Upchurch	493	Tony Green	870
Tony Green	443	Rufus Crawford	829
Mike Fuller	436	Keith Wright	789
Butch Johnson	401	John Dirden	780

Pro Bowl Game

(Memorial Coliseum, Los Angeles)

January 29 1979	National Conference	13	American Conference	7

NFL Playoffs

December 24	Philadelphia Eagles	13	at	Atlanta Falcons	14
December 24	Houston Oilers	17	at	Miami Dolphins	9
December 30	Atlanta Falcons	20	at	Dallas Cowboys	27
December 30	Denver Broncos	10	at	Pittsburgh Steelers	33
December 31	Minnesota Vikings	10	at	Los Angeles Rams	34
December 31	Houston Oilers	31	at	New England Patriots	14
January 7 1979	Dallas Cowboys	28	at	Los Angeles Rams	0
January 7 1979	Houston Oilers	5	at	Pittsburgh Steelers	34

Super Bowl XIII

(Orange Bowl, Miami)

January 21 1979	Pittsburgh Steelers	35	Dallas Cowboys	31

Individual Awards

AP MVP--Terry Bradshaw (Pittsburgh Steelers)
Bert Bell Trophy--Earl Campbell (Houston Oilers) [World Almanac]
Bert Bell Trophy--Terry Bradshaw (Pittsburgh Steelers)
George Halas Trophy--Randy Gradishaw (Denver Broncos)
Jim Thorpe Trophy--Earl Campbell (Houston Oilers)
P.F.W.A. MVP--Earl Campbell (Houston Oilers)
Pro Bowl MVP--Ahmad Rashad (Minnesota Vikings)
Super Bowl MVP--Terry Bradshaw (Pittsburgh Steelers)
U.P.I. AFC Coach of the Year--Walt Michaels(New York Jets)
U.P.I. AFC Player of the Year--Earl Campbell (Houston Oilers)
U.P.I. AFC Rookie of the Year--Earl Campbell (Houston Oilers)
U.P.I. NFC Coach of the Year--Dick Vermeil (Philadelphia Eagles)
U.P.I. NFC Player of the Year--Archie Manning (New Orleans Saints)
U.P.I. NFC Rookie of the Year--Bubba Baker (Detroit Lions)

Hall of Fame Inductees

Lance Alworth, Weeb Ewbank, Tuffy Leemans, Ray Nitschke, Larry Wilson

Rules

A defender is permitted to maintain contact with a receiver within five yards of the line of scrimmage but is restricted in contact beyond that point.

Notes

The NFL added a seventh official to its officiating crew.

Canadian Football League
Eastern Conference

Team Name	GP	W	L	T	PF	PA	Pts	Pct
Ottawa Rough Riders	16	11	5	0	395	261	22	.688
Montreal Alouettes	16	8	7	1	331	295	17	.531
Hamilton Tiger-Cats	16	5	10	1	225	403	11	.344
Toronto Argonauts	16	4	12	0	234	389	8	.250

Western Conference

Team Name	GP	W	L	T	PF	PA	Pts	Pct
Edmonton Eskimos	16	10	4	2	452	301	22	.688
Calgary Stampeders	16	9	7	3	381	311	21	.656
Winnipeg Blue Bombers	16	9	7	0	371	351	18	.563
British Columbia Lions	16	7	7	2	359	308	16	.500
Saskatchewan Roughriders	16	4	11	1	330	459	9	.281

Coaching Changes

Montreal--Joe Scanella 8-7-1; Hamilton--Tom Dimitroff 1-3-1, John Payne 4-7-0; Toronto--Leo Cahill 3-6-0, Bud Riley 1-6-0; Winnipeg--Ray Jauch 9-7-0; Saskatchewan--Jim Eddy 0-6-0, Walt Posadowski 4-5-1.

League Leaders

Yards Rushing		Yards Passing		Passing % (200 attempts)	
Mike Strickland	1306	Dieter Brock	3755	Tom Clements	63.6
Larry Key	1054	Jerry Tagge	3134	Conredge Holloway	61.7
Jim Washington	1032	Ron Lancaster	2677	Tom Wilkinson	60.6
Jim Sykes	1020	Tom Wilkinson	2394	Dieter Brock	59.8
Jim Germany	885	Jim Jones	2060	Jim Jones	58.7

Receiving Yards		Receptions		Points	
Tom Scott	1091	Joe Poplawski	75	Dave Cutler	167
Tony Gabriel	1070	Gord Paterson	69	Cyril McFall	163
Joe Poplawski	998	Tony Gabriel	67	Lui Passaglia	159
Waddel Smith	900	Tom Scott	66	Bernie Ruoff	149
Gord Paterson	866	Waddel Smith	59	J. T. Hay	136

All Star Game
(McMahon Stadium, Calgary)

June 3	Western Conference	24		Eastern Conference	12

Grey Cup Playoffs

November 11	Hamilton Tiger-Cats	20	at	Montreal Alouettes	35
November 12	Winnipeg Blue Bombers	4	at	Calgary Stampeders	38
November 18	Calgary Stampeders	13	at	Edmonton Eskimos	26
November 19	Montreal Alouettes	21	at	Ottawa Rough Riders	16
November 26	Edmonton Eskimos	20		Montreal Alouettes	13*

Individual Awards

Annis Stukus Trophy--Jack Gotta (Calgary Stampeders)
CFL All Star Game MVP--Brock Aynsley (Montreal Alouettes)
Tom Scott (Edmonton Eskimos)
Ray Odums (Calgary Stampeders)
Granville Liggins (Toronto Argonauts)
Dave Dryburgh Memorial Trophy--Dave Cutler (Edmonton Eskimos)
DeMarco-Becket Memorial Trophy--Al Wilson (British Columbia Lions)
Dr. Beattie Martin Trophy--Joe Poplawski (Winnipeg Blue Bombers)
Eddie James Memorial Trophy--Mike Strickland (Saskatchewan Roughriders)
Frank M. Gibson Trophy--Ben Zambiasi (Hamilton Tiger-Cats)
Grey Cup Most Outstanding Defensive Star--Dave Fennell (Edmonton Eskimos)
Grey Cup Most Outstanding Offensive Star--Tom Wilkinson (Edmonton Eskimos)
Grey Cup Most Valuable Canadian--Angelo Santucci (Edmonton Eskimos)
Jackie Parker Trophy--Joe Poplawski (Winnipeg Blue Bombers)
James P. McCaffrey Trophy--Randy Rhino (Montreal Alouettes)
Jeff Nicklin Memorial Trophy--Tom Wilkinson (Edmonton Eskimos)
Jeff Russel Memorial Trophy--Tony Gabriel (Ottawa Rough Riders)
Leo Dandurand Trophy--Jim Coode (Ottawa Rough Riders)
Lew Hayman Trophy--Tony Gabriel (Ottawa Rough Riders)
Norm Fieldgate Trophy--Dave Fennell (Edmonton Eskimos)
Schenley Award Most Outstanding Canadian--Tony Gabriel (Ottawa Rough Riders)
Schenley Award Most Outstanding Defensive Player--Dave Fennell (Edmonton Eskimos)

*Game played in Toronto

Schenley Award Most Outstanding Offensive Lineman--Jim Coode (Ottawa Rough Riders)
Schenley Award Most Outstanding Player--Tony Gabriel (Ottawa Rough Riders)
Schenley Award Most Outstanding Rookie--Joe Poplawski (Winnipeg Blue Bombers)

Hall of Fame Inductees

Ron Atchison, Paul Dojack, Harry McBrien, Kay Vaughan

HOCKEY
National Hockey League

Clarence Campbell Conference
Patrick Division

Team Name	GP	W	L	T	GF	GA	Pts	Pct
New York Islanders	80	48	17	15	334	270	111	.694
Philadelphia Flyers	80	45	20	15	296	200	105	.656
Atlanta Flames	80	34	27	19	274	252	87	.544
New York Rangers	80	30	37	13	279	280	73	.456

Smythe Division

Team Name	GP	W	L	T	GF	GA	Pts	Pct
Chicago Black Hawks	80	32	29	19	230	220	83	.519
Colorado Rockies	80	19	40	21	257	305	59	.369
Vancouver Canucks	80	20	43	17	239	320	57	.356
St. Louis Blues	80	20	47	13	195	304	53	.331
Minnesota North Stars	80	18	53	9	218	325	45	.281

Prince of Wales Conference

Norris Division

Team Name	GP	W	L	T	GF	GA	Pts	Pct
Montreal Canadiens	80	59	10	11	359	183	129	.806
Detroit Red Wings	80	32	34	14	252	266	78	.488
Los Angeles Kings	80	31	34	15	243	245	77	.481
Pittsburgh Penguins	80	25	37	18	254	321	68	.425
Washington Capitals	80	17	49	14	195	321	48	.300

Adams Division

Team Name	GP	W	L	T	GF	GA	Pts	Pct
Boston Bruins	80	51	18	11	333	218	113	.706
Buffalo Sabres	80	44	19	17	288	215	105	.656
Toronto Maple Leafs	80	41	29	10	271	237	92	.575
Cleveland Barons	80	22	45	13	230	325	57	.356

Coaching Changes

Rangers--Jean Guy Talbot 30-37-13; Chicago--Bob Pulford 32-29-19; Colorado--Pat Kelly 19-40-21; Vancouver--Orland Kurtenbach 20-43-17; St. Louis--Leo Boivin 11-36-7, Barclay Plager 9-11-6; Minnesota--Ted Harris 5-12-2, Andre Beaulieu 6-23-3, Lou Nanne 7-18-4; Detroit--Bobby Kromm 32-34-14; Los Angeles--Ron Stewart 31-34-15; Pittsburgh--John Wilson 25-37-18; Buffalo--Marcel Pronovost 44-19-17; Toronto--Roger Neilson 41-29-10.

League Leaders

Goals		Assists		Points	
Guy Lafleur	60	Bryan Trottier	77	Guy Lafleur	132
Mike Bossy	53	Guy Lafleur	72	Bryan Trottier	123
Steve Shutt	49	Darryl Sittler	72	Darryl Sittler	117
Lanny McDonald	47	Bobby Clarke	68	Jacques Lemaire	97
Bryan Trottier	46	Denis Potvin	64	Denis Potvin	94

Penalty Minutes		Plus/Minus (1,600 minutes)		GAA	
Dave Schultz	405	Guy Lafleur	73	Ken Dryden	2.05
Dave Williams	351	Larry Robinson	71	Bernie Parent	2.22
Dennis Polonich	254	Rick Smith	70	Glenn Resch	2.55
Randy Holt	249	Brad Park	68	Tony Esposito	2.63
Andre Dupont	225	Serge Savard	62	Don Edwards	2.64

Wins		Shutouts	
Don Edwards	38	Bernie Parent	7
Ken Dryden	37	Tony Esposito	5
Mike Palmateer	34	Don Edwards	5
Bernie Parent	29	Ken Dryden	5
Rogie Vachon	29	Mike Palmateer	5

All Star Game

(Memorial Auditorium, Buffalo)

January 24	Wales Conference	3	Campbell Conference	2

Stanley Cup Playoffs

April 11	Colorado Rockies	2	at	Philadelphia Flyers	3 [0:23]
April 11	Detroit Red Wings	5	at	Atlanta Flames	3
April 11	Los Angeles Kings	3	at	Toronto Maple Leafs	7
April 11	New York Rangers	1	at	Buffalo Sabres	4
April 13	Philadelphia Flyers	3	at	Colorado Rockies	1
April 13	Atlanta Flames	2	at	Detroit Red Wings	3
April 13	Toronto Maple Leafs	4	at	Los Angeles Kings	0
April 13	Buffalo Sabres	3	at	New York Rangers	4 [1:37]
April 15	New York Rangers	1	at	Buffalo Sabres	4
April 17	Chicago Black Hawks	1	at	Boston Bruins	6
April 17	Buffalo Sabres	1	at	Philadelphia Flyers	4
April 17	Detroit Red Wings	2	at	Montreal Canadiens	6
April 17	Toronto Maple Leafs	1	at	New York Islanders	4
April 19	Chicago Black Hawks	3	at	Boston Bruins	4 [1:50]
April 19	Buffalo Sabres	2	at	Philadelphia Flyers	3
April 19	Detroit Red Wings	4	at	Montreal Canadiens	2
April 19	Toronto Maple Leafs	2	at	New York Islanders	3 [2:50]
April 21	Boston Bruins	4	at	Chicago Black Hawks	3 [10:17]
April 21	Montreal Canadiens	4	at	Detroit Red Wings	2
April 21	New York Islanders	0	at	Toronto Maple Leafs	2
April 22	Philadelphia Flyers	1	at	Buffalo Sabres	4
April 23	Boston Bruins	5	at	Chicago Black Hawks	2
April 23	Philadelphia Flyers	4	at	Buffalo Sabres	2

April 23	Montreal Canadiens	8	at	Detroit Red Wings	0
April 23	New York Islanders	1	at	Toronto Maple Leafs	3
April 25	Buffalo Sabres	2	at	Philadelphia Flyers	4
April 25	Toronto Maple Leafs	1	at	New York Islanders	2 [8:02]
April 25	Montreal Canadiens	4	at	Detroit Red Wings	2
April 27	New York Islanders	2	at	Toronto Maple Leafs	5
April 29	Toronto Maple Leafs	2	at	New York Islanders	1 [4:13]
May 2	Toronto Maple Leafs	3	at	Montreal Canadiens	5
May 2	Philadelphia Flyers	2	at	Boston Bruins	3 [1:43]
May 4	Toronto Maple Leafs	2	at	Montreal Canadiens	3
May 4	Philadelphia Flyers	5	at	Boston Bruins	7
May 6	Montreal Canadiens	6	at	Toronto Maple Leafs	1
May 7	Boston Bruins	1	at	Philadelphia Flyers	3
May 9	Montreal Canadiens	2	at	Toronto Maple Leafs	0
May 9	Boston Bruins	4	at	Philadelphia Flyers	2
May 11	Philadelphia Flyers	3	at	Boston Bruins	6
May 13	Boston Bruins	1	at	Montreal Canadiens	4
May 16	Boston Bruins	2	at	Montreal Canadiens	3 [13:09]
May 18	Montreal Canadiens	0	at	Boston Bruins	4
May 21	Montreal Canadiens	3	at	Boston Bruins	4[6:22]
May 23	Boston Bruins	1	at	Montreal Canadiens	4
May 25	Montreal Canadiens	4	at	Boston Bruins	1

All Star Teams

First Team		Second Team
Ken Dryden	Goal	Don Edwards
Denis Potvin	Defense	Larry Robinson
Brad Park	Defense	Borje Salming
Bryan Trottier	Center	Darryl Sittler
Guy Lafleur	Right Wing	Mike Bossy
Clark Gillies	Left Wing	Steve Shutt

Individual Awards

Art Ross Trophy--Guy Lafleur (Montreal Canadiens)
Bill Masterton Trophy--Robert Goring (Los Angeles Kings)
Calder Memorial Trophy--Mike Bossy (New York Islanders)
Conn Smythe Trophy--Larry Robinson (Montreal Canadiens)
Frank J. Selke Trophy--Bob Gainey (Montreal Canadiens)
Hart Memorial Trophy--Guy Lafleur (Montreal Canadiens)
Jack Adams Award--Bobby Kromm (Detroit Red Wings)
James Norris Trophy--Denis Potvin (New York Islanders)
Lady Byng Memorial Trophy--Robert Goring (Los Angeles Kings)
Lester B. Pearson Award--Guy Lafleur (Montreal Canadiens)
Lester Patrick Trophy--Phil Esposito, Tom Fitzgerald, William Tutt, Bill Wirtz.
NHL All Star Game MVP--Billy Smith (New York Islanders)
Vezina Trophy--Ken Dryden and Michel Larocque (Montreal Canadiens)

Hall of Fame Inductees

Andy Bathgate, John Bickell, Jacques Plante, Sam Pollock, Marcel Pronovost, William Thayer Tutt

Rules

Teams requesting a stick measurement to be assessed a minor penalty in the event the measured stick does not violate the rules.

Notes

The National Hockey League set the age of players available for the amateur draft at 19.

World Hockey Association

Team Name	GP	W	L	T	GF	GA	Pts	Pct
Winnipeg Jets	80	50	28	2	381	270	102	.638
New England Whalers	80	44	31	5	335	269	93	.581
Houston Aeros	80	42	34	4	296	302	88	.550
Quebec Nordiques	80	40	37	3	349	347	83	.519
Edmonton Oilers	80	38	39	3	309	307	79	.494
Birmingham Bulls	80	36	41	3	287	314	75	.469
Cincinnati Stingers	80	35	42	3	298	332	73	.456
Indianapolis Racers	80	24	51	5	267	353	53	.331
Soviet "B" Team	8	3	4	1	27	36	7	.438
Czechoslovakia	8	1	6	1	21	40	3	.188

Coaching Changes

Winnipeg--Larry Hillman 50-28-2; Quebec--Marc Boileau 27-30-2, Maurice Filion 13-7-1; Edmonton--Glen Sather 38-39-3; Birmingham--Glen Sonmor 36-41-3; Cincinnati--Jacques Demers 35-42-3; Indianapolis--Ron Ingram 16-31-4, Bill Goldsworthy 8-20-1; Czechoslovakia--Stanislav Nevesely 1-6-1; Soviets.

League Leaders

Goals

Marc Tardif	65
Anders Hedberg	63
Robbie Ftorek	59
Real Cloutier	56
Bobby Hull	46

Assists

Marc Tardif	89
Ulf Nilsson	89
Andre Lacroix	77
Real Cloutier	73
Bobby Hull	71

Points

Marc Tardif	154
Real Cloutier	129
Ulf Nilsson	126
Anders Hedberg	122
Bobby Hull	117

Penalty Minutes

Steve Durbano	284
Frank Beaton	279
Gilles Bilodeau	258
Dave Hanson	241
Paul Stewart	241

GAA
(1,560 minutes)

Al Smith	3.22
Gary Bromley	3.30
Joe Daley	3.30
Louis Levasseur	3.30
Ernie Wakely	3.41

Wins

Al Smith	30
Ernie Wakely	28
Gary Bromley	25
John Garrett	24
Joe Daley	21

Shutouts

Michel Dion	4
Louis Levasseur	3
John Garrett	2
Don McLeod	2
Dave Dryden	2

All Star Game

(Colisee de Quebec, Quebec City)

January 17	Quebec Nordiques	5	All Stars	4

WHA Playoffs

April 14	Edmonton Oilers	4	at	New England Whalers	6
April 14	Birmingham Bulls	3	at	Winnipeg Jets	9
April 16	Quebec Nordiques	3	at	Houston Aeros	4 [7:19]
April 16	Edmonton Oilers	1	at	New England Whalers	4
April 16	Birmingham Bulls	3	at	Winnipeg Jets	8
April 18	Quebec Nordiques	5	at	Houston Aeros	4 [2:59]
April 19	New England Whalers	0	at	Edmonton Oilers	2
April 19	Winnipeg Jets	2	at	Birmingham Bulls	3
April 20	Houston Aeros	1	at	Quebec Nordiques	5
April 21	New England Whalers	9	at	Edmonton Oilers	1
April 21	Houston Aeros	0	at	Quebec Nordiques	3
April 21	Winnipeg Jets	5	at	Birmingham Bulls	1
April 23	Edmonton Oilers	1	at	New England Whalers	4
April 23	Quebec Nordiques	2	at	Houston Aeros	5
April 23	Birmingham Bulls	2	at	Winnipeg Jets	5
April 26	Houston Aeros	2	at	Quebec Nordiques	11
April 28	Quebec Nordiques	1	at	New England Whalers	5
April 30	Quebec Nordiques	3	at	New England Whalers	2
May 3	New England Whalers	5	at	Quebec Nordiques	4
May 5	New England Whalers	7	at	Quebec Nordiques	3
May 7	Quebec Nordiques	3	at	New England Whalers	6
May 12	Winnipeg Jets	4	at	New England Whalers	1
May 14	Winnipeg Jets	5	at	New England Whalers	2
May 19	New England Whalers	2	at	Winnipeg Jets	10
May 22	New England Whalers	3	at	Winnipeg Jets	5

All Star Teams

First Team		Second Team
Al Smith	Goal	Ernie Wakely
Lark-Erik Sjoberg	Defense	Rick Ley
Al Hamilton	Defense	Barry Long
Ulf Nilsson	Center	Robbie Ftorek
Anders Hedberg	Right Wing	Real Cloutier
Marc Tardif	Left Wing	Bobby Hull

Individual Awards

Ben Hatskin Trophy--Al Smith and Louis Levasseur (New England Whalers)
Bill Hunter Trophy--Marc Tardif (Quebec Nordiques)
Dennis Murphy Trophy--Lars-Erik Sjoberg (Winnipeg Jets)
Gordie Howe Trophy--Marc Tardif (Quebec Nordiques)
Lou Kaplan Trophy--Kent Nilsson (Winnipeg Jets)
Paul Deneau Trophy--Dave Keon (New England Whalers)
Robert Schmertz Trophy--Bill Dineen (Houston Aeros)
WHA All Star Game MVP--Marc Tardif (Quebec Nordiques)
Mark Howe (New England Whalers)
WHA MVP in Playoffs--Bobby Guindon (Winnipeg Jets)

Notes

The WHA moved its league offices to Hartford, Connecticut with Ben Hatskin as chairman of the board.
The teams of the WHA played games against touring Soviet and Czechoslovakian teams which counted in the league standings, a concept unique in North American sports.

SOCCER
North American Soccer League
National Conference
Eastern Division

Team Name	GP	W	L	GF	GA	BP	Pts	Pct
Cosmos	30	24	6	88	39	68	212	.785
Washington Diplomats	30	16	14	55	47	49	145	.537
Toronto Metro-Croatia	30	16	14	58	47	48	144	.533
Rochester Lancers	30	14	16	47	52	47	131	.485

Central Division

Team Name	GP	W	L	GF	GA	BP	Pts	Pct
Minnesota Kicks	30	17	13	58	43	54	156	.578
Tulsa Roughnecks	30	15	15	49	46	42	132	.489
Dallas Tornado	30	14	16	51	53	47	131	.485
Colorado Caribous	30	8	22	34	66	33	81	.300

Western Division

Team Name	GP	W	L	GF	GA	BP	Pts	Pct
Vancouver Whitecaps	30	24	6	68	29	55	199	.737
Portland Timbers	30	20	10	50	36	47	167	.610
Seattle Sounders	30	15	15	50	45	48	138	.511
Los Angeles Aztecs	30	9	21	36	69	34	88	.326

American Conference

Eastern Division

Team Name	GP	W	L	GF	GA	BP	Pts	Pct
New England Tea Men	30	19	11	62	39	51	165	.611
Tampa Bay Rowdies	30	18	12	63	48	57	165	.611
Fort Lauderdale Strikers	30	16	14	50	59	47	143	.530
Philadelphia Fury	30	12	18	40	58	39	111	.411

Central Division

Team Name	GP	W	L	GF	GA	BP	Pts	Pct
Detroit Express	30	20	10	68	36	56	176	.652
Chicago Sting	30	12	18	57	64	51	123	.456
Memphis Rogues	30	10	20	43	58	41	101	.374
Houston Hurricane	30	10	20	37	61	36	96	.356

Western Division

Team Name	GP	W	L	GF	GA	BP	Pts	Pct
San Diego Sockers	30	18	12	63	56	56	164	.607
California Surf	30	13	17	43	49	37	115	.426
Oakland Stompers	30	12	18	34	59	31	103	.381
San Jose Earthquakes	30	8	22	36	81	35	83	.307

Coaching Changes

Cosmos--Eddie Firmani 24-6; Washington--Gordon Bradley 16-14; Toronto--Domagoj Kapetnovic 16-14; Tulsa--Bill Foulkes 8-9, Alex Skotarek 7-6; Colorado--Dave Clements 6-14, Dan Wood 2-8; Vancouver--Tony Waiters 24-6; Portland--Don Megson 20-10; Los Angeles--Terry Fisher 5-8, Tommy Smith 3-13, Peter Short 1-0; New England--Noel Cantwell 19-11; Tampa Bay--Gordon Jago.

18-12; Philadelphia--Richard Dinnis 6-10, Alan Ball 6-8; Detroit--Ken Furphy 20-10; Chicago--Malcolm Musgrove 2-14, Willy Roy 10-4; Memphis--Eddie McCreadie 10-20; Houston--Timo Liekoski 10-20; San Diego--Hubert Vogelsinger 18-12; Oakland--Mirko Stojanovic 4-4, Ken Bracewell 7-13, Shep Messing and Dick Berg and Charlie Mrosko 1-1; San Jose--Gabbo Gavric 5-11, Terry Fisher 3-11

League Leaders

Goals		**Points**		**Shutouts**	
Giorgio Chinaglia	34	Giorgio Chinaglia	79	Phil Parkes	10
Mike Flanagan	30	Mike Flanagan	68	Colin Boulton	10
Trevor Francis	22	Trevor Francis	54	Mick Poole	9
Kevin Hector	21	Kevin Hector	52	Steve Hardwick	9
Jeff Bourne	21	Rodney Marsh	52	Tony Chursky	9

GAA
(1,350 minutes)

Phil Parkes	0.95
Erol Yasin	1.13
Mick Poole	1.16
Steve Hardwick	1.19
Kevin Keelan	1.24

NASL Playoffs

August 8	California Surf	1	at	San Diego Sockers	2
August 8	Chicago Sting	1	at	Tampa Bay Rowdies	3
August 8	Philadelphia Fury	0	at	Detroit Express	1
August 9	Fort Lauderdale Strikers	3	at	New England Tea Men	1
August 9	Toronto Metro-Croatia	0	at	Vancouver Whitecaps	4
August 9	Seattle Sounders	2	at	Cosmos	5
August 9	Washington Diplomats	1	at	Portland Timbers	2 [SO]
August 10	Tulsa Roughnecks	1	at	Minnesota Kicks	3
August 12	Vancouver Whitecaps	0	at	Portland Timbers	1
August 13	Detroit Express	3	at	Fort Lauderdale Strikers	4
August 14	Tampa Bay Rowdies	1	at	San Diego Sockers	0
August 14	Cosmos	2	at	Minnesota Kicks	9
August 16	Portland Timbers	2	at	Vancouver Whitecaps	1
August 16	Fort Lauderdale Strikers	0	at	Detroit Express	1
	Fort Lauderdale Strikers	1	at	Detroit Express	0 [SO]
August 16	San Diego Sockers	2	at	Tampa Bay Rowdies	1
	San Diego Sockers	0	at	Tampa Bay Rowdies	1 [SO]
August 16	Minnesota Kicks	0	at	Cosmos	4
	Minnesota Kicks	0	at	Cosmos	1 [SO]
August 18	Cosmos	1	at	Portland Timbers	0
August 20	Tampa Bay Rowdies	2	at	Fort Lauderdale Strikers	3
August 23	Portland Timbers	0	at	Cosmos	5
August 23	Fort Lauderdale	1	at	Tampa Bay Rowdies	3
	Fort Lauderdale	0	at	Tampa Bay Rowdies	1 [SO]
August 27	Tampa Bay Rowdies	1	at	Cosmos	3

All Star Teams

First Team		Second Team
Kevin Keelan	Goal	Alan Mayer
Carlos Alberto	Defender	Bruce Wilson
Mike England	Defender	Asene Auguste
Ray Evans	Defender	John Craven
Chris Turner	Defender	Alan Merrick
Franz Beckenbauer	Midfield	Vladislav Bogicevic
Gerry Daly	Midfield	Alan Ball
Rodney Marsh	Midfield	Ray Hudson
Mike Flanagan	Forward	Steve Hunt
Trevor Francis	Forward	Steve Wegerle
Giorgio Chinaglia	Forward	Kevin Hector

Individual Awards

Coach of the Year--Tony Waiters (Vancouver Whitecaps)
Lead Goalkeeper Award--Phil Parkes (Vancouver Whitecaps)
Most Valuable Player--Mike Flanagan (New England Tea Men)
NASL MVP in Playoffs --Dennis Tueart (New York Cosmos)
Rookie of the Year--Gary Etherington (New York Cosmos)
Top North American Player--Bob Lenarduzzi (Vancouver Whitecaps)
Top Offensive Player--Mike Flanagan (New England Tea-Men)
Top Defensive Player--Carlos Alberto (New York Cosmos)

Franchise Changes

NBA--New York Nets became the new Jersey Nets.
NASL--Team Hawaii became the Tulsa Roughnecks.
Las Vegas Quicksilvers became the San Diego Sockers.
St. Louis Stars became the California Surf.
Connecticut Bicentennials became the Oakland Stompers.

Other Sports

Horseracing--Kentucky Derby won by Affirmed (time 2:01.2, purse $186,900).
Heavyweight Boxing--Leon Spinks defeated Muhammad Ali in 15 rounds.
Muhammad Ali defeated Leon Spinks in 15 rounds (retired).
Larry Holmes defeated Ken Norton in 15 rounds (WBC).
Golf--U.S. Open won by Andy North with a score of 285.
Auto Racing--Indianapolis 500 won by Al Unser (ave. speed 161.363 MPH).
Tennis--U.S. Open won by Jimmy Connors in the men's singles.
U.S. Open won by Stan Smith and Bob Lutz in the men's doubles.
U.S. Open won by Chris Evert in the women's singles.
U.S. Open won by Martina Navratilova and Billie Jean King in the women's doubles.
U.S. Open won by Betty Stove and Frew McMillan in the mixed doubles.

Notes

Chris Evert won the U.S. Open for the fourth year in a row.
Affirmed became the second horse in a row to win Horseracing's Triple Crown after Seattle Slew won it the previous year.
Muhammad Ali regained the World Heavyweight Championship for the third time when he defeated Leon Spinks.

1979

BASEBALL
National League
East

Team Name	W	L	Pct	GB	R	OR
Pittsburgh Pirates	98	64	.605	-	775	643
Montreal Expos	95	65	.594	2	701	581
St. Louis Cardinals	86	76	.531	12	731	693
Philadelphia Phillies	84	78	.519	14	683	718
Chicago Cubs	80	82	.494	18	706	707
New York Mets	63	99	.389	35	593	706

West

Team Name	W	L	Pct	GB	R	OR
Cincinnati Reds	90	71	.559	-	731	644
Houston Astros	89	73	.549	1.5	583	582
Los Angeles Dodgers	79	83	.488	11.5	739	717
San Francisco Giants	71	91	.438	19.5	672	751
San Diego Padres	68	93	.422	22	603	681
Atlanta Braves	66	94	.413	23.5	669	763

Coaching Changes

St. Louis--Ken Boyer 86-76; Philadelphia--Danny Ozark 65-67, Dallas Green 19-11; Chicago--Herman Franks 78-77, Joey Amalfitano 2-5; Cincinnati--John McNamara 90-71; San Francisco--Joe Altobelli 81-79, Dave Bristol 10-12.

League Leaders

Batting Average
(440 at bats)

Keith Hernandez	.344
Pete Rose	.331
Ray Knight	.318
Steve Garvey	.315
Bob Horner	.314

Home Runs

Dave Kingman	48
Mike Schmidt	45
Dave Winfield	34
Bob Horner	33
Willie Stargell	32

RBI

Dave Winfield	118
Dave Kingman	115
Mike Schmidt	114
Steve Garvey	110
Keith Hernandez	105

Stolen Bases

Omar Moreno	77
Bill North	58
Dave Lopes	44
Frank Taveras	44
Rodney Scott	39

ERA
(162 innings)

J.R. Richard	2.71
Tom Hume	2.76
Dan Schatzeder	2.83
Burt Hooton	2.97
Joe Niekro	3.00

Wins

Joe Niekro	21
Phil Niekro	21
Rick Reuschel	18
J.R. Richard	18
Steve Carlton	18

Saves

Bruce Sutter	37
Kent Tekulve	31
Gene Garber	25
Joe Sambito	22
Gary Lavelle	20

Strikeouts

J.R. Richard	313
Steve Carlton	213
Phil Niekro	208
Bert Blyleven	172
Lynn McGlothen	147

NLCS

October 2	Pittsburgh Pirates	5	at	Cincinnati Reds	2 [11]
October 3	Pittsburgh Pirates	3	at	Cincinnati Reds	2 [10]
October 5	Cincinnati Reds	1	at	Pittsburgh Pirates	7

American League

East

Team Name	W	L	Pct	GB	R	OR
Baltimore Orioles	102	57	.642	-	757	582
Milwaukee Brewers	95	66	.590	8	807	722
Boston Red Sox	91	69	.569	11.5	841	711
New York Yankees	89	71	.556	13.5	734	672
Detroit Tigers	85	76	.528	18	770	738
Cleveland Indians	81	80	.503	22	760	805
Toronto Blue Jays	53	109	.327	50.5	613	862

West

Team Name	W	L	Pct	GB	R	OR
California Angels	88	74	.543	-	866	768
Kansas City Royals	85	77	.525	3	851	816
Texas Rangers	83	79	.512	5	750	698
Minnesota Twins	82	80	.506	6	764	725
Chicago White Sox	73	87	.456	14	730	748
Seattle Mariners	67	95	.414	21	711	820
Oakland Athletics	54	108	.333	34	573	860

Coaching Changes

New York--Bob Lemon 34-31, Billy Martin 55-40; Detroit--Les Moss 27-26, George "Sparky" Anderson 58-50; Cleveland--Jeff Torborg 43-52, Dave Garcia 38-28; California--Jim Fregosi 88-74; Texas--Pat Corrales 83-79; Chicago--Don Kessinger 46-60,Tony LaRussa 27-27; Oakland--Jim Marshall 54-108.

League Leaders

Batting Average (440 at bats)		Home Runs		RBI	
Fred Lynn	.333	Gorman Thomas	45	Don Baylor	139
George Brett	.329	Fred Lynn	39	Jim Rice	130
Brian Downing	.326	Jim Rice	39	Gorman Thomas	123
Jim Rice	.325	Ken Singleton	35	Fred Lynn	122
Al Oliver	.323	Bob Grich	30	Darrell Porter	112

Stolen Bases		ERA (162 innings)		Wins	
Willie Wilson	83	Ron Guidry	2.78	Mike Flanagan	23
Ron LeFlore	78	Tommy John	2.97	Tommy John	21
Julio Cruz	49	Dennis Eckersley	2.99	Jerry Koosman	20
Al Bumbry	37	Mike Flanagan	3.08	Ron Guidry	18
Elliot Wills	35	Jack Morris	3.27	Jack Morris	17

Saves		**Strikeouts**	
Mike Marshall	32	Nolan Ryan	223
Jim Kern	29	Ron Guidry	201
Aurelio Lopez	21	Mike Flanagan	190
Don Stanhouse	21	Ferguson Jenkins	164
Sid Monge	19	Jerry Koosman	157

All Star Game
(The Kingdome, Seattle)

July 17	National League	7		American League	6

ALCS

October 3	California Angels	3	at	Baltimore Orioles	6 [10]
October 4	California Angels	8	at	Baltimore Orioles	9
October 5	Baltimore Orioles	3	at	California Angels	4
October 6	Baltimore Orioles	8	at	California Angels	0

World Series

October 10	Pittsburgh Pirates	4	at	Baltimore Orioles	5
October 11	Pittsburgh Pirates	3	at	Baltimore Orioles	2
October 12	Baltimore Orioles	8	at	Pittsburgh Pirates	4
October 13	Baltimore Orioles	9	at	Pittsburgh Pirates	6
October 14	Baltimore Orioles	1	at	Pittsburgh Pirates	7
October 16	Pittsburgh Pirates	4	at	Baltimore Orioles	0
October 17	Pittsburgh Pirates	4	at	Baltimore Orioles	1

Individual Awards

Arch Ward Memorial Trophy--Dave Parker (Pittsburgh Pirates NL)
Baseball Writers Award--Keith Hernandez (St. Louis Cardinals NL)
Willie Stargell (Pittsburgh Pirates NL)
Don Baylor (California Angels AL)
Cy Young Award--Bruce Sutter (Chicago Cubs NL)
Mike Flanagan (Baltimore Orioles AL)
NLCS MVP--Willie Stargell (Pittsburgh Pirates NL)
Rookie of the Year--Rick Sutcliffe (Los Angeles Dodgers NL)
John Castino (Minnesota Twins AL)
Alfredo Griffin (Toronto Blue Jays AL)
Sporting News Executive of the Year--Hank Peters (Baltimore Orioles AL)
Sporting News Manager of the Year--Earl Weaver (Baltimore Orioles AL)
Sporting News Player of the Year--Keith Hernandez (St. Louis Cardinals NL)
Don Baylor (California Angels AL)
Sporting News Rookie of the Year--Jeff Leonard (Houston Astros NL)
Rick Sutcliffe (Los Angeles Dodgers NL)
Pat Putnam (Texas Rangers AL)
Mark Clear (California Angels AL)
World Series MVP--Willie Stargell (Pittsburgh Pirates NL)

Hall of Fame Inductees

Warren Giles, Willie Mays, Hack Wilson

Notes

New York Yankees catcher and captain Thurman Munson died when his private plane crashed on August 2, 1979.

BASKETBALL
National Basketball Association

Eastern Conference
Atlantic Division

Team Name	GP	W	L	PPGF	PPGA	Pct	GB
Washington Bullets	82	54	28	114.9	109.9	.659	-
Philadelphia 76ers	82	47	35	109.5	107.7	.573	7
New Jersey Nets	82	37	45	107.7	111.9	.451	17
New York Knickerbockers	82	31	51	107.7	111.1	.378	23
Boston Celtics	82	29	53	108.2	113.3	.354	25

Central Division

Team Name	GP	W	L	PPGF	PPGA	Pct	GB
San Antonio Spurs	82	48	34	119.3	114.1	.585	-
Houston Rockets	82	47	35	113.4	112.4	.573	1
Atlanta Hawks	82	46	36	109.1	107.1	.561	2
Cleveland Cavaliers	82	30	52	106.5	110.2	.366	18
Detroit Pistons	82	30	52	110.0	112.7	.366	18
New Orleans Jazz	82	26	56	108.3	114.6	.317	22

Western Conference

Midwest Division

Team Name	GP	W	L	PPGF	PPGA	Pct	GB
Kansas City Kings	82	48	34	113.1	110.2	.585	-
Denver Nuggets	82	47	35	110.7	109.5	.573	1
Indiana Pacers	82	38	44	108.6	110.2	.463	10
Milwaukee Bucks	82	38	44	114.1	111.8	.463	10
Chicago Bulls	82	31	51	104.7	108.7	.378	17

Pacific Division

Team Name	GP	W	L	PPGF	PPGA	Pct	GB
Seattle SuperSonics	82	52	30	106.6	103.9	.634	-
Phoenix Suns	82	50	32	115.4	111.7	.610	2
Los Angeles Lakers	82	47	35	112.9	109.9	.573	5
Portland Trail Blazers	82	45	37	108.4	107.1	.554	7
San Diego Clippers	82	43	39	113.1	114.9	.524	9
Golden State Warriors	82	38	44	105.1	104.8	.463	14

Coaching Changes

Philadelphia--Bill Cunningham 47-35; New York--Willis Reed 6-8, William Holzman 25-43; Boston--Tom Sanders 1-12, Dave Cowens 27-41; Detroit--Dick Vitale 30-52; Kansas City--Lowell "Cotton" Fitzsimmons 48-34; Denver--Larry Brown 28-25, Donnie Walsh 19-10; Chicago--Larry Costello 20-36, Scott Robertson 11-15; Seattle--Lenny Wilkens 52-30; San Diego--Gene Shue 43-39.

League Leaders

Field Goals		Free Throws		Assists	
George Gervin	947	Lloyd Free	654	Kevin Porter	1099
Marques Johnson	820	Moses Malone	599	Maurice Lucas	762
Paul Westphal	801	Cedric Maxwell	574	Norm Nixon	737
Lloyd Free	795	George McGinnis	509	Chris Ford	681
Kareem Abdul-Jabbar	777	John Drew	495	Paul Westphal	529

Points		Rebounds per Game	
George Gervin	2365	Moses Malone	17.6
Lloyd Free	2244	Rich Kelley	12.8
Moses Malone	2031	Kareem Abdul-Jabbar	12.8
Marques Johnson	1972	Artis Gilmore	12.7
Paul Westphal	1941	Jack Sikma	12.4

All Star Game

(Pontiac Silverdome, Pontiac, Michigan)

February 4	West Division	134		East Division	129

NBA Playoffs

April 10	Portland Trail Blazers	103	at	Phoenix Suns	107
April 10	Los Angeles Lakers	105	at	Denver Nuggets	110
April 11	New Jersey Nets	114	at	Philadelphia 76ers	122
April 11	Atlanta Hawks	109	at	Houston Rockets	106
April 13	Phoenix Suns	92	at	Portland Trail Blazers	96
April 13	Denver Nuggets	109	at	Los Angeles Lakers	121
April 13	Philadelphia 76ers	111	at	New Jersey Nets	101
April 13	Houston Rockets	91	at	Atlanta Hawks	100
April 15	Portland Trail Blazers	91	at	Phoenix Suns	101
April 15	Los Angeles Lakers	112	at	Denver Nuggets	111
April 15	Atlanta Hawks	89	at	Washington Bullets	103
April 15	Philadelphia 76ers	106	at	San Antonio Spurs	119
April 17	Los Angeles Lakers	101	at	Seattle SuperSonics	112
April 17	Kansas City Kings	99	at	Phoenix Suns	102
April 17	Atlanta Hawks	107	at	Washington Bullets	99
April 17	Philadelphia 76ers	120	at	San Antonio Spurs	121
April 18	Los Angeles Lakers	103	at	Seattle SuperSonics	108 [OT]
April 20	Washington Bullets	89	at	Atlanta Hawks	77
April 20	San Antonio Spurs	115	at	Philadelphia 76ers	123
April 20	Seattle SuperSonics	112	at	Los Angeles Lakers	118 [OT]
April 20	Phoenix Suns	91	at	Kansas City Kings	111
April 22	Washington Bullets	120	at	Atlanta Hawks	118 [OT]
April 22	San Antonio Spurs	115	at	Philadelphia 76ers	112
April 22	Seattle SuperSonics	117	at	Los Angeles Lakers	115
April 22	Kansas City Kings	93	at	Phoenix Suns	108
April 24	Atlanta Hawks	107	at	Washington Bullets	103
April 25	Los Angeles Lakers	100	at	Seattle SuperSonics	106
April 25	Phoenix Suns	108	at	Kansas City Kings	94
April 26	Philadelphia 76ers	120	at	San Antonio Spurs	97
April 26	Washington Bullets	86	at	Atlanta Hawks	104
April 27	Kansas City Kings	99	at	Phoenix Suns	120
April 29	Atlanta Hawks	94	at	Washington Bullets	100
April 29	San Antonio Spurs	90	at	Philadelphia 76ers	92
May 1	Phoenix Suns	93	at	Seattle SuperSonics	108
May 2	Philadelphia 76ers	108	at	San Antonio Spurs	111
May 4	San Antonio Spurs	118	at	Washington Bullets	97
May 4	Phoenix Suns	97	at	Seattle SuperSonics	103
May 6	San Antonio Spurs	95	at	Washington Bullets	115
May 6	Seattle SuperSonics	103	at	Phoenix Suns	113
May 8	Seattle SuperSonics	91	at	Phoenix Suns	100
May 9	Washington Bullets	114	at	San Antonio Spurs	116

May 11	Phoenix Suns	99	at	Seattle SuperSonics	93
May 11	Washington Bullets	102	at	San Antonio Spurs	118
May 13	Seattle SuperSonics	106	at	Phoenix Suns	105
May 13	San Antonio Spurs	103	at	Washington Bullets	107
May 16	Washington Bullets	108	at	San Antonio Spurs	100
May 17	Phoenix Suns	110	at	Seattle SuperSonics	114
May 18	San Antonio Spurs	105	at	Washington Bullets	107
May 20	Seattle SuperSonics	97	at	Washington Bullets	99
May 24	Seattle SuperSonics	92	at	Washington Bullets	82
May 27	Washington Bullets	95	at	Seattle SuperSonics	105
May 29	Washington Bullets	112	at	Seattle SuperSonics	114 [OT]
June 1	Seattle SuperSonics	97	at	Washington Bullets	93

All Star Teams

First Team	Second Team
Marques Johnson (Milwaukee Bucks)	Walter Davis (Phoenix Suns)
Elvin Hayes (Washington Bullets)	Bobby Dandridge (Washington Bullets)
Moses Malone (Houston Rockets)	Kareem Abdul-Jabbar (Los Angeles Lakers)
George Gervin (San Antonio Spurs)	Lloyd Free (San Diego Clippers)
Paul Westphal (Phoenix Suns)	Phil Ford (Kansas City Kings)

Individual Awards

Eddie Gottlieb Trophy--Phil Ford (Kansas City Kings)
Executive of the Year--Bob Ferry (Washington Bullets)
J. Walter Kennedy Citizenship Award--Calvin Murphy (Houston Rockets)
Maurice Podoloff Trophy--Moses Malone (Houston Rockets)
NBA All Star Game MVP--David Thompson (Denver Nuggets)
NBA Final MVP--Dennis Johnson(Seattle SuperSonics)
Red Auerbach Trophy--Lowell "Cotton" Fitzsimmons (Kansas City Kings)

Hall of Fame Inductees

Lester Harrison, Jerry Lucas, Oscar Robertson, Everett Shelton, Dallas Shirley, Jerry West

FOOTBALL
National Football League

National Conference
Eastern Division

Team Name	GP	W	L	T	PF	PA	Pct
Dallas Cowboys	16	11	5	0	371	313	.688
Philadelphia Eagles	16	11	5	0	339	282	.688
Washington Redskins	16	10	6	0	348	295	.625
New York Giants	16	6	10	0	237	323	.375
St. Louis Cardinals	16	5	11	0	307	358	.313

Central Division

Team Name	GP	W	L	T	PF	PA	Pct
Tampa Bay Buccaneers	16	10	6	0	273	237	.625
Chicago Bears	16	10	6	0	306	249	.625
Minnesota Vikings	16	7	9	0	259	337	.438
Green Bay Packers	16	5	11	0	246	316	.313
Detroit Lions	16	2	14	0	219	365	.125

Western Division

Los Angeles Rams	16	9	7	0	323	309	.563
New Orleans Saints	16	8	8	0	370	360	.500
Atlanta Falcons	16	6	10	0	300	388	.375
San Francisco 49ers	16	2	14	0	308	416	.125

American Conference

Eastern Division

Miami Dolphins	16	10	6	0	341	257	.625
New England Patriots	16	9	7	0	411	326	.563
New York Jets	16	8	8	0	337	383	.500
Buffalo Bills	16	7	9	0	268	279	.438
Baltimore Colts	16	5	11	0	271	351	.313

Central Division

Pittsburgh Steelers	16	12	4	0	416	262	.750
Houston Oilers	16	11	5	0	362	331	.688
Cleveland Browns	16	9	7	0	359	352	.563
Cincinnati Bengals	16	4	12	0	337	421	.250

Western Division

San Diego Chargers	16	12	4	0	411	246	.750
Denver Broncos	16	10	6	0	289	262	.625
Oakland Raiders	16	9	7	0	365	337	.563
Seattle Seahawks	16	9	7	0	378	372	.563
Kansas City Chiefs	16	7	9	0	238	262	.438

Coaching Changes

Giants--Ray Perkins 6-10-0; St. Louis--Bud Wilkinson 3-10-0, Larry Wilson 2-1-0; San Francisco--Bill Walsh 2-14-0; New England--Ron Erhardt 9-7-0; Cincinnati--Homer Rice 4-12-0; Oakland--Tom Flores 9-7-0.

League Leaders

Yards Rushing		**Yards Passing**		**Passing %** (300 attempts)	
Earl Campbell	1697	Dan Fouts	4082	Dan Fouts	62.6
Walter Payton	1610	Brian Sipe	3793	Ken Stabler	61.0
Ottis Anderson	1605	Terry Bradshaw	3724	Archie Manning	60.0
Wilbert Montgomery	1512	Jim Zorn	3661	Steve DeBerg	60.0
Mike Pruitt	1294	Steve DeBerg	3652	Greg Landry	59.1

Receiving Yards		**Receptions**		**Field Goals**	
Steve Largent	1237	Joe Washington	82	Mark Moseley	25
John Stallworth	1183	Ahmad Rashad	80	Tony Franklin	23
Ahmad Rashad	1156	Wallace Francis	74	John Smith	23
John Jefferson	1090	Rickey Young	72	Toni Fritsch	21
Wes Chandler	1069	Charlie Joiner	72	Uwe von Schamann	21

Punt Return Yards		Kickoff Return Yards	
J.T. Smith	612	Bruce Harper	1158
Mike Fuller	448	Nesby Glasgow	1126
Danny Reece	431	Jim Edwards	1103
Theo Bell	378	Tony Nathan	1016
Wally Henry	320	Roy Green	1005

Pro Bowl Game
(Aloha Stadium, Honolulu)

January 27 1980	National Conference	37		American Conference	27

NFL Playoffs

December 23	Chicago Bears	17	at	Philadelphia Eagles	27
December 23	Denver Broncos	7	at	Houston Oilers	13
December 29	Philadelphia Eagles	17	at	Tampa Bay Buccaneers	24
December 29	Houston Oilers	17	at	San Diego Chargers	14
December 30	Los Angeles Rams	21	at	Dallas Cowboys	19
December 30	Miami Dolphins	14	at	Pittsburgh Steelers	34
January 6 1980	Los Angeles Rams	9	at	Tampa Bay Buccaneers	0
January 6 1980	Houston Oilers	13	at	Pittsburgh Steelers	27

Super Bowl XIV
(Rose Bowl, Pasadena)

January 20 1980	Pittsburgh Steelers	31		Los Angeles Rams	19

Individual Awards

AP MVP--Earl Campbell (Houston Oilers)
Bert Bell Trophy--Ottis Anderson (St. Louis Cardinals) [World Almanac]
Bert Bell Trophy--Earl Campbell (Houston Oilers)
George Halas Trophy--Lee Roy Selmon (Tampa Bay Buccaneers)
Jim Thorpe Trophy--Earl Campbell (Houston Oilers)
P.F.W.A. MVP--Earl Campbell (Houston Oilers)
Pro Bowl MVP--Chuck Muncie (New Orleans Saints)
Super Bowl MVP--Terry Bradshaw (Pittsburgh Steelers)
U.P.I. AFC Coach of the Year--Sam Rutigliano (Cleveland Browns)
U.P.I. AFC Player of the Year--Dan Fouts (San Diego Chargers)
U.P.I. AFC Rookie of the Year--Jerry Butler (Buffalo Bills)
U.P.I. NFC Coach of the Year--Jack Pardee (Washington Redskins)
U.P.I. NFC Player of the Year--Ottis Anderson (St. Louis Cardinals)
U.P.I. NFC Rookie of the Year--Ottis Anderson (St. Louis Cardinals)

Hall of Fame Inductees

Dick Butkus, Yale Lary, Ron Mix, Johnny Unitas

Rules

The NFL prohibited the wearing of torn or altered pads and exposed pads which could be considered dangerous.

Canadian Football League
Eastern Conference

Team Name	GP	W	L	T	PF	PA	Pts	Pct
Montreal Alouettes	16	11	4	1	351	284	23	.719
Ottawa Rough Riders	16	8	6	2	349	315	18	.563
Hamilton Tiger-Cats	16	6	10	0	280	338	12	.375
Toronto Argonauts	16	5	11	0	234	352	10	.313

Western Conference

Team Name	GP	W	L	T	PF	PA	Pts	Pct
Edmonton Eskimos	16	12	2	2	495	219	26	.813
Calgary Stampeders	16	12	4	0	382	278	24	.750
British Columbia Lions	16	9	6	1	328	333	19	.594
Winnipeg Blue Bombers	16	4	12	0	283	340	8	.250
Saskatchewan Roughriders	16	2	14	0	194	437	4	.125

Coaching Changes

Hamilton--John Payne 6-10-0; Toronto--Forrest Gregg 5-11-0; Saskatchewan--Ron Lancaster 2-14-0.

League Leaders

Yards Rushing		Yards Passing		Passing % (200 attempts)	
David Green	1678	Tom Clements	2803	Tony Adams	61.2
Jim Germany	1324	Tony Adams	2692	Tom Wilkinson	58.3
Larry Key	1060	Joe Barnes	2456	Tom Clements	57.0
Jim Washington	918	Dieter Brock	2383	Ken Johnson	56.4
Ron Rowland	814	Warren Moon	2382	Dieter Brock	54.8

Receiving Yards		Receptions		Points	
Waddell Smith	1214	Waddell Smith	74	Bernie Ruoff	151
Brian Kelly	1098	Brian Kelly	61	Lui Passaglia	144
Mike Holmes	1034	Mike Holmes	60	Dave Cutler	140
Willie Armstead	968	Tom Forzani	58	J.T. Hay	113
Leif Petterson	838	Leif Petterson	56	Don Sweet	111

Grey Cup Playoffs

November 10	British Columbia Lions	2	at	Calgary Stampeders	37
November 11	Hamilton Tiger-Cats	26	at	Ottawa Rough Riders	29
November 17	Ottawa Rough Riders	6	at	Montreal Alouettes	17
November 18	Calgary Stampeders	7	at	Edmonton Eskimos	19
November 25	Edmonton Eskimos	17	at	Montreal Alouettes	9

Individual Awards

Annis Stukus Trophy--Hugh Campbell (Edmonton Eskimos)
Dave Dryburgh Memorial Trophy--Bernie Ruoff (Winnipeg Blue Bombers)
DeMarco-Becket Memorial Trophy--Mike Wilson (Edmonton Eskimos)
Dr. Beattie Martin Trophy--Dave Fennell (Edmonton Eskimos)
Eddie James Memorial Trophy--Jim Germany (Edmonton Eskimos)
Frank M. Gibson Trophy--Martin Cox (Ottawa Rough Riders)
Grey Cup Most Outstanding Defensive Player--Tom Cousineau (Montreal Alouettes)

Grey Cup Most Outstanding Offensive Player--David Green (Montreal Alouettes)
Grey Cup Most Valuable Canadian--Don Sweet (Montreal Alouettes)
Jackie Parker Trophy--Brian Kelly (Edmonton Eskimos)
James P. McCaffrey Trophy--Ben Zambiasi (Hamilton Tiger-Cats)
Jeff Nicklin Memorial Trophy--Waddell Smith (Edmonton Eskimos)
Jeff Russel Memorial Trophy--David Green (Montreal Alouettes)
Leo Dandurand Trophy--Ray Watrin (Montreal Alouettes)
Lew Hayman Trophy--Leif Petterson (Hamilton Tiger-Cats)
Norm Fieldgate Trophy--John Helton (Winnipeg Blue Bombers)
Schenley Award Most Outstanding Canadian--Dave Fennell (Edmonton Eskimos)
Schenley Award Most Outstanding Defensive Player--Ben Zambiasi (Hamilton Tiger-Cats)
Schenley Award Most Outstanding Offensive Lineman--Mike Wilson (Edmonton Eskimos)
Schenley Award Most Outstanding Player--David Green (Montreal Alouettes)
Schenley Award Most Outstanding Rookie--Brian Kelly (Edmonton Eskimos)

Hall of Fame Inductees

Norm Fieldgate, Garney Henley, Peter Neumann, George Reed

HOCKEY
National Hockey League

Clarence Campbell Conference
Patrick Division

Team Name	GP	W	L	T	GF	GA	Pts	Pct
New York Islanders	80	51	15	14	358	214	116	.725
Philadelphia Flyers	80	40	25	15	281	248	95	.594
New York Rangers	80	40	29	11	316	292	91	.569
Atlanta Flames	80	41	31	8	327	280	90	.563

Smythe Division

Team Name	GP	W	L	T	GF	GA	Pts	Pct
Chicago Black Hawks	80	29	36	15	244	277	73	.456
Vancouver Canucks	80	25	42	13	217	291	63	.394
St. Louis Blues	80	18	50	12	249	348	48	.300
Colorado Rockies	80	15	53	12	210	331	42	.263

Prince of Wales Conference

Norris Division

Team Name	GP	W	L	T	GF	GA	Pts	Pct
Montreal Canadiens	80	52	17	11	337	204	115	.719
Pittsburgh Penguins	80	36	31	13	281	279	85	.531
Los Angeles Kings	80	34	34	12	292	286	80	.500
Washington Capitals	80	24	41	15	273	338	63	.394
Detroit Red Wings	80	23	41	16	252	295	62	.388

Adams Division

Team Name	GP	W	L	T	GF	GA	Pts	Pct
Boston Bruins	80	43	23	14	316	270	100	.625
Buffalo Sabres	80	36	28	16	280	263	88	.550
Toronto Maple Leafs	80	34	33	13	267	252	81	.506
Minnesota North Stars	80	28	40	12	257	289	68	.425

Coaching Changes

Philadelphia--Bob McCammon 22-17-11, Pat Quinn 18-8-4; Rangers--Fred Shero 40-29-11; Vancouver--Harry Neale 25-42-13; St. Louis--Bob Plager 18-50-12; Colorado--Pat Kelly 3-14-4; Armand Guidolin 12-39-8; Los Angeles--Bob Berry 34-34-12; Washington--Danny Belisle 24-41-15; Buffalo--Marcel Pronovost 8-10-6, Billy Inglis 28-18-10; Minnesota--Harry Howell 3-6-2, Glen Sonmor 25-34-10.

League Leaders

Goals		**Assists**		**Points**	
Mike Bossy	69	Bryan Trottier	87	Bryan Trottier	134
Marcel Dionne	59	Guy Lafleur	77	Marcel Dionne	130
Guy Lafleur	52	Bob MacMillan	71	Guy Lafleur	129
Guy Chouinard	50	Marcel Dionne	71	Mike Bossy	126
Bryan Trottier	47	Denis Potvin	70	Bob MacMillan	108

Penalty Minutes		**Plus/Minus** (1,600 minutes)		**GAA**	
Dave Williams	298	Bryan Trottier	76	Ken Dryden	2.30
Dave Hutchison	235	Denis Potvin	71	Glenn Resch	2.50
Willi Plett	213	Mike Bossy	63	Bernie Parent	2.70
Dennis Polonich	208	Pierre Mondou	59	Michel Larocque	2.84
Garry Howatt	205	Clarke Gillies	57	Bill Smith	2.87

Wins		**Shutouts**	
Dan Bouchard	32	Ken Dryden	5
Ken Dryden	30	Mike Palmateer	4
Glenn Resch	26	Tony Esposito	4
Mike Palmateer	26	Bernie Parent	4
Don Edwards	26	Mario Lessard	4

Challenge Cup

(Madison Square Garden, New York)

February 8	NHL All Stars	4	Soviet All Stars	2
February 10	Soviet All Stars	5	NHL All Stars	4
February 11	Soviet All Stars	6	NHL All Stars	0

Stanley Cup Playoffs

April 10	Vancouver Canucks	3	at	Philadelphia Flyers	2
April 10	Toronto Maple Leafs	2	at	Atlanta Flames	1
April 10	Pittsburgh Penguins	4	at	Buffalo Sabres	3
April 10	Los Angeles Kings	1	at	New York Rangers	7
April 12	Philadelphia Flyers	6	at	Vancouver Canucks	4
April 12	Atlanta Flames	4	at	Toronto Maple Leafs	7
April 12	Buffalo Sabres	3	at	Pittsburgh Penguins	1
April 12	New York Rangers	2	at	Los Angeles Kings	1 [6:11]
April 14	Vancouver Canucks	2	at	Philadelphia Flyers	7
April 14	Pittsburgh Penguins	4	at	Buffalo Sabres	3 [0:47]
April 16	Boston Bruins	1	at	Montreal Canadiens	5
April 16	Pittsburgh Penguins	2	at	Boston Bruins	6
April 16	Chicago Black Hawks	2	at	New York Islanders	6
April 16	New York Rangers	2	at	Philadelphia Flyers	3 [0:44]

April 18	Toronto Maple Leafs	1	at	Montreal Canadiens	5
April 18	Pittsburgh Penguins	3	at	Boston Bruins	4
April 18	Chicago Black Hawks	0	at	New York Islanders	1 [2:31]
April 18	New York Rangers	7	at	Philadelphia Flyers	1
April 20	New York Islanders	4	at	Chicago Black Hawks	0
April 20	Philadelphia Flyers	1	at	New York Rangers	5
April 21	Montreal Canadiens	4	at	Toronto Maple Leafs	3 [5:25]
April 21	Boston Bruins	2	at	Pittsburgh Penguins	1
April 22	Montreal Canadiens	5	at	Toronto Maple Leafs	4 [4:14]
April 22	Boston Bruins	4	at	Pittsburgh Penguins	1
April 22	New York Islanders	3	at	Chicago Black Hawks	1
April 22	Philadelphia Flyers	0	at	New York Rangers	6
April 24	New York Rangers	8	at	Philadelphia Flyers	3
April 26	New York Rangers	4	at	New York Islanders	1
April 26	Boston Bruins	2	at	Montreal Canadiens	4
April 28	New York Rangers	3	at	New York Islanders	4 [8:02]
April 28	Boston Bruins	2	at	Montreal Canadiens	5
May 1	New York Islanders	1	at	New York Rangers	3
May 1	Montreal Canadiens	1	at	Boston Bruins	2
May 3	New York Islanders	3	at	New York Rangers	2 [3:40]
May 3	Montreal Canadiens	3	at	Boston Bruins	4 [3:46]
May 5	New York Rangers	4	at	New York Islanders	3
May 5	Toronto Maple Leafs	2	at	Montreal Canadiens	5
May 8	New York Islanders	1	at	New York Rangers	2
May 8	Montreal Canadiens	2	at	Boston Bruins	5
May 10	Boston Bruins	4	at	Montreal Canadiens	5 [9:33]
May 13	New York Rangers	4	at	Montreal Canadiens	1
May 15	New York Rangers	2	at	Montreal Canadiens	6
May 17	Montreal Canadiens	4	at	New York Rangers	1
May 19	Montreal Canadiens	4	at	New York Rangers	3 [7:25]
May 21	New York Rangers	1	at	Montreal Canadiens	4

All Star Teams

First Team		Second Team
Ken Dryden	Goal	Glenn Resch
Denis Potvin	Defense	Borje Salming
Larry Robinson	Defense	Serge Savard
Bryan Trottier	Center	Marcel Dionne
Guy Lafleur	Right Wing	Mike Bossy
Clark Gillies	Left Wing	Bill Barber

Individual Awards

Art Ross Trophy--Bryan Trottier (New York Islanders)
Bill Masterton Trophy--Serge Savard (Montreal Canadiens)
Calder Memorial Trophy--Bobby Smith (Minnesota North Stars)
Conn Smythe Trophy--Bob Gainey (Montreal Canadiens)
Frank J. Selke Trophy--Bob Gainey (Montreal Canadiens)
Hart Memorial Trophy--Bryan Trottier (New York Islanders)
Jack Adams Award--Al Arbour (New York Islanders)
James Norris Trophy--Denis Potvin (New York Islanders)
Lady Byng Memorial Trophy--Bob MacMillan (Atlanta Flames)
Lester B. Pearson Award--Marcel Dionne (Los Angeles Kings)
Lester Patrick Trophy--Bobby Orr
Vezina Trophy--Ken Dryden and Michel Larocque (Montreal Canadiens)

Hall of Fame Inductees

Harry Howell, Gordon Juckes, Bobby Orr, Henri Richard

World Hockey Association

Team Name	GP	W	L	T	GF	GA	Pts	Pct
Edmonton Oilers	80	48	30	2	340	266	98	.613
Quebec Nordiques	80	41	34	5	288	271	87	.544
Winnipeg Jets	80	39	35	6	307	306	84	.525
New England Whalers	80	37	34	9	298	287	83	.519
Cincinnati Stingers	80	33	41	6	274	284	72	.450
Birmingham Bulls	80	32	42	6	286	311	70	.438
Indianapolis Racers	25	5	18	2	78	130	12	.240
Soviet National Team	6	4	1	1	26	20	9	.750
Czechoslovakia Nationals	6	1	4	1	14	33	3	.250
Dinamo Moscow	1	0	1	0	1	4	0	.000

Coaching Changes

Quebec--Jacques Demers 41-34-5; New England--Bill Dineen 37-34-9; Cincinnati--Floyd Smith 33-41-6; Birmingham--John Brophy 32-42-6; Indianapolis--Pat Stapleton 5-18-2; Soviet Nationals--Boris Mayorov 4-1-1; Czechoslovakian Nationals--Stanislav Nevesely; Dinamo Moscow.

League Leaders

Goals		Assists		Points	
Real Cloutier	75	Robbie Ftorek	77	Real Cloutier	129
Morris Lukowich	65	Kent Nilsson	68	Robbie Ftorek	116
Peter Sullivan	46	Terry Ruskowski	66	Wayne Gretzky	110
Wayne Gretzky	46	Mark Howe	65	Mark Howe	107
Peter Marsh	43	Wayne Gretzky	64	Kent Nilsson	107

Penalty Minutes		GAA (1,560 minutes)		Wins	
Scott Campbell	248	Dave Dryden	2.89	Dave Dryden	41
Rick Vaive	248	Richard Brodeur	3.11	Richard Brodeur	25
Paul Baxter	240	Jim Corsi	3.30	Markus Mattsson	25
Barry Melrose	222	Al Smith	3.31	Mike Liut	23
Dave Hanson	212	Michel Dion	3.32	John Garrett	20

Shutouts	
Dave Dryden	3
Richard Brodeur	3
Mike Liut	3
Jim Corsi	3
Ed Mio	2

WHA-Moscow All Star Games

(Northlands Coliseum, Edmonton)

January 2	WHA All Stars	4	Moscow	2
January 4	WHA All Stars	4	Moscow	2
January 5	WHA All Stars	4	Moscow	3

WHA Playoffs

April 21	Cincinnati Stingers	3	at	New England Whalers	5
April 22	New England Whalers	3	at	Cincinnati Stingers	6
April 23	Winnipeg Jets	6	at	Quebec Nordiques	3
April 24	Cincinnati Stingers	1	at	New England Whalers	2
April 25	Winnipeg Jets	9	at	Quebec Nordiques	2
April 26	New England Whalers	2	at	Edmonton Oilers	6
April 27	Quebec Nordiques	5	at	Winnipeg Jets	9
April 27	New England Whalers	5	at	Edmonton Oilers	9
April 29	Quebec Nordiques	2	at	Winnipeg Jets	6
April 29	Edmonton Oilers	1	at	New England Whalers	4
May 1	Edmonton Oilers	1	at	New England Whalers	5
May 3	New England Whalers	2	at	Edmonton Oilers	5
May 6	Edmonton Oilers	4	at	New England Whalers	8
May 8	New England Whalers	3	at	Edmonton Oilers	6
May 11	Winnipeg Jets	3	at	Edmonton Oilers	1
May 13	Winnipeg Jets	3	at	Edmonton Oilers	2
May 15	Edmonton Oilers	8	at	Winnipeg Jets	3
May 16	Edmonton Oilers	2	at	Winnipeg Jets	3
May 18	Winnipeg Jets	2	at	Edmonton Oilers	10
May 20	Edmonton Oilers	3	at	Winnipeg Jets	7

All Star Teams

First Team		Second Teams
Dave Dryden	Goal	Richard Brodeur
Rick Ley	Defense	Dave Langevin
Rob Ramage	Defense	Paul Shmyr
Robbie Ftorek	Center	Wayne Gretzky
Real Cloutier	Right Wing	Blair MacDonald
Mark Howe	Left Wing	Morris Lukowich

Individual Awards

Ben Hatskin Trophy--Dave Dryden (Edmonton Oilers)
Bill Hunter Trophy--Real Cloutier (Quebec Nordiques)
Dennis Murphy Trophy--Rick Ley (New England Whalers)
Gordie Howe Trophy--Dave Dryden (Edmonton Oilers)
Lou Kaplan Trophy--Wayne Gretzky (Edmonton Oilers)
Paul Deneau Trophy--Kent Nilsson (Winnipeg Jets)
Robert Schmertz Trophy--John Brophy (Birmingham Bulls)
WHA MVP in Playoffs--Rich Preston (Winnipeg Jets)

Notes

This was the last season for the World Hockey Association.

SOCCER

North American Soccer League

National Conference

Eastern Division

Team Name	GP	W	L	GF	GA	BP	Pts	Pct
Cosmos	30	24	6	84	52	72	216	.800
Washington Diplomats	30	19	11	68	50	59	172	.637
Toronto Blizzard	30	14	16	52	65	49	133	.493
Rochester Lancers	30	15	15	43	57	42	132	.489

Central Division

Minnesota Kicks	30	21	9	67	48	58	184	.681
Dallas Tornado	30	17	13	53	51	50	152	.563
Tulsa Roughnecks	30	14	16	61	56	55	139	.515
Atlanta Chiefs	30	12	18	59	61	49	121	.488

Western Division

Vancouver Whitecaps	30	20	10	54	31	52	172	.637
Los Angeles Aztecs	30	18	12	62	47	54	162	.600
Seattle Sounders	30	13	17	58	52	47	125	.463
Portland Timbers	30	11	19	50	75	46	112	.415

American Conference

Eastern Division

Tampa Bay Rowdies	30	19	11	67	46	55	169	.626
Ft. Lauderdale Strikers	30	17	13	75	65	63	165	.611
Philadelphia Fury	30	10	20	55	60	51	111	.411
New England Tea Men	30	12	18	41	56	38	110	.407

Central Division

Houston Hurricane	30	22	8	61	46	55	187	.693
Chicago Sting	30	16	14	70	62	63	159	.589
Detroit Express	30	14	16	61	56	49	133	.493
Memphis Rogues	30	6	24	38	74	37	73	.270

Western Division

San Diego Sockers	30	15	15	59	55	50	140	.519
California Surf	30	15	15	53	56	50	140	.519
Edmonton Drillers	30	8	22	43	78	40	88	.326
San Jose Earthquakes	30	8	22	41	74	38	86	.319

Coaching Changes

New York--Eddie Firmani 9-2, Ray Klivecka 15-4; Toronto--Keith Eddy 14-16; Minnesota--Roy McCrohan 21-9; Tulsa--Alan Hinton 14-16; Atlanta--Dan Wood 12-18; Los Angeles--Rinus Michels 18-12; Philadelphia--Marko Valok 10-20; Chicago--Willy Roy 16-14; Memphis--Eddie McCreadie 2-6, Charlie Cooke 4-18; California--John Sewell 4-4, Peter Wall 11-11; Edmonton--Hans Kraay 6-19, Joe Petrone 2-3; San Jose--Terry Fisher 0-8, Peter Stubbe 8-14.

League Leaders

Goals		Points		Shutouts	
Giorgio Chinaglia	26	Oscar Fabbiani	58	Phil Parkes	7
Oscar Fabbiani	25	Giorgio Chinaglia	57	Colin Boulton	7
Alan Willey	21	Gerd Mueller	55	Paul Hammond	6
Karl-Heinz Granitza	20	David Robb	52	Volkmar Gross	6
Gerd Mueller	19	Jeff Bourne	51	Kevin Keelan	6

GAA
(1,350 minutes)

Phil Parkes	0.96
Victor Nogueira	1.26
Zeljko Bilecki	1.28
Mike Ivanow	1.39
Bill Irwin	1.45

NASL Playoffs

August 14	Houston Hurricane	1	at	Philadelphia Fury	2
August 15	Tampa Bay Rowdies	1	at	Detroit Express	0
August 15	Fort Lauderdale Strikers	0	at	Chicago Sting	2
August 15	Minnesota Kicks	1	at	Tulsa Roughnecks	2 [OT]
August 15	Vancouver Whitecaps	3	at	Dallas Tornado	2
August 15	Washington Diplomats	1	at	Los Angeles Aztecs	3
August 16	San Diego Sockers	4	at	California Surf	2
August 16	Cosmos	3	at	Toronto Blizzard	1
August 18	Chicago Sting	1	at	Fort Lauderdale Strikers	0
August 18	California Surf	2	at	San Diego Sockers	7
August 18	Dallas Tornado	1	at	Vancouver Whitecaps	2
August 19	Detroit Express	1	at	Tampa Bay Rowdies	3
August 19	Tulsa Roughnecks	2	at	Minnesota Kicks	1 [OT]
August 19	Los Angeles Aztecs	4	at	Washington Diplomats	3 [OT]
August 19	Toronto Blizzard	0	at	Cosmos	2
August 20	Philadelphia Fury	2	at	Houston Hurricane	1
August 22	Chicago Sting	0	at	San Diego Sockers	2
August 22	Vancouver Whitecaps	2	at	Los Angeles Aztecs	3 [SO]
August 23	Tampa Bay Rowdies	3	at	Philadelphia Fury	2 [SO]
August 23	Cosmos	0	at	Tulsa Roughnecks	3
August 25	San Diego Sockers	1	at	Chicago Sting	0
August 25	Philadelphia Fury	0	at	Tampa Bay Rowdies	1
August 25	Los Angeles Aztecs	0	at	Vancouver Whitecaps	1
MINI GAME	Los Angeles Aztecs	0	at	Vancouver Whitecaps	1
August 26	Tulsa Roughnecks	0	at	Cosmos	3
MINI GAME	Tulsa Roughnecks	1	at	Cosmos	3
August 29	Cosmos	0	at	Vancouver Whitecaps	2
August 30	Tampa Bay Rowdies	1	at	San Diego Sockers	2
September 1	Vancouver Whitecaps	2	at	Cosmos	3 [SO]
MINI GAME	Vancouver Whitecaps	1	at	Cosmos	0 [SO]
September 2	San Diego Sockers	2	at	Tampa Bay Rowdies	3 [SO]
MINI GAME	San Diego Sockers	0	at	Tampa Bay Rowdies	1
September 8	Vancouver Whitecaps	2		Tampa Bay Rowdies	1 *

*Game played in New York

All Star Teams

First Team		Second Team
Phil Parkes	Goal	Paul Hammond
Carlos Alberto	Defender	Marinho
Bruce Wilson	Defender	John Gorman
Mike Connell	Defender	Mihalj Keri
Wim Rijsbergen	Defender	Bob Lenarduzzi
Franz Beckenbauer	Midfield	Vladislav Bogicevic
Johan Neeskens	Midfield	Teofilo Cubillas
Ace Ntsoelengoe	Midfield	Alan Ball
Johan Cruyff	Forward	Oscar Fabbiani
Trevor Francis	Forward	Karl-Heinz Granitza
Giorgio Chinaglia	Forward	Gerd Mueller

Individual Awards

Coach of the Year--Timo Liekoski (Houston Hurricane)
Lead Goalkeeper Award--Phil Parkes (Vancouver Whitecaps)
Most Valuable Player--Johan Cruyff (Los Angeles Aztecs)
NASL-MVP in Playoffs--Alan Ball (Vancouver Whitecaps)
Rookie of the Year--Larry Hulcer (Los Angeles Aztecs)
Top Defensive Player--John Dempsey (Philadelphia Fury)
Nick Mijatovic (Rochester Lancers)
Top North American Player--Ricky Davis (New York Cosmos)
Top Offensive Player--Johan Cruyff (Los Angeles Aztecs)

Notes

Rochester goalie Shep Messing charged that Kevin Keelan of the New England Tea Men, suggested that the two teams give each other an extra goal in a late season game so both teams would make the playoffs.

Franchise Changes

NBA--Buffalo Braves became the San Diego Clippers.
NASL-Toronto Metro-Croatia became the Toronto Blizzard.
Colorado Caribous became the Atlanta Chiefs.
Oakland Stompers became the Edmonton Drillers

Other Sports

Horseracing--Kentucky Derby won by Spectacular Bid (time 2:02.4, purse $228,650).
Golf--U.S. Open won by Hale Irwin with a score of 284.
Auto Racing--Indianapolis 500 won by Rick Mears (ave. speed 158.899 MPH).
Tennis--U.S. Open won by John McEnroe in the men's singles.
U.S. Open won by John McEnroe and Peter Fleming in the men's doubles.
U.S. Open won by Tracy Austin in the women's singles.
U.S. Open won by Betty Stove and Wendy Turnbull in the women's doubles.
U.S. Open won by Greer Stevens and Bob Hewitt in the mixed doubles.

1980

BASEBALL
National League

East

Team Name	W	L	Pct	GB	R	OR
Philadelphia Phillies	91	71	.562	-	728	639
Montreal Expos	90	72	.556	1	694	629
Pittsburgh Pirates	83	79	.512	8	666	646
St. Louis Cardinals	74	88	.457	17	738	710
New York Mets	67	95	.414	24	611	702
Chicago Cubs	64	98	.395	27	614	728

West

Team Name	W	L	Pct	GB	R	OR
Houston Astros	93	70	.571	-	637	589
Los Angeles Dodgers	92	71	.564	1	663	591
Cincinnati Reds	89	73	.549	3.5	707	670
Atlanta Braves	81	80	.503	11	630	660
San Francisco Giants	75	86	.466	17	573	634
San Diego Padres	73	89	.451	19.5	591	654

Coaching Changes

Philadelphia--Dallas Green 91-71; St. Louis--Ken Boyer 18-33, Jack Krol 0-1, Dorrel "Whitey" Herzog 38-35, Albert"Red" Schoendienst 18-19; Chicago--Preston Gomez 38-52, Joey Amalfitano 26-45; San Francisco--Dave Bristol 75-86; San Diego--Jerry Coleman 73-89.

League Leaders

Batting Average
(440 at bats)

Bill Buckner	.324
Keith Hernandez	.321
Garry Templeton	.319
Arnold McBride	.309
Cesar Cedeno	.309

Home Runs

Mike Schmidt	48
Dale Murphy	35
Bob Horner	33
Dusty Baker	29
Gary Carter	29

RBI

Mike Schmidt	121
George Hendrick	109
Steve Garvey	106
Gary Carter	101
Keith Hernandez	99

Stolen Bases
(162 innings)

Ron LeFlore	97
Omar Moreno	96
Dave Collins	79
Rodney Scott	63
Gene Richards	61

ERA

Don Sutton	2.21
Steve Carlton	2.34
Jerry Reuss	2.52
Vida Blue	2.97
Steve Rogers	2.98

Wins

Steve Carlton	24
Joe Niekro	20
Jim Bibby	19
Jerry Reuss	18
Dick Ruthven	17

Saves

Bruce Sutter	28
Tom Hume	25
Rollie Fingers	23
Neil Allen	22
Rick Camp	22

Strikeouts

Steve Carlton	286
Nolan Ryan	200
Mario Soto	182
Phil Niekro	176
Bert Blyleven	168

NLCS

October 7	Houston Astros	1	at	Philadelphia Phillies	3
October 8	Houston Astros	7	at	Philadelphia Phillies	4 [10]
October 10	Philadelphia Phillies	0	at	Houston Astros	1 [10]
October 11	Philadelphia Phillies	5	at	Houston Astros	3
October 12	Philadelphia Phillies	8	at	Houston Astros	7

Notes

The Houston Astros defeated the Los Angeles Dodgers 7 to 1 in a playoff game for the West Division Championship of the National League.

American League

East

Team Name	W	L	Pct	GB	R	OR
New York Yankees	103	59	.636	-	820	662
Baltimore Orioles	100	62	.617	3	805	640
Milwaukee Brewers	86	76	.531	17	811	682
Boston Red Sox	83	77	.519	19	757	767
Detroit Tigers	84	78	.519	19	830	757
Cleveland Indians	79	81	.494	23	738	807
Toronto Blue Jays	67	95	.414	36	624	762

West

Team Name	W	L	Pct	GB	R	OR
Kansas City Royals	97	65	.599	-	809	694
Oakland Athletics	83	79	.512	14	686	642
Minnesota Twins	77	84	.478	19.5	670	724
Texas Rangers	76	85	.472	20.5	756	752
Chicago White Sox	70	90	.438	26	587	722
California Angels	65	95	.406	31	698	797
Seattle Mariners	59	103	.364	38	610	793

Coaching Changes

New York--Dick Howser 103-59; Milwaukee--Bob Rodgers 39-31, George Bamberger 47-45; Boston--Don Zimmer 82-73, John Pesky 1-4; Detroit--George "Sparky" Anderson 84-78; Cleveland--Dave Garcia 79-81; Toronto--Bob Mattick 67-95; Kansas City--Jim Frey 97-65; Oakland--Billy Martin 83-79; Minnesota--Gene Mauch 54-71, John Goryl 23-13; Chicago--Tony LaRussa 70-90; Seattle--Darrell Johnson 39-65, Maury Wills 20-38.

League Leaders

Batting Average (440 at bats)		Home Runs		RBI	
George Brett	.390	Reggie Jackson	41	Gary Cooper	122
Cecil Cooper	.352	Ben Oglivie	41	George Brett	118
Miguel Dilone	.341	Gorman Thomas	38	Ben Oglivie	118
Mickey Rivers	.333	Tony Armas	35	Al Oliver	117
Rod Carew	.341	Eddie Murray	32	Eddie Murray	116

Stolen Bases		**ERA** (162 innings)		**Wins**	
Rickey Henderson	100	Rudy May	2.47	Steve Stone	25
Willie Wilson	79	Mike Norris	2.54	Tommy John	22
Miguel Dilone	61	Britt Burns	2.84	Mike Norris	22
Julio Cruz	45	Matt Keough	2.92	Scott McGregor	20
Al Bumbry	44	Larry Gura	2.96	Dennis Leonard	20

Saves		**Strikeouts**	
Dan Quisenberry	33	Len Barker	187
Rich Gossage	33	Mike Norris	180
Ed Farmer	30	Ron Guidry	166
Tim Stoddard	26	Dennis Leonard	155
Tom Burgmeier	24	Floyd Bannister	155

All Star Game
(Dodger Stadium, Los Angeles)

July 8	National League	4		American League	2

ALCS

October 8	New York Yankees	2	at	Kansas City Royals	7
October 9	New York Yankees	2	at	Kansas City Royals	3
October 10	Kansas City Royals	4	at	New York Yankees	2

World Series

October 14	Kansas City Royals	6	at	Philadelphia Phillies	7
October 15	Kansas City Royals	4	at	Philadelphia Phillies	6
October 17	Philadelphia Phillies	3	at	Kansas City Royals	4
October 18	Philadelphia Phillies	3	at	Kansas City Royals	5
October 19	Philadelphia Phillies	4	at	Kansas City Royals	3
October 21	Kansas City Royals	1	at	Philadelphia Phillies	4

Individual Awards

ALCS MVP--Frank White (Kansas City Royals AL)
Arch Ward Memorial Trophy--Ken Griffey (Cincinnati Reds NL)
Baseball Writers Award--Mike Schmidt (Philadelphia Phillies NL)
George Brett (Kansas City Royals AL)
Cy Young Award--Steve Carlton (Philadelphia Phillies NL)
Steve Stone (Baltimore Orioles AL)
NLCS MVP--Manny Trillo (Philadelphia Phillies NL)
Rookie of the Year--Steve Howe (Los Angeles Dodgers NL)
Joe Charboneau (Cleveland Indians AL)
Sporting News Executive of the Year--Tal Smith (Houston Astros NL)
Sporting News Manager of the Year--Bill Virdon (Houston Astros NL)
Sporting News Pitcher of the Year--Steve Carlton (Philadelphia Phillies NL)
Steve Stone (Baltimore Orioles AL)
Sporting News Player of the Year--Mike Schmidt (Philadelphia Phillies NL)
George Brett (Kansas City Royals AL)
Sporting News Rookie of the Year--Lonnie Smith (Philadelphia Phillies NL)
Bill Gullickson (Montreal Expos NL)
Joe Charboneau (Cleveland Indians AL)
Britt Burns (Chicago White Sox AL)
World Series MVP--Mike Schmidt (Philadelphia Phillies NL)

Hall of Fame Inductees

Al Kaline, Chuck Klein, Duke Snider, Tom Yawkey

BASKETBALL
National Basketball Association

Eastern Conference
Atlantic Division

Team Name	GP	W	L	PPGF	PPGA	Pct	GB
Boston Celtics	82	61	21	113.5	105.7	.744	-
Philadelphia 76ers	82	59	23	109.1	104.9	.720	2
Washington Bullets	82	39	43	107.0	109.5	.476	22
New York Knickerbockers	82	39	43	114.0	115.0	.476	22
New Jersey Nets	82	34	48	108.3	109.5	.415	27

Central Division

Team Name	GP	W	L	PPGF	PPGA	Pct	GB
Atlanta Hawks	82	50	32	104.5	101.6	.610	-
Houston Rockets	82	41	41	110.8	110.6	.500	9
San Antonio Spurs	82	41	41	119.4	119.7	.500	9
Cleveland Cavaliers	82	37	45	114.1	113.8	.451	13
Indiana Pacers	82	37	45	111.2	111.9	.451	13
Detroit Pistons	82	16	66	108.9	117.2	.195	34

Western Conference

Midwest Division

Team Name	GP	W	L	PPGF	PPGA	Pct	GB
Milwaukee Bucks	82	49	33	110.1	106.1	.598	-
Kansas City Kings	82	47	35	108.0	104.9	.573	2
Chicago Bulls	82	30	52	107.5	110.2	.366	19
Denver Nuggets	82	30	52	108.3	112.7	.366	19
Utah Jazz	82	24	58	102.4	108.4	.293	25

Pacific Division

Team Name	GP	W	L	PPGF	PPGA	Pct	GB
Los Angeles Lakers	82	60	22	115.1	109.2	.732	-
Seattle SuperSonics	82	56	26	108.5	103.8	.683	4
Phoenix Suns	82	55	27	111.1	107.5	.671	5
Portland Trail Blazers	82	38	44	102.5	103.3	.463	22
San Diego Clippers	82	35	47	107.6	111.7	.427	25
Golden State Warriors	82	24	58	103.6	108.0	.293	36

Coaching Changes

Boston--Bill Fitch 61-21; New York William Holzman 39-43; Houston--Del Harris 41-4l; San Antonio--Doug Moe 33-33, Bob Bass 8-8; Cleveland Stan Albeck 37-45; Detroit--Dick Vitale 4-8, Richie Adubato 12-58; Chicago--Jerry Sloan 30-52; Denver--Donnie Walsh 30-52; Utah--Tom Nissalke 24-58; Los Angeles--Jack McKinney 10-4, Paul Westhead 50-18; Golden State--Al Attles 18-43, John Bach 6-15.

League Leaders

Field Goals		Free Throws		Assists	
George Gervin	1024	Lloyd Free	572	Mike Richardson	832
Julius Erving	838	Moses Malone	563	Nate Archibald	671
Kareem Abdul-Jabbar	835	Dan Issel	517	Norm Nixon	642
Otis Birdsong	781	George Gervin	505	Don Ford	610
Moses Malone	778	Reggie Theus	500	Foots Walker	607

Points		Rebounds Per Game	
George Gervin	2585	Swen Nater	15.0
Moses Malone	2119	Moses Malone	14.5
Julius Erving	2100	Wes Unseld	13.3
Lloyd Free	2055	Caldwell Jones	11.9
Kareem Abdul-Jabbar	2034	Elvin Hayes	11.1

All Star Game

(Capital Center, Landover, Maryland)

February 4	East Division	144	West Division	135 [OT]

NBA Playoffs

April 2	Washington Bullets	96	at	Philadelphia 76ers	111
April 2	Kansas City Kings	93	at	Phoenix Suns	96
April 2	San Antonio Spurs	85	at	Houston Rockets	95
April 2	Portland Trail Blazers	110	at	Seattle SuperSonics	120
April 4	Philadelphia 76ers	112	at	Washington Bullets	104
April 4	Phoenix Suns	96	at	Kansas City Kings	106
April 4	Houston Rockets	101	at	San Antonio Spurs	106
April 4	Seattle SuperSonics	95	at	Portland Trail Blazers	105
April 6	Kansas City Kings	99	at	Phoenix Suns	114
April 6	San Antonio Spurs	120	at	Houston Rockets	141
April 6	Portland Trail Blazers	86	at	Seattle SuperSonics	103
April 6	Atlanta Hawks	104	at	Philadelphia 76ers	107
April 8	Phoenix Suns	110	at	Los Angeles Lakers	119
April 8	Milwaukee Bucks	113	at	Seattle SuperSonics	114
April 9	Houston Rockets	101	at	Boston Celtics	119
April 9	Atlanta Hawks	92	at	Philadelphia 76ers	99
April 9	Phoenix Suns	128	at	Los Angeles Lakers	131
April 9	Milwaukee Bucks	114	at	Seattle SuperSonics	112
April 10	Philadelphia 76ers	93	at	Atlanta Hawks	105
April 11	Los Angeles Lakers	108	at	Phoenix Suns	105
April 11	Seattle SuperSonics	91	at	Milwaukee Bucks	95
April 11	Houston Rockets	75	at	Boston Celtics	95
April 13	Los Angeles Lakers	101	at	Phoenix Suns	127
April 13	Seattle SuperSonics	112	at	Milwaukee Bucks	107
April 13	Boston Celtics	100	at	Houston Rockets	81
April 13	Philadelphia 76ers	107	at	Atlanta Hawks	83
April 14	Boston Celtics	138	at	Houston Rockets	121
April 15	Atlanta Hawks	100	at	Philadelphia 76ers	105
April 15	Phoenix Suns	101	at	Los Angeles Lakers	126
April 15	Milwaukee Bucks	108	at	Seattle SuperSonics	97
April 18	Seattle SuperSonics	86	at	Milwaukee Bucks	85

April 18	Philadelphia 76ers	96	at	Boston Celtics	93
April 20	Milwaukee Bucks	94	at	Seattle SuperSonics	98
April 20	Philadelphia 76ers	90	at	Boston Celtics	96
April 22	Seattle SuperSonics	108	at	Los Angeles Lakers	107
April 23	Boston Celtics	97	at	Philadelphia 76ers	99
April 23	Seattle SuperSonics	99	at	Los Angeles Lakers	108
April 24	Boston Celtics	90	at	Philadelphia 76ers	102
April 25	Los Angeles Lakers	104	at	Seattle SuperSonics	100
April 27	Philadelphia 76ers	105	at	Boston Celtics	94
April 27	Los Angeles Lakers	98	at	Seattle SuperSonics	93
April 30	Seattle SuperSonics	105	at	Los Angeles Lakers	111
May 4	Philadelphia 76ers	102	at	Los Angeles Lakers	109
May 7	Philadelphia 76ers	107	at	Los Angeles Lakers	104
May 10	Los Angeles Lakers	111	at	Philadelphia 76ers	101
May 11	Los Angeles Lakers	102	at	Philadelphia 76ers	105
May 14	Philadelphia 76ers	103	at	Los Angeles Lakers	108
May 16	Los Angeles Lakers	123	at	Philadelphia 76ers	107

All Star Teams

First Team

Julius Erving (Philadelphia 76ers)
Larry Bird (Boston Celtics)
Kareem Abdul-Jabbar (Los Angeles Lakers)
George Gervin (San Antonio Spurs)
Paul Westphal (Phoenix Suns)

Second Team

Dan Roundfield (Atlanta Hawks)
Marques Johnson (Milwaukee Bucks)
Moses Malone (Houston Rockets)
Dennis Johnson (Seattle SuperSonics)
Gus Williams (Seattle SuperSonics)

Individual Awards

Eddie Gottlieb Trophy--Larry Bird (Boston Celtics)
Executive of the Year--Red Auerbach (Boston Celtics)
J. Walter Kennedy Citizenship Award--Austin Carr (Cleveland Cavaliers)
Maurice Podoloff Trophy--Kareem Abdul-Jabbar (Los Angeles Lakers)
NBA All Star Game MVP--George Gervin (San Antonio Spurs)
Red Auerbach Trophy--Bill Fitch (Boston Celtics)
NBA Finals MVP--Earvin Johnson (Los Angeles Lakers)

Hall of Fame Inductees

Thomas Barlow, Ferenc Hepp, J. Walter Kennedy, Arad McCutchan

FOOTBALL
National Football League

National Conference
Eastern Division

Team Name	GP	W	L	T	PF	PA	Pct
Philadelphia Eagles	16	12	4	0	384	222	.750
Dallas Cowboys	16	12	4	0	454	311	.750
Washington Redskins	16	6	10	0	251	293	.375
St. Louis Cardinals	16	5	11	0	299	350	.313
New York Giants	16	4	12	0	249	427	.250

Central Division

Minnesota Vikings	16	9	7	0	317	308	.563
Detroit Lions	16	9	7	0	334	272	.563
Chicago Bears	16	7	9	0	304	264	.438
Green Bay Packers	16	5	10	1	231	371	.344
Tampa Bay Buccaneers	16	5	10	1	271	341	.344

Western Division

Atlanta Falcons	16	12	4	0	405	272	.750
Los Angeles Rams	16	11	5	0	424	289	.688
San Francisco 49ers	16	6	10	0	320	415	.375
New Orleans Saints	16	1	15	0	289	487	.063

American Conference

Eastern Division

Buffalo Bills	16	11	5	0	320	260	.688
New England Patriots	16	10	6	0	441	325	.625
Miami Dolphins	16	8	8	0	266	305	.500
Baltimore Colts	16	7	9	0	355	387	.438
New York Jets	16	4	12	0	302	395	.250

Central Division

Cleveland Browns	16	11	5	0	357	310	.688
Houston Oilers	16	11	5	0	295	251	.688
Pittsburgh Steelers	16	9	7	0	352	313	.563
Cincinnati Bengals	16	6	10	0	244	312	.375

Western Division

San Diego Chargers	16	11	5	0	418	327	.688
Oakland Raiders	16	11	5	0	364	306	.688
Denver Broncos	16	8	8	0	310	323	.500
Kansas City Chiefs	16	8	8	0	319	336	.500
Seattle Seahawks	16	4	12	0	291	408	.250

Coaching Changes

St. Louis--Jim Hanifan 5-11-0; New Orleans--Dick Nolan 0-12-0, Dick Stanfel 1-3-0; Baltimore--Mike McCormack 7-9-0; Cincinnati--Forrest Gregg 6-10-0.

League Leaders

Yards Rushing		**Yards Passing**		**Passing %** (300 attempts)	
Earl Campbell	1934	Dan Fouts	4715	Ken Stabler	64.1
Walter Payton	1460	Brian Sipe	4132	Brian Sipe	60.8
Otis Anderson	1352	Archie Manning	3716	Craig Morton	60.8
William Andrews	1308	Tom Kramer	3582	Archie Manning	60.7
Billy Sims	1303	Steve Bartkowski	3544	Steve Fuller	60.3

Receiving Yards		Receptions		Field Goals	
John Jefferson	1340	Kellen Winslow	89	Ed Murray	27
Kellen Winslow	1290	Earl Cooper	83	John Smith	26
James Lofton	1226	Dwight Clark	82	Fred Steinfort	26
Charlie Joiner	1132	John Jefferson	82	Rolf Benirschke	24
Ahmad Rashad	1095	James Lofton	71	Nick Lowery	20

Punt Return Yards		Kickoff Return Yards	
J.T. Smith	581	Eddie Payton	1184
James Jones	548	Bruce Harper	1070
Mike Nelms	487	Horace Ivory	992
Ira Matthews	421	Gary Davis	951
Carl Roaches	384	Jim Rogers	930

Pro Bowl Game

(Aloha Stadium, Honolulu)

February 1 1981	National Conference	21		American Conference	7

NFL Playoffs

December 28	Los Angeles Rams	13	at	Dallas Cowboys	34
December 28	Houston Oilers	7	at	Oakland Raiders	27
January 3 1981	Minnesota Vikings	16	at	Philadelphia Eagles	31
January 3 1981	Buffalo Bills	14	at	San Diego Chargers	20
January 4 1981	Dallas Cowboys	30	at	Atlanta Falcons	27
January 4 1981	Oakland Raiders	14	at	Cleveland Browns	12
January 11 1981	Dallas Cowboys	7	at	Philadelphia Eagles	20
January 11 1981	Oakland Raiders	34	at	San Diego Chargers	27

Super Bowl XV

(Louisiana Superdome, New Orleans)

January 25 1981	Oakland Raiders	27	Philadelphia Eagles	10

Individual Awards

A.P. MVP--Brian Sipe (Cleveland Browns)
Bert Bell Trophy--Billy Sims (Detroit Lions) [World Almanac]
Bert Bell Trophy--Ron Jaworski (Philadelphia Eagles)
George Halas Trophy--Lester Hayes (Oakland Raiders)
Jim Thorpe Trophy--Earl Campbell (Houston Oilers)
P.F.W.A. MVP--Brian Sipe (Cleveland Browns)
Pro Bowl MVP--Eddie Murray (Detroit Lions)
Super Bowl MVP--Jim Plunkett (Oakland Raiders)
U.P.I. AFC Coach of the Year--Sam Rutigliano (Cleveland Browns)
U.P.I. AFC Player of the Year--Brian Sipe (Cleveland Browns)
U.P.I. AFC Rookie of the Year--Joe Cribbs (Buffalo Bills)
U.P.I. NFC Coach of the Year--Leeman Bennett (Atlanta Falcons)
U.P.I. NFC Player of the Year--Ron Jaworski (Philadelphia Eagles)
U.P.I. NFC Rookie of the Year--Billy Sims (Detroit Lions)

Hall of Fame Inductees

Jim Otto, Deacon Jones, Bob Lilly, Herb Adderley

Notes

The AFC-NFC Pro Bowl was played in Aloha Stadium in Honolulu, Hawaii; the first time the game was played in a non NFL city.
CBS television network paid $12 million dollars for the national radio rights to 26 regular and 10 post season NFL games for the 1980 to 1983 seasons.

Canadian Football League
Eastern Division

Team Name	GP	W	L	T	PF	PA	Pts	Pct
Hamilton Tiger-Cats	16	8	7	1	332	377	17	.531
Montreal Alouettes	16	8	8	0	356	375	16	.500
Ottawa Rough Riders	16	7	9	0	353	393	14	.438
Toronto Argonauts	16	6	10	0	334	358	12	.375

Western Division

Team Name	GP	W	L	T	PF	PA	Pts	Pct
Edmonton Eskimos	16	13	3	0	505	281	26	.813
Winnipeg Blue Bombers	16	10	6	0	394	387	20	.625
Calgary Stampeders	16	9	7	0	407	355	18	.563
British Columbia Lions	16	8	7	1	381	351	17	.531
Saskatchewan Roughriders	16	2	14	0	284	469	4	.125

Coaching Changes

Toronto--Willie Wood 6-10-0; Calgary--Ardell Wiegandt 9-7-0.

League Leaders

Yards Rushing		Yards Passing		Passing % (150 attempts)	
James Sykes	1263	Dieter Brock	4252	Joe Paopao	62.8
Richard Crump	1074	Warren Moon	3127	Dieter Brock	59.1
William Miller	1053	Mark Jackson	3041	Gerry Dattilio	57.6
Jim Germany	1019	Ken Johnson	3019	Mark Jackson	57.2
David Green	873	Gerry Dattilio	2892	Conredge Holloway	56.1

Receiving Yards		Receptions		Points	
Tom Scott	1245	Mike Holmes	79	Dave Cutler	158
Bob Gaddis	1112	Tom Scott	73	Lui Passaglia	147
Mike Holmes	1092	Bob Gaddis	68	Trevor Kennerd	142
Brian Kelly	922	James Sykes	57	Zenon Andrusyshyn	136
Joe Poplawski	897	Joe Poplawski	56	Bernie Ruoff	136

Grey Cup Playoffs

November 8	Ottawa Rough Riders	21	at	Montreal Alouettes	25
November 9	Calgary Stampeders	14	at	Winnipeg Blue Bombers	32
November 15	Winnipeg Blue Bombers	24	at	Edmonton Eskimos	34
November 16	Montreal Alouettes	13	at	Hamilton Tiger-Cats	24
November 23	Edmonton Eskimos	48		Hamilton Tiger-Cats	10*

*Game played in Toronto

Individual Awards

Annis Stukus Trophy--Ray Jauch (Winnipeg Blue Bombers)
Dave Dryburgh Memorial Trophy--Dave Cutler (Edmonton Eskimos)
DeMarco-Becket Memorial Trophy--Mike Wilson (Edmonton Eskimos)
Dr. Beattie Martin Trophy--Dave Fennell (Edmonton Eskimos)
Eddie James Memorial Trophy--Jimmy Sykes (Calgary Stampeders)
Frank M. Gibson Trophy--Dave Newman (Toronto Argonauts)
Grey Cup Most Outstanding Defensive Star--Dale Potter (Edmonton Eskimos)
Grey Cup Most Outstanding Offensive Star--Warren Moon (Edmonton Eskimos)
Grey Cup Most Valuable Canadian--Dale Potter (Edmonton Eskimos)
Jackie Parker Trophy--William Miller (Winnipeg Blue Bombers)
James P. McCaffrey Trophy--Tom Cousineau (Montreal Alouettes)
Jeff Nicklin Memorial Trophy--Dieter Brock (Winnipeg Blue Bombers)
Jeff Russel Memorial Trophy--Gerry Dattilio (Montreal Alouettes)
Leo Dandurand Trophy--Val Belcher (Ottawa Rough Riders)
Lew Hayman Trophy--Gerry Dattilio (Montreal Alouettes)
Norm Fieldgate Trophy--Dan Kepley (Edmonton Eskimos)
Schenley Award Most Outstanding Canadian--Gerry Dattilio (Montreal Alouettes)
Schenley Award Most Outstanding Defensive Player--Dan Kepley (Edmonton Eskimos)
Schenley Award Most Outstanding Offensive Lineman--Mike Wilson (Edmonton Eskimos)
Schenley Award Most Outstanding Player--Dieter Brock (Winnipeg Blue Bombers)
Schenley Award Most Outstanding Rookie--William Miller (Winnipeg Blue Bombers)

Hall of Fame Inductees

John Metras, Rollie Miles, Virgil Wagner, Harvey Wylie

Notes

The CFL signed a contract with Carling O'Keefe Breweries for $15.6 million dollars to televise CFL games for the 1981 to 1983 seasons.

HOCKEY
National Hockey League

Clarence Campbell Conference
Patrick Division

Team Name	GP	W	L	T	GF	GA	Pts	Pct
Philadelphia Flyers	80	48	12	20	237	237	116	.725
New York Islanders	80	39	28	13	281	247	91	.569
New York Rangers	80	38	32	10	308	284	86	.538
Atlanta Flames	80	35	32	13	282	269	83	.519
Washington Capitals	80	27	40	13	261	293	67	.419

Smythe Division

Team Name	GP	W	L	T	GF	GA	Pts	Pct
Chicago Black Hawks	80	34	27	19	247	250	87	.544
St. Louis Blues	80	34	34	12	266	278	80	.500
Vancouver Canucks	80	27	37	16	256	281	70	.438
Edmonton Oilers	80	28	39	13	301	322	69	.431
Colorado Rockies	80	19	48	13	234	308	51	.319
Winnipeg Jets	80	20	49	11	214	314	51	.319

Prince of Wales Conference

Norris Division

Montreal Canadiens	80	47	20	13	328	240	107	.669
Los Angeles Kings	80	30	36	14	290	313	74	.463
Pittsburgh Penguins	80	30	37	13	251	303	73	.456
Hartford Whalers	80	27	34	19	303	312	73	.456
Detroit Red Wings	80	26	43	11	268	306	63	.394

Adams Division

Buffalo Sabres	80	47	17	16	318	201	110	.688
Boston Bruins	80	46	21	13	310	234	105	.656
Minnesota North Stars	80	36	28	16	311	253	88	.550
Toronto Maple Leafs	80	35	40	5	304	327	75	.469
Quebec Nordiques	80	25	44	11	248	313	61	.381

Coaching Changes

Philadelphia--Pat Quinn 48-12-20; Atlanta--Al MacNeil 35-32-13; Washington--Dan Belisle 4-10-2; Gary Green 23-20-11; Chicago--Ed Johnston 34-27-19; St. Louis--Bob Plager 8-16-4, Gordon "Red" Berenson 26-18-8; Edmonton--Glen Sather 28-39-13; Colorado--Don Cherry 19-48-13; Winnipeg--Tom McVie 20-49-11; Montreal--Bernard Geoffrion 15-9-6, Claude Ruel 32-11-7; Hartford--Don Blackburn 27-34-19; Detroit--Bobby Kromm 24-36-11, Ted Lindsay 2-7-0; Buffalo--Scotty Bowman 47-17-16; Boston--Fred Creighton 40-20-13, Harry Sinden 6-1-0; Minnesota--Glen Sonmor 36-28-16; Toronto--Floyd Smith 30-33-5, Dick Duff 0-2-0, George Imlach 5-5-0; Quebec--Jacques Demers 25-44-11.

League Leaders

Goals		**Assists**		**Points**	
Charlie Simmer	56	Wayne Gretzky	86	Marcel Dionne	137
Danny Gare	56	Marcel Dionne	84	Wayne Gretzky	137
Blaine Stoughton	56	Guy Lafleur	75	Guy Lafleur	125
Marcel Dionne	53	Gil Perreault	66	Gil Perreault	106
Mike Bossy	51	Bryan Trottier	62	Mike Rogers	105

Penalty Minutes		**Plus/Minus**		**GAA** (1,600 minutes)	
Paul Holmgren	267	Jim Schoenfeld	60	Bob Sauve	2.36
Terry O'Reilly	265	Jim Watson	53	Denis Herron	2.51
Terry Ruskowski	252	Ray Bourque	52	Don Edwards	2.57
Paul Mulvey	240	Danny Gare	49	Pete Peeters	2.73
Willi Plett	231	Charlie Simmer	47	Gilles Gilbert	2.73

Wins		**Shutouts**	
Mike Liut	32	Tony Esposito	6
Tony Esposito	31	Bob Sauve	4
Pete Peeters	29	Gerry Cheevers	4
Don Edwards	27	Rogie Vachon	4
Gilles Meloche	27	Glenn Resch	3

All Star Game

(Joe Louis Arena, Detroit)

February 5	Wales Conference	6	Campbell Conference	3

Stanley Cup Playoffs

April 8	Toronto Maple Leafs	3	at	Minnesota North Stars	6
April 8	Edmonton Oilers	3	at	Philadelphia Flyers	4 [8:06]
April 8	St. Louis Blues	2	at	Chicago Black Hawks	3 [12:34]
April 8	Pittsburgh Penguins	4	at	Boston Bruins	2
April 8	Hartford Whalers	1	at	Montreal Canadiens	6
April 8	Los Angeles Kings	1	at	New York Islanders	8
April 8	Atlanta Flames	1	at	New York Rangers	2 [0:33]
April 8	Vancouver Canucks	1	at	Buffalo Sabres	2
April 9	Toronto Maple Leafs	2	at	Minnesota North Stars	7
April 9	Edmonton Oilers	1	at	Philadelphia Flyers	5
April 9	St. Louis Blues	1	at	Chicago Black Hawks	5
April 9	Hartford Whalers	4	at	Montreal Canadiens	8
April 9	Los Angeles Kings	6	at	New York Islanders	3
April 9	Atlanta Flames	1	at	New York Rangers	5
April 9	Vancouver Canucks	0	at	Buffalo Sabres	6
April 10	Pittsburgh Penguins	1	at	Boston Bruins	4
April 11	Minnesota North Stars	4	at	Toronto Maple Leafs	3 [0:32]
April 11	Philadelphia Flyers	3	at	Edmonton Oilers	2 [3:56]
April 11	Chicago Black Hawks	4	at	St. Louis Blues	1
April 11	Montreal Canadiens	4	at	Hartford Whalers	3 [0:291
April 11	New York Islanders	4	at	Los Angeles Kings	3 [6:55]
April 11	New York Rangers	2	at	Atlanta Flames	4
April 11	Buffalo Sabres	4	at	Vancouver Canucks	5
April 12	Boston Bruins	1	at	Pittsburgh Penguins	4
April 12	New York Islanders	6	at	Los Angeles Kings	0
April 12	New York Rangers	5	at	Atlanta Flames	2
April 12	Buffalo Sabres	3	at	Vancouver Canucks	1
April 13	Boston Bruins	8	at	Pittsburgh Penguins	3
April 14	Pittsburgh Penguins	2	at	Boston Bruins	6
April 16	Chicago Black Hawks	0	at	Buffalo Sabres	5
April 16	Minnesota North Stars	3	at	Montreal Canadiens	0
April 16	New York Islanders	2	at	Boston Bruins	1 [1:02]
April 16	New York Islanders	1	at	Philadelphia Flyers	2
April 17	Chicago Black Hawks	4	at	Buffalo Sabres	6
April 17	Minnesota North Stars	4	at	Montreal Canadiens	1
April 17	New York Islanders	5	at	Boston Bruins	4 [1:24]
April 17	New York Rangers	1	at	Philadelphia Flyers	4
April 19	Buffalo Sabres	2	at	Chicago Black Hawks	1
April 19	Montreal Canadiens	5	at	Minnesota North Stars	0
April 19	Boston Bruins	3	at	New York Islanders	5
April 19	Philadelphia Flyers	3	at	New York Rangers	0
April 20	Buffalo Sabres	3	at	Chicago Black Hawks	2
April 20	Montreal Canadiens	5	at	Minnesota North Stars	1
April 20	Philadelphia Flyers	3	at	New York Rangers	4
April 21	Boston Bruins	4	at	New York Islanders	3 [17:13]
April 22	Minnesota North Stars	2	at	Montreal Canadiens	6
April 22	New York Islanders	4	at	Boston Bruins	2
April 22	New York Rangers	1	at	Philadelphia Flyers	3
April 24	Montreal Canadiens	2	at	Minnesota North Stars	5
April 27	Minnesota North Stars	3	at	Montreal Canadiens	2
April 29	Minnesota North Stars	6	at	Philadelphia Flyers	5
April 29	New York Islanders	4	at	Buffalo Sabres	1
May 1	Minnesota North Stars	0	at	Philadelphia Flyers	8

May 1	New York Islanders	2	at	Buffalo Sabres	1 [1:20]
May 3	Buffalo Sabres	4	at	New York Islanders	7
May 4	Philadelphia Flyers	5	at	Minnesota North Stars	3
May 6	Buffalo Sabres	7	at	New York Islanders	4
May 6	Philadelphia Flyers	3	at	Minnesota North Stars	2
May 8	New York Islanders	0	at	Buffalo Sabres	2
May 8	Minnesota North Stars	3	at	Philadelphia Flyers	7
May 10	Buffalo Sabres	2	at	New York Islanders	5
May 13	New York Islanders	4	at	Philadelphia Flyers	3 [4:07]
May 15	New York Islanders	3	at	Philadelphia Flyers	8
May 17	Philadelphia Flyers	2	at	New York Islanders	6
May 19	Philadelphia Flyers	2	at	New York Islanders	5
May 22	New York Islanders	3	at	Philadelphia Flyers	6
May 24	Philadelphia Flyers	4	at	New York Islanders	5 [7:11]

All Star Teams

First Team		Second Team
Tony Esposito	Goal	Don Edwards
Larry Robinson	Defense	Borje Salming
Ray Bourque	Defense	Jim Schoenfeld
Marcel Dionne	Center	Wayne Gretzky
Guy Lafleur	Right Wing	Danny Gare
Charlie Simmer	Left Wing	Steve Shutt

Individual Awards

Art Ross Trophy--Marcel Dionne (Los Angeles Kings)
Bill Masterton Trophy--Al MacAdam (Minnesota North Stars)
Calder Memorial Trophy--Ray Bourque (Boston Bruins)
Conn Smythe Trophy--Bryan Trottier (New York Islanders)
Frank J. Selke Trophy--Bob Gainey (Montreal Canadiens)
Hart Memorial Trophy--Wayne Gretzky (Edmonton Oilers)
Jack Adams Award--Al Arbour (New York Islanders)
James Norris Trophy--Larry Robinson (Montreal Canadiens)
Lady Byng Memorial Trophy--Wayne Gretzky (Edmonton Oilers)
Lester B. Pearson Award--Marcel Dionne (Los Angeles Kings)
Lester Patrick Trophy--Bobby Clarke, Edward M. Snider, Fred Shero, 1980 U.S. Olympic Hockey Team.
NHL All Star Game MVP--Reggie Leach (Philadelphia Flyers)
Vezina Trophy--Bob Sauve and Don Edwards (Buffalo Sabres)

Hall of Fame Inductees

Jack Butterfield, Harry Lumley, Lynn Patrick, Lorne Worsley

Notes

Four former World Hockey Association clubs; the Edmonton Oilers, Hartford Whalers, Winnipeg Jets and Quebec Nordiques were absorbed into the National Hockey League.

SOCCER
North American Soccer League

National Conference
Eastern Division

Team Name	GP	W	L	GF	GA	BP	Pts	Pct
Cosmos	32	24	8	87	41	69	213	.740
Washington Diplomats	32	17	15	72	61	57	159	.552
Toronto Blizzard	32	14	18	49	65	44	128	.444
Rochester Lancers	32	12	20	42	67	37	109	.378
Central Division								
Dallas Tornado	32	18	14	57	58	49	157	.545
Minnesota Kicks	32	16	16	66	56	51	147	.510
Tulsa Roughnecks	32	15	17	56	62	49	139	.483
Atlanta Chiefs	32	7	25	34	84	32	74	.257
Western Division								
Seattle Sounders	32	25	7	74	31	57	207	.719
Los Angeles Aztecs	32	20	12	61	52	54	174	.604
Vancouver Whitecaps	32	16	16	52	47	43	139	.483
Portland Timbers	32	15	17	50	53	43	133	.462

American Conference

Eastern Division

Team Name	GP	W	L	GF	GA	BP	Pts	Pct
Tampa Bay Rowdies	32	19	13	61	50	54	168	.583
Ft. Lauderdale Strikers	32	18	14	61	55	55	163	.566
New England Tea Men	32	18	14	54	56	46	154	.535
Philadelphia Fury	32	10	22	42	68	38	98	.340
Central Division								
Chicago Sting	32	21	11	80	50	61	187	.649
Houston Hurricane	32	14	18	56	69	46	130	.451
Detroit Express	32	14	18	51	52	45	129	.448
Memphis Rogues	32	14	18	49	57	42	126	.438
Western Division								
Edmonton Drillers	32	17	15	58	51	47	149	.517
California Surf	32	15	17	61	67	54	144	.500
San Diego Sockers	32	16	16	53	51	44	140	.486
San Jose Earthquakes	32	9	23	45	68	41	95	.330

Coaching Changes

Cosmos--Hennes Weisweiler 24-8; Rochester--Ray Klivecka 3-4, Alex Perolli 9-16; Minnesota--Freddie Goodwin 14-9, Roy McCrohan 2-7; Tulsa--Charlie Mitchell 15-17; Seattle--Alan Hinton 25-7; Portland--Don Megson 4-6, Pete Warner 11-11; Ft. Lauderdale--Cor van der Hart 18-14; Philadelphia--Eddie Firmani 10-22; Houston--Eckhard Krautzun 14-18; Memphis--Charlie Cooke 14-18; Edmonton--Timo Liekoski 17-15; California--Peter Wall 15-17; San Diego--Hubert Vogelsinger 0-4, Hank Liotart 3-1, Ron Newman 13-11; San Jose--Bill Foulkes 9-23.

League Leaders

Goals		Points		GAA (1,440 minutes)	
Giorgio Chinaglia	32	Giorgio Chinaglia	77	Jack Brand	0.91
Luis Fernando	28	Karl-Heinz Granitza	64	H. Birkenmeier	1.14
Roger Davies	25	Roger Davies	61	Bruce Grobbelaar	1.19
Alan Green	25	Luis Fernando	60	Alfredo Anheilo	1.32
Karl-Heinz Granitza	19	Alan Green	59	Volkmar Gross	1.38

NASL Playoffs

August 27	Seattle Sounders	2	at	Vancouver Whitecaps	1
August 27	Los Angeles Aztecs	0	at	Washington Diplomats	1
August 27	Dallas Tornado	1	at	Minnesota Kicks	0
August 27	Chicago Sting	1	at	San Diego Sockers	2
August 27	Tampa Bay Rowdies	1	at	New England Tea Men	0
August 27	Edmonton Drillers	2	at	Houston Hurricane	1
August 28	Cosmos	3	at	Tulsa Roughnecks	1
August 28	Ft. Lauderdale Strikers	2	at	California Surf	1
August 30	Vancouver Whitecaps	1	at	Seattle Sounders	3
August 30	Washington Diplomats	1	at	Los Angeles Aztecs	2
MINI GAME	Washington Diplomats	0	at	Los Angeles Aztecs	2
August 30	San Diego Sockers	2	at	Chicago Sting	3
MINI GAME	San Diego Sockers	2	at	Chicago Sting	1
August 30	New England Tea Men	0	at	Tampa Bay Rowdies	4
August 31	Minnesota Kicks	0	at	Dallas Tornado	2
August 31	Tulsa Roughnecks	1	at	Cosmos	8
August 31	Houston Hurricane	1	at	Edmonton Drillers	0
MINI GAME	Houston Hurricane	0	at	Edmonton Drillers	1
August 31	California Surf	2	at	Ft. Lauderdale Strikers	0
MINI GAME	California Surf	0	at	Ft. Lauderdale Strikers	1
September 3	Seattle Sounders	0	at	Los Angeles Aztecs	3
September 3	Cosmos	3	at	Dallas Tornado	2
September 3	Ft. Lauderdale Strikers	1	at	Edmonton Drillers	0
September 4	Tampa Bay Rowdies	3	at	San Diego Sockers	6
September 5	Los Angeles Aztecs	0	at	Seattle Sounders	4
MINI GAME	Los Angeles Aztecs	2	at	Seattle Sounders	1
September 6	Edmonton Drillers	3	at	Ft. Lauderdale Strikers	2
MINI GAME	Edmonton Drillers	0	at	Ft. Lauderdale Strikers	2
September 7	Dallas Tornado	3	at	Cosmos	0
MINI GAME	Dallas Tornado	0	at	Cosmos	3
September 7	San Diego Sockers	0	at	Tampa Bay Rowdies	6
MINI GAME	San Diego Sockers	2	at	Tampa Bay Rowdies	1
September 11	Cosmos	2	at	Los Angeles Aztecs	1
September 11	Ft. Lauderdale Strikers	2	at	San Diego Sockers	1
September 13	Los Angeles Aztecs	1	at	Cosmos	3
September 13	San Diego Sockers	4	at	Ft. Lauderdale Strikers	2
MINI GAME	San Diego Sockers	0	at	Ft. Lauderdale Strikers	2
September 21	Cosmos	3	at	Ft. Lauderdale Strikers	0*

*Game played in Washington D.C.

Individual Awards

Coach of the Year--Alan Hinton (Seattle Sounders)
Lead Goalkeeper Award--Jack Brand (Seattle Sounders)
Most Valuable Player--Roger Davies (Seattle Sounders)
North American League Player of the Year--Jack Brand (Seattle Sounders)
Rookie of the Year--Jeff Durgan (New York Cosmos)

Franchise Changes

NBA--New Orleans Jazz became the Utah Jazz.

Other Sports

Horseracing--Kentucky Derby won by Genuine Risk (time 2.02, purse $250,550).
Heavyweight Boxing--Mike Weaver knocked-out John Tate in 15 rounds (WBA).
Golf--U.S. Open won by Jack Nicklaus with a score of 272.
Auto Racing--Indianapolis 500won by Johnny Rutherford (ave. speed 142.862 MPH).
Tennis--U.S. Open won by John McEnroe in the men's singles.
U.S. Open won by Bob Lutz and Stan Smith in the men's doubles.
U.S. Open won by Chris Evert Lloyd in the women's singles.
U.S. Open won by Billie Jean King and Martina Navratilova in the women's doubles.
U.S. Open won by Wendy Turnbull and Marty Riessen in the mixed doubles.

Notes

Genuine Risk became the first filly to win the Kentucky Derby since Regret won it in 1915.
Johnny Rutherford won his 3rd Indianapolis 500.
Chris Evert won her 5th U.S. Open women's singles championship.

1981

BASEBALL
National League
East

First Half

Team Name	W	L	Pct	GB	R	OR
Philadelphia Phillies	34	21	.618	-	249	
St. Louis Cardinals	30	20	.600	1.5	230	
Montreal Expos	30	25	.545	4	229	
Pittsburgh Pirates	25	23	.521	5.5	210	
New York Mets	17	34	.333	15	173	
Chicago Cubs	15	37	.288	17.5	179	

West

Team Name	W	L	Pct	GB	R	OR
Los Angeles Dodgers	36	21	.632	-	235	
Cincinnati Reds	35	21	.625	.5	263	
Houston Astros	28	29	.491	8	195	
Atlanta Braves	25	29	.463	9.5	200	
San Francisco Giants	27	32	.458	10	223	
San Diego Padres	23	33	.411	12.5	194	

Second Half

East

Team Name	W	L	Pct	GB	R	OR
Montreal Expos	30	23	.566	-	214	394
St. Louis Cardinals	29	23	.558	.5	234	417
Philadelphia Phillies	25	27	.481	4.5	242	472
New York Mets	24	28	.462	5.5	175	432
Chicago Cubs	23	28	.451	6	191	483
Pittsburgh Pirates	21	33	.389	9.5	197	394

West

Team Name	W	L	Pct	GB	R	OR
Houston Astros	33	20	.623	-	199	331
Cincinnati Reds	31	21	.596	1.5	201	440
San Francisco Giants	29	23	.588	3.5	204	414
Los Angeles Dodgers	27	26	.509	6	215	356
Atlanta Braves	25	27	.481	7.5	195	416
San Diego Padres	18	36	.333	15.5	188	455

Coaching Changes

Montreal--Dick Williams 44-37, Jim Fanning 16-11; St. Louis--Whitey Herzog 59-43; Chicago--Joey Amalfitano 38-65; San Francisco--Frank Robinson 56-55; San Diego--Frank Howard 41-69.

League Leaders

Batting Average (270 at bats)		Home Runs		RBI	
Bill Madlock	.341	Mike Schmidt	31	Mike Schmidt	91
Pete Rose	.325	Andre Dawson	24	George Foster	90
Dusty Baker	.320	George Foster	22	Bill Buckner	75
Mike Schmidt	.316	Dave Kingman	22	Gary Carter	68
Bill Buckner	.311	George Hendrick	18	Gary Matthews	67

Stolen Bases		ERA (110 innings)		Wins	
Tim Raines	71	Nolan Ryan	1.69	Tom Seaver	14
Omar Moreno	39	Bob Knepper	2.18	Fernando Valenzuela	13
Rodney Scott	30	Burt Hooton	2.28	Steve Carlton	13
Bill North	26	Jerry Reuss	2.29	Steve Rogers	12
Dave Collins	26	Steve Carlton	2.42	Dick Ruthven	12

Saves		Strikeouts	
Bruce Sutter	25	Fernando Valenzuela	180
Greg Minton	21	Steve Carlton	179
Neil Allen	18	Mario Soto	151
Rick Camp	17	Nolan Ryan	140
Tom Hume	13	Bill Gullickson	115

National League Playoffs

October 6	Los Angeles Dodgers	1	at	Houston Astros	3
October 7	Philadelphia Phillies	1	at	Montreal Expos	3
October 7	Los Angeles Dodgers	0	at	Houston Astros	1 [11]
October 8	Philadelphia Phillies	1	at	Montreal Expos	3
October 9	Montreal Expos	2	at	Philadelphia Phillies	6
October 9	Houston Astros	1	at	Los Angeles Dodgers	6
October 10	Montreal Expos	5	at	Philadelphia Phillies	6 [10]
October 10	Houston Astros	1	at	Los Angeles Dodgers	2
October 11	Montreal Expos	3	at	Philadelphia Phillies	0
October 11	Houston Astros	0	at	Los Angeles Dodgers	4
October 13	Montreal Expos	1	at	Los Angeles Dodgers	5
October 14	Montreal Expos	3	at	Los Angeles Dodgers	0
October 16	Los Angeles Dodgers	1	at	Montreal Expos	4
October 17	Los Angeles Dodgers	7	at	Montreal Expos	1
October 19	Los Angeles Dodgers	2	at	Montreal Expos	1

American League
East
First Half

Team Name	W	L	Pct	GB	R	OR
New York Yankees	34	22	.607	-	226	
Baltimore Orioles	31	23	.574	2	227	
Milwaukee Brewers	31	25	.554	3	246	
Detroit Tigers	31	26	.544	3.5	221	
Boston Red Sox	30	26	.536	4	256	
Cleveland Indians	26	24	.520	5	189	
Toronto Blue Jays	16	42	.276	19	186	

West

Oakland Athletics	37	23	.617	-	251
Texas Rangers	33	22	.600	1.5	268
Chicago White Sox	31	22	.585	2.5	250
California Angels	31	29	.517	6	268
Kansas City Royals	20	30	.400	12	181
Seattle Mariners	21	36	.368	14.5	214
Minnesota Twins	17	39	.304	18	180

Second Half

East

Milwaukee Brewers	31	22	.585	-	247	459
Boston Red Sox	29	23	.558	1.5	263	481
Detroit Tigers	29	23	.558	1.5	206	404
Baltimore Orioles	28	23	.549	2	202	437
Cleveland Indians	26	27	.491	5	242	442
New York Yankees	25	26	.490	5	195	343
Toronto Blue Jays	21	27	.438	7.5	143	466

West

Kansas City Royals	30	23	.566	-	216	405
Oakland Athletics	27	22	.551	1	207	403
Texas Rangers	24	26	.480	4.5	184	389
Minnesota Twins	24	29	.453	6	198	486
Seattle Mariners	23	29	.442	6.5	212	521
Chicago White Sox	23	30	.434	7	226	423
California Angels	20	30	.400	8.5	208	453

Coaching Changes

New York--Gene Michael 48-34, Bob Lemon 11-14; Milwaukee--Bob Rodgers 62-47; Boston--Ralph Houk 59-49; Kansas City--Jim Frey 30-40, Dick Howser 20-13; Texas--Don Zimmer 57-48; California--Jim Fregosi 22-25, Gene Mauch 29-34; Seattle--Maury Wills 6-18, Rene Lachemann 38-47; Minnesota--John Goryl 11-25, Bill Gardner 30-43.

League Leaders

Batting Average (270 at bats)		**Home Runs**		**RBI**	
Carney Lansford	.336	Eddie Murray	22	Eddie Murray	78
Kirk Gibson	.328	Dwight Evans	22	Tony Armas	76
Tom Paciorek	.326	Bob Grich	22	Ben Oglivie	72
Cecil Cooper	.320	Tony Armas	22	Dwight Evans	71
Rickey Henderson	.319	Gorman Thomas	21	Dave Winfield	68

Stolen Bases		**ERA** (110 innings)		**Wins**	
Rickey Henderson	56	Steve McCatty	2.32	Dennis Martinez	14
Julio Cruz	43	Sam Stewart	2.33	Jack Morris	14
Ron LeFlore	36	Dennis Lamp	2.41	Pete Vukovich	14
Willie Wilson	34	Tommy John	2.64	Steve McCatty	14
Miguel Dilone	29	Britt Burns	2.64	Scott McGregor	13

Saves		**Strikeouts**	
Rollie Fingers	28	Len Barker	127
Rich Gossage	20	Britt Burns	108
Dan Quisenberry	18	Bert Blyleven	107
Doug Corbett	17	Dennis Leonard	107
Kevin Saucier	13	Ron Guidry	104

All Star Game

(Municipal Stadium, Cleveland)

August 9	National League	5		American League	4

American League Playoffs

October 6	Oakland Athletics	4	at	Kansas City Royals	0
October 7	New York Yankees	5	at	Milwaukee Brewers	3
October 7	Oakland Athletics	2	at	Kansas City Royals	1
October 8	New York Yankees	3	at	Milwaukee Brewers	0
October 9	Milwaukee Brewers	5	at	New York Yankees	3
October 9	Kansas City Royals	1	at	Oakland Athletics	4
October 10	Milwaukee Brewers	2	at	New York Yankees	1
October 11	Milwaukee Brewers	3	at	New York Yankees	7
October 13	Oakland Athletics	1	at	New York Yankees	3
October 14	Oakland Athletics	3	at	New York Yankees	13
October 15	New York Yankees	4	at	Oakland Athletics	0

World Series

October 20	Los Angeles Dodgers	3	at	New York Yankees	5
October 21	Los Angeles Dodgers	0	at	New York Yankees	3
October 23	New York Yankees	4	at	Los Angeles Dodgers	5
October 24	New York Yankees	7	at	Los Angeles Dodgers	8
October 25	New York Yankees	1	at	Los Angeles Dodgers	2
October 28	Los Angeles Dodgers	9	at	New York Yankees	2

Individual Awards

ALCS MVP--Graig Nettles (New York Yankees AL)
Arch Ward Memorial Trophy--Gary Carter (Montreal Expos NL)
Baseball Writers Award--Mike Schmidt (Philadelphia Phillies NL)
Rollie Fingers (Milwaukee Brewers AL)
Cy Young Award--Fernando Valenzuela (Los Angeles Dodgers NL)
Rollie Fingers (Milwaukee Brewers AL)
NLCS MVP--Burt Hooton (Los Angeles Dodgers NL)
Rookie of the Year--Fernando Valenzuela (Los Angeles Dodgers NL)
Dave Righetti (New York Yankees AL)
Sporting News Executive of the Year--John McHale (Montreal Expos NL)
Sporting News Manager of the Year--Billy Martin (Oakland Athletics AL)
Sporting News Player of the Year--Andre Dawson (Montreal Expos NL)
Tony Armas (Oakland Athletics AL)
Sporting News Pitcher of the Year--Fernando Valenzuela (Los Angeles Dodgers NL)
Jack Morris (Detroit Tigers AL)
Sporting News Rookie of the Year--Tim Raines (Montreal Expos NL)
Fernando Valenzuela (Los Angeles Dodgers NL)
Rich Gedman (Boston Red Sox AL)
Dave Righetti (New York Yankees AL)
World Series MVP--Pedro Guerrero, Ron Cey and Steve Yeager (Los Angeles Dodgers NL)

Hall of Fame Inductees

George "Rube" Foster, Bob Gibson, Johnny Mize

Notes

The major league baseball season was interrupted by a seven week long player's strike. The strike was brought on by a dispute over the question of free agents. This was the first time the baseball season had been interrupted in its 106 year history. The first place teams at the time of the strike were declared first half winners and these teams would play a best of five playoff against the winners of the second half and if the same team won the second half as won the first half their opponent would be the team which finished second in the second half.

BASKETBALL
National Basketball Association

Eastern Conference
Atlantic Division

Team Name	GP	W	L	PPGF	PPGA	Pct	GB
Boston Celtics	82	62	20	109.9	104.0	.756	-
Philadelphia 76ers	82	62	20	111.7	103.8	.756	-
New York Knickerbockers	82	50	32	107.9	106.3	.610	12
Washington Bullets	82	39	43	105.6	105.6	.476	23
New Jersey Nets	82	24	58	106.9	113.0	.293	38

Central Division

Team Name	GP	W	L	PPGF	PPGA	Pct	GB
Milwaukee Bucks	82	60	22	113.1	105.9	.732	-
Chicago Bulls	82	45	37	109.0	107.0	.549	15
Indiana Pacers	82	44	38	107.6	106.2	.537	16
Atlanta Hawks	82	31	51	104.9	108.0	.378	29
Cleveland Cavaliers	82	28	54	105.7	110.6	.341	32
Detroit Pistons	82	21	61	99.7	106.0	.256	39

Western Conference

Midwest Division

Team Name	GP	W	L	PPGF	PPGA	Pct	GB
San Antonio Spurs	82	52	30	112.3	109.4	.634	-
Houston Rockets	82	40	42	108.3	107.9	.488	12
Kansas City Kings	82	40	42	106.9	106.9	.488	12
Denver Nuggets	82	37	45	121.8	122.3	.451	15
Utah Jazz	82	28	54	101.2	107.1	.341	24
Dallas Mavericks	82	15	67	101.5	109.9	.183	37

Pacific Division

Team Name	GP	W	L	PPGF	PPGA	Pct	GB
Phoenix Suns	82	57	25	110.0	104.5	.695	-
Los Angeles Lakers	82	54	28	111.2	107.3	.659	3
Portland Trail Blazers	82	45	37	110.7	109.8	.549	12
Golden State Warriors	82	39	43	109.8	111.0	.476	18
San Diego Clippers	82	36	46	106.5	108.1	.439	21
Seattle SuperSonics	82	34	48	104.0	105.7	.415	23

Coaching Changes

Washington--Gene Shue 39-43; New Jersey--Kevin Loughery 12-23, Bob MacKinnon 12-35; Indiana--Jack McKinney 44-38; Atlanta--Hubert Brown 31-48, Mike Fratello/Brendan Suhr 0-3; Cleveland--Bill Musselman 25-46, Don Delaney 3-8; Detroit--Scott Robertson 21-61; San Antonio--Stan Albeck 52-30; Denver--Donnie Walsh 11-20, Doug Moe 26-25; Dallas--Dick Motta 15-67; Los Angeles--Paul Westhead 54-28; Golden State--Al Attles 39-43; San Diego--Paul Silas 36-46.

League Leaders

Field Goals		Free Throws		Assists	
Adrian Dantley	909	Adrian Dantley	632	Kevin Porter	734
Mike Mitchell	853	Moses Malone	609	Norm Nixon	696
George Gervin	850	Lloyd Free	528	M.R. Richardson	627
Kareem Abdul-Jabbar	836	George Gervin	512	Nate Archibald	618
Moses Malone	806	David Thompson	489	Phil Ford	580

Points		Rebounds Per Game	
Adrian Dantley	2452	Moses Malone	14.8
Moses Malone	2222	Swen Nater	12.4
George Gervin	2221	Larry Smith	12.1
Kareem Abdul-Jabbar	2095	Larry Bird	10.9
Julius Erving	2014	Jack Sikma	10.4

All Star Game

(The Coliseum, Richfield, Ohio)

February 1	East Division	123	West Division	120

NBA Playoffs

Date	Team	Score		Team	Score
March 31	Chicago Bulls	90	at	N.Y. Knickerbockers	80
March 31	Indiana Pacers	108	at	Philadelphia 76ers	124
April 1	Houston Rockets	111	at	Los Angeles Lakers	107
April 1	Kansas City Kings	98	at	Portland Trail Blazers	97 [OT]
April 2	Philadelphia 76ers	96	at	Indiana Pacers	85
April 3	N.Y. Knickerbockers	114	at	Chicago Bulls	115 [OT]
April 3	Los Angeles Lakers	111	at	Houston Rockets	106
April 3	Portland Trail Blazers	124	at	Kansas City Kings	119 [OT]
April 5	Houston Rockets	89	at	Los Angeles Lakers	86
April 5	Kansas City Kings	104	at	Portland Trail Blazers	95
April 5	Milwaukee Bucks	122	at	Philadelphia 76ers	125
April 5	Chicago Bulls	109	at	Boston Celtics	121
April 7	Kansas City Kings	80	at	Phoenix Suns	102
April 7	Houston Rockets	107	at	San Antonio Spurs	98
April 7	Milwaukee Bucks	109	at	Philadelphia 76ers	99
April 7	Chicago Bulls	97	at	Boston Celtics	106
April 8	Kansas City Kings	88	at	Phoenix Suns	83
April 8	Houston Rockets	113	at	San Antonio Spurs	125
April 10	Philadelphia 76ers	108	at	Milwaukee Bucks	103
April 10	Boston Celtics	113	at	Chicago Bulls	107
April 10	Phoenix Suns	92	at	Kansas City Kings	93
April 10	San Antonio Spurs	99	at	Houston Rockets	112
April 12	Philadelphia 76ers	98	at	Milwaukee Bucks	109
April 12	Boston Celtics	109	at	Chicago Bulls	103

April 12	Phoenix Suns	95	at	Kansas City Kings	102
April 12	San Antonio Spurs	114	at	Houston Rockets	112
April 14	Houston Rockets	123	at	San Antonio Spurs	117
April 15	Milwaukee Bucks	99	at	Philadelphia 76ers	116
April 15	Kansas City Kings	89	at	Phoenix Suns	101
April 15	San Antonio Spurs	101	at	Houston Rockets	96
April 17	Philadelphia 76ers	86	at	Milwaukee Bucks	109
April 17	Phoenix Suns	81	at	Kansas City Kings	76
April 17	Houston Rockets	105	at	San Antonio Spurs	100
April 19	Milwaukee Bucks	98	at	Philadelphia 76ers	99
April 19	Kansas City Kings	95	at	Phoenix Suns	88
April 21	Philadelphia 76ers	105	at	Boston Celtics	104
April 21	Houston Rockets	97	at	Kansas City Kings	78
April 22	Philadelphia 76ers	99	at	Boston Celtics	118
April 22	Houston Rockets	79	at	Kansas City Kings	88
April 24	Boston Celtics	100	at	Philadelphia 76ers	110
April 24	Kansas City Kings	88	at	Houston Rockets	92
April 26	Boston Celtics	105	at	Philadelphia 76ers	107
April 26	Kansas City Kings	89	at	Houston Rockets	100
April 29	Houston Rockets	97	at	Kansas City Kings	88
April 29	Philadelphia 76ers	109	at	Boston Celtics	111
May 1	Boston Celtics	100	at	Philadelphia 76ers	98
May 3	Philadelphia 76ers	90	at	Boston Celtics	91
May 5	Houston Rockets	95	at	Boston Celtics	98
May 7	Houston Rockets	92	at	Boston Celtics	90
May 9	Boston Celtics	94	at	Houston Rockets	71
May 10	Boston Celtics	86	at	Houston Rockets	91
May 12	Houston Rockets	80	at	Boston Celtics	109
May 14	Boston Celtics	102	at	Houston Rockets	91

All Star Teams

First Team	Second Team
Julius Erving (Philadelphia 76ers)	Marques Johnson (Milwaukee Bucks)
Larry Bird (Boston Celtics)	Adrian Dantley (Utah Jazz)
Kareem Abdul-Jabbar (Los Angeles Lakers)	Moses Malone (Houston Rockets)
George Gervin (San Antonio Spurs)	Otis Birdsong (Kansas City Kings)
Dennis Johnson (Phoenix Suns)	Nate Archibald (Boston Celtics)

Individual Awards

Eddie Gottlieb Trophy--Darrell Griffith (Utah Jazz)
Executive of the Year--Jerry Colangelo (Phoenix Suns)
J. Walter Kennedy Citizenship Award--Mike Glenn (New York Knickerbockers)
Maurice Podoloff Trophy--Julius Erving (Philadelphia 76ers)
NBA All Star Game MVP--Nate Archibald (Boston Celtics)
NBA Finals MVP--Cedric Maxwell (Boston Celtics)
Red Auerbach Trophy--Jack McKinney (Indiana Pacers)

Hall of Fame Inductees

Everett Case, Al Duer, Clarence Gaines, Hal Greer, Slater Martin, Frank Ramsey, Willis Reed

FOOTBALL
National Football League

National Conference
Eastern Division

Team Name	GP	W	L	T	PF	PA	Pct
Dallas Cowboys	16	12	4	0	367	277	.750
Philadelphia Eagles	16	10	6	0	368	221	.625
New York Giants	16	9	7	0	295	257	.563
Washington Redskins	16	8	8	0	347	349	.500
St. Louis Cardinals	16	7	9	0	315	408	.438

Central Division

Team Name	GP	W	L	T	PF	PA	Pct
Tampa Bay Buccaneers	16	9	7	0	315	268	.563
Detroit Lions	16	8	8	0	397	322	.500
Green Bay Packers	16	8	8	0	324	361	.500
Minnesota Vikings	16	7	9	0	325	369	.438
Chicago Bears	16	6	10	0	253	324	.375

Western Division

Team Name	GP	W	L	T	PF	PA	Pct
San Francisco 49ers	16	13	3	0	357	250	.813
Atlanta Falcons	16	7	9	0	426	355	.438
Los Angeles Rams	16	6	10	0	303	351	.375
New Orleans Saints	16	4	12	0	207	378	.250

American Conference

Eastern Division

Team Name	GP	W	L	T	PF	PA	Pct
Miami Dolphins	16	11	4	1	345	275	.719
New York Jets	16	10	5	1	355	287	.656
Buffalo Bills	16	10	6	0	311	276	.625
Baltimore Colts	16	2	14	0	259	533	.125
New England Patriots	16	2	14	0	322	370	.125

Central Division

Team Name	GP	W	L	T	PF	PA	Pct
Cincinnati Bengals	16	12	4	0	421	304	.750
Pittsburgh Steelers	16	8	8	0	356	297	.500
Houston Oilers	16	7	9	0	281	355	.438
Cleveland Browns	16	5	11	0	276	375	.313

Western Division

Team Name	GP	W	L	T	PF	PA	Pct
San Diego Chargers	16	10	6	0	478	390	.625
Denver Broncos	16	10	6	0	321	289	.625
Kansas City Chiefs	16	9	7	0	343	290	.563
Oakland Raiders	16	7	9	0	273	343	.438
Seattle Seahawks	16	6	10	0	322	388	.375

Coaching Changes

Washington--Joe Gibbs 8-8-0; New Orleans--"Bum" Phillips 4-12-0; Houston--Ed Biles 7-9-0; Denver--Dan Reeves 10-6-0.

League Leaders

Yards Rushing		Yards Passing		Passing % (300 attempts)	
George Rogers	1674	Dan Fouts	4802	Joe Montana	63.7
Tony Dorsett	1646	Tom Kramer	3912	Ken Anderson	62.6
Billy Sims	1437	Brian Sipe	3876	Craig Morton	59.8
Wilbert Montgomery	1402	Steve Bartkowski	3829	Jim Zorn	59.4
Ottis Anderson	1376	Ken Anderson	3754	Dan Fouts	59.1

Receiving Yards		Receptions		Field Goals	
Alfred Jenkins	1354	Kellen Winslow	88	Rafael Septien	27
James Lofton	1294	Dwight Clark	85	Nick Lowery	26
Frank Lewis	1244	Ted Brown	83	Pat Leahy	25
Steve Largent	1224	William Andrews	81	Ed Murray	25
Charlie Joiner	1188	Joe Senser	79	Uwe von Schamann	24

Punt Return Yards		Kickoff Return Yards	
LeRoy Irvin	615	Stump Mitchell	1292
Frank Smith	528	Reg Smith	1143
Jeff Fisher	509	Mike Nelms	1099
Mike Nelms	492	James Brooks	949
Rob Martin	450	Fulton Walker	932

Pro Bowl Game

January 31 1982	American Conference	16	National Conference	13

NFL Playoffs

December 27	New York Giants	27	at	Philadelphia Eagles	21
December 27	Buffalo Bills	31	at	New York Jets	27
January 2 1982	Tampa Bay Buccaneers	0	at	Dallas Cowboys	38
January 2 1982	San Diego Chargers	41	at	Miami Dolphins	38 [OT]
January 3 1982	New York Giants	24	at	San Francisco 49ers	38
January 3 1982	Buffalo Bills	21	at	Cincinnati Bengals	28
January 10 1982	Dallas Cowboys	27	at	San Francisco	28
January 10 1982	San Diego Chargers	7	at	Cincinnati Bengals	27

Super Bowl XVI

(Pontiac Silverdome, Pontiac, Michigan)

January 24 1982	San Francisco 49ers	26	Cincinnati Bengals	21

Individual Awards

A.P. MVP--Ken Anderson (Cincinnati Bengals)
Bert Bell Trophy--Lawrence Taylor (New York Giants) [World Almanac]
Bert Bell Trophy--Ken Anderson (Cincinnati Bengals)
George Halas Trophy--Joe Klecko (New York Jets)
Jim Thorpe Trophy--Ken Anderson (Cincinnati Bengals)
P.F.W.A. MVP--Ken Anderson (Cincinnati Bengals)
Pro Bowl MVP--Kellen Winslow (San Diego Chargers)
Lee Roy Selmon (Tampa Bay Buccaneers)
Super Bowl MVP--Joe Montana (San Francisco 49ers)

U.P.I. AFC Coach of the Year--Forrest Gregg (Cincinnati Bengals)
U.P.I. AFC Player of the Year--Ken Anderson (Cincinnati Bengals)
U.P.I. AFC Rookie of the Year--Joe Delaney (Kansas City Chiefs)
U.P.I. NFC Coach of the Year--Bill Walsh (San Francisco 49ers)
U.P.I. NFC Player of the Year--Tony Dorsett (Dallas Cowboys)
U.P.I. NFC Rookie of the Year--George Rogers (New Orleans Saints)

Hall of Fame Inductees

Red Badgro, George Blanda, Willie Davis, Jim Ringo,

Notes

The National Football League owners adopted a disaster plan in the event a team was to be involved in a fatal accident.

Canadian Football League
Eastern Conference

Team Name	GP	W	L	T	PF	PA	Pts	Pct
Hamilton Tiger-Cats	16	11	4	1	414	335	23	.719
Ottawa Rough Riders	16	5	11	0	306	446	10	.313
Montreal Alouettes	16	3	13	0	267	518	6	.188
Toronto Argonauts	16	2	14	0	241	506	4	.125
Western Division								
Edmonton Eskimos	16	14	1	1	576	277	29	.906
Winnipeg Blue Bombers	16	11	5	0	517	299	22	.688
British Columbia Lions	16	10	6	0	438	377	20	.625
Saskatchewan Roughriders	16	9	7	0	431	371	18	.563
Calgary Stampeders	16	6	10	0	306	367	12	.375

Coaching Changes

Hamilton--Frank Kush 11-4-1; Montreal--Joe Scanella 1-9-0 , Jim Eddy 2-4-0; Toronto--Willie Wood 0-10-0, Tom Hudspeth 2-4-0; Saskatchewan--Joe Faragalli 9-7-0; Calgary--Ardell Wiegandt 6-7-0, Jerry Williams 0-3-0.

League Leaders

Yards Rushing		Yards Passing		Passing % (200 attempts)	
James Sykes	1107	Dieter Brock	4796	Warren Moon	62.7
Larry Key	1098	Tom Clements	4536	Dieter Brock	62.5
Dave Overstreet	952	Warren Moon	3959	Jordan Case	61.7
Jim Germany	861	Joe Paopao	3777	Ken Johnson	59.3
Cedric Minter	815	Ken Johnson	3364	Tom Clements	57.5

Receiving Yards		Receptions		Points	
Joey Walters	1715	Eugene Goodlow	100	Trevor Kennerd	185
Brian Kelly	1665	Joey Walters	91	Dave Cutler	175
Eugene Goodlow	1494	Joe Poplawski	84	Bernie Ruoff	152
Tyron Gray	1428	James Scott	81	Lui Passaglia	144
James Scott	1422	Brian Kelly	74	J.T. Hay	141

Grey Cup Playoffs

November 8	Montreal Alouettes	16	at	Ottawa Rough Riders	20
November 8	British Columbia Lions	15	at	Winnipeg Blue Bombers	11
November 15	Ottawa Rough Riders	17	at	Hamilton Tiger-Cats	13
November 15	British Columbia Lions	16	at	Edmonton Eskimos	22
November 22	Edmonton Eskimos	26	at	Ottawa Rough Riders	23*

Individual Awards

Annis Stukus Trophy--Joe Faragalli (Saskatchewan Roughriders)
Dave Dryburgh Memorial Trophy--Trevor Kennerd (Winnipeg Blue Bombers)
DeMarco-Becket Memorial Trophy--Larry Butler (Winnipeg Blue Bombers)
Dr. Beattie Martin Trophy--Joe Poplawski (Winnipeg Blue Bombers)
Eddie James Memorial Trophy--Jimmy Sykes (Calgary Stampeders)
Frank M. Gibson Trophy--Cedric Minter (Toronto Argonauts)
Grey Cup Most Outstanding Defensive Star--John Glassford (Ottawa Rough Riders)
Grey Cup Most Outstanding Offensive Star--J.C. Watts (Ottawa Rough Riders)
Grey Cup Most Outstanding Canadian--Neil Lumsden (Edmonton Eskimos)
Jackie Parker Trophy--Vince Goldsmith (Saskatchewan Roughriders)
James P. McCaffrey Trophy--Ben Zambiasi (Hamilton Tiger-Cats)
Jeff Nicklin Memorial Trophy--Dieter Brock (Winnipeg Blue Bombers)
Jeff Russel Memorial Trophy--Tom Clements (Hamilton Tiger-Cats)
Leo Dandurand Trophy--Val Belcher (Ottawa Rough Riders)
Lew Hayman Trophy--Tony Gabriel (Ottawa Rough Riders)
Norm Fieldgate Trophy--Dan Kepley (Edmonton Eskimos)
Schenley Award Most Outstanding Canadian--Joe Poplawski (Winnipeg Blue Bombers)
Schenley Award Most Outstanding Defensive Player--Dan Kepley (Edmonton Eskimos)
Schenley Award Most Outstanding Offensive Lineman--Larry Butler (Winnipeg Blue Bombers)
Schenley Award Most Outstanding Player--Dieter Brock (Winnipeg Blue Bombers)
Schenley Award Most Outstanding Rookie--Vince Goldsmith (Saskatchewan Roughriders)

Hall of Fame Inductees

Frank Clair, Eric Duggan, Gerry James, John O'Quinn

Notes

The Eastern and Western Conferences were officially dissolved but the East and West playing divisions were adopted. The teams played a complete inter-locking schedule for the first time.

HOCKEY
National Hockey League

Clarence Campbell Conference
Patrick Division

Team Name	GP	W	L	T	GF	GA	Pts	Pct
New York Islanders	80	48	18	14	355	260	110	.688
Philadelphia Flyers	80	41	24	15	313	249	97	.606
Calgary Flames	80	39	27	14	329	298	92	.575
New York Rangers	80	30	36	14	312	317	74	.463
Washington Capitals	80	26	36	18	286	317	70	.438

*Game played in Montreal

Smythe Division

St. Louis Blues	80	45	18	17	352	281	107	.669
Chicago Black Hawks	80	31	33	16	304	315	78	.488
Vancouver Canucks	80	28	32	20	289	301	76	.475
Edmonton Oilers	80	29	35	16	328	327	74	.463
Colorado Rockies	80	22	45	13	258	344	57	.356
Winnipeg Jets	80	9	57	14	246	400	32	.200

Prince of Wales Conference

Norris Division

Montreal Canadiens	80	45	22	13	332	232	103	.644
Los Angeles Kings	80	43	24	13	337	290	99	.619
Pittsburgh Penguins	80	30	37	13	302	345	73	.456
Hartford Whalers	80	21	41	18	292	372	60	.375
Detroit Red Wings	80	19	43	18	252	339	56	.350

Adams Division

Buffalo Sabres	80	39	20	21	237	250	99	.619
Boston Bruins	80	37	30	13	316	272	87	.544
Minnesota North Stars	80	35	28	17	291	263	87	.544
Quebec Nordiques	80	30	32	18	314	318	78	.488
Toronto Maple Leafs	80	28	37	15	322	367	71	.444

Coaching Changes

Calgary--Al MacNeil 39-27-14; Rangers--Fred Shero 4-13-4, Craig Patrick 26-23-10; Washington--Gary Green 26-36-18; St. Louis--Gordon "Red" Berenson 45-18-17; Chicago--Keith Magnuson 31-33-16; Edmonton--Bryan Watson 4-9-5, Glen Sather 25-26-11; Colorado--Billy MacMillan 22-45-13; Winnipeg--Tom McVie 1-20-7, Bill Sutherland 8-37-7; Montreal--Claude Ruel 45-22-13; Pittsburgh--Eddie Johnston 30-37-13; Hartford--Don Blackburn 15-29-16, Larry Pleau 6-12-2; Detroit--Ted Lindsay 3-14-3, Wayne Maxner 16-29-15; Buffalo--Roger Neilson 39-20-21; Boston--Gerry Cheevers 37-30-13; Quebec--Maurice Filion 1-3-2, Michel Bergeron 29-29-16; Toronto--Joe Crozier 13-22-5, Mike Nykoluk 15-15-10.

League Leaders

Goals		**Assists**		**Points**	
Mike Bossy	68	Wayne Gretzky	109	Wayne Gretzky	164
Marcel Dionne	58	Kent Nilsson	82	Marcel Dionne	135
Charlie Simmer	56	Marcel Dionne	77	Kent Nilsson	131
Wayne Gretzky	55	Bernie Federko	73	Mike Bossy	119
Rick Kehoe	55	Bryan Trottier	72	Dave Taylor	112

Penalty Minutes		**Plus/Minus**		**GAA** (1,600 minutes)	
Dave Williams	343	Marcel Dionne	17.0	Richard Sevigny	2.40
Paul Holmgren	306	Dave Taylor	15.3	Don Edwards	2.96
Chris Nilan	262	Wayne Gretzky	14.9	Pete Peeters	2.96
Jim Korn	246	Mark Howe	14.7	Glenn Resch	3.07
Behn Wilson	237	Brian Engblom	13.4	Bob Sauve	3.17

Wins		**Shutouts**	
Mario Lessard	35	Don Edwards	3
Mike Liut	33	Glenn Resch	3
Tony Esposito	29	Pete Peeters	2
Greg Millen	25	Mario Lessard	2
Rogie Vachon	25	Billy Smith	2

All Star Game

(The Forum, Los Angeles)

February 10	Campbell Conference	4	Wales Conference	1

Stanley Cup Playoffs

April 8	Minnesota North Stars	5	at	Boston Bruins	4 [3:34]
April 8	Pittsburgh Penguins	2	at	St. Louis Blues	4
April 8	Quebec Nordiques	4	at	Philadelphia Flyers	6
April 8	Vancouver Canucks	2	at	Buffalo Sabres	3 [5:00]
April 8	Chicago Black Hawks	3	at	Calgary Flames	4
April 8	Edmonton Oilers	6	at	Montreal Canadiens	3
April 8	Toronto Maple Leafs	2	at	New York Islanders	9
April 8	New York Rangers	3	at	Los Angeles Kings	1
April 9	Pittsburgh Penguins	6	at	St. Louis Blues	4
April 9	Quebec Nordiques	5	at	Philadelphia Flyers	8
April 9	Vancouver Canucks	2	at	Buffalo Sabres	5
April 9	Chicago Black Hawks	2	at	Calgary Flames	6
April 9	Minnesota North Stars	9	at	Boston Bruins	6
April 9	Edmonton Oilers	3	at	Montreal Canadiens	1
April 9	Toronto Maple Leafs	1	at	New York Islanders	5
April 9	New York Rangers	4	at	Los Angeles Kings	5
April 11	St. Louis Blues	5	at	Pittsburgh Penguins	4
April 11	Philadelphia Flyers	0	at	Quebec Nordiques	2
April 11	Buffalo Sabres	5	at	Vancouver Canucks	3
April 11	Boston Bruins	3	at	Minnesota North Stars	6
April 11	Calgary Flames	5	at	Chicago Black Hawks	4 [35:17]
April 11	Montreal Canadiens	2	at	Edmonton Oilers	6
April 11	New York Islanders	6	at	Toronto Maple Leafs	1
April 11	Los Angeles Kings	3	at	New York Rangers	10
April 12	St. Louis Blues	3	at	Pittsburgh Penguins	6
April 12	Philadelphia Flyers	3	at	Quebec Nordiques	4 [0:37]
April 12	Los Angeles Kings	3	at	New York Rangers	6
April 14	Pittsburgh Penguins	3	at	St. Louis Blues	4 [5:16]
April 14	Quebec Nordiques	2	at	Philadelphia Flyers	5
April 16	Minnesota North Stars	4	at	Buffalo Sabres	3 [0:22]
April 16	Calgary Flames	0	at	Philadelphia Flyers	4
April 16	Edmonton Oilers	2	at	New York Islanders	8
April 16	New York Rangers	3	at	St. Louis Blues	6
April 17	Minnesota North Stars	5	at	Buffalo Sabres	2
April 17	Calgary Flames	5	at	Philadelphia Flyers	4
April 17	Edmonton Oilers	3	at	New York Islanders	6
April 17	New York Rangers	6	at	St. Louis Blues	4
April 19	Buffalo Sabres	4	at	Minnesota North Stars	6
April 19	Philadelphia Flyers	1	at	Calgary Flames	2
April 19	New York Islanders	2	at	Edmonton Oilers	5
April 19	St. Louis Blues	3	at	New York Rangers	6

April 20	Buffalo Sabres	5	at	Minnesota North Stars	4 [16:32]
April 20	Philadelphia Flyers	4	at	Calgary Flames	5
April 20	New York Islanders	5	at	Edmonton Oilers	4 [5:41]
April 20	St. Louis Blues	1	at	New York Rangers	4
April 22	Minnesota North Stars	4	at	Buffalo Sabres	3
April 22	Calgary Flames	4	at	Philadelphia Flyers	9
April 22	Edmonton Oilers	4	at	New York Islanders	3
April 22	New York Rangers	3	at	St. Louis Blues	4
April 24	Philadelphia Flyers	3	at	Calgary Flames	2
April 24	New York Islanders	5	at	Edmonton Oilers	2
April 24	St. Louis Blues	4	at	New York Rangers	7
April 26	Calgary Flames	4	at	Philadelphia Flyers	1
April 28	New York Rangers	2	at	New York Islanders	5
April 28	Minnesota North Stars	4	at	Calgary Flames	1
April 30	New York Rangers	3	at	New York Islanders	7
April 30	Minnesota North Stars	2	at	Calgary Flames	3
May 2	New York Islanders	5	at	New York Rangers	1
May 3	Calgary Flames	4	at	Minnesota North Stars	6
May 5	New York Islanders	5	at	New York Rangers	2
May 5	Calgary Flames	4	at	Minnesota North Stars	7
May 7	Minnesota North Stars	1	at	Calgary Flames	3
May 9	Calgary Flames	3	at	Minnesota North Stars	5
May 12	Minnesota North Stars	3	at	New York Islanders	6
May 14	Minnesota North Stars	3	at	New York Islanders	6
May 17	New York Islanders	7	at	Minnesota North Stars	5
May 19	New York Islanders	2	at	Minnesota North Stars	4
May 21	Minnesota North Stars	1	at	New York Islanders	5

All Star Teams

First Team		Second Team
Mike Liut	Goal	Mario Lessard
Denis Potvin	Defense	Larry Robinson
Randy Carlyle	Defense	Ray Bourque
Wayne Gretzky	Center	Marcel Dionne
Mike Bossy	Right Wing	Dave Taylor
Charlie Simmer	Left Wing	Bill Barber

Individual Awards

Art Ross Trophy--Wayne Gretzky (Edmonton Oilers)
Bill Masterton Trophy--Blake Dunlop (St. Louis Blues)
Calder Memorial Trophy--Peter Stastny (Quebec Nordiques)
Conn Smythe Trophy--Robert Goring (New York Islanders)
Frank J. Selke Trophy--Bob Gainey (Montreal Canadiens)
Hart Memorial Trophy--Wayne Gretzky (Edmonton Oilers)
Jack Adams Award--Gordon Berenson (St. Louis Blues)
James Norris Trophy--Randy Carlyle (Pittsburgh Penguins)
Lady Byng Memorial Trophy--Rick Kehoe (Pittsburgh Penguins)
Lester B. Pearson Award--Mike Liut (St. Louis Blues)
Lester Patrick Trophy--Charles M. Schulz
NHL All Star Game MVP--Mike Liut (St. Louis Blues)
Vezina Trophy--Richard Sevigny and Denis Herron and Michel Larocque (Montreal Canadiens)

Hall of Fame Inductees

John Ashley, John Bucyk, Frank Mahovlich, Allan Stanley

SOCCER

North American Soccer League

Eastern Division

Team Name	GP	W	L	GF	GA	BP	Pts	Pct
Cosmos	32	23	9	80	49	64	200	.417
Montreal Manic	32	15	17	63	57	55	141	.294
Washington Diplomats	32	15	17	59	58	51	135	.281
Toronto Blizzard	32	7	25	39	82	37	77	.160

Northwest Division

Team Name	GP	W	L	GF	GA	BP	Pts	Pct
Vancouver Whitecaps	32	21	11	74	43	62	186	.388
Calgary Boomers	32	17	15	59	54	51	151	.315
Portland Timbers	32	17	15	52	49	45	141	.294
Seattle Sounders	32	15	17	60	62	51	137	.285
Edmonton Drillers	32	12	20	60	79	51	123	.256

Southern Division

Team Name	GP	W	L	GF	GA	BP	Pts	Pct
Atlanta Chiefs	32	17	15	62	60	53	151	.315
Ft. Lauderdale Strikers	32	18	14	54	46	44	144	.300
Jacksonville Teamen	32	18	14	51	46	41	141	.294
Tampa Bay Rowdies	32	15	17	63	64	53	139	.290

Central Division

Team Name	GP	W	L	GF	GA	BP	Pts	Pct
Chicago Sting	32	23	9	84	50	63	195	.406
Minnesota Kicks	32	19	13	63	57	55	163	.340
Tulsa Roughnecks	32	17	15	60	49	54	154	.321
Dallas Tornado	32	5	27	27	71	26	54	.113

Western Division

Team Name	GP	W	L	GF	GA	BP	Pts	Pct
San Diego Sockers	32	21	11	68	49	55	173	.360
Los Angeles Aztecs	32	19	13	53	55	48	160	.333
California Surf	32	11	21	60	77	51	117	.244
San Jose Earthquakes	32	11	21	44	78	42	108	.225

Coaching Changes

Montreal--Eddie Firmani 15-17; Washington--Ken Furphy 15-17; Vancouver--John Giles 21-11; Calgary--Al Miller 17-15; Portland--Vic Crowe 7-15; Atlanta--Dave Chadwick 17-15; Ft. Lauderdale--Eckhard Krautzun 18-14; Minnesota--Freddie Goodwin 19-13; Dallas--Mike Renshaw 5-27; San Diego--Ron Newman 21-11; Los Angeles--Claudio Coutinho 19-13; San Jose--Jim Gabriel 11-21; Jacksonville--Noel Cantwell 18-14.

League Leaders

Goals		Points		GAA (1,440 minutes)	
Giorgio Chinaglia	29	Giorgio Chinaglia	74	Arnie Mausser	1.21
Mike Stojanovic	23	Karl-Heinz Granitza	55	Jan van Beveren	1.29
Brian Kidd	22	Mike Stojanovic	52	Barry Siddall	1.30
Franz Gerber	20	Brian Kidd	52	Zeljko Bilecki	1.33
Karl-Heinz Granitza	19	Franz Gerber	50	Volkmar Gross	1.36

NASL Playoffs

August 22	Minnesota Kicks	3	at	Tulsa Roughnecks	1
August 22	San Diego Sockers	1	at	Portland Timbers	2
August 23	Vancouver Whitecaps	1	at	Tampa Bay Rowdies	4
August 23	Calgary Boomers	1	at	Ft. Lauderdale Strikers	3
August 23	Seattle Sounders	2	at	Chicago Sting	3
August 23	Atlanta Chiefs	2	at	Jacksonville Teamen	3
August 24	Los Angeles Aztecs	3	at	Montreal Manic	5
August 25	Jacksonville Teamen	2	at	Atlanta Chiefs	1
August 26	Tampa Bay Rowdies	1	at	Vancouver Whitecaps	0
August 26	Ft. Lauderdale Strikers	2	at	Calgary Boomers	0
August 26	Tulsa Roughnecks	0	at	Minnesota Kicks	1
August 26	Chicago Sting	0	at	Seattle Sounders	2
August 26	Portland Timbers	1	at	San Diego Sockers	5
August 27	Montreal Manic	2	at	Los Angeles Aztecs	3
August 30	Seattle Sounders	2	at	Chicago Sting	3
August 30	Montreal Manic	2	at	Los Angeles Aztecs	1
August 30	San Diego Sockers	2	at	Portland Timbers	0
September 2	Cosmos	6	at	Tampa Bay Rowdies	3
September 2	Minnesota Kicks	1	at	Ft. Lauderdale Strikers	3
September 2	Chicago Sting	2	at	Montreal Manic	3
September 2	San Diego Sockers	1	at	Jacksonville Teamen	2
September 5	Tampa Bay Rowdies	3	at	Cosmos	2
September 5	Montreal Manic	2	at	Chicago Sting	4
September 6	Ft. Lauderdale Strikers	3	at	Minnesota Kicks	0
September 6	Jacksonville Teamen	1	at	San Diego Sockers	2
September 9	Cosmos	2	at	Tampa Bay Rowdies	0
September 9	San Diego Sockers	3	at	Jacksonville Teamen	1
September 10	Montreal Manic	2	at	Chicago Sting	4
September 14	Cosmos	4	at	Ft. Lauderdale Strikers	3
September 14	Chicago Sting	1	at	San Diego Sockers	2
September 16	Ft. Lauderdale Strikers	1	at	Cosmos	4
September 16	San Diego Sockers	1	at	Chicago Sting	2
September 21	San Diego Sockers	0	at	Chicago Sting	1
September 26	Chicago Sting	1		Cosmos	0*

Individual Awards

Lead Goalkeeper Award--Arnie Mausser (Jacksonville Teamen)
NASL Final MVP--Frantz Mathieu (Chicago Sting)
Most Valuable Player--Giorgio Chinaglia (New York Cosmos)
North American Player of the Year--Mike Stojanovic (San Diego Sockers)
Rookie of the Year--Joe Morrone (Tulsa Roughnecks)

Franchise Changes

NHL--Atlanta Flames became the Calgary Flames.
NASL--Philadelphia Fury became the Montreal Manic.
Memphis Rogues became the Calgary Boomers.
New England Teamen became the Jacksonville Teamen.

*Game played in Toronto

Other Sports

Horseracing--Kentucky Derby won by Pleasant Colony (time 2:02, purse $317,200).
Golf--U.S. Open won by David Graham with a score of 273.
Auto Racing--Indianapolis 500 won by Bobby Unser (ave. speed 139.085 MPH).
Tennis--U.S. Open won by John McEnroe in the men's singles.
U.S. Open won by John McEnroe and Peter Fleming in the men's doubles.
U.S. Open won by Tracy Austin in the women's singles.
U.S. Open won by Annie Smith and Kathy Jordan in the women's doubles.
U.S. Open won by Annie Smith and Kevin Curren in the mixed doubles.

Notes

Bobby Unser joined his brother Al as a three time Indianapolis 500 winner.
John McEnroe won his third consecutive U.S. Open men's single championship.

1982

BASEBALL
National League

East

Team Name	W	L	Pct	GB	R	OR
St. Louis Cardinals	92	70	.568	-	685	609
Philadelphia Phillies	89	73	.549	3	664	654
Montreal Expos	86	76	.531	6	697	616
Pittsburgh Pirates	84	78	.519	8	724	696
Chicago Cubs	73	89	.451	19	676	709
New York Mets	65	97	.401	27	609	723

West

Team Name	W	L	Pct	GB	R	OR
Atlanta Braves	89	73	.549	-	739	702
Los Angeles Dodgers	88	74	.543	1	691	612
San Francisco Giants	87	75	.537	2	673	687
San Diego Padres	81	81	.500	8	675	658
Houston Astros	77	85	.475	12	569	620
Cincinnati Reds	61	101	.377	28	545	661

Coaching Changes

Philadelphia--Pat Corrales 89-73; Montreal--Jim Fanning 86-76; Chicago--Lee Elia 73-89; New York--George Bamberger 65-97; Atlanta--Joe Torre 89-73; San Diego--Dick Williams 81-81; Houston--Bill Virdon 49-62, Bob Lillis 28-23; Cincinnati--John McNamara 34-58, Russ Nixon 27-43.

League Leaders

Batting Average
(440 at bats)

Al Oliver	.331
Bill Madlock	.319
Leon Durham	.312
Lonnie Smith	.307
Bill Buckner	.306

Home Runs

Dave Kingman	37
Dale Murphy	36
Mike Schmidt	35
Bob Horner	32
Pedro Guerrero	32

RBI

Dale Murphy	109
Al Oliver	109
Bill Buckner	105
George Hendrick	104
Jack Clark	103

Stolen Bases

Tim Raines	78
Lonnie Smith	68
Omar Moreno	60
Mookie Wilson	58
Steve Sax	49

ERA
(162 innings)

Steve Rogers	2.40
Joe Niekro	2.47
Joaquin Andujar	2.47
Mario Soto	2.79
Fernando Valenzuela	2.87

Wins

Steve Carlton	23
Fernando Valenzuela	19
Steve Rogers	19
Jerry Reuss	18
Phil Niekro	17

Saves

Bruce Sutter	36
Greg Minton	30
Gene Garber	30
Jeff Reardon	26
Kent Tekulve	20

Strikeouts

Steve Carlton	286
Mario Soto	274
Nolan Ryan	245
Fernando Valenzuela	199
Steve Rogers	179

NLCS

October 7	Atlanta Braves	0	at	St. Louis Cardinals	7
October 9	Atlanta Braves	3	at	St. Louis Cardinals	4
October 10	St. Louis Cardinals	6	at	Atlanta Braves	2

American League

East

Team Name	W	L	Pct	GB	R	OR
Milwaukee Brewers	95	67	.586	-	891	717
Baltimore Orioles	94	68	.580	1	774	687
Boston Red Sox	89	73	.549	6	753	713
Detroit Tigers	83	79	.512	12	729	685
New York Yankees	79	83	.488	16	709	716
Cleveland Indians	78	84	.481	17	683	748
Toronto Blue Jays	78	84	.481	17	651	701

West

Team Name	W	L	Pct	GB	R	OR
California Angels	93	69	.574	-	814	670
Kansas City Royals	90	72	.556	3	784	717
Chicago White Sox	87	75	.537	6	786	710
Seattle Mariners	76	86	.469	17	651	712
Oakland Athletics	68	94	.420	25	691	819
Texas Rangers	64	98	.395	29	590	749
Minnesota Twins	60	102	.370	33	657	819

Coaching Changes

Milwaukee--Bob Rodgers 23-24, Harvey Kuenn 72-43; New York--Bob Lemon 6-8, Gene Michael 44-42, Clyde King 29-33; Toronto--Bobby Cox 78-84; California--Gene Mauch 93-69; Kansas City--Dick Howser 90-72; Seattle--Rene Lachmann 76-86; Texas--Don Zimmer 38-58, Darrell Johnson 26-40; Minnesota--Bill Gardner 60-102.

League Leaders

Batting Average
(440 at bats)

Willie Wilson	.332
Robin Yount	.331
Rod Carew	.319
Eddie Murray	.316
Cecil Cooper	.313

Home Runs

Reggie Jackson	39
Gorman Thomas	39
Dave Winfield	37
Ben Oglivie	34
Lance Parrish	32

RBI

Hal McRae	133
Cecil Cooper	121
Andre Thornton	116
Robin Yount	114
Gorman Thomas	112

Stolen Bases

Rickey Henderson	130
Damaso Garcia	54
Julio Cruz	46
Paul Molitor	41
Willie Wilson	37

ERA
(162 innings)

Rick Sutcliffe	2.96
Bob Stanley	3.10
Jim Palmer	3.13
Dan Petry	3.22
Dave Stieb	3.25

Wins

LaMarr Hoyt	19
Geoff Zahn	18
Larry Gura	18
Pete Vuckovich	18
Mike Caldwell	17

Saves		**Strikeouts**	
Dan Quisenberry	35	Floyd Bannister	209
Rich Gossage	30	Len Barker	187
Rollie Fingers	29	Dave Righetti	163
Bill Caudill	26	Ron Guidry	162
Ron Davis	22	John Tudor	146

All Star Game
(Olympic Stadium, Montreal)

July 13	National League	4		American League	1

ALCS

October 5	Milwaukee Brewers	3	at	California Angels	8
October 6	Milwaukee Brewers	2	at	California Angels	4
October 8	California Angels	3	at	Milwaukee Brewers	5
October 9	California Angels	5	at	Milwaukee Brewers	9
October 10	California Angels	3	at	Milwaukee Brewers	4

World Series

October 12	Milwaukee Brewers	10	at	St. Louis Cardinals	0
October 13	Milwaukee Brewers	4	at	St. Louis Cardinals	5
October 15	St. Louis Cardinals	6	at	Milwaukee Brewers	2
October 16	St. Louis Cardinals	5	at	Milwaukee Brewers	7
October 17	St. Louis Cardinals	4	at	Milwaukee Brewers	6
October 19	Milwaukee Brewers	1	at	St. Louis Cardinals	13
October 20	Milwaukee Brewers	3	at	St. Louis Cardinals	6

Individual Awards

ALCS MVP--Fred Lynn (California Angels AL)
Arch Ward Memorial Trophy--Dave Concepcion (Cincinnati Reds NL)
Baseball Writers Award--Dale Murphy (Atlanta Braves NL)
Robin Yount (Milwaukee Brewers AL)
Cy Young Award--Steve Carlton (Philadelphia Phillies NL)
Pete Vuckovich (Milwaukee Brewers AL)
NLCS MVP--Darrell Porter (St. Louis Cardinals NL)
Rookie of the Year--Steve Sax (Los Angeles Dodgers NL)
Cal Ripken(Baltimore Orioles AL)
Sporting News Executive of the Year--Harry Dalton (Milwaukee Brewers AL)
Sporting News Manager of the Year--Dorrel "Whitey" Herzog (St. Louis Cardinals NL)
Sporting News Pitcher of the Year--Steve Carlton (Philadelphia Phillies NL)
Dave Stieb (Toronto Blue Jays AL)
Sporting News Player of the Year--Dale Murphy (Atlanta Braves NL)
Robin Yount (Milwaukee Brewers AL)
Sporting News Rookie of the Year--Johnny Ray (Pittsburgh Pirates NL)
Steve Bedrosian (Atlanta Braves NL)
Cal Ripken (Baltimore Orioles AL)
Ed Vande Berg (Seattle Mariners AL)
World Series MVP--Darrell Porter (St. Louis Cardinals NL)

Hall of Fame Inductees

Hank Aaron, Happy Chandler, Travis Jackson, Frank Robinson

BASKETBALL

National Basketball Association

Eastern Conference
Atlantic Division

Team Name	GP	W	L	PPGF	PPGA	Pct	GB
Boston Celtics	82	63	19	112.0	105.6	.768	-
Philadelphia 76ers	82	58	24	111.2	105.5	.707	5
New Jersey Nets	82	44	38	106.7	106.0	.537	19
Washington Bullets	82	43	39	103.5	102.6	.524	20
New York Knickerbockers	82	33	49	106.2	108.9	.402	31

Central Division

Team Name	GP	W	L	PPGF	PPGA	Pct	GB
Milwaukee Bucks	82	55	27	108.4	102.9	.671	-
Atlanta Hawks	82	42	40	101.0	100.5	.512	13
Detroit Pistons	82	39	43	111.1	112.0	.476	16
Indiana Pacers	82	35	47	102.2	104.0	.427	20
Chicago Bulls	82	34	48	106.6	108.6	.415	21
Cleveland Cavaliers	82	15	67	103.2	111.7	.183	40

Western Conference

Midwest Division

Team Name	GP	W	L	PPGF	PPGA	Pct	GB
San Antonio Spurs	82	48	34	113.1	110.8	.585	-
Denver Nuggets	82	46	36	126.5	126.0	.561	2
Houston Rockets	82	46	36	105.9	105.9	.561	2
Kansas City Kings	82	30	52	107.1	110.2	.366	18
Dallas Mavericks	82	28	54	104.6	109.0	.341	20
Utah Jazz	82	25	57	110.9	116.6	.305	23

Pacific Division

Team Name	GP	W	L	PPGF	PPGA	Pct	GB
Los Angeles Lakers	82	57	25	114.6	109.8	.695	-
Seattle SuperSonics	82	52	30	107.3	103.1	.634	5
Phoenix Suns	82	46	36	106.2	102.7	.561	11
Golden State Warriors	82	45	37	110.9	109.8	.549	12
Portland Trail Blazers	82	42	40	109.8	109.2	.512	15
San Diego Clippers	82	17	65	108.5	115.9	.207	40

Coaching Changes

New Jersey--Larry Brown 44-38; Atlanta--Kevin Loughery 42-40; Chicago--Jerry Sloan 19-32, Phil Johnson 0-1, Rod Thorn 15-15; Cleveland--Don Delaney 4-11, Bob Koppenburg 0-3, Chuck Daly 9-32, Bill Musselman 2-21; Denver--Doug Moe 46-36; Utah--Tom Nissalke 8-12, Frank Layden 17-45; Los Angeles--Paul Westhead 7-4, Pat Riley 50-21.

League Leaders

Field Goals		Free Throws		Assists	
George Gervin	993	Adrian Dantley	648	Johnny Moore	762
Moses Malone	945	Moses Malone	630	Earvin Johnson	743
Adrian Dantley	904	George Gervin	555	Maurice Cheeks	667
Alex English	855	Dan Issel	546	Norm Nixon	652
Julius Erving	780	Kelly Tripucka	495	Rickey Green	630

Points		Rebounds Per Game	
George Gervin	2551	Moses Malone	14.7
Moses Malone	2520	Jack Sikma	12.7
Adrian Dantley	2457	Buck Williams	12.3
Alex English	2082	Mychal Thompson	11.7
Julius Erving	1974	Maurice Lucas	11.3

All Star Game

(The Meadowlands Arena, East Rutherford New Jersey)

January 31	East Division	120	West Division	118

NBA Playoffs

April 20	Washington Bullets	96	at	New Jersey Nets	83
April 20	Phoenix Suns	113	at	Denver Nuggets	129
April 21	Atlanta Hawks	76	at	Philadelphia 76ers	111
April 21	Houston Rockets	87	at	Seattle SuperSonics	102
April 23	Philadelphia 76ers	98	at	Atlanta Hawks	95
April 23	Seattle SuperSonics	70	at	Houston Rockets	91
April 23	New Jersey Nets	92	at	Washington Bullets	103
April 23	Denver Nuggets	110	at	Phoenix Suns	126
April 24	Phoenix Suns	124	at	Denver Nuggets	119
April 25	Houston Rockets	83	at	Seattle SuperSonics	104
April 25	Washington Bullets	91	at	Boston Celtics	109
April 25	Milwaukee Bucks	122	at	Philadelphia 76ers	125
April 27	Phoenix Suns	96	at	Los Angeles Lakers	115
April 27	San Antonio Spurs	95	at	Seattle SuperSonics	93
April 28	Washington Bullets	103	at	Boston Celtics	102
April 28	Milwaukee Bucks	108	at	Philadelphia 76ers	120
April 28	Phoenix Suns	98	at	Los Angeles Lakers	117
April 28	San Antonio Spurs	99	at	Seattle SuperSonics	114
April 30	Los Angles Lakers	114	at	Phoenix Suns	106
April 30	Seattle SuperSonics	97	at	San Antonio Spurs	99
May 1	Boston Celtics	92	at	Washington Bullets	83
May 1	Philadelphia 76ers	91	at	Milwaukee Bucks	92
May 2	Los Angeles Lakers	112	at	Phoenix Suns	107
May 2	Seattle SuperSonics	113	at	San Antonio Spurs	115
May 2	Boston Celtics	103	at	Washington Bullets	99 [OT]
May 2	Philadelphia 76ers	100	at	Milwaukee Bucks	93
May 5	San Antonio Spurs	109	at	Seattle SuperSonics	103
May 5	Washington Bullets	126	at	Boston Celtics	131 [OT]
May 5	Milwaukee Bucks	110	at	Philadelphia 76ers	98
May 7	Philadelphia 76ers	102	at	Milwaukee Bucks	90
May 9	Philadelphia 76ers	81	at	Boston Celtics	121

May 9	San Antonio Spurs	117	at	Los Angeles Lakers	128
May 11	San Antonio Spurs	101	at	Los Angeles Lakers	110
May 12	Philadelphia 76ers	121	at	Boston Celtics	113
May 14	Los Angeles Lakers	118	at	San Antonio Spurs	108
May 15	Los Angeles Lakers	128	at	San Antonio Spurs	123
May 15	Boston Celtics	97	at	Philadelphia 76ers	99
May 16	Boston Celtics	94	at	Philadelphia 76ers	119
May 19	Philadelphia 76ers	85	at	Boston Celtics	114
May 21	Boston Celtics	88	at	Philadelphia 76ers	75
May 23	Philadelphia 76ers	120	at	Boston Celtics	106
May 27	Los Angeles Lakers	124	at	Philadelphia 76ers	117
May 30	Los Angeles Lakers	94	at	Philadelphia 76ers	110
June 1	Philadelphia 76ers	108	at	Los Angeles Lakers	129
June 3	Philadelphia 76ers	101	at	Los Angeles Lakers	111
June 6	Los Angeles Lakers	102	at	Philadelphia 76ers	135
June 8	Philadelphia 76ers	104	at	Los Angeles Lakers	114

All Star Teams

First Team	Second Team
Larry Bird (Boston Celtics)	Alex English (Denver Nuggets)
Julius Erving (Philadelphia 76ers)	Bernard King (Golden State Warriors)
Moses Malone (Houston Rockets)	Robert Parish (Boston Celtics)
George Gervin (San Antonio Spurs)	Earvin Johnson (Los Angeles Lakers)
Gus Williams (Seattle SuperSonics)	Sidney Moncrief (Milwaukee Bucks)

Individual Awards

Eddie Gottlieb Trophy--Buck Williams (New Jersey Nets)
Executive of the Year--Bob Ferry (Washington Bullets)
J. Walter Kennedy Citizenship Award--Kent Benson (Detroit Pistons)
Maurice Podoloff Trophy--Moses Malone (Houston Rockets)
NBA All Star Came MVP--Larry Bird (Boston Celtics)
NBA Finals MVP--Earvin Johnson (Los Angeles Lakers)
Red Auerbach Trophy--Gene Shue (Washington Bullets)

Hall of Fame Inductees

Bill Bradley, Dave DeBusschere, Lloyd Leith, Dean Smith, Jack Twyman, Lou Wilke

FOOTBALL

National Football League
National Conference
Eastern Division

Team Name	GP	W	L	T	PF	PA	Pct
Washington Redskins	9	8	1	0	190	128	.889
Dallas Cowboys	9	6	3	0	126	145	.667
St. Louis Cardinals	9	5	4	0	135	170	.556
New York Giants	9	4	5	0	164	160	.444
Philadelphia Eagles	9	3	6	0	191	195	.333

Central Division

Green Bay Packers	9	5	3	1	226	169	.611
Minnesota Vikings	9	5	4	0	187	198	.556
Tampa Bay Buccaneers	9	5	4	0	158	178	.556
Detroit Lions	9	4	5	0	181	176	.444
Chicago Bears	9	3	6	0	141	174	.333

Western Division

Atlanta Falcons	9	5	4	0	183	199	.556
New Orleans Saints	9	4	5	0	129	160	.444
San Francisco 49ers	9	3	6	0	209	206	.333
Los Angeles Rams	9	2	7	0	200	250	.222

American Conference

Eastern Conference

Miami Dolphins	9	7	2	0	198	131	.778
New York Jets	9	6	3	0	245	166	.667
New England Patriots	9	5	4	0	143	157	.556
Buffalo Bills	9	4	5	0	150	154	.444
Baltimore Colts	9	0	8	1	113	236	.056

Central Division

Cincinnati Bengals	9	7	2	0	232	177	.778
Pittsburgh Steelers	9	6	3	0	204	146	.667
Cleveland Browns	9	4	5	0	140	182	.444
Houston Oilers	9	1	8	0	136	245	.111

Western Division

Los Angeles Raiders	9	8	1	0	260	200	.889
San Diego Chargers	9	6	3	0	288	221	.667
Seattle Seahawks	9	4	5	0	127	147	.444
Kansas City Chiefs	9	3	6	0	176	184	.333
Denver Broncos	9	2	7	0	148	226	.222

Coaching Changes

Chicago--Mike Ditka 3-6-0; New England--Ron Meyer 5-4-0; Baltimore--Frank Kush 0-8-1; Seattle--Jack Patera 0-2-0, Mike McCormack 4-3-0.

League Leaders

Yards Rushing		**Yards Passing**		**Passing %** (300 attempts)	
Freeman McNeil	786	Dan Fouts	2889	Ken Anderson	70.6
Tony Dorsett	745	Joe Montana	2613	Dan Fouts	61.8
Andra Franklin	701	Ken Anderson	2495	Joe Montana	61.6
Marcus Allen	697	Dan White	2079	Tom Kramer	57.1
Billy Sims	639	Ron Jaworski	2076	Doug Williams	53.4

Receiving Yards		Receptions		Field Goals	
Wes Chandler	1032	Dwight Clark	60	Mark Moseley	20
Dwight Clark	913	Kellen Winslow	54	Nick Lowery	19
Kellen Winslow	721	James Wilder	53	Bill Capece	18
Cris Collinsworth	700	Cris Collinsworth	49	Rolf Benirschke	16
Ozzie Newsome	633	Ozzie Newsome	49	Uwe von Schamann	15

Punt Return Yards		Kickoff Return Yards	
Rob Martin	275	James Brooks	749
Billy Johnson	273	Anthony Hancock	609
LeRoy Irvin	242	Rick Smith	567
Rick Upchurch	242	Mike Nelms	557
Tom Vigorito	192	Wally Henry	541

Pro Bowl Game

(Aloha Stadium, Honolulu)

February 6 1983	National Conference	20	American Conference	19

NFL Playoffs

January 8 1983	St. Louis Cardinals	16	at	Green Bay Packers	41
January 8 1983	Detroit Lions	7	at	Washington Redskins	31
January 8 1983	New England Patriots	13	at	Miami Dolphins	28
January 8 1983	Cleveland Browns	10	at	Los Angeles Raiders	27
January 9 1983	Tampa Bay Buccaneers	17	at	Dallas Cowboys	30
January 9 1983	Atlanta Falcons	24	at	Minnesota Vikings	30
January 9 1983	New York Jets	44	at	Cincinnati Bengals	17
January 9 1983	San Diego Chargers	31	at	Pittsburgh Steelers	28
January 15 1983	Minnesota Vikings	7	at	Washington Redskins	21
January 15 1983	New York Jets	17	at	Los Angeles Raiders	14
January 16 1983	Green Bay Packers	26	at	Dallas Cowboys	37
January 16 1983	San Diego Chargers	13	at	Miami Dolphins	34
January 22 1983	Dallas Cowboys	17	at	Washington Redskins	31
January 23 1983	New York Jets	0	at	Miami Dolphins	14

Super Bowl XVII

(Rose Bowl, Pasadena)

January 30 1983	Washington Redskins	27	Miami Dolphins	17

Individual Awards

A.P. MVP--Mark Moseley (Washington Redskins)
Bert Bell Trophy--Marcus Allen (Los Angeles Raiders) [World Almanac]
Bert Bell Trophy--Joe Theismann (Washington Redskins)
George Halas Trophy--Mark Gastineau (New York Jets)
P.F.W.A. MVP--Dan Fouts (San Diego Chargers)
Pro Bowl MVP--Dan Fouts (San Diego Chargers)
John Jefferson (Green Bay Packers)
Super Bowl MVP--John Riggins (Washington Redskins)
U.P.I. AFC Coach of the Year--Tom Flores (Los Angeles Raiders)
U.P.I. AFC Player of the Year--Dan Fouts (San Diego Chargers)
U.P.I. AFC Rookie of the Year--Marcus Allen (Los Angeles Raiders)
U.P.I. NFC Coach of the Year--Joe Gibbs (Washington Redskins)
U.P.I. NFC Player of the Year--Mark Moseley (Washington Redskins)
U.P.I. NFC Rookie of the Year--Jim McMahon (Chicago Bears)

Hall of Fame Inductees

Doug Atkins, Sam Huff, George Musso, Merlin Olsen

Notes

The NFL introduced a severance-pay system to aid players in career transitions, this was a first among professional sports leagues.
The league was also hit with a player's strike which followed on the heels of last year's baseball strike.

Canadian Football League
Eastern Division

Team Name	GP	W	L	T	PF	PA	Pts	Pct
Toronto Argonauts	16	9	6	1	426	426	19	.594
Hamilton Tiger-Cats	16	8	7	1	396	401	17	.531
Ottawa Rough Riders	16	5	11	0	376	462	10	.313
Montreal Concordes	16	2	14	0	267	502	4	.125

Western Division

Team Name	GP	W	L	T	PF	PA	Pts	Pct
Edmonton Eskimos	16	11	5	0	544	323	22	.688
Winnipeg Blue Bombers	16	11	5	0	444	352	22	.688
Calgary Stampeders	16	9	6	1	403	440	19	.594
British Columbia Lions	16	9	7	0	449	390	18	.563
Saskatchewan Roughriders	16	6	9	1	427	436	13	.406

Coaching Changes

Toronto--Bob O'Billovich 9-6-1; Hamilton--Bud Riley 8-7-1; Montreal--Joe Galat 2-14-0; Calgary--Jack Gotta 9-6-1.

League Leaders

Rushing Yards		Yards Passing		Passing % (150 attempts)	
Skip Walker	1141	Warren Moon	5000	Tom Clements	65.2
William Miller	1076	Tom Clements	4706	Roy DeWalt	60.9
James Sykes	1046	Conredge Holloway	4661	Warren Moon	59.2
Larry Key	820	Dieter Brock	4294	Conredge Holloway	58.9
John Henry White	624	Chris Isaac	3408	Dieter Brock	57.8

Receiving Yards		Receptions		Points	
Joey Walters	1692	Joey Walters	102	Dave Cutler	170
Tom Scott	1518	Tom Scott	91	Dave Ridgway	163
Terry Greer	1466	Nick Arakgi	89	Trevor Kennerd	149
Keith Baker	1282	Terry Greer	85	Bernie Ruoff	142
Rocky DiPietro	1160	Rocky DiPietro	85	Lui Passaglia	134

Grey Cup Playoffs

November 14	Calgary Stampeders	3	at	Winnipeg Blue Bombers	24
November 14	Ottawa Rough Riders	30	at	Hamilton Tiger-Cats	20
November 21	Winnipeg Blue Bombers	21	at	Edmonton Eskimos	24

November 21	Ottawa Rough Riders	7	at	Toronto Argonauts	44
November 28	Edmonton Eskimos	32	at	Toronto Argonauts	16

Individual Awards

Annis Stukus Trophy--Bob O'Billovich (Toronto Argonauts)
Dave Dryburgh Memorial Trophy--Dave Cutler (Edmonton Eskimos)
DeMarco-Becket Memorial Trophy--Lloyd Fairbanks (Calgary Stampeders)
Dr. Beattie Martin Trophy--Rick House (Winnipeg Blue Bombers)
Eddie James Memorial Trophy--William Miller (Winnipeg Blue Bombers)
Frank M. Gibson Trophy--Chris Isaac (Ottawa Rough Riders)
Grey Cup Most Outstanding Defensive Star--Dave Fennell (Edmonton Eskimos)
Grey Cup Most Outstanding Offensive Star--Warren Moon (Edmonton Eskimos)
Grey Cup Most Outstanding Canadian--Dave Fennell (Edmonton Eskimos)
Jackie Parker Trophy--Mervyn Fernandez (British Columbia Lions)
James P. McCaffrey Trophy--Zac Henderson (Toronto Argonauts)
Jeff Nicklin Memorial Trophy--Tom Scott (Edmonton Eskimos)
Jeff Russel Memorial Trophy--Conredge Holloway (Toronto Argonauts)
Leo Dandurand Trophy--Rudy Phillips (Ottawa Rough Riders)
Lew Hayman Trophy--Rocky DiPietro (Hamilton Tiger-Cats)
Norm Fieldgate Trophy--James Parker (Edmonton Eskimos)
Schenley Award Most Outstanding Canadian--Rocky DiPietro (Hamilton Tiger-Cats)
Schenley Award Most Outstanding Defensive Player--James Parker (Edmonton Eskimos)
Schenley Award Most Outstanding Offensive Lineman--Rudy Phillips (Ottawa Rough Riders)
Schenley Award Most Outstanding Player--Conredge Holloway (Toronto Argonauts)
Schenley Award Most Outstanding Rookie--Chris Isaac (Ottawa Rough Riders)

Hall of Fame Inductees

Willie Fleming, Ron Lancaster, Vince Scott, Buddy Tinsley

Notes

The CFL granted its first new franchise since 1954 when the Montreal Alouettes folded and were replaced by the Montreal Concorde.

HOCKEY

National Hockey League
Clarence Campbell Conference
Norris Division

Team Name	GP	W	L	T	GF	GA	Pts	Pct
Minnesota North Stars	80	37	23	20	346	288	94	.588
Winnipeg Jets	80	33	33	14	319	332	80	.500
St. Louis Blues	80	32	40	8	315	349	72	.450
Chicago Black Hawks	80	30	38	12	332	363	72	.450
Toronto Maple Leafs	80	20	44	16	298	380	56	.350
Detroit Red Wings	80	21	47	12	270	351	54	.338

Smythe Division

Team Name	GP	W	L	T	GF	GA	Pts	Pct
Edmonton Oilers	80	48	17	15	417	295	111	.694
Vancouver Canucks	80	30	33	17	290	286	77	.481
Calgary Flames	80	29	34	17	334	345	75	.469
Los Angeles Kings	80	24	41	15	314	369	63	.394
Colorado Rockies	80	18	49	13	241	362	49	.306

Prince of Wales Conference

Patrick Division

New York Islanders	80	54	16	10	385	250	118	.738
New York Rangers	80	39	27	14	316	306	92	.575
Philadelphia Flyers	80	38	31	11	325	313	87	.544
Pittsburgh Penguins	80	31	36	13	310	337	75	.469
Washington Capitals	80	26	41	13	319	338	65	.406

Adams Division

Montreal Canadiens	80	46	17	17	360	223	109	.681
Boston Bruins	80	43	27	10	323	285	96	.600
Buffalo Sabres	80	39	26	15	307	273	93	.581
Quebec Nordiques	80	33	31	16	356	345	82	.513
Hartford Whalers	80	21	41	18	264	351	60	.375

Coaching Changes

Winnipeg--Tom Watt 33-33-14; St. Louis--Gordon "Red" Berenson 28-35-6; Emile Francis 4-5-2; Chicago--Keith Magnuson 18-24-10, Bob Pulford 12-14-2; Toronto--Mike Nykoluk 20-44-16; Detroit--Wayne Maxner 18-39-12, Bill Dea 3-8-0; Edmonton--Glen Sather 48-17-15; Vancouver--Harry Neale 26-33-16, Roger Neilson 4-0-1; Los Angeles--Parker MacDonald 13-24-5, Don Perry 11-17-10; Colorado--Bert Marshall 3-17-4, Marshall Johnston 15-32-9; Rangers--Herb Brooks 39-27-14; Philadelphia--Pat Quinn 34-29-9, Bob McCammon 4-2-2; Washington--Gary Green 1-12-0, Roger Crozier 0-1-0, Bryan Murray 25-28-13; Montreal--Bob Berry 46-17-17; Buffalo--Scotty Bowman 18-11-7, Jim Roberts 21-15-9; Quebec--Michel Bergeron 33-31-16; Hartford--Larry Pleau 21-41-18.

League Leaders

Goals		**Assists**		**Points**	
Wayne Gretzky	92	Wayne Gretzky	120	Wayne Gretzky	212
Mike Bossy	64	Peter Stastny	93	Mike Bossy	147
Dennis Maruk	60	Denis Savard	87	Peter Stastny	139
Dino Ciccarelli	55	Mike Bossy	83	Dennis Maruk	136
Blaine Stoughton	52	Bryan Trottier	79	Bryan Trottier	129

Penalty Minutes		**Plus/Minus**		**GAA** (1,600 minutes)	
Dave Williams	341	Wayne Gretzky	81	Rick Wamsley	2.75
Glen Cochrane	329	Bryan Trottier	70	Billy Smith	2.97
Pat Price	322	Mike Bossy	69	Roland Melanson	3.23
Al Secord	303	Rod Langway	66	Grant Fuhr	3.31
Willi Plett	288	Larry Robinson	57	Richard Brodeur	3.35

Wins		**Shutouts**	
Billy Smith	32	Denis Herron	3
Grant Fuhr	28	Rick Wamsley	2
Mike Liut	28	Richard Brodeur	2
Dan Bouchard	27	Mike Liut	2
Don Edwards	26	Pat Riggin	2

All Star Game

(Capital Center, Landover, Maryland)

February 9	Wales Conference	4	Campbell Conference	2

Stanley Cup Playoffs

April 7	Chicago Black Hawks	3	at	Minnesota North Stars	2 [3:34]
April 7	Buffalo Sabres	1	at	Boston Bruins	3
April 7	Quebec Nordiques	1	at	Montreal Canadiens	5
April 7	St. Louis Blues	4	at	Winnipeg Jets	3
April 7	Pittsburgh Penguins	1	at	New York Islanders	8
April 7	Philadelphia Flyers	4	at	New York Rangers	1
April 7	Los Angeles Kings	10	at	Edmonton Oilers	8
April 7	Calgary Flames	3	at	Vancouver Canucks	5
April 8	Chicago Black Hawks	5	at	Minnesota North Stars	3
April 8	Buffalo Sabres	3	at	Boston Bruins	7
April 8	Quebec Nordiques	3	at	Montreal Canadiens	2
April 8	St. Louis Blues	2	at	Winnipeg Jets	5
April 8	Pittsburgh Penguins	2	at	New York Islanders	7
April 8	Philadelphia Flyers	3	at	New York Rangers	7
April 8	Los Angeles Kings	2	at	Edmonton Oilers	3 [6:20]
April 8	Calgary Flames	1	at	Vancouver Canucks	2 [14:20]
April 10	Boston Bruins	2	at	Buffalo Sabres	5
April 10	Montreal Canadiens	1	at	Quebec Nordiques	2
April 10	Minnesota North Stars	7	at	Chicago Black Hawks	1
April 10	Winnipeg Jets	3	at	St. Louis Blues	6
April 10	New York Islanders	1	at	Pittsburgh Penguins	2 [4:141
April 10	New York Rangers	4	at	Philadelphia Flyers	3
April 10	Edmonton Oilers	5	at	Los Angeles Kings	6 [2:35]
April 10	Vancouver Canucks	3	at	Calgary Flames	1
April 11	Boston Bruins	5	at	Buffalo Sabres	2
April 11	Montreal Canadiens	6	at	Quebec Nordiques	2
April 11	Minnesota North Stars	2	at	Chicago Black Hawks	5
April 11	Winnipeg Jets	2	at	St. Louis Blues	8
April 11	New York Islanders	2	at	Pittsburgh Penguins	5
April 11	New York Rangers	7	at	Philadelphia Flyers	5
April 12	Edmonton Oilers	3	at	Los Angeles Kings	2
April 13	Quebec Nordiques	3	at	Montreal Canadiens	2 [0:22]
April 13	Pittsburgh Penguins	3	at	New York Islanders	4 [6:191
April 13	Los Angeles Kings	7	at	Edmonton Oilers	4
April 15	Quebec Nordiques	3	at	Boston Bruins	4
April 15	Chicago Black Hawks	5	at	St. Louis Blues	4
April 15	New York Rangers	5	at	New York Islanders	4
April 15	Los Angeles Kings	2	at	Vancouver Canucks	3
April 16	Quebec Nordiques	4	at	Boston Bruins	8
April 16	Chicago Black Hawks	1	at	St. Louis Blues	3
April 16	New York Rangers	2	at	New York Islanders	7
April 16	Los Angeles Kings	3	at	Vancouver Canucks	2 [4:33]
April 18	Boston Bruins	2	at	Quebec Nordiques	3 [11:44]
April 18	St. Louis Blues	5	at	Chicago Black Hawks	6
April 18	New York Islanders	4	at	New York Rangers	3 [3:001
April 18	Vancouver Canucks	4	at	Los Angeles Kings	3 [1:23]
April 19	Boston Bruins	2	at	Quebec Nordiques	7
April 19	St. Louis Blues	4	at	Chicago Black Hawks	7
April 19	New York Islanders	5	at	New York Rangers	3

April 19	Vancouver Canucks	5	at	Los Angeles Kings	4
April 21	Quebec Nordiques	4	at	Boston Bruins	3
April 21	Chicago Black Hawks	2	at	St. Louis Blues	3 [3:28]
April 21	New York Rangers	4	at	New York Islanders	2
April 21	Los Angeles Kings	2	at	Vancouver Canucks	5
April 23	Boston Bruins	6	at	Quebec Nordiques	5 [10:54]
April 23	St. Louis Blues	0	at	Chicago Black Hawks	2
April 23	New York Islanders	5	at	New York Rangers	3
April 25	Quebec Nordiques	2	at	Boston Bruins	1
April 27	Quebec Nordiques	1	at	New York Islanders	4
April 27	Vancouver Canucks	2	at	Chicago Black Hawks	1 [28:58]
April 29	Quebec Nordiques	2	at	New York Islanders	5
April 29	Vancouver Canucks	1	at	Chicago Black Hawks	4
May 1	New York Islanders	5	at	Quebec Nordiques	4 [16:52]
May 1	Chicago Black Hawks	3	at	Vancouver Canucks	4
May 4	New York Islanders	4	at	Quebec Nordiques	2
May 4	Chicago Black Hawks	3	at	Vancouver Canucks	5
May 6	Vancouver Canucks	6	at	Chicago Black Hawks	2
May 8	Vancouver Canucks	5	at	New York Islanders	6 [19:58]
May 11	Vancouver Canucks	4	at	New York Islanders	6
May 13	New York Islanders	3	at	Vancouver Canucks	0
May 16	New York Islanders	3	at	Vancouver Canucks	1

All Star Teams

First Team		Second Team
Bill Smith	Goal	Grant Fuhr
Doug Wilson	Defense	Paul Coffey
Ray Bourque	Defense	Brian Engblom
Wayne Gretzky	Center	Bryan Trottier
Mike Bossy	Right Wing	Rick Middleton
Mark Messier	Left Wing	John Tonelli

Individual Awards

Art Ross Trophy--Wayne Gretzky (Edmonton Oilers)
Bill Masterton Trophy--Glenn Resch (Colorado Rockies)
Calder Memorial Trophy--Dale Hawerchuk (Winnipeg Jets)
Conn Smythe Trophy--Mike Bossy (New York Islanders)
Frank J. Selke Trophy--Steve Kasper (Boston Bruins)
Hart Memorial Trophy--Wayne Gretzky (Edmonton Oilers)
Jack Adams Award--Tom Watt (Winnipeg Jets)
James Norris Trophy--Doug Wilson (Chicago Black Hawks)
Lady Byng Memorial Trophy--Rick Middleton (Boston Bruins)
Lester B. Pearson Award--Wayne Gretzky (Edmonton Oilers)
Lester Patrick Trophy--Emile Francis
NHL All Star Game MVP--Mike Bossy (New York Islanders)
William M. Jennings Trophy--Rick Wamsley and Denis Herron (Montreal Canadiens)
Vezina Trophy--Bill Smith (New York Islanders)

Hall of Fame Inductees

Yvan Cournoyer, Emile Francis, Rod Gilbert, Norm Ullman

Notes

The NHL adopted an unbalanced schedule.

SOCCER

North American Soccer League

Eastern Division

Team Name	GP	W	L	GF	GA	BP	Pts	Pct
Cosmos	32	23	9	73	52	67	203	.423
Montreal Manic	32	19	13	60	43	49	159	.331
Toronto Blizzard	32	17	15	64	47	49	151	.315
Chicago Sting	32	13	19	56	67	53	129	.269

Southern Division

Team Name	GP	W	L	GF	GA	BP	Pts	Pct
Ft. Lauderdale Strikers	32	18	14	64	74	57	163	.340
Tulsa Roughnecks	32	16	16	69	57	59	151	.315
Tampa Bay Rowdies	32	12	20	47	77	42	112	.233
Jacksonville Tea Men	32	11	21	41	71	39	105	.219

Western Division

Team Name	GP	W	L	GF	GA	BP	Pts	Pct
Seattle Sounders	32	18	14	72	48	60	166	.346
San Diego Sockers	32	19	13	71	54	54	162	.338
Vancouver Whitecaps	32	20	12	58	48	46	160	.333
Portland Timbers	32	14	18	49	44	42	122	.254
San Jose Earthquakes	32	13	19	47	62	38	114	.238
Edmonton Drillers	32	11	21	38	65	33	93	.194

Coaching Changes

New York--Julio Mazzei 23-9; Toronto--Bobby Houghton 17-15; San Jose--Peter Short 13-19; Edmonton Roger Thompson 11-21; Tulsa--Terry Hennessey 16-16.

League Leaders

Goals		Points		GAA (1,440 minutes)	
Ricardo Alonso	21	Giorgio Chinaglia	55	Tino Lettieri	1.23
Giorgio Chinaglia	20	Karl-Heinz Granitza	49	Victor Nogueira	1.25
Karl-Heinz Granitza	20	Peter Ward	49	Paul Hammond	1.29
Peter Ward	18	Ricardo Alonso	46	Bill Irwin	1.32
Laurie Abrahams	17	Laurie Abrahams	44	Jan Moller	1.39

NASL Playoffs

August 25	Tulsa Roughnecks	0	at	Cosmos	5
August 25	Toronto Blizzard	2	at	Seattle Sounders	4
August 25	Ft. Lauderdale Strikers	2	at	Montreal Manic	3
August 25	Vancouver Whitecaps	1	at	San Diego Sockers	5
August 27	Seattle Sounders	1	at	Toronto Blizzard	2
August 28	Cosmos	0	at	Tulsa Roughnecks	1
August 29	Montreal Manic	0	at	Ft. Lauderdale Strikers	1
August 29	San Diego Sockers	0	at	Vancouver Whitecaps	1
September 1	Tulsa Roughnecks	0	at	Cosmos	1
September 1	Toronto Blizzard	2	at	Seattle Sounders	4
September 1	Montreal Manic	1	at	Ft. Lauderdale Strikers	4

September 2	Vancouver Whitecaps	1	at	San Diego Sockers	2
September 4	Ft. Lauderdale Strikers	2	at	Seattle Sounders	0
September 5	San Diego Sockers	1	at	Cosmos	2
September 8	Seattle Sounders	4	at	Ft. Lauderdale Strikers	3
September 8	Cosmos	2	at	San Diego Sockers	1
September 10	Ft. Lauderdale Strikers	0	at	Seattle Sounders	1
September 18	Cosmos	1		Seattle Sounders	0*

Individual Awards

Lead Goalkeeper Award--Tino Lettieri (Vancouver Whitecaps)
Most Valuable Player--Peter Ward (Seattle Sounders)

Notes

Howard J. Samuels replaced Phil Woosnam as President of the North American Soccer League on June 25.

Franchise Changes

NFL--Oakland Raiders became the Los Angeles Raiders.
CFL--Montreal Alouettes became the Montreal Concordes.

Other Sports

Horseracing--Kentucky Derby won by Gato del Sol (time 2:02.4, purse $428,850).
Heavyweight Boxing--Michael Dokes knocked-out Mike Weaver in 1 round (WBA).
Golf--U.S. Open won by Tom Watson with a score of 282.
Auto Racing--Indianapolis 500 won by Gordon Johncock (ave. speed 162.026 MPH).
Tennis--U.S. Open won by Jimmy Connors in the men's singles.
U.S. Open won by Kevin Curren and Steve Denton in the men's doubles.
U.S. Open won by Chris Evert Lloyd in the women's singles.
U.S. Open won by Rosemary Casals and Wendy Turnbull in the women's doubles.
U.S. Open won by Anne Smith and Kevin Curren in the mixed doubles.

*Game played in San Diego

1983

BASEBALL
National League
East

Team Name	W	L	Pct	GB	R	OR
Philadelphia Phillies	90	72	.556	-	696	635
Pittsburgh Pirates	84	78	.519	6	659	648
Montreal Expos	82	80	.506	8	677	646
St. Louis Cardinals	79	83	.488	11	679	710
Chicago Cubs	71	91	.438	19	701	719
New York Mets	68	94	.420	22	575	680

West

Team Name	W	L	Pct	GB	R	OR
Los Angeles Dodgers	91	71	.562	-	654	609
Atlanta Braves	88	74	.543	3	746	640
Houston Astros	85	77	.525	6	643	646
San Diego Padres	81	81	.500	10	653	653
San Francisco Giants	79	83	.488	12	687	697
Cincinnati Reds	74	88	.457	17	623	710

Coaching Changes

Philadelphia--Pat Corrales 43-42, Paul Owens 47-30; Montreal--Bill Virdon 82-80; Chicago--Lee Elia 54-69, Charlie Fox 17-22; New York--George Bamberger 16-30, Frank Howard 52-64; Houston--Bob Lillis 85-77; Cincinnati--Russ Nixon 74-88.

League Leaders

Batting Average

Bill Madlock	.323
Lonnie Smith	.321
Jose Cruz	.318
George Hendrick	.318
Ray Knight	.304

Home Runs

Mike Schmidt	40
Dale Murphy	36
Andre Dawson	32
Pedro Guerrero	32
Darrell Evans	30

RBI

Dale Murphy	121
Andre Dawson	113
Mike Schmidt	109
Pedro Guerrero	103
Terry Kennedy	98

Stolen Bases

Tim Raines	90
Alan Wiggins	66
Steve Sax	56
Mookie Wilson	54
Lonnie Smith	43

ERA
(160 innings)

Atlee Hammaker	2.25
John Denny	2.37
Bob Welch	2.65
Mario Soto	2.70
Alejandro Pena	2.75

Wins

John Denny	19
Mario Soto	17
Steve Rogers	17
Bill Gullickson	17
Charlie Lea	16

Saves

Lee Smith	29
Al Holland	25
Greg Minton	22
Bruce Sutter	21
Jeff Reardon	21

Strikeouts

Steve Carlton	275
Mario Soto	242
Larry McWilliams	199
Fernando Valenzuela	189
Nolan Ryan	183

NLCS

October 4	Philadelphia Phillies	1	at	Los Angeles Dodgers	0
October 5	Philadelphia Phillies	1	at	Los Angeles Dodgers	4
October 7	Los Angeles Dodgers	2	at	Philadelphia Phillies	7
October 8	Los Angeles Dodgers	2	at	Philadelphia Phillies	7

Notes

Steve Garvey ended his National League iron man streak at 1,207 games when he sat out a game on July 29th because of an injured thumb.

American League

East

Team Name	W	L	Pct	GB	R	OR
Baltimore Orioles	98	64	.605	-	799	652
Detroit Tigers	92	70	.568	6	789	679
New York Yankees	91	71	.562	7	770	703
Toronto Blue Jays	89	73	.549	9	795	726
Milwaukee Brewers	87	75	.537	11	764	708
Boston Red Sox	78	84	.481	20	724	775
Cleveland Indians	70	92	.432	28	704	785

West

Team Name	W	L	Pct	GB	R	OR
Chicago White Sox	99	63	.611	-	800	650
Kansas City Royals	79	83	.488	20	696	767
Texas Rangers	77	85	.475	22	639	609
Oakland Athletics	74	88	.457	25	708	782
Minnesota Twins	70	92	.432	29	709	822
California Angels	70	92	.432	29	722	779
Seattle Mariners	60	102	.370	39	558	740

Coaching Changes

Baltimore--Joe Altobelli 98-64; New York--Billy Martin 91-71; Milwaukee--Harvey Kuenn 87-75; Cleveland--Mike Ferraro 40-60, Pat Corrales 30-32; Texas--Doug Rader 77-85; Oakland--Steve Boros 74-88; California--John McNamara 70-92; Seattle--Rene Lachemann 26-47, Del Crandall 34-55.

League Leaders

Batting Average		**Home Runs**		**RBI**	
Wade Boggs	.361	Jim Rice	39	Jim Rice	126
Rod Carew	.339	Tony Armas	36	Cecil Cooper	126
Lou Whitaker	.320	Ron Kittle	35	Dave Winfield	116
Alan Trammell	.319	Eddie Murray	33	Lance Parrish	114
Cal Ripken	.318	Greg Luzinski	32	Eddie Murray	111

Stolen Bases		**ERA** (160 innings)		**Wins**	
Rickey Henderson	108	Rick Honeycutt	2.42	LaMarr Hoyt	24
Rudy Law	77	Mike Boddicker	2.77	Rich Dotson	22
Willie Wilson	59	Dave Stieb	3.04	Ron Guidry	21
Julio Cruz	57	Charlie Hough	3.18	Jack Morris	20
Bill Sample	44	Scott McGregor	3.18	Dan Petry	19

Saves		Strikeouts	
Dan Quisenberry	45	Jack Morris	232
Bob Stanley	33	Floyd Bannister	193
Ron Davis	30	Dave Stieb	187
Bill Caudill	26	Dave Righetti	169
Pete Ladd	25	Rick Sutcliffe	160

All Star Game

(Comiskey Park I, Chicago)

July 6	American League	13		National League	3

ALCS

October 5	Chicago White Sox	2	at	Baltimore Orioles	1
October 6	Chicago White Sox	0	at	Baltimore Orioles	4
October 7	Baltimore Orioles	11	at	Chicago White Sox	1
October 8	Baltimore Orioles	3	at	Chicago White Sox	0 [10]

World Series

October 11	Philadelphia Phillies	2	at	Baltimore Orioles	1
October 12	Philadelphia Phillies	1	at	Baltimore Orioles	4
October 14	Baltimore Orioles	3	at	Philadelphia Phillies	2
October 15	Baltimore Orioles	5	at	Philadelphia Phillies	4
October 16	Baltimore Orioles	5	at	Philadelphia Phillies	0

Individual Awards

ALCS MVP--Mike Boddicker (Baltimore Orioles AL)
Arch Ward Memorial Trophy--Fred Lynn (California Angels AL)
Baseball Writers Award--Dale Murphy (Atlanta Braves NL)
Cal Ripken (Baltimore Orioles AL)
Cy Young Award--John Denny (Philadelphia Phillies NL)
LaMarr Hoyt (Chicago White Sox AL)
NLCS MVP--Gary Matthews (Philadelphia Phillies NL)
Rookie of the Year--Darryl Strawberry (New York Mets NL)
Ron Kittle (Chicago White Sox AL)
Sporting News Executive of the Year--Hank Peters (Baltimore Orioles AL)
Sporting News Manager of the Year--Tony LaRussa (Chicago White Sox AL)
Sporting News Pitcher of the Year--John Denny (Philadelphia Phillies NL)
LaMarr Hoyt (Chicago White Sox AL)
Sporting News Player of the Year--Dale Murphy (Atlanta Braves NL)
Cal Ripken (Baltimore Orioles AL)
Sporting News Rookie of the Year--Darryl Strawberry (New York Mets NL)
Craig McMurty (Atlanta Braves NL)
Ron Kittle (Chicago White Sox AL)
Mike Boddicker (Baltimore Orioles AL)
World Series MVP--Rick Dempsey (Baltimore Orioles AL)

Hall of Fame Inductees

Walter Alston, George Kell, Juan Marichal, Brooks Robinson

BASKETBALL

National Basketball Association
Eastern Conference

Atlantic Division

Team Name	GP	W	L	PPGF	PPGA	Pct	GB
Philadelphia 76ers	82	65	17	112.1	104.4	.793	-
Boston Celtics	82	56	26	112.1	106.7	.683	9
New Jersey Nets	82	49	33	105.8	103.0	.598	16
New York Knickerbockers	82	44	38	100.0	97.5	.537	21
Washington Bullets	82	42	40	99.2	99.3	.512	23

Central Division

Team Name	GP	W	L	PPGF	PPGA	Pct	GB
Milwaukee Bucks	82	51	31	106.6	102.2	.622	-
Atlanta Hawks	82	43	39	101.6	102.6	.524	8
Detroit Pistons	82	37	45	112.7	113.1	.451	14
Chicago Bulls	82	28	54	111.0	115.9	.341	23
Cleveland Cavaliers	82	23	59	97.1	104.6	.280	28
Indiana Pacers	82	20	62	108.7	114.5	.244	31

Western Conference

Midwest Division

Team Name	GP	W	L	PPGF	PPGA	Pct	GB
San Antonio Spurs	82	53	29	114.3	110.7	.646	-
Denver Nuggets	82	45	37	123.2	122.6	.549	8
Kansas City Kings	82	45	37	113.8	112.3	.549	8
Dallas Mavericks	82	38	44	112.7	113.1	.463	15
Utah Jazz	82	30	52	109.0	113.2	.366	23
Houston Rockets	82	14	68	99.3	110.9	.171	39

Pacific Division

Team Name	GP	W	L	PPGF	PPGA	Pct	GB
Los Angeles Lakers	82	58	24	115.0	109.5	.707	-
Phoenix Suns	82	53	29	107.0	102.0	.646	5
Seattle SuperSonics	82	48	34	110.0	106.8	.585	10
Portland Trail Blazers	82	46	36	107.4	105.3	.561	12
Golden State Warriors	82	30	52	108.6	112.3	.366	28
San Diego Clippers	82	25	57	108.6	113.4	.305	33

Coaching Changes

New Jersey--Larry Brown 47-29, Bill Blair 2-4; New York--Hubie Brown 44-38; Chicago--Paul Westhead 28-54; Cleveland--Tom Nissalke 23-59; Utah--Frank Layden 30-52; Los Angeles--Pat Riley 58-24.

League Leaders

Field Goals		Free Throws		Assists	
Alex English	959	Moses Malone	600	Earvin Johnson	829
Kiki Vandeweghe	841	George Gervin	517	John Moore	753
Joe Carroll	785	Sidney Moncrief	499	Rickey Green	697
Mark Aguirre	767	Kiki Vandeweghe	489	Gus Williams	643
George Gervin	757	Reggie Theus	434	Isiah Thomas	634

Points		Rebounds Per Game	
Alex English	2326	Moses Malone	15.3
Kiki Vandeweghe	2186	Buck Williams	12.5
George Gervin	2043	Bill Laimbeer	12.1
Mark Aguirre	1979	Artis Gilmore	12.0
Reggie Theus	1953	Jack Sikma	11.4

All Star Game

(The Forum, Los Angeles)

February 13	East Division	132	West Division	123

NBA Playoffs

April 19	Atlanta Hawks	95	at	Boston Celtics	103
April 19	Denver Nuggets	108	at	Phoenix Suns	121
April 20	N.Y. Knickerbockers	118	at	New Jersey Nets	107
April 20	Portland Trail Blazers	108	at	Seattle SuperSonics	97
April 21	New Jersey Nets	99	at	N.Y. Knickerbockers	105
April 21	Phoenix Suns	99	at	Denver Nuggets	113
April 22	Seattle SuperSonics	96	at	Portland Trail Blazers	105
April 22	Boston Celtics	93	at	Atlanta Hawks	95
April 24	Atlanta Hawks	79	at	Boston Celtics	98
April 24	Denver Nuggets	117	at	Phoenix Suns	112 [OT]
April 24	N.Y. Knickerbockers	102	at	Philadelphia 76ers	112
April 24	Portland Trail Blazers	97	at	Los Angeles Lakers	118
April 26	Portland Trail Blazers	106	at	Los Angeles Lakers	112
April 26	Denver Nuggets	133	at	San Antonio Spurs	152
April 27	N.Y. Knickerbockers	91	at	Philadelphia 76ers	98
April 27	Milwaukee Bucks	116	at	Boston Celtics	95
April 27	Denver Nuggets	109	at	San Antonio Spurs	126
April 29	Los Angeles Lakers	115	at	Portland Trail Blazers	109 [OT]
April 29	San Antonio Spurs	127	at	Denver Nuggets	126 [OT]
April 29	Milwaukee Bucks	95	at	Boston Celtics	91
April 30	Philadelphia 76ers	107	at	N.Y. Knickerbockers	105
May 1	Los Angeles Lakers	95	at	Portland Trail Blazers	108
May 1	Philadelphia 76ers	105	at	N.Y. Knickerbockers	102
May 1	Boston Celtics	99	at	Milwaukee Bucks	107
May 2	San Antonio Spurs	114	at	Denver Nuggets	124
May 2	Boston Celtics	93	at	Milwaukee Bucks	107
May 3	Portland Trail Blazers	108	at	Los Angeles Lakers	116
May 4	Denver Nuggets	105	at	San Antonio Spurs	145
May 8	Milwaukee Bucks	109	at	Philadelphia 76ers	111
May 8	San Antonio Spurs	107	at	Los Angeles Lakers	119
May 10	San Antonio Spurs	122	at	Los Angeles Lakers	113

May 11	Milwaukee Bucks	81	at	Philadelphia 76ers	87
May 13	Los Angeles Lakers	113	at	San Antonio Spurs	100
May 14	Philadelphia 76ers	104	at	Milwaukee Bucks	96
May 15	Los Angeles Lakers	129	at	San Antonio Spurs	121
May 15	Philadelphia 76ers	94	at	Milwaukee Bucks	100
May 18	San Antonio Spurs	117	at	Los Angeles Lakers	112
May 18	Milwaukee Bucks	103	at	Philadelphia 76ers	115
May 20	Los Angeles Lakers	101	at	San Antonio Spurs	100
May 22	Los Angeles Lakers	107	at	Philadelphia 76ers	113
May 26	Los Angeles Lakers	93	at	Philadelphia 76ers	103
May 29	Philadelphia 76ers	111	at	Los Angeles Lakers	94
May 31	Philadelphia 76ers	115	at	Los Angeles Lakers	108

All Star Teams

First Team

Larry Bird (Boston Celtics)
Julius Erving (Philadelphia 76ers)
Moses Malone (Philadelphia 76ers)
Earvin Johnson (Los Angeles Lakers)
Sidney Moncrief (Milwaukee Bucks)

Second Team

Alex English (Denver Nuggets)
Buck Williams (New Jersey Nets)
Kareem Abdul-Jabbar (Los Angeles Lakers)
George Gervin (San Antonio Spurs)
Isiah Thomas (Detroit Pistons)

Individual Awards

Defensive Player of the Year--Sidney Moncrief (Milwaukee Bucks)
Eddie Gottlieb Trophy--Terry Cummings (San Diego Clippers)
Executive of the Year--Zollie Volchok (Seattle SuperSonics)
J. Walter Kennedy Citizenship Award--Julius Erving (Philadelphia 76ers)
Maurice Podoloff Trophy--Moses Malone (Philadelphia 76ers)
NBA All Star Game MVP--Julius Erving (Philadelphia 76ers)
NBA Finals MVP--Moses Malone (Philadelphia 76ers)
Red Auerbach Trophy--Don Nelson (Milwaukee Bucks)
Sixth Man Award--Bobby Jones (Philadelphia 76ers)

Hall of Fame Inductees

Clifford Fagan, Jack Gardner, John Havlicek, Sam Jones, Edward Steitz

FOOTBALL

National Football League
National Conference
Eastern Division

Team Name	GP	W	L	T	PF	PA	Pct
Washington Redskins	16	14	2	0	541	332	.875
Dallas Cowboys	16	12	4	0	479	360	.750
St. Louis Cardinals	16	8	7	1	374	428	.531
Philadelphia Eagles	16	5	11	0	233	322	.313
New York Giants	16	3	12	1	267	347	.219

Central Division

Team Name	GP	W	L	T	PF	PA	Pct
Detroit Lions	16	9	7	0	347	286	.562
Green Bay Packers	16	8	8	0	429	439	.500
Chicago Bears	16	8	8	0	311	301	.500
Minnesota Vikings	16	8	8	0	316	348	.500
Tampa Bay Buccaneers	16	2	14	0	241	380	.125

Western Division

San Francisco 49ers	16	10	6	0	432	293	.625
Los Angeles Rams	16	9	7	0	361	344	.562
New Orleans Saints	16	8	8	0	319	337	.500
Atlanta Falcons	16	7	9	0	370	389	.438

American Conference

Eastern Division

Miami Dolphins	16	12	4	0	389	250	.750
New England Patriots	16	8	8	0	274	289	.500
Buffalo Bills	16	8	8	0	283	351	.500
Baltimore Colts	16	7	9	0	264	354	.438
New York Jets	16	7	9	0	313	331	.438

Central Division

Pittsburgh Steelers	16	10	6	0	355	303	.625
Cleveland Browns	16	9	7	0	356	342	.562
Cincinnati Bengals	16	7	9	0	346	302	.438
Houston Oilers	16	2	14	0	288	460	.125

Western Division

Los Angeles Raiders	16	12	4	0	442	338	.750
Seattle Seahawks	16	9	7	0	403	397	.562
Denver Broncos	16	9	7	0	302	327	.562
San Diego Chargers	16	6	10	0	358	462	.375
Kansas City Chiefs	16	6	10	0	386	367	.375

Coaching Changes

Philadelphia--Marion Campbell 5-11-0; N.Y. Giants--Bill Parcels 3-12-1; L.A. Rams--John Robinson 9-7-0; Atlanta--Dan Henning 7-9-0; Buffalo--Kay Stephenson 8-8-0; N.Y. Jets--Joe Walton 7-9-0; Houston--Ed Biles 0-6-0, Chuck Studley 2-8-0; Seattle--Chuck Knox 9-7-0; Kansas City--John Mackovic 6-10-0.

League Leaders

Yards Rushing		Yards Passing		Passing % (300 attempts)	
Eric Dickerson	1808	Lynn Dickey	4458	Joe Montana	64.5
William Andrews	1567	Bill Kenney	4348	Steve Bartkowski	63.4
Curt Warner	1449	Danny White	3980	Dan Fouts	63.2
Walter Payton	1421	Joe Montana	3910	Danny White	62.7
John Riggins	1347	Joe Theismann	3714	Jim Plunkett	60.7

Receiving Yards		Receptions		Field Goals	
Mike Quick	1409	Todd Christensen	92	Ali Haji-Sheikh	35
Carlos Carson	1351	Ozzie Newsome	89	Mark Moseley	33
James Lofton	1300	Kellen Winslow	88	Raul Allegre	30
Todd Christensen	1247	Tim Smith	83	Gary Anderson	27
Roy Green	1227	Carlos Carson	80	Ray Wersching	25

Punt Return Yards		Kickoff Return Yards	
Greg Pruitt	666	Zachary Dixon	1171
Bill Johnson	489	Fulton Walker	962
Rick Smith	398	Rick Smith	916
Mark Clayton	392	Ron Fellows	855
Zach Thomas	368	Jarvis Redwine	838

Pro Bowl Game

(Aloha Stadium, Honolulu)

January 29 1984	National Conference	45		American Conference	3

NFL Playoffs

December 24	Denver Broncos	7	at	Seattle Seahawks	31
December 26	Los Angeles Rams	24	at	Dallas Cowboys	17
December 31	Detroit Lions	23	at	San Francisco 49ers	24
December 31	Seattle Seahawks	27	at	Miami Dolphins	20
January 1 1984	Los Angeles Rams	7	at	Washington Redskins	51
January 1 1984	Pittsburgh Steelers	10	at	Los Angeles Raiders	38
January 8 1984	San Francisco 49ers	21	at	Washington Redskins	24
January 8 1984	Seattle Seahawks	14	at	Los Angeles Raiders	30

Super Bowl XVIII

(Tampa Stadium, Tampa, Florida)

January 22 1984	Los Angeles Raiders	38	Washington Redskins	9

Individual Awards

A.P. MVP--Joe Theismann (Washington Redskins)
Bert Bell Trophy--Eric Dickerson (Los Angeles Rams) [World Almanac]
Bert Bell Trophy--John Riggins (Washington Redskins)
George Halas Trophy--Jack Lambert (Pittsburgh Steelers)
Jim Thorpe Trophy--Joe Thiesmann (Washington Redskins)
P.F.W.A. MVP--Joe Theismann (Washington Redskins)
Pro Bowl MVP--Joe Theismann (Washington Redskins)
Super Bowl MVP--Marcus Allen (Los Angeles Raiders NFL)
U.P.I. AFC Coach of the Year--Chuck Knox (Seattle Seahawks)
U.P.I. AFC Player of the Year--Curt Warner (Seattle Seahawks)
Rod Martin (Los Angeles Raiders)
U.P.I. AFC Rookie of the Year--Curt Warner (Seattle Seahawks)
U.P.I. NFC Coach of the Year--John Robinson (Los Angeles Rams)
U.P.I. NFC Player of the Year--Eric Dickerson (Los Angeles Rams)
Lawrence Taylor (New York Giants)
U.P.I. NFC Rookie of the Year--Eric Dickerson (Los Angeles Rams)

Hall of Fame Inductees

Bobby Bell, Sid Gillman, Sonny Jurgensen, Bobby Mitchell, Paul Warfield

Notes

George Halas the owner of the Chicago Bears died on Halloween night, Halas was the last surviving member of the NFL's second organizational meeting.

Canadian Football League
Eastern Division

Team Name	GP	W	L	T	PF	PA	Pts	Pct
Toronto Argonauts	16	12	4	0	452	328	24	.750
Ottawa Rough Riders	16	8	8	0	384	424	16	.500
Hamilton Tiger-Cats	16	5	10	1	389	498	11	.344
Montreal Concordes	16	5	10	1	367	447	11	.344

Western Division

Team Name	GP	W	L	T	PF	PA	Pts	Pct
British Columbia Lions	16	11	5	0	477	326	22	.688
Winnipeg Blue Bombers	16	9	7	0	412	402	18	.563
Edmonton Eskimos	16	8	8	0	450	377	16	.500
Calgary Stampeders	16	8	8	0	425	378	16	.500
Saskatchewan Roughriders	16	5	11	0	360	536	10	.313

Coaching Changes

Hamilton--Bud Riley 4-8-0, Al Bruno 1-2-1; British Columbia--Don Matthews 9-7-0; Winnipeg--Cal Murphy 9-7-0; Edmonton--Pete Kettela 4-4-0, Jackie Parker 4-4-0; Saskatchewan--Joe Faragalli 1-5-0, Rueben Berry 4-6-0.

League Leaders

Yards Rushing		**Yards Passing**		**Passing %** (150 attempts)	
Alvin Walker	1431	Warren Moon	5648	Roy DeWalt	62.2
John Shepherd	1069	Roy DeWalt	3637	John Evans	57.7
Willard Reaves	888	Conredge Holloway	3184	Tom Clements	57.4
Lester Brown	792	Dieter Brock	3133	Warren Moon	57.2
Ray Crouse	703	J.C. Watts	3089	Gerry Dattilio	56.8

Receiving Yards		**Reception**		**Points**	
Terry Greer	2003	Terry Greer	113	Lui Passaglia	191
Brian Kelly	1812	Brian Kelly	104	Trevor Kennerd	166
Ron Robinson	1379	Tom Scott	80	Bernie Ruoff	149
Mervyn Fernandez	1284	Mervyn Fernandez	78	Hank Ilesic	148
Tom Scott	1234	Sam Greene	75	Dave Cutler	143

All Star Game
(B.C. Place Stadium, Vancouver)

December 3	West Division	25	East Division	15

Grey Cup Playoffs

November 13	Edmonton Eskimos	22	at	Winnipeg Blue Bombers	49
November 13	Hamilton Tiger-Cats	33	at	Ottawa Rough Riders	31
November 20	Winnipeg Blue Bombers	21	at	British Columbia Lions	39
November 20	Hamilton Tiger-Cats	36	at	Toronto Argonauts	41
November 27	Toronto Argonauts	18	at	British Columbia Lions	17

Individual Awards

Annis Stukus Trophy--Cal Murphy (Winnipeg Blue Bombers)
CFL All Star Game MVP--Roy DeWalt (British Columbia Lions)
Dave Fennell (Edmonton Eskimos)
Dave Dryburgh Memorial Trophy--Lui Passaglia (British Columbia Lions)
DeMarco-Becket Memorial Trophy--John Bonk (Winnipeg Blue Bombers)
Dr. Beattie Martin Trophy--Paul Bennett (Winnipeg Blue Bombers)
Eddie James Memorial Trophy--Willard Reaves (Winnipeg Blue Bombers)
Frank M. Gibson Trophy--Johnny Shepherd (Hamilton Tiger-Cats)
Grey Cup Most Outstanding Defensive Star--Carl Brazley (Toronto Argonauts)
Grey Cup Most Outstanding Offensive Star--Joe Barnes (Toronto Argonauts)
Grey Cup Most Outstanding Canadian--Rick Klassen (British Columbia Lions)
Jackie Parker Trophy--Willard Reaves (Winnipeg Blue Bombers)
James P. McCaffrey Trophy--Greg Marshall (Ottawa Rough Riders)
Jeff Nicklin Memorial Trophy--Warren Moon (Edmonton Eskimos)
Jeff Russel Memorial Trophy--Terry Greer (Toronto Argonauts)
Leo Dandurand Trophy--Rudy Phillips (Ottawa Rough Riders)
Lew Hayman Trophy--Denny Ferdinand (Montreal Concordes)
Norm Fieldgate Trophy--Danny Bass (Calgary Stampeders)
Schenley Award Most Outstanding Canadian--Paul Bennett (Winnipeg Blue Bombers)
Schenley Award Most Outstanding Defensive Player--Greg Marshall (Ottawa Rough Riders)
Schenley Award Most Outstanding Offensive Lineman--Rudy Phillips (Ottawa Rough Riders)
Schenley Award Most Outstanding Player--Warren Moon (Edmonton Eskimos)
Schenley Award Most Outstanding Rookie--Johhny Shepherd (Hamilton Tiger-Cats)

Hall of Fame Inductees

Bud Grant, Herb Gray, Earl Lunsford, Don McPherson, Frank Morris

Notes

The CFL signed a three year, $33 million television contract with Carling O'Keefe Breweries.
This year s Grey Cup game was the first one to be played indoors when B.C. was defeated by Toronto 18-17 in Vancouver's B.C. Place Stadium.

United States Football League

Atlantic Division

Team Name	GP	W	L	T	PF	PA	Pct
Philadelphia Stars	18	15	3	0	379	204	.833
Boston Breakers	18	11	7	0	399	334	.611
New Jersey Generals	18	6	12	0	314	437	.333
Washington Federals	18	4	14	0	297	442	.222

Central Division

Team Name	GP	W	L	T	PF	PA	Pct
Michigan Panthers	18	12	6	0	451	337	.667
Chicago Blitz	18	12	6	0	456	271	.667
Tampa Bay Bandits	18	11	7	0	363	378	.611
Birmingham Stallions	18	9	9	0	343	346	.500

Pacific Division

Oakland Invaders	18	9	9	0	319	317	.500
Los Angeles Express	18	8	10	0	296	370	.444
Denver Gold	18	7	11	0	284	304	.389
Arizona Wranglers	18	4	14	0	261	442	.222

Coaching Changes

Philadelphia--Clare Peterson 15-3-0; Boston--Dick Coury 11-7-0; New Jersey--Chuck Fairbanks 6-12-0; Washington--Ray Jauch 4-14-0; Chicago--George Allen 12-6-0; Tampa Bay--Steve Spurrier 11-7-0; Birmingham--Rollie Dotsch 9-9-0; Oakland--John Ralston 9-9-0; Los Angeles--Hugh Campbell 8-10-0; Denver--Red Miller 4-7-0, Charley Armey 3-4-0; Michigan--Jim Stanley 12-6-0; Arizona--Doug Shavely 4-14-0.

League Leaders

Yards Rushing		**Yards Passing**		**Passing %** (300 attempts)	
Herschel Walker	1812	Fred Besana	3980	Fred Besana	62.7
Kelvin Bryant	1442	John Walton	3772	Bob Hebert	57.0
Ken Lacy	1180	Bob Hebert	3568	Chuck Fusina	56.5
Tim Spencer	1157	Bob Scott	2813	Greg Landry	56.3
Arthur Whittington	1043	Chuck Fusina	2718	John Walton	56.0

Receiving Yards	
Trumaine Johnson	1322
Danny Buggs	1146
Eric Truvillion	1080
Ray Chester	951
Ellis	716

USFL Playoffs

July 9	Chicago Blitz	38	at	Philadelphia Stars	44
July 10	Oakland Invaders	21	at	Michigan Panthers	37
July 17	Michigan Panthers	24	at	Philadelphia Stars	22*

Individual Awards

USFL Finals MVP--Bob Hebert (Michigan Panthers)

Notes

The United States Football League was organized this year and played a spring and summer schedule so as not to conflict with the NFL. Chet Simmons was named first Commissioner of the league.
Anthony Taylor of the Los Angeles Express became the first and only player to play in the NFL, CFL, WFL and the USFL.

*Game played in Denver

HOCKEY
National Hockey League

Clarence Campbell Conference

Norris Division

Team Name	GP	W	L	T	GF	GA	Pts	Pct
Chicago Black Hawks	80	47	23	10	338	268	104	.650
Minnesota North Stars	80	40	24	16	321	290	96	.600
Toronto Maple Leafs	80	28	40	12	293	330	68	.425
St. Louis Blues	80	25	40	15	285	316	65	.406
Detroit Red Wings	80	21	44	15	263	344	57	.356

Smythe Division

Team Name	GP	W	L	T	GF	GA	Pts	Pct
Edmonton Oilers	80	47	21	12	424	315	106	.663
Calgary Flames	80	32	34	14	321	317	78	.488
Vancouver Canucks	80	30	35	15	303	309	75	.469
Winnipeg Jets	80	33	39	8	311	333	74	.463
Los Angeles Kings	80	27	41	12	308	365	66	.413

Prince of Wales Conference

Patrick Division

Team Name	GP	W	L	T	GF	GA	Pts	Pct
Philadelphia Flyers	80	49	23	8	326	240	106	.663
New York Islanders	80	42	26	12	302	226	96	.600
Washington Capitals	80	39	25	16	306	283	94	.588
New York Rangers	80	35	35	10	306	287	80	.500
New Jersey Devils	80	17	49	14	230	338	48	.300
Pittsburgh Penguins	80	18	53	9	257	394	45	.281

Adams Division

Team Name	GP	W	L	T	GF	GA	Pts	Pct
Boston Bruins	80	50	20	10	327	228	110	.688
Montreal Canadiens	80	42	24	14	350	286	98	.613
Buffalo Sabres	80	38	29	13	318	285	89	.556
Quebec Nordiques	80	34	34	12	343	336	80	.500
Hartford Whalers	80	19	54	7	261	403	45	.281

Coaching Changes

Chicago--Orval Tessier 47-23-10; Minnesota--Glen Sonmor 22-13-9, Murray Oliver 18-11-7; St. Louis--Emile Francis 10-19-3, Barclay Plager 15-21-12; Detroit--Nick Polano 21-44-15; Calgary--Bob Johnson 32-34-14; Vancouver--Roger Neilson 30-35-15; Los Angeles--Don Perry 27-41-12; Philadelphia--Bob McCammon 49-23-8; Washington--Bryan Murray 39-25-16; New Jersey--Bill MacMillan 17-49-14; Buffalo--Scotty Bowman 38-29-13; Hartford--Larry Kish 12-32-5, Larry Pleau 4-13-1, John Cunniff 3-9-1.

League Leaders

Goals		Assists		Points	
Wayne Gretzky	71	Wayne Gretzky	125	Wayne Gretzky	196
Lanny McDonald	66	Denis Savard	85	Peter Stastny	124
Mike Bossy	60	Peter Stastny	77	Denis Savard	120
Michel Goulet	57	Paul Coffey	67	Mike Bossy	118
Marcel Dionne	56	Bobby Clarke	62	Barry Pederson	107

Penalty Minutes		Plus/Minus		GAA (1,600minutes)	
Randy Holt	275	Charlie Huddy	62	Pete Peeters	2.36
Dave Williams	265	Wayne Gretzky	60	Roland Melanson	2.66
Doug Wilson	258	Paul Coffey	52	Billy Smith	2.87
Brian Sutter	254	Ray Bourque	49	Pelle Lindbergh	2.98
Paul Baxter	238	Mark Howe	47	Murray Bannerman	3.10

Wins		Shutouts	
Pete Peeters	40	Pete Peeters	8
Andy Moog	33	Murray Bannerman	4
Rick Wamsley	27	Bob Froese	4
Bob Sauve	25	Pelle Lindbergh	3
Murray Bannerman	24	Ed Mio	2

All Star Game

(Nassau County Coliseum, New York)

February 8	Campbell Conference	9		Wales Conference	3

Stanley Cup Playoffs

April 5	Quebec Nordiques	3	at	Boston Bruins	4 [1:46]
April 5	New York Rangers	5	at	Philadelphia Flyers	3
April 6	St. Louis Blues	4	at	Chicago Black Hawks	2
April 6	Toronto Maple Leafs	4	at	Minnesota North Stars	5
April 6	Winnipeg Jets	3	at	Edmonton Oilers	6
April 6	Vancouver Canucks	3	at	Calgary Flames	4 [12:27]
April 6	Buffalo Sabres	1	at	Montreal Canadiens	0
April 6	Washington Capitals	2	at	New York Islanders	5
April 7	St. Louis Blues	2	at	Chicago Black Hawks	7
April 7	Toronto Maple Leafs	4	at	Minnesota North Stars	5 [5:03]
April 7	Winnipeg Jets	3	at	Edmonton Oilers	4
April 7	Vancouver Canucks	3	at	Calgary Flames	5
April 7	Quebec Nordiques	2	at	Boston Bruins	4
April 7	Buffalo Sabres	3	at	Montreal Canadiens	0
April 7	Washington Capitals	4	at	New York Islanders	2
April 7	New York Rangers	4	at	Philadelphia Flyers	3
April 9	Chicago Black Hawks	2	at	St. Louis Blues	1
April 9	Minnesota North Stars	3	at	Toronto Maple Leafs	6
April 9	Edmonton Oilers	4	at	Winnipeg Jets	3
April 9	Calgary Flames	4	at	Vancouver Canucks	5
April 9	Boston Bruins	1	at	Quebec Nordiques	2
April 9	Montreal Canadiens	2	at	Buffalo Sabres	4
April 9	Philadelphia Flyers	3	at	New York Rangers	9

April 9	New York Islanders	6	at	Washington Capitals	2
April 10	Chicago Black Hawks	5	at	St. Louis Blues	3
April 10	Minnesota North Stars	5	at	Toronto Maple Leafs	4 [8:05]
April 10	Calgary Flames	4	at	Vancouver Canucks	3 [1:06]
April 10	Boston Bruins	2	at	Quebec Nordiques	1
April 10	New York Islanders	6	at	Washington Capitals	3
April 14	Minnesota North Stars	2	at	Chicago Black Hawks	5
April 14	Calgary Flames	3	at	Edmonton Oilers	6
April 14	Buffalo Sabres	7	at	Boston Bruins	4
April 14	New York Rangers	1	at	New York Islanders	4
April 15	Minnesota North Stars	4	at	Chicago Black Hawks	7
April 15	Calgary Flames	1	at	Edmonton Oilers	5
April 15	Buffalo Sabres	3	at	Boston Bruins	5
April 15	New York Rangers	0	at	New York Islanders	5
April 17	Chicago Black Hawks	1	at	Minnesota North Stars	5
April 17	Edmonton Oilers	10	at	Calgary Flames	2
April 17	Boston Bruins	3	at	Buffalo Sabres	4
April 17	New York Islanders	6	at	New York Rangers	7
April 18	Chicago Black Hawks	4	at	Minnesota North Stars	3 [10:34]
April 18	Edmonton Oilers	5	at	Calgary Flames	6
April 18	Boston Bruins	6	at	Buffalo Sabres	2
April 18	New York Islanders	1	at	New York Rangers	3
April 20	Minnesota North Stars	2	at	Chicago Black Hawks	5
April 20	Calgary Flames	1	at	Edmonton Oilers	9
April 20	Buffalo Sabres	0	at	Boston Bruins	9
April 20	New York Rangers	2	at	New York Islanders	7
April 22	Boston Bruins	3	at	Buffalo Sabres	5
April 22	New York Islanders	5	at	New York Rangers	2
April 24	Buffalo Sabres	2	at	Boston Bruins	3 [1:52]
April 24	Chicago Black Hawks	4	at	Edmonton Oilers	8
April 26	New York Islanders	5	at	Boston Bruins	2
April 26	Chicago Black Hawks	2	at	Edmonton Oilers	8
April 28	New York Islanders	1	at	Boston Bruins	4
April 30	Boston Bruins	3	at	New York Islanders	7
May 1	Edmonton Oilers	3	at	Chicago Black Hawks	2
May 3	Boston Bruins	3	at	New York Islanders	8
May 3	Edmonton Oilers	6	at	Chicago Black Hawks	3
May 5	New York Islanders	1	at	Boston Bruins	5
May 7	Boston Bruins	4	at	New York Islanders	8
May 10	New York Islanders	2	at	Edmonton Oilers	0
May 12	New York Islanders	6	at	Edmonton Oilers	3
May 14	Edmonton Oilers	1	at	New York Islanders	5
May 17	Edmonton Oilers	2	at	New York Islanders	4

All Star Teams

First Team		Second Team
Pete Peeters	Goal	Roland Melanson
Mark Howe	Defense	Ray Bourque
Rod Langway	Defense	Paul Coffey
Wayne Gretzky	Center	Denis Savard
Mike Bossy	Right Wing	Lanny McDonald
Mark Messier	Left Wing	Michel Goulet

Individual Awards

Art Ross Trophy--Wayne Gretzky (Edmonton Oilers)
Bill Masterton Trophy--Lanny McDonald (Calgary Flames)
Calder Memorial Trophy--Steve Larmer (Chicago Black Hawks)
Conn Smythe Trophy--Billy Smith (New York Islanders)
Emery Edge Trophy--Charlie Huddy (Edmonton Oilers)
Frank J. Selke Trophy--Bobby Clarke (Philadelphia Flyers)
Hart Memorial Trophy--Wayne Gretzky (Edmonton Oilers)
Jack Adams Award--Orval Tessier (Chicago Black Hawks)
James Norris Trophy--Rod Langway (Washington Capitals)
Lady Byng Memorial Trophy--Mike Bossy (New York Islanders)
Lester B. Pearson Award--Wayne Gretzky (Edmonton Oilers)
Lester Patrick Trophy--Bill Torrey
NHL All Star Game MVP--Wayne Gretzky (Edmonton Oilers)
Vezina Trophy--Pete Peeters (Boston Bruins)
William-M. Jennings Trophy--Roland Melanson and Bill Smith (New York Islanders)

Hall of Fame Inductees

Ken Dryden, Bobby Hull, Stan Mikita, Harry Sinden

Rules

Number of players allowed to dress for a game is set at 18.

SOCCER

North American Soccer League

Eastern Division

Team Name	GP	W	L	GF	GA	BP	Pts	Pct
Cosmos	30	22	8	87	49	64	194	.431
Chicago Sting	30	15	15	66	73	57	147	.327
Toronto Blizzard	30	16	14	51	48	45	135	.300
Montreal Manic	30	12	18	58	71	52	124	.276
Southern Division								
Tulsa Roughnecks	30	17	13	56	49	47	145	.322
Ft. Lauderdale Strikers	30	14	16	60	63	54	136	.302
Tampa Bay Rowdies	30	7	23	48	87	41	83	.184
Team America	30	10	20	33	54	25	79	.176
Western Division								
Vancouver Whitecaps	30	24	6	63	34	51	187	.416
Golden Bay Earthquakes	30	20	10	71	54	55	169	.376
Seattle Sounders	30	12	18	62	61	51	119	.264
San Diego Sockers	30	11	19	53	65	42	106	.236

Coaching Changes

Montreal--Andy Lynch 12-18; Ft. Lauderdale--Dave Chadwick 14-16; Tampa Bay--Al Miller 7-23; Team America--Alkis Panagoulas 10-20; Golden Bay--Dan Popovic 20-10; Seattle--Laurie Calloway 12-18.

League Leaders

Points		**GAA**	
Roberto Cabanas	66	Tino Lettieri	0.86

NASL Playoffs

September 6	Montreal Manic	4	at	Cosmos	2
September 6	Ft. Lauderdale Strikers	2	at	Tulsa Roughnecks	3 [SO]
September 7	Chicago Sting	1	at	Golden Bay Earthquakes	6
September 8	Toronto Blizzard	0	at	Vancouver Whitecaps	1
September 10	Tulsa Roughnecks	4	at	Ft. Lauderdale Strikers	2
September 12	Cosmos	0	at	Montreal Manic	1
September 12	Golden Bay Earthquakes	0	at	Chicago Sting	1
September 12	Vancouver Whitecaps	3	at	Toronto Blizzard	4
September 14	Chicago Sting	2	at	Golden Bay Earthquakes	5
September 15	Toronto Blizzard	1	at	Vancouver Whitecaps	0
September 17	Toronto Blizzard	1	at	Golden Bay Earthquakes	0 [SO]
September 18	Montreal Manic	1	at	Tulsa Roughnecks	2 [SO]
September 22	Golden Bay Earthquakes	0	at	Toronto Blizzard	2
September 26	Tulsa Roughnecks	0	at	Montreal Manic	1
September 28	Montreal Manic	0	at	Tulsa Roughnecks	3
October 1	Tulsa Roughnecks	2		Toronto Blizzard	0 *

Individual Awards

Coach of the Year--Terry Hennessey (Tulsa Roughnecks)
Lead Goalkeeper Award--Tino Lettieri (Vancouver Whitecaps)
Most Valuable Player--Roberto Cabanas (New York Cosmos)
Soccer Bowl MVP--Niego Pesa (Tulsa Roughnecks)

Franchise Changes

NHL--Colorado Rockies became the New Jersey Devils.
NASL--San Jose Earthquakes became the Golden Bay Earthquakes.

Other Sports

Horseracing--Kentucky Derby won by Sonny's Halo (time 2:02.2, purse $426,000).
Heavyweight Boxing--Gerrie Coetzee knocked-out Michael Dokes in 10 rounds.
Golf--U.S. Open won by Larry Nelson with a score of 280.
Auto Racing--Indianapolis 500 won by Tom Sneva (ave. speed 162.117 MPH).
Tennis--U.S. Open won by Jimmy Connors in the men's singles.
U.S. Open won by John McEnroe and Peter Fleming in the men's doubles.
U.S. Open won by Martina Navritalova in the women's singles.
U.S. Open won by Martina Navritalova and Pam Shriver in the women's doubles.
U.S. Open won by Elizabeth Sayers and John Fitzgerald in the mixed doubles.

*Game played in Vancouver

1984

BASEBALL
National League
East

Team Name	W	L	Pct	GB	R	OR
Chicago Cubs	96	65	.596	-	762	658
New York Mets	90	72	.556	6.5	652	676
St. Louis Cardinals	84	78	.519	12.5	652	645
Philadelphia Phillies	81	81	.500	15.5	720	690
Montreal Expos	78	83	.484	18	593	585
Pittsburgh Pirates	75	87	.463	21.5	615	567

West

Team Name	W	L	Pct	GB	R	OR
San Diego Padres	92	70	.568	-	686	634
Atlanta Braves	80	82	.494	12	632	655
Houston Astros	80	82	.494	12	693	630
Los Angeles Dodgers	79	83	.488	13	580	600
Cincinnati Reds	70	92	.432	22	627	747
San Francisco Giants	66	96	.407	26	682	807

Coaching Changes

Chicago--Jim Frey 96-65; New York--Dave Johnson 90-72; Philadelphia--Paul Owens 81-81; Montreal--Bill Virdon 64-67, Jim Fanning 14-16; Cincinnati--Vern Rapp 51-70, Pete Rose 19-22; San Francisco--Frank Robinson 42-64, Danny Ozark 24-32.

League Leaders

Batting Average
(502 at bats)

Tony Gwynn	.351
Lee Lacy	.321
Charles Davis	.315
Ryne Sandberg	.314
Johnny Ray	.312

Home Runs

Dale Murphy	36
Mike Schmidt	36
Gary Carter	27
Darryl Strawberry	26
Ron Cey	25

RBI

Gary Carter	106
Mike Schmidt	106
Dale Murphy	100
Darryl Strawberry	97
Ron Cey	97

Stolen Bases

Tim Raines	75
Juan Samuel	72
Alan Wiggins	70
Lonnie Smith	50
Gary Redus	48

ERA
(162 innings)

Alejandro Pena	2.48
Dwight Gooden	2.60
Orel Hershiser	2.66
Rick Rhoden	2.72
John Candelaria	2.72

Wins

Joaquin Andujar	20
Mario Soto	18
Dwight Gooden	17
Rick Sutcliffe	16
Joe Niekro	16

Saves

Bruce Sutter	45
Lee Smith	33
Jesse Orosco	31
Al Holland	29
Rich Gossage	25

Strikeouts

Dwight Gooden	276
Fernando Valenzuela	240
Nolan Ryan	197
Mario Soto	185
Steve Carlton	163

NLCS

October 2	San Diego Padres	0	at	Chicago Cubs	13
October 3	San Diego Padres	2	at	Chicago Cubs	4
October 4	Chicago Cubs	1	at	San Diego Padres	7
October 6	Chicago Cubs	5	at	San Diego Padres	7
October 7	Chicago Cubs	3	at	San Diego Padres	6

American League
East

Team Name	W	L	Pct	GB	R	OR
Detroit Tigers	104	58	.642	-	829	643
Toronto Blue Jays	89	73	.549	15	750	696
New York Yankees	87	75	.537	17	758	679
Boston Red Sox	86	76	.531	18	810	764
Baltimore Orioles	85	77	.525	19	681	667
Cleveland Indians	75	87	.463	29	761	766
Milwaukee Brewers	67	94	.416	36.5	641	734

West

Team Name	W	L	Pct	GB	R	OR
Kansas City Royals	84	78	.519	-	673	686
California Angels	81	81	.500	3	696	697
Minnesota Twins	81	81	.500	3	673	675
Oakland Athletics	77	85	.475	7	738	796
Chicago White Sox	74	88	.457	10	679	736
Seattle Mariners	74	88	.457	10	682	774
Texas Rangers	69	92	.429	14.5	656	714

Coaching Changes

New York--Yogi Berra 87-75; Cleveland--Pat Corrales 75-87; Milwaukee Rene Lachemann 67-94; Oakland--Steve Boros 20-24, Jackie Moore 57-61; Seattle--Del Crandall 59-76, Chuck Cottier 15-12.

League Leaders

Batting Average (502 at bats)		**Home Runs**		**RBI**	
Don Mattingly	.343	Tony Armas	43	Tony Armas	123
Dave Winfield	.340	Dave Kingman	35	Jim Rice	122
Wade Boggs	.325	Andre Thornton	33	Dave Kingman	118
Buddy Bell	.315	Lance Parrish	33	Alvin Davis	116
Alan Trammell	.314	Dwayne Murphy	33	Eddie Murray	110

Stolen Bases		**ERA** (162 innings)		**Wins**	
Rickey Henderson	66	Mike Boddicker	2.79	Mike Boddicker	20
Dave Collins	60	Dave Stieb	2.83	Bert Blyleven	19
Brett Butler	52	Bert Blyleven	2.87	Jack Morris	19
Gary Pettis	48	Phil Niekro	3.09	Dan Petry	18
Willie Wilson	47	Geoff Zahn	3.12	Frank Viola	18

Saves		Strikeouts	
Dan Quisenberry	44	Mark Langston	204
Bill Caudill	36	Dave Stieb	198
Willie Hernandez	32	Mike Witt	196
Dave Righetti	31	Bert Blyleven	170
Ron Davis	29	Charlie Hough	164

All Star Game
(Candlestick Park, San Francisco)

July 10	National League	3		American League	1

ALCS

October 2	Detroit Tigers	8	at	Kansas City Royals	1
October 3	Detroit Tigers	5	at	Kansas City Royals	3 [11]
October 5	Kansas City Royals	0	at	Detroit Tigers	1

World Series

October 9	Detroit Tigers	3	at	San Diego Padres	2
October 10	Detroit Tigers	3	at	San Diego Padres	5
October 12	San Diego Padres	2	at	Detroit Tigers	5
October 13	San Diego Padres	2	at	Detroit Tigers	4
October 14	San Diego Padres	4	at	Detroit Tigers	8

Individual Awards

ALCS MVP--Kirk Gibson (Detroit Tigers AL)
Arch Ward Memorial Trophy--Gary Carter (Montreal Expos NL)
Baseball Writers Award--Ryne Sandberg (Chicago Cubs NL)
Willie Hernandez (Detroit Tigers AL)
Cy Young Award--Rick Sutcliffe (Chicago Cubs NL)
Willie Hernandez (Detroit Tigers AL)
NLCS MVP--Steve Garvey (San Diego Padres NL)
Rookie of the Year--Dwight Gooden (New York Mets NL)
Alvin Davis (Seattle Mariners AL)
Sporting News Executive of the Year--Dallas Green (Chicago Cubs NL)
Sporting News Manager of the Year--Jim Frey (Chicago Cubs NL)
Sporting News Pitcher of the Year--Rick Sutcliffe (Chicago Cubs NL)
Willie Hernandez (Detroit Tigers AL)
Sporting News Player of the Year--Ryne Sandberg (Chicago Cubs NL)
Don Mattingly (New York Yankees AL)
Sporting News Rookie of the Year--Juan Samuel (Philadelphia Phillies NL)
Dwight Gooden (New York Mets NL)
Alvin Davis (Seattle Mariners AL)
Mark Langston (Seattle Mariners AL)
World Series MVP--Alan Trammell (Detroit Tigers AL)

Hall of Fame Inductees

Lou Aparicio, Don Drysdale, Rick Ferrell, Harmon Killebrew, Harold "Pee Wee" Reese

Notes

Peter Ueberroth succeeded Bowie Kuhn as the new Commissioner of baseball and Bobby Brown succeeded Lee McPhail as President of the American League. Ueberroth had served as President of the Los Angeles Olympic Organizing Committee.

BASKETBALL

National Basketball Association

Eastern Conference
Atlantic Division

Team Name	GP	W	L	PPGF	PPGA	Pct	GB
Boston Celtics	82	62	20	112.1	105.6	.756	-
Philadelphia 76ers	82	52	30	107.8	105.6	.634	10
New York Knickerbockers	82	47	35	106.9	103.0	.573	15
New Jersey Nets	82	45	37	110.0	108.9	.549	17
Washington Bullets	82	35	47	102.7	105.6	.427	27

Central Division

Team Name	GP	W	L	PPGF	PPGA	Pct	GB
Milwaukee Bucks	82	50	32	105.7	101.5	.610	-
Detroit Pistons	82	49	33	117.1	113.5	.598	1
Atlanta Hawks	82	40	42	101.5	102.8	.488	10
Cleveland Cavaliers	82	28	54	102.3	106.5	.341	22
Chicago Bulls	82	27	55	103.7	108.9	.329	23
Indiana Pacers	82	26	56	104.5	109.3	.317	24

Western Conference

Midwest Division

Team Name	GP	W	L	PPGF	PPGA	Pct	GB
Utah Jazz	82	45	37	115.0	113.8	.549	-
Dallas Mavericks	82	43	39	110.4	110.0	.524	2
Denver Nuggets	82	38	44	123.7	124.8	.463	7
Kansas City Kings	82	38	44	110.0	111.5	.463	7
San Antonio Spurs	82	37	45	120.3	120.5	.451	8
Houston Rockets	82	29	53	110.6	113.7	.354	16

Pacific Division

Team Name	GP	W	L	PPGF	PPGA	Pct	GB
Los Angeles Lakers	82	54	28	115.6	111.8	.659	-
Portland Trail Blazers	82	48	34	113.1	109.6	.585	6
Seattle SuperSonics	82	42	40	108.1	108.3	.512	12
Phoenix Suns	82	41	41	111.0	110.1	.500	13
Golden State Warriors	82	37	45	109.9	113.3	.451	17
San Diego Clippers	82	30	52	110.7	114.0	.366	24

Coaching Changes

Boston--K.C. Jones 62-20; New Jersey--Stan Albeck 45-37; Detroit--Chuck Daly 49-33; Atlanta--Mike Fratello 40-42; Chicago--Kevin Loughery 27-55; San Antonio--Morris McHone 11-20, Bob Bass 26-25; Houston--Bill Fitch 29-53; Golden State--John Bach 37-45; San Diego--Jim Lynam 30-52.

League Leaders

Field Goals		Free Throws		Assists	
Mark Aguirre	925	Adrian Dantley	813	Isiah Thomas	914
Alex English	907	Moses Malone	545	Norm Nixon	914
Kiki Vandeweghe	895	Sidney Moncrief	529	Earvin Johnson	875
Adrian Dantley	802	Kiki Vandeweghe	494	Rickey Green	748
Bernard King	795	Jeff Ruland	466	Gus Williams	675

Points		Rebounds Per Game	
Adrian Dantley	2418	Moses Malone	13.4
Mark Aguirre	2330	Ray Williams	12.3
Kiki Vandeweghe	2295	Jeff Ruland	12.3
Alex English	2167	Bill Laimbeer	12.2
Bernard King	2027	Ralph Sampson	11.1

All Star Game

(McNichols Sports Arena, Denver)

January 29	East Division	154		West Division	145 [OT]

NBA Playoffs

April 17	Washington Bullets	83	at	Boston Celtics	91
April 17	Denver Nuggets	121	at	Utah Jazz	123
April 17	Atlanta Hawks	89	at	Milwaukee Bucks	105
April 17	Seattle SuperSonics	86	at	Dallas Mavericks	88
April 17	N.Y. Knickerbockers	94	at	Detroit Pistons	93
April 18	Phoenix Suns	113	at	Portland Trail Blazers	106
April 18	New Jersey Nets	116	at	Philadelphia 76ers	101
April 18	Kansas City Kings	105	at	Los Angeles Lakers	116
April 19	N.Y. Knickerbockers	105	at	Detroit Pistons	113
April 19	Washington Bullets	85	at	Boston Celtics	88
April 19	Denver Nuggets	132	at	Utah Jazz	116
April 19	Atlanta Hawks	87	at	Milwaukee Bucks	101
April 19	Seattle SuperSonics	95	at	Dallas Mavericks	92
April 20	Phoenix Suns	116	at	Portland Trail Blazers	122
April 20	New Jersey Nets	116	at	Philadelphia 76ers	102
April 20	Kansas City Kings	102	at	Los Angeles Lakers	109
April 21	Boston Celtics	108	at	Washington Bullets	111 [OT]
April 21	Milwaukee Bucks	94	at	Atlanta Hawks	103
April 21	Dallas Mavericks	94	at	Seattle SuperSonics	104
April 22	Utah Jazz	117	at	Denver Nuggets	121
April 22	Detroit Pistons	113	at	N.Y. Knickerbockers	120
April 22	Portland Trail Blazers	103	at	Phoenix Suns	106
April 22	Philadelphia 76ers	108	at	New Jersey Nets	100
April 22	Los Angeles Lakers	108	at	Kansas City Kings	102
April 24	Boston Celtics	99	at	Washington Bullets	96
April 24	Utah Jazz	129	at	Denver Nuggets	124
April 24	Milwaukee Bucks	97	at	Atlanta Hawks	100
April 24	Dallas Mavericks	107	at	Seattle SuperSonics	96
April 24	Portland Trail Blazers	113	at	Phoenix Suns	110
April 24	Philadelphia 76ers	110	at	New Jersey Nets	102
April 25	Detroit Pistons	119	at	N.Y. Knickerbockers	112

April 26	Denver Nuggets	111	at	Utah Jazz	127
April26	Atlanta Hawks	89	at	Milwaukee Bucks	118
April 26	Seattle SuperSonics	104	at	Dallas Mavericks	105 [OT]
April 26	Phoenix Suns	117	at	Portland Trail Blazers	105
April 26	New Jersey Nets	101	at	Philadelphia 76ers	98
April 27	N.Y. Knickerbockers	127	at	Detroit Pistons	123 [OT]
April 28	Dallas Mavericks	91	at	Los Angeles Lakers	134
April 29	N.Y. Knickerbockers	92	at	Boston Celtics	110
April 29	New Jersey Nets	106	at	Milwaukee Bucks	100
April 29	Phoenix Suns	95	at	Utah Jazz	105
May 1	Dallas Mavericks	101	at	Los Angeles Lakers	117
May 1	New Jersey Nets	94	at	Milwaukee Bucks	98
May 2	N.Y. Knickerbockers	102	at	Boston Celtics	116
May 2	Phoenix Suns	102	at	Utah Jazz	97
May 3	Milwaukee Bucks	100	at	New Jersey Nets	93
May 4	Boston Celtics	92	at	N.Y. Knickerbockers	100
May 4	Los Angeles Lakers	115	at	Dallas Mavericks	125
May 4	Utah Jazz	94	at	Phoenix Suns	106
May 5	Milwaukee Bucks	99	at	New Jersey Nets	106
May 6	Boston Celtics	113	at	N.Y. Knickerbockers	118
May 6	Los Angeles Lakers	122	at	Dallas Mavericks	115 [OT]
May 6	Utah Jazz	110	at	Phoenix Suns	111 [OT]
May 8	Dallas Mavericks	99	at	Los Angeles Lakers	115
May 8	New Jersey Nets	82	at	Milwaukee Bucks	94
May 8	Phoenix Suns	106	at	Utah Jazz	118
May 9	N.Y. Knickerbockers	99	at	Boston Celtics	121
May 10	Milwaukee Bucks	98	at	New Jersey Nets	97
May 10	Utah Jazz	82	at	Phoenix Suns	102
May 11	Boston Celtics	104	at	N.Y. Knickerbockers	106
May 12	Phoenix Suns	94	at	Los Angeles Lakers	110
May 13	N.Y. Knickerbockers	104	at	Boston Celtics	121
May 15	Milwaukee Bucks	96	at	Boston Celtics	119
May 15	Phoenix Suns	102	at	Los Angeles Lakers	118
May 17	Milwaukee Bucks	110	at	Boston Celtics	125
May 18	Los Angeles Lakers	127	at	Phoenix Suns	135 [OT]
May 19	Boston Celtics	109	at	Milwaukee Bucks	100
May 20	Los Angeles Lakers	126	at	Phoenix Suns	115
May 21	Boston Celtics	113	at	Milwaukee Bucks	122
May 23	Phoenix Suns	126	at	Los Angeles Lakers	121
May 23	Milwaukee Bucks	108	at	Boston Celtics	115
May 25	Los Angeles Lakers	99	at	Phoenix Suns	97
May 27	Los Angeles Lakers	115	at	Boston Celtics	109
May 31	Los Angeles Lakers	121	at	Boston Celtics	124 [OT]
June 3	Boston Celtics	104	at	Los Angeles Lakers	137
June 6	Boston Celtics	129	at	Los Angeles Lakers	125 [OT]
June 8	Los Angeles Lakers	103	at	Boston Celtics	121
June 10	Boston Celtics	108	at	Los Angeles Lakers	119
June 12	Los Angeles Lakers	102	at	Boston Celtics	111

All Star Teams

First Team	Second Team
Larry Bird (Boston Celtics)	Julius Erving (Philadelphia 76ers)
Bernard King (N.Y. Knickerbockers)	Adrian Dantley (Utah Jazz)
Kareem Abdul-Jabbar (Los Angeles Lakers)	Moses Malone (Philadelphia 76ers)
Earvin Johnson (Los Angeles Lakers)	Sidney Moncrief (Milwaukee Bucks)
Isiah Thomas (Detroit Pistons)	Jim Paxson (Portland Trail Blazers)

Individual Awards

Defensive Player of the Year--Sidney Moncrief (Milwaukee Bucks)
Eddie Gottlieb Trophy--Ralph Sampson (Houston Rockets)
Executive of the Year--Frank Layden (Utah Jazz)
J. Walter Kennedy Citizenship Award--Frank Layden (Utah Jazz)
Maurice Podoloff Trophy--Larry Bird (Boston Celtics)
NBA All-Star Game MVP--Isiah Thomas (Detroit Pistons)
NBA Finals MVP--Larry Bird (Boston Celtics)
Red Auerbach Trophy--Frank Layden (Utah Jazz)
Schick Award--Earvin Johnson (Los Angeles Lakers)
Sixth Man Award--Kevin McHale (Boston Celtics)

Hall of Fame Inductees

Senda Abbott, Harold Anderson, Al Cervi, Marv Harshman, Bertha Teague, Nate Thurmond, Margaret Wade

Notes

David Stern replaced Larry O'Brien as Commissioner of the National Basketball Association.

FOOTBALL
National Football League

National Conference
Eastern Division

Team Name	GP	W	L	T	PF	PA	Pct
Washington Redskins	16	11	5	0	426	310	.688
New York Giants	16	9	7	0	299	301	.563
St. Louis Cardinals	16	9	7	0	423	345	.563
Dallas Cowboys	16	9	7	0	308	308	.563
Philadelphia Eagles	16	6	9	1	275	339	.406

Central Division

Team Name	GP	W	L	T	PF	PA	Pct
Chicago Bears	16	10	6	0	325	248	.625
Green Bay Packers	16	8	8	0	390	309	.500
Tampa Bay Buccaneers	16	6	10	0	335	380	.375
Detroit Lions	16	4	11	1	283	408	.281
Minnesota Vikings	16	3	13	0	276	484	.188

Western Division

Team Name	GP	W	L	T	PF	PA	Pct
San Francisco 49ers	16	15	1	0	475	227	.938
Los Angeles Rams	16	10	6	0	346	316	.625
New Orleans Saints	16	7	9	0	298	361	.438
Atlanta Falcons	16	4	12	0	281	382	.250

American Conference

Eastern Division

Miami Dolphins	16	14	2	0	513	298	.875
New England Patriots	16	9	7	0	362	352	.563
New York Jets	16	7	9	0	332	364	.438
Indianapolis Colts	16	4	12	0	239	414	.250
Buffalo Bills	16	2	14	0	250	454	.125

Central Division

Pittsburgh Steelers	16	9	7	0	387	310	.563
Cincinnati Bengals	16	8	8	0	339	339	.500
Cleveland Browns	16	5	11	0	250	297	.313
Houston Oilers	16	3	13	0	240	437	.188

Western Division

Denver Broncos	16	13	3	0	353	241	.813
Seattle Seahawks	16	12	4	0	418	282	.750
Los Angeles Raiders	16	11	5	0	371	278	.688
Kansas City Chiefs	16	8	8	0	314	324	.500
San Diego Chargers	16	7	9	0	394	413	.438

Coaching Changes

Green Bay--Forrest Gregg 8-8-0; Minnesota--Les Steckel 3-13-0; New England--Ron Meyer 5-4-0, Raymond Berry 4-3-0; Indianapolis--Frank Kush 4-11-0, Hal Hunter 0-1-0; Cincinnati--Sam Wyche 8-8-0; Cleveland--Sam Rutigliano 1-7-0, Marty Schottenheimer 4-4-0; Houston--Hugh Campbell 3-13-0.

League Leaders

Yards Rushing		**Yards Passing**		**Passing %** (300 attempts)	
Eric Dickerson	2105	Dan Marino	5084	Joe Montana	64.6
Walter Payton	1684	Neil Lomax	4614	Dan Marino	64.2
James Wilder	1544	Phil Simms	4044	Dan Fouts	62.5
Gerald Riggs	1486	Dan Fouts	3740	Neil Lomax	61.6
Wendell Tyler	1262	Dave Krieg	3671	Gary Danielson	61.5

Receiving Yards		**Receptions**		**Field Goals**	
Roy Green	1555	Art Monk	106	Paul McFadden	30
John Stallworth	1395	Ozzie Newsome	89	Ray Wersching	25
Mark Clayton	1389	James Wilder	85	Mike Lansford	25
Art Monk	1372	John Stallworth	80	Mark Moseley	24
James Lofton	1361	Todd Christensen	80	Gary Anderson	24

Punt Return Yards		**Kickoff Return Yards**	
Louis Lipps	656	Lionel James	959
Dana McLemore	521	Darrin Nelson	891
Jeff Fisher	492	Mike Nelms	860
Greg Pruitt	473	Del Rodgers	843
Gary Allen	446	Michael Morton	835

Pro Bowl Game
(Aloha Stadium, Honolulu)

January 27 1985	American Conference	22		National Conference	14

NFL Playoffs

December 22	Los Angeles Raiders	7	at	Seattle Seahawks	13
December 23	New York Giants	16	at	Los Angeles Rams	13
December 29	Seattle Seahawks	10	at	Miami Dolphins	31
December 29	New York Giants	10	at	San Francisco 49ers	21
December 30	Pittsburgh Steelers	24	at	Denver Broncos	17
December 30	Chicago Bears	23	at	Washington Redskins	19
January 6 1985	Chicago Bears	0	at	San Francisco 49ers	23
January 6 1985	Pittsburgh Steelers	28	at	Miami Dolphins	45

Super Bowl XIX
(Stanford Stadium, Stanford, California)

January 20 1985	San Francisco 49ers	38		Miami Dolphins	16

Individual Awards

A.P. MVP--Dan Marino (Miami Dolphins)
Bert Bell Trophy--Louis Lipps (Pittsburgh Steelers) [World Almanac]
Bert Bell Trophy--Dan Marino (Miami Dolphins)
Dan McGuire Award--Mark Gastineau (New York Jets)
George Halas Trophy--Mike Haynes (Los Angeles Raiders)
Jim Thorpe Trophy--Dan Marino (Miami Dolphins)
P.F.W.A. MVP--Dan Marino (Miami Dolphins)
Super Bowl MVP--Joe Montana (San Francisco 49ers)
U.P.I. AFC Coach of the Year--Chuck Knox (Seattle Seahawks)
U.P.I. AFC Player of the Year--Dan Marino (Miami Dolphins)
Mark Gastineau (New York Jets)
U.P.I. AFC Rookie of the Year--Louis Lipps (Pittsburgh Steelers)
U.P.I. NFC Coach of the Year--Bill Walsh (San Francisco 49ers)
U.P.I. NFC Player of the Year--Eric Dickerson (Los Angeles Rams)
Mike Singletary (Chicago Bears)
U.P.I. Rookie of the Year--Paul McFadden (Philadelphia Eagles)

Hall of Fame Inductees

Billie Brown, Mike McCormack, Arnie Weinmeister

Canadian Football League
Eastern Division

Team Name	GP	W	L	T	PF	PA	Pts	Pct
Toronto Argonauts	16	9	6	1	461	361	19	.594
Hamilton Tiger-Cats	16	6	9	1	353	439	13	.406
Montreal Concordes	16	6	9	1	386	404	13	.406
Ottawa Rough Riders	16	4	12	0	354	507	8	.250

Western Division

Team Name	GP	W	L	T	PF	PA	Pts	Pct
British Columbia Lions	16	12	3	1	445	281	25	.781
Winnipeg Blue Bombers	16	11	4	1	523	309	23	.719
Edmonton Eskimos	16	9	7	0	464	443	18	.563
Saskatchewan Roughriders	16	6	9	1	348	479	13	.406
Calgary Stampeders	16	6	10	0	314	425	12	.375

Coaching Changes

Hamilton--Al Bruno 6-9-1; Edmonton--Jackie Parker 9-7-0; Saskatchewan--Rueben Berry 6-9-1; Calgary--Steve Burrato 6-10-0.

League Leaders

Yards Rushing		Yards Passing		Passing % (300 attempts)	
Willard Reaves	1733	Dieter Brock	3966	Tom Clements	62.5
Dwaine Wilson	1083	Tom Clements	3845	Joe Barnes	61.1
Larry Cowan	759	Roy DeWalt	3613	Roy DeWalt	59.0
Matt Dunigan	732	Matt Dunigan	3273	Joe Paopao	57.3
Lewis Walker	732	Joe Paopao	3270	Dieter Brock	57.0

Receiving Yards		Receptions		Points	
Mervyn Fernandez	1486	Craig Ellis	91	Lui Passaglia	167
Brian Kelly	1310	Mervyn Fernandez	89	Hank Ilesic	159
James Murphy	1220	Rocky DiPietro	71	Trevor Kennerd	152
Terry Greer	1189	Paul Pearson	71	Bernie Ruoff	145
Jeff Boyd	1106	James Murphy	70	J.T. Hay	135

Grey Cup Playoffs

November 4	Montreal Concordes	11	at	Hamilton Tiger-Cats	17
November 4	Edmonton Eskimos	20	at	Winnipeg Blue Bombers	55
November 11	Hamilton Tiger-Cats	14	at	Toronto Argonauts	13 [OT]
November 11	Winnipeg Blue Bombers	31	at	British Columbia Lions	14
November 18	Winnipeg Blue Bombers	47		Hamilton Tiger-Cats	17 *

Individual Awards

Annis Stukus Trophy--Cal Murphy (Winnipeg Blue Bombers)
Dave Dryburgh Memorial Trophy--Lui Passaglia (British Columbia Lions)
DeMarco-Becket Memorial Trophy--John Bonk (Winnipeg Blue Bombers)
Dr. Beattie Martin Trophy--Joe Poplawski (Winnipeg Blue Bombers)
Eddie James Memorial Trophy--Willard Reaves (Winnipeg Blue Bombers)
Frank M. Gibson Trophy--Dwaine Wilson (Montreal Concordes)
Grey Cup Most Outstanding Defensive Star--Tyrone Jones (Winnipeg Blue Bombers)
Grey Cup Most Outstanding Offensive Star--Tom Clements (Winnipeg Blue Bombers)
Grey Cup Most Outstanding Canadian--Sean Kehoe (Winnipeg Blue Bombers)
Jackie Parker Trophy--Stewart Hill (Edmonton Eskimos)
James P. McCaffrey Trophy--Harry Skipper (Montreal Concordes)
Jeff Nicklin Memorial Trophy--Willard Reaves (Winnipeg Blue Bombers)
Jeff Russel Memorial Trophy--Rufus Crawford (Hamilton Tiger-Cats)
Leo Dandurand Trophy--Dan Ferrone (Toronto Argonauts)
Lew Hayman Trophy--Nick Arakgi (Montreal Concordes)
Norm Fieldgate Trophy--James Parker (British Columbia Lions)
Schenley Award Most Outstanding Canadian--Nick Arakgi (Montreal Concordes)
Schenley Award Most Outstanding Defensive Player--James Parker (British Columbia Lions)
Schenley Award Most Outstanding Offensive Lineman--John Bonk (Winnipeg Blue Bombers)
Schenley Award Most Outstanding Player--Willard Reaves (Winnipeg Blue Bombers)
Schenley Award Most Outstanding Rookie--Dwaine Wilson (Montreal Concordes)

*Game played in Edmonton

Hall of Fame Inductees

Tom Brown, Terry Evanshen, Jake Gaudaur, Joe Kapp, Seymour Wilson

Notes

Doug Mitchell succeeded Jake Gaudaur as the Commissioner of the CFL. Mitchell is the CFL's sixth Commissioner.
The CFL eliminated the territorial exemption in its annual Canadian College draft.

United States Football League
Eastern Conference

Atlantic Division

Team Name	GP	W	L	T	PF	PA	Pct
Philadelphia Stars	18	16	2	0	479	225	.889
New Jersey Generals	18	14	4	0	430	312	.778
Pittsburgh Maulers	18	3	15	0	256	358	.167
Washington Federals	18	3	15	0	270	482	.167

Southern Division

Team Name	GP	W	L	T	PF	PA	Pct
Birmingham Stallions	18	14	4	0	557	316	.778
Tampa Bay Bandits	18	14	4	0	498	347	.778
New Orleans Breakers	18	8	10	0	348	395	.444
Memphis Showboats	18	7	11	0	320	455	.389
Jacksonville Bulls	18	6	12	0	327	455	.333

Western Conference

Central Division

Team Name	GP	W	L	T	PF	PA	Pct
Houston Gamblers	18	13	5	0	618	400	.722
Michigan Panthers	18	10	8	0	400	382	.556
San Antonio Gunslingers	18	7	11	0	309	325	.389
Oklahoma Outlaws	18	6	12	0	251	459	.333
Chicago Blitz	18	5	13	0	340	466	.278

Pacific Division

Team Name	GP	W	L	T	PF	PA	Pct
Los Angeles Express	18	10	8	0	338	373	.556
Arizona Wranglers	18	10	8	0	502	284	.556
Denver Gold	18	9	9	0	356	413	.500
Oakland Invaders	18	7	11	0	242	348	.389

Coaching Changes

New Jersey--Walt Michaels 14-4-0; Pittsburgh--Joe Pendry 3-15-0; New Orleans--Dick Coury 8-10-0; Memphis--Pepper Rodgers 7-11-0; Jacksonville--Lindy Infante 6-12-0; Houston--Jack Pardee 13-5-0; San Antonio--Gil Steinke 7-11-0; Oklahoma--Woody Widenhofer 6-12-0; Chicago--Marv Levy 5-13-0; Los Angeles--John Hadl 10-8-0; Arizona--George Allen 10-8-0; Denver--Craig Morton 9-9-0; John Ralston 0-3-0, Chuck Hutchison 7-8-0; Washington-0-1-0, Dick Bielski 3-14-0.

League Leaders

Yards Rushing		Yards Passing		Passing % (300 attempts)	
Joe Cribbs	1467	John Reaves	4092	Chuck Fusina	64.9
Kelvin Bryant	1406	Chuck Fusina	3837	Brian Sipe	59.1
Herschel Walker	1339	John Walton	3554	Robbie Mahfouz	58.3
Buford Jordan	1276	Cliff Stoudt	3121	Cliff Stoudt	57.9
Curtis Bledsoe	1080	Mike Hohensee	2766	Mike Hohensee	57.8

Receiving Yards	
Smith	1481
Joey Walters	1410
Eric Truvillion	1044
Marcus Anderson	994
Marvin Harvey	938

USFL Playoffs

June 30	New Jersey Generals	7	at	Philadelphia Stars	28
June 30	Michigan Panthers	21	at	Los Angeles Express	27 [OT]
July 1	Tampa Bay Bandits	17	at	Birmingham Stallions	36
July 1	Arizona Wranglers	17	at	Houston Gamblers	16
July 7	Arizona Wranglers	35	at	Los Angeles Express	23
July 8	Birmingham Stallions	10	at	Philadelphia Stars	20
July 15	Philadelphia Stars	23	at	Arizona Wranglers	3 *

HOCKEY

National Hockey League
Clarence Campbell Conference

Norris Division

Team Name	GP	W	L	T	GF	GA	Pts	Pct
Minnesota North Stars	80	39	31	10	345	344	88	.550
St. Louis Blues	80	32	41	7	293	316	71	.444
Detroit Red Wings	80	31	42	7	298	323	69	.431
Chicago Black Hawks	80	30	42	8	277	311	68	.425
Toronto Maple Leafs	80	26	45	9	303	387	61	.381

Smythe Division

Team Name	GP	W	L	T	GF	GA	Pts	Pct
Edmonton Oilers	80	57	18	5	446	314	119	.744
Calgary Flames	80	34	32	14	311	314	82	.513
Vancouver Canucks	80	32	39	9	306	328	73	.456
Winnipeg Jets	80	31	38	11	340	374	73	.456
Los Angeles Kings	80	23	44	13	309	376	59	.369

*Game played in Tampa

Wales Conference

Adams Division

Boston Bruins	80	49	25	6	336	261	104	.650
Buffalo Sabres	80	48	25	7	315	257	103	.644
Quebec Nordiques	80	42	28	10	360	278	94	.588
Montreal Canadiens	80	35	40	5	286	295	75	.469
Hartford Whalers	80	28	42	10	288	320	66	.413

Patrick Division

New York Islanders	80	50	26	4	357	269	104	.650
Washington Capitals	80	48	27	5	308	226	101	.631
Philadelphia Flyers	80	44	26	10	350	290	98	.613
New York Rangers	80	42	29	9	314	304	93	.581
New Jersey Devils	80	17	56	7	231	350	41	.256
Pittsburgh Penguins	80	16	58	6	254	390	38	.238

Coaching Changes

Minnesota--Bill Mahoney 39-31-10; St. Louis--Jacques Demers 32-41-7; Vancouver--Roger Neilson 17-26-5, Harry Neale 15-13-4; Winnipeg--Tom Watt 4-9-2, John Ferguson 2-3-0, Barry Long 25-26-9; Los Angeles--Don Perry 14-27-9, Rogatien Vachon 1-0-1, Roger Neilson 8-17-3; Montreal--Bob Berry 28-30-5, Jacques Lemaire 7-10-0; Hartford--Jack Evans 28-42-10; New Jersey--Bill MacMillan 2-18-0, Tom McVie 15-38-7; Pittsburgh--Lou Angotti 16-58-6.

League Leaders

Goals		Assists		Points	
Wayne Gretzky	87	Wayne Gretzky	118	Wayne Gretzky	205
Michel Goulet	56	Paul Coffey	86	Paul Coffey	126
Glenn Anderson	54	Barry Pederson	77	Michel Goulet	121
Tim Kerr	54	Peter Stastny	73	Peter Stastny	119
Jari Kurri	52	Bryan Trottier	71	Mike Bossy	118

Penalty Minutes		GAA (1,500 minutes)		Wins	
Chris Nilan	338	Pat Riggin	2.66	Grant Fuhr	30
Willi Plett	316	Tom Barrasso	2.84	Pete Peeters	29
Gary Rissling	297	Al Jensen	2.91	Dan Bouchard	29
Dave Williams	294	Doug Keans	3.10	Glen Hanlon	28
Jim Korn	257	Bob Froese	3.14	Bob Froese	28

Shutouts		Save %	
Pat Riggin	4	Roland Melanson	.902
Al Jensen	4	Billy Smith	.896
Mike Lint	3	Tom Barrasso	.893
Doug Keans	2	Rejean Lemelin	.893
Billy Smith	2	Glen Hanlon	.890

All Star Game

(Byrne Meadowlands Arena, East Rutherford, New Jersey)

January 31	Wales Conference	7	Campbell Conference	6

Stanley Cup Playoffs

April 4	Chicago Black Hawks	3	at	Minnesota North Stars	1
April 4	Montreal Canadiens	2	at	Boston Bruins	1
April 4	Quebec Nordiques	3	at	Buffalo Sabres	2
April 4	New York Rangers	1	at	New York Islanders	4
April 4	Philadelphia Flyers	2	at	Washington Capitals	4
April 4	Detroit Red Wings	2	at	St. Louis Blues	3
April 4	Winnipeg Jets	2	at	Edmonton Oilers	9
April 4	Vancouver Canucks	3	at	Calgary Flames	5
April 5	Montreal Canadiens	3	at	Boston Bruins	1
April 5	Quebec Nordiques	6	at	Buffalo Sabres	2
April 5	New York Rangers	3	at	New York Islanders	0
April 5	Philadelphia Flyers	2	at	Washington Capitals	6
April 5	Chicago Black Hawks	5	at	Minnesota North Stars	6
April 5	Detroit Red Wings	5	at	St. Louis Blues	3
April 5	Winnipeg Jets	4	at	Edmonton Oilers	5 [0:21]
April 5	Vancouver Canucks	2	at	Calgary Flames	4
April 7	Boston Bruins	0	at	Montreal Canadiens	5
April 7	Buffalo Sabres	1	at	Quebec Nordiques	4
April 7	New York Islanders	2	at	New York Rangers	7
April 7	Washington Capitals	5	at	Philadelphia Flyers	1
April 7	Minnesota North Stars	4	at	Chicago Black Hawks	1
April 7	St. Louis Blues	4	at	Detroit Red Wings	3 [37:07]
April 7	Edmonton Oilers	4	at	Winnipeg Jets	1
April 7	Calgary Flames	0	at	Vancouver Canucks	7
April 8	New York Islanders	4	at	New York Rangers	1
April 8	Minnesota North Stars	3	at	Chicago Black Hawks	4
April 8	St. Louis Blues	3	at	Detroit Red Wings	2 [2:42]
April 8	Calgary Flames	5	at	Vancouver Canucks	1
April 10	New York Rangers	2	at	New York Islanders	3 [8:56]
April 10	Chicago Black Hawks	1	at	Minnesota North Stars	4
April 12	Montreal Canadiens	2	at	Quebec Nordiques	4
April 12	Washington Capitals	3	at	New York Islanders	2
April 12	St. Louis Blues	1	at	Minnesota North Stars	2
April 12	Calgary Flames	2	at	Edmonton Oilers	5
April 13	Montreal Canadiens	4	at	Quebec Nordiques	1
April 13	Washington Capitals	4	at	New York Islanders	5 [7:35]
April 13	St. Louis Blues	4	at	Minnesota North Stars	3 [16:16]
April 13	Calgary Flames	6	at	Edmonton Oilers	5 [3:42]
April 15	Quebec Nordiques	1	at	Montreal Canadiens	2
April 15	New York Islanders	3	at	Washington Capitals	1
April 15	Minnesota North Stars	1	at	St. Louis Blues	3
April 15	Edmonton Oilers	3	at	Calgary Flames	2
April 16	Quebec Nordiques	4	at	Montreal Canadiens	3 [3:00]
April 16	New York Islanders	5	at	Washington Capitals	2
April 16	Minnesota North Stars	3	at	St. Louis Blues	2
April 16	Edmonton Oilers	5	at	Calgary Flames	3
April 18	Montreal Canadiens	4	at	Quebec Nordiques	0
April 18	Washington Capitals	3	at	New York Islanders	5
April 18	St. Louis Blues	0	at	Minnesota North Stars	6
April 18	Calgary Flames	5	at	Edmonton Oilers	4
April 20	Quebec Nordiques	3	at	Montreal Canadiens	5
April 20	Minnesota North Stars	0	at	St. Louis Blues	4
April 20	Edmonton Oilers	4	at	Calgary Flames	5 [1:04]

April 22	St. Louis Blues	3	at	Minnesota North Stars	4 [6:00]
April 22	Calgary Flames	4	at	Edmonton Oilers	7
April 24	New York Islanders	0	at	Montreal Canadiens	3
April 24	Minnesota North Stars	1	at	Edmonton Oilers	7
April 26	New York Islanders	2	at	Montreal Canadiens	4
April 26	Minnesota North Stars	3	at	Edmonton Oilers	4
April 28	Montreal Canadiens	2	at	New York Islanders	5
April 28	Edmonton Oilers	8	at	Minnesota North Stars	5
May 1	Montreal Canadiens	1	at	New York Islanders	3
May 1	Edmonton Oilers	3	at	Minnesota North Stars	1
May 3	New York Islanders	3	at	Montreal Canadiens	1
May 5	Montreal Canadiens	1	at	New York Islanders	4
May 10	Edmonton Oilers	1	at	New York Islanders	0
May 12	Edmonton Oilers	1	at	New York Islanders	6
May 15	New York Islanders	2	at	Edmonton Oilers	7
May 17	New York Islanders	2	at	Edmonton Oilers	7
May 19	New York Islanders	2	at	Edmonton Oilers	5

All Star Teams

First Team		Second Team
Tom Barrasso	Goal	Pat Riggin
Rod Langway	Defense	Paul Coffey
Ray Bourque	Defense	Denis Potvin
Wayne Gretzky	Center	Bryan
Trottier		
Mike Bossy	Right Wing	Jari Kurri
Michel Goulet	Left Wing	Mark Messier

Individual Awards

Art Ross Trophy--Wayne Gretzky (Edmonton Oilers)
Bill Masterton Trophy--Brad Park (Detroit Red Wings)
Calder Memorial Trophy--Tom Barrasso (Buffalo Sabres)
Conn Smythe Trophy--Mark Messier (Edmonton Oilers)
Emery Edge Trophy--Wayne Gretzky (Edmonton Oilers)
Frank J. Selke Trophy--Doug Jarvis (Washington Capitals)
Hart Memorial Trophy--Wayne Gretzky (Edmonton Oilers)
Jack Adams Award--Bryan Murray (Washington Capitals)
James Norris Trophy--Rod Langway (Washington Capitals)
Lady Byng Memorial Trophy--Mike Bossy (New York Islanders)
Lester B. Pearson Award--Wayne Gretzky (Edmonton Oilers)
Lester Patrick Trophy--John Ziegler and Art Ross.
NHL All-Star Game MVP--Don Maloney (New York Rangers)
Vezina Trophy--Tom Barrasso (Buffalo Sabres)
William M. Jennings Trophy--Al Jensen and Pat Riggin (Washington Capitals)

Hall of Fame Inductees

Phil Esposito, George Imlach, Jacques Lemaire, Jake Milford, Bernie Parent

Notes

The NHL adopted a five minute over-time period if the game ended in a tie after the expiration of regular time. The league abandoned over-time for the regular season games in 1942 because of travel restrictions during WW II.

SOCCER

North American Soccer League

Eastern Division

Team Name	GP	W	L	GF	GA	BP	Pts	Pct
Chicago Sting	24	13	11	50	49	44	120	.333
Toronto Blizzard	24	14	10	46	33	35	117	.325
Cosmos	24	13	11	43	42	39	115	.319
Tampa Bay Rowdies	24	9	15	43	61	35	87	.242

Western Division

Team Name	GP	W	L	GF	GA	BP	Pts	Pct
San Diego Sockers	24	14	10	51	42	40	118	.328
Vancouver Whitecaps	24	13	11	51	48	43	117	.325
Minnesota Strikers	24	14	10	40	44	35	115	.319
Tulsa Roughnecks	24	10	14	42	46	38	98	.272
Golden Bay Earthquakes	24	8	16	61	62	49	95	.264

Coaching Changes

New York--Eddie Firmani 13-11; Tampa Bay--Rodney Marsh 9-15; Vancouver--Alan Hinton 13-11; Minnesota--Dave Chadwick 14-10; Tulsa--Wim Suurbier 10-14.

League Leaders

Points		GAA	
Steve Zungul	50	Paul Hammond	1.16

NASL Playoffs

September 18	Vancouver Whitecaps	1	at	Chicago Sting	0 [SO]
September 18	Toronto Blizzard	2	at	San Diego Sockers	1
September 21	San Diego Sockers	0	at	Toronto Blizzard	1
September 23	Chicago Sting	3	at	Vancouver Whitecaps	1
September 29	Vancouver Whitecaps	3	at	Chicago Sting	4
October 1	Toronto Blizzard	1	at	Chicago Sting	2
October 3	Chicago Sting	3	at	Toronto Blizzard	2

Individual Awards

Lead Goalkeeper Award--Paul Hammond (Toronto Blizzard)
Most Valuable Player--Steve Zungul (Golden Bay Earthquakes)

Franchise Changes

NFL--Baltimore Colts became the Indianapolis Colts.
USFL--Boston Breakers became the New Orleans Breakers.
The Arizona and Chicago franchises were for all intents and purposes switched for each other.
NASL--Ft. Lauderdale Strikers became the Minnesota Strikers.

Other Sports

Horseracing--Kentucky Derby won by Swale (time 2:02.4, purse $537,000).

Heavyweight Boxing--Tim Witherspoon defeated Greg Page in 12 rounds (WBC).
Pinklon Thomas defeated Tim Witherspoon in 12 rounds (WBC).
Greg Page knocked-out Gerrie Coetzee in 8 rounds (WBA).

Golf --U.S. Open won by Fuzzy Zoeller with a score of 276.

Auto Racing--Indianapolis 500 won by Rick Mears (ave. speed 163.621 MPH).

Tennis--U.S. Open won by John McEnroe in the men's singles.
U.S. Open won by Tomas Smid and John Fitzgerald in the men's doubles.
U.S. Open won by Martina Navratilova in the women's singles.
U.S. Open won by Martina Navratilova and Pam Shriver in the women's doubles.
U.S. Open won by Manuela Maleeva and Tom Gullikson in the mixed doubles.

1985

BASEBALL
National League
East

Team Name	W	L	Pct	GB	R	OR
St. Louis Cardinals	101	61	.623	-	747	572
New York Mets	98	64	.605	3	695	568
Montreal Expos	84	77	.522	16.5	633	636
Chicago Cubs	77	84	.478	23.5	686	729
Philadelphia Phillies	75	87	.463	26	667	673
Pittsburgh Pirates	57	104	.354	43.5	568	708

West

Team Name	W	L	Pct	GB	R	OR
Los Angeles Dodgers	95	67	.586	-	682	579
Cincinnati Reds	89	72	.553	5.5	677	666
Houston Astros	83	79	.512	12	706	691
San Diego Padres	83	79	.512	12	650	622
Atlanta Braves	66	96	.407	29	632	781
San Francisco Giants	62	100	.383	33	556	674

Coaching Changes

Montreal--Buck Rodgers 84-77; Philadelphia--John Felske 75-87; Cincinnati--Pete Rose 89-72; Atlanta--Eddie Haas 50-71, Bobby Wine 16-25; San Francisco--Jim Davenport 56-88, Roger Craig 6-12.

League Leaders

Batting Average
(502 at bats)

Willie McGee	.353
Pedro Guerrero	.320
Tim Raines	.320
Tony Gwynn	.317
Dave Parker	.312

Home Runs

Dale Murphy	37
Dave Parker	34
Pedro Guerrero	33
Mike Schmidt	33
Gary Carter	32

RBI

Dave Parker	125
Dale Murphy	111
Tom Herr	110
Keith Moreland	106
Glenn Wilson	102

Stolen Bases

Vince Coleman	110
Tim Raines	70
Willie McGee	56
Juan Samuel	53
Ryne Sandberg	51

ERA
(162innings)

Dwight Gooden	1.53
John Tudor	1.93
Orel Hershiser	2.03
Rick Reuschel	2.27
Bob Welch	2.31

Wins

Dwight Gooden	24
John Tudor	21
Joaquin Andujar	21
Tom Browning	20
Orel Hershiser	19

Saves

Jeff Reardon	41
Lee Smith	33
Ted Power	27
Dave Smith	27
Rich Gossage	26

Strikeouts

Dwight Gooden	268
Mario Soto	214
Nolan Ryan	209
Fernando Valenzuela	208
Sid Fernandez	180

NLCS

October 9	St. Louis Cardinals	1	at	Los Angeles Dodgers	4
October 10	St. Louis Cardinals	2	at	Los Angeles Dodgers	8
October 12	Los Angeles Dodgers	2	at	St. Louis Cardinals	4
October 13	Los Angeles Dodgers	2	at	St. Louis Cardinals	12
October 14	Los Angeles Dodgers	2	at	St. Louis Cardinals	3
October 16	St. Louis Cardinals	7	at	Los Angeles Dodgers	5

American League

East

Team Name	W	L	Pct	GB	R	OR
Toronto Blue Jays	99	62	.615	-	759	588
New York Yankees	97	64	.602	2	839	660
Detroit Tigers	84	77	.522	15	729	688
Baltimore Orioles	83	78	.516	16	818	764
Boston Red Sox	81	81	.500	18.5	800	720
Milwaukee Brewers	71	90	.441	28	690	802
Cleveland Indians	60	102	.370	39.5	729	861

West

Team Name	W	L	Pct	GB	R	OR
Kansas City Royals	91	71	.562	-	687	639
California Angels	90	72	.556	1	732	703
Chicago White Sox	85	77	.525	6	736	720
Minnesota Twins	77	85	.475	14	705	782
Oakland Athletics	77	85	.475	14	757	787
Seattle Mariners	74	88	.457	17	719	818
Texas Rangers	62	99	.385	28.5	617	785

Coaching Changes

New York--Yogi Berra 6-10, Billy Martin 91-54; Baltimore--Joe Altobelli 29-26, Cal Ripken Sr. 1-0, Earl Weaver 53-52; Boston--John McNamara 81-81; Milwaukee--George Bamberger 71-90; California--Gene Mauch 90-72; Minnesota--Billy Gardner 27-35, Ray Miller 50-50; Oakland--Jackie Moore 77-85; Seattle--Chuck Cottier 74-88; Texas--Doug Rader 9-23, Bobby Valentine 53-76.

League Leaders

Batting Average (502 at bats)		Home Runs		RBI	
Wade Boggs	.368	Darrell Evans	40	Don Mattingly	145
George Brett	.335	Carlton Fisk	37	Eddie Murray	124
Don Mattingly	.324	Steve Balboni	36	Dave Winfield	114
Rickey Henderson	.314	Don Mattingly	35	Harold Baines	113
Brett Butler	.311	Gorman Thomas	32	George Brett	112

Stolen Bases		ERA (162 innings)		Wins	
Rickey Henderson	80	Dave Stieb	2.48	Ron Guidry	22
Gary Pettis	56	Charlie Leibrandt	2.69	Brett Saberhagen	20
Brett Butler	47	Brett Saberhagen	2.87	Frank Viola	18
Willie Wilson	43	Jim Key	3.00	Britt Burns	18
Lonnie Smith	40	Bert Blyleven	3.16	Charlie Leibrandt	17

Saves		Strikeouts	
Dan Quisenberry	37	Bert Blyleven	206
Bob James	32	Floyd Bannister	198
Donnie Moore	31	Jack Morris	191
Willie Hernandez	31	Bruce Hurst	189
Jay Howell	29	Mike Witt	180

All Star Game

(Hubert H. Humphrey Metrodome, Minneapolis)

July 16	National League	6		American League	1

ALCS

October 8	Kansas City Royals	1	at	Toronto Blue Jays	6
October 9	Kansas City Royals	5	at	Toronto Blue Jays	6 [10]
October 11	Toronto Blue Jays	5	at	Kansas City Royals	6
October 12	Toronto Blue Jays	3	at	Kansas City Royals	1
October 13	Toronto Blue Jays	0	at	Kansas City Royals	2
October 15	Kansas City Royals	5	at	Toronto Blue Jays	3
October 16	Kansas City Royals	6	at	Toronto Blue Jays	2

World Series

October 19	St. Louis Cardinals	3	at	Kansas City Royals	1
October 20	St. Louis Cardinals	4	at	Kansas City Royals	2
October 22	Kansas City Royals	6	at	St. Louis Cardinals	1
October 23	Kansas City Royals	0	at	St. Louis Cardinals	3
October 24	Kansas City Royals	6	at	St. Louis Cardinals	1
October 26	St. Louis Cardinals	1	at	Kansas City Royals	2
October 27	St. Louis Cardinals	0	at	Kansas City Royals	11

Individual Awards

ALCS MVP--George Brett (Kansas City Royals AL)
Arch Ward Memorial Trophy--LaMarr Hoyt (San Diego Padres NL)
Baseball Writers Award--Willie McGee (St. Louis Cardinals NL)
Don Mattingly (New York Yankees AL)
Cy Young Award--Dwight Gooden (New York Mets NL)
Bret Saberhagen (Kansas City Royals AL)
NLCS MVP--Ozzie Smith (St. Louis Cardinals NL)
Rookie of the Year--Vince Coleman (St. Louis Cardinals NL)
Sporting News Executive of the Year--John Schuerholz (Kansas City Royals AL)
Sporting News Manager of the Year--Bobby Cox (Toronto Blue Jays AL)
Sporting News Pitcher of the Year--Dwight Gooden (New York Mets NL)
Bret Saberhagen (Kansas City Royals AL)
Sporting News Player of the Year--Willie McGee (St. Louis Cardinals NL)
Don Mattingly (New York Yankees AL)
Sporting News Rookie of the Year--Vince Coleman (St. Louis Cardinals NL)
Tom Browning (Cincinnati Reds NL)
Ozzie Guillen (Chicago White Sox AL)
Teddy Higuera (Milwaukee Brewers AL)
World Series MVP--Bret Saberhagen (Kansas City Royals AL)

Hall of Fame Inductees

Lou Brock, Enos Slaughter, Arky Vaughan, Hoyt Wilhelm

Notes

In major league baseball a number of individual milestones were reached as Pete Rose passed Ty Cobb's number of lifetime hits with his 4,192nd hit. Nolan Ryan struck out his 4,000 batter and Tom Seaver and Phil Niekro both won their 300th game.

BASKETBALL

National Basketball Association

Eastern Conference
Atlantic Division

Team Name	GP	W	L	PPGF	PPGA	Pct	GB
Boston Celtics	82	63	19	114.8	108.1	.768	-
Philadelphia 76ers	82	58	24	112.9	108.8	.707	5
New Jersey Nets	82	42	40	109.5	109.2	.512	21
Washington Bullets	82	40	42	105.5	105.8	.488	23
New York Knickerbockers	82	24	58	105.2	109.8	.293	39

Central Division

Team Name	GP	W	L	PPGF	PPGA	Pct	GB
Milwaukee Bucks	82	59	23	110.9	104.0	.720	-
Detroit Pistons	82	46	36	116.0	113.5	.561	13
Chicago Bulls	82	38	44	108.7	109.6	.463	21
Cleveland Cavaliers	82	36	46	108.6	111.3	.439	23
Atlanta Hawks	82	34	48	106.6	108.1	.415	25
Indiana Pacers	82	22	60	108.3	114.5	.268	37

Midwest Division

Team Name	GP	W	L	PPGF	PPGA	Pct	GB
Denver Nuggets	82	52	30	120.0	117.6	.634	-
Houston Rockets	82	48	34	111.2	109.5	.585	4
Dallas Mavericks	82	44	38	111.2	109.0	.537	8
San Antonio Spurs	82	41	41	114.8	113.9	.500	11
Utah Jazz	82	41	41	109.0	109.1	.500	11
Kansas City Kings	82	31	51	114.8	117.5	.378	21

Pacific Division

Team Name	GP	W	L	PPGF	PPGA	Pct	GB
Los Angeles Lakers	82	62	20	118.2	110.9	.756	-
Portland Trail Blazers	82	42	40	115.5	112.1	.512	20
Phoenix Suns	82	36	46	108.0	110.1	.439	26
Los Angeles Clippers	82	31	51	107.1	111.6	.378	31
Seattle SuperSonics	82	31	51	102.1	107.6	.378	31
Golden State Warriors	82	22	60	110.4	117.7	.268	40

Coaching Changes

Cleveland--George Karl 36-46; Indiana--George Irvine 22-60; San Antonio--Lowell "Cotton" Fitzsimmons 41-41; Kansas City--Jack McKinney 1-8, Phil Johnson 30-43; L.A. Clippers--Jim Lynam 22-39, Don Chaney 9-12.

League Leaders

Field Goals		Free Throws		Assists	
Alex English	939	Moses Malone	737	Isiah Thomas	1123
Larry Bird	918	Michael Jordan	630	Earvin Johnson	968
Dominique Wilkins	853	Purvis Short	501	John Moore	816
Michael Jordan	837	Dominique Wilkins	486	Norm Nixon	711
Purvis Short	819	Artis Gilmore	484	John Bagley	697

Points		Rebounds Per Game	
Michael Jordan	2313	Moses Malone	13.1
Larry Bird	2295	Bill Laimbeer	12.4
Alex English	2262	Ray Williams	12.3
Dominique Wilkins	2217	Akeem Olajuwon	11.9
Purvis Short	2186	Mark Eaton	11.3

All Star Game

(Market Square Arena, Indianapolis)

February 10	West Division	140	East Division	129

NBA Playoffs

April 17	Washington Bullets	97	at	Philadelphia 76ers	104
April 18	Portland Trail Blazers	131	at	Dallas Mavericks	139 [OT]
April 18	Cleveland Cavaliers	123	at	Boston Celtics	126
April 18	New Jersey Nets	105	at	Detroit Pistons	125
April 18	Phoenix Suns	114	at	Los Angeles Lakers	142
April 18	San Antonio Spurs	111	at	Denver Nuggets	141
April 19	Chicago Bulls	100	at	Milwaukee Bucks	109
April 19	Utah Jazz	115	at	Houston Rockets	101
April 20	Cleveland Cavaliers	106	at	Boston Celtics	108
April 20	Phoenix Suns	130	at	Los Angeles Lakers	147
April 20	San Antonio Spurs	113	at	Denver Nuggets	111
April 20	Portland Trail Blazers	124	at	Dallas Mavericks	121 [OT]
April 21	Chicago Bulls	115	at	Milwaukee Bucks	122
April 21	Washington Bullets	94	at	Philadelphia 76ers	113
April 21	New Jersey Nets	111	at	Detroit Pistons	121
April 21	Utah Jazz	96	at	Houston Rockets	122
April 23	Boston Celtics	98	at	Cleveland Cavaliers	105
April 23	Los Angeles Lakers	119	at	Phoenix Suns	103
April 23	Denver Nuggets	115	at	San Antonio Spurs	112
April 23	Dallas Mavericks	109	at	Portland Trail Blazers	122
April 24	Milwaukee Bulls	107	at	Chicago Bulls	109
April 24	Detroit Pistons	116	at	New Jersey Nets	115
April 24	Houston Mavericks	104	at	Utah Jazz	112
April 24	Philadelphia 76ers	100	at	Washington Bullets	118
April 25	Boston Celtics	117	at	Cleveland Cavaliers	115
April 25	Dallas Mavericks	113	at	Portland Trail Blazers	115
April 26	Milwaukee Bucks	105	at	Chicago Bulls	97
April 26	Philadelphia 76ers	106	at	Washington Bullets	98
April 26	Denver Nuggets	111	at	San Antonio Spurs	116
April 26	Houston Rockets	96	at	Utah Jazz	94
April 27	Portland Trail Blazers	101	at	Los Angeles Lakers	125

April 28	Utah Jazz	104	at	Houston Rockets	97
April 28	San Antonio Spurs	99	at	Denver Nuggets	126
April 28	Detroit Pistons	99	at	Boston Celtics	133
April 28	Philadelphia 76ers	127	at	Milwaukee Bucks	105
April 30	Utah Jazz	113	at	Denver Nuggets	130
April 30	Detroit Pistons	114	at	Boston Celtics	121
April 30	Portland Trail Blazers	118	at	Los Angeles Lakers	134
April 30	Philadelphia 76ers	112	at	Milwaukee Bucks	108
May 2	Boston Celtics	117	at	Detroit Pistons	125
May 2	Utah Jazz	123	at	Denver Nuggets	131 [OT]
May 3	Los Angeles Lakers	130	at	Portland Trail Blazers	126
May 3	Milwaukee Bucks	104	at	Philadelphia 76ers	109
May 4	Denver Nuggets	123	at	Utah Jazz	131
May 5	Boston Celtics	99	at	Detroit Pistons	102
May 5	Los Angeles Lakers	107	at	Portland Trail Blazers	115
May 5	Milwaukee Bucks	112	at	Philadelphia 76ers	121
May 5	Denver Nuggets	125	at	Utah Jazz	118
May 7	Portland Trail Blazers	120	at	Los Angeles Lakers	139
May 7	Utah Jazz	104	at	Denver Nuggets	116
May 8	Detroit Pistons	123	at	Boston Celtics	130
May 10	Boston Celtics	123	at	Detroit Pistons	113
May 11	Denver Nuggets	122	at	Los Angeles Lakers	139
May 12	Philadelphia 76ers	93	at	Boston Celtics	108
May 14	Philadelphia 76ers	98	at	Boston Celtics	106
May 14	Denver Nuggets	136	at	Los Angeles Lakers	114
May 17	Los Angeles Lakers	136	at	Denver Nuggets	118
May 18	Boston Celtics	105	at	Philadelphia 76ers	94
May 19	Los Angeles Lakers	120	at	Denver Nuggets	116
May 19	Boston Celtics	104	at	Philadelphia 76ers	115
May 22	Denver Nuggets	109	at	Los Angeles Lakers	153
May 22	Philadelphia 76ers	100	at	Boston Celtics	102
May 27	Los Angeles Lakers	114	at	Boston Celtics	148
May 30	Los Angeles Lakers	109	at	Boston Celtics	102
June 2	Boston Celtics	111	at	Los Angeles Lakers	136
June 5	Boston Celtics	107	at	Los Angeles Lakers	105
June 7	Boston Celtics	111	at	Los Angeles Lakers	120
June 9	Los Angeles Lakers	111	at	Boston Celtics	100

All Star Teams

First Team

Larry Bird (Boston Celtics)
Bernard King (N.Y. Knickerbockers)
Moses Malone (Philadelphia 76ers)
Earvin Johnson (Los Angeles Lakers)
Isiah Thomas (Detroit Pistons)

Second Team

Terry Cummings (Milwaukee Bucks)
Ralph Sampson (Houston Rockets)
Kareem Abdul-Jabbar (Los Angeles Lakers)
Michael Jordan (Chicago Bulls)
Sidney Moncrief (Milwaukee Bucks)

Individual Awards

Defensive Player of the Year--Mark Eaton (Utah Jazz)
Eddie Gottlieb Trophy--Michael Jordan (Chicago Bulls)
Executive of the Year--Vince Boryla (Denver Nuggets)
J. Walter Kennedy Citizenship Award--Dan Issel (Denver Nuggets)
Maurice Podoloff Trophy--Larry Bird (Boston Celtics)
NBA All Star Game MVP--Ralph Sampson (Houston Rockets)

NBA Finals MVP--Kareem Abdul-Jabbar (Los Angeles Lakers)
Schick Award--Michael Jordan (Chicago Bulls)
Sixth Man Award--Kevin McHale (Boston Celtics)
Red Auerbach Trophy--Don Nelson (Milwaukee Bucks)

Hall of Fame Inductees

Fred Taylor, Stanley Watts

FOOTBALL

National Football League

National Conference
Eastern Division

Team Name	GP	W	L	T	PF	PA	Pct
Dallas Cowboys	16	10	6	0	357	333	.625
New York Giants	16	10	6	0	399	283	.625
Washington Redskins	16	10	6	0	297	312	.625
Philadelphia Eagles	16	7	9	0	286	310	.438
St. Louis Cardinals	16	5	11	0	278	414	.313

Central Division

Team Name	GP	W	L	T	PF	PA	Pct
Chicago Bears	16	15	1	0	456	198	.938
Green Bay Packers	16	8	8	0	337	355	.500
Minnesota Vikings	16	7	9	0	346	359	.438
Detroit Lions	16	7	9	0	307	366	.438
Tampa Bay Buccaneers	16	2	14	0	294	448	.125

Western Division

Team Name	GP	W	L	T	PF	PA	Pct
Los Angeles Rams	16	11	5	0	340	277	.688
San Francisco 49ers	16	10	6	0	411	263	.625
New Orleans Saints	16	5	11	0	294	401	.313
Atlanta Falcons	16	4	12	0	282	452	.250

American Conference

Eastern Division

Team Name	GP	W	L	T	PF	PA	Pct
Miami Dolphins	16	12	4	0	428	320	.750
New York Jets	16	11	5	0	393	264	.688
New England Patriots	16	11	5	0	362	290	.688
Indianapolis Colts	16	5	11	0	320	386	.313
Buffalo Bills	16	2	14	0	200	381	.125

Central Division

Team Name	GP	W	L	T	PF	PA	Pct
Cleveland Browns	16	8	8	0	287	294	.500
Cincinnati Bengals	16	7	9	0	441	437	.438
Pittsburgh Steelers	16	7	9	0	379	355	.438
Houston Oilers	16	5	11	0	284	412	.313

Western Division

Los Angeles Raiders	16	12	4	0	354	308	.750
Denver Broncos	16	11	5	0	380	329	.688
Seattle Seahawks	16	8	8	0	349	303	.500
San Diego Chargers	16	8	8	0	467	435	.500
Kansas City Chiefs	16	6	10	0	317	360	.375

Coaching Changes

Philadelphia--Marion Campbell 6-9-0, Fred Bruney 1-0-0; Minnesota--Bud Grant 7-9-0; Detroit--Darryl Rogers 7-9-0; Tampa Bay--Leeman Bennett 2-14-0; New Orleans--Bum Phillips 4-8-0, Wade Phillips 1-3-0; New England--Raymond Berry 11-5-0; Buffalo--Kay Stephenson 0-4-0; Indianapolis--Rod Dowhower 5-11-0; Hank Bullough 2-10-0; Cleveland--Marty Schottenheimer 8-8-0; Houston--Hugh Campbell 5-9-0, Jerry Glanville 0-2-0.

League Leaders

Yards Rushing		**Yards Passing**		**Passing %** (300 attempts)	
Marcus Allen	1759	Dan Marino	4137	Joe Montana	61.3
Gerald Riggs	1719	John Elway	3891	Ken O'Brien	60.9
Walter Payton	1551	Ken O'Brien	3888	Dieter Brock	59.7
Joe Morris	1336	Joe Montana	3653	Danny White	59.3
Freeman McNeil	1331	Dan Fouts	3638	Dan Marino	59.3

Receiving Yards		**Receptions**		**Field Goals**	
Steve Largent	1287	Roger Craig	92	Gary Anderson	33
Mike Quick	1247	Art Monk	91	Fuad Reveiz	33
Art Monk	1226	Lionel James	86	Kevin Butler	31
Wes Chandler	1199	Todd Christensen	82	Morten Anderson	31
Drew Hill	1169	Butch Woolfolk	80	Ed Murray	26

Punt Return Yards		**Kickoff Return Yards**	
Fulton Walker	692	Buster Rhymes	1345
Irving Fryar	520	Mike Martin	1104
Henry Ellard	501	Phil Freeman	1085
Robbie Martin	443	Herman Hunter	1047
Phil McConkey	442	Lorenzo Hampton	1020

Pro Bowl Game

(Aloha Stadium, Honolulu)

February 2 1986	National Conference	28	American Conference	24

NFL Playoffs

December 28	New England Patriots	26	at	New York Jets	14
December 29	San Francisco 49ers	3	at	New York Giants	17
January 4 1986	Dallas Cowboys	0	at	Los Angeles Rams	20
January 4 1986	Cleveland Browns	21	at	Miami Dolphins	24
January 5 1986	New York Giants	0	at	Chicago Bears	21
January 5 1986	New England Patriots	27	at	Los Angeles Raiders	20
January 12 1986	Los Angeles Rams	0	at	Chicago Bears	24
January 12 1986	New England Patriots	31	at	Miami Dolphins	14

Super Bowl XX

(Louisiana Superdome, New Orleans)

January	26 1986	Chicago Bears	46	New England Patriots	10

Individual Awards

A.P. MVP--Marcus Allen (Los Angeles Raiders)
Bert Bell Trophy--Eddie Brown (Cincinnati Bengals) [World Almanac]
Bert Bell Trophy--Walter Payton (Chicago Bears)
Dan McGuire Award--Phil Simms (New York Giants)
George Halas Trophy--Howie Long (Los Angeles Raiders)
Andre Tippett (New England Patriots)
Jim Thorpe Trophy--Walter Payton (Chicago Bears)
P.F.W.A. MVP--Marcus Allen (Los Angeles Raiders)
Super Bowl MVP--Richard Dent (Chicago Bears)
U.P.I. AFC Coach of the Year--Raymond Berry (New England Patriots)
U.P.I. AFC Player of the Year--Marcus Allen (Los Angeles Raiders)
Andre Tippett (New England Patriots)
U.P.I. AFC Rookie of the Year--Kevin Mack (Cleveland Browns)
U.P.I. NFC Coach of the Year--Mike Ditka (Chicago Bears)
U.P.I. NFC Player of the Year--Walter Payton (Chicago Bears)
Mike Singletary (Chicago Bears)
U.P.I. NFC Rookie of the Year--Jerry Rice (San Francisco 49ers)

Hall of Fame Inductees

Dan Fortmann, Frank Gatski, Joe Namath, Pete Rozelle, O.J. Simpson, Roger Staubach

Notes

The NFL extended the agreement for Honolulu's Aloha Stadium to host the Pro-Bowl game for the 1988, 1989 and 1990 seasons.

Canadian Football League

Eastern Division

Team Name	GP	W	L	T	PF	PA	Pts	Pct
Hamilton Tiger-Cats	16	8	8	0	377	315	16	.500
Montreal Concordes	16	8	8	0	284	332	16	.500
Ottawa Rough Riders	16	7	9	0	272	402	14	.438
Toronto Argonauts	16	6	10	0	344	397	12	.375

Western Division

Team Name	GP	W	L	T	PF	PA	Pts	Pct
British Columbia Lions	16	13	3	0	481	297	26	.813
Winnipeg Blue Bombers	16	12	4	0	500	259	24	.750
Edmonton Eskimos	16	10	6	0	432	373	20	.625
Saskatchewan Roughriders	16	5	11	0	320	462	10	.313
Calgary Stampeders	16	3	13	0	256	429	6	.188

Coaching Changes

Montreal--Joe Galat 6-8-0, Gary Durchik 2-0-0; Ottawa--Joe Moss 7-9-0; Winnipeg--Cal Murphy 9-3-0, Fred Glick 3-1-0; Calgary--Steve Burrato 0-5-0, Bud Riley 3-8-0; Saskatchewan--Jack Gotta 5-11-0.

League Leaders

Yards Rushing		Yards Passing		Passing % (150 attempts)	
Willard Reaves	1323	Roy DeWalt	4237	Conredge Holloway	66.1
Keyvan Jenkins	964	Tom Clements	3697	Roy DeWalt	63.2
Ken Hobart	928	Joe Barnes	3432	Homer Jordan	60.8
Matt Dunigan	737	Joe Paopao	3420	Tom Clements	60.4
J.C. Watts	710	Matt Dunigan	3410	Joe Paopao	60.4

Receiving Yards		Receptions		Points	
Mervyn Fernandez	1727	Craig Ellis	102	Trevor Kennerd	198
Jeff Boyd	1372	Mervyn Fernandez	95	Lui Passaglia	185
Terry Greer	1323	Ray Elgaard	79	Bernie Ruoff	154
Joe Poplawski	1271	Terry Greer	78	Tom Dixon	138
Ray Elgaard	1193	Jeff Boyd	76	John T. Hay	120

Grey Cup Playoffs

November 10	Edmonton Eskimos	15	at	Winnipeg Blue Bombers	22
November 10	Ottawa Rough Riders	20	at	Montreal Concordes	30
November 17	Winnipeg Blue Bombers	22	at	British Columbia Lions	42
November 17	Montreal Concordes	26	at	Hamilton Tiger-Cats	50
November 24	British Columbia Lions	37		Hamilton Tiger-Cats	24*

Individual Awards

Annis Stukus Trophy--Don Matthews (British Columbia Lions)
Dave Dryburgh Memorial Trophy--Trevor Kennerd (Winnipeg Blue Bombers)
DeMarco-Becket Memorial Trophy--Nick Bastaja (Winnipeg Blue Bombers)
Dr. Beattie Martin Trophy--Joe Poplawski (Winnipeg Blue Bombers)
Eddie James Memorial Trophy--Willard Reaves (Winnipeg Blue Bombers)
Frank M. Gibson Trophy--Nick Benjamin (Ottawa Rough Riders)
Grey Cup Most Outstanding Defensive Star--James Parker (British Columbia Lions)
Grey Cup Most Outstanding Offensive Star--Roy DeWalt (British Columbia Lions)
Grey Cup Most Outstanding Canadian--Lui Passaglia (British Columbia Lions)
Jackie Parker Trophy--Michael Gray (British Columbia Lions)
James P. McCaffrey Trophy--Paul Bennett (Hamilton Tiger-Cats)
Jeff Nicklin Memorial Trophy--Mervyn Fernandez (British Columbia Lions)
Jeff Russel Memorial Trophy--Ken Hobart (Hamilton Tiger-Cats)
Leo Dandurand Trophy--Dan Ferrone (Toronto Argonauts)
Lew Hayman Trophy--Paul Bennett (Hamilton Tiger-Cats)
Norm Fieldgate Trophy--Tyrone Jones (Winnipeg Blue Bombers)
Schenley Award Most Outstanding Canadian--Paul Bennett (Hamilton Tiger-Cats)
Schenley Award Most Outstanding Defensive Player--Tyrone Jones (Winnipeg Blue Bombers)
Schenley Award Most Outstanding Offensive Lineman--Nick Bastaja (Winnipeg Blue Bombers)
Schenley Award Most Outstanding Player--Mervyn Fernandez (British Columbia Lions)
Schenley Award Most Outstanding Rookie--Michael Gray (British Columbia Lions)

Hall of Fame Inductees

Tony Gabriel, Frank Rigney, Frank Tindall, William Zock

Rules

The CFL moved to adopt two five minute overtime halves for playoff games, replacing the two ten minute halves that had existed before.

*Game played in Montreal

United States Football League
Eastern Conference

Team Name	GP	W	L	T	PF	PA	Pct
Birmingham Stallions	18	13	5	0	436	299	.722
New Jersey Generals	18	11	7	0	418	377	.611
Memphis Showboats	18	11	7	0	428	337	.611
Baltimore Stars	18	10	7	1	368	260	.583
Tampa Bay Bandits	18	10	8	0	405	422	.556
Jacksonville Sharks	18	9	9	0	407	402	.500
Orlando Renegades	18	5	13	0	308	481	.278

Western Conference

Team Name	GP	W	L	T	PF	PA	Pct
Oakland Invaders	18	13	4	1	473	359	.750
Denver Gold	18	11	7	0	433	389	.611
Houston Gamblers	18	10	8	0	544	388	.556
Arizona Wranglers	18	8	10	0	376	405	.444
Portland Breakers	18	6	12	0	275	422	.333
San Antonio Gunslingers	18	5	13	0	296	436	.278
Los Angeles Express	18	3	15	0	266	456	.167

Coaching Changes

Baltimore--Jim Mora 10-7-1; Orlando--Lee Corso 5-13-0; Denver--Mouse Davis 11-7-0; Arizona--Frank Kush 8-10-0; Portland--Dick Coury 6-12-0; San Antonio--Jim Bates 3-9-0, Gil Steinke 2-4-0: Oakland--Charlie Sumner 13-14-1.

League Leaders

Yards Rushing		Yards Passing		Passing % (300 attempts)	
Herschel Walker	2411	Jim Kelly	4623	Jim Kelly	63.5
Mike Rozier	1361	John Reaves	4193	Chuck Fusina	61.1
Bill Johnson	1261	Bob Hebert	3811	Ed Luther	60.0
Gary Anderson	1207	Doug Williams	3673	Cliff Stoudt	59.9
Kelvin Bryant	1207	Chuck Fusina	3496	Bob Gagliano	57.3

Receiving Yards

Leonard Harris	1432
Johnson	1384
Anthony Carter	1323
Jim Smith	1322
Lewis	1207

USFL Playoffs

June 29	Houston Gamblers	20	at	Birmingham Stallions	22
June 30	Denver Gold	7	at	Memphis Showboats	48
June 30	Tampa Bay Bandits	27	at	Oakland Invaders	48
July 1	Baltimore Stars	20	at	New Jersey Generals	17
July 6	Oakland Invaders	28	at	Memphis Showboats	19
July 7	Baltimore Stars	28	at	Birmingham Stallions	14
July 14	Baltimore Stars	28	at	Oakland Invaders	24*

*Game played in East Rutherford, New Jersey

Individual Awards

Most Valuable Player--Herschel Walker (New Jersey Generals) [A.P., P.F.W.A. and Sporting News]

Notes

Harry Usher replaced Chet Simmons as Commissioner of the United States Football League on January 15 but this was the last season for the league.

HOCKEY

National Hockey League
Clarence Campbell Conference

Norris Division

Team Name	GP	W	L	T	GF	GA	Pts	Pct
St. Louis Blues	80	37	31	12	299	288	86	.538
Chicago BlackHawks	80	38	35	7	309	299	83	.519
Detroit Red Wings	80	27	41	12	313	357	66	.413
Minnesota North Stars	80	25	43	12	268	321	62	.388
Toronto Maple Leafs	80	20	52	8	253	358	48	.300

Smythe Division

Team Name	GP	W	L	T	GF	GA	Pts	Pct
Edmonton Oilers	80	49	20	11	401	298	109	.681
Winnipeg Jets	80	43	27	10	358	332	96	.600
Calgary Flames	80	41	27	12	363	302	94	.588
Los Angeles Kings	80	34	32	14	339	326	82	.513
Vancouver Canucks	80	25	46	9	284	401	59	.369

Prince of Wales Conference

Adams Division

Team Name	GP	W	L	T	GF	GA	Pts	Pct
Montreal Canadiens	80	41	27	12	309	262	94	.588
Quebec Nordiques	80	41	30	9	323	275	91	.569
Buffalo Sabres	80	38	28	14	290	237	90	.563
Boston Bruins	80	36	34	10	303	287	82	.513
Hartford Whalers	80	30	41	9	268	318	69	.431

Patrick Division

Team Name	GP	W	L	T	GF	GA	Pts	Pct
Philadelphia Flyers	80	53	20	7	348	241	113	.706
Washington Capitals	80	46	25	9	322	240	101	.631
New York Islanders	80	40	34	6	345	312	86	.538
New York Rangers	80	26	44	10	295	345	62	.388
New Jersey Devils	80	22	48	10	264	346	54	.338
Pittsburgh Penguins	80	24	51	5	276	385	53	.331

Coaching Changes

Chicago--Orval Tessier 22-28-3, Bob Pulford 16-7-4; Minnesota--Bill Mahoney 3-8-2, Glen Sonmor 22-35-10; Toronto--Dan Maloney 20-52-8; Winnipeg--Barry Long 43-27-10; Los Angeles--Pat Quinn 34-32-14; Vancouver--Bill LaForge 4-14-2, Harry Neale 21-32-7; Montreal--Jacques Lemaire 41-27-12; Boston--Gerry Cheevers 25-24-7, Harry Sinden 11-10-3; Philadelphia--Mike Keenan 53-20-7; New York Rangers--Herb Brooks 15-22-8, Craig Patrick 11-22-2; New Jersey--Doug Carpenter 22-48-10; Pittsburgh--Bob Berry 24-51-5.

League Leaders

Goals		Assists		Points	
Wayne Gretzky	73	Wayne Gretzky	135	Wayne Gretzky	208
Jari Kurri	71	Paul Coffey	84	Jari Kurri	135
Mike Bossy	58	Marcel Dionne	80	Dale Hawerckuk	130
Michel Goulet	55	Dale Hawerchuk	77	Marcel Dionne	126
John Ogrodnick	55	Bernie Federko	73	Paul Coffey	121

Penalty Minutes		GAA (1,500 minutes)		Wins	
Chris Nilan	358	Tom Barrasso	2.66	Pelle Lindbergh	40
Torrie Robertson	337	Pat Riggin	2.98	Brian Hayward	33
John Blum	263	Pelle Lindbergh	3.02	Rejean Lemelin	30
Tim Hunter	259	Steve Penney	3.08	Pat Riggin	28
Bob McGill	250	Bob Sauve	3.22	Murray Bannerman	27

Shutouts		Save %	
Tom Barrasso	5	Warren Skorodenski	.903
Warren Skorodenski	2	Pelle Lindbergh	.899
Steve Weeks	2	Andy Moog	.894
Kelly Hrudey	2	Mike Lint	.889
Mike Liut	2	Rejean Lemelin	.888

All Star Game

(Olympic Saddledome, Calgary)

February 12	Wales Conference	6		Campbell Conference	4

Stanley Cup Playoffs

April 10	Minnesota North Stars	3	at	St. Louis Blues	2
April 10	Boston Bruins	5	at	Montreal Canadiens	3
April 10	Buffalo Sabres	2	at	Quebec Nordiques	5
April 10	New York Rangers	4	at	Philadelphia Flyers	5 [8:01]
April 10	New York Islanders	3	at	Washington Capitals	4 [2:28]
April 10	Detroit Red Wings	5	at	Chicago Black Hawks	9
April 10	Los Angeles Kings	2	at	Edmonton Oilers	3 [3:01]
April 10	Calgary Flames	4	at	Winnipeg Jets	5 [7:56]
April 11	Minnesota North Stars	4	at	St. Louis Blues	3
April 11	Boston Bruins	3	at	Montreal Canadiens	5
April 11	Buffalo Sabres	2	at	Quebec Nordiques	3
April 11	New York Rangers	1	at	Philadelphia Flyers	3
April 11	New York Islanders	1	at	Washington Capitals	2 [1:23]
April 11	Detroit Red Wings	1	at	Chicago Black Hawks	6
April 11	Los Angeles Kings	2	at	Edmonton Oilers	4
April 11	Calgary Flames	2	at	Winnipeg Jets	5
April 13	St. Louis Blues	0	at	Minnesota North Stars	2
April 13	Montreal Canadiens	4	at	Boston Bruins	2
April 13	Quebec Nordiques	4	at	Buffalo Sabres	6
April 13	Philadelphia Flyers	6	at	New York Rangers	5
April 13	Washington Capitals	1	at	New York Islanders	2
April 13	Chicago Black Hawks	8	at	Detroit Red Wings	2
April 13	Edmonton Oilers	4	at	Los Angeles Kings	3 [0:46]

April 13	Winnipeg Jets	0	at	Calgary Flames	4
April 14	Montreal Canadiens	6	at	Boston Bruins	7
April 14	Quebec Nordiques	4	at	Buffalo Sabres	7
April 14	Washington Capitals	4	at	New York Islanders	6
April 14	Winnipeg Jets	5	at	Calgary Flames	3
April 16	Boston Bruins	0	at	Montreal Canadiens	1
April 16	Buffalo Sabres	5	at	Quebec Nordiques	6
April 16	New York Islanders	2	at	Washington Capitals	1
April 18	Quebec Nordiques	2	at	Montreal Canadiens	1 [12:23]
April 18	New York Islanders	0	at	Philadelphia Flyers	3
April 18	Minnesota North Stars	8	at	Chicago Black Hawks	5
April 18	Winnipeg Jets	2	at	Edmonton Oilers	4
April 20	Winnipeg Jets	2	at	Edmonton Oilers	5
April 21	Quebec Nordiques	4	at	Montreal Canadiens	6
April 21	New York Islanders	2	at	Philadelphia Flyers	5
April 21	Minnesota North Stars	2	at	Chicago Black Hawks	6
April 23	Montreal Canadiens	6	at	Quebec Nordiques	7 [18:36]
April 23	Philadelphia Flyers	5	at	New York Islanders	3
April 23	Chicago Black Hawks	5	at	Minnesota North Stars	3
April 23	Edmonton Oilers	5	at	Winnipeg Jets	4
April 25	Montreal Canadiens	3	at	Quebec Nordiques	1
April 25	Philadelphia Flyers	2	at	New York Islanders	6
April 25	Chicago Black Hawks	7	at	Minnesota North Stars	6 [1:57]
April 25	Edmonton Oilers	8	at	Winnipeg Jets	3
April 27	Quebec Nordiques	5	at	Montreal Canadiens	1
April 28	New York Islanders	0	at	Philadelphia Flyers	1
April 28	Minnesota North Stars	5	at	Chicago Black Hawks	4 [1:14]
April 30	Montreal Canadiens	5	at	Quebec Nordiques	2
April 30	Chicago Black Hawks	6	at	Minnesota North Stars	5 [15:41]
May 2	Quebec Nordiques	3	at	Montreal Canadiens	2 [2:22]
May 4	Chicago Black Hawks	2	at	Edmonton Oilers	11
May 5	Philadelphia Flyers	1	at	Quebec Nordiques	2 [6:20]
May 7	Chicago Black Hawks	3	at	Edmonton Oilers	7
May 7	Philadelphia Flyers	4	at	Quebec Nordiques	2
May 9	Edmonton Oilers	2	at	Chicago Black Hawks	5
May 9	Quebec Nordiques	2	at	Philadelphia Flyers	4
May 12	Edmonton Oilers	6	at	Chicago Black Hawks	8
May 12	Quebec Nordiques	5	at	Philadelphia Flyers	3
May 14	Chicago Black Hawks	5	at	Edmonton Oilers	10
May 14	Philadelphia Flyers	2	at	Quebec Nordiques	1
May 16	Edmonton Oilers	8	at	Chicago Black Hawks	2
May 16	Quebec Nordiques	0	at	Philadelphia Flyers	3
May 21	Edmonton Oilers	1	at	Philadelphia Flyers	4
May 23	Edmonton Oilers	3	at	Philadelphia Flyers	1
May 25	Philadelphia Flyers	3	at	Edmonton Oilers	4
May 28	Philadelphia Flyers	3	at	Edmonton Oilers	5
May 30	Philadelphia Flyers	3	at	Edmonton Oilers	8

All Star Teams

First Team		Second Team
Pelle Lindbergh	Goal	Tom Barrasso
Paul Coffey	Defense	Rod Langway
Ray Bourque	Defense	Doug Wilson
Wayne Gretzky	Center	Dale Hawerchuk
Jari Kurri	Right Wing	Mike Bossy
John Ogrodnick	Left Wing	John Tonelli

Individual Awards

Art Ross Trophy--Wayne Gretzky (Edmonton Oilers)
Bill Masterton Trophy--Anders Hedberg (New York Rangers)
Calder Memorial Trophy--Mario Lemieux (Pittsburgh Penguins)
Conn Smythe Trophy--Wayne Gretzky (Edmonton Oilers)
Dodge Performer of the Year--Wayne Gretzky (Edmonton Oilers)
Emery Edge Trophy--Wayne Gretzky (Edmonton Oilers)
Frank J. Selke Trophy--Craig Ramsay (Buffalo Sabres)
Hart Memorial Trophy--Wayne Gretzky (Edmonton Oilers)
Jack Adams Award--Mike Keenan (Philadelphia Flyers)
James Norris Trophy--Paul Coffey (Edmonton Oilers)
Lady Byng Memorial Trophy--Jari Kurri (Edmonton Oilers)
Lester B. Pearson Award--Wayne Gretzky (Edmonton Oilers)
Lester Patrick Trophy--Jack Butterfield and Arthur Wirtz
NHL All Star Game MVP--Mario Lemieux (Pittsburgh Penguins)
Vezina Trophy--Pelle Lindbergh (Philadelphia Flyers)
William M. Jennings Trophy--Tom Barrasso and Bob Sauve (Buffalo Sabres)

Hall of Fame Inductees

Gerry Cheevers, John Mariucci, Bert Olmstead, Rudy Pilous, Jean Ratelle

Franchise Changes

USFL--Philadelphia Stars became the Baltimore Stars.
Jacksonville Bulls became the Jacksonville Sharks.
New Orleans Breakers became the Portland Breakers.
NBA--San Diego Clippers became the Los Angeles Clippers.

Other Sports

Horseracing--Kentucky Derby won by Spend a Buck (time 2:00.2, purse $406,800).
Heavyweight Boxing--Tony Tubbs defeated Greg Page in 15 rounds (WBA).
Michael Spinx defeated Larry Holmes in 15 rounds (IBF).
Golf--U.S. Open won by Andy North with a score of 279.
Auto Racing--Indianapolis 500 won by Danny Sullivan (ave. speed 152.982 MPH).
Tennis--U.S. Open won by Ivan Lendl in the men's singles.
U.S. Open won by Ken Flach and Robert Seguso in the men's doubles.
U.S. Open won by Hana Mandlikova in the women's singles.
U.S. Open won by Claudia Kohde-Kilsch and Helena Sukova in the women's doubles.
U.S. open won by Martina Navratilova and Heinz Gundhardt in the mixed doubles.

1986

BASEBALL
National League
East

Team Name	W	L	Pct	GB	R	OR
New York Mets	108	54	.667	-	783	578
Philadelphia Phillies	86	76	.534	21.5	739	713
St. Louis Cardinals	79	82	.491	28.5	601	611
Montreal Expos	78	83	.484	29.5	637	688
Chicago Cubs	70	90	.438	37	680	781
Pittsburgh Pirates	64	98	.395	44	663	700

West

Team Name	W	L	Pct	GB	R	OR
Houston Astros	96	66	.593	-	654	569
Cincinnati Reds	86	76	.531	10	732	717
San Francisco Giants	83	79	.512	13	698	618
San Diego Padres	74	88	.457	22	656	723
Los Angeles Dodgers	73	89	.451	23	638	679
Atlanta Braves	72	89	.447	23.5	615	719

Coaching Changes

Chicago--Jim Frey 23-33, John Vukovich 1-1, Gene Michael 46-56; Pittsburgh--Jim Leyland 64-98; Houston--Hal Lanier 96-66; San Francisco--Roger Craig 83-79; San Diego--Steve Boros 74-88; Atlanta--Chuck Tanner 72-89.

League Leaders

Batting Average
(502 at bats)

Tim Raines	.334
Steve Sax	.332
Tony Gwynn	.329
Kevin Bass	.311
Keith Hernandez	.310

Home Runs

Mike Schmidt	37
Glenn Davis	31
Dave Parker	31
Dale Murphy	29
Eric Davis	27

RBI

Mike Schmidt	119
Dave Parker	116
Gary Carter	105
Glenn Davis	101
Von Hayes	98

Stolen Bases

Vince Coleman	107
Eric Davis	80
Tim Raines	70
Mariano Duncan	48
Bill Doran	42

ERA
(162 innings)

Mike Scott	2.22
Bob Ojeda	2.57
Ron Darling	2.81
Rick Rhoden	2.84
Dwight Gooden	2.84

Wins

Fernando Valenzuela	21
Mike Krukow	20
Bob Ojeda	18
Mike Scott	18
Dwight Gooden	17

Saves

Todd Worrell	36
Jeff Reardon	35
Dave Smith	33
Lee Smith	31
Steve Bedrosian	29

Strikeouts

Mike Scott	306
Fernando Valenzuela	242
Floyd Youmans	202
Dwight Gooden	200
Sid Fernandez	200

NLCS

October 8	New York Mets	0	at	Houston Astros	1
October 9	New York Mets	5	at	Houston Astros	1
October 11	Houston Astros	5	at	New York Mets	6
October 12	Houston Astros	3	at	New York Mets	1
October 14	Houston Astros	1	at	New York Mets	2 [12]
October 15	New York Mets	7	at	Houston Astros	6 [16]

American League
East

Team Name	W	L	Pct	GB	R	OR
Boston Red Sox	95	66	.590	-	794	696
New York Yankees	90	72	.556	5.5	797	738
Detroit Tigers	87	75	.537	8.5	798	714
Toronto Blue Jays	86	76	.531	9.5	889	733
Cleveland Indians	84	78	.519	11.5	831	841
Milwaukee Brewers	77	84	.478	18	667	734
Baltimore Orioles	73	89	.451	22.5	708	760

West

Team Name	W	L	Pct	GB	R	OR
California Angels	92	70	.568	-	786	684
Texas Rangers	87	75	.537	5	771	743
Kansas City Royals	76	86	.469	16	654	673
Oakland Athletics	76	86	.469	16	731	760
Chicago White Sox	72	90	.444	20	644	699
Minnesota Twins	71	91	.438	21	741	839
Seattle Mariners	67	95	.414	25	718	835

Coaching Changes

New York--Lou Piniella 90-72; Toronto--Jimy Williams 86-76; Milwaukee--George Bamberger 70-81, Tom Trebelhorn 7-3; Baltimore--Earl Weaver 73-89; Texas--Bobby Valentine 87-75; Oakland--Jackie Moore 29-44, Jeff Newman 2-8, Tony LaRussa 45-34; Kansas City--Dick Howser 41-48, Mike Ferraro 35-38; Chicago--Tony LaRussa 26-38, Doug Rader 1-1, Jim Fregosi 45-51; Minnesota--Ray Miller 59-80, Tom Kelly 12-11; Seattle--Chuck Cottier 9-19, Marty Martinez 0-1, Dick Williams 58-75.

League Leaders

Batting Average (502 at bats)		**Home Runs**		**RBI**	
Wade Boggs	.357	Jesse Barfield	40	Joe Carter	121
Don Mattingly	.352	Dave Kingman	35	Jose Canseco	117
Kirby Puckett	.328	Gary Gaetti	34	Don Mattingly	113
Pat Tabler	.326	Jose Canseco	33	Jim Rice	110
Jim Rice	.324	Rob Deer	33	Jesse Barfield	107

Stolen Bases		**ERA** (162 innings)		**Wins**	
Rickey Henderson	87	Roger Clemens	2.48	Roger Clemens	24
John Cangelosi	50	Ted Higuera	2.79	Jack Morris	21
Gary Pettis	50	Mike Witt	2.84	Ted Higuera	20
Kirk Gibson	34	Bruce Hurst	2.99	Mike Witt	18
Willie Wilson	34	Danny Jackson	3.20	Dennis Rasmussen	18

Saves		**Strikeouts**	
Dave Righetti	46	Mark Langston	245
Don Aase	34	Roger Clemens	238
Tom Henke	27	Jack Morris	223
Willie Hernandez	24	Bert Blyleven	215
Donnie Moore	21	Mike Witt	208

All Star Game

(The Astrodome, Houston)

July 15	American League	3		National League	2

ALCS

October 7	California Angels	8	at	Boston Red Sox	1
October 8	California Angels	2	at	Boston Red Sox	9
October 10	Boston Red Sox	3	at	California Angels	5
October 11	Boston Red Sox	3	at	California Angels	4 [11]
October 12	Boston Red Sox	7	at	California Angels	6 [11]
October 14	California Angels	4	at	Boston Red Sox	10
October 15	California Angels	1	at	Boston Red Sox	8

World Series

October 18	Boston Red Sox	1	at	New York Mets	0
October 19	Boston Red Sox	9	at	New York Mets	3
October 21	New York Mets	7	at	Boston Red Sox	1
October 22	New York Mets	6	at	Boston Red Sox	2
October 23	New York Mets	2	at	Boston Red Sox	4
October 25	Boston Red Sox	5	at	New York Mets	6 [10]
October 27	Boston Red Sox	5	at	New York Mets	8

Individual Awards

ALCS MVP--Marty Barrett (Boston Red Sox AL)
Arch Ward Memorial Trophy--Roger Clemens (Boston Red Sox AL)
Baseball Writers Award--Mike Schmidt (Philadelphia Phillies NL)
Roger Clemens (Boston Red Sox AL)
Cy Young Award--Mike Scott (Houston Astros NL)
Roger Clemens (Boston Red Sox AL)
NLCS MVP--Mike Scott (Houston Astros-NL)
Rookie of the Year--Todd Warrell (St. Louis Cardinals NL)
Jose Canseco (Oakland Athletics AL)
Sporting News Executive of the Year--Frank Cashen (New York Mets NL)
Sporting News Manager of the Year--Hal Lanier (Houston Astros NL)
John McNamara (Boston Red Sox AL)
Sporting News Pitcher of the Year--Mike Scott (Houston Astros NL)
Roger Clemens (Boston Red Sox AL)
Sporting News Player of the Year--Mike Schmidt (Philadelphia Phillies NL)
Don Mattingly (New York Yankees AL)
Sporting News Rookie of the Year--Bobby Thompson (San Francisco Giants NL)
Todd Warrell (St. Louis Cardinals NL)
Jose Canseco (Oakland Athletics AL)
Mark Eichhorn (Toronto Blue Jays AL)
World Series MVP--Ray Knight (New York Mets NL)

Hall of Fame Inductees

Bobby Doerr, Ernie Lombardi, Willie McCovey

BASKETBALL
National Basketball Association
Eastern Conference
Atlantic Division

Team Name	GP	W	L	PPGF	PPGA	Pct	GB
Boston Celtics	82	67	15	114.1	104.7	.817	-
Philadelphia 76ers	82	54	28	110.4	108.0	.659	13
Washington Bullets	82	39	43	103.0	104.8	.476	28
New Jersey Nets	82	39	43	109.1	111.1	.476	28
New York Knickerbockers	82	23	59	98.7	104.3	.280	44

Central Division

Team Name	GP	W	L	PPGF	PPGA	Pct	GB
Milwaukee Bucks	82	57	25	114.5	105.5	.695	-
Atlanta Hawks	82	50	32	108.6	106.2	.610	7
Detroit Pistons	82	46	36	114.2	113.0	.561	11
Chicago Bulls	82	30	52	109.3	113.1	.366	27
Cleveland Cavaliers	82	29	53	107.8	110.6	.354	28
Indiana Pacers	82	26	56	103.9	107.2	.317	31

Western Conference

Midwest Division

Team Name	GP	W	L	PPGF	PPGA	Pct	GB
Houston Rockets	82	51	31	114.4	111.8	.622	-
Denver Nuggets	82	47	35	114.8	113.5	.573	4
Dallas Mavericks	82	44	38	115.3	114.2	.537	7
Utah Jazz	82	42	40	108.2	108.5	.512	9
Sacramento Kings	82	37	45	108.8	111.9	.451	14
San Antonio Spurs	82	35	47	108.8	111.9	.427	16

Pacific Division

Team Name	GP	W	L	PPGF	PPGA	Pct	GB
Los Angeles Lakers	82	62	20	117.3	109.5	.756	-
Portland Trail Blazers	82	40	42	115.1	114.0	.488	22
Los Angeles Clippers	82	32	50	108.6	115.5	.390	30
Phoenix Suns	82	32	50	110.0	113.0	.390	30
Seattle SuperSonics	82	31	51	104.4	104.5	.378	31
Golden State Warriors	82	30	52	113.4	116.9	.366	32

Coaching Changes

Philadelphia--Matt Guokas 54-28; Washington--Gene Shue 32-37, Kevin Loughery 7-6; New Jersey--Dave Wohl 39-43; Chicago--Stan Albeck 30-52; Cleveland--George Karl 25-42, Gene Littles 4-11; Sacramento--Phil Johnson 37-45; Los Angeles Clippers--Don Chaney 32-50; Seattle--Bernie Bickerstaff 31-51.

League Leaders

Field Goals		Free Throws		Assists	
Alex English	951	Adrian Dantley	630	Earvin Johnson	907
Dominique Wilkins	888	Moses Malone	617	Isiah Thomas	830
Adrian Dantley	818	Dominique Wilkins	577	Reggie Theus	788
Mike Mitchell	802	Kiki Vandeweghe	523	Maurice Cheeks	753
Larry Bird	796	Alex English	511	"Sleepy" Floyd	746

Points		**Rebounds per Game**	
Alex-English	2414	Bill Laimbeer	13.1
Dominique Wilkins	2366	Charles Barkley	12.8
Adrian Dantley	2267	Buck Williams	12.0
Larry Bird	2115	Moses Malone	11.8
Kiki Vandeweghe	1962	Ralph Sampson	11.1

All Star Game

(Reunion Arena, Dallas)

February 9	East Division	139		West Division	132

NBA Playoffs

April 17	Chicago Bulls	104	at	Boston Celtics	123
April 17	Detroit Pistons	122	at	Atlanta Hawks	140
April 17	San Antonio Spurs	88	at	Los Angeles Lakers	135
April 17	Sacramento Kings	87	at	Houston Rockets	107
April 18	Portland Trail Blazers	126	at	Denver Nuggets	133
April 18	New Jersey Nets	107	at	Milwaukee Bucks	119
April 18	Washington Bullets	95	at	Philadelphia 76ers	94
April 18	Utah Jazz	93	at	Dallas Mavericks	101
April 19	Detroit Pistons	125	at	Atlanta Hawks	137
April 19	San Antonio Spurs	94	at	Los Angeles Lakers	122
April 19	Sacramento Kings	103	at	Houston Rockets	111
April 20	Portland Trail Blazers	108	at	Denver Nuggets	106
April 20	Utah Jazz	106	at	Dallas Mavericks	113
April 20	Chicago Bulls	131	at	Boston Celtics	135 [OT]
April 20	New Jersey Nets	97	at	Milwaukee Bucks	111
April 20	Washington Bullets	97	at	Philadelphia 76ers	102
April 22	Boston Celtics	122	at	Chicago Bulls	104
April 22	Milwaukee Bucks	118	at	New Jersey Nets	113
April 22	Philadelphia 76ers	91	at	Washington Bullets	86
April 22	Atlanta Hawks	97	at	Detroit Pistons	106
April 22	Houston Rockets	113	at	Sacramento Kings	98
April 22	Denver Nuggets	115	at	Portland Trail Blazers	104
April 23	Los Angeles Lakers	114	at	San Antonio Spurs	94
April 23	Dallas Mavericks	98	at	Utah Jazz	100
April 24	Philadelphia 76ers	111	at	Washington Bullets	116
April 24	Denver Nuggets	116	at	Portland Trail Blazers	112
April 25	Atlanta Hawks	114	at	Detroit Pistons	113 [OT]
April 25	Dallas Mavericks	117	at	Utah Jazz	113
April 26	Denver Nuggets	119	at	Houston Rockets	126
April 27	Washington Bullets	109	at	Philadelphia 76ers	134
April 27	Atlanta Hawks	91	at	Boston Celtics	103
April 27	Dallas Mavericks	116	at	Los Angeles Lakers	130
April 29	Philadelphia 76ers	118	at	Milwaukee Bucks	112
April 29	Atlanta Hawks	108	at	Boston Celtics	119
April 29	Denver Nuggets	101	at	Houston Rockets	119
April 30	Dallas Mavericks	113	at	Los Angeles Lakers	117
May 1	Philadelphia 76ers	107	at	Milwaukee Bucks	119
May 2	Boston Celtics	111	at	Atlanta Hawks	107
May 2	Los Angeles Lakers	108	at	Dallas Mavericks	110
May 2	Houston Rockets	115	at	Denver Nuggets	116
May 3	Milwaukee Bucks	103	at	Philadelphia 76ers	107

May 4	Boston Celtics	94	at	Atlanta Hawks	106
May 4	Los Angeles Lakers	118	at	Dallas Mavericks	120
May 4	Houston Rockets	111	at	Denver Nuggets	114 [OT]
May 5	Milwaukee Bucks	109	at	Philadelphia 76ers	104
May 6	Atlanta Hawks	99	at	Boston Celtics	132
May 6	Dallas Mavericks	113	at	Los Angeles Lakers	116
May 6	Denver Nuggets	103	at	Houston Rockets	131
May 7	Philadelphia 76ers	108	at	Milwaukee Bucks	113
May 8	Los Angeles Lakers	120	at	Dallas Mavericks	107
May 8	Houston Rockets	126	at	Denver Nuggets	122 [OT]
May 9	Milwaukee Bucks	108	at	Philadelphia 76ers	126
May 10	Houston Rockets	107	at	Los Angeles Lakers	119
May 11	Philadelphia 76ers	112	at	Milwaukee Bucks	113
May 13	Milwaukee Bucks	96	at	Boston Celtics	128
May 13	Houston Rockets	112	at	Los Angeles Lakers	102
May 15	Milwaukee Bucks	111	at	Boston Celtics	122
May 16	Los Angeles Lakers	109	at	Houston Rockets	117
May 17	Boston Celtics	111	at	Milwaukee Bucks	107
May 18	Los Angeles Lakers	95	at	Houston Rockets	105
May 18	Boston Celtics	111	at	Milwaukee Bucks	98
May 21	Houston Rockets	114	at	Los Angeles Lakers	112
May 26	Houston Rockets	100	at	Boston Celtics	112
May 29	Houston Rockets	95	at	Boston Celtics	117
June 1	Boston Celtics	104	at	Houston Rockets	106
June 3	Boston Celtics	106	at	Houston Rockets	103
June 5	Boston Celtics	96	at	Houston Rockets	111
June 8	Houston Rockets	97	at	Boston Celtics	114

All Star Teams

First Team

Larry Bird (Boston Celtics)
Dominique Wilkins (Atlanta Hawks)
Kareem Abdul-Jabbar (Los Angeles Lakers)
Earvin Johnson (Los Angeles Lakers)
Isiah Thomas (Detroit Pistons)

Second Team

Charles Barkley (Philadelphia 76ers)
Alex English (Denver Nuggets)
Akeem Olajuwon (Houston Rockets)
Sidney Moncrief (Milwaukee Bucks)
Alvin Robertson (San Antonio Spurs)

Individual Awards

Defensive Player of the Game--Alvin Robertson (San Antonio Spurs)
Eddie Gottlieb Trophy--Patrick Ewing (New York Knickerbockers)
Executive of the Year--Stan Kasten (Atlanta Hawks)
J. Walter Kennedy Citizenship Award--Michael Cooper (Los Angeles Lakers)
Rory Sparrow (New York Knickerbockers)
Maurice Podoloff Trophy--Larry Bird (Boston Celtics)
Most Improved Player--Alvin Robertson (San Antonio Spurs)
NBA All Star Game MVP--Isiah Thomas (Detroit Pistons)
NBA Finals MVP--Larry Bird(Boston Celtics)
Red Auerbach Trophy--Mike Fratello (Atlanta Hawks)
Schick Award--Charles Barkley (Philadelphia 76ers)
Sixth Man Award--Bill Walton (Boston Celtics)

Hall of Fame Inductees

Bill Cunningham, Tom Heinsohn, Bill Holzman, Zigmund Mihalik

FOOTBALL
National Football League

National Conference
Eastern Division

Team Name	GP	W	L	T	PF	PA	Pct
New York Giants	16	14	2	0	371	236	.875
Washington Redskins	16	12	4	0	368	296	.750
Dallas Cowboys	16	7	9	0	346	337	.438
Philadelphia Eagles	16	5	10	1	256	312	.344
St. Louis Cardinals	16	4	11	1	218	351	.281

Central Division

Team Name	GP	W	L	T	PF	PA	Pct
Chicago Bears	16	14	2	0	352	187	.875
Minnesota Vikings	16	9	7	0	398	273	.563
Detroit Lions	16	5	11	0	277	326	.313
Green Bay Packers	16	4	12	0	254	418	.250
Tampa Bay Buccaneers	16	2	14	0	239	473	.125

Western Division

Team Name	GP	W	L	T	PF	PA	Pct
San Francisco 49ers	16	10	5	1	374	247	.656
Los Angeles Rams	16	10	6	0	309	267	.625
Atlanta Falcons	16	7	8	1	280	280	.469
New Orleans Saints	16	7	9	0	288	287	.438

American Conference

Eastern Division

Team Name	GP	W	L	T	PF	PA	Pct
New England Patriots	16	11	5	0	412	307	.688
New York Jets	16	10	6	0	364	386	.625
Miami Dolphins	16	8	8	0	430	405	.500
Buffalo Bills	16	4	12	0	287	348	.250
Indianapolis Colts	16	3	13	0	229	400	.188

Central Division

Team Name	GP	W	L	T	PF	PA	Pct
Cleveland Browns	16	12	4	0	391	310	.750
Cincinnati Bengals	16	10	6	0	409	394	.625
Pittsburgh Steelers	16	6	10	0	307	336	.375
Houston Oilers	16	5	11	0	274	329	.313

Western Division

Team Name	GP	W	L	T	PF	PA	Pct
Denver Broncos	16	11	5	0	378	327	.688
Kansas City Chiefs	16	10	6	0	358	326	.625
Seattle Seahawks	16	10	6	0	366	293	.625
Los Angeles Raiders	16	8	8	0	323	346	.500
San Diego Chargers	16	4	12	0	335	396	.250

Coaching Changes

Philadelphia--Buddy Ryan 5-10-1; St. Louis--Gene Stallings 4-11-1; Minnesota--Jerry Burns 9-7-0; New Orleans--Jim Mora 7-9-0; Buffalo--Hank Bullough 1-6-0, Marv Levy 3-6-0; Indianapolis--Rod Dowhower 0-13-0, Ron Meyer 3-0-0; Houston--Jerry Glanville 5-11-0; San Diego--Don Coryell 1-7-0, Al Saunders 3-5-0.

League Leaders

Yards Rushing		**Yards Passing**		**Passing %** (300 attempts)	
Eric Dickerson	1821	Dan Marino	4746	Eric Hipple	63
Joe Morris	1516	Jay Schroeder	4109	Joe Montana	62
Curt Warner	1481	Boomer Esiason	3959	Tony Eason	62
Rueben Mayes	1353	Bernie Kosar	3854	Ken O'Brien	62
Walter Payton	1333	Ken O'Brien	3690	Dan Marino	61

Receiving Yards		**Receptions**		**Field Goals**	
Jerry Rice	1570	Todd Christensen	95	Tony Franklin	32
Stanley Morgan	1491	Jerry Rice	86	Kevin Butler	28
Mark Duper	1313	Al Toon	85	Matt Bahr	26
Gary Clark	1265	Stanley Morgan	84	Morten Andersen	26
Al Toon	1176	Roger Craig	81	Ray Wersching	25

Punt Return Yards		**Kickoff Return Yards**	
Vai Sikahema	522	Tim McGee	1007
Lew Barnes	482	Herman Hunter	1007
Gerald Wilhite	468	Gerald McNeil	997
Fulton Walker	440	Mel Gray	866
Pete Mandley	420	Vai Sikahema	847

Pro Bowl Game

(Aloha Stadium, Honolulu)

February 1 1987	American Conference	10	National Conference	6

NFL Playoffs

December 28	Kansas City Chiefs	15	at	New York Jets	35
December 28	Los Angeles Rams	7	at	Washington Redskins	19
January 3 1987	Washington Redskins	27	at	Chicago Bears	13
January 3 1987	New York Jets	20	at	Cleveland Browns	23 [OT]
January 4 1987	San Francisco 49ers	3	at	New York Giants	49
January 4 1987	New England Patriots	17	at	Denver Broncos	22
January 11 1987	Washington Redskins	0	at	New York Giants	17
January 11 1987	Denver Broncos	23	at	Cleveland Browns	20 [OT]

Super Bowl XXI

(Rose Bowl, Pasadena)

January 25 1987	New York Giants	39	Denver Broncos	20

Individual Awards

A.P. MVP--Lawrence Taylor (New York Giants)
Bert Bell Trophy--Rueben Mayes (New Orleans Saints) [World Almanac]
Bert Bell Trophy--Lawrence Taylor (New York Giants)

Dan McGuire Award--Reggie White (Philadelphia Eagles)
George Halas Trophy--Lawrence Taylor (New York Giants)
Jim Thorpe Trophy--Phil Simms (New York Giants)
P.F.W.A. MVP--Lawrence Taylor (New York Giants)
Super Bowl MVP--Phil Simms (New York Giants)
U.P.I. AFC Coach of the Year--Marty Schottenheimer (Cleveland Browns)
U.P.I. AFC Player of the Year--Curt Warner (Seattle Seahawks)
Rulon Jones (Denver Broncos)
U.P.I. AFC Rookie of the Year Leslie O'Neal (San Diego Chargers)
U.P.I. NFC Coach of the Year--Bill Parcells (New York Giants)
U.P.I. NFC Player of the Year--Eric Dickerson (Los Angeles Rams)
Lawrence Taylor (New York Giants)
U.P.I. NFC Rookie of the Year--Reuben Mayes (New Orleans Saints)

Hall of Fame Inductees

Paul Hornung, Ken Houston, Willie Lanier, Fran Tarkenton, Doak Walker

Notes

The NFL owners moved to adopt the limited use of video tape instant replays as an officiating aid. The NFL also banned the use of any piece of equipment displaying commercial names, personal messages or the names of any organizations.

Canadian Football League

Eastern Division

Team Name	GP	W	L	T	PF	PA	Pts	Pct
Toronto Argonauts	18	10	8	0	417	441	20	.556
Hamilton Tiger-Cats	18	9	8	1	405	366	19	.528
Montreal Alouettes	18	4	14	0	320	500	8	.222
Ottawa Rough Riders	18	3	14	1	346	514	7	.194

Western Division

Team Name	GP	W	L	T	PF	PA	Pts	Pct
Edmonton Eskimos	18	13	4	1	540	365	27	.750
British Columbia Lions	18	12	6	0	441	410	24	.667
Winnipeg Blue Bombers	18	11	7	0	545	387	22	.611
Calgary Stampeders	18	11	7	0	484	380	22	.611
Saskatchewan Roughriders	18	6	11	1	382	517	13	.361

Coaching Changes

Montreal--Gary Durchik 4-14-0; Winnipeg--Cal Murphy 11-7-0; Calgary--Bob Vespaziani 11-7-0.

League Leaders

Yards Rushing		Yards Passing		Passing % (150 attempts)	
Gary Allen	1153	Rick Johnson	4379	Tom Clements	67.5
Bob Johnson	869	Roy DeWalt	4057	John Hufnagel	59.0
Lester Brown	713	Matt Dunigan	3648	Joe Paopao	57.0
Walter Bender	618	John Hufnagel	3394	Mike Kerrigan	57.0
Chris Skinner	605	Brian Ransom	3204	Matt Dunigan	56.7

Receiving Yards		Receptions		Points	
James Murphy	1746	James Murphy	116	Tom Dixon	190
Ray Alexander	1590	James Hood	95	John T. Hay	181
James Hood	1411	Ray Alexander	88	Lui Passaglia	166
Perry Tuttle	1373	Rocky DiPietro	86	Paul Osbaldiston	165
Emanuel Tolbert	1286	Perry Tuttle	83	Lance Chomyc	157

Grey Cup Playoffs

November 15	Winnipeg Blue Bombers	14	at	British Columbia Lions	21
November 16	Toronto Argonauts	31	at	Hamilton Tiger-Cats	17
November 16	Calgary Stampeders	18	at	Edmonton Eskimos	27
November 23	Hamilton Tiger-Cats	42	at	Toronto Argonauts	25
November 23	British Columbia Lions	5	at	Edmonton Eskimos	41
November 30	Hamilton Tiger-Cats	39		Edmonton Eskimos	15*

Individual Awards

Annis Stukus Trophy--Al Bruno (Hamilton Tiger-Cats)
Dave Dryburgh Memorial Trophy--Tom Dixon (Edmonton Eskimos)
DeMarco-Becket Memorial Trophy--Roger Aldag (Saskatchewan Roughriders)
Dr. Beattie Martin Trophy--Joe Poplawski (Winnipeg Blue Bombers)
Eddie James Memorial Trophy--Gary Allen (Calgary Stampeders)
Frank M. Gibson Trophy--Willie Pless (Toronto Argonauts)
Grey Cup Most Outstanding Defensive Star--Grover Covington (Hamilton Tiger-Cats)
Grey Cup Most Outstanding Offensive Star--Mike Kerrigan (Hamilton Tiger-Cats)
Grey Cup Most Outstanding Canadian--Paul Osbaldiston (Hamilton Tiger-Cats)
Jackie Parker Trophy--Harold Hallman (Calgary Stampeders)
James P. McCaffrey Trophy--Brett Williams (Montreal Alouettes)
Jeff Nicklin Memorial Trophy--James Murphy (Winnipeg Blue Bombers)
Jeff Russel Memorial Trophy--James Hood (Montreal Alouettes)
Leo Dandurand Trophy--Miles Gorrell (Hamilton Tiger-Cats)
Lew Hayman Trophy--Rocky DiPietro (Hamilton Tiger-Cats)
Norm Fieldgate Trophy--James Parker (British Columbia Lions)
Schenley Award Most Outstanding Canadian--Joe Poplawski (Winnipeg Blue Bombers)
Schenley Award Most Outstanding Defensive Player--James Parker (British Columbia Lions)
Schenley Award Most Outstanding Offensive Lineman--Roger Aldag (Saskatchewan Roughriders)
Schenley Award Most Outstanding Player--James Murphy (Winnipeg Blue Bombers)
Schenley Award Most Outstanding Rookie--Harold Hallman (Calgary Stampeders)

Hall of Fame Inductees

Hec Crighton, John Helton, Don Luzzi, Roger Nelson, Jimmie Simpson

Rules

The CFL adopted the implementation of two five minute overtime halves in regular season games with no sudden death.

*Game played in Vancouver

HOCKEY

National Hockey League

Clarence Campbell Conference

Norris Division

Team Name	GP	W	L	T	GF	GA	Pts	Pct
Chicago Black Hawks	80	39	33	8	351	349	86	.538
Minnesota North Stars	80	38	33	9	327	305	85	.531
St. Louis Blues	80	37	34	9	302	291	83	.519
Toronto Maple Leafs	80	25	48	7	311	386	57	.356
Detroit Red Wings	80	17	57	6	266	415	40	.250

Smythe Division

Team Name	GP	W	L	T	GF	GA	Pts	Pct
Edmonton Oilers	80	56	17	7	426	310	119	.744
Calgary Flames	80	40	31	9	354	315	89	.556
Winnipeg Jets	80	26	47	7	295	372	59	.369
Vancouver Canucks	80	23	44	13	282	333	59	.369
Los Angeles Kings	80	23	49	8	284	389	54	.338

Prince of Wales Conference

Adams Division

Team Name	GP	W	L	T	GF	GA	Pts	Pct
Quebec Nordiques	80	43	31	6	330	289	92	.575
Montreal Canadiens	80	40	33	7	330	280	87	.544
Boston Bruins	80	37	31	12	311	288	86	.538
Hartford Whalers	80	40	36	4	332	302	84	.525
Buffalo Sabres	80	37	37	6	296	291	80	.500

Patrick Division

Team Name	GP	W	L	T	GF	GA	Pts	Pct
Philadelphia Flyers	80	53	23	4	335	241	110	.688
Washington Capitals	80	50	23	7	315	272	107	.669
New York Islanders	80	39	29	12	327	284	90	.563
New York Rangers	80	36	38	6	280	276	78	.488
Pittsburgh Penguins	80	34	38	8	313	305	76	.475
New Jersey Devils	80	28	49	3	300	374	59	.369

Coaching Changes

Chicago--Bob Pulford 39-33-8; Minnesota--Lorne Henning38-33-9; Detroit--Harry Neale 8-23-4, Brad Park 9-34-2; Winnipeg--Barry Long 19-41-6, John Ferguson 7-6-1; Vancouver--Tom Watt 23-44-13; Montreal--Jean Perron 40-33-7; Boston--Butch Goring 37-31-12; Buffalo--Jim Schoenfeld 19-19-5, Scotty Bowman 18-18-1; New York Rangers--Ted Sator 36-38-6.

League Leaders

Goals		Assists		Points	
Jari Kurri	68	Wayne Gretzky	163	Wayne Gretzky	215
Mike Bossy	61	Mario Lemieux	93	Mario Lemieux	141
Tim Kerr	58	Paul Coffey	90	Paul Coffey	138
Glenn Anderson	54	Peter Stastny	81	Jari Kurri	131
Michel Goulet	53	Neal Broten	76	Mike Bossy	123

Penalty Minutes		GAA (1,500 minutes)		Wins	
Joey Kocur	377	Bob Froese	2.55	John Vanbiesbrouck	31
Torrie Robertson	358	Al Jensen	3.18	Bob Froese	31
Dave Williams	320	Kelly Hrudey	3.21	Tom Barrasso	29
Tim Hunter	291	Clint Malarchuk	3.21	Rejean Lemelin	29
Rick Tocchet	284	John Vanbiesbrouck	3.32	Grant Fuhr	29

Shutouts		Save %	
Bob Froese	5	Bob Froese	.909
Clint Malarchuk	4	Kelly Hrudey	.906
Doug Soetaert	3	Clint Malarchuk	.895
John Vanbiesbrouck	3	Rick Wamsley	.894
Darren Jensen	2	Don Beaupre	.892

All Star Game

(Civic Center Coliseum, Hartford)

February 4	Wales Conference	4		Campbell Conference	3

Stanley Cup Playoffs

April 9	Hartford Whalers	3	at	Quebec Nordiques	2 [2:36]
April 9	St. Louis Blues	2	at	Minnesota North Stars	1
April 9	Boston Bruins	1	at	Montreal Canadiens	3
April 9	New York Rangers	6	at	Philadelphia Flyers	2
April 9	New York Islanders	1	at	Washington Capitals	3
April 9	Toronto Maple Leafs	5	at	Chicago Black Hawks	3
April 9	Vancouver Canucks	3	at	Edmonton Oilers	7
April 9	Winnipeg Jets	1	at	Calgary Flames	5
April 10	Hartford Whalers	4	at	Quebec Nordiques	1
April 10	Boston Bruins	2	at	Montreal Canadiens	3
April 10	New York Rangers	1	at	Philadelphia Flyers	2
April 10	New York Islanders	2	at	Washington Capitals	5
April 10	Toronto Maple Leafs	6	at	Chicago Black Hawks	4
April 10	St. Louis Blues	2	at	Minnesota North Stars	6
April 10	Vancouver Canucks	1	at	Edmonton Oilers	5
April 10	Winnipeg Jets	4	at	Calgary Flames	6
April 12	Quebec Nordiques	4	at	Hartford Whalers	9
April 12	Montreal Canadiens	4	at	Boston Bruins	3
April 12	Philadelphia Flyers	2	at	New York Rangers	5
April 12	Washington Capitals	3	at	New York Islanders	1
April 12	Chicago Black Hawks	2	at	Toronto Maple Leafs	7
April 12	Minnesota North Stars	3	at	St. Louis Blues	4
April 12	Edmonton Oilers	5	at	Vancouver Canucks	1

April 12	Calgary Flames	4	at	Winnipeg Jets	3 [8:25]
April 13	Philadelphia Flyers	7	at	New York Rangers	1
April 13	Minnesota North Stars	7	at	St. Louis Blues	4
April 15	St. Louis Blues	6	at	Minnesota North Stars	3
April 15	New York Rangers	5	at	Philadelphia Flyers	2
April 17	Hartford Whalers	4	at	Montreal Canadiens	1
April 17	New York Rangers	4	at	Washington Capitals	3 [1:16]
April 18	Toronto Maple Leafs	1	at	St. Louis Blues	6
April 18	Calgary Flames	4	at	Edmonton Oilers	1
April 19	Hartford Whalers	1	at	Montreal Canadiens	3
April 19	New York Rangers	1	at	Washington Capitals	8
April 20	Toronto Maple Leafs	3	at	St. Louis Blues	0
April 20	Calgary Flames	5	at	Edmonton Oilers	6 [1:04]
April 21	Montreal Canadiens	4	at	Hartford Whalers	1
April 21	Washington Capitals	6	at	New York Rangers	3
April 22	St. Louis Blues	2	at	Toronto Maple Leafs	5
April 22	Edmonton Oilers	2	at	Calgary Flames	3
April 23	Montreal Canadiens	1	at	Hartford Whalers	2 [1:07]
April 23	Washington Capitals	5	at	New York Rangers	6 [2:40]
April 24	St. Louis Blues	7	at	Toronto Maple Leafs	4
April 24	Edmonton Oilers	7	at	Calgary Flames	4
April 25	Hartford Whalers	3	at	Montreal Canadiens	5
April 25	New York Rangers	4	at	Washington Capitals	2
April 26	Toronto Maple Leafs	3	at	St. Louis Blues	4 [7:11]
April 26	Calgary Flames	4	at	Edmonton Oilers	1
April 27	Montreal Canadiens	0	at	Hartford Whalers	1
April 27	Washington Capitals	1	at	New York Rangers	2
April 28	St. Louis Blues	3	at	Toronto Maple Leafs	5
April 28	Edmonton Oilers	5	at	Calgary Flames	2
April 29	Hartford Whalers	1	at	Montreal Canadiens	2 [5:55]
April 30	Toronto Maple Leafs	1	at	St. Louis Blues	2
April 30	Calgary Flames	3	at	Edmonton Oilers	2
May 1	New York Rangers	1	at	Montreal Canadiens	2
May 2	St. Louis Blues	3	at	Calgary Flames	2
May 3	New York Rangers	2	at	Montreal Canadiens	6
May 4	St. Louis Blues	2	at	Calgary Flames	8
May 5	Montreal Canadiens	4	at	New York Rangers	3 [9:41]
May 6	Calgary Flames	5	at	St. Louis Blues	3
May 7	Montreal Canadiens	0	at	New York Rangers	2
May 8	Calgary Flames	2	at	St. Louis Blues	5
May 9	New York Rangers	1	at	Montreal Canadiens	3
May 10	St. Louis Blues	2	at	Calgary Flames	4
May 12	Calgary Flames	5	at	St. Louis Blues	6 [7:30]
May 14	St. Louis Blues	1	at	Calgary Flames	2
May 16	Montreal Canadiens	2	at	Calgary Flames	5
May 18	Montreal Canadiens	3	at	Calgary Flames	2[0:09]
May 20	Calgary Flames	3	at	Montreal Canadiens	5
May 22	Calgary Flames	0	at	Montreal Canadiens	1
May 24	Montreal Canadiens	4	at	Calgary Flames	3

All Star Teams

First Team		Second Team
John Vanbiesbrouck	Goal	Bob Froese
Paul Coffey	Defense	Larry Robinson
Mark Howe	Defense	Ray Bourque
Wayne Gretzky	Center	Mario Lemieux
Mike Bossy	Right Wing	Jari Kurri
Michel Goulet	Left Wing	Mats Naslund

Individual Awards

Art Ross Trophy--Wayne Gretzky (Edmonton Oilers)
Bill Masterton Trophy--Charlie Simmer (Boston Bruins)
Calder Memorial Trophy--Gary Suter (Calgary Flames)
Conn Smythe Trophy--Patrick Roy (Montreal Canadiens)
Dodge Performer of the Year--Wayne Gretzky (Edmonton Oilers)
Emery Edge Trophy--Mark Howe (Philadelphia Flyers)
Frank J. Selke Award--Troy Murray (Chicago Black Hawks)
Hart Memorial Trophy--Wayne Gretzky (Edmonton Oilers)
Jack Adams Award--Glen Sather (Edmonton Oilers)
James Norris Trophy--Paul Coffey (Edmonton Oilers)
Lady Byng Memorial Trophy--Mike Bossy (New York Islanders)
Lester B. Pearson Award--Mario Lemieux (Pittsburgh Penguins)
Lester Patrick Trophy--John MacInnes and Jack Riley.
NHL All Star Game MVP--Grant Fuhr (Edmonton Oilers)
Vezina Trophy--John Vanbiesbrouck (New York Rangers)
William M. Jennings Trophy--Bob Froese and Darren Jensen (Philadelphia Flyers)

Hall of Fame Inductees

Leo Boivin, William Hanley, Dave Keon, Serge Savard

Franchise Changes

CFL--Montreal Concordes became the Montreal Alouettes adopting the name that they had dropped in 1982.
NBA--Kansas City Kings became the Sacramento Kings.

Other Sports

Horseracing--Kentucky Derby won by Ferdinand (time 2;02.8, purse $609,400).
Heavyweight Boxing--Tim Witherspoon defeated Tony Tubbs in 15 rounds (WBA).
Trevor Berbick defeated Pinklon Thomas in 15 rounds (WBC).
Michael Spinx defeated Larry Holmes in 15 rounds (IBF).
Tim Witherspoon knocked-out Frank Bruno in 11 rounds (WBA).
Michael Spinx knocked-out Steffen Tangstad in 4 rounds (IBF).
Mike Tyson knocked-out Trevor Berbick in 2 rounds (WBC).
James Smith knocked out Tim Witherspoon in 1 round (WBA).
Golf--U.S. Open won by Ray Floyd with a score of 279.
Auto Racing--Indianapolis 500 won by Bobby Rahal (ave. speed 170.722 MPH).
Tennis--U.S. Open won by Ivan Lendl in the men's singles.
U.S. Open won by Andres Gomez and Slobodan Zivolinovic in the men's doubles.
U.S. open won by Martina Navratilova in the women's singles.
U.S. Open won by Martina Navratilova and Pam Shriver in the women's doubles.
U.S. Open won by Raffaella Reggi and Sergio Casal in the mixed doubles.

Notes

Bobby Rahal set a new record in the Indianapolis 500 with an average speed of 170.722 MPH

1987

BASEBALL

National League
East

Team Name	W	L	Pct	GB	R	OR
St. Louis Cardinals	95	67	.586	-	798	693
New York Mets	92	70	.568	3	823	698
Montreal Expos	91	71	.562	4	741	720
Philadelphia Phillies	80	82	.494	15	702	749
Pittsburgh Pirates	80	82	.494	15	723	744
Chicago Cubs	76	85	.472	18.5	720	801

West

Team Name	W	L	Pct	GB	R	OR
San Francisco Giants	90	72	.556	-	783	669
Cincinnati Reds	84	78	.519	6	783	752
Houston Astros	76	86	.469	14	648	678
Los Angeles Dodgers	73	89	.451	17	635	675
Atlanta Braves	69	92	.429	20.5	747	829
San Diego Padres	65	97	.401	25	668	763

Coaching Changes

Philadelphia--John Felske 29-32, Lee Elia 51-50; Chicago--Gene Michael 68-68, Frank Lucchesi 8-17; San Diego--Larry Bowa 65-97.

League Leaders

Batting Average
(502 at bats)

Tony Gwynn	.370
Pedro Guerrero	.338
Tim Raines	.330
John Kruk	.313
Dion James	.312

Home Runs

Andre Dawson	49
Dale Murphy	44
Darryl Strawberry	39
Eric Davis	37
Howard Johnson	36

RBI

Andre Dawson	137
Tim Wallach	123
Mike Schmidt	113
Jack Clark	106
Dale Murphy	105

Stolen Bases

Vince Coleman	109
Tony Gwynn	56
Billy Hatcher	53
Eric Davis	50
Tim Raines	50

ERA
(162 innings)

Nolan Ryan	2.76
Mike Dunne	3.03
Orel Hershiser	3.06
Rick Reuschel	3.09
Dwight Gooden	3.21

Wins

Rick Sutcliffe	18
Shane Rawley	17
Mike Scott	16
Orel Hershiser	16
Dwight Gooden	15

Saves

Steve Bedrosian	40
Lee Smith	36
Todd Worrell	33
John Franco	32
Roger McDowell	25

Strikeouts

Nolan Ryan	270
Mike Scott	233
Bob Welch	195
Orel Hershiser	190
Fernando Valenzuela	190

NLCS

October 6	San Francisco Giants	3	at	St. Louis Cardinals	5
October 7	San Francisco Giants	5	at	St. Louis Cardinals	0
October 9	St. Louis Cardinals	6	at	San Francisco Giants	5
October 10	St. Louis Cardinals	2	at	San Francisco Giants	4
October 11	St. Louis Cardinals	3	at	San Francisco Giants	6
October 13	San Francisco Giants	0	at	St. Louis Cardinals	1
October 14	San Francisco Giants	0	at	St. Louis Cardinals	6

Notes

Bart Giamatti succeeded Charles Feeney as President of the National League.

American League

East

Team Name	W	L	Pct	GB	R	OR
Detroit Tigers	98	64	.605	-	896	735
Toronto Blue Jays	96	66	.593	2	845	655
Milwaukee Brewers	91	71	.562	7	862	817
New York Yankees	89	73	.549	9	788	758
Boston Red Sox	78	84	.481	20	842	825
Baltimore Orioles	67	95	.414	31	729	880
Cleveland Indians	61	101	.377	37	742	957

West

Team Name	W	L	Pct	GB	R	OR
Minnesota Twins	85	77	.525	-	786	806
Kansas City Royals	83	79	.512	2	715	691
Oakland Athletics	81	81	.500	4	806	789
Seattle Mariners	78	84	.481	7	760	801
Chicago White Sox	77	85	.475	8	748	746
California Angels	75	87	.463	10	770	803
Texas Rangers	75	87	.463	10	823	849

Coaching Changes

Milwaukee--Tom Trebelhorn 91-71; Baltimore--Cal Ripken Sr. 67-95; Cleveland--Pat Corrales 31-56, Howard "Doc" Edwards 30-45; Minnesota--Tom Kelly 85-77; Kansas City--Bill Gardner 62-64, John Wathan 21-15; Oakland--Tony LaRussa 81-81; Seattle--Dick Williams 78-84; Chicago--Jim Fregosi 77-85.

League Leaders

Batting Average (502 at bats)		Home Runs		RBI	
Wade Boggs	.363	Mark McGwire	49	George Bell	134
Paul Molitor	.353	George Bell	47	Dwight Evans	123
Alan Trammell	.343	Darrell Evans	34	Mark McGwire	118
Kirby Puckett	.332	Dwight Evans	34	Wally Joyner	117
Don Mattingly	.327	Kent Hrbek	34	Don Mattingly	115

Stolen Bases		ERA (162 innings)		Wins	
Harold Reynolds	60	Jimmy Key	2.76	Roger Clemens	20
Willie Wilson	59	Frank Viola	2.90	Dave Stewart	20
Gary Redus	52	Roger Clemens	2.97	Mark Langston	19
Paul Molitor	45	Bret Saberhagen	3.36	Bret Saberhagen	18
Rickey Henderson	41	Jack Morris	3.38	Ted Higuera	18

Saves		Strikeouts	
Tom Henke	34	Mark Langston	262
Jeff Reardon	31	Roger Clemens	256
Dave Righetti	31	Ted Higuera	240
Dan Plesac	23	Charlie Hough	223
DeWayne Buice	17	Jack Morris	208

All Star Game
(Oakland-Alameda County Coliseum, Oakland)

July 14	National League	2		American League	0 [13]

ALCS

October 7	Detroit Tigers	5	at	Minnesota Twins	8
October 8	Detroit Tigers	3	at	Minnesota Twins	6
October 10	Minnesota Twins	6	at	Detroit Tigers	7
October 11	Minnesota Twins	5	at	Detroit Tigers	3
October 12	Minnesota Twins	9	at	Detroit Tigers	5

World Series

October 17	St. Louis Cardinals	1	at	Minnesota Twins	10
October 18	St. Louis Cardinals	4	at	Minnesota Twins	8
October 20	Minnesota Twins	1	at	St. Louis Cardinals	3
October 21	Minnesota Twins	2	at	St. Louis Cardinals	7
October 22	Minnesota Twins	2	at	St. Louis Cardinals	4
October 24	St. Louis Cardinals	5	at	Minnesota Twins	11
October 25	St. Louis Cardinals	2	at	Minnesota Twins	4

Individual Awards

ALCS MVP--Gary Gaetti (Minnesota Twins AL)
Arch Ward Memorial Trophy--Tim Raines (Montreal Expos NL)
Baseball Writers Award--Andre Dawson (Chicago Cubs NL)
George Bell (Toronto Blue Jays AL)
Cy Young Award--Steve Bedrosian (Philadelphia Phillies NL)
Roger Clemens (Boston Red Sox AL)
NLCS MVP--Jeff Leonard (San Francisco Giants NL)
Rookie of the Year--Benito Santiago (San Diego Padres NL)
Mark McGwire (Oakland Athletics AL)
Sporting News Executive of the Year--Al Rosen (San Francisco Giants NL)
Sporting News Manager of the Year--Buck Rogers (Montreal Expos NL)
George Anderson (Detroit Tigers AL)
Sporting News Pitcher of the Year--Rick Sutcliffe (Chicago Cubs NL)
Jimmy Key (Toronto Blue Jays AL)
Sporting News Player of the Year--Andre Dawson (Chicago Cubs NL)
George Bell (Toronto Blue Jays AL)
Sporting News Rookie of the Year--Benito Santiago (San Diego Padres NL)

Mike Dunne (Pittsburgh Pirates NL)
Mark McGwire (Oakland Athletics AL)
Mike Henneman (Detroit Tigers AL)
World Series MVP--Frank Viola (Minnesota Twins AL)

Hall of Fame Inductees

Ray Dandridge, Jim "Catfish" Hunter, Billy Williams

BASKETBALL
National Basketball Association

Eastern Conference
Atlantic Division

Team Name	GP	W	L	PPGF	PPGA	Pct	GB
Boston Celtics	82	59	23	112.6	106.0	.720	-
Philadelphia 76ers	82	45	37	106.5	106.6	.549	14
Washington Bullets	82	42	40	106.0	107.3	.512	17
New Jersey Nets	82	24	58	108.5	113.5	.293	35
New York Knickerbockers	82	24	58	103.8	110.0	.293	35

Central Division

Team Name	GP	W	L	PPGF	PPGA	Pct	GB
Atlanta Hawks	82	57	25	110.0	102.8	.695	-
Detroit Pistons	82	52	30	111.2	107.8	.634	5
Milwaukee Bucks	82	50	32	110.4	106.5	.610	7
Indiana Pacers	82	41	41	106.1	106.7	.500	16
Chicago Bulls	82	40	42	104.8	103.9	.488	17
Cleveland Cavaliers	82	31	51	104.4	108.2	.378	26

Western Conference

Midwest Division

Team Name	GP	W	L	PPGF	PPGA	Pct	GB
Dallas Mavericks	82	55	27	116.7	110.4	.671	-
Utah Jazz	82	44	38	107.9	107.5	.537	11
Houston Rockets	82	42	40	106.9	105.9	.512	13
Denver Nuggets	82	37	45	116.7	117.6	.451	18
Sacramento Kings	82	29	53	110.9	114.1	.354	26
San Antonio Spurs	82	28	54	108.3	113.4	.341	27

Pacific Division

Team Name	GP	W	L	PPGF	PPGA	Pct	GB
Los Angeles Lakers	82	65	17	117.8	108.5	.793	-
Portland Trail Blazers	82	49	33	117.9	114.8	.598	16
Golden State Warriors	82	42	40	112.0	114.4	.512	23
Seattle SuperSonics	82	39	43	113.7	113.3	.476	26
Phoenix Suns	82	36	46	111.1	113.5	.439	29
Los Angeles Clippers	82	12	70	104.5	115.9	.146	53

Coaching Changes

Washington--Kevin Loughery 42-40; New York--Hubie Brown 4-12, Bob Hill 20-46; Indiana--Jack Ramsay 41-41; Chicago--Doug Collins 40-42; Cleveland--Lenny Wilkens 31-51; Sacramento--Phil Johnson 14-32, Jerry Reynolds 15-21; San Antonio--Bob Weiss 28-54; Portland--Mike Schuler 49-33; Golden State--George Karl 42-40; Phoenix--John MacLeod 22-34, Dick Van Arsdale 14-12.

League Leaders

Field Goals		Free Throws		Assists	
Michael Jordan	1098	Michael Jordan	833	Earvin Johnson	977
Alex English	965	Dominique Wilkins	607	"Sleepy" Floyd	848
Dominique Wilkins	828	Moses Malone	570	Doc Rivers	823
Kiki Vandeweghe	808	Adrian Dantley	539	Isiah Thomas	813
Xavier McDaniel	806	Earvin Johnson	535	Terry Porter	715

Points		Rebounds Per Game	
Michael Jordan	3041	Charles Barkley	14.6
Alex English	2345	Charles Oakley	13.1
Dominique Wilkins	2294	Buck Williams	12.5
Kiki Vandeweghe	2122	James Donaldson	11.9
Larry Bird	2076	Bill Laimbeer	11.6

All Star Game

(Seattle Center Coliseum, Seattle)

February 8	West Division	154	East Division	149 [OT]

NBA Playoffs

April 23	Chicago Bulls	104	at	Boston Celtics	108
April 23	Denver Nuggets	95	at	Los Angeles Lakers	128
April 23	Golden State Warriors	85	at	Utah Jazz	99
April 23	Seattle SuperSonics	129	at	Dallas Mavericks	151
April 24	Philadelphia 76ers	104	at	Milwaukee Bucks	107
April 24	Washington Bullets	92	at	Detroit Pistons	106
April 24	Indiana Pacers	94	at	Atlanta Hawks	110
April 24	Houston Rockets	125	at	Portland Trail Blazers	115
April 25	Denver Nuggets	127	at	Los Angeles Lakers	139
April 25	Golden State Warriors	100	at	Utah Jazz	103
April 25	Seattle SuperSonics	112	at	Dallas Mavericks	110
April 26	Chicago Bulls	96	at	Boston Celtics	105
April 26	Philadelphia 76ers	125	at	Milwaukee Bucks	122 [OT]
April 26	Washington Bullets	85	at	Detroit Pistons	128
April 26	Indiana Pacers	93	at	Atlanta Hawks	94
April 26	Houston Rockets	98	at	Portland Trail Blazers	111
April 28	Boston Celtics	105	at	Chicago Bulls	94
April 28	Portland Trail Blazers	108	at	Houston Rockets	117
April 28	Dallas Mavericks	107	at	Seattle SuperSonics	117
April 29	Milwaukee Bucks	121	at	Philadelphia 76ers	120
April 29	Detroit Pistons	97	at	Washington Bullets	96
April 29	Atlanta Hawks	87	at	Indiana Pacers	96
April 29	Los Angeles Lakers	140	at	Denver Nuggets	103
April 29	Utah Jazz	95	at	Golden State Warriors	110
April 30	Portland Trail Blazers	101	at	Houston Rockets	113
April 30	Dallas Mavericks	98	at	Seattle SuperSonics	124
May 1	Milwaukee Bucks	118	at	Philadelphia 76ers	124
May 1	Atlanta Hawks	101	at	Indiana Pacers	97
May 1	Utah Jazz	94	at	Golden State Warriors	98
May 2	Seattle SuperSonics	111	at	Houston Rockets	106 [OT]
May 3	Philadelphia 76ers	89	at	Milwaukee Bucks	102

May 3	Golden State Warriors	118	at	Utah Jazz	113
May 3	Detroit Pistons	112	at	Atlanta Hawks	111
May 5	Golden State Warriors	116	at	Los Angeles Lakers	125
May 5	Seattle SuperSonics	99	at	Houston Rockets	97
May 5	Milwaukee Bucks	98	at	Boston Celtics	111
May 5	Detroit Pistons	102	at	Atlanta Hawks	115
May 6	Milwaukee Bucks	124	at	Boston Celtics	126
May 7	Houston Rockets	102	at	Seattle SuperSonics	84
May 7	Golden State Warriors	101	at	Los Angeles Lakers	116
May 8	Atlanta Hawks	99	at	Detroit Pistons	108
May 8	Boston Celtics	121	at	Milwaukee Bucks	126 [OT]
May 9	Houston Rockets	102	at	Seattle SuperSonics	117
May 9	Los Angeles Lakers	133	at	Golden State Warriors	108
May 10	Atlanta Hawks	88	at	Detroit Pistons	89
May 10	Boston Celtics	138	at	Milwaukee Bucks	137 [OT]
May 10	Los Angeles Lakers	121	at	Golden State Warriors	129
May 12	Golden State Warriors	106	at	Los Angeles Lakers	118
May 12	Seattle SuperSonics	107	at	Houston Rockets	112
May 13	Detroit Pistons	104	at	Atlanta Hawks	96
May 13	Milwaukee Bucks	129	at	Boston Celtics	124
May 14	Houston Rockets	125	at	Seattle SuperSonics	128 [OT]
May 15	Boston Celtics	111	at	Milwaukee Bucks	121
May 16	Seattle SuperSonics	87	at	Los Angeles Lakers	92
May 17	Milwaukee Bucks	113	at	Boston Celtics	119
May 19	Detroit Pistons	91	at	Boston Celtics	104
May 19	Seattle SuperSonics	104	at	Los Angeles Lakers	112
May 21	Detroit Pistons	101	at	Boston Celtics	110
May 23	Los Angeles Lakers	122	at	Seattle SuperSonics	121
May 23	Boston Celtics	104	at	Detroit Pistons	122
May 24	Boston Celtics	119	at	Detroit Pistons	145
May 25	Los Angeles Lakers	133	at	Seattle SuperSonics	102
May 26	Detroit Pistons	107	at	Boston Celtics	108
May 28	Boston Celtics	105	at	Detroit Pistons	113
May 30	Detroit Pistons	114	at	Boston Celtics	117
June 2	Boston Celtics	113	at	Los Angeles Lakers	126
June 4	Boston Celtics	122	at	Los Angeles Lakers	141
June 7	Los Angeles Lakers	103	at	Boston Celtics	109
June 9	Los Angeles Lakers	107	at	Boston Celtics	106
June 11	Los Angeles Lakers	108	at	Boston Celtics	123
June 14	Boston Celtics	93	at	Los Angeles Lakers	106

All Star Teams

First Team	Second Team
Larry Bird (Boston Celtics)	Dominique Wilkins (Atlanta Hawks)
Kevin McHale (Boston Celtics)	Charles Barkley (Philadelphia 76ers)
Akeem Olajuwon (Houston Rockets)	Moses Malone (Washington Bullets)
Earvin Johnson (Los Angeles Lakers)	Isiah Thomas (Detroit Pistons)
Michael Jordan (Chicago Bulls)	Lafayette Lever (Denver Nuggets)

Individual Awards

Defensive Player of the Year--Michael Cooper (Los Angeles Lakers)
Eddie Gottlieb Trophy--Chuck Person (Indiana Pacers)
Executive of the Year--Stan Kastern (Atlanta Hawks)

J. Walter Kennedy Citizenship Award--Isiah Thomas (Detroit Pistons)
Maurice Podoloff Trophy--Earvin Johnson (Los Angeles Lakers)
Most Improved Player--Dale Ellis (Seattle SuperSonics)
NBA All Star Game MVP--Tom Chambers (Seattle SuperSonics)
NBA Finals MVP--Earvin Johnson (Los Angeles Lakers)
Red Auerbach Trophy--Mike Schuler (Portland Trail Blazers)
Schick Award--Charles Barkley (Philadelphia 76ers)
Sixth Man Award--Ricky Pierce (Milwaukee Bucks)

Hall of Fame Inductees

Rick Barry, Clyde Frazier, Robert Houbregs, Pete Maravich, Robert Wanzer

FOOTBALL
National Football League

National Conference
Eastern Division

Team Name	GP	W	L	T	PF	PA	Pct
Washington Redskins	15	11	4	0	379	285	.733
Dallas Cowboys	15	7	8	0	340	348	.467
St. Louis Cardinals	15	7	8	0	362	368	.467
Philadelphia Eagles	15	7	8	0	337	380	.467
New York Giants	15	6	9	0	280	312	.400

Central Division

Team Name	GP	W	L	T	PF	PA	Pct
Chicago Bears	15	11	4	0	356	282	.733
Minnesota Vikings	15	8	7	0	336	335	.533
Green Bay Packers	15	5	9	1	255	300	.367
Detroit Lions	15	4	11	0	269	384	.267
Tampa Bay Buccaneers	15	4	11	0	286	360	.267

Western Division

Team Name	GP	W	L	T	PF	PA	Pct
San Francisco 49ers	15	13	2	0	459	253	.867
New Orleans Saints	15	12	3	0	422	283	.800
Los Angeles Rams	15	6	9	0	317	361	.400
Atlanta Falcons	15	3	12	0	205	436	.200

American Conference

Eastern Division

Team Name	GP	W	L	T	PF	PA	Pct
Indianapolis Colts	15	9	6	0	300	238	.600
New England Patriots	15	8	7	0	320	293	.533
Miami Dolphins	15	8	7	0	362	335	.533
Buffalo Bills	15	7	8	0	270	305	.467
New York Jets	15	6	9	0	334	360	.400

Central Division

Team Name	GP	W	L	T	PF	PA	Pct
Cleveland Browns	15	10	5	0	390	239	.667
Houston Oilers	15	9	6	0	345	349	.600
Pittsburgh Steelers	15	8	7	0	285	299	.533
Cincinnati Bengals	15	4	11	0	285	370	.267

Western Division

Denver Broncos	15	10	4	1	379	288	.700
Seattle Seahawks	15	9	6	0	371	314	.600
San Diego Chargers	15	8	7	0	253	317	.533
Los Angeles Raiders	15	5	10	0	301	289	.333
Kansas City Chiefs	15	4	11	0	273	388	.267

Coaching Changes

Tampa Bay--Ray Perkins 4-11-0; Atlanta--Marion Campbell 3-12-0; Indianapolis--Ron Meyer 9-6-0; Buffalo--Marv Levy 7-8-0; San Diego--Al Saunders 8-7-0; Kansas City--Frank Gansz 4-11-0.

League Leaders

Yards Rushing		Yards Passing		Passing % (300 attempts)	
Charles White	1374	Neil Lomax	3387	Joe Montana	66.8
Eric Dickerson	1288	Boomer Esiason	3321	Bernie Kosar	62.0
Curt Warner	985	Dan Marino	3245	Jim Kelly	60.0
Mike Rozier	957	John Elway	3198	Ken O'Brien	60.0
Rueben Mayes	917	Joe Montana	3054	Neil Lomax	59.4

Receiving Yards		Receptions		Field Goals	
J.T. Smith	1117	J.T. Smith	91	Morten Andersen	28
Jerry Rice	1078	Al Toon	68	Jim Breech	24
Gary Clark	1066	Roger Craig	66	Dean Biasucci	24
Carlos Carson	1044	Jerry Rice	65	Roger Ruzek	22
Drew Hill	989	Herschel Walker	60	Gary Anderson	22

Punt Return Yards		Kickoff Return Yards	
Vai Sikahema	550	Paul Palmer	923
Dennis McKinnon	405	Neal Guggemos	808
Lionel James	400	Vai Sikahema	761
Phil McKonkey	394	Gary Lee	719
Gerald McNeil	386	Sylvester Stamps	660

Pro Bowl Game

(Aloha Stadium, Honolulu)

February 7	American Conference	15	National Conference	6

NFL Playoffs

January 3 1988	Minnesota Vikings	44	at	New Orleans Saints	10
January 3 1988	Seattle Seahawks	20	at	Houston Oilers	23 [OT]
January 9 1988	Minnesota Vikings	36	at	San Francisco 49ers	24
January 9 1988	Indianapolis Colts	21	at	Cleveland Browns	38
January 10 1988	Washington Redskins	21	at	Chicago Bears	17
January 10 1988	Houston Oilers	10	at	Denver Broncos	34
January 17 1988	Minnesota Vikings	10	at	Washington Redskins	17
January 17 1988	Cleveland Browns	33	at	Denver Broncos	38

Super Bowl XXII

(San Diego/Jack Murphy Stadium, San Diego)

January 31 1988	Washington Redskins	42	Denver Broncos	10

Individual Awards

A.P. MVP--John Elway (Denver Broncos)
Bert Bell Trophy--Bo Jackson (Los Angeles Raiders) [World Almanac]
Bert Bell Trophy--Jerry Rice (San Francisco 49ers)
Dan McGuire Award--Bruce Smith (Buffalo Bills)
George Halas Trophy--Reggie White (Philadelphia Eagles)
Jim Thorpe Trophy--Jerry Rice (San Francisco 49ers)
P.F.W.A. MVP--Jerry Rice (San Francisco 49ers)
Super Bowl MVP--Doug Williams (Washington Redskins)
U.P.I. AFC Coach of the Year--Ron Meyer (Indianapolis Colts)
U.P.I. AFC Player of the Year--John Elway (Denver Broncos)
Bruce Smith (Buffalo Bills)
U.P.I. AFC Rookie of the Year--Shane Conlan (Buffalo Bills)
U.P.I. NFC Coach of the Year--Jim Mora (New Orleans Saints)
U.P.I. NFC Player of the Year--Jerry Rice (San Francisco 49ers)
Reggie White (Philadelphia Eagles)
U.P.I. NFC Rookie of the Year--Robert Awalt (St. Louis Cardinals)

Hall of Fame Inductees

Larry Csonka, Len Dawson, Joe Greene, John Henry Johnson, Jim Langer, Don Maynard, Gene Upshaw

Notes

The NFL season was shortened by 24 days due to a player's strike. The league also adopted a special pension payment plan to benefit the players not covered by the then current pension plan; covered were players who played at least five years in the league and retired before 1959.

Canadian Football League
Eastern Division

Team Name	GP	W	L	T	PF	PA	Pts	Pct
Winnipeg Blue Bombers	18	12	6	0	554	409	24	.667
Toronto Argonauts	18	11	6	1	484	427	23	.639
Hamilton Tiger-Cats	18	7	11	0	470	509	14	.389
Ottawa Rough Riders	18	3	15	0	377	598	6	.167

Western Division

Team Name	GP	W	L	T	PF	PA	Pts	Pct
British Columbia Lions	18	12	6	0	502	370	24	.667
Edmonton Eskimos	18	11	7	0	617	462	22	.611
Calgary Stampeders	18	10	8	0	453	517	20	.556
Saskatchewan Roughriders	18	5	12	1	364	529	11	.306

Coaching Changes

Winnipeg--Mike Riley 12-6-0; Ottawa--Fred Glick 3-15-0; British Columbia--Don Matthews 8-6-0, Larry Donovan 4-0-0; Edmonton--Jackie Parker 2-0-0, Joe Faragalli 9-7-0; Calgary--Bob Vespaziani 2-6-0, Lary Kuharich 8-2-0; Saskatchewan--John Gregory 5-12-1.

League Leaders

Yards Rushing		Yards Passing		Passing % (150attempts)	
Willard Reaves	1471	Tom Clements	4686	Kent Austin	59.6
Gill Fenerty	879	Roy DeWalt	3855	Tom Porras	59.6
Gary Allen	857	Tom Porras	3293	Roy DeWalt	57.1
Anthony Parker	635	Rick Worman	3021	Tom Clements	56.8
Cedric Minter	627	Todd Dillon	2901	John Congemi	55.6

Receiving Yards		Receptions		Points	
Brian Kelly	1626	Marc Lewis	94	Lui Passaglia	214
Steve Stapler	1516	Steve Stapler	85	Lance Chomyc	193
Larry Willis	1477	James Murphy	84	Trevor Kennerd	177
Jim Sandusky	1437	Jim Sandusky	80	Dave Ridgway	174
Darrell K. Smith	1392	Darrell K. Smith	79	John T. Hay	172

Grey Cup Playoffs

November 15	Hamilton Tiger-Cats	13	at	Toronto Argonauts	29
November 15	Calgary Stampeders	16	at	Edmonton Eskimos	30
November 22	Toronto Argonauts	19	at	Winnipeg Blue Bombers	3
November 22	Edmonton Eskimos	31	at	British Columbia Lions	7
November 29	Edmonton Eskimos	38		Toronto Argonauts	36*

Individual Awards

Annis Stukus Trophy--Bob O'Billovich (Toronto Argonauts)
Dave Dryburgh Memorial Trophy--Lui Passaglia (British Columbia Lions)
DeMarco-Becket Memorial Trophy--Bob Poley (Calgary Stampeders)
Dr. Beattie Martin Trophy--Nelson Martin (British Columbia Lions)
Eddie James Memorial Trophy--Gary Allen (Calgary Stampeders)
Frank M. Gibson Trophy--Gill Fenerty (Toronto Argonauts)
Grey Cup Most Outstanding Defensive Star--Stewart Hill (Edmonton Eskimos)
Grey Cup Most Outstanding Offensive Star--Damon Allen (Edmonton Eskimos)
Grey Cup Most Valuable Canadian--Milson Jones (Edmonton Eskimos)
Jackie Parker Trophy--Stanley Blair (Edmonton Eskimos)
James P. McCaffrey Award--James West (Winnipeg Blue Bombers)
Jeff Nicklin Memorial Trophy--Brian Kelly (Edmonton Eskimos)
Jeff Russel Memorial Trophy--Tom Clements (Winnipeg Blue Bombers)
Leo Dandurand Trophy--Chris Walby (Winnipeg Blue Bombers)
Lew Hayman Trophy--Scott Flagel (Winnipeg Blue Bombers)
Norm Fieldgate Trophy--Greg Stumon (British Columbia Lions)
Schenley Award Most Outstanding Canadian--Scott Flagel (Winnipeg Blue Bombers)
Schenley Award Most Outstanding Defensive Player--Greg Stumon (British Columbia Lions)
Schenley Award Most Outstanding Offensive Lineman--Chris Walby (Winnipeg Blue Bombers)
Schenley Award Most Outstanding Player--Tom Clements (Winnipeg Blue Bombers)
Schenley Award Most Outstanding Rookie--Gill Fenerty (Toronto Argonauts)

Hall of Fame Inductees

Harold Ballard, Dick Huffman, Bob Kramer, Angelo Mosca, Tom Wilkinson

*Game played in Vancouver

HOCKEY

National Hockey League

Clarence Campbell Conference
Norris Division

Team Name	GP	W	L	T	GF	GA	Pts	Pct
St. Louis Blues	80	32	33	15	281	293	79	.494
Detroit Red Wings	80	34	36	10	260	274	78	.488
Chicago Blackhawks	80	29	37	14	290	310	72	.450
Toronto Maple Leafs	80	32	42	6	286	319	70	.438
Minnesota North Stars	80	30	40	10	296	314	70	.438

Smythe Division

Team Name	GP	W	L	T	GF	GA	Pts	Pct
Edmonton Oilers	80	50	24	6	372	284	106	.663
Calgary Flames	80	46	31	3	318	289	95	.594
Winnipeg Jets	80	40	32	8	279	271	88	.550
Los Angeles Kings	80	31	41	8	318	341	70	.438
Vancouver Canucks	80	29	43	8	282	314	66	.413

Prince of Wales Conference

Adams Division

Team Name	GP	W	L	T	GF	GA	Pts	Pct
Hartford Whalers	80	43	30	7	287	270	93	.581
Montreal Canadiens	80	41	29	10	277	241	92	.575
Boston Bruins	80	39	34	7	301	276	85	.531
Quebec Nordiques	80	31	39	10	267	276	72	.450
Buffalo Sabres	80	28	44	8	280	308	64	.400

Patrick Division

Team Name	GP	W	L	T	GF	GA	Pts	Pct
Philadelphia Flyers	80	46	26	8	310	245	100	.625
Washington Capitols	80	38	32	10	285	278	86	.538
New York Islanders	80	35	33	12	279	281	82	.513
New York Rangers	80	34	38	8	307	323	76	.475
Pittsburgh Penguins	80	30	38	12	297	290	72	.450
New Jersey Devils	80	29	45	6	293	368	64	.400

Coaching Changes

St. Louis--Jacques Martin 32-33-15; Detroit--Jacques Demers 34-36-10; Toronto--John Brophy 32-42-6; Minnesota--Lorne Henning 30-39-9, Glen Sonmor 0-1-1; Winnipeg--Dan Maloney 40-32-8; Los Angeles--Pat Quinn 18-20-1, Mike Murphy 13-21-7; Boston--Butch Goring 7-5-1, Terry O'Reilly 32-29-6; Buffalo--Scotty Bowman 3-7-2, Craig Ramsay 4-15-2, Ted Sator 21-22-4; New York Islanders--Terry Simpson 35-33-12; New York Rangers--Ted Sator 5-10-4, Tom Webster 5-7-4, Phil Esposito 24-21-0.

League Leaders

Goals		Assists		Points	
Wayne Gretzky	62	Wayne Gretzky	121	Wayne Gretzky	183
Tim Kerr	58	Ray Bourque	72	Jari Kurri	108
Mario Lemieux	54	Mark Messier	70	Mario Lemieux	107
Jari Kurri	54	Bryan Trottier	64	Mark Messier	107
Dino Ciccarelli	52	Ron Francis	63	Doug Gilmour	105

Penalty Minutes		GAA (1,500 minutes)		Wins	
Tim Hunter	361	Brian Hayward	2.81	Ron Hextall	37
Dave Williams	358	Patrick Roy	2.93	Mike Liut	31
Brian Curran	356	Ron Hextall	3.00	Mike Vernon	30
Basil McRae	342	Dan Berthiaume	3.17	Andy Moog	28
Rick Tocchet	288	Glen Hanlon	3.18	Alain Chevrier	24

Shutouts		Save %	
Mike Liut	4	Ron Hextall	.902
Bill Ranford	3	Bob Sauve	.894
Tom Barrasso	2	Glen Hanlon	.893
Rejean Lemelin	2	Brian Hayward	.893
Allan Bester	2	Bill Ranford	.891

Rendez-Vous '87

(Colisee de Quebec, Quebec City)

February 11	NHL All Stars	4	USSR All Stars	3
February 13	USSR All Stars	5	NHL All Stars	3

Stanley Cup Playoffs

April 8	Toronto Maple Leafs	1	at	St. Louis Blues	3
April 8	Chicago Blackhawks	1	at	Detroit Red Wings	3
April 8	Los Angeles Kings	5	at	Edmonton Oilers	2
April 8	Winnipeg Jets	4	at	Calgary Flames	2
April 8	Quebec Nordiques	2	at	Hartford Whalers	3 [2:20]
April 8	Boston Bruins	2	at	Montreal Canadiens	6
April 8	New York Rangers	3	at	Philadelphia Flyers	0
April 8	New York Islanders	3	at	Washington Capitals	4
April 9	Toronto Maple Leafs	3	at	St. Louis Blues	2 [10:17]
April 9	Chicago Blackhawks	1	at	Detroit Red Wings	5
April 9	Los Angeles Kings	3	at	Edmonton Oilers	13
April 9	Winnipeg Jets	3	at	Calgary Flames	2
April 9	Quebec Nordiques	4	at	Hartford Whalers	5
April 9	Boston Bruins	3	at	Montreal Canadiens	4 [2:38]
April 9	New York Rangers	3	at	Philadelphia Flyers	8
April 9	New York Islanders	3	at	Washington Capitals	1
April 11	St. Louis Blues	5	at	Toronto Maple Leafs	3
April 11	Detroit Red Wings	4	at	Chicago Black Hawks	3 [4:51]
April 11	Edmonton Oilers	6	at	Los Angeles Kings	5
April 11	Calgary Flames	3	at	Winnipeg Jets	2 [3:531
April 11	Hartford Whalers	1	at	Quebec Nordiques	5
April 11	Montreal Canadiens	5	at	Boston Bruins	4

April 11	Philadelphia Flyers	3	at	New York Rangers	0
April 11	Washington Capitals	2	at	New York Islanders	0
April 12	St. Louis Blues	1	at	Toronto Maple Leafs	2
April 12	Detroit Red Wings	3	at	Chicago Blackhawks	1
April 12	Edmonton Oilers	6	at	Los Angeles Kings	3
April 12	Calgary Flames	3	at	Winnipeg Jets	4
April 12	Hartford Whalers	1	at	Quebec Nordiques	4
April 12	Montreal Canadiens	4	at	Boston Bruins	2
April 12	Philadelphia Flyers	3	at	New York Rangers	6
April 12	Washington Capitals	4	at	New York Islanders	1
April 14	Toronto Maple Leafs	2	at	St. Louis Blues	1
April 14	Los Angeles Kings	4	at	Edmonton Oilers	5
April 14	Winnipeg Jets	3	at	Calgary Flames	4
April 14	Quebec Nordiques	7	at	Hartford Whalers	5
April 14	New York Rangers	1	at	Philadelphia Flyers	3
April 14	New York Islanders	4	at	Washington Capitals	2
April 16	St. Louis Blues	0	at	Toronto Maple Leafs	4
April 16	Calgary Flames	1	at	Winnipeg Jets	6
April 16	Hartford Whalers	4	at	Quebec Nordiques	5 [6:05]
April 16	Philadelphia Flyers	5	at	New York Rangers	0
April 16	Washington Capitals	4	at	New York Islanders	5
April 18	New York Islanders	3	at	Washington Capitals	2 [68:47]
April 20	Quebec Nordiques	7	at	Montreal Canadiens	5
April 20	New York Islanders	2	at	Philadelphia Flyers	4
April 21	Toronto Maple Leafs	4	at	Detroit Red Wings	2
April 21	Winnipeg Jets	2	at	Edmonton Oilers	3 [0:36]
April 22	Quebec Nordiques	2	at	Montreal Canadiens	1
April 22	New York Islanders	2	at	Philadelphia Flyers	1
April 23	Toronto Maple Leafs	7	at	Detroit Red Wings	2
April 23	Winnipeg Jets	3	at	Edmonton Oilers	5
April 24	Montreal Canadiens	7	at	Quebec Nordiques	2
April 24	Philadelphia Flyers	4	at	New York Islanders	1
April 25	Detroit Red Wings	4	at	Toronto Maple Leafs	2
April 25	Edmonton Oilers	5	at	Winnipeg Jets	2
April 26	Montreal Canadiens	3	at	Quebec Nordiques	2 [5:30]
April 26	Philadelphia Flyers	6	at	New York Islanders	4
April 27	Detroit Red Wings	2	at	Toronto Maple Leafs	3 [9:31]
April 27	Edmonton Oilers	4	at	Winnipeg Jets	2
April 28	Quebec Nordiques	2	at	Montreal Canadiens	3
April 28	New York Islanders	2	at	Philadelphia Flyers	1
April 29	Toronto Maple Leafs	0	at	Detroit Red Wings	3
April 30	Montreal Canadiens	2	at	Quebec Nordiques	3
April 30	Philadelphia Flyers	2	at	New York Islanders	4
May 1	Detroit Red Wings	4	at	Toronto Maple Leafs	2
May 2	Quebec Nordiques	3	at	Montreal Canadiens	5
May 2	New York Islanders	1	at	Philadelphia Flyers	5
May 3	Toronto Maple Leafs	0	at	Detroit Red Wings	3
May 4	Montreal Canadiens	3	at	Philadelphia Flyers	4 [9:11]
May 5	Detroit Red Wings	3	at	Edmonton Oilers	1
May 6	Montreal Canadiens	5	at	Philadelphia Flyers	2
May 7	Detroit Red Wings	1	at	Edmonton Oilers	4
May 8	Philadelphia Flyers	4	at	Montreal Canadiens	3
May 9	Edmonton Oilers	2	at	Detroit Red Wings	1
May 10	Philadelphia Flyers	6	at	Montreal Canadiens	3

May 11	Edmonton Oilers	3	at	Detroit Red Wings	2
May 12	Montreal Canadiens	5	at	Philadelphia Flyers	2
May 13	Detroit Red Wings	3	at	Edmonton Oilers	6
May 14	Philadelphia Flyers	4	at	Montreal Canadiens	3
May 17	Philadelphia Flyers	2	at	Edmonton Oilers	4
May 20	Philadelphia Flyers	2	at	Edmonton Oilers	3 [6:50]
May 22	Edmonton Oilers	3	at	Philadelphia Flyers	5
May 24	Edmonton Oilers	4	at	Philadelphia Flyers	1
May 26	Philadelphia Flyers	4	at	Edmonton Oilers	3
May 28	Edmonton Oilers	2	at	Philadelphia Flyers	3
May 31	Philadelphia Flyers	1	at	Edmonton Oilers	3

All Star Teams

First Team		Second Team
Ron Hextall	Goal	Mike Liut
Ray Bourque	Defense	Larry Murphy
Mark Howe	Defense	Al MacInnis
Wayne Gretzky	Center	Mario Lemieux
Jari Kurri	Right Wing	Tim Kerr
Michel Goulet	Left Wing	Luc Robitaille

Individual Awards

Art Ross Trophy--Wayne Gretzky (Edmonton Oilers)
Bill Masterton Trophy--Doug Jarvis (Hartford Whalers)
Calder Memorial Trophy--Luc Robitaille (Los Angeles Kings)
Conn Smythe Trophy--Ron Hextall (Philadelphia Flyers)
Dodge Performer of the Year--Wayne Gretzky (Edmonton Oilers)
Emery Edge Trophy--Wayne Gretzky (Edmonton Oilers)
Frank J. Selke Trophy--Dave Poulin (Philadelphia Flyers)
Hart Memorial Trophy--Wayne Gretzky (Edmonton Oilers)
Jack Adams Award--Jacques Demers (Detroit Red Wings)
James Norris Trophy--Ray Bourque (Boston Bruins)
Lady Byng Memorial Trophy--Joe Mullen (Calgary Flames)
Lester B. Pearson Award--Wayne Gretzky (Edmonton Oilers)
Lester Patrick Trophy--Hobey Baker and Frank Mathers
Vezina Trophy--Ron Hextall (Philadelphia Flyers)

Hall of Fame Inductees

Bobby Clarke, Eddie Giacomin, Jacques Laperriere, Matt Pavelich

Rules

The NHL changed the off-side rule, eliminating the delayed off-side once the players of the offending team have cleared the opponents defensive zone.

Other Sports

Horseracing--Kentucky Derby won by Alysheba (time 2:02.2, purse $611,200).
Heavyweight Boxing--Mike Tyson defeated James Smith in 12 rounds (WBC, WBA).
Mike Tyson defeated Pinklon Thomas by TKO in 6 rounds (WBC, WBA).
Tony Tucker defeated Buster Douglas by TKO in 10 rounds (IBF).
Michael Spinks defeated Gerry Cooney by TKO in 5 rounds (IBF).
Mike Tyson defeated Tony Tucker in 12 rounds (IBF).
Mike Tyson defeated Tyrell Biggs in 7 rounds (WBA WBC IBF).
Golf--U.S. Open won by Scott Simpson with a score of 277.

Auto Racing--Indianapolis 500 won by Al Unser (ave. speed 162.175 MPH).
Tennis--U.S. Open won by Ivan Lendl in the men's singles.
U.S. Open won by Stefan Edberg and Anders Jarryd in the men's doubles.
U.S. Open won by Martina Navratilova in the women's singles.
U.S. Open won by Martina Navratilova and Pam Shriver in the women's doubles.
U.S. Open won by Martina Navratilova and Emilio Sanchez in the mixed doubles.

Notes

Al Unser won his 4th Indianapolis 500 auto race.
The Heavyweight boxing championships of all the major boxing organizations were consolidated when Mike Tyson defeated Tony Tucker for the IBF championship on August 1st.
The IBF recognized the winner of the fight between Tony Tucker and Buster Douglas as champion when Michael Spinks abandoned the title in a dispute with the organization.

1988

BASEBALL

National League
East

Team Name	W	L	Pct	GB	R	OR
New York Mets	100	60	.625	-	703	532
Pittsburgh Pirates	85	75	.531	15	651	616
Montreal Expos	81	81	.500	20	628	592
Chicago Cubs	77	85	.475	24	660	694
St. Louis Cardinals	76	86	.469	25	578	633
Philadelphia Phillies	65	96	.404	35.5	597	734

West

Team Name	W	L	Pct	GB	R	OR
Los Angeles Dodgers	94	67	.584	-	628	544
Cincinnati Reds	87	74	.540	7	641	596
San Diego Padres	83	78	.516	11	594	583
San Francisco Giants	83	79	.512	11.5	670	626
Houston Astros	82	80	.506	12.5	617	631
Atlanta Braves	54	106	.338	39.5	555	741

Coaching Changes

Chicago--Don Zimmer 77-85; Philadelphia--Lee Elia 60-92, John Vukovich 5-4; San Diego--Larry Bowa 16-30, Jack McKeon 67-48; Atlanta--Chuck Tanner 12-27, Russ Nixon 42-79.

League Leaders

Batting Average
(502 at bats)

Tony Gwynn	.313
Rafael Palmeiro	.307
Andre Dawson	.303
Andres Galarraga	.302
Gerald Perry	.300

Home Runs

Darryl Strawberry	39
Glenn Davis	30
Andres Galarraga	29
Will Clark	29
Kevin McReynolds	27

RBI

Will Clark	109
Darryl Strawberry	101
Andy Van Slyke	100
Bobby Bonilla	100
Kevin McReynolds	99

Stolen Bases

Vince Coleman	81
Gerald Young	65
Ozzie Smith	57
Otis Nixon	46
Chris Sabo	46

ERA
(162 innings)

Joe Magrane	2.18
David Cone	2.22
Orel Hershiser	2.26
Jose Rijo	2.39
Pascual Perez	2.44

Wins

Orel Hershiser	23
Danny Jackson	23
David Cone	20
Rick Reuschel	19
Dwight Gooden	18

Saves

John Franco	39
Jim Gott	34
Todd Worrell	32
Steve Bedrosian	28
Mark Davis	28

Strikeouts

Jose DeLeon	298
Nolan Ryan	228
David Cone	213
Mike Scott	190
Sid Fernandez	189

NLCS

October 4	New York Mets	3	at	Los Angeles Dodgers	2
October 5	New York Mets	3	at	Los Angeles Dodgers	6
October 8	Los Angeles Dodgers	4	at	New York Mets	8
October 9	Los Angeles Dodgers	5	at	New York Mets	4 [12]
October 10	Los Angeles Dodgers	7	at	New York Mets	4
October 11	New York Mets	5	at	Los Angeles Dodgers	1
October 12	New York Mets	0	at	Los Angeles Dodgers	6

Notes

The baseball umpires were told to strictly enforce the balk rule and as a result the season's record for balk calls was broken 41 days into the season.
The Cubs became the last team in major league baseball to install lights in their stadium thus allowing night games. The Cubs and Mets played the first official game on August 9th although the Cubs and Phillies had played in Wrigley Field the night before though the game was rained out.

American League

East

Team Name	W	L	Pct	GB	R	OR
Boston Red Sox	89	73	.549	-	813	689
Detroit Tigers	88	74	.543	1	703	658
Milwaukee Brewers	87	75	.537	2	682	616
Toronto Blue Jays	87	75	.537	2	763	680
New York Yankees	85	76	.528	3.5	772	748
Cleveland Indians	78	84	.481	11	666	731
Baltimore Orioles	54	107	.335	34.5	550	789

West

Team Name	W	L	Pct	GB	R	OR
Oakland Athletics	104	58	.642	-	800	620
Minnesota Twins	91	71	.562	13	759	672
Kansas City Royals	84	77	.522	19.5	704	648
California Angels	75	87	.463	29	714	771
Chicago White Sox	71	90	.441	32.5	631	757
Texas Rangers	70	91	.435	33.5	637	735
Seattle Mariners	68	93	.422	35.5	664	744

Coaching Changes

Boston--John McNamara 43-42, Joe Morgan 46-31; New York--Billy Martin 40-28, Lou Pinniella 45-48; Cleveland--Howard Edwards 78-84; Baltimore--Cal Ripken 0-6, Frank Robinson 54-101; Kansas City--John Wathan 84-77; California--Octavio Rojas 75-79, Lawrence Stubing 0-8; Seattle--Dick Williams 23-33, Jimmy Snyder 45-60.

League Leaders

Batting Average (502 at bats)		Home Runs		RBI	
Wade Boggs	.366	Jose Canseco	42	Jose Canseco	124
Kirby Puckett	.356	Fred McGriff	34	Kirby Puckett	121
Mike Greenwell	.325	Mark McGwire	32	Mike Greenwell	119
Dave Winfield	.322	Eddie Murray	28	Dwight Evans	111
Paul Molitor	.312	Gary Gaetti	28	Dave Winfield	107

Stolen Bases		ERA (162 innings)		Wins	
Rickey Henderson	93	Dave Stieb	2.04	Frank Viola	24
Gary Pettis	44	Allan Anderson	2.45	Dave Stewart	21
Paul Molitor	41	Ted Higuera	2.45	Mark Gubicza	20
Jose Canseco	40	Frank Viola	2.64	Bruce Hurst	18
Willie Wilson	35	Mark Gubicza	2.70	Greg Swindell	18

Saves		Strikeouts	
Dennis Eckersley	45	Roger Clemens	291
Jeff Reardon	42	Mark Langston	235
Doug Jones	37	Frank Viola	193
Bob Thigpen	34	Ted Higuera	192
Dan Plesac	30	Dave Stewart	192

All Star Game
(Riverfront Stadium, Cincinnati)

July 12	American League	2		National League	1

ALCS

October 5	Oakland Athletics	2	at	Boston Red Sox	1
October 6	Oakland Athletics	4	at	Boston Red Sox	3
October 8	Boston Red Sox	6	at	Oakland Athletics	10
October 9	Boston Red Sox	1	at	Oakland Athletics	4

World Series

October 15	Oakland Athletics	4	at	Los Angeles Dodgers	5
October 16	Oakland Athletics	0	at	Los Angeles Dodgers	6
October 18	Los Angeles Dodgers	1	at	Oakland Athletics	2
October 19	Los Angeles Dodgers	4	at	Oakland Athletics	3
October 20	Los Angeles Dodgers	5	at	Oakland Athletics	2

Individual Awards

ALCS MVP--Dennis Eckersley (Oakland Athletics AL)
Arch Ward Memorial Trophy--Terry Steinbach (Oakland Athletics AL)
Baseball Writers Award--Kirk Gibson (Los Angeles Dodgers NL)
Jose Canseco (Oakland Athletics AL)
Cy Young Award--Orel Hershiser (Los Angeles Dodgers NL)
Frank Viola (Minnesota Twins AL)
NLCS MVP--Orel Hershiser (Los Angeles Dodgers NL)
Rookie of the Year--Chris Sabo (Cincinnati Reds NL)
Walt Weiss (Oakland Athletics AL)
Sporting News Executive of the Year--Fred Claire (Los Angeles Dodgers NL)
Sporting News Manager of the Year--Tommy Lasorda (Los Angeles Dodgers NL)
Jim Leyland (Pittsburgh Pirates NL)
Tony LaRussa (Oakland Athletics AL)
Sporting News Pitcher of the Year--Orel Hershiser (Los Angeles Dodgers NL)
Frank Viola (Minnesota Twins AL)
Sporting News Player of the Year--Andy Van Slyke (Pittsburgh Pirates NL)
Jose Canseco (Oakland Athletics AL)
Sporting News Rookie of the Year--Mark Grace (Chicago Cubs NL)
Tim Belcher (Los Angeles Dodgers NL)
Walt Weiss (Oakland Athletics AL)
Bryan Harvey (California Angels AL)
World Series MVP--Orel Hershiser (Los Angeles Dodgers NL)

Hall of Fame Inductee

Willie Stargell

BASKETBALL

National Basketball Association

Eastern Conference
Atlantic Division

Team Name	GP	W	L	PPGF	PPGA	Pct	GB
Boston Celtics	82	57	25	113.6	107.7	.695	-
Washington Bullets	82	38	44	105.5	106.3	.463	19
New York Knickerbockers	82	38	44	105.5	106.0	.463	19
Philadelphia 76ers	82	36	46	105.7	107.1	.439	21
New Jersey Nets	82	19	63	100.4	108.5	.232	38

Central Division

Team Name	GP	W	L	PPGF	PPGA	Pct	GB
Detroit Pistons	82	54	28	109.2	104.1	.659	-
Atlanta Hawks	82	50	32	107.9	104.3	.610	4
Chicago Bulls	82	50	32	105.0	101.6	.610	4
Cleveland Cavaliers	82	42	40	104.5	103.7	.512	12
Milwaukee Bucks	82	42	40	106.1	105.5	.512	12
Indiana Pacers	82	38	44	104.6	105.4	.463	16

Western Conference

Midwest Division

Team Name	GP	W	L	PPGF	PPGA	Pct	GB
Denver Nuggets	82	54	28	116.7	112.7	.659	-
Dallas Mavericks	82	53	29	109.3	104.9	.646	1
Utah Jazz	82	47	35	108.5	104.8	.573	7
Houston Rockets	82	46	36	109.0	107.6	.561	8
San Antonio Spurs	82	31	51	113.6	118.5	.378	23
Sacramento Kings	82	24	58	108.0	113.7	.293	30

Pacific Division

Team Name	GP	W	L	PPGF	PPGA	Pct	GB
Los Angeles Lakers	82	62	20	112.8	107.0	.756	-
Portland Trail Blazers	82	53	29	116.1	111.5	.646	9
Seattle SuperSonics	82	44	38	111.4	109.3	.537	18
Phoenix Suns	82	28	54	108.5	113.0	.341	34
Golden State Warriors	82	20	62	107.0	115.3	.244	42
Los Angeles Clippers	82	17	65	98.8	109.1	.207	45

Coaching Changes

Washington--Kevin Loughery 8-19, Wes Unseld 30-25; New York--Rick Pitino 38-44; Philadelphia--Matt Guokas 20-23, Jim Lynam 16-23; New Jersey--Dave Wohl 2-13, Bob MacKinnon 10-29, Willis Reed 7-21; Milwaukee--Del Harris 42-40; Dallas--John MacLeod 53-29; Sacramento--Bill Russell 17-41, Jerry Reynolds 7-17; Phoenix--John Wetzel 28-54; Golden State--George Karl 16-48, Ed Gregory 4-14; Los Angeles Clippers--Gene Shue 17-65.

League Leaders

Field Goals		Free Throws		Assists	
Michael Jordan	1069	Michael Jordan	723	John Stockton	1128
Dominique Wilkins	909	Charles Barkley	714	Mark Jackson	868
Larry Bird	881	Karl Malone	552	Earvin Johnson	858
Karl Malone	858	Moses Malone	543	Terry Porter	831
Clyde Drexler	849	Dominique Wilkins	541	Doc Rivers	747

Points		Rebounds Per Game	
Michael Jordan	2868	Michael Cage	13.0
Dominique Wilkins	2397	Charles Oakley	13.0
Larry Bird	2275	Akeem Olajuwon	12.1
Karl Malone	2268	Karl Malone	12.0
Charles Barkley	2264	Buck Williams	11.9

All Star Game
(Chicago Stadium, Chicago)

February 7	East Division	138	West Division	133

NBA Playoffs

April 28	Washington Bullets	87	at	Detroit Pistons	96
April 28	Cleveland Cavaliers	93	at	Chicago Bulls	104
April 28	Houston Rockets	110	at	Dallas Mavericks	120
April 28	Utah Jazz	96	at	Portland Trail Blazers	108
April 29	N.Y. Knickerbockers	92	at	Boston Celtics	112
April 29	Milwaukee Bucks	107	at	Atlanta Hawks	110
April 29	San Antonio Spurs	110	at	Los Angeles Lakers	122
April 29	Seattle SuperSonics	123	at	Denver Nuggets	126
April 30	Washington Bullets	101	at	Detroit Pistons	102
April 30	Houston Rockets	119	at	Dallas Mavericks	108
April 30	Utah Jazz	114	at	Portland Trail Blazers	105
May 1	N.Y. Knickerbockers	102	at	Boston Celtics	128
May 1	Cleveland Cavaliers	101	at	Chicago Bulls	106
May 1	Milwaukee Bucks	97	at	Atlanta Hawks	104
May 1	San Antonio Spurs	112	at	Los Angeles Lakers	130
May 1	Seattle SuperSonics	111	at	Denver Nuggets	91
May 2	Detroit Pistons	106	at	Washington Bullets	114 [OT]
May 3	Chicago Bulls	102	at	Cleveland Cavaliers	110
May 3	Los Angeles Lakers	109	at	San Antonio Spurs	107
May 3	Denver Nuggets	125	at	Seattle SuperSonics	114
May 3	Dallas Mavericks	93	at	Houston Rockets	92
May 4	Boston Celtics	100	at	N.Y. Knickerbockers	109
May 4	Detroit Pistons	103	at	Washington Bullets	106
May 4	Atlanta Hawks	115	at	Milwaukee Bucks	123
May 4	Portland Trail Blazers	108	at	Utah Jazz	113
May 5	Chicago Bulls	91	at	Cleveland Cavaliers	97
May 5	Denver Nuggets	117	at	Seattle SuperSonics	127
May 5	Dallas Mavericks	107	at	Houston Rockets	97
May 6	Boston Celtics	102	at	N.Y. Knickerbockers	94
May 6	Atlanta Hawks	99	at	Milwaukee Bucks	105
May 6	Portland Trail Blazers	96	at	Utah Jazz	111

May 7	Seattle SuperSonics	96	at	Denver Nuggets	115
May 8	Washington Bullets	78	at	Detroit Pistons	99
May 8	Cleveland Cavaliers	101	at	Chicago Bulls	107
May 8	Milwaukee Bucks	111	at	Atlanta Hawks	121
May 8	Utah Jazz	91	at	Los Angeles Lakers	110
May 10	Chicago Bulls	82	at	Detroit Pistons	93
May 10	Utah Jazz	101	at	Los Angeles Lakers	97
May 10	Dallas Mavericks	115	at	Denver Nuggets	126
May 11	Atlanta Hawks	101	at	Boston Celtics	110
May 12	Chicago Bulls	105	at	Detroit Pistons	95
May 12	Dallas Mavericks	112	at	Denver Nuggets	108
May 13	Atlanta Hawks	97	at	Boston Celtics	108
May 13	Los Angeles Lakers	89	at	Utah Jazz	96
May 14	Detroit Pistons	101	at	Chicago Bulls	79
May 14	Denver Nuggets	107	at	Dallas Mavericks	105
May 15	Boston Celtics	92	at	Atlanta Hawks	110
May 15	Los Angeles Lakers	113	at	Utah Jazz	100
May 15	Denver Nuggets	103	at	Dallas Mavericks	124
May 15	Detroit Pistons	96	at	Chicago Bulls	77
May 16	Boston Celtics	109	at	Atlanta Hawks	118
May 17	Utah Jazz	109	at	Los Angeles Lakers	111
May 17	Dallas Mavericks	110	at	Denver Nuggets	106
May 18	Atlanta Hawks	112	at	Boston Celtics	104
May 18	Chicago Bulls	95	at	Detroit Pistons	102
May 19	Los Angeles Lakers	80	at	Utah Jazz	108
May 19	Denver Nuggets	95	at	Dallas Mavericks	108
May 20	Boston Celtics	102	at	Atlanta Hawks	100
May 21	Utah Jazz	98	at	Los Angeles Lakers	109
May 22	Atlanta Hawks	116	at	Boston Celtics	118
May 23	Dallas Mavericks	98	at	Los Angeles Lakers	113
May 25	Detroit Pistons	104	at	Boston Celtics	96
May 25	Dallas Mavericks	101	at	Los Angeles Lakers	123
May 26	Detroit Pistons	115	at	Boston Celtics	119 [OT]
May 27	Los Angeles Lakers	94	at	Dallas Mavericks	106
May 28	Boston Celtics	94	at	Detroit Pistons	98
May 29	Los Angeles Lakers	104	at	Dallas Mavericks	118
May 30	Boston Celtics	79	at	Detroit Pistons	78
May 31	Dallas Mavericks	102	at	Los Angeles Lakers	119
June 1	Detroit Pistons	102	at	Boston Celtics	96 [OT]
June 2	Los Angeles Lakers	103	at	Dallas Mavericks	105
June 3	Boston Celtics	90	at	Detroit Pistons	95
June 4	Dallas Mavericks	102	at	Los Angeles Lakers	117
June 7	Detroit Pistons	105	at	Los Angeles Lakers	93
June 9	Detroit Pistons	96	at	Los Angeles Lakers	108
June 12	Los Angeles Lakers	99	at	Detroit Pistons	86
June 14	Los Angeles Lakers	86	at	Detroit Pistons	111
June 16	Los Angeles Lakers	94	at	Detroit Pistons	104
June 19	Detroit Pistons	102	at	Los Angeles Lakers	103
June 21	Detroit Pistons	105	at	Los Angeles Lakers	108

All Star Teams

First Team	Second Team
Larry Bird (Boston Celtics)	Karl Malone (Utah Jazz)
Charles Barkley (Philadelphia 76ers)	Dominique Wilkins (Atlanta Hawks)
Akeem Olajuwon (Houston Rockets)	Patrick Ewing (N.Y. Knickerbockers)
Michael Jordan (Chicago Bulls)	Clyde Drexler (Portland Trail Blazers)
Earvin Johnson (Los Angeles Lakers)	John Stockton (Utah Jazz)

Individual Awards

Defensive Player of the Year--Michael Jordan (Chicago Bulls)
Eddie Gottlieb Trophy--Mark Jackson (New York Knickerbockers)
Executive of the Year--Jerry Krause (Chicago Bulls)
J. Walter Kennedy Citizenship Award--Alex English (Denver Nuggets)
Maurice Podoloff Trophy--Michael Jordan (Chicago Bulls)
Most Improved Player--Kevin Duckworth (Portland Trail Blazers)
NBA All Star Game MVP--Michael Jordan (Chicago Bulls)
NBA Finals MVP--James Worthy (Los Angeles Lakers)
Red Auerbach Trophy--Doug Moe (Denver Nuggets)
Schick Award--Charles Barkley (Philadelphia 76ers)
Sixth Man Award--Roy Tarpley (Dallas Mavericks)

Hall of Fame Inductees

Clyde Lovelette, Bobby McDermott, Ralph Miller, Wes Unseld

FOOTBALL

National Football League
National Conference
Eastern Division

Team Name	GP	W	L	T	PF	PA	Pct
Philadelphia Eagles	16	10	6	0	379	319	.625
New York Giants	16	10	6	0	359	304	.625
Washington Redskins	16	7	9	0	345	387	.438
Phoenix Cardinals	16	7	9	0	344	398	.438
Dallas Cowboys	16	3	13	0	265	381	.188

Central Division

Team Name	GP	W	L	T	PF	PA	Pct
Chicago Bears	16	12	4	0	312	215	.750
Minnesota Vikings	16	11	5	0	406	233	.688
Tampa Bay Buccaneers	16	5	11	0	261	350	.313
Detroit Lions	16	4	12	0	220	313	.250
Green Bay Packers	16	4	12	0	240	315	.250

Western Division

Team Name	GP	W	L	T	PF	PA	Pct
San Francisco 49ers	16	10	6	0	369	294	.625
Los Angeles Rams	16	10	6	0	407	293	.625
New Orleans Saints	16	10	6	0	312	283	.625
Atlanta Falcons	16	5	11	0	244	315	.313

American Conference

Eastern Division

Buffalo Bills	16	12	4	0	329	237	.750
Indianapolis Colts	16	9	7	0	354	315	.563
New England Patriots	16	9	7	0	250	284	.563
New York Jets	16	8	7	1	372	354	.531
Miami Dolphins	16	6	10	0	319	380	.375

Central Division

Cincinnati Bengals	16	12	4	0	448	329	.750
Cleveland Browns	16	10	6	0	304	288	.625
Houston Oilers	16	10	6	0	424	365	.625
Pittsburgh Steelers	16	5	11	0	336	421	.313

Western Division

Seattle Seahawks	16	9	7	0	339	329	.563
Denver Broncos	16	8	8	0	327	352	.500
Los Angeles Raiders	16	7	9	0	325	369	.438
San Diego Chargers	16	6	10	0	231	332	.375
Kansas City Chiefs	16	4	11	1	254	320	.281

Coaching Changes

Detroit--Darryl Rogers 2-9-0, Wayne Fontes 2-3-0; Green Bay--Lindy Infante 4-12-0; Los Angeles Raiders--Mike Shanahan 7-9-0.

League Leaders

Yards Rushing		**Yards Passing**		**Passing %** (300 attempts)	
Eric Dickerson	1659	Dan Marino	4434	Wade Wilson	61.4
Herschel Walker	1514	Jim Everett	3964	Joe Montana	59.9
Roger Craig	1502	Randall Cunningham	3808	Jim Everett	59.6
Greg Bell	1212	Boomer Esiason	3572	Jim Kelly	59.5
John Stephens	1168	Neil Lomax	3395	Bob Hebert	58.6

Receiving Yards		**Receptions**		**Field Goals**	
Henry Ellard	1414	Al Toon	93	Scott Norwood	32
Anthony Carter	1225	Mark Clayton	86	Gary Anderson	28
Rick Sanders	1148	Henry Ellard	86	Nick Lowery	27
Drew Hill	1141	Eric Martin	85	Mike Cofer	27
Mark Clayton	1129	J.T. Smith	83	Morten Anderson	26

Punt Return Yards		**Kickoff Return Yards**	
John Taylor	556	Tim Brown	1098
Leo Lewis	550	Bobby Edmonds	900
Tim Brown	444	Joe Cribbs	863
JoJo Townsell	409	Rod Woodson	850
Irving Fryar	398	Darryl Harris	833

Pro Bowl Game

(Aloha Stadium, Honolulu)

January 29 1989	National Conference	34		American Conference	3

NFL Playoffs

December 26	Los Angeles Rams	17	at	Minnesota Vikings	28
December 26	Houston Oilers	24	at	Cleveland Browns	23
December 31	Philadelphia Eagles	12	at	Chicago Bears	20
December 31	Seattle Seahawks	13	at	Cincinnati Bengals	21
January 1 1989	Minnesota Vikings	9	at	San Francisco 49ers	34
January 1 1989	Houston Oilers	10	at	Buffalo Bills	17
January 8 1989	San Francisco 49ers	28	at	Chicago Bears	3
January 8 1989	Buffalo Bills	10	at	Cincinnati Bengals	21

Super Bowl XXIII

(Joe Robbie Stadium, Miami)

January 22 1989	San Francisco 49ers	20		Cincinnati Bengals	16

Individual Awards

A.P. MVP--Boomer Esiason (Cincinnati Bengals)
Bert Bell Trophy--John Stephens (New England Patriots) [World Almanac]
Bert Bell Trophy--Randall Cunningham (Philadelphia Eagles)
Dan McGuire Award--Randall Cunningham (Philadelphia Eagles)
George Halas Trophy--Mike Singletary (Chicago Bears)
Jim Thorpe Trophy--Roger Craig (San Francisco 49ers)
P.F.W.A. MVP--Boomer Esiason (Cincinnati Bengals)
Super Bowl MVP--Jerry Rice (San Francisco 49ers)
U.P.I. AFC Coach of the Year--Marv Levy (Buffalo Bills)
U.P.I. AFC Player of the Year--Boomer Esiason (Cincinnati Bengals)
Bruce Smith (Buffalo Bills)
Cornelius Bennett (Buffalo Bills)
U.P.I. AFC Rookie of the Year--John Stephens (New England Patriots)
U.P.I. NFC Coach of the Year--Mike Ditka (Chicago Bears)
U.P.I. NFC Player of the Year--Roger Craig (San Francisco 49ers)
Mike Singletary (Chicago Bears)
U.P.I. NFC Rookie of the Year--Keith Jackson (Philadelphia Eagles)

Hall of Fame Inductees

Fred Biletnikoff, Mike Ditka, Jack Ham, Alan Page

Notes

The NFL replaced the 30 second clock with a 45 second clock, meaning a team would have 45 seconds from the time a ball is signaled dead until it is snapped on the succeeding play.

Canadian Football League

Eastern Division

Team Name	GP	W	L	T	PF	PA	Pts	Pct
Toronto Argonauts	18	14	4	0	571	326	28	.778
Winnipeg Blue Bombers	18	9	9	0	407	458	18	.500
Hamilton Tiger-Cats	18	9	9	0	478	465	18	.500
Ottawa Rough Riders	18	2	16	0	278	618	4	.111

Western Division

Edmonton Eskimos	18	11	7	0	477	408	22	.611
Saskatchewan Roughriders	18	11	7	0	525	452	22	.611
British Columbia Lions	18	10	8	0	489	417	20	.556
Calgary Stampeders	18	6	12	0	395	476	12	.333

Coaching Changes

Ottawa--Bob Webber 2-16-0; Edmonton--Joe Faragalli 11-7-0; British Columbia--Larry Donovan 10-8-0; Calgary--Lary Kuharich 6-12-0.

League Leaders

Yards Rushing		**Yards Passing**		**Passing %** (150 attempts)	
Orville Lee	1075	Gilbert Renfroe	4113	Kent Austin	58.5
Gill Fenerty	968	Matt Dunnigan	3776	Matt Dunnigan	56.9
Anthony Cherry	889	Tracy Ham	2840	Gilbert Renfroe	55.0
Anthony Parker	851	Mike Kerrigan	2764	Mike Kerrigan	55.0
Tim McCray	751	Tom Burgess	2575	Tracy Ham	54.6

Receiving Yards		**Receptions**		**Points**	
Dave Williams	1468	Dave Williams	83	Dave Ridgway	215
James Murphy	1409	James Murphy	76	Lance Chomyc	207
Emanuel Tolbert	1328	Larry Willis	73	Jerry Kauric	181
Larry Willis	1328	Darrel K. Smith	73	Paul Osbaldiston	178
Gerald Alphin	1307	Ray Elgaard	69	Trevor Kennerd	149

Grey Cup Playoffs

November 13	Hamilton Tiger-Cats	28	at	Winnipeg Blue Bombers	35
November 13	British Columbia Lions	42	at	Saskatchewan Roughriders	18
November 20	Winnipeg Blue Bombers	27	at	Toronto Argonauts	11
November 20	British Columbia Lions	37	at	Edmonton Eskimos	19
November 27	Winnipeg Blue Bombers	22		British Columbia Lions	21*

Individual Awards

Annis Stukus Trophy--Mike Riley (Winnipeg Blue Bombers)
CFL All Star Game MVP--Larry Willis (Calgary Stampeders)
CFL Award Most Outstanding Canadian--Ray Elgaard (Saskatchewan Roughriders)
CFL Award Most Outstanding Defensive Player--Grover Covington (Hamilton Tiger-Cats)
CFL Award Most Outstanding Offensive Lineman--Roger Aldag (Saskatchewan Roughriders)
CFL Award Most Outstanding Player--David Williams (British Columbia Lions)
CFL Award Most Outstanding Rookie--Orville Lee (Ottawa Rough Riders)
Dave Dryburgh Memorial Trophy--Dave Ridgway (Saskatchewan Roughriders)
DeMarco-Becket Memorial Trophy--Roger Aldag (Saskatchewan Roughriders)
Dr. Beattie Martin Trophy--Ray Elgaard (Saskatchewan Roughriders)
Eddie James Memorial Trophy--Anthony Cherry (British Columbia Lions)
Frank M. Gibson Trophy--Orville Lee (Ottawa Rough Riders)

*Game played in Ottawa

Grey Cup Most Outstanding Defensive Star--Michael Gray (Winnipeg Blue Bombers)
Grey Cup Most Outstanding Offensive Star--James Murphy (Winnipeg Blue Bombers)
Grey Cup Most Valuable Canadian--Bob Cameron (Winnipeg Blue Bombers)
Jackie Parker Trophy--Jeff Fairholm (Saskatchewan Roughriders)
James P. McCaffrey Trophy--Grover Covington (Hamilton Tiger-Cats)
Jeff Nicklin Memorial Trophy--David Williams (British Columbia Lions)
Jeff Russel Memorial Trophy--Earl Winfield (Hamilton Tiger-Cats)
Leo Dandurand Trophy--Ian Beckstead (Toronto Argonauts)
Lew Hayman Trophy--Orville Lee (Ottawa Rough Riders)
Norm Fieldgate Trophy--Danny Bass (Edmonton Eskimos)

Hall of Fame Inductees

Royal Copeland, Ed McQuarters, Tony Pajaczkowski, Ralph Sazio

HOCKEY

National Hockey League
Clarence Campbell Conference
Norris Division

Team Name	GP	W	L	T	GF	GA	Pts	Pct
Detroit Red Wings	80	41	28	11	322	269	93	.581
St. Louis Blues	80	34	38	8	278	294	76	.475
Chicago Blackhawks	80	30	41	9	284	328	69	.431
Toronto Maple Leafs	80	21	49	10	273	345	52	.325
Minnesota North Stars	80	19	48	13	242	349	51	.319

Smythe Division

Team Name	GP	W	L	T	GF	GA	Pts	Pct
Calgary Flames	80	48	23	9	397	305	105	.656
Edmonton Oilers	80	44	25	11	363	288	99	.619
Winnipeg Jets	80	33	36	11	292	310	77	.481
Los Angeles Kings	80	30	42	8	318	359	68	.425
Vancouver Canucks	80	25	46	9	272	320	59	.369

Prince of Wales Conference

Adams Division

Team Name	GP	W	L	T	GF	GA	Pts	Pct
Montreal Canadiens	80	45	22	13	298	238	103	.644
Boston Bruins	80	44	30	6	300	251	94	.588
Buffalo Sabres	80	37	32	11	283	305	85	.531
Hartford Whalers	80	35	38	7	249	267	77	.481
Quebec Nordiques	80	32	43	5	271	306	69	.431

Patrick Division

Team Name	GP	W	L	T	GF	GA	Pts	Pct
New York Islanders	80	39	31	10	308	267	88	.550
Washington Capitals	80	38	33	9	281	249	85	.531
Philadelphia Flyers	80	38	33	9	292	292	85	.531
New Jersey Devils	80	38	36	6	295	296	82	.513
New York Rangers	80	36	34	10	300	283	82	.513
Pittsburgh Penguins	80	36	35	9	319	316	81	.506

Coaching Changes

Chicago--Bob Murdoch 30-41-9; Minnesota--Herb Brooks 19-48-13; Calgary--Terry Crisp 48-23-9; Los Angeles--Mike Murphy 7-16-4, Rogatien Vachon 0-1-0, Robbie Ftorek 23-25-4; Vancouver--Bob McCammon 25-46-9; Boston--Terry O'Reilly 44-30-6; Buffalo--Ted Sator 37-32-11; Hartford--Jack Evans 22-25-7, Larry Pleau 13-13-0; Quebec--Andre Savard 10-13-1, Ron LaPointe 22-30-4; New Jersey--Doug Carpenter 21-24-5, Jim Schoenfeld 17-12-1; New York Rangers--Michel Bergeron 36-34-10; Pittsburgh--Pierre Creamer 36-35-9.

League Leaders

Goals		Assists		Points	
Mario Lemieux	70	Wayne Gretzky	109	Mario Lemieux	168
Craig Simpson	56	Mario Lemieux	98	Wayne Gretzky	149
Jimmy Carson	55	Denis Savard	87	Denis Savard	131
Luc Robitaille	53	Dale Hawerchuk	77	Dale Hawerchuk	121
Joe Nieuwendyk	51	Mark Messier	74	Luc Robitaille	111

Penalty Minutes		GAA (1,500 minutes)		Wins	
Bob Probert	398	Pete Peeters	2.78	Grant Fuhr	40
Basil McRae	378	Brian Hayward	2.86	Mike Vernon	39
Tim Hunter	337	Patrick Roy	2.90	Ron Hextall	30
Richard Zemlak	307	Rejean Lemelin	2.93	John Vanbiesbrouck	27
Chris Nilan	305	Greg Stefan	3.11	Tom Barrasso	25

Shutouts		Save %	
Glen Hanlon	4	Patrick Roy	.900
Clint Malarchuk	4	Pete Peeters	.898
Grant Fuhr	4	Tom Barrasso	.896
Patrick Roy	3	Kelly Hrudey	.896
Kelly Hrudey	3	Brian Hayward	.896

All Star Game

(St. Louis Arena, St. Louis)

February 9	Wales Conference	6		Campbell Conference	5

Stanley Cup Playoffs

April 6	Toronto Maple Leafs	6	at	Detroit Red Wings	2
April 6	Chicago Blackhawks	1	at	St. Louis Blues	5
April 6	Los Angeles Kings	2	at	Calgary Flames	9
April 6	Winnipeg Jets	4	at	Edmonton Oilers	7
April 6	Hartford Whalers	3	at	Montreal Canadiens	4
April 6	Buffalo Sabres	3	at	Boston Bruins	7
April 6	New Jersey Devils	3	at	New York Islanders	4 [6:11]
April 6	Philadelphia Flyers	4	at	Washington Capitals	2
April 7	Toronto Maple Leafs	2	at	Detroit Red Wings	6
April 7	Chicago Blackhawks	2	at	St. Louis Blues	3
April 7	Los Angeles Kings	4	at	Calgary Flames	6
April 7	Winnipeg Jets	2	at	Edmonton Oilers	3
April 7	Hartford Whalers	3	at	Montreal Canadiens	7
April 7	Buffalo Sabres	1	at	Boston Bruins	4
April 7	New Jersey Devils	3	at	New York Islanders	2

April 7	Philadelphia Flyers	4	at	Washington Capitals	5
April 9	Detroit Red Wings	6	at	Toronto Maple Leafs	3
April 9	St. Louis Blues	3	at	Chicago Black Hawks	6
April 9	Calgary Flames	2	at	Los Angeles Kings	5
April 9	Edmonton Oilers	4	at	Winnipeg Jets	6
April 9	Montreal Canadiens	4	at	Hartford Whalers	3
April 9	Boston Bruins	2	at	Buffalo Sabres	6
April 9	New York Islanders	0	at	New Jersey Devils	3
April 9	Washington Capitals	3	at	Philadelphia Flyers	4
April 9	Boston Bruins	2	at	Buffalo Sabres	6
April 10	Calgary Flames	7	at	Los Angeles Kings	3
April 10	Detroit Red Wings	8	at	Toronto Maple Leafs	0
April 10	St. Louis Blues	6	at	Chicago Black Hawks	5
April 10	Calgary Flames	7	at	Los Angeles Kings	3
April 10	Edmonton Oilers	5	at	Winnipeg Jets	3
April 10	Montreal Canadiens	5	at	Hartford Whalers	7
April 10	Boston Bruins	5	at	Buffalo Sabres	6 [5:32]
April 10	New York Islanders	5	at	New Jersey Devils	4 [15:07]
April 10	Washington Capitals	4	at	Philadelphia Flyers	5 [1:18]
April 12	Toronto Maple Leafs	6	at	Detroit Red Wings	5 [0:34]
April 12	Chicago Black Hawks	3	at	St. Louis Blues	5
April 12	Los Angeles Kings	4	at	Calgary Flames	6
April 12	Winnipeg Jets	2	at	Edmonton Oilers	6
April 12	Hartford Whalers	3	at	Montreal Canadiens	1
April 12	Buffalo Sabres	4	at	Boston Bruins	5
April 12	New Jersey Devils	4	at	New York Islanders	2
April 12	Philadelphia Flyers	2	at	Washington Capitals	5
April 14	Detroit Red Wings	5	at	Toronto Maple Leafs	3
April 14	Montreal Canadiens	2	at	Hartford Whalers	1
April 14	Boston Bruins	5	at	Buffalo Sabres	2
April 14	New York Islanders	5	at	New Jersey Devils	6
April 14	Washington Capitals	7	at	Philadelphia Flyers	2
April 16	Philadelphia Flyers	4	at	Washington Capitals	5 [5:57]
April 18	Boston Bruins	2	at	Montreal Canadiens	5
April 18	New Jersey Devils	1	at	Washington Capitals	3
April 19	St. Louis Blues	4	at	Detroit Red Wings	5
April 19	Edmonton Oilers	3	at	Calgary Flames	1
April 20	Boston Bruins	4	at	Montreal Canadiens	3
April 20	New Jersey Devils	5	at	Washington Capitals	2
April 21	St. Louis Blues	0	at	Detroit Red Wings	6
April 21	Edmonton Oilers	5	at	Calgary Flames	4 [7:54]
April 22	Montreal Canadiens	1	at	Boston Bruins	3
April 22	Washington Capitals	4	at	New Jersey Devils	10
April 23	Detroit Red Wings	3	at	St. Louis Blues	6
April 23	Calgary Flames	2	at	Edmonton Oilers	4
April 24	Montreal Canadiens	0	at	Boston Bruins	2
April 24	Washington Capitals	4	at	New Jersey Devils	1
April 25	Detroit Red Wings	3	at	St. Louis Blues	1
April 25	Calgary Flames	4	at	Edmonton Oilers	6
April 26	Boston Bruins	4	at	Montreal Canadiens	1
April 26	New Jersey Devils	3	at	Washington Capitals	1
April 27	St. Louis Blues	3	at	Detroit Red Wings	4
April 28	Washington Capitals	7	at	New Jersey Devils	2
April 30	New Jersey Devils	3	at	Washington Capitals	2

May 2	New Jersey Devils	3	at	Boston Bruins	5
May 3	Detroit Red Wings	1	at	Edmonton Oilers	4
May 4	New Jersey Devils	3	at	Boston Bruins	2 [17:46]
May 5	Detroit Red Wings	3	at	Edmonton Oilers	5
May 6	Boston Bruins	6	at	New Jersey Devils	1
May 7	Edmonton Oilers	2	at	Detroit Red Wings	5
May 8	Boston Bruins	1	at	New Jersey Devils	3
May 9	Edmonton Oilers	4	at	Detroit Red Wings	3 [11:02]
May 10	New Jersey Devils	1	at	Boston Bruins	7
May 11	Detroit Red Wings	4	at	Edmonton Oilers	8
May 12	Boston Bruins	3	at	New Jersey Devils	6
May 14	New Jersey Devils	2	at	Boston Bruins	6
May 18	Boston Bruins	1	at	Edmonton Oilers	2
May 20	Boston Bruins	2	at	Edmonton Oilers	4
May 22	Edmonton Oilers	6	at	Boston Bruins	3
May 24	Edmonton Oilers	3	at	Boston Bruins	3 *
May 26	Boston Bruins	3	at	Edmonton Oilers	6

All Star Teams

First Team		Second Team
Grant Fuhr	Goal	Patrick Roy
Ray Bourque	Defense	Gary Suter
Scott Stevens	Defense	Brad McCrimmon
Mario Lemieux	Center	Wayne Gretzky
Hakan Loob	Right Wing	Cam Neely
Luc Robitaille	Left Wing	Michel Goulet

Individual Awards

Art Ross Trophy--Mario Lemieux (Pittsburgh Penguins)
Bill Masterton Trophy--Bob Bourne (Los Angeles Kings)
Bud Light Man of the Year--Bryan Trottier (New York Islanders)
Calder Memorial Trophy--Joe Nieuwendyk (Calgary Flames)
Conn Smythe Trophy--Wayne Gretzky (Edmonton Oilers)
Dodge Performance of the Year--Mario Lemieux (Pittsburgh Penguins)
Dodge Performer of the Year--Mario Lemieux (Pittsburgh Penguins)
Dodge Ram Tough Award--Joe Nieuwendyk (Calgary Flames)
Emery Edge Trophy--Brad McCrimmon (Calgary Flames)
Frank J. Selke Trophy--Guy Carbonneau (Montreal Canadiens)
Hart Memorial Trophy--Mario Lemieux (Pittsburgh Penguins)
Jack Adams Award--Jacques Demers (Detroit Red Wings)
James Norris Trophy--Ray Bourque (Boston Bruins)
King Clancy Trophy--Lanny McDonald (Calgary Flames)
Lady Byng Memorial Trophy--Mats Naslund (Montreal Canadiens)
Lester B. Pearson Award--Mario Lemieux (Pittsburgh Penguins)
Lester Patrick Trophy--Keith Allen, Fred Cusick and Bob Johnson
NHL All Star Game MVP--Mario Lemieux (Pittsburgh Penguins)
William M. Jennings Trophy--Patrick Roy and Brian Hayward (Montreal Canadiens)
Vezina Trophy--Grant Fuhr (Edmonton Oilers)

Hall of Fame Inductees

Tony Esposito, George Hayes, Guy Lafleur, Buddy O'Connor, Brad Park, Ed Snider

*Game was called after 16:37 of the second period as Boston Gardens suffered a power failure.

Franchise Changes

NFL--St. Louis Cardinals became the Phoenix Cardinals.

Other Sports

Horseracing--Kentucky Derby won by Winning Colors (time 2:02.2, purse $611,200).
Heavyweight Boxing--Mike Tyson defeated Larry Holmes by TKO in 4 rounds (WBA, WBC, IBF).
Mike Tyson knocked-out Tony Tubbs in 2 rounds (WBA, WBC, IBF).
Mike Tyson knocked-out Michael Spinx in 1 round (WBA, WBC, IBF).
Golf--U.S. Open won by Curtis Strange with a score of 278.
Auto Racing--Indianapolis 500 won by Rick Mears (ave. speed 149.809 MPH).
Tennis--U.S. Open won by Mats Wilander in the men's singles.
U.S. Open won by Sergio Casal and Emilio Sanchez in the men's doubles.
U.S. Open won by Steffi Graf in the women's singles.
U.S. Open won by Gigi Fernandez and Robin White in the women's doubles.
U.S. Open won by Jana Novotna and Jim Pugh in the mixed doubles.

Notes

Winning Colors became only the third filly to win the Kentucky Derby.

1989

BASEBALL

National League
East

Team Name	W	L	Pct	GB	R	OR
Chicago Cubs	93	69	.574	-	702	623
New York Mets	87	75	.537	6	683	595
St. Louis Cardinals	86	76	.531	7	632	608
Montreal Expos	81	81	.500	12	632	630
Pittsburgh Pirates	74	88	.457	19	637	680
Philadelphia Phillies	67	95	.414	26	629	735

West

Team Name	W	L	Pct	GB	R	OR
San Francisco Giants	92	70	.568	-	699	600
San Diego Padres	89	73	.549	3	642	626
Houston Astros	86	76	.531	6	647	669
Los Angeles Dodgers	77	83	.481	14	554	536
Cincinnati Reds	75	87	.463	17	632	691
Atlanta Braves	63	97	.394	28	584	680

Coaching Changes

Philadelphia--Nick Leyva 67-95; San Diego--Jack McKeon 89-73; Houston--Art Howe 86-76; Cincinnati--Pete Rose 61-66, Tommy Helm 14-21; Atlanta--Russ Nixon 63-97.

League Leaders

Batting Average
(502 at bats)

Tony Gwynn	.336
Will Clark	.333
Mark Grace	.314
Pedro Guerrero	.311
Roberto Alomar	.295

Home Runs

Kevin Mitchell	47
Howard Johnson	36
Eric Davis	34
Glenn Davis	34
Ryne Sandberg	30

RBI

Kevin Mitchell	125
Pedro Guerrero	117
Will Clark	111
Eric Davis	101
Howard Johnson	101

Stolen Bases

Vince Coleman	65
Roberto Alomar	42
Juan Samuel	42
Howard Johnson	41
Tim Raines	41

ERA
(162 innings)

Scott Gerrelts	2.28
Orel Hershiser	2.31
Mark Langston	2.39
Ed Whitson	2.66
Bruce Hurst	2.69

Wins

Mike Scott	20
Greg Maddox	19
Mike Bielecki	18
Joe Magrane	18
Rick Reuschel	17

Saves

Mark Davis	44
Mitch Williams	36
John Franco	32
Tim Burke	28
Jay Howell	28

Strikeouts

Jose DeLeon	201
Tim Belcher	200
Sid Fernandez	198
David Cone	190
Bruce Hurst	179

NLCS

October 4	San Francisco Giants	11	at	Chicago Cubs	3
October 5	San Francisco Giants	5	at	Chicago Cubs	9
October 7	Chicago Cubs	4	at	San Francisco Giants	5
October 8	Chicago Cubs	4	at	San Francisco Giants	6
October 9	Chicago Cubs	2	at	San Francisco Giants	3

Notes

Bill White replaced Bart Giamatti as President of the National League.

American League

East

Team Name	W	L	Pct	GB	R	OR
Toronto Blue Jays	89	73	.549	-	731	651
Baltimore Orioles	87	75	.537	2	708	686
Boston Red Sox	83	79	.512	6	774	735
Milwaukee Brewers	81	81	.500	8	707	679
New York Yankees	74	87	.460	14.5	698	792
Cleveland Indians	73	89	.451	16	604	654
Detroit Tigers	59	103	.364	30	617	816

West

Team Name	W	L	Pct	GB	R	OR
Oakland Athletics	99	63	.611	-	712	576
Kansas City Royals	92	70	.568	7	690	635
California Angels	91	71	.562	8	669	578
Texas Rangers	83	79	.512	16	695	714
Minnesota Twins	80	82	.494	19	740	738
Seattle Mariners	73	89	.451	26	694	728
Chicago White Sox	69	92	.429	29.5	693	750

Coaching Changes

Toronto--Jimy Williams 12-24, Cito Gaston 77-49; Baltimore--Frank Robinson 87-75; Boston--Joe Morgan 83-79; New York--Dallas Green 56-65, Russell "Bucky" Dent 18-22; Cleveland--Howard "Doc" Edwards 65-78, John Hart 8-11; Detroit--George "Sparky" Anderson 50-94, Dick Tracewski 9-9; Kansas City-- John Wathan 92-70; California--Doug Rader 91-71; Seattle--Jim Lefebvre 73-89; Chicago--Jeff Torborg 69-92.

League Leaders

Batting Average (502 at bats)		**Home Runs**		**RBI**	
Kirby Puckett	.339	Fred McGriff	36	Ruben Sierra	119
Carny Lansford	.336	Joe Carter	35	Don Mattingly	113
Wade Boggs	.330	Mark McGwire	33	Nick Esasky	108
Robin Yount	.318	Bo Jackson	32	Bo Jackson	105
Julio Franco	.316	Nick Esasky	30	Joe Carter	105

Stolen Bases		**ERA** (162 innings)		**Wins**	
Rickey Henderson	77	Bret Saberhagen	2.16	Bret Saberhagen	23
Cecil Espy	45	Chuck Finley	2.57	Dave Stewart	21
Devon White	44	Bert Blyleven	2.73	Storm Davis	19
Gary Pettis	43	Kirk McCaskill	2.93	Mike Moore	19
Steve Sax	43	Chris Bosio	2.95	Jeff Ballard	18

Saves		**Strikeouts**	
Jeff Russell	38	Nolan Ryan	301
Bob Thigpen	34	Roger Clemens	230
Dennis Eckersley	33	Bret Saberhagen	193
Dan Plesac	33	Chris Bosio	173
Mike Schooler	33	Mark Gubicza	173

All Star Game

(Anaheim Stadium, Anaheim)

July 11	American League	5		National League	3

ALCS

October 3	Toronto Blue Jays	3	at	Oakland Athletics	7
October 4	Toronto Blue Jays	3	at	Oakland Athletics	6
October 6	Oakland Athletics	3	at	Toronto Blue Jays	7
October 7	Oakland Athletics	6	at	Toronto Blue Jays	5
October 8	Oakland Athletics	4	at	Toronto Blue Jays	3

World Series

October 14	San Francisco Giants	0	at	Oakland Athletics	5
October 15	San Francisco Giants	1	at	Oakland Athletics	5
October 27	Oakland Athletics	13	at	San Francisco Giants	7
October 28	Oakland Athletics	9	at	San Francisco Giants	6

Individual Awards

ALCS MVP--Rickey Henderson (Oakland Athletics AL)
Arch Ward Memorial Trophy--Bo Jackson (Kansas City Royals AL)
Baseball Writers Award--Kevin Mitchell (San Francisco Giants NL)
Robin Yount (Milwaukee Brewers AL)
Cy Young Award--Mark Davis (San Diego Padres NL)
Bret Saberhagen (Kansas City Royals AL)
NLCS MVP--Will Clark (San Francisco Giants NL)
Rookie of the Year--Jerome Walton (Chicago Cubs NL)
Gregg Olson (Baltimore Orioles AL)
Sporting News Executive of the Year--Roland Hemond (Baltimore Orioles AL)
Sporting News Manager of the Year--Don Zimmer (Chicago Cubs NL)
Frank Robinson (Baltimore Orioles AL)
Sporting News Pitcher of the Year--Mark Davis (San Diego Padres NL)
Bret Saberhagen (Kansas City Royals AL)
Sporting News Player of the Year--Kevin Mitchell (San Francisco Giants NL)
Ruben Sierra (Texas Rangers AL)
Sporting News Rookie of the Year--Jerome Walton (Chicago Cubs NL)
Andy Benes (San Diego Padres NL)
Craig Worthington (Baltimore Orioles AL)
Tom Gordon (Kansas City Royals AL)
World Series MVP--Dave Stewart (Oakland Athletics AL)

Hall of Fame Inductees

Al Barlick, Johnny Bench, Albert Schoendienst, Carl Yastrzemski

Notes

Bart Giamatti succeeded Peter Ueberroth as commissioner of baseball but died suddenly on September 1 and was replaced by Fay Vincent. Vincent became the last commissioner of major league baseball as the position was phased out in 1992 and replaced by the office of Chairman of the Executive Committee.

Half an hour before the start of game 3 of the World Series between Oakland and San Francisco, in San Francisco, an earthquake measuring 6.9 on the Richter scale rocked California's Bay area killing over 200 people and delaying the World Series for 11 days

BASKETBALL
National Basketball Association

Eastern Conference
Atlantic Division

Team Name	GP	W	L	PPGF	PPGA	Pct	GB
New York Knickerbockers	82	52	30	116.7	112.9	.634	-
Philadelphia 76ers	82	46	36	111.9	110.4	.561	6
Boston Celtics	82	42	40	109.2	108.1	.512	10
Washington Bullets	82	40	42	108.3	110.4	.488	12
New Jersey Nets	82	26	56	103.7	110.1	.317	26
Charlotte Hornets	82	20	62	104.5	113.0	.244	32

Central Division

Team Name	GP	W	L	PPGF	PPGA	Pct	GB
Detroit Pistons	82	63	19	106.6	100.8	.768	-
Cleveland Cavaliers	82	57	25	108.8	101.2	.695	6
Atlanta Hawks	82	52	30	111.0	106.1	.634	11
Milwaukee Bucks	82	49	33	108.9	105.3	.598	14
Chicago Bulls	82	47	35	106.4	105.0	.573	16
Indiana Pacers	82	28	54	106.9	111.1	.341	35

Western Conference

Midwest Division

Team Name	GP	W	L	PPGF	PPGA	Pct	GB
Utah Jazz	82	51	31	104.7	99.7	.622	-
Houston Rockets	82	45	37	108.5	107.5	.549	6
Denver Nuggets	82	44	38	118.0	116.3	.537	7
Dallas Mavericks	82	38	44	103.5	104.7	.463	13
San Antonio Spurs	82	21	61	105.5	112.8	.256	30
Miami Heat	82	15	67	97.8	109.0	.183	36

Pacific Division

Team Name	GP	W	L	PPGF	PPGA	Pct	GB
Los Angeles Lakers	82	57	25	114.7	107.5	.695	-
Phoenix Suns	82	55	27	118.6	110.9	.671	2
Seattle SuperSonics	82	47	35	112.1	109.2	.573	10
Golden State Warriors	82	43	39	116.6	116.9	.524	14
Portland Trail Blazers	82	39	43	114.6	113.1	.476	18
Sacramento Kings	82	27	55	105.5	111.0	.329	30
Los Angeles Clippers	82	21	61	106.2	116.2	.256	36

Coaching Changes

Philadelphia--Jim Lynam 46-36; Boston--Jimmy Rodgers 42-40; Washington--Wes Unseld 40-42; New Jersey--Willis Reed 26-56; Charlotte--Dick Harter 20-62; Indiana--Jack Ramsay 0-7, Mel Daniels 0-2, George Irvine 6-14, Dick Versace 22-31; Utah--Frank Layden 11-6, Jerry Sloan 40-25; Houston--Don Chaney 45-37; San Antonio--Larry Brown 21-61; Miami--Ron Rothstein 15-67; Phoenix--Lowell "Cotton" Fitzsimmons55-27; Golden State--Don Nelson 43-39; Portland--Mike Schuler 25-22, Rick Adelman 14-21; Sacramento--Jerry Reynolds 27-55; Los Angeles Clipper--Gene Shue 10-28, Don Casey 11-33.

League Leaders

Field Goals		**Free Throws**		**Assists**	
Michael Jordan	966	Karl Malone	703	John Stockton	1118
Alex English	924	Michael Jordan	674	Kevin Johnson	991
Dale Ellis	857	Charles Barkley	602	Earvin Johnson	988
Chris Mullin	830	Moses Malone	561	Terry Porter	770
Clyde Drexler	829	Earvin Johnson	513	Eric Floyd	709

Points		**Rebounds Per Game**	
Michael Jordan	2633	Akeem Olajuwon	13.5
Karl Malone	2326	Charles Barkley	12.5
Dale Ellis	2253	Robert Parish	12.5
Chris Mullin	2176	Moses Malone	11.8
Alex English	2175	Karl Malone	10.7

All Star Game

(The Astrodome, Houston)

February 12	West Division	143	East Division	134

NBA Playoffs

April 27	Philadelphia 76ers	96	at	N.Y. Knickerbockers	102
April 27	Milwaukee Bucks	92	at	Atlanta Hawks	100
April 27	Portland Trail Blazers	108	at	Los Angeles Lakers	128
April 27	Golden State Warriors	123	at	Utah Jazz	119
April 28	Boston Celtics	91	at	Detroit Pistons	101
April 28	Chicago Bulls	95	at	Cleveland Cavaliers	88
April 28	Denver Nuggets	103	at	Phoenix Suns	104
April 28	Houston Rockets	107	at	Seattle SuperSonics	111
April 29	Philadelphia 76ers	106	at	N.Y. Knickerbockers	107
April 29	Milwaukee Bucks	108	at	Atlanta Hawks	98
April 29	Golden State Warriors	99	at	Utah Jazz	91
April 30	Boston Celtics	95	at	Detroit Pistons	102
April 30	Chicago Bulls	88	at	Cleveland Cavaliers	96
April 30	Portland Trail Blazers	105	at	Los Angeles Lakers	113
April 30	Denver Nuggets	114	at	Phoenix Suns	132
April 30	Houston Rockets	97	at	Seattle SuperSonics	109
May 2	N.Y. Knickerbockers	116	at	Philadelphia76ers	115 [OT]
May 2	Detroit Pistons	100	at	Boston Celtics	85
May 2	Atlanta Hawks	113	at	Milwaukee Bucks	117 [OT]
May 2	Utah Jazz	106	at	Golden State Warriors	120
May 2	Phoenix Suns	130	at	Denver Nuggets	121
May 3	Cleveland Cavaliers	94	at	Chicago Bulls	101

May 3	Los Angeles Lakers	116	at	Portland Trail Blazers	108
May 3	Seattle SuperSonics	107	at	Houston Rockets	126
May 5	Cleveland Cavaliers	108	at	Chicago Bulls	105 [OT]
May 5	Atlanta Hawks	113	at	Milwaukee Bucks	106 [OT]
May 5	Seattle SuperSonics	98	at	Houston Rockets	96
May 6	Golden State	103	at	Phoenix Suns	130
May 7	Chicago Bulls	101	at	Cleveland Cavaliers	100
May 7	Milwaukee Bucks	96	at	Atlanta Hawks	92
May 7	Seattle SuperSonics	102	at	Los Angeles Lakers	113
May 9	Chicago Bulls	120	at	N.Y. Knickerbockers	109 [OT]
May 9	Golden State	127	at	Phoenix Suns	122
May 10	Milwaukee Bucks	80	at	Detroit Pistons	85
May 10	Seattle SuperSonics	108	at	Los Angeles Lakers	130
May 11	Chicago Bulls	97	at	N.Y. Knickerbockers	114
May 11	Phoenix Suns	113	at	Golden State Warriors	104
May 12	Milwaukee Bucks	92	at	Detroit Pistons	112
May 12	Los Angeles Lakers	91	at	Seattle SuperSonics	86
May 13	N.Y. Knickerbockers	88	at	Chicago Bulls	111
May 13	Phoenix Suns	135	at	Golden State Warriors	99
May 14	N.Y. Knickerbockers	93	at	Chicago Bulls	106
May 14	Detroit Pistons	110	at	Milwaukee Bucks	90
May 14	Los Angeles Lakers	97	at	Seattle SuperSonics	95
May 15	Detroit Pistons	96	at	Milwaukee Bucks	94
May 16	Chicago Bulls	114	at	N.Y. Knickerbockers	121
May 16	Golden State	104	at	Phoenix Suns	116
May 19	N.Y. Knickerbockers	111	at	Chicago Bulls	113
May 20	Phoenix Suns	119	at	Los Angeles Lakers	127
May 21	Chicago Bulls	94	at	Detroit Pistons	88
May 23	Phoenix Suns	95	at	Los Angeles Lakers	101
May 23	Chicago Bulls	91	at	Detroit Pistons	100
May 26	Los Angeles Lakers	110	at	Phoenix Suns	107
May 27	Detroit Pistons	97	at	Chicago Bulls	99
May 28	Los Angeles Lakers	122	at	Phoenix Suns	117
May 29	Detroit Pistons	86	at	Chicago Bulls	80
May 31	Chicago Bulls	85	at	Detroit Pistons	94
June 2	Detroit Pistons	103	at	Chicago Bulls	94
June 6	Los Angeles Lakers	97	at	Detroit Pistons	109
June 8	Los Angeles Lakers	105	at	Detroit Pistons	108
June 11	Detroit Pistons	114	at	Los Angeles Lakers	110
June 13	Detroit Pistons	105	at	Los Angeles Lakers	97

All Star Teams

First Team	Second Team	Third Team
Karl Malone	Tom Chambers	Dominique Wilkins
Charles Barkley	Chris Mullen	Terry Cummings
Akeem Olajuwon	Patrick Ewing	Robert Parish
Earvin Johnson	John Stockton	Dale Ellis
Michael Jordan	Kevin Johnson	Mark Price

Individual Awards

Defensive Player of the Game--Mark Eaton (Utah Jazz)
Eddie Gottlieb Trophy--Mitch Richmond (Golden State Warriors)
Executive of the Year--Jerry Colangelo (Phoenix Suns)

Good Hands Award--John Stockton (Utah Jazz)
J. Walter Kennedy Citizenship Award--Thurl Bailey (Utah Jazz)
Maurice Podoloff Trophy--Earvin Johnson (Los Angeles Lakers)
Most Improved Player--Kevin Johnson (Phoenix Suns)
NBA All Star Game MVP--Karl Malone (Utah Jazz)
NBA Finals MVP--Joe Dumars (Detroit Pistons)
Red Auerbach Trophy--Lowell "Cotton" Fitzsimmons (Phoenix Suns)
Schick Award--Michael Jordan (Chicago Bulls)
Sixth Man Award--Eddie Johnson (Phoenix Suns)

Hall of Fame Inductees

William Gates, K.C. Jones, Lenny Wilkens

Notes

Sharunas Marciulionis became the first Soviet born player to play in the NBA. Marciulionis went on to play 75 games for Golden State this season.
Denver Nuggets were sold to businessmen Bertram Lee and Peter Bynoe along with Comsat Video Enterprises for $65 million. Lee and Bynoe become the first black owners of a major league sports team.
N.B.C. acquired the rights to broadcast NBA games for four years for a $600 million price tag.

FOOTBALL

National Football League
National Conference

Eastern Division

Team Name	GP	W	L	T	PF	PA	Pct
New York Giants	16	12	4	0	348	252	.750
Philadelphia Eagles	16	11	5	0	342	274	.688
Washington Redskins	16	10	6	0	386	308	.625
Phoenix Cardinals	16	5	11	0	258	377	.313
Dallas Cowboys	16	1	15	0	204	393	.063

Central Division

Team Name	GP	W	L	T	PF	PA	Pct
Minnesota Vikings	16	10	6	0	351	275	.625
Green Bay Packers	16	10	6	0	362	356	.625
Detroit Lions	16	7	9	0	312	364	.438
Chicago Bears	16	6	10	0	358	377	.375
Tampa Bay Buccaneers	16	5	11	0	320	419	.313

Western Division

Team Name	GP	W	L	T	PF	PA	Pct
San Francisco 49ers	16	14	2	0	442	253	.875
Los Angeles Rams	16	11	5	0	426	344	.688
New Orleans Saints	16	9	7	0	386	301	.563
Atlanta Falcons	16	3	13	0	279	437	.188

American Conference

Eastern Division

Buffalo Bills	16	9	7	0	409	317	.563
Indianapolis Colts	16	8	8	0	298	301	.500
Miami Dolphins	16	8	8	0	331	379	.500
New England Patriots	16	5	11	0	297	391	.313
New York Jets	16	4	12	0	253	411	.250

Central Division

Cleveland Browns	16	9	6	1	334	254	.594
Houston Oilers	16	9	7	0	365	412	.563
Pittsburgh Steelers	16	9	7	0	265	326	.563
Cincinnati Bengals	16	8	8	0	404	285	.500

Western Division

Denver Broncos	16	11	5	0	362	226	.688
Kansas City Chiefs	16	8	7	1	318	286	.531
Los Angeles Raiders	16	8	8	0	315	297	.500
Seattle Seahawks	16	7	9	0	241	327	.438
San Diego Chargers	16	6	10	0	266	290	.375

Coaching Changes

Phoenix--Gene Stallings 5-6-0, Hank Kuhlmann 0-5-0; Dallas--Jim Johnson 1-15-0; Detroit--Wayne Fontes 7-9-0; San Francisco--George Seifert 14-2-0; Cleveland--Bud Carson 9-6-1; Kansas City--Marty Schottenheimer 8-7-1; Los Angeles Raiders--Mike Shanahan 1-3-0, Art Shell 7-5-0; San Diego--Dan Henning 6-10-0; Atlanta--Marion Campbell 3-9, Jim Hanifan 0-4.

League Leaders

Yards Rushing		Yards Passing		Passing % (300 attempts)	
Christian Okoye	1480	Don Majkowski	4318	Joe Montana	70.2
Barry Sanders	1470	Jim Everett	4310	Bobby Hebert	62.9
Eric Dickerson	1311	Dan Marino	3997	Steve DeBerg	60.5
Neal Anderson	1275	Mark Rypien	3768	Ken O'Brien	60.4
Dalton Hilliard	1262	Warren Moon	3631	Warren Moon	60.3

Receiving Yards		Receptions		Field Goals	
Jerry Rice	1483	Sterling Sharpe	90	Rich Karlis	31
Sterling Sharpe	1423	Andre Reed	88	Chip Lohmiller	29
Mark Carrier	1422	Mark Carrier	86	Mike Cofer	29
Henry Ellard	1382	Art Monk	86	David Treadwell	27
Andre Reed	1312	Jerry Rice	82	Tony Zendejas	25

Punt Return Yards		Kickoff Return Yards	
Dave Megett	582	James Dixon	1181
Walter Stanley	496	Rod Woodson	982
Gerald McNeil	496	Ron Brown	968
Leo Lewis	446	Vai Sikahema	874
Vai Sikahema	433	Deion Sanders	725

Pro Bowl Game

(Aloha Stadium, Honolulu)

February 4 1990	National Conference	27		American Conference	21

NFL Championship

December 31	Pittsburgh Steelers	26	at	Houston Oilers	23 [OT]
December 31	Los Angeles Rams	21	at	Philadelphia Eagles	7
January 6 1990	Buffalo Bills	30	at	Cleveland Browns	34
January 6 1990	Minnesota Vikings	13	at	San Francisco 49ers	41
January 7 1990	Pittsburgh Steelers	23	at	Denver Broncos	24
January 7 1990	Los Angeles Rams	19	at	New York Giants	13 [OT]
January 14 1990	Cleveland Browns	21	at	Denver Broncos	37
January 14 1990	Los Angeles Rams	3	at	San Francisco 49ers	30

Super Bowl XXIV

(Louisiana Superdome, New Orleans)

January 28 1990	San Francisco 49ers	55		Denver Broncos	10

Individual Awards

A.P. MVP--Joe Montana (San Francisco 49ers)
Bert Bell Trophy--Barry Sanders (Detroit Lions) [World Almanac]
Bert Bell Trophy--Joe Montana (San Francisco 49ers)
Dan McGuire Award--Jerry Gray (Los Angeles Rams)
George Halas Trophy--Tim Harris (Green Bay Packers)
Jim Thorpe Trophy--Joe Montana (San Francisco 49ers)
P.F.W.A. MVP--Joe Montana (San Francisco 49ers)
Super Bowl MVP--Joe Montana (San Francisco 49ers)
U.P.I. AFC Coach of the Year--Dan Reeves (Denver Broncos)
U.P.I. AFC Player of the Year--Christian Okoye (Kansas City Chiefs)
Michael Dean Perry (Cleveland Browns)
U.P.I. AFC Rookie of the Year--Derrick Thomas (Kansas City Chiefs)
U.P.I. NFC Coach of the Year--Lindy Infante (Green Bay Packers)
U.P.I. NFC Player of the Year--Joe Montana (San Francisco 49ers)
Keith Millard (Minnesota Vikings)
U.P.I. NFC Rookie of the Year--Barry Sanders (Detroit Lions)

Hall of Fame Inductees

Mel Blount, Terry Bradshaw, Art Shell, Willie Wood

Notes

When Pete Rozelle decided to retire on March 22 Paul Tagliabue succeeded him becoming the NFL's fifth Commissioner.

Canadian Football League
Eastern Division

Team Name	GP	W	L	T	PF	PA	Pts	Pct
Hamilton Tiger-Cats	18	12	6	0	519	517	24	.667
Toronto Argonauts	18	7	11	0	369	428	14	.389
Winnipeg Blue Bombers	18	7	11	0	408	462	14	.389
Ottawa Rough Riders	18	4	14	0	426	630	8	.222

Western Division

Edmonton Eskimos	18	16	2	0	644	302	32	.889
Calgary Stampeders	18	10	8	0	495	466	20	.556
Saskatchewan Roughriders	18	9	9	0	547	567	18	.500
British Columbia Lions	18	7	11	0	521	557	14	.389

Coaching Changes

Ottawa--Steve Goldman 4-14-0; British Columbia--Larry Donovan 0-4-0, Joe Galat 7-7-0.

League Leaders

Yards Rushing		**Yards Passing**		**Passing %** (100 attempts)	
Reggie Taylor	1503	Matt Dunnigan	4509	Kent Austin	56.7
Tim McCray	1285	Tracy Ham	4366	Matt Dunnigan	55.4
Gill Fenerty	1247	Sean Salisbury	4049	Todd Dillon	55.0
Derrick McAdoo	1039	Mike Kerrigan	3635	Tracy Ham	51.8
Tracy Ham	1005	Damon Allen	3093	Mike Kerrigan	51.0

Receiving Yards		**Receptions**		**Points**	
Tony Champion	1656	Tony Champion	95	Paul Osbaldiston	233
Gerald Alphin	1471	Don Narcisse	81	Jerry Kauric	224
Larry Willis	1451	Craig Ellis	80	Dave Ridgway	216
David Williams	1446	David Williams	79	Mark McLaughlin	202
Don Narcisse	1419	Eric Streater	76	Lui Passaglia	175

Grey Cup Playoffs

November 12	Winnipeg Blue Bombers	30	at	Toronto Argonauts	7
November 12	Saskatchewan Roughriders	33	at	Calgary Stampeders	26
November 19	Winnipeg Blue Bombers	10	at	Hamilton Tiger-Cats	14
November 19	Saskatchewan Roughriders	32	at	Edmonton Eskimos	21
November 26	Saskatchewan Roughriders	43		Hamilton Tiger-Cats	40*

Individual Awards

Annis Stukus Trophy--John Gregory (Saskatchewan Roughriders)
CFL Award Most Outstanding Canadian--Rocky DiPietro (Hamilton Tiger-Cats)
CFL Award Most Outstanding Defensive Player--Danny Bass (Edmonton Eskimos)
CFL Award Most Outstanding Offensive Lineman--Rod Connop (Edmonton Eskimos)
CFL Award Most Outstanding Player--Tracy Ham (Edmonton Eskimos)
CFL Award Most Outstanding Rookie--Stephen Jordan (Hamilton Tiger-Cats)
Dave Dryburgh Memorial Trophy--Jerry Kauric (Edmonton Eskimos)
DeMarco-Becket Memorial Trophy--Rod Connop (Edmonton Eskimos)
Dr. Beattie Martin Trophy--Jeff Fairholm (Saskatchewan Roughriders)
Eddie James Memorial Trophy--Reggie Taylor (Edmonton Eskimos)
Frank M. Gibson Trophy--Stephen Jordan (Hamilton Tiger-Cats)
Grey Cup Most Outstanding Defensive Star--Chuck Klingbeil (Saskatchewan Roughriders)
Grey Cup Most Outstanding Offensive Star--Kent Austin (Saskatchewan Roughriders)
Grey Cup Most Valuable Canadian--Dave Ridgway (Saskatchewan Roughriders)

*Game played in Toronto

Jackie Parker Trophy--Darrell Wallace (British Columbia Lions)
James P. McCaffrey Trophy--Greg Battle (Winnipeg Blue Bombers)
Jeff Nicklin Memorial Trophy--Tracy Ham (Edmonton Eskimos)
Jeff Russel Memorial Trophy--Tony Champion (Hamilton Tiger-Cats)
Leo Dandurand Trophy--Miles Gorrell (Hamilton Tiger-Cats)
Lew Hayman Trophy--Rocky DiPietro (Hamilton Tiger-Cats)
Norm Fieldgate Trophy--Danny Bass (Edmonton Eskimos)

Hall of Fame Inductees

Jerry Keeling, Karl Slocomb, Dave Thelen, Andy Tommy, Ted Urness

Notes

Bill Baker replaced Doug Mitchell to become President/Chief Operating Officer of the Canadian Football League.

HOCKEY
National Hockey League

Clarence Campbell Conference
Norris Division

Team Name	GP	W	L	T	GF	GA	Pts	Pct
Detroit Red Wings	80	34	34	12	313	316	80	.500
St. Louis Blues	80	33	35	12	275	285	78	.488
Minnesota North Stars	80	27	37	16	258	278	70	.438
Chicago Blackhawks	80	27	41	12	297	335	66	.413
Toronto Maple Leafs	80	28	46	6	259	342	62	.388

Smythe Division

Team Name	GP	W	L	T	GF	GA	Pts	Pct
Calgary Flames	80	54	17	9	354	226	117	.731
Los Angeles Kings	80	42	31	7	376	335	91	.569
Edmonton Oilers	80	38	34	8	325	306	84	.525
Vancouver Canucks	80	33	39	8	251	253	74	.463
Winnipeg Jets	80	26	42	12	300	355	64	.400

Prince of Wales Conference

Adams Division

Team Name	GP	W	L	T	GF	GA	Pts	Pct
Montreal Canadiens	80	53	18	9	315	218	115	.719
Boston Bruins	80	37	29	14	289	256	88	.550
Buffalo Sabres	80	38	35	7	291	299	83	.519
Hartford Whalers	80	37	38	5	299	290	79	.494
Quebec Nordiques	80	27	46	7	269	342	61	.381

Patrick Division

Team Name	GP	W	L	T	GF	GA	Pts	Pct
Washington Capitols	80	41	29	10	305	259	92	.575
Pittsburgh Penguins	80	40	33	7	347	349	87	.544
New York Rangers	80	37	35	8	310	307	82	.513
Philadelphia Flyers	80	36	36	8	307	285	80	.500
New Jersey Devils	80	27	41	12	281	325	66	.413
New York Islanders	80	28	47	5	265	325	61	.381

Coaching Changes

St. Louis--Brian Sutter 33-35-12; Minnesota--Pierre Page 27-37-16; Chicago--Mike Keenan 27-41-12; Toronto--John Brophy 11-20-2, George Armstrong 17-26-4; Los Angeles--Robbie Ftorek 42-31-7; Winnipeg--Dan Maloney 18-25-9, Rick Bowness 8-17-3; Montreal--Pat Burns 53-18-9; Hartford--Larry Pleau 37-38-5; Quebec--Ron LaPointe 11-20-2, Jean Perron 16-26-5; Pittsburgh--Gene Ubriaco 40-33-7; New York Rangers--Michel Bergeron 37-33-8, Phil Esposito 0-2-0; Philadelphia--Paul Holmgren 36-36-8; New Jersey--Jim Schoenfeld 27-41-12; New York Islanders--Terry Simpson 7-18-2, Al Arbour 21-29-3.

League Leaders

Goals		**Assists**		**Points**	
Mario Lemieux	85	Mario Lemieux	114	Mario Lemieux	199
Bernie Nicholls	70	Wayne Gretzky	114	Wayne Gretzky	168
Steve Yzerman	65	Steve Yzerman	90	Steve Yzerman	155
Wayne Gretzky	54	Paul Coffey	83	Bernie Nicholls	150
Joe Nieuwendyk	51	Bernie Nicholls	80	Rob Brown	115

Penalty Minutes		**GAA** (1,500 minutes		**Wins**	
Tim Hunter	375	Patrick Roy	2.47	Mike Vernon	37
Basil McRae	365	Mike Vernon	2.65	Patrick Roy	33
Dave Manson	352	Pete Peeters	2.85	Ron Hextall	30
Marty McSorley	350	Brian Hayward	2.90	John Vanbiesbrouck	28
Mike Hartman	316	Rick Wamsley	2.96	Kelly Hrudey	28

Shutouts		**Save %**	
Greg Millen	6	Patrick Roy	.908
Pete Peeters	4	Jon Casey	.900
Kirk McLean	4	Karl Takko	.899
Peter Sidorkiewicz	4	Mike Vernon	.897
Patrick Roy	4	Steve Weeks	.892

All Star Game

(Northlands Coliseum, Edmonton)

February 7	Campbell Conference	9	Wales Conference	5

Stanley Cup Playoffs

April 5	Minnesota North Stars	3	at	St. Louis Blues	4 [11:55]
April 5	Hartford Whalers	2	at	Montreal Canadiens	6
April 5	Buffalo Sabres	6	at	Boston Bruins	0
April 5	Philadelphia Flyers	2	at	Washington Capitals	3
April 5	New York Rangers	1	at	Pittsburgh Penguins	3
April 5	Chicago Blackhawks	2	at	Detroit Red Wings	3
April 5	Vancouver Canucks	4	at	Calgary Flames	3 [2:47]
April 5	Edmonton Oilers	4	at	Los Angeles Kings	3
April 6	Hartford Whalers	2	at	Montreal Canadiens	3
April 6	Buffalo Sabres	3	at	Boston Bruins	5
April 6	Philadelphia Flyers	3	at	Washington Capitals	2
April 6	New York Rangers	4	at	Pittsburgh Penguins	7
April 6	Chicago Blackhawks	5	at	Detroit Red Wings	4 [14:36]
April 6	Minnesota North Stars	3	at	St. Louis Blues	4 [5:30]

April 6	Vancouver Canucks	2	at	Calgary Flames	5
April 6	Edmonton Oilers	2	at	Los Angeles Kings	5
April 8	Montreal Canadiens	5	at	Hartford Whalers	4 [5:01]
April 8	Boston Bruins	4	at	Buffalo Sabres	2
April 8	Washington Capitals	4	at	Philadelphia Flyers	3 [0:51]
April 8	Pittsburgh Penguins	5	at	New York Rangers	3
April 8	Detroit Red Wings	2	at	Chicago Blackhawks	4
April 8	St. Louis Blues	5	at	Minnesota North Stars	3
April 8	Calgary Flames	4	at	Vancouver Canucks	0
April 8	Los Angeles Kings	0	at	Edmonton Oilers	4
April 9	Montreal Canadiens	4	at	Hartford Whalers	3 [15:12]
April 9	Boston Bruins	3	at	Buffalo Sabres	2
April 9	Washington Capitals	2	at	Philadelphia Flyers	5
April 9	Pittsburgh Penguins	4	at	New York Rangers	3
April 9	Detroit Red Wings	2	at	Chicago Blackhawks	3
April 9	St. Louis Blues	4	at	Minnesota North Stars	5
April 9	Calgary Flames	3	at	Vancouver Canucks	5
April 9	Los Angeles Kings	3	at	Edmonton Oilers	4
April 11	Buffalo Sabres	1	at	Boston Bruins	4
April 11	Philadelphia Flyers	8	at	Washington Capitals	5
April 11	Chicago Blackhawks	4	at	Detroit Red Wings	6
April 11	Minnesota North Stars	1	at	St. Louis Blues	6
April 11	Vancouver Canucks	0	at	Calgary Flames	4
April 11	Edmonton Oilers	2	at	Los Angeles Kings	4
April 13	Washington Capitals	3	at	Philadelphia Flyers	4
April 13	Detroit Red Wings	1	at	Chicago Blackhawks	7
April 13	Calgary Flames	3	at	Vancouver Canucks	6
April 13	Los Angeles Kings	4	at	Edmonton Oilers	1
April 15	Vancouver Canucks	3	at	Calgary Flames	4 [19:21]
April 15	Edmonton Oilers	3	at	Los Angeles Kings	6
April 17	Boston Bruins	2	at	Montreal Canadiens	3
April 17	Philadelphia Flyers	3	at	Pittsburgh Penguins	4
April 18	Chicago Blackhawks	3	at	St. Louis Blues	1
April 18	Los Angeles Kings	3	at	Calgary Flames	4 [7:47]
April 19	Boston Bruins	2	at	Montreal Canadiens	3 [12:24]
April 19	Philadelphia Flyers	4	at	Pittsburgh Penguins	2
April 20	Chicago Blackhawks	4	at	St. Louis Blues	5 [33:49]
April 20	Los Angeles Kings	3	at	Calgary Flames	8
April 21	Montreal Canadiens	5	at	Boston Bruins	4
April 21	Pittsburgh Penguins	4	at	Philadelphia Flyers	3 [12:08]
April 22	St. Louis Blues	2	at	Chicago Blackhawks	5
April 22	Calgary Flames	5	at	Los Angeles Kings	2
April 23	Montreal Canadiens	2	at	Boston Bruins	3
April 23	Pittsburgh Penguins	1	at	Philadelphia Flyers	4
April 24	St. Louis Blues	2	at	Chicago Blackhawks	3
April 24	Calgary Flames	5	at	Los Angeles Kings	3
April 25	Boston Bruins	2	at	Montreal Canadiens	3
April 25	Philadelphia Flyers	7	at	Pittsburgh Penguins	10
April 26	Chicago Blackhawks	4	at	St. Louis Blues	2
April 27	Pittsburgh Penguins	2	at	Philadelphia Flyers	6
April 29	Philadelphia Flyers	4	at	Pittsburgh Penguins	1
May 1	Philadelphia Flyers	3	at	Montreal Canadiens	1
May 2	Chicago Blackhawks	0	at	Calgary Flames	3
May 3	Philadelphia Flyers	0	at	Montreal Canadiens	3

May 4	Chicago Blackhawks	4	at	Calgary Flames	2
May 5	Montreal Canadiens	5	at	Philadelphia Flyers	1
May 6	Calgary Flames	5	at	Chicago Blackhawks	2
May 7	Montreal Canadiens	3	at	Philadelphia Flyers	0
May 8	Calgary Flames	2	at	Chicago Blackhawks	1 [15:05]
May 9	Philadelphia Flyers	2	at	Montreal Canadiens	1 [5:02]
May 10	Chicago Blackhawks	1	at	Calgary Flames	3
May 11	Montreal Canadiens	4	at	Philadelphia Flyers	2
May 14	Montreal Canadiens	2	at	Calgary Flames	3
May 17	Montreal Canadiens	4	at	Calgary Flames	2
May 19	Calgary Flames	3	at	Montreal Canadiens	4 [38:08]
May 21	Calgary Flames	4	at	Montreal Canadiens	2
May 23	Montreal Canadiens	2	at	Calgary Flames	3
May 25	Calgary Flames	4	at	Montreal Canadiens	2

All Star Teams

First Team		Second Team
Patrick Roy	Goal	Mike Vernon
Chris Chelios	Defense	Al MacInnis
Paul Coffey	Defense	Ray Bourque
Mario Lemieux	Center	Wayne Gretzky
Joe Mullen	Right Wing	Jari Kurri
Luc Robitaille	Left Wing	Gerard Gallant

Individual Awards

Art Ross Trophy--Mario Lemieux (Pittsburgh Penguins)
Bill Masterton Trophy--Tim Kerr (Philadelphia Flyers)
Bud Man of the Year--Lanny McDonald (Calgary Flames)
Calder Memorial Trophy--Brian Leetch (New York Rangers)
Conn Smythe Trophy--Al MacInnis (Calgary Flames)
Dodge Performance of the Year--Wayne Gretzky (Los Angeles Kings)
Dodge Performer of the Year--Mario Lemieux (Pittsburgh Penguins)
Dodge Ram Tough Award--Mario Lemieux (Pittsburgh Penguins)
Frank J. Selke Trophy--Guy Carbonneau (Montreal Canadiens)
Hart Memorial Trophy--Wayne Gretzky (Los Angeles Kings)
Jack Adams Award--Pat Burns (Montreal Canadiens)
James Norris Trophy--Chris Chelios (Montreal Canadiens)
King Clancy Trophy--Bryan Trottier (New York Islanders)
Lady Byng Memorial Trophy--Joe Mullen (Calgary Flames)
Lester B. Pearson Award--Steve Yzerman (Detroit Red Wings)
Lester Patrick Trophy--Dan Kelly, Lou Nanne, Lynn Patrick and Bud Poile
NHL All Star Game MVP--Wayne Gretzky (Los Angeles Kings)
Trico Goaltender Award--Patrick Roy (Montreal Canadiens)
Vezina Trophy--Patrick Roy (Montreal Canadiens)
William M. Jennings Trophy--Patrick Roy and Brian Hayward (Montreal Canadiens)

Hall of Fame Inductees

Father David Bauer, Alan Eagleson, Herb Lewis, Darryl Sittler, Vladislav Tretiak

Notes

Sergei Priakin became the first former Soviet National Team member to play in the NHL when he suited up for the Calgary Flames.

Other Sports

Horseracing--Kentucky Derby won by Sunday Silence (time 2:05, purse $574,000).

Heavyweight Boxing--Mike Tyson defeated Frank Bruno by TKO in 5 rounds (WBA, WBC, IBF).
Mike Tyson defeated Carl Williams by TKO in 1 round (WBA, WBC, IBF).

Golf--U.S. Open won by Curtis Strange with a score of 278.

Auto Racing--Indianapolis 500 won by Emerson Fittipaldi (ave. speed 167.581 MPH).

Tennis--U.S. Open won by Boris Becker in the men's singles.
U.S. Open won by John McEnroe and Mark Woodforde in the men's doubles.
U.S. Open won by Steffi Graf in the women's singles.
U.S. Open won by Martina Navratilova and Hana Mandlikova in the women's doubles.
U.S. Open won by Robin White and Shelby Cannon in the mixed doubles.

1990

BASEBALL
National League
East

Team Name	W	L	Pct	GB	R	OR
Pittsburgh Pirates	95	67	.586	-	733	619
New York Mets	91	71	.562	4	775	613
Montreal Expos	85	77	.525	10	662	598
Chicago Cubs	77	85	.475	18	690	774
Philadelphia Phillies	77	85	.475	18	646	729
St. Louis Cardinals	70	92	.432	25	599	698

West

Team Name	W	L	Pct	GB	R	OR
Cincinnati Reds	91	71	.562	-	693	597
Los Angeles Dodgers	86	75	.534	4.5	728	685
San Francisco Giants	85	77	.525	6	719	710
Houston Astros	75	87	.463	16	573	656
San Diego Padres	74	87	.460	16.5	673	673
Atlanta Braves	65	97	.401	26	682	821

Coaching Changes

New York--Davey Johnson 20-22, Bud Harrelson 71-49; St. Louis--Whitey Herzog 33-47, Red Schoendienst 13-11, Joe Torre 24-34 ; Cincinnati--Lou Piniella 91-71; San Diego--Jack McKeon 37-43, Greg Riddoch 38-44; Atlanta--Russ Nixon 25-40, Bobby Cox 40-57.

League Leaders

Batting Average

Willie McGee	.335
Eddie Murray	.330
Dave Magadan	.328
Lenny Dykstra	.325
Andre Dawson	.310

Home Runs

Ryne Sandberg	40
Darryl Strawberry	37
Kevin Mitchell	35
Matt Williams	33
Barry Bonds	33

RBI

Matt Williams	122
Bobby Bonilla	120
Joe Carter	115
Barry Bonds	114
Darryl Strawberry	108

Stolen Bases

Vince Coleman	77
Eric Yelding	64
Barry Bonds	52
Brett Butler	51
Otis Nixon	50

ERA

Danny Darwin	2.21
Zane Smith	2.55
Ed Whitson	2.60
Frank Viola	2.67
Jose Rijo	2.70

Wins

Doug Drabek	22
Ramon Martinez	20
Frank Viola	20
Dwight Gooden	19
Greg Maddox	15

Saves

John Franco	33
Randy Myers	31
Lee Smith	27
Craig Lefferts	23
Dave Smith	23

Strikeouts

David Cone	233
Ramon Martinez	223
Dwight Gooden	223
Frank Viola	182
Sid Fernandez	181

NLCS

October 4	Pittsburgh Pirates	4	at	Cincinnati Reds	3
October 5	Pittsburgh Pirates	1	at	Cincinnati Reds	2
October 8	Cincinnati Reds	6	at	Pittsburgh Pirates	3
October 9	Cincinnati Reds	5	at	Pittsburgh Pirates	3
October 10	Cincinnati Reds	2	at	Pittsburgh Pirates	3
October 12	Pittsburgh Pirates	1	at	Cincinnati Reds	2

American League
East

Team Name	W	L	Pct	GB	R	OR
Boston Red Sox	88	74	.543	-	699	664
Toronto Blue Jays	86	76	.531	2	767	661
Detroit Tigers	79	83	.488	9	750	754
Cleveland Indians	77	85	.475	11	732	737
Baltimore Orioles	76	85	.472	11.5	669	698
Milwaukee Brewers	73	88	.453	14.5	732	760
New York Yankees	67	95	.414	21	603	749

West

Team Name	W	L	Pct	GB	R	OR
Oakland Athletics	103	59	.636	-	733	570
Chicago White Sox	94	68	.580	9	682	633
Texas Rangers	83	78	.516	19.5	676	696
California Angels	80	82	.494	23	690	706
Seattle Mariners	77	85	.475	26	640	680
Kansas City Royals	75	86	.466	27.5	707	709
Minnesota Twins	74	88	.457	29	666	729

Coaching Changes

Toronto--Cito Gaston 86-76; Detroit--George "Sparky" Anderson 79-83; Cleveland--John McNamara 77-85; New York--Russell "Bucky" Dent 18-31, Stump Merrill 49-64.

League Leaders

Batting Average		Home Runs		RBI	
George Brett	.329	Cecil Fielder	51	Cecil Fielder	132
Rickey Henderson	.325	Mark McGwire	39	Kelly Gruber	118
Rafael Palmeiro	.319	Jose Canseco	37	Mark McGwire	108
Alan Trammell	.304	Fred McGriff	35	Jose Canseco	101
Wade Boggs	.302	Kelly Gruber	31	Ruben Sierra	96

Stolen Bases		ERA		Wins	
Rickey Henderson	65	Roger Clemens	1.93	Bob Welch	27
Steve Sax	43	Chuck Finley	2.40	Dave Stewart	22
Roberto Kelly	42	Dave Stewart	2.56	Roger Clemens	21
Alex Cole Jr.	40	Kevin Appier	2.76	Erik Hanson	18
Gary Pettis	38	Dave Stieb	2.93	Chuck Finley	18

Saves		**Strikeouts**	
Bobby Thigpen	57	Nolan Ryan	232
Dennis Eckersley	48	Bobby Witt	221
Doug Jones	43	Erik Hanson	211
Gregg Olson	37	Roger Clemens	209
Dave Righetti	36	Mark Langston	195

All Star Game

(Wrigley Field, Chicago)

July 10	American League	2		National League	0

ALCS

October 6	Oakland Athletics	9	at	Boston Red Sox	1
October 7	Oakland Athletics	4	at	Boston Red Sox	1
October 9	Boston Red Sox	1	at	Oakland Athletics	4
October 10	Boston Red Sox	1	at	Oakland Athletics	3

World Series

October 16	Oakland Athletics	0	at	Cincinnati Reds	7
October 17	Oakland Athletics	4	at	Cincinnati Reds	5 [10]
October 19	Cincinnati Reds	8	at	Oakland Athletics	3
October 20	Cincinnati Reds	2	at	Oakland Athletics	1

Individual Awards

ALCS MVP--Dave Stewart (Oakland Athletics AL)
Arch Ward Memorial Trophy--Julio Franco (Texas Rangers AL)
Baseball Writers Award--Barry Bonds (Pittsburgh Pirates NL)
Rickey Henderson (Oakland Athletics AL)
Cy Young Award--Doug Drabek (Pittsburgh Pirates NL)
Bob Welch (Oakland Athletics AL)
NLCS MVP--Rob Dibble (Cincinnati Reds NL)
Randy Myers (Cincinnati Reds NL)
Rookie of the Year--David Justice (Atlanta Braves NL)
Sandy Alomar (Cleveland Indians AL)
Sporting News Executive of the Year--Bob Quinn(Cincinnati Reds NL)
Sporting News Manager of the Year--Jim Leyland (Pittsburgh Pirates NL)
Jeff Torborg(Chicago White Sox AL)
Sporting News Pitcher of the Year--Doug Drabek (Pittsburgh Pirates NL)
Bob Welch (Oakland Athletics AL)
Sporting News Player of the Year--Barry Bonds (Pittsburgh Pirates NL)
Cecil Fielder (Detroit Tigers AL)
Sporting News Rookie of the Year--Sandy Alomar (Cleveland Indians AL)
Kevin Appier (Kansas City Royals AL)
David Justice (Atlanta Braves NL)
Mike Harkey (Chicago Cubs NL)
World Series MVP--Jose Rijo (Cincinnati Reds NL)

Hall of Fame Inductees

Joe Morgan, Jim Palmer

Notes

Jose Canseco signs baseball's first $5 million a year contract.
On August 31 Ken Griffey Sr. and Ken Griffey Jr. become the first father-son combination to play in the same game in Major League Baseball.

BASKETBALL
National Basketball Association

Eastern Conference
Atlantic Division

Team Name	GP	W	L	PPGF	PPGA	Pct	GB
Philadelphia 76ers	82	53	29	110.2	105.2	.646	-
Boston Celtics	82	52	30	110.0	106.0	.634	1
New York Knickerbockers	82	45	37	108.3	106.9	.549	8
Washington Bullets	82	31	51	107.7	109.9	.378	23
Miami Heat	82	18	64	100.6	110.3	.220	36
New Jersey Nets	82	17	65	100.1	108.0	.207	37

Central Division

Team Name	GP	W	L	PPGF	PPGA	Pct	GB
Detroit Pistons	82	59	23	104.3	98.3	.720	-
Chicago Bulls	82	55	27	1095	106.2	.671	4
Milwaukee Bucks	82	44	38	106.0	106.8	.537	15
Indiana Pacers	82	42	40	109.3	109.1	.512	17
Cleveland Cavaliers	82	42	40	102.6	102.9	.512	17
Atlanta Hawks	82	41	41	108.5	107.5	.500	18
Orlando Magic	82	18	64	110.9	119.8	.220	40

Western Conference

Midwest Division

Team Name	GP	W	L	PPGF	PPGA	Pct	GB
San Antonio Spurs	82	56	26	106.3	102.8	.683	-
Utah Jazz	82	55	27	106.8	102.0	.671	1
Dallas Mavericks	82	47	35	102.2	102.2	.573	9
Denver Nuggets	82	43	39	114.6	113.2	.524	13
Houston Rockets	82	41	41	106.7	105.3	.500	15
Minnesota Timberwolves	82	22	60	95.2	99.4	.268	34
Charlotte Hornets	82	19	63	100.4	108.2	.232	37

Pacific Division

Team Name	GP	W	L	PPGF	PPGA	Pct	GB
Los Angeles Lakers	82	63	19	110.7	103.9	.768	-
Portland Trail Blazers	82	59	23	114.2	107.9	.720	4
Phoenix Suns	82	54	28	114.9	107.8	.659	9
Seattle SuperSonics	82	41	41	106.9	105.9	.500	22
Golden State Warriors	82	37	45	116.3	119.4	.451	26
Los Angeles Clippers	82	30	52	103.8	107.2	.366	33
Sacramento Kings	82	23	59	101.7	106.8	.280	40

Coaching Changes

New York Knickerbockers--Stu Jackson 45-37; New Jersey--Bill Fitch 17-65; Chicago--Phil Jackson 55-27; Indiana--Dick Versace 42-40; Orlando--Matt Guokas 18-64; Utah--Jerry Sloan 55-27; Dallas--John MacLeod 5-6, Richie Adubato 42-29; Minnesota--Bill Musselman 22-60; Charlotte--Dick Harter 8-32, Gene Littles 11-31; Portland--Rick Adelman 59-23; Los Angeles Clippers--Don Casey 30-52; Sacramento--Jerry Reynolds 7-20, Dick Motta 16-39.

League Leaders

Field Goals		Free Throws		Assists per Game	
Michael Jordan	1034	Karl Malone	696	John Stockton	14.5
Patrick Ewing	922	David Robinson	613	Earvin Johnson	11.5
Karl Malone	914	Michael Jordan	593	Kevin Johnson	11.4
Tom Chambers	810	Earvin Johnson	567	Tyrone Bogues	10.7
Dominique Wilkins	810	Tom Chambers	557	Gary Grant	10.0

Points		Rebounds Per Game	
Michael Jordan	2753	Akeem Olajuwon	14.0
Karl Malone	2540	David Robinson	12.0
Patrick Ewing	2347	Charles Barkley	11.5
Tom Chambers	2201	Karl Malone	11.1
Dominique Wilkins	2138	Patrick Ewing	10.9

All Star Game

(Miami Arena, Miami)

February 11	East Division	130	West Division	113

NBA Playoffs

April 26	Indiana Pacers	92	at	Detroit Pistons	104
April 26	Cleveland Cavaliers	106	at	Philadelphia 76ers	111
April 26	N.Y. Knickerbockers	105	at	Boston Celtics	116
April 26	Denver Nuggets	103	at	San Antonio Spurs	119
April 26	Dallas Mavericks	102	at	Portland Trail Blazers	109
April 27	Milwaukee Bucks	97	at	Chicago Bulls	111
April 27	Houston Rockets	89	at	Los Angeles Lakers	101
April 27	Phoenix Suns	96	at	Utah Jazz	113
April 28	Indiana Pacers	87	at	Detroit Pistons	100
April 28	N.Y. Knickerbockers	128	at	Boston Celtics	157
April 28	Denver Nuggets	120	at	San Antonio Spurs	129
April 28	Dallas Mavericks	107	at	Portland Trail Blazers	114
April 29	Cleveland Cavaliers	101	at	Philadelphia 76ers	107
April 29	Milwaukee Bucks	102	at	Chicago Bulls	109
April 29	Houston Rockets	100	at	Los Angeles Lakers	104
April 29	Phoenix Suns	105	at	Utah Jazz	87
May 1	Detroit Pistons	108	at	Indiana Pacers	96
May 1	Philadelphia 76ers	95	at	Cleveland Cavaliers	122
May 1	Chicago Bulls	112	at	Milwaukee Bucks	119
May 1	Los Angeles Lakers	108	at	Houston Rockets	114
May 1	San Antonio Spurs	131	at	Denver Nuggets	120
May 2	Boston Celtics	99	at	N.Y. Knickerbockers	102
May 2	Utah Jazz	105	at	Phoenix Suns	120
May 2	Portland Trail-Blazers	106	at	Dallas Mavericks	92
May 3	Philadelphia 76ers	96	at	Cleveland Cavaliers	108
May 3	Chicago Bulls	110	at	Milwaukee Bucks	86
May 3	Los Angeles Lakers	109	at	Houston Rockets	88
May 4	Boston Celtics	108	at	N.Y. Knickerbockers	135
May 4	Utah Jazz	105	at	Phoenix Suns	94
May 5	Cleveland Cavaliers	97	at	Philadelphia 76ers	113
May 5	San Antonio Spurs	94	at	Portland Trail Blazers	107

May 6	N.Y. Knickerbockers	121	at	Boston Celtics	114
May 6	Phoenix Suns	104	at	Utah Jazz	102
May 7	Philadelphia 76ers	85	at	Chicago Bulls	96
May 8	N.Y. Knickerbockers	77	at	Detroit Pistons	112
May 8	Phoenix Suns	104	at	Los Angeles Lakers	102
May 8	San Antonio Spurs	112	at	Portland Trail Blazers	122
May 9	Philadelphia 76ers	96	at	Chicago Bulls	101
May 10	N.Y. Knickerbockers	97	at	Detroit Pistons	104
May 10	Phoenix Suns	100	at	Los Angeles Lakers	124
May 10	Portland Trail Blazers	98	at	San Antonio Spurs	121
May 11	Chicago Bulls	112	at	Philadelphia 76ers	118
May 12	Detroit Pistons	103	at	N.Y. Knickerbockers	111
May 12	Los Angeles Lakers	103	at	Phoenix Suns	117
May 12	Portland Trail Blazers	105	at	San Antonio Spurs	115
May 13	Detroit Pistons	102	at	N.Y. Knickerbockers	90
May 13	Chicago Bulls	111	at	Philadelphia 76ers	101
May 13	Los Angeles Lakers	101	at	Phoenix Suns	114
May 15	N.Y. Knickerbockers	84	at	Detroit Pistons	95
May 15	Phoenix Suns	106	at	Los Angeles Lakers	103
May 15	San Antonio Spurs	132	at	Portland Trail Blazers	138 [OT]
May 16	Philadelphia 76ers	99	at	Chicago Bulls	117
May 17	Portland Trail Blazers	97	at	San Antonio Spurs	112
May 19	San Antonio Spurs	105	at	Portland Trail Blazers	108 [OT]
May 20	Chicago Bulls	77	at	Detroit Pistons	86
May 21	Phoenix Suns	98	at	Portland Trail Blazers	100
May 22	Chicago Bulls	93	at	Detroit Pistons	102
May 23	Phoenix Suns	107	at	Portland Trail Blazers	108
May 25	Portland Trail Blazers	89	at	Phoenix Suns	123
May 26	Detroit Pistons	102	at	Chicago Bulls	109
May 27	Portland Trail Blazers	107	at	Phoenix Suns	119
May 28	Detroit Pistons	101	at	Chicago Bulls	108
May 29	Phoenix Suns	114	at	Portland Trail Blazers	120
May 30	Chicago Bulls	83	at	Detroit Pistons	97
May 31	Portland Trail Blazers	112	at	Phoenix Suns	109
June 1	Detroit Pistons	91	at	Chicago Bulls	109
June 3	Chicago Bulls	74	at	Detroit Pistons	93
June 5	Portland Trail Blazers	99	at	Detroit Pistons	105
June 7	Portland Trail Blazers	106	at	Detroit Pistons	105 [OT]
June 10	Detroit Pistons	121	at	Portland Trail Blazers	106
June 12	Detroit Pistons	112	at	Portland Trail Blazers	109
June 14	Detroit Pistons	92	at	Portland Trail Blazers	90

All Star Teams

First Team	Second Team	Third Team
Earvin Johnson	Akeem Olajuwon	David Robinson
Charles Barkley	John Stockton	Clyde Drexler
Karl Malone	Tom Chambers	Joe Dumars
Michael Jordan	Larry Bird	James Worthy
Patrick Ewing	Kevin Johnson	Chris Mullin

Individual Awards

Defensive Player of the Year--Dennis Rodman (Detroit Pistons)
Eddie Gottlieb Trophy--David Robinson (San Antonio Spurs)

Executive of the Year--Bob Bass (San Antonio Spurs)
Good Hands Award--Darrell Walker (Washington Bullets)
J. Walter Kennedy Citizenship Award--Doc Rivers (Atlanta Hawks)
Maurice Podoloff Trophy--Earvin Johnson (Los Angeles Lakers)
Most Improved Player--Rony Seikaly (Miami Heat)
NBA All Star Game MVP--Earvin Johnson (Los Angeles Lakers)
NBA Finals MVP--Isiah Thomas (Detroit Pistons)
Red Auerbach Trophy--Pat Riley (Los Angeles Lakers)
Schick Award--David Robinson (San Antonio Spurs)
Sixth Man Award--Ricky Pierce (Milwaukee Bucks)

Hall of Fame Inductees

Dave Bing, Elvin Hayes, Neil Johnston, Earl Monroe

FOOTBALL

National Football League
National Conference
Eastern Division

Team Name	GP	W	L	T	PF	PA	Pct
New York Giants	16	13	3	0	335	211	.813
Philadelphia Eagles	16	10	6	0	396	299	.625
Washington Redskins	16	10	6	0	381	301	.625
Dallas Cowboys	16	7	9	0	244	308	.438
Phoenix Cardinals	16	5	11	0	268	396	.313

Central Division

Team Name	GP	W	L	T	PF	PA	Pct
Chicago Bears	16	11	5	0	348	280	.688
Tampa Bay Buccaneers	16	6	10	0	264	367	.375
Detroit Lions	16	6	10	0	373	413	.375
Green Bay Packers	16	6	10	0	271	347	.375
Minnesota Vikings	16	6	10	0	351	326	.375

Western Division

Team Name	GP	W	L	T	PF	PA	Pct
San Francisco 49ers	16	14	2	0	353	239	.875
New Orleans Saints	16	8	8	0	274	275	.500
Los Angeles Rams	16	5	11	0	345	412	.313
Atlanta Falcons	16	5	11	0	348	365	.313

American Conference

Eastern Division

Team Name	GP	W	L	T	PF	PA	Pct
Buffalo Bills	16	13	3	0	428	263	.813
Miami Dolphins	16	12	4	0	336	242	.750
Indianapolis Colts	16	7	9	0	281	353	.438
New York Jets	16	6	10	0	295	345	.375
New England Patriots	16	1	15	0	181	446	.063

Central Division

Cincinnati Bengals	16	9	7	0	360	352	.563
Houston Oilers	16	9	7	0	405	307	.563
Pittsburgh Steelers	16	9	7	0	292	240	.563
Cleveland Browns	16	3	13	0	228	462	.188

Western Division

Los Angeles Raiders	16	12	4	0	337	268	.750
Kansas City Chiefs	16	11	5	0	369	257	.688
Seattle Seahawks	16	9	7	0	306	286	.563
San Diego Chargers	16	6	10	0	315	281	.375
Denver Broncos	16	5	11	0	331	374	.313

Coaching Changes

Phoenix--Joe Bugel 5-11-0; Tampa Bay--Ray Perkins 5-8-0, Richard Williamson 1-2-0; Atlanta--Jerry Glanville 5-11-0; New York Jets--Bruce Coslet 6-10-0; New England--Rod Rust 1-15-0; Houston--Jack Pardee 9-7-0; Cleveland--Bud Carson 2-7-0, Jim Shofner1-6-0; L.A. Raiders--Art Shell 12-4-0.

League Leaders

Yards Rushing		Yards Passing		Passing % (300 attempts)	
Barry Sanders	1304	Warren Moon	4689	Jim Kelly	63.3
Thurman Thomas	1297	Jim Everett	3989	Warren Moon	62.0
Marion Butts	1225	Joe Montana	3944	Joe Montana	61.7
Earnest Byner	1219	Dan Marino	3563	Dave Krieg	59.2
Bob Humphrey	1202	John Elway	3526	Phil Simms	59.2

Receiving Yards		Receptions		Field Goals	
Jerry Rice	1502	Jerry Rice	100	Nick Lowery	34
Henry Ellard	1294	Andre Rison	82	Chip Lohmiller	30
Andre Rison	1208	Keith Byars	81	Kevin Butler	26
Gary Clark	1112	Henry Ellard	76	David Treadwell	25
Sterling Sharpe	1105	Gary Clark	75	Mike Cofer	24

Punt Return Yards		Kickoff Return Yards	
Dave Meggett	467	Eric Metcalf	1052
John Bailey	399	Herschel Walker	966
Rod Woodson	398	Mel Gray	939
Clarence Verdin	396	Charles Wilson	798
Mel Gray	361	Rod Woodson	764

Pro Bowl Game

(Aloha Stadium, Honolulu)

February 3 1991	American Conference	23	National Conference	21

NFL Playoffs

January 5 1991	Kansas City Chiefs	16	at	Miami Dolphins	17
January 5 1991	Philadelphia Eagles	6	at	Washington Redskins	20
January 6 1991	Houston Oilers	14	at	Cincinnati Bengals	41
January 6 1991	New Orleans Saints	6	at	Chicago Bears	16
January 12 1991	Miami Dolphins	34	at	Buffalo Bills	44
January 12 1991	Washington Redskins	10	at	San Francisco 49ers	28
January 13 1991	Cincinnati Bengals	10	at	Los Angeles Raiders	20
January 13 1991	Chicago Bears	3	at	New York Giants	31
January 20 1991	Los Angeles Raiders	3	at	Buffalo Bills	51
January 20 1991	New York Giants	15	at	San Francisco 49ers	13

Super Bowl XXV

(Tampa Stadium, Tampa, Florida)

January 27 1991	New York Giants	20	Buffalo Bills	19

Individual Awards

A.P. MVP--Joe Montana (San Francisco 49ers)
Bert Bell Trophy--Eric Green (Pittsburgh Steelers) [World Almanac]
Bert Bell Trophy--Randall Cunningham (Philadelphia Eagles)
Dan McGuire Award--Jim Kelly (Buffalo Bills)
George Halas Trophy--Bruce Smith (Buffalo Bills)
Jim Thorpe Trophy--Warren Moon (Houston Oilers)
P.F.W.A. MVP--Randall Cunningham (Philadelphia Eagles)
Pete Rozelle Award--Ottis Anderson (New York Giants)
UPI AFC Coach of the Year--Art Shell (Los Angeles Raiders)
UPI AFC Player of the Year--Warren Moon (Houston Oilers)
Bruce Smith (Buffalo Bills)
UPI AFC Rookie of the Year--Richmond Webb (Miami Dolphins)
UPI NFC Coach of the Year--Jimmy Johnson (Dallas Cowboys)
UPI NFC Player of the Year--Randall Cunningham (Philadelphia Eagles)
Charles Haley (San Francisco 49ers)
UPI NFC Rookie of the Year--Mark Carrier (Chicago Bears)

Hall of Fame Inductees

Buck Buchanan, Bob Griese, Franco Harris, Ted Hendricks, Jack Lambert, Tom Landry, Bob St. Clair

Notes

CBS signed a deal to continue broadcasts of NFC games for four years. This costs the network over $1 billion, meanwhile NBC signs a four year $752 million deal for four years of AFC games.

Canadian Football League

Eastern Division

Team Name	GP	W	L	T	PF	PA	Pts	Pct
Winnipeg Blue Bombers	18	12	6	0	472	398	24	.667
Toronto Argonauts	18	10	8	0	689	538	20	.556
Ottawa Rough Riders	18	7	11	0	540	602	14	.389
Hamilton Tiger-Cats	18	6	12	0	476	628	12	.333

Western Division

Calgary Stampeders	18	11	6	1	588	566	23	.639
Edmonton Eskimos	18	10	8	0	612	510	20	.556
Saskatchewan Roughriders	18	9	9	0	557	592	18	.500
British Columbia Lions	18	6	11	1	520	620	11	.306

Coaching Changes

Toronto--Don Matthews 10-8-0; Hamilton--Al Bruno 4-8-0, Dave Beckman 2-4-0; Calgary--Wally Buono 11-6-1; British Columbia--Lary Kuharich 2-7-1, Jim Young 0-1-0, Bob O'Billovich 4-3-0.

League Leaders

Yards Rushing		**Yards Passing**		**Passing %** (200 attempts)	
Robert Mimbs	1341	Kent Austin	4404	Joe Paopao	61.2
Reggie Barnes	1260	Tracy Ham	4286	Kent Austin	58.3
Tracy Ham	1096	Tom Burgess	3958	Tom Burgess	57.5
Damon Allen	776	Damon Allen	3883	Matt Dunigan	55.0
Milson Jones	765	Mike Kerrigan	3655	Doug Flutie	52.8

Receiving Yards		**Receptions**		**Points**	
Darrell K. Smith	1826	Craig Ellis	106	Dave Ridgway	233
Craig Ellis	1654	Ray Elgaard	94	Paul Osbaldiston	212
Ray Elgaard	1494	Darrell K. Smith	93	Mark McLaughlin	209
Stephen Jones	1184	Don Narcisse	86	Lance Chomyc	200
Allen Pitts	1172	Lucius Floyd	73	Ray Macoritti	186

Grey Cup Playoffs

November 11	Ottawa Rough Riders	25	at	Toronto Argonauts	34
November 11	Saskatchewan Roughriders	27	at	Edmonton Eskimos	43
November 18	Toronto Argonauts	17	at	Winnipeg Blue Bombers	20
November 18	Edmonton Eskimos	43	at	Calgary Stampeders	23
November 25	Winnipeg Blue Bombers	50		Edmonton Eskimos	11*

Individual Awards

Annis Stukus Trophy--Mike Riley (Winnipeg Blue Bombers)
CFL Award Most Outstanding Canadian--Ray Elgaard (Saskatchewan Roughriders)
CFL Award Most Outstanding Defensive Player--Greg Battle (Winnipeg Blue Bombers)
CFL Award Most Outstanding Offensive Lineman--Jim Mills (British Columbia Lions)
CFL Award Most Outstanding Player--Mike Clemons (Toronto Argonauts)
CFL Award Most Outstanding Rookie--Reggie Barnes (Ottawa Rough Riders)
Dave Dryburgh Memorial Trophy--Dave Ridgway (Saskatchewan Roughriders)
DeMarco-Becket Memorial Trophy--Jim Mills (British Columbia Lions)
Dr. Beattie Martin Trophy--Ray Elgaard (Saskatchewan Roughriders)
Eddie James Memorial Trophy--Tracy Ham (Edmonton Eskimos)
Frank M. Gibson Trophy--Reggie Barnes (Ottawa Rough Riders)
Grey Cup Most Outstanding Defensive Star--Greg Battle (Winnipeg Blue Bombers)
Grey Cup Most Outstanding Offensive Star--Tom Burgess (Winnipeg Blue Bombers)
Grey Cup Most Valuable Canadian--Warren Hudson (Winnipeg Blue Bombers)

*Game played in Vancouver.

Jackie Parker Trophy--Lucius Floyd (Saskatchewan Roughriders)
James P. McCaffrey Trophy--Greg Battle (Winnipeg Blue Bombers)
Jeff Nicklin Memorial Trophy--Craig Ellis (Edmonton Eskimos)
Jeff Russel Memorial Trophy--Michael Clemons (Toronto Argonauts)
Leo Dandurand Trophy--Chris Walby (Winnipeg Blue Bombers)
Lew Hayman Trophy--Paul Osbaldiston (Hamilton Tiger-Cats)
Norm Fieldgate Trophy--Stewart Hill (Edmonton Eskimos)

Hall of Fame Inductees

Jim Corrigall, Dave Fennell, Eagle Keys, Marv Luster, Ken Preston

Notes

Donald Crump became Commissioner of the Canadian Football League replacing Bill Baker who had been President/Chief Operating Officer.

HOCKEY

National Hockey League

Clarence Campbell Conference
Norris Division

Team Name	GP	W	L	T	GF	GA	Pts	Pct
Chicago Blackhawks	80	41	33	6	316	294	88	.550
St. Louis Blues	80	37	34	9	295	279	83	.519
Toronto Maple Leafs	80	38	38	4	337	358	80	.500
Minnesota North Stars	80	36	40	4	284	291	76	.475
Detroit Red Wings	80	28	38	14	288	323	70	.438

Smythe Division

Team Name	GP	W	L	T	GF	GA	Pts	Pct
Calgary Flames	80	42	23	15	348	265	99	.619
Edmonton Oilers	80	38	28	14	315	283	90	.563
Winnipeg Jets	80	37	32	11	298	290	85	.531
Los Angeles Kings	80	34	39	7	338	337	75	.469
Vancouver Canucks	80	25	41	14	245	306	64	.400

Prince of Wales Conference

Adams Division

Team Name	GP	W	L	T	GF	GA	Pts	Pct
Boston Bruins	80	46	25	9	289	232	101	.631
Buffalo Sabres	80	45	27	8	286	248	98	.613
Montreal Canadiens	80	41	28	11	288	234	93	.581
Hartford Whalers	80	38	33	9	275	268	85	.531
Quebec Nordiques	80	12	61	7	240	407	31	.194

Patrick Division

Team Name	GP	W	L	T	GF	GA	Pts	Pct
New York Rangers	80	36	31	13	279	267	85	.531
New Jersey Devils	80	37	34	9	295	288	83	.519
Washington Capitals	80	36	38	6	284	275	78	.488
New York Islanders	80	31	38	11	281	288	73	.456
Pittsburgh Penguins	80	32	40	8	318	359	72	.450
Philadelphia Flyers	80	30	39	11	290	297	71	.444

Coaching Changes

Toronto--Doug Carpenter 38-38-4; Edmonton--John Muckler 38-28-14; Winnipeg--Bob Murdoch 37-32-11; Los Angeles--Tom Webster 28-30-7, Cap Raeder and Rick Wilson 6-9-0 (while Webster was recovering from surgery); Boston--Mike Milbury 46-25-9; Buffalo--Rick Dudley 45-27-8; Hartford--Rick Ley 38-33-9; Quebec--Michel Bergeron 12-61-7; New York Rangers--Roger Neilson 36-31-13; New Jersey--Jim Schoenfield 6-6-2, John Cunniff 31-28-7; Washington--Bryan Murray 18-24-4, Terry Murray 18-14-2; New York Islanders--Al Arbour 31-38-11; Pittsburgh--Gene Ubriaco 10-14-2, Craig Patrick 22-26-6.

League Leaders

Goals		**Assists**		**Points**	
Brett Hull	72	Wayne Gretzky	102	Wayne Gretzky	142
Steve Yzerman	62	Mark Messier	84	Mark Messier	129
Cam Neely	55	Adam Oates	79	Steve Yzerman	127
Brian Bellows	55	Mario Lemieux	78	Mario Lemieux	123
Pat LaFontaine	54	Paul Coffey	74	Brett Hull	113

Penalty Minutes		**GAA** (1,500 minutes)		**Wins**	
Basil McRae	351	Patrick Roy	2.53	Patrick Roy	31
Alan May	339	Mike Liut	2.53	Daren Puppa	31
Marty McSorley	322	Rejean Lemelin	2.81	Jon Casey	31
Troy Mallette	305	Daren Puppa	2.89	Andy Moog	24
Wayne Van Dorp	303	Andy Moog	2.89	Bill Ranford	24

Shutouts		**Save %**	
Mike Liut	4	Patrick Roy	.912
Andy Moog	3	Mike Liut	.905
Mark Fitzpatrick	3	Daren Puppa	.903
Patrick Roy	3	Clint Malarchuk	.903
Jon Casey	3	Mark Fitzpatrick	.898

All Star Game

(Civic Arena, Pittsburgh)

January 21	Wales Conference	12	Campbell Conference	7

Stanley Cup Playoffs

April 4	Minnesota North Stars	2	at	Chicago Blackhawks	1
April 4	Toronto Maple Leafs	2	at	St. Louis Blues	4
April 4	Los Angeles Kings	5	at	Calgary Flames	3
April 4	Winnipeg Jets	7	at	Edmonton Oilers	5
April 5	Hartford Whalers	4	at	Boston Bruins	3
April 5	Montreal Canadiens	1	at	Buffalo Sabres	4
April 5	New York Islanders	1	at	New York Rangers	2
April 5	Washington Capitals	5	at	New Jersey Devils	4 [5:34]
April 6	Minnesota North Stars	3	at	Chicago Blackhawks	5
April 6	Toronto Maple Leafs	2	at	St. Louis Blues	4
April 6	Los Angeles Kings	5	at	Calgary Flames	8
April 6	Winnipeg Jets	2	at	Edmonton Oilers	3 [4:21]
April 7	Hartford Whalers	1	at	Boston Bruins	3
April 7	Montreal Canadiens	3	at	Buffalo Sabres	0

April 7	New York Islanders	2	at	New York Rangers	5
April 7	Washington Capitals	5	at	New Jersey Devils	6
April 8	Chicago Blackhawks	2	at	Minnesota North Stars	1
April 8	St. Louis Blues	6	at	Toronto Maple Leafs	5 [6:04]
April 8	Calgary Flames	1	at	Los Angeles Kings	2 [8:37]
April 8	Edmonton Oilers	1	at	Winnipeg Jets	2
April 9	Boston Bruins	3	at	Hartford Whalers	5
April 9	Buffalo Sabres	1	at	Montreal Canadiens	2 [12:35]
April 9	New York Rangers	3	at	New York Islanders	4 [20:59]
April 9	New Jersey Devils	2	at	Washington Capitals	1
April 10	Chicago Blackhawks	0	at	Minnesota North Stars	4
April 10	St. Louis Blues	2	at	Toronto Maple Leafs	4
April 10	Calgary Flames	4	at	Los Angeles Kings	12
April 10	Edmonton Oilers	3	at	Winnipeg Jets	4 [21:08]
April 11	Boston Bruins	6	at	Hartford Whalers	5
April 11	Buffalo Sabres	4	at	Montreal Canadiens	2
April 11	New York Rangers	6	at	New York Islanders	1
April 11	New Jersey Devils	1	at	Washington Capitals	3
April 12	Minnesota North Stars	1	at	Chicago Blackhawks	5
April 12	Toronto Maple Leafs	3	at	St. Louis Blues	4
April 12	Los Angeles Kings	1	at	Calgary Flames	5
April 12	Winnipeg Jets	3	at	Edmonton Oilers	4
April 13	Hartford Whalers	2	at	Boston Bruins	3
April 13	Montreal Canadiens	4	at	Buffalo Sabres	2
April 13	New York Islanders	5	at	New York Rangers	6
April 13	Washington Capitals	4	at	New Jersey Devils	3
April 14	Chicago Blackhawks	3	at	Minnesota North Stars	5
April 14	Calgary Flames	3	at	Los Angeles Kings	4 [23:14]
April 14	Edmonton Oilers	4	at	Winnipeg Jets	3
April 15	Boston Bruins	2	at	Hartford Whalers	3 [12:30]
April 15	Buffalo Sabres	2	at	Montreal Canadiens	5
April 15	New Jersey Devils	2	at	Washington Capitals	3
April 16	Minnesota North Stars	2	at	Chicago Blackhawks	5
April 16	Winnipeg Jets	1	at	Edmonton Oilers	4
April 17	Hartford Whalers	1	at	Boston Bruins	3
April 18	St. Louis Blues	4	at	Chicago Blackhawks	3
April 18	Los Angeles Kings	0	at	Edmonton Oilers	7
April 19	Montreal Canadiens	0	at	Boston Bruins	1
April 19	Washington Capitals	3	at	New York Rangers	7
April 20	St. Louis Blues	3	at	Chicago Blackhawks	5
April 20	Los Angeles Kings	1	at	Edmonton Oilers	6
April 21	Montreal Canadiens	4	at	Boston Bruins	5 [3:42]
April 21	Washington Capitals	6	at	New York Rangers	3
April 22	Chicago Blackhawks	4	at	St. Louis Blues	5
April 22	Edmonton Oilers	5	at	Los Angeles Kings	4
April 23	Boston Bruins	6	at	Montreal Canadiens	3
April 23	New York Rangers	1	at	Washington Capitals	7
April 24	Chicago Blackhawks	3	at	St. Louis Blues	2
April 24	Edmonton Oilers	6	at	Los Angeles Kings	5 [4:42]
April 25	Boston Bruins	1	at	Montreal Canadiens	4
April 25	New York Rangers	3	at	Washington Capitals	4 [0:34]
April 26	St. Louis Blues	2	at	Chicago Blackhawks	3
April 27	Montreal Canadiens	1	at	Boston Bruins	3
April 27	Washington Capitals	2	at	New York Rangers	1 [6:48]

April 28	Chicago Blackhawks	2	at	St. Louis Blues	4
April 30	St. Louis Blues	2	at	Chicago Blackhawks	8
May 2	Chicago Blackhawks	2	at	Edmonton Oilers	5
May 3	Washington Capitals	3	at	Boston Bruins	5
May 4	Chicago Blackhawks	4	at	Edmonton Oilers	3
May 5	Washington Capitals	0	at	Boston Bruins	3
May 6	Edmonton Oilers	1	at	Chicago Blackhawks	5
May 7	Boston Bruins	4	at	Washington Capitals	1
May 8	Edmonton Oilers	4	at	Chicago Blackhawks	2
May 9	Boston Bruins	3	at	Washington Capitals	2
May 10	Chicago Blackhawks	3	at	Edmonton Oilers	4
May 12	Edmonton Oilers	8	at	Chicago Blackhawks	4
May 15	Edmonton Oilers	3	at	Boston Bruins	2 [55:13]
May 18	Edmonton Oilers	7	at	Boston Bruins	2
May 20	Boston Bruins	2	at	Edmonton Oilers	1
May 22	Boston Bruins	1	at	Edmonton Oilers	5
May 24	Edmonton Oilers	4	at	Boston Bruins	1

All Star Teams

First Team		Second Team
Patrick Roy	Goal	Daren Puppa
Ray Bourque	Defense	Paul Coffey
Al MacInnis	Defense	Doug Wilson
Mark Messier	Center	Wayne Gretzky
Brett Hull	Right Wing	Cam Neely
Luc Robitaille	Left Wing	Brian Bellows

Individual Awards

Alka-Seltzer Plus Award--Paul Cavallini (St. Louis Blues)
Art Ross Trophy--Wayne Gretzky (Los Angeles Kings)
Bill Masterton Trophy--Gord Kluzak (Boston Bruins)
Bud Man of the Year--Kevin Lowe (Edmonton Oilers)
Calder Memorial Trophy--Sergei Makarov (Calgary Flames)
Conn Smythe Trophy--Bill Ranford (Edmonton Oilers)
Dodge Performer of the Year--Pat LaFontaine (New York Islanders)
Dodge Ram Tough Award--Brett Hull (St. Louis Blues)
Frank J. Selke Trophy--Rick Meagher (St. Louis Blues)
Hart Memorial Trophy--Mark Messier (Edmonton Oilers)
Jack Adams Award--Bob Murdoch (Winnipeg Jets)
James Norris Trophy--Ray Bourque (Boston Bruins)
King Clancy Trophy--Kevin Lowe (Edmonton Oilers)
Lady Byng Memorial Trophy--Brett Hull (St. Louis Blues)
Lester B. Pearson Award--Mark Messier (Edmonton Oilers)
Lester Patrick Trophy--Len Ceglarski
NHL All Star Game MVP--Mario Lemieux (Pittsburgh Penguins)
Trico Goaltender Award--Patrick Roy (Montreal Canadiens)
Vezina Trophy--Patrick Roy (Montreal Canadiens)
William M. Jennings Trophy--Andy Moog and Rejean Lemelin (Boston Bruins)

Hall of Fame Inductees

Bill Barber, Fern Flaman, Gilbert Perreault, Bud Poile

Notes

St. Louis Blues sign Brett Hull to a contract worth $1.5 million a year, this is an increase of 1200% from his previous contract.

Other Sports

Horseracing--Kentucky Derby won by Unbridled (time 2;02, purse $581,000).

Heavyweight Boxing--James (Buster) Douglas knocked out Mike Tyson in 10 rounds (WBA, WBC, IBF),

Evander Holyfield knocked out James (Buster) Douglas in 3 rounds (WBA, WBC, IBF).

Golf--U.S. Open won by Hale Irwin in a playoff with Mike Donald on the first hole after scores of 280-280, 74-74.

Auto Racing--Indianapolis 500 won by Arie Luyendyk (ave. speed 185.981 MPH).

Tennis--U.S. Open won by Pete Sampras in the men's singles.
U.S. Open won by Gabriela Sabatini in the women's singles.
U.S. Open won by Pieter Aldrick and Danie Visser in the men's doubles.
U.S. Open won by Gigi Fernandez and Martina Navratilova in the women's doubles.
U.S. Open won by Elizabeth Smylie and Todd Woodbridge in the mixed doubles.

1991

BASEBALL
National League
East

Team Name	W	L	Pct	GB	R	OR
Pittsburgh Pirates	98	64	.605	-	768	632
St. Louis Cardinals	84	78	.519	14	651	648
Philadelphia Phillies	78	84	.481	20	629	680
Chicago Cubs	77	83	.481	20	695	734
New York Mets	77	84	.478	20.5	640	646
Montreal Expos	71	90	.441	26.5	579	655

West

Team Name	W	L	Pct	GB	R	OR
Atlanta Braves	94	68	.580	-	749	644
Los Angeles Dodgers	93	69	.574	1	665	565
San Diego Padres	84	78	.519	10	636	646
San Francisco Giants	75	87	.463	19	649	697
Cincinnati Reds	74	88	.457	20	689	691
Houston Astros	65	97	.401	29	605	717

Coaching Changes

St. Louis--Joe Torre 84-78; Philadelphia--Nick Leyva 4-9, Jim Fregosi 74-75; Chicago--Don Zimmer 18-19, Joe Altobelli 1-1, Jim Essian 58-63; New York--Bud Harrelson 74-80, Mike Cubbage 3-4; Montreal--Buck Rodgers 20-29, Tom Runnells 51-61; Atlanta--Bobby Cox 94-68; San Diego--Greg Riddoch 84-78.

League Leaders

Batting Average

Terry Pendleton	.319
Hal Morris	.318
Tony Gwynn	.317
Willie McGee	.312
Felix Jose	.305

Home Runs

Howard Johnson	38
Matt Williams	34
Ron Gant	32
Andre Dawson	31
Fred McGriff	31

RBI

Howard Johnson	117
Barry Bonds	116
Will Clark	116
Fred McGriff	106
Ron Gant	105

Stolen Bases

Marquis Grissom	76
Otis Nixon	72
Delino DeShields	56
Ray Lankford	44
Barry Bonds	43

ERA

Dennis Martinez	2.39
Jose Rijo	2.51
Tom Glavine	2.55
Tim Belcher	2.62
Pete Harnisch	2.70

Wins

John Smiley	20
Tom Glavine	20
Steve Avery	18
Ramon Martinez	17
Zane Smith	16

Saves

Lee Smith	47
Rob Dibble	31
John Franco	30
Mitch Williams	30
Dave Righetti	24

Strikeouts

David Cone	241
Greg Maddox	198
Tom Glavine	192
Pete Harnisch	172
Jose Rijo	172

NLCS

October 9	Atlanta Braves	1	at	Pittsburgh Pirates	5
October 10	Atlanta Braves	1	at	Pittsburgh Pirates	0
October 12	Pittsburgh Pirates	3	at	Atlanta Braves	10
October 13	Pittsburgh Pirates	3	at	Atlanta Braves	2 [10]
October 14	Pittsburgh Pirates	1	at	Atlanta Braves	0
October 16	Atlanta Braves	1	at	Pittsburgh Pirates	0
October 17	Atlanta Braves	4	at	Pittsburgh Pirates	0

Notes

The Montreal Expos were forced to play their final 9 home games on the road due to problems at Olympic Stadium.

American League

East

Team Name	W	L	Pct	GB	R	OR
Toronto Blue Jays	91	71	.562	-	684	622
Boston Red Sox	84	78	.519	7	731	712
Detroit Tigers	84	78	.519	7	817	794
Milwaukee Brewers	83	79	.512	8	799	744
New York Yankees	71	91	.438	20	674	777
Baltimore Orioles	67	95	.414	24	686	796
Cleveland Indians	57	105	.352	34	576	759

West

Team Name	W	L	Pct	GB	R	OR
Minnesota Twins	95	67	.586	-	776	652
Chicago White Sox	87	75	.537	8	758	681
Texas Rangers	85	77	.525	10	829	814
Oakland Athletics	84	78	.519	11	760	776
Seattle Mariners	83	79	.512	12	702	674
Kansas City Royals	82	80	.506	13	727	722
California Angels	81	81	.500	14	653	649

Coaching Changes

Toronto--Cito Gaston 72-57, Gene Tenace 19-14; New York--Stump Merrill 71-91; Baltimore--Frank Robinson 13-24, John Oates 54-71; Cleveland--John McNamara 25-52, Mike Hargrove 32-53; Kansas City--John Wathan 15-22, Bob Schaeffer 1-0, Hal McRae 66-58; California--Doug Rader 61-63, Buck Rodgers 20-18.

League Leaders

Batting Average		Home Runs		RBI	
Julio Franco	.341	Jose Canseco	44	Cecil Fielder	133
Wade Boggs	.332	Cecil Fielder	44	Jose Canseco	122
Willie Randolph	.327	Cal Ripken Jr.	34	Ruben Sierra	116
Ken Griffey Jr.	.327	Joe Carter	33	Cal Ripken	114
Paul Molitor	.325	Frank Thomas	32	Frank Thomas	109

Stolen Bases		**ERA**		**Wins**	
Rickey Henderson	58	Roger Clemens	2.62	Scott Erickson	20
Roberto Alomar	53	Tom Candiotti	2.65	Bill Gullickson	20
Tim Raines	51	Bill Wegman	2.84	Mark Langston	19
Luis Polonia	48	Jim Abbott	2.89	Chuck Finley	18
Milt Cuyler	41	Nolan Ryan	2.91	Roger Clemens	18

Saves		**Strikeouts**	
Bryan Harvey	46	Roger Clemens	241
Dennis Eckersley	43	Randy Johnson	228
Rick Aguilera	42	Nolan Ryan	203
Jeff Reardon	40	Jack McDowell	191
Jeff Montgomery	33	Mark Langston	183

All Star Game
(The Skydome, Toronto)

July 9	American League	4		National League	2

ALCS

October 8	Toronto Blue Jays	4	at	Minnesota Twins	5
October 9	Toronto Blue Jays	5	at	Minnesota Twins	2
October 11	Minnesota Twins	3	at	Toronto Blue Jays	2 [10]
October 12	Minnesota Twins	9	at	Toronto Blue Jays	3
October 13	Minnesota Twins	8	at	Toronto Blue Jays	5

World Series

October 19	Atlanta Braves	2	at	Minnesota Twins	5
October 20	Atlanta Braves	2	at	Minnesota Twins	3
October 22	Minnesota Twins	4	at	Atlanta Braves	5 [12]
October 23	Minnesota Twins	2	at	Atlanta Braves	3
October 24	Minnesota Twins	5	at	Atlanta Braves	14
October 26	Atlanta Braves	3	at	Minnesota Twins	4 [11]
October 27	Atlanta Braves	0	at	Minnesota Twins	1 [10]

Individual Awards

ALCS MVP--Kirby Puckett (Minnesota Twins AL)
Arch Ward Memorial Trophy--Cal Ripken Jr. (Baltimore Orioles AL)
Baseball Writers Award--Terry Pendleton (Atlanta Braves NL)
Cal Ripken Jr. (Baltimore Orioles AL)
Cy Young Award--Tom Glavine (Atlanta Braves NL)
Roger Clemens (Boston Red Sox AL)
NLCS MVP--Steve Avery (Atlanta Braves NL)
Rookie of the Year--Jeff Bagwell (Houston Astros NL)
Chuck Knoblauch (Minnesota Twins AL)
Sporting News Executive of the Year--Andy MacPhail (Minnesota Twins AL)
Sporting News Manager of the Year--Bobby Cox (Atlanta Braves NL)
Tom Kelly (Minnesota Twins AL)
Sporting News Pitcher of the Year--Tom Glavine (Atlanta Braves NL)
Roger Clemens (Boston Red Sox AL)
Sporting News Player of the Year--Barry Bonds (Pittsburgh Pirates NL)
Cal Ripken Jr. (Baltimore Orioles AL)

Sporting News Rookie of the Year--Jeff Bagwell (Houston Astros NL)
Al Osuna (Houston Astros NL)
Chuck Knoblauch (Minnesota Twins AL)
Juan Guzman (Toronto Blue Jays AL)
World Series MVP--Jack Morris (Minnesota Twins AL)

Hall of Fame Inductees

Rod Carew, Ferguson Jenkins, Tony Lazzeri, Gaylord Perry, Bill Veeck

Notes

Major League Baseball umpires staged a 2 day walkout at the beginning of the 1991 season.

BASKETBALL
National Basketball Association
Eastern Conference
Atlantic Division

Team Name	GP	W	L	PPGF	PPGA	Pct	GB
Boston Celtics	82	56	26	111.5	105.7	.683	-
Philadelphia 76ers	82	44	38	105.4	105.6	.537	12
New York Knickerbockers	82	39	43	103.1	103.3	.476	17
Washington Bullets	82	30	52	101.4	106.4	.366	26
New Jersey Nets	82	26	56	102.9	107.5	.317	30
Miami Heat	82	24	58	101.8	107.8	.293	32

Central Division

Team Name	GP	W	L	PPGF	PPGA	Pct	GB
Chicago Bulls	82	61	21	110.0	101.0	.744	-
Detroit Pistons	82	50	32	100.1	96.8	.610	11
Milwaukee Bucks	82	48	34	106.4	104.0	.585	13
Atlanta Hawks	82	43	39	109.8	109.0	.524	18
Indiana Pacers	82	41	41	111.7	112.1	.500	20
Cleveland Cavaliers	82	33	49	101.7	104.2	.402	28
Charlotte Hornets	82	26	56	102.8	108.0	.317	35

Western Conference

Midwest Division

Team Name	GP	W	L	PPGF	PPGA	Pct	GB
San Antonio Spurs	82	55	27	107.1	102.6	.671	-
Utah Jazz	82	54	28	104.0	100.7	.659	1
Houston Rockets	82	52	30	106.7	103.2	.634	3
Orlando Magic	82	31	51	105.9	109.9	.378	24
Minnesota Timberwolves	82	29	53	99.6	103.5	.354	26
Dallas Mavericks	82	28	54	99.9	104.5	.341	27
Denver Nuggets	82	20	62	119.9	130.8	.244	35

Pacific Division

Team Name	GP	W	L	PPGF	PPGA	Pct	GB
Portland Trail Blazers	82	63	19	114.7	106.0	.768	-
Los Angeles Lakers	82	58	24	106.3	99.6	.707	5
Phoenix Suns	82	55	27	114.0	107.5	.671	8
Golden State Warriors	82	44	38	116.6	115.0	.537	19
Seattle SuperSonics	82	41	41	106.6	105.4	.500	22
Los Angeles Clippers	82	31	51	103.5	107.0	.378	32
Sacramento Kings	82	25	57	96.7	103.5	.305	38

Coaching Changes

Boston--Chris Ford 56-26; New York--Stu Jackson 7-8, John McLeod 32-35; Atlanta--Bob Weiss 43-39; Indiana--Dick Versace 9-16, Bob Hill 32-25; Charlotte--Gene Littles 26-56; Dallas--Rich Adubato 28-54; Denver--Paul Westhead 20-62; L.A. Lakers--Mike Dunleavy 58-24; Seattle--K.C. Jones 41-41; L.A. Clippers--Mike Schuler 31-51; Sacramento--Dick Motta 25-57.

League Leaders

Field Goal %

Buck Williams	.602
Robert Parish	.598
Kevin Gamble	.587
Charles Barkley	.570
Vlade Divac	.565

Free Throw %

Reggie Miller	.918
Jeff Malone	.917
Ricky Pierce	.913
Kelly Tripucka	.910
Earvin Johnson	.906

Assists per Game

John Stockton	14.2
Earvin Johnson	12.5
Michael Adams	10.5
Kevin Johnson	10.1
Tim Hardaway	9.7

Points

Michael Jordan	2580
Karl Malone	2382
Patrick Ewing	2154
Chris Mullin	2107
Dominique Wilkins	2101

Rebounds per Game

David Robinson	13.0
Dennis Rodman	12.5
Charles Oakley	12.1
Karl Malone	11.8
Patrick Ewing	11.2

All Star Game

(Charlotte Coliseum, Charlotte)

February 10	East Division	116	West Division	114

NBA Championship

April 25	Utah Jazz	129	at	Phoenix Suns	90
April 25	Golden State Warriors	121	at	San Antonio Spurs	130
April 25	Houston Rockets	92	at	Los Angeles Lakers	94
April 25	New York Knickerbockers	85	at	Chicago Bulls	126
April 25	Philadelphia 76ers	99	at	Milwaukee Bucks	90
April 26	Seattle SuperSonics	102	at	Portland Trail Blazers	110
April 26	Indiana Pacers	120	at	Boston Celtics	127
April 26	Atlanta Hawks	103	at	Detroit Pistons	98
April 27	Utah Jazz	92	at	Phoenix Suns	102
April 27	Golden State Warriors	111	at	San Antonio Spurs	98
April 27	Houston Rockets	98	at	Los Angeles Lakers	109
April 27	Philadelphia 76ers	116	at	Milwaukee Bucks	112 [OT]
April 28	Seattle SuperSonics	106	at	Portland Trail Blazers	115
April 28	New York Knickerbockers	79	at	Chicago Bulls	89
April 28	Indiana Pacers	130	at	Boston Celtics	118
April 28	Atlanta Hawks	88	at	Detroit Pistons	101
April 30	Portland Trail Blazers	99	at	Seattle SuperSonics	102
April 30	Phoenix Suns	98	at	Utah Jazz	107
April 30	Los Angeles Lakers	94	at	Houston Rockets	90
April 30	Chicago Bulls	103	at	New York Knickerbockers	94
April 30	Milwaukee Bucks	100	at	Philadelphia 76ers	121
April 30	Detroit Pistons	103	at	Atlanta Hawks	91
May 1	San Antonio Spurs	106	at	Golden State Warriors	109
May 1	Boston Celtics	112	at	Indiana Pacers	105
May 2	Portland Trail Blazers	89	at	Seattle SuperSonics	101

May 2	Phoenix Suns	93	at	Utah Jazz	101
May 2	Detroit Pistons	111	at	Atlanta Hawks	123
May 3	San Antonio Spurs	97	at	Golden State Warriors	110
May 3	Boston Celtics	113	at	Indiana Pacers	116
May 4	Seattle SuperSonics	107	at	Portland Trail Blazers	119
May 4	Philadelphia 76ers	92	at	Chicago Bulls	105
May 5	Golden State Warriors	116	at	Los Angeles Lakers	125
May 5	Indiana Pacers	121	at	Boston Celtics	124
May 5	Atlanta Hawks	81	at	Detroit Pistons	113
May 6	Philadelphia 76ers	100	at	Chicago Bulls	112
May 7	Utah Jazz	97	at	Portland Trail Blazers	117
May 7	Detroit Pistons	86	at	Boston Celtics	75
May 8	Golden State Warriors	125	at	Los Angeles Lakers	124
May 9	Utah Jazz	116	at	Portland Trail Blazers	118
May 9	Detroit Pistons	103	at	Boston Celtics	109
May 10	Los Angeles Lakers	115	at	Golden State Warriors	112
May 10	Chicago Bulls	97	at	Philadelphia 76ers	99
May 11	Portland Trail Blazers	101	at	Utah Jazz	107
May 11	Boston Celtics	115	at	Detroit Pistons	83
May 12	Portland Trail Blazers	104	at	Utah Jazz	101
May 12	Los Angeles Lakers	123	at	Golden State Warriors	107
May 12	Chicago Bulls	101	at	Philadelphia 76ers	85
May 13	Boston Celtics	97	at	Detroit Pistons	104
May 14	Utah Jazz	96	at	Portland Trail Blazers	103
May 14	Golden State Warriors	119	at	Los Angeles Lakers	124 [OT]
May 14	Philadelphia 76ers	95	at	Chicago Bulls	100
May 15	Detroit Pistons	116	at	Boston Celtics	111
May 17	Boston Celtics	113	at	Detroit Pistons	117 [OT]
May 18	Los Angeles Lakers	111	at	Portland Trail Blazers	106
May 19	Detroit Pistons	83	at	Chicago Bulls	94
May 21	Los Angeles Lakers	98	at	Portland Trail Blazers	109
May 21	Detroit Pistons	97	at	Chicago Bulls	105
May 24	Portland Trail Blazers	92	at	Los Angeles Lakers	106
May 25	Chicago Bulls	113	at	Detroit Pistons	107
May 26	Portland Trail-Blazers	95	at	Los Angeles Lakers	116
May 27	Chicago Bulls	115	at	Detroit Pistons	94
May 28	Los Angeles Lakers	84	at	Portland Trail Blazers	95
May 30	Portland Trail Blazers	90	at	Los Angeles Lakers	91
June 2	Los Angeles Lakers	93	at	Chicago Bulls	91
June 5	Los Angeles Lakers	86	at	Chicago Bulls	107
June 7	Chicago Bulls	104	at	Los Angeles Lakers	96 [OT]
June 9	Chicago Bulls	97	at	Los Angeles Lakers	82
June 12	Chicago Bulls	108	at	Los Angeles Lakers	101

All Star Teams

First Team	Second Team	Third Team
Michael Jordan	Kevin Johnson	John Stockton
Earvin Johnson	Clyde Drexler	Joe Dumars
David Robinson	Patrick Ewing	Hakeem Olajuwon
Karl Malone	Dominique Wilkins	James Worthy
Charles Barkley	Chris Mullin	Bernard King

Individual Awards

Defensive Player of the Year--Dennis Rodman (Detroit Pistons)
Eddie Gottlieb Trophy--Derrick Coleman (New Jersey Nets)
Executive of the Year--Bucky Buckwalter (Portland Trail Blazers)
J. Walter Kennedy Citizenship Award--Kevin Johnson (Phoenix Suns)
Maurice Podoloff Trophy--Michael Jordan (Chicago Bulls)
Most Improved Player--Scott Skiles (Orlando Magic)
NBA All Star Game MVP--Charles Barkley (Philadelphia 76ers)
NBA Finals MVP--Michael Jordan (Chicago Bulls)
Red Auerbach Trophy--Don Chaney (Houston Rockets)
Schick Award--David Robinson (San Antonio Spurs)
Sixth Man Award--Detlef Schrempf (Indiana Pacers)

Hall of Fame Inductees

Nate Archibald, Dave Cowens, Larry Fleisher, Harry Gallatin, Bob Knight, Larry O'Brien, Boris Stankovic,

Notes

Earvin "Magic" Johnson announces his retirement from the game the after testing positive for the HIV virus. Johnson does return briefly to help the U.S. "Dream Team" win the 1992 Olympic Gold Medal in basketball. Johnson will return to the Los Angeles Laker line-up for the 1995-1996 season.

FOOTBALL

National Football League
National Conference
Eastern Division

Team Name	GP	W	L	T	PF	PA	Pct
Washington Redskins	16	14	2	0	485	224	.875
Dallas Cowboys	16	11	5	0	342	310	.688
Philadelphia Eagles	16	10	6	0	285	244	.625
New York Giants	16	8	8	0	281	297	.500
Phoenix Cardinals	16	4	12	0	196	344	.250

Central Division

Team Name	GP	W	L	T	PF	PA	Pct
Detroit Lions	16	12	4	0	339	295	.750
Chicago Bears	16	11	5	0	299	269	.688
Minnesota Vikings	16	8	8	0	301	306	.500
Green Bay Packers	16	4	12	0	273	313	.250
Tampa Bay Buccaneers	16	3	13	0	199	365	.188

Western Division

Team Name	GP	W	L	T	PF	PA	Pct
New Orleans Saints	16	11	5	0	341	211	.688
Atlanta Falcons	16	10	6	0	361	338	.625
San Francisco 49ers	16	10	6	0	393	239	.625
Los Angeles Rams	16	3	13	0	234	390	.188

American Conference

Eastern Division

Buffalo Bills	16	13	3	0	458	318	.813
New York Jets	16	8	8	0	314	293	.500
Miami Dolphins	16	8	8	0	343	349	.500
New England Patriots	16	6	10	0	211	305	.375
Indianapolis Colts	16	1	15	0	143	381	.063

Central Division

Houston Oilers	16	11	5	0	386	251	.688
Pittsburgh Steelers	16	7	9	0	292	344	.438
Cleveland Browns	16	6	10	0	293	298	.375
Cincinnati Bengals	16	3	13	0	263	435	.188

Western Division

Denver Broncos	16	12	4	0	304	235	.750
Kansas City Chiefs	16	10	6	0	322	252	.625
Los Angeles Raiders	16	9	7	0	298	297	.563
Seattle Seahawks	16	7	9	0	276	261	.438
San Diego Chargers	16	4	12	0	274	342	.250

Coaching Changes

Philadelphia--Rich Kotite 10-6-0; N.Y. Giants--Ray Handley 8-8-0; Tampa Bay--Richard Williamson 3-13-0; New England--Dick MacPherson 6-10-0; Indianapolis--Ron Meyer 0-5-0, Rick Venturi 1-10-0; Cleveland--Bill Belichick 6-10-0.

League Leaders

Yards Rushing		**Yards Passing**		**Passing %** (300 attempts)	
Emmitt Smith	1563	Warren Moon	4690	Troy Aikman	65.3
Barry Sanders	1548	Dan Marino	3970	Jim Kelly	64.1
Thurman Thomas	1407	Jim Kelly	3844	Bernie Kosar	62.1
Rodney Hampton	1059	Mark Rypien	3564	Warren Moon	61.7
Earnst Byner	1048	Bernie Kosar	3487	Jeff George	60.2

Receiving Yards		**Receptions**		**Field Goals**	
Michael Irvin	1523	Haywood Jeffries	100	Pete Stoyanovich	31
Gary Clark	1340	Michael Irvin	93	Chip Lohmiller	31
Jerry Rice	1206	Drew Hill	90	Jeff Jaeger	29
Haywood Jeffries	1181	Marv Cook	82	Roger Ruzek	28
Michael Haynes	1122	Andre Reed	81	David Treadwell	27

Punt Return Yards		**Kickoff Return Yards**	
Brian Mitchell	600	Mel Gray	929
Mel Gray	385	Dexter Carter	839
Willie Drewrey	360	Chris Warren	792
Tim Brown	330	Jon Vaughn	717
Rod Woodson	320	Nate Lewis	578

Pro Bowl Game

(Aloha Stadium, Honolulu)

February 2 1992	National Conference	21		American Conference	15

NFL Playoffs

December 28	Los Angeles Raiders	6	at	Kansas City Chiefs	10
December 28	Atlanta Falcons	27	at	New Orleans Saints	20
December 29	New York Jets	10	at	Houston Oilers	17
December 29	Dallas Cowboys	17	at	Chicago Bears	13
January 4 1992	Houston Oilers	24	at	Denver Broncos	26
January 4 1992	Atlanta Falcons	7	at	Washington Redskins	24
January 5 1992	Kansas City Chiefs	14	at	Buffalo Bills	37
January 5 1992	Dallas Cowboys	6	at	Detroit Lions	38
January 12 1992	Denver Broncos	7	at	Buffalo Bills	10
January 12 1992	Detroit Lions	10	at	Washington Redskins	41

Super Bowl XXVI

(Hubert H. Humphrey Metrodome, Minneapolis)

January 26 1992	Washington Redskins	37	Buffalo Bills	24

Individual Awards

A.P. MVP--Thurman Thomas (Buffalo Bills)
Bert Bell Trophy--Mike Croel (Denver Broncos) [World Almanac]
Bert Bell Trophy--Barry Sanders (Detroit Lions)
Dan McGuire Award--Michael Irvin (Dallas Cowboys)
George Halas Trophy--Pat Swilling (New Orleans Saints)
Jim Thorpe Trophy--Thurman Thomas (Buffalo Bills)
P.F.W.A. MVP--Thurman Thomas (Buffalo Bills)
Pete Rozelle Award--Mark Rypien (Washington Redskins)
U.P.I. AFC Coach of the Year--Dan Reeves (Denver Broncos)
U.P.I. AFC Player of the Year--Thurman Thomas (Buffalo Bills)
Cornelius Bennett (Buffalo Bills)
U.P.I. AFC Rookie of the Year--Mike Croel (Denver Broncos)
U.P.I. NFC Coach of the Year--Wayne Fontes (Detroit Lions)
U.P.I. NFC Player of the Year--Mark Rypien (Washington Redskins)
Reggie White (Philadelphia Eagles)
U.P.I. NFC Rookie of the Year--Lawrence Dawsey (Tampa Bay Buccaneers)

Hall of Fame Inductees

Earl Campbell, John Hannah, Stan Jones, Tex Schramm, Jan Stenerud

Canadian Football League

Eastern Division

Team Name	GP	W	L	T	PF	PA	Pts	Pct
Toronto Argonauts	18	13	5	0	647	526	26	.722
Winnipeg Blue Bombers	18	9	9	0	516	499	18	.500
Ottawa Rough Riders	18	7	11	0	522	577	14	.389
Hamilton Tiger-Cats	18	3	15	0	400	599	6	.167

Western Division

Edmonton Eskimos	18	12	6	0	671	569	24	.667
Calgary Stampeders	18	11	7	0	596	552	22	.611
British Columbia Lions	18	11	7	0	661	587	22	.611
Saskatchewan Roughriders	18	6	12	0	606	710	12	.333

Coaching Changes

Toronto--Adam Rita 13-5-0; Winnipeg--Darryl Rogers 9-9-0; Ottawa--Steve Goldman 0-4-0, Joe Faragalli 7-7-0; Hamilton--David Beckman 0-8-0, John Gregory 3-7-0; Edmonton--Ron Lancaster 12-6-0; British Columbia--Bob O'Billovich 11-7-0; Saskatchewan--John Gregory1-6-0, Don Matthews 5-6-0.

League Leaders

Yards Rushing		**Yards Passing**		**Passing %** (100 attempts)	
Robert Mimbs	1769	Doug Flutie	6619	Doug Flutie	63.8
Reggie Barnes	1486	Damon Allen	4275	Matt Dunigan	61.7
Jon Volpe	1395	Tom Burgess	4212	Danny Barrett	56.8
Reggie Taylor	1293	Kent Austin	4137	Warren Jones	55.7
Damon Allen	1036	Tracy Ham	3862	Kent Austin	54.5

Receiving Yards		**Receptions**		**Points**	
Allen Pitts	1764	Allen Pitts	118	Lance Chomyc	236
Ray Alexander	1605	Ray Alexander	104	Dave Ridgway	216
Matt Clark	1530	Lucius Floyd	84	Lui Passaglia	210
Darrell K. Smith	1399	Matt Clark	79	Mark McLaughlin	208
Raghib Ismail	1300	Don Narcisse	76	Terry Baker	202

Grey Cup Playoffs

November 10	Ottawa Rough Riders	8	at	Winnipeg Blue Bombers	26
November 10	British Columbia Lions	41	at	Calgary Stampeders	43
November 17	Winnipeg Blue Bombers	3	at	Toronto Argonauts	42
November 17	Calgary Stampeders	38	at	Edmonton Eskimos	36
November 24	Toronto Argonauts	36		Calgary Stampeders	21*

Individual Awards

Annis Stukus Trophy--Adam Rita (Toronto Argonauts)
Dave Dryburgh Memorial Trophy--Dave Ridgway (Saskatchewan Roughriders)
DeMarco-Becket Memorial Trophy--Jim Mills (British Columbia Lions)
Dr. Beattie Martin Trophy--Blake Marshall (Edmonton Eskimos)
Eddie James Memorial Trophy--Jon Volpe (British Columbia Lions)
Frank M. Gibson Trophy--Raghib Ismail (Toronto Argonauts)
G.M.C. Award Most Outstanding Canadian--Blake Marshall (Edmonton Eskimos)
G.M.C. Award Most Outstanding Defensive Player--Greg Battle (Winnipeg Blue Bombers)
G.M.C. Award Most Outstanding Offensive Lineman--Jim Mills (British Columbia Lions)
G.M.C. Award Most Outstanding Player--Doug Flutie (British Columbia Lions)
G.M.C. Award Most Outstanding Rookie--Jon Volpe (British Columbia Lions)
Grey Cup Most Valuable Canadian--David Sapunjis (Calgary Stampeders)
Grey Cup Most Valuable Player--Raghib Ismail (Toronto Argonauts)

*Game played in Winnipeg

Jackie Parker Trophy--Jon Volpe (British Columbia Lions)
James P. McCaffrey Trophy--Greg Battle (Winnipeg Blue Bombers)
Jeff Nicklin Memorial Trophy--Doug Flutie (British Columbia Lions)
Jeff Russel Memorial Trophy--Robert Mimbs (Winnipeg Blue Bombers)
Leo Dandurand Trophy--Chris Walby (Winnipeg Blue Bombers)
Lew Hayman Trophy--Lance Chomyc (Toronto Argonauts)
Norm Fieldgate Trophy--Will Johnson (Calgary Stampeders)

Hall of Fame Inductees

Tom Hinton, Brian Kelly, Norm Kimball, Jim Young

World League of American Football

Team Name	GP	W	L	T	PF	PA	Pct
European Division							
London Monarchs	10	9	1	0	310	121	.900
Barcelona Dragons	10	8	2	0	206	126	.800
Frankfurt Galaxy	10	7	3	0	155	139	.700
North American East							
NY-NJ Knights	10	5	5	0	257	155	.500
Orlando Thunder	10	5	5	0	242	286	.500
Montreal Machine	10	4	6	0	145	244	.400
Raleigh-Durham Skyhawks	10	0	10	0	123	300	.000
North American West							
Birmingham Fire	10	5	5	0	140	140	.500
San Antonio Riders	10	4	6	0	176	196	.400
Sacramento Surge	10	3	7	0	179	226	.300

Coaching

London--Larry Kennan 9-1-0; Barcelona--Jack Bicknell 8-2-0; Frankfurt--Jack Elway 7-3-0; NY/NJ--Darrel Davis 5-5-0; Orlando--Don Matthews 5-5-0; Montreal--Jacques Dussault 4-6-0; Raleigh/Durham--Roman Gabriel 0-10-0; Birmingham--Chan Gailey 5-5-0; San Antonio--Mike Riley 4-6-0; Sacramento--Kay Stephenson 3-7-0

League Leaders

Passing

	Attempts	Completions	Yards
Stan Gelbaugh	303	189	2655
Scott Erney	158	79	1186
Jeff Graham	272	157	2407
Kerwin Bell	325	181	2214
Mike Elkins	312	153	2068

Receptions		Receiving Yards		Rushing Yards	
Judd Garrett	71	Jon Horton	931	Eric Wilkerson	717
B. Williams	59	B. Williams	811	Baker	648
Carl Parker	52	Carl Parker	801	Ricky Blake	554
Jon Horton	43	Gene Taylor	745	Elroy Harris	540
Lonnie Turner	41	Monty Gilbreath	643	Ricky Johnson	423

WLAF Championship

June 1	Barcelona Dragons	10	at	Birmingham Fire	3
June 2	London Monarchs	42	at	NY-NJ Knights	26
June 9	Barcelona Dragons	0	at	London Monarchs	21

HOCKEY

National Hockey League

Clarence Campbell Conference
Norris Division

Team Name	GP	W	L	T	GF	GA	Pts	Pct
Chicago Blackhawks	80	49	23	8	284	211	106	.663
St. Louis Blues	80	47	22	11	310	250	105	.656
Detroit Red Wings	80	34	36	8	273	298	76	.475
Minnesota North Stars	80	27	39	14	256	266	68	.425
Toronto Maple Leafs	80	23	46	11	241	318	57	.356

Smythe Division

Team Name	GP	W	L	T	GF	GA	Pts	Pct
Los Angeles Kings	80	46	24	10	340	254	102	.638
Calgary Flames	80	46	26	8	344	263	100	.625
Edmonton Oilers	80	37	37	6	272	272	80	.500
Vancouver Canucks	80	28	43	9	243	315	65	.406
Winnipeg Jets	80	26	43	11	260	288	63	.394

Prince of Wales Conference

Adams Division

Team Name	GP	W	L	T	GF	GA	Pts	Pct
Boston Bruins	80	44	24	12	299	264	100	.625
Montreal Canadiens	80	39	30	11	273	249	89	.556
Buffalo Sabres	80	31	30	19	292	278	81	.506
Hartford Whalers	80	31	38	11	238	276	73	.456
Quebec Nordiques	80	16	50	14	236	354	46	.288

Patrick Division

Team Name	GP	W	L	T	GF	GA	Pts	Pct
Pittsburgh Penguins	80	41	33	6	342	305	88	.550
New York Rangers	80	36	31	13	297	265	85	.531
Washington Capitals	80	37	36	7	258	258	81	.506
New Jersey Devils	80	32	33	15	272	264	79	.494
Philadelphia Flyers	80	33	37	10	252	267	76	.475
New York Islanders	80	25	45	10	223	290	60	.375

Coaching Changes

Detroit--Bryan Murray 34-36-8; Minnesota--Bob Gainey 27-39-14; Toronto--Doug Carpenter 1-9-1, Tom Watt 22-37-10; Los Angeles--Tom Webster 46-24-10; Calgary--Doug Risebrough 46-26-8; Vancouver--Bob McCammon 19-30-5, Pat Quinn 9-13-4; Quebec--Dave Chambers 16-50-14; Pittsburgh--Bob Johnson 41-33-6; N.Y. Rangers--Roger Neilson 36-31-13; Washington--Terry Murray 37-36-7; New Jersey--John Cunniff 28-28-11, Tom McVie 4-5-4.

League Leaders

Goals

Brett Hull	86
Cam Neely	51
Theoren Fleury	51
Steve Yzerman	51
Mike Gartner	49

Assists

Wayne Gretzky	122
Adam Oates	90
Al MacInnis	75
Ray Bourque	73
Mark Recchi	73

Points

Wayne Gretzky	163
Brett Hull	131
Adam Oates	115
Mark Recchi	113
John Cullen	110

Penalty Minutes

Rob Ray	350
Mike Peluso	320
Bob Probert	315
Gino Odjick	296
Craig Berube	293

GAA
(1,200 minutes)

Ed Belfour	2.47
Don Beaupre	2.64
Patrick Roy	2.71
Andy Moog	2.87
Pete Peeters	2.88

Wins
(1,200 minutes)

Ed Belfour	43
Mike Vernon	31
Tim Cheveldae	30
Vincent Riendeau	29
Tom Barrasso	27

Shutouts

Don Beaupre	5
Andy Moog	4
Bob Essensa	4
Ed Belfour	4
John Vanbiesbrouck	3

Save %

Ed Belfour	.910
Patrick Roy	.906
Mike Richter	.903
Pete Peeters	.902
Kelly Hrudey	.900

All Star Game
(The Stadium, Chicago)

January 19	Campbell Conference	11	Wales Conference	5

Stanley Cup Playoffs

April 3	Hartford Whalers	5	at	Boston Bruins	2
April 3	Buffalo Sabres	5	at	Montreal Canadiens	7
April 3	New Jersey Devils	3	at	Pittsburgh Penguins	1
April 3	Washington Capitals	1	at	New York Rangers	2
April 4	Minnesota North Stars	4	at	Chicago Blackhawks	3 [4:14]
April 4	Detroit Red Wings	6	at	St. Louis Blues	3
April 4	Vancouver Canucks	6	at	Los Angeles Kings	5
April 4	Edmonton Oilers	3	at	Calgary Flames	1
April 5	Hartford Whalers	3	at	Boston Bruins	4
April 5	Buffalo Sabres	4	at	Montreal Canadiens	5
April 5	New Jersey Devils	4	at	Pittsburgh Penguins	5 [8:521
April 5	Washington Capitals	3	at	New York Rangers	0
April 6	Minnesota North Stars	2	at	Chicago Blackhawks	5
April 6	Detroit Red Wings	2	at	St. Louis Blues	4
April 6	Vancouver Canucks	2	at	Los Angeles Kings	3 [11:081
April 6	Edmonton Oilers	1	at	Calgary Flames	3
April 7	Boston Bruins	6	at	Hartford Whalers	3
April 7	Montreal Canadiens	4	at	Buffalo Sabres	5
April 7	Pittsburgh Penguins	4	at	New Jersey Devils	3
April 7	New York Rangers	6	at	Washington Capitals	0
April 8	Chicago Blackhawks	6	at	Minnesota North Stars	5
April 8	St. Louis Blues	2	at	Detroit Red Wings	5
April 8	Los Angeles Kings	1	at	Vancouver Canucks	2 [3:12]

April 8	Calgary Flames	3	at	Edmonton Oilers	4
April 9	Boston Bruins	3	at	Hartford Whalers	4
April 9	Montreal Canadiens	4	at	Buffalo Sabres	6
April 9	Pittsburgh Penguins	1	at	New Jersey Devils	4
April 9	New York Rangers	2	at	Washington Capitals	3
April 10	Chicago Blackhawks	1	at	Minnesota North Stars	3
April 10	St. Louis Blues	3	at	Detroit Red Wings	4
April 10	Los Angeles Kings	6	at	Vancouver Canucks	1
April 10	Calgary Flames	2	at	Edmonton Oilers	5
April 11	Hartford Whalers	1	at	Boston Bruins	6
April 11	Buffalo Sabres	3	at	Montreal Canadiens	4 [5:56]
April 11	New Jersey Devils	4	at	Pittsburgh Penguins	2
April 11	Washington Capitals	5	at	New York Rangers	4 [6:44]
April 12	Minnesota North Stars	6	at	Chicago Blackhawks	0
April 12	Detroit Red Wings	1	at	St. Louis Blues	6
April 12	Vancouver Canucks	4	at	Los Angeles Kings	7
April 12	Edmonton Oilers	3	at	Calgary Flames	5
April 13	Boston Bruins	3	at	Hartford Whalers	1
April 13	Montreal Canadiens	5	at	Buffalo Sabres	1
April 13	Pittsburgh Penguins	4	at	New Jersey Devils	3
April 13	New York Rangers	2	at	Washington Capitals	4
April 14	Chicago Blackhawks	1	at	Minnesota North Stars	3
April 14	St. Louis Blues	3	at	Detroit Red Wings	0
April 14	Los Angeles Kings	4	at	Vancouver Canucks	1
April 14	Calgary Flames	2	at	Edmonton Oilers	1 [4:40]
April 15	New Jersey Devils	0	at	Pittsburgh Penguins	4
April 16	Detroit Red Wings	2	at	St. Louis Blues	3
April 16	Edmonton Oilers	5	at	Calgary Flames	4 [6:58]
April 17	Montreal Canadiens	1	at	Boston Bruins	2
April 17	Washington Capitals	4	at	Pittsburgh Penguins	2
April 18	Minnesota North Stars	2	at	St. Louis Blues	1
April 18	Edmonton Oilers	3	at	Los Angeles Kings	4 [2:13]
April 19	Montreal Canadiens	4	at	Boston Bruins	3 [0:27]
April 19	Washington Capitals	6	at	Pittsburgh Penguins	7 [8:10]
April 20	Minnesota North Stars	2	at	St. Louis Blues	5
April 20	Edmonton Oilers	4	at	Los Angeles Kings	3 [24:48]
April 21	Boston Bruins	3	at	Montreal Canadiens	2
April 21	Pittsburgh Penguins	3	at	Washington Capitals	1
April 22	St. Louis Blues	1	at	Minnesota North Stars	5
April 22	Los Angeles Kings	3	at	Edmonton Oilers	4[20:48]
April 23	Boston Bruins	2	at	Montreal Canadiens	6
April 23	Pittsburgh Penguins	3	at	Washington Capitals	1
April 24	St. Louis Blues	4	at	Minnesota North Stars	8
April 24	Los Angeles Kings	2	at	Edmonton Oilers	4
April 25	Montreal Canadiens	1	at	Boston Bruins	4
April 25	Washington Capitals	1	at	Pittsburgh Penguins	4
April 26	Minnesota North Stars	2	at	St. Louis Blues	4
April 26	Edmonton Oilers	2	at	Los Angeles Kings	5
April 27	Boston Bruins	2	at	Montreal Canadiens	3 [17:47]
April 28	St. Louis Blues	2	at	Minnesota North Stars	3
April 28	Los Angeles Kings	3	at	Edmonton Oilers	4 [16:57]
May 1	Pittsburgh Penguins	3	at	Boston Bruins	6
May 2	Minnesota North Stars	3	at	Edmonton Oilers	1
May 3	Pittsburgh Penguins	4	at	Boston Bruins	5 [8:14]

May 4	Minnesota North Stars	2	at	Edmonton Oilers	7
May 5	Boston Bruins	1	at	Pittsburgh Penguins	4
May 6	Edmonton Oilers	3	at	Minnesota North Stars	7
May 7	Boston Bruins	1	at	Pittsburgh Penguins	4
May 8	Edmonton Oilers	1	at	Minnesota North Stars	5
May 9	Pittsburgh Penguins	7	at	Boston Bruins	2
May 10	Minnesota North Stars	3	at	Edmonton Oilers	2
May 11	Boston Bruins	3	at	Pittsburgh Penguins	5
May 15	Minnesota North Stars	5	at	Pittsburgh Penguins	4
May 17	Minnesota North Stars	1	at	Pittsburgh Penguins	4
May 19	Pittsburgh Penguins	1	at	Minnesota North Stars	3
May 21	Pittsburgh Penguins	5	at	Minnesota North Stars	3
May 23	Minnesota North Stars	4	at	Pittsburgh Penguins	6
May 25	Pittsburgh Penguins	8	at	Minnesota North Stars	0

All Star Teams

First Team		Second Team
Ed Belfour	Goal	Patrick Roy
Ray Bourque	Defense	Chris Chelios
Al MacInnis	Defense	Brian Leetch
Wayne Gretzky	Center	Adam Oates
Brett Hull	Right Wing	Cam Neely
Luc Robitaille	Left Wing	Kevin Stevens

Individual Awards

Alka Seltzer Plus Award--Marty McSorley (Los Angeles Kings)
Theoren Fleury (Calgary Flames)
Art Ross Trophy--Wayne Gretzky (Los Angeles Kings)
Bill Masterton Trophy--Dave Taylor (Los Angeles Kings)
Bud Man of the Year--Kevin Dineen (Hartford Whalers)
Calder Memorial Trophy--Ed Belfour (Chicago Blackhawks)
Conn Smythe Trophy--Mario Lemieux (Pittsburgh Penguins)
Dodge Ram Tough Award--Brett Hull (St. Louis Blues)
Frank J. Selke Trophy--Dirk Graham (Chicago Blackhawks)
Hart Memorial Trophy--Brett Hull (St. Louis Blues)
Jack Adams Award--Brian Sutter (St. Louis Blues)
James Norris Trophy--Ray Bourque (Boston Bruins)
King Clancy Trophy--Dave Taylor (Los Angeles Kings)
Lady Byng Memorial Trophy--Wayne Gretzky (Los Angeles Kings)
Lester B. Pearson Award--Brett Hull (St. Louis Blues)
Lester Patrick Trophy--Rod Gilbert and Mike Illitch
NHL All Star Game MVP--Vincent Damphousse (Toronto Maple Leafs)
Pro-Set NHL Player of the Year--Brett Hull (St. Louis Blues)
Trico Goaltender Award--Ed Belfour (Chicago Blackhawks)
Vezina Trophy--Ed Belfour (Chicago Blackhawks)
William M. Jennings Trophy--Ed Belfour (Chicago Blackhawks)

Hall of Fame Inductees

Neil Armstrong, Mike Bossy, Scotty Bowman, Denis Potvin, Bob Pulford, Clint Smith

Other Sports

Horseracing--Kentucky Derby won by Strike the Gold (time 2:03, purse $655,800).

Heavyweight Boxing--Evander Holyfield defeated George Foreman in 12 rounds (WBC, WBA, IBF).

Golf--U.S. Open won by Payne Stewart in a playoff with Scott Simpson with scores of 282-282, 75-77.

Auto Racing--Indianapolis 500 won by Rick Mears (ave. speed 176.457 MPH).

Tennis--U.S. Open won by Stefan Edberg in the men's singles.
U.S. Open won by John Fitzgerald and Anders Jarryd in the men's doubles.
U.S. Open won by Monica Seles in the women's singles.
U.S. Open won by Pam Shriver and Natalia Zvereva in the women's doubles.
U.S. Open won by Manon Bollegraf and Tom Nijssen in the mixed doubles.

Notes

Two spectators were killed by lightning in two different PGA events.

Willy T. Ribbs becomes the first black driver to qualify for a starting berth in the Indianapolis 500.

1992

BASEBALL
National League
East

Team Name	W	L	Pct	GB	R	OR
Pittsburgh Pirates	96	66	.593	-	693	595
Montreal Expos	87	75	.537	9	648	581
St. Louis Cardinals	83	79	.512	13	631	604
Chicago Cubs	78	84	.481	18	593	624
New York Mets	72	90	.444	24	599	653
Philadelphia Phillies	70	92	.432	26	686	717

West

Team Name	W	L	Pct	GB	R	OR
Atlanta Braves	98	64	.605	-	682	569
Cincinnati Reds	90	72	.556	8	660	609
San Diego Padres	82	80	.506	16	617	636
Houston Astros	81	81	.500	17	608	668
San Francisco Giants	72	90	.444	26	574	647
Los Angeles Dodgers	63	99	.389	35	548	636

Coaching Changes

Montreal--Tom Runnells 17-20, Felipe Alou 70-55; Chicago--Jim Lefevre 78-84; New York--Jeff Torborg 72-90; Philadelphia--Jim Fregosi 70-92; San Diego--Greg Riddoch 78-72, Jim Riggleman 4-8.

League Leaders

Batting Average
(502 at bats)

Gary Sheffield	.330
Andy Van Slyke	.324
John Kruk	.323
Bip Roberts	.323
Tony Gwynn	.317

Home Runs

Fred McGriff	35
Barry Bonds	34
Gary Sheffield	33
Darren Daulton	27
Dave Hollins	27

RBI

Darren Daulton	109
Terry Pendleton	105
Fred McGriff	104
Barry Bonds	103
Gary Sheffield	100

Stolen Bases

Marquis Grissom	78
Delino DeShields	46
Steve Finley	44
Bip Roberts	44
Ozzie Smith	43

ERA
(162 innings)

Bill Swift	2.08
Bob Tewksbury	2.16
Greg Maddox	2.18
Curt Schilling	2.35
Dennis Martinez	2.47

Wins

Tom Glavine	20
Greg Maddox	20
Bob Tewksbury	16
Mike Morgan	16
Ken Hill	16

Saves

Lee Smith	43
Randy Myers	38
John Wetteland	37
Doug Jones	36
Mitch Williams	29

Strikeouts

John Smoltz	215
David Cone	214
Greg Maddox	199
Sid Fernandez	193
Doug Drabek	177

NLCS

October 6	Pittsburgh Pirates	1	at	Atlanta Braves	5
October 7	Pittsburgh Pirates	5	at	Atlanta Braves	13
October 9	Atlanta Braves	2	at	Pittsburgh Pirates	3
October 10	Atlanta Braves	6	at	Pittsburgh Pirates	4
October 11	Atlanta Braves	1	at	Pittsburgh Pirates	7
October 13	Pittsburgh Pirates	13	at	Atlanta Braves	4
October 14	Pittsburgh Pirates	2	at	Atlanta Braves	3

Notes

Ryne Sandberg signs a 5 year $30.5 million contract with the Chicago Cubs.
Barry Bonds signs a 6 year $43.75 million deal with the San Francisco Giants.
Bud Selig is named chairman of baseball's executive council taking over the duties of baseball Commissioner.

American League
East

Team Name	W	L	Pct	GB	R	OR
Toronto Blue Jays	96	66	.593	-	780	682
Milwaukee Brewers	92	70	.568	4	740	604
Baltimore Orioles	89	73	.549	7	705	656
Cleveland Indians	76	86	.469	20	674	746
New York Yankees	76	86	.469	20	733	746
Detroit Tigers	75	87	.463	21	791	794
Boston Red Sox	73	89	.451	23	599	669

West

Team Name	W	L	Pct	GB	R	OR
Oakland Athletics	96	66	.593	-	745	672
Minnesota Twins	90	72	.556	6	747	653
Chicago White Sox	86	76	.531	10	738	690
Texas Rangers	77	85	.475	19	682	753
California Angels	72	90	.444	24	579	671
Kansas City Royals	72	90	.444	24	610	667
Seattle Mariners	64	98	.395	32	679	799

Coaching Changes

Toronto--Cito Gaston 96-66; Milwaukee--Phil Garner 92-70; Baltimore--John Oates 89-73; Cleveland--Mike Hargrove 76-86; New York--Buck Showalter 76-86; Boston--Butch Hobson 73-89; Chicago--Gene Lamont 86-76; Texas--Bobby Valentine 45-41, Toby Harrah 32-44; California--Buck Rodgers 33-40, John Wathan 39-50; Kansas City--Hal McRae 72-90; Seattle--Bill Plummer 64-98.

League Leaders

Batting Average (502 at bats)		Home Runs		RBI	
Edgar Martinez	.343	Juan Gonzalez	43	Cecil Fielder	124
Kirby Puckett	.329	Mark McGwire	42	Joe Carter	119
Frank Thomas	.323	Cecil Fielder	35	Frank Thomas	115
Paul Molitor	.320	Albert Belle	34	George Bell	112
Shane Mack	.315	Joe Carter	34	Albert Belle	112

Stolen Bases		ERA (162 innings)		Wins	
Ken Lofton	66	Roger Clemens	2.41	Jack Morris	21
Pat Listach	54	Kevin Appier	2.46	Kevin Brown	21
Brady Anderson	53	Mike Mussina	2.54	Jack McDowell	20
Luis Polonia	51	Juan Guzman	2.64	Mike Mussina	18
Roberto Alomar	49	Jim Abbott	2.77	Roger Clemens	18

Saves		Strikeouts	
Dennis Eckersley	51	Randy Johnson	241
Rick Aguilera	41	Melido Perez	218
Jeff Montgomery	39	Roger Clemens	208
Greg Olson	36	Juan Guzman	179
Tom Henke	34	Jack McDowell	178

All Star Game

(San Diego/Jack Murphy Stadium, San Diego)

July 14	American League	13	National League	6

ALCS

October 7	Oakland Athletics	4	at	Toronto Blue Jays	3
October 8	Oakland Athletics	1	at	Toronto Blue Jays	3
October 10	Toronto Blue Jays	7	at	Oakland Athletics	5
October 11	Toronto Blue Jays	7	at	Oakland Athletics	6 [11]
October 12	Toronto Blue Jays	2	at	Oakland Athletics	6
October 14	Oakland Athletics	2	at	Toronto Blue Jays	9

World Series

October 17	Toronto Blue Jays	1	at	Atlanta Braves	3
October 18	Toronto Blue Jays	5	at	Atlanta Braves	4
October 20	Atlanta Braves	2	at	Toronto Blue Jays	3
October 21	Atlanta Braves	1	at	Toronto Blue Jays	2
October 22	Atlanta Braves	7	at	Toronto Blue Jays	2
October 24	Toronto Blue Jays	4	at	Atlanta Braves	3 [11]

Individual Awards

ALCS MVP--Roberto Alomar (Toronto Blue Jays AL)
Arch Ward Memorial Trophy--Ken Griffey Jr. (Seattle Mariners NL)
Baseball Writers Award--Barry Bonds (Pittsburgh Pirates NL)
Dennis Eckersley (Oakland Athletics AL)
Cy Young Award-- Greg Maddox (Chicago Cubs NL)
Dennis Eckersley (Oakland Athletics AL)
NLCS MVP--John Smoltz (Atlanta Braves NL)
Rookie of the Year--Eric Karros (Los Angeles Dodgers NL)
Pat Listach (Milwaukee Brewers AL)
Sporting News Executive of the Year--Dan Duquette (Montreal Expos NL)
Sporting News Manager of the Year--Jim Leyland (Pittsburgh Pirates NL)
Tony LaRussa (Oakland Athletics AL)
Sporting News Pitcher of the Year--Greg Maddox (Chicago Cubs NL)
Dennis Eckersley (Oakland Athletics AL)
Sporting News Player of the Year--Gary Sheffield (San Diego Padres NL)

Sporting News Rookie of the Year--Eric Karros (Los Angeles Dodgers NL)
Tim Wakefield (Pittsburgh Pirates NL)
Pat Listach (Milwaukee Brewers AL)
Cal Eldred (Milwaukee Brewers AL)
World Series MVP--Pat Borders (Toronto Blue Jays AL)

Hall of Fame Inductees

Rollie Fingers, Bill McGowan, Hal Newhouser, Tom Seaver

BASKETBALL

National Basketball Association
Eastern Conference
Atlantic Division

Team Name	GP	W	L	PPGF	PPGA	Pct	GB
Boston Celtics	82	51	31	106.6	103.0	.622	-
New York Knickerbockers	82	51	31	101.6	97.7	.622	-
New Jersey Nets	82	40	42	105.4	107.1	.488	11
Miami Heat	82	38	44	105.0	109.2	.463	13
Philadelphia 76ers	82	35	47	101.9	103.2	.427	16
Washington Bullets	82	25	57	102.4	106.8	.305	26
Orlando Magic	82	21	61	101.6	108.5	.256	30

Central Division

Team Name	GP	W	L	PPGF	PPGA	Pct	GB
Chicago Bulls	82	67	15	109.9	99.5	.817	-
Cleveland Cavaliers	82	57	25	108.9	103.4	.695	10
Detroit Pistons	82	48	34	98.9	96.9	.585	19
Indiana Pacers	82	40	42	112.2	110.3	.488	27
Atlanta Hawks	82	38	44	106.2	107.7	.463	29
Charlotte Hornets	82	31	51	109.5	113.4	.378	36
Milwaukee Bucks	82	31	51	105.0	106.7	.378	36

Western Conference

Midwest Division

Team Name	GP	W	L	PPGF	PPGA	Pct	GB
Utah Jazz	82	55	27	108.3	101.9	.671	-
San Antonio Spurs	82	47	35	104.0	100.6	.573	8
Houston Rockets	82	42	40	102.0	103.7	.512	13
Denver Nuggets	82	24	58	99.7	107.6	.293	31
Dallas Mavericks	82	22	60	97.6	105.3	.268	33
Minnesota Timberwolves	82	15	67	100.5	107.5	.183	40

Pacific Division

Team Name	GP	W	L	PPGF	PPGA	Pct	GB
Portland Trail Blazers	82	57	25	111.4	104.1	.695	-
Golden State Warriors	82	55	27	118.7	114.8	.671	2
Phoenix Suns	82	53	29	112.1	106.2	.646	4
Seattle SuperSonics	82	47	35	106.5	104.7	.573	10
Los Angeles Clippers	82	45	37	102.9	101.9	.549	12
Los Angeles Lakers	82	43	39	100.4	101.5	.524	14
Sacramento Kings	82	29	53	104.3	110.3	.347	28

Coaching Changes

New York--Pat Riley 51-31; Miami--Kevin Loughery 38-44; Indiana--Bob Hill 40-42; Charlotte--Allan Bristow 31-51; Milwaukee--Del Harris 8-9, Frank Hamblen 23-42; San Antonio--Larry Brown 21-17, Bob Bass 26-18; Houston--Don Chaney 26-26, Rudy Tomjanovich 16-14; Minnesota--Jimmy Rodgers 15-67; Seattle--K.C. Jones 18-18, Bob Kloppenburg 2-2, George Karl 27-15; Clippers Mike Schuler 21-24, Mack Calvin 1-1, Larry Brown 23-12; Sacramento--Dick Motta 7-18, Rex Hughes 22-35.

League Leaders

Field Goal %		Free Throw %		Assists Per Game	
Buck Williams	.604	Mark Price	.947	John Stockton	13.7
Otis Thorpe	.592	Larry Bird	.926	Kevin Johnson	10.7
Horace Grant	.578	Ricky Pierce	.916	Tim Hardaway	10.0
Brad Daugherty	.570	Rolando Blackman	.898	Muggsy Bogues	9.1
Michael Page	.566	Jeff Malone	.898	Mark Jackson	8.6

Points		Rebounds per Game	
Michael Jordan	2404	Dennis Rodman	18.7
Karl Malone	2272	Kevin Willis	15.5
Chris Mullins	2074	Dikembe Mutombo	12.3
Patrick Ewing	1970	David Robinson	12.2
Clyde Drexler	1903	Hakeem Olajuwon	12.1

All Star Game

(Orlando Arena, Orlando)

February 9	West Division	153		East Division	113

NBA Playoffs

April 23	Los Angeles Lakers	102	at	Portland Trail Blazers	115
April 23	Seattle SuperSonics	117	at	Golden State warriors	109
April 23	New Jersey Nets	113	at	Cleveland Cavaliers	120
April 23	Indiana Pacers	113	at	Boston Celtics	124
April 24	Detroit Pistons	75	at	N.Y. Knickerbockers	109
April 24	Los Angeles Clippers	97	at	Utah Jazz	115
April 24	San Antonio Spurs	111	at	Phoenix Suns	117
April 24	Miami Heat	94	at	Chicago Bulls	113
April 25	Los Angeles Lakers	79	at	Portland Trail Blazers	101
April 25	Seattle SuperSonics	101	at	Golden State Warriors	115
April 25	New Jersey Nets	96	at	Cleveland Cavaliers	118
April 25	Indiana Pacers	112	at	Boston Celtics	119 [OT]
April 26	Los Angeles Clippers	92	at	Utah Jazz	103
April 26	San Antonio Spurs	107	at	Phoenix Suns	119
April 26	Miami Heat	90	at	Chicago Bulls	120
April 26	Detroit Pistons	89	at	N.Y. Knickerbockers	88
April 27	Boston Celtics	102	at	Indiana Pacers	98
April 28	Golden State Warriors	128	at	Seattle SuperSonics	129
April 28	Utah Jazz	88	at	Los Angeles Clippers	98
April 28	Cleveland Cavaliers	104	at	New Jersey Nets	109
April 28	N.Y. Knickerbockers	90	at	Detroit Pistons	87 [OT]
April 29	Portland Trail Blazers	119	at	Los Angeles Lakers	121 [OT]
April 29	Phoenix Suns	101	at	San Antonio Spurs	92

April 29	Chicago Bulls	119	at	Miami Heat	114
April 30	Golden State Warriors	116	at	Seattle SuperSonics	119
April 30	Cleveland Cavaliers	98	at	New Jersey Nets	89
May 1	N.Y. Knickerbockers	82	at	Detroit Pistons	86
May 2	Boston Celtics	76	at	Cleveland Cavaliers	101
May 3	Portland Trail Blazers	102		Los Angeles Lakers	76 *
May 3	Los Angeles Clippers	115		Utah Jazz	107 **
May 3	Detroit Pistons	87	at	N.Y. Knickerbockers	94
May 4	Los Angeles Clippers	89	at	Utah Jazz	98
May 4	Boston Celtics	104	at	Cleveland Cavaliers	98
May 5	N.Y. Knickerbockers	94	at	Chicago Bulls	89
May 5	Phoenix Suns	111	at	Portland Trail Blazers	113
May 6	Seattle SuperSonics	100	at	Utah Jazz	108
May 7	Phoenix Suns	119	at	Portland Trail Blazers	126
May 7	N.Y. Knickerbockers	78	at	Chicago Bulls	86
May 8	Seattle SuperSonics	97	at	Utah Jazz	103
May 8	Cleveland Cavaliers	107	at	Boston Celtics	110
May 9	Portland Trail Blazers	117	at	Phoenix Suns	124
May 9	Chicago Bulls	94	at	N.Y. Knickerbockers	86
May 10	Utah Jazz	98	at	Seattle SuperSonics	104
May 10	Chicago Bulls	86	at	N.Y. Knickerbockers	93
May 10	Cleveland Cavaliers	114	at	Boston Celtics	112 [OT]
May 11	Phoenix Suns	151	at	Portland Trail Blazers	153 [OT]
May 12	Utah Jazz	89	at	Seattle SuperSonics	83
May 12	N.Y. Knickerbockers	88	at	Chicago Bulls	96
May 13	Boston Celtics	98	at	Cleveland Cavaliers	114
May 14	Phoenix Suns	106	at	Portland Trail Blazers	118
May 14	Seattle SuperSonics	100	at	Utah Jazz	111
May 14	Chicago Bulls	86	at	N.Y. Knickerbockers	100
May 15	Cleveland Cavaliers	91	at	Boston Celtics	122
May 16	Utah Jazz	88	at	Portland Trail Blazers	113
May 17	N.Y. Knickerbockers	81	at	Chicago Bulls	103
May 17	Boston Celtics	104	at	Cleveland Cavaliers	122
May 19	Utah Jazz	102	at	Portland Trail Blazers	119
May 19	Cleveland Cavaliers	89	at	Chicago Bulls	103
May 21	Cleveland Cavaliers	107	at	Chicago Bulls	81
May 22	Portland Trail Blazers	89	at	Utah Jazz	97
May 23	Chicago Bulls	105	at	Cleveland Cavaliers	96
May 24	Portland Trail Blazers	112	at	Utah Jazz	121
May 25	Chicago Bulls	85	at	Cleveland Cavaliers	99
May 26	Utah Jazz	121	at	Portland Trail Blazers	127 [OT]
May 27	Cleveland Cavaliers	89	at	Chicago Bulls	112
May 28	Portland Trail Blazers	105	at	Utah Jazz	97
May 29	Chicago Bulls	99	at	Cleveland Cavaliers	94
June 3	Cleveland Cavaliers	89	at	Chicago Bulls	122
June 5	Portland Trail Blazers	115	at	Chicago Bulls	104 [OT]
June 7	Chicago Bulls	94	at	Portland Trail Blazers	84
June 10	Chicago Bulls	88	at	Portland Trail Blazers	93
June 12	Chicago Bulls	119	at	Portland Trail Blazers	106
June 14	Portland Trail Blazers	93	at	Chicago Bulls	97

*Game played in Las Vegas
**Game played in Anaheim

All Star Teams

First Team	Second Team	Third Team
Michael Jordan	Tim Hardaway	Mark Price
Clyde Drexler	John Stockton	Kevin Johnson
David Robinson	Patrick Ewing	Brad Daugherty
Karl Malone	Scottie Pippen	Dennis Rodman
Chris Mullin	Charles Barkley	Kevin Willis

Individual Awards

Defensive Player of the Year--David Robinson (San Antonio Spurs)
Eddie Gottlieb Trophy--Larry Johnson (Charlotte Hornets)
Executive of the Year--Wayne Embry (Cleveland Cavaliers)
J. Walter Kennedy Citizenship Award--Earvin Johnson (Los Angeles Lakers)
Maurice Podoloff Trophy--Michael Jordan (Chicago Bulls)
Most Improved Player--Pervis Ellison (Washington Bullets)
NBA All Star Game MVP--Earvin Johnson (Los Angeles Lakers)
NBA Finals M.V.P.--Michael Jordan (Chicago Bulls)
Red Auerbach Trophy--Don Nelson (Golden State Warriors)
Schick Award--Dennis Rodman (Detroit Pistons)
Sixth Man Award--Detlef Schrempf (Indiana Pacers)

Hall of Famee Inductees

Sergei Belov, Lou Carnesecca, Lucy Harris, Connie Hawkins, Bob Lanier, Al McGuire, Jack Ramsay, Nera White, Phil Woolpert

FOOTBALL

National Football League

National Conference
Eastern Division

Team Name	GP	W	L	T	PF	PA	Pct
Dallas Cowboys	16	13	3	0	409	243	.813
Philadelphia Eagles	16	11	5	0	354	245	.688
Washington Redskins	16	9	7	0	300	255	.563
New York Giants	16	6	10	0	306	367	.375
Phoenix Cardinals	16	4	12	0	243	332	.250

Central Division

Team Name	GP	W	L	T	PF	PA	Pct
Minnesota Vikings	16	11	5	0	374	249	.688
Green Bay Packers	16	9	7	0	276	296	.563
Tampa Bay Buccaneers	16	5	11	0	267	365	.313
Chicago Bears	16	5	11	0	295	361	.313
Detroit Lions	16	5	11	0	273	332	.313

Western Division

Team Name	GP	W	L	T	PF	PA	Pct
San Francisco 49ers	16	14	2	0	431	236	.875
New Orleans Saints	16	12	4	0	330	202	.750
Atlanta Falcons	16	6	10	0	327	414	.375
Los Angeles Rams	16	6	10	0	313	383	.375

American Conference

Eastern Division

Miami Dolphins	16	11	5	0	340	281	.688
Buffalo Bills	16	11	5	0	381	283	.688
Indianapolis Colts	16	9	7	0	216	302	.563
New York Jets	16	4	12	0	220	315	.250
New England Patriots	16	2	14	0	205	363	.125

Central Division

Pittsburgh Steelers	16	11	5	0	299	225	.688
Houston Oilers	16	10	6	0	352	258	.625
Cleveland Browns	16	7	9	0	272	275	.438
Cincinnati Bengals	16	5	11	0	274	364	.313

Western Division

San Diego Chargers	16	11	5	0	335	241	.688
Kansas City Chiefs	16	10	6	0	348	282	.625
Denver Broncos	16	8	8	0	262	329	.500
Los Angeles Raiders	16	7	9	0	249	281	.438
Seattle Seahawks	16	2	14	0	140	312	.125

Coaching Changes

Minnesota--Dennis Green 11-5-0; Green Bay--Mike Holmgren 9-7-0; Tampa Bay--Sam Wyche 5-11-0; L.A. Rams--Chuck Knox 6-10-0; Indianapolis--Ted Marchibroda 9-7-0; Pittsburgh--Bill Cowher 11-5-0; Cincinnati--David Shula 5-11-0; San Diego--Bobby Ross 11-5-0; Seattle--Tom Flores 2-14-0; New England--Dick MacPherson 0-8-0, Dante Scarnecchia 2-6-0.

League Leaders

Yards Rushing		**Yards Passing**		**Passing %** (300 attempts)	
Emmitt Smith	1713	Dan Marino	4116	Steve Young	66.7
Barry Foster	1690	Steve Young	3465	Warren Moon	64.7
Thurman Thomas	1487	Jim Kelly	3457	Brett Favre	64.1
Barry Sanders	1352	Troy Aikman	3445	Troy Aikman	63.8
Lorenzo White	1226	Stan Humphries	3356	Randall Cunningham	60.7

Receiving Yards		**Receptions**		**Field Goals**	
Sterling Sharpe	1461	Sterling Sharpe	108	Pete Stoyanovich	30
Michael Irvin	1396	Andre Rison	93	Chip Lohmiller	30
Jerry Rice	1201	Haywood Jeffries	90	Morten Andersen	29
Andre Rison	1119	Jerry Rice	84	Gary Anderson	28
Fred Barnett	1083	Curtis Duncan	82	John Carney	26

Punt Return Yards		**Kickoff Return Yards**	
Kelvin Martin	532	Deion Sanders	1067
Vai Sikahema	503	Mel Gray	1006
Dale Carter	398	Clarence Verdin	815
Tim Brown	383	John Bailey	690
Rod Woodson	364	Randy Baldwin	675

Pro Bowl Game

(Aloha Stadium, Honolulu)

February 7 1993	American Conference	23		National Conference	20

NFL Playoffs

January 2 1993	Washington Redskins	24	at	Minnesota Vikings	7
January 2 1993	Kansas City Chiefs	0	at	San Diego Chargers	17
January 3 1993	Houston Oilers	38	at	Buffalo Bills	41 [OT]
January 3 1993	Philadelphia Eagles	36	at	New Orleans Saints	20
January 9 1993	Buffalo Bills	24	at	Pittsburgh Steelers	3
January 9 1993	Washington Redskins	13	at	San Francisco 49ers	20
January 10 1993	Philadelphia Eagles	10	at	Dallas Cowboys	34
January 10 1993	San Diego Chargers	0	at	Miami Dolphins	31
January 17 1993	Dallas Cowboys	30	at	San Francisco 49ers	20
January 17 1993	Buffalo Bills	29	at	Miami Dolphins	10

Super Bowl XXVII

(Rose Bowl, Pasadena)

January 31 1993	Dallas Cowboys	52		Buffalo Bills	17

Individual Awards

A.P. MVP--Steve Young (San Francisco 49ers)
Bert Bell Trophy--Dale Carter (Kansas City Chiefs) [World Almanac]
Bert Bell Trophy--Steve Young (San Francisco 49ers)
Dan McGuire Award-- Steve Tasker (Buffalo Bills)
George Halas Trophy--Junior Seau (San Diego Chargers)
Jim Thorpe Trophy--Steve Young (San Francisco 49ers)
P.F.W.A. MVP--Steve Young (San Francisco 49ers)
Pete Rozelle Award--Troy Aikman (Dallas Cowboys)
U.P.I. AFC Coach of the Year--Bobby Ross (San Diego Chargers)
U.P.I. AFC Player of the Year--Barry Foster (Pittsburgh Steelers)
Junior Seau (San Diego Chargers)
U.P.I. AFC Rookie of the Year--Dale Carter (Kansas City Chiefs)
U.P.I. NFC Coach of the Year--Dennis Green (Minnesota Vikings)
U.P.I. NFC Player of the Year--Steve Young (San Francisco 49ers)
Chris Dolman (Minnesota Vikings)
U.P.I. NFC Rookie of the Year--Robert Jones (Dallas Cowboys)

Hall of Fame Inductees

Lem Barney, Al Davis, John Mackey, John Riggins

Canadian Football League
Eastern Division

Team Name	GP	W	L	T	PF	PA	Pts	Pct
Winnipeg Blue Bombers	18	11	7	0	507	499	22	.611
Hamilton Tiger-Cats	18	11	7	0	536	514	22	.611
Ottawa Rough Riders	18	9	9	0	484	439	18	.500
Toronto Argonauts	18	6	12	0	469	523	12	.333

Western Division

Calgary Stampeders	18	13	5	0	607	430	26	.722
Edmonton Eskimos	18	10	8	0	552	515	20	.556
Saskatchewan Roughriders	18	9	9	0	505	545	18	.500
British Columbia Lions	18	3	15	0	472	667	6	.167

Coaching Changes

Winnipeg--Urban Bowman 11-7-0; Hamilton--John Gregory 11-7-0; Ottawa--Ron Smeltzer 9-9-0; Toronto--Adam Rita 3-8-0, Dennis Meyer 3-4-0; Saskatchewan--Don Matthews 9-9-0.

League Leaders

Yards Rushing		**Yards Passing**		**Passing %** (200 attempts)	
Mike Richardson	1153	Kent Austin	6225	Kent Austin	59.6
Jon Volpe	941	Doug Flutie	5945	Doug Flutie	57.6
Reggie Barnes	926	Tom Burgess	4026	Danny Barrett	56.2
Damon Allen	831	Damon Allen	3858	Tom Burgess	54.0
Darren Joseph	711	Tracy Ham	3655	Tracy Ham	51.6

Receiving Yards		**Receptions**		**Points**	
Allen Pitts	1591	Allen Pitts	103	Mark McLaughlin	208
Ray Elgaard	1444	Ray Elgaard	91	Troy Westwood	199
Stephen Jones	1400	Darren Flutie	90	Paul Osbaldiston	196
Jeff Fairholm	1344	Don Narcisse	80	Terry Baker	184
Darren Flutie	1336	Jim Sandusky	78	Dave Ridgway	165

Grey Cup Playoffs

November 15	Ottawa Rough Riders	28	at	Hamilton Tiger-Cats	29
November 15	Saskatchewan Roughriders	20	at	Edmonton Eskimos	22
November 22	Hamilton Tiger-Cats	11	at	Winnipeg Blue Bombers	59
November 22	Edmonton Eskimos	22	at	Calgary Stampeders	23
November 29	Calgary Stampeders	24		Winnipeg Blue Bombers	10*

Individual Awards

Annis Stukus Trophy--Wally Buono (Calgary Stampeders)
Dave Dryburgh Memorial Trophy--Mark McLaughlin (Calgary Stampeders)
DeMarco-Becket Memorial Trophy--Vic Stevenson (Saskatchewan Roughriders)
Dr. Beattie Martin Trophy--Ray Elgaard (Saskatchewan Roughriders)
Eddie James Memorial Trophy--Jon Volpe (British Columbia Lions)
Frank M. Gibson Trophy--Mike Richardson (Winnipeg Blue Bombers)
G.M.C. Award Most Outstanding Canadian--Ray Elgaard (Saskatchewan Roughriders)
G.M.C. Award Most Outstanding Defensive Player--Willie Pless (Edmonton Eskimos)
G.M.C. Award Most Outstanding Offensive Lineman--Rob Smith (Ottawa Rough Riders)
G.M.C. Award Most Outstanding Player--Doug Flutie (Calgary Stampeders)
G.M.C. Award Most Outstanding Rookie--Michael Richardson (Winnipeg Blue Bombers)
Grey Cup Most Valuable Canadian--Dave Sapunjis (Calgary Stampeders)
Grey Cup Most Valuable Player--Doug Flutie (Calgary Stampeders)
Jackie Parker Trophy--Bruce Covernton (Calgary Stampeders)

*Game played in Toronto

James P. McCaffrey Award--Angelo Snipes (Ottawa Rough Riders)
Jeff Nicklin Memorial Trophy--Doug Flutie (Calgary Stampeders)
Jeff Russel Memorial Trophy--Angelo Snipes (Ottawa Rough Riders)
Leo Dandurand Trophy--Rob Smith (Ottawa Rough Riders)
Lew Hayman Trophy--Ken Evraire (Hamilton Tiger-Cats)
Norm Fieldgate Trophy--Willie Pless (Edmonton Eskimos)

Hall of Fame Inductees

Ken Charlton, Ellison Kelly, Don Sutherin, Ralph Cooper,

World Football League
European Division

Team Name	GP	W	L	T	PF	PA	Pct
Barcelona Dragons	10	5	5	0	104	161	.500
Frankfurt Galaxy	10	3	7	0	150	257	.300
London Monarchs	10	2	7	1	178	203	.250
North American East							
Orlando Thunder	10	8	2	0	247	127	.800
NY-NJ Knights	10	6	4	0	284	188	.600
Montreal Machine	10	2	8	0	175	274	.200
Ohio Glory	10	1	9	0	132	230	.100
North American West							
Sacramento Surge	10	8	2	0	250	152	.800
Birmingham Fire	10	7	2	1	192	165	.750
San Antonio Riders	10	7	3	0	195	150	.700

Coaching Changes

London--Ray Willsey 2-7-1; Orlando--Galen Hall 8-2-0; Ohio--Larry Little 1-9-0.

League Leaders

Passing

	Attempts	Completions	Yards
David Archer	317	194	2964
Reggie Slack	215	140	1898
Michael Proctor	193	113	1478
Mike Perez	147	86	985
Mike Johnson	257	144	1760

Receptions		Receiving Yards		Rushing Yards	
Willie Wilson	65	Eddie Brown	1011	Ivory Lee Brown	767
Willie Bonyer	57	Bernard Ford	833	Amir Rasul	572
Joe Howard Johnson	56	Willie Wilson	776	Darryl Clack	517
Judd Garrett	55	Willie Bonyer	706	Mike Pringle	507
T. Woods	51	Joe Howard Johnson	687	J. Alexander	501

WFL Playoffs

May 30	Birmingham Fire	7	at	Orlando Thunder	45
May 31	Barcelona Dragons	15	at	Sacramento Surge	17

June 6	Sacramento Surge 21	Orlando Thunder	17*

HOCKEY

National Hockey League
Clarence Campbell Conference
Norris Division

Team Name	GP	W	L	T	GF	GA	Pts	Pct
Detroit Red Wings	80	43	25	12	320	256	98	.613
Chicago Blackhawks	80	36	29	15	257	236	87	.544
St. Louis Blues	80	36	33	11	279	266	83	.519
Minnesota North Stars	80	32	42	6	246	278	70	.438
Toronto Maple Leafs	80	30	43	7	234	294	67	.419

Smythe Division

Team Name	GP	W	L	T	GF	GA	Pts	Pct
Vancouver Canucks	80	42	26	12	285	250	96	.600
Los Angeles Kings	80	35	31	14	287	296	84	.525
Edmonton Oilers	80	36	34	10	295	297	82	.513
Winnipeg Jets	80	33	32	15	251	244	81	.506
Calgary Flames	80	31	37	12	296	305	74	.463
San Jose Sharks	80	17	58	5	219	359	39	.244

Prince of Wales Conference

Adams Division

Team Name	GP	W	L	T	GF	GA	Pts	Pct
Montreal Canadiens	80	41	28	11	267	207	93	.581
Boston Bruins	80	36	32	12	270	275	84	.525
Buffalo Sabres	80	31	37	12	289	299	74	.463
Hartford Whalers	80	26	41	13	247	283	65	.406
Quebec Nordiques	80	20	48	12	255	318	52	.325

Patrick Division

Team Name	GP	W	L	T	GF	GA	Pts	Pct
New York Rangers	80	50	25	5	321	246	105	.656
Washington Capitals	80	45	27	8	330	275	98	.613
Pittsburgh Penguins	80	39	32	9	343	308	87	.544
New Jersey Devils	80	38	31	11	289	259	87	.544
New York Islanders	80	34	35	11	291	299	79	.494
Philadelphia Flyers	80	32	37	11	252	273	75	.469

Coaching Changes

Toronto--Tom Watt 30-43-7; Edmonton--Ted Green 36-34-10; Winnipeg--John Paddock 33-32-15; Calgary--Doug Risebrough 25-31-9, Guy Charron 6-6-3; San Jose--George Kingston 17-58-5; Boston--Rick Bowness 36-32-12; Hartford--Jim Roberts 26-41-13; Quebec--Dave Chambers 3-14-1, Pierre Page 17-34-11; Pittsburgh--Scotty Bowman 39-32-9; New Jersey--Tom McVie 38-31-11; Philadelphia--Paul Holmgren 8-14-2, Bill Dineen 24-23-9; Vancouver--Pat Quinn 42-26-12; Buffalo--Rick Dudley 9-15-4, John Muckler 22-22-8.

*Game played in Montreal

League Leaders

Goals		Assists		Points	
Brett Hull	70	Wayne Gretzky	90	Mario Lemieux	131
Kevin Stevens	54	Mario Lemieux	87	Kevin Stevens	123
Gary Roberts	53	Brian Leetch	80	Wayne Gretzky	121
Jeremy Roenick	53	Adam Oates	79	Brett Hull	109
Pat LaFontaine	46	Dale Hawerchuk	75	Luc Robitaille	107

Penalty Minutes		GAA (25 games)		Wins	
Mike Peluso	408	Patrick Roy	2.36	Kirk McLean	38
Rob Ray	354	Ed Belfour	2.70	Tim Cheveldae	38
Gino Odjick	348	Kirk McLean	2.74	Patrick Roy	36
Ronnie Stern	338	John Vanbiesbrouck	2.85	Don Beaupre	29
Link Gaetz	326	Bob Essensa	2.88	Andy Moog	28

Shutouts		Save %	
Bob Essensa	5	Patrick Roy	.914
Ed Belfour	5	Curtis Joseph	.910
Kirk McLean	5	Bob Essensa	.910
Patrick Roy	5	John Vanbiesbrouck	.910
Mike Richter	3	Kirk McLean	.901

All Star Game

(The Spectrum, Philadelphia)

January 18	Campbell Conference	10		Wales Conference	6

Stanley Cup Playoffs

April 18	Minnesota North Stars	4	at	Detroit Red Wings	3
April 18	St. Louis Blues	1	at	Chicago Blackhawks	3
April 18	Winnipeg Jets	3	at	Vancouver Canucks	2
April 18	Edmonton Oilers	3	at	Los Angeles Kings	1
April 19	Hartford Whalers	0	at	Montreal Canadiens	2
April 19	Buffalo Sabres	3	at	Boston Bruins	2
April 19	New Jersey Devils	1	at	New York Rangers	2
April 19	Pittsburgh Penguins	1	at	Washington Capitals	3
April 20	Minnesota North Stars	4	at	Detroit Red Wings	2
April 20	St. Louis Blues	5	at	Chicago Blackhawks	3
April 20	Winnipeg Jets	2	at	Vancouver Canucks	3
April 20	Edmonton Oilers	5	at	Los Angeles Kings	8
April 21	Hartford Whalers	2	at	Montreal Canadiens	5
April 21	Buffalo Sabres	2	at	Boston Bruins	3 [11:14]
April 21	New Jersey Devils	7	at	New York Rangers	3
April 21	Pittsburgh Penguins	2	at	Washington Capitals	6
April 22	Detroit Red Wings	5	at	Minnesota North Stars	4 [1:15]
April 22	Chicago Blackhawks	4	at	St. Louis Blues	5 [23:33]
April 22	Vancouver Canucks	2	at	Winnipeg Jets	4
April 22	Los Angeles Kings	3	at	Edmonton Oilers	4
April 23	Montreal Canadiens	2	at	Hartford Whalers	5
April 23	Boston Bruins	3	at	Buffalo Sabres	2
April 23	New York Rangers	1	at	New Jersey Devils	3

April 23	Washington Capitals	4	at	Pittsburgh Penguins	6
April 24	Detroit Red Wings	4	at	Minnesota North Stars	5
April 24	Chicago Black Hawks	5	at	St. Louis Blues	3
April 24	Vancouver Canucks	1	at	Winnipeg Jets	3
April 24	Los Angeles Kings	4	at	Edmonton Oilers	3
April 25	Montreal Canadiens	1	at	Hartford Whalers	3
April 25	Boston Bruins	5	at	Buffalo Sabres	4 [2:08]
April 25	New York Rangers	3	at	New Jersey Devils	0
April 25	Washington Capitals	7	at	Pittsburgh Penguins	2
April 26	Minnesota North Stars	0	at	Detroit Red Wings	3
April 26	St. Louis Blues	4	at	Chicago Blackhawks	6
April 26	Winnipeg Jets	2	at	Vancouver Canucks	8
April 26	Edmonton Oilers	5	at	Los Angeles Kings	2
April 27	Hartford Whalers	4	at	Montreal Canadiens	7
April 27	Buffalo Sabres	2	at	Boston Bruins	0
April 27	New Jersey Devils	5	at	New York Rangers	8
April 27	Pittsburgh Penguins	5	at	Washington Capitals	2
April 28	Detroit Red Wings	1	at	Minnesota North Stars	0 [16:13]
April 28	Chicago Blackhawks	2	at	St. Louis Blues	1
April 28	Vancouver Canucks	8	at	Winnipeg Jets	3
April 28	Los Angeles Kings	0	at	Edmonton Oilers	3
April 29	Montreal Canadiens	1	at	Hartford Whalers	2 [0:24]
April 29	Boston Bruins	3	at	Buffalo Sabres	9
April 29	New York Rangers	3	at	New Jersey Devils	5
April 29	Washington Capitals	4	at	Pittsburgh Penguins	6
April 30	Minnesota North Stars	2	at	Detroit Red Wings	5
April 30	Winnipeg Jets	0	at	Vancouver Canucks	5
May 1	Hartford Whalers	2	at	Montreal Canadiens	3 [25:26]
May 1	Buffalo Sabres	2	at	Boston Bruins	3
May 1	New Jersey Devils	4	at	New York Rangers	8
May 1	Pittsburgh Penguins	3	at	Washington Capitals	1
May 2	Chicago Blackhawks	2	at	Detroit Red Wings	1
May 3	Edmonton Oilers	4	at	Vancouver Canucks	3 [8:36]
May 3	Boston Bruins	6	at	Montreal Canadiens	4
May 3	Pittsburgh Penguins	4	at	New York Rangers	2
May 4	Chicago Blackhawks	3	at	Detroit Red Wings	1
May 4	Edmonton Oilers	0	at	Vancouver Canucks	4
May 5	Boston Bruins	3	at	Montreal Canadiens	2 [3:12]
May 5	Pittsburgh Penguins	2	at	New York Rangers	4
May 6	Detroit Red Wings	4	at	Chicago Blackhawks	5
May 6	Vancouver Canucks	2	at	Edmonton Oilers	5
May 7	Montreal Canadiens	2	at	Boston Bruins	3
May 7	New York Rangers	6	at	Pittsburgh Penguins	5 [1:291
May 8	Detroit Red Wings	0	at	Chicago Blackhawks	1
May 8	Vancouver Canucks	2	at	Edmonton Oilers	3
May 9	Montreal Canadiens	0	at	Boston Bruin	2
May 9	New York Rangers	4	at	Pittsburgh Penguins	5 [2:47]
May 10	Edmonton Oilers	3	at	Vancouver Canucks	4
May 11	Pittsburgh Penguins	3	at	New York Rangers	2
May 12	Vancouver Canucks	0	at	Edmonton Oilers	3
May 13	New York Rangers	1	at	Pittsburgh Penguins	5
May 16	Edmonton Oilers	2	at	Chicago Blackhawks	8
May 17	Boston Bruins	3	at	Pittsburgh Penguins	4 [9:44]
May 18	Edmonton Oilers	2	at	Chicago Blackhawks	4

May 19	Boston Bruins	2	at	Pittsburgh Penguins	5
May 20	Chicago Blackhawks	4	at	Edmonton Oilers	3 [2:451
May 21	Pittsburgh Penguins	5	at	Boston Bruins	1
May 22	Chicago Blackhawks	5	at	Edmonton Oilers	1
May 23	Pittsburgh Penguins	5	at	Boston Bruins	1
May 26	Chicago Blackhawks	4	at	Pittsburgh Penguins	5
May 28	Chicago Blackhawks	1	at	Pittsburgh Penguins	3
May 30	Pittsburgh Penguins	1	at	Chicago Blackhawks	0
June 1	Pittsburgh Penguins	6	at	Chicago Blackhawks	5

All Star Teams

First Team		Second Team
Patrick Roy	Goal	Kirk McLean
Brian Leetch	Defense	Phil Housley
Ray Bourque	Defense	Scott Stevens
Mark Messier	Center	Mario Lemieux
Brett Hull	Right Wing	Mark Recchi
Kevin Stevens	Left Wing	Luc Robitaille

Individual Awards

Alka-Seltzer Plus Award--Paul Ysebaert (Detroit Red Wings)
Art Ross Trophy--Mario Lemieux (Pittsburgh Penguins)
Bill Masterton Trophy--Mark Fitzpatrick (New York Islanders)
Bud Man of the Year--Ryan Walter (Vancouver Canucks)
Calder Memorial Trophy--Pavel Bure (Vancouver Canucks)
Conn Smythe Trophy--Mario Lemieux (Pittsburgh Penguins)
Frank J. Selke Trophy--Guy Carbonneau (Montreal Canadiens)
Hart Memorial Trophy--Mark Messier (New York Rangers)
Jack Adams Award--Pat Quinn (Vancouver Canucks)
James Norris Trophy--Brian Leetch (New York Rangers)
King Clancy Trophy--Ray Bourque (Boston Bruins)
Lady Byng Memorial Trophy--Wayne Gretzky (Los Angeles Kings)
Lester B. Pearson Award--Mark Messier (New York Rangers)
Lester Patrick Trophy--Al Arbour, Art Berglund and Lou Lamoriello
NHL All Star Game MVP--Brett Hull (St. Louis Blues)
Pro Set NHL Player of the Year--Mario Lemieux (Pittsburgh Penguins)
Vezina Trophy--Patrick Roy (Montreal Canadiens)
William M. Jennings Trophy--Patrick Roy (Montreal Canadiens)

Hall of Fame Inductees

Keith Allen, Marcel Dionne, Woody Dumart, Bob Gainey, Bob Johnson, Frank Mathers, Lanny McDonald

Notes

John Ziegler resigns as NHL President and is replaced by Gil Stein.
NHL players vote to strike with 5 days remaining in the regular season. The players finish the season after sitting out 10 days.
Manon Rheaume became the first woman to play in an NHL exhibition game, playing 1 period as her Tampa Bay Lightning played St. Louis on September 23.

Other Sports

Horseracing--Kentucky Derby won by Lil E. Tee (time 2:04, purse $724,800).

Heavyweight Boxing--Evander Holyfield defeated Bert Cooper in 7 rounds (WBA, WBC, IBF).
Evander Holyfield defeated Larry Holmes in 12 rounds (WBA, WBC, IBF).

Golf--U.S. Open won by Tom Kite with a score of 285.

Auto Racing-- Indianapolis 500 won by Al Unser Jr. (ave. speed 134.479 MPH).

Tennis--U.S. Open won by Stefan Edberg defeated Pete Sampras in the men's singles.
U.S. Open won by Jim Grabb and Richey Reneberg in the men's doubles.
U.S. Open won by Monica Seles in the women's singles.
U.S. Open won by Gigi Fernandez and Natalia Zvereva in the women's doubles.
U.S. Open won Nicole Provis and Mark Woodforde in the mixed doubles.

Notes

Former heavyweight boxing champ Mike Tyson is found guilty of rape and sentenced to 6 years in prison and fined $30,000.

Lyn St. James became the oldest woman and driver to be named Indianapolis 500 rookie of the year.

1993

BASEBALL
National League
East

Team Name	W	L	Pct	GB	R	OR
Philadelphia Phillies	97	65	.599	-	877	740
Montreal Expos	94	68	.580	3	732	682
St. Louis Cardinals	87	75	.537	10	758	744
Chicago Cubs	84	78	.519	13	738	739
Pittsburgh Pirates	75	87	.463	22	707	806
Florida Marlins	64	98	.395	33	581	724
New York Mets	59	103	.364	38	672	744

West

Team Name	W	L	Pct	GB	R	OR
Atlanta Braves	104	58	.642	-	767	559
San Francisco Giants	103	59	.636	1	808	636
Houston Astros	85	77	.525	19	716	630
Los Angeles Dodgers	81	81	.500	23	675	662
Cincinnati Reds	73	89	.451	31	722	785
Colorado Rockies	67	95	.414	37	758	967
San Diego Padres	61	101	.377	43	679	772

Coaching Changes

Montreal--Felipe Alou 94-68; Florida--Rene Lachemann 64-98; New York--Jeff Torborg 13-25, Dallas Green 46-78; San Francisco--Dusty Baker 103-59; Cincinnati--Tony Perez 20-24, Davey Johnson 53-65; Colorado--Don Baylor 67-95; San Diego--Jim Riggleman 61-101.

League Leaders

Batting Average
(502 at bats)

Andres Galarraga	.370
Tony Gwynn	.358
Gregg Jefferies	.342
Barry Bonds	.336
Mark Grace	.325

Home Runs

Barry Bonds	46
Dave Justice	40
Matt Williams	38
Fred McGriff	37
Ron Gant	36

RBI

Barry Bonds	123
Dave Justice	120
Ron Gant	117
Mike Piazza	112
Matt Williams	110

Stolen Bases

Chuck Carr	58
Marquis Grissom	53
Otis Nixon	47
Gregg Jefferies	46
Darren Lewis	46

ERA
(162 innings)

Greg Maddux	2.36
Jose Rijo	2.48
Mark Portugal	2.77
Bill Swift	2.82
Steve Avery	2.94

Wins

Tom Glavine	22
John Burkett	22
Bill Swift	21
Greg Maddox	20
Mark Portugal	18

Saves

Randy Myers	53
Rod Beck	48
Bryan Harvey	45
Lee Smith	43
Mitch Williams	43

Strikeouts

Jose Rijo	227
John Smoltz	208
Greg Maddox	197
Curt Schilling	186
Pete Harnisch	185

NLCS

October 6	Atlanta Braves	3	at	Philadelphia Phillies	4
October 7	Atlanta Braves	14	at	Philadelphia Phillies	3
October 9	Philadelphia Phillies	4	at	Atlanta Braves	9
October 10	Philadelphia Phillies	2	at	Atlanta Braves	1
October 11	Philadelphia Phillies	4	at	Atlanta Braves	3 [10]
October 13	Atlanta Braves	3	at	Philadelphia Phillies	6

American League

East

Team Name	W	L	Pct	GB	R	OR
Toronto Blue Jays	95	67	.586	-	847	742
New York Yankees	88	74	.543	7	821	761
Baltimore Orioles	85	77	.525	10	786	745
Detroit Tigers	85	77	.525	10	899	837
Boston Red Sox	80	82	.494	15	686	698
Cleveland Indians	76	86	.469	19	790	813
Milwaukee Brewers	69	93	.426	26	733	792

West

Team Name	W	L	Pct	GB	R	OR
Chicago White Sox	94	68	.580	-	776	664
Texas Rangers	86	76	.531	8	835	751
Kansas City Royals	84	78	.519	10	675	694
Seattle Mariners	82	80	.506	12	734	731
California Angels	71	91	.438	23	684	770
Minnesota Twins	71	91	.438	23	693	830
Oakland Athletics	68	94	.420	26	715	846

Coaching Changes

Texas--Kevin Kennedy 86-76; Seattle--Lou Piniella 82-80; California--Buck Rodgers 71-91.

League Leaders

Batting Average (502 at bats)		**Home Runs**		**RBI**	
John Olerud	.363	Juan Gonzalez	46	Albert Belle	129
Paul Molitor	.332	Ken Griffey	45	Frank Thomas	128
Roberto Alomar	.326	Frank Thomas	41	Joe Carter	121
Kenny Lofton	.325	Albert Belle	38	Juan Gonzalez	118
Carlos Baerga	.321	Rafael Palmeiro	37	Cecil Fielder	117

Stolen Bases		**ERA** (162 innings)		**Wins**	
Mark Lofton	70	Kevin Appier	2.56	Jack McDowell	22
Roberto Alomar	55	Wilson Alvarez	2.95	Randy Johnson	19
Luis Polonia	55	Jimmy Key	3.00	Pat Hentgen	19
Rickey Henderson	53	Alex Fernandez	3.13	Jimmy Key	18
Chad Curtis	48	Frank Viola	3.14	Kevin Appier	18

Saves		Strikeouts	
Duane Ward	45	Randy Johnson	308
Jeff Montgomery	45	Mark Langston	196
Tom Henke	40	Juan Guzman	194
Roberto Hernandez	38	David Cone	191
Dennis Eckersley	36	Chuck Finley	187

All Star Game

(Oriole Park at Camden Yards, Baltimore)

July 13	American League	9		National League	3

ALCS

October 5	Toronto Blue Jays	7	at	Chicago White Sox	3
October 6	Toronto Blue Jays	3	at	Chicago White Sox	1
October 8	Chicago White Sox	6	at	Toronto Blue Jays	1
October 9	Chicago White Sox	7	at	Toronto Blue Jays	4
October 10	Chicago White Sox	3	at	Toronto Blue Jays	5
October 12	Toronto Blue Jays	6	at	Chicago White Sox	3

World Series

October 16	Philadelphia Phillies	5	at	Toronto Blue Jays	8
October 17	Philadelphia Phillies	6	at	Toronto Blue Jays	4
October 19	Toronto Blue Jays	10	at	Philadelphia Phillies	3
October 20	Toronto Blue Jays	15	at	Philadelphia Phillies	14
October 21	Toronto Blue Jays	0	at	Philadelphia Phillies	2
October 23	Philadelphia Phillies	6	at	Toronto Blue Jays	8

Individual Awards

ALCS MVP--Dave Stewart (Toronto Blue Jays AL)
Arch Ward Memorial Trophy--Kirby Puckett (Minnesota Twins AL)
Baseball Writers Award--Barry Bonds (San Francisco Giants NL)
Frank Thomas (Chicago White Sox AL)
Cy Young Award--Greg Maddox (Atlanta Braves NL)
Jack McDowell (Chicago White Sox AL)
NLCS MVP--Curt Schilling (Philadelphia Phillies NL)
Rookie of the Year--Mike Piazza (Los Angeles Dodgers NL)
Tim Salmon (California Angels AL)
Sporting News Executive of the Year--Lee Thomas (Philadelphia Phillies NL)
Sporting News Manager of the Year--Bobby Cox (Atlanta Braves NL)
John Oates (Baltimore Orioles AL)
Sporting News Pitcher of the Year--Greg Maddox (Atlanta Braves NL)
Jack McDowell (Chicago White Sox AL)
Sporting News Player of the Year--Frank Thomas (Chicago White Sox AL)
Sporting News Rookie of the Year--Mike Piazza (Los Angeles Dodgers NL)
Kirk Rueter (Montreal Expos NL)
Tim Salmon (California Angels AL)
Aaron Sele (Boston Red Sox AL)
World Series MVP--Paul Molitor (Toronto Blue Jays AL)

Hall of Fame Inductees

Reggie Jackson

Notes

Baseball owners vote to realign each league into three divisions for the following season.

BASKETBALL

National Basketball Association
Eastern Conference
Atlantic Division

Team Name	GP	W	L	PPGF	PPGA	Pct	GB
New York Knickerbockers	82	60	22	101.6	95.4	.732	-
Boston Celtics	82	48	34	103.7	102.8	.585	12
New Jersey Nets	82	43	39	102.8	101.6	.524	17
Orlando Magic	82	41	41	105.5	104.2	.500	19
Miami Heat	82	36	46	103.6	104.7	.439	24
Philadelphia 76ers	82	26	56	104.3	110.1	.317	34
Washington Bullets	82	22	60	101.9	108.9	.268	38

Central Division

Team Name	GP	W	L	PPGF	PPGA	Pct	GB
Chicago Bulls	82	57	25	105.2	98.9	.695	-
Cleveland Cavaliers	82	54	28	107.7	101.3	.659	3
Charlotte Hornets	82	44	38	110.1	110.4	.537	13
Atlanta Hawks	82	43	39	107.5	108.4	.524	14
Indiana Pacers	82	41	41	107.8	106.1	.500	16
Detroit Pistons	82	40	42	100.6	102.0	.488	17
Milwaukee Bucks	82	28	54	102.3	106.1	.341	29

Western Conference

Midwest Division

Team Name	GP	W	L	PPGF	PPGA	Pct	GB
Houston Rockets	82	55	27	104.0	99.8	.671	-
San Antonio Spurs	82	49	33	105.5	102.8	.598	6
Utah Jazz	82	47	35	106.2	104.0	.573	8
Denver Nuggets	82	36	46	105.2	106.9	.439	19
Minnesota Timberwolves	82	19	63	98.1	105.9	.232	36
Dallas Mavericks	82	11	71	99.3	114.5	.134	44

Pacific Division

Team Name	GP	W	L	PPGF	PPGA	Pct	GB
Phoenix Suns	82	62	20	113.4	106.7	.756	-
Seattle SuperSonics	82	55	27	108.3	101.3	.671	7
Portland Trail Blazers	82	51	31	108.5	105.4	.622	11
Los Angeles Clippers	82	41	41	107.1	106.8	.500	21
Los Angeles Lakers	82	39	43	104.2	105.5	.476	23
Golden State Warriors	82	34	48	109.9	110.9	.415	28
Sacramento Kings	82	25	57	107.9	111.1	.305	37

Coaching Changes

New Jersey--Chuck Daly 43-39; Philadelphia--Doug Moe 19-37, Fred Carter 7-19; Detroit--Ron Rothstein 40-42; Milwaukee--Mike Dunleavy 28-54; Houston--Rudy Tomjanovich 55-27; San Antonio--Jerry Tarkanian 9-11, Rex Hughes 1-0, John Lucas 39-22; Denver--Dan Issel 36-46; Minnesota--Jimmy Rodgers 6-23, Sidney Lowe 13-40; Phoenix--Paul Westphal 62-20; Seattle--George Karl 55-27; Clippers--Larry Brown 41-41; Lakers--Randy Pfund 39-43; Sacramento--Garry St. Jean 25-57; Dallas--Rich Adubato 2-27, Gar Heard 9-44.

League Leaders

Field Goal %		Free Throw %		Assists per Game	
Cedric Ceballos	.576	Mark Price	.948	John Stockton	12.0
Brad Daugherty	.571	Chris Jackson	.935	Tim Hardaway	10.6
Dale Davis	.568	Eddie Johnson	.911	Scott Skiles	9.4
Shaquille O'Neal	.562	Mike Williams	.907	Mark Jackson	8.8
Otis Thorpe	.558	Scott Skiles	.892	Tyrone Bogues	8.8

Points		Rebounds per Game	
Michael Jordan	2541	Dennis Rodman	18.3
Karl Malone	2217	Shaquille O'Neal	13.9
Hakeem Olajuwon	2140	Dikembe Mutombo	13.0
Dominique Wilkins	2121	Hakeem Olajuwon	13.0
Patrick Ewing	1959	Kevin Willis	12.9

All Star Game

(Delta Center, Salt Lake City)

February 21	West Division	135	East Division	132 [OT]

NBA Playoffs

April 29	New Jersey Nets	98	at	Cleveland Cavaliers	114
April 29	Charlotte Hornets	101	at	Boston Celtics	112
April 29	Los Angeles Clippers	94	at	Houston Rockets	117
April 29	San Antonio Spurs	87	at	Portland Trail Blazers	86
April 30	Indiana Pacers	104	at	N.Y. Knickerbockers	107
April 30	Atlanta Hawks	90	at	Chicago Bulls	114
April 30	Los Angeles Lakers	107	at	Phoenix Suns	103
April 30	Utah Jazz	85	at	Seattle SuperSonics	99
May 1	New Jersey Nets	101	at	Cleveland Cavaliers	99
May 1	Charlotte Hornets	99	at	Boston Celtics	98 [OT]
May 1	Los Angeles Clippers	95	at	Houston Rockets	83
May 1	San Antonio Spurs	96	at	Portland Trail Blazers	105
May 2	Indiana Pacers	91	at	N.Y. Knickerbockers	101
May 2	Atlanta Hawks	102	at	Chicago Bulls	117
May 2	Los Angeles Lakers	86	at	Phoenix Suns	81
May 2	Utah Jazz	89	at	Seattle SuperSonics	85
May 3	Boston Celtics	89	at	Charlotte Hornets	119
May 3	Houston Rockets	111	at	Los Angeles Clippers	99
May 4	N.Y. Knickerbockers	93	at	Indiana Pacers	116
May 4	Chicago Bulls	98	at	Atlanta Hawks	88
May 4	Phoenix Suns	107	at	Los Angeles Lakers	102
May 4	Seattle SuperSonics	80	at	Utah Jazz	90
May 5	Cleveland Cavaliers	93	at	New Jersey Nets	84
May 5	Boston Celtics	103	at	Charlotte Hornets	104
May 5	Houston Rockets	90	at	Los Angeles Clippers	93
May 5	Portland Trail Blazers	101	at	San Antonio Spurs	107
May 6	N.Y. Knickerbockers	109	at	Indiana Pacers	100 [OT]
May 6	Phoenix Suns	101	at	Los Angeles Lakers	86
May 6	Seattle SuperSonics	93	at	Utah Jazz	80
May 7	Cleveland Cavaliers	79	at	New Jersey Nets	96
May 7	Portland Trail Blazers	97	at	San Antonio Spurs	100

May 8	Los Angeles Clippers	80	at	Houston Rockets	84
May 8	Utah Jazz	92	at	Seattle SuperSonics	100
May 9	New Jersey Nets	89	at	Cleveland Cavaliers	99
May 9	Los Angeles Lakers	104	at	Phoenix Suns	112
May 9	Charlotte Hornets	95	at	N.Y. Knickerbockers	111
May 11	Cleveland Cavaliers	84	at	Chicago Bulls	91
May 11	Houston Rockets	90	at	Seattle SuperSonics	99
May 11	San Antonio Spurs	89	at	Phoenix Suns	98
May 12	Charlotte Hornets	101	at	N.Y. Knickerbockers	105
May 13	Cleveland Cavaliers	85	at	Chicago Bulls	104
May 13	Houston Rockets	100	at	Seattle SuperSonics	111
May 13	San Antonio Spurs	103	at	Phoenix Suns	109
May 14	N.Y. Knickerbockers	106	at	Charlotte Hornets	110
May 15	Chicago Bulls	96	at	Cleveland Cavaliers	90
May 15	Seattle SuperSonics	79	at	Houston Rockets	97
May 15	Phoenix Suns	96	at	San Antonio Spurs	111
May 16	N.Y. Knickerbockers	94	at	Charlotte Hornets	92
May 16	Seattle SuperSonics	92	at	Houston Rockets	103
May 16	Phoenix Suns	103	at	San Antonio Spurs	117
May 17	Chicago Bulls	103	at	Cleveland Cavaliers	101
May 18	Charlotte Hornets	101	at	N.Y. Knickerbockers	105
May 18	Houston Rockets	95	at	Seattle SuperSonics	120
May 18	San Antonio Spurs	97	at	Phoenix Suns	109
May 20	Seattle SuperSonics	90	at	Houston Rockets	103
May 20	Phoenix Suns	102	at	San Antonio Spurs	100
May 22	Houston Rockets	100	at	Seattle SuperSonics	103[OT]
May 23	Chicago Bulls	90	at	N.Y. Knickerbockers	98
May 24	Seattle SuperSonics	91	at	Phoenix Suns	105
May 25	Chicago Bulls	91	at	N.Y. Knickerbockers	96
May 26	Seattle SuperSonics	103	at	Phoenix Suns	99
May 28	Phoenix Suns	104	at	Seattle SuperSonics	97
May 29	N.Y. Knickerbockers	83	at	Chicago Bulls	103
May 30	Phoenix Suns	101	at	Seattle SuperSonics	120
May 31	N.Y. Knickerbockers	95	at	Chicago Bulls	105
June 1	Seattle SuperSonics	114	at	Phoenix Suns	120
June 2	Chicago Bulls	97	at	N.Y. Knickerbockers	94
June 3	Phoenix Suns	102	at	Seattle SuperSonics	118
June 4	N.Y. Knickerbockers	88	at	Chicago Bulls	96
June 5	Seattle SuperSonics	110	at	Phoenix Suns	123
June 9	Chicago Bulls	100	at	Phoenix Suns	92
June 11	Chicago Bulls	111	at	Phoenix Suns	108
June 13	Phoenix Suns	129	at	Chicago Bulls	121 [OT]
June 16	Phoenix Suns	105	at	Chicago Bulls	111
June 18	Phoenix Suns	108	at	Chicago Bulls	98
June 20	Chicago Bulls	99	at	Phoenix Suns	98

All Star Teams

First Team	Second Team	Third Team
Michael Jordan	John Stockton	Tim Hardaway
Mark Price	Joe Dumars	Drazen Petrovic
Hakeem Olajuwon	Patrick Ewing	David Robinson
Charles Barkley	Dominique Wilkins	Scottie Pippen
Karl Malone	Larry Johnson	Derrick Coleman

Individual Awards

Defensive Player of the Year--Hakeem Olajuwon (Houston Rockets)
Eddie Gottlieb Trophy--Shaquille O'Neal (Orlando Magic)
Executive of the Year--Jerry Colangelo (Phoenix Suns)
IBM Award--Hakeem Olajuwon (Houston Rockets)
J. Walter Kennedy Citizenship Award--Terry Porter (Portland Trail Blazers)
Maurice Podoloff Trophy--Charles Barkley (Phoenix Suns)
Most Improved Player--Chris Jackson (Denver Nuggets)
NBA All Star Game MVP--Karl Malone (Utah Jazz)
John Stockton (Utah Jazz)
NBA Finals M.V.P.--Michael Jordan (Chicago Bulls)
Sixth Man Award--Cliff Robinson (Portland Trail Blazers)
Red Auerbach Trophy--Pat Riley (New York Knickerbockers)

Hall of Fame Inductees

Walt Bellamy, Julius Erving, Dan Issel, Dick McGuire, Ann Meyers, Calvin Murphy, Juliana Semenova, Bill Walton

FOOTBALL

National Football League
National Conference
Eastern Division

Team Name	GP	W	L	T	PF	PA	Pct
Dallas Cowboys	16	12	4	0	376	229	.750
New York Giants	16	11	5	0	288	205	.688
Philadelphia Eagles	16	8	8	0	293	315	.500
Phoenix Cardinals	16	7	9	0	326	269	.438
Washington Redskins	16	4	12	0	230	345	.250

Central Division

Team Name	GP	W	L	T	PF	PA	Pct
Detroit Lions	16	10	6	0	298	292	.625
Minnesota Vikings	16	9	7	0	277	290	.563
Green Bay Packers	16	9	7	0	340	282	.563
Chicago Bears	16	7	9	0	234	230	.438
Tampa Bay Buccaneers	16	5	11	0	237	376	.313

Western Division

Team Name	GP	W	L	T	PF	PA	Pct
San Francisco 49ers	16	10	6	0	473	295	.625
New Orleans Saints	16	8	8	0	317	343	.500
Atlanta Falcons	16	6	10	0	316	385	.375
Los Angeles Rams	16	5	11	0	221	367	.313

American Conference

Eastern Division

Team Name	GP	W	L	T	PF	PA	Pct
Buffalo Bills	16	12	4	0	329	242	.750
Miami Dolphins	16	9	7	0	349	351	.563
New York Jets	16	8	8	0	270	247	.500
New England Patriots	16	5	11	0	238	286	.313
Indianapolis Colts	16	4	12	0	189	378	.250

Central Division

Houston Oilers	16	12	4	0	368	238	.750
Pittsburgh Steelers	16	9	7	0	308	281	.563
Cleveland Browns	16	7	9	0	304	307	.438
Cincinnati Bengals	16	3	13	0	187	319	.188

Western Division

Kansas City Chiefs	16	11	5	0	328	291	.688
Los Angeles Raiders	16	10	6	0	306	326	.625
Denver Broncos	16	9	7	0	373	284	.563
San Diego Chargers	16	8	8	0	322	290	.500
Seattle Seahawks	16	6	10	0	280	314	.375

Coaching Changes

N.Y. Giants--Dan Reeves 11-5-0; Washington--Richie Petitbon 4-12-0; Chicago--Dave Wannstedt 7-9-0; New England--Bill Parcells 5-11-0; Denver--Wade Phillips 9-7-0.

League Leaders

Yards Rushing		**Yards Passing**		**Passing %** (300 attempts)	
Emmitt Smith	1486	John Elway	4030	Troy Aikman	69.1
Jerome Bettis	1429	Steve Young	4023	Steve Young	68.0
Thurman Thomas	1315	Boomer Esiason	3421	John Elway	63.2
Eric Pegram	1185	Jim Kelly	3382	Phil Simms	61.8
Barry Sanders	1115	Brett Favre	3303	Steve Beuerlein	61.7

Receiving Yards		**Receptions**		**Field Goals**	
Jerry Rice	1503	Sterling Sharpe	112	Jeff Jaeger	35
Michael Irvin	1330	Jerry Rice	98	Jason Hanson	34
Sterling Sharpe	1274	Michael Irvin	88	Chris Jacke	31
Andre Rison	1242	Andre Rison	86	John Carney	31
Tim Brown	1180	Cris Carter	86	Al Del Greco	29

Punt Return Yards		**Kickoff Return Yards**	
Tyrone Hughes	503	Clarence Verdin	1050
Tim Brown	465	Tony Smith	948
Eric Metcalf	464	O.J. McDuffie	755
Glyn Milburn	425	Tyrone Hughes	753
Dexter Carter	411	John Bailey	699

Pro Bowl Game

(Aloha Stadium, Honolulu)

February 6 1994	National Conference	17	American Conference	3

NFL Playoffs

January 8 1994	Pittsburgh Steelers	24	at	Kansas City Chiefs	27 [OT]
January 8 1994	Green Bay Packers	28	at	Detroit Lions	24
January 9 1994	Minnesota Vikings	10	at	New York Giants	17
January 9 1994	Denver Broncos	24	at	Los Angeles Raiders	42

January 15 1994	Los Angeles Raiders	23	at	Buffalo Bills	29
January 15 1994	New York Giants	3	at	San Francisco 49ers	44
January 16 1994	Green Bay Packers	17	at	Dallas Cowboys	27
January 16 1994	Kansas City Chiefs	28	at	Houston Oilers	20
January 23 1994	Kansas City Chiefs	13	at	Buffalo Bills	30
January 23 1994	San Francisco 49ers	21	at	Dallas Cowboys	38

Super Bowl XXVIII
(Georgia Dome, Atlanta)

January 30 1994	Dallas Cowboys	30	Buffalo Bills	13

Individual Awards

A.P. MVP--Emmitt Smith (Dallas Cowboys)
Bert Bell Trophy--Emmitt Smith (Dallas Cowboys)
Dan McGuire Award--Andre Rison (Atlanta Falcons)
George Halas Trophy--Bruce Smith (Buffalo Bills)
Jim Thorpe Trophy--Emmitt Smith (Dallas Cowboys)
P.F.W.A. MVP--Emmitt Smith (Dallas Cowboys)
Pete Rozelle Award--Emmitt Smith (Dallas Cowboys)
U.P.I. AFC Coach of the Year--Marv Levy (Buffalo Bills)
U.P.I. AFC Player of the Year--John Elway (Denver Broncos)
Rod Woodson (Pittsburgh Steelers)
U.P.I. AFC Rookie of the Year--Rick Mirer (Seattle Seahawks)
U.P.I. NFC Coach of the Year--Dan Reeves (New York Giants)
U.P.I. NFC Player of the Year--Emmitt Smith (Dallas Cowboys)
Eric Allen (Philadelphia Eagles)
U.P.I. NFC Rookie of the Year--Jerome Bettis (Los Angeles Rams)

Hall of Fame Inductees

Dan Fouts, Larry Little, Chuck Noll, Walter Payton, Bill Walsh

Canadian Football League
Eastern Division

Team Name	**GP**	**W**	**L**	**T**	**PF**	**PA**	**Pts**	**Pct**
Winnipeg Blue Bombers	18	14	4	0	646	421	28	.778
Hamilton Tiger-Cats	18	6	12	0	316	567	12	.333
Ottawa Rough Riders	18	4	14	0	387	517	8	.222
Toronto Argonauts	18	3	15	0	390	593	6	.167

Western Division

Team Name	**GP**	**W**	**L**	**T**	**PF**	**PA**	**Pts**	**Pct**
Calgary Stampeders	18	15	3	0	646	418	30	.833
Edmonton Eskimos	18	12	6	0	507	372	24	.667
Saskatchewan Roughriders	18	11	7	0	511	495	22	.611
British Columbia Lions	18	10	8	0	574	583	20	.556
Sacramento Gold Miners	18	6	12	0	498	509	12	.333

Coaching Changes

Winnipeg--Cal Murphy 14-4-0; Toronto--Dennis Meyer 1-9-0, Bob O'Billovich 2-6-0; British Columbia--Dave Ritchie 10-8-0; Sacramento--Kay Stephenson 6-12-0.

League Leaders

Yards Rushing		Yards Passing (200 attempts)		Passing %	
Mike Richardson	925	Doug Flutie	6092	Doug Flutie	59.2
Damon Allen	920	David Archer	6023	David Archer	57.5
Bruce Perkins	812	Kent Austin	5754	Danny Barrett	57.1
Mike Oliphant	760	Tom Burgess	5063	Kent Austin	56.6
Mike Saunders	683	Matt Dunigan	4682	Matt Dunigan	55.7

Receiving Yards		Receptions		Points	
Dave Sapunjis	1484	Dave Sapunjis	103	Mark McLaughlin	215
Ray Elgaard	1393	Rod Harris	90	Troy Westwood	209
Jeff Fairholm	1391	Ray Elgaard	89	Dave Ridgway	196
Rod Harris	1379	David Williams	84	Lui Passaglia	176
Ed Brown	1378	Don Narcisse	83	Sean Fleming	166

Grey Cup Playoffs

November 14	Saskatchewan Roughriders	13	at	Edmonton Eskimos	51
November 14	British Columbia Lions	9	at	Calgary Stampeders	17
November 14	Ottawa Rough Riders	10	at	Hamilton Tiger-Cats	21
November 21	Edmonton Eskimos	29	at	Calgary Stampeders	15
November 21	Hamilton Tiger-Cats	19	at	Winnipeg Blue Bombers	20
November 28	Edmonton Eskimos	33	at	Winnipeg Blue Bombers	23*

Hall of Fame Inductees

Peter Dalla Riva, Sam Berger, Herm Harrison, Whit Tucker,

Individual Awards

Annis Stukus Trophy--Wally Buono (Calgary Stampeders)
CFL Award Most Outstanding Canadian--Dave Sapunjis (Calgary Stampeders)
CFL Award Most Outstanding Defensive Player--Jearld Baylis (Saskatchewan Roughriders)
CFL Award Most Outstanding Offensive Lineman--Chris Walby (Winnipeg Blue Bombers)
CFL Award Most Outstanding Player--Doug Flutie (Calgary Stampeders)
CFL Award Most Outstanding Rookie--Mike O'Shea (Hamilton Tiger-Cats)
Dr. Beattie Martin Trophy--David Sapunjis (Calgary Stampeders)
Grey Cup Most Valuable Canadian--Sean Fleming (Edmonton Eskimos)
Grey Cup Most Valuable Player--Damon Allen (Edmonton Eskimos)
Dave Dryburgh Memorial Trophy-- Mark McLaughlin (Calgary Stampeders)
DeMarco-Becket Memorial Trophy--Bruce Covernton (Calgary Stampeders)
Eddie James Memorial Trophy--Damon Allen (Edmonton Eskimos)
Frank M. Gibson Trophy--Michael O'Shea (Hamilton Tiger-Cats)
Jackie Parker Trophy--Brian Wiggins (Calgary Stampeders)
James P. McCaffrey Award--Elfrid Payton (Winnipeg Blue Bombers)
Jeff Nicklin Memorial Trophy--Doug Flutie (Calgary Stampeders)
Jeff Russel Memorial Trophy--Matt Dunigan (Winnipeg Blue Bombers)
Leo Dandurand Trophy--Chris Walby (Winnipeg Blue Bombers)
Lew Hayman Trophy--Gerald Wilcox (Winnipeg Blue Bombers)
Norm Fieldgate Trophy--Jearld Baylis (Saskatchewan Roughriders)

*Game played in Calgary

HOCKEY

National Hockey League

Clarence Campbell Conference
Norris Division

Team Name	GP	W	L	T	GF	GA	Pts	Pct
Chicago Blackhawks	84	47	25	12	279	230	106	.631
Detroit Red Wings	84	47	28	9	369	280	103	.613
Toronto Maple Leafs	84	44	29	11	288	241	99	.589
St. Louis Blues	84	37	36	11	282	278	85	.506
Minnesota North Stars	84	36	38	10	272	293	82	.488
Tampa Bay Lightning	84	23	54	7	245	332	53	.315

Smythe Division

Team Name	GP	W	L	T	GF	GA	Pts	Pct
Vancouver Canucks	84	46	29	9	346	278	101	.601
Calgary Flames	84	43	30	11	322	282	97	.578
Los Angeles Kings	84	39	35	10	338	340	88	.524
Winnipeg Jets	84	40	37	7	322	320	87	.518
Edmonton Oilers	84	26	50	8	242	337	60	.357
San Jose Sharks	84	11	71	2	218	414	24	.143

Prince of Wales Conference

Adams Division

Team Name	GP	W	L	T	GF	GA	Pts	Pct
Boston Bruins	84	51	26	7	332	268	109	.649
Quebec Nordiques	84	47	27	10	351	300	104	.619
Montreal Canadiens	84	48	30	6	326	280	102	.607
Buffalo Sabres	84	38	36	10	335	297	86	.512
Hartford Whalers	84	26	52	6	284	369	58	.345
Ottawa Senators	84	10	70	4	202	395	24	.143

Patrick Division

Team Name	GP	W	L	T	GF	GA	Pts	Pct
Pittsburgh Penguins	84	56	21	7	367	268	119	.708
Washington Capitals	84	43	34	7	325	286	93	.554
New York Islanders	84	40	37	7	335	297	87	.518
New Jersey Devils	84	40	37	7	308	299	87	.518
Philadelphia Flyers	84	36	37	11	319	319	83	.494
New York Rangers	84	34	39	11	304	308	79	.470

Coaching Changes

Chicago--Darryl Sutter 47-25-12; Toronto--Pat Burns 44-29-11; St. Louis--Bob Plager 4-6-1, Bob Berry 33-30-10; Tampa Bay--Terry Crisp 23-54-7; Calgary--Dave King 43-30-11; Los Angeles--Barry Melrose 39-35-10; Boston--Brian Sutter 51-26-7; Quebec--Pierre Page 47-27-10; Montreal--Jacques Demers 48-30-6; Buffalo--John Muckler 38-36-10; Hartford--Paul Holmgren 26-52-6; Ottawa--Rick Bowness 10-70-4; New Jersey--Herb Brooks 40-37-7; Philadelphia--Bill Dineen 36-37-11; New York Rangers--Roger Neilson 19-17-4, Ron Smith 15-22-7.

League Leaders

Goals		Assists		Points	
Alexander Mogilny	76	Adam Oates	97	Mario Lemieux	160
Teemu Selanne	76	Doug Gilmour	95	Pat LaFontaine	148
Mario Lemieux	69	Pat LaFontaine	95	Adam Oates	142
Luc Robitaille	63	Mario Lemieux	91	Steve Yzerman	137
Pavel Bure	60	Craig Janney	82	Teemu Selanne	132

Penalty Minutes		GAA (27 games)		Wins (27 games)	
Marty McSorley	399	Felix Potvin	2.50	Tom Barrasso	43
Gino Odjick	370	Ed Belfour	2.59	Ed Belfour	41
Tie Domi	344	Tom Barrasso	3.01	Andy Moog	37
Nick Kypreos	325	Curtis Joseph	3.02	Tim Cheveldae	34
Mike Peluso	318	Kay Whitmore	3.10	Bob Essensa	33

Shutouts		Save %	
Ed Belfour	7	Curtis Joseph	.911
Tommy Soderstrom	5	Felix Potvin	.910
John Vanbiesbrouck	4	Ed Belfour	.906
Tom Barrasso	4	Tom Barrasso	.901
Tim Cheveldae	4	John Vanbiesbrouck	.900

All Star Game

(The Forum, Montreal)

February 6	Wales Conference	16	Campbell Conference	6

Stanley Cup Playoffs

April 18	Buffalo Sabres	5	at	Boston Bruins	4 [11:03]
April 18	Montreal Canadiens	2	at	Quebec Nordiques	3 [16:49]
April 18	New Jersey Devils	3	at	Pittsburgh Penguins	6
April 18	New York Islanders	1	at	Washington Capitals	3
April 19	Winnipeg Jets	2	at	Vancouver Canucks	4
April 19	Los Angeles Kings	6	at	Calgary Flames	3
April 19	St. Louis Blues	4	at	Chicago Blackhawks	3
April 19	Toronto Maple Leafs	3	at	Detroit Red Wings	6
April 20	Buffalo Sabres	4	at	Boston Bruins	0
April 20	Montreal Canadiens	1	at	Quebec Nordiques	4
April 20	New Jersey Devils	0	at	Pittsburgh Penguins	7
April 20	New York Islanders	5	at	Washington Capitals	4 [34:50]
April 21	Winnipeg Jets	2	at	Vancouver Canucks	3
April 21	Los Angeles Kings	4	at	Calgary Flames	9
April 21	St. Louis Blues	2	at	Chicago Blackhawks	0
April 21	Toronto Maple Leafs	2	at	Detroit Red Wings	6
April 22	Boston Bruins	3	at	Buffalo Sabres	4 [1:05]
April 22	Quebec Nordiques	1	at	Montreal Canadiens	2 [10:30]
April 22	Pittsburgh Penguins	4	at	New Jersey Devils	3
April 22	Washington Capitals	3	at	New York Islanders	4 [4:46]
April 23	Vancouver Canucks	4	at	Winnipeg Jets	5
April 23	Calgary Flames	5	at	Los Angeles Kings	2
April 23	Chicago Blackhawks	0	at	St. Louis Blues	3

April 23	Detroit Red Wings	2	at	Toronto Maple Leafs	4
April 24	Boston Bruins	5	at	Buffalo Sabres	6 [4:48]
April 24	Quebec Nordiques	2	at	Montreal Canadiens	3
April 24	Pittsburgh Penguins	1	at	New Jersey Devils	4
April 24	Washington Capitals	3	at	New York Islanders	4 [25:40]
April 25	Vancouver Canucks	3	at	Winnipeg Jets	1
April 25	Calgary Flames	1	at	Los Angeles Kings	3
April 25	Chicago Blackhawks	3	at	St. Louis Blues	4 [10:43]
April 25	Detroit Red Wings	2	at	Toronto Maple Leafs	3
April 26	Montreal Canadiens	5	at	Quebec Nordiques	4 [8:17]
April 26	New Jersey Devils	3	at	Pittsburgh Penguins	5
April 26	New York Islanders	4	at	Washington Capitals	6
April 27	Winnipeg Jets	4	at	Vancouver Canucks	3 [6:18]
April 27	Los Angeles Kings	9	at	Calgary Flames	4
April 27	Toronto Maple Leafs	5	at	Detroit Red Wings	4 [2:05]
April 28	Quebec Nordiques	2	at	Montreal Canadiens	6
April 28	Washington Capitals	3	at	New York Islanders	5
April 29	Vancouver Canucks	4	at	Winnipeg Jets	3 [4:30]
April 29	Calgary Flames	6	at	Los Angeles Kings	9
April 29	Detroit Red Wings	7	at	Toronto Maple Leafs	3
May 1	Toronto Maple Leafs	4	at	Detroit Red Wings	3 [2:35]
May 2	New York Islanders	3	at	Pittsburgh Penguins	2
May 2	Buffalo Sabres	3	at	Montreal Canadiens	4
May 2	Los Angeles Kings	2	at	Vancouver Canucks	5
May 3	St. Louis Blues	0	at	Toronto Maple Leafs	1
May 4	New York Islanders	0	at	Pittsburgh Penguins	3
May 4	Buffalo Sabres	3	at	Montreal Canadiens	4 [2:50]
May 5	Los Angeles Kings	6	at	Vancouver Canucks	3
May 5	St. Louis Blues	2	at	Toronto Maple Leafs	1 [23:03]
May 6	Pittsburgh Penguins	3	at	New York Islanders	1
May 6	Montreal Canadiens	4	at	Buffalo Sabres	3 [8:28]
May 7	Vancouver Canucks	4	at	Los Angeles Kings	7
May 7	Toronto Maple Leafs	3	at	St. Louis Blues	4
May 8	Pittsburgh Penguins	5	at	New York Islanders	6
May 8	Montreal Canadiens	4	at	Buffalo Sabres	3 [11:37]
May 9	Vancouver Canucks	7	at	Los Angeles Kings	2
May 9	Toronto Maple Leafs	4	at	St. Louis Blues	1
May 10	New York Islanders	3	at	Pittsburgh Penguins	6
May 11	Los Angeles Kings	4	at	Vancouver Canucks	3 [26:31]
May 11	St. Louis Blues	1	at	Toronto Maple Leafs	5
May 12	Pittsburgh Penguins	5	at	New York Islanders	7
May 13	Vancouver Canucks	3	at	Los Angeles Kings	5
May 13	Toronto Maple Leafs	1	at	St. Louis Blues	2
May 14	New York Islanders	4	at	Pittsburgh Penguins	3
May 15	St. Louis Blues	0	at	Toronto Maple Leafs	6
May 16	New York Islanders	1	at	Montreal Canadiens	4
May 17	Los Angeles Kings	1	at	Toronto Maple Leafs	4
May 18	New York Islanders	3	at	Montreal Canadiens	4 [26:21]
May 19	Los Angeles Kings	3	at	Toronto Maple Leafs	2
May 20	Montreal Canadiens	2	at	New York Islanders	1 [12:34]
May 21	Toronto Maple Leafs	2	at	Los Angeles Kings	4
May 22	Montreal Canadiens	1	at	New York Islanders	4
May 23	Toronto Maple Leafs	4	at	Los Angeles Kings	2
May 24	New York Islanders	2	at	Montreal Canadiens	5

May 25	Los Angeles Kings	2	at	Toronto Maple Leafs	3 [19:20]
May 27	Toronto Maple Leafs	4	at	Los Angeles Kings	5 [1:41]
May 29	Los Angeles Kings	5	at	Toronto Maple Leafs	4
June 1	Los Angeles Kings	4	at	Montreal Canadiens	1
June 3	Los Angeles Kings	2	at	Montreal Canadiens	3 [0:51]
June 5	Montreal Canadiens	4	at	Los Angeles Kings	3 [0:34]
June 7	Montreal Canadiens	3	at	Los Angeles Kings	2 [14:37]
June 9	Los Angeles Kings	1	at	Montreal Canadiens	4

All Star Teams

First Team		Second Team
Ed Belfour	Goal	Tom Barrasso
Chris Chelios	Defense	Larry Murphy
Ray Bourque	Defense	Al Iafrate
Mario Lemieux	Center	Pat LaFontaine
Teemu Selanne	Right Wing	Alexander Mogilny
Luc Robitaille	Left Wing	Kevin Stevens

Individual Awards

Alka Seltzer Plus Award--Mario Lemieux (Pittsburgh Penguins)
Art Ross Trophy--Mario Lemieux (Pittsburgh Penguins)
Bill Masterton Trophy--Mario Lemieux (Pittsburgh Penguins)
Calder Memorial Trophy--Teemu Selanne (Winnipeg Jets)
Conn Smythe Trophy--Patrick Roy (Montreal Canadiens)
Frank J. Selke Trophy--Doug Gilmour (Toronto Maple Leafs)
Hart Memorial Trophy--Mario Lemieux (Pittsburgh Penguins)
Jack Adams Award--Pat Burns (Toronto Maple Leafs NHL)
James Norris Trophy--Chris Chelios (Chicago Blackhawks)
King Clancy Trophy--Dave Poulin (Boston Bruins)
Lady Byng Memorial Trophy--Pierre Turgeon (New York Islanders)
Lester B. Pearson Award--Mario Lemieux (Pittsburgh Penguins)
Lester Patrick Trophy--Frank Boucher, Mervyn Dutton, Bruce McNall, Gil Stein
NHL All Star Game M.V.P.--Mike Gartner (New York Rangers)
Vezina Trophy--Ed Belfour (Chicago Blackhawks)
William M. Jennings Trophy--Ed Belfour (Chicago Blackhawks)

Hall of Fame Inductees

John D'Amico, Frank Griffiths, Seymour Knox III, Guy Lapointe, Edgar Laprade, Fred Page, Steve Shutt, Billy Smith

Notes

Wayne Gretzky signs a three year $25.5 million contract with the Los Angeles Kings.
NHL commissioner Gary Bettman begins an investigations into rumors that the Ottawa Senators intentionally lost their final game of the season to secure the first overall draft pick of 1994.Bettman will eventually clear the Senators of any wrong doing but fines former owner Bruce Firestone over $100,000 for comments he made which Bettman judged were detrimental to the league.

Other Sports

Horseracing--Kentucky Derby won by Sea Hero (time 2:02.4, purse $735,900).

Heavyweight Boxing--Riddock Bowe defeated Michael Dokes by TKO in 1 round (WBA, WBC, IBF).
Lennox Lewis defeated Tony Tucker by unanimous decision in 12 rounds (WBC).
Riddock Bowe defeated Jesse Ferguson by TKO in 2 rounds (WBA, IBF).
Lennox Lewis defeated Frank Bruno by TKO in 7 rounds (WBC).

Golf--U.S. Open won by Lee Janzen with a score of 272.

Auto Racing--Indianapolis 500 won by Emerson Fittipaldi (ave speed 157.207 MPH).

Tennis--U.S. Open won by Pete Sampras in the men's singles.
U.S. Open won by Ken Flach and Rick Leach in the men's doubles.
U.S. Open won by Steffi Graf in the women's singles.
U.S. Open won by Arantxa Sanchez Vicario and Helena Sukova in the women's doubles.
U.S. Open won by Helena Sukova and Todd Woodbridge in the mixed doubles.

Notes

German worker Gunter Parche is given a two year suspended sentence for his attack on tennis star Monica Seles during a match. Parche a fan of Seles' rival Steffi Graf, gets off easier than Seles who will not return to competitive tennis until the 1995 season.

1994

BASEBALL

National League

East

Team Name	W	L	Pct	GB	R	OR
Montreal Expos	74	40	.649	-	585	454
Atlanta Braves	68	46	.596	6	542	448
New York Mets	55	58	.487	18.5	506	526
Philadelphia Phillies	54	61	.470	20.5	521	497
Florida Marlins	51	64	.443	23.5	468	576

Central

Team Name	W	L	Pct	GB	R	OR
Cincinnati Reds	66	48	.579	-	609	490
Houston Astros	66	49	.574	.5	602	503
St. Louis Cardinals	53	61	.465	13	535	621
Pittsburgh Pirates	53	61	.465	13	466	580
Chicago Cubs	49	64	.434	16.5	500	549

West

Team Name	W	L	Pct	GB	R	OR
Los Angeles Dodgers	58	56	.509	-	532	509
San Francisco Giants	55	60	.478	3.5	504	500
Colorado Rockies	53	64	.453	6.5	573	638
San Diego Padres	47	70	.402	12.5	479	531

Coaching Changes

N.Y. Mets--Dallas Green 55-58; Cincinnati--Davey Johnson 66-48; Houston--Terry Collins 66-49; Chicago--Tom Trebelhorn 49-64.

League Leaders

Batting Average		Home Runs		RBI	
Tony Gwynn	.394	Matt Williams	43	Jeff Bagwell	116
Jeff Bagwell	.368	Jeff Bagwell	39	Matt Williams	96
Moises Alou	.339	Barry Bonds	37	Dante Bichette	95
Hal Morris	.335	Fred McGriff	34	Fred McGriff	94
Kevin Mitchell	.326	Andres Galarraga	31	Mike Piazza	92

Stolen Bases		ERA		Wins	
Craig Biggio	39	Greg Maddux	1.56	Ken Hill	16
Deion Sanders	38	Bret Saberhagen	2.74	Greg Maddux	16
Marquis Grissom	36	Doug Drabek	2.84	Bret Saberhagen	14
Chuck Carr	32	Jeff Fassero	2.99	Danny Jackson	14
Darren Lewis	30	Shane Reynolds	3.05	Tom Glavine	13

Saves		Strikeouts	
John Franco	30	Andy Benes	189
Rod Beck	28	Jose Rijo	171
Doug Jones	27	Greg Maddux	156
John Wetteland	25	Bret Saberhagen	143
Greg McMichael	21	Pedro Martinez	142

Playoffs

Due to the player's strike there were no playoffs held this year.

American League

East

Team Name	W	L	Pct	GB	R	OR
New York Yankees	70	43	.619	-	670	534
Baltimore Orioles	63	49	.563	6.5	589	497
Toronto Blue Jays	55	60	.478	16	566	579
Boston Red Sox	54	61	.470	17	552	621
Detroit Tigers	53	62	.461	18	652	671

Central

Team Name	W	L	Pct	GB	R	OR
Chicago White Sox	67	46	.593	-	633	498
Cleveland Indians	66	47	.584	1	679	562
Kansas City Royals	64	51	.557	4	574	532
Minnesota Twins	53	60	.469	14	594	688
Milwaukee Brewers	53	62	.461	15	547	586

West

Team Name	W	L	Pct	GB	R	OR
Texas Rangers	52	62	.456	-	613	697
Oakland Athletics	51	63	.447	1	549	589
Seattle Mariners	49	63	.438	2	569	616
California Angels	47	68	.409	5.5	543	660

Coaching Changes

None.

League Leaders

Batting Average		Home Runs		RBI	
Paul O'Neill	.359	Ken Griffey Jr.	40	Kirby Puckett	112
Albert Belle	.357	Frank Thomas	38	Joe Carter	103
Frank Thomas	.353	Albert Belle	36	Albert Belle	101
Kenny Lofton	.349	Jose Canseco	31	Frank Thomas	101
Wade Boggs	.342	Cecil Fielder	28	Julio Franco	98

Stolen Bases		ERA		Wins	
Kenny Lofton	60	Steve Ontiveros	2.65	Jimmy Key	17
Vince Coleman	50	Roger Clemens	2.85	David Cone	16
Otis Nixon	42	David Cone	2.94	Mike Mussina	16
Chuck Knoblauch	35	Mike Mussina	3.06	Ben McDonald	14
Brady Anderson	31	Randy Johnson	3.19	Randy Johnson	13

Saves		**Strikeouts**	
Lee Smith	33	Randy Johnson	204
Jeff Montgomery	27	Roger Clemens	168
Rick Aguilera	23	Chuck Finley	148
Dennis Eckersley	19	Pat Hentgen	147
Bobby Ayala	18	Kevin Appier	145

All Star Game

(Three Rivers Stadium, Pittsburgh)

July 12	National League	8	American League	7

Playoffs

Due to the player's strike there were no playoffs held this year.

Individual Awards

ALCS M.V.P.--No Award
Arch Ward Memorial Trophy--Fred McGriff (Atlanta Braves NL)
Baseball Writers Award--Jeff Bagwell (Houston Astros NL)
Frank Thomas (Chicago White Sox AL)
Cy Young Award--Greg Maddux (Atlanta Braves NL)
David Cone (Kansas City Royals AL)
NLCS MVP--No Award
Rookie of the Year--Raul Mondesi (Los Angeles Dodgers NL)
Bob Hamelin (Kansas City Royals AL)
Sporting News Executive of the Year--John Hart (Cleveland Indians AL)
Sporting News Manager of the Year--Felipe Alou (Montreal Expos NL)
Buck Showalter (New York Yankees AL)
Sporting News Pitcher of the Year--Greg Maddux (Atlanta Braves NL)
Jimmy Key (New York Yankees AL)
Sporting News Player of the Year--Jeff Bagwell (Houston Astros NL)
Sporting News Rookie of the Year--Raul Mondesi (Los Angeles Dodgers NL)
Steve Trachsel (Chicago Cubs NL)
Bob Hamelin (Kansas City Royals AL)
Brian Anderson (California Angels AL)
World Series MVP--No Award

Hall of Fame Inductees

Steve Carlton, Leo Durocher, Phil Rizzuto

Notes

Both the National League and the American League split into three divisions this year. Each divisional winner plus a wild card team from each league were to participate in the playoffs but on August 12 the major league players went on strike, canceling 669 games remaining in the regular season and all post season play.

BASKETBALL

National Basketball Association

Eastern Conference
Atlantic Division

Team Name	GP	W	L	PPGF	PPGA	Pct	GB
New York Knickerbockers	82	57	25	98.5	91.5	.695	-
Orlando Magic	82	50	32	105.7	101.8	.610	7
New Jersey Nets	82	45	37	103.2	101.0	.549	12
Miami Heat	82	42	40	103.4	100.7	.512	15
Boston Celtics	82	32	50	100.8	105.1	.390	25
Philadelphia 76ers	82	25	57	98.0	105.6	.305	32
Washington Bullets	82	24	58	100.4	107.7	.293	33

Central Division

Team Name	GP	W	L	PPGF	PPGA	Pct	GB
Atlanta Hawks	82	57	25	101.4	96.2	.695	-
Chicago Bulls	82	55	27	98.0	94.9	.671	2
Indiana Pacers	82	47	35	101.0	97.5	.573	10
Cleveland Cavaliers	82	47	35	101.2	97.1	.573	10
Charlotte Hornets	82	41	41	106.5	106.7	.500	16
Detroit Pistons	82	20	62	96.9	104.7	.244	37
Milwaukee Bucks	82	20	62	96.9	103.4	.244	37

Western Conference

Midwest Division

Team Name	GP	W	L	PPGF	PPGA	Pct	GB
Houston Rockets	82	58	24	101.1	96.8	.707	-
San Antonio Spurs	82	55	27	100.0	94.8	.671	3
Utah Jazz	82	53	29	101.9	97.7	.646	5
Denver Nuggets	82	42	40	100.3	98.8	.512	16
Minnesota Timberwolves	82	20	62	96.7	103.6	.244	38
Dallas Mavericks	82	13	69	95.1	103.8	.159	45

Pacific Division

Team Name	GP	W	L	PPGF	PPGA	Pct	GB
Seattle SuperSonics	82	63	19	105.9	96.9	.768	-
Phoenix Suns	82	56	26	108.2	103.4	.683	7
Golden State Warriors	82	50	32	107.9	106.1	.610	13
Portland Trail Blazers	82	47	35	107.3	104.6	.573	16
Los Angeles Lakers	82	33	49	100.4	104.7	.402	30
Sacramento Kings	82	28	54	101.1	106.9	.341	35
Los Angeles Clippers	82	27	55	103.0	108.7	.329	36

Coaching Changes

Orlando--Brian Hill 50-32; Philadelphia--Fred Carter 25-57; Atlanta--Lenny Wilkens 57-25; Indiana--Larry Brown 47-35; Cleveland--Mike Fratello 47-35; Detroit--Don Chaney 20-62; San Antonio--John Lucas 55-27; Minnesota--Sidney Lowe 20-62; Dallas--Quinn Buckner 13-69; L.A. Lakers--Randy Pfund 27-37, Bill Bertka 1-1, Earvin Johnson 5-11; L.A. Clippers--Bob Weiss 27-55.

League Leaders

Field Goal %		Free Throw %		Assists per Game	
Shaquille O'Neal	.599	Mahmoud Abdul-Rauf	.956	John Stockton	12.6
Dikembe Mutombo	.569	Reggie Miller	.908	Muggsy Bogues	10.1
Otis Thorpe	.561	Ricky Pierce	.896	Mookie Blaylock	9.7
Chris Webber	.552	Sedale Threatt	.890	Ken Anderson	9.6
Shawn Kemp	.538	Mark Price	.888	Kevin Johnson	9.5

Points		Rebounds per Game	
David Robinson	2383	Dennis Rodman	17.3
Shaquille O'Neal	2377	Shaquille O'Neal	13.2
Hakeem Olajuwon	2184	Kevin Willis	12.0
Karl Malone	2063	Hakeem Olajuwon	11.9
Patrick Ewing	1939	Olden Polynice	11.9

All Star Game

(Target Center, Minneapolis)

February 13	East Division	127	West Division	118

NBA Playoffs

April 28	Miami Heat	93	at	Atlanta Hawks	88
April 28	Cleveland Cavaliers	96	at	Chicago Bulls	104
April 28	Indiana Pacers	89	at	Orlando Magic	88
April 28	Denver Nuggets	82	at	Seattle SuperSonics	106
April 28	Utah Jazz	89	at	San Antonio Spurs	106
April 29	New Jersey Nets	80	at	N.Y. Knickerbockers	91
April 29	Portland Trail Blazers	104	at	Houston Rockets	114
April 29	Golden State Warriors	104	at	Phoenix Suns	111
April 30	Miami Heat	86	at	Atlanta Hawks	104
April 30	Indiana Pacers	103	at	Orlando Magic	101
April 30	Utah Jazz	96	at	San Antonio Spurs	84
April 30	Denver Nuggets	87	at	Seattle SuperSonics	97
May 1	New Jersey Nets	81	at	N.Y. Knickerbockers	90
May 1	Cleveland Cavaliers	96	at	Chicago Bulls	105
May 1	Portland Trail Blazers	104	at	Houston Rockets	115
May 1	Golden State Warriors	111	at	Phoenix Suns	117
May 2	Orlando Magic	86	at	Indiana Pacers	99
May 2	Seattle SuperSonics	93	at	Denver Nuggets	110
May 3	Atlanta Hawks	86	at	Miami Heat	90
May 3	Chicago Bulls	95	at	Cleveland Cavaliers	92
May 3	Houston Rockets	115	at	Portland Trail Blazers	118
May 4	N.Y. Knickerbockers	92	at	New Jersey Nets	93
May 4	Phoenix Suns	140	at	Golden State Warriors	133
May 4	San Antonio Spurs	72	at	Utah Jazz	105
May 5	Atlanta Hawks	103	at	Miami Heat	89
May 5	Seattle SuperSonics	85	at	Denver Nuggets	94 [OT]
May 5	San Antonio Spurs	90	at	Utah Jazz	95
May 6	N.Y. Knickerbockers	102	at	New Jersey Nets	92
May 6	Houston Rockets	92	at	Portland Trail Blazers	89
May 7	Denver Nuggets	98	at	Seattle SuperSonics	94 [OT]
May 8	Miami Heat	91	at	Atlanta Hawks	102

May 8	Chicago Bulls	86	at	N.Y. Knickerbockers	90
May 8	Phoenix Suns	91	at	Houston Rockets	87
May 10	Denver Nuggets	91	at	Utah Jazz	100
May 10	Indiana Pacers	96	at	Atlanta Hawks	85
May 11	Chicago Bulls	91	at	N.Y. Knickerbockers	96
May 11	Phoenix Suns	124	at	Houston Rockets	117 [OT]
May 12	Denver Nuggets	94	at	Utah Jazz	104
May 12	Indiana Pacers	69	at	Atlanta Hawks	92
May 13	N.Y. Knickerbockers	102	at	Chicago Bulls	104
May 13	Houston Rockets	118	at	Phoenix Suns	102
May 14	Utah Jazz	111	at	Denver Nuggets	109 [OT]
May 14	Atlanta Hawks	81	at	Indiana Pacers	101
May 15	N.Y. Knickerbockers	83	at	Chicago Bulls	95
May 15	Houston Rockets	107	at	Phoenix Suns	96
May 15	Utah Jazz	82	at	Denver Nuggets	83
May 15	Atlanta Hawks	86	at	Indiana Pacers	102
May 17	Phoenix Suns	86	at	Houston Rockets	109
May 17	Denver Nuggets	109	at	Utah Jazz	101
May 17	Indiana Pacers	76	at	Atlanta Hawks	88
May 18	Chicago Bulls	86	at	N.Y. Knickerbockers	87
May 19	Houston Rockets	89	at	Phoenix Suns	103
May 19	Utah Jazz	91	at	Denver Nuggets	94
May 19	Atlanta Hawks	79	at	Indiana Pacers	98
May 20	N.Y. Knickerbockers	79	at	Chicago Bulls	93
May 21	Phoenix Suns	94	at	Houston Rockets	104
May 21	Denver Nuggets	81	at	Utah Jazz	91
May 22	Chicago Bulls	77	at	N.Y. Knickerbockers	87
May 23	Utah Jazz	88	at	Houston Rockets	100
May 24	Indiana Pacers	89	at	N.Y. Knickerbockers	100
May 25	Utah Jazz	99	at	Houston Rockets	104
May 26	Indiana Pacers	78	at	N.Y. Knickerbockers	89
May 27	Houston Rockets	86	at	Utah Jazz	95
May 28	N.Y. Knickerbockers	68	at	Indiana Pacers	88
May 29	Houston Rockets	80	at	Utah Jazz	78
May 30	N.Y. Knickerbockers	77	at	Indiana Pacers	83
May 31	Utah Jazz	83	at	Houston Rockets	94
June 1	Indiana Pacers	93	at	N.Y. Knickerbockers	86
June 3	N.Y. Knickerbockers	98	at	Indiana Pacers	91
June 5	Indiana Pacers	90	at	N.Y. Knickerbockers	94
June 8	N.Y. Knickerbockers	78	at	Houston Rockets	85
June 10	N.Y. Knickerbockers	91	at	Houston Rockets	83
June 12	Houston Rockets	93	at	N.Y. Knickerbockers	89
June 15	Houston Rockets	82	at	N.Y. Knickerbockers	91
June 17	Houston Rockets	84	at	N.Y. Knickerbockers	91
June 19	N.Y. Knickerbockers	84	at	Houston Rockets	86
June 22	N.Y. Knickerbockers	84	at	Houston Rockets	90

All Star Teams

First Team	Second Team	Third Team
Scottie Pippen	Shawn Kemp	Derrick Coleman
Karl Malone	Charles Barkley	Dominique Wilkins
Hakeem Olajuwon	David Robinson	Shaquille O'Neal
John Stockton	Mitch Richmond	Mark Price
Latrell Sprewell Kevin Johnson	Gary Payton	

Individual Awards

Defensive Player of the Year--Hakeem Olajuwon (Houston Rockets)
Eddie Gottlieb Trophy--Chris Webber (Golden State Warriors)
Executive of the Year--Bob Whitsitt (Seattle SuperSonics)
IBM Award--David Robinson (San Antonio Spurs)
J. Walter Kennedy Citizenship Award--Joe Dumars (Detroit Pistons)
Maurice Podoloff Trophy--Hakeem Olajuwon (Houston Rockets)
Most Improved Player--Don MacLean (Washington Bullets)
NBA All-Star Game MVP--Scottie Pippen (Chicago Bulls)
NBA Finals MVP--Hakeem Olajuwon (Houston Rockets)
Red Auerbach Trophy--Lenny Wilkens (Atlanta Hawks)
Sixth Man Award--Dell Curry (Charlotte Hornets)

Hall of Fame Inductees

Carol Blazejowski, Denny Crum, Chuck Daly, Buddy Jeannette, Cesare Rubini

FOOTBALL

National Football League

National Conference
Eastern Division

Team Name	GP	W	L	T	PF	PA	Pct
Dallas Cowboys	16	12	4	0	414	248	.750
New York Giants	16	9	7	0	279	305	.563
Arizona Cardinals	16	8	8	0	235	267	.500
Philadelphia Eagles	16	7	9	0	308	308	.438
Washington Redskins	16	3	13	0	320	412	.188

Central Division

Team Name	GP	W	L	T	PF	PA	Pct
Minnesota Vikings	16	10	6	0	356	314	.625
Green Bay Packers	16	9	7	0	382	287	.563
Detroit Lions	16	9	7	0	357	342	.563
Chicago Bears	16	9	7	0	271	307	.563
Tampa Bay Buccaneers	16	6	10	0	251	351	.375

Western Division

Team Name	GP	W	L	T	PF	PA	Pct
San Francisco 49ers	16	13	3	0	505	296	.813
New Orleans Saints	16	7	9	0	348	407	.438
Atlanta Falcons	16	7	9	0	317	385	.438
Los Angeles Rams	16	4	12	0	286	365	.250

American Conference

Eastern Division

Miami Dolphins	16	10	6	0	389	327	.625
New England Patriots	16	10	6	0	351	312	.625
Indianapolis Colts	16	8	8	0	307	320	.500
Buffalo Bills	16	7	9	0	340	356	.438
New York Jets	16	6	10	0	264	320	.375

Central Division

Pittsburgh Steelers	16	12	4	0	316	234	.750
Cleveland Browns	16	9	7	0	319	298	.563
Cincinnati Bengals	16	3	13	0	276	406	.188
Houston Oilers	16	2	14	0	226	352	.125

Western Division

San Diego Chargers	16	11	5	0	381	306	.688
Kansas City Chiefs	16	9	7	0	319	298	.563
Los Angeles Raiders	16	9	7	0	303	327	.563
Denver Broncos	16	7	9	0	347	396	.438
Seattle Seahawks	16	6	10	0	287	323	.375

Coaching Changes

Dallas--Barry Switzer 12-4-0; Arizona--Buddy Ryan 8-8-0; Washington--Norv Turner 3-13-0; Atlanta--June Jones 7-9-0; N.Y. Jets 6-10-0; Houston--Jack Pardee 1-9-0, Jeff Fisher 1-5-0.

League Leaders

Yards Rushing		**Yards Passing**		**Passing %** (300 attempts)	
Barry Sanders	1883	Drew Bledsoe	4555	Steve Young	70.3
Chris Warren	1545	Dan Marino	4453	Troy Aikman	64.5
Emmitt Smith	1484	Warren Moon	4264	Jim Everett	64.1
Natrone Means	1350	Steve Young	3969	Jim Kelly	63.6
Marshall Faulk	1282	Brett Favre	3882	Dan Marino	62.6

Receiving Yards		**Receptions**		**Field Goals**	
Jerry Rice	1499	Chris Carter	122	John Carney	34
Terance Mathis	1342	Jerry Rice	112	Fuad Reveiz	34
Tim Brown	1309	Terance Mathis	111	Jason Elam	30
Andre Reed	1303	Ben Coates	96	Doug Pelfry	28
Irving Fryar	1270	Sterling Sharpe	94	Morten Andersen	28

Punt Return Yards		**Kickoff Return Yards**	
Tim Brown	487	Tyrone Hughes	1556
Darrien Gordon	475	Brian Mitchell	1478
Brian Mitchell	452	Andre Coleman	1293
Jeff Snyder	381	Mel Gray	1276
Glyn Milburn	379	Kevin Williams	1148

Pro Bowl Game
(Aloha Stadium, Honolulu)

February 5 1995	American Conference	41	National Conference	13

NFL Playoffs

December 31	Detroit Lions	12	at	Green Bay Packers	16
December 31	Kansas City Chiefs	17	at	Miami Dolphins	27
January 1 1995	New England Patriots	13	at	Cleveland Browns	20
January 1 1995	Chicago Bears	35	at	Minnesota Vikings	18
January 7 1995	Cleveland Browns	9	at	Pittsburgh Steelers	29
January 7 1995	Chicago Bears	15	at	San Francisco 49ers	44
January 8 1995	Green Bay Packers	9	at	Dallas Cowboys	35
January 8 1995	Miami Dolphins	21	at	San Diego Chargers	22
January 15 1995	San Diego Chargers	17	at	Pittsburgh Steelers	13
January 15 1995	Dallas Cowboys	28	at	San Francisco 49ers	38

Super Bowl XXIX
(Joe Robbie Stadium, Miami)

January 29 1995	San Francisco 49ers	49	San Diego Chargers	26

Individual Awards
A.P. MVP--Steve Young (San Francisco 49ers)
Bert Bell Trophy--Steve Young (San Francisco 49ers)
Dan McGuire Award--Marshall Faulk (Indianapolis Colts)
George Halas Trophy--
Jim Thorpe Trophy--
P.F.W.A. MVP--Steve Young (San Francisco 49ers)
Pete Rozelle Award--Steve Young (San Francisco 49ers)
U.P.I. AFC Coach of the Year--Bill Parcells (New England Patriots)
U.P.I. AFC Player of the Year--Dan Marino (Miami Dolphins)
Greg Lloyd (Pittsburgh Steelers)
U.P.I. AFC Rookie of the Year--Marshall Faulk (Indianapolis Colts)
U.P.I. NFC Coach of the Year--Dave Wannstedt (Chicago Bears)
U.P.I. NFC Player of the Year--Steve Young (San Francisco 49ers)
Charles Haley (Dallas Cowboys)
U.P.I. NFC Rookie of the Year--Bryant Young (San Francisco 49ers)

Hall of Fame Inductees
Tony Dorsett, Bud Grant, Jimmy Johnson, Leroy Kelly, Jackie Smith, Randy White

Canadian Football League

Eastern Division

Team Name	GP	W	L	T	PF	PA	Pts	Pct
Winnipeg Blue Bombers	18	13	5	0	651	572	26	.722
Baltimore CFLers	18	12	6	0	561	431	24	.667
Toronto Argonauts	18	7	11	0	504	578	14	.389
Ottawa Rough Riders	18	4	14	0	480	642	8	.222
Hamilton Tiger-Cats	18	4	14	0	435	562	8	.222
Shreveport Pirates	18	3	15	0	330	662	6	.167

Western Division

Calgary Stampeders	18	15	3	0	698	355	30	.833
Edmonton Eskimos	18	13	5	0	518	398	26	.722
Saskatchewan Roughriders	18	12	6	0	508	453	24	.667
British Columbia Lions	18	10	7	1	603	457	21	.583
Sacramento Gold Miners	18	9	8	1	436	436	19	.528
Las Vegas Posse	18	5	13	0	444	622	10	.278

Coaching Changes

Baltimore--Don Matthews 12-6-0; Toronto--Bob O'Billovich 7-11-0; Ottawa--Adam Rita 4-14-0; Hamilton--John Gregory 1-5-0; Don Sutherin 3-9-0; Shreveport--Forrest Gregg 3-15-0; Saskatchewan--Ray Jauch 12-6-0; Las Vegas--Ron Meyer 5-13-0.

League Leaders

Yards Rushing		Yards Passing		Passing % (200 attempts)	
Mike Pringle	1972	Doug Flutie	5726	Reggie Slack	61.8
Cory Philpot	1461	Tracy Ham	4348	Doug Flutie	61.2
Blaise Bryant	1289	Kent Austin	4193	Matt Dunigan	58.5
Troy Mills	1230	Danny Barrett	4173	Kent Austin	57.6
Mike Saunders	1205	Matt Dunigan	3985	Tracy Ham	53.9

Receiving Yards		Receptions		Points	
Allen Pitts	2036	Allen Pitts	126	Troy Westwood	213
Darren Flutie	1731	Darren Flutie	111	Sean Fleming	206
Gerald Wilcox	1624	Gerald Wilcox	111	Mark McLoughlin	199
Chris Armstrong	1586	Rod Harris	88	Donald Igwebuike	184
Paul Masotti	1280	Ray Alexander	85	Terry Baker	182

Grey Cup Playoffs

November 12	Toronto Argonauts	15	at	Baltimore CFLers	34
November 12	British Columbia Lions	24	at	Edmonton Eskimos	23
November 13	Ottawa Rough Riders	16	at	Winnipeg Blue Bombers	26
November 13	Saskatchewan Roughriders	3	at	Calgary Stampeders	36
November 20	Baltimore CFLers	14	at	Winnipeg Blue Bombers	12
November 20	British Columbia Lions	37	at	Calgary Stampeders	36
November 27	Baltimore CFLers	23	at	British Columbia Lions	26

Individual Awards

Annis Stukus Trophy--Don Matthews (Baltimore CFLers)
CFL Award Most Outstanding Canadian--Gerald Wilcox (Winnipeg Blue Bombers)
CFL Award Most Outstanding Defensive Player Willie Pless (Edmonton Eskimos)
CFL Award Most Outstanding Offensive Lineman--Rocco Romano (Calgary Stampeders)
CFL Award Most Outstanding Player--Doug Flutie (Calgary Stampeders)
CFL Award Most Outstanding Rookie--Matt Goodwin (Baltimore CFLers)
Dave Dryburgh Memorial Trophy--Seam Fleming (Edmonton Eskimos)
DeMarco-Becket Memorial Trophy--Rocco Romano (Calgary Stampeders)
Dr. Beattie Martin Trophy--Larry Wruck (Edmonton Eskimos)
Eddie James Memorial Trophy--Cory Philpot (British Columbia Lions)
Frank M. Gibson Trophy--Matt Goodwin (Baltimore CFLers)
Grey Cup Most Valuable Canadian--Lui Passaglia (British Columbia Lions)

Grey Cup Most Valuable Player--Karl Anthony (Baltimore CFLers)
Jackie Parker Trophy--Carlos Huerta (Las Vegas Posse)
James P. McCaffrey Award--Tim Cofield (Hamilton Tiger-Cats)
Jeff Nicklin Memorial Trophy--Doug Flutie (Calgary Stampeders)
Jeff Russel Memorial Trophy--Mike Pringle (Baltimore CFLers)
Leo Dandurand Trophy--Shar Pourdanesh (Baltimore CFLers)
Lew Hayman Trophy--Gerald Wilcox (Winnipeg Blue Bombers)
Norm Fieldgate Trophy--Willie Pless (Edmonton Eskimos)

Hall of Fame Inductees

Bill Baker, Tom Clements,Gene Gaines, Don McNaughton

HOCKEY

National Hockey League
Western Conference
Pacific Division

Team Name	GP	W	L	T	GF	GA	Pts	Pct
Calgary Flames	84	42	29	13	302	256	97	.577
Vancouver Canucks	84	41	40	3	279	276	85	.506
San Jose Sharks	84	33	35	16	252	265	82	.488
Anaheim Mighty Ducks	84	33	46	5	229	251	71	.423
Los Angeles Kings	84	27	45	12	294	322	66	.393
Edmonton Oilers	84	25	45	14	261	305	64	.381

Central Division

Team Name	GP	W	L	T	GF	GA	Pts	Pct
Detroit Red Wings	84	46	30	8	356	275	100	.595
Toronto Maple Leafs	84	43	29	12	280	243	98	.583
Dallas Stars	84	42	29	13	286	265	97	.577
St. Louis Blues	84	40	33	11	270	283	91	.542
Chicago Blackhawks	84	39	36	9	254	240	87	.518
Winnipeg Jets	84	24	51	9	245	344	57	.339

Eastern Conference

Atlantic Division

Team Name	GP	W	L	T	GF	GA	Pts	Pct
New York Rangers	84	52	24	8	299	231	112	.667
New Jersey Devils	84	47	25	12	307	220	106	.631
Washington Capitals	84	39	35	10	277	263	88	.524
New York Islanders	84	36	36	12	282	264	84	.500
Florida Panthers	84	33	34	17	233	233	83	.494
Philadelphia Flyers	84	35	39	10	294	315	80	.476
Tampa Bay Lightning	84	30	43	11	224	251	71	.423

Northeast Division

Team Name	GP	W	L	T	GF	GA	Pts	Pct
Pittsburgh Penguins	84	44	27	13	299	285	101	.601
Boston Bruins	84	42	29	13	289	252	97	.577
Montreal Canadiens	84	41	29	14	283	248	96	.571
Buffalo Sabres	84	43	32	9	282	218	95	.565
Quebec Nordiques	84	34	42	8	277	292	76	.452
Hartford Whalers	84	27	48	9	227	288	63	.375
Ottawa Senators	84	14	61	9	201	397	37	.220

Coaching Changes

San Jose--Kevin Constantine 33-35-16; Edmonton--Ted Green 3-18-3, Glen Sather 22-27-11; Detroit--Scotty Bowman 46-30-8; Dallas--Bob Gainey 42-29-13; St. Louis--Bob Berry 40-33-11; New York Rangers--Mike Keenan 52-24-8; New Jersey--Jacques Lemaire 47-25-12; Washington--Terry Murray 20-23-4, Jim Schoenfeld 19-12-6; Florida--Roger Neilson 33-34-17; Philadelphia--Terry Simpson 35-39-10; Pittsburgh--Ed Johnston 44-27-13; Hartford--Paul Holmgren 4-11-2, Pierre McGuire 23-37-7.

League Leaders

Goals		**Assists**		**Points**	
Pavel Bure	60	Wayne Gretzky	92	Wayne Gretzky	130
Brett Hull	57	Doug Gilmour	84	Sergei Federov	120
Sergei Federov	56	Adam Oates	80	Adam Oates	112
Dave Andreychuk	53	Sergei Zubov	77	Doug Gilmour	111
Brendan Shanahan	52	Ray Bourque	71	Pavel Bure	107

Penalty Minutes		**GAA** (2,500 minutes)		**Wins**	
Tie Domi	347	Dominik Hasek	1.95	Mike Richter	42
Shane Churla	333	Martin Brodeur	2.40	Ed Belfour	37
Warren Rychel	322	Patrick Roy	2.50	Curtis Joseph	36
Craig Berube	305	John Vanbiesbrouck	2.53	Patrick Roy	35
Kelly Chase	278	Mike Richter	2.57	Felix Potvin	34

Shutouts		**Save %**	
Dominik Hasek	7	Dominik Hasek	.930
Patrick Roy	7	John Vanbiesbrouck	.924
Ed Belfour	7	Patrick Roy	.918
Ron Hextall	5	Martin Brodeur	.915
Mike Richter	5	Mark Fitzpatrick	.913

All Star Game

(Madison Square Garden, New York)

January 22	Eastern Conference	9		Western Conference	8

Stanley Cup Playoffs

April 16	Montreal Canadiens	2	at	Boston Bruins	3
April 17	St. Louis Blues	3	at	Dallas Stars	5
April 17	New York Islanders	0	at	New York Rangers	6
April 17	Washington Capitals	5	at	Pittsburgh Penguins	3
April 17	Buffalo Sabres	2	at	New Jersey Devils	0
April 18	San Jose Sharks	5	at	Detroit Red Wings	4
April 18	Vancouver Canucks	5	at	Calgary Flames	0
April 18	Chicago Blackhawks	1	at	Toronto Maple Leafs	5
April 18	Montreal Canadiens	3	at	Boston Bruins	2
April 18	New York Islanders	0	at	New York Rangers	6
April 19	Washington Capitals	1	at	Pittsburgh Penguins	2
April 19	Buffalo Sabres	1	at	New Jersey Devils	2
April 20	San Jose Sharks	0	at	Detroit Red Wings	4
April 20	Vancouver Canucks	5	at	Calgary Flames	7
April 20	Chicago Blackhawks	0	at	Toronto Maple Leafs	1 [2:15]

April 20	St. Louis Blues	2	at	Dallas Stars	4
April 21	New York Rangers	5	at	New York Islanders	1
April 21	Pittsburgh Penguins	0	at	Washington Capitals	2
April 21	New Jersey Devils	2	at	Buffalo Sabres	1
April 21	Boston Bruins	6	at	Montreal Canadiens	3
April 22	Detroit Red Wings	3	at	San Jose Sharks	2
April 22	Calgary Flames	4	at	Vancouver Canucks	2
April 22	Dallas Stars	5	at	St. Louis Blues	4 [8:34]
April 23	Pittsburgh Penguins	1	at	Washington Capitals	4
April 23	Detroit Red Wings	3	at	San Jose Sharks	4
April 23	Toronto Maple Leafs	4	at	Chicago Blackhawks	5
April 23	New Jersey Devils	3	at	Buffalo Sabres	5
April 23	Boston Bruins	2	at	Montreal Canadiens	5
April 24	Calgary Flames	3	at	Vancouver Canucks	2
April 24	Toronto Maple Leafs	3	at	Chicago Blackhawks	4 [1:23]
April 24	Dallas Stars	2	at	St. Louis Blues	1
April 24	New York Rangers	5	at	New York Islanders	2
April 25	Washington Capitals	2	at	Pittsburgh Penguins	3
April 25	Buffalo Sabres	3	at	New Jersey Devils	5
April 25	Montreal Canadiens	2	at	Boston Bruins	1 [17:18]
April 26	Detroit Red Wings	4	at	San Jose Sharks	6
April 26	Vancouver Canucks	2	at	Calgary Flames	1 [7:15]
April 26	Chicago Blackhawks	0	at	Toronto Maple Leafs	1
April 27	Pittsburgh Penguins	3	at	Washington Capitals	6
April 27	New Jersey Devils	0	at	Buffalo Sabres	1 [65:43]
April 27	Boston Bruins	3	at	Montreal Canadiens	2
April 28	San Jose Sharks	1	at	Detroit Red Wings	7
April 28	Calgary Flames	2	at	Vancouver Canucks	3 [16:43]
April 28	Toronto Maple Leafs	1	at	Chicago Blackhawks	0
April 29	Buffalo Sabres	1	at	New Jersey Devils	2
April 29	Montreal Canadiens	3	at	Boston Bruins	5
April 30	San Jose Sharks	3	at	Detroit Red Wings	2
April 30	Vancouver Canucks	4	at	Calgary Flames	3 [22:20]
May 1	Washington Capitals	3	at	New York Rangers	6
May 1	Boston Bruins	2	at	New Jersey Devils	1
May 2	San Jose Sharks	3	at	Toronto Maple Leafs	2
May 2	Vancouver Canucks	6	at	Dallas Stars	4
May 3	Washington Capitals	2	at	New York Rangers	5
May 3	Boston Bruins	6	at	New Jersey Devils	5 [9:08]
May 4	San Jose Sharks	1	at	Toronto Maple Leafs	5
May 4	Vancouver Canucks	3	at	Dallas Stars	0
May 5	New York Rangers	3	at	Washington Capitals	0
May 5	New Jersey Devils	4	at	Boston Bruins	2
May 6	Toronto Maple Leafs	2	at	San Jose Sharks	5
May 6	Dallas Stars	4	at	Vancouver Canucks	3
May 7	New York Rangers	2	at	Washington Capitals	4
May 7	New Jersey Devils	5	at	Boston Bruins	4
May 8	Toronto Maple Leafs	8	at	San Jose Sharks	3
May 8	Dallas Stars	1	at	Vancouver Canucks	2
May 9	Washington Capitals	3	at	New York Rangers	4
May 9	Boston Bruins	0	at	New Jersey Devils	2
May 10	Toronto Maple Leafs	2	at	San Jose Sharks	5
May 10	Dallas Stars	2	at	Vancouver Canucks	4
May 11	New Jersey Devils	5	at	Boston Bruins	3

May 12	San Jose Sharks	2	at	Toronto Maple Leafs	3 [8:53]
May 14	San Jose Sharks	2	at	Toronto Maple Leafs	4
May 15	New Jersey Devils	4	at	New York Rangers	3 [35:23]
May 16	Vancouver Canucks	2	at	Toronto Maple Leafs	3 [16:55]
May 17	New Jersey Devils	0	at	New York Rangers	4
May 18	Vancouver Canucks	4	at	Toronto Maple Leafs	3
May 19	New York Rangers	3	at	New Jersey Devils	2 [26:13]
May 20	Toronto Maple Leafs	0	at	Vancouver Canucks	4
May 21	New York Rangers	1	at	New Jersey Devils	3
May 22	Toronto Maple Leafs	0	at	Vancouver Canucks	2
May 23	New Jersey Devils	4	at	New York Rangers	1
May 24	Toronto Maple Leafs	3	at	Vancouver Canucks	4 [20:14]
May 25	New York Rangers	4	at	New Jersey Devils	2
May 27	New Jersey Devils	1	at	New York Rangers	2 [24:24]
May 31	Vancouver Canucks	3	at	New York Rangers	2 [19:26]
June 2	Vancouver Canucks	1	at	New York Rangers	3
June 4	New York Rangers	4	at	Vancouver Canucks	1
June 7	New York Rangers	4	at	Vancouver Canucks	2
June 9	Vancouver Canucks	6	at	New York Rangers	3
June 11	New York Rangers	1	at	Vancouver Canucks	4
June 14	Vancouver Canucks	2	at	New York Rangers	3

All Star Teams

First Team		Second Team
Dominik Hasek	Goal	John Vanbiesbrouck
Ray Bourque	Defense	Al MacInnis
Kevin Stevens	Defense	Brian Leetch
Sergei Federov	Center	Wayne Gretzky
Pavel Bure	Right Wing	Cam Neely
Brendan Shanahan	Left Wing	Adam Graves

Individual Awards

Alka-Seltzer Plus Award--Scott Stevens (New Jersey Devils)
Art Ross Trophy--Wayne Gretzky (Los Angeles Kings)
Bill Masterton Trophy--Cam Neely (Boston Bruins)
Calder Memorial Trophy--Martin Brodeur (New Jersey Devils)
Conn Smythe Trophy--Brian Leetch (New York Rangers)
Frank J. Selke Trophy--Sergei Federov (Detroit Red Wings)
Hart Memorial Trophy--Sergei Federov (Detroit Red Wings)
Jack Adams Award--Jacques Lemaire (New Jersey Devils)
James Norris Trophy--Ray Bourque (Boston Bruins)
King Clancy Trophy--Adam Graves (New York Rangers)
Lady Byng Memorial Trophy--Wayne Gretzky (Los Angeles Kings)
Lester B. Pearson Award--Sergei Federov (Detroit Red Wings)
Lester Patrick Trophy--Wayne Gretzky, Robert Ridder
NHL All-Star Game MVP--Mike Richter (New York Rangers)
Vezina Trophy--Dominik Hasek (Buffalo Sabres)
William M. Jennings Trophy--Dominik Hasek and Grant Fuhr (Buffalo Sabres)

Hall of Fame Inductees

Lionel Conacher, Brian O'Neill, Harry Watson

Franchise Changes

NFL--Phoenix Cardinals changed their name to Arizona Cardinals.
NHL--Minnesota North Stars became the Dallas Stars.

Other Sports

Horseracing--Kentucky Derby won by Go for Gin (time 2:03.6, purse $628,800).
Heavyweight Boxing--Michael Moorer won by a majority decision in 12 rounds over Evander Holyfield (IBF, WBA).
Lennox Lewis defeated Phil Jackson by TKO in 8 rounds (WBC).
Oliver McCall defeated Lennox Lewis by TKO in 2 rounds (WBC).
Golf--U.S. Open won by Ernie Els with a score of 279.
Auto racing--Indianapolis 500 won by Al Unser Jr. (ave. speed 160.872 MPH).
Tennis--U.S. Open won by Andre Agassi in the men's singles.
U.S. Open won by Jacco Eltingh and Paul Haarhuis in the men's doubles.
U.S. Open won by Arantxa Sanchez Vicario in the women's singles.
U.S. Open won by Jana Novotna and Arantxa Sanchez Vicario in the women's doubles.
U.S. Open won by Elna Reinach and Patrick Galbraith in the mixed doubles.

1995

BASEBALL

National League

East

Team Name	W	L	Pct	GB	R	OR
Atlanta Braves	90	54	.625	-	645	671
New York Mets	69	75	.479	21	657	618
Philadelphia Phillies	69	75	.479	21	615	658
Florida Marlins	67	76	.469	22.5	673	673
Montreal Expos	66	78	.458	24	621	638

Central

Team Name	W	L	Pct	GB	R	OR
Cincinnati Reds	85	59	.590	-	747	623
Houston Astros	76	68	.528	9	747	674
Chicago Cubs	73	71	.507	12	693	671
St. Louis Cardinals	62	81	.434	22.5	563	658
Pittsburgh Pirates	58	86	.403	27	629	736

West

Team Name	W	L	Pct	GB	R	OR
Los Angeles Dodgers	78	66	.542	-	634	609
Colorado Rockies	77	67	.535	1	785	783
San Diego Padres	70	74	.486	8	668	672
San Francisco Giants	67	77	.465	11	652	776

Coaching Changes

Chicago--Jim Riggleman 73-71; San Diego--Bruce Bochy 70-74.

League Leaders

Batting Average		Home Runs		RBI	
Tony Gwynn	.368	Dante Bichette	40	Dante Bichette	128
Mike Piazza	.346	Sammy Sosa	36	Sammy Sosa	119
Dante Bichette	.340	Larry Walker	36	Andres Galarraga	106
Derek Bell	.334	Barry Bonds	33	Jeff Conine	105
Mark Grace	.326	Vinny Castilla	32	Eric Karros	105

Stolen Bases		ERA		Wins	
Quilvio Veras	56	Greg Maddux	1.63	Greg Maddux	19
Barry Larkin	51	Hideo Nomo	2.54	Pete Schourek	18
Delino DeShields	39	Andy Ashby	2.94	Ramon Martinez	17
Steve Finley	36	Ismael Valdez	3.05	Tom Glavine	16
Reggie Sanders	36	Joey Hamilton	3.08	Pat Rapp	14

Saves		Strikeouts	
John Franco	40	Hideo Nomo	236
Randy Myers	38	John Smoltz	193
Tom Henke	36	Greg Maddux	181
Rod Beck	33	Shane Reynolds	175
Heathcliff Slocumb	32	Pedro Martinez	174

NLCS

October 3	Cincinnati Reds	7	at	Los Angeles Dodgers	5
October 3	Atlanta Braves	5	at	Colorado Rockies	4
October 4	Cincinnati Reds	5	at	Los Angeles Dodgers	4
October 4	Atlanta Braves	7	at	Colorado Rockies	4
October 6	Los Angeles Dodgers	1	at	Cincinnati Reds	10
October 6	Colorado Rockies	7	at	Atlanta Braves	5
October 7	Colorado Rockies	4	at	Atlanta Braves	10
October 10	Atlanta Braves	2	at	Cincinnati Reds	1 [11]
October 11	Atlanta Braves	6	at	Cincinnati Reds	2 [10]
October 13	Cincinnati Reds	2	at	Atlanta Braves	5
October 14	Cincinnati Reds	0	at	Atlanta Braves	6

American League

East

Team Name	W	L	Pct	GB	R	OR
Boston Red Sox	86	58	.597	-	791	698
New York Yankees	79	65	.549	7	745	688
Baltimore Orioles	71	73	.493	15	704	640
Detroit Tigers	60	84	.417	26	654	844
Toronto Blue Jays	56	88	.389	30	642	777
Central						
Cleveland Indians	100	44	.694	-	840	607
Kansas City Royals	70	74	.486	30	629	691
Chicago White Sox	68	76	.472	32	755	758
Milwaukee Brewers	65	79	.451	35	740	747
Minnesota Twins	56	88	.389	44	703	889
West						
Seattle Mariners	78	66	.542	-	796	708
California Angels	78	66	.542	-	801	697
Texas Rangers	74	70	.514	4	691	720
Oakland Athletics	67	77	.465	11	730	761

Coaching Changes

Boston--Kevin Kennedy 86-58: Baltimore--Phil Regan 71-73; Kansas City--Bob Boone 70-74; Chicago--Gene Lamont 11-20, Terry Bevington 57-56; California--Marcel Lachemann 78-66; Texas--Johnny Oates 74-70.

League Leaders

Batting Average		Home Runs		RBI	
Edgar Martinez	.356	Albert Belle	50	Albert Belle	126
Chuck Knoblauch	.333	Jay Buhner	40	Mo Vaughn	126
Tim Salmon	.330	Frank Thomas	40	Jay Buhner	121
Wade Boggs	.324	Mark McGwire	39	Edgar Martinez	113
Eddie Murray	.323	Mo Vaughn	39	Frank Thomas	111

Stolen Bases		ERA		Wins	
Kenny Lofton	54	Randy Johnson	2.48	Mike Mussina	19
Tom Goodwin	50	Tim Wakefield	2.95	Randy Johnson	18
Otis Nixon	50	Dennis Martinez	3.08	David Cone	18
Chuck Knoblauch	46	Mike Mussina	3.29	Kenny Rogers	17
Vince Coleman	42	Kenny Rogers	3.38	Orel Hershiser	16

Saves		Strikeouts	
Jose Mesa	46	Randy Johnson	294
Lee Smith	37	Todd Stottlemyre	205
Rick Aguilera	32	Chuck Finley	195
Roberto Hernandez	32	David Cone	191
John Wetteland	31	Kevin Appier	185

All Star Game

(The Ballpark in Arlington, Arlington, Texas)

July 11	National League	3		American League	2

ALCS

October 3	Seattle Mariners	6	at	New York Yankees	9
October 3	Boston Red Sox	4	at	Cleveland Indians	5 [13]
October 4	Seattle Mariners	5	at	New York Yankees	7 [15]
October 4	Boston Red Sox	0	at	Cleveland Indians	4
October 6	New York Yankees	4	at	Seattle Mariners	7
October 6	Cleveland Indians	8	at	Boston Red Sox	2
October 7	New York Yankees	8	at	Seattle Mariners	11
October 8	New York Yankees	5	at	Seattle Mariners	6 [11]
October 10	Cleveland Indians	2	at	Seattle Mariners	3
October 11	Cleveland Indians	5	at	Seattle Mariners	2
October 13	Seattle Mariners	5	at	Cleveland Indians	2 [11]
October 14	Seattle Mariners	0	at	Cleveland Indians	7
October 15	Seattle Mariners	2	at	Cleveland Indians	3
October 17	Cleveland Indians	4	at	Seattle Mariners	0

World Series

October 21	Cleveland Indians	2	at	Atlanta Braves	3
October 22	Cleveland Indians	3	at	Atlanta Braves	4
October 24	Atlanta Braves	6	at	Cleveland Indians	7 [11]
October 25	Atlanta Braves	5	at	Cleveland Indians	2
October 26	Atlanta Braves	4	at	Cleveland Indians	5
October 28	Cleveland Indians	0	at	Atlanta Braves	1

Individual Awards

ALCS MVP--Orel Hershiser (Cleveland Indians)
Baseball Writers Award--

NLCS MVP--Mike Devereaux (Atlanta Braves)
Rookie of the Year--Hideo Nomo (Los Angeles Dodgers)
Marty Cordova (Minnesota Twins)
Sporting News Executive of the Year--John Hart (Cleveland Indians)
Sporting News Manager of the Year--Don Baylor (Colorado Rockies)
Mike Hargrove (Cleveland Indians)
Sporting News Pitcher of the Year--Greg Maddux (Atlanta Braves)
Randy Johnson (Seattle Mariners)
Sporting News Player of the Year--Albert Belle (Cleveland Indians)
Sporting News Rookie of the Year--Chipper Jones (Atlanta Braves)
Hideo Nomo (Los Angeles Dodgers)
Garrett Anderson (California Angels)
Julian Tavarez (Cleveland Indians)
Arch Ward Memorial Trophy--Jeff Conine (Florida Marlins)
World Series MVP--Tom Glavine (Atlanta Braves)
Cy Young Award--Greg Maddux (Atlanta Braves)
Randy Johnson (Seattle Mariners)

Hall of Fame Inductees

Richie Ashburn, Leon Day, William Hulbert, Mike Schmidt, Vic Willis

Notes

The Seattle mariners defeated the California Angels 9 to 1 in Seattle on October 2 to decide the champion of the West Division.

BASKETBALL

National Basketball Association

Eastern Conference
Atlantic Division

Team Name	GP	W	L	PPGF	PPGA	Pct	GB
Orlando Magic	82	57	25	110.9	103.8	.695	-
New York Knickerbockers	82	55	27	98.2	95.1	.671	2
Boston Celtics	82	35	47	102.8	104.7	.427	22
Miami Heat	82	32	50	101.1	102.8	.390	25
New Jersey Nets	82	30	52	98.1	101.2	.366	27
Philadelphia 76ers	82	24	58	95.4	101.2	.293	33
Washington Bullets	82	21	61	100.5	106.1	.256	36

Central Division

Team Name	GP	W	L	PPGF	PPGA	Pct	GB
Indiana Pacers	82	52	30	99.2	95.5	.634	-
Charlotte Hornets	82	50	32	100.6	97.3	.610	2
Chicago Bulls	82	47	35	101.5	96.7	.573	5
Cleveland Cavaliers	82	43	39	90.5	89.8	.524	9
Atlanta Hawks	82	42	40	96.6	95.3	.512	10
Milwaukee Bucks	82	34	48	99.3	103.7	.415	17
Detroit Pistons	82	28	54	98.2	105.5	.341	24

Western Conference

Midwest Division

San Antonio Spurs	82	62	20	106.6	100.6	.756	-
Utah Jazz	82	60	22	106.4	98.4	.732	2
Houston Rockets	82	47	35	103.5	101.4	.573	15
Denver Nuggets	82	41	41	101.3	100.5	.500	21
Dallas Mavericks	82	36	46	103.2	106.1	.439	26
Minnesota Timberwolves	82	21	61	94.2	103.2	.256	41

Pacific Division

Phoenix Suns	82	59	23	110.6	106.8	.720	-
Seattle SuperSonics	82	57	25	110.4	102.2	.695	2
Los Angeles Lakers	82	48	34	105.1	105.3	.585	11
Portland Trail Blazers	82	44	38	103.1	99.2	.537	15
Sacramento Kings	82	39	43	98.2	99.2	.476	20
Golden State Warriors	82	26	56	105.7	111.1	.317	33
Los Angeles Clippers	82	17	65	96.7	105.8	.207	42

Coaching Changes

Miami--Kevin Loughery 17-29, Alvin Gentry 15 21; New Jersey--Butch Beard 30-52; Philadelphia--John Lucas 24-58; Washington--Jim Lynam 21-61; San Antonio Bob Hill 62-20; Denver Dan Issel 18-16, Gene Littles 3-13 Bernie Bickerstaff 20-12; Dallas--Dick Motta 36-46; Minnesota--Bill Blair 21-61; Los Angeles Lakers--Del Harris 48-34; Portland--P.J. Carlesimo 44-38; Golden State--Don Nelson 14-31, Bob Lanier 12-25; Los Angeles Clippers Bill Fitch 17-65.

League Leaders

Field Goal %		**Free Throw %**		**Assists per Game**	
Chris Gatling	.633	Spud Webb	.934	John Stockton	12.3
Shaquille O'Neal	.583	Mark Price	.914	Kenny Anderson	9.4
Horace Grant	.567	Dana Barros	.899	Tim Hardaway	9.3
Otis Thorpe	.565	Reggie Miller	.897	Rod Strickland	8.8
Dale Davis	.563	Tyrone Bogues	.889	Tyrone Bogues	8.7

Points		**Rebounds per Game**	
Shaquille O'Neal	2315	Dennis Rodman	16.8
David Robinson	2238	Dikembe Mutombo	12.5
Karl Malone	2187	Shaquille O'Neal	11.4
Hakeem Olajuwon	2005	Patrick Ewing	11.0
Jamal Mashburn	1926	Shawn Kemp	10.9

All Star Game

(America West Arena, Phoenix)

February 12	Western Division	139	Eastern Division	112

NBA Playoffs

April 27	Atlanta Hawks	82	at	Indiana Pacers	90
April 27	Cleveland Cavaliers	79	at	N.Y. Knickerbockers	103
April 27	Houston Rockets	100	at	Utah Jazz	102

April 27	Los Angeles Lakers	71	at	Seattle SuperSonics	96
April 28	Boston Celtics	77	at	Orlando Magic	124
April 28	Chicago Bulls	108	at	Charlotte Hornets	100 [OT]
April 28	Denver Nuggets	88	at	San Antonio Spurs	104
April 28	Portland Trail Blazers	102	at	Phoenix Suns	129
April 29	Cleveland Cavaliers	90	at	N.Y. Knickerbockers	84
April 29	Houston Rockets	140	at	Utah Jazz	126
April 29	Los Angeles Lakers	84	at	Seattle SuperSonics	82
April 30	Atlanta Hawks	97	at	Indiana Pacers	105
April 30	Boston Celtics	99	at	Orlando Magic	92
April 30	Chicago Bulls	89	at	Charlotte Hornets	106
April 30	Denver Nuggets	96	at	San Antonio Spurs	122
April 30	Portland Trail Blazers	94	at	Phoenix Suns	103
May 1	N.Y. Knickerbockers	83	at	Cleveland Cavaliers	81
May 1	Seattle SuperSonics	101	at	Los Angeles Lakers	105
May 2	Indiana Pacers	105	at	Atlanta Hawks	89
May 2	Charlotte Hornets	80	at	Chicago Bulls	103
May 2	San Antonio Spurs	99	at	Denver Nuggets	95
May 2	Phoenix Suns	117	at	Portland Trail Blazers	109
May 3	Orlando Magic	82	at	Boston Celtics	77
May 3	Utah Jazz	95	at	Houston Rockets	82
May 4	N.Y. Knickerbockers	93	at	Cleveland Cavaliers	80
May 4	Charlotte Hornets	84	at	Chicago Bulls	85
May 4	Seattle SuperSonics	110	at	Los Angeles Lakers	114
May 5	Boston Celtics	92	at	Orlando Magic	95
May 5	Utah Jazz	106	at	Houston Rockets	123
May 6	Los Angeles Lakers	110	at	San Antonio Spurs	94
May 7	Houston Rockets	95	at	Utah Jazz	91
May 7	Indiana Pacers	107	at	N.Y. Knickerbockers	105
May 7	Chicago Bulls	91	at	Orlando Magic	94
May 8	Los Angeles Lakers	90	at	San Antonio Spurs	97 [OT]
May 9	Indiana Pacers	77	at	N.Y. Knickerbockers	96
May 9	Houston Rockets	108	at	Phoenix Suns	130
May 10	Chicago Bulls	104	at	Orlando Magic	94
May 11	N.Y. Knickerbockers	95	at	Indiana Pacers	97 [OT]
May 11	Houston Rockets	94	at	Phoenix Suns	118
May 12	Orlando Magic	110	at	Chicago Bulls	101
May 12	San Antonio Spurs	110	at	Los Angeles Lakers	94
May 13	N.Y. Knickerbockers	84	at	Indiana Pacers	98
May 13	Phoenix Suns	85	at	Houston Rockets	118
May 14	Orlando Magic	95	at	Chicago Bulls	106
May 14	Phoenix Suns	114	at	Houston Rockets	110
May 14	San Antonio Spurs	80	at	Los Angeles Lakers	71
May 16	Chicago Bulls	95	at	Orlando Magic	103
May 16	Houston Rockets	103	at	Phoenix Suns	97 [OT]
May 16	Los Angeles Lakers	98	at	San Antonio Spurs	96 [OT]
May 17	Indiana Pacers	95	at	N.Y. Knickerbockers	96
May 18	Orlando Magic	108	at	Chicago Bulls	102
May 18	Phoenix Suns	103	at	Houston Rockets	116
May 18	San Antonio Spurs	100	at	Los Angeles Lakers	88
May 19	N.Y. Knickerbockers	92	at	Indiana Pacers	82
May 20	Houston Rockets	115	at	Phoenix Suns	114
May 21	Indiana Pacers	97	at	N.Y. Knickerbockers	95
May 22	Houston Rockets	94	at	San Antonio Spurs	93

May 23	Indiana Pacers	101	at	Orlando Magic	105
May 24	Houston Rockets	106	at	San Antonio Spurs	96
May 25	Indiana Pacers	114	at	Orlando Magic	119
May 26	San Antonio Spurs	107	at	Houston Rockets	102
May 27	Orlando Magic	100	at	Indiana Pacers	105
May 28	San Antonio Spurs	103	at	Houston Rockets	81
May 29	Orlando Magic	93	at	Indiana Pacers	94
May 30	Houston Rockets	111	at	San Antonio Spurs	90
May 31	Indiana Pacers	106	at	Orlando Magic	108
June 1	San Antonio Spurs	95	at	Houston Rockets	100
June 2	Orlando Magic	96	at	Indiana Pacers	123
June 4	Indiana Pacers	81	at	Orlando Magic	105
June 7	Houston Rockets	120	at	Orlando Magic	118 [OT]
June 9	Houston Rockets	117	at	Orlando Magic	106
June 11	Orlando Magic	103	at	Houston Rockets	106
June 14	Orlando Magic	101	at	Houston Rockets	113

All Star Teams

First Team	Second Team	Third Team
Karl Malone	Charles Barkley	Dennis Rodman
Scottie Pippen	Shawn Kemp	Detlef Schrempf
David Robinson	Shaquille O'Neal	Hakeem Olajuwon
John Stockton	Gary Payton	Reggie Miller
Anfernee Hardaway	Mitch Richmond	Clyde Drexler

Individual Awards

Court Vision Award--Muggsy Bogues (Charlotte Hornets)
Eddie Gottlieb Trophy--Grant Hill (Detroit Pistons)
Jason Kidd (Dallas Mavericks)
IBM Award--David Robinson (San Antonio Spurs)
J. Walter Kennedy Citizenship Award--Joe O'Toole (Atlanta Hawks)
Maurice Podoloff Trophy--David Robinson (San Antonio Spurs)
NBA All-Star Game MVP--Mitch Richmond (Sacramento Kings)
NBA Defensive Player of the Year--Dikembe Mutombo (Denver Nuggets)
NBA Executive of the Year--Jerry West (Los Angeles Lakers)
NBA Finals MVP--Hakeem Olajuwon (Houston Rockets)
NBA Most Improved Player--Dana Barros (Philadelphia 76ers)
Red Auerbach Trophy--Del Harris (Los Angeles Lakers)
Sixth Man Award--Anthony Mason (New York Knickerbockers)

Hall of Fame Inductees

Kareem Abdul-Jabbar, Anne Donovan, Aleksandr Gomelsky, John Kundla, Vern Mikkelsen, Cheryl Miller, Earl Strom,

FOOTBALL

National Football League
National Conference
Eastern Division

Team Name	GP	W	L	T	PF	PA	Pct
Dallas Cowboys	16	12	4	0	435	291	.750
Philadelphia Eagles	16	10	6	0	318	338	.615
Washington Redskins	16	6	10	0	326	359	.375
New York Giants	16	5	11	0	290	340	.313
Arizona Cardinals	16	4	12	0	275	422	.250

Central Division

Team Name	GP	W	L	T	PF	PA	Pct
Green Bay Packers	16	11	5	0	404	314	.689
Detroit Lions	16	10	6	0	436	336	.625
Chicago Bears	16	9	7	0	392	360	.563
Minnesota Vikings	16	8	8	0	412	385	.500
Tampa Bay Buccaneers	16	7	9	0	238	335	.438

Western Division

Team Name	GP	W	L	T	PF	PA	Pct
San Francisco 49ers	16	11	5	0	457	258	.688
Atlanta Falcons	16	9	7	0	362	349	.563
St. Louis Rams	16	7	9	0	309	418	.438
Carolina Panthers	16	7	9	0	289	325	.438
New Orleans Saints	16	7	9	0	319	348	.438

American Conference

Eastern Division

Team Name	GP	W	L	T	PF	PA	Pct
Buffalo Bills	16	10	6	0	350	335	.625
Indianapolis Colts	16	9	7	0	331	316	.563
Miami Dolphins	16	9	7	0	398	332	.563
New England Patriots	16	6	10	0	294	377	.375
New York Jets	16	3	13	0	233	384	.188

Central Division

Team Name	GP	W	L	T	PF	PA	Pct
Pittsburgh Steelers	16	11	5	0	407	327	.689
Cincinnati Bengals	16	7	9	0	349	374	.438
Houston Oilers	16	7	9	0	348	324	.438
Cleveland Browns	16	5	11	0	289	356	.313
Jacksonville Jaguars	16	4	12	0	275	404	.250

Western Division

Team Name	GP	W	L	T	PF	PA	Pct
Kansas City Chiefs	16	13	3	0	358	241	.813
San Diego Chargers	16	9	7	0	321	323	.563
Seattle Seahawks	16	8	8	0	363	366	.500
Denver Broncos	16	8	8	0	388	345	.500
Oakland Raiders	16	8	8	0	348	332	.500

Coaching Changes

Philadelphia--Ray Rhodes 10-6-0; St. Louis--Rich Brooks 7-9-0; Carolina--Dom Capers 7-9-0; New York Jets--Rich Kotite 3-13-0; Houston--Jeff Fisher 7-9-0; Jacksonville--Tom Coughlin 4-12-0; Seattle--Dennis Erickson 8-8-0; Denver--Mike Shanahan 8-8-0; Oakland--Mike White 8-8-0.

League Leaders

Yards Rushing		**Yards Passing**		**Passing %** (300 attempts)	
Emmitt Smith	1773	Brett Favre	4413	Steve Young	66.9
Barry Sanders	1500	Scott Mitchell	4338	Troy Aikman	64.8
Curtis Martin	1487	Warren Moon	4228	Dan Marino	64.1
Chris Warren	1346	Jeff George	4143	Jim Harbaugh	63.7
Terry Allen	1309	John Elway	3970	Chris Chandler	63.2

Receivng Yards		**Receptions**		**Field Goals**	
Jerry Rice	1848	Herman Moore	123	Norm Johnson	34
Isaac Bruce	1781	Jerry Rice	122	Jason Elam	31
Herman Moore	1686	Chris Carter	122	Steve Christie	31
Michael Irvin	1603	Isaac Bruce	119	Morten Andersen	31
Robert Brooks	1497	Michael Irvin	111	Greg Davis	30

Punt Return Yards		**Kickoff Return Yards**	
Tamarick Vanover	540	Tyrone Hughes	1617
Eric Guliford	475	Andre Coleman	1411
Andre Hastings	474	Brian Mitchell	1408
Dave Meggett	383	Ernie Mills	1306
Eric Metcalf	383	Glyn Milburn	1269

Pro Bowl Game

(Aloha Stadium, Honolulu)

February 4 1996	National Conference	20	American Conference	13

NFL Playoffs

December 30	Miami Dolphins	22	at	Buffalo Bills	37
December 30	Detroit Lions	37	at	Philadelphia Eagles	58
December 31	Atlanta Falcons	20	at	Green Bay Packers	37
December 31	Indianapolis Colts	35	at	San Diego Chargers	20
January 6 1996	Buffalo Bills	21	at	Pittsburgh Steelers	40
January 6 1996	Green Bay Packers	27	at	San Francisco49ers	17
January 7 1996	Philadelphia Eagles	11	at	Dallas Cowboys	30
January 7 1996	Indianapolis Colts	10	at	Kansas City Chiefs	7
January 14 1996	Green Bay Packers	27	at	Dallas Cowboys	38
January 14 1996	Indianapolis Colts	16	at	Pittsburgh Steelers	20

Super Bowl XXX

(Sun Devil Stadium Tempe, Arizona)

January 28 1996	Dallas Cowboys	27	Pittsburgh Steelers	17

Awards

A.P. MVP--Brett Favre (Green Bay Packers)
Dan McGuire Award--Jerry Rice (San Francisco 49ers)

Hall of Fame Inductees

Jim Finks,Henry Jordan, Steve Largent, Lee Roy Selmon, Kellen Winslow

Canadian Football League

Northern Division

Team Name	GP	W	L	T	PF	PA	Pts	Pct
Calgary Stampeders	18	15	3	0	631	404	30	.833
Edmonton Eskimos	18	13	5	0	599	359	26	.722
British Columbia Lions	18	10	8	0	535	470	20	.556
Hamilton Tiger-Cats	18	8	10	0	427	509	16	.444
Winnipeg Blue Bombers	18	7	11	0	404	653	14	.389
Saskatchewan Roughriders	18	6	12	0	422	451	12	.333
Toronto Argonauts	18	4	14	0	376	519	8	.222
Ottawa Rough Riders	18	3	15	0	348	685	6	.167

Southern Division

Team Name	GP	W	L	T	PF	PA	Pts	Pct
Baltimore Stallions	18	15	3	0	541	369	30	.833
San Antonio Texans	18	12	6	0	630	457	24	.667
Birmingham Barracudas	18	10	8	0	548	518	20	.556
Memphis Mad Dogs	18	9	9	0	346	364	18	.500
Shreveport Pirates	18	5	13	0	465	514	10	.278

Coaching Changes

Hamilton--Don Sutherin 8-10-0; Toronto--Mike Faragalli 2-7-0, Bob O'Billovich 2-7-0; Ottawa--Jim Gilstrap 3-15-0; San Antonio--Kay Stephenson 12-6-0; Birmingham--Jack Pardee 10-8-0; Memphis Pepper Rogers 9-9-0.

League Leaders

Yards Rushing		Yards Passing		Passing % (200 attempts)	
Mike Pringle	1791	Matt Dunigan	4911	Doug Flutie	67.2
Cory Philpot	1308	Danny McManus	4655	Jeff Garcia	63.2
Martin Patton	1040	David Archer	4471	Kerwin Bell	62.1
Mike Saunders	1030	Billy Joe Tolliver	3767	David Archer	61.4
Mike Clemons	836	Jeff Garcia	3358	Kent Austin	59.7

Receiving Yards		Receptions		Points	
Dave Sapunjis	1655	Donald Narcisse	123	Roman Anderson	235
Marcus Grant	1559	Dave Sapunjis	111	Carlos Huerta	228
Earl Winfield	1496	Allen Pitts	100	Mark McLoughlin	220
Allen Pitts	1492	Earl Winfield	92	Sean Fleming	207
Joseph Horn	1415	Marcus Grant	84	Lui Passaglia	194

Playoffs

November 4	Winnipeg Blue Bombers	21	at	Baltimore Stallions	36
November 4	Hamilton Tiger-Cats	13	at	Calgary Stampeders	30
November 5	Birmingham Barracudas	9	at	San Antonio Texans	52
November 5	British Columbia Lions	15	at	Edmonton Eskimos	26

November 12	San Antonio Texans	11	at	Baltimore Stallions	21
November 12	Edmonton Eskimos	4	at	Calgary Stampeders	37
November 19	Baltimore Stallions	37		Calgary Stampeders	20*

Individual Awards

Annis Stukus Trophy--Don Matthews (Baltimore Stallions)
Chrysler Award M.V.P.--Mike Pringle (Baltimore Stallions)
Chrysler Award Most Valuable-Canadian--Dave Sapunjis (Calgary Stampeders)
Chrysler Award Most Valuable Offensive Lineman--Mike Withycombe (Baltimore Stallions)
Chrysler Award Most Valuable Defensive Player--Willie Pless (Edmonton Eskimos)
Chrysler Award Rookie of the Year--Shalon Baker (Edmonton Eskimos)
Chrysler Grey Cup M.V.P.--Tracy Ham (Baltimore Stallions)
Dave Dryburgh Memorial Trophy--Mark McLoughlin (Calgary Stampeders)
DeMarco-Becket Memorial Trophy--Jamie Taras (British Columbia Lions)
Dr. Beattie Martin Trophy--Larry Wruck (Edmonton Eskimos)
Eddie James Memorial Trophy--Cory Philpot (British Columbia Lions)
Frank M. Gibson Trophy--Chris Wright (Baltimore Stallions)
Jackie Parker Trophy--Shalon baker (Edmonton Eskimos)
James P. McCaffrey Award--Tim Cofield (Memphis Mad Dogs)
Jeff Nicklin Memorial Trophy--Dave Sapunjis (Calgary Stampeders)
Leo Dandurand Trophy--Mike Withycombe (Baltimore Stallions)
Lew Hayman Trophy--Dave Sapunjis (Calgary Stampeders)
Norm Fieldgate Trophy--Willie Pless (Edmonton Eskimos)
Terry Evanshen Award--Mike Pringle (Baltimore Stallions)
R.C.A. Grey Cup Canadian Player of the Game--Dave Sapunjis (Calgary Stampeders)

Hall of Fame Inductees

Dieter Brock, Greg Fulton, Tom Grant,

HOCKEY
National Hockey League

Western Conference
Central Division

Team Name	GP	W	L	T	GF	GA	Pts	Pct
Detroit Red Wings	48	33	11	4	180	117	70	.729
St. Louis Blues	48	28	15	5	178	135	61	.635
Chicago Blackhawks	48	24	19	5	156	115	53	.552
Toronto Maple Leafs	48	21	19	8	135	146	50	.521
Dallas Stars	48	17	23	8	136	135	42	.438
Winnipeg Jets	48	16	25	7	157	177	39	.406

Pacific Division

Team Name	GP	W	L	T	GF	GA	Pts	Pct
Calgary Flames	48	24	17	7	163	135	55	.573
Vancouver Canucks	48	18	18	12	153	143	48	.500
San Jose Sharks	48	19	25	4	129	161	42	.438
Los Angeles Kings	48	16	23	9	142	174	41	.427
Edmonton Oilers	48	17	27	4	136	182	38	.396
Anaheim Mighty Ducks	48	16	27	5	125	164	37	.385

*Game played in Regina.

Eastern Conference

Northeast Division

Quebec Nordiques	48	30	13	5	185	134	65	.677
Pittsburgh Penguins	48	29	16	3	181	158	61	.635
Boston Bruins	48	27	18	3	150	127	57	.594
Buffalo Sabres	48	22	19	7	130	119	51	.531
Hartford Whalers	48	19	24	5	127	141	43	.448
Montreal Canadiens	48	18	23	7	125	148	43	.448
Ottawa Senators	48	9	34	5	116	174	23	.240

Atlantic Division

Philadelphia Flyers	48	28	16	4	150	132	60	.625
Washington Capitals	48	22	18	8	136	120	52	.542
New Jersey Devils	48	22	18	8	136	121	52	.542
New York Rangers	48	22	23	3	139	134	47	.490
Florida Panthers	48	20	22	6	115	127	46	.479
Tampa Bay Lightning	48	17	28	3	120	144	37	.385
New York Islanders	48	15	28	5	126	158	35	.365

Coaching Changes

St. Louis--Mike Keenan 28-15-5; Winnipeg--John Paddock 9-18-6, Terry Simpson 7-7-1; Vancouver--Rick Ley 18-18-12; Los Angeles--Barry Melrose 13-21-7, Rogatien Vachon 3-2-2; Edmonton--George Burnett 12-20-3, Ron Low 5-7-1; Quebec--Marc Crawford 30-13-5; Hartford--Paul Holmgren 19-24-5; Philadelphia--Terry Murray 28-16-4; Washington--Jim Schoenfeld 22-18-8; New York Rangers--Colin Campbell 22-23-3; New York Islanders--Lorne Henning 15-28-5.

League Leaders

Goals		Assists		Points	
Peter Bondra	34	Ron Francis	48	Jaromir Jagr	70
Jaromir Jagr	32	Paul Coffey	44	Eric Lindros	70
Ray Sheppard	30	Joe Sakic	43	Alexi Zhamnov	65
Owen Nolan	30	Eric Lindros	41	Joe Sakic	62
Alexi Zhamnov	30	Adam Oates	41	Ron Francis	59

Penalty Minutes		GAA (780 minutes)		Wins	
Enrico Ciccone	225	Dominik Hasek	2.11	Ken Wregget	25
Shane Churla	186	Rick Tabaracci	2.11	Ed Belfour	22
Bryan Marchment	184	Jim Carey	2.13	Trevor Kidd	22
Craig Berube	173	Chris Osgood	2.26	Curtis Joseph	20
Rob Ray	173	Ed Belfour	2.28	Mike Vernon	19

Shutouts		Save % (780 minutes)	
Dominik Hasek	5	Dominik Hasek	.930
Ed Belfour	5	Chris Osgood	.917
Jim Carey	4	Jocelyn Thibeault	.917
Blaine Lacher	4	Andy Moog	.915
Arturs Irbe	4	John Vanbiesbrouck	.914

All Star Game

There was no all star game this year due to the players' strike.

Stanley Cup Playoffs

May 6	New York Rangers	4	at	Quebec Nordiques	5
May 6	Washington Capitals	5	at	Pittsburgh Penguins	4
May 7	Dallas Stars	3	at	Detroit Red Wings	4
May 7	San Jose Sharks	5	at	Calgary Flames	4
May 7	Vancouver Canucks	1	at	St. Louis Blues	2
May 7	Toronto Maple Leafs	5	at	Chicago Blackhawks	3
May 7	Buffalo Sabres	3	at	Philadelphia Flyers	4 [11:06]
May 7	New Jersey Devils	5	at	Boston Bruins	0
May 8	New York Rangers	8	at	Quebec Nordiques	3
May 8	Buffalo Sabres	1	at	Philadelphia Flyers	3
May 8	Washington Capitals	3	at	Pittsburgh Penguins	5
May 8	New Jersey Devils	3	at	Boston Bruins	0
May 9	Dallas Stars	1	at	Detroit Red Wings	4
May 9	San Jose Sharks	5	at	Calgary Flames	4 [12:21]
May 9	Vancouver Canucks	5	at	St. Louis Blues	3
May 9	Toronto Maple Leafs	3	at	Chicago Blackhawks	0
May 10	Quebec Nordiques	3	at	New York Rangers	4
May 10	Philadelphia Flyers	1	at	Buffalo Sabres	3
May 10	Pittsburgh Penguins	2	at	Washington Capitals	6
May 10	Boston Bruins	3	at	New Jersey Devils	2
May 11	Detroit Red Wings	5	at	Dallas Stars	1
May 11	Calgary Flames	9	at	San Jose Sharks	2
May 11	St. Louis Blues	1	at	Vancouver Canucks	6
May 11	Chicago Blackhawks	3	at	Toronto Maple Leafs	2
May 12	Quebec Nordiques	2	at	New York Rangers	3 [8:09]
May 12	Philadelphia Flyers	4	at	Buffalo Sabres	2
May 12	Pittsburgh Penguins	2	at	Washington Capitals	6
May 12	Boston Bruins	0	at	New Jersey Devils	1 [8:51]
May 13	Calgary Flames	6	at	San Jose Sharks	4
May 13	St. Louis Blues	5	at	Vancouver Canucks	2
May 13	Chicago Blackhawks	3	at	Toronto Maple Leafs	1
May 14	Detroit Red Wings	1	at	Dallas Stars	4
May 14	New York Rangers	2	at	Quebec Nordiques	4
May 14	Buffalo Sabres	4	at	Philadelphia Flyers	6
May 14	Washington Capitals	5	at	Pittsburgh Penguins	6 [4:30]
May 14	New Jersey Devils	3	at	Boston Bruins	2
May 15	Dallas Stars	1	at	Detroit Red Wings	3
May 15	San Jose Sharks	0	at	Calgary Flames	5
May 15	Vancouver Canucks	6	at	St. Louis Blues	5 [1:48]
May 15	Toronto Maple Leafs	2	at	Chicago Blackhawks	4
May 16	Quebec Nordiques	2	at	New York Rangers	4
May 16	Pittsburgh Penguins	7	at	Washington Capitals	1
May 17	Calgary Flames	3	at	San Jose Sharks	5
May 17	St. Louis Blues	8	at	Vancouver Canucks	2
May 17	Chicago Blackhawks	4	at	Toronto Maple Leafs	5 [10:00]
May 18	Washington Capitals	0	at	Pittsburgh Penguins	3
May 19	San Jose Sharks	5	at	Calgary Flames	4 [21:54]
May 19	Vancouver Canucks	5	at	St. Louis Blues	3
May 19	Toronto Maple Leafs	2	at	Chicago Blackhawks	5
May 20	New Jersey Devils	2	at	Pittsburgh Penguins	3

May 21	San Jose Sharks	0	at	Detroit Red Wings	6
May 21	Vancouver Canucks	1	at	Chicago Blackhawks	2 [9:04]
May 21	New York Rangers	4	at	Philadelphia Flyers	5 [7:03]
May 22	New York Rangers	3	at	Philadelphia Flyers	4 [00:25]
May 22	New Jersey Devils	4	at	Pittsburgh Penguins	2
May 23	San Jose Sharks	2	at	Detroit Red Wings	6
May 23	Vancouver Canucks	0	at	Chicago Blackhawks	2
May 24	Philadelphia Flyers	5	at	New York Rangers	2
May 24	Pittsburgh Penguins	1	at	New Jersey Devils	5
May 25	Detroit Red Wings	6	at	San Jose Sharks	2
May 25	Chicago Blackhawks	3	at	Vancouver Canucks	2 [6:22]
May 26	Philadelphia Flyers	4	at	New York Rangers	1
May 26	Pittsburgh Penguins	1	at	New jersey Devils	2 [18:36]
May 27	Detroit Red Wings	6	at	San Jose Sharks	2
May 27	Chicago Blackhawks	4	at	Vancouver Canucks	3 [5:35]
May 28	New Jersey Devils	4	at	Pittsburgh Penguins	1
June 1	Chicago Blackhawks	1	at	Detroit Red Wings	2 [1:01]
June 3	New Jersey Devils	4	at	Philadelphia Flyers	1
June 4	Chicago Blackhawks	2	at	Detroit Red Wings	3
June 5	New Jersey Devils	5	at	Philadelphia Flyers	2
June 6	Detroit Red Wings	4	at	Chicago Blackhawks	3 [29:25]
June 7	Philadelphia Flyers	3	at	New Jersey Devils	2 [4:19]
June 8	Detroit Red Wings	2	at	Chicago Blackhawks	5
June 10	Philadelphia Flyers	4	at	New Jersey Devils	2
June 11	Chicago Blackhawks	1	at	Detroit Red Wings	2 [22:25]
June 11	New Jersey Devils	3	at	Philadelphia Flyers	2
June 13	Philadelphia Flyers	2	at	New Jersey Devils	4
June 17	New Jersey Devils	2	at	Detroit Red Wings	1
June 19	New Jersey Devils	4	at	Detroit Red Wings	2
June 22	Detroit Red Wings	2	at	New Jersey Devils	5
June 24	Detroit Red Wings	2	at	New Jersey Devils	5

All Star Teams

First Team		Second Team
Dominik Hasek	Goal	Ed Belfour
Paul Coffey	Defense	Ray Bourque
Chris Chelios	Defense	Larry Murphy
Eric Lindros	Center	Alexei Zhamnov
Jaromir Jagr	Right Wing	Theoren Fleury
John LeClair	Left Wing	Keith Tkachuk

Individual Awards

Jack Adams Award--Marc Crawford (Quebec Nordiques)
Alka-Seltzer Plus Award--Ron Francis (Pittsburgh Penguins)
Art Ross Trophy--Jaromir Jagr (Pittsburgh Penguins)
Calder Memorial Trophy--Peter Forsberg (Quebec Nordiques)
King Clancy Trophy--Joe Nieuwendyk (Calgary Flames)
Conn Smythe Trophy--Claude Lemieux (New Jersey Devils)
Hart Memorial Trophy--Eric Lindros (Philadelphia Flyers)
William M. Jennings Trophy--Ed Belfour (Chicago Blackhawks)
Lady Byng Memorial Trophy--Ron Francis (Pittsburgh Penguins)
Lester Patrick Award--Joe Mullen, Brian Mullen, Bob Fleming
Bill Masterton Trophy--Pat LaFontaine (Buffalo Sabres)

NHL All-Star Game MVP--Game was canceled due to the players strike.
James Norris Trophy--Paul Coffey (Detroit Red Wings)
Lester B. Pearson Award--Eric Lindros (Philadelphia Flyers)
Frank J. Selke Trophy--Ron Francis (Pittsburgh Penguins)
Vezina Trophy--Dominik Hasek (Buffalo Sabres)

Hall of Fame Inductees

Bun Cook, Larry Robinson, Gunter Sebetzki, Bill Torrey

Franchise Changes

NFL--Los Angeles Rams became St. Louis Rams.
CFL--Baltimore CFLers became Baltimore Stallions.
CFL--Sacramento Gold Miners became San Antonio Texans.

Other Sports

Horseracing--Kentucky Derby won by Thunder Gulch (time 2:01.2, purse $707,400).
Heavyweight Boxing--George Foreman defeated Michael Moorer in 10 rounds by a knockout (IBF, WBA).
Oliver McCall defeated Larry Holmes in a 12 round unanimous decision (WBC).
George Foreman defeated Axel Schulz in a 12 round majority decision (IBF).
Bruce Seldon defeated Joe Hipp in a 10 round TKO (WBA).
Frank Bruno defeated Oliver McCall in a 12 round unanimous decision (WBC).
Golf--U.S. Open won by Corey Pavin with a score of 280.
Auto Racing--Indianapolis 500 won by Jacques Villeneuve (ave speed 153.616 MPH).
Tennis--U.S. Open won by Pete Sampras in the men's singles.
U.S. Open won by Todd Woodbridge and Mark Woodforde in the men's doubles.
U.S. Open won by Steffi Graf in the women's singles.
U.S. Open won by Gigi Fernandez and Natasha Zvereva in the women's doubles.
U.S. open won by Meredith McGrath and M. Lucena in the mixed doubles.

1996

BASKETBALL
National Basketball Association

Eastern Conference
Atlantic Division

Team Name	GP	W	L	PPGF	PPGA	Pct	GB
Orlando Magic	82	60	22	104.5	99.0	.732	-
New York Knickerbockers	82	47	35	97.2	94.9	.573	13
Miami Heat	82	42	40	96.5	95.0	.512	18
Washington Bullets	82	39	43	102.5	101.5	.476	21
Boston Celtics	82	33	49	103.6	107.0	.402	27
New Jersey Nets	82	30	52	93.7	97.9	.366	30
Philadelphia 76ers	82	18	64	94.5	104.5	.220	42

Central Division

Team Name	GP	W	L	PPGF	PPGA	Pct	GB
Chicago Bulls	82	72	10	105.2	92.9	.878	-
Indiana Pacers	82	52	30	99.3	96.1	.634	20
Cleveland Cavaliers	82	47	35	91.1	88.5	.573	25
Atlanta Hawks	82	46	36	98.3	97.1	.561	26
Detroit Pistons	82	46	36	95.4	92.9	.561	26
Charlotte Hornets	82	41	41	102.8	103.4	.500	31
Milwaukee Bucks	82	25	57	95.6	100.9	.305	47
Toronto Raptors	82	21	61	97.5	105.0	.256	51

Western Conference

Midwest Division

Team Name	GP	W	L	PPGF	PPGA	Pct	GB
San Antonio Spurs	82	59	23	103.4	97.1	.720	-
Utah Jazz	82	55	27	102.5	95.9	.671	4
Houston Rockets	82	48	34	102.5	100.7	.585	11
Denver Nuggets	82	35	47	97.7	100.4	.427	24
Minnesota Timberwolves	82	26	56	97.9	103.2	.317	33
Dallas Mavericks	82	26	56	102.5	107.5	.317	33
Vancouver Grizzlies	82	15	67	89.8	99.8	.183	44

Pacific Division

Team Name	GP	W	L	PPGF	PPGA	Pct	GB
Seattle SuperSonics	82	64	18	104.5	96.7	.780	-
Los Angeles Lakers	82	53	29	102.9	98.5	.646	11
Portland Trail Blazers	82	44	38	99.3	97.0	.537	20
Phoenix Suns	82	41	41	104.3	104.0	.500	23
Sacramento Kings	82	39	43	99.5	102.3	.476	25
Golden State Warriors	82	36	46	101.6	103.1	.439	28
Los Angeles Clippers	82	29	53	99.4	103.0	.354	35

Coaching Changes

New York--Don Nelson 34-25, Jeff van Gundy 13-10; Miami--Pat Riley 42-40; Boston--M.L. Carr 33-49; Detroit--Doug Collins 46-36; Toronto--Brendan Malone 21-61; Denver--Bernie Bickerstaff 35-47; Minnesota--Bill Blair 6-14, Flip Saunders 20-42; Vancouver--Brian Winters 15-67; Phoenix--Paul Westphal 14-19, Lowell "Cotton" Fitzsimmons 27-22; Golden State--Rick Adelman 36-46.

League Leaders

Field Goal %		Free Throw %		Assists per Game	
Gheorghe Muresan	.584	Mahmoud Abdul-Rauf	.930	John Stockton	11.2
Chris Gatling	.575	Jeff Hornacek	.893	Jason Kidd	9.7
Shaquille O'Neal	.573	Terrell Brandon	.887	Avery Johnson	9.6
Anthony Mason	.563	Dana Barros	.884	Rod Strickland	9.6
Shawn Kemp	.561	Brent Price	.874	Damon Stoudamire	9.3

Points		Rebounds per Game	
Michael Jordan	2491	Dennis Rodman	14.9
Karl Malone	2106	David Robinson	12.2
David Robinson	2051	Dikembe Mutombo	11.8
Hakeem Olajuwon	1936	Charles Barkley	11.6
Mitch Richmond	1872	Shawn Kemp	11.4

All Star Game

(Alamodome, San Antonio)

February 11	Eastern Division	129	Western Division	118

NBA Playoffs

April 25	Atlanta Hawks	92	at	Indiana Pacers	80
April 25	New York Knickerbockers	106	at	Cleveland Cavaliers	83
April 25	Portland Trail Blazers	102	at	Utah Jazz	110
April 25	Houston Rockets	87	at	Los Angeles Lakers	83
April 26	Miami Heat	85	at	Chicago Bulls	102
April 26	Detroit Pistons	92	at	Orlando Magic	112
April 26	Sacramento Kings	85	at	Seattle SuperSonics	97
April 26	Phoenix Suns	98	at	San Antonio Spurs	120
April 27	Atlanta Hawks	94	at	Indiana Pacers	102 [OT]
April 27	New York Knickerbockers	84	at	Cleveland Cavaliers	80
April 27	Portland Trail Blazers	90	at	Utah Jazz	105
April 27	Houston Rockets	94	at	Los Angeles Lakers	104
April 28	Miami Heat	75	at	Chicago Bulls	106
April 28	Detroit Pistons	77	at	Orlando Magic	92
April 28	Sacramento Kings	90	at	Seattle SuperSonics	81
April 28	Phoenix Suns	105	at	San Antonio Spurs	110
April 29	Indiana Pacers	83	at	Atlanta Hawks	90
April 29	Utah Jazz	91	at	Portland Trail Blazers	94 [OT]
April 30	Los Angeles Lakers	98	at	Houston Rockets	104
April 30	Orlando Magic	101	at	Detroit Pistons	98
April 30	Seattle SuperSonics	96	at	Sacramento Kings	89
May 1	Cleveland Cavaliers	76	at	New York Knickerbockers	81
May 1	Utah Jazz	90	at	Portland Trail Blazers	98
May 1	Chicago Bulls	112	at	Miami Heat	91
May 1	San Antonio Spurs	93	at	Phoenix Suns	94
May 2	Indiana Pacers	83	at	Atlanta Hawks	75
May 2	Los Angeles Lakers	94	at	Houston Rockets	102
May 2	Seattle SuperSonics	101	at	Sacramento Kings	87
May 3	San Antonio Kings	116	at	Phoenix Suns	98
May 4	Houston Rockets	75	at	Seattle SuperSonics	108

May 5	Atlanta Hawks	89	at	Indiana Pacers	87
May 5	Portland Trail Blazers	64	at	Utah Jazz	102
May 5	New York Knickerbockers	84	at	Chicago Bulls	91
May 6	Houston Rockets	101	at	Seattle SuperSonics	105
May 7	New York Knickerbockers	80	at	Chicago Bulls	91
May 7	Utah Jazz	95	at	San Antonio Spurs	75
May 8	Atlanta Hawks	105	at	Orlando Magic	117
May 9	Utah Jazz	77	at	San Antonio Spurs	88
May 10	Seattle SuperSonics	115	at	Houston Rockets	112
May 10	Atlanta Hawks	94	at	Orlando Magic	120
May 11	Chicago Bulls	99	at	New York Knickerbockers	102 [OT]
May 11	San Antonio Spurs	75	at	Utah Jazz	105
May 12	Seattle SuperSonics	114	at	Houston Rockets	107 [OT]
May 12	Chicago Bulls	94	at	New York Knickerbockers	91
May 12	San Antonio Spurs	86	at	Utah Jazz	101
May 12	Orlando Magic	103	at	Atlanta Hawks	96
May 13	Orlando Magic	99	at	Atlanta Hawks	104
May 14	New York Knickerbockers	81	at	Chicago Bulls	94
May 14	Utah Jazz	87	at	San Antonio Spurs	98
May 15	Atlanta Hawks	88	at	Orlando Magic	96
May 16	San Antonio Spurs	81	at	Utah Jazz	108
May 18	Utah Jazz	72	at	Seattle SuperSonics	102
May 19	Orlando Magic	83	at	Chicago Bulls	121
May 20	Utah Jazz	87	at	Seattle SuperSonics	91
May 21	Orlando Magic	88	at	Chicago Bulls	93
May 24	Seattle SuperSonics	76	at	Utah Jazz	96
May 25	Chicago Bulls	86	at	Orlando Magic	67
May 26	Seattle SuperSonics	88	at	Utah Jazz	86
May 27	Chicago Bulls	106	at	Orlando Magic	101
May 28	Utah Jazz	98	at	Seattle SuperSonics	95 [OT]
May 30	Seattle SuperSonics	83	at	Utah Jazz	118
June 2	Utah Jazz	86	at	Seattle SuperSonics	90
June 5	Seattle SuperSonics	90	at	Chicago Bulls	107
June 7	Seattle SuperSonics	88	at	Chicago Bulls	92
June 9	Chicago Bulls	108	at	Seattle SuperSonics	84
June 12	Chicago Bulls	86	at	Seattle SuperSonics	107
June 14	Chicago Bulls	78	at	Seattle SuperSonics	89
June 16	Seattle SuperSonics	75	at	Chicago Bulls	87

All Star Teams

First Team	Second Team	Third Team
Scotty Pippen	Shawn Kemp	Charles Barkley
Karl Malone	Hakeem Olajuwon	Juwon Howard
David Robinson	Grant Hill	Shaquille O'Neal
Michael Jordan	Gary Payton	Mitch Richmond
Anfernee Hardaway	John Stockton	Reggie Miller

Individual Awards

Court Vision Award--
Eddie Gottlieb Trophy--Damon Stoudamire (Toronto Raptors)
IBM Award--
J. Walter Kennedy Citizenship Award--
Maurice Podoloff Trophy--Michael Jordan (Chicago Bulls)

NBA All Star Game MVP--Michael Jordan (Chicago Bulls)
NBA Defensive Player of the Year--
NBA Executive of the Year--
NBA Finals MVP--Michael Jordan (Chicago Bulls)
NBA Most Improved Player--
Red Auerbach Trophy--
Sixth Man Award--Toni Kukoc (Chicago Bulls)

HOCKEY

National Hockey League

Western Conference
Central Division

Team Name	GP	W	L	T	GF	GA	Pts	Pct
Detroit Red Wings	82	62	13	7	325	181	131	.799
Chicago Blackhawks	82	40	28	14	273	220	94	.573
Toronto Maple Leafs	82	34	36	12	247	252	80	.488
St. Louis Blues	82	32	34	16	219	248	80	.488
Winnipeg Jets	82	36	40	6	275	291	78	.476
Dallas Stars	82	26	42	14	227	280	66	.402

Pacific Division

Team Name	GP	W	L	T	GF	GA	Pts	Pct
Colorado Avalanche	82	47	25	10	326	240	104	.634
Calgary Flames	82	34	37	11	241	240	79	.482
Vancouver Canucks	82	32	35	15	278	278	79	.482
Anaheim Mighty Ducks	82	35	39	8	234	247	78	.476
Edmonton Oilers	82	30	44	8	240	304	68	.415
Los Angeles Kings	82	24	40	18	256	302	66	.402
San Jose Sharks	82	20	55	7	252	357	47	.287

Eastern Conference
Northeast Division

Team Name	GP	W	L	T	GF	GA	Pts	Pct
Pittsburgh Penguins	82	49	29	4	362	284	102	.622
Boston Bruins	82	40	31	11	282	269	91	.555
Montreal Canadiens	82	40	32	10	265	248	90	.549
Hartford Whalers	82	34	39	9	237	259	77	.470
Buffalo Sabres	82	33	42	7	247	262	73	.445
Ottawa Senators	82	18	59	5	191	291	41	.250

Atlantic Division

Team Name	GP	W	L	T	GF	GA	Pts	Pct
Philadelphia Flyers	82	45	24	13	282	208	103	.628
New York Rangers	82	41	27	14	272	237	96	.585
Florida Panthers	82	41	31	10	254	234	92	.561
Washington Capitals	82	39	32	11	234	204	89	.543
Tampa Bay Lightning	82	38	32	12	238	248	88	.537
New Jersey Devils	82	37	33	12	215	202	86	.524
New York Islanders	82	22	50	10	229	315	54	.329

Coaching Changes

Chicago--Craig Hartsburg 40-28-14; Toronto--Pat Burns 25-30-10, Nick Beverley 9-6-2; Winnipeg--Terry Simpson 36-40-6; Dallas--Bob Gainey 11-19-9, Ken Hitchcock 15-23-5; Colorado--Marc Crawford 47-25-10; Calgary--Pierre Page 34-37-11; Vancouver--Rick Ley 29-32-15, Pat Quinn 3-3-0; Edmonton--Ron Low 30-44-8; Los Angeles--Larry Robinson 24-40-18; San Jose--Kevin Constantine 3-18-4, Jim Wiley 17-37-3; Boston--Steve Kasper 40-31-11; Montreal--Jacques Demers 0-4-0, Steve Shutt and Jacques Laperriere 0-1-0, Mario Tremblay 40-27-10; Hartford--Paul Holmgren 5-6-1, Paul Maurice 29-33-8; Buffalo--Ted Nolan 33-42-7; Ottawa--Rick Bowness 6-13-0, Dave Allison 2-22-1, Jacques Martin 10-24-4; Florida--Doug MacLean 41-31-10; New York Islanders--Mike Milbury 22-50-10.

League Leaders

Goals		**Assists**		**Points**	
Mario Lemieux	69	Mario Lemieux	92	Mario Lemieux	161
Jaromir Jagr	62	Ron Francis	92	Jaromir Jagr	149
Alexander Mogilny	55	Jaromir Jagr	87	Joe Sakic	120
Peter Bondra	52	Peter Forsberg	86	Ron Francis	119
Joe Sakic	51	Wayne Gretzky	79	Peter Forsberg	116

Penalty Minutes		**GAA** (2,500 minutes)		**Wins**	
Matthew Barnaby	335	Ron Hextall	2.17	Chris Osgood	39
Enrico Ciccone	306	Chris Osgood	2.17	Jim Carey	35
Tie Domi	297	Jim Carey	2.26	Martin Brodeur	34
Brad May	295	Martin Brodeur	2.34	Ron Hextall	31
Rob Ray	287	Daren Puppa	2.46	Felix Potvin	30

Shutouts		**Save %** (2,500 minutes)	
Jim Carey	9	Dominik Hasek	.920
Martin Brodeur	6	Daren Puppa	.918
Chris Osgood	5	Guy Hebert	.914
Daren Puppa	5	Ron Hextall	.913
Jeff Hackett	4	Martin Brodeur	.911

All Star Game

(Fleet Center, Boston)

January 21	Eastern Conference	5	Western Conference	4

Stanley Cup Playoffs

April 16	Vancouver Canucks	2	at	Colorado Avalanche	5
April 16	St. Louis Blues	3	at	Toronto Maple Leafs	1
April 16	Tampa Bay Lightning	3	at	Philadelphia Flyers	7
April 16	Montreal Canadiens	3	at	New York Rangers	2 [5:04]
April 17	Winnipeg Jets	1	at	Detroit Red Wings	4
April 17	Calgary Flames	1	at	Chicago Blackhawks	4
April 17	Washington Capitals	6	at	Pittsburgh Penguins	4
April 17	Boston Bruins	3	at	Florida Panthers	6
April 18	Vancouver Canucks	5	at	Colorado Avalanche	4
April 18	St. Louis Blues	4	at	Toronto Maple Leafs	5 [4:02]
April 18	Tampa Bay Lightning	2	at	Philadelphia Flyers	1 [9:05]
April 18	Montreal Canadiens	5	at	New York Rangers	3

April 19	Winnipeg Jets	0	at	Detroit Red Wings	4
April 19	Calgary Flames	0	at	Chicago Blackhawks	3
April 19	Washington Capitals	5	at	Pittsburgh Penguins	3
April 20	Colorado Avalanche	4	at	Vancouver Canucks	0
April 21	Detroit Red Wings	1	at	Winnipeg Jets	4
April 21	Chicago Blackhawks	7	at	Calgary Flames	5
April 21	Toronto Maple Leafs	2	at	St. Louis Blues	3 [1:24]
April 21	Philadelphia Flyers	4	at	Tampa Bay Lightning	5 [2:13]
April 21	New York Rangers	2	at	Montreal Canadiens	1
April 22	Colorado Avalanche	3	at	Vancouver Canucks	4
April 22	Pittsburgh Penguins	4	at	Washington Capitals	1
April 22	Boston Bruins	2	at	Florida Panthers	6
April 23	Detroit Red Wings	6	at	Winnipeg Jets	1
April 23	Chicago Blackhawks	2	at	Calgary Flames	1 [50:02]
April 23	Toronto Maple Leafs	1	at	St. Louis Blues	5
April 23	Philadelphia Flyers	4	at	Tampa Bay Lightning	1
April 23	New York Rangers	4	at	Montreal Canadiens	3
April 24	Pittsburgh Penguins	3	at	Washington Capitals	2 [79:15]
April 24	Florida Panthers	4	at	Boston Bruins	2
April 25	Vancouver Canucks	4	at	Colorado Avalanche	5 [00:51]
April 25	St. Louis Blues	4	at	Toronto Maple Leafs	5 [7:31]
April 25	Tampa Bay Lightning	1	at	Philadelphia Flyers	4
April 25	Florida Panthers	2	at	Boston Bruins	6
April 26	Winnipeg Jets	3	at	Detroit Red Wings	1
April 26	Washington Capitals	1	at	Pittsburgh Penguins	4
April 26	Montreal Canadiens	2	at	New York Rangers	3
April 27	Colorado Avalanche	3	at	Vancouver Canucks	2
April 27	Toronto Maple Leafs	1	at	St. Louis Blues	2
April 27	Philadelphia Flyers	6	at	Tampa Bay Lightning	1
April 27	Boston Bruins	3	at	Florida Panthers	4
April 28	Detroit Red Wings	4	at	Winnipeg Jets	1
April 28	Pittsburgh Penguins	3	at	Washington Capitals	2
April 28	New York Rangers	5	at	Montreal Canadiens	3
May 2	Chicago Blackhawks	3	at	Colorado Avalanche	2 [6:29]
May 2	Florida Panthers	2	at	Philadelphia Flyers	0
May 3	St. Louis Blues	2	at	Detroit Red Wings	3
May 3	New York Rangers	3	at	Pittsburgh Penguins	4
May 4	Chicago Blackhawks	1	at	Colorado Avalanche	5
May 4	Florida Panthers	2	at	Philadelphia Flyers	3
May 5	St. Louis Blues	3	at	Detroit Red Wings	8
May 5	New York Rangers	6	at	Pittsburgh Penguins	3
May 6	Colorado Avalanche	3	at	Chicago Blackhawks	4 [00:46]
May 7	Philadelphia Flyers	3	at	Florida Panthers	1
May 7	Pittsburgh Penguins	3	at	New York Rangers	2
May 8	Detroit Red Wings	4	at	St. Louis Blues	5 [3:23]
May 8	Colorado Avalanche	3	at	Chicago Blackhawks	2 [44:33]
May 9	Philadelphia Flyers	3	at	Florida Panthers	4 [4:06]
May 9	Pittsburgh Penguins	4	at	New York Rangers	1
May 10	Detroit Red Wings	0	at	St. Louis Blues	1
May 11	Chicago Blackhawks	1	at	Colorado Avalanche	4
May 11	New York Rangers	3	at	Pittsburgh Penguins	7
May 12	St. Louis Blues	3	at	Detroit Red Wings	2
May 12	Florida Panthers	2	at	Philadelphia Flyers	1 [28:05]
May 13	Colorado Avalanche	4	at	Chicago Blackhawks	3 [25:18]

May 14	Philadelphia Flyers	1	at	Florida Panthers	4
May 14	Detroit Red Wings	4	at	St. Louis Blues	2
May 16	St. Louis Blues	0	at	Detroit Red Wings	1 [21:15]
May 18	Florida Panthers	5	at	Pittsburgh Penguins	1
May 19	Colorado Avalanche	3	at	Detroit Red Wings	2 [17:31]
May 20	Florida Panthers	2	at	Pittsburgh Penguins	3
May 21	Colorado Avalanche	3	at	Detroit Red Wings	0
May 23	Detroit Red Wings	6	at	Colorado Avalanche	4
May 24	Pittsburgh Penguins	2	at	Florida Panthers	5
May 25	Detroit Red Wings	2	at	Colorado Avalanche	4
May 26	Pittsburgh Penguins	2	at	Florida Panthers	1
May 27	Colorado Avalanche	2	at	Detroit Red Wings	5
May 29	Florida Panthers	0	at	Pittsburgh Penguins	3
May 29	Detroit Red Wings	1	at	Colorado Avalanche	4
May 30	Pittsburgh Penguins	3	at	Florida Panthers	4
June 1	Florida Panthers	3	at	Pittsburgh Penguins	1
June 4	Florida Panthers	1	at	Colorado Avalanche	3
June 6	Florida Panthers	1	at	Colorado Avalanche	8
June 8	Colorado Avalanche	3	at	Florida Panthers	2
June 10	Colorado Avalanche	1	at	Florida Panthers	0 [44:31]

All Star Teams

First Team		Second Team
Jim Carey	Goal	Chris Osgood
Chris Chelios	Defense	Brian Leetch
Ray Bourque	Defense	Vladimir Konstantinov
Mario Lemieux	Center	Eric Lindros
Jaromir Jagr	Right Wing	Alexander Mogilny
Paul Kariya	Left Wing	John LeClair

Individual Awards

Jack Adams Award--Scotty Bowman (Detroit Red Wings)
Alka Seltzer Plus Award--
Art Ross Trophy--Mario Lemieux (Pittsburgh Penguins)
Calder Memorial Trophy--Daniel Alfredsson (Ottawa Senators)
King Clancy Trophy--Kris King (Winnipeg Jets)
Conn Smythe Trophy--Joe Sakic (Colorado Avalanche)
Hart Memorial Trophy--Mario Lemieux (Pittsburgh Penguins)
William M. Jennings Trophy--Chris Osgood and Mike Vernon (Detroit Red Wings)
Lady Byng Memorial Trophy--Paul Kariya (Anaheim Mighty Ducks)
Lester Patrick Award--
Bill Masterton Trophy--Gary Roberts (Calgary Flames)
NHL All Star Game MVP--Raymond Bourque (Boston Bruins)
James Norris Trophy--Chris Chelios (Chicago Black Hawks)
Lester B. Pearson Award--Mario Lemieux (Pittsburgh Penguins)
Frank J. Selke Trophy--Sergei Fedorov (Detroit Red Wings)
Vezina Trophy--Jim Carey (Washington Capitals)

Franchise Changes

NHL--Quebec Nordiques became Colorado Avalanche.

Other Sports

Auto Racing--Indianapolis 500 won by Buddy Lazier (ave. speed 147.956 M.P.H.).
Horseracing--Kentucky Derby won by Grindstone (purse $1,000,000, time 2:01).
Golf--U.S. Open won by Steve Jones with a score of 278.

Individual Team Statistics

AKRON FIRESTONE NON-SKIDS

Home City: Akron, Ohio
Home Arena:
Origin of Name: The team was sponsored by the Firestone Tire Company and named after a brand of their tires.

Regular Season Record

Season	League	GP	W	L	PPGF	PPGA	Pct	GB
1937-1938	NBL	18	14	4	40.1	34.0	.778	-
1938-1939	NBL	27	24	3	44.6	35.9	.889	-
1939-1940	NBL	27	18	9	44.2	40.8	.667	-
1940-1941	NBL	24	13	11	42.3	40.4	.542	5
TOTAL:	4 years	96	69	27				5
AVERAGE:		24	17	7	42.8	37.8	.719	1

Playoff Record

Season	GP	W	L	PPGF	PPGA	Result
1937-1938	2	0	2	26.0	31.5	Lost to Akron Goodyear in 1st round.
1938-1939	5	3	2	40.0	36.8	**Won NBL championship.**
1939-1940	8	5	3	43.9	44.8	**Won NBL championship.**
1940-1941	2	0	2	34.5	38.5	Lost to Oshkosh in 1st round.
TOTAL:	17	8	9			
AVERAGE:	4	2	2	36.1	37.9	

COACHING HISTORY: 1937-1941 Paul Sheeks 69-27-.719

AKRON GOODYEAR WINGFOOTS

Home City: Akron, Ohio
Home Arena: Goodyear Hall
Origin of Name: The team was sponsored by the Goodyear Tire Company and named after a brand of their tires.

Regular Season Record

Season	League	GP	W	L	PPGF	PPGA	Pct	GB
1937-1938	NBL	18	13	5	35.8	27.7	.722	1
1938-1939	NBL	28	14	14	34.1	35.5	.500	10.5
1939-1940	NBL	28	14	14	37.4	37.0	.500	4.5
1940-1941	NBL	24	11	13	38.6	38.8	.458	7
1941-1942	NBL	24	15	9	45.4	40.8	.625	5
TOTAL:	5 years	122	67	55				28
AVERAGE:		24	13	11	38.3	36.0	.549	6

Playoff Record

Season	GP	W	L	PPGF	PPGA	Result
1937-1938	5	4	1	31.6	31.2	**Won NBL championship.**

COACHING HISTORY: 1937-1939 Lefty Byers 27-19-.587; 1939-1942 Ray Detrick 40-36-.526

AKRON INDIANS
(were Akron Pros)

Home City: Akron, Ohio
Home Arena:
Origin of Name:

Regular Season Record

Season	League	GP	W	L	T	PF	PA	Pct
1926	NFL	8	1	4	3	23	89	.313

COACHING HISTORY: Fritz Pollard & Rube Ursella 1-4-3-.313

AKRON PROS
(became Akron Indians)

Home City: Akron, Ohio
Home Field:
Origin of Name: The team was officially the Akron Professional Football Club.

Regular Season Record

Season	League	GP	W	L	T	PF	PA	Pct
1922	NFL	10	3	5	2	146	95	.375
1923	NFL	7	1	6	0	25	74	.143
1924	NFL	8	2	6	0	59	132	.250
1925	NFL	8	4	2	2	65	51	.667
TOTAL:	4 years	33	10	19	4	295	352	
AVERAGE:		8	2	5	1	74	88	.364

COACHING HISTORY:1922 Brooke Brewer & Paul Sheeks 3-5-2-.375; 1923 Carl Cramer 1-6-0-.143; 1924 Jim Flower 2-6-0-.250; 1925 Fritz Pollard 0-2-0-.000; 1925 George Berry 4-0-2-.833

ALBERTA OILERS
(became Edmonton Oilers)

Home City: Edmonton, Alberta
Home Arena: Edmonton Gardens Capacity: 5,200 [1973]
Origin of Name: The name was picked in a Name the Team Contest and chosen because of Edmonton's and Alberta's large petrochemical industry.

Regular Season Record

Season	League	GP	W	L	T	GF	GA	Pts	Pct
1972-1973	WHA	78	38	37	3	269	256	79	.506

COACHING HISTORY: Ray Kinasewich 38-37-3-.506

ALTOONA PRIDE

Home City: Altoona, Pennsylvania
Home Field: Columbia Park
Origin of Name:

Regular Season Record

Season	League	GP	W	L	Pct	GB	R	OR
1884	UA	25	6	19	.240	44	90	216

COACHING HISTORY: Ed Curtis 6-19-.240

ANAHEIM AMIGOS

Home City: Anaheim, California
Home Court: Convention Center
Origin of Name: The name was chosen in a Name the Team Contest.

Regular Season Record

Season	League	GP	W	L	PPGF	PPGA	Pct	GB
1968	ABA	78	25	53	111.6	116.1	.321	23

COACHING HISTORY: Al Brightman 12-24-.333; Harry Dinnel 13-29-.310

ANAHEIM MIGHTY DUCKS

Home City: Anaheim, California
Home Arena: Arrowhead Pond — Capacity: 17,174 [1995]
Origin of Name: The name was suggested by the Disney movie "The Mighty Ducks". The franchise is owned by the Disney Corporation.

Regular Season Record

Season	League	GP	W	L	T	GF	GA	Pts	Pct
1993-1994	NHL	84	33	46	5	229	251	71	.423
1994-1995	NHL	48	16	27	5	125	164	37	.385
1995-1996	NHL	82	35	39	8	234	247	78	.476
TOTAL:	3 years	214	84	112	18	588	662	186	
AVERAGE:		71	28	37	6	196	221	62	.435

COACHING HISTORY: 1993-present Ron Wilson

ANDERSON DUFFEY PACKERS

Home City: Anderson, Indiana
Home Court: The team played some games in Chicago Stadium
Origin of Name: The team was sponsored by Duffey's Inc. a meat packing plant owned by I.W. Duffey.

Regular Season Record

Season	League	GP	W	L	PPGF	PPGA	Pct	GB
1946-1947	NBL	44	24	20	59.7	58.5	.545	4
1947-1948	NBL	60	42	18	65.0	59.4	.700	2
1948-1949	NBL	64	49	15	72.1	63.1	.766	-
1949-1950	NBL	64	37	27	87.3	83.6	.578	2
TOTAL:	4 years	232	152	80				8
AVERAGE:		58	38	20	71.0	66.2	.655	2

Playoff Record

Season	GP	W	L	PPGF	PPGA	Result
1947-1948	6	4	2	69.0	65.3	Lost to Rochester in 2nd round.
1948-1949	7	6	1	78.7	71.6	**Won NBL championship.**
1949-1950	8	4	4	75.5	74.8	Lost to Minneapolis in 3rd round.
TOTAL:	21	14	7			
AVERAGE:	7	5	2	74.4	70.6	

COACHING HISTORY: 1946-1949 Murray Mendenhall 115-53-.685; 1949-1950 Howie Schultz 21-14-.600; 1949-1950 Ike Duffey 1-2-.333; 1949-1950 Doxie Moore 15-11-.577

ARIZONA CARDINALS

(were Phoenix Cardinals)

Home City: Tempe, Arizona
Home Stadium: Sun Devil Stadium — Capacity: 73,269 [1995]
Origin of Name: The team was formerly known as the Phoenix Cardinals.

Regular Season Record

Season	League	GP	W	L	T	PF	PA	Pct
1994	NFL	16	8	8	0	235	267	.500
1995	NFL	16	4	12	0	275	422	.250
TOTAL:	2 years	32	12	20	0	510	689	
AVERAGE:		16	6	10	0	255	345	.375

COACHING HISTORY: 1994-1995 Buddy Ryan 12-20-0-.375

ARIZONA WRANGLERS

Home City: Tempe, Arizona
Home Stadium: Sun Devil Stadium — Capacity: 72,000 [1985]
Origin of Name: The name was chosen in a Name the Team Contest.

Regular Season Record

Season	League	GP	W	L	T	PF	PA	Pct
1983	USFL	18	4	14	0	261	442	.222
1984	USFL	18	10	8	0	502	284	.556
1985	USFL	18	8	10	0	376	405	.471
TOTAL:	3 years	54	22	32	0	1139	1131	
AVERAGE:		18	7	11	0	380	377	.407

Playoff Record

Season	GP	W	L	PF	PA	Result
1984	3	2	1	55	62	Lost to Philadelphia in USFL final game.

COACHING HISTORY: 1983 Doug Shively 4-14-0-.222; 1984 George Allen 10-8-0-.556; 1985 Frank Kush 8-10-0-.471

ATLANTA APOLLOS

Home City: Atlanta, Georgia
Home Stadium: Atlanta Fulton County Stadium — Capacity: 51,383 [1973]
Origin of Name: According to team President Bill Putnam, Apollos "is a name associated with success" and like the space program "we feel our new soccer program is headed for new horizons, adventure, intrigue and courage."

Regular Season Record

Season	League	GP	W	L	T	GF	GA	BP	Pts	Pct
1973	NASL	19	3	9	7	23	40	23	62	.363

COACHING HISTORY: Ken Bracewell 3-9-7-.363

ATLANTA BRAVES
(were Milwaukee Braves)

Home City: Atlanta, Georgia
Home Field: Atlanta-Fulton County Stadium * (1966-to present) Capacity: 52,709 [1995]
Origin of Name: The team kept the same name when it moved to Atlanta from Milwaukee.

			Regular Season Record					
Season	**League**	**GP**	**W**	**L**	**Pct**	**GB**	**R**	**OR**
1966	NL	162	85	77	.525	10	782	683
1967	NL	162	77	85	.475	24.5	631	640
1968	NL	162	81	81	.500	16	514	549
1969	NL	162	93	69	.574	-	691	631
1970	NL	162	76	86	.469	26	736	772
1971	NL	162	82	80	.506	8	643	699
1972	NL	154	70	84	.455	25	628	730
1973	NL	161	76	85	.472	22.5	799	774
1974	NL	162	88	74	.543	14	661	563
1975	NL	161	67	94	.416	40.5	584	739
1976	NL	162	70	92	.432	32	620	700
1977	NL	162	61	101	.377	37	678	895
1978	NL	162	69	93	.426	26	600	750
1979	NL	160	66	94	.413	23.5	669	763
1980	NL	161	81	80	.503	11	630	660
1981	NL	106	50	56	.472	NA	395	416
1982	NL	162	89	73	.549	-	739	702
1983	NL	162	88	74	.543	3	746	640
1984	NL	162	80	82	.494	12	632	655
1985	NL	162	66	96	.407	29	632	781
1986	NL	161	72	89	.447	23.5	615	719
1987	NL	161	69	92	.429	20.5	747	829
1988	NL	160	54	106	.338	39.5	555	741
1989	NL	160	63	97	.394	28	584	680
1990	NL	162	65	97	.401	26	682	821
1991	NL	162	98	64	.605	-	768	632
1992	NL	162	98	64	.605	-	682	569
1993	NL	162	104	58	.642	-	767	559
1994	NL	114	68	46	.596	6	542	448
1995	NL	144	90	54	.625	-	645	540
TOTAL:	30 years	4719	2296	2423		503.5	19597	20280
AVERAGE:		157	76	81	.487	17	653	649

*Originally Atlanta Stadium from 1966 to 1974

Playoff Record

Season	GP	W	L	R	OR	Result
1969	3	0	3	15	27	Lost NLCS to New York.
1982	3	0	3	5	17	Lost NLCS to St. Louis.
1991	14	7	7	48	36	Lost to Minnesota in World Series.
1992	13	6	7	54	52	Lost to Toronto in World Series.
1993	6	2	4	33	23	Lost NLCS to Philadelphia.
1995	14	11	3	69	43	**Won World Series.**
TOTAL:	53	26	27	224	198	
AVERAGE:	9	4	5	37	33	

COACHING HISTORY: 1966 Bobby Bragan 52-59-.468; 1966-67 Bill Hitchcock 110-100-.524; 1967 Ken Silvestri 0-3-.000; 1968-72 Lum Harris 379-373-.504; 1972-74 Eddie Matthews 149-161-.481; 1974-75 Clyde King 97-101-.490; 1975 Connie Ryan 8-18-.308; 1976-77 Dave Bristol 130-192-.404; 1977 Ted Turner 0-1-.000; 1977 Vern Benson 1-0-1.000; 1978-81 Bobby Cox 266-323-.452; 1982-84 Joe Torre 257-229-.529; 1985 Eddie Haas 50-71-.413; 1985 Bobby Wine 16-25-.390; 1986-88 Chuck Tanner 153-208-.424; 1988-90 Russ Nixon 128-216-.372; 1990-present-Bobby Cox

ATLANTA CHIEFS

Home City: Atlanta, Georgia
Home Stadium: Atlanta-Fulton County Stadium Capacity: 51,383 [1972]
Origin of Name: The name was selected as a tie in to the Atlanta Braves of the National League of baseball as the two teams had the same backers.

Regular Season Record

Season	League	GP	W	L	T	GF	GA	BP	Pts	Pct
1967	NPSL	31	10	12	9	51	46	NA	135	.484
1968	NASL	31	18	7	6	50	32	48	174	.624
1969	NASL	16	11	2	3	46	20	34	109	.757
1970	NASL	24	11	8	5	53	33	42	123	.569
1971	NASL	24	12	7	5	35	29	33	120	.556
1972	NASL	14	5	6	3	19	18	17	56	.444
TOTAL:	6 years	140	67	42	31	254	178	174	717	
AVERAGE:		23	11	7	5	42	30	29	120	.569

Playoff Record

Season	GP	W	L	T	GF	GA	Result
1968	4	2	0	2	6	2	**Won NASL championship.**
1971	5	3	2	0	6	7	Lost to Dallas in NASL championship game.
TOTAL:	9	5	2	2	12	9	
AVERAGE:	5	3	1	1	6	5	

COACHING HISTORY: 1967-68 Phil Woosnam 28-19-15-.554; 1969 Vic Crowe 11-2-2-.757; 1970-72 Vic Rouse 28-21-13

ATLANTA CHIEFS
(were Colorado Caribous)

Home City: Atlanta, Georgia
Home Stadium: Atlanta-Fulton County Stadium — Capacity: 52,522 [1979]
Origin of Name: Named after previous NASL team.

Regular Season Record

Season	League	GP	W	L	GF	GA	BP	Pts	Pct
1979	NASL	30	12	18	59	61	49	121	.448
1980	NASL	32	7	25	34	84	32	74	.257
1981	NASL	32	17	15	62	60	53	151	.315
TOTAL:	3 years	94	36	58	155	205	134	346	
AVERAGE:		31	12	19	52	68	45	115	.343

Playoff Record

Season	GP	W	L	GF	GA	Result
1981	2	0	2	3	5	Lost to Jacksonville in 1st round.

COACHING HISTORY: 1979-80 Dan Wood 19-43; 1981 Dave Chadwick 17-15

ATLANTA FALCONS

Home City: Atlanta, Georgia
Home Stadium: Atlanta-Fulton County Stadium* (1966-1991) — Capacity: 59,643 [1990]
Georgia Dome (1992-present) — Capacity: 71,228 [1995]
Origin of Name: The name was chosen in a radio sponsored contest.

Regular Season Record

Season	League	GP	W	L	T	PF	PA	Pct
1966	NFL	14	3	11	0	204	437	.214
1967	NFL	14	1	12	1	175	422	.077
1968	NFL	14	2	12	0	170	389	.143
1969	NFL	14	6	8	0	276	268	.429
1970	NFL	14	4	8	2	206	261	.333
1971	NFL	14	7	6	1	274	277	.538
1972	NFL	14	7	7	0	269	274	.500
1973	NFL	14	9	5	0	318	224	.643
1974	NFL	14	3	11	0	111	271	.214
1975	NFL	14	4	10	0	240	289	.286
1976	NFL	14	4	10	0	172	312	.286
1977	NFL	14	7	7	0	179	129	.500
1978	NFL	16	9	7	0	240	290	.563
1979	NFL	16	6	10	0	300	388	.375
1980	NFL	16	12	4	0	405	272	.750
1981	NFL	16	7	9	0	426	355	.438
1982	NFL	9	5	4	0	183	199	.556

*Originally Atlanta Stadium from 1966 to 1974.

1983	NFL	16	7	9	0	370	389	.438
1984	NFL	16	4	12	0	281	382	.250
1985	NFL	16	4	12	0	282	452	.250
1986	NFL	16	7	8	1	280	280	.469
1987	NFL	15	3	12	0	205	436	.200
1988	NFL	16	5	11	0	244	315	.313
1989	NFL	16	3	13	0	279	437	.188
1990	NFL	16	5	11	0	348	365	.313
1991	NFL	16	10	6	0	361	338	.625
1992	NFL	16	6	10	0	327	414	.375
1993	NFL	16	6	10	0	316	385	.375
1994	NFL	16	7	9	0	317	385	.438
1995	NFL	16	9	7	0	362	349	.563
TOTAL:	30 years	448	172	271	5	8120	9984	
AVERAGE:		15	6	9	0	271	333	.390

Playoff Record

Season	GP	W	L	PF	PA	Result
1978	2	1	1	34	40	Lost to Dallas in NFC playoffs.
1980	1	0	1	27	30	Lost to Dallas in NFC playoffs.
1982	1	0	1	24	30	Lost to Minnesota in NFC 1st round.
1991	2	1	1	34	44	Lost to Washington in NFC semifinals.
1995	1	0	1	20	37	Lost to Green Bay in NFC semifinals.
TOTAL:	7	2	5	139	181	
AVERAGE:	2	1	1	28	36	

COACHING HISTORY: 1966-68 Norb Hecker 4-26-1-.145; 1968-74 Norm Van Brocklin 37-49-3-.433; 1974-76 Marion Campbell 6-19-0-.240; 1976 Pat Peppler 3-6-0-.333; 1977-82 Leeman Bennett 47-44-0-.516; 1983-86 Dan Henning 22-41-1-.352; 1987-89 Marion Campbell 11-36-0-.234; 1990-93 Jerry Glanville 27-37-0-.422; 1994-present June Jones

ATLANTA FLAMES
(became Calgary Flames)

Home City: Atlanta, Georgia
Home Arena: The Omni — Capacity: 15,191 [1980]
Origin of Name: The name was chosen in a Name the Team Contest and suggested by the burning of Atlanta during the American Civil War by General Sherman.

Regular Season Record

Season	League	GP	W	L	T	GF	GA	Pts	Pct
1972-1973	NHL	78	25	38	15	191	239	65	.417
1973-1974	NHL	78	30	34	14	214	238	74	.474
1974-1975	NHL	80	34	31	15	243	233	83	.519
1975-1976	NHL	80	35	33	12	262	237	82	.513
1976-1977	NHL	80	34	34	12	264	265	80	.500
1977-1978	NHL	80	34	27	19	274	252	87	.544
1978-1979	NHL	80	41	31	8	327	280	90	.563
1979-1980	NHL	80	35	32	13	282	269	83	.519
TOTAL:	8 years	636	268	260	108	2057	2013	644	
AVERAGE:		80	34	33	13	257	252	81	.506

Playoff Record

Season	GP	W	L	GF	GA	Result
1973-1974	4	0	4	6	17	Lost to Philadelphia in quarter finals.
1975-1976	2	0	2	1	3	Lost to Los Angeles in preliminary round.
1976-1977	3	1	2	7	11	Lost to Los Angeles in preliminary round.
1977-1978	2	0	2	5	8	Lost to Detroit in preliminary round.
1978-1979	2	0	2	5	9	Lost to Toronto in preliminary round.
1979-1980	4	1	3	8	14	Lost to N.Y. Rangers in preliminary round.
TOTAL:	17	2	15	32	62	
AVERAGE:	3	0	3	5	10	

COACHING HISTORY: 1972-1975 Bernie Geoffrion 77-92-39-.464; 1975-1979 Fred Creighton 156-136-56-.529; 1979-1980 Al MacNeil 35-32-13-.519

ATLANTA HAWKS
(were St. Louis Hawks)

Home City: Atlanta, Georgia
Home Court: Alexander Memorial Coliseum (1969-1972) Capacity: 7,166
The Omni (1972-present) Capacity: 16,365 [1995]
Origin of Name: The team kept the same nickname when it moved to Atlanta from St. Louis.

Regular Season Record

Season	League	GP	W	L	PPGF	PPGA	Pct	GB
1968-1969	NBA	82	48	34	111.3	109.4	.585	7
1969-1970	NBA	82	48	34	117.6	117.2	.585	-
1970-1971	NBA	82	36	46	114.0	115.8	.439	6
1971-1972	NBA	82	36	46	109.5	111.3	.439	2
1972-1973	NBA	82	46	36	112.4	112.3	.561	6
1973-1974	NBA	82	35	47	108.6	110.0	.427	12
1974-1975	NBA	82	31	51	105.1	106.5	.378	29
1975-1976	NBA	82	29	53	102.6	105.5	.354	20
1976-1977	NBA	82	31	51	102.4	106.4	.378	18
1977-1978	NBA	82	41	41	103.7	103.9	.500	11
1978-1979	NBA	82	46	36	109.1	107.1	.561	2
1979-1980	NBA	82	50	32	104.5	101.6	.610	-
1980-1981	NBA	82	31	51	104.9	108.0	.378	29
1981-1982	NBA	82	42	40	101.0	100.5	.512	13
1982-1983	NBA	82	43	39	101.6	102.6	.524	8
1983-1984	NBA	82	40	42	101.5	102.8	.488	10
1984-1985	NBA	82	34	48	106.6	108.1	.415	25
1985-1986	NBA	82	50	32	108.6	106.2	.610	7
1986-1987	NBA	82	57	25	110.0	102.8	.695	-
1987-1988	NBA	82	50	32	107.9	104.3	.610	4
1988-1989	NBA	82	52	30	111.0	106.1	.634	11
1989-1990	NBA	82	41	41	108.5	107.5	.500	18
1990-1991	NBA	82	43	39	109.8	109.0	.524	18
1991-1992	NBA	82	38	44	106.2	107.7	.463	29
1992-1993	NBA	82	43	39	107.5	108.4	.524	14
1993-1994	NBA	82	57	25	101.4	96.2	.695	-
1994-1995	NBA	82	42	40	96.6	95.3	.512	10

1995-1996	NBA	82	46	36	98.3	97.1	.561	26
TOTAL:	28 years	2296	1186	1110				335
AVERAGE:		82	42	40	106.6	106.0	.517	12

Playoff Record

Season	GP	W	L	PPGF	PPGA	Result
1968-1969	11	5	6	102.5	101.8	Lost Division final to Los Angeles.
1969-1970	9	4	5	114.3	114.0	Lost Division final to Los Angeles.
1970-1971	5	1	4	104.6	110.0	Lost Conference semifinal to New York.
1971-1972	6	2	4	113.0	121.2	Lost Conference semifinal to Boston.
1972-1973	6	2	4	106.8	114.7	Lost Conference semifinal to Boston.
1977-1978	2	0	2	98.5	105.0	Lost 1st round series to Washington.
1978-1979	9	5	4	100.6	99.7	Lost Conference semifinals to Washington.
1979-1980	5	1	4	96.8	102.2	Lost Conference semifinals to Philadelphia.
1981-1982	2	0	2	85.5	104.5	Lost 1st round series to Philadelphia.
1982-1983	3	1	2	89.7	98.0	Lost 1st round series to Boston.
1983-1984	5	2	3	93.6	103.0	Lost 1st round series to Milwaukee.
1985-1986	9	4	5	111.0	113.9	Lost Conference semifinals to Boston.
1986-1987	9	4	5	100.1	99.4	Lost Conference semifinals to Detroit.
1987-1988	12	6	6	108.6	107.2	Lost Conference semifinals to Boston.
1988-1989	5	2	3	103.2	103.8	Lost 1st round series to Milwaukee.
1990-1991	5	2	3	97.2	105.2	Lost 1st round series to Detroit.
1992-1993	3	0	3	93.3	109.7	Lost 1st round series to Chicago.
1993-1994	11	5	6	90.4	90.1	Lost Conference semifinals to Indiana.
1994-1995	3	0	3	89.3	100.0	Lost 1st round series to Indiana.
1995-1996	10	4	6	92.7	97.0	Lost Conference semifinal to Orlando.
TOTAL:	130	50	80			
AVERAGE:	7	3	4	101.4	104.5	

COACHING HISTORY: 1968-1972 Richie Guerin 168-160-.512; 1972-1976 Lowell "Cotton" Fitzsimmons 140-180-.438; 1976 Gene Tormohlen 1-7-.125; 1976-1981 Hubie Brown 199-208-.489; 1981-1983 Kevin Loughery 85-79-.518; 1981 Mike Fratello 0-3-.000; 1983-1990 Mike Fratello 324-250-.564; 1990-1993 Bob Weiss 124-122-.504; 1993-present Lenny Wilkens

BALTIMORE BAYS

Home City: Baltimore, Maryland
Home Stadium: Memorial Stadium — Capacity: 52,185 [1968]
Origin of Name: The team was named after the nearby Chesapeake Bay.

Regular Season Record

Season	League	GP	W	L	T	GF	GA	BP	Pts	Pct
1967	NPSL	32	14	9	9	53	47	NA	162	.563
1968	NASL	32	13	16	3	42	43	41	128	.444
1969	NASL	16	2	13	1	27	56	27	42	.292
TOTAL:	3 years	80	29	38	13	122	146	68	332	
AVERAGE:		27	10	13	4	41	49	23	111	.457

Playoff Record

Season	GP	W	L	T	GF	GA	Result
1967	2	1	1	0	2	4	Lost final series to Oakland.

COACHING HISTORY: 1967 Doug Millward 14-9-9-.563; 1968-1969 Gordon Jago 15-29-4-.394

BALTIMORE BLADES
(were Michigan Stags)

Home City: Baltimore, Maryland
Home Arena: Baltimore Civic Center Capacity: 11,329 [1975]
Origin of Name: The team was named by league executives after the league took over the operations of the club and moved them to Baltimore.

Regular Season Record

Season	League	GP	W	L	T	GF	GA	Pts	Pct
1974-1975	WHA	35	7	27	1	98	162	15	.214

COACHING HISTORY: John Wilson 7-27-1-.214

BALTIMORE BULLETS

Home City: Baltimore, Maryland
Home Court:
Origin of Name: The team kept its nickname after it jumped from the minor league American Basketball League to the BAA

Regular Season Record

Season	League	GP	W	L	PPGF	PPGA	Pct	GB
1947-1948	BAA	48	28	20	74.4	70.5	.583	1
1948-1949	BAA	60	29	31	83.6	82.2	.483	9
1949-1950	NBA	68	25	43	73.1	78.7	.368	28
1950-1951	NBA	66	24	42	82.0	84.3	.364	16
1951-1952	NBA	66	20	46	81.5	89.0	.303	20
1952-1953	NBA	70	16	54	84.4	90.9	.229	31
1953-1954	NBA	72	16	56	78.3	85.1	.222	28
TOTAL:	7 years	450	158	292				133
AVERAGE:		64	23	42	79.6	83.0	.351	19

Playoff Record

Season	GP	W	L	PPGF	PPGA	Result
1947-1948	12	9	3	76.8	74.3	**Won championship of BAA**.
1948-1949	3	1	2	85.0	89.3	Lost 1st round series to New York.
TOTAL:	15	10	5			
AVERAGE:	7	5	2	80.9	81.8	

COACHING HISTORY: 1947-1951 Buddy Jeannette 96-117-.451; 1951 Walt Budko 10-19-.345; 1952 Fred Scolari 12-27-.308; 1952-1953 Chick Reiser 8-22-.267; 1953-1954 Clair Bee 32-107-.230

BALTIMORE BULLETS
(were Chicago Zephyrs)
(became Capital Bullets)

Home City: Baltimore, Maryland
Home Court: Baltimore Civic Center Capacity: 12,289
Origin of Name: Named after previous NBA team.

Regular Season Record

Season	League	GP	W	L	PPGF	PPGA	Pct	GB
1963-1964	NBA	80	31	49	111.9	113.6	.388	17
1964-1965	NBA	80	37	43	113.6	115.8	.463	12
1965-1966	NBA	80	38	42	118.3	119.5	.475	7
1966-1967	NBA	81	20	61	115.5	122.0	.247	48
1967-1968	NBA	82	36	46	117.4	117.8	.439	26
1968-1969	NBA	82	57	25	116.4	112.1	.695	-
1969-1970	NBA	82	50	32	120.7	118.6	.610	10
1970-1971	NBA	82	42	40	112.9	112.3	.512	-
1971-1972	NBA	82	38	44	107.1	108.3	.463	-
1972-1973	NBA	82	52	30	105.0	101.6	.634	-
TOTAL:	10 years	813	401	412				120
AVERAGE:		81	40	41	113.9	114.2	.493	12

Playoff Record

Season	GP	W	L	PPGF	PPGA	Result
1964-1965	10	5	5	115.2	113.3	Lost Division finals to St. Louis.
1965-1966	3	0	3	107.7	113.0	Lost Division semifinals to St. Louis.
1968-1969	4	0	4	104.4	113.5	Lost Division semifinals to New York.
1969-1970	7	3	4	105.0	106.6	Lost Division semifinals to New York.
1970-1971	18	8	10	103.7	102.8	Lost championship series to Milwaukee.
1971-1972	6	2	4	96.8	105.8	Lost Conference semifinals to New York.
1972-1973	5	1	4	95.6	103.8	Lost Conference semifinals to New York.
TOTAL:	53	19	34			
AVERAGE:	8	3	5	104.1	108.4	

COACHING HISTORY: 1963-1964 Bob Leonard 80-31-49-.388; 1964-1965 Buddy Jeannette 80-37-43-.463; 1965-1966 Paul Seymour 80-38-42-.475; 1966-1967 Mike Farmer 9-1-8-.111; 1966-1967 Buddy Jeannette 16-3-13-.188; 1967-1973 Gene Shue 548-291-257-.531

BALTIMORE CFLers
(became Baltimore Stallions)

Home City: Baltimore, Maryland
Home Stadium: Memorial Stadium Capacity: 54,600 [1994]
Origin of Name: The team was supposed to be called the Colts after the previous NFL team, however the Indianapolis Colts of the NFL obtained a court injunction preventing them from using the name. The team adopted the unofficial nickname of CFLers for the 1994 season.

Regular Season Record

Season	League	GP	W	L	T	PF	PA	Pts	Pct
1994	CFL	18	12	6	0	561	431	24	.667

Playoff Record

Season	GP	W	L	PF	PA	Result
1994	3	2	1	71	53	Lost Grey Cup game to British Columbia.

COACHING HISTORY: 1994 Don Matthews 12-6-0-.667

BALTIMORE COLTS

Home City: Baltimore, Maryland
Home Stadium: Memorial Stadium (1947-1948) Capacity: 60,000 [1947]
Babe Ruth Stadium (1949-1950) Capacity: 24,000 [1949]
Origin of Name: The name was chosen in a Name the Team Contest and chosen from several hundred entries.

Regular Season Record

Season	League	GP	W	L	T	PF	PA	Pct
1947	AAFC	14	2	11	1	167	377	.179
1948	AAFC	14	7	7	0	333	327	.500
1949	AAFC	12	1	11	0	172	341	.083
1950	NFL	12	1	11	0	213	462	.083
TOTAL:	4 years	52	11	40	1	885	1507	
AVERAGE:		13	3	10	0	221	377	.221

COACHING HISTORY: 1947-1949 Cecil Isbell 9-22-1-.297; 1949 Walt Driskill 1-7-0-.125; 1950 Clem Crowe 1-11-0-.083

BALTIMORE COLTS

(were Dallas Texans)
(became Indianapolis Colts)

Home City: Baltimore, Maryland
Home Stadium: Memorial Stadium Capacity: 60,763 [1983]
Origin of Name: The team was named after the team which played in the AAFC and the NFL from 1947 to 1950.

Regular Season Record

Season	League	GP	W	L	T	PF	PA	Pct
1953	NFL	12	3	9	0	182	350	.250
1954	NFL	12	3	9	0	131	279	.250
1955	NFL	12	5	6	1	214	239	.458
1956	NFL	12	5	7	0	270	322	.417
1957	NFL	12	7	5	0	303	235	.583
1958	NFL	12	9	3	0	381	203	.750
1959	NFL	12	9	3	0	374	251	.750
1960	NFL	12	6	6	0	288	234	.500
1961	NFL	14	8	6	0	302	307	.571
1962	NFL	14	7	7	0	293	288	.500
1963	NFL	14	8	6	0	316	285	.571
1964	NFL	14	12	2	0	428	225	.857
1965	NFL	14	10	3	1	389	284	.750
1966	NFL	14	9	5	0	314	226	.643
1967	NFL	14	11	1	2	394	198	.857
1968	NFL	14	13	1	0	402	144	.929
1969	NFL	14	8	5	1	279	268	.607
1970	NFL	14	11	2	1	321	234	.821
1971	NFL	14	10	4	0	313	140	.714
1972	NFL	14	5	9	0	235	252	.357

1973	NFL	14	4	10	0	226	341	.286
1974	NFL	14	2	12	0	190	329	.143
1975	NFL	14	10	4	0	395	269	.714
1976	NFL	14	11	3	0	417	246	.786
1977	NFL	14	10	4	0	295	221	.714
1978	NFL	16	5	11	0	239	421	.313
1979	NFL	16	5	11	0	271	351	.313
1980	NFL	16	7	9	0	355	387	.438
1981	NFL	16	2	14	0	259	533	.125
1982	NFL	9	0	8	1	113	236	.056
1983	NFL	16	7	9	0	264	354	.438
TOTAL:	31 years	423	222	194	7	9153	8652	
AVERAGE:		14	7	7	0	295	279	.533

Playoff Record

Season	GP	W	L	PF	PA	Result
1958	1	1	0	23	17	Lost NFL championship game to New York.
1959	1	1	0	31	16	Lost NFL championship game to New York.
1964	1	0	1	0	27	Lost NFL championship game to Cleveland.
1968	3	2	1	65	30	Lost Super Bowl game to New York.
1970	3	3	0	60	30	**Won Super Bowl.**
1971	2	1	1	20	24	Lost AFC championship game to Miami.
1975	1	0	1	10	28	Lost AFC playoffs to Pittsburgh.
1976	1	0	1	14	40	Lost AFC playoffs to Pittsburgh.
1977	1	0	1	31	37	Lost AFC playoffs to Oakland.
TOTAL:	14	8	6	254	249	
AVERAGE:	2	1	1	28	28	

COACHING HISTORY: 1953 Keith Molesworth 3-9-0-.250; 1954-62 Weeb Ewbank 61-52-1-.539; 1963-69 Don Shula 73-26-4-.728; 1970-72 Don McCafferty 26-11-1-.697; 1972 John Sandusky 4-5-0-.444; 1973-74 Howard Schnellenberger 4-13-0-.235; 1974 Joe Thomas 2-9-0-.182; 1975-79 Ted Marchibroda 41-36-0-.532; 1980-81 Mike McCormack 9-23-0-.281; 1982-83 Frank Kush 7-17-1-.300

BALTIMORE COMETS
(became San Diego Jaws)

Home City: Baltimore, Maryland
Home Stadium: Memorial Stadium — Capacity: 53,208 [1974]
Origin of Name:

Regular Season Record

Season	League	GP	W	L	T	GF	GA	BP	Pts	Pct
1974	NASL	20	10	8	2	42	46	39	105	.583
1975	NASL	22	9	13	0	34	52	33	87	.439
TOTAL:	2 years	42	19	21	2	76	98	72	192	
AVERAGE:		21	9	10	1	38	49	36	96	.452

Playoff Record

Season	GP	W	L	T	PF	PA	Result
1974	1	0	1	0	0	1	Lost 1st round game to Boston.

COACHING HISTORY: 1974-1976 Doug Millward 9-10-1-.452

BALTIMORE ORIOLES

Home City: Baltimore, Maryland
Home Field: Newington Park (1882) Capacity: 5,000
Oriole Park (1882-1899) Capacity: 6,000
Origin of Name: The team was named after Maryland's state bird.

Regular Season Record

Season	League	GP	W	L	Pct	GB	R	OR
1882	AA	73	19	54	.260	32.5	273	515
1883	AA	96	28	68	.292	37	471	742
1884	AA	106	63	43	.594	11.5	636	515
1885	AA	109	41	68	.376	36.5	541	683
1886	AA	131	48	83	.366	41	625	878
1887	AA	135	77	58	.570	18	975	861
1888	AA	137	57	80	.416	36	653	779
1889	AA	135	70	65	.519	22	791	795
1890	AA	133	41	92	.308	47.5	674	925
1891	AA	135	72	63	.533	21	850	798
1892	NL	147	46	101	.313	54.5	779	1020
1893	NL	130	60	70	.462	26.5	820	893
1894	NL	128	89	39	.695	-	1171	820
1895	NL	130	87	43	.669	-	1009	646
1896	NL	129	90	39	.698	-	995	662
1897	NL	130	90	40	.692	2	964	674
1898	NL	149	96	53	.644	6	933	623
1899	NL	148	86	62	.581	15	827	691
TOTAL:	18 years	2281	1160	1121		407	13987	13520
AVERAGE:		127	65	62	.509	23	777	751

COACHING HISTORY: 1882 Henry Myers 19-54-.260; 1883-1891 Bill Barnie 461-545-.461; 1890 Jim Kennedy 26-73-.263; 1891-1892 George Van Haltren 5-16-.238; 1892 John Waltz 0-2-.000; 1892-1898 Ned Hanlon 557-369-.602; 1899 John McGraw 86-62-.581

BALTIMORE ORIOLES
(became New York Highlanders)

Home City: Baltimore, Maryland
Home Field: Oriole Park Capacity: 8,500
Origin of Name: The team was named after the Maryland state bird and the previous National League team.

Regular Season Record

Season	League	GP	W	L	Pct	GB	R	OR
1901	AL	133	68	65	.511	13.5	761	750
1902	AL	138	50	88	.362	34	715	850
TOTAL:	2 years	271	118	153		47.5	1476	1600
AVERAGE:		136	59	77	.435	24	738	800

COACHING HISTORY: 1901-1902 John McGraw 96-99-.492; 1902 Wilbert Robinson 22-54-.289

BALTIMORE ORIOLES

Home City: Baltimore, Maryland
Home Court:
Origin of Name: The team was named after the baseball teams that had played at various times in the city.

Regular Season Record

Season	League	GP	W	L	Pct
1926-1927	ABL	42	6	36	048

COACHING HISTORY: Johnny Beckman 6-36-.143

BALTIMORE ORIOLES
(were St. Louis Browns)

Home City: Baltimore, Maryland
Home Field: Memorial Stadium (1954-1991) Capacity: 54,017 [1988]
Camden Yards (1992-present) Capacity: 48,262 [1995]
Origin of Name: Named after previous professional baseball teams.

Regular Season Record

Season	League	GP	W	L	Pct	GB	R	OR
1954	AL	154	54	100	.351	57	483	668
1955	AL	154	57	97	.370	39	540	754
1956	AL	154	69	85	.448	28	571	705
1957	AL	152	76	76	.500	21	597	588
1958	AL	153	74	79	.484	17.5	521	575
1959	AL	154	74	80	.481	20	551	621
1960	AL	154	89	65	.578	8	682	606
1961	AL	162	95	67	.586	14	691	588
1962	AL	162	77	85	.475	19	652	680
1963	AL	162	86	76	.531	18.5	644	621
1964	AL	162	97	65	.599	2	679	567
1965	AL	162	94	68	.580	8	641	578
1966	AL	160	97	63	.606	-	755	601
1967	AL	161	76	85	.472	15.5	654	592
1968	AL	162	91	71	.562	12	579	497
1969	AL	162	109	53	.673	-	779	517
1970	AL	162	108	54	.667	-	792	574
1971	AL	158	101	57	.639	-	742	530
1972	AL	154	80	74	.519	5	519	430
1973	AL	162	97	65	.599	-	754	561
1974	AL	162	91	71	.562	-	659	612
1975	AL	159	90	69	.566	4.5	682	553
1976	AL	162	88	74	.543	10.5	619	598
1977	AL	161	97	64	.602	2.5	719	653
1978	AL	161	90	71	.559	9	659	633
1979	AL	159	102	57	.642	-	757	582
1980	AL	162	100	62	.617	3	805	640
1981	AL	105	59	46	.562	NA	429	437
1982	AL	162	94	68	.580	1	774	687

1983	AL	162	98	64	.605	-	799	652
1984	AL	162	85	77	.525	19	681	667
1985	AL	161	83	78	.516	16	818	764
1986	AL	162	73	89	.451	22.5	708	760
1987	AL	162	67	95	.414	31	729	880
1988	AL	161	54	107	.335	34.5	550	789
1989	AL	162	87	75	.537	2	708	686
1990	AL	161	76	85	.472	11.5	669	698
1991	AL	162	67	95	.414	24	686	796
1992	AL	162	89	73	.549	7	705	656
1993	AL	162	85	77	.525	10	786	745
1994	AL	112	63	49	.563	6.5	589	497
1995	AL	144	71	73	.493	15	704	640
TOTAL:	42 years	6594	3510	3084		514	28061	26478
AVERAGE:		157	84	73	.532	12.5	668	630

Playoff Record

Season	GP	W	L	R	OR	Result
1966	4	4	0	13	2	Lost World Series to Los Angeles.
1969	8	4	4	25	20	Lost World Series to New York.
1970	8	7	1	60	30	**Won World Series.**
1971	10	6	4	39	30	Lost World Series to Pittsburgh.
1973	5	2	3	15	15	Lost ALCS to Oakland.
1974	4	1	3	7	11	Lost ALCS to Oakland.
1979	11	6	5	52	47	Lost World Series to Pittsburgh.
1983	9	7	2	37	12	**Won World Series.**
TOTAL:	59	37	22	248	167	
AVERAGE:	7	4	3	31	21	

COACHING HISTORY: 1954 Jimmy Dykes 54-100-.351; 1955-1961 Paul Richards 523-529-.497; 1961 Lum Harris 11-20-.351; 1962-1963 Billy Hitchcock 163-161-.503; 1964-1968 Hank Bauer 407-318-.561; 1968-1982 Earl Weaver 1354-919-.596; 1983-1985 Joe Altobelli 212-167-.560; 1985 Cal Ripken Sr. 1-0-1.000; 1985-1986 Earl Weaver 126-141-.472; 1987-1988 Cal Ripken Sr. 67-101-.399; 1988-1991 Frank Robinson 230-285-.447; 1991-1994 John Oates 291-270-.519; 1995-present Phil Regan

BALTIMORE STALLIONS

(were Baltimore CFLers)
(became Montreal Alouettes)

Home City: Baltimore, Maryland
Home Stadium: Memorial Stadium Capacity: 54,600 [1995]
Origin of Name: This was a takeoff of the name Colts which the team was not allowed by the NFL to use.

Regular Season Record

Season	League	GP	W	L	T	PF	PA	Pts	Pct
1995	CFL	18	15	3	0	541	369	30	.833

Playoff Record

Season	GP	W	L	PF	PA	Result
1995	3	3	0	94	52	**Won Grey Cup.**

COACHING HISTORY: 1995 Don Matthews 15-3-0-.833

BALTIMORE STARS
(were Philadelphia Stars)

Home City: College Park, Maryland
Home Stadium: Byrd Stadium Capacity: 45,000 [1985]
Origin of Name: The team kept the same nickname when it moved to Baltimore.

Regular Season Record

Season	League	GP	W	L	T	PF	PA	Pct
1985	USFL	18	10	7	1	368	260	.583

Playoff Record

Season	GP	W	L	PF	PA	Result
1985	3	3	0	76	55	**Won USFL championship.**

COACHING HISTORY: Jim Mora 10-7-1-.583

BALTIMORE TERRAPINS

Home City: Baltimore, Maryland
Home Field: Terrapin Park * Capacity: 16,000 [1914]
Origin of Name: Named after the turtles which are found in abundance in the area.

Regular Season Record

Season	League	GP	W	L	Pct	GB	R	OR
1914	FL	154	84	70	.545	4.5	645	628
1915	FL	154	47	107	.305	40	550	760
TOTAL:	2 years	308	131	177		44.5	1195	1388
AVERAGE:		154	66	88	.425	22	598	694

COACHING HISTORY: 1914-1915 Otto Knabe 131-177-.425

BALTIMORE UNIONS

Home City: Baltimore, Maryland
Home Field: Madison Avenue Grounds **
Origin of Name: Named Unions because they belonged to the Union Association.

Regular Season Record

Season	League	GP	W	L	Pct	GB	R	OR
1884	UA	105	58	47	.552	32	662	627

COACHING HISTORY: Charlie Levis 53-35-.602; Bill Henderson 5-12-.294

*Also known as Oriole Park V
**Also known as Belair Lot

BARCELONA DRAGONS

Home City: Barcelona, Spain
Home Stadium: Montjuic Stadium — Capacity: 42,000 [1991]
Origin of Name:

Regular Season Record

Season	League	GP	W	L	T	PF	PA	Pct
1991	WLAF	10	8	2	0	206	126	.800
1992	WFL	10	5	5	0	104	161	.500
TOTAL:	2 years	20	13	7	0	310	287	
AVERAGE:		10	7	3	0	155	144	.650

COACHING HISTORY: 1991-1992 Jack Bicknell 13-7-0-.650

Playoff Record

Season	GP	W	L	PF	PA	Result
1991	2	1	1	10	24	Lost WLAF final game.
1992	1	0	1	15	17	Lost WFL 1st round game.
TOTAL:	3	1	2	25	41	
AVERAGE:	2	1	1	12	21	

BIRMINGHAM AMERICANS
(became Birmingham Vulcans)

Home City: Birmingham, Alabama
Home Stadium: Legion Field — Capacity: 72,000 [1974]
Origin of Name: The name was chosen by the team executives.

Regular Season Record

Season	League	GP	W	L	T	PF	PA	Pct
1974	WFL	20	15	5	0	500	394	.750

Playoff Record

Season	GP	W	L	PF	PA	Result
1974	2	2	0	44	40	**Won WFL championship game.**

COACHING HISTORY: Jack Gotta 15-5-0-.750

BIRMINGHAM BARRACUDAS

Home City: Birmingham, Alabama
Home Stadium: Legion Field — Capacity: 75,017 [1995]
Origin of Name:

Regular Season Record

Season	League	GP	W	L	T	PF	PA	Pts	Pct
1995	CFL	18	10	8	0	548	518	20	.556

Playoff Record

Season	GP	W	L	PF	PA	Result
1995	1	0	1	9	52	Lost Southern Division playoff to San Antonio.

COACHING HISTORY: 1995 Jack Pardee 10-8-0-.556

BIRMINGHAM BULLS
(were Toronto Toros)

Home City: Birmingham, Alabama
Home Arena: Birmingham-Jefferson Civic Center Coliseum Capacity: 16,500 [1977]
Origin of Name: Toro is the Spanish word for Bull and is much more euphonious when combined with Birmingham than Toros would be.

Regular Season Record

Season	League	GP	W	L	T	GF	GA	Pts	Pct
1976-1977	WHA	81	31	46	4	289	309	66	.407
1977-1978	WHA	80	36	41	3	287	314	75	.469
1978-1979	WHA	80	32	42	6	286	311	70	.438
TOTAL:	3 years	241	99	129	13	862	934	211	
AVERAGE:		80	33	43	4	287	311	70	.438

Playoff Record

Season	GP	W	L	GF	GA	Result
1977-1978	5	1	4	12	29	Lost 1st round series to Winnipeg.

COACHING HISTORY: 1976-1977 Gilles Leger 7-16-1-.313; 1976-1977 Pat Kelly 24-30-3-.447; 1977-1978 Glen Sonmor 36-41-3-.469; 1978-1979 John Brophy 32-42-6-.438

BIRMINGHAM FIRE

Home City: Birmingham, Alabama
Home Stadium: Legion Field Capacity: 72,000 [1974]
Origin of Name:

Regular Season Record

Season	League	GP	W	L	T	PF	PA	Pct
1991	WLAF	10	5	5	0	140	140	.500
1992	WFL	10	7	2	1	192	165	.750
TOTAL:	2 years	20	12	7	1	332	305	
AVERAGE:		10	6	4	0	166	153	.625

Playoff Record

Season	GP	W	L	PF	PA	Result
1991	1	0	1	3	10	Lost 1st round playoff game to Barcelona.
1992	1	0	1	7	45	Lost 1st round playoff game to Orlando.
TOTAL:	2	0	2	10	55	
AVERAGE:	1	0	1	5	28	

COACHING HISTORY: 1991-1992 Chan Gailey 12-7-1-.625

BIRMINGHAM STALLIONS

Home City: Birmingham, Alabama
Home Stadium: Legion Field Capacity: 72,000 [1975]
Origin of Name: The name was chosen in a Name the Team Contest.

Regular Season Record

Season	League	GP	W	L	T	PF	PA	Pct
1983	USFL	18	9	9	0	343	346	.500
1984	USFL	18	14	4	0	557	316	.778
1985	USFL	18	13	5	0	436	299	.722
TOTAL:	3 years	54	36	18	0	1336	961	
AVERAGE:		18	12	6	0	445	320	.667

Playoff Record

Season	GP	W	L	PF	PA	Result
1984	2	1	1	46	37	Lost semifinal game to Philadelphia.
1985	2	1	1	36	48	Lost semifinal game to Baltimore.
TOTAL:	4	2	2	82	85	
AVERAGE:	2	1	1	41	43	

COACHING HISTORY: 1983-1985 Rollie Dotsch 36-18-0-.667

BIRMINGHAM VULCANS
(were Birmingham Americans)

Home City: Birmingham, Alabama
Home Stadium: Legion Field Capacity: 72,000 [1975]
Origin of Name: The name was already registered by prospective NFL owners and when they didn't get a franchise they let the WFL owners use it.

Regular Season Record

Season	League	GP	W	L	T	PF	PA	Pct
1975	WLF	12	9	3	0	257	186	.750

COACHING HISTORY: Marvin Bass 9-3-0-.750

BOSTON BEACONS

Home City: Boston, Massachusetts
Home Stadium: Fenway Park Capacity: 33,375 [1968]
Origin of Name: The name was suggested by Boston's famous Beacon hill.

Regular Season Record

Season	League	GP	W	L	T	GF	GA	BP	Pts	Pct
1968	NASL	32	9	17	6	51	69	49	121	.420

COACHING HISTORY: Jack Mansell 9-17-6-.420

BOSTON BEANEATERS

(were Boston Red Caps)
(became Boston Doves)

Home City: Boston, Massachusetts
Home Field: South End Grounds I (1883-1894)
South End Grounds II (1895-1906) Capacity: 6,800 [1888]
Origin of Name: The name was chosen because of Boston's nickname of Beantown.

Regular Season Record

Season	League	GP	W	L	Pct	GB	R	OR
1883	NL	98	63	35	.643	-	669	456
1884	NL	111	73	38	.658	10.5	684	468
1885	NL	112	46	66	.411	41	528	589
1886	NL	117	56	61	.479	30.5	657	661
1887	NL	121	61	60	.504	16.5	831	792
1888	NL	134	70	64	.522	15.5	669	619
1889	NL	128	83	45	.648	1	826	626
1890	NL	133	76	57	.571	12	763	593
1891	NL	138	87	51	.630	-	847	658
1892	NL	150	102	48	.680	-	862	649
1893	NL	129	86	43	.667	-	1008	795
1894	NL	132	83	49	.629	8	1222	1002
1895	NL	131	71	60	.542	16.5	907	826
1896	NL	131	74	57	.565	17	860	761
1897	NL	132	93	39	.705	-	1025	665
1898	NL	149	102	47	.685	-	872	614
1899	NL	152	95	57	.625	8	858	645
1900	NL	138	66	72	.478	17	778	739
1901	NL	138	69	69	.500	20.5	530	556
1902	NL	137	73	64	.533	29	571	515
1903	NL	138	58	80	.420	32	575	661
1904	NL	153	55	98	.359	51	491	752
1905	NL	154	51	103	.331	54.5	467	733
1906	NL	151	49	102	.325	66.5	408	646
TOTAL:	24 years	3207	1742	1465		447	17908	16021
AVERAGE:		134	73	61	.543	19	746	668

COACHING HISTORY: 1883 Jack Burdock 31-26-.544; 1883-1888 John Morrill 338-333-.504; 1889 Jim Hart 83-45-.648; 1890-1901 Frank Selee 1004-649-.607; 1902-1904 Al Buckenberger 186-242-.435; 1905-1906 Fred Tenney 100-205-.328

BOSTON BEES

(were Boston Braves)
(became Boston Braves)

Home City: Boston, Massachusetts
Home Field: Braves Field Capacity: 45,000 [1939]
Origin of Name: The name was chosen from over 1,300 different entries in a Name the Team Contest.

Season	League	GP	W	L	Pct	GB	R	OR
			Regular Season Record					
1936	NL	154	71	83	.461	21	631	715
1937	NL	152	79	73	.520	16	579	556
1938	NL	152	77	75	.507	12	561	618
1939	NL	151	63	88	.417	32.5	572	659
1940	NL	152	65	87	.428	34.5	623	745
TOTAL:	5years	761	355	406		116	2966	3293
AVERAGE:		152	71	81	.466	23	593	659

COACHING HISTORY: 1936-1937 Bill McKechnie 150-156-.409; 1938-1940 Casey Stengel 205-250-.451

BOSTON BRAVES

(were Boston Pilgrims)
(became Milwaukee Braves)

Home City: Boston, Massachusetts
Home Field: South End Grounds (1912-1914)
Braves Field (1915-1952) Capacity: 40,000 [1915]
Origin of Name; The team got its name because then owner Jim Gaffney was directly involved in the Tammany Society, a patriotic and charitable society founded in New York City founded in 1789. The members of the Society were known as braves.

Season	League	GP	W	L	Pct	GB	R	OR
			Regular Season Record					
1912	NL	153	52	101	.340	52	693	873
1913	NL	151	69	82	.457	31.5	641	690
1914	NL	153	94	59	.614	-	657	548
1915	NL	152	83	69	.546	7	582	545
1916	NL	152	89	63	.586	4	542	453
1917	NL	153	72	81	.471	25.5	536	558
1918	NL	124	53	71	.427	28.5	424	469
1919	NL	139	57	82	.410	38.5	465	563
1920	NL	152	62	90	.408	30	523	670
1921	NL	153	79	74	.516	15	721	697
1922	NL	153	53	100	.346	39.5	596	822
1923	NL	154	54	100	.351	41.5	636	798
1924	NL	154	53	100	.346	40	520	800
1925	NL	153	70	83	.458	25	708	802
1926	NL	152	66	86	.434	22	624	719
1927	NL	154	60	94	.390	34	651	771
1928	NL	153	50	103	.327	44.5	631	878
1929	NL	154	56	98	.364	43	657	876
1930	NL	154	70	84	.455	22	693	835
1931	NL	154	64	90	.416	37	533	680
1932	NL	154	77	77	.500	13	649	655
1933	NL	154	83	71	.539	9	552	531
1934	NL	151	78	73	.517	16	683	714
1935	NL	153	38	115	.248	61.5	575	852
1941	NL	154	62	92	.403	38	592	720
1942	NL	148	59	89	.399	44	515	645

1943	NL	153	68	85	.444	36.5	465	612
1944	NL	154	65	89	.422	40	593	674
1945	NL	152	67	85	.441	30	721	728
1946	NL	153	81	72	.529	15.5	630	592
1947	NL	154	86	68	.558	8	701	622
1948	NL	153	91	62	.595	-	739	584
1949	NL	154	75	79	.487	22	706	719
1950	NL	154	83	71	.539	8	785	736
1951	NL	154	76	78	.494	20.5	723	662
1952	NL	153	64	89	.418	32	569	651
TOTAL:	36 years	5464	2459	3005		974.5	22231	24744
AVERAGE:		152	68	84	.450	27	618	687

Playoff Record

Season	**GP**	**W**	**L**	**R**	**OR**	**Result**
1914	4	4	0	16	6	**Won World Series**.
1948	6	2	4	17	17	Lost World Series to Cleveland.
TOTAL:	10	6	4	33	23	
AVERAGE:	5	3	2	17	12	

COACHING HISTORY: 1912 Johnny Kling 52-101-.340; 1913-1920 George Stallings 579-597-.492; 1921-1923 Fred Mitchell 186-274-.404; 1924-1927 Dave Bancroft 249-363-.407; 1928 Jack Slattery 11-20-.355; 1928 Rogers Hornsby 39-83-.320; 1929 Judge Fuchs 56-98-.364; 1930-1935 Bill McKechnie 410-510-.446; 1941-1943 Casey Stengel 189-266-.415; 1944-1945 Bob Coleman 107-138-.437; 1945 Del Bissonette 25-36-.410; 1946-1951 Bill Southworth 444-383-.537; 1951-1952 Tommy Holmes 61-69-.469; 1952 Charlie Grimm 51-67-.432

BOSTON BRAVES

Home City: Boston, Massachusetts
Home Stadium: Braves Field — Capacity: 40,000 [1915]
Origin of Name: The team was called Braves because they played in Braves Field.

Regular Season Record

Season	**League**	**GP**	**W**	**L**	**T**	**PF**	**PA**	**Pct**
1932	NFL	10	4	4	2	55	79	.500

COACHING HISTORY: Lud Wray 4-4-2-.500

BOSTON BREAKERS

(became New Orleans Breakers)

Home City: Boston Massachusetts
Home Stadium: Nickerson Field — Capacity: 21,000 [1983]
Origin of Name: The name was chosen in a Name the Team Contest.

Regular Season Record

Season	**League**	**GP**	**W**	**L**	**T**	**PF**	**PA**	**Pct**
1983	USFL	18	11	7	0	399	334	.611

COACHING HISTORY: Dick Coury 11-7-0-.611

BOSTON BRUINS

Home City: Boston, Massachusetts
Home Arena: Boston Arena (1924-1928) Capacity: 6,200
Boston Garden (1928-1994) Capacity: 14,448 [1994]
Fleet Center (1995-present) Capacity: 17,565 [1995]
Origin of Name: Named by team owner Charles F. Adams.

			Regular Season Record						
Season	League	GP	W	L	T	GF	GA	Pts	Pct
1924-1925	NHL	30	6	24	0	49	119	12	.200
1925-1926	NHL	36	17	15	4	92	85	38	.528
1926-1927	NHL	44	21	20	3	97	89	45	.511
1927-1928	NHL	44	20	13	11	77	70	51	.580
1928-1929	NHL	44	26	13	5	89	52	57	.648
1929-1930	NHL	44	38	5	1	179	98	77	.875
1930-1931	NHL	44	28	10	6	143	90	62	.705
1931-1932	NHL	48	15	21	12	122	117	42	.438
1932-1933	NHL	48	25	15	8	124	88	58	.604
1933-1934	NHL	48	18	25	5	111	130	41	.427
1934-1935	NHL	48	26	16	6	129	112	58	.604
1935-1936	NHL	48	22	20	6	92	83	50	.521
1936-1937	NHL	48	23	18	7	120	110	53	.552
1937-1938	NHL	48	30	11	7	142	89	67	.698
1938-1939	NHL	48	36	10	2	156	76	74	.771
1939-1940	NHL	48	31	12	5	170	98	67	.698
1940-1941	NHL	48	27	8	13	168	102	67	.698
1941-1942	NHL	48	25	17	6	160	118	56	.583
1942-1943	NHL	50	24	17	9	195	176	57	.570
1943-1944	NHL	50	19	26	5	223	268	43	.430
1944-1945	NHL	50	16	30	4	179	219	36	.360
1945-1946	NHL	50	24	18	8	167	156	56	.560
1946-1947	NHL	60	26	23	11	190	175	63	.525
1947-1948	NHL	60	23	24	13	167	168	59	.369
1948-1949	NHL	60	29	23	8	178	163	66	.550
1949-1950	NHL	70	22	32	16	198	228	60	.429
1950-1951	NHL	70	22	30	18	178	197	62	.443
1951-1952	NHL	70	25	29	16	162	176	66	.471
1952-1953	NHL	70	28	29	13	152	172	69	.493
1953-1954	NHL	70	32	28	10	177	181	74	.529
1954-1955	NHL	70	23	26	21	169	188	67	.479
1955-1956	NHL	70	23	34	13	147	185	59	.421
1956-1957	NHL	70	34	24	12	195	174	80	.571
1957-1958	NHL	70	27	28	15	199	194	69	.493
1958-1959	NHL	70	32	29	9	205	215	73	.521
1959-1960	NHL	70	28	34	8	220	241	64	.457
1960-1961	NHL	70	15	42	13	176	254	43	.307
1961-1962	NHL	70	15	47	8	177	306	38	.271
1962-1963	NHL	70	14	39	17	198	281	45	.321
1963-1964	NHL	70	18	40	12	170	212	48	.343
1964-1965	NHL	70	21	43	6	166	253	48	.343
1965-1966	NHL	70	21	43	6	174	275	48	.343
1966-1967	NHL	70	17	43	10	182	253	44	.314

1967-1968	NHL	74	37	27	10	259	216	84	.568
1968-1969	NHL	76	42	18	16	303	221	100	.658
1969-1970	NHL	76	40	17	19	277	216	99	.651
1970-1971	NHL	78	57	14	7	399	207	121	.776
1971-1972	NHL	78	54	13	11	330	204	119	.763
1972-1973	NHL	78	51	22	5	330	235	107	.686
1973-1974	NHL	78	52	17	9	349	221	113	.724
1974-1975	NHL	80	40	26	14	345	245	94	.588
1975-1976	NHL	80	48	15	17	313	237	113	.706
1976-1977	NHL	80	49	23	8	312	240	106	.663
1977-1978	NHL	80	51	18	11	333	218	113	.706
1978-1979	NHL	80	43	23	14	316	270	100	.625
1979-1980	NHL	80	46	21	13	310	234	105	.656
1980-1981	NHL	80	37	30	13	316	272	87	.544
1981-1982	NHL	80	43	27	10	323	285	96	.600
1982-1983	NHL	80	50	20	10	327	228	110	.688
1983-1984	NHL	80	49	25	6	336	261	104	.650
1984-1985	NHL	80	36	34	10	303	287	82	.513
1985-1986	NHL	80	37	31	12	311	288	86	.538
1986-1987	NHL	80	39	34	7	301	276	85	.531
1987-1988	NHL	80	44	30	6	300	251	94	.588
1988-1989	NHL	80	37	29	14	289	256	88	.550
1989-1990	NHL	80	46	25	9	289	232	101	.631
1990-1991	NHL	80	44	24	12	299	264	100	.625
1991-1992	NHL	80	36	32	12	270	275	84	.525
1992-1993	NHL	84	51	26	7	332	268	109	.649
1993-1994	NHL	84	42	29	13	289	252	97	.577
1994-1995	NHL	48	27	18	3	150	127	57	.594
1995-1996	NHL	82	40	31	11	282	269	91	.555
TOTAL:	72 years	4730	2280	1753	697	15657	14091	5269	
AVERAGE:		66	32	24	10	217	196	74	.557

Playoff Record

Season	**GP**	**W**	**L**	**T**	**GF**	**GA**	**Result**
1926-1927	8	2	2	4	16	13	Lost Stanley Cup final to Ottawa.
1927-1928	2	0	1	1	2	5	Lost semifinals to N.Y. Rangers.
1928-1929	5	5	0	0	9	3	**Won Stanley Cup**.
1929-1930	6	3	3	0	14	12	Lost Stanley Cup final to Montreal.
1930-1931	5	2	3	0	13	13	Lost semifinals to Montreal.
1932-1933	5	2	3	0	7	9	Lost semifinals to Toronto.
1935-1936	2	1	1	0	6	8	Lost quarterfinals to Toronto.
1936-1937	3	1	2	0	6	8	Lost quarterfinals to the Maroons.
1937-1938	3	0	3	0	3	6	Lost semifinals to Toronto.
1938-1939	12	8	4	0	26	18	**Won Stanley Cup**.
1939-1940	6	2	4	0	9	15	Lost semifinals to New York.
1940-1941	11	8	3	0	27	23	**Won Stanley Cup**.
1941-1942	5	2	3	0	10	16	Lost semifinals to Detroit.
1942-1943	9	4	5	0	23	33	Lost Stanley Cup finals to Detroit.
1944-1945	7	3	4	0	22	22	Lost semifinals to Detroit.
1945-1946	10	5	5	0	29	29	Lost Stanley Cup finals to Montreal.
1946-1947	5	1	4	0	10	16	Lost semifinals to Montreal.
1947-1948	5	1	4	0	13	20	Lost semifinals to Toronto.
1948-1949	5	1	4	0	10	16	Lost semifinals to Toronto.

1950-1951	6	1	4	1	5	17	Lost semifinals to Toronto.
1951-1952	7	3	4	0	12	18	Lost semifinals to Montreal.
1952-1953	11	5	6	0	30	37	Lost Stanley Cup finals to Montreal.
1953-1954	4	0	4	0	4	16	Lost semifinals to Montreal.
1954-1955	5	1	4	0	9	16	Lost semifinals to Montreal.
1956-1957	10	5	5	0	21	29	Lost Stanley Cup finals to Montreal.
1957-1958	12	6	6	0	42	32	Lost Stanley Cup finals to Montreal.
1958-1959	7	3	4	0	21	20	Lost semifinals to Toronto.
1967-1968	4	0	4	0	8	15	Lost quarterfinals to Montreal.
1968-1969	10	6	4	0	40	20	Lost semifinals to Montreal.
1969-1970	14	12	2	0	63	33	**Won Stanley Cup**.
1970-1971	7	3	4	0	26	28	Lost quarterfinals to Montreal.
1971-1972	15	12	3	0	64	34	**Won Stanley Cup**.
1972-1973	5	1	4	0	11	22	Lost quarterfinals to N.Y. Rangers.
1973-1974	16	10	6	0	58	44	Lost Cup finals to Philadelphia.
1974-1975	3	1	2	0	15	12	Lost preliminary round to Chicago.
1975-1976	12	5	7	0	38	33	Lost semifinals to Philadelphia.
1976-1977	14	8	6	0	50	48	Lost Stanley Cup finals to Montreal.
1977-1978	15	10	5	0	53	42	Lost Stanley Cup finals to Montreal.
1978-1979	11	7	4	0	36	32	Lost semifinals to Montreal.
1979-1980	10	4	6	0	35	33	Lost quarterfinals to N.Y. Islanders.
1980-1981	3	0	3	0	13	20	Lost preliminary round to Minnesota.
1981-1982	11	6	5	0	43	39	Lost quarterfinals to Quebec.
1982-1983	17	9	8	0	65	61	Lost semifinals to N.Y. Islanders.
1983-1984	3	0	3	0	2	10	Lost semifinals to Montreal.
1984-1985	5	2	3	0	17	19	Lost semifinals to Montreal.
1985-1986	3	0	3	0	6	10	Lost semifinals to Montreal.
1986-1987	4	0	4	0	11	19	Lost semifinals to Montreal.
1987-1988	23	12	10	1	85	72	Lost Stanley Cup finals to Edmonton.
1988-1989	12	5	7	0	29	30	Lost Division finals to Montreal.
1989-1990	21	13	8	0	62	59	Lost Stanley Cup finals to Edmonton.
1990-1991	19	10	9	0	60	62	Lost Conference finals to Pittsburgh.
1991-1992	15	8	7	0	40	51	Lost Conference finals to Pittsburgh.
1992-1993	4	0	4	0	12	19	Lost semifinals to Buffalo.
1993-1994	13	6	7	0	39	42	Lost semifinals to New Jersey.
1994-1995	5	1	4	0	5	14	Lost quarterfinals to New Jersey.
1995-1996	5	1	4	0	16	22	Lost quarterfinals to Florida.
TOTAL:	475	227	241	7	1401	1415	
AVERAGE:	8	4	4	0	25	25	

COACHING HISTORY:1924-1928 Art Ross 64-72-18-.474; 1928-1929 Cy Denneny 26-13-5-.648; 1929-1934 Art Ross 124-76-32-.603; 1935-1936 Frank Patrick 48-36-12-.563; 1936-1939 Art Ross 89-39-16-.674; 1939-1940 Ralph Weiland 58-20-18-.698; 1941-1946 Art Ross 84-90-24-.485; 1945-1949 Aubrey Clapper 102-88-40-.530; 1949-1950 George Boucher 22-32-16-.429; 1950-1955 Lynn Patrick 117-130-63-.479; 1955-1961 Milt Schmidt 172-203-85-.466; 1961-1963 Phil Watson 16-55-13-.268; 1963-1966 Milt Schmidt 73-157-36-.342; 1966-1970 Harry Sinden 136-105-55-.552; 1970-1973 Tom Johnson 142-43-23-.738; 1973-1975 Armand Guidolin 72-23-9-.736; 1974-1979 Don Cherry 231-105-64-.658; 1979-1980 Fred Creighton 40-20-13-.637; 1979-1980 Harry Sinden 6-1-0-.857; 1980-1985 Gerry Cheevers 204-126-46-.604; 1985-1986 Harry Sinden 11-10-3-.521; 1985-1987 Butch Goring 44-36-13-.543; 1986-1989 Terry O'Reilly 113-88-26-.555; 1989-1991 Mike Milbury 90-49-21-.628; 1991-1992 Rick Bowness 36-32-12-.525; 1992-1995 Brian Sutter 120-73-23-.609; 1995-present Steve Kasper

A game between Edmonton and Boston in the 1987-1988 playoffs was suspended due to power failure in Boston Garden, the above statistics include totals from this game.

BOSTON BULLDOGS

(were Pottsville Maroons)

Home City: Boston, Massachusetts
Home Stadium:
Origin of Name: Named after teams which had previously played in the area.

Regular Season Record

Season	League	GP	W	L	T	PF	PA	Pct
1929	NFL	8	4	4	0	98	73	.500

COACHING HISTORY: Dick Rauch 4-4-0-.500

BOSTON CELTICS

Home City: Boston, Massachusetts
Home Court: Boston Garden (1946-present) Capacity: 14,890 [1994]
Fleet Center (1995-present) Capacity: 18,400 [1995]
Origin of Name: Named by team owner Walter Brown.

Regular Season Record

Season	League	GP	W	L	PPGF	PPGA	Pct	GB
1946-1947	BAA	60	22	38	60.1	65.0	.367	27
1947-1948	BAA	48	20	28	68.8	72.7	.417	7
1948-1949	BAA	60	25	35	76.6	79.5	.417	13
1949-1950	NBA	68	22	46	79.7	82.2	.324	31
1950-1951	NBA	69	39	30	85.2	85.5	.565	2.5
1951-1952	NBA	66	39	27	91.3	87.3	.591	1
1952-1953	NBA	71	46	25	88.1	85.8	.648	1.5
1953-1954	NBA	72	42	30	87.7	85.4	.583	2
1954-1955	NBA	72	36	36	101.4	101.5	.500	7
1955-1956	NBA	72	39	33	106.0	105.3	.542	6
1956-1957	NBA	72	44	28	105.5	100.2	.611	-
1957-1958	NBA	72	49	23	109.9	104.4	.681	-
1958-1959	NBA	72	52	20	116.4	109.9	.722	-
1959-1960	NBA	75	59	16	124.5	116.2	.787	-
1960-1961	NBA	79	57	22	119.7	114.1	.722	-
1961-1962	NBA	80	60	20	121.1	111.9	.750	-
1962-1963	NBA	80	58	22	118.8	111.6	.725	-
1963-1964	NBA	80	59	21	113.0	105.1	.738	-
1964-1965	NBA	80	62	18	112.8	104.5	.775	-
1965-1966	NBA	80	54	26	112.7	107.8	.675	1
1966-1967	NBA	81	60	21	119.3	111.3	.741	8
1967-1968	NBA	82	54	28	116.1	112.0	.659	8
1968-1969	NBA	82	48	34	111.0	105.4	.585	9
1969-1970	NBA	82	34	48	114.9	116.8	.415	26
1970-1971	NBA	82	44	38	117.2	115.1	.537	8
1971-1972	NBA	82	56	26	115.6	110.8	.683	-
1972-1973	NBA	82	68	14	112.7	104.5	.829	-

1973-1974	NBA	82	56	26	109.0	105.1	.683	-
1974-1975	NBA	82	60	22	106.5	100.8	.732	-
1975-1976	NBA	82	54	28	106.2	103.9	.659	-
1976-1977	NBA	82	44	38	104.5	106.5	.537	6
1977-1978	NBA	82	32	50	105.7	107.7	.390	23
1978-1979	NBA	82	29	53	108.2	113.3	.354	25
1979-1980	NBA	82	61	21	113.5	105.7	.744	-
1980-1981	NBA	82	62	20	109.9	104.0	.756	-
1981-1982	NBA	82	63	19	112.0	105.6	.768	-
1982-1983	NBA	82	56	26	112.1	106.7	.683	9
1983-1984	NBA	82	62	20	112.1	105.6	.756	-
1984-1985	NBA	82	63	19	114.8	108.1	.768	-
1985-1986	NBA	82	67	15	114.1	104.7	.817	-
1986-1987	NBA	82	59	23	112.6	106.0	.720	-
1987-1988	NBA	82	57	25	113.6	107.7	.695	-
1988-1989	NBA	82	42	40	109.2	108.1	.512	10
1989-1990	NBA	82	52	30	110.0	106.0	.634	1
1990-1991	NBA	82	56	26	111.5	105.7	.683	-
1991-1992	NBA	82	51	31	106.6	103.0	.622	-
1992-1993	NBA	82	48	34	103.7	102.8	.585	12
1993-1994	NBA	82	32	50	100.8	105.1	.390	25
1994-1995	NBA	82	35	47	102.8	104.7	.427	22
1995-1996	NBA	82	33	49	103.6	107.0	.402	27
TOTAL:	50 years	3887	2422	1465				318
AVERAGE:		78	48	30	104.0	100.8	.623	6

Playoff Record

Season	**GP**	**W**	**L**	**PPGF**	**PPGA**	**Result**
1947-1948	3	1	2	75.7	79.0	Lost quarterfinals to Chicago.
1950-1951	2	0	2	73.5	87.5	Lost semifinals to New York.
1951-1952	3	1	2	96.3	94.3	Lost semifinals to New York.
1952-1953	6	3	3	88.7	89.0	Lost Division finals to New York.
1953-1954	6	2	4	87.0	89.2	Lost Division finals to Syracuse.
1954-1955	7	3	4	105.3	106.4	Lost Division finals to Syracuse.
1955-1956	3	1	2	101.7	98.7	Lost semifinals to Syracuse.
1956-1957	10	7	3	111.7	104.5	**Won NBA championship**.
1957-1958	11	6	5	106.5	101.5	Lost championship series to St. Louis.
1958-1959	11	8	3	123.3	116.5	**Won NBA championship**.
1959-1960	13	8	5	113.2	107.4	**Won NBA championship**.
1960-1961	10	8	2	120.7	109.1	**Won NBA championship**.
1961-1962	14	8	6	114.9	110.1	**Won NBA championship**.
1962-1963	13	8	5	118.1	115.9	**Won NBA championship**.
1963-1964	10	8	2	103.4	97.2	**Won NBA championship**.
1964-1965	12	8	4	117.3	109.3	**Won NBA championship**.
1965-1966	17	11	6	115.8	110.3	**Won NBA championship**.
1966-1967	9	4	5	115.7	117.3	Lost Division finals to Philadelphia.
1967-1968	19	12	7	114.6	111.6	**Won NBA championship**.
1968-1969	18	12	6	107.8	104.7	**Won NBA championship**.
1971-1972	11	5	6	112.9	112.4	Lost Conference finals to New York.
1972-1973	13	7	6	108.1	106.5	Lost Conference finals to New York.
1973-1974	18	12	6	102.4	96.8	**Won NBA championship**.
1974-1975	11	6	5	107.1	107.1	Lost Conference final to Washington.
1975-1976	18	12	6	100.7	97.7	**Won NBA championship**.

1976-1977	9	5	4	104.0	106.2	Lost semifinals to Philadelphia.
1979-1980	9	5	4	102.4	96.7	Lost Conference final to Philadelphia.
1980-1981	17	12	5	103.4	97.3	**Won NBA championship**.
1981-1982	12	7	5	105.8	94.5	Lost Conference final to Philadelphia.
1982-1983	7	2	5	96.0	99.1	Lost semifinals to Milwaukee.
1983-1984	23	15	8	110.9	106.7	**Won NBA championship.**
1984-1985	21	13	8	113.1	110.5	Lost championship series to L.A.
1985-1986	18	15	3	114.4	104.1	**Won NBA championship**.
1986-1987	23	13	10	113.1	114.2	Lost championship series to L.A.
1987-1988	17	9	8	103.5	102.6	Lost Conference finals to Detroit.
1988-1989	3	0	3	90.3	101.0	Lost 1st round series to Detroit.
1989-1990	5	2	3	118.8	118.2	Lost 1st round series to New York.
1990-1991	11	5	6	110.4	109.2	Lost semifinals to Detroit.
1991-1992	10	6	4	107.1	107.0	Lost semifinals to Cleveland.
1992-1993	4	1	3	100.5	105.8	Lost 1st round series to Charlotte.
1994-1995	4	1	3	86.3	98.3	Lost 1st round series to Orlando.
TOTAL:	461	272	189			
AVERAGE:	11	7	4	98.6	96.7	

COACHING HISTORY: 1946-1948 John Russell 42-66-.389; 1948-1950 Alvin Julian 47-81-.367; 1950-1966 Red Auerbach 795-397-.670; 1966-1969 Bill Russell 162-83-.661; 1969-1978 Tom Heinsohn 427-263-.619; 1978-1979 Tom Sanders 23-39-.371; 1978-1979 Dave Cowens 27-41-.397; 1979-1983 Bill Fitch 242-86-.738; 1983-1988 K.C. Jones 308-102-.751; 1989-1991 Jimmy Rodgers 94-70-.573; 1991-1995 Chris Ford 234-201-.538; 1995-present M.L. Carr

BOSTON DOVES

(were Boston Beaneaters)
(became Boston Pilgrims)

Home City: Boston, Massachusetts
Home Field: South End Grounds II — Capacity: 6,800
Origin of Name: The team was known as the Doves while the team president was George Dovey.

Regular Season Record

Season	**League**	**GP**	**W**	**L**	**Pct**	**GB**	**R**	**OR**
1907	NL	148	58	90	.392	47	503	651
1908	NL	154	63	91	.409	36	537	621
TOTALS:	2years	302	121	181		83	1040	1272
AVERAGE:		151	61	90	.401	41.5	520	636

COACHING HISTORY: 1907 Fred Tenney 58-90-.392; 1908 Joe Kelley 63-91-.409

BOSTON MINUTEMEN

Home City: Boston, Massachusetts
Home Field: Nickerson Field — Capacity: 12,500 [1974]
Origin of Name: Name was picked in a contest and was named after the minutemen who served in Massachusetts and other New England colonies prior to and during the American Revolution.

Regular Season Record

Season	**League**	**GP**	**W**	**L**	**T**	**GF**	**GA**	**BP**	**Pts**	**Pct**
1974	NASL	20	10	9	1	36	23	31	94	.522
1975	NASL	22	13	9	0	41	29	38	114	.576

1976	NASL	24	7	17	0	35	64	32	74	.343
TOTAL:	3 years	66	30	35	1	112	116	101	282	
AVERAGE:		22	10	12	0	37	39	34	94	.475

Playoff Record

Season	GP	W	L	T	GF	GA	Result
1974	2	1	1	0	1	2	Lost 2nd round game to Los Angeles.
1975	1	0	1	0	1	2	Lost 1st round game to Miami.
TOTAL:	3	1	2	0	2	4	
AVERAGE:	2	1	1	0	1	2	

COACHING HISTORY: 1974-1976 Hubert Vogelsinger 28-22-1; 1976 John Bertos 6-11-0

BOSTON PATRIOTS

(became New England Patriots)

Home City: Boston, Massachusetts
Home Stadium: Nickerson Field (Boston University) [1960-62] Capacity: 17,369
Fenway Park [1963-1968] Capacity: 33,379 [1971]
Alumni Stadium (Boston College)[1969] Capacity: 26,000
Harvard Stadium[1970] Capacity: 37,300 [1970]
Origin of Name: The name was picked in a contest sponsored by a local newspaper

Regular Season Record

Season	League	GP	W	L	T	PF	PA	Pct
1960	AFL	14	5	9	0	286	349	.357
1961	AFL	14	9	4	1	413	313	.679
1962	AFL	14	9	4	1	346	295	.679
1963	AFL	14	7	6	1	327	257	.536
1964	AFL	14	10	3	1	365	297	.750
1965	AFL	14	4	8	2	244	302	.357
1966	AFL	14	8	4	2	315	283	.643
1967	AFL	14	3	10	1	280	389	.250
1968	AFL	14	4	10	0	229	406	.286
1969	AFL	14	4	10	0	266	316	.286
1970	AFL	14	2	12	0	149	361	.143
TOTAL:	11 years	154	65	80	9	3220	3568	
AVERAGE:		14	6	7	1	293	324	.451

Playoff Record

Season	GP	W	L	PF	PA	Result
1963	1	0	1	10	51	Lost AFL championship to San Diego.

COACHING HISTORY: 1960-1961 Lou Saban 7-12-0-.368; 1961-1968 Mike Holovak 52-46-9-.528; 1969-1970 Clive Rush 5-16-0-.238; 1970 John Mazur 1-6-0-.143

BOSTON PILGRIMS

(were Boston Doves)
(became Boston Braves)

Home City: Boston, Massachusetts
Home Field: South End Grounds III
Origin of Name: The name was chosen to honor the Pilgrims who landed at Plymouth Rock.

Regular Season Record

Season	League	GP	W	L	Pct	GB	R	OR
1909	NL	153	45	108	.294	65.5	427	681
1910	NL	153	53	100	.346	50.5	495	700
1911	NL	151	44	107	.291	54	699	1020
TOTAL:	3years	457	142	315		170	1621	2401
AVERAGE:		152	47	105	.311	56.5	540	800

COACHING HISTORY: 1909 Frank Bowerman 23-55-.295; 1909 Harry Smith 22-53-.293; 1910 Fred Lake 53-100-.346; 1911 Fred Tenney 44-107-.291

BOSTON PURITANS
(were Boston Puritans)
(became Boston Red Sox)

Home City: Boston, Massachusetts
Home Field: Huntington Avenue Grounds Capacity: 9,000 [1901]
Origin of Name: Puritans was selected to honor the Colonial heritage of the area.

Regular Season Record

Season	League	GP	W	L	Pct	GB	R	OR
1905	AL	152	78	74	.513	16	583	557
1906	AL	154	49	105	.318	45.5	462	711
TOTAL:	2years	306	127	179		61.5	1045	1268
AVERAGE:		153	64	89	.415	31	523	634

COACHING HISTORY: 1905-1906 Jimmy Collins 122-166-.424; 1906 Charles Stahl 5-13-.278

BOSTON RED CAPS
(became Boston Beaneaters)

Home City: Boston, Massachusetts
Home Field: South End Grounds I
Origin of Name: The name was adopted because the team wore red caps.

Regular Season Record

Season	League	GP	W	L	Pct	GB	R	OR
1876	NL	70	39	31	.557	15	471	450
1877	NL	60	42	18	.700	-	419	263
1878	NL	60	41	19	.683	-	298	241
1879	NL	84	54	30	.643	5	562	348
1880	NL	84	40	44	.476	27	416	456
1881	NL	83	38	45	.458	17.5	349	410
1882	NL	84	45	39	.536	10	472	414
TOTAL:	7 years	525	299	226		74.5	2987	2582
AVERAGE:		75	43	32	.570	11	427	369

COACHING HISTORY: 1876-1881 Harry Wright 254-187-.576; 1882 John Morrill 45-39-.536

BOSTON REDS

Home City: Boston, Massachusetts
Home Field: Congress Street Park
Origin of Name:

Regular Season Record

Season	League	GP	W	L	Pct	GB	R	OR
1890	PL	129	81	48	.628	-	992	767
1891	AA	135	93	42	.689	-	1028	675
TOTAL:	2 years	264	174	90		-	2020	1440
AVERAGE:		132	87	45	.659	-	1010	720

COACHING HISTORY: 1890 Michael Kelly 81-48-.628; 1891 Arthur Irwin 93-42-.689

BOSTON REDSKINS
(were Boston Braves)
(became Washington Redskins)

Home City: Boston, Massachusetts
Home Stadium: Fenway Park Capacity: 27,000
Origin of Name: According to legend during the first season, the team coached by Native American, Lone Star Dietz, signed several Native players and for an early season game the entire team showed up wearing war paint, feathers and headdresses, and thus the name was born.

Regular Season Record

Season	League	GP	W	L	T	PF	PA	Pct
1933	NFL	12	5	5	2	103	97	.500
1934	NFL	12	6	6	0	107	94	.500
1935	NFL	11	2	8	1	65	123	.227
1936	NFL	12	7	5	0	149	110	.583
TOTAL:	4 years	47	20	24	3	424	424	
AVERAGE:		12	5	6	1	106	106	.458

Playoff Record

Season	GP	W	L	T	PF	PA	Result
1936	1	0	1	0	6	21	Lost championship game to Green Bay.

COACHING HISTORY: 1933-1934 Lone Star Dietz 11-11-2-.500; 1935 Eddie Casey 2-8-1-.227; 1936 Ray Flaherty 7-5-0-.583

BOSTON RED SOX
(were Boston Puritans)

Home City: Boston, Massachusetts
Home Field: Huntington Avenue Grounds (1907-1911) Capacity: 9,000 [1901]
Fenway Park (1912 to present) Capacity: 33,871 [1995]
Origin of Name: The name was changed to Red Sox from Puritans after the new owner of the team, John Taylor, decided the team needed a flashier name. The team at the time wore red stockings.

Regular Season Record

Season	League	GP	W	L	Pct	GB	R	OR
1907	AL	151	49	102	.325	43.5	505	690
1908	AL	154	75	79	.487	15.5	563	515
1909	AL	151	88	63	.583	9.5	590	561
1910	AL	153	81	72	.529	22.5	637	564
1911	AL	153	78	75	.510	24	680	647
1912	AL	152	105	47	.691	-	800	544
1913	AL	150	79	71	.527	15.5	630	607
1914	AL	153	91	62	.595	8.5	588	511
1915	AL	151	101	50	.669	-	668	499
1916	AL	154	91	63	.591	-	548	480
1917	AL	152	90	62	.592	9	556	453
1918	AL	126	75	51	.595	-	473	381
1919	AL	137	66	71	.482	20.5	565	552
1920	AL	153	72	81	.471	25.5	651	699
1921	AL	154	75	79	.487	23.5	668	696
1922	AL	154	61	93	.396	33	598	769
1923	AL	152	61	91	.401	37	584	809
1924	AL	154	67	87	.435	25	725	801
1925	AL	152	47	105	.309	49.5	639	921
1926	AL	153	46	107	.301	44.5	562	835
1927	AL	154	51	103	.331	59	597	856
1928	AL	153	57	96	.373	43.5	589	770
1929	AL	154	58	96	.377	48	605	803
1930	AL	154	52	102	.338	50	612	814
1931	AL	152	62	90	.408	45	625	800
1932	AL	154	43	111	.279	64	566	915
1933	AL	149	63	86	.423	34.5	700	758
1934	AL	152	76	76	.500	24	820	775
1935	AL	153	78	75	.510	16	718	732
1936	AL	154	74	80	.481	28.5	775	764
1937	AL	152	80	72	.526	21	821	775
1938	AL	149	88	61	.591	9.5	902	751
1939	AL	151	89	62	.589	17	890	795
1940	AL	154	82	72	.532	8	872	825
1941	AL	154	84	70	.545	17	865	750
1942	AL	152	93	59	.612	9	761	594
1943	AL	152	68	84	.447	29	563	607
1944	AL	154	77	77	.500	12	739	676
1945	AL	154	71	83	.461	17.5	599	674
1946	AL	154	104	50	.675	-	792	594
1947	AL	154	83	71	.539	14	720	669
1948	AL	155	96	59	.619	1	907	720
1949	AL	154	96	58	.623	1	896	667
1950	AL	154	94	60	.610	4	1027	804
1951	AL	154	87	67	.565	11	804	725
1952	AL	154	76	78	.494	19	668	658
1953	AL	153	84	69	.549	16	656	632
1954	AL	154	69	85	.448	42	700	728
1955	AL	154	84	70	.545	12	755	652
1956	AL	154	84	70	.545	13	780	751
1957	AL	154	82	72	.532	16	721	668

1958	AL	154	79	75	.513	13	697	691
1959	AL	154	75	79	.487	19	726	696
1960	AL	154	65	89	.422	32	658	775
1961	AL	162	76	86	.469	33	729	792
1962	AL	160	76	84	.475	19	707	756
1963	AL	161	76	85	.472	28	666	704
1964	AL	162	72	90	.444	27	688	793
1965	AL	162	62	100	.383	40	669	791
1966	AL	162	72	90	.444	26	655	731
1967	AL	162	92	70	.568	-	722	614
1968	AL	162	86	76	.531	17	614	611
1969	AL	162	87	75	.537	22	743	736
1970	AL	162	87	75	.537	21	786	722
1971	AL	162	85	77	.525	18	691	667
1972	AL	155	85	70	.548	.5	640	620
1973	AL	162	89	73	.549	8	738	647
1974	AL	162	84	78	.519	7	696	661
1975	AL	160	95	65	.594	-	796	709
1976	AL	162	83	79	.512	15.5	716	660
1977	AL	161	97	64	.602	22	859	712
1978	AL	163	99	64	.607	1	796	657
1979	AL	160	91	69	.569	11.5	841	711
1980	AL	160	83	77	.519	19	757	767
1981	AL	108	59	49	.546	NA	519	481
1982	AL	162	89	73	.549	6	753	713
1983	AL	162	78	84	.481	20	724	775
1984	AL	162	86	76	.531	18	810	764
1985	AL	162	81	81	.500	18.5	800	720
1986	AL	161	95	66	.590	-	794	696
1987	AL	162	78	84	.481	20	842	825
1988	AL	162	89	73	.549	-	813	689
1989	AL	162	83	79	.512	6	774	735
1990	AL	162	88	74	.543	-	699	664
1991	AL	162	84	78	.519	7	731	712
1992	AL	162	73	89	.451	23	599	669
1993	AL	162	80	82	.494	15	686	698
1994	AL	115	54	61	.470	17	552	621
1995	AL	144	86	58	.597	-	791	698
TOTAL:	89 years	13754	6982	6772		1658	62752	61919
AVERAGE:		154	78	76	.508	18.5	705	696

Playoff Record

Season	GP	W	L	R	OR	Result
1912	7	4	3	25	31	**Won World Series.**
1915	5	4	1	12	10	**Won World Series.**
1916	5	4	1	21	13	**Won World Series.**
1918	6	4	2	9	10	**Won World Series.**
1946	7	3	4	20	28	Lost World Series to St. Louis.
1967	7	3	4	21	25	Lost World Series to St. Louis.
1975	10	6	4	48	35	Lost World Series to Cincinnati.
1986	14	7	7	68	62	Lost World Series to New York.
1988	4	0	4	11	20	Lost ALCS to Oakland.
1990	4	0	4	4	20	Lost ALCS to Oakland.

1995	3	0	3	6	17	Lost Division playoffs to Cleveland.
TOTAL:	72	35	37	245	271	
AVERAGE:	7	3	4	22	25	

COACHING HISTORY: 1907 Cy Young 3-4-.429; 1907 George Huff 3-5-.375; 1907 Bob Unglaub 8-20-.286; 1907-1908 Deacon McGuire 98-123-.443; 1908-1909 Fred Lake 110-80-.579; 1910-1911 Patsy Donovan 159-147-.520; 1912-1913 Jake Stahl 144-88-.621; 1913-1916 Bill Carrigan 323-205-.612; 1917 Jack Barry 90-62-.592; 1918-1920 Ed Barrow 213-203-.512; 1921-1922 Hugh Duffy 136-172-.442; 1923 Frank Chance 61-91-.401; 1924-1926 Lee Fohl 160-299-.349; 1927-1929 Bill Carrigan 166-295-.360; 1930 Heinie Wagner 52-102-.338; 1931-1932 Shano Collins 73-136-.349; 1932-1933 Marty McManus 95-151-.386; 1934 Bucky Harris 76-76-.500; 1935-1947 Joe Cronin 1071-916-.539; 1948-1950 Joe McCarthy 224-147-.604; 1950-1951 Steve O'Neill 149-97-.606; 1952-1954 Lou Boudreau 229-232-.497; 1955-1962 Pinky Higgins 543-541-.501; 1959 Rudy York 0-1-.000; 1959-1960 Bill Jurges 78-83-.484; 1963-1964 John Pesky 146-175-.455; 1964-1966 Bill Herman 128-182-.413; 1966 Pete Runnels 8-8 .500; 1967-1969 Dick Williams 260-217-.545; 1969 Ed Popowski 5-4-.556; 1970-1973 Ed Kasko 346-295-.540 1974-1976 Darrell Johnson 220-188-.539; 1976-1980 Don Zimmer 411-304-.575; 1980 John Pesky 1-4-.200; 1981-1984 Ralph Houk 312-282-.525; 1985-1988 John McNamara 297-273-.521; 1988-1991 Joe Morgan 301-262 .535; 1992-1994 Butch Hobson 207-232-.472; 1995-present Kevin Kennedy

BOSTON ROVERS

Home City: Boston, Massachusetts
Home Stadium: Manning Bowl
Origin of Name: The team was represented by the Shamrock Rovers of Dublin.

Regular Season Record

Season	League	GP	W	L	T	GF	GA	Pts	Pct
1967	USA	12	2	7	3	12	26	7	.292

COACHING HISTORY: Liam Tuohy 2-7-3-.292

BOSTON SOMERSETS
(became Boston Puritans)

Home City: Boston, Massachusetts
Home Field: Huntington Avenue Grounds — Capacity: 9,000 [1901]
Origin of Name: The team was named after owner Charles Somers

Regular Season Record

Season	League	GP	W	L	Pct	GB	R	OR
1901	AL	136	79	57	.581	4	759	608
1902	AL	137	77	60	.562	6.5	664	600
1903	AL	138	91	47	.659	-	707	505
1904	AL	154	95	59	.617	-	608	466
TOTAL:	4 years	565	342	223		10.5	2738	2179
AVERAGE:		141	85	56	.603	2.5	685	545

Playoff Record

Season	GP	W	L	R	OR	Result
1903	8	5	3	39	24	**Won World Series.**

COACHING HISTORY: 1901-1904 Jimmy Collins 342-223-.605

BOSTON UNIONS

Home City: Boston, Massachusetts
Home Field: Union Park *
Origin of Name: The team played in the Union Association and adopted the name of the league as their own.

			Regular Season Record					
Season	**League**	**GP**	**W**	**L**	**Pct**	**GB**	**R**	**OR**
1884	UA	109	58	51	.532	34	636	558

COACHING HISTORY: Tim Murnane 8-17-.320; Tom Furniss 4-6-.400; Jake Morse 46-28-.622

BOSTON WHIRLWINDS

Home City: Boston, Massachusetts
Home Court:
Origin of Name: The team was called Whirlwinds after a successful barnstorming team of the era.

		Regular Season Record				
Season	**League**	**GP**	**W**	**L**	**Pct**	**GB**
1925-1926	ABL	16	6	10	.375	6

COACHING RECORD:

BOSTON YANKS
(became New York Bulldogs)

Home City: Boston, Massachusetts
Home Stadium: Fenway Park (1944-1945) Capacity: 35,000 [1944]
Braves Field (1946-1948)
Origin of Name: Owner Ted Collins wanted a team in Yankee Stadium but kept the name when the franchise was awarded to Boston.

			Regular Season Record					
Season	**League**	**GP**	**W**	**L**	**T**	**PF**	**PA**	**Pct**
1944	NFL	10	2	8	0	82	233	.200
1945	NFL	10	3	6	1	123	211	.350
1946	NFL	11	2	8	1	189	273	.227
1947	NFL	12	4	7	1	168	256	.375
1948	NFL	12	3	9	0	174	372	.250
TOTAL:	5 years	55	14	38	3	736	1345	
AVERAGE:		11	3	7	1	147	269	.282

COACHING HISTORY: 1944-1946 Herb Kopf 7-22-2-.258; 1947-1948 Clipper Smith 7-16-1-.313

*Also known as Dartmouth Grounds

BRITISH COLUMBIA LIONS

Home City: Vancouver, British Columbia
Home Stadium: Empire Stadium (1954-1982) Capacity: 30,229
B.C. Place Stadium (1983-present) Capacity: 59,478 [1995]
Origin of Name: The Lions are the twin mountain peaks which symbolically guard Vancouver and its harbor. They are the city's most prominent natural feature.

Regular Season Record

Season	League	GP	W	L	T	PF	PA	Pts	Pct
1954	CRU	16	1	15	0	100	345	2	.063
1955	CRU	16	5	11	0	211	330	10	.313
1956	CFC	16	6	10	0	251	361	12	.375
1957	CFC	16	4	11	1	284	369	9	.281
1958	CFL	16	3	13	0	202	399	6	.188
1959	CFL	16	9	7	0	306	301	18	.563
1960	CFL	16	5	9	2	296	356	12	.375
1961	CFL	16	1	13	2	215	393	4	.125
1952	CFL	16	7	9	0	346	342	14	.438
1963	CFL	16	12	4	0	387	232	24	.750
1964	CFL	16	11	2	3	328	168	25	.781
1965	CFL	16	6	9	1	286	273	13	.406
1966	CFL	16	5	11	0	254	269	10	.313
1967	CFL	16	3	12	1	239	319	7	.219
1968	CFL	16	4	11	1	217	318	9	.281
1969	CFL	16	5	11	0	235	335	10	.313
1970	CFL	16	6	10	0	295	384	12	.375
1971	CFL	16	6	9	1	282	363	13	.406
1972	CFL	16	5	11	0	254	380	10	.313
1973	CFL	16	5	9	2	261	328	12	.375
1974	CFL	16	8	8	0	306	299	16	.500
1975	CFL	16	6	10	0	276	331	12	.375
1976	CFL	16	5	9	2	308	336	12	.375
1977	CFL	16	10	6	0	369	326	20	.625
1978	CFL	16	7	7	2	359	308	16	.500
1979	CFL	16	9	6	1	328	333	19	.594
1980	CFL	16	8	7	1	381	351	17	.531
1981	CFL	16	10	6	0	438	377	20	.625
1982	CFL	16	9	7	0	449	390	18	.563
1983	CFL	16	11	5	0	477	326	22	.688
1984	CFL	16	12	3	1	445	281	25	.781
1985	CFL	16	13	3	0	481	297	26	.813
1986	CFL	18	12	6	0	441	410	24	.667
1987	CFL	18	12	6	0	502	370	24	.667
1988	CFL	18	10	8	0	489	417	20	.556
1989	CFL	18	7	11	0	521	557	14	.389
1990	CFL	18	6	11	1	520	620	11	.306
1991	CFL	18	11	7	0	661	587	22	.611
1992	CFL	18	3	15	0	472	667	6	.167
1993	CFL	18	10	8	0	574	583	20	.556
1994	CFL	18	10	7	1	603	457	21	.583
1995	CFL	18	10	8	0	535	470	20	.556

TOTAL:	42 years	692	308	361	23	15184	15658	639	
AVERAGE:		16	7	9	0	362	373	14	.462

Playoff Record

Season	GP	W	L	PF	PA	Result
1959	2	0	2	15	61	Lost semifinals to Edmonton.
1963	4	2	2	73	42	Lost Grey Cup to Hamilton.
1964	4	3	1	101	62	**Won Grey Cup**.
1969	1	0	1	21	35	Lost semifinals to Calgary.
1973	1	0	1	13	33	Lost semifinals to Saskatchewan.
1974	1	0	1	14	24	Lost semifinals to Saskatchewan.
1977	2	1	1	34	70	Lost Division finals to Edmonton.
1979	1	0	1	2	37	Lost semifinals to Calgary.
1981	2	1	1	31	33	Lost Division finals to Edmonton.
1983	2	1	1	56	39	Lost Grey Cup game to Toronto.
1984	1	0	1	14	31	Lost Division finals to Winnipeg.
1985	2	2	0	79	46	**Won Grey Cup**.
1986	2	1	1	26	55	Lost Division finals to Edmonton.
1987	1	0	1	7	31	Lost Division finals to Edmonton.
1988	3	2	1	100	59	Lost Grey Cup game to Winnipeg.
1991	1	0	1	41	43	Lost semifinals to Calgary.
1993	1	0	1	9	17	Lost semifinals to Calgary.
1994	3	3	0	87	82	**Won Grey Cup**.
1995	1	0	1	15	26	Lost semifinals to Edmonton.
TOTAL:	35	16	19	738	826	
AVERAGE:	2	1	1	39	43	

COACHING HISTORY: 1954-1955 Annis Stukus 6-26-0-.188; 1956-1958 Clem Crowe 10-27-1-.276; 1958 Dan Edwards 3-7-0-.300; 1959-1961 Wayne Robinson 14-23-3-.388; 1961-1967 Dave Skrien 42-45-5-.484; 1967-1969 Jim Champion 8-28-2-.237; 1969-1970 Jackie Parker 10-12-0-.455; 1971-1975 Eagle Keys 25-42-3-.379; 1975-1976 Cal Murphy 10-14-2-.423; 1977-1982 Vic Rapp 53-39-4-.573; 1983-1987 Don Matthews 56-23-1-.706; 1987-1989 Larry Donovan 14-12-0-.538; 1989 Joe Galat 7-7-0-.500; 1990 Lary Kuharich 2-7-1-.250; 1990 Jim Young 0-1-0-.000; 1990-1992 Bob O'Billovich 18-25-0-.419; 1993-present Dave Ritchie

BROOKLYN AMERICANS
(were New York Americans)

Home City: New York, New York
Home Arena: Madison Square Gardens III Capacity: 15,925
Origin of Name: The team kept the same nickname when it became the Brooklyn Americans in an attempt to draw more fans from the Brooklyn area.

Regular Season Record

Season	League	GP	W	L	T	GF	GA	Pts	Pct
1941-1942	NHL	48	16	29	3	133	175	35	.365

COACHING HISTORY: Mervyn Dutton 16-29-3-.365

BROOKLYN ARCADIANS

Home City: Brooklyn, New York
Home Court: Arcadia Hall — Capacity: 3,000
Origin of Name: The team was named after the place where they played their home games.

Regular Season Record

Season	League	GP	W	L	Pct
1925-1926	ABL	30	19	11	.633
1926-1927	ABL	42	32	10	.762
TOTAL:	2 years	72	51	21	
AVERAGE:		36	26	10	.708

Playoff Record

Season	GP	W	L	Result
1925-1926	3	0	3	Lost final series to Cleveland.
1926-1927	3	3	0	**Won ABL championship**.
TOTAL:	6	3	3	
AVERAGE:	3	2	1	

COACHING HISTORY: 1925-1926 Gary Schmeelk 19-11-.633; 1926-1927 Not Available

BROOKLYN BRIDEGROOMS
(merged with Baltimore in 1890)

Home City: Brooklyn, New York
Home Field: Washington Park I — Capacity: 2,000
Origin of Name:

Regular Season Record

Season	League	GP	W	L	Pct	GB	R	OR
1884	AA	104	40	64	.385	33.5	476	644
1885	AA	112	53	59	.473	26	624	650
1886	AA	137	76	61	.555	16	832	832
1887	AA	134	60	74	.448	34.5	904	918
1888	AA	140	88	52	.629	6.5	758	584
1889	AA	137	93	44	.679	-	995	706
TOTAL:	6 years	764	410	354		116.5	4589	4334
AVERAGE:		127	68	59	.537	19.5	765	722

COACHING HISTORY: 1884 George Taylor 40-64-.385; 1885 Joe Doyle 13-20-.394; 1885 Charlie Hackett 15-25-.375; 1885-1887 Charlie Byrne 161-149-.519; 1888-1889 Bill McGunnigle 181-96-.653

BROOKLYN BRIDEGROOMS
(became Brooklyn Superbas)

Home City: Brooklyn, New York
Home Field: Washington Park I (1890) — Capacity: 2,000
Eastern Park (1891-1897)
Washington Park II (1898) — Capacity: 3,000
Origin of Name: The team was named Bridegrooms after three players got married in the summer of 1889.

Regular Season Record

Season	League	GP	W	L	Pct	GB	R	OR
1890	NL	129	86	43	.667	-	884	620
1891	NL	137	61	76	.445	25.5	765	820
1892	NL	154	95	59	.617	9	935	733
1893	NL	128	65	63	.508	20.5	775	845
1894	NL	131	70	61	.534	20.5	1021	1007
1895	NL	131	71	60	.542	16.5	867	834
1896	NL	131	58	73	.443	33	692	764
1897	NL	132	61	71	.462	32	802	845
1898	NL	145	54	91	.372	46	638	811
TOTAL:	9 years	1218	621	597		203	7379	7279
AVERAGE:		135	69	66	.510	22.5	820	809

COACHING HISTORY: 1890 Bill McGunnigle 86-43-.667; 1891-1892 Monte Ward 156-135-.536; 1893-1896 Dave Foutz 264-257-.507; 1897-1898 Bill Barnie 76-91-.455; 1898 Mike Griffin 1-3-.250; 1898 Charlie Ebbets 38-68-.358

BROOKLYN DODGERS

(were Brooklyn Superbas)
(became Los Angeles Dodgers)

Home City: Brooklyn, New York
Home Field: Washington Park II (1911-1912) Capacity: 3,000
Ebbets Field (1913-1957) Capacity: 31,497
Roosevelt Stadium (1957) Capacity: 24,167
Origin of Name: The name had its origins in the name given turn-of-the-century Brooklinites by the residents of New York who called them "Trolley Dodgers."

Regular Season Record

Season	League	GP	W	L	Pct	GB	R	OR
1911	NL	150	64	86	.427	33.5	539	659
1912	NL	153	58	95	.379	46	651	748
1913	NL	149	65	84	.436	34.5	595	613
1914	NL	154	75	79	.487	19.5	622	612
1915	NL	152	80	72	.526	10	536	560
1916	NL	154	94	60	.610	-	585	467
1917	NL	151	70	81	.464	26.5	511	566
1918	NL	126	57	69	.452	25.5	360	459
1919	NL	140	69	71	.493	27	525	513
1920	NL	154	93	61	.604	-	660	528
1921	NL	152	77	75	.507	16.5	667	681
1922	NL	154	76	78	.494	17	743	754
1923	NL	154	76	78	.494	19.5	753	741
1924	NL	154	92	62	.597	1.5	717	675
1925	NL	153	68	85	.444	27	786	866
1926	NL	153	71	82	.464	17.5	623	705
1927	NL	153	65	88	.425	28.5	541	619
1928	NL	153	77	76	.503	17.5	665	640
1929	NL	153	70	83	.458	28.5	755	888
1930	NL	154	86	68	.558	6	871	738
1931	NL	152	79	73	.520	21	681	673

1932	NL	154	81	73	.526	9	752	747
1933	NL	153	65	88	.425	26.5	617	695
1934	NL	152	71	81	.467	23.5	748	795
1935	NL	153	70	83	.458	29.5	711	767
1936	NL	154	67	87	.435	25	662	752
1937	NL	153	62	91	.405	33.5	616	772
1938	NL	149	69	80	.463	18.5	704	710
1939	NL	153	84	69	.549	12.5	708	645
1940	NL	153	88	65	.575	12	697	621
1941	NL	154	100	54	.649	-	800	581
1942	NL	154	104	50	.675	2	742	510
1943	NL	153	81	72	.529	23.5	716	674
1944	NL	154	63	91	.409	42	690	832
1945	NL	154	87	67	.565	11	795	724
1946	NL	156	96	60	.615	2	701	570
1947	NL	154	94	60	.610	-	77	466
1948	NL	154	84	70	.545	7.5	744	667
1949	NL	154	97	57	.630	-	879	651
1950	NL	154	89	65	.578	2	847	724
1951	NL	157	97	60	.618	1	855	672
1952	NL	153	96	57	.627	-	775	603
1953	NL	154	105	49	.682	-	955	689
1954	NL	154	92	62	.597	5	778	740
1955	NL	153	98	55	.641	-	857	650
1956	NL	154	93	61	.604	-	720	601
1957	NL	154	84	70	.545	11	690	591
TOTAL:	47 years	7162	3779	3383		720	32222	31154
AVERAGE:		152	80	72	.528	15.5	686	663

Playoff Record

Season	**GP**	**W**	**L**	**R**	**OR**	**Result**
1916	5	1	4	13	21	Lost World Series to Boston.
1920	7	2	5	8	21	Lost World Series to Cleveland.
1941	5	1	4	11	17	Lost World Series to New York.
1947	7	3	4	29	38	Lost World Series to New York.
1949	5	1	4	14	21	Lost World Series to New York.
1952	7	3	4	20	26	Lost World Series to New York.
1953	6	2	4	27	33	Lost World Series to New York.
1955	7	4	3	31	26	**Won World Series.**
1956	7	3	4	25	33	Lost World Series to New York.
TOTAL:	56	20	36	178	236	
AVERAGE:	6	2	4	20	26	

COACHING HISTORY: 1911-1913 Bill Dahlen 187-265-.414; 1914-1931 Wilbert Robinson 1375-1341-.506; 1932-1933 Max Carey 146-161-.476; 1934-1936 Casey Stengel 208-251-.453; 1937-1938 Burleigh Grimes 131-171-.434; 1939-1948 Leo Durocher 787-598-.568; 1947 Clyde Sukeforth 1-0-1.000; 1947-1950 Burt Shotton 363-252-.590; 1951-1953 Chuck Dressen 298-166-.642; 1954-1957 Walter Alston 367-248-.597

BROOKLYN DODGERS
(became Brooklyn Tigers)

Home City: Brooklyn, New York
Home Stadium: Ebbets Field — Capacity: 31,497
Origin of Name: Named after the baseball team.

Regular Season Record

Season	League	GP	W	L	T	PF	PA	Pct
1930	NFL	12	7	4	1	154	59	.625
1931	NFL	14	2	12	0	64	199	.143
1932	NFL	12	3	9	0	63	131	.250
1933	NFL	10	5	4	1	93	54	.550
1934	NFL	11	4	7	0	61	153	.364
1935	NFL	12	5	6	1	90	141	.458
1936	NFL	12	3	8	1	92	161	.292
1937	NFL	11	3	7	1	82	174	.318
1938	NFL	11	4	4	3	131	161	.500
1939	NFL	11	4	6	1	108	219	.409
1940	NFL	11	8	3	0	186	120	.727
1941	NFL	11	7	4	0	158	127	.636
1942	NFL	11	3	8	0	100	168	.273
1943	NFL	10	2	8	0	65	234	.200
TOTAL:	14 years	159	60	90	9	1447	2101	
AVERAGE:		11	4	6	1	103	150	.406

COACHING HISTORY: 1930 Al Jolley 7-4-1-.625; 1931 John Depler 2-12-0-.143; 1932 Benny Friedman 3-9-0-.250; 1933-1934 Cap McEwen 9-11-1-.452; 1935-1936 Paul Schissler 8-14-2-.375; 1937-1939 Potsy Clark 11-17-5-.409; 1940-1941 Jock Sutherland 15-7-0-.682; 1942 Mike Getto 3-8-0-.273; 1943 Pete Cawthorn 2-8-0-.200

BROOKLYN DODGERS

Home City: Brooklyn, New York
Home Stadium: Ebbets Field — Capacity: 31,497
Origin of Name: Named after the baseball team.

Regular Season Record

Season	League	GP	W	L	T	PF	PA	Pct
1946	AAFC	14	3	10	1	226	339	.250
1947	AAFC	14	3	10	1	181	340	.250
1948	AAFC	14	2	12	0	253	387	.143
TOTAL:	3 years	42	8	32	2	660	1066	
AVERAGE:		14	3	10	1	220	355	.214

COACHING HISTORY: 1946 Mal Stevens 2-4-1-.357; 1946-1947 Cliff Battles 4-16-1-.214; 1948 Carl Voyles 2-12-0-.143

BROOKLYN LIONS

Home City: Brooklyn, New York
Home Stadium: Ebbets Field Capacity: 31,497
Origin of Name:

Regular Season Record

Season	League	GP	W	L	T	PF	PA	Pct
1926	NFL	11	3	8	0	60	150	.273

COACHING HISTORY: Robert Berryman 3-8-0-.273

BROOKLYN SUPERBAS
(were Brooklyn Bridegrooms)
(became Brooklyn Dodgers)

Home City: Brooklyn, New York
Home Field: Washington Park II Capacity: 3,000
Origin of Name: The team was named Superbas when the team was managed by Ned Hanlon because there was a popular vaudeville team at the time named Hanlon's Superbas.

Regular Season Record

Season	League	GP	W	L	Pct	GB	R	OR
1899	NL	148	101	47	.682	-	892	658
1900	NL	136	82	54	.603	-	816	722
1901	NL	136	79	57	.581	9.5	744	600
1902	NL	138	75	63	.543	27.5	564	519
1903	NL	136	70	66	.515	19	666	674
1904	NL	153	56	97	.366	50	497	614
1905	NL	152	48	104	.316	56.5	506	807
1906	NL	152	66	86	.434	50	495	620
1907	NL	148	65	83	.439	40	446	522
1908	NL	154	53	101	.344	46	375	515
1909	NL	153	55	98	.359	55.5	442	627
1910	NL	154	64	90	.416	40	497	622
TOTAL:	12 years	1760	814	946		394	6940	7500
AVERAGE:		147	68	79	.463	33	578	625

COACHING HISTORY: 1899-1905 Ned Hanlon 511-488-.512; 1906-1908 Patrick Donovan 184-270-.405; 1909 Harry Lumley 55-98-.359; 1910 Bill Dahlen 64-90-.416

BROOKLYN TIGERS
(were Brooklyn Dodgers)

Home City: Brooklyn, New York
Home Stadium: Ebbets Field Capacity: 31,497
Origin of Name:

Regular Season Record

Season	League	GP	W	L	T	PF	PA	Pct
1944	NFL	10	0	10	0	69	166	.000

COACHING HISTORY: Pete Cawthorn & Ed Kuhale & Frank Bridges 0-10-0-.000

BROOKLYN TIP-TOPS

Home City: Brooklyn, New York
Home Field: Washington Park II Capacity: 3,000
Origin of Name: The team was owned by the Ward brothers, owners of the Ward Baking Co. and makers of Tip Top bread.

Regular Season Record

Season	League	GP	W	L	Pct	GB	R	OR
1914	FL	154	77	77	.500	11.5	662	677
1915	FL	152	70	82	.461	16	647	673
TOTAL:	2 years	306	147	159		27.5	1309	1350
AVERAGE:		153	74	79	.480	14	655	675

COACHING HISTORY: 1914 Bill Bradley 77-77-.500; 1915 Lee Magee 53-64-.453; 1915 John Ganzel 17-18-.486

BROOKLYN VISITATIONS
(merged with Washington in 1928)

Home City: Brooklyn, New York
Home Court: Arcadia Hall Capacity: 3,000
Origin of Name: The team was named after the church in which they were organized.

Regular Season Record

Season	League	GP	W	L	Pct
1927-1928	ABL	31	19	12	.613
1928-1929	ABL	41	25	16	.610
1929-1930	ABL	54	30	24	.556
1930-1931	ABL	37	22	15	.595
TOTAL:	4 years	163	96	67	
AVERAGE:		41	24	17	.589

Playoff Record

Season	GP	W	L	Result
1930-1931	6	4	2	**Won ABL championship.**

COACHING HISTORY:

BROOKLYN WONDERS

Home City: Brooklyn, New York
Home Field: Eastern Park
Origin of Name: The team was owned by John Ward who owned the Wonder Bread Co.

Regular Season Record

Season	League	GP	W	L	Pct	GB	R	OR
1890	PL	132	76	56	.576	6.5	964	893

COACHING HISTORY: Monte Ward 76-56-.576

BUFFALO ALL AMERICANS
(became Buffalo Bisons)

Home City: Buffalo, New York
Home Stadium:
Origin of Name: The team had six players from Walter Camp's All-American selections. Camp was active in revising the rules by which football was played and in 1889 began making his All-American selections.

Regular Season Record

Season	League	GP	W	L	T	PF	PA	Pct
1922	NFL	10	5	4	1	87	41	.550
1923	NFL	11	4	4	3	81	43	.500
TOTAL:	2 years	21	9	8	4	168	84	
AVERAGE:		11	5	4	2	84	42	.524

COACHING HISTORY:1922-1923 Tom Hughitt 9-8-4-.524

BUFFALO BILLS
(were Buffalo Bisons)

Home City: Buffalo, New York
Home Stadium: Civic Stadium Capacity: 32,000
Origin of Name: The name was chosen in a Name the Team Contest because of its connection with Buffalo Bill Cody.

Regular Season Record

Season	League	GP	W	L	T	PF	PA	Pct
1947	AAFC	14	8	4	2	320	288	.643
1948	AAFC	14	7	7	0	360	358	.500
1949	AAFC	12	5	5	2	236	256	.500
TOTAL:	3 years	40	20	16	4	916	902	
AVERAGE:		13	7	5	1	305	301	.577

Playoff Record

Season	GP	W	L	PF	PA	Result
1948	2	1	1	35	66	Lost AAFC championship to Cleveland.

COACHING HISTORY: 1947-1948 Red Dawson 15-11-2-.571; 1949 Red Dawson & Clem Crowe 5-5-2-.500

BUFFALO BILLS

Home City: Buffalo, New York (1960-1972)
Orchard Park, New York (1973-
Home Stadium: War Memorial Stadium (1960-1972) Capacity: 45,748
Rich Stadium (1973-present) Capacity: 80,024 [1995]
Origin of Name: The team was named by then owner Ralph Wilson, after previous Buffalo teams.

Regular Season Record

Season	League	GP	W	L	T	PF	PA	Pct
1960	AFL	14	5	8	1	296	303	.393
1961	AFL	14	6	8	0	294	342	.429
1962	AFL	14	7	6	1	309	272	.536
1963	AFL	14	7	6	1	304	291	.536
1964	AFL	14	12	2	0	400	242	.857
1965	AFL	14	10	3	1	313	226	.750
1966	AFL	14	9	4	1	358	225	.679
1967	AFL	14	4	10	0	237	285	.286
1968	AFL	14	1	12	1	199	367	.107
1969	AFL	14	4	10	0	230	359	.286
1970	NFL	14	3	10	1	204	337	.250
1971	NFL	14	1	13	0	184	394	.071
1972	NFL	14	4	9	1	257	377	.321
1973	NFL	14	9	5	0	259	230	.643
1974	NFL	14	9	5	0	264	244	.643
1975	NFL	14	8	6	0	420	355	.571
1976	NFL	14	2	12	0	245	363	.143
1977	NFL	14	3	11	0	160	313	.214
1978	NFL	16	5	11	0	302	354	.313
1979	NFL	16	7	9	0	268	279	.438
1980	NFL	16	11	5	0	320	260	.688
1981	NFL	16	10	6	0	311	276	.625
1982	NFL	9	4	5	0	150	154	.444
1983	NFL	16	8	8	0	283	351	.500
1984	NFL	16	2	14	0	250	454	.125
1985	NFL	16	2	14	0	200	381	.125
1986	NFL	16	4	12	0	287	348	.250
1987	NFL	15	7	8	0	270	305	.467
1988	NFL	16	12	4	0	329	237	.750
1989	NFL	16	9	7	0	409	317	.563
1990	NFL	16	13	3	0	428	263	.813
1991	NFL	16	13	3	0	458	318	.813
1992	NFL	16	11	5	0	381	283	.688
1993	NFL	16	12	4	0	329	242	.750
1994	NFL	16	7	9	0	340	356	.438
1995	NFL	16	10	6	0	350	335	.625
TOTAL:	36 years	532	251	273	8	10598	11038	
AVERAGE:		15	7	8	0	294	307	.479

Playoff Record

Season	GP	W	L	PF	PA	Result
1964	1	1	0	20	7	**Won AFL championship**.
1965	1	1	0	23	0	**Won AFL championship**.
1966	1	0	1	7	31	Lost AFL championship to Kansas City.
1974	1	0	1	14	32	Lost Divisional semifinals to Pittsburgh.
1980	1	0	1	14	20	Lost Divisional semifinals to San Diego.
1981	2	1	1	52	55	Lost Divisional semifinals to Cincinnati.
1988	2	1	1	27	31	Lost AFC championship to Cincinnati.
1989	1	0	1	30	34	Lost Divisional semifinals to Cleveland.
1990	3	2	1	114	57	Lost Super Bowl to N.Y. Giants
1991	3	2	1	71	58	Lost Super Bowl to Washington.

1992	4	3	1	111	103	Lost Super Bowl to Dallas.
1993	3	2	1	72	66	Lost Super Bowl to Dallas.
1995	2	1	1	58	62	Lost Divisional semifinal to Pittsburgh.
TOTAL:	25	14	11	613	556	
AVERAGE:	2	1	1	47	43	

COACHING HISTORY: 1960-1961 Buster Ramsey 11-16-1-.411; 1962-1965 Lou Saban 36-17-3-.670; 1966-1968 Joe Collier 13-16-1-.450; 1968 Harvey Johnson 1-10-1-.125; 1969-1970 John Rauch 7-20-1-.268; 1971 Harvey Johnson 1-13-0-.071; 1972-1976 Lou Saban 32-28-1-.524; 1976-1977 Jim Ringo 3-20-0-.130; 1978-1982 Chuck Knox 37-36-0-.507; 1983-1985 Kay Stephenson 10-26-0-.278; 1985-1986 Hank Bullough 3-16-0-.158; 1986-present Marv Levy

BUFFALO BISONS

Home City: Buffalo, New York
Home Field: Riverside Park (1879-1883)
Olympic Park (1884-1885) Capacity: 6,000
Origin of Name: The team used the nickname associated with other teams which had played in the area

Regular Season Record

Season	League	GP	W	L	Pct	GB	R	OR
1879	NL	78	46	32	.590	10	394	365
1880	NL	82	24	58	.293	42	331	502
1881	NL	83	45	38	.542	10.5	440	447
1882	NL	84	45	39	.536	10	500	461
1883	NL	97	52	45	.536	10.5	614	576
1884	NL	111	64	47	.577	19.5	700	626
1885	NL	112	38	74	.339	49	495	761
TOTAL:	7 years	647	314	333		151.5	3474	3738
AVERAGE:		92	45	47	.485	21.5	496	534

COACHING HISTORY: 1879 John Clapp 46-32-.590; 1880 Bill McGunnigle 4-13-.235; 1880 Sam Crane 20-45-.308; 1881-1884 Jim O'Rourke 206-169-.549; 1885 Jack Chapman 12-19-.387; 1885 George Hughson 18-33-.353; 1885 Pud Galvin 8-22-.267

BUFFALO BISONS

Home City: Buffalo, New York
Home Field: Olympic Park II
Origin of Name: The team adopted the name which had been used by previous Buffalo based teams.

Regular Season Record

Season	League	GP	W	L	Pct	GB	R	OR
1890	PL	132	36	96	.273	46.5	793	1199

COACHING HISTORY: Jack Rowe 36-96-.273

BUFFALO BISONS
(were Buffalo All-Americans)

Home City: Buffalo, New York
Home Stadium:
Origin of Name: Named after previous teams in the area.

			Regular Season Record					
Season	**League**	**GP**	**W**	**L**	**T**	**PF**	**PA**	**Pct**
1924	NFL	11	6	5	0	120	140	.545
1925	NFL	9	1	6	2	33	113	.222
1926	NFL	10	4	4	2	53	62	.500
1927	NFL	5	0	5	0	8	123	.000
TOTAL:	4 years	35	11	20	4	214	438	
AVERAGE:		9	3	5	1	54	110	.389

COACHING HISTORY: 1924 Tom Hughitt 6-5-0-.545; 1925 Walt Koppisch 1-6-2-.222; 1926 Jim Kendrick 4-4-2-.500; 1927 George Patterson 0-5-0-.000

BUFFALO BISONS

Home City: Buffalo, New York
Home Stadium:
Origin of Name: Named after previous teams in the area.

			Regular Season Record					
Season	**League**	**GP**	**W**	**L**	**T**	**PF**	**PA**	**Pct**
1929	NFL	9	1	7	1	48	142	.167

COACHING HISTORY: Al Jolley 1-7-1-.167

BUFFALO BISONS

Home City: Buffalo, New York
Home Court:
Origin of Name: Named after previous teams in the area.

			Regular Season Record					
Season	**League**	**GP**	**W**	**L**	**PPGF**	**PPGA**	**Pct**	**GB**
1938	NBL	9	3	6	29.1	30.6	.333	6.5

COACHING HISTORY: Allie Heerdt 3-6-.333

BUFFALO BISONS
(merged with Tri-Cities Blackhawks in 1947)

Home City: Buffalo, New York
Home Court: Memorial Auditorium
Origin of Name: Named after previous teams in the Buffalo area.

Regular Season Record

Season	League	GP	W	L	PPGF	PPGA	Pct	GB
1946-1947	NBL	12	4	8	49.1	51.8	.333	16

COACHING HISTORY: Nat Hickey 4-8-.333

BUFFALO BISONS
(became Buffalo Bills)

Home City: Buffalo, New York
Home Stadium: Civic Stadium Capacity: 32,000
Origin of Name: Named after previous professional football teams in Buffalo.

Regular Season Record

Season	League	GP	W	L	T	PF	PA	Pct
1946	AAFC	14	3	10	1	249	370	.250

COACHING HISTORY: Red Dawson 3-10-1-.250

BUFFALO BLUES
(also known as Buf-Feds)

Home City: Buffalo, New York
Home Field: Federal League Park Capacity: 20,000
Origin of Name: The team wearing blue uniforms played in the Federal League and were sometimes known as the Buf-Feds.

Regular Season Record

Season	League	GP	W	L	Pct	GB	R	OR
1914	FL	151	80	71	.530	7	620	602
1915	FL	152	74	78	.487	12	574	634
TOTAL:	2 years	303	154	149		19	1194	1236
AVERAGE:		152	77	75	.508	9.5	597	618

COACHING HISTORY: 1914-1915 Larry Schlafly 94-100-.485; 1915 Walter Blair 1-1-.500; 1915 Harry Lord 59-48-.551

BUFFALO BRAVES

Home City: Buffalo, New York
Home Court: Memorial Auditorium Capacity: 17,300
Origin of Name: The name was chosen in a Name the Team Contest. More than 14,000 submissions were received.

Regular Season Record

Season	League	GP	W	L	PPGF	PPGA	Pct	GB
1970-1971	NBA	82	22	60	105.5	112.1	.268	30
1971-1972	NBA	82	22	60	102.0	111.3	.268	34
1972-1973	NBA	82	21	61	103.3	112.5	.256	47
1973-1974	NBA	82	42	40	111.6	111.8	.512	14

1974-1975	NBA	82	49	33	107.8	105.6	.598	11
1975-1976	NBA	82	46	36	107.3	106.4	.561	8
1976-1977	NBA	82	30	52	105.0	109.5	.366	20
1977-1978	NBA	82	27	55	105.3	109.0	.329	28
TOTAL:	8 years	656	259	397				192
AVERAGE:		82	32	50	106.0	109.8	.395	24

Playoff Record

Season	GP	W	L	PPGF	PPGA	Result
1973-1974	6	2	4	104.0	106.7	Lost semifinals to Boston.
1974-1975	7	3	4	102.0	106.1	Lost semifinals to Washington.
1975-1976	9	4	5	103.2	107.7	Lost semifinals to Boston.
TOTAL:	22	9	13			
AVERAGE:	7	3	4	103.1	106.8	

COACHING HISTORY: 1971-1972 Dolph Schayes 22-61-.265; 1972 John McCarthy 22-59-.272; 1973-1976 Jack Ramsay 158-170-.428; 1977 Tates Locke 16-30-.348; 1977 Bob MacKinnon 3-4-.429; 1977 Joe Mullaney 11-18-.379; 1978 Lowell "Cotton" Fitzsimmons 27-55-.329

BUFFALO GERMANS

Home City: Buffalo, New York
Home Court:
Origin of Name: The team was named after a very successful amateur team first organized in 1895.

Regular Season Record

Season	League	GP	W	L	Pct
1926	ABL	30	10	20	.333

COACHING HISTORY: Allie Heerdt 10-20-.333

BUFFALO SABRES

Home City: Buffalo, New York
Home Arena: Memorial Auditorium (1970-1996) Capacity: 16,230 [1995]
(1996-present) Capacity:
Origin of Name: The name was chosen in a Name the Team Contest.

Regular Season Record

Season	League	GP	W	L	T	GF	GA	Pts	Pct
1970-1971	NHL	78	24	39	15	217	291	63	.404
1971-1972	NHL	78	16	43	19	203	289	51	.327
1972-1973	NHL	78	37	27	14	257	219	88	.564
1973-1974	NHL	78	32	34	12	242	250	76	.487
1974-1975	NHL	80	49	16	15	354	240	113	.706
1975-1976	NHL	80	46	21	13	339	240	105	.656
1976-1977	NHL	80	48	24	8	301	220	104	.650
1977-1978	NHL	80	44	19	17	288	215	105	.656
1978-1979	NHL	80	36	28	16	280	263	88	.550
1979-1980	NHL	80	47	17	16	318	201	110	.688
1980-1981	NHL	80	39	20	21	327	250	99	.619

1981-1982	NHL	80	39	26	15	307	273	93	.581
1982-1983	NHL	80	38	29	13	318	285	89	.556
1983-1984	NHL	80	48	25	7	315	257	103	.644
1984-1985	NHL	80	38	28	14	290	237	90	.563
1985-1986	NHL	80	37	37	6	296	291	80	.500
1986-1987	NHL	80	28	44	8	280	308	64	.400
1987-1988	NHL	80	37	32	11	283	305	85	.531
1988-1989	NHL	80	38	35	7	291	299	83	.519
1989-1990	NHL	80	45	27	8	286	248	98	.613
1990-1991	NHL	80	31	30	19	292	278	81	.506
1991-1992	NHL	80	31	37	12	289	299	74	.463
1992-1993	NHL	84	38	36	10	335	297	86	.512
1993-1994	NHL	84	43	32	9	282	218	95	.565
1994-1995	NHL	48	22	19	7	130	119	51	.531
1995-1996	NHL	82	33	42	7	247	262	73	.445
TOTAL:	26 years	2050	964	767	319	7367	6654	2247	
AVERAGE:		79	37	30	12	283	256	86	.549

Playoff Record

Season	GP	W	L	GF	GA	Result
1972-1973	6	2	4	16	21	Lost quarterfinals to Montreal.
1974-1975	17	10	7	53	58	Lost Stanley Cup final to Philadelphia.
1975-1976	9	4	5	25	29	Lost quarterfinals to N.Y. Islanders.
1976-1977	6	2	4	21	19	Lost quarterfinals to N.Y. Islanders.
1977-1978	8	3	5	22	22	Lost quarterfinals to Philadelphia.
1978-1979	3	1	2	9	9	Lost preliminary round to Pittsburgh.
1979-1980	14	9	5	48	36	Lost semifinals to N.Y. Islanders.
1980-1981	8	4	4	30	30	Lost quarterfinals to Minnesota.
1981-1982	4	1	3	11	17	Lost preliminary round to Boston.
1982-1983	10	7	3	31	35	Lost quarterfinals to Boston.
1983-1984	3	0	3	5	13	Lost semifinals to Quebec.
1984-1985	5	2	3	22	22	Lost semifinals to Quebec.
1987-1988	6	2	4	22	28	Lost semifinals to Boston.
1988-1989	5	1	4	14	16	Lost semifinals to Boston.
1989-1990	6	2	4	13	17	Lost semifinals to Montreal.
1990-1991	6	2	4	24	29	Lost semifinals to Montreal.
1991-1992	7	3	4	24	19	Lost semifinals to Boston.
1992-1993	8	4	4	31	28	Lost Division finals to Montreal.
1993-1994	7	3	4	14	14	Lost quarterfinals to New Jersey.
1994-1995	5	1	4	13	18	Lost quarterfinals to Philadelphia.
TOTAL:	143	63	80	448	480	
AVERAGE:	7	3	4	22	24	

COACHING HISTORY: 1970-1972 George Imlach 32-62-25-.374; 1972 Floyd Smith 0-1-0-.000; 1972-1974 Joe Crozier 77-80-35-.492; 1974-1977 Floyd Smith 143-61-36-.671; 1977-1979 Marcel Pronovost 52-29-23-.611; 1979 Bill Inglis 28-18-10-.589; 1979-1980 Scotty Bowman 47-17-16-.688; 1980-1981 Roger Neilson 39-20-21-.619; 1981 Jim Roberts 21-15-9-.567; 1981-1987 Scotty Bowman 164-117-44-.572; 1986 Jim Schoenfeld 19-19-5-.500; 1986-1989 Ted Sator 96-89-22-.513; 1989-1992 Rick Dudley 85-72-31-.535; 1991-1995 John Muckler 125-109-34-.530; 1995-present Ted Nolan

CALGARY BOOMERS
(were Memphis Rogues)

Home City: Calgary, Alberta
Home Field: McMahon Stadium Capacity: 34,828 [1981]
Origin of Name: Calgary was considered a "boom" town in the 1970's because of the emergence of Alberta's oil industry.

Regular Season Record

Season	League	GP	W	L	GF	GA	BP	Pts	Pct
1981	NASL	32	17	15	59	54	51	151	.315

Playoff Record

Season	GP	W	L	GF	GA	Result
1981	2	0	2	1	5	Lost 1st round series to Ft. Lauderdale.

COACHING HISTORY: AL Miller 17-15

CALGARY COWBOYS
(were Vancouver Blazers)

Home City: Calgary, Alberta
Home Arena: Stampede Corral Capacity: 6,492
Origin of Name: The name was chosen because Calgary is the home of the world famous Calgary Stampede.

Regular Season Record

Season	League	GP	W	L	T	GF	GA	Pts	Pct
1975-1976	WHA	80	41	35	4	307	282	86	.538
1976-1977	WHA	81	31	43	7	252	296	69	.426
TOTAL:	2 years	161	72	78	11	559	578	155	
AVERAGE:		80	36	39	5	280	289	77	.481

Playoff Record

Season	GP	W	L	GF	GA	Result
1975-1976	10	5	5	36	37	Lost semifinal round to Winnipeg.

COACHING HISTORY: 1975-1977 Joe Crozier 72-78-11-.481

CALGARY FLAMES
(were Atlanta Flames)

Home City: Calgary, Alberta
Home Arena: Stampede Corral (1980-1983) Capacity: 6,492 [1980]
Canadian Airlines Saddledome (1983-present) Capacity: 20,000 [1995]
Origin of Name: The team kept the same nickname after it moved from Atlanta to Calgary.

Regular Season Record

Season	League	GP	W	L	T	GF	GA	Pts	Pct
1980-1981	NHL	80	39	27	14	329	298	92	.575
1981-1982	NHL	80	29	34	17	334	345	75	.469
1982-1983	NHL	80	32	34	14	321	317	78	.488
1983-1984	NHL	80	34	32	14	311	314	82	.513
1984-1985	NHL	80	41	27	12	363	302	94	.588
1985-1986	NHL	80	40	31	9	354	315	89	.556
1986-1987	NHL	80	46	31	3	318	289	95	.594
1987-1988	NHL	80	48	23	9	397	305	105	.656
1988-1989	NHL	80	54	17	9	354	226	117	.731
1989-1990	NHL	80	42	23	15	348	265	99	.619
1990-1991	NHL	80	46	26	8	344	263	100	.625
1991-1992	NHL	80	31	37	12	296	305	74	.463
1992-1993	NHL	84	43	30	11	322	282	97	.578
1993-1994	NHL	84	42	29	13	302	256	97	.578
1994-1995	NHL	48	24	17	7	163	135	55	.573
1995-1996	NHL	82	34	37	11	241	240	79	.482
TOTAL:	16 years	1258	625	455	178	5097	4457	1428	
AVERAGE:		79	39	29	11	319	279	89	.568

Playoff Record

Season	GP	W	L	GF	GA	Result
1980-1981	16	9	7	54	61	Lost semifinal round to Minnesota.
1981-1982	3	0	3	5	10	Lost preliminary round to Vancouver.
1982-1983	9	4	5	30	49	Lost quarterfinals to Edmonton.
1983-1984	11	6	5	41	46	Lost quarterfinals to Edmonton.
1984-1985	4	1	3	13	15	Lost 1st round series to Winnipeg.
1985-1986	22	12	10	81	69	Lost Stanley Cup final to Montreal.
1986-1987	6	2	4	15	22	Lost 1st round series to Winnipeg.
1987-1988	9	4	5	41	36	Lost quarterfinals to Edmonton.
1988-1989	22	16	6	82	55	**Won Stanley Cup**.
1989-1990	6	2	4	24	29	Lost 1st round series to Los Angeles.
1990-1991	7	3	4	20	22	Lost 1st round series to Edmonton.
1992-1993	6	2	4	28	33	Lost 1st round series to Los Angeles.
1993-1994	7	3	4	20	23	Lost 1st round series to Vancouver.
1994-1995	7	3	4	35	26	Lost 1st round series to San Jose.
1995-1996	4	0	4	7	16	Lost 1st round series to Chicago.
TOTAL:	139	67	72	496	512	
AVERAGE:	9	4	5	33	34	

COACHING HISTORY: 1980-1982 Al MacNeil 68-61-31-.522; 1982-1987 Bob Johnson 193-155-52-.548; 1987-1990 Terry Crisp 144-63-33-.669; 1990-1992 Doug Risebrough 71-57-17-.548; 1991-1992 Guy Charron 6-6-3-.500; 1992-1995 Dave King 109-76-31-.576; 1995-present Pierre Page

The Canadian Airlines Saddledome was known as Olympic Saddledome from 1983 to 1994.

CALGARY STAMPEDERS

Home City: Calgary, Alberta
Home Stadium: Mewata Stadium (1950-1959) Capacity: 12,000
McMahon Stadium (1960-present) Capacity: 37,317 [1995]
Origin of Name: Named after the world famous Calgary Stampede.

Regular Season Record

Season	League	GP	W	L	T	PF	PA	Pts	Pct
1950	CRU	14	4	10	0	152	251	8	.286
1951	CRU	14	4	10	0	205	299	8	.286
1952	CRU	16	7	9	0	293	340	14	.438
1953	CRU	16	3	12	1	190	313	7	.219
1954	CRU	16	8	8	0	271	165	16	.500
1955	CRU	16	4	12	0	209	299	8	.250
1956	CFC	16	4	12	0	229	410	8	.250
1957	CFC	16	6	10	0	221	413	12	.375
1958	CFL	16	6	9	1	314	312	13	.406
1959	CFL	16	8	8	0	356	301	16	.500
1960	CFL	16	6	8	2	374	404	14	.438
1961	CFL	16	7	9	0	300	311	14	.438
1962	CFL	16	9	6	1	352	335	19	.594
1963	CFL	16	10	4	2	427	323	22	.688
1964	CFL	16	12	4	0	352	249	24	.750
1965	CFL	16	12	4	0	340	243	24	.750
1966	CFL	16	6	9	1	227	259	13	.406
1967	CFL	16	12	4	0	382	219	24	.750
1968	CFL	16	10	6	0	412	249	20	.625
1969	CFL	16	9	7	0	327	314	18	.563
1970	CFL	16	9	7	0	293	209	18	.563
1971	CFL	16	9	6	1	290	218	19	.594
1972	CFL	16	6	10	0	331	394	12	.375
1973	CFL	16	6	10	0	214	368	12	.375
1974	CFL	16	6	10	0	285	305	12	.375
1975	CFL	16	6	10	0	387	363	12	.375
1976	CFL	16	2	12	2	316	442	6	.188
1977	CFL	16	4	12	0	241	327	8	.250
1978	CFL	16	9	4	3	381	311	21	.656
1979	CFL	16	12	4	0	382	278	24	.750
1980	CFL	16	9	7	0	407	355	18	.563
1981	CFL	16	6	10	0	306	367	12	.375
1982	CFL	16	9	6	1	403	440	19	.594
1983	CFL	16	8	8	0	425	378	16	.500
1984	CFL	16	6	10	0	314	425	12	.375
1985	CFL	16	3	13	0	256	429	6	.188
1986	CFL	18	11	7	0	484	380	22	.611
1987	CFL	18	10	8	0	453	517	20	.556
1988	CFL	18	6	12	0	395	476	12	.333
1989	CFL	18	10	8	0	495	466	20	.556
1990	CFL	18	11	6	1	588	566	23	.639
1991	CFL	18	11	7	0	596	552	22	.611
1992	CFL	18	13	5	0	607	430	26	.722
1993	CFL	18	15	3	0	646	418	30	.833

1994	CFL	18	15	3	0	698	355	30	.833
1995	CFL	18	15	3	0	631	404	30	.833
TOTAL:	46 years	752	374	362	16	16757	16182	764	
AVERAGE:		16	8	8	0	364	352	16	.508

Playoff Record

Season	**GP**	**W**	**L**	**T**	**PF**	**PA**	**Result**
1952	2	1	1	0	38	42	Lost semifinal round to Edmonton.
1957	2	0	1	1	16	28	Lost semifinal round to Winnipeg.
1960	2	0	2	0	28	70	Lost semifinal round to Edmonton.
1961	4	1	3	0	42	83	Lost Division final to Winnipeg.
1962	5	3	2	0	81	52	Lost Division final to Winnipeg.
1963	2	1	1	0	47	48	Lost semifinals to Saskatchewan.
1964	5	3	2	0	114	107	Lost Division finals to B.C.
1965	3	1	2	0	50	43	Lost Division finals to Winnipeg.
1967	3	1	2	0	37	39	Lost Division final to Saskatchewan.
1968	4	3	1	0	107	49	Lost Grey cup game to Ottawa.
1969	3	1	2	0	59	74	Lost Division final to Saskatchewan.
1970	5	3	2	0	72	68	Lost Grey Cup game to Montreal.
1971	3	3	0	0	67	53	**Won Grey Cup**.
1978	2	1	1	0	51	30	Lost Division final to Edmonton.
1979	2	1	1	0	44	21	Lost Division final to Edmonton.
1980	1	0	1	0	14	32	Lost semifinals to Winnipeg.
1982	1	0	1	0	3	24	Lost semifinals to Winnipeg.
1987	1	0	1	0	16	30	Lost semifinals to Edmonton.
1989	1	0	1	0	26	33	Lost semifinals to Saskatchewan.
1990	1	0	1	0	23	43	Lost Division final to Edmonton.
1991	3	2	1	0	102	113	Lost Grey Cup game to Toronto.
1992	2	2	0	0	47	32	**Won Grey Cup**.
1993	2	1	1	0	32	38	Lost Division final to Edmonton.
1994	2	1	1	0	72	40	Lost Division final to B.C.
1995	3	2	1	0	87	54	Lost Grey Cup game to Baltimore.
TOTAL:	64	31	32	1	1275	1246	
AVERAGE:	2	1	1	0	51	50	

COACHING HISTORY: 1950-1952 Les Lear 15-29-0-.341; 1953 Bob Snyder 3-12-1-.219; 1954 Larry Seemering 8-8-0-.500: 1955-1956 Jack Hennemier 6-14-0-.300; 1956-1960 Otis Douglas 23-40-1-.367; 1960 Steve Owen 5-5-2-.500: 1961-1964 Bobby Dobbs 38-23-3-.617; 1965-1968 Jerry Williams 40-23-1-.633; 1969-1973 Jim Duncan 38-38-1-.500; 1973-1975 Jim Wood 11-18-0-.379; 1975-1976 Bob Baker 2-13-1-.156; 1976 Joe Tiller 2-3-1-.417; 1977-1979 Jack Gotta 25-20-3-.552; 1980-1981 Ardell Wiegandt 15-14-0-.517; 1981 Jerry Williams 0-3-0-.000; 1982-1983 Jack Gotta 17-14-1-.547; 1984-1985 Steve Burrato 6-15-0-.286; 1985 Bud Riley 3-8-0-.273; 1986-1987 Bob Vespaziani 13-13-0-.500; 1987-1989 Lary Kuharich 24-22-0-.522; 1990-present Wally Buono

CALGARY TIGERS

Home City: Calgary, Alberta
Home Arena: Victoria Arena — Capacity: 5,000 [1924]
Origin of Name:

Regular Season Record

Season	League	GP	W	L	T	GF	GA	Pts	Pct
1921-1922	WCHA	24	14	10	0	75	62	28	.583
1922-1923	WCHA	30	12	18	0	91	106	24	.400
1923-1924	WCHA	30	18	11	1	83	72	37	.617
1924-1925	WCHL	28	17	11	0	96	80	34	.607
1925-1926	WHL	30	10	17	3	71	80	23	.383
TOTAL:	5years	142	71	67	4	416	400	146	
AVERAGE:		28	14	13	1	83	80	29	.514

Playoff Record

Season	GP	W	L	T	GF	GA	Result
1921-1922	2	0	1	1	1	2	Lost semifinal to Regina.
1923-1924	7	3	3	1	15	18	Lost playoff with Vancouver.
1924-1925	2	0	1	1	1	3	Lost WHL final to Victoria.
TOTAL:	11	3	5	3	17	23	
AVERAGE:	4	1	2	1	6	8	

COACHING HISTORY: 1921-1923 Barney Stanley 14-10-0-.583; 1922-1926 Herb Gardiner 57-57-4-.500

CALIFORNIA ANGELS
(were Los Angeles Angels)

Home City: Anaheim, California
Home Field: Dodger Stadium(1965) Capacity: 56,000 [1965]
Anaheim Stadium (1966-present) Capacity: 64,593 [1995]
Origin of Name: The team kept the same name when it moved from Los Angeles to Anaheim.

Regular Season Record

Season	League	GP	W	L	Pct	GB	R	OR
1965	AL	162	75	87	.463	27	527	569
1966	AL	162	80	82	.494	18	604	643
1967	AL	161	84	77	.522	7.5	567	587
1968	AL	162	67	95	.414	36	498	615
1969	AL	162	71	91	.438	26	528	652
1970	AL	162	86	76	.531	12	631	630
1971	AL	162	76	86	.469	25.5	511	576
1972	AL	155	75	80	.484	18	454	533
1973	AL	162	79	83	.488	15	629	657
1974	AL	162	68	94	.420	22	618	657
1975	AL	161	72	89	.447	25.5	628	723
1976	AL	162	76	86	.469	14	550	631
1977	AL	162	74	88	.457	28	675	695
1978	AL	162	87	75	.537	5	691	666
1979	AL	162	88	74	.543	-	866	768
1980	AL	160	65	95	.406	31	698	797
1981	AL	110	51	59	.464	NA	476	453
1982	AL	162	93	69	.574	-	814	670
1983	AL	162	70	92	.432	29	722	779
1984	AL	162	81	81	.500	3	696	697
1985	AL	162	90	72	.556	1	732	703

1986	AL	162	92	70	.568	-	786	684
1987	AL	162	75	87	.463	10	770	803
1988	AL	162	75	87	.463	29	714	771
1989	AL	162	91	71	.562	8	669	578
1990	AL	162	80	82	.494	23	690	706
1991	AL	162	81	81	.500	14	653	649
1992	AL	162	72	90	.444	24	579	671
1993	AL	162	71	91	.438	23	684	770
1994	AL	115	47	68	.409	5.5	543	660
1995*	AL	144	78	66	.542	-	801	697
TOTAL:	31 years	4894	2370	2524		480	20004	20690
AVERAGE:		158	76	82	.483	15.5	645	667

Playoff Record

Season	GP	W	L	R	OR	Result
1979	4	1	3	15	26	Lost ALCS to Baltimore.
1982	5	2	3	23	23	Lost ALCS to Milwaukee.
1986	7	3	4	30	41	Lost ALCS to Boston.
TOTAL:	16	6	10	68	90	
AVERAGE:	5	2	3	23	30	

COACHING HISTORY: 1965-1969 Bill Rigney 317-369-.462; 1969-1971 Harold Phillips 222-225-.497; 1972 Del Rice 75-80-.484; 1973-1974 Bobby Winkles 111-129-.463; 1974-1976 Dick Williams 147-194-.431; 1976-1977 Norm Sherry 76-71-.517; 1977-1978 Dave Garcia 60-67-.472; 1978-1981 Jim Fregosi 237-248-.489; 1981-1982 Gene Mauch 122-103-.542; 1983-1984 John McNamara 151-173-.466; 1985-1987 Gene Mauch 257-229-.529; 1988 Octavio Rojas 75-79-.487; 1988 Lawrence Stubing 0-8-.000; 1989-1991 Doug Rader 232-216-.518; 1991-1994 Buck Rodgers 140-172-.449; 1992 John Wathan 39-50-.438; 1994-present Marcel Lachemann

CALIFORNIA GOLDEN SEALS

(were Oakland Seals)
(became Cleveland Barons)

Home City: Oakland, California
Home Arena: Alameda County Coliseum — Capacity: 12,500 [1974]
Origin of Name: See Oakland Seals.

Regular Season Record

Season	League	GP	W	L	T	GF	GA	Pts	Pct
1970-1971	NHL	78	20	53	5	199	320	45	.288
1971-1972	NHL	78	21	39	18	216	288	60	.385
1972-1973	NHL	78	16	46	16	213	323	48	.308
1973-1974	NHL	78	13	55	10	195	342	36	.231
1974-1975	NHL	80	19	48	13	212	316	51	.319
1975-1976	NHL	80	27	42	11	250	278	65	.406
TOTAL:	6 years	472	116	283	73	1285	1867	305	
AVERAGE:		78	19	47	12	214	311	50	.323

COACHING HISTORY: 1970-1975 Fred Glover 45-131-28-.289; 1971-1972 Vic Stasiuk 21-38-16-.387; 1972-1973 Gary Young 2-7-3-.292; 1973-1975 Marshall Johnston 13-45-11-.268; 1974-1975 Bill McCreary 8-20-4-.313; 1975-1976 Jack Evans 27-42-11-.406

*Defeated by Seattle 9 to 1 in a playoff with Seattle to determine 1st place.

CALIFORNIA SURF
(were St. Louis Stars)

Home City: Anaheim, California
Home Stadium: Anaheim Stadium Capacity: 43,250 [1977]
Origin of Name: The name was chosen by team executives.

Regular Season Record

Season	League	GP	W	L	GF	GA	BP	Pts	Pct
1978	NASL	30	13	17	43	49	37	115	.426
1979	NASL	30	15	15	53	56	50	140	.519
1980	NASL	32	15	17	61	67	54	144	.500
1981	NASL	32	11	21	60	77	51	117	.260
TOTAL:	4 years	124	54	70	217	249	192	516	
AVERAGE:		31	14	17	54	62	48	129	.404

Playoff Record

Season	GP	W	L	GF	GA	Result
1978	1	0	1	1	2	Lost 1st round series to San Diego.
1979	2	0	2	4	11	Lost 1st round series to San Diego.
1980	3	1	2	3	3	Lost 1st round series to Ft. Lauderdale.
TOTAL:	6	1	5	8	16	
AVERAGE:	2	0	2	3	5	

COACHING HISTORY: 1978-1979 John Sewell 17-21; 1979-1981 Peter Wall 37-49

CANTON BULLDOGS
(became Cleveland Bulldogs)

Home City: Canton, Ohio
Home Stadium: Lakeside Park
Origin of Name: The team was named after previous Canton teams tracing their origins back to at least 1906.

Regular Season Record

Season	League	GP	W	L	T	PF	PA	Pct
1922	NFL	12	10	0	2	184	15	.917
1923	NFL	12	11	0	1	246	19	.958
TOTAL:	2years	24	21	0	3	430	34	
AVERAGE:		12	10	0	2	215	17	.938

COACHING HISTORY: 1922-1923 Guy Chamberlin 21-0-3-.938

CANTON BULLDOGS

Home City: Canton, Ohio
Home Stadium: Lakeside Park
Origin of Name: Named after previous NFL team.

Regular Season Record

Season	League	GP	W	L	T	PF	PA	Pct
1925	NFL	8	4	4	0	50	73	.500
1926	NFL	13	1	9	3	46	161	.192
TOTAL:	2years	21	5	13	3	96	234	
AVERAGE:		11	3	6	2	48	117	.310

COACHING HISTORY: 1925 Harry Robb 4-4-0-.500; 1926 Harry Robb & Pete Henry 1-9-3-.192

CAPITAL BULLETS

(were the Baltimore Bullets)
(became Washington Bullets)

Home City: Landover, Maryland
Home Court: Capital Center Capacity: 17,500 [1974]
Origin of Name: The team kept the same name when it moved from Baltimore.

Regular Season Record

Season	League	GP	W	L	PPGF	PPGA	Pct	GB
1973-1974	NBA	82	47	35	101.9	100.4	.573	

Playoff Record

Season	GP	W	L	PPGF	PPGA	Result
1973-1974	7	3	4	95.1	94.0	Lost semifinals to New York.

COACHING HISTORY: K.C. Jones 47-35-.573

CAROLINA COUGARS

Home City: Greensboro, North Carolina (the team also played some home games in Charlotte and Raleigh)
Home Court: Greensboro Coliseum Capacity: 15,500 [1974]
Origin of Name: Named by general manager Don DeJardin.

Regular Season Record

Season	League	GP	W	L	PPGF	PPGA	Pct	GB
1969-1970	ABA	84	42	42	106.8	107.0	.500	17
1970-1971	ABA	84	34	50	115.3	119.4	.405	21
1971-1972	ABA	84	35	49	114.8	118.1	.417	33
1972-1973	ABA	84	57	27	115.6	110.7	.679	-
1973-1974	ABA	84	47	37	110.5	107.0	.560	8
TOTAL:	5years	420	215	205				79
AVERAGE:		84	43	41	112.6	112.4	.512	16

Playoff Record

Season	GP	W	L	PPGF	PPGA	Result
1969-1970	4	0	4	103.8	112.8	Lost 1st round series to Indiana.
1972-1973	12	7	5	108.0	106.0	Lost 2nd round series to Kentucky.

1973-1974	4	0	4	106.8	116.3	Lost 1st round series to Kentucky.
TOTAL:	20	7	13			
AVERAGE:	7	2	5	106.2	111.7	

COACHING HISTORY: 1969-1971 Bones McKinney 59-67-.468; 1971 Jerry Steele 17-25-.405; 1971-1972 Tom Meschery 35-49-.417; 1972-1974 Larry Brown 104-64-.619

CAROLINA PANTHERS

Home City: Charlotte, North Carolina
Home Stadium: Memorial Stadium (Clemson University) Capacity: 81,473 [1995]
Origin of Name:

Regular Season Record

Season	League	GP	W	L	T	PF	PA	Pct
1995	NFL	16	7	9	0	289	325	.438

COACHING HISTORY: 1995-present Dom Capers

CHARLOTTE HORNETS
(were Charlotte Stars)

Home City: Charlotte, North Carolina
Home Stadium: American Legion Stadium Capacity: 22,315 [1975]
Origin of Name: Hornets is a popular name for teams in Carolina.

Regular Season Record

Season	League	GP	W	L	T	PF	PA	Pct
1975	WFL	11	6	5	0	225	199	.545

COACHING HISTORY: Bob Gibson 6-5-0-.545

CHARLOTTE HORNETS

Home City: Charlotte, North Carolina
Home Court: Charlotte Coliseum Capacity: 23,698 [1995]
Origin of Name: The name has long been associated with teams from Charlotte.

Regular Season Record

.Season	League	GP	W	L	PPGF	PPGA	Pct	GB
1988-1989	NBA	82	20	62	104.5	113.0	.244	32
1989-1990	NBA	82	19	63	100.4	108.2	.232	37
1990-1991	NBA	82	26	56	102.8	108.0	.317	35
1991-1992	NBA	82	31	51	109.5	113.4	.378	36
1992-1993	NBA	82	44	38	110.1	110.4	.537	13
1993-1994	NBA	82	41	41	106.5	106.7	.500	16
1994-1995	NBA	82	50	32	100.6	97.3	.610	2
1995-1996	NBA	82	41	41	102.8	103.4	.500	31
TOTAL:	8 years	656	272	384				202
AVERAGE:		82	34	48	104.7	107.6	.415	25

Playoff Record

Season	GP	W	L	PPGF	PPGA	Result
1992-1993	9	4	5	102.4	102.6	Lost semifinals to New York.
1994-1995	4	1	3	92.5	96.3	Lost 1st round series to Chicago.
TOTAL:	13	5	8			
AVERAGE:	7	3	4	99.4	100.7	

COACHING HISTORY: 1988-1989 Dick Harter 28-94-.230; 1989-1991 Gene Littles 37-87-.298; 1991-1996 Allan Bristow 207-203-.509; 1996-present

CHARLOTTE STARS

(became Charlotte Hornets)
(moved from New York part way through the season)

Home City: Charlotte, North Carolina
Home Stadium: American Legion Stadium Capacity: 22,315 [1974]
Origin of Name: The team kept the same nickname when it moved from New York to Charlotte.

Regular Season Record

Season	League	GP	W	L	T	PF	PA	Pct
1974	WFL	9	7	2	0	302	72	.778

COACHING HISTORY: Babe Parilli 7-2-0-.778

CHICAGO-PITTSBURGH

(Chicago team was known as the Unions)

Home City: Chicago, Illinois
Pittsburgh, Pennsylvania
Home Field: Lakefront Park and Chicago Cricket Grounds
Origin of Name: This was merger of the Chicago and Pittsburgh franchises.

Regular Season Record

Season	League	GP	W	L	Pct	GB	R	OR
1884	UA	91	41	50	.451	42	438	482

COACHING HISTORY: Ed Hengle 34-39-.466; Joe Battin 1-5-.167; Joe Ellick 6-6-.500

CHICAGO-PITTSBURGH

Home City: Chicago, Illinois
Pittsburgh, Pennsylvania
Home Stadium: Comiskey Park (Chicago) Capacity: 52,000
Forbes Field (Pittsburgh) Capacity: 35,000
Origin of Name: This was a merger of the Pittsburgh Steelers and the Chicago Cardinals

Regular Season Record

Season	League	GP	W	L	T	PF	PA	Pct
1944	NFL	10	0	10	0	108	328	.000

COACHING RECORD: Phil Handler and Walt Kiesling 0-10-0-.000

CHICAGO AMERICAN GEARS

Home City: Chicago, Illinois
Home Court: Chicago Stadium
Origin of Name: The team was sponsored by the American Gear Company.

Regular Season Record

Season	League	GP	W	L	PPGF	PPGA	Pct	GB
1944-1945	NBL	30	14	16	51.6	53.9	.467	5
1945-1946	NBL	34	17	17	48.4	51.6	.500	4
1946-1947	NBL	44	26	18	58.4	54.3	.591	2
TOTAL:	3 years	108	57	51				11
AVERAGE:		36	19	17	52.8	53.3	.528	4

Playoff Record

Season	GP	W	L	PPGF	PPGA	Result
1944-1945	3	1	2	37.7	51.7	Lost 1st round series to Sheboygan.

COACHING HISTORY: 1944-1945 Jack Tierney 14-16-.467; 1945-1946 Swede Roos 17-17-.500; 1946-1947 Davey Banks 4-4-.500; 1946-1947 Harry Foote 4-4-.500; 1946-1947 Bob McDermott 18-10-.643

CHICAGO BEARS

Home City: Chicago, Illinois
Home Stadium: Wrigley Field (1922-1970) Capacity: 37,741 [1973]
Soldier Field (1971 to present) Capacity: 66,950 [1995]
Origin of Name: The team was named the Bears to create a relationship with the National League Cubs.

Regular Season Record

Season	League	GP	W	L	T	PF	PA	Pct
1922	NFL	12	9	3	0	123	44	.750
1923	NFL	12	9	2	1	123	35	.792
1924	NFL	11	6	1	4	136	55	.727
1925	NFL	17	9	5	3	158	96	.618
1926	NFL	16	12	1	3	216	63	.844
1927	NFL	14	9	3	2	149	98	.714
1928	NFL	13	7	5	1	182	85	.577
1929	NFL	14	4	8	2	110	207	.357
1930	NFL	14	9	4	1	169	71	.679
1931	NFL	13	8	5	0	145	92	.615
1932	NFL	14	7	1	6	160	44	.714
1933	NFL	13	10	2	1	133	82	.808
1934	NFL	13	13	0	0	286	86	1.000
1935	NFL	12	6	4	2	192	106	.583
1936	NFL	12	9	3	0	222	94	.750
1937	NFL	11	9	1	1	201	100	.864
1938	NFL	11	6	5	0	194	148	.545
1939	NFL	11	8	3	0	298	157	.727
1940	NFL	11	8	3	0	238	152	.727

1941	NFL	11	10	1	0	396	147	.909
1942	NFL	11	11	0	0	376	84	1.000
1943	NFL	10	8	1	1	303	157	.850
1944	NFL	10	6	3	1	258	172	.650
1945	NFL	10	3	7	0	192	235	.300
1946	NFL	11	8	2	1	289	193	.773
1947	NFL	12	8	4	0	363	241	.667
1948	NFL	12	10	2	0	375	151	.833
1949	NFL	12	9	3	0	332	218	.750
1950	NFL	12	9	3	0	279	207	.750
1951	NFL	12	7	5	0	286	282	.583
1952	NFL	12	5	7	0	245	326	.417
1953	NFL	12	3	8	1	218	262	.292
1954	NFL	12	8	4	0	301	279	.667
1955	NFL	12	8	4	0	294	251	.667
1956	NFL	12	9	2	1	363	246	.792
1957	NFL	12	5	7	0	203	211	.417
1958	NFL	12	8	4	0	298	230	.667
1959	NFL	12	8	4	0	252	196	.667
1960	NFL	12	5	6	1	194	299	.458
1961	NFL	14	8	6	0	326	302	.571
1962	NFL	14	9	5	0	321	287	.643
1963	NFL	14	11	1	2	301	144	.857
1964	NFL	14	5	9	0	260	379	.357
1965	NFL	14	9	5	0	409	275	.643
1966	NFL	14	5	7	2	234	272	.429
1967	NFL	14	7	6	1	239	218	.536
1968	NFL	14	7	7	0	250	333	.500
1969	NFL	14	1	13	0	210	339	.071
1970	NFL	14	6	8	0	256	261	.429
1971	NFL	14	6	8	0	185	276	.429
1972	NFL	14	4	9	1	225	275	.321
1973	NFL	14	3	11	0	195	334	.214
1974	NFL	14	4	10	0	152	279	.286
1975	NFL	14	4	10	0	191	379	.286
1976	NFL	14	7	7	0	253	216	.500
1977	NFL	14	9	5	0	255	253	.643
1978	NFL	16	7	9	0	253	274	.438
1979	NFL	16	10	6	0	306	249	.625
1980	NFL	16	7	9	0	304	264	.438
1981	NFL	16	6	10	0	253	324	.375
1982	NFL	9	3	6	0	141	174	.333
1983	NFL	16	8	8	0	311	301	.500
1984	NFL	16	10	6	0	325	248	.625
1985	NFL	16	15	1	0	456	198	.938
1986	NFL	16	14	2	0	352	187	.875
1987	NFL	15	11	4	0	356	282	.733
1988	NFL	16	12	4	0	312	215	.750
1989	NFL	16	6	10	0	358	377	.375
1990	NFL	16	11	5	0	348	280	.688
1991	NFL	16	11	5	0	299	269	.688
1992	NFL	16	5	11	0	295	361	.313
1993	NFL	16	7	9	0	234	230	.438
1994	NFL	16	9	7	0	271	307	.563

1995	NFL	16	9	7	0	392	360	.563
TOTAL:	74 years	993	572	382	39	19080	15924	
AVERAGE:		13	8	5	0	258	215	.596

Playoff Record

Season	GP	W	L	PF	PA	Result
1933	1	1	0	23	21	**Won NFL championship**.
1934	1	0	1	13	30	Lost championship game to N.Y. Giants
1937	1	0	1	21	28	Lost championship game to Washington.
1940	1	1	0	73	0	**Won NFL championship**.
1941	2	2	0	70	23	**Won NFL championship**.
1942	1	0	1	6	14	Lost championship game to Washington.
1943	1	1	0	41	21	**Won NFL championship**.
1946	1	1	0	24	14	**Won NFL championship**.
1950	1	0	1	14	24	Lost Conference playoff to Los Angeles.
1956	1	0	1	7	47	Lost championship game to N.Y. Giants.
1963	1	1	0	14	10	**Won NFL championship**.
1977	1	0	1	7	37	Lost Divisional playoff to Dallas.
1979	1	0	1	17	27	Lost 1st round game to Philadelphia.
1984	2	1	1	23	42	Lost NFC championship to San Francisco.
1985	3	3	0	91	10	**Won Super Bowl**.
1986	1	0	1	13	27	Lost Divisional playoff to Washington.
1987	1	0	1	17	21	Lost Divisional playoff to Washington.
1988	2	1	1	23	40	Lost NFC championship to San Francisco.
1990	1	0	1	3	31	Lost semifinals to N.Y. Giants.
1991	1	0	1	13	17	Lost Wild Card game to Dallas.
1994	2	1	1	50	62	Lost semifinals to San Francisco.
TOTAL:	27	13	14	563	546	
AVERAGE:	2	1	1	27	26	

COACHING HISTORY: 1922-1929 George Halas 70-29-16-.678; 1930-1932 Ralph Jones 24-10-7-.671; 1933-1942 George Halas 89-24-4-.778; 1942-1945 Johnsos, Anderson and Driscoll 21-12-2-.629; 1945-1955 George Halas 78-43-2-.642; 1956-1957 Paddy Driscoll 14-9-1-.604; 1958-1967 George Halas 76-53-6-.585; 1968-1971 Jim Dooley 20-36-0-.357; 1972-1974 Abe Gibron 11-30-1-.274; 1975-1977 Jack Pardee 20-22-0-.476; 1978-1981 Neill Armstrong 30-34-0-.469; 1982-1992 Mike Ditka 106-62-0-.631; 1993-present Dave Wannstedt

CHICAGO BLACKHAWKS

(Team known as Black Hawks until 1986)

Home City: Chicago, Illinois
Home Arena: Chicago Coliseum (1926-1929) — Capacity: 5,000
Chicago Stadium (1929-1994) — Capacity: 17,317 [1994]
United Center (1994-present) — Capacity: 20,500 [1995]
Origin of Name: The team was named after the Blackhawks Field Gun Battalion commanded by original team owner Major Frederick McLaughlin during World War I.

Regular Season Record

Season	League	GP	W	L	T	GF	GA	Pts	Pct
1926-1927	NHL	44	19	22	3	115	116	41	.466
1927-1928	NHL	44	7	34	3	68	134	17	.193

1928-1929	NHL	44	7	29	8	33	85	22	.250
1929-1930	NHL	44	21	18	5	117	111	47	.534
1930-1931	NHL	44	24	17	3	108	78	51	.580
1931-1932	NHL	48	18	19	11	86	101	47	.490
1932-1933	NHL	48	16	20	12	88	101	44	.458
1933-1934	NHL	48	20	17	11	88	83	51	.531
1934-1935	NHL	48	26	17	5	118	88	57	.594
1935-1936	NHL	48	21	19	8	93	92	50	.521
1936-1937	NHL	48	14	27	7	99	131	35	.365
1937-1938	NHL	48	14	25	9	97	139	37	.385
1938-1939	NHL	48	12	28	8	91	132	32	.333
1939-1940	NHL	48	23	19	6	112	120	52	.542
1940-1941	NHL	48	16	25	7	112	139	39	.407
1941-1942	NHL	48	22	23	3	145	155	47	.490
1942-1943	NHL	50	17	18	15	179	180	49	.490
1943-1944	NHL	50	22	23	5	178	187	49	.490
1944-1945	NHL	50	13	30	7	141	194	33	.330
1945-1946	NHL	50	23	20	7	200	178	53	.530
1946-1947	NHL	60	19	37	4	193	274	42	.350
1947-1948	NHL	60	20	34	6	195	225	46	.383
1948-1949	NHL	60	21	31	8	173	211	50	.417
1949-1950	NHL	70	22	38	10	203	244	54	.386
1950-1951	NHL	70	13	47	10	171	280	36	.257
1951-1952	NHL	70	17	44	9	158	241	43	.307
1952-1953	NHL	70	27	28	15	169	175	69	.493
1953-1954	NHL	70	12	51	7	133	242	31	.221
1954-1955	NHL	70	13	40	17	161	235	43	.307
1955-1956	NHL	70	19	39	12	155	216	50	.357
1956-1957	NHL	70	16	39	15	169	225	47	.336
1957-1958	NHL	70	24	39	7	163	202	55	.393
1958-1959	NHL	70	28	29	13	197	208	69	.493
1959-1960	NHL	70	28	29	13	191	180	69	.493
1960-1961	NHL	70	29	24	17	198	180	75	.536
1961-1962	NHL	70	31	26	13	217	186	75	.536
1962-1963	NHL	70	32	21	17	194	178	81	.579
1963-1964	NHL	70	36	22	12	218	169	84	.600
1964-1965	NHL	70	34	28	8	224	176	76	.543
1965-1966	NHL	70	37	25	8	240	187	82	.586
1966-1967	NHL	70	41	17	12	264	170	94	.671
1967-1968	NHL	74	32	26	16	212	222	80	.571
1968-1969	NHL	76	34	33	9	280	246	77	.507
1969-1970	NHL	76	45	22	9	250	170	99	.651
1970-1971	NHL	78	49	20	9	277	184	107	.686
1971-1972	NHL	78	46	17	15	256	166	107	.686
1972-1973	NHL	78	42	27	9	284	225	93	.596
1973-1974	NHL	78	41	14	23	272	164	105	.673
1974-1975	NHL	80	37	35	8	268	241	82	.513
1975-1976	NHL	80	32	30	18	254	261	82	.513
1976-1977	NHL	80	26	43	11	240	298	63	.394
1977-1978	NHL	80	32	29	19	230	220	83	.519
1978-1979	NHL	80	29	36	15	244	277	73	.456
1979-1980	NHL	80	34	27	19	241	250	87	.544
1980-1981	NHL	80	31	33	16	304	315	78	.488
1981-1982	NHL	80	30	38	12	332	363	72	.450

1982-1983	NHL	80	47	23	10	338	268	104	.650
1983-1984	NHL	80	30	42	8	277	311	68	.425
1984-1985	NHL	80	38	35	7	309	299	83	.519
1985-1986	NHL	80	39	33	8	351	350	86	.538
1986-1987	NHL	80	29	37	14	290	310	72	.450
1987-1988	NHL	80	30	41	9	284	328	69	.431
1988-1989	NHL	80	27	41	12	297	335	66	.413
1989-1990	NHL	80	41	33	6	316	294	88	.550
1990-1991	NHL	80	49	23	8	284	211	106	.663
1991-1992	NHL	80	36	29	15	257	236	87	.544
1992-1993	NHL	84	47	25	12	279	230	106	.631
1993-1994	NHL	84	39	36	9	254	240	87	.518
1994-1995	NHL	48	24	19	5	156	115	53	.552
1995-1996	NHL	82	40	28	14	273	220	94	.573
TOTAL:	70 years	4664	1930	2013	721	14163	14297	4581	
AVERAGE:		67	28	29	10	202	204	66	.491

Playoff Record

Season	GP	W	L	T	GF	GA	Result
1926-1927	2	0	2	0	5	10	Lost quarterfinals to Boston.
1929-1930	2	0	2	0	2	3	Lost quarterfinals to Montreal.
1930-1931	9	5	3	1	15	13	Lost Stanley Cup final to Montreal.
1931-1932	2	1	1	0	2	6	Lost quarterfinals to Toronto.
1933-1934	8	6	1	1	19	12	**Won Stanley Cup**.
1934-1935	2	0	1	1	0	1	Lost quarterfinals to Maroons.
1935-1936	2	1	1	0	5	7	Lost quarterfinals to Americans.
1937-1938	10	7	3	0	26	21	**Won Stanley Cup**.
1939-1940	2	0	2	0	3	5	Lost quarterfinals to Toronto.
1940-1941	5	2	3	0	10	12	Lost semifinals to Detroit.
1941-1942	3	1	2	0	7	5	Lost quarterfinals to Boston.
1943-1944	9	4	5	0	25	24	Lost Stanley Cup final to Montreal.
1945-1946	4	0	4	0	7	26	Lost semifinals to Montreal.
1952-1953	7	3	4	0	14	18	Lost semifinals to Montreal.
1958-1959	6	2	4	0	16	22	Lost semifinals to Montreal.
1959-1960	4	0	4	0	6	14	Lost semifinals to Montreal.
1960-1961	12	8	4	0	35	27	**Won Stanley Cup**.
1961-1962	12	6	6	0	34	31	Lost Stanley Cup final to Toronto.
1962-1963	6	2	4	0	19	25	Lost semifinals to Detroit.
1963-1964	7	3	4	0	18	24	Lost semifinals to Detroit.
1964-1965	14	7	7	0	35	37	Lost Stanley Cup final to Montreal.
1965-1966	6	2	4	0	10	22	Lost semifinals to Detroit.
1966-1967	6	2	4	0	14	18	Lost semifinals to Toronto.
1967-1968	11	5	6	0	28	34	Lost semifinals to Montreal.
1969-1970	8	4	4	0	26	28	Lost semifinals to Boston.
1970-1971	18	11	7	0	59	42	Lost Stanley Cup final to Montreal.
1971-1972	8	4	4	0	23	25	Lost semifinals to N.Y. Rangers.
1972-1973	16	10	6	0	60	53	Lost Stanley Cup final to Montreal.
1973-1974	11	6	5	0	30	35	Lost semifinals to Boston.
1974-1975	8	3	5	0	22	35	Lost quarterfinals to Buffalo.
1975-1976	4	0	4	0	3	13	Lost quarterfinals to Montreal.
1976-1977	2	0	2	0	3	7	Lost preliminary to Islanders.
1977-1978	4	0	4	0	9	19	Lost quarterfinals to Boston.
1978-1979	4	0	4	0	3	14	Lost quarterfinals to Islanders.

1979-1980	7	3	4	0	19	20	Lost quarterfinals to Buffalo.
1980-1981	3	0	3	0	9	15	Lost preliminary to Calgary.
1981-1982	15	8	7	0	50	51	Lost semifinals to Vancouver.
1982-1983	13	7	6	0	49	51	Lost semifinals to Edmonton.
1983-1984	5	2	3	0	14	18	Lost 1st round series to Minnesota.
1984-1985	15	9	6	0	81	81	Lost semifinals to Edmonton.
1985-1986	3	0	3	0	9	18	Lost 1st round series to Toronto.
1986-1987	4	0	4	0	6	15	Lost 1st round series to Detroit.
1987-1988	5	1	4	0	17	22	Lost 1st round series to St. Louis.
1988-1989	16	9	7	0	52	45	Lost semifinals to Calgary.
1989-1990	20	10	10	0	69	65	Lost semifinals to Edmonton.
1990-1991	6	2	4	0	16	23	Lost 1st round series to Minnesota.
1991-1992	18	12	6	0	65	48	Lost Stanley Cup final to Pittsburgh.
1992-1993	4	0	4	0	6	13	Lost 1st round series to St. Louis.
1993-1994	6	2	4	0	10	15	Lost 1st round series to Toronto.
1994-1995	16	9	7	0	45	39	Lost semifinals to Detroit.
1995-1995	10	6	4	0	30	28	Lost quarterfinals to Colorado.
TOTAL:	400	185	212	3	1140	1255	
AVERAGE:	8	4	4	0	22	25	

COACHING HISTORY: 1926-1927 Pete Muldoon 19-22-3-.466; 1927-1928 Barney Stanley 4-17-2-.217; 1927-1928 Hugh Lehman 3-17-1-.167; 1928-1929 Herb Gardiner 7-29-8-.250; 1929-1930 Tom Shaughnessy 10-8-3-.548; 1929-1930 Bill Tobin 11-10-2-.522; 1930-1931 Dick Irvin 24-17-3-.580; 1931-1933 Emil Iverson 26-28-17-.486; 1933-1934 Tommy Gorman 28-28-17-.500; 1934-1937 Clem Laughlin 61-63-20-.493; 1937-1939 Bill Stewart 22-35-12-.406; 1938-1944 Paul Thompson 104-127-41-.458; 1944-1947 John Gottselig 62-96-20-.404; 1947-1950 Charlie Conacher 56-83-22-.416; 1950-1952 Ebbie Goodfellow 30-91-19-.282; 1952-1954 Sid Abel 39-79-22-.357; 1954-1955 Frank Eddolls 13-40-17-.307; 1955-1956 Dick Irvin 19-39-12-.357; 1956-1957 Tommy Ivan 16-39-15-.336: 1957-1963 Rudy Pilous 172-168-80-.505; 1963-1977 Billy Reay 516-335-171-.589; 1976-1977 Bill White 16-24-6-.413; 1977-1979 Bob Pulford 61-65-34-.488; 1979-1980 Eddie Johnston 34-27-19-.544; 1980-1982 Keith Magnuson 49-57-26-.470; 1981-1982 Bob Pulford 12-14-2-.464; 1982-1985 Orval Tessier 99-93-21-.514; 1985-1987 Bob Pulford 84-77-26-.519; 1987-1988 Bob Murdoch 30-41-9-.431; 1988-1992 Mike Keenan 153-126-41-.542; 1992-1995 Darryl Sutter 110-80-26-.569; 1995-present Craig Hartsburg

CHICAGO BLITZ

Home City: Chicago, Illinois
Home Stadium: Soldier Field Capacity: 65,077 [1984]
Origin of Name: The name was chosen in a Name the Team Contest and chosen from over 20,000 entries.

Regular Season Record

Season	League	GP	W	L	T	PF	PA	Pct
1983	USFL	18	12	6	0	456	271	.667
1984	USFL	18	5	13	0	340	466	.278
TOTAL:	2years	36	17	19	0	796	737	
AVERAGE:		18	8	10	0	398	369	.472

Playoff Record

Season	GP	W	L	PF	PA	Result
1983	1	0	1	38	44	Lost semifinal game to Philadelphia.

COACHING HISTORY: 1983 George Allen 12-6-0-.667; 1984 Marv Levy 5-13-0-.278

CHICAGO BRUINS

Home City: Chicago, Illinois
Home Court: Chicago Stadium
Origin of Name: The team was named Bruins because it was owned by Chicago Bears owner George Halas and he wanted to create an association between the Bears and the Bruins.

			Regular Season Record		
Season	**League**	**GP**	**W**	**L**	**Pct**
1925-1926	ABL	30	9	21	.300
1926-1927	ABL	42	13	29	.310
1927-1928	ABL	49	13	36	.265
1928-1929	ABL	41	19	22	.463
1929-1930	ABL	54	29	25	.537
1930-1931	ABL	37	18	19	.486
TOTAL:	6 years	253	101	152	
AVERAGE:		42	17	25	.399

				Playoff Record		
Season	**GP**	**W**	**L**	**PF**	**PA**	**Result**
1930-1931	1	0	1	16	20	Lost playoff game to Ft. Wayne.

COACHING HISTORY: 1925-1929 George Halas 54-108-.333; 1929-1931 Not available

CHICAGO BRUINS

Home City: Chicago, Illinois
Home Court: Chicago Stadium
Origin of Name: Named after previous ABL team, as this team was also owned by George Halas.

			Regular Season Record					
Season	**League**	**GP**	**W**	**L**	**PPGF**	**PPGA**	**Pct**	**GB**
1939-1940	NBL	28	14	14	36.8	36.4	.500	1
1940-1941	NBL	24	11	13	38.0	37.2	.458	7
1941-1942	NBL	23	8	15	41.8	44.6	.348	11.5
TOTAL:	3 years	75	33	42				19.5
AVERAGE:		25	11	14	38.9	39.4	.440	6.5

COACHING HISTORY: 1939-1940 Sam Lifschulz 14-14-.500; 1940-1941 Frank Linskey 11-13-.458; 1941-1942 Jack Tierny 8-15-.348

CHICAGO BULLS

Home City: Chicago, Illinois
Home Court: Chicago Amphitheater (1966-1967) — Capacity: 11,002
Chicago Stadium (1967-1994) — Capacity: 18,676 [1994]
United Center (1994-present) — Capacity: 21,500 [1995]
Origin of Name: The name was chosen by team executives.

Regular Season Record

Season	League	GP	W	L	PPGF	PPGA	Pct	GB
1966-1967	NBA	81	33	48	113.2	116.9	.407	11
1967-1968	NBA	82	29	53	109.5	113.5	.354	27
1968-1969	NBA	82	33	49	104.7	106.9	.402	22
1969-1970	NBA	82	39	43	114.9	116.7	.476	9
1970-1971	NBA	82	51	31	110.6	105.4	.622	15
1971-1972	NBA	82	57	25	111.2	102.9	.695	6
1972-1973	NBA	82	51	31	104.1	100.6	.622	9
1973-1974	NBA	82	54	28	102.0	98.7	.659	5
1974-1975	NBA	82	47	35	98.1	95.0	.573	-
1975-1976	NBA	82	24	58	95.9	98.8	.293	14
1976-1977	NBA	82	44	38	98.9	98.0	.537	6
1977-1978	NBA	82	40	42	103.9	104.8	.488	8
1978-1979	NBA	82	31	51	104.7	108.7	.378	17
1979-1980	NBA	82	30	52	107.5	110.2	.366	19
1980-1981	NBA	82	45	37	109.0	107.0	.549	15
1981-1982	NBA	82	34	48	106.6	108.6	.415	21
1982-1983	NBA	82	28	54	111.0	115.9	.341	23
1983-1984	NBA	82	27	55	103.7	108.9	.329	23
1984-1985	NBA	82	38	44	108.7	109.6	.463	21
1985-1986	NBA	82	30	52	109.31	13.1	.366	27
1986-1987	NBA	82	40	42	104.8	103.9	.488	17
1987-1988	NBA	82	50	32	105.0	101.6	.610	4
1988-1989	NBA	82	47	35	106.4	105.0	.573	16
1989-1990	NBA	82	55	27	109.5	106.2	.671	4
1990-1991	NBA	82	61	21	110.0	101.0	.744	-
1991-1992	NBA	82	67	15	109.9	99.5	.817	-
1992-1993	NBA	82	57	25	105.2	98.9	.695	-
1993-1994	NBA	82	55	27	98.0	94.9	.671	2
1994-1995	NBA	82	47	35	101.5	96.7	.573	5
1995-1996	NBA	82	72	10	105.2	92.9	.878	-
TOTAL:	30 years	2459	1316	1143				346
AVERAGE:		82	44	38	106.1	104.7	.535	12

Playoff Record

Season	GP	W	L	PPGF	PPGA	Result
1966-1967	3	0	3	104.3	115.3	Lost Division semifinal to St. Louis.
1967-1968	5	1	4	99.4	106.6	Lost Division semifinal to Los Angeles.
1969-1970	5	1	4	110.8	118.4	Lost Division semifinal to Atlanta.
1970-1971	7	3	4	101.3	104.0	Lost Division semifinal to Los Angeles.
1971-1972	4	0	4	100.5	110.5	Lost Division semifinal to Los Angeles.
1972-1973	7	3	4	98.0	100.9	Lost Division semifinal to Los Angeles.
1973-1974	11	4	7	94.0	100.6	Lost Conference final to Milwaukee.
1974-1975	13	7	6	101.8	100.6	Lost Conference final to Golden State.
1976-1977	3	1	2	96.0	102.0	Lost 1st round series to Portland.
1980-1981	6	2	4	103.5	107.2	Lost Conference semifinal to Boston.
1984-1985	4	1	3	105.3	110.8	Lost 1st round series to Milwaukee.
1985-1986	3	0	3	113.0	126.7	Lost 1st round series to Boston.
1986-1987	3	0	3	98.0	106.0	Lost 1st round series to Boston.
1987-1988	10	4	6	94.8	98.9	Lost Conference semifinal to Detroit.
1988-1989	17	9	8	99.6	99.4	Lost Conference final to Detroit.

1989-1990	16	10	6	102.0	98.4	Lost Conference final to Detroit.
1990-1991	17	15	2	103.9	92.2	**Won NBA championship**.
1991-1992	22	15	7	100.4	94.2	**Won NBA championship**.
1992-1993	19	15	4	102.4	96.5	**Won NBA championship**.
1993-1994	10	6	4	93.6	90.8	Lost semifinal series to New York.
1994-1995	10	5	5	98.4	97.4	Lost semifinal series to Orlando.
1995-1996	18	15	3	97.4	86.7	**Won NBA championship**.
TOTAL:	213	117	96			
AVERAGE:	9	5	4	100.6	102.2	

COACHING HISTORY: 1966-1968 John Kerr 62-101-.380; 1968-1976 Dick Motta 356-300-.543; 1976-1978 Ed Badger 88-80-.524; 1978-1979 Larry Costello 20-36-.357; 1978-1979 Scott Robertson 11-15-.423; 1979-1982 Jerry Sloan 94-121-.437; 1981-1982 Phil Johnson 0-1-.000; 1981-1982 Rod Thorn 15-15-.500; 1982-1983 Paul Westhead 28-54-.341; 1983-1985 Kevin Loughery 65-99-.396; 1985-1986 Stan Albeck 30-52-.366; 1986-1989 Doug Collins 137-109-.557; 1990-present Phil Jackson

CHICAGO CARDINALS

(became St. Louis Cardinals)
(merged with Pittsburgh Steelers for the 1944 season)

Home City: Chicago, Illinois
Home Stadium: Comiskey Park (1922-1925) Capacity: 28,000
Normal Field (1926-1928) Capacity: 7,500
Comiskey Park (1929-1959) Capacity: 52,000
Origin of Name: The team was named Cardinals because of the color of their uniforms which were a faded maroon color.

Regular Season Record

Season	**League**	**GP**	**W**	**L**	**T**	**PF**	**PA**	**Pct**
1922	NFL	11	8	3	0	96	50	.727
1923	NFL	12	8	4	0	161	56	.667
1924	NFL	10	5	4	1	90	67	.550
1925	NFL	14	11	2	1	230	65	.821
1926	NFL	12	5	6	1	74	98	.458
1927	NFL	11	3	7	1	69	134	.318
1928	NFL	6	1	5	0	7	107	.167
1929	NFL	13	6	6	1	154	83	.500
1930	NFL	13	5	6	2	128	132	.462
1931	NFL	9	5	4	0	120	128	.556
1932	NFL	10	2	6	2	72	114	.300
1933	NFL	11	1	9	1	52	101	.136
1934	NFL	11	5	6	0	80	84	.455
1935	NFL	12	6	4	2	99	97	.583
1936	NFL	12	3	8	1	74	143	.292
1937	NFL	11	5	5	1	135	165	.500
1938	NFL	11	2	9	0	111	168	.182
1939	NFL	11	1	10	0	84	254	.091
1940	NFL	11	2	7	2	139	222	.273
1941	NFL	11	3	7	1	127	197	.318
1942	NFL	11	3	8	0	98	209	.273
1943	NFL	10	0	10	0	95	238	.000
1945	NFL	10	1	9	0	98	228	.100

1946	NFL	11	6	5	0	260	198	.545
1947	NFL	12	9	3	0	306	231	.750
1948	NFL	12	11	1	0	395	226	.917
1949	NFL	12	6	5	1	360	301	.542
1950	NFL	12	5	7	0	233	287	.417
1951	NFL	12	3	9	0	210	287	.250
1952	NFL	12	4	8	0	172	221	.333
1953	NFL	12	1	10	1	190	337	.125
1954	NFL	12	2	10	0	183	347	.167
1955	NFL	12	4	7	1	224	252	.375
1956	NFL	12	7	5	0	240	182	.583
1957	NFL	12	3	9	0	200	299	.250
1958	NFL	12	2	9	1	261	356	.208
1959	NFL	12	2	10	0	234	324	.167
TOTAL:	37 years	420	156	243	21	5861	6988	
AVERAGE:		11	4	7	0	158	189	.387

Playoff Record

Season	GP	W	L	PF	PA	Result
1947	1	1	0	28	21	**Won NFL championship**.
1948	1	0	1	0	7	Lost championship game to Philadelphia.
TOTAL:	2	1	1	28	28	
AVERAGE:	1	1	0	14	14	

COACHING HISTORY: 1922 John Driscoll 8-3-0-.727; 1923-1924 Arnold Horween 13-8-1-.614; 1925-1926 Norman Barry 16-8-2-.654; 1927 Guy Chamberlin 3-7-1-.318; 1928 Fred Gillies 1-5-0-.167; 1929 Dewey Scanlon 6-6-1-.500; 1930-1931 Ernie Nevers 10-9-2-.524; 1931 LeRoy Andrews 0-1-0-.000; 1932 Jack Chevigny 2-6-2-.300; 1933-1934 Paul Schissler 6-15-1-.295; 1935-1938 Milan Creighton 16-26-4-.391; 1939 Ernie Nevers 1-10-0-.091; 1940-1942 Jim Conzelman 8-22-3-.288; 1943 Phil Handler 0-10-0-.000; 1945 Phil Handler 1-9-0-.100; 1946-1948 Jim Conzelman 27-10-0-.730; 1949 Phil Handler, Buddy Parker 2-4-0-.333; 1949 Buddy Parker 4-1-1-.750; 1950-1951 Curly Lambeau 7-15-0-.318; 1951 Phil Handler, Cecil Isbell 1-1-0-.500; 1952 Joe Kuharich 4-8-0-.333; 1953-1954 Joe Stydahar 3-20-1-.146; 1955-1957 Ray Richards 14-21-1-.403; 1958-1959 Frank Ivy 4-19-1-.188

CHICAGO COLTS
(were Chicago White Stockings)
(became Chicago Orphans)

Home City: Chicago, Illinois
Home Field: West Side Grounds Capacity: 16,000
Origin of Name: The team was called the Colts after manager Cap Anson appeared in a stage play called the "Runaway Colt."

Regular Season Record

Season	League	GP	W	L	Pct	GB	R	OR
1894	NL	132	57	75	.432	34	1041	1066
1895	NL	130	72	58	.554	15	866	854
1896	NL	128	71	57	.555	18.5	815	799
1897	NL	132	59	73	.447	34	832	894
TOTAL:	4 years	522	259	263		101.5	3554	3613
AVERAGE:		131	65	66	.496	25.5	889	903

COACHING HISTORY: 1894-1897 Cap Anson 259-263-.496

CHICAGO COUGARS

Home City: Chicago, Illinois
Home Arena: International Amphitheater Capacity: 9,000 [1975]
Origin of Name:

Regular Season Record

Season	League	GP	W	L	T	GF	GA	Pts	Pct
1972-1973	WHA	78	26	50	2	245	295	54	.346
1973-1974	WHA	78	38	35	5	271	273	81	.519
1974-1975	WHA	78	30	47	1	261	312	61	.391
TOTAL:	3 years	234	94	132	8	777	880	196	
AVERAGE:		78	31	44	3	259	293	65	.417

Playoff Record

Season	GP	W	L	GF	GA	Result
1973-1974	18	8	10	67	90	Lost WHA final to Houston.

COACHING HISTORY: 1972-1973 Marcel Pronovost 26-50-2-.346; 1973-1975 Pat Stapleton 68-82-6-.455

CHICAGO CUBS
(were Chicago Orphans)

Home City: Chicago, Illinois
Home Field: West Side Grounds (1899-1915) Capacity: 16,000
Wrigley Field (1916-present) Capacity: 38,712 [1995]*
Origin of Name: The team was named the Cubs by sportswriters George Rice and Fred Hayner because the team had so many young players on it.

Regular Season Record

Season	League	GP	W	L	Pct	GB	R	OR
1899	NL	148	75	73	.507	26	812	763
1900	NL	140	65	75	.464	19	635	751
1901	NL	139	53	86	.381	37	578	698
1902	NL	137	68	69	.496	34	530	501
1903	NL	138	82	56	.594	8	695	594
1904	NL	153	93	60	.608	13	597	517
1905	NL	153	92	61	.601	13	667	442
1906	NL	152	116	36	.763	-	704	381
1907	NL	152	107	45	.704	-	570	390
1908	NL	154	99	55	.643	-	625	457
1909	NL	153	104	49	.680	6.5	632	376
1910	NL	154	104	50	.675	-	711	497
1911	NL	154	92	62	.597	7.5	757	607
1912	NL	150	91	59	.607	11.5	756	666
1913	NL	153	88	65	.575	13.5	720	640

*Originally Weeghman Park from 1914 to 1917 then Cubs Park from 1918 to 1925.

1914	NL	154	78	76	.506	16.5	605	638
1915	NL	153	73	80	.477	17.5	570	620
1916	NL	153	67	86	.438	26.5	520	541
1917	NL	154	74	80	.481	24	552	553
1918	NL	129	84	45	.651	-	538	391
1919	NL	140	75	65	.536	21	454	407
1920	NL	154	75	79	.487	18	619	635
1921	NL	153	64	89	.418	30	668	773
1922	NL	154	80	74	.519	13	771	808
1923	NL	154	83	71	.539	12.5	756	704
1924	NL	153	81	72	.529	12	698	699
1925	NL	154	68	86	.442	27.5	723	773
1926	NL	154	82	72	.532	7	682	602
1927	NL	153	85	68	.556	8.5	750	661
1928	NL	154	91	63	.591	4	714	615
1929	NL	152	98	54	.645	-	982	758
1930	NL	154	90	64	.584	2	998	870
1931	NL	154	84	70	.545	17	828	710
1932	NL	154	90	64	.584	-	720	633
1933	NL	154	86	68	.558	6	646	536
1934	NL	151	86	65	.570	8	705	639
1935	NL	154	100	54	.649	-	847	597
1936	NL	154	87	67	.565	5	755	603
1937	NL	154	93	61	.604	3	811	682
1938	NL	152	89	63	.586	-	713	598
1939	NL	154	84	70	.545	13	724	678
1940	NL	154	75	79	.487	25.5	681	636
1941	NL	154	70	84	.455	30	666	670
1942	NL	154	68	86	.442	38	591	665
1943	NL	153	74	79	.484	30.5	632	600
1944	NL	154	75	79	.487	30	702	669
1945	NL	154	98	56	.636	-	735	532
1946	NL	153	82	71	.536	14.5	626	581
1947	NL	154	69	85	.448	25	567	722
1948	NL	154	64	90	.416	27.5	597	706
1949	NL	154	61	93	.396	36	593	773
1950	NL	153	64	89	.418	26.5	643	772
1951	NL	154	62	92	.403	34.5	614	750
1952	NL	154	77	77	.500	19.5	628	631
1953	NL	154	65	89	.422	40	633	835
1954	NL	154	64	90	.416	33	700	766
1955	NL	153	72	81	.471	26	626	713
1956	NL	154	60	94	.390	33	597	708
1957	NL	154	62	92	.403	33	628	722
1958	NL	154	72	82	.468	20	709	725
1959	NL	154	74	80	.481	13	673	688
1960	NL	154	60	94	.390	35	634	776
1961	NL	154	64	90	.416	29	689	800
1962	NL	162	59	103	.364	42.5	632	827
1963	NL	162	82	80	.506	17	570	578
1964	NL	162	76	86	.469	17	649	724
1965	NL	162	72	90	.444	25	635	723
1966	NL	162	59	103	.364	36	644	809
1967	NL	161	87	74	.540	14	702	624

1968	NL	162	84	78	.519	13	612	611
1969	NL	162	92	70	.568	8	720	611
1970	NL	162	84	78	.519	5	806	679
1971	NL	162	83	79	.512	14	637	648
1972	NL	155	85	70	.548	11	685	567
1973	NL	161	77	84	.478	5	614	655
1974	NL	162	66	96	.407	22	669	826
1975	NL	162	75	87	.463	17.5	712	827
1976	NL	162	75	87	.463	26	611	728
1977	NL	162	81	81	.500	20	692	739
1978	NL	161	79	83	.488	11	664	724
1979	NL	162	80	82	.494	18	706	707
1980	NL	162	64	98	.395	27	614	728
1981	NL	103	38	65	.369	NA	370	483
1982	NL	162	73	89	.451	19	676	709
1983	NL	162	71	91	.438	19	701	719
1984	NL	161	96	65	.596	-	762	658
1985	NL	161	77	84	.478	23.5	686	729
1986	NL	160	70	90	.438	37	680	781
1987	NL	161	76	85	.472	18.5	720	801
1988	NL	162	77	85	.475	24	660	694
1989	NL	162	93	69	.574	-	702	623
1990	NL	162	77	85	.475	18	690	774
1991	NL	160	77	83	.481	20	695	734
1992	NL	162	78	84	.481	18	593	624
1993	NL	162	84	78	.519	13	738	739
1994	NL	113	49	64	.434	16.5	500	549
1995	NL	144	73	71	.507	12	693	671
TOTAL:	97 years	14932	7576	7356		1668	64942	64067
AVERAGE:		154	78	76	.507	17	670	660

Playoff Record

Season	GP	W	L	T	R	OR	Result
1906	6	2	4	0	18	22	Lost World Series to White Sox.
1907	5	4	0	1	19	6	**Won World Series**.
1908	5	4	1	0	24	15	**Won World Series**.
1910	5	1	4	0	15	35	Lost World Series to Philadelphia.
1918	6	2	4	0	10	9	Lost World Series to Boston.
1929	5	1	4	0	17	26	Lost World Series to Philadelphia.
1932	4	0	4	0	19	37	Lost World Series to New York.
1935	6	2	4	0	18	21	Lost World Series to Detroit.
1938	4	0	4	0	9	22	Lost World Series to New York.
1945	7	3	4	0	29	32	Lost World Series to Detroit.
1984	5	2	3	0	26	22	Lost NLCS to San Diego
1989	5	1	4	0	22	30	Lost NLCS to San Francisco.
TOTAL:	63	22	40	1	226	277	
AVERAGE:	5	2	3	0	19	23	

COACHING HISTORY: 1899 Tom Burns 75-73-.507; 1900-1901 Tom Loftus 118-161-.423; 1902-1905 Frank Selee 295-223-.569; 1905-1912 Frank Chance 753-379-.665; 1913 Johnny Evers 88-65-.575; 1914 Hank O'Day 78-76-.506; 1915 Roger Bresnahan 73-80-.477; 1916 Joe Tinker 67-86-.438; 1917-1920 Fred Mitchell 308-269-.534; 1921 Johnny Evers 42-56-.429; 1921-1925 Bill Killefer 299-292-.506; 1925 Walter Maranville 23-30-.434; 1925 George Gibson 12-14-.462;

1926-1930 Joe McCarthy 442-321-.579; 1930-1932 Rogers Hornsby 141-114-.553; 1932-1938 Charlie Grimm 525-371-.586; 1938-1940 Charles Hartnett 203-176-.536; 1941-1944 Jim Wilson 213-258-.452; 1944 Roy Johnson 0-1-.000; 1944-1949 Charlie Grimm 406-402-.502; 1949-1951 Frank Frisch 141-196-.418; 1951-1953 Phil Cavarretta 169-213-.442; 1954-1956 Stan Hack 196-265-.425; 1957-1959 Bob Scheffing 208-254-.450; 1960 Charlie Grimm 6-11-.353; 1960 Lou Boudreau 54-83-.394; 1961 Avitus Himsl 10-21-.323; 1961 Harry Craft 7-9-.438; 1961-1962 Elvin Tappe 46-69-.400; 1961-1962 Lou Klein 17-25-.405; 1962 Charlie Metro 43-69-.384; 1963-1965 Bob Kennedy 182-198-.479; 1965 Lou Klein 48-58-.453; 1966-1972 Leo Durocher 535-526-.504; 1972-1974 Walter Lockman 157-162-.492; 1974-1976 Jim Marshall 175-218-.445; 1977-1979 Herman Franks 237-241-.496; 1979-1981 Joey Amalfitano 66-115-.365; 1980 Preston Gomez 38-52-.422; 1982-1983 Lee Elia 127-158-.446; 1983 Charlie Fox 17-22-.436; 1984-1986 Jim Frey 196-182-.519; 1986 John Vukovich 1-1-.500; 1986-1987 Gene Michael 114-124-.479; 1987 Frank Lucchesi 8-17-.320; 1988-1991 Don Zimmer 265-258-.507; 1991 Joe Altobelli 1-1-.500; 1991 Jim Essian 58-63-.479; 1992 -1993 Jim Lefevre 162-162-.500; 1994 Tom Trebelhorn 49-64-.434; 1995-present Jim Riggleman

CHICAGO FIRE

Home City: Chicago, Illinois
Home Stadium: Soldier Field — Capacity: 55,049 [1974]
Origin of Name: The team was named by owner Tom Origer and suggested by the infamous Great Chicago Fire of 1871.

Regular Season Record

Season	League	GP	W	L	T	PF	PA	Pct
1974	WFL	19	7	12	0	446	600	.368

COACHING HISTORY: Jim Spavital 7-12-0-.368

CHICAGO HORNETS
(were Chicago Rockets)

Home City: Chicago, Illinois
Home Stadium: Soldier Field
Origin of Name: Named by team executives, James C. Thompson, Lee A. Freeman and Irvin Rooks.

Regular Season Record

Season	League	GP	W	L	T	PF	PA	Pct
1949	AAFC	12	4	8	0	179	268	.333

COACHING HISTORY: Ray Flaherty 4-8-0-.333

CHICAGO MUSTANGS

Home City: Chicago, Illinois
Home Field: Comiskey Park — Capacity: 46,550 [1967]
Origin of Name: The name was chosen to reflect a "spirited" team and was represented by Cagliari of Italy.

Regular Season Record

Season	League	GP	W	L	T	GF	GA	BP	Pts	Pct
1967	USA	12	3	2	7	20	14	NA	13	.542
1968	NASL	32	13	10	9	68	68	59	164	.569
TOTAL:	2 years	44	16	12	16	88	82	59	177	
AVERAGE:		22	8	6	8	44	41	30	89	

COACHING HISTORY: 1967 Manlio Scopigno 3-2-7-.542; 1968 George Meyer 13-10-9-.569

CHICAGO ORPHANS
(were Chicago Colts)
(became Chicago Cubs)

Home City: Chicago, Illinois
Home Field: West Side Grounds — Capacity: 16,000
Origin of Name: The team was named Orphans after manager Cap Anson left the club.

Regular Season Record

Season	League	GP	W	L	Pct	GB	R	OR
1898	NL	150	85	65	.567	17.5	828	679

COACHING HISTORY: Tom Burns 85-65-.567

CHICAGO PACKERS
(became Chicago Zephyrs)

Home City: Chicago, Illinois
Home Court: The Amphitheater — Capacity: 8,300
Origin of Name: The name was chosen by club executives.

Regular Season Record

Season	League	GP	W	L	PPGF	PPGA	Pct	GB
1961-1962	NBA	80	18	62	110.9	119.4	.225	36

COACHING HISTORY: Jim Pollard 18-62-.225

CHICAGO PIRATES

Home City: Chicago, Illinois
Home Field: South Side Park II
Origin of Name:

Regular Season Record

Season	League	GP	W	L	Pct	GB	R	OR
1890	PL	137	75	62	.547	10	886	770

COACHING HISTORY: Charlie Comiskey 75-62-.547

CHICAGO ROCKETS
(became Chicago Hornets)

Home City: Chicago, Illinois
Home Stadium: Soldier Field
Origin of Name: The name was chosen by team executives.

Regular Season Record

Season	League	GP	W	L	T	PF	PA	Pct
1946	AAFC	14	5	6	3	263	315	.464
1947	AAFC	14	1	13	0	263	425	.071
1948	AAFC	14	1	13	0	202	439	.071
TOTAL:	3 years	42	7	32	3	728	1179	
AVERAGE:		14	2	11	1	243	393	.202

COACHING HISTORY: 1946 Dick Haley 1-1-1-.500; 1946 Bob Dove & Ned Mathews & Willie Wilkin 2-2-1-.500; 1946 Pat Boland 2-3-1-.417; 1947 Jim Crowley 0-10-0-.000; 1947 Hamp Pool 1-3-0-.250; 1948 Ed McKeever 1-13-0-.071

CHICAGO SPURS

Home City: Chicago, Illinois
Home Field: Soldier Field
Origin of Name:

Regular Season Record

Season	League	GP	W	L	T	GF	GA	Pts	Pct
1967	NPSL	32	10	11	11	50	55	142	.493

COACHING HISTORY: Alan Rogers 10-11-11-.493

CHICAGO STAGS

Home City: Chicago, Illinois
Home Court: Chicago Stadium Capacity: 19,000
Origin of Name: The name was chosen by team executives.

Regular Season Record

Season	League	GP	W	L	PPGF	PPGA	Pct	GB
1946-1947	BAA	61	39	22	77.0	73.3	.639	-
1947-1948	BAA	48	28	20	75.8	73.2	.583	1
1948-1949	BAA	60	38	22	84.0	80.0	.633	7
1949-1950	NBA	68	40	28	78.7	77.1	.588	11
TOTAL:	4 years	237	145	92				19
AVERAGE:		59	36	23	78.9	75.9	.612	5

Playoff Record

Season	GP	W	L	PPGF	PPGA	Result
1946-1947	11	5	6	70.8	70.6	Lost 2nd round series to Philadelphia.
1947-1948	7	3	4	74.6	76.3	Lost 3rd round series to Baltimore.

1948-1949	2	0	2	81.0	92.5	Lost 1st round series to Minneapolis.
1949-1950	3	0	3	70.3	82.0	Lost 2nd round series to Minneapolis.
TOTAL:	23	8	15			
AVERAGE:	6	2	4	74.2	80.4	

COACHING HISTORY: 1946-1949 Ole Olsen 95-63-.601; 1948-1950 Phil Brownstein 50-29-.633

CHICAGO STING

Home City: Chicago, Illinois
Home Field: Soldier Field (1977,1979-1980) Capacity: 54,000 [1980]
Wrigley Field (1978,1980,1982-1984) Capacity: 37,741 [1980]
Comiskey Park (1981,1984) Capacity: 44,492
Origin of Name: The team may have been named after the 1973 movie *The Sting* which was set in 1930's era Chicago. Team owner Lee B. Stern named the team.

Regular Season Record

Season	**League**	**GP**	**W**	**L**	**GF**	**GA**	**BP**	**Pts**	**Pct**
1975	NASL	22	12	10	39	33	34	106	.535
1976	NASL	24	15	9	52	32	42	132	.611
1977	NASL	26	10	16	31	43	28	88	.376
1978	NASL	30	12	18	57	64	51	123	.456
1979	NASL	30	16	14	70	62	63	159	.589
1980	NASL	32	21	11	80	50	61	187	.649
1981	NASL	32	23	9	84	50	63	195	.433
1982	NASL	32	13	19	56	67	53	129	.287
1983	NASL	30	15	15	66	73	57	147	.327
1984	NASL	24	13	11	50	49	44	120	.333
TOTAL:	10 years	282	150	132	585	523	496	1386	
AVERAGE:		28	15	13	59	52	50	139	.427

Playoff Record

Season	**GP**	**W**	**L**	**GF**	**GA**	**Result**
1976	1	0	1	2	3	Lost 1st round series to Toronto.
1978	1	0	1	1	3	Lost 1st round series to Tampa.
1979	4	2	2	3	3	Lost 2nd round series to San Diego.
1980	3	1	2	5	6	Lost 1st round series to San Diego.
1981	10	7	3	23	16	**Won championship of NASL.**
1983	3	1	2	4	11	Lost 1st round series to Golden Bay.
1984	5	4	1	12	8	**Won championship of NASL.**
TOTAL:	27	15	12	50	50	
AVERAGE:	4	2	2	7	7	

COACHING HISTORY: 1975-1977 Bill Foulkes 26-29; 1977-1984 Willy Roy 117-89; 1978 Malcolm Musgrove 2-14

CHICAGO STUDEBAKERS

Home City: Chicago, Illinois
Home Court:
Origin of Name: The team was sponsored by the local Studebaker plant as the plant workers were exempt from war duty and many former stars got jobs at the plant.

Regular Season Record

Season	League	GP	W	L	PPGF	PPGA	Pct	GB
1942-1943	NBL	23	8	15	48.2	50.8	.348	9

COACHING HISTORY: John Jordan 8-15-.348

CHICAGO WHALES

Home City: Chicago, Illinois
Home Field: Weeghman Park — Capacity: 14,000 [1914]
Origin of Name: The name was chosen in a Name the Team Contest.

Regular Season Record

Season	League	GP	W	L	Pct	GB	R	OR
1914	FL	154	87	67	.565	1.5	621	517
1915	FL	152	86	66	.566	-	641	538
TOTAL:	2 years	306	173	133		1.5	1262	1055
AVERAGE:		153	87	66	.565	.5	631	528

COACHING HISTORY: 1914-1915 Joe Tinker 173-133-.565

CHICAGO WHITE SOX

Home City: Chicago, Illinois
Home Field: Southside Park 3 (1901-1910) — Capacity: 15,000
Comiskey Park I* (1910-1990) — Capacity: 43,931 [1989]
Comiskey Park II (1991-present) — Capacity: 44,321 [1995]
Origin of Name: The team was named after the National League's Chicago White Stockings and the name was then abbreviated to White Sox.

Regular Season Record

Season	League	GP	W	L	Pct	GB	R	OR
1901	AL	136	83	53	.610	-	819	632
1902	AL	134	74	60	.552	8	675	602
1903	AL	137	60	77	.438	30.5	516	613
1904	AL	154	89	65	.578	6	600	482
1905	AL	152	92	60	.605	2	613	443
1906	AL	151	93	58	.616	-	570	460
1907	AL	151	87	64	.576	5.5	584	475
1908	AL	152	88	64	.579	1.5	535	480
1909	AL	152	78	74	.513	20	494	465
1910	AL	153	68	85	.444	35.5	456	495
1911	AL	151	77	74	.510	24	717	627
1912	AL	154	78	76	.506	28	640	647
1913	AL	152	78	74	.513	17.5	486	492
1914	AL	154	70	84	.455	30	487	568
1915	AL	154	93	61	.604	9.5	717	509

*Originally White Sox Park from 1910 to 1912 then Comiskey Park from 1913 to 1961 then White Sox Park again from 1962 to 1975 then Comiskey Park from 1976 to 1990.

1916	AL	154	89	65	.578	2	601	500
1917	AL	154	100	54	.649	-	657	464
1918	AL	124	57	67	.460	17	457	443
1919	AL	140	88	52	.629	-	668	534
1920	AL	154	96	58	.623	2	794	666
1921	AL	154	62	92	.403	36.5	683	858
1922	AL	154	77	77	.500	17	691	691
1923	AL	154	69	85	.448	30	692	741
1924	AL	153	66	87	.431	25.5	793	858
1925	AL	154	79	75	.513	18.5	811	771
1926	AL	153	81	72	.529	9.5	730	665
1927	AL	153	70	83	.458	39.5	662	708
1928	AL	154	72	82	.468	29	656	725
1929	AL	152	59	93	.388	46	627	792
1930	AL	154	62	92	.403	40	729	884
1931	AL	153	56	97	.366	51.5	704	939
1932	AL	151	49	102	.325	56.5	667	897
1933	AL	150	67	83	.447	31	683	814
1934	AL	152	53	99	.349	47	704	946
1935	AL	152	74	78	.487	19.5	738	750
1936	AL	151	81	70	.536	20	920	873
1937	AL	154	86	68	.558	16	780	730
1938	AL	148	65	83	.439	32	709	752
1939	AL	154	85	69	.552	22.5	755	737
1940	AL	154	82	72	.532	8	735	672
1941	AL	154	77	77	.500	24	638	649
1942	AL	148	66	82	.446	34	538	609
1943	AL	154	82	72	.532	16	573	594
1944	AL	154	71	83	.461	18	543	662
1945	AL	149	71	78	.477	15	596	633
1946	AL	154	74	80	.481	30	562	595
1947	AL	154	70	84	.455	27	553	661
1948	AL	152	51	101	.336	44.5	559	814
1949	AL	154	63	91	.409	34	648	737
1950	AL	154	60	94	.390	38	625	749
1951	AL	154	81	73	.526	17	714	644
1952	AL	154	81	73	.526	14	610	568
1953	AL	154	89	65	.578	11.5	716	592
1954	AL	154	94	60	.610	17	711	521
1955	AL	154	91	63	.591	5	725	557
1956	AL	154	85	69	.552	12	776	634
1957	AL	154	90	64	.584	8	707	566
1958	AL	154	82	72	.532	10	634	615
1959	AL	154	94	60	.610	-	669	588
1960	AL	154	87	67	.565	10	741	617
1961	AL	162	86	76	.531	23	765	726
1962	AL	162	85	77	.525	11	707	658
1963	AL	162	94	68	.580	10.5	683	544
1964	AL	162	98	64	.605	1	642	501
1965	AL	162	95	67	.586	7	647	555
1966	AL	162	83	79	.512	15	574	517
1967	AL	162	89	73	.549	3	531	491
1968	AL	162	67	95	.414	36	463	527
1969	AL	162	68	94	.420	29	625	723

1970	AL	162	56	106	.346	42	633	822
1971	AL	162	79	83	.488	22.5	617	597
1972	AL	154	87	67	.565	5.5	566	535
1973	AL	162	77	85	.475	17	652	705
1974	AL	160	80	80	.500	9	684	721
1975	AL	161	75	86	.466	22.5	655	703
1976	AL	161	64	97	.398	25.5	586	745
1977	AL	162	90	72	.556	12	844	771
1978	AL	161	71	90	.441	20.5	634	731
1979	AL	160	73	87	.456	14	730	748
1980	AL	160	70	90	.438	26	587	722
1981	AL	106	54	52	.509	NA	476	423
1982	AL	162	87	75	.537	6	786	710
1983	AL	162	99	63	.611	-	800	650
1984	AL	162	74	88	.457	10	679	736
1985	AL	162	85	77	.525	6	736	720
1986	AL	162	72	90	.444	20	644	699
1987	AL	162	77	85	.475	8	748	746
1988	AL	161	71	90	.441	32.5	631	757
1989	AL	161	69	92	.429	29.5	693	750
1990	AL	162	94	68	.580	9	682	633
1991	AL	162	87	75	.537	8	758	681
1992	AL	162	86	76	.531	10	738	690
1993	AL	162	94	68	.580	-	776	664
1994	AL	113	67	46	.593	-	633	498
1995	AL	144	68	76	.472	32	755	758
TOTAL:	95 years	14612	7363	7249		1742.5	62753	62162
AVERAGE:		154	78	76	.504	18.5	661	654

Playoff Record

Season	**GP**	**W**	**L**	**R**	**OR**	**Result**
1906	6	4	2	22	18	**Won World Series.**
1917	6	4	2	21	17	**Won World Series.**
1919	8	3	5	20	35	Lost World Series to Cincinnati.
1959	6	2	4	23	21	Lost World Series to Los Angeles.
1983	4	1	3	3	19	Lost ALCS to Baltimore.
1993	6	2	4	23	26	Lost ALCS to Toronto.
TOTAL:	36	16	20	112	136	
AVERAGE:	6	3	3	19	23	

COACHING HISTORY: 1901-1902 Clark Griffith 157-113-.581; 1903-1904 James Callahan 82-[illegible]5-.463; 1904-1908 Fielder Jones 427-293-.593; 1909 Billy Sullivan 78-74-.513; 1910-1911 Hugh Duffy 145-159-.477; 1912-1914 James Callahan 226-234-.491; 1915-1918 Clarence Rowland 339-247-.578; 1919-1923 William Gleason 392-364-.519: 1924 Johnny Evers 66-87-.431; 1925-1926 Eddie Collins 160-147-.521; 1927-1928 Ray Schalk 102-125-.449; 1928-1929 Lena Blackburne 99-133-.427; 1930-1931 Owen Bush 118-189-.384; 1932-1934 Lew Fonseca 120-198-.377; 1934-1946 Jimmy Dykes 899-938-.489; 1946-1948 Ted Lyons 185-245-.430; 1949-1950 Jack Onslow 71-113-.386; 1950 John Corriden 52-72-.419; 1951-1954 Paul Richards 342-265-.563; 1954-1956 Marty Marion 179-138-.565; 1957-1965 Al Lopez 811-615-.569; 1966-1968 Eddie Stanky 206-197-.511; 1968 Les Moss 0-2-.000 1968-1969 Al Lopez 41-57-.418; 1969-1970 Don Gutteridge 109-172-.388; 1970 Bill Adair 4-6-.400; 1970-1975 Charles Tanner 401-414-.492; 1976 Paul Richards 64-97-.398; 1977-1978 Bob Lemon 124-112-.525; 1978 Larry Doby 37-50-.425; 1979 Don Kessinger 46-60-.434; 1979-1986 Tony LaRussa 522-510-.506; 1986 Doug Rader

1-1-.500; 1986-1988 Jim Fregosi 193-226-.461; 1989-1991 Jeff Torborg 250-235-.515; 1992-1995 Gene Lamont 258-210-.551; 1995-present Terry Bevington

CHICAGO WHITE STOCKINGS
(became Chicago Colts)

Home City: Chicago, Illinois
Home Field: State Street Grounds (1876-1877)
Lakefront Park (1878-1884)
West Side Park (1885-1891) Capacity: 16,000
Brotherhood Park (1891-1893)
Origin of Name: The team originally wore white stockings.

Regular Season Record

Season	League	GP	W	L	Pct	GB	R	OR
1876	NL	66	52	14	.788	-	624	257
1877	NL	59	26	33	.441	15.5	366	375
1878	NL	60	30	30	.500	11	371	331
1879	NL	79	46	33	.582	10.5	437	411
1880	NL	84	67	17	.798	-	538	317
1881	NL	84	56	28	.667	-	550	379
1882	NL	84	55	29	.655	-	604	353
1883	NL	98	59	39	.602	4	679	540
1884	NL	112	62	50	.554	22	834	647
1885	NL	112	87	25	.777	-	834	470
1886	NL	124	90	34	.726	-	900	555
1887	NL	121	71	50	.587	6.5	813	716
1888	NL	135	77	58	.570	9	734	659
1889	NL	132	67	65	.508	19	867	814
1890	NL	137	84	53	.613	6	847	692
1891	NL	135	82	53	.607	3.5	832	730
1892	NL	146	70	76	.479	30	635	735
1893	NL	127	56	71	.441	29	829	874
TOTAL:	18years	1895	1137	758		166	12294	9855
AVERAGE:		105	63	42	.600	9	683	548

COACHING HISTORY: 1876-1877 Al Spalding 78-47-.624; 1878 Bob Ferguson 30-30-.500; 1879-1893 Cap Anson 1029-681-.602

Playoff Record

Season	GP	W	L	T	R	OR	Result
1885	7	3	3	1	38	36	**Co-Winner of World Series.**
1886	6	2	4	0	28	38	Lost World Series.
TOTAL:	13	5	7	1	66	74	
AVERAGE:	7	3	4	0	33	37	

CHICAGO WIND
(were Chicago Fire)

Home City: Chicago, Illinois
Home Stadium: Soldier Field Capacity: 55,701 [1975]
Origin of Name: The name was picked because of Chicago's nickname of "The Windy City."

Regular Season Record

Season	League	GP	W	L	T	PF	PA	Pct
1975	WFL	5	1	4	0	67	124	.200

COACHING HISTORY: Abe Gibron 1-4-0-.200

CHICAGO ZEPHYRS
(were Chicago Stags)
(became Baltimore Bullets)

Home City: Chicago, Illinois
Home Court: Chicago Coliseum Capacity: 7,100
Origin of Name: The name was chosen in a Name the Team Contest and meant to reflect on Chicago's reputation as the "Windy City". Zephyr is any soft gentle wind.

Regular Season Record

Season	League	GP	W	L	PPGF	PPGA	Pct	GB
1962-1963	NBA	80	25	55	109.9	113.9	.313	28

COACHING HISTORY: Jack McMahon 12-26-.316; Bob Leonard 13-29-.310

CINCINNATI BENGALS

Home City: Cincinnati, Ohio
Home Stadium: Nippert Stadium (1968-1969) Capacity: 26,500
Riverfront Stadium (1970-present) Capacity: 60,389 [1995]
Origin of Name: Paul Brown named the team after previous minor-pro football teams that had played in Cincinnati.

Regular Season Record

Season	League	GP	W	L	T	PF	PA	Pct
1968	NFL	14	3	11	0	215	329	.214
1969	NFL	14	4	9	1	280	367	.321
1970	NFL	14	8	6	0	312	255	.571
1971	NFL	14	4	10	0	284	265	.286
1972	NFL	14	8	6	0	299	229	.571
1973	NFL	14	10	4	0	286	231	.714
1974	NFL	14	7	7	0	283	259	.500
1975	NFL	14	11	3	0	340	246	.786
1976	NFL	14	10	4	0	335	210	.714
1977	NFL	14	8	6	0	238	235	.571
1978	NFL	16	4	12	0	252	284	.250
1979	NFL	16	4	12	0	337	421	.250
1980	NFL	16	6	10	0	244	312	.375
1981	NFL	16	12	4	0	421	304	.750
1982	NFL	9	7	2	0	232	177	.778
1983	NFL	16	7	9	0	346	302	.438
1984	NFL	16	8	8	0	339	339	.500
1985	NFL	16	7	9	0	441	437	.438
1986	NFL	16	10	6	0	409	394	.625
1987	NFL	15	4	11	0	285	370	.267

1988	NFL	16	12	4	0	448	329	.750
1989	NFL	16	8	8	0	404	285	.500
1990	NFL	16	9	7	0	360	352	.563
1991	NFL	16	3	13	0	263	435	.188
1992	NFL	16	5	11	0	274	364	.313
1993	NFL	16	3	13	0	187	319	.188
1994	NFL	16	3	13	0	276	406	.188
1995	NFL	16	7	9	0	349	374	.438
TOTAL:	28 years	420	192	227	1	8739	8830	
AVERAGE:		15	7	8	0	312	315	.458

Playoff Record

Season	**GP**	**W**	**L**	**PF**	**PA**	**Result**
1970	1	0	1	0	17	Lost Divisional playoff to Baltimore.
1973	1	0	1	16	34	Lost Divisional playoff to Miami.
1975	1	0	1	28	31	Lost Divisional playoff to Oakland.
1981	3	2	1	76	54	Lost Super Bowl to San Francisco.
1982	1	0	1	44	17	Lost 1st round series to N.Y. Jets.
1988	3	2	1	58	43	Lost Super Bowl to San Francisco.
1990	2	1	1	51	34	Lost semifinal round to L.A. Raiders.
TOTAL:	12	5	7	273	230	
AVERAGE:	2	1	1	39	33	

COACHING HISTORY: 1968-1975 Paul Brown 55-56-1-.496; 1976-1978 Bill Johnson 18-15-0-.545; 1978-1979 Homer Rice 8-19-0-.296; 1980-1983 Forrest Gregg 32-25-0-.561; 1984-1991 Sam Wyche 61-66-.480; 1992-present David Shula

CINCINNATI COMELLOS

(merged with Richmond in 1938 and then disbanded)

Home City: Cincinnati, Ohio
Home Court:
Origin of Name:

Regular Season Record

Season	**League**	**GP**	**W**	**L**	**PPGF**	**PPGA**	**Pct**	**GB**
1937-1938	NBL	7	2	5	29.1	37.6	.286	6.5

COACHING HISTORY: Bob McConachie, John Wiethe

CINCINNATI KELLY'S KILLERS

(merged with Milwaukee in 1891)

Home City: Cincinnati Ohio
Home Field: Pendleton Grounds
Origin of Name: The team was coached by Michael Kelly.

Regular Season Record

Season	**League**	**GP**	**W**	**L**	**Pct**	**GB**	**R**	**OR**
1891	AA	136	64	72	.471	29.5	776	799

COACHING HISTORY: Michael Kelly 43-57-.430; Charlie Cushman 21-15-.583

CINCINNATI OUTLAW REDS

Home City: Cincinnati, Ohio
Home Field: Bank Street Grounds
Origin of Name: The team played in the "outlaw" Union Association but also wanted to create an association with the National League Reds.

Regular Season Record

Season	League	GP	W	L	Pct	GB	R	OR
1884	UA	105	69	36	.657	21	703	466

COACHING HISTORY: Dan O'Leary 33-29-.532; Sam Crane 36-7-.837

CINCINNATI RED LEGS

(were Cincinnati Reds)
(became Cincinnati Reds)

Home City: Cincinnati, Ohio
Home Field: Crosley Field Capacity: 30,000 [1948]
Origin of Name: The Cincinnati Reds briefly changed their name to Red Legs during the communist scare of the 1940's when it was not good form for anything to be called Reds.

Regular Season Record

Season	League	GP	W	L	Pct	GB	R	OR
1944	NL	154	89	65	.578	16	573	537
1945	NL	154	61	93	.396	37	536	694
TOTAL:	2 years	308	150	158		53	1109	1231
AVERAGE:		154	75	79	.487	26.5	555	616

COACHING HISTORY:1944-1945 Bill McKechnie 150-158-.487

CINCINNATI REDS

Home City: Cincinnati, Ohio
Home Field: Avenue Grounds (1876-1879)
Bank Street Grounds (1880)
Origin of Name: The name is short for Red Stockings.

Regular Season Record

Season	League	GP	W	L	Pct	GB	R	OR
1876	NL	65	9	56	.138	42.5	238	579
1877	NL	57	15	42	.263	25.5	291	485
1878	NL	60	37	23	.617	4	333	281
1879	NL	80	43	37	.538	14	485	464
1880	NL	80	21	59	.263	44	296	472
TOTAL:	5 years	342	125	217		130	1643	2281
AVERAGE:		68	25	43	.365	26	329	456

COACHING HISTORY: 1876 Charlie Gould 9-56-.138; 1877 Lip Pike 3-11-.214; 1877 Bob Addy 12-31-.279; 1878-1879 Cal McVey 72-52-.581; 1879 Deacon White 8-8-.500; 1880 John Clapp 21-59-.263

CINCINNATI REDS

(temporarily changed name to Red Legs in 1944 and 1945)

Home City: Cincinnati, Ohio
Home Field: Redland Field I *(1890-1901)
Palace of the Fans (1902-1911)
Crosley Field * (1912-1970) Capacity: 29,603 [1958]
Riverfront Stadium (1970-present) Capacity: 52,952 [1995]
Origin of Name: The name is short for Red Stockings.

Regular Season Record

Season	League	GP	W	L	Pct	GB	R	OR
1890	NL	132	77	55	.583	10.5	753	633
1891	NL	137	56	81	.409	30.5	646	790
1892	NL	150	82	68	.547	20	766	731
1893	NL	128	65	63	.508	20.5	759	814
1894	NL	130	55	75	.423	35	910	1085
1895	NL	130	66	64	.508	21	903	854
1896	NL	127	77	50	.606	12	783	620
1897	NL	132	76	56	.576	17	763	705
1898	NL	152	92	60	.605	11.5	831	740
1899	NL	150	83	67	.553	19	856	770
1900	NL	139	62	77	.446	21.5	703	745
1901	NL	139	52	87	.374	38	561	818
1902	NL	140	70	70	.500	33.5	632	566
1903	NL	139	74	65	.532	16.5	764	749
1904	NL	153	88	65	.575	18	692	547
1905	NL	153	79	74	.516	26	736	691
1906	NL	151	64	87	.424	51.5	530	582
1907	NL	153	66	87	.431	41.5	524	514
1908	NL	154	73	81	.474	26	488	542
1909	NL	153	77	76	.503	33.5	603	599
1910	NL	154	75	79	.487	29	620	665
1911	NL	153	70	83	.458	29	682	700
1912	NL	153	75	78	.490	29	656	722
1913	NL	153	64	89	.418	37.5	607	714
1914	NL	154	60	94	.390	34.5	530	671
1915	NL	154	71	83	.461	20	516	585
1916	NL	153	60	93	.392	33.5	505	622
1917	NL	154	78	76	.506	20	601	611
1918	NL	128	68	60	.531	15.5	538	496
1919	NL	140	96	44	.686	-	578	402
1920	NL	153	82	71	.536	10.5	639	569
1921	NL	153	70	83	.458	24	618	649
1922	NL	154	86	68	.558	7	766	677
1923	NL	154	91	63	.591	4.5	708	629
1924	NL	153	83	70	.542	10	649	579
1925	NL	153	80	73	.523	15	690	643
1926	NL	154	87	67	.565	2	747	651

*Redland Field was originally known as League Park from 1890 to 1893 and Crosley Field was known as Redland Field II from 1912 to 1933.

1927	NL	153	75	78	.490	18.5	643	653
1928	NL	152	78	74	.513	16	648	686
1929	NL	154	66	88	.429	33	686	760
1930	NL	154	59	95	.383	33	665	857
1931	NL	154	58	96	.377	43	592	742
1932	NL	154	60	94	.390	30	575	715
1933	NL	152	58	94	.382	33	496	643
1934	NL	151	52	99	.344	42	590	801
1935	NL	153	68	85	.444	31.5	646	772
1936	NL	154	74	80	.481	18	722	760
1937	NL	154	56	98	.364	40	612	707
1938	NL	150	82	68	.547	6	723	634
1939	NL	154	97	57	.630	-	767	595
1940	NL	153	100	53	.654	-	707	528
1941	NL	154	88	66	.571	12	616	564
1942	NL	152	76	76	.500	29	527	545
1943	NL	154	87	67	.565	18	608	543
1946	NL	154	67	87	.435	30	523	570
1947	NL	154	73	81	.474	21	681	755
1948	NL	153	64	89	.418	27	588	752
1949	NL	154	62	92	.403	35	627	770
1950	NL	153	66	87	.431	24.5	654	734
1951	NL	154	68	86	.442	28.5	559	667
1952	NL	154	69	85	.448	27.5	615	659
1953	NL	154	68	86	.442	37	714	788
1954	NL	154	74	80	.481	23	729	763
1955	NL	154	75	79	.487	23.5	761	684
1956	NL	154	91	63	.591	2	775	658
1957	NL	154	80	74	.519	15	747	781
1958	NL	154	76	78	.494	16	695	621
1959	NL	154	74	80	.481	13	764	738
1960	NL	154	67	87	.435	28	640	692
1961	NL	154	93	61	.604	-	710	653
1962	NL	162	98	64	.605	3.5	802	685
1963	NL	162	86	76	.531	13	648	594
1964	NL	162	92	70	.568	1	660	566
1965	NL	162	89	73	.549	8	825	704
1966	NL	160	76	84	.475	18	692	702
1967	NL	162	87	75	.537	14.5	604	563
1968	NL	162	83	79	.512	14	690	673
1969	NL	162	89	73	.549	4	798	768
1970	NL	162	102	60	.630	-	775	681
1971	NL	162	79	83	.488	11	586	581
1972	NL	154	95	59	.617	-	707	557
1973	NL	162	99	63	.611	-	741	557
1974	NL	162	98	64	.605	4	776	631
1975	NL	162	108	54	.667	-	840	586
1976	NL	162	102	60	.630	-	857	633
1977	NL	162	88	74	.543	10	802	725
1978	NL	161	92	69	.571	2.5	710	688
1979	NL	161	90	71	.559	-	731	644
1980	NL	162	89	73	.549	32	707	670
1981	NL	108	66	42	.611	NA	464	440
1982	NL	162	61	101	.377	28	545	661

1983	NL	162	74	88	.457	17	623	710
1984	NL	162	70	92	.432	22	627	747
1985	NL	161	89	72	.553	5.5	677	666
1986	NL	162	86	76	.531	10	732	717
1987	NL	162	84	78	.519	6	783	752
1988	NL	161	87	74	.540	7	641	596
1989	NL	162	75	87	.463	17	632	691
1990	NL	162	91	71	.562	-	693	597
1991	NL	162	74	88	.457	20	689	691
1992	NL	162	90	72	.556	8	660	609
1993	NL	162	73	89	.451	31	722	785
1994	NL	114	66	48	.579	-	609	490
1995	NL	144	85	59	.590	-	747	623
TOTAL:	104 years	15850	8044	7806		1885	70253	69453
AVERAGE:		152	77	75	.508	18	676	668

Playoff Record

Season	GP	W	L	R	OR	Result
1919	8	5	3	35	20	**Won World Series**.
1939	4	0	4	8	20	Lost World Series to New York.
1940	7	4	3	22	28	**Won World Series**.
1961	5	1	4	13	27	Lost World Series to New York.
1970	8	4	4	29	36	Lost World Series to Baltimore.
1972	12	6	6	40	31	Lost World Series to Oakland.
1973	5	2	3	8	23	Lost NLCS to New York.
1975	10	7	3	48	37	**Won World Series**.
1976	7	7	0	41	19	**Won World Series**.
1979	3	0	3	5	15	Lost NLCS to Pittsburgh.
1990	10	8	2	42	23	**Won World Series**.
1995	7	3	4	27	29	Lost NLCS to Atlanta.
TOTAL:	86	47	39	318	308	
AVERAGE:	7	4	3	27	26	

COACHING HISTORY: 1890-1891 Tom Loftus 133-136-.494; 1892-1894 Charlie Comiskey 202-206-.495; 1895-1899 William Ewing 394-297-.570; 1900 Bob Allen 62-77-.446; 1901-1902 John McPhee 79-124-.389; 1902 Frank Bancroft 10-7-.588; 1902-1905 Joe Kelley 274-230-.544; 1906-1907 Ned Hanlon 130-170-.433; 1908 John Ganzel 73-81-.474: 1909-1911 Clark Griffith 222-238-.483; 1912 Hank O'Day 75-78-.490; 1913 Joe Tinker 64-89-.418; 1914-1916 Charles Herzog 165-226-.422; 1916 Ivy Wingo 1-1-.500; 1916-1918 Christy Mathewson 164-176-.482; 1918 Heinie Groh7-3-.700; 1919-1923 Pat Moran 425-329-.564; 1924-1929 Jack Hendricks 469-450-.510; 1930-1932 Dan Howley 177-285-.383; 1933 Owen Bush 58-94-.382; 1934 Bob O'Farrell 26-58-.310; 1934 Burt Shotton 1-0-1.000; 1934-1937 Chuck Dressen 245-284-.463; 1937 Bobby Wallace 5-20-.200; 1938-1946 Bill McKechnie 597-474-.557; 1947-1948 John Neun 117-137-.461; 1948-1949 William Walters 81-123-.397; 1949-1952 Luke Sewell 174-234-.426; 1952 Earl Bruckner 3-2-.600; 1952-1953 Rogers Hornsby 91-106-.462; 1953 Buster Mills 4-4-.500: 1954-1958 George Tebbets 372-357-.510; 1958 Jimmy Dykes 24-17-.585; 1959 Mayo Smith 35-45-.438; 1959-1964 Fred Hutchinson 443-372-.544; 1964-1965 Dick Sisler 121-94-.563; 1966-1969 Dave Bristol 335-311-.519: 1970-1978 George Anderson 863-586-.596; 1979-1982 John McNamara 279-244-.533; 1982-1983 Russ Nixon 101-131-.435; 1984 Vern Rapp 51-70-.421; 1984-1989 Pete Rose 426-388-.523; 1989 Tommy Helm 14-21-.400: 1990-1992 Lou Piniella 255-231-.525; 1993 Tony Perez 20-24-.455; 1993-present Davey Johnson

CINCINNATI REDS

(merged with St. Louis in 1934)

Home City: Cincinnati, Ohio
Home Field:
Origin of Name: The team was named after the baseball team.

Regular Season Record

Season	League	GP	W	L	T	PF	PA	Pct
1933	NFL	10	3	6	1	38	110	.350
1934	NFL	8	0	8	0	10	243	.000
TOTAL:	2 years	18	3	14	1	48	353	
AVERAGE:		9	1	7	1	24	177	.194

COACHING HISTORY: 1933 Al Jolley 0 3 0 .000; 1933 Mike Palm 3 3 1 .500; 1934 Algy Clark 0-8-0-.000

CINCINNATI RED STOCKINGS

Home City: Cincinnati, Ohio
Home Field: Bank Street Grounds (1882-1883)
League Park I (1884-1889)
Origin of Name: The team wore red stockings.

Regular Season Record

Season	League	GP	W	L	Pct	GB	R	OR
1882	AA	80	55	25	.688	-	489	268
1883	AA	98	61	37	.622	5	662	413
1884	AA	109	68	41	.624	8	754	512
1885	AA	112	63	49	.563	16	642	575
1886	AA	138	65	73	.471	27.5	883	865
1887	AA	135	81	54	.600	14	892	745
1888	AA	134	80	54	.597	11.5	745	628
1889	AA	139	76	63	.547	18	897	769
TOTAL:	8 years	945	549	396		100	5964	4775
AVERAGE:		118	69	49	.581	12.5	746	597

COACHING HISTORY: 1882-1884 Pop Snyder 141-38-.788; 1884 Will White 43-25-.632; 1885-1886 O.P. Caylor 128-122-.512; 1887-1889 Gus Schmelz 237-171-.581

CINCINNATI ROYALS

(were Rochester Royals)
(became Kansas City-Omaha Kings)

Home City: Cincinnati, Ohio
Home Court: Cincinnati Gardens Capacity: 11,438
Origin of Name: The team kept the same name when it moved from Rochester to Cincinnati.

Regular Season Record

Season	League	GP	W	L	PPGF	PPGA	Pct	GB
1957-1958	NBA	72	33	39	101.7	103.1	.458	8

1958-1959	NBA	72	19	53	103.1	112.0	.264	30
1959-1960	NBA	75	19	56	111.1	117.4	.253	27
1960-1961	NBA	79	33	46	117.9	121.3	.418	18
1961-1962	NBA	80	43	37	123.1	121.3	.538	11
1962-1963	NBA	80	42	38	119.0	117.8	.525	16
1963-1964	NBA	80	55	25	114.7	109.7	.688	4
1964-1965	NBA	80	48	32	114.2	111.9	.600	14
1965-1966	NBA	80	45	35	117.8	116.6	.563	10
1966-1967	NBA	81	39	42	117.1	117.4	.481	29
1967-1968	NBA	82	39	43	116.6	117.4	.476	23
1968-1969	NBA	82	41	41	114.5	115.6	.500	16
1969-1970	NBA	82	36	46	117.3	120.2	.439	24
1970-1971	NBA	82	33	49	116.0	119.2	.402	9
1971-1972	NBA	82	30	52	107.8	111.8	.366	8
TOTAL:	15 years	1189	555	634				247
AVERAGE:		79	37	42	114.1	115.5	.467	16

Playoff Record

Season	GP	W	L	PPGF	PPGA	Result
1957-1958	2	0	2	96.0	112.0	Lost semifinals to Detroit.
1961-1962	4	1	3	117.3	115.0	Lost semifinals to Detroit.
1962-1963	12	6	6	121.2	122.6	Lost Division finals to Boston.
1963-1964	10	4	6	105.8	107.4	Lost Division finals to Boston.
1964-1965	4	1	3	111.0	116.5	Lost semifinals to Philadelphia.
1965-1966	5	2	3	110.2	114.8	Lost semifinals to Boston.
1966-1967	4	1	3	105.5	118.0	Lost semifinals to Philadelphia.
TOTAL:	41	15	26			
AVERAGE:	6	2	4	109.6	115.2	

COACHING HISTORY: 1957-1959 Bobby Wanzer 36-74-.327; 1959-1960 Tom Marshall 35-94-.271; 1960-1963 Charlie Wolf 118-121-.494; 1963-1967 Jack McMahon 187-134-.583; 1967-1969 Ed Jucker 80-84-.488; 1969-1972 Bob Cousy 99-147-.402

CINCINNATI STINGERS

Home City: Cincinnati, Ohio
Home Arena: Riverfront Coliseum Capacity: 16,500 [1976]
Origin of Name: The team name was chosen in a Name the Team Contest. The team received over 1,250 entries.

Regular Season Record

Season	League	GP	W	L	T	GF	GA	Pts	Pct
1975-1976	WHA	80	35	44	1	285	340	71	.444
1976-1977	WHA	81	39	37	5	354	303	83	.512
1977-1978	WHA	80	35	42	3	298	332	73	.456
1978-1979	WHA	80	33	41	6	274	284	72	.450
TOTAL:	4 years	321	142	164	15	1211	1259	299	
AVERAGE:		80	35	41	4	303	315	74	.466

Playoff Record

Season	GP	W	L	GF	GA	Result
1976-1977	4	0	4	9	19	Lost quarterfinals to Indianapolis.
1978-1979	3	1	2	10	10	Lost preliminary round to New England.
TOTAL:	7	1	6	19	29	
AVERAGE:	4	1	3	10	20	

COACHING HISTORY: 1975-1977 Terry Slater 74-81-6-.478; 1977-1978 Jacques Demers 35-42-3-.456; 1978-1979 Floyd Smith 33-41-6-.450

CLEVELAND ALLMEN TRANSFERS

Home City: Cleveland, Ohio
Home Court:
Origin of Name: The team was sponsored by the Allmen Transfer Company.

Regular Season Record

Season	League	GP	W	L	PPGF	PPGA	Pct	GB
1944-1945	NBL	30	13	17	51.0	51.0	.433	12
1945-1946	NBL	33	4	29	46.1	56.4	.121	21.5
TOTAL:	2 years	63	17	46				33.5
AVERAGE:		32	9	23	48.6	53.7	.270	17

Playoff Record

Season	GP	W	L	PPGF	PPGA	Round
1944-1945	2	0	2	50.5	68.0	Lost 1st round series to Fort Wayne.

COACHING HISTORY: 1944-1946 Jeff Carlin 17-46-.270

CLEVELAND BARONS
(merged with Minnesota after the 1977-1978 season)

Home City: Richfield, Ohio
Home Arena: The Coliseum Capacity: 18,544 [1977]
Origin of Name: The team was named after the American Hockey League team which had played in the city for many years.

Regular Season Record

Season	League	GP	W	L	T	GF	GA	Pts	Pct
1976-1977	NHL	80	25	42	13	240	383	63	.394
1977-1978	NHL	80	22	45	13	230	325	57	.356
TOTAL:	2 years	160	47	87	26	470	708	120	
AVERAGE:		80	24	43	13	235	354	60	.375

COACHING HISTORY: 1976-1978 Jack Evans 47-87-26-.375

CLEVELAND BLUES

Home City: Cleveland, Ohio
Home Field: National League Park
Origin of Name:

Regular Season Record

Season	League	GP	W	L	Pct	GB	R	OR
1879	NL	82	27	55	.329	31	322	461
1880	NL	84	47	37	.560	20	387	337
1881	NL	84	36	48	.429	20	392	414
1882	NL	82	42	40	.512	12	402	411
1883	NL	97	55	42	.567	7.5	476	443
1884	NL	112	35	77	.313	49	458	716
TOTAL:	6 years	541	242	299		139.5	2437	2782
AVERAGE:		90	40	50	.447	23	406	464

COACHING HISTORY: 1879-1880 Jim McCormick 74-92-.446; 1881 Mike McGeary 36-48-.429; 1882 Ford Evans 42-40-.512: 1883 Frank Bancroft 55-42-.567; 1884 Charlie Hackett 35-77-.313

CLEVELAND BLUES

Home City: Cleveland, Ohio
Home Field: Spider Park
Origin of Name: The team got its nickname from the color of their uniforms.

Regular Season Record

Season	League	GP	W	L	Pct	GB	R	OR
1887	AA	131	39	92	.298	54	729	1112
1888	AA	132	50	82	.379	40.5	651	839
TOTAL:	2 years	263	89	174		94.5	1380	1951
AVERAGE:		132	45	87	.338	47	690	976

COACHING HISTORY: 1887-1888 Jimmy Williams 58-191-.233; 1888 Tom Lofthus 31-41-.431

CLEVELAND BLUES
(were Cleveland Bronchos)
(became Cleveland Naps)

Home City: Cleveland, Ohio
Home Field: League Park I — Capacity: 9,000
Origin of Name: Called Blues because of the color of their uniform.

Regular Season Record

Season	League	GP	W	L	Pct	GB	R	OR
1902	AL	136	69	67	.507	14	686	667
1903	AL	140	77	63	.550	15	639	578
1904	AL	151	86	65	.570	7.5	647	482
TOTAL:	3 years	427	232	195		36.5	1972	1727
AVERAGE:		142	77	65	.543	12	657	576

COACHING HISTORY: 1902-1904 Bill Armour 232-195-.543

CLEVELAND BRONCHOS
(became Cleveland Blues)

Home City: Cleveland, Ohio
Home Field: League Park I — Capacity: 9,000
Origin of Name:

Regular Season Record

Season	League	GP	W	L	Pct	GB	R	OR
1901	AL	137	55	82	.401	28.5	666	831

COACHING HISTORY: Jim McAleer 55-82-.401

CLEVELAND BROWNS
(became Baltimore Ravens)

Home City: Cleveland, Ohio
Home Stadium: Cleveland Stadium * — Capacity: 78,512 [1995]
Origin of Name: The team was named Browns either after Paul Brown who coached the team for the first several seasons.

Regular Season Record

Season	League	GP	W	L	T	PF	PA	Pct
1946	AAFC	14	12	2	0	423	137	.857
1947	AAFC	14	12	1	1	410	185	.893
1948	AAFC	14	14	0	0	389	190	1.000
1949	AAFC	12	9	1	2	339	171	.833
1950	NFL	12	10	2	0	310	144	.833
1951	NFL	12	11	1	0	331	152	.917
1952	NFL	12	8	4	0	310	213	.667
1953	NFL	12	11	1	0	348	162	.917
1954	NFL	12	9	3	0	336	162	.750
1955	NFL	12	9	2	1	349	218	.792
1956	NFL	12	5	7	0	167	177	.417
1957	NFL	12	9	2	1	269	172	.792
1958	NFL	12	9	3	0	302	217	.750
1959	NFL	12	7	5	0	270	214	.583
1960	NFL	12	8	3	1	362	217	.708
1961	NFL	14	8	5	1	319	270	.607
1962	NFL	14	7	6	1	291	257	.536
1963	NFL	14	10	4	0	343	262	.714
1964	NFL	14	10	3	1	415	293	.750
1965	NFL	14	11	3	0	363	325	.786
1966	NFL	14	9	5	0	403	259	.643
1967	NFL	14	9	5	0	334	297	.643
1968	NFL	14	10	4	0	394	273	.714
1969	NFL	14	10	3	1	351	300	.750
1970	NFL	14	7	7	0	286	265	.500
1971	NFL	14	9	5	0	285	273	.643
1972	NFL	14	10	4	0	268	249	.714

*Originally Municipal Stadium from 1932 to 1974.

1973	NFL	14	7	5	2	234	255	.571
1974	NFL	14	4	10	0	251	344	.286
1975	NFL	14	3	11	0	218	372	.214
1976	NFL	14	9	5	0	267	287	.643
1977	NFL	14	6	8	0	269	267	.429
1978	NFL	16	8	8	0	334	356	.500
1979	NFL	16	9	7	0	359	352	.563
1980	NFL	16	11	5	0	357	310	.688
1981	NFL	16	5	11	0	276	375	.313
1982	NFL	9	4	5	0	140	182	.444
1983	NFL	16	9	7	0	356	342	.562
1984	NFL	16	5	11	0	250	297	.313
1985	NFL	16	8	8	0	287	294	.500
1986	NFL	16	12	4	0	391	310	.750
1987	NFL	15	10	5	0	390	239	.667
1988	NFL	16	10	6	0	304	288	.625
1989	NFL	16	9	6	1	334	254	.594
1990	NFL	16	3	13	0	228	462	.188
1991	NFL	16	6	10	0	293	298	.375
1992	NFL	16	7	9	0	272	275	.438
1993	NFL	16	7	9	0	304	307	.438
1994	NFL	16	9	7	0	319	298	.563
1995	NFL	16	5	11	0	289	356	.313
TOTAL:	50 years	704	419	272	13	15689	13174	
AVERAGE:		14	8	6	0	314	263	.604

Playoff Record

Season	GP	W	L	PF	PA	Result
1946	1	1	0	14	9	**Won AAFC championship**
1947	1	1	0	14	3	**Won AAFC championship**
1948	1	1	0	49	7	**Won AAFC championship**
1949	1	1	0	21	7	**Won AAFC championship**
1950	2	2	0	38	31	**Won NFL championship**.
1951	1	0	1	17	24	Lost championship game to Los Angeles.
1952	1	0	1	7	17	Lost championship game to Detroit.
1953	1	0	1	16	17	Lost championship game to Detroit.
1954	1	1	0	56	10	**Won NFL championship**.
1955	1	1	0	38	14	**Won NFL championship**.
1957	1	0	1	14	59	Lost championship game to Detroit.
1958	1	0	1	0	10	Lost Conference playoff to N.Y. Giants.
1964	1	1	0	27	0	**Won NFL championship**.
1965	1	0	1	12	23	Lost championship game to Green Bay.
1967	1	0	1	14	52	Lost Conference playoff to Dallas.
1968	2	1	1	31	54	Lost NFL championship to Baltimore.
1969	2	1	1	45	41	Lost NFL championship to Minnesota.
1971	1	0	1	3	20	Lost Divisional playoff to Baltimore.
1972	1	0	1	14	20	Lost Divisional playoff to Miami.
1980	1	0	1	12	14	Lost Divisional playoff to Oakland.
1982	1	0	1	10	27	Lost 1st round playoff to L.A. Raiders.
1985	1	0	1	21	24	Lost Divisional playoff to Miami.
1986	2	1	1	40	40	Lost AFC championship to Denver.
1987	2	1	1	71	59	Lost AFC championship to Denver.
1988	1	0	1	23	24	Lost 1st round playoff to Houston.

1994	2	1	1	29	42	Lost Division semifinals to Pittsburgh.
TOTAL:	32	14	18	636	648	
AVERAGE:	2	1	1	24	25	

COACHING HISTORY: 1946-1962 Paul Brown 158-48-8-.757; 1963-1970 Blanton Collier 76-34-2-.688; 1971-1974 Nick Skorich 30-24-2-.554; 1975-1977 Forrest Gregg 18-23-0-.439; 1977 Dick Modzelewski 0-1-0-.000; 1978-1984 Sam Rutigliano 47-50-0-.485; 1984-1988 Marty Schottenheimer 44-27-0-.620; 1989-1990 Bud Carson 11-13-1-.460; 1990 Jim Shofner 1-6-0-.143; 1991-1995 Bill Belichick 34-46-0-.425

CLEVELAND BULLDOGS
(were Canton Bulldogs)
(became Canton Bulldogs)

Home City: Cleveland, Ohio
Home Stadium:
Origin of Name: The team kept the same name after it moved from Canton.

Regular Season Record

Season	League	GP	W	L	T	PF	PA	Pct
1924	NFL	9	7	1	1	229	60	.833

COACHING HISTORY: Guy Chamberlin 7-1-1-.833

CLEVELAND BULLDOGS

Home City: Cleveland, Ohio
Home Stadium:
Origin of Name: Named after the previous NFL team.

Regular Season Record

Season	League	GP	W	L	T	PF	PA	Pct
1927	NFL	13	8	4	1	209	107	.654

COACHING HISTORY: LeRoy Andrews 8-4-1-.654

CLEVELAND CAVALIERS

Home City: Cleveland, Ohio (1970-1974)
Richfield, Ohio (1975-1994)
Cleveland, Ohio (1994-present)
Home Court: Cleveland Arena (1970-1974) Capacity: 11,000 [1974]
The Coliseum (1975-1994) Capacity: 20,273 [1994]
Gund Arena (1994-present) Capacity: 20,562 [1995]
Origin of Name: The name was chosen in a Name the Team Contest sponsored by a local newspaper.

Regular Season Record

Season	League	GP	W	L	PPGF	PPGA	Pct	GB
1970-1971	NBA	82	15	67	102.1	113.3	.183	27
1971-1972	NBA	82	23	59	105.8	113.4	.280	15

1972-1973	NBA	82	32	50	102.7	105.3	.390	20
1973-1974	NBA	82	29	53	100.3	104.6	.354	18
1974-1975	NBA	82	40	42	99.0	99.4	.488	20
1975-1976	NBA	82	49	33	101.7	99.2	.598	-
1976-1977	NBA	82	43	39	102.1	101.0	.524	6
1977-1978	NBA	82	43	39	104.4	103.9	.524	9
1978-1979	NBA	82	30	52	106.5	110.2	.366	18
1979-1980	NBA	82	37	45	114.1	113.8	.451	13
1980-1981	NBA	82	28	54	105.7	110.6	.341	32
1981-1982	NBA	82	15	67	103.2	111.7	.183	40
1982-1983	NBA	82	23	59	97.1	104.6	.280	28
1983-1984	NBA	82	28	54	102.3	106.5	.341	22
1984-1985	NBA	82	36	46	108.6	111.3	.439	23
1985-1986	NBA	82	29	53	107.8	110.6	.354	28
1986-1987	NBA	82	31	51	104.4	108.2	.378	26
1987-1988	NBA	82	42	40	104.5	103.7	.512	12
1988-1989	NBA	82	57	25	108.8	101.2	.695	6
1989-1990	NBA	82	42	40	102.6	102.9	.512	17
1990-1991	NBA	82	33	49	101.7	104.2	.402	28
1991-1992	NBA	82	57	25	108.9	103.4	.695	10
1992-1993	NBA	82	54	28	107.7	101.3	.659	3
1993-1994	NBA	82	47	35	101.2	97.1	.573	10
1994-1995	NBA	82	43	39	90.5	89.8	.524	9
1995-1996	NBA	82	47	35	91.1	88.5	.573	25
TOTAL:	26 years	2132	953	1179				465
AVERAGE:		82	37	45	103.3	104.5	.447	18

Playoff Record

Season	**GP**	**W**	**L**	**PPGF**	**PPGA**	**Result**
1975-1976	13	6	7	92.0	92.7	Lost Conference finals to Boston.
1976-1977	3	1	2	96.3	98.7	Lost 1st round series to Washington.
1977-1978	2	0	2	110.5	120.5	Lost 1st round series to New York.
1984-1985	4	1	3	112.3	112.3	Lost 1st round series to Boston.
1987-1988	5	2	3	100.4	102.0	Lost 1st round series to Chicago.
1988-1989	5	2	3	97.2	98.0	Lost 1st round series to Chicago.
1989-1990	5	2	3	106.8	104.4	Lost 1st round series to Philadelphia.
1991-1992	17	9	8	103.6	101.1	Lost Conference final to Chicago.
1992-1993	9	3	6	92.0	97.6	Lost Conference semifinal to Chicago.
1993-1994	3	0	3	94.7	101.3	Lost 1st round series to Chicago.
1994-1995	4	1	3	82.5	90.8	Lost 1st round series to New York.
1995-1996	3	0	3	79.7	90.3	Lost 1st round series to New York.
TOTAL:	73	27	46			
AVERAGE:	6	2	4	99.0	101.8	

COACHING HISTORY: 1970-1980 Bill Fitch 304-434-.412; 1979-1980 Stan Albeck 37-45-.451; 1980-1982 Bill Musselman 27-67-.287; 1980-1982 Don Delaney 7-19-.269; 1981-1982 Bob Koppenburg 0-3-.000; 1981-1982 Chuck Daly 9-32-.220; 1982-1984 Tom Nissalke 51-113-.311; 1984-1986 George Karl 61-88-.409; 1985-1986 Gene Littles 4-11-.267; 1986-1993 Lenny Wilkens 316-258-.551; 1993-present Mike Fratello

CLEVELAND CHASE BRASS

Home City: Cleveland, Ohio
Home Court:
Origin of Name: The team was sponsored by the Chase Brass Company of Cleveland.

Regular Season Record

Season	League	GP	W	L	PPGF	PPGA	Pct	GB
1943-1944	NBL	18	3	15	42.1	48.4	.167	13

COACHING HISTORY: Vito Kubilus 3-15-.167

Playoff Record

Season	GP	W	L	PPGF	PPGA	Result
1943-1944	2	0	2	53.0	34.0	Lost 1st round series to Fort Wayne.

CLEVELAND CRUSADERS

(became Minnesota Fighting Saints)

Home City: Richfield, Ohio
Home Arena: The Coliseum Capacity: 18,500 [1975]
Origin of Name: The name was chosen in a Name the Team Contest.

Regular Season Record

Season	League	GP	W	L	T	GF	GA	Pts	Pct
1972-1973	WHA	78	43	32	3	287	239	89	.571
1973-1974	WHA	78	37	32	9	266	264	83	.532
1974-1975	WHA	78	35	40	3	236	258	73	.468
1975-1976	WHA	80	35	40	5	273	279	75	.469
TOTAL:	4 years	314	150	144	20	1062	1040	320	
AVERAGE:		78	37	36	5	266	260	80	.510

Playoff Record

Season	GP	W	L	GF	GA	Result
1972-1973	9	5	4	33	22	Lost semifinal round to New England.
1973-1974	5	1	4	9	18	Lost quarterfinal round to Toronto.
1974-1975	5	1	4	14	24	Lost quarterfinal round to Houston.
1975-1976	3	0	3	6	14	Lost preliminary round to New England.
TOTAL:	22	7	15	62	78	
AVERAGE:	6	2	4	16	20	

COACHING HISTORY: 1972-1974 Bill Needham 80-64-12-.551; 1974-1975 John Hanna 14-18-1-.439; 1974-1975 Jack Vivian 21-22-2-.489; 1975-1976 John Wilson 35-40-5-.469

CLEVELAND INDIANS
(were Cleveland Molly McGuires)

Home City: Cleveland, Ohio
Home Field: League Park II (1915-1946) Capacity: 22,500 [1939]
Cleveland Stadium (1932-1993) * Capacity: 74,483 [1993]
Jacobs Field (1994-present) Capacity: 42,865 [1995]
Origin of Name: The name was chosen in a Name the Team Contest and was chosen to honor former player Louis Sockalexis the first full-blooded native American to play in the major leagues.

Regular Season Record

Season	League	GP	W	L	Pct	GB	R	OR
1915	AL	152	57	95	.375	44.5	539	670
1916	AL	154	77	77	.500	14	630	621
1917	AL	154	88	66	.571	12	584	543
1918	AL	129	73	56	.566	3.5	510	447
1919	AL	139	84	55	.604	3.5	634	535
1920	AL	154	98	56	.636	-	857	642
1921	AL	154	94	60	.610	4.5	925	712
1922	AL	154	78	76	.506	16	768	817
1923	AL	153	82	71	.536	16.5	888	746
1924	AL	153	67	86	.438	24.5	755	814
1925	AL	154	70	84	.455	27.5	782	810
1926	AL	154	88	66	.571	3	738	612
1927	AL	153	66	87	.431	43.5	668	766
1928	AL	154	62	92	.403	39	674	830
1929	AL	152	81	71	.533	24	717	736
1930	AL	154	81	73	.526	21	890	915
1931	AL	154	78	76	.506	30	885	833
1932	AL	152	87	65	.572	19	845	747
1933	AL	151	75	76	.497	23.5	654	669
1934	AL	154	85	69	.552	16	814	763
1935	AL	153	82	71	.536	12	776	739
1936	AL	154	80	74	.519	22.5	921	862
1937	AL	154	83	71	.539	19	817	768
1938	AL	152	86	66	.566	13	847	782
1939	AL	154	87	67	.565	20.5	797	700
1940	AL	154	89	65	.578	1	710	637
1941	AL	154	75	79	.487	26	677	668
1942	AL	154	75	79	.487	28	590	659
1943	AL	153	82	71	.536	15.5	600	577
1944	AL	154	72	82	.468	17	643	677
1945	AL	145	73	72	.503	11	557	548
1946	AL	154	68	86	.442	36	537	637
1947	AL	154	80	74	.519	17	687	588
1948	AL	155	97	58	.626	-	840	568
1949	AL	154	89	65	.578	8	675	574
1950	AL	154	92	62	.597	6	806	654
1951	AL	154	93	61	.604	5	696	594
1952	AL	154	93	61	.604	2	763	606

*Originally Municipal Stadium from 1932-1974.

1953	AL	154	92	62	.597	8.5	770	627
1954	AL	154	111	43	.721	-	746	504
1955	AL	154	93	61	.604	3	698	601
1956	AL	154	88	66	.571	9	712	581
1957	AL	153	76	77	.497	21.5	682	722
1958	AL	153	77	76	.503	14.5	694	635
1959	AL	154	89	65	.578	5	745	646
1960	AL	154	76	78	.494	21	667	693
1961	AL	161	78	83	.484	30.5	737	752
1962	AL	162	80	82	.494	16	682	745
1963	AL	162	79	83	.488	25.5	635	702
1964	AL	162	79	83	.488	20	689	693
1965	AL	162	87	75	.537	15	663	613
1966	AL	162	81	81	.500	17	574	586
1967	AL	162	75	87	.463	17	559	613
1968	AL	161	86	75	.534	16.5	516	504
1969	AL	161	62	99	.385	46.5	573	717
1970	AL	162	76	86	.469	32	649	675
1971	AL	162	60	102	.370	43	543	747
1972	AL	156	72	84	.462	14	472	519
1973	AL	162	71	91	.438	26	679	826
1974	AL	162	77	85	.475	14	662	694
1975	AL	159	79	80	.497	15.5	688	703
1976	AL	159	81	78	.509	16	615	615
1977	AL	161	71	90	.441	28.5	676	739
1978	AL	159	69	90	.434	29	639	694
1979	AL	161	81	80	.503	22	760	805
1980	AL	160	79	81	.494	23	738	807
1981	AL	103	52	51	.505	NA	431	442
1982	AL	162	78	84	.481	17	683	748
1983	AL	162	70	92	.432	28	704	785
1984	AL	162	75	87	.463	29	761	766
1985	AL	162	60	102	.370	39.5	729	861
1986	AL	162	84	78	.519	11.5	831	841
1987	AL	162	61	101	.377	37	742	957
1988	AL	162	78	84	.481	11	666	731
1989	AL	162	73	89	.451	16	604	654
1990	AL	162	77	85	.475	11	732	737
1991	AL	162	57	105	.352	34	576	759
1992	AL	162	76	86	.469	20	674	746
1993	AL	162	76	86	.469	19	790	813
1994	AL	113	66	47	.584	1	679	562
1995	AL	144	100	44	.694	-	840	607
TOTAL:	81 years	12540	6375	6165		1468.5	56601	55833
AVERAGE:		155	79	76	.508	18	699	689

Season	GP	W	L	R	OR	Result
			Playoff Record			
1920	7	5	2	17	8	**Won World Series.**
1948	6	4	2	17	17	**Won World Series.**
1954	4	0	4	9	21	Lost World Series to New York.
1995	15	9	6	59	41	Lost World Series to Atlanta.
TOTAL:	32	18	14	102	87	
AVERAGE:	8	5	3	26	22	

COACHING HISTORY: 1915 Joe Birmingham 12-16-.429; 1915-1919 Lee Fohl 328-312-.513; 1919-1926 Tris Speaker 616-520-.542; 1927 Jack McCallister 66-87-.431; 1928-1933 Roger Peckinpaugh 415-402-.508; 1933-1935 Walter Johnson 180-168-.517; 1935-1937 Steve O'Neil 199-168-.542; 1938-1940 Ossie Vitt 262-198-.570; 1941 Roger Peckinpaugh 75-79-.487; 1942-1950 Lou Boudreau 728-649-.529; 1951-1956 Al Lopez 570-354-.617; 1957 Kerby Farrell 76-77-.497; 1958 Bob Bragan 31-36-.463; 1958-1960 Joe Gordon 184-151-.549; 1960 Joyner White 1-0-1.000; 1960-1961 Jim Dykes 104-114-.477; 1961 Mel Harder 0-1-.000; 1962 Mel McGaha 80-82-.494; 1963-1966 George Tebbetts 311-298-.511; 1966 George Strickland 15-24-.385; 1967 Joe Adcock 75-87-.463; 1968-1971 Alvin Dark 266-321-.453; 1971 John Lipon 18-41-.305; 1972-1974 Ken Aspromonte 220-260-.458; 1975-1977 Frank Robinson 186-189-.496; 1977-1979 Jeff Torborg 157-201-.439; 1979-1982 Dave Garcia 247-244-.503; 1983 Mike Ferraro 40-60-.400; 1983-1987 Pat Corrales 280-355-.441; 1987-1989 Howard Edwards 173-207-.455; 1989 John Hart 8-11-.421; 1990-1991 John McNamara 102-137-.427; 1991-present Mike Hargrove

CLEVELAND INDIANS

Home City: Cleveland, Ohio
Home Stadium:
Origin of Name: Named after the American League baseball team.

Season	League	GP	W	L	T	PF	PA	Pct
			Regular Season Record					
1923	NFL	11	1	10	0	49	247	.091

COACHING HISTORY: Gene Edwards 1-10-0-.091

CLEVELAND INDIANS

Home City: Cleveland, Ohio
Home Stadium:
Origin of Name: Named after the American League baseball team.

Season	League	GP	W	L	T	PF	PA	Pct
			Regular Season Record					
1931	NFL	10	2	8	0	45	137	.200

COACHING HISTORY: Harry Workman 2-8-0-.200

CLEVELAND INFANTS

Home City: Cleveland, Ohio
Home Field: Brotherhood Park
Origin of Name:

Regular Season Record

Season	League	GP	W	L	Pct	GB	R	OR
1890	PL	130	55	75	.423	26.5	849	1027

COACHING HISTORY: Jay Faatz 10-25-.286; Henry Larkin 27-33-.450; Patsy Tebeau 18-17-.514

CLEVELAND MOLLY McGUIRES

(were Cleveland Naps)
(became Cleveland Indians)

Home City: Cleveland, Ohio
Home Field: League Park II — Capacity: 21,414
Origin of Name: Named after former manager James McGuire.

Regular Season Record

Season	League	GP	W	L	Pct	GB	R	OR
1912	AL	153	75	78	.490	30.5	680	681
1913	AL	152	86	66	.566	9.5	631	529
1914	AL	153	51	102	.333	48.5	538	708
TOTAL:	3 years	458	212	246		88.5	1849	1918
AVERAGE:		153	71	82	.463	29.5	616	639

COACHING HISTORY: 1912 Harry Davis 54-71-.432; 1912-1914 Joe Birmingham 158-175-.474

CLEVELAND NAPS

(were Cleveland Blues)
(became Cleveland Molly McGuires)

Home City: Cleveland, Ohio
Home Field: League Park I (1905-1909) — Capacity: 9,000
League Park II (1910-1911) — Capacity: 21,414
Origin of Name: The team was named Naps when Napoleon Lajoie became the player-manager.

Regular Season Record

Season	League	GP	W	L	Pct	GB	R	OR
1905	AL	154	76	78	.494	19	559	582
1906	AL	153	89	64	.582	5	663	482
1907	AL	152	85	67	.559	8	528	523
1908	AL	154	90	64	.584	.5	570	471
1909	AL	153	71	82	.464	27.5	519	543
1910	AL	152	71	81	.467	32	539	654
1911	AL	153	80	73	.523	22	691	709
TOTAL:	7 years	1071	562	509		114	4069	3964
AVERAGE:		153	80	73	.525	16	581	566

COACHING HISTORY: 1905-1909 Napoleon Lajoie 397-330-.546; 1909-1911 James McGuire 91-117-.438; 1911 George Stovall 74-62-.544

CLEVELAND RAMS
(became Los Angeles Rams)

Home City: Cleveland, Ohio
Home Stadium: Municipal Stadium Capacity: 85,703
Origin of Name: The name was chosen during a meeting of the owners and sportswriters.

Regular Season Record

Season	League	GP	W	L	T	PF	PA	Pct
1937	NFL	11	1	10	0	175	207	.091
1938	NFL	11	4	7	0	131	215	.364
1939	NFL	11	5	5	1	195	164	.500
1940	NFL	11	4	6	1	171	191	.409
1941	NFL	11	2	9	0	116	244	.182
1942	NFL	11	5	6	0	150	207	.455
1944	NFL	10	4	6	0	188	224	.400
1945	NFL	10	9	1	0	244	136	.900
TOTAL: 8 years		86	34	50	2	1370	1588	
AVERAGE:		11	5	6	0	171	199	.407

Playoff Record

Season	GP	W	L	PF	PA	Result
1945	1	1	0	15	14	**Won NFL championship**.

COACHING HISTORY: 1937-1938 Hugo Bezdek 1-13-0-.071; 1938 Art Lewis 4-4-0-.500; 1939-1942 Dutch Clark 16-26-2-.386; 1944 Buff Donelli 4-6-0-.400; 1945 Adam Walsh 9-1-0-.900

CLEVELAND REBELS

Home City: Cleveland, Ohio
Home Court:
Origin of Name:

Regular Season Record

Season	League	GP	W	L	PPGF	PPGA	Pct	GB
1946-1947	BAA	60	30	30	70.9	71.8.	500	8.5

Playoff Record

Season	GP	W	L	PPGF	PPGA	Result
1946-1947	3	1	2	74.0	76.7	Lost 1st round series to New York.

COACHING HISTORY: Dutch Dehnert 17-20-.459: Roy Clifford 13-10-.565

CLEVELAND ROSENBLUMS

Home City: Cleveland, Ohio
Home Court: Cleveland Auditorium Capacity: 20,000
Origin of Name: The team was sponsored by department store owner Max Rosenblum.

Regular Season Record

Season	League	GP	W	L	Pct	GB
1925-1926	ABL	30	23	7	.767	NA
1926-1927	ABL	42	26	16	.619	NA
1927-1928	ABL	51	22	29	.431	5
1928-1929	ABL	42	29	13	.690	NA
1929-1930	ABL	54	35	19	.648	NA
1930-1931	ABL	12	6	6	.500	NA
TOTAL:	6 years	231	141	90		NA
AVERAGE:		39	24	15	.610	

Playoff Record

Season	GP	W	L	Result
1925-1926	3	3	0	**Won ABL championship**.
1926-1927	3	0	3	Lost ABL championship series to Brooklyn.
1927-1928	2	0	2	Lost 1st round series to Fort Wayne.
1928-1929	4	4	0	**Won ABL championship**.
1929-1930	5	4	1	**Won ABL championship**.
TOTAL:	17	11	6	
AVERAGE:	3	2	1	

COACHING HISTORY: 1925-1927 Marty Friedman 49-23-.681; 1927-1930 Dave Kerr 86-86-.500; 1930-1931 Not Available

CLEVELAND SPIDERS

Home City: Cleveland, Ohio
Home Field: National League Park II (1889-1890)
League Park I (1891-1899) Capacity: 9,000
Origin of Name: Averaging five foot eight inches and 149 pounds (according to available statistics) the team got its nickname from the physique of its players.

Regular Season Record

Season	League	GP	W	L	Pct	GB	R	OR
1889	NL	133	61	72	.459	25.5	656	720
1890	NL	132	44	88	.333	43.5	630	832
1891	NL	139	65	74	.468	22.5	835	888
1892	NL	149	93	56	.624	8.5	855	613
1893	NL	128	73	55	.570	12.5	976	839
1894	NL	129	68	61	.527	21.5	932	896
1895	NL	130	84	46	.646	3	917	720
1896	NL	128	80	48	.625	9.5	840	650
1897	NL	131	69	62	.527	23.5	773	680
1898	NL	149	81	68	.544	21	730	683
1899	NL	154	20	134	.130	84	529	1252
TOTAL: 11 years		1502	738	764		275	8673	8773
AVERAGE:		137	67	70	.491	25	788	798

COACHING HISTORY: 1889 Tom Lofthus 61-72-.459; 1890 Gus Schmelz 21-55-.276; 1890-1891 Bob Leadley 54-67-.446: 1891-1898 Patsy Tebeau 582-436-.572; 1899 Lave Cross 8-30-.211; 1899 Joe Quinn 12-104-.103

CLEVELAND STOKERS

Home City: Cleveland, Ohio
Home Stadium: Municipal Stadium Capacity: 74,056 [1967]
Origin of Name: Most of the teams in the USA were represented by English professional teams and Cleveland was represented by the Stoke City Potters.

Regular Season Record

Season	League	GP	W	L	T	GF	GA	BP	Pts	Pct
1967	USA	12	5	3	4	19	13	NA	14	.583
1968	NASL	32	14	7	11	62	44	58	175	.569
TOTAL:	2 years	44	19	10	15	81	57	58	189	
AVERAGE:		22	10	5	7	41	29	29	95	

Playoff Record

Season	GP	W	L	T	GF	GA	Result
1968	2	0	1	1	2	3	Lost 1st round series to Atlanta.

COACHING HISTORY: 1967 Tony Waddington 5-3-4-.583; 1968 Norman Low 14-7-11-.569

CLEVELAND WHITE HORSES

(were Warren Penn Oilers until mid 1939)
(became Detroit Eagles)

Home City: Cleveland, Ohio
Home Court:
Origin of Name:

Regular Season Record

Season	League	GP	W	L	PPGF	PPGA	Pct	GB
1939	NBL	9	5	4	38.1	39.6	.556	10

COACHING HISTORY: Gerry Archibald5-4-.556

COBALT SILVER KINGS

Home City: Cobalt, Ontario
Home Rink:
Origin of Name: The team was named Silver Kings because of the silver mines around Cobalt.

Regular Season Record

Season	League	GP	W	L	T	GF	GA	Pts	Pct
1909-1910	NHA	12	4	8	0	79	104	8	.333

COACHING HISTORY:

COLORADO AVALANCHE
(were Quebec Nordiques)

Home City: Denver, Colorado
Home Arena: McNichols Sports Arena Capacity: 16,061 [1995]
Origin of Name: After extensive market research the team was named by Comsat Video Enterprises the group which had purchased the team and moved it from Quebec City.

Regular Season Record

Season	League	GP	W	L	T	GF	GA	Pts	Pct
1995-1996	NHL	82	47	25	10	326	240	104	.634

Playoff Record

Season	GP	W	L	GF	GA	Result
1995-1996	22	16	6	80	51	**Won Stanley Cup**

COACHING HISTORY: 1995-present Marc Crawford

COLORADO CARIBOUS
(became the Atlanta Chiefs)

Home City: Denver, Colorado,
Home Stadium: Mile High Stadium Capacity: 63,500 [1978]
Origin of Name:

Regular Season Record

Season	League	GP	W	L	GF	GA	BP	Pts	Pct
1978	NASL	30	8	22	34	66	33	81	.300

COACHING HISTORY: Dave Clements 6-14; Dan Wood 2-8

COLORADO ROCKIES
(were Kansas City Scouts)
(became New Jersey Devils)

Home City: Denver, Colorado
Home Arena: McNichols Sports Arena Capacity: 16,401 [1977]
Origin of Name: The name was picked because of Denver's proximity to the Rocky Mountains and in the words of one of their owners the name sounded mean and aggressive.

Regular Season Record

Season	League	GP	W	L	T	GF	GA	Pts	Pct
1976-1977	NHL	80	20	46	14	226	307	54	.338
1977-1978	NHL	80	19	40	21	257	305	59	.369
1978-1979	NHL	80	15	53	12	210	331	42	.263
1979-1980	NHL	80	19	48	13	234	308	51	.319
1980-1981	NHL	80	22	45	13	258	344	57	.356
1981-1982	NHL	80	18	49	13	241	362	49	.306
TOTAL:	6 years	480	113	281	86	1426	1957	312	
AVERAGE:		80	19	47	14	238	326	52	.325

Playoff Record

Season	GP	W	L	GF	GA	Result
1977-1978	2	0	2	3	6	Lost preliminary round to Philadelphia.

COACHING HISTORY: 1976-1977 John Wilson 20-46-14-.338; 1977-1979 Pat Kelly 22-54-25-.342; 1978-1979 Armand Guidolin 12-39-8-.271; 1979-1980 Don Cherry 19-48-13-.319; 1980-1981 Bill MacMillan 22-45-13-.356; 1981-1982 Bert Marshall 3-17-4-.208; 1981-1982 Marshall Johnston 15-32-9-.348

COLORADO ROCKIES

Home City: Denver, Colorado
Home Stadium: Mile High Stadium (1993-1994) Capacity: 76,100 [1993]
Coors Field (1995-present) Capacity: 50,100 [1995]
Origin of Name: The Colorado Baseball Partnership, the team's ownership group, named the team.

Regular Season Record

Season	League	GP	W	L	Pct	GB	R	OR
1993	NL	162	67	95	.414	37	758	967
1994	NL	117	53	64	.453	6.5	573	638
1995	NL	144	77	67	.535	1	785	783
TOTAL:	3 years	423	197	226		44.5	2116	2388
AVERAGE:		141	66	75	.466	15	705	796

Playoff Record

Season	GP	W	L	R	OR	Result
1995	4	1	3	19	27	Lost National League playoffs to Atlanta.

COACHING HISTORY: 1993-present Don Baylor

COLUMBUS ATHLETIC SUPPLY

Home City: Columbus, Ohio
Home Court:
Origin of Name: The team was sponsored by the Columbus Athletic Supply Company.

Regular Season Record

Season	League	GP	W	L	PPGF	PPGA	Pct	GB
1937-1938	NBL	13	1	12	25.6	38.7	.077	10.5

COACHING HISTORY: Cookie Cunningham 1-12-.077

COLUMBUS DISCOVERERS

Home City: Columbus, Ohio
Home Field: Recreation Park Capacity: 6,500
Origin of Name: Named after the famous explorer Christopher Columbus.

Regular Season Record

Season	League	GP	W	L	Pct	GB	R	OR
1883	AA	97	32	65	.330	33.5	476	659
1884	AA	108	69	39	.639	6.5	585	459
TOTAL:	2 years	205	101	104		40	1061	1118
AVERAGE:		103	51	52	.493	20	531	559

COACHING HISTORY: 1883 Horace Phillips 32-65-.330; 1884 Gus Schmelz 69-39-.639

COLUMBUS DISCOVERERS

Home City: Columbus, Ohio
Home Field: Recreation Park Capacity: 6,500
Origin of Name: Named after the previous American Association team.

Regular Season Record

Season	League	GP	W	L	Pct	GB	R	OR
1889	AA	138	60	78	.435	33.5	779	924
1890	AA	134	79	55	.590	10	831	617
1891	AA	137	61	76	.445	33	702	777
TOTAL:	3 years	409	200	209		76.5	2312	2318
AVERAGE:		136	67	69	.489	25.5	771	773

COACHING HISTORY: 1889-1890 Al Buckenberger 102-120-.459; 1890-1891 Gus Schmelz 98-89-.524

COLUMBUS PANHANDLES
(became Columbus Tigers)

Home City: Columbus, Ohio
Home Stadium:
Origin of Name: The team was originally composed of employees of the Panhandle Division of the Pennsylvania Railroad.

Regular Season Record

Season	League	GP	W	L	T	PF	PA	Pct
1922	NFL	7	0	7	0	18	156	.000

COACHING HISTORY: Frank Nesser 0-7-0-.000

COLUMBUS TIGERS
(were Columbus Panhandles)

Home City: Columbus, Ohio
Home Stadium:
Origin of Name:

Regular Season Record

Season	League	GP	W	L	T	PF	PA	Pct
1923	NFL	10	5	4	1	119	35	.550
1924	NFL	8	4	4	0	91	68	.500
1925	NFL	9	0	9	0	28	124	.000
1926	NFL	7	1	6	0	26	93	.143
TOTAL:	4 years	34	10	23	1	264	320	
AVERAGE:		9	3	6	0	66	80	.309

COACHING HISTORY: 1923 Gus Tebell 4-2-0-.667; 1923 Pete Stinchcomb 1-2-1-.375; 1924-1925 Jim Weaver 4-13-0-.235: 1926 John Heldt 1-6-0-.143

CONNECTICUT BICENTENNIALS

(were Hartford Bicentennials)
(became Oakland Stompers)

Home City: New Haven, Connecticut
Home Stadium: Yale Bowl — Capacity: 70,874 [1977]
Origin of Name: The team kept the same nickname when it moved from Hartford to New Haven.

Regular Season Record

Season	League	GP	W	L	GF	GA	BP	Pts	Pct
1977	NASL	26	7	19	34	65	30	72	.308

COACHING HISTORY: Bobby Thomson 1-12; Malcolm Musgrove 6-7

CZECHOSLOVAKIA

Home City: Prague, Czechoslovakia *
Home Arena: The team played all its games in North America.
Origin of Name: This was the Czechoslovakian National hockey team.

Regular Season Record

Season	League	GP	W	L	T	GF	GA	Pts	Pct
1977-1978	WHA	8	1	6	1	21	40	3	.188
1978-1979	WHA	6	1	4	1	14	33	3	.250
TOTAL:	2 years	14	2	10	2	35	73	6	
AVERAGE:		7	1	5	1	18	37	3	.214

COACHING HISTORY: 1977-1979 Stanislav Nevesely 2-10-2-.214

DALLAS CHAPARRALS

(changed name to Texas Chaparrals for the 1971 season)

Home City: Dallas, Texas
Home Court: Moody Coliseum (1968-1973) — Capacity: 8,500
Memorial Auditorium (1968-1973) — Capacity: 8,088
Origin of Name: The team was named by one of the team's investors after one of the hotel rooms where the team executives held one of their meetings. Chaparral are low thorny shrubs.

Regular Season Record

Season	League	GP	W	L	PPGF	PPGA	Pct	GB
1967-1968	ABA	78	46	32	109.9	108.6	.590	2
1968-1969	ABA	78	41	37	111.0	111.7	.526	19
1969-1970	ABA	84	45	39	120.0	118.1	.536	6
1971-1972	ABA	84	42	42	104.4	104.3	.500	18
1972-1973	ABA	84	28	56	110.7	115.1	.333	27
TOTAL:	5 years	408	202	206				72
AVERAGE:		82	41	41	111.2	111.6	.495	14

Playoff Record

Season	GP	W	L	PPGF	PPGA	
1967-1968	8	4	4	108.8	107.5	Lost 2nd round series to New Orleans.
1968-1969	7	3	4	115.0	114.6	Lost 1st round series to New Orleans.
1969-1970	6	2	4	124.7	125.7	Lost 1st round series to Los Angeles.
1971-1972	4	0	4	97.8	104.5	Lost 1st round series to Utah.
TOTAL:	25	9	16			
AVERAGE:	6	2	4	111.6	113.1	

COACHING HISTORY: 1967-1970 Cliff Hagan 109-90-.548; 1969-1970 Max Williams 23-18-.561; 1971-1972 Tom Nissalke 42-42-.500; 1972-1973 Babe McCarthy 24-48-.333; 1972-1973 Dave Brown 4-8-.333

DALLAS COWBOYS

Home City: Dallas, Texas (1960-1970)
Irving, Texas (1971-present)
Home Stadium: Cotton Bowl (1960-1970) Capacity: 72,000
Texas Stadium (1971-present) Capacity: 63,812 [1995]
Origin of Name: The name was chosen by the team owners.

Regular Season Record

Season	League	GP	W	L	T	PF	PA	Pct
1960	NFL	12	0	11	1	177	369	.042
1961	NFL	14	4	9	1	236	380	.321
1962	NFL	14	5	8	1	398	402	.393
1963	NFL	14	4	10	0	305	378	.286
1964	NFL	14	5	8	1	250	289	.393
1965	NFL	14	7	7	0	325	280	.500
1966	NFL	14	10	3	1	445	239	.750
1967	NFL	14	9	5	0	342	268	.643
1968	NFL	14	12	2	0	431	186	.857
1969	NFL	14	11	2	1	369	223	.821
1970	NFL	14	10	4	0	299	221	.714
1971	NFL	14	11	3	0	406	222	.786
1972	NFL	14	10	4	0	319	240	.714
1973	NFL	14	10	4	0	382	203	.714
1974	NFL	14	8	6	0	297	235	.571
1975	NFL	14	10	4	0	350	268	.714
1976	NFL	14	11	3	0	296	194	.786
1977	NFL	14	12	2	0	345	212	.857

1978	NFL	16	12	4	0	384	208	.750
1979	NFL	16	11	5	0	371	313	.688
1980	NFL	16	12	4	0	454	311	.750
1981	NFL	16	12	4	0	367	277	.750
1982	NFL	9	6	3	0	126	145	.667
1983	NFL	16	12	4	0	541	332	.875
1984	NFL	16	9	7	0	308	308	.563
1985	NFL	16	10	6	0	357	333	.625
1986	NFL	16	7	9	0	346	337	.438
1987	NFL	15	7	8	0	340	348	.467
1988	NFL	16	3	13	0	265	381	.188
1989	NFL	16	1	15	0	204	393	.063
1990	NFL	16	7	9	0	244	308	.438
1991	NFL	16	11	5	0	342	310	.688
1992	NFL	16	13	3	0	409	243	.813
1993	NFL	16	12	4	0	376	229	.750
1994	NFL	16	12	4	0	414	248	.750
1995	NFL	16	12	4	0	435	291	.750
TOTAL:	36 years	530	318	206	6	12255	10124	
AVERAGE:		15	9	6	0	340	281	.606

Playoff Record

Season	**GP**	**W**	**L**	**PF**	**PA**	**Result**
1966	1	0	1	27	34	Lost championship game to Green Bay.
1967	2	1	1	69	35	Lost Conference championship to Cleveland.
1968	1	0	1	20	31	Lost Conference championship to Cleveland.
1969	1	0	1	14	38	Lost Conference championship to Cleveland.
1970	3	2	1	35	26	Lost Super Bowl to Baltimore.
1971	3	3	0	58	18	**Won Super Bowl**.
1972	2	1	1	33	54	Lost NFC championship to Washington.
1973	2	1	1	37	43	Lost NFC championship to Minnesota.
1975	3	2	1	71	42	Lost Super Bowl to Pittsburgh.
1976	1	0	1	12	14	Lost Divisional playoff to Los Angeles.
1977	3	3	0	87	23	**Won Super Bowl**.
1978	3	2	1	86	55	Lost Super Bowl to Pittsburgh.
1979	1	0	1	19	21	Lost Divisional playoff to Los Angeles.
1980	3	2	1	71	60	Lost NFC championship to Philadelphia.
1981	2	1	1	65	28	Lost NFC championship to San Francisco.
1982	3	2	1	84	74	Lost NFC championship to Washington.
1983	1	0	1	17	24	Lost 1st round game to Los Angeles.
1985	1	0	1	0	20	Lost 1st round game to Los Angeles.
1991	2	1	1	23	51	Lost semifinal game to Detroit.
1992	3	3	0	116	47	**Won Super Bowl**.
1993	3	3	0	95	51	**Won Super Bowl**.
1994	2	1	1	63	47	Lost Conference playoff to San Francisco.
1995	3	3	0	95	55	**Won Super Bowl**.
TOTAL:	49	31	18	1197	891	
AVERAGE:	2	1	1	52	39	

COACHING HISTORY: 1960-1988 Tom Landry 250-162-6-.605; 1989-1993 Jim Johnson 44-36-0-.550; 1994-present Barry Switzer

DALLAS MAVERICKS

Home City: Dallas, Texas
Home Court: Reunion Arena — Capacity: 17,502 [1995]
Origin of Name: The name was chosen in a Name the Team Contest.

Regular Season Record

Season	League	GP	W	L	PPGF	PPGA	Pct	GB
1980-1981	NBA	82	15	67	101.5	109.9	.183	37
1981-1982	NBA	82	28	54	104.6	109.0	.341	20
1982-1983	NBA	82	38	44	112.7	113.1	.463	15
1983-1984	NBA	82	43	39	110.4	110.0	.524	2
1984-1985	NBA	82	44	38	111.2	109.0	.537	8
1985-1986	NBA	82	44	38	115.3	114.2	.537	7
1986-1987	NBA	82	55	27	116.7	110.4	.671	-
1987-1988	NBA	82	53	29	109.3	104.9	.646	1
1988-1989	NBA	82	38	44	103.5	104.7	.463	13
1989-1990	NBA	82	47	35	102.2	102.2	.573	9
1990-1991	NBA	82	28	54	99.9	104.5	.341	27
1991-1992	NBA	82	22	60	97.6	105.3	.268	33
1992-1993	NBA	82	11	71	99.3	114.5	.134	44
1993-1994	NBA	82	13	69	95.1	103.8	.159	45
1994-1995	NBA	82	36	46	103.2	106.1	.439	26
1995-1996	NBA	82	26	56	102.5	107.5	.317	33
TOTAL:	16 years	1312	541	771				320
AVERAGE:		82	34	48	105.3	108.1	.412	20

Playoff Record

Season	GP	W	L	PPGF	PPGA	Result
1983-1984	10	4	6	101.7	108.8	Lost semifinal to Los Angeles.
1984-1985	4	1	3	120.5	123.0	Lost 1st round series to Portland.
1985-1986	10	5	5	110.8	112.1	Lost semifinal to Los Angeles.
1986-1987	4	1	3	116.5	120.5	Lost 1st round series to Seattle.
1987-1988	17	10	7	107.9	108.0	Lost Conference final to Los Angeles.
1989-1990	3	0	3	100.3	109.7	Lost 1st round series to Portland.
TOTAL:	48	21	27			
AVERAGE:	8	4	4	109.6	113.7	

COACHING HISTORY: 1980-1987 Dick Motta 267-307-.465; 1987-1990 John MacLeod 96-79-.549; 1989-1993 Richie Adubato 106-228-.317; 1992-1993 Gar Heard 9-44-.170; 1993-1994 Quinn Buckner 13-69-.159; 1994-present Dick Motta

DALLAS STARS

(were Minnesota North Stars)

Home City: Dallas, Texas
Home Arena: Reunion Arena — Capacity: 16,924 [1995]
Origin of Name: The team basically kept the same nickname after moving to Dallas from Minnesota, but being based in Texas obviously couldn't be called North Stars.

Regular Season Record

Season	League	GP	W	L	T	GF	GA	Pts	Pct
1993-1994	NHL	84	42	29	13	286	265	97	.577
1994-1995	NHL	48	17	23	8	136	135	42	.438
1995-1996	NHL	82	26	42	14	227	280	66	.402
TOTAL:	3 years	214	85	94	35	649	680	205	
AVERAGE:		71	28	31	12	216	227	68	.479

Playoff Record

Season	GP	W	L	GF	GA	Result
1993-1994	9	5	4	27	28	Lost quarterfinal series to Vancouver.
1994-1995	5	1	4	10	17	Lost 1st round series to Detroit.
TOTAL:	14	6	8	37	45	
AVERAGE:	7	3	4	19	23	

COACHING HISTORY: 1993-1996 Bob Gainey 70-71-30; 1995-present Ken Hitchcock

DALLAS TEXANS

(were--New York Yanks)
(became Baltimore Colts)

Home City: Dallas, Texas
Home Stadium: Cotton Bowl — Capacity: 72,000
Origin of Name: The team was based in Texas.

Regular Season Record

Season	League	GP	W	L	T	PF	PA	Pct
1952	NFL	12	1	11	0	182	427	.083

COACHING HISTORY: Jim Phelan 1-11-0-.083

DALLAS TEXANS

(became Kansas City Chiefs)

Home City: Dallas, Texas
Home Stadium: Cotton Bowl — Capacity: 72,000
Origin of Name: Named by team owner Lamar Hunt.

Regular Season Record

Season	League	GP	W	L	T	PF	PA	Pct
1960	AFL	14	8	6	0	362	253	.571
1961	AFL	14	6	8	0	334	343	.429
1962	AFL	14	11	3	0	389	233	.786
TOTAL:	3 years	42	25	17	0	1085	829	
AVERAGE:		14	8	6	0	362	276	.595

Playoff Record

Season	GP	W	L	PF	PA	Result
1962	1	1	0	20	17	**Won AFL championship**.

COACHING HISTORY: Hank Stram 25-17-.595

DALLAS TORNADO

Home City: Dallas Texas
Home Stadium: Cotton Bowl (1967-1970)
Texas Stadium (1971-1976, 1981) Capacity: 65,101
Ownby Stadium (1977-1980) Capacity: 23,783
Origin of Name: The team was named by club executives and represented in its first year by Dundee F.C. of Dundee Scotland.

Regular Season Record

Season	League	GP	W	L	T	GF	GA	BP	Pts	Pct
1967	USA	12	3	6	3	14	23	-	9	.375
1968	NASL	32	2	26	4	28	109	28	52	.181
1969	NASL	16	8	6	2	32	31	28	82	.569
1970	NASL	24	8	12	4	39	39	32	92	.426
1971	NASL	24	10	6	8	38	24	35	119	.551
1972	NASL	14	6	5	3	15	12	15	60	.476
1973	NASL	19	11	4	4	36	25	33	111	.649
1974	NASL	20	9	8	3	39	27	37	100	.556
1975	NASL	22	9	13	-	33	38	29	83	.419
1976	NASL	24	13	11	-	44	45	39	117	.542
1977	NASL	26	18	8	-	56	37	53	161	.688
1978	NASL	30	14	16	-	51	53	47	131	.485
1979	NASL	30	17	13	-	53	51	50	152	.563
1980	NASL	32	18	14	-	57	58	49	157	.545
1981	NASL	32	5	27	-	27	27	26	54	.113
TOTAL:	15 years	357	151	175	31	562	599	501	1480	
AVERAGE:		24	10	12	2	37	40	33	99	.446

Playoff Record

Season	GP	W	L	T	GF	GA	
1971	6	4	2	0	13	7	**Won NASL championship**.
1972	1	0	1	0	0	1	Lost 1st round series to New York.
1973	2	1	1	0	1	2	Lost championship game to Philadelphia.
1974	2	1	1	0	4	3	Lost 2nd round series to Miami.
1976	2	1	1	0	2	2	Lost 2nd round series to San Jose.
1977	2	0	2	0	2	8	Lost 1st round series to Los Angeles.
1979	2	0	2	0	3	5	Lost 1st round series to Vancouver.
1980	5	3	2	0	8	6	Lost 2nd round series to New York.
TOTAL:	22	10	12	0	33	34	
AVERAGE:	3	1	2	0	4	4	

COACHING HISTORY: 1967 Jerry Kerr 3-6-3-.375; 1968 Bob Kap; 1968 Keith Spurgeon; 1969-1975 Ron Newman 61-54-24: 1976-1980 Al Miller 80-62; 1981 Mike Renshaw 5-27

DAYTON METROS

Home City: Dayton, Ohio
Home Court:
Origin of Name: Metros was a short form for Metropolitans

Season	League	GP	W	L	PPGF	PPGA	Pct	GB
			Regular Season Record					
1938	NBL	13	2	11	31.5	37.6	.154	9.5

COACHING HISTORY: Bill Hosket 2-11-.154

DAYTON RENS

(Detroit Vagabond Kings became the Dayton Rens midway through the 1949 season)

Home City: Dayton, Ohio
Home Court: The team played only road games.
Origin of Name: When the Detroit team disbanded midway through the 1949 season its record was assumed by the New York Rens, a powerful all-black touring team and the team played its few home games in Dayton Ohio. Rens was short for Renaissance.

Season	League	GP	W	L	PPGF	PPGA	Pct	GB
			Regular Season Record					
1948-1949	NBL	40	14	26	56.7	61.7	.350	30.5

COACHING HISTORY: Pop Gates 14-26-.350

DAYTON TRIANGLES

Home City: Dayton, Ohio
Home Stadium:
Origin of Name: The team was sponsored by a triangle of plants in downtown Dayton.

Season	League	GP	W	L	T	PF	PA	Pct
			Regular Season Record					
1922	NFL	8	4	3	1	80	62	.563
1923	NFL	8	1	6	1	16	95	.188
1924	NFL	8	2	6	0	45	148	.250
1925	NFL	8	0	7	1	3	84	.063
1926	NFL	6	1	4	1	15	82	.250
1927	NFL	8	1	6	1	15	58	.188
1928	NFL	7	0	7	0	9	131	.000
1929	NFL	6	0	6	0	7	136	.000
TOTAL:	8 years	59	9	45	5	190	796	
AVERAGE:		7	1	5	1	24	100	.195

COACHING HISTORY: 1922-1926 Carl Storck 8-26-4-.263; 1927 Lou Mahrt 1-6-1-.188; 1928-1929 Fay Abbott 0-13-0-.000

DENVER BRONCOS

Home City: Denver, Colorado
Home Stadium: Mile High Stadium Capacity: 76,273 [1995]
Origin of Name: The name was picked in a Name the Team Contest.

Regular Season Record

Season	League	GP	W	L	T	PF	PA	Pct
1960	AFL	14	4	9	1	309	393	.321
1961	AFL	14	3	11	0	251	432	.214
1962	AFL	14	7	7	0	353	334	.500
1963	AFL	14	2	11	1	301	473	.179
1964	AFL	14	2	11	1	240	438	.179
1965	AFL	14	4	10	0	303	392	.286
1966	AFL	14	4	10	0	196	381	.286
1967	AFL	14	3	11	0	256	409	.214
1968	AFL	14	5	9	0	255	404	.357
1969	AFL	14	5	8	1	297	344	.393
1970	NFL	14	5	8	1	253	264	.393
1971	NFL	14	4	9	1	203	275	.321
1972	NFL	14	5	9	0	325	350	.357
1973	NFL	14	7	5	2	354	296	.571
1974	NFL	14	7	6	1	302	294	.536
1975	NFL	14	6	8	0	254	307	.429
1976	NFL	14	9	5	0	315	206	.643
1977	NFL	14	12	2	0	274	148	.857
1978	NFL	16	10	6	0	282	198	.625
1979	NFL	16	10	6	0	289	262	.625
1980	NFL	16	8	8	0	310	323	.500
1981	NFL	16	10	6	0	321	289	.625
1982	NFL	9	2	7	0	148	226	.222
1983	NFL	16	9	7	0	302	327	.562
1984	NFL	16	13	3	0	353	241	.813
1985	NFL	16	11	5	0	380	329	.688
1986	NFL	16	11	5	0	378	327	.688
1987	NFL	15	10	4	1	379	288	.700
1988	NFL	16	8	8	0	327	352	.500
1989	NFL	16	11	5	0	362	226	.688
1990	NFL	16	5	11	0	331	374	.313
1991	NFL	16	12	4	0	304	235	.750
1992	NFL	16	8	8	0	262	329	.500
1993	NFL	16	9	7	0	373	284	.563
1994	NFL	16	7	9	0	347	396	.438
1995	NFL	16	8	8	0	388	345	.500
TOTAL:	36 years	532	256	266	10	10877	11491	
AVERAGE:		15	7	8	0	302	319	.491

Playoff Record

Season	GP	W	L	PF	PA	Result
1977	3	2	1	64	65	Lost Super Bowl to Dallas.
1978	1	0	1	10	33	Lost Divisional playoff to Pittsburgh.
1979	1	0	1	7	13	Lost 1st round playoff to Houston.
1983	1	0	1	7	31	Lost 1st round playoff to Seattle.

*Known as Bears Stadium from 1960 to 1966

1984	1	0	1	17	24	Lost Divisional playoff to Pittsburgh.
1986	3	2	1	65	76	Lost Super Bowl to N.Y. Giants.
1987	3	2	1	82	85	Lost Super Bowl to Washington.
1989	3	2	1	71	99	Lost Super Bowl to San Francisco.
1991	2	1	1	33	34	Lost AFC championship to Buffalo.
1993	1	0	1	24	42	Lost Wild Card game to L.A. Raiders.
TOTAL:	19	9	10	380	502	
AVERAGE:	2	1	1	38	50	

COACHING HISTORY: 1960-1961 Frank Filchock 7-20-1-.268; 1962-1964 Jack Faulkner 9-22-1-.297; 1964-1966 Mac Speedie 6-19-1-.250; 1966 Ray Malavasi 4-8-0-.333; 1967-1971 Lou Saban 20-42-3-.331; 1971 Jerry Smith 2-3-0-.400; 1972-1976 John Ralston 34-33-3-.507; 1977-1980 Red Miller 40-22-0-.645; 1981-1992 Dan Reeves 110-73-1-.601; 1993-1994 Wade Phillips 16-16-0-.500; 1995-present Mike Shanahan

DENVER DYNAMOS

(became Minnesota Kicks)

Home City: Denver, Colorado
Home Stadium: Mile High Stadium Capacity: 51,706 [1975]
Origin of Name: The team was named after the famous Moscow Dynamo sports teams.

Regular Season Record

Season	League	GP	W	L	T	GF	GA	BP	Pts	Pct
1974	NASL	20	5	15	0	21	42	19	49	.272
1975	NASL	22	9	13	-	37	42	31	85	.429
TOTAL:	2 years	42	14	28	0	58	84	50	134	
AVERAGE:		21	7	14	0	29	42	25	67	.354

COACHING HISTORY: 1974 Ken Bracewell 5-15-0-.272; 1975 John Young 9-13-.429

DENVER GOLD

Home City: Denver, Colorado
Home Stadium: Mile High Stadium Capacity: 75,123 [1984]
Origin of Name: Named for Colorado's gold mining industry.

Regular Season Record

Season	League	GP	W	L	T	PF	PA	Pct
1983	USFL	18	7	11	0	284	304	.389
1984	USFL	18	9	9	0	356	413	.500
1985	USFL	18	11	7	0	433	389	.611
TOTAL:	3 years	54	27	27	0	1073	1106	
AVERAGE:		18	9	9	0	358	369	.500

Playoff Record

Season	GP	W	L	PF	PA	Result
1985	1	0	1	7	48	Lost 1st round game to Memphis.

COACHING HISTORY: 1983 Red Miller 4-7-0-.364; 1983 Charley Armey 3-4-0-.429; 1984 Craig Morton 9-9-0-.500; 1985 Mouse Davis 11-7-0-.611

DENVER NUGGETS

Home City: Denver, Colorado
Home Court:
Origin of Name: Named for Colorado's gold mining industry

Regular Season Record

Season	League	GP	W	L	PPGF	PPGA	Pct	GB
1948-1949	NBL	62	18	44	58.2	64.1	.290	18
1949-1950	NBA	62	11	51	77.7	89.1	.177	27
TOTAL:	2 years	124	29	95				45
AVERAGE:		62	14	47	68.0	76.6	.238	23

COACHING HISTORY: 1948-1949 Ralph Bishop 18-44-.290; 1949-1950 Jim Darden 11-51-.177

DENVER NUGGETS
(were Denver Rockets)

Home City: Denver, Colorado
Home Court: Auditorium Arena (1974-1975) Capacity: 6,841 [1974]
McNichols Sports Arena (1975-present) Capacity: 17,171 [1995]
Origin of Name: Named after previous area team.

Regular Season Record

Season	League	GP	W	L	PPGF	PPGA	Pct	GB
1974-1975	ABA	84	65	19	118.7	111.4	.774	-
1975-1976	ABA	84	60	24	121.9	115.9	.714	-
1976-1977	NBA	82	50	32	112.6	107.4	.610	-
1977-1978	NBA	82	48	34	111.8	110.9	.585	-
1978-1979	NBA	82	47	35	110.7	109.5	.573	1
1979-1980	NBA	82	30	52	108.3	112.7	.366	19
1980-1981	NBA	82	37	45	121.8	122.3	.451	15
1981-1982	NBA	82	46	36	126.5	126.0	.561	2
1982-1983	NBA	82	45	37	123.2	122.6	.549	8
1983-1984	NBA	82	38	44	123.7	124.8	.463	7
1984-1985	NBA	82	52	30	120.0	117.6	.634	-
1985-1986	NBA	82	47	35	114.8	113.5	.573	4
1986-1987	NBA	82	37	45	116.7	117.6	.451	18
1987-1988	NBA	82	54	28	116.7	112.7	.659	-
1988-1989	NBA	82	44	38	118.0	116.3	.537	7
1989-1990	NBA	82	43	39	114.6	113.2	.524	13
1990-1991	NBA	82	20	62	119.9	130.8	.244	35
1991-1992	NBA	82	24	58	99.7	107.6	.293	31
1992-1993	NBA	82	36	46	105.2	106.9	.439	19
1993-1994	NBA	82	42	40	100.3	98.8	.512	16
1994-1995	NBA	82	41	41	101.3	100.5	.500	21
1995-1996	NBA	82	35	47	97.7	100.4	.427	24
TOTAL:	22 years	1808	941	867				240
AVERAGE:		82	43	39	113.8	113.6	.520	11

Playoff Record

Season	GP	W	L	PPGF	PPGA	Result
1974-1975	13	7	6	114.9	116.2	Lost 2nd round game to Indiana.
1975-1976	13	6	7	116.1	117.2	Lost championship to New York.
1976-1977	6	2	4	104.8	106.5	Lost Conf. semifinal to Portland.
1977-1978	13	6	7	110.6	113.6	Lost Conference final to Seattle.
1978-1979	3	1	2	110.0	112.7	Lost 1st round series to Los Angeles.
1981-1982	3	1	2	119.3	121.0	Lost 1st round series to Phoenix.
1982-1983	8	3	5	116.9	124.5	Lost Conf. semifinal to San Antonio.
1983-1984	5	2	3	121.8	122.4	Lost 1st round series to Utah.
1984-1985	15	8	7	122.0	120.1	Lost Conference final to L.A. Lakers.
1985-1986	10	5	5	114.5	117.8	Lost Conf. semifinal to Houston.
1986-1987	3	0	3	108.3	135.7	Lost 1st round series to L.A. Lakers.
1987-1988	11	5	6	110.8	113.2	Lost Conf. semifinal to Dallas.
1988-1989	3	0	3	112.7	122.0	Lost 1st round series to Phoenix.
1989-1990	3	0	3	114.3	126.3	Lost 1st round series to San Antonio.
1993-1994	12	6	6	94.3	96.3	Lost Conference semifinals to Utah.
1994-1995	3	0	3	93.0	108.3	Lost 1st round series to San Antonio.
TOTAL:	124	52	72			
AVERAGE:	8	3	5	111.7	116.7	

COACHING HISTORY: 1974-1979 Larry Brown 251-134-.652; 1978-1981 Donnie Walsh 60-82-.423; 1980-1990 Doug Moe 432-357-.548; 1990-1992 Paul Westhead 44-120-.268; 1992-1994 Dan Issel 102-108-.486; 1994-1995 Gene Littles 3-13; 1994-present Bernie Bickerstaff

DENVER ROCKETS

(became Denver Nuggets)

Home City: Denver, Colorado
Home Court: Auditorium Arena Capacity: 6,841 [1974]
Origin of Name: The owner of the team also owned Rocket Truck Lines and named the team after the trucking company.

Regular Season Record

Season	League	GP	W	L	PPGF	PPGA	Pct	GB
1967-1968	ABA	78	45	33	105.7	101.5	.577	3
1968-1969	ABA	78	44	34	114.9	113.4	.564	16
1969-1970	ABA	84	51	33	115.4	111.1	.607	-
1970-1971	ABA	84	30	54	118.6	122.7	.357	28
1971-1972	ABA	84	34	50	111.9	113.1	.405	26
1972-1973	ABA	84	47	37	110.8	107.6	.560	8
1973-1974	ABA	84	37	47	113.2	115.7	.440	14
TOTAL:	7 years	576	288	288				95
AVERAGE:		82	41	41	112.9	112.2	.500	14

Playoff Record

Season	GP	W	L	PPGF	PPGA	Result
1967-1968	5	2	3	101.4	107.0	Lost 1st round series to New Orleans.
1968-1969	7	3	4	110.7	119.3	Lost 1st round series to Oakland.
1969-1970	12	5	7	120.9	117.8	Lost 2nd round series to Los Angeles.
1971-1972	7	3	4	101.1	100.9	Lost 1st round series to Indiana.

1972-1973	5	1	4	98.2	106.4	Lost 1st round series to Indiana.
TOTAL:	36	14	22			
AVERAGE:	7	3	4	106.5	110.3	

COACHING HISTORY: 1967-1969 Bob Bass 89-67-.571; 1969-1970 John McClendon 9-19-.321; 1969-1971 Joe Belmont 45-24-.652; 1970-1971 Stan Albeck 27-44-.380; 1971-1974 Alex Hannum 118-134-.468

DENVER SPURS

(became Ottawa Civics during the 1975-1976 season)

Home City: Denver, Colorado
Home Arena: McNichols Sports Arena — Capacity: 16,900 [1975]
Origin of Name: Named after the previous year's minor league team.

Regular Season Record

Season	League	GP	W	L	T	GF	GA	Pts	Pct
1975-1976	WHA	34	14	19	1	114	142	29	.426

COACHING HISTORY: Jean Guy Talbot 14-19-1-.426

DETROIT CARDINALS

Home City: Detroit, Michigan
Home Stadium: Olympia Stadium
Origin of Name:

Regular Season Record

Season	League	GP	W	L	Pct	GB
1927-1928	ABL	18	5	13	.278	11

COACHING HISTORY:

DETROIT COUGARS

(became Detroit Falcons)

Home City: Detroit, Michigan
Home Arena: Border Cities Arena (1926-1927) — Capacity: 3,200
Olympia Stadium (1927-1930) — Capacity: 16,700
Origin of Name: The team was named Cougars because it consisted of many players from the previous years Victoria Cougars of the Western Hockey League.

Regular Season Record

Season	League	GP	W	L	T	GF	GA	Pts	Pct
1926-1927	NHL	44	12	28	4	76	105	28	.318
1927-1928	NHL	44	19	19	6	88	79	44	.500
1928-1929	NHL	44	19	16	9	72	63	47	.534
1929-1930	NHL	44	14	24	6	117	133	34	.386
TOTAL:	4 years	176	64	87	25	353	380	153	
AVERAGE:		44	16	22	6	88	95	38	.435

Playoff Record

Season	GP	W	L	T	GF	GA	Result
1928-1929	2	0	2	0	2	7	Lost quarterfinal series to Toronto.

COACHING HISTORY: 1926-1927 Art Duncan 12-28-4-.318; 1927-1930 Jack Adams 52-59-21-.473

The Cougars played their first season in Windsor, Ontario until the Olympia Stadium was completed.

DETROIT COUGARS

Home City: Detroit, Michigan
Home Stadium: Tiger Stadium Capacity: 53,089 [1967]
Origin of Name: The team was represented by the Glentoran Club of Belfast.

Regular Season Record

Season	League	GP	W	L	T	GF	GA	BP	Pts	Pct
1967	USA	12	3	3	6	11	18	-	12	.500
1968	NASL	31	6	21	4	48	65	40	88	.315
TOTAL:	2 years	43	9	24	10	59	83	40	100	
AVERAGE:		22	5	12	5	30	42	20	50	

COACHING HISTORY: 1967 John Colrain 3-3-6-.500; 1968 Len Julians; 1968 Andre Nagy

DETROIT EAGLES

(were the Cleveland White Horses)

Home City: Detroit, Michigan
Home Court:
Origin of Name:

Regular Season Record

Season	League	GP	W	L	PPGF	PPGA	Pct	GB
1939-1940	NBL	27	17	10	39.8	36.6	.630	1
1940-1941	NBL	24	12	12	40.5	43.7	.500	6
TOTAL:	2 years	51	29	22				7
AVERAGE:		26	15	11	40.2	40.2	.569	4

Playoff Record

Season	GP	W	L	PPGF	PPGA	Result
1939-1940	3	1	2	39.7	43.7	Lost 1st round series to Akron Firestone.
1940-1941	3	1	2	34.0	36.0	Lost 1st round series to Sheboygan.
TOTAL:	6	2	4			
AVERAGE:	3	1	2	36.9	39.9	

COACHING HISTORY: 1939-1940 Gerry Archibald 17-10-.630; 1940-1941 Dutch Dehnert 12-12-.500

DETROIT EXPRESS

Home City: Detroit, Michigan
Home Stadium: Pontiac Silverdome — Capacity: 80,638 [1980]
Origin of Name:

Regular Season Record

Season	League	GP	W	L	GF	GA	BP	Pts	Pct
1978	NASL	30	20	10	68	36	56	176	.652
1979	NASL	30	14	16	61	56	49	133	.493
1980	NASL	32	14	18	51	52	45	129	.448
TOTAL:	3 years	92	48	44	180	144	150	438	
AVERAGE:		31	16	15	60	48	50	146	.529

Playoff Record

Season	GP	W	L	T	GF	GA	Result
1978	4	2	2	0	5	5	Lost 2nd round series to Ft. Lauderdale.
1979	2	0	2	0	1	4	Lost 1st round series to Tampa.
TOTAL:	6	2	4	0	6	9	
AVERAGE:	3	1	2	0	3	5	

COACHING HISTORY: 1978-1980 Ken Furphy 48-44

DETROIT FALCONS

(were Detroit Cougars)
(became Detroit Red Wings)

Home City: Detroit, Michigan
Home Arena: Olympia Stadium — Capacity: 16,700
Origin of Name: The name was picked in a Name the Team Contest sponsored by a newspaper.

Regular Season Record

Season	League	GP	W	L	T	GF	GA	Pts	Pct
1930-1931	NHL	44	16	21	7	102	105	39	.443
1931-1932	NHL	48	18	20	10	95	108	46	.479
1932-1933	NHL	48	25	15	8	111	93	58	.604
TOTAL:	3 years	140	59	56	25	308	306	143	
AVERAGE:		47	20	19	8	103	102	48	.511

Playoff Record

Season	GP	W	L	T	GF	GA	Result
1931-1932	2	0	1	1	1	3	Lost 1st round series to Maroons.
1932-1933	4	2	2	0	8	8	Lost semifinal round to N.Y. Rangers.
TOTAL:	6	2	3	1	9	11	
AVERAGE:	3	1	2	0	5	6	

COACHING HISTORY: 1930-1933 Jack Adams 59-56-25-.511

DETROIT FALCONS

Home City: Detroit, Michigan
Home Court: Olympia Stadium
Origin of Name:

Season	League	GP	W	L	PPGF	PPGA	Pct	GB
			Regular Season Record					
1946-1947	BAA	60	20	40	63.3	65.3	.333	18.5

COACHING HISTORY: Glenn Curtis 12-22-.353; Cincy Sachs 8-18-.308

DETROIT GEMS

Home City: Detroit, Michigan
Home Court:
Origin of Name: The team was owned by a local jeweler.

Season	League	GP	W	L	PPGF	PPGA	Pct	GB
			Regular Season Record					
1946-1947	NBL	44	4	40	47.6	63.0	.091	24

COACHING HISTORY: Joel Mason 3-13-.188; Fred Campbell 1-27-.036

DETROIT LIONS
(were Portsmouth Spartans)

Home City: Detroit, Michigan (1937-1974)
Pontiac, Michigan (1975-present)
Home Stadium: University of Detroit Stadium (1934-1937) Capacity: 25,000
Tiger Stadium * (1938-1974) Capacity: 54,468
Pontiac Silverdome ** (1975-present) Capacity: 80,365 [1995]
Origin of Name: The name was picked in a radio sponsored contest.

Season	League	GP	W	L	T	PF	PA	Pct
			Regular Season Record					
1934	NFL	13	10	3	0	238	59	.769
1935	NFL	12	7	3	2	191	111	.667
1936	NFL	12	8	4	0	235	102	.667
1937	NFL	11	7	4	0	180	105	.636
1938	NFL	11	7	4	0	119	108	.636
1939	NFL	11	6	5	0	145	150	.545
1940	NFL	11	5	5	1	138	153	.500
1941	NFL	11	4	6	1	121	195	.409
1942	NFL	11	0	11	0	38	263	.000
1943	NFL	10	3	6	1	178	218	.350
1944	NFL	10	6	3	1	216	151	.650

*Known as Navin Field from 1934 to 1937 and then Briggs Stadium from 1938 to 1960.
**Known as Pontiac Metropolitan Stadium in 1975.

1945	NFL	10	7	3	0	195	194	.700
1946	NFL	11	1	10	0	142	310	.091
1947	NFL	12	3	9	0	231	305	.250
1948	NFL	12	2	10	0	200	407	.167
1949	NFL	12	4	8	0	237	259	.333
1950	NFL	12	6	6	0	321	285	.500
1951	NFL	12	7	4	1	336	259	.625
1952	NFL	12	9	3	0	344	192	.750
1953	NFL	12	10	2	0	271	205	.833
1954	NFL	12	9	2	1	337	189	.792
1955	NFL	12	3	9	0	230	275	.250
1956	NFL	12	9	3	0	300	188	.750
1957	NFL	12	8	4	0	251	231	.667
1958	NFL	12	4	7	1	261	276	.375
1959	NFL	12	3	8	1	203	275	.292
1960	NFL	12	7	5	0	239	212	.583
1961	NFL	14	8	5	1	270	258	.607
1962	NFL	14	11	3	0	315	177	.786
1963	NFL	14	5	8	1	326	265	.393
1964	NFL	14	7	5	2	280	260	.571
1965	NFL	14	6	7	1	257	295	.464
1966	NFL	14	4	9	1	206	317	.321
1967	NFL	14	5	7	2	260	259	.429
1968	NFL	14	4	8	2	207	241	.357
1969	NFL	14	9	4	1	259	188	.679
1970	NFL	14	10	4	0	347	202	.714
1971	NFL	14	7	6	1	341	286	.536
1972	NFL	14	8	5	1	339	290	.607
1973	NFL	14	6	7	1	271	247	.464
1974	NFL	14	7	7	0	256	270	.500
1975	NFL	14	7	7	0	245	262	.500
1976	NFL	14	6	8	0	262	220	.429
1977	NFL	14	6	8	0	183	252	.429
1978	NFL	16	7	9	0	290	300	.438
1979	NFL	16	2	14	0	219	365	.125
1980	NFL	16	9	7	0	334	272	.563
1981	NFL	16	8	8	0	397	322	.500
1982	NFL	9	4	5	0	181	176	.444
1983	NFL	16	9	7	0	347	286	.562
1984	NFL	16	4	11	1	283	408	.281
1985	NFL	16	7	9	0	307	366	.438
1986	NFL	16	5	11	0	277	326	.313
1987	NFL	15	4	11	0	269	384	.267
1988	NFL	16	4	12	0	220	313	.250
1989	NFL	16	7	9	0	312	364	.438
1990	NFL	16	6	10	0	373	413	.375
1991	NFL	16	12	4	0	339	295	.750
1992	NFL	16	5	11	0	273	332	.313
1993	NFL	16	10	6	0	298	292	.625
1994	NFL	16	9	7	0	357	342	.563
1995	NFL	16	10	6	0	436	336	.625
TOTAL:	62 years	830	393	412	25	16033	15858	
AVERAGE:		13	6	7	0	259	256	.489

Playoff Record

Season	GP	W	L	PF	PA	Result
1935	1	1	0	26	7	Lost championship game to N.Y. Giants.
1952	2	2	0	48	28	**Won NFL championship**.
1953	1	1	0	17	16	**Won NFL championship**.
1954	1	0	1	10	56	Lost championship game to Cleveland.
1957	2	2	0	90	41	**Won NFL championship**.
1970	1	0	1	0	5	Lost Divisional playoff to Dallas.
1982	1	0	1	7	31	Lost 1st round game to Washington.
1983	1	0	1	23	24	Lost Divisional playoff to San Francisco.
1991	2	1	1	48	47	Lost NFC championship to Washington.
1993	1	0	1	24	28	Lost Wild Card game to Green Bay.
1994	1	0	1	12	16	Lost Wild Card game to Green Bay.
1995	1	0	1	37	58	Lost Wild Card game to Philadelphia.
TOTAL:	15	7	8	342	357	
AVERAGE:	2	1	1	29	30	

COACHING HISTORY: 1934-1936 Potsy Clark 25-10-2-.703; 1937-1938 Dutch Clark 14-8-0-.636; 1939 Gus Henderson 6-5-0.545; 1940 Potsy Clark 5-5-1-.500; 1941-1942 Bill Edwards 4-9-1-.321; 1942 John Karcis 0-8-0-.000; 1943-1947 Gus Dorais 20-31-2-.396; 1948-1950 Bo McMillin 12-24-0-.333; 1951-1956 Buddy Parker 47-23-2-.667; 1957-1964 George Wilson 53-45-6-.538; 1965-1966 Harry Gilner 10-16-2-.393; 1967-1972 Joe Schmidt 43-34-7-.554; 1973 Don McCafferty 6-7-1-.464; 1974-1976 Rick Forzano 15-17-0-.469; 1976-1977 Tom Hudspeth 11-13-0-.458; 1978-1984 Monte Clark 43-61-1-.414; 1985-1988 Darryl Rogers 18-40-0-.310; 1988-present Wayne Fontes

DETROIT PALUSKI POST FIVE

Home City: Detroit, Michigan
Home Court:
Origin of Name: The team was sponsored by Pulaski Post No. 270.

Regular Season Record

Season	League	GP	W	L	Pct
1925-1926	ABL	30	8	22	.267

COACHING HISTORY:

DETROIT PANTHERS

Home City: Detroit, Michigan
Home Stadium:
Origin of Name: The team may have been named Panthers to identify with the American League baseball team Tigers.

Regular Season Record

Season	League	GP	W	L	T	PF	PA	Pct
1925	NFL	12	8	2	2	129	39	.750
1926	NFL	12	4	6	2	107	70	.417
TOTAL:	2 years	24	12	8	4	236	109	
AVERAGE:		12	6	4	2	118	55	.583

COACHING HISTORY: 1925-1926 Jimmy Conzelman 12-8-4-.583

DETROIT PISTONS
(were Fort Wayne Pistons)

Home City: Detroit, Michigan (1957-1978)
Pontiac, Michigan (1978-1988)
Auburn Hills, Michigan (1988-
Home Court: Olympia Stadium (1957-1961) Capacity: 14,000
Cobo Arena (1961-1978) Capacity: 11,147 [1978]
The Silverdome (1978-1988) Capacity: 22,366 [1986]
The Palace (1988-present) Capacity: 21,454 [1995]
Origin of Name: The team kept the same name when it moved from Fort Wayne.

Regular Season Record

Season	League	GP	W	L	PPGF	PPGA	Pct	GB
1957-1958	NBA	72	33	39	105.3	107.7	.458	8
1958-1959	NBA	72	28	44	105.1	106.6	.389	21
1959-1960	NBA	75	30	45	111.6	115.0	.400	16
1960-1961	NBA	79	34	45	118.6	121.0	.430	17
1961-1962	NBA	80	37	43	115.4	117.1	.463	17
1962-1963	NBA	80	34	46	113.9	117.6	.425	19
1963-1964	NBA	80	23	57	107.8	115.5	.288	25
1964-1965	NBA	80	31	49	108.5	111.9	.388	18
1965-1966	NBA	80	22	58	110.3	117.2	.275	23
1966-1967	NBA	81	30	51	111.3	116.8	.370	14
1967-1968	NBA	82	40	42	118.6	120.6	.488	22
1968-1969	NBA	82	32	50	114.1	117.3	.390	25
1969-1970	NBA	82	31	51	112.8	116.1	.378	29
1970-1971	NBA	82	45	37	110.1	110.9	.549	21
1971-1972	NBA	82	26	56	109.1	115.9	.317	37
1972-1973	NBA	82	40	42	110.3	110.0	.488	20
1973-1974	NBA	82	52	30	104.4	100.3	.634	7
1974-1975	NBA	82	40	42	98.9	100.3	.488	7
1975-1976	NBA	82	36	46	104.9	106.0	.439	2
1976-1977	NBA	82	44	38	109.4	110.4	.537	6
1977-1978	NBA	82	38	44	109.0	110.2	.463	10
1978-1979	NBA	82	30	52	110.0	112.7	.366	18
1979-1980	NBA	82	16	66	108.9	117.2	.195	34
1980-1981	NBA	82	21	61	99.7	106.0	.256	39
1981-1982	NBA	82	39	43	111.1	112.0	.476	16
1982-1983	NBA	82	37	45	112.7	113.1	.451	14
1983-1984	NBA	82	49	33	117.1	113.5	.598	1
1984-1985	NBA	82	46	36	116.0	113.5	.561	13
1985-1986	NBA	82	46	36	114.2	113.0	.561	11
1986-1987	NBA	82	52	30	111.2	107.8	.634	5
1987-1988	NBA	82	54	28	109.2	104.1	.659	-
1988-1989	NBA	82	63	19	106.6	100.8	.768	-
1989-1990	NBA	82	59	23	104.3	98.3	.720	-
1990-1991	NBA	82	50	32	100.1	96.8	.610	11
1991-1992	NBA	82	48	34	98.9	96.9	.585	19
1992-1993	NBA	82	40	42	100.6	102.0	.488	17
1993-1994	NBA	82	20	62	96.9	104.7	.244	37

1994-1995	NBA	82	28	54	98.2	105.5	.341	24
1995-1996	NBA	82	46	36	95.4	92.9	.561	26
TOTAL:	39 years	3157	1470	1687				649
AVERAGE:		81	38	43	108.2	110.9	.466	17

Playoff Record

Season	GP	W	L	PPGF	PPGA	Result
1957-1958	7	3	4	105.3	108.4	Lost Division finals to St. Louis.
1958-1959	3	1	2	102.7	108.0	Lost Division semifinal to Minneapolis.
1959-1960	2	0	2	105.5	113.5	Lost Division semifinal to Minneapolis.
1960-1961	5	2	3	117.4	120.8	Lost Division semifinal to Los Angeles.
1961-1962	10	5	5	115.3	120.4	Lost Division finals to Los Angeles.
1962-1963	4	1	3	103.5	111.8	Lost Division semifinal to St. Louis.
1967-1968	6	2	4	110.0	115.5	Lost Division semifinal to Boston.
1973-1974	7	3	4	95.0	92.7	Lost Conference semifinal to Chicago.
1974-1975	3	1	2	97.3	98.7	Lost 1st round series to Seattle.
1975-1976	9	4	5	110.3	115.1	Lost Conf. semifinal to Golden State.
1976-1977	3	1	2	101.3	112.3	Lost 1st round series to Golden State.
1983-1984	5	2	3	112.2	111.6	Lost 1st round series to New York.
1984-1985	9	5	4	115.3	117.1	Lost Conference semifinal to Boston.
1985-1986	4	1	3	116.5	122.0	Lost 1st round series to Atlanta.
1986-1987	15	10	5	109.3	103.3	Lost Conference final to Boston.
1987-1988	23	14	9	99.7	95.2	Lost final series to L.A. Lakers.
1988-1989	17	15	2	100.6	92.9	**Won NBA championship**.
1989-1990	20	15	5	101.8	94.9	**Won NBA championship**.
1990-1991	15	7	8	101.1	102.2	Lost Conference final to Chicago.
1991-1992	5	2	3	84.8	92.6	Lost 1st round series to New York.
1995-1996	3	0	3	89.0	101.7	Lost 1st round series to Orlando.
TOTAL:	175	94	81			
AVERAGE:	8	4	4	104.4	103.9	

COACHING HISTORY: 1957-1958 Charles Eckman 9-16-.360; 1957-1960 Ephraim Rocha 65-88-.425; 1959-1963 Dick McGuire 122-158-.436; 1963-1965 Charles Wolf 25-66-.275; 1964-1967 Dave DeBusschere 79-143-.356; 1966-1969 Donnie Butcher 52-60-.464; 1968-1969 Paul Seymour 22-38-.367; 1969-1972 Butch van Breda Kolff 82-94-.466; 1971-1973 Earl Lloyd 22-55-.286; 1972-1976 Ray Scott 147-134-.523; 1975-1978 Herb Brown 72-74-.493; 1977-1978 Bob Kauffman 29-29-.500; 1978-1980 Dick Vitale 34-60-.362; 1979-1980 Rich Adubato 12-58-.171; 1980-1983 Scotty Robertson 97-149-.394; 1983-1992 Chuck Daly 467-271-.633; 1992-1993 Ron Rothstein 40-42-.488; 1993-1995t Don Chaney 48-116-.293; 1995-present Doug Collins

DETROIT RED WINGS
(were Detroit Falcons)

Home City: Detroit, Michigan
Home Arena: Olympia Stadium (1934-1979) — Capacity: 16,700 [1979]
Joe Louis Arena (1979-present) — Capacity: 19,275 [1995]
Origin of Name: When Jack Norris bought the team in 1935 he named the team Red Wings in honor of the Winged Wheelers a team he had played for in his youth in Montreal. Norris also adopted the Winged Wheelers team logo for his new team.

Regular Season Record

Season	League	GP	W	L	T	GF	GA	Pts	Pct
1933-1934	NHL	48	24	14	10	113	98	58	.604
1934-1935	NHL	48	19	22	7	127	114	45	.469
1935-1936	NHL	48	24	16	8	124	103	56	.583
1936-1937	NHL	48	25	14	9	128	102	59	.615
1937-1938	NHL	48	12	25	11	99	133	35	.365
1938-1939	NHL	48	18	24	6	107	128	42	.438
1939-1940	NHL	48	16	26	6	90	126	38	.396
1940-1941	NHL	48	21	16	11	112	102	53	.552
1941-1942	NHL	48	19	25	4	140	147	42	.438
1942-1943	NHL	50	25	14	11	169	124	61	.610
1943-1944	NHL	50	26	18	6	214	177	58	.580
1944-1945	NHL	50	31	14	5	218	161	67	.670
1945-1946	NHL	50	20	20	10	146	159	50	.500
1946-1947	NHL	60	22	27	11	190	193	55	.458
1947-1948	NHL	60	30	18	12	187	148	72	.600
1948-1949	NHL	60	34	19	7	195	145	75	.625
1949-1950	NHL	70	37	19	14	229	164	88	.629
1950-1951	NHL	70	44	13	13	236	139	101	.721
1951-1952	NHL	70	44	14	12	215	133	100	.714
1952-1953	NHL	70	36	16	18	222	133	90	.643
1953-1954	NHL	70	37	19	14	191	132	88	.629
1954-1955	NHL	70	42	17	11	204	134	95	.679
1955-1956	NHL	70	30	24	16	183	148	76	.543
1956-1957	NHL	70	38	20	12	198	157	88	.629
1957-1958	NHL	70	29	29	12	176	207	70	.500
1958-1959	NHL	70	25	37	8	167	218	58	.414
1959-1960	NHL	70	26	29	15	186	197	67	.479
1960-1961	NHL	70	25	29	16	195	215	66	.471
1961-1962	NHL	70	23	33	14	184	219	60	.429
1962-1963	NHL	70	32	25	13	200	194	77	.550
1963-1964	NHL	70	30	29	11	191	204	71	.507
1964-1965	NHL	70	40	23	7	224	175	87	.621
1965-1966	NHL	70	31	27	12	221	194	74	.529
1966-1967	NHL	70	27	39	4	212	241	58	.414
1967-1968	NHL	74	27	35	12	245	257	66	.446
1968-1969	NHL	76	33	31	12	239	221	78	.513
1969-1970	NHL	76	40	21	15	246	199	95	.625
1970-1971	NHL	78	22	45	11	209	308	55	.353
1971-1972	NHL	78	33	35	10	261	262	76	.487
1972-1973	NHL	78	37	29	12	265	243	86	.551
1973-1974	NHL	78	29	39	10	255	319	68	.436
1974-1975	NHL	80	23	45	12	259	335	58	.363
1975-1976	NHL	80	26	44	10	226	300	62	.388
1976-1977	NHL	80	16	55	9	183	309	41	.256
1977-1978	NHL	80	32	34	14	252	266	78	.488
1978-1979	NHL	80	23	41	16	252	295	62	.388
1979-1980	NHL	80	26	43	11	268	306	63	.394
1980-1981	NHL	80	19	43	18	252	339	56	.350
1981-1982	NHL	80	21	47	12	270	351	54	.338
1982-1983	NHL	80	21	44	15	263	344	57	.356
1983-1984	NHL	80	31	42	7	298	323	69	.431

1984-1985	NHL	80	27	41	12	313	357	66	.413
1985-1986	NHL	80	17	57	6	266	415	40	.250
1986-1987	NHL	80	34	36	10	260	274	78	.488
1987-1988	NHL	80	41	28	11	322	269	93	.581
1988-1989	NHL	80	34	34	12	313	316	80	.500
1989-1990	NHL	80	28	38	14	288	323	70	.438
1990-1991	NHL	80	34	36	8	273	298	76	.475
1991-1992	NHL	80	43	25	12	320	256	98	.613
1992-1993	NHL	84	47	28	9	369	280	103	.613
1993-1994	NHL	84	46	30	8	356	275	100	.595
1994-1995	NHL	48	33	11	4	180	117	70	.729
1995-1996	NHL	82	62	13	7	325	181	131	.799
TOTAL:	63 years	4348	1867	1804	675	13821	13702	4409	
AVERAGE:		69	30	28	11	219	217	71	.507

Playoff Record

Season	**GP**	**W**	**L**	**T**	**GF**	**GA**	**Result**
1933-1934	9	4	5	0	18	21	Lost Stanley Cup final to Chicago.
1935-1936	7	6	1	0	24	12	**Won Stanley Cup**.
1936-1937	10	6	4	0	22	16	**Won Stanley Cup**.
1938-1939	6	3	3	0	16	15	Lost semifinal series to Toronto.
1939-1940	5	2	3	0	11	12	Lost semifinal series to Toronto.
1940-1941	9	4	5	0	17	20	Lost Stanley Cup final to Boston.
1941-1942	12	7	5	0	36	38	Lost Stanley Cup final to Toronto.
1942-1943	10	8	2	0	36	22	**Won Stanley Cup**.
1943-1944	5	1	4	0	8	17	Lost semifinal series to Chicago.
1944-1945	14	7	7	0	31	31	Lost Stanley Cup final to Toronto.
1945-1946	5	1	4	0	10	16	Lost semifinal series to Boston.
1946-1947	5	1	4	0	14	18	Lost semifinal series to Toronto.
1947-1948	10	6	4	0	24	30	Lost Stanley Cup final to Toronto.
1948-1949	11	4	7	0	22	26	Lost Stanley Cup final to Toronto.
1949-1950	14	7	7	0	32	28	**Won Stanley Cup**.
1950-1951	6	2	4	0	12	13	Lost semifinal series to Montreal.
1951-1952	8	8	0	0	24	5	**Won Stanley Cup**.
1952-1953	6	2	4	0	21	21	Lost semifinal series to Boston.
1953-1954	12	8	4	0	29	20	**Won Stanley Cup.**
1954-1955	11	8	3	0	41	26	**Won Stanley Cup**.
1955-1956	10	5	5	0	23	28	Lost Stanley Cup final to Montreal.
1956-1957	5	1	4	0	14	15	Lost semifinal series to Boston.
1957-1958	4	0	4	0	6	19	Lost semifinal series to Montreal.
1959-1960	6	2	4	0	16	20	Lost semifinal series to Toronto.
1960-1961	11	6	5	0	27	27	Lost Stanley Cup final to Chicago.
1962-1963	11	5	6	0	36	36	Lost Stanley Cup final to Toronto.
1963-1964	14	7	7	0	41	40	Lost Stanley Cup final to Toronto.
1964-1965	7	3	4	0	19	23	Lost semifinal series to Chicago.
1965-1966	12	6	6	0	36	28	Lost Stanley Cup final to Montreal.
1969-1970	4	0	4	0	8	16	Lost quarterfinal series to Chicago.
1977-1978	7	3	4	0	18	29	Lost quarterfinal series to Montreal.
1983-1984	4	1	3	0	12	13	Lost 1st round series to St. Louis.
1984-1985	3	0	3	0	8	23	Lost 1st round series to Chicago.
1986-1987	16	9	7	0	45	40	Lost semifinal series to Edmonton.
1987-1988	16	9	7	0	69	57	Lost semifinal series to Edmonton.
1988-1989	6	2	4	0	18	25	Lost 1st round series to Chicago.

1990-1991	7	3	4	0	20	24	Lost 1st round series to St. Louis.
1991-1992	11	4	7	0	29	30	Lost quarterfinal series to Chicago.
1992-1993	7	3	4	0	30	24	Lost 1st round series to Toronto.
1993-1994	7	3	4	0	27	21	Lost 1st round series to San Jose.
1994-1995	18	12	6	0	61	44	Lost Stanley Cup final to New Jersey.
1995-1996	19	10	9	0	58	46	Lost semifinal series to Colorado.
TOTAL:	380	189	191	0	1069	1035	
AVERAGE:	9	4	5	0	25	25	

COACHING HISTORY: 1933-1947 Jack Adams 302-275-115-.520; 1947-1954 Tommy Ivan 262-380-90-.419; 1954-1958 Jimmy Skinner 123-78-46-.591; 1957-1968 Sid Abel 302-318-117-.489; 1968-1970 Bill Gadsby 35-32-12-.519; 1969-1970 Sid Abel 38-20-15-.623; 1970-1971 Ned Harkness 9-7-3-.553; 1970-1972 Doug Barkley 16-46-8-.286; 1971-1973 John Wilson 67-56-22-.538; 1973-1974 Ted Garvin 2-9-1-.208; 1973-1977 Alex Delvecchio 82-130-32-.402; 1975-1976 Doug Barkley 7-15-4-.346; 1976-1977 Larry Wilson 3-29-4-.139; 1977-1980 Bobby Kromm 79-111-41-.431; 1979-1981 Ted Lindsay 5-21-3-.224; 1980-1982 Wayne Maxner 34-68-27-.368; 1981-1982 Bill Dea 3-8-0-.273; 1982-1985 Nick Polano 79-127-34-.400; 1985-1986 Harry Neale 8-23-4-.286; 1985-1986 Brad Park 9-34-2-.222; 1986-1990 Jacques Demers 137-136-47-.502; 1990-1993 Bryan Murray 124-91-29-.568; 1993-present Scotty Bowman

DETROIT TIGERS

Home City: Detroit, Michigan
Home Field: Bennett Park (1901-1911) Capacity: 8,500[1901]
Tiger Stadium* (1912-present) Capacity: 52,416[1995]
Origin of Name: The team was called Tigers because the stockings they originally wore resembled the stockings worn by the Princeton Tigers.

Regular Season Record

Season	**League**	**GP**	**W**	**L**	**Pct**	**GB**	**R**	**OR**
1901	AL	135	74	61	.548	8.5	742	696
1902	AL	135	52	83	.385	30.5	566	657
1903	AL	136	65	71	.478	25	567	539
1904	AL	152	62	90	.408	32	505	627
1905	AL	153	79	74	.516	15.5	511	608
1906	AL	149	71	78	.477	21	518	596
1907	AL	150	92	58	.613	-	696	519
1908	AL	153	90	63	.588	-	645	552
1909	AL	152	98	54	.645	-	666	493
1910	AL	154	86	68	.558	18	679	580
1911	AL	154	89	65	.578	13.5	831	777
1912	AL	153	69	84	.451	36.5	720	768
1913	AL	153	66	87	.431	30	624	720
1914	AL	153	80	73	.523	19.5	615	618
1915	AL	154	100	54	.649	2.5	778	573
1916	AL	154	87	67	.565	4	673	573
1917	AL	153	78	75	.510	21.5	639	577
1918	AL	126	55	71	.437	20	473	555
1919	AL	140	80	60	.571	8	620	582
1920	AL	154	61	93	.396	37	651	832
1921	AL	153	71	82	.464	27	883	852
1922	AL	154	79	75	.513	15	828	791
1923	AL	154	83	71	.539	16	831	741

1924	AL	154	86	68	.558	6	849	796
1925	AL	154	81	73	.526	16.5	903	829
1926	AL	154	79	75	.513	12	793	830
1927	AL	153	82	71	.536	27.5	845	805
1928	AL	154	68	86	.442	33	744	804
1929	AL	154	70	84	.455	36	926	928
1930	AL	154	75	79	.487	27	783	833
1931	AL	154	61	93	.396	47	651	836
1932	AL	151	76	75	.503	29.5	799	787
1933	AL	154	75	79	.487	25	722	733
1934	AL	154	101	53	.656	-	958	708
1935	AL	151	93	58	.616	-	919	665
1936	AL	154	83	71	.539	19.5	921	871
1937	AL	154	89	65	.578	13	935	841
1938	AL	154	84	70	.545	16	862	795
1939	AL	154	81	73	.526	26.5	849	762
1940	AL	154	90	64	.584	-	888	717
1941	AL	154	75	79	.487	26	686	743
1942	AL	154	73	81	.474	30	589	587
1943	AL	154	78	76	.506	20	632	560
1944	AL	154	88	66	.571	1	658	581
1945	AL	153	88	65	.575	-	633	565
1946	AL	154	92	62	.597	12	704	567
1947	AL	154	85	69	.552	12	714	642
1948	AL	154	78	76	.506	18.5	700	726
1949	AL	154	87	67	.565	10	751	655
1950	AL	154	95	59	.617	3	837	713
1951	AL	154	73	81	.474	25	685	741
1952	AL	154	50	104	.325	45	557	738
1953	AL	154	60	94	.390	40.5	695	923
1954	AL	154	68	86	.442	43	584	664
1955	AL	154	79	75	.513	17	775	658
1956	AL	154	82	72	.532	15	789	699
1957	AL	154	78	76	.506	20	614	614
1958	AL	154	77	77	.500	15	659	606
1959	AL	154	76	78	.494	18	713	732
1960	AL	154	71	83	.461	26	633	644
1961	AL	162	101	61	.623	8	841	671
1962	AL	161	85	76	.528	10.5	758	692
1963	AL	162	79	83	.488	25.5	700	703
1964	AL	162	85	77	.525	14	699	678
1965	AL	162	89	73	.549	13	680	602
1966	AL	162	88	74	.543	10	719	698
1967	AL	162	91	71	.562	1	683	587
1968	AL	162	103	59	.636	-	671	492
1969	AL	162	90	72	.556	19	701	601
1970	AL	162	79	83	.488	29	666	731
1971	AL	162	91	71	.562	12	701	645
1972	AL	156	86	70	.551	-	558	514
1973	AL	162	85	77	.525	12	642	674
1974	AL	162	72	90	.444	19	620	768
1975	AL	159	57	102	.358	37.5	570	786
1976	AL	161	74	87	.460	24	609	709
1977	AL	162	74	88	.457	26	714	751

1978	AL	162	86	76	.531	13.5	714	653
1979	AL	161	85	76	.528	18	770	738
1980	AL	162	84	78	.519	19	830	757
1981	AL	109	60	49	.550	NA	427	404
1982	AL	162	83	79	.512	12	729	685
1983	AL	162	92	70	.568	6	789	679
1984	AL	162	104	58	.642	-	829	643
1985	AL	161	84	77	.522	15	729	688
1986	AL	162	87	75	.537	8.5	798	714
1987	AL	162	98	64	.605	-	896	735
1988	AL	162	88	74	.543	1	703	658
1989	AL	162	59	103	.364	30	617	816
1990	AL	162	79	83	.488	9	750	754
1991	AL	162	84	78	.519	7	817	794
1992	AL	162	75	87	.463	21	791	794
1993	AL	162	85	77	.525	10	899	837
1994	AL	115	53	62	.461	18	652	671
1995	AL	144	60	84	.417	26	654	844
TOTAL:	95 years	14653	7569	7084		1607	68142	65890
AVERAGE:		154	80	74	.517	17	717	694

Playoff Record

Season	**GP**	**W**	**L**	**T**	**R**	**OR**	**Result**
1907	5	0	4	1	6	19	Lost World Series to Chicago.
1908	5	1	4	0	15	24	Lost World Series to Chicago.
1909	7	3	4	0	28	34	Lost World Series to Pittsburgh.
1934	7	3	4	0	23	34	Lost World Series to St. Louis.
1935	6	4	2	0	21	18	**Won World Series.**
1940	7	3	4	0	28	22	Lost World Series to Cincinnati.
1945	7	4	3	0	32	29	**Won World Series.**
1968	7	4	3	0	34	30	**Won World Series.**
1972	5	2	3	0	10	13	Lost ALCS to Oakland.
1984	8	7	1	0	37	20	**Won World Series.**
1987	5	1	4	0	23	34	Lost ALCS to Minnesota.
TOTAL:	69	32	36	1	257	277	
AVERAGE:	6	3	3	0	23	25	

COACHING HISTORY: 1901 George Stallings 74-61-.548; 1902 Frank Dwyer 52-83-.385; 1903-1904 Ed Barrow 97-117-.453; 1904 Bobby Lowe 30-44-.405; 1905-1906 Bill Armour 150-152-.497; 1907-1920 Hugh Jennings 1131-972-.538; 1921-1926 Ty Cobb 479-444-.519; 1927-1928 George Moriarty 150-157-.489; 1929-1933 Stanley Harris 355-410-.464; 1933 Del Baker 2-0-1.000; 1934-1938 Mickey Cochrane 413-297-.582; 1938-1942 Del Baker 356-317-.529; 1943-1948 Steve O'Neill 509-414-.551; 1949-1952 Robert Rolfe 278-256-.521; 1952-1954 Fred Hutchinson 155-235-.397; 1955-1956 Stanley Harris 161-147-.523; 1957-1958 Jack Tighe 99-104-.488; 1958-1959 Bill Norman 58-64-.475; 1959-1960 Jimmy Dykes 118-115-.506; 1960 Bill Hitchcock 1-0-1.000; 1960 Joe Gordon 26-31-.456; 1961-1963 Bob Scheffing 210-173-.548; 1963-1966 Charles Dressen 245-207-.542; 1966 Bob Swift 32-25-.561; 1967-1970 Mayo Smith 363-285-.560; 1971-1973 Billy Martin 253-208-.549; 1973 Joe Schultz 9-10-.474; 1974-1978 Ralph Houk 363-443-.450; 1979 Les Moss 27-26-.509; 1989 Dick Tracewski 9-9-.500; 1979-1995 George "Sparky" Anderson 1324-1239-.517; 1996-Buddy Bell

*Tiger stadium was known as Navin Field from 1912 to 1937, then Briggs Stadium from 1938 to 1960.

DETROIT VAGABOND KINGS

(became Dayton Rens part way through the 1949 season)

Home City: Detroit, Michigan
Home Court: NONE
Origin of Name: The team owned by King Boring, had no home arena so they were considered vagabonds

Regular Season Record

Season	League	GP	W	L	PPGF	PPGA	Pct	GB
1948-1949	NBL	19	2	17	61.1	75.2	.105	NA

COACHING HISTORY: Del Loranger 2-17-.105

DETROIT WHEELS

Home City: Ypsilanti, Michigan
Home Stadium: Rynearson Stadium Capacity: 19,800 [1974]
Origin of Name: The name was chosen by the team and chosen to reflect Detroit's image as the "motor city".

Regular Season Record

Season	League	GP	W	L	T	PF	PA	Pct
1974	WFL	14	1	13	0	209	358	.071

COACHING HISTORY: Dan Boisture 1-13-0-.071

DETROIT WOLVERINES

Home City: Detroit, Michigan
Home Field: Recreation Park
Origin of Name: Named after Michigan's state animal.

Regular Season Record

Season	League	GP	W	L	Pct	GB	R	OR
1881	NL	84	41	43	.488	15	439	429
1882	NL	83	42	41	.506	12.5	407	488
1883	NL	98	40	58	.408	23	524	650
1884	NL	112	28	84	.250	56	445	736
1885	NL	108	41	67	.380	44	514	582
1886	NL	123	87	36	.707	2.5	829	538
1887	NL	124	79	45	.637	-	969	714
1888	NL	131	68	63	.519	16	721	629
TOTAL:	8 years	863	426	437		169	4848	4766
AVERAGE:		108	53	55	.494	21	606	596

Playoff Record

Season	GP	W	L	R	OR	Result
1887	15	10	5	73	54	**Won World Series.**

COACHING HISTORY: 1881-1882 Fred Bancroft 83-84-.497; 1883-1884 Jack Chapman 68-142-.324; 1885 Charlie Morton 18-39-.316; 1885-1888 Bill Watkins 238-154-.607; 1888 Bob Leadley 19-18-.514

DETROIT WOLVERINES

Home City: Detroit, Michigan
Home Stadium:
Origin of Name: Named after previous National League baseball team and Michigan's state animal.

Regular Season Record

Season	League	GP	W	L	T	PF	PA	Pct
1928	NFL	10	7	2	1	189	76	.750

COACHING HISTORY: LeRoy Andrews 7-2-1-.750

DINAMO MOSCOW

Home City: Moscow, U.S.S.R.
Home Arena: Played all games in North America
Origin of Name: This was the Moscow Dinamo team of the Soviet National League.

Regular Season Record

Season	League	GP	W	L	T	GF	GA	Pts	Pct
1978-1979	WHA	1	0	1	0	1	4	0	.000

COACHING HISTORY:

DULUTH ESKIMOS
(became Duluth Kelleys)
(were Duluth Kelleys)

Home City: Duluth, Minnesota
Home Stadium: The team played only road games.
Origin of Name: The team received their nickname because a local clothier gave the team mackinaws with ERNIE NEVERS ESKIMOS printed on the back and the team changed names accordingly. Nevers was a star player for the Eskimos.

Regular Season Record

Season	League	GP	W	L	T	PF	PA	Pct
1923	NFL	7	4	3	0	35	33	.571
1926	NFL	14	6	5	3	113	81	.536
1927	NFL	9	1	8	0	68	134	.111
TOTAL:	3 years	30	11	16	3	216	248	
AVERAGE:		10	4	5	1	72	83	.417

COACHING HISTORY: 1923 Joe Sternaman 4-3-0-.571; 1926 Dewey Scanlon 6-5-3-.536; 1927 Ernie Nevers 1-8-0-.111

DULUTH KELLEYS
(were Duluth Eskimos)
(became Duluth Eskimos)

Home City: Duluth, Minnesota
Home Stadium: The team played only road games.
Origin of Name: The team was sponsored by the Kelley Duluth Hardware Store.

Regular Season Record

Season	League	GP	W	L	T	PF	PA	Pct
1924	NFL	6	5	1	0	56	16	.833
1925	NFL	3	0	3	0	6	25	.000
TOTAL:	2 years	9	5	4	0	62	41	
AVERAGE:		5	3	2	0	31	21	.556

COACHING HISTORY: 1924-1925 Dewey Scanlon 5-4-0-.556

EDMONTON DRILLERS

(were Oakland Stompers)

Home City: Edmonton, Alberta
Home Field: Commonwealth Stadium (1979-1981) Capacity,.42,500[1980]
Clarke Stadium:(1982) Capacity: 22,343
Origin of Name: The name was chosen in a Name the Team Contest in which the team received over 4,000 entries and announced March 8 1979. The name was meant to honor Edmonton's large petrochemical industry.

Regular Season Record

Season	League	GP	W	L	GF	GA	BP	Pts	Pct
1979	NASL	30	8	22	43	78	40	88	.326
1980	NASL	32	17	15	58	51	47	149	.517
1981	NASL	32	12	20	60	79	51	123	.256
1982	NASL	32	11	21	38	65	33	93	.194
TOTAL:	4 years	126	48	78	199	273	171	453	
AVERAGE:		32	12	20	50	68	43	113	.298

Playoff Record

Season	GP	W	L	GF	GA	Result
1980	6	3	3	6	7	Lost 2nd round series to Ft. Lauderdale.

COACHING HISTORY: 1979 Hans Kraay 6-19; 1979 Joe Petrone 2-3; 1980-1981 Timo Liekoski 28-33; 1981 Joe Petrone 1-2; 1982 Roger Thompson 11-21

EDMONTON ESKIMOS

Home City: Edmonton, Alberta
Home Arena: Edmonton Arena Capacity: 7,000
Origin of Name: Eskimos (or Esquimaux) is a name long associated with Edmonton as it is the most northerly major city in North America outside Alaska.

Regular Season Record

Season	League	GP	W	L	T	GF	GA	Pts	Pct
1921-1922	WCHA	24	15	9	0	117	76	30	.625
1922-1923	WCHA	30	19	10	1	112	90	39	.650
1923-1924	WCHA	30	11	15	4	69	81	26	.433
1924-1925	WCHL	28	14	13	1	97	109	29	.518
1925-1926	WHL	30	19	11	0	94	77	38	.633
TOTAL:	5 years	142	78	58	6	489	433	162	
AVERAGE:		29	16	12	1	98	87	33	.570

Playoff Record

Season	GP	W	L	T	GF	GA	Result
1921-1922	2	0	1	1	2	3	Lost WCHL championship to Regina.
1922-1923	4	1	2	1	5	6	Lost Stanley Cup playoff to Ottawa.
1925-1926	2	0	1	1	3	5	Lost WHL championship to Victoria.
TOTAL:	8	1	4	3	10	14	
AVERAGE:	2	0	1	1	3	5	

COACHING HISTORY: 1921-1926 Ken McKenzie 78-58-6-.570

EDMONTON ESKIMOS

Home City: Edmonton, Alberta
Home Stadium: Clarke Stadium (1950-1977) Capacity: 22,343 [1974]
Commonwealth Stadium (1978-present) Capacity: 60,081 [1995]
Origin of Name: Named after the team which challenged for the Grey Cup in 1921. Eskimos was a popular name for teams in the area in the early part of the century.

Regular Season Record

Season	League	GP	W	L	T	PF	PA	Pts	Pct
1950	CRU	14	7	7	0	201	197	14	.500
1951	CRU	14	8	6	0	306	262	16	.571
1952	CRU	16	9	6	1	291	280	19	.594
1953	CRU	16	12	4	0	276	157	24	.750
1954	CRU	16	11	5	0	255	163	22	.688
1955	CRU	16	14	2	0	286	117	28	.875
1956	CFC	16	11	5	0	358	235	22	.688
1957	CFC	16	14	2	0	475	142	28	.875
1958	CFL	16	9	6	1	312	292	19	.594
1959	CFL	16	10	6	0	370	221	20	.625
1960	CFL	16	10	6	0	318	225	20	.625
1961	CFL	16	10	5	1	334	257	21	.656
1962	CFL	16	6	9	1	310	346	13	.406
1963	CFL	16	2	14	0	220	425	4	.125
1964	CFL	16	4	12	0	223	458	8	.250
1965	CFL	16	5	11	0	257	400	10	.313
1966	CFL	16	6	9	1	251	328	13	.406
1967	CFL	16	9	6	1	266	246	19	.594
1968	CFL	16	8	7	1	228	288	17	.531
1969	CFL	16	5	11	0	241	246	10	.313
1970	CFL	16	9	7	0	282	287	18	.563
1971	CFL	16	6	10	0	237	305	12	.375
1972	CFL	16	10	6	0	380	368	20	.625
1973	CFL	16	9	5	2	329	284	20	.625
1974	CFL	16	10	5	1	345	247	21	.656
1975	CFL	16	12	4	0	432	370	24	.750
1976	CFL	16	9	6	1	311	367	19	.594
1977	CFL	16	10	6	0	412	320	20	.625
1978	CFL	16	10	4	2	452	301	22	.688
1979	CFL	16	12	2	2	495	219	26	.813
1980	CFL	16	13	3	0	505	281	26	.813
1981	CFL	16	14	1	1	576	277	29	.906

1982	CFL	16	11	5	0	544	323	22	.688
1983	CFL	16	8	8	0	450	377	16	.500
1984	CFL	16	9	7	0	464	443	18	.563
1985	CFL	16	10	6	0	432	373	20	.625
1986	CFL	18	13	4	1	540	365	27	.750
1987	CFL	18	11	7	0	617	462	22	.611
1988	CFL	18	11	7	0	477	408	22	.611
1989	CFL	18	16	2	0	644	302	32	.889
1990	CFL	18	10	8	0	612	510	20	.556
1991	CFL	18	12	6	0	671	569	24	.667
1992	CFL	18	10	8	0	552	515	20	.556
1993	CFL	18	14	4	0	646	421	28	.778
1994	CFL	18	13	5	0	518	398	26	.722
1995	CFL	18	13	5	0	599	359	26	.722
TOTAL:	46 years	752	455	280	17	18300	14736	927	
AVERAGE:		16	10	6	0	398	320	20	.614

Playoff Record

Season	GP	W	L	PF	PA	Result
1950	4	2	2	59	68	Lost Division final to Winnipeg.
1951	4	2	2	42	43	Lost Division final to Saskatchewan.
1952	6	3	3	105	110	Lost Grey Cup to Toronto.
1953	3	1	2	66	58	Lost Division final to Winnipeg.
1954	4	3	1	51	45	**Won Grey Cup**.
1955	3	3	0	89	31	**Won Grey Cup**.
1956	4	3	1	143	69	**Won Grey Cup**.
1957	3	1	2	16	40	Lost Division final to Winnipeg.
1958	5	3	2	102	72	Lost Division final to Winnipeg.
1959	4	2	2	80	50	Lost Division final to Winnipeg.
1960	6	4	2	106	73	Lost Grey Cup to Ottawa.
1961	2	1	1	26	27	Lost Division semifinal to Calgary.
1966	1	0	1	8	16	Lost Division semifinal to Winnipeg.
1967	1	0	1	5	21	Lost Division semifinal to Saskatchewan.
1968	1	0	1	13	29	Lost Division semifinal to Calgary.
1970	1	0	1	9	16	Lost Division semifinal to Calgary.
1972	1	0	1	6	8	Lost Division semifinal to Saskatchewan.
1973	2	1	1	43	45	Lost Grey Cup to Ottawa.
1974	2	1	1	38	47	Lost Grey Cup to Montreal.
1975	2	2	0	39	26	**Won Grey Cup**.
1976	2	1	1	27	35	Lost Division final to Saskatchewan.
1977	2	1	1	44	42	Lost Grey Cup to Montreal.
1978	2	2	0	46	26	**Won Grey Cup**.
1979	2	2	0	36	16	**Won Grey Cup**.
1980	2	2	0	82	34	**Won Grey Cup**.
1981	2	2	0	48	39	**Won Grey Cup**.
1982	2	2	0	56	37	**Won Grey Cup**.
1983	1	0	1	22	49	Lost Division semifinal to Winnipeg.
1984	1	0	1	10	55	Lost Division semifinal to Winnipeg.
1985	1	0	1	15	22	Lost Division semifinal to Winnipeg.
1986	3	2	1	83	62	Lost Grey Cup to Hamilton.
1987	3	3	0	99	59	**Won Grey Cup**.
1988	1	0	1	19	37	Lost Division final to B.C.
1989	1	0	1	21	32	Lost Division final to Saskatchewan.

1990	3	2	1	97	100	Lost Grey Cup to Winnipeg.
1991	1	0	1	36	38	Lost Division final to Calgary.
1992	2	1	1	44	43	Lost Division final to Calgary.
1993	3	3	0	113	51	**Won Grey Cup**.
1994	1	0	1	23	24	Lost Division final to B.C.
1995	2	1	1	30	52	Lost Division final to Calgary.
TOTAL:	96	56	40	1997	1747	
AVERAGE:	2	1	1	50	44	

COACHING HISTORY: 1950-1951 Annis Stukus 15-13-0-.536; 1952 Frank Filchock 9-6-1-.594; 1953 Darrell Royal 12-4-0-.750; 1954-1957 Frank Ivy 50-14-0-.781; 1958 Sam Lyle 9-6-1-.594; 1959-1963 Eagle Keys 38-40-2-.488; 1964-1969 Neil Armstrong 37-56-3-.401; 1970-1976 Ray Jauch 65-43-4-.598; 1977-1982 Hugh Campbell 70-21-5-.755; 1983 Pete Kettela 4-4-0-.500; 1983-1987 Jackie Parker 38-21-1-.642; 1987-1990 Joe Faragalli 46-24-0-.657; 1991-present Ron Lancaster

EDMONTON OILERS
(were Alberta Oilers)

Home City: Edmonton, Alberta
Home Arena: Edmonton Gardens (1973-1974) — Capacity: 7,200 [1974]
Edmonton Coliseum *(1974-present) — Capacity:17,503 [1994]
Origin of Name: See Alberta Oilers.

Regular Season Record

Season	**League**	**GP**	**W**	**L**	**T**	**GF**	**GA**	**Pts**	**Pct**
1973-1974	WHA	78	38	37	3	268	269	79	.506
1974-1975	WHA	78	36	38	4	279	279	76	.487
1975-1976	WHA	81	27	49	5	268	345	59	.364
1976-1977	WHA	81	34	43	4	243	304	72	.444
1977-1978	WHA	80	38	39	3	309	307	79	.494
1978-1979	WHA	80	48	30	2	340	266	98	.613
1979-1980	NHL	80	28	39	13	301	322	69	.431
1980-1981	NHL	80	29	35	16	328	327	74	.463
1981-1982	NHL	80	48	17	15	417	295	111	.694
1982-1983	NHL	80	47	21	12	424	315	106	.663
1983-1984	NHL	80	57	18	5	446	314	119	.744
1984-1985	NHL	80	49	20	11	401	298	109	.681
1985-1986	NHL	80	56	17	7	426	310	119	.744
1986-1987	NHL	80	50	24	6	372	284	106	.663
1987-1988	NHL	80	44	25	11	363	288	99	.619
1988-1989	NHL	80	38	34	8	325	306	84	.525
1989-1990	NHL	80	38	28	14	315	283	90	.563
1990-1991	NHL	80	37	37	6	272	272	80	.500
1991-1992	NHL	80	36	34	10	295	297	82	.513
1992-1993	NHL	84	26	50	8	242	337	60	.357
1993-1994	NHL	84	25	45	14	261	305	64	.381
1994-1995	NHL	48	17	27	4	136	182	38	.396
1995-1996	NHL	82	30	44	8	240	304	68	.415
TOTAL:	23 years	1816	876	751	189	7271	6809	1941	
AVERAGE:		79	38	33	8	316	296	84	.534

Playoff Record

Season	GP	W	L	GF	GA	Result
1973-1974	5	1	4	14	22	Lost quarterfinal series to Minnesota.
1975-1976	4	0	4	11	22	Lost quarterfinal series to Winnipeg.
1976-1977	5	1	4	16	20	Lost quarterfinal series to Houston.
1977-1978	5	1	4	9	23	Lost quarterfinal series to New England.
1978-1979	13	6	7	58	50	Lost final series to Winnipeg.
1979-1980	3	0	3	6	12	Lost preliminary series to Philadelphia.
1980-1981	9	5	4	35	35	Lost quarterfinal series to N.Y. Islanders.
1981-1982	5	2	3	23	27	Lost preliminary series to Los Angeles.
1982-1983	16	11	5	80	50	Lost Stanley Cup final to N.Y. Islanders.
1983-1984	19	15	4	94	56	**Won Stanley Cup**.
1984-1985	18	15	3	98	57	**Won Stanley Cup**.
1985-1986	10	6	4	41	30	Lost quarterfinal series to Calgary.
1986-1987	21	16	5	87	57	**Won Stanley Cup**.
1987-1988	18	16	2	87	56	**Won Stanley Cup**.
1988-1989	7	3	4	20	25	Lost 1st round series to Los Angeles.
1989-1990	22	16	6	93	60	**Won Stanley Cup**.
1990-1991	18	9	9	57	60	Lost semifinal series to Minnesota.
1991-1992	16	8	8	49	54	Lost semifinal series to Chicago.
TOTAL:	214	131	83	878	716	
AVERAGE:	12	7	5	49	40	

COACHING HISTORY: 1973-1975 Brian Shaw 68-63-6-.518; 1974-1976 Bill Hunter 15-33-4-.327; 1975-1976 Clare Drake 18-28-2-.396; 1975-1976 Armand Guidolin 25-36-2-.413; 1976-1989 Glen Sather 537-317-106-.615; 1980-1981 Bryan Watson 4-9-5-.361; 1989-1991 John Muckler 75-65-20-.531; 1991-1993 Ted Green 65-102-21-.402; 1993-1994 Glen Sather 22-27-11-.458; 1994-1995 George Burnett 12-20-3-.386; 1994-present Ron Low

*Known as Northlands Coliseum from 1974 to 1994.

EVANSVILLE CRIMSON GIANTS

Home City: Evansville, Indiana
Home Stadium:
Origin of Name:

Regular Season Record

Season	League	GP	W	L	T	PF	PA	Pct
1922	NFL	3	0	3	0	6	88	.000

COACHING HISTORY: Frank Fausch 0-3-0-.000

FLINT DOW A.C.'s

Home City: Midland, Michigan
Flint Michigan
Home Court:
Origin of Name: The team was sponsored by the Dow Athletic Club

Regular Season Record

Season	League	GP	W	L	PPGF	PPGA	Pct	GB
1947-1948	NBL	60	8	52	58.4	69.4	.133	36

COACHING HISTORY: Jim Walsh 0-2-.000; Matt Zunic 8-50-.138

FLORIDA BLAZERS

Home City: Orlando, Florida
Home Stadium: Tangerine Bowl Stadium — Capacity: 70,363
Origin of Name:

Regular Season Record

Season	League	GP	W	L	T	PF	PA	Pct
1974	WFL	20	14	6	0	419	280	.700

COACHING HISTORY: Jack Pardee 14-6-0-.700

Playoff Record

Season	GP	W	L	PF	PA	Result
1974	3	2	1	57	40	Lost championship game to Birmingham.

FLORIDA MARLINS

Home City: Miami, Florida
Home Stadium: Joe Robbie Stadium — Capacity: 47,226 [1995]
Origin of Name: The name reflects the regional nature of the team.

Regular Season Record

Season	League	GP	W	L	Pct	GB	R	OR
1993	NL	162	64	98	.395	33	581	724
1994	NL	115	51	64	.443	23.5	468	576
1995	NL	143	67	76	.469	22.5	673	673
TOTAL:	3 years	420	182	238		79	1722	1973
AVERAGE:		140	61	79	.433	26.5	574	658

COACHING HISTORY: 1993-present Rene Lachemann

FLORIDA PANTHERS

Home City: Miami, Florida
Home Arena: Miami Arena (1993-present) — Capacity: 14,703 [1995]
Origin of Name: The name was chosen by the team officials in honor of the endangered Panthers which inhabit the Everglades.

Regular Season Record

Season	League	GP	W	L	T	GF	GA	Pts	Pct
1993-1994	NHL	84	33	34	17	233	233	83	.494
1994-1995	NHL	48	20	22	6	115	127	46	.479

1995-1996	NHL	82	41	31	10	254	234	92	.561
TOTAL:	3 years	214	94	87	33	602	594	221	
AVERAGE:		72	31	30	11	201	198	73	.516

Playoff Record

Season	GP	W	L	GF	GA	Result
1995-1996	22	12	10	61	57	Lost Stanley Cup final to Colorado.

COACHING HISTORY: 1993-1995 Roger Neilson 53-56-23-.489; 1995-present Doug MacLean

FLORIDIANS

(were Miami Floridians)

Home City: Miami, Florida
Home Court: Miami Beach Convention Hall
Origin of Name: The team played its home games in Florida

Regular Season Record

Season	League	GP	W	L	PPGF	PPGA	Pct	GB
1970-1971	ABA	84	37	47	114.0	115.6	.440	18
1971-1972	ABA	84	36	48	112.8	114.3	.429	32
TOTAL:	2 years	168	73	95				50
AVERAGE:		84	37	47	113.4	115.0	.435	25

Playoff Record

Season	GP	W	L	PPGF	PPGA	Result
1970-1971	6	2	4	112.5	114.2	Lost 1st round series to Kentucky.
1971-1972	4	0	4	106.5	118.0	Lost 1st round series to Virginia.
TOTAL:	10	2	8			
AVERAGE:	5	1	4	109.5	116.1	

COACHING HISTORY: 1970-1971 Hal Blitman 18-30-.375; 1970-1972 Bob Bass 55-65-.458

FT. LAUDERDALE STRIKERS

(were Miami Toros)
(became Minnesota Strikers)

Home City: Ft. Lauderdale, Florida
Home Field: Lockhart Stadium — Capacity: 19,600 [1980]
Origin of Name: The team was named Strikers because striker is a soccer term for a forward player.

Regular Season Record

Season	League	GP	W	L	GF	GA	BP	Pts	Pct
1977	NASL	26	19	7	49	29	47	161	.688
1978	NASL	30	16	14	50	59	47	143	.530
1979	NASL	30	17	13	75	65	63	165	.611
1980	NASL	32	18	14	61	55	55	163	.566
1981	NASL	32	18	14	54	46	44	144	.300
1982	NASL	32	18	14	64	74	57	163	.340

1983	NASL	30	14	16	60	63	54	136	.302
TOTAL:	7 years	212	120	92	413	391	367	1075	
AVERAGE:		30	17	13	59	56	52	154	.435

Playoff Record

Season	GP	W	L	GF	GA	Result
1977	2	0	2	5	11	Lost 1st round series to New York.
1978	7	5	2	12	11	Lost 3rd round series to Tampa.
1979	2	0	2	0	3	Lost 1st round series to Chicago.
1980	10	6	4	14	14	Lost championship series to New York.
1981	6	4	2	15	10	Lost 3rd round series to new York.
1982	6	3	3	12	9	Lost 2nd round series to Seattle.
1983	2	0	2	4	7	Lost 1st round series to Tulsa.
TOTAL:	35	18	17	62	65	
AVERAGE:	5	2	3	9	9	

COACHING HISTORY: 1977-1979 Ron Newman 52-34; 1980 Cor van der Hart 18-14; 1981-1982 Eckhard Krautzen 36-28;1983 Dave Chadwick 14-16

FT. WAYNE CASEYS

(became Ft. Wayne Hoosiers)

Home City: Ft. Wayne, Indiana
Home Court:
Origin of Name: The team was sponsored by the Knights of Columbus (K.C.'s).

Regular Season Record

Season	League	GP	W	L	Pct
1925-1926	ABL	30	13	17	.433

COACHING HISTORY:

FT. WAYNE HOOSIERS

(were Ft. Wayne Caseys)

Home City: Ft. Wayne, Indiana
Home Court:
Origin of Name: The team was named Hoosiers because Indiana is known as the Hoosier State.

Regular Season Record

Season	League	GP	W	L	Pct
1926-1927	ABL	42	23	19	.548
1927-1928	ABL	51	27	24	.529
1928-1929	ABL	42	29	13	.690
1929-1930	ABL	54	25	29	.463
1930-1931	ABL	38	24	14	.632
TOTAL:	5 years	227	128	99	
AVERAGE:		45	26	19	.564

Playoff Record

Season	GP	W	L	Result
1927-1928	6	3	3	Lost championship series to New York.
1928-1929	4	0	4	Lost championship series to Cleveland.
1930-1931	7	3	4	Lost championship series to Brooklyn.
TOTAL:	17	6	11	
AVERAGE:	6	2	4	

COACHING HISTORY: 1926-1927 Not Available; 1927-1928 Frank Morgenweck 27-24-.529; 1928-1931 Not Available

FORT WAYNE PISTONS

(were Fort Wayne Zollner Pistons)
(became Detroit Pistons)

Home City: Fort Wayne, Indiana
Home Court: Memorial Coliseum — Capacity: 9,306
Origin of Name: See Fort Wayne Zollner Pistons.

Regular Season Record

Season	League	GP	W	L	PPGF	PPGA	Pct	GB
1956-1957	NBA	72	34	38	96.4	98.7	.472	-**

Playoff Record

Season	GP	W	L	PPGF	PPGA	Result
1956-1957	2	0	2	117.5	120.5	Lost Division semifinal to Minneapolis.

COACHING HISTORY: Charlie Eckman 34-38-.472

**Lost 103 to 115 to St. Louis in a playoff for first place.

FORT WAYNE ZOLLNER PISTONS

(became Fort Wayne Pistons)

Home City: Fort Wayne, Indiana
Home Court: North Side High School Gym (1948-1952) — Capacity: 3,800
Memorial Coliseum (1952-1957) — Capacity: 9,306
Origin of Name: The team was named after team president Fred Zollner, the owner of a large piston manufacturing plant.

Regular Season Record

Season	League	GP	W	L	PPGF	PPGA	Pct	GB
1937-1938	NBL	20	13	7	40.4	31.6	.650	2
1941-1942	NBL	24	15	9	47.0	44.4	.625	5
1942-1943	NBL	23	17	6	51.1	46.4	.739	-
1943-1944	NBL	22	18	4	47.2	41.2	.818	-
1944-1945	NBL	30	25	5	56.9	50.2	.833	-
1945-1946	NBL	34	26	8	58.7	51.0	.765	-
1946-1947	NBL	44	25	19	58.3	55.6	.568	6
1947-1948	NBL	60	40	20	59.9	56.9	.667	4

1948-1949	BAA	60	22	38	74.3	77.5	.367	23
1949-1950	NBA	68	40	28	79.3	77.9	.588	11**
1950-1951	NBA	68	32	36	84.1	86.0	.471	12
1951-1952	NBA	66	29	37	78.0	80.1	.439	12
1952-1953	NBA	69	36	33	81.0	81.1	.522	11.5
1953-1954	NBA	72	40	32	77.0	76.1	.556	6
1954-1955	NBA	72	43	29	92.4	90.0	.597	-
1955-1956	NBA	72	37	35	94.4	93.7	.514	-
TOTAL:	16 years	804	458	346				92.5
AVERAGE:		51	29	22	67.5	65.0	.570	6

Playoff Record

Season	GP	W	L	PPGF	PPGA	Result
1941-1942	6	3	3	49.5	50.0	Lost championship series to Oshkosh.
1942-1943	6	3	3	42.3	40.7	Lost championship series to Sheboygan.
1943-1944	5	5	0	49.0	37.0	**Won NBL championship**.
1944-1945	7	5	2	58.7	50.4	**Won NBL championship**.
1945-1946	4	1	3	53.0	57.5	Lost 1st round series to Rochester.
1946-1947	8	4	4	54.3	51.5	Lost 2nd round series to Rochester.
1947-1948	4	1	3	58.3	66.0	Lost 1st round series to Rochester.
1949-1950	4	2	2	82.5	86.0	Lost Division final to Minneapolis.
1950-1951	3	1	2	80.7	95.0	Lost Division semifinal to Rochester.
1951-1952	2	0	2	82.0	93.5	Lost Division semifinal to Rochester.
1952-1953	8	4	4	76.4	80.1	Lost Division final to Minneapolis.
1953-1954	2	0	2	73.0	85.5	Lost Division playoff to Minneapolis.
1954-1955	11	6	5	93.6	91.5	Lost championship series to Syracuse.
1955-1956	10	4	6	92.8	92.2	Lost championship series to Philadelphia.
TOTAL:	80	39	41			
AVERAGE:	6	3	3	67.9	69.8	

COACHING HISTORY: 1937-1938 Byron Evard 13-7-.650; 1941-1949 Carl Bennet 159-70-.694; 1946-1947 Bobby McDermott 7-7-.500; 1948-1949 Curly Armstrong 22-32-.407; 1949-1951 Murray Mendenhall 72-64-.529; 1951-1954 Paul Birch 105-102-.507; 1954-1956 Charlie Eckman 80-64-.556

**Defeated Chicago 86-69 in a playoff game to determine third place.

FRANKFORD YELLOW JACKETS

Home City: Philadelphia, Pennsylvania
Home Stadium: Frankford Stadium
Origin of Name: The team was named after several local football teams that had played in the area since 1913.

Regular Season Record

Season	League	GP	W	L	T	PF	PA	Pct
1924	NFL	14	11	2	1	326	109	.821
1925	NFL	20	13	7	0	190	169	.650
1926	NFL	16	14	1	1	236	49	.906
1927	NFL	18	6	9	3	155	166	.417
1928	NFL	16	11	3	2	175	84	.750
1929	NFL	18	9	4	5	129	128	.639

1930	NFL	18	4	13	1	113	321	.250
1931	NFL	8	1	6	1	13	99	.188
TOTAL:	8 years	128	69	45	14	1337	1125	
AVERAGE:		16	9	6	1	167	141	.594

COACHING HISTORY: 1924 Robert Berryman 11-2-1-.821; 1925-1926 Guy Chamberlin 27-8-1-.764; 1927 Adolph Youngstrom 4-5-2-.455; 1927 Charley Moran 2-4-1-.357; 1928 Ed Weir 11-3-2-.750; 1929-1931 Russell Behman 14-23-7-.398

FRANKFURT GALAXY

Home City: Frankfurt, Germany
Home Stadium: Waldstadion — Capacity: 54,000 [1991]
Origin of Name:

Regular Season Record

Season	League	GP	W	L	T	PF	PA	Pct
1991	WLAF	10	7	3	0	155	139	.700
1992	WFL	10	3	7	0	150	257	.300
TOTAL:	2 years	20	10	10	0	305	396	
AVERAGE:		10	5	5	0	153	198	.500

COACHING HISTORY:1991-1992 Jack Elway 10-10-0-.500

GOLDEN BAY EARTHQUAKES
(were San Jose Earthquakes)

Home City: San Jose, California
Home Field:. Spartan Stadium — Capacity: 17,500
Origin of Name: The area is well known for its earthquakes

Regular Season Record

Season	League	GP	W	L	GF	GA	BP	Pts	Pct
1983	NASL	30	20	10	71	54	55	169	.376
1984	NASL	24	8	16	61	62	49	95	.264
TOTAL:	2 years	54	28	26	132	116	104	264	
AVERAGE:		27	14	13	66	58	52	132	.326

Playoff Record

Season	GP	W	L	GF	GA	Result
1983	5	2	3	11	7	Lost 2nd round series to Toronto.

COACHING HISTORY: 1983-1984 Don Popovic-28-26

GOLDEN STATE WARRIORS
(were San Francisco Warriors)

Home City: Oakland, California
Home Court: Oakland Coliseum Arena — Capacity: 15,025 [1995]
Origin of Name: The team kept the same nickname when it moved from San Francisco.

Regular Season Record

Season	League	GP	W	L	PPGF	PPGA	Pct	GB
1971-1972	NBA	82	51	31	108.2	107.4	.622	18
1972-1973	NBA	82	47	35	108.8	105.7	.573	13
1973-1974	NBA	82	44	38	109.9	107.3	.537	3
1974-1975	NBA	82	48	34	108.5	105.2	.585	-
1975-1976	NBA	82	59	23	109.8	103.1	.720	-
1976-1977	NBA	82	46	36	110.9	107.7	.561	7
1977-1978	NBA	82	43	39	106.1	105.7	.524	15
1978-1979	NBA	82	38	44	105.1	104.8	.463	14
1979-1980	NBA	82	24	58	103.6	108.0	.293	36
1980-1981	NBA	82	39	43	109.8	111.0	.476	18
1981-1982	NBA	82	45	37	110.9	109.8	.549	12
1982-1983	NBA	82	30	52	108.6	112.3	.366	28
1983-1984	NBA	82	37	45	109.9	113.3	.451	17
1984-1985	NBA	82	22	60	110.4	117.7	.268	40
1985-1986	NBA	82	30	52	113.4	116.9	.366	32
1986-1987	NBA	82	42	40	112.0	114.4	.512	23
1987-1988	NBA	82	20	62	107.0	115.3	.244	42
1988-1989	NBA	82	43	39	116.6	116.9	.524	14
1989-1990	NBA	82	37	45	116.3	119.4	.451	26
1990-1991	NBA	82	44	38	116.6	115.0	.537	19
1991-1992	NBA	82	55	27	118.7	114.8	.671	2
1992-1993	NBA	82	34	48	109.9	110.9	.415	28
1993-1994	NBA	82	50	32	107.9	106.1	.610	13
1994-1995	NBA	82	26	56	105.7	111.1	.317	33
1995-1996	NBA	82	36	46	101.6	103.1	.439	28
TOTAL:	25 years	2050	990	1060				481
AVERAGE:		82	40	42	109.8	110.5	.483	19

Playoff Record

Season	GP	W	L	PPGF	PPGA	Result
1971-1972	5	1	4	100.6	112.0	Lost Conference semifinal to Milwaukee.
1972-1973	11	5	6	97.9	105.7	Lost Conference final to Los Angeles.
1974-1975	17	12	5	100.2	94.9	**Won NBA championship**.
1975-1976	13	7	6	112.1	106.3	Lost Conference final to Phoenix.
1976-1977	10	5	5	105.6	103.7	Lost Conference semifinal to Los Angeles.
1986-1987	10	4	6	107.1	111.7	Lost Conference semifinal to Lakers.
1988-1989	8	4	4	109.9	116.5	Lost Conference semifinal to Phoenix.
1990-1991	9	4	5	114.4	115.9	Lost Conference semifinal to Lakers.
1991-1992	4	1	3	117.0	116.5	Lost 1st round series to Seattle.
1993-1994	3	0	3	116.0	122.7	Lost 1st round series to Phoenix.
TOTAL:	90	43	47			
AVERAGE:	9	4	5	107.6	109.7	

COACHING HISTORY: 1971-1983 Al Attles 508-455-.528; 1979-1980 John Bach 6-15-.288; 1983-1986 John Bach 89-157-.362; 1986-1988 George Karl 146-58788-.397; 1987-1988 Ed Gregory 18-4-14-.222; 1988-1995 Don Nelson 277 260 .516; 1994-1995 Bob Lanier 12-25-.324; 1995-present Rick Adelman

GREEN BAY PACKERS

Home City: Milwaukee, Wisconsin
Green Bay, Wisconsin
Home Stadium: County Stadium(1953-1993) Capacity: 56,051 (Milwaukee) [1993]
Hagemeister Brewery Park (1922) (Green Bay)
Bellevue Park (1923-1924) (Green Bay)
City Stadium I (1925-1956) Capacity: 24,800 (Green Bay)
Lambeau Field (1957-present)** Capacity: 60,790 (Green Bay) [1995]
Origin of Name: The team was first sponsored by the Acme Packing Company of Green Bay.

Regular Season Record

Season	League	GP	W	L	T	PF	PA	Pct
1922	NFL	11	4	4	3	70	54	.550
1923	NFL	10	7	2	1	85	34	.750
1924	NFL	11	7	4	0	108	38	.636
1925	NFL	13	8	5	0	151	110	.615
1926	NFL	13	7	3	3	151	61	.654
1927	NFL	10	7	2	1	113	43	.750
1928	NFL	13	6	4	3	120	92	.577
1929	NFL	13	12	0	1	198	22	.962
1930	NFL	14	10	3	1	234	111	.750
1931	NFL	14	12	2	0	291	87	.857
1932	NFL	14	10	3	1	152	63	.750
1933	NFL	13	5	7	1	170	107	.423
1934	NFL	13	7	6	0	156	112	.538
1935	NFL	12	8	4	0	181	96	.667
1936	NFL	12	10	1	1	248	118	.875
1937	NFL	11	7	4	0	220	122	.636
1938	NFL	11	8	3	0	223	118	.727
1939	NFL	11	9	2	0	233	153	.818
1940	NFL	11	6	4	1	238	155	.591
1941	NFL	11	10	1	0	258	120	.909
1942	NFL	11	8	2	1	300	215	.773
1943	NFL	10	7	2	1	264	172	.750
1944	NFL	10	8	2	0	238	141	.800
1945	NFL	10	6	4	0	258	173	.600
1946	NFL	11	6	5	0	148	158	.545
1947	NFL	12	6	5	1	274	210	.542
1948	NFL	12	3	9	0	154	290	.250
1949	NFL	12	2	10	0	114	329	.167
1950	NFL	12	3	9	0	244	406	.250
1951	NFL	12	3	9	0	254	375	.250
1952	NFL	12	6	6	0	295	312	.500
1953	NFL	12	2	9	1	200	338	.208
1954	NFL	12	4	8	0	234	251	.333
1955	NFL	12	6	6	0	258	276	.500
1956	NFL	12	4	8	0	264	342	.333
1957	NFL	12	3	9	0	218	311	.250
1958	NFL	12	1	10	1	193	382	.125
1959	NFL	12	7	5	0	248	246	.583
1960	NFL	12	8	4	0	332	209	.667
1961	NFL	14	11	3	0	391	223	.786

1962	NFL	14	13	1	0	415	148	.929
1963	NFL	14	11	2	1	369	206	.821
1964	NFL	14	8	5	1	342	245	.607
1965	NFL	14	10	3	1	316	224	.750
1966	NFL	14	12	2	0	335	163	.857
1967	NFL	14	9	4	1	332	209	.679
1968	NFL	14	6	7	1	281	227	.464
1969	NFL	14	8	6	0	269	221	.571
1970	NFL	14	6	8	0	196	293	.429
1971	NFL	14	4	8	2	274	298	.357
1972	NFL	14	10	4	0	304	226	.714
1973	NFL	14	5	7	2	202	259	.429
1974	NFL	14	6	8	0	210	206	.429
1975	NFL	14	4	10	0	226	285	.286
1976	NFL	14	5	9	0	218	299	.357
1977	NFL	14	4	10	0	134	219	.286
1978	NFL	16	8	7	1	249	269	.531
1979	NFL	16	5	11	0	246	316	.313
1980	NFL	16	5	10	1	231	371	.344
1981	NFL	16	8	8	0	324	361	.500
1982	NFL	9	5	3	1	226	169	.611
1983	NFL	16	8	8	0	429	439	.500
1984	NFL	16	8	8	0	390	309	.500
1985	NFL	16	8	8	0	337	355	.500
1986	NFL	16	4	12	0	254	418	.250
1987	NFL	15	5	9	1	255	300	.367
1988	NFL	16	4	12	0	240	315	.250
1989	NFL	16	10	6	0	362	356	.625
1990	NFL	16	6	10	0	271	347	.375
1991	NFL	16	4	12	0	273	313	.250
1992	NFL	16	9	7	0	276	296	.563
1993	NFL	16	9	7	0	340	282	.563
1994	NFL	16	9	7	0	382	287	.563
1995	NFL	16	11	5	0	404	314	.689
TOTAL:	74 years	979	511	433	35	18393	16720	
AVERAGE:		13	7	6	0	249	226	.540

Playoff Record

Season	GP	W	L	PF	PA	Result
1936	1	1	0	21	6	**Won NFL championship.**
1938	1	0	1	17	23	Lost NFL championship to N.Y. Giants.
1939	1	1	0	27	0	**Won NFL championship.**
1941	1	0	1	14	33	Lost Division playoff to Chicago Bears.
1944	1	1	0	14	7	**Won NFL championship.**
1960	1	0	1	13	17	Lost NFL championship to Philadelphia.
1961	1	1	0	37	0	**Won NFL championship.**
1962	1	1	0	16	7	**Won NFL championship.**
1965	2	2	0	36	22	**Won NFL championship.**
1966	2	2	0	69	37	**Won NFL championship.**
1967	3	3	0	82	38	**Won NFL championship.**
1972	1	0	1	3	16	Lost Divisional playoff to Washington.
1982	2	1	1	67	53	Lost 2nd round playoff to Dallas.
1993	2	1	1	45	51	Lost Divisional semifinal to Dallas.

1994	2	1	1	25	47	Lost Divisional semifinal to Dallas.
1995	3	2	1	91	75	Lost Conference final to Dallas.
TOTAL:	25	17	8	577	432	
AVERAGE:	2	1	1	36	27	

COACHING HISTORY: 1922-1949 Curly Lambeau 206-102-20-.658; 1950-1953 Gene Ronzani 14-31-1-.315; 1953 Hugh Devore & Ray McLean 0-2-0-.000; 1954-1957 Lisle Blackbourn 17-31-0-.354; 1958 Ray McLean 1-10-1-.125; 1959-1967 Vince Lombardi 89-29-4-.746; 1968-1970 Phil Bengston 20-21-1-.488; 1971-1974 Dan Devine 25-27-4-.482; 1975-1983 Bart Starr 52-76-3-.408; 1984-1987 Forrest Gregg 25-37-1-.405; 1988-1991 Lindy Infante 24-40-0-.375; 1992-present Mike Holmgren

*The Packers have played some home games in Milwaukee every year from 1933 to 1952 including Borchert Field, State Fair Park and Marquette Stadium, then County Stadium from 1953 to 1994.
**Lambeau Field was known as City Stadium II from 1957 to 1964.

HAILEYBURY COMETS

Home City: Haileybury, Ontario
Home Arena:
Origin of Name: Probably named after the comet discovered by Edmund Halley.

			Regular Season Record						
Season	**League**	**GP**	**W**	**L**	**T**	**GF**	**GA**	**Pts**	**Pct**
1909-1910	NHA	12	4	8	0	77	83	8	.333

COACHING HISTORY:

HAMILTON TIGER-CATS

Home City: Hamilton, Ontario
Home Stadium: Ivor Wynne Stadium Capacity: 29,183 [1995]
Origin of Name: The team was formed from an amalgamation of the Hamilton Tigers of the IRFU and the Hamilton Wildcats of the ORFU.

			Regular Season Record						
Season	**League**	**GP**	**W**	**L**	**T**	**PF**	**PA**	**Pts**	**Pct**
1950	CRU	12	7	5	0	231	217	14	.583
1951	CRU	12	7	5	0	229	131	14	.583
1952	CRU	12	9	2	1	268	162	19	.792
1953	CRU	14	8	6	0	229	247	16	.571
1954	CRU	14	9	5	0	275	207	18	.643
1955	CRU	12	8	4	0	271	193	16	.667
1956	CFC	14	7	7	0	383	385	14	.500
1957	CFC	14	10	4	0	250	189	20	.714
1958	CFL	14	10	3	1	291	235	21	.750
1959	CFL	14	10	4	0	298	162	20	.714
1960	CFL	14	4	10	0	273	377	8	.286
1961	CFL	14	10	4	0	340	393	20	.714
1962	CFL	14	9	4	1	358	286	19	.679
1963	CFL	14	10	4	0	312	214	20	.714

1964	CFL	14	10	3	1	329	201	21	.750
1965	CFL	14	10	4	0	281	153	20	.714
1966	CFL	14	9	5	0	264	160	18	.643
1967	CFL	14	10	4	0	250	195	20	.714
1968	CFL	14	6	7	1	262	292	13	.464
1969	CFL	14	8	5	1	307	315	17	.607
1970	CFL	14	8	5	1	292	279	17	.607
1971	CFL	14	7	7	0	242	246	14	.500
1972	CFL	14	11	3	0	372	262	22	.786
1973	CFL	14	7	7	0	304	263	14	.500
1974	CFL	16	7	9	0	279	313	14	.438
1975	CFL	16	5	10	1	284	395	11	.344
1976	CFL	16	8	8	0	269	348	16	.500
1977	CFL	16	5	11	0	283	394	10	.313
1978	CFL	16	5	10	1	225	403	11	.344
1979	CFL	16	6	10	0	280	338	12	.375
1980	CFL	16	8	7	1	332	377	17	.531
1981	CFL	16	11	4	1	414	335	23	.719
1982	CFL	16	8	7	1	396	401	17	.531
1983	CFL	16	5	10	1	389	498	11	.344
1984	CFL	16	6	9	1	353	439	13	.406
1985	CFL	16	8	8	0	377	315	16	.500
1986	CFL	18	9	8	1	405	366	19	.528
1987	CFL	18	7	11	0	470	509	14	.389
1988	CFL	18	9	9	0	478	465	18	.500
1989	CFL	18	12	6	0	519	517	24	.667
1990	CFL	18	6	12	0	476	628	12	.333
1991	CFL	18	3	15	0	400	599	6	.167
1992	CFL	18	11	7	0	536	514	22	.611
1993	CFL	18	6	12	0	316	567	12	.333
1994	CFL	18	4	14	0	435	562	8	.222
1995	CFL	18	8	10	0	427	509	16	.444
TOTAL:	46 years	700	361	324	15	15254	15556	737	
AVERAGE:		15	8	7	0	332	338	16	.526

Playoff Record

Season	GP	W	L	T	PF	PA	Result
1950	2	1	1	0	19	35	Lost Division final to Toronto.
1951	4	1	3	0	47	56	Lost Division final to Ottawa.
1952	3	1	2	0	40	45	Lost Division final to Toronto.
1953	3	3	0	0	71	29	**Won Grey Cup**.
1954	2	0	2	0	28	38	Lost Division final to Montreal.
1955	1	0	1	0	28	32	Lost Division semifinal to Toronto.
1956	3	1	2	0	108	99	Lost Division final to Montreal.
1957	3	3	0	0	88	18	**Won Grey Cup**.
1958	3	2	1	0	82	49	Lost Grey Cup game to Winnipeg.
1959	3	1	2	0	33	45	Lost Grey Cup game to Winnipeg.
1961	3	1	2	0	69	48	Lost Grey Cup game to Winnipeg.
1962	3	2	1	0	85	66	Lost Grey Cup game to Winnipeg.
1963	3	2	1	0	84	45	**Won Grey Cup**.
1964	3	1	2	0	63	72	Lost Grey Cup game to B.C.
1965	3	3	0	0	57	36	**Won Grey Cup**.
1966	3	1	2	0	41	86	Lost Division final to Ottawa.

1967	3	3	0	0	61	4	**Won Grey Cup**.
1968	1	0	1	0	21	33	Lost Division semifinal to Toronto.
1969	1	0	1	0	9	15	Lost Division semifinal to Toronto.
1970	2	0	2	0	26	43	Lost Division final to Montreal.
1971	3	1	1	1	48	44	Lost Division final to Toronto.
1972	3	2	1	0	43	37	**Won Grey Cup**.
1974	1	0	1	0	19	21	Lost Division semifinal to Ottawa.
1975	1	0	1	0	12	35	Lost Division semifinal to Montreal.
1976	2	1	1	0	38	17	Lost Division final to Ottawa.
1978	1	0	1	0	20	35	Lost Division semifinal to Montreal.
1979	1	0	1	0	26	29	Lost Division semifinal to Ottawa.
1980	2	1	1	0	34	61	Lost Grey Cup game to Edmonton.
1981	1	0	1	0	13	17	Lost Division final to Ottawa.
1982	1	0	1	0	20	30	Lost Division semifinal to Ottawa.
1983	2	1	1	0	69	72	Lost Division final to Toronto.
1984	3	2	1	0	48	71	Lost Grey Cup game to Winnipeg.
1985	2	1	1	0	74	63	Lost Grey Cup game to B.C.
1986	3	2	1	0	98	71	**Won Grey Cup**.
1987	1	0	1	0	13	29	Lost Division semifinal to Toronto.
1988	1	0	1	0	28	35	Lost Division semifinal to Winnipeg.
1989	2	1	1	0	54	53	Lost Grey cup game to Saskatchewan.
1992	2	1	1	0	40	87	Lost Division final to Winnipeg.
1993	2	1	1	0	40	30	Lost Division final to Winnipeg.
1995	1	0	1	0	13	30	Lost Division final to Calgary.
TOTAL:	87	40	46	1	1810	1761	
AVERAGE:	2	1	1	0	45	44	

COACHING HISTORY: 1950-1955 Carl Voyles 48-27-1-.638; 1956-1962 Jim Trimble 60-36-2-.622; 1963-1967 Ralph Sazio 49-20-1-.707; 1968-1970 Joe Restic 22-17-3-.560; 1971 Al Darrow 7-7-0-.500; 1972-1975 Jerry Williams 30-28-0-.517; 1975 Bob Krouse 0-1-1-.250; 1976 George Dickson 0-2-07.000; 1976-1977 Bob Shaw 13-17-0-.433; 1978 Tom Dimitroff 1-3-1-.300; 1978-1980 John Payne 18-24-1-.430; 1981 Frank Kush 11-4-1-.719; 1982-1983 Bud Riley 12-15-1-.446; 1983-1990 Al Bruno 56-61-3-.479; 1990-1991 David Beckman 2-12-0-.143; 1991-1994 John Gregory 21-31-0-.404; 1994-present Don Sutherin

HAMILTON TIGERS

(became New York Americans)

Home City: Hamilton, Ontario
Home Arena: Hamilton Arena
Origin of Name: Named by team executives after a senior team which won the Allan Cup in 1919.

Regular Season Record

Season	**League**	**GP**	**W**	**L**	**T**	**GF**	**GA**	**Pts**	**Pct**
1920-1921	NHL	24	6	18	0	92	132	12	.250
1921-1922	NHL	24	7	17	0	88	105	14	.292
1922-1923	NHL	24	6	18	0	81	110	12	.250
1923-1924	NHL	24	9	15	0	63	68	18	.375
1924-1925	NHL	30	19	10	1	90	60	39	.650
TOTAL:	5 years	126	47	78	1	414	475	95	
AVERAGE:		25	9	16	0	83	95	19	.377

Playoff Record*

*The team's players went on strike for more money at season's end and did not compete in the playoffs.

COACHING HISTORY: 1920-1922 Paul Thompson 13-35-0-.271; 1922-1923 Art Ross 6-18-0-.250; 1923-1924 Percy Lesueur 9-15-0-.375; 1924-1925 Jimmy Gardner 19-10-1-.650

HAMMOND CALUMET BUCCANEERS

Home City: Hammond, Indiana
Home Court:
Origin of Name: The team was owned by fans in Hammond, Calumet City and the surrounding area.

Regular Season Record

Season	League	GP	W	L	PPGF	PPGA	Pct	GB
1948-1949	NBL	62	21	41	61.0	64.9	.339	17

Playoff Record

Season	GP	W	L	PPGF	PPGA	Result
1948-1949	2	0	2	67.5	76.0	Lost 1st round series to Syracuse.

COACHING HISTORY: Bob Carpenter 11-16-.407; George Sobek 10-25-.286

HAMMOND CIESAR ALL-AMERICANS

(were Whiting Ciesar All-Americans)

Home City: Hammond, Indiana
Home Court:
Origin of Name: The team kept the same nickname when it moved from Whiting to Hammond.

Regular Season Record

Season	League	GP	W	L	PPGF	PPGA	Pct	GB
1938-1939	NBL	28	4	24	36.0	42.1	.143	13
1939-1940	NBL	28	9	19	36.9	40.8	.321	6
1940-1941	NBL	24	6	18	38.6	44.4	.250	12
TOTAL:	3 years	80	19	61	31			
AVERAGE:		27	7	20	37.2	42.4	.238	10

COACHING HISTORY: 1938-1939 Whitey Wickhorst 4-24-.143; 1939-1940 Lou Boudreau 1-4-.200; 1939-1940 Eddie Ciesar 0-2-.000; 1939-1940 Leo Bereolos 8-13-.381; 1940-1941 Carl Anderson 6-18-.250

HAMMOND PROS

Home City: Hammond, Indiana
Home Stadium:
Origin of Name: As with all teams with the name of Pros, the name is a shortened version of professional.

Regular Season Record

Season	League	GP	W	L	T	PF	PA	Pct
1922	NFL	6	0	5	1	0	69	.000
1923	NFL	7	1	5	1	14	59	.214
1924	NFL	5	2	2	1	18	45	.500
1925	NFL	5	1	4	0	23	87	.200
1926	NFL	4	0	4	0	3	56	.000
TOTAL:	5 years	27	4	20	3	58	316	
AVERAGE:		5	1	4	0	12	63	.204

COACHING HISTORY: 1922 Not Available; 1923-1925 Fritz Pollard 4-10-2-.313; 1925-1926 Doc Young 0-5-0-.000

HARTFORD BICENTENNIALS
(became Connecticut Bicentennials)

Home City: Hartford, Connecticut
Home Stadium: Dillon Stadium
Origin of Name: Adopted the name because the team was formed around the time of the U.S.A.'s bicentennial.

Regular Season Record

Season	League	GP	W	L	GF	GA	BP	Pts	Pct
1975	NASL	22	6	16	27	51	25	61	.308
1976	NASL	24	12	12	37	56	35	107	.495
TOTAL:	2 years	46	18	28	64	107	60	168	
AVERAGE:		23	9	14	32	54	30	84	.406

COACHING HISTORY: 1975-1976 Manfred Schellscheidt 8-19; 1976 Bobby Thompson 10-9

HARTFORD BLUES

Home City: Hartford, Connecticut
Home Field: Hartford Baseball Grounds*
Origin of Name: The team was named after the color of their uniforms

Regular Season Record

Season	League	GP	W	L	Pct	GB	R	OR
1876	NL	68	47	21	.691	6	429	261
1877	NL	58	31	27	.534	10	341	311
TOTAL:	2 years	126	78	48		16	770	572
AVERAGE:		63	39	24	.619	8	385	286

COACHING HISTORY: 1876-1877 Bob Ferguson 78-48-.619

*Played all their home games in 1877 in Brooklyn, New York.

HARTFORD BLUES

Home City: Hartford, Connecticut
Home Stadium:
Origin of Name:

Season	League	GP	W	L	T	PF	PA	Pct
			Regular Season Record					
1926	NFL	10	3	7	0	57	99	.300

COACHING HISTORY: Jack Keough 3-7-0-.300

HARTFORD WHALERS
(were New England Whalers)

Home City: Hartford, Connecticut
Home Arena: Hartford Civic Center II Capacity: 15,635 [1995]
Origin of Name: The name was chosen by team executives because of Hartford's whaling history.

Regular Season Record

Season	League	GP	W	L	T	GF	GA	Pts	Pct
1979-1980	NHL	80	27	34	19	303	312	73	.456
1980-1981	NHL	80	21	41	18	222	372	60	.375
1981-1982	NHL	80	21	41	18	264	351	60	.375
1982-1983	NHL	80	19	54	7	261	403	45	.281
1983-1984	NHL	80	28	42	10	288	320	66	.413
1984-1985	NHL	80	30	41	9	268	318	69	.431
1985-1986	NHL	80	40	36	4	332	302	84	.525
1986-1987	NHL	80	43	30	7	287	270	93	.581
1987-1988	NHL	80	35	38	7	249	267	77	.481
1988-1989	NHL	80	37	38	5	299	290	79	.494
1989-1990	NHL	80	38	33	9	275	268	85	.531
1990-1991	NHL	80	31	38	11	238	276	73	.456
1991-1992	NHL	80	26	41	13	247	283	65	.406
1992-1993	NHL	84	26	52	6	284	369	58	.345
1993-1994	NHL	84	27	48	9	227	288	63	.375
1994-1995	NHL	48	19	24	5	127	141	43	.448
1995-1996	NHL	82	34	39	9	237	259	77	.470
TOTAL:	17 years	1338	502	670	166	4408	5089	1170	
AVERAGE:		79	30	39	10	259	299	70	.437

Playoff Record

Season	GP	W	L	GF	GA	Result
1979-1980	3	0	3	8	18	Lost preliminary series to Montreal.
1985-1986	10	4	6	29	23	Lost quarterfinal series to Montreal.
1986-1987	6	2	4	19	27	Lost Division semifinal to Quebec.
1987-1988	6	2	4	20	23	Lost Division semifinal to Montreal.
1988-1989	4	0	4	11	18	Lost Division semifinal to Montreal.
1989-1990	7	3	4	21	23	Lost Division semifinal to Boston.
1990-1991	6	2	4	17	24	Lost Division semifinal to Boston.
1991-1992	7	3	4	18	21	Lost Division semifinal to Montreal.
TOTAL:	49	16	33	143	177	
AVERAGE:	6	2	4	18	22	

COACHING RECORD: 1979-1981 Don Blackburn 42-63-35-.425; 1980-1983 Larry Pleau 31-66-21-.352; 1982-1983 Larry Kish 12-32-5-.296; 1982-1983 John Cunniff 3-9-1-.269; 1983-1988 Jack Evans 163-174-37-.485; 1987-1989 Larry Pleau 50-51-5-.495; 1989-1991 Rick Ley 69-71-20-.494; 1991-1992 Jim Roberts 26-41-13-.406; 1992-1993 Paul Holmgren 30-63-8-.337; 1993-1994 Pierre McGuire 23-37-7-.396; 1994-present Paul Holmgren 24-30-6-.450; 1995-present Paul Maurice

HAWAIINS, The

Home City: Honolulu, Hawaii
Home Stadium: Honolulu Stadium — Capacity: 23,000 [1975]
Origin of Name: The team was based in Hawaii.

Regular Season Record

Season	League	GP	W	L	T	PF	PA	Pct
1974	WFL	20	9	11	0	413	422	.450
1975	WFL	11	4	7	0	210	281	.364
TOTAL:	2 years	31	13	18	0	623	703	
AVERAGE:		16	7	9	0	312	352	.419

Playoff Record

Season	GP	W	L	PF	PA	Result
1974	2	1	1	53	36	Lost 2nd round series to Birmingham.

COACHING HISTORY: 1974-1975 Mike Gaddings 13-18-0-.419

HOUSTON AEROS

Home City: Houston, Texas
Home Arena: Sam Houston Coliseum (1972-1975) — Capacity: 9,000 [1972]
The Summit (1975-1978) — Capacity: 15,256 [1977]
Origin of Name: The name was chosen because of Houston's association with the aerospace industry.

Regular Season Record

Season	League	GP	W	L	T	GF	GA	Pts	Pct
1972-1973	WHA	78	39	35	4	284	269	82	.526
1973-1974	WHA	78	48	25	5	318	219	101	.647
1974-1975	WHA	78	53	25	0	369	247	106	.679
1975-1976	WHA	80	53	27	0	341	263	106	.663
1976-1977	WHA	80	50	24	6	320	241	106	.663
1977-1978	WHA	80	42	34	4	296	302	88	.550
TOTAL:	6 years	474	285	170	19	1928	1541	589	
AVERAGE:		79	48	28	3	321	257	99	.621

Playoff Record

Season	GP	W	L	GF	GA	Result
1972-1973	10	4	6	26	30	Lost semifinal series to Winnipeg.
1973-1974	14	12	2	71	35	**Won WHA championship**.

1974-1975	13	12	1	61	26	**Won WHA championship**.
1975-1976	17	8	9	56	63	Lost WHA final series to Winnipeg.
1976-1977	11	6	5	43	40	Lost semifinal series to Winnipeg.
1977-1978	6	2	4	16	29	Lost 1st round series to Quebec.
TOTAL:	71	44	27	273	223	
AVERAGE:	12	7	5	46	37	

COACHING HISTORY: 1972-1978 Bill Dineen 285-170-19-.621

HOUSTON ASTROS
(were Houston Colt 45's)

Home City: Houston, Texas
Home Field: The Astrodome Capacity: 54,313 [1995]
Origin of Name: The team was named Astros after the Astrodome opened in 1965.

Regular Season Record

Season	**League**	**GP**	**W**	**L**	**Pct**	**GB**	**R**	**OR**
1965	NL	162	65	97	.401	32	569	711
1966	NL	162	72	90	.444	23	612	695
1967	NL	162	69	93	.426	32.5	626	742
1968	NL	162	72	90	.444	25	510	588
1969	NL	162	81	81	.500	12	676	668
1970	NL	162	79	83	.488	23	744	763
1971	NL	162	79	83	.488	11	585	567
1972	NL	153	84	69	.549	10.5	708	636
1973	NL	162	82	80	.506	17	681	672
1974	NL	162	81	81	.500	21	653	632
1975	NL	161	64	97	.398	43.5	664	711
1976	NL	162	80	82	.494	22	625	657
1977	NL	162	81	81	.500	17	680	650
1978	NL	162	74	88	.457	21	605	634
1979	NL	162	89	73	.549	1.5	583	582
1980	NL	163	93	70	.571	-	637	589
1981	NL	110	61	49	.555	NA	394	331
1982	NL	162	77	85	.475	12	569	620
1983	NL	162	85	77	.525	6	643	646
1984	NL	162	80	82	.494	12	693	630
1985	NL	162	83	79	.512	12	706	691
1986	NL	162	96	66	.593	-	654	569
1987	NL	162	76	86	.469	14	648	678
1988	NL	162	82	80	.506	12.5	617	631
1989	NL	162	86	76	.531	6	647	669
1990	NL	162	75	87	.463	16	573	656
1991	NL	162	65	97	.401	29	605	717
1992	NL	162	81	81	.500	17	608	668
1993	NL	162	85	77	.525	19	716	630
1994	NL	115	66	49	.574	.5	602	503
1995	NL	144	76	68	.528	9	747	674
TOTAL:	31 years	4896	2419	2477		476.5	19580	19810
AVERAGE:		158	78	80	.494	15.5	632	639

Playoff Record

Season	GP	W	L	R	OR	Result
1980	5	2	3	19	20	Lost NLCS to Philadelphia.
1981	5	2	3	6	13	Lost Division series to Los Angeles.
1986	6	2	4	17	21	Lost NLCS to New York.
TOTAL:	16	6	10	42	54	
AVERAGE:	5	2	3	14	18	

COACHING HISTORY: 1965 Luman Harris 65-97-.401; 1966-1968 Grady Hatton 164-221-.426; 1968-1972 Harry Walker 355-353-.501; 1972 Francis Parker 1-0-1.000; 1972-1973 Leo Durocher 98-95-.508; 1974-1975 Preston Gomez 128-161-.443; 1975-1982 Bill Virdon 544-522-.510; 1982-1985 Bob Lillis 276-261-.514; 1986-1988 Hal Lanier 254-232-.523; 1989-1993 Art Howe 307-341-.474; 1994-present Terry Collins

HOUSTON COLT 45's

(became Houston Astros)

Home City: Houston, Texas
Home Field: Colt Stadium — Capacity: 32,601 [1962]
Origin of Name: The name was chosen in a Name the Team Contest.

Regular Season Record

Season	League	GP	W	L	Pct	GB	R	OR
1962	NL	160	64	96	.400	36.5	592	717
1963	NL	162	66	96	.407	33	464	640
1964	NL	162	66	96	.407	27	495	628
TOTAL:	3 years	484	196	288		96.5	1551	1985
AVERAGE:		161	65	96	.405	32	517	662

COACHING HISTORY: 1962-1964 Harry Craft 191-280-.406; 1964 Luman Harris 5-8-.385

HOUSTON GAMBLERS

Home City: Houston Texas
Home Stadium: The Astrodome — Capacity: 50,496 [1984]
Origin of Name: The name was chosen by Jerry Argovitz, one of the co-owners of the team.

Regular Season Record

Season	League	GP	W	L	T	PF	PA	Pct
1984	USFL	18	13	5	0	618	400	.722
1985	USFL	18	10	8	0	544	388	.556
TOTAL:	2 years	36	23	13	0	1162	788	
AVERAGE:		18	12	6	0	581	394	.639

Playoff Record

Season	GP	W	L	PF	PA	Result
1984	1	0	1	16	17	Lost 1st round series to Arizona.
1985	1	0	1	20	22	Lost 1st round series to Birmingham.
TOTAL:	2	0	2	36	39	
AVERAGE:	1	0	1	18	20	

COACHING HISTORY: 1984-1985 Jack Pardee 23-13-0-.639

HOUSTON HURRICANE

Home City: Houston, Texas
Home Stadium: The Astrodome Capacity: 35,443
Origin of Name: The name was chosen in a Name the Team Contest.

Regular Season Record

Season	League	GP	W	L	GF	GA	BP	Pts	Pct
1978	NASL	30	10	20	37	61	36	96	.356
1979	NASL	30	22	8	61	46	55	187	.693
1980	NASL	32	14	18	51	52	45	129	.448
TOTAL:	3 years	92	46	46	149	159	136	412	
AVERAGE:		31	16	15	50	53	45	137	.498

Playoff Record

Season	GP	W	L	GF	GA	Result
1979	2	0	2	2	4	Lost 1st round series to Philadelphia.
1980	3	1	2	2	3	Lost 1st round series to Edmonton.
TOTAL:	5	1	4	4	7	
AVERAGE:	3	1	2	2	4	

COACHING HISTORY: 1978-1979 Timo Liekoski 32-28-.524; 1980 Eckhard Krautzun 14-18-.448

HOUSTON MAVERICKS

Home City: Houston, Texas
Home Court: Sam Houston Coliseum Capacity: 9,300
Origin of Name: The name is synonymous with Texas. Sam Maverick was a Texan who fought for Texas independence.

Regular Season Record

Season	League	GP	W	L	PPGF	PPGA	Pct	GB
1967-1968	ABA	78	29	49	103.5	107.8	.372	19
1968-1969	ABA	78	23	55	111.3	117.0	.295	37
TOTAL:	2 years	156	52	104				56
AVERAGE:		78	26	52	107.4	112.4	.333	28

Playoff Record

Season	GP	W	L	PPGF	PPGA	Result
1967-1968	3	0	3	103.3	114.0	Lost 1st round series to Dallas.

COACHING HISTORY: 1967-1969 Slater Martin 32-58-.356; 1968-1969 Jim Weaver 20-46-.303

HOUSTON OILERS

Home City: Houston, Texas
Home Stadium: Jeppesen Stadium (1960-1964) Capacity: 23,500
Rice University Stadium (1965-1967) Capacity: 70,000
The Astrodome (1968-present) Capacity: 59,969 [1995]
Origin of Name: The team was named by then owner Bud Adams Jr. chosen to reflect on one of Houston's major industries.

			Regular Season Record					
Season	**League**	**GP**	**W**	**L**	**T**	**PF**	**PA**	**Pct**
1960	AFL	14	10	4	0	379	285	.714
1961	AFL	14	10	3	1	513	242	.750
1962	AFL	14	11	3	0	387	270	.786
1963	AFL	14	6	8	0	302	372	.429
1964	AFL	14	4	10	0	310	355	.286
1965	AFL	14	4	10	0	298	429	.286
1966	AFL	14	3	11	0	335	396	.214
1967	AFL	14	9	4	1	258	199	.679
1968	AFL	14	7	7	0	303	248	.500
1969	AFL	14	6	6	2	278	279	.500
1970	NFL	14	3	10	1	217	352	.250
1971	NFL	14	4	9	1	251	330	.321
1972	NFL	14	1	13	0	164	380	.071
1973	NFL	14	1	13	0	199	467	.071
1974	NFL	14	7	7	0	236	282	.500
1975	NFL	14	10	4	0	293	226	.714
1976	NFL	14	5	9	0	222	273	.357
1977	NFL	14	8	6	0	299	230	.571
1978	NFL	16	10	6	0	283	298	.625
1979	NFL	16	11	5	0	362	331	.688
1980	NFL	16	11	5	0	295	251	.688
1981	NFL	16	7	9	0	281	355	.438
1982	NFL	9	1	8	0	136	245	.111
1983	NFL	16	2	14	0	288	460	.125
1984	NFL	16	3	13	0	240	437	.188
1985	NFL	16	5	11	0	284	412	.313
1986	NFL	16	5	11	0	274	329	.313
1987	NFL	15	9	6	0	345	349	.600
1988	NFL	16	10	6	0	424	365	.625
1989	NFL	16	9	7	0	365	412	.563
1990	NFL	16	9	7	0	405	307	.563
1991	NFL	16	11	5	0	386	251	.688
1992	NFL	16	10	6	0	352	258	.625
1993	NFL	16	12	4	0	368	238	.750
1994	NFL	16	2	14	0	226	352	.125
1995	NFL	16	7	9	0	348	324	.438
TOTAL:	36 years	532	243	283	6	10906	11589	
AVERAGE:		15	7	8	0	303	322	.462

Playoff Record

Season	GP	W	L	PF	PA	Result
1960	1	1	0	24	16	**Won AFL championship.**
1961	1	1	0	10	3	**Won AFL championship.**
1962	1	0	1	17	20	Lost AFL championship to Dallas.
1967	1	0	1	7	40	Lost AFL championship to Oakland.
1969	1	0	1	7	56	Lost Divisional playoff to Oakland.
1978	3	2	1	53	74	Lost AFC championship to Pittsburgh.
1979	3	2	1	43	48	Lost AFC championship to Pittsburgh.
1980	1	0	1	7	27	Lost 1st round playoff to Oakland.
1987	2	1	1	33	54	Lost Divisional playoff to Denver.
1988	2	1	1	34	40	Lost Divisional playoff to Buffalo.
1989	1	0	1	23	26	Lost Wild Card game to Pittsburgh.
1990	1	0	1	14	41	Lost Wild Card game to Cincinnati.
1991	2	1	1	41	36	Lost Conference semifinal to Denver.
1992	1	0	1	38	41	Lost Wild Card game to Buffalo.
1993	1	0	1	20	28	Lost Conference semifinal to Kansas City.
TOTAL:	22	9	13	371	550	
AVERAGE:	2	1	1	25	37	

COACHING HISTORY: 1960-1961 Lou Rymkus 11-7-1-.605; 1961 Wally Lemm 9-0-0-1.000; 1962-1963 Frank Ivy 17-11-0-.607; 1964 Sammy Baugh 4-10-0-.286; 1965 Hugh Taylor 4-10-0-.286; 1966-1970 Wally Lemm 28-38-4-.429; 1971 Ed Hughes 4-9-1-.321; 1972-1973 Bill Peterson 1-18-07.053; 1973-1974 Sid Gillman 8-15-0-348; 1975-1980 Bum Phillips 55-35-0-.611; 1981-1983 Ed Biles 8-23-0-.258; 1983 Chuck Studley 2-8-0-.200; 1984-1985 Hugh Campbell 8-22-0-.267; 1986-1989 Jerry Glanville 33-30-0-.524; 1990-1994 Jack Pardee 43-31-0-.581; 1994-present Jeff Fisher

HOUSTON ROCKETS
(were San Diego Rockets)

Home City: Houston, Texas
Home Court: Hofheinz Pavilion (1971-1975) — Capacity: 10,218
Hofheinz Pavilion & Hemisfair Arena (1972-1973) — Capacity: 10,446
The Summit (1975-present) — Capacity: 16,661 [1995]
Origin of Name: The team kept the same nickname when it moved from San Diego to Houston.

Regular Season Record

Season	League	GP	W	L	PPGF	PPGA	Pct	GB
1971-1972	NBA	82	34	48	109.7	111.2	.415	35
1972-1973	NBA	82	33	49	112.8	114.5	.402	19
1973-1974	NBA	82	32	50	107.4	107.6	.390	15
1974-1975	NBA	82	41	41	103.9	102.9	.500	19
1975-1976	NBA	82	40	42	106.2	107.0	.488	9
1976-1977	NBA	82	49	33	106.4	104.8	.598	-
1977-1978	NBA	82	28	54	103.8	107.8	.341	24
1978-1979	NBA	82	47	35	113.4	112.4	.573	1
1979-1980	NBA	82	41	41	110.8	110.6	.500	9
1980-1981	NBA	82	40	42	108.3	107.9	.488	12
1981-1982	NBA	82	46	36	105.9	105.9	.561	2
1982-1983	NBA	82	14	68	99.3	110.9	.171	39
1983-1984	NBA	82	29	53	110.6	113.7	.354	16

1984-1985	NBA	82	48	34	111.2	109.5	.585	4
1985-1986	NBA	82	51	31	114.4	111.8	.622	-
1986-1987	NBA	82	42	40	106.9	105.9	.512	13
1987-1988	NBA	82	46	36	109.0	107.6	.561	8
1988-1989	NBA	82	45	37	108.5	107.5	.549	6
1989-1990	NBA	82	41	41	106.7	105.3	.500	15
1990-1991	NBA	82	52	30	106.7	103.2	.634	3
1991-1992	NBA	82	42	40	102.0	103.7	.512	13
1992-1993	NBA	82	55	27	104.0	99.8	.671	-
1993-1994	NBA	82	58	24	101.1	96.8	.707	-
1994-1995	NBA	82	47	35	103.5	101.4	.573	15
1995-1996	NBA	82	48	34	102.5	100.7	.585	11
TOTAL:	25 years	2050	1049	1001				288
AVERAGE:		82	42	40	107.0	106.8	.512	12

Playoff Record

Season	**GP**	**W**	**L**	**PPGF**	**PPGA**	**Result**
1974-1975	8	3	5	108.5	107.9	Lost Conference semifinal to Boston.
1976-1977	12	6	6	108.9	108.8	Lost Conference final to Philadelphia.
1978-1979	2	0	2	98.5	104.5	Lost 1st round series to Atlanta.
1979-1980	7	2	5	102.1	109.0	Lost Conference semifinal to Boston.
1980-1981	21	12	9	98.0	98.5	Lost championship series to Boston.
1981-1982	3	1	2	87.0	92.0	Lost 1st round series to Seattle.
1984-1985	5	2	3	104.0	104.2	Lost 1st round series to Utah.
1985-1986	20	13	7	111.3	107.5	Lost championship series to Boston.
1986-1987	10	5	5	109.7	108.1	Lost Conference semifinal to Seattle.
1987-1988	4	1	3	104.5	107.0	Lost 1st round series to Dallas.
1988-1989	4	1	3	106.5	106.3	Lost 1st round series to Seattle.
1989-1990	4	1	3	97.8	105.5	Lost 1st round series to L.A. Lakers.
1990-1991	3	0	3	93.3	99.0	Lost 1st round series to L.A. Lakers.
1992-1993	12	6	6	97.8	96.3	Lost Conference semifinal to Seattle.
1993-1994	23	15	8	97.1	94.0	**Won NBA championship**.
1994-1995	22	15	7	107.0	104.2	**Won NBA championship**.
1995-1996	8	3	5	97.8	102.6	Lost Conference semifinal to Seattle.
TOTAL:	168	86	82			
AVERAGE:	10	5	5	101.8	102.5	

COACHING HISTORY:1971-1973 Tex Winter 51-78-.395; 1972-1976 John Egan 129-152-.459; 1976-1979 Tom Nissalke 124-122-.504; 1979-1983 Del Harris 141-187-.430; 1983-1988 Bill Fitch 216-194-.527; 1988-1992 Don Chaney 164-134-.550; 1991-present Rudy Tomjanovich

HOUSTON STARS

Home City: Houston, Texas
Home Stadium: The Astrodome Capacity: 46,000 [1967]
Origin of Name: The team was represented by the Bangu Soccer Club of Rio de Janiero.

Regular Season Record

Season	**League**	**GP**	**W**	**L**	**T**	**GF**	**GA**	**BP**	**Pts**	**Pct**
1967	USA	12	4	4	4	19	18	NA	12	.500
1968	NASL	32	14	12	6	58	41	48	150	.521
TOTAL:	2 years	44	18	16	10	77	59	48	162	
AVERAGE:		22	9	8	5	39	30	24	81	.409

COACHING HISTORY: 1967 Matim Francisco 4-4-4; 1968 Geza Henni 14-12-6

HOUSTON TEXANS
(became Shreveport Steamers)

Home City: Houston Texas
Home Stadium: The Astrodome — Capacity: 44,500 [1974]
Origin of Name: The team was based in Texas

Regular Season Record

Season	League	GP	W	L	T	PF	PA	Pct
1974	WFL	12	3	8	1	113	269	.292

COACHING HISTORY: Jim Garrett 3-8-1-.292

INDIANA PACERS

Home City: Indianapolis, Indiana
Home Court: State Fairgrounds (1967-1974) — Capacity: 9,147 [1974]
Market Square Arena (1974-present) — Capacity: 16,530 [1995]
Origin of Name: The name was chosen by team executives.

Regular Season Record

Season	League	GP	W	L	PPGF	PPGA	Pct	GB
1967-1968	ABA	78	38	40	109.6	109.4	.487	16
1968-1969	ABA	78	44	34	119.6	115.5	.564	-
1969-1970	ABA	84	59	25	113.2	109.8	.702	-
1970-1971	ABA	84	58	26	119.1	113.1	.690	-
1971-1972	ABA	84	47	37	112.9	110.3	.560	13
1972-1973	ABA	84	51	33	114.7	112.5	.607	4
1973-1974	ABA	84	46	38	105.8	105.0	.548	5
1974-1975	ABA	84	45	39	112.8	111.7	.536	20
1975-1976	ABA	84	39	45	112.9	112.6	.464	21
1976-1977	NBA	82	36	46	106.8	108.6	.439	14
1977-1978	NBA	82	31	51	108.6	111.1	.378	17
1978-1979	NBA	82	38	44	108.6	110.2	.463	10
1979-1980	NBA	82	37	45	111.2	111.9	.451	13
1980-1981	NBA	82	44	38	107.6	106.2	.537	16
1981-1982	NBA	82	35	47	102.2	104.0	.427	20
1982-1983	NBA	82	20	62	108.7	114.5	.244	31
1983-1984	NBA	82	26	56	104.5	109.3	.317	24
1984-1985	NBA	82	22	60	108.3	114.5	.268	37
1985-1986	NBA	82	26	56	103.9	107.2	.317	31
1986-1987	NBA	82	41	41	106.1	106.7	.500	16
1987-1988	NBA	82	38	44	104.6	105.4	.463	16
1988-1989	NBA	82	28	54	106.9	111.1	.341	35
1989-1990	NBA	82	42	40	109.3	109.1	.512	17
1990-1991	NBA	82	41	41	111.7	112.1	.500	20
1991-1992	NBA	82	40	42	112.2	110.3	.488	27
1992-1993	NBA	82	41	41	107.8	106.1	.500	16
1993-1994	NBA	82	47	35	101.0	97.5	.573	10

1994-1995	NBA	82	52	30	99.2	95.5	.634	-
1995-1996	NBA	82	52	30	99.3	96.1	.634	20
TOTAL:	29 years	2384	1164	1220				469
AVERAGE:		82	40	42	108.6	108.5	.488	16

Playoff Record

Season	GP	W	L	PPGF	PPGA	Result
1967-1968	3	0	3	116.3	133.3	Lost 1st round series to Pittsburgh.
1968-1969	16	9	7	127.9	123.9	Lost championship series to Oakland.
1969-1970	15	12	3	114.6	107.5	**Won ABA championship**.
1970-1971	11	7	4	108.2	107.8	Lost 2nd round series to Utah.
1971-1972	20	12	8	108.4	107.3	**Won ABA championship**.
1972-1973	18	12	6	102.5	100.8	**Won ABA championship**.
1973-1974	14	7	7	100.4	101.6	Lost 2nd round series to Utah.
1974-1975	18	9	9	108.8	108.4	Won championship series to Kentucky.
1975-1976	3	1	2	105.7	105.0	Lost 1st round series to Kentucky.
1989-1990	3	0	3	91.7	104.0	Lost 1st round series to Detroit.
1990-1991	5	2	3	118.4	118.8	Lost 1st round series to Boston.
1991-1992	3	0	3	107.7	115.0	Lost 1st round series to Boston.
1992-1993	4	1	3	102.8	102.5	Lost 1st round series to New York.
1993-1994	16	10	6	90.3	87.4	Lost Conference final to New York.
1994-1995	17	10	7	98.6	97.5	Lost Conference final to Orlando.
1995-1996	5	2	3	87.0	88.0	Lost 1st round series to Atlanta.
TOTAL:	171	94	77			
AVERAGE:	11	6	5	105.3	106.3	

COACHING HISTORY: 1967-1969 Larry Staverman 40-47-.460; 1968-1980 Bob Leonard 529-456-.537; 1980-1984 Jack McKinney 125-203-.381; 1984-1986 George Irvine 48-116-.293; 1986-1989 Jack Ramsay 79-92-.462; 1988-1989 Mel Daniels 0-2-.000; 1988-1989 George Irvine 6-14-.300; 1988-1991 Dick Versace 51-56-.477; 1991-1993 Bob Hill 113-108-.511; 1993-present Larry Brown

INDIANAPOLIS COLTS

(were Baltimore Colts)

Home City: Indianapolis, Indiana
Home Stadium: RCA Dome * Capacity: 60,272 [1995]
Origin of Name: The team kept the same nickname when it moved from Baltimore to Indianapolis.

Regular Season Record

Season	League	GP	W	L	T	PF	PA	Pct
1984	NFL	16	4	12	0	239	414	.250
1985	NFL	16	5	11	0	320	386	.313
1986	NFL	16	3	13	0	229	400	.188
1987	NFL	15	9	6	0	300	238	.600
1988	NFL	16	9	7	0	354	315	.563
1989	NFL	16	8	8	0	298	301	.500
1990	NFL	16	7	9	0	281	353	.438
1991	NFL	16	1	15	0	143	381	.063
1992	NFL	16	9	7	0	216	302	.563
1993	NFL	16	4	12	0	189	378	.250

1994	NFL	16	8	8	0	307	320	.500
1995	NFL	16	9	7	0	331	316	.563
TOTAL:	12 years	191	76	115	0	3207	4104	
AVERAGE:		16	6	10	0	267	342	.398

Playoff Record

Season	GP	W	L	PF	PA	Result
1987	1	0	1	21	38	Lost Divisional playoff to Cleveland.
1995	3	2	1	61	47	Lost Conference final to Pittsburgh.
TOTAL:	4	2	2	82	85	
AVERAGE:	2	1	1	41	43	

COACHING HISTORY: 1984 Frank Kush 4-11-0-.267; 1984 Hal Hunter 0-1-0-.000; 1985-1986 Rod Dowhower 5-24-0-.172: 1986-1991 Ron Meyer 36-35-0-.507; 1991 Rick Venturi 1-10-0-.090; 1992-present Ted Marchibroda

*Known as Hoosier Dome from 1984 to 1994.

INDIANAPOLIS FEDERAL HOOSIERS

Home City: Indianapolis, Indiana
Home Field: West Washington Street Park * Capacity: 20,000 [1914]
Origin of Name: The team got its nickname because this Federal League team played in the Hoosier State.

Regular Season Record

Season	League	GP	W	L	Pct	GB	R	OR
1914	FL	153	88	65	.575	-	762	622

COACHING HISTORY: Bill Phillips 88-65-.575

*Also known as Federal League Park.

INDIANAPOLIS HOOSIERS

Home City: Indianapolis, Indiana
Home Field: South Street Park
Origin of Name: The team played in the Hoosier State.

Regular Season Record

Season	League	GP	W	L	Pct	GB	R	OR
1878	NL	60	24	36	.400	17	293	328

COACHING HISTORY: John Clapp 24-36-.400

INDIANAPOLIS HOOSIERS

Home City: Indianapolis, Indiana
Home Field: Bruce Park
Origin of Name: The team played in Indiana which is known as the Hoosier State.

Season	League	GP	Regular Season Record W	L	Pct	GB	R	OR
1884	AA	107	29	78	.271	46	462	755

COACHING HISTORY: Jim Gifford 25-59-.298; Bill Watkins 4-19-.174

INDIANAPOLIS HOOSIERS

Home City: Indianapolis, Indiana
Home Field: Bruce Park (Sundays only in 1887)
Tinker Park (1887-1889)*
Origin of Name: See above.

Season	League	GP	Regular Season Record W	L	Pct	GB	R	OR
1887	NL	126	37	89	.294	43	628	965
1888	NL	135	50	85	.370	36	603	731
1889	NL	134	59	75	.440	28	819	894
TOTAL:	3 years	395	146	249		107	2050	2590
AVERAGE:		132	49	83	.370	36	683	863

COACHING HISTORY: 1887 Walter Burnham 6-22-.214; 1887 Fred Thomas 11-18-.379; 1887 Horace Fogel 20-49-.290; 1888 Harry Spence 50-85-.370; 1889 Frank Bancroft 25-42-.373; 1889 Jack Glasscock 34-33-.507

*Also known as 7th Street Park II

INDIANAPOLIS JETS
(were Indianapolis Kautskys)

Home City: Indianapolis, Indiana
Home Court:
Origin of Name:

Season	League	GP	Regular Season Record W	L	PPGF	PPGA	Pct	GB
1948-1949	BAA	60	18	42	74.7	79.4	.300	27

COACHING HISTORY: Bruce Hale 4-13-.235; Burl Friddle 14-29-.326

INDIANAPOLIS KAUTSKYS

Home City: Indianapolis, Indiana
Home Court:
Origin of Name: The team was named after owner Frank Kautsky.

Season	League	GP	Regular Season Record W	L	PPGF	PPGA	Pct	GB
1937-1938	NBL	13	4	9	36.3	37.7	.308	7.5
1938-1939	NBL	26	13	13	43.3	43.6	.500	3

1939-1940	NBL	28	9	19	41.5	45.6	.321	9.5
1941-1942	NBL	23	12	11	41.5	41.2	.522	7.5
TOTAL:	4 years	90	38	52				27.5
AVERAGE:		23	10	13	41.3	42.8	.388	6.5

Playoff Record

Season	GP	W	L	PPGF	PPGA	Result
1941-1942	2	0	2	40.5	52.0	Lost 1st round to Oshkosh.

COACHING HISTORY: 1937-1938 Frank Kautsky 4-9-.308; 1938-1940 Bob Nipper 22-32-.407; 1941-1942-(unknown)

INDIANAPOLIS KAUTSKYS

(became Indianapolis Jets)

Home City: Indianapolis, Indiana
Home Court:
Origin of Name: The team was owned by Frank Kautsky.

Regular Season Record

Season	League	GP	W	L	PPGF	PPGA	Pct	GB
1945-1946	NBL	32	10	22	46.4	49.8	.313	10
1946-1947	NBL	44	27	17	56.9	53.1	.614	1
1947-1948	NBL	59	24	35	60.2	63.2	.407	18.5
TOTAL:	3 years	135	61	74				29.5
AVERAGE:		45	20	25	54.5	55.4	.452	10

Playoff Record

Season	GP	W	L	PPGF	PPGA	Result
1946-1947	5	2	3	63.6	68.0	Lost 1st round to Chicago.
1947-1948	4	1	3	69.0	72.8	Lost 1st round to Tri-Cities.
TOTAL:	9	3	6			
AVERAGE:	5	2	3	66.3	70.4	

COACHING HISTORY: 1945-1946 Nat Hickey 10-22-.313; 1946-1947 Ernie Andres 21-13-.618; 1946-1947 Bob Dietz & Herm Schaefer 6-4-.600; 1947-1948 Glenn Curtis 2-2-.500; 1947-1948 Leo Klier 1-1-.500; 1947-1948 Bruce Hale 21-32-.396

INDIANAPOLIS OLYMPIANS

Home City: Indianapolis, Indiana
Home Court: Butler University
Origin of Name: The team consisted of the 1948 Olympic gold medal winning team from the University of Kentucky.

Regular Season Record

Season	League	GP	W	L	PPGF	PPGA	Pct	GB
1949-1950	NBA	64	39	25	85.8	82.1	.609	-
1950-1951	NBA	68	31	37	81.7	84.1	.456	13
1951-1952	NBA	66	34	32	82.9	82.8	.515	7

1952-1953	NBA	71	28	43	74.6	77.4	.394	20.5
TOTAL:	4 years	269	132	137				40.5
AVERAGE:		67	33	34	81.3	81.6	.493	10

Playoff Record

Season	GP	W	L	PPGF	PPGA	Result
1949-1950	6	3	3	78.5	81.5	Lost Division final to Anderson.
1950-1951	3	1	2	89.7	89.3	Lost Division semifinal to Minneapolis.
1951-1952	2	0	2	78.5	86.0	Lost Division semifinal to Minneapolis.
1952-1953	2	0	2	74.0	83.0	Lost Division semifinal to Minneapolis.
TOTAL:	13	4	9			
AVERAGE:	3	1	2	80.2	85.0	

COACHING HISTORY: 1949-1951 Cliff Barker 70-62-.530; 1951-1953 Herm Schaeffer 62-75-.453

INDIANAPOLIS RACERS

Home City: Indianapolis, Indiana
Home Arena: Market Square Arena — Capacity: 16,042 [1975]
Origin of Name: The name was suggested because Indianapolis is the home of the most prestigious automobile race in North America, the Indianapolis 500. The name was chosen in a Name the Team Contest in which the club received over 4,000 entries.

Regular Season Record

Season	League	GP	W	L	T	GF	GA	Pts	Pct
1974-1975	WHA	78	18	57	3	216	338	39	.250
1975-1976	WHA	80	35	39	6	245	247	76	.475
1976-1977	WHA	81	36	37	8	276	305	80	.494
1977-1978	WHA	80	24	51	5	267	353	53	.331
1978-1979	WHA	25	5	18	2	78	130	12	.240
TOTAL:	5 years	344	118	202	24	1082	1373	260	
AVERAGE:		69	24	40	5	216	275	53	.378

Playoff Record

Season	GP	W	L	GF	GA	Result
1975-1976	7	3	4	15	18	Lost quarterfinal series to New England.
1976-1977	9	5	4	33	34	Lost semifinal series to Quebec.
TOTAL:	16	8	8	48	52	
AVERAGE:	8	4	4	24	26	

COACHING HISTORY: 1974-1975 Gerry Moore 18-57-3-.250; 1975-1977 Jacques Demers 71-76-14-.484; 1977-1978 Ron Ingram 16-31-4-.353; 1977-1978 Bill Goldsworthy 8-20-1-.293; 1978-1979 Pat Stapleton 5-18-2-.240

JACKSONVILLE BULLS
(became Jacksonville Sharks)

Home City: Jacksonville, Florida
Home Stadium: Gator Bowl — Capacity: 70,000 [1984]
Origin of Name: The name was chosen in a Name the Team Contest.

Regular Season Record

Season	League	GP	W	L	T	PF	PA	Pct
1984	USFL	18	6	12	0	327	455	.333

COACHING HISTORY: Lindy Infante 6-12-0-.333

JACKSONVILLE EXPRESS
(were Jacksonville Sharks)

Home City: Jacksonville, Florida
Home Stadium: Gator Bowl Capacity: 70,000 [1975]
Origin of Name:

Regular Season Record

Season	League	GP	W	L	T	PF	PA	Pct
1975	WFL	11	6	5	0	227	247	.545

COACHING HISTORY: Charlie Tate 6-5-0-.545

JACKSONVILLE JAGUARS

Home City: Jacksonville, Florida
Home Stadium: Jacksonville Municipal Stadium* Capacity: 73,000 [1995]
Origin of Name: Touchdown Jacksonville !, the ownership group responsible for securing the new franchise announced December 6, 1991 that the team would be named Jaguars.

Regular Season Record

Season	League	GP	W	L	T	PF	PA	Pct
1995	NFL	16	4	12	0	275	404	.250

COACHING HISTORY: 1995-present Tom Coughlin

*Built on the site of and incorporated parts of the old Gator Bowl Stadium

JACKSONVILLE SHARKS
(became Jacksonville Express)

Home City: Jacksonville, Florida
Home Stadium: Gator Bowl Capacity: 70,000 [1974]
Origin of Name:

Regular Season Record

Season	League	GP	W	L	T	PF	PA	Pct
1974	WFL	14	4	10	0	258	358	.286

COACHING HISTORY: Bud Asher 2-4-0-.333; Charlie Tate 2-6-0-.250

JACKSONVILLE SHARKS
(were Jacksonville Bulls)

Home City: Jacksonville, Florida
Home Stadium: Gator Bowl — Capacity: 70,000 [1985]
Origin of Name:

Regular Season Record

Season	League	GP	W	L	T	PF	PA	Pct
1985	USFL	18	9	9	0	407	402	.500

COACHING HISTORY: Lindy Infante 9-9-0-.500

JACKSONVILLE TEAMEN
(were New England Teamen)

Home City: Jacksonville, Florida
Home Field: Gator Bowl — Capacity: 70,000 [1982]
Origin of Name: The team kept the same nickname when it moved from the New England area to Jacksonville.

Regular Season Record

Season	League	GP	W	L	GF	GA	BP	Pts	Pct
1981	NASL	32	18	14	51	46	41	141	.294
1982	NASL	32	11	21	41	71	39	105	.219
TOTAL:	2 years	64	29	35	92	117	80	246	
AVERAGE:		32	15	17	46	59	40	123	.256

Playoff Record

Season	GP	W	L	GF	GA	Result
1981	5	3	2	8	8	Lost 2nd round series to San Diego.

COACHING HISTORY: 1981-1982 Noel Cantwell 29-35-.256

KANKAKEE GALLAGHER TROJANS

Home City: Kankakee, Illinois
Home Court:
Origin of Name: Most of the players were from the Gallagher Business School and the team used the name of the school.

Regular Season Record

Season	League	GP	W	L	PPGF	PPGA	Pct	GB
1937-1938	NBL	14	3	11	33.3	53.3	.214	9

COACHING HISTORY: Don Betourne 3-11-.214

KANSAS CITY ATHLETICS
(were Philadelphia Athletics)
(became Oakland Athletics)

Home City: Kansas City, Missouri
Home Field: Municipal Stadium Capacity: 32,561 [1964]
Origin of Name: The team kept the same nickname when it moved from Philadelphia.

Regular Season Record

Season	League	GP	W	L	Pct	GB	R	OR
1955	AL	154	63	91	.409	33	638	911
1956	AL	154	52	102	.338	45	619	831
1957	AL	153	59	94	.386	38.5	563	710
1958	AL	154	73	81	.474	19	642	713
1959	AL	154	66	88	.429	28	681	760
1960	AL	154	58	96	.377	39	615	756
1961	AL	161	61	100	.379	47.5	683	863
1962	AL	162	72	90	.444	24	745	837
1963	AL	162	73	89	.451	31.5	615	704
1964	AL	162	57	105	.352	42	621	836
1965	AL	162	59	103	.364	43	585	755
1966	AL	160	74	86	.463	23	564	648
1967	AL	161	62	99	.385	29.5	533	660
TOTAL:	13 years	2053	829	1224		443	8104	9984
AVERAGE:		158	64	94	.404	34	623	768

COACHING HISTORY: 1955-1957 Lou Boudreau 151-260-.367; 1957-1959 Harry Craft 162-196-.453; 1960 Bob Elliot 58-96-.377; 1961 Joe Gordon 26-43-.377; 1961-1962 Hank Bauer 107-147-.421; 1963-1964 Ed Lopat 90-124-.421; 1964-1965 Mel McGaha 45-91-.331; 1965 Haywood Sullivan 54-82-.397; 1966-1967 Alvin Dark 126-155-.448: 1967 Luke Appling 10-30-.250

KANSAS CITY BLUES
(were New York Metropolitans)

Home City: Kansas City, Missouri
Home Field: Association Park I (1888)
Exposition Park (1889)
Origin of Name: As with most teams with colors in their name the team was probably named after the color of their uniforms.

Regular Season Record

Season	League	GP	W	L	Pct	GB	R	OR
1888	AA	132	43	89	.326	47.5	579	896
1889	AA	137	55	82	.401	38	852	1031
TOTAL:	2 years	269	98	171		85.5	1431	1927
AVERAGE:		135	49	86	.364	43	716	964

COACHING HISTORY: 1888 Dave Rowe 14-35-.286; 1888 Sam Barkley 26-43-.377; 1888-1889 Bill Watkins 58-93-.384

KANSAS CITY CHIEFS
(were Dallas Texans)

Home City: Kansas City, Missouri
Home Stadium: Municipal Stadium (1963-1971) Capacity: 47,000 [1971]
Arrowhead Stadium (1972-present) Capacity: 79,101 [1995]
Origin of Name: The team was named by owner Lamar Hunt.

Regular Season Record

Season	League	GP	W	L	T	PF	PA	Pct
1963	AFL	14	5	7	2	347	263	.429
1964	AFL	14	7	7	0	366	306	.500
1965	AFL	14	7	5	2	322	285	.571
1966	AFL	14	11	2	1	448	276	.821
1967	AFL	14	9	5	0	408	254	.643
1968	AFL	14	12	2	0	371	170	.857
1969	AFL	14	11	3	0	359	177	.786
1970	NFL	14	7	5	2	272	244	.571
1971	NFL	14	10	3	1	302	208	.750
1972	NFL	14	8	6	0	287	254	.571
1973	NFL	14	7	5	2	231	192	.571
1974	NFL	14	5	9	0	233	293	.357
1975	NFL	14	5	9	0	282	341	.357
1976	NFL	14	5	9	0	290	376	.357
1977	NFL	14	2	12	0	225	349	.143
1978	NFL	16	4	12	0	243	327	.250
1979	NFL	16	7	9	0	238	262	.438
1980	NFL	16	8	8	0	319	336	.500
1981	NFL	16	9	7	0	343	290	.563
1982	NFL	9	3	6	0	176	184	.333
1983	NFL	16	6	10	0	386	367	.375
1984	NFL	16	8	8	0	314	324	.500
1985	NFL	16	6	10	0	317	360	.375
1986	NFL	16	10	6	0	358	326	.625
1987	NFL	15	4	11	0	273	388	.267
1988	NFL	16	4	11	1	254	320	.281
1989	NFL	16	8	7	1	318	286	.531
1990	NFL	16	11	5	0	369	257	.688
1991	NFL	16	10	6	0	322	252	.625
1992	NFL	16	10	6	0	348	282	.625
1993	NFL	16	11	5	0	328	291	.688
1994	NFL	16	9	7	0	319	298	.563
1995	NFL	16	13	3	0	358	241	.813
TOTAL:	33 years	490	252	226	12	10,326	9379	
AVERAGE:		15	8	7	0	313	284	.527

Playoff Record

Season	GP	W	L	PF	PA	Result
1966	2	1	1	41	42	Lost Super Bowl to Green Bay.
1968	1	0	1	6	41	Lost Division playoff to Oakland.
1969	3	3	0	53	20	**Won Super Bowl.**
1971	1	0	1	24	27	Lost Division playoff to Miami.

1986	1	0	1	15	35	Lost 1st round playoff to N.Y. Jets.
1990	1	0	1	16	17	Lost Wild Card game to Miami.
1991	2	1	1	24	43	Lost Conference semifinal to Buffalo.
1992	1	0	1	0	17	Lost Wild Card game to San Diego.
1993	3	2	1	68	74	Lost Conference final to Buffalo.
1994	1	0	1	17	27	Lost 1st round game to Miami.
1995	1	0	1	7	10	Lost Conference semifinal to Indianapolis.
TOTAL:	17	7	10	271	353	
AVERAGE:	2	1	1	25	32	

COACHING HISTORY: 1963-1974 Hank Stram 99-59-10-.619; 1975-1977 Paul Wiggin 11-24-0-.314; 1977 Tom Bettio 1-6-0-.143; 1978-1982 Marv Levy 31-42-0-.425; 1983-1986 John Mackovic 30-34-0-.469; 1987-1988 Frank Gansz 8-22-1-.274; 1989-present Marty Schottenheimer

KANSAS CITY COWBOYS

Home City: Kansas City, Missouri
Home Field: Association Park I
Origin of Name: The name was chosen to reflect the western heritage of the area.

Regular Season Record

Season	**League**	**GP**	**W**	**L**	**Pct**	**GB**	**R**	**OR**
1886	NL	121	30	91	.248	58.5	494	872

COACHING HISTORY: Dave Rowe 30-91-.248

KANSAS CITY COWBOYS

Home City: Kansas City, Missouri
Home Stadium: The team played only road games.
Origin of Name: See Above.

Regular Season Record

Season	**League**	**GP**	**W**	**L**	**T**	**PF**	**PA**	**Pct**
1924	NFL	9	2	7	0	46	124	.222
1925	NFL	8	2	5	1	65	97	.313
1926	NFL	11	8	3	0	76	53	.727
TOTAL:	3 years	28	12	15	1	187	274	
AVERAGE:		9	4	5	0	62	91	.446

COACHING HISTORY: LeRoy Andrews 12-15-1-.446

KANSAS CITY KINGS

(were Kansas City-Omaha Kings)
(became Sacramento Kings)

Home City: Kansas City, Missouri
Home Court: Kemper Arena Capacity: 16,642 [1984]
Origin of Name: The team kept the same nickname from its previous locations.

Regular Season Record

Season	League	GP	W	L	PPGF	PPGA	Pct	GB
1975-1976	NBA	82	31	51	103.3	106.2	.378	7
1976-1977	NBA	82	40	42	107.7	106.8	.488	10
1977-1978	NBA	82	31	51	109.5	111.4	.378	17
1978-1979	NBA	82	48	34	113.1	110.2	.585	-
1979-1980	NBA	82	47	35	108.0	104.9	.573	2
1980-1981	NBA	82	40	42	106.9	106.9	.488	12
1981-1982	NBA	82	30	52	107.1	110.2	.366	18
1982-1983	NBA	82	45	37	113.8	112.3	.549	8
1983-1984	NBA	82	38	44	110.0	111.5	.463	7
1984-1985	NBA	82	31	51	114.8	117.5	.378	21
TOTAL:	10 years	820	381	439				102
AVERAGE:		82	38	44	109.4	109.8	.465	10

Playoff Record

Season	GP	W	L	PPGF	PPGA	Result
1978-1979	5	1	4	99.2	105.8	Lost Conference semifinal to Phoenix.
1979-1980	3	1	2	99.3	102.0	Lost 1st round series to Phoenix.
1980-1981	15	7	8	91.7	94.9	Lost Conference final to Houston.
1983-1984	3	0	3	103.0	111.0	Lost 1st round series to Los Angeles.
TOTAL:	26	9	17			
AVERAGE:	6	2	4	98.3	103.4	

COACHING HISTORY: 1975-1978 Phil Johnson 84-117-.418; 1977-1978 Larry Staverman 18-27-.400; 1978-1984 Lowell "Cotton" Fitzsimmons 248-244-.504; 1984-1985 Jack McKinney 1-8-.111; 1984-1985 Phil Johnson 30-43-.411.

KANSAS CITY-OMAHA KINGS

(were Cincinnati Royals)
(became Kansas City Kings)

Home City: Kansas City, Missouri
Omaha, Nebraska
Home Court: Municipal Auditorium (Kansas City) Capacity: 9,929 [1975]
Omaha Civic Auditorium (Omaha) Capacity: 9,144 [1975]
Origin of Name: The name was chosen in a Name the Team Contest.

Regular Season Record

Season	League	GP	W	L	PPGF	PPGA	Pct	GB
1972-1973	NBA	82	36	46	107.6	110.5	.439	24
1973-1974	NBA	82	33	49	102.0	105.8	.402	26
1974-1975	NBA	82	44	38	101.4	101.6	.537	3
TOTAL:	3 years	246	113	133				53
AVERAGE:		82	38	44	103.7	106.0	.459	18

Playoff Record

Season	GP	W	L	PPGF	PPGA	Result
1974-1975	6	2	4	91.8	98.0	Lost Conference semifinal to Chicago.

COACHING HISTORY: 1972-1974 Bob Cousy 42-60-.412; 1973-1974 Draff Young 0-4-.000; 1973-1975 Phil Johnson 71-69-.507

KANSAS CITY PACKERS

Home City: Kansas City, Missouri
Home Field: Federal League Park * Capacity: 12,000 [1914]
Origin of Name: The name was chosen due to the fact Kansas City is the home of a major livestock show and is well known for its packing plants.

Season	League	GP	Regular Season Record W	L	Pct	GB	R	OR
1914	FL	151	67	84	.444	20	644	683
1915	FL	153	81	72	.529	5.5	547	551
TOTAL:	2 years	304	148	156		25.5	1191	1234
AVERAGE:		152	74	78	.487	13	596	617

COACHING HISTORY: 1914-1915 George Stovall 148-156-.487

*Also known as Gordon and Koppel Field

KANSAS CITY ROYALS

Home City: Kansas City, Missouri
Home Field: Municipal Stadium (1969-1972) Capacity:,35,561 [1971]
Ewing Kauffman Stadium (1973-present)* Capacity: 40,625 [1995]
Origin of Name: The name was chosen in a Name the Team Contest.

Season	League	GP	Regular Season Record W	L	Pct	GB	R	OR
1969	AL	162	69	93	.426	28	586	688
1970	AL	162	65	97	.401	33	611	705
1971	AL	161	85	76	.528	16	603	566
1972	AL	154	76	78	.494	16.5	580	545
1973	AL	162	88	74	.543	6	754	752
1974	AL	162	77	85	.475	13	667	662
1975	AL	162	91	71	.562	7	710	649
1976	AL	162	90	72	.556	-	713	611
1977	AL	162	102	60	.630	-	822	651
1978	AL	160	90	70	.568	-	743	634
1979	AL	162	85	77	.525	3	851	816
1980	AL	162	97	65	.599	-	809	694
1981	AL	103	50	53	.485	NA	397	405
1982	AL	162	90	72	.556	3	784	717
1983	AL	162	79	83	.488	20	696	767
1984	AL	162	84	78	.519	-	673	686
1985	AL	162	91	71	.562	-	687	639
1986	AL	162	76	86	.469	16	654	673
1987	AL	162	83	79	.512	2	715	691
1988	AL	161	84	77	.522	19.5	704	648
1989	AL	162	92	70	.568	7	690	635
1990	AL	161	75	86	.466	27.5	707	709
1991	AL	162	82	80	.506	13	727	722
1992	AL	162	72	90	.444	24	610	667
1993	AL	162	84	78	.519	10	675	694

1994	AL	115	64	51	.557	4	574	532
1995	AL	144	70	74	.486	30	629	691
TOTAL:	27 years	4237	2191	2046		298.5	18371	17849
AVERAGE:		157	81	76	.517	11	680	661

Playoff Record

Season	GP	W	L	R	OR	Result
1976	5	2	3	24	23	Lost ALCS to New York.
1977	5	2	3	22	21	Lost ALCS to New York.
1978	4	1	3	17	19	Lost ALCS to New York.
1980	9	5	4	37	33	Lost World Series to Philadelphia.
1981	3	0	3	2	10	Lost Divisional playoff to Oakland.
1984	3	0	3	4	14	Lost ALCS to Detroit.
1985	14	8	6	54	38	**Won World Series**.
TOTAL:	43	18	25	160	158	
AVERAGE:	6	2	4	23	23	

COACHING RECORD: 1969 Joe Gordon 69-93-.426; 1970 Charlie Metro 19-35-.352; 1970-1972 Bob Lemon 207-216-.489; 1973-1975 Jack McKeon 215-205-.512; 1975-1979 Dorrel "Whitey" Herzog 408-304-.573; 1980-1981 Jim Frey127-105-.547; 1981-1986 Dick Howser 405-365-.526; 1986 Mike Ferraro 35-38-.479; 1987 Bill Gardner 62-64-.493; 1987-1991 John Wathan 287-270-.515; 1991 Bob Schaeffer 1-0-1.000; 1991-1994 Hal McRae 286-277-.508; 1995-present Bob Boone

*Known as Royals Stadium from 1973 to 1992

KANSAS CITY SCOUTS
(became Colorado Rockies)

Home City: Kansas City, Missouri
Home Arena: Crosby-Kemper Arena Capacity: 16,500 [1975]
Origin of Name: The team was named in honor of the scouts who left with the wagon trains going westward from Kansas City.

Regular Season Record

Season	League	GP	W	L	T	GF	GA	Pts	Pct
1974-1975	NHL	80	15	54	11	184	328	41	.256
1975-1976	NHL	80	12	56	12	190	351	36	.225
TOTAL:	2 years	160	27	110	23	374	679	77	
AVERAGE:		80	14	55	11	187	340	39	.241

COACHING HISTORY: 1974-1976 Armand Guidolin 26-84-15-.268; 1975-1976 Sid Abel 0-3-0-.000; 1975-1976 Ed Bush 1-23-8-.156

KANSAS CITY SPURS
(were Chicago Spurs)

Home City: Kansas City, Missouri
Home Stadium:
Origin of Name: The team kept the same nickname after moving from Chicago.

Regular Season Record

Season	League	GP	W	L	T	GF	GA	BP	Pts	Pct
1968	NASL	32	16	11	5	61	43	47	158	.549
1969	NASL	16	10	2	4	53	28	38	110	.764
1970	NASL	24	8	10	6	42	44	34	100	.463
TOTAL:	3 years	72	34	23	15	156	115	119	368	
AVERAGE:		24	11	8	5	52	38	40	123	.568

Playoff Record

Season	GP	W	L	T	GF	GA	Result
1968	2	0	1	1	1	2	Lost 1st round series to San Diego.

COACHING HISTORY: 1968-1969 Janos Bedl 26-13-9-.620; 1970 Alan Rogers 8-10-6-.463

KANSAS CITY UNIONS

Home City: Kansas City, Missouri
Home Field: Athletic Park Capacity: 4,000
Origin of Name: Most of the teams in the league adopted the name of the league as their own.

Regular Season Record

Season	League	GP	W	L	Pct	GB	R	OR
1884	UA	79	16	63	.203	61	311	618

COACHING HISTORY: Ted Sullivan 16-63-.203

KENOSHA MAROONS

Home City: Kenosha, Wisconsin
Home Stadium:
Origin of Name: The team received its name from the color of their uniforms.

Regular Season Record

Season	League	GP	W	L	T	PF	PA	Pct
1924	NFL	6	0	5	1	18	127	.083

COACHING HISTORY: Earl Potteiger 0-5-1-.083

KENTUCKY COLONELS

Home City: Louisville, Kentucky
Home Court: University of Kentucky Memorial Coliseum (1967-1972)
Freedom Hall (1973-1976) Capacity: 16,933 [1975]
Origin of Name: The name is a popular nickname in Kentucky.

Regular Season Record

Season	League	GP	W	L	PPGF	PPGA	Pct	GB
1967-1968	ABA	78	36	42	104.5	105.2	.462	18
1968-1969	ABA	78	42	36	111.2	111.0	.538	2

1969-1970	ABA	84	45	39	113.5	112.5	.536	14
1970-1971	ABA	84	44	40	122.3	122.1	.524	11
1971-1972	ABA	84	68	16	116.0	107.0	.810	-
1972-1973	ABA	84	56	28	111.9	105.5	.667	1
1973-1974	ABA	84	53	31	107.4	103.3	.631	2
1974-1975	ABA	84	58	26	108.9	101.7	.690	-
1975-1976	ABA	84	46	38	111.0	110.2	.548	14
TOTAL:	9 years	744	448	296				62
AVERAGE:		83	50	33	111.9	108.7	.602	7

Playoff Record

Season	GP	W	L	PPGF	PPGA	Result
1967-1968	5	2	3	102.2	105.2	Lost 1st round series to Minnesota.
1968-1969	7	3	4	110.7	113.7	Lost 1st round series to Indiana.
1969-1970	12	5	7	111.5	112.9	Lost 2nd round series to Indiana.
1970-1971	19	11	8	120.6	121.6	Lost championship series to Utah.
1971-1972	6	2	4	100.0	103.3	Lost 1st round series to New York.
1972-1973	19	11	8	104.6	100.3	Lost championship series to Indiana.
1973-1974	8	4	4	103.5	104.6	Lost 2nd round series to New York.
1974-1975	15	12	3	106.6	99.0	**Won ABA championship**.
1975-1976	10	5	5	113.8	113.4	Lost 2nd round series to Denver.
TOTAL:	101	55	46			
AVERAGE:	11	6	5	108.2	108.2	

COACHING HISTORY: 1967-1968 John Givens 5-12-.294; 1968-1971 Gene Rhodes 128-110-.538; 1970-1971 Alex Groza 2-0-1.000; 1970-1971 Frank Ramsey 32-35-.478; 1971-1973 Joe Mullaney 124-44-.738; 1973-1974 Babe McCarthy 53-31-.631; 1974-1976 Hubie Brown 104-64-.619

LAS VEGAS POSSE

Home City: Las Vegas, Nevada
Home Stadium: Sam Boyd Stadium — Capacity: 31,000 [1994]
Origin of Name: The name was entered in a Name the Team Contest by Janet Negrete of Las Vegas because in her words when she moved to Las Vegas it was "just a cowboy town." Five other entries were received with the name Posse but Negrete was declared winner because she also chose the colors.

Regular Season Record

Season	League	GP	W	L	T	PF	PA	Pts	Pct
1994	CFL	18	5	13	0	444	622	10	.278

COACHING HISTORY: 1994 Ron Meyer 5-13-0-.278

LAS VEGAS QUICKSILVERS

(were San Diego Jaws)
(became San Diego Sockers)

Home City: Las Vegas, Nevada
Home Field: Las Vegas Stadium — Capacity: 16,000
Origin of Name:

Regular Season Record

Season	League	GP	W	L	GF	GA	BP	Pts	Pct
1977	NASL	26	11	15	38	44	37	103	.440

COACHING HISTORY: Derek Trevis 10-10; Jim Fryatt 1-5

LONDON MONARCHS

Home City: London, England
Home Stadium: Wembley Stadium — Capacity: 63,500 [1991]
Origin of Name: London is the seat of the British monarchy.

Regular Season Record

Season	League	GP	W	L	T	PF	PA	Pct
1991	WLAF	10	9	1	0	310	121	.900
1992	WFL	10	2	7	1	178	203	.250
TOTAL:	2 years	20	11	8	1	488	324	
AVERAGE:		10	6	4	0	244	162	.575

Playoff Record

Season	GP	W	L	PF	PA	Result
1991	2	2	0	63	26	**Won WLAF championship**.

COACHING HISTORY: 1991 Larry Kennan 9-1-0-.900; 1992 Ray Willsey 2-7-1-.250

LOS ANGELES ANGELS
(became California Angels)

Home City: Los Angeles, California
Home Field: Wrigley Field (California) (1961) — Capacity: 20,457 [1961]
Dodger Stadium (1962-1965) — Capacity: 56,000 [1964]
Origin of Name: The team was named after the Pacific Coast League team, which was based in the "City of Angels."

Regular Season Record

Season	League	GP	W	L	Pct	GB	R	OR
1961	AL	161	70	91	.435	38.5	744	784
1962	AL	162	86	76	.531	10	718	706
1963	AL	161	70	91	.435	34	597	660
1964	AL	162	82	80	.506	17	544	551
TOTAL:	4 years	646	308	338		99.5	2603	2701
AVERAGE:		162	77	85	.477	25	651	675

COACHING HISTORY: 1961-1964 Bill Rigney 308-338-.477

LOS ANGELES AZTECS

Home City: Los Angeles, California
Home Field: Los Angeles Memorial Coliseum (1977; 1981) — Capacity: 90,000 [1977]
Rose Bowl (1978-1980) — Capacity: 106,721 [1979]
Origin of Name: The name was chosen to attract some of the large Mexican-American population living in Los Angeles.

Regular Season Record

Season	League	GP	W	L	T	GF	GA	BP	Pts	Pct
1974	NASL	20	11	7	2	41	36	38	110	.611
1975	NASL	22	12	10	-	42	33	35	107	.540
1976	NASL	24	12	12	-	43	44	36	108	.500
1977	NASL	26	15	11	-	65	54	57	147	.628
1978	NASL	30	9	21	-	36	69	34	88	.326
1979	NASL	30	18	12	-	62	47	54	162	.600
1980	NASL	32	20	12	-	61	52	54	174	.604
1981	NASL	32	19	13	-	53	55	48	160	.333
TOTAL:	8 years	216	116	98	2	403	390	356	1056	
AVERAGE:		27	15	12	0	50	49	45	132	.494

Playoff Record

Season	GP	W	L	GF	GA	Result
1974	2	2	0	6	3	**Won NASL championship**.
1975	1	0	1	1	2	Lost 1st round series to St. Louis.
1976	1	0	1	0	2	Lost 1st round series to Dallas.
1977	5	3	2	11	7	Lost 3rd round series to Seattle.
1979	5	3	2	10	8	Lost 2nd round series to Vancouver.
1980	8	4	4	11	12	Lost 3rd round series to New York.
1981	3	1	2	7	9	Lost 1st round series to Montreal.
TOTAL:	25	13	12	46	43	
AVERAGE:	4	2	2	7	6	

COACHING HISTORY: 1974 Alex Perolli 11-7-2-.611; 1975-1978 Terry Fisher 44-41; 1978 Tommy Smith 3-13; 1978 Peter Short 1-0; 1979-1980 Rinus Michels 38-24; 1981 Claudio Coutinho 19-13

LOS ANGELES BUCCANEERS

Home City: Los Angeles, California
Home Stadium: The team only played road games
Origin of Name:

Regular Season Record

Season	League	GP	W	L	T	PF	PA	Pct
1926	NFL	10	6	3	1	77	57	.650

COACHING HISTORY: Brick Muller & Tut Imlay 6-3-1-.650

LOS ANGELES CHARGERS

(became San Diego Chargers)

Home City: Los Angeles, California
Home Stadium: Los Angeles Memorial Coliseum Capacity: 92,604
Origin of Name: The team was originally owned by Baron Hilton the owner of the Carte Blanche credit card company.

Regular Season Record

Season	League	GP	W	L	T	PF	PA	Pct
1960	AFL	14	10	4	0	373	336	.714

Playoff Record

Season	GP	W	L	PF	PA	Result
1960	1	0	1	16	24	Lost championship game to Houston.

COACHING HISTORY: Sid Gillman 10-4-0-.714

LOS ANGELES CLIPPERS
(were San Diego Clippers)

Home City: Los Angeles, California
Home Court: Los Angeles Sports Arena (1984-present) Capacity: 16,021 [1995]
Arrowhead Pond (1995-present) Capacity: 18,198 [1995]
Origin of Name: The team kept the same nickname when it moved from San Diego.

Regular Season Record

Season	League	GP	W	L	PPGF	PPGA	Pct	GB
1984-1985	NBA	82	31	51	107.1	111.6	.378	31
1985-1986	NBA	82	32	50	108.6	115.5	.390	30
1986-1987	NBA	82	12	70	104.5	115.9	.146	53
1987-1988	NBA	82	17	65	98.8	109.1	.207	45
1988-1989	NBA	82	21	61	106.2	116.2	.256	36
1989-1990	NBA	82	30	52	103.8	107.2	.366	33
1990-1991	NBA	82	31	51	103.5	107.0	.378	32
1991-1992	NBA	82	45	37	102.9	101.9	.549	12
1992-1993	NBA	82	41	41	107.1	106.8	.500	21
1993-1994	NBA	82	27	55	103.0	108.7	.329	36
1994-1995	NBA	82	17	65	96.7	105.8	.207	42
1995-1996	NBA	82	29	53	99.4	103.0	.354	35
TOTAL:	12 years	984	333	651				406
AVERAGE:		82	28	54	103.5	109.0	.338	34

Playoff Record

Season	GP	W	L	PPGF	PPGA	Result
1991-1992	5	2	3	98.2	102.2	Lost 1st round series to Utah.
1992-1993	5	2	3	92.2	97.0	Lost 1st round series to Houston.
TOTAL:	10	4	6			
AVERAGE:	5	2	3	95.2	99.6	

COACHING HISTORY: 1984-1985 Jim Lynam 22-39-.361; 1984-1987 Don Chaney 53-132-.286; 1987-1989 Gene Shue 27-93-.225; 1988-1990 Don Casey 41-85-.325; 1990-1992 Mike Schuler 53-76-.411; 1991-1992 Mack Calvin 1-1-.500; 1991-1993 Larry Brown 64-53-.547; 1993-1994 Bob Weiss 27-55-.329; 1994-present Bill Fitch

LOS ANGELES DODGERS
(were Brooklyn Dodgers)

Home City: Los Angeles, California
Home Field: Memorial Coliseum (1958-1961) Capacity: 94,600 [1959]
Dodger Stadium (1962-present) Capacity: 56,000 [1995]
Origin of Name: The team kept the same nickname when it moved to Los Angeles from Brooklyn.

			Regular Season Record					
Season	**League**	**GP**	**W**	**L**	**Pct**	**GB**	**R**	**OR**
1958	NL	154	71	83	.461	21	668	761
1959	NL	156	88	68	.564	-	705	670
1960	NL	154	82	72	.532	13	662	593
1961	NL	154	89	65	.578	4	735	697
1962	NL	165	102	63	.618	1	842	697
1963	NL	162	99	63	.611	-	640	550
1964	NL	162	80	82	.494	13	614	572
1965	NL	162	97	65	.599	-	608	521
1966	NL	162	95	67	.586	-	606	490
1967	NL	162	73	89	.451	28.5	519	595
1968	NL	162	76	86	.469	21	470	509
1969	NL	162	85	77	.525	8	645	561
1970	NL	161	87	74	.540	14.5	749	684
1971	NL	162	89	73	.549	1	663	587
1972	NL	155	85	70	.548	10.5	584	527
1973	NL	161	95	66	.590	3.5	675	565
1974	NL	162	102	60	.630	-	798	561
1975	NL	162	88	74	.543	20	648	534
1976	NL	162	92	70	.568	10	608	543
1977	NL	162	98	64	.605	-	769	582
1978	NL	162	95	67	.586	-	727	573
1979	NL	162	79	83	.488	11.5	739	717
1980	NL	163	92	71	.564	1	663	591
1981	NL	110	63	47	.573	NA	450	356
1982	NL	162	88	74	.543	1	691	612
1983	NL	162	91	71	.562	-	654	609
1984	NL	162	79	83	.488	13	580	600
1985	NL	162	95	67	.586	-	682	579
1986	NL	162	73	89	.451	23	638	679
1987	NL	162	73	89	.451	17	635	675
1988	NL	161	94	67	.584	-	628	544
1989	NL	160	77	83	.481	14	554	536
1990	NL	161	86	75	.534	4.5	728	685
1991	NL	162	93	69	.574	1	665	565
1992	NL	162	63	99	.389	35	548	636
1993	NL	162	81	81	.500	23	675	662
1994	NL	114	58	56	.509	-	532	509
1995	NL	144	78	66	.542	-	634	609
TOTAL:	38 years	5999	3231	2768		313	24631	22536
AVERAGE:		158	85	73	.539	8	648	593

Playoff Record

Season	GP	W	L	R	OR	Result
1959	6	4	2	21	23	**Won World Series.**
1963	4	4	0	12	4	**Won World Series.**
1965	7	4	3	24	20	**Won World Series.**
1966	4	0	4	2	13	Lost World Series to Baltimore.
1974	9	4	5	31	26	Lost World Series to Oakland.
1977	10	5	5	50	40	Lost World Series to New York.
1978	10	5	5	44	53	Lost World Series to New York.
1981	16	10	6	55	38	**Won World Series.**
1983	4	1	3	8	16	Lost NLCS to Philadelphia.
1985	6	2	4	23	29	Lost NLCS to St. Louis.
1988	12	8	4	52	38	**Won World Series.**
1995	3	0	3	10	22	Lost playoff series to Cincinnati.
TOTAL:	91	47	44	332	322	
AVERAGE:	8	4	4	28	27	

COACHING HISTORY: 1958-1976 Walter Alston 1675-1367-.551; 1977-present Tom Lasorda

LOS ANGELES DONS

Home City: Los Angeles, California
Home Stadium: Los Angeles Coliseum — Capacity: 103,000 [1946]
Origin of Name: The team's name was chosen by the owner, to reflect the Spanish heritage of the area and perhaps not coincidentally the owner was actor Don Ameche.

Regular Season Record

Season	League	GP	W	L	T	PF	PA	Pct
1946	AAFC	14	7	5	2	305	290	.571
1947	AAFC	14	7	7	0	328	256	.500
1948	AAFC	14	7	7	0	258	305	.500
1949	AAFC	12	4	8	0	253	322	.333
TOTAL:	4 years	54	25	27	2	1144	1173	
AVERAGE:		14	6	7	1	286	293	.481

COACHING HISTORY: 1946-1947 Dud Degroot 12-10-2-.542; 1947 Mel Hein & Ted Shipkey 2-2-0-.500; 1948-1949 Jim Phelan 11-15-0-.423

LOS ANGELES EXPRESS

Home City: Los Angeles, California
Home Stadium: Los Angeles Coliseum — Capacity: 92,516 [1985]
Origin of Name: Name chosen in a Name the Team Contest.

Regular Season Record

Season	League	GP	W	L	T	PF	PA	Pct
1983	USFL	18	8	10	0	296	370	.444
1984	USFL	18	10	8	0	338	373	.556
1985	USFL	18	3	15	0	266	456	.167
TOTAL:	3 years	54	21	33	0	900	1199	
AVERAGE:		18	7	11	0	300	400	.389

Playoff Record

Season	GP	W	L	PF	PA	Result
1984	2	1	1	50	56	Lost 2nd round game to Arizona.

COACHING HISTORY: 1983 Hugh Campbell 8-10-0-.444; 1984-1985 John Hadl 13-23-0-.361

LOS ANGELES KINGS

Home City: Inglewood, California
Home Arena: Long Beach Sports Arena (1967-1968) Capacity: 11,168 [1968]
Los Angeles Sports Arena (1967-1968) Capacity: 11,325 [1968]
The Great Western Forum (1967-present) * Capacity: 16,005 [1995]
Origin of Name: The name was chosen by owner Jack Kent Cooke from names submitted in a Name the Team contest.

Regular Season Record

Season	League	GP	W	L	T	GF	GA	Pts	Pct
1967-1968	NHL	74	31	33	10	200	224	72	.486
1968-1969	NHL	76	24	42	10	185	260	58	.382
1969-1970	NHL	76	14	52	10	168	290	38	.250
1970-1971	NHL	78	25	40	13	239	303	63	.404
1971-1972	NHL	78	20	49	9	206	305	49	.314
1972-1973	NHL	78	31	36	11	232	245	73	.468
1973-1974	NHL	78	33	33	12	233	231	78	.500
1974-1975	NHL	80	42	17	21	269	185	105	.656
1975-1976	NHL	80	38	33	9	263	265	85	.531
1976-1977	NHL	80	34	31	15	271	241	83	.519
1977-1978	NHL	80	31	34	15	243	245	77	.481
1978-1979	NHL	80	34	34	12	292	286	80	.500
1979-1980	NHL	80	30	36	14	290	313	74	.463
1980-1981	NHL	80	43	24	13	337	290	99	.619
1981-1982	NHL	80	24	41	15	314	369	63	.394
1982-1983	NHL	80	27	41	12	308	365	66	.413
1983-1984	NHL	80	23	44	13	309	376	59	.369
1984-1985	NHL	80	34	32	14	339	326	82	.513
1985-1986	NHL	80	23	49	8	284	389	54	.338
1986-1987	NHL	80	31	41	8	318	341	70	.438
1987-1988	NHL	80	30	42	8	318	359	70	.438
1988-1989	NHL	80	42	31	7	376	335	91	.569
1989-1990	NHL	80	34	39	7	338	337	75	.469
1990-1991	NHL	80	46	24	10	340	254	102	.638
1991-1992	NHL	80	35	31	14	287	296	84	.525
1992-1993	NHL	84	39	35	10	338	340	88	.524
1993-1994	NHL	84	27	45	12	294	322	66	.393
1994-1995	NHL	48	16	23	9	142	174	41	.427
1995-1996	NHL	82	24	40	18	256	302	66	.402
TOTAL:	29 years	2276	885	1052	339	7989	8568	2111	
AVERAGE:		78	31	36	11	275	295	73	.463

Playoff Record

Season	GP	W	L	GF	GA	Result
1967-1968	7	3	4	21	26	Lost quarterfinal series to Minnesota.
1968-1969	11	4	7	28	41	Lost semifinal series to St. Louis.
1973-1974	5	1	4	7	10	Lost quarterfinal series to Chicago.
1974-1975	3	1	2	6	7	Lost preliminary series to Toronto.
1975-1976	9	5	4	17	27	Lost quarterfinal series to Boston.
1976-1977	9	4	5	35	37	Lost quarterfinal series to Boston.
1977-1978	2	0	2	3	11	Lost preliminary series to Toronto.
1978-1979	2	0	2	2	9	Lost preliminary series to N.Y. Rangers.
1979-1980	4	1	3	10	21	Lost preliminary series to N.Y. Islanders.
1980-1981	4	1	3	12	23	Lost preliminary series to N.Y. Rangers.
1981-1982	10	4	6	41	42	Lost quarterfinal series to Vancouver.
1984-1985	3	0	3	11	7	Lost preliminary series to Edmonton.
1986-1987	5	1	4	20	32	Lost preliminary series to Edmonton.
1987-1988	5	1	4	18	30	Lost preliminary series to Calgary.
1988-1989	11	4	7	36	42	Lost quarterfinal series to Calgary.
1989-1990	10	4	6	39	48	Lost quarterfinal series to Edmonton.
1990-1991	12	6	6	46	37	Lost quarterfinal series to Edmonton.
1991-1992	6	2	4	18	23	Lost preliminary series to Edmonton.
1992-1993	24	13	11	93	91	Lost Stanley Cup final series to Montreal.
TOTAL:	142	55	87	463	564	
AVERAGE:	7	3	4	24	30	

COACHING HISTORY: 1967-1969 Leonard "Red" Kelly 55-75-20-.433; 1969-1970 Hal Laycoe 5-18-1-.229; 1969-1970 John Wilson 9-34-9-.260; 1970-1972 Larry Regan 27-47-14-.386; 1971-1972 Fred Glover 18-42-8-.324; 1972-1977 Bob Pulford 178-150-68-.535; 1977-1978 Ron Stewart 31-34-15-.481; 1978-1981 Bob Berry 107-94-39-.527; 1981-1982 Parker MacDonald 13-24-5-.369; 1981-1984 Don Perry 52-85-31-.402; 1983-1984 Rogatien Vachon 1-0-1-.750; 1983-1984 Roger Neilson 8-17-3-.339; 1984-1987 Pat Quinn 75-101-28-.436; 1986-1988 Mike Murphy 20-37-11-.375; 1987-1988 Rogatien Vachon 0-1-0-.000; 1987-1989 Robbie Ftorek 65-56-11-.534; 1989-1990 Cap Raeder & Rick Wilson 6-9-0-.400; 1989-1992 Tom Webster 114-92-33-.546; 1992-1995 Barry Melrose 79-101-29; 1994-1995 Rogatien Vachon 3-2-2-.571; 1995-present Larry Robinson

*Originally known as the Forum from 1967-1988

LOS ANGELES LAKERS

(were Minneapolis Lakers)

Home City: Inglewood, California
Home Arena: The Los Angeles Sports Arena (1960-1967) Capacity: 14,781 [1966]
The Great Western Forum (1967-present) Capacity: 17,505 [1995]
Origin of Name: The team kept the same nickname when it moved to L.A. from Minneapolis.

Regular Season Record

Season	League	GP	W	L	PPGF	PPGA	Pct	GB
1960-1961	NBA	79	36	43	114.0	114.1	.456	15
1961-1962	NBA	80	54	26	118.5	120.0	.675	-
1962-1963	NBA	80	53	27	115.5	112.4	.663	-
1963-1964	NBA	80	42	38	109.7	108.7	.525	6
1964-1965	NBA	80	49	31	111.9	109.9	.613	-

1965-1966	NBA	80	45	35	119.5	116.4	.563	-
1966-1967	NBA	81	36	45	120.5	120.2	.444	8
1967-1968	NBA	82	52	30	121.2	115.6	.634	4
1968-1969	NBA	82	55	27	112.2	108.1	.671	-
1969-1970	NBA	82	46	36	113.7	111.8	.561	2
1970-1971	NBA	82	48	34	114.8	111.7	.585	-
1971-1972	NBA	82	69	13	121.0	108.7	.841	-
1972-1973	NBA	82	60	22	111.7	103.2	.732	-
1973-1974	NBA	82	47	35	109.2	108.3	.573	-
1974-1975	NBA	82	30	52	103.2	107.2	.366	18
1975-1976	NBA	82	40	42	106.9	106.8	.488	19
1976-1977	NBA	82	53	29	106.9	104.1	.646	-
1977-1978	NBA	82	45	37	110.3	107.6	.549	13
1978-1979	NBA	82	47	35	112.9	109.9	.573	5
1979-1980	NBA	82	60	22	115.1	109.2	.732	-
1980-1981	NBA	82	54	28	111.2	107.3	.659	3
1981-1982	NBA	82	57	25	114.6	109.8	.695	-
1982-1983	NBA	82	58	24	115.0	109.5	.707	-
1983-1984	NBA	82	54	28	115.6	111.8	.659	-
1984-1985	NBA	82	62	20	118.2	110.9	.756	-
1985-1986	NBA	82	62	20	117.3	109.5	.756	-
1986-1987	NBA	82	65	17	117.8	108.5	.793	-
1987-1988	NBA	82	62	20	112.8	107.0	.756	-
1988-1989	NBA	82	57	25	114.7	107.5	.695	-
1989-1990	NBA	82	63	19	110.7	103.9	.768	-
1990-1991	NBA	82	58	24	106.3	99.6	.707	5
1991-1992	NBA	82	43	39	100.4	101.5	.524	14
1992-1993	NBA	82	39	43	104.2	105.5	.476	23
1993-1994	NBA	82	33	49	100.4	104.7	.402	30
1994-1995	NBA	82	48	34	105.1	105.3	.585	11
1995-1996	NBA	82	53	29	102.9	98.5	.646	11
TOTAL:	36 years	2938	1835	1103				187
AVERAGE:		82	51	31	112.1	108.8	.625	5

Playoff Record

Season	GP	W	L	PPGF	PPGA	Result
1960-1961	12	6	6	117.0	115.6	Lost Division final to St. Louis.
1961-1962	13	7	6	117.7	116.7	Lost championship series to Boston.
1962-1963	13	6	7	113.0	110.8	Lost championship series to Boston.
1963-1964	5	2	3	101.2	107.0	Lost Division semifinal to St. Louis.
1964-1965	11	5	6	114.3	119.1	Lost championship series to Boston.
1965-1966	14	7	7	116.6	116.3	Lost championship series to Boston.
1966-1967	3	0	3	108.3	119.7	Lost Div. semifinal to San Francisco.
1967-1968	15	10	5	113.5	108.9	Lost championship series to Boston.
1968-1969	18	11	7	103.4	99.1	Lost championship series to Boston.
1969-1970	18	11	7	114.0	110.1	Lost championship series to New York.
1970-1971	12	5	7	99.7	103.8	Lost Conference final to Milwaukee.
1971-1972	15	12	3	106.6	103.4	**Won NBA championship**.
1972-1973	17	9	8	103.4	99.2	Lost championship series to New York.
1973-1974	5	1	4	93.0	106.0	Lost Conference semifinal to Milwaukee.
1976-1977	11	4	7	103.4	104.2	Lost Conference final to Portland.
1977-1978	3	1	2	99.0	104.0	Lost 1st round series to Seattle.
1978-1979	8	3	5	109.4	110.6	Lost Conference semifinal to Seattle.

1979-1980	16	12	4	110.6	106.3	**Won NBA championship**.
1980-1981	3	1	2	101.3	102.0	Lost 1st round series to Houston.
1981-1982	14	12	2	115.4	109.4	**Won NBA championship**.
1982-1983	15	8	7	109.7	109.1	Lost championship series to Philadelphia.
1983-1984	22	14	8	111.8	104.8	Lost championship series to Boston.
1984-1985	19	15	4	126.3	116.2	**Won NBA championship**.
1985-1986	14	8	6	115.5	107.9	Lost Conference final to Houston.
1986-1987	18	15	3	120.6	109.2	**Won NBA championship**.
1987-1988	24	15	9	105.7	103.0	**Won NBA championship**.
1988-1989	15	11	4	110.5	105.1	Lost championship series to Detroit.
1989-1990	9	4	5	106.1	103.6	Lost Conference semifinal to Phoenix.
1990-1991	16	12	4	123.2	122.1	Lost championship series to Chicago.
1991-1992	4	1	3	94.5	109.3	Lost 1st round series to Portland.
1992-1993	5	2	3	97.0	100.8	Lost 1st round series to Phoenix.
1994-1995	10	5	5	92.5	96.6	Lost Conf. semifinal to San Antonio.
1995-1996	4	1	3	94.8	96.8	Lost 1st round series to Houston.
TOTAL:	401	236	165			
AVERAGE:	12	7	5	108.5	108.1	

COACHING HISTORY: 1960-1967 Fred Schaus 315-245-.563; 1967-1969 Butch van Breda Kolff 107-57-.652; 1969-1971 Joe Mullaney 94-70-.573; 1971-1976 Bill Sharman 246-164-.600; 1976-1979 Jerry West 145-101-.589; 1979-1980 Jack McKinney 10-4-.714; 1979-1982 Paul Westhead 111-50-.689; 1981-1990 Pat Riley 533-194-.733; 1990-1992 Mike Dunleavy 101-63-.616; 1992-1994 Randy Pfund 67-80-.456; 1993-1994 Earvin Johnson 5-12-.294; 1994-present Del Harris

*Known as the Forum from 1967-1988

LOS ANGELES RAIDERS
(were Oakland Raiders)
(became Oakland Raiders)

Home City: Los Angeles, California
Home Stadium: Memorial Stadium Capacity: 67,800 [1994]
Origin of Name: The team kept the same nickname when it moved from Oakland to L.A.

Regular Season Record

Season	**League**	**GP**	**W**	**L**	**T**	**PF**	**PA**	**Pct**
1982	NFL	9	8	1	0	260	200	.889
1983	NFL	16	12	4	0	442	338	.750
1984	NFL	16	11	5	0	371	278	.688
1985	NFL	16	12	4	0	354	308	.750
1986	NFL	16	8	8	0	323	346	.500
1987	NFL	15	5	10	0	301	289	.333
1988	NFL	16	7	9	0	325	369	.438
1989	NFL	16	8	8	0	315	297	.500
1990	NFL	16	12	4	0	337	268	.750
1991	NFL	16	9	7	0	298	297	.563
1992	NFL	16	7	9	0	249	281	.438
1993	NFL	16	10	6	0	306	326	.625
1994	NFL	16	9	7	0	303	327	.563
TOTAL:	13 years	200	118	82	0	4184	3924	
AVERAGE:		15	9	6	0	322	302	.590

Playoff Record

Season	GP	W	L	PF	PA	Result
1982	2	1	1	41	27	Lost 2nd round playoff to N.Y. Jets.
1983	3	3	0	106	33	**Won Super Bowl**.
1984	1	0	1	7	13	Lost 1st round playoff to Seattle.
1985	1	0	1	20	27	Lost Divisional playoff to New England.
1990	2	1	1	23	61	Lost Conference semifinal to Cincinnati
1991	1	0	1	6	10	Lost Wild Card game to Kansas City.
1993	2	1	1	65	53	Lost Conference semifinal to Buffalo.
TOTAL:	12	6	6	268	224	
AVERAGE:	2	1	1	38	32	

COACHING HISTORY: 1982-1987 Tom Flores 56-32-0-.636; 1988-1989 Mike Shanahan 8-12-0-.400; 1989-1994 Art Shell 54-38-0-.587

LOS ANGELES RAMS

(were Cleveland Rams)
(became St. Louis Rams)

Home City: Los Angeles, California (1946-1979)
Anaheim, California (1980-1994)
Home Stadium: Memorial Coliseum (1946-1979) Capacity: 90,000 [1979]
Anaheim Stadium (1980-1994) Capacity: 69,008 [1994]
Origin of Name: The team kept the same nickname when it moved from Cleveland to California.

Regular Season Record

Season	League	GP	W	L	T	PF	PA	Pct
1946	NFL	11	6	4	1	277	257	.600
1947	NFL	12	6	6	0	259	214	.500
1948	NFL	12	6	5	1	327	269	.545
1949	NFL	12	8	2	2	360	239	.800
1950	NFL	12	9	3	0	466	309	.750
1951	NFL	12	8	4	0	392	261	.667
1952	NFL	12	9	3	0	349	234	.750
1953	NFL	12	8	3	1	366	236	.727
1954	NFL	12	6	5	1	314	285	.545
1955	NFL	12	8	3	1	260	231	.727
1956	NFL	12	4	8	0	291	307	.333
1957	NFL	12	6	6	0	307	278	.500
1958	NFL	12	8	4	0	344	278	.667
1959	NFL	12	2	10	0	242	315	.167
1960	NFL	12	4	7	1	265	297	.364
1961	NFL	14	4	10	0	263	333	.286
1962	NFL	14	1	12	1	220	334	.077
1963	NFL	14	5	9	0	210	350	.357
1964	NFL	14	5	7	2	283	339	.417
1965	NFL	14	4	10	0	269	328	.286
1966	NFL	14	8	6	0	289	212	.571
1967	NFL	14	11	1	2	398	196	.917
1968	NFL	14	10	3	1	312	200	.769
1969	NFL	14	11	3	0	320	243	.786
1970	NFL	14	9	4	1	325	202	.692

1971	NFL	14	8	5	1	313	260	.615
1972	NFL	14	6	7	1	291	286	.464
1973	NFL	14	12	2	0	388	178	.857
1974	NFL	14	10	4	0	263	181	.714
1975	NFL	14	12	2	0	312	135	.857
1976	NFL	14	10	3	1	351	190	.750
1977	NFL	14	10	4	0	302	146	.714
1978	NFL	16	12	4	0	316	245	.750
1979	NFL	16	9	7	0	323	309	.563
1980	NFL	16	11	5	0	424	289	.688
1981	NFL	16	6	10	0	303	351	.375
1982	NFL	9	2	7	0	200	250	.222
1983	NFL	16	9	7	0	361	344	.563
1984	NFL	16	10	6	0	346	316	.625
1985	NFL	16	11	5	0	340	277	.688
1986	NFL	16	10	6	0	309	267	.625
1987	NFL	15	6	9	0	317	361	.400
1988	NFL	16	10	6	0	407	293	.625
1989	NFL	16	11	5	0	426	344	.688
1990	NFL	16	5	11	0	345	412	.313
1991	NFL	16	3	13	0	234	390	.188
1992	NFL	16	6	10	0	313	383	.375
1993	NFL	16	5	11	0	221	367	.313
1994	NFL	16	4	12	0	286	385	.250
TOTAL:	49 years	681	364	299	18	15399	13706	
AVERAGE:		14	8	6	0	314	280	.548

Playoff Record

Season	GP	W	L	PF	PA	Result
1949	1	0	1	0	14	Lost championship game to Philadelphia.
1950	2	1	1	52	44	Lost championship game to Cleveland.
1951	1	1	0	24	17	**Won NFL championship**.
1952	1	0	1	21	31	Lost Conference playoff to Detroit.
1955	1	0	1	14	38	Lost championship game to Cleveland.
1967	1	0	1	7	28	Lost Conference championship to Green Bay.
1969	1	0	1	20	23	Lost Conference championship to Minnesota.
1973	1	0	1	16	27	Lost Divisional playoff to Dallas.
1974	2	1	1	29	24	Lost NFC championship to Minnesota.
1975	2	1	1	42	60	Lost NFC championship to Dallas.
1976	2	1	1	27	36	Lost NFC championship to Minnesota.
1977	1	0	1	7	14	Lost Divisional playoff to Minnesota.
1978	2	1	1	34	38	Lost NFC championship to Dallas.
1979	3	2	1	49	50	Lost Super Bowl game to Pittsburgh.
1980	1	0	1	13	34	Lost 1st round playoff to Dallas.
1983	2	1	1	31	68	Lost Divisional playoff to Washington.
1984	1	0	1	13	16	Lost 1st round playoff to N.Y. Giants.
1985	2	1	1	20	24	Lost NFC championship to Chicago.
1986	1	0	1	7	19	Lost 1st round playoff to Washington.
1988	1	0	1	17	28	Lost 1st round playoff to Minnesota.
1989	3	2	1	43	50	Lost Conference final to San Francisco.
TOTAL:	32	12	20	486	683	
AVERAGE:	2	1	1	23	33	

COACHING HISTORY: 1946 Adam Walsh 6-4-1-.600; 1947 Bob Snyder 6-6-0-.500; 1948-1949 Clark Shaughnessy 14-7-3-.646; 1950-1952 Joe Stydahar 17-8-0-.680; 1952-1954 Hamp Pool 23-10-2-.686; 1955-1959 Sid Gillman 28-31-1-.475; 1960-1962 Bob Waterfield 9-24-1-.279; 1962-1965 Harland Svare 14-31-3-.323; 1966-1970 George Allen 49-17-4-.729; 1971-1972 Tommy Prothro 14-12-2-.536; 1973-1977 Chuck Knox 54-15-1-.779; 1978-1982 Ray Malavasi 40-33-0-.548; 1983-1991 John Robinson 88-55-.615; 1992-1994 Chuck Knox 15-33-0-.313

LOS ANGELES SHARKS

(became Michigan Stags)

Home City: Los Angeles, California
Home Arena: Los Angeles Sports Arena — Capacity: 14,700 [1972]
Origin of Name:

Regular Season Record

Season	League	GP	W	L	T	GF	GA	Pts	Pct
1972-1973	WHA	78	37	35	6	259	250	80	.513
1973-1974	WHA	78	25	53	0	239	339	50	.321
TOTAL:	2 years	156	62	88	6	498	589	130	
AVERAGE:		78	31	44	3	249	295	65	.417

Playoff Record

Season	GP	W	L	GF	GA	Result
1972-1973	6	2	4	16	23	Lost quarterfinal series to Houston.

COACHING HISTORY: 1972-1974 Terry Slater 42-49-6-.464; 1973-1974 Ted McCaskill 20-39-0-.339

LOS ANGELES STARS

(were Anaheim Amigos)
(became Utah Stars)

Home City: Los Angeles, California
Home Court: Los Angeles Sports Arena — Capacity: 11,325 [1968]
Origin of Name:

Regular Season Record

Season	League	GP	W	L	PPGF	PPGA	Pct	GB
1968-1969	ABA	78	33	45	114.4	117.5	.423	27
1969-1970	ABA	84	43	41	113.7	113.9	.512	8
TOTAL:	2 years	162	76	86				35
AVERAGE:		81	38	43	114.1	115.7	.469	18

Playoff Record

Season	GP	W	L	PPGF	PPGA	Result
1969-1970	17	10	7	116.5	117.7	Lost championship series to Indiana.

COACHING HISTORY: 1968-1970 Bill Sharman 76-86-.469

LOS ANGELES TOROS
(became San Diego Toros)

Home City: Los Angeles, California
Home Field: Memorial Coliseum Capacity: 103,000
Origin of Name:

Regular Season Record

Season	League	GP	W	L	T	GF	GA	Pts	Pct
1967	NPSL	32	7	15	10	42	61	114	.396

COACHING HISTORY: Max Wozniak 7-15-10-.396

LOS ANGELES WOLVES

Home City: Los Angeles, California
Home Field: Memorial Coliseum Capacity: 103,000
Origin of Name: As with most of the USA clubs the team was represented by a European professional club, Los Angeles being represented by Wolverhampton.

Regular Season Record

Season	League	GP	W	L	T	GF	GA	BP	Pts	Pct
1967	USA	12	5	2	5	21	14	-	15	.625
1968	NASL	32	11	13	8	55	52	49	139	.483
TOTAL:	2 years	44	16	15	13	76	66	49	154	
AVERAGE:		22	8	7	7	38	33	25	77	

Playoff Record

Season	GP	W	L	T	GF	GA	Result
1967	1	1	0	0	5	6	**Won USA championship**.

COACHING HISTORY: 1967 Ronnie Allen 5-2-5-.625; 1968 Ray Wood 11-13-8-.483

LOUISVILLE BRECKS

Home City: Louisville, Kentucky
Home Stadium:
Origin of Name: The team was originally a boy's neighborhood team known as The Floyd and Brecks.

Regular Season Record

Season	League	GP	W	L	T	PF	PA	Pct
1922	NFL	4	1	3	0	13	140	.250
1923	NFL	3	0	3	0	0	83	.000
TOTAL:	2 years	7	1	6	0	13	223	
AVERAGE:		4	1	3	0	7	112	.071

COACHING HISTORY: 1922 Hubert Wiggs 1-3-0-.250; 1923 Jim Kendrick 0-3-0-.000

LOUISVILLE COLONELS

Home City: Louisville, Kentucky
Home Field: National League Park
Origin of Name: Colonels is a popular nickname and image in Louisville

Regular Season Record

Season	League	GP	W	L	Pct	GB	R	OR
1876	NL	66	30	36	.455	22	280	344
1877	NL	60	35	25	.583	7	339	288
TOTAL:	2 years	126	65	61		29	619	632
AVERAGE:		63	33	30	.516	14.5	310	316

COACHING HISTORY: 1876 Chick Fulmer 30-36-.455; 1877 Jack Chapman 35-25-.583

LOUISVILLE COLONELS

(were Louisville Eclipse)
(merged with the Pittsburgh Pirates in 1900)

Home City: Louisville, Kentucky
Home Field: Eclipse Park I (1892-1893)
Eclipse Park II (1893-1899)
Origin of Name: Named after previous National League team.

Regular Season Record

Season	League	GP	W	L	Pct	GB	R	OR
1892	NL	152	63	89	.414	40	649	804
1893	NL	125	50	75	.400	34	759	942
1894	NL	130	36	94	.277	54	692	1001
1895	NL	131	35	96	.267	52.5	698	1090
1896	NL	131	38	93	.290	53	653	997
1897	NL	130	52	78	.400	40	669	859
1898	NL	151	70	81	.464	33	728	833
1899	NL	152	75	77	.493	28	827	775
TOTAL:	8 years	1102	419	683		334.5	5675	7301
AVERAGE:		138	53	85	.380	42	709	913

COACHING HISTORY: 1892 Jack Chapman 23-35-.397; 1892 Fred Pfeffer 40-54-.426; 1893-1894 Bill Barnie 86-169-.337; 1895-1896 John McCloskey 44-130-.253; 1896 Bill McGunnigle 29-59-.330; 1897 Jim Rogers 17-26-.395; 1897-1899 Fred Clarke 180-210-.462

LOUISVILLE COLONELS

Home City: Louisville, Kentucky
Home Stadium: The team actually operated out of Chicago
Origin of Name: See Above

Regular Season Record

Season	League	GP	W	L	T	PF	PA	Pct
1926	NFL	4	0	4	0	0	108	.000

COACHING HISTORY: Len Sachs 0-4-0-.000

LOUISVILLE ECLIPSE

(became Louisville Colonels)

Home City: Louisville, Kentucky
Home Field: Eclipse Park I
Origin of Name: The name was chosen to honor American Eclipse a famous horse retired to stud in Kentucky.

Regular Season Record

Season	League	GP	W	L	Pct	GB	R	OR
1882	AA	80	42	38	.525	13	443	352
1883	AA	97	52	45	.536	13.5	564	562
1884	AA	108	68	40	.630	7.5	573	425
1885	AA	112	53	59	.473	26	564	598
1886	AA	136	66	70	.485	25.5	833	805
1887	AA	136	76	60	.559	19.5	956	854
1888	AA	135	48	87	.356	44	689	870
1889	AA	138	27	111	.196	66.5	632	1091
1890	AA	132	88	44	.667	-	819	588
1891	AA	139	55	84	.396	40	713	890
TOTAL:	10 years	1213	575	638		255.5	6786	7035
AVERAGE:		121	57	64	.474	25.5	679	704

Playoff Record

Season	GP	W	L	T	R	OR	Result
1890	7	3	3	1	32	38	Lost World Series to Brooklyn.

COACHING HISTORY: 1882 John Dyler 6-7-.462 ; 1882-1883 Bill Reccius 36-28-.563; 1882-1883 Leech Maskrey 36-29-.554; 1883-1884 Joe Gerhardt 55-37-.598; 1884 Mike Walsh 29-22-.569; 1885-1886 Jim Hart 119-129-.480; 1887 John Kelly 76-60-.559; 1888 John Kerins 11-32-.256; 1888 Mordecai Davidson 37-55-.402; 1889 Thomas Esterbrook 2-8-.200; 1889 William Wolf 15-51-.227; 1889 Dan Shannon 9-43-.173; 1889-1891 Jack Chapman 144-137-.512

MEMPHIS MAD DOGS

Home City: Memphis, Tennessee
Home Stadium: Liberty Bowl — Capacity: 63,068 [1995]
Origin of Name:

Regular Season Record

Season	League	GP	W	L	T	PF	PA	Pts	Pct
1995	CFL	18	9	9	0	346	364	18	.500

COACHING HISTORY: 1995 Pepper Rogers 9-9-0-.500

MEMPHIS PROS

(were New Orleans Buccaneers)
(became Memphis Tams)

Home City: Memphis, Tennessee
Home Court: Mid-South Coliseum — Capacity: 10,945
Origin of Name: The name was chosen by team owner P.L. Blake.

Regular Season Record

Season	League	GP	W	L	PPGF	PPGA	Pct	GB
1970-1971	ABA	84	41	43	109.2	109.9	.488	17
1971-1972	ABA	84	26	58	107.5	113.0	.310	34
TOTAL:	2 years	168	67	101				51
AVERAGE:		84	34	50	108.4	111.5	.399	26

Playoff Record

Season	GP	W	L	PPGF	PPGA	Result
1970-1971	4	0	4	98.3	103.3	Lost 1st round series to Indiana.

COACHING HISTORY: 1970-1972 Babe McCarthy 67-101-.399

MEMPHIS ROGUES

(became Calgary Boomers)

Home City: Memphis, Tennessee
Home Field: Liberty Bowl Capacity: 50,164 [1979]
Origin of Name:

Regular Season Record

Season	League	GP	W	L	GF	GA	BP	Pts	Pct
1978	NASL	30	10	20	43	58	41	101	.374
1979	NASL	30	6	24	38	74	37	73	.270
1980	NASL	32	14	18	49	57	42	126	.438
TOTAL:	3 years	92	30	62	130	189	120	300	
AVERAGE:		31	10	21	43	63	40	100	.362

COACHING HISTORY: 1978-1979 Eddie McCreadie 12-26; 1979-1980 Charlie Cooke 18-36

MEMPHIS SHOWBOATS

Home City: Memphis, Tennessee
Home Stadium: Liberty Bowl Capacity: 50,164 [1985]
Origin of Name: The team was named after the Mississippi Riverboats which traveled through the area in the mid 1800's.

Regular Season Record

Season	League	GP	W	L	T	PF	PA	Pct
1984	USFL	18	7	11	0	320	455	.389
1985	USFL	18	11	7	0	428	337	.611
TOTAL:	2 years	36	18	18	0	748	792	
AVERAGE:		18	9	9	0	374	396	.500

Playoff Record

Season	GP	W	L	PF	PA	Result
1985	2	1	1	67	35	Lost 2nd round series to Oakland.

COACHING HISTORY: 1984-1985 Pepper Rodgers 18-18-0-.500

MEMPHIS SOUNDS
(were Memphis Tams)

Home City: Memphis, Tennessee
Home Court: Mid-South Coliseum — Capacity: 10,945 [1975]
Origin of Name: The name was chosen because musician Isaac Hayes was one of the owners.

Regular Season Record

Season	League	GP	W	L	PPGF	PPGA	Pct	GB
1974-1975	ABA	84	27	57	103.6	108.9	.321	31

COACHING HISTORY: Joe Mullaney 27-57-.321

MEMPHIS SOUTHMEN

Home City: Memphis, Tennessee
Home Stadium: Memphis Memorial Stadium — Capacity: 50,000 [1975]
Origin of Name: The team was originally to have been called the Toronto Northmen but due to opposition from the Canadian Football League, John Bassett the team's owner moved the team to Memphis and called them the Southmen.

Regular Season Record

Season	League	GP	W	L	T	PF	PA	Pct
1974	WFL	20	17	3	0	629	365	.850
1975	WFL	11	7	4	0	254	206	.636
TOTAL:	2 years	31	24	7	0	883	571	
AVERAGE:		16	12	4	0	442	286	.774

Playoff Record

Season	GP	W	L	PF	PA	Result
1974	1	0	1	15	18	Lost 2nd round series to Florida.

COACHING HISTORY: 1974-1975 John McVay 24-7-0-.774

MEMPHIS TAMS
(were Memphis Pros)
(became Memphis Sounds)

Home City: Memphis, Tennessee
Home Court: Mid-South Coliseum — Capacity: 10,945 [1974]
Origin of Name: The name was chosen in a Name the Team contest and stood for Tennessee, Arkansas and Mississippi which all surround Memphis.

Regular Season Record

Season	League	GP	W	L	PPGF	PPGA	Pct	GB
1972-1973	ABA	84	24	60	111.5	118.1	.286	33
1973-1974	ABA	84	21	63	101.2	108.2	.250	34
TOTAL:	2 years	168	45	123				67
AVERAGE:		84	23	61	106.4	113.2	.268	34

COACHING HISTORY: 1972-1973 Bob Bass 24-60-.286; 1973-1974 Butch Van Breda Kolff 21-63-.250

MIAMI DOLPHINS

Home City: Miami, Florida
Home Stadium: Orange Bowl (1966-1986) Capacity: 75,206 [1986]
Joe Robbie Stadium (1987-present) Capacity: 74,916 [1995]
Origin of Name: The team's nickname was picked in a Name the Team Contest.

Regular Season Record

Season	League	GP	W	L	T	PF	PA	Pct
1966	AFL	14	3	11	0	213	362	.214
1967	AFL	14	4	10	0	219	407	.286
1968	AFL	14	5	8	1	276	355	.385
1969	AFL	14	3	10	1	233	332	.231
1970	NFL	14	10	4	0	297	228	.714
1971	NFL	14	10	3	1	315	174	.769
1972	NFL	14	14	0	0	385	171	1.000
1973	NFL	14	12	2	0	343	150	.857
1974	NFL	14	11	3	0	327	216	.786
1975	NFL	14	10	4	0	357	222	.714
1976	NFL	14	6	8	0	263	264	.429
1977	NFL	14	10	4	0	313	197	.714
1978	NFL	16	11	5	0	372	254	.688
1979	NFL	16	10	6	0	341	257	.625
1980	NFL	16	8	8	0	266	305	.500
1981	NFL	16	11	4	1	345	275	.719
1982	NFL	9	7	2	0	198	131	.778
1983	NFL	16	12	4	0	389	250	.750
1984	NFL	16	14	2	0	513	298	.875
1985	NFL	16	12	4	0	428	320	.750
1986	NFL	16	8	8	0	430	405	.500
1987	NFL	15	8	7	0	362	335	.533
1988	NFL	16	6	10	0	319	380	.375
1989	NFL	16	8	8	0	331	379	.500
1990	NFL	16	12	4	0	336	242	.750
1991	NFL	16	8	8	0	343	349	.500
1992	NFL	16	11	5	0	340	281	.688
1993	NFL	16	9	7	0	349	351	.563
1994	NFL	16	10	6	0	389	327	.625
1995	NFL	16	9	7	0	398	332	.563
TOTAL:	30 years	448	272	172	4	9990	8549	
AVERAGE:		15	9	6	0	333	285	.612

Playoff Record

Season	GP	W	L	PF	PA	Result
1970	1	0	1	14	21	Lost Divisional playoff to Oakland.
1971	3	2	1	51	48	Lost Super Bowl to Dallas.
1972	3	3	0	55	38	**Won Super Bowl.**
1973	3	3	0	85	33	**Won Super Bowl.**
1974	1	0	1	26	28	Lost Divisional playoff to Oakland.

1978	1	0	1	9	17	Lost 1st round playoff to Houston.
1979	1	0	1	14	34	Lost Divisional playoff to Pittsburgh.
1981	1	0	1	38	41	Lost Divisional playoff to San Diego.
1982	4	3	1	93	53	Lost Super Bowl to Washington.
1983	1	0	1	20	27	Lost Divisional playoff to Seattle.
1984	3	2	1	92	76	Lost Super Bowl to San Francisco.
1985	2	1	1	38	52	Lost AFC championship to New England.
1990	2	1	1	51	60	Lost Conference semifinal to Buffalo.
1992	2	1	1	41	29	Lost Conference final to Buffalo.
1994	2	1	1	48	39	Lost Conference semifinal to San Diego.
1995	1	0	1	22	37	Lost 1st round playoff to Buffalo.
TOTAL:	31	17	14	697	633	
AVERAGE:	2	1	1	44	40	

COACHING HISTORY: 1966-1969 George Wilson 15-39-2-.286; 1970-1995 Don Shula 257-133-2-.658; 1996-present Jimmy Johnson

MIAMI FLORIDIANS
(were Minnesota Muskies)
(became Floridians)

Home City: Miami, Florida
Home Court: Miami Beach Convention Hall
Origin of Name: The name was chosen because the team was based in Florida.

Regular Season Record

Season	League	GP	W	L	PPGF	PPGA	Pct	GB
1968-1969	ABA	78	43	35	115.5	115.1	.551	1
1969-1970	ABA	84	23	61	113.2	118.3	.274	36
TOTAL:	2 years	162	66	96				37
AVERAGE:		81	33	48	114.4	116.7	.407	19

Playoff Record

Season	GP	W	L	PPGF	PPGA	Result
1968-1969	12	5	7	111.3	115.6	Lost 2nd round series to Indiana.

COACHING HISTORY: 1968-1970 Jim Pollard 48-50-.490; 1969-1970 Hal Blitman 18-46-.281

MIAMI GATOS
(were Washington Darts)
(became Miami Toros)

Home City: Miami, Florida
Home Field:
Origin of Name: Gatos is the Spanish word for cat.

Regular Season Record

Season	League	GP	W	L	T	GF	GA	BP	Pts	Pct
1972	NASL	14	3	8	3	17	32	17	44	.349

COACHING HISTORY: Sal DeRosa, Norm Sutherland

MIAMI HEAT

Home City: Miami, Florida
Home Court: Miami Arena — Capacity: 15,200 [1995]
Origin of Name: The nickname was chosen in a Name the Team Contest.

Regular Season Record

Season	League	GP	W	L	PPGF	PPGA	Pct	GB
1988-1989	NBA	82	15	67	97.8	109.0	.183	36
1989-1990	NBA	82	18	64	100.6	110.3	.220	36
1990-1991	NBA	82	24	58	101.8	107.8	.293	32
1991-1992	NBA	82	38	44	105.0	109.2	.463	13
1992-1993	NBA	82	36	46	103.6	104.7	.439	24
1993-1994	NBA	82	42	40	103.4	100.7	.512	15
1994-1995	NBA	82	32	50	101.1	102.8	.390	25
1995-1996	NBA	82	42	40	96.5	95.0	.512	18
TOTAL:	8 years	656	247	409				199
AVERAGE:		82	31	51	101.2	104.9	.377	22

Playoff Record

Season	GP	W	L	PPGF	PPGA	Result
1991-1992	3	0	3	99.3	117.3	Lost 1st round series to Chicago.
1993-1994	5	2	3	89.8	96.6	Lost 1st round series to Atlanta.
1995-1996	3	0	3	83.7	106.7	Lost 1st round series to Chicago.
TOTAL:	11	2	9			
AVERAGE:	4	1	3	90.7	105.0	

COACHING HISTORY: 1988-1991 Ron Rothstein 57-189-.232; 1991-1995 Kevin Loughery 133-159-.455; 1994-1995 Alvin Gentry 15-21-.417; 1995-present Pat Riley

MIAMI SEAHAWKS

Home City: Miami, Florida
Home Stadium: Orange Bowl Stadium
Origin of Name:

Regular Season Record

Season	League	GP	W	L	T	PF	PA	Pct
1946	AAFC	14	3	11	0	167	378	.214

COACHING HISTORY: Jack Meagher 1-5-0-.167; Hamp Pool 2-6-0-.250

MIAMI TOROS

(were Miami Gatos)
(became Fort Lauderdale Strikers)

Home City: Miami, Florida
Home Field: Orange Bowl — Capacity: 80,045 [1976]
Origin of Name: The team was named by new owner Joe Robbie.

Regular Season Record

Season	League	GP	W	L	T	GF	GA	BP	Pts	Pct
1973	NASL	19	8	5	6	26	21	22	88	.515
1974	NASL	20	9	5	6	38	24	35	107	.594
1975	NASL	22	14	8	-	47	30	39	123	.621
1976	NASL	24	6	18	-	29	58	28	63	.292
TOTAL:	4 years	85	37	36	12	140	133	124	381	
AVERAGE:		21	9	9	3	47	33	31	95	.498

Playoff Record

Season	GP	W	L	GF	GA	Result
1974	2	1	1	6	5	Lost championship game to Los Angeles.
1975	2	1	1	2	4	Lost 2nd round series to Tampa Bay.
TOTAL:	4	2	2	8	9	
AVERAGE:	2	1	1	4	4	

COACHING HISTORY: 1973-1974 John Young 17-10-12-.556; 1975-1976 Greg Meyers 20-26-.449

MICHIGAN PANTHERS

(merged with Oakland for the 1985 season)

Home City: Pontiac, Michigan
Home Stadium: Pontiac Silverdome — Capacity: 80,638 [1984]
Origin of Name: The name was chosen to fit in with Detroit's other professional sports teams, the Lions and Tigers.

Regular Season Record

Season	League	GP	W	L	T	PF	PA	Pct
1983	USFL	18	12	6	0	451	337	.667
1984	USFL	18	10	8	0	400	382	.556
TOTAL:	2 years	36	22	14	0	851	719	
AVERAGE:		18	11	7	0	426	360	.611

Playoff Record

Season	GP	W	L	PF	PA	Result
1983	2	2	0	61	43	**Won USFL championship**.
1984	1	0	1	21	27	Lost 1st round series to Los Angeles.
TOTAL:	3	2	1	82	70	
AVERAGE:	2	1	1	41	35	

COACHING HISTORY: 1983-1984 Jim Stanley 22-14-0

MICHIGAN STAGS

(were Los Angeles Sharks)
(became Baltimore Blades)

Home City: Detroit, Michigan
Home Arena: Cobo Hall — Capacity: 10,500 [1975]
Origin of Name:

Regular Season Record

Season	League	GP	W	L	T	GF	GA	Pts	Pct
1974-1975	WHA	43	14	26	3	107	179	31	.360

COACHING HISTORY: John Wilson 14-26-3-.360

MILWAUKEE BADGERS

Home City: Milwaukee, Wisconsin
Home Stadium:
Origin of Name: The name was chosen because Wisconsin's nickname is the Badger State. The badger is Wisconsin's state animal.

Regular Season Record

Season	League	GP	W	L	T	PF	PA	Pct
1922	NFL	9	2	4	3	51	71	.389
1923	NFL	12	7	2	3	100	49	.708
1924	NFL	13	5	8	0	142	188	.385
1925	NFL	6	0	6	0	7	191	.000
1926	NFL	9	2	7	0	41	66	.222
TOTAL:	5 years	49	16	27	6	341	565	
AVERAGE:		10	3	6	1	68	113	.388

COACHING HISTORY: 1922 Fritz Pollard 2-4-3-.389; 1923-1924 Jimmy Conzelman 12-10-5-.537; 1925-1926 John Bryan 2-13-0-.133

MILWAUKEE BRAVES

(were Boston Braves)
(became Atlanta Braves)

Home City: Milwaukee, Wisconsin
Home Field: County Stadium Capacity: 43,911 [1953]
Origin of Name: The team kept the same nickname when it moved from Boston to Milwaukee.

Regular Season Record

Season	League	GP	W	L	Pct	GB	R	OR
1953	NL	154	92	62	.597	13	738	589
1954	NL	154	89	65	.578	8	670	556
1955	NL	154	85	69	.552	13.5	743	668
1956	NL	154	92	62	.597	1	709	569
1957	NL	154	95	59	.617	-	772	613
1958	NL	154	92	62	.597	-	675	541
1959	NL	156	86	70	.551	2	724	623
1960	NL	154	88	66	.571	7	724	658
1961	NL	154	83	71	.539	10	712	656
1962	NL	162	86	76	.531	15.5	730	665
1963	NL	162	84	78	.519	15	677	603
1964	NL	162	88	74	.543	5	803	744
1965	NL	162	86	76	.531	11	708	633
TOTAL:	13 years	2036	1146	890		101	9385	8118
AVERAGE:		157	88	68	.563	8	722	624

Playoff Record

Season	GP	W	L	R	OR	Result
1957	7	4	3	23	25	**Won World Series.**
1958	7	3	4	25	29	Lost World Series to New York.
TOTAL:	14	7	7	48	54	
AVERAGE:	7	4	3	24	27	

COACHING HISTORY: 1953-1956 Charlie Grimm 290-218-.571; 1956-1959 Fred Haney 341-231-.596; 1960-1961 Charles Dressen 159-124-.562; 1961-1962 George Tebbetts 98-89-.524; 1963-1965 Bob Bragan 258-228-.531

MILWAUKEE BREWERS
(merged with Cincinnati in 1891)

Home City: Milwaukee, Wisconsin
Home Field: Athletic Park — Capacity: 10,000
Origin of Name: The name was chosen because Milwaukee is well known for its many breweries.

FOR RECORD SEE CINCINNATI KELLY'S KILLERS

MILWAUKEE BREWERS
(became St. Louis Browns)

Home City: Milwaukee, Wisconsin
Home Field: Milwaukee Park
Origin of Name: Named after previous baseball teams.

Regular Season Record

Season	League	GP	W	L	Pct	GB	R	OR
1901	AL	137	48	89	.350	35.5	641	828

COACHING HISTORY: Hugh Duffy 48-89-.350

MILWAUKEE BREWERS
(were Seattle Pilots)

Home City: Milwaukee, Wisconsin
Home Field: County Stadium — Capacity: 53,192 [1995]
Origin of Name: Named after previous American League team.

Regular Season Record

Season	League	GP	W	L	Pct	GB	R	OR
1970	AL	162	65	97	.401	33	613	751
1971	AL	161	69	92	.429	32	534	609
1972	AL	156	65	91	.417	21	493	595
1973	AL	162	74	88	.457	23	708	731
1974	AL	162	76	86	.469	15	647	660
1975	AL	162	68	94	.420	28	675	792
1976	AL	161	66	95	.410	32	570	655
1977	AL	162	67	95	.414	33	639	765
1978	AL	162	93	69	.574	6.5	804	650

1979	AL	161	95	66	.590	8	807	722
1980	AL	162	86	76	.531	17	811	682
1981	AL	109	62	47	.569	NA	493	459
1982	AL	162	95	67	.586	-	891	717
1983	AL	162	87	75	.537	11	764	708
1984	AL	161	67	94	.416	36.5	641	734
1985	AL	161	71	90	.441	28	690	802
1986	AL	161	77	84	.478	18	667	734
1987	AL	162	91	71	.562	7	862	817
1988	AL	162	87	75	.537	2	682	616
1989	AL	162	81	81	.500	8	707	679
1990	AL	161	73	88	.453	14.5	732	760
1991	AL	162	83	79	.512	8	799	744
1992	AL	162	92	70	.568	4	740	604
1993	AL	162	69	93	.426	26	733	792
1994	AL	115	53	62	.461	15	547	586
1995	AL	144	65	79	.451	35	740	747
TOTAL:	26 years	4081	1977	2104		461.5	17989	18111
AVERAGE:		157	76	81	.484	17.5	692	697

Playoff Record

Season	**GP**	**W**	**L**	**R**	**OR**	**Result**
1981	5	2	3	13	19	Lost Divisional playoff to New York.
1982	12	6	6	56	62	Lost World Series to St. Louis.
TOTAL:	17	8	9	69	81	
AVERAGE:	9	4	5	35	41	

COACHING HISTORY: 1970-1972 Dave Bristol 144-209-.408; 1972 Roy McMillan 1-1-.500; 1972-1975 Del Crandall 272-338-.446; 1976-1977 Alex Grammas 133-190-.412; 1978-1980 George Bamberger 235-180-.566; 1980-1982 Bob Rodgers 124-102-.549; 1982-1983 Harvey Kuenn 159-118-.574; 1984 Rene Lachemann 67-94-.416; 1985-1986 George Bamberger 141-171-.452; 1986-1991 Tom Trebelhorn 422-397-.515; 1992-present Phil Garner

MILWAUKEE BUCKS

Home City: Milwaukee, Wisconsin
Home Court: Milwaukee Arena (1968-1988)* — Capacity: 10,746 [1974]
Bradley Center (1988-present) — Capacity: 18,633 [1995]
Origin of Name: The name was chosen in a Name the Team Contest

Regular Season Record

Season	**League**	**GP**	**W**	**L**	**PPGF**	**PPGA**	**Pct**	**GB**
1968-1969	NBA	82	27	55	110.2	115.4	.329	30
1969-1970	NBA	82	56	26	118.8	114.2	.683	4
1970-1971	NBA	82	66	16	118.4	106.2	.805	-
1971-1972	NBA	82	63	19	114.6	103.5	.768	-
1972-1973	NBA	82	60	22	107.2	99.0	.732	-
1973-1974	NBA	82	59	23	107.1	99.0	.720	-
1974-1975	NBA	82	38	44	100.7	100.5	.463	9
1975-1976	NBA	82	38	44	101.8	103.3	.463	-
1976-1977	NBA	82	30	52	108.4	111.5	.366	20
1977-1978	NBA	82	44	38	112.4	113.0	.537	4

1978-1979	NBA	82	38	44	114.1	111.8	.463	10
1979-1980	NBA	82	49	33	110.1	106.1	.598	-
1980-1981	NBA	82	60	22	113.1	105.9	.732	-
1981-1982	NBA	82	55	27	108.4	102.9	.671	-
1982-1983	NBA	82	51	31	106.6	102.2	.622	-
1983-1984	NBA	82	50	32	105.7	101.5	.610	-
1984-1985	NBA	82	59	23	110.9	104.0	.720	-
1985-1986	NBA	82	57	25	114.5	105.5	.695	-
1986-1987	NBA	82	50	32	110.4	106.5	.610	7
1987-1988	NBA	82	42	40	106.1	105.5	.512	12
1988-1989	NBA	82	49	33	108.9	105.3	.598	14
1989-1990	NBA	82	44	38	106.0	106.8	.537	15
1990-1991	NBA	82	48	34	106.4	104.0	.585	13
1991-1992	NBA	82	31	51	105.0	106.7	.378	36
1992-1993	NBA	82	28	54	102.3	106.1	.341	29
1993-1994	NBA	82	20	62	96.9	103.4	.244	37
1994-1995	NBA	82	34	48	99.3	103.7	.415	17
1995-1996	NBA	82	25	57	95.6	100.9	.305	47
TOTAL:	28 years	2296	1271	1025				304
AVERAGE:		82	45	37	107.8	105.5	.554	11

Playoff Record

Season	GP	W	L	PPGF	PPGA	Result
1969-1970	10	5	5	113.4	113.4	Lost Division final to New York.
1970-1971	14	12	2	109.1	94.6	**Won NBA championship**.
1971-1972	11	6	5	108.7	102.3	Lost Conference final to Los Angeles.
1972-1973	6	2	4	99.2	96.7	Lost Conf. semifinal to Golden State.
1973-1974	16	11	5	101.0	95.4	Lost championship series to Boston.
1975-1976	3	1	2	112.3	113.3	Lost 1st round series to Detroit.
1977-1978	9	5	4	112.4	109.8	Lost Conference semifinal to Denver.
1979-1980	7	3	4	102.3	101.4	Lost Conference semifinal to Seattle.
1980-1981	7	3	4	107.0	104.4	Lost Conf. semifinal to Philadelphia.
1981-1982	6	2	4	102.5	106.0	Lost Conf. semifinal to Philadelphia.
1982-1983	9	5	4	101.6	98.8	Lost Conference final to Philadelphia.
1983-1984	16	8	8	102.5	101.7	Lost Conference final to Boston.
1984-1985	8	3	5	109.0	111.3	Lost Conf. semifinal to Philadelphia.
1985-1986	14	7	7	109.8	112.2	Lost Conference final to Boston.
1986-1987	12	6	6	118.2	117.7	Lost Conference semifinal to Boston.
1987-1988	5	2	3	108.6	109.8	Lost 1st round series to Atlanta.
1988-1989	9	3	6	97.2	102.1	Lost Conference semifinal to Detroit.
1989-1990	4	1	3	101.0	110.5	Lost 1st round series to Chicago.
TOTAL:	166	85	81			
AVERAGE:	9	5	4	106.4	105.6	

COACHING HISTORY: 1968-1977 Larry Costello 410-264-.608; 1977-1987 Don Nelson 540-344-.611; 1987-1992 Del Harris 191-154-.554; 1991-1992 Frank Hamblen 23-42-.354; 1992-present Mike Dunleavy

*Also known as The Mecca

MILWAUKEE GRAYS

Home City: Milwaukee, Wisconsin
Home Field: Milwaukee Base-Ball Grounds
Origin of Name: The team was named for the color of their uniforms.

Regular Season Record

Season	League	GP	W	L	Pct	GB	R	OR
1878	NL	60	15	45	.250	26	256	386

COACHING HISTORY: Jack Chapman 15-45-.250

MILWAUKEE HAWKS

(were Tri-Cities Blackhawks)
(became St. Louis Hawks)

Home City: Milwaukee, Wisconsin
Home Court: Milwaukee Arena Capacity: 11,000
Origin of Name: The name was a short form of Blackhawks, the teams previous nickname.

Regular Season Record

Season	League	GP	W	L	PPGF	PPGA	Pct	GB
1951-1952	NBA	66	17	49	73.2	81.2	.258	24
1952-1953	NBA	71	27	44	75.9	78.8	.380	21.5
1953-1954	NBA	72	21	51	70.0	75.3	.292	31
1954-1955	NBA	72	26	46	87.4	90.4	.361	17
TOTAL:	4 years	281	91	190				93.5
AVERAGE:		70	23	47	76.6	81.4	.324	23.5

COACHING HISTORY: 1951-1952 Doxie Moore 17-49-.258; 1952-1954 Fuzzy Levane 38-79-.325; 1953-1955 Red Holzman 36-62-.367

MILWAUKEE UNIONS

Home City: Milwaukee, Wisconsin
Home Field: Wright Street Grounds
Origin of Name: Like so many teams in the Union Association this team adopted the nickname of Unions.

Regular Season Record

Season	League	GP	W	L	Pct	GB	R	OR
1884	UA	12	8	4	.667	35.5	53	34

COACHING HISTORY: Tom Lofthus 8-4-.667

MINNEAPOLIS LAKERS

(became Los Angeles Lakers)

Home City: Minneapolis, Minnesota
Home Court: Minneapolis Auditorium (1948-1958) Capacity: 10,000
Minneapolis Armory (1959-1960)
Origin of Name: The team was named Lakers because Minnesota is well known for its over 15,000 lakes.

Regular Season Record

Season	League	GP	W	L	PPGF	PPGA	Pct	GB
1947-1948	NBL	60	43	17	64.1	56.6	.717	-
1948-1949	BAA	60	44	16	84.0	76.7	.733	1
1949-1950	NBA	68	51	17	84.1	75.7	.750	-
1950-1951	NBA	68	44	24	82.8	77.4	.647	-
1951-1952	NBA	66	40	26	85.6	79.5	.606	1
1952-1953	NBA	70	48	22	85.3	79.2	.686	-
1953-1954	NBA	72	46	26	81.7	78.3	.639	-
1954-1955	NBA	72	40	32	95.6	94.5	.556	3
1955-1956	NBA	72	33	39	99.3	100.2	.458	4
1956-1957	NBA	72	34	38	102.3	103.1	.472	-
1957-1958	NBA	72	19	53	105.1	111.5	.264	22
1958-1959	NBA	72	33	39	106.0	107.3	.458	16
1959-1960	NBA	75	25	50	107.3	111.4	.333	21
TOTAL:	13 years	899	500	399				68
AVERAGE:		69	38	31	91.0	88.6	.556	5

Playoff Record

Season	GP	W	L	PPGF	PPGA	Result
1947-1948	10	8	2	75.8	67.3	**Won NBL championship**.
1948-1949	10	8	2	80.3	73.9	**Won BAA championship**.
1949-1950	13	11	2	84.0	75.5	**Won NBA championship**.
1950-1951	7	3	4	79.3	82.1	Lost Division final to Rochester.
1951-1952	13	9	4	82.3	78.9	**Won NBA championship**.
1952-1953	12	9	3	82.9	77.7	**Won NBA championship**.
1953-1954	13	9	4	80.3	74.1	**Won NBA championship**.
1954-1955	7	3	4	94.9	96.0	Lost Division final to Ft. Wayne.
1955-1956	3	1	2	121.0	102.3	Lost Division semifinal to St. Louis.
1956-1957	5	2	3	117.8	120.4	Lost Division final to St. Louis.
1958-1959	13	6	7	106.5	111.0	Lost championship series to Boston.
1959-1960	9	5	4	104.1	106.0	Lost Division final to St. Louis.
TOTAL:	115	74	41			
AVERAGE:	10	6	4	92.4	88.8	

COACHING HISTORY: 1947-1959 John Kundla 466-319-.594; 1957-1958 George Mikan 9-30-.231; 1959-1960 John Castellani 11-25-.306; 1959-1960 Jim Pollard 14-25-.359

MINNEAPOLIS MARINES

Home City: Minneapolis, Minnesota
Home Stadium:
Origin of Name:

Regular Season Record

Season	League	GP	W	L	T	PF	PA	Pct
1922	NFL	4	1	3	0	19	40	.250
1923	NFL	9	2	5	2	48	87	.333
1924	NFL	6	0	6	0	14	108	.000
TOTAL:	3 years	19	3	14	2	81	235	
AVERAGE:		6	1	4	1	27	78	.211

COACHING HISTORY: 1922 Not Available; 1923 Harry Mehre 2-5-2-.333; 1924 Joe Brandy 0-6-0-.000

MINNEAPOLIS REDJACKETS

Home City: Minneapolis, Minnesota
Home Stadium:
Origin of Name:

Regular Season Record

Season	League	GP	W	L	T	PF	PA	Pct
1929	NFL	10	1	9	0	42	185	.100
1930	NFL	9	1	7	1	27	165	.167
TOTAL:	2 years	19	2	16	1	69	350	
AVERAGE:		10	1	8	1	35	175	.132

COACHING HISTORY: 1929 Herb Joesting 1-9-0-.100; 1930 George Gibson 1-7-1-.167

MINNESOTA FIGHTING SAINTS

Home City: St. Paul, Minnesota
Home Arena: St. Paul Auditorium (1972-1973) Capacity: 8,000 [1972]
St. Paul Civic Center (1972-1976) Capacity: 16,180 [1972]
Origin of Name:

Regular Season Record

Season	League	GP	W	L	T	GF	GA	Pts	Pct
1972-1973	WHA	78	38	37	3	250	269	79	.506
1973-1974	WHA	78	44	32	2	332	275	90	.577
1974-1975	WHA	78	42	33	3	308	279	87	.558
1975-1976	WHA	59	30	25	4	211	212	64	.542
TOTAL:	4 years	293	154	127	12	1101	1035	320	
AVERAGE:		73	38	32	3	275	259	80	.548

Playoff Record

Season	GP	W	L	GF	GA	Result
1972-1973	5	1	4	16	23	Lost quarterfinal series to Winnipeg.
1973-1974	11	6	5	39	40	Lost semifinal series to Houston.
1974-1975	12	6	6	44	42	Lost quarterfinal series to Quebec.
TOTAL:	28	13	15	99	105	
AVERAGE:	9	4	5	33	35	

COACHING HISTORY: 1972-1973 Glen Sonmor 38-37-3-.506; 1973-1976 Harry Neale 116-90-9-.560

MINNESOTA FIGHTING SAINTS
(were Cleveland Crusaders)

Home City: St. Paul, Minnesota
Home Arena: St. Paul Civic Center Capacity: 15,705 [1977]
Origin of Name: The team was named after the previous WHA team.

Regular Season Record

Season	League	GP	W	L	T	GF	GA	Pts	Pct
1976-1977	WHA	42	19	18	5	136	129	43	.512

COACHING HISTORY: Glen Sonmor 19-18-5-.512

MINNESOTA KICKS
(were Denver Dynamos)

Home City: Minneapolis, Minnesota
Home Field: Memorial Stadium (University of Minnesota) Capacity: 56,725 [1977]
Origin of Name: The team name was chosen in a Name the Team Contest.

Regular Season Record

Season	League	GP	W	L	GF	GA	BP	Pts	Pct
1976	NASL	24	15	9	54	33	48	138	.639
1977	NASL	26	16	10	44	36	41	136	.581
1978	NASL	30	17	13	58	43	54	156	.578
1979	NASL	30	21	9	67	48	58	184	.681
1980	NASL	32	16	16	66	56	51	147	.510
1981	NASL	32	19	13	63	57	55	163	.340
TOTAL:	6 years	174	104	70	352	273	307	924	
AVERAGE:		29	17	12	59	46	51	154	.526

Playoff Record

Season	GP	W	L	GF	GA	Result
1976	3	2	1	6	4	Lost 3rd round series to San Jose.
1977	2	0	2	1	3	Lost 1st round series to Seattle.
1978	4	2	2	12	8	Lost 2nd round series to New York.
1979	2	0	2	2	4	Lost 1st round series to Tulsa.
1980	2	0	2	0	3	Lost 1st round series to Dallas.
1981	4	2	2	5	7	Lost 2nd round series to Ft. Lauderdale.
TOTAL:	17	6	11	26	29	
AVERAGE:	3	1	2	4	5	

COACHING HISTORY: 1976-1978 Freddie Goodwin 48-32-.597; 1979-1980 Roy McCrohan 23-16; 1980-1981 Freddie Goodwin 33-22

MINNESOTA MUSKIES
(became Miami Floridians)

Home City: Minneapolis, Minnesota
Home Court: Metropolitan Sports Center Capacity: 15,499
Origin of Name: The name was chosen because the Muskie (a fish) abound in the lakes of Minnesota.

Regular Season Record

Season	League	GP	W	L	PPGF	PPGA	Pct	GB
1967-1968	ABA	78	50	28	108.6	104.7	.641	4

Playoff Record

Season	GP	W	L	PPGF	PPGA	Result
1967-1968	10	4	6	109.2	109.7	Lost 2nd round series to Pittsburgh.

COACHING HISTORY: Jim Pollard 50-28-.641

MINNESOTA NORTH STARS
(became Dallas Stars)

Home City: Bloomington, Minnesota
Home Arena: Met Center * Capacity: 15,174 [1992]
Origin of Name: North Stars was one of the many entries submitted in a Name the Team Contest. Minnesota's official nickname is "North Star State."

Regular Season Record

Season	League	GP	W	L	T	GF	GA	Pts	Pct
1967-1968	NHL	74	27	32	15	191	226	69	.466
1968-1969	NHL	76	18	43	15	189	270	51	.336
1969-1970	NHL	76	19	35	22	224	257	60	.395
1970-1971	NHL	78	28	34	16	191	223	72	.462
1971-1972	NHL	78	37	29	12	191	191	86	.551
1972-1973	NHL	78	37	30	11	254	230	85	.549
1973-1974	NHL	78	23	38	17	235	195	63	.404
1974-1975	NHL	80	23	50	7	221	341	53	.331
1975-1976	NHL	80	20	53	7	195	303	47	.294
1976-1977	NHL	80	23	39	18	240	310	64	.400
1977-1978	NHL	80	18	53	9	218	325	45	.281
1978-1979	NHL	80	28	40	12	257	289	68	.425
1979-1980	NHL	80	36	28	16	311	253	88	.550
1980-1981	NHL	80	35	28	17	291	263	87	.544
1981-1982	NHL	80	37	23	20	346	288	94	.588
1982-1983	NHL	80	40	24	16	321	290	96	.600
1983-1984	NHL	80	39	31	10	345	344	88	.550
1984-1985	NHL	80	25	43	12	268	321	62	.388
1985-1986	NHL	80	38	33	9	327	305	85	.531
1986-1987	NHL	80	30	40	10	296	314	70	.438
1987-1988	NHL	80	19	48	13	242	349	51	.319
1988-1989	NHL	80	27	37	16	258	278	70	.438
1989-1990	NHL	80	36	40	4	284	291	76	.475
1990-1991	NHL	80	27	39	14	256	266	68	.425
1991-1992	NHL	80	32	42	6	246	278	70	.438
1992-1993	NHL	84	36	38	10	272	293	82	.488
TOTAL:	26 years	2062	758	970	334	6669	7293	1850	
AVERAGE:		79	29	37	13	257	281	71	.449

Playoff Record

Season	GP	W	L	GF	GA	Result
1967-1968	14	7	7	48	39	Lost semifinal series to St. Louis.
1969-1970	6	2	4	16	20	Lost quarterfinal series to St. Louis.
1970-1971	12	6	6	35	42	Lost semifinal series o Montreal.
1971-1972	7	3	4	19	19	Lost quarterfinal series to St. Louis.

1972-1973	6	2	4	12	14	Lost quarterfinal series to Philadelphia.
1976-1977	2	0	2	3	11	Lost preliminary series to Buffalo.
1979-1980	15	8	7	49	57	Lost semifinal series to Philadelphia.
1980-1981	19	12	7	84	74	Lost Stanley Cup final to N.Y. Islanders.
1981-1982	4	1	3	14	14	Lost preliminary series to Chicago.
1982-1983	9	4	5	34	40	Lost quarterfinal series to Chicago.
1983-1984	16	7	9	47	53	Lost semifinal series to Edmonton.
1984-1985	9	5	4	38	38	Lost quarterfinal series to Chicago.
1985-1986	5	2	3	20	18	Lost preliminary series to St. Louis.
1988-1989	5	1	4	15	23	Lost preliminary series to St. Louis.
1989-1990	7	3	4	18	21	Lost preliminary series to Chicago.
1990-1991	23	14	9	81	75	Lost Stanley Cup final to Pittsburgh.
1991-1992	7	3	4	19	23	Lost preliminary series to Detroit.
TOTAL:	166	80	86	552	581	
AVERAGE:	10	5	5	33	34	

COACHING HISTORY: 1967-1970 Wren Blair 48-66-33-.439; 1968-1969 John Muckler 6-22-7-.271; 1969-1970 Charlie Burns 10-22-12-.364; 1970-1975 Jackie Gordon 116-124-50-.486; 1973-1974 Parker MacDonald 20-30-11-.418; 1974-1975 Charlie Burns 12-27-2-.317; 1975-1978 Ted Harris 48-104-27-.344; 1977-1978 Andre Beaulieu 6-23-3-.234; 1977-1978 Lou Nanne 7-18-4-.310; 1978-1979 Harry Howell 3-6-2-.364; 1978-1983 Glen Sonmor 155-126-72-.541; 1982-1983 Murray Oliver 18-11-7-.597; 1983-1985 Bill Mahoney 64-74-22-.469; 1985-1987 Lorne Henning 68-72-18-.487; 1986-1987 Glen Sonmor 0-1-1-.250; 1987-1988 Herb Brooks 19-48-13-.319; 1988-1990 Pierre Page 63-77-20-.456; 1990-1993 Bob Gainey 95-119-30-.451

*Originally known as Metropolitan Sports Center from 1967 to 1982.

MINNESOTA PIPERS
(were Pittsburgh Pipers)
(became Pittsburgh Pipers)

Home City: Minneapolis, Minnesota
Home Court: Metropolitan Sports Center — Capacity: 15,500 [1968]
Origin of Name: The team kept the same name when it moved from Pittsburgh.

Regular Season Record

Season	League	GP	W	L	PPGF	PPGA	Pct	GB
1968-1969	ABA	78	36	42	114.3	114.2	.462	8

Playoff Record

Season	GP	W	L	PPGF	PPGA	Result
1968-1969	7	3	4	110.6	112.3	Lost 1st round series to Miami.

COACHING HISTORY: Jim Harding 20-12-.625; Vern Mikkelsen 6-7-.462; Gus Young 10-23-.303

MINNESOTA STRIKERS
(were Ft. Lauderdale Strikers)

Home City: Bloomington, Minnesota
Home Field: Hubert H. Humphrey Metrodome — Capacity: 54,711
Origin of Name: The team kept the same nickname when it moved to Bloomington from Ft. Lauderdale.

Regular Season Record

Season	League	GP	W	L	GF	GA	BP	Pts	Pct
1984	NASL	24	14	10	40	44	35	115	.319

COACHING HISTORY: Dave Chadwick 14-10

MINNESOTA TIMBERWOLVES

Home City: Minneapolis, Minnesota
Home Court: Hubert H. Humphrey Metrodome (1989-1990) Capacity: 23,000 [1990]
Target Center (1990-present) Capacity: 19,006 [1995]
Origin of Name: The name was chosen in a Name the Team Contest.

Regular Season Record

Season	League	GP	W	L	PPGF	PPGA	Pct	GB
1989-1990	NBA	82	22	60	95.2	99.4	.268	34
1990-1991	NBA	82	29	53	99.6	103.5	.354	26
1991-1992	NBA	82	15	67	100.5	107.5	.183	40
1992-1993	NBA	82	19	63	98.1	105.9	.232	36
1993-1994	NBA	82	20	62	96.7	103.6	.244	38
1994-1995	NBA	82	21	61	94.2	103.2	.256	41
1995-1996	NBA	82	26	56	97.9	103.2	.317	33
TOTAL:	7 years	574	152	422				248
AVERAGE:		82	22	60	97.5	103.8	.265	35

COACHING HISTORY: 1989-1991 Bill Musselman 51-113-.311; 1991-1993 Jimmy Rodgers 21-90-.189; 1992-1994 Sidney Lowe 33-102-.244; 1994-1996 Bill Blair 27-75-.265; 1995-present Flip Saunders

MINNESOTA TWINS

(were Washington Senators)

Home City: Bloomington, Minnesota (1960-1981)
Minneapolis, Minnesota (1982-present)
Home Field: Metropolitan Stadium (1960-1981) Capacity: 45,919 [1975]
Hubert H. Humphrey Metrodome (1982-present) Capacity: 55,883 [1995]
Origin of Name: The team was named for the twin cities of Minneapolis and St. Paul.

Regular Season Record

Season	League	GP	W	L	Pct	GB	R	OR
1961	AL	160	70	90	.438	38	707	778
1962	AL	162	91	71	.562	5	798	713
1963	AL	161	91	70	.565	13	767	602
1964	AL	162	79	83	.488	20	737	678
1965	AL	162	102	60	.630	-	774	600
1966	AL	162	89	73	.549	9	663	581
1967	AL	162	91	71	.562	1	671	590
1968	AL	162	79	83	.488	24	562	546
1969	AL	162	97	65	.599	-	790	618
1970	AL	162	98	64	.605	-	744	605
1971	AL	160	74	86	.463	26.5	654	670

1972	AL	154	77	77	.500	15.5	537	535
1973	AL	162	81	81	.500	13	738	692
1974	AL	162	82	80	.506	8	673	669
1975	AL	159	76	83	.478	20.5	724	736
1976	AL	162	85	77	.525	5	743	704
1977	AL	161	84	77	.522	17.5	867	776
1978	AL	162	73	89	.451	19	666	678
1979	AL	162	82	80	.506	6	764	725
1980	AL	161	77	84	.478	19.5	670	724
1981	AL	109	41	68	.376	NA	378	486
1982	AL	162	60	102	.370	33	657	819
1983	AL	162	70	92	.432	29	709	822
1984	AL	162	81	81	.500	3	673	675
1985	AL	162	77	85	.475	14	705	782
1986	AL	162	71	91	.438	21	741	839
1987	AL	162	85	77	.525	-	786	806
1988	AL	162	91	71	.562	13	759	672
1989	AL	162	80	82	.494	19	740	738
1990	AL	162	74	88	.457	29	666	729
1991	AL	162	95	67	.586	-	776	652
1992	AL	162	90	72	.556	6	747	653
1993	AL	162	71	91	.438	23	693	830
1994	AL	113	53	60	.469	14	594	688
1995	AL	144	56	88	.389	44	703	889
TOTAL:	35 years	5532	2773	2759		508.5	24576	24300
AVERAGE:		158	79	79	.501	14.5	702	694

Playoff Record

Season	GP	W	L	R	OR	Result
1965	7	3	4	20	24	Lost World Series to Los Angeles.
1969	3	0	3	5	16	Lost ALCS to Baltimore.
1970	3	0	3	10	27	Lost ALCS to Baltimore.
1987	12	8	4	72	49	**Won World Series.**
1991	12	8	4	47	44	**Won World Series.**
TOTAL:	37	19	18	154	160	
AVERAGE:	7	4	3	31	32	

COACHING HISTORY: 1961 Harry Lavagetto 29-45-.392; 1961-1967 Sam Mele 518-427-.548; 1967-1968 Cal Ermer 145-129-.529; 1969 Billy Martin 97-65-.599; 1970-1972 Bill Rigney 208-184-.531; 1972-1975 Frank Quilici 280-287-.494; 1976-1980 Gene Mauch 378-394-.490; 1980-1981 John Goryl 34-38-.472; 1981-1985 Bill Gardner 268-353-.432; 1985-1986 Ray Miller 109-130-.456; 1986-present Tom Kelly

MINNESOTA VIKINGS

Home City: Bloomington, Minnesota (1961-1981)
Minneapolis, Minnesota (1982-present)
Home Stadium: Metropolitan Stadium (1961-1981) Capacity: 48,446 [1981]
Hubert H. Humphrey Metrodome (1982-present) Capacity: 63,000 [1995]
Origin of Name: The team was named by the teams first G.M. Bert Rose, because of Minnesota's large Scandinavian population.

Regular Season Record

Season	League	GP	W	L	T	PF	PA	Pct
1961	NFL	14	3	11	0	285	407	.214
1962	NFL	14	2	11	1	254	410	.179
1963	NFL	14	5	8	1	309	390	.393
1964	NFL	14	8	5	1	355	296	.607
1965	NFL	14	7	7	0	383	403	.500
1966	NFL	14	4	9	1	292	304	.321
1967	NFL	14	3	8	3	233	294	.321
1968	NFL	14	8	6	0	282	242	.571
1969	NFL	14	12	2	0	379	133	.857
1970	NFL	14	12	2	0	335	143	.857
1971	NFL	14	11	3	0	245	139	.786
1972	NFL	14	7	7	0	301	252	.500
1973	NFL	14	12	2	0	296	168	.857
1974	NFL	14	10	4	0	310	195	.714
1975	NFL	14	12	2	0	377	180	.857
1976	NFL	14	11	2	1	305	176	.821
1977	NFL	14	9	5	0	231	227	.643
1978	NFL	16	8	7	1	294	306	.531
1979	NFL	16	7	9	0	259	337	.438
1980	NFL	16	9	7	0	317	308	.563
1981	NFL	16	7	9	0	325	369	.438
1982	NFL	9	5	4	0	187	198	.556
1983	NFL	16	8	8	0	316	348	.500
1984	NFL	16	3	13	0	276	484	.188
1985	NFL	16	7	9	0	346	359	.438
1986	NFL	16	9	7	0	398	273	.563
1987	NFL	15	8	7	0	336	335	.533
1988	NFL	16	11	5	0	406	233	.688
1989	NFL	16	10	6	0	351	275	.625
1990	NFL	16	6	10	0	351	326	.375
1991	NFL	16	8	8	0	301	306	.500
1992	NFL	16	11	5	0	374	249	.688
1993	NFL	16	9	7	0	277	290	.563
1994	NFL	16	10	6	0	356	314	.625
1995	NFL	16	8	8	0	412	385	.500
TOTAL:	35 years	518	280	229	9	11054	10054	
AVERAGE:		15	8	7	0	316	287	.549

Playoff Record

Season	GP	W	L	PF	PA	Result
1968	1	0	1	14	24	Lost Conference championship to Baltimore.
1969	3	2	1	57	50	Lost Super Bowl to Kansas City.
1970	1	0	1	14	17	Lost Divisional playoff to San Francisco.
1971	1	0	1	12	20	Lost Divisional playoff to Dallas.
1973	3	2	1	61	54	Lost Super Bowl to Miami.
1974	3	2	1	50	40	Lost Super Bowl to Pittsburgh.
1975	1	0	1	14	17	Lost Divisional playoff to Dallas.
1976	3	2	1	73	65	Lost Super Bowl to Oakland.
1977	2	1	1	20	30	Lost NFC championship to Dallas.
1978	1	0	1	10	34	Lost Divisional playoff to Los Angeles.

1980	1	0	1	16	31	Lost Divisional playoff to Philadelphia.
1982	2	1	1	37	45	Lost 2nd round playoff to Washington.
1987	3	2	1	90	51	Lost NFC championship to Washington.
1988	2	1	1	37	51	Lost Divisional playoff to San Francisco.
1989	1	0	1	13	41	Lost Conference semifinal to San Francisco.
1992	1	0	1	7	24	Lost 1st round game to Washington.
1993	1	0	1	10	17	Lost 1st round game to N.Y. Giants.
1994	1	0	1	18	35	Lost 1st round game to Chicago.
TOTAL:	31	13	18	553	646	
AVERAGE:	2	1	1	31	36	

COACHING HISTORY: 1961-1966 Norm Van Brocklin 29-51-4-.369; 1967-1983 Bud Grant 151-87-5-.632; 1984 Les Steckel 3-13-0-.188; 1985 Bud Grant 7-9-0-.438; 1986-1991 Jerry Burns 52-43-0-.547; 1992-present Dennis Green

MONTREAL ALOUETTES
(became Montreal Concordes)
(were Montreal Concordes)

Home City: Montreal, Quebec
Home Stadium: Molson Stadium [McGill University] (1950-1968, 1972)
Autostade (1969-1971, 1973-1976) Capacity: 33,212 [1974]
Olympic Stadium (1977-1981, 1986) Capacity: 58,500 [1986]
Origin of Name: The English translation of Alouette is lark.

Regular Season Record

Season	**League**	**GP**	**W**	**L**	**T**	**PF**	**PA**	**Pts**	**Pct**
1950	CRU	12	6	6	0	192	261	12	.500
1951	CRU	12	3	9	0	146	286	6	.250
1952	CRU	12	2	10	0	136	278	4	.167
1953	CRU	14	8	6	0	292	229	16	.571
1954	CRU	14	11	3	0	341	148	22	.786
1955	CRU	12	9	3	0	388	214	18	.750
1956	CFC	14	10	4	0	478	361	20	.714
1957	CFC	14	6	8	0	287	301	12	.429
1958	CFL	14	7	6	1	265	269	15	.536
1959	CFL	14	6	8	0	193	305	12	.429
1960	CFL	14	5	9	0	340	458	10	.357
1961	CFL	14	4	9	1	213	225	9	.321
1962	CFL	14	4	7	3	308	309	11	.393
1963	CFL	14	6	8	0	277	297	12	.429
1964	CFL	14	6	8	0	192	264	12	.429
1965	CFL	14	5	9	0	183	215	10	.357
1966	CFL	14	7	7	0	156	215	14	.500
1967	CFL	14	2	12	0	166	302	4	.143
1968	CFL	14	3	9	2	234	327	8	.286
1969	CFL	14	2	10	2	304	395	6	.214
1970	CFL	14	7	6	1	246	279	15	.536
1971	CFL	14	6	8	0	226	248	12	.429
1972	CFL	14	4	10	0	246	353	8	.286
1973	CFL	14	7	6	1	273	238	15	.536
1974	CFL	16	9	5	2	339	271	20	.625
1975	CFL	16	9	7	0	353	345	18	.563

1976	CFL	16	7	8	1	305	273	15	.469
1977	CFL	16	11	5	0	311	245	22	.688
1978	CFL	16	8	7	1	331	295	17	.531
1979	CFL	16	11	4	1	351	284	23	.719
1980	CFL	16	8	8	0	356	375	16	.500
1981	CFL	16	3	13	0	267	518	6	.188
1986	CFL	18	4	14	0	320	500	8	.222
TOTAL:	33 years	474	206	252	16	9015	9883	428	
AVERAGE:		14	6	8	0	273	299	13	.451

Playoff Record

Season	**GP**	**W**	**L**	**PF**	**PA**	**Result**
1953	2	0	2	23	59	Lost Division final to Hamilton.
1954	3	2	1	63	54	Won Eastern Division final series.
1955	2	1	1	57	70	Lost Grey Cup game to Edmonton.
1956	3	2	1	105	112	Lost Grey Cup game to Edmonton.
1957	3	1	2	35	71	Lost Division final to Hamilton.
1958	1	0	1	12	26	Lost Division semifinal to Ottawa.
1959	1	0	1	0	43	Lost Division semifinal to Ottawa.
1960	1	0	1	14	30	Lost Division semifinal to Ottawa.
1962	3	1	2	56	75	Lost Division final to Hamilton.
1963	1	0	1	5	17	Lost Division semifinal to Ottawa.
1964	1	0	1	0	27	Lost Division semifinal to Ottawa.
1965	1	0	1	7	36	Lost Division semifinal to Ottawa.
1966	1	0	1	14	24	Lost Division semifinal to Hamilton.
1970	4	4	0	82	43	**Won Grey Cup**.
1972	1	0	1	11	14	Lost Division semifinal to Ottawa.
1973	2	1	1	46	33	Lost Division final to Ottawa.
1974	2	2	0	34	11	**Won Grey Cup**.
1975	3	2	1	63	31	Lost Grey Cup game to Edmonton.
1976	1	0	1	0	23	Lost Division semifinal to Hamilton.
1977	2	2	0	62	24	**Won Grey Cup**.
1978	3	2	1	69	56	Lost Grey Cup game to Edmonton.
1979	2	1	1	26	23	Lost Grey Cup game to Edmonton.
1980	2	1	1	38	45	Lost Division final to Hamilton.
1981	1	0	1	16	20	Lost Division semifinal to Ottawa.
TOTAL:	46	22	24	838	967	
AVERAGE:	2	1	1	35	40	

COACHING HISTORY: 1950-1951 Lew Hayman 9-15-0-.375; 1952-1959 Doug "Peahead " Walker 59-48-1-.551; 1960-1962 Perry Moss 13-25-4-.357; 1963-1966 Jim Trimble 24-32-0-.429; 1967 Darrell Mudra 2-12-0-.143; 1968-1969 Kay Dalton 5-19-4-.250; 1970-1972 Sam Etcheverry 17-24-1-.417; 1973-1977 Marv Levy 43-31-4-.577; 1978-1981 Joe Scanella 28-28-2-.500; 1981 Jim Eddy 2-4-0-.333; 1986 Gary Durchik 4-14-0-.222

MONTREAL ALOUETTES

(were Baltimore Stallions)

Home City: Montreal, Quebec
Home Stadium: Olympic Stadium Capacity:
Origin of name: The name was chosen by team owner Jim Speros on February 7, 1996 and named in honor of the previous CFL team.

Season	League	GP	Regular Season Record W	L	T	PF	PA	Pts	Pct

The team begins play in the 1996 season.

COACHING HISTORY:

MONTREAL CANADIENS

Home City: Montreal, Quebec
Home Arena: Jubilee Arena Capacity: 3,200 [1909]
Origin of Name: The team was named by club founder J. Ambrose O'Brien and was originally called "Club de Hockey Canadien".

Season	League	GP	Regular Season Record W	L	T	GF	GA	Pts	Pct
1909-1910	NHA	12	2	10	0	59	100	4	.167

COACHING HISTORY:

MONTREAL CANADIENS

Home City: Montreal, Quebec
Home Arena: Jubilee Arena (1910-1913: 1918-1920) Capacity: 3,200
Westmount Arena (1913-1918) Capacity: 6,000
Mount Royal Arena (1920-1926) Capacity: 6,750
Montreal Forum I (1926-1968) Capacity: 15,500
Montreal Forum II (1968-1996) Capacity: 17,959 [1995]
Molson Center (1996-present) Capacity: 21,450 [1995]
Origin of Name: The team was named after "Club Athletique Canadien" a French Canadian sports club owned by team owner George Kennedy, and also after the previous NHA team founded and named by J. Ambrose O'Brien.

Season	League	GP	Regular Season Record W	L	T	GF	GA	Pts	Pct
1910-1911	NHA	16	8	8	0	66	62	16	.500
1911-1912	NHA	18	8	10	0	59	66	16	.444
1912-1913	NHA	20	9	11	0	83	81	18	.450
1913-1914	NHA	20	13	7	0	85	65	26	.650
1914-1915	NHA	20	6	14	0	65	81	12	.300
1915-1916	NHA	24	16	7	1	104	76	33	.688
1916-1917	NHA	20	10	10	0	89	80	20	.500
1917-1918	NHL	22	13	9	0	115	84	26	.591
1918-1919	NHL	18	10	8	0	88	78	20	.556
1919-1920	NHL	24	13	11	0	129	113	26	.542
1920-1921	NHL	24	13	11	0	112	99	26	.542
1921-1922	NHL	24	12	11	1	88	94	25	.521
1922-1923	NHL	24	13	9	2	73	61	28	.583
1923-1924	NHL	24	13	11	0	59	48	26	.542
1924-1925	NHL	30	17	11	2	93	56	36	.600
1925-1926	NHL	36	11	24	1	79	108	23	.319
1926-1927	NHL	44	28	14	2	99	67	58	.659

1927-1928	NHL	44	26	11	7	116	48	59	.670
1928-1929	NHL	44	22	7	15	71	43	59	.670
1929-1930	NHL	44	21	14	9	142	114	51	.580
1930-1931	NHL	44	26	10	8	129	89	60	.682
1931-1932	NHL	48	25	16	7	128	111	57	.594
1932-1933	NHL	48	18	25	5	92	115	41	.427
1933-1934	NHL	48	22	20	6	99	101	50	.521
1934-1935	NHL	48	19	23	6	110	145	44	.458
1935-1936	NHL	48	11	26	11	82	123	33	.344
1936-1937	NHL	48	24	18	6	115	111	54	.563
1937-1938	NHL	48	18	17	13	123	128	49	.510
1938-1939	NHL	48	15	24	9	115	146	39	.406
1939-1940	NHL	48	10	33	5	90	167	25	.260
1940-1941	NHL	48	16	26	6	121	147	38	.396
1941-1942	NHL	48	18	27	3	134	173	39	.406
1942-1943	NHL	50	19	19	12	181	191	50	.500
1943-1944	NHL	50	38	5	7	234	109	83	.830
1944-1945	NHL	50	38	8	4	228	121	80	.800
1945-1946	NHL	50	28	17	5	172	134	61	.610
1946-1947	NHL	60	34	16	10	189	138	78	.650
1947-1948	NHL	60	20	29	11	147	169	51	.425
1948-1949	NHL	60	28	23	9	152	126	65	.542
1949-1950	NHL	70	29	22	19	164	150	77	.550
1950-1951	NHL	70	25	30	15	173	184	65	.464
1951-1952	NHL	70	34	26	10	195	164	78	.557
1952-1953	NHL	70	28	23	19	155	148	75	.536
1953-1954	NHL	70	35	24	11	195	141	81	.579
1954-1955	NHL	70	41	18	11	228	157	93	.664
1955-1956	NHL	70	45	15	10	222	131	100	.714
1956-1957	NHL	70	35	23	12	210	155	82	.586
1957-1958	NHL	70	43	17	10	250	158	96	.686
1958-1959	NHL	70	39	18	13	258	158	91	.650
1959-1960	NHL	70	40	18	12	255	178	92	.657
1960-1961	NHL	70	41	19	10	254	188	92	.657
1961-1962	NHL	70	42	14	14	259	166	98	.700
1962-1963	NHL	70	28	19	23	225	183	79	.564
1963-1964	NHL	70	36	21	13	209	167	85	.607
1964-1965	NHL	70	36	23	11	211	185	83	.593
1965-1966	NHL	70	41	21	8	239	173	90	.643
1966-1967	NHL	70	32	25	13	202	188	77	.550
1967-1968	NHL	74	42	22	10	236	167	94	.635
1968-1969	NHL	76	46	19	11	271	202	103	.678
1969-1970	NHL	76	38	22	16	244	201	92	.605
1970-1971	NHL	78	42	23	13	291	216	97	.622
1971-1972	NHL	78	46	16	16	307	205	108	.692
1972-1973	NHL	78	52	10	16	329	184	120	.769
1973-1974	NHL	78	45	24	9	293	240	99	.635
1974-1975	NHL	80	47	14	19	374	225	113	.706
1975-1976	NHL	80	58	11	11	337	174	127	.794
1976-1977	NHL	80	60	8	12	387	171	132	.825
1977-1978	NHL	80	59	10	11	359	183	129	.806
1978-1979	NHL	80	52	17	11	337	204	115	.719
1979-1980	NHL	80	47	20	13	328	240	107	.669
1980-1981	NHL	80	45	22	13	332	232	103	.644

1981-1982	NHL	80	46	17	17	360	223	109	.681
1982-1983	NHL	80	42	24	14	350	286	98	.613
1983-1984	NHL	80	35	40	5	286	295	75	.469
1984-1985	NHL	80	41	27	12	309	262	94	.588
1985-1986	NHL	80	40	33	7	330	280	87	.544
1986-1987	NHL	80	41	29	10	277	241	92	.575
1987-1988	NHL	80	45	22	13	298	238	103	.644
1988-1989	NHL	80	53	18	9	315	218	115	.719
1989-1990	NHL	80	41	28	11	288	234	93	.581
1990-1991	NHL	80	39	30	11	273	249	89	.556
1991-1992	NHL	80	41	28	11	267	207	93	.581
1992-1993	NHL	84	48	30	6	326	280	102	.607
1993-1994	NHL	84	41	29	14	283	248	96	.571
1994-1995	NHL	48	18	23	7	125	148	43	.448
1995-1996	NHL	82	40	32	10	265	248	90	.549
TOTAL:	86 years	5028	2649	1624	755	17137	13543	6053	
AVERAGE:		58	31	18	9	199	157	71	.602

Playoff Record

Season	GP	W	L	T	GF	GA	Result
1913-1914	2	1	1	0	2	6	Lost championship series to Toronto.
1915-1916	5	3	2	0	15	13	**Won Stanley Cup**.
1916-1917	6	2	4	0	18	29	Lost Stanley Cup final to Seattle.
1917-1918	2	1	1	0	7	10	Lost League playoff to Toronto.
1918-1919	10	6	3	1	36	37	Stanley Cup final canceled.
1922-1923	2	1	1	0	2	3	Lost League playoff to Ottawa.
1923-1924	6	6	0	0	19	6	**Won Stanley Cup**.
1924-1925	6	3	3	0	13	18	Lost Stanley Cup final to Victoria.
1926-1927	4	1	1	2	3	6	Lost semifinal series to Ottawa.
1927-1928	2	0	1	1	2	3	Lost semifinal series to Maroons.
1928-1929	3	0	3	0	2	5	Lost semifinal series to Boston.
1929-1930	6	5	0	1	14	6	**Won Stanley Cup**.
1930-1931	10	6	4	0	23	21	**Won Stanley Cup**.
1931-1932	4	1	3	0	9	13	Lost semifinal series to Rangers.
1932-1933	2	0	1	1	5	8	Lost quarterfinal series to Rangers.
1933-1934	2	0	1	1	3	4	Lost quarterfinal series to Chicago.
1934-1935	2	0	1	1	5	6	Lost quarterfinal series to Rangers.
1936-1937	5	2	3	0	8	13	Lost semifinal series to Detroit.
1937-1938	3	1	2	0	8	11	Lost quarterfinal series to Chicago.
1938-1939	3	1	2	0	5	8	Lost quarterfinal series to Detroit.
1940-1941	3	1	2	0	7	8	Lost quarterfinal series to Chicago.
1941-1942	3	1	2	0	8	8	Lost quarterfinal series to Detroit.
1942-1943	5	1	4	0	17	18	Lost semifinal series to Boston.
1943-1944	9	8	1	0	39	14	**Won Stanley Cup**.
1944-1945	6	2	4	0	21	15	Lost semifinal series to Toronto.
1945-1946	9	8	1	0	45	20	**Won Stanley Cup**.
1946-1947	11	6	5	0	29	23	Lost Stanley Cup final to Toronto.
1948-1949	7	3	4	0	14	17	Lost semifinal series to Detroit.
1949-1950	5	1	4	0	7	15	Lost semifinal series to Rangers
1950-1951	11	5	6	0	23	25	Lost Stanley Cup final to Toronto.
1951-1952	11	4	7	0	20	23	Lost Stanley Cup final to Detroit.
1952-1953	12	8	4	0	34	23	**Won Stanley Cup**.
1953-1954	11	7	4	0	28	18	Lost Stanley Cup final to Detroit.

1954-1955	12	7	5	0	36	36	Lost Stanley Cup final to Detroit.
1955-1956	10	8	2	0	42	18	**Won Stanley Cup**.
1956-1957	10	8	2	0	37	18	**Won Stanley Cup**.
1957-1958	10	8	2	0	35	20	**Won Stanley Cup**.
1958-1959	11	8	3	0	40	25	**Won Stanley Cup**.
1959-1960	8	8	0	0	29	11	**Won Stanley Cup**.
1960-1961	6	2	4	0	15	16	Lost semifinal series to Chicago.
1961-1962	6	2	4	0	13	19	Lost semifinal series to Chicago.
1962-1963	5	1	4	0	6	14	Lost semifinal series to Toronto.
1963-1964	7	3	4	0	14	17	Lost semifinal series to Toronto.
1964-1965	13	8	5	0	35	26	**Won Stanley Cup**.
1965-1966	10	8	2	0	33	20	**Won Stanley Cup**.
1966-1967	10	6	4	0	30	25	Lost Stanley Cup final to Toronto.
1967-1968	13	12	1	0	48	25	**Won Stanley Cup**.
1968-1969	14	12	2	0	43	26	**Won Stanley Cup**.
1970-1971	20	12	8	0	75	63	**Won Stanley Cup**.
1971-1972	6	2	4	0	14	19	Lost quarterfinal series to Rangers.
1972-1973	17	12	5	0	73	52	**Won Stanley Cup**.
1973-1974	6	2	4	0	17	21	Lost quarterfinal series to Rangers.
1974-1975	11	6	5	0	49	30	Lost semifinal series to Buffalo.
1975-1976	13	12	1	0	44	26	**Won Stanley Cup**.
1976-1977	14	12	2	0	54	23	**Won Stanley Cup**.
1977-1978	15	12	3	0	58	29	**Won Stanley Cup**.
1978-1979	16	12	4	0	63	41	**Won Stanley Cup**.
1979-1980	10	6	4	0	39	26	Lost quarterfinal series to Minnesota.
1980-1981	3	0	3	0	6	15	Lost preliminary series to Edmonton.
1981-1982	5	2	3	0	16	11	Lost preliminary series to Quebec.
1982-1983	3	0	3	0	2	8	Lost preliminary series to Buffalo.
1983-1984	15	9	6	0	42	32	Lost semifinal series to Islanders
1984-1985	12	6	6	0	43	41	Lost quarterfinal series to Quebec.
1985-1986	20	15	5	0	56	41	**Won Stanley Cup**.
1986-1987	17	10	7	0	67	54	Lost semifinal series to Philadelphia.
1987-1988	11	5	6	0	33	35	Lost quarterfinal series to Boston.
1988-1989	21	14	7	0	67	51	Lost Stanley Cup final to Calgary.
1989-1990	11	5	6	0	31	29	Lost quarterfinal series to Boston.
1990-1991	13	7	6	0	47	42	Lost quarterfinal series to Boston.
1991-1992	11	4	7	0	29	32	Lost quarterfinal series to Boston.
1992-1993	20	16	4	0	66	51	**Won Stanley Cup**.
1993-1994	7	3	4	0	20	22	Lost preliminary series to Boston.
1995-1996	6	2	4	0	17	19	Lost preliminary series to Rangers.
TOTAL:	636	382	246	8	1975	1582	
AVERAGE:	9	5	4	0	27	22	

COACHING HISTORY: 1910-1920 George Kennedy 106-95-1-.527; 1920-1925 Leo Dandurand 68-53-5-.560; 1925-1932 Cecil Hart 159-96-49-.604; 1932-1935 Newsy Lalonde 45-53-14-.464; 1934-1935 Leo Dandurand 14-15-3-.484; 1935-1936 Sylvio Mantha 11-26-11-.344; 1936-1939 Cecil Hart 48-53-25-.480; 1938-1939 Jules Dugal 9-6-3-.583; 1939-1940 Alfred Lepine 10-33-5-.260; 1940-1955 Dick Irvin 431-313-152-.566; 1955-1968 Hector Blake 500-255-159-.634; 1968-1971 Claude Ruel 95-49-31-.631; 1970-1971 Al MacNeil 31-15-9-.645; 1971-1979 Scotty Bowman 419-110-105-.744; 1979-1980 Bernie Geoffrion 15-9-6-.600; 1979-1981 Claude Ruel 77-33-20-.669; 1981-1984 Bob Berry 116-71-36-.601; 1983-1985 Jacques Lemaire 48-37-12-.557; 1985-1988 Jean Perron 126-84-30-.588; 1988-1992 Pat Burns 174-104-42-.609; 1992-1996 Jacques Demers 107-86-27-.548; 1995-1996 Steve Shutt and Jacques Laperriere 0-1-0-.000; 1995-present Mario Tremblay

MONTREAL CONCORDE
(were Montreal Alouettes)
(became Montreal Alouettes)

Home City: Montreal, Quebec
Home Stadium: Olympic Stadium Capacity: 58,500 [1985]
Origin of Name: Named after the supersonic transport plane which first flew in 1976.

Regular Season Record

Season	League	GP	W	L	T	PF	PA	Pts	Pct
1982	CFL	16	2	14	0	267	502	4	.125
1983	CFL	16	5	10	1	367	447	11	.344
1984	CFL	16	6	9	1	386	404	13	.406
1985	CFL	16	8	8	0	284	332	16	.500
TOTAL:	4 years	64	21	41	2	1304	1685	44	
AVERAGE:		16	5	10	1	326	421	11	.344

Playoff Record

Season	GP	W	L	PF	PA	Result
1984	1	0	1	11	17	Lost Division semifinal to Hamilton.
1985	2	1	1	56	70	Lost Division final to Hamilton.
TOTAL:	3	1	2	67	87	
AVERAGE:	2	1	1	34	44	

COACHING HISTORY: 1982-1985 Joe Galat 19-41-2-.323; 1985 Gary Durchik 2-0-0-1.000

MONTREAL EXPOS

Home City: Montreal, Quebec
Home Stadium: Jarry Park (1969-1976) Capacity: 28,456 [1969]
Olympic Stadium (1977-present) Capacity: 46,500 [1995]
Origin of Name: The team was named after Expo '67, the World's Fair held in Montreal in 1967.

Regular Season Record

Season	League	GP	W	L	Pct	GB	R	OR
1969	NL	162	52	110	.321	48	582	791
1970	NL	162	73	89	.451	16	687	807
1971	NL	161	71	90	.441	25.5	622	729
1972	NL	156	70	86	.449	26.5	513	609
1973	NL	162	79	83	.488	3.5	668	702
1974	NL	161	79	82	.491	8.5	662	657
1975	NL	162	75	87	.463	17.5	601	690
1976	NL	162	55	107	.340	46	531	734
1977	NL	162	75	87	.463	26	665	736
1978	NL	162	76	86	.469	14	633	611
1979	NL	160	95	65	.594	2	701	581
1980	NL	162	90	72	.556	1	694	629
1981	NL	108	60	48	.556	NA	443	394
1982	NL	162	86	76	.531	6	697	616
1983	NL	162	82	80	.506	8	677	646
1984	NL	161	78	83	.484	18	593	585

1985	NL	161	84	77	.522	16.5	633	636
1986	NL	161	78	83	.484	29.5	637	688
1987	NL	162	91	71	.562	4	741	720
1988	NL	162	81	81	.500	20	628	592
1989	NL	162	81	81	.500	12	632	630
1990	NL	162	85	77	.525	10	662	598
1991	NL	161	71	90	.441	26.5	579	655
1992	NL	162	87	75	.537	9	648	581
1993	NL	162	94	68	.580	3	732	682
1994	NL	114	74	40	.649	-	585	454
1995	NL	144	66	78	.458	24	621	638
TOTAL:	27 years	4240	2088	2152		421	17067	17391
AVERAGE:		157	77	80	.492	16	632	644

Playoff Record

Season	GP	W	L	R	OR	Result
1981	10	5	5	26	29	Lost NLCS to Los Angeles.

COACHING HISTORY: 1969-1975 Gene Mauch 499-627-.443; 1976 Karl Kuehl 43-85-.336; 1976 Charlie Fox 12-22-.353; 1977-1981 Dick Williams 380-347-.523; 1981-1982 Jim Fanning 102-87-.540; 1983-1984 Bill Virdon 146-147-.498; 1984 Jim Fanning 14-16-.467; 1985-1991 Buck Rodgers 520-499-.510; 1991-1992 Tom Runnells 68-81-.456; 1992-present Felipe Alou

MONTREAL MACHINE

Home City: Montreal, Quebec
Home Stadium: Olympic Stadium — Capacity: 61,000 [1991]
Origin of Name:

Regular Season Record

Season	League	GP	W	L	T	PF	PA	Pct
1991	WLAF	10	4	6	0	145	244	.400
1992	WFL	10	2	8	0	175	274	.200
TOTAL:	2 years	20	6	14	0	320	518	
AVERAGE:		10	3	7	0	160	259	.300

COACHING HISTORY: 1991-1992 Jacques Dussault 6-14-0-.300

MONTREAL MANIC
(were Philadelphia Fury)

Home City: Montreal, Quebec
Home Field: Olympic Stadium — Capacity: 58,500
Origin of Name: The team was named for the Manicouagan River in northern Quebec.

Regular Season Record

Season	League	GP	W	L	GF	GA	BP	Pts	Pct
1981	NASL	32	15	17	63	57	55	141	.294
1982	NASL	32	19	13	60	43	49	159	.331
1983	NASL	30	12	18	58	71	52	124	.276
TOTAL:	3 years	94	46	48	181	171	156	424	
AVERAGE:		31	15	16	60	57	52	141	.301

Playoff Record

Season	GP	W	L	GF	GA	Result
1981	6	3	3	16	17	Lost 2nd round series to Chicago.
1982	3	1	2	4	7	Lost 1st round series to Fort Lauderdale.
1983	5	3	2	7	7	Lost 2nd round series to Tulsa.
TOTAL:	14	7	7	27	31	
AVERAGE:	5	2	3	9	10	

COACHING HISTORY: 1981-1982 Eddie Firmani 34-30; 1983 Andy Lynch 12-18

MONTREAL MAROONS

Home City: Montreal, Quebec
Home Arena: Montreal Forum Capacity: 15,500
Origin of Name: Like many other teams the team was named after the color of their uniforms.

Regular Season Record

Season	League	GP	W	L	T	GF	GA	Pts	Pct
1924-1925	NHL	30	9	19	2	45	65	20	.333
1925-1926	NHL	36	20	11	5	91	73	45	.625
1926-1927	NHL	44	20	20	4	71	68	44	.500
1927-1928	NHL	44	24	14	6	96	77	54	.614
1928-1929	NHL	44	15	20	9	67	65	39	.443
1929-1930	NHL	44	23	16	5	141	114	51	.580
1930-1931	NHL	44	20	18	6	105	106	46	.523
1931-1932	NHL	48	19	22	7	142	139	45	.469
1932-1933	NHL	48	22	20	6	135	119	50	.521
1933-1934	NHL	48	19	18	11	117	122	49	.510
1934-1935	NHL	48	24	19	5	123	92	53	.552
1935-1936	NHL	48	22	16	10	114	106	54	.563
1936-1937	NHL	48	22	17	9	126	110	53	.552
1937-1938	NHL	48	12	30	6	101	149	30	.313
TOTAL:	14 years	622	271	260	91	1474	1405	633	
AVERAGE:		44	19	18	7	105	100	45	.509

Playoff Record

Season	GP	W	L	T	GF	GA	Result
1925-1926	8	5	1	2	18	8	**Won Stanley Cup**.
1926-1927	2	0	1	1	1	2	Lost quarterfinal series to Canadiens.
1927-1928	9	5	3	1	12	8	Lost Stanley Cup final to Rangers.
1929-1930	4	1	3	0	5	11	Lost semifinal series to Boston.
1930-1931	2	0	2	0	1	8	Lost quarterfinal series to Rangers.
1931-1932	4	1	1	2	6	5	Lost semifinal series to Toronto.
1932-1933	2	0	2	0	2	5	Lost quarterfinal series to Detroit.
1933-1934	4	1	2	1	4	7	Lost semifinal series to Chicago.
1934-1935	7	5	0	2	16	8	**Won Stanley Cup**.
1935-1936	3	0	3	0	1	6	Lost semifinal series to Detroit.
1936-1937	5	2	3	0	8	11	Lost semifinal series to Rangers.
TOTAL:	50	20	21	9	74	79	
AVERAGE:	5	2	2	1	7	7	

COACHING HISTORY: 1924-1929 Eddie Gerard 88-84-26-.510; 1929-1931 Duncan Munro 37-29-10-.553; 1930-1931 George Boucher 6-5-1-.542; 1931-1932 Sprague Cleghorn 19-22-7-.469; 1932-1934 Eddie Gerard 41-38-17-.516; 1934-1938 Tommy Gorman 74-71-29-.509; 1937-1938 "King" Clancy 6-11-1-.361

MONTREAL OLYMPIQUES

Home City: Montreal, Quebec
Home Field: The Autostade [1971,1973] Capacity: 33,212 [1974
Molson Stadium (McGill University) [1972]
Origin of Name: Les Olympiques de Montreal were named such because Montreal had been awarded the 1976 Olympic Games.

Regular Season Record

Season	League	GP	W	L	T	GF	GA	BP	Pts	Pct
1971	NASL	24	4	15	5	29	58	26	65	.301
1972	NASL	14	4	5	5	19	20	18	57	.452
1973	NASL	19	5	10	4	25	32	22	64	.374
TOTAL:	3 years	57	13	30	14	73	110	66	186	
AVERAGE:		19	4	10	5	24	37	22	62	.363

COACHING HISTORY: 1971 Renato Tofani 4-15-5-.301; 1972-1973 Graham Adams 9-15-9-.407

MONTREAL SHAMROCKS

Home City: Montreal, Quebec
Home Arena: Wood Avenue Arena Capacity: 4,300
Origin of Name: The team was originally the Montreal Crystals of the Amateur Hockey Association and when the team became affiliated with the Shamrock Amateur Athletic Association they changed their name to Shamrocks.

Regular Season Record

Season	League	GP	W	L	T	GF	GA	Pts	Pct
1908-1909	ECHA	12	2	10	0	56	103	4	.167
1909-1910	NHA	12	3	8	1	52	95	7	.292
TOTAL:	2 years	24	5	18	1	108	198	11	
AVERAGE:		12	3	9	0	54	99	6	.229

COACHING HISTORY:

MONTREAL WANDERERS

Home City: Montreal, Quebec
Home Arena: Wood Avenue Arena Capacity: 4,300
Origin of Name:

Regular Season Record

Season	League	GP	W	L	T	GF	GA	Pts	Pct
1908-1909	ECHA	12	9	3	0	82	61	18	.750
1909-1910	NHA	12	11	1	0	91	41	22	.917

1910-1911	NHA	16	7	9	0	73	88	14	.438
1911-1912	NHA	18	9	9	0	95	96	18	.500
1912-1913	NHA	20	10	10	0	93	90	20	.500
1913-1914	NHA	20	7	13	0	102	125	14	.350
1914-1915	NHA	20	14	6	0	127	82	28	.700
1915-1916	NHA	24	10	14	0	90	116	20	.417
1916-1917	NHA	20	5	15	0	94	137	10	.250
1917-1918	NHL	6	1	5	0	17	35	2	.167
TOTAL:	10 years	168	83	85	0	864	871	166	
AVERAGE:		17	8	9	0	86	87	16	.494

Playoff Record

Season	GP	W	L	GF	GA	Result
1908-1909	2	1	1	13	10	Won playoff series with Edmonton.
1909-1910	1	1	0	7	3	**Won Stanley Cup**.
1914-1915	2	1	1	1	4	Lost championship series with Ottawa.
TOTAL:	5	3	2	21	17	
AVERAGE:	2	1	1	7	6	

COACHING HISTORY: 1910-1911 Dick Boon 7-9-0-.438; 1917-1918 Art Ross 1-5-0-.167

MOOSE JAW ORPHANS

(Saskatoon Sheiks became Moose Jaw Orphans-in mid 1921-1922 season)

Home City: Moose Jaw, Saskatchewan
Home Arena:
Origin of Name: Named Orphans because the team was homeless when they left Saskatoon.

Regular Season Record

Season	League	GP	W	L	T	GF	GA	Pts	Pct
1921-1922	WCHA	10	1	9	0	24	60	2	.100

COACHING HISTORY:

NEW ENGLAND PATRIOTS

(were Boston Patriots)

Home City: Foxboro, Massachusetts
Home Stadium: Foxboro Stadium* Capacity: 60,290 [1995]
Origin of Name: The team kept the same nickname after moving from Boston to Foxboro.

Regular Season Record

Season	League	GP	W	L	T	PF	PA	Pct
1971	NFL	14	6	8	0	238	325	.429
1972	NFL	14	3	11	0	192	446	.214
1973	NFL	14	5	9	0	258	300	.357
1974	NFL	14	7	7	0	348	289	.500
1975	NFL	14	3	11	0	258	358	.214
1976	NFL	14	11	3	0	376	236	.786
1977	NFL	14	9	5	0	278	217	.643
1978	NFL	16	11	5	0	358	286	.688

1979	NFL	16	9	7	0	411	326	.563
1980	NFL	16	10	6	0	441	325	.625
1981	NFL	16	2	14	0	322	370	.125
1982	NFL	9	5	4	0	143	157	.556
1983	NFL	16	8	8	0	274	289	.500
1984	NFL	16	9	7	0	362	352	.563
1985	NFL	16	11	5	0	362	290	.688
1986	NFL	16	11	5	0	412	307	.688
1987	NFL	15	8	7	0	320	293	.533
1988	NFL	16	9	7	0	250	284	.563
1989	NFL	16	5	11	0	297	391	.313
1990	NFL	16	1	15	0	181	446	.063
1991	NFL	16	6	10	0	211	305	.375
1992	NFL	16	2	14	0	205	363	.125
1993	NFL	16	5	11	0	238	286	.313
1994	NFL	16	10	6	0	351	312	.625
1995	NFL	16	6	10	0	294	377	.375
TOTAL:	25 years	378	172	206	0	7380	7930	
AVERAGE:		15	7	8	0	295	317	.461

Playoff Record

Season	GP	W	L	PF	PA	Result
1976	1	0	1	21	24	Lost Divisional playoff to Oakland.
1978	1	0	1	14	31	Lost Divisional playoff to Houston.
1982	1	0	1	13	28	Lost 1st round series to Miami.
1985	4	3	1	94	94	Lost Super Bowl game to Chicago.
1986	1	0	1	17	22	Lost Divisional playoff to Denver.
1994	1	0	1	13	20	Lost Wild Card game to Cleveland.
TOTAL:	9	3	6	172	219	
AVERAGE:	2	1	1	29	37	

COACHING HISTORY: 1971-1972 John Mazur 8-15-0-.348; 1972 Phil Bengtson 1-4-0-.200; 1973-1978 Chuck Fairbanks 46-39-0-.541; 1978 Ron Erhardt & Hank Bullough 0-1-0-.000; 1979-1981 Ron Erhardt 21-27-0-.438; 1982-1984 Ron Meyers 18-15-0-.545; 1984-1989 Raymond Berry 48-38-0-.558; 1990 Rod Rust 1-15-0-.063; 1991-1992 Dick MacPherson 6-18-0-.250; 1992 Dante Scarnecchia 2-6-0-.250; 1993-present Bill Parcells

*Originally known as Schaefer Stadium from 1971 to 1982 and then Sullivan Stadium from 1983 to 1989.

NEW ENGLAND TEA MEN
(became Jacksonville Tea Men)

Home City: Foxboro, Massachusetts
Home Stadium: Schaefer Stadium — Capacity: 61,279 [1980]
Origin of Name: The team was owned by the Lipton Tea Company.

Regular Season Record

Season	League	GP	W	L	GF	GA	BP	Pts	Pct
1978	NASL	30	19	11	62	39	51	165	.611
1979	NASL	30	12	18	41	56	38	110	.407

1980	NASL	32	18	14	54	56	46	154	.535
TOTAL:	3 years	92	49	43	157	151	135	429	
AVERAGE:		31	16	15	52	50	45	143	.518

Playoff Record

Season	GP	W	L	GF	GA	Result
1978	1	0	1	1	3	Lost 1st round game to Fort Lauderdale.
1980	2	0	2	0	5	Lost 1st round game to Tampa Bay.
TOTAL:	3	0	3	1	8	
AVERAGE:	2	0	2	1	4	

COACHING HISTORY: 1978-1980 Noel Cantwell 49-43

NEW ENGLAND WHALERS
(became Hartford Whalers)

Home City: Boston, Massachusetts (1972-1974)
Springfield, Massachusetts (1974-1975, 1977-1979)
Hartford, Connecticut (1974-1978)

Home Arena: Boston Garden (1972-1974) Capacity: 14,994 [1972]
West Springfield Big E (1974-1975) Capacity: 5,513 [1974]
Hartford Civic Center (1974-1978) Capacity: 10,507 [1974]
Springfield Civic Center (1977-1979) Capacity: 7,725 [1977]

Origin of Name: The name was picked because the New England area is well known as a whaling area and chosen by team executives.

Regular Season Record

Season	League	GP	W	L	T	GF	GA	Pts	Pct
1972-1973	WHA	78	46	30	2	318	263	94	.603
1973-1974	WHA	78	43	31	4	291	260	90	.577
1974-1975	WHA	78	43	30	5	274	279	91	.583
1975-1976	WHA	80	33	40	7	255	290	73	.456
1976-1977	WHA	81	35	40	6	275	290	76	.469
1977-1978	WHA	80	44	31	5	335	269	93	.581
1978-1979	WHA	80	37	34	9	298	287	83	.519
TOTAL:	7 years	555	281	236	38	2046	1938	600	
AVERAGE:		79	40	34	5	292	277	85	.538

Playoff Record

Season	GP	W	L	GF	GA	Result
1972-1973	15	12	3	30	48	**Won WHA championship**.
1973-1974	7	3	4	23	24	Lost quarterfinal series to Chicago.
1974-1975	6	2	4	17	28	Lost quarterfinal series to Minnesota.
1975-1976	17	10	7	54	40	Lost semifinal series to Houston.
1976-1977	5	1	4	14	23	Lost quarterfinal series to Quebec.
1977-1978	14	8	6	56	47	Lost championship series to Winnipeg.
1978-1979	10	5	5	39	42	Lost semifinal series to Edmonton.
TOTAL:	74	41	33	233	252	
AVERAGE:	11	6	5	33	36	

COACHING HISTORY: 1972-1973 Jack Kelley 46-30-2-.603; 1973-1975 Ron Ryan 83-59-9-.579; 1974-1976 Jack Kelley 17-18-3-.487; 1975-1976 Don Blackburn 14-18-3-.443; 1975-1978 Harry Neale 84-77-12-.520; 1978-1979 Bill Dineen 37-34-9-.519

NEW JERSEY AMERICANS
(became New York Nets)

Home City: Teaneck, New Jersey
Home Court: Teaneck Armory Capacity: 3,500
Origin of Name: The team adopted the league name as their own.

Regular Season Record

Season	**League**	**GP**	**W**	**L**	**PPGF**	**PPGA**	**Pct**	**GB**
1967-1968	ABA	78	36	42	110.8	112.4	.462	18

COACHING HISTORY: Max Zaslofsky 36-42-.462

NEW JERSEY DEVILS
(were Colorado Rockies)

Home City: East Rutherford, New Jersey
Home Arena: Meadowlands Arena Capacity: 19,040 [1995]
Origin of Name: The name was suggested by the mythical Jersey Devil, a creature that first appeared in 1735. Rumors continue circulating about it to the present day.

Regular Season Record

Season	**League**	**GP**	**W**	**L**	**T**	**GF**	**GA**	**Pts**	**Pct**
1982-1983	NHL	80	17	49	14	230	338	48	.300
1983-1984	NHL	80	17	56	7	231	350	41	.256
1984-1985	NHL	80	22	48	10	264	346	54	.338
1985-1986	NHL	80	28	49	3	300	374	59	.369
1986-1987	NHL	80	29	45	6	293	368	64	.400
1987-1988	NHL	80	38	36	6	295	296	82	.513
1988-1989	NHL	80	27	41	12	281	325	66	.413
1989-1990	NHL	80	37	34	9	295	288	83	.519
1990-1991	NHL	80	32	33	15	272	264	79	.494
1991-1992	NHL	80	38	31	11	289	259	87	.544
1992-1993	NHL	84	40	37	7	308	299	87	.518
1993-1994	NHL	84	47	25	12	307	220	106	.631
1994-1995	NHL	48	22	18	8	136	121	52	.542
1995-1996	NHL	82	37	33	12	215	202	86	.524
TOTAL:	14 years	1098	431	535	132	3716	4050	994	
AVERAGE:		78	31	38	9	266	289	71	.453

Playoff Record

Season	**GP**	**W**	**L**	**GF**	**GA**	**Result**
1987-1988	20	11	9	67	71	Lost semifinal series to Boston.
1989-1990	6	2	4	18	21	Lost preliminary series to Washington.
1990-1991	7	3	4	21	21	Lost preliminary series to Pittsburgh.
1991-1992	7	3	4	25	28	Lost preliminary series to Rangers.
1992-1993	5	1	4	13	23	Lost preliminary series to Pittsburgh.

1993-1994	20	11	9	52	49	Lost semifinal series to Rangers.
1994-1995	20	16	4	67	34	**Won Stanley Cup.**
TOTAL:	85	47	38	263	247	
AVERAGE:	12	7	5	38	35	

COACHING HISTORY: 1982-1984 Billy MacMillan 19-67-14-.260; 1983-1984 Tom McVie 15-38-7-.308; 1984-1988 Doug Carpenter 100-166-24-.386; 1987-1990 Jim Schoenfeld 50-59-15-.464; 1989-1991 John Cunniff 59-56-18-.511; 1991-1992 Tom McVie 42-36-15-.532; 1992-4993 Herb Brooks 40-37-7-.518; 1993-present Jacques Lemaire

NEW JERSEY GENERALS

Home City: East Rutherford, New Jersey
Home Stadium: Giants Stadium Capacity: 76,891 [1984]
Origin of Name: The name was chosen by team executives to indicate the regional nature of the franchise .

Regular Season Record

Season	League	GP	W	L	T	PF	PA	Pct
1983	USFL	18	6	12	0	314	437	.333
1984	USFL	18	14	4	0	430	312	.778
1985	USFL	18	11	7	0	418	377	.611
TOTAL:	3 years	54	31	23	0	1162	1126	
AVERAGE:		18	10	8	0	387	375	.556

Playoff Record

Season	GP	W	L	PF	PA	Result
1984	1	0	1	17	28	Lost 1st round game to Philadelphia.
1985	1	0	1	17	20	Lost 1st round game to Baltimore.
TOTAL:	2	0	2	34	48	
AVERAGE:	1	0	1	17	24	

COACHING HISTORY: 1983 Chuck Fairbanks 6-12-0-.333; 1984-1985 Walt Michaels 25-11-0-.694

NEW JERSEY KNIGHTS

(New York Golden Blades became the Knights in mid 1974 season)

Home City: Cherry Hill, New Jersey
Home Arena: Cherry Hill Arena — Capacity: 4,000
Origin of Name: The name was chosen by the league.

Season	League	GP	W	L	T	GF	GA	Pts	Pct
			Regular Season Record						
1973-1974	WHA	58	26	30	2	221	233	54	.466

COACHING HISTORY: Harry Howell 26-30-2-.466

NEW JERSEY NETS

(were New York Nets)

Home City: Piscataway, New Jersey (1977-1981)
East Rutherford, New Jersey (1981-present)
Home Court: Rutgers Athletic Center (1977-1981) — Capacity: 9,050 [1980]
Byrne Meadowlands Arena (1981-present) — Capacity: 20,039 [1995]
Origin of Name: The team kept the same nickname after moving from New York to New Jersey.

Season	League	GP	W	L	PPGF	PPGA	Pct	GB
			Regular Season Record					
1977-1978	NBA	82	24	58	106.7	112.5	.293	31
1978-1979	NBA	82	37	45	107.7	111.9	.451	17
1979-1980	NBA	82	34	48	108.3	109.5	.415	27
1980-1981	NBA	82	24	58	106.9	113.0	.293	38
1981-1982	NBA	82	44	38	106.7	106.0	.537	19
1982-1983	NBA	82	49	33	105.8	103.0	.598	16
1983-1984	NBA	82	45	37	110.0	108.9	.549	17
1984-1985	NBA	82	42	40	109.5	109.2	.512	21
1985-1986	NBA	82	39	43	109.1	111.1	.476	28
1986-1987	NBA	82	24	58	108.5	113.5	.293	35
1987-1988	NBA	82	19	63	100.4	108.5	.232	38
1988-1989	NBA	82	26	56	103.7	110.1	.317	26
1989-1990	NBA	82	17	65	100.1	108.0	.207	36
1990-1991	NBA	82	26	56	102.9	107.5	.317	30
1991-1992	NBA	82	40	42	105.4	107.1	.488	11
1992-1993	NBA	82	43	39	102.8	101.6	.524	17
1993-1994	NBA	82	45	37	103.2	101.0	.549	12
1994-1995	NBA	82	30	52	98.1	101.2	.366	27
1995-1996	NBA	82	30	52	93.7	97.9	.366	30
TOTAL:	19 years	1558	638	920				476
AVERAGE:		82	34	48	104.7	107.4	.409	25

Playoff Record

Season	GP	W	L	PPGF	PPGA	Result
1978-1979	2	0	2	107.5	116.5	Lost 1st round series to Philadelphia.
1981-1982	2	0	2	87.5	99.5	Lost 1st round series to Washington.
1982-1983	2	0	2	103.0	111.5	Lost 1st round series to New York.
1983-1984	11	5	6	101.2	100.7	Lost Conf. semifinal to Milwaukee.
1984-1985	3	0	3	110.3	120.7	Lost 1st round series to Detroit.
1985-1986	3	0	3	105.7	116.0	Lost 1st round series to Milwaukee.
1991-1992	4	1	3	101.8	110.0	Lost 1st round series to Cleveland.
1992-1993	5	2	3	93.6	96.8	Lost 1st round series to Cleveland.
1993-1994	4	1	3	86.5	93.8	Lost 1st round series to New York.
TOTAL:	36	9	27			
AVERAGE:	4	1	3	99.7	107.3	

COACHING HISTORY: 1977-1981 Kevin Loughery 107-174-.381; 1980-1981 Bob MacKinnon 12-35-.255; 1981-1983 Larry Brown 91-67-.576; 1982-1983 Bill Blair 2-4-.333; 1983-1985 Stan Albeck 87-77-.530; 1985-1988 Dave Wohl 65-114-.363; 1987-1988 Bob MacKinnon 10-29-.256; 1987-1989 Willis Reed 33-77-.300; 1989-1992 Bill Fitch 83-163-.337; 1992-1994 Chuck Daly 88-76-.537; 1994-1996 Butch Beard 60-104-.366; 1996-present

NEW ORLEANS BREAKERS

(were Boston Breakers)
(became Portland Breakers)

Home City: New Orleans, Louisiana
Home Stadium: Louisiana Superdome — Capacity: 71,330 [1984]
Origin of Name: The team kept the same nickname when it moved from Boston to New Orleans.

Regular Season Record

Season	League	GP	W	L	T	PF	PA	Pct
1984	USFL	18	8	10	0	348	395	.444

COACHING HISTORY: Dick Coury 8-10-0-.444

NEW ORLEANS BUCCANEERS

(became Memphis Pros)

Home City: New Orleans, Louisiana
Home Court: Loyola University Fieldhouse — Capacity: 6,425
Origin of Name:

Regular Season Record

Season	League	GP	W	L	PPGF	PPGA	Pct	GB
1967-1968	ABA	78	48	30	111.7	106.9	.615	-
1968-1969	ABA	78	46	32	116.1	112.7	.590	14
1969-1970	ABA	84	42	42	107.9	107.1	.500	9
TOTAL:	3 years	240	136	104				23
AVERAGE:		80	45	35	111.9	108.9	.563	8

Playoff Record

Season	GP	W	L	PPGF	PPGA	Result
1967-1968	17	10	7	109.2	106.5	Lost championship series to Pittsburgh.
1968-1969	11	4	7	115.0	119.0	Lost 2nd round series to Oakland.
TOTAL:	28	14	14			
AVERAGE:	14	7	7	112.1	112.8	

COACHING HISTORY: 1967-1970 Babe McCarthy 136-104-.563

NEW ORLEANS JAZZ

(became Utah Jazz)

Home City: New Orleans, Louisiana
Home Court: Municipal Auditorium (1974-1975) Capacity: 7,853
Louisiana Superdome (1974-1979) Capacity: 47,284
Origin of Name: The name was chosen because New Orleans is well known for its jazz music, and was chosen in a Name the Team Contest.

Regular Season Record

Season	League	GP	W	L	PPGF	PPGA	Pct	GB
1974-1975	NBA	82	23	59	101.5	109.3	.280	37
1975-1976	NBA	82	38	44	104.1	105.0	.463	11
1976-1977	NBA	82	35	47	104.6	107.4	.427	14
1977-1978	NBA	82	39	43	107.6	109.5	.476	13
1978-1979	NBA	82	26	56	108.3	114.6	.317	22
TOTAL:	5 years	410	161	249				97
AVERAGE:		82	32	50	105.2	109.2	.393	19

COACHING HISTORY: 1974-1975 Scotty Robertson 1-14-.067; 1974-1975 Elgin Baylor 0-1-.000; 1974-1977 Butch van Breda Kolff 74-100-.425; 1976-1979 Elgin Baylor 86-134-.391

NEW ORLEANS SAINTS

Home City: New Orleans, Louisiana
Home Stadium: Tulane Stadium (1967-1974) Capacity: 80,985 [1974]
Louisiana Superdome (1975-present) Capacity: 69,065 [1995]
Origin of Name: Named Saints because the team's fight song was "When the Saints Go Marching In" and the franchise was awarded on All Saints Day in 1966.

Regular Season Record

Season	League	GP	W	L	T	PF	PA	Pct
1967	NFL	14	3	11	0	233	379	.214
1968	NFL	14	4	9	1	246	327	.321
1969	NFL	14	5	9	0	311	393	.357
1970	NFL	14	2	11	1	172	347	.179
1971	NFL	14	4	8	2	266	347	.357
1972	NFL	14	2	11	1	215	361	.179
1973	NFL	14	5	9	0	163	312	.357
1974	NFL	14	5	9	0	166	263	.357
1975	NFL	14	2	12	0	165	360	.143
1976	NFL	14	4	10	0	253	346	.286

1977	NFL	14	3	11	0	232	336	.214
1978	NFL	16	7	9	0	281	298	.438
1979	NFL	16	8	8	0	370	360	.500
1980	NFL	16	1	15	0	291	487	.063
1981	NFL	16	4	12	0	207	378	.250
1982	NFL	9	4	5	0	129	160	.444
1983	NFL	16	8	8	0	319	337	.500
1984	NFL	16	7	9	0	298	361	.438
1985	NFL	16	5	11	0	294	401	.313
1986	NFL	16	7	9	0	288	287	.438
1987	NFL	15	12	3	0	422	283	.800
1988	NFL	16	10	6	0	312	283	.625
1989	NFL	16	9	7	0	386	301	.563
1990	NFL	16	8	8	0	274	275	.500
1991	NFL	16	11	5	0	341	211	.688
1992	NFL	16	12	4	0	330	202	.750
1993	NFL	16	8	8	0	317	343	.500
1994	NFL	16	7	9	0	348	407	.438
1995	NFL	16	7	9	0	319	348	.438
TOTAL:	29 years	434	174	255	5	7948	9493	
AVERAGE:		15	6	9	0	274	327	.401

Playoff Record

Season	GP	W	L	PF	PA	Result
1987	1	0	1	10	44	Lost 1st round game to Minnesota.
1990	1	0	1	6	16	Lost Wild Card game to Chicago.
1991	1	0	1	20	27	Lost Wild Card game to Atlanta.
1992	1	0	1	20	36	Lost Wild Card game to Philadelphia.
TOTAL:	4	0	4	56	123	
AVERAGE:	1	0	1	14	31	

COACHING HISTORY: 1967-1970 Tom Fears 13-34-2-.286; 1970-1972 J.D. Roberts 7-25-3-.243; 1973-1975 John North 11-23-0-.324; 1975 Ernie Hefferle 1-7-0-.125; 1976-1977 Hank Stram 7-21-0-.250; 1978-1980 Dick Nolan 15-29-0-.341; 1980 Dick Stanfel 1-3-0-.250; 1981-1985 "Bum" Phillips 27-42-0-.391; 1985 Wade Phillips 1-3-0-.250; 1986-present Jim Mora

NEW WESTMINSTER ROYALS

(became Portland Rosebuds)

Home City: New Westminster, British Columbia
Home Arena: Vancouver Arena Capacity: 10,500
Origin of Name:

Regular Season Record

Season	League	GP	W	L	T	GF	GA	Pts	Pct
1911-1912	PCHA	15	9	6	0	78	77	18	.600
1912-1913	PCHA	15	6	9	0	67	74	12	.400
1913-1914	PCHA	16	7	9	0	75	81	14	.438
TOTAL:	3 years	46	22	24	0	220	232	44	
AVERAGE:		15	7	8	0	73	77	14	.478

COACHING HISTORY: 1911-1912 Jimmy Gardiner 9-6-0-.600; 1912-1914 Not Available

*A new arena had been planned for New Westminster but it was never completed and the team played all its home games in Vancouver.

NEW YORK AMERICANS

(were Hamilton Tigers)
(became Brooklyn Americans)

Home City: New York, New York
Home Arena: Madison Square Garden III — Capacity: 15,925
Origin of Name:

Regular Season Record

Season	League	GP	W	L	T	GF	GA	Pts	Pct
1925-1926	NHL	36	12	20	4	68	89	28	.389
1926-1927	NHL	44	17	25	2	82	91	36	.409
1927-1928	NHL	44	11	27	6	63	128	28	.318
1928-1929	NHL	44	19	13	12	53	53	50	.568
1929-1930	NHL	44	14	25	5	113	161	33	.375
1930-1931	NHL	44	18	16	10	76	74	46	.523
1931-1932	NHL	48	16	24	8	95	142	40	.417
1932-1933	NHL	48	15	22	11	91	118	41	.427
1933-1934	NHL	48	15	23	10	104	132	40	.417
1934-1935	NHL	48	12	27	9	100	142	33	.344
1935-1936	NHL	48	16	25	7	109	122	39	.406
1936-1937	NHL	48	15	29	4	122	161	34	.354
1937-1938	NHL	48	19	18	11	110	111	49	.510
1938-1939	NHL	48	17	21	10	119	157	44	.458
1939-1940	NHL	48	15	29	4	196	140	34	.354
1940-1941	NHL	48	8	29	11	99	186	27	.281
TOTAL:	16 years	736	239	373	124	1600	2007	602	
AVERAGE:		46	15	23	8	100	125	38	.409

Playoff Record

Season	GP	W	L	T	GF	GA	Result
1928-1929	2	0	1	1	0	1	Lost quarterfinal series to Rangers.
1935-1936	5	2	3	0	10	11	Lost semifinal series to Toronto.
1937-1938	6	3	3	0	13	12	Lost semifinal series to Chicago.
1938-1939	2	0	2	0	0	6	Lost quarterfinal series to Toronto.
1939-1940	3	1	2	0	7	9	Lost quarterfinal series to Detroit.
TOTAL:	18	6	11	1	30	39	
AVERAGE:	3	1	2	0	6	8	

COACHING HISTORY: 1925-1926 Tommy Gorman 12-20-4-.389; 1926-1927 Edouard Lalonde 17-25-2-.409; 1927-1928 Wilf Green 11-27-6-.318; 1928-1929 Tommy Gorman 19-13-12-.568; 1929-1930 Lionel Conacher 14-25-5-.375; 1930-1932 Eddie Gerard 34-40-18-.467; 1932-1935 Joe Simpson 42-72-30-.396; 1935-1941 Mervyn Dutton 90-151-47-.394

NEW YORK BULLDOGS
(were Boston Yanks)
(became New York Yanks)

Home City: New York, New York
Home Stadium: Polo Grounds — Capacity: 55,987
Origin of Name: The team was named by owner Ted Collins.

Regular Season Record

Season	League	GP	W	L	T	PF	PA	Pct
1949	NFL	12	1	10	1	153	368	.125

COACHING HISTORY: Charley Ewart 1-10-1-.125

NEW YORK CELTICS
(were Brooklyn Arcadians)

Home City: New York, New York
Home Court: Madison Square Garden III — Capacity: 15,925
Origin of Name: Due to poor attendance the Brooklyn team disbanded in 1927 and its record was assumed by the powerful barnstorming New York Celtic team.

Regular Season Record

Season	League	GP	W	L	Pct	GB
1927-1928	ABL	49	40	9	.899	-

Playoff Record

Season	GP	W	L	Result
1927-1928	6	5	1	**Won ABL championship**

COACHING HISTORY: John Whitty 40-9-.899

NEW YORK COSMOS
(were known as the Cosmos from 1977 to 1984)

Home City: New York, New York (1971-1976)
East Rutherford, New Jersey (1977-1984)
Home Stadium: Yankee Stadium (1971, 1976) — Capacity: 63,800
Hofstra Stadium (1972-1973) — Capacity:
Downing Stadium (1974-1975)* — Capacity: 21,000
Giants Stadium (1977-1984) — Capacity: 76,891 [1984]
Origin of Name: The name was chosen in a Name the Team Contest.

Regular Season Record

Season	League	GP	W	L	T	GF	GA	BP	Pts	Pct
1971	NASL	24	9	10	5	51	55	48	117	.542
1972	NASL	14	7	3	4	28	16	23	77	.611
1973	NASL	19	7	5	7	31	23	28	91	.532
1974	NASL	20	4	14	2	28	40	28	58	.322
1975	NASL	22	10	12	-	39	38	31	91	.460

1976	NASL	24	16	8	-	65	34	52	148	.685
1977	NASL	26	15	11	-	60	39	50	140	.598
1978	NASL	30	24	6	-	88	39	68	212	.785
1979	NASL	30	24	6	-	84	52	72	216	.800
1980	NASL	32	24	8	-	87	41	69	213	.740
1981	NASL	32	23	9	-	80	49	64	200	.417
1982	NASL	32	23	9	-	73	52	67	203	.423
1983	NASL	30	22	8	-	87	49	64	194	.431
1984	NASL	24	13	11	-	43	42	39	115	.319
TOTAL:	14 years	359	221	120	18	844	569	703	2075	
AVERAGE:		26	16	9	1	60	41	50	148	.527

Playoff Record

Season	**GP**	**W**	**L**	**T**	**GF**	**GA**	**Result**
1971	2	0	2	0	0	3	Lost 1st round series to Atlanta.
1972	2	2	0	0	3	1	**Won NASL championship**.
1973	1	0	1	0	0	1	Lost 1st round series to Dallas.
1976	2	1	1	0	3	3	Lost 2nd round game to Tampa Bay.
1977	6	6	0	0	22	8	**Won NASL championship**.
1978	7	6	1	0	21	12	**Won NASL championship**.
1979	8	5	3	0	14	10	Lost 3rd round series to Vancouver.
1980	8	7	1	0	25	9	**Won NASL championship**.
1981	6	4	2	0	18	11	Lost championship series to Chicago.
1982	6	5	1	0	11	3	**Won NASL championship**.
1983	2	0	2	0	2	5	Lost 1st round series to Montreal.
TOTAL:	50	36	14	0	119	66	
AVERAGE:	5	4	1	0	12	6	

COACHING HISTORY: 1971-1977 Gordon Bradley 57-54-18; 1976 Ken Furphy 8-6; 1977-1979 Eddie Firmani 36-11; 1979 Ray Klivecka 15-4; 1980-1981 Hennes Weisweiler 47-17; 1982-1983 Julio Mazzei 45-17; 1984 Eddie Firmani 13-11

*Also known as Triborough Stadium

NEW YORK GENERALS

Home City: New York, New York
Home Stadium: Yankee Stadium — Capacity: 67,000 [1967]
Origin of Name: The team was originally sponsored by RKO-GENERAL and adopted their name.

Regular Season Record

Season	**League**	**GP**	**W**	**L**	**T**	**GF**	**GA**	**BP**	**Pts**	**Pct**
1967	NPSL	32	11	13	8	60	58	NA	143	.496
1968	NASL	32	12	8	12	62	54	36	164	.569
TOTAL:	2 years	64	23	21	20	122	112	36	307	
AVERAGE:		32	12	10	10	61	56	18	154	.535

COACHING HISTORY: 1967-1968 Freddie Goodwin 23-21-20-

NEW YORK GIANTS
(were New York Gothams)
(became San Francisco Giants)

Home City: New York, New York
Home Field: Polo Grounds I (1886-1888) Capacity: 21,000
Manhattan Field (1889-1890) Capacity:
Polo Grounds II (1891-1957) Capacity: 55,987
Origin of Name: The team name was coined by then manager Jim Mutrie who said his players played like "Giants" after a particularly successful road trip.

Regular Season Record

Season	League	GP	W	L	Pct	GB	R	OR
1886	NL	119	75	44	.630	12.5	692	558
1887	NL	123	68	55	.553	10.5	816	723
1888	NL	131	84	47	.641	-	659	479
1889	NL	126	83	43	.659	-	935	708
1890	NL	131	63	68	.481	24	713	698
1891	NL	132	71	61	.538	13	754	711
1892	NL	151	71	80	.470	31.5	811	826
1893	NL	132	68	64	.515	19.5	941	845
1894	NL	132	88	44	.667	3	940	789
1895	NL	131	66	65	.504	21.5	852	834
1896	NL	131	64	67	.489	27	829	821
1897	NL	131	83	48	.634	9.5	895	695
1898	NL	150	77	73	.513	25.5	837	800
1899	NL	150	60	90	.400	42	734	863
1900	NL	138	60	78	.435	23	713	823
1901	NL	137	52	85	.380	37	544	755
1902	NL	136	48	88	.353	53.5	401	589
1903	NL	139	84	55	.604	6.5	729	548
1904	NL	153	106	47	.693	-	744	476
1905	NL	153	105	48	.686	-	780	504
1906	NL	152	96	56	.632	20	625	508
1907	NL	153	82	71	.536	25.5	573	511
1908	NL	154	98	56	.636	1	652	458
1909	NL	153	92	61	.601	18.5	621	546
1910	NL	154	91	63	.591	13	715	545
1911	NL	153	99	54	.647	-	756	542
1912	NL	151	103	48	.682	-	823	571
1913	NL	152	101	51	.664	-	684	502
1914	NL	154	84	70	.545	10.5	672	576
1915	NL	152	69	83	.454	21	582	628
1916	NL	152	86	66	.566	7	597	503
1917	NL	154	98	56	.636	-	635	457
1918	NL	124	71	53	.573	10.5	480	423
1919	NL	140	87	53	.621	9	605	470
1920	NL	154	86	68	.558	7	682	543
1921	NL	153	94	59	.614	-	840	637
1922	NL	154	93	61	.604	-	852	658
1923	NL	153	95	58	.621	-	854	679
1924	NL	153	93	60	.608	-	857	641
1925	NL	152	86	66	.566	8.5	736	702

1926	NL	151	74	77	.490	13.5	663	668
1927	NL	154	92	62	.597	2	817	720
1928	NL	154	93	61	.604	2	807	653
1929	NL	151	84	67	.556	13.5	897	709
1930	NL	154	87	67	.565	5	959	814
1931	NL	152	87	65	.572	13	768	599
1932	NL	154	72	82	.468	18	755	706
1933	NL	152	91	61	.599	-	636	515
1934	NL	153	93	60	.608	2	760	583
1935	NL	153	91	62	.595	8.5	770	675
1936	NL	154	92	62	.597	-	742	621
1937	NL	152	95	57	.625	-	732	602
1938	NL	150	83	67	.553	5	705	637
1939	NL	151	77	74	.510	18.5	703	685
1940	NL	152	72	80	.474	27.5	663	659
1941	NL	153	74	79	.484	25.5	667	706
1942	NL	152	85	67	.559	20	675	600
1943	NL	153	55	98	.359	49.5	558	713
1944	NL	154	67	87	.435	38	682	773
1945	NL	152	78	74	.513	19	668	700
1946	NL	154	61	93	.396	36	612	685
1947	NL	154	81	73	.526	13	830	761
1948	NL	154	78	76	.506	13.5	780	704
1949	NL	154	73	81	.474	24	736	693
1950	NL	154	86	68	.558	5	735	643
1951	NL	157	98	59	.624	-	781	641
1952	NL	154	92	62	.597	4.5	722	639
1953	NL	154	70	84	.455	35	768	747
1954	NL	154	97	57	.630	-	732	550
1955	NL	154	80	74	.519	18.5	702	673
1956	NL	154	67	87	.435	26	540	650
1957	NL	154	69	85	.448	26	643	701
TOTAL:	72 years	10645	5874	4771		993	52368	46570
AVERAGE:		148	82	66	.552	14	727	647

Playoff Record

Season	GP	W	L	T	R	OR	Result
1888	10	6	4	0	64	60	**Won World Series.**
1889	9	6	3	0	73	52	**Won World Series.**
1894	4	4	0	0	33	11	**Won Temple Cup.**
1905	5	4	1	0	15	3	**Won World Series.**
1911	6	2	4	0	13	27	Lost World Series to Philadelphia.
1912	8	3	4	1	31	25	Lost World Series to Boston.
1913	5	1	4	0	15	23	Lost World Series to Philadelphia.
1917	6	2	4	0	17	21	Lost World Series to Chicago.
1921	8	5	3	0	29	22	**Won World Series.**
1922	5	4	0	1	18	11	**Won World Series.**
1923	6	2	4	0	17	30	Lost World Series to Yankees.
1924	7	3	4	0	27	26	Lost World Series to Washington.
1933	5	4	1	0	16	11	**Won World Series.**
1936	6	2	4	0	23	43	Lost World Series to Yankees.
1937	5	1	4	0	12	28	Lost World Series to Yankees.
1951	6	2	4	0	18	29	Lost World Series to Yankees.

1954	4	4	0	0	21	9	Won World Series.
TOTAL:	105	55	48	2	442	431	
AVERAGE:	6	3	3	0	26	25	

COACHING HISTORY: 1886-1891 Jim Mutrie 444-318-.583; 1892 Pat Powers 71-80-.470; 1893-1894 Monte Ward 156-108-.591; 1895 George Davis 17-17-.500; 1895 Jack Doyle 31-31-.500; 1895 Harvey Watkins 18-17-.514; 1896 Arthur Irwin 38-53-.418; 1896-1898 Bill Joyce 177-122-,.,592; 1898 Cap Anson 9-13-.409; 1899 John Day 30-40-.429; 1899 Fred Hoey 30-50-.375; 1900 William Ewing 21-41-.339; 1900-1901 George Davis 91-122-.427; 1902 Horace Fogel 18-23-.439; 1902 George Smith 5-27-.156; 1902-1932 John McGraw 2658-1823-.593; 1932-1941 Bill Terry 823-661-.555; 1942-1948 Mel Ott 454-530-.461; 1948-1955 Leo Durocher 647-523-.553; 1956-1957 Bill Rigney 136-172-.442

NEW YORK GIANTS

Home City: New York, New York
Home Field: Polo Grounds IV Capacity: 16,000 [1891]
Origin of Name: The team was named after their National League counterparts.

Regular Season Record

Season	League	GP	W	L	Pct	GB	R	OR
1890	PL	131	74	57	.565	8	1018	875

COACHING HISTORY: William Ewing 74-57-.565

NEW YORK GIANTS

Home City: New York, New York (1925-1973, 1975)
New Haven, Connecticut (1973-1974)
East Rutherford, New Jersey (1976-
Home Stadium: Polo Grounds II (1925-1955) Capacity: 55,200
Yankee Stadium I (1956-1973) Capacity: 63,800
Yale Bowl (1973-1974) Capacity: 70,896
Shea Stadium (1975) Capacity: 60,372
Giants Stadium: (1976-present) Capacity: 77,716 [1995]
Origin of Name: The team was named after the baseball team with which they shared the Polo Grounds.

Regular Season Record

Season	League	GP	W	L	T	PF	PA	Pct
1925	NFL	12	8	4	0	122	67	.667
1926	NFL	13	8	4	1	147	45	.654
1927	NFL	13	11	1	1	197	20	.885
1928	NFL	13	4	7	2	79	136	.385
1929	NFL	14	12	1	1	298	77	.893
1930	NFL	17	13	4	0	308	98	.765
1931	NFL	14	7	6	1	154	100	.536
1932	NFL	12	4	6	2	93	113	.417
1933	NFL	14	11	3	0	244	101	.786
1934	NFL	13	8	5	0	147	107	.615
1935	NFL	12	9	3	0	180	96	.750
1936	NFL	12	5	6	1	115	163	.458

1937	NFL	11	6	3	2	128	109	.636
1938	NFL	11	8	2	1	194	79	.773
1939	NFL	11	9	1	1	168	85	.864
1940	NFL	11	6	4	1	131	133	.591
1941	NFL	11	8	3	0	238	114	.727
1942	NFL	11	5	5	1	155	139	.500
1943	NFL	10	6	3	1	197	170	.650
1944	NFL	10	8	1	1	206	75	.850
1945	NFL	10	3	6	1	179	198	.350
1946	NFL	11	7	3	1	236	162	.682
1947	NFL	12	2	8	2	190	309	.250
1948	NFL	12	4	8	0	297	388	.333
1949	NFL	12	6	6	0	287	298	.500
1950	NFL	12	10	2	0	268	150	.833
1951	NFL	12	9	2	1	254	161	.792
1952	NFL	12	7	5	0	234	231	.583
1953	NFL	12	3	9	0	179	277	.250
1954	NFL	12	7	5	0	293	184	.583
1955	NFL	12	6	5	1	267	223	.542
1956	NFL	12	8	3	1	264	197	.708
1957	NFL	12	7	5	0	254	211	.583
1958	NFL	12	9	3	0	246	183	.750
1959	NFL	12	10	2	0	284	170	.833
1960	NFL	12	6	4	2	271	261	.600
1961	NFL	14	10	3	1	368	220	.769
1962	NFL	14	12	2	0	398	283	.857
1963	NFL	14	11	3	0	448	280	.786
1964	NFL	14	2	10	2	241	399	.167
1965	NFL	14	7	7	0	270	338	.500
1966	NFL	14	1	12	1	263	501	.077
1967	NFL	14	7	7	0	369	379	.500
1968	NFL	14	7	7	0	294	325	.500
1969	NFL	14	6	8	0	264	298	.429
1970	NFL	14	9	5	0	301	270	.643
1971	NFL	14	4	10	0	228	362	.286
1972	NFL	14	8	6	0	331	247	.571
1973	NFL	14	2	11	1	226	362	.179
1974	NFL	14	2	12	0	195	299	.143
1975	NFL	14	5	9	0	216	306	.357
1976	NFL	14	3	11	0	170	250	.214
1977	NFL	14	5	9	0	181	265	.357
1978	NFL	16	6	10	0	264	298	.375
1979	NFL	16	6	10	0	237	323	.375
1980	NFL	16	4	12	0	249	425	.250
1981	NFL	16	9	7	0	295	257	.563
1982	NFL	9	4	5	0	164	160	.444
1983	NFL	16	3	12	1	267	347	.219
1984	NFL	16	9	7	0	299	301	.563
1985	NFL	16	10	6	0	399	283	.625
1986	NFL	16	14	2	0	371	236	.875
1987	NFL	15	6	9	0	280	312	.400
1988	NFL	16	10	6	0	359	304	.625
1989	NFL	16	12	4	0	348	252	.750
1990	NFL	16	13	3	0	335	211	.813

1991	NFL	16	8	8	0	281	297	.500
1992	NFL	16	6	10	0	306	367	.375
1993	NFL	16	11	5	0	288	205	.688
1994	NFL	16	9	7	0	279	305	.563
1995	NFL	16	5	11	0	290	340	.313
TOTAL:	71 years	952	506	414	32	17578	16237	
AVERAGE:		13	7	6	0	248	229	.548

Playoff Record

Season	GP	W	L	PF	PA	Result
1933	1	0	1	21	23	Lost championship game to Bears.
1934	1	1	0	30	13	**Won NFL championship**.
1935	1	0	1	7	26	Lost championship game to Detroit.
1938	1	1	0	23	17	**Won NFL championship**.
1939	1	0	1	0	27	Lost championship game to Green Bay.
1941	1	0	1	9	37	Lost championship game to Bears.
1943	1	0	1	0	28	Lost Divisional playoff to Washington.
1944	1	0	1	7	14	Lost championship game to Green Bay.
1946	1	0	1	14	24	Lost championship game to Bears.
1950	1	0	1	3	8	Lost Conference playoff to Cleveland.
1956	1	1	0	47	7	**Won NFL championship**.
1958	2	1	1	27	23	Lost championship game to Baltimore.
1959	1	0	1	16	35	Lost championship game to Baltimore.
1961	1	0	1	0	37	Lost championship game to Green Bay.
1962	1	0	1	7	16	Lost championship game to Green Bay.
1963	1	0	1	10	14	Lost championship game to Chicago.
1981	2	1	1	51	59	Lost Divisional playoff to San Francisco.
1984	2	1	1	26	34	Lost Divisional playoff to San Francisco.
1985	2	1	1	17	24	Lost Divisional playoff to Chicago.
1986	3	3	0	105	23	**Won Super Bowl**.
1989	1	0	1	13	19	Lost Conference semifinal to Rams.
1990	3	3	0	66	35	**Won Super Bowl**.
1993	2	1	1	20	54	Lost Conference semifinal to San Francisco.
TOTAL:	32	14	18	519	597	
AVERAGE:	2	1	1	23	26	

COACHING HISTORY: 1925 Bob Folwell 8-4-0-.667; 1926 Joe Alexander 8-4-1-.654; 1927-1928 Earl Potteiger 15-8-3-.635; 1929-1930 LeRoy Andrews 24-5-1-.817; 1930 Benny Friedman 2-0-0-1.000; 1931-1953 Steve Owen 151-100-17-.595; 1954-1960 Jim Lee Howell 52-27-4-.651; 1961-1968 Allie Sherman 57-51-4-.527; 1969-1973 Alex Webster 29-40-1-.421; 1974-1976 Bill Arnsparger 7-28-0-.200; 1976-1978 John McVay 14-23-0-.378; 1979-1982 Ray Perkins 23-34-0-.404; 1983-1990 Bill Parcells 77-49-17.610; 1991-1992 Ray Handley 14-18-0-.438; 1993-present Dan Reeves

NEW YORK GOLDEN BLADES

(were New York Raiders)
(became New Jersey Knights in mid 1974)

Home City: New York, New York
Home Arena: Madison Square Garden IV — Capacity: 17,500 [1973]
Origin of Name:

Season	League	GP	W	L	T	GF	GA	Pts	Pct
			Regular Season Record						
1973-1974	WHA	20	6	12	2	47	80	14	.350

COACHING HISTORY: Camille Henry 6-12-2-.350

NEW YORK GOTHAMS

(were Troy Trojans)
(became New York Giants)

Home City: New York, New York
Home Field: Polo Grounds I Capacity: 21,000
Origin of Name: Named Gothams because New York is sometimes known as Gotham.

Season	League	GP	W	L	Pct	GB	R	OR
			Regular Season Record					
1883	NL	96	46	50	.479	16	530	577
1884	NL	112	62	50	.554	22	693	623
1885	NL	112	85	27	.759	2	691	370
TOTAL:	3 years	320	193	127		40	1914	1570
AVERAGE:		107	64	43	.603	13	638	523

COACHING HISTORY: 1883 John Clapp 46-50-.479; 1884 James Price 56-42-.571; 1884 Monte Ward 6-8-.429; 1885 Jim Mutrie 85-27-.759

NEW YORK HAKOAHS

Home City: New York, New York
Home Court: St. Nicholas Arena
Origin of Name: The team played under the colors of the Hakoah Club in New York.

Season	League	GP	W	L	Pct
			Regular Season Record		
1928-1929	ABL	43	18	25	.419

COACHING HISTORY:

NEW YORK HIGHLANDERS

(were Baltimore Orioles)
(became New York Yankees)

Home City: New York, New York
Home Field: Hilltop Park Capacity:15,000
Origin of Name: The name was suggested due to the fact the team's ball park was situated on high ground.

Season	League	GP	W	L	Pct	GB	R	OR
			Regular Season Record					
1903	AL	134	72	62	.537	17	579	573
1904	AL	151	92	59	.609	1.5	598	526

1905	AL	149	71	78	.477	21.5	587	644
1906	AL	151	90	61	.596	3	643	544
1907	AL	148	70	78	.473	21	604	671
1908	AL	154	51	103	.331	39.5	458	700
1909	AL	151	74	77	.490	23.5	591	580
1910	AL	151	88	63	.583	14.5	629	502
1911	AL	152	76	76	.500	25.5	686	726
1912	AL	152	50	102	.329	55	632	839
TOTAL:	10 years	1493	734	759		222	6007	6305
AVERAGE:		149	73	76	.492	22	601	631

COACHING HISTORY: 1903-1908 Clark Griffith 419-370-.531; 1908 Norman Elberfeld 27-71-.276; 1909-1910 George Stallings 153-138-.526; 1910-1911 Hal Chase 85-78-.521; 1912 Harry Wolverton 50-102-.329

NEW YORK ISLANDERS

Home City: Uniondale, New York
Home Arena: Nassau Veteran's Memorial Coliseum — Capacity: 16,297 [1995]
Origin of Name: The name was chosen by owner Roy Boe.

			Regular Season Record						
Season	**League**	**GP**	**W**	**L**	**T**	**GF**	**GA**	**Pts**	**Pct**
1972-1973	NHL	78	12	60	6	170	347	30	.192
1973-1974	NHL	78	19	41	18	182	247	56	.359
1974-1975	NHL	80	33	25	22	264	221	88	.550
1975-1976	NHL	80	42	21	17	297	190	101	.631
1976-1977	NHL	80	47	21	12	288	196	106	.663
1977-1978	NHL	80	48	17	15	334	270	111	.694
1978-1979	NHL	80	51	15	14	358	214	116	.725
1979-1980	NHL	80	39	28	13	281	247	91	.569
1980-1981	NHL	80	48	18	14	355	260	110	.688
1981-1982	NHL	80	54	16	10	385	250	118	.738
1982-1983	NHL	80	42	26	12	302	226	96	.600
1983-1984	NHL	80	50	26	4	357	269	104	.650
1984-1985	NHL	80	40	34	6	345	312	86	.538
1985-1986	NHL	80	39	29	12	327	284	90	.563
1986-1987	NHL	80	35	33	12	279	281	82	.513
1987-1988	NHL	80	39	31	10	308	267	88	.550
1988-1989	NHL	80	28	47	5	265	325	61	.381
1989-1990	NHL	80	31	38	11	281	288	73	.456
1990-1991	NHL	80	25	45	10	223	290	60	.375
1991-1992	NHL	80	34	35	11	291	299	79	.494
1992-1993	NHL	84	40	37	7	335	297	87	.518
1993-1994	NHL	84	36	36	12	282	264	84	.500
1994-1995	NHL	48	15	28	5	126	158	35	.365
1995-1996	NHL	82	22	50	10	229	315	54	.329
TOTAL:	24 years	1894	869	757	268	6864	6317	2006	
AVERAGE:		79	36	32	11	286	263	83	.530

Season	GP	W	L	GF	GA	Result
			Playoff Record			
1974-1975	17	9	8	47	45	Lost semifinal series to Philadelphia.
1975-1976	13	7	6	43	39	Lost semifinal series to Montreal.
1976-1977	12	8	4	36	32	Lost semifinal series to Montreal.
1977-1978	7	3	4	13	16	Lost quarterfinal series to Toronto.
1978-1979	10	6	4	27	21	Lost semifinal series to Rangers.
1979-1980	21	15	6	88	66	**Won Stanley Cup**.
1980-1981	18	15	3	97	48	**Won Stanley Cup**.
1981-1982	19	15	4	85	52	**Won Stanley Cup**.
1982-1983	20	15	5	94	53	**Won Stanley Cup**.
1983-1984	21	12	9	62	60	Lost championship series to Edmonton.
1984-1985	10	4	6	25	28	Lost quarterfinal series to Philadelphia.
1985-1986	3	0	3	4	11	Lost preliminary series to Washington.
1986-1987	14	7	7	35	42	Lost quarterfinal series to Philadelphia.
1987-1988	6	2	4	18	23	Lost preliminary series to New Jersey.
1989-1990	5	1	4	13	22	Lost preliminary series to Rangers.
1992-1993	18	9	9	58	65	Lost semifinal series to Montreal.
1993-1994	4	0	4	3	22	Lost preliminary series to Rangers.
TOTAL:	218	128	90	748	645	
AVERAGE:	13	8	5	44	38	

COACHING HISTORY: 1972-1973 Phil Goyette 6-40-4-.160; 1972-1973 Earl Ingarfield 6-20-2-.250; 1973-1986 Al Arbour 552-317-169-.613; 1986-1989 Terry Simpson 81-82-24-.497; 1988-1994 Al Arbour 187-220-54-.464; 1994-1995 Lorne Henning 15-28-5-.365; 1995-present Mike Milbury

NEW YORK JETS

(were New York Titans)

Home City: New York, New York (1963-1983)
East Rutherford, New Jersey (1984-present)
Home Stadium: Polo Grounds (1963) Capacity: 55,987
Shea Stadium (1964-1983) Capacity: 60,372 [1983]
Giants Stadium (1984-present) Capacity: 77,716 [1995]
Origin of Name: The name was chosen by the team owners.

Season	League	GP	W	L	T	PF	PA	Pct
			Regular Season Record					
1963	AFL	14	5	8	1	249	399	.385
1964	AFL	14	5	8	1	278	315	.385
1965	AFL	14	5	8	1	285	303	.385
1966	AFL	14	6	6	2	322	312	.500
1967	AFL	14	8	5	1	371	329	.615
1968	AFL	14	11	3	0	419	280	.786
1969	AFL	14	10	4	0	353	269	.714
1970	NFL	14	4	10	0	255	286	.286
1971	NFL	14	6	8	0	212	299	.429
1972	NFL	14	7	7	0	367	324	.500
1973	NFL	14	4	10	0	240	306	.286
1974	NFL	14	7	7	0	279	300	.500
1975	NFL	14	3	11	0	258	433	.214

1976	NFL	14	3	11	0	169	383	.214
1977	NFL	14	3	11	0	191	300	.214
1978	NFL	16	8	8	0	359	364	.500
1979	NFL	16	8	8	0	337	383	.500
1980	NFL	16	4	12	0	302	395	.250
1981	NFL	16	10	5	1	355	287	.656
1982	NFL	9	6	3	0	245	166	.667
1983	NFL	16	7	9	0	313	331	.438
1984	NFL	16	7	9	0	332	364	.438
1985	NFL	16	11	5	0	393	264	.688
1986	NFL	16	10	6	0	364	386	.625
1987	NFL	15	6	9	0	334	360	.400
1988	NFL	16	8	7	1	372	354	.531
1989	NFL	16	4	12	0	253	411	.250
1990	NFL	16	6	10	0	295	345	.375
1991	NFL	16	8	8	0	314	293	.500
1992	NFL	16	4	12	0	220	315	.250
1993	NFL	16	8	8	0	270	247	.500
1994	NFL	16	6	10	0	264	320	.375
1995	NFL	16	3	13	0	233	384	.188
TOTAL:	33years	490	211	271	8	9803	10807	
AVERAGE:		15	7	8	0	297	327	.439

Playoff Record

Season	GP	W	L	PF	PA	Result
1968	2	2	0	43	30	**Won Super Bowl.**
1969	1	0	1	6	13	Lost Divisional playoff to Kansas City.
1981	1	0	1	27	31	Lost 1st round game to Buffalo.
1982	3	2	1	61	45	Lost AFC championship to Miami.
1985	1	0	1	14	26	Lost 1st round game to New England.
1986	2	1	1	55	38	Lost Divisional playoff to Cleveland.
1991	1	0	1	10	17	Lost Wild Card game to Houston.
TOTAL:	11	5	6	216	200	
AVERAGE:	2	1	1	31	29	

COACHING HISTORY: 1963-1973 Weeb Ewbank 71-77-6-.481; 1974-1975 Charley Winner 9-14-0-.391; 1975 Ken Shipp 1-4-0-.200; 1976 Lou Holtz 3-10-0-.231; 1976 Mike Holovak 0-1-0-.000; 1977-1982 Walt Michaels 39-47-1-.454; 1983-1989 Joe Walton 53-57-1-.482; 1990-1993 Bruce Coslet 26-38-0-.406; 1994-present Pete Carroll 6-10-0-.375; 1995-present Rich Kotite

NEW YORK KNICKERBOCKERS

Home City: New York, New York
Home Court: 69th Regiment Armory (1946-1947) Capacity: 5,000
Madison Square Garden III (1946-1968) Capacity: 18,496
Madison Square Garden IV (1968-present) Capacity: 19,763 [1995]
Origin of Name: The name was chosen by owner Ned Irish. Knickerbockers is a name long associated with New York City.

Regular Season Record

Season	League	GP	W	L	PPGF	PPGA	Pct	GB
1946-1947	BAA	60	33	27	64.7	64.0	.550	16

1947-1948	BAA	48	26	22	74.5	71.4	.542	1
1948-1949	BAA	60	32	28	79.2	77.7	.533	6
1949-1950	NBA	68	40	28	80.7	78.6	.588	13
1950-1951	NBA	66	36	30	85.8	85.4	.545	4
1951-1952	NBA	66	37	29	85.0	84.2	.561	3
1952-1953	NBA	70	47	23	85.5	80.3	.671	-
1953-1954	NBA	72	44	28	79.0	79.1	.611	-
1954-1955	NBA	72	38	34	92.7	92.6	.528	5
1955-1956	NBA	72	35	37	100.2	100.6	.486	10
1956-1957	NBA	72	36	36	100.8	100.9	.500	8
1957-1958	NBA	72	35	37	112.1	110.8	.486	14
1958-1959	NBA	72	40	32	110.3	110.1	.556	12
1959-1960	NBA	75	27	48	117.3	119.6	.360	32
1960-1961	NBA	79	21	58	113.7	120.1	.266	36
1961-1962	NBA	80	29	51	114.8	119.7	.363	31
1962-1963	NBA	80	21	59	110.5	117.7	.263	37
1963-1964	NBA	80	22	58	112.2	119.6	.275	37
1964-1965	NBA	80	31	49	107.4	111.1	.388	31
1965-1966	NBA	80	30	50	116.7	119.3	.375	25
1966-1967	NBA	81	36	45	116.4	119.4	.444	32
1967-1968	NBA	82	43	39	116.1	114.3	.524	19
1968-1969	NBA	82	54	28	110.8	105.2	.659	3
1969-1970	NBA	82	60	22	115.0	105.9	.732	-
1970-1971	NBA	82	52	30	110.1	105.0	.634	-
1971-1972	NBA	82	48	34	107.1	104.7	.585	8
1972-1973	NBA	82	57	25	105.0	98.2	.695	11
1973-1974	NBA	82	49	33	101.3	98.5	.598	7
1974-1975	NBA	82	40	42	100.4	101.7	.488	20
1975-1976	NBA	82	38	44	102.7	103.9	.463	16
1976-1977	NBA	82	40	42	108.6	108.6	.488	10
1977-1978	NBA	82	43	39	113.4	114.0	.524	12
1978-1979	NBA	82	31	51	107.7	111.1	.378	23
1979-1980	NBA	82	39	43	114.0	115.1	.476	22
1980-1981	NBA	82	50	32	107.9	106.3	.610	12
1981-1982	NBA	82	33	49	106.2	108.9	.402	30
1982-1983	NBA	82	44	38	100.0	97.5	.537	21
1983-1984	NBA	82	47	35	106.9	103.0	.573	15
1984-1985	NBA	82	24	58	105.2	109.8	.293	39
1985-1986	NBA	82	23	59	98.7	104.3	.280	44
1986-1987	NBA	82	24	58	103.8	110.0	.293	35
1987-1988	NBA	82	38	44	105.5	106.0	.463	19
1988-1989	NBA	82	52	30	116.7	112.9	.634	-
1989-1990	NBA	82	45	37	108.3	106.9	.549	8
1990-1991	NBA	82	39	43	103.1	103.3	.476	17
1991-1992	NBA	82	51	31	101.6	97.7	.622	-
1992-1993	NBA	82	60	22	101.6	95.4	.732	-
1993-1994	NBA	82	57	25	98.5	91.5	.695	-
1994-1995	NBA	82	55	27	98.2	95.1	.671	2
1995-1996	NBA	82	47	35	97.2	94.9	.573	13
TOTAL:	50 years	3883	1979	1904				759
AVERAGE:		78	40	38	102.6	102.2	.510	15

Season	GP	W	L	Playoff Record PPGF	PPGA	Result
1946-1947	5	2	3	70.6	75.2	Lost semifinal series to Philadelphia
1947-1948	3	1	2	79.0	79.3	Lost quarterfinal series to Baltimore.
1948-1949	6	3	3	83.5	83.3	Lost Division final to Washington.
1949-1950	5	3	2	87.2	85.6	Lost Division final to Syracuse.
1950-1951	14	8	6	83.4	83.6	Lost championship series to Rochester.
1951-1952	14	8	6	86.9	88.5	Lost championship series to Minneapolis.
1952-1953	11	6	5	83.0	80.9	Lost championship series to Minneapolis.
1953-1954	4	0	4	79.0	87.5	Lost playoff series to Syracuse.
1954-1955	3	1	2	104.0	111.0	Lost Division semifinal to Boston.
1955-1956	1	0	1	77.0	82.0	Lost playoff game to Syracuse.
1958-1959	2	0	2	119.0	130.0	Lost Division semifinal to Syracuse.
1966-1967	4	1	3	112.5	121.3	Lost Division semifinal to Boston.
1967-1968	6	2	4	113.5	117.8	Lost Division semifinal to Philadelphia.
1968-1969	10	6	4	106.5	103.4	Lost Division final to Boston.
1969-1970	19	12	7	110.5	106.8	**Won NBA championship**.
1970-1971	12	7	5	101.1	102.3	Lost Conference final to Baltimore.
1971-1972	16	9	7	106.6	101.9	Lost championship series to Los Angeles.
1972-1973	17	12	5	103.8	98.8	**Won NBA championship**.
1973-1974	12	5	7	94.4	99.4	Lost Conference final to Boston.
1974-1975	3	1	2	92.0	104.3	Lost 1st round series to Houston.
1977-1978	6	2	4	110.7	119.8	Lost Conf. semifinal to Philadelphia.
1980-1981	2	0	2	97.0	102.5	Lost 1st round series to Chicago.
1982-1983	6	2	4	103.8	104.7	Lost Conf. semifinal to Philadelphia.
1983-1984	12	6	6	106.6	111.5	Lost Conference semifinal to Boston.
1987-1988	4	1	3	99.3	110.5	Lost 1st round series to Boston.
1988-1989	9	5	4	106.8	108.7	Lost Conference semifinal to Chicago.
1989-1990	10	4	6	105.0	111.0	Lost Conference semifinal to Detroit.
1990-1991	3	0	3	86.0	106.0	Lost 1st round series to Chicago.
1991-1992	12	6	6	90.3	89.3	Lost Conference semifinal to Chicago.
1992-1993	15	9	6	99.0	99.5	Lost Conference final to Chicago.
1993-1994	25	14	11	88.8	87.7	Lost championship series to Houston.
1994-1995	11	6	5	93.3	89.4	Lost Conference semifinal to Indiana.
1995-1996	8	4	4	88.6	88.5	Lost Conference semifinal to Chicago.
TOTAL:	290	146	144			
AVERAGE:	8	4	4	95.6	98.4	

COACHING HISTORY: 1946-1947 Neil Cohalan 33-27-.550; 1947-1956 Joe Lapchick 326-247-.569; 1955-1958 Vince Boryla 80-85-.485; 1958-1960 Andrew Levane 48-51-.485; 1959-1961 Carl Braun 40-87-.315; 1961-1965 Eddie Donovan 85-193-.306; 1964-1966 Harry Gallatin 25-38-.397; 1965-1968 Dick McGuire 75-102-.424; 1967-1977 Red Holzman 466-317-.595; 1977-1979 Willis Reed 49-47-.510; 1978-1982 Red Holzman 147-167-.468; 1982-1987 Hubie Brown 142-202-.413; 1986-1987 Bob Hill 20-46-.303; 1987-1989 Rick Pitino 90-74-.549; 1989-1991 Stu Jackson 52-45-.536; 1990-1991 John McLeod 32-35-.478; 1991-1995 Pat Riley 223-105-.680; 1995-1996 Don Nelson 34-25-.576, 1995-present Jeff van Gundy

NEW YORK METROPOLITANS
(became Kansas City Blues)

Home City: New York, New York
Home Field: Polo Grounds I (1883-1885) Capacity: 21,000
Metropolitan Park (1884 some games)
St. George Ground (1886-1887)
Origin of Name:

Regular Season Record

Season	League	GP	W	L	Pct	GB	R	OR
1883	AA	96	54	42	.563	11	498	405
1884	AA	107	75	32	.701	-	734	423
1885	AA	108	44	64	.407	33	526	688
1886	AA	135	53	82	.393	38	628	766
1887	AA	133	44	89	.331	50	754	1093
TOTAL:	5 years	579	270	309		132	3140	3375
AVERAGE:		116	54	62	.466	26.5	628	675

Playoff Record

Season	GP	W	L	R	OR	Result
1884	3	0	3	3	21	Lost World Series to Providence.

COACHING HISTORY: 1883-1884 Jim Mutrie 129-74-.635; 1885-1886 Jim Gifford 50-76-.397; 1886-1887 Bob Ferguson 53-94-.361; 1887 Dave Orr 28-36-.438; 1887 O.P. Caylor 10-29-.256

NEW YORK METS

Home City: New York, New York
Home Field: Polo Grounds V (1962-1963) Capacity: 56,000 [1953]
Shea Stadium (1964-present) Capacity: 55,601 [1995]
Origin of Name: The name is short for Metropolitans and was named for the American Association team from the 1880's.

Regular Season Record

Season	League	GP	W	L	Pct	GB	R	OR
1962	NL	160	40	120	.250	60.5	617	948
1963	NL	162	51	111	.315	48	501	774
1964	NL	162	53	109	.327	40	569	776
1965	NL	162	50	112	.309	47	495	752
1966	NL	161	66	95	.410	28.5	587	761
1967	NL	162	61	101	.377	40.5	498	672
1968	NL	162	73	89	.451	24	473	499
1969	NL	162	100	62	.617	-	632	541
1970	NL	162	83	79	.512	6	695	630
1971	NL	162	83	79	.512	14	588	550
1972	NL	156	83	73	.532	13.5	528	578
1973	NL	161	82	79	.509	-	608	588
1974	NL	162	71	91	.438	17	572	646
1975	NL	162	82	80	.506	10.5	646	625

1976	NL	162	86	76	.531	15	615	538
1977	NL	162	64	98	.395	37	587	663
1978	NL	162	66	96	.407	24	607	690
1979	NL	162	63	99	.389	35	593	706
1980	NL	162	67	95	.414	24	611	702
1981	NL	103	41	62	.398	NA	348	432
1982	NL	162	65	97	.401	27	609	723
1983	NL	162	68	94	.420	22	575	680
1984	NL	162	90	72	.556	6.5	652	676
1985	NL	162	98	64	.605	3	695	568
1986	NL	162	108	54	.667	-	783	578
1987	NL	162	92	70	.568	3	823	698
1988	NL	160	100	60	.625	-	703	532
1989	NL	162	87	75	.537	6	683	595
1990	NL	162	91	71	.562	4	775	613
1991	NL	161	77	84	.478	20.5	640	646
1992	NL	162	72	90	.444	24	599	653
1993	NL	162	59	103	.364	38	672	744
1994	NL	113	55	58	.487	18.5	506	526
1995	NL	144	69	75	.479	21	657	618
TOTAL:	34 years	5369	2496	2873		678	20742	21921
AVERAGE:		158	73	85	.465	20	610	645

Playoff Record

Season	GP	W	L	R	OR	Result
1969	8	7	1	42	24	**Won World Series.**
1973	12	6	6	47	29	Lost World Series to Oakland.
1986	13	8	5	53	44	**Won World Series.**
1988	7	3	4	27	31	Lost NLCS to Los Angeles.
TOTAL:	40	24	16	169	128	
AVERAGE:	10	6	4	42	32	

COACHING HISTORY: 1962-1965 Casey Stengel 175-404-.302; 1965-1967 Wes Westrum 142-237-.375; 1967 Francis Parker 4-7-.364; 1968-1971 Gil Hodges 339-309-.523; 1972-1975 Yogi Berra 292-296-.497; 1975 Roy McMillan 26-27-.491; 1976-1977 Joe Frazier 101-105-.490; 1977-1981 Joe Torre 286-421-.405; 1982-1983 George Bamberger 81-127-.389; 1983 Frank Howard 52-64-.448; 1984-1990 Dave Johnson 595-417-.588; 1990-1991 Bud Harrelson 145-129-.529; 1991 Mike Cubbage 3-4-.429; 1992-1993 Jeff Torborg 85-115-.425; 1993-present Dallas Green

NEW YORK MUTUALS

Home City: New York, New York
Home Field: Capitoline Grounds
Origin of Name: The club was organized in the firehouse of the Mutual Hook and Ladder Company No. 1 in 1857.

Regular Season Record

Season	League	GP	W	L	Pct	GB	R	OR
1876	NL	56	21	35	.375	26	260	412

COACHING HISTORY: Bill Cammeyer 21-35-.375

NEW YORK NETS

(were New Jersey Americans)
(became New Jersey Nets)

Home City: Commack, New York (1968-1969)
West Hempstead, New York (1969-1971)
Uniondale, New York (1971-1977)
Home Court: Long Island Arena (1968-1969) Capacity: 6,500
Island Garden (1969-1971) Capacity: 5,200
Nassau Veteran's Memorial Coliseum (1971-1977) Capacity: 15,934 [1977]
Origin of Name: The name was chosen as a tie in to the other New York teams, the Jets and the Mets.

Regular Season Record

Season	League	GP	W	L	PPGF	PPGA	Pct	GB
1968-1969	ABA	78	17	61	108.5	117.2	.218	27
1969-1970	ABA	84	39	45	108.9	109.8	.464	20
1970-1971	ABA	84	40	44	111.0	111.6	.476	15
1971-1972	ABA	84	44	40	112.8	112.4	.524	24
1972-1973	ABA	84	30	54	103.6	110.1	.357	27
1973-1974	ABA	84	55	29	109.4	104.0	.655	-
1974-1975	ABA	84	58	26	111.1	103.4	.690	-
1975-1976	ABA	84	55	29	111.8	108.8	.655	5
1976-1977	NBA	82	22	60	95.9	102.7	.268	28
TOTAL:	9 years	748	360	388				146
AVERAGE:		83	40	43	108.1	108.9	.481	16

Playoff Record

Season	GP	W	L	PPGF	PPGA	Result
1969-1970	7	3	4	111.7	114.0	Lost 1st round series to Kentucky.
1970-1971	6	2	4	119.3	121.7	Lost 1st round series to Virginia.
1971-1972	19	10	9	107.5	109.6	Lost championship series to Indiana.
1972-1973	5	1	4	104.4	112.8	Lost 1st round series to Indiana.
1973-1974	14	12	2	106.9	96.1	**Won ABA championship**.
1974-1975	5	1	4	102.4	108.2	Lost 1st round series to St. Louis.
1975-1976	13	8	5	111.2	111.2	**Won ABA championship**.
TOTAL:	69	37	32			
AVERAGE:	10	5	5	109.1	110.5	

COACHING HISTORY: 1968-1969 Max Zaslofsky 17-61-.218; 1969-1970 York Larese 39-45-.464; 1970-1973 Lou Carnesecca 114-138-.452; 1973-1977 Kevin Loughery 190-188-.503

NEW YORK-NEW JERSEY KNIGHTS

Home City: East Rutherford, New Jersey
Home Stadium: Giants Stadium Capacity: 77,152 [1991]
Origin of Name:

Regular Season Record

Season	League	GP	W	L	T	PF	PA	Pct
1991	WLAF	10	5	5	0	257	155	.500

1992	WFL	10	6	4	0	284	188	.600
TOTAL:	2 years	20	11	9	0	541	343	
AVERAGE:		10	6	4	0	271	172	.550

Playoff Record

Season	GP	W	L	PF	PA	Result
1991	1	0	1	26	42	Lost 1st round game to London.

COACHING HISTORY: 1991-1992 Darrell Davis 11-9-0-.550

NEW YORK RAIDERS

(became New York Golden Blades)

Home City: New York, New York
Home Arena: Madison Square Gardens IV — Capacity: 17,500 [1972]
Origin of Name:

Regular Season Record

Season	League	GP	W	L	T	GF	GA	Pts	Pct
1972-1973	WHA	78	33	43	2	303	334	68	.436

COACHING HISTORY: Camille Henry 33-43-2-.436

NEW YORK RANGERS

Home City: New York, New York
Home Arena: Madison Square Garden III (1926-1968) — Capacity: 15,925
Madison Square Garden IV (1968-present) — Capacity: 18,200 [1995]
Origin of Name: The team was named after the Texas Rangers. The president of Madison Square Garden and one of the men responsible for bringing the Rangers to New York was Tex Rickard and the team was unofficially known as "Tex's Rangers" after Rickard's home state police.

Regular Season Record

Season	League	GP	W	L	T	GF	GA	Pts	Pct
1926-1927	NHL	44	25	13	6	95	72	56	.636
1927-1928	NHL	44	19	16	9	94	79	47	.534
1928-1929	NHL	44	21	13	10	72	65	52	.591
1929-1930	NHL	44	17	17	10	136	143	44	.500
1930-1931	NHL	48	23	17	8	134	112	54	.563
1931-1932	NHL	48	23	17	8	134	112	54	.563
1932-1933	NHL	48	23	17	8	135	107	54	.563
1933-1934	NHL	48	21	19	8	120	113	50	.521
1934-1935	NHL	48	22	20	6	137	139	50	.521
1935-1936	NHL	48	19	17	12	91	96	50	.521
1936-1937	NHL	48	19	20	9	117	106	47	.490
1937-1938	NHL	48	27	15	6	149	96	60	.625
1938-1939	NHL	48	26	16	6	149	105	58	.604
1939-1940	NHL	48	27	11	10	136	77	64	.667
1940-1941	NHL	48	21	19	8	143	125	50	.521
1941-1942	NHL	48	29	17	2	177	143	60	.625
1942-1943	NHL	50	11	31	8	161	253	30	.313

1943-1944	NHL	50	6	39	5	162	310	17	.170
1944-1945	NHL	50	11	29	10	154	147	32	.320
1945-1946	NHL	50	13	28	9	144	191	35	.350
1946-1947	NHL	60	22	32	6	167	186	50	.417
1947-1948	NHL	60	21	26	13	176	201	55	.458
1948-1949	NHL	60	18	31	11	133	172	47	.392
1949-1950	NHL	70	28	31	11	170	189	67	.479
1950-1951	NHL	70	20	29	21	169	201	61	.438
1951-1952	NHL	70	23	34	13	192	219	59	.421
1952-1953	NHL	70	17	37	16	152	211	50	.357
1953-1954	NHL	70	29	31	10	161	182	68	.486
1954-1955	NHL	70	17	35	18	150	210	52	.371
1955-1956	NHL	70	32	28	10	204	203	74	.529
1956-1957	NHL	70	26	30	14	184	227	66	.471
1957-1958	NHL	70	32	25	13	195	188	77	.550
1958-1959	NHL	70	26	32	12	201	217	64	.457
1959-1960	NHL	70	17	38	15	187	247	49	.350
1960-1961	NHL	70	22	38	10	204	248	54	.386
1961-1962	NHL	70	26	32	12	195	207	64	.457
1962-1963	NHL	70	22	36	12	211	233	56	.400
1963-1964	NHL	70	22	38	10	186	242	54	.386
1964-1965	NHL	70	20	38	12	179	246	52	.371
1965-1966	NHL	70	18	41	11	195	261	47	.336
1966-1967	NHL	70	30	28	12	188	189	72	.514
1967-1968	NHL	74	39	23	12	226	183	90	.608
1968-1969	NHL	76	41	26	9	231	196	91	.599
1969-1970	NHL	76	38	22	16	246	189	92	.605
1970-1971	NHL	78	49	18	11	259	177	109	.699
1971-1972	NHL	78	48	17	13	317	192	109	.699
1972-1973	NHL	78	47	23	8	298	208	102	.654
1973-1974	NHL	78	40	24	14	300	251	94	.603
1974-1975	NHL	80	37	29	14	319	276	88	.550
1975-1976	NHL	80	29	42	9	262	333	67	.419
1976-1977	NHL	80	29	37	14	272	310	72	.450
1977-1978	NHL	80	30	37	13	279	280	73	.456
1978-1979	NHL	80	40	29	11	316	292	91	.569
1979-1980	NHL	80	38	32	10	308	284	86	.538
1980-1981	NHL	80	30	36	14	312	317	74	.463
1981-1982	NHL	80	39	27	14	316	306	92	.575
1982-1983	NHL	80	35	35	10	306	287	80	.500
1983-1984	NHL	80	42	29	9	314	304	93	.581
1984-1985	NHL	80	26	44	10	295	345	62	.388
1985-1986	NHL	80	36	38	6	280	276	78	.488
1986-1987	NHL	80	34	38	8	307	323	76	.475
1987-1988	NHL	80	36	34	10	300	283	82	.513
1988-1989	NHL	80	37	35	8	310	307	82	.513
1989-1990	NHL	80	36	31	13	279	267	85	.531
1990-1991	NHL	80	36	31	13	297	265	85	.531
1991-1992	NHL	80	50	25	5	321	246	105	.656
1992-1993	NHL	84	34	39	11	304	308	79	.470
1993-1994	NHL	84	52	24	8	299	231	112	.667
1994-1995	NHL	48	22	23	3	139	134	47	.490
1995-1996	NHL	82	41	27	14	272	237	96	.585
TOTAL:	70 years	4668	1982	1956	730	14723	14677	4694	

AVERAGE:	66	28	28	10	210	210	66	.503

Playoff Record

Season	GP	W	L	T	GF	GA	Result
1926-1927	2	0	1	1	1	3	Lost semifinal series to Boston.
1927-1928	9	5	3	1	16	12	**Won Stanley Cup**.
1928-1929	6	3	2	1	5	5	Lost Stanley Cup final to Boston.
1929-1930	4	1	2	1	7	7	Lost semifinal series to Canadiens.
1930-1931	4	2	2	0	8	4	Lost semifinal series to Chicago.
1931-1932	7	3	4	0	23	27	Lost Stanley Cup final to Toronto.
1932-1933	8	6	1	1	25	13	**Won Stanley Cup**.
1933-1934	2	0	1	1	1	2	Lost quarterfinal series to Maroons.
1934-1935	4	1	1	2	10	10	Lost semifinal series to Maroons.
1936-1937	9	6	3	0	18	10	Lost Stanley Cup final to Detroit.
1937-1938	3	1	2	0	7	8	Lost quarterfinal series to Americans.
1938-1939	7	3	4	0	12	14	Lost semifinal series to Boston.
1939-1940	12	8	4	0	29	20	**Won Stanley Cup**.
1940-1941	3	1	2	0	6	6	Lost quarterfinal series to Detroit.
1941-1942	6	2	4	0	12	13	Lost semifinal series to Toronto.
1947-1948	6	2	4	0	12	17	Lost semifinal series to Detroit.
1949-1950	12	7	5	0	32	29	Lost Stanley Cup final to Detroit.
1955-1956	5	1	4	0	9	24	Lost semifinal series to Montreal.
1956-1957	5	1	4	0	12	22	Lost semifinal series to Montreal.
1957-1958	6	2	4	0	16	28	Lost semifinal series to Boston.
1961-1962	6	2	4	0	15	22	Lost semifinal series to Toronto.
1966-1967	4	0	4	0	8	14	Lost semifinal series to Montreal.
1967-1968	6	2	4	0	12	18	Lost quarterfinal series to Chicago.
1968-1969	4	0	4	0	7	16	Lost quarterfinal series to Montreal.
1969-1970	6	2	4	0	16	25	Lost quarterfinal series to Boston.
1970-1971	13	7	6	0	30	36	Lost semifinal series to Chicago.
1971-1972	16	10	6	0	52	41	Lost Stanley Cup final to Boston.
1972-1973	10	5	5	0	33	26	Lost semifinal series to Chicago.
1973-1974	13	7	6	0	38	39	Lost quarterfinal series to Philadelphia.
1974-1975	3	1	2	0	13	10	Lost preliminary series to Islanders.
1977-1978	3	1	2	0	6	11	Lost preliminary series to Buffalo.
1978-1979	18	11	7	0	66	42	Lost Stanley Cup final to Montreal.
1979-1980	9	4	5	0	21	23	Lost quarterfinal series to Philadelphia.
1980-1981	14	7	7	0	60	56	Lost semifinal series to Islanders.
1981-1982	10	5	5	0	39	42	Lost quarterfinal series to Islanders.
1982-1983	9	5	4	0	33	37	Lost quarterfinal series to Islanders.
1983-1984	5	2	3	0	14	13	Lost preliminary series to Islanders.
1984-1985	3	0	3	0	10	14	Lost preliminary series to Philadelphia.
1985-1986	16	8	8	0	47	55	Lost semifinal series to Montreal.
1986-1987	6	2	4	0	13	22	Lost preliminary series to Philadelphia.
1988-1989	4	0	4	0	11	19	Lost preliminary series to Pittsburgh.
1989-1990	10	5	5	0	37	35	Lost quarterfinal series to Washington.
1990-1991	6	2	4	0	16	16	Lost preliminary series to Washington.
1991-1992	13	6	7	0	47	49	Lost quarterfinal series to Pittsburgh.
1993-1994	23	16	7	0	81	50	**Won Stanley Cup**.
1994-1995	10	4	6	0	35	37	Lost quarterfinal series to Philadelphia.
1995-1996	11	5	6	0	34	38	Lost quarterfinal series to Pittsburgh.
TOTAL:	371	174	189	8	1055	1080	
AVERAGE:	8	4	4	0	22	23	

COACHING HISTORY: 1926-1939 Lester Patrick 285-217-106-.556; 1939-1949 Frank Boucher 167-243-77-.422; 1948-1950 Lynn Patrick 40-51-16-.449; 1950-1952 Neil Colville 26-41-26-.419; 1951-1953 Bill Cook 34-59-24-.393; 1953-1954 Frank Boucher 12-20-6-.395; 1953-1955 Murray Patrick 34-46-22-.441; 1955-1960 Phil Watson 119-124-52-.492; 1959-1961 Alf Pike 36-67-22-.376; 1961-1962 Doug Harvey 26-32-12-.457; 1962-1963 Murray Patrick 11-19-4-.382; 1962-1966 George Sullivan 58-103-35-.385; 1965-1975 Emile Francis 347-209-98-.606; 1968-1969 Bernie Geoffrion 22-18-3-.547; 1973-1974 Larry Popein 18-14-9-.549; 1975-1976 Ron Stewart 15-20-4-.436; 1975-1977 John Ferguson 43-59-19-.434; 1977-1978 Jean-Guy Talbot 30-37-13-.456; 1978-1981 Fred Shero 82-74-25-.522; 1980-1981 Craig Patrick 26-23-10-.525; 1981-1985 Herb Brooks 131-113-41-.532; 1984-1985 Craig Patrick 11-22-2-.343; 1985-1987 Ted Sator 41-48-10-.465; 1986-1987 Tom Webster 5-7-4-.438; 1986-1987 Phil Esposito 24-21-0-.533; 1987-1989 Michel Bergeron 73-67-18-.519; 1988-1989 Phil Esposito 0-2-0-.000; 1989-1992 Roger Neilson 141-104-35-.566; 1992-1993 Ron Smith 15-22-7-.420; 1993-1994 Mike Keenan 52-24-8-.667; 1994-present Colin Campbell

NEW YORK SKYLINERS

Home City: New York, New York
Home Field: Yankee Stadium — Capacity: 67,000 [1967]
Origin of Name: May have adopted the name in tribute to the city's famous skyline. The team was represented by the Cerro club of Montevideo, Uruguay.

			Regular Season Record						
Season	**League**	**GP**	**W**	**L**	**T**	**GF**	**GA**	**Pts**	**Pct**
1967	USA	12	2	4	6	15	17	10	.417

COACHING HISTORY: Ondino Vierra 2-4-6-.417

NEW YORK STARS
(became Charlotte Stars)

Home City: New York, New York
Home Stadium: Downing Stadium * — Capacity: 21,000
Origin of Name: The team was named by coach Babe Parilli.

			Regular Season Record					
Season	**League**	**GP**	**W**	**L**	**T**	**PF**	**PA**	**Pct**
1974	WFL	11	3	8	0	165	278	.273

COACHING HISTORY: Babe Parilli 3-8-0-.273

*Also known as Triborough Stadium

NEW YORK TITANS
(became New York Jets)

Home City: New York, New York
Home Stadium: Polo Grounds — Capacity: 55,987
Origin of Name: Named by team owner Harry Wismer in an attempt to compete against the New York Giants of the NFL.

Season	League	GP	W	L	T	PF	PA	Pct
		Regular Season Record						
1960	AFL	14	7	7	0	382	399	.500
1961	AFL	14	7	7	0	301	390	.500
1962	AFL	14	5	9	0	278	423	.357
TOTAL:	3 years	42	19	23	0	961	1212	
AVERAGE:		14	6	8	0	320	404	.452

COACHING HISTORY: 1960-1961 Sammy Baugh 14-14-0-.500; 1962 "Bulldog" Turner 5-9-0-.357

NEW YORK YANKEES
(were New York Highlanders)

Home City: New York, New York
Home Field: Polo Grounds V (1913-1922) Capacity:38,000 [1919]
Yankee Stadium I (1923-1913) Capacity:67,224 [1958]
Shea Stadium (1974-1975) Capacity:55,101 [1975]
Yankee Stadium II (1976-present) Capacity:57,545 [1995]
Origin of Name: According to some baseball historians the team's nickname was originated by Jim Price of the NEW YORK PRESS.

Season	League	GP	W	L	Pct	GB	R	OR
		Regular Season Record						
1913	AL	151	57	94	.377	38	529	669
1914	AL	154	70	84	.455	30	536	550
1915	AL	152	69	83	.454	32.5	583	596
1916	AL	154	80	74	.519	11	575	561
1917	AL	153	71	82	.464	28.5	524	560
1918	AL	123	60	63	.488	13.5	491	474
1919	AL	139	80	59	.576	7.5	582	514
1920	AL	154	95	59	.617	3	839	629
1921	AL	153	98	55	.641	-	948	708
1922	AL	154	94	60	.610	-	758	618
1923	AL	152	98	54	.645	-	823	622
1924	AL	152	89	63	.586	2	798	667
1925	AL	154	69	85	.448	28.5	706	774
1926	AL	154	91	63	.591	-	847	713
1927	AL	154	110	44	.714	-	975	599
1928	AL	154	101	53	.656	-	894	685
1929	AL	154	88	66	.571	18	899	775
1930	AL	154	86	68	.558	16	1062	898
1931	AL	153	94	59	.614	13.5	1067	760
1932	AL	154	107	47	.695	-	1002	724
1933	AL	150	91	59	.607	7	927	768
1934	AL	154	94	60	.610	7	842	669
1935	AL	149	89	60	.597	3	818	632
1936	AL	153	102	51	.667	-	1065	731
1937	AL	154	102	52	.662	-	979	671
1938	AL	152	99	53	.651	-	966	710
1939	AL	151	106	45	.702	-	967	556
1940	AL	154	88	66	.571	2	817	671

1941	AL	154	101	53	.656	-	830	631
1942	AL	154	103	51	.669	-	801	507
1943	AL	154	98	56	.636	-	669	542
1944	AL	154	83	71	.539	6	674	617
1945	AL	152	81	71	.533	6.5	676	606
1946	AL	154	87	67	.565	17	684	547
1947	AL	154	97	57	.630	-	794	568
1948	AL	154	94	60	.610	2.5	857	633
1949	AL	154	97	57	.630	-	829	637
1950	AL	154	98	56	.636	-	914	691
1951	AL	154	98	56	.636	-	798	621
1952	AL	154	95	59	.617	-	727	557
1953	AL	151	99	52	.656	-	801	547
1954	AL	154	103	51	.669	8	805	563
1955	AL	154	96	58	.623	-	762	569
1956	AL	154	97	57	.630	-	857	631
1957	AL	154	98	56	.636	-	723	534
1958	AL	154	92	62	.597	-	759	577
1959	AL	154	79	75	.513	15	687	647
1960	AL	154	97	57	.630	-	746	627
1961	AL	162	109	53	.673	-	827	612
1962	AL	162	96	66	.593	-	817	680
1963	AL	161	104	57	.646	-	714	547
1964	AL	162	99	63	.611	-	730	577
1965	AL	162	77	85	.475	25	611	604
1966	AL	159	70	89	.440	26.5	611	612
1967	AL	162	72	90	.444	20	522	621
1968	AL	162	83	79	.512	20	536	531
1969	AL	161	80	81	.497	28.5	562	587
1970	AL	162	93	69	.574	15	680	612
1971	AL	162	82	80	.506	21	648	641
1972	AL	155	79	76	.510	6.5	557	527
1973	AL	162	80	82	.494	17	641	610
1974	AL	162	89	73	.549	2	671	623
1975	AL	160	83	77	.519	12	681	588
1976	AL	159	97	62	.610	-	730	575
1977	AL	162	100	62	.617	-	831	651
1978	AL	163	100	63	.613	-	735	582
1979	AL	160	89	71	.556	13.5	734	672
1980	AL	162	103	59	.636	-	820	662
1981	AL	107	59	48	.551	NA	421	343
1982	AL	162	79	83	.488	16	709	716
1983	AL	162	91	71	.562	7	770	703
1984	AL	162	87	75	.537	17	758	679
1985	AL	161	97	64	.602	2	839	660
1986	AL	162	90	72	.556	5.5	797	738
1987	AL	162	89	73	.549	9	788	758
1988	AL	161	85	76	.528	3.5	772	748
1989	AL	161	74	87	.460	14.5	698	792
1990	AL	162	67	95	.414	21	603	749
1991	AL	162	71	91	.438	20	674	777
1992	AL	162	76	86	.469	20	733	746
1993	AL	162	88	74	.543	7	821	761
1994	AL	113	70	43	.619	-	670	534

1995	AL	144	79	65	.549	7	745	688
TOTAL:	83 years	12841	7358	5483		672.5	62668	52862
AVERAGE:		155	89	66	.573	8	755	637

Playoff Record

Season	GP	W	L	T	R	OR	Result
1921	8	3	5	0	22	29	Lost World Series to Giants.
1922	5	0	4	1	11	18	Lost World Series to Giants.
1923	6	4	2	0	30	17	**Won World Series**.
1926	7	3	4	0	21	31	Lost World Series to St. Louis.
1927	4	4	0	0	23	10	**Won World Series**.
1928	4	4	0	0	27	10	**Won World Series**.
1932	4	4	0	0	37	19	**Won World Series**.
1936	6	4	2	0	43	23	**Won World Series**.
1937	5	4	1	0	28	12	**Won World Series**.
1938	4	4	0	0	22	9	**Won World Series**.
1939	4	4	0	0	20	8	**Won World Series**.
1941	5	4	1	0	17	11	**Won World Series**.
1942	5	1	4	0	18	23	Lost World Series to St. Louis.
1943	5	4	1	0	17	9	**Won World Series**.
1947	7	4	3	0	38	29	**Won World Series**.
1949	5	4	1	0	21	14	**Won World Series**.
1950	4	4	0	0	11	5	**Won World Series**.
1951	6	4	2	0	29	18	**Won World Series**.
1952	7	4	3	0	26	20	**Won World Series**.
1953	6	4	2	0	33	27	**Won World Series**.
1955	7	3	4	0	26	31	Lost World Series to Brooklyn.
1956	7	4	3	0	33	25	**Won World Series**.
1957	7	3	4	0	25	23	Lost World Series to Milwaukee.
1958	7	4	3	0	29	25	**Won World Series**.
1960	7	3	4	0	55	27	Lost World Series to Pittsburgh.
1961	5	4	1	0	27	13	**Won World Series**.
1962	7	4	3	0	20	21	**Won World Series**.
1963	4	0	4	0	4	12	Lost World Series to Los Angeles.
1964	7	3	4	0	33	32	Lost World Series to St. Louis.
1976	9	3	6	0	31	46	Lost World Series to Cincinnati.
1977	11	7	4	0	47	50	**Won World Series**.
1978	10	7	3	0	55	40	**Won World Series**.
1980	3	0	3	0	6	14	Lost ALCS to Kansas City.
1981	14	8	6	0	61	44	Lost World Series to Los Angeles.
1995	5	2	3	0	33	35	Lost Division playoff to Seattle.
TOTAL:	217	126	90	1	979	780	
AVERAGE:	6	4	2	0	28	22	

COACHING HISTORY: 1913-1914 Frank Chance 118-170-.410; 1914 Roger Peckinpaugh 9-8-.529; 1915-1917 Bill Donovan 220-239-.479; 1918-1929 Miller Huggins 1067-719-.597; 1929 Art Fletcher 6-5-.545; 1930 Bob Shawkey 86-68-.558; 1931-1946 Joe McCarthy 1460-867-.627; 1946 Bill Dickey 57-48-.543; 1946 Johnny Neun 8-6-.571; 1947-1948 Stanley Harris 191-117-.620; 1949-1960 Casey Stengel 1149-696-.623; 1961-1963 Ralph Houk 309-176-.637; 1964 Yogi Berra 99-63-.611; 1965-1966 Johnny Keane 81-101-.445; 1966-1973 Ralph Houk 635-630-.502; 1974-1975 Bill Virdon 142-124-.534; 1975-1979 Billy Martin 334-232-.590; 1978 Dick Howser 0-1-.000; 1978-1979 Bob Lemon 82-51-.617; 1980 Dick Howser 103-59-.636; 1981-1982 Bob Lemon 17-22-.436; 1981-1982 Gene Michael 92-76-.548; 1982 Clyde King 29-33-.468; 1983 Billy Martin

91-71-.562; 1984-1985 Yogi Berra 93-85-.522; 1985 Billy Martin 91-54-.628; 1986-1988 Lou Pinniella 224-193-.537; 1988 Billy Martin 40-28-.588; 1989 Dallas Green 56-65-.463; 1989-1990 Russell Dent 36-53-.404; 1990-1991 Stump Merrill 120-155-.436; 1992-present Buck Showalter

NEW YORK YANKEES

Home City: New York, New York
Home Stadium: Yankee Stadium Capacity: 67,224
Origin of Name: The team was called Yankees because they played in Yankee Stadium.

Regular Season Record

Season	League	GP	W	L	T	PF	PA	Pct
1927	NFL	16	7	8	1	143	174	.469
1928	NFL	13	4	8	1	103	179	.346
TOTAL:	2 years	29	11	16	2	246	353	
AVERAGE:		15	6	8	1	123	177	.414

COACHING HISTORY: 1927 Ralph Scott 7-8-1-.469; 1928 Dick Rauch 4-8-1-.346

NEW YORK YANKEES

Home City: New York, New York
Home Stadium: Yankee Stadium I Capacity: 63,800
Origin of Name: The team was owned by Dan Topping, the owner of the baseball Yankees and named after them.

Regular Season Record

Season	League	GP	W	L	T	PF	PA	Pct
1946	AAFC	14	10	3	1	270	192	.750
1947	AAFC	14	11	2	1	378	239	.821
1948	AAFC	14	6	8	0	265	301	.429
1949	AAFC	12	8	4	0	196	206	.667
TOTAL:	4 years	54	35	17	2	1109	938	
AVERAGE:		14	9	4	1	277	235	.667

Playoff Record

Season	GP	W	L	PF	PA	Result
1946	1	0	1	9	14	Lost championship game to Cleveland.
1947	1	0	1	3	14	Lost championship game to Cleveland.
TOTAL:	2	0	2	12	28	
AVERAGE:	1	0	1	6	14	

COACHING HISTORY: 1946-1948 Ray Flaherty 23-11-2-.667; 1948-1949 Red Strader 12-10-0-.545

NEW YORK YANKS

(were New York Bulldogs)
(became Dallas Texans)

Home City: New York, New York
Home Stadium: Yankee Stadium I Capacity: 63,800
Origin of Name: Adapted from previous sports teams in the city.

Regular Season Record

Season	League	GP	W	L	T	PF	PA	Pct
1950	NFL	12	7	5	0	366	367	.583
1951	NFL	12	1	9	2	241	382	.167
TOTAL:	2 years	24	8	14	2	607	749	
AVERAGE:		12	4	7	1	304	375	375

COACHING HISTORY: 1950-1951 Red Strader 8-14-2-.375

NEWARK PEPPERS

Home City: Harrison, New Jersey
Home Field: Harrison Field — Capacity: 21,000 [1915]
Origin of Name:

Regular Season Record

Season	League	GP	W	L	Pct	GB	R	OR
1915	FL	152	80	72	.526	6	585	562

COACHING HISTORY: Bill Phillips 26-27-.491; Bill McKechnie 54-45-.545

NEWARK TORNADOES
(were Orange Tornadoes)

Home City: Newark, New Jersey
Home Stadium: Newark Velodrome
Origin of Name: The team kept the same name when it moved from Orange to Newark.

Regular Season Record

Season	League	GP	W	L	T	PF	PA	Pct
1930	NFL	12	1	10	1	51	190	.125

COACHING HISTORY: John Depler 1-10-1-.125

OAKLAND ATHLETICS
(were Kansas City Athletics)

Home City: Oakland, California
Home Field: Oakland Alameda County Coliseum — Capacity: 47,313 [1995]
Origin of Name: The team kept the same nickname when it moved from Kansas City to Oakland.

Regular Season Record

Season	League	GP	W	L	Pct	GB	R	OR
1968	AL	162	82	80	.506	21	569	544
1969	AL	162	88	74	.543	9	740	678
1970	AL	162	89	73	.549	9	678	593
1971	AL	161	101	60	.627	-	691	564
1972	AL	155	93	62	.600	-	604	457
1973	AL	162	94	68	.580	-	758	615
1974	AL	162	90	72	.556	-	689	551

1975	AL	162	98	64	.605		758	606
1976	AL	161	87	74	.540	2.5	686	598
1977	AL	161	63	98	.391	38.5	605	749
1978	AL	162	69	93	.426	23	532	690
1979	AL	162	54	108	.333	34	573	860
1980	AL	162	83	79	.512	14	686	642
1981	AL	109	64	45	.587	NA	458	403
1982	AL	162	68	94	.420	25	691	819
1983	AL	162	74	88	.457	25	708	782
1984	AL	162	77	85	.475	7	738	796
1985	AL	162	77	85	.475	14	757	787
1986	AL	162	76	86	.469	16	731	760
1987	AL	162	81	81	.500	4	806	789
1988	AL	162	104	58	.642	-	800	620
1989	AL	162	99	63	.611	-	712	576
1990	AL	162	103	59	.636	-	733	570
1991	AL	162	84	78	.519	11	760	776
1992	AL	162	96	66	.593	-	745	672
1993	AL	162	68	94	.420	26	715	846
1994	AL	114	51	63	.447	1	549	589
1995	AL	144	67	77	.465	11	730	761
TOTAL:	28 years	4407	2280	2127		291	19202	18693
AVERAGE:		157	81	76	.517	10	686	668

Playoff Record

Season	GP	W	L	R	OR	Result
1971	3	0	3	7	15	Lost ALCS to Baltimore.
1972	12	7	5	29	31	**Won World Series.**
1973	12	7	5	36	39	**Won World Series.**
1974	9	7	2	27	18	**Won World Series.**
1975	3	0	3	6	18	Lost ALCS to Boston.
1981	6	3	3	14	22	Lost ALCS to New York.
1988	9	5	4	31	32	Lost World Series to Los Angeles.
1989	9	8	1	58	35	**Won World Series.**
1990	8	4	4	28	26	Lost World Series to Cincinnati.
1992	6	2	4	24	31	Lost ALCS to Toronto.
TOTAL:	77	43	34	260	267	
AVERAGE:	7	4	3	26	27	

COACHING HISTORY: 1968 Bob Kennedy 82-80-.506; 1969 Hank Bauer 80-69-.537; 1969-1970 John McNamara 97-78-.554; 1971-1973 Dick Williams 288-190-.603; 1974-1975 Alvin Dark 188-136-.580; 1976 Charles Tanner 87-74-.540; 1977-1978 Jack McKeon 71-105-.403; 1977-1978 Bobby Winkles 61-86-.415; 1979 Jim Marshall 54-108-.333; 1980-1982 Billy Martin 215-218-.497; 1983-1984 Steve Boros 94-112-.456; 1984-1986 Jackie Moore 163-190 .462; 1986 Jeff Newman 2-8-.200; 1986-1995 Tony LaRussa 798-673-.542; 1996-present Art Howe

OAKLAND CLIPPERS

Home City: Oakland, California
Home Field: Oakland Coliseum Capacity: 50,000
Origin of Name: The name was suggested by the clipper ships that made the city their home port.

Regular Season Record

Season	League	GP	W	L	T	GF	GA	BP	Pts	Pct
1967	NPSL	32	19	8	5	64	34	NA	185	.642
1968	NASL	32	18	8	6	71	38	59	185	.642
TOTAL:	2 years	64	37	16	11	135	72	59	370	
AVERAGE:		32	19	8	5	68	36	30	185	.642

Playoff Record

Season	GP	W	L	T	GF	GA	Result
1967	2	1	1	0	4	2	**Won NPSL championship.**

COACHING HISTORY: 1967-1968 Ivan Toplak 37-16-11-.642

OAKLAND INVADERS

Home City: Oakland, California
Home Stadium: Oakland Coliseum Capacity: 54,615 [1984]
Origin of Name: The name was adopted to rival the NFL's Raiders.

Regular Season Record

Season	League	GP	W	L	T	PF	PA	Pct
1983	USFL	18	9	9	0	319	317	.500
1984	USFL	18	7	11	0	242	348	.389
1985	USFL	18	13	4	1	473	359	.750
TOTAL:	3 years	54	29	24	1	1034	1024	
AVERAGE:		18	10	8	0	345	341	.546

Playoff Record

Season	GP	W	L	PF	PA	Result
1983	1	0	1	21	37	Lost 1st round game to Michigan.
1985	3	2	1	100	74	Lost championship game to Baltimore.
TOTAL:	4	2	2	121	111	
AVERAGE:	2	1	1	61	56	

COACHING HISTORY: 1983-1984 John Ralston 9-12-0-.429; 1984 Chuck Hutchison 7-8-0-.467; 1985 Charlie Sumner 13-4-1-.750

OAKLAND OAKS
(became Washington Capitols)

Home City: Oakland, California
Home Court: Oakland County Coliseum Capacity: 12,500
Origin of Name: The was name was adopted from the Pacific Coast League baseball team.

Regular Season Record

Season	League	GP	W	L	PPGF	PPGA	Pct	GB
1967-1968	ABA	78	22	56	110.8	117.4	.282	26
1968-1969	ABA	78	60	18	126.5	118.1	.769	-
TOTAL:	2 years	156	82	74				26
AVERAGE:		78	41	37	118.7	117.8	.526	13

Playoff Record

Season	GP	W	L	PPGF	PPGA	Result
1968-1969	16	12	4	124.8	117.3	**Won ABA championship.**

COACHING HISTORY: 1967-1968 Bruce Hale 22-56-.282; 1968-1969 Alex Hannum 60-18-.769

OAKLAND RAIDERS
(became Los Angeles Raiders)

Home City: San Francisco, California (1960-1961)
Oakland, California (1962-1981)
Home Stadium: Kesar Stadium (1960) Capacity: 59,636
Candlestick Park (1961) Capacity: 42,500
Frank Youell Field (1962-1965) Capacity: 20,000
Oakland-Alameda County Coliseum (1966-1981) Capacity: 54,615 [1981]
Origin of Name: The name was chosen by team executives.

Regular Season Record

Season	League	GP	W	L	T	PF	PA	Pct
1960	AFL	14	6	8	0	319	388	.429
1961	AFL	14	2	12	0	237	458	.143
1962	AFL	14	1	13	0	213	370	.071
1963	AFL	14	10	4	0	363	288	.714
1964	AFL	14	5	7	2	303	350	.417
1965	AFL	14	8	5	1	298	239	.615
1966	AFL	14	8	5	1	315	288	.615
1967	AFL	14	13	1	0	468	233	.929
1968	AFL	14	12	2	0	453	233	.857
1969	AFL	14	12	1	1	377	242	.923
1970	NFL	14	8	4	2	300	293	.667
1971	NFL	14	8	4	2	344	278	.667
1972	NFL	14	10	3	1	365	248	.750
1973	NFL	14	9	4	1	292	175	.679
1974	NFL	14	12	2	0	355	228	.857
1975	NFL	14	11	3	0	375	255	.786
1976	NFL	14	13	1	0	350	237	.929
1977	NFL	14	11	3	0	351	230	.786
1978	NFL	16	9	7	0	311	283	.563
1979	NFL	16	9	7	0	365	337	.563
1980	NFL	16	11	5	0	364	306	.688
1981	NFL	16	7	9	0	273	343	.438
TOTAL:	22 years	316	195	110	11	7391	6302	
AVERAGE:		14	9	5	0	336	286	.634

Playoff Record

Season	GP	W	L	PF	PA	Result
1967	1	1	0	40	7	Lost Super Bowl to Green Bay.
1968	2	1	1	64	33	Lost AFL championship to N.Y. Jets.
1969	2	1	1	63	24	Lost AFL championship to Kansas City.
1970	2	1	1	38	41	Lost AFC championship to Baltimore.

1972	1	0	1	7	13	Lost Divisional playoff to Pittsburgh.
1973	2	1	1	43	41	Lost AFC championship to Miami.
1974	2	1	1	41	50	Lost AFC championship to Pittsburgh.
1975	2	1	1	41	44	Lost AFC championship to Pittsburgh.
1976	3	3	0	80	42	**Won Super Bowl**.
1977	2	1	1	54	51	Lost AFC championship to Denver.
1980	4	4	0	102	56	**Won Super Bowl**
TOTAL:	23	15	8	573	402	
AVERAGE:	2	1	1	52	37	

COACHING HISTORY: 1960 Eddie Erdelatz 6-8-0--143; 1961-1962 Marty Feldman 2-17-0-.105; 1962 Red Conkright 1-8-0-.111; 1963-1965 Al Davis 23-16-3-.583; 1966-1968 John Rauch 33-8-1-.779; 1969-1978 John Madden 103-32-7-.750; 1979-1981 Tom Flores 27-21-0-.563

OAKLAND RAIDERS

(were Los Angeles Raiders)

Home City: Oakland, California
Home Stadium: Oakland Alameda County Coliseum Capacity: 54,587 [1995]
Origin of Name: The team kept the same nickname when it moved from Los Angeles to Oakland.

Regular Season Record

Season	League	GP	W	L	T	PF	PA	Pct
1995	NFL	16	8	8	0	348	332	.500

COACHING HISTORY: 1995-present Mike White

OAKLAND SEALS

(became California Golden Seals)

Home City: Oakland, California
Home Arena: Oakland Alameda County Coliseum Capacity: 12,500
Origin of Name: Named after the semi-professional Western Hockey League team of the previous year based in San Francisco.

Regular Season Record

Season	League	GP	W	L	T	GF	GA	Pts	Pct
1967-1968	NHL	74	15	42	17	153	219	47	.318
1968-1969	NHL	76	29	36	11	219	251	69	.454
1969-1970	NHL	76	22	40	14	169	243	58	.372
TOTAL:	3 years	226	66	118	42	541	713	174	
AVERAGE:		75	22	39	14	180	238	58	.385

Playoff Record

Season	GP	W	L	GF	GA	Result
1968-1969	7	3	4	25	23	Lost quarterfinal series to Los Angeles.
1969-1970	4	0	4	6	12	Lost quarterfinal series to Pittsburgh.
TOTAL:	11	3	8	31	35	
AVERAGE:	6	2	4	16	18	

COACHING HISTORY: 1967-1968 Bert Olmstead 11-37-16-.297; 1967-1968 Gord Fashoway 4-5-1-.450; 1968-1970 Fred Glover 51-76-25-.418

OAKLAND STOMPERS

(were Connecticut Bicentennials)
(became Edmonton Drillers)

Home City: Oakland, California
Home Field: Oakland Alameda County Coliseum — Capacity: 54,037 [1978]
Origin of Name: The name was chosen to honor California's wine making industry.

Regular Season Record

Season	League	GP	W	L	GF	GA	BP	Pts	Pct
1978	NASL	30	12	18	34	59	31	103	.381

COACHING HISTORY: Mirko Stojanovic 4-4; Ken Bracewell 7-13; Shep Messing & Dick Berg & Charlie Mrosko 1-1

OHIO GLORY

Home City: Columbus, Ohio
Home Stadium: Ohio Stadium (Ohio State University) — Capacity: 86,071 [1992]
Origin of Name:

Regular Season Record

Season	League	GP	W	L	T	PF	PA	Pct
1992	WFL	10	1	9	0	132	230	.100

COACHING HISTORY: Larry Little 1-9-0-.100

OKLAHOMA OUTLAWS

(merged with Arizona for the 1985 season)

Home City: Tulsa, Oklahoma
Home Stadium: Skelly Stadium — Capacity: 40,235 [1984]
Origin of Name: The name was chosen by team executives.

Regular Season Record

Season	League	GP	W	L	T	PF	PA	Pct
1984	USFL	18	6	12	0	251	459	.333

COACHING HISTORY: Woody Widenhofer 6-12-0-.333

OORANG INDIANS

Home City: Marion, Ohio
Home Stadium:
Origin of Name: The team was composed entirely of native Americans

Regular Season Record

Season	League	GP	W	L	T	PF	PA	Pct
1922	NFL	8	2	6	0	51	184	.250
1923	NFL	11	1	10	0	49	247	.045
TOTAL:	2 years	19	3	16	0	100	431	
AVERAGE:		10	2	8	0	50	216	.079

COACHING HISTORY: 1922-1923 Jim Thorpe 3-16-0-.079

ORANGE TORNADOES

(became Newark Tornadoes)

Home City: Orange, New Jersey
Home Stadium: Casey Stadium
Origin of Name: The team was also known as the Orange A.C.'s.

Regular Season Record

Season	League	GP	W	L	T	PF	PA	Pct
1929	NFL	11	3	4	4	35	80	.455

COACHING HISTORY: John Depler 3-4-4-.455

ORLANDO MAGIC

Home City: Orlando, Florida
Home Court: Orlando Arena Capacity: 15,998 [1995]
Origin of Name: The team name was chosen in a contest sponsored by the club and the ORLANDO SENTINEL.

Regular Season Record

Season	League	GP	W	L	PPGF	PPGA	Pct	GB
1989-1990	NBA	82	18	64	110.9	119.8	.220	40
1990-1991	NBA	82	31	51	105.9	109.9	.378	24
1991-1992	NBA	82	21	61	101.6	108.5	.256	30
1992-1993	NBA	82	41	41	105.5	104.2	.500	19
1993-1994	NBA	82	50	32	105.7	101.8	.610	7
1994-1995	NBA	82	57	25	110.9	103.8	.695	-
1995-1996	NBA	82	60	22	104.5	99.0	.732	-
TOTAL:	7 years	574	278	296				120
AVERAGE:		82	40	42	106.4	106.7	.484	17

Playoff Record

Season	GP	W	L	PPGF	PPGA	Result
1993-1994	3	0	3	91.7	97.0	Lost 1st round series to Indiana.
1994-1995	21	11	10	102.4	101.1	Lost championship series to Houston.
1995-1996	12	7	5	98.3	96.7	Lost Conference final to Chicago.
TOTAL:	36	18	18			
AVERAGE:	12	6	6	100.1	99.3	

COACHING HISTORY: 1989-1993 Matt Guokas 111-217-.338; 1993-present Brian Hill

ORLANDO RENEGADES

(were Washington Federals)

Home City: Orlando, Florida
Home Stadium: Orlando Stadium — Capacity: 50,000
Origin of Name: The team was named by owner Donald Dizney. In his words "Any time you comb your hair a little different you have to have a little renegade blood in you. And we hope to be a little different."

Regular Season Record

Season	League	GP	W	L	T	PF	PA	Pct
1985	USFL	18	5	13	0	308	481	.278

COACHING HISTORY: Lee Corso 5-13-0

ORLANDO THUNDER

Home City: Orlando, Florida
Home Stadium: Florida Citrus Bowl — Capacity: 52,300 [1992]
Origin of Name:

Regular Season Record

Season	League	GP	W	L	T	PF	PA	Pct
1991	WLAF	10	5	5	0	242	286	.500
1992	WFL	10	8	2	0	247	127	.800
TOTAL:	2 years	20	13	7	0	489	413	
AVERAGE:		10	7	3	0	245	207	.650

Playoff Record

Season	GP	W	L	PF	PA	Result
1992	2	1	1	62	28	Lost championship game to Sacramento.

COACHING HISTORY: 1991 Don Matthews 5-5-0-.500; 1992 Galen Hall 8-2-0-.800

OSHKOSH ALL-STARS

Home City: Oshkosh, Wisconsin
Home Court: South Park Junior High School Gym — Capacity: 2,200
Origin of Name:

Regular Season Record

Season	League	GP	W	L	PPGF	PPGA	Pct	GB
1937-1938	NBL	14	12	2	49.1	35.2	.857	-
1938-1939	NBL	28	17	11	41.2	36.1	.607	-
1939-1940	NBL	28	15	13	42.7	40.2	.536	-
1940-1941	NBL	24	18	6	42.2	37.1	.750	-
1941-1942	NBL	24	20	4	49.3	40.7	.833	-
1942-1943	NBL	23	11	12	44.4	44.2	.478	6
1943-1944	NBL	22	7	15	42.1	43.5	.318	11
1944-1945	NBL	30	12	18	46.9	48.2	.400	7

1945-1946	NBL	34	19	15	53.4	49.2	.559	2
1946-1947	NBL	44	28	16	58.0	55.3	.636	-
1947-1948	NBL	60	29	31	59.7	59.6	.483	14
1948-1949	NBL	64	37	27	60.9	59.0	.578	-
TOTAL:	12 years	395	225	170				40
AVERAGE:		33	19	14	49.2	45.7	.570	3

Playoff Record

Season	GP	W	L	PPGF	PPGA	Result
1937-1938	5	3	2	35.0	33.2	Lost championship series to Akron.
1938-1939	5	2	3	36.8	40.0	Lost championship series to Akron.
1939-1940	8	4	4	44.1	39.5	Lost championship series to Akron.
1940-1941	5	5	0	45.6	36.2	**Won NBL championship**.
1941-1942	5	4	1	53.4	49.6	**Won NBL championship**.
1942-1943	2	0	2	42.5	53.0	Lost 1st round series to Sheboygan.
1943-1944	3	1	2	30.7	34.7	Lost 1st round series to Sheboygan.
1945-1946	5	2	3	51.6	51.6	Lost 1st round series to Sheboygan.
1946-1947	7	3	4	50.3	50.1	Lost 2nd round series to Chicago.
1947-1948	4	1	3	51.4	70.0	Lost 1st round series to Minneapolis.
1948-1949	7	3	4	68.4	68.3	Lost 2nd round series to Anderson.
TOTAL:	56	28	28			
AVERAGE:	5	3	2	46.3	47.8	

COACHING HISTORY: 1937-1949 Lon Darling 196-147-.571; 1948-1949 Gene Englund 29-23-.558

OTTAWA CIVICS
(were Denver Spurs)

Home City: Ottawa, Ontario
Home Arena: Ottawa Civic Center Capacity: 9,355 [1976]
Origin of Name: The team was named after the arena in which they played their home games.

Regular Season Record

Season	League	GP	W	L	T	GF	GA	Pts	Pct
1975-1976	WHA	7	0	7	0	20	30	0	.000

COACHING HISTORY: Jean-Guy Talbot 0-7-0-.000

OTTAWA NATIONALS
(became Toronto Toros)

Home City: Ottawa, Ontario
Home Arena: Ottawa Civic Center Capacity: 9,300 [1972]
Origin of Name: The team took the name because they were the nation's capital.

Regular Season Record

Season	League	GP	W	L	T	GF	GA	Pts	Pct
1972-1973	WHA	78	35	39	4	279	301	74	.474

Playoff Record

Season	GP	W	L	GF	GA	Result
1972-1973	5	1	4	16	24	Lost quarterfinal series to New England.

COACHING HISTORY: Billy Harris 35-39-4-.474

OTTAWA ROUGH RIDERS

Home City: Ottawa, Ontario
Home Stadium: Frank Clair Stadium * Capacity: 30,927 [1995]
Origin of Name: The team adopted the name from the lumberjacks who rode the logs down the Ottawa River.

Regular Season Record

Season	League	GP	W	L	T	PF	PA	Pts	Pct
1950	CRU	12	4	7	1	182	231	9	.375
1951	CRU	12	7	5	0	218	197	14	.583
1952	CRU	12	5	7	0	200	238	10	.417
1953	CRU	14	7	7	0	266	238	14	.500
1954	CRU	14	2	12	0	129	337	4	.143
1955	CRU	12	3	9	0	174	337	6	.250
1956	CFC	14	7	7	0	326	359	14	.500
1957	CFC	14	8	6	0	326	237	16	.571
1958	CFL	14	6	8	0	233	243	12	.429
1959	CFL	14	8	6	0	275	217	16	.571
1960	CFL	14	9	5	0	400	283	18	.643
1961	CFL	14	8	6	0	359	285	16	.571
1962	CFL	14	6	7	1	339	302	13	.464
1963	CFL	14	9	5	0	326	284	18	.643
1964	CFL	14	8	5	1	313	228	17	.607
1965	CFL	14	7	7	0	300	234	14	.500
1966	CFL	14	11	3	0	278	177	22	.786
1967	CFL	14	9	4	1	337	207	19	.679
1968	CFL	14	9	3	2	416	271	20	.714
1969	CFL	14	11	3	0	399	298	22	.786
1970	CFL	14	4	10	0	255	279	8	.286
1971	CFL	14	6	8	0	291	277	12	.429
1972	CFL	14	11	3	0	298	228	22	.786
1973	CFL	14	9	5	0	275	234	18	.643
1974	CFL	16	7	9	0	261	271	14	.438
1975	CFL	16	10	5	1	394	280	21	.656
1976	CFL	16	9	6	1	411	346	19	.594
1977	CFL	16	8	8	0	368	344	16	.500
1978	CFL	16	11	5	0	395	261	22	.688
1979	CFL	16	8	6	2	349	315	18	.563
1980	CFL	16	7	9	0	353	393	14	.438
1981	CFL	16	5	11	0	306	446	10	.313
1982	CFL	16	5	11	0	376	462	10	.313
1983	CFL	16	8	8	0	384	424	16	.500
1984	CFL	16	4	12	0	354	507	8	.250
1985	CFL	16	7	9	0	272	402	14	.438
1986	CFL	18	3	14	1	346	514	7	.194

1987	CFL	18	3	15	0	377	598	6	.167
1988	CFL	18	2	16	0	278	618	4	.111
1989	CFL	18	4	14	0	426	630	8	.222
1990	CFL	18	7	11	0	540	602	14	.389
1991	CFL	18	7	11	0	522	577	14	.389
1992	CFL	18	9	9	0	484	439	18	.500
1993	CFL	18	4	14	0	387	517	8	.222
1994	CFL	18	4	14	0	480	642	8	.222
1995	CFL	18	3	15	0	348	685	6	.167
TOTAL:	46 years	700	309	380	11	15326	16494	629	
AVERAGE:		15	7	8	0	333	359	14	.449

Playoff Record

Season	GP	W	L	T	PF	PA	Result
1951	4	4	0	0	92	47	**Won Grey Cup**.
1956	1	0	1	0	21	46	Lost Division semifinal to Hamilton.
1957	1	0	1	0	15	24	Lost Division semifinal to Montreal.
1958	3	1	2	0	40	66	Lost Division final to Hamilton.
1959	3	2	1	0	67	26	Lost Division final to Hamilton.
1960	4	4	0	0	100	61	**Won Grey Cup**.
1961	1	0	1	0	19	43	Lost Division semifinal to Toronto.
1962	1	0	1	0	17	18	Lost Division semifinal to Montreal.
1963	3	2	1	0	52	68	Lost Division final to Hamilton.
1964	3	2	1	0	65	39	Lost Division final to Hamilton.
1965	3	1	2	0	56	42	Lost Division final to Hamilton.
1966	3	2	1	0	86	46	Lost Grey Cup game to Saskatchewan.
1967	3	1	2	0	41	59	Lost Division final to Hamilton.
1968	3	2	1	0	71	48	**Won Grey Cup**
1969	3	2	1	0	75	36	**Won Grey Cup**.
1971	1	0	1	0	4	23	Lost Division semifinal to Hamilton.
1972	3	2	1	0	41	41	Lost Division final to Hamilton.
1973	2	2	0	0	45	32	**Won Grey Cup**.
1974	2	1	1	0	25	33	Lost Division final to Montreal.
1975	1	0	1	0	10	20	Lost Division final to Montreal.
1976	2	2	0	0	40	35	**Won Grey Cup**.
1977	2	1	1	0	39	37	Lost Division final to Montreal.
1978	1	0	1	0	16	21	Lost Division final to Montreal.
1979	2	1	1	0	35	43	Lost Division final to Montreal.
1980	1	0	1	0	21	25	Lost Division semifinal to Montreal.
1981	3	2	1	0	60	55	Lost Grey Cup game to Edmonton.
1982	2	1	1	0	37	64	Lost Division final to Toronto.
1983	1	0	1	0	31	33	Lost Division semifinal to Hamilton.
1985	1	0	1	0	20	30	Lost Division semifinal to Montreal.
1990	1	0	1	0	25	34	Lost Division semifinal to Toronto.
1991	1	0	1	0	8	26	Lost Division semifinal to Winnipeg.
1992	1	0	1	0	28	29	Lost Division semifinal to Hamilton.
1993	1	0	1	0	10	21	Lost Division semifinal to Hamilton
1994	1	0	1	0	16	26	Lost Division semifinal to Winnipeg.
TOTAL:	68	35	33	0	1328	1297	
AVERAGE:	2	1	1	0	39	38	

COACHING HISTORY: 1950 Wally Masters 4-7-1-.375; 1951-1954 Clem Crowe 21-31-0-.404; 1955 Chan Caldwell 3-9-0-.250; 1956-1969 Frank Clair 116-75-5-.605; 1970-1973 Jack

Gotta 30-26-0-.536; 1974-1984 George Brancato 82-90-4-.477; 1985-1986 Joe Moss 10-23-1-.309; 1987 Fred Glick 3-15-0-.167; 1988 Bob Webber 2-16-0-.111; 1989-1991 Steve Goldman 11-25-0-..306; 1991 Joe Faragalli 7-7-0-.500; 1992-1993 Ron Smeltzer 13-23-0-.361; 1994 Adam Rita 4-14-0-.222; 1995-1996 Jim Gilstrap 3-17-0; 1996-present John Payne

*Known as Lansdowne Park from 1950 to 1992

OTTAWA SENATORS
(became St. Louis Eagles)

Home City: Ottawa, Ontario
Home Arena: Laurier Avenue Arena (1909-1923) Capacity: 7,500
Ottawa Auditorium (1923-1934) Capacity: 10,000
Origin of Name: The team was named Senators because Ottawa is the capital city of Canada.

Regular Season Record

Season	League	GP	W	L	T	GF	GA	Pts	Pct
1908-1909	ECHA	12	10	2	0	117	63	20	.833
1909-1910	NHA	12	9	3	0	89	66	18	.750
1910-1911	NHA	16	13	3	0	122	69	26	.813
1911-1912	NHA	18	9	9	0	99	93	18	.500
1912-1913	NHA	20	9	11	0	87	81	18	.450
1913-1914	NHA	20	11	9	0	65	71	22	.550
1914-1915	NHA	20	14	6	0	74	65	28	.700
1915-1916	NHA	24	13	11	0	78	72	26	.542
1916-1917	NHA	20	15	5	0	119	63	30	.750
1917-1918	NHL	22	9	13	0	102	114	18	.409
1918-1919	NHL	18	12	6	0	71	53	24	.667
1919-1920	NHL	24	19	5	0	121	64	38	.792
1920-1921	NHL	24	14	10	0	97	75	28	.583
1921-1922	NHL	24	14	8	2	106	84	30	.625
1922-1923	NHL	24	14	9	1	77	54	29	.604
1923-1924	NHL	24	16	8	0	74	54	32	.667
1924-1925	NHL	30	17	12	1	83	66	35	.583
1925-1926	NHL	36	24	8	4	77	42	52	.722
1926-1927	NHL	44	30	10	4	86	69	64	.727
1927-1928	NHL	44	20	14	10	78	57	50	.568
1928-1929	NHL	44	14	17	13	54	67	41	.466
1929-1930	NHL	44	21	15	8	138	118	50	.568
1930-1931	NHL	44	10	30	4	91	142	24	.273
1932-1933	NHL	48	11	27	10	88	131	32	.333
1933-1934	NHL	48	13	29	6	115	143	32	.333
TOTAL:	25 years	704	361	280	63	2308	1976	785	
AVERAGE:		28	14	11	3	92	79	31	.558

Playoff Record

Season	GP	W	L	T	GF	GA	Result
1909-1910	4	4	0	0	36	15	Won playoff series from Edmonton.
1910-1911	2	2	0	0	20	8	**Won Stanley Cup**.
1914-1915	5	1	4	0	12	27	Lost Stanley Cup final to Vancouver.
1916-1917	2	1	1	0	6	7	Lost playoff series to Canadiens.
1918-1919	5	1	4	0	18	26	Lost playoff series to Canadiens.

1919-1920	5	3	2	0	15	11	**Won Stanley Cup**.
1920-1921	7	5	2	0	19	12	**Won Stanley Cup**.
1921-1922	2	0	1	1	4	5	Lost playoff series to Toronto.
1922-1923	8	6	2	0	16	10	**Won Stanley Cup**
1923-1924	2	0	2	0	2	5	Lost playoff series to Canadiens.
1925-1926	2	0	1	1	1	2	Lost playoff series to Maroons.
1926-1927	6	3	0	3	12	4	**Won Stanley Cup**.
1927-1928	2	0	2	0	1	3	Lost quarterfinal series to Maroons.
1929-1930	2	0	1	1	3	6	Lost quarterfinal series to Rangers.
TOTAL:	54	26	22	6	165	141	
AVERAGE:	4	2	2	0	12	10	

COACHING HISTORY: 1908-1909 Bruce Stuart 10-2-0-.833; 1910-1911 Pud Glass 13-3-0-.813; 1914-1915 Frank Shaughnessy 14-6-0-.700; 1915-1916 Alf Smith 13-11-0-.542; 1916-1918 Eddie Gerard 24-18-0-.571; 1918-1919 Alf Smith 12-6-0-.667; 1919-1926 Pete Green 118-60-8-.656; 1926-1929 Dave Gill 64-41-27-.587; 1929-1931 Edouard Lalonde 31-45-12-.420; 1932-1933 Cyril Denneny 11-27-10-.333; 1933-1934 George Boucher 13-29-6-.333

OTTAWA SENATORS

Home City: Ottawa, Ontario
Home Arena: Ottawa Civic Center (1992-1996) Capacity: 10,575 [1995]
Corel Center (1996-present) Capacity: 18,500 [1996]
Origin of Name: The team was named in honor of the previous NHL team based in Ottawa.

Regular Season Record

Season	**League**	**GP**	**W**	**L**	**T**	**GF**	**GA**	**Pts**	**Pct**
1992-1993	NHL	84	10	70	4	202	395	24	.143
1993-1924	NHL	84	14	61	9	201	397	37	.220
1994-1995	NHL	48	9	34	5	116	174	23	.240
1995-1996	NHL	82	18	59	5	191	291	41	.250
TOTAL:	4 years	298	51	224	23	710	1257	125	
AVERAGE:		75	13	56	6	178	314	32	.210

COACHING HISTORY: 1992-1996 Rick Bowness 39-178-18-.204; 1995-1996 Dave Allison 2-22-1-.100; 1995-present Jacques Martin

PATERSON CRESCENTS
(were Paterson Whirlwinds)

Home City: Paterson, New Jersey
Home Court: Arcola Park
Origin of Name:

Regular Season Record

Season	**League**	**GP**	**W**	**L**	**Pct**	**GB**
1930-1931	ABL	18	9	9	.500	3.5

COACHING HISTORY:

PATERSON WHIRLWINDS
(became Paterson Crescents)

Home City: Paterson, New Jersey
Home Court: Arcola Park
Origin of Name:

Regular Season Record

Season	League	GP	W	L	Pct
1928-1929	ABL	37	9	28	.243
1929-1930	ABL	54	18	36	.333
TOTAL:	2 years	91	27	64	
AVERAGE:		46	14	32	.297

COACHING HISTORY:

PHILADELPHIA ATHLETICS

Home City: Philadelphia, Pennsylvania
Home Field: Athletics Park
Origin of Name: The team traces its roots to the mid 1800's, taking the name of a local social club.

Regular Season Record

Season	League	GP	W	L	Pct	GB	R	OR
1876	NL	59	14	45	.237	34.5	378	534

COACHING HISTORY: Al Wright 14-45-.237

PHILADELPHIA ATHLETICS

Home City: Philadelphia, Pennsylvania
Home Field: Oakdale Park (1882)
Athletics Park
Origin of Name: Named after previous National League team.

Regular Season Record

Season	League	GP	W	L	Pct	GB	R	OR
1882	AA	75	41	34	.547	11.5	406	389
1883	AA	98	66	32	.673	-	720	547
1884	AA	107	61	46	.570	14	700	546
1885	AA	112	55	57	.491	24	764	691
1886	AA	135	63	72	.467	28	772	942
1887	AA	133	64	69	.481	30	893	890
1888	AA	133	81	52	.609	10	827	594
1889	AA	133	75	58	.564	16	880	787
1890	AA	132	54	78	.409	34	702	945
1891	AA	139	73	66	.525	22	817	794
TOTAL:	10 years	1197	633	564		189.5	7481	7125
AVERAGE:		120	63	57	.529	19	748	713

COACHING HISTORY: 1882 Charlie Mason 21-15-.583; 1882-1883 Lew Simmons 86-51-.632; 1884-1885 Charlie Mason 45-44-.506; 1884-1891 Bill Sharsig 344-306-.529; 1885 Lon Knight 16-19-.457; 1886 Lew Simmons 41-55-.427; 1887 Frank Bancroft 22-25-.468; 1891 George Wood 54-46-.540; 1891 Bill Barnie 4-3-.571

PHILADELPHIA ATHLETICS
(became Kansas City Athletics)

Home City: Philadelphia, Pennsylvania
Home Field: Columbia Park (1901-1908) Capacity: 9,500 [1901]
Shibe Park (1909-1954)* Capacity: 33,156 [1953]
Origin of Name: Named after previous National League and American Association teams.

			Regular Season Record					
Season	**League**	**GP**	**W**	**L**	**Pct**	**GB**	**R**	**OR**
1901	AL	136	74	62	.544	9	805	760
1902	AL	136	83	53	.610	-	775	636
1903	AL	135	75	60	.556	14.5	597	519
1904	AL	151	81	70	.536	12.5	557	503
1905	AL	148	92	56	.622	-	617	486
1906	AL	145	78	67	.538	12	561	536
1907	AL	145	88	57	.607	1.5	582	509
1908	AL	153	68	85	.444	22	487	554
1909	AL	153	95	58	.621	3.5	600	414
1910	AL	150	102	48	.680	-	672	439
1911	AL	151	101	50	.669	-	861	601
1912	AL	152	90	62	.592	15	780	656
1913	AL	153	96	57	.627	-	794	593
1914	AL	152	99	53	.651	-	749	520
1915	AL	152	43	109	.283	58.5	545	890
1916	AL	153	36	117	.235	54.5	447	776
1917	AL	153	55	98	.359	44.5	527	691
1918	AL	128	52	76	.406	24	412	563
1919	AL	140	36	104	.257	52	459	742
1920	AL	154	48	106	.312	50	555	831
1921	AL	153	53	100	.346	45	657	894
1922	AL	154	65	89	.422	29	705	830
1923	AL	152	69	83	.454	29	661	761
1924	AL	152	71	81	.467	20	685	778
1925	AL	152	88	64	.579	8.5	830	714
1926	AL	150	83	67	.553	6	677	570
1927	AL	154	91	63	.591	19	841	726
1928	AL	153	98	55	.641	2.5	829	615
1929	AL	150	104	46	.693	-	901	615
1930	AL	154	102	52	.662	-	951	751
1931	AL	152	107	45	.704	-	858	626
1932	AL	154	94	60	.610	13	981	752
1933	AL	151	79	72	.523	19.5	875	853
1934	AL	150	68	82	.453	31	764	838
1935	AL	149	58	91	.389	34	710	869
1936	AL	153	53	100	.346	49	714	1045
1937	AL	151	54	97	.358	46.5	699	854
1938	AL	152	53	99	.349	46	726	956

1939	AL	152	55	97	.362	51.5	711	1022
1940	AL	154	54	100	.351	36	703	932
1941	AL	154	64	90	.416	37	713	840
1942	AL	154	55	99	.357	48	549	801
1943	AL	154	49	105	.318	49	497	717
1944	AL	154	72	82	.468	17	525	594
1945	AL	150	52	98	.347	34.5	494	638
1946	AL	154	49	105	.318	55	529	680
1947	AL	154	78	76	.506	19	633	614
1948	AL	154	84	70	.545	12.5	729	735
1949	AL	154	81	73	.526	16	726	725
1950	AL	154	52	102	.338	46	670	913
1951	AL	154	70	84	.455	28	736	745
1952	AL	154	79	75	.513	16	664	723
1953	AL	154	59	95	.383	41.5	632	799
1954	AL	154	51	103	.331	60	542	875
TOTAL:	54 years	8134	3886	4248		1338.5	36499	38619
AVERAGE:		151	72	79	.478	25	676	715

Playoff Record

Season	**GP**	**W**	**L**	**R**	**OR**	**Result**
1905	5	1	4	3	15	Lost World Series to New York.
1910	5	4	1	35	15	**Won World Series.**
1911	6	4	2	27	13	**Won World Series.**
1913	5	4	1	23	15	**Won World Series.**
1914	4	0	4	6	16	Lost World Series to Boston.
1929	5	4	1	26	17	**Won World Series.**
1930	6	4	2	21	12	**Won World Series.**
1931	7	3	4	22	19	Lost World Series To St. Louis.
TOTAL:	43	24	19	163	122	
AVERAGE:	5	3	2	20	15	

COACHING HISTORY: 1901-1950 Connie Mack 3627-3891-.482; 1951-1953 Jimmy Dykes 208-254-.450; 1954 Eddie Joost 51-103-.331

*Known as Connie Mack Stadium from 1953 to 1954.

PHILADELPHIA ATOMS

Home City: Philadelphia, Pennsylvania
Home Stadium: Veterans Stadium — Capacity: 55,730 [1973]
Origin of Name: The name was chosen in a Name the Team contest.

Regular Season Record

Season	**League**	**GP**	**W**	**L**	**T**	**GF**	**GA**	**BP**	**Pts**	**Pct**
1973	NASL	19	9	2	8	29	14	26	104	.608
1974	NASL	20	8	11	1	25	25	23	74	.411
1975	NASL	22	10	12	-	33	42	30	90	.455
1976	NASL	24	8	16	-	32	49	32	80	.370
TOTAL:	4 years	85	35	41	9	119	130	111	348	
AVERAGE:		21	9	10	2	30	33	28	87	.455

Playoff Record

Season	GP	W	L	T	GF	GA	Result
1973	2	2	0	0	5	0	**Won NASL championship**.

COACHING HISTORY: 1973-1975 Al Miller 27-25-9-.488; 1976 Jesus Ponce 8-16-.370

PHILADELPHIA BELL

Home City: Philadelphia, Pennsylvania
Home Stadium: John F. Kennedy Stadium Capacity: 90,000 [1975]
Origin of Name: The name was suggested by one of the teams investors. The name was no doubt chosen because of Philadelphia's connection to the famous Liberty Bell.

Regular Season Record

Season	League	GP	W	L	T	PF	PA	Pct
1974	WFL	19	8	11	0	491	413	.421
1975	WFL	11	4	7	0	195	237	.364
TOTAL:	2 years	30	12	18	0	686	650	
AVERAGE:		15	6	9	0	343	325	.400

Playoff Record

Season	GP	W	L	PF	PA	Result
1974	1	0	1	3	18	Lost 1st round game to Florida.

COACHING HISTORY: 1974 Ron Waller 8-11-0-.421; 1975 Willie Wood 4-7-0-.364

PHILADELPHIA BLAZERS
(became Vancouver Blazers)

Home City: Philadelphia, Pennsylvania
Home Arena: Convention Hall Capacity: 9,000 [1972]
Origin of Name:

Regular Season Record

Season	League	GP	W	L	T	GF	GA	Pts	Pct
1972-1973	WHA	78	38	40	0	288	305	76	.487

Playoff Record

Season	GP	W	L	GF	GA	Result
1972-1973	4	0	4	6	19	Lost quarterfinal series to Cleveland.

COACHING HISTORY: John McKenzie 1-6-0-.143; Phil Watson 37-34-0-.521

PHILADELPHIA BLUE JAYS
(were Philadelphia Phillies)
(became Philadelphia Phillies)

Home City: Philadelphia, Pennsylvania
Home Stadium: Shibe Park Capacity: 32,750 [1947]
Origin of Name: When the team was bought in 1943 the new owners changed the name in an attempt to create a new image but the name didn't stick.

Regular Season Record

Season	League	GP	W	L	Pct	GB	R	OR
1943	NL	154	64	90	.416	41	571	676
1944	NL	153	61	92	.399	43.5	539	658
TOTAL:	2 years	307	125	182		84.5	1110	1334
AVERAGE:		154	63	91	.407	42	555	667

COACHING HISTORY: 1943 Stanley Harris 64-90-.416; 1944 Fred Fitzsimmons 61-92-.399

PHILADELPHIA EAGLES

(Pittsburgh Steelers and Philadelphia Eagles merged for the 1943 season)

Home City: Philadelphia, Pennsylvania
Home Stadium: Baker Bowl (1933-1935) Capacity: 18,800
Municipal Stadium (1936-1939, 1941) Capacity: 73,702
Shibe Park (1940, 1942, 1944-1957)* Capacity: 33,608
Franklin Field (1958-1970) Capacity: 60,546 [1970]
Veterans Stadium (1971-present) Capacity: 65,178 [1995]
Origin of Name: The team was named in honor of the eagle which was on the emblem of the National Recovery Administration of the New Deal.

Regular Season Record

Season	League	GP	W	L	T	PF	PA	Pct
1933	NFL	9	3	5	1	77	158	.389
1934	NFL	11	4	7	0	127	85	.364
1935	NFL	11	2	9	0	60	179	.182
1936	NFL	12	1	11	0	51	206	.083
1937	NFL	11	2	8	1	86	177	.227
1938	NFL	11	5	6	0	154	164	.455
1939	NFL	11	1	9	1	105	200	.136
1940	NFL	11	1	10	0	111	211	.091
1941	NFL	11	2	8	1	119	218	.227
1942	NFL	11	2	9	0	134	239	.182
1944	NFL	10	7	1	2	267	131	.800
1945	NFL	10	7	3	0	272	133	.700
1946	NFL	11	6	5	0	231	220	.545
1947	NFL	12	8	4	0	308	242	.667
1948	NFL	12	9	2	1	376	156	.792
1949	NFL	12	11	1	0	364	134	.917
1950	NFL	12	6	6	0	254	141	.500
1951	NFL	12	4	8	0	234	264	.333
1952	NFL	12	7	5	0	252	271	.583
1953	NFL	12	7	4	1	352	215	.625
1954	NFL	12	7	4	1	284	230	.625
1955	NFL	12	4	7	1	248	231	.375
1956	NFL	12	3	8	1	143	215	.292
1957	NFL	12	4	8	0	173	230	.333
1958	NFL	12	2	9	1	235	306	.208
1959	NFL	12	7	5	0	268	278	.583
1960	NFL	12	10	2	0	321	246	.833
1961	NFL	14	10	4	0	361	297	.714
1962	NFL	14	3	10	1	282	356	.250

1963	NFL	14	2	10	2	242	381	.214
1964	NFL	14	6	8	0	312	313	.429
1965	NFL	14	5	9	0	363	359	.357
1966	NFL	14	9	5	0	326	340	.643
1967	NFL	14	6	7	1	351	409	.464
1968	NFL	14	2	12	0	202	351	.143
1969	NFL	14	4	9	1	279	377	.321
1970	NFL	14	3	10	1	241	332	.231
1971	NFL	14	6	7	1	221	302	.464
1972	NFL	14	2	11	1	145	352	.179
1973	NFL	14	5	8	1	310	393	.393
1974	NFL	14	7	7	0	242	217	.500
1975	NFL	14	4	10	0	225	302	.286
1976	NFL	14	4	10	0	165	286	.286
1977	NFL	14	5	9	0	220	207	.357
1978	NFL	16	9	7	0	270	250	.563
1979	NFL	16	11	5	0	339	282	.688
1980	NFL	16	12	4	0	384	222	.688
1981	NFL	16	10	6	0	368	221	.625
1982	NFL	9	3	6	0	191	195	.333
1983	NFL	16	5	11	0	233	322	.313
1984	NFL	16	6	9	1	278	320	.406
1985	NFL	16	7	9	0	286	310	.438
1986	NFL	16	5	10	1	256	312	.344
1987	NFL	15	7	8	0	337	380	.467
1988	NFL	16	10	6	0	379	319	.625
1989	NFL	16	11	5	0	342	274	.688
1990	NFL	16	10	6	0	396	299	.625
1991	NFL	16	10	6	0	285	244	.625
1992	NFL	16	11	5	0	354	245	.688
1993	NFL	16	8	8	0	293	315	.500
1994	NFL	16	7	9	0	308	308	.438
1995	NFL	16	10	6	0	318	338	.615
TOTAL:	62 years	826	367	436	23	15710	16210	
AVERAGE:		13	6	7	0	253	261	.458

Playoff Record

Season	**GP**	**W**	**L**	**PF**	**PA**	**Result**
1947	2	1	1	42	28	Lost championship game to Cardinals
1948	1	1	0	7	0	**Won NFL championship**.
1949	1	1	0	14	0	**Won NFL championship**.
1960	1	1	0	17	13	**Won NFL championship**.
1978	1	0	1	13	14	Lost 1st round game to Atlanta.
1979	2	1	1	44	41	Lost Divisional playoff to Tampa Bay.
1980	3	2	1	61	50	Lost Super Bowl to Oakland.
1981	1	0	1	21	27	Lost 1st round playoff to N.Y. Giants.
1988	1	0	1	12	20	Lost Divisional playoff to Chicago.
1989	1	0	1	7	21	Lost Wild Card game to L.A. Rams.
1990	1	0	1	6	20	Lost Wild Card game to Washington.
1992	2	1	1	46	54	Lost Conference semifinal to Dallas.
1995	2	1	1	69	67	Lost Conference semifinal to Dallas.
TOTAL:	19	9	10	359	355	
AVERAGE:	2	1	1	28	27	

COACHING HISTORY: 1933-1935 Lud Wray 9-21-1-.306; 1936-1940 Bert Bell 10-44-2-.196; 1941-1950 Greasy Neale 58-39-4-.594; 1951 Bo McMillin 2-0-0-.1.000; 1951 Wayne Millner 2-8-0-.200; 1952-1955 Jim Trimble 25-20-3-.552; 1956-1957 Hugh Devore 7-16-1-.313; 1958-1960 Buck Shaw 19-16-1-.542; 1961-1963 Nick Skorich 15-24-3-.393; 1964-1968 Joe Kuharich 28-41-1-.407; 1969-1971 Jerry Williams 7-22-2-.258; 1971-1972 Ed Khayat 8-15-2-.360; 1973-1975 Mike McCormack 16-25-1-.393; 1976-1982 Dick Vermeil 54-47-0-.535; 1983-1985 Marion Campbell 17-29-1-.372; 1985 Fred Bruney 1-0-0-1.000; 1986-1990 Buddy Ryan 43-35-1-.551; 1991-1994 Rich Kotite 36-28-0-.563; 1995-present Ray Rhodes

PHILADELPHIA FLYERS

Home City: Philadelphia, Pennsylvania
Home Arena: CoreStates Spectrum* Capacity: 17,380 [1995]
Origin of Name: The name was chosen in a Name the Team Contest.

Regular Season Record

Season	League	GP	W	L	T	GF	GA	Pts	Pct
1967-1968	NHL	74	31	32	11	173	179	73	.493
1968-1969	NHL	76	20	35	21	174	225	61	.401
1969 1970	NHL	76	17	35	24	197	225	58	.382
1970-1971	NHL	78	28	33	17	207	225	73	.468
1971-1972	NHL	78	26	38	14	200	236	66	.423
1972-1973	NHL	78	37	30	11	296	256	85	.545
1973-1974	NHL	78	50	16	12	273	164	112	.718
1974-1975	NHL	80	51	18	11	293	181	113	.706
1975-1976	NHL	80	51	13	16	348	209	118	.738
1976-1977	NHL	80	48	16	16	323	213	112	.700
1977-1978	NHL	80	45	20	15	296	200	105	.656
1978-1979	NHL	80	40	25	15	281	248	95	.594
1979-1980	NHL	80	48	12	20	237	254	116	.725
1980-1981	NHL	80	41	24	15	313	249	97	.606
1981-1982	NHL	80	38	31	11	325	313	87	.544
1982-1983	NHL	80	49	23	8	326	240	106	.663
1983-1984	NHL	80	44	26	10	350	290	98	.613
1984-1985	NHL	80	53	20	7	348	241	113	.706
1985-1986	NHL	80	53	23	4	335	241	110	.688
1986-1987	NHL	80	46	26	8	310	245	100	.625
1987-1988	NHL	80	38	33	9	292	292	85	.531
1988-1989	NHL	80	36	36	8	307	285	80	.500
1989-1990	NHL	80	30	39	11	290	297	71	.444
1990-1991	NHL	80	33	37	10	252	267	76	.475
1991-1992	NHL	80	32	37	11	252	273	75	.469
1992-1993	NHL	84	36	37	11	319	319	83	.494
1993-1994	NHL	84	35	39	10	294	315	80	.476
1994-1995	NHL	48	28	16	4	150	132	60	.625
1995-1996	NHL	82	45	24	13	282	208	103	.628
TOTAL:	29 years	2276	1129	794	353	8043	7022	2611	
AVERAGE:		78	39	27	12	277	242	90	.574

Playoff Record

Season	GP	W	L	GF	GA	Result
1967-1968	7	3	4	17	17	Lost quarterfinal series to St. Louis.

1968-1969	4	0	4	3	17	Lost quarterfinal series to St. Louis.
1970-1971	4	0	4	8	20	Lost quarterfinal series to Chicago.
1972-1973	11	5	6	27	31	Lost semifinal series to Montreal.
1973-1974	17	12	5	54	36	**Won Stanley Cup**.
1974-1975	17	12	5	53	34	**Won Stanley Cup**.
1975-1976	16	8	8	61	49	Lost championship series to Montreal.
1976-1977	10	4	6	27	32	Lost semifinal series to Boston.
1977-1978	12	7	5	37	35	Lost semifinal series to Boston.
1978-1979	8	3	5	23	37	Lost quarterfinal series to Rangers.
1979-1980	19	13	6	80	53	Lost championship series to N.Y. Islanders.
1980-1981	12	6	6	48	39	Lost quarterfinal series to Calgary.
1981-1982	4	1	3	15	19	Lost preliminary series to N.Y. Rangers.
1982-1983	3	0	3	9	18	Lost preliminary series to N.Y. Rangers.
1983-1984	3	0	3	5	15	Lost preliminary series to Washington.
1984-1985	19	12	7	61	54	Lost championship series to Edmonton.
1985-1986	5	2	3	15	18	Lost preliminary series to N.Y. Rangers.
1986-1987	26	15	11	85	73	Lost championship series to Edmonton.
1987-1988	7	3	4	25	31	Lost preliminary series to Washington.
1988-1989	19	10	9	64	60	Lost semifinal series to Montreal.
1994-1995	15	10	5	50	43	Lost semifinal series to New Jersey.
1995-1996	12	6	6	37	28	Lost quarterfinal series to Florida.
TOTAL:	250	132	118	804	759	
AVERAGE:	11	6	5	38	35	

COACHING HISTORY: 1967-1969 Keith Allen 51-67-32-.447; 1969-1971 Vic Stasiuk 45-68-41-.425; 1971-1978 Fred Shero 308-151-95-.642; 1978-1979 Bob McCammon 22-17-11-.550; 1978-1982 Pat Quinn 141-73-48-.630; 1981-1984 Bob McCammon 97-51-20-.637; 1984-1988 Mike Keenan 190-102-28-.638; 1988-1992 Paul Holmgren 107-126-31-.464; 1991-1993 Bill Dineen 60-60-20-.500; 1993-1994 Terry Simpson 35-39-10-.476; 1994-present Terry Murray

*Known as The Spectrum from 1967 to 1994.

PHILADELPHIA FURY

(became Montreal Manic)

Home City: Philadelphia, Pennsylvania
Home Stadium: Veterans Stadium — Capacity: 66,052 [1980]
Origin of Name:

Regular Season Record

Season	**League**	**GP**	**W**	**L**	**GF**	**GA**	**BP**	**Pts**	**Pct**
1978	NASL	30	12	18	40	58	39	111	.411
1979	NASL	30	10	20	55	60	51	111	.411
1980	NASL	32	10	22	42	68	38	98	.340
TOTAL:	3 years	92	32	60	137	186	128	320	
AVERAGE:		31	11	20	46	62	43	107	.386

Playoff Record

Season	**GP**	**W**	**L**	**GF**	**GA**	**Result**
1979	4	2	2	6	6	Lost 2nd round series to Tampa Bay.

COACHING HISTORY: 1978 Richard Dinnis 6-10; 1978 Alan Ball 6-8; 1979 Marko Valok 10-20; 1980 Eddie Firmani 10-22

PHILADELPHIA KEYSTONES

Home City: Philadelphia, Pennsylvania
Home Field: Keystone Park
Origin of Name: The name was chosen because Pennsylvania is known as the Keystone State.

			Regular Season Record					
Season	League	GP	W	L	Pct	GB	R	OR
1884	UA	67	21	46	.313	50	414	545

COACHING HISTORY: Fergy Malone 11-30-.268; Tom Pratt 10-16-.385

PHILADELPHIA PHILLIES

(were Worcester Brown Stockings)
(known as Philadelphia Blue Jays from 1943 to 1944)

Home City: Philadelphia, Pennsylvania
Home Field: Recreation Park (1883-1886)
Philadelphia Baseball Grounds (1887-1894)
Baker Bowl (1895-1938) Capacity: 18,800 [1895]
Shibe Park (1938-1970) Capacity: 33,608 [1961]
Veterans Stadium (1971-present) Capacity: 64,538 [1995]
Origin of Name: The team was originally called Fillies.

			Regular Season Record					
Season	League	GP	W	L	Pct	GB	R	OR
1883	NL	98	17	81	.173	46	437	887
1884	NL	112	39	73	.348	45	549	824
1885	NL	110	56	54	.509	30	513	511
1886	NL	114	71	43	.623	14	621	498
1887	NL	123	75	48	.610	3.5	901	702
1888	NL	130	69	61	.531	14.5	535	509
1889	NL	127	63	64	.496	20.5	742	748
1890	NL	132	78	54	.591	9.5	823	707
1891	NL	137	68	69	.496	18.5	756	773
1892	NL	153	87	66	.569	16.5	860	690
1893	NL	129	72	57	.558	14	1011	841
1894	NL	128	71	57	.555	18	1143	966
1895	NL	131	78	53	.595	9.5	1068	957
1896	NL	130	62	68	.477	28.5	890	891
1897	NL	132	55	77	.417	38	752	792
1898	NL	149	78	71	.523	24	823	784
1899	NL	152	94	58	.618	9	916	743
1900	NL	138	75	63	.543	8	810	792
1901	NL	140	83	57	.593	7.5	668	543
1902	NL	137	56	81	.409	46	484	649
1903	NL	135	49	86	.363	39.5	618	743
1904	NL	152	52	100	.342	53.5	571	782
1905	NL	152	83	69	.546	21.5	708	603
1906	NL	153	71	82	.464	45.5	530	568
1907	NL	147	83	64	.565	21.5	514	481
1908	NL	154	83	71	.539	16	503	446

1909	NL	153	74	79	.484	36.5	514	518
1910	NL	153	78	75	.510	25.5	674	682
1911	NL	152	79	73	.520	19.5	658	673
1912	NL	152	73	79	.480	30.5	670	689
1913	NL	151	88	63	.583	12.5	693	636
1914	NL	154	74	80	.481	20.5	651	673
1915	NL	152	90	62	.592	-	589	463
1916	NL	153	91	62	.595	2.5	581	489
1917	NL	152	87	65	.572	10	578	501
1918	NL	123	55	68	.447	26	430	507
1919	NL	137	47	90	.343	47.5	510	699
1920	NL	153	62	91	.405	30.5	565	714
1921	NL	154	51	103	.331	43.5	617	919
1922	NL	153	57	96	.373	35.5	738	920
1923	NL	154	50	104	.325	45.5	748	1008
1924	NL	151	55	96	.364	37	676	849
1925	NL	153	68	85	.444	27	812	930
1926	NL	151	58	93	.384	29.5	687	900
1927	NL	154	51	103	.331	43	678	903
1928	NL	152	43	109	.283	51	660	957
1929	NL	153	71	82	.464	27.5	897	1032
1930	NL	154	52	102	.338	40	944	1199
1931	NL	154	66	88	.429	35	684	828
1932	NL	154	78	76	.506	12	844	796
1933	NL	152	60	92	.395	31	607	760
1934	NL	149	56	93	.376	37	675	794
1935	NL	153	64	89	.418	35.5	685	871
1936	NL	154	54	100	.351	38	726	874
1937	NL	153	61	92	.399	34.5	724	869
1938	NL	150	45	105	.300	43	550	840
1939	NL	151	45	106	.298	50.5	553	856
1940	NL	153	50	103	.327	50	494	750
1941	NL	154	43	111	.279	57	501	793
1942	NL	151	42	109	.278	62.5	394	706
1945	NL	154	46	108	.299	52	548	865
1946	NL	154	69	85	.448	28	560	705
1947	NL	154	62	92	.403	32	589	687
1948	NL	154	66	88	.429	25.5	591	729
1949	NL	154	81	73	.526	16	662	668
1950	NL	154	91	63	.591	-	722	624
1951	NL	154	73	81	.474	23.5	648	644
1952	NL	154	87	67	.565	9.5	657	552
1953	NL	154	83	71	.539	22	716	666
1954	NL	154	75	79	.487	22	659	614
1955	NL	154	77	77	.500	21.5	675	666
1956	NL	154	71	83	.461	22	668	738
1957	NL	154	77	77	.500	18	623	656
1958	NL	154	69	85	.448	23	664	762
1959	NL	154	64	90	.416	23	599	725
1960	NL	154	59	95	.383	36	546	691
1961	NL	154	47	107	.305	46	584	796
1962	NL	161	81	80	.503	20	705	759
1963	NL	162	87	75	.537	12	642	578
1964	NL	162	92	70	.568	1	693	632

1965	NL	161	85	76	.528	11.5	654	667
1966	NL	162	87	75	.537	8	696	640
1967	NL	162	82	80	.506	19.5	612	581
1968	NL	162	76	86	.469	21	543	615
1969	NL	162	63	99	.389	37	645	745
1970	NL	161	73	88	.453	15.5	594	730
1971	NL	162	67	95	.414	30	558	688
1972	NL	156	59	97	.378	37.5	503	635
1973	NL	162	71	91	.438	11.5	642	717
1974	NL	162	80	82	.494	8	676	701
1975	NL	162	86	76	.531	6.5	735	694
1976	NL	162	101	61	.623	-	770	557
1977	NL	162	101	61	.623	-	847	668
1978	NL	162	90	72	.556	-	708	586
1979	NL	162	84	78	.519	14	683	718
1980	NL	162	91	71	.562	-	728	639
1981	NL	107	59	48	.551	NA	491	472
1982	NL	162	89	73	.549	3	664	654
1983	NL	162	90	72	.556	-	696	635
1984	NL	162	81	81	.500	15.5	720	690
1985	NL	162	75	87	.463	26	667	673
1986	NL	162	86	76	.534	21.5	739	713
1987	NL	162	80	82	.494	15	702	749
1988	NL	161	65	96	.404	35.5	597	734
1989	NL	162	67	95	.414	26	629	735
1990	NL	162	77	85	.475	18	646	729
1991	NL	162	78	84	.481	20	629	680
1992	NL	162	70	92	.432	26	686	717
1993	NL	162	97	65	.599	-	877	740
1994	NL	115	54	61	.470	20.5	521	497
1995	NL	144	69	75	.479	21	615	658
TOTAL:	111 years	16633	7776	8857		2666	73977	79442
AVERAGE:		150	70	80	.468	24	666	716

Playoff Record

Season	**GP**	**W**	**L**	**R**	**OR**	**Result**
1915	5	1	4	10	12	Lost World series to Boston.
1950	4	0	4	5	11	Lost World Series to New York.
1976	3	0	3	11	19	Lost NLCS to Cincinnati.
1977	4	1	3	14	22	Lost NLCS to Los Angeles.
1978	4	1	3	17	21	Lost NLCS to Los Angeles.
1980	11	7	4	47	42	**Won World Series**.
1981	5	2	3	14	16	Lost Divisional playoff to Montreal.
1983	9	4	5	25	26	Lost World series to Baltimore.
1993	12	6	6	59	78	Lost World Series to Toronto.
TOTAL:	57	22	35	202	247	
AVERAGE:	6	2	3	22	27	

COACHING HISTORY: 1883 Bob Ferguson 4-13-.235; 1883 Blondie Purcell 13-68-.160; 1884-1893 Harry Wright 678-589-.535; 1894-1895 Arthur Irwin 149-110-.575; 1896 Billy Nash 62-68-.477; 1897-1898 George Stallings 74-104-.416; 1898-1902 Bill Shettsline 367-303-.548; 1903 Chief Zimmer 49-86-.363; 1904-1906 Hugh Duffy 206-251-.451; 1907-1909 Bill Murray 240-214-.529; 1910-1914 Charles Dooin 392-370-.514; 1915-1918 Pat Moran 323-257-.557; 1919

Jack Coombs 18-44-.290; 1919-1920 Clifford Cravath 91-137-.399; 1921 Bill Donovan 31-71-.304; 1921-1922 Irvin Wilhelm 77-128-.376; 1923-1926 Art Fletcher 231-378-.379; 1927 John McInnis 51-103-.331; 1928-1933 Burt Shotton 370-549-.403; 1934-1938 Jimmie Wilson 280-477-.370; 1938 Hans Lobert 0-2-.000; 1939-1941 James Prothro 138-320-.301; 1942 Hans Lobert 42-109-.278; 1945 Fred Fitzsimmons 17-50-.254; 1945-1948 Ben Chapman 197-277-.416; 1948 Allen Cooke 6-5-.545; 1948-1952 Eddie Sawyer 296-293-.503; 1952-1954 Steve O'Neill 182-140-.565; 1954 Terry Moore 35-42-.455; 1955-1958 Mayo Smith 264-281-.484; 1958-1960 Eddie Sawyer 94-132-.416; 1960 Andy Cohen 1-0-1.000; 1960-1968 Gene Mauch 645-684-.485; 1968-1969 George Myatt 21-35-.375; 1968-1969 Bob Skinner 92-123--.428; 1970-1972 Frank Lucchesi 166-233-.416; 1972 Paul Owens 33-47-.413; 1973-1979 Danny Ozark 594-510-.538; 1979-1981 Dallas Green 169-130-.565; 1982-1983 Pat Corrales 132-115-.534; 1983-1984 Paul Owens 128-111-.536; 1985-1987 John Felske 190-195-.494; 1987-1988 Lee Elia 111-142-.439; 1988 John Vukovich 5-4-.556; 1989-1991 Nick Leyva 148-189-.439; 1991-present Jim Fregosi

PHILADELPHIA-PITTSBURGH

(Philadelphia Eagles and Pittsburgh Steelers merged for the 1943 season)

Home City: Philadelphia, Pennsylvania
Pittsburgh, Pennsylvania
Home Stadium: Forbes Field — Capacity: 35,000
Origin of Name: This was a merger of the Philadelphia and Pittsburgh teams.

Regular Season Record

Season	League	GP	W	L	T	PF	PA	Pct
1943	NFL	10	5	4	1	225	230	.550

COACHING HISTORY: Greasy Neale & Walt Kiesling 5-4-1-.550

PHILADELPHIA QUAKERS

Home City: Philadelphia, Pennsylvania
Home Field: Brotherhood Park* — Capacity: 17,200
Origin of Name: Philadelphia had been first settled primarily by Quakers.

Regular Season Record

Season	League	GP	W	L	Pct	GB	R	OR
1890	PL	131	68	63	.519	14	941	855

COACHING HISTORY: Ben Hilt 17-19-.472; Jim Fogarty 30-19-.612; Charlie Buffinton 21-25-.457

*Also known as Forepaugh Park

PHILADELPHIA QUAKERS

(were Pittsburgh Pirates)

Home City: Philadelphia, Pennsylvania
Home Arena: Philadelphia Arena — Capacity: 5,000
Origin of Name: The name was chosen in a bid to attract some of the large Quaker population of Pennsylvania to the games.

Regular Season Record

Season	League	GP	W	L	T	GF	GA	Pts	Pct
1930-1931	NHL	44	4	36	4	76	184	12	.136

COACHING HISTORY: Cooper Smeaton 4-36-4-.136

PHILADELPHIA 76ers

(were Syracuse Nationals)

Home City: Philadelphia, Pennsylvania
Home Court: Convention Hall (1963-1967) Capacity: 12,000
CoreStates Spectrum (1967-present)* Capacity: 18,168 [1995]
Origin of Name: The name was suggested because of Philadelphia's role in the founding of the United States in 1776, and submitted in a Name the Team Contest.

Regular Season Record

Season	League	GP	W	L	PPGF	PPGA	Pct	GB
1963-1964	NBA	80	34	46	112.2	116.5	.425	25
1964-1965	NBA	80	40	40	112.5	112.7	.500	22
1965-1966	NBA	80	55	25	117.3	112.7	.688	-
1966-1967	NBA	81	68	13	125.2	115.8	.840	-
1967-1968	NBA	82	62	20	122.6	114.0	.756	-
1968-1969	NBA	82	55	27	118.9	113.8	.671	2
1969-1970	NBA	82	42	40	121.9	118.5	.512	18
1970-1971	NBA	82	47	35	114.8	113.3	.573	5
1971-1972	NBA	82	30	52	112.2	115.9	.366	26
1972-1973	NBA	82	9	73	104.1	116.2	.110	59
1973-1974	NBA	82	25	57	101.2	107.5	.305	31
1974-1975	NBA	82	34	48	99.8	102.8	.415	26
1975-1976	NBA	82	46	36	106.5	106.3	.561	8
1976-1977	NBA	82	50	32	110.2	106.2	.610	-
1977-1978	NBA	82	55	27	114.7	109.6	.671	-
1978-1979	NBA	82	47	35	109.5	107.7	.573	7
1979-1980	NBA	82	59	23	109.1	104.9	.720	2
1980-1981	NBA	82	62	20	111.7	103.8	.756	-
1981-1982	NBA	82	58	24	111.2	105.5	.707	5
1982-1983	NBA	82	65	17	112.1	104.4	.793	-
1983-1984	NBA	82	52	30	107.8	105.6	.634	10
1984-1985	NBA	82	58	24	112.9	108.8	.707	5
1985-1986	NBA	82	54	28	110.4	108.0	.659	13
1986-1987	NBA	82	45	37	106.5	106.6	.549	14
1987-1988	NBA	82	36	46	105.7	107.1	.439	21
1988-1989	NBA	82	46	36	111.9	110.4	.561	6
1989-1990	NBA	82	53	29	110.2	105.2	.646	-
1990-1991	NBA	82	44	38	105.4	105.6	.537	12
1991-1992	NBA	82	35	47	101.9	103.2	.427	16
1992-1993	NBA	82	26	56	104.3	110.1	.317	34
1993-1994	NBA	82	25	57	98.0	105.6	.305	32
1994-1995	NBA	82	24	58	95.4	100.4	.293	33
1995-1996	NBA	82	18	64	94.5	104.5	.220	42
TOTAL:	33 years	2699	1459	1240				474
AVERAGE:		82	44	38	106.2	105.6	.541	14

Playoff Record

Season	GP	W	L	PPGF	PPGA	Result
1963-1964	5	2	3	113.2	118.4	Lost Division semifinal to Cincinnati.
1964-1965	11	6	5	111.8	111.6	Lost Division final to Boston.
1965-1966	5	1	4	104.0	113.6	Lost Division final to Boston.
1966-1967	15	11	4	121.7	112.3	**Won NBA championship**.
1967-1968	13	7	6	113.7	113.0	Lost Divisional final to Boston.
1968-1969	5	1	4	106.0	116.4	Lost Division semifinal to Boston.
1969-1970	5	1	4	113.4	123.8	Lost Division semifinal to Milwaukee.
1970-1971	7	3	4	109.0	112.4	Lost Conference semifinal to Baltimore.
1975-1976	3	1	2	114.3	108.3	Lost 1st round series to Buffalo.
1976-1977	19	10	9	107.6	107.4	Lost championship series to Portland.
1977-1978	10	6	4	114.4	108.8	Lost Conference final to Washington.
1978-1979	9	5	4	112.7	109.2	Lost Conference semifinal to San Antonio.
1979-1980	18	12	6	102.8	100.6	Lost championship series to Los Angeles.
1980-1981	16	9	7	104.3	104.4	Lost Conference final to Boston.
1981-1982	21	12	9	105.7	104.4	Lost championship series to Los Angeles.
1982-1983	13	12	1	105.8	99.3	**Won NBA championship**.
1983-1984	5	2	3	103.8	107.0	Lost 1st round series to New Jersey.
1984-1985	13	8	5	107.1	104.7	Lost Conference final to Boston
1985-1986	12	6	6	109.5	106.7	Lost Conference semifinal to Milwaukee.
1986-1987	5	2	3	112.4	114.0	Lost 1st round series to Milwaukee.
1988-1989	3	0	3	105.7	108.3	Lost 1st round series to New York.
1989-1990	10	4	6	102.1	107.1	Lost Conference semifinal to Chicago.
1990-1991	8	4	4	100.9	102.1	Lost Conference semifinal to Chicago.
TOTAL:	231	125	106			
AVERAGE:	10	5	5	108.8	109.3	

COACHING HISTORY: 1963-1966 Dolph Schayes 129-111-.538; 1966-1968 Alex Hannum 130-33-.798; 1968-1972 Jack Ramsay 174-154-.530; 1972-1973 Roy Rubin 4-47-.078; 1972-1973 Kevin Loughery 5-26-.161; 1973-1978 Gene Shue 157-177-.470; 1977-1985 Bill Cunningham 454-196-.698; 1985-1988 Matt Guokas 119-88-.575; 1987-1992 Jim Lynam 194-173-.529; 1992-1993 Doug Moe 19-37-.339; 1992-1994 Fred Carter 32-76-.296; 1994-present John Lucas

*Known as The Spectrum from 1967 to 1994.

PHILADELPHIA SPARTANS

Home City: Philadelphia, Pennsylvania
Home Stadium: Temple Stadium
Origin of Name:

Regular Season Record

Season	League	GP	W	L	T	GF	GA	Pts	Pct
1967	NPSL	32	14	9	9	53	43	157	.545

COACHING HISTORY: John Szep 14-9-9-.545

PHILADELPHIA STARS
(became Baltimore Stars)

Home City: Philadelphia, Pennsylvania
Home Stadium: Veterans Stadium — Capacity: 72,204 [1984]
Origin of Name: Name was chosen in a Name the Team Contest.

Regular Season Record

Season	League	GP	W	L	T	PF	PA	Pct
1983	USFL	18	15	3	0	379	204	.833
1984	USFL	18	16	2	0	479	225	.889
TOTAL:	2 years	36	31	5	0	858	429	
AVERAGE:		18	16	2	0	429	215	.861

Playoff Record

Season	GP	W	L	PF	PA	Result
1983	2	1	1	66	62	Lost championship game to Michigan.
1984	3	3	0	71	30	**Won USFL championship.**
TOTAL:	5	4	1	137	92	
AVERAGE:	3	2	1	69	46	

COACHING HISTORY: 1983-1984 Jim Mora 31-5-0-.861

PHILADELPHIA WARRIORS

Home City: Philadelphia, Pennsylvania
Home Court: Philadelphia Arena
Origin of Name:

Regular Season Record

Season	League	GP	W	L	Pct
1926-1927	ABL	42	24	18	.571
1927-1928	ABL	51	30	21	.588
TOTAL:	2 years	93	54	39	
AVERAGE:		47	27	20	.581

COACHING HISTORY: 1926-1927 Eddie Gottlieb 24-18-.571; 1927-1928 Not Available

PHILADELPHIA WARRIORS
(became San Francisco Warriors)

Home City: Philadelphia, Pennsylvania
Home Court: Philadelphia Arena (1946-1952) — Capacity: 7,777
Convention Hall (1952-1962) — Capacity: 9,200
Philadelphia Arena (1952-1962) — Capacity: 7,777
Origin of Name: The team adopted the name of previous teams which had played in Philadelphia.

Regular Season Record

Season	League	GP	W	L	PPGF	PPGA	Pct	GB
1946-1947	BAA	60	35	25	68.6	65.2	.583	14

1947-1948	BAA	48	27	21	73.4	72.1	.563	-
1948-1949	BAA	60	28	32	83.7	83.4	.467	10
1949-1950	NBA	68	26	42	73.3	76.4	.382	27
1950-1951	NBA	66	40	26	85.4	81.6	.606	-
1951-1952	NBA	66	33	33	86.5	87.8	.500	7
1952-1953	NBA	69	12	57	80.2	88.9	.174	34.5
1953-1954	NBA	72	29	43	78.2	80.4	.403	15
1954-1955	NBA	72	33	39	93.2	93.5	.458	10
1955-1956	NBA	72	45	27	103.1	98.8	.625	-
1956-1957	NBA	72	37	35	100.4	98.8	.514	7
1957-1958	NBA	72	37	35	104.3	104.4	.514	12
1958-1959	NBA	72	32	40	103.3	106.3	.444	20
1959-1960	NBA	75	49	26	118.6	116.4	.653	10
1960-1961	NBA	79	46	33	121.0	120.1	.582	11
1961-1962	NBA	80	49	31	125.4	122.7	.613	11
TOTAL:	16 years	1103	558	545				188.5
AVERAGE:		69	35	34	93.7	93.6	.506	12

Playoff Record

Season	GP	W	L	PPGF	PPGA	Result
1946-1947	10	8	2	75.3	69.4	**Won BAA championship**.
1947-1948	13	6	7	71.7	66.0	Lost championship series to Baltimore.
1948-1949	2	0	2	74.0	86.0	Lost Division semifinal to Washington.
1949-1950	2	0	2	64.5	76.0	Lost Division semifinal to Syracuse.
1950-1951	2	0	2	83.5	90.5	Lost Division semifinal to Syracuse.
1951-1952	3	1	2	85.3	93.7	Lost Division semifinal to Syracuse.
1955-1956	10	7	3	104.6	98.4	**Won NBA championship**.
1956-1957	2	0	2	88.0	97.0	Lost Division semifinal to Syracuse.
1957-1958	8	3	5	94.8	96.9	Lost Division final to Boston.
1959-1960	9	4	5	113.9	112.0	Lost Division final to Boston.
1960-1961	3	0	3	108.0	112.0	Lost Division semifinal to Syracuse.
1961-1962	12	6	6	106.1	106.8	Lost Division final to Boston.
TOTAL:	76	35	41			
AVERAGE:	6	3	3	89.1	92.1	

COACHING HISTORY: 1946-1955 Eddie Gottlieb 263-318-.453; 1955-1958 George Senesky 119-97-.551; 1958-1959 Al Cervi 32-40-.444; 1959-1961 Neil Johnston 95-59-.617; 1961-1962 Frank McGuire 49-31-.613

PHOENIX CARDINALS

(were St. Louis Cardinals)
(became Arizona Cardinals)

Home City: Tempe, Arizona
Home Stadium: Sun Devil Stadium — Capacity: 72,000 [1992]
Origin of Name: The team kept the same nickname when the team moved from St. Louis to Arizona.

Regular Season Record

Season	League	GP	W	L	T	PF	PA	Pct
1988	NFL	16	7	9	0	344	398	.438
1989	NFL	16	5	11	0	258	377	.313

1990	NFL	16	5	11	0	268	396	.313
1991	NFL	16	4	12	0	196	344	.250
1992	NFL	16	4	12	0	243	332	.250
1993	NFL	16	7	9	0	326	269	.438
TOTAL:	6 years	96	32	64	0	1635	2116	
AVERAGE:		16	5	11	0	273	353	.333

COACHING HISTORY: 1988-1989 Gene Stallings 12-20-0-.375; 1990-1993 Joe Bugel 20-44-0-.313

PHOENIX ROADRUNNERS

Home City: Phoenix, Arizona
Home Arena: Veteran's Memorial Coliseum Capacity: 12,600 [1976]
Origin of Name: The team was named after the previous Western Hockey League team.

Regular Season Record

Season	League	GP	W	L	T	GF	GA	Pts	Pct
1974-1975	WHA	78	39	31	8	300	265	86	.551
1975-1976	WHA	80	39	35	6	302	287	84	.525
1976-1977	WHA	80	28	48	4	281	383	60	.375
TOTAL:	3 years	238	106	114	18	883	935	230	
AVERAGE:		79	35	38	6	294	312	76	.483

Playoff Record

Season	GP	W	L	GF	GA	Result
1974-1975	5	1	4	12	23	Lost quarterfinal series to Quebec.
1975-1976	5	2	3	13	16	Lost preliminary series to San Diego.
TOTAL:	10	3	7	25	39	
AVERAGE:	5	2	3	13	20	

COACHING HISTORY: 1974-1976 Sandy Hucul 78-66-14-.538; 1976-1977 Al Rollins 28-48-4-.375

PHOENIX SUNS

Home City: Phoenix, Arizona
Home Court: Arizona Veteran's Memorial Coliseum (1968-1992) Capacity: 14,487 [1992]
America West Arena (1992-present) Capacity: 19,023 [1995]
Origin of Name: The name was chosen in a Name the Team Contest.

Regular Season Record

Season	League	GP	W	L	PPGF	PPGA	Pct	GB
1968-1969	NBA	82	16	66	111.7	120.5	.195	39
1969-1970	NBA	82	39	43	119.3	121.1	.476	9
1970-1971	NBA	82	48	34	113.8	111.9	.585	18
1971-1972	NBA	82	49	33	116.3	110.8	.598	14
1972-1973	NBA	82	38	44	111.6	112.9	.463	22
1973-1974	NBA	82	30	52	107.9	111.5	.366	17
1974-1975	NBA	82	32	50	101.2	103.6	.390	16
1975-1976	NBA	82	42	40	105.1	104.5	.512	17

1976-1977	NBA	82	34	48	104.9	104.2	.415	19
1977-1978	NBA	82	49	33	112.3	108.6	.598	9
1978-1979	NBA	82	50	32	115.4	111.7	.610	2
1979-1980	NBA	82	55	27	111.1	107.5	.671	5
1980-1981	NBA	82	57	25	110.0	104.5	.695	-
1981-1982	NBA	82	46	36	106.2	102.7	.561	11
1982-1983	NBA	82	53	29	107.0	102.0	.646	5
1983-1984	NBA	82	41	41	111.0	110.1	.500	13
1984-1985	NBA	82	36	46	108.0	110.1	.439	26
1985-1986	NBA	82	32	50	110.0	113.0	.390	30
1986-1987	NBA	82	36	46	111.1	113.5	.439	29
1987-1988	NBA	82	28	54	108.5	113.0	.341	34
1988-1989	NBA	82	55	27	118.6	110.9	.671	2
1989-1990	NBA	82	54	28	114.9	107.8	.659	9
1990-1991	NBA	82	55	27	114.0	107.5	.671	8
1991-1992	NBA	82	53	29	112.1	106.2	.646	4
1992-1993	NBA	82	62	20	113.4	106.7	.756	-
1993-1994	NBA	82	56	26	108.2	103.4	.683	7
1994-1995	NBA	82	59	23	110.6	106.8	.720	-
1995-1996	NBA	82	41	41	104.3	104.0	.500	23
TOTAL:	28 years	2296	1246	1050				388
AVERAGE:		82	45	37	106.8	105.2	.543	14

Playoff Record

Season	**GP**	**W**	**L**	**PPGF**	**PPGA**	**Result**
1969-1970	7	3	4	108.3	114.3	Lost Div. semifinal to Los Angeles.
1975-1976	19	10	9	105.5	106.6	Lost championship series to Boston.
1977-1978	2	0	2	96.5	102.5	Lost 1st round series to Milwaukee.
1978-1979	15	9	6	103.1	100.3	Lost Conference final to Seattle.
1979-1980	8	3	5	109.6	110.4	Lost Conf. semifinal to Los Angeles.
1980-1981	7	3	4	91.7	89.0	Lost Conf. semifinal to Kansas City.
1981-1982	7	2	5	110.0	116.6	Lost Conf. semifinal to Los Angeles.
1982-1983	3	1	2	110.7	112.7	Lost 1st round series to Denver.
1983-1984	17	9	8	109.0	109.2	Lost Conf. final to Los Angeles.
1984-1985	3	0	3	115.7	136.0	Lost 1st round series to Lakers.
1988-1989	12	7	5	118.3	111.3	Lost Conf. final to Lakers.
1989-1990	16	9	7	108.1	105.1	Lost Conference final to Portland.
1990-1991	4	1	3	95.8	107.3	Lost 1st round series to Utah.
1991-1992	8	4	4	118.5	117.1	Lost Conf. semifinal to Portland.
1992-1993	24	13	11	104.8	104.0	Lost championship series to Chicago.
1993-1994	10	6	4	106.4	107.9	Lost Conf. semifinal to Houston.
1994-1995	10	6	4	111.0	106.9	Lost Conf. semifinal to Houston.
1995-1996	4	1	3	98.8	109.8	Lost 1st round series to San Antonio.
TOTAL:	176	87	89			
AVERAGE:	10	5	5	107.0	109.3	

COACHING HISTORY: 1968-1970 Johnny Kerr 31-89-.258; 1969-1970 Jerry Colangelo 24-20-.545; 1970-1972 Lowell "Cotton" Fitzsimmons 97-67-.591; 1972-1973 Butch van Breda Kolff 3-4-.429; 1972-1973 Jerry Colangelo 35-40-.467; 1973-1987 John MacLeod 579-543-.516; 1986-1987 Dick Van Arsdale 14-12-.538; 1987-1988 John Wetzel 28-54-.341; 1988-1992 Lowell "Cotton" Fitzsimmons 217-111-.662; 1992-1996 Paul Westphal 191-88-.685; 1995-present Lowell "Cotton" Fitzsimmons

PITTSBURGH ALLEGHENYS

(became Pittsburgh Innocents)

Home City: Pittsburgh, Pennsylvania
Home Field: Exposition Park (1882-1884)
Recreation Park (1885-1889) Capacity:17,000 [1884]
Origin of Name: The name was taken from the Allegheny River or Allegheny Mountains, both in Pennsylvania.

Regular Season Record

Season	League	GP	W	L	Pct	GB	R	OR
1882	AA	78	39	39	.500	15	428	418
1883	AA	98	31	67	.316	35	525	728
1884	AA	108	30	78	.278	45.5	406	725
1885	AA	111	56	55	.505	22.5	547	539
1886	AA	137	80	57	.584	12	810	647
1887	NL	124	55	69	.444	24	621	750
1888	NL	134	66	68	.493	19.5	534	580
1889	NL	132	61	71	.462	25	726	801
TOTAL:	8 years	922	418	504		198.5	4597	5188
AVERAGE:		115	52	63	.453	25	575	649

COACHING HISTORY: 1882-1883 Al Pratt 51-59-.464; 1883 Ormond Butler 17-36-.321; 1883-1884 Joe Battin 3-14-.176; 1884 George Creamer 2-7-.222; 1884 Denny McKnight 12-17-.414; 1884 Bob Ferguson 5-21-.192; 1884-1889 Horace Phillips 295-322-.478; 1889 Fred Dunlap 7-9-.438; 1889 Ned Hanlon 26-19-.578

PITTSBURGH BURGHERS

Home City: Pittsburgh, Pennsylvania
Home Field: Exposition Park
Origin of Name:

Regular Season Record

Season	League	GP	W	L	Pct	GB	R	OR
1890	PL	128	60	68	.469	20.5	835	892

COACHING HISTORY: Ned Hanlon 60-68-.469

PITTSBURGH CONDORS

(were Pittsburgh Pipers)

Home City: Pittsburgh, Pennsylvania
Home Court: Civic Arena Capacity: 12,500 [1970]
Origin of Name: The name was chosen by team General Manager Marty Blake.

Regular Season Record

Season	League	GP	W	L	PPGF	PPGA	Pct	GB
1970-1971	ABA	84	36	48	119.1	121.8	.429	19
1971-1972	ABA	84	25	59	119.2	126.4	.298	43
TOTAL:	2 years	168	61	107				62
AVERAGE:		84	31	53	119.2	124.1	.363	31

COACHING HISTORY: 1970-1972 Jack McMahon 40-54-.426; 1971-1972 Mark Binstein 21-43-.328

PITTSBURGH INNOCENTS

(were Pittsburgh Allegheny's)
(became Pittsburgh Pirates)

Home City: Pittsburgh, Pennsylvania
Home Field: Recreation Park — Capacity: 17,000 [1884]
Origin of Name: The team was named Innocents when they moved to the National League from the American Association.

Regular Season Record

Season	League	GP	W	L	Pct	GB	R	OR
1890	NL	136	23	113	.169	66.5	597	1235

COACHING HISTORY: Guy Hecker 23-113-.169

PITTSBURGH IRONMEN

Home City: Pittsburgh, Pennsylvania
Home Court: Duquesne Gardens
Origin of Name: The name was suggested by Pittsburgh's large iron and steel industry.

Regular Season Record

Season	League	GP	W	L	PPGF	PPGA	Pct	GB
1946-1947	BAA	60	15	45	61.2	67.6	.250	23.5

COACHING HISTORY: Paul Birch 15-45-.250

PITTSBURGH MAULERS

(merged with Baltimore for the 1985 season)

Home City: Pittsburgh, Pennsylvania
Home Stadium: Three Rivers Stadium — Capacity: 50,350 [1984]
Origin of Name: The name was a tribute to the city's steelworkers.

Regular Season Record

Season	League	GP	W	L	T	PF	PA	Pct
1984	USFL	18	3	15	0	256	358	.167

COACHING HISTORY: Joe Pendry 3-15-0-.167

PITTSBURGH PENGUINS

Home City: Pittsburgh, Pennsylvania
Home Arena: Civic Arena — Capacity: 17,181 [1995]
Origin of Name: The name was picked in a Name the Team Contest.

Regular Season Record

Season	League	GP	W	L	T	GF	GA	Pts	Pct
1967-1968	NHL	74	27	34	13	195	216	67	.453
1968-1969	NHL	76	20	45	11	189	252	51	.336
1969-1970	NHL	76	26	38	12	182	238	64	.421
1970-1971	NHL	78	21	37	20	221	240	62	.397
1971-1972	NHL	78	26	38	14	220	258	66	.423
1972-1973	NHL	78	32	37	9	257	265	73	.468
1973-1974	NHL	78	28	41	9	242	273	65	.417
1974-1975	NHL	80	37	28	15	326	289	89	.556
1975-1976	NHL	80	35	33	12	339	303	82	.513
1976-1977	NHL	80	34	33	13	240	252	81	.506
1977-1978	NHL	80	25	37	18	254	321	68	.425
1978-1979	NHL	80	36	31	13	281	279	85	.531
1979-1980	NHL	80	30	37	13	251	303	73	.456
1980-1981	NHL	80	30	37	13	302	345	73	.456
1981-1982	NHL	80	31	36	13	310	337	75	.469
1982-1983	NHL	80	18	53	9	257	394	45	.281
1983-1984	NHL	80	16	58	6	254	390	38	.238
1984-1985	NHL	80	24	51	5	276	385	53	.331
1985-1986	NHL	80	34	38	8	313	305	76	.475
1986-1987	NHL	80	30	38	12	297	290	72	.450
1987-1988	NHL	80	36	35	9	319	316	81	.506
1988-1989	NHL	80	40	33	7	347	349	87	.544
1989-1990	NHL	80	32	40	8	318	359	72	.450
1990-1991	NHL	80	41	33	6	342	305	88	.550
1991-1992	NHL	80	39	32	9	343	308	87	.544
1992-1993	NHL	84	56	21	7	367	268	119	.708
1993-1994	NHL	84	44	27	13	299	285	101	.601
1994-1995	NHL	48	29	16	3	181	158	61	.635
1995-1996	NHL	82	49	29	4	362	284	102	.622
TOTAL:	29 years	2276	926	1046	304	8084	8567	2156	
AVERAGE:		78	32	36	10	279	295	74	.474

Playoff Record

Season	GP	W	L	GF	GA	Result
1969-1970	10	6	4	22	25	Lost semifinal series to St. Louis.
1971-1972	4	0	4	8	14	Lost quarterfinal series to Chicago.
1974-1975	9	5	4	27	27	Lost quarterfinal series to N.Y. Islanders.
1975-1976	3	1	2	3	8	Lost preliminary series to Toronto.
1976-1977	3	1	2	10	13	Lost preliminary series to Toronto.
1978-1979	7	2	5	16	25	Lost quarterfinal series to Boston.
1979-1980	5	2	3	14	21	Lost preliminary series to Boston.
1980-1981	5	2	3	21	20	Lost preliminary series to St. Louis.
1981-1982	5	2	3	13	22	Lost preliminary series to N.Y. Islanders.
1988-1989	11	7	4	43	42	Lost quarterfinal series to Philadelphia.
1990-1991	24	16	8	95	68	**Won Stanley Cup**.
1991-1992	21	16	5	83	63	**Won Stanley Cup**.
1992-1993	12	7	5	50	37	Lost quarterfinal series to N.Y. Islanders.
1993-1994	6	2	4	12	20	Lost preliminary series to Washington.
1994-1995	12	5	7	37	43	Lost quarterfinal series to New Jersey.

1995-1996	18	11	7	57	52	Lost semifinal series to Florida.
TOTAL:	155	85	70	511	500	
AVERAGE:	9	5	4	32	31	

COACHING HISTORY: 1967-1969 George Sullivan 47-79-24-.393; 1969-1973 Leonard Kelly 90-132-52-.423; 1972-1974 Ken Schinkel 29-49-8-.384; 1973-1976 Marc Boileau 66-61-24-.517; 1975-1977 Ken Schinkel 54-43-20-.547; 1977-1980 John Wilson 91-105-44-.471; 1980-1983 Eddie Johnston 79-126-35-.402; 1983-1984 Lou Angotti 16-58-6-.238; 1984-1987 Bob Berry 88-127-25-.419; 1987-1988 Pierre Creamer 36-35-9-.506; 1988-1990 Gene Ubriaco 50-47-9-.514; 1989-1990 Craig Patrick 22-26-6-.463; 1990-1991 Bob Johnson 41-33-6-.550; 1991-1993 Scotty Bowman 95-53-16-.628; 1993-present Ed Johnston

PITTSBURGH PHANTOMS

Home City: Pittsburgh, Pennsylvania
Home Stadium: Forbes Field
Origin of Name:

Regular Season Record

Season	League	GP	W	L	T	GF	GA	Pts	Pct
1967	NPSL	31	10	14	7	59	74	132	.473

COACHING HISTORY: Janos Bedl, Co Prins, Pepino Gruber

PITTSBURGH PIPERS

(were Minnesota Pipers)
(became Minnesota Pipers)

Home City: Pittsburgh, Pennsylvania
Home Court: Pittsburgh Civic Arena Capacity: 16,164
Origin of Name: The name was chosen by team owner Gene Rubin because he liked the sound of it.

Regular Season Record

Season	League	GP	W	L	PPGF	PPGA	Pct	GB
1967-1968	ABA	78	54	24	111.9	108.7	.692	-
1969-1970	ABA	84	29	55	112.4	117.0	.345	30
TOTAL:	2 years	162	83	79				30
AVERAGE:		81	42	39	112.2	112.9	.512	15

Playoff Record

Season	GP	W	L	PPGF	PPGA	Result
1967-1968	15	11	4	117.4	112.4	**Won ABA championship.**

COACHING HISTORY: 1967-1968 Vince Cazetta 54-24-.692; 1969-1970 John Clark 14-25-.359; 1969-1970 Buddy Jeannette 15-30-.333

PITTSBURGH PIRATES
(were Pittsburgh Innocents)

Home City: Pittsburgh, Pennsylvania
Home Field: Exposition Park (1891-1909)
Forbes Field (1909-1970) Capacity: 35,000 [1960]
Three Rivers Stadium (1970-present) Capacity: 49,972 [1995]
Origin of Name: The team was named Pirates after the team pirated two star players away from Philadelphia of the American Association.

Regular Season Record

Season	League	GP	W	L	Pct	GB	R	OR
1891	NL	135	55	80	.407	30.5	679	744
1892	NL	153	80	73	.523	23.5	802	796
1893	NL	129	81	48	.628	5	970	766
1894	NL	130	65	65	.500	25	955	972
1895	NL	132	71	61	.538	17	811	787
1896	NL	129	66	63	.512	24	787	741
1897	NL	131	60	71	.458	32.5	676	835
1898	NL	148	72	76	.486	29.5	634	694
1899	NL	149	76	73	.510	25.5	834	765
1900	NL	139	79	60	.568	4.5	733	612
1901	NL	139	90	49	.647	-	776	534
1902	NL	139	103	36	.741	-	775	440
1903	NL	140	91	49	.650	-	792	613
1904	NL	153	87	66	.569	19	675	586
1905	NL	153	96	57	.627	9	692	569
1906	NL	153	93	60	.608	23.5	622	464
1907	NL	154	91	63	.591	17	634	507
1908	NL	154	98	56	.636	1	585	474
1909	NL	152	110	42	.724	-	701	448
1910	NL	153	86	67	.562	17.5	655	576
1911	NL	154	85	69	.552	14.5	744	560
1912	NL	151	93	58	.616	10	751	565
1913	NL	149	78	71	.523	21.5	673	585
1914	NL	154	69	85	.448	25.5	503	540
1915	NL	154	73	81	.474	18	557	520
1916	NL	154	65	89	.422	29	484	586
1917	NL	154	51	103	.331	47	464	594
1918	NL	125	65	60	.520	17	466	411
1919	NL	139	71	68	.511	24.5	472	466
1920	NL	154	79	75	.513	14	530	552
1921	NL	153	90	63	.588	4	692	595
1922	NL	154	85	69	.552	8	865	736
1923	NL	154	87	67	.565	8.5	786	696
1924	NL	153	90	63	.588	3	724	588
1925	NL	153	95	58	.621	-	912	715
1926	NL	153	84	69	.549	4.5	769	689
1927	NL	154	94	60	.610	-	817	659
1928	NL	152	85	67	.559	9	837	704
1929	NL	153	88	65	.575	10.5	904	780
1930	NL	154	80	74	.519	12	891	928
1931	NL	154	75	79	.487	26	636	691

1932	NL	154	86	68	.558	4	701	711
1933	NL	154	87	67	.565	5	667	619
1934	NL	150	74	76	.493	19.5	735	713
1935	NL	153	86	67	.562	13.5	743	647
1936	NL	154	84	70	.545	8	804	718
1937	NL	154	86	68	.558	10	704	646
1938	NL	150	86	64	.573	2	707	630
1939	NL	153	68	85	.444	28.5	666	721
1940	NL	154	78	76	.506	22.5	809	783
1941	NL	154	81	73	.526	19	690	643
1942	NL	147	66	81	.449	36.5	585	631
1943	NL	154	80	74	.519	25	669	605
1944	NL	153	90	63	.588	14.5	744	662
1945	NL	154	82	72	.532	16	753	686
1946	NL	154	63	91	.409	34	552	668
1947	NL	154	62	92	.403	32	744	817
1948	NL	154	83	71	.539	8.5	706	699
1949	NL	154	71	83	.461	26	681	760
1950	NL	153	57	96	.373	33.5	681	857
1951	NL	154	64	90	.416	32.5	689	845
1952	NL	154	42	112	.273	54.5	515	793
1953	NL	154	50	104	.325	55	622	887
1954	NL	154	53	101	.344	44	557	845
1955	NL	154	60	94	.390	38.5	560	767
1956	NL	154	66	88	.429	27	588	653
1957	NL	154	62	92	.403	33	586	696
1958	NL	154	84	70	.545	8	662	607
1959	NL	154	78	76	.506	9	651	680
1960	NL	154	95	59	.617	-	734	593
1961	NL	154	75	79	.487	18	694	675
1962	NL	161	93	68	.578	8	706	626
1963	NL	162	74	88	.457	25	567	595
1964	NL	162	80	82	.494	13	663	636
1965	NL	162	90	72	.556	7	675	580
1966	NL	162	92	70	.568	3	759	641
1967	NL	162	81	81	.500	20.5	679	693
1968	NL	162	80	82	.494	17	583	532
1969	NL	162	88	74	.543	12	725	652
1970	NL	162	89	73	.549	-	729	664
1971	NL	162	97	65	.599	-	788	599
1972	NL	155	96	59	.619	-	691	512
1973	NL	162	80	82	.494	2.5	704	693
1974	NL	162	88	74	.543	-	751	657
1975	NL	161	92	69	.571	-	712	565
1976	NL	162	92	70	.568	9	708	630
1977	NL	162	96	66	.593	5	734	665
1978	NL	161	88	73	.547	1.5	684	637
1979	NL	162	98	64	.605	-	775	643
1980	NL	162	83	79	.512	8	666	646
1981	NL	102	46	56	.451	NA	407	394
1982	NL	162	84	78	.519	8	724	696
1983	NL	162	84	78	.519	6	659	648
1984	NL	162	75	87	.463	21.5	615	567
1985	NL	161	57	104	.354	43.5	568	708

1986	NL	162	64	98	.395	44	663	700
1987	NL	162	80	82	.494	15	723	744
1988	NL	160	85	75	.531	15	651	616
1989	NL	162	74	88	.457	19	637	680
1990	NL	162	95	67	.586	-	733	619
1991	NL	162	98	64	.605	-	768	632
1992	NL	162	96	66	.593	-	693	595
1993	NL	162	75	87	.463	22	707	806
1994	NL	114	53	61	.465	13	466	580
1995	NL	144	58	86	.403	27	629	736
TOTAL:	105 years	16010	8332	7678		1653.5	72406	68927
AVERAGE:		152	79	73	.520	16	690	656

			Playoff Record			
Season	**GP**	**W**	**L**	**R**	**OR**	**Result**
1900	4	1	3	15	15	Lost NL championship to Brooklyn.
1903	8	3	5	24	39	Lost World Series to Boston.
1909	7	4	3	34	28	**Won World Series**.
1925	7	4	3	25	26	**Won World Series**.
1927	4	0	4	10	23	Lost World Series to New York.
1960	7	4	3	27	55	**Won World Series**.
1970	3	0	3	3	9	Lost NLCS to Cincinnati.
1971	11	7	4	47	39	**Won World Series**.
1972	5	2	3	15	19	Lost NLCS to Cincinnati.
1974	4	1	3	10	20	Lost NLCS to Los Angeles.
1975	3	0	3	7	19	Lost NLCS to Cincinnati.
1979	10	7	3	47	31	**Won World Series**.
1990	6	2	4	15	20	Lost NLCS to Cincinnati.
1991	7	3	4	12	19	Lost NLCS to Atlanta.
1992	7	3	4	35	34	Lost NLCS to Atlanta.
TOTAL:	93	41	52	326	396	
AVERAGE:	6	3	3	22	26	

COACHING HISTORY: 1891 Ned Hanlon 31-47-.397; 1891 Bill McGunnigle 24-33-.421; 1892 Tom Burns 25-30-.455; 1892-1894 Al Buckenberger 189-146-.564; 1894-1896 Connie Mack 149-134-.527; 1897 Patsy Donovan 60-71-.458; 1898-1899 Bill Watkins 80-92-.465; 1899 Patsy Donovan 68-57-.544; 1900-1915 Fred Clarke 1422-969-.595; 1916-1917 James Callahan 85-129-.397; 1917 Honus Wagner 1-4-.200; 1917-1919 Hugo Bezdek 166-187-.470; 1920-1922 George Gibson 201-171-.540; 1922-1926 Bill McKechnie 409-293-.583; 1927-1929 Owen Bush 246-178-.580; 1929-1931 Jewel Ens 176-167-.513; 1932-1934 George Gibson 200-159-.557; 1934-1939 Harold Traynor 457-406-.530; 1940-1946 Frankie Frisch 539-528-.505; 1946 Virgil Davis 1-2-.333; 1947 Billy Herman 61-92-.399; 1947 Bill Burwell 1-0-1.000; 1948-1952 Billy Meyer 317-452-.412; 1953-1955 Fred Haney 163-299-.353; 1956-1957 Bobby Bragan 102-155-.397; 1957-1964 Danny Murtaugh 605-547-.525; 1965-1967 Harry Walker 224-184-.549; 1967 Danny Murtaugh 39-39-.500; 1968-1969 Larry Shepard 164-155-.514; 1969 Alex Grammas 4-1-.800; 1970-1971 Danny Murtaugh 186-138-.574; 1972-1973 Bill Virdon 163-128-.560; 1973-1976 Danny Murtaugh 285-226-.558; 1977-1985 Charles Tanner 711-685-.509; 1986-present Jim Leyland

PITTSBURGH PIRATES
(became Philadelphia Quakers)

Home City: Pittsburgh, Pennsylvania
Home Arena: Duquesne Gardens
Origin of Name: The team was named after the National League baseball team.

Regular Season Record

Season	League	GP	W	L	T	GF	GA	Pts	Pct
1925-1926	NHL	36	19	16	1	82	70	39	.542
1926-1927	NHL	44	15	26	3	79	108	33	.375
1927-1928	NHL	44	19	17	8	67	76	46	.523
1928-1929	NHL	44	9	27	8	46	80	26	.295
1929-1930	NHL	44	5	36	3	102	185	13	.148
TOTAL:	5 years	212	67	122	23	376	519	157	
AVERAGE:		42	13	24	5	75	104	31	.370

Playoff Record

Season	GP	W	L	T	GF	GA	Result
1925-1926	2	0	1	1	4	6	Lost 1st round series to Montreal.
1927-1928	2	1	1	0	4	6	Lost quarterfinal series to Rangers.
TOTAL:	4	1	2	1	8	12	
AVERAGE:	2	1	1	0	2	6	

COACHING HISTORY: 1925-1929 Ogilvie Cleghorn 62-86-20-.429; 1929-1930 Frank Frederickson 5-36-3-.148

PITTSBURGH PIRATES
(became Pittsburgh Steelers)

Home City: Pittsburgh, Pennsylvania
Home Stadium: Forbes Field Capacity: 35,000
Origin of Name: Named after National League baseball team.

Regular Season Record

Season	League	GP	W	L	T	PF	PA	Pct
1933	NFL	11	3	6	2	67	208	.364
1934	NFL	12	2	10	0	51	206	.167
1935	NFL	12	4	8	0	100	209	.333
1936	NFL	12	6	6	0	98	187	.500
1937	NFL	11	4	7	0	122	145	.364
1938	NFL	11	2	9	0	79	169	.182
TOTAL:	6 years	69	21	46	2	517	1124	
AVERAGE:		12	4	8	0	86	187	.319

COACHING HISTORY: 1933 Jap Douds 3-6-2-.364; 1934 Luby DiMelio 2-10-0-.167; 1935-1936 Joe Bach 10-14-0-.417; 1937-1938 Johnny Blood 6-16-0-.273

PITTSBURGH PIRATES

Home City: Pittsburgh, Pennsylvania
Home Court:
Origin of Name: The owners showed great originality by naming their team Pirates which was named after the National League baseball team.

Regular Season Record

Season	League	GP	W	L	PPGF	PPGA	Pct	GB
1937-1938	NBL	13	8	5	37.3	33.4	.615	3.5
1938-1939	NBL	27	13	14	36.9	39.3	.481	11
TOTAL:	2 years	40	21	19				14.5
AVERAGE:		20	11	9	37.1	36.4	.525	7

COACHING HISTORY: 1937-1939 Dudey Moore 21-19-.525

PITTSBURGH RAIDERS

Home City: Pittsburgh, Pennsylvania
Home Court:
Origin of Name:

Regular Season Record

Season	League	GP	W	L	PPGF	PPGA	Pct	GB
1944-1945	NBL	30	7	23	48.7	55.5	.233	18

COACHING HISTORY: Joe Urso 7-23-.233

PITTSBURGH REBELS

Home City: Pittsburgh, Pennsylvania
Home Stadium: Exposition Park
Origin of Name: The team changed its name when it changed its managers from Harry Gessler to Ennis "Rebel" Oakes.

Regular Season Record

Season	League	GP	W	L	Pct	GB	R	OR
1914	FL	150	64	86	.427	22.5	605	698
1915	FL	153	86	67	.562	.5	592	524
TOTAL:	2 years	303	150	153		23	1197	1222
AVERAGE:		152	75	77	.493	11.5	599	611

COACHING HISTORY: 1914 Harry Gessler 6-12-.333; 1914-1915 Ennis Oakes 144-141-.505

PITTSBURGH STEELERS

(were Pittsburgh Pirates)
(Pittsburgh merged with Philadelphia in 1943 and Chicago in 1944)

Home City: Pittsburgh, Pennsylvania
Home Stadium: Forbes Field * (1939-1963) Capacity: 35,000
Pitt Stadium * (1958-1969) Capacity: 54,500
Three Rivers Stadium (1970) Capacity: 59,600 [1995]
Origin of Name: The team name was chosen in a contest sponsored by the owners.

Regular Season Record

Season	League	GP	W	L	T	PF	PA	Pct
1939	NFL	11	1	9	1	114	216	.136
1940	NFL	11	2	7	2	60	178	.273
1941	NFL	11	1	9	1	103	276	.136
1942	NFL	11	7	4	0	167	119	.636
1945	NFL	10	2	8	0	79	220	.200
1946	NFL	11	5	5	1	136	117	.500
1947	NFL	12	8	4	0	240	259	.667
1948	NFL	12	4	8	0	200	243	.333
1949	NFL	12	6	5	1	224	214	.542
1950	NFL	12	6	6	0	180	195	.500
1951	NFL	12	4	7	1	183	235	.375
1952	NFL	12	5	7	0	300	273	.417
1953	NFL	12	6	6	0	211	263	.500
1954	NFL	12	5	7	0	219	263	.417
1955	NFL	12	4	8	0	195	285	.333
1956	NFL	12	5	7	0	217	250	.417
1957	NFL	12	6	6	0	161	178	.500
1958	NFL	12	7	4	1	261	230	.625
1959	NFL	12	6	5	1	257	216	.542
1960	NFL	12	5	6	1	240	275	.458
1961	NFL	14	6	8	0	295	287	.429
1962	NFL	14	9	5	0	312	363	.643
1963	NFL	14	7	4	3	321	295	.607
1964	NFL	14	5	9	0	253	315	.357
1965	NFL	14	2	12	0	202	397	.143
1966	NFL	14	5	8	1	316	347	.393
1967	NFL	14	4	9	1	281	320	.321
1968	NFL	14	2	11	1	244	397	.179
1969	NFL	14	1	13	0	218	404	.071
1970	NFL	14	5	9	0	210	272	.357
1971	NFL	14	6	8	0	246	292	.429
1972	NFL	14	11	3	0	343	175	.786
1973	NFL	14	10	4	0	347	210	.714
1974	NFL	14	10	3	1	305	189	.750
1975	NFL	14	12	2	0	373	162	.857
1976	NFL	14	10	4	0	342	138	.714
1977	NFL	14	9	5	0	283	243	.643
1978	NFL	16	14	2	0	356	195	.875
1979	NFL	16	12	4	0	416	262	.750
1980	NFL	16	9	7	0	352	313	.563
1981	NFL	16	8	8	0	356	297	.500
1982	NFL	9	6	3	0	204	146	.667
1983	NFL	16	10	6	0	355	303	.625
1984	NFL	16	9	7	0	387	310	.563
1985	NFL	16	7	9	0	379	355	.438
1986	NFL	16	6	10	0	307	336	.375
1987	NFL	15	8	7	0	285	299	.533
1988	NFL	16	5	11	0	336	421	.313
1989	NFL	16	9	7	0	265	326	.563
1990	NFL	16	9	7	0	292	240	.563
1991	NFL	16	7	9	0	292	344	.438

1992	NFL	16	11	5	0	299	225	.688
1993	NFL	16	9	7	0	308	281	.563
1994	NFL	16	12	4	0	316	234	.750
1995	NFL	16	11	5	0	407	327	.689
TOTAL:	55 years	751	371	363	17	14550	14525	
AVERAGE:		14	7	7	0	265	264	.505

Playoff Record

Season	GP	W	L	PF	PA	Result
1947	1	0	1	0	21	Lost Division playoff to Philadelphia.
1972	2	1	1	30	28	Lost AFC championship to Miami.
1973	1	0	1	14	33	Lost Divisional playoff to Oakland.
1974	3	3	0	72	33	**Won Super Bowl.**
1975	3	3	0	65	37	**Won Super Bowl.**
1976	2	1	1	47	38	Lost AFC championship to Oakland.
1977	1	0	1	21	34	Lost Division playoff to Denver.
1978	3	3	0	102	46	**Won Super Bowl.**
1979	3	3	0	92	46	**Won Super Bowl.**
1982	1	0	1	28	31	Lost 1st round playoff to San Diego.
1983	1	0	1	10	38	Lost Division playoff to L.A. Raiders.
1984	2	1	1	52	62	Lost AFC championship to Miami.
1989	2	1	1	49	47	Lost Conference semifinal to Denver.
1992	1	0	1	3	24	Lost Conference semifinal to Buffalo.
1993	1	0	1	24	27	Lost Wild Card game to Kansas City.
1994	2	1	1	42	26	Lost Conference final to San Diego.
1995	3	2	1	77	64	Lost Super Bowl to Dallas.
TOTAL:	32	19	13	728	635	
AVERAGE:	2	1	1	43	37	

COACHING HISTORY: 1939 Johnny Blood 0-3-0-.000; 1939-1940 Walt Kiesling 3-13-3-.237; 1941 Bert Bell 0-2-0-.000; 1941 Buff Donelli 0-5-0-.000; 1941-1942 Walt Kiesling 1-2-1-.375; 1945 Jim Leonard 2-8-0-.200; 1946-1947 Jock Sutherland 13-10-1-.563; 1948-1951 Johnny Michelosen 20-26-2-.438; 1952-1953 Joe Bach 11-13-0-.458; 1954-1956 Walt Kiesling 14-22-0-.389; 1957-1964 Buddy Parker 51-47-6-.519; 1965 Mike Nixon 2-12-0-.143; 1966-1968 Bill Austin 11-28-3-.298; 1969-1991 Chuck Noll 193-148-1-7.566; 1992-present Bill Cowher

*The Steelers played games in both Forbes Field and Pitt Stadium from 1958 to 1963.

PORTLAND BREAKERS

(were New Orleans Breakers)

Home City: Portland, Oregon
Home Stadium: Civic Stadium Capacity: 32,500
Origin of Name: The team kept the same nickname when it moved from New Orleans to Portland.

Regular Season Record

Season	League	GP	W	L	T	PF	PA	Pct
1985	USFL	18	6	12	0	275	422	.333

COACHING HISTORY: Dick Coury 6-12-0-.333

PORTLAND ROSEBUDS
(were New Westminster Royals)
(became Victoria Aristocrats)

Home City: Portland, Oregon
Home Arena:
Origin of Name: Portland has long been known as "The Rose City."

Regular Season Record

Season	League	GP	W	L	T	GF	GA	Pts	Pct
1914-1915	PCHA	18	9	9	0	91	83	18	.500
1915-1916	PCHA	18	13	5	0	71	50	26	.722
1916-1917	PCHA	24	9	15	0	114	112	18	.375
1917-1918	PCHA	18	7	11	0	63	75	14	.389
TOTAL:	4 years	78	38	40	0	339	320	76	
AVERAGE:		20	10	10	0	85	80	19	.487

Playoff Record

Season	GP	W	L	T	GF	GA	Result
1915-1916	5	2	3	0	13	15	Lost Stanley Cup final to Canadiens.

COACHING HISTORY: 1914-1917 Pete Muldoon; 1916-1917 Tom Scott; 1917-1918 Not Available

PORTLAND ROSEBUDS
(were Regina Capitals)

Home City: Portland, Oregon
Home Arena: Portland Arena
Origin of Name: Named after previous PCHA team.

Regular Season Record

Season	League	GP	W	L	T	GF	GA	Pts	Pct
1925-1926	WHL	30	12	16	2	84	110	26	.433

COACHING HISTORY: Pete Muldoon 12-16-2-.433

PORTLAND STORM
(became Portland Thunder)

Home City: Portland, Oregon
Home Stadium: Portland Civic Stadium — Capacity: 29,010 [1974]
Origin of Name:

Regular Season Record

Season	League	GP	W	L	T	PF	PA	Pct
1974	WFL	20	7	12	1	264	426	.375

COACHING HISTORY: Dick Coury 7-12-1-.375

PORTLAND THUNDER

(were Portland Storm)

Home City: Portland, Oregon
Home Stadium: Portland Civic Stadium — Capacity: 33,000 [1975]
Origin of Name: Team executives announced May 14, 1975 that the name of the team would be changed to Thunder.

Regular Season Record

Season	League	GP	W	L	T	PF	PA	Pct
1975	WFL	11	4	7	0	213	239	.364

COACHING HISTORY: Greg Barton 1-5-0-.167; Bob Brodhead 1-1-0-.500; Joe Gardi 2-1-0-.667.

PORTLAND TIMBERS

Home City: Portland, Oregon
Home Field: Portland Civic Stadium — Capacity: 33,000 [1978]
Origin of Name: Named by team officials because of the Portland areas large forest industry.

Regular Season Record

Season	League	GP	W	L	GF	GA	BP	Pts	Pct
1975	NASL	22	16	6	43	27	42	138	.697
1976	NASL	24	8	16	23	40	23	71	.329
1977	NASL	26	10	16	39	42	38	98	.419
1978	NASL	30	20	10	50	36	47	167	.619
1979	NASL	30	11	19	50	75	46	112	.415
1980	NASL	32	15	17	50	53	43	133	.462
1981	NASL	32	17	15	52	49	45	141	.294
1982	NASL	32	14	18	49	44	42	122	.254
TOTAL:	8 years	228	111	117	356	366	326	982	
AVERAGE:		29	14	15	45	46	41	123	.403

Playoff Record

Season	GP	W	L	T	GF	GA	Result
1975	3	2	1	0	3	3	Lost championship series to Tampa Bay.
1978	5	3	2	0	5	8	Lost 3rd round series to New York.
1981	3	1	2	0	3	8	Lost 1st round series to San Diego.
TOTAL:	11	6	5	0	11	19	
AVERAGE:	4	2	2	0	4	6	

COACHING HISTORY: 1975-1976 Vic Crowe 24-22-.505; 1977 Brian Tiler 10-16-.419; 1978-1980 Don Megson 35-35; 1980 Pete Warner 11-11; 1981-1982 Vic Crowe 31-33

PORTLAND TRAIL BLAZERS

Home City: Portland, Oregon
Home Court: Memorial Coliseum (1970-1995) — Capacity: 12,888 [1994]
Rose Garden (1995-present) — Capacity: 20,340 [1995]
Origin of Name: The name was chosen in a Name the Team Contest.

Regular Season Record

Season	League	GP	W	L	PPGF	PPGA	Pct	GB
1970-1971	NBA	82	29	53	115.5	120.0	.354	19
1971-1972	NBA	82	18	64	106.8	116.5	.220	51
1972-1973	NBA	82	21	61	106.2	112.4	.256	39
1973-1974	NBA	82	27	55	106.8	111.6	.329	20
1974-1975	NBA	82	38	44	103.8	103.3	.463	10
1975-1976	NBA	82	37	45	104.1	105.3	.451	22
1976-1977	NBA	82	49	33	111.7	106.2	.598	4
1977-1978	NBA	82	58	24	107.7	101.5	.707	-
1978-1979	NBA	82	45	37	108.4	107.1	.549	7
1979-1980	NBA	82	38	44	102.5	103.3	.463	22
1980-1981	NBA	82	45	37	110.7	109.8	.549	12
1981-1982	NBA	82	42	40	109.8	109.2	.512	15
1982-1983	NBA	82	46	36	107.4	105.3	.561	12
1983-1984	NBA	82	48	34	113.1	109.6	.585	6
1984-1985	NBA	82	42	40	115.5	112.1	.512	20
1985-1986	NBA	82	40	42	115.1	114.0	.488	22
1986-1987	NBA	82	49	33	117.9	114.8	.598	16
1987-1988	NBA	82	53	29	116.1	111.5	.646	9
1988-1989	NBA	82	39	43	114.6	113.1	.476	18
1989-1990	NBA	82	59	23	114.2	107.9	.720	42
1990-1991	NBA	82	63	19	114.7	106.0	.768	-
1991-1992	NBA	82	57	25	111.4	104.1	.695	-
1992-1993	NBA	82	51	31	108.5	105.4	.622	11
1993-1994	NBA	82	47	35	107.3	104.6	.573	16
1994-1995	NBA	82	44	38	103.1	99.2	.537	15
1995-1996	NBA	82	44	38	99.3	97.0	.537	20
TOTAL:	26 years	2132	1129	1003				428
AVERAGE:		82	43	39	109.7	108.1	.530	16

Playoff Record

Season	GP	W	L	PPGF	PPGA	Result
1976-1977	19	14	5	107.4	102.7	**Won NBA championship**.
1977-1978	6	2	4	96.7	98.3	Los Conference semifinal to Seattle.
1978-1979	3	1	2	96.7	100.0	Lost 1st round series to Phoenix.
1979-1980	3	1	2	100.3	106.0	Lost 1st round series to Seattle.
1980-1981	3	1	2	105.3	107.0	Lost 1st round series to Kansas City.
1982-1983	7	3	4	105.9	107.0	Lost Conf. semifinal to Los Angeles.
1983-1984	5	2	3	109.8	112.4	Lost 1st round series to Phoenix.
1984-1985	9	4	5	119.1	124.1	Lost Conf. semifinal to Los Angeles.
1985-1986	4	1	3	112.5	117.5	Lost 1st round series to Denver.
1986-1987	4	1	3	108.8	113.3	Lost 1st round series to Houston.
1987-1988	4	1	3	104.3	108.5	Lost 1st round series to Utah.
1988-1989	3	0	3	107.0	119.0	Lost 1st round series to Lakers.
1989-1990	11	2	9	107.1	109.4	Lost NBA final to Detroit.
1990-1991	16	9	7	103.9	102.6	Lost Conference final to Lakers.
1991-1992	21	13	8	110.0	106.6	Lost NBA final to Chicago.
1992-1993	4	1	3	97.3	97.5	Lost 1st round series to San Antonio.
1993-1994	4	1	3	103.8	109.0	Lost 1st round series to Houston.
1994-1995	3	0	3	101.7	116.3	Lost 1st round series to Phoenix

1995-1996	5	2	3	89.6	99.6	Lost 1st round series to Utah.
TOTAL:	134	59	75			
AVERAGE:	7	3	4	105.1	108.1	

COACHING HISTORY: 1970-1972 Rolland Todd 41-97-.297; 1971-1972 Stu Inman 6-20-.231; 1972-1974 Jack McCloskey 48-116-.293; 1974-1976 Lenny Wilkens 75-89-.457; 1976-1986 Jack Ramsay 453-367-.552; 1986-1989 Mike Schuler 127-84-.602; 1988-1994 Rick Adelman 291-154-.654; 1994-present P.J. Carlesimo

PORTSMOUTH SPARTANS

(became Detroit Lions)

Home City: Portsmouth, Ohio
Home Stadium: Spartan Stadium Capacity: 8,200
Origin of Name: The team may have been named after the stadium in which they played their home games.

Regular Season Record

Season	League	GP	W	L	T	PF	PA	Pct
1930	NFL	14	5	6	3	176	161	.464
1931	NFL	14	11	3	0	175	77	.786
1932	NFL	12	6	2	4	116	71	.667
1933	NFL	11	6	5	0	128	87	.545
TOTAL:	4 years	51	28	16	7	595	396	
AVERAGE:		13	7	4	2	149	99	.618

COACHING HISTORY: 1930 Hal Griffen 5-6-3-.464; 1931-1933 George Clark 23-10-4-.676

POTTSVILLE MAROONS

(became Boston Bulldogs)

Home City: Pottsville, Pennsylvania
Home Stadium:
Origin of Name: The name was chosen because of the color of the player's uniforms.

Regular Season Record

Season	League	GP	W	L	T	PF	PA	Pct
1925	NFL	12	10	2	0	270	45	.833
1926	NFL	13	10	2	1	155	29	.808
1927	NFL	13	5	8	0	80	163	.385
1928	NFL	10	2	8	0	74	134	.200
TOTAL:	4 years	48	27	20	1	579	371	
AVERAGE:		12	7	5	0	145	93	.573

COACHING HISTORY: 1925-1927 Dick Rauch 25-12-1-.671; 1928 Pete Henry 2-8-0-.200

PROVIDENCE GRAYS

Home City: Providence, Rhode Island
Home Field: Messer Park
Origin of Name: The players wore gray uniforms

Regular Season Record

Season	League	GP	W	L	Pct	GB	R	OR
1878	NL	60	33	27	.550	8	353	337
1879	NL	84	59	25	.702	-	612	355
1880	NL	84	52	32	.619	15	419	299
1881	NL	84	47	37	.560	9	447	426
1882	NL	84	52	32	.619	3	463	356
1883	NL	98	58	40	.592	5	636	436
1884	NL	112	84	28	.750	-	665	388
1885	NL	110	53	57	.482	33	442	531
TOTAL:	8 years	716	438	278		73	4037	3128
AVERAGE:		90	55	35	.612	9	505	391

Playoff Record

Season	GP	W	L	R	OR	Result
1884	3	3	0	21	3	Won World Series.

COACHING HISTORY: 1878 George Ware 33-27-.550; 1879 George Wright 59-25-.702; 1880-1881 Jim Bullock 69-49-.585; 1881 Bob Morrow 30-20-.600; 1882-1883 Harry Wright 110-72-.604; 1884-1885 Frank Bancroft 137-85-.617

PROVIDENCE STEAM ROLLERS

Home City: Providence, Rhode Island
Home Stadium: Providence Cycledrome Capacity: 14,000
Origin of Name: The name was chosen by co-founder Charles Coppen when he overheard a fan say Providence steamrolled its foes.

Regular Season Record

Season	League	GP	W	L	T	PF	PA	Pct
1925	NFL	12	6	5	1	111	101	.542
1926	NFL	13	5	7	1	83	103	.423
1927	NFL	14	8	5	1	105	88	.607
1928	NFL	11	8	1	2	128	42	.818
1929	NFL	12	4	6	2	107	117	.417
1930	NFL	11	6	4	1	90	125	.591
1931	NFL	11	4	4	3	78	127	.500
TOTAL:	7 years	84	41	32	11	702	703	
AVERAGE:		12	6	5	1	100	100	.542

COACHING HISTORY: 1925 Archie Golembeski 6-5-1-.542; 1926 Jim Laird 5-7-1-.423; 1927-1930 Jim Conzelman 26-16-6-.604; 1931 Ed Robinson 4-4-3-.500

PROVIDENCE STEAMROLLERS

Home City: Providence, Rhode Island
Home Court: Providence Auditorium
Origin of Name: Named after previous NFL team.

Regular Season Record

Season	League	GP	W	L	PPGF	PPGA	Pct	GB
1946-1947	BAA	60	28	32	72.5	74.2	.467	21
1947-1948	BAA	48	6	42	69.1	80.7	.125	21
1948-1949	BAA	60	12	48	78.5	87.6	.200	26
TOTAL:	3 years	168	46	122				68
AVERAGE:		56	15	41	73.4	80.8	.274	23

COACHING HISTORY: 1946-1947 Bob Morris 28-32-.467; 1947-1948 Hank Soar 2-17-.105; 1947-1948 Nat Hickey 4-25-.138; 1948-1949 Ken Loeffler 12-48-.200

QUEBEC BULLDOGS

Home City: QuebecCity, Quebec
Home Arena: Quebec Coliseum
Origin of Name.

Regular Season Record

Season	League	GP	W	L	T	GF	GA	Pts	Pct
1908-1909	ECHA	12	3	9	0	78	106	6	.250

COACHING HISTORY:

QUEBEC BULLDOGS

Home City: Quebec City, Quebec
Home Arena: Quebec Coliseum
Origin of Name: Named after previous ECHA team.

Regular Season Record

Season	League	GP	W	L	T	GF	GA	Pts	Pct
1910-1911	NHA	16	4	12	0	65	97	8	.250
1911-1912	NHA	18	10	8	0	81	79	20	.556
1912-1913	NHA	20	16	4	0	112	75	32	.800
1913-1914	NHA	20	12	8	0	111	73	24	.600
1914-1915	NHA	20	11	9	0	85	85	22	.550
1915-1916	NHA	24	10	12	2	91	98	22	.458
1916-1917	NHA	20	10	10	0	97	126	20	.500
TOTAL:	7 years	138	73	63	2	642	633	148	
AVERAGE:		20	10	9	1	92	90	21	.536

Playoff Record

Season	GP	W	L	T	GF	GA	Result
1911-1912	2	2	0	0	17	3	Won Stanley Cup.
1912-1913	2	2	0	0	20	5	Won Stanley Cup.
TOTAL:	4	4	0	0	37	8	
AVERAGE:	2	2	0	0	19	4	

COACHING HISTORY: 1910-1911 Not Available; 1911-1912 C. Nolan 10-8-0-.556; 1912-1913 Joe Malone 16-4-0-.800; 1913-1917 Not Available

QUEBEC BULLDOGS
(became Hamilton Tigers)

Home City: Quebec City, Quebec
Home Arena: Quebec Coliseum
Origin of Name: According to *NHL 75th Anniversary Commemorative Book* the team was formally called the Athletics but the team was more often referred to as the Bulldogs by the press and fans.

Regular Season Record

Season	League	GP	W	L	T	GF	GA	Pts	Pct
1919-1920	NHL	24	4	20	0	91	177	8	.167

COACHING HISTORY: Mike Quinn 4-20-0-.167

QUEBEC NORDIQUES
(became Colorado Avalanche)

Home City: Quebec City, Quebec
Home Arena: Le Colisee de Quebec Capacity: 15,399 [1995]
Origin of Name: The name was chosen in a contest sponsored by a local sportsmen's club.

Regular Season Record

Season	League	GP	W	L	T	GF	GA	Pts	Pct
1972-1973	WHA	78	33	40	5	276	313	71	.455
1973-1974	WHA	78	38	36	4	306	280	80	.513
1974-1975	WHA	78	46	32	0	331	299	92	.590
1975-1976	WHA	81	50	27	4	371	316	104	.642
1976-1977	WHA	81	47	31	3	353	295	97	.599
1977-1978	WHA	80	40	37	3	349	347	83	.519
1978-1979	WHA	80	41	34	5	288	271	87	.544
1979-1980	NHL	80	25	44	11	248	313	61	.381
1980-1981	NHL	80	30	32	18	314	318	78	.488
1981-1982	NHL	80	33	31	16	356	345	82	.513
1982-1983	NHL	80	34	34	12	343	336	80	.500
1983-1984	NHL	80	42	28	10	360	278	94	.588
1984-1985	NHL	80	41	30	9	323	275	91	.569
1985-1986	NHL	80	43	31	6	330	289	92	.575
1986-1987	NHL	80	31	39	10	267	276	72	.450
1987-1988	NHL	80	32	43	5	271	306	69	.431
1988-1989	NHL	80	27	46	7	269	342	61	.381
1989-1990	NHL	80	12	61	7	240	407	31	.194
1990-1991	NHL	80	16	50	14	236	354	46	.288
1991-1992	NHL	80	20	48	12	255	318	52	.325
1992-1993	NHL	84	47	27	10	351	300	104	.619
1993-1994	NHL	84	34	42	8	277	292	76	.452
1994-1995	NHL	48	30	13	5	185	134	65	.677
TOTAL:	23 years	1812	792	836	184	6899	7004	1768	
AVERAGE:		78	34	36	8	300	305	77	.488

Playoff Record

Season	GP	W	L	GF	GA	Result
1974-1975	15	8	7	55	48	Lost WHA final to Houston.
1975-1976	5	1	4	15	23	Lost quarterfinal series to Calgary.
1976-1977	17	12	5	79	56	**Won WHA championship**.
1977-1978	11	5	6	43	41	Lost semifinal series to New England.
1978-1979	4	0	4	30	12	Lost semifinal series to Winnipeg.
1980-1981	5	2	3	17	22	Lost preliminary series to Philadelphia.
1981-1982	16	7	9	48	60	Lost semifinal series to N.Y. Islanders.
1982-1983	4	1	3	8	11	Lost preliminary series to Boston.
1983-1984	9	5	4	26	25	Lost quarterfinal series to Montreal.
1984-1985	18	9	9	58	63	Lost semifinal series to Philadelphia.
1985-1986	3	0	3	7	16	Lost preliminary series to Hartford.
1986-1987	13	7	6	48	45	Lost quarterfinal series to Montreal.
1992-1993	6	2	4	16	19	Lost preliminary series to Montreal.
1994-1995	6	2	4	19	25	Lost preliminary series to N.Y. Rangers.
TOTAL:	132	61	71	469	466	
AVERAGE:	9	4	5	34	34	

COACHING HISTORY: 1972-1973 Maurice Richard 1-1-0-.500; 1972-1973 Maurice Filion 32-39-5-.454; 1973-1974 Jacques Plante 38-36-4-.513; 1974-1976 Jean-Guy Gendron 96-59-4-.616; 1976-1978 Marc Boileau 74-61-5-.546; 1977-1978 Maurice Filion 13-7-1-.643; 1978-1980 Jacques Demers 66-78-16-.463; 1980-1981 Maurice Filion 1-3-2-.333; 1980-1987 Michel Bergeron 253-222-79-.528; 1987-1988 Andre Savard 10-13-1-.438; 1987-1989 Ron LaPointe 33-50-6-.404; 1988-1989 Jean Perron 16-26-5-.394; 1989-1990 Michel Bergeron 12-61-7-.194; 1990-1992 Dave Chambers 19-64-15-.270; 1991-1994 Pierre Page 98-103-29-.489; 1994-1995 Marc Crawford 30-13-5-.677.

RACINE LEGIONS

Home City: Racine, Wisconsin
Home Stadium:
Origin of Name: The team was sponsored by the local American Legion.

Regular Season Record

Season	League	GP	W	L	T	PF	PA	Pct
1922	NFL	11	6	4	1	122	56	.591
1923	NFL	10	4	4	2	86	86	.500
1924	NFL	10	4	4	3	69	47	.500
TOTAL:	3 years	31	14	12	6	277	189	
AVERAGE:		11	5	4	2	92	63	.548

COACHING HISTORY: 1922 Babe Ruetz 6-4-1-.591; 1923-1924

RACINE TORNADOES

Home City: Racine, Wisconsin
Home Stadium:
Origin of Name:

Regular Season Record

Season	League	GP	W	L	T	PF	PA	Pct
1926	NFL	5	1	4	0	8	92	.200

COACHING HISTORY: Hank Gillo & Wallace Barr 1-4-0-.200

RALEIGH-DURHAM SKYHAWKS

Home City: Raleigh, North Carolina
Home Stadium: Carter-Finley Stadium Capacity: 53,500 [1991]
Origin of Name:

Regular Season Record

Season	League	GP	W	L	T	PF	PA	Pct
1991	WLAF	10	0	10	0	123	300	.000

COACHING HISTORY: Roman Gabriel 0-10-0-.000

REGINA CAPITALS
(became Portland Rosebuds)

Home City: Regina, Saskatchewan
Home Arena: Regina Stadium
Origin of Name: The team may have been named Capitals because Regina is the capital city of Saskatchewan.

Regular Season Record

Season	League	GP	W	L	T	GF	GA	Pts	Pct
1921-1922	WCHA	24	14	10	0	94	78	28	.583
1922-1923	WCHA	30	16	14	0	93	97	32	.533
1923-1924	WCHA	30	17	11	2	83	67	36	.600
1924-1925	WCHL	28	8	20	0	82	123	16	.286
TOTAL:	4 years	112	55	55	2	352	365	112	
AVERAGE:		28	14	14	0	88	91	28	.500

Playoff Record

Season	GP	W	L	T	GF	GA	Result
1921-1922	6	3	2	1	7	8	Lost playoff series to Vancouver.
1922-1923	2	0	1	1	3	4	Lost WCHL playoff to Edmonton.
1923-1924	2	0	1	1	2	4	Lost WCHL playoff to Calgary.
TOTAL:	10	3	4	3	12	16	
AVERAGE:	3	1	1	1	4	5	

COACHING HISTORY: 1921-1922 Wes Champ 14-10-0-.583; 1922-1925 Russell Stanley 41-45-2-.466

RENFREW CREAMERY KINGS

Home City: Renfrew, Ontario
Home Arena: Renfrew Arena Capacity: 2,500
Origin of Name: The team acquired its name because Renfrew was a well known dairy town.

			Regular Season Record						
Season	**League**	**GP**	**W**	**L**	**T**	**GF**	**GA**	**Pts**	**Pct**
1909-1910	NHA	12	8	3	1	96	54	17	.708
1910-1911	NHA	16	8	8	0	91	101	16	.500
TOTAL:	2 years	28	16	11	1	187	155	33	
AVERAGE:		14	8	6	0	94	78	16	.589

COACHING HISTORY:

RICHMOND KING CLOTHIERS

(merged with Cincinnati Comellos in 1938)

Home City: Richmond, Indiana
Home Court:
Origin of Name: The team was sponsored by King Clothiers.

			Regular Season Record					
Season	**League**	**GP**	**W**	**L**	**PPGF**	**PPGA**	**Pct**	**GB**
1937-1938	NBL	3	1	2	29.1	37.6	.333	5.5

COACHING HISTORY: Bob McConachie 1-2-.333

RICHMOND VIRGINIAS

Home City: Richmond, Virginia
Home Field: Virginia Park
Origin of Name: The team adopted the states name as its own.

			Regular Season Record					
Season	**League**	**GP**	**W**	**L**	**Pct**	**GB**	**R**	**OR**
1884	AA	42	12	30	.286	30.5	194	294

COACHING HISTORY: Felix Moses 12-30-.286

ROCHESTER BEAU BRUMMELS

Home City: Rochester, New York
Home Field: Culver Field Capacity: 4,200
Origin of Name: The team acquired its name because of its uniforms.

			Regular Season Record					
Season	**League**	**GP**	**W**	**L**	**Pct**	**GB**	**R**	**OR**
1890	AA	126	63	63	.500	22	709	711

COACHING HISTORY: Pat Powers 63-63-.500

ROCHESTER CENTRALS

Home City: Rochester, New York
Home Court:
Origin of Name: The team was originally formed by a group of boys who attended school in the Central Avenue area of Rochester.

Regular Season Record

Season	League	GP	W	L	Pct
1925-1926	ABL	30	18	12	.600
1926-1927	ABL	42	14	28	.333
1927-1928	ABL	52	24	28	.462
1928-1929	ABL	40	18	22	.450
1929-1930	ABL	54	33	21	.611
1930-1931	ABL	34	15	19	.441
TOTAL:	6 years	252	122	130	
AVERAGE:		42	20	22	.484

Playoff Record

Season	GP	W	L	PF	PA	Result
1929-1930	5	1	4	81	96	Lost championship series to Cleveland.

COACHING HISTORY: 1925-1929 Not Available; 1929-1930 Frank Morgenweck 33-21; 1930-1931 Not Available

ROCHESTER JEFFERSONS

Home City: Rochester, New York
Home Stadium:
Origin of Name:

Regular Season Record

Season	League	GP	W	L	T	PF	PA	Pct
1922	NFL	5	0	4	1	13	76	.100
1923	NFL	2	0	2	0	0	116	.000
1924	NFL	7	0	7	0	7	156	.000
1925	NFL	7	0	6	1	26	111	.071
TOTAL:	4 years	21	0	19	2	46	459	
AVERAGE:		5	0	5	0	11	115	.048

COACHING HISTORY: 1922-1923 Leo Lyons 0-6-1-.071; 1924-1925 Jerry Noonan 0-13-1-.036

ROCHESTER LANCERS

Home City: Rochester, New York
Home Field: Holleder Stadium Capacity: 20,000
Origin of Name: The team kept the same name when it moved from the American Soccer League to the North American Soccer League.

Regular Season Record

Season	League	GP	W	L	T	GF	GA	BP	Pts	Pct
1970	NASL	24	9	9	6	41	45	39	111	.514
1971	NASL	24	13	5	6	48	31	45	141	.653
1972	NASL	14	6	5	3	20	22	19	64	.508
1973	NASL	19	4	9	6	17	27	17	59	.345
1974	NASL	20	8	10	2	23	30	23	77	.428
1975	NASL	22	6	16	-	29	49	28	64	.323
1976	NASL	24	13	11	-	36	32	36	114	.528
1977	NASL	26	11	15	-	34	41	33	99	.423
1978	NASL	30	14	16	-	47	52	47	131	.485
1979	NASL	30	15	15	-	43	57	42	132	.489
1980	NASL	32	12	20	-	42	67	37	109	.378
TOTAL:	11 years	265	111	131	23	380	453	366	1101	
AVERAGE:		24	10	12	2	35	41	33	100	.462

Playoff Record

Season	GP	W	L	T	GF	GA	Result
1970	2	1	1	0	4	3	Lost championship series to Washington.
1971	3	1	2	0	4	6	Lost 1st round series to Dallas.
1972	1	0	1	0	0	2	Lost 1st round series to St. Louis.
1976	1	0	1	0	1	2	Lost 1st round series to Toronto.
1977	5	3	2	0	5	6	Lost 3rd round series to New York.
TOTAL:	12	5	7	0	14	19	
AVERAGE:	2	1	1	0	3	4	

COACHING HISTORY: 1970 Alex Perolli; 1970 Charles Schiano; 1970-1971 Sal DeRosa; 1972 Adolfo Gori 6-5-3-.508; 1973 Sal DeRosa 4-9-6-.345; 1974 Bill Hughes; 1974 John Petrossi; 1974-1975 Ted Dumitru; 1976-1979 Don Popovic 53-57; 1980 Ray Klivecka 3-4; 1980 Alex Perolli 9-16

ROCHESTER ROYALS

(became Cincinnati Royals)

Home City: Rochester, New York
Home Court: Edgarton Park Arena (1946-1955) Capacity: 5,000
Rochester War Memorial (1955-1957) Capacity: 10,000
Origin of Name: The name was chosen in a Name the Team Contest.

Regular Season Record

Season	League	GP	W	L	PPGF	PPGA	Pct	GB
1945-1946	NBL	34	24	10	56.8	50.8	.706	2
1946-1947	NBL	44	31	13	62.9	56.5	.705	-
1947-1948	NBL	60	44	16	64.6	58.2	.733	-
1948-1949	BAA	60	45	15	84.0	77.4	.750	-
1949-1950	NBA	68	51	17	82.4	74.6	.750	-
1950-1951	NBA	68	41	27	84.6	81.7	.603	3
1951-1952	NBA	66	41	25	86.2	82.9	.621	-
1952-1953	NBA	70	44	26	86.3	83.5	.629	4
1953-1954	NBA	72	44	28	79.8	77.3	.611	2
1954-1955	NBA	72	29	43	90.8	92.4	.403	14

1955-1956	NBA	72	31	41	95.8	98.7	.431	6
1956-1957	NBA	72	31	41	93.4	95.6	.431	3
TOTAL:	12 years	758	456	302				34
AVERAGE:		63	38	25	80.6	77.5	.602	3

Playoff Record

Season	GP	W	L	PPGF	PPGA	Result
1945-1946	7	6	1	59.6	52.0	**Won NBL championship**
1946-1947	11	6	5	63.5	61.3	Lost championship series to Chicago.
1947-1948	11	6	5	68.7	65.5	Lost championship series to Minneapolis.
1948-1949	4	2	2	73.3	68.8	Lost Division final to Minneapolis.
1949-1950	3	0	3	79.3	82.3	Lost Division semifinal to Ft. Wayne.
1950-1951	14	9	5	83.9	77.2	**Won NBA championship**.
1951-1952	6	3	3	83.3	80.7	Lost Division final to Minneapolis.
1952-1953	3	1	2	75.0	74.0	Lost Division semifinal to Ft. Wayne.
1953-1954	6	3	3	80.2	83.2	Lost Division final to Minneapolis.
1954-1955	3	1	2	94.0	97.7	Lost Division semifinal to Minneapolis.
TOTAL:	68	37	31			
AVERAGE:	7	4	3	76.1	74.5	

COACHING HISTORY: 1945-1946 Les Harrison 24-10-.765; 1946-1947 Ed Malanowicz & Les Harrison 31-13-.705; 1947-1948 Eddie Malanowicz 44-16-.733; 1948-1955 Les Harrison 295-181-.620; 1955-1957 Bobby Wanzer 62-82-.431

ROCK ISLAND INDEPENDENTS

Home City: Rock Island, Illinois
Home Stadium:
Origin of Name:

Regular Season Record

Season	League	GP	W	L	T	PF	PA	Pct
1922	NFL	7	4	2	1	154	27	.643
1923	NFL	8	2	3	3	84	62	.438
1924	NFL	10	6	2	2	98	44	.700
1925	NFL	11	5	3	3	99	58	.591
TOTAL:	4 years	36	17	10	9	435	191	
AVERAGE:		9	4	3	2	109	48	.597

COACHING HISTORY: 1922 Jim Conzelman 4-2-1-.643; 1923 Dale Sies 2-3-3-.438; 1924 John Armstrong 6-2-2-.700; 1925 Rube Ursella 5-3-3-.591

SACRAMENTO GOLD MINERS

(became San Antonio Texans)

Home City: Sacramento, California
Home Stadium: Hornet Field — Capacity: 24,000 [1994]
Origin of Name: The name was chosen by the team owners.

Regular Season Record

Season	League	GP	W	L	T	PF	PA	Pts	Pct
1993	CFL	18	6	12	0	498	509	12	.333
1994	CFL	18	9	8	1	436	436	19	.528
TOTAL:	2 years	36	15	20	1	934	945	31	
AVERAGE:		18	8	10	0	467	473	16	.431

COACHING HISTORY: 1993-1994 Kay Stephenson 15-20-1-.431

SACRAMENTO KINGS
(were Kansas City Kings)

Home City: Sacramento, California
Home Court: ARCO Arena I (1985-1988) Capacity: 10,333 [1987]
ARCO Arena II (1988-present) Capacity: 17,317 [1995]
Origin of Name: The team kept the same nickname when it moved from Kansas City to Sacramento.

Regular Season Record

Season	League	GP	W	L	PPGF	PPGA	Pct	GB
1985-1986	NBA	82	37	45	108.8	111.9	.451	14
1986-1987	NBA	82	29	53	110.9	114.1	.354	26
1987-1988	NBA	82	24	58	108.0	113.7	.293	30
1988-1989	NBA	82	27	55	105.5	111.0	.329	30
1989-1990	NBA	82	23	59	101.7	106.8	.280	40
1990-1991	NBA	82	25	57	96.7	103.5	.305	38
1991-1992	NBA	82	29	53	104.3	110.3	.347	28
1992-1993	NBA	82	25	57	107.9	111.1	.305	37
1993-1994	NBA	82	28	54	101.1	106.9	.341	35
1994-1995	NBA	82	39	43	98.2	99.2	.476	20
1995-1996	NBA	82	39	43	99.5	102.3	.476	25
TOTAL:	11 years	902	325	577				323
AVERAGE:		82	30	52	103.9	108.3	.360	29

Playoff Record

Season	GP	W	L	PPGF	PPGA	Result
1985-1986	3	0	3	96.0	110.3	Lost 1st round series to Houston.
1995-1996	4	1	3	87.8	93.8	Lost 1st round series to Seattle.
TOTAL	7	1	6			
AVERAGE	3	0	3	91.3	100.9	

COACHING HISTORY: 1985-1987 Phil Johnson 51-77-.398; 1986-1990 Jerry Reynolds 56-113-.331; 1987-1988 Bill Russell 17-41-.293; 1989-1992 Dick Motta 48-114-.296; 1991-1992 Rex Hughes 22-35-.386; 1992-present Garry St. Jean

SACRAMENTO SURGE

Home City: Sacramento, California
Home Stadium: Charles Hughes Stadium (1991) Capacity: 23,000 [1991]
Hornet Stadium (1992) Capacity: 29,500 [1992]
Origin of Name:

Regular Season Record

Season	League	GP	W	L	T	PF	PA	Pct
1991	WLAF	10	3	7	0	179	226	.300
1992	WFL	10	8	2	0	250	152	.800
TOTAL:	2 years	20	11	9	0	429	378	
AVERAGE:		10	6	4	0	215	189	.550

Playoff Record

Season	GP	W	L	PF	PA	Result
1992	2	2	0	38	32	Won WLAF championship.

COACHING HISTORY: 1991-1992 Kay Stephenson 11-9-0-.550

ST. LOUIS BLUES

Home City: St. Louis, Missouri
Home Arena: St. Louis Arena (1967-1994)* Capacity: 17,188 [1994]
Kiel Center (1994-present) Capacity: 19,260 [1995]
Origin of Name: The team name was suggested by the W.C. Handy ballad "The St. Louis Blues" and chosen by team owner Sid Solomon, Jr.

Regular Season Record

Season	League	GP	W	L	T	GF	GA	Pts	Pct
1967-1968	NHL	74	27	31	16	177	191	70	.473
1968-1969	NHL	76	37	25	14	204	157	88	.579
1969-1970	NHL	76	37	27	12	224	179	86	.566
1970-1971	NHL	78	34	25	19	223	208	87	.558
1971-1972	NHL	78	28	39	11	247	247	67	.429
1972-1973	NHL	78	32	34	12	233	251	76	.487
1973-1974	NHL	78	26	40	12	206	248	64	.410
1974-1975	NHL	80	35	31	14	269	267	84	.525
1975-1976	NHL	80	29	37	14	249	290	72	.450
1976-1977	NHL	80	32	39	9	239	276	73	.456
1977-1978	NHL	80	20	47	13	195	304	53	.331
1978-1979	NHL	80	18	50	12	249	348	48	.300
1979-1980	NHL	80	34	34	12	266	278	80	.500
1980-1981	NHL	80	45	18	17	352	281	107	.669
1981-1982	NHL	80	32	40	8	315	349	72	.450
1982-1983	NHL	80	25	40	15	285	316	65	.406
1983-1984	NHL	80	32	41	7	293	316	71	.444
1984-1985	NHL	80	37	31	12	299	288	86	.538
1985-1986	NHL	80	37	34	9	302	291	83	.531
1986-1987	NHL	80	32	33	15	281	293	79	.494
1987-1988	NHL	80	34	38	8	278	294	76	.475
1988-1989	NHL	80	33	35	12	275	285	78	.488
1989-1990	NHL	80	37	34	9	295	279	83	.519
1990-1991	NHL	80	47	22	11	310	250	105	.656
1991-1992	NHL	80	36	33	11	279	266	83	.519
1992-1993	NHL	84	37	36	11	282	278	85	.506
1993-1994	NHL	84	40	33	11	270	283	91	.542

1994-1995	NHL	48	28	15	5	178	135	61	.635
1995-1996	NHL	82	32	34	16	219	248	80	.488
TOTAL:	29 years	2276	953	976	347	7455	7696	2253	
AVERAGE:		79	33	34	12	257	265	78	.495

Playoff Record

Season	**GP**	**W**	**L**	**GF**	**GA**	**Result**
1967-1968	18	8	10	42	50	Lost Stanley Cup final to Montreal.
1968-1969	12	8	4	36	20	Lost Stanley Cup final to Montreal.
1969-1970	16	8	8	46	46	Lost Stanley Cup final to Boston.
1970-1971	6	2	4	15	16	Lost quarterfinal series to Minnesota.
1971-1972	11	4	7	27	47	Lost semifinal series to Boston.
1972-1973	5	1	4	9	22	Lost quarterfinal series to Chicago.
1974-1975	2	0	2	6	9	Lost preliminary series to Pittsburgh.
1975-1976	3	1	2	8	7	Lost preliminary series to Buffalo.
1976-1977	4	0	4	4	19	Lost quarterfinal series to Montreal.
1979-1980	3	0	3	4	12	Lost preliminary series to Chicago.
1980-1981	11	5	6	42	50	Lost quarterfinal series to N.Y. Rangers.
1981-1982	10	5	5	39	36	Lost quarterfinal series to Chicago.
1982-1983	4	1	3	10	16	Lost preliminary series to Chicago.
1983-1984	11	6	5	30	31	Lost quarterfinal series to Minnesota.
1984-1985	3	0	3	5	9	Lost preliminary series to Minnesota.
1985-1986	19	10	9	64	70	Lost semifinal series to Calgary.
1986-1987	6	2	4	12	15	Lost preliminary series to Toronto.
1987-1988	10	5	5	36	38	Lost quarterfinal series to Detroit.
1988-1989	10	5	5	35	34	Lost quarterfinal series to Chicago.
1989-1990	12	7	5	42	44	Lost quarterfinal series to Chicago.
1990-1991	13	6	7	41	42	Lost quarterfinal series to Minnesota.
1991-1992	6	2	4	19	23	Lost preliminary series to Chicago.
1992-1993	11	7	4	24	28	Lost quarterfinal series to Toronto.
1993-1994	4	0	4	10	16	Lost preliminary series to Dallas.
1994-1995	7	3	4	27	27	Lost preliminary series to Vancouver.
1995-1996	13	7	6	37	37	Lost quarterfinal series to Detroit.
TOTAL:	230	103	127	670	764	
AVERAGE:	9	4	5	26	29	

COACHING HISTORY: 1967-1968 Lynn Patrick 4-10-2-.313; 1967-1971 Scotty Bowman 110-83-45-.557; 1970-1973 Al Arbour 42-40-25-.509; 1971-1972 Sid Abel 3-6-1-.350; 1971-1972 Bill McCreary 6-14-4-.333; 1972-1974 Jean-Guy Talbot 52-53-15-.496; 1973-1975 Lou Angotti 6-20-6-.281; 1974-1976 Lynn Patrick 4-5-1-.450; 1974-1976 Garry Young 41-41-16-.500; 1975-1976 Leo Boivin 17-17-9-.500; 1976-1977 Emile Francis 32-39-9-.456; 1977-1978 Leo Boivin 11-36-7-.269; 1977-1980 Barclay Plager 35-77-22-.343; 1979-1982 Gordon Berenson 99-71-31-.570; 1981-1983 Emile Francis 14-24-5-.384; 1982-1983 Barclay Plager 15-21-12-.438; 1983-1986 Jacques Demers 106-106-28-.500; 1986-1988 Jacques Martin 66-71-23-.484; 1988-1992 Brian Sutter 153-124-43-.545; 1992-1993 Bob Plager 4-6-1-.409; 1992-1994 Bob Berry 73-63-21-.532; 1994-present Mike Keenan

*St. Louis Arena was known as the Checkerdome from 1977-1982 while the team was owned by the Ralston-Purina Company.

ST. LOUIS BOMBERS

Home City: St. Louis, Missouri
Home Court: St. Louis Arena
Origin of Name:

Regular Season Record

Season	League	GP	W	L	PPGF	PPGA	Pct	GB
1946-1947	BAA	61	38	23	66.6	64.1	.623	1
1947-1948	BAA	48	29	19	71.5	69.5	.604	-
1948-1949	BAA	60	29	31	75.8	79.4	.483	16
1949-1950	NBA	68	26	42	73.7	76.5	.382	25
TOTAL:	4 years	237	122	115				42
AVERAGE:		59	30	29	71.9	72.4	.515	11

Playoff Record

Season	GP	W	L	PPGF	PPGA	Result
1946-1947	3	1	2	66.7	66.3	Lost quarterfinal series to Philadelphia.
1947-1948	7	3	4	58.9	69.9	Lost semifinal series to Philadelphia.
1948-1949	2	0	2	64.0	79.5	Lost Division semifinal to Rochester.
TOTAL:	12	4	8			
AVERAGE:	4	1	3	63.2	71.9	

COACHING HISTORY: 1946-1948 Ken Loeffler 67-42-.615; 1948-1950 Grady Lewis 55-73-.430

ST. LOUIS BROWNS
(became St. Louis Cardinals)

Home City: St. Louis, Missouri
Home Field: Sportsman's Park (1882-1891) Capacity: 12,000 [1886]
Robison Field (1892-1897) Capacity: 14,500 [1893]
Origin of Name: The team wore brown stockings.

Regular Season Record

Season	League	GP	W	L	Pct	GB	R	OR
1882	AA	80	37	43	.463	18	399	496
1883	AA	98	65	33	.663	1	549	409
1884	AA	107	67	40	.626	8	658	539
1885	AA	112	79	33	.705	-	677	461
1886	AA	139	93	46	.669	-	944	592
1887	AA	135	95	40	.704	-	1131	761
1888	AA	135	92	43	.681	-	789	501
1889	AA	135	90	45	.667	2	957	680
1890	AA	136	78	58	.574	12	870	736
1891	AA	138	86	52	.623	8.5	976	753
1892	NL	150	56	94	.373	46	703	922
1893	NL	132	57	75	.432	30.5	745	829
1894	NL	132	56	76	.424	35	771	954
1895	NL	131	39	92	.298	48.5	747	1032
1896	NL	130	40	90	.308	50.5	593	929

1897	NL	131	29	102	.221	63.5	588	1083
TOTAL:	16 years	2021	1059	962		323.5	12097	11677
AVERAGE:		126	66	60	.524	20	756	730

Playoff Record

Season	GP	W	L	T	R	OR	Result
1885	7	3	3	1	36	38	**Co-Winner of World Series.**
1886	6	4	2	0	38	28	**Won World Series.**
1887	15	5	10	0	54	73	Lost World Series to Detroit.
1888	10	4	6	0	60	64	Lost World series to N.Y. Giants
TOTAL:	38	16	21	1	188	203	
AVERAGE:	9	4	5	0	47	51	

COACHING HISTORY: 1882 Ned Cuthbert 37-43-.463; 1882 Ed Brown 10-11-.476; 1883 Ted Sullivan 53-27-.663; 1883 Charlie Comiskey 12-6-.667; 1884 Jimmy Williams 67-40-.626; 1885-1889 Charlie Comiskey 449-207-.684; 1890 Tom McCarthy 13-13-.500; 1890 James Roseman 32-19-.627; 1890 Charles Campau 33-26-.559;1891 Charlie Comiskey 86-52-.623; 1892 Chris Von Der Ahe 56-94-.373; 1893 Bill Watkins 57-75-.432; 1894 George Miller 56-76-.424; 1895 Al Buckenberger 16-23-.410; 1895 Joe Quinn 13-27-.325; 1895 Lew Phelan 8-21-.276; 1895-1897 Chris Von Der Ahe 3-16-.158; 1896 Harry Diddlebock 7-11-.389; 1896 Arlie Latham 0-2-.000; 1896 Roger Connor 9-37-.196; 1896-1897 Tommy Dowd 30-63-.323; 1897 Hugh Nicol 9-29-.237; 1897 Bill Hallman 13-46-.220

ST. LOUIS BROWNS

(were Milwaukee Brewers)
(became Baltimore Orioles)

Home City: St. Louis, Missouri
Home Field: Sportsman's Park II (1902-1908) Capacity: 18,000 [1907]
Sportsman's Park III (1909-1953) Capacity: 34,450 [1953]
Origin of Name: The team was named Browns because of the brown trim on their uniforms.

Regular Season Record

Season	League	GP	W	L	Pct	GB	R	OR
1902	AL	136	78	58	.574	5	619	607
1903	AL	139	65	74	.468	26.5	500	525
1904	AL	152	65	87	.428	29	481	604
1905	AL	153	54	99	.353	40.5	509	606
1906	AL	149	76	73	.510	16	565	501
1907	AL	152	69	83	.454	24	538	560
1908	AL	152	83	69	.546	6.5	543	478
1909	AL	150	61	89	.407	36	443	574
1910	AL	154	47	107	.305	57	454	778
1911	AL	152	45	107	.296	56.5	567	810
1912	AL	154	53	101	.344	53	556	790
1913	AL	153	57	96	.373	39	528	642
1914	AL	153	71	82	.464	28.5	523	614
1915	AL	154	63	91	.409	39.5	521	693
1916	AL	154	79	75	.513	12	591	545
1917	AL	154	57	97	.370	43	511	687
1918	AL	124	60	64	.484	14	426	448

1919	AL	139	67	72	.482	20.5	535	567
1920	AL	153	76	77	.497	21.5	797	766
1921	AL	154	81	73	.526	17.5	835	845
1922	AL	154	93	61	.604	1	867	643
1923	AL	152	74	78	.487	24	688	720
1924	AL	152	74	78	.487	17	764	797
1925	AL	153	82	71	.536	15	897	909
1926	AL	154	62	92	.403	29	682	845
1927	AL	153	59	94	.386	50.5	724	904
1928	AL	154	82	72	.532	19	772	742
1929	AL	152	79	73	.520	26	733	713
1930	AL	154	64	90	.416	38	751	886
1931	AL	154	63	91	.409	45	722	870
1932	AL	154	63	91	.409	44	736	898
1933	AL	151	55	96	.364	43.5	669	820
1934	AL	152	67	85	.441	33	674	800
1935	AL	152	65	87	.428	28.5	718	930
1936	AL	152	57	95	.375	44.5	804	1064
1937	AL	154	46	108	.299	56	715	1023
1938	AL	152	55	97	.362	44	755	962
1939	AL	154	43	111	.279	64.5	733	1035
1940	AL	154	67	87	.435	23	757	882
1941	AL	154	70	84	.455	31	765	823
1942	AL	151	82	69	.543	19.5	730	637
1943	AL	152	72	80	.474	25	596	604
1944	AL	154	89	65	.578	-	684	587
1945	AL	151	81	70	.536	6	597	548
1946	AL	154	66	88	.429	38	621	711
1947	AL	154	59	95	.383	38	564	744
1948	AL	153	59	94	.386	37	671	849
1949	AL	154	53	101	.344	44	667	913
1950	AL	154	58	96	.377	40	684	916
1951	AL	154	52	102	.338	46	611	882
1952	AL	154	64	90	.416	31	604	733
1953	AL	154	54	100	.351	46.5	555	778
TOTAL:	52 years	7881	3416	4465		1633	33552	38808
AVERAGE:		152	66	86	.433	31.5	645	746

Playoff Record

Season	GP	W	L	R	OR	Result
1944	6	2	4	12	16	Lost World Series to Cardinals

COACHING HISTORY: 1902-1909 Jimmy McAleer 551-632-.466; 1910 Jack O'Connor 47-107-.305; 1911-1912 Bobby Wallace 57-134-.298; 1912-1913 George Stovall 91-158-.365; 1913 Jimmy Austin 2-6-.250; 1913-1915 Branch Rickey 139-179-.437; 1916-1918 Fielder Jones 159-196-.448; 1918 Jimmy Austin 6-8-.429; 1918-1920 Jimmy Burke 172-181-.487; 1921-1923 Lee Fohl 225-183-.551; 1923 Jimmy Austin 23-29-.442; 1924-1926 George Sisler 218-241-.475; 1927-1929 Dan Howley 220-239-.479; 1930-1933 Bill Lillefer 224-331-.404; 1933 Allen Sothoron 1-3-.250; 1933-1937 Rogers Hornsby 234-351-.400; 1937 Jim Bottomley 21-58-.266; 1938 Charley Street 55-97-.362; 1939-1941 Fred Haney 125-227-.355; 1941-1946 Luke Sewell 432-410-.513; 1947 Herold Ruel 59-95-.383; 1948-1951 Zack Taylor 222-393-.361; 1952 Rogers Hornsby 22-28-.440; 1952-1953 Marty Marion 96-162-.372

ST. LOUIS BROWNS

Home City: St. Louis, Missouri
Home Stadium:
Origin of Name: Named after the American League baseball team.

Regular Season Record

Season	League	GP	W	L	T	PF	PA	Pct
1923	NFL	7	1	4	2	14	39	.286

COACHING HISTORY: Ollie Kraehe 1-4-2-.286

ST. LOUIS CARDINALS
(were St. Louis Browns)

Home City: St. Louis, Missouri
Home Field: Robison Field (1898-1920) Capacity: 15,200 [1899]
Sportsman's Park II (1920-1966) * Capacity: 30,500 [1954]
Busch Stadium (1966-present) ** Capacity: 57,000 [1995]
Origin of Name: Named by St. Louis sports writer Willie McHale because the team wore uniforms with red trim on them.

Regular Season Record

Season	League	GP	W	L	Pct	GB	R	OR
1898	NL	150	39	111	.260	63.5	571	929
1899	NL	151	84	67	.556	18.5	819	739
1900	NL	140	65	75	.464	19	744	748
1901	NL	140	76	64	.543	14.5	792	689
1902	NL	134	56	78	.418	44.5	517	695
1903	NL	137	43	94	.314	46.5	505	762
1904	NL	154	75	79	.487	31.5	602	595
1905	NL	154	58	96	.377	47.5	534	741
1906	NL	150	52	98	.347	63	475	620
1907	NL	153	52	101	.340	55.5	419	607
1908	NL	154	49	105	.318	50	372	624
1909	NL	152	54	98	.355	56	583	728
1910	NL	153	63	90	.412	40.5	637	717
1911	NL	149	75	74	.503	22	671	745
1912	NL	153	63	90	.412	41	659	825
1913	NL	150	51	99	.340	49	523	756
1914	NL	153	81	72	.529	13	558	540
1915	NL	153	72	81	.471	18.5	590	601
1916	NL	153	60	93	.392	33.5	476	629
1917	NL	152	82	70	.539	15	531	568
1918	NL	129	51	78	.395	33	454	534
1919	NL	137	54	83	.394	40.5	463	552
1920	NL	154	75	79	.487	18	675	682
1921	NL	153	87	66	.569	7	809	681
1922	NL	154	85	69	.552	8	863	819
1923	NL	153	79	74	.516	16	746	732
1924	NL	154	65	89	.422	28.5	740	750
1925	NL	153	77	76	.503	18	828	764

1926	NL	154	89	65	.578	-	817	678
1927	NL	153	92	61	.601	1.5	754	665
1928	NL	154	95	59	.617	-	807	636
1929	NL	152	78	74	.513	20	831	806
1930	NL	154	92	62	.597	-	1004	784
1931	NL	154	101	53	.656	-	815	614
1932	NL	154	72	82	.468	18	684	717
1933	NL	153	82	71	.536	9.5	687	609
1934	NL	153	95	58	.621	-	799	656
1935	NL	154	96	58	.623	4	829	625
1936	NL	154	87	67	.565	5	795	794
1937	NL	154	81	73	.526	15	789	733
1938	NL	151	71	80	.470	17.5	725	721
1939	NL	153	92	61	.601	4.5	779	633
1940	NL	153	84	69	.549	16	747	699
1941	NL	153	97	56	.634	2.5	734	589
1942	NL	154	106	48	.688	-	755	482
1943	NL	154	105	49	.682	-	679	475
1944	NL	154	105	49	.682	-	772	490
1945	NL	154	95	59	.617	3	756	583
1946	NL	156	98	58	.628	-	712	545
1947	NL	154	89	65	.578	5	780	634
1948	NL	154	85	69	.552	6.5	742	646
1949	NL	154	96	58	.623	1	766	616
1950	NL	153	78	75	.510	12.5	693	670
1951	NL	154	81	73	.526	15.5	683	671
1952	NL	154	88	66	.571	8.5	677	630
1953	NL	154	83	71	.539	22	768	713
1954	NL	154	72	82	.468	25	799	790
1955	NL	154	68	86	.442	30.5	654	757
1956	NL	154	76	78	.494	17	678	698
1957	NL	154	87	67	.565	8	737	666
1958	NL	154	72	82	.468	20	619	704
1959	NL	154	71	83	.461	16	641	725
1960	NL	154	86	68	.558	9	639	616
1961	NL	154	80	74	.519	13	703	668
1962	NL	162	84	78	.519	17.5	774	664
1963	NL	162	93	69	.574	6	747	628
1964	NL	162	93	69	.574	-	715	652
1965	NL	161	80	81	.497	16.5	707	674
1966	NL	162	83	79	.512	12	571	577
1967	NL	161	101	60	.627	-	695	557
1968	NL	162	97	65	.599	-	583	472
1969	NL	162	87	75	.537	13	595	540
1970	NL	162	76	86	.469	13	744	747
1971	NL	162	90	72	.556	7	739	699
1972	NL	156	75	81	.481	21.5	568	600
1973	NL	162	81	81	.500	1.5	643	603
1974	NL	161	86	75	.534	1.5	677	643
1975	NL	162	82	80	.506	10.5	662	689
1976	NL	162	72	90	.444	29	629	671
1977	NL	162	83	79	.512	18	737	688
1978	NL	162	69	93	.426	21	600	657
1979	NL	162	86	76	.531	12	731	693

1980	NL	162	74	88	.457	17	738	710
1981	NL	102	59	43	.578	NA	464	417
1982	NL	162	92	70	.568	-	685	609
1983	NL	162	79	83	.488	11	679	710
1984	NL	162	84	78	.519	12.5	652	645
1985	NL	162	101	61	.623	-	747	572
1986	NL	161	79	82	.491	28.5	601	611
1987	NL	162	95	67	.586	-	798	693
1988	NL	162	76	86	.469	25	578	633
1989	NL	162	86	76	.531	7	632	608
1990	NL	162	70	92	.432	25	599	698
1991	NL	162	84	78	.519	14	651	648
1992	NL	162	83	79	.512	13	631	604
1993	NL	162	87	75	.537	10	758	744
1994	NL	114	53	61	.465	13	535	621
1995	NL	143	62	81	.434	22.5	563	658
TOTAL:	98 years	15077	7730	7347		1636	66433	64745
AVERAGE:		154	79	75	.513	16.5	678	661

Playoff Record

Season	GP	W	L	R	OR	Result
1926	7	4	3	31	21	**Won World Series.**
1928	4	0	4	10	27	Lost World Series to New York.
1930	6	2	4	12	21	Lost World Series to Philadelphia.
1931	7	4	3	19	22	**Won World Series.**
1934	7	4	3	34	23	**Won World Series.**
1942	5	4	1	23	18	**Won World Series.**
1943	5	1	4	9	17	Lost World Series to New York.
1944	6	4	2	16	12	**Won World Series.**
1946	7	4	3	28	20	**Won World Series.**
1964	7	4	3	32	33	**Won World Series.**
1967	7	4	3	25	21	**Won World Series.**
1968	7	3	4	27	34	Lost World Series to Detroit.
1982	10	7	3	56	38	**Won World Series.**
1985	13	7	6	42	51	Lost World series to Kansas City.
1987	14	7	7	49	61	Lost World Series to Minnesota.
TOTAL:	112	59	53	413	419	
AVERAGE:	7	4	3	28	28	

COACHING HISTORY: 1898 Tim Hurst 39-111-.260; 1899-1900 Patsy Tebeau 132-122-.520; 1900 Louie Heilbroner 17-20-.459; 1901-1903 Patrick Donovan 175-236-.426; 1904-1905 Charles Nichols 94-108-.465; 1905 Jimmy Burke 17-32-.347; 1905 Stanley Robison 22-35-.386; 1906-1908 John McCloskey 153-304-.335; 1909-1912 Roger Bresnahan 255-352-.420; 1913-1917 Miller Huggins 346-415-.455; 1918 Jack Hendricks 51-78-.395; 1919-1925 Branch Rickey 458-485-.486; 1925-1926 Rogers Hornsby 153-116-.569; 1927 Bob O'Farrell 92-61-.601; 1928-1929 Bill McKechnie 128-88-.593; 1929 Bill Southworth 43-45-.489; 1929-1933 Charles Street 313-242-.564; 1933-1938 Frank Frisch 457-354-.564; 1938 Mike Gonzalez 9-8-.529; 1939-1940 Ray Blades 107-85-.557; 1940 Mike Gonzalez 0-5-.000; 1940-1945 Bill Southworth 577-301-.657; 1946-1950 Eddie Dyer 446-325-.578; 1951 Marty Marion 81-73-.526; 1952-1955 Eddie Stanky 260-238-.522; 1955 Harry Walker 51-67-.432; 1956-1958 Fred Hutchinson 232-220-.513; 1958 Stank Hack 3-7-.300; 1959-1961 Solomen Hemus 190-192-.497; 1961-1964 John Keane 317-249-.560; 1965-1976 Albert Schoendienst 1010-925-.522; 1977-1978 Vern Rapp 89-89-.500; 1978 Jack Krol 1-1-.500; 1978-1980 Ken Boyer 166-191-.465; 1980 Jack Krol 0-1-.000; 1980 Albert

Schoendienst 18-19-.486; 1980-1990 Dorrel "Whitey" Herzog 822-728-.530; 1990 Albert Schoendienst 13-11-.542; 1990-1995 Joe Torre 393-408-.491; 1996-present Tony LaRussa

*Sportsman's Park II named Busch Stadium from 1953-1966
**Busch Stadium was known as Busch Memorial Stadium from 1966 to 1982.

ST. LOUIS CARDINALS
(were Chicago Cardinals)
(became Phoenix Cardinals)

Home City: St. Louis, Missouri
Home Stadium: Busch Stadium (1960-1965) Capacity: 34,000
Busch Memorial Stadium (1966-1987) Capacity: 51,392 [1986]
Origin of Name: The team kept the same name when it moved from Chicago to St. Louis.

Regular Season Record

Season	League	GP	W	L	T	PF	PA	Pct
1960	NFL	12	6	5	1	288	230	.542
1961	NFL	14	7	7	0	279	267	.500
1962	NFL	14	4	9	1	287	361	.321
1963	NFL	14	9	5	0	341	283	.643
1964	NFL	14	9	3	2	357	331	.714
1965	NFL	14	5	9	0	296	309	.357
1966	NFL	14	8	5	1	264	265	.607
1967	NFL	14	6	7	1	333	356	.464
1968	NFL	14	9	4	1	325	289	.679
1969	NFL	14	4	9	1	314	389	.321
1970	NFL	14	8	5	1	325	228	.607
1971	NFL	14	4	9	1	231	279	.321
1972	NFL	14	4	9	1	193	303	.321
1973	NFL	14	4	9	1	286	365	.321
1974	NFL	14	10	4	0	285	218	.714
1975	NFL	14	11	3	0	356	276	.786
1976	NFL	14	10	4	0	309	267	.714
1977	NFL	14	7	7	0	272	287	.500
1978	NFL	16	6	10	0	248	296	.375
1979	NFL	16	5	11	0	307	358	.313
1980	NFL	16	5	11	0	299	350	.313
1981	NFL	16	7	9	0	315	408	.438
1982	NFL	9	5	4	0	135	170	.556
1983	NFL	16	8	7	1	374	428	.531
1984	NFL	16	9	7	0	423	345	.563
1985	NFL	16	5	11	0	278	414	.313
1986	NFL	16	4	11	1	218	351	.281
1987	NFL	15	7	8	0	362	368	.467
TOTAL:	28 years	402	186	202	14	8300	8791	
AVERAGE:		14	7	7	0	296	314	.480

Playoff Record

Season	GP	W	L	PF	PA	Result
1974	1	0	1	14	30	Lost Divisional playoff to Minnesota.
1975	1	0	1	23	35	Lost Divisional playoff to Los Angeles.

1982	1	0	1	16	41	Lost 1st round playoff to Green Bay.
TOTAL:	3	0	3	53	106	
AVERAGE:	1	0	1	18	35	

COACHING HISTORY: 1960-1961 Frank Ivy 11-12-1-.479; 1961 Chuck Drulis & Ray Prochaska & Ray Willsey 2-0-0-1.000; 1962-1965 Wally Lemm 27-26-3-.509; 1966-1970 Charley Winner 35-30-5-.536; 1971-1972 Bob Hollway 8-18-2-.321; 1973-1977 Don Coryell 42-27-1-.607; 1978-1979 Bud Wilkinson 9-20-0-.310; 1979 Larry Wilson 2-1-0-.667; 1980-1985 Jim Hanifan 39-49-1-.444; 1986-1987 Gene Stallings 11-19-1-.371

ST. LOUIS EAGLES
(were Ottawa Senators)

Home City: St. Louis, Missouri
Home Arena: St. Louis Arena Capacity: 12,600
Origin of Name:

Regular Season Record

Season	League	GP	W	L	T	GF	GA	Pts	Pct
1934-1935	NHL	48	11	31	6	86	144	28	.292

COACHING HISTORY: Eddie Gerard 2-11-0-.154; George Boucher 9-20-6-.343

ST. LOUIS GUNNERS
(Cincinnati Reds folded with 3 games remaining in 1934 season and the Gunners were formed)

Home City: St. Louis, Missouri
Home Stadium:
Origin of Name: The team was purchased from its Cincinnati owners by the St. Louis Gunners an independent team operating in the area.

Regular Season Record

Season	League	GP	W	L	T	PF	PA	Pct
1934	NFL	3	1	2	0	27	61	.333

COACHING HISTORY: Mike Palm 1-2-0-.333

ST. LOUIS HAWKS
(were Milwaukee Hawks)
(became Atlanta Hawks)

Home City: St. Louis, Missouri
Home Court: Kiel Auditorium Capacity: 10,000
Origin of Name: The team kept the same name when it moved from Milwaukee to St. Louis.

Regular Season Record

Season	League	GP	W	L	PPGF	PPGA	Pct	GB
1955-1956	NBA	72	33	39	96.6	98.0	.458	4
1956-1957	NBA	72	34	38	98.5	98.6	.472	-
1957-1958	NBA	72	41	31	107.5	106.2	.569	-
1958-1959	NBA	72	49	23	108.8	105.1	.681	-

1959-1960	NBA	75	46	29	113.4	110.7	.613	-
1960-1961	NBA	79	51	28	118.8	114.1	.646	-
1961-1962	NBA	80	29	51	118.9	122.1	.363	25
1962-1963	NBA	80	48	32	109.6	107.8	.600	5
1963-1964	NBA	80	46	34	110.0	108.4	.575	2
1964-1965	NBA	80	45	35	108.8	105.8	.563	4
1965-1966	NBA	80	36	44	111.4	112.0	.450	9
1966-1967	NBA	81	39	42	113.6	115.2	.481	5
1967-1968	NBA	82	56	26	113.0	110.3	.683	-
TOTAL:	13 years	1005	553	452				54
AVERAGE:		77	42	35	109.9	108.8	.550	4

Playoff Record

Season	GP	W	L	PPGF	PPGA	Result
1955-1956	9	4	5	93.2	103.0	Lost Division final to Ft. Wayne.
1956-1957	10	6	4	113.8	115.4	Lost championship series to Boston.
1957-1958	11	8	3	109.5	107.0	**Won NBA championship**.
1958-1959	6	2	4	108.0	100.8	Lost Divisional final to Minneapolis.
1959-1960	14	7	7	105.7	107.3	Lost championship series to Boston.
1960-1961	12	5	7	111.9	117.1	Lost championship series to Boston.
1962-1963	11	6	5	110.9	109.5	Lost Division final to Los Angeles.
1963-1964	12	6	6	106.1	106.5	Lost Division final to San Francisco.
1964-1965	4	1	3	109.0	113.3	Lost Division semifinal to Baltimore.
1965-1966	10	6	4	114.0	115.4	Lost Division final to Los Angeles.
1966-1967	9	5	4	114.4	113.4	Lost Division final to San Francisco.
1967-1968	6	2	4	111.3	110.0	Lost Division semifinal to San Francisco.
TOTAL:	114	58	56			
AVERAGE:	10	5	5	109.0	109.8	

COACHING HISTORY: 1955-1957 Red Holzman 47-58-.448; 1956-1957 Slater Martin 5-3-.625; 1956-1958 Alex Hannum 56-47-.544; 1958-1959 Andy Phillip 6-4-.600; 1958-1960 Ed MacAuley 89-48-.650; 1960-1962 Paul Seymour 56-37-.602; 1961-1962 Fuzzy Levane 20-40-.333; 1961-1962 Bob Pettit 4-2-.667; 1962-1965 Harry Gallatin 111-82-.575; 1964-1968 Richie Guerin 159-131-.548

ST. LOUIS MAROONS

Home City: St. Louis, Missouri
Home Field: Lucas Park (1884) — Capacity: 10,000 [1884]
Robison Field (1885-1886) — Capacity: 18,000
Origin of Name: The team was named for the color of their uniforms.

Regular Season Record

Season	League	GP	W	L	Pct	GB	R	OR
1884	UA	113	94	19	.832	-	887	429
1885	NL	108	36	72	.333	49	390	593
1886	NL	122	43	79	.352	46	547	712
TOTAL:	3 years	343	173	170		95	1824	1734
AVERAGE:		114	58	56	.504	32	608	578

COACHING HISTORY: 1884-1885 Henry Lucas 130-91-.588; 1886 Gus Schmelz 43-79-.352

ST. LOUIS RAMS
(were Los Angeles Rams)

Home City: St. Louis, Missouri
Home Stadium: Busch Stadium (1995) — Capacity: 59,022 [1995]
Trans World Dome (1995-present) — Capacity: 67,000 [1995]
Origin of Name: The team kept the same nickname when it moved from Los Angeles to St. Louis.

Regular Season Record

Season	League	GP	W	L	T	PF	PA	Pct
1995	NFL	16	7	9	0	309	418	.438

COACHING HISTORY: 1995-present Rich Brooks

ST. LOUIS REDS

Home City: St. Louis, Missouri
Home Field: Sportsman's Park — Capacity 18,000
Athletic Park — Capacity: 9,000
Origin of Name: The team may have been named for the color of their uniforms.

Regular Season Record

Season	League	GP	W	L	Pct	GB	R	OR
1876	NL	64	45	19	.703	6	386	229
1877	NL	60	28	32	.467	14	284	318
TOTAL:	2 years	124	73	51		20	670	547
AVERAGE:		62	37	25	.589	10	335	274

COACHING HISTORY: 1876 Harmon Dehlman 45-19-.703; 1877 John Lucas 14-12-.538; 1877 George McManus 14-20-.412

ST. LOUIS SPIRITS
(also known as Spirits of St. Louis)

Home City: St. Louis, Missouri
Home Court: St. Louis Arena — Capacity: 18,006
Origin of Name: The team was named by club executives.

Regular Season Record

Season	League	GP	W	L	PPGF	PPGA	Pct	GB
1974-1975	ABA	84	32	52	109.0	113.4	.381	26
1975-1976	ABA	84	35	49	108.9	112.1	.417	25
TOTAL:	2 years	168	67	101				51
AVERAGE:		84	34	50	109.0	112.8	.399	26

Playoff Record

Season	GP	W	L	PPGF	PPGA	Result
1974-1975	10	5	5	116.0	117.7	Lost 2nd round series to Kentucky.

COACHING HISTORY: 1974-1975 Bob MacKinnon 32-52-.381; 1975-1976 Rod Thorn 20-27-.426; 1975-1976 Joe Mullaney 15-22-.405

ST. LOUIS STARS
(became California Surf)

Home City: St. Louis, Missouri
Home Field: Francis Field (1967) Capacity: 10,000 [1967]
Busch Stadium (1968-1977) Capacity: 49,450 [1968]
Origin of Name: The team name was chosen in a Name the Team Contest.

Regular Season Record

Season	League	GP	W	L	T	GF	GA	BP	Pts	Pct
1967	NPSL	32	14	11	7	54	57	NA	156	.542
1968	NASL	32	14	12	6	58	41	48	150	.521
1969	NASL	16	3	11	2	24	47	23	47	.326
1970	NASL	24	5	17	2	26	71	24	60	.278
1971	NASL	24	6	13	5	37	47	35	86	.398
1972	NASL	14	7	4	3	20	14	18	69	.548
1973	NASL	19	7	7	5	27	27	25	82	.480
1974	NASL	20	4	15	1	27	42	27	54	.300
1975	NASL	22	13	9	-	38	34	37	115	.581
1976	NASL	24	5	19	-	28	57	28	58	.269
1977	NASL	26	12	14	-	33	35	32	104	.444
TOTAL:	11 years	253	90	132	31	372	472	297	981	
AVERAGE:		23	8	12	3	34	43	27	89	.431

Playoff Record

Season	GP	W	L	GF	GA	Result
1972	2	1	1	3	2	Lost championship series to New York.
1975	2	1	1	2	2	Lost 2nd round series to Portland.
1977	1	0	1	0	1	Lost playoff game to Rochester.
TOTAL:	5	2	3	5	5	
AVERAGE:	2	1	1	2	2	

COACHING HISTORY: 1967-1968 Rudi Gutendorf 28-23-13; 1969-1970 Robert Kehoe; 1970 Don Range; 1971 George Meyer 1971-1973 Casey Frankiewicz; 1974-1977 John Sewell 34-57-1

ST. LOUIS TERRIERS

Home City: St. Louis, Missouri
Home Field: Handlan's Park Capacity: 15,000 [1915]
Origin of Name:

Regular Season Record

Season	League	GP	W	L	Pct	GB	R	OR
1914	FL	151	62	89	.411	25	565	697
1915	FL	154	87	67	.565	-	634	528
TOTAL:	2 years	305	149	156		25	1199	1225
AVERAGE:		153	75	78	.489	12.5	600	613

COACHING HISTORY: 1914 Mordecai "Three Finger" Brown 50-63-.442; 1914-1915 Fielder Jones 99-93-.516

ST. PAUL SAINTS

Home City: St. Paul, Minnesota
Home Field: The team played only road games
Origin of Name:

Regular Season Record

Season	League	GP	W	L	Pct	GB	R	OR
1884	UA	8	2	6	.250	39.5	24	57

COACHING HISTORY: A.M. Thompson 2-6-.250

SAN ANTONIO GUNSLINGERS

Home City: San Antonio, Texas
Home Stadium: Alamo Stadium Capacity: 32,000
Origin of Name: The name was picked in a Name the Team Contest

Regular Season Record

Season	League	GP	W	L	T	PF	PA	Pct
1984	USFL	18	7	11	0	309	325	.389
1985	USFL	18	5	13	0	296	436	.278
TOTAL:	2 years	36	12	24	0	605	761	
AVERAGE:		18	6	12	0	303	381	.333

COACHING HISTORY: 1984-1985 Gil Steinke 9-15-0-.375; 1985 Jim Bates 3-9-0-.250

SAN ANTONIO RIDERS

Home City: San Antonio, Texas
Home Stadium: Alamo Stadium (1991) Capacity: 25,000 [1991]
Bobcat Field (1992) Capacity: 23,000 [1992]
Origin of Name:

Regular Season Record

Season	League	GP	W	L	T	PF	PA	Pct
1991	WLAF	10	4	6	0	176	196	.400
1992	WFL	10	7	3	0	195	150	.700
TOTAL:	2 years	20	11	9	0	371	346	
AVERAGE:		10	6	4	0	186	173	.550

COACHING HISTORY: 1991-1992 Mike Riley 11-9-0-.550

SAN ANTONIO SPURS
(were Dallas Chaparrals)

Home City: San Antonio, Texas
Home Court: HemisFair Arena (1973-1993) Capacity: 15,908 [1992]
Alamodome (1993-present) Capacity: 20,500 [1994]
Origin of Name: The name was chosen in a Name the Team Contest.

Regular Season Record

Season	League	GP	W	L	PPGF	PPGA	Pct	GB
1973-1974	ABA	84	45	39	97.6	96.7	.536	6
1974-1975	ABA	84	51	33	113.4	109.2	.607	14
1975-1976	ABA	84	50	34	115.6	111.6	.595	10
1976-1977	NBA	82	44	38	115.0	114.4	.537	5
1977-1978	NBA	82	52	30	114.5	111.1	.634	-
1978-1979	NBA	82	48	34	119.3	114.1	.585	-
1979-1980	NBA	82	41	41	119.4	119.7	.500	9
1980-1981	NBA	82	52	30	112.3	109.4	.634	-
1981-1982	NBA	82	48	34	113.1	110.8	.585	-
1982-1983	NBA	82	53	29	114.3	110.7	.646	-
1983-1984	NBA	82	37	45	120.3	120.5	.451	8
1984-1985	NBA	82	41	41	114.8	113.9	.500	11
1985-1986	NBA	82	35	47	111.2	113.1	.427	16
1986-1987	NBA	82	28	54	108.3	113.4	.341	27
1987-1988	NBA	82	31	51	113.6	118.5	.378	23
1988-1989	NBA	82	21	61	105.5	112.3	.256	30
1989-1990	NBA	82	56	26	106.3	102.8	.683	-
1990-1991	NBA	82	55	27	107.1	102.6	.671	-
1991-1992	NBA	82	47	35	104.0	100.6	.573	8
1992-1993	NBA	82	49	33	105.5	102.8	.598	6
1993-1994	NBA	82	55	27	100.0	94.8	.671	3
1994-1995	NBA	82	62	20	106.6	100.6	.756	-
1995-1996	NBA	82	59	23	103.4	97.1	.720	-
TOTAL:	23 years	1892	1060	832				176
AVERAGE:		82	46	36	110.5	108.8	.560	8

Playoff Record

Season	GP	W	L	PPGF	PPGA	Result
1973-1974	7	3	4	100.9	101.7	Lost 1st round series to Indiana.
1974-1975	6	2	4	108.0	112.3	Lost 1st round series to Indiana.
1975-1976	7	3	4	107.6	106.3	Lost 1st round series to New York.
1976-1977	2	0	2	101.5	108.5	Lost 1st round series to Boston.
1977-1978	6	2	4	107.8	108.0	Lost Conference semifinal to Washington.
1978-1979	14	7	7	108.8	109.4	Lost Conference final to Washington.
1979-1980	3	1	2	103.7	112.3	Lost 1st round series to Houston.
1980-1981	7	3	4	107.7	109.7	Lost Conference semifinal to Houston.
1981-1982	9	4	5	107.3	111.6	Lost Conference final to Los Angeles.
1982-1983	11	6	5	121.0	116.7	Lost Conference final to Los Angeles.
1984-1985	5	2	3	110.2	120.8	Lost 1st round series to Denver.
1985-1986	3	0	3	92.0	123.7	Lost 1st round series to Lakers.
1987-1988	3	0	3	109.7	120.3	Lost 1st round series to Lakers.
1989-1990	10	6	4	117.0	111.8	Lost Conference semifinal to Portland.
1990-1991	4	1	3	107.8	112.8	Lost 1st round series to Golden State.
1991-1992	3	0	3	103.3	112.3	Lost 1st round series to Phoenix.
1992-1993	10	5	5	100.7	100.6	Lost Conference semifinal to Phoenix.
1993-1994	4	1	3	88.0	96.3	Lost 1st round series to Utah.
1994-1995	15	9	6	99.1	94.9	Lost Conference final to Houston.
1995-1996	10	5	5	94.2	96.8	Lost Conference semifinal to Utah.
TOTAL:	139	60	79			
AVERAGE:	7	3	4	104.5	108.4	

COACHING HISTORY: 1973-1975 Tom Nissalke 62-49-.559; 1974-1976 Bob Bass 84-57-.596; 1976-1980 Doug Moe 177-135-.567; 1979-1980 Bob Bass 8-8-.500; 1980-1983 Stan Albeck 153-93-.622; 1983-1984 Morris McHone 11-20-.355; 1983-1984 Bob Bass 26-25-.510; 1984-1986 Lowell "Cotton" Fitzsimmons 76-88-.463; 1986-1988 Bob Weiss 59-105-.360; 1988-1992 Larry Brown 153-131-.539; 1991-1992 Bob Bass 26-18-.591; 1992-1993 Jerry Tarkanian 9-11-.450; 1992-1993 Rex Hughes 1-0-1.000; 1992-1994 John Lucas 94-49-.657; 1994-present Bob Hill

SAN ANTONIO TEXANS

(were Sacramento Gold Miners)

Home City: San Antonio, Texas
Home Stadium: The Alamodome — Capacity: 59,000 [1995]
Origin of Name: The team adopted the state's name as its own.

Regular Season Record

Season	League	GP	W	L	T	PF	PA	Pts	Pct
1995	CFL	18	12	6	0	630	457	24	.667

Playoff Record

Season	GP	W	L	PF	PA	Result
1995	2	1	1	63	30	Lost Division final to Baltimore.

COACHING HISTORY: 1995 Kay Stephenson 12-6-0-.667

SAN ANTONIO THUNDER

(became Team Hawaii)

Home City: San Antonio, Texas
Home Stadium: Alamo Stadium — Capacity: 22,500 [1975]
Origin of Name: The name was chosen in a Name the Team Contest.

Regular Season Record

Season	League	GP	W	L	GF	GA	BP	Pts	Pct
1975	NASL	22	6	16	24	46	23	59	.298
1976	NASL	24	12	12	38	32	35	107	.495
TOTAL:	2 years	46	18	28	62	78	58	166	
AVERAGE:		23	9	14	31	39	29	83	.401

COACHING HISTORY: 1975 Alex Perolli 1-8; 1975-1976 Don Batie 17-20

SAN ANTONIO WINGS

Home City: San Antonio, Texas
Home Stadium: Alamo Stadium — Capacity: 22,500 [1975]
Origin of Name:

Regular Season Record

Season	League	GP	W	L	T	PF	PA	Pct
1975	WFL	13	7	6	0	364	268	.538

COACHING HISTORY: Perry Moss 7-6-0-.538

SAN DIEGO CHARGERS
(were Los Angeles Chargers)

Home City: San Diego, California
Home Stadium: Balboa Stadium (1961-1966) Capacity: 34,000
San Diego/Jack Murphy Stadium (1967-present) Capacity: 60,789 [1995]
Origin of Name: The team kept the same nickname when it moved from Los Angeles to San Diego.

Regular Season Record

Season	League	GP	W	L	T	PF	PA	Pct
1961	AFL	14	12	2	0	396	219	.857
1962	AFL	14	4	10	0	314	392	.286
1963	AFL	14	11	3	0	399	256	.785
1964	AFL	14	8	5	1	341	300	.607
1965	AFL	14	9	2	3	340	227	.750
1966	AFL	14	7	6	1	335	284	.536
1967	AFL	14	8	5	1	360	352	.607
1968	AFL	14	9	5	0	382	310	.643
1969	AFL	14	8	6	0	288	276	.571
1970	NFL	14	5	6	3	282	278	.464
1971	NFL	14	6	8	0	311	341	.429
1972	NFL	14	4	9	1	264	344	.321
1973	NFL	14	2	11	1	188	386	.179
1974	NFL	14	5	9	0	212	285	.357
1975	NFL	14	2	12	0	189	345	.143
1976	NFL	14	6	8	0	248	285	.429
1977	NFL	14	7	7	0	222	205	.500
1978	NFL	16	9	7	0	355	309	.563
1979	NFL	16	12	4	0	411	246	.750
1980	NFL	16	11	5	0	418	327	.688
1981	NFL	16	10	6	0	478	390	.625
1982	NFL	9	6	3	0	288	221	.667
1983	NFL	16	6	10	0	358	462	.375
1984	NFL	16	7	9	0	394	413	.438
1985	NFL	16	8	8	0	467	435	.500
1986	NFL	16	4	12	0	335	396	.250
1987	NFL	15	8	7	0	253	317	.533
1988	NFL	16	6	10	0	231	332	.375
1989	NFL	16	6	10	0	266	290	.375
1990	NFL	16	6	10	0	315	281	.375
1991	NFL	16	4	12	0	274	342	.250
1992	NFL	16	11	5	0	335	241	.688
1993	NFL	16	8	8	0	322	290	.500
1994	NFL	16	11	5	0	381	306	.688
1995	NFL	16	9	7	0	321	323	.563
TOTAL:	35 years	518	255	252	11	11273	11006	
AVERAGE:		15	8	7	0	322	314	.503

Playoff Record

Season	GP	W	L	PF	PA	Result
1961	1	0	1	3	10	Lost championship game to Houston.
1963	1	1	0	51	10	**Won AFL championship**.
1964	1	0	1	7	20	Lost championship game to Buffalo.
1965	1	0	1	0	23	Lost championship game to Buffalo.
1979	1	0	1	14	17	Lost Divisional playoff to Houston.
1980	2	1	1	47	48	Lost AFC championship to Oakland.
1981	2	1	1	48	65	Lost AFC championship to Cincinnati.
1982	2	1	1	44	62	Lost 2nd round series to Miami.
1992	2	1	1	17	31	Lost Conference semifinal to Miami.
1994	3	2	1	65	83	Lost Super Bowl game to San Francisco.
1995	1	0	1	20	35	Lost Wild Card game to Indianapolis.
TOTAL:	17	7	10	316	404	
AVERAGE:	2	1	1	29	37	

COACHING HISTORY: 1961-1969 Sid Gillman 82-48-6-.625; 1969-1970 Charlie Waller 9-7-3-.553; 1971 Sid Gillman 4-6-0-.400; 1971-1973 Harland Svare 7-17-2-.308; 1973 Ron Waller 1-5-0-.167; 1974-1978 Tommy Prothro 21-39-0-.350; 1978-1986 Don Coryell 69-56-0-.552; 1986-1988 Al Saunders 17-22-0-.436; 1989-1991 Dan Henning 16-32-0-.333; 1992-present Bobby Ross

SAN DIEGO CLIPPERS

(were Buffalo Bisons)
(became Los Angeles Clippers)

Home City: San Diego, California
Home Court: San Diego Sports Arena — Capacity: 13,841 [1984]
Origin of Name: The name was chosen in a Name the Team Contest

Regular Season Record

Season	League	GP	W	L	PPGF	PPGA	Pct	GB
1978-1979	NBA	82	43	39	113.1	114.9	.524	9
1979-1980	NBA	82	35	47	107.6	111.7	.427	25
1980-1981	NBA	82	36	46	106.5	108.1	.439	21
1981-1982	NBA	82	17	65	108.5	115.9	.207	40
1982-1983	NBA	82	25	57	108.6	113.4	.305	33
1983-1984	NBA	82	30	52	110.7	114.0	.366	24
TOTAL:	6 years	492	186	306				152
AVERAGE:		82	31	51	109.2	113.0	.378	25

COACHING HISTORY: 1978-1980 Gene Shue 78-86-.476; 1980-1983 Paul Silas 78-168-.317; 1983-1984 Jim Lynam 30-52-.366

SAN DIEGO CONQUISTADORS

(became San Diego Sails)

Home City: San Diego, California
Home Court: Peterson Gym at San Diego State (1972-73) — Capacity: 4,200 [1972]
San Diego Sports Arena (1973-1975) — Capacity: 13,600 [1974]
Origin of Name: The name was chosen in a Name the Team Contest.

Regular Season Record

Season	League	GP	W	L	PPGF	PPGA	Pct	GB
1972-1973	ABA	84	30	54	109.0	113.3	.357	25
1973-1974	ABA	84	37	47	107.0	107.5	.440	14
1974-1975	ABA	84	31	53	109.0	115.5	.369	34
TOTAL:	3 years	252	98	154				73
AVERAGE:		84	33	51	108.3	112.1	.389	24

Playoff Record

Season	GP	W	L	PPGF	PPGA	Result
1972-1973	4	0	4	94.8	106.8	Lost 1st round series to Utah.

COACHING HISTORY: 1972-1973 K.C. Jones 30-54-.357; 1973-1974 Wilt Chamberlain 37-47-.440; 1974-1975 Alex Groza 15-23-.395; 1974-1975 Beryl Shipley 16-30-.348

SAN DIEGO JAWS

(were Baltimore Comets)
(became Las Vegas Quicksilvers)

Home City: San Diego, California
Home Stadium: San Diego Stadium Capacity: 50,000
Origin of Name: The name was no doubt suggested by Steven Spielberg's hit movie *Jaws* which had been released the previous year.

Regular Season Record

Season	League	GP	W	L	GF	GA	BP	Pts	Pct
1976	NASL	24	9	15	29	47	28	82	.380

COACHING HISTORY: Derek Trevis 9-15-.380

SAN DIEGO MARINERS

(were New Jersey Knights)

Home City: San Diego, California
Home Arena: San Diego Sports Arena Capacity: 13,039
Origin of Name: The name was chosen to reflect the city's maritime heritage.

Regular Season Record

Season	League	GP	W	L	T	GF	GA	Pts	Pct
1974-1975	WHA	78	43	31	4	326	268	90	.577
1975-1976	WHA	80	36	38	6	303	290	78	.488
1976-1977	WHA	81	40	37	4	284	283	84	.519
TOTAL:	3 years	239	119	106	14	913	841	252	
AVERAGE:		80	40	35	5	304	280	84	.527

Playoff Record

Season	GP	W	L	GF	GA	Result
1974-1975	10	4	6	34	44	Lost semifinal series to Houston.
1975-1976	11	5	6	33	39	Lost quarterfinal series to Houston.
1976-1977	7	3	4	19	28	Lost quarterfinal series to Winnipeg.
TOTAL:	28	12	16	86	111	
AVERAGE:	9	4	5	29	37	

COACHING HISTORY: 1974-1975 Harry Howell 43-31-4-.577; 1975-1977 Ron Ingram 76-75-10-.503

SAN DIEGO PADRES

Home City: San Diego, California
Home Field: San Diego/Jack Murphy Stadium* Capacity: 59,700 [1995]
Origin of Name: The team was named after the previous Pacific Coast League team.

Regular Season Record

Season	League	GP	W	L	Pct	GB	R	OR
1969	NL	162	52	110	.321	41	468	746
1970	NL	162	63	99	.389	39	681	788
1971	NL	161	61	100	.379	28.5	486	610
1972	NL	153	58	95	.379	36.5	488	665
1973	NL	162	60	102	.370	39	548	770
1974	NL	162	60	102	.370	42	541	830
1975	NL	162	71	91	.438	37	552	683
1976	NL	162	73	89	.451	29	570	662
1977	NL	162	69	93	.426	29	692	834
1978	NL	162	84	78	.519	11	591	598
1979	NL	161	68	93	.422	22	603	681
1980	NL	162	73	89	.451	19.5	591	654
1981	NL	110	41	69	.373	NA	382	455
1982	NL	162	81	81	.500	8	675	658
1983	NL	162	81	81	.500	10	653	653
1984	NL	162	92	70	.568	-	686	634
1985	NL	162	83	79	.512	12	650	622
1986	NL	162	74	88	.457	22	656	723
1987	NL	162	65	97	.401	25	668	763
1988	NL	161	83	78	.516	11	594	583
1989	NL	162	89	73	.549	3	642	626
1990	NL	161	74	87	.460	16.5	673	673
1991	NL	162	84	78	.519	10	636	646
1992	NL	162	82	80	.506	16	617	636
1993	NL	162	61	101	.377	43	679	772
1994	NL	117	47	70	.402	12.5	479	531
1995	NL	144	70	74	.486	8	668	672
TOTAL:	27 years	4246	1899	2347		570.5	16169	18168
AVERAGE:		157	70	87	.447	21	599	673

Playoff Record

Season	GP	W	L	R	OR	Result
1984	10	4	6	37	49	Lost World Series to Detroit.

COACHING HISTORY: 1969-1972 Preston Gomez 180-316-.363; 1972-1973 Don Zimmer 114-190-.375; 1974-1977 John McNamara 224-310-.419; 1977 Al Dark 49-55-.471; 1978-1979 Roger Craig 152-171-.471; 1980 Jerry Coleman 73-89-.451; 1981 Frank Howard 41-69-.373; 1982-1985 Dick Williams 337-311-.520; 1986 Steve Boros 74-88-.457; 1987-1988 Larry Bowa 81-127-.389; 1988-1990 Jack McKeon 193-164-.541; 1990-1992 Greg Riddoch 200-194-.508; 1992-1994 Jim Riggleman 112-179-.385; 1995-present Bruce Bochy

*Known as San Diego Stadium from 1969 to 1981.

SAN DIEGO ROCKETS
(became Houston Rockets)

Home City: San Diego, California
Home Court: San Diego Sports Arena — Capacity: 14,000
Origin of Name: The name was chosen in a Name the Team Contest.

Regular Season Record

Season	League	GP	W	L	PPGF	PPGA	Pct	GB
1967-1968	NBA	82	15	67	112.4	121.0	.183	41
1968-1969	NBA	82	37	45	115.3	115.5	.451	18
1969-1970	NBA	82	27	55	118.7	121.8	.329	21
1970-1971	NBA	82	40	42	113.2	113.4	.488	8
TOTAL:	4 years	328	119	209				88
AVERAGE:		82	30	52	114.9	117.9	.363	22

Playoff Record

Season	GP	W	L	PPGF	PPGA	Result
1968-1969	6	2	4	106.2	108.7	Lost Division semifinal to Atlanta.

COACHING HISTORY: 1967-1970 Jack McMahon 61-129-.321; 1970-1971 Alex Hannum 58-80-.420

SAN DIEGO SAILS
(were San Diego Conquistadors)

Home City: San Diego, California
Home Court: San Diego Sports Arena — Capacity: 14,000 [1976]
Origin of Name: The name was chosen because of the areas maritime history.

Regular Season Record

Season	League	GP	W	L	PPGF	PPGA	Pct	GB
1975-1976	ABA	11	3	8	98.8	103.5	.273	36.5

COACHING HISTORY: Bill Musselman 3-8-.273

SAN DIEGO SOCKERS
(were Las Vegas Quicksilvers)

Home City: San Diego, California
Home Stadium: San Diego/Jack Murphy Stadium Capacity: 52,675 [1984]
Origin of Name: The word socker is a variation of the word soccer and was probably chosen for that reason.

Regular Season Record

Season	League	GP	W	L	GF	GA	BP	Pts	Pct
1978	NASL	30	18	12	63	56	56	164	.607
1979	NASL	30	15	15	59	55	50	140	.519
1980	NASL	32	16	16	53	51	44	140	.486
1981	NASL	32	21	11	68	49	55	173	.360
1982	NASL	32	19	13	71	54	54	162	.338
1983	NASL	30	11	19	53	65	42	106	.236
1984	NASL	24	14	10	51	42	40	118	.328
TOTAL:	7 years	210	114	96	418	372	341	1003	
AVERAGE:		30	16	14	60	53	49	143	.386

Playoff Record

Season	GP	W	L	GF	GA	Result
1978	4	2	2	4	4	Lost 2nd round series to Tampa Bay.
1979	7	5	2	18	9	Lost 3rd round series to Tampa Bay.
1980	9	5	4	19	21	Lost 3rd round series to Ft. Lauderdale.
1981	9	5	4	17	13	Lost 3rd round series to Chicago.
1982	5	2	3	9	7	Lost 2nd round series to New York.
1984	2	0	2	1	3	Lost 1st round series to Toronto.
TOTAL:	36	19	17	68	57	
AVERAGE:	6	3	3	11	9	

COACHING HISTORY: 1978-1980 Hubert Vogelsinger 33-31; 1980 Hank Liotart 3-1; 1980-1984 Ron Newman 78-64

SAN DIEGO TOROS
(were Los Angeles Toros)

Home City: San Diego, California
Home Stadium:
Origin of Name: The team kept the same nickname after moving to San Diego from Los Angeles.

Regular Season Record

Season	League	GP	W	L	T	GF	GA	BP	Pts	Pct
1968	NASL	32	18	8	6	65	38	60	186	.646

Playoff Record

Season	GP	W	L	T	GF	GA	Result
1968	4	1	1	2	2	4	Lost championship series to Atlanta.

COACHING HISTORY: George Curtis, Angel Papadopolus

SAN FRANCISCO 49ers

Home City: San Francisco, California
Home Stadium: Kezar Stadium (1946-1970) Capacity: 59,636
3Com Park(1971-present)* Capacity: 68,491 [1995]
Origin of Name: The team was named by the team owners and was suggested by the California Gold Rush of 1849.

Regular Season Record

Season	League	GP	W	L	T	PF	PA	Pct
1946	AAFC	14	9	5	0	307	189	.643
1947	AAFC	14	8	4	2	327	264	.643
1948	AAFC	14	12	2	0	495	248	.857
1949	AAFC	12	9	3	0	416	227	.750
1950	NFL	12	3	9	0	213	300	.250
1951	NFL	12	7	4	1	255	205	.625
1952	NFL	12	7	5	0	285	221	.583
1953	NFL	12	9	3	0	372	237	.750
1954	NFL	12	7	4	1	313	251	.625
1955	NFL	12	4	8	0	216	298	.333
1956	NFL	12	5	6	1	233	284	.458
1957	NFL	12	8	4	0	260	264	.667
1958	NFL	12	6	6	0	257	324	.500
1959	NFL	12	7	5	0	255	237	.583
1960	NFL	12	7	5	0	208	205	.583
1961	NFL	14	7	6	1	346	272	.538
1962	NFL	14	6	8	0	282	331	.429
1963	NFL	14	2	12	0	198	391	.143
1964	NFL	14	4	10	0	236	330	.286
1965	NFL	14	7	6	1	421	402	.536
1966	NFL	14	6	6	2	320	325	.500
1967	NFL	14	7	7	0	273	337	.500
1968	NFL	14	7	6	1	303	310	.536
1969	NFL	14	4	8	2	277	319	.357
1970	NFL	14	10	3	1	352	267	.750
1971	NFL	14	9	5	0	300	216	.643
1972	NFL	14	8	5	1	353	249	.607
1973	NFL	14	5	9	0	262	319	.357
1974	NFL	14	6	8	0	226	236	.429
1975	NFL	14	5	9	0	255	286	.357
1976	NFL	14	8	6	0	270	190	.571
1977	NFL	14	5	9	0	220	260	.357
1978	NFL	16	2	14	0	219	350	.125
1979	NFL	16	2	14	0	308	416	.125
1980	NFL	16	6	10	0	320	415	.375
1981	NFL	16	13	3	0	357	250	.813
1982	NFL	9	3	6	0	209	206	.333
1983	NFL	16	10	6	0	432	293	.625
1984	NFL	16	15	1	0	475	227	.938
1985	NFL	16	10	6	0	411	263	.625
1986	NFL	16	10	5	1	374	247	.656
1987	NFL	15	13	2	0	459	253	.867
1988	NFL	16	10	6	0	369	294	.625

1989	NFL	16	14	2	0	442	253	.875
1990	NFL	16	14	2	0	353	239	.875
1991	NFL	16	10	6	0	393	239	.625
1992	NFL	16	14	2	0	431	236	.875
1993	NFL	16	10	6	0	473	295	.625
1994	NFL	16	13	3	0	505	296	.813
1995	NFL	16	11	5	0	457	258	.688
TOTAL:	50 years	704	394	295	15	16293	13824	
AVERAGE:		14	8	6	0	326	276	.556

Playoff Record

Season	GP	W	L	PF	PA	Result
1949	1	0	1	7	21	Lost championship game to Cleveland.
1957	1	0	1	27	31	Lost Conference playoff to Detroit.
1970	2	1	1	27	31	Lost NFC championship to Dallas.
1971	2	1	1	27	34	Lost NFC championship to Dallas.
1972	1	0	1	28	30	Lost Divisional playoff to Dallas.
1981	3	3	0	92	72	**Won Super Bowl.**
1983	2	1	1	45	47	Lost NFC championship to Washington.
1984	3	3	0	82	26	**Won Super Bowl.**
1985	1	0	1	3	17	Lost 1st round playoff to Giants.
1986	1	0	1	3	49	Lost Divisional playoff to Giants.
1987	1	0	1	24	36	Lost Divisional playoff to Minnesota.
1988	3	3	0	82	28	**Won Super Bowl.**
1989	3	3	0	126	26	**Won Super Bowl.**
1990	2	1	1	41	25	Lost Conference final to Giants.
1992	2	1	1	40	43	Lost Conference final to Dallas.
1993	2	1	1	65	41	Lost Conference final to Dallas.
1994	3	3	0	131	69	**Won Super Bowl.**
1995	1	0	1	17	27	Lost Conference semifinal to Green Bay.
TOTAL:	34	21	13	867	653	
AVERAGE:	2	1	1	48	36	

COACHING HISTORY: 1946-1954 Lawrence Shaw 71-39-4-.640; 1955 Norman Strader 4-8-0-.333; 1956-1958 Frank Albert 19-16-1-.542; 1959-1963 Howard Hickey 27-27-1-.500; 1963-1967 Jack Christiansen 26-38-3-.410; 1968-1975 Dick Nolan 54-53-5-.504; 1976 Monte Clark 8-6-0-.571; 1977 Ken Meyer 5-9-0-.357; 1978 Pete McCulley 1-8-0-.111; 1978 Fred O'Connor 1-6-0-.143; 1979-1988 Bill Walsh 92-59-1-.609; 1989-present George Seifert

*Known as Candlestick Park from 1971 to 1994.

SAN FRANCISCO GIANTS
(were New York Giants)

Home City: San Francisco, California
Home Field: Seals Stadium (1958-1959) Capacity: 22,900 [1958]
Candlestick Park (1960-present) Capacity: 62,000 [1995]
Origin of Name: The team kept the same nickname when it moved from New York to San Francisco.

Regular Season Record

Season	League	GP	W	L	Pct	GB	R	OR
1958	NL	154	80	74	.519	12	727	698
1959	NL	154	83	71	.539	4	705	613
1960	NL	154	79	75	.513	16	671	631
1961	NL	154	85	69	.552	8	773	655
1962	NL	165	103	62	.624	-	878	690
1963	NL	162	88	74	.543	11	725	641
1964	NL	162	90	72	.556	3	656	587
1965	NL	162	95	67	.586	2	682	593
1966	NL	161	93	68	.578	1.5	675	626
1967	NL	162	91	71	.562	10.5	652	551
1968	NL	162	88	74	.543	9	599	529
1969	NL	162	90	72	.556	3	713	636
1970	NL	162	86	76	.531	16	831	826
1971	NL	162	90	72	.556	-	706	644
1972	NL	155	69	86	.445	26.5	662	649
1973	NL	162	88	74	.543	11	739	702
1974	NL	162	72	90	.444	30	634	723
1975	NL	161	80	81	.497	27.5	659	671
1976	NL	162	74	88	.457	28	595	686
1977	NL	162	75	87	.463	23	673	711
1978	NL	162	89	73	.549	6	613	594
1979	NL	162	71	91	.438	19.5	672	751
1980	NL	161	75	86	.466	17	573	634
1981	NL	111	56	55	.505	NA	427	414
1982	NL	162	87	75	.537	2	673	687
1983	NL	162	79	83	.488	12	687	697
1984	NL	162	66	96	.407	26	682	807
1985	NL	162	62	100	.383	33	556	674
1986	NL	162	83	79	.512	13	698	618
1987	NL	162	90	72	.556	-	783	669
1988	NL	162	83	79	.512	11.5	670	626
1989	NL	162	92	70	.568	-	699	600
1990	NL	162	85	77	.525	6	719	710
1991	NL	162	75	87	.463	19	649	697
1992	NL	162	72	90	.444	26	574	647
1993	NL	162	103	59	.636	1	808	636
1994	NL	115	55	60	.478	3.5	504	500
1995	NL	144	67	77	.465	11	652	776
TOTAL:	38 years	6001	3089	2912		448.5	25594	24799
AVERAGE:		158	81	77	.515	12	674	653

Playoff Record

Season	GP	W	L	R	OR	Result
1962	7	3	4	21	20	Lost World Series to New York.
1971	4	1	3	15	24	Lost NLCS to Pittsburgh.
1987	7	3	4	23	23	Lost NLCS to St. Louis.
1989	9	4	5	44	54	Lost World Series to Oakland.
TOTAL:	27	11	16	103	121	
AVERAGE:	7	3	4	26	30	

COACHING HISTORY: 1958-1960 Bill Rigney 196-170-.536; 1960 Tom Sheehan 46-50-.479; 1961-1964 Alvin Dark 366-277-.569; 1965-1968 Herman Franks 367-280-.567; 1969-1970 Clyde King 109-97-.529; 1970-1974 Charlie Fox 348-325-.517; 1974-1975 Wes Westrum 118-129-.478; 1976 Bill Rigney 74-88-.457; 1977-1979 Joe Altobelli 245-239-.506; 1979-1980 Dave Bristol 85-98-.464; 1981-1984 Frank Robinson 264-277-.488; 1984 Danny Ozark 24-32-.429; 1985 Jim Davenport 56-88-.389; 1985-1992 Roger Craig 586-566-.509; 1993-present Dusty Baker

SAN FRANCISCO GOLDEN GATE GALES

Home City: San Francisco, California
Home Stadium: Kesar Stadium
Origin of Name: The name was suggested by the city's famous Golden Gate Bridge and the club was represented by the ADO Club from the Netherlands.

Regular Season Record

Season	League	GP	W	L	T	GF	GA	Pts	Pct
1967	USA	12	5	4	3	25	19	13	.542

COACHING HISTORY: Ernst Happel 5-4-3-.542

SAN FRANCISCO WARRIORS

(were Philadelphia Warriors)
(became Golden State Warriors)

Home City: San Francisco, California
Home Court: Cow Palace (1962-1964) Capacity: 13,862
Civic Auditorium (1964-1966) Capacity: 7,500
USF Memorial Gym (1964-1966) Capacity: 6,000
Cow Palace (1966-1967) Capacity: 13,862
Civic Auditorium (1966-1967) Capacity: 7,500
Oakland Coliseum Arena (1966-1967) Capacity: 15,000
Cow Palace (1967-1971) Capacity: 14,500
Origin of Name: The team kept the same nickname when they moved to San Francisco from Philadelphia.

Regular Season Record

Season	League	GP	W	L	PPGF	PPGA	Pct	GB
1962-1963	NBA	80	31	49	118.5	120.6	.388	22
1963-1964	NBA	80	48	32	107.7	102.6	.600	-
1964-1965	NBA	80	17	63	105.8	112.0	.213	32
1965-1966	NBA	80	35	45	115.5	118.2	.438	10
1966-1967	NBA	81	44	37	122.4	119.5	.543	-
1967-1968	NBA	82	43	39	117.0	117.6	.524	13
1968-1969	NBA	82	41	41	109.1	110.7	.500	14
1969-1970	NBA	82	30	52	111.1	115.6	.366	18
1970-1971	NBA	82	41	41	107.1	108.5	.500	7
TOTAL:	9 years	729	330	399				116
AVERAGE:		81	37	44	112.7	113.9	.453	13

Playoff Record

Season	GP	W	L	PPGF	PPGA	Result
1963-1964	12	5	7	106.5	105.3	Lost championship series to Boston.
1966-1967	15	9	6	118.3	117.1	Lost championship series to Philadelphia.
1967-1968	10	4	6	110.1	115.0	Lost Division final to Los Angeles.
1968-1969	6	2	4	94.7	105.7	Lost Division semifinal to Los Angeles.
1970-1971	5	1	4	96.0	113.0	Lost Conference semifinal to Milwaukee.
TOTAL:	48	21	27			
AVERAGE:	10	4	6	105.1	111.2	

COACHING HISTORY: 1962-1963 Bob Feerick 31-49-.388; 1963-1966 Alex Hannum 100-140-.417; 1966-1968 Bill Sharman 87-76-.534; 1968-1970 George Lee 63-71-.470; 1969-1971 Al Attles 49-63-.438

SAN JOSE EARTHQUAKES
(became Golden Bay Earthquakes)

Home City: San Jose, California
Home Field: Spartan Stadium Capacity: 18,155 [1976]
Origin of Name: The name was picked because of the areas proximity to the San Andreas Fault and chosen by club General Manager Dick Berg.

Regular Season Record

Season	League	GP	W	L	T	GF	GA	BP	Pts	Pct
1974	NASL	20	9	8	3	43	38	40	103	.572
1975	NASL	22	8	14	-	37	48	35	83	.419
1976	NASL	24	14	10	-	47	30	39	123	.569
1977	NASL	26	14	12	-	37	44	35	119	.509
1978	NASL	30	8	22	-	36	81	35	83	.307
1979	NASL	30	8	22	-	41	74	38	86	.319
1980	NASL	32	9	23	-	45	68	41	95	.330
1981	NASL	32	11	21	-	44	78	42	108	.225
1982	NASL	32	13	19	-	47	62	38	114	.238
TOTAL:	9 years	248	94	151	3	377	523	343	914	
AVERAGE:		28	11	17	0	42	58	38	102	.349

Playoff Record

Season	GP	W	L	GF	GA	Result
1974	1	0	1	0	3	Lost 1st round game to Dallas.
1976	2	1	1	3	3	Lost 2nd round game to Minnesota.
1977	1	0	1	1	2	Lost 1st round game to Los Angeles.
TOTAL:	4	1	3	4	8	
AVERAGE:	1	0	1	1	2	

COACHING HISTORY: 1974-1978 Gabbo Gavric 43-41; 1974-1975 Ivan Toplak 7-14-3; 1978-1979 Terry Fisher 3-19; 1979 Peter Stubbe 8-14; 1980 Bill Foulkes 9-23; 1981 Jim Gabriel 11-21; 1982 Peter Short 13-19

SAN JOSE SHARKS

Home City: Daly City, California (1991-1993)
San Jose, California (1993-present)
Home Arena: Cow Palace (1991-1993) Capacity: 10,800 [1992]
San Jose Arena (1993-present) Capacity: 17,190 [1995]
Origin of Name: The name was chosen in a Name the Team Contest.

Regular Season Record

Season	League	GP	W	L	T	GF	GA	Pts	Pct
1991-1992	NHL	80	17	58	5	219	359	39	.244
1992-1993	NHL	84	11	71	2	218	414	24	.143
1993-1994	NHL	84	33	35	16	252	265	82	.488
1994-1995	NHL	48	19	25	4	129	161	42	.438
1995-1996	NHL	82	20	55	7	252	357	47	.287
TOTAL:	5 years	378	100	244	34	1070	1556	234	
AVERAGE:		76	20	49	7	214	311	47	.310

Playoff Record

Season	GP	W	L	GF	GA	Result
1993-1994	14	7	7	42	53	Lost quarterfinal series to Toronto.
1994-1995	11	4	7	32	59	Lost quarterfinal series to Detroit.
TOTAL:	25	11	14	74	112	
AVERAGE:	13	6	7	37	56	

COACHING HISTORY: 1991-1993 George Kingston 28-129-7-.192; 1993-1996 Kevin Constantine 55-78-24-.427; 1995-present Jim Wiley

SASKATCHEWAN ROUGHRIDERS

Home City: Regina, Saskatchewan
Home Stadium: Taylor Field Capacity: 27,637 [1995]
Origin of Name: The name was adopted because a contingent of North West Mounted Police officers who played 2 rugby matches in Winnipeg in 1890 were referred to as "Roughriders" due to their occupation of breaking horses used by the force. The name survived the various primitive early teams and leagues.

Regular Season Record

Season	League	GP	W	L	T	PF	PA	Pts	Pct
1950	CRU	14	7	7	0	207	177	14	.500
1951	CRU	14	8	6	0	277	219	16	.571
1952	CRU	16	3	13	0	216	363	6	.188
1953	CRU	16	8	7	1	243	239	17	.531
1954	CRU	16	10	4	2	239	204	22	.688
1955	CRU	16	10	6	0	270	245	20	.625
1956	CFC	16	10	6	0	353	272	20	.625
1957	CFC	16	3	12	1	276	438	7	.219
1958	CFL	16	7	7	2	320	324	16	.500
1959	CFL	16	1	15	0	212	567	2	.063
1960	CFL	16	2	12	2	205	422	6	.188
1961	CFL	16	5	10	1	211	314	11	.344

1962	CFL	16	8	7	1	268	336	17	.531
1963	CFL	16	7	7	2	223	266	16	.500
1964	CFL	16	9	7	0	330	282	18	.563
1965	CFL	16	8	7	1	276	277	17	.531
1966	CFL	16	9	6	1	351	318	19	.594
1967	CFL	16	12	4	0	346	282	24	.750
1968	CFL	16	12	3	1	345	223	25	.781
1969	CFL	16	13	3	0	392	261	26	.813
1970	CFL	16	14	2	0	369	206	28	.875
1971	CFL	16	9	6	1	347	316	19	.594
1972	CFL	16	8	8	0	330	283	16	.500
1973	CFL	16	10	6	0	360	287	20	.625
1974	CFL	16	9	7	0	305	289	18	.563
1975	CFL	16	10	5	1	373	390	21	.656
1976	CFL	16	11	5	0	427	238	22	.688
1977	CFL	16	8	8	0	330	389	16	.500
1978	CFL	16	4	11	1	330	459	9	.281
1979	CFL	16	2	14	0	194	437	4	.125
1980	CFL	16	2	14	0	284	469	4	.125
1981	CFL	16	9	7	0	431	371	18	.563
1982	CFL	16	6	9	1	427	436	13	.406
1983	CFL	16	5	11	0	360	536	10	.313
1984	CFL	16	6	9	1	348	479	13	.406
1985	CFL	16	5	11	0	320	462	10	.313
1986	CFL	18	6	11	1	382	517	13	.361
1987	CFL	18	5	12	1	364	529	11	.306
1988	CFL	18	11	7	0	525	452	22	.611
1989	CFL	18	9	9	0	547	567	18	.500
1990	CFL	18	9	9	0	557	592	18	.500
1991	CFL	18	6	12	0	606	710	12	.333
1992	CFL	18	9	9	0	505	545	18	.500
1993	CFL	18	11	7	0	511	495	22	.611
1994	CFL	18	12	6	0	508	453	24	.667
1995	CFL	18	6	12	0	422	451	12	.333
TOTAL:	46 years	752	354	376	22	16022	17387	730	
AVERAGE:		16	8	8	0	348	378	16	.486

Playoff Record

Season	GP	W	L	T	PF	PA	Result
1950	1	0	1	0	1	24	Lost Division final to Edmonton.
1951	4	2	2	0	56	59	Lost Grey Cup game to Ottawa.
1953	2	1	1	0	23	60	Lost Division final to Winnipeg.
1954	2	0	1	1	25	27	Lost Division semifinal to Winnipeg.
1955	2	1	1	0	16	24	Lost Division semifinal to Winnipeg.
1956	5	2	3	0	92	119	Lost Division final to Edmonton.
1958	2	0	2	0	12	58	Lost Division semifinal to Edmonton.
1962	2	0	2	0	7	43	Lost Division semifinal to Calgary.
1963	5	2	3	0	69	110	Lost Division final to B.C.
1964	2	1	1	0	40	76	Lost Division semifinal to Calgary.
1965	1	0	1	0	9	15	Lost Division semifinal to Winnipeg.
1966	3	3	0	0	64	40	**Won Grey Cup**.
1967	5	3	2	0	61	66	Lost Grey Cup game to Hamilton.
1968	2	0	2	0	12	57	Lost Division final to Calgary.

1969	3	2	1	0	64	53	Lost Grey Cup game to Ottawa.
1970	3	1	2	0	36	46	Lost Division final to Calgary.
1971	3	1	2	0	76	76	Lost Division final to Calgary.
1972	3	2	1	0	45	43	Lost Grey Cup game to Hamilton.
1973	2	1	1	0	56	38	Lost Division final to Edmonton.
1974	2	1	1	0	51	45	Lost Division final to Edmonton.
1975	2	1	1	0	60	54	Lost Division final to Edmonton.
1976	2	1	1	0	43	36	Lost Grey Cup game to Ottawa.
1988	1	0	1	0	18	42	Lost Division semifinal to B.C.
1989	3	3	0	0	108	87	**Won Grey Cup**.
1990	1	0	1	0	27	43	Lost Division semifinal to Edmonton.
1992	1	0	1	0	20	22	Lost Division semifinal to Edmonton.
1993	1	0	1	0	13	51	Lost Division semifinal to Edmonton.
1994	1	0	1	0	3	36	Lost Division semifinal to Calgary.
TOTAL:	66	28	37	1	1107	1450	
AVERAGE:	2	1	1	0	40	52	

COACHING HISTORY: 1950 Fred Grant 7-7-0-.500; 1951 H. Smith 8-6-0-.571; 1952 Glenn Dobbs 3-13-0-.188; 1953-1957 Frank Filchock 41-35-4-.538; 1958-1959 George Terlep 7-16-2-.320; 1959 Frank Tripucka 1-6-0-.143; 1960 Ken Carpenter 2-12-2-.188; 1961-1962 Steve Owen 13-17-2-.438; 1963-1964 Bob Shaw 16-14-2-.531; 1965-1970 Eagle Keys 68-25-3-.724; 1971-1972 Dave Skrien 17-14-1-.547; 1973-1976 John Payne 40-23-1-.633; 1977-1978 Jim Eddy 8-14-0-.364; 1978 Walt Posadowski 4-5-1-.450; 1979-1980 Ron Lancaster 4-28-0-.125; 1981-1983 Joe Faragalli 16-21-1-.434; 1983-1984 Rueben Berry 10-15-1-.404; 1985-1986 Jack Gotta 11-22-1-.338; 1987-1991 John Gregory 35-43-1-.449; 1991-1993 Don Matthews 25-22-0-.532; 1994-1995 Ray Jauch 18-18-0-.500; 1996-present Jim Daley

SASKATOON CRESCENTS
(were Saskatoon Sheiks)

Home City: Saskatoon, Saskatchewan
Home Arena: Saskatoon Arena
Origin of Name:

Regular Season Record

Season	League	GP	W	L	T	GF	GA	Pts	Pct
1923-1924	WCHA	30	15	12	3	91	73	33	.550
1924-1925	WCHL	28	16	11	1	102	75	33	.589
1925-1926	WHL	30	18	11	1	93	64	37	.617
TOTAL:	3 years	88	49	34	5	286	212	103	
AVERAGE:		29	16	11	2	95	71	34	.585

Playoff Record

Season	GP	W	L	T	GF	GA	Result
1924-1925	2	0	1	1	4	6	Lost WCHL playoff to Victoria.
1925-1926	2	0	1	1	3	4	Lost WHL playoff to Victoria.
TOTAL:	4	0	2	2	7	10	
AVERAGE:	2	0	1	1	4	5	

COACHING HISTORY: 1923-1926 Edouard Lalonde 49-34-5-.585

SASKATOON SHEIKS

(became Saskatoon Crescents)
(became Moose Jaw Orphans mid way through the 1921-1922 season)

Home City: Saskatoon, Saskatchewan
Home Arena: Saskatoon Arena
Origin of Name:

Regular Season Record

Season	League	GP	W	L	T	GF	GA	Pts	Pct
1921-1922	WCHA	14	4	10	0	43	77	8	.286
1922-1923	WCHA	30	8	20	2	91	125	18	.300
TOTAL:	2 years	44	12	30	2	134	202	26	
AVERAGE:		22	6	15	1	67	101	13	.295

COACHING HISTORY: 1921-1922 Bob Pinder 4-10-0-.286; 1922-1923 Edouard Lalonde 8-20-2-.300

SEATTLE MARINERS

Home City: Seattle, Washington
Home Field: The Kingdome Capacity: 59,166 [1995]
Origin of Name: The name was chosen in a Name the Team Contest and was adopted to honor the nautical tradition of the area.

Regular Season Record

Season	League	GP	W	L	Pct	GB	R	OR
1977	AL	162	64	98	.395	38	624	855
1978	AL	160	56	104	.350	35	614	834
1979	AL	162	67	95	.414	21	711	820
1980	AL	162	59	103	.364	38	610	793
1981	AL	109	44	65	.404	NA	426	521
1982	AL	162	76	86	.469	17	651	712
1983	AL	162	60	102	.370	39	558	740
1984	AL	162	74	88	.457	10	682	774
1985	AL	162	74	88	.457	17	719	818
1986	AL	162	67	95	.414	25	718	835
1987	AL	162	78	84	.481	7	760	801
1988	AL	161	68	93	.422	35.5	664	744
1989	AL	162	73	89	.451	26	694	728
1990	AL	162	77	85	.475	26	640	680
1991	AL	162	83	79	.512	12	702	674
1992	AL	162	64	98	.395	32	679	799
1993	AL	162	82	80	.506	12	734	731
1994	AL	112	49	63	.438	2	569	616
1995	AL	144	78	66	.542	-	796	708
TOTAL:	19 years	2954	1293	1661		392.5	12551	14183
AVERAGE:		155	68	87	.438	20.5	661	746

Playoff Record

Season	GP	W	L	R	OR	Result
1995	11	5	6	47	56	Lost ALCS to Cleveland.

COACHING HISTORY: 1977-1980 Darrell Johnson 226-362-.384; 1980-1981 Maury Wills 26-56-.317; 1981-1983 Rene Lachmann 140-180-.438; 1983-1984 Del Crandall 93-131-.415; 1984-1986 Chuck Cottier 98-119-.452; 1986 Marty Martinez 0-1-.000; 1986-1988 Dick Williams 159-192-.453; 1988 Jimmy Snyder 45-60-.429; 1989-1991 Jim Lefebvre 233-253-.479; 1992 Bill Plummer 64-98-.395; 1993-present Lou Piniella

SEATTLE METROPOLITANS

Home City: Seattle, Washington
Home Arena: Seattle Arena
Origin of Name:

Regular Season Record

Season	League	GP	W	L	T	GF	GA	Pts	Pct
1915-1916	PCHA	18	9	9	0	68	67	18	.500
1916-1917	PCHA	24	16	8	0	125	80	32	.667
1917-1918	PCHA	18	11	7	0	67	65	22	.611
1918-1919	PCHA	20	11	9	0	66	46	22	.550
1919-1920	PCHA	22	12	10	0	59	55	24	.545
1920-1921	PCHA	24	12	11	1	77	68	25	.521
1921-1922	PCHA	24	12	11	1	65	64	25	.521
1922-1923	PCHA	30	15	15	0	100	106	30	.500
1923-1924	PCHA	30	14	16	0	84	99	28	.467
TOTAL:	9 years	210	112	96	2	711	650	226	
AVERAGE:		23	12	11	0	79	72	24	.538

Playoff Record

Season	GP	W	L	T	GF	GA	Result
1916-1917	4	3	1	0	23	11	**Won Stanley Cup**.
1917-1918	2	0	1	1	2	3	Lost PCHA playoff to Vancouver.
1918-1919	7	3	3	1	26	15	Stanley Cup final canceled.
1919-1920	7	3	4	0	18	18	Lost Stanley Cup final to Ottawa.
1920-1921	2	0	2	0	2	13	Lost PCHA playoff to Vancouver.
1921-1922	2	0	2	0	0	2	Lost PCHA playoff to Vancouver.
1923-1924	2	0	1	1	3	4	Lost PCHA playoff to Vancouver.
TOTAL:	26	9	14	3	74	66	
AVERAGE:	4	1	2	1	11	9	

COACHING HISTORY: 1915-1916 Not Available; 1916-1924 Pete Muldoon 103-87-2-.542

SEATTLE PILOTS
(became Milwaukee Brewers)

Home City: Seattle, Washington
Home Field: Sick's Stadium — Capacity: 25,420 [1969]
Origin of Name: The name was chosen in a Name the Team Contest.

Regular Season Record

Season	League	GP	W	L	Pct	GB	R	OR
1969	AL	162	64	98	.395	33	639	799

COACHING HISTORY: Joseph Schultz 64-98-.395

SEATTLE SEAHAWKS

Home City: Seattle, Washington
Home Stadium: The Kingdome (1976-present) Capacity: 66,400 [1995]
Husky Stadium (1994) Capacity: 72,500 [1995]
Origin of Name: The name was chosen in a Name the Team Contest.

Regular Season Record

Season	League	GP	W	L	T	PF	PA	Pct
1976	NFL	14	2	12	0	229	429	.143
1977	NFL	14	5	9	0	282	373	.357
1978	NFL	16	9	7	0	345	358	.563
1979	NFL	16	9	7	0	378	372	.563
1980	NFL	16	4	12	0	291	408	.250
1981	NFL	16	6	10	0	322	388	.375
1982	NFL	9	4	5	0	127	147	.444
1983	NFL	16	9	7	0	403	397	.562
1984	NFL	16	12	4	0	418	282	.750
1985	NFL	16	8	8	0	349	303	.500
1986	NFL	16	10	6	0	366	293	.625
1987	NFL	15	9	6	0	371	314	.600
1988	NFL	16	9	7	0	339	329	.563
1989	NFL	16	7	9	0	241	327	.438
1990	NFL	16	9	7	0	306	286	.563
1991	NFL	16	7	9	0	276	261	.438
1992	NFL	16	2	14	0	140	312	.125
1993	NFL	16	6	10	0	280	314	.375
1994	NFL	16	6	10	0	287	323	.375
1995	NFL	16	8	8	0	363	366	.500
TOTAL:	20 years	308	141	167	0	6113	6582	
AVERAGE:		15	7	8	0	306	329	.458

Playoff Record

Season	GP	W	L	PF	PA	Result
1983	3	2	1	72	57	Lost AFC championship to Raiders.
1984	2	1	1	23	38	Lost Divisional playoff to Miami.
1987	1	0	1	20	23	Lost 1st round playoff to Houston.
1988	1	0	1	13	23	Lost Divisional playoff to Cincinnati.
TOTAL:	7	3	4	128	141	
AVERAGE:	2	1	1	32	35	

COACHING HISTORY: 1976-1982 Jack Patera 35-59-0-.372; 1982 Mike McCormack 4-3-0-.571; 1983-1991 Chuck Knox 35-108-0-.245; 1992-1994 Tom Flores 14-34-0-.292; 1995-present Dennis Erickson

SEATTLE SOUNDERS

Home City: Seattle, Washington
Home Stadium: Memorial Stadium (1974-1975) Capacity: 18,000 [1975]
Seattle Kingdome (1976-1983) Capacity: 64,752 [1983]
Origin of Name: The name was chosen in a Name the Team Contest and suggested by the fact Seattle is on Puget Sound.

Regular Season Record

Season	League	GP	W	L	T	GF	GA	BP	Pts	Pct
1974	NASL	20	10	7	3	37	17	32	101	.561
1975	NASL	22	15	7	-	42	28	39	129	.652
1976	NASL	24	14	10	-	40	31	39	123	.569
1977	NASL	26	14	12	-	43	34	39	123	.526
1978	NASL	30	15	15	-	50	45	48	138	.511
1979	NASL	30	13	17	-	58	52	47	125	.463
1980	NASL	32	25	7	-	74	31	57	207	.719
1981	NASL	32	15	17	-	60	62	51	137	.285
1982	NASL	32	18	14	-	64	74	57	163	.340
1983	NASL	30	12	18	-	62	61	51	119	.264
TOTAL:	10 years	278	151	124	3	530	435	460	1365	
AVERAGE:		28	15	13	0	53	44	46	137	.445

Playoff Record

Season	GP	W	L	GF	GA	Result
1975	1	0	1	1	2	Lost 1st round series to Portland.
1976	2	1	1	1	3	Lost 2nd round series to Minnesota.
1977	6	5	1	10	4	Lost championship series to New York.
1978	1	0	1	2	5	Lost 1st round series to New York.
1980	5	3	2	10	7	Lost 2nd round series to Los Angeles.
1981	3	1	2	6	6	Lost 1st round series to Chicago.
1982	7	4	3	14	12	Lost preliminary series to New York.
TOTAL:	25	14	11	44	39	
AVERAGE:	4	2	2	6	6	

COACHING HISTORY: 1974-1976 John Best 39-24-3-.594; 1977-1979 Jim Gabriel 42-44-.499; 1980-1982 Alan Hinton 58-38; 1983 Laurie Calloway 12-18

SEATTLE SUPERSONICS

Home City: Seattle, Washington
Home Court: Seattle Center Coliseum (1967-1978) Capacity: 14,098 [1978]
Kingdome (1978-1985) Capacity: 40,192 [1985]
The Coliseum (1985-present) Capacity: 14,250 [1993]
Tacoma Dome (1994-1995) Capacity: 19,000 [1994]
Key Arena at Seattle Center (1995-present) Capacity: 17,100 [1995]
Origin of Name: The name was chosen in a Name the Team Contest.

Regular Season Record

Season	League	GP	W	L	PPGF	PPGA	Pct	GB
1967-1968	NBA	82	23	59	118.7	125.1	.280	33

1968-1969	NBA	82	30	52	112.1	116.6	.366	25
1969-1970	NBA	82	36	46	116.9	119.5	.439	12
1970-1971	NBA	82	38	44	115.0	117.0	.463	10
1971-1972	NBA	82	47	35	109.2	108.8	.573	22
1972-1973	NBA	82	26	56	103.7	109.6	.317	34
1973-1974	NBA	82	36	46	107.0	109.5	.439	11
1974-1975	NBA	82	43	39	103.1	103.1	.524	5
1975-1976	NBA	82	43	39	106.4	106.7	.524	16
1976-1977	NBA	82	40	42	104.0	105.5	.488	13
1977-1978	NBA	82	47	35	104.5	102.9	.573	11
1978-1979	NBA	82	52	30	106.6	103.9	.634	-
1979-1980	NBA	82	56	26	108.5	103.8	.683	4
1980-1981	NBA	82	34	48	104.0	105.7	.415	23
1981-1982	NBA	82	52	30	107.3	103.1	.634	5
1982-1983	NBA	82	48	34	110.0	106.8	.585	10
1983-1984	NBA	82	42	40	108.1	108.3	.512	12
1984-1985	NBA	82	31	51	102.1	107.6	.378	31
1985-1986	NBA	82	31	51	104.4	104.5	.378	31
1986-1987	NBA	82	39	43	113.7	113.3	.476	26
1987-1988	NBA	82	44	38	111.4	109.3	.537	18
1988-1989	NBA	82	47	35	112.1	109.2	.573	10
1989-1990	NBA	82	41	41	106.9	105.9	.500	22
1990-1991	NBA	82	41	41	106.6	105.4	.500	22
1991-1992	NBA	82	47	35	106.5	104.7	.573	10
1992-1993	NBA	82	55	27	108.3	101.3	.671	7
1993-1994	NBA	82	63	19	105.9	96.9	.768	-
1994-1995	NBA	82	57	25	110.4	102.2	.695	2
1995-1996	NBA	82	64	18	104.5	96.7	.780	-
TOTAL:	29 years	2378	1253	1125				425
AVERAGE:		82	43	39	108.2	107.3	.527	15

Playoff Record

Season	GP	W	L	PPGF	PPGA	Result
1974-1975	9	4	5	99.4	104.7	Lost Conference semifinal to Golden Bay.
1975-1976	6	2	4	107.3	113.2	Lost Conference semifinal to Phoenix.
1977-1978	22	13	9	102.9	102.5	Lost championship series to Washington.
1978-1979	17	12	5	104.6	102.1	**Won NBA championship**.
1979-1980	15	7	8	102.2	103.0	Lost Conference final to Los Angeles.
1981-1982	8	3	5	99.5	97.3	Lost Conference semifinal to San Antonio.
1982-1983	2	0	2	96.5	106.5	Lost 1st round series to Portland.
1983-1984	5	2	3	97.0	97.2	Lost 1st round series to Dallas.
1986-1987	14	7	7	110.1	112.1	Lost Conference final to Lakers.
1987-1988	5	2	3	114.2	114.8	Lost 1st round series to Denver.
1988-1989	8	3	5	102.0	107.1	Lost Conference semifinal to Lakers.
1990-1991	5	2	3	103.6	106.4	Lost 1st round series to Portland.
1991-1992	9	4	5	105.6	108.6	Lost Conference semifinal to Utah.
1992-1993	18	10	8	105.8	104.3	Lost Conference final to Phoenix.
1993-1994	5	2	3	95.0	94.2	Lost 1st round series to Denver.
1994-1995	4	1	3	97.3	93.5	Lost 1st round series to Lakers.
1995-1996	21	13	8	94.0	92.7	Lost championship series to Chicago.
TOTAL:	173	87	86			
AVERAGE:	10	5	5	102.1	103.5	

COACHING HISTORY: 1967-1969 Al Bianchi 53-111-.323; 1969-1972 Lenny Wilkins 121-125-.492; 1972-1973 Tom Nissalke 13-32-.289; 1972-1973 Bucky Buckwalter 13-24-.351; 1973-1977 Bill Russell 162-166-.494; 1977-1978 Bob Hopkins 5-17-.227; 1977-1985 Lenny Wilkins 357-277-.563; 1985-1990 Bernie Bickerstaff 202-208-.493; 1990-1992 K.C. Jones 59-59-.500; 1991-1992 Bob Kloppenburg 2-2-.500; 1991-present George Karl

SHEBOYGAN REDSKINS

Home City: Sheboygan, Wisconsin
Home Court:
Origin of Name:

Regular Season Record

Season	League	GP	W	L	PPGF	PPGA	Pct	GB
1938-1939	NBL	28	11	17	35.6	37.5	.393	6
1939-1940	NBL	28	15	13	36.7	38.3	.536	-
1940-1941	NBL	24	13	11	36.1	34.7	.542	5
1941-1942	NBL	24	10	14	39.3	42.4	.417	10
1942-1943	NBL	23	12	11	43.2	43.7	.522	5
1943-1944	NBL	22	14	8	41.5	40.9	.636	4
1944-1945	NBL	30	19	11	49.8	46.0	.633	-
1945-1946	NBL	34	21	13	51.0	48.2	.618	-
1946-1947	NBL	44	26	18	54.5	53.0	.591	2
1947-1948	NBL	60	23	37	56.8	60.9	.383	20
1948-1949	NBL	64	35	29	62.0	61.7	.547	2
1949-1950	NBA	62	22	40	82.4	87.8	.355	16
TOTAL:	12 years	443	221	222				70
AVERAGE:		37	18	19	49.5	49.6	.499	6

Playoff Record

Season	GP	W	L	PPGF	PPGA	Result
1939-1940	3	1	2	32.0	38.0	Lost 1st round series to Oshkosh.
1940-1941	6	2	4	36.7	42.2	Lost championship series to Oshkosh.
1942-1943	5	4	1	47.2	42.8	**Won NBL championship**.
1943-1944	6	2	4	36.8	38.5	Lost championship series to Ft. Wayne.
1944-1945	8	4	4	50.9	48.5	Lost championship series to Ft. Wayne.
1945-1946	8	3	5	50.5	56.4	Lost championship series to Rochester.
1946-1947	5	2	3	46.0	47.6	Lost 1st round series to Oshkosh.
1948-1949	2	0	2	55.5	67.0	Lost 1st round series to Tri-Cities.
1949-1950	3	1	2	88.0	87.3	Lost 1st round series to Indianapolis.
TOTAL:	46	19	27			
AVERAGE:	5	2	3	49.3	52.0	

COACHING HISTORY: 1938-1939 Doc Schutte 11-17-.393; 1939-1942 Frank Zummach 38-38-.500; 1942-1944 Carl Roth 26-19-.578; 1944-1946 Dutch Dehnert 40-24-.625; 1946-1948 Doxie Moore 49-55-.471; 1948-1950 Kenny Suesens 57-69-.452

SHREVEPORT PIRATES

Home City: Shreveport, Louisiana
Home Stadium: Independence Stadium — Capacity: 40,000 [1995]
Origin of Name: In the words of team President, Lonie Glieberman, the name was chosen because he considered them to be a "pirate team in a pirate league".

Regular Season Record

Season	League	GP	W	L	T	PF	PA	Pts	Pct
1994	CFL	18	3	15	0	330	662	6	.167
1995	CFL	18	5	13	0	465	514	10	.278
TOTAL:	2 Years	36	8	28	0	795	1176	16	
AVERAGE:		18	4	14	0	398	588	8	.222

COACHING HISTORY: 1994-1995 Forrest Gregg 8-28-0-.222

SHREVEPORT STEAMERS

(were Houston Texans)

Home City: Shreveport, Louisiana
Home Stadium: State Fair Stadium — Capacity: 48,000
Origin of Name: Name chosen in a Name the Team Contest in which the club reportedly received over 40,000 entries.

Regular Season Record

Season	League	GP	W	L	T	PF	PA	Pct
1974	WFL	8	4	4	0	127	146	.500
1975	WFL	12	5	7	0	276	313	.417
TOTAL:	2 years	20	9	11	0	403	459	
AVERAGE:		10	5	5	0	202	230	.450

COACHING HISTORY: 1974 Jim Garret 4-4-0-.500; 1975 Marshall Taylor 5-7-0-.417

SOUTHERN CALIFORNIA SUN

Home City: Anaheim, California
Home Stadium: Anaheim Stadium — Capacity: 69,008
Origin of Name: The name was chosen in a Name the Team Contest.

Regular Season Record

Season	League	GP	W	L	T	PF	PA	Pct
1974	WFL	20	13	7	0	486	341	.650
1975	WFL	12	7	5	0	354	341	.583
TOTAL:	2 years	32	20	12	0	840	682	
AVERAGE:		16	10	6	0	420	341	.625

Playoff Record

Season	GP	W	L	PF	PA	Result
1974	1	0	1	14	34	Lost 1st round series to Hawaiins.

COACHING HISTORY: 1974-1975 Tom Fears 20-12-0-.625

SOVIET "B" TEAM

Home City: Moscow, USSR
Home Arena: The team only played road games.
Origin of Name:

			Regular Season Record						
Season	**League**	**GP**	**W**	**L**	**T**	**GF**	**GA**	**Pts**	**Pct**
1977-1978	WHA	8	3	4	1	27	36	7	.438

COACHING HISTORY: Vladimir Yurzinov 3-4-1-.438

SOVIET NATIONAL TEAM

Home City: Moscow, USSR
Home Arena: The team only played road games.
Origin of Name: This was the Soviet National team which would compete in the Olympics in 1980.

			Regular Season Record						
Season	**League**	**GP**	**W**	**L**	**T**	**GF**	**GA**	**Pts**	**Pct**
1978-1979	WHA	6	4	1	1	26	20	9	.750

COACHING HISTORY: Boris Mayorov 4-1-1-.750

SPOKANE CANARIES
(were Victoria Aristocrats)

Home City: Spokane, Washington
Home Arena: Spokane Arena
Origin of Name:

			Regular Season Record						
Season	**League**	**GP**	**W**	**L**	**T**	**GF**	**GA**	**Pts**	**Pct**
1916-1917	PCHA	23	8	15	0	89	143	16	.348

COACHING HISTORY: Lester Patrick 8-15-0-.348

STATEN ISLAND STAPLETONS

Home City: New York, New York
Home Field: Thompson Athletic Stadium Capacity: 12,000
Origin of Name: Stapleton is one of the communities making up the New York City burrough of Staten Island.

			Regular Season Record					
Season	**League**	**GP**	**W**	**L**	**T**	**PF**	**PA**	**Pct**
1929	NFL	10	3	4	3	89	65	.450
1930	NFL	12	5	5	2	95	112	.500
1931	NFL	11	4	6	1	79	118	.409
1932	NFL	12	2	7	3	77	173	.292
TOTAL:	4 years	45	14	22	9	340	468	
AVERAGE:		11	4	5	2	85	117	.411

COACHING HISTORY: 1929-1930 Doug Wycoff 8-9-5-.477; 1931 Hinky Haines 4-6-1-.409; 1932 Hal Hanson 2-7-3-.292

SYRACUSE ALL-AMERICANS

Home City: Syracuse, New York
Home Court:
Origin of Name:

Regular Season Record

Season	League	GP	W	L	Pct	GB
1929-1930	ABL	24	4	20	.167	13

COACHING HISTORY:

SYRACUSE NATIONALS
(became Philadelphia 76ers)

Home City: Syracuse, New York
Home Court: State Fair Coliseum (1949-1951) Capacity: 7,500
Onodaga County War Memorial (1951-1963) Capacity: 8,000
Origin of Name: The club used the league's nickname as its own.

Regular Season Record

Season	League	GP	W	L	PPGF	PPGA	Pct	GB
1946-1947	NBL	44	21	23	55.8	55.5	.477	10
1947-1948	NBL	60	24	36	59.3	62.5	.400	20
1948-1949	NBL	63	40	23	66.5	63.8	.635	8.5
1949-1950	NBA	64	51	13	84.8	76.7	.797	-
1950-1951	NBA	66	32	34	86.1	85.5	.485	8
1951-1952	NBA	66	40	26	86.7	82.2	.606	-
1952-1953	NBA	71	47	24	85.6	81.3	.662	12
1953-1954	NBA	72	42	30	83.5	78.6	.583	2
1954-1955	NBA	72	43	29	91.1	89.7	.597	-
1955-1956	NBA	72	35	37	96.9	96.9	.486	10
1956-1957	NBA	72	38	34	99.7	101.1	.528	6
1957-1958	NBA	72	41	31	107.2	105.1	.569	8
1958-1959	NBA	72	35	37	113.1	109.1	.486	17
1959-1960	NBA	75	45	30	118.9	116.4	.600	14
1960-1961	NBA	79	38	41	121.3	119.2	.481	19
1961-1962	NBA	80	41	39	120.7	118.4	.513	19
1962-1963	NBA	80	48	32	121.6	117.8	.600	10
TOTAL:	17 years	1180	661	519				163.5
AVERAGE:		69	39	30	94.0	91.8	.560	10

Playoff Record

Season	GP	W	L	PPGF	PPGA	Result
1946-1947	4	1	3	58.3	60.8	Lost 1st round series to Rochester.
1947-1948	3	0	3	59.3	74.7	Lost 1st round series to Anderson.
1948-1949	6	3	3	74.8	75.3	Lost championship series to Anderson.
1949-1950	11	6	5	81.0	79.9	Lost championship series to Minneapolis.

1950-1951	7	4	3	88.7	87.6	Lost Division final to New York.
1951-1952	7	3	4	93.3	90.6	Lost Division final to New York.
1952-1953	2	0	2	93.0	99.0	Lost Division semifinal to Boston.
1953-1954	13	9	4	81.5	80.0	Lost championship series to Minneapolis.
1954-1955	11	7	4	97.2	94.0	**Won NBA championship**.
1955-1956	8	4	4	101.6	108.0	Lost Division final to Philadelphia.
1956-1957	5	2	3	93.8	97.4	Lost Division final to Boston.
1957-1958	3	1	2	89.0	92.7	Lost Division semifinal to Philadelphia.
1958-1959	9	5	4	120.6	123.0	Lost Division final to Boston.
1959-1960	3	1	2	109.7	122.0	Lost Division semifinal to Philadelphia.
1960-1961	8	4	4	108.4	117.9	Lost Division final to Boston.
1961-1962	5	2	3	99.2	105.4	Lost Division semifinal to Philadelphia.
1962-1963	5	2	3	120.8	125.2	Lost Division semifinal to Cincinnati.
TOTAL:	110	54	56			
AVERAGE:	6	3	3	92.4	96.1	

COACHING HISTORY: 1946-1948 Ben Borgmann 45-59-.433; 1948-1957 Al Cervi 334-224-.599; 1956-1960 Paul Seymour 155-124-.556; 1960-1963 Alex Hannum 127-112-.531

SYRACUSE STARS

Home City: Syracuse, New York
Home Field: Newell Park
Lakeside Park (Sundays only)
Origin of Name:

Regular Season Record

Season	**League**	**GP**	**W**	**L**	**Pct**	**GB**	**R**	**OR**
1879	NL	70	22	48	.314	30	276	462

COACHING HISTORY: Mike Dorgan 22-48-.314

SYRACUSE STARS

Home City: Syracuse, New York
Home Field: Star Park
Origin of Name:

Regular Season Record

Season	**League**	**GP**	**W**	**L**	**Pct**	**GB**	**R**	**OR**
1890	AA	127	55	72	.433	30.5	698	831

COACHING HISTORY: George Frazer 55-72-.433

TAMPA BAY BANDITS

Home City: Tampa, Florida
Home Stadium: Tampa Stadium — Capacity: 72,126 [1984]
Origin of Name: Named by team owner John Bassett.

Regular Season Record

Season	League	GP	W	L	T	PF	PA	Pct
1983	USFL	18	11	7	0	363	378	.611
1984	USFL	18	14	4	0	498	347	.778
1985	USFL	18	10	8	0	405	422	.556
TOTAL:	3 years	54	35	19	0	1266	1147	
AVERAGE:		18	12	6	0	422	382	.648

Playoff Record

Season	GP	W	L	PF	PA	Result
1984	1	0	1	17	36	Lost 1st round series to Birmingham.
1985	1	0	1	27	48	Lost 1st round series to Oakland.
TOTAL:	2	0	2	44	84	
AVERAGE:	1	0	1	22	42	

COACHING HISTORY: 1983-1985 Steve Spurrier 35-19-0-.648

TAMPA BAY BUCCANEERS

Home City: Tampa, Florida
Home Stadium: Tampa Stadium — Capacity: 74,296 [1995]
Origin of Name: The name was picked in a Name the Team Contest.

Regular Season Record

Season	League	GP	W	L	T	PF	PA	Pct
1976	NFL	14	0	14	0	125	412	.000
1977	NFL	14	2	12	0	103	223	.143
1978	NFL	16	5	11	0	241	259	.313
1979	NFL	16	10	6	0	273	237	.625
1980	NFL	16	5	10	1	271	341	.344
1981	NFL	16	9	7	0	315	268	.563
1982	NFL	9	5	4	0	158	178	.556
1983	NFL	16	2	14	0	241	380	.125
1984	NFL	16	6	10	0	335	380	.375
1985	NFL	16	2	14	0	294	448	.125
1986	NFL	16	2	14	0	239	473	.125
1987	NFL	15	4	11	0	286	360	.267
1988	NFL	16	5	11	0	261	350	.313
1989	NFL	16	5	11	0	320	393	.313
1990	NFL	16	6	10	0	264	367	.375
1991	NFL	16	3	13	0	199	365	.188
1992	NFL	16	5	11	0	267	365	.313
1993	NFL	16	5	11	0	237	376	.313
1994	NFL	16	6	10	0	251	351	.375
1995	NFL	16	7	9	0	238	335	.438
TOTAL:	20 years	308	94	213	1	4918	6861	
AVERAGE:		15	5	10	0	246	343	.307

Playoff Record

Season	GP	W	L	PF	PA	Result
1979	2	1	1	24	26	Lost NFC championship to Los Angeles.
1981	1	0	1	0	38	Lost Divisional playoff to Dallas.
1982	1	0	1	17	30	Lost 1st round playoff to Dallas.
TOTAL:	4	1	3	41	94	
AVERAGE:	1	0	1	14	31	

COACHING HISTORY: 1976-1984 John McKay 44-88-1-.335; 1985-1986 Leeman Bennett 4-28-0-.125; 1987-1990 Ray Perkins 19-41-0-.317; 1990-1991 Richard Williamson 4-15-0-.211; 1992-1995 Sam Wyche 23-41-0-.359; 1996-present Tony Dungy

TAMPA BAY LIGHTNING

Home City: Tampa, Florida (1992-1993)
St. Petersburg, Florida (1993-present)
Home Arena: Expo Hall (1992-1993) Capacity: 10,400 [1993]
ThunderDome (1993-present) Capacity: 26,000 [1995]
Origin of Name: The name was chosen by General Manager Phil Esposito after witnessing an electrical storm.

Regular Season Record

Season	League	GP	W	L	T	GF	GA	Pts	Pct
1992-1993	NHL	84	23	54	7	245	332	53	.315
1993-1994	NHL	84	30	43	11	224	251	71	.423
1994-1995	NHL	48	17	28	3	120	144	37	.385
1995-1996	NHL	82	38	32	12	238	248	88	.537
TOTAL:	4 years	298	108	157	33	827	975	249	
AVERAGE:		74	27	39	8	207	244	62	.418

Playoff Record

Season	GP	W	L	GF	GA	Result
1995-1996	6	2	4	13	26	Lost preliminary series to Philadelphia

COACHING HISTORY: 1992-present Terry Crisp

TAMPA BAY ROWDIES

Home City: Tampa, Florida
Home Stadium: Tampa Stadium Capacity: 72,126 [1984]
Origin of Name: The name was chosen in a Name the Team Contest.

Regular Season Record

Season	League	GP	W	L	GF	GA	BP	Pts	Pct
1975	NASL	22	16	6	46	27	39	135	.682
1976	NASL	24	18	6	58	30	46	154	.713
1977	NASL	26	14	12	55	45	47	131	.560
1978	NASL	30	18	12	63	48	57	165	.611
1979	NASL	30	19	11	67	46	55	169	.626
1980	NASL	32	19	13	61	50	54	168	.583

1981	NASL	32	15	17	63	64	53	139	.290
1982	NASL	32	12	20	47	77	42	112	.233
1983	NASL	30	7	23	48	87	41	83	.184
1984	NASL	24	9	15	43	61	35	87	.242
TOTAL:	10 years	282	147	135	551	535	469	1343	
AVERAGE:		28	15	13	55	54	47	134	.414

Playoff Record

Season	GP	W	L	GF	GA	Result
1975	3	3	0	6	0	**Won NASL championship**.
1976	2	1	1	3	3	Lost 2nd round series to Toronto.
1977	1	0	1	0	3	Lost 1st round series to New York.
1978	8	5	3	13	10	Lost championship series to New York.
1979	8	6	2	14	9	Lost championship series to New York.
1980	5	3	2	15	8	Lost 2nd round series to San Diego.
1981	5	3	2	11	11	Lost 2nd round series to New York.
TOTAL:	32	21	11	62	44	
AVERAGE:	5	3	2	9	6	

COACHING HISTORY: 1975-1977 Eddie Firmani 41-15; 1977 John Boyle 7-9; 1978-1982 Gordon Jago 83-73; 1983 Al Miller 7-23; 1984 Rodney Marsh 9-15

TEAM AMERICA

Home City: Washington, D.C.
Home Stadium: Robert F. Kennedy Memorial Stadium Capacity: 55,031,[1983]
Origin of Name: The team was to have been the nucleus of the next American national team.

Regular Season Record

Season	League	GP	W	L	GF	GA	BP	Pts	Pct
1983	NASL	30	10	20	33	54	25	79	.176

COACHING HISTORY: Alkis Panagoulas 10-20

TEAM HAWAII

(were San Antonio Thunder)
(became Tulsa Roughnecks)

Home City: Honolulu, Hawaii
Home Stadium: Aloha Stadium (University of Hawaii) Capacity: 50,000 [1977]
Origin of Name: The team was based in Hawaii

Regular Season Record

Season	League	GP	W	L	GF	GA	BP	Pts	Pct
1977	NASL	26	11	15	45	59	41	106	.453

COACHING HISTORY: Hubert Vogelsinger 8-9; Charlie Mitchell 3-6

TEXAS CHAPARRALS

(were Dallas Chaparrals)
(became Dallas Chaparrals)

Home City: Dallas, Texas
Home Court: Moody Coliseum — Capacity: 8,500
Memorial Auditorium — Capacity: 8,088
Origin of Name: The team changed its name from Dallas Chaparrals in an attempt to create regional support for the team.

Regular Season Record

Season	League	GP	W	L	PPGF	PPGA	Pct	GB
1970-1971	ABA	84	30	54	121.5	124.5	.357	28

Playoff Record

Season	GP	W	L	PPGF	PPGA	Result
1970-1971	4	0	4	107.5	125.8	Lost 1st round series to Utah.

COACHING HISTORY: Max Williams 5-14-.263; Bill Blakeley 25-40-.385

TEXAS RANGERS

(were Washington Senators)

Home City: Arlington, Texas
Home Field: Arlington Stadium (1972-1993) — Capacity: 43,521 [1993]
The Ballpark in Arlington (1994-present) — Capacity: 49,292 [1995]
Origin of Name: The name was chosen in honor of the famous law enforcement agency.

Regular Season Record

Season	League	GP	W	L	Pct	GB	R	OR
1972	AL	154	54	100	.351	38.5	461	628
1973	AL	162	57	105	.352	37	619	844
1974	AL	160	84	76	.525	5	690	698
1975	AL	162	79	83	.488	19	714	733
1976	AL	162	76	86	.469	14	616	652
1977	AL	162	94	68	.580	8	767	657
1978	AL	162	87	75	.537	5	692	632
1979	AL	162	83	79	.512	5	750	698
1980	AL	161	76	85	.472	20.5	756	752
1981	AL	105	57	48	.543	NA	452	389
1982	AL	162	64	98	.395	29	590	749
1983	AL	162	77	85	.475	22	639	609
1984	AL	161	69	92	.429	14.5	656	714
1985	AL	161	62	99	.385	28.5	617	785
1986	AL	162	87	75	.537	5	771	743
1987	AL	162	75	87	.463	10	823	849
1988	AL	161	70	91	.435	33.5	637	735
1989	AL	162	83	79	.512	16	695	714
1990	AL	161	83	78	.516	19.5	676	696
1991	AL	162	85	77	.525	10	829	814
1992	AL	162	77	85	.475	19	682	753

1993	AL	162	86	76	.531	8	835	751
1994	AL	114	52	62	.456	-	613	697
1995	AL	144	74	70	.514	4	691	720
TOTAL:	24 years	3750	1791	1959		371	16271	17012
AVERAGE:		156	75	81	.477	15.5	678	709

COACHING HISTORY: 1972 Ted Williams 54-100-.351; 1973 Dorrel "Whitey" Herzog 47-91-.341; 1973 Del Wilber 1-0-1.000; 1973-1975 Billy Martin 137-141-.493; 1975-1977 Frank Lucchesi 142-149-.488; 1977 Eddie Stanky 1-0-1.000; 1977 Connie Ryan 2-4-.333; 1977-1978 Bill Hunter 146-108-.575; 1978-1980 Pat Corrales 160-164-.494; 1981-1982 Don Zimmer 95-106-.473; 1982 Darrell Johnson 26-40-.394; 1983-1985 Doug Rader 155-200-.437; 1985-1992 Bobby Valentine 581-604-.490; 1992 Toby Harrah 32-44-.421; 1993-1994 Kevin Kennedy 138-138-.500; 1995-present Johnny Oates

TOLEDO BLUE STOCKINGS

Home City: Toledo, Ohio
Home Field: League Park — Capacity: 4,000
Tri-State Fairgrounds
Origin of Name: The team wore blue stockings.

Regular Season Record

Season	League	GP	W	L	Pct	GB	R	OR
1884	AA	104	46	58	.442	27.5	463	571

COACHING HISTORY: Charlie Morton 46-58-.442

TOLEDO JEEPS

Home City: Toledo, Ohio
Home Court: Toledo Sports Arena
Origin of Name: The team was sponsored by the workers' recreation program of Willys Jeep factory in Toledo.

Regular Season Record

Season	League	GP	W	L	PPGF	PPGA	Pct	GB
1946-1947	NBL	44	21	23	57.3	56.0	.477	10
1947-1948	NBL	59	22	37	55.8	57.1	.373	21.5
TOTAL:	2 years	103	43	60				31.5
AVERAGE:		52	22	30	56.6	56.6	.417	16

Playoff Record

Season	GP	W	L	PPGF	PPGA	Result
1946-1947	5	2	3	45.8	56.4	Lost 1st round series to Ft. Wayne.

COACHING HISTORY: 1946-1948 Julie Rivlin 43-60-.417

TOLEDO JIM WHITE CHEVROLETS

Home City: Toledo, Ohio
Home Court:
Origin of Name: The team was sponsored by a local Chevrolet dealership.

Regular Season Record

Season	League	GP	W	L	PPGF	PPGA	Pct	GB
1941-1942	NBL	24	3	21	39.7	51.2	.125	17
1942-1943	NBL	4	0	4	38.8	48.0	.000	7.5
TOTAL:	2 years	28	3	25				24.5
AVERAGE:		14	2	12	39.3	49.6	.107	12

COACHING HISTORY: 1941-1942 Tommy Edwards 3-21-.125; 1942-1943 Sid Goldberg 0-4-.000

TOLEDO MAROONS

Home City: Toledo, Ohio
Home Stadium:
Origin of Name: The team received its name from the color of their jerseys.

Regular Season Record

Season	League	GP	W	L	T	PF	PA	Pct
1922	NFL	9	5	2	2	94	59	.667
1923	NFL	7	2	3	2	23	60	.429
TOTAL:	2 years	16	7	5	4	117	119	
AVERAGE:		8	4	2	2	59	60	.563

COACHING HISTORY: 1922 Gil Falcon 5-2-2-.667; 1923 Clarence Horning 2-3-2-.429

TOLEDO MAUMEES

Home City: Toledo, Ohio
Home Field: Speranza Park Capacity: 5,500
Origin of Name: Speranza Park was located near the mouth of the Maumee River.

Regular Season Record

Season	League	GP	W	L	Pct	GB	R	OR
1890	AA	132	68	64	.515	20	739	689

COACHING HISTORY: Charlie Morton 68-64-.515

TOLEDO REDMAN TOBACCOS

Home City: Toledo, Ohio
Home Court:
Origin of Name: The team was sponsored by the Pinkerton Tobacco Co. one of their brands being Red Man Tobacco.

Regular Season Record

Season	League	GP	W	L	Pct
1930-1931	ABL	36	12	24	.333

COACHING HISTORY:

TORONTO ARENAS
(were Toronto Blueshirts)
(became Toronto St. Patricks)

Home City: Toronto, Ontario
Home Arena: Mutual Street Arena Capacity: 8,000
Origin of Name: The team was named Arenas because the team was purchased by the directors of the Mutual Street Arena and named after the Arena.

Regular Season Record

Season	League	GP	W	L	T	GF	GA	Pts	Pct
1917-1918	NHL	22	13	9	0	108	109	26	.591
1918-1919	NHL	18	5	13	0	64	92	10	.278
TOTAL:	2 years	40	18	22	0	172	201	36	
AVERAGE:		20	9	11	0	86	101	18	.450

Playoff Record

Season	GP	W	L	T	GF	GA	Result
1917-1918	7	4	3	0	28	28	**Won Stanley Cup**.

COACHING HISTORY: 1917-1919 Dick Carroll 18-22-0-.450

TORONTO ARGONAUTS

Home City: Toronto, Ontario
Home Stadium: Varsity Stadium (1950-1958) Capacity: 27,000
Exhibition Stadium* (1959-1988) Capacity: 54,530 [1987]
Skydome (1989-present) Capacity: 53,595 [1995]
Origin of Name: The team was formed in 1873 by the Toronto Argonaut Rowing Club

Regular Season Record

Season	League	GP	W	L	T	PF	PA	Pts	Pct
1950	CRU	12	6	5	1	291	187	13	.542
1951	CRU	12	7	5	0	226	205	14	.583
1952	CRU	12	7	4	1	265	191	15	.625
1953	CRU	14	5	9	0	172	249	10	.357
1954	CRU	14	6	8	0	212	265	12	.429
1955	CRU	12	4	8	0	239	328	8	.333
1956	CFC	14	4	10	0	331	413	8	.286
1957	CFC	14	4	10	0	274	410	8	.286
1958	CFL	14	4	10	0	266	308	8	.286
1959	CFL	14	4	10	0	192	274	8	.286
1960	CFL	14	10	4	0	370	265	20	.714
1961	CFL	14	7	6	1	255	258	15	.536
1962	CFL	14	4	10	0	259	378	8	.286
1963	CFL	14	3	11	0	202	310	6	.214
1964	CFL	14	4	10	0	243	332	8	.286
1965	CFL	14	3	11	0	193	360	6	.214
1966	CFL	14	5	9	0	182	271	10	.357
1967	CFL	14	5	8	1	252	266	11	.393
1968	CFL	14	9	5	0	284	266	18	.643

1969	CFL	14	10	4	0	406	280	20	.714
1970	CFL	14	8	6	0	329	290	16	.571
1971	CFL	14	10	4	0	289	248	20	.714
1972	CFL	14	3	11	0	254	298	6	.214
1973	CFL	14	7	5	2	265	231	16	.571
1974	CFL	16	6	9	1	281	314	13	.406
1975	CFL	16	5	10	1	261	324	11	.343
1976	CFL	16	7	8	1	289	354	15	.469
1977	CFL	16	6	10	0	251	266	12	.375
1978	CFL	16	4	12	0	234	389	8	.250
1979	CFL	16	5	11	0	234	352	10	.313
1980	CFL	16	6	10	0	334	358	12	.375
1981	CFL	16	2	14	0	241	506	4	.125
1982	CFL	16	6	9	1	426	426	13	.594
1983	CFL	16	12	4	0	452	328	24	.750
1984	CFL	16	9	6	1	461	361	19	.594
1985	CFL	16	6	10	0	344	397	12	.375
1986	CFL	18	10	8	0	417	441	20	.556
1987	CFL	18	11	6	1	484	427	23	.639
1988	CFL	18	14	4	0	571	326	28	.778
1989	CFL	18	7	11	0	369	428	14	.389
1990	CFL	18	10	8	0	689	538	20	.556
1991	CFL	18	13	5	0	647	526	26	.722
1992	CFL	18	6	12	0	469	523	12	.333
1993	CFL	18	3	15	0	390	593	6	.167
1994	CFL	18	7	11	0	504	578	14	.389
1995	CFL	18	4	14	0	376	519	8	.222
TOTAL:	46 years	700	298	390	12	14975	16157	608	
AVERAGE:		15	7	8	0	326	351	13	.434

Playoff Record

Season	GP	W	L	T	PF	PA	Result
1950	4	3	1	0	91	32	**Won Grey Cup**.
1951	2	1	1	0	28	31	Lost Division semifinal to Hamilton.
1952	5	4	1	0	100	66	**Won Grey Cup**.
1955	2	1	1	0	68	66	Lost Division final to Montreal.
1960	2	0	2	0	41	54	Lost division final to Ottawa.
1961	3	2	1	0	70	74	Lost Division semifinal to Ottawa.
1967	1	0	1	0	22	38	Lost Division semifinal to Ottawa.
1968	3	2	1	0	60	68	Lost Division final to Ottawa.
1969	3	2	1	0	40	55	Lost Division final to Ottawa.
1970	1	0	1	0	7	16	Lost Division semifinal to Montreal.
1971	3	1	1	1	51	39	Lost Grey Cup game to Calgary.
1973	1	0	1	0	10	32	Lost Division semifinal to Montreal.
1977	1	0	1	0	16	21	Lost Division semifinal to Ottawa.
1982	2	1	1	0	60	39	Lost Grey Cup game to Edmonton.
1983	2	2	0	0	59	53	**Won Grey Cup**.
1984	1	0	1	0	13	14	Lost Division final to Hamilton.
1986	2	1	1	0	56	59	Lost Division final to Hamilton.
1987	3	2	1	0	84	54	Lost Grey Cup game to Edmonton.
1988	1	0	1	0	11	27	Lost Division final to Winnipeg.
1989	1	0	1	0	7	30	Lost Division semifinal to Winnipeg.
1990	2	1	1	0	51	45	Lost Division final to Winnipeg.

1991	2	2	0	0	78	24	**Won Grey Cup**.
1994	1	0	1	0	15	34	Lost Division semifinal to Baltimore.
TOTAL:	48	25	22	1	1038	971	
AVERAGE:	2	1	1	0	45	42	

COACHING HISTORY: 1950-1954 Frank Clair 31-31-2-.500; 1955-1956 Bill Swiacki 8-18-0-.308; 1957-1959 Hampton Pool 9-23-0-.281; 1959 Steve Owen 3-7-0-.300; 1960-1962 Lou Agase 17-13-1-.565; 1962-1964 Norbert Wirkowski 11-28-0-.282; 1965-1966 Bob Shaw 8-20-0-.286; 1967-1972 Leo Cahill 45-38-1-.542; 1973-1974 John Rauch 10-9-2-.524; 1974 Joe Moss 3-5-1-.389; 1975-1976 Russ Jackson 12-18-2-.406; 1977-1978 Leo Cahill 9-16-0-.360; 1978 Bud Riley 1-6-0-.143; 1979 Forrest Gregg 5-11-0-.313; 1980-1981 Willie Wood 6-20-0-.231; 1981 Tom Hudspeth 2-4-0-.333; 1982-1989 Bob O'Billovich 75-58-3-.563; 1990 Don Matthews 10-8-0-.556; 1991-1992 Adam Rita 16-13-0-.552; 1992-1993 Dennis Meyer 4-13-0-.235; 1993-1994 Bob O'Billovich 9-17-0-.346; 1995 Mike Faragalli 2-7-0; 1995 Bob O'Billovich 2-7-0; 1996-present Don Matthews

Known as C.N.E. Stadium until 1973

TORONTO BLIZZARD

(were Toronto Metro Croatia)

Home City: Toronto, Ontario
Home Stadium: Exhibition Stadium — Capacity: 54,472 [1980]
Origin of Name: Since many people associate Canada with cold and blizzards the name was chosen by team officials.

Regular Season Record

Season	**League**	**GP**	**W**	**L**	**GF**	**GA**	**BP**	**Pts**	**Pct**
1979	NASL	30	14	16	52	65	49	133	.493
1980	NASL	32	14	18	49	65	44	128	.444
1981	NASL	32	7	25	39	82	37	77	.160
1982	NASL	32	17	15	64	47	49	151	.315
1983	NASL	30	16	14	51	48	45	135	.300
1984	NASL	24	14	10	46	33	35	117	.325
TOTAL:	6 years	180	82	98	301	340	259	741	
AVERAGE:		30	14	16	50	57	43	124	.318

Playoff Record

Season	**GP**	**W**	**L**	**GF**	**GA**	**Result**
1979	2	0	2	1	5	Lost 1st round series to New York.
1982	3	1	2	6	9	Lost 1st round series to Seattle.
1983	6	4	2	8	6	Lost championship series to Tulsa.
1984	4	2	2	6	6	Lost championship series to Chicago.
TOTAL:	15	7	8	21	26	
AVERAGE:	4	2	2	5	6	

COACHING HISTORY: 1979-1981 Keith Eddy 35-59; 1981 Dave Turnet 3-10; 1982-1984 Bobby Houghton 47-39

TORONTO BLUE JAYS

Home City: Toronto, Ontario
Home Field: Exhibition Stadium (1977-1989) Capacity: 43,737 [1978]
Skydome (1989-present) Capacity: 50,300 [1995]
Origin of Name: The club's name was picked in a Name the Team Contest.

Regular Season Record

Season	League	GP	W	L	Pct	GB	R	OR
1977	AL	161	54	107	.335	45.5	605	822
1978	AL	161	59	102	.366	40	590	775
1979	AL	162	53	109	.327	50.5	613	862
1980	AL	162	67	95	.414	36	624	762
1981	AL	106	37	69	.349	NA	329	466
1982	AL	162	78	84	.481	17	651	701
1983	AL	162	89	73	.549	9	795	726
1984	AL	162	89	73	.549	15	750	696
1985	AL	161	99	62	.615	-	759	588
1986	AL	162	86	76	.531	9.5	889	733
1987	AL	162	96	66	.593	2	845	655
1988	AL	162	87	75	.537	2	763	680
1989	AL	162	89	73	.549	-	731	651
1990	AL	162	86	76	.531	2	767	661
1991	AL	162	91	71	.562	-	684	622
1992	AL	162	96	66	.593	-	780	682
1993	AL	162	95	67	.586	-	847	742
1994	AL	115	55	60	.478	16	566	579
1995	AL	144	56	88	.389	30	642	777
TOTAL:	19 years	2954	1462	1492		274.5	13230	13180
AVERAGE:		155	77	78	.495	14.5	696	694

Playoff Record

Season	GP	W	L	R	OR	Result
1985	7	3	4	25	26	Lost ALCS to Kansas City.
1989	5	1	4	21	26	Lost ALCS to Oakland.
1991	5	1	4	19	27	Lost ALCS to Minnesota.
1992	12	8	4	48	44	**Won World Series.**
1993	12	8	4	71	59	**Won World Series**
TOTAL:	41	21	20	184	182	
AVERAGE:	8	4	4	37	36	

COACHING HISTORY: 1977-1979 Roy Hartsfield 166-318-.343; 1980-1981 Bob Mattick 104-164-.388; 1982-1985 Bobby Cox 355-292-.549; 1986-1989 Jimy Williams 281-241-.538; 1991 Gene Tenace 19-14-.576; 1989-present Cito Gaston

TORONTO BLUESHIRTS
(became Toronto Arenas)

Home City: Toronto, Ontario
Home Arena
Origin of Name: The team wore blue uniforms.

Regular Season Record

Season	League	GP	W	L	T	GF	GA	Pts	Pct
1912-1913	NHA	20	9	11	0	86	95	18	.450
1913-1914	NHA	20	13	7	0	93	65	26	.650
1914-1915	NHA	20	8	12	0	66	84	16	.400
1915-1916	NHA	24	9	14	1	97	98	19	.396
1916-1917	NHA	14	7	7	0	64	61	14	.500
TOTAL:	5 years	98	46	51	1	406	403	93	
AVERAGE:		19	9	10	0	81	81	19	.474

Playoff Record

Season	GP	W	L	GF	GA	Result
1913-1914	5	4	1	19	10	**Won Stanley Cup**.

COACHING HISTORY: 1912-1913 Bruce Ridpath 0-3-0-.000; 1912-1915 Jack Marshall 30-27-0-.526; 1915-1917 Not Available

TORONTO CITY

Home City: Toronto, Ontario
Home Stadium: Varsity Stadium
Origin of Name: The team played it's home games in Toronto and was represented by the Hibernian team of Edinburgh, Scotland.

Regular Season Record

Season	League	GP	W	L	T	GF	GA	Pts	Pct
1967	USA	12	4	3	5	23	17	13	.542

COACHING HISTORY: Bob Shankly 4-3-5-.542

TORONTO FALCONS

Home City: Toronto, Ontario
Home Stadium: Varsity Stadium
Origin of Name: The team was named after the Toronto Italia-Falcons of the Eastern Canada Professional Soccer League.

Regular Season Record

Season	League	GP	W	L	T	GF	GA	BP	Pts	Pct
1967	NPSL	32	10	17	5	59	70	NA	127	.441
1968	NASL	32	13	13	6	55	69	48	144	.500
TOTAL:	2 years	64	23	30	11	114	139	48	271	
AVERAGE:		32	12	15	5	57	70	24	136	.470

COACHING HISTORY: 1967 Hector Mariano 10-17-5-.441; 1968 Laddie Kubala 13-13-6-.500

TORONTO HUSKIES

Home City: Toronto, Ontario
Home Court: Maple Leaf Gardens — Capacity: 14,640 [1947]
Origin of Name:

Regular Season Record

Season	League	GP	W	L	PPGF	PPGA	Pct	GB
1946-1947	BAA	60	22	38	66.6	71.0	.367	27

COACHING HISTORY: Ed Sadowski 3-9-.250; Lew Hayman 0-1-.000; Dick Fitzgerald 2-1-.667; Red Rolfe 17-27-.386

TORONTO MAPLE LEAFS
(were Toronto St. Patricks)

Home City: Toronto, Ontario
Home Arena: Mutual Street Arena (1927-1931) Capacity: 8,000
Maple Leaf Gardens (1931-present) Capacity: 15,846 [1995]
Origin of Name: Owner Conn Smythe chose the name because it was emblematic of Canada and previous Canadian Olympic hockey teams had worn it on their uniforms.

Regular Season Record

Season	League	GP	W	L	T	GF	GA	Pts	Pct
1926-1927	NHL	44	15	24	5	79	94	35	.398
1927-1928	NHL	44	18	18	8	89	88	44	.500
1928-1929	NHL	44	21	18	5	85	69	47	.534
1929-1930	NHL	44	17	21	6	116	124	40	.455
1930-1931	NHL	44	22	13	9	118	99	53	.602
1931-1932	NHL	48	23	18	7	133	127	53	.552
1932-1933	NHL	48	24	18	6	119	111	54	.563
1933-1934	NHL	48	26	13	9	174	119	61	.635
1934-1935	NHL	48	30	14	4	157	111	64	.667
1935-1936	NHL	48	23	19	6	126	106	52	.542
1936-1937	NHL	48	22	21	5	119	115	49	.510
1937-1938	NHL	48	24	15	9	151	127	57	.594
1938-1939	NHL	48	19	20	9	114	107	47	.490
1939-1940	NHL	48	25	17	6	134	110	56	.583
1940-1941	NHL	48	28	14	6	145	99	62	.646
1941-1942	NHL	48	27	18	3	158	136	57	.594
1942-1943	NHL	50	22	19	9	198	159	53	.530
1943-1944	NHL	50	23	23	4	214	174	50	.500
1944-1945	NHL	50	24	22	4	183	161	52	.520
1945-1946	NHL	50	19	24	7	174	185	45	.450
1946-1947	NHL	60	31	19	10	209	172	72	.600
1947-1948	NHL	60	32	15	13	182	143	77	.642
1948-1949	NHL	60	22	25	13	147	161	57	.475
1949-1950	NHL	70	31	27	12	176	173	74	.529
1950-1951	NHL	70	41	16	13	212	138	95	.679
1951-1952	NHL	70	29	25	16	168	157	74	.529
1952-1953	NHL	70	27	30	13	156	167	67	.479
1953-1954	NHL	70	32	24	14	152	131	78	.557
1954-1955	NHL	70	24	24	22	147	135	70	.500
1955-1956	NHL	70	24	33	13	153	181	61	.436
1956-1957	NHL	70	21	34	15	174	192	57	.407
1957-1958	NHL	70	21	38	11	192	226	53	.379
1958-1959	NHL	70	27	32	11	189	201	65	.464
1959-1960	NHL	70	35	26	9	199	195	79	.564

1960-1961	NHL	70	39	19	12	234	176	90	.643
1961-1962	NHL	70	37	22	11	232	180	85	.607
1962-1963	NHL	70	35	23	12	221	180	82	.586
1963-1964	NHL	70	33	25	12	192	172	78	.557
1964-1965	NHL	70	30	26	14	204	173	74	.529
1965-1966	NHL	70	34	25	11	208	187	79	.564
1966-1967	NHL	70	32	27	11	204	211	75	.536
1967-1968	NHL	74	33	31	10	209	176	76	.514
1968-1969	NHL	76	35	26	15	234	217	85	.559
1969-1970	NHL	76	29	34	13	222	242	71	.455
1970-1971	NHL	78	37	33	8	248	211	82	.526
1971-1972	NHL	78	33	31	14	209	208	80	.513
1972-1973	NHL	78	27	41	10	247	279	64	.410
1973-1974	NHL	78	35	27	16	274	230	86	.551
1974-1975	NHL	80	31	33	16	280	309	78	.488
1975-1976	NHL	80	34	31	15	294	276	83	.519
1976-1977	NHL	80	33	32	15	301	285	81	.506
1977-1978	NHL	80	41	29	10	271	237	92	.575
1978-1979	NHL	80	34	33	13	267	252	81	.506
1979-1980	NHL	80	35	40	5	304	327	75	.469
1980-1981	NHL	80	28	37	15	322	367	71	.444
1981-1982	NHL	80	20	44	16	298	380	56	.350
1982-1983	NHL	80	28	40	12	293	330	68	.425
1983-1984	NHL	80	26	45	9	303	387	61	.381
1984-1985	NHL	80	20	52	8	253	358	48	.300
1985-1986	NHL	80	25	48	7	311	386	57	.356
1986-1987	NHL	80	32	42	6	286	319	70	.438
1987-1988	NHL	80	21	49	10	273	345	52	.325
1988-1989	NHL	80	28	46	6	259	342	62	.388
1989-1990	NHL	80	38	38	4	337	358	80	.500
1990-1991	NHL	80	23	46	11	241	318	57	.356
1991-1992	NHL	80	30	43	7	234	294	67	.419
1992-1993	NHL	84	44	29	11	288	241	99	.589
1993-1994	NHL	84	43	29	12	280	243	98	.583
1994-1995	NHL	48	21	19	8	135	146	50	.521
1995-1996	NHL	82	34	36	12	247	252	80	.488
TOTAL:	70 years	4664	1987	1968	709	14457	14387	4683	
AVERAGE:		66	28	28	10	207	206	66	.502

Playoff Record

Season	**GP**	**W**	**L**	**T**	**GF**	**GA**	**Result**
1928-1929	4	2	2	0	8	5	Lost semifinal series to Rangers.
1930-1931	2	0	1	1	3	4	Lost quarterfinal series to Chicago.
1931-1932	7	5	1	1	28	15	**Won Stanley Cup**.
1932-1933	9	4	5	0	14	18	Lost Stanley Cup to Rangers.
1933-1934	5	2	3	0	12	11	Lost semifinal series to Detroit.
1934-1935	7	3	4	0	11	12	Lost Stanley Cup to Maroons.
1935-1936	9	4	5	0	25	27	Lost Stanley Cup to Detroit.
1936-1937	2	0	2	0	1	5	Lost quarterfinal series to Rangers.
1937-1938	7	4	3	0	14	13	Lost Stanley Cup to Chicago.
1938-1939	10	5	5	0	22	20	Lost Stanley Cup to Boston.
1939-1940	10	6	4	0	21	19	Lost Stanley Cup to Rangers.
1940-1941	7	3	4	0	17	15	Lost semifinal series to Boston.

1941-1942	13	8	5	0	25	31	**Won Stanley Cup**.
1942-1943	6	2	4	0	17	20	Lost semifinal series to Detroit.
1943-1944	5	1	4	0	6	23	Lost semifinal series to Montreal.
1944-1945	13	8	5	0	24	30	**Won Stanley Cup**.
1946-1947	11	8	3	0	31	27	**Won Stanley Cup**.
1947-1948	9	8	1	0	38	20	**Won Stanley Cup**.
1948-1949	9	8	1	0	28	15	**Won Stanley Cup**.
1949-1950	7	3	4	0	11	10	Lost semifinal series to Detroit.
1950-1951	11	8	2	1	30	15	**Won Stanley Cup**.
1951-1952	4	0	4	0	3	13	Lost semifinal series to Detroit.
1953-1954	5	1	4	0	8	15	Lost semifinal series to Detroit.
1954-1955	4	0	4	0	6	14	Lost semifinal series to Detroit.
1955-1956	5	1	4	0	10	14	Lost semifinal series to Detroit.
1958-1959	12	5	7	0	32	39	Lost Stanley Cup to Montreal.
1959-1960	10	4	6	0	25	31	Lost Stanley Cup to Montreal.
1960-1961	5	1	4	0	8	15	Lost semifinal series to Detroit.
1961-1962	12	8	4	0	40	30	**Won Stanley Cup**.
1962-1963	10	8	2	0	31	16	**Won Stanley Cup**.
1963-1964	14	8	6	0	39	31	**Won Stanley Cup**.
1964-1965	6	2	4	0	14	17	Lost semifinal series to Montreal.
1965-1966	4	0	4	0	6	15	Lost semifinal series to Montreal.
1966-1967	12	8	4	0	35	30	**Won Stanley Cup**.
1968-1969	4	0	4	0	5	24	Lost quarterfinal series to Boston.
1970-1971	6	2	4	0	15	16	Lost quarterfinal series to Rangers.
1971-1972	5	1	4	0	10	18	Lost quarterfinal series to Boston.
1973-1974	4	0	4	0	9	17	Lost quarterfinal series to Boston.
1974-1975	7	2	5	0	13	21	Lost quarterfinal series to Philadelphia.
1975-1976	10	5	5	0	31	36	Lost quarterfinal series to Philadelphia.
1976-1977	9	4	5	0	31	29	Lost quarterfinal series to Philadelphia
1977-1978	13	6	7	0	33	32	Lost semifinal series to Montreal.
1978-1979	6	2	4	0	19	24	Lost quarterfinal series to Montreal.
1979-1980	3	0	3	0	8	17	Lost preliminary series to Minnesota.
1980-1981	3	0	3	0	4	20	Lost preliminary series to Islanders.
1982-1983	4	1	3	0	18	18	Lost preliminary series to Minnesota.
1985-1986	10	6	4	0	40	33	Lost quarterfinal series to St. Louis.
1986-1987	13	7	6	0	33	32	Lost quarterfinal series to Detroit.
1987-1988	6	2	4	0	20	32	Lost preliminary series to Detroit.
1989-1990	5	1	4	0	16	20	Lost preliminary series to St. Louis.
1992-1993	21	11	10	0	69	63	Lost semifinal series to Los Angeles.
1993-1994	18	9	9	0	50	47	Lost semifinal series to Vancouver.
1994-1995	7	3	4	0	20	22	Lost preliminary series to Chicago.
1995-1996	6	2	4	0	15	21	Lost preliminary series to St. Louis.
TOTAL:	426	202	221	3	1102	1177	
AVERAGE:	8	4	4	0	20	22	

COACHING HISTORY: 1926-1931 Conn Smythe 72-81-25-.475; 1930-1932 Art Duncan 21-16-10-.553; 1931-1940 Dick Irvin 216-152-59-.575; 1940-1950 Clarence Day 259-206-81-.549; 1950-1953 Joe Primeau 97-71-42-.562; 1953-1956 Francis "King" Clancy 80-90-40-.476; 1956-1957 Howie Meeker 21-34-15-.407; 1957-1959 Billy Reay 26-50-14-.367; 1958-1969 George Imlach 358-269-123-.559; 1966-1967 Francis "King" Clancy 7-1-2-.800; 1969-1973 John McLellan 117-136-42-.468; 1971-1972 Francis "King" Clancy 9-3-3-.700; 1973-1977 Leonard Kelly 129-129-62-.500; 1977-1079 Roger Neilson 75-62-23-.541; 1979-1980 Floyd Smith 30-33-5-.478; 1979-1980 Dick Duff 0-2-0-.000; 1979-1980 George Imlach 5-5-0-.500; 1980-1981 Joe Crozier 13-22-5-.388; 1980-1984 Mike Nykoluk 89-144-47-.402; 1984-1986 Dan Maloney 45-

100-15-.328; 1986-1989 John Brophy 64-111-18-.378; 1988-1989 George Armstrong 17-26-4-.404; 1989-1991 Doug Carpenter 39-47-5-.456; 1990-1992 Tom Watt 52-80-17-.406; 1992-1996 Pat Burns 133-107-41; 1995-1996 Nick Beverley 9-6-2;

TORONTO METRO CROATIA

(were Toronto Metros)
(became Toronto Blizzard)

Home City: Toronto, Ontario
Home Stadium: Varsity Stadium [1975-1978] Capacity: 27,000
Lamport Stadium [1976] Capacity: 9,000
Origin of Name: The name was an attempt by the team management to draw the large ethnic population of Toronto to the games.

Regular Season Record

Season	League	GP	W	L	GF	GA	BP	Pts	Pct
1975	NASL	22	13	9	39	28	36	114	.576
1976	NASL	24	15	9	38	30	33	123	.569
1977	NASL	26	13	13	42	38	37	115	.491
1978	NASL	30	16	14	58	47	48	144	.533
TOTAL:	4years	102	57	45	177	143	154	496	
AVERAGE:		25	14	11	44	36	39	124	.540

Playoff Record

Season	GP	W	L	GF	GA	Result
1975	1	0	1	0	1	Lost 1st round series to Tampa Bay.
1976	4	4	0	10	3	**Won NASL championship**.
1977	2	0	2	2	0	Lost 1st round series to Rochester.
1978	1	0	1	0	4	Lost 1st round series to Vancouver.
TOTAL:	8	4	4	12	8	
AVERAGE:	2	1	1	3	2	

COACHING HISTORY: 1975-1976 Ivan Markovic 23-15; 1976 Domagoj Kapetanovic 5-3; 1977 Ivan Sangullian 13-13-.491; 1978 Domagoj Kapetanovic 16-14-.533

TORONTO METROS

(became Toronto Metro-Croatia)

Home City: Toronto, Ontario
Home Stadium: Varsity Stadium Capacity: 27,000
Origin of Name:

Regular Season Record

Season	League	GP	W	L	T	GF	GA	BP	Pts	Pct
1971	NASL	24	5	10	9	32	47	32	89	.412
1972	NASL	14	4	6	4	18	22	17	53	.421
1973	NASL	19	6	4	9	32	18	26	89	.520
1974	NASL	20	9	10	1	30	31	30	87	.483
TOTAL:	4years	77	24	30	23	112	118	105	318	
AVERAGE:		19	6	7	6	28	30	26	80	.459

Playoff Record

Season	GP	W	L	T	GF	GA	Result
1973	1	0	1	0	0	3	Lost 1st round series to Philadelphia

COACHING HISTORY: 1971-1972 Graham Leggat 9-16-13-.415; 1973-1974 Arthur Rodrigues 15-14-10-.501

TORONTO ONTARIOS

(were Toronto Tecumsehs)
(changed name to Shamrocks in mid 1914-1915)

Home City: Toronto, Ontario
Home Arena: Arena Gardens
Origin of Name: The team played in the Province of Ontario.

Regular Season Record

Season	League	GP	W	L	T	GF	GA	Pts	Pct
1913-1914	NHA	20	4	16	0	61	118	8	.200
1914-1915	NHA	20	7	13	0	76	96	14	.350
TOTAL:	2years	40	11	29	0	137	214	22	
AVERAGE:		20	6	14	0	69	107	11	.275

COACHING HISTORY: 1913-1915 Jim Murphy 11-29-0-.275

TORONTO RAPTORS

Home City: Toronto, Ontario
Home Court: The Skydome Capacity: 22,911 [1995]
Origin of Name: The name was officially chosen in a Name the Team Contest, but it was reported the name was registered the same day that the contest was announced. The name was an attempt to cash in on the dinosaur craze of the 1990's brought on by director Steven Spielberg's mega movie hit "Jurassic Park".

Regular Season Record

Season	League	GP	W	L	PPGF	PPGA	Pct	GB
1995-1996	NBA	82	21	61	97.5	105.0	.256	51

COACHING HISTORY: 1995-1996 Brendan Malone 21-61-.256; 1996-present Darrell Walker

TORONTO ST. PATRICKS

(were Toronto Arenas)
(became Toronto Maple Leafs)

Home City: Toronto, Ontario
Home Arena: Mutual Street Arena Capacity: 8,000
Origin of Name: The team was named St. Patricks in an attempt to attract Toronto's large Irish population to the games.

Regular Season Record

Season	League	GP	W	L	T	GF	GA	Pts	Pct
1919-1920	NHL	24	12	12	0	119	106	24	.500
1920-1921	NHL	24	15	9	0	105	100	30	.625
1921-1922	NHL	24	13	10	1	98	97	27	.563
1922-1923	NHL	24	13	10	1	82	88	27	.563
1923-1924	NHL	24	10	14	0	59	85	20	.417
1924-1925	NHL	30	19	11	0	90	84	38	.633
1925-1926	NHL	36	12	21	3	92	114	27	.375
TOTAL:	7years	186	94	87	5	645	674	193	
AVERAGE:		26	13	12	1	92	96	27	.519

Playoff Record

Season	GP	W	L	T	GF	GA	Result
1920-1921	2	0	2	0	0	7	Lost NHL playoff series to Ottawa.
1921-1922	7	4	2	1	21	13	**Won Stanley Cup**.
1924-1925	2	0	2	0	2	5	Lost NHL playoff series to Canadiens.
TOTAL:	11	4	6	1	23	25	
AVERAGE:	3	1	2	0	8	8	

COACHING HISTORY: 1919-1920 Frank Heffernan 5-7-0-.417; 1919-1920 Harry Sproule 7-5-0-.583; 1920-1921 Dick Carroll 15-9-0.625; 1921-1922 Eddie Powers 13-10-1-.563; 1922-1923 Charlie Querrie 3-3-0-.500; 1922-1923 Jack Adams 10-7-1-.583; 1923-1926 Eddie Powers 41-46-3-.472

TORONTO SHAMROCKS

(see Toronto Ontarios)

TORONTO TECUMSEHS

(became Toronto Ontarios)

Home City: Toronto, Ontario
Home Arena: Arena Gardens
Origin of Name: Tecumseh was an American Indian leader who fought on the British side during the War of 1812.

Regular Season Record

Season	League	GP	W	L	T	GF	GA	Pts	Pct
1912-1913	NHA	20	7	13	0	59	98	14	.350

COACHING HISTORY:

TORONTO TOROS

(were Ottawa Nationals)
(became Birmingham Bulls)

Home City: Toronto, Ontario
Home Arena: Maple Leaf Gardens Capacity: 16,316 [1975]
Origin of Name: The name was chosen because Toros is a shortened form of the name Toronto.

Regular Season Record

Season	League	GP	W	L	T	GF	GA	Pts	Pct
1973-1974	WHA	78	41	33	4	304	272	86	.551
1974-1975	WHA	78	43	33	2	349	304	88	.564
1975-1976	WHA	81	24	52	5	335	398	53	.327
TOTAL:	3years	237	108	118	11	988	974	227	
AVERAGE:		79	36	39	4	329	325	76	.479

Playoff Record

Season	GP	W	L	GF	GA	Result
1973-1974	12	7	5	45	43	Lost semifinal series to Chicago.
1974-1975	6	2	4	27	29	Lost quarterfinal series to San Diego.
TOTAL:	18	9	9	72	72	
AVERAGE:	9	5	4	36	36	

COACHING HISTORY: 1973-1975 Bill Harris 63-50-5-.555; 1974-1975 Bob LeDuc 21-16-1-.566; 1975-1976 Bob Baun 15-35-5-.318; 1975-1976 Gilles Leger 9-17-0-.346

TRENTON BENGALS

Home City: Trenton, New Jersey
Home Court:
Origin of Name: The team was originally the Passaic Bengal Tigers a local basketball team which had played in the area in the preceding year.

Regular Season Record

Season	League	GP	W	L	Pct
1928-1929 ABL	40	16	24	.400	

COACHING HISTORY:

TRI-CITIES BLACKHAWKS

(merged with Buffalo in mid 1946-1947)
(became Milwaukee Hawks)

Home City: Moline, Illinois
Rock Island, Illinois
Davenport, Iowa
Home Court: Wharton Field House (Moline) Capacity: 6,000
Origin of Name:

Regular Season Record

Season	League	GP	W	L	PPGF	PPGA	Pct	GB
1946-1947	NBL	32	15	17	49.1	51.8	.469	10
1947-1948	NBL	60	30	30	60.9	61.1	.500	13
1948-1949	NBL	64	36	28	65.1	62.4	.563	1
1949-1950	NBA	64	29	35	83.0	83.6	.453	10
1950-1951	NBA	68	25	43	84.3	88.1	.368	19
TOTAL:	5years	288	135	153				53
AVERAGE:		58	27	31	68.5	69.4	.469	11

Playoff Record

Season	GP	W	L	PPGF	PPGA	Result
1947-1948	6	3	3	71.5	76.2	Lost 2nd round series to Minneapolis.
1948-1949	6	3	3	66.3	64.3	Lost 2nd round series to Oshkosh.
1949-1950	3	1	2	74.7	86.0	Lost Division semifinal to Anderson.
TOTAL:	15	7	8			
AVERAGE:	5	2	3	70.8	75.5	

COACHING HISTORY:1946-1948 Nat Hickey 23-29-.442; 1947-1949 Bobby McDermott 47-38-.553; 1948-1950 Roger Potter 12-14-.462; 1949-1950 Red Auerbach 28-29-.491; 1950-1951 Dave McMillan 9-14-.391; 1950-1951 Johnny Logan 2-1-.667; 1950-1951 Mike Todorovich 14-28-.333

TROY TROJANS

(became New York Gothams)

Home City: Troy, New York
Home Field: Putnam Grounds (1879)
Center Island Grounds (1880-1881)
Troy Ball Club Grounds (1882) Capacity: 3,000
Origin of Name: The residents of Troy are called Trojans.

Regular Season Record

Season	League	GP	W	L	Pct	GB	R	OR
1879	NL	75	19	56	.253	35.5	321	543
1880	NL	83	41	42	.494	25.5	392	438
1881	NL	84	39	45	.464	17	399	429
1882	NL	83	35	48	.422	19.5	430	522
TOTAL:	4years	325	134	191		97.5	1542	1932
AVERAGE:		81	33	48	.412	24.5	386	483

COACHING HISTORY: 1879 Horace Phillips 12-46-.207; 1879-1882 Bob Ferguson 122-1.45-.457

TULSA ROUGHNECKS

(were Team Hawaii)

Home City: Tulsa, Oklahoma
Home Stadium: Skelly Stadium Capacity: 40,235 [1984]
Origin of Name: The name was chosen to honor Oklahoma's oil industry.

Regular Season Record

Season	League	GP	W	L	GF	GA	BP	Pts	Pct
1978	NASL	30	15	15	49	46	42	132	.489
1979	NASL	30	14	16	61	56	55	139	.515
1980	NASL	32	15	17	56	62	49	139	.483
1981	NASL	32	17	15	60	49	54	154	.321
1982	NASL	32	16	16	69	57	59	151	.315
1983	NASL	30	17	13	56	49	47	145	.322

1984	NASL	24	10	14	42	46	38	98	.272
TOTAL:	7years	210	104	106	393	365	344	958	
AVERAGE:		30	15	15	56	52	49	137	.369

Playoff Record

Season	**GP**	**W**	**L**	**GF**	**GA**	**Result**
1978	1	0	1	1	3	Lost 1st round series to Minnesota.
1979	5	3	2	8	8	Lost 2nd round series to New York.
1980	2	0	2	2	11	Lost 1st round series to New York.
1981	2	0	2	1	4	Lost 1st round series to Minnesota.
1982	3	1	2	1	6	Lost 1st round series to New York.
1983	6	5	1	14	6	**Won NASL championship.**
TOTAL:	19	9	10	27	38	
AVERAGE:	3	1	2	4	6	

COACHING HISTORY: 1978 Bill Foulkes 8-9; 1978 Alex Skotarek 7-6; 1979 Alan Hinton 14-16; 1980-1981 Charlie Mitchell 32-32; 1982-1983 Terry Hennessey 33-29; 1984 Wim Suurbier 10-14

228th BATTALION

Home City: Toronto, Ontario
Home Arena:
Origin of Name: The Northern Fusiliers (228th Battalion) recruited several hockey stars from Ontario and formed a team which competed in the National Hockey Association in the 1916-1917 season. The regiment was called overseas during the season and didn't complete the schedule.

Regular Season Record

Season	**League**	**GP**	**W**	**L**	**T**	**GF**	**GA**	**Pts**	**Pct**
1916-1917	NHA	14	6	8	0	73	69	12	.429

COACHING HISTORY: L.W. Reade 6-8-0-.429

UTAH JAZZ
(were New Orleans Jazz)

Home City: Salt Lake City, Utah
Las Vegas, Nevada (1983-1984)
Home Court: Salt Palace (1979-1983) Capacity: 12,201 [1980]
Salt Palace (1983-1984) Capacity: 12,201 [1980]
Thomas-Mack Center (1983-1984) Capacity: 18,500 [1984]
Salt Palace (1985-1991) Capacity: 12,616 [1991]
Delta Center (1991-present) Capacity: 19,911 [1995]
Origin of Name: The team kept the same nickname when it moved to Salt Lake City from New Orleans.

Regular Season Record

Season	**League**	**GP**	**W**	**L**	**PPGF**	**PPGA**	**Pct**	**GB**
1979-1980	NBA	82	24	58	102.4	108.4	.293	25
1980-1981	NBA	82	28	54	101.2	107.1	.341	24
1981-1982	NBA	82	25	57	110.9	116.6	.305	23

1982-1983	NBA	82	30	52	109.0	113.2	.366	23
1983-1984	NBA	82	45	37	115.0	113.8	.549	-
1984-1985	NBA	82	41	41	109.0	109.1	.500	11
1985-1986	NBA	82	42	40	108.2	108.5	.512	9
1986-1987	NBA	82	44	38	107.9	107.5	.537	11
1987-1988	NBA	82	47	35	108.5	104.8	.573	7
1988-1989	NBA	82	51	31	104.7	99.7	.622	-
1989-1990	NBA	82	55	27	106.8	102.0	.671	1
1990-1991	NBA	82	54	28	104.0	100.7	.659	1
1991-1992	NBA	82	55	27	108.3	101.9	.671	-
1992-1993	NBA	82	47	35	106.2	104.0	.573	8
1993-1994	NBA	82	53	29	101.9	97.7	.646	5
1994-1995	NBA	82	60	22	106.4	98.4	.732	2
1995-1996	NBA	82	55	27	102.5	95.9	.671	4
TOTAL:	17 years	1394	756	638				154
AVERAGE:		82	44	38	106.7	105.3	.537	9

Playoff Record

Season	GP	W	L	PPGF	PPGA	Result
1983-1984	11	5	6	110.7	111.9	Lost Conference semifinal to Phoenix.
1984-1985	10	4	6	111.0	114.5	Lost Conference semifinal to Denver.
1985-1986	4	1	3	103.0	107.3	Lost 1st round series to Dallas.
1986-1987	5	2	3	100.8	102.2	Lost 1st round series to Golden State.
1987-1988	11	6	5	103.4	102.4	Lost Conference semifinal to Los Angeles.
1988-1989	3	0	3	105.3	114.0	Lost 1st round series to Golden State.
1989-1990	5	2	3	102.4	103.8	Lost 1st round series to Phoenix.
1990-1991	9	4	5	105.1	102.9	Lost Conference semifinal to Portland.
1991-1992	16	9	7	102.9	102.5	Lost Conference final to Portland.
1992-1993	5	2	3	87.2	91.4	Lost 1st round series to Seattle.
1993-1994	16	8	8	94.3	92.3	Lost Conference final to Houston.
1994-1995	5	2	3	104.0	108.0	Lost 1st round series to Houston.
1995-1996	18	10	8	95.2	87.6	Lost Conference final to Seattle.
TOTAL:	118	55	63			
AVERAGE:	9	4	5	100.8	100.9	

COACHING HISTORY: 1979-1982 Tom Nissalke 60-124-.326; 1981-1989 Frank Layden 277-294-.485; 1988-present Jerry Sloan

UTAH STARS
(were Los Angeles Stars)

Home City: Salt Lake City, Utah
Home Court: Salt Palace Capacity: 12,201 [1975]
Origin of Name: The team kept the same nickname when it moved to Salt Lake City from Los Angeles.

Regular Season Record

Season	League	GP	W	L	PPGF	PPGA	Pct	GB
1970-1971	ABA	84	57	27	119.0	111.9	.679	1
1971-1972	ABA	84	60	24	117.8	112.1	.714	-
1972-1973	ABA	84	55	29	115.6	110.0	.655	-
1973-1974	ABA	84	51	33	105.1	104.7	.607	-

1974-1975	ABA	84	38	46	101.3	102.9	.452	27
1975-1976	ABA	16	4	12	114.9	116.6	.125	34
TOTAL:	6 years	436	265	171				62
AVERAGE:		73	44	29	112.3	109.7	.608	10

Playoff Record

Season	GP	W	L	PPGF	PPGA	Result
1970-1971	18	12	6	120.8	113.7	**Won ABA championship**.
1971-1972	11	7	4	110.3	107.8	Lost 2nd round series to Indiana.
1972-1973	10	6	4	107.3	103.4	Lost 2nd round series to Indiana.
1973-1974	18	9	9	102.3	99.8	Lost championship series to New York.
1974-1975	6	2	4	118.8	118.5	Lost 1st round series to Denver.
TOTAL:	63	36	27			
AVERAGE:	12	7	5	111.9	108.6	

COACHING HISTORY: 1970-1971 Bill Sharman 57-27-.679; 1971-1973 LaDell Andersen 115-53-.685; 1973-1974 Joe Mullaney 51-33-.607; 1974-1975 Bucky Buckwalter 24-32-.429; 1974-1976 Tom Nissalke 18-26-.409

VANCOUVER BLAZERS

(were Philadelphia Blazers)
(became Calgary Cowboys)

Home City: Vancouver, British Columbia
Home Arena: Pacific Coliseum — Capacity: 15,569 [1975]
Origin of Name: The team kept the same nickname when it moved to Vancouver from Philadelphia.

Regular Season Record

Season	League	GP	W	L	T	GF	GA	Pts	Pct
1973-1974	WHA	78	27	50	1	278	345	55	.353
1974-1975	WHA	78	37	39	2	256	270	76	.487
TOTAL:	2years	156	64	89	3	534	615	131	
AVERAGE:		78	32	45	1	267	308	65	.420

COACHING HISTORY: 1973-1974 John McKenzie 3-4-0-.429; 1973-1974 Phil Watson 3-9-0-.250; 1973-1974 Andy Bathgate 21-37-1-.364; 1974-1975 Joe Crozier 37-39-2-.487

VANCOUVER CANUCKS

Home City: Vancouver, British Columbia
Home Arena: Pacific Coliseum (1970-1995) — Capacity: 16,150 [1994]
General Motors Place (1995-present) — Capacity: 19,000 [1995]
Origin of Name: The team was named after the minor pro Western Hockey League team of the 1960's.

Regular Season Record

Season	League	GP	W	L	T	GF	GA	Pts	Pct
1970-1971	NHL	78	24	46	8	229	296	56	.359
1971-1972	NHL	78	20	50	8	203	297	48	.308
1972-1973	NHL	78	22	47	9	233	339	53	.340

1973-1974	NHL	78	24	43	11	224	296	59	.378
1974-1975	NHL	80	38	32	10	271	254	86	.538
1975-1976	NHL	80	33	32	15	271	272	81	.506
1976-1977	NHL	80	25	42	13	235	294	63	.394
1977-1978	NHL	80	20	43	17	239	320	57	.356
1978-1979	NHL	80	25	42	13	217	291	63	.394
1979-1980	NHL	80	27	37	16	256	281	70	.438
1980-1981	NHL	80	28	32	20	289	301	76	.475
1981-1982	NHL	80	30	33	17	290	286	77	.481
1982-1983	NHL	80	30	35	15	303	309	75	.469
1983-1984	NHL	80	32	39	9	306	328	73	.456
1984-1985	NHL	80	25	46	9	284	401	59	.369
1985-1986	NHL	80	23	44	13	282	333	59	.369
1986-1987	NHL	80	29	43	8	282	314	66	.413
1987-1988	NHL	80	25	46	9	272	320	59	.369
1988-1989	NHL	80	33	39	8	251	253	74	.463
1989-1990	NHL	80	25	41	14	245	306	64	.400
1990-1991	NHL	80	28	43	9	243	315	65	.406
1991-1992	NHL	80	42	26	12	285	250	96	.600
1992-1993	NHL	84	46	29	9	346	278	101	.601
1993-1994	NHL	84	41	40	3	279	276	85	.506
1994-1995	NHL	48	18	18	12	153	148	48	.500
1995-1996	NHL	82	32	35	15	278	278	79	.482
TOTAL:	26 years	2050	745	1003	302	6766	7636	1792	
AVERAGE:		79	29	39	11	260	294	69	.437

Playoff Record

Season	GP	W	L	GF	GA	Result
1974-1975	5	1	4	9	20	Lost quarterfinal series to Montreal.
1975-1976	2	0	2	4	8	Lost preliminary series to Islanders.
1978-1979	3	1	2	9	15	Lost preliminary series to Philadelphia.
1979-1980	4	1	3	7	15	Lost preliminary series to Buffalo.
1980-1981	3	0	3	7	13	Lost preliminary series to Buffalo.
1981-1982	17	11	6	57	50	Lost Stanley Cup final to Islanders.
1982-1983	4	1	3	14	17	Lost preliminary series to Calgary.
1983-1984	4	1	3	13	14	Lost preliminary series to Calgary.
1985-1986	3	0	3	5	17	Lost preliminary series to Edmonton.
1988-1989	7	3	4	20	26	Lost preliminary series to Calgary.
1990-1991	6	2	4	16	26	Lost preliminary series to Los Angeles.
1991-1992	13	6	7	44	35	Lost quarterfinal series to Edmonton.
1992-1993	12	6	6	46	43	Lost quarterfinal series to Los Angeles.
1993-1994	24	15	9	78	61	Lost Stanley Cup final to Rangers.
1994-1995	11	4	7	33	38	Lost quarterfinal series to Chicago.
1995-1996	6	2	4	17	24	Lost preliminary series to Colorado.
TOTAL:	124	54	70	379	422	
AVERAGE:	8	4	4	24	26	

COACHING HISTORY: 1970-1972 Hal Laycoe 44-96-16-.333; 1972-1973 Vic Stasiuk 22-47-9-.340; 1973-1974 Bill McCreary 9-25-7-.305; 1973-1977 Phil Maloney 95-105-32-.478; 1976-1978 Orland Kurtenbach 36-62-27-.396; 1978-1982 Harry Neale 106-144-65-.440; 1981-1984 Roger Neilson 51-61-21-.462; 1983-1985 Harry Neale 36-45-117.451; 1984-1985 Bill LaForge 4-14-2-.250; 1985-1987 Tom Watt 52-87-21-.391; 1987-1991 Bob McCammon 102-156-36-.408;

1990-1994 Pat Quinn 138-108-28-.555; 1994-1996 Rick Ley 47-50-27-.488, 1995-present Pat Quinn

VANCOUVER GRIZZLIES

Home City: Vancouver, British Columbia
Home Court: General Motors Place (1995-present) Capacity: 20,004 [1995]
Origin of Name: According to team General Manager Stu Jackson the name was chosen to reflect "the powerful nature of the team, the culture, geography and heritage of Western Canada and an indigenous species".

Regular Season Record

Season	League	GP	W	L	PPGF	PPGA	Pct	GB
1995-1996	NBA	82	15	67	89.8	99.8	.183	44

COACHING HISTORY: 1995-present Brian Winters

VANCOUVER MAROONS
(were Vancouver Millionaires)

Home City: Vancouver, British Columbia
Home Arena: Denman Street Arena Capacity: 10,500
Origin of Name: As with most clubs with "colorful" names the team was named after their uniforms color.

Regular Season Record

Season	League	GP	W	L	T	GF	GA	Pts	Pct
1922-1923	PCHA	30	17	12	1	116	88	35	.583
1923-1924	PCHA	30	13	16	1	87	80	27	.450
1924-1925	WCHL	28	12	16	0	91	102	24	.429
1925-1926	WHL	30	10	18	2	64	90	22	.367
TOTAL:	4 years	118	52	62	4	358	360	108	
AVERAGE:		30	13	16	1	90	90	27	.458

Playoff Record

Season	GP	W	L	T	GF	GA	Result
1922-1923	6	2	4	0	12	13	Lost playoff series to Ottawa.
1923-1924	7	2	4	1	14	18	Lost playoff series to Canadiens.
TOTAL:	13	4	8	1	26	31	
AVERAGE:	6	2	4	0	13	16	

COACHING HISTORY: 1922-1926 Frank Patrick 52-62-4-.458

VANCOUVER MILLIONAIRES
(became Vancouver Maroons)

Home City: Vancouver, British Columbia
Home Arena: Denman Street Arena Capacity: 10,500
Origin of Name: The team adopted the unofficial nickname of the Renfrew team of the NHA who were sometimes known as the Millionaires because of their high payroll.

Regular Season Record

Season	League	GP	W	L	T	GF	GA	Pts	Pct
1911-1912	PCHA	15	7	8	0	102	94	14	.467
1912-1913	PCHA	16	7	9	0	84	89	14	.438
1913-1914	PCHA	15	6	9	0	76	83	12	.400
1914-1915	PCHA	17	13	4	0	115	71	26	.765
1915-1916	PCHA	18	9	9	0	75	69	18	.500
1916-1917	PCHA	23	14	9	0	131	124	28	.607
1917-1918	PCHA	18	9	9	0	70	60	18	.500
1918-1919	PCHA	20	12	8	0	72	55	24	.600
1919-1920	PCHA	22	11	11	0	75	65	22	.500
1920-1921	PCHA	24	13	11	0	86	78	26	.542
1921-1922	PCHA	24	12	12	0	77	68	24	.500
TOTAL:	11 years	212	113	99	0	963	856	226	
AVERAGE:		19	10	9	0	88	78	20	.533

Playoff Record

Season	GP	W	L	T	GF	GA	Result
1914-1915	3	3	0	0	26	8	**Won Stanley Cup**.
1917-1918	7	3	3	1	24	20	Lost Stanley Cup final to Toronto.
1918-1919	2	1	1	0	5	7	Lost PCHA championship to Seattle.
1919-1920	2	1	1	0	3	7	Lost PCHA championship to Seattle.
1920-1921	7	4	3	0	25	14	Lost Stanley Cup final to Ottawa.
1921-1922	9	5	4	0	16	18	Lost Stanley Cup final to Toronto.
TOTAL:	30	17	12	1	99	74	
AVERAGE:	5	3	2	0	17	12	

COACHING HISTORY: 1911-1922 Frank Patrick 113-99-0-.533

VANCOUVER ROYALS

Home City: Vancouver, British Columbia
Home Stadium: Empire Stadium
Origin of Name: The team was represented by the Sunderland Club of the English League.

Regular Season Record

Season	League	GP	W	L	T	GF	GA	BP	Pts	Pct
1967	USA	12	3	4	5	20	28	-	11	.458
1968	NASL	32	12	15	5	51	60	49	136	.472
TOTAL:	2 years	44	15	19	10	71	88	49	147	
AVERAGE:		22	8	9	5	36	44	25	74	.471

COACHING HISTORY: 1967 Ian McCall 3-4-5-.458; 1968 Ferenc Puskas 12-15-5-.472

VANCOUVER WHITECAPS

Home City: Vancouver, British Columbia
Home Stadium: Empire Stadium (1974-1982) Capacity: 32,759 [1975]
B.C. Place Stadium (1983-1984) Capacity: 59,421 [1984]
Origin of Name: The name was chosen due to the fact Vancouver is surrounded by white capped mountains and white capped ocean waves.

Regular Season Record

Season	League	GP	W	L	T	GF	GA	BP	Pts	Pct
1974	NASL	20	5	11	4	29	30	28	70	.389
1975	NASL	22	11	11	-	38	28	33	99	.500
1976	NASL	24	14	10	-	38	30	36	120	.556
1977	NASL	26	14	12	-	43	46	40	124	.530
1978	NASL	30	24	6	-	68	29	55	199	.737
1979	NASL	30	20	10	-	54	34	52	172	.637
1980	NASL	32	16	16	-	52	47	43	139	.483
1981	NASL	32	21	11	-	74	43	62	186	.388
1982	NASL	32	20	12	-	58	48	46	160	.333
1983	NASL	30	24	6	-	63	34	51	187	.416
1984	NASL	24	13	11	-	51	48	43	117	.325
TOTAL:	11years	302	182	116	4	568	417	489	1573	
AVERAGE:		28	17	11	-	52	38	44	143	.459

Playoff Record

Season	GP	W	L	GF	GA	Result
1976	1	0	1	0	1	Lost 1st round series to Seattle.
1977	1	0	1	0	2	Lost 1st round series to Seattle.
1978	3	1	2	5	3	Lost 2nd round series to Portland.
1979	9	7	2	16	10	**Won NASL championship**.
1980	2	0	2	2	5	Lost 1st round series to Seattle.
1981	2	0	2	1	5	Lost 1st round series to Tampa Bay.
1982	3	1	2	3	7	Lost 1st round series to San Diego.
1983	3	1	2	4	5	Lost 1st round series to Toronto.
1984	3	1	2	5	7	Lost 1st round series to Chicago.
TOTAL:	27	11	16	36	45	
AVERAGE:	3	1	2	4	5	

COACHING HISTORY: 1974-1975 Jim Easton 16-22-4-.447; 1976-1977 Eckhard Krautzun 17-13; 1977 Holger Osieck 0-3; 1978-1980 Tony Waiters 60-32; 1981-1983 John Giles 65-29; 1984 Alan Hinton 13-11

VICTORIA ARISTOCRATS

(were Victoria Senators)
(became Spokane Canaries)

Home City: Victoria, British Columbia
Home Arena: Victoria Arena Capacity: 4,000
Origin of Name:

Regular Season Record

Season	League	GP	W	L	T	GF	GA	Pts	Pct
1912-1913	PCHA	15	10	5	0	68	56	20	.667
1913-1914	PCHA	15	10	5	0	80	67	20	.667
1914-1915	PCHA	17	4	13	0	64	116	8	.235
1915-1916	PCHA	18	5	13	0	74	102	10	.278
TOTAL:	4 years	65	29	36	0	286	341	58	
AVERAGE:		16	7	9	0	72	85	14	.446

Playoff Record

Season	GP	W	L	T	GF	GA	Result
1913-1914	3	0	3	0	8	13	Lost Stanley Cup final to Toronto.

COACHING HISTORY: 1912-1916 Lester Patrick 29-36-0.446

VICTORIA ARISTOCRATS

(were Portland Rosebuds)
(became Victoria Cougars)

Home City: Victoria, British Columbia
Home Arena: Victoria Arena Capacity: 4,000
Origin of Name: The team was named after the previous PCHA team.

Regular Season Record

Season	League	GP	W	L	T	GF	GA	Pts	Pct
1918-1919	PCHA	20	7	13	0	44	81	14	.350
1919-1920	PCHA	22	10	12	0	57	71	20	.455
TOTAL:	2years	42	17	25	0	101	152	34	
AVERAGE:		21	9	12	0	51	76	17	.405

COACHING HISTORY: 1918-1920 Lester Patrick 17-25-0-.425

VICTORIA COUGARS

(were Victoria Aristocrats)

Home City: Victoria, British Columbia
Home Arena: Victoria Arena Capacity: 4,000
Origin of Name:

Regular Season Record

Season	League	GP	W	L	T	GF	GA	Pts	Pct
1920-1921	PCHA	24	10	13	1	71	88	21	.438
1921-1922	PCHA	24	11	12	1	61	71	23	.479
1922-1923	PCHA	30	16	14	0	94	85	32	.533
1923-1924	PCHA	30	11	18	1	78	103	23	.383
1924-1925	WCHL	28	16	12	0	84	63	32	.571
1925-1926	WHL	30	15	11	4	68	53	34	.567
TOTAL:	6years	166	79	80	7	456	463	165	
AVERAGE:		27	13	13	1	76	77	27	.497

Playoff Record

Season	GP	W	L	T	GF	GA	Result
1922-1923	2	1	1	0	3	5	Lost PCHA playoff to Vancouver.
1924-1925	8	5	1	2	25	13	**Won Stanley Cup**.
1925-1926	8	3	3	2	12	16	Lost Stanley Cup final to Maroons.
TOTAL:	18	9	5	4	40	34	
AVERAGE:	6	3	2	1	13	11	

COACHING HISTORY: 1920-1926 Lester Patrick 79-80-7-.497

VICTORIA SENATORS
(became Victoria Aristocrats)

Home City: Victoria, British Columbia
Home Arena: Victoria Arena — Capacity: 4,000
Origin of Name:

Regular Season Record

Season	League	GP	W	L	T	GF	GA	Pts	Pct
1911-1912	PCHA	16	7	9	0	81	90	14	.438

COACHING HISTORY: Lester Patrick 7-9-0-.438

VIRGINIA SQUIRES
(were Washington Capitols)

Home City: Norfolk, Virginia
Home Court: Norfolk Scope — Capacity: 10,600 [1975]
Origin of Name:

Regular Season Record

Season	League	GP	W	L	PPGF	PPGA	Pct	GB
1970-1971	ABA	84	55	29	123.3	119.7	.655	-
1971-1972	ABA	84	45	39	118.9	118.0	.536	23
1972-1973	ABA	84	42	42	115.4	115.8	.500	15
1973-1974	ABA	84	28	56	106.4	111.3	.333	27
1974-1975	ABA	84	15	69	99.0	109.5	.179	43
1975-1976	ABA	83	15	68	106.9	116.6	.181	44.5
TOTAL:	6 years	503	200	303				152.5
AVERAGE:		84	33	51	111.7	115.2	.398	25

Playoff Record

Season	GP	W	L	PPGF	PPGA	Result
1970-1971	12	6	6	124.0	123.6	Lost 2nd round series to Kentucky.
1971-1972	11	7	4	117.2	109.7	Lost 2nd round series to New York.
1972-1973	5	1	4	103.2	112.0	Lost 1st round series to Kentucky.
TOTAL:	28	14	14			
AVERAGE:	9	5	4	114.8	115.1	

COACHING HISTORY: 1970-1976 Al Bianchi 186-241-.436; 1975-1976 Mack Calvin 0-6-.000; 1975-1976 Bill Musselman 4-22-.154; 1975-1976 Jack Ankerson 1-1-.500; 1975-1976 Zelmo Beatty 9-33-.214

WARREN PENN OILERS
(became Cleveland White Horses)

Home City: Warren, Pennsylvania
Home Court: Beaty Junior High School Gym — Capacity: 900
Origin of Name: The team received its name because it was sponsored by the Hyvis Oil Company.

Regular Season Record

Season	League	GP	W	L	PPGF	PPGA	Pct	GB
1937-1938	NBL	12	3	9	26.5	38.6	.250	8
1938-1939	NBL	19	9	10	38.1	39.6	.474	11
TOTAL:	2years	31	12	19				19
AVERAGE:		16	6	10	32.3	39.1	.387	9.5

COACHING HISTORY: 1937-1939 Gerry Archibald 12-19-.387

WASHINGTON BULLETS
(were Capital Bullets)

Home City: Landover, Maryland
Home Court: U.S. Air Arena (1974-present) * Capacity: 18,756 [1995]
Baltimore Arena (1988-present) Capacity: 12,289 [1995] (4 games a year)
Origin of Name: The team kept the same nickname when they moved from Baltimore to Landover.

Regular Season Record

Season	League	GP	W	L	PPGF	PPGA	Pct	GB
1974-1975	NBA	82	60	22	104.7	97.5	.732	-
1975-1976	NBA	82	48	34	102.8	100.4	.585	1
1976-1977	NBA	82	48	34	105.5	104.5	.585	1
1977-1978	NBA	82	44	38	110.3	109.4	.537	8
1978-1979	NBA	82	54	28	114.9	109.9	.659	-
1979-1980	NBA	82	39	43	107.0	109.5	.476	22
1980-1981	NBA	82	39	43	105.6	105.6	.476	23
1981-1982	NBA	82	43	39	103.5	102.6	.524	20
1982-1983	NBA	82	42	40	99.2	99.3	.512	23
1983-1984	NBA	82	35	47	102.7	105.6	.427	27
1984-1985	NBA	82	40	42	105.5	105.8	.488	23
1985-1986	NBA	82	39	43	103.0	104.8	.476	28
1986-1987	NBA	82	42	40	106.0	107.3	.512	17
1987-1988	NBA	82	38	44	105.5	106.3	.463	19
1988-1989	NBA	82	40	42	108.3	110.4	.488	12
1989-1990	NBA	82	31	51	107.7	109.9	.378	22
1990-1991	NBA	82	30	52	101.4	106.4	.366	26
1991-1992	NBA	82	25	57	102.4	106.8	.305	26
1992-1993	NBA	82	22	60	101.9	108.9	.268	38
1993-1994	NBA	82	24	58	100.4	107.7	.293	33
1994-1995	NBA	82	21	61	100.5	106.1	.256	36
1995-1996	NBA	82	39	43	102.5	101.5	.476	21
TOTAL:	22 years	1804	843	961				426
AVERAGE:		82	38	44	104.6	105.7	.467	19

Playoff Record

Season	GP	W	L	PPGF	PPGA	Result
1974-1975	17	8	9	102.8	100.2	Lost championship series to Golden State.
1975-1976	7	3	4	91.7	91.1	Lost Conference semifinal to Cleveland.
1976-1977	9	4	5	104.3	104.7	Lost Conference semifinal to Houston.
1977-1978	21	14	7	107.6	103.9	**Won NBA championship**.
1978-1979	19	9	10	101.6	102.9	Lost championship series to Seattle.

1979-1980	2	0	2	100.0	111.5	Lost 1st round series to Philadelphia.
1981-1982	7	3	4	100.1	101.7	Lost Conference semifinal to Boston.
1983-1984	4	1	3	93.8	96.5	Lost 1st round series to Boston.
1984-1985	4	1	3	101.8	105.8	Lost 1st round series to Philadelphia.
1985-1986	5	2	3	100.6	106.4	Lost 1st round series to Philadelphia.
1986-1987	3	0	3	91.0	110.3	Lost 1st round series to Detroit.
1987-1988	5	2	3	97.2	101.2	Lost 1st round series to Detroit.
TOTAL:	103	47	56			
AVERAGE:	9	4	5	99.4	103.0	

COACHING HISTORY: 1974-1976 K.C. Jones 108-56-.659; 1976-1980 Dick Motta 185-143-.564; 1980-1986 Gene Shue 231-248-.482; 1985-1988 Kevin Loughery 57-65-.467; 1987-1994 Wes Unseld 204-348-.370; 1994-present Jim Lynam

*Known as Capital Center from 1974 to 1993.

WASHINGTON CAPITALS

Home City: Landover, Maryland
Home Arena: U.S. Air Arena * Capacity: 18,130 [1995]
Origin of Name: The name was chosen in a Name the Team Contest.

Regular Season Record

Season	League	GP	W	L	T	GF	GA	Pts	Pct
1974-1975	NHL	80	8	67	5	181	446	21	.131
1975-1976	NHL	80	11	59	10	224	394	32	.200
1976-1977	NHL	80	24	42	14	221	307	62	.388
1977-1978	NHL	80	17	49	14	195	321	48	.300
1978-1979	NHL	80	24	41	15	273	338	63	.394
1979-1980	NHL	80	27	40	13	261	293	67	.419
1980-1981	NHL	80	26	36	18	286	317	70	.438
1981-1982	NHL	80	26	41	13	319	338	65	.406
1982-1983	NHL	80	39	25	16	306	283	94	.588
1983-1984	NHL	80	48	27	5	308	226	101	.631
1984-1985	NHL	80	46	25	9	322	240	101	.631
1985-1986	NHL	80	50	23	7	315	272	107	.669
1986-1987	NHL	80	38	32	10	285	278	86	.538
1987-1988	NHL	80	38	33	9	281	249	85	.531
1988-1989	NHL	80	41	29	10	305	259	92	.575
1989-1990	NHL	80	36	38	6	284	275	78	.488
1990-1991	NHL	80	37	36	7	258	258	81	.506
1991-1992	NHL	80	45	27	8	330	275	98	.613
1992-1993	NHL	84	43	34	7	325	286	93	.554
1993-1994	NHL	84	39	35	10	277	263	88	.524
1994-1995	NHL	48	22	18	8	136	120	52	.542
1995-1996	NHL	82	39	32	11	234	204	89	.543
TOTAL:	22 years	1738	724	789	225	5926	6242	1673	
AVERAGE:		79	33	36	10	269	284	76	.481

Playoff Record

Season	GP	W	L	GF	GA	Result
1982-1983	4	1	3	11	19	Lost preliminary series to Islanders.

1983-1984	8	4	4	28	25	Lost quarterfinal series to Islanders.
1984-1985	5	2	3	12	14	Lost preliminary series to Islanders.
1985-1986	9	5	4	36	24	Lost quarterfinal series to Rangers.
1986-1987	7	3	4	19	19	Lost preliminary series to Islanders.
1987-1988	14	7	7	54	50	Lost quarterfinal series to New Jersey.
1988-1989	6	2	4	19	25	Lost preliminary series to Philadelphia.
1989-1990	15	8	7	49	48	Lost semifinal series to Boston.
1990-1991	11	5	6	29	35	Lost quarterfinal series to Pittsburgh.
1991-1992	7	3	4	27	25	Lost preliminary series to Pittsburgh.
1992-1993	6	2	4	22	23	Lost preliminary series to Islanders.
1993-1994	11	5	6	32	32	Lost quarterfinal series to Rangers.
1994-1995	7	3	4	26	29	Lost preliminary series to Pittsburgh.
1995-1996	6	2	4	17	21	Lost preliminary series to Pittsburgh.
TOTAL:	116	52	64	381	389	
AVERAGE:	8	4	4	27	28	

COACHING HISTORY: 1974-1975 Jim Anderson 4-45-5-.120; 1974-1975 George Sullivan 2-17-0-.105; 1974-1976 Milt Schmidt 5-33-5-.174; 1975-1978 Tom McVie 49-122-33-.321; 1978-1980 Danny Belisle 28-51-17-.380; 1979-1982 Gary Green 50-78-29-.411; 1981-1982 Roger Crozier 0-1-0-.000; 1981-1990 Bryan Murray 343-246-83-.572; 1989-1994 Terry Murray 163-134-28-.545; 1994-present Jim Schoenfeld

*Known as Capital Center from 1974 to 1993

WASHINGTON CAPITOLS

Home City: Washington, D.C.
Home Court: Uline Arena
Origin of Name: As with other teams based in Washington and Ottawa the team seems to have been named because of the fact the cities were the seats of national government.

Regular Season Record

Season	**League**	**GP**	**W**	**L**	**PPGF**	**PPGA**	**Pct**	**GB**
1946-1947	BAA	60	49	11	73.8	63.9	.817	-
1947-1948	BAA	48	28	20	73.7	71.1	.58	3
1948-1949	BAA	60	38	22	81.8	79.4	.633	-
1949-1950	NBA	68	32	36	76.5	77.4	.471	21
1950-1951	NBA	35	10	25	81.3	86.0	.286	14.5
TOTAL:	5 years	271	157	114				38.5
AVERAGE:		54	31	23	77.4	75.6	.579	8

Playoff Record

Season	**GP**	**W**	**L**	**PPGF**	**PPGA**	**Result**
1946-1947	6	2	4	62.8	67.8	Lost semifinal series to Chicago.
1947-1948	1	1	0	72.0	75.0	Lost Division tiebreaker to Chicago.
1948-1949	11	6	5	77.3	77.5	Lost championship series to Minneapolis.
1949-1950	2	0	2	85.0	96.5	Lost Division semifinal to New York.
TOTAL:	20	9	11			
AVERAGE:	5	2	3	74.3	79.2	

COACHING HISTORY:1946-1949 Red Auerbach 115-53-.685; 1949-1950 Bob Feerick 32-36-.471; 1950-1951 Bones McKinney 10-25-.286

WASHINGTON CAPITOLS
(were Oakland Oaks)
(became Virginia Squires)

Home City: Washington, D.C.
Home Court: Washington Arena
Origin of Name: Named by team owner Earl Foreman.

Regular Season Record

Season	League	GP	W	L	PPGF	PPGA	Pct	GB
1969-1970	ABA	84	44	40	118.2	118.8	.524	7

Playoff Record

Season	GP	W	L	PPGF	PPGA	Result
1969-1970	7	3	4	120.7	127.6	Lost 1st round series to Denver.

COACHING HISTORY: Al Bianchi 44-40-.524

WASHINGTON DARTS
(became Miami Gatos)

Home City: Washington, D.C.
Home Field: Catholic University Stadium (some games)
Origin of Name: The team kept the same nickname when it transferred from the semi-professional American Soccer League to the NASL

Regular Season Record

Season	League	GP	W	L	T	GF	GA	BP	Pts	Pct
1970	NASL	24	14	6	4	52	29	41	137	.634
1971	NASL	24	8	6	10	36	34	33	111	.514
TOTAL:	2years	48	22	12	14	88	63	74	248	
AVERAGE:		24	11	6	7	44	32	37	124	.574

Playoff Record

Season	GP	W	L	GF	GA	Result
1970	2	1	1	3	4	Lost championship series to Rochester.

COACHING HISTORY: 1970 Lincoln Phillips 14-6-4-.634; 1971 Alan Rogers 8-6-10-.514

WASHINGTON DIPLOMATS

Home City: Washington, D.C.
Home Stadium: RFK Memorial Stadium Capacity: 55,031 [1975]
Origin of Name: The name was chosen by the wife of the team president.

Regular Season Record

Season	League	GP	W	L	T	GF	GA	BP	Pts	Pct
1974	NASL	20	7	12	1	29	36	25	70	.389
1975	NASL	22	12	10	-	42	47	40	112	.566

1976	NASL	24	14	10	-	46	38	42	126	.583
1977	NASL	26	10	16	-	32	49	32	92	.393
1978	NASL	30	16	14	-	55	47	49	145	.537
1979	NASL	30	19	11	-	68	50	59	172	.637
1980	NASL	32	17	15	-	72	61	57	159	.552
1981	NASL	32	15	17	-	59	58	51	135	.281
TOTAL:	8years	216	110	105	1	403	386	355	1011	
AVERAGE:		27	14	13	0	50	48	44	126	.473

Playoff Record

Season	GP	W	L	T	GF	GA	Result
1976	1	0	1	0	0	2	Lost 1st round series to New York.
1978	1	0	1	0	0	1	Lost 1st round series to Portland.
1979	2	0	2	0	4	7	Lost 1st round series to Los Angeles.
1980	3	1	2	0	2	4	Lost 1st round series to Los Angeles.
TOTAL:	7	1	6	0	6	14	
AVERAGE:	2	0	2	0	2	3	

COACHING HISTORY: 1974-1977 Dennis Viollet 39-41-1; 1977 Alan Spavin 4-7; 1978-1980 Gordon Bradley 52-40; 1981 Ken Furphy 15-17

WASHINGTON FEDERALS

Home City: Washington, D.C.
Home Stadium: RFK Memorial Stadium Capacity: 55,031 [1984]
Origin of Name: The name was chosen because Washington is sometimes called the Federal City.

Regular Season Record

Season	League	GP	W	L	T	PF	PA	Pct
1983	USFL	18	4	14	0	297	442	.222
1984	USFL	18	3	15	0	270	482	.167
TOTAL:	2years	36	7	29	0	567	924	
AVERAGE:		18	4	14	0	284	462	.194

COACHING HISTORY: 1983-1984 Ray Jauch 4-15-0-.211; 1984 Dick Bielske 3-14-0-.176

WASHINGTON NATIONALS

Home City: Washington, D.C.
Home Field: Union Association Park* Capacity:6,000
Origin of Name: Most teams in the city adopted names which reflected it's role in the National government.

Regular Season Record

Season	League	GP	W	L	Pct	GB	R	OR
1884	UA	112	47	65	.420	46.5	572	679

COACHING HISTORY: Mike Scanlon 47-65-.420

*Also known as Capitol Grounds

WASHINGTON NATIONALS

Home City: Washington, D.C.
Home Field: Athletic Park
Origin of Name: See above

Season	League	GP	W	L	Pct	GB	R	OR
			Regular Season Record					
1884	AA	63	12	51	.190	41	248	481

COACHING HISTORY: Holly Hollingshead 12-51-.190

WASHINGTON PALACE FIVE
(merged with Brooklyn in mid 1927-1928)

Home City: Washington, D.C.
Home Court:
Origin of Name: The name was chosen because the team was owned by George Marshall, owner of the Palace Laundry.

Season	League	GP	W	L	Pct
			Regular Season Record		
1925-1926	ABL	30	22	8	.733
1926-1927	ABL	42	30	12	.714
1927-1928	ABL	20	6	14	.300
TOTAL:	3years	92	58	34	
AVERAGE:		31	19	12	.630

COACHING HISTORY: 1925-1926 Ray Kennedy 22-8-.733; 1926-1928 Not Available

WASHINGTON REDSKINS
(were Boston Redskins)

Home City: Washington, D.C.
Home Stadium: Griffith Stadium (1937-1960) Capacity: 35,000
RFK Stadium (1960-present) Capacity: 56,454 [1995]
Origin of Name: The team kept the same nickname when it moved from Boston to Washington.

Season	League	GP	W	L	T	PF	PA	Pct
			Regular Season Record					
1937	NFL	11	8	3	0	195	120	.727
1938	NFL	11	6	3	2	148	154	.636
1939	NFL	11	8	2	1	242	94	.773
1940	NFL	11	9	2	0	245	142	.818
1941	NFL	11	6	5	0	176	174	.545
1942	NFL	11	10	1	0	227	102	.909
1943	NFL	10	6	3	1	229	137	.650
1944	NFL	10	6	3	1	169	180	.650
1945	NFL	10	8	2	0	209	121	.800
1946	NFL	11	5	5	1	171	191	.500
1947	NFL	12	4	8	0	295	367	.333

1948	NFL	12	7	5	0	291	287	.583
1949	NFL	12	4	7	1	268	339	.375
1950	NFL	12	3	9	0	232	326	.250
1951	NFL	12	5	7	0	183	296	.833
1952	NFL	12	4	8	0	240	287	.333
1953	NFL	12	6	5	1	208	215	.542
1954	NFL	12	3	9	0	207	432	.250
1955	NFL	12	8	4	0	246	222	.667
1956	NFL	12	6	6	0	183	225	.500
1957	NFL	12	5	6	1	251	230	.458
1958	NFL	12	4	7	1	214	268	.375
1959	NFL	12	3	9	0	185	350	.250
1960	NFL	12	1	9	2	178	309	.167
1961	NFL	14	1	12	1	174	392	.107
1962	NFL	14	5	7	2	305	376	.429
1963	NFL	14	3	11	0	279	398	.214
1964	NFL	14	6	8	0	307	305	.429
1965	NFL	14	6	8	0	257	301	.429
1966	NFL	14	7	7	0	351	355	.500
1967	NFL	14	5	6	3	347	353	.464
1968	NFL	14	5	9	0	249	358	.357
1969	NFL	14	7	5	2	307	319	.571
1970	NFL	14	6	8	0	297	314	.429
1971	NFL	14	9	4	1	276	190	.679
1972	NFL	14	11	3	0	336	218	.786
1973	NFL	14	10	4	0	325	198	.714
1974	NFL	14	10	4	0	320	196	.714
1975	NFL	14	8	6	0	325	276	.571
1976	NFL	14	10	4	0	291	217	.714
1977	NFL	14	9	5	0	196	189	.643
1978	NFL	16	8	8	0	273	283	.500
1979	NFL	16	10	6	0	348	295	.625
1980	NFL	16	6	10	0	261	293	.375
1981	NFL	16	8	8	0	347	349	.500
1982	NFL	9	8	1	0	190	128	.889
1983	NFL	16	14	2	0	541	332	.875
1984	NFL	16	11	5	0	426	310	.688
1985	NFL	16	10	6	0	297	312	.625
1986	NFL	16	12	4	0	368	296	.750
1987	NFL	15	11	4	0	379	285	.733
1988	NFL	16	7	9	0	345	387	.438
1989	NFL	16	10	6	0	386	308	.625
1990	NFL	16	10	6	0	381	301	.625
1991	NFL	16	14	2	0	485	224	.875
1992	NFL	16	9	7	0	300	255	.563
1993	NFL	16	4	12	0	230	345	.250
1994	NFL	16	3	13	0	320	412	.188
1995	NFL	16	6	10	0	326	359	.375
TOTAL:	59years	793	414	358	21	16337	15997	
AVERAGE:		13	7	6	0	277	271	.535

Playoff Record

Season	GP	W	L	PF	PA	Result
1937	1	1	0	28	21	**Won NFL championship**.
1940	1	0	1	0	73	Lost championship game to Bears.
1942	1	1	0	14	6	**Won NFL championship**.
1943	2	1	1	49	41	Lost championship game to Bears.
1945	1	0	1	14	15	Lost championship game to Cleveland.
1971	1	0	1	20	24	Lost Divisional playoff to San Francisco.
1972	3	2	1	49	20	Lost Super Bowl to Miami.
1973	1	0	1	20	27	Lost Divisional playoff to Minnesota.
1974	1	0	1	10	19	Lost Divisional playoff to Los Angeles.
1976	1	0	1	20	35	Lost Divisional playoff to Minnesota.
1982	4	4	0	110	48	**Won Super Bowl**.
1983	3	2	1	84	66	Lost Super Bowl to Raiders.
1984	1	0	1	19	23	Lost Divisional playoff to Chicago.
1986	3	2	1	46	37	Lost NFC championship to Giants.
1987	3	3	0	80	37	**Won Super Bowl**.
1990	2	1	1	30	34	Lost Conference semifinal to San Francisco.
1991	3	3	0	102	41	**Won Super Bowl**.
1992	2	1	1	37	27	Lost Conference semifinal to San Francisco.
TOTAL:	34	21	13	732	594	
AVERAGE:	2	1	1	41	33	

COACHING HISTORY: 1937-1942 Ray Flaherty 47-16-3-.735; 1943 Arthur Bergman 6-3-1-.650; 1944-1945 Dudley DeGroot 14-5-1-.725; 1946-1948 Glen Edwards 16-18-1-.471; 1949 John Whelchel 3-3-1-.500; 1949-1951 Herman Ball 4-16-0-.200; 1951 Dick Todd 5-4-0-.556; 1952-1953 Earl Lambeau 10-13-1-.438; 1954-1958 Joe Kuharich 26-32-2-.450; 1959-1960 Mike Nixon 4-18-2-.208; 1961-1965 Bill McPeak 21-46-3-.321; 1966-1968 Otto Graham 17-22-3-.440; 1969 Vince Lombardi 7-5-2-.571; 1971-1977 George Allen 67-30-1-.689; 1978-1980 Jack Pardee 24-24-0-.500; 1981-1992 Joe Gibbs 124-60-.674; 1993 Richie Petitbon 4-12-0-.250; 1994-present Norv Turner

WASHINGTON SENATORS

Home City: Washington, D.C.
Home Field: Capitol Park* Capacity: 6,000
Origin of Name: The name was chosen because of Washington's position as the seat of the American government.

Regular Season Record

Season	League	GP	W	L	Pct	GB	R	OR
1886	NL	120	28	92	.233	60	445	791
1887	NL	122	46	76	.377	32	601	818
1888	NL	134	48	86	.358	37.5	482	731
1889	NL	124	41	83	.331	41	632	892
TOTAL:	4years	500	163	337		170.5	2160	3232
AVERAGE:		125	41	84	.326	43	540	808

COACHING HISTORY: 1886 Mike Scanlon 13-66-.165; 1886-1887 John Gaffney 61-102-.374; 1888 Walter Hewitt 12-29-.293; 1888 Ted Sullivan 36-57-.387; 1889 John Morrill 13-39-.250; 1889 Arthur Irwin 28-44-.389

*Also known as Swampoodle Grounds

WASHINGTON SENATORS

Home City: Washington, D.C.
Home Field: Griffith Stadium** Capacity: 6,500
Origin of Name: The team was named after the previous National League team.

Regular Season Record

Season	League	GP	W	L	Pct	GB	R	OR
1891	AA	135	43	92	.319	50	691	1067
1892	NL	151	58	93	.384	44.5	731	869
1893	NL	129	40	89	.310	46	722	1032
1894	NL	132	45	87	.341	46	882	1122
1895	NL	128	43	85	.336	43	837	1048
1896	NL	131	58	73	.443	33	818	920
1897	NL	132	61	71	.462	32	781	793
1898	NL	152	51	101	.336	52.5	704	939
1899	NL	152	54	98	.355	49	743	983
TOTAL:	9years	1242	453	789		396	6909	8773
AVERAGE:		138	50	88	.365	44	768	975

COACHING HISTORY: 1891 Sam Trott 4-8-.333; 1891 Charles Snyder 23-46-.333; 1891 Dan Shannon 12-25-.324; 1891 Sandy Griffin 4-13-.235; 1892 Bill Barnie 13-21-.382; 1892 Arthur Irwin 34-46-.425; 1892 Danny Richardson 11-26-.297; 1893 Jim O'Rourke 40-89-.310; 1894-1897 Gus Schmelz 155-270-.365; 1897-1898 Tom Brown 55-59-.482; 1898 Jack Doyle 20-24-.455; 1898 James McCuire 19-49-.279; 1898-1899 Arthur Irwin 63-113-.358

**Also known as Boundary Field

WASHINGTON SENATORS
(became Minnesota Twins)

Home City: Washington, D.C.
Home Field: American League Park (1901-1902)
Griffith Stadium (1903-1960) Capacity: 27,410 [1961]
Origin of Name: Named after the previous National League team.

Regular Season Record

Season	League	GP	W	L	Pct	GB	R	OR
1901	AL	134	61	73	.455	21	683	771
1902	AL	136	61	75	.449	22	709	790
1903	AL	137	43	94	.314	47.5	438	691
1904	AL	151	38	113	.252	55.5	437	743
1905	AL	151	64	87	.424	29.5	560	613
1906	AL	150	55	95	.367	37.5	518	670
1907	AL	151	49	102	.325	43.5	505	690
1908	AL	152	67	85	.441	22.5	479	530
1909	AL	152	42	110	.276	56	382	655
1910	AL	151	66	85	.437	36.5	498	552
1911	AL	154	64	90	.416	38.5	624	760
1912	AL	152	91	61	.599	14	698	581
1913	AL	154	90	64	.584	6.5	596	566
1914	AL	154	81	73	.526	19	572	519

1915	AL	153	85	68	.556	17	571	492
1916	AL	153	76	77	.497	14.5	534	543
1917	AL	153	74	79	.484	25.5	543	566
1918	AL	128	72	56	.563	4	461	392
1919	AL	140	56	84	.400	32	533	570
1920	AL	152	68	84	.447	29	723	802
1921	AL	153	80	73	.523	18	704	738
1922	AL	154	69	85	.448	25	650	706
1923	AL	153	75	78	.490	23.5	720	747
1924	AL	154	92	62	.597	-	755	613
1925	AL	151	96	55	.636	-	829	669
1926	AL	150	81	69	.540	8	802	761
1927	AL	154	85	69	.552	25	782	730
1928	AL	154	75	79	.487	26	718	705
1929	AL	152	71	81	.467	34	730	776
1930	AL	154	94	60	.610	8	892	689
1931	AL	154	92	62	.597	16	843	691
1932	AL	154	93	61	.604	14	840	716
1933	AL	152	99	53	.651	-	850	665
1934	AL	152	66	86	.434	34	729	806
1935	AL	153	67	86	.438	27	823	903
1936	AL	153	82	71	.536	20	889	799
1937	AL	153	73	80	.477	28.5	757	841
1938	AL	151	75	76	.497	23.5	814	873
1939	AL	152	65	87	.428	41.5	702	797
1940	AL	154	64	90	.416	26	665	811
1941	AL	154	70	84	.455	31	728	798
1942	AL	151	62	89	.411	39.5	653	817
1943	AL	153	84	69	.549	13.5	666	595
1944	AL	154	64	90	.416	25	592	664
1945	AL	154	87	67	.565	1.5	622	562
1946	AL	154	76	78	.494	28	608	706
1947	AL	154	64	90	.416	33	496	675
1948	AL	153	56	97	.366	40	578	796
1949	AL	154	50	104	.325	47	584	868
1950	AL	154	67	87	.435	31	690	813
1951	AL	154	62	92	.403	36	672	764
1952	AL	154	78	76	.506	17	598	608
1953	AL	152	76	76	.500	23.5	687	614
1954	AL	154	66	88	.429	45	632	680
1955	AL	154	53	101	.344	43	598	789
1956	AL	154	59	95	.383	38	652	924
1957	AL	154	55	99	.357	43	603	808
1958	AL	154	61	93	.396	31	553	747
1959	AL	154	63	91	.409	31	619	701
1960	AL	154	73	81	.474	24	672	696
TOTAL:	60 years	9088	4223	4865		1590.5	39061	42157
AVERAGE:		151	70	81	.465	26.5	651	703

Playoff Record

Season	GP	W	L	R	OR	Result
1924	7	4	3	26	27	**Won World Series**.
1925	7	3	4	26	25	Lost World Series to Pittsburgh.

1933	5	1	4	11	16	Lost World Series to New York.
TOTAL:	19	8	11	63	68	
AVERAGE:	6	3	3	21	23	

COACHING HISTORY: 1901 Jimmy Manning 61-73-.455; 1902-1903 Tom Lofthus 104-169-.381; 1904 Malachi Kittredge 1-16-.059; 1904 Patrick Donovan 37-97-.276; 1905-1906 Jake Stahl 119-182-.395; 1907-1909 Joe Cantillon 158-297-.347; 1910-1911 Jim McAleer 130-175-.426; 1912-1920 Clark Griffith 693-646-.518; 1921 George McBride 80-73-.523; 1922 Clyde Milan 69-85-.448; 1923 Owen Bush 75-78-.490; 1924-1928 Stanley Harris 429-334-.562; 1929-1932 Walter Johnson 350-264-.570; 1933-1934 Joe Cronin 165-139-.543; 1935-1942 Stanley Harris 558-663-.457; 1943-1947 Ossie Bluege 375-394-.488; 1948-1949 Joe Kuhel 106-201-.345; 1950-1954 Stanley Harris 349-419-.454; 1955-1957 Charles Dressen 117-212-.356; 1957-1960 Harry Lavagetto 247-348-.415

WASHINGTON SENATORS
(became Texas Rangers)

Home City: Washington, D.C.
Home Field: Griffith Stadium (1961) — Capacity: 27,410 [1961]
RFK Stadium (1962-1971) — Capacity: 45,016 [1971]
Origin of Name: Named after the previous American League team.

Regular Season Record

Season	**League**	**GP**	**W**	**L**	**Pct**	**GB**	**R**	**OR**
1961	AL	161	61	100	.379	47.5	618	776
1962	AL	161	60	101	.373	35.5	599	716
1963	AL	162	56	106	.346	48.5	578	812
1964	AL	162	62	100	.383	37	578	733
1965	AL	162	70	92	.432	32	591	721
1966	AL	159	71	88	.447	25.5	557	659
1967	AL	161	76	85	.472	15.5	550	637
1968	AL	161	65	96	.404	37.5	524	665
1969	AL	162	86	76	.531	23	694	644
1970	AL	162	70	92	.432	38	626	689
1971	AL	159	63	96	.396	38.5	537	660
TOTAL:	11 years	1772	740	1032		378.5	6452	7712
AVERAGE:		161	67	94	.418	34.5	587	701

COACHING HISTORY: 1961-1963 James Vernon 135-227-.373; 1963-1967 Gil Hodges 321-445-.419; 1968 Jim Lemon 65-96-.404; 1969-1971 Ted Williams 219-264-.453

WASHINGTON WHIPS

Home City: Washington, D.C.
Home Field: D.C. Stadium
Origin of Name: The name was chosen in a Name the Team Contest. The team was represented by the Aberdeen Club of Scotland.

Regular Season Record

Season	**League**	**GP**	**W**	**L**	**T**	**GF**	**GA**	**BP**	**Pts**	**Pct**
1967	USA	12	5	2	5	19	11	-	15	.625

1968	NASL	32	15	10	7	63	53	56	167	.580
TOTAL:	2 years	44	20	12	12	82	64	56	182	
AVERAGE:		22	10	6	6	41	32	28	91	.583

Playoff Record

Season	GP	W	L	GF	GA	Result
1967	1	0	1	5	6	Lost championship game to Los Angeles.

COACHING HISTORY: 1967 Ed Turnbull 5-2-5-.625; 1968 Andre Nagy; 1968 Hicabi Emerkli

WATERLOO HAWKS

Home City: Waterloo, Iowa
Home Court:
Origin of Name:

Regular Season Record

Season	League	GP	W	L	PPGF	PPGA	Pct	GB
1948-1949	NBL	62	30	32	58.9	59.2	.484	6
1949-1950	NBA	62	19	43	79.4	84.9	.306	19
TOTAL:	2 years	124	49	75				25
AVERAGE:		62	25	37	69.2	72.1	.395	13

COACHING HISTORY: 1948-1950 Charley Shipp 38-59-.392; 1949-1950 Jack Smiley 11-16-.407

WHITING CIESAR ALL-AMERICANS

(became Hammond Ciesar All-Americans)

Home City: Whiting, Indiana
Home Court:
Origin of Name: The team was owned by Eddie Ciesar.

Regular Season Record

Season	League	GP	W	L	PPGF	PPGA	Pct	GB
1937-1938	NBL	15	12	3	41.3	37.3	.800	.5

Playoff Record

Season	GP	W	L	PPGF	PPGA	Result
1937-1938	2	0	2	35.5	40.5	Lost 1st round series to Oshkosh.

COACHING HISTORY: Whitey Wickhorst 12-3-.800

WILMINGTON QUICKSTEPS

Home City: Wilmington, Delaware
Home Field: Union Association Park
Origin of Name: This was the minor league Eastern League team which won the championship in 1884 before moving to the Union Association to replace the Philadelphia Keystones.

Regular Season Record

Season	League	GP	W	L	Pct	GB	R	OR
1884	UA	18	2	16	.111	44.5	35	114

COACHING HISTORY: Joe Simmons 2-16-.111

WINNIPEG BLUE BOMBERS

Home City: Winnipeg, Manitoba
Home Stadium: Osborne Stadium (1950-1952)
Winnipeg Stadium (1953-present) Capacity: 32,675 [1995]
Origin of Name: The name was coined by reporter Vince Leah who called the team the "Blue Bombers of Western Football" from a Grantland Rice description of Joe Louis a.k.a. The Brown Bomber.

Regular Season Record

Season	League	GP	W	L	T	PF	PA	Pts	Pct
1950	CRU	14	10	4	0	221	156	20	.714
1951	CRU	14	8	6	0	303	311	16	.571
1952	CRU	16	12	3	1	394	211	25	.781
1953	CRU	16	8	8	0	226	226	16	.500
1954	CRU	16	8	6	2	202	190	18	.563
1955	CRU	16	7	9	0	210	195	14	.438
1956	CFC	16	9	7	0	315	228	18	.563
1957	CFC	16	12	4	0	406	300	24	.750
1958	CFL	16	13	3	0	361	182	26	.813
1959	CFL	16	12	4	0	418	272	24	.750
1960	CFL	16	14	2	0	453	239	28	.875
1961	CFL	16	13	3	0	360	251	26	.813
1962	CFL	16	11	5	0	385	291	22	.688
1963	CFL	16	7	9	0	302	325	14	.438
1964	CFL	16	1	14	1	270	397	3	.094
1965	CFL	16	11	5	0	301	262	22	.688
1966	CFL	16	8	7	1	264	230	17	.531
1967	CFL	16	4	12	0	212	414	8	.250
1968	CFL	16	3	13	0	210	374	6	.188
1969	CFL	16	3	12	1	192	359	7	.219
1970	CFL	16	2	14	0	184	332	4	.125
1971	CFL	16	7	8	1	366	349	15	.469
1972	CFL	16	10	6	0	401	300	20	.625
1973	CFL	16	4	11	1	267	315	9	.281
1974	CFL	16	8	8	0	258	350	16	.500
1975	CFL	16	6	8	2	340	383	14	.438
1976	CFL	16	10	6	0	384	316	20	.625
1977	CFL	16	10	6	0	382	336	20	.625
1978	CFL	16	9	7	0	371	351	18	.563
1979	CFL	16	4	12	0	283	340	8	.250
1980	CFL	16	10	6	0	394	387	20	.625
1981	CFL	16	11	5	0	517	299	22	.688
1982	CFL	16	11	5	0	444	352	22	.688
1983	CFL	16	9	7	0	412	402	18	.563
1984	CFL	16	11	4	1	523	309	23	.719

1985	CFL	16	12	4	0	500	259	24	.750
1986	CFL	18	11	7	0	545	387	22	.611
1987	CFL	18	12	6	0	554	409	24	.667
1988	CFL	18	9	9	0	407	458	18	.500
1989	CFL	18	7	11	0	408	462	14	.438
1990	CFL	18	12	6	0	472	398	24	.667
1991	CFL	18	9	9	0	516	499	18	.500
1992	CFL	18	11	7	0	507	499	22	.611
1993	CFL	18	14	4	0	646	421	28	.778
1994	CFL	18	13	5	0	651	572	26	.722
1995	CFL	18	7	11	0	404	653	14	.389
TOTAL:	46 years	752	413	328	11	17141	15551	837	
AVERAGE:		16	9	7	0	373	338	18	.557

Playoff Record

Season	GP	W	L	T	PF	PA	Result
1950	4	2	2	0	67	48	Lost Grey Cup game to Toronto.
1951	1	0	1	0	1	4	Lost Division semifinal to Edmonton.
1952	3	1	2	0	51	52	Lost Division final to Edmonton.
1953	7	4	3	0	148	105	Lost Grey Cup game to Hamilton.
1954	5	2	2	1	47	50	Lost Division final to Edmonton.
1955	4	1	3	0	36	71	Lost Division final to Edmonton.
1956	2	1	1	0	26	50	Lost Division semifinal to Saskatchewan.
1957	6	3	2	1	75	62	Lost Grey Cup game to Hamilton.
1958	4	3	1	0	95	72	**Won Grey Cup**.
1959	3	3	0	0	56	26	**Won Grey Cup**.
1960	3	1	2	0	29	30	Lost Division final to Edmonton.
1961	3	3	0	0	78	29	**Won Grey Cup**.
1962	4	3	1	0	73	65	**Won Grey Cup**.
1965	5	3	2	0	74	81	Lost Grey Cup game to Hamilton.
1966	3	1	2	0	42	43	Lost Division final to Saskatchewan.
1971	1	0	1	0	23	34	Lost Division semifinal to Saskatchewan.
1972	1	0	1	0	24	27	Lost Division final to Saskatchewan.
1975	1	0	1	0	24	42	Lost Division semifinal to Saskatchewan.
1976	1	0	1	0	12	14	Lost Division semifinal to Edmonton.
1977	1	0	1	0	32	33	Lost Division semifinal to B.C.
1978	1	0	1	0	4	38	Lost Division semifinal to Calgary.
1980	2	1	1	0	56	48	Lost Division final to Edmonton.
1981	1	0	1	0	11	15	Lost Division semifinal to B.C.
1982	2	1	1	0	45	27	Lost Division final to Edmonton.
1983	2	1	1	0	70	61	Lost Division final to B.C.
1984	3	3	0	0	133	51	**Won Grey Cup**.
1985	2	1	1	0	44	57	Lost Division final to B.C.
1986	1	0	1	0	14	21	Lost Division semifinal to B.C.
1987	1	0	1	0	3	19	Lost Division final to Toronto.
1988	3	3	0	0	84	60	**Won Grey Cup**.
1989	2	1	1	0	40	21	Lost Division final to Hamilton.
1990	2	2	0	0	70	28	**Won Grey Cup**.
1991	2	1	1	0	29	50	Lost Division final to Toronto.
1992	2	1	1	0	69	35	Lost Grey Cup game to Calgary.
1993	2	1	1	0	43	52	Lost Grey Cup game to Edmonton.
1994	2	1	1	0	38	30	Lost Division final to Baltimore.

1995	1	0	1	0	21	36	Lost Division semifinal to Baltimore.
TOTAL:	93	48	43	2	1787	1587	
AVERAGE:	2	1	1	0	48	43	

COACHING HISTORY: 1950 Frank Larson 10-4-0-.714; 1951-1953 George Trafton 28-17-1-.620; 1954-1956 Allie Sherman 24-22-2-.521; 1957-1966 Bud Grant 102-56-2-.644; 1967-1969 Joe Zaleski 10-37-1-.219; 1970-1973 Jim Spavital 23-39-2-.375; 1974-1977 Bud Riley 34-28-2-.547; 1978-1982 Ray Jauch 45-35-0-.563; 1983-1986 Cal Murphy 40-21-1-.653; 1985 Fred Glick 3-1-0-.750; 1987-1990 Mike Riley 40-32-0-.556; 1991 Darryl Rogers 9-9-0-.500; 1992 Urban Bowman 11-7-0-.611; 1993-present Cal Murphy

WINNIPEG JETS
(became Phoenix Coyotes)

Home City: Winnipeg, Manitoba
Home Arena: Winnipeg Arena Capacity: 15,393 [1995]
Origin of Name: Team owner Ben Hatskin was a friend of New York Jets owner Sonny Werblin and named the team in honor of them.

Regular Season Record

Season	League	GP	W	L	T	GF	GA	Pts	Pct
1972-1973	WHA	78	43	31	4	285	249	90	.577
1973-1974	WHA	78	34	39	5	264	296	73	.468
1974-1975	WHA	78	38	35	5	322	293	81	.519
1975-1976	WHA	81	52	27	2	345	254	106	.654
1976-1977	WHA	80	46	32	2	366	291	94	.588
1977-1978	WHA	80	50	28	2	381	270	102	.638
1978-1979	WHA	80	39	35	6	307	306	84	.525
1979-1980	NHL	80	20	49	11	214	314	51	.319
1980-1981	NHL	80	9	57	14	246	400	32	.200
1981-1982	NHL	80	33	33	14	319	332	80	.500
1982-1983	NHL	80	33	39	8	311	333	74	.463
1983-1984	NHL	80	31	38	11	340	374	73	.456
1984-1985	NHL	80	43	27	10	358	332	96	.600
1985-1986	NHL	80	26	47	7	295	372	59	.369
1986-1987	NHL	80	40	32	8	279	271	88	.550
1987-1988	NHL	80	33	36	11	292	310	77	.481
1988-1989	NHL	80	26	42	12	300	355	64	.400
1989-1990	NHL	80	37	32	11	298	290	85	.531
1990-1991	NHL	80	26	43	11	260	288	63	.394
1991-1992	NHL	80	33	32	15	251	244	81	.506
1992-1993	NHL	84	40	37	7	322	320	87	.518
1993-1994	NHL	84	24	51	9	245	344	57	.339
1994-1995	NHL	48	16	25	7	157	177	39	.406
1995-1996	NHL	82	36	40	6	275	291	78	.476
TOTAL:	24 years	1893	808	887	198	7032	7306	1814	
AVERAGE:		79	34	37	8	293	304	76	.479

Playoff Record

Season	GP	W	L	GF	GA	Result
1972-1973	14	9	5	55	49	Lost championship series to New England.
1973-1974	4	0	4	9	23	Lost quarterfinal series o Houston.

1975-1976	13	12	1	68	35	**Won WHA championship**.
1976-1977	20	11	9	80	73	Lost championship series to Quebec.
1977-1978	9	8	1	53	20	**Won WHA championship**.
1978-1979	10	8	2	51	38	**Won WHA championship**.
1981-1982	4	1	3	13	20	Lost preliminary series to St. Louis.
1982-1983	3	0	3	9	14	Lost preliminary series to Edmonton.
1983-1984	3	0	3	7	18	Lost preliminary series to Edmonton.
1984-1985	8	3	5	26	35	Lost quarterfinal series to Chicago.
1985-1986	3	0	3	8	15	Lost preliminary series to Calgary.
1986-1987	10	4	6	31	32	Lost quarterfinal series to Edmonton.
1987-1988	5	1	4	17	25	Lost preliminary series to Edmonton.
1989-1990	7	3	4	22	24	Lost preliminary series to Edmonton.
1991-1992	7	3	4	17	29	Lost preliminary series to Vancouver.
1992-1993	6	2	4	17	21	Lost preliminary series to Vancouver.
1995-1996	6	2	4	10	20	Lost preliminary series to Detroit.
TOTAL:	132	67	65	493	491	
AVERAGE:	8	4	4	29	29	

COACHING HISTORY: 1972-1975 Bobby Hull 81-79-9-.506; 1974-1975 Rudy Pilous 34-26-5-.562; 1975-1977 Bobby Kromm 98-59-4-.621; 1977-1979 Larry Hillman 89-63-8-.581; 1979-1981 Tom McVie 21-69-18-.278; 1980-1981 Bill Sutherland 8-37-7-.221; 1981-1984 Tom Watt 70-81-24-.469; 1983-1984 John Ferguson 2-3-0-.400; 1983-1986 Barry Long 87-94-25-.483; 1985-1986 John Ferguson 7-6-1-.536; 1986-1989 Dan Maloney 91-93-28-.495; 1988-1989 Rick Bowness 8-17-3-.339; 1989-1991 Bob Murdoch 63-75-22-.463; 1991-1995 John Paddock 106-138-37-.443; 1994-1996 Terry Simpson 43-47-7-.479

WORCESTER BROWN STOCKINGS
(became Philadelphia Phillies)

Home City: Worcester, Massachusetts
Home Field: Agricultural Grounds
Origin of Name: The players wore brown stockings.

Regular Season Record

Season	**League**	**GP**	**W**	**L**	**Pct**	**GB**	**R**	**OR**
1880	NL	83	40	43	.482	26.5	412	370
1881	NL	82	32	50	.390	23	410	492
1882	NL	84	18	66	.214	37	379	652
TOTAL:	3years	249	90	159		86.5	1201	1514
AVERAGE:		83	30	53	.361	29	400	505

COACHING HISTORY: 1880 Frank Bancroft 40-43-.482; 1881-1882 Freeman Brown 36-69-.343; 1882 Tommy Bond 5-22-.185; 1882 Jack Chapman 9-25-.265

YOUNGSTOWN BEARS
(were Pittsburgh Pirates)

Home City: Youngstown, Ohio
Home Court:
Origin of Name:

Regular Season Record

Season	League	GP	W	L	PPGF	PPGA	Pct	GB
1945-1946	NBL	33	13	20	46.6	50.5	.394	12.5
1946-1947	NBL	44	12	32	53.5	60.1	.273	19
TOTAL:	2 years	77	25	52				31.5
AVERAGE:		39	13	26	50.1	55.3	.325	16

COACHING HISTORY: 1945-1946 Paul Birch 13-20-.394; 1946-1947 Frank Shannon 12-32-.273

Bibliography

ALBERTA ON ICE, Gary W. Zeman, 1985, Westweb Press, Edmonton, Alberta.

AMERICAN ENCYCLOPEDIA OF SOCCER, Zander Hollander, 1980, Beaverbooks, Pickering, Ontario.

BALLPARKS OF NORTH AMERICA, Michael Benson, 1989, McFarland & Company Inc., Jefferson, North Carolina.

BOOK OF WINNERS, Clair Walter, 1979, Harcourt, Brace, Jovanovich, New York, New York.

CAN YOU NAME THAT TEAM ? David B. Biesel, 1991, Scarecrow Press Inc. Metuchen New Jersey.

CANADIAN FOOTBALL LEAGUE GUIDE; Published annually by the Canadian Football League; Compiled by the CFL Media/Public Relations Department.

COMPLETE HISTORICAL AND STATISTICAL REFERENCE TO THE WORLD HOCKEY ASSOCIATION, Scott Adam Surgent, 1995, Xaler Press, Temple Arizona.

ENCYCLOPEDIA OF FOOTBALL, 16th Revised Edition; Roger Treat, A.S. Barnes & Co. Inc. Cranbury, N.J.

ENCYCLOPEDIA OF PRO BASKETBALL TEAM HISTORIES, Peter C. Bjarkman, 1994, Carroll and Graf Publishers New York, New York

FAMOUS FIRST FACTS AND RECORDS, Joseph Nathan Kane, 1975, Ace Books, New York, New York.

FUNK AND WAGNALLS NEW ENCYCLOPEDIA, 1975, New York, New York

GOODYEAR STORY, Maurice O'Reilly, 1983, The Benjamin Company Inc. Elmsford, New York

GREAT BASEBALL FEATS, FACTS & FIRSTS, David Nemec, 1989, Penguin Books Canada Limited, Markham, Ontario.

GREEN CATHEDRALS, Phillip J. Lowry, 1992, Addison Wesley Publishing Co. Inc.

HOCKEY ENCYCLOPEDIA (THE COMPLETE RECORD OF PROFESSIONAL ICE HOCKEY), Stan Fischler and Shirley Walton Fischler , 1983, MacMillan Publishing Company New York, New York.

INFORMATION PLEASE SPORTS ALMANAC, Mike Meserole, Published annually by The Houghton Mifflin Company.

KYLE ROTE JR'S COMPLETE BOOK OF SOCCER, Kyle Rote Jr., and Basil Kane, 1978 Simon & Schuster, New York, New York.

MACMILLAN BASEBALL ENCYCLOPEDIA ,1976, MacMillan Publishing Co. Inc., Special Editorial Consultant--Joseph L. Reichler.

NATIONAL HOCKEY LEAGUE OFFICIAL GUIDE AND RECORD BOOK; Published annually by the NHL Communications Department and the member clubs of the NHL.

NBA'S OFFICIAL ENCYCLOPEDIA OF PRO BASKETBALL, Zander Hollander, 1981 New American Library/NAL Books, New York, New York.

NHL 75th ANNIVERSARY COMMEMORATIVE BOOK, Edited by Dan Diamond, 1991, McClelland & Stewart, Toronto, Ontario

OFFICIAL NATIONAL FOOTBALL LEAGUE 1989 RECORD & FACT BOOK; Compiled by the NFL Public Relations Department and Seymour Siwoff, Elias Sports Bureau, 1989, Workman Publishing Co. New York, New York;

OFFICIAL NFL ENCYCLOPEDIA OF PRO FOOTBALL, Compiled by the Creative Services Division of NFL Properties, Inc., 1982 NAL Books, Scarborough, Ontario;

$1 LEAGUE (THE RISE AND FALL OF THE USFL) Jim Byrne, 1986, Prentice Hall Press New York, New York.

100 YEARS OF CANADIAN FOOTBALL, Gordon Currie, 1968, Pagurian Press Limited Toronto, Ontario.

THE PATRICKS: HOCKEY'S ROYAL FAMILY, Eric Whitehead, 1983, Formac Publishing, Halifax, Nova Scotia.

PROFESSIONAL SPORTS TEAM HISTORIES, Edited by Michael L. Leblanc, 1994, Gale Research Inc.

SPORTING NEWS OFFICIAL NBA GUIDE , The Sporting News; edited by Alex Sachare and David Sloan, 1989

SPORTS ENCYCLOPEDIA PRO BASEBALL, David S. Neft, and Richard M. Cohen, 1989 St. Martin's Press, New York, New York.

SPORTS ENCYCLOPEDIA PRO BASKETBALL , David S. Neft, Roland T. Johnson, Richard M. Cohen and Jordan A. Deutsch, 1975, Grosset and Dunlap, New York, New York.

SPORTS ENCYCLOPEDIA PRO FOOTBALL, David S. Neft, Roland T. Johnson, Richard M. Cohen and Jordan A. Deutsch, 1974, Grosset and Dunlap, New York, New York.

STORY OF BASKETBALL, John Devaney, 1976, Random House New York, New York

TRAIL OF THE STANLEY CUP, Charles L. Coleman, 1964, Kendall/ Hall Publishing Company Dubuque, Iowa.

WHA PRO HOCKEY 76-77, Dan Proudfoot, 1976, Pocket Books, Simon & Schuster Canada Ltd., Markham, Ontario.

WORLD ALMANAC AND BOOK OF FACTS, published annually by Pharos Books, New York, New York.

NEWSPAPERS AND PERIODICALS

Calgary Herald, Edmonton Journal, Edmonton Sun, The Hockey News, Montreal Gazette, New York Times, Toronto Globe and Mail, Sports Illustrated, Hockey Digest, The Sporting News

Also special thanks to the public relations departments of the following teams.
Arizona Cardinals, Atlanta Falcons, Atlanta Hawks, Buffalo Bills, Calgary Flames, Calgary Stampeders, California Angels, Chicago White Sox, Cincinnati Bengals, Cleveland Cavaliers, Colorado Rockies, Dallas Cowboys, Dallas Mavericks, Dallas Stars, Denver Broncos, Denver Nuggets, Detroit Lions, Detroit Red Wings, Edmonton Eskimos, Edmonton Oilers, Florida Panthers, Golden State Warriors, Green Bay Packers, Hamilton Tiger-Cats, Houston Astros, Houston Oilers, Houston Rockets, Kansas City Chiefs, Kansas City Royals, Los Angeles Dodgers, Los Angeles Lakers, Los Angeles Kings, Miami Dolphins, Milwaukee Brewers, Montreal Canadiens, Montreal Expos, New Jersey Devils, New York Giants, New York Islanders, New York Jets, New York Mets, Ottawa Senators, Philadelphia Eagles, Pittsburgh Penguins, Pittsburgh Steelers, Quebec Nordiques, Sacramento Gold Miners, St. Louis Cardinals, San Diego Chargers, San Diego Mariners, Saskatchewan Roughriders, Seattle Mariners, Seattle Seahawks, Tampa Bay Lightning, Toronto Argonauts, Toronto Blue Jays, Toronto Maple Leafs, Washington Bullets, Washington Capitals, Winnipeg Blue Bombers.